Blackstone's Statutes Series

copy 5
X

BSL
CMML
CLA

Trusted by millions

For your **course**, your **exam**

Blackstone's Statutes

EU T...
Legis...

Nigel Foster

✓ Edited by s...
✓ Trusted in ...

OXFORD

The University of Law
incorporating The College of Law

This book must be returned to the library on or before the last date stamped below. Failure to do so will result in a fine.

14 AUG 2017

University of Law
14 Store Street
London
WC1E 7DE

Bloomsbury Library	Moorgate Library
T: 01483 216387	T: 01483 216371
library-bloomsbury@law.ac.uk	library-moorgate@law.ac.uk

Bu...

www.oxfordtextbooks.co.uk/statutes/

COMMERCIAL LAW

TEXT, CASES, AND MATERIALS

FIFTH EDITION

MA CLARKE

RJA HOOLEY

RJC MUNDAY

LS SEALY

AM TETTENBORN

PG TURNER

OXFORD

UNIVERSITY PRESS

OXFORD
UNIVERSITY PRESS

Great Clarendon Street, Oxford, OX2 6DP,
United Kingdom

Oxford University Press is a department of the University of Oxford.
It furthers the University's objective of excellence in research, scholarship,
and education by publishing worldwide. Oxford is a registered trade mark of
Oxford University Press in the UK and in certain other countries

Fourth edition 2009
Fifth edition 2017
Impression: 1

Published in the United States of America by Oxford University Press
198 Madison Avenue, New York, NY 10016, United States of America

British Library Cataloguing in Publication Data
Data available

Library of Congress Control Number: 2017931323

ISBN 978-0-19-969208-8

Printed in Great Britain by
Bell & Bain Ltd., Glasgow

PREFACE TO THE FIFTH EDITION

It is with great pleasure that Len Sealy and Richard Hooley welcome Malcolm Clarke, Roderick Munday, Andrew Tettenborn and Peter Turner as authors of the fifth edition of this book. All are acknowledged experts in their chosen fields; all bring immense experience of teaching both undergraduate and graduate students.

Our aim in writing this new edition is the same as it was with all previous editions: to provide a book that combines extracts from the cases and other materials with a substantial commentary that helps put those extracts in context and stimulates thought about their significance.

There have been many developments in the eight years since the last edition, which we have attempted to take on board. We have also taken the opportunity to review the areas of commercial law covered. The result is a slightly leaner book than the last edition, but which remains resolutely focused on those areas of modern commercial practice that a student is likely to come across when studying English commercial law.

The responsibilities of authorship have been divided between us as follows:

Malcolm Clarke: Chapter 27

Richard Hooley: Chapters 1, 16, 17, 18, 19, 20, 21, 24, 25, and 26

Roderick Munday: Chapters 4, 5, 6, and 7

Len Sealy: Chapter 28

Andrew Tettenborn: Chapters 2, 3, 8, 9, 10, 11, 12, 13, 14, and 15

Peter Turner: Chapters 22 and 23

We have tried to state the law as it stood from sources available to us on 1 September 2016.

We are very grateful to the staff at Oxford University Press, particularly John Carroll, Joy Ruskin-Tompkins, and Sarah Stephenson, for their help and encouragement in the writing and production of this fifth edition.

MAC
RJAH
RJCM
LSS
AMT
PGT
September 2016

NEW TO THIS EDITION

Analysis of the latest developments in case law, including:

- *Armstrong DLW GmbH v Winnington Networks Ltd* and *Devani v Republic of Kenya* on personal property law;
- *Mohamud v WM Morrison Supermarkets Plc* (Supreme Court) on vicarious liability;
- *Kelly v Fraser* (Privy Council) and *Thanakharn Kasikorn Thai Chamkat (Mahachon) v Akai Holdings Ltd* (Hong Kong Court of Final Appeal) on apparent authority;
- *Sinclair Investments (UK) Ltd v Versailles Trade Finance Ltd* (Court of Appeal) and *European Ventures LLP v Cedar Capital Partners LLC* (Supreme Court) on agent's secret profits;
- *Novoship (UK) Ltd v Mikhaylyuk* on bribery of agents;
- *Bailey v Angove's Pty Ltd* (Supreme Court) on irrevocable agencies;
- *Blankley v Central Manchester and Manchester Children's University Hospital NHS Trust* (Court of Appeal) on intervening mental incapacity and termination of agency;
- *PST Energy 7 Shipping LLC Product Shipping & Trading SA v OW Bunker Malta Ltd* (Supreme Court) on what is a sale of goods and action for the price;
- *Trebor Bassett Holdings Ltd v ADT Fire & Security Plc* (Court of Appeal) clarifying the boundary between goods and services;
- *Summers v Harvard* (Court of Appeal) and *Fadallah v Pollak* on transfer of title by a non-owner;
- *BSS Group Plc v Makers (UK) Ltd* (Court of Appeal), *The Mercini Lady* (Court of Appeal) and *Proton Energy Group SA v Orlen Lietuva* on interpretation of ss 13 and 14 of the Sale of Goods Act 1979;
- *Bunge SA v Nidera BV* (Supreme Court) on damages for non-delivery of goods;
- *Tidal Energy Ltd v Bank of Scotland Plc* (Court of Appeal) on duties of payer's bank in an electronic funds transfer;
- *Taurus Petroleum v State Oil Marketing Co of Iraq* (Court of Appeal); *Fortis Bank SA/NV v Indian Overseas Bank* (Court of Appeal); *Société Générale v Saad Trading; Bulgrains & Co Ltd v Shinhan Bank; Alternative Power Solution Ltd v Central Electricity Board* (Privy Council) and other cases on letters of credit and demand guarantees;
- *Wuhan Guoyu Logistics Group Co Ltd v Emporiki Bank of Greece* (Court of Appeal) on distinguishing between true demand and suretyship guarantees;
- *Bassano v Toft* on pledges; *Your Response Ltd v Datateam Business Media Ltd* (Court of Appeal) and *Spencer v S Frances Ltd* on liens;
- *Cukurova Finance International v Alfa Telecom Turkey Ltd* (Privy Council), *Gray v G-T-P Group Ltd* and *USA v Nolan* (Supreme Court) on the Financial Collateral Arrangements (No 2) Regulations;
- *Online Catering Ltd v Acton* (Court of Appeal) on bills of sale;

- *Versloot Dredging v HDI Gerling Industrie Versicherung AG* (Supreme Court) on fraudulent device rule and insurance claims.

Discussion of new legislation, including:

- Consumer Rights Act 2015;
- Insurance Act 2015;
- Modern Slavery Act 2015;
- Small Business, Enterprise and Employment Act 2015;
- Third Parties (Rights against Insurers) Act 2010;
- Bribery Act 2010;
- Payment Services Regulations 2009.

Other new features include:

- Chapter 1 (Introduction) includes a new section on the impact of Brexit on English commercial law;
- Chapter 22 (Assignment of choses in action) reorganised and rewritten;
- Chapter 28 (Insolvency) includes discussion of new out-of-court bankruptcy procedure, debt relief orders, and pre-pack administrations.

CONTENTS

Acknowledgements   xvi

Table of cases   xviii

Table of legislation   li

PART I   INTRODUCTION

1 An introduction to commercial law   3

1 The nature of commercial law   3

2 The function of commercial law   8

3 The historical development of commercial law   14

4 The sources of commercial law   20

5 The role of equity in commercial law   28

6 Public law in the commercial arena   33

7 The philosophy and concepts of commercial law   36

8 The codification of commercial law   44

9 The challenges for commercial law in the twenty-first century   46

10 The impact of Brexit on English commercial law   51

2 Basic concepts of personal property   54

1 The distinction between real and personal property   54

2 Types of personal property   55

3 What is property?   56

4 What are the characteristics of property rights?   59

5 The significance of property rights   61

6 Types of property rights in chattels   65

7 Ownership of chattels   66

8 Acquisition and transfer of legal and equitable ownership in chattels 68

9 Possession of chattels   69

10 The protection of possession   72

11 Attornment in respect of chattels   76

12 Transfer of possession   78

13 The importance of possession   78

14 Acquisition and transfer of legal and equitable ownership in choses
    in action and intangibles   80
15 The remedies for recovery of, and interference with, personal property   81
16 Equitable property   89

3 Bailment   92
1 What is bailment?   92
2 Types of bailment   92
3 Three requirements for a bailment   94
4 The bailee's liability   97
5 The burden of proof   100
6 Bailment and third parties   101

PART II   THE LAW OF AGENCY

4 Introduction   107
1 The legal concept of agency   107

5 Creation of agency, and the authority of the agent   125
1 Creation of the agency relationship   125
2 Authority of the agent   127

6 Relations with third parties   168
1 Disclosed agency   168
2 Undisclosed agency   200

7 Relations between principal and agent   224
1 Duties of the agent   224
2 Rights of the agent   256
3 Termination of agency   270

PART III   DOMESTIC SALES LAW

8 Introduction and definitions   297
1 Introduction   297
2 The Sale of Goods Act and the general law   298
3 The application of the Sale of Goods Act   299
4 Definitions   300
5 Sale of goods distinguished from other transactions   312
6 Formation of the contract of sale   325

9 **Passing of the property in the goods as between seller and buyer**   327

1 Significance of the passing of property   327

2 Rules for determining when the property passes   330

3 Passing of property, acceptance, and rejection   358

4 Risk and property   361

5 Statutory provisions relating to perishing of specific goods   367

6 Frustration of sale of goods contracts   379

10 **Transfer of title**   381

1 The rule *nemo dat quod non habet*   381

2 First exception: estoppel   384

3 Second exception: sale under the Factors Act 1889, s 2   394

4 Third exception: sale under a voidable title   404

5 Fourth exception: sale by seller continuing in possession   407

6 Fifth exception: sale by buyer in possession   412

7 Sixth exception: sale by unpaid seller under SGA 1979, s 48   421

8 Seventh exception: private purchase of motor vehicle held on hire-purchase   421

9 Eighth exception: sale under general powers of sale or court order   421

11 **Seller's obligations as to quality**   423

1 Introduction: express and implied terms as to quality, and their effect   423

2 The implied condition that the goods will correspond with their description (s 13)   425

3 Implied terms as to quality and fitness in general   434

4 Implied condition that goods are of satisfactory quality: s 14(2)   435

5 Implied condition as to fitness for purpose (s 14(3))   441

6 Terms implied in sales of goods by sample (s 15)   448

7 Contractual modification of the seller's obligations as to quality   450

8 Product liability   454

12 **Performance of the contract**   455

1 Duties of the seller   455

2 Duties of the buyer   463

13 **Remedies of the seller**   476

1 Action for the price   476

2 Action for damages for non-acceptance   479

3 Recovery or forfeiture of a deposit   482

4 Specific performance   483

5 Remedies of an unpaid seller against the goods: lien, stoppage in transit, and resale   483

6 Retention of title clauses   497

14 Remedies of the buyer   515

1 Introduction   515

2 Buyer's action for damages for non-delivery   515

3 Buyer's action for damages for late delivery   523

4 The buyer's action for damages for breach of warranty   524

5 The buyer's right to recover the price of goods not delivered,
   or validly rejected   526

6 Specific performance   527

PART IV   INTERNATIONAL SALES

15 International sales   533

1 Introduction   533

2 Typical export transactions and INCOTERMS   534

3 Sales involving sea carriage   535

4 FOB contracts   537

5 FAS contracts   542

6 CIF contracts   543

7 Variants of the CIF contract   552

8 DAP contracts (sometimes called 'ex ship' or 'arrival' contracts)   552

9 FCA, CIP, and similar contracts   555

10 Payment in international sales transactions   557

11 International sales: the future   558

PART V   PAYMENT METHODS

16 Modern payment systems   563

1 Introduction   563

2 The nature of a funds transfer   564

3 Terminology   568

4 Credit/debit transfers   569

5 Clearing and settlement   576

6 Clearing systems and clearing rules   580

7 Duties of the banks involved in a funds transfer   582

8 Countermand   609

9 Completion of payment   611

10 Unwanted payments   619

17 Payment cards 624

1 Introduction 624

2 Types of payment card 624

3 Contractual networks 627

4 The regulation of contractual relationships 635

5 Liability for unauthorised transaction 639

6 Connected lender liability 641

18 Negotiable instruments 644

1 Introduction 644

2 Definition of a negotiable instrument 645

3 How instruments come to be negotiable 651

4 Types of negotiable instrument 654

5 Advantages of a negotiable instrument 655

19 Bills of exchange 659

1 The use of bills of exchange 659

2 The Bills of Exchange Act 1882 659

3 Definition of a bill of exchange 661

4 Transfer of a bill of exchange 665

5 Persons entitled to the benefit of the obligation on the bill 675

6 Liability on the bill of exchange: general principles 691

7 Liability on the bill: specific parties 699

8 Enforcement of the bill 703

9 Discharge of the bill 706

10 Mistaken payment 708

20 Cheques and other instruments 727

1 Cheques 727

2 Promissory notes 759

3 Banker's drafts 762

4 Travellers' cheques 762

PART VI THE FINANCING OF INTERNATIONAL TRADE

21 The financing of international trade 767

1 Documentary bills 768

2 Documentary credits 769

3 Standby credits, performance bonds, and guarantees   839
4 Other financing methods   854
5 Export credit guarantees   856

PART VII   ASSIGNMENT AND RECEIVABLES FINANCING

22 Assignment of choses in action   859
1 Introduction   859
2 'Chose in action' and 'assignment'   860
3 Existing and assignable choses in action   862
4 Intention to assign   887
5 Writing   900
6 Notice   910
7 Effects of assignment   931
8 Obstacles to enforcement   943

23 Receivables financing   948
1 General introduction   948
2 Financing by sale   958
3 Financing by secured transactions   977
4 Other doctrines affecting assigned receivables   1001
5 Reform   1002
6 International factoring   1003

PART VIII   COMMERCIAL CREDIT AND SECURITY

24 Introduction   1007
1 Commercial credit   1007
2 Security   1009

25 Possessory security   1024
1 Pledge   1024
2 Lien   1040
3 Reform   1058

26 Non-possessory security   1059
1 Mortgage   1059
2 Equitable charge   1068

3 Equitable lien   1077

4 Statutory control   1077

5 Reform   1085

PART IX   PRINCIPLES OF INSURANCE LAW

27 Insurance   1089

1 Introduction   1089

2 Formation of the contract   1091

3 Content and interpretation of the contract   1095

4 Liability of the insurer   1097

5 Rights of the insurer   1099

6 Marine insurance   1100

7 Insurance claims   1100

PART X   INSOLVENCY LAW

28 Insolvency   1105

1 Introduction   1105

2 The basic objectives of insolvency law   1106

3 The various definitions of insolvency   1108

4 Insolvency procedures   1109

Index   1139

ACKNOWLEDGEMENTS

Grateful acknowledgement is made to all the authors and publishers of copyright material which appears in this book, and in particular to the following for permission to reprint material from the sources indicated.

Extracts from *Law Commission Reports*, Committee Reports, and other government papers are Crown copyright material and are reproduced under Class Licence Number C2006010631 with the permission of the Controller of OPSI and the Queen's Printer.

Brill for extracts from Tony Weir: 'The Common Law System' in *International Encyclopedia of Comparative Law*, Vol II, ch 2, Part III.

Cambridge Law Journal for extracts from Kevin Gray: 'Property in Thin Air', CLJ 252 (1991).

Canadian Bar Association for extract from G H L Fridman: 'The Demise of Watteau v Fenwick: Sign-o-Lite Ltd v Metropolitan Life Insurance Co' 70 *Canadian Bar Review* 329 (1991).

Council for Law Reporting for New South Wales for extract from the *New South Wales Law Reports* (NSWLR): *Grey v Australian Motorists and General Insurance Co Pty Ltd* [1976] 1 NSWLR 669—reproduced with permission.

Incorporated Council of Law Reporting for extracts from the Law Reports: Appeal Cases (AC), Chancery Division (Ch), King's Bench Division (KB), Queen's Bench Division (QB), and Weekly Law Reports (WLR).

Informa Law for extracts from the *Lloyd's Law Reports* (LLR).

Israel Law Review Association and the author for extract from A Barak: 'The Nature of the Negotiable Instrument', 18 *Israel LR* 49 (1983).

John Wiley & Sons Ltd for extracts from *Modern Law Review*: FE Dowrick: 'The Relationship of Principal and Agent' (1954) 17 MLR 24; R Goode: 'The Codification of Commercial Law' (1988) 14 Mon LR 135; G Battersby and AD Preston: 'The Concepts of "Property", "Title" and "Owner" used in the Sale of Goods Act 1893' (1972) 35 MLR 268—reproduced with permission via PLSclear.

Oxford University Press for extracts from R Goode: 'Reflections on the Harmonization of Commercial Law' in R Cranston and R Goode (eds): *Commercial and Consumer Law— National and International Dimensions* (OUP, 1993); L Sealy and S Worthington: *Cases and Materials in Company Law* (11e, OUP, 2016); Kevin J Gray: *Elements of Land Law* (1e, 1987); and from *Oxford Journal of Legal Studies*: E P Ellinger: 'Bank's liability for paying fraudulently issued cheques', 5 OJLS 293 (1985).

RELX (UK) Ltd trading as LexisNexis for extracts from Law Reports: Butterworths Company Law Cases (BCLC) and All ER.

Thomson Reuters (Professional) Australia Limited for extracts from the Commonwealth Law Reports: *Norman v Federal Comr of Taxation* (1963) 109 CLR 9, High Court of Australia; *McRae v Commonwealth Disposals Commission* (1950) 84 CLR 377, High Court of Australia; *Equuscorp Pty Ltd v Haxton* (2012) 246 CLR 498, High Court of Australia- reproduced with permission.

Thomson Reuters (Professional) UK Limited for extracts from CM Schmitthoff: 'The Concept of Economic Law in England' [1966] JBL 309; 'Civil and Commercial Law: A Distinction Worth Making' 102 LQR 569; 'Equity's Place in the Law of Commerce' 114 LQR 214; 'Ownership and Obligation in Commercial Transactions' 103 LQR 433; *Re London Wine Co (Shippers) Ltd* [1986] PCC 121; *Wells v First National Commercial Bank* [1998] PNLR 552; R Goode: 'Commercial Law in an International Environment: Towards the Next Millennium' in R Goode: *Commercial Law in the Next Millennium* (1998); and Palmer: *Bailment* (2009)—reproduced with permission via PLSclear.

Every effort has been made to trace and contact copyright holders prior to publication but this has not been possible in every case. If notified, the publisher will undertake to rectify any errors or omissions at the earliest opportunity.

TABLE OF CASES

Page references printed in **bold** indicate where a case is set out.

Abbey National Building Society v Cann [1991] 1 AC 56;
[1990] 2 WLR 832; [1990] 1 All ER 1085...1073
Abbey National Plc v JSF Finance & Currency Exchange
Co Ltd [2006] EWCA Civ 328...**683**
Abbott v Condici Ltd [2005] 2 Lloyd's Rep 450...278
Aberdeen Railway Co v Blaikie Bros (1854) 1 Macq
461...**234**
ABN Amro Commercial Finance Plc v McGinn [2014]
EWHC 1674 (Comm)...844
Abou-Rahmah v Abacha [2005] EWHC 2662 (QB);
[2006] 1 All ER (Comm) 247...**608**
Abou-Rahmah v Abacha [2006] EWCA Civ 1492;
[2007] 1 All ER (Comm) 827; [2007] 1 Lloyd's Rep
115...**608**, 716
Adams, Re [2004] EWHC 2739 (QB)...**867–8**
Adams v Morgan & Co [1924] 1 KB 751...268
Adamson & Sons v Liverpool and London and Globe
Insurance Co Ltd [1953] 2 Lloyd's Rep 355...1101
Addison v Gandassequi (1812) 4 Taunt 574; 128 ER
454...176, 217
Advanced Technology Structures Ltd v Cray Valley
Products Ltd [1993] BCLC 723...874
AE Lindsay & Co Ltd v Cook [1953] 1 Lloyd's Rep
328...815
AEG (UK) v Lewis [1993] 2 Bank LR 119...677
Aegeon, The see Agapitos v Agnew (The
Aegeon) (No 1)
AerCap Partners 1 Ltd v Avia Asset Management
AB [2010] EWHC 2431 (Comm); [2010] 2 CLC
578...**480–1**
AG Securities v Vaughan [1990] 1 AC 417; [1988] 3
WLR 1205; [1988] 3 All ER 1058...952, 954
Agapitos v Agnew (The Aegeon) (No 1) [2002] EWCA
Civ 247; [2003] QB 556; [2002] 3 WLR 616...1101
Agip (Africa) Ltd v Jackson [1991] Ch 547; [1991] 3
WLR 116; [1992] 4 All ER 451...**718–25**
Agnew v Inland Revenue Commissioner [2001]
UKPC 28; [2001] 2 AC 710; [2001] 3 WLR 454
(PC)...956, **985–7**, 992, 997–1000, **1071–2**
Agra & Masterman's Bank ex p Asiatic Banking Corp,
Re (1867) LR 2 Ch App 391...774
AIB Finance Ltd v Debtors [1998] 2 All ER 929...1067
AIB Group (UK) Plc v Mark Redler & Co Solicitors
[2014] UKSC 58; [2015] AC 1503; [2014] 3 WLR
1367...31, 89–90
Aiden Shipping Co Ltd v Interbulk Ltd (The Vimeira) (No
2) [1986] AC 965; [1986] 2 WLR 1051; [1986] 2 All
ER 409...874
Aiken v Short (1856) 1 Hurl & N 210; 156 ER
1180...709
Aiken v Stewart Wrightson Members Agency Ltd [1995]
1 WLR 1281; [1995] 3 All ER 449...254
Aiolos, The see Central Insurance Co Ltd v Seacalf
Shipping Corp (The Aiolos)

Air Studios (Lyndhurst) Ltd (t/a Air Entertainment Group)
v Lombard North Central Plc [2012] EWHC 3162
(QB); [2013] 1 Lloyd's Rep 63...517, 522
Air Transworld Ltd v Bombardier Inc [2012] EWHC 243
(Comm); [2012] 2 All ER (Comm) 60...**450**
Akbar Khan v Attar Singh [1936] 2 All ER 545
(PC)...645, **760–1**
Aktor, The see PT Berlian Laju Tanker TBK v Nuse
Shipping Ltd (The Aktor)
A L Underwood Ltd v Bank of Liverpool and Martins
[1924] 1 KB 775...744, 746, 755
Alan Ramsay Sales & Marketing Ltd v Typhoo Tea Ltd
[2016] EWHC 486 (Comm); [2016] 4 WLR 59...278
Albazero, The see Owners of Cargo Laden on Board the
Albacruz v Owners of the Albazero
Albemarle Supply Co Ltd v Hind & Co [1928] 1 KB
307...1051–2, **1055–7**
Albright & Wilson UK Ltd v Biachem Ltd [2002] UKHL
37; [2002] 2 All ER (Comm) 753; [2003] 1 CLC
637...438
Aldridge v Johnson (1857) 7 El & Bl 885; 119 ER
1476...306, 313–14, 316, 352, 355
Alecos M, The see Sealace Shipping Co Ltd v
Oceanvoice Ltd (The Alecos M)
Alexander v Gardner (1835) 1 Bing NC 671; 131 ER
1276...346
Alfred C Toepfer v Continental Grain Co [1974] 1
Lloyd's Rep 11...451
Ali v Top Marques Car Rental Ltd [2006] EWHC 109
(Ch)...1081
Aliakmon, The see Leigh & Sillivan Ltd v Aliakmon
Shipping Co Ltd (The Aliakmon)
Allam & Co Ltd v Europa Poster Services Ltd [1968] 1
WLR 638; [1968] 1 All ER 826...251
Allen v Royal Bank of Canada (1925) 95 LJPC 17...629
Allen v Smith (1862) 12 CB NS 638; 142 ER
1293...1056
Alliance Bank Ltd v Broom (1864) 2 Drew & Sm 289; 62
ER 631...677
Allied Marine Transport v Vale do Rio Doce Navegacao
SA (The Leonidas D) [1985] 1 WLR 925; [1985] 2 All
ER 796...812
Allseas International Management v Panroy Bulk
Transport SA (The Star Gazer and The Star Delta)
[1985] 1 Lloyd's Rep 370...529
Alpha Trading Ltd v Dunnshaw-Patten [1981]
QB 290; [1981] 2 WLR 169; [1981] 1 All ER
482...265
Alternative Power Solution Ltd v Central Electricity
Board [2014] UKPC 31; [2015] 1 WLR 697; [2014] 4
All ER 882 (PC)...801
Aluminium Industrie Vaassen BV v Romalpa Aluminium
Ltd [1976] 1 WLR 676; [1976] 2 All ER 552...32,
115, 325, 328, 334, **498–500**, 502, 507, 514

AMB Generali Holding AG v SEB Trygg Liv Holding AB [2005] EWCA Civ 1327; [2006] 1 WLR 2276; [2006] 1 All ER 437...132, 136, 158, 197–8, 293

AMB Imballaggi Plastici Srl v Pacflex Ltd [1999] CLC 1391; 1999] 2 All ER (Comm) 249...115, 121

American Accord, The *see* United City Merchants (Investments) Ltd v Royal Bank of Canada (The American Accord)

American Cyanamid Co v Ethicon Ltd (No 1) [1975] AC 396; [1975] 2 WLR 316; [1975] 1 All ER 504...801

Anangel Atlas Compañia Naviera SA v Ishikawajima-Harima Heavy Industries Co (No 1) [1990] 1 Lloyd's Rep 167...243–4

Anchor Line (Henderson Bros) Ltd, Re [1937] Ch 483; [1937] 2 All ER 823...338

Ancona v Marks (1862) 7 Hurl & N 686; 158 ER 645...163

Andrabell Ltd, Re [1984] 3 All ER 407...504–5

Andrews v Ramsay & Co [1903] 2 KB 635...245

Angara Maritime Ltd v OceanConnect UK Ltd [2010] EWHC 619 (QB); [2011] 1 Lloyd's Rep 61...417, 512

Anglo African Shipping Co of New York Inc v J Mortner Ltd [1962] 1 Lloyd's Rep 610...118

Annangel Glory Compañia Naviera SA v M Golodetz Ltd (The Annangel Glory) [1988] 1 Lloyd's Rep 45...1021

Annangel Glory, The *see* Annangel Glory Compañia Naviera SA v M Golodetz Ltd (The Annangel Glory)

Anns v Merton LBC [1978] AC 728; [1977] 2 WLR 1024; [1977] 2 All ER 492...229, 599

Anstyanax, The *see* Panagiotis Stravelakis v Rocco Guiseppe and Figli SNC (The Astyanax)

Antaios Compañia Naviera SA v Salen Rederierna AB (The Antaios) [1985] AC 191; [1984] 3 WLR 592; [1984] 3 All ER 229...21

Appleton v Binks (1804) 5 East 148; 102 ER 1025...190

Arab Bank Ltd v Ross [1952] 2 QB 216; [1952] 1 All ER 709...681, **684–6**

Arbuthnot v Norton (1846) 5 Moo PC 219 (PC); 13 ER 474...869

Archer v Stone (1898) 78 LT 34...207, 213

Architects of Wine Ltd (In Liquidation) v Barclays Bank Plc [2007] EWCA Civ 239; [2007] 2 All ER (Comm) 285; [2007] 2 Lloyd's Rep 471...**752–7**

Archivent Sales & Development Ltd v Strathclyde Regional Council 1985 SLT 154; 27 BLR 98...417, 512

Arcos Ltd v EA Ronaasen & Son [1933] AC 470...**427–8**, 429–30, 432

Arctic Shipping Co Ltd v Mobilia AB (The Tatra) [1990] 2 Lloyd's Rep 51...145

Argo Fund Ltd v Essar Steel Ltd [2006] EWCA Civ 241; [2006] 2 All ER (Comm) 104; [2006] 2 Lloyd's Rep 134...885

Argos, The (1873) LR 5 PC 134...154

Armagas Ltd v Mundogas SA (The Ocean Frost) [1985] 3 WLR 640; [1985] 3 All ER 795...174

Armagas Ltd v Mundogas SA (The Ocean Frost) [1986] AC 717; [1986] 2 WLR 1063; [1986] 2 All ER 385; [1985] 1 Lloyd's Rep 1...116, 136, 138, 140, 142–3, 146, 245

Armagh Shoes Ltd, Re [1984] BCLC 405...1072

Armitage v Nurse [1998] Ch 241; [1997] 3 WLR 1046; [1997] 2 All ER 705...32, 232

Armory v Delamirie (1722) 1 Str 505; 93 ER 664...73–4

Armour v Thyssen Edelstahlwerke AG [1991] 2 AC 339; [1990] 3 WLR 810; [1990] 3 All ER 481...1015

Armstrong DLW GmbH v Winnington Networks Ltd [2012] EWHC 10 (Ch); [2013] Ch 156; [2012] 3 WLR 835...55–6, **87–8**

Armstrong v Jackson [1917] 2 KB 822...**233–4**

Armstrong v Stokes (1872) LR 7 QB 598...172–3, 201, **221–2**

Armstrong v Strain [1952] 1 KB 232; [1952] 1 All ER 139; [1952] 1 TLR 82...175

Arnhold Karberg & Co v Blythe Green Jourdain & Co [1916] 1 KB 495...547, 549

Arnold v Britton [2015] UKSC 36; [2015] AC 1619; [2015] 2 WLR 1593...22

Arpad, The (No 2) [1934] P 189...522

Asfar & Co v Blundell [1896] 1 QB 123...369

Ashby v Tolhurst [1937] 2 KB 242; [1937] 2 All ER 837...94

Ashford Shire Council v Dependable Motors Pty Ltd [1961] AC 336; [1960] 3 WLR 999; [1961] 1 All ER 96 (PC)...129

Ashington Piggeries Ltd v Christopher Hill Ltd [1972] AC 441; [1971] 2 WLR 1051; [1971] 1 All ER 847...432-4, 661

Asian v Murphy [1990] 1 WLR 766; [1989] 3 All ER 130...954

Astley Industrial Trust Ltd v Miller [1968] 2 All ER 36...**399–400**, 1033

Aston FFI (Suisse) SA v Louis Dreyfus Commodities Suisse SA [2015] EWHC 80 (Comm); [2015] 1 All ER (Comm) 985; [2015] 1 Lloyd's Rep 413...538

Astro Amo Compañia Naviera SA v Elf Union SA and First National City Bank (The Zographia M) [1976] 2 Lloyd's Rep 382...611

Astro Exito Navegacion SA v Southland Enterprise Co (The Messiniaki Tolmi) (No 2) [1983] 2 AC 787; [1983] 3 WLR 130; [1983] 2 All ER 725...483

Aswan Engineering Establishment Co v Lupdine Ltd [1987] 1 WLR 1; [1987] 1 All ER 135...446

Atari Corp (UK) Ltd v Electronics Boutique Stores (UK) Ltd [1998] QB 539; [1998] 2 WLR 66; [1998] 1 All ER 1010...92, 350

Athenaeum Life Assurance Society v Pooley *see* Official Manager of the Athenaeum Life Assurance Society v Pooley

Atkinson v Cotesworth (1825) 3 B & C 647; 107 ER 873...223

Atlantic Computer Systems Plc, Re [1992] Ch 505; [1992] 2 WLR 367; [1992] 1 All ER 476...1012

Attorney General v Blake [2001] 1 AC 268; [2000] 3 WLR 625; [2000] 4 All ER 385...241

Attorney General of Belize v Belize Telecom Ltd [2009] UKPC 10; [2009] 1 WLR 1988; [2009] 2 All ER 1127 (PC)...258

Attorney General of Hong Kong v Nai-Keung (Daniel Chan) [1987] 1 WLR 1339 (PC)...565–6

Attorney General of Hong Kong v Reid [1994] 1 AC 324; [1993] 3 WLR 1143; [1994] 1 All ER 1 (PC)...114, 240–1, **246–7**, 255

Attorney-General for Ceylon v Silva [1953] 1 Lloyd's Rep 563; [1953] AC 461 (PC)...138–9

Australian Mutual Provident Society v Derham (1979) 39 FLR 165...740

Autobiography Ltd v Byrne [2005] EWHC 213 (Ch)...678

Automatic Bottle Makers Ltd, Re [1926] Ch 412...1072

AVX Ltd v EGM Solders Ltd Times 7 July 1982...95

Awilco of Oslo A/S v Fulvia SpA di Navigazione of Cagliari (The Chikuma) [1981] 1 WLR 314; [1981] 1 All ER 652...564, 612

Ayala Holdings Ltd (No 2), Re [1996] 1 BCLC 467...886

Ayr Harbour Trustees v Oswald (1883) 8 App Cas 623...34

B Johnson & Co (Builders) Ltd, Re [1955] Ch 634; [1955] 3 WLR 269; [1955] 2 All ER 775...1118–20

B Liggett (Liverpool) Ltd v Barclays Bank Ltd [1928] 1 KB 48...736, 759

Babcock v Lawson (1880) 5 QBD 284...1033–4

Bailey v Angove's Pty Ltd [2016] UKSC 47; [2016] 1 WLR 3179...33, **272–5**

Bain v Fothergill (1874) LR 7 HL 158...305

Baines v National Provincial Bank Ltd (927) 96 LJKB 801...740

Baird Textiles Holdings Ltd v Marks and Spencer plc [2001] EWCA Civ 274; [2002] 1 All ER (Comm) 737; [2001] CLC 999...**146**

Baker v JE Clark & Co (Transport) UK Ltd [2006] EWCA Civ 464; [2006] Pens LR 131...232

Balfour v Official Manager of Sea Fire Life Assurance Company (1857) 3 CB NS 300; 140 ER 756...865

Ball v Dunsterville (1791) 4 Term Rep 313; 100 ER 1038...126

Balmoral Group Ltd v Borealis (UK) Ltd [2006] EWHC 1900 (Comm); [2006] 2 Lloyd's Rep 629...437

Balsamo v Medici [1984] 1 WLR 951; [1984] 2 All ER 304...255

Banco Central SA v Lingoss & Falce Ltd (The Raven) [1980] 2 Lloyd's Rep 266...947

Banco Santander SA v Bayfern Ltd [2000] 1 All ER (Comm) 776...774

Bank of America v Arnell [1999] Lloyd's Rep Bank 399...723, 725

Bank of Baroda v Vysya Bank Ltd [1994] 2 Lloyd's Rep 87...771, 823, **833–8**

Bank of Credit & Commerce Hong Kong Ltd (In Liquidation) v Sonali Bank [1995] 1 Lloyd's Rep 227...771

Bank of Credit and Commerce International (Overseas) Ltd v Akindele [2001] Ch 437; [2000] 3 WLR 1423...90

Bank of Credit and Commerce International SA (In Liquidation) v Ali (No 1) [2001] UKHL 8; [2002] 1 AC 251; [2001] 2 WLR 735...1095

Bank of Credit and Commerce International SA (No 8), Re [1998] AC 214; [1997] 4 All ER 568; [1996] Ch 245...9, 65, **972–5**, 984, **1069**

Bank of England v Vagliano Bros [1891] AC 107...298, **660**, **667–9**, 686, 698, 739

Bank of India v Morris [2005] EWCA Civ 693; [2005] BCC 739...1134

Bank Mellat v HM Treasury [2013] UKSC 39; [2014] AC 700; [2013] 3 WLR 179...35

Bank Melli Iran v Barclays Bank (Dominion Colonial & Overseas) [1951] 2 Lloyd's Rep 367...780, **823**

Bank of Montreal v Dominion Gresham Guarantee and Casualty Co Ltd [1930] AC 659 (PC)...759

Bank of Montreal v Exhibit and Trading Co (1906) 11 Com Cas 250...686

Bank Negara Indonesia 1946 v Lariza (Singapore) Pte Ltd [1988] AC 583; [1988] 2 WLR 374 (PC)...777

Bank of Nova Scotia v Hellenic Mutual War Risk Association (Bermuda) Ltd (The Good Luck) [1992] 1 AC 233; [1991] 2 WLR 1279; [1991] 3 All ER 1...1095

Bank Russo Iran v Gordon Woodroffe & Co (1972) 116 SJ 921...831, 845

Bank of Scotland v Alfred Truman (A Firm) [2005] EWHC 583 (QB); [2005] CCLR 3...641

Bank of Scotland Plc v Targetfollow Properties Holdings Ltd [2010] EWHC 3606 (Ch); [2013] BCC 817...**1114–15**

Bank Tejarat v Hong Kong and Shanghai Banking Corp (CI) Ltd [1995] 1 Lloyd's Rep 239...724

Bankers Trust Co v State Bank of India [1991] 2 Lloyd's Rep 443...826

Bankes v Jarvis [1903] 1 KB 549; [1903] All ER Rep 656...945

Bankway Properties Ltd v Penfold-Dunsford [2001] EWCA Civ 528; [2001] 1 WLR 1369...955

Banque Belge pour l'Etranger v Hambrouck [1921] 1 KB 321...**721–3**

Banque de l'Indochine et de Suez SA v JH Rayner (Mincing Lane) Ltd [1983] QB 711; [1983] 2 WLR 841; [1983] 1 All ER 1137...784, **828–30**

Banque Financière de la Cite SA (formerly Banque Keyser Ullmann SA) v Westgate Insurance Co (formerly Hodge General & Mercantile Co Ltd) [1991] 2 AC 249; [1990] 3 WLR 364; [1990] 2 All ER 947...1093

Banque Saudi Fransi v Lear Siegler Services Inc [2006] EWCA Civ 1130; [2007] 1 All ER (Comm) 67...852

Barbados Trust Co Ltd (formerly CI Trustees (Asia Pacific) Ltd) v Bank of Zambia [2007] EWCA Civ 148; [2007] 2 All ER (Comm) 444; [2007] 1 Lloyd's Rep 495...61, 884–5, 887, **891–900**

Barber v Meyerstein (1870) LR 4 HL 317...536, 1028

Barber v NWS Bank plc [1996] 1 WLR 641; [1996] 1 All ER 906...461

Barclays Bank Ltd v Aschaffenburger Zellstoffwerke AG [1967] 1 Lloyd's Rep 387...**689**, 769

Barclays Bank Ltd v Astley Industrial Trust Ltd [1970] 2 QB 527; [1970] 2 WLR 876; [1970] 1 All ER 719...688, **751**, 769

Barclays Bank Ltd v Quistclose Investments Ltd [1970] AC 567; [1968] 3 WLR 1097...32, 89–90, **1126–7**

Barclays Bank Ltd v WJ Simms Son & Cooke (Southern) Ltd [1980] QB 677; [1980] 2 WLR 218; [1979] 3 All ER 522...**708–14**, 717

Barclays Bank Plc v Bank of England [1985] 1 All ER 385; [1985] FLR 209...581, 590, 595, 611, **730–3**

Barclays Bank Plc v Stuart Landon Ltd [2001] EWCA Civ 140...1081

Barclays Mercantile Business Finance Ltd v Mawson (Inspector of Taxes) [2004] UKHL 51; [2005] 1 AC 684; [2004] 3 WLR 1383; [2005] 1 All ER 97...956

Barclays Mercantile Business Finance Ltd v Sibec Developments Ltd [1992] 1 WLR 1253; [1993] 2 All ER 195...83

Baring v Corrie (1818) 2 B & Ald 137; 106 ER
    317...117, 218–19, 1048
Barker v Greenwood; (1837) 2 Y & C Ex 414; 160 ER
    458...174
Barker v Stickney [1919] 1 KB 121...55
Barn Crown Ltd, Re [1995] 1 WLR 147; [1994] 2 BCLC
    186...1129
Barr v Gibson (1838) 3 M & W 390; 150 ER 1196...371
Barratt v Davies [1996] 2 Lloyd's Rep 1...1100
Barrett McKenzie & Co Ltd v Escada (UK) Ltd [2001]
    ECC 50; [2001] Eu LR 567...284
Barrett v Deere (1828) Mood & M 200; 173 ER
    1131...135
Barron v Fitzgerald (1840) 6 Bing NC 201; 133
    ER 79...269
Barros Mattos Junior v MacDaniels Ltd [2004] EWHC
    1188 (Ch); [2005] 1 WLR 247; [2004] 3 All ER
    299...716
Barrow, Lane & Ballard Ltd v Phillip Phillips & Co [1929]
    1 KB 574...**368–9**, 372
Barry v Heathcote Ball & Co (Commercial Auctions) Ltd
    [2000] 1 WLR 1962; [2001] 1 All ER 944...181
Bassano v Toft [2014] EWHC 377 (QB); [2014] ECC
    14...51, 664, **1033–4**, 1084
Bastone & Firminger Ltd v Nasima Enterprises (Nigeria)
    Ltd [1996] CLC 1902...768
Batra v Ebrahim [1982] 2 Lloyd's Rep 11n...803
Bavins & Sims v London & South Western Bank Ltd
    [1900] 1 QB 270...81, 735
Bawejem Ltd v MC Fabrications Ltd [1999] 1 All ER
    (Comm) 377...935–6
Bayerische Vereinsbank AG v National Bank of Pakistan
    [1997] 1 Lloyd's Rep 59...816, 826–7
Beale v Taylor [1967] 1 WLR 1193; [1967] 3 All ER
    253...425, 431
Bechuanaland Exploration Co v London Trading Bank
    Ltd [1898] 2 QB 658...654
Becket, Re [1918] 2 Ch 72...256
Bedford Insurance Co Ltd v Instituto de Resseguros do
    Brasil [1985] QB 966; [1984] 3 WLR 726; [1984] 3 All
    ER 766...163, 165
Behn v Burness (1863) 3 B & S 751; 122 ER 281...428
Behnke v Bede Shipping Co Ltd [1927] 1 KB 649...529
Behrend & Co Ltd v Produce Brokers Co Ltd [1920] 3 KB
    530...**465**, 527
Belding v Read (1865) 3 Hurl & C 955; 159 ER
    812...962–3
Bell Electrical Ltd v Aweco Appliance Systems GmbH
    & Co KG [2002] EWHC 872 (QB); [2002] CLC
    1246...120, **278–9**
Bellamy v Marjoribanks (1852) 7 Ex 389; 155 ER
    999...729
Belmont Park Investments Pty Ltd v BNY Corporate
    Trustee Services Ltd [2011] UKSC 38; [2012] 1
    AC 383...10
Bem Dis A Turk Ticaret S/A TR v International Agri Trade
    Co Ltd (The Selda) [1999] 1 All ER (Comm) 619...480
Bence Graphics International Ltd v Fasson UK Ltd [1998]
    QB 87; [1997] 3 WLR 205; [1997] 1 All ER 979...525
Bence v Shearman [1898] 2 Ch 582...913
Benjamin Cope & Sons Ltd, Re [1914] 1 Ch 800...1072
Bennett v Cooper (1846) 9 Beav 252; 50 ER 340...963
Bentley v Craven (1853) 18 Beav 75; 52 ER 29...234–5

Bentley v Gaisford [1997] QB 627; [1997] 2 WLR 401;
    [1997] 1 All ER 842...1048
Benton v Campbell, Parker & Co Ltd [1925] 2 KB
    410...189, 192
Berger v Gill & Duffus [1984] AC 382; [1984] 2 WLR 95;
    [1984] 1 All ER 438...545, 552
Berkeley v Hardy (1826) 5 B & C 355; 108 ER 132...126
Bernal v Pim (1835) 1 Gale 17...1043
Beverley Acceptances Ltd v Oakley [1982] RTR
    417...401
BG Global Energy Ltd (formerly BG International (NSW)
    Ltd) v Talisman Sinopec Energy UK Ltd (formerly
    Talisman Energy (UK) Ltd) [2015] EWHC 110
    (Comm)...885
Bhoja Trader, The *see* Intraco Ltd v Notis Shipping Corp
    of Liberia (The Bhoja Trader)
Bibby Factors Northwest Ltd v HFD Ltd [2015] EWCA
    Civ 1908; [2016] 1 Lloyd's Rep 517...944
Bickerton v Burrell (1816) 5 M & S 383; 105 ER
    1091...192–3
Biddell Bros v E Clemens Horst Co [1911] 1 KB
    214...549
Biggerstaff v Rowatt's Wharf Ltd [1896] 2 Ch
    93...944, 1074
Bilbie v Lumley (1802) 2 East 469; 102 ER 448...713
Bim Kemi AB v Blackburn Chemicals Ltd (No 1) [2001]
    EWCA Civ 457; [2001] 2 Lloyd's Rep 93...946
Bird v Brown (1850) 4 Ex 786; 154 ER 1433...164, 166
Bird & Co (London) Ltd v Thomas Cook & Son Ltd
    [1937] 2 All ER 227...685
Bishopsgate Investment Management Ltd (In
    Liquidation) v Homan [1995] Ch 211; [1994] 3 WLR
    1270; [1995] 1 All ER 347...724
Bishopsgate Motor Finance Corp Ltd v Transport Brakes
    Ltd [1949] 1 KB 322; [1949] 1 All ER 37...**383–4**
Bissell & Co v Fox Bros Co (1885) 53 LT 193...739
Blackburn Bobbin Co Ltd v TW Allen & Sons Ltd [1918]
    2 KB 467...**377–8**
Blackburn v Scholes (1810) 2 Camp 341; 170 ER
    1177...274
Blakely Ordnance Co, Re (1867) LR 3 Ch App 154...947
Blankenstein, The *see* Damon Compañía Naviera SA v
    Hapag-Lloyd International SA (The Blankenstein)
Blankley v Central Manchester and Manchester
    Children's University Hospitals NHS Trust [2015]
    EWCA Civ 18; [2015] 1 WLR 4307; [2016] 3 All ER
    382...**290–2**
Blue Sky One Ltd v Blue Airways LLC [2009] EWHC
    3314 (Comm)...82
Blyth Shipbuilding & Dry Docks Co Ltd, Re (No 3) [1926]
    Ch 494...328, 338, 359
Boardman v Phipps [1967] 2 AC 46; [1966] 3 WLR
    1009; [1966] 3 All ER 721...108, 231, 234,
    236, 240–1
Bobbett v Pinkett (1876) 1 Ex D 368...729
Bolivinter Oil SA v Chase Manhattan Bank NA [1984] 1
    WLR 392; [1984] 1 All ER 351; [1984] 1 Lloyd's Rep
    251...**800**, 851
Bolkiah v KPMG [1999] 2 AC 222; [1999] 2 WLR 215;
    [1999] 1 All ER 517...**239**
Bolt & Nut Co (Tipton) Ltd v Rowlands Nicholls & Co Ltd
    [1964] 2 QB 10; [1964] 2 WLR 98; [1964] 1 All ER
    137...629

Bolton Partners v Lambert (1889) 41 Ch D 295...**163–7**

Bominflot Bunkergesellschaft für Mineralole mbH &
   Co KG v Petroplus Marketing AG (The Mercini Lady)
   [2010] EWCA Civ 1145; [2011] 2 All ER (Comm)
   522; [2010] 2 CLC 637...**439, 451–2**

Bominflot Bunkergesellschaft für Mineralole mbH &
   Co KG v Petroplus Marketing AG (The Mercini Lady)
   [2012] EWHC 3009 (Comm); [2013] 1 All ER (Comm)
   610; [2013] 1 Lloyd's Rep 360...362

Bond v Barrow Haematite Steel Co [1902] 1 Ch
   353...867

Bond Worth Ltd, Re [1980] Ch 228; [1979] 3 WLR 629;
   [1979] 3 All ER 919...**500–1, 505–8**, 1043, 1069

Bondina Ltd v Rollaway Shower Blinds Ltd [1986] 1 WLR
   517; [1986] 1 All ER 564...**693–4**

Bonita, & The Charlotte (1861) Lush 252; 167 ER
   111...158

Booth Steamship Co Ltd v Cargo Fleet Iron Co Ltd
   [1916] 2 KB 570...491

Borag, The see Compañía Financiera Soleada SA v
   Hamoor Tanker Corp Inc (The Borag)

Borden (UK) Ltd v Scottish Timber Products Ltd [1981]
   Ch 25; [1979] 3 WLR 672; [1979] 3 All ER 961...337,
   502–4, **508–9, 514**

Borealis AB (formerly Borealis Petrokemi AB and Statoil
   Petrokemi AB) v Stargas Ltd (The Berge Sisar)
   [2001] UKHL 17; [2002] 2 AC 205; [2001] 2 WLR
   1118...78, 537

Borrowman Phillips & Co v Free & Hollis (1878) 4 QBD
   500...**466–7**

Boscawen v Bajwa [1996] 1 WLR 328; [1995] 4 All ER
   769...718

Boston Deep Sea Fishing and Ice Co v Ansell (1888) 39
   Ch D 339...**241–3**, 266, 275

Boston Deep Sea Fishing and Ice Co v Farnham [1957] 1
   WLR 1051; [1957] 3 All ER 204...162

Bourne v Colodense [1985] ICR 291...874

Bovis International Inc (formerly L/M International
   Construction Inc) v Circle Ltd Partnership (1995) 49
   Con LR 12...905

Bowes v Shand [1967] 1 WLR 1193; [1967] 3 All ER 253
   (1877) 2 App Cas 455...**426–7, 429–30**, 458

Bowmaker Ltd v Wycombe Motors Ltd [1946] KB 505;
   [1946] 2 All ER 113...1049, 1051–3

Bowmakers Ltd v Barnet Instruments Ltd [1945] KB 65;
   [1944] 2 All ER 579...805

Box v Barclays Bank plc [1998] Lloyd's Rep Bank
   185...725

Boyter v Thomson [1995] 2 AC 628; [1995] 3 WLR 36;
   [1995] 3 All ER 135...203, 435–6

Bradford Advance Co Ltd v Ayers [1924] WN
   152...1084

Braithwaite v Thomas Cook Travellers Cheques
   [1989] QB 553; [1989] 3 WLR 213; [1989] 1 All ER
   235...763

Bramhill v Edwards [2004] EWCA Civ 403; [2004] 2
   Lloyd's Rep 653...437

Brandao v Barnett (1846) 3 CB 519; (1846) 12 Cl & F; 8
   ER 1622 787...653, 1048

Brandeis Brokers Ltd v Black [2001] 2 All ER (Comm)
   980; [2001] 2 Lloyd's Rep 359...231–2

Branwhite v Worcester Works Finance Ltd [1969] 1 AC
   552; [1968] 3 WLR 760; [1968] 3 All ER 104...**108**

Braymist Ltd v Wise Finance Co Ltd [2002] EWCA Civ
   127; [2002] Ch 273; [2002] 3 WLR 322...161, 191–2

Brazil v Durant International Corp [2015] UKPC 35;
   [2016] AC 297; [2015] 3 WLR 599 (PC)...724, 726

Brebner v Henderson 1925 SC 643; 1925 SLT 473...185

Bremer Vulkan Schiffbau und Maschinenfabrik v South
   India Shipping Corp Ltd [1981] AC 909; [1981] 2
   WLR 141; [1981] 1 All ER 289...13

Brennan v Bolt Burden [2004] EWCA Civ 1017; [2005]
   QB 303; [2004] 3 WLR 1321...198

Brian Cooper & Co v Fairview Estates (Investments)
   [1987] 1 EGLR 18...261

Brice v Bannister (1878) 3 QBD 569...866, 904, 913

Bridges & Salmon Ltd v Owner of The Swan (The Swan)
   [1968] 1 Lloyd's Rep 5...**185–8**

Brightlife Ltd, Re [1987] Ch 200; [1987] 2 WLR 197;
   [1986] 3 All ER 673...984, 992, 996–8, 1076

Brimnes, The see Tenax Steamship Co v Owners of the
   Motor Vessel Brimnes (The Brimnes)

Bristol & West Building Society v Mothew (t/a Stapley &
   Co) [1998] Ch 1; [1997] 2 WLR 436; [1996] 4 All ER
   698...**230**, 238

Bristol & West Plc v Bartlett [2002] EWCA Civ 1181;
   [2003] 1 WLR 284; [2002] 4 All ER 544...1067

Bristol Airport Plc v Powdrill [1990] Ch 744; [1990]
   2 WLR 1362; [1990] 2 All ER 493...66, **1014,
   1041, 1054**

Bristol Tramways Carriage Co Ltd v Fiat Motors Ltd
   [1910] 2 KB 831...436, 442

British Bank of the Middle East v Sun Life Assurance Co
   of Canada (UK) [1983] 2 Lloyd's Rep 9...138–40

British Eagle International Airlines Ltd v Compagnie
   Nationale Air France [1975] 1 WLR 758; [1975] 2 All
   ER 390...**1107–8**

British Energy Power & Energy Trading Ltd v Credit
   Suisse [2007] EWHC 1428 (Comm); [2007] 2 Lloyd's
   Rep 427...884

British Motor Trade Association v Salvadori [1949] Ch
   556; [1949] 1 All ER 208...64

British and North European Bank Ltd v Zalzstein [1927]
   2 KB 92...616

British Thomson-Houston Co Ltd v Federated European
   Bank Ltd [1932] 2 KB 176...130, 138

Britten Norman Ltd (In Liquidation) v State Ownership
   Fund of Romania [2000] Lloyd's Rep Bank
   315...802, 852

Britvic Soft Drinks Ltd v Messer UK Ltd [2002] EWCA Civ
   548; [2002] 2 All ER (Comm) 321; [2002] 2 Lloyd's
   Rep 326...303, 437, 447, 526

Brogden v Metropolitan Railway Co (1877) 2 App Cas
   666...159

Brook v Hook (1871) LR 6 Ex 89...163, 696, 698

Browne v Hare (1859) 4 Hurl & N 822; 157 ER
   1067...356, 538

Browning v Provincial Insurance Co of Canada (1873) LR
   5 PC 263...217–18

Brownton Ltd v Edward Moore Inbucom Ltd [1985] 3
   All ER 499...874

Brumark Investments Ltd, Re [2001] UKPC 28; [2001] 2
   AC 710; [2001] 3 WLR 454 (PC)...985

Brush Aggregates Ltd, Re (1983) 1 BCC 98904; [1983]
   BCLC 320...984

Bryant v Flight (1839) 5 M & W 114; 151 ER 49...257

BS Brown & Sons Ltd v Craiks Ltd [1970] 1 WLR 752;
   [1970] 1 All ER 823…436–7
BSS Group Plc v Makers (UK) Ltd (t/a Allied Services)
   [2011] EWCA Civ 809; [2011] TCLR 7…442–4
Buchler v Talbot [2004] UKHL 9; [2004] 2 AC
   298…1013, 1074
Budberg v Jerwood (1934) 51 TLR 99…396
Bulfied v Foamier (1895) 11 TLR 282…245
Bulgrains & Co Ltd v Shinhan Bank [2013] EWHC 2498
   (QB)…781, 826
Bullen v Swan Electric Engraving Co (1906) 22 TLR
   275…364
Buller v Harrison (1777) 2 Cowp 565; 98 ER 1243…716
Bunge Corp v Vegetable Vitamin Foods (Pte) Ltd [1985]
   1 Lloyd's Rep 613…779, 815
Bunge SA v Nidera BV (formerly Nidera
   Handelscompagnie BV) [2013] EWCA Civ 1628;
   [2014] 1 Lloyd's Rep 404…379
Bunge SA v Nidera BV (formerly Nidera
   Handelscompagnie BV) [2015] UKSC 43; [2015] 3 All
   ER 1082…379, 482, 515–16, 520–2
Burlinson v Hall (1884) 12 QBD 347…905–6
Burnside v Dayrell (1849) 3 Ex 224; 154 ER 825…126
Business Computers Ltd v Anglo-African Leasing Ltd
   [1977] 1 WLR 578; [1977] 2 All ER 741…514, 944–6
Butterworth v Kingsway Motors [1954] 1 WLR 1286;
   [1954] 2 All ER 694…460
Butwick v Grant [1924] 2 KB 483…174

C Sharpe & Co Ltd v Nosawa & Co [1917] 2 KB
   814…517
Cadogan Petroleum Plc v Tolley [2011] EWHC 2286
   (Ch); [2015] WTLR 1505…247
Cahn v Pockett's Bristol Channel Steam Packet Co Ltd
   [1899] 1 QB 643…768
Caja de Ahorros del Mediterraneo v Gold Coast Ltd
   [2001] EWCA Civ 1806; [2002] 1 All ER (Comm)
   142; [2002] CLC 397…843
Caldicott ex p *see* Hart ex p Caldicott, Re
Calico Printers' Association Ltd v Barclays Bank Ltd
   (1931) 39 Ll L Rep 51…252–4, 588, 768
Camdex International Ltd v Bank of Zambia (No 1)
   [1998] QB 22; [1996] 3 WLR 759; [1996] 3 All ER
   431…870, 874
Cammell Laird & Co Ltd v Manganese Bronze & Brass
   Co Ltd [1934] AC 402…442–3
Campanari v Woodburn (1854) 15 CB 400; 139 ER
   480…270–1, 293, 610
Campbell v Mirror Group Newspapers Ltd [2004] UKHL
   22; [2004] 2 AC 457; [2004] 2 WLR 1232…35
Campden Hill Ltd v Chakrani [2005] EWHC 911 (Ch);
   [2005] NPC 65…714
Caparo Industries Plc v Dickman [1990] 2 AC 605;
   [1990] 2 WLR 358; [1990] 1 All ER 568…600–1
Cape Asbestos Co Ltd v Lloyds Bank Ltd [1921] WN
   274…775
Capital and Counties Bank Ltd v Gordon [1903] AC
   240…734, 738–40, 752
Capital Fire Insurance Association, Re (1883) 24 Ch D
   408…1049
Car & Universal Finance Co Ltd v Caldwell [1965]
   1 QB 525; [1964] 2 WLR 600; [1964] 1 All ER
   290…407, 414

Cardinal Financial Investment Corp v Central Bank of
   Yemen (No 1) [2001] Lloyd's Rep Bank 1…762
Cargill International SA v Bangladesh Sugar & Food
   Industries Corp [1996] 4 All ER 563; [1996] 2 Lloyd's
   Rep 524…848–51, 853
Carlos v Fancourt (1794) 5 Term Rep 482; 101 ER
   272…645
Carlos Federspiel & Co SA v Charles Twigg & Co Ltd
   [1957] 1 Lloyd's Rep 240…351, 354–6, 539
Carlos Soto SAU v AP Moller-Maersk AS [2015] EWHC
   458 (Comm); [2015] 2 All ER (Comm) 382; [2015] 1
   Lloyd's Rep 537…416, 546
Carmichael's Case *see* Hannan's Empress Gold Mining
   and Development Co, Re
Carpenters Co v British Mutual Banking Co Ltd [1938] 1
   KB 511; [1937] 3 All ER 811…737–40, 758
Carreras Rothmans Ltd v Freeman Mathews Treasure Ltd
   (In Liquidation) [1985] Ch 207; [1984] 3 WLR 1016;
   [1985] 1 All ER 155…1069, 1127
Carter v Wake (1877) 4 Ch D 605…1028, 1039
Carter Commercial Developments Ltd, Re [2002] BCC
   803; [2002] BPIR 1053…1054
Castellain v Preston (1883) 11 QBD 380…1098–9
Castle v Playford (1872) LR 7 Ex 98…346–7, 377, 554
Caterpillar Motoren GmbH & Co KG v Mutual Benefits
   Assurance Co [2015] EWHC 2304 (Comm); [2016] 2
   All ER (Comm) 322…844
Catlin v Bell (1815) 4 Camp 183; 171 ER 59…252
Cebora SNC v SIP (Industrial Products) [1976] 1 Lloyd's
   Rep 271…656, 688–9
Cehave NV v Bremer Handelsgesellschaft mbH (The
   Hansa Nord) [1976] QB 44; [1975] 3 WLR 447;
   [1975] 3 All ER 739…423, 428, 466
Celtic Extraction Ltd (In Liquidation), Re [2001] Ch 475;
   [2000] 2 WLR 991; [1999] 4 All ER 684…61
Central Estates (Belgravia) Ltd v Woolgar (No 2) [1972]
   1 WLR 1048; [1972] 3 All ER 610…607
Central Insurance Co Ltd v Seacalf Shipping Corp (The
   Aiolos) [1983] 2 Lloyd's Rep 25…933
Central Newbury Car Auctions Ltd v Unity Finance Ltd
   [1957] 1 QB 371; [1956] 3 WLR 1068; [1956] 3 All
   ER 905…388–90, 392
CEP Holdings Ltd v Steni AS [2009] EWHC 2447
   (QB)…885
Chabbra Corp Pte Ltd v Owners of the Jag Shakti (The
   Jag Shakti) [1986] AC 337; [1986] 2 WLR 87; [1986]
   1 All ER 480 (PC)…74
Chaigley Farms Ltd v Crawford Kaye & Grayshire Ltd (t/a
   Leylands) [1996] BCC 957…505
Chamberlain v Young and Tower [1893] 2 QB
   206…664–5
Chapleo v Brunswick Permanent Building Society (No
   2) (1881) 6 QBD 696…143, 198
Chapman (t/a Chapman & Co Solicitors) v Wilson
   [2010] EWHC 1746 (Ch)…1079
Chappell v Bray (1860) 6 Hurl & N 145; 158 ER 60…275
Chappell v Somers & Blake [2003] EWHC 1644 (Ch);
   [2004] Ch 19; [2003] 3 WLR 1233…90
Charge Card Services Ltd, Re [1987] Ch 150; (1986) 2
   BCC 99371…316, 632–3, 968–75
Charge Card Services Ltd (No 2), Re [1989] Ch 497;
   [1988] 3 WLR 764; [1988] 3 All ER 702…627–32,
   658, 816

Charles v Blackwell (1877) 2 CPD 151...734–5

Chartbrook Ltd v Persimmon Homes Ltd [2009] UKHL 38...21

Charter v Sullivan [1957] 2 QB 117; [1957] 2 WLR 528; [1957] 1 All ER 809...480, 482

Chase Manhattan Bank NA v Israel-British Bank (London) Ltd [1981] Ch 105; [1980] 2 WLR 202; [1979] 3 All ER 1025...725–6, 1127

Chasen Ryder & Co v Hedges [1993] 08 EG 119; [1993] NPC 6...261

Chatfields-Martin Walker Ltd v Lombard North Central Plc [2014] EWHC 1222 (QB)...**385–6**, 391

Chaudhry v Prabhakar [1989] 1 WLR 29; [1988] 3 All ER 718...**225–9**

Chelmsford Auctions Ltd v Poole [1973] QB 542; [1973] 2 WLR 219; [1973] 1 All ER 810...192

Cherry Tree Investments Ltd v Landmain Ltd [2012] EWCA Civ 736; [2013] Ch 305; [2013] 2 WLR 481...22

Chikuma, The see Awilco of Oslo A/S v Fulvia SpA di Navigazione of Cagliari (The Chikuma)

China-Pacific SA v Food Corp of India (The Winson) [1982] AC 939; [1981] 3 WLR 860; [1981] 3 All ER 688...98, **152–7**

Choko Star, The see Industrie Chimiche Italia Centrale and Cerealfin SA v Alexander G Tsavliris & Sons Maritime Co (The Choko Star)

Chow Yoong Hong v Choong Fah Rubber Manufactory [1962] AC 209; [1962] 2 WLR 43; [1961] 3 All ER 1163 (PC)...953, 967–8

Christie v Taunton Delmard Lane & Co [1893] 2 Ch 175...944

Churchill and Sim v Goddard [1937] 1 KB 92; [1936] 1 All ER 675...**679–80**

Cia de Seguros Imperio v Heath (REBX) Ltd (formerly CE Heath & Co (America) Ltd) [2001] 1 WLR 112; [2000] 2 All ER (Comm) 787...230

Citibank NA v MBIA Assurance SA [2006] EWHC 3215 (Ch)...32

Citibank NA v MBIA Assurance SA [2007] EWCA Civ 11; [2007] 1 All ER (Comm) 475; [2008] 1 BCLC 376...232

City Fur Manufacturing Co Ltd v Fureenbond (Brokers) London Ltd [1937] 1 All ER 799...**71–2**

Ciudad de Pasto, The see Mitsui & Co Ltd v Flota Mercante Grancolombiana SA (The Ciudad de Pasto and The Ciudad de Neiva)

CL Nye Ltd, Re [1971] Ch 442; [1970] 3 WLR 158; [1970] 3 All ER 1061...1081

Claridge v South Staffordshire Tramway Co [1892] 1 QB 422...**72–3**

Clark Boyce v Mouat [1994] 1 AC 428; [1993] 3 WLR 1021; [1993] 4 All ER 268 (PC)...238

Clarke, Re (1887) 36 Ch D 348...963

Clarke v Earl of Dunraven (The Satanita) [1897] AC 59...581

Clarkson Booker Ltd v Andjel [1964] 2 QB 775; [1964] 3 WLR 466; [1964] 3 All ER 260...**213–17**

Clay v Yates (1856) 1 Hurl & N 73; 156 ER 1123...**323–4**

Claydon v Bradley [1987] 1 WLR 521; [1987] 1 All ER 522...645, 664, 761

Cleadon Trust Ltd, [1939] Ch 286; [1938] 4 All ER 518...736

Clegg v Andersson (t/a Nordic Marine) [2003] EWCA Civ 320; [2003] 1 All ER (Comm) 721; [2003] 2 Lloyd's Rep 32...437, 472

Clerk v Laurie (1857) 2 Hurl & N 199; 157 ER 83...272

Clerke v Martin (1702) 2 Ld Raym 757; 92 ER 6...**651–3**

Clifford Chance v Silver [1992] 2 Bank LR 11...688, 692

Clough Mill Ltd v Martin [1985] 1 WLR 111; [1984] 3 All ER 982...95, 501–2, **509–11**

Clutton v George Attenborough & Son [1897] AC 90...671

Coastal (Bermuda) Petroleum Ltd v VTT Vulcan Petroleum SA (No 2) (The Marine Star) [1994] 2 Lloyd's Rep 629...522

Coates v Lewes (1808) 1 Camp 444; 170 ER 1015...223

Cobbe v Yeoman's Row Management Ltd [2008] UKHL 55; [2008] 1 WLR 1752; [2008] 4 All ER 713...31

Cobec Brazilian Trading & Warehousing Corp v Toepfer [1983] 2 Lloyd's Rep 386...465

Cocks v Masterman (1829) 9 B & C 902; 109 ER 335...709, 711–12, 714, 734

Coggs v Bernard (1703) 1 Salk 26; 91 ER 25...74, 97–8

Coggs v Bernard (1703) 2 Ld Raym 909; 92 ER 107...**92–3**, 1024–5, 1036

Cohen v Kittell (1889) 22 QBD 680...225

Cohen v Roche [1927] 1 KB 169...528

Coldman v Hill [1919] 1 KB 443...100

Cole v North Western Bank (1875) LR 10 CP 354...396

Coleman's Depositories Ltd and Life & Health Assurance Association's Arbitration, Re [1907] 2 KB 798...1101

Collen v Wright (1857) 8 El & Bl 647; 120 ER 241...**194–7**

Colley v Overseas Exporters (1919) Ltd [1921] 3 KB 302...474, **476–9**, 539

Collins v Associated Greyhound Racecourses Ltd [1930] 1 Ch 1...201

Collyer v Isaacs (1881) 19 Ch D 342...**886**

Colombiana, The see Compañia Colombiana de Seguros v Pacific Steam Navigation Co (The Colombiana)

Colonial Bank v Cady and Williams (1890) 15 App Cas 267...651

Colonial Bank v Exchange Bank of Yarmouth, Nova Scotia (1885) 11 App Cas 84 (PC)...720

Colonial Bank v Whinney (1885) 30 Ch D 261...55, 860

Colonial Mutual General Insurance Co Ltd v ANZ Banking Group (New Zealand) Ltd [1995] 1 WLR 1140; [1995] 3 All ER 987 (PC)...912

Colonial Trusts Corp ex p Bradshaw, Re (1879) 15 Ch D 465...989

Colour Quest Ltd v Total Downstream UK Plc [2010] EWCA Civ 180; [2011] QB 86; [2010] 3 WLR 1192...90

Comdel Commodities Ltd v Siporex Trade SA [1997] 1 Lloyd's Rep 424...851

Comerford v Britannic Assurance Co Ltd (1908) 24 TLR 593...170

Commercial Banking Co of Sydney Ltd v Mann [1961] AC 1; [1960] 3 WLR 726; [1960] 3 All ER 482 (PC)...762

Commercial Banking Co of Sydney Ltd v Jalsard Pty [1973] AC 279; [1972] 3 WLR 566 (PC)...**818–19**, 821

Commercial Factors Ltd v Maxwell Printing Ltd [1994] NZLR 724...9

Commerzbank AG v Gareth Price-Jones [2003] EWCA
Civ 1663...715

Commission Car Sales (Hastings) v Saul [1957] NZLR
144...496

Commissioner of Public Works v Hills [1906] AC
368...851

Commonwealth Trust Ltd v Akotey [1926] AC 72
(PC)...**393**

Compañia Colombiana de Seguros v Pacific Steam
Navigation Co (The Colombiana) [1965] 1 QB 101;
[1964] 2 WLR 484; [1964] 1 All ER 216...872

Compañia Financiera Soleada SA v Hamoor Tanker Corp
Inc (The Borag) [1980] 1 Lloyd's Rep 111...269

Company (No 005009 of 1987) ex p Copp, Re (1988) 4
BCC 424; [1989] BCLC 13...998

Compaq Computer Ltd v Abercorn Group Ltd (t/a Osiris)
[1991] BCC 484...511, **917–20, 927–8**

Compass Group UK and Ireland Ltd (t/a Medirest) v Mid
Essex Hospital Services NHS Trust [2013] EWCA Civ
200; [2013] BLR 265...42

Comptoir d'Achat et de Vente du Boerenbond Belge SA
v Luis de Ridder Limitada (The Julia) [1949] AC 293;
[1949] 1 All ER 269...535, **553–5**

Conley, Re [1938] 2 All ER 127...1064

Conn v Westminster Motor Insurance Association
[1966] 1 Lloyd's Rep 407...1096

Contigroup Cos Inc v Glencore AG [2004] EWHC 2750
(Comm); [2005] 1 Lloyd's Rep 241...**523–4**

Continental Caoutchou and Gutta Percha Co v
Kleinwort Sons & Co (1903) 8 Com Cas 277...616

Cooke v Haddon (1862) 3 F & F 229; 176 ER 103...1037

Cooke & Sons v Eshelby (1887) 12 App Cas
271...**218–21**

Cooper v Micklefield Coal and Lime Co Ltd (1912) 107
LT 457...884

Cooper v Pure Fishing (UK) Ltd (formerly Outdoor
Technology Group (UK) Ltd) [2004] EWCA Civ 375;
[2004] 2 Lloyd's Rep 518...279

Copp ex p, Re *see* Company (No 005009 of 1987) ex p
Copp, Re

Cordova Land Co Ltd v Victor Bros Inc [1966] 1 WLR
793...439

Corporacion Nacional del Cobre de Chile v Sogemin
Metals Ltd [1997] 1 WLR 1396; [1997] 2 All ER
917...248

Cosslett (Contractors) Ltd, Re [1998] Ch 495; [1998] 2
WLR 131; [1997] 4 All ER 115...980, 1014, 1041,
1043, **1069**

Cosslett (Contractors) Ltd (In Administration) (No 2), Re
[2001] UKHL 58; [2002] 1 AC 336; [2001] 3 WLR
1347...992, 998

Costello v Chief Constable of Derbyshire Constabulary
[2001] EWCA Civ 381; [2001] 1 WLR 1437; [2001] 3
All ER 150...75–6

Couchman v Hill [1947] KB 554; [1947] 1 All ER
103...428

Coulter v Chief Constable of Dorset [2003] EWHC 3391
(Ch); [2004] 1 WLR 1425...888

Coulthard v Disco Mix Club Ltd [2000] 1 WLR 707;
[1999] 2 All ER 457...230

County Homesearch Co (Thames & Chilterns) Ltd
v Cowham [2008] EWCA Civ 26; [2008] 1 WLR
909...260–1

Couturier v Hastie (1856) 5 HL Cas 673; 10 ER
1065...**369–71**

Crane v Sky In-Home Service Ltd [2007] EWHC 66
(Ch); [2007] 2 All ER (Comm) 599; [2007] 1 CLC
389...121, 276, 279

Crantrave Ltd (In Liquidation) v Lloyds Bank Plc
[2000] QB 917; [2000] 3 WLR 877; [2000] 4 All ER
473...736

Crears v Hunter (1887) 19 QBD 341...677

Crédit Agricole Corp and Investment Bank v
Papadimitriou [2015] UKPC 13; [2015] 1 WLR 4265;
[2015] 2 All ER 974...726

Crédit Agricole Indosuez v Chailease Finance Corp
[2000] 1 All ER (Comm) 399...**784–5**

Crédit Agricole Indosuez v Generale Bank (No 2) [1999]
2 All ER (Comm) 1016...822

Crédit Agricole Indosuez v Muslim Commercial Bank Ltd
[2000] 1 All ER (Comm) 172...**823**

Crédit Industriel et Commercial v China Merchants Bank
[2002] EWHC 973 (Comm); [2002] 2 All ER (Comm)
427...783, 785, 821, 827

Credit Lyonnais Bank Nederland NV (now Generale
Bank Nederland NV) v Export Credits Guarantee
Department [1998] 1 Lloyd's Rep 19...700

Credit Lyonnais Bank Nederland NV v Export Credits
Guarantee Department [2000] 1 AC 486; [1999] 2
WLR 540; [1999] 1 All ER 929...116, 174

Crédit Suisse (Monaco) SA v Attar [2004] EWHC 374
(Comm)...714

Crema v Cenkos Securities plc [2010] EWCA Civ 1444;
[2011] 1 WLR 2066; [2011] 2 All ER (Comm) 676...23

Criterion Properties Plc v Stratford UK Properties LLC
[2004] UKHL 28; [2004] 1 WLR 1846...132, 144

Crocker Horlock Ltd v B Lang & Co Ltd [1949] 1 All ER
526...266

Crockfords Club Ltd v Mehta [1992] 1 WLR 355; [1992]
2 All ER 748...658

Crocs Europe BV v Anderson (t/a Spectrum Agencies
(A Partnership)) [2012] EWCA Civ 1400; [2013] 1
Lloyd's Rep 1...276

Crouch v Crédit Foncier of England Ltd (1873) LR 8 QB
374...571, **649–50**, 654

CTI Group Inc v Transclear SA (The Mary Nour) [2008]
EWCA Civ 856; [2009] 2 All ER (Comm) 25...378

Cuckmere Brick Co v Mutual Finance [1971]
Ch 949; [1971] 2 WLR 1207; [1971] 2 All ER
633...116, **1120–1**

Cukurova Finance International Ltd v Alfa Telecom
Turkey Ltd [2009] UKPC 19; [2009] 3 All ER 849
(PC)...1065, 1068

Cundy v Lindsay (1878) 3 App Cas 459; [1878] All ER
Rep 1149...345, **401, 404–7**

Cunliffe-Owen v Teather and Greenwood [1967] 1 WLR
1421; [1967] 3 All ER 561...23, 131

Curlewis v Birkbeck (1863) 3 F & F 894; 176 ER
406...293

Curran v Newpark Cinemas Ltd [1951] 1 All ER
295...926, **928–31**

Currie v Misa (1875) LR 10 Ex 153...678

Curtain Dream Plc, Re [1990] BCC 341; [1990] BCLC
925...319, 954

Curtice v London City & Midland Bank Ltd [1908] 1 KB
293...610

Curwen v Milburn (1889) 42 Ch D 424...972
Customs and Excise Commissioners v Diners Club Ltd
   [1989] 1 WLR 1196; [1989] 2 All ER 385...633
Customs and Excise Commissioners v Everwine Ltd
   [2003] EWCA Civ 953; (2003) 147 SJLB 870...335
Customs and Excise Commissioners v FDR Ltd [2000]
   STC 672...567, 633
Customs and Excise Commissioners v National
   Westminster Bank Plc (Authorisation: Mistake)
   [2002] EWHC 2204 (Ch); [2003] 1 All ER (Comm)
   327...564, 607, **619–22**
CVG Siderurgicia del Orinoco SA v London Steamship
   Owners Mutual Insurance Association Ltd (The
   Vainqueur Jose) [1979] 1 Lloyd's Rep 557...1101
Czarnikow-Rionda Sugar Trading Inc v Standard Bank
   London Ltd [1999] 1 All ER (Comm) 890...789,
   800–1, 852

D & C Builders Ltd v Rees [1966] 2 QB 617; [1966] 2
   WLR 288; [1965] 3 All ER 837...658
Da Rocha-Afodu v Mortgage Express Ltd [2014] EWCA
   Civ 454; [2014] 2 P & CR DG10...99
Dallas, Re [1904] 2 Ch 385...916–17, 920, 965
Dalmare SpA v Union Maritime Ltd [2012] EWHC 3537
   (Comm); [2013] 2 All ER 870; [2013] 1 CLC 59...452
Daly v Lime Street Underwriting Agencies [1987] 2 FTLR
   277...274
Damon Compañía Naviera SA v Hapag-Lloyd
   International SA (The Blankenstein) [1985] 1 WLR
   435; [1985] 1 All ER 475...482–3
Daraydan Holdings Ltd v Solland International Ltd
   [2004] EWHC 622 (Ch); [2005] Ch 119...244, 247
Daun v City of London Brewery Co (1869) LR 8
   Eq 155...23
Daun v Simmins (1879) 41 LT 783...151
David T Boyd & Co v Louis Louca [1973] 1 Lloyd's Rep
   209...538
Davies v Rees (1886) 17 QBD 408...1084
Davis Contractors Ltd v Fareham Urban DC [1956] AC
   696; [1956] 3 WLR 37; [1956] 2 All ER 145...372
Davison v Donaldson (1882) 9 QBD 623...174
Dawson v Great Northern & City Railway Co [1905] 1
   KB 260...941
Dawson (Clapham) Ltd v H & G Dutfield [1936] 2 All ER
   232...313, **315**
Dawsons Ltd v Bonnin [1922] 2 AC 413...1093
De Bussche v Alt (1878) 8 Ch D 286; 38 LT
   370...**250–1**, 253–4
De Franco v Commissioner of Police of the Metropolis
   Times 8 May 1987...75
De Mattos v Gibson (1859) 4 De G & J 276; 45 ER
   108...64–5
De Mattos v Saunders (1872) LR 7 CP 570...947
Dearle v Hall (1828) 3 Russ 1; 38 ER 475...**913–20**,
   927, 1001
Debenham's Ltd v Perkins (1925) 133 LT 252...**176–8**
Debenhams Retail Plc v Customs and Excise
   Commissioners [2005] EWCA Civ 892; [2005] STC
   1155...634
Debs v Sibec Developments Ltd [1990] RTR 91...386, 401
Debtor (No 229 of 1927), Re [1927] 2 Ch 367...243
Demby Hamilton & Co Ltd v Barden [1949] 1 All ER
   435...**363–4**

Den Norske Bank ASA v Acemex Management Co Ltd
   (The Tropical Reefer) [2003] EWCA Civ 1559; [2004]
   1 All ER (Comm) 904; [2004] 1 Lloyd's Rep 1...1067
Dennant v Skinner & Collom [1948] 2 KB 164; [1948] 2
   All ER 29...**339–40**
Denny v Conklin [1913] 3 KB 177...924
Deposit Protection Board v Barclays Bank Plc [1994]
   2 AC 367; [1994] 2 WLR 732; [1994] 2 All ER
   577...567, 889, 907, 914, 934
Deposit Protection Board v Dalia see Deposit Protection
   Board v Barclays Bank Plc
Deutsche Morgan Grenfell Group Plc v Inland Revenue
   Commissioners [2006] UKHL 49; [2007] 1 AC 558;
   [2006] 3 WLR 781...713
Devani v Kenya [2015] EWHC 3535 (Admin)...77, 95
Deverges v Sandeman Clark & Co [1902] 1 Ch
   579...**1065–6**
Devonald v Rosser & Sons [1906] 2 KB 728...654
Dextra Bank & Trust Co Ltd v Bank of Jamaica [2002] 1
   All ER (Comm) 193 (PC)...683, 692, 715–16
DF Mount v Jay & Jay (Provisions) Co [1960] 1 QB 159;
   [1959] 3 WLR 537; [1959] 3 All ER 307...417, **420**,
   485, **487–9**
DFC Financial Services Ltd v Coffey [1991] 2 NZLR 513;
   [1991] BCC 218 (PC)...1076
Dhak v Insurance Co of North America (UK) Ltd [1996]
   1 WLR 936; [1996] 2 All ER 609...1095
Diamond v Graham [1968] 1 WLR 1061; [1968] 2 All ER
   909...**679–81**
Diamond Alkali Export Corp v Bourgeois [1921] 3 KB
   443...544
Diana Prosperity, The see Reardon Smith Ltd v Yngvar
   Hensen Tangen (The Diana Prosperity)
Dickinson v Lilwal (1815) 4 Camp 279; 171 ER 89...274
Dies v British & International Mining & Finance Corp Ltd
   [1939] 1 KB 724...321–2
Director General of Fair Trading v First National Bank
   plc [2001] UKHL 52; [2002] 1 AC 481; [2001] 3 WLR
   1297...42
Dirks v Richards (1842) 4 Man & G 574; 134 ER
   236...1056
Discount Records Ltd v Barclays Bank Ltd [1975] 1 WLR
   315; [1975] 1 All ER 1071...788, 800
Dix v Grainger (1922) 12 Ll L Rep 194...813
Dixon v Bovill (1856) 19 D (HL) 9; (1856) 3 Marq 1...649
Dixon v Stansfeld (1850) 10 CB 398...269
Do-Buy 925 Ltd v National Westminster Bank Plc [2010]
   EWHC 2862 (QB)...634
Don Commercials Ltd v Lancaster Trucks Ltd Unreported
   14 December 1994...431
Don King Productions Inc v Warren (No 1) [2000] Ch
   291; [1999] 3 WLR 276; [1999] 2 All ER 218...31,
   884, **890–2**, 895, 900
Donald v Suckling (1866) LR 1 QB 585...**1035–8**, 1041
Donaldson v Donaldson (1854) Kay 711; 69 ER
   303...921
Donegal International Ltd v Zambia [2007] EWHC 197
   (Comm); [2007] 1 Lloyd's Rep 397...245
Donoghue v Stevenson [1932] AC 56 2...227–9, 254,
   392, 454
Doosan Babcock Ltd v Comercializadora de Equipos
   y Materiales Mabe Lda (formerly Mabe Chile Lda)
   [2013] EWHC 3201 (TCC); [2014] BLR 33...789

Doward, Dickson & Co v Williams & Co (1890) 6 TLR 316...273

Downsview Nominees Ltd v First City Corporation Ltd [1993] AC 295; [1993] 2 WLR 86; [1993] 3 All ER 626 (PC)...**1059**, 1066, **1118–21**

Drake v Thos Agnew & Sons Ltd [2002] EWHC 294 (QB)...431

Drew v Nunn (1879) 4 QBD 661...**287–92**

Drummond & Sons v Van Ingen & Co (1887) 12 App Cas 284...**448–9**

DTC (CNC) Ltd v Gary Sergeant & Co [1996] 1 WLR 797; [1996] 2 All ER 369...1049

Du Jardin v Beadman Bros Ltd [1952] 2 QB 712; [1952] 2 All ER 160...401

Dublin City Distillery Ltd v Doherty [1914] AC 823...77, 1027, 1029, 1031–2, 1040

Duke of Portland v Baird and Co (1865) 4 M 10...882

Duncan Fox & Co v North & South Wales Bank (1880) 6 App Cas 1...701

Dunhill v Burgin (Nos 1 and 2) [2014] UKSC 18; [2014] 1 WLR 933; [2014] 2 All ER 364...**290–1**

Dunton Properties Ltd v Coles, Knapp & Kennedy Ltd (1959) 174 EG 723...237

Durham Bros v Robertson [1898] 1 QB 765...**903–5**, 914

Durham Fancy Goods Ltd v Michael Jackson (Fancy Goods) Ltd [1968] 2 QB 839; [1968] 3 WLR 225; [1968] 2 All ER 987...695

Durkin v DSG Retail Ltd [2014] UKSC 21; [2014] 1 WLR 1148; [2014] 2 All ER 715...641

Dyster v Randall & Sons [1926] Ch 932...**207–8**, 212

E Pfeiffer Weinkellerei-Weineinkauf GmbH & Co v Arbuthnot Factors Ltd [1988] 1 WLR 150...511, 918, 920, 927

East West Corp v DKBS 1912 [2003] EWCA Civ 83; [2003] QB 1509; [2003] 3 WLR 916; [2003] 1 All ER (Comm) 524...78, 80, 96

Eastern Distributors Ltd v Goldring [1957] 2 QB 600; [1957] 3 WLR 237; [1957] 2 All ER 525...319, 386, 392

Easton v London Joint Stock Bank (1886) 34 Ch D 95...651, 654

Economides v Commercial Union Assurance Co Plc [1998] QB 587; [1997] 3 WLR 1066; [1997] 3 All ER 636...1094

E D & F Man Ltd v Nigerian Sweets & Confectionery Co [1977] 2 Lloyd's Rep 50...629, 816

Edelstein v Schuler & Co [1902] 2 KB 144...654

Edmunds v Bushell (1866) LR 1 QB 97...147

Edward Owen Engineering Ltd v Barclays Bank International Ltd [1978] QB 159; [1977] 3 WLR 764; [1978] 1 All ER 976...791, 796, 831, 842, **845–8**, 851

Edwards v International Connection (UK) Ltd [2006] EWCA Civ 662...121

Edwards v Newland & Co [1950] 2 KB 534; [1950] 1 All ER 1072...99

Egan Lawson Ltd v Standard Life Assurance Co [2001] 1 EGLR 27...261

Egyptian International Foreign Trade Co v Soplex Wholesale Supplies Ltd and PS Refson SL Co Ltd (The Raffaella) [1985] 2 Lloyd's Rep 36...**136–9**

Eide UK Ltd v Lowndes Lambert Group Ltd [1999] QB 199; [1998] 3 WLR 643; [1998] 1 All ER 946...1049

El Amria, The [1982] 2 Lloyd's Rep 28...540

El Awadi v Bank of Credit and Commerce International SA Ltd [1990] 1 QB 606; [1989] 3 WLR 220; [1989] 1 All ER 242...763

Elafi, The *see* Karlshamns Oljefabriker A/B v Eastport Navigation Corp (The Elafi)

Ellenborough, Re [1903] 1 Ch 697...864

Ellerman Lines Ltd v Lancaster Maritime Co Ltd (The Lancaster) [1980] 2 Lloyd's Rep 497...927

Elliott v Kemp (1840) 7 M & W 306; 151 ER 783...79

Ellis v Torrington [1920] 1 KB 399...872, 876

Elphick v Barnes (1880) 5 CPD 321...350

Elvin & Powell Ltd v Plummer Roddis (1933) 50 TLR 158...95, 99

EM Bowden's Patents Syndicate Ltd v Herbert Smith & Co [1904] 2 Ch 86...932

Emerald Meats (London) Ltd v AIB Group (UK) Plc [2002] EWCA Civ 460...741

Empresa Exportadora De Azucar (CUBAZUCAR) v Industria Azucarera Nacional SA (IANSA) (The Playa Larga and Marble Islands) [1983] 2 Lloyd's Rep 171...462

English and Scottish Mercantile Investment Co Ltd v Brunton [1892] 2 QB 700...**1072–3**

Enka Insaat Ve Sanayi AS v Banca Popolare dell'Alto Adige SpA [2009] EWHC 2410 (Comm)...853

Epps v Rothnie [1945] KB 562; [1946] 1 All ER 146...205

Equitable Trust Co of New York v Dawson Partners Ltd (1927) 27 Ll L Rep 49...558, 589, **778–9**, 823

Esal (Commodities) Ltd and Reltor Ltd v Oriental Credit Ltd and Wells Fargo Bank NA [1985] 2 Lloyd's Rep 546...842

Esso Petroleum Co Ltd v Craft [1996] CLY 744...572

Esso Petroleum Co Ltd v Customs and Excise Commissioners [1976] 1 WLR 1; [1976] 1 All ER 117...313

Esso Petroleum Co Ltd v Milton [1997] 1 WLR 938; [1997] 1 WLR 1060; [1997] 2 All ER 593...**571–5**

Esteban De Comas v Jacobus Cornelus Prost and George Charles Adolphus Kohler (1865) 3 Moo PC NS 158; 16 ER 59...273

Euro Commercial Leasing Ltd v Cartwright & Lewis [1995] BCC 830; [1995] 2 BCLC 618...1057

Euro-Diam Ltd v Bathurst [1990] 1 QB 1; [1988] 2 WLR 517; [1988] 2 All ER 23...805

European Asian Bank AG v Punjab and Sind Bank [1981] 2 Lloyd's Rep 651...834, 836

European Asian Bank AG v Punjab and Sind Bank (No 2) [1983] 1 WLR 642...128, 819

European Ventures LLP v Cedar Capital Partners LLC [2014] UKSC 45; [2015] AC 250; [2014] 3 WLR 535...114, 241, 248, 255

Evans v Bicknell (1801) 6 Ves Jr 174; 31 ER 998...914

Evans v Rival Granite Quarries Ltd [1910] 2 KB 979...991, **1071–2**

Explora Group Plc v Hesco Bastion Ltd [2005] EWCA Civ 646...266, 898

Eyles v Ellis (1827) 4 Bing 112; 130 ER 710...612, 616–18

F v West Berkshire Health Authority [1990] 2 AC 1;
  [1989] 2 WLR 1025; [1989] 2 All ER 545...156

F&C Alternative Investments (Holdings) Ltd v Barthelemy
  (No 2) [2011] EWHC 1731 (Ch); [2012] Ch 613;
  [2012] 3 WLR 10...**231**

Fadallah v Pollak [2013] EWHC 3159 (QB)...**397,
  410, 415–16**

Fairfax Gerrard Holdings Ltd v Capital Bank Plc [2006]
  EWHC 3439 (Comm); [2007] 1 Lloyd's Rep 171...419

Fairstar Heavy Transport NV v Adkins [2013] EWCA Civ
  886; [2013] 2 CLC 272...250

Fairvale Ltd v Sabharwal [1992] 2 EGLR 27...259

Falcke v Gray (1859) 4 Drew 651; 62 ER 250...529

Falcke v Scottish Imperial Insurance Co (1886) 34 Ch D
  234...157

Farina v Home (1846) 16 M & W 119; 153 ER 1124...77

Farley Health Products Ltd v Babylon Trading Co Times
  29 July 1987...197

Farquharson Bros & Co v King & Co [1902] AC
  325...143, 145, **381–3**, 385, **387–8**, 392–3

Federal Commerce & Navigation Co Ltd v Molena Alpha
  Inc (The Nanfri) [1979] AC 757; [1978] 3 WLR 991;
  [1979] 1 All ER 307...812

Fellus v National Westminster Bank plc (1983) 133 NLJ
  766...763

Fern Computer Consultancy Ltd v Intergraph Cadworx
  & Analysis Solutions Inc [2014] EWHC 2908 (Ch);
  [2015] 1 Lloyd's Rep 1...121

Ferryways NV v Associated British Ports (The Humber
  Way) [2008] EWHC 225 (Comm); [2008] 2 All ER
  (Comm) 504...205

FHR European Ventures LLP v Cedar Capital Partners
  LLC [2014] UKSC 45; [2015] AC 250; [2014] 3
  WLR 535...33

FHR European Ventures LLP v Mankarious [2013] EWCA
  Civ 17; [2014] Ch 1; [2013] 3 WLR 466...247

Ficom SA v Sociedad Cadex Ltda [1980] 2 Lloyd's Rep
  118...812

Finlan v Eyton Morris Winfield (A Firm) [2007] EWHC
  914 (Ch); [2007] 4 All ER 143...888

Fiona Trust & Holding Corp v Privalov [2007] UKHL 40;
  [2008] 1 Lloyd's Rep 254...249

Fiona Trust v Privalov [2010] EWHC 758 (Comm)...244

Fiorentino Comm Giuseppe Srl v Farnesi [2005] EWHC
  160 (Ch); [2005] 1 WLR 3718; [2005] 2 All ER
  737...695

Firbank's Executors v Humphreys (1886) 18
  QBD 54...195

First Energy (UK) Ltd v Hungarian International Bank Ltd
  [1993] 2 Lloyd's Rep 194...132, 135, 139–41, 143

Fisher Reeves & Co Ltd v Armour & Co Ltd [1920] 3 KB
  614...471

Fisher v Smith (1878) 4 App Cas 1...255, 1043

Fitzalan-Howard v Hibbert [2009] EWHC 2855 (QB);
  [2010] PNLR 11...726

Flame SA v Glory Wealth Shipping Pty Ltd [2013] EWHC
  3153 (Comm); [2014] QB 1080...482, 522

Fleet v Murton (1871) LR 7 QB 126...189

Fleming v Bank of New Zealand [1900] AC 577 (PC)...167

Flightline Ltd v Edwards [2003] EWCA Civ 63; [2003] 1
  WLR 1200; [2003] 3 All ER 1200...1064

Flood v Shand Construction Ltd [1997] CLC 588; 81 BLR
  31; 54 Con LR 125...885

Florence Land and Public Works Co, Re [1878] 10 Ch D
  530...989, 999

Foley v Hill (1848) 2 HL Cas 28; 9 ER 1002...564

Folkes v King [1923] 1 KB 282...**400–1**

Forbes v Marshall (1855) 11 Ex 166; 156 ER 788...685

Force India Formula One Team Ltd v 1 Malaysia Racing
  Team Sdn Bhd [2012] EWHC 616 (Ch); [2012]
  RPC 29...58

Forestal Minosa v Oriental Credit Ltd [1986] 1 WLR 631;
  [1986] 2 All ER 400...773

Formby Bros v Formby (1910) 102 LT 116...204

Forsythe International (UK) Ltd v Silver Shipping Co Ltd
  (The Saetta) [1994] 1 WLR 1334; [1994] 1 All ER
  851...64, 83, 417, 419, 512

Forth v Simpson (1849) 13 QB 680; 116 ER
  1423...**1042–3**, 1057

Forthright Finance Ltd v Carlyle Finance Ltd [1997] 4 All
  ER 90; [1997] CCLR 84...318

Fortis Bank SA/NV v Indian Overseas Bank [2009] EWHC
  2303 (Comm); [2010] 1 Lloyd's Rep 227...776

Fortis Bank SA/NV v Indian Overseas Bank [2011] EWCA
  Civ 58; [2011] 2 All ER (Comm) 288; [2011] 2 Lloyd's
  Rep 33...**773, 828**

Fortis Bank SA/NV v Indian Overseas Bank [2011] EWHC
  538 (Comm) [2011] 2 Lloyd's Rep 190...828, 830

Foskett v McKeown [2001] 1 AC 102; [2000] 2 WLR
  1299; [2000] 3 All ER 97...249, 567, 718, 724–6

Foster v Bates (1843) 12 M & W 226; 152
  ER 1180...293

Foster v Cockerell (1835) 3 Cl & F 456;
  6 ER 1508...917

Four Point Garage Ltd v Carter [1985]
  3 All ER 12...417

Fowler v Hollins (1872) LR 7 QB 616...84

Foxtons Ltd v Bicknell [2008] EWCA Civ 419; [2008] 2
  EGLR 23...**261**

Fragano v Long (1825) 4 B & C 219; 107 ER 1040...346

Franklin v Neate (1844) 13 M & W 480; 153 ER
  200...**1038**

Frans Maas (UK) Ltd v Samsung Electronics (UK) Ltd
  [2004] EWHC 1502 (Comm); [2005] 2 All ER (Comm)
  783; [2004] 2 Lloyd's Rep 251...175, 453

Fraser v BN Furman (Productions) Ltd [1967] 1 WLR 898;
  [1967] 3 All ER 57...225

Fraser v Equitorial Shipping Co Ltd and Equitorial Lines
  Ltd (The Ijaolo) [1979] 1 Lloyd's Rep 103...**1014–16**

Fred Drughorn Ltd v Rederiaktiebolaget Transatlantic
  [1919] AC 203...**204–5**

Freeman & Lockyer v Buckhurst Park Properties (Mangal)
  Ltd [1964] 2 QB 480; [1964] 2 WLR 618; [1964] 1 All
  ER 630...**127**, 129–30, 132–8, 145, 203

French v Gething [1922] 1 KB 236...72

Frith v Frith [1906] AC 254 (PC)...**271–3**, 275

Frost Express, The *see* Seatrade Groningen BV v Geest
  Industries Ltd (The Frost Express)

Frost v Aylesbury Dairy Co [1905] 1 KB 608...442, 447

Fullerton v Provincial Bank of Ireland [1903] AC
  309...677

Future Express, The [1992] 2 Lloyd's Rep 79...78

FW Moore & Co Ltd v Landauer & Co [1921] 2 KB
  519...**428–30**

Fyffes Group Ltd v Templeman [2000] 2 Lloyd's Rep
  643...248

G & H Montague GmbH (formerly Grunzweig und Hartmann Montage GmbH) v Irvani [1990] 1 WLR 667; [1990] 2 All ER 225...702

G & T Earle Ltd v Hemsworth Rural Distict Council (1928) 44 TLR 758...863–4

G(A) v G(T) [1970] 2 QB 643; [1970] 3 WLR 132; [1970] 3 All ER 546...126

Gadd v Houghton (1876) 1 Ex D 357...184–5, 187

Galaxy Energy International Ltd v Murco Petroleum Ltd (The Seacrown) [2013] EWHC 3720 (Comm); [2013] 2 CLC 1007...523

Galloway v Guardian Royal Exchange (UK) Ltd [1999] Lloyd's Rep IR 209...1101

Garcia v Page & Co Ltd (1936) 55 Ll L Rep 391...**810–13**

Garnac Grain Co Inc v HMF Faure and Fairclough Ltd [1968] AC 1130; [1967] 3 WLR 143; [1967] 2 All ER 353...**108**, 126, 223

Garnham, Harris & Elton v Ellis Ltd (Alfred W) (Transport) Ltd [1967] 1 WLR 940; [1967] 2 All ER 940; [1967] 2 Lloyd's Rep 22...99

Garriock and Others v John Walker (1873) 1 R 100...154

Gatoil International Inc v Tradax Petroleum Ltd (The Rio Sun) [1985] 1 Lloyd's Rep 350...462

Gaussen v Morton (1830) 10 B & C 731; 109 ER 622...273

Gedding v Marsh [1920] 1 KB 668...438

General Trading Co and Van Stolk's Commissiehandel, Re (1911) 16 Com Cas 95...550

Geofizika DD v MMB International Ltd [2009] EWHC 1675 (Comm); [2009] 2 All ER (Comm) 1034; [2010] 1 Lloyd's Rep 458...544

George Barker (Transport) Ltd v Eynon [1974] 1 WLR 462; [1974] 1 All ER 900...946

George Inglefield Ltd, Re [1933] Ch 1...950, 952–4, 966

George v Clagett (1797) 7 Term Rep 359; 101 ER 1019...218–19

Gerald McDonald & Co v Nash & Co [1924] AC 625...702

Gerard v Lewis (1867) LR 2 CP 305...889

Gewa Chartering BV v Remco Shipping Lines Ltd (The Remco) [1984] 2 Lloyd's Rep 205...193, 213

Gian Singh & Co Ltd v Banque de l'Indochine [1974] 1 WLR 1234; [1974] 2 All ER 754 (PC)...792, **820**

Gibaud v Great Eastern Railway Co [1921] 2 KB 426...99

Gibbon v Pease [1905] 1 KB 810...250

Giblin v McMullen (1868) LR 2 PC 317...97

Gibson v Jeyes (1801) 6 Ves Jr 266; 31 ER 1044...235

Gibson v Minet (1824) 130 ER 206...611

Giles v Thompson [1994] 1 AC 142; [1993] 2 WLR 908; [1993] 3 All ER 321...869, 871, 876

Gill & Duffus SA v Berger & Co Inc (No 2) [1982] 1 Lloyd's Rep 101...451

Gillett v Hill (1834) 2 Cr & M 530; 149 ER 871...366

Gillett v Peppercorne (1840) 3 Beav 78; 49 ER 31...234

Gillott's Settlement, Re [1934] Ch 97...888

Gisborne v Burton [1989] QB 390; [1988] 3 WLR 921; [1988] 3 All ER 760...954

GKN Contractors Ltd v Lloyds Bank Plc (1985) 30 BLR 48...822, 852

GL Saunders Ltd (In Liquidation), Re [1986] 1 WLR 215...1122

Glasscock v Balls (1889) 24 QBD 13...**707**

Glaxo Group Ltd v Dowelhurst Ltd [2004] EWCA Civ 290; [2005] ETMR 104...**556–7**

Glegg v Bromley [1912] 3 KB 474...863, 872

Glencore Energy UK Ltd v Cirrus Oil Services Ltd [2014] EWHC 87 (Comm); [2014] 1 All ER (Comm) 513; [2014] 2 Lloyd's Rep 1...**481**

Glencore Energy UK Ltd v Transworld Oil Ltd [2010] EWHC 141 (Comm); [2010] 1 CLC 284...517

Glencore Grain Ltd v Agros Trading Co Ltd [1999] 2 All ER (Comm) 288...947

Glencore Grain Rotterdam BV v Lebanese Organisation for International Commerce (The Lorico) [1997] 4 All ER 514; [1997] 2 Lloyd's Rep 386; [1997] CLC 1274...**811–12**, 815

Glencore International AG v Bank of China [1996] 1 Lloyd's Rep 135...773, 782, 784–5

Glencore International AG v Metro Trading International Inc (No 2) [2001] 1 All ER (Comm) 103; [2001] 1 Lloyd's Rep 284; [2001] CLC 1732...316–17

Glencore International AG v MSC Mediterranean Shipping Co SA [2015] EWHC 1989 (Comm); [2015] 2 Lloyd's Rep 508...83

Glenie v Bruce Smith [1908] 1 KB 263...684

Glicksman v Lancashire & General Assurance Co Ltd [1927] AC 139...1093

Godts v Rose (1855) 17 CB 229; 139 ER 1058...76

Goel v Pick [2006] EWHC 833 (Ch); [2007] 1 All ER 982...861

Goldcorp Exchange Ltd (In Receivership), Re [1995] 1 AC 74; [1994] 3 WLR 199; [1994] 2 All ER 806...30, 334, 336, 351

Golden Ocean Group Ltd v Salgaocar Mining Industries Pvt Ltd [2012] EWCA Civ 265; [2012] 1 WLR 3674; [2012] 1 Lloyd's Rep 542...51, 663–4

Golden Strait Corp v Nippon Yusen Kubishka Kaisha (The Golden Victory) [2007] UKHL 12; [2007] 2 AC 353; [2007] 2 WLR 691...11

Gomba Holdings (UK) Ltd v Homan [1986] 1 WLR 1301; [1986] 3 All ER 94...**1117–18**

Goodwin v Robarts (1875) LR 10 Exch 337; (1876) 1 App Cas 476...645, **652–3**

Gordon (Brigitte) v Gordon (Andrew Granville) [2002] EWCA Civ 1884...1046

Gordon v Harper (1796) 7 Term Rep 9; 101 ER 828...79

Gordon v London City and Midland Bank Ltd *see* Capital and Counties Bank Ltd v Gordon

Gordon v Strange (1847) 1 Ex 477; 154 ER 203...657

Gorringe v Irwell India Rubber and Gutta Percha Works (1886) 34 Ch D 128...**913, 918**

Gosling v Anderson (1972) EGD 709...175

Gosse Millard Ltd v Canadian Government Merchant Marine Ltd (The Canadian Highlander) [1929] AC 223...101

Graham v Johnson (1869) LR 8 Eq 36...946

Grain Union Co SA v Hans Larsen A/S (1933) 46 Ll L Rep 246...351

Gran Gelato Ltd v Richcliff (Group) Ltd [1992] Ch 560; [1992] 2 WLR 867; [1992] 1 All ER 865...181

Grant v Australian Knitting Mills Ltd [1936] AC 85 (PC)...425

Grant v Vaughan (1764) 3 Burr 1516; 97 ER 957...664

Granville Oil & Chemicals Ltd v Davis Turner & Co Ltd [2003] EWCA Civ 570; [2003] 1 All ER (Comm) 819; [2003] 2 CLC 418...453

Gray v Barr [1971] 2 QB 554; [1971] 2 WLR 1334; [1971] 2 All ER 949...1090

Gray v G-T-P Group Ltd [2010] EWHC 1772 (Ch); [2011] BCC 869; [2011] 1 BCLC 313...1074

Gray v Haig & Sons (1855) 20 Beav 219; 52 ER 587...250

Gray v Smith [2013] EWHC 4136 (Comm); [2014] 2 All ER (Comm) 359...422

Gray's Inn Construction Co Ltd, Re [1980] 1 WLR 711; [1980] 1 All ER 814...**1127–9**

Great Elephant Corp v Trafigura Beheer BV [2013] EWCA Civ 905; [2013] 2 All ER (Comm) 992; [2013] 2 CLC 185...462

Great Northern Railway Co v Swaffield (1874) LR 9 Ex 132...154, 157

Grébert-Borgnis v J & W Nugent (1885) 15 QBD 85...523

Green v All Motors Ltd [1917] 1 KB 625...1051, 1055

Greenwood v Martins Bank Ltd [1933] AC 51...**697–8**

Greer v Downs Supply Co [1927] 2 KB 28...**208**, 221

Griffin v Weatherby (1868) LR 3 QB 753...890

Griffiths v Peter Conway Ltd [1939] 1 All ER 685...445

Griffiths v Yorkshire Bank Ltd [1994] 1 WLR 1427...1073

Griffon Shipping LLC v Firodi Shipping Ltd [2013] EWCA Civ 1567; [2014] 1 All ER (Comm) 593; [2014] 1 CLC 1...483

Grosvenor Casinos Ltd v National Bank of Abu Dhabi [2008] EWHC 511 (Comm); [2008] 2 All ER (Comm) 112...768

Group Josi Re Co SA v Walbrook Insurance Co Ltd [1996] 1 WLR 1152; [1996] 1 All ER 791...797, 801, **804–5**, 852

Grover & Grover Ltd v Matthews [1910] 2 KB 401...165

Grovewood Holdings Plc v James Capel & Co Ltd [1995] Ch 80; [1995] 2 WLR 70; [1994] 4 All ER 417...886

Guinness plc v Saunders [1990] 2 AC 663; [1990] 2 WLR 324; [1990] 1 All ER 652...241

GUS Property Management Ltd v Littlewoods Mail Order Stores Ltd 1982 SC (HL) 157; 1982 SLT 533...941

Gwembe Valley Development Co Ltd v Koshy (No 3) [2003] EWCA Civ 1478; [2004] 1 BCLC 131...232

H & K (Medway) Ltd, Re [1997] 1 WLR 1422; [1997] 2 All ER 321...1073

H Parsons (Livestock) Ltd v Uttley Ingham & Co Ltd [1978] QB 791; [1977] 3 WLR 990; [1978] 1 All ER 525...526

Habib Bank Ltd v Central Bank of Sudan [2006] EWHC 1767 (Comm); [2007] 1 WLR 470; [2006] 2 Lloyd's Rep 412...824

Habibsons Bank Ltd v Standard Chartered Bank (Hong Kong) Ltd [2010] EWCA Civ 1335; [2011] QB 943...699

Habton Farms v Nimmo [2002] EWHC 102 (QB)...141

Habton Farms v Nimmo [2003] EWCA Civ 68; [2004] QB 1; [2003] 3 WLR 633...200

Hackett v Advanced Medical Computer Systems Ltd [1999] CLC 160...279

Hadenfayre v British National Insurance Society [1984] 2 Lloyd's Rep 393...1093, 1100

Hadley v Baxendale (1854) 9 Ex 341; 156 ER 145...198, **480**, 482, 515, 520, 523, 525, 813

Hadley v Henry (1896) 22 VLR 230...685

Hagedorn v Oliverson (1814) 2 M & S 485; 105 ER 461...162–3

Halesowen Presswork & Assemblies v Westminster Bank Ltd [1972] AC 785; [1971] 1 QB 1; [1970] 3 WLR 625; [1970] 3 All ER 473...969, 971, 973

Halifax Building Society v Thomas [1996] Ch 217; [1996] 2 WLR 63; [1995] 4 All ER 673...247

Hallett's Estate, Re (1880) 13 Ch D 696...498–9, 502, 721

Halliday v Holgate (1868) LR 3 Ex 299...904, 1025, 1037–8

Haly v Howlett & Sons [1917] 1 KB 337...367

Hamer v Sharp (1874) LR 19 Eq 108...131

Hamilton, Re (1921) 124 LT 737...921

Hamilton v Papakura DC [2002] UKPC 9; [2002] 2 NZLR 308 (PC)...447

Hammonds v Barclay (1802) 2 East 227; 102 ER 356...**1040–1**

Hamzeh Malas & Sons v British Imex Industries Ltd [1958] 2 QB 127; [1958] 2 WLR 100; [1958] 1 All ER 262...558, 772, **786–7**, 845

Hanak v Green [1958] 2 QB 9; [1958] 2 WLR 755; [1958] 2 All ER 141...945

Hannan's Empress Gold Mining and Development Co, Re (Carmichael's Case) [1896] 2 Ch 643...272, 274

Hansa Nord, The *see* Cehave NV v Bremer Handelsgesellschaft mbH (The Hansa Nord)

Hansson v Hamel & Horley Ltd [1922] 2 AC 36...**550–1**

Harding v Harding (1886) 17 QBD 442...905

Harding Maughan Hambly Ltd v Cie Européenne de Courtage d'Assurance SA [2000] 1 All ER (Comm) 225; [2000] 1 Lloyd's Rep 316; [2000] CLC 524...261

Hardwick ex p Hubbard, Re (1886) 17 QBD 690...**1038**, 1040

Hardy & Co (London) Ltd v Hillerns & Fowler [1923] 2 KB 490...360–1, 472

Hare v Henty (1861) 10 CB NS 65; 142 ER 374...16, 581, 590, 595–7, 611, 733

Harlingdon and Leinster Enterprises Ltd v Christopher Hull Fine Art Ltd [1991] 1 QB 564; [1990] 3 WLR 13; [1990] 1 All ER 737...**430–1**

Harlow & Jones Ltd v Panex (International) Ltd [1967] 2 Lloyd's Rep 509...480

Harlow and Jones v American Express Bank and Creditanstalt-Bankverein [1990] 2 Lloyd's Rep 343...768, 773

Harmer v Armstrong [1934] Ch 65...170, 895, 932

Harper & Co v Vigers Bros [1909] 2 KB 549...193

Harrold v Plenty [1901] 2 Ch 314...1028, 1065

Hart ex p Caldicott, Re (1884) 25 Ch D 716...971

Hartley v Hymans [1920] 3 KB 475...458

Harvey Jones Ltd v Woolwich plc *see* Smith v Lloyds TSB Bank Plc

Hasan v Willson [1977] 1 Lloyd's Rep 431...678–80, 683, 762

Hatton v Car Maintenance Co Ltd [1915] 1 Ch 621...**1044**

Haugesund Kommune v Depfa ACS Bank [2010] EWCA Civ 579; [2012] QB 549; [2012] 2 WLR 199...716

Hawtayne v Bourne Hawtayne (Public Officer of the Western District Banking Company) v Bourne (1841) 7 M & W 595; 151 ER 905...156

Hayward v Zurich Insurance Co Plc [2016] UKSC 48; [2016] 3 WLR 637; [2016] 4 All ER 628...1102

Hazell v Hammersmith and Fulham London Borough Council [1992] 2 AC 1; [1990] 2 QB 697...9–11, 33, 174

Head v Tattersall (1871) LR 7 Ex 7...359, **364–5**

Heald v Kenworthy (1855) 10 Ex 739; 156 ER 638...172–3, 221

Heap v Motorists' Advisory Agency Ltd [1923] 1 KB 577...403

Heard v Pilley (1869) LR 4 Ch App 548...126

Hedley Byrne & Co Ltd v Heller & Partners Ltd [1964] AC 465; [1963] 3 WLR 101; [1963] 2 All ER 575...175, 227, 229, 254, 392, 599, 601–3

Heinl v Jyske Bank (Gibraltar) Ltd [1999] Lloyd's Rep Bank 511...144

Helby v Matthews [1895] AC 471...318, 413

Helstan Securities Ltd v Hertfordshire CC [1978] 3 All ER 262...869–70, 880, 882–4

Hely-Hutchinson v Brayhead Ltd [1968] 1 QB 549; [1967] 3 WLR 1408; [1967] 3 All ER 98...**129–31**, 136, 138

Henderson & Co v Williams [1895] 1 QB 521...**385**

Henderson Sons & Co Ltd v Wallace and Pennell (1902) 40 SLR 70...665

Henderson v Merrett Syndicates Ltd (No 1) [1995] 2 AC 145; [1994] 3 WLR 761; [1994] 3 All ER 506...225, **231**, 238, 254, 599

Hendry v Chartsearch Ltd [1998] CLC 1382...885, 935

Hendy Lennox (Industrial Engines) Ltd v Grahame Puttick Ltd [1984] 1 WLR 485; [1984] 2 All ER 152...**509**

Henry Kendall & Sons v William Lillico & Sons Ltd [1969] 2 AC 31; [1968] 3 WLR 110; [1968] 2 All ER 444...436, 442

Herkules Piling Ltd v Tilbury Construction Ltd (1992) 32 Con LR 112; (1992) 61 BLR 107...913

Hermione, The [1922] P 162...224

Heron II, The *see* Koufos v C Czarnikow Ltd (The Heron II)

Heseltine v Simmons [1892] 2 QB 547...1079

Hewison, Assignees of George Mickle, and John Mickle v Guthrie (1836) 2 Bing NC 755; 132 ER 290...1049

Heyman v Flewker (1863) 13 CB NS 519; 143 ER 205...396

Hibernian Bank Ltd v Gysin [1939] 1 KB 483; [1939] 1 All ER 166...**673–4**, 728

Hichens Harrison Woolston & Co v Jackson & Sons [1943] AC 266; [1943] 1 All ER 128...189

Higgins v Senior (1841) 8 M & W 834; 151 ER 1278...187

Highway Foods International Ltd (In Administrative Receivership), Re [1995] BCC 271; [1995] 1 BCLC 209...417, 501, 512

HIH Casualty & General Insurance Ltd v Chase Manhattan Bank [2003] UKHL 6; [2003] 1 All ER (Comm) 349; [2003] 2 Lloyd's Rep 61...174–5

Hill v Peters [1918] 2 Ch 273...918–19

Hillas & Co Ltd v Arcos Ltd (1932) 43 Ll L Rep 359; (1932) 147 LT 503...326

Hilton v Barker Booth & Eastwood [2005] UKHL 8; [2005] 1 WLR 567; [2005] 1 All ER 651...238

Hilton v Tucker (1888) 39 Ch D 669...**1028**, **1030–1**

Hinde v Whitehouse (1806) 7 East 558; 103 ER 216...117

Hindley & Co v East Indian Produce Co [1973] 2 Lloyd's Rep 515...**548–50**

Hine Bros v Steamship Insurance Syndicate Ltd (1895) 72 LT 79...174

Hiort v Bott (1874) LR 9 Ex 86...99

Hippisley v Knee Bros [1905] 1 KB 1...239–40

Hitch v Stone (Inspector of Taxes) [2001] EWCA Civ 63; [2001] STC 214...955

HMV Fields Properties Ltd v Bracken Self Selection Fabrics Ltd 1991 SLT 31; 1990 SCLR 677...622

HO Brandt & Co v HN Morris & Co [1917] 2 KB 784...189

Hodges & Sons v Hackbridge Park Residential Hotel Ltd [1940] 1 KB 404; [1939] 4 All ER 347...260

Hogan v London Irish Rugby Football Club Trading Ltd Unreported 20 December 1999...158

Hollicourt (Contracts) Ltd (In Liquidation) v Bank of Ireland [2001] Ch 555; [2001] 2 WLR 290; [2001] 1 All ER 289...1130

Hollins v Fowler (1875) LR 7 HL 757...103

Holmes, Re (1885) 29 Ch D 786...917

Holmes v Governor of Brixton Prison [2004] EWHC 2020 (Admin); [2005] 1 WLR 1857; [2005] 1 All ER 490...619

Holmes v Payne [1930] 2 KB 301...1099

Holroyd v Marshall (1862) 10 HL Cas 191; 11 ER 999...68, 501, 886, **960–3**, 1020, 1063–4, 1069–70, 1078

Homburg Houtimport BV v Agrosin Private Ltd (The Starsin) [1999] 2 All ER (Comm) 591; [2000] 1 Lloyd's Rep 85...136

Homburg Houtimport BV v Agrosin Private Ltd (The Starsin) [2003] UKHL 12; [2004] 1 AC 715; [2003] 2 WLR 711...136

Homes v Smith [2000] Lloyd's Rep Bank 139...658

Hong Kong and Shanghai Banking Corp Ltd v GD Trade Co Ltd [1998] CLC 238...664

Hong Kong and Shanghai Banking Corp Ltd v Kloeckner & Co AG [1990] 2 QB 514; [1990] 3 WLR 634; [1989] 3 All ER 513...809

Hongkong Fir Shipping Co Ltd v Kawasaki Kisen Kaisha Ltd (The Hongkong Fir) [1962] 2 QB 26; [1962] 2 WLR 474; [1962] 1 All ER 474...424, 429, 469

Hongkong Fir, The *see* Hongkong Fir Shipping Co Ltd v Kawasaki Kisen Kaisha Ltd (The Hongkong Fir)

Honourable Society of the Middle Temple v Lloyds Bank Plc [1999] 1 All ER (Comm) 193...741–2, 755, 757, 759

Hopkins v TL Dallas Group Ltd [2004] EWHC 1379 (Ch); [2005] 1 BCLC 543...132, 144

Hopkinson v Forster (1874) LR 19 Eq 74...889

Horn v Minister of Food [1948] 2 All ER 1036...368

Hornsby v Clark Kenneth Leventhal [1998] PNLR 635...116

Houghland v RR Low (Luxury Coaches) Ltd [1962] 1 QB 694; [1962] 2 WLR 1015; [1962] 2 All ER 159...97–**101**, 226, 228

Hounslow LBC v Twickenham Garden Developments Ltd [1971] Ch 233; [1970] 3 WLR 538; [1970] 3 All ER 326...1046

Hovenden & Sons v Milhof (1900) 83 LT 41...244–5
Howard v Harris (1884) Cab & El 253...99
Howe Richardson Scale Co v Polimex-Cekop [1978] 1 Lloyd's Rep 161...842, 847
Howell v Coupland (1876) 1 QBD 258...373–5
HR & S Sainsbury Ltd v Street [1972] 1 WLR 834; [1972] 3 All ER 1127...**374–5**
HSBC Rail (UK) Ltd v Network Rail Infrastructure Ltd (formerly Railtrack Plc) [2005] EWCA Civ 1437; [2006] 1 WLR 643; [2006] 1 All ER 343...83
Hudson v Granger (1821) 5 B & Ald 27; 106 ER 1103...174
Hughes v Pendragon Sabre Ltd (t/a Porsche Centre Bolton) [2016] EWCA Civ 18; [2016] 1 Lloyd's Rep 311...517, 522
Hughes v Pump House Hotel Co Ltd (No 1) [1902] 2 KB 190...**906**
Humber Way, The see Ferryways NV v Associated British Ports (The Humber Way)
Humble v Hunter (1848) 12 QB 310; 116 ER 885...204–6
Hunter v Canary Wharf Ltd [1997] AC 655; [1997] 2 WLR 684; [1997] 2 All ER 426...85
Hunter v Moss [1993] 1 WLR 934...334
Hunter v Moss [1994] 1 WLR 452; [1994] 3 All ER 215...334
Hurstanger Ltd v Wilson [2007] EWCA Civ 299; [2007] 1 WLR 2351; [2007] 4 All ER 1118...245, 249
Hussain v Brown (No 1) [1996] 1 Lloyd's Rep 627...1094
Hutchinson v Tatham (1873) LR 8 CP 482...188
Huth & Co v Lamport (1886) 16 QBD 735...1056
Hyundai Heavy Industries Co Ltd v Papadopoulos [1980] 1 WLR 1129; [1980] 2 All ER 29...**321–3**

Ian Stach Ltd v Baker Bosly Ltd [1958] 2 QB 130; [1958] 2 WLR 419; [1958] 1 All ER 542...778, 813, 815
IE Contractors Ltd v Lloyds Bank Plc [1990] 2 Lloyd's Rep 496...853
IIG Capital LLC v Van der Merwe [2008] EWCA Civ 542; [2008] 2 All ER (Comm) 1173; [2008] 2 Lloyd's Rep 187...844
Ijaolo, The see Fraser v Equitorial Shipping Co Ltd and Equitorial Lines Ltd (The Ijaolo)
Illingworth v Houldsworth [1904] AC 355...990
Imperial Bank of Canada v Bank of Hamilton [1903] AC 49 (PC)...711–12
Importers Co Ltd v Westminster Bank Ltd [1927] 2 KB 297...741
Independent Automatic Sales, Ltd v Knowles & Foster [1962] 1 WLR 974; [1962] 3 All ER 27...**981–4**
Indian Oil Corp Ltd v Greenstone Shipping SA (Panama) (The Ypatianna) [1988] QB 345; [1987] 3 WLR 869; [1987] 3 All ER 893...315
Industrial Development Consultants Ltd v Cooley [1972] 1 WLR 443; [1972] 2 All ER 162...240
Industrial Finance Syndicate Ltd v Lind see Lind, Re
Industrie Chimiche Italia Centrale and Cerealfin SA v Alexander G Tsavliris & Sons Maritime Co (The Choko Star) (1990) [1990] 1 Lloyd's Rep 516...157
Industries and General Mortage Co Ltd v Lewis [1949] 2 All ER 573...243–4
Ing Re (UK) Ltd v R & V Versicherung AG [2006] EWHC 1544 (Comm); [2006] 2 All ER (Comm) 870; [2007] 1 BCLC 108...136, 139, 158

Inglis v Robertson [1898] AC 616...77, 1027–8
Ingmar GB Ltd v Eaton Leonard Inc (formerly Eaton Leonard Technologies Inc) [2001] CLC 1825; [2002] ECC 5; [2001] Eu LR 755...267
Inland Revenue Commissioners v Crossman [1937] AC 26; [1936] 1 All ER 762...281
Inland Revenue Commissioners v Goldblatt [1972] Ch 498; [1972] 2 WLR 953; [1972] 2 All ER 202...1122
Inland Revenue Commissioners v McGuckian [1997] 1 WLR 991; [1997] 3 All ER 817...955
Innes v Sir T Wallace Dunlop, Bart (1800) 8 Term Rep 595; 101 ER 1565...649
Insurance Corp of Ireland v Dunluce Meats [1991] NI 286...691–2
Interfoto Picture Library Ltd v Stiletto Visual Programmes Ltd [1989] QB 433; [1988] 2 WLR 615; [1988] 1 All ER 348...41
International Contract Co, Re (Pickering's Claim) (1871) LR 6 Ch App 525...170
International Factors v Rodriguez [1979] QB 351; [1978] 3 WLR 877; [1979] 1 All ER 17...967
International Finance Corp v DSNL Offshore Ltd [2005] EWHC 1844 (Comm); [2007] 2 All ER (Comm) 305...529, 1042
International Railway Co v Niagra Parks Commission [1941] AC 328; [1941] 2 All ER 456...188
Intertradex SA v Lesieur-Tourteaux Sarl [1977] 2 Lloyd's Rep 146...376, **378**
Intraco Ltd v Notis Shipping Corp of Liberia (The Bhoja Trader) [1981] 2 Lloyd's Rep 256...851–2
Investors Compensation Scheme Ltd v West Bromwich Building Society (No 1) [1998] 1 WLR 896; [1998] 1 All ER 98...20, 22, 843–4, 861, 1095
Ireland v Livingston (1872) LR 5 HL 395...118, **128**
Irvine & Co v Watson & Sons (1880) 5 QBD 414...**171–3**, 222
Ismail v Richards Butler [1996] QB 711; [1996] 3 WLR 129; [1996] 2 All ER 506...1048

J & H Ritchie Ltd v Lloyd Ltd [2007] UKHL 9; [2007] 1 WLR 670; [2007] 2 All ER 353...361, **472–4**
J Lauritzen AS v Wijsmuller BV (The Super Servant Two) [1990] 1 Lloyd's Rep 1...376
J Pereira Fernandes SA v Mehta [2006] EWHC 813 (Ch); [2006] 1 WLR 1543...51
Jackson v Rotax Motor & Cycle Co [1910] 2 KB 937...436
Jackson v Royal Bank of Scotland [2005] UKHL 3; [2005] 1 WLR 377; [2005] 2 All ER 71...777
Jackson v Union Marine Insurance Co (1874) LR 10 CP 125...377
Jacobs v Morris [1902] 1 Ch 816...129
Jacobus Marler Estates Ltd v Marler (1913) 85 LJPC 167n...235
Jade International Steel Stahl und Eisen GmbH & Co KG v Robert Nicholas (Steels) Ltd [1978] QB 917; [1978] 3 WLR 39; [1978] 3 All ER 104...684, **690–1**
Jag Shakti, The see Chabbra Corp Pte Ltd v Owners of the Jag Shakti (The Jag Shakti)
James Finlay & Co Ltd v NV Kwik Hoo Tung Handel Maatschappij [1929] 1 KB 400; [1928] All ER Rep 110...551

James Miller & Partners Ltd v Whitworth Street Estates (Manchester) Ltd [1970] AC 583; [1970] 2 WLR 728; [1970] 1 All ER 796...**1000**

James Talcott Ltd v John Lewis & Co Ltd [1940] 3 All ER 592...**910–12**

Jarl Tra AB v Convoys Ltd [2003] EWHC 1488 (Comm); [2003] 2 Lloyd's Rep 459...**1044**

Jeavons ex p Mackay, Re (1873) LR 8 Ch App 643...**972, 1108**

Jebara v Ottoman Bank [1927] 2 KB 254...**157**

Jeffries v Great Western Railway Co (1856) 5 El & Bl 802; 119 ER 680...**73**

Jenkins v Hutchinson (1849) 13 QB 744; 116 ER 1448...**191**

Jeremy D Stone Consultants Ltd v National Westminster Bank Plc [2013] EWHC 208 (Ch)...**716**

Jerome v Bentley [1952] 2 All ER 114...**150, 383**

Jetivia SA v Bilta (UK) Ltd (In Liquidation) [2015] UKSC 23; [2016] AC 1; [2015] 2 WLR 1168...**1134**

Jewson Ltd v Boyhan [2003] EWCA Civ 1030; [2004] 1 Lloyd's Rep 505...**436, 441, 446**

JH Rayner & Co Ltd v Hambros Bank Ltd [1943] KB 37; [1942] 2 All ER 694...**558, 780, 823**

Joachimson (N) (a firm) v Swiss Bank Corp [1921] 3 KB 110; (1921) 6 Ll L Rep 435...**621**

Joel v Law Union & Crown Insurance Co [1908] 2 KB 863...**1091**

John McCann & Co v Pow [1974] 1 WLR 1643; [1975] 1 All ER 129...**256**

Johnson, Assignee of Mathew Cumming, a Bankrupt v Stear (1863) 15 CB NS 330; 143 ER 812...**1035**

Johnston v Reading (1893) 9 TLR 200...**150**

Jones ex p Nichols, Re (1883) 22 Ch D 782...**904**

Jones v Churcher [2009] EWHC 722 (QB); [2009] 2 Lloyd's Rep 94...**716**

Jones v Gordon (1877) 2 App Cas 616...**43, 687–8**

Jones v Marshall (1889) 24 QBD 269...**1039**

Jones v Selby (1710) Prec Ch 300; 24 ER 143...**1030**

Joseph v Lyons (1884) 15 QBD 280...**1079**

Josephs v Pebrer (1825) 3 B & C 639; 107 ER 870...**266**

Jugoslavenska Linijska Plovidba v Hulsman (t/a Brusse & Sippel Import-Export) (The Primorje) [1980] 2 Lloyd's Rep 74...**187**

Julia, The *see* Comptoir d'Achat et de Vente du Boerenbond Belge SA v Luis de Ridder Limitada (The Julia)

Justice v Wynne (1860) 121 Ch R 289...**916**

K/S Merc-Scandia XXXXII v Lloyd's Underwriters (The Mercandian Continent) [2001] EWCA Civ 1275; [2001] Lloyd's Rep IR 802...**1101**

Kanchenjunga, The *see* Motor Oil Hellas (Corinth) Refineries SA v Shipping Corp of India (The Kanchenjunga)

Karak Rubber Co Ltd v Burden (No 2) [1972] 1 WLR 602; [1972] 1 All ER 1210; [1972] 1 Lloyd's Rep 73...**588**

Karlshamns Oljefabriker A/B v Eastport Navigation Corp (The Elafi) [1982] 1 All ER 208; [1981] 2 Lloyd's Rep 679...**337**

Kayford Ltd (In Liquidation), Re [1975] 1 WLR 279; [1975] 1 All ER 604...32, **1124–6**

KBC Bank v Industrial Steels (UK) Ltd [2001] 1 All ER (Comm) 409...**831**

Keene v Thomas [1905] 1 KB 136...**1051**

Keighley Maxsted & Co v Durant (t/a Bryan Durant & Co) [1901] AC 240...150, **159–61, 201–3**

Kelcey, Re [1899] 2 Ch 530...**1017**

Kelly v Cooper [1993] AC 205; [1992] 3 WLR 936 (PC)...**30, 231, 235–9, 266**

Kelly v Fraser [2012] UKPC 25; [2013] 1 AC 450; [2012] 3 WLR 1008 (PC)...**141–3**

Kelly v Solari (1841) 9 M & W 54; 152 ER 24...**709**

Kelner v Baxter (1866) LR 2 CP 174...**161**

Kendal v Wood (1870) LR 6 Ex 243...**708**

Kendall v Hamilton (1879) 4 App Cas 504...**217**

Keppel v Wheeler [1927] 1 KB 577...**237**

Kerrison v Glyn Mills Currie & Co (1911) 81 LJ KB 465...**709**

Khouj v Acropolis Capital Partners Ltd [2016] EWHC 2120 (Comm) 53...**108**

Kidderminster Corp v Hardwick (1873) LR 9 Ex 13...**166**

Kimber Coal Co Ltd v Stone & Rolfe Ltd [1926] AC 414; (1926) 24 Ll L Rep 429...**185**

Kinahan & Co Ltd v Parry [1911] 1 KB 459...**151**

King v Tunnock Ltd 2000 SC 424...**283–4**

King and Boyd v Porter [1925] NI 107...**705**

Kingscroft Insurance Co v HS Weavers (Underwriting) Agencies [1993] 1 Lloyd's Rep 187...**114**

Kirk v Blurton (1841) 9 M & W 284...**685**

Kirkham v Attenborough [1897] 1 QB 201...**347–8**

Kleinwort Benson Ltd v Lincoln City Council [1999] 2 AC 349; [1998] 3 WLR 1095...**11, 22, 144, 198, 713**

Kleinwort Sons & Co v Dunlop Rubber Co (1907) 97 LT 263...**709**

Knight Machinery (Holdings) Ltd v Rennie 1994 SC 338; 1995 SLT 166...**453**

Knotz v Fairclough Dodd & Jones Ltd [1952] 1 Lloyd's Rep 226...**812**

Koenigsblatt v Sweet [1923] 2 Ch 314...**158**

Kofi Sunkersette Obu v A Strauss & Co Ltd [1951] AC 243 (PC)...**257–9**

Kolmar Group AG v Traxpo Enterprises Pvt Ltd [2010] EWHC 113 (Comm); [2011] 1 All ER (Comm) 46; [2010] 2 Lloyd's Rep 653...**815**

Komercni Banka AS v Stone & Rolls Ltd [2002] EWHC 2263 (Comm); [2003] 1 Lloyd's Rep 383...**831**

Korea Exchange Bank Ltd v Debenhams (Central Buying) Ltd [1979] 1 Lloyd's Rep 548...**664**

Koufos v C Czarnikow Ltd (The Heron II) [1969] 1 AC 350; [1967] 3 WLR 1491; [1967] 3 All ER 686...**523**

Kredietbank Antwerp v Midland Bank Plc [1999] 1 All ER (Comm) 801...**782–5**

Kreditbank Cassel GmbH v Schenkers Ltd [1927] 1 KB 826...**696**

Kronman & Co v Steinberger (1922) 10 Ll L Rep 39...**812**

Kronos Worldwide Ltd v Sempra Oil Trading Sarl [2004] EWCA Civ 3; [2004] 1 All ER (Comm) 915; [2004] 1 CLC 136...**812**

Kum v Wah Tat Bank Ltd [1971] 1 Lloyd's Rep 439 (PC)...**8, 23, 650**

Kursell v Timber Operators & Contractors Ltd [1927] 1 KB 298...304, **307–8, 340–1**

Kwei Tek Chao (t/a Zung Fu Co) v British Traders & Shippers Ltd [1954] 2 QB 459; [1954] 2 WLR 365; [1954] 1 All ER 779…**359–61**, 365, 538, 545, **551**

Kydon Compañia Naviera SA v National Westminster Bank Ltd (The Lena) [1981] 1 Lloyd's Rep 68…827

L French & Co Ltd v Leeston Shipping Co Ltd [1922] 1 AC 451…265

Lacave & Co v Crédit Lyonnais [1897] 1 QB 148…734

Laconia, The *see* Mardorf Peach & Co Ltd v Attica Sea Carriers Corp of Liberia (The Laconia)

Lage v Siemens Bros & Co Ltd (1932) 42 Ll L Rep 252…269

Lamb v Attenborough (1862) 1 B & S 831; 121 ER 922…396

Lamb v Evans [1893] 1 Ch 218…239

Lambert v Cooperative Insurance Society Ltd [1975] 2 Lloyd's Rep 485…1094

Lampet's Case (1612) 10 Co Rep 46; 77 ER 994…865

Lancashire County Council v Municipal Mutual Insurance Ltd [1997] QB 897; [1996] 3 WLR 493; [1996] 3 All ER 545…1095

Lancaster, The *see* Ellerman Lines Ltd v Lancaster Maritime Co Ltd (The Lancaster)

Lancore Services Ltd v Barclays Bank Plc [2009] EWCA Civ 752; [2010] 1 All ER 763…633

Land Development Association, Re (1888) 39 Ch D 259…616

Langton v Higgins (1859) 4 Hurl & N 402; 157 ER 896…355

Larner v Fawcett [1950] 2 All ER 727…422, 1054

Law Debenture Trust Corp v Ural Caspian Oil Corp Ltd [1993] 1 WLR 138; [1993] 2 All ER 355…65

Law Debenture Trust Corp v Ural Caspian Oil Corp Ltd [1995] Ch 152; [1994] 3 WLR 1221; [1995] 1 All ER 157…64

Lazenby Garages v Wright [1976] 1 WLR 459; [1976] 2 All ER 770…481

Lee v Butler [1893] 2 QB 318…**413–14**, 419

Lee v Griffin (1861) 1 B & S 272; 121 ER 716…323–4

Lees v Nuttall (1829) 1 Russ & M 53; 39 ER 21…250

Legard v Hodges (1792) 1 Ves Jr 477; 30 ER 447…963

Legg v Evans and Wheelton (1840) 6 M & W 36; 151 ER 311…1041

Lehman Brothers International (Europe) (In Administration), Re [2012] EWHC 2997 (Ch); [2014] 2 BCLC 295…1017, 1042, 1075

Leigh & Sillivan Ltd v Aliakmon Shipping Co Ltd (The Aliakmon) [1986] AC 785; [1986] 2 WLR 902; [1986] 2 All ER 145…63, 79, **328–30**, 362

Lena, The *see* Kydon Compañia Naviera SA v National Westminster Bank Ltd (The Lena)

Leonard v Wilson (1834) 2 Cr & M 589; 149 ER 895…685

Leonidas D, The *see* Allied Marine Transport v Vale do Rio Doce Navegacao SA (The Leonidas D)

L'Estrange v L'Estrange (1850) 13 Beav 281; 51 ER 108…866

Lett v Morris (1831) 4 Sim 607; 58 ER 227…866

Lewis v Averay [1972] 1 QB 198; [1971] 3 WLR 603; [1971] 3 All ER 907…**404–6**

Lewis v Clay (1897) 67 LJQB 224…683

Lewis v Madocks (1803) 8 Ves Jr 150; 32 ER 310…962

Lewis v Nicholson and Parker (1852) 18 QB 503; 118 ER 190…**179–81**, 196

Lewis v Thomas [1919] 1 KB 319…1079

Lexmead (Basingstoke) Ltd v Lewis [1982] AC 225; [1981] 2 WLR 713; [1981] 1 All ER 1185…**440–1**

Leyland Daf, Re *see* Buchler v Talbot

Libyan Arab Foreign Bank v Bankers Trust Co [1989] QB 728; [1989] 3 WLR 314; [1989] 3 All ER 252…564, 567, 612

Libyan Arab Foreign Bank v Manufacturers Hanover Trust (No 2) [1989] 1 Lloyd's Rep 608…612

Lickbarrow v Mason (1787) 2 Term Rep 63 6 East 20n…382–3, 388, 393

Light v Ty Europe Ltd [2003] EWCA Civ 1238; [2004] 1 Lloyd's Rep 693…120, 256, 278

Lilley (Assignees of Bennett) v Barnsley and Another (1844) 1 Car & K 344; 174 ER 839…1046

Lilley v Doubleday (1881) 7 QBD 510…99

Lily, Wilson & Co v Smales, Eeles & Co [1892] 1 QB 456…198

Lind, Re [1915] 2 Ch 345…81, 886, 1020

Linden Gardens Trust Ltd v Lenesta Sludge Disposal Ltd [1994] 1 AC 85; [1993] 3 WLR 408; [1993] 3 All ER 417…869, **878–84**, 889, 896–7, 935–7, 941–3

Lindon Tricotagefabrik v White & Meacham [1975] 1 Lloyd's Rep 384…356

Lindsay v O'Loughnane [2010] EWHC 529 (QB); [2012] BCC 153…663

Linklaters v HSBC Bank Plc [2003] EWHC 1113 (Comm); [2003] 2 Lloyd's Rep 545…741–2, 752, 758

Lipkin Gorman v Karpnale Ltd [1991] 2 AC 548; [1991] 3 WLR 10; [1992] 4 All ER 512…714–16, 831

Lister & Co v Stubbs (1890) 45 Ch D 1…240–1, **245–7**

Lister v Romford Ice and Cold Storage Co Ltd [1957] AC 555; [1957] 2 WLR 158; [1957] 1 All ER 125…1099

Liversidge v Broadbent (1859) 4 Hurl & N 603; 157 ER 978…890

Lloyd v Grace, Smith & Co [1912] AC 716…116, 174

Lloyds & Scottish Finance v Cyril Lord Carpet Sales [1992] BCLC 609…952–4, 956–8, **965–6**, 968

Lloyds Bank Ltd v Bank of America National Trust and Savings Association [1938] 2 KB 147; [1938] 2 All ER 63…770, 1033

Lloyds Bank Ltd v Chartered Bank of India Australia and China [1929] 1 KB 40; [1928] All ER Rep 285…744, 755–6

Lloyds Bank Ltd v Cooke [1907] 1 KB 794…665, 683

Lloyds Bank Ltd v EB Savory & Co [1933] AC 201…739, 755

Lloyds Bank plc v Independent Insurance Co Ltd [2000] QB 110; [1999] 2 WLR 986; [1999] 1 All ER 8…136, 713, 717

Lloyds Bank v Suisse Bankverein (1912) 107 LT 309; aff'd (1913) 108 LT 143 (CA)…150

Loescher v Dean [1950] Ch 491; [1950] 2 All ER 124…1057

Logicrose Ltd v Southend United Football Club Ltd (No 2) [1988] 1 WLR 1256…249

Lomax Leisure Ltd (In Liquidation) v Miller [2007] EWHC 2508 (Ch); [2008] 1 BCLC 262…678

London, Birmingham and South Staffordshire Banking Company, Re (1865) 34 Beav 332; 55 ER 663…629

London & County Banking Co Ltd v London & River Plate Bank Ltd (1887) 20 QBD 232...654

London and County (A & D) Ltd v Wilfred Sportsman Ltd [1971] Ch 764; [1970] 3 WLR 418; [1970] 2 All ER 600...607

London Export Corpn Ltd v Jubilee Coffee Roasting Co [1958] 1 WLR 661; [1958] 2 All ER 411...23

London Flight Centre (Stansted) Ltd v Osprey Aviation Ltd [2002] BPIR 1115...1055

London and Globe Finance Corp, Re [1902] 2 Ch 416...1049

London Joint Stock Bank Ltd v Macmillan [1918] AC 777...698, 736

London Joint Stock Bank Ltd v Simmons [1892] AC 201...43

London, Provincial and Southwestern Bank Ltd v Buszard (1918) 35 TLR 142...610

London Wine Co (Shippers), Re [1986] PCC 121...77, **331–4**, 336, 1029

Longman v Hill (1891) 7 TLR 639...214

Lonsdale v Howard & Hallam Ltd [2007] UKHL 32; [2007] 1 WLR 2055...119, **278–86**

Lord Strathcona Steamship Co Ltd v Dominion Coal Co Ltd [1926] AC 108...65

Lothian v Jenolite Ltd 1969 SC 111; 1970 SLT 31...237

Lotus Cars Ltd v Southampton Cargo Handling Plc (The Rigoletto) [2000] 2 All ER (Comm) 705...103

Louis Dreyfus Trading Ltd v Reliance Trading Ltd [2004] EWHC 525 (Comm); [2004] 2 Lloyd's Rep 243...462

Lovegrove, Re [1935] Ch 464...954

Lowe v W Machell Joinery Ltd [2011] EWCA Civ 794; [2012] 1 All ER (Comm) 153...442

Lowther v Harris [1927] 1 KB 393...**395–6**, **400–1**

Lubbe v Cape plc [2000] 1 WLR 1545; [2000] 4 All ER 268...838

Lukoil Mid-East Ltd v Barclays Bank Plc [2016] EWHC 166 (TCC); [2016] BLR 162...853

Lumsden & Co v London Trustee Savings Bank [1971] 1 Lloyd's Rep 114...734

Lunn v Thornton (1845) 1 CB 379; 135 ER 587...68, 864

Lupton v White (1808) 15 Ves Jr 432; 33 ER 817...249

Luxor (Eastbourne) Ltd v Cooper [1941] AC 108; [1941] 1 All ER 33...**261–5**, 275

Lyell v Kennedy (No 4) (1887) 18 QBD 796...164

Lyle (BS) v Rosher [1959] 1 WLR 8; [1958] 3 All ER 597...**918–19**

Lynch v Dalzell (1729) 4 Bro PC 431; 2 ER 292...884

Lysaght v Edwards (1876) 2 Ch D 499...69

M & J Marine Engineering Services Co Ltd v Shipshore Ltd [2009] EWHC 2031 (Comm)...517

M & J Polymers Ltd v Imerys Minerals Ltd [2008] EWHC 344 (Comm); [2008] 1 All ER (Comm) 893; [2008] 1 CLC 276...479

McArdle, Re [1951] Ch 669; [1951] 1 All ER 905...865

Macaura v Northern Assurance Co Ltd [1925] AC 619...1090

McCandless Aircraft LC v Payne [2010] EWHC 1835 (QB)...482

McCullagh v Lane Fox & Partners (1995) 49 Con LR 124...**181–2**

Macdonald v Pollock (No 2) [2012] CSIH 12; [2012] 1 Lloyd's Rep 425; 2013 SC 22...435, 438

McDougall v Aeromarine of Emsworth Ltd [1958] 1 WLR 1126; [1958] 3 All ER 431...**358–9**, 464

McEntire v Crossley Brothers Ltd [1895] AC 457...954, 956, 1015

McEwan & Sons v Smith (1849) 2 HL Cas 309; 9 ER 1109...1027

Mackay, Re *see* Jeavons ex p Mackay, Re

Mackay v Dick (1881) 6 App Cas 251; (1881) 8 R (HL) 37...**42**, 478

Mackersy v Ramsays, Bonars & Co (1843) 9 Cl & F 818; 8 ER 628...255

Macmillan Inc v Bishopsgate Investment Trust Plc (No 3) [1995] 1 WLR 978; [1995] 3 All ER 747...917

MacNiven (Inspector of Taxes) v Westmoreland Investments Ltd [2001] UKHL 6; [2003] 1 AC 311; [2001] 2 WLR 377; [2001] 1 All ER 865...956

McPherson v Watt (1877) 3 App Cas 254...235

Macpherson Train & Co Ltd v Howard Ross & Co Ltd [1955] 1 WLR 640; [1955] 2 All ER 445...432, 458

Madden v Kempster (1807) 1 Camp 12; 170 ER 859...1043

Mahesan S/O Thambiah v Malaysia Government Officers' Cooperative Housing Society [1979] AC 374; [1978] 2 WLR 444; [1978] 2 All ER 405...244, 247

Mahkutai, The [1996] AC 650; [1996] 3 WLR 1; [1996] 3 All ER 502...102

Mahonia Ltd v JP Morgan Chase Bank (No 1) [2003] EWHC 1927 (Comm); [2003] 2 Lloyd's Rep 911...789, **806–9**, 852

Makdessi v Cavendish Square Holdings BV [2015] UKSC 67; [2016] AC 1172; [2015] 3 WLR 1373...10, 483

Managers of the Metropolitan Asylums Board v Kingham & Sons (1890) 6 TLR 217...165

Manaifest Lipkowy, The *see* Marcan Shipping (London) v Polish Steamship Co (The Manifest Lipkowy)

Manbré Saccharine Co Ltd v Corn Products Co Ltd [1919] 1 KB 198...464, 477, **544–8**

Manchester Brewery Co v Coombs [1901] 2 Ch 608...870

Manchester Sheffield and Lincolnshire Railway Co v North Central Wagon Co (1888) 13 App Cas 554...1084

Manchester Trust v Furness, Withy & Co [1895] 2 QB 539...28, 33, 135

Manifatture Tessile Laniera Wooltex v Ashley Ltd [1979] 2 Lloyd's Rep 28...471

Mann v Forrester (1814) 4 Camp 60; 171 ER 20...269

Manni Investments Co Ltd v Eagle Star Life Assurance Co Ltd [1997] AC 749; [1997] 2 WLR 945; [1997] 3 All ER 352...**21–2**, 596, 912, 925

Maple Flock Co Ltd v Universal Furniture Products (Wembley) Ltd [1934] 1 KB 148...**468–9**

Maran Road Saw Mill v Austin Taylor & Co *see* Ng Chee Chong, Ng Weng Chong, Ng Cheng and Ng Yew (A Firm t/a Maran Road Saw Mill) v Austin Taylor & Co

Marathon Electrical Manufacturing Corp v Mashreqbank PSC [1997] 2 BCLC 460; [1997] CLC 1090...809, 868, 947

Marcan Shipping (London) v Polish Steamship Co (The Manifest Lipkowy) [1989] 2 Lloyd's Rep 138...265

Marcel (Furriers) v Tapper [1953] 1 WLR 49; [1953] 1 All ER 15...323

Marchant v Morton Down & Co [1901] 2 KB 829...908, 918, 927

Marconi Communications International Ltd v PT Pan Indonesia Bank TBK [2005] EWCA Civ 422; [2005] 2 All ER (Comm) 325...838

Marcq v Christie Manson & Woods Ltd (t/a Christie's) [2003] EWCA Civ 731; [2004] QB 286; [2003] 3 WLR 980...96, 103, 1044

Mardorf Peach & Co Ltd v Attica Sea Carriers Corp of Liberia (The Laconia) [1976] QB 835; [1977] AC 850; [1977] 2 WLR 286; [1977] 1 All ER 545...11, 604–7, 617–19

Marfani & Co v Midland Bank [1968] 1 WLR 956; [1968] 2 All ER 573...83, 733, 752–3, 759

Margarine Union GmbH v Cambay Prince Steamship Co (The Wear Breeze) [1969] 1 QB 219; [1967] 3 WLR 1569; [1967] 3 All ER 775...329

Margetson & Jones, Re [1897] 2 Ch 314...197

Marine Star, The see Coastal (Bermuda) Petroleum Ltd v VTT Vulcan Petroleum SA (No 2) (The Marine Star)

Maritime National Fish Ltd v Ocean Trawlers Ltd [1935] AC 524 (PC)...376

Marks & Spencer Plc v Freshfields Bruckhaus Deringer [2004] EWCA Civ 741; [2005] PNLR 4...238

Marquess of Bute v Barclays Bank Ltd [1955] 1 QB 202; [1954] 3 WLR 741; [1954] 3 All ER 365...735

Marsh v Commissioner of Police [1945] KB 43; [1944] 2 All ER 392...1053

Marsh v Joseph [1897] 1 Ch 213...158

Marshall v Glanvill [1917] 2 KB 87...274

Marshall v Green (1875) 1 CPD 35...305

Martell v Consett Iron Co Ltd [1955] Ch 363; [1955] 2 WLR 463; [1955] 1 All ER 481...872

Martin v Duffy [1985] NI 417; [1985] 11 NIJB 80...419

Martin-Baker Aircraft Co v Canadian Flight Equipment [1955] 2 QB 556; [1955] 3 WLR 212; [1955] 2 All ER 722...275

Martin-Smith v Williams [1999] EMLR 571...256

Marubeni Hong Kong and South China Ltd v Mongolia [2005] EWCA Civ 395; [2005] 1 WLR 2497; [2005] 2 All ER (Comm) 288...844

Mary Nour, The see CTI Group Inc v Transclear SA (The Mary Nour)

Mash & Murrell Ltd v Joseph I Emanuel Ltd [1962] 1 WLR 16...362, 368, **439**

Mason v Burningham [1949] 2 KB 545; [1949] 2 All ER 134...463

Mason v Clifton (1863) 3 F & F 899; 176 ER 408...266

Massai Aviation Services v Attorney General for the Bahamas [2007] UKPC 12 (PC)...859, 874

Master v Miller (1791) 4 Term Rep 320; 100 ER 1042...865

Mathew v TM Sutton Ltd [1994] 1 WLR 1455; [1994] 4 All ER 793...75, 1026, 1039

Matsuda v Waldorf Hotel Co Ltd (1910) 27 TLR 153...1046

May & Butcher Ltd v R [1934] 2 KB 17; [1929] All ER Rep 679...326

Maynegrain Pty Ltd v Compafina Bank (1984) 58 ALJR 389 (PC)...223

MC Bacon Ltd (No 1), Re [1990] BCC 78; [1990] BCLC 324...**1131–3**

MCC Proceeds Inc v Lehman Brothers International (Europe) [1998] 4 All ER 675...66, 83, 90, 422

Mears v London & South Western Railway Co (1862) 11 CB NS 850; 142 ER 1029...80, 83

Mechanisations (Eaglescliffe) Ltd, Re [1966] Ch 20; [1965] 2 WLR 702; [1964] 3 All ER 840...1081

Medforth v Blake [2000] Ch 86; [1999] 3 WLR 922; [1999] 3 All ER 97...1067, **1121–2**

Mediterranean Salvage & Towage Ltd v Seamar Trading & Commerce Inc [2009] EWCA Civ 531; [2010] 1 All ER (Comm) 1...258

Melachrino v Nickoll & Knight [1920] 1 KB 693...**518–19**

Mercandian Continent, The see K/S Merc-Scandia XXXXII v Lloyd's Underwriters (The Mercandian Continent)

Mercantile Bank of India Ltd v Central Bank of India Ltd [1938] AC 287; [1938] 1 All ER 52 (PC)...390–1, 1033

Mercantile Credit Co Ltd v Hamblin [1965] 2 QB 242; [1964] 3 WLR 798; [1964] 3 All ER 592...319, 392, 665

Mercantile International Group Plc v Chuan Soon Huat Industrial Group Ltd [2002] EWCA Civ 288; [2002] 1 All ER (Comm) 788; [2002] CLC 913...115, 121

Mercedes-Benz Finance Ltd v Clydesdale Bank Plc 1997 SLT 905; [1998] Lloyd's Rep 249; [1997] CLC 81...567

Mercer v Craven Grain Storage Ltd [1994] CLC 328...67, 95, 317

Mercini Lady, The see Bominflot Bunkergesellschaft für Mineralole mbH & Co KG v Petroplus Marketing AG (The Mercini Lady)

Mercuria Energy Trading Pte Ltd v Citibank NA [2015] EWHC 1481 (Comm); [2015] 1 CLC 999...76–7, 456

Meretz Investments NV v ACP Ltd [2006] EWHC 74 (Ch); [2007] Ch 197; [2007] 2 WLR 403; [2006] 3 All ER 1029...1066

Meritz Fire & Marine Insurance Co Ltd v Jan de Nul NV [2011] EWCA Civ 827; [2012] 1 All ER (Comm) 182; [2011] 2 Lloyd's Rep 379; [2011] 2 CLC 842...841, 844

Merrett v Babb [2001] EWCA Civ 214; [2001] QB 1174; [2001] 3 WLR 1...182

Mersey Steel and Iron Co Ltd v Naylor, Benzon & Co (1884) 9 App Cas 434...457

Messiniaki Tolmi, The see Astro Exito Navegacion SA v Southland Enterprise Co (The Messiniaki Tolmi) (No 2)

Meyerstein v Barber (1866) LR 2 CP 38...1028–9

Michael Elliott & Partners v UK Land [1991] 1 EGLR 39...259

Michael Gerson (Leasing) Ltd v Wilkinson [2001] QB 514; [2000] 3 WLR 1645; [2001] 1 All ER 148...76, 78, **410–12**, 417

Microbeads AC v Vinhurst Road Markings Ltd [1975] 1 WLR 218; [1975] 1 All ER 529...462

Middleton v Pollock ex p Elliott (1876) 2 Ch D 104...921

Midland Bank Ltd v RV Harris Ltd [1963] 1 WLR 1021; [1963] 2 All ER 685...684, 752

Midland Bank Ltd v Reckitt [1933] AC 1...129, 746

Midland Bank Ltd v Seymour [1955] 2 Lloyd's Rep 147...**817–19**

Midland Bank Trust Co Ltd v Hett, Stubbs & Kemp [1979] Ch 384; [1978] 3 WLR 167; [1978] 3 All ER 571...181, 225

Milan Tramways Co ex p Theys, Re (1884) 25 Ch D
   587...947
Miles v McIlwraith (1883) 8 App Cas 120 (PC)...150
Miliangos v George Frank (Textiles) Ltd [1976] AC 443;
   [1975] 3 WLR 758; [1975] 3 All ER 801...475
Millar, Son & Co v Radford (1903) 19 TLR 575...**259–60**
Miller v Beal (1879) 27 WR 403...259
Miller v Race (1758) 1 Burr 452; 97 ER 398...649
Mills v Charlesworth [1892] AC 231...1078
Minories Finance v Afribank Nigeria Ltd [1995] 1 Lloyd's
   Rep 134...768
Mirabita v Imperial Ottoman Bank (1878) 3 Ex D
   164...354
Mitchell v Ealing LBC [1979] QB 1; [1978] 2 WLR 999;
   [1978] 2 All ER 779...99
Mitsui & Co Ltd v Flota Mercante Grancolombiana SA
   (The Ciudad de Pasto and The Ciudad de Neiva)
   [1988] 1 WLR 1145; [1989] 1 All ER 951...538, **540–2**
MK International Development Co v Housing Bank
   [1991] 1 Bank LR 74...664, 678, 680–1, 688
Mocatta v Bell (1857) 24 Beav 585; 53 ER 483...1033
Modelboard Ltd v Outer Box Ltd (In Liquidation) [1992]
   BCC 945; [1993] BCLC 623...504
Mohamud v Wm Morrison Supermarkets Plc [2016]
   UKSC 11; [2016] AC 677; [2016] 2 WLR 821...116
Momm (t/a Delbrueck & Co) v Barclays Bank
   International Ltd [1977] QB 790; [1977] 2 WLR 407;
   [1976] 3 All ER 588...589, **612–19**, 621
Monkland v Jack Barclay Ltd [1951] 2 KB 252; [1951] 1
   All ER 714...379
Montgomerie v United Kingdom Mutual Steamship
   Association [1891] 1 QB 370...**168–71**, 179, 188
Montrod Ltd v Grundkötter Fleischvertriebs GmbH
   [2001] EWCA Civ 1954; [2002] 1 WLR 1975; [2002]
   3 All ER 697...225, 788, **794–7**, 802
Moody v Condor Insurance Ltd [2006] EWHC 100 (Ch);
   [2006] 1 WLR 1847; [2006] 1 All ER 934...170
Moor v Anglo-Italian Bank (1879) 10 Ch D 681...989
Moorcock, The (1889) 14 PD 64; [1886–90] All ER Rep
   530...630, 1050
Moore v Piretta PTA Ltd [1999] 1 All ER 174; [1998] CLC
   992...267, 277
Moorgate Mercantile Co Ltd v Twitchings [1977] AC
   890; [1976] 3 WLR 66; [1976] 2 All ER 641...**391–3**
Moralice (London) Ltd v ED and F Man [1954] 2 Lloyd's
   Rep 526...779
Mordaunt Bros v British Oil and Cake Mills [1910] 2 KB
   502...**485–7**
Mores v Conham (1609) Owen 123; 74 ER 946...1036
Morgan v Ashcroft [1938] 1 KB 49; [1937] 3 All
   ER 92...709
Morgan v Russell & Sons [1909] 1 KB 357...305
Morison v London County & Westminster Bank Ltd
   [1914] 3 KB 356...693, 696, 735, 739, 744
Morley v Hay (1828) 3 Man & Ry KB 396...1057
Morrell v Wootten (1852) 16 Beav 197; 51 ER
   753...**921–2**
Morris v CW Martin & Sons Ltd [1966] 1 QB 716; [1965]
   3 WLR 276; [1965] 2 All ER 725...94, 96, 102–3
Morris v Kanssen [1946] AC 459; [1946] 1 All ER
   586...130
Morris, Assignees of Smith, Bankrupts v Cleasby (1816)
   4 M & S 566; 105 ER 943...118

Morrison & Co Ltd v Shaw Savill & Albion Co Ltd [1916]
   2 KB 783...99
Morritt ex p Official Receiver, Re (1886) 18 QBD
   222...1066
Moseley v Cressey's Co (1865) LR 1 Eq 405...1061
Moss v Sweet (1851) 16 QB 493; 117 ER 968...348
Moss Steamship Co Ltd v Whinney [1912] AC
   254...1118
Motis Exports Ltd v Dampskibsselskabet AF 1912 A/S
   (No 1) [2000] 1 All ER (Comm) 91; [2000] 1 Lloyd's
   Rep 211...83, 536
Motor Oil Hellas (Corinth) Refineries SA v Shipping Corp
   of India (The Kanchenjunga) [1990] 1 Lloyd's Rep
   391...467
Mount I, The *see* Raiffeisen Zentralbank Osterreich AG v
   Five Star General Trading LLC (The Mount I)
Movitex Ltd v Bulfield (1986) 2 BCC 99403; [1988]
   BCLC 104...232
MSC Mediterranean Shipping Co SA v Cottonex
   Anstalt [2015] EWHC 283 (Comm); [2015] 2 All ER
   (Comm) 614...42
MSC Mediterranean Shipping Co SA v Cottonex
   Anstalt [2016] EWCA Civ 789; [2016] 2 Lloyd's
   Rep 494...42
Mucklow v Mangles (1808) 1 Taunt 318; 127 ER
   856...**353**
Muldoon v Wood Unreported, 1 April 1998...223
Muller Maclean & Co v Leslie & Anderson (1921) 8 Ll L
   Rep 328...481
Mulliner v Florence (1878) 3 QBD 484...1057
Murphy v Brentwood District Council [1991] 1 AC 398;
   [1990] 3 WLR 414; [1990] 2 All ER 908...599
Mustapha v Wedlake [1891] WN 201...1030
MW High Tech Projects UK Ltd v Biffa Waste Services Ltd
   [2015] EWHC 949 (TCC); [2015] 1 CLC 449...789

N & J Vlassopulos Ltd v Ney Shipping Ltd (The Santa
   Carina) [1977] 1 Lloyd's Rep 478...**188–90**
Nahum v Royal Holloway and Bedford New College
   [1999] EMLR 252...260
Nanfri, The *see* Federal Commerce & Navigation Co Ltd
   v Molena Alpha Inc (The Nanfri)
Nanka-Bruce v Commonwealth Trust Ltd [1926] AC 77
   (PC)...**344–5**
Nanwa Gold Mines Ltd, Re [1955] 1 WLR 1080; [1955]
   3 All ER 219...1061, 1125
Nash v Dix (1898) 78 LT 445...207, 213
National Bank v Silke [1891] 1 QB 435...674, 728
National Bank of Commerce v National Westminster
   Bank Plc [1990] 2 Lloyd's Rep 514...735
National Bank of Egypt v Hannevig's Bank Ltd (1919) 1
   Ll L Rep 69...824
National Bank of New Zealand v Walpole and Patterson
   [1975] 2 NZLR 7...734
National Coal Board v Gamble [1959] 1 QB 11; [1958] 3
   WLR 434; [1958] 3 All ER 203...345
National Employers' Mutual General Insurance
   Association Ltd v Elphinstone [1929] WN 135...252
National Employers' Mutual General Insurance
   Association Ltd v Jones [1990] 1 AC 24; [1988] 2
   WLR 952; [1988] 2 All ER 425...**419–20**
National Oilwell (UK) Ltd v Davy Offshore Ltd [1993] 2
   Lloyd's Rep 582...162, 165, 209

National Phonographic Co Ltd v Edison-Bell Consolidated Phonographic Co Ltd [1908] 1 Ch 335...64

National Provincial & Union Bank of England v Charnley [1924] 1 KB 431...971, 973

National Provincial Bank of England v Harle (1881) 6 QBD 626...903

National Provincial Bank Ltd v Ainsworth [1965] AC 1175; [1965] 3 WLR 1; [1965] 2 All ER 472...59

National Westminster Bank Ltd v Barclays Bank International Ltd [1975] QB 654; [1975] 2 WLR 12; [1974] 3 All ER 834...603, 711–12, 735

National Westminster Bank Ltd v Halesowen Presswork and Assemblies Ltd [1972] AC 785; [1972] 2 WLR 455; [1972] 1 All ER 641...1137

National Westminster Bank Plc v Jones [2001] 1 BCLC 98...**955**

National Westminster Bank Plc v Kapoor [2011] EWCA Civ 1083; [2012] 1 All ER 1201...907, **933–4**

National Westminster Bank Plc v Somer International (UK) Ltd [2001] EWCA Civ 970; [2002] QB 1286; [2002] 3 WLR 64; [2002] 1 All ER 198...716

National Westminster Bank Plc v Spectrum Plus Ltd [2005] UKHL 41; [2005] 2 AC 680; [2005] 3 WLR 58; [2005] 4 All ER 209...956–7, 985, **988–1000**, 1071–2, 1076

Neste Oy v Lloyds Bank Plc [1983] 2 Lloyd's Rep 658...1127

New Bullas Trading Ltd, Re [1994] BCC 36; [1994] 1 BCLC 485...985, 987, 993–5

New Zealand and Australian Land Co v Watson (1881) 7 QBD 374...254

New Zealand Netherlands Society 'Oranje' v Kuys [1973] 1 WLR 1126; [1973] 2 All ER 1222 (PC)...236

Newcastle International Airport Ltd v Eversheds LLP [2012] EWHC 2648 (Ch); [2013] PNLR 5...145

Newfoundland v Newfoundland Railway Co (1888) 13 App Cas 199 (PC)...945–6

Newland Shipping and Forwarding Ltd v Toba Trading FZC [2014] EWHC 661 (Comm)...526

Newtons of Wembley Ltd v Williams [1965] 1 QB 560; [1964] 3 WLR 888; [1964] 3 All ER 532...407, **414–15, 418–19**

Ng Chee Chong, Ng Weng Chong, Ng Cheng and Ng Yew (A Firm t/a Maran Road Saw Mill) v Austin Taylor & Co [1975] 1 Lloyd's Rep 156...629, 816

Niblett Ltd v Confectioners Materials Co Ltd [1921] 3 KB 387...437, 461

Nicolls v Bastard (1835) 2 Cr M & R 659; 150 ER 279...75

Niru Battery Manufacturing Co v Milestone Trading Ltd (No 1) [2002] EWHC 1425 (Comm); [2002] 2 All ER (Comm) 705...715–16

Niru Battery Manufacturing Co v Milestone Trading Ltd (No 1) [2003] EWCA Civ 1446; [2004] QB 985; [2004] 2 WLR 1415; [2004] 1 All ER (Comm) 193...831

Nisshin Shipping Co Ltd v Cleaves & Co Ltd [2003] EWHC 2602 (Comm); [2004] 1 All ER (Comm) 481; [2004] 1 Lloyd's Rep 38...259

Noblett v Hopkinson [1905] 2 KB 214...356

Noel v Poland [2001] 2 BCLC 645; [2002] Lloyd's Rep IR 30...182

Nokes v Doncaster Amalgamated Collieries Ltd [1940] AC 1014; [1940] 3 All ER 549...870, 879

Norfolk CC v Secretary of State for the Environment [1973] 1 WLR 1400; [1973] 3 All ER 673...145

Norglen Ltd (In Liquidation) v Reeds Rains Prudential Ltd [1999] 2 AC 1; [1997] 3 WLR 1177; [1998] 1 All ER 218...887, 955

North and South Insurance Corp Ltd v National Provincial Bank Ltd [1936] 1 KB 328...665

North and South Trust Co v Berkeley [1971] 1 WLR 470; [1971] 1 All ER 980...23, 235, 237

North & South Wales Bank Ltd v Macbeth [1908] AC 137...670

North Central Wagon Finance Co Ltd v Brailsford [1962] 1 WLR 1288; [1962] 1 All ER 502...1084

North Star Shipping Ltd v Sphere Drake Insurance Plc [2006] EWCA Civ 378; [2006] 2 All ER (Comm) 65...1093

North Western Bank Ltd v John Poynter Son & MacDonalds [1895] AC 56...1033

Northern Bank Ltd v Ross [1990] BCC 883...984

Norwich Union Fire Insurance Society Ltd v WMH Price Ltd [1934] AC 455 (PC)...709

Notara v Henderson (1872) LR 7 QB 225...154

Nova (Jersey) Knit Ltd v Kammgarn Spinnerei GmbH [1977] 1 WLR 713; [1977] 2 All ER 463...572, 574, **656–7**

Novaknit Hellas SA v Kumar Bros International Ltd [1998] Lloyd's Rep Bank 287; [1998] CLC 971...664

Novoship (UK) Ltd v Mikhaylyuk [2015] EWHC 992 (Comm)...**243–4**

Nsubuga v Commercial Union Assurance Co Plc [1998] 2 Lloyd's Rep 682...1101

NW Robbie & Co Ltd v Witney Warehouse Co Ltd [1963] 1 WLR 1324; [1963] 3 All ER 613...946

Oasis Merchandising Services Ltd (In Liquidation), Re [1998] Ch 170; [1997] 2 WLR 764; [1997] 1 All ER 1009...886

Obestain Inc v National Mineral Development Corp Ltd (The Sanix Ace) [1987] 1 Lloyd's Rep 465...74

OBG Ltd v Allan [2007] UKHL 21; [2008] 1 AC 1; [2007] 2 WLR 920...58, 64, 79, **84–9**, 225, 735, 742, 1041

Ocean Frost, The *see* Armagas Ltd v Mundogas SA (The Ocean Frost)

Odessa, The [1916] 1 AC 145 (PC)...1025, **1038–9**

Offer-Hoar v Larkstore Ltd [2005] EWHC 2742 (TCC); [2006] PNLR 17...936

Offer-Hoar v Larkstore Ltd [2006] EWCA Civ 1079; [2006] 1 WLR 2926...**936–43**

Office of Fair Trading v Lloyds TSB Bank Plc [2006] EWCA Civ 268; [2007] QB 1; [2006] 3 WLR 452...637, 641

Office of Fair Trading v Lloyds TSB Bank Plc [2007] UKHL 48; [2008] 1 AC 316; [2007] 3 WLR 733...642

Official Assignee of Madras v Mercantile Bank of India Ltd [1935] AC 53 (PC)...77–8, **1026–7**, 1029

Official Custodian for Charities v Mackey (No 2) [1985] 1 WLR 1308; [1985] 2 All ER 1016...61

Official Manager of the Athenaeum Life Assurance Society v Pooley (1858) 3 De G & J 294; 44 ER 1281...943–4

Offshore International SA v Banco Central SA [1977] 1 WLR 399; [1976] 3 All ER 749; [1976] 2 Lloyd's Rep 402…836–7

Old Grovebury Manor Farm Ltd v W Seymour Plant Sales & Hire Ltd (No 2) [1979] 1 WLR 1397; [1979] 3 All ER 504…883

Olds Discount Co Ltd v Cohen [1938] 3 All ER 281n…966

Olds Discount Co Ltd v John Playfair Ltd [1938] 3 All ER 275…957–8, 966

Oliver v Court (1820) 8 Price 127…234

Oliver v Davis [1949] 2 KB 727; [1949] 2 All ER 353…**676–8**, 680

Ollett v Jordan [1918] 2 KB 41…340

On Demand Information Plc (In Administrative Receivership) v Michael Gerson (Finance) Plc [2001] 1 WLR 155; [2000] 4 All ER 734…64

On Demand Information Plc (In Administrative Receivership) v Michael Gerson (Finance) Plc [2002] UKHL 13; [2003] 1 AC 368; [2002] 2 WLR 919…64

Online Catering Ltd v Acton [2010] EWCA Civ 58; [2011] QB 204…1078–9

Oppenheimer v Attenborough & Sons [1908] 1 KB 221…401

Orbit Mining & Trading Co Ltd v Westminster Bank Ltd [1963] 1 QB 794; [1962] 3 WLR 1256; [1962] 3 All ER 565…633, 664

Orient Co v Brekke & Howlid [1913] 1 KB 531…544

Orion Finance Ltd v Crown Financial Management Ltd (No 1) [1994] BCC 897; [1994] 2 BCLC 607…886

Orion Finance Ltd v Crown Financial Management Ltd (No 1) [1996] BCC 621; [1996] 2 BCLC 78…**957**

O'Sullivan v Williams [1992] 3 All ER 385…75

Otis Vehicle Rentals Ltd (formerly Brandrick Hire (Birmingham) Ltd) v Ciceley Commercials Ltd (Damages) [2002] EWCA Civ 1064…475, 477

Overbrooke Estates Ltd v Glencombe Properties Ltd [1974] 1 WLR 1335; [1974] 3 All ER 511…144

Owners of the Borvigilant v Owners of the Romina G [2003] EWCA Civ 935; [2003] 2 All ER (Comm); [2003] 2 Lloyd's Rep 520…167

Owners of Cargo Laden on Board the Albacruz v Owners of the Albazero [1977] AC 774; [1976] 3 WLR 419; [1976] 3 All ER 129…546

Owners of Cargo Lately Laden on Board the Siskina v Distos Compania Naviera SA [1979] AC 210; [1977] 3 WLR 818; [1977] 3 All ER 803…801

Ozalid Group (Export) Ltd v African Continental Bank Ltd [1979] 2 Lloyd's Rep 231…831

P & O Nedlloyd BV v Arab Metals Co (The UB Tiger) [2006] EWCA Civ 1717; [2007] 1 WLR 2288; [2007] 2 All ER (Comm) 401…483

Pacific & General Insurance Co Ltd v Hazell [1997] LRLR 65; [1997] BCC 400…274–5

Pacific Associates v Baxter [1990] 1 QB 993; [1989] 3 WLR 1150; [1989] 2 All ER 159…602

Pacific Motor Auctions Pty Ltd v Motor Credits (Hire Finance) Ltd [1965] AC 867; [1965] 2 WLR 881; [1965] 2 All ER 105 (PC)…402, **408–10**, 416

Pacific Trading Co Ltd v Robert O Wiener & Co (1923) 14 Ll L Rep 51…432

Page v Combined Shipping & Trading Co Ltd [1997] 3 All ER 656; [1996] CLC 1952…119, 282

Pain, Re [1919] 1 Ch 38…909

Palk v Mortgage Services Funding Plc [1993] Ch 330; [1993] 2 WLR 415; [1993] 2 All ER 481…1065

Palmer v Carey [1926] AC 703 (PC)…971, 1016, 1062, 1064

Palmer v Temple (1839) 9 Ad & El 508; 112 ER 1304…322

Pan Ocean Shipping Co Ltd v Creditcorp Ltd (The Trident Beauty) [1994] 1 WLR 161; [1994] 1 All ER 470…947

Panagiotis Stravelakis v Rocco Guiseppe and Figli SNC (The Astyanax) [1985] 2 Lloyd's Rep 109…205

Panama New Zealand and Australian Royal Mail Co, Re (1870) LR 5 Ch App 318…986, 989

Pangood Ltd v Barclay Brown & Co Ltd [1999] 1 All ER (Comm) 460; [1999] Lloyd's Rep IR 405…254

Pankhania v Hackney LBC [2002] EWHC 2441 (Ch); [2002] NPC 123…198

Panoutsos v Raymond Hadley Corp of New York [1917] 2 KB 473…813

Papamichael v National Westminster Bank Plc (No 2) [2003] EWHC 164 (Comm); [2003] 1 Lloyd's Rep 341…726

Parker, Re (1882) 21 Ch D 408…269

Parker v British Airways Board [1982] QB 1004; [1982] 2 WLR 503; [1982] 1 All ER 834…76

Parker v McKenna (1874) LR 10 Ch App 96…233

Parks v Esso Petroleum Co Ltd [2000] ECC 45; [2000] Eu LR 25; (1999) 18 Tr LR 232…120

Parsons (Livestock) Ltd v Uttley Ingham & Co Ltd [1978] QB 791; [1977] 3 WLR 990; [1978] 1 All ER 525…324

Patel v Standard Chartered Bank [2001] Lloyd's Rep Bank 229…128, 698

Paterson v Gandasequi (1812) 15 East 62; 104 ER 768…176

Patrick & Co Ltd v Russo-British Grain Export Co Ltd [1927] 2 KB 535…515, 518, 522–3

Paul & Frank v Discount Bank (Overseas) [1967] Ch 348; [1966] 3 WLR 490; [1966] 2 All ER 922…**982–4**

Pavia & Co SpA v Thurmann Nielsen [1952] 2 QB 84; [1952] 1 All ER 492…**813–14**

Paxton v Courtnay (1860) 2 F & F 131; 175 ER 991…23

Peachdart Ltd, Re [1984] Ch 131; [1983] 3 WLR 878; [1983] 3 All ER 204…**503–4**

Peacock v Pursell (1863) 14 CB NS 728; 143 ER 630…705

Pears (Newark) Ltd v Omega Proteins Ltd [2009] EWHC 1070 (Comm); [2009] 2 Lloyd's Rep 339…437

Pearse v Green (1819) 1 Jac & W 135; 37 ER 327…250

Pearson v Rose & Young Ltd [1951] 1 KB 275; [1950] 2 All ER 1027…**398–9**, 401

Penn v Bristol and West Building Society [1997] 1 WLR 1356; [1997] 3 All ER 470…199

Pennington v Reliance Motor Works Ltd [1923] 1 KB 127…1056–7

Pereira Fernandes SA v Mehta [2006] EWHC 813 (Ch); [2006] 1 WLR 1543…663

Performing Right Society Ltd v London Theatre of Varieties Ltd [1924] AC 1…928, 932–3

Permanent Houses (Holdings) Ltd, Re (1989) 5 BCC 151…984

Petrofina (UK) Ltd v Magnaload Ltd [1984] QB 127; [1983] 3 WLR 805; [1983] 3 All ER 35…1090

Petrograde Inc v Stinnes GmbH [1995] 1 Lloyd's Rep 142...464

Petrologic Capital SA v Banque Cantonale de Genéve [2012] EWHC 453 (Comm); [2012] ILPr 20...772

Petromec Inc v Petroleo Brasileiro SA Petrobras (No 3) [2005] EWCA Civ 891; [2006] 1 Lloyd's Rep 121...42, 248

Petrotrade Inc v Smith (Vicarious Liability) [2000] 1 Lloyd's Rep 486...244–5

Phelps v Spon Smith & Co (Preliminary Issues) [2001] BPIR 326...**901**

Philip Collins Ltd v Davis [2000] 3 All ER 808...716

Philip Head & Sons Ltd v Showfronts Ltd [1970] 1 Lloyd's Rep 140...324, **341–4**, 352

Phillips v Brooks Ltd [1919] 2 KB 243...405

Phonogram Ltd v Lane [1982] QB 938; [1981] 3 WLR 736; [1981] 3 All ER 182...**191**

Photo Production Ltd v Securicor Transport Ltd [1980] AC 827; [1980] 2 WLR 283; [1980] 1 All ER 556...452

Pignataqro v Gilroy [1919] 1 KB 459...**353–5**

Pigot v Cubley (1864) 15 CB NS 701; 143 ER 960...**1065**

Pigot's Case [1614] All ER Rep 50; 77 ER 1177; 80 ER 1096; (1614) 2 Bulst 246; (1614) 11 Co Rep 26...**699**

Pinnock, Assignees of Charles Bean, a Bankrupt v Harrison (1838) 3 M & W 532; 150 ER 1256...**1046**

Pinnock Bros v Lewis & Peat Ltd [1923] 1 KB 690...430

Pinto Leite and Nephews, Re [1929] 1 Ch 221...945

Pioneer Concrete (UK) Ltd v National Employers Mutual General Insurance Association Ltd [1985] 2 All ER 395...**1101**

Pioneer Container, The [1994] 2 AC 324; [1994] 3 WLR 1; [1994] 2 All ER 250 (PC)...94, **96**, 102

Pioneer Shipping Ltd v BTP Tioxide Ltd (The Nema) (No 2) [1982] AC 724; [1981] 3 WLR 292; [1981] 2 All ER 1030...22

Pitcher v Rawlins (1872) LR 7 Ch App 259...920

Pitt v Holt [2013] UKSC 26; [2013] 2 AC 108; [2013] 2 WLR 1200...713

PJ Pipe & Valve Co Ltd v Audco India Ltd [2005] EWHC 1904 (QB); [2006] Eu LR 368...120, 267

PK Airfinance Sarl v Alpstream AG [2015] EWCA Civ 1318; [2015] 2 WLR 875...1066

Plasticmoda Societa Per Azioni v Davidsons (Manchester) Ltd [1952] 1 Lloyd's Rep 527...815

Playa Larga, The *see* Empresa Exportadora De Azucar (CUBAZUCAR) v Industria Azucarera Nacional SA (IANSA) (The Playa Larga and Marble Islands)

Pole v Leask (1862) 33 LJ Ch 155...126

Polhill v Walter (1832) 3 B & Ad 114; 110 ER 43...194

Pollway Ltd v Abdullah [1974] 1 WLR 493; [1974] 2 All ER 381...680

Poole v Smith's Car Sales (Balham) Ltd [1962] 1 WLR 744; [1962] 2 All ER 482...**348–50**

Pople v Evans [1969] 2 Ch 255; [1968] 3 WLR 97; [1968] 2 All ER 743...202

Port Line v Ben Line Steamers [1958] 2 QB 146; [1958] 2 WLR 551; [1958] 1 All ER 787...65

Port Swettenham Authority v TW Wu & Co Sdn Bhd [1979] AC 580; [1978] 3 WLR 530; [1978] 3 All ER 337 (PC)...98, 101

Portman Building Society v Hamlyn Taylor Neck [1998] 4 All ER 202...716

Portuguese Consolidated Copper Mines Ltd, Re (1890) 45 Ch D 16...165

Potton Homes Ltd v Coleman Contractors (Overseas) Ltd (1984) 28 BLR 19...**851–2**

Powell v Braun [1954] 1 WLR 401; [1954] 1 All ER 484...259

Powell v Evan Jones & Co [1905] 1 KB 11; 92 LT 430...253, 255

Powell v Wiltshire [2004] EWCA Civ 534; [2005] QB 117; [2004] 3 WLR 666...387

Power Curber International Ltd v National Bank of Kuwait SAK [1981] 1 WLR 1233; [1981] 3 All ER 607...838

Prager v Blatspiel, Stamp and Heacock Ltd [1924] 1 KB 566...156–7

Preist v Last [1903] 2 KB 148...442, **444**

Prenn v Simmonds [1971] 1 WLR 1381; [1971] 3 All ER 237...20

Prentis Donegan & Partners Ltd v Leeds and Leeds Co Inc [1998] 2 Lloyd's Rep 326...254

Presentaciones Musicales SA v Secunda [1994] Ch 271; [1994] 2 WLR 660; [1994] 2 All ER 737...166

Price v Neal (1762) 3 Burr 1354; 97 ER 871...711

Price Meats Ltd v Barclays Bank plc [2000] 2 All ER (Comm) 346...698

Prideaux v Criddle (1869) LR 4 QB 455...590

Priestly v Fernie (1863) 3 Hurl & C 977; 159 ER 820...178, 217

Primorje, The *see* Jugoslavenska Linijska Plovidba v Hulsman (t/a Brusse & Sippel Import-Export) (The Primorje)

Produce Brokers Co Ltd v Olympia Oil & Cake Co Ltd [1917] 1 KB 320...367, 548

Produce Marketing Consortium (In Liquidation) Ltd, Re (No 2) (1989) 5 BCC 569; [1989] BCLC 520...**1134–7**

Proton Energy Group SA v Orlen Lietuva [2013] EWHC 2872 (Comm); [2014] 1 All ER (Comm) 972...**432–4**

PST Energy 7 Shipping LLC Product Shipping & Trading SA v OW Bunker Malta Ltd [2016] UKSC 23; [2016] AC 1034; [2016] 2 WLR 1193...**300–2**, 337, 476–7, 479, 512

PT Berlian Laju Tanker TBK v Nuse Shipping Ltd (The Aktor) [2008] EWHC 1330 (Comm); [2008] 2 All ER (Comm) 784; [2008] 1 CLC 967...564

Punjab National Bank v De Boinville 1 WLR 1138; [1992] 3 All ER 104; [1992] 1 Lloyd's Rep 7...181, 187

Purnell v Paine [1918] 2 Ch 72...256

Pyrene Co Ltd v Scindia Steam Navigation Co Ltd [1954] 2 QB 402; [1954] 2 WLR 1005; [1954] 2 All ER 158...**539–40**

Pyxis Special Shipping Co Ltd v Dritsas & Kaglis Bros (The Scaplake) [1978] 2 Lloyd's Rep 380...217

R v Adams (Christopher) [2003] EWCA Crim 3620...568

R v Chester and North Wales Legal Aid Area Office (No 12) ex p Floods of Queensferry Ltd [1998] 1 WLR 1496; [1998] BCC 685; [1998] 2 BCLC 436...935

R v International Stock Exchange of the United Kingdom and the Republic of Ireland Ltd ex p Else (1982) Ltd [1993] QB 534; [1993] 2 WLR 70; [1993] 1 All ER 420...34

R v Life Assurance Unit Trust Regulatory Organisation ex p Ross [1993] QB 17; [1992] 3 WLR 549; [1993] 1 All ER 545...34

R v Lloyd's of London ex p Briggs [1993] 1 Lloyd's Rep 176...34

R v Monopolies and Mergers Commission ex p Argyll Group Plc [1986] 1 WLR 763; [1986] 2 All ER 257...35

R v Panel on Takeovers and Mergers ex p Datafin Plc [1987] QB 815; [1987] 2 WLR 699; [1987] 1 All ER 564...34–5

R v Preddy (John Crawford) [1996] AC 815; [1996] 3 WLR 255; [1996] 3 All ER 481...**565–8**

R v Randall (Daniel Gilbert) (1811) Russ & Ry 195; 168 ER 756...665

R v Richards (1811) Russ & Ry 193; 168 ER 755...665

R v Secretary of State for Transport ex p Factortame [1990] 2 AC 85; [1989] 2 WLR 997; [1989] 2 All ER 692...25

R v Walbrook (Martin) (1994) 15 Cr App R (S) 783; [1994] Crim LR 613...**868**

R v Wheeler (Stephen Godfrey) (1991) 92 Cr App R 279...**461**

R v Williams (Jacqueline) Unreported 30 July 1993...565

Rabone v Williams (1785) 7 Term Rep 360n...218

Raffaella, The *see* Egyptian International Foreign Trade Co v Soplex Wholesale Supplies Ltd and PS Refson SL Co Ltd (The Raffaella)

Raiffeisen Zentralbank Osterreich AG v Five Star General Trading LLC (The Mount I) [2001] EWCA Civ 68; [2001] QB 825; [2001] 2 WLR 1344...58–9, 886, 902, 907

Railton v Hodgson (1804) 4 Taunt 576n...191

Rainbow v Howkins [1904] 2 KB 322...199

Rainy Sky SA v Kookmin Bank [2011] UKSC 50; [2011] 1 WLR 2900; [2012] 1 All ER 1137...844

Rama Corp Ltd v Proved Tin & General Investments Ltd [1952] 2 QB 147; [1952] 1 All ER 554...**132–5**, 145

Ramazotti v Bowering & Arundell (1859) 7 CB NS 851; 141 ER 1050...223

Ramchurn Mullick v Luchmeechund Radakissen and Gobind Doss (1854) 9 Moo PC 46; 14 ER 215 (PC)...727

Ramsay v Margrett [1894] 2 QB 18...72

Ramsey v Hartley [1977] 1 WLR 686; [1977] 2 All ER 673...886

Rasbora Ltd v JCL Marine Ltd [1977] 1 Lloyd's Rep 645...889

Rashdall v Ford (1866) LR 2 Eq 750...198

Rasnoimport V/O v Guthrie & Co Ltd [1966] 1 Lloyd's Rep 1...198

Raven, The *see* Banco Central SA v Lingoss & Falce Ltd (The Raven)

Rayner v Grote 153 ER 888; (1846) 15 M & W 359...**192–3**

Rayner v Preston (1881) 18 Ch D 1...69

RD Harbottle (Mercantile) Ltd v National Westminster Bank Ltd [1978] QB 146; [1977] 3 WLR 752; [1977] 2 All ER 862...787, 846–7, 852

RE Jones Ltd v Waring and Gillow Ltd [1926] AC 670...**683**, 692, 709, 716, 762

Read v Anderson (1884) 13 QBD 779...275

Read v Brown (1888) 22 QBD 128...927

Real Meat Co Ltd (In Receivership), Re [1996] BCC 254...1075

Reardon Smith Ltd v Yngvar Hensen Tangen (The Diana Prosperity) [1976] 1 WLR 989; [1976] 3 All ER 570...20, **428–9**

Reddall v Union Castle Mail Steamship Co (1914) 84 LJKB 360...**490–1**

Reed Publishing Holdings Limited, Reed Properties Limited and IPC Magazines Limited v Kings Reach Investments Ltd Unreported 25 May 1983...882–3

Reeves v Capper (1838) 5 Bing NC 136; 132 ER 1057...**1032**, 1034

Refuge Assurance Co Ltd v Kettlewell [1909] AC 243...174

Regal (Hastings) Ltd v Gullivar [1967] 2 AC 134; [1942] 1 All ER 378...264

Regent ohG Aisestadt & Barig v Francesco of Jermyn Street Ltd [1981] 3 All ER 327...469

Rekstin v Severo Sibirsko Gosudarstvennoe Akcionernoe Obschestvo Komseverputj [1933] 1 KB 47; [1932] All ER Rep 534...588–9, 612, 616–18, 930

Relfo Ltd (In Liquidation) v Varsani [2014] EWCA Civ 360; [2015] 1 BCLC 14...724

Remco, The *see* Gewa Chartering BV v Remco Shipping Lines Ltd (The Remco)

Resolute Maritime Inc v Nippon Kaiji Kyokai (The Skopas) [1983] 1 WLR 857; [1983] 2 All ER 1...175

R G Grain Trade LLP (UK) v Feed Factors International Ltd [2011] EWHC 1889 (Comm); [2011] 2 Lloyd's Rep 433...**423**

Rhodes v Allied Dunbar (Pension Services) Ltd [1987] 1 WLR 1703; [1988] 1 All ER 524...917

Rhodes v Fielder, Jones and Harrison (1919) 89 LJKB 159...**267–8**

Rhodes v Forwood (1876) 1 App Cas 256...265, 274, 276

Rhodian River Shipping Co SA v Halla Maritime Corp [1984] 1 Lloyd's Rep 373...150

Richmond Gate Property Co, Re [1965] 1 WLR 335; [1964] 3 All ER 936...259

Rickford v Ridge (1810) 2 Camp 537; 170 ER 1243...590

Rio Su, The *see* Gatoil International Inc v Tradax Petroleum Ltd (The Rio Sun)

Riyad Bank v Ahli United Bank (UK) Plc [2006] EWCA Civ 780; [2006] 2 All ER (Comm) 777; [2006] 2 Lloyd's Rep 292...255

Robert A Munro & Co Ltd v Meyer [1930] 2 KB 312...469

Roberts v Gill & Co [2010] UKSC 22; [2011] 1 AC 240; [2010] 2 WLR 1227...**932–4**

Roberts v Ogilby (1821) 9 Price 269; 147 ER 89...126

Robins & Co v Gray [1895] 2 QB 501...1053

Robinson v Graves [1935] 1 KB 579...323–4

Robinson v Mollett (1875) LR 7 HL 802...118, 131

Robinson v Unicos Property Corp [1962] 1 WLR 520; [1962] 2 All ER 24...933

Robot Arenas Ltd v Waterfield [2010] EWHC 115 (QB)...99

Rodick v Gandell (1852) 1 De GM & G 763; 42 ER 749...1062

Rogers v Challis (1859) 27 Beav 175; 54 ER 68...1017, 1064

Rogers v Kelly (1809) 2 Camp 123; 170 ER 1102...86

Rohde v Thwaites (1827) 6 B & C 388; 108 ER 495...354

Rolfe Lubell & Co (a firm) v Keith [1979] 1 All ER 860...**694–5**

Rolls-Royce Power Engineering plc v Ricardo Consulting Engineers Ltd [2003] EWHC 2871 (TCC); [2004] 2 All ER (Comm) 129...**208–11**

Romer & Haslam, Re [1893] 2 QB 286...629

Rose v Watson (1864) 10 HL Cas 672; 11 ER 1187...1077

Rosenbaum v Belson [1900] 2 Ch 267...131

Ross v London County Westminster & Parr's Bank Ltd [1919] 1 KB 678...755

Ross T Smyth & Co Ltd v TD Bailey Son & Co (1940) 45 Com Cas 292; (1940) 67 Ll L Rep 147...540–1, **545–6**

Rother Iron Works Ltd v Canterbury Precision Engineers Ltd [1974] QB 1; [1973] 2 WLR 281; [1973] 1 All ER 394...946

Rothschild v Brookman (1831) 5 Bli NS 165; 5 ER 273...234

Rowland v Divall [1923] 2 KB 500...330, **459–61**, 463, 526

Royal Bank of Scotland Group Plc v Customs and Excise Commissioners (Reciprocity Fees) [2002] STC 575; 2002 SLT 664...634

Royal Bank of Scotland Plc v Cassa di Risparmio delle Provincie Lombarde SA [1992] 1 Bank LR 251...773

Royal British Bank v Turquand (1856) 6 El & Bl 327; 119 ER 886...696

Royal Brunei Airlines Sdn Bhd v Tan [1995] 2 AC 378; [1995] 3 WLR 64; [1995] 3 All ER 97 (PC)...91

Royal Products Ltd v Midland Bank Ltd [1981] 2 Lloyd's Rep 194...**586–9**, 609, 621

Rumsey v North-Eastern Railway Company (1863) 14 CB NS; 143 ER 596 641...1056

Rushforth v Hadfield (1805) 6 East 519...**1047**

Rushforth v Hadfield (1806) 7 East 224; 103 ER 86...**1048**

Rust v McNaught and Co Ltd [1918] 144 LT Jo 440...1057

RV Ward Ltd v Bignall [1967] 1 QB 534; [1967] 2 WLR 1050; [1967] 2 All ER 449...343, **492–6**

Ryall v Rowles (1750) 1 Ves Sen 165; 28 ER 490...915

Rye v Rye [1962] AC 496; [1962] 2 WLR 361; [1962] 1 All ER 146...975

Sachs v Miklos [1948] 2 KB 23; [1948] 1 All ER 67...157

Saetta, The see Forsythe International (UK) Ltd v Silver Shipping Co Ltd (The Saetta)

Safa Ltd v Banque du Caire [2000] 2 All ER (Comm) 567...657, 809, 852

Sagal (t/a Bunz UK) v Atelier Bunz GmbH [2009] EWCA Civ 700; [2009] 4 All ER 1253; [2009] 2 Lloyd's Rep 303...121

Said v Butt [1920] 3 KB 497...**206–7**, 212–13

Sainsbury's Supermarkets Ltd v Mastercard Inc [2015] EWHC 3472 (Ch); [2016] CAT 11...**632**, 634

St Albans District Council v International Computers Ltd [1996] 4 All ER 481...303, 325, 453

Saint Gobain Building Distribution Ltd (t/a International Decorative Surfaces) v Hillmead Joinery (Swindon) Ltd [2015] BLR 555...453

St Martins Property Corp Ltd v Sir Robert McAlpine & Sons see Linden Gardens Trust Ltd v Lenesta Sludge Disposal Ltd

Saipol SA v Inerco Trade SA [2014] EWHC 2211 (Comm); [2015] 1 Lloyd's Rep 26...525–6

Salda, The see Bem Dis A Turk Ticaret S/A TR v International Agri Trade Co Ltd (The Selda)

Salomon v Salomon & Co Ltd [1897] AC 22...990

Salter v Finning Ltd [1997] AC 473; [1996] 3 WLR 190; [1996] 3 All ER 398...445

Salton v New Beeston Cycle Co [1900] 1 Ch 43...196

Sandeman Coprimar SA v Transitos y Transportes Integrales SL [2003] EWCA Civ 113; [2003] QB 1270; [2003] 2 WLR 1496; [2003] 3 All ER 108...**102**

Sanders Bros v Maclean & Co (1883) 11 QBD 327...41

Sang Stone Hamoon Jonoub Co Ltd v Baoyue Shipping Co Ltd [2015] EWHC 2288 (Comm); [2016] 1 Lloyd's Rep 320...102

Sanix Ace, The see Obestain Inc v National Mineral Development Corp Ltd (The Sanix Ace)

Santa Carina, The see N & J Vlassopulos Ltd v Ney Shipping Ltd (The Santa Carina)

Santley v Wilde [1899] 2 Ch 474...1059

Satanita, The see Clarke v Earl of Dunraven (The Satanita)

Saunders (Inspector of Taxes) v Pilcher [1949] 2 All ER 1097...303

Sayer v Wagstaff (1844) 14 LJ Ch 116...629

Scandinavian Trading Tanker Co AB v Flota Petrolera Ecuatoriana (The Scaptrade) [1983] 2 AC 694; [1983] 3 WLR 203; [1983] 2 All ER 763...42

Scaplake, The see Pyxis Special Shipping Co Ltd v Dritsas & Kaglis Bros (The Scaplake)

Scaptrade, The see Scandinavian Trading Tanker Co AB v Flota Petrolera Ecuatoriana

Scarf v Jardine (1882) 7 App Cas 345; [1882] All ER Rep 651...214, 216, 293

Scarfe v Morgan (1838) 4 M & W 270; 150 ER 1430...1045, 1056

Scarisbrick v Parkinson (1869) 20 LT 175...256

Schmaling v Thomlinson (1815) 6 Taunt 147; 128 ER 989...251

Schmaltz v Avery (1851) 16 QB 655; 117 ER 1031...193

Schroeder Music Publishing Co Ltd v Macaulay [1974] 1 WLR 1308; [1974] 3 All ER 616...20

Scotland v British Credit Trust Ltd [2014] EWCA Civ 790; [2015] 1 All ER 708; [2015] 1 All ER (Comm) 401...642

Scottish Equitable Plc v Derby [2001] EWCA Civ 369; [2001] 3 All ER 818; [2001] 2 All ER (Comm) 274...714, 716

Sea-Cargo Skips AS v State Bank of India [2013] EWHC 177 (Comm); [2013] 2 Lloyd's Rep 477...853

Seaconsar (Far East) Ltd v Bank Markazi Jomhouri Islami Iran (Service Outside Jurisdiction) [1993] 1 Lloyd's Rep 236...**780–1**

Seacrown, The see Galaxy Energy International Ltd v Murco Petroleum Ltd (The Seacrown)

Sealace Shipping Co Ltd v Oceanvoice Ltd (The Alecos M) [1991] 1 Lloyd's Rep 120...522

Seath & Co v Moore (1886) LR 11 App Cas 350...342

Seatrade Groningen BV v Geest Industries Ltd (The Frost Express) [1996] 2 Lloyd's Rep 375...187

Selangor United Rubber Estates Ltd v Cradock (No 3) [1968] 1 WLR 1555; [1968] 2 All ER 1073...89, 588

Sellers v London Counties Newspapers [1951] 1 KB 784; [1951] 1 All ER 544...266

Semenza v Brinsley (1865) 18 CB NS 467; 144 ER 526...219

Sempra Metals Ltd (formerly Metallgesellschaft Ltd) v Inland Revenue Commissioners [2007] UKHL 34; [2008] 1 AC 561; [2007] 3 WLR 354...479, 713

Shalson v Russo [2003] EWHC 1637 (Ch); [2005] Ch 281; [2005] 2 WLR 1213...725

Shamia v Joory [1958] 1 QB 448; [1958] 2 WLR 84; [1958] 1 All ER 111...890, 921

Shamji v Johnson Matthey Bankers [1986] BCLC 178; [1991] BCLC 36...**1115–17**

Sharman v Brandt (1871) LR 6 QB 720...193

Shaw v Commissioner of Police of the Metropolis [1987] 1 WLR 1332; [1987] 3 All ER 405...387

Shearman (t/a Charles Shearman Agencies) v Hunter Boot Ltd [2014] EWHC 47 (QB); [2014] 1 All ER (Comm) 689; [2014] 1 CLC 240...277

Sheffield (Earl of) v London Joint Stock Bank Ltd (1888) 13 App Cas 333...654

Shell UK Ltd v Total UK Ltd [2010] EWCA Civ 180; [2011] QB 86; [2010] 3 WLR 1192...70

Shell-Mex and BP Ltd v Manchester Garages Ltd [1971] 1 WLR 612; [1971] 1 All ER 841...952

Shipley v Marshall (1863) 14 CB NS 566; 143 ER 567...981

Shipton, Anderson & Co v Weil Bros & Co [1912] 1 KB 574...458, 464

Shipway v Broadwood [1899] 1 QB 369...245

Shogun Finance Ltd v Hudson [2003] UKHL 62; [2004] 1 AC 919; [2003] 3 WLR 1371; [2004] 1 All ER 215...401, 407

Short v Packman (1831) 2 B & Ad 962; 109 ER 1400...191

Siebe Gorman & Co Ltd v Barclays Bank Ltd [1979] 2 Lloyd's Rep 142...948, 987–8, 991–2, 994–6, 998, 1000, 1082

Sigma Finance Corp (In Administration), Re [2009] UKSC 2; [2010] 1 All ER 571; [2010] BCC 40...21–2

Silven Properties Ltd v Royal Bank of Scotland Plc [2003] EWCA Civ 1409; [2004] 1 WLR 997; [2004] 4 All ER 484...1066–7

Simaan General Contracting Co v Pilkington Glass Ltd (No 2) [1988] QB 758; [1988] 2 WLR 761; [1988] 1 All ER 791...255

Simmons v London Joint Stock Bank [1891] 1 Ch 270...650

Simon Carves Ltd v Ensus UK Ltd [2011] EWHC 657 (TCC); [2011] BLR 340...**788–9**, 852

Simpson v Norfolk and Norwich University Hospital NHS Trust [2011] EWCA Civ 1149; [2012] QB 640; [2012] 2 WLR 873...862, 878

Sims v Bond (1833) 5 B & Ad 389; 110 ER 834...219, 223

Sinason-Teicher Inter-American Grain Corp v Oilcakes and Oilseeds Trading Co [1954] 1 WLR 1394; [1954] 3 All ER 468...814–15

Sinclair Investment Holdings SA v Versailles Trade Finance Ltd (In Administrative Receivership) [2005] EWCA Civ 722; [2006] 1 BCLC 60...725

Sinclair Investments (UK) Ltd v Versailles Trade Finance Ltd (In Administration) [2011] EWCA Civ 347; [2012] Ch 453; [2011] 3 WLR 1153...241, 247–8

Sinclair v Brougham [1914] AC 398; [1914] All ER Rep 622...721

Singer Manufacturing Co v London & South Western Railway Co [1894] 1 QB 833...1050–2

Singh v Sardar Investments Ltd [2002] EWCA Civ 1706; [2002] NPC 134...199

Siporex Trade SA v Banque Indosuez [1986] 2 Lloyd's Rep 146...843

Sirius International Insurance Co (Publ) v FAI General Insurance Ltd [2003] EWCA Civ 470; [2003] 1 WLR 2214; [2004] 1 All ER 308; [2003] 1 All ER (Comm) 865...788

Siskina, The *see* Owners of Cargo Lately Laden on Board the Siskina v Distos Compañía Naviera SA

Siu Yin Kwan v Eastern Insurance Co Ltd [1994] 2 AC 199; [1994] 2 WLR 370; [1994] 1 All ER 213 (PC)...**200–3**, 205, 209–11, 213

Skandinaviska Kreditaktie Bolaget v Barclays Bank (1925) 22 Ll L Rep 523...824

Sky Petroleum Ltd v VIP Petroleum Ltd [1974] 1 WLR 576; [1974] 1 All ER 954...528

Slater v Hoyle & Smith Ltd [1920] 2 KB 11...525

Slingsby v District Bank Ltd (Manchester) [1931] 2 KB 588...736, 745–7

Slingsby v District Bank Ltd (Manchester) [1932] 1 KB 544...740, 745–7

Smart v Sandars (1848) 5 CB 895; 136 ER 1132...272–3

SMC Electronics Ltd v Akhter Computers Ltd [2001] 1 BCLC 433...131

Smith v Chadwick (1882) 20 Ch D 27...1093

Smith v Henniker-Major & Co [2002] EWCA Civ 762; [2003] Ch 182; [2002] 3 WLR 1848...158–9, 166

Smith v Lloyds TSB Bank Plc [2001] QB 541; [2000] 3 WLR 1725; [2001] 1 All ER 424; [2000] 2 All ER (Comm) 693...699, 735–6, **742–8**, 758

Smith v Reliance Water Controls Ltd (Damages) [2004] EWHC 1016 (QB)...267

Smith v Union Bank of London (1875) LR 10 QB 291...735, 740

Smith, Bailey Palmer v Howard & Hallam Ltd [2005] EWHC 2790 (QB); [2006] Eu LR 578...284

Smout v Ilbery (1842) 10 M & W 1; 152 ER 357...194–6, 270

Snook v London and West Riding Investments Ltd [1967] 2 QB 786; [1967] 2 WLR 1020; [1967] 1 All ER 518...**952**, 955

Sobell Industries Ltd v Cory Bros & Co Ltd (Sadikoglu Bros, Third Parties) [1955] 2 Lloyd's Rep 82...118

Société Cooperative Suisse des Céréales et Matières Fourrageres v La Plata Cereal Co SA (1947) 80 Ll L Rep 530...376

Société des Industries Metallurgiques SA v Bronx Engineering Co [1975] 1 Lloyd's Rep 465...529

Société Générale SA v Saad Trading [2011] EWHC 2424 (Comm); [2011] 2 CLC 629...775, 822–3

Société Eram Shipping Co Ltd v Compagnie Internationale de Navigation [2003] UKHL 30; [2004] 1 AC 260; [2003] 3 WLR 21...839

Society of Lloyd's v Canadian Imperial Bank of Commerce [1993] 2 Lloyd's Rep 579...800

Society of Lloyd's v Leighs [1997] CLC 759...274

Socimer International Bank Ltd v Standard Bank London Ltd [1988] 1 Lloyd's Rep 558...42

Soeximex SAS v Agrocorp International Pte Ltd [2011]
   EWHC 2743 (Comm); [2012] 1 Lloyd's Rep 52...813
Solly v Rathbone (1814) 2 M & S 298; 105 ER
   392...251, 269
Solo Industries UK Ltd v Canara Bank [2001] EWCA Civ
   1059; [2001] 1 WLR 1800; [2001] 2 All ER (Comm)
   217...657, 809, 852
Soproma SpA v Marine & Animal By-Products Corp
   [1966] 1 Lloyd's Rep 367...816
Sorrell v Finch [1977] AC 728; [1976] 2 WLR 833;
   [1976] 2 All ER 371...117
Soules CAF v PT Transap (Indonesia) [1999] 1 Lloyd's
   Rep 917...466
South Australian Insurance Co v Randell (1871) LR 3 PC
   101 (PC)...95, 316–17
South Lanarkshire Council v Aviva Insurance Ltd [2016]
   CSOH 83...844
South Tyneside MBC v Svenska International Plc [1995]
   1 All ER 545...715
Southcote v Southcote (1647) Al 80; 82 ER 926...1024
Southern Livestock Producers Ltd, Re [1964] 1 WLR 24;
   [1963] 3 All ER 801...1045
Southwark LBC v IBM UK Ltd [2011] EWHC 549 (TCC);
   135 Con LR 136...303, 325
Soward v Palmer (1818) 8 Taunt 277; 129 ER 390...705
Spain v Christie Manson & Woods Ltd [1986] 1 WLR
   1120; [1986] 3 All ER 28...861
Specialist Plant Services Ltd v Braithwaite Ltd (1987) 3
   BCC 119; [1987] BCLC 1...511
Spectrum Plus Ltd (In Liquidation), Re see National
   Westminster Bank plc v Spectrum Plus Ltd
Spencer v Clarke (1878) 9 Ch D 137...916
Spencer v S Franses Ltd [2011] EWHC 1269
   (QB)...1046, 1057
Spiliada Maritime Corp v Cansulex Ltd (The Spiliada)
   [1987] AC 460; [1986] 3 WLR 972; [1986] 3 All ER
   843...838
Spiro v Lintern [1973] 1 WLR 1002; [1973] 3 All ER
   319...145–6
Spleithoff's Bevrachtingskantoor BV v Bank of China Ltd
   [2015] EWHC 999 (Comm); [2016] 1 All ER (Comm)
   1034...844
Spooner v Sandilands (1842) 1 Y & C Ch 390; 62 ER
   939...272
Springer v Great Western Railway Co [1921] 1 KB
   257...156
Stadium Finance Ltd v Robbins [1962] 2 QB 664; [1962]
   3 WLR 453; [1962] 2 All ER 633...401–2
Staffs Motor Guarantee Ltd v British Wagon Co Ltd
   [1934] 2 KB 305...400, 409
Standard Bank London Ltd v Bank of Tokyo Ltd [1995] 2
   Lloyd's Rep 169...824
Standard Chartered Bank Ltd v Walker [1982] 1 WLR
   1410; [1982] 3 All ER 938...1121
Standard Chartered Bank v Dorchester LNG (2) Ltd
   [2014] EWCA Civ 1382; [2016] QB 1; [2014] 2 CLC
   740...512, 830
Standard Chartered Bank v Pakistan National Shipping
   Corp (No 2) [2002] UKHL 43; [2003] 1 AC 959; [2002]
   3 WLR 1547; [2000] 1 All ER (Comm) 1...182, 831
Standing v Bowring (1885) 31 Ch D 282...921, 930
Stanley v English Fibres Industries Ltd (1899) 68 LJQB
   839...923–4

Stapylton Fletcher Ltd (In Administrative Receivership),
   Re [1994] 1 WLR 1181; [1995] 1 All ER 192...30,
   67, 334
Star Gazer, The see Allseas International Management
   v Panroy Bulk Transport SA (The Star Gazer and The
   Star Delta)
Starkey v Bank of England [1903] AC 114...196
State Trading Corp of India Ltd v ED & F Man
   (Sugar) and State Bank of India [1981] Com LR
   235...849, 852
State Trading Corp of India Ltd v M Golodetz & Co Inc
   Ltd [1989] 2 Lloyd's Rep 277...839
Steel Wing Co Ltd, Re [1921] 1 Ch 349...907
Steels & Busks Ltd v Bleecker Bik & Co [1956] 1 Lloyd's
   Rep 228...448–50
Stein, Forbes & Co v County Tailoring Co (1916) 86 LKJB
   448...479
Sterns Ltd v Vickers Ltd [1923] 1 KB 78...357, **366–7**, 398
Stevens v Biller (1883) 25 Ch D 31...117
Stevenson v Rogers [1999] QB 1028; [1999] 2 WLR
   1064; [1999] 1 All ER 613...435
Stevenson, Assignees of Collis, a Bankrupt v Blakelock,
   Gentleman (1813) 1 M & S 535; 105 ER 200...1057
Stewart Chartering Ltd v Owners of the Ship Peppy
   [1997] 2 Lloyd's Rep 722...239
Stocznia Gdanska SA v Latvian Shipping Co [1998] 1
   WLR 574; [1998] 1 All ER 883...323
Stoddart v Union Trust Ltd [1912] 1 KB 181...946
Stoneleigh Finance Ltd v Phillips [1965] 2 QB 537;
   [1965] 2 WLR 508; [1965] 1 All ER 513...955
Street v Mountford [1985] AC 809; [1985] 2 WLR 877;
   [1985] 2 All ER 289...952, 954, 957, 998
Stroud Architectural Services Ltd v John Laing
   Construction Ltd [1994] BCC 18...508
Stubbs v Slater [1910] 1 Ch 632...**1065–6**
Stucley, Re [1906] 1 Ch 67...1077
Summers v Havard [2011] EWCA Civ 764; [2011] 2
   Lloyd's Rep 283...**402–3**
Summers v Solomon (1857) 7 El & Bl 879; 119 ER
   1474...143
Sumner Permain & Co v Webb & Co [1922] 1
   KB 55...445
Sunbolf v Alford (1838) 3 M & W 248; 150 ER 1135...1046
Suncorp Insurance and Finance v Milano Assicurazioni
   SpA [1993] 2 Lloyd's Rep 225...139, 159
Super Servant Two, The see J Lauritzen AS v Wijsmuller
   BV (The Super Servant Two)
Surrey Asset Finance Ltd v National Westminster Bank
   Times 30 November 2000...735
Surrey Breakdown Ltd v Knight [1999] RTR 84...157
Sutcliffe v Chief Constable of West Yorkshire (1995)
   159 JP 770; [1996] RTR 86...98
Sutherland v Royal Bank of Scotland Plc 1997 SLT 329;
   [1997] 6 Bank LR 132...619
Swan v North British Australasian Co (1863) 2 Hurl & C
   175; 159 ER 73...144, 392
Swan, The see Bridges & Salmon Ltd v Owner of The
   Swan (The Swan)
Swift v Dairywise Farms Ltd (No 1) [2000] 1 WLR 1177;
   [2000] 1 All ER 320...58, 61
Swiss Bank Corp v Lloyds Bank Ltd [1982] AC 584;
   [1981] 2 WLR 893; [1981] 2 All ER 449...65, 919,
   1061–4, **1068**, 1127

Swotbooks.com Ltd v Royal Bank of Scotland Plc [2011] EWHC 2025 (QB)...736, 780, 822

Symington & Co v Union Insurance Society of Canton Ltd (1928) 97 LJKB 646...1097

Syrett v Egerton [1957] 1 WLR 1130; [1957] 3 All ER 331...1017

Sze Hai Tong Bank v Rambler Cycle Co [1959] AC 576; [1959] 3 WLR 214; [1959] 3 All ER 182 (PC)...536

T and L Sugars Ltd v Tate and Lyle Industries Ltd [2015] EWHC 2696 (Comm)...715

Tai Hing Cotton Mill Ltd v Kamsing Knitting Factory [1979] AC 91; [1978] 2 WLR 62; [1978] 1 All ER 515 (PC)...520

Tai Hing Cotton Mill Ltd v Liu Chong Hing Bank Ltd (No 1) [1986] AC 80; [1985] 3 WLR 317; [1985] 2 All ER 947 (PC)...671, 736

Tailby v Official Receiver (1888) 13 App Cas 523...69, 81, 501, 864–5, 886, **961–4**, 982, 991, 993, 1017, 1020, 1064, 1069–70

Talbot v Von Boris [1911] 1 KB 854...683

Tamarind International Ltd v Eastern Natural Gas (Retail) Ltd [2000] CLC 1397...121

Tancred v Delagoa Bay & East Africa Railway (1889) 23 QBD 239...903, 905, 930

Tandrin Aviation Holdings Ltd v Aero Toy Store LLC [2010] EWHC 40 (Comm); [2010] 2 Lloyd's Rep 668...482

Tanks & Vessels Industries Ltd v Devon Cider Co Ltd [2009] EWHC 1360 (Ch)...82

Tappenden (t/a English & American Autos) v Artus [1964] 2 QB 185; [1963] 3 WLR 685; [1963] 3 All ER 213...**1041, 1049–52**

Target Holdings Ltd v Redferns [1996] AC 421; [1995] 3 WLR 352; [1995] 3 All ER 785...**31**, 895–6

Tate, Re ex p Moffatt (1841) 2 Mont D & De G 170...1053

Tatlock v Harris (1789) 3 Term Rep 174; 100 ER 517...889

Tatra, The *see* Arctic Shipping Co Ltd v Mobilia AB (The Tatra)

Tatung (UK) Ltd v Galex Telesure Ltd (1989) 5 BCC 325...502, 511

Taurus Petroleum Ltd v State Oil Marketing Co of the Ministry of Oil, Iraq [2013] EWHC 3494 (Comm); [2014] 1 All ER (Comm) 942; [2014] 1 Lloyd's Rep 432...772

Taurus Petroleum Ltd v State Oil Marketing Co of the Ministry of Oil, Iraq [2015] EWCA Civ 835; [2016] 2 All ER (Comm) 1037; [2016] 1 Lloyd's Rep 42...830, 838

Taxation Commissioners v English Scottish and Australian Bank Ltd [1920] AC 683 (PC)...754

Tayeb v HSBC Bank Plc [2004] EWHC 1529 (Comm); [2004] 4 All ER 1024; [2005] 1 CLC 866...581, 596, 608

Taylor v Blakelock (1886) 32 Ch D 560...920

Taylor v Caldwell (1863) 3 B & S 826; 122 ER 309...377

Taylor v Hamer [2002] EWCA Civ 1130; [2003] 1 P & CR DG6...529

Taylor v Plumer (1815) 3 M & S 562; 105 ER 721...721, 723

Taylor v Robinson (1818) 2 Moore CP 730...269

Technocrats International Inc v Fredic Ltd (No 1) [2004] EWHC 692 (QB)...902

Technotrade Ltd v Larkstore Ltd *see* Offer-Hoar v Larkstore Ltd

Teheran-Europe Co Ltd v ST Belton (Tractors) Ltd (No 1) [1968] 2 QB 545; [1968] 3 WLR 205; [1968] 2 All ER 886...171, 188–9, 201–3, 205, 210, **445–6**

Temple Legal Protection Ltd v QBE Insurance (Europe) Ltd [2009] EWCA Civ 453; [2010] 1 All ER (Comm) 703; [2009] Lloyd's Rep IR 544...273

Tenax Steamship Co v Owners of the Motor Vessel Brimnes (The Brimnes) [1973] 1 WLR 386; [1973] 1 All ER 769...564, 605, 612

Tenax Steamship Co v Owners of the Motor Vessel Brimnes (The Brimnes) [1975] QB 929; [1974] 3 WLR 613; [1974] 3 All ER 88...564, 570, 605, 612, 617–18

Test Claimants in the FII Group Litigation v Revenue and Customs Commissioners [2014] EWHC 4302 (Ch); [2015] STC 1471...715

Thackwell v Barclays Bank plc [1986] 1 All ER 676...759

Thai Airways International Public Co Ltd v KI Holdings Co Ltd (formerly Koito Industries Ltd) [2015] EWHC 1250 (Comm); [2016] 1 All ER (Comm) 675...522

Thames Guaranty Ltd v Campbell [1985] QB 210; [1984] 3 WLR 109; [1984] 2 All ER 585...1063

Thames Valley Power Ltd v Total Gas & Power Ltd [2005] EWHC 2208 (Comm); [2006] 1 Lloyd's Rep 441...379, **527–8**

Themehelp Ltd v West [1996] QB 84; [1995] 3 WLR 751; [1995] 4 All ER 215...799, 801–2, 852

Thomas v Hewes (1834) 2 Cr & M 519; 149 ER 866...180

Thomas v Houston Corbett & Co [1969] NZLR 151...709

Thomas v Kelly (1888) 13 App Cas 506...1078

Thomas Cheshire & Co v Vaughan Bros & Co [1920] 3 KB 240...255

Thomas Gabriel & Sons v Churchill and Sim [1914] 3 KB 1272...118

Thompson v Robinson (1859) 27 Beav 486; 54 ER 192...482

Thomson v Davenport (1829) 9 B & C 78; 109 ER 30...172–3, **175–6**, 179, 217, 222

Thorndike v Hunt (1859) 3 De G & J 563; 44 ER 1386...920

Three Rivers DC v Bank of England (No 1) [1996] QB 292; [1995] 3 WLR 650; [1995] 4 All ER 312...933–4

Tidal Energy Ltd v Bank of Scotland Plc [2014] EWCA Civ 1107; [2015] 2 All ER 15; [2014] 2 CLC 124...581, 583, **586–97**, 611

Tiedemann and Ledermann Freres Arbitration, Re [1899] 2 QB 66...167

Tigana Ltd v Decoro Ltd [2003] EWHC 23 (QB); [2003] ECC 23; [2003] Eu LR 189...278, 284

Tigress, The (1863) Brown & Lush 38; (1863) 32 LJPM & A 97; 167 ER 286...**489–90**

Timpson's Executors v Yerbury (Inspector of Taxes) [1936] 1 KB 645; [1936] 1 All ER 186...921–2

Tinsley v Milligan [1994] 1 AC 340; [1993] 3 WLR 126; [1993] 3 All ER 65...804

Tolhurst v Associated Portland Cement Manufacturers (1900) Ltd [1903] AC 414...870

Tom Shaw & Co v Moss Empires Ltd (1908) 25 TLR 190...882–3, 897

Tony Mekwin MTV & Co v National Westminster Bank Plc [1998] CCLR 22...635

Torkington v Magee [1902] 2 KB 427...860, **907–9**

Toulmin v Millar (1887) 58 LT 96...260

Tradax Internacional SA v Goldschmidt SA [1977] 2 Lloyd's Rep 604...466

Tradigrain SA v State Trading Corp of India [2005] EWHC 2206 (Comm); [2006] 1 All ER (Comm) 197...853–4

Trafalgar House Construction (Regions) Ltd v General Surety & Guarantee Co Ltd [1996] AC 199; [1995] 3 WLR 204; [1995] 3 All ER 737...849

Trans Trust SPRL v Danubian Trading Co Ltd [1952] 2 QB 297; [1952] 1 All ER 970...558, 812–13

Transco Plc v United Utilities Water Plc [2005] EWHC 2784 (QB)...83

Transcontainer Express v Custodian Security [1988] 1 Lloyd's Rep 128...79

Transport & General Credit Co Ltd v Morgan [1939] Ch 531; [1939] 2 All ER 17...1077

Trebor Bassett Holdings Ltd v ADT Fire & Security Plc [2012] EWCA Civ 1158; [2012] BLR 441...**320–1**, 323

Tredegar Iron & Coal Co v Hawthorn Bros & Co (1902) 18 TLR 716...481

Trendtex Trading Corp v Crédit Suisse [1982] AC 679; [1981] 3 WLR 766; [1981] 3 All ER 520...**871–5, 877–8**

Trident Beauty, The *see* Pan Ocean Shipping Co Ltd v Creditcorp Ltd (The Trident Beauty)

Trident International Ltd v Barlow [2000] BCC 602; [1999] 2 BCLC 506...1043–4

Trident Turboprop (Dublin) Ltd v First Flight Couriers Ltd [2009] EWCA Civ 290; [2010] QB 86; [2009] 3 WLR 861...453

Triffit Nurseries (a firm) v Salads Etcetera Ltd [1999] 1 All ER (Comm) 110; [1999] 1 Lloyd's Rep 697...274

Tropical Reefer, The *see* Den Norske Bank ASA v Acemex Management Co Ltd (The Tropical Reefer)

Truk (UK) Ltd v Tokmakidis GmbH [2000] 2 All ER (Comm) 594; [2000] 1 Lloyd's Rep 543...**470–1**

Trustee of the Property of FC Jones & Sons (A Firm) v Jones [1997] Ch 159; [1997] 1 WLR 51...723, 726

TSB Bank of Scotland Ltd v Welwyn Hatfield DC and Council of the London Borough of Brent [1993] 2 Bank LR 267...564, 620, 623

TTI Team Telecom International Ltd v Hutchison 3G UK Ltd [2003] EWHC 762 (TCC); [2003] 1 All ER (Comm) 914...788, 852

Tubantia, The (No 2) [1924] P 78...71

Tudor Marine Ltd v Tradax Export SA (The Virgo) [1976] 2 Lloyd's Rep 135...187

Turcan, Re (1888) 40 Ch D 5...880–1, 883, 894, 896, 936

Turkiye IS Bankasi AS v Bank of China [1996] 2 Lloyd's Rep 611...796, 800

Turkiye IS Bankasi AS v Bank of China [1998] 1 Lloyd's Rep 250...851–2

Turley v Bates (1863) 2 Hurl & C 200; 159 ER 83...345

Turner v Goldsmith [1891] 1 QB 544...265, 276

Turner v Royal Bank of Scotland Plc [1999] 2 All ER (Comm) 664...581

Turpin v Bilton (1843) 5 Man & G 455; 134 ER 641...224

Twinsectra Ltd v Yardley [1999] Lloyd's Rep Bank 438...725

Twinsectra Ltd v Yardley [2002] UKHL 12; [2002] 2 AC 164; [2002] 2 WLR 802...32, 89, 91, 1127

Twyne's case [1774] All ER Rep 303; 76 ER 809; (1601) 3 Co Rep 80...915

TXU Europe Group Plc (In Administration), Re [2003] EWHC 3105 (Ch); [2004] 1 BCLC 519...1064

Tyrrell v Bank of London (1862) 10 HL Cas 26; 11 ER 934...235

UB Tiger, The *see* P&O Nedlloyd BV v Arab Metals Co (The UB Tiger)

UBS AG (London Branch) v Kommunale Wasserwerke Leipzig GmbH [2014] EWHC 3615 (Comm)...108

Ugland Trailer, The *see* Welsh Irish Ferries Ltd, Re (The Ugland Trailer)

Ulster Swift Ltd v Taunton Meat Haulage Ltd [1977] 1 WLR 625; [1977] 3 All ER 641...101

Underwood Ltd v Burgh Castle Brick & Cement Syndicate [1922] 1 KB 343...**304–5, 340–1**, 343

Unique Mariner, The [1978] 1 Lloyd's Rep 438...156

United Bank of Kuwait v Hammoud [1988] 1 WLR 1051; [1988] 3 All ER 418...139

United Bank of Kuwait plc v Sahib [1997] Ch 107; [1996] 3 WLR 372; [1996] 3 All ER 215...916, 1064

United Central Bakeries Ltd v Spooner Industries Ltd [2013] CSOH 150...445

United City Merchants (Investments) Ltd v Royal Bank of Canada (The American Accord) [1983] 1 AC 168; [1982] 2 WLR 1039; [1982] 2 All ER 720...771, **789–94**, 796–7, 799, **802–5**, 807

United Kingdom Mutual Steamship Assurance Association v Nevill (1887) 19 QBD 110...206

United States v Dollfus Mieg et Cie SA [1952] AC 582; [1952] 1 All ER 572...70, 72

United States v Nolan [2015] UKSC 63; [2016] AC 463; [2015] 3 WLR 1105...1068

United Trading Corp SA v Allied Arab Bank Ltd [1985] 2 Lloyd's Rep 554...**801, 822**

Universal Steam Navigation Co Ltd v James McKelvie & Co [1923] AC 492; (1923) 15 Ll L Rep 99...**182–5, 187–9**

Urquhart Lindsay & Co Ltd v Eastern Bank Ltd [1922] 1 KB 318; (1921) 9 Ll L Rep 572...558, 830

Uzeinterimpex JSC v Standard Bank Plc [2008] EWCA Civ 819; [2008] Bus LR 1762; [2008] 2 Lloyd's Rep 456...854

Vacwell Ltd v BDH Chemicals Ltd [1971] 1 QB 88; [1969] 3 WLR 927; [1969] 3 All ER 1681...454

Vainqueur Jose, The *see* CVG Siderurgicia del Orinoco SA v London Steamship Owners Mutual Insurance Association Ltd (The Vainqueur Jose)

Vallejo v Wheeler (1774) 1 Cowp 143; 98 ER 1012...**11**

Valpy v Gibson (1847) 4 CB 837; 136 ER 737...**484–5**

Van Den Hurk v R Martens & Co Ltd (In Liquidation) [1920] 1 KB 850...525

Van Lynn Developments Ltd v Pelias Construction Co Ltd [1969] 1 QB 607; [1968] 3 WLR 1141; [1968] 3 All ER 824...**923–6**

Van Praagh v Everidge [1902] 2 Ch 266...274

Vandepitte v Preferred Accident Insurance Corp of New York [1933] AC 70 (PC)...891, 897–900, 932

Varley v Whipp [1900] 1 QB 513...**340, 432**

Velos Group Ltd v Harbour Insurance Services Ltd [1997] 2 Lloyd's Rep 461...254

Versloot Dredging BV v HDI Gerling Industrie Versicherung AG [2013] EWHC 1666 (Comm); [2013] 2 All ER (Comm) 465; [2013] 2 Lloyd's Rep 131...**1101–2**

Versloot Dredging BV v HDI Gerling Industrie Versicherung AG [2016] UKSC 45; [2017] AC 1; [2016] 3 WLR 543...**1101–2**

VFS Financial Services Ltd v JF Plant Tyres Ltd [2013] EWHC 346 (QB); [2013] 1 WLR 2987...313, 316

Vic Mill Ltd, Re [1913] 1 Ch 465...**480, 482**

Vick v Vogle Gapes Ltd [2006] EWHC 1665 (QB)...267

Victoria Laundry (Windsor) v Newman Industries [1949] 2 KB 528; [1949] 1 All ER 997...**524**

Vimeira, The *see* Aiden Shipping Co Ltd v Interbulk Ltd (The Vimeira) (No 2)

Vinden v Hughes [1905] 1 KB 795...669–70

Virago, The *see* Tudor Marine Ltd v Tradax Export SA (The Virgo)

Visconde des Olivaes ex p *see* Pinto Leite and Nephews, Re

Vitol SA v Conoil plc [2009] EWHC 1144 (Comm); [2009] 2 Lloyd's Rep 466...463

Vossloh AG v Alpha Trains (UK) Ltd [2010] EWHC 2443 (Ch); [2011] 2 All ER (Comm) 307...**844**

Wahbe Tamari & Sons Ltd v Sociedade Geral de Fibras Cafes e Productos Coloniais Lda (Colprogeca) [1969] 2 Lloyd's Rep 18...776

Wait, Re [1927] 1 Ch 606...**69, 298–9,** 306, 314, 328, 331, 334, 336, 374, 527, 546, 1042, 1077

Wait v Baker (1848) 2 Ex 1; 154 ER 380...**352,** 355

Wait & James v Midland Bank (1926) 24 Ll L Rep 313; (1926) 31 Com Cas 172...333, 337

Wake v Harrop (1862) 1 Hurl & C 202; 158 ER 859...187

Walford v Miles [1992] 2 AC 128; [1992] 2 WLR 174...41

Walker v Bradford Old Bank Ltd (1884) 12 QBD 511...866

Wallace v Woodgate (1824) 1 Car & P 575; 171 ER 1323...1057

Wallis v Russell [1902] 2 IR 585; (1902) 36 ILTR 67...442

Wallis Son & Wells v Pratt & Haynes [1911] AC 394...451–2

Walsh v Whitcomb (1797) 2 Esp 565; 170 ER 456...272–3

Walter v James (1871) LR 6 Ex 124...164

Walter & Sullivan v J Murphy & Sons [1955] 2 QB 584; [1955] 2 WLR 919; [1955] 1 All ER 843...907

Ward v Duncombe [1893] AC 369...917–19

Ward v Turner (1752) 1 Ves Sen 378; 28 ER 555...1030

Ward & Co v Wallis [1900] 1 QB 675...709

Wardar's (Import & Export) Co Ltd v W Norwood & Sons Ltd [1968] 2 QB 663; [1968] 2 WLR 1440; [1968] 2 All ER 602...**356–8**

Warehousing and Forwarding Co of East Africa Ltd v Jafferali & Sons Ltd [1964] AC 1; [1963] 3 WLR 489; [1963] 3 All ER 571...165

Warinco AG v Samor SpA [1977] 2 Lloyd's Rep 582; [1979] 1 Lloyd's Rep 450...**457**

Warlow v Harrison (1859) 1 El & El 309; 120 ER 925...**610–11**

Warner Bros Records Inc v Rollgreen Ltd [1976] QB 430; [1975] 2 WLR 816; [1975] 2 All ER 105...**934**

Warren (t/a On-line Cartons and Print) v Drukkerij Flach BV [2014] EWCA Civ 993; [2015] 1 Lloyd's Rep 111...278

Warwick v Nairn (1855) 10 Ex 762; 156 ER 648...575

Watford Electronics Ltd v Sanderson CFL Ltd [2001] EWCA Civ 317; [2001] 1 All ER (Comm) 696...11

Watson v Davies [1931] 1 Ch 455...165

Watson v King (1815) 4 Camp 272; 171 ER 87...292

Watson v Mid Wales Railway Co (1867) LR 2 CP 593...945

Watson v Swann (1862) 11 CB NS 756; 142 ER 993...**162**

Watteau v Fenwick [1893] 1 QB 346...**146–51**

Waugh v HB Clifford & Sons Ltd [1982] Ch 374; [1982] 2 WLR 679; [1982] 1 All ER 1095...117, 131, 136

Way v Latilla [1937] 3 All ER 759...256–9

Way's Trusts, Re (1864) 2 De GJ & S 365; 46 ER 416...921

Wear Breeze, The *see* Margarine Union GmbH v Cambay Prince Steamship Co (The Wear Breeze)

Webb v Chief Constable of Merseyside [2000] QB 427; [2000] 2 WLR 546; [2000] 1 All ER 209...75–6

Weddell v JA Pearce & Major (A Firm) [1988] Ch 26; [1987] 3 WLR 592; [1987] 3 All ER 624...933

Weiner v Gill [1906] 2 KB 574...**348**

Weiner v Harris [1910] 1 KB 285...**395**

Welch v Royal Exchange Assurance [1939] 1 KB 294; [1938] 4 All ER 289...1101

Weld-Blundell v Synott [1940] 2 KB 107; [1940] 2 All ER 580...710

Weldon v GRE Linked Life Assurance [2000] 2 All ER (Comm) 914...570

Wells v First National Commercial Bank [1998] PNLR 552...**598–600,** 603

Welsh Development Agency v Export Finance Co Ltd [1992] BCC 270; [1992] BCLC 148...161, 212, 319, **950–7, 967–8,** 999, 1016, 1078

Welsh Irish Ferries Ltd, Re (The Ugland Trailer) [1986] Ch 471; [1985] 3 WLR 610...1021

Wertheim v Chicoutimi Pulp Co [1911] AC 301 (PC)...523

West Bromwich Building Society v Wilkinson [2005] UKHL 44; [2005] 1 WLR 2303; [2005] 4 All ER 97...1067

Westacre Investments Inc v Jugoimport SPDR Holding Co Ltd [1999] QB 740; [1998] 3 WLR 770; [1998] 4 All ER 570...808

Westdeutsche Landesbank Girozentrale v Islington LBC [1996] AC 669; [1996] 2 WLR 802; [1996] 2 All ER 961...31–2, 713, 725

Westerbrook Resources Ltd v Globe Metallurgical Inc [2009] EWCA Civ 310; [2009] 2 All ER (Comm) 1060; [2009] 2 Lloyd's Rep 224...464

Westminster Bank Ltd v Hilton (1926) 136 LT 315...610, 719

Westminster Bank Ltd v Zang [1966] AC 182; [1966] 2 WLR 110; [1966] 1 All ER 114...**684, 748–51**

WF Harrison & Co v Burke [1956] 1 WLR 419; [1956] 2 All ER 169...**922–6**

Wheatley v Silkstone & Haigh Moor Coal Co (1885) 29
   Ch D 715…1072
Whistler v Forster (1863) 14 CB NS 248; 143 ER
   441…673
White v Jones [1995] 2 AC 207; [1995] 2 WLR 187;
   [1995] 1 All ER 691…599–603
White & Carter (Councils) Ltd v McGregor [1962] AC
   413; [1962] 2 WLR 17; [1961] 3 All ER 1178…41–2
Whittingstall v King (1882) 46 LT 520…926
Whitworth Street Estates (Manchester) Ltd v James
   Miller & Partners Ltd [1970] AC 583; [1970] 2 WLR
   728; [1970] 1 All ER 796…956
Wiehe v Dennis Bros (1913) 29 TLR 250…**363–4**
Wilbraham v Snow (1668) 2 Saund 47; 85 ER 624…73
Wilkie v Scottish Aviation Ltd 1956 SC 198…259
William Brandt's Sons & Co v Dunlop Rubber Co Ltd
   [1905] AC 454…**887–8**, 901, 903, 910, 932–3
William Gaskell Group Ltd v Highley [1993] BCC 200;
   [1994] 1 BCLC 197…997
William H Muller & Co (London) Ltd v Lethem [1928]
   AC 34; 138 LT 241…253
Williams v Allsup (1861) 10 CB NS 417; 142 ER
   514…**1050–2**
Williams v Atlantic Assurance Co Ltd [1933] 1 KB 81…907
Williams v Central Bank of Nigeria [2014] UKSC 10;
   [2014] AC 1189; [2014] 2 WLR 355…724
Williams v Earle (1868) LR 3 QB 739…883
Williams v Natural Life Health Foods Ltd [1998] 1 WLR
   830; [1998] 2 All ER 577…182
Williams v North China Insurance Co (1876) 1 CPD
   757…165
Williams v Reynolds (1865) 6 B & S 495; 122 ER
   1278…**516–18**
Williams Bros v ET Agius Ltd [1914] AC 510…517
Williamson v Rider [1963] 1 QB 89; [1962] 3 WLR 119;
   [1962] 2 All ER 268…664
Willingale (Inspector of Taxes) v International
   Commercial Bank Ltd [1978] AC 834; [1978] 2 WLR
   452; [1978] 1 All ER 754…968
Wilson v Anderton (1830) 1 B & Ad 450; 109 ER
   855…490
Wilson v Brett 152 ER 737; (1843) 11 M & W 113…97
Wilson v First County Trust Ltd (No 2) [2003] UKHL 40;
   [2004] AC 816…35
Wilson v Lombank Ltd [1963] 1 WLR 1294; [1963] 1 All
   ER 740…72, 76, 1043
Wilson v Rickett Cockerell & Co Ltd [1954] 1 QB 598;
   [1954] 2 WLR 629; [1954] 1 All ER 868…438
Wilson v Tumman (1843) 6 Man & G 236; 134 ER
   879…159
Wilson & Meeson v Pickering [1946] KB 422; [1946] 1
   All ER 394…665
Wilson, Smithett & Cope Ltd v Terruzzi [1976] QB 683;
   [1976] 2 WLR 418; [1976] 1 All ER 817…803
Wiltshire v Sims (1808) 1 Camp 258; 170 ER 949…170
Wimble, Sons & Co v Rosenberg & Sons [1913] 3 KB
   743…539
Wincanton Ltd v P & O Trans European Ltd [2001]
   EWCA Civ 227; [2001] CLC 962…95
Winicofsky v Army & Navy General Assurance
   Association Ltd (1919) 88 LJKB 1111…1098
Winkfield, The [1902] P 42; [1902] All ER Rep 346…58,
   72–4, 75

Winson, The see China-Pacific SA v Food Corp of India
   (The Winson)
Withers v Reynolds (1831) 2 B & Ad 882; 109 ER
   1370…**456–7**
Withers LLP v Rybak [2011] EWCA Civ 1419; [2012] 1
   WLR 1748; [2012] 2 All ER 616…1057
WJ Alan & Co Ltd v El Nasr Export & Import Co
   [1972] 2 QB 189; [1972] 2 WLR 800; [1972]
   2 All ER 127…629–30, 632, 805, 813, 816
WL Thompson Ltd v R Robinson (Gunmakers) Ltd [1955]
   Ch 177; [1955] 2 WLR 185; [1955] 1 All ER 154…480
Wolstenholm v Sheffield Union Banking Co (1886) 54
   LT 746…269
Wolverhampton & Walsall Railway Co v London & North
   Western Railway Co (1873) LR 16 Eq 433…964
Woodhouse AC Israel Cocoa SA v Nigerian Produce
   Marketing Co Ltd [1972] AC 741; [1972] 2 WLR
   1090; [1972] 2 All ER 271…128
Woodroffes (Musical Instruments) Ltd [1986] Ch 366;
   [1985] 3 WLR 543; [1985] 2 All ER 908…1075
Woodworth v Conroy [1976] QB 884; [1976] 2 WLR
   338; [1976] 1 All ER 107…1049
Wookey v Pole (1820) 4 B & Ald 1; 106 ER 839…665
Woolcott v Sun Alliance and London Insurance Ltd
   [1978] 1 WLR 493; [1978] 1 All ER 1253; [1978] 1
   Lloyd's Rep 629…1093
Woolfall & Rimmer Ltd v Moyle [1942] 1 KB 66; [1941]
   3 All ER 304…1096
Worcester Works Finance Ltd v Cooden Engineering Co
   Ltd [1972] 1 QB 210; [1971] 3 WLR 661; [1971] 3 All
   ER 708…410
Workers Trust & Merchant Bank Ltd v Dojap Investments
   Ltd [1993] AC 573; [1993] 2 WLR 702; [1993] 2 All
   ER 370 (PC)…851
Workman Clark & Co Ltd v Lloyd Brazileno [1908] 1 KB
   968…477–8
Wormell v RHM Agricultural (East) Ltd [1986] 1 WLR
   336; [1986] 1 All ER 769…437, 447
Worwood v Leisure Merchandising Services Ltd [2002] 1
   BCLC 249…1066
Wrightson v McArthur & Hutchisons (1919) Ltd [1921] 2
   KB 807…**1030–1**, 1040
WS Tankship II BV v Kwangju Bank Ltd [2011] EWHC
   3103 (Comm)…844
WT Ramsay Ltd v Inland Revenue Commissioners [1982]
   AC 300; [1981] 2 WLR 449; [1981] 1 All ER 865…955
Wuhan Guoyu Logistics Group Co Ltd v Emporiki Bank
   of Greece SA [2012] EWCA Civ 1679; [2013] 1 All ER
   (Comm) 1191; [2012] 2 CLC 986…840–4, 854

X-Fab Semiconductor Foundries AG v Plessey
   Semiconductors Ltd [2014] EWHC 1574 (QB)…82

Yam Seng Pte Ltd v International Trade Corp Ltd [2013]
   EWHC 111 (QB); [2013] 1 All ER (Comm) 1321…42
Yasuda Fire & Marine Insurance Co of Europe Ltd v
   Orion Marine Insurance Underwriting Agency Ltd
   [1995] QB 174; [1995] 2 WLR 49; [1995] 3 All ER
   211…125, 250
Yearworth v North Bristol NHS Trust [2009] EWCA Civ
   37; [2010] QB 1; [2009] 3 WLR 118…94, 303
Yeoman Credit Ltd v Gregory [1963] 1 WLR 343; [1963]
   1 All ER 245…**704–5**

Yeung Kai Yung v Hong Kong and Shanghai Banking
    Corp [1981] AC 787; [1980] 3 WLR 950; [1980] 2 All
    ER 599 (PC)...**181**
Yona International Ltd v La Réunion Française SA
    d'Assurances et de Réassurances [1996] 2 Lloyd's
    Rep 84...159
Yonge v Toynbee [1910] 1 KB 215...**194–7, 291–2**
York Corp v Henry Leetham & Sons Ltd [1924] 1
    Ch 557...34
York Products Pty v Gilchrist Watt & Sanderson Pty
    [1970] 1 WLR 1262; [1970] 3 All ER 825...96, 102
Yorkshire Bank Plc v Hall [1999] 1 WLR 1713; [1999] 1
    All ER 879...1121
Yorkshire Bank Plc v Lloyds Bank Plc [1999] 1 All ER
    (Comm) 154...736
Yorkshire Railway Wagon Co v Maclure (1882) 21 Ch D
    309...955
Yorkshire Woolcombers Association Ltd, Re [1903] 2 Ch
    284...986, 990, 997, 999, 1072
Young and Marten Ltd v McManus Childs Ltd [1969]
    1 AC 454; [1968] 3 WLR 630; [1968] 2 All ER
    1169...321
Young v Gordon (1896) 23 R 419...**688**
Young v Kitchin (1878) 3 Ex D 127...947
Your Response Ltd v Datateam Business Media Ltd
    [2014] EWCA Civ 281; [2015] QB 41; [2014] 3 WLR
    887; [2014] CP Rep 31...79, 303, 1041–2
Ypatianna, The *see* Indian Oil Corp Ltd v Greenstone
    Shipping SA (Panama) (The Ypatianna)
Yuen Kun Yeu v Attorney-General of Hong Kong [1989]
    AC 288; [1988] AC 175 (PC)...229

Zenziper Grains and Feed Stuffs v Bulk Trading
    Corporation Limited [2000] All ER (D) 2139; [2001]
    CLC 496...555
Zim Israel Navigation Co Ltd v Effy Shipping Corp [1972]
    1 Lloyd's Rep 18...**616**
Zographia M, The *see* Astro Amo Compañia Naviera
    SA v Elf Union SA and First National City Bank (The
    Zographia M)

AUSTRALIA

Associated Alloys Pty Ltd v ACN 001 452 106 Pty Ltd
    (2000) 202 CLR 558 (HCAus)...511, 958
Attorney-General v Blake [1998] Ch 439
    (HCAus)...230, 234
Australasian Conference Association Ltd v Mainline
    Constructions Pty Ltd (In Liquidation) [1978] 141 CLR
    335 (HCAus)...850
Bolwell Fibreglass Pty Ltd v Foley [1984] VR 97
    (HCAus)...1046
Broad v Stamp Duties Commissioner [1980] 2 NSWLR
    40 (HCAus)...972
Campbells Cash and Carry Pty Ltd v Fostif Pty Ltd (2006)
    229 CLR 386 (HCAus)...876
Channon v English, Scottish & Australian Bank (1918)
    18 SR (NSW) 30...729
Chapman Bros v Verco Bros & Co Ltd (1933) 49 CLR
    306 (HCAus)...95
Clark v Macourt [2013] HCA 56; (2013) 253 CLR 1
    (HCAus)...525
Commissioners of State Savings Bank v Permewan
    Wright & Co 19 CLR 457 (HCAus)...754

Comptroller of Stamps (Vic) v Howard Smith (1936) 54
    CLR 614 (SCNSW)...921
Cossill v Strangman [1963] NSWR 1694 (SCNSW)...926
Davison v Vickery's Motors Ltd (1925) 37 CLR 1
    (HCAus)...167
Devefi Pty Ltd v Mateffy Pearl Nagy Pty Ltd [1993] RPC
    493 (FedCA(Aust))...870, 884, 890
Equuscorp Pty Ltd v Haxton (2012) 246 CLR 498
    (HCAus)...**875–8**
Estate of McClure, Re (1947) 48 SR (NSW) 93...972
Federal Commissioner of Taxation v Everett (1980) 143
    CLR 440 (HCAus)...909
Fire Nymph Products Ltd v The Heating Centre Property
    Ltd (1992) 7 ACSR 365...1076
Fisher v Automobile Finance Co of Australia Ltd (1928)
    41 CLR 167 (HCAus)...1053
Gamer's Motor Centre (Newcastle) Pty Ltd v Natwest
    Wholesale Australia Pty Ltd [1987] HCA 30; 163 CLR
    236 (HCAus)...410
GE Crane Pty Ltd v Federal Commissioner of Taxation
    (1971) 126 CLR 177 (HCAus)...936, 966
Golden Mile Property Investments Pty Ltd (In liquidation)
    v Cudgegong Australia Pty Ltd [2015] NSWCA 100;
    (2015) NSWLR 237 (SCNSW)...965
Grey v Australian Motorists and General
    Insurance Co Pty Ltd [1976] 1 NSWLR 669
    (CANSW)...921, **929–31**
Grimaldi v Chameleon Mining NL (No 2) [2012] FCAFC
    6 (FCAus)...247
Hart v Barnes (1982) 7 ACLR 310...998
Hospital Products Ltd v United States Surgical Corp [1984]
    HCA 64;(1984) 156 CLR 41 (HCAus)...28–9, 237
International Leasing Corpn (Victoria) Ltd v Aiken [1967]
    2 NSWLR 427; 85 WNNSW 766...930
International Paper Co v Spicer (1906) 4 CLR 739
    (HCAus)...150
LJ Hooker Ltd v WJ Adams Estates Ltd 138 CLR 52;
    (1977) 51 ALJR 413 (HCAus)...261
McRae v Commonwealth Disposals Commission (1950)
    84 CLR 377 (HCAus)...**370–2**
Maynegrain Pty Ltd v Compafina Bank [1982] 2 NSWLR
    141 (CANSW)...77, 203, 223, **1029**
Miller Associates (Australia) Pty Ltd v Bennington Pty Ltd
    (1975) 7 ALR 144 (SCNSW)...673
Ministry for Supply v Serviceman's Cooperative
    Joinery Manufacturers Ltd (1951) 82 CLR 621
    (HCAus)...479
Mutual Pools & Staff Pty Ltd v Commonwealth (1994)
    179 CLR 155 (HCAus)...877
NM Superannuation Pty Ltd v Hughes (1992) 7 ACSR
    105 (SCNSW)...167
Norman v Federal Commissionner of Taxation (1963)
    109 CLR 9 (HCAus)...**862, 864–8, 886**, 930
Olsson v Dyson (1969) 120 CLR 365 (HCAus)...889
Palette Shoes Pty Limited v Krohn (1937) 58 CLR 1
    (FCAus)...953
Palgo Holding Pty Ltd v Gowans [2005] HCA 28; (2005)
    221 CLR 249 (HCAus)...958
Parsons v R (1999) 73 ALJR 270 (HCAus)...568
Porter v Latec Finance (Qld) Pty Ltd (1964) 111 CLR 177
    (HCQld)...710
Shepherd v Federal Taxation Commissioner (1965) 113
    CLR 385 (HCAus)...863–4

Smith v Commercial Banking Co of Sydney Ltd (1910)
    11 CLR 667...740
Sutherland Shire Council v Heyman (1985) 157 CLR
    424; 60 ALR 1 (HCAus)...600
UTC Ltd (in liquidation) v NZI Securities Australia Ltd
    (1991) 4 WAR 349...921
Vered v Inscorp Holding Ltd (1993) 31 NSWLR 209
    (SCNSW)...1041
Woodhall Ltd v Pipeline Authority [1979] 141 CLR 443
    (HCAus)...850

CANADA

713860 Ontario Ltd v Royal Trust Corp of Canada
    Unreported 22 January 1996 (OntCA)...158
Bank of Nova Scotia v Angelica-Whitewear Ltd [1987] 1
    SCR 59...799
Becherer v Asher (1896) 23 OAR 202 (OntCA)...150
BMP Global Distribution Inc v Bank of Nova Scotia
    [2009] 1 SCR 504 (SupCt Can)...723
Boma Manufacturing Ltd v Canadian Imperial Bank
    of Commerce (1996) 140 DLR (4th) 463 (SupCt
    Can)...670–2
Canadian Laboratory Supplies Ltd v Englehard Industries
    Ltd (1979) 97 DLR (3d) 1 (SupCt Can)...139
Crampsey v Deveney (1969) 2 DLR (3d) 161(SupCt
    Can)...158
Jirna Ltd v Mister Donut of Canada Ltd (1973) DLR (3d)
    303 (SupCt Can)...233
McKillop & Benjafield v Alexander (1912) 45 SCR 551
    (SCCan)...884
McLaughlin v Gentiles (1919) 51 DLR 383; 46 OLR 477
    (OntAD)...150
Massey Harris Co Ltd v Bond [1930] 2 DLR 57; [1930] 1
    WWR 72 (AltaSC)...150
Newell v Royal Bank of Canada (1997) 147 DLR (4th)
    257 (CANS)...698
Norberg v Wynrib [1992] 2 SCR 226...28
QNS Paper Co Ltd v Chartwell Shipping Ltd [1989] 2
    SCR 683...190
Royal Bank of Canada v Concrete Column Clamps
    (1961) Ltd (1976) 74 DLR (3d) 26 (SupCt Can)...762
Royal Bank of Canada v Stangl (1992) 32 AWCS (3d) 17
    (HCOnt)...608
Sign-O-Lite Ltd v Metropolitan Life Insurance Co (1991)
    70 Can Bar Rev 329 (BritColCA)...**147–9**

COURT OF JUSTICE OF THE EUROPEAN UNION

Honyvem Informazioni Commerciali Srl v Mariella De
    Zotti (Case C-465/04) EU:C:2006:199; [2006] ECR
    I-02879...282
Ingmar GB Ltd v Eaton Leonard Technologies Inc (Case
    C-381/98) EU:C:2000:605; [2001] 1 All ER (Comm)
    329; [2000] ECR I-9305; [2001] 1 CMLR 9...119, 282
Poseidon Chartering BV v Marianne Zeeschip VOF (Case
    C-3/304) EU:C:2006:176; [2007] Bus LR 446; [2006]
    2 Lloyd's Rep 105; [2006] ECR I-2505...120

HONG KONG

Hing Yip Hing Fat Co Ltd v Daiwa Bank Ltd [1991] 2
    HKLR 35...781, 827
Thanakharn Kasikorn Thai Chambit (Mahachon)
    v Akai Holdings Ltd (In Liquidation) [2010]
    HKCFA 64...141, 145

IRELAND

Flynn v Mackin [1974] IR 101...316
Keenan Bros Ltd, Re [1986] BCLC 242 (SCIre)...992, 997
Kenny v Ireland ROC Ltd [2005] IEHC 241...120
TE Potterton Ltd v Northern Bank Ltd [1995] 4 Bank LR
    179 (HCIre)...603

NEW ZEALAND

Contemporary Cottages (NZ) Ltd v Margin Traders Ltd
    [1981] 2 NZLR 114 (HCNZ)...**984**
Covacich v Riordan [1994] 2 NZLR 502 (HCNZ)...1076
Dovey v Bank of New Zealand [2000] 3 NZLR 641
    (NZCA)...567, 622
Greymouth Gas Kaimiro Ltd v Swift Energy New Zealand
    [2010] NZSC 117 (SCNZ)...**885**
James Cook Hotel Ltd v Canx Corporation Services
    Ltd [1989] 3 NZLR 213; [1989] LRC (Comm) 518
    (HCNZ)...658
LC Fowler & Sons Ltd v St Stephens College Board of
    Governors [1991] 3 NZLR 304...217
Len Vidgen Ski & Leisure Ltd v Timaru Marine Supplies
    (1982) Ltd [1986] 1 NZLR 349...511
Manurewa Transport Ltd, Re [1971] NZLR 909
    (HCNZ)...1076
Mitchell v Jones (1905) 24 NZLR 932...409
Oldfield Asphalts Ltd v Grovedale Coolstores (1994) Ltd
    [1998] 3 NZLR 479...369
Pongakawa Sawmill Ltd v New Zealand Forest
    Productions Ltd [1992] 3 NZLR 304...505
Supercool Refrigeration and Air Conditioning (In
    Receivership and Liquidation) v Hoverd Industries Ltd
    [1994] 3 NZLR 300 (HCNZ)...992
Weddell New Zealand Ltd, Re (1996) 5 NZBLC
    104055...505

SINGAPORE

Beam Technology (MFG) Pty Ltd v Standard Chartered
    Bank [2003] 1 SLR 597 (CASing)...**797–9**
Lambias (Importers and Exporters) Co Pty Ltd v Hong
    Kong and Shanghai Banking Corp [1993] 2 SLR 751
    (HCSing)...796
Profindo Pte Ltd v Abani Trading Pte Ltd [2013] SGHC
    10; [2013] 1 Lloyd's Rep 370 (HCSing)...538

SOUTH AFRICA

B & H Engineering v First National Bank of SA Ltd 1995
    (2) SA 279 (A) (SCASAfr)...717
Paiges v Van Ryn Gold Mines Estates Ltd 1920 AD 600
    (SCSAfr)...882
Stapleberg v Barclays Bank 1963 (3) SA 120...740

UNITED STATES

Ayers v Franch (1874) 41 Conn R 142...86
Far Eastern Textile Ltd v City National Bank and Trust
    430 F Supp 193 (SD Ohio 1977)...778
Kremen v Online Classified Inc (2003) 337 F 3d 1024...85
Phillips Puerto Rico v Tradax Petroleum 782 F 2d 314
    (1985)...362
Sztejn v J Henry Schroder Banking Corp 31 NYS 2d 631
    (1941)...791, 807, 845
Transamerica Delaval Inc v Citibank NA 545 F Supp 200
    (SDNY 1982)...778

TABLE OF LEGISLATION

STATUTES

United Kingdom

Agricultural Holdings Act 1948...954
Arbitration Act 1889...553
Arbitration Act 1934...553
Arbitration Act 1996...13
Banking Act 1979
  s 47...759
Banking Act 1989...47
  s 89...637
Banking Act 2009
  s 255...1068
  s 256...1068
Bankruptcy Act 1861
  s 137...981
Bankruptcy Act 1883...1105
Bankruptcy Act 1914...1105
  s 31...970–1
  s 44(1)...1131
Bills of Exchange Act 1882...15, 43, 297, 572, 649,
  651, 659–61
  Pt 4A...581, 733, 742
  s 1(2)(b)...762
  s 1(2)(d)...762
  s 2...663, 671, 675, 680, 682, 692, 749
  s 3...661, 727
  s 3(1)...645, 663, 665–6, 669, 673, 680, 736, 762–3
  s 5(2)...663, 692, 761–2
  s 7(1)...664
  s 7(2)...664
  s 7(3)...660, 664, 666, 669–70, 672
  s 7(c)...700
  s 8...674, 734
  s 8(1)...650, 673
  s 8(3)...666
  s 8(4)...672, 675
  s 9(1)...664
  s 10(1)...664
  s 11...664
  s 12...43
  s 16(1)...702
  s 18...299
  s 19...702
  s 20...665, 684, 702
  s 20(1)...665
  s 20(2)...665
  s 21...680
  s 21(1)...681, 692
  s 21(2)...683, 692
  s 21(2)(a)...692
  s 21(3)...692, 735
  s 22...676
  s 22(1)...692
  s 23...170, 692, 699

s 24...671, 675, 685, 696–7, 699, 708, 736, 752
s 25...170, 693
s 26...186, 693
s 26(1)...170, 693
s 26(2)...694
s 27...676–7
s 27(1)...681
s 27(1)(a)...661, 680
s 27(1)(b)...678
s 27(2)...675, 678–81, 688
s 27(3)...688, 751, 1053
s 28(1)...685
s 29...685
s 29(1)...43, 682–4, 686, 688, 748, 947
s 29(1)(a)...708
s 29(1)(b)...688, 708, 751
s 29(2)...688–9
s 29(3)...684, 689–91
s 30(1)...676
s 30(2)...43, 682–3
s 31(2)...666
s 31(3)...672, 702
s 31(4)...673
s 34(1)...666
s 34(2)...666
s 34(3)...666
s 34(4)...672
s 35...675
s 36(1)...675, 708
s 36(3)...685, 708
s 38(1)...675, 681
s 38(2)...681–2, 688, 947
s 39...703
s 40...703
s 43(1)...703
s 43(2)...703, 832
s 44(1)...702
s 44(2)...703
s 44(3)...703
s 45...703–4
s 45(2)...705, 741
s 46(1)...704
s 47(1)...703
s 47(2)...690, 832
s 48...705–6, 712
s 49...705, 712
s 50...712
s 50(2)...706, 712
s 50(2)(c)...706, 712
s 51(2)...706
s 52...299
s 52(1)...704
s 52(4)...706
s 53(1)...567, 700, 889
s 54...669

s 54(1)...676, 700
s 54(2)...701
s 54(2)(a)...663, 669
s 55(1)...701
s 55(1)(a)...676
s 55(2)...685, 701
s 55(2)(a)...676
s 55(2)(b)...663, 698–9
s 55(2)(c)...708
s 56...701
s 57...700
s 58...703
s 58(2)...702
s 58(3)...702, 708
s 59...671, 675, 735
s 59(1)...43, 675, 701, 706
s 59(2)...701
s 59(3)...701
s 60...43, 736–40, 758
s 61...706
s 62...706
s 62(2)...298
s 63...706
s 64...699, 729, 733, 744–8
s 64(1)...699, 735–6, 743–7
s 68(5)...157
s 73...727, 763
s 74...703, 705
s 74(1)...741
s 74(2)...741
s 74A...733
s 76(1)...728
s 76(2)...728
s 77...729
s 77(2)...729
s 77(3)...729
s 77(4)...729
s 77(5)...729
s 77(6)...729
s 78...729
s 79(2)...43, 729
s 80...43, 736–7, 741, 744–5, 758, 762
s 81...665, 674–5, 728, 752
s 81A...575, 736
s 81A(1)...672, 675, 727–8, 736–7, 741, 748, 752,
    758, 762
s 81A(2)...737
s 82...738–40, 745
s 83...763
s 83(1)...759–60
s 86...705
s 87...705
s 87(1)...761
s 88(1)...676
s 89...705
s 89(1)...708, 761
s 89(2)...761
s 89(3)...761
s 89B...581
s 89E(1)...742
s 90...43, 686
s 91(1)...170, 692
s 95...660
s 97(2)...661

ss 73-82...727
ss 83-89...761
ss 89A-89F...663
Bills of Lading Act 1855
    s 1...62, 537
Bills of Sale Act 1877...943
Bills of Sale Act 1878...976, 1060, 1070, 1077–80
    s 3...1079
    s 4...1078
    s 10...1079
    s 11...1079
Bills of Sale Act 1882...319, 1060, 1070, 1077–80
    s 3...1078
    s 4...1079
    s 5...1079–80
    s 7...1085
    s 7A...1067
    s 7A(1)...1085
    s 9...1084
    s 12...1084
    s 13...1085
    s 15...1079
Bills of Sale Act (1878) Amendment
    Act 1882...1084–5
    s 7...1066
    s 8...1018
    s 13...1067
Bretton Woods Agreements Act 1945...802
Bribery Act 2010
    s 1...249
    s 2...249
    s 6...249
    s 7...249
    s 10...249
Carriage of Goods by Sea Act 1971...539
Carriage of Goods by Sea Act 1992...11, 329
    s 1(5)...559
    s 2...62, 537, 546
    s 2(1)...63–4
    s 3...537
Cheques Act 1957
    s 1...43, 737, 740, 762
    s 2...684, 749–50
    s 3...749–50
    s 4...43, 85, 734, 738, 748–9, 752–3, 756–9, 762
    s 4(1)...752
    s 4(2)...758
    s 4(2)(b)...737
    s 4(2)(c)...737
    s 4(2)(d)...737
    s 4(3)...758
    s 5...660, 737, 762
    s 6(2)...650
Cheques Act 1992...727, 758
    s 3...758
Civil Aviation Act 1982
    s 88...1041
Civil Liability (Contribution) Act 1978...269,
    454, 742
    s 3...178
Companies Act 1900...1080
Companies Act 1948
    s 95...510, 981–2
    s 95(2)(e)...981
    s 227...1128

Companies Act 1985...137, 951, 980
  Pt XII...918, 1023
  s 36C(1)...161
  s 221(1)...1136
  s 221(2)(a)...1136
  s 247(3)...1111
  s 349(4)...695
  s 395...886, 951, 974, 990
  s 396...990
  s 396(1)(e)...974
Companies Act 1989...137
  Pt VII...1108
Companies Act 2006...1080–4
  Pt 10...232
  Pt 21...80, 870
  Pt 25...318–19, 501–2, 507, 510, 918, 956, 959,
    977, 980, 1001–2, 1015, 1023, 1077, 1080
  s 17...137
  s 28...137
  s 39(1)...126, 137, 692
  s 40...134, 137
  s 40(2)(b)(i)...137
  s 40(2)(b)(ii)...137
  s 40(2)(b)(iii)...137
  s 41...137
  s 51...695
  s 51(1)...191–2, 695
  s 83...695
  s 84...695
  s 127...1129
  s 170...232
  s 170(3)...232
  s 170(4)...232
  s 174...230
  s 175...232
  s 176...233
  s 177...233
  s 178...232
  s 178(2)...230
  s 182...233
  s 232...232
  s 544...80, 870
  s 859A...501, 951, 974, 979, 1042, 1058, 1060,
    1075, 1077, 1080, 1084
  s 859A(6)...979–80, 1080
  s 859C...1080
  s 859D(2)(c)...1073
  s 859E...1080
  s 859F...1080–1
  s 859H...951, 980, 1060, 1075, 1077, 1081, 1084
  s 859H(4)...1081
  s 859I(4)...1081
  s 859I(6)...1081
  s 859L...1082
  s 859M...1081
  s 859N...1081
  s 859Q...1082
  s 860...977–8, 981–2, 984
  s 860(7)(a)...978
  s 860(7)(f)...977–8
  s 860(7)(g)...977
  s 860(7)(i)...978
  s 861...978, 981–2
  s 874...886, 978, 981–2
  s 874(1)...977

  s 895A...1018
  s 895H...1018
  s 1282...1013, 1074
Company Directors Disqualification Act
  1986...1111
Competition Act 1998...24, 122
Consumer Credit Act 1974...16, 24, 414, 636–8,
  1008–9, 1084
  Pt V...637
  s 4(b)...640
  s 7A...1085
  s 9(1)...1008
  s 12(b)...641–2
  s 12(c)...641–2
  s 14(1)...636, 639
  s 14(1)(a)...638
  s 14(1)(b)...636–8
  s 14(2)...636–8
  s 14(3)...636–8
  s 51...636
  s 56...642
  s 56(2)...642
  s 60(1)...664
  s 66...636, 639–40
  s 70(2)...1041
  s 73(5)...1041
  s 75...637, 641–2
  s 75(1)...641–2
  s 75(2)...641
  s 75(3)...641–2
  s 75(3)(c)...641
  s 75(4)...641
  s 75A...642
  s 83...639–40
  s 84...639–40
  s 84(2)...639
  s 84(3)...639
  s 87...1067
  s 87(1)...1085
  s 88...1067
  s 88(2)...1085
  s 89...1067, 1085
  s 105(1)...1064
  s 114(1)...1039
  s 114(3)...1040
  s 116(1)...1040
  s 121(1)...1040
  s 123...762
  s 123(1)...689
  s 123(3)...689
  s 124...762
  s 125(1)...689
  s 125(4)...689
  s 129(1)(a)...1040
  s 171(4)(b)...639
  s 187(3A)...637, 641
  s 189(1)...1039
  ss 114-122...1039
  ss 117-122...1040
  ss 140A-140C...1009
Consumer Credit Act 2006
  s 2...1009
Consumer Insurance (Disclosure and Representations)
  Act 2012...1090, 1092
  s 6(2)...1093

Consumer Protection Act 1987...16, 24
  Pt 1...454
Consumer Rights Act 2015...7, 16, 24, 99, 232, 254,
  297, 300, 424, 454
  Pt 2...635, 1097
  s 2...10, 635
  s 7...99
  s 8...99
  s 9...99
  s 10...99
  s 13...99
  s 62(1)...1097
  s 63(1)...736
  s 65...1097
  s 66(1)(a)...1097
  s 70...1097
  Sch 2...736
  Sch 3...1097
Contracts (Applicable Law) Act 1990...833, 836
  s 2(1)...833
  s 3(1)...833
Contracts (Rights of Third Parties) Act 1999...102, 203,
  259, 454, 581, 598, 626, 1098
  s 1(1)...170, 255, 608
  s 1(1)(b)...608
  s 1(2)...170, 772
  s 1(3)...161
  s 1(6)...102
Conveyancing Act 1881
  s 12...930–1
Copyright, Designs and Patents Act 1988
  s 90...870
Courts and Legal Services Act 1990
  s 58...871
  s 58A...871
Criminal Justice Act 1988...596, 867
Criminal Law Act 1967
  s 13(1)...872
  s 14...870
  s 14(1)...872
  s 14(2)...872
Deregulation Act 2015...1106
Electronic Communications Act 2000...50, 663
  s 8...51, 663
Enduring Powers of Attorney Act 1985...275, 292
Enterprise Act 2002...24, 1073, 1105, 1110–12,
  1116, 1122–3
  s 250...1013, 1074
  s 251...998
  s 252...1013
Enterprise and Regulatory Reform Act
  2013...1106, 1110
  s 71(3)...976
Estate Agents Act 1979
  s 3...239
  s 21...239
European Communities Act 1972
  s 2(1)...25
Exchange Control Act 1947...1061
Factors Act 1823...1027
Factors Act 1825...1027
Factors Act 1842...1027
Factors Act 1877...1027

Factors Act 1889...85, 117, 348, 650, 1027
  s 1...397
  s 1(1)...394, 397
  s 1(4)...1028
  s 2...394–404, 415, 418–19, 1033, 1053
  s 2(1)...43, 394–5, 397, 401, 418
  s 2(2)...398
  s 2(3)...398
  s 3...1027–8
  s 8...43, 408, 414, 1053
  s 9...43, 408, 412–15, 417–19, 768, 1053
  s 16...421
  s 20A...421
  s 24...394, 410–12, 650
  s 25(1)...394
  s 47...420
  s 47(1)...420
Fair Trading Act 1973...16
Financial Services Act 2012...35
Financial Services (Banking Reform) Act 2013...728
  s 40...581
Financial Services and Markets Act 2000...24, 35,
  239, 1091
  s 147...239
Fires Prevention (Metropolis) Act 1774
  s 83...1098
Forgery Act 1913...696
Forgery and Counterfeiting Act 1981...696, 698
  s 1...696
  s 9...696
  s 9(1)(d)...696
Hire-Purchase Act 1964
  Pt III...421, 461
  s 27...43, 391, 414
  s 28...43
  s 29...43
Hotel Proprietors Act 1956
  s 1(1)...1046
  s 2(2)...1046
Human Rights Act 1998...35
  s 3...35
  s 4...35
  s 6(1)...35
  s 6(3)...35
Innkeepers Act 1878
  s 1...1053
Insolvency Act 1976
  s 72A...1074
Insolvency Act 1985...1105
  s 176ZA...1074
  Sch B1...1074
Insolvency Act 1986...934, 1105
  Pt 7A...1109
  Pt I...1111
  Pt II...1109, 1111
  Pt III...1115
  Pt IV...1123
  Pt IX...1110
  Pt VIII...1109
  s 1...1111
  s 15...1113
  s 29(1)...1116
  s 29(2)...1116, 1123

s 30...1117
s 31...1117
s 40...990, 1073, 1122
s 40(2)...996
s 72A...1069, 1112
s 72A(1)...1013
s 74(2)(f)...1137
s 122(1)(f)...1124
s 123(1)...1125
s 123(2)...1124
s 127...886, 965, 1127–8, 1130
s 128...1128, 1130
s 165(2)...886
s 167(1)...886
s 175...990, 1137
s 175(2)(b)...996, 1073
s 176A...1013, 1122, 1137
s 176ZA...1013
s 178...1127
s 212...1133
s 213...1133–5
s 214...1133–4, 1136
s 214(1)...1136
s 214(2)...1136
s 214(3)...1136
s 214(6)...1109
s 234(3)...85
s 238...951, 1084, 1130–2
s 238(4)...1132
s 239...951, 1084, 1125, 1130–1
s 244...951, 1130
s 245...951, 991, 1073, 1075, 1130
s 246(2)...1049, 1054
s 246(3)...1054
s 248(b)...1040, 1054
s 249...1130
s 251...1074
s 284(4)...293
s 284(5)...293
s 314(1)...886
s 323...970–1
s 339...1084
s 340...1084
s 344...943, 951, 959, 976, 1078
s 386...1137
s 423...951, 1130
s 424...951
s 425...951
s 435...1130
s 436...66
ss 72B-72H...1069, 1074
ss 263H-263O...1110
Sch 1...1112
Sch 4...886, 1124
Sch 5...886
Sch 6...1073, 1110, 1137
Sch A1...1111
Sch B1...1012, 1040, 1054, 1057, 1073–4, 1112,
    1114–15
Insolvency Act 2000...1105
Insurance Act 2015...1090, 1096
s 2(1)...1092
s 3...1092

s 3(4)...1092
s 3(5)...1092
s 4...1092
s 5...1092
s 6...1092
s 8...1092
s 9(2)...1093
s 10(1)...1096
s 10(2)...1096
s 10(3)...1096
s 10(4)...1096
s 12(1)...1102
s 12(2)...1102
s 15...1096, 1102
s 16...1092, 1096, 1102
s 17...1092, 1096, 1102
ss 2-8...1092
Sch 1...1092
Land Registration Act 2002
s 23(1)(a)...1060
Late Payment of Commercial Debts (Interest) Act
    1998...479
Law of Property Act 1925...1117
s 51...303
s 53(1)...69, 126
s 53(1)(c)...901, 1064, 1069
s 54...126
s 56(1)...170
s 61(1)...303
s 85...1060, 1069
s 86...1060, 1069
s 87...1069
s 91...1066
s 101...1067
s 101(1)...1066
s 103...1066
s 109...1067
s 136...80, 655, 870, 875, 888, 901–3, 905, 907–
    10, 920, 922–3, 925–8, 930–1, 935, 938, 943,
    980, 1060
s 136(1)...927–9, 931
s 137(1)...916, 918
Law of Property (Miscellaneous Provisions) Act 1989
s 1...170
s 1(1)(c)...126
s 2...303
s 2(1)...1064
s 3...305
Sch 1...170
Law Reform (Contributory Negligence) Act 1945...440
Law Reform (Frustrated Contracts) Act 1943
s 2(5)(c)...380
s 7...380
Life Assurance Act 1774...1090
Limitation Act 1980
s 3(2)...79
s 20...1067
s 35...932
Limited Liability Partnerships Act 2000...1070
Local Government Act 1988
s 17...34
Local Government Act 1999
s 3(1)...34

Local Government (Contracts) Act 1997...34
Localism Act 2011...34
Marine Insurance Act 1906...15, 659, 1090, 1100
   s 17...43
Mental Capacity Act 2005...275
   s 9(1)...275
   s 13...275
   s 14...292
   s 14(5)...198
   s 66...275
   ss 5-8...158
   Sch 4...275
Merchant Shipping Act 1995
   s 224(1)...157
Misrepresentation Act 1967
   s 2(1)...175
Modern Slavery Act 2015
   s 54...36
Partnership Act 1890...15
   s 5...117
Pensions Act 1995
   s 91...869
Policies of Assurance Act 1867...80
   s 1...870
Powers of Attorney Act 1971
   s 4...275
   s 4(1)...273
   s 5...292-3
   s 5(1)...198
   s 7(1)...170, 191
   s 10...129
   Sch 1...129
Preferential Payments in Bankruptcy Amendment
   Act 1897
   s 2...990, 996
   s 3...990, 996
Proceeds of Crime Act 2002...867
Promissory Notes Act 1704...24, 651-3
Sale of Goods Act 1893...15, 297-8, 304-5, 429, 659
   s 1(1)...310
   s 1(2)...506
   s 1(3)...310
   s 2...310
   s 2(1)...308, 330
   s 2(3)...497
   s 2(4)...310, 327
   s 2(5)...310, 327
   s 4...323
   s 5(2)...305, 374-5, 488
   s 5(3)...305
   s 6...367-72, 375
   s 7...328, 367-75
   s 9...326
   s 9(1)...326
   s 9(2)...326
   s 10...464
   s 10(1)...456, 494
   s 10(2)...458
   s 11(2)...464
   s 11(3)...340, 466
   s 11(4)...469
   s 12...455
   s 12(1)...459-61, 463

s 12(2)(a)...462-3
s 12(2)(b)...462-3
s 12(3)...305, 308, 459, 462
s 12(4)...462-3
s 12(5)...463
s 12(5A)...459
s 13...340, 466
s 14...340, 466
s 14(1)...441, 443-4
s 14(2)...340
s 15...466
s 15A...466, 552
s 16...351, 365, 546
s 17...348, 358, 497, 546
s 18...307, 339-40, 342-3, 347-50, 354-5, 358,
   362, 489, 506, 538, 556
s 19...546
s 19(1)...358, 538
s 19(2)...358, 538
s 19(3)...497
s 20...328, 355, 357, 458, 506
s 20(1)...362-3
s 20(2)...363
s 20(3)...363
s 20A...307, 314, 328, 365, 367
s 21...381-2, 387-8
s 21(1)...384, 387
s 22...305
s 23...404, 407
s 24...305, 330, 409, 496-7
s 25...348
s 25(1)...305, 330, 408, 506
s 25(2)...412, 488
s 27...455, 463, 474
s 28...330, 339, 455-6, 463, 474, 493-4
s 29(1)...458
s 29(2)...458
s 29(4)...456
s 29(5)...458
s 29(6)...458
s 30...458, 464-5
s 30(1)...469
s 30(2)...468
s 30(2A)...458, 464, 466, 469, 552
s 30(2B)...464
s 31...458
s 31(1)...465
s 31(2)...467
s 32(1)...458
s 32(3)...458
s 33...368, 458
s 34...472
s 35...360, 464, 469
s 35(1)...470
s 35(1)(b)...472
s 35(2)...470
s 35(4)...470
s 35(6)...472
s 35(6)(b)...471-2
s 35(7)...472
s 35A...472
s 35A(3)...472
s 37(1)...463, 482

s 38...495
s 38(1)...484
s 38(1)(a)...484
s 38(2)...325
s 39...484, 494
s 39(1)...483–4, 493, 495
s 39(1)(a)...339
s 39(1)(c)...494, 496
s 39(2)...483, 488–9, 493
s 41(1)...484
s 41(2)...484
s 42...484
s 43(1)...484–5
s 43(1)(a)...489
s 43(2)...484
s 45...489
s 45(4)...489
s 46...489
s 46(1)-(3)...489
s 46(4)...489
s 47...485–9
s 47(2)...488
s 48...491–6
s 48(1)...491–2
s 48(2)...305, 308, 492–3, 496–7
s 48(3)...491–3, 496
s 48(4)...491–3, 496
s 49...478
s 49(1)...328, 474
s 49(2)...330, 474–5
s 50...328, 515
s 50(1)...479
s 50(2)...480
s 50(3)...480–2
s 51...327–8, 515, 522
s 51(1)...479
s 51(2)...515, 522–3
s 51(3)...515–18, 520, 523
s 52...327, 483, 527
s 52(1)...527
s 53...524
s 53(1)(c)...522
s 53(2)...525
s 53(3)...525
s 54...482, 523
s 59...458, 546
s 61...310
s 61(1)...305–8
s 61(2)...374–5
s 61(4)...489
s 62...310
s 62(1)...311, 506
s 62(4)...319
ss 16-19...330, 381
ss 21-25...308
ss 21-26...311
ss 38-48...494
ss 44-46...489
Sale of Goods Act 1979...7, 15, 39, 43, 297, 301
s 1(5)...300
s 2(1)...300
s 2(3)...301
s 2(4)...302

s 2(5)...68, 302
s 2(6)...68, 301
s 5(1)...68
s 5(3)...337
s 6...371
s 11...424
s 11(3)...452
s 13...423–34, 438
s 13(1)...431, 446
s 13(3)...425
s 14...320, 423–4, 432, 434, 438, 440
s 14(1)...434, 446
s 14(2)...203, 425, 435–7, 439, 441–2, 447–8,
    452, 657
s 14(2)(c)...448
s 14(2A)...436
s 14(2B)...436, 449
s 14(2B)(a)...321, 436
s 14(2C)...442
s 14(2C)(b)...438
s 14(3)...203, 439, 441–8, 657
s 14(4)...434
s 14(5)...203, 435–6
s 15...423–4, 434, 448–50
s 15(1)...448
s 15(2)...448–9
s 15(2)(a)...448–50
s 15(2)(c)...438, 448–9
s 15A...424
s 16...331, 333, 335, 337
s 17...68, 80, 333, 337–8, 501
s 17(2)...337
s 18...68, 80, 333, 337–41, 439
s 19(2)...536, 540–2
s 19(3)...557, 768
s 20A...67, 335–7
s 20A(4)...335
s 20A(5)...335
s 20A(6)...335
s 20B...335–7
s 21(2)(a)...394
s 21(2)(b)...421
s 22...43, 422
s 23...43
s 24...43, 80, 400, 416–18, 650, 1053
s 25...43, 80, 650, 768, 1053
s 25(1)...318, 401, 412–17, 419–20, 488, 512
s 28...476
s 29(4)...76
s 30...428
s 35...323
s 35(6)(a)...473
s 35A...657
s 41...1041
s 42...1041
s 43...1041
s 47...43, 488
s 47(2)...650
s 48...421, 1053
s 48(2)...1057
s 49...476–7
s 49(1)...476, 512
s 49(2)...476–7

s 50...516
s 50(3)...480
s 51...516
s 51(2)...516
s 55(1)...424
s 61(1)...302, 335–6, 411
s 61(3)...43
s 61(4)...1109
s 62(1)...449
ss 12-15...316, 318–19
ss 12-15A...313
ss 13-15...114
ss 17-20A...323
ss 39-46...80
Sale of Goods Act 1995
    s 20B...1029
Sale of Goods (Amendment) Act 1994...297, 309
Sale of Goods (Amendment) Act
    1995...297, 1029
    s 2(2)...307
    s 20A...299, 1029
Sale and Supply of Goods Act 1994...297, 473
Senior Courts Act 1981
    s 35A...479
    s 49...934
    s 51...874
Small Business, Enterprise and Employment Act
    2015...1106
    s 1...887, 1002–3
    s 13...581, 663, 733, 742
Social Security Administration Act 1992
    s 187...869
Stamp Act 1853
    s 19...734, 738–9
    s 60...734
Statute of Frauds 1677...256
    s 4...663–4, 702
    s 17...297
Statute of Frauds Amendment Act 1928
    s 6...663
Stock Transfer Act 1963...80
Stock Transfer Act 1982...80
Supply of Goods (Implied Terms) Act 1973...16
    s 8...459
    ss 8-12...318
Supply of Goods and Services
    Act 1982...99, 312, 316, 470
    s 2...459
    s 3...423
    s 4...323, 423
    s 5...423
    s 8...423
    s 9...423
    s 10...423
    s 11...423
    s 13...323
    s 15...258, 326
    ss 1-5A...323
    ss 2-5A...313
Supreme Court of Judicature Act 1873...861
    s 25...906, 908
    s 25(6)...655, 865–6, 870, 888, 901,
        903, 907–8, 927, 929, 931

Theft Act 1968
    s 3...572
    s 4(1)...565–6
    s 15...568
    s 15(1)...565–7
    s 15A...568
Theft (Amendment) Act 1996...568
Third Parties (Rights against Insurers) Act
    1930...1090, 1099
Third Parties (Rights against Insurers) Act
    2010...1090, 1099
Torts (Interference with Goods) Act 1977
    s 2(2)...83, 101
    s 3...54, 82
    s 7...79
    s 8...76, 79
    s 8(1)...67
    s 11(1)...759
    s 11(2)...1034
    s 12...157, 422, 1053
    s 13...157, 422, 1053
    Sch 1...157
Trade Descriptions Act 1968...16
Trade Descriptions Act 1972...16
Trustee Act 2000
    ss 11-23...251
Trustee Delegation Act 1999...251
Unfair Contract Terms Act 1977...10, 16, 99, 232, 254,
    297, 424, 450, 635
    s 1(2)...10
    s 3...780, 822
    s 6...452
    s 6(1)(a)...461
    s 7...453
    s 11(1)...453
    s 11(2)...453
    s 13...452–3
    s 13(1)(c)...736
    s 14...452
    s 15...452
    s 26...10, 453
    s 27...10, 453
    Sch 1...10
    Sch 2...453
Uniform Laws on International Sales
    Act 1967...533
Unsolicited Goods and Services Act 1971...16

Australia

Cheques Act 1986...729
Cheques and Payment Orders Act 1986...729
Goods Act 1928 (Victoria)
    s 11...371
Introduction Agents Act 2001 (Queensland)
    s 8(1)(a)...108
Personal Property Securities Act 2009
    (Commonwealth)...318, 1076
    s 12...498
Sale of Goods Act 1923 (NSW)
    s 28(1)...409

Belgium

Loi du 11 juillet 2013 sur le gage...513

Bermuda

Charge and Security (Special Provisions)
  Act 1990...975

Canada

Personal Property Security Act 1993 (Sask)...1022

Cayman Islands

Property (Miscellaneous Provisions) Law 1994...975

France

Loi no 91-593 du 25 juin 1991
  art 12...280

Germany

Civil Code...44
  art 242...38
  art 929...337
  art 932...384
  art 935...384
  art 985...82

Hong Kong

Theft Ordinance 1980
  s 5(1)...566
Third Parties (Rights Against Insurers) Ordinance
  1951...212

Israel

Bills of Exchange Ordinance...661

New Zealand

Personal Property Securities Act 1999...1076
Sale of Goods Act 1895...409

Singapore

Civil Law Act
  s 9A...975

United States

American Uniform Commercial
  Code (UCC)...5–6, 330
  art 2...6
  art 4...6
  art 4A...6, 568–9
  art 5(rev)...6
  art 6(rev)...6
  art 7...6
  art 8(rev)...6
  art 9...39, 318, 1022, 1083
  art 9(rev)...6
  s 1-102(2)...6
  s 1-203...38
  s 2-304(1)...315
  s 2-403...394
  s 2-615...376
  s 4-407...717
  s 5-105...772
  s 5-109(a)...799
  s 5-110(a)...832
  s 5-115...799
  s 9-109(a)(1)...498

STATUTORY INSTRUMENTS

Bretton Woods Agreements Order in Council 1946
  (SR & O 1946/36)...790, 802–5
Civil Procedure Rules 1998 (SI 1998/3132)
  Pt 6...833
  Pt 24...571
  Pt 25.1...1054
  Pt 25.1(c)(v)...1054
  r 58.1(2)...6, 12
  r 63A 1(3)...12
Commercial Agents (Council Directive) Regulations
  1993 (SI 1993/3053)...115, 119, 126
  Pt III...266
  reg 1(2)...119
  reg 1(3)...119
  reg 1(3)(b)...119
  reg 2(1)...119–21, 266
  reg 2(2)...121
  reg 2(3)...121
  reg 2(4)...121
  reg 3(1)...43, 122, 224, 233
  reg 3(2)...224, 233
  reg 4(1)...43, 122
  reg 5(1)...233
  reg 6(1)...266
  reg 6(3)...266
  regs 6-12...122
  reg 7(1)...266
  reg 7(1)(b)...267
  reg 7(2)...267
  regs 7-12...266
  reg 8...267
  reg 10(1)...267
  reg 10(2)...267
  reg 10(4)...267
  reg 13(1)...126
  reg 13(2)...126
  regs 13-16...122
  reg 14...276
  reg 15...276
  reg 15(2)...276
  reg 16...276
  reg 17...279
  reg 17(1)...276–7
  reg 17(2)...277, 280, 282
  reg 17(2)(a)...282
  reg 17(2)(b)...283
  reg 17(3)...267, 277, 280–4
  reg 17(3)(a)...277
  reg 17(4)...277
  reg 17(5)...277–8
  reg 17(6)...277, 281
  reg 17(8)...278
  reg 17(9)...279
  regs 17-19...122
  reg 18...278–9
  reg 18(a)...278–9
  reg 18(b)...278
  reg 18(b)(i)...278
  reg 19...279
  reg 20...122–3
  reg 20(3)...123
  regs 3-5...121

Companies Act 2006 (Amendment of Part 25)
   Regulations 2013 (SI 2013/600)...977, 1002,
   1023, 1080
Company, Limited Liability Partnership and Business
   (Names and Trading Disclosures) Regulations 2015
   (SI 2015/17)
   reg 24(1)(b)...695
   reg 24(1)(c)...695
   reg 28(1)...695
Concession Contracts Regulations 2016 (SI 2016/
   273)...34
Consumer Contracts (Information, Cancellation and
   Additional Charges) Regulations 2013 (SI 2013/
   3134)...16
Consumer Protection (Distance Selling) Regulations
   2000 (SI 2000/2334)
   reg 3...641
   reg 5...641
Cross-Border Insolvency Regulations 2006
   (SI 2006/1030)...1106
Electronic Commerce (EC Directive) Regulations 2002
   (SI 2002/2013)...50
Electronic Money Regulations 2011
   (SI 2011/99)...627
Electronic Signatures Regulations 2002 (SI 2002/
   318)...50
Financial Collateral Arrangements (No 2)
   Regulations 2003 (SI 2003/3226)...580, 978,
   1065, 1068
   reg 3...979, 1018, 1084
   reg 3(1)...1067, 1074
   reg 3(2)...1074
   reg 4(3)...910
   reg 4(4)...1084
   reg 8...1012
   reg 17...1068
   reg 18(2)...1068
   reg 18(3)...1068
Financial Markets and Insolvency Regulations 1991 (SI
   1991/880)...1108
Financial Markets and Insolvency (Settlement Finality)
   Regulations 1999 (SI 1999/2979)...580, 1108
Financial Markets and Insolvency (Settlement Finality
   and Financial Collateral Arrangements) (Amendment)
   Regulations 2010 (SI 2010/2993)...1074
Financial Services and Markets Act 2000 (Regulated
   Activities) Order 2001 (RAO) (SI 2001/544)
   art 60H...1009
   art 60L...1008
   arts 60C-60HA...1009
   arts 60C(3)-(7)...1009
Insolvency (Prescribed Part) Order 2003 (SI 2003/
   2097)...1074
Insolvency Rules 1986 (SI 1986/1925)
   r 4 90...970, 973-4
Money Laundering Regulations 2007 (SI 2007/
   2157)...752
Payment Services Regulations 2009 (SI 2009/209)...569,
   582, 639
   Pt 5...639-40
   Pt 6...639-41
   reg 2(1)...583, 639
   reg 33(1)...582

reg 34...639
reg 35...639
reg 51(1)...582
reg 52...639
reg 52(a)...636
reg 53(3)...639
reg 55(1)...584
reg 55(2)...584
reg 55(4)...610
regs 56-59...639
reg 56...641
reg 57...640-1
reg 57(1)(b)...640
reg 57(2)...640
reg 58...641
reg 58(1)(b)...636
reg 59...641
reg 59(1)...584-5, 640
reg 59(2)...584-5, 640
reg 59(3)...609
reg 60(1)...640
reg 60(2)...640
reg 61...639-41
reg 61(a)...584
reg 61(b)...584
reg 62(1)...640
reg 62(2)...640
reg 62(3)...641
reg 63...639
reg 63(2)...584
reg 64(4)...610
reg 65(1)...610
reg 67...610
reg 68(1)...585
reg 68(2)...585
reg 68(3)(b)...585
reg 70(1)...583
reg 70(5)...584
reg 70(6)...584-5
reg 73...582
reg 73(1)...585
reg 73(2)...585
reg 74(2)...583, 585
reg 75...583-4
reg 75(2)...583
reg 75(4)...583
reg 75(5)...585
reg 76...583
reg 76(2)...584-5
reg 76(3)...585
reg 76(4)...585
reg 76(5)...584-5
reg 77...584-5
reg 78...584-5
reg 79...583-5
reg 120(1)...582
reg 120(3)...582
Sch 1...639
Public Contracts Regulations 2015 (SI 2015/102)...34
Rules of the Supreme Court (Revision) 1965 (SI 1965/
   1776)
   r 1(1)...833
   r 1(d)...833

Unfair Terms in Consumer Contracts Regulations 1999
(SI 1999/2083)...43, 232, 256, 1097
reg 3(1)...233
reg 3(2)...232
reg 4(1)...233
reg 5(1)...233
Utilities Contracts Regulations 2016 (SI 2016/274)...34

EU LEGISLATION

Convention on the Law Applicable to Contractual
Obligations 1980 (Rome Convention)...832–3
art 3...833
art 4(1)...837
art 4(2)...837–8
art 4(3)...837
art 4(5)...833, 836–8
art 10(b)...834
art 11(d)...834
Directive 85/374 on the approximation of the laws
regulations and administrative provisions of the
Member States concerning liability for defective
products...454
Directive 86/653 on the coordination of the laws of the
Member States relating to self-employed commercial
agents...119
art 1(2)...120
art 3(1)...43
art 4(1)...43
art 17...279
art 17(2)...280
art 17(2)(a)...282
art 17(2)(b)...283
art 17(3)...280–1, 284
art 17(6)...281
art 47(3)...282
Directive 93/13 on unfair terms in consumer
contracts...43
Directive 98/26 on settlement finality in payment and
securities settlement systems
art 3(1)...579
art 3(2)...579–80
art 3(3)...580
art 5...580
art 6(1)...580
art 7...580
Directive 99/93 on a Community framework for
electronic signatures...50
Directive 2000/32 on certain legal aspects of
information society services, in particular electronic
commerce, in the Internal Market (Electronic
Commerce Directive)
art 9...50
Directive 2002/47 on financial collateral
arrangements...580, 1067
art 4...976
Directive 2002/92 on insurance mediation...1091
Directive 2005/29 concerning unfair business-to-
consumer commercial practices in the internal
market...16
Directive 2007/64 on payment services in the internal
market amending Directives 97/7, 2002/65, 2005/60
and 2006/48 and repealing Directive 97/5...528

Directive 2008/48 on credit agreements for consumers
and repealing Council Directive 87/102 (Consumer
Credit Directive)...1040
Directive 2011/83 on consumer rights...16
Directive 2015/2366 on payment services in the internal
market amending Directives 2002/65, 2009/110 and
2013/36 and Regulation 1093/2010, and repealing
Directive 2007/64...569, 582
Directive 2016/97 on insurance distribution
(recast)...1091
Regulation 1/2003 on the implementation of the rules
on competition laid down in articles 81 and 82 of
the Treaty...123
Regulation 44/2001 on jurisdiction and the recognition
and enforcement of judgments in civil and
commercial matters (Brussels I)...1102
Regulation 330/2010 on the application of article
101(3) of the Treaty on the Functioning of the
European Union to categories of vertical agreements
and concerted practices...123
Regulation 593/2008 on the law applicable to
contractual obligations (Rome I)...52
art 4...832
art 4(1)(b)...832, 839
art 4(2)...839
art 4(3)...832–3
art 19(1)...832
art 19(2)...832
Regulation 864/2007 on the law applicable to non-
contractual obligations (Rome II)...52
Regulation 910/2014 on electronic identification and
trust services for electronic transactions in the
internal market and repealing Directive 1999/93
(eIDAS Regulation)...50
Regulation 1215/2012 on jurisdiction and the
recognition and enforcement of judgments in civil
and commercial matters...52, 1102
Regulation 2015/848 on insolvency proceedings...1106
Regulation 2790/99 on the application of article 81(3)
of the Treaty to categories of vertical agreements and
concerted practices
art 4...123
art 5...123
Treaty of Amsterdam 1997
art 85...122
art 86...122
Treaty on the Functioning of the European Union 2007
art 101...122
art 101(1)...122–3
art 101(3)...123
art 102...122
Treaty of Lisbon 2009
art 81...122
art 82...122

INTERNATIONAL LAW INSTRUMENTS

Cape Town Convention *see* Convention on International
Interests in Mobile Equipment CMR Convention *see*
Convention on the Contract for the International
Carriage of Goods by Road Convention on the
Contract for the International Carriage of Goods by
Road 1956 (CMR Convention)...101, 103

Convention on International Interests in Mobile
    Equipment 2001 (Cape Town Convention)...27,
    855–6, 1013, 1023
Convention for the Unification of Certain Rules for
    International Carriage by Air 1999 (Montreal
    Convention)...101, 103, 556
Convention for the Unification of Certain Rules relating
    to International Carriage by Air 1929 (Warsaw
    Convention)...101, 103, 556
European Convention for the Protection of Human
    Rights and Fundamental Freedoms 1950...35
    art 6...35
    art 6(1)...35
    art 8...35
    art 10...35
    art 11...35
    Protocol I
        art 1...35
Geneva Convention on Agency in the International Sale
    of Goods 1983...26, 123
    art 1(1)...123
    art 1(3)...124
    art 2(1)...123–4
    art 2(2)...124
    art 3...124
    art 7(1)...43
Geneva Convention Providing a Uniform Law For Bills
    of Exchange and Promissory Notes 1930 (League of
    Nations)...19
Hague Convention on Choice of Court Agreements
    2005...53
Hague Convention relating to a Uniform Law on the
    International Sale of Goods 1964...19
International Standby Practices (ISP98)...840, 844, 854
Model Law on Secured Transactions (EBRD)...1023
Montreal Convention 1999 *see* Convention for the
    Unification of Certain Rules for International
    Carriage by Air
Protocol to the Convention on International Interests
    in Mobile Equipment on Matters Specific to Aircraft
    Equipment 2001...855–6, 1023
UNCITRAL Convention on the Assignment of
    Receivables in International Trade 2001...27, 1003
    art 11...887
UNCITRAL Legislative Guide on Secured Transactions
    2007...1003
UNCITRAL Model Law on Electronic Commerce
    1996...50
UNCITRAL Model Law on Electronic Signatures
    2001...50
UNCITRAL Model Law on International Commercial
    Arbitration 1985...13, 27
UNCITRAL Model Law on secured transactions
    2016...1023
UNIDROIT Convention on International Factoring
    1988...27, 1003
    art 6...887
UNIDROIT Convention on International Financial Leasing
    1988...26–7
    art 3(1)...855
    art 8...855
    art 10...855
    art 12(5)...855

UNIDROIT Model Law on Leasing 2008...855
United Nations Convention on Contracts for the
    International Sale of Goods 1980 (Vienna
    Convention)...19, 26–7, 123, 533
United Nations Convention on Independent
    Guarantees and Stand-by Letters of Credit 1995
    (UNCITRAL)...27, 854
United Nations Convention on International Bills
    of Exchange and International Promissory Notes
    1988...26
Vienna Sales Convention *see* United Nations
    Convention on Contracts for the International Sale
    of Goods
Warsaw Convention 1929 *see* Convention for the
    Unification of Certain Rules relating to International
    Carriage by Air

UNIFORM RULES

eUCP *see* Uniform Customs and Practice
    for Documentary Credits for Electronic
    Presentation (eUCP)
International Standby Practices (ISP98)...840, 844, 854
Principles of International Commercial Contracts 2004
    (UNIDROIT)
    art 9.1.9...887
Uniform Customs and Practice for Documentary Credits
    for Electronic Presentation (eUCP)
    art e2(b)...773
    art e12...822
Uniform Customs and Practice for Documentary Credits
    (UCP) 1962 Revision
    art 7...820
Uniform Customs and Practice for Documentary Credits
    (UCP) 1974
    Revision...972
Uniform Customs and Practice for Documentary Credits
    (UCP500)...796, 798
    art 13(a)...820
    art 13(b)...825–6
    art 14(d)(i)...827
    art 14(d)(ii)...827
    art 37(c)...784
Uniform Customs and Practice for Documentary Credits
    (UCP600)...767, 772–3, 817
    art 1...773
    art 2...770, 774, 776, 783
    art 3...776
    art 4(a)...786
    art 5...786, 791
    art 6(a)...770
    art 6(b)...774
    art 6(c)...832
    art 6(d)(i)...815
    art 6(d)(ii)...815
    art 6(e)...815
    art 7...823
    art 7(a)...776, 824
    art 7(b)...815
    art 7(c)...775
    art 8(a)...776, 824
    art 8(b)...815
    art 9...792
    art 9(a)...776

art 10(a)...776
art 12(a)...770, 776
art 12(b)...774
art 12(c)...770, 776
art 13(b)(iii)...824
art 13(c)...824
art 14...783, 819, 825
art 14(a)...820–1, 825
art 14(b)...821, 825–7
art 14(c)...815
art 14(d)...783
art 14(e)...784
art 14(f)...783
art 14(g)...821
art 14(h)...821
art 15...825
art 15(a)...825
art 15(b)...825
art 15(c)...825
art 16...825, 827–8
art 16(a)...826
art 16(b)...826
art 16(c)...826
art 16(c)(ii)...782, 826–7
art 16(c)(iii)...828

art 16(d)...782, 825–7
art 16(f)...827–8, 831
art 17...785
art 17(d)...785
art 17(e)...786
art 20(b)...785
art 29...816
art 29(a)...816
art 29(b)...816
art 34...792, 821, 823
art 35...822
art 36...816, 822
art 37...822
art 38...776
Uniform Rules for Bank Payment
    Obligations (ICC)
    art 39...777
    art 40(j)...781
Uniform Rules for Bank-to-Bank Reimbursement under
    Documentary
    Credits (ICC)...824
Uniform Rules for Collections (ICC)...768, 773
Uniform Rules for Demand Guarantees (URDG)
    (ICC)...844, 854
Uniform Rules for Forfaiting (URF800)...855

PART I

INTRODUCTION

Chapter 1   An introduction to commercial law   3
Chapter 2   Basic concepts of personal property   54
Chapter 3   Bailment   92

CHAPTER 1

AN INTRODUCTION TO COMMERCIAL LAW

1 THE NATURE OF COMMERCIAL LAW

What is commercial law? In the absence of any established legal definition of commercial law, writers on the subject have put forward various definitions of their own. These include the following:

> 'Commercial law' is an expression incapable of strict definition, but it is used to comprehend all that portion of the law of England which is more especially concerned with commerce, trade and business.
>
> (HW Disney, *The Elements of Commercial Law* (1931), p 1)

> The object of commerce is to deal in merchandise and, if we adopt this criterion, commercial law can be defined as the special rules which apply to contracts for the sale of goods and to such contracts as are ancillary thereto, namely, contracts for the carriage and insurance of goods and contracts the main purpose of which is to finance the carrying out of contracts of sale.
>
> (HC Gutteridge, 'Contract and Commercial Law' (1935) 51 LQR 117)

Professor Sir Roy Goode, the leading academic commercial lawyer in the country, has described commercial law as 'that branch of law which is concerned with rights and duties arising from the supply of goods and services in the way of trade' (E McKendrick, *Goode on Commercial Law* (5th edn, 2016), p 8).[1] This makes it a subject of wide compass, embracing

---

[1] Roy Goode first published his classic textbook on commercial law in 1982. Professor Ewan McKendrick took over responsibility for preparation of the 4th and 5th editions. The book has had a profound impact on the way commercial law is taught and practised in this country. Professor Goode's enormous contribution to the development of the subject is reflected in a series of essays written by leading academics and practitioners to mark his retirement as Norton Rose Professor of English Law in the University of Oxford: see R Cranston (ed), *Making Commercial Law—Essays in Honour of Roy Goode* (1997). It is also reflected in the number of times his work is cited in this book! *Goode on Commercial Law* is essential reading for every student of the subject.

many different areas of English law; a point made by Professor Goode in his 1997 Hamlyn Lectures when he said:

> In my own perception commercial law represents the totality of the law's response to mercantile disputes. It encompasses all those principles, rules and statutory provisions, of whatever kind and from whatever source, which bear on the private law rights and obligations of parties to commercial transactions, whether between themselves or in their relationship with others.
>
> Thus commercial law draws for its sustenance on all the great streams of law that together make up the corpus of English jurisprudence, with the law of contract as its core, whilst equity acts now as its handmaiden, now as the keeper of its conscience. The great judicial reformer Brougham was surely right to describe commercial law as 'far purer and free from defects than any other part of the system'.
>
> (R Goode, *Commercial Law in the Next Millennium* (1998), pp 8–9)

The thread running through these various definitions of commercial law is the mercantile nature of the subject. Commercial law *is* the law of commerce. It is concerned with commercial transactions, ie transactions in which both parties deal with each other in the course of business. The sale of goods, where both seller and buyer are acting in the course of business, is the paradigm commercial transaction. However, there are many other types of commercial transaction, for example contracts for the carriage of goods, contracts for the insurance of goods, contracts for the finance of sale transactions, equipment leasing agreements, receivables financing arrangements, and so on.

Many different spheres of commercial activity fall within the ambit of commercial law. It is not possible, or desirable, to draw up an exhaustive list of the contents of the subject. Commercial law is a pragmatic and responsive subject which looks to facilitate the commercial practices of the business community. As those practices change and develop, often to accommodate new technology, the contents of commercial law may change and develop with them. A rigid definition of the scope of the subject would only inhibit this process.

'The Codification of Commercial Law' by R Goode
(1988) 14 Mon LR 135 at 141–143

III WHAT SHOULD GO INTO A COMMERCIAL CODE?

On one view, this is simply another way of posing the question: what is commercial law? Some would even ask: does commercial law exist? Having taught the subject for nearly two decades I desperately hope it does! But what goes into it is another matter. For my purposes I shall treat commercial law as that body of law which governs commercial transactions, that is, agreements and arrangements between professionals for the provision and acquisition of goods, services and facilities in the way of trade. Commercial law as thus defined possesses four characteristics. It is based on transactions, not on institutions; it is concerned primarily with dealings between merchants, in the broad sense of professionals as opposed to consumers; it is centred on contract and on the usages of the market; and it is concerned with a large mass of transactions in which each participant is a regular player, so that the transactions are typical and in large measure repetitive and lend themselves to a substantial measure of standardised treatment. On this basis we would expect commercial law in the sense in which I have used it to exclude consumer law as a *lex specialis* involving non-professionals; to exclude for the most part obligations of a kind normally derived from non-contractual sources of law such as tort, equity, bankruptcy and trusts; and to exclude the law governing institutional structures such as partnerships, corporations, banks, insurance companies, and the like. This is not to say that these are unsuitable subjects for codification, merely that they do not belong in a *commercial* code, which is concerned with contracts and with the dynamics of goods and services moving in the stream of trade rather than with the general law of obligations and the statics of institutional structure and organisation . . .

(i) Types of transaction to be covered

Central to commercial law is that most common of contracts, the contract of sale, with its associated contracts of carriage, warehousing, insurance and finance. But the modern view of commercial law embodies a wider perspective, embracing equipment leasing, receivables financing, payment systems, personal property security, rights to investment securities, and a range of other commercial transactions not derived from a contract of sale. It is also necessary for a modern commercial code to accommodate new technology, in particular the teletransmission of trade and financial data, and new systems for clearing dealings in money, commodities and securities.

In deciding what items from a shopping list should be included in a commercial code, two points must be borne in mind. First, commercial law is not an abstraction, it is a tool for its users, whose needs will vary from place to place according to national practices, tradition and the level of sophistication of its business and financial institutions. No country should slavishly copy the sophisticated model represented by the American *Uniform Commercial Code*, which is designed for a country of fifty jurisdictions and some two hundred million inhabitants addicted to lawyers and litigation. Secondly, where the business community has codified trade usage this may make legislation both unnecessary and unhelpful. For example, there would seem little need to codify the law relating to documentary credits in view of the adoption around the world of the Uniform Customs and Practice.

(ii) The application of a commercial code to non-commercial transactions

While the emphasis of the *Uniform Commercial Code* is on commercial transactions, the draftsmen, preserving the common law tradition, made no attempt to exclude non-commercial contracts from its ambit. The formal separation of civil and commercial transactions to be found in some civil law systems has never been adopted by the common law and even those civil law jurisdictions that have it are said to have experienced difficulties. What the *Uniform Commercial Code* does do is to identify certain rules which apply solely to dealings between merchants and others which are restricted to transactions involving consumers. This is a sensible approach, for many of the Code rules are equally appropriate for commercial and non-commercial transactions, and little purpose is served by leaving the latter to remain governed by the vagaries of the common law.

(iii) Transactions omitted from the Uniform Commercial Code

Of some interest is the omission from the *Uniform Commercial Code* of major types of commercial transaction which one might expect to find covered in a code of this kind. Examples are guarantees, commercial agency, banking transactions (other than those relating to cheques) and insurance contracts. One explanation of the omission of these is that the function of the *Uniform Commercial Code* was seen not so much as codifying the commercial law in general but rather as bringing together in revised and integrated form those branches of commercial law which had already been codified in uniform laws prepared under the aegis of the National Conference of Commissions on Uniform State Laws. It may also be noted that, whether by accident or by design, the types of contract selected for inclusion in the code and its statutory predecessors are those which had been allowed to develop with the minimum interference of equity, whereas guarantees, agency, duties of bankers to customers and third parties and contracts of insurance are heavily underpinned by concepts of equitable obligation, reflecting the fact that the parties are involved not merely in a contract but in a continuing relationship and, moreover, a relationship attracting fiduciary duties. The Code, on the other hand, is concerned primarily with short-term, discrete contracts; it is not directed to on-going relationships, nor has it anything to say about the special problems of long-term contracts, problems which are relational, not purely contractual.

There is in my view no necessary reason why the rights and duties of the various parties arising from contracts of guarantee, commercial agency and the like should not be dealt with in a commercial code; indeed, their inclusion would do much to dispel the widespread ignorance of these matters prevailing among lawyers as well as laymen . . .

NOTES

1. Although written with the specific purpose of stating what should go into a commercial code, this extract offers a sharp insight into the nature of commercial law generally. Unlike most civil law systems, and unlike the United States with its Uniform Commercial Code, English law has no comprehensive commercial code. Professor Goode advocates that there should be one. The issue is considered further below at pp 44–46.

2. The American Uniform Commercial Code (UCC) is a model statute sponsored by the National Conference of Commissioners on Uniform State Laws and the American Law Institute. The first official text of the UCC was approved by its sponsors and the American Bar Association in 1952 and it has been revised on several occasions since. The UCC has been fully adopted by all the US states except Louisiana (which has a civil law tradition). The stated purpose of the UCC is 'to simplify, clarify and modernize the law governing commercial transactions; to permit the continued expansion of commercial practices through custom usage and agreement of the parties; to make uniform the law among the various jurisdictions' (s 1–102(2)). It covers a wide range of commercial activity: sales (Art 2); leases (Art 2A); negotiable instruments (rev Art 3); bank deposits and collections (Art 4); wholesale wire transfers (Art 4A); letters of credit (rev Art 5); bulk transfers and bulk sales (rev Art 6); warehouse receipts, bills of lading, and other documents of title (Art 7); investment securities (rev Art 8); secured transactions (rev Art 9). The UCC has been a great success. Much of the credit for this must go to the Code's chief architect, Professor Karl N Llewellyn. Professor Llewellyn's desire to avoid unnecessary theorisation and keep the Code as close to business reality as possible has made the UCC extremely workable.

3. Professor Goode asks: does commercial law exist? His entertaining answer disguises the importance of the question. It is sometimes argued that commercial law consists of no more than a collection of distinct subjects (eg agency, sales, negotiable instruments, security) each possessing its own rules but with no common thread of principle running through them. If this is true, 'commercial law' is merely a label which is useful for gathering together diverse material with no obvious home of its own, so as to aid exposition on a lecture course or in a textbook, or for the better organisation of the business of the High Court of Justice (see the Civil Procedure Rules 1998, r 58.1(2), set out below at p 12, defining the business suitable to be heard by the Commercial Court), but no more. On the other hand, if there are common principles running through the law's response to those spheres of commercial activity which fall within the ambit of 'commercial law', the subject gains an existence of its own. Those common principles may then be used for the better understanding of the subject and as important guides when facing new problems not previously the subject of judicial decisions. Professor Goode firmly believes that such unifying principles do exist (see the extract which appears below at pp 36–41). We agree with him, but note that those principles are not so easy to identify. There is no neat body of uniform rules unique to commercial transactions. Unlike most civil law systems, English common law does not make any formal distinction between commercial and non-commercial transactions (statute may do so, see, eg, the way that the Consumer Rights Act 2015 makes separate provision for consumer sales and takes them out of the Sale of Goods Act 1979, which applies to commercial sale of goods and documentary sales), although there is some evidence that English judges do distinguish between commercial law and civil law generally when deciding cases. Compare the following extracts.

'The Common Law System' by Tony Weir in *International Encyclopedia of Comparative Law*, Vol II, Ch 2, Part III, para 146

Resistance of judges and jurists.—Holdsworth (History V 147) said that 'the distinctive character of the rules of commercial law, and their adaptability to the ever changing needs of new commercial conditions, have caused them to preserve many characteristic features unknown in other departments of the common law'. This statement is, however, open to doubt. It has already been seen that the common law adapted increasingly slowly, when at all, to the changing needs and practices of commerce. Legislation was frequently called for and 'the necessity of such recourse . . . seems to argue a failure on the part of the lawyers to adjust to the views of commerce'. Furthermore, it is not at all clear that the rules of commercial law are really very different in substance from the rules of civil law. Some transactions, of course, will be entered only by merchants as, for example, marine insurance. But the rules of marine insurance, though different from those of land insurance, are surprisingly little different. Other transactions, such as sale of goods, are entered by merchants and private citizens alike. In such cases the common law studiously avoids making different rules for the two cases, although it may well be that the same rules are applied somewhat differently.

Indicative of the dislike of the judges for treating commercial law as special is their readiness to analogise from the commercial to the private sphere. The liability of the shipowner to the cargo-owner for damage to the goods is compared with the liability of the employer to the employee injured at work; whether a stevedore can claim the sea carrier's limitation of liability for damaging the cargo is related to whether a bus driver can claim his employer's immunity in a question with a passenger who falls off a bus.

In a difficult case concerning a time-voyage charterparty the House of Lords were pressed with the analogy of the consumer taking a car on hire-purchase; and of deviation from the contract by sea-carrier and dry-cleaner one judge said 'both are governed by and *only* by the general law relating to contracts' (judicial emphasis). The judges do not think of commercial law as a separate part of the law or they would not analogise so widely.

The same is true of jurists. Textbooks on the law of contract juxtapose, almost without comment, contracts in restraint of marriage and contracts in restraint of trade; both are treated simply as promises which are unenforceable on the grounds of public policy, and the distinction between civil law and commercial law is simply not perceived or, by not being mentioned, is actually obscured. More particularly, a decision of the Court of Appeal in 1906 has met with almost unanimous condemnation from academic writers. The Court decided that whereas a person was bound who carelessly permitted himself to be deceived into signing a negotiable instrument, subsequently negotiated, a person was not bound who similarly signed a non-negotiable instrument, it being supposed in both cases that the person signing the document believed himself to be signing a document of a quite different kind.

Writers think that the distinction between a negotiable instrument and a non-negotiable instrument is unsound. Yet almost any lawyer with a sense of the needs of commerce would find the distinction worth considering. Most significant of all indications that common lawyers do not consider commercial law as distinct from civil law is the fact that in English law the general part of contract is huge, and the differences between the specific types of contract always underplayed.

'Civil and Commercial Law: A Distinction Worth Making' by G Samuel
(1986) 102 LQR 569 at 577–578

At first sight it is very easy to answer the question whether the common lawyer recognises the distinction between civil and commercial law. As Weir has observed, the 'phrase 'commercial law' is by no means unknown to English lawyers or unused by them,' but 'if asked what it contrasted with rather than what it contained [the English lawyer] would have no answer at all.' No doubt, then, the academic could write a monograph on the topic and the practitioner would see an important procedural significance in cases which attracted the label; yet if either the academic or the practitioner was asked whether it would be of significance that the parties, or a party, to a property or contractual transaction fall(s) into the class of *commerçant* the likely response would be in the negative. However such a response might well have to be qualified on reflection. Despite Maine, it is not beneath the dignity of a modern court to link ownership with mercantile status nor to measure liability by reference to the 'commercial man' or 'men of business or professional men'; and legislation for some time now has been prepared to place a litigant (including the state) into a business class if his activities are of a certain kind. The status of a party, whether it is defined directly or indirectly, can have a bearing on the application and interpretation of private law rules.

Moreover the status test is, as the Continental lawyer will testify, only one approach. If one looks at the other test, that of the type of transaction, then the problem for the English lawyer becomes more acute: for although topics like contract and tort do not on the whole like formally to distinguish between the status of the parties, the fact that the relationship or transaction is a commercial one can be of great significance. This transaction approach is, not surprisingly, of relevance in legislation, particularly in legislation recognising consumer interests; yet the common law must by no means be overlooked. Thus in bailment relationships the fact that the bailment is a 'commercial one' can be of importance in the determination of a restitution claim for the bailee's expenses; and in the law of contract not only must 'commercial reality' be on occasions openly recognised as an aid to the interpretation and application of a rule like consideration but the fact that the contract itself is a mercantile one can have important implications with regard to implied terms or agency. Furthermore in the tort relationship of duty of care a business context is to be differentiated from the social gathering when the focus is upon advice given or statements made; and in deciding upon the validity of an assignment of a cause of action much will depend upon whether the assignee has 'a genuine commercial interest' in enforcing the claim. The fact, then, that the act or transaction is a 'commercial' or 'business' one in that it involves, say, a mercantile contract, a commercial interest or a business context may well have a direct bearing upon the outcome of some contract, tort and property cases.

2 THE FUNCTION OF COMMERCIAL LAW

In *Kum v Wah Tat Bank Ltd* [1971] 1 Lloyd's Rep 439 at 444, Lord Devlin stated that:

The function of the commercial law is to allow, so far as it can, commercial men to do business in the way they want to do it and not to require them to stick to forms that they may think to be outmoded. The common law is not bureaucratic.

This statement captures the fundamental purpose of commercial law: the facilitation of commercial transactions, ie transactions between parties dealing with each other in the course of business. This purpose generally underlies the reasoning of the judges in cases involving commercial disputes. As Lord Goff once wrote in an article analysing the objectives of the judges when interpreting commercial contracts ([1984] LMCLQ 382 at 391):

> Our only desire is to give sensible commercial effect to the transaction. We are there to help business-men, not to hinder them: we are there to give effect to their transactions, not to frustrate them: we are there to oil the wheels of commerce, not to put a spanner in the works, or even grit in the oil.

Often the judges are simply giving their seal of approval to techniques developed by practising commercial lawyers who use the law as a 'malleable resource which can be used instrumentally to achieve their clients' ends' (R Cranston, 'Doctrine and Practice in Commercial Law' in K Hawkins (ed), *The Human Face of Law—Essays in Honour of Donald Harris* (1997), p 199). As Professor Cranston observes (ibid, pp 218–219):

> The practising lawyers are the main creative element, reacting to the needs of their clients; the courts then respond to the devices which the lawyers develop, approving (with or without qualification) or disapproving. Importantly, common law courts have in the main approved—instead of being too concerned with elaborate edifices or logical consistency, common law courts have crafted doctrinal lines consistent with commercial needs in a largely pragmatic manner (eg R Chorley, 'Liberal Trends in Present-Day Commercial Law' (1940) 1 MLR 272).

This was the stance taken by Lord Hoffmann in *Re Bank of Credit and Commerce International SA (No 8)* [1998] AC 214, where the House of Lords had to consider whether it was legally possible for a bank to take an effective charge over its own customer's credit balance, a matter of common commercial practice, when he declared (at 228):

> I think that the Courts should be very slow to declare a practice of the commercial community to be conceptually impossible.[2]

Lord Hoffmann, delivering a judgment with which all their Lordships agreed, went on to hold that there was no reason why a bank could not take a charge over its own customer's deposit. However, the decision has been criticised by no less than Professor Goode, usually a strong advocate of commercial realism in judicial decision making, as 'showing how a determined jurist can surmount apparently insuperable conceptual problems in order to arrive at what he perceives to be a sensible commercial result' (RM Goode, *Commercial Law in the Next Millennium* (1998), p 69). The case highlights the tension that can exist when a court bends established legal doctrine, in this case the meaning of the concept of proprietary interest, to fit commercial needs (for further details, see below, p 972).

Only in exceptional cases will the court relegate commercial needs to the back seat (described as 'a misalignment of commercial law and commercial practice': G Villalta Puig [2012] LMCLQ 317). This happened in *Hazell v Hammersmith and Fulham London Borough Council* [1992] 2 AC 1, where the House of Lords held that local authorities did not have the capacity to enter into swap transactions[3] with the result that such transactions concluded

---

[2] This echoes the famous dictum of Hammond J in *Commercial Factors Ltd v Maxwell Printing Ltd* [1994] NZLR 724 at 727 that good commercial law should follow good commercial practice.

[3] There are various types of swap transactions, eg interest rate swaps, currency swaps, etc. This case was concerned with interest rate swaps which, in their simplest form, involve 'an agreement between two parties by which each agrees to pay the other on a specified date or dates an amount calculated by reference to the

between banks and other financial institutions with local authorities were void *ab initio*.[4] The result of this decision was that the local authorities were allowed to walk away from the swap agreements they had freely entered into. Although swap transactions are normal everyday occurrences in the financial markets, and are recognised as a valuable mechanism for the effective management of debt, so far as their Lordships were concerned swaps were highly speculative in character and the ratepayers of Hammersmith and Fulham had to be protected from having public funds used in this way. The decision caused great concern in the City of London, and was condemned as damaging the City's reputation as a world financial centre, especially with foreign banks which had entered into swap transactions with local authorities in good faith. It may be best explained as a case of 'public law trumping commercial law' (R Cranston, 'Doctrine and Practice in Commercial Law' in K Hawkins (ed), *The Human Face—Essays in Honour of Donald Harris* (1997), p 217).

Businessmen have special needs. First, they demand that their agreements be upheld. Secondly, they require the decisions of the courts on commercial issues to be predictable so that they know where they stand. Thirdly, they need the law to be flexible enough to take account of their latest business practices. Fourthly, they want their disputes resolved quickly, inexpensively, and effectively. Both in its substance and in its procedure, commercial law attempts to facilitate commercial transactions by endeavouring to meet these special needs of the business community.

As to the first need (upholding commercial bargains), the courts adopt a non-interventionist approach with regard to commercial contracts. The judges work on the assumption that there is equality of bargaining power between commercial men. This assumption underpins two basic principles of commercial law: freedom of contract and sanctity of contract. As the late Professor Schmitthoff wrote ([1966] JBL 309 at 315):

> The basis of commercial law is the contractual principle of autonomy of the parties' will. Subject to the ultimate reservation of public policy, the parties are free to arrange their affairs as they like.

In other words, '[d]espite statutory inroads, party autonomy is at the heart of English commercial law' (*Belmont Park Investments Pty Ltd v BNY Corporate Trustee Services Ltd* [2011] UKSC 38, [2012] 1 AC 383 at [103], per Lord Collins). The law's respect for autonomy is much stronger in the case of commercial transactions, especially those 'between properly advised parties of comparable bargaining power' (*Cavendish Square Holding BV v El Makdessi* [2015] UKSC 67, [2015] 3 WLR 1373 at [35], per Lords Neuberger and Sumption), than it is for consumer transactions, where legislation is often required to redress a perceived imbalance in bargaining power between the 'trader' and the 'consumer' (see how those terms are defined in the Consumer Rights Act 2015, s 2). It is significant that even though the Unfair Contract Terms Act 1977 (UCTA 1977), which regulates exclusion and limitation of liability clauses in non-consumer contracts, extends to commercial contracts in general, several key types of commercial contract are excluded from its scope, for example contracts of insurance, contracts of carriage of goods by sea, international supply contracts, and contracts governed by English law by party choice alone (UCTA 1977, ss 1(2), 26, 27, and Sch 1). Similarly, even

---

interest which would have accrued over a given period on the same notional principal sum assuming different rates of interest are payable in each case' (*Hazell v Hammersmith and Fulham London Borough Council* [1990] 2 QB 697 at 739–741, Div Ct).

[4] For a review of the swaps litigation and fallout following it, see E McKendrick, 'Local Authorities and Swaps: Undermining the Market?' in R Cranston (ed), *Making Commercial Law* (1997), Ch 9.

where the 1977 Act applies, a term is unlikely to be struck down as unreasonable where the contract was made between commercial parties of roughly equal bargaining power following genuine negotiation between them (*Watford Electronics Ltd v Sanderson* [2001] EWCA Civ 317, [2001] 1 All ER (Comm) 696).

As to the second need (predictability of legal decisions on commercial issues), the courts have consistently promoted considerations of 'certainty', in the sense of predictability, of outcome over those of fairness and justice. In *Vallejo v Wheeler* (1774) 1 Cowp 143 at 153 Lord Mansfield said: 'In all mercantile transactions the great object should be certainty: and therefore, it is of more consequence that a rule be certain, than whether the rule is established one way or the other. Because speculators in trade then know what ground to go upon.' More recently, in *Mardorf Peach & Co Ltd v Attica Sea Carriers Corpn of Liberia, The Laconia* [1977] AC 850 at 878, Lord Salmon stated tersely that: 'Certainty is of primary importance in all commercial transactions.' Sometimes the courts forget this. The majority decision of the House of Lords in *Kleinwort Benson Ltd v Lincoln City Council* [1999] 2 AC 349, which allows a payer to rely on the retrospective effect of a change in the law arising from a subsequent judicial decision to recover money paid decades earlier, on the ground that it was paid under a mistake, even though it was paid under a settled view of the law at that time, may be criticised for failing to take into account the fundamental principles of certainty and finality in commercial transactions. The same criticism can be made of *The Golden Victory* [2007] UKHL 12, [2007] 2 WLR 691, where a majority of the House of Lords ignored the usual rule that damages are assessed at the time of breach of contract and, applying the principle of 'fair compensation', held that there was an exception to this rule when subsequent events, known to the court, had reduced the value of the contractual rights in question. But the contract that had been repudiated in this case was a charterparty, a commercial contract par excellence, and we must agree with the powerful dissent of Lord Bingham who pointed out (at [1]) that 'the [majority's] decision undermines the quality of certainty which is a traditional strength and major selling point of English commercial law'. In some (but not all) cases, commercial parties are able to reduce or eliminate legal uncertainty, or allocate the risk arising from uncertainty, through contract terms (I MacNeil (2009) 13 Edin LR 68 at 80). But this will often depend on the quality (and cost) of the legal advice available to them.

Traditionally, the third need (flexibility to accommodate new commercial practices) has been met by judicial recognition of mercantile custom and usage. Courts take mercantile custom and usage into account when interpreting commercial contracts. However, not every trade custom and usage will be recognised by the courts, and the presence of a well-drafted contract usually leaves little scope for reference to it (P Devlin (1951) 14 MLR 249 at 251). A trade custom or usage will not be received by the court unless it can be shown to be reasonable, to be consistent with the express terms of the contract, and to be universally recognised in the trade as a binding custom (see below, p 22). This last requirement can often be difficult to prove. Where the courts are unable to take account of mercantile practice, so that the smooth operation of commercial transactions is being frustrated by the courts, Parliament may intervene to remedy the situation. For example, see the Carriage of Goods by Sea Act 1992, which avoids problems of privity of contract by allowing the buyer, sub-buyer, or consignee of goods, as the lawful holder of the bill of lading (or certain other documents commonly used in sea transport), the right to sue the carrier on the contract of carriage (see below, p 537). But contrast, the stance taken by the government after *Hazell v Hammersmith and Fulham London Borough Council* [1992] 2 AC 1 (above), when it refused to introduce retrospective legislation reversing the House of Lords' decision that swap transactions concluded by banks with local authorities were *ultra vires* the local authorities (perhaps venting its displeasure at the fact that the banks had assisted the local authorities to avoid government controls on their expenditure).

The fourth need (speedy, inexpensive, and efficient dispute resolution) is met, to a greater or lesser degree, by the practice and procedures of the Commercial Court and the availability of commercial arbitration. The Commercial Court has jurisdiction to try 'commercial claims', defined in r 58.1(2) of the Civil Procedure Rules 1998 to mean:

> any claim arising out of the transaction of trade and commerce and includes any claim relating to: (a) a business document or contract, (b) the export or import of goods, (c) the carriage of goods by land, sea, air or pipeline, (d) the exploitation of oil and gas reserves or other natural resources, (e) insurance and re-insurance, (f) banking and financial services, (g) the operation of markets and exchanges, (h) the purchase and sale of commodities, (i) the construction of ships, (j) business agency, and (k) arbitration.

The Commercial Court is a separate court of the Queen's Bench Division of the High Court staffed by judges who are experienced arbiters of commercial disputes.[5] The rules of the Commercial Court are flexible and operate with the minimum of formality. The judges of the Commercial Court have developed procedures which meet the needs of court users: for example, injunctions to prevent defendants from disposing of their assets (a 'freezing injunction') and orders allowing seizure of evidence which might otherwise be destroyed (a 'search order'). Many of the procedures of the Commercial Court, together with efficient case management techniques developed by commercial court judges, were adopted by Lord Woolf in his blueprint for reform of civil litigation in general (*Access to Justice, Final Report*, July 1996), and have found their way into the Civil Procedure Rules 1998.

On 1 October 2015, a new Financial List of the High Court opened for business. A claim may be brought in the Financial List if it:

(1) principally relates to loans, project finance, banking transactions, derivatives and complex financial products, financial benchmark, capital, or currency controls, bank guarantees, bonds, debt securities, private equity deals, hedge fund disputes, sovereign debt, or clearing and settlement, and is for more than £50 million or equivalent;

(2) requires particular expertise in the financial markets; or

(3) raises issues of general importance to the financial markets.

The 'financial markets' for these purposes 'include the fixed income markets (covering repos, bonds, credit derivatives, debt securities and commercial paper generally), the equity markets, the derivatives markets, the loan markets, the foreign currency markets, and the commodities markets' (Civil Procedure Rules, r 63A.1(3)).

In essence, the Financial List focuses on the provision of wholesale financial service. In a speech given in July 2015, announcing the establishment of a new Financial List, Lord Thomas, the Lord Chief Justice, stressed that it was designed both to promote access to the courts and the expertise of trial judges (the List is staffed by judges of the Chancery

---

[5] It seems that one of the main reasons for establishing the Commercial List in 1895 was the outrage caused by the incompetence of Mr Justice JC Lawrence in his conduct of the trial in *Rose v Bank of Australasia* [1894] AC 687, a claim by a shipowner for general average contribution from cargo-owners. According to a note written by Sir Francis Mackinnon in the Law Quarterly Review ((1944) 60 LQR 323), Lawrence J was 'a stupid man, a very ill-equipped lawyer, and a bad judge' who 'knew as much about the principles of general average as a Hindoo about figure-skating'. The transcript of Lawrence J's judgment is reproduced in 'Mr Justice Lawrence: The 'True Begetter' of the English Commercial Court' by VV Veeder QC in (1994) 110 LQR 292.

Division and the Commercial Court with expertise in financial market disputes) and to avoid costly and time-consuming litigation (mainly through a new hypothetical test case procedure that will provide authoritative guidance on financial market issues before disputes have arisen). For comment on the introduction of the Financial List, see G McMeel [2016] LMCLQ 1.

Litigation can be slow and prove costly, and it is generally thought that arbitration provides a quicker and cheaper alternative for dispute resolution. There are a number of other reasons why the parties to a commercial dispute may opt for arbitration as opposed to litigation: these include more flexible procedures, confidentiality, the availability of arbitrators who have personal experience of the trade in which the dispute has arisen, and the fact that there is only a limited right of appeal against arbitration awards thus ensuring that the dispute is not prolonged by a long appeal process. To ensure that arbitration continues to provide fair, speedy, and cost-effective resolution of disputes by an impartial tribunal, English arbitration law was overhauled by the Arbitration Act 1996, which reflects as far as possible the structure, language, and spirit of the UN Commission on International Trade Law (UNCITRAL) Model Law on International Commercial Arbitration (1985). Interestingly, in his Bailii Lecture 2016, Lord Thomas, the Lord Chief Justice, observed (with regret) that the popularity of arbitration, coupled with a tightening up of the right of appeal from arbitral awards in 1979 (by statute) and in 1981 (by Lords Denning and Diplock through interpretation of that statute), has resulted in the Commercial Court having fewer opportunities to develop and explain English commercial law, especially with regard to the construction of standard form commercial contracts, which often contain arbitration clauses (Lord Thomas, 'Developing Commercial Law Through the Courts: Rebalancing the Relationship Between the Courts and Arbitration' (9 March 2016), published at http://www.bailii.org).

Sir John Donaldson MR (later Lord Donaldson) once described the courts and the arbitrators respectively as the public and private sectors of the administration of justice industry (*Bremer Vulkan Schiffbau und Maschinenfabrik v South India Shipping Corpn Ltd* [1981] AC 909 at 921). Both sectors of the industry have striven to meet the needs of the business community and in doing so have attracted many foreign litigants and arbitrants to have their disputes resolved in this jurisdiction. Recent analysis (by Portland Legal Disputes) of Commercial Court decisions shows that foreign nationals accounted for 63 per cent of 562 litigants in the 12 months ending March 2015. The data found that there were 71 countries represented in the Commercial Court in the 12-month period, with 23 litigants from Russia and 20 from Kazakhstan. UK courts attract litigants from all over the world because they are considered a safe and neutral forum overseen by an independent judiciary and, unlike the United States, civil cases do not have juries. In a speech given in July 2015 by Lord Thomas, the Lord Chief Justice, he said that the UK courts were respected globally for their expertise, independence, knowledge of markets, and incorruptibility. This is good news for 'UK PLC' as it is estimated that litigation at the Commercial Court brings in invisible earnings of around £1 billion a year.

Potential litigants and arbitrants also have an array of alternative dispute resolution (ADR) procedures available to them (eg conciliation, mediation, minitrials, early neutral evaluation). Unlike litigation or arbitration, ADR processes are non-binding (which some perceive as a disadvantage), but they tend to be more informal, flexible, and cheaper than traditional dispute resolution machinery (clear advantages). ADR is particularly useful where the parties to the dispute have a continuing relationship which would be placed in jeopardy by the more hostile, adversarial, environment of litigation or arbitration.

QUESTIONS

1.   Why do you think that English commercial law has been so accommodating to the needs of the business community?

2.   Does the business community's need for 'certainty' and its need for 'flexibility' conflict? If it does, how can that conflict be resolved? (See G Villalta Puig, 'The Misalignment of Commercial Law and Commercial Practice' [2012] LMCLQ 317.)

3.   Is there always equality of bargaining power between business enterprises?

3 THE HISTORICAL DEVELOPMENT OF COMMERCIAL LAW

(a) The *lex mercatoria*

Modern commercial law has its roots in the *lex mercatoria* (law merchant) of the Middle Ages. During that period merchants would travel with their goods to fairs and markets across Europe. Their disputes would be settled by special local courts, such as the courts of the fairs and boroughs and the staple courts, where judge and jury would be merchants themselves. These merchant courts would decide cases quickly, apply flexible rules of evidence and procedure, and uphold principles of good faith and fairness. There was also a willingness to recognise new mercantile practices. It was during this period that some of the most important features of modern commercial law were developed: the bill of exchange, the charterparty and the bill of lading, the concepts of assignability and negotiability, the acceptance of stoppage in transit, and general average.

The traditional (somewhat romanticised) view of the *lex mercatoria* was of an international law of commerce based on the general customs and practices of merchants which were common throughout Europe and applied almost uniformly by the merchant courts in different countries. Professor Emily Kadens (in E Kadens, 'The Myth of the Customary Law Merchant' (2012) 90 Tex L Rev 1152 at 1158) has convincingly argued that this view is unsupported by evidence and that:

> To the extent that merchants did indeed invent a special set of uniform and universal rules governing long-distance trade across pre-modern Europe, those legal rules usually arose from contract and legislation rather than from custom. Commercial custom did exist, but it was primarily local.

England contributed relatively little to the development of the substantive law merchant during this period. Modern legal historians have revealed that in medieval England the *lex mercatoria* did not develop as a separate body of law distinct from the common law, but that it constituted 'the factual matrix within which certain types of contract are made' (JH Baker, 'The Law Merchant as a Source of English Law' in W Swadling and G Jones (eds), *The Search for Principle: Essays in Honour of Lord Goff* (1999), p 96). Its rules were mainly procedural. As Professor John Baker has explained (JH Baker, 'The Law Merchant and the Common Law' (1979) 38 CLJ 295 at 301):

> The medieval law merchant was not so much a corpus of mercantile practice or commercial law as an expeditious procedure especially adapted for the needs of men who could not tarry for the common law.

(b) *The lex mercatoria* and the common law

In the fifteenth and sixteenth centuries most of the business of the merchant courts was taken over by the Court of Admiralty, which continued to recognise the *lex mercatoria*. But in the seventeenth century the commercial jurisdiction of the Admiralty Court was itself taken over by the common law courts. This was mainly due to the work of Sir Edward Coke. As the merchant courts were by then defunct, the common law courts captured most of the nation's mercantile litigation. In an attempt to keep that business, the common law courts adopted some of the rules of the *lex mercatoria*. But it was not until the late seventeenth and eighteenth centuries that the *lex mercatoria* was fully incorporated into the common law. This was largely done through the work of Sir John Holt (Chief Justice from 1689 to 1710) and Lord Mansfield (Chief Justice from 1756 to 1788). Holt CJ was responsible for important developments in the law relating to negotiable instruments, bailment, and agency. But he was too conservative in outlook to complete the process of incorporation of the *lex mercatoria* into the common law (eg see his judgment in *Clerke v Martin* (1702) 2 Ld Raym 757: below, p 651). It was left to Lord Mansfield to complete this task and earn himself the accolade of 'founder of the commercial law of this country' (*Lickbarrow v Mason* (1787) 2 Term Rep 63 at 73, per Buller J). As the late Professor Schmitthoff wrote:

> ... the reform which Lord Mansfield carried out when sitting with his special jury men at Guildhall in London was ostensibly aimed at the simplification of commercial procedure but was, in fact, much more: its purpose was the creation of a body of substantive commercial law, logical, just, modern in character and at the same time in harmony with the principles of the common law. It was due to Lord Mansfield's genius that the harmonisation of commercial custom and the common law was carried out with an almost complete understanding of the requirements of the commercial community, and the fundamental principles of the old law and that that marriage of ideas proved acceptable to both merchants and lawyers.
>
> (CM Schmitthoff, 'International Business Law, A New Law Merchant' in RSJ Macdonald (ed), *Current Law and Social Problems* (1961), p 137)

(c) The age of commercial codification

The development of commercial law through the common law led to a complex, and sometimes conflicting, mass of case law. In the nineteenth century there was a call for rationalisation of the law through codification. This process was achieved not by an all-embracing commercial code but through the codification of certain defined areas of commercial law. It resulted from the work of some exceptional draftsmen. Sir Mackenzie Chalmers drafted the Bills of Exchange Act 1882, the Sale of Goods Act 1893, and the Marine Insurance Act 1906. Sir Frederick Pollock drafted the Partnership Act 1890. All of these statutes remain in force today—though the Sale of Goods Act 1893 has been re-enacted with several amendments as the Sale of Goods Act 1979 (and the 1979 Act was itself amended in 1994, 1995, 2002, and 2015, although it still retains most of the essential features of the 1893 Act). A fine testimony to the work of these great draftsmen. For an historical account of the codification of commercial law in Victorian Britain, see A Rodgers (1992) 109 LQR 570.

(d) The rise of consumerism

The next great era of change came with the development of the welfare state after the Second World War. During this period there was a move away from the principles of freedom and sanctity of contract (and the laissez-faire economics upon which those principles were based) which had dominated Victorian thinking, towards those of social responsibility and the protection of the economically weaker against the economically stronger. This change is reflected in the expansion of consumer protection legislation in recent years: see especially the Trade Descriptions Acts 1968 and 1972, the Unsolicited Goods and Services Act 1971, the Fair Trading Act 1973, the Supply of Goods (Implied Terms) Act 1973, the Consumer Credit Act 1974, the Unfair Contract Terms Act 1977 (since restricted to non-consumer contracts), the Consumer Protection Act 1987, and the Consumer Rights Act 2015, together with a host of delegated legislation, often implementing EU consumer protection initiatives, including, most significantly, the Consumer Protection from Unfair Trading Regulations 2008 (SI 2008/1277) which implemented EC Directive 2005/29 concerning unfair business-to-consumer commercial practices, and the Consumer Contracts (Information, Cancellation and Additional Charges) Regulations 2013 (SI 2013/3134) which implemented (in part) EU Directive 2011/83 on consumer rights.

It is important to get some idea of the relationship between consumer law and commercial law (as defined at the start of this chapter). Some see consumer law as an application of general commercial law principles in a specific context, although greatly amended by special consumer legislation (see F Reynolds, 'The Applicability of General Rules of Private Law to Consumer Disputes' in S Andermann et al (eds), *Law and the Weaker Party* (1982), Vol 2, pp 93–110). But the differences between the two seem much more fundamental than this approach suggests. Whereas commercial law is concerned with transactions in which both parties deal with each other in the course of business, consumer law is primarily concerned with transactions between ordinary individuals (consumers) and those who provide goods and services on a commercial basis. Whereas commercial law is based on the premise that businessmen are of roughly equal bargaining power, consumer law assumes that the consumer and business enterprise are economically unequal. Whilst commercial law is happy for businessmen to regulate their own affairs through mercantile usage, usage plays only a peripheral role in consumer transactions (a consumer may be bound by the reasonable usage of the market in which the business provider of goods or services deals, for example 'a man who employs a banker is bound by the usage of bankers': *Hare v Henty* (1861) 10 CBNS 65, 142 ER 374 at 379). These fundamental differences in philosophy mean that whereas commercial law is non-interventionist and essentially pragmatic in nature, consumer law intrudes into contracts made between consumer and business supplier and is essentially an instrument of social policy.

Consumer protection law has developed into a subject worthy of study in its own right. We do not intend to deal with the subject in this book. Those students who would like to study consumer protection law further are referred to the following books: C Scott and J Black, *Cranston's Consumers and the Law* (3rd edn, 2000); B Harvey and D Parry, *The Law of Consumer Protection and Fair Trading* (6th edn, 2000); and G Woodroffe and R Lowe, *Consumer Law and Practice* (9th edn, 2013).

(e) A new *lex mercatoria*?

In the seventeenth and eighteenth centuries the *lex mercatoria* was incorporated into the national laws of Europe. This meant that commercial law in England, and in other countries, lost much of its international character. However, in the second half of the twentieth century there was a growing call for the harmonisation of the principles and rules of commercial law governing international transactions. (The extract which follows gives you some idea of the arguments for and against harmonisation.) This process of harmonisation led to the development of what is now known as transnational commercial law (students of the subject are well served by R Goode, H Kronke, and E McKendrick, *Transnational Commercial Law: Text, Cases, and Materials* (2nd edn, 2015)). Harmonisation of national commercial law has taken place in a number of ways (see generally, R Goode, 'Reflections on the Harmonization of Commercial Law' in R Cranston and R Goode (eds), *Commercial and Consumer Law—National and International Dimensions* (1993), Ch 1). First, there has been the work of bodies such as the Hague Conference on Private International Law, the International Institute for the Unification of Private Law (UNIDROIT), UNCITRAL, the International Chamber of Commerce (ICC), the Council of Europe, and the European Union. These bodies have sought to harmonise national laws relating to specific areas of international trade, including the international sale of goods, international factoring and financial leasing, international payment mechanisms, international shipping laws, international commercial arbitration, the assignment of receivables in international trade, and international security interests in mobile equipment. Harmonisation has been achieved through a variety of mechanisms—conventions, model laws, uniform rules, codification of custom and usage or of trade terms, and model contracts. Secondly, there has been harmonisation through the uncodified international trade usage of merchants. Some scholars have argued that uncodified international trade usage constitutes a new *lex mercatoria*, ie an autonomous international set of principles and rules which govern international transactions without the need for their incorporation into a contract or the support of national laws. In a sense they are right, for at the heart of the *lex mercatoria* is the idea that the law is fashioned by the mercantile community. But uncodified international trade usage falls short of true *lex mercatoria* for it only has legal force by virtue of its express or implied incorporation into contract, or its reception into national law, or supranational law (eg EU law), through judicial recognition or legislation, and not simply by dint of its mere existence (as convincingly argued by Professor Goode in (1997) 46 ICLQ 1). Nevertheless, uncodified international trade practice remains important even when it has not reached the status of law. Professor Goode ((2005) 54 ICLQ 539 at 549) explains as follows:

> As law the *lex mercatoria* consists of binding usage and depends in the last resort on recognition by national law. As observed practice the *lex mercatoria* is not dependent on external legal recognition at all, for it is not truly *lex*. It simply exists, and it is effective because business people in the relevant community perceive its observance as necessary to the fair and efficient conduct of business, so that the sanction for failure to follow the practice is not a legal sanction but opprobrium from fellow businessmen, their unwillingness to deal with the culprit and, in the last resort, expulsion from the relevant mercantile community. *Lex mercatoria* as practice is thus almost as potent as true law, and this is why it has been described by some leading scholars as operating at the periphery of the legal process and as soft law but not real law.

Thirdly, there has been both the conscious and unconscious borrowing of legal concepts from foreign law by judges in different countries. This has been described as 'judicial parallelism' (see R Goode, *Commercial Law in the Next Millennium* (1998), pp 92–93). Fourthly, the work of scholars has also been influential in the development of transnational commercial law, especially the two different (though overlapping) groups of scholars who worked on the UNIDROIT *Principles of International Commercial Contracts* (1st edn, 1994; 2nd edn, 2004) and the *Principles of European Contract Law* (Part I, 1995; Parts I and II, 2000; Part III, 2003) prepared by the Commission on European Contract Law. The former are designed for worldwide application, but are restricted to commercial contracts of an international character: the latter are designed for contracts within Europe, but cover contracts generally, whether domestic or international and whether commercial or non-commercial. Both sets of principles take the form of restatements similar to those prepared by the American Law Institute in the United States. Neither set of principles has the force of law (they represent 'soft law'), although each is available to contracting parties for incorporation into their contracts, and each can be used by courts and tribunals when seeking the best solution to a contract problem or simply filling in gaps in existing international conventions.

The Draft Common Frame of Reference (DCFR) is a more ambitious project promoted by the European Commission and involving scholars from across Europe (see C von Bar, E Clive, and H Schulte-Nolke (eds), *Principles, Definitions and Model Rules of European Private Law* (2009)). The DCFR is split into ten books covering various aspects of private law, including contracts. The 'academic' DCFR could be used as the basis for a 'political' CFR designed as a toolbox for legislators and having the potential to develop into a European Civil Code. The European Commission also proposed a new Regulation on a Common European Sales Law (CELS) which, as originally drafted, would have covered cross-border transactions for the sale of goods, for the supply of digital content, and for related services (COM (2011) 635 final). The CELS drew heavily on the DCFR. But the proposal met with significant opposition (see, eg, S Whittaker (2012) 75 MLR 578) and was later withdrawn. The European Commission's focus is now on enhancement of its digital single market strategy.

R Goode, 'Reflections on the Harmonization of Commercial Law' in R Cranston and R Goode (eds), *Commercial and Consumer Law— National and International Dimensions* (1993), pp 24–27

The advantages of harmonizing law relating to international transactions would seem fairly evident even to the layman. But given the reluctance of businessmen, their legal advisers, and their legislatures to modify their national law in favour or harmonization measures, it is perhaps worthwhile restating the advantages of harmonization. The harmonizing measure:

(1) may fill a legal vacuum by providing rules in a field where national law was previously non-existent or obscure;

(2) substitutes a single law for a proliferation of national laws and thus within the given field dispenses with the need to resort to conflict-of-laws rules and the opportunity these give for forum shopping;

(3) is usually available in several languages, official or unofficial, and is therefore more readily accessible than a national law;

(4) by reason of (1) and (2), facilitates conversance with its provisions and saves time and expense;

(5) provides a neutral law for parties to a contract neither of whom is willing to accept the law of the other's country;

(6) offers a legal regime more attuned to international transactions than domestic law, since it reflects the influence of many legal systems, whereas domestic law is focused on internal transactions and may thus be less accommodating on international dealings;

(7) operates as part of the law of each ratifying State, so that the courts of each such State take judicial notice of it and is established by legal argument, not by the expensive and time-consuming process of adducing expert evidence, often from a different jurisdiction;

(8) facilitates a common market.

Despite these manifold advantages it is often hard to persuade the commercial community even to take an interest in proposals for harmonization affecting their sphere of business, still less to give the proposals their support. Why is this so? Numerous reasons possessing varying degrees of persuasiveness are advanced.

Traditionally the first and principal line of attack is that existing domestic law is better or, if not better, is at least well known and understood. This may be true but presupposes that the law in question is the one which will govern the contract, whereas the reality is that for every contract governed by that law there will be another contract governed by a foreign law with which the party concerned may be unfamiliar, which is in a foreign language he does not understand, and which, when put to the test, may prove demonstrably inferior not only to his own law but to the proposed uniform law.

A second line of attack is that the proposed harmonizing measure is inadequate in scope. Thus the Vienna Sales Convention has been criticized for excluding questions relating to the validity of the contract of sale, the transfer of property, or the resolution of property disputes between the seller or buyer and a third party. The response of those engaged in the arduous labours which led to the conclusion of the Convention is no doubt not dissimilar to that of the scholar who writes a book on the doctrine of unconscionability in contract law and is then taken to task by a reviewer for his failure to cover breach and termination—in other words, for not writing a different book. Some limits have to be set to any project. How they are set is a difficult question to which I shall return, but those who decry as too narrow the scope of a Convention running to over a hundred Articles must surely embody the resuscitated spirit of Oliver Twist who will always cry for more.

Then, of course, there is the inevitable criticism of the drafting. If ever I get to Heaven (which my friends tell me is unlikely) one of my first requests will be to witness The Perfect Draft. Such a thing is certainly not to be found on this earth; yet those who pick to pieces the open texture or verbal infelicities of an international Convention rarely pause to consider how, when legislation prepared in a single legal system is generally so verbose, obscure, and generally badly drafted, one can reasonably expect more of the product of many hands drawn from widely differing legal systems with different cultures, legal structures, and methods of legal reasoning and decision-making, entailing maximum flexibility, co-operation, and compromise.

This is not to say that all criticism is unjustified. There are good Conventions and bad Conventions. The good ones are those which, for all their rough edges, are found to work and are widely used. The bad ones do not work and are rightly neglected. The Geneva Convention on Bills of Exchange is an example of an excellent Convention which has functioned extremely effectively and has been widely adopted. By contrast, the Uniform Law for International Sales, the forlorn predecessor of the Vienna Sales Convention, is an indifferent product which has not attracted support.

But behind the expressed reasons for antagonism or inertia in the face of proposals for harmonization lies a more fundamental consideration. It is human nature to be antipathetic to change. Let me render this more accurately. It is human nature to advocate change in someone else's affairs whilst vigorously opposing its necessity in one's own. The force of this NIMBY (Not in my backyard) approach, as it has become known in England, should not be underestimated. Few individuals or institutions are truly resistant to it. Even academics, who are supposed to embody the quintessence of detached assessment, somehow respond with a lack of enthusiasm when it is suggested that their own methods of teaching, research, or organization might benefit from review.

This inherent resistance to change is exacerbated by the low priority accorded by our law schools to the teaching of comparative law and, in England, by an unwillingness to grapple with foreign languages, itself both a cause and a consequence of English becoming the new lingua franca. If the harmonization process is to have any hope of acceleration it is essential for law schools to reduce their preoccupation with national law and their assumption of its superiority over other legal systems and to revert at least in some degree to the internationalism of medieval law teaching. It is primarily by the spreading of awareness of foreign legal systems among our students that we can hope to accelerate the process of harmonization and to produce practitioners and judges of the future prepared to look beyond the horizon of their own legal system. In his outstanding study of unification ['The International Unification of Private Law' in *International Encyclopedia of Comparative Law*, Vol II, Ch 5, p 16] that great French comparativist the late Professor Réne David exposed the kernel of the matter with his customary elegance and felicity:

Legal theory suffocates within the frontiers of a State. Like all science its prosperity requires a cosmopolitan atmosphere; only schools of a low intellectual level can exist in a country with closed frontiers, training narrow-minded practitioners, mere pawns to carry out decrees of power. Universality is necessary to legal theory, and it is a factor favourable to the unification of law.

4 THE SOURCES OF COMMERCIAL LAW

(a) Contracts

The law of contract lies at the heart of commercial law. In the world of commerce, goods and services are supplied pursuant to the terms of contracts made between businessmen. Sometimes each term of the contract will have been individually negotiated by the parties. But in many cases there will have been little or no negotiation as to the precise terms of the agreement beyond those terms relating to subject matter and price. In such cases the parties prefer to use standard form contracts to embody their bargain and thereby save time and money that would otherwise have been spent on the negotiation of each term. So long as the standard form contract is made between businessmen, and not between an ordinary person and the business provider of goods and services, the courts are reluctant to interfere with the principles of freedom and sanctity of contract. This is particularly true of those standard form contracts drawn up by trade associations and adopted by their members, for example bills of lading, charterparties, policies of insurance, and contracts of sale in the commodity markets. As Lord Diplock said in *Schroeder Music Publishing Co Ltd v Macaulay* [1974] 1 WLR 1308 at 1316: 'The standard clauses in these contracts have been settled over the years by negotiation by representatives of the commercial interests involved and have been widely adopted because experience has shown that they facilitate the conduct of trade.'

Some types of standard form contract have been the subject of detailed legal analysis. A jurisprudence has grown up around them giving many of their terms legally predictable meanings. Lord Goff has even gone so far as to suggest that those standard form contracts which are widely used throughout the world (eg the Lloyd's standard marine policy, the various forms of charterparty, and commodity trade contracts) each form the basis of their own separate commercial code ([1993] JCL 1 at 3). See also CM Schmitthoff ((1968) 17 ICLQ 551) discussing the harmonisation of international trade law by means of standard form contracts.

The courts are often called upon to construe the terms of commercial contracts. Most cases before the Commercial Court turn on points of construction of such contracts. The task of the court is to discover the mutual intention of the parties as revealed by their written contract, which is the outward manifestation of that intention. In the past the courts took a literalist approach to construction; however, in recent years, mainly as a result of the speeches of Lord Wilberforce in *Prenn v Simmonds* [1971] 1 WLR 1381 and *Reardon Smith Ltd v Yngvar Hansen Tangen, The Diana Prosperity* [1976] 1 WLR 989, there has been a shift to a contextual approach to construction, which allows a court to construe a commercial contract in a commercially sensible way. The principles by which contractual documents are nowadays construed were restated by Lord Hoffmann in *Investors Compensation Scheme Ltd v West Bromwich Building Society* [1998] 1 WLR 896 at 912–913 as follows:

(1) Interpretation is the ascertainment of the meaning which the document would convey to a reasonable person having all the background knowledge which would reasonably have been available to the parties in the situation in which they were at the time of the contract.

(2) The background was famously referred to by Lord Wilberforce as the 'matrix of fact,' but this phrase is, if anything, an understated description of what the background may include. Subject to the requirement that it should have been reasonably available to the parties and to the exception to be mentioned next, it includes absolutely anything which would have affected the way in which the language of the document would have been understood by a reasonable man.

(3) The law excludes from the admissible background the previous negotiations of the parties and their declarations of subjective intent. They are admissible only in an action for rectification. The law makes this distinction for reasons of practical policy and, in this respect only, legal interpretation differs from the way we would interpret utterances in ordinary life. The boundaries of this exception are in some respects unclear. But this is not the occasion on which to explore them.

(4) The meaning which a document (or any other utterance) would convey to a reasonable man is not the same thing as the meaning of its words. The meaning of words is a matter of dictionaries and grammars; the meaning of the document is what the parties using those words against the relevant background would reasonably have been understood to mean. The background may not merely enable the reasonable man to choose between the possible meanings of words which are ambiguous but even (as occasionally happens in ordinary life) to conclude that the parties must, for whatever reason, have used the wrong words or syntax: see *Mannai Investments Co. Ltd. v. Eagle Star Life Assurance Co. Ltd.* [1997] A.C. 749.

(5) The 'rule' that words should be given their 'natural and ordinary meaning' reflects the common sense proposition that we do not easily accept that people have made linguistic mistakes, particularly in formal documents. On the other hand, if one would nevertheless conclude from the background that something must have gone wrong with the language, the law does not require judges to attribute to the parties an intention which they plainly could not have had. Lord Diplock made this point more vigorously when he said in *Antaios Compania Naviera S.A. v. Salen Rederierna A.B.* [1985] A.C. 191, 201:

'if detailed semantic and syntactical analysis of words in a commercial contract is going to lead to a conclusion that flouts business commonsense, it must be made to yield to business commonsense.'

Lord Justice Lewison, writing extra-judicially in his textbook *The Interpretation of Contracts* (6th edn, 2015), has also referred to a sixth principle of contractual interpretation. In *Re Sigma Finance Corp* [2009] 2 UKSC 2, [2010] BCC 40 at [12], Lord Mance, approving Lord Neuberger's dissenting judgment in the Court of Appeal, said:

Lord Neuberger was right to observe that the resolution of an issue of interpretation in a case like the present is an iterative process, involving 'checking each of the rival meanings against other provisions of the document and investigating its commercial consequences.'

Lord Hoffmann's restatement is the starting point for a judge construing the terms of a commercial contract. But questions remain. Three stand out. The first question relates to the rule that excludes evidence of pre-contractual negotiations when interpreting a contract. Despite sustained criticism of this exclusionary rule (see, eg, G McMeel (2003) 119 LQR 272, Lord Nicholls (2005) 121 LQR 577), the House of Lords declared in *Chartbrook Ltd v Persimmon Homes Ltd* [2009] UKHL 38, [2009] 1 AC 1101 that it remains part of English

Law (but evidence of previous negotiations may be admitted to establish that a background fact is known to the parties, or to support a claim for rectification or estoppel by convention). The need for certainty (and the avoidance of the increased cost of litigation) was held to be paramount.

The second question relates to reliance on 'background' material available to the original contracting parties when rights and obligations under the contract in question are transferred to a third party (eg because those contractual rights and obligations are part of a tradable financial instrument) who does not have access to that material. Lord Collins addressed the issue in *Re Sigma Finance Corp*, above, at [37]:

> this is not the type of case where the background or matrix of fact is or ought to be relevant, except in the most generalised way. I do not consider, therefore, that there is much assistance to be derived from the principles of interpretation re-stated by Lord Hoffmann in the familiar passage in *Investors Compensation Scheme Ltd v West Bromwich Building Society* ... In this type of case it is the wording of the instrument which is paramount. The instrument must be interpreted as a whole in the light of the commercial intention which may be inferred from the face of the instrument and from the nature of the debtor's business. Detailed semantic analysis must give way to business common sense.

A similarly restrictive approach to the admission of background material is to be applied when interpreting a contract in a public document, for example on the registration of a security charge over a company's property (see *Cherry Tree Investments Ltd v Landmain Ltd* [2012] EWCA Civ 736, [2013] Ch 305).

The third question relates to the relationship between the express language used by the parties in a commercial contract and the court's reliance on 'commercial common sense' to interpret those words. The danger is that in striving to interpret the contract in a commercially sensible way, the court might end up rewriting the bargain reached by the parties. There is no doubt that the courts generally favour a commercially sensible interpretation (*Mannai Investment Co Ltd v Eagle Star Life Assurance Co Ltd* [1997] AC 749 at 771). But there are limits to this approach. The purpose of interpretation 'is to identify what the parties have agreed, not what the court thinks they should have agreed', and so 'the reliance placed in some cases on commercial common sense and surrounding circumstances . . . should not be invoked to undervalue the importance of the language of the provision which is to be construed' (*Arnold v Britton* [2015] UKSC 36, [2015] 2 WLR 1593 at [20] and [17], per Lord Neuberger). This is of utmost importance where a commercial contract incorporates standard industry terms; for as Lord Diplock said in *Pioneer Shipping Ltd v BTP Tioxide Ltd, The Nema* [1982] AC 724 at 737:

> it is in the interests alike of justice and of the conduct of commercial transactions that those standard terms should be construed ... as giving rise to similar legal rights and obligations in all [cases] in which the events [that] have given rise to the dispute do not differ from one another in some relevant respect. It is only if parties to commercial contracts can rely upon a uniform commercial construction being given to standard terms that they can prudently incorporate them in their contracts without the need for detailed negotiation or discussion.

(b) Custom and usage

'In the field of commercial law . . . the custom of merchants has always been a fruitful source of law' (*Kleinwort Benson Ltd v Lincoln City Council* [1999] 2 AC 349 at 394, per Lord Lloyd).

A custom is a rule which has obtained the force of law in a particular locality and a usage is the settled practice of a particular trade or profession (see, generally, *Halsbury's Laws of England* (5th edn, 2012), Vol 32, paras 1 and 50). In fact, the courts often pay scant regard to the technical distinctions between custom and usage and use the terms interchangeably (but see *Halsbury*, ibid, para 5 as to the main points of distinction).

A court may admit evidence of a trade custom or usage to imply a term into a commercial contract. For these purposes the custom or usage must be one the court will recognise, for only then will the custom or usage become a legally binding obligation. As Ungoed-Thomas J stated in *Cunliffe-Owen v Teather and Greenwood* [1967] 1 WLR 1421 at 1438–1439:

> 'Usage' is apt to be used confusingly in the authorities, in two senses, (1) a practice, and (2) a practice which the court will recognise. 'Usage' as a practice which the court will recognise is a mixed question of fact and law. For the practice to amount to such a recognised usage, it must be certain, in the sense that the practice is clearly established; it must be notorious, in the sense that it is so well known, in the market in which it is alleged to exist, that those who conduct business in that market contract with the usage as an implied term; and it must be reasonable. The burden lies on those alleging 'usage' to establish it. . . .
>
> A party to a contract is bound by usages applicable to it as certain, notorious and reasonable, although not known to him. If the practice, though certain and notorious, is unreasonable, it of course follows that it cannot constitute a usage which the court will enforce as a usage. Nevertheless if a party knows of such a practice and agrees to it, then though unreasonable, he is bound by it. . . .

A custom or usage is not reasonable unless it is fair and proper and such as reasonable, honest, and right-minded men would adopt (*Paxton v Courtnay* (1860) 2 F & F 131, per Keating J). For example, in *North and South Trust Co v Berkeley* [1971] 1 WLR 470, Donaldson J held that the practice of Lloyd's underwriters to use Lloyd's insurance brokers, who placed business with them, as their agents in communications with claims assessors was wholly unreasonable and incapable of being a legal usage. The practice was held to be unreasonable because it conflicted with a basic principle of the law of agency that an agent (the broker) cannot act at the same time for two opposing principals (the assured and the underwriters) without their consent (see below, p 235).

The custom or usage must not be inconsistent with the express or implied terms of the contract (*Kum v Wah Tat Bank Ltd* [1971] 1 Lloyd's Rep 439), or with the nature of the contract as a whole (*London Export Corpn Ltd v Jubilee Coffee Roasting Co* [1958] 1 WLR 661 at 675, per Jenkins LJ). Furthermore, the custom or usage must not be unlawful (*Daun v City of London Brewery Co* (1869) LR 8 Eq 155 at 161).

A trade custom or usage must be distinguished from a mere market practice. A market practice, however much repeated, does not affect legal relations unless it is a recognised (ie legally binding) usage. Nevertheless, a market practice is not entirely without legal affect. In *Crema v Cenkos Securities plc* [2010] EWCA Civ 1444, [2011] 1 WLR 2066, Aikens LJ (at [42]–[43]) and Morritt C (at [70]) stated that a court was entitled to have regard to 'market practice' falling short of a trade custom or usage, if that was relevant background knowledge, for the purpose of construing the terms of the contract.

So far we have considered the incorporation of trade custom and usage into the law via contract. Incorporation into the contract may be as a result of an express term or, as we have just seen, an implied term, and 'once a usage has been recognized in decisions the courts may well be prepared to take judicial notice of it in subsequent cases, but even then it is only upon the basis that the parties must be supposed to have intended to contract with reference to the usage' (E McKendrick, *Goode on Commercial Law* (5th edn, 2016), p 13, fn 60). Statutory codification of custom and usage is also a form of incorporation; although in most cases the custom and usage will have already been recognised by the courts before codification (as occurred with the major codifying statutes of the late nineteenth century, referred to above at p 15; cf the Promissory Notes Act 1704, referred to below at p 651).

(c) National legislation

Primary and secondary legislation play an important role in the regulation of commercial transactions. Traditionally, commercial legislation has been designed to give effect to the free will of the parties to a commercial transaction and thereby promote the free flow of trade. The codifying statutes of the second half of the nineteenth and early part of the twentieth centuries were designed to do this (see above, p 15). But other, more recent, legislation has been of a much more intrusive character, designed to promote social and economic policies of the state rather than the free will of the parties to a commercial transaction. Examples include recent banking and financial services legislation (eg the Financial Services and Markets Act 2000 and the raft of legislation that followed the global financial crisis of 2007–2009), ever-increasing consumer protection legislation (eg the Consumer Credit Act 1974, the Consumer Protection Act 1987, and the Consumer Rights Act 2015), and those statutes regulating monopolies, restrictive trade practices, and mergers (eg the Competition Act 1998 and the Enterprise Act 2002). The late Professor Schmitthoff described interventionist legislation of this type as forming a body of 'economic law'.

'The Concept of Economic Law in England' by CM Schmitthoff
[1966] JBL 309 at 315, 318–319

An English lawyer, if pressed for a definition, would state that economic law comprises the regulation of state interference with the affairs of commerce, industry and finance. He would see the distinction between commercial law and economic law in their fundamental attitude to commerce. The basis of commercial law is the contractual principle of autonomy of the parties' will. Subject to the ultimate reservation of public policy, the parties are free to arrange their affairs as they like. The underlying philosophy of economic law is economic *dirigism*, ie, the idea that the paternalistic state may limit the autonomy of the parties' will in the public interest. Economic law should thus be placed between commercial law and administrative law; it shares with the former its concern with economic affairs and with the latter its governmental technique.

From this point of view, England has its fair share of economic law. Indeed, as state planning asserts itself in a constantly more consistent pattern, economic law develops into the discipline which reflects the transition to a planned and directed free market economy. Its importance is growing and full academic recognition cannot be withheld from it indefinitely.

What are the divisions of English economic law? This subject can be arranged into the law relating to:

1 financial regulation,
2 competitive economic regulation,
3 prices and incomes regulation, and
4 consumer protection regulation . . .

THE CHARACTERISTICS OF ENGLISH ECONOMIC LAW
English economic law shows two characteristics. First, it has evolved the central concept of public interest and, secondly, its fabric is very different from that of other branches of law.

It has been pointed out elsewhere that, unlike public policy, the term 'public interest' does not carry an inherent element of opprobrium. 'The new concept of public interest is used to indicate the wide—and growing—area in which Parliament has regulated certain activities of private persons in the social and economic sphere because it considers such regulation to be desirable for the common weal.' The concept of public interest is thus a socio-political concept. In the legislation relating to restrictive trade practices and resale price maintenance the notion of public interest is clearly defined; it operates in this manner that certain restrictive trade arrangements are generally declared to be prohibited by Parliament as being contrary to the public interest but that the relevant enactments establish closely defined grounds on which those arrangements can be justified; these grounds are known as the 'gateways' to legality . . .

Secondly, the fabric of economic law is different from that of other branches of law. The normal technique of the legislator in commercial law is to place at the disposal of the parties certain legal institutions, to regulate their effect and to leave it to the parties to adopt the statutory scheme or to modify it as desired. Enactments pertaining to economic law are constructed differently. They are of mandatory rather than permissive character. They embody Governmental policy, and do so in considerable detail . . . The detailed incorporation of Government policy into statutes gives English economic law its peculiar flavour.

NOTE

The term 'economic law', as used by Professor Schmitthoff, must not be confused with what is called the law and economics movement which has become prominent in US and Canadian law schools. This movement focuses on the application of economic theory to matters of legal concern. It uses economic concepts of market incentives, utility maximisation, and allocative efficiency to analyse legal institutions, concepts, and rules, including those relevant to commercial law: see JS Ziegel, 'What Can the Economic Analysis of Law Teach Commercial and Consumer Law Scholars?' in R Cranston and R Goode (eds), *Commercial and Consumer Law* (1993), Ch 12 and the literature footnoted therein.

(d) European Union law

The EU comprises 28 Member States including the UK, which joined the EU's predecessor, the European Economic Community (the EEC was replaced by the European Community in 1993), on 1 January 1973. On 23 June 2016, a majority voted in a national referendum for the UK to withdraw from the EU, and the government thereafter declared its intention to end the UK's membership of the EU. The future relationship between the UK and the EU has yet to be decided, and so the analysis which follows is based on the legal relationship at the time of writing, ie in August 2016.

EU law is a separate legal system, distinct from, though closely linked to, the national legal systems of Member States (see, generally, TC Hartley, *The Foundations of European Union Law* (8th edn, 2014), Part 2). It has had a profound impact on UK law. Section 2(1) of the European Communities Act 1972 provides that directly effective EU law must be recognised and enforced in the UK. It is now well settled that where there is a conflict between directly effective EU law and national law, including Acts of Parliament, EU law prevails (*R v Secretary of State for Transport, ex p Factortame* [1990] 2 AC 85, HL).

So far as the commercial world is concerned, the influence of EU law has mainly been felt in the area of regulatory law, for example there have been various EU Directives dealing with the harmonisation of bank regulation across Member States. By contrast, the EU has been relatively inactive in the area of private rights of those involved in commercial, as opposed to consumer, transactions. As Professor Goode observes (*Commercial Law in the Next Millennium* (1998), pp 88–89):

> It is an interesting phenomenon that the impact of European Community law on the private rights of parties to commercial transactions, as opposed to transactions with consumers, has so far been almost negligible. If we leave on one side EC conventions of a general character, such as the Rome Convention on the law applicable to contractual obligations and the Brussels and related conventions on jurisdiction and the enforcement of judgments, it is hard to recall any measure of significance in the field of private commercial law other than the Directive on commercial agents, which certainly introduced concepts novel to English law, such as the non-excludable right of a commercial agent to compensation or an indemnity on termination of his agency. So what we have is mainly a public law superstructure which, outside commercial agency, has not so far been underpinned by any measures to harmonise, for example, the law of obligations or the law governing dealings in commercial assets.

Professor Goode believes (at p 89) that 'the European Union has been wise to exercise restraint in this regard, for there are other agencies whose remit is universal rather than regional and whose products are more focused on the private law of commercial transactions'. (We turn to the work of these agencies in the next section.) Nevertheless, as we have seen already (see above, p 18), in 2009 a group of scholars, working under the auspices of the European Commission, published the DCFR, which covers various aspects of private law, including contract law. The DCFR has the potential to develop into a European Civil Code. On the other hand, the European Commission's proposal for a new Regulation on a Common European Sales Law (COM (2011) 635 final) met with significant opposition and was later withdrawn. The European Commission's focus is now on enhancement of its digital single market strategy.

(e) International conventions, model laws, uniform rules, and uniform trade terms

We have already examined the various forces behind the harmonisation of international trade law (see above, pp 16–20). The two methods of harmonisation which have had the greatest impact are, on the one hand, international conventions and model laws, favoured by international intergovernmental bodies such as UNIDROIT and UNCITRAL (sometimes collectively, though inaccurately, referred to as 'international legislation': see CM Schmitthoff, *Commercial Law in a Changing Economic Climate* (2nd edn, 1981), p 22) and, on the other hand, uniform rules and uniform trade terms, especially those promoted by the ICC, a non-governmental body.

International conventions only have the force of law in England if incorporated into our national law by legislation. A convention must be incorporated in its entirety into domestic law, save for those parts of it covered by permitted reservations and declarations. Even then the convention may be 'voluntary' to the extent that the parties to a commercial transaction can exclude the operation of its provisions. Examples of harmonising conventions include the Vienna Convention on Contracts for the International Sale of Goods (1980) (see below, p 533), the Geneva Convention on Agency in the International Sale of Goods (1983) (see below, p 123), the UN Convention on International Bills of Exchange and International Promissory Notes (1988), the Ottawa Conventions on International Factoring and International

Financial Leasing (1988) (see below, p 1003 and p 855), the UN Convention on Independent Guarantees and Standby Letters of Credit (1995) (see below, p 854), the UN Convention on the Assignment of Receivables in International Trade (2001) (see below, p 1003), and the Cape Town Convention on International Interests in Mobile Equipment (2001) (see below, p 1013). Of these conventions, only the Cape Town Convention has been ratified by the UK (in 2015), although there have been conventions on the carriage of goods by road, rail, sea, and air which have been incorporated into the law of the UK. The current attitude against ratification is reflected in the words of Mr Justice (later Lord) Hobhouse who wrote in (1990) 106 LQR 530 at 533, with specific reference to the Vienna Sales Convention, as follows:

> These conventions are inevitably and confessedly drafted as multi-cultural compromises between different schemes of law. Consequently they will normally have less merit than most of the individual legal systems from which they have been derived. They lack coherence and consistency. They create problems about their scope. They introduce uncertainty where no uncertainty existed before. They probably deprive the law of those very features which enable it to be an effective tool for the use of international commerce.

For a point-by-point rebuttal of these, and other, criticisms made by Lord Hobhouse, see J Steyn (later Lord Steyn), 'A Kind of Esperanto?' in PBH Birks (ed), *The Frontiers of Liability* (1994), Vol 2, Ch 1. More generally, see the extract from Professor Goode's paper 'Reflections on the Harmonization of Commercial Law' which appears above at pp 18–20. The Vienna Sales Convention has been adopted by 84 states (as of 29 December 2015), but not the UK. The convention has been adopted by most of the world's other leading trading nations.

A model law has no legal force as such: it merely provides a model which a state can adopt in whole or in part, with or without amendment. A good example is the UNCITRAL Model Law on International Commercial Arbitration (1985). Although the UK did not adopt this model law in its entirety, it clearly influenced the way the Arbitration Act 1996 was drafted (see above, p 13).

Uniform rules and uniform trade terms only have the force of law when incorporated into a contract either expressly or by a previous course of dealing or by custom or usage of the trade. Examples of such harmonising measures include the INCOTERMS (2010 revision) (see below, p 534), the Uniform Rules for Demand Guarantees (2010 Revision) (see below, p 854), and the Uniform Customs and Practice for Documentary Credits (2007 revision) (see below, p 772), all of which have been sponsored by the ICC. Typically, uniform rules and uniform trade terms codify existing trade practice and usage.

QUESTION

In his Law Quarterly Review note (106 LQR 530), Lord Hobhouse distinguished between international conventions which establish international safety standards, recognise and protect intellectual property rights, and govern the rights and liability of carriers in international carriage, all of which he saw as having an important and valuable role to play in the commercial world, and those conventions, like the Vienna Sales Convention, which he disliked for 'seeking to legislate for the ordinary law governing the basic elements of commercial relationships'. Do you think Lord Hobhouse was right to make such a distinction? Can you draw any parallels with the way the EU has legislated with regard to commercial law (see above)?

5 THE ROLE OF EQUITY
IN COMMERCIAL LAW

Westdeutsche Landesbank Girozentrale v Islington London Borough Council
[1996] AC 669, House of Lords

> **Lord Browne-Wilkinson:** . . . My Lords, wise judges have often warned against the wholesale importation into commercial law of equitable principles inconsistent with the certainty and speed which are essential requirements for the orderly conduct of business affairs.

'Equity's Place in the Law of Commerce' by Sir Peter Millett
(1998) 114 LQR 214 at 214–217 (footnotes omitted)

Equity's place in the law of commerce, long resisted by commercial lawyers, can no longer be denied. What they once opposed through excessive caution they now embrace with excessive enthusiasm. I propose to consider the reasons for this development, and then to examine the two principal concepts which equity deploys in the commercial field: the fiduciary duty and the constructive trust.

Even twenty years ago there was still a widely held belief, by no means confined to common lawyers, that equity had no place in the world of commerce. Businessmen need speed and certainty; these do not permit a detailed and leisurely examination of the parties' conduct. Commerce needs the kind of bright line rules which the common law provides and which equity abhors. Resistance to the intrusion of equity into the business world is justified by concern for the certainty and security of commercial transactions. Such considerations led Lindley LJ over a century ago to give his well-known warning against the extension of the equitable doctrine of constructive notice to commercial transactions [*Manchester Trust v Furness, Withy & Co* [1885] 2 QB 539, 545]. This is often repeated like a mantra. But it is inaccurate and its influence has been harmful. The purchase of land and the giving of a bank guarantee are both commercial transactions; yet the doctrine of constructive notice applies to both. In fact Lindley LJ was speaking of the doctrine of constructive notice as it was developed by the Court of Chancery in relation to land, with its many refinements and its insistence on a proper investigation of title in every case. This cannot be applied without modification to transactions where there is no recognised procedure for investigating title. The principal modification is to insist on the need to show that the circumstances were such as to put the transferee on inquiry; and in an ordinary commercial context this is very difficult to establish.

While the purchaser of land and the bank which takes a guarantee are not immune from equity's intervention, however, they are not fiduciaries. This is not because the transactions in question are commercial; it is because the relationships to which they are parties are exclusively commercial. In Canada and Australia there has been a tendency to extend applications of equitable doctrines to commercial transactions through the concepts of constructive trust and fiduciary obligations more widely than we would do. But the pendulum is swinging back again, at least in Australia. The rejection of any fiduciary relationship by the High Court of Australia in an ordinary commercial distributorship agreement in *Hospital Products Ltd v United States Surgical Corpn* (1984) 156 CLR 41 marks a welcome insistence on principle. The situation in Canada is rather less satisfactory, perhaps because only lip service appears to have been paid to the valuable comment of Sopinka J [in *Norberg v Wynrib* [1992] 2 SCR 226 at 312] that:

Fiduciary duties should not be superimposed on . . . [c]ommon law duties to improve the nature or extent of the remedy.

There has to be a proper import licence. Moreover, there is a different licence for each doctrine. In Australia Dawson J [in *Hospital Products Ltd v United States Surgical Corpn*, above, 149] has warned of the:

. . . undesirability of extending fiduciary duties to commercial relationships and the anomaly of imposing those duties where the parties are at arms' length from one another.

If this warning is not observed then equity's place in the commercial world will be put at risk: it will be found to do more harm than good. When the question is concerned with the imposition of fiduciary duties, the distinction is not between commercial and non-commercial *transactions*, a distinction which Lehane has described as 'a red herring' [P Finn (ed), *Essays in Equity* (1985), p 104], but between commercial and non- commercial *relationships*.

It is of course far too late to suppose that the body of law which owes its origin to family and friendship cannot be introduced into the market place without making some kind of category mistake. It is no longer possible to dispute Sir Anthony Mason's extrajudicial observation [in A Mason, 'The Place of Equity and Equitable Remedies in the Contemporary Common Law World' (1994) 110 LQR 238 at 238] that the concepts, doctrines, principles and remedies developed by the old Court of Chancery:

. . . have extended beyond the old boundaries into new territory where no Lord Chancellor's foot has previously left its imprint . . . Equitable doctrines and reliefs have penetrated the citadels of business and commerce long thought, at least by common lawyers, to be immune from the intrusion of such principles.

Three things have combined to bring about this development. First, there is the growing complexity and professionalism of commercial life which have accompanied the change from an industrial to a service economy and the growth of the financial services industry. Much commerce today is based on trust; on each side of a commercial arms' length transaction there are likely to be relationships of trust and confidence. As a result, the modern fiduciary is usually a professional. He expects to be paid for his services, and he expects to be liable (and to be covered by appropriate insurance) if he performs his duties negligently. The picture of the trustee or fiduciary as an old friend of the family who has gratuitously volunteered his services is long obsolete. Principles of equity designed to mitigate the severity of its rules as they bore on the well-meaning amateur are incongruous when applied to the paid professional.

We ought to stop repeating the inaccurate incantation that equity does not permit a trustee to profit from his trust. Of course it does. What it forbids is his making a *secret or uncovenanted* profit from his trust. We also need to reconsider the propriety of including the standard form of trustee exemption clause which exempts the trustee from liability for loss or damage not caused by his own dishonesty. The view is widely held that these clauses have gone too far, and that trustees who charge for their services and who, as professional men, would not dream of excluding liability for ordinary professional negligence, should not be able to rely on a trustee exemption clause which excludes liability for gross negligence. Jersey introduced a law in 1989 which denies effect to a trustee exemption clause which purports to absolve a trustee from liability for his own 'fraud, wilful misconduct or gross negligence'. The subject is presently under consideration in this country by the Trust Law Committee under the chairmanship of Sir John Vinelott and its proposals will be awaited with interest.

Secondly, there has never been a greater need to impose on those who engage in commerce the high standards of conduct which equity demands. The common law insists on honesty, diligence, and the due performance of contractual obligations. But equity insists on nobler and subtler qualities: loyalty, fidelity, integrity, respect for confidentiality, and the disinterested discharge of obligations of trust and confidence. It exacts higher standards than those of the market place, where the end justifies the means and the old virtues of loyalty, fidelity and responsibility are admired less than the idols of 'success, self-interest, wealth, winning and not getting caught'. It is unrealistic to expect that employees can be given incentives through enormous bonuses without undermining their business ethics. It is hardly necessary to say more on this subject in a year in which we have seen employees in the financial services industry, enticed by the prospect of even larger bonuses, threaten not only to leave their employer for a competitor but to take their entire teams of junior staff with them; and in which we have seen a takeover bidder make use, possibly of stolen documents, but certainly of confidential information belonging to the target company, with major City firms apparently regarding such conduct as acceptable.

Thirdly, plaintiffs and their advisers have discovered the apparent advantages of alleging breach of trust or fiduciary duty, with the result that a statement of claim is considered to be seriously deficient if it does not contain inappropriate references to these concepts which are often scattered throughout the pleadings with complete abandon.

At first equity lawyers looked with disdain at their common law colleagues who were obviously using equitable concepts without any understanding of their proper scope. More recently, however, we have been challenged to define these expressions, and to our dismay have realised that we cannot agree on their meanings. We have been forced to re-examine our terminology and reconsider our own concepts. The process is a continuing one and is marked by considerable controversy. It has, however, been greatly assisted by a number of academic monographs on particular concepts as subrogation, fiduciary obligations, and constructive and resulting trusts, which are required reading for anyone seriously interested in the concepts on which the development of equity into the next century depends.

NOTES

1.   There are several reasons why a claimant might wish to assert breach of a fiduciary duty against a defendant. First, it may allow him to take advantage of more flexible equitable tracing rules. Secondly, it may enable him to assert a proprietary claim and thereby gain priority over other creditors in the event of the defendant's insolvency, or maintain a claim to profits. Thirdly, he may be able to benefit from more flexible rules as to recovery of compensation for loss and so avoid the common law rules of causation and remoteness of damages. Fourthly, there are more favourable limitation periods in equity than at common law.

2.   English courts have resisted the temptation to impose fiduciary obligations on parties to a purely commercial relationship who deal with each other at arm's length and can be expected to look after their own interests. There are various modern examples of this approach: see *Kelly v Cooper* [1993] AC 205, PC (below, p 235); *Re Stapylton Fletcher Ltd* [1994] 1 WLR 1181 (below, p 334); and *Re Goldcorp Exchange Ltd* [1995] 1 AC 74, PC (below, p 334). Where businessmen have defined their relationship in the terms of a contract freely negotiated between them, the courts should hesitate before interfering with their bargain. By the terms of their contract each party has accepted certain risks, including the risk of the other party's insolvency before completing performance of the contract, and the law should be slow to confer additional rights upon them through the medium of equitable intervention. This does not mean that a commercial relationship and a fiduciary relationship are mutually exclusive, but it does mean that it is necessary to show something more, in terms of a relationship of trust and confidence, influence, or confidentiality, before a court will impose a fiduciary relationship on top of a commercial one. The imposition of a fiduciary relationship brings with it the obligation to act selflessly, something which is usually out of place in the adversarial world of commerce.

3.   In *Westdeutsche*, Lord Browne-Wilkinson warned against the wholesale importation of equitable principles into the common law, and in *Cobbe v Yeoman's Row Management Ltd* [2008] UKHL 55, [2008] 1 WLR 1752 at [81], Lord Walker referred to 'the general principle that the court shall be very slow to introduce uncertainty into commercial transactions by the over-ready use of equitable concepts'. Nevertheless, we can see from the extract taken from Sir Peter (now Lord) Millett's article that equity has the potential to play an important role in commerce. English courts may be slow to *impose* fiduciary obligations on parties to arm's length commercial transactions, but they are quick to give effect to fiduciary obligations which are *expressly intended* by the parties. In *Don King Productions Inc v Warren* [2000] Ch 291 at 317, the facts of which appear below at p 890, Lightman J referred to the warning of Lord Browne-Wilkinson in *Westdeutsche* and continued: 'There can however be no sustainable objection on these grounds to the recognition of a trust if the parties have manifested their intention to create it, *a fortiori* when this is necessary to achieve justice between the parties.' In that case the subject matter of the trust was a management and promotion contract made between a boxer and his manager, which, it was argued, could not be held on trust by the manager for his business partner because normal trust rules would have allowed the partner to interfere in the management of the contract and this was quite contrary to the personal nature of the contract. On appeal, the Court of Appeal dismissed this objection and held that although the benefit of the contract was held on trust, normal trust rules had to be modified in this context, so that the partner could not insist on rendering vicarious performance of the personal obligations arising under the contract ([2000] Ch 291 at 335–336). Their Lordships relied on the observations of Lord Browne-Wilkinson in *Target Holdings Ltd v Redferns* [1996] AC 421 at 435, when he said:

> In my judgment it is in any event wrong to lift wholesale the detailed rules developed in the context of traditional trusts and then seek to apply them to trusts of quite a different kind. In the modern world the trust has become a valuable device in commercial and financial dealings. The fundamental principles of equity apply as much to such trusts as they do to the traditional trusts in relation to which those principles were originally formulated. But in my judgment it is important, if the trust is not to be rendered commercially useless, to distinguish between the basic principles of trust law and those specialist rules developed in relation to traditional trusts which are applicable only to such trusts and the rationale of which has no application to trusts of quite a different kind.

Lord Browne-Wilkinson's distinction between 'traditional' and 'commercial' trusts has proved controversial, but it is one that the courts have, on the whole, been prepared to maintain (see *AIB Group (UK) plc v Mark Redler & Co Solicitors* [2014] UKSC 58, [2015] AC 1503 at [70] and [102]).

4.   There are numerous examples of parties to commercial and financial transactions intending to apply the doctrines of equity and trusts. In many cases the parties wish to take advantage of one particular aspect of the trust, namely the 'insolvency ring fence' which affords priority to claimants over general creditors of the defendant. Trusts are regularly used, for example, in the international financial markets (see, generally, D Hayton, H Piggott, and J Benjamin [2002] JIBFL 23). In secured syndicated loans the security interest is invariably held by a trustee on behalf of the lenders. In international bond issues a trustee is appointed to safeguard the interests of the bondholders and to act on their behalf in policing and, if necessary, enforcing payment of the bonds. A global custodian may declare that it holds a pool of assets on trust, the terms of which are to meet the claims of the global custodian itself and for the client. The main feature of trusts used in commercial and financial arrangements is that the rights and duties of the parties are determined on the basis of the contractual documents. The contractual arrangements dominate the fiduciary concepts inherent in the trust. The risk with this approach is that the contract may strip the arrangement of the core features necessary for it to be characterised as a trust in the first place (described in *Armitage v Nurse* [1998] Ch 241 at 253, as the 'irreducible core'). However, the English courts seem reluctant to recharacterise 'commercial trusts' in this way (see, eg, *Citibank NA v MBIA Assurance SA* [2006] EWHC 3215 (Ch), noted by A Trukhtanov (2007) 123 LQR 342). The fear is that an interventionist approach would introduce an element of uncertainty which might undermine the predominant position of the City of London as a world financial market. On financial and commercial uses of trusts, see D Hayton (ed), *Modern International Developments in Trust Law* (1999) and S Degeling and J Edelman (eds), *Equity in Commercial Law* (2005).

5.   The role of equity is particularly important where money is lent, or payment made for goods in advance of delivery, or goods supplied before payment, and the borrower, seller, or purchaser, as the case may be, subsequently becomes insolvent before performing his side of the bargain. Any claim in contract, or for recovery of the price on a total failure of consideration, or in debt, is only a personal claim against the general assets of the insolvent person. As a personal claim it will abate with the claims of other creditors in the insolvency. On the other hand, if the payer or supplier can establish an equitable proprietary interest in the money paid or goods supplied, he will gain priority over other creditors in the insolvency. Thus, where the payer can show that the money paid is held by the recipient subject to a trust in his favour, the payer will be able to withdraw *his* assets from those available in the insolvency: see, for example, *Barclays Bank Ltd v Quistclose Investments Ltd* [1970] AC 567 (money lent for a specified purpose held on trust for the lender when the purpose failed; the nature of the trust is explained in *Twinsectra Ltd v Yardley* [2002] UKHL 12, [2002] 2 AC 164, see, especially, Lord Millett at [77]–[102]); *Re Kayford Ltd* [1975] 1 WLR 279 (customers' prepayments for goods held on trust in favour of the customers). Where goods are supplied before payment, the supplier may be able to rely upon a reservation of title clause to make the purchaser a trustee of the goods, their product, or the proceeds of their sale, until he is paid in full—a claim which may involve tracing in equity: see *Aluminium Industrie Vaassen BV v Romalpa Aluminium Ltd* [1976] 1 WLR 676, and those cases considered below at pp 497–514. See, generally, W Goodhart and G Jones (1980) 43 MLR 489; R Goode (1987) 103 LQR 433 at 434–447.

6.   In each case referred to in Note 5 above, the claimant relied on his pre-existing right of property to bring a proprietary claim against the defendant. However, there are cases which suggest that, in appropriate circumstances, the English courts may create a trust or lien if the defendant's conduct is unconscionable and will not be deterred from doing so by the absence of a 'proprietary base'. There are dicta in a number of cases which tentatively suggest that an English court might follow the approach taken in a number of Commonwealth countries, for example Canada and Australia, and recognise the remedial constructive trust which allows the court to grant, by way of remedy, a proprietary right to someone who, beforehand, had no proprietary right. Significantly, in *Westdeutsche Landesbank Girozentrale v Islington London Borough Council* [1996] AC 669 at 716, Lord Browne-Wilkinson expressly left open the door to future recognition of the remedial constructive trust in English law. However, that door appears to have been firmly shut by the

Supreme Court in *FHR European Ventures LLP v Cedar Capital Partners LLC* [2014] UKSC 45, [2015] AC 250 at [47], where Lord Neuberger accepted that the remedial constructive trust is 'not part of English law' (and for a similarly robust refusal to impose property rights based merely upon 'a judgment of the relative moral merits of the parties', see *Bailey v Angove's Pty Ltd* [2016] UKSC 47 at [28], per Lord Sumption). This should not displease commercial lawyers for the remedial constructive trust would give the court a wide discretion to vary property rights whenever it considers it just to so and thereby introduce new and unwelcome risks into commercial dealings.

7. The courts have traditionally opposed the application of the equitable standard of constructive notice to commercial transactions. As Lindley LJ stated forcefully in *Manchester Trust Ltd v Furness* [1895] 2 QB 539 at 545:

> ... as regards the extension of the equitable doctrines of constructive notice to commercial transactions, the Courts have always set their faces resolutely against it. The equitable doctrines of constructive notice are common enough in dealing with land and estates, with which the Court is familiar; but there have been repeated protests against the introduction into commercial transactions of anything like an extension of those doctrines, and the protest is founded on perfect good sense. In dealing with estates in land title is everything, and it can be leisurely investigated; in commercial transactions possession is everything, and there is no time to investigate title; and if we were to extend the doctrine of constructive notice to commercial transactions we should be doing infinite mischief and paralyzing the trade of the country.

Lord Millett identifies the flaws in this approach (see extract above). He is right to do so. It has been convincingly argued by David Fox ([1998] CLJ 391) that constructive notice does not always require the same detailed level of inquiry that purchasers of land are expected to observe; on the contrary, the standard of inquiry varies from one transaction to another, and reasonable conduct must be measured against the standard practice of that business or trade. Fox continues (at 395):

> Notice can be sensitive to the demands of commercial dealing where speed and security of transaction are important. Recent authority supports this more flexible view. The conduct of a bank receiving a deposit of misappropriated trust money should be measured against the standard of inquiry that could reasonably be expected of a banker not a purchaser of land. Likewise the facts that raise the duty of inquiry may differ from one kind of property transfer to another. Outside land transactions inquiries need not be made as a matter of routine. A commercial recipient may only be put on inquiry if the facts immediately known to him make it glaringly obvious that some impropriety is afoot.

6 PUBLIC LAW IN THE COMMERCIAL ARENA

A commercial lawyer cannot afford to ignore the impact of public law on commercial interests. Public law impacts on commercial interests in at least three different ways.

First, public bodies or local authorities may themselves enter into commercial transactions. Public authorities whose powers derive from statute are subject to the doctrine of *ultra vires*, which is designed to protect the public funds entrusted to such bodies. For example, in *Hazell v Hammersmith and Fulham London Borough Council* [1992] 2 AC 1, the House of

Lords held that banks which entered into interest rate swaps with local authorities could not sue on their contracts when they were held to be *ultra vires* the local authorities. The effect of this decision, and others like it, caused considerable uncertainty amongst those financial institutions which dealt with local authorities. Fearing that this uncertainty would inhibit financial institutions from entering into commercial relationships with local authorities, the government introduced legislation to provide them with reassurance and to facilitate the policy of encouraging the Private Finance Initiative (PFI), partnerships, and other contractual relationships between local authorities and the private sector: see the Local Government (Contracts) Act 1997 and the Localism Act 2011.

Other public law principles may come into conflict with the fundamental principles of freedom and sanctity of contract which are so prized in the commercial world. In the case of public authorities, the principle of freedom of contract is limited by legislation (see the Local Government Act 1988, s 17 and the Local Government Act 1999, s 3(1)) and regulations implementing EU Directives on public sector contracts (see the Public Contracts Regulations 2015 (SI 2015/102); the Utilities Contracts Regulations 2016 (SI 2016/274); the Concession Contracts Regulations 2016 (SI 2016/273)), as well as the general principles governing the exercise of discretionary powers. There are particularly rigid controls on advertising and tendering procedures (see, generally, S Arrowsmith, *The Law of Public and Utilities Procurement* (3ed edn, 2014)). The principle of sanctity of contract can come into conflict with the public law principle that a court will not enforce a term of a contract which has the effect of fettering a public body's statutory discretion (*Ayr Harbour Trustees v Oswald* (1883) 8 App Cas 623; *York Corpn v Henry Leetham & Sons Ltd* [1924] 1 Ch 557).

Secondly, we have already seen how areas of commercial activity are regulated by statute or through the use of statutory powers (see above, p 24). This is particularly true of the financial markets, where it is vital to have regulation which is both predictable, so as to avoid uncertainty, and yet sufficiently flexible to accommodate new business products and practices (an important point made by R Goode, *Commercial Law in the Next Millennium* (1998), pp 44–52). Flexibility can be achieved by giving a regulator wide discretionary powers, but the price for this is the increased risk of arbitrary and unfair decisions. It is here that public law has a vital role to play through what has become known as 'commercial judicial review' (see, generally, J Black, P Muchlinski, and P Walker (eds), *Commercial Regulation and Judicial Review* (1998)). The 'path-breaking decision' (per HWR Wade (1987) 103 LQR 323 at 327) was *R v Panel on Take-overs and Mergers, ex p Datafin plc* [1987] QB 815. There the Court of Appeal held that decisions of the takeover panel, a private body which monitored a code of rules, promulgated by itself, governing company takeovers and mergers, but which had neither statutory nor governmental powers, were susceptible to judicial review on the ground that the panel had wide de facto powers which it exercised in the public sphere. (Since May 2006 the panel and its rules have had a statutory basis.) The case is important because it extends judicial review to regulatory bodies operating in the commercial sphere which do not exercise statutory or prerogative powers, although there must be a 'public element' and the body must not derive its power solely through consensual submission to its jurisdiction (*Datafin*, at 838). Thus, decisions of self-regulatory organisations set up under the (now repealed) Financial Services Act 1986 to regulate sectors of the financial markets (see, eg, *R v Life Assurance Unit Trust Regulatory Authority, ex p Ross* [1993] QB 17), and even those of the Stock Exchange (*R v International Stock Exchange of the United Kingdom and the Republic of Ireland Ltd, ex p Else (1982) Ltd* [1993] QB 534), have been held to be amenable to judicial review (but contrast *R v Lloyd's of London, ex p Briggs* [1993] 1 Lloyd's Rep 176, where the Court of Appeal held that there could be no review of powers exercised by Lloyd's over its members when

Lloyd's exercised those powers solely by virtue of a contractual agreement with its members). Furthermore, the Prudential Regulation Authority and the Financial Conduct Authority, the key regulators of the financial services industry under the Financial Services and Markets Act 2000 (as amended by the Financial Services Act 2012), themselves private companies but with statutory powers, are also subject to judicial review. However, the danger that arises through the extension of judicial review into the commercial sphere is that it causes uncertainty in the markets and delays commercial transactions as decisions of regulatory bodies are challenged in the courts. Sir John Donaldson MR identified the danger in *Datafin* (at 840), and stated that, save in a case of a breach of natural justice, judicial review in such cases should be 'historic rather than contemporaneous', with the court giving declaratory guidance as to future conduct and leaving existing decisions alone (at 842). In one exceptional case, the Court of Appeal relied, inter alia, on the need for finality and certainty in the financial markets, when justifying its decision to refuse relief against an *ultra vires* delegation of power to the chairman of the Monopolies and Mergers Commission (*R v Monopolies and Mergers Commission, ex p Argyll Group* [1986] 1 WLR 763).

Thirdly, the Human Rights Act 1998 has had an impact upon commercial interests, although not as great, nor as negative, as some initially feared (see CA Gearty and J Phillips, 'The Human Rights Act and Business: Friend or Foe?' [2012] LMCLQ 487). The Act incorporates the European Convention for the Protection of Human Rights and Fundamental Freedoms into English law. It does this by three mechanisms. First, by requiring the courts to construe all legislation 'so far as it is possible to do so . . . in a way which is compatible with the Convention rights' (s 3). Secondly, by introducing a procedure whereby the courts can declare legislation incompatible with the Convention rights, leaving it to Parliament to amend the legislation should it wish to do so (s 4). Thirdly, by making it unlawful for a public authority to act in a way which is incompatible with a Convention right (s 6(1)). The Act provides that a 'public authority' includes 'a court or tribunal' (s 6(3)). This means that the Convention inevitably affects such matters as the exercise of judicial discretion, and the development of the common law. The Act does not expressly give private citizens a direct horizontal right of action against each other based on breach of the Convention rights, but it does inevitably have an indirect horizontal effect in the manner in which courts and tribunals deal with proceedings between private parties and there is already evidence of this occurring (see, eg, *Wilson v First National Trust Ltd (No 2)* [2003] UKHL 40, [2004] 1 AC 816; *Campbell v Mirror Group Newspapers Ltd* [2004] UKHL 22, [2004] 2 AC 457). The degree to which the Act affects legal relations between private individuals is controversial (see, eg, at one extreme, HWR Wade (2000) 116 LQR 217, arguing for full horizontal effect and, at the other, R Buxton (2000) 116 LQR 48, denying that the Act creates private law rights, and for a view somewhere in between these two extremes, N Bamforth (2001) 117 LQR 34).

The provisions of the Convention of most relevance to the protection of commercial interests are: (1) the right to property (Protocol No 1, art 1: see, eg, *Bank Mellat v HM Treasury (No 2)* [2013] UKSC 39, [2014] AC 700, where a majority of the Supreme Court held that HM Treasury had breached the human rights of Bank Mellat, a large Iranian bank, by making an Order in Council, under its statutory powers, that prevented the Bank Mellat carrying on its business in the UK because HM Treasury believed that the Iranian bank was engaged in facilitating the development of nuclear weapons by Iran); (2) the right of access to a court (an inherent element of the notion of a fair trial embodied in art 6(1)); (3) the right to a fair trial in relation to the determination of a person's civil rights and obligations or of any criminal charges brought against him (art 6); (4) the right to freedom of expression (art 10); (5) the right to respect for privacy (art 8); and (6) the right of freedom of association (art 11): see P Duffy,

'The Protection of Commercial Interests Under the European Convention on Human Rights' in R Cranston (ed), *Making Commercial Law—Essays in Honour of Roy Goode* (1997), Ch 23.

The relationship between human rights and commerce was again highlighted by the Modern Slavery Act 2015. Section 54 of the Act came into force on 20 October 2015. It requires commercial organisations that supply goods or services, have a global turnover of £36 million or more, and carry on business in the UK, to publish a slavery and human trafficking statement each financial year that sets out the steps they have taken, if any, to ensure that modern slavery (including slavery, servitude, forced or compulsory labour, and human trafficking) is not taking place in their business operations or supply chains. The new statement must be published on the organisation's website with a link in a prominent place on its homepage. If an organisation fails to produce a statement, the Secretary of State may seek an injunction requiring it to comply. Failure to comply with the injunction could result in an unlimited fine as punishment for contempt of court. Damage to the organisation's commercial reputation is also likely to result from non-compliance with the legislation.

7 THE PHILOSOPHY AND CONCEPTS OF COMMERCIAL LAW

'The Codification of Commercial Law' by R Goode
(1988) 14 Mon LR 135 at 147–155

. . . *[A]re* there concepts of commercial law? Or is commercial law no more than an aggregation of the different rules governing particular forms of commercial contract, with no linking themes of any kind? If this is the case, and if it is what we want, then a commercial code is not for us. I believe that commercial law does exist and that it embodies a philosophy, not always very coherent but nonetheless present, and fundamental concepts, not always very clearly articulated but nonetheless helping to implement that philosophy and to serve the needs of the business community. By the philosophy of commercial law I mean those underlying assumptions of fairness and utility which inform commercial law and run like a thread through its different branches. By concepts of commercial law I mean those principles of law, whether the common law or legislation, which are a particular response to the needs of the commercial community and thus apply with special vigour to commercial transactions, even though they are capable of application to non-commercial dealings.

VI THE PHILOSOPHY AND CONCEPTS OF COMMERCIAL LAW

The primary function of commercial law, in the sense in which I use that term, is to accommodate the legitimate practices and expectations of the business community in relation to their commercial dealings. This sounds much easier than it is. Business law reflects commercial life, and life is not simple. The law and the judges have to balance a range of competing values, the relative weight of which varies not only from one legal system to another but from one age to another within a single jurisdiction. Those who criticise the *Uniform Commercial Code* for appearing to face all ways at once are correct in the accusation but unfair in the criticism, for the Code does no more than reflect the fact that desirable objectives often pull in opposite directions and require conflicting treatments. The problem for the law maker is much the same as that confronting two consultants treating the same patient, one for diabetes which requires insulin and another for hypoglycaemia which reacts adversely to insulin.

1. The philosophy of commercial law

There would seem to me to be eight principles which together make up the philosophy of commercial law. They are: . . .

(a) Party autonomy

The general philosophy of the common law is that businessmen should be free to make their own law. A contract is a contract. A party is entitled to the benefit of his bargain and to the strict performance of conditions of the contract, whether they relate to the time of performance or the description or quality of what is to be tendered as performance. Only where contract terms are so restrictive, oppressive or otherwise incompatible with society's goals as to offend against the public interest should the courts intervene to curb the sanctity of contract. One reason for upholding contracts is a philosophical one, that of freedom under the law, including the freedom to fetter one's own freedom. Another is that the enforcement of contractual undertakings helps to promote security and predictability, a matter of some importance to the business world. Hence the *Uniform Commercial Code* makes it clear, in section 1–102(2)(b) and (3), that freedom of contract is a principle of the Code. But freedom of contract cannot be absolute, and the Code itself contains numerous specific restrictions, as well as a general bar on contracting out of the obligations of good faith, diligence, reasonableness and care. The circumstances which are considered to justify legislative or judicial interference in the bargain of the parties to a commercial transaction vary widely according to the *mores* of the particular society, the familiarity of the judges with the problems of business life and the relative importance of a particular State as an international centre of commerce or finance . . . The view in London, as I see it, may be broadly expressed in these terms: 'business life is rough and tough; if you can't take care of yourself or don't know what you're doing, you shouldn't get into it in the first place!' In other words, in a contest between contract and equity in a commercial dispute, contract wins almost every time; and I suspect that one reason why foreigners so frequently select English law, rather than Continental law, to govern their contracts and English courts to adjudicate their disputes is that they know where they stand on the law and can rely on judges experienced in commercial transactions to give effect to their understanding. Related to the contract/equity conflict is the tension between conflicting goals expressed in the opposing maxims of international law, *pacta sunt servanda* and *rebus sic stantibus*. It takes a great deal to persuade an English court that change of circumstances modifies or discharges even a long-term contract.

(b) Predictability

The business world attaches high importance to the predictability of judicial decisions on legal issues. The weight given by a legal system to the need for predictability compared with equity and flexibility will, of course, vary from jurisdiction to jurisdiction and will depend in no small measure on the volume of business and of dispute resolution a particular State has or wishes to attract. A reasonable degree of predictability is needed in the commercial world because so much planning and so many transactions, standardised or high in value, are undertaken on the basis that the courts will continue to follow the rules laid down in preceding cases. But every businessman and his lawyer knows that there are tides in judicial philosophy, that every action ultimately produces a reaction, that a form of liability denied by one generation of judges will be vigorously developed by the next . . .

(c) Flexibility

Needless to say, the man of affairs wishes to have his cake and eat it; to be given predictability on the one hand and flexibility to accommodate new practices and developments on the other. Karl Llewellyn was acutely aware of the need to accommodate these opposing goals in the *Uniform Commercial Code;* and he sought, with a fair measure of success, to achieve that accommodation by building into the Code a range of flexible words and concepts to encourage the organic growth of Code law whilst trusting the courts to observe the general policies and philosophy of the Code as a whole. Thus we find references to 'the continued expansion of commercial practices through custom, usage and agreement of the parties' and to 'obligations of good faith, diligence, reasonableness and care' as well as the preservation of general principles of law and equity. In England the courts are on the whole very responsive to the needs of the business community and reluctant to deny recognition to the legal efficacy of commercial instruments and practices in widespread use. As in the Army, there are two opposing but equally effective techniques to avoid bringing disaster on your head from on high. One is to keep out of the way, proceed in stealth and hope that no one will know you are there, still less what you are doing. The other is the exact opposite, namely to promote your activities with a fanfare of trumpets, persuade the rest of the corps to join you and then defy the authorities to upset such a large number of people and such a huge volume of business by declaring it illegal! In the international markets the latter technique seems to work rather well, always so long as one does not come up against a rural judge whose main interests lie in equity and the avoidance of unconscionable bargains!

(d) Good faith

The attitude of the common law to the question of good faith in contracts is curiously ambivalent and is fashioned by English legal history. In civil law jurisdictions the duty of good faith is inherent not only in contractual but in pre-contractual relationships. Particularly vigorous is the general requirement of good faith embodied in [Art] 242 of the German *Civil Code*, which has given rise to a mass of doctrine and jurisprudence and is widely applied. Section 1–203 of the *Uniform Commercial Code* provides that:

> Every contract or duty within this Act imposes an obligation of good faith in its performance or enforcement.

By contrast, good faith is not a general requirement of English law for the enforcement of *legal* rights or the exercise of *legal* remedies. A party can exercise a right to terminate a contract for breach even though it causes him no loss and his sole motive is to escape the consequences of a bad bargain; and a party able to perform a contract without need of the other party's co-operation can in general proceed with performance against the other party's wishes, and even when that party no longer has an interest in the performance, and then claim payment of the contract sum. Where good faith does surface in commercial transactions is in a priority dispute or where some equitable right or remedy is involved. It is surely high time that English law adopted a general principle of good faith and cast off its historical shackles.

(e) The encouragement of self-help

Compared to continental legal systems, the common law is remarkably indulgent towards self-help. Acceleration clauses can be invoked, contracts can be terminated or rescinded, goods repossessed, liens and rights of contractual set-off exercised, receivers and managers appointed and securities realised, all without any need for judicial approval, the only limiting factor (in the absence of special legislation) being that one must not commit a breach of the peace. There seems no pressure to modify this approach in relation to commercial transactions, nor, with the enormous pressure of work on courts all over the world, does a change seem particularly necessary or desirable. Civilised self-help has the advantages of speed, efficiency, flexibility and cheapness upon which the smooth functioning of business life so much depends.

(f) The facilitation of security aspects

As an aspect of the common law's attitude towards self-help, but also an independent characteristic, we may note that—again by comparison with continental systems—it is extremely favourable to the creation of security interests. Security can be taken over almost any kind of asset, tangible or intangible, usually with little or no formality; it can cover present and future property without the need for specific description; and it can secure present and future indebtedness. The creditor has the option of security by possession, ownership (mortgage) or mere charge. He has the facility of appointing a receiver over the entirety of a debtor company's assets, with full powers to take over and manage the company's business, without the creditor being in any way responsible for his receiver's acts or omissions so long as the creditor does not intervene in the conduct of the receivership. Moreover, one of the particular features of insolvency law is that it recognizes and protects interests created and perfected under non-insolvency rules, so that in general a security interest will be accepted as having priority over the claims of the general body of unsecured creditors in the debtor's bankruptcy or winding up.

One of the criticisms levelled against Article 9 was that it was *too* favourable to secured creditors and gave inadequate consideration to the claims of the general body of unsecured creditors. But the balance of the interests of secured and unsecured creditors is primarily a function of insolvency law, not of commercial law, for so long as the debtor is solvent the existence of security is of no moment to the unsecured creditor, who can take a judgment and enforce it by execution.

(g) The protection of vested rights

(h) The protection of innocent third parties

These two well established principles of commercial law do, of course, run in opposite directions. The first reflects a general feeling that an owner should not lose his property without fault; the second, that innocent buyers (including incumbrancers) should be protected against proprietary rights of which they have no notice, in order to ensure the free flow of goods in the stream of trade. Like most legal systems, English law faces both ways. Its starting position is the *nemo dat* principle but its *Sale of Goods Act* moves towards the civilian principle *possession vaut titre*. Third parties may also acquire overriding rights where the holder of a prior security interest has failed to perfect it by registration. No ordering of priorities can do justice in every case, but the position in English law has probably become more incoherent than under most legal systems. Certainly we would expect a commercial code to provide a reasonably rational balance between competing interests and one which, as under the *Uniform Commercial Code*, moves away from distinctions between legal and equitable interests. A rational law should seek to embody two principles: first, that no one should suffer loss or subordination of his rights without fault; secondly, that no one should be affected by a prior interest of which he has neither knowledge nor the means of acquiring knowledge. These two competing principles can be harmonised in some measure by registration requirements, which on the one hand provide the owner of an interest with a means of protecting it and on the other allow third parties to ignore a registrable interest which is unregistered. But we cannot prescribe registration of all real rights, and the problem then is to establish the general, or residuary, rule. For residuary cases I believe the interests of commerce require the civilian principle of *possession vaut titre* rather than the common law principle *nemo dat quod non habet*. A party who puts an article of commerce, tangible or intangible, into the stream of trade must take his chances. This is simply an application in the field of property rights of the policy that dictates that equity should be slow to interfere in commercial transactions.

2. The concepts of commercial law

(a) The concept of a market

As one would expect in a body of law concerned with dealings among merchants, the concept of a market is central to commercial law. By this is meant not necessarily a physical market in which traders strike bargains *in praesenti* on the floor of the market but a mechanism for bringing together substantial numbers of participants who deal in commodities, securities or money and who make a market by acting both as buyers and as sellers at prices determined by supply and demand. With the advent of telecommunications physical markets are steadily giving way to markets established by computer networks in which the participants are linked to each other and to a central system operated by the relevant exchange for striking bargains and displaying market prices. Commercial law is influenced by the concept of a market in a variety of ways. Parties dealing in a market are deemed to contract with reference to its established and reasonable customs and usages, which can have the effect of giving a special meaning to ordinary words, of importing rights and obligations not normally implied, of permitting tolerances in performance which would not be accepted in the general law of contract and of expanding or restricting remedies for a shortfall in performance, as where a small deficiency in quantity or quality is compensatable by an allowance against the price, to the exclusion of the remedy of termination of the contract. The market price is taken as the reference point in computing damages against a seller who fails to deliver or a buyer who fails to accept the subject-matter of the contract, and a party who reduces his loss by a subsequent sale at a higher price or a subsequent purchase at a lower price is not normally required to bring this saving into account, contrary to the normal contract rules as to mitigation of damages.

The problem for commercial law is to define the manner in which a usage of the market is to be established, a matter that can be of great difficulty but on which much may turn. . . .

(b) The importance of customs or usages of a trade or locality

Even without a market a court will recognize established customs or usages, such as those of a particular trade or locality, where the circumstances indicate that the parties were contracting by reference to the custom or usage. The enforceability of abstract payment undertakings is an important example to which I shall allude in more detail shortly.

(c) The importance of a course of dealing

Since traders are often concerned in a continuous and consistent course of dealing with each other, it is taken for granted that the usual terms apply, whether or not spelled out in the contract. Terms implied by a course of dealing are thus a fruitful source of implication into commercial contracts.

(d) The concept of negotiability

A key feature of commercial law is its recognition of the need for the ready marketability of commercial assets, in particular goods, money obligations and securities. Hence the development of documents of title and negotiable instruments and securities, the delivery of which (with any necessary indorsement) passes constructive possession (goods) or legal title (instruments and securities) to the underlying rights. Hence also the rule, confined to negotiable instruments, that a holder in due course acquires a title free from equities and defects in the title of his transferor. The concept of negotiability derives from the old law merchant and is a particular characteristic of commercial law. Its importance in facilitating dealings with goods in transit and with negotiable securities may be expected to decline as systems evolve for the paperless transfer of goods and securities, an evolution which the draftsman of a commercial code will have to be ready to accommodate. The same is true of negotiable instruments payable at sight or on demand, since these are payment documents rather than credit instruments and in relative terms are gradually giving way to electronic funds transfers. By contrast, term instruments may be expected to retain their vigour, since there seems no reasonable prospect of devising a commercially viable system for replicating electronically the negotiability of a paper document.

(e) The enforceability of abstract payment undertakings

General contract law requires a promise not made under seal to be supported by consideration if it is to be enforceable. But all kinds of legal magic can be worked by mercantile usage. It is generally accepted—though to this day there are no English decisions directly on the point—that certain types of payment undertaking become binding when communicated to the beneficiary, despite the absence of any consideration or any act of reliance on the part of the beneficiary. I refer in particular to the obligations of a bank issuing a documentary credit, a standby credit and a performance bond or guarantee. The contracts engendered by such undertakings are of a peculiar kind, since they are neither unilateral nor bilateral in the ordinary sense, they involve no acceptance of an offer and no consideration. Exactly what types of payment undertaking will be so enforced remains a matter of conjecture. Is this privileged status confined to undertakings by banks? And if so, which types of undertaking? The answer apparently lies in mercantile custom and usage, a force so powerful that it can sweep aside without argument what is generally considered to be a basic principle of contract law.

I hope I have demonstrated to your satisfaction that there *is* a philosophy of commercial law and there *are* concepts of commercial law which mark out commercial transactions for special treatment. Other concepts may suggest themselves as desirable, such as the irrevocability of firm offers in dealings between merchants. But my purpose is not to produce an exhaustive catalogue, simply to refute the notion still current in some circles that commercial law is merely an aggregation of rules governing particular classes of transaction with no common threads calling for an integrated codification.

NOTES

1.   When commercial people deal with each other, they usually do so in a spirit of trust and confidence. As Bowen LJ put it in *Sanders Bros v Maclean & Co* (1883) 11 QBD 327 at 343:

> Credit, not distrust, is the basis of commercial dealing; mercantile genius consists principally in knowing whom to trust and with whom to deal, and commercial intercourse and communication is no more based on the supposition of fraud than it is on the supposition of forgery.

Yet English law knows no general doctrine of good faith (*Walford v Miles* [1992] 2 AC 128 at 138, per Lord Ackner). Under the common law a party may enforce his *legal* rights and exercise his *legal* remedies without regard to any general requirement of good faith: there is no rule against abuse of rights (see the dictum of Lord Reid in *White & Carter (Councils) Ltd v McGregor* [1962] AC 413 at 430). Some academic commentators would like to change this by introducing a general principle of good faith into English contract law (see, eg, R Brownsword (1994) 7 JCL 197, (1996) 49 CLP 111, and his *Contract Law: Themes for the Twenty-First Century* (2nd edn, 2006), Ch 5). Others question the need for such wholesale incorporation of a principle of good faith, preferring instead to rely on an incremental approach towards good faith principles. As Bingham LJ stated in *Interfoto Picture Library Ltd v Stiletto Visual Programmes Ltd* [1988] QB 433 at 439:

> In many civil law systems, and perhaps in most legal systems outside the common law world, the law of obligations recognises and enforces an overriding principle that in making and carrying out contracts parties should act in good faith. This does not simply mean that they should not deceive each other, a principle which any legal system must recognise; its effect is perhaps most aptly conveyed by such metaphorical colloquialisms as 'playing fair,' 'coming clean' or 'putting one's cards face upwards on the table.' It is in essence a principle of fair and open dealing....
>
> English law has, characteristically, committed itself to no such overriding principle but has developed piecemeal solutions in response to demonstrated problems of unfairness. Many examples could be given. Thus equity has intervened to strike down unconscionable bargains. Parliament has stepped in to regulate the imposition of exemption clauses and the form of certain hire-purchase agreements. The common law also has made its contribution, by holding that certain classes of contract require the utmost good faith, by treating as irrecoverable what purport to be agreed estimates of damage but are in truth a disguised penalty for breach, and in many other ways.

There is no doubt that good faith plays an important role in priority disputes (eg the protection given to a good faith purchaser or incumbrancer) and also where *equitable* rights or remedies are involved (reflected in the general maxims of equity 'he who seeks equity must do equity' and 'he who comes to equity must come with clean hands'). However, there is a strong case for keeping a general principle of good faith out of the common law, especially in the case of commercial transactions (see RM Goode, *Commercial Law in the Next Millennium* (1998), pp 19–20). First, what do we mean by good faith? The concept seems impossible to define with any degree of precision (see the range of different attempts at definition in J Beatson and D Friedmann (eds), *Good Faith and Fault in Contract Law* (1995)). Good faith means different things in different jurisdictions and within different legal traditions (F Reynolds [2002] LMCLQ 182 at 197; and see also *Director General of Fair Trading v First National Bank plc* [2001] UKHL 52, [2002] 1 AC 481 at [17], per Lord Bingham: 'The member states [of the EU] have no common concept of fairness or good faith'). Secondly, the uncertain scope of the concept would make it difficult to predict the outcome of legal disputes, something valued by the commercial community. Thirdly, a general concept of good faith seems unnecessary when there are a number of alternative mechanisms already available to the courts to regulate the conduct of negotiations and the performance of contracts. The following concepts can all be added to the list of regulatory mechanisms set out by Bingham LJ in *Interfoto v Stiletto*: election, estoppel, waiver, relief against forfeiture (although the House of Lords denied its application to a commercial contract—a time charter—in *The Scaptrade* [1983] 2 AC 694), the *contra proferentem* rule, the willingness of the courts to imply a duty of co-operation on a contracting party in order to achieve a common goal of the contract (*Mackay v Dick* (1881) 6 App Cas 251 at 263), the requirement that in exceptional cases an innocent party ought to accept a repudiation and mitigate his loss (*White & Carter (Councils) Ltd v McGregor* [1962] AC 413, HL; cf *MSC Mediterranean Shipping Co SA v Cottonex Anstalt* [2015] EWHC 283 (Comm) at [97]–[98], per Leggatt J, where the principle is placed within a wider context of good faith, but see also Moore-Bick LJ's criticism of Leggatt J's approach on appeal at [2016] EWCA Civ 789 at [45]), and control of the exercise of contractual discretion through the implication of a term that the discretion must be exercised in good faith for the purpose for which it was conferred, and must not be exercised arbitrarily, capriciously, perversely, or irrationally (see, eg, *Socimer International Bank Ltd v Standard Bank London Ltd* [1988] 1 Lloyd's Rep 558 at 575–577, CA; but such a term will not be implied to control the exercise of an absolute contractual right: see *Mid Essex Hospital Services NHS Trust v Compass Group UK and Ireland Ltd* [2013] EWCA Civ 200 at [83], [140]).

Nevertheless, in recent years the courts have tended to enforce expressly assumed obligations to act in good faith (*Mid Essex*, above) and have even shown some willingness to give effect to expressly assumed obligations to negotiate in good faith (see, eg, *Petromec Inc v Petroleo Brasileiro SA Petrobras (No 3)* [2005] EWCA Civ 891, [2006] 1 Lloyd's Rep 121 at [115]–[121], per Longmore LJ, *obiter*). In these cases, certainty has had to yield to the principle of giving effect to the parties' agreement in accordance with the principle of party autonomy (M Arden (2013) 30 JCL 199 at 211). Whether the courts will imply obligations of good faith into commercial contracts is a different matter. In recent years, following the lead taken by Leggatt J in *Yam Seng Pte Ltd v International Trade Corpn Ltd* [2013] EWHC 111 (QB), [2013] 1 All ER (Comm) 1321, the courts have sometimes been prepared to imply a duty of good faith into 'relational' contracts (ie agreements to govern long-term relationships such as distributorship agreements) on the ground that it reflects the intention of the parties. Nevertheless, the general rule in commercial contracts is that 'if the parties wish to impose such a duty [of good faith] they must do so expressly' (*Mid Essex*, above, at [105], per Jackson LJ).

A requirement of good faith does feature in some of the most important pieces of English commercial legislation, although here it emerges as a subjective standard of honesty rather than an objective one of fair dealing. Both the Bills of Exchange Act 1882 (BEA) and the Sale of Goods Act 1979 (SGA) demand the exercise of good faith before certain rights, particularly those rights protecting third party purchasers, can be acquired (see BEA, ss 12, 29(1), 30(2), 59(1), 60, 79(2), 80; SGA, ss 22–25, 47). Both statutes define good faith in terms of 'honesty in fact' (BEA, s 90; SGA, s 61(3)), although it is clear that wilfully turning a blind eye to one's own suspicions is evidence of dishonesty (*Jones v Gordon* (1877) 2 App Cas 616 at 629, per Lord Blackburn, see below, p 687; *London Joint Stock Bank v Simmons* [1892] AC 201 at 221, per Lord Herschell). See also the Factors Act 1889, ss 2(1), 8 and 9; the Marine Insurance Act 1906, s 17; the Cheques Act 1957, ss 1 and 4; and the Hire-Purchase Act 1964, ss 27–29.

References in statutes to standards of good faith, particularly in the objective sense of fair dealing, are likely to increase with the harmonisation of commercial law in the EU (see, eg, EC Directive 1986/653 on Self-Employed Commercial Agents, arts 3(1) and 4(1), as implemented by the Commercial Agents (Council Directive) Regulations 1993 (SI 1993/3053), regs 3(1) and 4(1)) and the harmonisation of world trade law (see, eg, the Vienna Convention on Contracts for the International Sale of Goods (1980), art 7(1), not yet ratified by the UK). It comes as no surprise that art 1.7 of the UNIDROIT *Principles of International Commercial Contracts* (above, p 17), and also art 1.201(1) of the *Principles of European Contract Law* (above, p 17), prepared by the Commission on European Contract Law, demand that 'each party must act in accordance with good faith and fair dealing'. The concept is already embedded in English consumer law with the implementation of EC Directive 93/13 on Unfair Terms in Consumer Contracts, which polices 'unfair terms' in consumer contracts, through, first, the Unfair Terms in Consumer Contracts Regulations 1999 (SI 1999/2083) and then, more recently, Part 2 of the Consumer Rights Act 2015, which in October 2015 repealed and replaced the 1999 Regulations.

2. Professor Goode returned to the subject of the influence of the concept of a market on the development of commercial law when delivering the 33rd Lionel Cohen Lecture in 1990 (see R Goode (1990) 24 Israel Law Review 185, later published in [1991] LMCLQ 177). He argued (at 186; at 178) that:

> . . . the needs and practices of the market are driving English contract and commercial law, in particular by forcing the evolution of new techniques for the creation and transfer of rights, by applying old concepts to new situations and by modifying and expanding rules of law both to accommodate legitimate business expectations and to protect the stability and integrity of the market.

The English courts have generally been good at doing this, but there have been some notable exceptions. We have already seen how the uncertainty created by the decision of the House of Lords in *Hazell v Hammersmith and Fulham London Borough Council* [1992] 2 AC 1 (above, p 9), the swaps case, seriously dented the City of London's reputation with foreign investors. This led directly to the Bank of England setting up the Legal Risk Review Committee and then, on the Committee's recommendation, the Financial Law Panel, and, in 2002, following on from the closure of the Financial Law Panel, the Financial Markets Law Committee, whose function is to identify issues of legal uncertainty in the framework of the wholesale financial markets which might give rise to material risks, and to consider how such issues can be addressed. The Financial Markets Law Committee has been tasked with the provision of seminars to those specialist commercial and chancery judges who are designated to hear cases on the Financial List of the High Court, which was established in October 2015 (see above, p 12). The Financial List is designed to deal (inter alia) with disputes, and also hypothetical test cases, which raise issues of general importance to the financial markets.

8 THE CODIFICATION OF COMMERCIAL LAW

You will have realised by reading this far that there have been calls for the codification of English commercial law. Those who make that call, such as Professor Goode, do not ask for codification along Victorian lines, where there were virtually no links between the co-dified statutes. On the contrary, the modern advocates of codification want a comprehensive commercial code along the lines of the US UCC (above, p 6). An English commercial code would embody 'a set of principles and main rules for a handful of key commercial transactions—sale, secured transactions, intermediated securities and electronic funds transfer, and perhaps agency and suretyship guarantees, together with a set of general provisions—that would be regularly reviewed and could be amended by some fast-track procedure' (R Goode (2007) 123 LQR 602 at 605–606). Such a code would contain statements of principle and would not attempt to deal in detail with every problem that might arise in commerce.

The case for codification can be summarised as follows: it simplifies the law and makes it easily accessible; the process of codification highlights areas of weakness in the existing law; it enables the law to be modernised and reduces ambiguities and inconsistencies between statutes; and it provides an integrated body of commercial law of which the various branches are linked by common concepts, a coherent philosophy, and a consistent terminology. It is said that the net effect of commercial codification will be to improve the law and also produce savings in time, effort, and money for those who must advise on it and comply with it. See, generally, R Goode (1988) 14 Mon LR 135 at 137–140, upon which this summary is based (and also the extract from Professor Goode's 1997 Hamlyn Lecture 'Commercial Law in an International Environment: Towards the Next Millennium' which appears below at p 46). Professor Goode is not alone in calling for an English commercial code (see also Mrs Justice Arden [1997] CLJ 516, especially at 530–534).

Yet there has been no call for a commercial code from the vast majority of our commercial judges or practitioners (Lord Goff (1992) 5 JCL 1 at 3; although Lord Goff has since declared that he has come 'to entertain new thoughts about codification' (1997) 46 ICLQ 745 at 751). The opponents of such general codification say that it is unnecessary, inflexible, and contrary to our common law tradition of responding to the changing needs of the business community as they arise. Furthermore, there is the perceived danger that codification will stifle the ability of judges to develop the law (but this has not occurred in Germany where there is a Civil Code (the BGB): see Lord Goff (1997) 46 ICLQ 745 at 751–752). Of course, those who see commercial law as an amalgam of distinct subjects, and who deny that there are any general principles of commercial law, see the whole process of general codification as meaningless.

As the next extract illustrates, there have been similar calls for wholesale codification of international trade law.

'The Codification of the Law of International Trade' by CM Schmitthoff

[1985] JBL 34 at 41–43

. . . [W]e have to consider whether the creation of a world code on international trade law—a task which, as I have already observed, undoubtedly would fall to UNCITRAL—would be beneficial and feasible. Three questions have here to be examined: what would be the purpose of such codification, what would be the method of it, and what would be the contents of such a code?

As regards the benefits of such codification, they would be, in my view, considerable. Probably the greatest benefit would be that such a code would offer countries in the course of development a compact package deal. If they adopt the code, they would at once have the most modern and comprehensive legal instrument for the conduct of their international business. Secondly, it would be possible to establish in a general part of such code certain principles which should apply to all international trade transactions. I am thinking here, eg of the obligation of good faith in the performance and enforcement of an international contract, as it is laid down in paragraph 1–203 of the American Uniform Commercial Code. Other equitable rules of the American Code's General Provisions may likewise be suitable for incorporation into a general part of a world code, eg those on severability of an invalid provision, or those on a liberal construction, according to the underlying purposes and policies, in this context, of international Conventions or other international instruments.

Further, a code of international trade law could deal with certain general questions which affect all international trade contracts, such as the effect of telecommunications and the determination of a universal unit of accounts for international conventions, ie the Special Drawing Rights of the World Bank. Lastly, the creation of a code on international trade law would emphasise the inherent unity of the work of UNCITRAL and other formulating agencies in their efforts to harmonise and unify the legal regulation of international trade on a worldwide basis. This inherent unit is not always clearly discernible in the present state of development as these organisations have often to deal with highly specialised topics of relatively small ambit.

As to the method of codification, little has to be said. It is obvious that the empirical method has to be adopted. The code would thus be nothing more than a technical legal instrument of consolidation.

As to its contents, the code would necessarily have to be built on existing measures of unification. It would have to include, in an integrated manner, the United Nations Conventions so far promulgated and other international measures widely accepted by the practice. It should not be limited to measures sponsored by UNCITRAL but should include suitable texts drafted by other formulating agencies and approved by UNCITRAL. But this may not be enough. A general part would have to be provided, bracketing together the substantive parts. In addition, some further specific subjects may have to be included in order to make the code comprehensive and workable in practice. I have indicated elsewhere what I would consider to be the substance of such a code. I said [CM Schmitthoff, *Commercial Law in a Changing Economic Climate* (2nd edn, 1981), p 30]:

> If the Unidroit project on the Code of International Trade Law and the ICC scheme on trade usages are joined together with the United Nations Convention on Contracts for the International Sale of Goods, the ICC Uniform Customs and Practice on Documentary Credits and the Uniform Rules for Collections, the United Nations Hamburg Rules on the Carriage of Goods by Sea, and the UNCITRAL Arbitration Rules, the basis of a world code on international trade is already laid. What has to be done, is to weld together these disjoined pieces of unification into a logical, integrated work and to supplement it by unifications which are still extant, such as the proposed uniform law on international bills of exchange and promissory notes, the regulation of the international contracts of forwarding and warehousing, and other relevant topics.

In the result, the creation of a uniform world code on international trade law would, in my view, serve a useful purpose and, having regard to the existing and planned unificatory measures, is a feasible proposition.

NOTE

Professor Schmitthoff is not referring to the piecemeal harmonisation of trade law that has already taken place via international conventions and codes. He is calling for a worldwide code of international trade. Like Professor Goode, he points to the US UCC as proof that such a code is not a utopian goal. Such a code would create a new *lex mercatoria*.

QUESTION

Given the UK's past track record with regard to ratification of international conventions which seek to harmonise specific areas of international trade law (see above, p 26), would you expect the UK to be in the vanguard of states lobbying for a worldwide code as proposed by Professor Schmitthoff? (Try not to laugh too loud when answering this question!) If not, why not?

9 THE CHALLENGES FOR COMMERCIAL LAW IN THE TWENTY-FIRST CENTURY

'Commercial Law in an International Environment: Towards the Next Millennium' in R Goode, *Commercial Law in the Next Millennium* (1998), pp 96–104 (footnotes omitted)

What are the challenges for commercial law as we approach the 21st century? I have already referred to the importance of harmonisation, whether in the form of hard law, such as an international convention, or of contractually incorporated rules, such as those issued by the ICC, or of so-called soft law, as exemplified by the two international restatements of contract previously mentioned. In this concluding part of the final Hamlyn lecture I should like, first, to consider some of the legal implications of new technology, secondly, to comment on the changing approach to commercial dispute resolution, and, thirdly, to offer some more general reflections on the present shape of English commercial law.

TECHNOLOGICAL DEVELOPMENTS

In debates concerning the legal implications of an electronic business environment there is an unfortunate tendency to over-emphasise the technology and to assume that it automatically changes everything so far as legal relationships are concerned. This is a myth which I am anxious to dispel. Whether one is dealing with electronic funds transfer, the dematerialisation or immobilisation of securities or the use of electronic bills of lading, it is necessary to ask why, if the message is broadly the same, its legal significance should be affected by the medium through which it is sent. My heart warmed to a member of the audience at an International Bar Association gathering in Vienna some years ago who asked what, conceptually, was the difference between a funds transfer effected as the result of communication across the ether and the delivery of a sack of notes or gold carried over the shoulder from one place to another. This is a very perceptive question and one that needs to be addressed. Of course, it can be said that there are legal instruments, such as a bill of exchange or a bill of lading, which depend for their legal efficacy on a writing and a signature. The shipping conventions, for example, all refer to a signed bill of lading. But what is really at stake is an authenticated message, and modern legal definitions of writing and signature allow for any medium of communication and any proper system of authentication so long as the message is capable of being reproduced in tangible form. Moreover, even where it is necessary to interpret international conventions as requiring a physical, signed document, in most cases the desired effects of those conventions can be achieved by a contractual incorporation of the convention rules, which will thus apply as terms of the contract.

What, then, is so special about the medium? Why should electronic transmissions necessitate different rules of law? These questions are worth asking because in many cases we find the same rules apply to electronic transactions as to written ones. For example, the basic concepts of payment and the revocability of a payment instruction remain unchanged, though some tweaking of the rules is needed and this is usually achieved by rules of the clearing house. But computer technology does have an impact on legal rules and legal risk. Copyright issues have to be considered. Rules must be devised to govern the payment systems themselves, the rights and obligations of the parties and the allocation of risk where the system fails or is improperly accessed. The ease and speed with which large sums can be moved around the world in an electronic environment creates the potential for large-scale losses through fraud or system failure. There was a celebrated event many years ago in New York when a clearing bank appeared to become increasingly insolvent as the day drew to a close. It transpired that a computer, with the malignity of intent that characterised the last weeks of the master computer HAL in 2001, was debiting the bank with all its outflows but failing to credit it with its inflows. The problems was dealt with by deferring the daily settlement for a few hours, during which time the defect was rectified. But imagine the consequences if it had not been.

There are also public law implications of electronic trading, particularly in the field of regulation. Data protection has become an increasingly complex field; so also has the legal treatment of digital cash. Is a person who holds value in an electronic purse to be treated as a depositor for the purpose of the Banking Act because of his right to require the bank issuing the electronic value to redeem it? Probably not in most cases, but the issue continues to be debated. How is control to be exercised over regulated activities where these are conducted through the Internet? How are we to establish in which jurisdiction relevant acts have occurred? And what is the position if one of the ingredients of an offence is committed in this country and the other or others abroad? These are matters yet to be resolved; they add a new dimension to the task of the regulator.

The resolution of commercial disputes

So far tonight I have concentrated on substantive law. But as I have remarked earlier in this lecture series, the procedure for the resolution of commercial disputes is itself of vital importance. It is no use having legal rights if they cannot readily be enforced and if disputes cannot be fairly and expeditiously resolved. It is generally considered that our central courts—in particular the specialist Commercial Court and the more general courts of the Queen's Bench and Chancery Divisions—provide a good, often an excellent, service to commercial users. Even so, over time the delays and expense associated with litigation led to the growth of commercial arbitration. This was seen as fast, flexible, informal, private, relatively inexpensive and conducive to finality. This is still true of a considerable amount of arbitration, particularly in the commodities field. But it has to be said that much commercial arbitration has become almost indistinguishable from litigation. Arbitral proceedings, particularly with a three-person tribunal in an international arbitration, can be very protracted and a good deal more expensive than litigation. We do at least have the benefit of a modern Arbitration Act ordered in a logical arrangement and expressed in plain English. The Act follows the spirit of the UNCITRAL Model Law more closely than had at one time been envisaged, though Scotland was still bolder in its adoption of the Model Law. Even so, there is much dissatisfaction with arbitration and a growing drift towards alternative dispute resolution methods, such as mediation and the mini-trial. In the early days of ADR experienced arbitrators were inclined to be dismissive, taking the rather lofty view that it would no doubt work well enough in family disputes but would be quite unsuited to disputes of a commercial character. That view is increasingly seen as misplaced and ADR is growing. It is a great deal quicker and cheaper. Of course, it may not be successful, but most hearings appear to end in agreement. Of equal importance is the fact that ADR is designed to be non-confrontational, to expose the real reason, rather than the ostensible reason, for the parties' disagreement and to offer the prospects of continuance of their relationship instead of the acceptance of its breakdown. Moreover, because ADR is not fettered by legal rights and remedies and can facilitate non-legal forms of relief, such as the offer of a substitute contract to the aggrieved party or the resuscitation of an agreement that has been legally ended. What the commercial community has not yet fully appreciated is the importance of laying down procedures in advance at the contract stage by which principals not previously involved in the handling of the dispute and with the authority to negotiate are brought into discussions at an early stage with a view to avoiding a breakdown of the relationship rather than simply assuming the breakdown and alleviating it consequences....

The present state of English commercial law

I have said that we need to become more outward-looking, more international in our approach to international conventions. But what of the internal state of English commercial law? How well placed are we to undertake the challenges of change as we enter the next millennium? Here I have to say that for many years now the judiciary seems to have been more attuned than the legislature to the need to keep abreast of legal thought and dynamics in the international community. The courts have shown an ever-increasing readiness to look to patterns of judicial lawmaking in other legal systems for solutions to help resolve complex issues of legal policy. Law, like friendship, has to be constantly cultivated and regularly renewed. When I visit other common law countries, and in particular Canada and the United States, I am immensely impressed with their concern to keep their commercial law up to date and with the enormous energy and legal creativity which their academic and practising lawyers bring to bear to modernise and keep under regular review their laws governing commercial transactions. Pride of place must go to the American Uniform Commercial Code. Admittedly this is powerfully driven by the need for harmonisation among 50 jurisdictions, a motive power we lack; but it is clear that the Americans take the health of their law very seriously indeed. And when I return to England I feel, as always, uplifted by the remarkably high standard in which our judiciary is held but depressed by the state of our statute book and by our inertia and complacent belief in the innate superiority of English commercial law. I believe that at the legislative level we have shamefully neglected our commercial law for as long as I can remember....

How is it that we feel able to embark on the 21st century with commercial law statutes passed in the 19th? How can we seriously expect to confront the problems of modern commerce with legislation enacted in the era of the steam coach, which had to be preceded by a man with a red flag; when the aeroplane, television, the computer and spacecraft were all in the future? Our version of a well-known aphorism is: if it's broken, don't fix it! And as if this were not bad enough, there are whole areas of the law relating to commercial transactions on which we have virtually no legislation whatsoever: nothing on funds transfers or payment systems, nothing on indirect holdings of immobilised securities, nothing on warehouse receipts and no up-to-date and integrated treatment of documents of title generally. And we are the world's leading financial centre! As so often in so many areas, when Parliament is inert it is the courts that have to come to the rescue; and it is only because of the commercial awareness of our judges and the high standing they enjoy with foreigners that we are able to manage. Surely it is not too much to ask that commercial law statutes be reviewed at least once every 25 years; and when more than a century has elapsed without significant change, we can reasonably assume that it is time to replace the entire legislation and begin again.

> 'Ah love! Could thou and I with Fate conspire
> To grasp this sorry Scheme of Things entire,
> Would not we shatter it to bits—and then
> Re-mould it nearer to the Heart's Desire!'

My strong preference is for a commercial code of the kind so successfully adopted throughout the United States. A commercial code has many advantages. It gathers together in one place the rules governing the major forms of commercial transaction and thereby makes the law accessible both to lawyers and to laymen. At present we have to resort to textbooks. Helpful though they may be, they are no substitute for a code, for within a given subject they analyse each principle and rule separately, so that these are diffused across the entire work and are not available to the reader in one place as with the code.

A commercial code is also an exportable product. Even if not taken over in its entirety, it can provide the inspiration for a modern commercial law elsewhere and particularly in developing countries and those that have moved or are moving to a market economy. A code integrates what are at present a disparate collection of statutes, unconnected to each other, replacing them with provisions which cover the field as a whole, in which each part is linked to the others and which are bedded down on a set of general provisions governing all transactions to which the code applies. The very process of preparing a commercial code helps to expose the inadequacies and inconsistencies of the present law and provides an opportunity for commerce, industry and finance to identify weaknesses and to suggest what is needed to overcome them. There are other benefits. Transactions could be conducted more efficiently, legal rules would be much more susceptible to developing business needs than they are now and much time currently spent in digging for particles of commercial law and then arduously assembling them into a coherent principle would be saved.

The preparation of a code would involve several years of effort and a not inconsiderable expense; but that is the price to be paid for a quality product and it is surely a price worth paying. We continue to suffer from false economies in the shape of quick fixes that come unstuck, of half-baked legislation in other areas which has to be corrected, of a philosophy which counts nothing as worth doing unless it can be done quickly and produce an immediate return. But if industry does not shirk at devoting large sums of money and years of research to producing quality products, surely the lawmakers, for a fraction of the cost, can do the same. But if such a project is to succeed it must engage the interest and the involvement not only of academic and practising lawyers but of businessmen in industry, commerce and finance. They must be willing to join the lawyers in such an enterprise, to put their shoulders behind the wheel and, having helped to produce the modern legislation we so desperately need, to urge on government the importance of enacting it.

My final plea is for a greater academic commitment to commercial law. We need more, many more, academic lawyers in the field than we currently possess. Particularly do we need young scholars of an enquiring turn of mind, interested in the workings of commercial practice as well as the development of theory, who can advance the boundaries of knowledge and take our students forward into the next age of commercial law. They will find a warm welcome not only from their colleagues but from practitioners, who are only too happy to share their expertise, and from the judges, who from the House of Lords downwards have, in recent years in particular, been generous in acknowledging the contribution of scholarly writings to their decisions. The academic community is in turn indebted to Bench and Bar for reasoned arguments and judgments which form the basis of much of our teaching and research and which often possess such a combination of creative thinking and intellectual rigour as to make some of us wonder if it is not the members of the practising profession who are often the true scholars!

We have come a long way from the ancient caravan trade and the medieval market, from the runner and the carrier pigeon to instantaneous global communication, from the longboat and the Phoenician round ship to the Japanese oil tanker, from dealings in physical assets to dealings in derivatives and other bundles of intangible rights. Yet the basis of our commerce remains as it was in early times: an organised, regulated market with an efficient clearing and settlement system, a procedure for the fair and expeditious resolution of disputes and a high degree of predictability of outcomes on issues of legal entitlement and obligation. It is a matter for some astonishment that although our legislation governing commercial transactions is archaic, foreigners continue to resort to English law and to English courts, while our own mercantile community remains able to structure agreements and relationships to produce almost any commercially desirable result, and to fashion new financial and commercial instruments, confident in the belief that these will be upheld and that the reasonable usages of merchants will be respected. But that is the genius of English commercial law.

NOTES

1. In 1996, UNCITRAL adopted a Model Law on Electronic Commerce. Most countries which have dealt with or propose to deal with e-commerce have based their legislation on or have at least purported to make it consistent with this Model Law. In 2001, UNCITRAL also adopted a Model Law on Electronic Signatures.

2. In 1999, the EU adopted Directive 99/93 on a framework for electronic signatures ([2000] OJ LI3/12), and this was followed in 2000 by Directive 00/31 on certain legal aspects of information society services, in particular electronic commerce, in the Internal Market ([2000] OJ L178/1). Regulation (EU) No 910/2014 of 23 July 2014 (the eIDAS Regulation) has direct effect in EU Member States from 1 July 2016. The eIDAS Regulation repeals the Electronic Signatures Directive and establishes an EU-wide legal framework for electronic signatures, as well as for electronic seals, electronic time stamps, electronic registered delivery services, and website authentication.

3. Implementation of the Electronic Signatures Directive in the UK has been through the Electronic Communications Act 2000 and the Electronic Signatures Regulations 2002 (SI 2002/318). This establishes a legal framework for electronic signatures. The eIDAS Regulation does not require UK law to be modified. The Electronic Communications Act 2000 and the Electronic Signatures Regulations 2002 comply with it. Parts of the E-Commerce Directive have been implemented by the Electronic Commerce (EC Directive) Regulations 2002 (SI 2002/ 2013), together with four statutory instruments relating to financial services. The Directive and the Regulations address three main areas: (1) liberalising the European Economic Area internal market in e-commerce services; (2) requiring providers of e-commerce services to incorporate certain features into their online ordering process and to provide particular information to users; and (3) defining the liability of online intermediaries such as internet service providers (see, generally, G Smith and A Hand [2002] NLJ 1597).

4. In December 2001, the Law Commission published its Advice to Government entitled *Electronic Commerce: Formal Requirements in Commercial Transactions* (for a useful summary, see H Beale and L Griffiths [2002] LMCLQ 467). The Law Commission had considered whether law reform was required to prevent formal requirements in various commercial transactions hindering the development of electronic commerce. There was particular concern as to whether specific measures were needed to implement art 9 of the E-Commerce Directive, which requires that:

> Member States shall ensure that their legal system allows contracts to be concluded by electronic means. Member States shall in particular ensure that the legal requirements applicable to the contractual process neither create obstacles for the use of electronic contracts nor result in such contracts being deprived of legal effectiveness and validity on account of their having been made electronically.

The advice focused on the international sale and carriage of goods and the associated banking and insurance transactions. The Law Commission concluded (as summarised in Part 10 of the advice) that:

- statutory requirements for 'writing' and a 'signature' were generally capable of being satisfied by emails (later confirmed in *J Pereira Fernandes SA v Mehta* [2006] EWHC 813 (Ch), [2006] 1 WLR 1543 at [31]: see also *Golden Ocean Group Ltd v Salgaocar Mining Industries Pvt Ltd* [2012] EWCA Civ 265, [2012] 1 Lloyd's Rep 542 at [32]; *Bassano v Toft* [2014] EWHC 377 (QB), [2014] ECC 14 at [43]–[44]) and by website trading (but not by Electronic Data Interchange);
- because English law seldom imposes such formal requirements in a contractual context, it was only in very rare cases that the statute book conflicts with the obligations imposed by art 9 of the Electronic Commerce Directive;
- general reform of the statute book was not therefore required; and
- where particular statutory rules did conflict with the requirements of the E-Commerce Directive, an order under s 8 of the Electronic Communications Act 2000 could be used to make context-specific reform. Section 8 gives ministers the authority to review statutes and related legislation that require documents to be in writing and to amend them by way of secondary legislation 'in such manner as [the minister] may think fit for the purpose of authorising or facilitating the use of electronic communications or electronic storage'.

QUESTION

Why is it in the national interest for English law to keep up to date with, and reflect, modern trading practices?

10 THE IMPACT OF BREXIT ON ENGLISH COMMERCIAL LAW

In a national referendum held on 23 June 2016, a majority voted in favour of the UK withdrawing from the EU, and the government thereafter declared its intention to end the UK's membership of the EU. The process of the UK leaving the EU is commonly referred to as 'Brexit'. The future legal relationship of the UK to the EU is uncertain and will turn on arrangements to be negotiated by the UK and agreed by the other Member States. At the time of writing, the UK remains a Member State of the EU and it is likely to remain a Member State for some time as the complex issues thrown up by Brexit are resolved. This book is written on the premise that the UK is a member of the EU and that the status of EU legislation in the law of England and Wales remains unchanged.

We are reminded of the observations made by Professor Goode in *Commercial Law in the Next Millennium* (1998) (see above, p 26) that:

> It is an interesting phenomenon that the impact of European Community law on the private rights of parties to commercial transactions, as opposed to transactions with consumers, has so far been almost negligible. If we leave on one side EC conventions of a general character, such as the Rome Convention on the law applicable to contractual obligations and the Brussels and related conventions on jurisdiction and the enforcement of judgments, it is hard to recall any measure of significance in the field of private commercial law other than the Directive on commercial agents, which certainly introduced concepts novel to English law, such as the non-excludable right of a commercial agent to compensation or an indemnity on termination of his agency. So what we have is mainly a public law superstructure which, outside commercial agency, has not so far been underpinned by any measures to harmonise, for example, the law of obligations or the law governing dealings in commercial assets.

We agree with these observations and, because of them, believe that Brexit will have a relatively minor impact on the substantive content of English commercial (as opposed to consumer) law.

Two further questions remain to be answered. What will be the impact of Brexit on the parties' choice of English law as the governing law of their commercial contracts? Currently, all EU countries apply the same set of rules to determine the governing law of both contractual (the Rome I Regulation (EC) No 593/2008) and non-contractual (the Rome II Regulation (EC) No 864/2007) obligations. Both Regulations require the court in question to give effect to the parties' express choice of law in most cases, regardless of whether the contracting parties are located in a Member State and regardless of whether the parties have chosen the law of a Member State. Although Rome I and Rome II may no longer apply in the UK following Brexit, we believe that commercial parties are still likely to choose English law to govern their contracts and also their non-contractual obligations. There are three main reasons for this. First, English contract law as applied between commercial parties is largely unaffected by EU law. Secondly, the main reasons why English law is currently a popular choice of law in international commercial contracts are almost entirely unconnected with the UK's membership of the EU, for example the emphasis on party autonomy, predictability, and flexibility (see above, p 10). Thirdly, following Brexit, the choice of English law is very likely to continue to be enforced by both English courts (which have a long-standing practice of respecting party autonomy when it comes to choice of English contractual governing law clauses) and the courts of other Member States of the EU (as Rome I and Rome II will continue to apply in the courts of EU Member States).

What will be the impact of Brexit on choice of English jurisdiction clauses in international commercial contracts? Currently, the recast EU Brussels I Regulation (Regulation (EU) No 1215/2012) determines which court has jurisdiction over a particular matter and also provides for reciprocal recognition across the EU of judgments of the courts of Member States. Again, we believe it unlikely that there will to be a move away from English jurisdiction clauses because the reasons for their choice by commercial parties largely remain unaffected by Brexit. We have already touched on some of the reasons why overseas litigants bring their disputes before the English Commercial Court (see above, p 13), for example the quality and independence of the judiciary, as well as the fact that the English courts are best placed to resolve disputes under English law. Again, we think it highly likely that English jurisdiction clauses and English judgments will be enforced post-Brexit in the majority of cases, even if it turns out (in a worst-case scenario) that no reciprocal regime is put in place (albeit this may be a more time-consuming and costly process). Where the parties have chosen an exclusive English jurisdiction clause, it is likely that a reciprocal enforcement regime will be put in place post-Brexit as the UK is likely to sign up to the 2005 Hague Convention on Choice of Court Agreements (the EU signed up to the Convention on behalf of Member States, other than Denmark, on 1 October 2015).

CHAPTER 2

BASIC CONCEPTS OF PERSONAL PROPERTY

In this chapter, we shall examine some basic concepts of personal property law: the nature of personal property, the characteristics and significance of property rights, ownership, and possession.[1] It is important to understand these concepts as commercial law is primarily concerned with dealings in personal property, for example the sale of goods, the exploitation of intangible property, the use of negotiable instruments, and the factoring of debts.

1 THE DISTINCTION BETWEEN REAL AND PERSONAL PROPERTY

The common law distinguishes between real property and personal property. In general terms, real property is land and all things built on land. Personal property is all the property that is left after real property has been subtracted from the class of property taken as a whole.[2] Personal property is, therefore, a residual class of property.

The reason for the division is historical. In the Middle Ages the common law allowed an owner who had been wrongfully dispossessed of freehold land to bring an action, called a real action, to recover the land itself. On the other hand, an owner of personal property could not bring an action to recover the property itself; he was restricted to a personal action for damages against the person who had wrongfully deprived him of it. This procedural distinction still formally applies today. But it is of much less importance, since 1854 courts have had a discretion to order delivery of goods back to their owner (see now the Torts (Interference with Goods) Act 1977, s 3).

The law treats real and personal property differently. For example, specific performance will rarely be ordered when a buyer fails to deliver goods, whereas it is the usual remedy when a vendor fails to complete a contract for the sale of land; there are different rules for the

---

[1] See, generally, RM Goode, *Commercial Law* (5th edn, 2016) ('Goode'), Ch 2 (a masterly survey on which much that follows is based). For an excellent short commentary on the law of personal property, see MG Bridge, *Personal Property Law* (4th edn, 2015) ('Bridge'). Students are well served with Sarah Worthington's *Personal Property Law: Text, Cases, and Materials* (2000). For more detailed analysis, see AP Bell, *Modern Law of Personal Property in England and Ireland* (1989) ('Bell'). For a stimulating collection of essays dealing with many of the areas covered in this chapter, see N Palmer and E McKendrick (eds), *Interests in Goods* (2nd edn, 1998).

[2] Subject to one exception. For historical reasons a lease of land, having its origins in contract, is technically personal, not real, property. But this is of no practical importance today.

creation and *inter vivos* transfer of interests in real property (where formalities are required) and personal property (where few formalities are required); and, as we have seen, whereas the wrongfully dispossessed owner of real property may recover it as a matter of course, the recovery of personal property *in specie* rather than a money substitute for it is subject to the court's discretion. But why are real and personal property treated so differently? Professor Goode points to the different characteristics of the two types of property: land is generally immovable, relatively permanent, readily split into multiple interests, primarily acquired for use, and not intended to circulate in the flow of trade; on the other hand, personal property moves freely in the world of commerce, usually has a relatively short life, has a primary value measured in money, and does not readily lend itself to division into multiple interests (Goode, paras 2.17–2.18). He concludes:

> . . . land is governed primarily by property law concepts, goods and choses in action by commercial law concepts; land law is concerned essentially with status, commercial law with obligations. But . . . many rules of property law apply equally well to land and chattels.

2 TYPES OF PERSONAL PROPERTY

Personal property, sometimes called 'chattels personal',[3] is traditionally divided into choses in possession (known to civil lawyers as tangible movables) and choses in action (intangible movables): see *Colonial Bank v Whinney* (1885) 30 Ch D 261 at 285, per Fry LJ.

While choses in possession include goods and money, choses in action (defined in greater detail below at p 860) encompass a broader spectrum of intangible personal property consisting of private law claims assertible by action in court. As intangible property, they can helpfully be divided into two categories: documentary intangibles and pure intangibles (for a good summary see *Armstrong DLW GmbH v Winnington Networks Ltd* [2012] EWHC 10 (Ch), [2013] Ch 156 at [47]). Documentary intangibles are at bottom intangible rights to money, goods, or other assets. But they are distinguished by the fact that those rights are embodied in a physical document, and that the right which the document represents may be pledged or otherwise transferred simply by delivery of the document, together with any necessary indorsement. Examples of documentary intangibles include bills of lading, negotiable instruments, documentary letters of credit, and policies of insurance. Pure intangibles, by contrast, are those choses in action that are not documentary intangibles. Examples of pure intangibles include debts, securities, and rights to sue under a contract.

It should be noted that intellectual property rights such as copyright, patents, trade marks, and related rights technically fall under the heading of choses in action (eg *Barker v Stickney* [1919] 1 KB 121 at 132, per Scrutton LJ). However, intellectual property forms a subject in its own right and will not be considered further in this book. (Those interested in the subject should consult L Bently and B Sherman, *Intellectual Property Law* (4th edn, 2013) or WR Cornish, D Llewelyn, and T Aplin, *Intellectual Property* (8th edn, 2013).)

While it is traditional to divide personal property into choses in possession and choses in action, it is now clear that there are rights which fall into neither category, but nevertheless

---

[3] Leasehold land, being technically a form of personal property, is sometimes referred to by the archaic term 'chattel real'. This need not concern us here.

remain personal property. The most important instance of these is a permit issued by a public authority allowing the holder to do something otherwise forbidden: for example, an export quota, a petroleum exploration licence, or an EU carbon emission allowance. Property of this sort is often subject to its own unique rules; for example, as to transfer or the remedies available against third parties who interfere with it. A useful discussion of this subject appears in *Armstrong DLW GmbH v Winnington Networks Ltd* [2012] EWHC 10 (Ch), [2013] Ch 156, referred to below at p 87.

We have already noted that personal property is defined in negative terms, ie all property that is left after real property has been subtracted from the class of property taken as a whole. This means that anything that can be described as property, so long as it is not real property, is personal property. As Andrew Bell has observed: 'the list [of personal property] is an open-ended one: any novel phenomenon that is recognised as property will in practice be classified as personal property' (Bell, p 1). So, what is property?

3 WHAT IS PROPERTY?

Crossley Vaines on Personal Property by E Tyler and N Palmer (eds)
(5th edn, 1973), p 3

> 'Property' is a word of different meanings. It may mean a thing owned (my watch or my house is 'my property'); it may mean ownership itself as when I speak of my 'property' in my watch which may pass to the person to whom I sell the watch before I actually hand the watch over or it may even mean an interest in a thing less than ownership but nevertheless conferring certain rights, as when we speak of the 'property' or 'special property' of a bailee in the thing bailed . . . In English law, therefore, 'property' comprehends tangibles and intangibles, movables and immovables; it means a tangible thing (land or chattel) itself, or rights in respect of that thing, or rights, such as a debt, in relation to which no tangible thing exists.

Elements of Land Law by K Gray
(1st edn, 1987), pp 8–14

> #### THE MEANING OF PROPERTY
> It is important at the outset to dispel one common lay notion concerning 'property'. Non-lawyers (and sometimes lawyers) speak loosely of property as the thing which is owned. While this usage is harmless enough in day-to-day speech, it has the effect of obscuring certain salient features of property as a legal phenomenon, for semantically 'property' is the condition of being 'proper' to (or belonging to) a particular person.
>
> #### (1) Property is not a 'thing' but a 'relationship'
> It was the philosopher, Jeremy Bentham, who had to remind lawyers that property is not a thing but a relationship. Bentham pointed out that 'in common speech in the phrase the object of a man's property, the words the object of are commonly left out; and by an ellipsis, which, violent as it is, is now become more familiar than the phrase at length, they have made that part of it which consists of the words a man's property perform the office of the whole.' More recently Professor Macpherson has drawn attention to the way in which, in the transition from the pre-capitalist world to the world of the exchange economy, the distinction between a right to a thing (ie the

legal relation) and the thing itself, became blurred. 'The thing itself became, in common parlance, the property'.

(a) Potential multiplicity of competing users

At one level of analysis, then, 'property' is a relation between the owner and the thing (ie between a 'subject' and an 'object'). However, as has already been suggested, it is unreal to think simply in terms of 'the' owner of any particular thing. It is possible for conflicting claims to be brought by two or more 'subjects' in respect of the same 'object', and therefore the property lawyer is almost always concerned with the relative merits of different claims. In order to establish what belongs to, or is 'proper' to, any particular 'subject', he must first analyse the legal relations between a number of competing subjects vis à vis the same object. A further level of complexity arises because any particular 'object' of property may itself be capable of sustaining a wide variety of different (but not necessarily conflicting) claims. This is demonstrated most clearly in the case of land. Land may, for instance, be the object of a multiplicity of claims made simultaneously by an owner-occupier, a tenant, a building society, a neighbour who enjoys a right of way or restrictive covenant, or even by a spouse who has certain rights not to be evicted from the property.

(b) A network of 'property' relationships

In the ultimate analysis the law of property is concerned with entire networks of legal relationship existing between individuals in respect of things. 'Property' is thus the name given to the bundles of mutual rights and obligations which prevail between 'subjects' in respect of certain 'objects', and the study of property law accordingly becomes an inquiry into a variety of socially defined relationships and morally conditioned obligations. This relational view highlights certain characteristics of property which are essential to any real understanding of land law.

Professor Bruce Ackerman has spoken of the need to disabuse law students of their primitive lay notions regarding ownership. In the words of Ackerman, 'only the ignorant think it meaningful to talk about owning things free and clear of further obligation'. Instead of defining the relationship between a person and 'his' things, property law considers the 'way rights to use things may be parcelled out amongst a host of competing resource users'. Ackerman points out that each resource user is conceived as holding 'a bundle of rights vis à vis other potential users' and that the ways in which user rights may be legally packaged and distributed are 'wondrously diverse'. Ackerman concludes that

> it is probably never true that the law assigns to any single person the right to use any thing in absolutely any way he pleases. Hence, it risks serious confusion to identify any single individual as the owner of any particular thing. At best, this locution may sometimes serve as identifying the holder of that bundle of rights which contains a range of entitlements more numerous or more valuable than the bundle held by any other person with respect to the thing in question. Yet, like all shorthands, talk about 'the' property owner invites the fallacy of misplaced concreteness, of reification. Once one begins to think sloppily, it is all too easy to start thinking that 'the' property owner, by virtue of being 'the' property owner, must necessarily own a particular bundle of rights over a thing. And this is to commit the error that separates layman from lawyer. For the fact (or is it the law?) of the matter is that property is not a thing, but a set of legal relations between persons governing the use of things.

(2) Property is a dynamic relationship

If property is a relationship, it is a dynamic relationship; the content of the relationship is liable to change. The 'subjects' of property may differ from one social era to another. The 'objects' of property are likewise liable to fluctuate with the passage of time and the emergence of new economic conditions. Above all, the ideology of property is profoundly influenced by changing factors of social, political and economic philosophy.

(a) The changing 'subjects' of property

An element of social control is exercised over the property relation in every society, in that each social group to a greater or lesser extent determines for itself the categories of person who may be recognised as the potential 'subjects' of property. In some societies of the past various classes of labourer or serf (eg slaves) were excluded from legal competence as potential 'subjects' of property. Even until relatively recently in England, the married woman was deprived of capacity to hold a legal title in her own name. However, the present century has seen the 'emergence of a property-owning, particularly a real-property-mortgaged-to-a-building-society-owning, democracy.' The years of greater affluence following the World Wars brought about, in the words of Lord Wilberforce, 'the extension, beyond the paterfamilias, of rights of ownership, itself following from the diffusion of property and earning capacity.' Less obviously this diffusion of ownership rights has accentuated the demand that other kinds of right should be recognised as 'proprietary' rights on behalf of less advantaged social groups. Those, for instance, who are not owners of the homes in which they live may wish to assert that their occupation rights (eg as tenants) represent a proprietary status equivalent to that of the owner-occupier.

NOTE

Three important points emerge from the extract taken from Professor Gray's textbook on land law. These points are just as relevant to the commercial lawyer as they are to the (real) property lawyer. The points are:

(1) Property is not a thing but rather a set of legal relations existing between persons in respect of things (Ackerman would regard the editors of *Crossley Vaines* as guilty of 'sloppy thinking' because they define property, inter alia, as 'a thing owned').

(2) Property is a relative, not an absolute, concept. For example, S sells goods to B1 and then sells the same goods to B2. Here both B1 and B2 have some kind of property in the goods; but their rights conflict, and the law ultimately has to prefer one or the other. Again, imagine that O has goods carried on S's ship. Both O and S have proprietary rights in the goods (eg O can sue S for damage to them, while S can sue third parties who interfere with them: see *The Winkfield* [1902] P 42, p 72).

(3) Property is a dynamic relationship. Both the 'subjects' and 'objects' of property may change. Whether a person has property rights in respect of an object may be of great practical significance to the commercial lawyer. For example, is confidential information property? (probably not: *OBG Ltd v Allan* [2007] UKHL 21, [2008] 1 AC 1 at [275], per Lord Walker ('information, even if it is confidential, cannot properly be regarded as a form of property'); also *Force India Formula One Team Ltd v 1 Malaysia Racing Team Sdn Bhd* [2012] EWHC 616 (Ch), [2012] RPC 29 at [376], per Arnold J; and P Kohler and N Palmer, 'Information as Property' in N Palmer and E McKendrick (eds), *Interests in Goods* (2nd edn, 1998), Ch 1.) Again, can a state concession like EU milk quotas be regarded as property, so as (for example) to be capable of being the subject matter of a trust in favour of a creditor or lender? (The answer here is yes: *Swift v Dairywise Farms Ltd* [2000] 1 WLR 1177 at 1185, per Jacob J.) Yet again, is a debt such as a bank deposit a mere personal obligation, or does it have enough of property about it to make it capable of being the subject of a charge by the creditor (account holder) in favour of the debtor (the bank)? (See below, pp 968–976.) And if the same debt is assigned, but there is an argument over the validity of the assignment, is this a matter of the law of obligations or the law of property? (See, eg, *Raiffeisen Zentralbank Österreich AG v Five Star Trading*

LLC [2001] EWCA CIV 68, [2001] QB 825, where the point was important in order to establish which system of law applied in a cross-border transaction.)

4 WHAT ARE THE CHARACTERISTICS OF PROPERTY RIGHTS?

The commercial world has always been concerned with the buying and selling of commodities, be they goods, ideas, debts, or shares. To facilitate this process, the law has limited the number of property interests that can exist in relation to the commodity in question and ensured that each interest is clearly defined, easily discoverable by third parties, and readily convertible into money (see, especially, *National Provincial Bank Ltd v Ainsworth* [1965] AC 1175 at 1247–1248, per Lord Wilberforce). However, as one commentator has put it, 'it is increasingly apparent that there is more to life than buying and selling, and that this is just as true of commercial life as it is of social and domestic life' (A Clarke, 'Property Law: Re-Establishing Diversity' (1997) 50 CLP 119 at 121). Commodities are bought and sold, but they can, for example, just as easily be made the subject of a bailment or security transaction. Put simply, commerce does sometimes require things simply to be bought and sold as commodities, in which case the first priority is free alienability, but 'at other times it requires us to do more complex things with them, and in those cases alienability is relatively unimportant' (Clarke, ibid, p 122). In the extract which follows, Professor Gray is also critical of our preoccupation with alienability and searches for an alternative hallmark of 'property'.

'Property in Thin Air' by K Gray
[1991] CLJ 252 at 292–295

IV. 'PROPERTY' AS CONTROL OVER ACCESS
And so continues our search for the inner mystery of 'property'. Let us look back and see how far we have got since we started. There is no real likelihood that we have arrived at our destination, for the quest for the essential nature of 'property' has beguiled thinkers for many centuries. The essence of 'property' is indeed elusive. That is why, in a sense, we have tried to catch the concept by surprise by asking not 'What is property?' but rather 'What is not property?' We have started from the other end of the earth—both geographically and conceptually—and we have deliberately come by the direction which seemed least probable. But along the way we may have discovered something of value. We may have discovered the irreducible conditions which underlie any claim of 'property'.

The classic common law criteria of 'property' have tended to rest a twin emphasis on the assignability of the benefits inherent in a resource and on the relative permanence of those benefits if unassigned. Before a right can be admitted within the category of 'property' it must, according to Lord Wilberforce in *National Provincial Bank Ltd v Ainsworth*, be 'definable, identifiable by third parties, capable in its nature of assumption by third parties, and have some degree of permanence or stability'. This preoccupation with assignability of benefit and enforceability of burden doubtless owes much to the fact that the formative phases of the common law concept of property coincided with a remarkable culture of bargain and exchange. Non-transferable rights or rights which failed on transfer were simply not 'property'. Within the crucible of transfer lawyers affected to demarcate rights of 'property' from rights founded in contract and tort or, for that matter, from human rights and civil liberties. Only brief reflection is required in order to perceive the horrible circularity of such hallmarks of 'property'. If naively we ask which rights are proprietary, we are told that they are those rights which are assignable to and enforceable against third parties. When we then ask which rights these may be, we are told that they comprise, of course, the rights which are traditionally identified as 'proprietary'. 'Property' is 'property' because it is 'property': property status and proprietary consequence confuse each other in a deadening embrace of cause and effect.

Nor have the philosophers given significantly greater assistance in explaining the phenomenon of 'property'. Perhaps inevitably lawyers have concentrated their attention on locating the ownership of 'property', this task of identification assuming vital significance in a legal culture dominated by transfer and conveyance. By contrast philosophers have directed their efforts principally towards rationalising the institution of 'property'. While lawyers discuss who owns what, philosophers ask why anyone can legitimately claim to own anything. Justificatory theories of 'property' range diversely from appeals to the investment of labour or the existence of a social contract to arguments based upon first occupancy, utility or personhood. A pervasive influence in all philosophical thinking on 'property' is still the brooding omnipresence of John Locke. But Locke's concentration on original acquisition ill suits legal discourse in a modern world which is based on derivative acquisition and in which original acquisition (except perhaps in the area of intellectual property) is now virtually impossible. Even Locke himself cannot have believed that in late 17th century England the 'Commons' still contained many unappropriated acorns yet to be 'picket up under an Oak' or apples to be 'gathered from the Trees in the Wood', even if he did think that 'property' in such things was 'fixed' by the labour invested in their 'first gathering'. As Walton Hamilton noted much later, Locke's natural state is 'a curious affair, peopled with the Indians of North America and run by the scientific principles of his friend Sir Isaac Newton'.

In their respective preoccupations with resource allocation and institutional justification, lawyers and philosophers alike have largely failed to identify the characteristic hallmark of the common law notion of 'property'. If our own travels in search of 'property' have indicated one thing, it is that the criterion of 'excludability' gets us much closer to the core of 'property' than does the conventional legal emphasis on the assignability or enforceability of benefits. For 'property' resides not in consumption of benefits but in control over benefits. 'Property' is not about enjoyment of access but about control over access. 'Property' is the power-relation constituted by the state's endorsement of private claims to regulate the access of strangers to the benefits of particular resources. If, in respect of a given claimant and a given resource, the exercise of such regulatory control is physically impracticable or legally abortive or morally or socially undesirable, we say that such a claimant can assert no 'property' in that resource and for that matter can lose no 'property' in it either. Herein lies an important key to the 'propertiness' of property.

…

The concept of excludability thus takes us some way towards discovering a rationally defensible content in the term 'property'. The differentiation of excludable and non-excludable resources points up the irreducible elements which lie at the core of the 'property' notion. But these irreducibles, once isolated and identified, leave little if anything of value to be gathered from the traditional indicia of 'property'. The concept of excludability does not, of course, resolve entirely the issue of justice in holdings; it merely demarcates the categories of resource in which it is possible to claim 'property'. It sets outer limits on claims of 'property', but provides no criteria for justifying such claims on behalf of particular individuals—except to the extent that we accept the initially unpalatable (but historically attested) proposition that the sustained assertion of effective control over access to the benefits of a resource tends ultimately to be constitutive of 'property' in that resource. The precise allocation of 'property' in excludable resources is left to be determined—is indeed constantly formulated and reformulated—by various kinds of social and moral consensus over legitimate modes of acquisition and the relative priority of competing claims. This consensus is reinforced by a machinery of legal recognition and enforcement which thus adds or withholds the legitimacy of state sanction in relation to individual assertions of 'property'.

NOTES

1.   Something may be 'property' for some purposes but not others. For example, it may not be freely transferable, but nevertheless be susceptible to being held on trust (see, eg, *Swift v Dairywise Farms Ltd* [2000] 1 WLR 1177 (EU milk quota) and *Barbados Trust Co Ltd v Bank of Zambia* [2007] EWCA Civ 148, [2007] 2 All ER (Comm) 445 (bond transferable only in limited circumstances)).

2.   A vast literature on the meaning of 'property', and the justification of private property, has been produced by lawyers, philosophers, and political scientists: recent examples include J Waldron, *The Right to Private Property* (1990); JE Penner, *The Idea of Property in Law* (2000); JW Harris, *Property and Justice* (2002). You are encouraged to read K Gray, 'Equitable Property' (1994) 47 CLP 157.

QUESTIONS

1.   A buys a car from B. Can A exclude others from the car? What if the car had been stolen by B and the true owner wants it back? Does A have 'property' in the car? The sale of goods by a non-owner is considered below in Chapter 10.

2.   D owes £100 to C. Can C exclude others from the debt? If D erroneously pays the debt to E, the debt still exists and C continues to look to D for payment. Therefore, does C have 'property' in the debt? Should C perhaps be able to sue E on the ground that E has received payment on account of something 'belonging' to C? (Cf *Official Custodian of Charities v Mackey* [1985] 1 WLR 1308 at 1314–1315, per Nourse J.)

3.   It is illegal to engage in waste management in England without a licence from the Environment Agency. The licence once granted cannot be transferred. Is the licence nevertheless 'property'? Why might it matter? (See *Re Celtic Extraction Ltd (In Liquidation)* [2001] Ch 475.)

5   THE SIGNIFICANCE OF PROPERTY RIGHTS

'Ownership and Obligation in Commercial Transactions' by RM Goode
(1987) 103 LQR 433 at 433–435, 436–438

I INTRODUCTION

In common with other legal systems, English law sharply distinguishes property rights from mere personal rights to the delivery or transfer of an asset. I own property; I am owed performance of a transfer obligation. Ownership attracts several advantages, and some disadvantages, in law, and is frequently a condition precedent to the assertion of contractual rights. If I own an asset in the possession of another who becomes bankrupt, I can withdraw it from the reach of his creditors; if I am owed a purely personal obligation to transfer the asset to me I have no right to remove it from the common pool. As owner of a chattel I am entitled to a remedy in tort for negligence if it is carelessly damaged or destroyed by another. Ownership also carries with it a right to possession, where no one else has a better right, and is protected by the law of torts, in particular the tort of conversion. If I own goods, I bear the burden of accidental loss or damage. The transfer of ownership is in general a condition of the seller's right to sue for the price under a contract of sale of goods; and the acquisition of ownership is a prerequisite to certain statutory transfers of contractual rights, such as the transfer of the shipper's rights under a bill of lading to a consignee or indorsee under section 1 of the Bills of Lading Act 1855 [since replaced by s 2 of the Carriage of Goods by Sea Act 1992] . . .

II OWNERSHIP IN INSOLVENCY

(i) Practical importance of the question

In the commercial world the distinction between ownership of an asset and a purely personal right to acquire an asset, eg under a contract, is usually of little significance so long as the debtor is traceable and solvent, for the interest of a commercial creditor in the performance of a transfer undertaking is usually monetary rather than in ownership for its own sake, and if the debtor (using this term in the broad sense of an obligor) fails to deliver then the creditor can simply obtain what is due to him, either in cash or in kind, by suing for it and enforcing any resulting judgment.

It is upon the debtor's insolvency that the distinction between ownership and a personal right to an asset becomes of crucial significance, for it is a basic policy of insolvency law to adopt the non-bankruptcy ordering of rights and thus to respect proprietary rights held by another prior to the debtor's bankruptcy. Hence in principle the estate available for distribution among the general body of creditors is limited to the debtor's own assets. Owners and secured creditors can withdraw from the pool the assets they own or over which they have security, whilst unsecured creditors are left to prove in competition with each other for such crumbs as remain after proprietary rights, the expenses of the insolvency proceedings and the claims of preferential creditors have been satisfied.

It follows that the degree in which the law is willing to recognise rights as proprietary rather than merely personal is of great moment to unsecured creditors, for every extension of the concept of ownership erodes the debtor's estate and thus reduces the significance of the hallowed principle of pari passu distribution. Conversely, every condition precedent attached by the law to the acquisition of ownership represents a pitfall for the would-be investor and the would-be secured creditor who lays out his money in the expectation of receiving in exchange some proprietary interest in the debtor's patrimony . . .

(iii) The growth of equitable property rights

Property and obligation at law

The common law (in its narrow sense) sharply distinguished transfers of property from mere personal undertakings. A transfer from A to B had to relate to an existing asset in which A had a subsisting interest, and the transfer itself had to be in proper form. Except in the case of a contract for the sale of existing goods, where the agreement was effective by itself to transfer title, an agreement for transfer conferred no proprietary rights on the intended transferee even if he had parted with his money. A purported transfer by A to B of A's after-acquired property was at best a contract and could not of itself operate to vest the property in B even after A had acquired it; a new act of transfer was necessary after the acquisition. Similarly, a transfer by A to C to hold on trust for B conferred no interest on B, for the conveyance was not made to him.

These common law rules still apply in relation to the transfer of a legal title, save for the special case of contracts of sale of goods, in relation to which the Sale of Goods Act prescribes the automatic transfer of title to future goods upon their acquisition by the seller, if the parties so agree.

Property and obligation in equity

Under the influence of equity the distinction between property rights in an asset and personal rights to an asset became blurred. Acting on the basis that equity treats as done that which ought to be done, courts of equity came to regard an unperfected agreement to assign as an assignment which became perfected by payment of the consideration; they upheld the assignment of future property as effective on acquisition by the debtor without the need for any new act of transfer; they recognised the interest of the beneficiary under a passive trust as a proprietary interest; and they accorded proprietary status to the right of an owner of an asset to trace the products and proceeds of dispositions by the owner's bailee.

Even after all this the ingenuity of the equity lawyers was not exhausted. A person might succeed to a claim by assignment or by subrogation. Equity also came to recognise the existence of proprietary rights not in a specific asset but in a shifting fund of assets, as exemplified by the interest of the beneficiary under an active trust and of a debenture holder under a floating charge, and these interests became included in the category of proprietary rights having priority over the claims of unsecured creditors.

The development of the resulting trust and the constructive trust led to the recognition of proprietary rights in a variety of situations in which one person improperly held assets or benefits to which another had a better right. Among the events that have been held to attract these forms of trust are the payment of money for a purpose which has failed, the payment of money under a mistake of fact and the acquisition of an asset by the defendant from a third party, or the retention of such an asset, in breach of the defendant's fiduciary duty to the plaintiff.

Finally, even a 'mere equity,' such as a right to rescind (eg for fraud or misrepresentation) a contract under which the bankrupt acquired an asset can be asserted against his trustee, thus removing the asset from the general body of creditors even after the commencement of bankruptcy.

The result of this equitable development is that most obligations owed by B to A to transfer an asset to A are proprietary in nature rather than merely personal, though often A has a personal right to the asset running concurrently with his proprietary interest in it. It is unusual to find a situation in which B has a duty to make over to A an asset still in B's hands without A thereby enjoying equitable ownership of the asset. In equity, the obligation to transfer, whatever its source, is itself a transfer provided that the obligation is not merely contingent, the subject-matter is identifiable and the consideration is in due course paid. The one outstanding exception to this rule is the contract of sale of goods, where the buyer either acquires legal title or acquires nothing beyond a mere contract right. This exception reflects not only the universality of the contract of sale of goods, which makes it undesirable to complicate the contract by equitable ownership, but the fact that under a contract of sale title passes by agreement, and except where this is reserved to secure payment a seller who has not reached the stage of passing legal title usually intends to reserve a right to dispose of the goods elsewhere.

NOTES

1.   The rule that only someone with a proprietary right can sue in tort is illustrated by *Leigh & Sillivan Ltd v Aliakmon Shipping Co Ltd, The Aliakmon* [1986] AC 785. Carriers negligently damaged steel coils which shippers had agreed to sell to buyers, at a time when the buyers bore the risk of damage but had not yet become owners. The buyers' action in tort failed (today they would have a statutory contract claim— see the Carriage of Goods by Sea Act

1992, s 2(1)—but that is by the by). Lord Brandon, with whose speech all their Lordships agreed, stated (at 809) that:

> . . . there is a long line of authority for a principle of law that, in order to enable a person to claim in negligence for loss caused to him by reason of loss of or damage to property, he must have had either the legal ownership of or a possessory title to the property concerned at the time the loss or damage occurred, and it is not enough for him to have only had contractual rights in relation to such property which have been adversely affected by the loss of or damage to it.

2. A property right binds third parties generally. If A Ltd sells fuel to B Ltd, reserving title to it until paid, and B transfers it to C Ltd before it has paid A, A's rights in the fuel remain and hence A can demand that C account to A unless C is protected by an exception to the rule *nemo dat quod non habet* (on which, see below, p 412): see, eg, *The Saetta* [1994] 1 WLR 1334. Again, if A leases a chattel from B it seems that he obtains a proprietary right in it; hence if B sells the chattel to C, C must respect A's right as lessee. See Robert Walker LJ in *On Demand Information Plc v Michael Gerson (Finance) Plc* [2001] 1 WLR 155 at 171: 'Contractual rights which entitle the hirer to indefinite possession of chattels so long as the hire payments are duly made, and which qualify and limit the owner's general property in the chattels, cannot aptly be described as purely contractual rights.' (The decision was later reversed in the House of Lords, but on unrelated grounds: *On Demand Information Plc v Michael Gerson (Finance) Plc* [2002] UKHL 13, [2003] 1 AC 368). By contrast, a mere obligation binds only the parties to it. So if B undertakes a personal contractual obligation towards A to use an asset in a particular way for A's benefit, but then sells it to C, C and later purchasers are generally free to use it as they wish without regard to A's rights (eg *Law Debenture Trust Corpn v Ural Caspian Oil Corpn Ltd* [1995] Ch 152).

3. Nevertheless there are a few cases of commercial significance where even a third party may be held liable for interfering with the performance of obligations. Two are well established. One is the rule that if C knowingly induces B to break his obligations to A—for example, by buying property from B in the knowledge that B has contracted to sell to A exclusively—he will be liable to A (eg *British Motor Trade Association v Salvadori* [1949] Ch 556). Such liability depends on the purchaser intending to induce the breach (see *OBG Ltd v Allan* [2007] UKHL 21, [2008] 1 AC 1 at [8] and [62], per Lord Hoffmann). Secondly, C will be liable if he uses unlawful means with intent to prevent B performing his obligation to A—for example, by deceiving a manufacturer's distributor into supplying goods to non-authorised buyers. (See *National Phonograph Co Ltd v Edison-Bell Consolidated Phonograph Co Ltd* [1908] 1 Ch 335; *OBG Ltd v Allan* [2007] UKHL 21, [2008] 1 AC 1 at [45]–[64], per Lord Hoffmann.)

4. In addition, there is a line of authority which suggests that, in certain circumstances, an agreement by A to use personal property for the benefit of B—for example, an agreement to time-charter a ship—may of itself limit the right of a third party purchaser C to do as he wishes with the asset concerned, even in the absence of any intent to harm the claimant. In *De Mattos v Gibson* (1858) 4 De G & J 276, the owner of a ship time-chartered it and then mortgaged it; the mortgagee was aware of the charterparty. The mortgagee sought to sell the ship without regard to the charterer's rights to its use. The charterer successfully obtained an interlocutory injunction. Knight Bruce LJ said (at 282):

> Reason and justice seem to prescribe that, at least as a general rule, where a man, by gift or purchase, acquires property from another, with knowledge of a previous contract, lawfully and for valuable consideration made by him with a third person, to use and employ the property for

> a particular purpose in a specified manner, the acquirer shall not, to the material damage of the third person, in opposition to the contract and inconsistently with it, use and employ the property in a manner not allowable to the giver or seller. This rule, applicable alike in general as I conceive to moveable and immoveable property, and recognized and adopted, as I apprehend, by the English law, may, like other general rules, be liable to exceptions arising from special circumstances; but I see at present no room for any exception in the instance before us.

At the full hearing, Lord Chelmsford refused the injunction for other reasons. Seventy years later the Privy Council in *Lord Strathcona Steamship Co Ltd v Dominion Coal Co* [1926] AC 108 similarly restrained the purchaser of a ship from using it inconsistently with a time charter granted by the previous owner. But the existence of any such principle as enunciated by Knight Bruce LJ is doubtful. Diplock J in *Port Line Ltd v Ben Line Steamers Ltd* [1958] 2 QB 146 thought the *Strathcona* case wrongly decided. Although in *Swiss Bank Corpn v Lloyds Bank Ltd* [1979] Ch 548 (reversed on other grounds [1982] AC 584), Browne-Wilkinson J thought the *De Mattos* principle represented good law and explained it in terms of the equitable counterpart of the tort of knowing interference with contractual rights (which is wrong as the two are doctrinally distinct and subject to different requirements: see A Tettenborn [1982] CLJ 58 at 82–83), Hoffmann J in *Law Debenture Trust Corpn plc v Ural Caspian Oil Corpn Ltd* [1993] 1 WLR 138 at 144 (affirmed on other grounds [1995] Ch 152), thought that it permitted 'no more than the grant of a negative injunction to restrain the third party from doing acts which would be inconsistent with performance of the contract by the original contracting party'. In short, the *De Mattos* principle is surrounded by confusion and uncertainty. See A Tettenborn, 'Covenants, Privity of Contract, and the Purchaser of Personal Property' [1982] CLJ 58 and A Clarke, '*De Mattos v Gibson* Again' [1992] LMCLQ 448.

QUESTION

In *Re Bank of Credit & Commerce International SA (No 8)* [1998] AC 214 (see below, p 972), where the House of Lords indicated that it was conceptually possible for a bank to take a charge over its own indebtedness to one of its customers, Lord Hoffmann described a 'proprietary interest' in terms of anything which is binding on an assignee or a liquidator or trustee in bankruptcy (at 227). Was he right to do so? See R Goode, 'Charge-Backs and Legal Fictions' (1998) 114 LQR 178 at 179.

6 TYPES OF PROPERTY RIGHTS IN CHATTELS

English law recognises only two types of property rights over chattels at common law: (1) ownership, and (2) possession for a limited interest, including liens (below, p 1040), bailments (Chapter 3), and rights arising under pledges (below, p 1024). All other rights exist only in equity, for example the rights of a beneficiary under a trust, mere charges (see below, p 1068), non-possessory liens (below, p 1077), and a mortgagor's right of redemption (below, p 1064).

As a general rule, all these rights display the two traditional characteristics of property rights: they are assignable, and they are enforceable against third parties. But this may not always be the case. For example, in certain circumstances common law property rights may be overridden; furthermore, equitable rights may be defeated by a bona fide purchaser for value without notice in the case of personal property in commercial circulation as much as with land (*MCC Proceeds Inc v Lehman Brothers International (Europe) Ltd* [1998] 4 All ER 675). This confirms what we have already noted: namely, that property rights are relative, and not absolute.

7 OWNERSHIP OF CHATTELS

Honoré defines ownership 'as the *greatest possible interest in a thing which a mature system of law recognizes*' (AM Honoré, 'Ownership' in AG Guest (ed), *Oxford Essays in Jurisprudence* (1961), p 108, his emphasis). Ownership carries with it a bundle of rights, and some obligations, which Honoré describes as the 'standard incidents of ownership' and which he lists (at p 113) as follows: 'the right to possess, the right to use, the right to manage, the right to the income of the thing, the right to the capital, the right to security, the rights or incidents of transmissibility and absence of term, the prohibition of harmful use, liability to execution, and the incident of residuarity'. For criticism of Honoré's analysis, see P Eleftheriadis, 'The Analysis of Property Rights' (1996) 16 OJLS 31.

Residuarity is the vital feature here. A person can be described as 'owner' even though the other listed incidents of ownership are not present. A caterpillar tractor belonging to an equipment leasing company A, for example, may be subject to a charge to a bank B which has extensive rights to control dealings with it, and at the same time leased out to a lessee C which has the right to its physical use. Nevertheless A indubitably remains the owner, since it is A's right that will remain even if the charge is paid off and the lease comes to an end, thus eliminating the rights of B and C. In essence, therefore, ownership is the residue of legal rights in an asset left in a person after lesser rights have been granted to others (Honoré, pp 126–128).

(a) Legal and equitable ownership

In many commercial contexts we are simply concerned with outright legal ownership, where no issue of equitable rights arises. Such ownership is normally in one person alone, but may also be shared concurrently between two or more. However, it is not possible for legal ownership of a chattel to be split in the sense that a smaller legal interest is carved out of it. This is why an *agreement* by which a chattel is let on lease or rental confers no legal—or equitable[4]—interest on the lessee: only on taking delivery does the lessee acquire a limited legal interest in the chattel by virtue of his *possession*.

Alternatively, legal ownership may be vested in one person and equitable ownership vested in another, as where A (legal owner) holds goods or securities on trust for B (equitable owner). Furthermore, equitable interests are not subject to the same restrictions as legal interests on the types of interest that may be created. Provided it is sufficiently certain, almost any right

---

[4] The view of Browne-Wilkinson V-C in *Bristol Airport plc v Powdrill* [1990] Ch 744 at 759, that the right of a lessee to delivery of possession of an aircraft under a chattel lease constituted 'property' for the purposes of s 436 of the Insolvency Act 1986, on the ground that 'the "lessee" has at least an equitable right of some kind in that aircraft', cannot easily be reconciled with these basic principles of personal property law. See criticisms of RM Goode, *Principles of Corporate Insolvency Law* (4th edn, 2011), 11–60.

over personal property can be created that human ingenuity can conceive. It follows that while lesser interests such as usufructs recognised in European civil law jurisdictions cannot exist at common law, they can still in English law be created in equity.

(b) Interest and title

> A person's interest in an asset denotes the quantum of rights over it which he enjoys against other persons, though not necessarily against all other persons. His title measures the strength of the interest he enjoys in relation to others . . .
>
> (Goode, para 2.21)

Both the true owner of an asset and the person who is in possession of it *animo domini* (ie with the intent of exercising the rights of an owner over it) have an independent legal *interest* in the asset. Each has title to the absolute interest in the asset and each may assert his interest against a third party, so long as the third party does not have a better title. However, as against each other, the true owner has an *absolute* (or indefeasible) title to the asset and the possessor only a *relative* title. The possessor may not assert his title against the true owner, nor anyone deriving title from him or acting with his authority. It is also possible in some cases for a third party to defend an action for wrongful interference brought by someone with a possessory title on the ground that the claimant is not the true owner (Torts (Interference with Goods) Act 1977, s 8(1): see below, p 75).

The concept of relativity of title also applies to equitable interests. But it should be noted that an equitable interest is also liable to be overridden by a transfer of the legal interest to a bona fide purchaser for value without notice. See generally, D Fox, 'Relativity of Title at Law and in Equity' [2006] CLJ 330, and, especially, at pp 351–361, on the relativity of equitable titles.

(c) Co-ownership

Personal property may be the subject of co-ownership at law and in equity. Although legal ownership is otherwise indivisible (see above), two or more persons may be the legal co-owners of a chattel as joint tenants or as tenants in common. If co-owners are joint tenants and one dies, his share passes to the others by survivorship; but in the case of tenants in common, the deceased's share forms part of his estate and passes under his will or on his intestacy. The former is rare in the commercial context, except in the case of trustees; the latter is more frequent. Such co-ownership can happen where two investors (for example) are co-proprietors of a racehorse. More topically, it also arises where the owner of goods in bulk (eg a ship-load of soya beans) sells an undivided part of that bulk to a buyer who pays for it: see s 20A of the Sale of Goods Act 1979 (below, p 335); and where chattels belonging to two owners are mixed to form an indistinguishable mass. Examples of the latter are *Re Stapylton Fletcher Ltd* [1994] 1 WLR 1181, where a wine merchant who segregated wine purchased by customers from his own trading stock and stored it in composite stacks was held to have constituted the customers tenants in common; and *Mercer v Craven Grain Storage Ltd* [1994] CLC 328, where, in the case of grain deposited by farmers with a grain storage company in a common stock, it was held that all the farmers were tenants in common of the commingled mass.

8 ACQUISITION AND TRANSFER OF LEGAL AND EQUITABLE OWNERSHIP IN CHATTELS

(a) Legal ownership

Legal ownership in chattels may be acquired by any of the following means.

(1) By taking possession of an existing thing which does not have an owner. One example is taking possession of a wild animal or bird; a more commercial and contemporary one is taking air from the atmosphere with a view to manufacturing compressed oxygen from it.

(2) By bringing a new thing into existence. This mode of acquisition of legal ownership is particularly relevant where goods are manufactured from raw materials: for example, carpets from fibre, or soft drinks from water and flavouring. Prima facie, the manufacturer will be the legal owner of the newly manufactured product. However, the position is complicated where the manufacturer has made the new product from material supplied under a contract of sale which reserves ownership of the material in the supplier until payment. Such reservation of title clauses may even purport to claim ownership of the finished product. Further difficulties arise where the finished product is manufactured from material supplied by different suppliers each relying on their own reservation of title clause to claim ownership of the finished product. These issues are fully explored below, at pp 508–512.

(3) Most importantly, by consensual transfer of a thing from the existing owner: in the case of chattels, by gift, sale, or exchange. The typical form of transfer in the commercial world is by sale. At common law, where there is a contract of sale, ownership may be transferred by mere agreement (see now Sale of Goods Act, ss 17, 18; below, p 337). At common law it was probably impossible to give effect to an agreement to transfer after-acquired property (ie property which the transferor did not yet own or possess); there had to be some new act of transfer after the property had been acquired (*Lunn v Thornton* (1845) 1 CB 379). But today, in the case of contracts for the sale of goods, ownership of future goods will automatically transfer to the buyer when those goods have been acquired by the seller, if the parties have so agreed (Sale of Goods Act 1979, ss 2(5), (6), 5(1)). In the case of transfers not by sale, for example by gift or exchange, the rules are by contrast much stricter. The transfer must be effected by the delivery of possession or by a deed, and there must be an intention to make a present, not future, transfer of ownership (see Goode, paras 2.30–2.31).

(4) By transfer which overrides the rights of the existing owner. The general rule is *nemo dat quod non habet*. However, there are exceptions to the *nemo dat* rule which allow A to transfer to B a good title to C's goods without the latter's consent. The rule and its exceptions are considered below in Chapter 10.

(5) By operation of law when goods become fixtures or accessions or through confusion or commingling. See PBH Birks, 'Mixtures' and H Bennett, 'Attachment of Chattels to Land' in N Palmer and E McKendrick (eds), *Interests in Goods* (2nd edn, 1998), Chs 9 and 11 respectively.

(6) By operation of law on death or insolvency (see Bell, Chs 17, 18).

(b) Equitable ownership

Equitable ownership of chattels may be acquired either by a transaction whose effect is to create a new equitable interest, or by transfer of an existing equitable interest.

A new equitable interest in goods may be created by any one of the following means.

(1) By declaration of trust. The owner of an asset either declares himself to hold it on trust for the transferee, or transfers it at law to a third party to hold on trust for the transferee.

(2) By an agreement to transfer legal ownership (see generally *Holroyd v Marshall* (1862) 10 HLC 191 at 209, per Lord Westbury). This only applies, however, if the agreement is on principle specifically enforceable, since the transferee's equitable title arises by virtue of the rule that equity regards as done that which ought to have been done. As a result the rule does not apply to sales of ordinary commercial chattels: *Re Wait* [1927] 1 Ch 606. The conditions which must exist for such a transfer to operate are that the obligation is not merely contingent; that the subject matter is identifiable; and that the consideration is in due course paid. The intended transferee cannot assert an inchoate interest against the intended transferor or third parties until he pays the price and converts that interest into full equitable ownership, which is then deemed to relate back to the time the agreement was made (RM Goode, 'Ownership and Obligation in Commercial Transactions' (1987) 103 LQR 433 at 437, fn; *Lysaght v Edwards* (1876) 2 Ch D 499; *Rayner v Preston* (1881) 18 Ch D 1). Similarly, when there has been an agreement to transfer an after-acquired asset, the transferee has an inchoate interest which attaches to the asset when it is acquired by the transferor with effect from the date of the agreement (*Holroyd v Marshall* (1862) 10 HLC 191, above; cf *Tailby v Official Receiver* (1888) 13 App Cas 523, below, p 961).

(3) By a purported present transfer of an after-acquired asset for value, assuming the contract is susceptible of specific performance. Even if the Sale of Goods Act does not apply, once the asset is acquired the equitable interest will vest in the transferee. See *Holroyd v Marshall* (1862) 10 HLC 191 at 211, per Lord Westbury.

An existing equitable interest in goods may be transferred by written assignment or declaration of trust (for the requirement of writing, see the Law of Property Act 1925, s 53(1)(c).

9 POSSESSION OF CHATTELS

An Essay on Possession in the Common Law by F Pollock and RS Wright
(1888), pp 26–28

THE NATURE OF POSSESSION

Throughout our inquiry we have to bear in mind that the following elements are quite distinct in conception, and, though very often found in combination, are also separable and often separated in practice. They are

i. Physical control, detention, or *de facto* possession. This, as an actual relation between a person and a thing, is matter of fact. Nevertheless questions which the Court must decide as matter of law arise as to the proof of the facts.

ii. Legal possession, the state of being a possessor in the eye of the law. This is a definite legal relation of the possessor to the thing possessed. In its most normal and obvious form, it coexists with the fact of physical control, and with other facts making the exercise of that control rightful. But it may exist either with or without detention, and either with or without a rightful origin.

A tailor sends to JS's house a coat which JS has ordered. JS puts on the coat, and then has both physical control and rightful possession in law.

JS takes off the coat and gives it to a servant to take back to the tailor for some alterations. Now the servant has physical control (in this connexion generally called 'custody' by our authorities) and JS still has the possession in law.

While the servant is going on his errand, Z assaults him and robs him of the coat. Z is not only physically master of the coat, but, so soon as he has complete control of it, he has possession in law, though a wrongful possession. To see what is left to JS we must look to the next head.

iii. Right to possess or to have legal possession. This includes the right to physical possession. It can exist apart from both physical and legal possession; it is, for example, that which remains to a rightful possessor immediately after he has been wrongfully dispossessed. It is a normal incident of ownership or property, and the name of 'property' is often given to it. Unlike possession itself, it is not necessarily exclusive. A may have the right to possess a thing as against B and every one else, while B has at the same time a right to possess it as against every one except A. So joint tenants have both single possession and a single joint right to possess, but tenants in common have a single possession with several rights to possess. When a person having right to possess a thing acquires the physical control of it, he necessarily acquires legal possession also.

Right to possess, when separated from possession, is often called 'constructive possession'. The correct use of the term would seem to be coextensive with and limited to those cases where a person entitled to possess is (or was) allowed the same remedies as if he had really been in possession. But it is also sometimes specially applied to the cases where the legal possession is with one person and the custody with his servant, or some other person for the time being in a like position; and sometimes it is extended to other cases where legal possession is separated from detention.

'Actual possession' as opposed to 'constructive possession' is in the same way an ambiguous term. It is most commonly used to signify physical control, with or without possession in law. 'Bare possession' is sometimes used with the same meaning. 'Lawful possession' means a legal possession which is also rightful or at least excusable; this may be consistent with a superior right to possess in some other person.

The whole terminology of the subject, however, is still very loose and unsettled in the books, and the reader cannot be too strongly warned that careful attention must in every case be paid to the context.

NOTES

1. In *United States of America & Republic of France v Dollfus Mieg et Cie SA and Bank of England* [1952] AC 582 at 605, Earl Jowitt observed that 'English law has never worked out a completely logical and exhaustive definition of possession'. As Andrew Bell explains (Bell, p 34):

> The truth is that 'possession' has no single meaning: it is used in different senses in different contexts. This is perfectly reasonable, for the essence of possession is control, but the degree of control required for a particular rule will depend on the purpose of that rule. This flexibility has its price, however, the price of uncertainty.

Despite the fact that many eminent jurists have expended much energy developing various theories to explain the concept of possession (see, eg, DR Harris, 'The Concept of Possession in English Law' in AG Guest (ed), *Oxford Essays in Jurisprudence* (1961), Ch 4; and see, generally, RWM Dias, *Jurisprudence* (5th edn, 1985), Ch 13), the subject remains an enigma. It lacks even an agreed terminology to explain the various forms of possession. The warning given by Pollock and Wright at the end of the extract (above) remains as relevant today as it was in 1888.

2. (a) *De facto possession* Physical control of a chattel may not create possession in law. To constitute possession in law, physical control must be coupled with an intention to exclude others. As Pollock and Wright observe (at p 20): 'Possession in fact, with the manifest intent of sole and exclusive dominion, always imports possession in law.' Control in fact may be acquired by taking physical possession of the chattel itself or possession of an object which gives physical control of the chattel, for example the key or swipe card, or possibly a PIN number, granting access to the warehouse in which the chattel is stored (possession of a key to a container or to a building has been variously described by the courts as giving 'actual', 'constructive', or 'symbolic' possession of the chattels contained therein: see below, pp 77–78). The degree of control necessary to acquire possession will be relative to the nature of the chattel. For example, in *The Tubantia* [1924] P 78, the plaintiffs carried out salvage work on a wreck lying in 100 feet of water in the North Sea. They had cut a hole into a hold, buoyed the wreck, and recovered some of the cargo when the defendants, a rival salvage company, interrupted their work. Sir Henry Drake P held that the plaintiffs had possession of the wreck and were entitled to an injunction and damages against the defendants for trespass. Although the plaintiffs had only been able to work on the wreck for short periods, with long interruptions because of the weather, the President was satisfied that '[t]here was the use and occupation of which the subject matter was capable'. Finally, it should be noted that the degree of control needed to acquire possession may not have to be maintained for possession to continue (see, eg, Bridge, pp 33–34; Bell, pp 35–36). Once acquired, possession is deemed to continue unless it is acquired by someone else or it is abandoned (Harris, op cit, p 73).

(b) *Legal possession* In the examples given by Pollock and Wright, JS has legal possession of the coat when he has both ownership and physical control of it. JS maintains legal possession when he gives up physical control to his employee (servant). The employee does not acquire legal possession of the coat because although he has physical control (or custody) of it, he does not have the necessary intention to control. However, if the employee took possession of the coat for a limited interest of his own, for example as a pledge for unpaid wages, he would acquire legal possession of it. As possession is indivisible, JS would have lost legal possession to the employee taking possession for a limited interest. Similarly, Z, the thief, acquires legal possession of the coat, and JS loses such possession, when he steals it from the employee. However, Z holds possession with the intention of asserting ownership rights. Therefore, Z's possession *animo domini* gives him an absolute legal interest in and a relative title to the coat. (See above, p 67; also L Tan, *Personal Property Law* (2014), para 3.006).

The question of the employee's possession (or lack of it) may have practical implications. Suppose an employee of a security company receives a parcel of diamonds in the course of his employment for loading onto a secure van, but negligently loses them before they can be loaded. Because he has no possession, he cannot be held personally liable as bailee to the owner of the diamonds: the latter can only sue the employers. See the colourful old stage-coach case of *Cavenagh v Such* (1815) 1 Price 328.

(c) *Right to possess or to have legal possession* Where a bailee holds possession of a chattel for his own interest, for example as a pledgee, the bailor maintains a right to possess but he does not have legal possession of the chattel (see Pollock and Wright, op cit, p 20). Like ownership, possession is indivisible and can only be held and transferred entire. But where the bailee holds possession for the bailor's interest, as in the case of a warehouse-man holding property to the bailor's order, the bailor and bailee will share legal possession and the bailor may be said to have constructive possession of the chattel (see *City Fur*

Manufacturing Co Ltd v Fureenbond (Brokers) London Ltd [1937] 1 All ER 799 at 802, per Branson J).

Constructive possession may even operate in favour of a person with a mere possessory title. For example, in *Wilson v Lombank Ltd* [1963] 1 All ER 740, W purchased a car from someone who had no title to sell. W took the car to a garage for repairs. The repairs were completed but whilst the car was awaiting collection a representative of L Ltd (who were not the true owners of the car) removed it from the garage in error. Hinchcliffe J held that W was in possession of the car and could sue L Ltd for trespass. W had a possessory title to the car which the garage held as bailees at will. Therefore, W had constructive possession of the car when it was in the actual possession of the garage. See also *United States of America & Republic of France v Dollfus Mieg et Cie SA and Bank of England* [1952] AC 582 at 611, per Lord Porter.

3. In cases of doubt over who has possession of property, for example when the property is on premises which are jointly occupied, the owner is presumed to be the person in possession of it (*Ramsay v Margrett* [1894] 2 QB 18; *French v Gething* [1922] 1 KB 236).

10 THE PROTECTION OF POSSESSION

The Winkfield

[1902] P 42, Court of Appeal

The facts appear from Collins MR's judgment.

> **Collins MR:** This is an appeal from the order of Sir Francis Jeune dismissing a motion made on behalf of the Postmaster-General in the case of *The Winkfield*.
>
> The question arises out of a collision which occurred on April 5, 1900, between the steamship *Mexican* and the steamship *Winkfield*, and which resulted in the loss of the former with a portion of the mails which she was carrying at the time.
>
> The owners of the *Winkfield* under a decree limiting liability to £32,514 17s 10d (£32,514.89) paid that amount into court, and the claim in question was one by the Postmaster-General on behalf of himself and the Postmasters-General of Cape Colony and Natal to recover out of that sum the value of letters, parcels, etc, in his custody as bailee and lost on board the *Mexican*.
>
> The case was dealt with by all parties in the Court below as a claim by a bailee who was under no liability to his bailor for the loss in question, as to which it was admitted that the authority of *Claridge v South Staffordshire Tramway Co* ([1892] 1 QB 422) was conclusive, and the President accordingly, without argument and in deference to that authority, dismissed the claim. The Postmaster-General now appeals.
>
> The question for decision, therefore, is whether *Claridge*'s case was well decided. I emphasize this because it disposes of a point which was faintly suggested by the respondents, and which, if good, would distinguish *Claridge*'s case, namely, that the applicant was not himself in actual occupation of the things bailed at the time of the loss. This point was not taken below, and having regard to the course followed by all parties on the hearing of the motion, I think it is not open to the respondents to make it now, and I therefore deal with the case upon the footing upon which it was dealt with on the motion, namely, that it is covered by *Claridge*'s case. I assume, therefore, that the subject-matter of the bailment was in the custody of the Postmaster-General as bailee at the time of the accident. For the reasons which I am about to state I am of opinion

that *Claridge*'s case was wrongly decided, and that the law is that in an action against a stranger for loss of goods caused by his negligence, the bailee in possession can recover the value of the goods, although he would have had a good answer to an action by the bailor for damages for the loss of the thing bailed.

It seems to me that the position, that possession is good against a wrongdoer and that the latter cannot set up the *jus tertii* unless he claims under it, is well established in our law, and really concludes this case against the respondents. As I shall shew presently, a long series of authorities establishes this in actions of trover and trespass at the suit of a possessor. And the principle being the same, it follows that he can equally recover the whole value of the goods in an action on the case for their loss through the tortious conduct of the defendant. I think it involves this also, that the wrongdoer who is not defending under the title of the bailor is quite unconcerned with what the rights are between the bailor and bailee, and must treat the possessor as the owner of the goods for all purposes quite irrespective of the rights and obligations as between him and the bailor.

I think this position is well established in our law, though it may be that reasons for its existence have been given in some of the cases which are not quite satisfactory. I think also that the obligation of the bailee to the bailor to account for what he has received in respect of the destruction or conversion of the thing bailed has been admitted so often in decided cases that it cannot now be questioned; and, further, I think it can be shewn that the right of the bailee to recover cannot be rested on the ground suggested in some of the cases, namely, that he was liable over to the bailor for the loss of the goods converted or destroyed. It cannot be denied that since the case of *Armory v Delamirie* ((1722) 1 Stra 505), not to mention earlier cases from the Year Books onward, a mere finder may recover against a wrongdoer the full value of the thing converted. That decision involves the principle that as between possessor and wrongdoer the presumption of law is, in the words of Lord Campbell in *Jeffries v Great Western Rly Co* ((1856) 5 E & B 802,806), 'that the person who has possession has the property.' In the same case he says: 'I am of opinion that the law is that a person possessed of goods as his property has a good title as against every stranger, and that one who takes them from him, having no title in himself, is a wrongdoer, and cannot defend himself by shewing that there was title in some third person, for *against a wrongdoer possession is title*. The law is so stated by the very learned annotator in his note to *Wilbraham v Snow* ((1670) 2 Wms Saund 47f).' Therefore it is not open to the defendant, being a wrongdoer, to inquire into the nature or limitation of the possessor's right, and unless it is competent for him to do so the question of his relation to, or liability towards, the true owner cannot come into the discussion at all; and, therefore, as between those two parties full damages have to be paid without any further inquiry. The extent of the liability of the finder to the true owner not being relevant to the discussion between him and the wrongdoer, the facts which would ascertain it would not have been admissible in evidence, and therefore the right of the finder to recover full damages cannot be made to depend upon the extent of his liability over to the true owner. To hold otherwise would, it seems to me, be in effect to permit a wrongdoer to set up a *jus tertii* under which he cannot claim. But, if this be the fact in the case of a finder, why should it not be equally the fact in the case of a bailee? Why, as against a wrongdoer, should the nature of the plaintiff's interest in the thing converted be any more relevant to the inquiry, and therefore admissible in evidence, than in the case of a finder? It seems to me that neither in one case nor the other ought it to be competent for the defendant to go into evidence on that matter.

[His Lordship then reviewed several cases showing that a bailee had an unqualified right to sue the wrongdoer. He continued:]

The ground of the decision in *Claridge*'s case was that the plaintiff in that case, being under no liability to his bailor, could recover no damages, and though for the reasons I have already given I think this position is untenable, it is necessary to follow it out a little further....

Holmes CJ in his admirable lectures on the Common Law, in the chapter devoted to bailments, traces the origin of the bailee's right to sue and recover the whole value of chattels converted, and arrives at the clear conclusion that the bailee's obligation to account arose from the fact that he was originally the only person who could sue, though afterwards by an extension, not perhaps quite logical, the right to sue was conceded to the bailor also. He says at p 167: 'At first the bailee was answerable to the owner because he was the only person who could sue; now it was said he could sue because he was answerable to the owner.' And again at p 170: 'The inverted explanation of Beaumanoir will be remembered, that the bailee could sue because he was answerable over, in place of the original rule that he was answerable over so strictly because only he could sue.' ... But long after the decision of *Coggs v Bernard*, which classified the obligations of bailees, the bailee has, nevertheless, been allowed to recover full damages against a wrongdoer, where the facts would have afforded a complete answer for him against his bailor. The cases above cited are instances of this. In each of them the bailee would have had a good answer to an action by his bailor; for in none of them was it suggested that the act of the wrongdoer was traceable to negligence on the part of the bailee. I think, therefore, that the statement drawn, as I have said, from the Year Books may be explained, as Holmes CJ explains it, but whether that be the true view of it or not, it is clear that it has not been treated as law in our Courts . . . . Therefore, as I said at the outset, and as I think I have now shewn by authority, the root principle of the whole discussion is that, as against a wrongdoer, possession is title. The chattel that has been converted or damaged is deemed to be the chattel of the possessor and of no other, and therefore its loss or deterioration is his loss, and to him, if he demands it, it must be recouped. His obligation to account to the bailor is really not ad rem in the discussion. It only comes in after he has carried his legal position to its logical consequence against a wrongdoer, and serves to soothe a mind disconcerted by the notion that a person who is not himself the complete owner should be entitled to receive back the full value of the chattel converted or destroyed. There is no inconsistency between the two positions; the one is the complement of the other. As between bailee and stranger possession gives title—that is, not a limited interest, but absolute and complete ownership, and he is entitled to receive back a complete equivalent for the whole loss or deterioration of the thing itself. As between bailor and bailee the real interests of each must be inquired into, and, as the bailee has to account for the thing bailed, so he must account for that which has become its equivalent and now represents it. What he has received above his own interest he has received to the use of his bailor. The wrongdoer, having once paid full damages to the bailee, has an answer to any action by the bailor.

[**Stirling** and **Mathew LJJ** concurred.]

NOTES

1. This case shows that possession (there a bailee's possession) is sufficient to meet the requirement that a claimant in an action for trespass or conversion must have been in possession of the chattel at the time of the interference alleged against the wrongdoer. Despite having only a limited interest in the chattel, the possessor is entitled, at common law, to recover the full market value of the chattel against the wrongdoer (see too the antique decision in *Armory v Delamirie* (1722) 1 Strange 505, and also *The Sanix Ace* [1987] 1 Lloyd's Rep 465). In *The Jag Shakti* [1986] AC 337, the Privy Council applied *The Winkfield* to a bailee who had merely a right to immediate possession of the goods at the time of the wrong (criticised in N Palmer, *Bailment* (3rd edn, 2009), pp 342–351, and also in his essay 'Possessory Title' in N Palmer and E McKendrick (eds), *Interests in Goods* (2nd edn, 1998), pp 68–71).

2. The rule in *The Winkfield* can be expressed as a rule that it is not open to a wrongdoer to plead that some third party has a better title than the claimant (sometimes known as the rule excluding the *ius tertii*). But in three exceptional situations the wrongdoer may raise another person's superior title to the chattel as a defence against an action brought by the possessor. These are as follows:

(a) when the wrongdoer defends the action on behalf of, and with the authority of, the true owner;

(b) when the wrongdoing was committed with the authority of the true owner;

(c) when the wrongdoer has, since the time of the wrongdoing, become the owner of the goods.

3. Where a claimant sues on the basis of mere possession, it is irrelevant that his possession was obtained wrongfully or even by theft: *Costello v Chief Constable of Derbyshire Constabulary* [2001] EWCA Civ 381, [2001] 1 WLR 1437 at [31].

4. Having recovered in full from the wrongdoer, a possessor may subtract the value (if any) of his own interest, but he must pay the surplus to the owner (*The Winkfield*). It seems that any such surplus in the possessor's hands is held on trust: see *Mathew v TM Sutton Ltd* [1994] 4 All ER 793 where a pledgee was deemed to hold surplus sale proceeds on trust. See N Palmer, 'Possessory Title' in N Palmer and E McKendrick (eds), *Interests in Goods* (2nd edn, 1998), pp 67–68). Why do you think it matters whether the bailor has a proprietary or personal claim against the bailee?

5. When goods are subject to a bailment there is a further rule. If the bailee recovers damages in full from the wrongdoer no action may later be maintained by the bailor, even if he would otherwise be able to sue (*Nicolls v Bastard* (1835) 2 Cr M & R 659 at 660, per Parke B). Conversely, the bailee will be prevented from recovering against the wrongdoer if the bailor has already done so (*O'Sullivan v Williams* [1992] 3 All ER 385). This can work unfairness if bailor or bailee (as the case may be) sues, then dissipates the money and goes bankrupt.

6. *The Winkfield* must also be read in the light of ss 7 and 8 of the Torts (Interference with Goods) Act 1977. This allows a wrongdoer to insist, when sued, on joining all other possible claimants whom he can identify so that they may recover according to their actual interests. Where a given potential claimant X is not joined, s 7(3) obliges the possessor, if he recovers, to account to X 'to such an extent to avoid double liability'. Should X later bring his own claim, with the result that the wrongdoer pays twice, s 7(4) imposes a duty on X, if he has received payment from the first claimant, to reimburse the wrongdoer to the extent of his unjust enrichment. Section 8 allows the wrongdoer to set up a third party Y's superior title as a defence to the claimant's claim if he can identify Y (and probably also on condition that he joins Y as a party to the action (*De Franco v Metropolitan Police Comr* (1987) The Times, 8 May, per Lloyd LJ). But if he cannot identify Y he must pay in full, even if it is clear that the claimant with possession is not in fact owner. This is what happened in *Costello v Chief Constable of Derbyshire Constabulary* [2001] EWCA Civ 381, [2001] 1 WLR 1437, where it was clear that the goods in question had been stolen, but no one knew from whom.

QUESTIONS

1. B steals A's car. C later steals the same car from B. Can B assert a possessory title against C and sue him in conversion? See *Costello v Chief Constable of Derbyshire Constabulary* [2001] EWCA Civ 381, [2001] 1 WLR 1437; *Webb v Chief Constable of Merseyside Police*

[2000] QB 427, CA; *Parker v British Airways Board* [1982] QB 1004 at 1010, per Donaldson LJ; cf the Torts (Interference with Goods) Act 1977, s 8 (see below, pp 00–00), but s 8 is of no assistance where the third party with a better title than the claimant cannot be identified. What if controlled drugs and not a car had been stolen in this question? See *Costello*, above at [15], per Lightman J. For useful notes (on *Costello*), see J Getzler, 'Unclean Hands and the Doctrine of *Jus Tertii*' (2001) 117 LQR 565; D Fox, 'Enforcing a Possessory Title to a Stolen Car' [2002] CLJ 27; G Battersby, 'Acquiring Title by Theft' (2002) 65 MLR 603.

2. In *Wilson v Lombank Ltd*, above, Hinchcliffe J held that the garage did not have a lien on the car. Why was this important to the eventual outcome of the case?

11 ATTORNMENT IN RESPECT OF CHATTELS

Attornment (see D Sheehan, *The Principles of Personal Property Law* (2011), Ch 10) is an important commercial application of the concept of constructive possession. Attornment is the process by which a person (the attornor) holding actual possession of a chattel for himself or another person (under the terms of a bailment), later undertakes to hold possession of the goods for someone else (the attornee). The attornor must give his undertaking *to the attornee* (*Godts v Rose* (1855) 17 CB 229; Sale of Goods Act 1979, s 29(4)) and, once given, the attornee is deemed to have constructive possession of the chattel. Attornment most frequently arises where goods sold by A to B are held by C, who is a warehouseman or carrier (but attornment may not involve a third party as where, for example, A retains possession of goods he has sold to B under a sale and leaseback arrangement, and A acknowledges that he holds the goods for B: see *Michael Gerson (Leasing) Ltd v Wilkinson* [2001] QB 514, CA, especially at [28], per Clarke LJ). C will attorn to B when he acknowledges, with A's assent, that he henceforth holds the goods for B.

Mercuria Energy Trading Pte Ltd v Citibank NA
[2015] EWHC 1481 (Comm)

Mercuria, who were metal dealers, owned a quantity of raw metal in Chinese warehouses. As part of a financing deal, it sold this metal to Citibank on the basis that it would buy it back at a higher price at a later date, at which time it was the duty of the bank to 'deliver' the metal back to it. Doubts having arisen as to the authenticity of the metal, or indeed as to whether it existed at all, Citibank argued that it could nevertheless satisfy its duty to redeliver (ie transfer possession of) the metal to Mercuria merely by handing over receipts addressed to it by the warehouse owners. The court disagreed.

Phillips J:
    57. It will be apparent from the above that (absent the transfer of a document of title to the goods, namely, a bill of lading) it is only when a warehouse operator itself attorns to the buyer that delivery is effected. It is at that point that the third party becomes bailee for the buyer and the buyer acquires constructive possession of the goods. In particular, it is well established that the transfer by the seller to the buyer of a 'warrant' or 'receipt' issued by the warehouse operator in respect of the goods does not in itself effect delivery, even if that document promises delivery to the seller's order or to his assigns....

59. Thus an attornment by the warehouse operator is a necessary element in the transfer of constructive possession from the seller to the buyer and, as delivery is by definition the transfer of possession, it is also a condition of delivery. The position can be contrasted with the more straightforward situation where the goods are in the possession of the seller, in which case the manner in which possession is to be transferred (including the buyer obtaining constructive possession) is purely a matter for agreement between the parties.

60. In the present case, Citi accepts that the warehouse receipts which it tendered to Mercuria were not documents of title … Accordingly, applying the established principles set out above, the tender of those warehouse receipts on 22 July 2014 did not result in Mercuria obtaining constructive possession of the metal and therefore did not effect delivery …

(a) Attornment in respect of part of a bulk

Can there be attornment in respect of an unidentified part of a bulk? For example, if A sells to B an unidentified part of a bulk held in C's warehouse, can the acknowledgement by C that it now holds the goods partly for B give constructive joint possession to B?

Older authority denied this, and limited the effect of such acknowledgement ('quasi-attornment'—see RM Goode, *Proprietary Rights in Insolvency and Sales Transactions* (3rd edn, 2009), para 1–26) to an estoppel preventing C, if sued by B, from denying that it held the requisite goods on his behalf and was therefore liable to hand over to B the quantity in question. See *Re London Wine Co (Shippers) Ltd* [1986] PCC 121 and *Maynegrain Pty Ltd v Compafina Bank* [1982] 2 NSWLR 141, Court of Appeal of New South Wales (reversed on another ground (1984) 58 ALJR 389, PC), noted by F Reynolds (1984) 4 OJLS 434. But a more recent case holds that attornment can create constructive possession even of part of a bulk: see *Devani v Republic of Kenya* [2015] EWHC 3535 (Admin) at [22].

The point may matter in one situation. Imagine that a bulk commodity such as oil is held, undifferentiated, at C's storage facility; that A owns an undivided share in it; and that C on A's instructions acknowledges that it holds A's share on behalf of B, a bank or financier lending money to A on the security of that share. If the financier thereby obtains constructive possession it will have a valid pledge: if not, it will not (see *Dublin City Distillery Ltd v Doherty* [1914] AC 823: below, p 1031, and cf *Inglis v Robertson* [1898] AC 616). In terms of practicality there is much to be said for upholding B's possession and hence the validity of its pledge. This was one of the essential points at issue in *Devani v Republic of Kenya* [2015] EWHC 3535 (Admin), referred to above.

(b) Documents and attornment

The possession of a document of title to goods held by a third party does not usually carry with it constructive possession of the goods themselves (*Dublin City Distillery Ltd v Doherty* [1914] AC 823: below, p 1031). Thus a delivery warrant issued by a warehouseman or other bailee requires attornment by the warehouseman or bailee before the transferee takes constructive possession of the goods referred to therein (*Farina v Home* (1846) 16 M &W 119).

An important exception to this rule arises in the case of a bill of lading (see below, p 536), which is the only true document of title recognised at common law (*Official Assignee of Madras v Mercantile Bank of India* [1935] AC 53 at 59, per Lord Wright: below, p 1026). The holder of a bill of lading is deemed to have constructive, or more likely symbolic, possession of the goods referred to therein, so long as the bill of lading has been properly transferred to him by delivery or by delivery and indorsement as required (the case for symbolic, as opposed to constructive, possession has been persuasively argued by Michael Bools in his excellent book *The Bill of Lading: A Document of Title to Goods* (1997), Ch 7). No attornment is required after the transferee has received delivery of the bill of lading, so long as it was delivered to him with the *intention* that he is to be given constructive or symbolic possession of the goods (see *The Future Express* [1992] 2 Lloyd's Rep 79 at 95–96, per HH Judge Diamond QC, approved on this point [1993] 2 Lloyd's Rep 542 at 550, CA. It may be that this is because issue of the bill of lading carries with it a transferable attornment by the carrier: see *Borealis AB v Stargas Ltd, The Berge Sisar* [2001] UKHL 17, [2002] 2 AC 205 at [18], per Lord Hobhouse, although in *East West Corpn v DKBS 1912* [2003] EWCA Civ 83, [2003] 1 All ER (Comm) 525 at [42], Mance LJ described this as 'a difficult area'; see further RM Goode, *Proprietary Rights in Insolvency and Sales Transactions* (3rd edn, 2009), paras 1–22 ff; Bools, above, pp 153–156).

12 TRANSFER OF POSSESSION

Although the transfer of possession of a chattel may be effected by unilateral assumption (eg the taking of ownerless property, or even theft), the most common method is voluntary transfer, effected by actual or constructive delivery. Actual delivery transfers actual physical possession of the chattel. Constructive delivery transfers control of the chattel to the deliveree, usually without giving him actual possession. Constructive delivery by A to B may take place in any one of the following ways:

(1) where A, being in actual possession of the chattel, agrees to hold it as bailee or agent for B (see *Michael Gerson (Leasing) Ltd v Wilkinson* [2001] QB 514, CA);

(2) where a third party C, being in actual possession of the chattel as bailee for A, attorns to B with A's consent (see above, p 76);

(3) where B is already in possession of the chattel as bailee or agent for A and A agrees that B shall thenceforth hold it for himself;

(4) where A transfers a genuine document of title, such as a bill of lading, to B (see above);

(5) where a seller A hands them to a carrier for the purpose of transmission to a buyer B: Sale of Goods Act 1979, s 32(1);

(6) where A transfers to B an object giving physical control of the chattel, such as a key (or swipe card) to the warehouse where the goods are stored (but see above, p 71).

Delivery is considered further below at p 1026. See also *Official Assignee of Madras v Mercantile Bank of India Ltd* [1935] AC 53 at 58–59, per Lord Wright: below, p 1026.

13 THE IMPORTANCE OF POSSESSION

Before considering the commercial importance of possession, it is worth making a few preliminary observations. First, possession is only relevant to chattels capable of physical manipulation. Goods, money, and documentary intangibles are all capable of physical possession; but a pure intangible is not, and the same almost certainly goes for digitised products such as software or a database (see S Green, 'Can a Digitized Product be the Subject of Conversion?' [2006] LMCLQ 568 and compare *Your Response Ltd v Datateam Business Media Ltd* [2014] EWCA Civ 281, [2015] QB 41). Secondly, an agreement to give possession, as opposed to ownership, cannot of itself create any kind of proprietary right at law or in equity. It cannot create it at law because legal possession cannot be transferred by agreement; it cannot create it in equity because there is no such thing as equitable possession (possession being an entirely common law concept). Thirdly, susceptibility to possession may govern other matters such as remedies. So intangibles cannot be made the subject of an action in conversion (*OBG Ltd v Allan* [2007] UKHL 21, [2008] 1 AC 1, on which see S Green, 'To Have and to Hold? Conversion and Intangible Property' (2008) 71 MLR 114); and there can be no lien over an intangible asset such as a database (*Your Response Ltd v Datateam Business Media Ltd* [2014] EWCA Civ 281, [2015] QB 41).

However, even in the light of these limitations, the concept of possession remains important for the following reasons.

(1) Possession is prima facie evidence of ownership (though see *Elliott v Kemp* (1840) 7 M & W 306). Possession may also be relevant to the acquisition of legal ownership under the law of limitation (Limitation Act 1980, s 3(2)).

(2) A person in possession has available to him the remedies of conversion and trespass to goods, independently of whether he is also owner. See above, p 72. This can be important in the case of persons such as carriers and holders of liens over goods. It can also be vital in the case of goods held on trust. Here the trustee in possession can sue for the benefit of the equitable owner and recover the loss suffered by the latter; indeed, the beneficial owner can himself force the issue if he is prepared to join the trustee as a party to the action. See *Shell UK Ltd v Total UK Ltd* [2010] EWCA Civ 180, [2011] QB 86. At common law it seems that the person with possessory title could generally recover independently of where the true loss actually lay: but see now ss 7 and 8 of the Torts (Interference with Goods) Act 1977.

(3) Not only is possession generally sufficient to allow a claimant to sue for conversion and trespass to goods; in both cases proof of possession, or an immediate right to possession, is actually necessary to allow the claimant to sue at all, even where he is in fact owner (see, generally, N Palmer, 'Possessory Title' in N Palmer and E McKendrick (eds), *Interests in Goods* (2nd edn, 1998), Ch 3). In an action for trespass the goods must have been in possession, or bailor under a bailment at will, at the time of the alleged interference (Bridge, p 86). As regards conversion, the claimant must have either been in actual possession, or had an immediate proprietary right to possession; in the absence of this his action will fail (*Gordon v Harper* (1796) 7 Term Rep 9). The same rule applies to an action in negligence for damage to goods: *The Aliakmon* [1986] AC 785 at 809, per Lord Brandon. In *Shell UK Ltd v Total UK Ltd* [2010] EWCA Civ 180, [2011] QB 86, a beneficial owner of oil installations without possession or the right to possession was allowed to sue when they were negligently damaged, but it seems only because the installations were held on trust for it and the trustee, who did have possessory rights, was joined as a party to the action (see at [128]–[142], per Waller LJ).

(4) Where goods are bailed the situation is complex. If the bailment is at the will of the bailor, the latter will have a right to immediate possession. Since a bailment to a carrier is presumed to be revocable at will, the goods owner will normally be able to pursue possessory remedies against persons injuring or interfering with the goods (*Transcontainer Express Ltd v Custodian Security Ltd* [1988] 1 Lloyd's Rep 128, CA). Similarly, a cargo owner will retain a right to immediate possession where he transfers a bill of lading to a bank, named as consignee, to hold as his agent, whether or not the effect of that transfer was to confer on the

bank a sufficient possessory interest for it to pursue claims in bailment (*East West Corpn v DKBS 1912* [2003] EWCA Civ 83, [2003] QB 1509 at [39], CA). But where the bailment is for a fixed term, or to a pledgee, the bailor has no right to immediate possession.

(5) An owner without possession or the right to it (in the case of conversion) or without possession or the status of a bailor at will (in the case of trespass to goods) is relegated to a claim in tort for 'reversionary injury', that is, for any damage done to his reversionary interest. On this see *Mears v London & South Western Rly Co* (1862) 11 CBNS 850, and below, p 83.

(6) Possession may be relevant to the transfer of legal ownership. Although the passing of property under a contract of sale depends on mere intention and does not require delivery (Sale of Goods Act 1979, ss 17, 18, below, p 336), in other contexts ownership of chattels can be transferred only by delivery of possession or the execution of a deed. This can be important in the case of transfers without consideration, and in contracts of exchange (eg counter-trade, where two commodities are exchanged for each other).

(7) Several exceptions to the *nemo dat* rule turn on one or other party having possession of goods (eg Sale of Goods Act 1979, ss 24, 25: below, pp 407 ff and 412 ff).

(8) Possession may be relevant in cases of insolvency. Where the buyer of goods becomes insolvent, an unpaid seller may still be able to exercise a lien on the goods, despite property in the goods having passed to the buyer, if he retains possession of them, or a right to stop the goods in transit if they have not yet reached the buyer's possession (Sale of Goods Act 1979, ss 39–46). Furthermore, where the buyer takes possession of goods under an agreement for sale, and the seller later becomes insolvent, the buyer has a right to retain possession of the goods and may complete the transaction by tendering the price (RM Goode, *Proprietary Rights and Insolvency in Sales Transactions* (3rd edn, 2009), paras 1–15 to 1–17).

14 ACQUISITION AND TRANSFER OF LEGAL AND EQUITABLE OWNERSHIP IN CHOSES IN ACTION AND INTANGIBLES

(a) Legal ownership

Intangibles being non-physical, the concepts of taking possession or manufacturing a new thing are clearly not applicable to them. It follows that the only means of acquisition worth discussing is consensual transfer.

This is subject to its own rules, entirely separate from those applicable to chattels. Essentially all means of consensual transfer of choses in action and other intangibles are statutory. For choses in action in general, the procedure is laid down in s 136 of the Law of Property Act 1925, requiring transfer in writing with written notice to the debtor. A number of particular choses in action and other intangibles have particular means laid down by statute: for example, the Policies of Assurance Act 1867 for life insurance policies or the Stock Transfer Acts 1963 and 1982 and the Companies Act 2006, s 544 and Part 21 for company securities. For further details, see below, Chapter 22.

(b) Equitable ownership

Equitable ownership of choses in action may be acquired either by means not dissimilar to those applicable to chattels (above, p 80), or alternatively by equitable assignment.

Thus a new equitable interest in intangibles may be created by any one of the following means.

(1) By declaration of trust. The owner of an intangible either declares himself to hold it on trust for the transferee, or transfers it at law to a third party to hold on trust for the transferee.

(2) By a contract for value to transfer ownership (see generally *Tailby v Official Receiver* (1888) 13 App Cas 523 and *Re Lind* [1915] 2 Ch 345). When there has been an agreement to transfer an after-acquired chose in action, the transferee has an inchoate interest which attaches to the asset when it is acquired by the transferor with effect from the date of the agreement (*Tailby v Official Receiver* (1888) 13 App Cas 523, above). This is a very common device used to create security over receivables (see below, p 961).

(3) By a purported present transfer for value of an after-acquired chose in action for value (*Tailby v Official Receiver* (1888) 13 App Cas 523 at 531–532, per Lord Herschell).

(4) By equitable assignment.

See generally Chapter 23, below, where this matter is covered in more detail.

15 THE REMEDIES FOR RECOVERY OF, AND INTERFERENCE WITH, PERSONAL PROPERTY

In order to comprehend English commercial law, it is necessary to have some understanding of the remedies available to the owner or possessor of personal property, both tangible (choses in possession) and intangible (choses in action and other intangibles) when that property is interfered with or wrongfully withheld.

(a) Choses in possession (including documentary intangibles)

We begin with physical things. This category also includes documentary intangibles, such as cheques and bills of lading, since they are embodied in a physical piece of paper, even though their value is dependent solely on the rights represented by the physical document (see *Bavins, Jr & Sims v London & South Western Bank Ltd* [1900] 1 QB 270).

'Conversion, Tort and Restitution' by A Tettenborn in N Palmer and E McKendrick (eds), *Interests in Goods*
(2nd edn, 1998), p 825

> Conversion is one of the mysteries, or perhaps embarrassments, of English law. Universities tend not to teach it; judges themselves have professed not to know about it; writers on tort deal with it, but more or less apologetically, as something not really their concern.

Something peculiar is obviously going on; put shortly, the nub of the problem is that no-one has ever sat down seriously to consider what conversion is *for*. True, it is classified as a tort: but that is only for historical reasons and for lack of anywhere else to file it. In fact it is trying to do not one, but three very different jobs at the same time; it is (1) standing in as a kind of surrogate *vindicatio*, allowing owners to get back their property or its value from a wrongful possessor (call this the 'recovery function'); (2) acting to compensate owners for losses caused by past misdealings with their property (tort proper); and (3) on occasion reversing unjust enrichment arising from the property or proceeds which have got into the wrong hands (restitution).

NOTES

1. Recovery of property In most legal systems an owner of tangible property is given a simple cause of action, independent of the law of tort, to recover it from a wrongful possessor. Typical is the provision of art 985 the German Civil Code:

The owner is entitled to demand the surrender of his thing from the person in possession of it.

English law does not follow this sensible and straightforward route. Instead, it chooses to reach the same result using a more convoluted procedure. It provides that a possessor of goods who fails without justification to give them up on demand to the owner thereby commits a tort (conversion); that this renders the possessor liable to pay damages in tort to the owner; that the measure of those damages is presumptively the value of the goods, plus any other losses flowing from the possessor's wrongful retention; and that those damages can be mitigated by the return of the goods as demanded (for the painful details see A Tettenborn, 'Damages in Conversion—The Exception or the Anomaly?' [1993] CLJ 128).

In addition, the court has since 1854 had a statutory discretionary power, if requested by the claimant, to order the defendant to return the goods themselves without the option of paying their value (see now the Torts (Interference with Goods) Act 1977, s 3). This power will often not be exercised in respect of ordinary articles of commerce, such as ordinary industrial machinery: see, eg, *Tanks & Vessels Industries Ltd v Devon Cider Co Ltd* [2009] EWHC 1360 (Ch) at [55]. But courts are inclined to order return where goods are 'commercially unique', ie otherwise hard to buy on the market within a reasonable time (as in the case of jumbo jets: see *Blue Sky One Ltd v Blue Airways LLC* [2009] EWHC 3314 (Comm) at [314]–[316], per Beatson J). Very significantly for commercial law, the courts also now accept that where a defendant is of doubtful solvency a specific order may be appropriate, thus essentially giving the claimant a guaranteed preference over other creditors: see *Blue Sky One Ltd v Blue Airways LLC*, above, at [309] and *X-Fab Semiconductor Foundries AG v Plessey Semiconductors Ltd* [2014] EWHC 1574 (QB) at [32].

2. Interference with property Where goods are damaged or interfered with, the owner has a number of torts at his disposal. For details, see *Clerk & Lindsell on Torts* (21st edn, 2016), paras 17–01 to 17–05.

Negligence: in the case of damage to the goods, then provided the owner has in addition to ownership either possession or the right to immediate possession and in addition can prove fault in the defendant, he can simply sue in negligence.

Conversion: in the case where the goods are deliberately consumed or destroyed, or where they are received, bought, sold, or otherwise dealt with in such a way as to amount to a usurpation of his rights, the owner may be able to sue the person responsible for such dealings in conversion. Although conversion lies only in respect of deliberate acts, it is not necessary for the claimant to prove fault in the defendant (see *Marfani & Co Ltd v Midland Bank Ltd* [1968] 1 WLR 956 at 970–971, per Diplock LJ). Thus a person who receives, consumes, or disposes of property without being entitled to do so remains liable to pay its value even if he no longer has the property and did not know, and had no reason to think, that he was not entitled to act as he did. This can be commercially significant. For example, a shipowner innocently taking over and consuming the bunkers (fuel) in a ship on termination of a charter may find itself liable to the persons who sold them to the charterer on reservation of title terms and were never paid (see *The Saetta* [1994] 1 All ER 851, p 000 below). Again, a carrier handing over goods against a forged bill of lading or fake electronic delivery order is liable to the true owner for the full value of the goods despite all care having been taken. See *Motis Exports Ltd v Dampskibsselskabet AF 1912* [2000] 1 Lloyd's Rep 211 and *Glencore International AG v MSC Mediterranean Shipping Co SA* [2015] EWHC 1989 (Comm), [2015] 2 Lloyd's Rep 508 (below, pp 536).

There is one exception to the rule that conversion lies only for deliberate acts. Under s 2(2) of the Torts (Interference with Goods) Act 1977 a bailor can sue a bailee who fails to produce the goods in conversion: the bailee will then be automatically liable unless he can show that the goods were lost owing to some cause for which he was not responsible. For bailment, see below, Chapter 3.

Trespass to goods: trespass to goods covers all unjustified deliberate physical interference with goods in another's possession. It is thus wider than conversion, covering as it does (for example) moving or damaging goods, even though this may not be a dealing amounting to a usurpation of the owner's rights. It is narrower than conversion, however, in that it only covers acts done to goods not already in the defendant's possession: so (for instance) the carrier who delivers goods to a non-owner is guilty of conversion but not trespass. As with conversion, a defendant can be liable for trespass even though he did not know, and had no reason to know, that he was not entitled to act as he did. This tort can also be of commercial significance. A carrier inadvertently collecting the wrong cargo will commit it, as will a construction company if, having been told to shut off given utilities during work, it inadvertently shuts off others as well or instead (see *Transco Plc v United Utilities Water Plc* [2005] EWHC 2784 (QB).

Reversionary injury: negligence, conversion, and trespass to goods contain important limitations as to who can sue. In the case of negligence and conversion, title to sue is limited to a person with either possession or an immediate right to possession (an example of the latter being where a finance company has the right to repossess goods in the hands of a hirer following non-payment of instalments: see *Barclays Mercantile Business Finance Ltd v Sibec Developments Ltd* [1992] 1 WLR 1253). With trespass it is limited to a person with actual (ie physical or constructive) possession. To protect the position of an owner without the necessary possessory right, the law has developed the tort of 'reversionary injury'. This allows such a person, if he can prove what would otherwise be the elements of negligence, conversion, or trespass to goods, to recover for any actual damage done to his reversionary interest. On this see *Mears v London & South Western Rly Co* (1862) 11 CBNS 850; *HSBC Rail (UK) Ltd v Network Rail Infrastructure Ltd* [2005] EWCA Civ 1437, [2006] 1 All ER (Comm) 345; and see generally, A Tettenborn, 'Reversionary Damage to Chattels' [1994] CLJ 326). But this does not extend to a mere equitable owner: *MCC Proceeds Inc v Lehman Bros International (Europe)* [1998] 4 All ER 675, CA, adopting arguments made by A Tettenborn [1996] CLJ 36. The availability of the action for reversionary injury is particularly significant where a third party interferes with goods that were at the time hired out to a user, or were subject to a finance lease or lease-purchase or conditional sale agreement.[5] This is because in all these cases it is likely that the owner will have neither possession nor an immediate right to it, and therefore the action for reversionary injury will be his only means of suing the third party interferer.

(b) Choses in action and other intangibles

OBG Ltd v Allan

[2007] UKHL 21, [2008] 1 AC 1, House of Lords

In this decision, a number of cases raising related issues were appealed together. In *OBG v Allan* itself, a receiver was appointed by a creditor of OBG, but there was a technical invalidity in his appointment. Unknown to anyone, therefore, he had no right of any kind to interfere in the company's property. The receiver interfered in the performance of certain contracts entered into by OBG, and in essence gave up OBG's right to make a profit out of performing them. Later OBG, through its liquidator, sued the liquidator for having 'converted' the chose in action represented by those contracts. The issue raised was therefore: were the remedies available for interference with choses in possession also available for choses in action? The Court of Appeal said no, and the appeal was dismissed on that point.

> **Lord Hoffmann**:
>
> 94. The case in conversion was unanimously rejected by all the judges who heard the *OBG* case and it might therefore be sufficient to say that I agree with them. But the claim was given considerable prominence in argument, with a good deal of reference to North American authorities, and I shall therefore deal with it at greater length.
>
> 95. Everyone agrees that conversion is historically a tort against a person's interest in a chattel, being derived from the action for trover, which included a fictitious allegation that the plaintiff had lost the chattel and that the defendant had found it. Secondly, and consistently with its ancient origin, conversion is a tort of strict liability. Anyone who converts a chattel, that is to say, does an act inconsistent with the rights of the owner, however innocent he may be, is liable for the loss caused which, if the chattel has not been recovered by the owner, will usually be the value of the goods. *Fowler v Hollins* (1872) LR 7 QB 616 was a claim for conversion of bales of cotton bought in good faith through a broker in Liverpool. The purchasers were nevertheless held strictly liable. Cleasby B said robustly, at p 639, that:
>
>> the liability under it is founded upon what has been regarded as a salutary rule for the protection of property, namely, that persons deal with the property in chattels or exercise acts of ownership over them at their peril.
>
> 96. Advising the House of Lords on appeal from this decision, Blackburn J was more sympathetic. He said, *Hollins v Fowler* (1875) LR 7 HL 757, 765 that the result was hard on the innocent purchasers but added:

---

[5] Under a finance lease, goods are leased by a financier to a user for a period which may be as long as their useful life; in a hire-purchase agreement they are leased for a shorter period with an option granted to the hirer to buy them for a sum, often nominal, at the end of it. Under a conditional sale arrangement the price is payable by instalments, with ownership reserved in the seller until all have been paid. In all these cases the commercial object of the transaction, whatever its form, is the provision of finance; and in all of them the total sums payable to the financier approximate to the amount of capital finance provided, plus finance charges and interest.

If, as is quite possible, the changes in the course of business since the principles of law were established make them cause great hardships or inconvenience, it is the province of the legislature to alter the law.

97. Parliament has responded with legislation such as the Factors Act 1889 (52 & 53 Vict c 45), section 4 of the Cheques Act 1957 (which protects a collecting bank against liability for conversion of a cheque to which its customer had no title) and section 234(3) of the Insolvency Act 1986, which, in the absence of negligence, protects an administrative receiver who 'seizes or disposes of any property which is not property of the company' against liability. But there are no such protective provisions in relation to anything other than chattels. Why not? Obviously because Parliament thought them to be unnecessary. It would never have occurred to Parliament that strict liability for conversion could exist for anything other than chattels. The whole of the statutory modification of the law of conversion has been on the assumption that it applies only to chattels. There has been no discussion of the question of whether an extension of conversion to choses in action would require a corresponding or even greater degree of protection for people acting in good faith.

98. Mr Randall, who appeared for OBG, drew attention to paras 829 and 830 of the Report of the Review Committee on Insolvency Law and Practice (the Cork Committee) (1982) (Cmnd 8558), which endorsed a recommendation of the Jenkins Committee (Cmnd 1749) (1962) that the court should be given power to relieve an invalidly appointed receiver from liability for acts which would have been lawful if the appointment had been valid. Parliament has not given effect to this recommendation. He suggested that this omission should be regarded as somehow justifying a drastic extension of the liability of such receivers for conversion. The fallacy in this reasoning does not need to be underlined.

99. By contrast with the approving attitude of Cleasby B to the protection of rights of property in chattels, it is a commonplace that the law has always been very wary of imposing any kind of liability for purely economic loss. The economic torts which I have discussed at length are highly restricted in their application by the requirement of an intention to procure a breach of contract or to cause loss by unlawful means. Even liability for causing economic loss by negligence is very limited. Against this background, I suggest to your Lordships that it would be an extraordinary step suddenly to extend the old tort of conversion to impose strict liability for pure economic loss on receivers who were appointed and acted in good faith. Furthermore, the effects of such a change in the law would of course not stop there. *Hunter v Canary Wharf Ltd* [1997] AC 655, 694 contains a warning from Lord Goff of Chieveley (and other of their Lordships) against making fundamental changes to the law of tort in order to provide remedies which, if they are to exist at all, are properly the function of other parts of the law.

...

101. Mr Randall relied upon authorities in Canada and the US. I can find no discussion in the Canadian cases of whether a claim for conversion can be made in respect of a chose in action. These cases are analysed by Peter Gibson LJ in his judgment in the Court of Appeal [2005] QB 762, 777–778 and I do not think that I should lengthen this judgment by adding to his comments. For the reasons which he gives, I derive no assistance from them. There are certainly cases in the US which support Mr Randall's submission and which form part of the profligate extension of tort law which has occurred in that country. Perhaps the most remarkable is the decision of the Federal Court of Appeals (9th Circuit) in *Kremen v Online Classifieds Inc* (2003) 337 F 3d 1024, in which it was held that a publicly-funded company which provided gratuitous registration of internet domain names could be liable in conversion, on a footing of strict liability, for transferring a registered name[6] to a third party, having

---

6 For those interested, the domain in question was http://www.sex.com.

acted in good faith on the authority of a forged letter. The court held that the domain name was intangible property which could be converted in the same way as a chattel and that the registration company could be liable for its value. I have no difficulty with the proposition that a domain name may be intangible property, like a copyright or trade mark, but the notion that a registrar of such property can be strictly liable for the common law tort of conversion is, I think, foreign to English law.

102. The American cases make a good deal of the line of authority, which in England goes back to the beginning of the 19th century or earlier, by which a person who misappropriates a document which constitutes or evidences title to a debt can be liable in conversion for the face value of the document. Surely, it was said, in such cases the action is in substance for conversion of the debt, a chose in action, and if that is right, then why not have conversion of any chose in action?

103. But the document cases have been recognised to be an anomaly created by the judges to solve a particular problem, namely that a person who wrongfully secures payment of money due to another cannot be sued by the true creditor for money had and received to his use. That is because the creditor is not the owner of the money. The wrongful payment was treated as a matter between the paying party and the recipient which did not affect the creditor's position. Thus in *Rogers v Kelly* (1809) 2 Camp 123 a bank had mistakenly paid the defendant some money which the plaintiff had deposited. Lord Ellenborough said: 'There is no privity between the parties to this suit. The plaintiff's claim is on the bankers, and they must seek their remedy against the defendant the best way they can.'

104. But in cases in which the title to the debt was evidenced by a negotiable instrument, or even in some cases where it was not negotiable, the wrongful misappropriation of the document could cause actual loss to the true creditor, who might not be able to recover the debt. That left a gap in the law. The judges filled it by treating the misappropriation as a conversion of a chattel equal in value to the debt which it evidenced....

107.... I would therefore dismiss the liquidator's appeal.

Lady Hale (dissenting):

309. In a logical world, there would be such a proprietary remedy for the usurpation of all forms of property. The relevant question should be, not 'is there a proprietary remedy?', but 'is what has been usurped property?' Rights of action were not seen as property in the 15th and 16th centuries when the tort of conversion was first developing. The essential feature of property is that it has an existence independent of a particular person: it can be bought and sold, given and received, bequeathed and inherited, pledged or seized to secure debts, acquired (in the olden days) by a husband on marrying its owner. So great was the medieval fear of maintenance that the law took a very long time to recognise any right of action (even a reversionary right to tangible property) as having this quality: see W S Holdsworth, 'The History of the Treatment of Choses in Action by the Common Law' (1920) 33 Harvard Law Review 997. But it is noteworthy that, when new forms of chose in action which could be assigned were developed during the 17th and 18th centuries, the remedy of conversion was adapted to accommodate them: it did so by pretending that the document or other token representing or evidencing the obligation had the same value as the obligation itself.

310. The point was well made by Park CJ, in the Supreme Court of Errors in the State of Connecticut, in *Ayres v French* (1874) 41 Conn R 142, 150:

> There is really no difference in any important respect between [a share of stock] and other kinds of personal property. A man purchases a share of stock and pays one hundred dollars for it. He afterwards purchases a horse, and pays the same price. The one was bought in the market as readily as the other and can be sold and delivered as readily. The one can be

> pledged as collateral security as easily as the other; as easily attached to secure a debt; and its value as easily estimated. The one enriches a man as much as the other, and fills as important a place in the inventory of his estate.

Once the law recognises something as property, the law should extend a proprietary remedy to protect it. Our law is prepared, according to *Clerk & Lindsell*, to apply the remedy of conversion to 'any document which is specially prepared in the ordinary course of business as evidence of a debt or obligation': see *Clerk & Lindsell on Torts*, 19th ed (2006), para 17–35. The reliance on a document or some other tangible token of the existence of the obligation may be understandable as a relic of the history, but it is not principled. It is at once too wide and too narrow. There may be a document evidencing an obligation of a purely personal kind, which ought not to attract a proprietary remedy. On the other hand, there are many debts and some other obligations which can now be readily assigned, attached, form part of an insolvent estate, and enjoy all the other characteristics of property, but which are not represented by a specific document. It is not surprising that the law has not yet taken the logical step of applying the same principle to them, because it is much more difficult wrongly to deprive someone of his rights of action than it is to deprive him of his wallet or his coat. But, to my mind, it is no greater step for the law to do this than it is for the law to recognise that photographs of the Douglas wedding enjoy the same protection as more conventional trade secrets. It is not only entirely consistent with principle. It is inconsistent with principle not to do so.

311. The facts of the *OBG* case make the point more clearly than I could ever do. The defendants took control over all the company's assets. They entered the company's premises and changed the locks. They took charge of all its plant and machinery and other chattels. They had no right to do so. No one disputes that they are strictly liable in trespass to land and conversion no matter how bona fide their belief that they were entitled to do this. They also took charge of the company's business and closed it down. The judge found that the company was doomed, so that there was no goodwill to be attached to disposing of it as a going concern. But among the company's assets were the debts and other contractual liabilities it was owed. The judge found that the defendants obtained less for these assets than would have been obtained in an orderly winding up. This is not improbable. The receivers' obligations and priorities were different from those of the company, its other creditors and shareholders. They might well result in lower realisations than the company might have achieved for itself. Accepting, as we must, the judge's findings on this, it makes no sense that the defendants should be strictly liable for what was lost on the tangible assets but not for what was lost on the intangibles.

Armstrong DLW GmbH v Winnington Networks Ltd
[2012] EWHC 10 (Ch), [2013] Ch 156, Chancery Division

An EUA is a proprietary EU permit allowing the holder to emit 1 tonne of CO_2, something otherwise illegal under environmental protection laws. EUAs have no physical existence, being controlled electronically through national registries; but they may be fairly freely transferred, bought, and sold. As a result of an email fraud perpetrated by a third party, a large number of EUAs were transferred from Armstrong's account to that of Winnington and subsequently sold on to good faith purchasers. The question in this case was whether Armstrong could recover the value of the 'stolen' EUAs from Winnington, through whose hands the EUAs had passed and who had good reason to suspect something might be amiss. Stephen Morris QC, sitting as a deputy judge, held that the answer was yes.

Stephen Morris QC:

88.... In my judgment, there is no reason why, in an appropriate case, a claimant does not have a personal claim at law to vindicate his legal proprietary rights in respect of a chose in action or form of other intangible property. Nor does any authority preclude such a claim.

...

90.... I do not accept that the proprietary restitutionary claim has to be characterised as, or brought in the form of, an action for money had and received.

...

93.... [T]he fact that there can be no claim in conversion in respect of choses in action or other intangibles does not mean that there can be no proprietary restitutionary claim in respect of choses in action or other intangibles. Conversion is a strict liability tort with no room for defences of bona fide purchase. That is not the position with a proprietary restitutionary claim. Lord Hoffmann's observations in *OBG Ltd v Allan* [2008] AC 1, paras [95]–[97], [102]–[106], on the statutory modification of the law of conversion and on the extension of conversion to documentary intangibles are to be seen in the context of whether, as a matter of policy, there should be strict liability in respect of such documents and thus for choses in action (and not whether there should be no claim at law at all). There is no reason why the law should provide protection for land, chattels, documentary intangibles and money but not for other intangibles.

94. In my judgment, as a matter of authority and principle, if and where legal title remains with the claimant, a proprietary restitutionary claim at common law is available in respect of receipt by the defendant of a chose in action or other intangible property.

NOTES

1. As a result of *OBG v Allan* above, it is now clear that, save for documentary intangibles, intangible property is not subject to the remedial scheme applicable to choses in possession. There can therefore be no claim for conversion of, or trespass to, a chose in action or intangible property, still less a claim for reversionary injury to it. Furthermore, insofar as a claim is brought in negligence, the claimant will not be able to point to any physical damage, and therefore will have to show that his case is one of the exceptional ones where there is a duty of care in respect of pure economic loss (see eg *Clerk & Lindsell on Torts* (21st edn, 2016), paras 8–93 to 8–125).

2. It remains to be seen what remedies are available for interference with intangibles. The position seems to be the following.

(a) Recovery: this question does not arise as regards intangibles. Recovery presupposes a claimant who is entitled and a defendant in possession. This is clearly inapplicable in the case of an intangible, where there can be no possession divorced from entitlement.

(b) Interference: in *Armstrong v Winnington*, above, it was held that where A without justification receives an intangible from B in circumstances where B ceases to be entitled to enforce it, B has a 'proprietary restitutionary claim' against A for its value. This claim is not dependent on proof of fault, but A can escape liability on proof that he is a good faith buyer for value and without notice of B's rights. In *Armstrong v Winnington* (at [122]), it was said that notice included knowingly turning a blind eye to the possibility of wrongdoing, and also the case where, on the facts actually known to this defendant, a reasonable person would either have appreciated that the transaction was probably fraudulent or improper, or would have made inquiries or sought advice which would have revealed the probability of impropriety.

Besides the liability under a 'proprietary restitutionary claim' referred to in *Armstrong v Winnington*, interference with the enforcement or exercise of an intangible right may also amount to one or more of the 'economic torts', notably inducement of breach of contract and causing loss by unlawful means. See above, pp 64.

QUESTIONS

1. Is the English scheme of liability for interference with property satisfactory? If not, why not?

2. Do you agree with Baroness Hale in *OBG v Allan* that 'In a logical world, there would be … a proprietary remedy for the usurpation of all forms of property'?

16 EQUITABLE PROPERTY

Trusts are today vitally important in commercial law, and go well beyond the traditional field of investments held by trustees. Very informative in this context is P Millett, 'Equity's Place in The Law of Commerce' (1998) 114 LQR 214.

For example, money lent for a particular purpose may well be entrusted to the borrower on terms that until the purpose is satisfied it is held on trust for the lender, as happened in cases such as *Barclays Bank Ltd v Quistclose Investments Ltd* [1970] AC 567 and *Twinsectra Ltd v Yardley* [2002] UKHL 12, [2002] 2 AC 164. Again, in very many commercial conveyancing transactions mortgage monies are held by solicitors on trust to be paid out if, and only if, certain criteria are satisfied: if such monies are misapplied, remedies for breach of trust become relevant, as happened in *AIB Group (UK) Plc v Mark Redler & Co* [2014] UKSC 58, [2015] AC 1503. More prosaically, almost every pension fund in the land is set up through the medium of an express trust. Most individual shareholdings in publicly quoted companies are now 'dematerialised': ie the shares themselves are vested at law in a central custodian/trustee, with individual shareholders having merely an equitable interest. (For further details of the latter, see J Benjamin, *Financial Law* (2008), Ch 19.)

Moreover, this development is not confined to express trusts. When a company director or agent has control over assets belonging to the company or the principal, for certain purposes he is treated as if he were a trustee of those assets, with the company or principal playing the part of beneficiary. See generally E Lim, 'Directors' Fiduciary Duties: A New Analytical Framework' (2013) 129 LQR 242 and, for example, *Selangor United Rubber Estates Ltd v Cradock (No 3)* [1968] 1 WLR 1555.

In all these cases, the remedies available for protection of equitable property may become relevant, and we need to mention them briefly here.

(a) Claims to trust assets

So long as assets remain subject to the trust, any beneficiary of that trust has a right to sue to ensure that they are applied according to its terms and not disbursed contrary to those terms. This can be commercially very important for two reasons. One is that trust assets remain trust assets even in the hands of third parties, unless they are good faith purchasers for value without notice. The other is that assets held subject to a trust are not subject to the insolvency rules, thus protecting the beneficiary's rights in them. The point was illustrated in *Barclays Bank Ltd v Quistclose Investments Ltd* [1970] AC 567. Money lent to R Ltd, then in dire financial straits, for a particular purpose was credited to R's bank account on the basis that pending the fulfilment of the stipulated purpose it was to be held on trust for the lender. It was held that neither R's creditors nor the bank could lay claim to the money when R collapsed before the purpose could be fulfilled: the money went back to the lender.

(b) Claims for breach of trust

Where property held subject to a trust is paid out contrary to the terms of the trust, any beneficiary has on principle a claim to have the trust fund reconstituted by the trustee. This claim may well coexist with a parallel claim in contract or tort (eg where a solicitor entrusted with funds negligently pays them to the wrong person). Nevertheless, the principles on which the courts act are entirely different, the burden of proof is different, and in certain cases the amount payable by the trustee may be substantially greater in the former case. See generally M Carn, 'Clarifying the Law for Breach of Commercial Trusts' (2014) 4 Tr L Int 226 and *AIB Group (UK) Plc v Mark Redler & Co* [2014] UKSC 58, [2015] AC 1503.

(c) Claims for damage by third parties to trust property

The common law technically does not recognise equitable interests. It follows that where property is held on trust, no action lies at common law at the suit of the beneficiary for negligence, conversion, or trespass to goods (see *MCC Proceeds Inc v Lehman Bros International (Europe)* [1998] 4 All ER 675 and A Tettenborn, 'Trust Property and Conversion: An Equitable Confusion' [1996] CLJ 36). However, this is not very significant. The trustee can sue, and can recover substantial damages on behalf of the beneficiary (compare *Chappell v Somers & Blake* [2003] EWHC 1644 (Ch), [2004] Ch 19 at [27]–[28]); furthermore, it seems that the beneficiary can force this result by suing himself and joining the trustee as a party to the action (see *Colour Quest Ltd v Total Downstream UK Plc* [2010] EWCA Civ 180, [2011] QB 86 at [128] ff).

(d) Claims for unconscionable receipt and dishonest assistance

The rule in section (c) above is helpful when the wrongdoer is unconnected with the trustee. But it cannot help the beneficiary where the trustee cannot sue at all because he has himself collaborated with the third party in the misdealings concerned. Nevertheless, in this situation the beneficiary has two causes of action available to him in equity.

(1) Unconscionable receipt of trust property. A third party unjustifiably receiving trust property with knowledge of its status becomes liable in equity to account for its value to the beneficiary of the trust. This is a personal liability, and subsists even after he has lost or disposed of the property itself. The degree of knowledge required in the recipient is fairly vague: but it must be 'such as to make it unconscionable for him to retain the benefit of the receipt'. (See *Bank of Credit and Commerce International (Overseas) Ltd v Akindele* [2001] Ch 437 at 455, per Nourse LJ.) This can be of particular significance where agents or company directors misuse funds under their control and pay them to third parties (as happened in the

Akindele case, above). For further details, see G Virgo, *Principles of Equity and Trusts* (2nd edn, 2016), pp 681 ff.

(2) Dishonest assistance. Even without receiving trust property, a third party may assist a trustee in committing a breach of trust. If he does so he is again liable to account in equity to the beneficiary or beneficiaries for any loss suffered. In order to be liable the defendant must have acted 'dishonestly, or with a lack of probity': something that means 'simply not acting as an honest person would in the circumstances'. (See *Royal Brunei Airlines Sdn Bhd v Tan* [1995] 2 AC 378 at 389, per Lord Nicholls.) Like knowing receipt, this can be significant in the commercial context, for example where loan monies held on trust have been misused but the trustee who misused them is not himself worth suing (cf *Twinsectra Ltd v Yardley* [2002] UKHL 12, [2002] 2 AC 164). See Virgo, above, pp 699 ff.

CHAPTER 3

BAILMENT

1 WHAT IS BAILMENT?

We have already made a number of references to bailment[1] in the previous chapters. But what is bailment? In their treatise *An Essay on Possession in the Common Law* (1888), Pollock and Wright wrote (at p 163):

> . . . any person is to be considered as a bailee who otherwise than as a servant either receives possession of a thing from another or consents to receive or hold possession of a thing for another upon an undertaking with the other person either to keep and return or deliver to him the specific thing or to (convey and) apply the specific thing according to the directions antecedent or future of the other person.

Bailment is thus a transaction under which A, a bailee, lawfully receives possession of goods from B, a bailor, for some purpose. Examples from commercial law include warehousing, carriage, the deposit of property to have work done on it, leasing, and pledge. Again, a buyer under a sale or return transaction is, pending acceptance or rejection, a bailee of the goods: see *Atari Corpn (UK) Ltd v Electronics Boutique Stores (UK) Ltd* [1998] QB 539, CA.

A Bell, 'The Place of Bailment in the Modern Law of Obligations' in N Palmer and E McKendrick (eds), *Interests in Goods* (2nd edn, 1998), stresses, at p 488, following an examination of obligations to which bailments give rise, that 'bailment is indeed an independent source of obligations and . . . in moving away from contract, bailment has not in the process been simply absorbed by the law of tort'.

2 TYPES OF BAILMENT

Coggs v Bernard
(1703) 2 Ld Raym 909, Court of King's Bench

> **Holt CJ**: . . . And there are six sorts of bailments. The first sort of bailment is, a bare naked bailment of goods, delivered by one man to another to keep for the use of the bailor; and

---

[1] What follows deals with certain aspects of the law of bailment. For more detailed coverage, see generally N Palmer, *Bailment* (3rd edn, 2009 ('Palmer'); Bell, Ch 5. By contrast, see G McMeel, 'The Redundancy of Bailment' [2003] LMCLQ 169, for the interesting, if somewhat heretical, view that bailment does not constitute

this I call a *depositum*, and it is that sort of bailment which is mentioned in *Southcote's* case ((1601) Cro Eliz 815). The second sort is, when goods or chattels that are useful, are lent to a friend gratis, to be used by him; and this is called *commodatum*, because the thing is to be restored *in specie*. The third sort is, when goods are left with the bailee to be used by him for hire; this is called *locatio et conductio*, and the lender is called locator, and the borrower conductor. The fourth sort is, when goods or chattels are delivered to another as a pawn, to be a security to him for money borrowed of him by the bailor; and this is called in Latin *vadium*, and in English a pawn or a pledge. The fifth sort is when goods or chattels are delivered to be carried, or something is to be done about them for a reward to be paid by the person who delivers them to the bailee, who is to do the thing about them. The sixth sort is when there is a delivery of goods or chattels to somebody, who is to carry them, or do something about them gratis, without any rewards for such his work or carriage, which is this present case. I mention these things, not so much that they are all of them so necessary in order to maintain the proposition which is to be proved, as to clear the reason of the obligation, which is upon persons in cases of trust.

Bailment by NE Palmer

(3rd edn, 2009), para 3–003

Although there seems to have been no particular reason for the order in which these six varieties of bailment were enumerated, it cannot be denied that Holt CJ's descriptive classification corresponded with the major contemporary manifestations of the bailor–bailee relationship and proved markedly influential upon subsequent discussions of the subject. Even today, it is not easy to think of types of bailment that are not accommodated by his categorisation, and the broad sweep of his analysis is one which has been adopted, with certain refinements, in the present treatment of the subject. Nevertheless, Holt CJ's division is governed by a fundamentally consensual concept of bailment and by the most obvious social or commercial examples of that concept. It therefore pays no regard to the more hybrid or peripheral kinds of bailment and, by leaving them out altogether, suggests that they do not belong to the realm of bailment at all. Admittedly, this observation is based in part upon developments which have occurred since *Coggs v Bernard*, and is therefore a statement of Holt CJ's failure to foresee these developments rather than a criticism of his failure to observe them as a contemporary force. The fact remains that a large number of bailments, of a more or less orthodox character, are excluded from his classification. These include bailments by finding, bailments which arise upon a wrongful or mistaken seizure of property, 'mutual loans', bailments which arise when a landlord levies distress upon his tenant's goods or when a finance company calls in its security, bailments existing between an owner of goods and a sub-bailee, and bailments which, although redounding to the mutual benefit of the parties, are not the product of a direct bargain or do not involve a 'reward to be paid' from bailor to bailee or vice-versa. Nor is it clear that certain bailments of a more modern but conventional kind (such as the contract of hire-purchase, the conditional sale arising by virtue of a title retention clause, the issue of a ticket to a railway passenger on condition that he surrender it at the end of his journey, the custody of a will by the testator's solicitor, the delivery of a manuscript to a publisher, or the delivery of a tool to a workman in order that he can perform certain work with it) can find a place within the foregoing classification. Although it would be unfair to criticise Holt

an independent concept but is better explained in terms of general principles of contract, tort, unjust enrichment, and property. See also GS McBain, 'Modernising and Codifying the Law of Bailment' [2008] JBL 1.

CJ's analysis merely for failing to be watertight or comprehensive, it seems that if the value of classification rests in the earmarking of variant obligations within a basic unitary concept, the analysis is not complete. By concentrating exclusively upon the kinds of bailment that arise from some privity or bargain inter parties, the learned Chief Justice's approach neglects the extended or constructive bailment; by concentrating upon the more conventional types of consensual bailment he neglects certain others which fall within the consensual definition; and by stressing only the elements of purpose and reward he discounts certain other criteria which may affect the obligations of the parties.

NOTES

1. There have been numerous attempts to classify the various types of bailment (they are reviewed by Palmer, paras 3–004 to 3–009). None is entirely satisfactory. Nevertheless, it is common practice amongst textbook writers to divide bailments into two categories: gratuitous bailments (eg where you lend this book to a friend to use without charge) and bailments for reward (eg warehousing, carriage, hire, hire-purchase, and pledge). In certain circumstances, it may also be important to ascertain whether the bailment is for a fixed term or is determinable at the will of the bailor (see earlier, p 79).

2. Where bailment arises out of a contract between bailor and bailee, as is usually the case, the contractual incidents will supplement those that arise out of the proprietary relationship of bailor and bailee. But there does not have to be a contract between the parties for one to become the bailee of the other. For example, where the bailor consents, the bailee may bail the chattel to another person, who becomes the sub-bailee of the original bailor even though there is no contract between them (*Morris v CW Martin & Sons Ltd* [1966] 1 QB 716; *The Pioneer Container* [1994] 2 AC 324). Where there is a non-contractual bailment, the rights and duties of the bailor and the bailee *inter se* may be defined according to the general law of tort. However, it seems that bailment also gives rise to obligations which are independent of both contract and tort, and that there is such a thing as a cause of action in bailment (see *The Pioneer Container* [1994] 2 AC 324 at 343–344, per Lord Goff; *Yearworth v North Bristol NHS Trust* [2009] EWCA Civ 37, [2010] QB 1 at [48], per Lord Judge CJ; Palmer, paras 1–47 to 1–105; A Bell, 'The Place of Bailment in the Modern Law of Obligations' in N Palmer and E McKendrick (eds), *Interests in Goods* (2nd edn, 1998), Ch 19.

3 THREE REQUIREMENTS FOR A BAILMENT

There are three requirements: (1) transfer of possession; (2) ownership remaining in the bailor, or at least not passing to the bailee; and (3) consent by the bailee.

(1) Transfer of possession. Possession lies at the heart of bailment: without a bailee in possession there can be no bailment. In *Ashby v Tolhurst* [1937] 2 KB 242, for example, the owner of a car left it in a private car park. Later the attendant negligently allowed a thief to drive off in the vehicle. The car park owners would not be liable in tort for what was essentially a failure to protect the car from theft, but would be liable if they were bailees. Reversing the trial judge, the Court of Appeal correctly held that they were not bailees: as

the court realised, putting your car on someone's land is not the same thing as putting it into his hands.

(2) Ownership not passing to the bailee. It is essential to bailment that at the end of the bailment the bailee must redeliver the chattel to the bailor or deal with it according to the bailor's instructions. Imagine that A receives a quantity of some commodity such as wheat or oil from B on the basis that its duty is to hand back at a later time not those goods but the same quantity of identical goods. In such a case there is no bailment but a passing of title to A followed by a duty in A to pass title back to B (see *South Australian Insurance Co v Randell* (1869) LR 3 PC 101 and *Wincanton Ltd v P & O Trans European Ltd* [2001] CLC 962 at [19], per Dyson LJ). Another example arises from some contracts to transport oil or gas by pipeline, which can take the form of a duty, not to transport anything but simply to accept a certain quantity of hydrocarbons at one end and discharge an equivalent amount at the other. In neither of these cases is there a bailment. The point can be very important if the 'bailee' becomes insolvent. See the Australian decision in *Chapman Bros v Verco Bros & Co Ltd* (1933) 49 CLR 306 (a case of a grain company taking wheat into storage against a mere obligation to deliver equivalent wheat later: when the company became insolvent, the original owner of the wheat had a mere unsecured claim and thus received nothing).

However, so long as the bailee has not become owner of the goods, the relationship can remain one of bailment. Hence, a buyer under a reservation of title clause may hold as bailee, even though given the power to sell to a sub-buyer or use the goods for manufacturing, unless and until it exercises that power (*Clough Mill Ltd v Martin* [1985] 1 WLR 111 at 116, per Robert Goff LJ). Again, provided that the person in actual possession does not become owner, there can be a bailment of commingled goods belonging to several owners, even though in such a case the bailee's obligation is not to redeliver particular goods but simply to account to each owner for a given quantity rather than particular goods. So in *Mercer v Craven Grain Storage Ltd* [1994] CLC 328 (noted by L Smith, 'Bailment with Authority to Mix—And Substitute' (1995) 111 LQR 10), the House of Lords held that a grain storage society was bailee of grain deposited by a number of farmers, even though the grain delivered by any particular farmer was commingled with grain delivered by others, creating an indistinguishable mass subject to continual additions and withdrawals; in that case the relevant agreement specified that 'the grain shall remain the property of the grower'. See too *Devani v Republic of Kenya* [2015] EWHC 3535 (Admin) at [17] (concerning a similar arrangement over oil storage in a tank farm).

(3) Consent by the bailee. For a bailment in the ordinary sense to exist, the bailee must consent to take possession of the chattel. If he does not, for instance when goods are sent to his premises by mistake (as in *AVX Ltd v EGM Solders Ltd* (1982) The Times, 7 July or *Elvin & Powell Ltd v Plummer Roddis* (1933) 50 TLR 158), he is known as an 'involuntary bailee' and his duty is not that of the ordinary bailee but is limited to a duty to act in good faith as regards the goods (see below, p 99).

Can there be a bailment where the *bailor* has not consented to the bailee having possession of the chattel? Traditionally, bailment has been explained on the basis of mutual consent (see, eg, Pollock and Wright, op cit, p 163: above). More recently, however, the view has been accepted that, whether or not the bailor consents to a bailment relationship, 'any person who voluntarily assumes possession of goods belonging to another will be held to owe at least the principal duties of the bailee at common law' (Palmer, p 37).

The Pioneer Container

[1994] 2 AC 324, Privy Council

Owners of cargo consigned from the United States to Hong Kong (bailors) were held to have consented to an exclusive jurisdiction clause in a contract concluded between the carrier (bailee) and a sub-carrier (sub-bailee) employed to carry the goods over the last stage of the voyage from Taiwan to Hong Kong.

Lord Goff: In truth, at the root of this question lies a doctrinal dispute of a fundamental nature, which is epitomised in the question: is it a prerequisite of a bailment that the bailor should have consented to the bailee's possession of the goods? An affirmative answer to this question (which is the answer given by Bell, *Modern Law of Personal Property in England and Ireland*, at pp 88–89) leads to the conclusion that, if the owner seeks to hold a sub-bailee responsible to him as bailee, he has to accept all the terms of the sub-bailment, warts and all; for either he will have consented to the sub-bailment on those terms or, if not, he will (by holding the sub-bailee liable to him as bailee) be held to have ratified all the terms of the sub-bailment. A negative answer to the question is however supported by other writers, notably by Palmer, *Bailment*, at pp 31 et seq., where Professor Palmer cites a number of examples of bailment without the consent of the owner, and by Professor Tay in her article 'The Essence of Bailment: Contract, Agreement or Possession?' (1966) 5 Sydney Law Review 239. On this approach, a person who voluntarily takes another person's goods into his custody holds them as bailee of that person (the owner); and he can only invoke, for example, terms of a sub-bailment under which he received the goods from an intermediate bailee as qualifying or otherwise affecting his responsibility to the owner if the owner consented to them. It is the latter approach which, as their Lordships have explained, has been adopted by English law and, with English law, the law of Hong Kong.

   Their Lordships wish to add that this conclusion, which flows from the decisions in *Morris v CW Martin & Sons Ltd* [1966] 1 QB 716 and [*York Products Pty Ltd v Gilchrist Watt & Sanderson Pty Ltd* [1970] 1 WLR 1262], produces a result which in their opinion is both principled and just. They incline to the opinion that a sub-bailee can only be said for these purposes to have voluntarily taken into his possession the goods of another if he has sufficient notice that a person other than the bailee is interested in the goods so that it can properly be said that (in addition to his duties to the bailee) he has, by taking the goods into his custody, assumed towards that other person the responsibility for the goods which is characteristic of a bailee. This they believe to be the underlying principle. Moreover, their Lordships do not consider this principle to impose obligations on the sub-bailee which are onerous or unfair, once it is recognised that he can invoke against the owner terms of the sub-bailment which the owner has actually (expressly or impliedly) or even ostensibly authorised. In the last resort the sub-bailee may, if necessary and appropriate, be able to invoke against the bailee the principle of warranty of authority.

See, too, Mance LJ in *East West Corpn v DKBS 1912* [2003] EWCA Civ 83, [2003] QB 1509 at [24] and [26]: 'What is fundamental is not contract, but the *bailee's* consent . . . the essence of bailment is the bailee's voluntary possession of another's goods.'

   However, the participation of the bailor remains important in one respect. As pointed out in *The Pioneer Container*, the bailee owes the duties of a bailee only to those of whom he is aware as possible bailors. Hence it has been held, applying *The Pioneer Container*, that there is no bailment if the bailee is wholly unaware of the existence of the bailor. See *Marcq v Christie, Manson & Woods Ltd* [2003] EWCA Civ 731, [2004] QB 286, where after an auctioneer took possession of painting from X unaware that it had been stolen from Y, the Court of Appeal held no bailor–bailee relationship arose between Y and the auctioneer.

4　THE BAILEE'S LIABILITY

The bailee owes the bailor a duty to take reasonable care of the bailed chattel. This duty of care is central to their relationship. But does the standard of care required of the bailee vary according to whether the bailment is gratuitous or for reward?

Houghland v RR Low (Luxury Coaches) Ltd
[1962] 1 QB 694, Court of Appeal

Returning from a trip to Jersey, Mrs H and her husband boarded one of the defendants' coaches at Southampton. Their suitcase was loaded into the boot of the coach, which was locked by the driver. On the way the coach stopped at Ternhill, Shropshire, for tea. After tea the driver was unable to restart the coach and so he called for a relief coach which arrived some three hours later. During this period the coach stood unattended in the dark. When the relief coach arrived, the driver supervised the loading of the passengers' luggage into it. The unloading of the luggage from the first coach and its transfer to the relief coach was done by the passengers themselves without supervision. The boot of the relief coach was locked. The relief coach continued the journey stopping occasionally to allow passengers to disembark. When the coach arrived at its final destination, Hoylake, Cheshire, Mrs H and her husband could not find their suitcase. Mrs H sued the defendants alleging negligence.

Ormerod LJ: The judge, according to the note that we have of his judgment . . . found in the first place that the driver of the coach was a bailee of the suitcase, and that the bailment was a gratuitous bailment. I am not sure that there is any evidence for the latter finding; and indeed, I might well, I think, have come to a different conclusion. . . .

The judge then found that it was probably at Ternhill that the suitcase was either taken or lost, and in the circumstances he decided that the defendants were liable to pay the plaintiff £82 10s 11d (£82.54).

The objection made to the judgment, as I understand it, is that, as this was a gratuitous bailment, the high degree of negligence required, otherwise called gross negligence in some of the cases, has not been established; that the judge made no finding of negligence, and that, in the circumstances, the judgment should not stand. I am bound to say that I am not sure what is meant by the term 'gross negligence' which has been in use for a long time in cases of this kind. There is no doubt, of course, that it is a phrase which has been commonly used in cases of this sort since the time of *Coggs v Bernard*, when the distinction was made in a judgment of Lord Holt CJ ((1703) 2 Ld Raym 909, 913) which has been frequently referred to and cited; but as we know from the judgment of Lord Chelmsford in *Giblin v McMullen* ((1868) LR 2 PC 317, 336) that it was said, after referring to the use of the term 'gross negligence' over a long period: 'At last, Lord Cranworth (then Baron Rolfe) in the case of *Wilson v Brett* ((1843) 11 M & W 113, 115) objected to it, saying that he "could see no difference between negligence and gross negligence; that it was the same thing, with the addition of a vituperative epithet." And this critical observation has been since approved of by other eminent judges.'

For my part, I have always found some difficulty in understanding just what was 'gross negligence,' because it appears to me that the standard of care required in a case of bailment, or any other type of case, is the standard demanded by the circumstances of that particular case. It seems to me that to try and put a bailment, for instance, into a watertight compartment—such as gratuitous bailment on the one hand, and bailment for reward on the other—is to overlook the fact that there might well be an infinite variety of cases, which might come into one or the other category. The question that we have to consider in a case of this kind, if it is necessary to consider negligence, is whether in the circumstances of this particular case a sufficient standard of care has been observed by the defendants or their servants.

Willmer LJ: I agree, and there is not much that I wish to add. In my judgment, this appeal fails on the facts. In saying that I do not think that it makes any difference whether the case is put in detinue, or whether it is treated as an action on the case for negligence. Whichever be the correct approach, it has been admitted in argument that the plaintiff, by proving the delivery of the suitcase at Southampton and its non-return on the arrival of the coach at Hoylake, made out a prima facie case....

... [T]he defendants could discharge the burden upon them by showing that, although they could not put their finger on what actually did happen to the suitcase, nevertheless, whatever did occur occurred notwithstanding all reasonable care having been exercised by them throughout the whole of the journey. Clearly the judge was not satisfied that they had proved the exercise of any such degree of care throughout the whole of the journey. On the evidence, particularly having regard to his preference for the plaintiff's evidence as against that called for the defendants, it was plainly open to him to come to that conclusion. All we know is that, in relation to the stop at Ternhill, this coach was apparently standing deserted in the middle of the night for a period of three hours. When the relief coach arrived, and the time came to transfer the luggage, this was done apparently with only the one member of the defendants' staff supervising the reloading on the second coach, and with no supervision at all over the discharge of the luggage from the first coach. In those circumstances, it is only too clear that the defendants entirely failed to show that throughout the period, when they had this suitcase in their custody, they exercised reasonable care.

I, therefore, agree that this appeal must fail.

[**Danckwerts LJ** concurred on this point.]

NOTES

1. In *Houghland v RR Low (Luxury Coaches) Ltd* above, the Court of Appeal held that the same test applies to all types of bailment, whether gratuitous or for reward. In *Sutcliffe v Chief Constable of West Yorkshire* [1996] RTR 86, the Court of Appeal followed the *Houghland* case, with Otton LJ making it clear (at 90) that 'no distinction is to be drawn between a gratuitous bailment and one for reward': the bailee's standard of care was that required by the circumstances of the particular case.

It must be admitted, however, that there remain traces of an older approach. Holt CJ in *Coggs v Bernard*, above, suggested (at 915) that different duties might be owed by different kinds of bailee. In *Port Swettenham Authority v TG Wu & Co Sdn Bhd* [1979] AC 580, the Privy Council continued to distinguish between the standard of care expected of a bailee for reward and that expected of a gratuitous bailee; whilst in *The Winson* [1982] AC 939 at 960, Lord Diplock declared that the lower standard of care of a gratuitous bailee is 'too well known and too well-established to call for any citation of authority'. The matter is therefore still open. There is, however, much to be said for the view that, although rigid distinctions cannot be drawn, the professional status of the bailee, or lack of it, should be in account as forming part of the 'circumstances of the particular case', with a higher duty in practice attaching to the professional bailee. See generally A Bell, 'The Place of Bailment in the Modern Law of Obligations' in N Palmer and E McKendrick (eds), *Interests in Goods* (2nd edn, 1998), p 477).

2. Despite the stance taken by the Court of Appeal in *Houghland v RR Low (Luxury Coaches) Ltd*, there remain a number of other reasons for the courts to distinguish between contractual and gratuitous bailments.

First, the Supply of Goods and Services Act 1982 (and, in consumer cases, the Consumer Rights Act 2015) only applies to contractual bailments. The 1982 Act contains provisions relating to the bailee's duty of care (when the contract is for the supply of services in the course of business: s 13) and the bailor's obligations to the bailee (when the contract is for the hire of goods: ss 7–10).

Secondly, there may be contractual exemption clauses which exclude or limit the bailee's duties, subject to those controls contained in the Unfair Contract Terms Act 1977 (and, in consumer cases, the Consumer Rights Act 2015). If they are contained in a contract between bailor and bailee, the matter is straightforward. If it is sought to apply these clauses against or in favour of those who are not party to the contract, the position is more complicated: see Section 6 below.

3. In certain circumstances, the bailee's liability for loss or damage to the bailed chattel may be strict. Strict liability generally arises as follows.

(a) Where the bailee is a common carrier, unless the loss or damage to the goods is caused by an excepted peril, for example an Act of God, inherent vice, etc. This is of little if any importance today, since few if any contemporary carriers retain the status of common carriers.

(b) Where the bailee 'deviates' in the conduct of the bailment: for example, by storing the chattel somewhere other than the place agreed (*Lilley v Doubleday* (1881) 7 QBD 510); or by entrusting the chattel without authority to a third person (*Edwards v Newland & Co* [1950] 2 KB 534); or by wrongfully refusing to return the chattel, or negligently failing to return it, when called upon to do so by the bailor at the end of the bailment (*Mitchell v Ealing London Borough Council* [1979] QB 1; or by carrying the chattel otherwise than by the agreed route, unless there is no causative link between the deviation and loss or damage to the chattel (*Morrison & Co Ltd v Shaw, Savill and Albion Co Ltd* [1916] 2 KB 783). (Deviation in the conduct of the bailment also has other consequences: it amounts to a repudiatory breach and gives the bailor an immediate right to possess the chattel; where the deviation is so serious as to amount to a blatant disregard of the bailor's interests, it may constitute conversion by the bailee (*Garnham, Harris and Elton Ltd v Alfred W Ellis (Transport) Ltd* [1967] 2 Lloyd's Rep 22); and the bailee will generally lose the protection of any contractual exclusion clauses (*Gibaud v Great Eastern Rly Co* [1921] 2 KB 426; see also Bell, pp 115–118).)

4. It is traditionally said that an 'involuntary bailee' will not be liable for mere negligence (*Howard v Harris* (1884) Cab & El 253: theatre manager not liable for loss of unsolicited script of play sent to him by playwright) and that his sole duty is to refrain from intentional destruction or damage of the goods (*Hiort v Bott* (1874) LR 9 Exch 86 at 90, per Bramwell B, *obiter*; *Elvin & Powell Ltd v Plummer Roddis* (1933) 50 TLR 158). This may apparently include getting rid of goods that reasonably seem unwanted: *Robot Arenas Ltd v Waterfield* [2010] EWHC 115 (QB). However, the matter is not beyond controversy. A minority view holds that an involuntary bailee of goods should owe a duty of care towards their owner, although the standard of care, which will vary according to what is reasonable in all the circumstances of the case, will generally be an undemanding one given that the involuntary bailee did not agree to have the goods in the first place (Palmer, para 13–013; see too *Da Rocha-Afodu v Mortgage Express Ltd* [2014] EWCA Civ 454 at [44]–[50], per Arden LJ).

5 THE BURDEN OF PROOF

Houghland v RR Low (Luxury Coaches) Ltd
[1962] 1 QB 694, Court of Appeal

For the facts, see above, p 97. One issue that arose was where the burden of proof lay: was it up to Mr & Mrs H to prove that the coach company had been at fault in losing their luggage, or did the company have to prove lack of negligence?

Ormerod LJ: … It has been admitted by Mr Somerset Jones on behalf of the defendants that this is a case where a prima facie case has been established by the plaintiff. If that be so, I find it difficult to appreciate that there can be any grounds for appeal. Mr Somerset Jones has endeavoured to establish, and he has done it by reference to authority, that to found a prima facie case is not sufficient—that there must, in addition, be affirmative evidence before the plaintiff can succeed. I am bound to say that is a doctrine which rather surprises me. If a prima facie case is once established, it is something which may be rebutted easily, but it can only be rebutted by evidence, and that is not present in this case; and therefore, the prima facie case having been established, still remains.

Supposing that the claim is one in detinue, then it would appear that once the bailment has been established, and once the failure of the bailee to hand over the articles in question has been proved, there is a prima facie case, and the plaintiff is entitled to recover, unless the defendant can establish to the satisfaction of the court a defence; and that, I think, is very clear from the words used by Bankes LJ in *Coldman v Hill* ([1919] 1 KB 443, 449) in a passage that appears to me to be important in this case: 'I think the law still is that if a bailee is sued in detinue only, it is a good answer for him to say that the goods were stolen without any default on his part, as the general bailment laid in the declaration pledges the plaintiff to the proof of nothing except that the goods were in the defendant's hands and were wrongfully detained.' So far, so good, but it is, of course, in those circumstances for the defendants to establish affirmatively, not only that the goods were stolen, but that they were stolen without default on their part; in other words, that there was no negligence on their part in the care which they took of the goods.

Applying that principle here, Mr Somerset Jones has been at pains to point out that the judge has made no finding that these goods were in fact stolen. The only view that the judge has expressed on the point is: 'It is impossible to say what happened to this suitcase when it was lost on its journey,' and with that I am bound to agree. It was put on the coach at Southampton, and it was not in the boot of the relief coach when it arrived at Hoylake. The judge has come to the conclusion that, on the probabilities, and again I agree with him, something happened to that suitcase when the transfer took place at Ternhill, or when the coach was delayed for some considerable period of time there. There seems to be no doubt that for something like three hours in the darkness that coach remained there unattended.

In these circumstances, I find it difficult to appreciate what substance there is in the complaint made by Mr Somerset Jones that in this case the judge, in treating this as a case of detinue, was in error. But let us suppose for a moment that the issue here is an issue in negligence: then he admits, and I think properly admits, that there is a prima facie case against the defendants derived from the fact that the suitcase was found by the judge to have been put on the coach at Southampton, and was not on the second coach when it arrived at its destination at Hoylake. In those circumstances, it is for the defendants to adduce evidence which will rebut a presumption of negligence.

…

In the circumstances, I fail to see where the judge went wrong, and I would dismiss this appeal.

Willmer LJ: I agree, and there is not much that I wish to add. In my judgment, this appeal fails on the facts. In saying that I do not think that it makes any difference whether the case is put in detinue, or whether it is treated as an action on the case for negligence. Whichever be the correct approach, it has been admitted in argument that the plaintiff, by proving the delivery of the suitcase at Southampton and its non-return on the arrival of the coach at Hoylake, made out a prima facie case. That prima facie case stands unless and until it is rebutted. The burden was on the defendants to adduce evidence in rebuttal. They could discharge that burden by proving what in fact did happen to the suitcase, and by showing that what did happen happened without any default on their part. They certainly did not succeed in doing that, for the judge was left in the position that he simply did not know what did happen to the suitcase.

[**Danckwerts LJ** concurred.]

NOTES

1. For other cases demonstrating the reversal of the burden of proof in bailment cases, see *Ulster-Swift Ltd v Taunton Meat Haulage Ltd* [1977] 1 WLR 625 at 636, per Megaw LJ and *Port Swettenham Authority v TW Wu & Co Sdn Bhd* [1979] AC 580.

2. This principle is particularly important commercially in carriage cases. All that the claimant has to prove is that the goods were taken over in good condition and delivered damaged (or not delivered at all): it is then up to the carrier to prove if it can that the loss or damage was caused by a factor for which it was not responsible. See, for example, *Gosse Millerd Ltd v Canadian Government Merchant Marine Ltd* [1929] AC 223 at 234, per Lord Hailsham. This principle, it should be noted, also applies to a number of other international carriage regimes: for instance, to international carriage by sea under the Hague–Visby Rules, to carriage by road under the Convention on the Contract for the International Carriage of Goods by Road (CMR Convention), and to carriage by air under the Warsaw Convention 1929 and the Montreal Convention 1999.

3. The reference to detinue needs explaining. Where a bailee cannot produce the goods bailed to him, the bailor can sue the bailee for breach of bailment; but he may alternatively sue for the tort of conversion (see above, p 81). In either case, the burden remains on the bailee to explain the loss. Until 1977 (and hence in 1966 when *Houghland*'s case was decided) the bailor sued, not in conversion, but for the separate tort of detinue: but by s 2 of the Torts (Interference with Goods) Act 1977 the tort of detinue was suppressed and replaced in this connection with a statutory liability in conversion.

6 BAILMENT AND THIRD PARTIES

Not only a bailor can create a bailment: a bailee may himself create a further bailment, known as a sub-bailment. An example is where a carrier in possession of goods (the bailee) subcontracts the carriage for part of the transit to a different carrier (sub-bailee), or where goods in the hands of a repairer (bailee) are physically entrusted to a specialist subcontractor (sub-bailee). Such an arrangement generally creates no privity of contract between goods owner and sub-bailee, but nevertheless gives rise to duties of care owed by the sub-bailee directly to the owner.

(a) The terms of the sub-bailment and the goods owner

What we have just said immediately raises a further question. If the sub-bailment contains specific terms regulating the sub-bailee's liability or putting duties on the sub-bailee, is the owner bound by, and can it enforce, those terms?

(1) Is the owner bound? In *The Pioneer Container* [1994] 2 AC 324, the Privy Council held that a sub-bailee who knows that the goods are not the bailee's goods can rely on a term of the sub-bailment where the bailor has expressly or impliedly consented to that term or if the bailee has ostensible authority to include the term in the sub-bailment. In that case, the term was an exclusive jurisdiction clause: but the principle equally applies to an exception clause (see, eg, *Morris v CW Martin & Sons Ltd* [1966] 1 QB 716 and *York Products Pty Ltd v Gilchrist Watt & Sanderson Pty Ltd* [1970] 1 WLR 1262) and to provisions allowing the sub-bailee to take reasonable steps with regard to uncollected goods (*Sang Stone Hamoon Jonoub Co Ltd v Baoyue Shipping Co Ltd* [2015] EWHC 2288 (Comm), [2016] 1 Lloyd's Rep 320).

(2) In the converse case, can the owner invoke the terms of the sub-bailment for its own benefit? The answer is yes, in two cases. One is where the bailee has the owner's express or implied authority to contract on its behalf with the sub-bailee. In *Sandeman Coprimar SA v Transitos y Transportes Integrales SL* [2003] EWCA Civ 113, [2003] QB 1270 at [62], Lord Phillips MR, delivering the judgment of the court, said (at [63]):

> Where a bailee had the consent, and thus the authority, of the bailor to enter into a sub-bailment on particular terms and does so, and where those terms purport to govern the relationship not merely between the sub-bailee and the bailee, but between the sub-bailee and bailor, it seems to us that all the elements of a collateral contract binding the sub-bailee and the bailor will be present, for there will be privity, via the agency of the bailee, and no difficulty in identifying consideration, at least if the terms are capable of resulting in benefit to each of the parties.

The other case is where a term in the contract between bailee and sub-bailee expressly or impliedly purports to enure to the benefit of the goods owner. In this case, the latter may be able to invoke the provisions of the Contracts (Rights of Third Parties) Act 1999 to enforce the term for its own benefit. For the details of this Act, see for example J Beatson, A Burrows, and J Cartwright, *Anson's Law of Contract* (29th edn, 2010), pp 624 ff. This point could be commercially significant. Imagine, for example, that a subcontracted carrier of frozen meat contracts with the main carrier to maintain a given temperature, but fails to do so and the meat deteriorates as a result. The 1999 Act might well allow a direct action by the owner against the subcontracted carrier for any loss suffered.

(b) The terms of the bailment and the sub-bailee

Conversely, the sub-bailee may also benefit from a clause in the main contract, such as one exempting him from liability (although much turns on the construction of the clause in question: see *The Mahkutai* [1996] AC 650, PC). Since the abolition of the strict rule of privity of contract in 1999, this rule can now also be based on s 1(6) of the Contracts (Rights of Third Parties) Act 1999.

But where the sub-bailee speaks for himself, for example by issuing a shipping note direct to the bailor, the terms of that note will take precedence where they are inconsistent with the terms of contract between the bailor and the bailee (*Lotus Cars Ltd v Southampton Cargo Handling plc* [2000] 2 All ER (Comm) 705 at [49], per Rix LJ).

(c) The liability of the bailee for the fault of the sub-bailee

Apart from what we have said above, it should always be remembered that where a bailee of goods creates a sub-bailment, the bailee is presumptively liable for the negligence of the sub-bailee, even in the absence of personal fault himself. See, for example, *Morris v CW Martin & Sons Ltd* [1966] 1 QB 716 at 725–728, per Lord Denning MR. This is a rule of some importance in the case of carriage and warehousing contracts, since it allows the goods owner in almost all cases to sue the person with whom he has contracted if there has been damage caused by fault, without regard to whose fault was responsible. It should also be remembered that many international transport conventions apply a similar rule: examples include the Hague–Visby Rules (carriage by sea), the CMR Convention (international carriage by road within Europe and neighbouring states), and the Warsaw and Montreal Conventions (carriage by air). It goes without saying that in such cases the bailor who has been held liable can, subject to any terms in the contract between it and the sub-bailee, recover an indemnity from the latter.

QUESTIONS

1.   Henty Ltd, retail jewellers, took a large diamond to diamond cutters Piercy Ltd to be cut, for a fee. Piercy told Henty's employee to return and collect it the next day. Piercy cut the diamond, locked it in their safe, and locked up for the night. That night a thief broke into Piercy's workshop, forced the safe, and stole the diamond. Will Piercy be liable to Henty for this loss? Would your answer be different if Piercy's employee had been tricked into handing over the diamond to the thief, who had falsely but convincingly claimed to be Henty's van driver and had produced a cleverly forged letter of authority from Henty? Again, would it make any difference to your answer if the thief had executed his fraud some six months after Henty had delivered the diamond to Piercy and, in the interim, Piercy had constantly urged Henty to come and collect it?

2.   Electron plc, a manufacturer of electrical goods, arranged to store a large consignment of valuable products in Securestore Ltd's warehouse in Manchester. Electron paid all storage charges in advance and warned Securestore to have the components ready for it to collect in six months' time. After the goods had been delivered to Securestore's warehouse, Securestore sold them to Transtech plc, another manufacturer of electrical products in Leeds, and employed Cargosure Ltd, a firm of hauliers, to transport them to Transtech's factory. During the transit, Cargosure's lorry was blown over by freak hurricane-force winds; it and its cargo were completely destroyed. What rights, if any, does Electron have against Securestore and/ or Cargosure? See the Notes above and also *Hollins v Fowler* (1875) LR 7 HL 757 at 766–767; *Marcq v Christie, Manson & Woods Ltd* [2003] EWCA Civ 731, [2004] QB 286 at [53].

PART II

THE LAW OF AGENCY

Chapter 4   Introduction   107
Chapter 5   Creation of agency, and the authority of the agent   125
Chapter 6   Relations with third parties   168
Chapter 7   Relations between principal and agent   224

INTRODUCTION

1 THE LEGAL CONCEPT OF AGENCY

(a) Definitions of agency

> Agency is the fiduciary relationship that arises when one person (a 'principal') manifests assent to another person (an 'agent') that the agent shall act on the principal's behalf and subject to the principal's control, and the agent manifests or otherwise consents so to act.
>
> (American Law Institute, *Restatement of the Law of Agency* (3rd edn, 2006), para 1.01)

> Agency is the fiduciary relationship which exists between two persons, one of whom expressly or impliedly manifests assent that the other should act on his behalf so as to affect his relations with third parties, and the other of whom similarly manifests assent so to act or so acts pursuant to the manifestation.
>
> (FMB Reynolds, *Bowstead and Reynolds on Agency* (20th edn, 2014), art 1(1))

> Agency is the relationship that exists between two persons when one, called the *agent*, is considered in law to represent the other, called the *principal*, in such a way as to be able to affect the principal's legal position in respect of strangers to the relationship by the making of contracts or the disposition of property.
>
> (GHL Fridman, *The Law of Agency* (7th edn, 1996), p 11)

NOTES

1. Any concise definition of the concept of agency must be treated with care.[1] Striving for brevity, the definition is likely to be flawed by errors and omissions which may make it misleading. For instance, in art 1(4) *Bowstead and Reynolds* additionally recognises that the relationship of principal and agent may sometimes exist where a person acts on behalf of a

---

[1] In this and the succeeding chapters dealing with the law of agency, the following abbreviations are used in referring to standard textbooks:

Bowstead and Reynolds: Peter G Watts, *Bowstead and Reynolds on Agency* (20th edn, 2014);
Fridman: GHL Fridman, *The Law of Agency* (7th edn, 1996);
Munday: RJC Munday *Agency: Law and Principles* (3rd edn, 2016).

principal but has *no* authority to affect the principal's relations with third parties, provided that the relationship is a fiduciary one. This would cover, say, an introduction agent (an agent whose activities are specifically regulated in some jurisdictions: for example, the Introduction Agents Act 2001 (Queensland), in which s 8(1)(a) defines an introduction agent as 'a person who carries on a business of providing, or offering to provide, an introduction service…'). Nevertheless, the definitions set out above do provide a starting point from which to begin our assessment of the theoretical basis of agency.

2.   Various theories have been advanced to explain the concept of agency (they are reviewed in *Bowstead and Reynolds*, Ch 1). The definition provided in *Bowstead and Reynolds*, which is based on that given in the US *Restatement* (3rd edn, 2006), focuses on the manifestation of assent to the agency by both the principal and the agent. In most cases the principal agrees to the agent acting on his behalf and the agent agrees to do so. *Bowstead and Reynolds* designates this the 'paradigm case' (para 1–011). The consent theory, however, breaks down when we move away from the paradigm case. The theory fails to take account of the fact that agency can also arise in cases where the agent only enjoys apparent authority (below, pp 132–146), irrespective of, and sometimes contrary to, the wishes of the parties (see, eg, *Boardman v Phipps* [1967] 2 AC 46, where the House of Lords held that an agency relationship existed even though there was no consent by the principal). Such cases can only be brought within the consent theory by a strained construction of the term 'consent' (cf *Bowstead and Reynolds*, para 1–013: 'the authority stems from the principal's objectively determined assent'; see also G McMeel (2000) 116 LQR 387, 392: 'qualified by the objective principle, the consent theory of agency is capable of explaining the majority of agency cases'). Nor is there consent where agency arises by operation of law, notably in cases of agency of necessity (below, pp 152–158). Furthermore, the consent theory is liable to turn the question of whether an agency relationship exists into a question of fact (ie if there is consent, there is agency), when it is really a question of law. In the words of Lord Pearson in *Garnac Grain Co Inc v HMF Faure and Fairclough Ltd* [1968] AC 1130 at 1137:

> [the parties] will be held to have consented *if they have agreed to what amounts in law to such a relationship*, even if they do not recognise it themselves and even if they have professed to disclaim it. (Emphasis added)

Lord Wilberforce, in *Branwhite v Worcester Works Finance Ltd* [1969] 1 AC 552 at 587, endorsed Lord Pearson's statement. Having quoted this passage, Lord Wilberforce went on to say:

> The significant words, for the present purpose, are 'if they have agreed to what amounts in law to such a relationship…' These I understand as pointing to the fact that, while agency must ultimately derive from consent, the consent need not necessarily be to the relationship of principal and agent itself (indeed the existence of it may be denied) but may be to a state of fact upon which the law imposes the consequences which result from agency. It is consensual, not contractual.

These passages are commonly quoted, and applied, in practice: for example, *UBS AG (London Branch) v Kommunale Wasserwerke Leipzig GmbH* [2014] EWHC 3615 (Comm), Males J; *Khouj v Acropolis Capital Partners Ltd* [2016] EWHC 2120 (Comm), Knowles J.

3.   Fridman's definition of agency is based on a power–liability analysis of the relationship between the principal and agent. The power–liability analysis focuses on the agent's power to alter the principal's *legal* relations with third parties (in particular by making contracts on behalf of the principal or by disposing of the principal's property) and the principal's consequent liability to have his relations so altered. The power–liability relationship of the principal and agent is best explained by Professor Dowrick in the next extract.

'The Relationship of Principal and Agent' by FE Dowrick
(1954) 17 MLR 24 at 36–38

The essential characteristic of an agent is that he is invested with a legal power to alter his principal's legal relations with third persons: the principal is under a correlative liability to have his legal relations altered. It is submitted that this power-liability relation is the essence of the relationship of principal and agent. The rules which normally attach to the parties, the normal incidents of the relation, are ancillary to this power-liability relation. To satisfy principals' claims in a myriad of cases the judges have imposed on agents certain rules constituting safeguards against the abuse of their powers. To satisfy agents' claims for reimbursement the judges have granted certain rights to agents. But the parties, the best judges of their own interests, may exclude these normal incidents of the relation by their agreement. This power-liability relation, which, it is contended, is the nucleus of the relation of principal and agent, needs to be examined more closely. A power-liability relation is one of the fundamental legal relations. It exists between two persons, A and B, when A has the ability, conferred on him by law, by his own acts to alter B's legal relations. Agency is but one of the numerous kinds of power-liability relations recognised in our legal system. The distinctive feature of the agency power-liability relation is that the power of the one party to alter the legal relations of the other party is a reproduction of the power possessed by the latter to alter his own legal position. In other words, the power conferred by law on the agent is a facsimile of the principal's own power. This is to be inferred from the main principles of the law of agency, notably the following: when an agent acts on behalf of his principal in a legal transaction and uses the principal's name, the result in law is that the principal's legal position is altered but the agent himself drops out of the transaction: persons who are not themselves *sui juris* may nevertheless have the power to act as agents for persons who are: the power of an agent to bind his principal is limited to the power of the principal to bind himself: if the powers of the principal to alter his own legal relations are ended by his death, insanity, or bankruptcy, the agent's powers are terminated automatically . . .

   At this juncture it is tempting to define the relation of principal and agent as that existing between two legal persons, P and A, when A is invested with a legal power to alter P's legal relations which is a facsimile of the legal power possessed by P himself, and further to proceed to distinguish the relation from such other special legal relations as master-servant and trustee-beneficiary on the simple ground that in the latter relations this power-liability nexus is not essential. But in common law special legal relations are not to be confined within the strait-jackets of definitions; *elegantia juris* may be achieved only at the expense of the dynamic element in our law. Moreover the distinctions between agency and these other special legal relations cannot be so sharply drawn. Suffice it to assert that in mid-twentieth-century English law the nucleus of the rules in the doctrine of principal and agent is this power-liability relation.

NOTES

1. The terms 'power' and 'authority' should not be confused. As Professor Dowrick has emphasised (op cit, p 37 fn):

> A power is a legal concept: it connotes the ability of a person to alter legal relations by doing some act: an agent's power is such an ability existing in the eyes of the law. Authority is a matter of fact: it connotes that one person has given instructions or permission to another to act on his behalf. The legal attribute of an agent, his power, may be called into being by the fact that he has his principal's authority to act, but it may be called into being by other facts, such as the necessity of the case.

2. It is clear, therefore, that the principal cannot actually confer power on his agent. As Professor Montrose has explained ((1938) 16 Can Bar Rev 757 at 761):

> The term power . . . is a legal relation, one which exists by virtue of a legal rule. The power of an agent is not strictly conferred by the principal but by the law: the principal and agent do the acts which bring the rule into operation, as a result of which the agent acquires a power.

The legal rule will be brought into operation if the principal actually authorises the agent to do certain acts. Once the legal rule comes into operation the agent will be vested with power to affect the principal's legal relations with third parties. Even if the principal does not give the agent any authority, or the agent exceeds his authority, the legal rule may still be brought into operation and vest the agent with power. In such circumstances, public policy will determine the existence and extent of the agent's power to affect his principal's relations (see, generally, WA Seavey (1920) 29 Yale LJ 859 and JL Montrose, op cit, p 761). For further jurisprudential discussion of the power–liability relation, see WN Hohfeld, *Fundamental Legal Conceptions as Applied in Judicial Reasoning* (1923), pp 50–60; WM Dias, *Jurisprudence* (5th edn, 1985), pp 33–39; M Kramer, 'Rights without Trimmings' in M Kramer, N Simmonds, and H Steiner (eds), *A Debate over Rights* (1998), pp 7–22; W Edmundson, *An Introduction to Rights* (2nd edn, 2012), pp 71–82.

3. Explaining agency in terms of a power–liability relationship appears to avoid the criticisms which we have already made of those definitions based on the consent of the parties (see above, p 108). However, the danger with an explanation which focuses on the agent's power to affect the principal's relations with third parties is that it shifts attention away from the *internal* relationship between the principal and agent to the *external* relationship between the principal and third party. It must always be remembered that agency is a triangular relationship between principal, agent, and third party. The law of agency is as much concerned with the relationship between the principal and agent (eg the agent's right to remuneration or indemnity from the principal; the agent's fiduciary duties owed to the principal) as it is concerned with the relationship between the principal and third party. The triangular relationship between principal, agent, and third party is highlighted in the next extract, taken from an article by Professor McMeel in which he subjects the power–liability analysis, advanced by Professor Dowrick, to penetrating criticism.

'Philosophical Foundations of the Law of Agency' by G McMeel
(2000) 116 LQR 387 at 393–396

> The seminal instance of 'power-liability' analysis is acknowledged to be Hohfeld in *Fundamental Legal Conceptions* which first appeared in 1913:
>
> > ...X has the power to create contractual obligations of various kinds. Agency cases are likewise instructive. By use of some metaphorical expression such as the Latin, *qui facit per alium, facit per se*, the true nature of agency relations is only too frequently obscured. The creation of the agency relation involves, inter alia, the grant of legal powers to the so-called agent, and the creation of correlative liabilities in the principal. That is to say, one party P has the power to create agency powers in another party A,—for example, the power to convey X's property, the power to impose (so-called) contractual obligations on P, the power to 'receive' title to property so that it shall vest in P, and so forth.
>
> This discussion was contextualised in Hohfeld's conceptual critique of attempts to reduce most legal relationships simply to rights and duties. Instead, he proposed four categories of rights together with their jural correlatives and opposites. First, true *rights*; correlative: *duty*; opposite: no rights. Secondly, *privilege*; correlative: *no right*; opposite: duty. Thirdly, *power*; correlative: *liability*; opposite: disability. Fourthly, *immunity*; correlative: *disability*; opposite: liability. Further, Hohfeld suggests the nearest synonym for 'power' is '(legal) ability'. Note in the extract, Hohfeld first mentions the ability to enter into contracts. Prior to that, he instanced the example of the power to dispose of one's own property.
>
> It is clearly correct at this level of generality to classify agency reasoning as a species of legal power or ability. It was an important insight of Hart's jurisprudence that modern systems of law are constituted as much by power-conferring rules (both in the public and private spheres) as by duty-imposing norms. Such 'facilitative institutions' constitute a large segment of private law, not just contract and commercial law, but also corporate law, trusts and succession. In the particular context of agency, the deployment of conceptual tools such as 'power' and 'liability' merits close analysis. Note that Dowrick speaks of the agent having the power to affect the principal's legal relations, and the principal coming under a correlative liability to the third party. Contrast the earlier analysis of Hohfeld which more accurately captures the existence of two distinct legal powers. First, the *principal's power* to confer upon an agent the power to act upon his behalf. This results, in Pollock's graphic phrase, in the law recognising that '...by agency the individual's legal personality is multiplied in space'. Note multiplication: nothing in agency doctrine forbids a principal from acting personally in respect of the business entrusted to the agent. Secondly and consequently, the *agent's power* to act upon the principal's behalf and to impose obligations on him *vis-à-vis* third parties, within the scope of his authority. Further, contrary to Dowrick's, but consistent with Hohfeld's formulation, there are two separate liabilities. First, the *principal's*: having conferred power upon the agent, he is subject to obligations and liabilities to third parties under the transactions thereby effected. Secondly, the *agent's*: if he chooses to act in accordance with the powers entrusted to him, he must do so in accordance with the legal consequences which attend agency. He must act with reasonable care and skill and he is subject to the stringency of the fiduciary regime. The first of these two distinct power-liability relationships is explicit in Hohfeld's formulation, and the second (it is submitted) is implicit in it.
>
> Pursuing the critique of Dowrick's elision a little further it is submitted that, the true explanation of even simple legal phenomena may require complex analysis—a spider's web [of] conceptually

distinct relations. Where there is a contractual regime between principal and agent, the agent may be bound to act and the principal bound to remunerate, yielding a relationship of the Hofeldian claim-rights and duties. To this framework must be added the claim-right/duty *vinculum juris* which results between principal and third party. Note that the triangular relationship involved in agency requires rejection of Dowrick's over-simplification. It is superseded by at least three logically distinct relationships. Whatever lip service is paid to the (simplified) power-liability analysis, in practice textbooks do regard agency in this way. The details of the rules of the three sides of the triangular nexus—principal/agent; agent/contractor; contractor/principal—are analysed separately. Therefore, it is submitted, true Hohfeldian analysis yields a complex nexus of relationships at a conceptual level. Much modern agency theory fails to do justice to the Hohfeldian scheme.

So why the shift in emphasis between Hohfeld's and Dowrick's analysis? Hohfeld's discussion needs to be contextualised in his discussion of other 'facilitative institutions': agency is treated alongside the general ability to contract, and to dispose of property interests by acts of transmissive consent. The discussion is not directed to non-core instances of agency, such as apparent authority or agency of necessity, but seems to envisage only actual authority. Contrast Dowrick and other 'externalised theories' which are directed to incorporating the miscellaneous examples of non-standard doctrine into a single grand theory of agency. Therefore the double power-liability analysis of Hohfeld (which is only apt to cover consensual manifestations of agency) is transmuted into a single power-liability analysis. The agent is invested with power to affect the principal's legal relations. Therefore it is the task of jurists to enumerate the instances where the law recognises such power: there is no need to focus upon consensual instances. The principal, consequently, is under liability to any third parties who deal with the legally constituted agent: his consent is not conclusive of this legal determination. The reformulated power-liability analysis is seen as having three key strengths. First, it unites the various instances of agency into a single formulation which applies to each equally, without having to recognise any particular example (such as consensual agency) as the paradigm case. Secondly, it emphasises that the recognition of the relationship of agency is a matter of law, and not simply a determination of the facts. The answer to the legal question posed depends upon considerations of public policy generally, and is not simply focused upon consent. Thirdly, in contradistinction to the consensual model which concentrates upon the linear relationship between principal and agent, the power-liability model focuses upon the triangular configuration which is a hallmark of true agency. Rather than being attentive solely to the 'internal relationship' between principal and agent, consideration is paid to the 'external relationship' between principal/agent and contractor.

The strengths of the 'power-liability' analysis are clear, but weaknesses soon begin to surface. Is it not the case that the conceptual elegance of the resulting model is bought at the expense of under-elaboration of doctrine? Whether the agent is invested with power is treated as being a question of public policy. However once it is admitted that evidence of the principal's consent to the agent wielding power on his behalf is a sufficient public policy reason to recognise agency, there is serious danger of the 'power-liability' model collapsing into the qualified consensual approach. Further, by de-emphasising Hohfeld's 'power-to-invest-another-with-power' approach, the modern power-liability model overlooks the paradigm instance of responsibility, in favour of more marginal cases. Most significantly the refined model does not advert to the responsibilities of the agent in discharging the functions conferred upon him, such as duties of competence and fidelity. A favourite case with power-liability theorists, *Boardman v. Phipps*, where there was no consent (and no possibility of consent) to the actions of the 'self-appointed' agents, was concerned not with the liability of the principal, but the liability of the agent for breach of fiduciary duty. Therefore, like many simple models, the power-liability analysis only presents one perspective on a multi-dimensional phenomenon. This was inevitable when the aim of 'power-liability' theorists was to reduce agency relationships to the lowest common denominator.

NOTES

1. McMeel (at p 396) considers that:

> The danger of a modern 'power-liability' analysis of agency collapsing into a qualified consensual model, is not accidental. Its location on a slippery slope is inevitable and understandable once it is appreciated that the 'power-liability' and the 'consensual' model are not opposing accounts of the same legal doctrine. Rather they are examples of different types of legal theory. In truth, rather than being in opposition to one another, the two theories are readily reconcilable.

McMeel regards the 'power–liability' model as an example of 'ontological', 'conceptual', or 'descriptive' theorising, whereas he sees the 'consensual' model as a species of a 'normative', 'justificatory', or 'presumptive' analysis (see pp 396–399). In his view (expressed at p 398), '[n]othing in the "power-liability" analysis contradicts the "consensual model" and vice-versa'.

2. McMeel places a 'qualified consent' model at the heart of his analysis of the nature of agency (at pp 400–401):

> Modern contract law is at its core consensual, but is supplemented by principles which protect injurious reliance. Turning back to agency, it is submitted that a consensual model, supplemented by protection of misplaced reliance, can account for all the legally recognised instances of actual and apparent authority . . . With regard to other agency doctrines, ratification or *post hoc* authority can be regarded as a matter of commercial reality, recognising that authorisation as a matter of mercantile practice may not always be neatly contemporaneous with the initial transaction. Similarly, the agent's liability for breach of warranty of authority can be seen as an archetypal instance of legal protection for misplaced reliance upon the deed or words of others.

McMeel acknowledges that agency of necessity is more difficult to account for, but regards true agency of necessity (ie where the necessitous intervener creates contractual rights and obligations between principal and third party) as so rare 'that it seems misguided to distort the conceptual account of the nature of agency just in order to accommodate it' (at p 409).

3. In response, it is submitted that while actual consent lies at the heart of most agency cases, this can just as readily be seen as one of several 'triggers' that activate the legal rule vesting the agent with power to affect the principal's legal relations with third parties. The power–liability theory embraces cases of actual consent and also what McMeel describes as cases involving 'protection of misplaced reliance'. We shall see (at pp 132–146) that in cases of apparent authority the principal may become exposed to contractual liabilities to a third party without the benefit of reciprocal rights (hence the need for ratification). This, it is suggested, is a public policy response to acts or omissions of the principal that are far removed from anything that can in reality (as opposed to by some legal fiction) be described as 'consent'. Even the objective principle when applied to contract formation allows both parties (including the party whose intentions have been objectively assessed) to enforce the resultant contract. Finally, it is submitted that the consent theory cannot stand on its own two feet: it requires support from at least two sources. The first is that it must be 'supplemented by the principle protecting misplaced reliance (or the policy favouring an objective reading of commercial communications)'; the second is that 'it is further supplemented by instances of policy motivated recognitions of agency' (McMeel, p 410).

(b) Agency distinguished from other relationships

We have seen how Professor Dowrick distinguished agency from other power–liability relationships. But what are those other relationships?

Agency and the trust Agents and trustees are similar in many ways. They can, for example, both affect the legal position of those persons with whose affairs they are dealing and are both accountable to their principals for any profits derived from their position. These similarities, however, mask an important conceptual difference between the two institutions. Whereas an agent acts for another, a trustee holds property for another. This means that the beneficial owner of the property held in trust will usually be able to enforce his rights against the trustee on a proprietary basis, whereas a principal may only be able to enforce his rights against an agent on a personal basis (although the principal may have a proprietary remedy against an agent who has breached his fiduciary duties: see, eg, *A-G for Hong Kong v Reid* [1994] 1 AC 324, PC; *European Ventures LLP v Cedar Capital Partners LLC* [2014] UKSC 45, [2014] 3 WLR 535, SC. See further Munday, paras 8.44–8.48). Furthermore, whereas an agent represents his principal to the outside world, the trustee does not represent the beneficiary and so cannot create contractual relations between that beneficiary and third parties. For further differences between agency and trusts, see Fridman, pp 23–27.

Finally, it is important to note that a normal principal and agent relationship does not of itself give rise to a trust relationship (*Kingscroft Insurance Co Ltd v HS Weavers (Underwriting) Agencies Ltd* [1993] 1 Lloyd's Rep 187 at 191, per Harman J). Whether there is a simultaneous trust relationship between the principal and agent will depend on the intentions of the parties, which are usually ascertained from the terms of the agency contract (see *Bowstead and Reynolds*, para 6–040).

Agency and bailment Bailment occurs when there is the delivery or transfer of a chattel (or other item of personal property) by one person (the bailor) to another (the bailee) with a specific mandate which requires the identical item to be delivered up to the bailor or to be dealt with in a particular way by the bailee (see above, pp 92 ff). There are two important features which distinguish agency and bailment; namely:

(1) whilst the bailee merely exercises, with leave of the bailor, certain powers over the bailed property, unlike the agent, the bailee does not represent the bailor; and

(2) the bailee cannot enter into contracts on the bailor's behalf, although he may have power to do things which are reasonably incidental to his use of the goods which he holds (eg to have the property repaired) and thereby make the bailor liable to a third party (see, eg, *Tappenden v Artus* [1964] 2 QB 185).

Agency and sale Consider the following situations.

(1) A asks B to acquire goods for him, and B is held to be A's agent. In these circumstances A will be privy to any contract B makes with his supplier; B will not be liable for failing to acquire the goods if he has used his best endeavours to do so; and B will not be liable if the goods prove defective so long as he exercised due care and skill in his purchase from the third party. On the other hand, if B agrees to obtain the goods and resell them to A there will be no privity between A and B's supplier; B will be absolutely liable to A if he does not obtain the goods; and B will also be liable to A for defects in the goods (under express terms of the contract of sale, or under terms implied by the Sale of Goods Act 1979, ss 13–15).

(2) C agrees to dispose of D's goods, and C is held to be D's agent. In these circumstances D will be privy to any contract of sale made by C with a third party; D (not C) will be liable to the third party on the contract of sale for defects in the goods; and if the third party pays C, who fails to account to D for the money, the third party will only be discharged if C was authorised to receive his payment on behalf of D. On the other hand, if C is held to have purchased the goods from D, there will be no privity between D and the third party; C (not D) will be liable to the third party on the contract of sale for defects in the goods; and the third party's liability will be discharged if he pays C.

The importance of distinguishing between agency and sale is clear. Nevertheless, it may not always be easy to draw the distinction. In the world of commerce the term 'agent' is often used without regard to its legal meaning (eg a car dealer may describe himself as the 'agent' of a particular manufacturer, but it is probably the case that he purchases the vehicles from the manufacturer and resells them to his own customers). However, the distinction can be made according to whether the 'agent' intended to act on his own behalf or on behalf of someone else. If the evidence shows that he intended to act on his own behalf he cannot be an agent, for an agency relationship can only arise when one person intends to act on behalf of another. Of particular relevance to this issue is the extent to which the 'agent' is accountable to the 'principal' for monies received by him, and also whether the resale price is fixed by the 'agent' or the 'principal'. But no single factor need be decisive of the issue and each case must be examined on its facts. Thus, in *AMB Imballaggi Plastici SRL v Pacflex Ltd* [1999] CLC 1391, the Court of Appeal held that a price 'mark up' was a telling factor pointing to the conclusion that a party was not an agent but a principal and thus not a 'commercial agent' within reg 2(1) of the Commercial Agents (Council Directive) Regulations 1993 (see below, p 119). On the other hand, in *Mercantile International Group plc v Chuan Soon Huat Industrial Group Ltd* [2002] EWCA Civ 288, [2002] CLC 913, the Court of Appeal reached the opposite conclusion. There, the claimant (agent) charged more to third parties than it confirmed to the defendant (principal). The mark up, whose amount was unknown to and uncontrolled by the defendant, was retained by the claimant, who received no other commission for its services. The Court of Appeal held that there was an agency relationship between the claimant and the defendant as there was documentation (agreed not to be a sham) which purported to describe the relationship between claimant, defendant, and third parties in these terms. The court held that the absence of such documentation in *AMB Imballaggi* distinguished that case from this. Rix LJ did note (at 791), however, that it was 'common ground that the word "agent" can be carelessly and indiscriminately used, and that the test is ultimately one of substance rather than form'.

Agency, distributorship, and franchising When a manufacturer supplies goods to a distributor or a franchisee that person may be described as a 'selling agent' or 'exclusive agent' of the manufacturer. Often the distributor/franchisee will have agreed to promote the sale of the manufacturer's goods and be prohibited from selling goods of rival manufacturers (which may raise restraint of trade and UK and EU competition law issues: see below, pp 122–123). Yet, whatever the extent of the additional obligations the distributor/franchisee has contractually undertaken, the central relationship between the parties is usually one of sale not agency. This is because the distributor/franchisee will buy the goods from the manufacturer and resell them to his own customers. All the same, difficult issues of agency law are raised when the contract of sale between the manufacturer and the distributor/franchisee contains reservation of title clauses, authorising the distributor/franchisee to sell the goods as agent for the manufacturer (see *Aluminium Industrie Vaassen BV v Romalpa Aluminium Ltd* [1976] 1 WLR 676, considered below at pp 498 ff; FMB Reynolds (1978) 94 LQR 224 at 235–238).

Agency, servants, and independent contractors As some servants (or employees) and some independent contractors have agency powers, whereas others do not, there may be little practical value in attempting to distinguish these persons from agents (see *Bowstead and Reynolds*, para 1–030; cf Fridman, pp 31–37). The issue tends to arise in the context of vicarious liability. The principle upon which vicarious liability depends is well established: 'It is that the wrong of the servant or agent for which the master or principal is liable is one committed in the case of a servant in the course of his employment, and in the case of an agent in the course of his authority' (*Crédit Lyonnais Bank Nederland NV v Export Credits Guarantee Department* [2000] 1 AC 486 at 494, per Lord Woolf MR). Vicarious liability will also now apply whenever an employee's activities are so closely connected with his employment that it would be just to hold the employer liable: *Mohamud v WM Morrison Supermarkets plc* [2016] UKSC 11, [2016] AC 677. Where an employee also acts as his employer's agent, there may be a question as to whether the course of his employment is coextensive with the course of his authority, actual or apparent. It seems likely that an employee who acts within the scope of his actual or apparent authority also acts within the course of his employment. However, it is possible to envisage situations where the agent acts outside the scope of his actual or apparent authority, but within the course of his employment. Is the employer to be held vicariously liable for his employee's torts in the latter case? The answer to this question depends on the nature of the tort (see especially *Armagas Ltd v Mundogas SA, The Ocean Frost* [1986] AC 717, CA and HL). In cases of deceit, or other torts where the claimant relies on a representation made by the employee, the employer will only be held vicariously liable where the employee acts within the scope of his actual or apparent authority. Thus in *Lloyd v Grace, Smith & Co* [1912] AC 716, a clerk, employed by a firm of solicitors, fraudulently persuaded a widow to transfer her property to him and was able to do this because of the position he had been placed in by his employer. The House of Lords held the firm of solicitors vicariously liable for the clerk's fraud on the ground that he had acted within the scope of his apparent authority. By contrast, in *Hornsby v Clark Kenneth Leventhal* [1998] PNLR 635, the Court of Appeal held that a firm of accountants was not vicariously liable for the fraud of their employee where the claimant had known that the business conducted by the employee in his employer's time, and on the employer's premises, was not the business of his employer. On the other hand, where the tort involves no reliance by the claimant upon a representation of the employee, for example those torts involving intentional or negligent physical acts by the employee, then the employer will be held vicariously liable where all the features of the wrong which were necessary to make the employee liable occurred in the course of his employment (*Crédit Lyonnais Bank Nederland NV v Export Credits Guarantee Department*, above) or were so closely connected with the employee's employment that it would be just to hold the employer liable (*Mohamud v WM Morrison Supermarkets plc*, above).

Finally, it is important to note that the relationships between agency and (1) trusts, (2) bailment, (3) distributors/franchisees, and (4) servants/independent contractors, are not mutually exclusive, for example a trustee *may* also have agency powers in appropriate circumstances, an agent *may* hold money or property as trustee or bailee. The relationship between agency and sale, however, is mutually exclusive; as the editor of *Bowstead and Reynolds* states (para 1–032): 'in respect of a particular transaction a person cannot be acting as agent if (without appropriate disclosure) he is a buyer from or seller to his principal and vice versa'.

(c) Examples of types of agent

There are many different types of agent. They include:

(1) auctioneers, who are agents for the seller, but may also be agents for the buyer for certain purposes (*Hinde v Whitehouse* (1806) 7 East 558);

(2) directors, who are agents of the company when they act collectively as a board of directors (although the company's articles of association usually provide also for delegation of some, or all, of the board's functions to individual directors);

(3) partners, who are agents of the firm and their other partners for the purpose of the business of the partnership (Partnership Act 1890, s 5); and

(4) solicitors and counsel, who are agents of their clients when, inter alia, they effect a compromise of matters connected with, but not merely collateral to, the litigation in question (*Waugh v HB Clifford & Sons Ltd* [1982] Ch 374).

There are other types of 'agent' who may have little or no power to change their principal's legal relations with third parties but nevertheless owe fiduciary obligations to their principal. Estate agents are an example of this type of agent, for their powers are extremely limited. Whilst they may have power to make representations about the property (*Sorrell v Finch* [1977] AC 728 at 753), they have no power to make a contract between their client and the prospective purchaser, unless specifically authorised to do so. Such agents do not fit into the power–liability analysis of agency outline by Professor Dowrick (above, pp 109–110) and have been described by one commentator as 'anomalous' (Fridman, p 13 fn) and by another as 'incomplete' (*Bowstead and Reynolds*, para 1–019).

We shall now turn to those agents who play a particular role in commercial transactions.

Factors   The term 'factor' was used to a great extent up to the nineteenth century and is now important for the understanding of cases from that era. A factor was an agent who was given possession or control of goods to sell on behalf of his principal. He usually sold the goods in his own name without disclosing the name of his principal (*Baring v Corrie* (1818) 2 B & Ald 137), although he would remain a factor if he sold the goods in his principal's name (*Stevens v Biller* (1883) 25 Ch D 31). Those who purchased goods from the factor could often rely on his apparent authority to sell them, or his apparent ownership of them, to validate any disposition which had not been authorised by the factor's principal. The term 'factor' is little used in its traditional sense today (although see below, p 958, for the term being used in a different sense). The Factors Act 1889 introduced the term 'mercantile agent' to cover those persons (including factors) who were accorded a statutory power to make unauthorised dispositions which would bind their principals (see below, p 394). It is now more important to identify a person as a mercantile agent than it is to identify him as a factor. For a legal history of the factor, see RJC Munday (1977) 6 Anglo-American LR 221.

Brokers   A broker is a negotiator who makes contracts between buyers and sellers of goods. Unlike a factor, the broker is not given possession or control of the goods he sells and he may not sell those goods in his own name (*Baring v Corrie*, above). But it should be noted that there are other types of broker, for example stockbroker, insurance broker, and credit broker (considered by Fridman, p 38).

Del credere agent   A *del credere* agent, in return for an extra commission, undertakes to indemnify the principal should the latter suffer loss as a result of the failure of a customer, introduced by the agent, to pay the purchase price of the goods sold, when the price is ascertained and due (*Morris v Cleasby* (1816) 4 M & S 566). A *del credere* agent can only be made liable to pay the price of the goods on default or insolvency of the buyer; the principal is not entitled to litigate with a *del credere* agent any disputes arising out of the performance of the contract of sale made by the agent (*Thomas Gabriel & Sons v Churchill and Sim* [1914] 3 KB 1272). *Del credere* agents are of particular use to exporters who are uncertain of the financial risks and creditworthiness of overseas buyers introduced by the agent. *Del credere* agencies are something of a rarity nowadays. The modern practice is for an exporter to rely instead on documentary credits (see below, p 769 ff), credit guarantees (see below, p 839 ff), and confirmations (see immediately below) to secure payment from overseas buyers.

Confirming houses   A confirming house usually acts as an agent for an overseas buyer who wishes to import goods. As such the confirming house may do one of the following:

(1)   purchase goods in the domestic market as agent for the overseas buyer without itself becoming liable to the seller on the contract of sale;

(2)   buy from the seller as principal and then resell to the overseas buyer;

(3)   act as agent of the overseas buyer with regard to the contract of sale but also enter into a collateral contract with the seller under which the confirming house undertakes liability for the solvency of, and performance of the contract of sale by, the overseas buyer: this is known as 'confirmation' (see *Sobell Industries Ltd v Cory Bros & Co* [1955] 2 Lloyd's Rep 82); and

(4)   purchase from the seller as principal and yet remain as an agent in relation to the overseas buyer (*Anglo-African Shipping Co of New York Inc v J Mortner Ltd* [1962] 1 Lloyd's Rep 610, may well be an example of this). For further discussion, see DJ Hill (1972) J Mar L & Com 307.

Commission agents   A commission agent (sometimes called 'commission merchant') contracts with third parties as a principal in his own name, although all contracts will be made by the agent on behalf of his own principal. As a consequence, the commission agent creates privity of contract between himself and the third party (not between his principal and the third party), yet remains in an agency relationship with his own principal. Although this type of agency is well established in civil law countries (where it is called 'indirect representation'), it has not been generally recognised in English law (early recognition by Blackburn J in *Ireland v Livingston* (1872) LR 5 HL 395 and *Robinson v Mollett* (1875) LR 7 HL 802 has found little support in more recent cases: see *Bowstead and Reynolds*, para 1–021). One reason why this type of agency has not been assimilated into English law is that it does not sit easily, if at all, with the traditional agency theory that the hallmark of an agent is his power to alter the principal's legal relations with third parties and then drop out of the transaction himself. However, whilst English law has not been prepared to recognise a general category of 'commission agent', in commercial practice certain agents do enter into contracts with third parties as principals and yet remain in an agency relationship with their own principal (see example (4) under 'Confirming houses', above). The doctrine of undisclosed principal is loosely analogous to the civil law contract of commission (where 'commission' refers to the entrusting of a task to the agent and not the method of payment), although, unlike a commission agent, the agent of an undisclosed principal makes his principal liable and entitled on the contract, subject to the rules of election and merger (FMB Reynolds (1978) 94 LQR 224 at 234). For a powerful argument in support of recognition of the commission agent in English law, see DJ Hill (1968) 31 MLR 623; see also [1964] JBL 304; [1967] JBL 122; cf Fridman, pp 30, 49–50).

(d) Agency law and the EU

(i) Self-employed commercial agents

On 1 January 1994 the Commercial Agents (Council Directive) Regulations 1993 (SI 1993/ 3053, as amended), implementing EC Directive 86/653 on self-employed commercial agents, came into force. The EC Directive was drafted in response to a perceived need to protect self-employed commercial agents against exploitation by their principals. In *Page v Combined Shipping and Trading Co Ltd* [1996] CLC 1952 at 1956, Staughton LJ said that the preamble to the Directive suggested that 'commercial agents are a down-trodden race, and need and should be afforded protection against their principals' (although in *Lonsdale v Howard & Hallam Ltd* [2007] UKHL 32, [2007] 1 WLR 2055 at [19], Lord Hoffmann observed that Staughton LJ's comment was made 'with more than a touch of irony' and constituted 'generalities which do not help one to decide what protection is sufficient to give effect to the policy of the Directive'). Through the terms of the Directive, and its implementing Regulations, commercial agents have been given protection against their principals in a way which treats them more as employees than as the independent contractors, which most of them in fact are. This represents a new departure for English law. Hitherto, English law has not singled out any particular category of agent for special protection: the common law rules as to the relationship between principal and agent being based on freedom of contract.

The Regulations govern the relations between commercial agents and their principals and, unless the parties have agreed that the agency agreement is to be governed by the law of another Member State, apply in relation to the activities of commercial agents in Great Britain (reg 1(2), (3)). Regulation l(3)(b) confirms that an agent who performs his duties outside Great Britain but within another Member State of the European Economic Area, under an agreement governed by English law, falls within the Regulations, provided the law of that other Member State implementing the Directive allows the parties to agree that the agency contract is to be governed by the law of a different Member State. The Regulations also have extra-territorial effect. In Case C-381/98 *Ingmar GB Ltd v Eaton Leonard Technologies Inc* [2001] 1 CMLR 9, an English agent conducted activities in the UK for a Californian principal under an agency contract which the parties expressly chose to be governed by Californian law. The English Court of Appeal asked the European Court of Justice for a preliminary ruling on whether the Regulations lay down mandatory rules which should apply regardless of the choice of law. The ECJ held that they do. Since the purpose of the Directive is to protect commercial agents on a uniform basis throughout the Community (as it then was), 'It must therefore be held that it is essential for the Community legal order that a principal established in a non-member country, whose commercial agent carries on his activity within the Community, cannot evade those provisions by the simple expedient of a choice-of-law clause' (para 25). The rights given by the Directive must be applied whenever the commercial agent carries on business in a Member State, irrespective of the law chosen by the parties to govern their contract. For criticism of this decision, see Verhagen (2002) 51 ICLQ 135.

A commercial agent is defined in the Regulations as 'a self-employed intermediary who has continuing authority to negotiate the sale or purchase of goods on behalf of another person (the "principal"), or to negotiate and conclude the sale or purchase of goods on behalf of and in the name of that principal' (reg 2(1)). Several points emerge from this definition.

(1) The agent must be self-employed. This means that the agent must be what the common law would describe as an 'independent contractor'. Hence a company or a partnership

can be a commercial agent (*Bell Electrical Ltd v Aweco Appliance Systems GmbH & Co KG* [2002] EWHC 872 (QB), [2002] CLC 1246 at [50], per Elias J).

(2) The agent must have 'continuing authority'. This means that an agent appointed for a single transaction would fall outside the definition of a commercial agent. However, the European Court of Justice has held, in a preliminary ruling, that where a self-employed intermediary has authority to conclude a single contract, subsequently extended over several years, the condition in art 1(2) of the Directive (same definition of 'commercial agent' as found in reg 2(1)) that the authority be 'continuing' required that the principal should have conferred continuing authority on that intermediary to negotiate successive extensions to that contract; the mere fact that the intermediary maintained relations with the principal throughout the contractual period was, in itself, insufficient to demonstrate such authority (Case C-3/04 *Poseidon Chartering BV v Marianne Zeeschip VOF* [2006] 2 Lloyd's Rep 105). In *Light v Ty Europe Ltd* [2003] EWCA Civ 1238, [2004] 1 Lloyd's Rep 693, the Court of Appeal held that a sub-agent, who had contracted with the principal's agent and not with the principal himself, could have continuing authority to act for the principal and so fall within the definition of a commercial agent in reg 2(1), but that as there was no direct contractual relationship between them, the sub-agent could not rely on the rights and obligations laid down by the Regulations as against the principal. The decision may be criticised for failing to adopt a purposive approach to the construction of legislation which is based on a European Directive. The Court of Appeal left open the question whether a sub-agent could claim under the Regulations against the agent (Ward LJ was prepared to contemplate that he could). The problem for the sub-agent with this claim is that it may prove difficult to convince a court that he has continuing authority to negotiate sales on behalf of the agent as opposed to the real principal.

(3) The agent must have continuing authority to 'negotiate' on behalf of the principal. In *Parks v Esso Petroleum Co Ltd* (1999) 19 Tr LR 232, the Court of Appeal held that a person selling fuel under a licence at a self-service petrol station did not 'negotiate' with motorists who bought petrol, and hence was not a commercial agent: he did not 'deal with, manage or conduct' (the *Oxford English Dictionary* definition of 'negotiate') the sales to motorists since he neither took part in their choice and self-service nor provided any skill or consideration. The decision has been criticised for its narrow interpretation of what is meant by negotiation (see S Saintier [2001] JBL 540). By contrast, the Irish High Court took a broader view of 'negotiate' in *Kenny v Ireland ROC Ltd* [2005] IEHC 241, where, again, the question was whether an agent who ran a self-service petrol station had authority to 'negotiate' on behalf of his principal. Clark J held the agent to be a commercial agent because he exercised a 'limited but not insignificant autonomy' over the way the forecourt and shop were run and in his relations with some suppliers. It seems that Mr Kenny enjoyed a higher degree of responsibility and autonomy than Mr Parks and so the two cases are distinguishable on that ground. However, Clark J went further and said (at [6.1]) that insofar as the decision in *Parks* was to be taken as implying that it was not possible for a person to be a commercial agent when that person exercised skill in attracting customers, but where the ultimate transaction was by self-service and payment, he would not find the judgment persuasive and would not follow it. There is evidence of this broader view now finding favour this side of the Irish Sea. In *PJ Pipe & Valve Co v Audco India Ltd* [2005] EWHC 1904 (QB), [2006] Eu LR 368, Fulford J held that an agent who introduced customers to his principal, but had no authority to negotiate price or bind his principal to a sale agreement, was nevertheless a commercial agent because he contributed to the development of goodwill in his principal's business. This approach to

the meaning of 'negotiate' is to be welcomed for it gives effect to the purpose of the legislation, which is to protect an agent who builds up business goodwill within a particular area for his principal (see further C Gardiner [2007] JBL 412 at 414–420).

(4) A person who buys and sells as principal, and therefore acts on his own behalf and not on behalf of another, is not a commercial agent within the Regulations. A distributor purchasing goods from a manufacturer and selling the goods on at an increased price (the 'mark-up') is a good example of this (*AMB Imballaggi Plastici SRL v Pacflex Ltd* [1999] CLC 1391, CA). Similarly, an agent who contracts directly with a purchaser in his own name rather than in the name of the principal cannot be said to be acting on behalf of another (*Sagal (t/a Bunz UK) v Atelier Bunz GmbH* [2009] EWCA Civ 700, [2009] 2 Lloyd's Rep 303). Charging a mark-up, it should be said, will not always prove decisive of the issue; other factors, for example the contractual documentation, may indicate an agency relationship despite the presence of a mark-up (*Mercantile International Group plc v Chuan Soon Huat Industrial Group Ltd* [2002] EWCA Civ 288, [2002] CLC 913, CA: see above, p 115).

A few commercial agents (ie those whose activities are unpaid, those who work on commodity exchanges and in commodity markets, and Crown Agents for Overseas Governments) are expressly excluded from the Regulations (reg 2(2)). This exclusion also extends to anyone whose activities as a commercial agent are considered as *secondary* (reg 2(3), (4)). The Directive contemplates that the activities of the person as agent are secondary when they are not his primary activities as compared to the rest of his business. However, the Schedule to the Regulations seems to contemplate a different test involving only an assessment of the agent's arrangements with the principal and not a comparison with the agent's other business (which is how Morison J applied the test in *Tamarind International Ltd v Eastern Natural Gas (Retail) Ltd* [2000] CLC 1397. See also *Fern Computer Consultancy Ltd v Intergraph Cadworx & Analysis Solutions Inc* [2014] EWHC 2908 (Ch), [2015] 1 Lloyd's Rep 1 at [97]–[103], per Mann J). In *Crane v Sky In-Home Service Ltd* [2007] EWHC 66 (Ch), [2007] 1 CLC 389, where the agent's activities (which related to the sale of Sky box packages) were held to be secondary, Briggs J (at [59]) considered that the Schedule was 'directed at distinguishing between a relationship where the agent develops goodwill...which passes to the principal, and one where that does not happen'. The Court of Appeal has highlighted the (apparently unintentional) inconsistency between the Directive and the Schedule to the Regulations, and called for speedy amendment to bring the Regulations in line with the Directive (*AMB Imballaggi Plastici*, above); nevertheless, the UK's power to make special provision in the Schedule has recently been affirmed (*Crane*, above, at [41]).

The Regulations contain a rebuttable presumption that the activities of mail order catalogue agents for consumer goods and consumer credit agents are secondary (Sch, para 5). There is, however, some uncertainty as to the burden of proof in general. A number of Scottish cases have placed the burden of proof on the person alleging that he is a commercial agent, but this was doubted by the English Court of Appeal in *Edwards v International Connection (UK) Ltd* [2006] EWCA Civ 662, where it was tentatively suggested that if a purported commercial agent can show that reg 2(1) applies to him it might be for the other party to show that the agent's activities are secondary within reg 2(4) and the Schedule. (See further Munday, paras 1.54–1.63.)

The main effects of the Regulations will be referred to at appropriate points in the chapters which follow. At this stage, by way of summary, it should be noted that the Regulations cover such matters as the rights and duties of the principal and commercial agent (regs 3–5), remuneration of the commercial agent (regs 6–12), termination of the agency agreement (regs 13–16), the agent's right to an indemnity or compensation on termination of the agency agreement (regs 17–19), and restraint of trade clauses (reg 20). In many respects these provisions merely reflect the existing position at common law, although English lawyers will find the requirement that each party acts dutifully and *in good faith* towards the other somewhat unfamiliar (regs 3(1) and 4(1): see A Tosato [2013] LMCLQ 544 and (2016) 36 OJLS 661; also below, p 233). However, the introduction of the agent's right to compensation on termination of his agency, above and beyond any claim he may have for damages for breach of contract by the principal, does mark a radical new departure from existing common law principles.

(ii) Competition law

Articles 101 and 102 of the Consolidated version of the Treaty on the Functioning of the European Union (prior to the Treaty of Lisbon 2007, which entered into force in 2009, these were numbered arts 81 and 82; and prior to the Treaty of Amsterdam (1997), which came into force in 1999, they were arts 85 and 86 respectively) are the main EU competition provisions. Article 101(1) prohibits, as incompatible with the internal market, all agreements between undertakings that may affect trade between Member States and which have as their object or effect the prevention, restriction, or distortion of competition within the internal market. Article 102 prohibits, as incompatible with the internal market, any abuse by one or more undertakings of a dominant position within the internal market or a substantial part of it, insofar as it affects trade between Member States. The UK's Competition Act 1998 mirrors these provisions. It is beyond the scope of this book to consider the provisions of the Treaty that relate to competition, or the similar provisions in the Competition Act 1998 in any detail (see, generally, R Whish and D Bailey, *Competition Law* (8th edn, 2015), for detailed discussion).

The majority of agency agreements will fall outside the purview of art 101(1). The European Commission's *Guidelines on Vertical Restraints* ([2000] OJ C130/1) define agency agreements as those that cover a situation where one person negotiates and/or concludes contracts on behalf of another for the purchase or sale of goods or services, by or from the principal (para 12). In the case of a 'genuine' agency agreement, art 101 does not apply to the obligations imposed on the agent, but in the case of a 'non-genuine' agency agreement it may do. The factor which determines whether art 101(1) applies is, regardless of how many principals an agent is acting for, 'the financial or commercial risk borne by the agent in relation to the activities for which he has been appointed as an agent by the principal' (para 13). In essence, the more the agent accepts risk, the more likely it is that the agreement falls within art 101(1). However, even a 'genuine' agency agreement may be caught by art 101(1) where it contains exclusivity provisions which could foreclose access to the market (para 19), or if it facilitates collusion, in the form of an anti-competitive agreement or concerted practice (para 20).

The practice has been to overlook agreements of minor importance that infringe art 101(1) under a *de minimis* principle, which is declared to 'provide a safe harbour for agreements between undertakings which the Commission considers to have non-appreciable effects on competition' (see the Commission's De Minimis Notice of 2014; revised version 3 June 2015, C (2014) 4136 final). Broadly, vertical agreements concluded by non-competing concerns whose individual market share is under 15 per cent will usually fall within this classification, provided that such agreements do not contain restrictions, listed as hardcore restrictions, in any current or future Commission Block Exemption Regulation.

Any agency agreement falling within art 101(1) may still be eligible for block exemption under the European Commission's Regulation on Vertical Agreements and Concerted Practices (originally Regulation 2790/99 ([1999] OJ L336/21), on which see R Whish (2000) 37 CMLR 887; replaced in June 2010 by an amended Regulation 330/2010 ([2010] OJ L102)). To qualify for a block exemption it is necessary for the agency agreement to avoid the 'hard-core' restrictions set out in art 4 of the Regulation (ie certain types of severely anti-competitive restrictions such as minimum and resale prices, and certain types of territorial protection) and 'non-compete' provisions of the kind set out in art 5 of the Regulation.

It used to be possible for the European Commission to grant individual exemption to a vertical agreement which infringed art 101(1)'s predecessor and was ineligible for block exemption under Regulation 2790/99. The agreement had to satisfy the terms of what is now art 101(3); that is, contribute to improving the production or distribution of goods or promote technical and economic progress, while allowing consumers a fair share of the resulting benefit. However, the system of notifying agreements to the Commission for individual exemption was abolished in May 2004 under Regulation 1/2003. Henceforth, national courts and national competition authorities are to apply the provisions of art 101(3) to vertical (and any other) agreements.

By reg 20 of the Commercial Agents (Council Directive) Regulations 1993 (above, p 119), a restraint of trade clause restricting the right of a commercial agent to act as such after termination of an agency contract will only be valid if, and to the extent that, it is in writing; it relates to the geographical area, or to both the group of customers and the geographical area, and to the kind of goods in respect of which the commercial agent has a right to act; it is reasonable from the point of view of the principal and the commercial agent and their common customers; and it does not apply for a period of more than two years after the termination of the agency contract. The restraint of trade clause would also be subject to the common law on restraint of trade agreements (as to which, see E Peel, *Treitel's Law of Contract* (14th edn, 2015), paras 11–062 ff): see reg 20(3).

(e) Harmonisation of agency law

To facilitate the unification of international trade law, a diplomatic conference held in Geneva in 1983, and attended by delegations from 58 countries, approved a Convention on Agency in the International Sale of Goods. The Convention, based on a draft prepared by the International Institute for the Unification of Private Law (UNIDROIT), supplements the rules contained in the 1980 Vienna Convention on Contracts for the International Sale of Goods (see below, p 533). Like the Vienna Convention, the Geneva Convention will enter into force when ratified by ten states (art 33(1)). Neither Convention has been ratified by the UK.

The Geneva Convention only applies where:

(1) the agent has authority or purports to have authority on behalf of the principal to conclude a contract for the sale of goods with a third party (art 1(1));

(2) the principal and the third party have their places of business in different states (art 2(1)); and

(3) the agent has his place of business in a contracting state or the rules of private international law lead to the application of the law of a contracting state (art 2(1)).

If the third party neither knows, nor ought to have known, that the agent was acting as an agent, then the Convention will only apply if the agent and the third party had their places of business in different states and if the requirements of art 2(1) are satisfied (art 2(2)). Certain types of agency, for example the agency of a dealer on a stock, commodity, or other exchange, fall outside the provisions of the Convention (art 3).

The Geneva Convention is concerned only with relations between the principal or agent, on the one hand, and the third party, on the other (art 1(3)). The Convention does not regulate the internal relationship between the principal and the agent. This omission, which was necessary to ensure the adoption of the Convention, may reduce the practical importance of the Geneva Convention (MJ Bonell (1984) 32 Am J Comp L 717 at 747). However, within its stated object, the Convention does represent an impressive attempt to assimilate the different common law and civil law rules of agency. For detailed analysis of the Geneva Convention, see M Evans [1984] Unif L Rev 74; and Bonell, op cit, which reproduces the text of the Convention.

CHAPTER 5

CREATION OF AGENCY, AND THE AUTHORITY OF THE AGENT

1 CREATION OF THE AGENCY RELATIONSHIP

The relationship of principal and agent may be created in the four following ways:

(1) by express or implied agreement between principal and agent;

(2) under the doctrine of apparent authority (see below, pp 132–146);

(3) by operation of law (see below, pp 152–158); and

(4) by ratification of an unauthorised agent's acts by the principal (see below, pp 158–167).

Agency arising out of agreement will always be consensual, but it need not be contractual. An agency may be gratuitous. Even in the commercial context, the agency may not be contractual (although this is rare). As Coleman J said in *Yasuda Fire & Marine Insurance Co of Europe Ltd v Orion Marine Insurance Underwriting Agency Ltd* [1995] QB 174 at 185:

> Although in modern commercial transactions agencies are almost invariably founded upon a contract between principal and agent, there is no necessity for such a contract to exist. It is sufficient if there is consent by the principal to the exercise by the agent of authority and consent by the agent to his exercising such authority on behalf of the principal.

The main differences between a purely consensual and a contractual agency are: (1) the presence or absence of consideration; and (2) the fact that if an agency is contractual, the agent is usually under an *obligation* to carry out his functions and the principal is under a corresponding obligation to remunerate him. The agent's contractual right to remuneration, it should be noted, must be distinguished from his right to an indemnity for loss and expense incurred in the execution of his duties. The right to an indemnity arises by operation of law, irrespective of any agreement between the parties (see below, p 267).

The agreement between the principal and agent may be expressed orally, in writing, or by deed (usually taking the form of a 'power of attorney'). In general, creation of an agency requires no formality. Indeed, an agent may be appointed orally even when he is appointed to make a contract which has to be in writing or evidenced in writing, as with a contract for the purchase of land or a contract of guarantee (*Heard v Pilley* (1869) 4 Ch App 548). There are, however, statutory provisions that exceptionally require certain transactions to be evidenced in writing (eg Law of Property Act 1925, ss 53(1) and 54). Additionally, if an agent is appointed to *execute* a deed, his appointment, too, must have been by deed (*Berkeley v Hardy* (1826) 5 B & C 355), unless the agent executes the deed in the presence of the principal (*Ball v Dunsterville* (1791) 4 Term Rep 313). In contrast, under s 1(1)(c) of the Law of Property (Miscellaneous Provisions) Act 1989 a deed is no longer required to authorise *delivery* of a deed.

Under the Commercial Agents (Council Directive) Regulations 1993 (above, p 119), a commercial agent and his principal are each entitled to receive from the other, on request, a signed written statement of the terms of the agency contract, including any terms agreed after the creation of the agency contract (reg 13(1)). This does not mean that the agency contract must be in writing, but it does require each party to provide the other with a written record of its terms. This right may not be waived (reg 13(2)).

Agreement between the principal and agent need not be express. It may be implied by their conduct (see *Garnac Grain Co Inc v HMF Faure and Fairclough Ltd* [1968] AC 1130 at 1137, per Lord Pearson). For example, the consent of the principal may be implied by the fact that he appointed a person to a position in which he would usually act as agent for the person who appoints him (see *Pole v Leask* (1862) 33 LJ Ch 155 at 161–162). Alternatively, the principal may simply acquiesce in the acts of another. Consent, however, will not be presumed merely from the principal's silence, unless other factors indicate that he acquiesced in the agency (*Burnside v Dayrell* (1849) 3 Exch 224). The consent of the agent may be inferred from the fact that he purports to act on behalf of the principal (*Roberts v Ogilby* (1821) 9 Price 269), although merely doing what the principal requests will not invariably imply the existence of an agency relationship. As Powell observed (*The Law of Agency* (2nd edn, 1961), p 297):

> Suppose, for example, that A is about to buy for himself a racehorse called Saucy Sally and receives [an email] from P: 'Buy Saucy Sally for me at £900.' Must it be supposed that A's subsequent purchase of the horse, even at £900, makes A P's agent with a liability to deliver the horse to P? Or that P's authorisation imposes on A any obligation to communicate to P his refusal to act as P's agent? If, therefore, the indication of A's consent is to be the performance of an act by A, that act must show unequivocally that A has consented to act as P's agent.

Finally, it should be noted that any person who is capable of consenting can act as an agent, even though he has only limited or no contractual capacity himself (although any contractual liability to his principal or a third party would depend on his contractual capacity). In general, the principal will only be bound by the contracts and acts of his agent if the principal has capacity to contract or to do the act himself (*G(A) v G(T)* [1970] 2 QB 643 at 652, per Lord Denning MR; on contracts made by agents acting on behalf of principals suffering from latent mental incapacity, see P Watts [2015] CLJ 140). See also s 39(1) of the Companies Act 2006 for an example of an exception to this rule: 'the validity of an act done by a company shall not be called into question on the ground of lack of capacity by reason of anything in the company's constitution'.

QUESTION

Adam writes to Bill asking him to purchase a particular Ming vase on his behalf and promising to reimburse Bill the cost of the purchase. Before Bill receives the letter, Bill purchases the vase as a birthday present for Adam and gives it to him. The next day Bill receives Adam's letter and now seeks to recover the cost of the vase from Adam.

Advise Bill. Would it make any difference to your answer if Bill had bought the vase in anticipation of receiving instructions from Adam to do so, rather than as a present for him? See *Bowstead and Reynolds*, paras 2–032 to 2–033.

2 AUTHORITY OF THE AGENT

The relationship between the 'power' and 'authority' of an agent was considered in the previous chapter (above, p 110). Nevertheless, you will see from what follows that the term 'authority' is not always used in its strict sense.

(a) Actual authority

Whether an agent has authority is a question of fact. If the principal has given prior consent to the agent acting on his behalf then the agent can be said to have 'actual' authority. Actual authority will be conferred on the agent by the principal under the terms of the agreement or contract between them. As Diplock LJ stated in *Freeman and Lockyer v Buckhurst Park Properties (Mangal) Ltd* [1964] 2 QB 480 at 502:

> An 'actual' authority is a legal relationship between principal and agent created by a consensual agreement to which they alone are parties. Its scope is to be ascertained by applying ordinary principles of construction of contracts, including any proper implications from the express words used, the usages of the trade, or the business between the parties.

Ascertaining the scope of the agent's actual authority is important. As a general rule, only if the agent acts within the scope of his actual authority is he entitled to an indemnity from his principal (and the same applies to any remuneration due under a contract of agency). Moreover, if the agent acts outside his actual authority he may be liable to his principal for breach of contract (see below, p 224), or liable to a third party for breach of his implied warranty of authority (see below, pp 194–200). The position would be altered if the principal later adopted or ratified the agent's unauthorised actions (see below, pp 158–167 and 199).

(i) *Express actual authority*

Ireland v Livingston
(1872) LR 5 HL 395, House of Lords

Livingston wrote to Ireland asking him to ship 500 tons of sugar. The letter continued: 'Fifty tons more or less of no moment, if it enables you to get a suitable price.' Ireland shipped 400 tons in one vessel, presumably intending to ship the rest in another vessel. Livingston refused to accept the 400 tons and wrote to Ireland to cancel any further shipment. The House of Lords held that Livingston was bound to accept the sugar.

Lord Chelmsford: My Lords, the difference of opinion which has prevailed amongst the Judges in this case, shews that the order given to the Plaintiffs by the Defendant in his letter of the 25th of July, 1864 (upon which the question principally turns) is of doubtful construction; and this, in my mind, is a sufficient ground in itself for bringing me to the conclusion at which I have arrived...

Now it appears to me that if a principal gives an order to an agent in such uncertain terms as to be susceptible of two different meanings, and the agent *bona fide* adopts one of them and acts upon it, it is not competent to the principal to repudiate the act as unauthorized because he meant the order to be read in the other sense of which it is equally capable. It is a fair answer to such an attempt to disown the agents' authority to tell the principal that the departure from his intention was occasioned by his own fault, and that he should have given his order in clear and unambiguous terms. This view of the case will, in my opinion, dispense with the necessity of determining which is the more correct construction of the contract, that which was adopted unanimously by the Court of Queen's Bench, and by two of the Judges of the Exchequer Chamber, or that which the four other Judges of the Exchequer Chamber considered to be the right interpretation of it. It is sufficient for the justification of the Plaintiffs, that the meaning which they affixed to the order of the Defendant is, that which is sanctioned by so many learned Judges. It would be most unjust, after the Plaintiffs have honestly acted upon what they conceived to be the wishes of the Defendant, as expressed in his order, that he should be allowed to repudiate the whole transaction and throw the loss of it upon the Plaintiffs in order (as his correspondence shews) to escape from a speculation which had become a losing one in consequence of the market prices of sugars having fallen.

The short ground upon which I think the case may be disposed of, renders it unnecessary for me to express my opinion as to the proper interpretation of the letters upon which the Courts below have proceeded...

The Plaintiffs have construed the meaning of the Defendant's language in a manner for which there was a reasonable excuse, if not a complete justification, and with an honest desire to perform their duty to him, and have obeyed his order according to their understanding of its meaning.

[**Lords Westbury** and **Colonsay** delivered concurring opinions.]

NOTES

1. In *Woodhouse AC Israel Cocoa Ltd SA v Nigerian Produce Marketing Co Ltd* [1972] AC 741 at 772, Lord Salmon observed that 'in 1872 there were no means by which an agent, at the other end of the world, receiving ambiguous instructions, could communicate with his principal in London to clear up any doubt about their meaning before carrying out his duty to act upon them promptly'. With the speed of modern communications it is most unlikely that an agent would be deemed to have a reasonable excuse to adopt one interpretation of patently ambiguous instructions without first clarifying those instructions with his principal (*European Asian Bank AG v Punjab and Sind Bank (No 2)* [1983] 1 WLR 642 at 656, per Robert Goff LJ). As Toulson J observed in *Patel v Standard Chartered Bank* [2001] Lloyd's Rep Bank 229 at [36], 'the critical question is not limited to whether the agent's interpretation was reasonable; it is whether he behaved reasonably in acting upon that interpretation'.

2. In *Ireland v Livingston* the principal's instruction was conveyed to the agent in a letter. Where the authority of an agent has been conferred in a document not under seal, or has been given orally, the instruction will be construed liberally, with regard to the purpose

of the agency and to the usages of trade or business (*Ashford Shire Council v Dependable Motors Pry Ltd* [1961] AC 336, PC). If the authority is contained in a deed, the stricter rules of construction apply. In particular, this will mean that (a) authority will be limited to the purpose for which it was given (*Midland Bank Ltd v Reckitt* [1933] AC 1), and (b) general words of appointment will be restricted by other specific words which describe the particular acts the agent is authorised to perform (*Jacobs v Morris* [1902] 1 Ch 816). The construction of powers of attorney, however, which must adopt the form of a deed under which a principal confers authority upon an agent to perform certain acts or functions on the principal's behalf, follows different principles provided that the power has been executed in accordance with the formula set out in Sch 1 to the Powers of Attorney Act 1971. Section 10 of the Powers of Attorney Act then provides that if a general power of attorney has been drawn up in the statutory form, or in a similar manner, and expressed to be made under the Act, it confers on the donee of the power authority to do on behalf of the donor, ie the principal, 'anything which he can lawfully do by an attorney'. Thus, if the words are unqualified, the only restriction on the agent's authority will be by virtue of any incapacity of his principal.

(ii) Implied actual authority

Hely-Hutchinson v Brayhead Ltd
[1968] 1 QB 549, Court of Appeal

Richards was the chairman of Brayhead. To the knowledge, and with the acquiescence, of Brayhead's board, he also acted as the company's de facto managing director. Brayhead held shares in another company, Perdio Electronics Ltd. To encourage Hely-Hutchinson to inject funds into Perdio, Richards, in his capacity as chairman of Brayhead, wrote to him undertaking to indemnify him for any loss he might incur as a result of lending money to Perdio or guaranteeing any loan made to Perdio. In reliance on this undertaking, Hely-Hutchinson advanced £45,000 to Perdio. Subsequently, Perdio went into liquidation and Hely-Hutchinson had to pay off a company loan which he had guaranteed. Hely-Hutchinson sought to recover that sum, along with the £45,000 lent to Perdio, from Brayhead. He relied on the terms of Brayhead's letter of indemnity. This raised the question of Richards' authority to bind the company. Roskill J upheld Hely-Hutchinson's claim on the ground that Richards had ostensible or apparent authority to bind Brayhead. The Court of Appeal dismissed Brayhead's appeal on the ground that Richards had implied actual authority to bind Brayhead.

> **Lord Denning MR**: I need not consider at length the law on the authority of an agent, actual, apparent, or ostensible. That has been done in the judgments of this court in *Freeman & Lockyer v Buckhurst Park Properties (Mangal) Ltd* ([1964] 2 QB 480). It is there shown that actual authority may be express or implied. It is *express* when it is given by express words, such as when a board of directors pass a resolution which authorises two of their number to sign cheques. It is *implied* when it is inferred from the conduct of the parties and the circumstances of the case, such as when the board of directors appoint one of their number to be managing director. They thereby impliedly authorise him to do all such things as fall within the usual scope of that office. Actual authority, express or implied, is binding as between the company and the agent, and also as between the company and others, whether they are within the company or outside it.

Ostensible or apparent authority is the authority of an agent as it *appears* to others. It often coincides with actual authority. Thus, when the board appoint one of their number to be managing director, they invest him not only with implied authority, but also with ostensible authority to do all such things as fall within the usual scope of that office. Other people who see him acting as managing director are entitled to assume that he has the usual authority of a managing director. But sometimes ostensible authority exceeds actual authority. For instance, when the board appoint the managing director, they may expressly limit his authority by saying he is not to order goods worth more than £500 without the sanction of the board. In that case his *actual* authority is subject to the £500 limitation, but his *ostensible* authority includes all the usual authority of a managing director. The company is bound by his ostensible authority in his dealings with those who do not know of the limitation. He may himself do the 'holding-out.' Thus, if he orders goods worth £1,000 and signs himself 'Managing Director for and on behalf of the company,' the company is bound to the other party who does not know of the £500 limitation, see *British Thomson-Houston Co Ltd v Federated European Bank Ltd* ([1932] 2 KB 176), which was quoted for this purpose by Pearson LJ in *Freeman & Lockyer* (at 499). Even if the other party happens himself to be a director of the company, nevertheless the company may be bound by the ostensible author-ity. Suppose the managing director orders £1,000 worth of goods from a new director who has just joined the company and does not know of the £500 limitation, not having studied the minute book, the company may yet be bound. Lord Simonds in *Morris v Kanssen* ([1946] AC 459 at 475–476), envisaged that sort of case, which was considered by Roskill J in the present case.

Apply these principles here. It is plain that Mr Richards had no express authority to enter into these two contracts on behalf of the company: nor had he any such authority implied from the nature of his office. He had been duly appointed chairman of the company but that office in itself did not carry with it authority to enter into these contracts without the sanction of the board. But I think he had authority implied from the conduct of the parties and the circumstances of the case. The judge did not rest his decision on implied authority, but I think his findings necessarily carry that consequence. The judge finds that Mr Richards acted as *de facto* managing director of Brayhead. He was the chief executive who made the final decision on any matter concerning finance. He often committed Brayhead to contracts without the knowledge of the board and reported the matter afterwards. The judge said:

> I have no doubt that Mr. Richards was, by virtue of his position as *de facto* managing director of Brayhead or, as perhaps one might more compendiously put it, as Brayhead's chief executive, the man who had, in Diplock LJ's words, 'actual authority to manage' ([1964] 2 QB 480 at 505) and he was acting as such when he signed those two documents.

And later he said:

> . . . the board of Brayhead knew of and acquiesced in Mr. Richards acting as *de facto* managing director of Brayhead.

The judge held that Mr Richards had ostensible or apparent authority to make the contract, but I think his findings carry with it the necessary inference that he had also actual authority, such authority being implied from the circumstance that the board by their conduct over many months had acquiesced in his acting as their chief executive and committing Brayhead Ltd to contracts without the necessity of sanction from the board.

[**Lords Wilberforce** and **Pearson** delivered concurring judgments.]

NOTES

1. Implied actual authority may arise in any of the following forms.

(a) Incidental authority, ie an agent has implied actual authority to do everything necessary for, or ordinarily incidental to, the effective execution of his express authority in the usual way. For example, in one case an agent instructed to sell a house was held to have incidental authority to sign the agreement of sale (*Rosenbaum v Belson* [1900] 2 Ch 267) and, in another case, an agent employed to promote sales of his principal's goods was held to have incidental authority to enter into commission agreements with third parties (*SMC Electronics Ltd v Akhter Computers Ltd* [2001] 1 BCLC 433, CA). In contrast, it has been held that an agent who is instructed to 'find a purchaser', not to 'sell', has no incidental authority to conclude a contract (*Hamer v Sharp* (1874) LR 19 Eq 108). In each case the scope of the agent's incidental authority turned on construction of his express authority.

(b) Usual authority, ie an agent has implied actual authority to do what is usual in his trade, profession, or business for the purpose of carrying out his authority or anything necessary or incidental thereto. For example, if the board of directors appoint someone to be managing director 'they thereby impliedly authorise him to do all such things as fall within the usual scope of that office' (*Hely-Hutchinson v Brayhead Ltd*, above, p 130, per Lord Denning MR). A solicitor's authority to compromise litigation is a further example of this form of implied actual authority (*Waugh v HB Clifford & Sons Ltd* [1982] Ch 374, CA; see generally G Fridman (1987) 36 UNB LJ 9 at 24–40). For further examples, see *Bowstead and Reynolds*, paras 3–024 and 3–027.

(c) Customary authority, ie an agent has implied actual authority to act in accordance with the usages and customs of the particular place, market, or business in which he is employed, so long as those usages or customs are reasonable and lawful. A usage or custom will be unreasonable if it is inconsistent with the instructions given by the principal to the agent, or with the nature of the principal and agent relationship itself. A principal will only be bound by an unreasonable usage or custom if he had actual notice of it at the time he conferred authority on the agent (*Robinson v Mollett* (1875) LR 7 HL 802). Whether an illegal usage or custom can bind a principal, who is aware of the illegality, probably depends on the nature of the illegality (*Bowstead and Reynolds*, para 3–036). For the definition of 'usage', see *Cunliffe-Owen v Teather and Greenwood* [1967] 1 WLR 1421 at 1438–1439, per Ungoed-Thomas J.

(d) Implied actual authority may be inferred from the conduct of the parties and the circumstances of the case. For example, in *Hely-Hutchinson* Lord Denning MR held that Richards' authority was to be 'implied from the conduct of the parties and the circumstances of the case' (above, p 130). It should be noted that, unlike the types of implied authority considered under paras (a)–(c) above, the type of implied authority considered in this paragraph corresponds to the creation of an agency relationship by implied agreement (above, p 125).

2. An agent cannot have *actual* authority when he exceeds an express limit on his authority or when he does something which his principal has expressly prohibited. This means that the principal can prevent implied actual authority arising by expressly restricting his agent's authority. However, the principal will continue to be bound by prohibited acts of his agent if (a) those acts fall within the authority which an agent of that type would usually possess

(usual authority), and (b) the third party dealing with the agent is not aware of restrictions which the principal has placed on the agent's authority. Here the agent's usual authority will not be a form of implied actual authority (because of the prohibition), rather it goes to invest the agent with apparent authority (see *First Energy (UK) Ltd v Hungarian International Bank Ltd* [1993] 2 Lloyd's Rep 194 at 201, per Steyn LJ; *AMB Generali Holding AG v SEB Trygg Liv Holding AB* [2005] EWCA Civ 1237, [2006] 1 WLR 2276 at [32], per Buxton LJ). To avoid terminological confusion, it is important to note that the expression 'usual authority' can be used in these two very different senses, and is probably best restricted to them (see RTH Stone [1993] JBL 325 at 336–337). Unfortunately, as we shall soon discover, it can also be used in a third sense (below, p 146).

3.   An agent has no actual authority to bind his principal when he acts fraudulently or in furtherance of his own interests (*Hopkins v TL Dallas Group Ltd* [2004] EWHC 1389 (Ch), [2005] 1 BCLC 543 at [89], per Lightman J). An agent acting within the scope of his apparent authority may bind his principal when he acts fraudulently or in furtherance of his own interests (ibid). But where the person dealing with an agent knows, or has reason to believe, that the contract or transaction is not in the commercial interests of the agent's principal, it is likely to be very difficult for the person to assert with any credibility that he believed the agent had actual authority and lack of such belief will prevent him claiming the agent had apparent authority (*Criterion Properties plc v Stratford UK Properties LLC* [2004] UKHL 28, [2004] 1 WLR 1846 at [31], per Lord Scott).

(b) Apparent authority

Rama Corpn Ltd v Proved Tin and General Investments Ltd
[1952] 2 QB 147, Queen's Bench Division

The facts are irrelevant.

> **Slade J**: Ostensible or apparent authority...is merely a form of estoppel, indeed, it has been termed agency by estoppel, and you cannot call in aid an estoppel unless you have three ingredients: (i) a representation, (ii) reliance on the representation, and (iii) an alteration of your position resulting from such reliance.

Freeman & Lockyer v Buckhurst Park Properties (Mangal) Ltd
[1964] 2 QB 480, Court of Appeal

K and H formed the defendant company to purchase and resell a large estate. K and H, together with their nominees, were the directors of the company. The articles of association of the company contained a power to appoint a managing director, but none was appointed. Nevertheless, to the knowledge, and with the acquiescence, of the board, K acted as de facto managing director and entered into contracts on the company's behalf. On one occasion K employed a firm of architects to apply for planning permission to develop the estate and to do other work in that connection. K had no actual authority to do this and when the architects claimed their fees from the defendant company an issue arose as to whether K had apparent authority to bind it. The trial judge held that K had such apparent authority. The Court of Appeal dismissed the company's appeal from that decision.

Diplock LJ: . . . We are concerned in the present case with the authority of an agent to create contractual rights and liabilities between his principal and a third party whom I will call 'the contractor.' This branch of the law has developed pragmatically rather than logically owing to the early history of the action of assumpsit and the consequent absence of a general *jus quaesitum tertii* in English law. But it is possible (and for the determination of this appeal I think it is desirable) to restate it upon a rational basis.

It is necessary at the outset to distinguish between an 'actual' authority of an agent on the one hand, and an 'apparent' or 'ostensible' authority on the other. Actual authority and apparent authority are quite independent of one another. Generally they co-exist and coincide, but either may exist without the other and their respective scopes may be different. As I shall endeavour to show, it is upon the apparent authority of the agent that the contractor normally relies in the ordinary course of business when entering into contracts.

An 'actual' authority is a legal relationship between principal and agent created by a consensual agreement to which they alone are parties. Its scope is to be ascertained by applying ordinary principles of construction of contracts, including any proper implications from the express words used, the usages of the trade, or the course of business between the parties. To this agreement the contractor is a stranger; he may be totally ignorant of the existence of any authority on the part of the agent. Nevertheless, if the agent does enter into a contract pursuant to the 'actual' authority, it does create contractual rights and liabilities between the principal and the contractor. . . .

An 'apparent' or 'ostensible' authority, on the other hand, is a legal relationship between the principal and the contractor created by a representation, made by the principal to the contractor, intended to be and in fact acted upon by the contractor, that the agent has authority to enter on behalf of the principal into a contract of a kind within the scope of the 'apparent' authority, so as to render the principal liable to perform any obligations imposed upon him by such contract. To the relationship so created the agent is a stranger. He need not be (although he generally is) aware of the existence of the representation but he must not purport to make the agreement as principal himself. The representation, when acted upon by the contractor by entering into a contract with the agent, operates as an estoppel, preventing the principal from asserting that he is not bound by the contract. It is irrelevant whether the agent had actual authority to enter into the contract.

In ordinary business dealings the contractor at the time of entering into the contract can in the nature of things hardly ever rely on the 'actual' authority of the agent. His information as to the authority must be derived either from the principal or from the agent or from both, for they alone know what the agent's actual authority is. All that the contractor can know is what they tell him, which may or may not be true. In the ultimate analysis he relies either upon the representation of the principal, that is, apparent authority, or upon the representation of the agent, that is, warranty of authority.

The representation which creates 'apparent' authority may take a variety of forms of which the commonest is representation by conduct, that is, by permitting the agent to act in some way in the conduct of the principal's business with other persons. By so doing the principal represents to anyone who becomes aware that the agent is so acting that the agent has authority to enter on behalf of the principal into contracts with other persons of the kind which an agent so acting in the conduct of his principal's business has usually 'actual' authority to enter into.

In applying the law as I have endeavoured to summarise it to the case where the principal is not a natural person, but a fictitious person, namely, a corporation, two further factors arising from the legal characteristics of a corporation have to be borne in mind. The first is that the capacity of a corporation is limited by its constitution, that is, in the case of a company incorporated under the Companies Act, by its memorandum and articles of association; the second is that a corporation cannot do any act, and that includes making a representation, except through its agent.

[Diplock LJ examined certain aspects of the *ultra vires* and constructive notice doctrines—now repealed: see note 5 below—and continued:]

The second characteristic of a corporation, namely, that unlike a natural person it can only make a representation through an agent, has the consequence that in order to create an estoppel between the corporation and the contractor, the representation as to the authority of the agent which creates his 'apparent' authority must be made by some person or persons who have 'actual' authority from the corporation to make the representation. Such 'actual' authority may be conferred by the constitution of the corporation itself, as, for example, in the case of a company, upon the board of directors, or it may be conferred by those who under its constitution have the powers of management upon some other person to whom the constitution permits them to delegate authority to make representations of this kind. It follows that where the agent upon whose 'apparent' authority the contractor relies has no 'actual' authority from the corporation to enter into a particular kind of contract with the contractor on behalf of the corporation, the contractor cannot rely upon the agent's own representation as to his actual authority. He can rely only upon a representation by a person or persons who have actual authority to manage or conduct that part of the business of the corporation to which the contract relates.

The commonest form of representation by a principal creating an 'apparent' authority of an agent is by conduct, namely, by permitting the agent to act in the management or conduct of the principal's business. Thus, if in the case of a company the board of directors who have 'actual' authority under the memorandum and articles of association to manage the company's business permit the agent to act in the management or conduct of the company's business, they thereby represent to all persons dealing with such agent that he has authority to enter on behalf of the corporation into contracts of a kind which an agent authorised to do acts of the kind which he is in fact permitted to do usually enters into in the ordinary course of such business. The making of such a representation is itself an act of management of the company's business. *Prima facie* it falls within the 'actual' authority of the board of directors, and unless the memorandum or articles of the company either make such a contract *ultra vires* the company or prohibit the delegation of such authority to the agent,[1] the company is estopped from denying to anyone who has entered into a contract with the agent in reliance upon such 'apparent' authority that the agent had authority to contract on behalf of the company.

If the foregoing analysis of the relevant law is correct, it can be summarised by stating four conditions which must be fulfilled to entitle a contractor to enforce against a company a contract entered into on behalf of the company by an agent who had no actual authority to do so. It must be shown:

(1) that a representation that the agent had authority to enter on behalf of the company into a contract of the kind sought to be enforced was made to the contractor;

(2) that such representation was made by a person or persons who had 'actual' authority to manage the business of the company either generally or in respect of those matters to which the contract relates;

(3) that he (the contractor) was induced by such representation to enter into the contract, that is, that he in fact relied upon it; and

(4) that under its memorandum or articles of association the company was not deprived of the capacity either to enter into a contract of the kind sought to be enforced or to delegate authority to enter into a contract of that kind to the agent.[2]

---

[1] These remarks must now be read in the light of s 40 of the Companies Act 2006: see note 5 below.

[2] This fourth requirement is now irrelevant, in the light of the reforms mentioned in the preceding footnote, unless the 'contractor' cannot bring himself within s 40, eg because he was not dealing in good faith.

The confusion which, I venture to think, has sometimes crept into the cases is in my view due to a failure to distinguish between these four separate conditions, and in particular to keep steadfastly in mind (a) that the only 'actual' authority which is relevant is that of the persons making the representation relied upon, and (b) that the memorandum and articles of association of the company are always relevant (whether they are in fact known to the contractor or not) to the questions (i) whether condition (2) is fulfilled, and (ii) whether condition (4) is fulfilled, and (but only if they are in fact known to the contractor) may be relevant (iii) as part of the representation on which the contractor relied. ...

In the present case the findings of fact by the county court judge are sufficient to satisfy the four conditions, and thus to establish that [K] had 'apparent' authority to enter into contracts on behalf of the company for their services in connection with the sale of the company's property, including the obtaining of development permission with respect to its use. The judge found that the board knew that [K] had throughout been acting as managing director in employing agents and taking other steps to find a purchaser. They permitted him to do so, and by such conduct represented that he had authority to enter into contracts of a kind which a managing director or an executive director responsible for finding a purchaser would in the normal course be authorised to enter into on behalf of the company. Condition (1) was thus fulfilled. The articles of association conferred full powers of management on the board. Condition (2) was thus fulfilled. The plaintiffs, finding [K] acting in relation to the company's property as he was authorised by the board to act, were induced to believe that he was authorised by the company to enter into contracts on behalf of the company for their services in connection with the sale of the company' s property, including the obtaining of development permission with respect to its use. Condition (3) was thus fulfilled. The articles of association, which contained powers for the board to delegate any of the functions of management to a managing director or to a single director, did not deprive the company of capacity to delegate authority to [K], a director, to enter into contracts of that kind on behalf of the company. Condition (4) was thus fulfilled.

I think the judgment was right, and would dismiss the appeal.

[**Willmer** and **Pearson LJJ** delivered concurring judgments.]

NOTES

1. Apparent authority can operate: (a) to create authority where there was none before; (b) to enlarge an agent's actual authority; (c) to clothe an agent with authority where he would usually have actual authority but for the existence of a restriction unknown to the third party; and (d) to extend an agent's authority beyond termination of the agency relationship. An example of (a) is *Barrett v Deere* (1828) Mood & M 200, where A entered P's counting house and acted as if entrusted with the conduct of P's business. Payment of a debt to A was held to be good payment to P because, although A was a stranger to P and not his agent, P allowed A to enter his business premises and appear to be responsible for the conduct of that business. An example of (b) is *First Energy (UK) Ltd v Hungarian International Bank Ltd* [1993] 2 Lloyd's Rep 194, where a senior regional manager of a bank was held to have had apparent authority to convey head office approval of a certain type of loan, when he had neither actual authority to grant that type of loan nor to convey head office approval of it (a difficult case, considered in detail below at p 140). An example of (c) is *Manchester Trust v Furness* [1895] 2 QB 539, where a charterparty provided that the ship's master, appointed by the owners, was to sign bills of lading as agent of the charterers only, but the owners were nevertheless held liable on a bill of lading signed by the master

because the third party holder of the bill of lading, who was unaware of the restriction, was entitled to assume that the usual situation applied, namely that the master was the agent of the owner. An example of (d) is *AMB Generali Holding AG v SEB Trygg Liv Holding AB* [2005] EWCA Civ 1237, [2006] 1 WLR 2276, where H (the agent) resigned as a director of a company (the principal) but was held to have apparent authority to bind the company to arbitration proceedings after his resignation because of a general representation from his appointment as director that he had all the usual authority of the post, and also from specific representations by the company. The effect of these various representations was held to have survived H's resignation until the third party was put on notice of it, and no further representation by the company was needed for apparent authority to continue after cessation of the director's actual authority.

2.   For the interrelationship between implied actual authority and apparent authority, see *Hely-Hutchinson v Brayhead Ltd*, above, p 129; and *Waugh v HB Clifford & Sons Ltd* [1982] Ch 374, CA.

3.   There has been some debate as to whether or not apparent authority is 'real' authority (see *Bowstead and Reynolds*, para 8–028 for references to the relevant literature). It has been submitted by some writers that, like actual authority, apparent authority is based on consent and is, therefore, real authority. These writers concentrate on the objective appearance of consent as manifested in the principal's representations and conduct (eg see M Conant (1968) 47 Nebr L Rev 678 at 681–686; FMB Reynolds (1994) 110 LQR 21 at 22; G McMeel (2000) 116 LQR 387 at 407). The objective consent theory, however, has not found favour with the English courts. Since the *Freeman and Lockyer* decision, English courts have almost invariably referred to apparent authority as a form of estoppel (eg *Egyptian International Foreign Trade Co v Soplex Wholesale Supplies Ltd and PS Refson SL Co Ltd, The Raffaella* [1985] 2 Lloyd's Rep 36 at 41, CA; *Armagas Ltd v Mundogas SA* [1986] AC 717 at 777, HL; *Lloyds Bank plc v Independent Insurance Co Ltd* [2000] QB 110 at 121–122, CA; *AMB Generali Holdings AB v SEB Trygg Liv Holding AB* [2005] EWCA Civ 1237, [2006] 1 Lloyd's Rep 318 at [31]–[32], CA; *Ing Re (UK) Ltd v R & V Versicherung AG* [2006] EWHC 1544 (Comm), [2007] 1 BCLC 108 at [99], per Toulson J). In *Homburg Houtimport BV v Agrosin Private Ltd* [2000] 1 Lloyd's Rep 85 at 95, Coleman J said that apparent authority was based on 'a substantially similar public policy foundation...as for estoppel by representation', namely 'unconscionability' (on appeal [2001] 1 Lloyd's Rep 437, CA, and [2003] UKHL 12, [2004] 1 AC 715, but without reference to this point). As such, apparent authority cannot be real authority; rather, it creates the appearance of authority which, for policy reasons, the law recognises as giving the agent power to affect the legal relations of the principal (see above, p 130). For an interesting historical survey of how the basis of an agent's external authority changed from that of general authority, a form of actual authority derived from status, to that of apparent authority, in the form of a holding-out by the principal to the third party, as business practices changed in the nineteenth century, see I Brown [2006] JBL 391.

4.   Although this debate may appear somewhat academic, it does have practical significance. Some of the consequences of the agent having actual authority, as opposed to apparent authority, have already been considered (above, p 127). Furthermore, as a form of estoppel, apparent authority can only make the principal liable under any contract made by his agent; it cannot give the principal an independent cause of action unless he ratifies his agent's unauthorised act (although the editor of *Bowstead and Reynolds*, at para 8–029, submits that the principal should be able to make counterclaims and raise defences against any action brought against him by the third party on the unauthorised contract). If apparent authority was true authority, the principal could sue and be sued on the contract (Powell, op cit, p 70; Conant, op cit, p 683).

5. In *Freeman and Lockyer*, Diplock LJ considered how limitations in a company's constitution could affect the capacity of the company to do acts and the power of the board to delegate authority to an agent. (Prior to the coming into force of the relevant provisions of the Companies Act 2006, a company's constitution was made up of its memorandum of association and its articles of association. Under s 17 of the 2006 Act a company's constitution is now defined to include its articles of association and not its memorandum of association: see s 28 for companies formed under the old Companies Acts.) These comments must now be considered in the light of changes to the law made first in 1989, through amendment of the Companies Act 1985, and now to be found in the Companies Act 2006, which has repealed and replaced the 1985 Act. In most cases limitations on the company's capacity and on the board's power to delegate are no longer relevant. Section 39(1) of the Companies Act 2006 provides that 'the validity of an act done by a company shall not be called into question on the ground of lack of capacity by reason of anything in the company's constitution'. This provision effectively abolishes the *ultra vires* doctrine. Section 40(1) of the Companies Act 2006 extends the protection for third parties by providing that 'in favour of a person dealing with a company in good faith, the power of the directors to bind the company, or authorise others to do so, shall be deemed to be free of any limitation under the company's constitution'. Under s 40(2)(b)(i), a third party is not bound to inquire whether there is any limitation on the powers of the directors to bind the company or authorise others to do so; under s 40(2)(b)(ii), a third party is presumed to have acted in good faith unless the contrary is proved; and, under s 40(2)(b)(iii), a third party shall not be deemed to have acted in bad faith merely because he actually knows that a transaction is beyond the directors' powers under the company's constitution. The net effect of these provisions is that the doctrine of constructive notice (whereby a person dealing with a company was deemed to have notice of that company's constitutional documents) has effectively been abolished. The protection offered by s 40, however, is not intended to allow directors and their associates to take advantage of the company. To this end, s 41 alters the presumptions found in s 40 where a transaction is with a director or a person connected with a director. For further discussion of the rules relating to corporate capacity and the authority of a company's agents, see L Sealy and S Worthington, *Cases and Materials in Company Law* (10th edn, 2013), Ch 3.

The requirements for apparent authority were summarised by Slade J in the *Rama* case (above, p 132) as (i) representation, (ii) reliance, (iii) alteration of position.

(i) Representation

Egyptian International Foreign Trade Co v Soplex Wholesale Supplies Ltd and PS Refson & Co Ltd, The Raffaella
[1985] 2 Lloyd's Rep 36, Court of Appeal

The plaintiffs sued the defendant bank on a letter of guarantee signed solely by the bank's credit manager, Mr Booth. At the trial it was common ground that, under the bank's internal rules, Mr Booth did not have actual authority to bind the bank to the guarantee on his sole signature (although at the time he signed the guarantee Mr Booth had assured the plaintiffs' representative that one signature was sufficient to do this). The trial judge, and the Court of Appeal, held that Mr Booth had apparent authority to bind the bank to the guarantee by virtue of his designation as credit manager and because of what the bank had permitted him to do in the past.

Browne-Wilkinson LJ: I have so far ignored the representation made by Mr Booth that 'in London one signature is sufficient'. [Counsel] submitted that a principal cannot be held liable as a result of the agent holding himself out as possessing an authority he does not in fact possess: he relied on remarks to that effect in the *Freeman & Lockyer* case ([1964] 2 QB 480 at p 505, *A-G for Ceylon v Silva* [1953] 1 Lloyd's Rep 563, [1953] AC 461 at pp 571 and 479, *The British Bank of the Middle East case* ([1983] 2 Lloyd's Rep 9) and *Armagas Ltd v Mundogas SA* [1985] 1 Lloyd's Rep 1. As at present advised, I am not satisfied that the principle to be derived from those cases is as wide as [counsel] suggests: they were all cases or *dicta* dealing with the position where the agent had neither authority to enter into the transaction nor authority to make representations on behalf of the principal. It is obviously correct that an agent who has no actual or apparent authority either (a) to enter into a transaction or (b) to make representations as to the transaction cannot hold himself out as having authority to enter into the transaction so as to affect the principal's position. But, suppose a company confers actual or apparent authority on X to make representations and X erroneously represents to a third party that Y has authority to enter into a transaction; why should not such a representation be relied upon as part of the holding out of Y by the company? By parity of reasoning, if a company confers actual or apparent authority on A to make representations on the company's behalf but no actual authority on A to enter into the specific transaction, why should a representation made by A as to his authority not be capable of being relied on as one of the acts of holding out? There is substantial authority that it can be: see *British Thomson-Houston Co Ltd v Federated European Bank Ltd* [1932] 2 KB 176, especially at p 182 (where the only holding out was an erroneous representation by the agent that he was managing director); and the *Freeman & Lockyer* case *per* Lord Justice Pearson at p 499; *Hely-Hutchinson v Brayhead Ltd* [1968] 1 QB 549 *per* Lord Denning MR at p 593A–D. If, as I am inclined to think, an agent with authority to make representations can make a representation that he has authority to enter into a transaction, then the Judge was entitled to hold, as he did, that Mr Booth, as the representative of Refson in charge of the transaction, had implied or apparent authority to make the representation that only one signature was required and that this representation was a relevant consideration in deciding whether Refson had held out Mr Booth as having authority to sign the undertaking. However, since it is not necessary to decide this point for the purposes of this appeal, I express no concluded view on it.

Kerr LJ: In this summary I have deliberately made no reference to one other matter concerning the letter of July 26, although Mr Sharobeem [one of the plaintiffs] undoubtedly placed some reliance on it. This was Mr Booth's assurance, in answer to Mr Sharobeem's question, that he was authorized to sign the letter by himself. The recent decision of this Court in *Armagas Ltd v Mundogas SA* shows that, when a third party is aware that an agent has no actual authority to do a particular act, then the agent's untrue subsequent assurance that he has obtained the necessary authority cannot possibly invest him with any apparent authority for this purpose. In the argument before us this situation was aptly referred to as one where the agent is seeking to pull himself up by his own bootstraps. The present case is different, because it is conceded that the plaintiffs had no reason to doubt Mr Booth's authority at any point. Nevertheless, I would not, as at present advised, accept the argument of Mr Johnson QC that the plaintiffs derive some additional support from Mr Booth's assurance to Mr Sharobeem. As I see it, the issue as to Mr Booth's apparent authority must be resolved with the same result even if this question had not been asked and answered as it was, and I therefore prefer to leave this matter there.

[**Lawton LJ** delivered a concurring judgment.]

NOTES

1. The representation that the agent has authority must be made by the principal and not by the agent himself (*A-G for Ceylon v Silva* [1953] AC 461 at 479, PC). As Lord Donaldson MR said in *United Bank of Kuwait v Hammoud* [1988] 1 WLR 1051 at 1066, 'it is trite law that an agent cannot ordinarily confer ostensible authority on himself. He cannot pull himself up by his own shoe laces.' However, the representation may be made by another (intermediate) agent with actual authority to make such a representation (*Bowstead and Reynolds*, para 8–019). Difficult questions arise as to whether an intermediate agent with no actual authority to make representations can nevertheless have apparent authority to make such representation. Similarly, one could ask whether an agent can have apparent authority to make representations about his own authority.

2. In *Ing Re (UK) Ltd v R & V Versicherung AG* [2006] EWHC 1544 (Comm), [2007] 1 BCLC 108 at [90], Toulson J held that the doctrine of apparent authority was based on estoppel by representation and would apply where the principal (P) represented or caused to be represented to a third party (T) that an agent (A) had authority to act on P's behalf, and T dealt with A as P's agent on the faith of that representation. He continued (at [100]):

> I accept that the same principle can also apply at one remove where T relies on a representation made by an agent having ostensible (but not actual) authority to make such a representation on behalf of P. Thus, where P represents or causes it to be represented to T that A1 has authority to represent to T that A2 has authority to act on P's behalf, and T deals with A2 as P's agent on the faith of such representations, P is bound by A2's acts to the same extent as if he had the authority which he was represented as having. The critical requirement is that A2's authority must be able to be traced back to the principal by a representation or chain of representations upon which T acted and whose authenticity P is estopped from denying by his representation through words or conduct. There is little case law on this variant of the doctrine, but I agree with the statement in *Bowstead and Reynolds on Agency*, 17th ed (2001) at para 8–021:
>
>> It seems correct in principle to say that an agent can have apparent authority to make representations as to the authority of other agents, provided that his own authority can finally be traced back to a representation by the principal or to a person with actual authority from the principal to make it.

In almost all cases the intermediate agent (A1) will have apparent authority because he has usual authority to do the act in question but his authority has been limited by his principal's secret reservation (*British Bank of the Middle East v Sun Life Assurance Co of Canada (UK) Ltd* [1983] 2 Lloyd's Rep 9, HL, is consistent with this view: see note 4 below). If an intermediate agent does not usually have authority to do the act, the third party would normally be put on inquiry should the intermediate agent represent that another agent is authorised to do it (see note 3 below).

3. The same principles apply to the question whether an agent can ever make representations about his own authority. In principle, an agent can have apparent authority to make representations as to his own authority (*The Raffaella, obiter*, above at p 137; *First Energy (UK) Ltd v Hungarian International Bank Ltd* [1993] 2 Lloyd's Rep 194; also *Canadian Laboratory Supplies Ltd v Engelhard Industries Ltd* (1979) 97 DLR (3d) 1 at 10, Supreme Court of Canada). But such cases will be extremely rare (*Suncorp Insurance and Finance v Milano Assicurazioni SpA* [1993] 2 Lloyd's Rep 225 at 232, per Waller J). Unless the agent would usually have authority to do the act in question, it will be very difficult for the third party to rely

on a specific representation of the agent's authority to act, as the third party would normally have been put on inquiry as to the actual limitation on the agent's authority (Fridman, p 125). This point is illustrated by *Armagas Ltd v Mundogas SA* [1986] AC 717. In this case, the third party knew that the agent had no general authority to enter into the transaction in question. It was held by both the Court of Appeal and the House of Lords that, with this knowledge, the third party could not rely on the agent's representation of his own authority to enter into this particular transaction, even though the principal had employed the agent in a senior position in its organisation. With regard to any specific representation of authority made by the principal, Lord Keith stated (at 777):

> It must be a most unusual and peculiar case where an agent who is known to have no general authority to enter into transactions of a certain type can by reason of circumstances created by the principal reasonably be believed to have specific authority to enter into a particular transaction of that type. The facts in the present case fall far short of establishing such a situation.

4.   *First Energy (UK) Ltd v Hungarian International Bank Ltd* [1993] 2 Lloyd's Rep 194 (noted by FMB Reynolds (1994) 110 LQR 21) was such an exceptional case. The senior manager in charge of the Manchester office of the defendant bank (as the plaintiff company's representative knew) had no actual authority to sanction a credit facility for the plaintiff. However, the senior manager wrote and signed (alone) a letter offering to provide the plaintiff with finance. He had no actual authority to do this either, as such a letter should have been signed by two bank officials. Nevertheless, the Court of Appeal held that the senior manager had apparent authority, by virtue of the usual authority associated with his position, to communicate such an offer on behalf of the bank—ie to inform the plaintiff that head office approval had been given for the offer to be made—and so the bank was bound. The Court of Appeal stressed that the decision was consistent with the reasonable expectations of the parties and that it was unrealistic to expect the plaintiff to have checked with the bank's head office as to whether an employee as senior as this manager had actually obtained necessary approval to make the offer. This decision may be contrasted with *British Bank of the Middle East v Sun Life Assurance Co of Canada (UK) Ltd* [1983] 2 Lloyd's Rep 9 (noted by J Collier [1984] CLJ 26), where the House of Lords held that a branch manager of an insurance company had no usual authority to represent to the plaintiff that a junior employee had actual authority to execute undertakings to pay money to the bank. The evidence was that all such undertakings were in practice executed by insurance companies at their head office. Whereas the plaintiff in *First Energy* could rely on the fact that the senior manager had usual authority to sign and send letters on the bank's behalf (the plaintiff being unaware of the bank's restriction on that authority), the plaintiff in *British Bank of the Middle East* could not do the same because of the limited nature of the branch manager's usual authority.

The protection of the third party is limited in this type of case to the extent of the usual authority of the agent, which is itself governed by what would normally be implied between principal and agent, something of which the third party may be quite ignorant, despite the fact that he may have acted reasonably. This may seem harsh on the third party (as the *British Bank of the Middle East* case illustrates), especially where he deals with an agent who is just one cog in a large impersonal corporate machine, when it is unreasonable to expect the third party to make intrusive inquiries about the agent's authority. This has led one commentator to suggest that 'there should be a realignment of the rules of apparent authority to focus attention primarily upon the *agent's* conduct, as seen from the third party's perspective, rather than the *principal's* conduct in creating the appearance of authority. The reasonable reliance of the third party on the apparent normality of the agent's acts should thus be dominant' (I Brown [1995] JBL 360 at 372). Prima facie, the *First Energy* decision seems to offer some support to this alternative approach: after all, Steyn LJ did stress in his judgment (at 196) that 'a theme that runs through our law of contract is that the reasonable expectations of honest men must be protected'. Yet his Lordship also emphasised (at 204) that he decided the case on 'orthodox principles', and the traditional requirements of representation and reliance also underpin the reasoning of Evans and Nourse LJJ, the two other members of the court. *First Energy* may be an exceptional case. Indeed, in *Habton Farms v Nimmo* (25 January 2002, unreported) at [101], upheld on appeal [2003] EWCA Civ 68, [2004] QB 1, HH Judge Behrens described it as 'a very special case on its own facts'. More recently Lord Neuberger NPJ, in the Hong Kong Court of Final Appeal, said that the judgments in *First Energy* 'illustrate how the law struggles to reconcile principle and predictability with commercial reality and fairness', underlining the 'inadvisability of seeking to lay down any rigid principles in this area' (*Thanakharn Kasikorn Thai Chamkat (Mahachon) v Akai Holdings Ltd (in liquidation)* [2010] HKCFA 64 at [70]). Certainly, it is over-optimistic to herald *First Energy* as the harbinger of a new approach to apparent authority.

Kelly v Fraser

[2012] UKPC 25, [2013] 1 AC 450, Privy Council (Jamaica)

First Energy fell to be considered by the Privy Council in *Kelly v Fraser*. In this case the transfer value of a member of a pension plan had been transferred to a new pension plan when the member, F, changed employment. Owing to the fact that the transfer was conducted by M, a senior employee of the human resources department of the employer who sponsored the pension plan, the pension plan's trustees had not been involved in the process and were completely unaware both of the transfer request and of the receipt and investment of the transfer funds. The Board was required to rule whether, under these circumstances, the transfer value had been properly received and held to the account of the relevant pension plan. More particularly, since the transfer had boosted F's funds in the pension plan, was F entitled to a commensurate share in the distribution of the surplus when the scheme was eventually wound up? Without disputing that they could have lawfully approved the transaction had they known of it, the trustees sought to take advantage of their oversight and applied for a declaration that they were entitled to distribute the fund without taking into account this additional transfer effected by M, which they had not endorsed. The question for the Board was whether the representations made by M, a senior employee of the sponsoring company's occupational pension scheme, informing F that whatever steps needed to be taken to carry out this transaction regularly had been duly performed, fell within the apparent authority of an agent acting such as to bind the principal—*in specie* the trustees.

M had never professed to have authorised the acceptance of the transfer funds himself, but the plan could hardly have been operated if he did not enjoy authority to write letters informing contributors that they had been duly accepted and in respect of what contributions. Moreover, with or without the trustees' approval, the transfer funds were in fact accepted, and accruals to the transfer funds notified in successive benefit statements. The trustees could only disclaim this and treat the transfer funds for some purposes as if they had been received and for other purposes as if they had not if it appeared that F had not relied to his detriment upon the agent's representations. This contention was not open to the trustees as it could be inferred that F was worse off by having been led to believe that his transfer fund had been duly invested than he would have been if he had not been told this and had raised the issue at the time.

Having concluded that the evidence unequivocally implied that all internal approvals, including those required of the trustees, had been obtained, the opinion of the Board continued:

Lord Sumption:

AUTHORITY TO MAKE THE REPRESENTATIONS

11. The Board approaches the question whether the trustees were bound by these statements on the footing that neither Mr Masters nor anyone else in the employee benefits division had authority of any kind to approve the transfer into the plan. Nor did they purport to have done so. Equally, none of them had any actual authority to tell Mr Fraser that everything was in order if it was not. The question, therefore, is whether they had ostensible authority to tell Mr Fraser that whatever steps needed to be taken to carry out his transaction regularly had been duly performed, if they had no authority to perform those steps themselves.

12. The question could hardly have arisen in this form but for certain observations of Goff LJ in the Court of Appeal in *Armagas Ltd v Mundogas SA (The Ocean Frost)* [1986] AC 717, and of Lord Keith of Kinkel, delivering the leading speech in the House of Lords in the same case. *The Ocean Frost* was a decision on complex and extraordinary facts.... Goff LJ, delivering the leading judgment [in the Court of Appeal], considered that there was no basis for concluding on the facts of that case that, by appointing [Mr Magelssen] as vice-president and chartering manager, Mundogas had held him out as having power to make the particular representations relied upon: see pp 730–732. This was because the only authority of Mr Magelssen that would serve Armagas's purposes was authority to enter into the charterparty, as he had purported to do. The principals of Armagas knew that Mr Magelssen was not authorised to do that without the specific and express authority of his superiors. He cannot therefore have had any ostensible authority to do it simply by virtue of the appointments that he held in Mundogas. To say that he had ostensible authority by virtue of those appointments to communicate that he had express authority to contract was only another [way] of saying he had ostensible authority to contract. Every agent who enters into a contract thereby asserts that he has authority, but that alone cannot be enough to bind his principal. The House of Lords affirmed the decision of the Court of Appeal and endorsed Goff LJ's analysis. Lord Keith, who delivered the sole reasoned speech, declared [1986] AC 717, 779 that he was not willing to accept:

> the general proposition that ostensible authority of an agent to communicate agreement by his principal to a particular transaction is conceptually different from ostensible authority to enter into that particular transaction.

Like Goff LJ, Lord Keith thought, at p 777, that while it was conceptually possible to have a case of 'ostensible specific authority to enter into a particular transaction', such cases were bound to be rare. It is clear that the whole of this analysis is dependent on the fact that in *The Ocean Frost* the agent was in reality holding out himself as having authority to do a specific thing that the third party knew that he had no general authority to do. Such cases are necessarily fact-sensitive. *The Ocean Frost* is not authority for the broader proposition that a person without authority of any kind to enter into a transaction cannot as a matter of law occupy a position in which he has ostensible authority to tell a third party that the proper person has authorised it.

13. To take an obvious example, the company secretary does not have the actual authority which the board of directors has, but he is likely to have its ostensible authority by virtue of his functions to communicate what the board has decided or to authenticate documents which record what it has decided. The ordinary authority to communicate a company's authorisation of a transaction will generally be more widely distributed than that, especially in a bureaucratically complex organisation and in the case of routine transactions. It is not at all uncommon for the authority to approve transactions to be limited to a handful of very senior officers, but for their approval to be communicated in the ordinary course of the company's administration by others whose function it is to do that....

14. In *First Energy (UK) Ltd v Hungarian International Bank Ltd* [1993] 2 Lloyd's Rep 194...the Court of Appeal held that...there is...'no requirement that the authority to communicate decisions should be commensurate with the authority to enter into a transaction of the kind in question on behalf of the principal' (at 206).

15. It is clear from the judgments in *First Energy* that the Court of Appeal regarded their approach in that case as being wholly consistent with the law stated by Lord Keith in *Armagas Ltd v Mundogas SA* [1986] AC 717. In the Board's opinion, they were right to regard them as consistent. Lord Keith's speech remains the classic statement of the relevant legal principles. An agent cannot be said to have authority solely on the basis that he has held himself out as having it. It is, however, perfectly possible for the proper authorities of a company (or, for that matter, any other principal) to organise its affairs in such a way that subordinates who would not have authority to approve a transaction are nevertheless held out by those authorities as the persons who are to communicate to outsiders the fact that it has been approved by those who are authorised to approve it or that some particular agent has been duly authorised to approve it. These are representations which, if made by someone held out by the company to make representations of that kind, may give rise to an estoppel. Every case calls for a careful examination of its particular facts.

NOTE

See further JL Yap [2014] JBL 72; P-W Lee (2014) 26 SAcLJ 258.

Other points to note about the representation are:

(a) It can be express (oral or in writing); or implied from a course of dealing (eg in *Summers v Solomon* (1857) 7 E & B 879, where P employed A to run his jewellery shop and regularly paid for jewellery ordered by A from TP for resale in the shop: P was held liable to pay for jewellery ordered by A from TP after A had left P's employment since the previous course of dealings had led TP to believe that A had authority to pledge his credit, and P had not informed TP that that authority had terminated); or implied from conduct, such as putting the agent in a position that carries with it usual authority (above, p 131); or by entrusting the agent with the indicia of ownership of property (see below, p 146).

(b) It must be made to the particular third party who deals with the agent, or to the public at large when it would be expected that members of the general public would be likely to deal with the agent (*Farquharson Bros & Co v King & Co* [1902] AC 325 at 341, per Lord Lindley).

(c) It once had to be of fact and not of law (*Chapleo v Brunswick Permanent Building Society* (1881) 6 QBD 696). This distinction must now be reviewed in the light of

Kleinwort Benson Ltd v Lincoln City Council [1999] 2 AC 349, where the House of Lords allowed recovery in restitution of money paid under mistake of law. The *Kleinwort Benson* decision has had an impact outside the law of restitution, so that a contract may be *void* for mistake of law or *rescinded* for a misrepresentation of law. It has been argued, however, that it should not be applied to the present rule, which is concerned with the *creation* of contractual rights (see E Peel, *Treitel's Law of Contract* (14th edn, 2015), para 16–023).

(d) It must be that the 'agent' is authorised to act as agent and not as principal (see below, pp 146–152).

(e) It must be made intentionally or, possibly, negligently (*Bowstead and Reynolds*, para 8–016; Fridman, p 118).

(ii) Reliance

The third party must have relied on the representation. There must be a causal connection between the representation and the third party's dealing with the agent. Furthermore, in cases of representation by negligence, the principal's breach of duty of care owed to the third party must be the proximate cause of his damage (*Swan v North British Australasian Co Ltd* (1863) 2 H & C 175).

   The third party will not be able to say he relied on the representation if he knew, or ought to have known, of the restriction on the agent's authority. In the words of Nourse LJ in *Heinl v Jyske Bank (Gibraltar) Ltd* [1999] Lloyd's Rep Bank 511 at 521, 'the knowledge of the other party unclothes [the agent] of ostensible authority to contract on behalf of the principal'. In *Overbrooke Estates Ltd v Glencombe Properties Ltd* [1974] 1 WLR 1335, a purchaser of land at an auction failed to establish that the seller was bound by a misrepresentation relating to the property made by his agent (the auctioneer) before the sale. Before any contract was formed, and before any representation was made, the purchaser had been in possession of the conditions of sale of the property which contained a clause to the effect that the auctioneer had no authority to give representations or warranties. Brightman J held that the purchaser 'knew, or ought to have known, that [the auctioneer] had no authority to make or give any representation or warranty in relation to this property'.

   Contracts or transactions that appear to run against the commercial interests of the principal must be treated with especial caution by the third party. As Lord Scott warned in *Criterion Properties plc v Stratford UK Properties LLC* [2004] UKHL 28, [2004] 1 WLR 1846 at [31]: 'if a person dealing with an agent knows or has reason to believe that the contract or transaction is contrary to the commercial interests of the agent's principal, it is likely to be very difficult for the person to assert with any credibility that he believed the agent did have actual authority. Lack of such a belief would be fatal to a claim that the agent had apparent authority.' Thus, in *Hopkins v TL Dallas Group Ltd* [2004] EWHC 1379 (Ch), [2005] 1 BCLC 543, a director (A) signed letters of undertaking on behalf of his company (P), agreeing to pay sums totalling just under £1 million to another company (T), in discharge of indebtedness owed to T by a further company (X), a company with which P had no connection. Lightman J held that the transaction was not binding on P. First, A was held to have had no actual authority because he was acting contrary to his principal's interests. Secondly, A was held to have had no apparent authority because the director acting for the company receiving the undertakings (T) knew that A was not acting in the interests of his company (P). Lightman J stated (at [96]) that, even if there was no actual knowledge of the breach of fiduciary duty by A, the director acting for the company to whom the undertakings were given (T) was 'on the clearest notice that the transactions were both abnormal and suspicious and required confirmation of their propriety and regularity'.

This proposition ought not to be pressed too far, however. As Lord Neuberger NPJ declared in an influential judgment in the Hong Kong Court of Final Appeal, *Thanakharn Kasikorn Thai Chamkat (Mahachon) v Akai Holdings Ltd (in liquidation)* [2010] HKCFA 64 at [75], 'once a third party has established that the alleged agent had apparent authority, . . . and that the third party has entered into a contract with the alleged agent on behalf of the principal, then, in the absence of any evidence or indication to the contrary, it would be an unusual case where reliance was not presumed'. A third party could therefore rely on an agent's appearance of authority unless its 'belief in that connection was dishonest or irrational (which includes turning a blind eye and being reckless)' (at [62]). (See also Proudman J in *Newcastle International Airport Ltd v Eversheds LLP* [2012] EWHC 2648 (Ch), [2013] PNLR 5, esp at [115].)

(iii) Alteration of position

Must the third party alter his position to his detriment? There are cases going either way (eg *Rama Corpn v Proved Tin and General Investments*, above at p 132, and *Freeman and Lockyer v Buckhurst Park (Mangal) Properties Ltd*, above at p 132 call simply for an alteration of position; *Farquharson Bros & Co v King & Co* [1902] AC 325, and *Norfolk County Council v Secretary of State for the Environment* [1973] 1 WLR 1400, call for detrimental reliance). The need for detriment is consistent with the strict requirements of an estoppel, but in one of the more recent cases on apparent authority Gatehouse J held that '[t]he only detriment that has to be shown . . . is the entering into the contract': *The Tatra* [1990] 2 Lloyd's Rep 51 at 59.

(iv) Subsequent conduct of the principal

The principal may be bound by a contract, even though the requirements of apparent authority are not satisfied, if he is precluded by his *subsequent* conduct from denying that the contract was made on his behalf. In *Spiro v Lintern* [1973] 1 WLR 1002, a wife contracted to sell her husband's house. The wife had no actual authority to do this and, because she appeared to be the owner of the house (not her husband's agent), she had no apparent authority. However, after the contract was entered into the husband neither stated that his wife was acting without his authority nor indicated that he was not willing for the sale to proceed. On the contrary, the husband allowed the purchaser to incur various expenses with regard to the property. In an action for specific performance of the contract, the Court of Appeal held the husband was estopped from denying that his wife had authority to sell the house on his behalf. As Buckley LJ stated (at 1011):

> If A sees B acting in the mistaken belief that A is under some binding obligation to him and in a manner consistent only with the existence of such an obligation, which would be to B's disadvantage if A were thereafter to deny the obligation, A is under a duty to B to disclose the non-existence of the supposed obligation.

Buckley LJ emphasised that detrimental reliance was necessary for this type of estoppel (contrast this with apparent authority, above) but held that the purchaser had acted to his detriment by incurring expenses.

There is a difference between the estoppel that operates in a case like *Spiro v Lintern* and the estoppel that operates in a case of apparent authority. It was identified by Mance LJ in *Baird Textiles Holdings Ltd v Marks and Spencer plc* [2001] EWCA Civ 274, [2001] CLC 999 at [90] as follows:

> The doctrine of apparent or ostensible authority also rests on the ability of an estoppel to preclude a person (A) who has held out another person (B) as his agent to a third person (C) from denying the existence of such authority or therefore the validity of a contract purportedly made by B on A's behalf with C. A may also estop himself after the event from denying that B was acting as his agent in contracting with C: *Spiro v Lintern* [1973] 1 WLR 1002. But in these situations there is either a purported or an actual legal relationship created by the conduct of B and C, to which A is estopped from denying that he is party. In the former situation, he is estopped from denying the existence of a collateral condition of the validity of such relationship (authority). In the latter, he is estopped from denying that B was acting as his undisclosed agent in making an actual contract.

QUESTIONS

1. In *Armagas Ltd v Mundogas SA* (above, p 140), would the third party have any remedy against the 'agent'?

2. Philip, a businessman, employs Alice as his personal assistant. Alice has held similar posts with other employers and is told by Philip 'do for me what you have always done as a personal assistant for your previous employers, but never book me on a plane as I hate flying'. A few weeks later, forgetting Philip's restriction, Alice rings up EasiAir and books Philip on a flight to Manchester to attend an important business meeting which he would not have had time to attend unless he travelled by plane. When he finds out about the flight, Philip refuses to go and is now being sued by EasiAir for the cost of his ticket. Advise Philip. Would it make any difference if the person who dealt with the booking at EasiAir had dealt with Philip before and knew he hated flying?

(c) Usual authority

Watteau v Fenwick
[1893] 1 QB 346, Queen's Bench Division

The facts appear from the judgment of Wills J.

> **Lord Coleridge CJ:** The judgment which I am about to read has been written by my brother Wills, and I entirely concur in it.
>
> **Wills J:** The plaintiff sues the defendants for the price of cigars supplied to the Victoria Hotel, Stockton-upon-Tees. The house was kept, not by the defendants, but by a person named Humble, whose name was over the door. The plaintiff gave credit to Humble, and to him alone, and had never heard of the defendants. The business, however, was really the defendants', and they had put Humble into it to manage it for them, and had forbidden him to buy cigars on credit. The

cigars, however, were such as would usually be supplied to and dealt in at such an establishment. The learned county court judge held that the defendants were liable. I am of opinion that he was right.

There seems to be less of direct authority on the subject than one would expect. But I think that the Lord Chief Justice during the argument laid down the correct principle, *viz*, once it is established that the defendant was the real principal, the ordinary doctrine as to principal and agent applies—that the principal is liable for all the acts of the agent which are within the authority usually confided to an agent of that character, notwithstanding limitations, as between the principal and the agent, put upon that authority. It is said that it is only so where there has been a holding out of authority—which cannot be said of a case where the person supplying the goods knew nothing of the existence of a principal. But I do not think so. Otherwise, in every case of undisclosed principal, or at least in every case where the fact of there being a principal was undisclosed, the secret limitation of authority would prevail and defeat the action of the person dealing with the agent and then discovering that he was an agent and had a principal.

But in the case of a dormant partner it is clear law that no limitation of authority as between the dormant and active partner will avail the dormant partner as to things within the ordinary authority of a partner. The law of partnership is, on such a question, nothing but a branch of the general law of principal and agent, and it appears to me to be undisputed and conclusive on the point now under discussion.

The principle laid down by the Lord Chief Justice, and acted upon by the learned county court judge, appears to be identical with that enunciated in the judgments of Cockburn CJ and Mellor J in *Edmunds v Bushell* ((1865) LR 1 QB 97), the circumstances of which case, though not identical with those of the present, come very near to them. There was no holding out, as the plaintiff knew nothing of the defendant. I appreciate the distinction drawn by Mr Finlay in his argument, but the principle laid down in the judgments referred to, if correct, abundantly covers the present case. I cannot find that any doubt has ever been expressed that it is correct, and I think it is right, and that very mischievous consequences would often result if that principle were not upheld.

In my opinion this appeal ought to be dismissed with costs.

Appeal dismissed.

'The Demise of *Watteau v Fenwick: Sign-O-Lite Ltd v Metropolitan Life Insurance Co*' by GHL Fridman

(1991) 70 Can Bar Rev 329 at 329–333

INTRODUCTION

In the law of agency the most difficult and controversial decision is that of Wills J in *Watteau v Fenwick*[1] It has been criticised by commentators[2] and distinguished or not followed by judges.[3] Several years ago an English judge described the case as puzzling, the argument for the plaintiff as fallacious, and the doctrine of the case as one that courts should be wary about following.[4]

The case concerned the liability of an undisclosed principal for unauthorised contracts entered into by the principal's agent...

The problem with this case is the logical one of saying that someone who is not known to be an agent can be regarded as having been held out by a principal as having an apparent authority, culled from what was usual or customary in the business in which the agent was engaged,[5] to contract in the way he did, although he lacked any actual authority to do so.[6] Since the doctrine of apparent authority is based upon a principal's holding out someone as his agent with authority to act on his, that is, the principal's behalf,[7] it is difficult to conceive of a case of undisclosed agency as involving the application of the doctrine of apparent authority. One who is not apparently an agent cannot logically be said to have been held out as having any authority at all, whether based on custom, what is usual, or otherwise. The only logical way in which such a conclusion can be reached is by starting from the premise that anyone who employs an agent and does not disclose that he is an agent, inferentially accepts liability for any and every transaction into which the undisclosed agent enters as long as such transaction has a connection with the business or other activity which has been entrusted to the undisclosed agent. The difficulty about this, however, from a practical, if not a logical point of view, is that it would expose the undisclosed principal to a potentially very wide, almost limitless liability for what the agent does. This might protect third parties transacting with the agent. It would mean that the principal has accepted a very great risk by employing an agent and allowing him to appear to be the principal.[8]

Not surprisingly other decisions have taken a contrary view of such a situation. They have held that the act of an undisclosed agent would not make an undisclosed principal liable, even where the act or acts in question related to the authority which, unknown to the third party, had been given to the agent.[9] These decisions hold that, if there has been a limitation placed on the agent's authority by the undisclosed principal, this will bind the third party dealing with the agent, even though the third party was unaware that he was dealing with an agent, and, therefore, was necessarily ignorant of any such limitations. What is surprising, however, is that no decision has firmly and decisively held that *Watteau v Fenwick* was wrong and should be discredited. Such a decision can now be found in the judgment of the British Columbia Court of Appeal in *Sign-O-Lite Plastics Ltd v Metropolitan Life Insurance Co.*[10]

SIGN-O-LITE PLASTICS LTD v METROPOLITAN LIFE INSURANCE CO

The facts in this case were as follows. In 1978 the plaintiff contracted with Calbax Properties Ltd for the renting of an electronic sign to be installed and maintained by the plaintiff at the Market Mall shopping centre in Calgary. This rental agreement was to last for 61 months. It contained a clause providing for automatic renewal for a further term of 60 months in the event that neither party communicated a contrary intention to the other, in writing, more than 30 days before the end of the first term. By virtue of that clause the agreement was renewed in 1984. Prior to that date, however, the defendant, in two stages, acquired ownership of the company which owned and controlled the shopping mall in which the sign was displayed. As part of this transaction the defendants agreed to assume the 1978 rental agreement between Calbax Properties Ltd and the plaintiff. When the defendant acquired ownership of the mall it was agreed with The Baxter Group Ltd that the latter should manage the mall as agent for the defendant. For that purpose the Baxter Group Ltd was given limited authority to enter into contracts on behalf of its principal, the defendants. The plaintiff knew nothing of the change of ownership of the mall. In other words the plaintiff was unaware of the existence of an undisclosed principal of The Baxter Group Ltd. In 1985, after the automatic renewal of the rental agreement in accordance with the original terms of 1978, The Baxter Group Ltd entered into a new rental agreement with the plaintiff intended by both parties to replace the original agreement. At that time the plaintiff believed, as it had every reason to believe, that it was dealing with a different corporate form of the same owner with which the plaintiff had originally contracted in 1978. The new agreement was one which The Baxter Group Ltd had not authority to contract. This was because (a) it did not disclose that The Baxter Group Ltd was acting as agent for the defendant, and (b) it did not provide for cancellation on 60 days' notice. As a result of various later transactions, which are not relevant to the problem in this case, the plaintiff eventually sued the defendant for damages for breach of contract, that is, the contract entered into in 1985 (not the original contract of 1978). At the trial the plaintiff was unsuccessful in establishing liability under the 1985 agreement, and was awarded damages on the 1978 contract. The defendant appealed and the plaintiff cross-appealed.

Two issues were before the court. The first was whether the defendant could be liable, as an undisclosed principal. This raised directly the question whether *Watteau v Fenwick* was good law and was part of the law in British Columbia. After considering the language of Wills J in *Watteau v Fenwick* and the subsequent case-law in which that decision had been rejected in Ontario[11] (as well as in Alberta[12]), Wood JA delivering the judgment of the court, declared that the reports he had researched were 'bereft of any hint that *Watteau v Fenwick* should be considered good law'.[13] In view of the decisions to which reference has been made earlier, it is hardly a matter for surprise that Wood JA should have reached that conclusion.

Wills J had said in 1883 that once it was established that a defendant was a real principal, the ordinary doctrine as to principal and agent applied—that the principal was liable for all the acts of the agent that were within the authority usually confided to an agent of that character, notwithstanding limitations as between the principal and agent upon that authority.[14] In 1919 in *McLaughlin v Gentles*,[15] Hodgins J A of the Ontario Court of Appeal said:

It seems to me to be straining the doctrine of ostensible agency or holding out to apply it in a case where the fact of agency and the holding out were unknown to the person dealing with the so-called agent at the time, and to permit that person, when he discovered that his purchaser was only an agent, to recover against the principal, on the theory that the latter was estopped from denying that he authorized the purchase. It appears to me that the fact that there was a limitation of authority is at least as important as the fact that the purchaser was an agent.

For reasons previously mentioned, the opinion of Hodgins JA is undoubtedly preferable to that of Wills J. But, as Wood JA said in the *Sign-O-Lite* case:[16]

It is astonishing that, after all these years, an authority of such doubtful origin, and of such unanimously unfavourable reputation, should still be exhibiting signs of life and disturbing the peace of mind of trial judges.

It was time to end any uncertainty that might linger as to its proper place in the law of agency. He had no difficulty in concluding that the doctrine set out in *Watteau v Fenwick* was not part of the law of British Columbia. On that ground the plaintiff's cross-appeal failed: the defendant was not liable as an undisclosed principal on the 1985 contract.

Although this case dealt only with the law of British Columbia, it does not appear unreasonable to conclude, in light of this decision and the earlier Ontario cases referred to therein, that in common law Canada generally, whatever the state of the law in England, the doctrine of *Watteau v Fenwick* is defunct. It is to be hoped that the same will ultimately prove to be the situation in England. There is every indication that when the time comes for a court to do so, it will give the same short shrift to the decision of Wills J as it has now received at the hands of the British Columbia Court of Appeal.

FOOTNOTES:

1 [1893] 1 QB 346 (QBD).

2 FMB Reynolds [*Bowstead and Reynolds on Agency* (18th edn, 2006), paras 3–006, 8–079]; GHL Fridman, *Law of Agency* [(7th edn, 1996), pp 69–76]; R Powell *Law of Agency* (2nd edn, 1961), pp 75–78; SJ Stoljar *Law of Agency* (6th edn, 1990), pp 60–66; AL Goodhart and CJ Hamson, *Undisclosed Principals in Contract* (1932) 4 Camb LJ 320; JA Hornby *The Usual Authority of An Agent* [1961] Camb LJ 239.

3 *Miles v McIlwraith* (1883) 8 App Cas 120 (PC); *Becherer v Asher* (1896) 23 OAR 202 (Ont CA); *McLaughlin v Gentles* (1919) 51 DLR 383,46 OLR 477 (Ont App Div); *Massey Harris Co Ltd v Bond* [1930] 2 DLR 57, [1930] 1 WWR 72 (Alta SC). See also *Johnston v Reading* (1893) 9 TLR 200 (QBD); *Lloyd's Bank v Suisse Bankverein* (1912) 107 LT 309, aff'd (1913) 108 LT 143 (CA); *Jerome v Bentley* [1952] 2 All ER 114 (QBD); *International Paper Co v Spicer* (1906) 4 CLR 739 (Aust HC).

4 *Rhodian River Shipping Co SA v Halla Maritime Corp* [1984] 1 Lloyd's Rep 373, at pp 378–379 (QBD), per Bingham J. Curiously, this case was not referred to in the British Columbia decision that is now under discussion.

5 Bowstead, *op cit*, footnote 2, [paras 3–005 and 3–006]; Fridman, *op cit*, footnote 2, [pp 69–76, 122–128].

6 On actual authority see Bowstead, *ibid*, [paras 3–001 to 3–004]; Fridman, *ibid*, [pp 62–64].

7 See the authorities cited *supra*, footnote 5.

8 It also seems to be rejected by the decision of the House of Lords in *Keighley Maxsted & Co v Durant* [1901] AC 240, on which see Bowstead, *op cit*, footnote 2, [para 2–061]; Fridman, *op cit*, footnote 2, [pp 89–90].

9 See, eg *McLaughlin v Gentles*, *supra*, footnote 3: cf *Keighley Maxsted & Co v Durant*, *supra*, footnote 8.

10 (1990) 73 DLR (4th) 541, 49 BCLR (2d) 183 (BCCA).

11 *McLaughlin v Gentles*, *supra*, footnote 3; *Massey Harris Co Ltd v Bond*, *supra*, footnote 3.

12 *Massey Harris Co Ltd v Bond*, *ibid*.

13 *Supra*, footnote 10, at pp 548 (DLR), 191 (BCLR).

14 *Watteau v Fenwick*, *supra*, footnote 1, at pp 348–349.

15 *Supra*, footnote 3, at pp 394–395 (DLR), 490 (OLR).

16 *Supra*, footnote 10, at pp 548 (DLR), 191 (BCLR).

NOTES

1.   A number of theories have been advanced in an attempt to explain *Watteau v Fenwick:* apparent authority (AL Goodhart and CJ Hamson [1931] CLJ 320 at 336; but see above for Fridman's response); 'inherent agency power' (*Restatement of the Law of Agency* (2nd edn, 1958), paras 8A, 140; but see M Conant (1968) 47 Nebraska LR 678 at 686, and the concept is not used in the third edition of the *Restatement*, although art 2.06 retains a rule similar to the effect of *Watteau v Fenwick*); an independent type of usual authority (*Bowstead and Reynolds*, para 3–005; R Powell, *Law of Agency* (2nd edn, 1961), p 78; but see also *Bowstead and Reynolds*, para 8–077); by analogy with the doctrine of vicarious liability in tort (E Peel, *Treitel's Law of Contract* (14th edn, 2015), para 16–030; but see J Collier [1985] CLJ 363 at 365); and as an extension of the doctrine of apparent ownership (Conant, op cit, pp 687–688; but see J Hornby [1961] CLJ 239 at 246). All these theories are open to criticism and none provides a satisfactory explanation of the case. If *Watteau v Fenwick* can be explained at all,

it may be necessary to go outside the realm of agency and see it as an example of estoppel by conduct (but not of agency created by estoppel): 'what Fenwick represented by leaving Humble in charge was not that Humble was Fenwick's agent, but rather *that Humble and the owner of the Victoria Hotel (whoever that might he) were one and the same person.* By putting someone in charge of their business in such a way that he seemed to be the proprietor of it, they gave Watteau the impression that they, as owners of the hotel, were not a distinct legal entity from the person Watteau did business with' (A Tettenborn [1998] CLJ 274 at 279). Alternatively, it may be better simply to regard the decision as a product of its time, when the actual, general authority of a manager of a business was enough to make the principal responsible to a third party for his agent's acts, irrespective of internal restrictions on the agent's authority (see I Brown [2004] JBL 391 at 407–412).

2.   Whatever the theoretical basis of the decision, it is submitted that there are good policy reasons against holding an undisclosed principal liable to a third party when the principal's agent exceeds his actual authority (contrast Collier, op cit, p 364, who describes *Watteau v Fenwick* as 'eminently just'). It must be remembered that *Watteau v Fenwick* places the undisclosed principal under a personal liability; it does not give him any right to sue the third party (*Bowstead and Reynolds*, para 8–077). Furthermore, if the agent exceeds his actual authority, the principal cannot sue the third party under the doctrine of undisclosed principal (below, p 202); neither can he rely on ratification of the agent's acts, as an undisclosed principal cannot ratify (below, p 159). It seems unjust that the principal should have a liability without a right of action, especially when he never wished to be bound by such a contract in the first place. However, by analogy with the doctrine of apparent authority, if the principal is sued on a contract made by his agent, he can probably make counterclaims as well as adduce defences, as opposed to suing on the contract of his own motion (see above, p 136). The issue remains undecided.

3.   Whatever the faults of the decision, *Watteau v Fenwick* has not been overruled in England. However, the limits of the case are clear. First, 'there should be an existing agency relationship, and the agent should be of such a character that it is possible to identify the "usual" powers that such an agent will have' (RTH Stone [1993] JBL 325 at 328). Identifying the 'usual' powers of any one category of agent may not be easy: 'late twentieth-century business practices do not enable a facile classification of stereotypical agents with concomitant, standard authorities' (I Brown [1995] JBL 360 at 367). Secondly, *Watteau v Fenwick* will not apply where the agent acts for himself and not for his principal (this is why *Kinahan & Co Ltd v Parry* [1910] 2 KB 389, where *Watteau v Fenwick* was followed, was reversed on appeal: [1911] 1 KB 459), or where the third party knows, or ought reasonably to know, of the restriction on the agent's authority (*Daun v Simmins* (1879) 41 LT 783, CA).

QUESTIONS

1.   In *Watteau v Fenwick*, could Watteau have sued Humble for the price of the cigars?

2.   Pippa appoints Audrey as her general manager for the purchase of houses in Leeds, instructing Audrey, however, not to disclose the existence of the agency, and not to purchase except on a surveyor's report. Audrey discloses her position to Tessa, withholding, however, the requirement of a surveyor's report and purchases houses in Leeds from Tessa as agent for Pippa without a surveyor's report. Is Pippa liable to Tessa for the price of the houses? See Montrose (1939) 17 Can Bar Rev 693 at 710–711; Hornby [1961] CLJ 239 at 240 fn.

3.   Article 2.2.4 of the UNIDROIT *Principles of International Commercial Contracts* (2004) (see above, p 123) provides as follows:

(1) Where an agent acts within the scope of its authority and the third party neither knew nor ought to have known that the agent was acting as an agent, the acts of the agent shall affect only the relations between the agent and the third party.

(2) However, where such an agent, when contracting with the third party on behalf of a business, represents itself to be the owner of that business, the third party, upon discovery of the real owner of the business, may exercise also against the latter the rights it has against the agent.

What reason could there be for retaining the exception in art 2.2.4(2)? Can you think of an alternative way of protecting the third party in such circumstances? See *Bowstead and Reynolds*, para 8–077.

(d) Authority by operation of law

(i) Agency of necessity

Bowstead and Reynolds on Agency **by Peter G Watts**
(20th edn, 2014), art 33

DOCTRINE OF AGENCY OF NECESSITY

(1) A person may have authority to act on behalf of another in certain cases where he is faced with an emergency in which the property or interests of that other are in imminent jeopardy and it becomes necessary, in order to preserve the property or interest, so to act.

(2) In some cases this authority may entitle him to affect his principal's legal position by making contracts or disposing of property. In others it may merely entitle him to reimbursement of expenses or indemnity against liabilities incurred in so acting, or to a defence against a claim that what he did was wrongful as against the person for whose benefit he acted.

China-Pacific SA v Food Corpn of India, The Winson
[1982] AC 939, House of Lords

The defendant cargo owner chartered a ship to carry wheat from the United States to Bombay. During the voyage the ship stranded on a reef. The ship's managing agents (in effect the ship's master) then entered into a Lloyd's Standard Form of Salvage Agreement No Cure—No Pay (known as the Lloyd's open form) with the plaintiffs, who were professional salvors. To assist the salvage operation, the salvors unloaded several parcels of wheat and shipped them to Manila. To protect the wheat from deterioration, the salvors contracted with various depositaries to warehouse it at the salvors' expense. The salvors then looked to the cargo owner for reimbursement of these storage charges. Lloyd J's decision to hold the cargo owner liable to reimburse the salvors was reversed by the Court of Appeal. The House of Lords upheld the salvors' appeal against the Court of Appeal's ruling, restoring the judgment of Lloyd J.

Lord Diplock: Lloyd's open form is expressed by clause 16 to be signed by the master 'as agent for the vessel her cargo and freight and the respective owners thereof and binds each (but not the one for the other or himself personally) to the due performance thereof.' The legal nature of the relationship between the master and the owner of the cargo aboard the vessel in signing the agreement on the latter's behalf is often though not invariably an agency of necessity. It arises only when salvage services by a third party are necessary for the preservation of the cargo. Whether one person is entitled to act as agent of necessity for another person is relevant to the question whether circumstances exist which in law have the effect of conferring on him authority to create contractual rights and obligations between that other person and a third party that are directly enforceable by each against the other. It would, I think, be an aid to clarity of legal thinking if the use of the expression 'agent of necessity' were confined to contexts in which this was the question to be determined and not extended, as it often is, to cases where the only relevant question is whether a person who without obtaining instructions from the owner of goods incurs expense in taking steps that are reasonably necessary for their preservation is in law entitled to recover from the owner of the goods the reasonable expenses incurred by him in taking those steps. Its use in this wider sense may, I think, have led to some confusion in the instant case, since where reimbursement is the only relevant question all of those conditions that must be fulfilled in order to entitle one person to act on behalf of another in creating direct contractual relationships between that other person and a third party may not necessarily apply.

In the instant case it is not disputed that when the Lloyd's open form was signed on January 22, 1975, the circumstances that existed at that time were such as entitled the master to enter into the agreement on the cargo owner's behalf as its agent of necessity. The rendering of salvage services under the Lloyd's open agreement does not usually involve the salvor's taking possession of the vessel or its cargo from the shipowner; the shipowner remains in possession of both ship and cargo while salvage services are being carried out by the salvors on the ship. But salvage services may involve the transfer of possession of cargo from the shipowner to the salvors, and will do so in a case of stranding as respects part of the cargo if it becomes necessary to lighten the vessel in order to refloat her. When, in the course of salvage operations cargo is off-loaded from the vessel by which the contract of carriage was being performed and conveyed separately from that vessel to a place of safety by means (in the instant case, barges) provided by the salvor, the direct relationship of bailor and bailee is created between cargo owner and salvor as soon as the cargo is loaded on vessels provided by the salvor to convey it to a place of safety; and all the mutual rights and duties attaching to that relationship at common law apply, save in so far as any of them are inconsistent with the express terms of the Lloyd's open agreement...

My Lords, in the courts below and in argument before your Lordships there has been some discussion as to whether on their obtaining possession of the cargo from the shipowner the relationship of the salvors to the cargo owner was that of bailee or sub-bailee. A sub-bailee is one to whom actual possession of goods is transferred by someone who is not himself the owner of the goods but has a present right to possession of them as bailee of the owner. In the instant case Lloyd J and the Court of Appeal were of the view that the salvors were bailees of the cargo owner, and this was, in my view also, plainly right. They would only be sub-bailees of the cargo owner if the contract to render salvage services to the cargo under Lloyd's open form had been signed by the master as agent for the shipowner only. This was plainly not the case. The contract was one under which the salvors' remuneration in respect of salvage services to the cargo was a liability of the cargo owner, not of the shipowner, and security for such remuneration could be required by the salvors to be given by the cargo owner alone; so the only consideration for salvage services rendered to the cargo by salvors under Lloyd's open form came from the cargo owner. The only sub-bailments involved in the instant case were those effected by the salvors themselves with the depositaries when they deposited the salved wheat for safe keeping at Manila....

Upon the assumption, whether correct or not, to which I have already referred as being that upon which this case has been argued throughout, that the salvage services which the salvors had contracted to render to the cargo owner came to an end as respects each parcel of salved wheat when it arrived at a place of safety in Manila Harbour, the legal relationship of bailor and bailee between cargo owner and salvors nevertheless continued to subsist until possession of the wheat was accepted by the cargo owner from the depositaries who had been the salvors' sub-bailees. Subject always to the question of the salvors' right to the provision of security before removal of the salved wheat from Manila, with which I shall deal separately later, the bailment which up to the conclusion of the salvage services had been a bailment for valuable consideration became a gratuitous bailment; and so long as that relationship of bailor and bailee continued to subsist the salvors, under the ordinary principles of the law of bailment too well known and too well-established to call for any citation of authority, owed a duty of care to the cargo owner to take such measures to preserve the salved wheat from deterioration by exposure to the elements as a man of ordinary prudence would take for the preservation of his own property. For any breach of such duty the bailee is liable to his bailor in damages for any diminution in value of the goods consequent upon his failure to take such measures; and if he fulfils that duty he has, in my view, a correlative right to charge the owner of the goods with the expenses reasonably incurred in doing so.

My Lords, as I have already said, there is not any direct authority as to the existence of this correlative right to reimbursement of expenses in the specific case of a salvor who retains possession of cargo after the salvage services rendered by him to that cargo have ended; but Lloyd J discerned what he considered to be helpful analogous applications of the principle of the bailee's right to reimbursement in *Cargo ex Argos* (1873) LR 5 PC 134, from which I have taken the expression 'correlative right,' and in *Great Northern Rly Co v Swaffield* (1874) LR 9 Exch 132. Both these were cases of carriage of goods in which the carrier/bailee was left in possession of the goods after the carriage contracted for had terminated. Steps necessary for the preservation of the goods were taken by the bailee in default of any instructions from owner/bailor to do otherwise. To these authorities I would add *Notara v Henderson* (1872) LR 7 QB 225, in which the bailee was held liable in damages for breach of his duty to take steps necessary for the preservation of the goods, and the Scots case of *Garriock v Walker* (1873) 1 R 100 in which the bailee recovered the expenses incurred by him in taking such steps. Although in both these cases, which involved carriage of goods by sea, the steps for the prevention of deterioration of the cargo needed to be taken before the contract voyage was completed, the significance of the Scots case is that the cargo owner was on the spot when the steps were taken by the carrier/bailee and did not acquiesce in them. Nevertheless, he took the benefit of them by taking delivery of the cargo thus preserved at the conclusion of the voyage.

In the instant case the cargo owner was kept informed of the salvors' intentions as to the storage of the salved wheat upon its arrival in Manila; it made no alternative proposals; it made no request to the salvors for delivery of any of the wheat after its arrival at Manila, and a request made by the salvors to the cargo owner through their solicitors on February 25,1975, after the arrival of the second of the six parcels, to take delivery of the parcels of salved wheat on arrival at Manila remained unanswered and uncomplied with until after notice of abandonment of the charter voyage had been received by the cargo owner from the shipowner.

The failure of the cargo owner as bailor to give any instructions to the salvors as its bailee although it was fully apprised of the need to store the salved wheat under cover on arrival at Manila if it was to be preserved from rapid deterioration was, in the view of Lloyd J, sufficient to attract the application of the principle to which I have referred above and to entitle the salvors to recover from the cargo owner their expenses in taking measures necessary for its preservation. For my part I think that in this he was right and the Court of Appeal, who took the contrary view, were wrong. It is, of course, true that in English law a mere stranger cannot compel an owner of goods to pay for a benefit bestowed upon him against his will; but this latter principle does not apply where there is a pre-existing legal relationship between the owner of the goods and the bestower of the benefit, such as that of bailor and bailee, which imposes upon the bestower of the benefit a legal duty of care in respect of the preservation of the goods that is owed by him to their owner.

In the Court of Appeal Megaw LJ, as I understand his judgment, with which Bridge and Cumming-Bruce LJJ expressed agreement, was of opinion that, in order to entitle the salvors to reimbursement of the expenses incurred by them in storing the salvaged wheat at Manila up to April 24,1975, they would have to show not only that, looked at objectively, the measures that they took were necessary to preserve it from rapid deterioration, but, in addition, that it was impossible for them to communicate with the cargo owner to obtain from him such instructions (if any) as he might want to give. My Lords, it may be that this would have been so if the question in the instant case had been whether the depositaries could have sued the cargo owner directly for their contractual storage charges on the ground that the cargo owner was party as principal to the contracts of storage made on its behalf by the salvors as its agents of necessity; for English law is economical in recognising situations that give rise to agency of necessity. In my view, inability to communicate with the owner of the goods is not a condition precedent to the bailee's own right to reimbursement of his expenses. The bailor's failure to give any instructions when apprised of the situation is sufficient.

So, on the cargo owner's main propositions of law in this appeal, I think it fails and that on these points the Court of Appeal was wrong in reversing Lloyd J.

[**Lord Simon of Glaisdale** held that the salvors' right of reimbursement arose by implication from the Lloyd's open form agreement and from the common law of bailment. He continued]:

Agency of necessity. Lloyd J decided in favour of the salvor on the further ground that he was the cargo owner's agent of necessity and as such entitled to reimbursement of the expenses in issue. The Court of Appeal held that there was no agency of necessity.

One of the ways in which an agency of necessity can arise is where A is in possession of goods the property of B, and an emergency arises which places those goods in imminent jeopardy: If A cannot obtain instructions from B as to how he should act in such circumstances, A is bound to take without authority such action in relation to the goods as B, as a prudent owner, would himself have taken in the circumstances. The relationship between A and B is then known as an 'agency of necessity,' A being the agent and B the principal. This was the situation described by Lloyd J and denied by the Court of Appeal.

Issues as to agency of necessity generally arise forensically when A enters into a contract with C in relation to the goods, the question being whether B is bound by that contract. The purely terminological suggestion that, in order to avoid confusion, 'agent of necessity' should be confined to such contractual situations does not involve that other relevant general incidents of agency are excluded from the relationship between A and B. In particular, if A incurs reasonable expenses in safeguarding B's goods in a situation of emergency, A is entitled to be reimbursed by B: . . .

To confine 'agent of necessity' terminologically to the contractual situations is justified by the fact that the law of bailment will often resolve any issue between alleged principal and agent of necessity, as it has done here. But sometimes the law of agency will be more useful: for example, if available here it would obviate any problem about the correlation of performance of a duty of care with a claim for reimbursement, since an agent is undoubtedly entitled to an indemnity for expenses incurred reasonably to benefit his principal.

However, I respectfully agree with the Court of Appeal [1981] QB 403, 424 that:

The relevant time, for the purpose of considering whether there was a necessity, or an emergency . . . is . . . the time when the existence of the supposed emergency became apparent. The emergency would be the arrival, or expected arrival, of salved cargo at Manila, with no arrangements for its off-loading or for its preservation in proper storage having been made or put in hand. There never was, so far as one can ascertain from the evidential matter here, such an emergency.

In addition to the factual difficulty in treating the case as one of agency of necessity, there are legal difficulties in the way of the salvor. For an agency of necessity to arise, the action taken must be necessary for the protection of the interests of the alleged principal, not of the agent; the alleged agent must have acted *bona fide* in the interests of the alleged principal:... The Court of Appeal [1981] QB 403, 425 held that the salvor's purpose in storing the salved cargo was to maintain his lien on it. This was assuredly at least in part the salvor's purpose. The law does not seem to have determined in this context what ensues where interests are manifold or motives mixed: it may well be that the court will look to the interest mainly served or to the dominant motive. In view of the opinion I have formed on the rights arising by implication from the Lloyd's open form and from the common law bailment, it is unnecessary to come to any conclusion on these issues.

[**Lords Keith of Kinkel**, **Lord Roskill**, and **Lord Brandon of Oakbrook** concurred with Lord Diplock.]

NOTES

1.   Traditionally, the courts have not distinguished between cases where an agent of necessity creates a contractual relationship between his principal and a third party and those where the agent of necessity simply seeks reimbursement from the principal, or looks to defend an action for wrongful interference with the principal's goods. However, the distinction was made by Lord Diplock in *The Winson* and we shall adopt it here (cf E Peel, *Treitel's Law of Contract* (14th edn, 2015), para 16–042; A Burrows, *The Law of Restitution* (3rd edn, 2011), pp 473–474).

2.   (a) *True agents of necessity* In such cases the agent has power to affect the legal relations of his principal. The agent may contract with third parties on behalf of his principal and he may dispose of his principal's property. The agent will have a defence if sued by his principal, and he may be able to claim reimbursement from the principal for expenses incurred. However, agency of necessity will only arise if:

(a)   it is impossible or impracticable for the agent to communicate with the principal (*Springer v Great Western Rly Co* [1921] 1 KB 257 at 265, per Bankes LJ)—improved methods of communication in the modern commercial world mean that this requirement is now rarely met;

(b)   the action is necessary for the benefit of the principal (*Prager v Blatspiel, Stamp and Heacock Ltd* [1924] 1 KB 566 at 571, per McCardie J);

(c)   the agent acts bona fide in the interests of the principal (*Prager v Blatspiel*, above, at 572);

(d)   the action taken by the agent is reasonable and prudent (*F v West Berkshire Health Authority* [1990] 2 AC 1 at 76, per Lord Goff); and

(e)   the principal has not given the agent express instructions to the contrary (see *Bowstead and Reynolds*, para 4–005: 'this follows from the fact that [agency of necessity] does not operate where the principal can be consulted. The inference is that the principal could forbid the action at the time: if so, he can do so in advance').

The traditional (possibly only) example of a true agent of necessity is the master of a ship who acts in an emergency to save the ship or the cargo (*Hawtayne v Bourne* (1841) 7 M & W 595 at 599, per Parke B). Sometimes it is possible to explain the master's agency in terms of implied actual authority, for example when he signs a salvage contract on behalf of the shipowner (*The Unique Mariner* [1978] 1 Lloyd's Rep 438). On other occasions it may only be possible to explain the master's action in terms of necessity, for example in *The Choko Star* [1990] 1 Lloyd's Rep 516 the Court of Appeal stressed that the ship's master had no implied actual authority to sign a salvage agreement on behalf of cargo owners, but he could do so as an agent of necessity (noted by RJC Munday [1991] LMCLQ 1; I Brown (1992) 55 MLR 414). But now see s 224(1) of the Merchant Shipping Act 1995 implementing art 6(2) of the International Convention on Salvage of 1989, which gives the master wide powers, including the power to sign a salvage contract for the cargo.

There has been considerable debate as to whether true agency of necessity is restricted to cases of the carriage of goods by sea. For conflicting dicta, see *Prager v Blatspiel, Stamp and Heacock Ltd* [1924] 1 KB 566 at 569–571, per McCardie J; and *Jebara v Ottoman Bank* [1927] 2 KB 254 at 270–271, per Scrutton LJ. However, it has been established that agency of necessity also extends to the carriage or storage of perishable goods or livestock on land (*Great Northern Rly Co v Swaffield* (1874) LR 9 Exch 132; *Sachs v Miklos* [1948] 2 KB 23) and there seems no reason why non-perishable goods should not be included in this category, although such cases are likely to be rare. The dicta of Lord Simon in *The Winson* appear to support this broader approach (above). See also ss 12 and 13 of and Sch 1 to the Torts (Interference with Goods) Act 1977 (conferring a power of sale on bailees of goods in specified circumstances). Cf *Bowstead and Reynolds*, para 4–006 and Fridman, pp 142–143, who submit that these non-maritime cases are more appropriately dealt with as part of the law of restitution, ie under category (b) below.

(b) *Agents who act for another in circumstances of necessity and seek reimbursement or look to defend themselves against an action for interference with the principal's property* The *Winson* provides an example of this type of agent. Lord Diplock did not think it necessary that such an agent need comply with all the strict rules as apply to true agents of necessity (above, p 153) and this view is supported by *Bowstead and Reynolds* (para 4–005). Whether this type of agency is confined to situations where there is a pre-existing relationship (contractual or otherwise) between the principal and agent is a difficult question to answer. In *The Winson* such a relationship existed, ie that of bailor and bailee. It is really a question for the law of restitution. English law has traditionally set itself against a general principle (outside the law of maritime salvage) entitling a stranger who protects or benefits the property of another to seek reimbursement or claim a lien (see the classic dictum of Bowen LJ in *Falcke v Scottish Imperial Insurance Co* (1886) 34 Ch D 234 at 248–249). The long-established right of an acceptor of a bill of exchange for honour to seek reimbursement from the drawer would appear to be an exception to this general rule (Bills of Exchange Act 1882, s 68(5)). However, recent developments in the law of restitution indicate that a stranger who intervenes in an emergency will have a good claim if (a) there was a pressing emergency which compelled intervention without the property owner's authority; (b) he acted reasonably and in the best interests of the property owner; (c) he was not able to obtain the 'principal's' instructions; and (d) (possibly) he is a professional performing a professional service (see R Goff and G Jones, *The Law of Unjust Enrichment* (8th edn, 2011), para 17–013). In *Surrey Breakdown Ltd v Knight* [1999] RTR 84, Sir Christopher Staughton, speaking *obiter*, described this more flexible approach to the availability of a restitutionary claim as representing the modern law. In that case the police called in a garage to pull a stolen car out of a pond. The garage did so and later claimed the cost of this service, and subsequent storage charges, from the car's owner. The Court of Appeal rejected the claim on the ground that the facts of the case did not meet condition (a): there was no pressing emergency compelling intervention without the car owner's authority. For further reading, see *Goff and Jones*, above, Ch 18; A Burrows,

The Law of Restitution (3rd edn, 2011), Ch 18; G Virgo, *Principles of the Law of Restitution* (3rd edn, 2015), Ch 12.

3. Sections 5–8 of the Mental Capacity Act 2005 create a statutory form of agency of necessity for mentally incapacitated persons (see *Bowstead and Reynolds*, para 4–012). It enables a person to intervene on behalf of a mentally incapacitated person to pledge that person's credit in connection with his care or treatment, and to use that person's money and/or seek indemnity in respect of acts done for that purpose. This regime does not affect the operation of a lasting power of attorney that may have been drawn up by the mentally incapacitated person before the incapacity arose.

QUESTION

'Agency by estoppel is really agency by operation of law' (Fridman, p 19). Discuss.

(e) Ratification

If a person (the 'agent') acts without authority, or exceeds his authority, his actions cannot bind the person (the 'principal') on whose behalf he purports to act. Subsequently, however, the principal may ratify the agent's acts. Ratification validates the agent's actions with effect from the time those actions took place. As Lord Sterndale MR expressed matters in *Koenigsblatt v Sweet* [1923] 2 Ch 314 at 325: 'Ratification...is equivalent to an antecedent authority.' The doctrine is to some extent anomalous and the courts seem keen to keep it in check (*Smith v Henniker-Major & Co* [2002] EWCA Civ 762, [2002] Ch 182 at [61], per Robert Walker LJ).

   Ratification may be express or implied from the principal's unequivocal conduct. In *Hogan v London Irish Rugby Football Trading Ltd* (20 December 1999, unreported), the defendants were held to have ratified oral agreements made by A, their chief coach and director of rugby, with the players, by allowing them to represent the club and turn up for training, and by continuing to pay them at the rate agreed with A. If ratification is to be implied from the principal's conduct, he must usually be shown to have had full knowledge of the agent's unauthorised acts and to have enjoyed a real choice as to whether or not he wished to adopt them (*The Bonita; The Charlotte* (1861) 1 Lush 252). This means that the principal must have had knowledge of what the agent has done; it does not mean that he needs to know that the agent lacked authority to do it (*Ing Re (UK) Ltd v R & V Versicherung AG* [2006] EWHC 1544 (Comm), [2007] 1 BCLC 108 at [155]–[157]). Ignorance of the law will not allow the principal to avoid the effect of an act that, objectively viewed, exposes him to liability to third parties (*AMB Generali Holdings AB v SEB Trygg Liv Holding AB* [2005] EWCA Civ 1237, [2006] 1 Lloyd's Rep 318 at [43]). However, a principal with incomplete knowledge may be held to have ratified the unauthorised acts of his agent if it can be shown that he took a risk as to how the circumstances might turn out (*Marsh v Joseph* [1897] 1 Ch 213). Silence or inactivity alone will not amount to ratification as they do not provide clear and unequivocal evidence of the principal's approval and adoption of his agent's actions (*Crampsey v Deveney* (1969) 2 DLR (3d) 161 at 164, per Judson J; *713860 Ontario Ltd v Royal Trust Corpn of Canada* (22 January 1996, unreported), per Wilson J, an Ontario case cited in Munday at para 6.28, and since upheld on appeal (1 March 1999, unreported). Silence or inactivity, however, may amount to ratification where they are coupled with other factors: for example, where the principal is aware of all the material facts and appreciates that he is regarded as having accepted the position of principal, and he takes no steps to disown that character within a reasonable time, or adopts no means of asserting his rights at the earliest possible time (*Suncorp Insurance and Finance v Milano Assicurazioni SpA* [1993] 2 Lloyd's Rep 225 at 234–235, per Waller J; *Yona International Ltd v La Réunion Française SA d'Assurances et de Réassurances* [1996] 2 Lloyd's Rep 84 at 103, per Moore-Bick J). A party wishing to ratify a transaction must adopt it in its entirety, although adoption of part of a transaction may be held to amount to ratification of the whole (*Smith v Henniker-Major & Co*, above, at [56], per Robert Walker LJ).

The principal can only ratify acts which the agent purported to do on the principal's behalf. As the next case illustrates, if the agent purports to act on his own behalf the principal cannot ratify.

Keighley, Maxsted & Co v Durant

[1901] AC 240, House of Lords

Keighley, Maxsted & Co (KM) instructed Roberts, a corn merchant, to buy wheat at a certain price on the joint account of themselves and Roberts. Roberts could not buy at this price, but he agreed to purchase wheat from Durant at a higher price. Although Roberts intended to buy the wheat on behalf of himself and KM, he bought it in his own name without informing Durant that he was also acting for KM. KM then purported to ratify the agreement. The price was not paid to Durant who claimed to hold KM liable on the contract. Day J dismissed the action, but he was reversed by the Court of Appeal. The House of Lords allowed an appeal from the Court of Appeal's decision.

Lord Macnaghten: As a general rule, only persons who are parties to a contract, acting either by themselves or by an authorized agent, can sue or be sued on the contract. A stranger cannot enforce the contract, nor can it be enforced against a stranger. That is the rule; but there are exceptions. The most remarkable exception, I think, results from the doctrine of ratification as established in English law. That doctrine is thus stated by Tindal CJ in *Wilson v Tumman* ((1843) 6 Man & G 236 at 242): 'That an act done, *for another*, by a person, not assuming to act for himself, but for such other person, though without any precedent authority whatever, becomes the act of the principal, if subsequently ratified by him, is the known and well-established rule of law. In that case the principal is bound by the act, whether it be for his detriment or his advantage, and whether it be founded on a tort or on a contract, to the same effect as by, and with all the consequences which follow from, the same act done by his *previous* authority.' And so by a wholesome and convenient fiction, a person ratifying the act of another, who, without authority, has made a contract openly and avowedly on his behalf, is deemed to be, though in fact he was not, a party to the contract. Does the fiction cover the case of a person who makes no avowal at all, but assumes to act for himself and for no one else? If Tindal CJ's statement of the law is accurate, it would seem to exclude the case of a person who may intend to act for another, but at the same time keeps his intention locked up in his own breast; for it cannot be said that a person who so conducts himself does assume to act for anybody but himself. But ought the doctrine of ratification to be extended to such a case? On principle I should say certainly not. It is, I think, a well-established principle in English law that civil obligations are not to be created by, or founded upon, undisclosed intentions. That is a very old principle. Lord Blackburn, enforcing it in the case of *Brogden v Metropolitan Rly Co* ((1877) 2 App Cas 666 at 692), traces it back to the year-books of Edward IV (17 Edw 4, 2, pl 2) and to a quaint judgment of Brian CJ: 'It is common learning,' said that Chief Justice, who was a great authority in those days, 'that the thought of a man is not triable, for the Devil has not knowledge of man's thoughts.' Sir E Fry quotes the same observation in his work on Specific Performance, s 295, p 133, 3rd edn. It is, I think, a sound maxim—at least, in its legal aspect: and in my opinion it is not to be put aside or disregarded merely because it may be that, in a case like the present, no injustice might be done to the actual parties to the contract by giving effect to the undisclosed intentions of a would-be agent.

Lord Shand: The question which arises on this state of the facts is whether, where a person who has avowedly made a contract for himself (1) without a suggestion that he is acting to any extent for another (an undisclosed principal), and (2) without any authority to act for another, can effectually bind a third party as principal, or as a joint obligant with himself, to the person with whom he contracted, by the fact that in his own mind merely he made a contract in the hope and expectation that his contract would be ratified or shared by the person as to whom he entertained that hope and expectation. I am clearly of opinion, with all respect to the majority of the Court of Appeal, that he cannot. The only contract actually made is by the person himself and for himself, and it seems to me to be conclusive against the argument for the respondents, that if their reasoning were sound it would be in his power, on an averment of what was passing in his own mind, to make the contract afterwards either one for himself only, as in fact it was, or one affecting or binding on another as a contracting party, even although he had no authority for this. The result would be to give one of two contracting parties in his option, merely from what was passing in his own mind and not disclosed, the power of saying the contract was his alone, or a contract in which others were bound with him. That, I think, he certainly cannot do in any case where he had no authority, when he made the contract, to bind any one but himself.

Lord Davey: The argument seems to be that as the law permits an undisclosed principal, on whose behalf a contract has been made, to sue and be sued on the contract, and as the effect of ratification is equivalent to a previous mandate, a person who ratifies a contract intended but not expressed to be made on his behalf is in the same position as any other undisclosed principal. Further, it is said that whether the intention of the contractor be expressed or not, its existence is mere matter of evidence, and once it is proved the conclusion ought to follow. Romer LJ held that on principle it ought to be held that ratification (in the case before the Court) is possible, and that to hold the contrary would be to establish an anomaly in the law, and moreover a useless one. My Lords, I cannot agree. There is a wide difference between an agency existing at the date of the contract which is susceptible of proof, and a repudiation of which by the agent would be fraudulent, and an intention locked up in the mind of the contractor, which he may either abandon or act on at his own pleasure, and the ascertainment of which involves an inquiry into the state of his mind at the date of the contract. Where the intention to contract on behalf of another is expressed in the contract, it passes from the region of speculation into that of fact, and becomes irrevocable. In what sense, it may be asked, does a man contract for another, when it depends on his own will whether he will give that other the benefit of the contract or not? In the next place, the rule which permits an undisclosed principal to sue and be sued on a contract to which he is not a party, though well settled, is itself an anomaly, and to extend it to the case of a person who accepts the benefit of an undisclosed intention of a party to the contract would, in my opinion, be adding another anomaly to the law, and not correcting an anomaly.

Lord Lindley: That ratification when it exists is equivalent to a previous authority is true enough (subject to some exceptions which need not be referred to). But, before the one expression can be substituted for the other, care must be taken that ratification is established.

It was strongly contended that there was no reason why the doctrine of ratification should not apply to undisclosed principals in general, and that no one could be injured by it if it were so applied. I am not convinced of this. But in this case there is no evidence in existence that, at the time when Roberts made his contract, he was in fact acting, as distinguished from intending to act, for the defendants as possible principals, and the decision appealed from, if affirmed, would introduce a very dangerous doctrine. It would enable one person to make a contract between two others by creating a principal and saying what his own undisclosed intentions were, and these could not be tested.

[**The Earl of Halsbury LC**, and **Lords James of Hereford**, **Brampton**, and **Robertson** delivered concurring opinions.]

NOTES

1. The decision of the House of Lords in *Keighley, Maxsted & Co v Durant* has been described as 'peremptory and short-sighted' (I Brown [2004] JBL 391 at 394). Can you think why? For criticism of the rule precluding ratification of an undisclosed principal, see A Rochvarg (1989) 34 McGill LJ 286. The rule has been abandoned in the third edition of the US *Restatement of the Law of Agency* (para 4.03 and Comment b). But the rule is well established in English law and unlikely to be altered in the near future: in *Welsh Development Agency v Export Finance Co Ltd* [1992] BCLC 148 at 158, Dillon LJ described it as 'clear law'.

2. In *Keighley, Maxsted & Co v Durant* the undisclosed principal evaded liability. But in *Spiro v Lintern* (discussed above, p 145), where *Keighley, Maxsted & Co v Durant* was followed and applied, the undisclosed principal was held liable to the third party, even though the agent had acted beyond her actual authority. How did this liability arise?

3. As a general rule, an undisclosed principal may sue and be sued on a contract made by an agent acting *within* the scope of his actual authority (see below, p 202).

(i) Other requirements for ratification

(1) The principal must be in existence at the time of the agent's act. Thus a newly incorporated company cannot ratify a prior contract made by its promoters (*Kelner v Baxter* (1866) LR 2 CP 174), although the contract will normally take effect as one between the third party and the promoter allowing both parties to sue and be sued on it (Companies Act 2006, s 51(1); *Braymist Ltd v Wise Finance Co Ltd* [2002] EWCA Civ 127, [2002] Ch 273, applying the identically worded Companies Act 1985, s 36C(1)). The Contracts (Rights of Third Parties) Act 1999 (below, p 170) does not change this requirement even though s 1(3) provides that a 'third party' may enforce a term of a contract to which he is not a party despite the fact that he is not in existence when the contract is entered into. The disclosed principal should not be regarded as a 'third party' for these purposes as he is a party to the contract and able to enforce it as promisee. The way round the problem would be for the agent to be made a party to a contract that included provision for a third party beneficiary, ie the non-existent principal (E Peel, *Treitel's Law of Contract* (14th edn, 2015), para 16–062). Alternatively, a novation (see below, p 889) could take place once the principal has come into existence. Neither solution involves ratification.

(2) According to Willes J in *Watson v Swann* (1862) 11 CBNS 756 at 771:

> To entitle a person to sue upon a contract, it must clearly be shown that he himself made it, or that it was made on his behalf by an agent authorised to act for him. The law obviously requires that the person for whom the agent professes to act must be a person capable of being ascertained at the time. It is not necessary that he should be named; but there must be such a description of him as shall amount to a reasonable designation of the person intended to be bound by the contract.

In that case, an agent was instructed to effect a general policy of insurance on goods for a principal. The agent was unable to do this, so he declared the goods on the back of a general policy of insurance which he had previously effected for himself. Later, when the goods had been lost, the principal sued on the policy. It was held that the principal could not recover on the policy because it was not made on his behalf. At the time the policy was effected by the agent the principal was not even known to him.

The narrow scope of Willes J's dicta has been criticised (see, eg, *Bowstead and Reynolds*, para 2–065; *Markesinis and Munday: An Outline of the Law of Agency* (4th edn, 1998), p 69). In fact policies of marine insurance may be taken out 'for and on behalf of any person interested' and such persons can ratify even though not named on the policy (*Hagedorn v Oliverson* (1814) 2 M & S 485). The reasoning underlying this broader approach was set out by Coleman J in *National Oilwell (UK) Ltd v Davy Offshore Ltd* [1993] 2 Lloyd's Rep 582 at 596–597 (a non-marine insurance case):

> Where at the time when the contract of insurance was made the principal assured or other contracting party had no actual authority to bind the other party to the contract of insurance, but the policy is expressed to insure not only the principal assured but also a class of others who are not identified in that policy, a party who at the time when the policy was effected could have been ascertained to qualify as a member of that class can ratify and sue on the policy as co-assured if at that time it was intended by the principal assured or other contracting party to create privity of contract with the insurer on behalf of that party.

Evidence as to whether in any particular case the principal assured or other contracting party did have the requisite intention may be provided by the terms of the policy itself, by the terms of any contract between the principal assured or other contracting party and the alleged co-assured, and by any other admissible material showing what was subjectively intended by the principal assured.

There seems no good reason to restrict the application of Coleman J's propositions to insurance law. As the editor of *Markesinis and Munday* observed (at p 70): 'If third parties (eg underwriters) are willing to contract under such terms and if principals are prepared to ratify such contracts, there seems no reason why the law should refuse to give effect to the parties' collective wishes, not least because it serves an obvious commercial convenience.' See also F Reynolds, 'Some Agency Problems in Insurance Law' in FD Rose (ed), *Consensus Ad Idem* (1996), pp 82–83.

(3) The principal must have been competent at the time when the act was done by the agent: for example, a principal who was an enemy alien at the time of the agent's act could not ratify: *Boston Deep Sea Fishing and Ice Co Ltd v Farnham (Inspector of Taxes)* [1957] 1 WLR 1051. The principal must also have capacity at the date of the purported ratification, for instance a principal cannot ratify if he is an enemy alien at the date of purported ratification, even though he was not one at the time the act was done.

(4) An act which is void *ab initio* (eg on grounds of illegality or because it is a nullity) cannot be ratified. In the leading case of *Brook v Hook* (1871) LR 6 Exch 89 a distinction was drawn between voidable acts, which can be ratified, and void acts, which cannot. However, as unauthorised acts cannot properly be described as voidable (if anything, they could be described as void), such a general distinction seems unsatisfactory. *Brook v Hook* involved forgery of the principal's signature on a promissory note by his agent. It was held that the principal could not ratify the agent's act as the signature was a nullity. It is submitted that the case is better explained as one where, by forging the principal's signature, the agent did not purport to act on behalf of the principal; quite the contrary, the agent purported to be the principal himself (E Peel, *Treitel's Law of Contract* (14th edn, 2015), para 16–046). Furthermore, a principal cannot ratify an unauthorised contract which is prohibited by statute (*Bedford Insurance Co Ltd v Instituto de Resseguros do Brasil* [1985] QB 966 at 986), but otherwise a principal can ratify an unlawful act.

(ii) Effect of ratification

Bolton Partners v Lambert
(1889) 41 Ch D 295

Lambert made an offer to Scratchley, an agent of Bolton Partners, to take the lease of certain properties. The offer was accepted by Scratchley on behalf of Bolton Partners, though he had no authority to do so. Lambert withdrew the offer before Bolton Partners ratified Scratchley's acceptance. Bolton Partners claimed specific performance of the contract. Affirming the decision of Kekewich J, the Court of Appeal held that Bolton Partners were entitled to specific performance of the contract.

> **Cotton LJ:** But then it is said that on January 13, 1887, the Defendant entirely withdrew the offer he had made. Of course the withdrawal could not be effective, if it were made after the contract had become complete. As soon as an offer has been accepted the contract is complete. But it is said that there could be a withdrawal by the Defendant on January 13 on this ground, that the offer of the Defendant had been accepted by *Scratchley*, a director of the Plaintiff company, who was not authorized to bind the company by acceptance of the offer, and therefore that until the company ratified *Scratchley's* act there was no acceptance on behalf of the company binding on the company, and therefore the Defendant could withdraw his offer. Is that so? The rule as to ratification by a principal of acts done by an assumed agent is that the ratification is thrown back to the date of the act done, and that the agent is put in the same position as if he had had authority to do the act at the time the act was done by him. Various cases have been referred to as laying down this principle, but there is no case exactly like the present one. The case of *Hagedorn v Oliverson* ((1814) 2 M & S 485) is a strong case of the application of the principle. It was there pointed out how favourable the rule was to the principal, because till ratification he was not bound, and he had an option to adopt or not to adopt what had been done. In that case the plaintiff had effected an insurance on a ship in which another person was interested, and it was held that long after the ship had been lost the other person might adopt the act of the plaintiff, though done without authority, so as to enable the plaintiff to sue upon the policy. Again, in *Ancona v Marks* ((1862) 7 H & N 686), where a bill was indorsed to and sued on in the name of *Ancona*, who had given no authority for that purpose, yet it was held that *Ancona* could, after the action had been brought, ratify what had been done, and that the subsequent ratification was equivalent to a prior authority so as to entitle *Ancona* to sue upon the bill. It was

said by [counsel for the defendant] that in that case there was a previously existing liability of the defendant towards some person; but the liability of the defendant to *Ancona* was established by *Ancona's* authorizing and ratifying the act of the agent, and a previously existing liability to others did not affect the principle laid down.

The rule as to ratification is of course subject to some exceptions. An estate once vested cannot be divested, nor can an act lawful at the time of its performance be rendered unlawful, by the application of the doctrine of ratification. The case of *Walter v James* ((1871) LR 6 Exch 124) was relied on by the Appellant, but in that case there was an agreement between the assumed agent of the defendant and the plaintiff to cancel what had been done before any ratification by the defendant; in the present case there was no agreement made between *Scratchley* and the Defendant that what had been done by *Scratchley* should be considered as null and void.

The case of *Bird v Brown* ((1850) 4 Exch 786), which was also relied on by the Appellant, is distinguishable from this case. There it was held that the ratification could not operate to divest the ownership which had previously vested in the purchaser by the delivery of the goods before the ratification of the alleged *stoppage in transitu*. So also in *Lyell v Kennedy* ((1887) 18 QBD 796) the plaintiff, who represented the lawful heir, desired, after the defendant *Kennedy* had acquired a title to the estate by means of the *Statute of Limitations*, and after the title of the heir was gone, to ratify the act *of Kennedy* as to the receipt of rents, so as to make the estate vest in the heir. In my opinion none of these cases support the Appellant's contention.

I think the proper view is that the acceptance by *Scratchley* did constitute a contract, subject to its being shewn that *Scratchley* had authority to bind the company. If that were not shewn there would be no contract on the part of the company, but when and as soon as authority was given to *Scratchley* to bind the company the authority was thrown back to the time when the act was done by *Scratchley*, and prevented the Defendant withdrawing his offer, because it was then no longer an offer, but a binding contract.

Lindley LJ: The question is what is the consequence of the withdrawal of the offer after acceptance by the assumed agent but before the authority of the agent has been ratified? Is the withdrawal in time? It is said on the one hand that the ordinary principle of law applies, viz, that an offer may be withdrawn before acceptance. That proposition is of course true. But the question is—acceptance by whom? It is not a question whether a mere offer can be withdrawn, but the question is whether, when there has been in fact an acceptance which is in form an acceptance by a principal through his agent, though the person assuming to act as agent has not then been so authorized, there can or cannot be a withdrawal of the offer before the ratification of the acceptance? I can find no authority in the books to warrant the contention that an offer made, and in fact accepted by a principal through an agent or otherwise, can be withdrawn. The true view on the contrary appears to be that the doctrine as to the retrospective action of ratification is applicable.

Lopes LJ: An important point is raised with regard to the withdrawal of the offer before ratification in this case.

If there had been no withdrawal of the offer this case would have been simple. The ratification by the Plaintiffs would have related back to the time of the acceptance of the Defendant's offer by *Scratchley*, and the Plaintiffs would have adopted a contract made on their behalf.

It is said that there was no contract which could be ratified, because *Scratchley* at the time he accepted the Defendant's offer had no authority to act for the Plaintiffs. Directly *Scratchley* on behalf and in the name of the Plaintiffs accepted the Defendant's offer I think there was a contract made by *Scratchley* assuming to act for the Plaintiffs, subject to proof by the Plaintiffs that *Scratchley* had that authority.

The Plaintiffs subsequently did adopt the contract, and thereby recognised the authority of their agent *Scratchley*. Directly they did so the doctrine of ratification applied and gave the same effect to the contract made by *Scratchley* as it would have had if *Scratchley* had been clothed with a precedent authority to make it.

If *Scratchley* had acted under a precedent authority the withdrawal of the offer by the Defendant would have been inoperative, and it is equally inoperative where the Plaintiffs have ratified and adopted the contract of the agent. To hold otherwise would be to deprive the doctrine of ratification of its retrospective effect. To use the words of Martin B in *Brook v Hook* ((1871) LR 6 Exch 89 at 96), the ratification would not be 'dragged back as it were, and made equipollent to a prior command.'

I have nothing to add with regard to the other points raised. I agree with what has been said on those points. The appeal must be dismissed.

NOTES

1. The effect of the rule in *Bolton Partners v Lambert* is limited in a number of ways.

(a) Ratification must take place within a reasonable time after acceptance of the offer by the unauthorised person: *Managers of the Metropolitan Asylums Board v Kingham & Sons* (1890) 6 TLR 217. What is a reasonable time will depend on the facts of the case. The third party offeror may abridge the time within which the ratification must take place by informing the principal of his wish to withdraw from the contract (*Re Portuguese Consolidated Copper Mines Ltd* (1890) 45 Ch D 16). There is dictum by Fry LJ in the *Metropolitan Asylums Board* case that 'reasonable time can never extend after the time at which the contract is to commence'. But this dictum has since been disapproved, and can no longer be considered as valid (see, eg, *Bedford Insurance Co Ltd v Instituto de Resseguros do Brasil* [1985] QB 966 at 987, per Parker J). It has long been established that a policy of marine insurance may be ratified after loss (*Williams v North China Insurance Co* (1876) 1 CPD 757), and it has more recently been suggested that the same rule applies to non-marine insurance (*National Oilwell (UK) Ltd v Davy Offshore Ltd* [1993] 2 Lloyd's Rep 582 at 607–608; cf *Grover & Grover Ltd v Matthews* [1910] 2 KB 401). If ratification after loss is contemplated by the terms of the contract this should be allowed.

(b) The rule in *Bolton Partners v Lambert* will not apply if the third party's offer was expressly made subject to ratification (*Metropolitan Asylums Board v Kingham*, above, at 218, per Fry LJ), or the third party's acceptance was expressly made subject to ratification (*Watson v Davies* [1931] 1 Ch 455 at 469, per Maugham J), or the '[third] party to the contract has intimation of the limitation of the agent's authority' (*Warehousing and Forwarding Co of East Africa Ltd v Jafferali & Sons Ltd* [1964] AC 1 at 9, per Lord Guest). In all such cases the third party may withdraw his offer at any time before the principal ratifies the agent's unauthorised acceptance.

(c) It has been stated by Fridman (Fridman, p 102) that 'although, following *Bolton Partners v Lambert*, the contract which is ratified is considered to have been in existence from the moment when the agent in fact made it with the third party, none the less it has been held that ratification will not entitle the principal to sue for any breach of contract which may have occurred *before* the time for ratification'.

Fridman cites the case of *Kidderminster Corpn v Hardwick* (1873) LR 9 Exch 13. He continues:

> ... if the third party, between the time of the agent's acceptance and the principal's ratification does something which, in effect, makes the contract between the third party and the principal virtually non-existent (eg commencing to work for another employer, after having agreed to work for the principal) then the third party will be able to have all the advantages of revocation or withdrawal of his offer, even though he cannot technically revoke or withdraw it.

Tan finds this difficult to accept (see (2003) 117 LQR 626 at 632–634), and of *Kidderminster* he says:

> It is clear that it provides no such support. Rather than absolving a third party from liability for breaches prior to ratification, *Kidderminster* suggests more fundamentally that the third party may withdraw from its obligations altogether prior to any ratification by the principal. It therefore challenges the very basis of *Bolton Partners v Lambert* instead of merely limiting its effect.

The two cases are indeed irreconcilable (and it should be noted that *Kidderminster* was not referred to in *Bolton Partners v Lambert*).

(d)   The agent and the third party may cancel the unauthorised transaction by mutual consent: *Walter v James* (1871) LR 6 Exch 124.

(e)   Ratification is not effective where to permit it would unfairly prejudice a third party, and in particular where: (i) it is essential to the validity of an act that it should be done within a certain time: the act cannot be ratified after the expiration of that time, to the prejudice of any third party; and (ii) ratification may not be recognised if it will affect proprietary rights which have arisen in favour of the third party or others claiming through him since the act of the unauthorised agent (*Bowstead and Reynolds*, art 19). Thus, in *Bird v Brown* (1850) 4 Exch 786, the agent of a consignor of goods, acting without authority, gave notice of stoppage in transit on his principal's behalf. The goods arrived at their destination and were demanded by the trustee in bankruptcy of the consignee. It was held that the consignor could not later ratify the stoppage in transit and so divest the property in the goods, as this had in the meantime vested in the consignee's trustee in bankruptcy. The decision should be contrasted with *Presentaciones Musicales SA v Secunda* [1994] Ch 271 (noted by I Brown (1994) 110 LQR 531). There, a solicitor issued a writ within the limitation period but without his client's authority. The client later purported to ratify the solicitor's action, even though the limitation period had since expired. The Court of Appeal held the ratification to be effective. The court held that as an unauthorised issue of a writ was not a complete nullity, it could be ratified after the expiration of the limitation period. Dillon and Nourse LJJ (at 280–281) distinguished *Bird v Brown* as a case where 'the act done by the self-appointed agent, before the crucial date, had no effect in law unless ratified'. The third member of the court, Roch LJ, simply regarded *Bird v Brown* as authority for the rule that ratification will not be allowed to deprive a third party of any property rights which have vested in him before ratification (see also the explanation of the case given by Cotton LJ in *Bolton Partners v Lambert*, above). The issue is considered further by C-H Tan in (2001) 117 LQR 626. In each case it is important to assess whether there has been unfair prejudice to the third party; even a relatively small amount of prejudice coupled with a long delay before ratification may be unfair (*Smith v Henniker-Major & Co* [2002] EWCA Civ 762, [2003] Ch 182 at [82], per

Robert Walker LJ, *obiter*). Moreover, it has been held by the Court of Appeal that there is no absolute rule that a contract cannot be ratified if the effect of ratification would be to divest an accrued property right, although the court did go on to accept that in the vast majority of cases it would be unjust to the third party to give effect to a ratification if this was the result (*Owners of the ship 'Borvigilant' v Owners of the ship 'Romina G'* [2003] EWCA Civ 935, [2003] 2 Lloyd's Rep 520 at [70] and [87]).

2.   *Bolton Partners v Lambert* has been criticised for putting the third party in a worse position than he would have been in if he had made his offer direct to the principal, for then he could have withdrawn the offer before the principal accepted it (WA Seavey (1920) 29 Yale LJ 859 at 891). The case was specifically not followed in *Fleming v Bank of New Zealand* [1900] AC 577, PC, and was disapproved of in the dissenting judgment of Isaacs J in *Davison v Vickery's Motors Ltd* (1925) 37 CLR 1, High Court of Australia. The case has more recently been criticised by the Supreme Court of New South Wales in *NM Superannuation Pty Ltd v Hughes* (1992) 7 ACSR 105 at 115–117, per Cohen J. Furthermore, most jurisdictions in the United States allow the third party to withdraw his offer before ratification and the 1983 Geneva Convention on Agency in the International Sale of Goods (above, p 123) allows a third party to withdraw before ratification if, at the time of contracting, he was unaware of the agent's lack of authority (art 15(2)).

Yet *Bolton Partners v Lambert* may not be as prejudicial to the third party as first appears. As we have seen, there are a number of exceptions to the rule. Furthermore, it must be remembered that if the principal ratifies the contract the third party gets what he bargained for, and that if he does not ratify, the third party can sue the agent for breach of warranty of authority. The real prejudice to the third party is the possibility of uncertainty whilst waiting to see whether the principal will ratify the contract or not. However, as we have seen, even this period may be curtailed if the third party serves notice on the principal of his wish to withdraw from the contract (above, p 165).

QUESTIONS

1.   Why should an undisclosed principal be prohibited from ratifying the unauthorised acts of his agent?

2.   Adam contracts with Ted, telling him that he is acting on behalf of Paul. In fact, Adam is acting on his own behalf. Can Paul ratify the contract? See *Re Tiedemann & Ledermann Frères* [1899] 2 QB 66.

CHAPTER 6

RELATIONS WITH THIRD PARTIES

We have seen how an agent has power to affect the legal relations of his principal with regard to third parties (above, p 127). Typically the agent will do this by contracting on behalf of the principal or by disposing of the principal's property. In this chapter we shall focus on the effect of contracts made by agents; the unauthorised disposition of property by an agent is considered in Chapter 10.

When considering the rights and liabilities arising under a contract made by an agent, it is important to ascertain whether the agent was acting for a disclosed or undisclosed principal. A *disclosed* principal is one of whose existence the third party is aware at the time of contracting with the agent. If the name of the principal is known to the third party then the principal is described as 'named'. If the third party does not know the principal's name, but knows of his existence, the principal is described as 'unnamed'.[1] Whether named or unnamed the principal remains disclosed. On the other hand, if the third party is unaware of the existence of the principal at the time he contracts with the agent, ie the third party thinks the agent is contracting on his own behalf and not for someone else, the principal is described as *undisclosed*.

1 DISCLOSED AGENCY

(a) Relations between principal and third party

(i) The general rule

Montgomerie v United Kingdom Mutual Steamship Association

[1891] 1 QB 370, Queen's Bench Division

Montgomerie was the part-owner of a ship which he insured with the defendant mutual insurance association. The policy of insurance was effected by Perry, Raines & Co who acted as Montgomerie's agent. Perry, Raines & Co was a member of the association. Montgomerie

---

[1] The words 'identified' and 'unidentified' are used in preference to 'named' and 'unnamed' in the third edition of the US *Restatement of the Law of Agency* (2006). Like Professor Reynolds before him, Professor Watts adopts the terminology in the twentieth edition (2014) of *Bowstead and Reynolds on Agency*, and notes that the change reflects the fact than an unnamed principal may nevertheless be identified (see para 1–037).

was not, and his name did not appear on the policy. When Montgomerie sued the association to recover a loss on the ship, the association claimed that the terms of the policy expressly excluded their liability to anyone other than a member of the association. Wright J gave judgment for the association.

> **Wright J:** There is no doubt whatever as to the general rule as regards an agent, that where a person contracts as agent for a principal the contract is the contract of the principal, and not that of the agent; and, *prima facie*, at common law the only person who may sue is the principal, and the only person who can be sued is the principal. To that rule there are, of course, many exceptions. First, the agent may be added as the party to the contract if he has so contracted, and is appointed as the party to be sued. Secondly, the principal may be excluded in several other cases. He may be excluded if the contract is made by a deed *inter partes*, to which the principal is no party. In that case, by ancient rule of common law, it does not matter whether the person made a party is or is not an agent...Another exception is as regards bills and notes. If a person who is an agent makes himself a party in writing to a bill or note, by the law merchant a principal cannot be added. Another exception is that by usage, which is treated as forming part of the contract or of the law merchant, where there is a foreign principal, generally speaking the agent in England is the party to the contract, and not the foreign principal; but this is subject to certain limitations. Then a principal's liability may be limited, though not excluded. If the other party elects to sue the agent, he cannot afterwards sue the principal. Again, where the principal is an undisclosed principal, he must, if he sues, accept the facts as he finds them at the date of his disclosure, so far as those facts are consistent with reasonable and proper conduct on the part of the other party. Again, if the principal is sued, he is entitled to an allowance for payments which he may have made to his agent if the other party gave credit originally to that agent. Also, and this is very important, in all cases the parties can by their express contract provide that the agent shall be the person liable either concurrently with or to the exclusion of the principal, or that the agent shall be the party to sue either concurrently with or to the exclusion of the principal...
>
> ...The question, then, is, Have the parties so contracted that Montgomerie and his co-plaintiffs cannot sue, the alternative being that the action should have been brought in the name of Perry, Raines & Co? I have come to the conclusion that the parties have so contracted. I think that the rules annexed to the policy and the articles of association which are incorporated with the policy shew plainly that it was the intention of the parties that the association should look to the member only for contribution, and should have to deal with and be entitled to say that they would deal with the member only in respect of the settlements of losses.

NOTES

1.   Montgomerie was an undisclosed principal, but the statement made by Wright J as to the normal relationship between the principal and the third party applies to disclosed principals generally.

2.   Where the agent acts within the scope of his authority on behalf of a disclosed principal, direct contractual relations are established between the principal and the third party. If the agent acts within the scope of his actual authority (express or implied), or the principal

---

Whilst this is undoubtedly true, we shall continue to use the terms 'named' and 'unnamed' principals as this is how the English courts have traditionally referred to them (and how they are described in the extracts from the judgments that appear in this chapter).

subsequently ratifies the agent's unauthorised acts, the principal may sue and be sued on the contract. In contrast, as we have already seen, where the agent has only apparent authority the principal will be liable on the contract made by his agent but he will not be able to sue upon it himself, unless he ratifies his agent's unauthorised act (above, p 158). Where the agent acts without authority, and there is no ratification, the principal will incur no liability to the third party (eg *Comerford v Britannic Assurance Co Ltd* (1908) 24 TLR 593; *Wiltshire v Sims* (1808) 1 Camp 258).

3.   There are two exceptional situations in which a disclosed principal will not be privy to a contract made by his agent acting within the scope of his authority.

First, when the agent contracts by a deed *inter partes* the principal will not be able to sue and be sued on the contract unless he is described in the deed as a party to it and the deed is executed in his name (*Re International Contract Co, Pickering's Claim* (1871) 6 Ch App 525— but where the deed is not *inter partes*, the principal can sue on it if he is a covenantee: *Moody v Condor Insurance Ltd* [2006] EWHC 100 (Ch), [2006] 1 WLR 1847). However, this general rule is itself subject to a number of exceptions:

(a)   if the agent who contracts by deed contracts as trustee for the principal then the principal can sue on the deed (*Harmer v Armstrong* [1934] Ch 65);

(b)   under s 7(1) of the Powers of Attorney Act 1971, as amended by s 1 of and Sch 1, para 7(1) to the Law of Property (Miscellaneous Provisions) Act 1989, if the agent was appointed by a power of attorney, and he acts within the scope of his authority, he may execute the deed in his own name and the principal may sue on it (for detailed consideration of this section, see *Bowstead and Reynolds*, para 8–087); and

(c)   under s 56(1) of the Law of Property Act 1925, a principal may acquire an interest in land or other property, or the benefit of any condition, right of entry, covenant, or agreement over or respecting land or other property, even though he is not named as a party to the conveyance or instrument (but note that the ambit of this section has been restrictively construed by the courts: see J Beatson, A Burrows, and J Cartwright, *Anson's Law of Contract* (29th edn, 2010), pp 642–643);

(d)   under s 1(1) of the Contracts (Rights of Third Parties) Act 1999, a person who is not a party to a contract may in his own right enforce a term of a contract if (i) the contract expressly provides that he may or (ii) the term purports to confer a benefit on him (unless, in the case of (ii), it is apparent from a proper construction of the contract that the parties did not intend to give him enforceable rights: s 1(2)). This provision would allow a disclosed principal to enforce a term of a contract made by deed, which expressly so provides or which confers a benefit on him, even though he is not a party to it and the deed is not executed in his name.

Secondly, a principal cannot be made liable on any negotiable instrument unless his signature appears on it (Bills of Exchange Act 1882, s 23). However, the principal will be liable on the instrument if his signature is written on the document by someone acting by or with his authority (1882 Act, s 91(1)). If the agent signs the instrument with the principal's name, the principal will be bound. But difficulties can arise when the agent uses a representative signature: see s 26(1) of the 1882 Act; considered below, pp 693–695. A signature by procuration will put the third party on notice that the agent's authority to sign is limited and the principal will only be bound by the signature if the agent was acting within the scope of his actual authority: s 25.

4. There is no longer a presumption that an agent contracting for a foreign principal does so personally and cannot establish privity of contract between the principal and the third party. In *Teheran-Europe Co Ltd v ST Belton (Tractors) Ltd* [1968] 2 QB 545, the Court of Appeal held that modern commercial usage does not raise such a presumption. But the foreign character of the principal is not irrelevant, for as Diplock LJ said (at 558):

> . . . the fact that the principal is a foreigner is one of the circumstances to be taken into account in determining whether or not the other party to the contract was willing, or led the agent to believe that he was willing, to treat as a party to the contract the agent's principal, and, if he was so willing, whether the mutual intention of the other party and the agent was that the agent should be personally entitled to sue and liable to be sued on the contract as well as his principal. But it is only one of many circumstances, and as respects the creation of privity of contract between the other party and the principal its weight may be minimal, particularly in a case such as the present where the terms of payment are cash before delivery and no credit is extended by the other party to the principal. It may have considerably more weight in determining whether the mutual intention of the other party and the agent was that the agent should be personally liable to be sued as well as the principal, particularly if credit has been extended by the other party.

See also RJC Munday (1977) 6 Anglo-American LR 221 at 235–240; FMB Reynolds (1983) 36 CLP 119 at 126–127.

5. *Montgomerie v United Mutual Steamship Association* provides an example of a 'commission agent', ie someone who contracts with the third party as principal yet makes the contract on behalf of his own principal (above, p 168).

The dicta of Wright J in *Montgomerie v United Mutual Steamship Association* make it clear that, as a general rule, where an agent makes a contract on behalf of a disclosed principal he can neither sue nor be sued on that contract. The textbook writers usually express this result in the maxim that the agent 'drops out' of the transaction (see, eg, *Bowstead and Reynolds*, para 9–002; Munday, para 10.17, Fridman, p 122). The maxim must be treated with caution, especially outside the area of contract (see R Stevens [2005] LMCLQ 101). There is no specific rule of agency law which says the agent will automatically 'drop out' and escape liability. The agent can neither sue nor be sued on the contract because where the agency is disclosed it is objectively apparent to the third party that the other contracting party is the principal and not the agent (the reverse is true where the agency is undisclosed). This is an application of the general law of contract. Furthermore, even though the agent cannot sue or be sued on the contract where the agency is disclosed, the rights and liabilities of the principal and the third party may still be affected by the agent in a number of ways.

(ii) Settlement with the agent

Irvine & Co v Watson & Sons
(1880) 5 QBD 414, Court of Appeal

W & Sons employed C, a broker, to purchase oil for them. C purchased the oil from I & Co with payment to be by 'cash on or before delivery'. At the time of purchase C informed I & Co that he was buying for principals, although he did not reveal the name of his principals. I & Co delivered the oil to C without payment, and W & Sons, not knowing that I & Co had not been paid, in good faith paid C. C did not pay I & Co, who then sued W & Sons for the price. Bowen J gave judgment for I & Co. W & Sons appealed.

Bramwell LJ: I am of opinion that the judgment must be affirmed. The facts of the case are shortly these: The plaintiffs sold certain casks of oil, and on the face of the contract of sale Conning appeared as the purchaser. But the plaintiffs knew that he was only an agent buying for principals, for he told them so at the time of the sale, therefore they knew that they had a right against somebody besides Conning. On the other hand, the defendants knew that somebody or other had a remedy against them, for they had authorized Conning, who was an ordinary broker, to pledge their credit, and the invoice specified the goods to have been bought '*per* John Conning.' Then, that being so, the defendants paid the broker; and the question is whether such payment discharged them from their liability to the plaintiffs. I think it is impossible to say that it discharged them, unless they were misled by some conduct of the plaintiffs into the belief that the broker had already settled with the plaintiffs, and made such payment in consequence of such belief. But it is contended that the plaintiffs here did mislead the defendants into such belief, by parting with the possession of the oil to Conning without getting the money. The terms of the contract were 'cash on or before delivery,' and it is said that the defendants had a right to suppose that the sellers would not deliver unless they received payment of the price at the time of delivery. I do not think, however, that that is a correct view of the case. The plaintiffs had a perfect right to part with the oil to the broker without insisting strictly upon their right to prepayment, and there is, in my opinion, nothing in the facts of the case to justify the defendants in believing that they would so insist. No doubt if there was an invariable custom in the trade to insist on prepayment where the terms of the contract entitled the seller to it, that might alter the matter; and in such case noninsistence on prepayment might discharge the buyer if he paid the broker on the faith of the seller already having been paid. But that is not the case here; the evidence before Bowen J shews that there is no invariable custom to that effect.

Apart from all authorities, then, I am of opinion that the defendants' contention is wrong, and upon looking at the authorities, I do not think that any of them are in direct conflict with that opinion. It is true that in *Thomson v Davenport* ((1829) 9 B & C 78) both Lord Tenterden and Bayley J suggest in the widest terms that a seller is not entitled to sue the undisclosed principal on discovering him, if in the meantime the state of account between the principal and the agent has been altered to the prejudice of the principal. But it is impossible to construe the *dicta* of those learned judges in that case literally; it would operate most unjustly to the vendor if we did. I think the judges who uttered them did not intend a strictly literal interpretation to be put on their words. But whether they did or no, the opinion of Parke B in *Heald v Kenworthy* ((1855) 10 Exch 739) seems to me preferable; it is this, that 'If the conduct of the seller would make it unjust for him to call upon the buyer for the money, as for example, where the principal is induced by the conduct of the seller to pay his agent the money on the faith that the agent and seller have come to a settlement on the matter, or if any representation to that effect is made by the seller, either by words or conduct, the seller cannot afterwards throw off the mask and sue the principal'. That is in my judgment a much more accurate statement of the law. But then the defendants rely on the case *of Armstrong v Stokes* ((1872) LR 7 QB 598). Now that is a very remarkable case; it seems to have turned in some measure upon the peculiar character filled by Messrs Ryder as commission merchants. The Court seemed to have thought it would be unreasonable to hold that Messrs Ryder had not authority to receive the money. I think upon the facts of that case that the agents would have been entitled to maintain an action for the money against the defendant, for as commission merchants they were not mere agents of the buyer. Moreover the present case is a case, which Blackburn J there expressly declines to decide. He expressly draws a distinction between a case in which, as in *Armstrong v Stokes*, the seller at the time of the sale supposes the agent to be himself a principal, and gives credit to him alone, and one in which, as here, he knows that the person with whom he is dealing has a principal behind, though he does not know who that principal is.

It is to my mind certainly difficult to understand that distinction, or to see how the mere fact of the vendor knowing or not knowing that the agent has a principal behind can affect the liability of that principal. I should certainly have thought that his liability would depend upon what he himself knew, that is to say whether he knew that the vendor had a claim against him and would look to him for payment in the agent's default. But it is sufficient here that the defendants did know that the sellers had a claim against them, unless the broker had already paid for the goods.

Baggallay LJ: ... What then was the effect of that payment? If the *dicta* in *Thomson v Davenport* are to be taken as strictly correct, they certainly go a long way to support the defendants' contention. But it is to be observed that they were mere *dicta*, and quite unnecessary to the decision. The largeness of those *dicta* has since been dissented from by Parke B, in the case of *Heald v Kenworthy*, and with his dissent I entirely agree. He sought to limit the qualification of the general rule to cases, in which the seller by some conduct has misled the buyer into believing that a settlement has been made with the agent. And if that limitation is correct, I am of opinion that there is no such payment here as would discharge the defendants.

But reliance is placed upon the case *of Armstrong v Stokes* as establishing the doctrine that the buyer is released from liability, if he pays the agent at a time at which the seller still gives credit to the agent—and it is contended that as that state of facts existed here, the defendants are accordingly discharged. But I think that is not the true view of the decision in *Armstrong v Stokes*. It must be accepted with reference to the particular circumstances of that case. There at the time of the payment by the principal to the brokers, the sellers still gave credit to the brokers and to the brokers alone. But that is not the case here; the plaintiffs it is true gave credit to Conning, but they did not give him exclusive credit. I do not think I am running counter to any of the decided cases in thinking that this judgment must be affirmed.

[**Brett LJ** considered *Thomson v Davenport* and the limitation placed on the dicta in that case by the judgment of Parke B in *Heald v Kenworthy* and continued:]

...But it is suggested that that limitation was overruled in *Armstrong v Stokes*. I think, however, that the Court there did not intend to overrule it, but to treat the case before them as one to which the limitation did not apply. I think they noticed the peculiar character of Manchester commission merchants. Probably their decision means this, that, when the seller deals with the agent as sole principal, and the nature of the agent's business is such that the buyer ought to believe that the seller has so dealt, in such a case it would be unjust to allow the seller to recover from the principal after he paid the agent. Or it may perhaps be that Blackburn J, finding the wider qualification in the very case which lays down the general rule, felt himself bound by the terms of that qualification, and applied them to the case before him.

If the case of *Armstrong v Stokes* arises again, we reserve to ourselves sitting here the right of reconsidering it.

The only other question is whether the present case falls within the qualification as limited by Parke B, whether there was any misleading conduct on the part of the plaintiffs. But the only thing relied on by the defendants on that point was the noninsistence on prepayment by the plaintiffs. And I do not think that that amounted to laches, or was such an act as would justify the defendants in supposing that Conning had already paid the plaintiffs.

NOTES

1. When the principal is disclosed the estoppel theory is generally accepted as explaining those exceptional cases where the right of the third party is affected by the principal having paid or otherwise settled with the agent (see also *Davison v Donaldson* (1882) 9 QBD 623, CA). Cf when the principal is undisclosed, see below, pp 218–221.

2. Mere delay by the third party in enforcing his claim against the principal is not usually sufficient to give rise to an estoppel, unless there are other factors which make the delay misleading to the principal (see *Davison v Donaldson*, above).

A disclosed principal is not bound by the *third party* making payment to or settling with the agent, unless the agent had actual or apparent authority to receive the payment or settle on behalf of the principal (*Butwick v Grant* [1924] 2 KB 483; cf when the principal is undisclosed, see below, p 221). The third party will only be discharged if payment is made in the manner which the agent is authorised to accept, for example if the agent is authorised to accept payment in cash, payment by bill of exchange will not discharge the third party (*Hine Bros v Steamship Insurance Syndicate Ltd* (1895) 72 LT 79). If the agent is not authorised to receive payment but he does so and pays over the money to the principal, the principal will be deemed to have ratified the agent's actions and the third party will be discharged. Exceptionally, if the agent has a lien over the principal's goods for a debt owed to him by the principal, and the agent, acting within his authority, sells the goods to a third party who pays the agent (who has no authority to receive payment), the third party can set off the principal's debt to the agent against the price of the goods which remains owing to the principal (*Hudson v Granger* (1821) 5 B & Ald 27).

(iii) Set-off and other defences available against the agent

The third party is entitled to set up against the disclosed principal all defences which arise out of the contract itself and all defences which are available against the principal himself (eg set-off, the fact that the principal is an enemy alien): *Bowstead and Reynolds*, art 79(1) and commentary thereon. Defences and set-off which the third party may have against the agent personally and which are unconnected with the contract made by the agent are not available against the disclosed principal (unless set-off is authorised by the principal: *Barker v Greenwood* (1837) 2 Y & C Ex 414).

Particular difficulties arise when the third party seeks to rely on the deceit or other misrepresentation of the agent against the principal. If the principal instigates or ratifies the agent's action, he will be held personally liable to the third party. The principal will also be held liable for the agent's deceit or other misrepresentation if the agent was acting within the scope of his actual or apparent authority at the time he made the representation: *Lloyd v Grace, Smith & Co* [1912] AC 716, HL; *Armagas Ltd v Mundogas SA* [1985] 3 WLR 640, CA; affd [1986] AC 717; *Crédit Lyonnais Bank Nederland NV v Export Credits Guarantee Department* [2000] 1 AC 486, HL: see above, p 116. In such circumstances, the principal will be liable even if he did not know of the agent's actions (*Refuge Assurance Co Ltd v Kettlewell* [1909] AC 243) and even if the agent was acting for his own benefit and not for the benefit of the principal (*Lloyd v Grace, Smith & Co*, above). There is uncertainty as to whether a principal can exclude liability for his agent's fraud in inducing the making of a contract. What is clear is that the law, on public policy grounds, does not permit a contracting party to exclude liability for his own fraud, and so it is submitted that the contracting party should not be able to exclude liability for his agent's deceit either. The issue did not have to be resolved in *HIH*

Casualty & General Insurance Ltd v Chase Manhattan Bank [2003] UKHL 6, [2003] 2 Lloyd's Rep 61, where the House of Lords held (at [16]) that a party seeking to exonerate himself from the consequences of his agent's fraud (assuming that is legally possible) must do so 'in clear and unmistakable terms on the face of the contract' and that general words will not be effective. Nevertheless, it would appear that general words may be effective to cover fraud in the performance (as opposed to the formation) of the contract by an agent (*Frans Maas (UK) Ltd v Samsung (UK) Ltd* [2004] EWHC 1502 (Comm), [2004] 2 Lloyd's Rep 251 at [152]).

The principal will not be liable in deceit if the agent made an innocent misrepresentation and the principal, who would have known the representation to be false, did not know it had been made (*Armstrong v Strain* (1951) 1 TLR 856; affd [1952] 1 KB 232). However, in such circumstances the principal would be liable to the third party under s 2(1) of the Misrepresentation Act 1967 if the third party had contracted with the principal in reliance upon the agent's misrepresentation (*Gosling v Anderson* (1972) EGD 709; although the agent would not be liable to the third party under the statute: *Resolute Maritime Inc v Nippon Kaiji Kyokai* [1983] 1 WLR 857). The principal may also be liable to the third party in negligence on the basis of *Hedley Byrne & Co Ltd v Heller & Partners Ltd* [1964] AC 465, or liable for any negligent misstatement made by the agent when acting within the scope of his authority, if it can be established that the principal and/or the agent owed the third party a duty of care.

Where the third party sues the principal on the contract made through the agent, the principal, whether disclosed or undisclosed, should be able to raise all defences arising out of the transaction with the agent, and defences personal to himself, but not defences personal to the agent: *Bowstead and Reynolds*, art 79(3). For example, the principal could allege the contract is void for mistake or voidable for misrepresentation, but he could not rely on the fact that the agent is a minor.

(iv) Merger and election

Thomson v Davenport

(1829) 9 B & C 78, Court of King's Bench

M'Kune, a 'general Scotch agent' in Liverpool, ordered a quantity of glass and earthenware from Davenport & Co, dealers in Liverpool, for Thomson, who lived in Dumfries. At the time he placed the order M'Kune informed Davenport & Co that he was acting for a principal but he did not reveal the principal's name. The goods were invoiced and debited to M'Kune, but he became bankrupt. Davenport & Co thereupon sued Thomson for the price of the goods supplied. The jury of the Borough Court of Liverpool delivered a verdict in favour of Davenport & Co. The Court of King's Bench affirmed that decision.

Lord Tenderden CJ: I am of opinion that the direction give by the learned recorder in this case was right, and that the verdict was also right. I take it to be a general rule, that if a person sells goods (supposing at the time of the contract he is dealing with a principal), but afterwards discovers that the person with whom he has been dealing is not the principal in the transaction, but agent for a third person, though he may in the mean time have debited the agent with it, he may afterwards recover the amount from the real principal; subject, however, to this qualification, that the state of the account between the principal and the agent is not altered to the prejudice of the principal. On the other hand, if at the time of the sale the seller knows, not only that the person who is nominally dealing with him is not principal but agent, and also knows who the principal really is, and, notwithstanding all that knowledge, chooses to make the agent his debtor, dealing with him and him alone, then, according to the cases of *Addison v Gandassequi* ((1812) 4 Taunt 574), and *Paterson v Gandasequi* ((1812) 15 East 62), the seller cannot afterwards, on the failure of the agent, turn round and charge the principal, having once made his election at the time when he had the power of choosing between the one and the other. The present is a middle case. At the time of the dealing for the goods, the plaintiffs were informed that M'Kune, who came to them to buy the goods, was dealing for another, that is, that he was an agent, but they were not informed who the principal was. They had not, therefore, at that time the means of making their election. It is true that they might, perhaps, have obtained those means if they had made further enquiry; but they made no further enquiry. Not knowing who the principal really was, they had not the power at that instant of making their election. That being so, it seems to me that this middle case falls in substance and effect within the first proposition which I have mentioned, the case of a person not known to be an agent; and not within the second, where the buyer is not merely known to be agent, but the name of his principal is also known.

[**Bayley J** delivered a concurring judgment.]

Littledale J: The general principle of law is, that the seller shall have his remedy against the principal, rather than against any other person. Where goods are bought by an agent, who does not at the time disclose that he is acting as agent; the vendor, although he has debited the agent, may upon discovering the principal, resort to him for payment. But if the principal be known to the seller at the time when he makes the contract, and he, with a full knowledge of the principal, chooses to debit the agent, he thereby makes his election, and cannot afterwards charge the principal. Or if in such case he debits the principal, he cannot afterwards charge the agent. There is a third case; the seller may, in his invoice and bill of parcels, mention both principal and agent: he may debit A as a purchaser for goods bought through B, his agent. In that case, he thereby makes his election to charge the principal, and cannot afterwards resort to the agent. The general principle is, that the seller shall have his remedy against the principal, although he may by electing to take the agent as his debtor, abandon his right against the principal. The present case differs from any of those which I have mentioned. Here the agent purchased the goods in his own name. The name of the principal was not then known to the seller, but it afterwards came to his knowledge. It seems to me to be more consistent with the general principle of law, that the seller shall have his remedy against the principal, rather than against any other person, to hold in this case that the seller, who knew that there was a principal, but did not know who that principal was, may resort to him as soon as he is discovered. Here the agent did not communicate to the seller sufficient information to enable him to debit any other individual. The seller was in the same situation, as if at the time of the contract he had not known that there was any principal besides the person with whom he was dealing, and had afterwards discovered that the goods had been purchased on account of another; and, in that case, it is clear that he might have charged the principal. It is said, that he ought to have ascertained by enquiry of the agent who the principal was, but I think that he was not bound to make such enquiry, and that by debiting the agent with the price of the goods, he has not precluded himself from resorting to the principal, whose name was not disclosed to him... For the reasons already given, I think the plaintiff is entitled to recover.

[**Parke J**, having been concerned as counsel in the case, gave no opinion.]

Debenham's Ltd v Perkins

(1925) 133 LT 252, King's Bench Division

In March, April, and June 1922 Mrs Perkins purchased various items from Debenham's Ltd (the plaintiffs). In May 1922 Mrs Perkins separated from her husband. The plaintiffs obtained judgment against Mrs Perkins for the items purchased after her separation. They then sued her husband for the price of those items sold to Mrs Perkins before her separation alleging that she acted as his agent. The county court judge entered judgment for the husband on the ground that the plaintiffs had elected to proceed to judgment against the wife. The plaintiffs appealed and Scrutton and Bankes LJJ, sitting as additional judges of the King's Bench Division, allowed the appeal.

Scrutton LJ: When an agent acts for a disclosed principal, it may be that the agent makes himself or herself personally liable as well as the principal. But in such a case the person with whom the contract is made may not get judgment against both. He may get judgment against the principal or he may get judgment against the agent who is liable as principal, but once he has got judgment against either the principal or the agent who has the liability of the principal, he cannot then proceed against the other party who might be liable on the contract if proceedings had been taken against him or her first. This is sometimes explained by the doctrine of election and sometimes by the doctrine that when one has merged a contract in a judgment, one can have only one judgment, and, having merged the contract in the judgment, one cannot use the contract to get a second judgment. It is unnecessary to consider which is right.

In this case the tradesman first of all sued the married woman for nine dated items, claiming for a lump sum the price of the goods sold and delivered. As far as we can surmise what happened at the trial—and I understand that counsel are agreed as to what did happen at the trial in this case—the judge took the view that as to the first four items in date the wife was the agent of a principal, the husband, and not herself personally liable, and therefore judgment could not be entered against her, but he decided that as to the last five items the wife was then living separately and not with her husband, and she was not acting as his agent, but was personally liable. Then comes a very odd fact, that having held that she was not acting as agent for her husband, so that there was no defence and she was personally liable, in some way, which I do not understand, the learned judge, on a third-party procedure, held that the husband was found to indemnify the wife. The learned judge is so experienced a judge that one cannot help thinking that there is something one does not know which must have led him to take that view. Anyhow, as far as the case against the wife was concerned, the result of that procedure was that the tradesman failed to recover anything under the first four items and succeeded in getting a judgment for the amount of the last five items, though they were not specifically set out in the judgment. Whereupon the tradesman, desiring to get his money from somebody, sued the husband for the first three items. Thereupon objection was taken, which I understand can be put in this way: the plaintiff sued for one cause of action, and although it is quite true he did not get what he wanted, he got a judgment for part of that cause of action. Having taken judgment against the one person for the cause of action, he cannot use the cause of action to try to get a judgment against another party. The cause of action, the contract, is merged in the judgment.

But it appears to me that there are really two causes of action, not one, in this case. There is a cause of action against the wife who is liable personally, there is a cause of action against another person supposed to be acting by the agency of the wife, for different items, at different times, resulting in claims of different amounts. It seems to me, therefore, that this claim for one sum as a debt is really the result of two causes of action. If that is so, the fact that the plaintiff has got judgment against the wife on one cause of action does not merge the cause of action on which he has failed to get judgment, and which still remains available against the person against whom that cause of action should properly be brought.

Another way, perhaps, of putting it, though I think it also involves treating the matter as two causes of action, is that a plaintiff does not elect to sue one of two people alternatively liable, because he brings a proceeding against the other which fails, and in which he does not get judgment. He terminates the liability of the person alternatively liable only if he brings an action against his or her alternate and gets judgment, so that having got judgment against the one, the person who is alternatively liable is discharged . . .

On the best consideration, therefore, that I can give to the matter, it seems to me that the judgment obtained in the first action was for a cause of action different from the one which is now being sued, and that therefore the tradesman ought not to be estopped from continuing to sue the husband for those items not included in the first account. I quite appreciate that the husband says that he has defences which the County Court judge in the first action ought to have appreciated, and which he is going to raise when he is able to put all the facts before the court. We are not, therefore, deciding for the moment who is going to succeed when this action is tried, but only that the judge was premature in stopping the action on the ground either of an election or of *res judicata*.

[**Bankes LJ** delivered a concurring judgment.]

NOTES

1. The doctrines of merger and election only become relevant if the agent is personally liable on the main contract he makes with the third party. Remember, in cases of disclosed agency the agent does not normally become personally liable on the contract (above, pp 168–171). But for those exceptional occasions when the agent may contract personally, see below, pp 179–194.

2. In most cases where an agent has been held to contract personally the courts have held the agent's liability to be in the alternative to that of the principal: for example, see *Debenham's Ltd v Perkins*, above, where the assumption of alternative liability underlies Scrutton LJ's judgment. Yet this approach is open to severe criticism. As the editor of *Markesinis and Munday: An Outline of the Law of Agency* (4th edn, 1998) observed (p 150):

. . . even if one is endeavouring to read the intentions of the third party at the time when he concludes his contract with the agent acting for a named or unnamed principal, there is no strong reason to presume that he will always opt for the alternative liability of the agent and the principal rather than for their joint and several liability. After all, joint liability is both more advantageous to the third party and, legally, might appear more conventional. In short, Scrutton LJ's basic assumption in *Debenham's Ltd v Perkins* may be unrealistic and, arguably, contradict the most probable intentions of the parties to the contract.

3. Merger occurs when the third party obtains judgment against the principal, or the agent, when they are both liable in the alternative. Judgment against one releases the other. This is because there is only a single obligation and two judgments cannot arise out of a single obligation. It used to be the case that judgment against one of two joint debtors released the other, but this is no longer the law (Civil Liability (Contribution) Act 1978, s 3). Similarly, if the principal and agent are jointly and severally liable on the contract, judgment against one will not release the other. It should be noted that the doctrine of merger can apply even if the third party does not know of the existence of the principal (and, *a fortiori*, the principal's identity) at the time he obtained judgment against the agent (*Priestly v Fernie* (1865) 3 H & C 977). In this respect merger differs significantly from election.

4.   When the principal and agent are liable in the alternative on the contract with the third party, the third party may elect to hold one of them exclusively liable and thereby be barred from suing the other. As with merger, election will not apply if the principal and agent are jointly and severally liable or liable on separate causes of action. The election must be clear and unequivocal. Obtaining judgment against the principal or the agent is clearly the best evidence of election (although strictly speaking this will constitute a merger of actions), and it seems that giving exclusive credit to the agent will suffice (see *Thomson v Davenport*). In each case it is a question of fact whether there has been a clear and unequivocal act giving rise to an election (see further below, pp 213–216). Furthermore, as illustrated by *Thomson v Davenport*, the third party must have full knowledge of the facts, including the identity of the principal, before he can be said to have elected.

5.   The doctrines of merger and election raise a number of difficult issues. Reynolds wrote an excellent article on the subject in (1970) 86 LQR 318 (developed further in his commentary to art 82 of *Bowstead and Reynolds*). Of particular interest is his view that many of the decisions on election in disclosed agency (including *Thomson v Davenport*) are cases involving contract formation rather than concerning election at all, for example that the disclosed principal was never liable on the contract at all as it was made solely with the agent. There is much to commend this approach, and it may be embraced by the courts at some point in the future. However, for the present, the courts are likely to continue to decide cases according to the familiar, well-entrenched concepts of alternative liability and election.

QUESTION

A bought some goods from T, representing that he was acting on behalf of P Ltd. T charged the price to A's account, but when A became insolvent, T sued P Ltd for the money. Can P Ltd successfully argue that, by debiting A, T made an effective election and can no longer sue P Ltd? Would your answer be different if A, when buying the goods, had made it clear that he was acting for a principal whose identity he refused to disclose?

(b)   Relations between agent and third party

(i)   *The general rule*

Montgomerie v United Kingdom Mutual Steamship Association
[1891] 1 QB 370, Queen's Bench Division

See above, pp 168–169.

Lewis v Nicholson and Parker
(1852) 18 QB 503, Court of Queen's Bench

Lewis was the mortgagee of a bankrupt's property. Nicholson and Parker were solicitors to assignees of the bankrupt. Purporting to act 'on behalf of the assignees' Nicholson and Parker entered into an agreement with Lewis to sell the bankrupt's property and pay Lewis those sums owed to him out of the proceeds of sale. Although the property was sold Lewis was not paid. In fact, it turned out that Nicholson and Parker did not have the authority of the assignees to enter into this particular transaction. Lewis therefore brought an action against the solicitors personally for breach of the agreement.

Lord Campbell CJ: ...Looking at the two letters which constitute the contract, I think it appears on the face of them, that the defendants did not intend to make themselves personally liable on the contract, but to make a contract between the plaintiff and the assignees. It is quite clear that the plaintiff's solicitor, to whom the letter of 26th August was addressed, was not himself a contracting party, but was acting as agent, making a contract for the plaintiff: and I think that the true construction of the letters is that the defendants also were not contracting parties, but acting as agents for the assignees, making a contract for them, and, as I think, personally contracting that they had authority to make a contract binding the assignees. The letter expresses that, in consideration of the plaintiff consenting to the sale, 'we hereby, on behalf of the assignees, consent.' My brother Shee in effect asks us to read the contract as if the words on behalf of the assignees were not there; but they are there; and the nature of facts shews that they were meant to express a contract by the assignees; for it was the consent of the assignees to pay over the money that was material to the plaintiff. The answer refers to 'the undertaking given by you herein, and contained in your letter.' That however does not shew that it was understood by the writer to be a personal undertaking by the defendants, but merely refers to the undertaking as made in their letter, and by them. I think therefore that, looking at these two letters which form the contract, it appears to have been the intention of both parties that the consent should be that of the assignees, not that of the defendants...

Then the other point is to be considered. I think the facts raise it, as the trade assignee had no authority to make the official assignee personally liable on such a collateral contract. He might give assent, binding on both, to the disposal of the goods or money; but this goes much beyond such authority. So, the principals not being bound, the question arises whether the defendants are liable in this form of action. In the note to *Thomas v Hewes* ((1834) 2 Cr & M 519, 530, note (e), 4 Tyr 335, 338), it is stated to have been said by Bayley B that 'where an agent makes a contract in the name of his principal, and it turns out that the principal is not liable from the want of authority in the agent to make such contract, the agent is personally liable on the contract.' That is a high authority; but I must dissent from it. It is clear that it cannot apply where the contract is peculiarly personal; otherwise this absurdity would follow, that, if A, professing to have but not having authority from B, made a contract that B should marry C, C might sue A for breach of promise of marriage, even though they were of the same sex....I think in no case where it appears that a man did not intend to bind himself, but only to make a contract for a principal, can he be sued as principal, merely because there was no authority. He is liable, if there was any fraud, in an action for deceit, and, in my opinion, as at present advised, on an implied contract that he had authority, whether there was fraud or not. In either way he may be made liable for the damages occasioned by the absence of authority. But I think that to say he is liable as principal is to make a contract, not to construe it. I think therefore that these defendants were liable, but not in this action.

Erle J: The first question is, what is the true construction of this contract. Looking at the terms of the instruments, and the circumstances under which they were written, I think the construction is that the defendants made a contract between the plaintiff and the assignees, and signed it as agents of the assignees...

I also think that the defendants had not the authority of both assignees to make the contract. The question therefore arises, are they liable as principals on the contract, though intending and expressing an intention to act only as agents in making it? I think they are not. I think that, in general, no contract is made by the law contrary to the intention of the parties. The definition of a contract is that it is the mutual intention of the two parties. There is a class of what are called implied contracts, such as the promise to pay money had and received to the plaintiffs use: but, when it is said that such a contract is implied contrary to the intent of the person receiving the money, it is in truth only a technical mode of naming the remedy which the law gives against that wrongdoer. I know of no case in which what is properly called a contract is made by the law contrary to the intent of the parties.

[**Wightman** and **Crompton JJ** delivered concurring judgments.]

NOTES

1. Although the general rule is that the agent 'drops out' of any contract made on behalf of his disclosed principal, the mere fact that a person acts as agent does not prevent him being liable to the third party. As Lord Scarman said in *Yeung Kai Yung v Hong Kong and Shanghai Banking Corpn* [1981] AC 787 at 795, PC:

It is not the case that, if a principal is liable, his agent cannot be. The true principle of law is that a person is liable for his engagements (as for his torts) even though he acts for another, unless he can show that by the law of agency he is to be held to have expressly or impliedly negatived his personal liability.

2. The agent may be liable and entitled on the main contract made with the third party (see below) or on a collateral contract (eg in an auction without reserve, there is a collateral contract between the auctioneer and the highest bidder, consisting of an offer by the auctioneer to sell to the highest bidder and an acceptance of that offer when the bid is made: *Barry v Heathcote Ball & Co (Commercial Auctions) Ltd* [2000] 1 WLR 1962, CA). Even if not liable on the main contract, the agent may be liable for breach of warranty of authority (as recognised by Lord Campbell CJ in *Lewis v Nicholson and Parker*, also see below, p 194).

3. The agent may be personally liable in tort (see, generally, *Bowstead and Reynolds*, paras 9–115 to 9–125; R Stevens [2005] LMCLQ 101 at 102 ff). As Hobhouse LJ said in *McCullagh v Lane Fox & Partners* (1995) 49 Con LR 124 at 144:

An agent or an employee, owes a duty of care to his principal in relation to the transaction on which he is employed, which can be both contractual and tortious (*Midland Bank Trust Co Ltd v Hett, Stubbs & Kemp* [1979] Ch 384). But, in performing his agency, he may put himself in a position where he owes a duty of care to the person with whom he is dealing on behalf of his principal and be liable to him as well if he makes a careless misrepresentation or does a careless act which causes loss, damage or injury to the third party. Where personal injury is involved, no problem arises. An agent or employee who drives his employer's vehicle on his employer's business carelessly is liable to someone who is injured as a result. The same applies to careless acts causing property damage and can in principle apply to acts causing financial loss.

In *Punjab National Bank v De Boinville* [1992] 1 Lloyd's Rep 7, it was held that employees of an insurance broker engaged by the plaintiffs owed a direct duty of care in tort to the plaintiffs. In *McCullagh v Lane Fox & Partners*, above, the Court of Appeal said that in principle an estate agent employed by the vendor of property could owe a duty of care to the purchaser in respect of statements about the property, although no such duty was owed on the facts. But in *Gran Gelato Ltd v Richcliff (Group) Ltd* [1992] Ch 560, Nicholls V-C declined to impose a duty of care on the vendor's solicitor in answering inquiries before contract—a case which, according to Hobhouse LJ in *McCullagh v Lane Fox & Partners*, above, is probably best restricted to solicitors in conveyancing transactions (see, generally, C Passmore (1996) 146 NLJ 409). The key question is whether there has been an assumption of responsibility by the agent towards the third party. As Watts notes, '[U]ntil someone comes up with a principled and workable alternative,... judges should continue to treat an assumption of responsibility as the foundation of liability for negligent statements.' ((2012) 128 LQR 260 at 274. See *Williams v Natural Life Health Foods Ltd* [1998] 1 WLR 830, HL; cf *Merrett v Babb* [2001] EWCA Civ 214, [2001] QB 1174, where a majority of the Court of Appeal distinguished *Williams* on the basis that it was concerned with the liability of a director of a limited company: such a restrictive interpretation was later rejected by Lord Hoffmann in *Standard Chartered Bank v Pakistan National Shipping Corpn (Nos 2 and 4)* [2002] UKHL 43, [2003] 1 AC 959 at [23], who held that *Williams* had nothing to do with company law but was 'an application of the law of principal and agent to the requirement of assumption of responsibility under the *Hedley Byrne* principle'). But this reasoning does not apply in cases of deceit, where liability does not turn on the existence of any assumption of responsibility or special relationship between claimant and defendant. The making by an agent of a knowingly false statement relied on by the person to whom it was made is a tort on the part of the agent (*Noel v Poland* [2001] 2 BCLC 645 at [21], per Toulson J). Moreover, agents may be personally liable for deceit notwithstanding the liability of their principals. In *Standard Chartered Bank v Pakistan National Shipping Corpn (Nos 2 and 4)*, above, a company director, who made a fraudulent misrepresentation within the scope of his employment, was held by the House of Lords to be personally liable in deceit even though his statements were made in a representative capacity (which resulted in the company also being held liable in deceit). The case is noted by B Parker [2003] LMCLQ 1 and by R Grantham [2003] CLJ 15. See also N Campbell and J Armour [2003] CLJ 290, who put the case (which we support) that questions of a corporate agent's liability do not turn on some special principle of company law but on 'the established rules relating to the particular head of liability, with due regard paid to the defendant's capacity as an agent' (at 291).

(ii) When will the agent be liable on the contract made on behalf of his principal?

(a) Contracts in writing

Universal Steam Navigation Co Ltd v James McKelvie & Co
[1923] AC 492, House of Lords

A charterparty was entered into between TH Seed & Co Ltd, as agents for the owners of the vessel, and 'James McKelvie & Co, Newcastle-on-Tyne, Charterers'. The charterparty was signed: 'For and on behalf of James McKelvie & Co (as agents). JA McKelvie'. When sued for breach of the charterparty, McKelvie & Co claimed to have acted as agents for an Italian company, and denied that they were personally liable on the contract. The Court of Appeal entered judgment for McKelvie & Co. The House of Lords dismissed the owners' appeal from that decision.

Viscount Cave LC: My Lords, apart from authority, I should feel no doubt whatever as to the correctness of the judgment of the Court of Appeal. If the respondents had signed the charterparty without qualification, they would of course have been personally liable to the shipowners; but by adding to their signature the words 'as agents' they indicated clearly that they were signing only as agents for others and had no intention of being personally bound as principals. I can imagine no other purpose for which these words could have been added; and unless they had that meaning, they appear to me to have no sense or meaning at all.

When the cases are examined, it appears that the weight of authority is in favour of the above view.

Lord Shaw of Dunfermline: The first question is in what character Messrs McKelvie signed this document? I see no ground whatsoever for denying effect to the express word 'agents': it was undoubtedly in that character that the contract was signed: there is as little ground for cutting out the express character in which it was signed as for cutting out the signature itself.

The second question is, whether, although thus denominating themselves as 'agents,' Messrs McKelvie were yet signing a contract which by its terms made them principals therein. But its terms do not refer to either 'principals' or 'agents'; the body of the document can be applied to either category. As for the names of the parties, I hold that the names of McKelvie followed by 'Charterers' with nothing said of agency, is definitely stamped with agency by the express affirmation of the signature.

A third view is suggested—namely, that they were *ex concessu* agents, but yet were principals over and above. This answers itself. Such a confused and unusual situation would require the clearest words to make it intelligible and effective. As at present advised, I have doubts as to whether this could be done...

But I desire to say that in my opinion the appending of the word 'agents' to the signature of a party to a mercantile contract is, in all cases, the dominating factor in the solution of the problem of principal or agent. A highly improbable and conjectural case (in which this dominating factor might be overcome by other parts of the contract) may by an effort of the imagination be figured, but, apart from that, the appending of the word 'agent' to the signature is a conclusive assertion of agency, and a conclusive rejection of the responsibility of a principal, and is and must be accepted in that twofold sense by the other contracting party.

Lord Sumner: ...I agree that for many years past it has, I believe, been generally understood in business, that to add 'as agents' to the signature is all that is necessary to save a party, signing for a principal, from personal liability on the contract, and I agree also that, even as a matter of construction, when a signature so qualified is attached to a general printed form with blanks filled in ad hoc, preponderant importance attaches to the qualification in comparison with printed clauses or even with manuscript insertions in the form. It still, however, remains true, that the qualifying words 'as agents' are a part of the contract and must be construed with the rest of it. They might have been expressed as a separate clause eg 'it is further agreed that the party signing this charter as charterer does so as agent for an undisclosed principal'—and that clause would obviously have to be construed. They are a form of words and not a mere part of the act of signifying assent and closing a negotiation by duly attaching a name. They purport to limit and explain a liability, and not merely to identify the person signing or to justify the inscription of a name by the hand of another person than the owner of it. They are more than the addition of 'junior' or 'Revd.' to the signature, which serves to identify the signatory by distinguishing him from others. They are more than a mere 'per procuration,' which only alleges authority to write another's name...

...It has sometimes been said that when 'agents' is the word added to the signature, it is a mere word of description, and so does not qualify the liability which the act of signing imports. I question this explanation. One's signature is not the place in which to advertise one's calling, nor is 'agent' ordinarily used to describe a trade, as 'tailor' or 'butcher' would be. I have no doubt that, when people add 'agent' to a signature to a contract, they are trying to escape personal liability, but are unaware that the attempt will fail. The result, however, is the same. When words added to a signature in themselves qualify liability, it is because, as words, they can be so construed in conjunction with the contract as a whole.

In construing the words 'as agents,' there is a distinction to be taken. Though it may be somewhat subtle, it has been mentioned in the older cases. Do the words 'as agents' mean 'and as agents,' or 'only as agents'? The positive affirmation, that I sign 'as agent'—that is, for another—is formally consistent with my signing for myself as well. If the act of signing raises a presumption of personal assent and obligation, which has to be sufficiently negatived or qualified by apt words, are the words 'as agent' apt or sufficient to exclude personal liability? For myself, I think that, standing alone, they are. To say 'as agent,' meaning thereby 'also as agent' for some one undisclosed, is substantially useless. If the agent refuses to disclose, the opposite party is no better off. If the statement is true, the rights and liabilities of the principal can be established at any time by proof. The statement only acquires a business efficacy as distinct from a formal content, if it means 'I am not liable but someone else is and he only,' and this is what I think it does mean.

Unless, then, something is to be found to the contrary in the earlier part of this charter, the qualification 'as agents' appears to me to relieve Messrs McKelvie & Co from personal liability on the contract.

Lord Parmoor: . . . The words 'as agents' are, in my opinion, clearly words of qualification and not of description. They denote, in unambiguous language, that the respondents did not sign as principals, and did not intend to incur personal liability. The signature applies to the whole contract, and to every term in the contract. I think it would not be admissible to infer an implied term, or implied terms, in the contract inconsistent with the limitation of liability directly expressed in the qualification of the signature, since the effect of such an implication would be to contradict an express term of the contract. It is not impossible that by plain words in the body of the document, persons signing 'as agents,' may expressly undertake some form of personal liability as principals, but I can find no trace of any intention of the respondents to incur any such liability in the charterparty, which is in question in the present appeal . . .

Different considerations arise when a person signs a contract without qualification, and the question is raised whether he is to be deemed as contracting personally, or as agent only. In such a case the intention of the parties is to be discovered from the contract itself, and the rule laid down in *Smith's Leading Cases* has been adopted as the rule to be followed. 'That where a person signs a contract in his own name, without qualification, he is prima facie to be deemed to be a person contracting personally, and in order to prevent this liability from attaching, it must be apparent from the other portions of the document that he did not intend to bind himself as principal.' I agree with Atkin LJ that it would tend to confusion to consider these cases in a case in which the signature itself has been expressly qualified.

Atkin LJ, in giving his decision in the present case, says: 'If the words qualify the signature, they qualify the assent, and nothing more matters.' I do not understand Atkin LJ to exclude the possibility that a person, signing 'as agent,' may nevertheless in the same document expressly undertake some form of personal liability. Such a possibility does not, in my opinion, affect the value of the rule as laid down by Atkin LJ, or its acceptance as an accurate guide in the construction of contracts, not regulated by statute, or considerations of a special character. The rule accords with the *dictum* of Mellish LJ in *Gadd v Houghton* ((1876) 1 Ex D 357 at 360), 'when the signature comes at the end you apply it to everything which occurs throughout the contract.'

In my opinion the appeal should be dismissed with costs.

Bridges & Salmon Ltd v The Swan (Owner), The Swan

[1968] 1 Lloyd's Rep 5, Admiralty Division

The plaintiffs were two firms of boat repairers claiming against the defendant, Mr JD Rodger, for the cost of repairs to the *Swan*. The *Swan* was owned by Mr Rodger but at all material times the vessel had been on hire to JD Rodger Ltd. Mr Rodger was a director of, and shareholder in, JD Rodger Ltd and acted as agent of the company when it ordered repairs to be carried out to the vessel by the plaintiffs. The repairs in question had been ordered partly orally and partly in writing on the company's headed notepaper, signed 'JD Rodger, Director'. At all times the plaintiffs knew that Mr Rodger was the company's agent but they also knew that he was the vessel's owner. The plaintiffs claimed that Mr Rodger was personally liable on the repair contracts, the company having become insolvent.

Brandon J: Where A contracts with B on behalf of a disclosed principal C, the question whether both A and C are liable on the contract or only C depends on the intention of the parties. That intention is to be gathered from (1) the nature of the contract, (2) its terms and (3) the surrounding circumstances . . . The intention for which the Court looks is not the subjective intention of A or of B. Their subjective intentions may differ. The intention for which the Court looks is an objective intention of both parties, based on what two reasonable businessmen making a contract of that nature, in those terms and in those surrounding circumstances, must be taken to have intended.

Where a contract is wholly in writing, the intention depends on the true construction, having regard to the nature of the contract and the surrounding circumstances, of the document or documents in which the contract is contained. Where, as in the present case, the contract is partly oral and partly in writing, the intention depends on the true effect, having regard again to the nature of the contract and the surrounding circumstances, of the oral and written terms taken together.

Many of the decided cases on questions of this kind relate to contracts wholly in writing. But it seems to me that, in principle, there can be no difference in the approach to the problem, whether the contract concerned is wholly in writing or partly in writing and partly oral. In either case the terms of the contract must be looked at and their true effect ascertained. I therefore think that, although I am here concerned with contracts which are partly oral and partly written, I can nevertheless properly seek guidance from decided cases on contracts wholly in writing.

. . . [A] distinction has been drawn between cases in which a person contracts expressly as agent and those in which, although he describes himself as an agent, he does not contract expressly as such.

Where it is stated in the contract that a person makes it 'as agent for', or 'on account of', or 'on behalf of', or simply 'for', a principal, or where words of that kind are added after such person's signature, he is not personally liable: *Gadd v Houghton & Co* (1876) 1 Ex D 357; *Universal Steam Navigation Co Ltd v James McKelvie & Co* [1923] AC 492; *Kimber Coal Co Ltd v Stone and Rolfe Ltd* [1926] AC 414, 24 Ll L Rep 429.

Where such words are not used but the person is merely stated to be an agent, or the word 'agent' is just added after his signature, the result is uncertain, because it is not clear whether the word is used as a qualification or merely as a description: see *Gadd v Houghton & Co, supra, per* James LJ at p 359; and *Universal Steam Navigation Co Ltd v James McKelvie & Co, supra, per* Lord Sumner at p 501. In general it would seem that in such a case the person does not avoid personal liability, although there may be exceptions to this general rule depending on the other terms of the contract or the surrounding circumstances.

Where a person contracts as agent for a company and does nothing more than add the word 'director' or 'secretary' after his signature, it seems that he does not avoid personal liability: *Brebner v Henderson* 1925 SC 643. This was a Scottish Appeal to the Court of Session which turned on the construction of s 26 of the Bills of Exchange Act, 1882, but I think the reasoning is applicable to a similar situation at common law.

Bearing in mind the distinctions drawn in the authorities to which I have referred, I return to an analysis of the facts in the present case. It seems to me that the defendant did not ever contract expressly as agent in the sense of saying either orally or in writing that he was acting 'as agent for', or 'on account of, or 'on behalf of, or 'for' the company. What he did was to describe himself to both plaintiffs at an earlier stage as 'Mr Rodger, of J D Rodger Ltd', and later to write the written orders on the company's notepaper and add the word 'Director' to his signature. On the other hand, the plaintiffs' subsequent conduct shows that they understood clearly that the bills for their work were to be sent to the company. It has been argued with force for the defendant that this shows that the plaintiffs understood the defendant to be contracting 'on account of the company and it was to the company alone that they were giving credit. I am not sure, however, that this is the only interpretation to be put on the facts, for it is possible for a person to give credit to a principal without at the same time giving exclusive credit to him.

On this analysis, which takes no account of any special factor arising from the surrounding circumstances, the present case appears to be somewhat near the borderline, with strong arguments available either way. But, as indicated earlier, the surrounding circumstances must also be looked at, and when looked at seem to me to assist considerably in the resolution of the problem.

The main surrounding circumstance, in my view, is that the defendant was at all material times the owner of the *Swan* and that both plaintiffs dealt with him either in the knowledge or on the correct assumption that this was so. The consequence of the defendant being the owner of the *Swan* was that he had a personal interest in the repairs in addition to his interest as director of the company in that the effect of the repairs was to preserve or to improve his own property. In particular, the repairs finally ordered and now sued for were of such an extent and character that they must greatly have increased the value of the vessel. All this was, or must be taken to have been, apparent both to Mr Pearce and to Mr Salmon [the managers of the respective plaintiffs].

The difficulty in the present case seems to me to arise mainly from the fact that the defendant had these two roles, one as director of the company which was operating the *Swan*, and the other as her owner. The defendant claims that, in all his dealings with the first and second plaintiffs in connection with repairs to the *Swan*, he was playing solely the first role. But the question is whether he made it clear to the two managers concerned, by his words oral or written, or his conduct, that this was so, or led them to suppose that he was playing the role of owner as well.

It seems to me that, when a person who is known or correctly assumed to be the owner of a boat, has discussions with a repairing company's manager about repairs to her, it is natural for the manager to assume that, if an order for the repairs is placed, that person will accept personal liability for them as such owner unless he makes the contrary clear beyond doubt. In the present case the defendant did make it clear to both Mr Pearce and Mr Salmon that the accounts for the work should be sent to the company. But the question is whether he made it clear to them at the same time that, although he was the owner of the boat and would therefore derive personal benefit from the repairs, he was nevertheless disowning any personal liability to pay for the work. Unless he did so it seems to me that they were entitled to assume that, while he was placing the order for the company to whom the account was to be sent, he remained also personally liable on the contract.

Approaching the matter in that way I have come to the conclusion that nothing said orally at any time to Mr Pearce, whether by the skipper or engineer of the *Swan* or by the defendant, and nothing contained in the written order to the second plaintiffs dated October 14, 1966, did make it clear beyond doubt that the defendant, although owner of the vessel, was disowning personal liability for the cost of the repairs which he was ordering.

> I have reached a similar conclusion with regard to the first plaintiffs, although in their case the question of anything significant being said to Mr Salmon by anyone other than the defendant does not arise.
>
> In the result, the decision which I have come to, after considering the nature and terms of the two contracts, and the surrounding circumstances, is that both plaintiffs are entitled to succeed on the second of the three points argued on their behalf, namely, that the defendant, though contracting as agent, did not do so solely as agent but in such a way as to be also personally liable.

NOTES

1. Whether an agent is liable on a contract in writing made on behalf of a disclosed principal depends on the objective intention of the parties, ie of the agent and third party. It is axiomatic to say that each case turns on the construction of the document in question. As Hobhouse J has emphasised: 'each contract has to be construed in its own context and having regard to the whole of its terms' (*Punjab National Bank v De Boinville* [1992] 1 Lloyd's Rep 7 at 12, see also Staughton LJ in the same case at 31). Furthermore, it is important to note that contracts made by deed, bills of exchange, promissory notes, and cheques are governed by their own rules (see below, pp 190–191).

2. Whilst generalisations as to the effect of particular words and phrases must be dangerous (*Bowstead and Reynolds*, para 9–037), the following principles offer some general guidance.

(a) If the agent signs the contract in his own name without more, he will be deemed to have contracted personally, unless he can rely on any term of the contract which *plainly* shows he was merely contracting as agent (eg *Gadd v Houghton & Co* (1876) 1 Ex D 357, CA, where brokers signed a contract of sale in their own name without qualification, but were not held personally liable as they were described in the body of the contract as selling 'on account of' someone else; cf *Tudor Marine Ltd v Tradax Export SA, The Virgo* [1976] 2 Lloyd's Rep 135, CA; *Jugoslavenska Linijska Plovidba v Hulsman (t/a Brusse & Sippel Import-Export), The Primorje* [1980] 2 Lloyd's Rep 74; *Seatrade Groningen BV v Geest Industries Ltd, The Frost Express* [1996] 2 Lloyd's Rep 375, CA).

(b) If an agent signs as 'agent', 'broker', 'director', etc, this may amount to no more than a description and not a qualification of his personal liability, unless a contrary intention can be established from the whole of the contract or from the surrounding circumstances (see *Universal Steam Navigation Co v McKelvie*, above, per Lord Sumner; *The Swan*, above).

(c) If the agent clearly indicates by a qualification added to his signature that he is contracting solely as agent, he will not be held personally liable (although see Lord Shaw's reference to a 'highly improbable and conjectural case' in *Universal Steam Navigation Co v McKelvie*, above; see also note 3 below as to the effect of extrinsic evidence of custom or usage).

3. The terms of the written contract indicating that the agent contracted personally cannot be contradicted by parol or other extrinsic evidence (*Higgins v Senior* (1841) 8 M & W 834). However, the agent may have an equitable defence to an action by the third party if he can establish an extrinsic agreement between himself and the third party that he should not be made personally liable (*Wake v Harrop* (1862) 1 H & C 202; *Bowstead and Reynolds*, para 9-040; cf Fridman, p 241). Nevertheless, parol evidence of custom or usage may be introduced to show that the agent is personally liable on a contract, when he does not appear otherwise to be so. Provided that the parol evidence does not contradict the terms of the written agreement, the personal liability of the agent may be established in this way (eg *Hutchinson v Tatham* (1873) LR 8 CP 482, where parol evidence of trade usage was admitted to show that the agent, who signed a charterparty 'as agents to merchants', was liable if the name of the principal was not disclosed in a reasonable time).

4.   When an agent is held personally liable on the contract he concludes with the third party, the question arises as to whether he is solely liable or whether he is liable together with his principal. The liability of both principal and agent will often accord with commercial expectations, and there is certainly evidence that the courts have been willing to hold that the agent has undertaken liability as well as the principal (eg see *International Rly Co v Niagara Parks Commission* [1941] AC 328 at 342; *Montgomerie v UK Mutual Steamship Association*, above at p 168; *The Swan*, above at p 185; *Teheran-Europe Co Ltd v ST Belton (Tractors) Ltd*, above at p 171; see also FMB Reynolds (1969) 85 LQR 92). Such cases, however, are probably still to be regarded as exceptional (they are often explained as turning on special trade custom) and it is more likely that the agent will either be held solely liable as principal or not liable at all (see *Universal Steam Navigation Co v McKelvie*, above at p 182, per Lord Shaw; Reynolds, op cit, p 94). There is much that remains uncertain and unsatisfactory in this area (see, in particular, the cases on election: discussed above at pp 175–179). Finally, it should be noted that the terms of the agent's liability will constitute an important issue whenever the agent undertakes personal liability to the third party; the issue is not restricted to contracts in writing.

5.   See PN Legh-Jones (1969) 32 MLR 325, who argues that *The Swan* was wrongly decided.

(b) Oral contracts

N & J Vlassopulos Ltd v Ney Shipping Ltd, The Santa Carina
[1977] 1 Lloyd's Rep 478, Court of Appeal

The defendants, who were brokers on the Baltic Exchange, telephoned the plaintiffs, who were also brokers there, and asked them to supply bunkers to the vessel *Santa Carina*. Bunkers were supplied but the plaintiffs' invoice remained unpaid. The plaintiffs then brought an action to recover the price from the defendants. The defendants denied liability on the grounds that they were acting merely as agents for their principals, the time charterers of the *Santa Carina*, and that although the plaintiffs did not know the identity of the principals, they did know that the defendants acted as agents. Reversing Mocatta J, the Court of Appeal gave judgment for the defendants.

> **Lord Denning MR:** On the facts I have stated, it is clear that Vlassopulos, the brokers for the suppliers, knew that Ney, the brokers for the time charterers, were ordering the fuel simply as agents. They were agents either for the owners or the time charterers of the vessels. The brokers for the suppliers knew they were agents. They received a telephone message saying: 'Please supply this fuel oil to the vessel'. But they knew it was from the agents as agents.
>
> The Judge held that the brokers who ordered the fuel were personally liable. He was much influenced by the cases where a person gives a written order for goods or signs a written contract when he is known to be acting as an agent. Nevertheless, although he is known to be acting as an agent, he will be liable on that order or liable on that contract if he signs in his own personal name

without qualification. That is settled by cases both in this Court and in the House of Lords: see *H O Brandt & Co v H N Morris & Co Ltd* [1917] 2 KB 784 at p 796 *per* Lord Justice Scrutton, and *Hichens, Harrison, Woolston & Co v Jackson & Sons* [1943] AC 266 at p 273 *per* Lord Atkin. In order to exclude his liability he has to append to his signature some such words as 'as agent only' or 'for and on behalf' of or such exclusion must be apparent elsewhere in the document. That is clear from *Universal Steam Navigation Co v James McKelvie & Co* [1923] AC 492 at pp 505–506.

The Judge thought that those cases on written orders and written contracts should be applied to the present case of an oral contract. He felt that if there is an oral conversation on the telephone, as in this case ordering bunkers, the broker is liable unless he uses some express words so as to show that he is acting as agent only and is not to be held personally liable. He said ([1976] 2 Lloyd's Rep 223 at p 226):

> Thus some words must be used to indicate that the agent is not himself undertaking any financial obligation or liability.

I have no doubt that those cases on written orders and written contracts arose out of the old rule of evidence whereby it was not permissible to admit oral evidence to alter or contradict a written contract. Those cases still apply today to written orders and written contracts. But they do not apply to oral orders or oral contracts. At any rate not so rigidly. In many cases if a man, who is an agent for another, orders goods or makes a contract by word of mouth, but does not disclose the name or standing of his principal (so that his credit is unknown to the other contracting party) the agent himself is liable to pay for the goods or to fulfil the contract. It may be that the other contracting party knows that the man is only an agent, but, as he does not know who the principal is, it is to be inferred that he does not rely on the credit of the principal but looks to the agent. That, I think, is the thought underlying the dictum of Mr Justice Salter in *Benton v Campbell, Parker & Co Ltd* [1925] 2 KB 410 at p 414, and the *American Restatement on Agency* in the comment to para 321. But in other cases that may not be the proper inference. There are cases where, although the man who supplied the goods knows that the other is an agent and does not know his principal, nevertheless he is content to look to the credit of that principal whoever he may be. This is something which Lord Justice Diplock contemplated in the case of *Teheran-Europe Co Ltd v S T Belton (Tractors) Ltd* [1968] 2 QB 545. He said that

> . . . he may be willing to treat as a party to the contract anyone on whose behalf the agent may have been authorised to contract . . .

This applies particularly to the case of a broker. As Mr Justice Blackburn said in *Fleet v Murton* (1871) LR 7 QB 126 at p 131.

> . . . I take it that there is no doubt at all, in principle, that a broker, as such, merely dealing as broker and not as purchaser of the article, makes a contract from the very nature of things between the buyer and the seller and he is not himself either buyer or seller.

It seems to me that the present case falls into that second category. It was known to both sides that the agents, Ney Shipping Ltd, were only brokers. They were brokers ordering bunkers for a vessel. It was obvious that they were only agents, and they were ordering bunkers for the time charterers or the owners of a vessel. They had often done it before. The accounts for the fuel had always been paid by the principals either directly or through the brokers. It cannot be supposed that the brokers were ever intended to be personally liable. The suppliers would look to the time charterers or the owners, whoever they might be, they being the people to be relied upon. Although they were not named or specified or disclosed, they would be the people to whom the suppliers would look for payment of the oil.

It is just the same, it seems to me, as if the brokers had given a written order for the bunkers and added to their signatures 'as agents only'. In that case they would not have been personally liable. Nor should they be liable in this case when it was done by word of mouth and when the inference from the conduct and the whole of the circumstances was that they were ordering the fuel as agents only.

It can be tested by taking the converse case. Suppose the fuel had been of bad quality and the engines of the ship had been damaged, or the ship delayed, could the brokers Ney Shipping have sued for damages? Or the brokers Vlassopulos have been made liable in damages? Clearly not. It would be for the principals on either side to have sued. So here the brokers Vlassopulos could not sue for the price, nor the brokers Ney be liable for it.

I know that in many trades there is a custom by which the broker is liable. Those cases rest on a custom of the trade. There was no such custom alleged or proved in respect of the brokers on the Baltic Exchange. It seems to me that, in the circumstances of this case, the proper inference is that the agents here were, when they gave the telephone message, giving it as agents only. By their conduct it is to be inferred that it was just the same as if they had given a written order excluding their personal liability and the suppliers looked to the owners or time charterers of the vessel who were the people really liable. It is the unfortunate fact that they have proved insolvent or unable to pay, but it seems to me that that is not a sufficient ground for now making the brokers liable. I would therefore allow the appeal and give judgment for the defendant.

[**Roskill** and **Lawton LJJ** delivered concurring judgments.]

NOTES

1.   With oral contracts it is a question of fact in each particular case whether it was intended that the agent should or should not be entitled to sue, and/or be held personally liable, on the contract. The agent's failure to name his principal is merely one factor, albeit a significant one, for the court to take into account when assessing whether the agent intended to contract personally.

2.   In *The Santa Carina*, Lord Denning referred to the rule contained in the second edition of the US *Restatement of the Law of Agency* (1958), which provides that when the agent acts for a principal whose existence is known but who is not identified at the time of contracting, the agent is, unless otherwise agreed, a party to the contract. The same rule is now to be found in para 6.02 of the third edition of the *Restatement* (2006). However, the Court of Appeal declined to apply such a general rule to unwritten contracts under English law (and the Supreme Court of Canada has done the same in respect of written contracts: *QNS Paper Co Ltd v Chartwell Shipping Ltd* [1989] 2 SCR 683). *The Santa Carina* has been criticised by Professor Reynolds, who argues for a prima facie rule (applicable to both written and unwritten contracts) making the agent liable together with the unnamed principal unless it is absolutely clear that the person concerned acted as agent only. Reynolds submits that because there is no such prima facie rule the courts have caused confusion by wrongly classifying unnamed principal cases as undisclosed principal cases so as to prevent the agent avoiding personal liability. See FMB Reynolds (1983) 36 CLP 119, and also *Bowstead and Reynolds*, para 9–016.

(c) Deeds

If an agent contracts by deed, he will be personally liable so long as he is a party to the deed and has executed it in his own name. In these circumstances, the agent will be liable even if he is described in the deed as acting for and on behalf of a named principal (*Appleton v Binks*

(1804) 5 East 148). As to the possible effect of s 7(1) of the Powers of Attorney Act 1971 (as amended) on this rule, see Fridman, pp 220–221, 231; *Bowstead and Reynolds*, paras 8–087 and 9–048.

(d) Negotiable instruments
Special rules apply in cases where an agent has signed a bill of exchange, promissory note, or cheque. These rules are considered below at pp 692–695.

(e) Agents for foreign principals
See above, p 171.

(f) Agents for fictitious or non-existent principals
First, at common law, an agent who purports to act for a non-existent or fictitious principal may be held personally liable on the contract. Whether the agent is liable will turn on the objective construction of the terms of the contract by the court. Even if the parties did not intend the agent to be liable on the contract, he may still be held liable for breach of warranty of authority, in deceit, or, possibly, for negligent misstatement.

Secondly, by statute, where a contract purports to be made by or on behalf of a company, at a time when the company has not yet been formed, then subject to any agreement to the contrary, the contract has effect as a contract made with the person purporting to act for the company or as agent for it, and he is personally liable on the contract accordingly: s 51(1) of the Companies Act 2006 (above, p 161). If the agent is to avoid liability under the statute there must be 'a clear exclusion of personal liability': signing the contract 'for and on behalf of X Ltd' would not be enough (*Phonogram Ltd v Lane* [1982] QB 938 at 944, per Lord Denning MR). It has been held that s 51(1) also entitles the person or agent purporting to act for the unformed company to enforce the contract against the other party unless such enforcement is otherwise precluded by the ordinary principles governing contractual arrangements (*Braymist Ltd v Wise Finance Co Ltd* [2002] EWCA Civ 127, [2002] Ch 273, applying the identically worded Companies Act 1985, s 36C(1)). See, generally, A Griffiths (1993) 13 LS 241, and also C Twigg-Flesner (2001) 22 Co Law 274.

Thirdly, where it turns out that the agent is in fact his own principal, there is authority that the apparent agent can be held personally liable on the contract (*Railton v Hodgson* (1804) 4 Taunt 576n; *Jenkins v Hutchinson* (1849) 13 QB 744; cf *Bowstead and Reynolds*, paras 9–090 and 9–091, where it is argued that liability on a collateral warranty would be more appropriate).

(g) Statute
A statutory provision may make an agent personally liable on a contract made on behalf of his principal, for example s 51(1) of the Companies Act 2006 (considered immediately above).

(iii) When will the agent be entitled to sue on the contract made on behalf of his principal?

The agent will be entitled to sue on the contract made on behalf of his disclosed principal in any of the following circumstances.

(1) Where it is the intention of the parties that the agent should have rights as well as liabilities on the contract (eg *Short v Spackman* (1831) 2 B & Ad 962).

(2) Where the agent's right of action arises out of a collateral contract with the third party (although, strictly, this does not allow the agent to sue on the main contract).

(3) Where the agent has some special property in the subject matter of the contract, or possesses a lien over it, or has a beneficial interest in completion of the contract, he may sue the third party. For example, the auctioneer's right to sue the highest bidder for the price stems from his special property in, or lien over, the subject matter of the sale he effects (*Benton v Campbell Parker & Co* [1925] 2 KB 410 at 416, per Salter J); although the right of action actually arises under a collateral contract between the auctioneer and the highest bidder (*Chelmsford Auctions Ltd v Poole* [1973] QB 542 at 548–549, per Lord Denning MR).

(4) Where the agent purports to contract on behalf of a company yet to be formed, the agent may be entitled as well as liable on the contract under s 51(1) of the Companies Act 2006 (as was held to be the case by the Court of Appeal in *Braymist Ltd v Wise Finance Co Ltd* [2002] EWCA Civ 127, [2002] Ch 273: see above).

What if it turns out that the agent is in fact his own principal?

Rayner v Grote
(1846) 15 M & W 359, Court of Exchequer

The plaintiff, purporting to act for a named principal, contracted in writing to sell certain goods to the defendant. After discovering that the plaintiff was in fact the real principal, the defendant accepted delivery and paid for part of the goods. The plaintiff then sued the defendant for non-acceptance of the remainder of the goods. The Court of Exchequer (Pollock CB, Rolfe B, and Alderson B) upheld the verdict of the jury in favour of the plaintiff.

> **Alderson B** (delivering the judgment of the court): . . . At the time when this contract was made, the plaintiff was himself the real principal in the transaction; and although the contract on the face of it appeared to have been made by him as agent for another party, there was evidence given at the trial, tending strongly to shew, that when the first parcel of the goods was delivered to and accepted by the defendants, the name of the plaintiff as the principal was then fully known to the defendants: and we think that it was then properly left to the jury to infer from the evidence, that the defendants, with the full knowledge of the facts, had received that portion of the goods, and that all parties then treated the contract as one made with the plaintiff as the principal in the transaction. The defendants' counsel, in the argument, contended against this view of the case, and cited the case of *Bickerton v Burrell* as an authority that the plaintiff could not sue in such a case in his own name. That case is indeed in one respect stronger than the present, inasmuch as that was an action for money had and received, whereas this is a case of an executory contract. If, indeed, the contract had been wholly unperformed, and one which the plaintiff, by merely proving himself to be the real principal, was seeking to enforce, the question might admit of some doubt. In many such cases, such as, for instance, the case of contracts in which the skill or solvency of the person who is named as the principal may reasonably be considered as a material ingredient in the contract, it is clear that the agent cannot then shew himself to be the real principal, and sue in his own name; and perhaps it may be fairly urged that this, in all executory contracts, if wholly unperformed, or if partly performed without the knowledge of who is the real principal, may be the general rule. But the facts of this case raise a totally different question, as the jury must be taken to have found, under the learned Judge's direction, that this contract has been in part

performed, and that part performance accepted by the defendants with full knowledge that the plaintiff was not the agent, but the real principal. If so, we think the plaintiff may, after that, very properly say that they cannot refuse to complete that contract, by receiving the remainder of the goods, and paying the stipulated price for them. And it may be observed that this case is really distinguishable from *Bickerton v Burrell*, on the very ground on which that case was decided; for here, at all events, before action brought and trial had, the defendants knew that the plaintiff was the principal in the transaction. Perhaps it may be doubted whether that case was well decided on such a distinction, as it may fairly be argued that it would have been quite sufficient to prevent any possible inconvenience or injustice, and more in accordance with former authorities, if the Court had held that a party named as agent, under such circumstances as existed in that case, was entitled, on shewing himself to be the real principal, to maintain the action, the defendant being, however, allowed to make any defence to which he could shew himself to be entitled, either as against the plaintiff or as against the person named as principal by the plaintiff in the contract. It is not, however, necessary for us, in the present case, to question the authority of that decision.

NOTES

1. In *Bickerton v Burrell* (1816) 5 M & S 383, it was held that the plaintiff, having signed a contract as agent for a named principal, could not sue as the real principal, at all events unless he had given notice to the defendant of his true status in advance of bringing the action.

2. It would appear from the dictum of Alderson B in *Rayner v Grote* that an agent who purports to act for a *named* principal may nevertheless sue on the contract as the real principal provided that the agent has informed the third party that he acted on his own behalf, or the third party has otherwise become aware of the true position, *and* the identity of the principal was immaterial to the making of the contract by the third party. The fact that the defendant in *Rayner v Grote*, after discovering that the agent was the real principal, affirmed the contract by accepting delivery and paying for part of the goods, indicated to the court that he did not regard the principal's identity as material. Alderson B also suggested in *Rayner v Grote* that, whenever the contract remained entirely executory, the agent should not be allowed to sue in his own name. However, so long as the identity of the principal is not material to the third party, it is doubtful that there is anything to be gained by preventing the agent from suing on an entirely executory contract once the third party is aware of the true position.

3. Alderton B's dictum was cited with approval by Webster J in *Gewa Chartering BV v Remco Shipping Lines Ltd, The Remco* [1984] 2 Lloyd's Rep 205. In that case an agent, purporting to act on behalf of a named principal, entered into a contract for the charter of a ship. Later the agent revealed himself to be the real principal. Webster J held that the agent could not enforce the contract since the other contracting party, the shipowner, regarded the identity of the charterer as material (because the charterer was responsible for payment of freight). It could be shown that the shipowner would not have agreed to the same terms if it had known that the agent was really the principal.

4. There have been a number of cases where an agent, who purports to act for an *unnamed* principal, has been allowed to reveal himself as the real principal and sue on the contract, on the ground that the personal characteristics of the supposed principal cannot have influenced the third party (see *Schmaltz v Avery* (1851) 16 QB 655; *Harper & Co v Vigers Bros* [1909] 2 KB 549; cf *Sharman v Brandt* (1871) LR 6 QB 720). For criticism of this line of authority, see *Bowstead and Reynolds*, paras 9–095 and 9–096.

QUESTION

Arnold contracts purportedly on behalf of Percy, a noted dog breeder, to buy a valuable prize poodle from Thomas. During the negotiations, Thomas says to Arnold: 'I am surprised that a reputable breeder like Percy is acting through a spiv like you.' Arnold is in fact acting for himself. Two weeks after the conclusion of this contract, Arnold telephones Thomas and admits that he is really the purchaser. At first, Thomas accepts the situation philosophically; but after consulting a lawyer, Daisy, he refuses to deliver up the poodle. Advise Arnold.

(iv) Breach of warranty of authority

Bowstead and Reynolds on Agency by Peter G Watts
(20th edn, 2014), art 105(1)

> Where a person, by words or conduct, represents that he has actual authority to act on behalf of another, and a third party is induced by such representation to act in a manner in which he would not have acted if such representation had not been made, the first-mentioned person is deemed to warrant that the representation is true, and is liable for any loss caused to such third party by a breach of that implied warranty, even if he acted in good faith, under a mistaken belief that he had such authority.

Yonge v Toynbee
[1910] 1 KB 215, Court of Appeal

Solicitors were instructed by Toynbee to defend an action for libel and slander threatened against him by Yonge. Before the action was commenced, and unknown to his solicitors, Toynbee became insane and was certified as being of unsound mind. On commencement of the action the solicitors entered an appearance, delivered a defence, and engaged in certain interlocutory proceedings. Subsequently, the solicitors discovered that Toynbee was insane and informed Yonge of that fact. Yonge then applied to have the appearance and all subsequent proceedings struck out and for the solicitors to pay personally his costs of the action, on the ground that they had acted for Toynbee without authority. The Master ordered the appearance and subsequent proceedings to be struck out but refused to make an order that Yonge's costs should be paid by the solicitors personally. The Court of Appeal allowed Yonge's appeal against the Master's refusal to make an order for costs against the solicitors.

> **Buckley LJ:** The interesting and important question in this case is as to the extent to which the principle *of Smout v Ilbery* ((1842) 10 M & W 1) remains good law after the decision in *Collen v Wright* ((1857) 8 E & B 647). In *Smout v Ilbery* Alderson B, in giving the judgment of the Court, dealt with the authorities under three heads: First, the case where the agent made a fraudulent misrepresentation as to his authority with an intention to deceive. In such case the agent is, of course, personally responsible. Secondly, the case where the agent without fraud, but untruly in fact, represented that he had authority when he had none, instancing under this head *Polhill v Walter* ((1832) 3 B & Ad 114). In that case A, having no authority from B to accept a bill on his behalf, did accept it as by his procuration, *bona fide* believing that B would retrospectively approve that which he was doing. In such case again the agent is personally liable, for he induced the other

party to enter into a contract on a misrepresentation of a fact within his own knowledge. The third class is where the agent *bona fide* believes that he has, but in fact has not, authority. This third class the learned Baron seems to subdivide into two heads—the first where the agent never had authority, but believed that he had (eg when he acted on a forged warrant of attorney which he thought to be genuine), and the second where the agent had in fact full authority originally, but that authority had come to an end without any knowledge, or means of knowledge, on the part of the agent that such was the fact. The latter was the state of facts in *Smout v Ilbery*. I understand *Smout v Ilbery* not to dispute that in the former of these last two cases (that is, where the agent never had authority) he is liable, but to hold that in the latter (namely, where he originally had authority, but that authority has ceased without his having knowledge, or means of knowledge, that it has ceased) he is not liable. The principle is stated in the following words: 'If, then, the true principle derivable from the cases is, that there must be some wrong or omission of right on the part of the agent, in order to make him personally liable on a contract made in the name of his principal, it will follow that the agent is not responsible in such a case as the present. And to this conclusion we have come.' It seems to me that, if that principle be the true principle, then the former of the last two mentioned cases ought to have been resolved in the same way as the latter. I can see no distinction in principle between the case where the agent never had authority and the case where the agent originally had authority, but that authority has ceased without his knowledge or means of knowledge. In the latter case as much as in the former the proposition, I think, is true that without any *mala fides* he has at the moment of acting represented that he had an authority which in fact he had not. In my opinion he is then liable on an implied contract that he had authority, whether there was fraud or not. That this is the true principle is, I think, shewn by passages which I will quote from judgments in three which I have selected out of the numerous cases upon this subject. In *Collen v Wright* Willes J in giving the judgment of the Court uses the following language: 'I am of opinion that a person who induces another to contract with him, as the agent of a third party, by an unqualified assertion of his being authorized to act as such agent, is answerable to the person who so contracts for any damages which he may sustain by reason of the assertion of authority being untrue...The fact that the professed agent honestly thinks that he has authority affects the moral character of his act; but his moral innocence, so far as the person whom he has induced to contract is concerned, in no way aids such person or alleviates the inconvenience and damage which he sustains. The obligation arising in such a case is well expressed by saying that a person professing to contract as agent for another, impliedly, if not expressly, undertakes to or promises the person who enters into such contract, upon the faith of the professed agent being duly authorized, that the authority which he professes to have does in point of fact exist.' This language is equally applicable to each of the two classes of cases to which I have referred. The language is not, in my opinion, consistent with maintaining that which *Smout v Ilbery* had laid down as the true principle, that there must be some wrong or omission of right on the part of the agent in order to make him liable. The question is not as to his honesty or *bona fides*. His liability arises from an implied undertaking or promise made by him that the authority which he professes to have does in point of fact exist. I can see no difference of principle between the case in which the authority never existed at all and the case in which the authority once existed and has ceased to exist. In *Firbank's Executors v Humphreys* ((1886) 18 QBD 54 at 60) the rule is thus stated by Lord Esher:

> The rule to be deduced is that, where a person by asserting that he has the authority of the principal induces another person to enter into any transaction which he would not have entered into but for that assertion, and the assertion turns out to be untrue, to the injury of the person to whom it is made, it must be taken that the person making it undertook that it was true, and he is liable personally for the damage that has occurred.

Lastly, Lord Davey in *Starkey v Bank of England* ([1903] AC 114 at 119), after stating that the rule extends to every transaction of business into which a third party is induced to enter by a representation that the person with whom he is doing business has the authority of some other person, rejects the argument that the rule in *Collen v Wright* does not extend to cases where the supposed agent did not know that he had no authority, and had not the means of finding out; cites Lord Campbell's language in *Lewis v Nicholson* ((1852) 18 QB 503), that the agent 'is liable, if there was any fraud, in an action for deceit, and, in my opinion, as at present advised, on an implied contract that he had authority, whether there was fraud or not'; and concludes by saying that in his opinion 'it is utterly immaterial for the purpose of the application of this branch of the law whether the supposed agent knew of the defect of his authority or not.'

The result of these judgments, in my opinion, is that the liability of the person who professes to act as agent arises (a) if he has been fraudulent, (b) if he has without fraud untruly represented that he had authority when he had not, and (c) also where he innocently misrepresents that he has authority where the fact is either (1) that he never had authority or (2) that his original authority has ceased by reasons of facts of which he has not knowledge or means of knowledge. Such last-mentioned liability arises from the fact that by professing to act as agent he impliedly contracts that he has authority, and it is immaterial whether he knew of the defect of his authority or not.

This implied contract may, of course, be excluded by the facts of the particular case. If, for instance, the agent proved that at the relevant time he told the party with whom he was contracting that he did not know whether the warrant of attorney under which he was acting was genuine or not, and would not warrant its validity, or that his principal was abroad and he did not know whether he was still living, there will have been no representation upon which the implied contract will arise. This may have been the *ratio decidendi* in *Smout v Ilbery* as expressed in the passage 'The continuance of the life of the principal was, under these circumstances, a fact equally within the knowledge of both contracting parties'; and this seems to be the ground upon which *Story on Agency*, s 265a, approves the decision. The husband had left England for China in May, 1839, a time in the history of the world when communication was not what it is now, and the Court seems to have decided upon the ground that the butcher who supplied the goods knew that the facts were such that the wife did not, because she could not, take upon herself to affirm that he was alive. If so, there was no implied contract. The principle, as stated in the words I have quoted, may have been meant to be, but is not in words, rested upon that ground, and, if it is to be understood as it seems to have been understood in *Salton v New Beeston Cycle Co* ([1900] 1 Ch 43), it is not, I think, consistent with *Collen v Wright*. The true principle as deduced from the authorities I have mentioned rests, I think, not upon wrong or omission of right on the part of the agent, but upon implied contract.

The facts here are that the solicitors originally had authority to act for Mr Toynbee; that that authority ceased by reason of his unsoundness of mind; that, subsequently, they on October 30, 1908, undertook to appear, and on November 6 appeared, in the first action, and, after that was discontinued, did on December 21 undertake to appear, and did on December 30 enter an appearance, in the second action; and that they subsequently, on February 22, 1909, delivered a defence pleading privilege, and denying the slander, and did not until April 5 inform the plaintiff that, as the fact was, their client had become of unsound mind. During all this time they were putting the plaintiff to costs, and these costs were incurred upon the faith of their representation that they had authority to act for the defendant. They proved no facts addressed to shew that implied contract was excluded.

It has been pressed upon us that a solicitor is an agent of a special kind with an obligation towards his client to continue to take on his behalf all proper steps in the action. The particular nature of his agency is not, I think, very material. On the other hand it must be borne in mind that after August 21, when the defendant Toynbee wrote to the plaintiffs solicitors, referring them

to Messrs Wontner & Sons, the plaintiff could not consistently with professional etiquette communicate personally with the defendant. During the period from August, 1908, to April, 1909, the
solicitors had the means of knowing and did not in fact ascertain that the defendant had become
of unsound mind. In the interval they did acts which amounted to representations on their part
that they were continuing to stand in a position in which they were competent to bind the defendant. This was not the case. They are liable, in my judgment, upon an implied warranty or contract
that they had an authority which they had not.

For these reasons I think that the appellant is entitled to succeed and to have an order against
the solicitors for damages, and the measure of damage is, no doubt, the amount of the plaintiff's costs thrown away in the action. The appeal, therefore, should be allowed with costs here
and below.

Swinfen Eady J: I wish to add that in the conduct of litigation the Court places much reliance
upon solicitors, who are its officers; it issues writs at their instance, and accepts appearances for
defendants which they enter, as a matter of course, and without questioning their authority; the
other parties to the litigation also act upon the same footing, without questioning or investigating
the authority of the solicitor on the opposite side; and much confusion and uncertainty would be
introduced if a solicitor were not to be under any liability to the opposite party for continuing to act
without authority in cases where he originally possessed one... The manner in which business is
ordinarily conducted requires that each party should be able to rely upon the solicitor of the other
party having obtained a proper authority before assuming to act. It is always open to a solicitor to
communicate as best he can with his own client, and obtain from time to time such authority and
instructions as may be necessary. But the solicitor on the other side does not communicate with his
opponent's client, and, speaking generally, it is not proper for him to do so, as was pointed out by
Kekewich J in *Re Margetson & Jones* ([1897] 2 Ch 314). It is in my opinion essential to the proper
conduct of legal business that a solicitor should be held to warrant the authority which he claims
of representing the client; if it were not so, no one would be safe in assuming that his opponent's
solicitor was duly authorized in what he said or did, and it would be impossible to conduct legal
business upon the footing now existing; and, whatever the legal liability may be, the Court, in exercising the authority which it possesses over its own officers, ought to proceed upon the footing that
a solicitor assuming to act, in an action, for one of the parties to the action warrants his authority.

[**Vaughan Williams LJ** delivered a concurring judgment.]

NOTES

1. Despite the fact that it was held in *Yonge v Toynbee* that the agent's liability to the third
party was contractual, debate has continued as to the nature of an agent's liability to a third
party when acting without authority. Various alternative theories have been advanced, including those based on quasi-contract, negligent misstatement, and estoppel, but none withstand
close scrutiny (see Fridman, pp 244–247, who concludes that 'the true nature and basis of
this anomalous liability is... uncertain and unclear'). In *Farley Health Products Ltd v Babylon
Trading Co* (1987) The Times, 29 July, Sir Neil Lawson thought that liability for breach of
warranty of authority was *sui generis*, not being a claim in contract or tort. However, it is submitted that the best explanation, which reflects the reasoning of Willes J in *Collen v Wright*
(1857) 7 E & B 301, and of the Court of Appeal in *Yonge v Toynbee*, is that the agent's liability
is based on a collateral contract made with the third party (*AMB Generali Holding AG v SEB
Trygg Liv Holding AB* [2005] EWCA Civ 1237, [2006] 1 WLR 2276 at [60], per Buxton LJ).
Furthermore, the damages awarded for breach of an agent's warranty of authority will be

assessed on normal *Hadley v Baxendale* (1854) 9 Exch 341 principles (see note 5 below), thus reflecting the contractual nature of the liability (although if the agent has been fraudulent or negligent the third party can ask for damages to be assessed on a different basis).

2. An agent may be liable for breach of warranty of authority whether he is fraudulent, negligent, or innocent. Liability is strict and may operate harshly on an agent who is innocently unaware of the initial absence, or subsequent termination, of his authority. However, the harshness of the rule is mitigated in the following respects.

(a) The agent will not be liable where the third party knew, or ought to have known, that the agent was not warranting his authority (eg *Lilly, Wilson & Co v Smales, Eeles & Co* [1892] 1 QB 456, where it was held that trade custom should have put the third party on notice that the agent was not warranting his authority).

(b) It used to be that the agent's representation of authority had to be one of fact and not of law (eg *Rashdall v Ford* (1866) LR 2 Eq 750, where directors of a statutory company, with no borrowing powers on a true construction of the incorporating statute, were held to have made a representation of law, and not of fact, when they purported to borrow from a third party). However, it is often difficult to distinguish representations of fact from representations of law, and at least in one area, namely recovery of money paid by mistake, the distinction had been abolished (*Kleinwort Benson Ltd v Lincoln City Council* [1999] 2 AC 349, HL). In the light of this development, which the Court of Appeal has said 'now permeates the law of contract' (*Brennan v Bolt Burden* [2004] EWCA Civ 1017, [2005] QB 303 at [10]), the distinction made between an agent's representation of fact and his representation of law may no longer apply (the distinction has been removed in other areas of contract law, eg it has been held that a contract may be rescinded for a misrepresentation of law: *Pankhania v Hackney London Borough Council* [2002] EWHC 2441 (Ch), [2002] NPC 123 at [57]).

(c) Under s 5(1) of the Powers of Attorney Act 1971, a donee of a power of attorney who acts in pursuance of the power at a time when it has been revoked does not, by reason of the revocation, incur any liability (either to the donor or to any other person) if at the time he did not know that the power had been revoked. The protection afforded by s 5(1) also extends to the donee of a lasting power of attorney (Mental Capacity Act 2005, s 14(5)).

(d) The agent's warranty is limited. It is that he has authority to make the contract or enter into the transaction; it is not that the contract or transaction will be performed by his principal, or that the principal is solvent (*AMB Generali Holding AG v SEB Trygg Liv Holding AB* [2005] EWCA Civ 1237, [2006] 1 WLR 2276 at [60] ff, per Buxton LJ: held solicitor conducting proceedings only gives a warranty that he has a client who exists and has authorised proceedings; he does not give a warrant as to his client's name, or that he has a good cause of action or is solvent). This means that if the principal is insolvent, the third party cannot recover more from the agent than he could have recovered from the principal, had the agent had authority.

3. Liability for breach of warranty of authority may extend very widely indeed. Not only may the agent be liable for breach of warranty of his own authority but he may also be liable if he warrants the authority of someone else (*Chapleo v Brunswick Permanent Building Society* (1881) 6 QBD 696). Furthermore, the agent may be held liable to a person unknown to him but who nevertheless relied upon his representation, for example the indorsee of a bill of exchange or a bill of lading (see *Rasnoimport V/O v Guthrie & Co Ltd* [1966] 1 Lloyd's Rep 1, where Mocatta J said at 13: 'I can see nothing extravagant or heterodox in holding that the implied warranty of authority...was given by the defendants to all whom they could reasonably foresee would become such indorsees and became actionable by such persons on proof of their having acted in reliance upon the warranty and having suffered damage thereby'—but see FMB Reynolds (1967) 80 LQR 189 for criticism of this decision). The third party need not be induced to transact with the purported principal as a result of the agent's warranty of authority, although this is the paradigm case; he may provide consideration for the agent's warranty by entering into a transaction with someone else. Thus, in *Penn v Bristol and West Building Society* [1997] 1 WLR 1356, when a solicitor mistakenly thought he had authority to act for both joint owners of a house, and held himself out as such to another solicitor who, as he was aware, acted for both the prospective purchaser and the building society which was lending money to finance the purchase, the Court of Appeal held that the solicitor's warranty of authority was given to both the purchaser and the building society which acted in reliance on that promise by lending the money to the purchaser.

4.   Will an agent with no actual authority be in breach of his warranty of authority if he has apparent authority or if the principal subsequently ratifies his actions? Treitel submits that the agent would not be liable for breach of his warranty of authority in either of these circumstances (E Peel, *Treitel's Law of Contract* (14th edn, 2015), para 16–082, relying, inter alia, on *Rainbow v Howkins* [1904] 2 KB 322). This is a questionable contention. The agent professes that he has authority and this must be taken to mean that he has actual authority. This is because apparent authority is no authority at all but merely a condition which calls into being the power of an 'agent' to alter the legal relations of his 'principal' (see above, pp 132–146). All the same, the fact that the agent has apparent authority is significant because it avoids loss to the third party which would otherwise result from the agent's breach of warranty of authority. If the third party can hold the principal to the contract or transaction affected by the agent on grounds of the latter's apparent authority, the third party will have suffered no loss by reason of the agent's breach of warranty of authority (see, eg, *Drew v Nunn* (1879) 4 QBD 661, below at p 287; but the point was not considered in *Yonge v Toynbee*). A similar conclusion can be reached with regard to the principal's ratification of an agent's unauthorised acts. Ratification is not retrospective for all purposes (above, pp 166–167) and so it is better to regard the agent as technically in breach of his warranty of authority, even though the third party's loss will be limited if the principal ratifies the agent's acts (although the third party could still have incurred loss in pursuing the agent before ratification by the principal).

5.   The measure of damages for breach of warranty of authority is the contract measure (see note 1 above). Lord Esher MR put the matter as follows in *Firbank's Executors v Humphreys* (1886) 18 QBD 54 at 60:

> The damages under the general rule are arrived at by considering the difference in the position he [the person acting in reliance on the warranty] would have been in had the representation been true and the position he is actually in inconsequence of its being untrue.

This involves a comparison between the position the third party would have been in had the agent had the principal's authority and the position he was actually in, given the absence of that authority. The assessment may not always work in the third party's favour. In *Singh v Sardar Investments Ltd* [2002] EWCA Civ 1706, [2002] NPC 134, the claimants entered into a contract to purchase shop premises from the defendant company. They dealt with one of two brothers who owned the company. It turned out that the brother had no authority to enter into the contract on the company's behalf. The claimants brought an action against him for breach of warranty of authority and claimed damages for loss of bargain, together with the rent they would have received by letting out the upper floors. The Court of Appeal upheld the trial judge's award of only nominal damages. The Court of Appeal held that even if the contract had been authorised the company would have been entitled to rescind it as the claimants were not in a position to fund the purchase at the time of completion.

6. Although the prima facie rule is that damages for breach of warranty of authority fall to be assessed at the date of the breach, this is not an absolute rule. Damages may be assessed at another date if it is more just to do so. The issue arose in *Habton Farms v Nimmo* [2003] EWCA Civ 68, [2004] QB 1. The defendant, a bloodstock agent, purporting to act on behalf of a certain racehorse owner, concluded an agreement with the claimant sellers for the purchase of a horse for £70,000. The agent was unauthorised and the owner refused to take delivery of the horse. The sellers did not accept the owner's 'repudiation' of the purported contract and made no immediate effort to sell the horse. The horse was still in the sellers' possession when, four weeks after the delivery date, it contracted peritonitis and died. The sellers sued the agent for breach of warranty of authority. They claimed damages of £70,000. The agent argued that the damages should be nil as on the day the contract was concluded (ie the date the agent breached his warranty of authority), there was no difference between the contract price and the market price of the horse. The Court of Appeal, by a majority, rejected that submission and held that the correct measure of damages was £70,000. The majority (Clarke and Auld LJ: see, especially, at [127]) held that if the contract had proceeded, the sellers would have divested themselves of the ownership, possession, and risk of harm to the horse in return for the price some four weeks before the horse died. Their Lordships held that the sellers should not be put in any worse position than they would have been in if there had been a contract simply because it transpired that they were entitled to damages for the agent's breach of warranty of authority and not to the notional sale price against the owner. The case was to be distinguished from one where a seller accepts the notional buyer's repudiation and sells elsewhere at a lower market price, when the measure of damages would be the contract price less the market value normally identified as that sale price.

2 UNDISCLOSED AGENCY

(a) Relations between principal and third party

(i) *The general rule*

Siu Yin Kwan v Eastern Insurance Co Ltd
[1994] 2 AC 199, Privy Council

The facts appear below at pp 211–212.

Lord Lloyd of Berwick (delivering the advice of the Privy Council (Lords Templeman, Mustill, Woolf, Lloyd of Berwick and Sir Thomas Eichelbaum)): . . . The main features of the law relating to an undisclosed principal have been settled since at least the end of the 18th century. A hundred years later, in 1872, Blackburn J said in *Armstrong v Stokes* (1872) LR 7 QB 598, 604 that it had often been doubted whether it was originally right to hold that an undisclosed principal was liable to be sued on the contract made by an agent on his behalf, but added that 'doubts of this kind come now too late'.

For present purposes the law can be summarised shortly. (1) An undisclosed principal may sue and be sued on a contract made by an agent on his behalf, acting within the scope of his actual authority. (2) In entering into the contract, the agent must intend to act on the principal's behalf. (3) The agent of an undisclosed principal may also sue and be sued on the contract. (4) Any defence which the third party may have against the agent is available against his principal. (5) The terms of the contract may, expressly or by implication, exclude the principal's right to sue, and his liability to be sued. The contract itself, or the circumstances surrounding the contract, may show that the agent is the true and only principal.

The origin of, and theoretical justification for, the doctrine of the undisclosed principal has been the subject of much discussion by academic writers. Their Lordships would especially mention the influential article by Goodhart and Hamson 'Undisclosed Principals in Contract' [1932] 4 CLJ 320, commenting on the then recent case of *Collins v Associated Greyhound Racecourses Ltd* [1930] 1 Ch 1. It seems to be generally accepted that, while the development of this branch of the law may have been anomalous, since it runs counter to fundamental principles of privity of contract, it is justified on grounds of commercial convenience.

The present case is concerned with the fifth of the features noted above. The law in that connection was stated by Diplock LJ in *Teheran-Europe Co Ltd v ST Belton (Tractors) Ltd* [1968] 2 QB 545, 555:

> Where an agent has…actual authority and enters into a contract with another party intending to do so on behalf of his principal, it matters not whether he discloses to the other party the identity of his principal, or even that he is contracting on behalf of a principal at all, if the other party is willing or leads the agent to believe that he is willing to treat as a party to the contract anyone on whose behalf the agent may have been authorised to contract. In the case of an ordinary commercial contract such willingness of the other party may be assumed by the agent unless either the other party manifests his unwillingness or there are other circumstances which should lead the agent to realise that the other party was not so willing.

Keighley, Maxsted & Co v Durant

[1901] AC 240, House of Lords

The facts appear above at p 159.

> **Lord Lindley:**…[A]s a contract is constituted by the concurrence of two or more persons and by their agreement to the same terms, there is an anomaly in holding one person bound to another of whom he knows nothing and with whom he did not, in fact, intend to contract. But middlemen, through whom contracts are made, are common and useful in business transactions, and in the great mass of contracts it is a matter of indifference to either party whether there is an undisclosed principal or not. If he exists it is, to say the least, extremely convenient that he should be able to sue and be sued as a principal, and he is only allowed to do so upon terms which exclude injustice.

NOTES

1. The general rule is that an undisclosed principal can sue and be sued on a contract made on his behalf by his agent acting within the scope of his actual authority. This doctrine is widely regarded as anomalous because it gives the undisclosed principal rights, and subjects him to liabilities, that arise under a contract to which he was not originally privy. As Sir Frederick Pollock once commented in (1887) 3 LQR 358 at 359:

> The plain truth ought never to be forgotten—that the whole law as to the rights and liabilities of an undisclosed principal is inconsistent with the elementary doctrines of the law of contract. The right of one person to sue another on a contract not really made with the person suing is unknown to every other legal system except that of England and America.

The anomalous nature of the doctrine has also been recognised by other academic commentators (see, eg, OW Holmes, 'The History of Agency' in *Selected Essays in Anglo-American Legal History* (1909), Vol 3, Part 6, p 404; JH Barr (1909) 18 Yale LJ 443) and by the courts (see, eg, *Siu Yin Kwan v Eastern Insurance Co Ltd* [1994] 2 AC 199 at 207, per Lord Lloyd, extract above; *Keighley, Maxsted & Co v Durant* [1901] AC 240 at 261, per Lord Lindley, extract above). However, the undisclosed principal doctrine developed before theories of contract law requiring (objectively determined) consent of the parties became established, and this has led Tan Cheng-Han (2004) 120 LQR 480, to submit (at 485) that 'it makes no more sense to say that the undisclosed principal doctrine is anomalous when measured by contract principles than it is to say that the doctrine of privity of contract is anomalous because it is inconsistent with the undisclosed principal doctrine'.

2. Numerous theories have been advanced to explain the doctrine: they are usefully reviewed by A Rochvarg (1989) 34 McGill LJ 286 at 298–314. The theories which have received most attention are those based on trust and assignment. It has been argued that the agent is trustee for the undisclosed principal (see JB Ames, 'Undisclosed Principal: His Rights and Liabilities' (1909) 18 Yale LJ 443), but it was held by Ungoed-Thomas J in *Pople v Evans* [1969] 2 Ch 255 at 264, in the context of the *res judicata* doctrine, that 'there is no trust relationship between any of the parties which can be recognised as between the third party on the one hand and the principal and agent, or either of them, on the other hand'. The assignment theory was advanced in an influential article written by AL Goodhart and CJ Hamson, 'Undisclosed Principals in Contract' [1932] CLJ 320, where it was suggested that the contract originally made between the agent (not the principal) and the third party was automatically transferred to the undisclosed principal by 'a primitive and highly restricted form of assignment' (at 352). However, the analogy is not perfect for, unlike assignment, the undisclosed principal doctrine involves the transfer of liabilities as well as rights and, furthermore, there is no event which can be regarded as an assignment. For further differences between the undisclosed principal doctrine and assignment, see R Powell, *The Law of Agency* (2nd edn, 1961), pp 165–166. For these reasons, the assignment theory was firmly rejected by the Privy Council in *Siu Yin Kwan v Eastern Insurance Co Ltd*, above, at 210, per Lord Lloyd. Tan (2004) 120 LQR 480, advanced (at 501–505) a theory based on the existence of an implied contract between a third party and an undisclosed principal. He relies on a dictum of Diplock LJ in *Teheran-Europe Co Ltd v ST Belton (Tractors) Ltd* [1968] 2 QB 545 at 555 (see above, p 201), that ordinarily the third party in a commercial contract is willing to treat as a party to the contract anyone on whose behalf the agent may have been authorised to contract. The idea is that the third party *intends* to contract with the undisclosed principal. But this theory is open to the criticism that, because the third party is unaware of the undisclosed principal's existence, he can have no intention to contract with him. Of course, anyone who enters into a contract could have an undisclosed principal behind him, but that is to imply an intention to contract on the basis of a mere possibility.

3. The lack of any watertight legal explanation of the undisclosed principal doctrine does not appear to have unduly troubled the courts, which have applied the doctrine in a wide variety of contexts. For example, in *Boyter v Thomson* [1995] 2 AC 628, the House of Lords held that under s 14(5) of the Sale of Goods Act 1979, where a buyer purchases goods from an agent acting for an undisclosed principal, the buyer was entitled to sue the undisclosed principal for breach of the implied conditions set out under s 14(2) and (3) in respect of the unseaworthiness of a boat that was the subject matter of the sale. As Lord Jauncey explained (at 632): 'When the subsection applies the normal common law rules of principal and agent also apply.' The courts have been prepared to justify the doctrine simply on grounds of commercial convenience (see *Keighley, Maxsted & Co v Durant*, above, per Lord Lindley; *Teheran-Europe Co Ltd v Belton (Tractors) Ltd* [1968] 2 QB 545 at 552, per Lord Denning MR; *Siu Yin Kwan v Eastern Insurance Co Ltd*, above, at 207, per Lord Lloyd; cf *Freeman & Lockyer v Buckhurst Park Properties (Mangal) Ltd* [1964] 2 QB 480 at 503, per Diplock LJ—above at p 132). This pragmatic approach is to be welcomed, but it has meant that certain aspects of the application of the undisclosed principal doctrine remain unclear, for example the effect of a disposition of goods to the agent of an undisclosed principal (considered by the Court of Appeal of New South Wales in *Maynegrain Pty Ltd v Compafina Bank* [1982] 2 NSWLR 141; reversed on the facts by the Privy Council (1984) 58 ALJR 389, noted by FMB Reynolds (1984) 4 OJLS 434).

4. For an account of the historical development of the undisclosed principal doctrine, see AL Goodhart and CJ Hamson [1932] CLJ 320; SJ Stoljar, *The Law of Agency* (1961), pp 204–211. For a comparative treatment of the subject, see W Muller-Freienfels (1953) 16 MLR 299 and (1955) 18 MLR 33.

QUESTIONS

1. Peter employs Alan to contract with Ted, instructing him to do so in his own name. Ted suspects Alan may be acting for a principal as it is known in the trade that Alan sometimes contracts for himself and sometimes for others. But without making any inquiry as to Alan's status, Ted contracts with him. Peter has now revealed himself to be Alan's principal but Ted wants to hold Alan personally liable on the contract as the agent of an undisclosed principal. Was Peter really an 'undisclosed' principal? See FMB Reynolds (1983) 36 CLP 119 at 122–128; *Bowstead and Reynolds*, para 8–073.

2. The Contracts (Rights of Third Parties) Act 1999 makes it possible for a third party to rely on a term of a contract to which he was not a party (privy). But the Act does not confer rights on an undisclosed principal. Can you see why?

(ii) Exclusion of the undisclosed principal

Look again at Lord Lloyd's fifth principle in the *Siu Yin Kwan v Eastern Insurance Co Ltd* (see extract above, at p 201).

(a) By the terms of the contract

An undisclosed principal is not allowed to intervene where this would be inconsistent with the terms of the contract.

Fred Drughorn Ltd v Rederiaktiebolaget Trans-Atlantic
[1919] AC 203, House of Lords

An undisclosed principal claimed to be entitled to sue on a charterparty signed by its agent as 'charterer'. Affirming the decision of the Court of Appeal, the House of Lords held that evidence was admissible to establish that the agent had contracted on behalf of the principal.

Viscount Haldane: My Lords, by the law of England if B contracts with C *prima facie* that is a contract between these two only, but if at the time B entered into the contract he was really acting as agent for A, then evidence is generally admissible to show that A was the principal, and A can take advantage of the contract as if it had been actually made between himself and C . . .

But, my Lords, the principle is limited by [a] consideration, about which . . . there is no doubt, and the applicability of which to the present case is beyond question. In *Humble v Hunter* ((1848) 12 QB 310) it was approved, although it was not necessary to give a decision on the point, and also in *Formby Bros v Formby* ((1910) 102 LT 116) and in other cases. These are authorities for the proposition that evidence of authority of an outside principal is not admissible, if to give such evidence would be to contradict some term in the contract itself. It was held in *Humble v Hunter*, that where a charterer dealt with someone described as the owner, evidence was not admissible to show that some other person was the owner. That is perfectly intelligible. The question is not before us now, but I see no reason to question that where you have the description of a person as the owner of property, and it is a term of the contract that he should contract as owner of that property, you cannot show that another person is the real owner. That is not a question of agency—that is a question of property.

My Lords, in the same way in *Formby Bros v Formby* the term was 'proprietor,' and 'proprietor' was treated in the opinion of the Court of Appeal as on the same footing as the expression 'owner.' But, my Lords, we are not dealing with that case here. The principle remains, but the question is whether the principle applies to a charterparty where the person who says that he signed only as agent describes himself as the charterer.

My Lords, there may be something to be said from the heading of the charterparty in this case, and the reference to the company which claims to have been his principal, for the proposition that, reading the document as a whole, there is evidence that he intended to convey that he was acting as agent for somebody else; but whether that is so or not the term 'charterer' is a very different term from the term 'owner' or the term 'proprietor.' A charterer may be and *prima facie* is merely entering into a contact. A charterparty is not a lease—it is a chattel that is being dealt with, a chattel that is essentially a mere subject of contract; and although rights of ownership or rights akin to ownership may be given under it *prima facie* it is a contract for the hiring or use of the vessel. Under these circumstances it is in accordance with ordinary business common-sense and custom that charterers should be able to contract as agents for undisclosed principals who may come in and take the benefit of the charterparty.

But, my Lords, it is said that in this charterparty the terms are such as to exclude that notion. Why is that said to be so? Because the term 'charterer' is used. Well, I have already commented upon that. It is said that the term 'charterer' was meant simply to describe a particular person who is to carry out the nomination of arbitrators and everything else which is contained in the charterparty—to give orders which can only be given by one person, and that for the working out of the charterparty it is essential to treat the person so contracting as designated as a person whose identity cannot be varied or contradicted.

My Lords, the answer is that the principal may take that place, and that the company, in this case acting through its agent, whoever that agent may be, will be in the same position as the charterer contracting originally. There is nothing in that position inconsistent with the stipulations of this charterparty, and therefore it appears to me that the qualifying principle of *Humble v Hunter*, that you shall not contradict the instrument by giving evidence of agency, has no application in this case.

[**Lords Shaw of Dunfermline** and **Wrenbury** concurred. **Lord Sumner** delivered a concurring opinion.]

NOTES

1. In *Humble v Hunter* (1848) 12 QB 310, a son chartered out a vessel owned by his mother but signed the charterparty as 'CJ Humble Esq, owner of the good ship or vessel called the *Ann*'. It was held that the mother could not enforce the contract as undisclosed principal on the basis that she was in fact the shipowner, since the description of her son as 'owner' was inconsistent with this. The House of Lords' decision in *Drughorn*'s case clearly limits the effect of *Humble v Hunter* (in *Epps v Rothnie* [1945] KB 562 at 565, Scott LJ went so far as to suggest that *Humble v Hunter* had been overruled by *Drughorn*'s case). In *Siu Yin Kwan v Eastern Insurance Co Ltd* [1994] 2 AC 199, *Drughorn*'s case was relied on by Lord Lloyd (delivering the advice of the Privy Council) when he stated, albeit by way of *obiter dictum*, that the fact that the agent was described in an employer's liability policy as the employer did not exclude the right of the undisclosed principal (the actual employer) to intervene. As Lord Lloyd said (at 209): 'If courts are too ready to construe written contracts as contradicting the right of the undisclosed principal to intervene, it would go far to destroy the beneficial assumption in commercial cases, to which Diplock J referred to in *Teheran-Europe Co Ltd v ST Belton (Tractors) Ltd* [1968] 2 QB 545, 555 [set out above, p 201].' It is now likely to be only in exceptional cases that the undisclosed principal's intervention will be held inconsistent with the terms of the contract, and possibly only in cases where the agent can be construed to have contracted as the owner of property. But see *Panagiotis Stravelakis v Rocco Giuseppe and Figli SNC, The Astyanax* [1985] 2 Lloyd's Rep 109, where the Court of Appeal held that the description of one party to a charterparty as 'disponent owner' of a vessel was neutral, but that the surrounding circumstances and the course of negotiations were inconsistent with that party contracting as mere agent on behalf of the registered owners of the vessel. On the other hand, in *Ferryways NV v Associated British Ports* [2008] EWHC 225 (Comm), [2008] 1 Lloyd's Rep 639, a case in which a port owner/operator denied liability to F for payments following the death of an employee of A for which ABP was liable, Teare J held that the words 'as the employers' did not exclude the intervention of the undisclosed principal as 'there is no express provision that [A] is the only person to have the rights and obligations of an employer under the contract of employment' (at [56]).

2. In cases such as those we have just considered, the test which determines whether the undisclosed principal can intervene is whether the agent has impliedly contracted that there is no principal behind him. If the agent has given such an implied undertaking the undisclosed principal may not intervene (AL Goodhart and CJ Hamson [1932] CLJ 320 at 327 and 342; *Bowstead and Reynolds*, para 8–079). However, it is always open to exclude the possibility of intervention by an undisclosed principal through an express term that the agent is the real and only principal (*United Kingdom Mutual Steamship Assurance Association v Nevill* (1887) 19 QBD 110).

QUESTION

In *Humble v Hunter*, could the mother have intervened if she had been co-owner of the vessel with her son? See Goodhart and Hamson, op cit, p 327.

(b) Other circumstances

If the third party can show that he wanted to deal with the agent and with no one else, the undisclosed principal cannot intervene. This may be because of some particular attribute of the agent or some reason why the third party does not wish to deal with the undisclosed principal.

Said v Butt

[1920] 3 KB 497, King's Bench Division

Said wished to attend the first night of a new play to be staged at the Palace Theatre. He knew that the theatre owners would not sell a ticket to him because of an existing dispute with them over allegations Said had made concerning the sale of tickets by the theatre. Said therefore asked his friend Pollock to buy a ticket for him. When Said arrived at the theatre for the performance, Butt (the managing director) refused him admittance. Said sued Butt for wrongfully inducing the owners of the theatre to commit a breach of contract.

> **McCardie J:** ...A first night at the Palace Theatre is, as with other theatres, an event of great importance. The result of a first night may make or mar a play. If the play be good, then word of its success may be spread, not only by the critics, but by members of the audience. The nature and social position and influence of the audience are of obvious importance. First nights have become to a large extent a species of private entertainment given by the theatrical proprietors and management to their friends and acquaintances, and to influential persons, whether critics or otherwise. The boxes, stalls and dress circle are regarded as parts of the theatre which are subject to special allocation by the management. Many tickets for those parts may be given away. The remaining tickets are usually sold by favour only. A first night, therefore, is a special event, with special characteristics. As the plaintiff himself stated in evidence, the management only disposes of first night tickets for the stalls and dress circle to those whom it selects. I may add that it is scarcely likely to choose those who are antagonistic to the management; or who have attacked the character of the theatre officials... The Palace Theatre officials had no idea that they were selling a ticket to an agent of the plaintiff. If they had known it, they would at once have refused to supply a ticket. I find as a fact that the plaintiff used the name of Mr Pollock in order to disguise that he himself was the purchaser; and I also find that the plaintiff well knew that the Palace Theatre would not have sold him personally a ticket for December 23, 1919. I am satisfied that Mr Pollock himself was aware of the above-mentioned circumstances. I may point out that a theatre stands on a wholly different footing from a public inn, or a public service such as a railway. A public inn, for example, is under a common law duty to supply to all who come provided that accommodation exists; and provided also that the guest is of proper character and behaviour. But a theatre stands upon a wholly different footing. It may sell or refuse to sell tickets at its own option. The public cannot compel a theatre to grant admission.

Under these circumstances, the question is whether the plaintiff, as an undisclosed principal of Mr Pollock, can claim that a binding contract existed between the Palace Theatre, Ltd, and himself.

[His Lordship then considered the authorities dealing with the effect of mistake as to the identity of a contracting party and continued:]

In my opinion the defendant can rightly say, upon the special circumstances of this case, that no contract existed on December 23, 1919, upon which the plaintiff could have sued the Palace Theatre. The personal element was here strikingly present. The plaintiff knew that the Palace Theatre would not contract with him for the sale of a seat for December 23. They had expressly refused to do so. He was well aware of their reasons. I hold that by the mere device of utilizing the name and services of Mr Pollock, the plaintiff could not constitute himself a contractor with the Palace Theatre against their knowledge, and contrary to their express refusal. He is disabled from asserting that he was the undisclosed principal of Mr Pollock.

It follows, therefore, that the plaintiff has failed to prove that the defendant caused any breach of a contract between the Palace Theatre, Ltd, and himself.

I realize, however, that the question is one of difficulty . . .

Dyster v Randall & Sons

[1926] Ch 932, Chancery Division

Dyster knowing that Randall and Sons would not sell certain land to him (because they distrusted him), procured his friend Crossley to purchase the land for him without disclosing that he was acting on Dyster's behalf. When Randall and Sons discovered that Crossley had been acting for Dyster, they sought to resist specific performance of the contract of sale of the land on the grounds that they had been deceived by Dyster.

Lawrence J: . . . [I]t is essential to bear in mind that the agreement which the plaintiff seeks to enforce is not one in which any personal qualifications possessed by Crossley formed a material ingredient, but is a simple agreement for sale of land in consideration of a lump sum to be paid on completion. It is an agreement which the defendants would have entered into with any other person. It is well settled that the benefit of such an agreement is assignable and that the assignee can enforce specific performance of it. If Crossley had entered into the agreement on his own behalf (as the defendants believed he had) he could immediately have assigned it to the plaintiff and the defendants would have been bound to convey the plots to the plaintiff. Moreover, as Crossley had not, before signing the agreement, disclosed the fact that he was acting as agent, he was liable under it as principal and the defendants could have compelled him to complete the purchase.

Further, it is to be noted that in this case there was no direct misrepresentation such as there was in *Archer v Stone* ((1898) 78 LT 34). Crossley was not asked by the defendants whether he was buying for the plaintiff and he made no statement to the defendants on the subject. The real question therefore is whether Crossley's silence, in the circumstances, amounted to a misrepresentation which renders the agreement unenforceable in this Court. In my judgment mere non-disclosure as to the person actually entitled to the benefit of a contract for the sale of real estate does not amount to misrepresentation, even though the contracting party knows that, if the disclosure were made, the other party would not enter into the contract; *secus*, if the contract were one in which some personal consideration formed a material ingredient: see *Nash v Dix* ((1898) 78 LT 445) and *Said v Butt* ([1920] 3 KB 497). In *Nash v Dix* North J held that the ostensible purchaser was acting on his own account and not as agent, but it appears to me that the learned judge would have arrived at the same conclusion if the alleged agency had been established. In *Said v Butt* McCardie J relied entirely on the personal consideration which entered into the contract and would obviously have decided otherwise if the personal element had been absent. I therefore hold that the first ground relied upon by the defendants does not afford a good defence to the plaintiffs claim to specific performance.

Greer v Downs Supply Co
[1927] 2 KB 28, Court of Appeal

Downs Supply Co (the respondent) purchased timber from Godwin for £29, it being agreed that the respondent should have the right to set off against the price the sum of £17 owed by Godwin to the respondent. Godwin was in fact acting for an undisclosed principal (the appellant) who sought to intervene on the contract. The Court of Appeal held that the undisclosed principal had no right of action on the contract.

Scrutton LJ: . . . The appellant issued a plaint for goods sold and delivered, and the original orders given by the respondent to Godwin were furnished as particulars of the contract of sale. When a plaintiff claims as an undisclosed principal the question sometimes arises whether the contract was made with the agent for reasons personal to the agent which induced the other party to contract with the agent to the exclusion of his principal or any one else. When the learned judge at the trial found that the respondent knew nothing about the appellant and honestly believed he was contracting with Godwin and when it was proved that he was contracting with Godwin because Godwin was his debtor, there was an end of the case for the appellant at the trial.

[**Bankes** and **Lawrence LJJ** delivered concurring judgments.]

Rolls-Royce Power Engineering plc v Ricardo Consulting Engineers Ltd
[2003] EWHC 2871 (TCC), [2004] 2 All ER (Comm) 129, Technology and Construction Court

Allen Power Engineering Ltd (Allen) was a wholly-owned subsidiary of Rolls-Royce Power Engineering Plc (RRPE). Under the terms of management agreements controlling the relationship between Allen and RRPE, Allen acted as RRPE's agent in respect of a range of activities. Allen entered into a collaborative agreement with Ricardo Consulting Engineers Ltd (Ricardo) for the development of a new engine (the 'definitive design contract'). The contract followed on from an earlier agreement entered into by the same parties (the 'concept design contract'). An issue arose as to whether Allen entered into the definitive design contract as agent for RRPE, as undisclosed principal, so as to enable RRPE to sue Ricardo on that contract.

Judge Seymour QC (sitting as a judge of the High Court):
   49. It was common ground between Mr. Marrin and Mr. Fenwick that the principles of law to be applied in answering Issue 1 in the light of my findings of fact relevant to that issue were those

summarised by Lord Lloyd of Berwick in giving the advice of the Privy Council in *Siu v Eastern Insurance Co. Ltd* [1994] 2 AC 199 at p 207:—

> For present purposes the law can be summarised shortly. (1) An undisclosed principal may sue and be sued on a contract made by an agent on his behalf acting within the scope of his actual authority. (2) In entering into the contract, the agent must intend to act on the principal's behalf. (3) The agent of an undisclosed principal may also sue and be sued on the contract. (4) Any defence which the third party may have against the agent is available against his principal. (5) The terms of the contract may, expressly or by implication, exclude the principal's right to sue, and his liability to be sued. The contract itself or the circumstances surrounding the contract, may show that the agent is the true and only principal.

50. It was in the light of the principles summarised by Lord Lloyd in the passage quoted in the previous paragraph that Mr. Fenwick and Mr. Sutherland identified as relevant to Issue 1 the question 'In entering into the Definitive Design Contract, did Allen intend to act on RRPE's behalf?' I accept as accurate the submissions of Mr. Fenwick and Mr. Sutherland as to the state of the evidence in relation to that question, even following cross-examination. The fact is that there was no evidence that at the time of the making of the Definitive Design Contract anyone at the Allen end gave any thought whatever to the issue on whose behalf Allen was acting in entering into the contract. . . . Thus if it were necessary, in order for a party claiming to be an undisclosed principal to be able to sue on a contract made by his alleged agent, for the agent subjectively at the moment of contracting to have considered that it was acting on behalf of the supposed undisclosed principal, no one within Allen, on the evidence led before me, had that subjective intention in respect of the making of the Definitive Design Contract. That said, at the time the Definitive Design Contract was made the Second Management Agreement was in place. It was a perfectly lawful agreement and there is no obvious reason why effect should not be given to it according to its terms. Thus, if the question were whether, objectively, at the moment at which the Definitive Design Contract was made, arrangements were in place which had the effect that, as between Allen and RRPE, the Definitive Design Contract was to be taken as having been made by Allen on behalf of RRPE, the answer would be affirmative.

51. My attention was drawn by Mr. Marrin, in the context of the question whether the intention of an agent said to have been acting for an undisclosed principal to enter into the relevant contract as agent was to be ascertained objectively or subjectively, to a decision of Colman J, *National Oilwell (UK) Ltd. v. Davy Offshore Ltd* [1993] 2 Lloyd's Rep 582. A major issue in the case, relevant to the alleged counterclaim of the defendant, was whether the plaintiff and the defendant were co-assured. In the context of that issue it was necessary for Colman J to consider and to analyse various previous decisions relating to co-assurance. In the course of that analysis one question upon which the learned judge had to form a view was as to how intention to enter into a policy of insurance on behalf of other parties might be demonstrated. On that point Colman J said, at page 597:

> (3) Evidence as to whether in any particular case the principal assured or other contracting party did have the requisite intention may be provided by the terms of the policy itself by the terms of any contract between the principal assured or other contracting party and the alleged co-assured or by any other admissible material showing what was subjectively intended by the principal assured.

Mr Marrin accepted that the relevant intention was subjective, as Colman J suggested, but submitted that the Second Management Agreement was, in Colman J's terms 'any contract between the [agent, in this case] . . . and the alleged [principal]' which demonstrated the requisite intention subjectively.

52. I agree with Colman J that the relevant intention needs to be proved subjectively. Unless that were so, the second of Lord Lloyd's principles adds nothing to the first, in effect that the contract must have been made by the supposed agent acting within the scope of his actual authority. However, I reject the submission of Mr Marrin that in the present case the terms of the Second Management Agreement provide the requisite proof of the subjective intention of Allen to enter into the Definitive Design Contract on behalf of RRPE. In the passage which I have quoted from his judgment it seems to me that the focus of Colman J's attention was on the need for proof of subjective intention, and he was contemplating that an agreement in appropriate terms made at an appropriate date between the policy holder and the supposed co-assured could provide proof of such subjective intention. That is, in my judgment, a considerable distance from his view having been that, having regard to arrangements previously made which were not present to anyone's mind when the relevant contract were made, the necessary subjective intention was demonstrated. As I have already indicated, in my judgment in the present case Allen has not proved that it consciously intended at the time the Definitive Design Contract was made to enter into it on behalf of RRPE.

53. There is an even more fundamental objection to a finding that Allen entered into the Definitive Design Contract as agent for RRPE and that depends upon the fifth of Lord Lloyd's principles. He himself went on later on page 207 of his speech to say:—

> The present case is concerned with the fifth of the features noted above. The law in that connection was stated by Diplock LJ in *Teheran-Europe Co Ltd v ST Belton (Tractors) Ltd* [1968] 2 QB 545, 555:
>
> > Where an agent has . . . actual authority and enters into a contract with another party intending to do so on behalf of his principal, it matters not whether he discloses to the other party the identity of his principal, or even that he is contracting on behalf of a principal at all, if the other party is willing or leads the agent to believe that he is willing to treat as a party to the contract anyone on whose behalf the agent may have been authorised to contract. In the case of an ordinary commercial contract such willingness of the other party may be assumed unless either the other party manifests his unwillingness or there are other circumstances which should lead the agent to realise that the other party was not so willing.

. . .

56. Mr. Fenwick and Mr. Sutherland submitted, correctly in my judgment, first that the formulation of Diplock LJ approved by the Privy Council in *Siu v Eastern Insurance Co Ltd* did not postulate that unwillingness to treat as a party to the contract anyone on whose behalf the agent may have been authorised to act had to be manifested by means of a term of the contract, and second that the issue was not whether Ricardo would have had an objection to contracting with the party alleged to be the actual undisclosed principal, RRPE, but whether Ricardo was unwilling to take the risk of contracting with anyone whomsoever on whose behalf Allen may have been authorised to act. Their position was, essentially, that the fact that the nature of the services to be provided by Ricardo under the Definitive Design Contract involved employees of Ricardo working in collaboration with employees of Allen in pursuit of a common objective of developing a new engine design for Allen and providing for a transfer of technology made plain that this was not an ordinary commercial contract, but one in respect of which it was inconceivable that the particular identities of the respective contracting parties was not of the greatest significance to the other. A number of witnesses called on behalf of the Claimants spoke of the high reputation of Ricardo and the high regard in which it was held as a result of experience of dealing with it over a number of years. On the Ricardo side Mr. Monaghan indicated that it was important to Ricardo to be committing itself to collaborate not with any party which might appear and claim the benefit of the Definitive

Design Contract, but with Allen. At paragraph 32 of his witness statement, a passage as to which he was not cross-examined, he said:

> I have been asked whether it was of any significance to Ricardo that it was contracting with WHA rather than anyone else. The answer is that this was of significance. Both the Concept and the Definitive Design contracts were for a collaborative project, in which Ricardo were to work closely with (and to train) the client throughout these design development stages. We agreed to do this (and prepared our budget) on the basis that it was WHA's personnel, at WHA's premises, who were the client. WHA were well known to us and we thought that the intended collaboration was workable on the terms set out in the proposal documents, and was likely to be worthwhile (in the sense that the project was likely to be profitable to Ricardo both financially and in terms of adding to Ricardo's profile and portfolio). Obviously the same would not necessarily be the case with any and every other engineering firm or company.

I accept that evidence.

57. Moreover, the conclusion of the Definitive Design Contract obviously has to be viewed in the context that it was the successor to and the logical continuation of the work done, apparently successfully, under the Concept Design Contract. It thus was intended to build upon work already done in collaboration between identified individuals who had no doubt developed satisfactory personal relationships in the course of the earlier work. The background of the earlier successful work and the satisfactory working relationships established during the course of it was, as it seems to me, essential to the decision of Ricardo to agree to a continuation. Had the earlier work been fraught with difficulties at a practical level it is impossible sensibly to contemplate that the Definitive Design Contract would have been made. Consequently in my judgment the Definitive Design Contract was manifestly one which was not an ordinary commercial contract and, moreover, was one which was made in circumstances such that, had anyone at Allen given the matter any attention, they would have realised that Ricardo was not willing to, contract with anyone other than Allen.

58. In the result I find that the answer to Issue 1 as formulated is that Allen did not enter into the Definitive Design Contract as agent for RRPE as undisclosed principal so as to enable RRPE to sue Ricardo on the Definitive Design Contract or Allen to recover damages quantified by reference to the loss allegedly sustained by RRPE....

NOTES

1. The non-assignable nature of a contract normally provides evidence that the parties intended to exclude the intervention of an undisclosed principal, but this is not an absolute rule. In the somewhat unusual case of *Siu Yin Kwan v Eastern Insurance Co Ltd* [1994] 2 AC 199, shipping agents insured in their own name the employers of the crew of a ship, the *Osprey*, against liability. The insurers had dealt with the shipping agents before and knew that they did not own the ship, but it was just about conceivable that they might have employed the crew. (This would have been rare as the owners, not the shipping agents, would have been expected to employ the crew, but the trial judge found that he could not be satisfied that the insurers knew that the agents were not the employers of the crew and this explains why the case was treated as one involving an undisclosed principal and not, as would have been more usual in a case such as this, as one of a disclosed but unnamed principal.) The actual employers were the owners of the ship, but they were not mentioned in the proposal form or the policy. Owing to the negligence of the owners, the *Osprey* sank in a typhoon with the loss of two crew members. As the owners were insolvent, the relatives of the dead crew members sued the insurers under the Third Parties (Rights against Insurers) Ordinance of Hong Kong (the UK has similar legislation: see below, p 1090). The success of that action depended on whether the owners could themselves have enforced the policy. The Privy Council held that the owners would have been able to intervene on the contract of insurance as undisclosed principals and that the relatives were entitled to recover against the insurers. Although a non-marine insurance contract (such as an employer's liability policy) is personal in the sense that it is not assignable, the Privy Council held that this did not prevent the intervention of the owners as undisclosed principals in this case because the trial judge had found as a fact that the identity of the actual employer was a matter of indifference to the insurer and not material to the risk. More generally, the Board said (*obiter*) that a contract of insurance was not a personal contract in the sense of a contract to paint a portrait and that an undisclosed principal could intervene on such a contract so long as disclosures relevant to the risk had been made. The case is usefully noted by A Tettenborn [1994] CLJ 223 and also by J Halladay [1994] LMCLQ 174. See further, F Reynolds, 'Some Agency Problems in Insurance Law' in FD Rose (ed), *Consensus Ad Idem* (1996), especially pp 89–95.

2.   Whether the undisclosed principal will be prohibited from intervening in cases where the third party would not have dealt with the principal if he had known that the agent was acting for him is a moot point. *Said v Butt* certainly appears to support the exclusion of the undisclosed principal doctrine in these circumstances. In that case there was no express term of the contract excluding the principal's intervention and the contract itself could not be described as a personal contract, unless a ticket for a first night performance is regarded as non-assignable (and even then, as we have just seen, this may not be decisive of the issue). It is submitted that it is best to regard *Said v Butt* as wrongly decided. This task is made somewhat easier by reason of the fact that McCardie J's judgment is based on the erroneous premise that the contract was made between the third party and the undisclosed principal (the correct analysis is that the undisclosed principal intervenes in a contract originally made between the third party and the agent: *Welsh Development Agency v Export Finance Co Ltd* [1992] BCLC 148 at 173, 182, CA; see also AL Goodhart and CJ Hamson [1932] CLJ 320 at 346–352; *Bowstead and Reynolds*, para 8–069; cf Tan Cheng-Han (2004) 120 LQR 480 at 486–496, who argues that the contract is with the undisclosed principal). Dicta in *Dyster v Randall and Sons* that personality may prevent the undisclosed principal's intervention if it is a 'material ingredient' or 'strikingly present', to use McCardie J's words in *Said v Butt*, should be rejected in so far as they purport to go beyond the circumstances prohibiting intervention as set out under note 1 above (see Goodhart and Hamson, op cit, pp 349–352). Allowing an additional exception to the undisclosed principal doctrine merely heaps a further anomaly upon an anomaly (ie the doctrine itself). Furthermore, whatever the dicta in *Dyster v Randall and Sons*, the result was clear: the mere fact that the third party would not have dealt with the undisclosed principal was not enough to prevent the principal's intervention.

However, for a strong defence of *Said v Butt*, see E Peel, *Treitel's Law of Contract* (14th edn, 2015), para 16–060, where it is argued that 'an undisclosed principal should not be allowed to intervene if he knows that the third party does not want to deal with him'; Glanville Williams (1945) 23 Can Bar Rev 380 at 406–412 submits that 'ordinary ideas of fair dealing' lie at the heart of the decision. Professor Reynolds had said that 'this is one of the comparatively few areas in common law where a principle of good faith might provide reasoning not otherwise available' (A Burrows (ed), *English Private Law* (2nd edn, 2007), para 9.76). English law does not recognise a general principle of good faith (see above, pp 38 ff).

3.   The problem raised by *Said v Butt* will be avoided if it can be shown that the person the third party dealt with was acting as principal and not agent. In *Nash v Dix* (1898) 78 LT 445, the defendants did not wish to sell a Congregational chapel to a committee of Roman Catholics. Instead they sold the chapel to the plaintiff but later refused to complete the transaction when they discovered the plaintiff was going to on-sell it to the Roman Catholic Committee. North J ordered specific performance of the contract of sale on the grounds that the plaintiff was not an agent of the committee but was purchasing the chapel for himself with a view to resale at a profit.

4.   If the contract between the agent and the third party was induced by the agent's misrepresentation, the principal cannot enforce it against the third party: *Archer v Stone* (1898) 78 LT 34 (third party asked agent if he was acting for S and he untruthfully denied that he was).

QUESTIONS

1.   Why is *Siu Yin Kwan v Eastern Insurance Co Ltd* such an unusual case?

2.   What can an insurer do to prevent the intervention of an undisclosed principal on a contract of insurance?

3.   If Said had gone to the Palace Theatre to buy a ticket saying it was for a friend, could he have later revealed that his friend was in fact himself? See *The Remco* [1984] 2 Lloyd's Rep 205, above, p 193.

4.   Thelma sells her whole crop of strawberries to Agatha. Unknown to Thelma, Agatha is acting as agent for Louise, who Thelma blames for the breakdown of her marriage and has sworn she would never do business with. Before payment, Agatha becomes insolvent and Thelma discovers that Louise is the principal behind her. Thelma now wishes to hold Louise liable for the price. Can Louise successfully resist Thelma's claim on grounds of personality? Contrast Munday, paras 10.57–10.58, and Fridman, pp 263–264, with *Bowstead and Reynolds*, para 8–079.

(c) Deeds, bills of exchange, and promissory notes

An undisclosed principal cannot sue or be sued on a deed *inter partes*, nor can he be made liable on any negotiable instrument (see above, p 170).

(iii) *Particular aspects of the relationship between undisclosed principal and third party*

The rights and liabilities of the undisclosed principal and third party may be affected by the agent in a number of ways.

(a) Merger and election

Clarkson Booker Ltd v Andjel
[1964] 2 QB 775, Court of Appeal

Andjel purchased airline tickets on credit from Clarkson Booker Ltd (the plaintiffs), who were travel agents. In fact, Andjel was acting for an undisclosed principal, Peters & Milner

Ltd (P & M). Subsequently, on being informed that Andjel was acting for P & M, the plaintiffs wrote to both principal and agent threatening proceedings unless the amount due was paid. Payment was not made and the plaintiffs started proceedings against P & M. However, the plaintiffs were then informed that P & M were insolvent and about to be put into liquidation. The plaintiffs accordingly did not proceed further with their action against the principal, P & M, but started proceedings against the agent, Andjel. Andjel resisted the claim on the ground that the plaintiffs had elected to hold the principal exclusively liable and, therefore, were precluded from proceeding against him, the agent. The county court judge gave judgment for the plaintiffs. Andjel's appeal from that decision was dismissed by the Court of Appeal.

Willmer LJ: . . . [T]he point is taken for the defendant that the plaintiffs, having elected to start proceedings against Peters & Milner Ltd, are now debarred from asserting their claim against the defendant. The contention on behalf of the defendant is that this is a case of true election in that, with full knowledge of the facts, the plaintiffs deliberately and unequivocally chose to pursue their right against the principals, which was a right inconsistent with their right against the defendant as agent. Reliance is placed on a statement contained in *Powell on Agency*, 2nd edn (1961), p 270, where the following is put forward as proposition (v): 'T (a third party) starts proceedings against P (the principal) or A (the agent). The initiation of proceedings against P or A is strong evidence of election, though not necessarily conclusive. That is so whether T issues a writ or files proof of his debt in bankruptcy proceedings.' This proposition is not accepted by the plaintiffs as a correct statement of the law. It is submitted on their behalf that a plaintiff is barred only if he has sued one or other (ie, principal or agent) to judgment. It is conceded that he cannot then proceed against the other. But that, it is said, is not a true case of election; the remedy is barred because the cause of action has merged in the judgment. It is contended that nothing short of judgment against the principal is sufficient to bar the plaintiffs' remedy against the agent. In the present case it is said that there has been nothing amounting either in law or in fact to an election, so as to preclude the present action against the defendant.

The judge, in dealing with this aspect of the case, quoted at some length from the speech of Lord Blackburn in *Scarf v Jardine* ((1882) 7 App Cas 345 at 354–362). I need not quote again the passage from Lord Blackburn. Suffice it to say that he expressed the view that there could be no more unequivocal act than instituting proceedings against one of two possible debtors; this, he thought, amounted to a final election to treat that debtor as liable so as to preclude the plaintiff thereafter from suing the other debtor . . .

I cannot, of course, do other than attach the greatest possible weight to the decision of the House of Lords in *Scarf v Jardine*, particularly the reasoning of Lord Blackburn. But I do not understand him to mean that where proceedings have once been commenced against one of two possible debtors a plaintiff is necessarily precluded as a matter of law from subsequently taking proceedings against the other. Indeed, Mr Hamilton freely conceded that there must be some cases at least where the mere issue of a writ could not be held to amount to a binding election—for instance, where it is issued for the purpose of preventing limitation time from running out. Similarly, it has been held that an abortive writ issued against a company not yet incorporated at the time when the order for the plaintiffs' services was given did not amount to a binding election so as to preclude a subsequent action against the agents through whom the order was given: see *Longman v Hill* ((1891) 7 TLR 639). But even allowing for such exceptional cases it is clear that the institution of proceedings against either agent or principal is at least strong evidence of an election such as, if not rebutted, will preclude subsequent proceedings against the other. In other words, it raises a *prima facie* case of election . . .

Having regard to those authorities, I think that the judge in the present case was plainly right in regarding the question before him as one of fact. But it has been argued that he came to a wrong conclusion on the facts. Since the relevant evidence is all contained in the correspondence, we have been invited to review his findings and to draw our own inferences from the correspondence. In a case such as the present we are clearly entitled to take this course, for we are in as good a position to draw inferences as was the judge.

In the light of the authorities to which I have referred, I approach the question to be decided on the basis that the institution of proceedings against Peters & Milner Ltd affords at least *prima facie* evidence of an election on the part of the plaintiffs to look only to them for payment of their debt. The question is whether there is any sufficient evidence to rebut the *prima facie* inference that arises from the institution of those proceedings.

In order to constitute an election which will bar the present proceedings against the defendant, the decision to sue Peters & Milner Ltd must, in the first place, be shown to have been taken with full knowledge of all the relevant facts. In the circumstances of this case I feel no difficulty on this point, for it cannot be suggested that when the plaintiffs made their decision to sue Peters & Milner Ltd they were in any way ignorant of their rights against the defendant.

But, secondly, it must be shown that the decision to institute proceedings against Peters & Milner Ltd was a truly unequivocal act if it is to preclude the plaintiffs from subsequently suing the defendant. This, I think, involves looking closely at the context in which the decision was taken, for any conclusion must be based on a review of all the relevant circumstances. One highly relevant circumstance is the fact that it was the defendant to whom the plaintiffs gave credit, as they had done over previous transactions. The correspondence shows that down to the letters of July 26 the plaintiffs throughout were looking to the defendant for payment of their debt, ie, to the person to whom they had given credit, although they also adumbrated a possible claim against Peters & Milner Ltd. On July 26, as I have already stated, they caused letters to be written to both the defendant and Peters & Milner Ltd, threatening proceedings against each. Clearly, up to that time there was no election to proceed only against the latter.

The whole case for the defendant rests on the fact that on August 8, having taken instructions, the plaintiffs' solicitors wrote to Peters & Milner Ltd announcing their intention 'to obtain judgment' against them. It is true that they did not at that time write any similar letter to the defendant, but they did not then or at any other time ever withdraw their threat to take proceedings against him. There is not, and could not be, any suggestion that the defendant was in any way prejudiced by the course which the plaintiffs took, or that he was in any sense lulled into a false sense of security.

Had the plaintiffs carried out their threat to obtain judgment against Peters & Milner Ltd they would, of course, have been precluded from subsequently taking proceedings against the defendant, for their cause of action would then have been merged in the judgment obtained against Peters & Milner Ltd. But in fact the plaintiffs took no step against Peters & Milner Ltd beyond the issue and service of the writ. Upon being informed of the proposal to put the company into liquidation they took no further action whatsoever against that company. They did not, for instance (as in *Scarf v Jardine* and other cases cited), seek to prove in the liquidation; instead they proceeded to give effect forthwith to their already announced, and never withdrawn, threat to sue the defendant.

On the whole, though I regard the case as being very near the borderline, I find myself unable to disagree with the conclusion arrived at by the judge. I do not think that the plaintiffs, by the mere institution of proceedings against Peters & Milner Ltd, made such an unequivocal election as to debar them from taking the present proceedings against the defendant.

I would accordingly dismiss the appeal.

[**Davies LJ** concurred.]

Russell LJ: The defendant having contracted as agent for an undisclosed principal, the plaintiffs were entitled to enforce the contract either against the defendant on the footing that he was contracting and liable as principal, or against the principal on the footing that the defendant was not liable, being merely an agent. The plaintiffs could not enforce the contract against both. Their right against the defendant and their right against the principal were inconsistent rights. At some stage the plaintiffs had to elect to avail themselves of one of those inconsistent rights and abandon the other. The question is whether the correct conclusion from the facts of this case is that, prior to the issue of their writ against the defendant, the plaintiffs had so elected. If they had, the election crystallised their rights, and they could not sue the defendant. The judge concluded that they had not so elected.

What were the facts? . . .

Was the judge on those facts wrong in concluding that the plaintiffs had not elected to treat the principal as liable in exoneration of the defendant?

It was reluctantly (although rightly) accepted by counsel for the defendant that the service of a writ against the principal *per se* does not show an election. Statements by Lord Blackburn in [*Scarf v Jardine* (1882) 7 App Cas 345 at 360] cannot be taken as establishing that position in law. It would be in some respects convenient if it were so, as tending to certainty in the application of the law, but even that would not resolve the problems that would arise in the case of a single writ against the principal and agent claiming in the alternative, or in the case of simultaneous or substantially simultaneous writs. The position is that in every case the external acts of the plaintiff must lead to the conclusion, as a matter of fact, that the plaintiff has settled to a choice involving abandonment of his option to enforce his right against one party. I have no doubt that in a given case this may be shown without his proceeding to the length of obtaining a judgment; indeed, if judgment is obtained against either principal or agent, this is more than election, though frequently referred to as election: the judgment supersedes the contractual right against either, and if obtained against the agent precludes action against the principal even if the plaintiff was ignorant of his existence and therefore unable to elect. Further, I have no doubt that, in assessing the facts of a particular case in pursuit of a conclusion on the question of election, the fact of the service of a writ against one and not against the other points significantly towards a decision to exonerate the other. A letter may assert a claim and demand satisfaction, but it is not capable of bearing fruit, even if wholly ignored by the recipient, whereas service of a writ is the first step in actual enforcement of the claim, to be ignored by the recipient at his peril. On the other hand, it is in terms a statement that the plaintiff makes a claim against the defendant. As I have said, it does not necessarily involve abandonment of a similar alternative claim against another possible defendant. It would not do so if there were a simultaneous writ against the other. Nor would it do so if the plaintiff were simultaneously expressly informing the other that the alternative claim was not abandoned. Nor would it do so if simultaneously the plaintiff was maintaining vis-a-vis the other the attitude that he might be looked to for liability on the contract.

What of the present case? It is said for the defendant that the letters of July 26 maintained the alternative claim against each, and that by contrast the writ against one demonstrated the exoneration of the other as a matter of election. I am not on the whole persuaded by this. I do not think that the letter to the principal's solicitors (as such) of August 3 can really be regarded as any less a determination to enforce the right against the principal than the subsequent issue and service of the writ on the principal, but that letter was contemporaneous with correspondence which demonstrates a retention of the right to claim against the defendant. In those circumstances, I am not able to conclude that the facts demonstrate that the plaintiffs finally elected to rely on the liability of the principal under the contract in exoneration of the agent. Consequently, I agree that this appeal fails.

NOTES

1. In cases of undisclosed agency the third party is able to sue both the agent on the contract made with him and also the principal because of the special rule of law operating in this situation. 'But because the third party has only purported to make one contract with one person, to enter into a single obligation, these two rights of action are commonly said to be alternative': FMB Reynolds (1970) 86 LQR 317 at 320.

2. There is clear authority that the doctrine of merger applies to cases of undisclosed agency when the third party proceeds to judgment against the principal or the agent (*Priestly v Fernie* (1865) 3 H & C 977; *Kendall v Hamilton* (1879) 4 App Cas 504 at 514–515, per Lord Cairns LC). For further consideration of the doctrine of merger, see above, p 175.

3. It is clear from *Clarkson Booker v Andjel* that in cases of undisclosed agency there can be election by means of an unequivocal act short of obtaining judgment against the principal or the agent. What constitutes an election is a question of fact to be decided in the circumstances of the case. Commencing legal proceedings against one party provides prima facie evidence of election, but it is not conclusive (as shown by *Clarkson Booker v Andjel*; applied in *Pyxis Special Shipping Co Ltd v Dritsas & Kaglis Bros Ltd, The Scaplake* [1978] 2 Lloyd's Rep 380; cf *Cyril Lord Carpet Sales Ltd v Browne* (1966) 111 Sol Jo 51, where the Court of Appeal held the commencement of proceedings against the agent was an election barring action against the principal). Debiting one party has also been held to provide evidence of election (*Addison v Gandassequi* (1812) 4 Taunt 574; cf *Thomson v Davenport* (1829) 9 B & C 78).

4. There is no doubt that in most cases where election is invoked, the plea fails. In fact Reynolds submits that in cases of undisclosed agency where the plea has succeeded, and was based on an act short of judgment, the doctrine of estoppel, and not election, may provide the real explanation for those decisions (see (1970) 86 LQR 318 at 323–328). He submits that:

> . . . it is open to the courts to make articulate the proposition that, short of a judgment, a plaintiff will only lose his right against one party by a representation of fact that the contract is with the other or has been performed by the other, or by a representation of intention not to enforce his right against that one, in either case acted on by that party in such a way that it would be detrimental to him if the plaintiff changed his mind. The clearest case of such detriment would occur when the representation or conduct induced the principal to settle with the agent, but it may be that other cases could arise.

See further his commentary to art 82 of *Bowstead and Reynolds*, and see E Peel, *Treitel's Law of Contract* (14th edn, 2015), para 16–076, who also supports the estoppel theory. A New Zealand judge has stated that 'the doctrine of election is frequently misnamed. Rather, it is to be regarded as being an instance of waiver (or estoppel or release)': *LC Fowler & Sons Ltd v St Stephens College Board of Governors* [1991] 3 NZLR 304 at 308, per Thomas J (noted approvingly by F Reynolds [1994] JBL 149).

(b) Set-off and other defences available against the agent

As a general rule, when an undisclosed principal intervenes on his agent's contract the third party may set up against him any defences, including personal set-off of debts, which would be available to him against the agent provided that those defences accrued before the third party had notice of the principal's existence (*Browning v Provincial Insurance Co of Canada*

(1873) LR 5 PC 263 at 272–273; *Rabone v Williams* (1785) 7 Term Rep 360n). However, as the next case illustrates, the third party's rights of set-off appear to be subject to an important restriction.

Cooke & Sons v Eshelby

(1887) 12 App Cas 271, House of Lords

Livesey & Co, a firm of brokers, who were in fact acting on behalf of an undisclosed principal, sold cotton to Cooke & Sons (the appellants). The price not being paid, Eshelby (the respondent), the trustee in bankruptcy of the undisclosed principal, claimed it from Cooke & Sons. Cooke & Sons attempted to set off against the price a debt owed to them by Livesey & Co. Cooke & Sons knew that Livesey & Co were in the habit of dealing both for principals and on their own account but at the time of the sale in question they had no belief whether Livesey & Co were acting as agents or not. Affirming the decision of the Court of Appeal, the House of Lords held that there was no right of set-off.

> **Lord Halsbury LC:** My Lords, in this case a merchant in Liverpool effected two sales through his brokers. The brokers effected the sales in their own names. The appellants, the merchants with whom these contracts were made, knew the brokers to be brokers, and that it was their practice to sell in their own names in transactions in which they were acting only as brokers. They also knew that the brokers were in the habit of buying and selling for themselves. The appellants with commendable candour admit that they are unable to say that they believed the brokers to be principals; they knew they might be either one or the other; they say that they dealt with the brokers as principals, but at the same time they admit that they had no belief one way or the other whether they were dealing with principals or brokers.
>
> It appears to me that the principle upon which this case must be decided has been so long established that in such a state of facts as I have recited the legal result cannot be doubtful. The ground upon which all these cases have been decided is that the agent has been permitted by the principal to hold himself out as the principal, and that the person dealing with the agent has believed that the agent was the principal, and has acted on that belief. With reference to both those propositions, namely, first, the permission of the real principal to the agent to assume his character, and with reference to the fact whether those dealing with the supposed principal have in fact acted upon the belief induced by the real principal's conduct, various difficult questions of fact have from time to time arisen; but I do not believe that any doubt has ever been thrown upon the law as decided by a great variety of judges for something more than a century. The cases are all collected in the notes to *George v Clagett* ((1797) 7 Term Rep 359).
>
> In *Baring v Corrie* ((1818) 2 B & Ald 137), in 1818, Lord Tenterden had before him a very similar case to that which is now before your Lordships, and although in that case the Court had to infer what we have here proved by the candid admission of the party, the principle upon which the case was decided is precisely that which appears to me to govern the case now before your Lordships. Lord Tenterden says of the persons who were in that case insisting that they had a right to treat the brokers as principals: 'They knew that Coles & Co acted both as brokers and merchants, and if they meant to deal with them as merchants, and to derive a benefit from so dealing with them, they ought to have inquired whether in this transaction they acted as brokers or not; but they made no inquiry.' And Bayley J says: 'When Coles & Co stood at least in an equivocal situation, the defendants ought in common honesty, if they bought the goods with a view to cover their own debt, to have asked in what character they sold the goods in question. I therefore cannot think

that the defendants believed, when they bought the goods, that Coles & Co sold them on their own account. And if so, they can have no defence to the present action.'

I am therefore of opinion that the judgment of the Court of Appeal was right. The selling in his own name by a broker is only one fact, and by no means a conclusive fact, from which, in the absence of other circumstances, it might be inferred that he was selling his own goods. Upon the facts proved or admitted in this case the fact of selling in the broker's name was neither calculated to induce nor did in fact induce that belief.

Lord Watson: . . . According to the practice of the Liverpool cotton market with which the appellants were familiar, brokers in the position of Livesey Sons & Co buy and sell both for themselves and for principals; and in the latter case they transact, sometimes in their own name without disclosing their agency, and at other times in the name of their principal. In their answer to an interrogation by the plaintiff touching their belief that Livesey Sons & Co were acting on behalf of principals in the two transactions in question, the appellants say: 'We had no belief upon the subject. We dealt with Livesey Sons & Co as principals, not knowing whether they were acting as brokers on behalf of principals or on their own account as the principals.'

That is a very candid statement, but I do not think any other answer could have been honestly made by persons who, at the time of the transactions, were cognisant of the practice followed by members of the Liverpool Cotton Association. A sale by a broker in his own name to persons having that knowledge, does not convey to them an assurance that he is selling on his own account; on the contrary it is equivalent to an express intimation that the cotton is either his own property or the property of a principal who has employed him as an agent to sell. A purchaser who is content to buy on these terms cannot, when the real principal comes forward, allege that the broker sold the cotton as his own. If the intending purchaser desires to deal with the broker as a principal and not as an agent in order to secure a right to set-off, he is put upon his inquiry. Should the broker refuse to state whether he is acting for himself or for a principal, the buyer may decline to enter into the transaction. If he chooses to purchase without inquiry, or notwithstanding the broker's refusal to give information, he does so with notice that there may be a principal for whom the broker is acting as agent; and should that ultimately prove to be the fact, he has, in my opinion, no right to set off his indebtedness to the principal against debts owing to him by the agent.

It was argued for the appellants, that in all cases where a broker, having authority to that effect, sells in his own name for an undisclosed principal, the purchaser, at the time when the principal is disclosed, is entitled to be placed in the same position as if the agent had contracted on his own account. That was said to be the rule established by *George v Clagett* ((1797) 7 Term Rep 359), *Sims v Bond* ((1833) 5 B & Ad 389) and subsequent cases. It is clear that Livesey Sons & Co were not mere brokers or middlemen, but were agents within the meaning of these authorities, and if the argument of the appellants were well founded they would be entitled to prevail in this appeal, because in that case their right of set-off had arisen before July 20, 1883, when they first had notice that Maximos was the principal.

I do not think it necessary to enter into a minute examination of the authorities, which were fully discussed in the arguments addressed to us. The case of *George v Clagett* ((1797) 7 Term Rep 359) has been commented upon and its principles explained in many subsequent decisions, and notably in *Baring v Corrie* ((1818) 2 B & Ald 137), *Semenza v Brinsley* ((1865) 18 CBNS 467), and *Borries v Imperial Ottoman Bank* ((1873) LR 9 CP 38). These decisions appear to me to establish conclusively that, in order to sustain the defence pleaded by the appellants, it is not enough to shew that the agent sold in his own name. It must be shewn that he sold the goods as his own, or, in other words, that the circumstances attending the sale were calculated to induce, and did induce, in the mind of the purchaser a reasonable belief that the agent was selling on his own account and not for an undisclosed principal; and it must also be shewn that the agent was enabled to appear as the real contracting party by the conduct, or by the authority, express or implied, of the principal. The rule thus explained is intelligible and just; and I agree with Bowen LJ that it rests upon the doctrine of estoppel. It would be inconsistent with fair dealing that a latent principal should by his own act or omission lead a purchaser to rely upon a right of set-off against the agent as the real seller, and should nevertheless be permitted to intervene and deprive the purchaser of that right at the very time when it had become necessary for his protection.

Lord Fitzgerald: I concur with my noble and learned friend [Lord Watson] in adopting at once the decision and the reasons of the Court of Appeal. I have, however, some hesitation in accepting the view that the decisions rest on the doctrine of estoppel. Estoppel *in pais* involves considerations not necessarily applicable to the case before us. There is some danger in professing to state the principle on which a line of decisions rests, and it seems to me to be sufficient to say in the present case that Maximos did not in any way wilfully or otherwise mislead the defendants (Cooke & Sons) or induce them to believe that Livesey & Co were the owners of the goods or authorized to sell them as their own, or practice any imposition on them. The defendants were not in any way misled.

NOTES

1.   Although it is arguable that *Cooke & Sons v Eshelby* might really be a case of an unnamed, as opposed to an undisclosed, principal (because the third party knew there was a risk that the brokers might be acting for a principal), it is generally treated as an undisclosed principal case: see FMB Reynolds (1983) 36 CLP 119 at 126 and 133.

2.   In *Cooke & Sons v Eshelby* the House of Lords held that an undisclosed principal would not be bound by the third party's rights of set-off against the agent unless the principal had misled the third party by allowing the agent to appear as the principal. This estoppel approach may be criticised on two grounds. First, it is difficult to see how the third party can rely on the representation of a person of whose existence he is unaware. Secondly, it could be said that in all cases of undisclosed agency the agent is held out to be the principal.

3.   A preferable approach would be to allow the third party a right of set-off in all cases where he lacks notice of the principal's existence. The undisclosed principal would then intervene on his agent's contract subject to the third party's rights of set-off in much the same way as the assignee of a chose in action takes subject to equities. But what of the case where an undisclosed principal instructs his agent to contract in the principal's name and yet the agent disobeys that instruction and contracts in his own name? On the estoppel theory the principal would not be bound by set-off, whereas under this alternative approach he would be bound. This result, however, may not be as unjust as it may at first appear. It is not the third party's fault that the agent disobeys his instructions, whereas it could be argued that by choosing to deal through an agent the principal takes the risk that the agent may exceed his authority and act as though he is the principal: R Powell, *The Law of Agency* (2nd edn, 1961), p 177; SR Derham [1985] CLJ 384 at 399.

4.   A key element of both the estoppel and subject-to-equities approaches to set-off is that the third party must not have notice of the existence of a principal at the time he contracted with the agent, or at the time that the debt available for setting off accrued if that was later. On the estoppel approach, notice would mean that the third party's prejudice would not have been caused by the principal's conduct. On the subject-to-equities approach, notice would mean that there would not be an equity in favour of the third party. But what is meant by

'notice'? Is it restricted to actual notice? In *Cooke & Sons v Eshelby* Lord Watson referred to the third party's 'reasonable belief that the agent was selling on his own account and not for an undisclosed principal'. Furthermore, there appears to be common law support for the view that the third party will be put on notice of the principal's existence if the circumstances are such as to put the third party on inquiry as to the status of the agent and he fails to make an inquiry (see Derham, op cit, pp 390–395 and the cases cited therein). This common law duty of inquiry should not be confused with the separate equitable doctrine of constructive notice which has no place in commercial transactions (see, eg, *Greer v Downs Supply Co* [1927] 2 KB 28; Derham, op cit, p 391: although the statement in the text should be read in conjunction with that appearing above at p 208. On this basis, even if the House of Lords had applied the subject-to-equities approach to set-off in *Cooke & Sons v Eshelby*, the third party (Cooke & Sons) would probably still have been denied a right of set-off. Cooke & Sons were aware of the risk that the brokers could have been acting for a principal, yet they failed to inquire as to what was the true position.

For defences available to the principal against an action brought by the third party, see above, p 217.

QUESTION

Was it really necessary for the Court of Appeal to consider the personal nature of the contract in *Greer v Downs Supply Co* (above, p 208), or could the court have simply held the third party to have a right of set-off against the undisclosed principal?

(c) Settlement with the agent

Armstrong v Stokes
(1872) LR 7 QB 598, Court of Queen's Bench

R & Co were commission merchants who sometimes acted for themselves and sometimes as agents for others. A was a merchant who had dealings with R & Co on a number of occasions but had never inquired whether R & Co were acting for themselves or on behalf of others. On one occasion A sold shirts on credit to R & Co when R & Co were acting as agents for S. A delivered the shirts to R & Co who sent them to S. S paid R & Co but R & Co did not pay A. On discovering that R & Co were acting as agents for S, A sued S for the price. The Court of Queen's Bench held that the action failed.

Blackburn J (delivering the judgment of the court): . . . [In *Heald v Kenworthy* (1855) 10 Exch 739 at 745] Parke B lays down generally that 'if a person orders an agent to make a purchase for him, he is bound to see that the agent pays the debt; and giving the agent money for that purpose does not amount to payment, unless the agent pays it accordingly.' After commenting on several of the cases already referred to, he concludes: 'I think that there is no authority for saying that a payment made to the agent precludes the seller from recovering from the principal, unless it appears that he has induced the principal to believe that a settlement has been made with the agent.' He states this as generally true wherever a principal has allowed himself to be made a party to a contract, and makes no exception as to the case where the other side made the contract with the agent believing him to be principal, and continued in such belief till after the payment was made. He certainly does not in terms say that there is no qualification of the principle he lays down when applicable to such a case; but recollecting how careful Parke B always was to lay down what he thought to be the law fully and with accuracy, we think the counsel for the plaintiff were justified in arguing that Parke B thought the exception did not exist. And this is, in our opinion, a weighty authority in favour of the plaintiff's contention, more especially as Pollock CB assents in his judgment to the remark thrown out by Parke B during the argument, and afterwards more elaborately stated by him in his judgment. And Alderson B, in his judgment, appears entirely to assent to the judgment of Parke B.

We think that we could not, without straining the evidence, hold in this case that the plaintiff had induced the defendants to believe that he (the plaintiff) had settled with J & O Ryder at the time when the defendants paid them.

This makes it necessary to determine whether we agree in what we think was the opinion of Parke B, acquiesced in by Pollock CB and Alderson B.

We think that, if the rigid rule thus laid down were to be applied to those who were only discovered to be principals after they had fairly paid the price to those whom the vendor believed to be the principals, and to whom alone the vendor gave credit, it would produce intolerable hardship. It may be said, perhaps truly, this is the consequence of that which might originally have been a mistake, in allowing the vendor to have recourse at all against one to whom he never gave credit, and that we ought not to establish an illogical exception in order to cure a fault in a rule. But we find an exception (more or less extensively expressed) always mentioned in the very cases that lay down the rule; and without deciding anything as to the case of a broker, who avowedly acts for a principal (though not necessarily named), and confining ourselves to the present case, which is one in which, to borrow Lord Tenterden's phrase in *Thomson v Davenport* ((1829) 9 B & C 78 at 86), the plaintiff sold the goods to Ryder & Co, 'supposing at the time of the contract he was dealing with a principal,' we think such an exception is established.

We wish to be understood as expressing no opinion as to what would have been the effect of the state of the accounts between the parties if J & O Ryder had been indebted to the defendants on a separate account, so as to give rise to a set-off or mutual credit between them. We confine our decision to the case where the defendants, after the contract was made, and in consequence of it, *bona fide* and without moral blame, paid J & O Ryder at a time when the plaintiff still gave credit to J & O Ryder, and knew of no one else. We think that after that it was too late for the plaintiff to come upon the defendants.

On this ground we make the rule absolute to enter the verdict for the defendants.

NOTES

1.   Contrast *Armstrong v Stokes* with *Irvine & Co v Watson & Sons* (1880) 5 QBD 414, above at p 171. In *Irvine & Co v Watson & Sons* the principal was disclosed, whereas in *Armstrong v Stokes* the principal was undisclosed. Unlike the case of a disclosed principal, the general rule for an undisclosed principal appears to be that he can avoid liability to the third party if he settles with his own agent. When the principal is disclosed he can only avoid such liability if the third party induced him to settle with the agent. However, if the existence of the principal is unknown to the third party it is difficult to see how he can have induced the principal to settle with the agent.

2.   *Armstrong v Stokes* has been subjected to considerable criticism, for example see *Irvine & Co v Watson*, above at p 172, per Bramwell LJ. In fact, it could be said to be logically indefensible, and most unlikely to be followed by the courts today (see Munday, para 10.72, and Fridman, p 267: '*Armstrong v Stokes* . . . is not a good authority today'). Reynolds, however, has been less critical of the rule that an undisclosed principal will be discharged from liability to the third party if he settles with the agent. In (1983) 36 CLP 119 at 134, he submits that:

> ...for a true undisclosed principal situation this might seem again a reasonable rule. The principal has utilised the services of an intermediary who in the transaction into which he has entered has raised no expectation of the accountability of a principal. Surely the principal's duty is performed by keeping the intermediary in funds: if the third party loses, it is because of his misplaced trust in the intermediary. There is no need to make the principal the insurer.

Treitel, with some justice, submits that the argument advanced by Reynolds proves too much. For as Peel (and Treitel before him) notes: 'whenever an undisclosed principal is sued the third party gets a windfall of this kind' (E Peel, *Treitel's Law of Contract* (14th edn, 2015), para 16–065).

When the third party pays or settles with an agent acting for an undisclosed principal the third party will be discharged from liability to the principal if he was unaware of the principal's existence at the time of payment or settlement (*Coates v Lewes* (1808) 1 Camp 444). However, as in the case of set-off, the third party can only rely on this defence if the principal's conduct induced him to believe that the agent was the principal in the transaction (eg *Ramazotti v Bowring* (1859) 7 CBNS 851). For criticism of this requirement in the context of set-off, see above, p 220.

(b) Relations between the agent and the third party

As the third party contracts in the first instance with the agent and not the undisclosed principal (see above, p 201), it is not surprising to discover that the agent may sue and be sued on that contract (*Sims v Bond* (1833) 5 B & Ad 389 at 393, per Denman CJ). Indeed, in *Muldoon v Wood* (1 April 1998, unreported), Sir John Knox, sitting in the Court of Appeal, described the fact that the agent may be sued on the contract as 'elementary law'. If the agent sues the third party on the contract, the third party can set up against him any defence which would have been available against the undisclosed principal, including the fraud of the principal (*Garnac Grain Co Inc v HMF Faure & Fairclough Ltd* [1966] 1 QB 650; reversed on other grounds by the Court of Appeal [1966] 1 QB 650 at 685–668; affirmed by the House of Lords [1968] AC 1130; however, set-off may not always be available to the third party: see Fridman, pp 271–272). But should the undisclosed principal intervene on the contract the agent loses his right of action against the third party (*Atkinson v Cotesworth* (1825) 3 B & C 647; *aliter* if the agent has a lien or other interest over the goods which form the subject matter of the contract).

Even if the principal intervenes on the contract the agent remains liable to the third party until the third party elects whether to hold the principal or the agent liable (above, pp 213–217). In cases of undisclosed agency, the principal and the agent are liable on the contract in the alternative (*Maynegrain Pty Ltd v Compafina Bank* [1982] 2 NSWLR 141 at 150, per Hope JA; reversed on the facts by the Privy Council (1984) 58 ALJR 389).

CHAPTER 7

RELATIONS BETWEEN PRINCIPAL AND AGENT

In most cases the rights and duties of an agent derive either from a contract made between the principal and agent or from the fiduciary nature of their relationship. But they may also derive from other sources, for example tort, statute, or the law of restitution. See generally, FE Dowrick (1954) 17 MLR 24.

Most agencies are consensual. But some arise because of the apparent or usual authority of the agent (above, pp 132–146 and pp 146–152), or through necessity (above, pp 152–158). Such agencies are non-consensual and it remains uncertain as to whether they give rise to the normal incidents of a principal–agent relationship. They probably do not (see R Powell, *The Law of Agency* (2nd edn, 1961), pp 295–296, fn 4; cf Dowrick, op cit, pp 26–27, fn 15).

1 DUTIES OF THE AGENT

(a) Duty to perform his undertaking and obey instructions

If an agent has entered into a bilateral contract with his principal he must do what he has undertaken to do. For example, in *Turpin v Bilton* (1843) 5 Man & G 455 an agent agreed to insure his principal's ship. He failed to do so, which meant that when the ship was lost the principal was uninsured. It was held that the agent was liable for breach of contract.

When performing his undertaking the agent must obey the lawful and reasonable instructions of his principal, even though he genuinely believes that departing from those instructions would be in his principal's best interests (*The Hermione* [1922] P 162: in the case of a 'commercial agent', defined above at p 119, see the Commercial Agents (Council Directive) Regulations 1993 (SI 1993/3053), reg 3(1), (2), set out below at p 233). But a professional agent, such as a solicitor, may be under a duty to warn and advise the principal of any risks inherent in his instructions. For what happens when the instructions are ambiguous, see above, pp 127–128.

In summary, the agent must follow, and not exceed, the terms of his authority, whether they be express or implied (including those terms implied from custom and usage). But an agent is not obliged to do anything that is illegal, or which, at common law or by statute, is null and void (*Cohen v Kittell* (1889) 22 QBD 680; cf *Fraser v BN Furman (Productions) Ltd* [1967] 1 WLR 898).

On the other hand, if the agent acts under a unilateral contract he is under no duty to do anything at all. Similarly, a gratuitous agent is not bound to do anything, unless his failure to act gives rise to liability in tort. Generally, failure to act does not give rise to tortious liability unless it can be said that there has been an assumption of responsibility to act (see *Henderson v Merrett Syndicates Ltd* [1995] 2 AC 145, and also *Bowstead and Reynolds*, para 6–029). It is arguable, but as yet undecided, that if an agent has agreed to act and then changes his mind, he may be held to have assumed responsibility to the principal to warn him that his intentions have changed (see R Powell, *The Law of Agency* (2nd edn, 1961), pp 302–303; R Bradgate, *Commercial Law* (3rd edn, 2000), para 6.2.1.1; but contrast Fridman, pp 156–157).

There is some uncertainty as to the nature and extent of the agent's liability to his principal where the agent exceeds his actual authority and, by virtue of his apparent authority, causes the principal to be bound by a disadvantageous contract with a third party. Where there is no contract between principal and agent it is possible that the agent's liability might arise in tort (see *Montrod v Grundkötter Fleischvertriebs GmbH* [2001] EWCA Civ 1954, [2002] 1 WLR 1975). But Lord Hoffmann doubts this, saying that the agent might be liable on an implied contract, but not outside contract (*OGB Ltd v Allan* [2007] UKHL 21, [2007] 2 WLR 920 at [93]; see also P Watts (2007) 123 LQR 519).

(b) Duty of care and skill

A contractually rewarded agent owes a duty to his principal to exercise reasonable care and skill in the performance of his undertaking. The duty can be both contractual and tortious (*Midland Bank Trust Co Ltd v Hett, Stubbs & Kemp* [1979] Ch 384, solicitor held liable to his client in contract and in tort). The availability of a concurrent action in tort has been affirmed by the House of Lords in *Henderson v Merrett Syndicates Ltd* [1995] 2 AC 145 (where the reasoning in *Midland Bank Trust Co Ltd v Hett, Stubbs & Kemp* was approved). Whether the agent complies with the duty is a question of fact. But what is the standard of care which the agent must exercise? Does the same duty and standard of care apply to a gratuitous agent? The next case provides some answers to these questions.

Chaudhry v Prabhakar
[1989] 1 WLR 29, Court of Appeal

Chaudhry (C), who had just passed her driving test, asked Prabhakar (P), a close friend, to find a second-hand car, which had not been involved in an accident, for her to buy. P agreed to do so for no payment. C knew nothing about cars but P, though not a qualified mechanic, did know something about them. P found a car offered for sale by someone who was a car sprayer and panel beater. P noticed that the bonnet of the car had been repaired but he made no inquiries as to whether the car had been involved in an accident. P recommended that C should buy the car and, in answer to C's specific inquiry, informed her that the car had not been involved in an accident. C bought the car. When C later discovered that the car had been involved in an accident and was unroadworthy, she sued P for breach of a duty of care.

The trial judge gave judgment for C. P appealed but his appeal was dismissed by the Court of Appeal.

Stuart-Smith LJ: Mr Hoyle on behalf of the appellant first defendant accepts that he was under a duty of care to the plaintiff, but he submitted that the judge had imposed too high a standard of care, and when the correct standard was applied the first defendant was not in breach. In the forefront of his argument is the proposition that the first defendant was a gratuitous or unpaid agent and that the duty on such a person is to take such care towards his principal as he would in relation to his own affairs and to exhibit such skill as he actually possesses. He further submitted that this standard is an entirely subjective one. This appears to mean in the context of this case that if the first defendant would have bought the car himself, as he said he would, and is an honest man as the judge found him to be, he cannot be held liable because he has acted up to the standard expected of an unpaid agent.

I cannot accept this; the degree of care and skill owed by a gratuitous agent is stated by *Bowstead on Agency*, 15th edn (1985), art 44(3), p 152 to be:

> . . . such skill and care as persons ordinarily exercise in their own affairs or, where the agent has expressly or impliedly held himself out to his principal as possessing skill adequate to the performance of a particular undertaking, such skill and care as would normally be shown by one possessing that skill.

But I am quite satisfied that this is an objective standard and is not simply to be measured by the agent's honest statement that he would have similarly acted if he had been transacting the business on his own account, however foolish that may be. For my part, I would prefer to state an agent's duty of care as that which may reasonably be expected of him in all the circumstances. This was the approach of the Court of Appeal in *Houghland v R R Low (Luxury Coaches) Ltd* [1962] 1 QB 694 on the somewhat analogous case of a gratuitous bailee. Ormerod LJ said, at p 698:

> For my part, I have always found some difficulty in understanding just what was 'gross negligence,' because it appears to me that the standard of care required in a case of bailment, or any other type of case, is the standard demanded by the circumstances of that particular case. It seems to me that to try and put a bailment, for instance, into a watertight compartment—such as gratuitous bailment on the one hand, and bailment for reward on the other—is to overlook the fact that there might well be an infinite variety of cases, which might come into one or the other category. The question that we have to consider in a case of this kind, if it is necessary to consider negligence, is whether in the circumstances of this particular case a sufficient standard of care has been observed by the defendants or their servants.

I have no doubt that one of the relevant circumstances is whether or not the agent is paid. If he is, the relationship is a contractual one and there may be express terms upon which the parties can rely. Moreover, if a paid agent exercised any trade, profession or calling, he is required to exercise the degree of skill and diligence reasonably to be expected of a person exercising such trade, profession or calling, irrespective of the degree of skill he may possess. Where the agent is unpaid, any duty of care arises in tort. Relevant circumstances would be the actual skill and experience that the agent had, though, if he has represented such skill and experience to be greater than it in fact is and the principal has relied on such representation, it seems to me to be reasonable to expect him to show that standard of skill and experience which he claims he possesses. Moreover, the fact that principal and agent are friends does not in my judgment affect the existence of the duty of care, though conceivably it may be a relevant circumstance in considering the degree or standard of care.

Mr Scott on behalf of the plaintiff has submitted that the duty of care arises not only because of the relationship of principal and agent, but also under the doctrine enunciated in *Hedley Byrne & Co Ltd v Heller & Partners Ltd* [1964] AC 465. The House of Lords held that a negligent, though honest, misrepresentation, spoken or written, may give rise to an action for damage for financial loss caused thereby, apart from any contract or fiduciary relationship, since the law will imply a duty of care when a party seeking information from a party possessed of special skill trusts him to exercise care, and that party knew, or ought to have known that reliance was being placed on his skill and judgment.

When considering the question of whether a duty of care arises, the relationship between the parties is material. If they are friends, the true view may be that the advice or representation is made upon a purely social occasion and the circumstances show that there has not been a voluntary assumption of responsibility.

Lord Reid in *Hedley Byrne & Co Ltd v Heller & Partners Ltd* said, at pp 482–483:

> The law ought so far as possible to reflect the standards of the reasonable man, and that is what *Donoghue v Stevenson* [1932] AC 562 sets out to do. The most obvious difference between negligent words and negligent acts is this. Quite careful people often express definite options on social or informal occasions even when they see that others are likely to be influenced by them: and they often do that without taking that care which they would take if asked for their opinion professionally or in a business connection. The appellant agrees that there can be no duty of care on such occasions, and we were referred to American and South African authorities where that is recognised, although their law appears to have gone much further than ours has yet done.

But where, as in this case, the relationship of principal and agent exists, such that a contract comes into existence between the principal and the third party, it seems to me that, at the very least, this relationship is powerful evidence that the occasion is not a purely social one, but, to use Lord Reid's expression, is in a business connection. Indeed the relationship between the parties is one that is equivalent to contract, to use the words of Lord Devlin, at p 530, save only for the absence of consideration.

It seems to me that all the necessary ingredients are here present. The plaintiff clearly relied upon the first defendant's skill and judgment, and, although it may not have been great, it was greater than hers and was quite sufficient for the purpose of asking the appropriate questions of the second defendant. The first defendant also knew that the plaintiff was relying on him; indeed he told her that she did not need to have it inspected by a mechanic and she did not do so on the strength of his recommendation. It was clearly in a business connection, because he knew that she was there and then going to commit herself to buying the car for £4,500 through his agency.

If, as I think, the duty of care in this case can equally be said to arise under the *Hedley Byrne* principle, then logically the standard of care, or the nature and extent of the duty, should be the same as that required of an unpaid agent. And this is an additional reason why I prefer to state the duty as I have, namely, to take such care as is reasonably to be expected of him in all the circumstances.

Stocker LJ: This appeal does not raise any question as to whether or not any duty was owed at all, since it was conceded that the defendant was a gratuitous agent and owed the appropriate duty. On the facts of this particular case I agree that the concession was properly made, though the incidence of the duty may be a matter of dispute.

In many cases in which actionable negligence is claimed in respect of the voluntary giving of advice, the first question that arises is whether any duty of care is owed in respect of such advice where the relationship of the parties is such that no voluntary assumption of legal responsibility was intended or can properly be imputed and where the giving of the advice was motivated solely out of friendship. Thus, in my view, in the absence of other factors giving rise to such a duty, the giving of advice sought in the context of family, domestic or social relationships will not in itself give rise to any duty in respect of such advice. The existence of the duty would depend upon all the circumstances in which the advice was sought or tendered. This problem does not arise in this case because of the concession referred to that the duty of care did exist. Whether the duty arises out of a gratuitous agency or by reason of the extension of the *Donoghue v Stevenson* [1932] AC 562 principle to economic loss sustained as a result of negligent advice as enunciated in *Hedley Byrne & Co Ltd v Heller & Partners Ltd* [1964] AC 465, on the facts of this case, even if the existence of the duty had not been conceded, I should, for my part, have felt bound to conclude that it did exist.

The first defendant accepted the task of finding a motor car suitable for the plaintiff in respect of which a specific characteristic was stipulated—viz that it had not been involved in an accident. The first defendant purported to have done so and stated specifically in answer to the plaintiffs question that it had not been involved in any accident and assured that there was no need to have it examined by a mechanic. He gave her information with regard to its provenance which was incorrect since he did not know the vendor before seeing the car. In making these assertions to the plaintiff he went beyond what was required of him in his capacity as a friend, and it seems to me he owed a duty of care to the plaintiff. The issue arising on this appeal, therefore, relates not to the existence of a duty of care but to its extent.

Mr Hoyle submits that the duty was that of a gratuitous agent which is stated in *Bowstead on Agency*, 15th edn, art 44(3) to be: 'Such skill and care as persons ordinarily exercise in their own affairs'. I doubt whether this is an adequate formulation, at least in the circumstances of this case, when applied to advice given to another. However, even if it be the appropriate duty, the words 'ordinarily exercise[d] in their own affairs' seems to me to postulate an objective and not a subjective standard. If a subjective standard be correct, then in my view the duty so expressed becomes virtually meaningless and would cover circumstances in which no care at all had been taken. Objectively regarded, there was sufficient evidence before the judge from which he could properly conclude that the first defendant did not exercise such care, and the fact that he honestly asserted that he would have been happy to purchase the car himself begs the question rather than resolving it. In my view, the fact that he did not ask the vendor specifically whether or not the car had been involved in any accident did not itself establish a breach provided that he had reasonable grounds for belief that it had not and if he had such reasonable grounds it would not necessarily follow that his assertion to this effect to the plaintiff amounted to actionable negligence. This, however, is to consider this aspect of his advice to her in isolation. He did not, in fact, contrary to his assertion, know the vendor. He did not ask for, or examine, any registration documents, nor make any inquiries as to the previous owner of the car or its provenance. He bought it from a person whose trade was that of a panel beater and observed that the car had a crumpled bonnet. In my view, any purchaser of a car in these circumstances, however naive, would be put on inquiry. Thus, judged even by the standard of care for which Mr Hoyle contends, if objectively considered, the first defendant failed to discharge it.

In my opinion, in the circumstances such as prevailed here, a more appropriate test is that suggested by Ormerod LJ in *Houghland v RR Low (Luxury Coaches) Ltd* [1962] 1 QB 694, 698: 'whether in the circumstances of this particular case a sufficient standard of care has been observed.' On either formulation of the duty, in my view, the first defendant failed to discharge the duty and was accordingly liable for actionable negligence as the judge has found.

I have sympathy for the first defendant. He was, as the judge found, acting honestly and without any apparent motive to mislead the plaintiff. Common prudence would indicate that he should have explained the circumstances in which he obtained the car and not voluntarily have accepted a duty which otherwise might well not have been imposed upon him.

May LJ: The real questions in this case, looked at with common sense and avoiding unnecessary legal jargon, were, first, did the friend seeking the car owe the intending purchaser any duty of care in and about his search; secondly, if he did, what was its nature and extent; thirdly, did he commit any breach of that duty causing the plaintiff any damage?

As Stuart-Smith and Stocker LJJ have recorded in their judgments, counsel for the first defendant conceded that his client owed the intending purchaser at least the duty to take such care in and about her business, namely, the search for a suitable car for her, as he would have about his own affairs had he been looking for a car for himself. In the light of the more cautious approach taken in recent cases by the House of Lords and the Privy Council to the question whether a duty of care exists, as expressed by Lord Wilberforce in the familiar passage from his speech in *Anns v Merton London Borough Council* [1978] AC 728, 751–752—see, for instance, the opinion of the Privy Council in *Yuen Kun Yeu v A-G of Hong Kong* [1988] AC 175—I for my part respectfully doubt whether counsel's concession in the instant case was rightly made in law. I do not find the conclusion that one must impose upon a family friend looking out for a first car for a girl of 26 a *Donoghue v Stevenson* duty of care in and about his quest, enforceable with all the formalities of the law of tort, entirely attractive.

Nor do I think, on the facts of this case, that but for the concession one can apply to the young man's answer to the girl's inquiry about the car's history:

>...the principle that a duty of care arises where a party is asked for and gives gratuitous advice upon a matter within his particular skill or knowledge and knows or ought to have known that the person asking for the advice will rely upon it and act accordingly

see *Yuen Kun Yeu v A-G of Hong Kong* [1988] AC 175, 192, referring to the effect of *Hedley Byrne & Co Ltd v Heller & Partners Ltd* [1964] AC 465. To do so in this and similar cases will make social relations and responsibilities between friends unnecessarily hazardous.

However the concession was made, and I agree with Stuart-Smith and Stocker LJJ that we must accordingly decide this appeal on that basis. In those circumstances I think that one is driven to the conclusion that the findings by the deputy judge that the plaintiff did ask the first defendant if the car had been involved in an accident, that he had answered that it had not without any direct inquiry to the vendor, whereas in truth it had been involved in a serious accident and been extensively but unskillfully repaired, inevitably led to the conclusion that the first defendant did breach his conceded duty of care and that the plaintiff suffered the damage alleged in consequence.

I too would therefore dismiss this appeal.

NOTES

1.   *Chaudhry v Prabhakar* seems to put paid to the traditional view that there are different standards of care as between gratuitous agents and agents for reward; the Court of Appeal having made it clear that the required standard of any agent is such as is reasonable in all the circumstances. The standard of care will vary with the facts of any particular case and the fact that the agent is acting gratuitously or for reward is simply one of the factors to be taken into account (see Stuart-Smith LJ, above; cf Powell, op cit, p 304). Other factors include whether the agent for reward exercises any trade, profession, or calling, and where the agent is unpaid, the skill and experience which he has or represents himself as having (see Stuart-Smith LJ, above).

2.   *Chaudhry v Prabhakar* leaves one important question without a clear answer: when will a gratuitous agent owe a duty of care to his principal? Remember, some doubt was expressed over whether counsel was right to concede the existence of a duty of care in that case (see May LJ,

above). See *Markesinis and Munday: An Outline of the Law of Agency* (4th edn, 1998), p 97. A further question could be asked: was it really necessary to treat Prabhakar as a gratuitous agent at all? See NE Palmer [1992] SPTL Reporter 35 at 36, who sees *Chaudhry v Prabhakar* as a straightforward case of liability for negligent advice.

(c) Duties arising from the fiduciary nature of the agency relationship

Agents are normally subject to fiduciary duties. This is because the agent has power to affect the legal relations of his principal and the principal normally places trust and confidence in the agent with regard to the exercise of that power. In these circumstances, equity will intervene and subject the agent to fiduciary duties so as to protect the principal from any abuse of power by the agent.[1] The core duties are those of loyalty and fidelity. As Millett LJ said in *Bristol and West Building Society v Mothew* [1998] Ch 1 at 18:

> A fiduciary is someone who has undertaken to act for or on behalf of another in a particular matter in circumstances which give rise to a relationship of trust and confidence. The distinguishing obligation of a fiduciary is the obligation of loyalty. The principal is entitled to the single-minded loyalty of the fiduciary. This core liability has several facets. A fiduciary must act in good faith; he must not make a profit out of his trust; he must not place himself in a position where his duty and his interest may conflict; he may not act for his own benefit or the benefit of a third person without the informed consent of his principal. This is not intended to be an exhaustive list, but it is sufficient to indicate the nature of fiduciary obligations. They are the defining characteristics of the fiduciary.

Fiduciary duties are proscriptive in nature: they tell the fiduciary what he must not do, they do not tell him what he ought to do (*A-G v Blake* [1998] Ch 439 at 455, per Lord Woolf MR; *Breen v Williams* (1996) 186 CLR 71, High Court of Australia, noted by R Nolan (1997) 113 LQR 220). A fiduciary may be subject to positive duties at common law and in equity, for example an agent must act with care and skill, but this is not a fiduciary duty—in the case of a company director, this duty is now codified in the Companies Act 2006 (s 174), which also confirms that it is not a fiduciary duty (s 178(2)). Even the simple duty to account, central though it is, is not a fiduciary duty (*Coulthard v Disco Mix Club Ltd* [2000] 1 WLR 707 at 728, per Sher QC, sitting as a deputy judge; and see also *Compañía de Seguros Imperio v Health (REBX) Ltd* [2001] 1 WLR 112, CA). As Millett LJ said in the *Mothew* case (at 16), 'not every breach of a duty by a fiduciary is a breach of fiduciary duty'.

Despite the fact that most agents are fiduciaries, some are not, and those that are may not act in a fiduciary capacity for all purposes. As Professor Dowrick has noted: 'if P appoints A to be his agent merely to sign a memorandum and places no particular trust in A, the doctrine of fiduciary relations and the incidents of agency which derive from this equitable doctrine would not apply' ((1954) 17 MLR 24 at 31–32). However, the term 'non-fiduciary agent' is probably best avoided for, as *Bowstead and Reynolds* states (at para 6–037), it seems better to say that where an agent does not act in a fiduciary capacity (eg because he simply carries

---

[1] For a detailed discussion of the nature of fiduciary relationships and the topics considered in this section generally, see R Flannigan [2004] JBL 277; M Conaglen (2005) 121 LQR 452; R Flannigan (2006) 122 LQR 449; R Lee (2007) 27 OJLS 327; J Edelman (2010) 126 LQR 302; L Smith (2014) 130 LQR 608.

out specific instructions), this is a reflection of the scope of his duties and the boundaries of the equitable rules.

The extent of the fiduciary duties of an agent may vary from case to case ('Fiduciaries are not all required, like the victims of Procrustes, to lie on a bed of the same length': *Brandeis Brokers Ltd v Black* [2001] 2 Lloyd's Rep 359 at 367, per Toulson J). As Lord Upjohn said in *Boardman v Phipps* [1967] 2 AC 46 at 123: 'Rules of equity have to be applied to such a great diversity of circumstances that they can be stated only in the most general terms and applied with particular attention to the exact circumstances of each case.' Lord Browne-Wilkinson made a similar observation in *Kelly v Cooper* [1993] AC 205 at 214–215 (below, pp 235–237), and later in *Henderson v Merrett Syndicates Ltd* [1995] 2 AC 145 at 206 he said:

> The phrase 'fiduciary duties' is a dangerous one, giving rise to a mistaken assumption that all fiduciaries owe the same duties in all circumstances. That is not the case. Although, so far as I am aware, every fiduciary is under a duty not to make a profit from his position (unless such profit is authorised), the fiduciary duties owed, for example, by an express trustee are not the same as those owed by an agent. Moreover, and more relevantly, the extent and nature of the fiduciary duties owed in any particular case fall to be determined by reference to any underlying contractual relationship between the parties. Thus, in the case of an agent employed under a contract, the scope of his fiduciary duties is determined by the terms of the underlying contract. Although an agent is, in the absence of contractual provision, in breach of his fiduciary duties if he acts for another who is in competition with his principal, if the contract under which he is acting authorises him to do so, the normal fiduciary duties are modified accordingly: see *Kelly v Cooper* [1993] AC 205, and the cases there cited. The existence of a contract does not exclude the co-existence of concurrent fiduciary duties (indeed, the contract may well be their source); but the contract can and does modify the extent and nature of the general duty that would otherwise arise.

Sales J neatly summarised fiduciary duties, in a passage subsequently adopted by J McGhee, *Snell's Equity* (33rd edn, 2015), para 7–005, as 'obligations imposed by law as a reaction to particular circumstances of responsibility assumed by one person in respect of the conduct of the affairs of another': *F&C Alternative Investments (Holdings) Ltd v Barthelemy (No 2)* [2011] EWHC 1731 (Ch), [2012] Ch 613 at [225]. Earlier in his judgment (at [223]), he had said:

> Fiduciary obligations may arise in a wide range of business relationships, where a substantial degree of control over the property or affairs of one person is given to another person. Very often, of course, a contract may lie at the heart of such a business relationship, and then a question arises about the way in which fiduciary obligations may be imposed alongside the obligations spelled out in the contract. In making their contract, the parties will have bargained for a distribution of risk and for the main standards of conduct to be applied between them. In commercial contexts, care has to be taken in identifying any fiduciary obligations which may arise that the court does not distort the bargain made by the parties: see the observation by Lord Neuberger of Abbotsbury writing extrajudicially in 'The Stuffing of Minerva's Owl? Taxonomy and Taxidermy in Equity' [2009] CLJ 537, 543 … The touchstone is to ask what obligations of a fiduciary character may reasonably be expected to apply in the particular context, where the contract between the parties will usually provide the major part of the contextual framework in which that question arises.

As fiduciary duties of an agent arise in equity, and do not depend upon any contract made between the principal and agent, those duties may apply to both contractual and gratuitous agents alike (contrary dicta of Lord Browne-Wilkinson in *Kelly v Cooper* and *Henderson v Merrett Syndicates*, suggesting that fiduciary duties stem from contract, should be treated with caution). However, the principal and agent may incorporate fiduciary duties into any contract made between them, or, alternatively, exclude or modify those duties from their relationship by the terms of their contract. The exclusion or modification of fiduciary duties is controlled by both common law and statute. At common law, where an agent seeks by a contract term to reserve power to act in a way inconsistent with the agency he must either acknowledge his agency and disclose the potential conflict of interest so as to obtain his principal's consent to it, or he must make it clear that the obligation undertaken is not one of agency at all (see *Bowstead and Reynolds*, para 6–056). In the latter case the clause must give a precise indication of the capacity in which he acts and one that states that he may on occasions change his role is probably ineffective for the purpose (*Brandeis Brokers Ltd v Black*, above, p 369). A contract clause seeking to modify or exclude an agent's fiduciary duties may also be caught by the Consumer Rights Act 2015 (situations formerly governed by the Unfair Contract Terms Act 1977, and on occasion by the Unfair Terms in Consumer Contracts Regulations 1999: see below, p 424). For consideration of the special problems raised when directors contract out of their fiduciary duties, see s 232 of the Companies Act 2006 (provisions protecting directors from liability); *Movitex Ltd v Bulfield* [1988] BCLC 104 (distinction between duties and disabilities of directors); *Gwembe Valley Development Co Ltd v Koshy (No 3)* [2003] EWCA Civ 1478, [2004] 1 BCLC 131 at [104]–[109] (that distinction was 'a needless complication'); and note that the Companies Act 2006, in its statutory statement of director's duties, abandons the distinction between duties and disabilities. As to trustee exemption clauses, see *Armitage v Nurse* [1998] Ch 241 (danger of reducing the obligations of a trustee beyond the 'irreducible core of obligations'); *Citibank NA v MBIA Assurance SA* [2007] EWCA Civ 11, [2008] 1 BCLC 376 (refusal to re-characterise 'commercial trust' on ground that trustee's obligations had been reduced beyond 'irreducible core'); *Baker v JE Clark & Co (Transport) Ltd* [2006] EWCA Civ 464, [2006] Pens LR 131 (Unfair Contract Terms Act 1977 and Unfair Terms in Consumer Contracts Regulations 1999 did not apply to trust instruments because a trust instrument is not a 'contract'); and Law Commission Report No 301, *Trustee Exemption Clauses* (2006) (provisional recommendation to prohibit professional trustees from relying on clauses to exclude or limit liability for breach of trust arising from negligence was abandoned in final report).

Two categories of agent deserve special mention at this stage: company directors and commercial agents.

Company directors: Part 10, Chapter 2, of the Companies Act 2006 codifies the common law and equitable duties applying to company directors. Section 170 sets out the scope and nature of the codified general duties owed by a director of a company to the company. The section makes it clear that the statutory duties described in Chapter 2 have been put in place to replace the common law rules and equitable principles from which they are derived (s 170(3)). However, s 170(4) requires the court to have regard to the existing interpretation and the continuing development of the common law rules and equitable principles on which the statutory duties are based when interpreting those duties. Furthermore, s 178 preserves the common law and equitable rules as to remedies for breach of the statutory duties and makes it clear that most of the codified general duties of directors remain fiduciary in character.

There are three general provisions in the 2006 Act designed to reformulate and codify the fiduciary duties owed by directors to their companies. First, s 175 lays down a duty to avoid conflicts of interest so far as third parties are concerned (the 'no conflict' and 'no profit' rules—see below—are replaced by a single rule). Secondly, s 176 sets out a duty not to accept benefits from third parties (ie not to accept bribes or secret commission). Thirdly, s 177 requires a director to declare any direct or indirect interest he has in a proposed transaction or arrangement with the company. If the director fails to declare his interest, and the company enters into the impugned transaction, the director is under a new and continuing duty to disclose his interest (s 182).

Commercial agents: the Commercial Agents (Council Directive) Regulations 1993 lay down duties for commercial agents as defined therein (see above, p 119). Such duties generally reflect those duties which already arise at common law and in equity.[2] By reg 3(1) a commercial agent must 'in performing his activities look after the interests of his principal and act dutifully and in good faith'. In particular he must: (a) make proper efforts to negotiate and, where appropriate, conclude the transactions he is instructed to take care of; (b) communicate to his principal all the necessary information available to him; and (c) comply with reasonable instructions given by his principal (reg 3(2)). The parties may not derogate from these duties (reg 5(1)). See further A Tosato (2016) 36 OJLS 661.

(i) Specific fiduciary duties of an agent

The most important fiduciary duties which may be owed by an agent towards his principal are the following.

(a) Duty not to put himself in a position where his duties as agent conflict with his own interests, or the interests of another principal

Armstrong v Jackson
[1917] 2 KB 822, King's Bench Division

Armstrong instructed Jackson, a stockbroker, to buy shares in a certain company for him. Although Jackson pretended to purchase the shares on the open market, he actually sold his own shares in the company to Armstrong. On discovering the truth some years later, Armstrong claimed to have the transaction set aside. McCardie J upheld the claim and ordered Jackson to repay all sums paid by Armstrong for the shares.

> **McCardie J**:...First as to the claim to avoid the transaction. It is obvious that the defendant gravely failed in his duty to the plaintiff. He was instructed to buy shares. But he never carried out his mandate. A broker who is employed to buy shares cannot sell his own shares unless he makes a full and accurate disclosure of the fact to his principal, and the principal, with a full knowledge, gives his assent to the changed position of the broker. The rule is one not merely of law but of obvious morality. As was said by Lord Cairns in *Parker v McKenna* ((1874) 10 Ch App 96 at 118), 'No man can in this Court, acting as an agent, be allowed to put himself into a position in which his interest and his duty will be in conflict.' Now a broker who secretly sells his own shares is in a wholly false position. As vendor it is to his interest to sell his shares at the highest price. As broker it is his clear duty to the principal to buy at the lowest price and to give unbiassed and independent advice (if such be asked) as to the time when and the price at which shares shall be bought, or

---

[2] Although attempts to impose fiduciary duties on principals have proved largely unsuccessful (see *Jirna Ltd v Mister Donut of Canada Ltd* (1973) 40 DLR (3d) 303, Supreme Court of Canada), the principal of a commercial agent must act 'dutifully and in good faith' towards his agent: Commercial Agents (Council Directive) Regulations 1993, reg 4(1). The parties may not derogate from this regulation: reg 5(1).

whether they shall be bought at all. The law has ever required a high measure of good faith from an agent. He departs from good faith when he secretly sells his own property to the principal. The rule has long been the same, both at law and equity: see *Story on Agency*, s 210. It matters not that the broker sells at the market price, or that he acts without intent to defraud: see *Bentley v Craven* ((1853) 18 Beav 75). The prohibition of the law is absolute. It will not allow an agent to place himself in a situation which, under ordinary circumstances, would tempt a man to do that which is not the best for his principal: see *per* Romilly MR in *Bentley v Craven*. The Court will not enter into discussion as to the propriety of the price charged by the broker, nor is it material to inquire whether the principal has or has not suffered a loss. If the breach of duty by the broker be shown, the Court will set aside the transaction: see *Gillett v Peppercorne* ((1840) 3 Beav 78). The rule was strikingly illustrated in the case of *Rothschild v Brookman* ((1831) 5 Bli NS 165 at 197). The facts in that case were not dissimilar to the facts in the present action. The House of Lords (affirming the Court below) set aside transactions in which the agent had secretly acted as principal. In giving his opinion Lord Wynford (formerly Best CJ) used these words: 'If any man who is to be trusted places himself in a condition in which he has an opportunity of taking advantage of his employer, by placing himself in such a situation, whether acting fairly or not, he must suffer the consequence of his situation. Such is the jealousy which the law of England entertains against any such transactions.' ...

The position of principal and agent gives rise to particular and onerous duties on the part of the agent, and the high standard of conduct required from him springs from the fiduciary relationship between his employer and himself. His position is confidential. It readily lends itself to abuse. A strict and salutary rule is required to meet the special situation. The rules of English law as they now exist spring from the strictness originally required by Courts of Equity in cases where the fiduciary relationship exists. Those requirements are superadded to the common law obligations of diligence and skill: see *per* Lord Cranworth in *Aberdeen Rly Co v Blaikie Bros* ((1854) 1 Macq 461 at 471 ff) and *per curiam* in *Oliver v Court* ((1820) 8 Price 127 at 161).

NOTES

1.   In *Aberdeen Rly Co v Blaikie Bros* (1854) 1 Macq 461 at 471, Lord Cranworth LC provided a classic description of the 'no conflict' rule when he said:

> It is a rule of universal application that no one, having [fiduciary] duties to discharge, shall be allowed to enter into engagements in which he has, or can have, a personal interest conflicting, or which may possibly conflict, with the interests of those whom he is bound to protect.

The rule is strictly applied whenever there is an actual conflict of interest and duty or whenever there is 'a real sensible possibility of conflict' (*Boardman v Phipps* [1967] 2 AC 46 at 124, per Lord Upjohn). The fact that the agent has acted in good faith, and produced a benefit for the principal, is irrelevant to the application of the rule (see, eg, *Boardman v Phipps*, below at p 240). The rationale behind the rule is that the agent must be deterred from the temptation to place his own interests above those of his principal. However, the agent's duty of loyalty, which stems from the trust and confidence placed in him by his principal, will end on termination of his agency. Thus, in *A-G v Blake* [1998] Ch 439, the Court of Appeal held that a former employee of the Secret Intelligence Service did not owe a continuing duty of loyalty to his employer after he left the service. It further held that the former employee would continue to be subject to a separate fiduciary obligation to maintain the confidentiality of information imparted to him in confidence, as long as the information had not become public knowledge, which it had in this case (there was no appeal on this issue, but the House of Lords held the former employee liable to account for profits made in breach of his express undertaking not to divulge any official information gained as a result of his employment: [2001] 1 AC 268). The former agent will also continue to owe fiduciary obligations to his former principal where he continues to have influence over the principal which he exploits for his own benefit. This is a different category of fiduciary relationship than one stemming from either trust and confidence or from confidentiality: it is a relationship of ascendancy and dependency (see Millett LJ, as he then was, writing extra-judicially, in (1998) 114 LQR 214 at 219–220).

2. *Armstrong v Jackson* illustrates one facet of the no conflict rule, ie an agent instructed to purchase property must not sell his own property to the principal. Another facet of the rule is that an agent instructed to sell his principal's property must not buy it himself (*McPherson v Watt* (1877) 3 App Cas 254, where the House of Lords held that the agent had breached the rule when he purchased the property in his brother's name). Where an agent deals with his principal in breach of duty, the principal may rescind the contract (assuming there are no bars to rescission, eg restitution is impossible, intervention of third party rights, affirmation of the contract evidenced by lapse of time after discovering the truth). Alternatively, the principal may affirm the contract and claim an account of any profit made by the agent (*Bentley v Craven* (1853) 18 Beav 75). Special rules apply, however, when the agent sells property to the principal. If the agent sells property which he acquired after the creation of the agency relationship then he must account to the principal for any profit (*Tyrrell v Bank of London* (1862) 10 HL Cas 26). If the agent already owned the property before the agency was created he will not be accountable for any profit but he will have to pay compensation for any loss caused to the principal (*Jacobus Marler Estates Ltd v Marler* (1913) 85 LJPC 167n). See *Bowstead and Reynolds*, para 6–068; see also P Watts [1992] LMCLQ 439.

3. There will be no breach of duty if the agent makes full disclosure of all material facts to the principal and obtains the principal's consent before placing himself in a position where his interests and duty conflict (*North and South Trust Co v Berkeley* [1971] 1 WLR 470 at 484–485, per Donaldson J). When an agent sells his own property to the principal, or buys the principal's property from him, the agent must also show that the price was fair and that he did not abuse his position in any way (*Gibson v Jeyes* (1801) 6 Ves 266). Furthermore, as we have already seen, the no conflict rule may be excluded by the terms of any contract made between the principal and agent (above, p 231). Exclusion of the duty may be by express or implied terms of the contract (*Kelly v Cooper* [1993] AC 205, below).

So far we have examined the no conflict rule in terms of the agent's duty not to put himself in a position where his duty to his principal conflicts with his own interests. However, the rule also prevents the agent from placing himself in a position where he owes a duty to another person which is inconsistent with his duty to his principal (see *North and South Trust Co v Berkeley* [1971] 1 WLR 470 at 484–485, per Donaldson J; see also the case next cited).

Kelly v Cooper

[1993] AC 205, Privy Council

Kelly instructed Coopers, a firm of estate agents, to sell his house ('Caliban'). Brant, the owner of an adjacent house ('Vertigo'), also instructed Coopers to sell his house. Coopers showed Perot, a prospective purchaser, around both houses and Perot made an offer for Vertigo, which was accepted by Brant. Perot then offered to buy Caliban. Coopers did not inform Kelly of the agreement to buy Vertigo. In ignorance of the agreement made between Perot and Brant, Kelly accepted Perot's offer and the sales of both houses were completed. Kelly later brought an action against Coopers claiming that they were in breach of their duties in: (1) failing to disclose material information to him; and (2) placing themselves in a position where there was a conflict between their duty of disclosure to Kelly and their own interest in ensuring they obtained commission on both houses.

> **Lord Browne-Wilkinson** (delivering the advice of the Privy Council (Lords Keith of Kinkel, Ackner, Browne-Wilkinson, Mustill, and Slynn of Hadley), held that Perot's interest in buying both houses was a material factor which could have influenced the negotiations for the price at which Caliban was sold. His Lordship continued):
>
> In the view of the Board the resolution of this case depends upon two fundamental propositions: first, agency is a contract made between principal and agent; second, like every other contract, the rights and duties of the principal and agent are dependent upon the terms of the contract between them, whether express or implied. It is not possible to say that all agents owe the same duties to their principals: it is always necessary to have regard to the express or implied terms of the contract...
>
> In a case where a principal instructs as selling agent for his property or goods a person who to his knowledge acts and intends to act for other principals selling property or goods of the same description, the terms to be implied into such agency contract must differ from those to be implied where an agent is not carrying on such general agency business. In the case of estate agents, it is their business to act for numerous principals: where properties are of a similar description, there will be a conflict of interest between the principals each of whom will be concerned to attract potential purchasers to their property rather than that of another. Yet, despite this conflict of interest, estate agents must be free to act for several competing principals otherwise they will be unable to perform their function. Yet it is normally said that it is a breach of an agent's duty to act for competing principals. In the course of acting for each of their principals, estate agents will acquire information confidential to that principal. It cannot be sensibly suggested that an estate agent is contractually bound to disclose to any one of his principals information which is confidential to another of his principals. The position as to confidentiality is even clearer in the case of stockbrokers who cannot be contractually bound to disclose to their private clients inside information disclosed to the brokers in confidence by a company for which they also act. Accordingly in such cases there must be an implied term of the contract with such an agent that he is entitled to act for other principals selling competing properties and to keep confidential the information obtained from each of his principals.
>
> Similar considerations apply to the fiduciary duties of agents. The existence and scope of these duties depends upon the terms on which they are acting. In *New Zealand Netherlands Society Oranje Inc v Kuys* [1973] 1 WLR 1126, 1129–1130, Lord Wilberforce, in giving the judgment of this Board, said:
>
> > The obligation not to profit from a position of trust, or, as it is sometimes relevant to put it, not to allow a conflict to arise between duty and interest, is one of strictness. The strength, and indeed the severity, of the rule has recently been emphasised by the House of Lords: *Boardman v Phipps* [1967] 2 AC 46. It retains its vigour in all jurisdictions where the principles of equity are applied. Naturally it has different applications in different contexts. It applies, in principle, whether the case is one of a trust, express or implied, of partnership, of directorship of a limited company, of principal and agent, or master and servant, but the precise scope of it must be moulded according to the nature of the relationship. As Lord Upjohn said in *Boardman v Phipps* at p 123: 'Rules of equity have to be applied to such a great diversity of circumstances that they

can be stated only in the most general terms and applied with particular attention to the exact circumstances of each case.'

In *Hospital Products Ltd v United States Surgical Corpn* (1986) 156 CLR 41, 97, Mason J in the High Court of Australia said:

> That contractual and fiduciary relationships may co-exist between the same parties has never been doubted. Indeed, the existence of a basic contractual relationship has in many situations provided a foundation for the erection of a fiduciary relationship. In these situations it is the contractual foundation which is all important because it is the contract that regulates the basic rights and liabilities of the parties. The fiduciary relationship, if it is to exist at all, must accommodate itself to the terms of the contract so that it is consistent with, and conforms to, them. The fiduciary relationship cannot be superimposed upon the contract in such a way as to alter the operation which the contract was intended to have according to its true construction.

Thus, in the present case, the scope of the fiduciary duties owed by the defendants to the plaintiff (and in particular the alleged duty not to put themselves in a position where their duty and their interest conflicted) are to be defined by the terms of the contract of agency.

Applying those considerations to the present case, their Lordships are of the view that since the plaintiff was well aware that the defendants would be acting also for other vendors of comparable properties and in so doing would receive confidential information from those other vendors, the agency contract between the plaintiff and the defendants cannot have included either (a) a term requiring the defendants to disclose such confidential information to the plaintiff or (b) a term precluding the defendants acting for rival vendors or (c) a term precluding the defendants from seeking to earn commission on the sale of the property of a rival vendor.

Their Lordships are therefore of opinion that the defendants committed no breach of duty, whether contractual or fiduciary, by failing to reveal to the plaintiff Mr Perot's interest in buying Vertigo, since such information was confidential to Mr Brant. Nor did the fact that the defendants had a direct financial interest in securing a sale of Vertigo constitute a breach of fiduciary duty since the contract of agency envisaged that they might have such a conflict of interest.

This decision is consistent with *Lothian v Jenolite Ltd* 1969 SC 111 and does not conflict with any of the other authorities to which their Lordships were referred. The failure of estate agents to communicate material information to their principals which was held to exist in *Keppel v Wheeler* [1927] 1 KB 577 and *Dunton Properties Ltd v Coles, Knapp & Kennedy Ltd* (1959) 174 EG 723 related to information received by the estate agents in their capacity as agents of the principal who was complaining and was therefore not subject to any duty of confidentiality owed by the agents to other persons.

North and South Trust Co v Berkeley [1971] 1 WLR 470 raised quite a different problem. The plaintiff was insured under a policy which had been effected by brokers. The insured had made a claim against the insurers. The brokers then accepted instructions from the insurers (ie a person having a contrary interest to that of the insured) to obtain a report from assessors. Having obtained such report, the brokers refused to disclose it to their original principals, the assured. Donaldson J rightly held that this was a breach of duty by the brokers to their principals. In that case, there was nothing in the circumstances to justify the implication of any term in the agency between the assured and the brokers that the brokers should be free to act for the opposing party, the insurers. . . .

As to the defendants' claim for commission, even if a breach of fiduciary duty by the defendants had been proved, they would not thereby have lost their right to commission unless they had acted dishonestly. In *Keppel v Wheeler* [1927] 1 KB 577 the agents admitted an honest breach of fiduciary duty by mistake and yet were entitled to their commission. In the present case the plaintiff did not allege, nor did the judge find, any bad faith by the defendants. Even on the view the judge took therefore there was no ground for depriving the defendants of their commission.

NOTES

1. *Kelly v Cooper* has its critics. In [1994] JBL 144 at 149, Professor Reynolds writes:

> The rather brusque reasoning and the citation of two cases on commercial distributors, seems to deny fiduciary obligations to all and to leave everything to express and even implied terms of the contract. Variable as the degree of fiduciary liability is, such reasoning cannot be appropriate to agency law in general. And it would be most unfortunate if it was taken as a *carte blanche* for persons acting in potentially inconsistent capacities in the area of financial services.

See also the criticisms of I Brown (1993) 109 LQR 206. However, the contractual approach to the exclusion and modification of fiduciary duties has subsequently been echoed by Lord Jauncey, delivering the advice of the Privy Council, in *Clark Boyce v Mouat* [1994] 1 AC 428 at 436, by Lord Browne-Wilkinson in *Henderson v Merrett Syndicates Ltd* [1995] 2 AC 145 at 206 (see above, p 231), and by Lord Walker in *Hilton v Barker Booth & Eastwood (a firm)* [2005] UKHL 8, [2005] 1 WLR 567 at [30]. It has also found favour with the Law Commission (see Note 3 below).

2. *Kelly v Cooper* is a case of unrelated agencies, ie Coopers were not acting as agents for competing principals *in the same transaction*. Implied consent to the agent acting for competing principals was to be derived from the particular business context (an estate agent is known to act for many parties). But in other areas of business activity, for example where the agent is a solicitor, the normal requirement of undivided loyalty may apply even where the agent acts for two principals in different matters (*Marks & Spencer plc v Freshfields Bruckhaus Deringer* [2004] EWCA Civ 741, [2005] PNLR 4). It is most unlikely that a court will imply a term to enable an agent to act for opposing principals in the same transaction. In such circumstances the agent would have to obtain the fully informed consent *of both* principals to his continuing to act for both of them. For example, in *Clark Boyce v Mouat* [1994] 1 AC 428, the Privy Council held that a solicitor was entitled to act for both parties in a transaction even where their interests might conflict, provided that he obtained the informed consent of both parties to his so acting. Sometimes, even disclosure will not save the agent when he has put himself in a position 'where he cannot fulfil his obligations to one without failing in his obligations to the other' (*Bristol & West Building Society v Mothew* [1998] Ch 1 at 19, per Millett LJ). The agent has only himself to blame for not having refused to act for one of the principals in the first place. For example, in *Hilton v Barker Booth & Eastwood* [2005] UKHL 8, [2005] 1 WLR 567, the House of Lords held a solicitor liable for having put himself in a position where he owed irreconcilable duties to two clients when acting for them in the same transaction: one duty to the claimant to reveal information in his possession that might affect the claimant's interests, and one duty to the other client not to disclose discreditable facts about him without his consent.

3. The problems facing fiduciaries owing duties to opposing clients are of long standing but they have been highlighted by the growth of multifunction fiduciaries, especially in the financial services industry. With the abolition of single-capacity trading in the mid-1980s following 'Big Bang', it became possible for large firms and banking groups to offer a range of financial services to their customers. This has increased the potential for conflicts of interest. For example, the corporate finance department of a bank may be advising with regard to a rumoured bid from an anonymous bidder, whilst the corporate advisory department of the same bank may be advising the bidder. In these circumstances the bank may be in breach of its duty of confidentiality or its duty to give 'undivided loyalty' to each client, even though it has complied with regulatory rules made pursuant to the Financial Services and Markets Act 2000. It is by no means certain how far, if at all, such regulatory rules have modified traditional fiduciary duties. The issue was addressed in 1995 by the Law Commission in their report on *Fiduciary Duties and Regulatory Rules* (Report No 236; summarised by H McVea [1997] CfiLR 123). The Law Commission followed the *Kelly v Cooper* line, endorsing the use of contractual techniques for modifying the scope of fiduciary duties and general advanced disclosure clauses. The Law Commission also recommended the introduction of a legislative 'safe harbour' which would allow multifunctional fiduciaries in the financial services industry to rely on compliance with regulatory rules as an excuse for deviation from the strict fiduciary obligations imposed by common law. The government decided against the inclusion of such a provision in the Financial Services and Markets Act 2000. It stated that, in the light of recent case law (in particular, *Prince Jefri Bolkiah v KPMG* [1999] 2 AC 222):

> [i]t is the Government's firm belief that the courts would be unlikely to hold that someone could successfully sue an authorised person for breach of fiduciary duties where the authorised person has complied with [Financial Services Authority] rules, which, of course, are made under Parliament's delegated statutory powers. (*Hansard*, HL, col 1409, 9 May 2000.)

This is probably an over-optimistic generalisation, but it is submitted that regulatory rules do offer the courts a guide to the scope of fiduciary obligations in this context.

4. Although not applicable in *Kelly v Cooper*, s 21 of the Estate Agents Act 1979 imposes a duty of disclosure on estate agents who have a personal interest in land about which they negotiate. Failure to disclose such an interest does not render the agent liable to any criminal or civil sanction, but it may lead to disqualification under s 3 of the Act.

5. Lord Browne-Wilkinson said that an agent who was in breach of fiduciary duty would not lose his right to commission unless he acted dishonestly. These *obiter* comments have been criticised for being too narrow in scope (*Stewart Chartering Ltd v Owners of the Ship Peppy* [1997] 2 Lloyd's Rep 722 at 729, per David Steel QC, sitting as a deputy High Court judge). Where there is no dishonesty, the real question is whether the agent's breach of duty goes to the root of the obligations he has undertaken to his principal. If it does, he loses his right to commission, albeit he acted honestly, unless the agent effects severable transactions (*Hippisley v Knee Bros* [1905] 1 KB 1, CA). For further discussion, see below, p 266.

The no conflict rule is probably the most important of the agent's fiduciary duties. Many of the other fiduciary duties owed by the agent (see below) can be regarded as particular applications of the no conflict rule.

(b) Duty not to make a secret profit

Unless he makes full disclosure to his principal and obtains his consent, the agent may not use his position as agent, nor his principal's property or confidential information, to make a profit for himself.

The following cases illustrate how the no secret profit rule operates:

(1) *Lamb v Evans* [1893] 1 Ch 218: L, the proprietor of a trades directory, employed canvassers to obtain advertisements from traders to be inserted in the directory. L discovered

that some of the canvassers were proposing to assist a rival publication after their agreement with L had come to an end. The Court of Appeal held that the canvassers were 'not entitled to use for the purposes of any other publication the materials which, while in the plaintiff's employment, they had obtained for the purpose of his publication'.

(2) *Hippisley v Knee Bros* [1905] 1 KB 1: H employed KB as agents to sell goods on commission. H also agreed to pay KB's out-of-pocket expenses. KB sold the goods and charged H with the cost of printing and advertising. KB claimed the full cost even though they had received a discount from those who had provided these services. At all times KB acted honestly and in accordance with trade custom (of which H had no knowledge). The Court of Appeal held that KB were in breach of duty and had to account for the discount as a secret profit. KB, however, were allowed to keep their commission on the sale because they had acted in good faith and their breach of duty was only incidental to the sale itself.

(3) *Boardman v Phipps* [1967] 2 AC 46: B, a solicitor, and TP, acting together as agents for the trustees of an estate, attended the annual general meeting of a company in which the estate had a minority holding of shares. Later, they obtained information about share prices from the company. They formed the opinion that the company could be made more profitable and, acting honestly and without concealment (but not having first obtained the 'informed consent' of all the trustees), used their own money to bid for and eventually to acquire a controlling interest in it. Ultimately, they succeeded in making considerable profits for both themselves and the estate from capital distributions on their respective holdings of shares. By a majority of three to two, the House of Lords held that they must account to the trust for the profit that they had made from their own investments: the profit had been made by reason of their fiduciary position as agents and by reason of the opportunity and the knowledge which had come to them while acting in that capacity.

Where the agent breaches his duty not to make a secret profit, he must account to the principal for that profit. A duty to account is a personal liability, but it appears that the agent may also hold his secret profit on constructive trust for the principal (ie the principal has a proprietary remedy). The two key advantages of a proprietary remedy are that it entitles the principal to any enhancement in the value of the secret profit, for example where the agent has used his secret profit to purchase land which has increased in value, and that it gives the principal priority over the agent's unsecured creditors should the agent become insolvent (to the clear detriment of those other creditors). For a long time it appeared that if the agent had used his principal's property to make a secret profit then such profit was held on constructive trust, but if the profit had been made without the use of the principal's property the agent was only personally accountable to the principal (see *Industrial Development Consultants Ltd v Cooley* [1972] 1 WLR 443; *Lister & Co v Stubbs* (1890) 45 Ch D 1).

It was always difficult to explain *Boardman v Phipps* on this reasoning. In that case the House of Lords did not distinguish between accountability and constructive trust (in fact there was no need to do so as B, the solicitor, was solvent) and the agents were held liable to account for their profits *and* hold them on constructive trust even though they did not use their principal's property to acquire those profits. The case has often been explained on the ground that confidential information is a special form of trust property (as some of their Lordships thought it was). However, in *A-G for Hong Kong v Reid* [1994] 1 AC 324, the Privy Council held that an agent holds a bribe (which is a secret profit) on constructive trust for his principal. Although Lord Templeman, delivering the advice of the Privy Council, did not specifically address the question of whether a secret profit would normally be held on constructive trust when it was not a bribe, his reasoning, and the fact that he cited *Boardman v Phipps* with approval, suggested that it too would be held on trust by the agent. The Court of Appeal, in *Sinclair Investments (UK) Ltd v Versailles Trade Finance Ltd* [2012] Ch 453, declined to follow the Privy Council's opinion in *A-G for Hong Kong v Reid*, preferring to affirm the view embodied in *Lister & Co v Stubbs* that a beneficiary has no proprietary interest in secret profits made by his fiduciary. This decision was strongly criticised, and two years later the Supreme Court, in *European Ventures LLP v Cedar Capital Partners LLC* [2014] 3 WLR 535, overturned the Court of Appeal's ruling in *Sinclair Investments*, determining that a principal is entitled not merely to an equitable account in respect of any secret profit made by the fiduciary but also to the beneficial ownership of the benefit (for further discussion, see below, p 248).

If the agent has used confidential information to acquire a benefit, the principal may seek an injunction to restrain the agent making further use of the information and, in the case of a contractual agency, claim damages for breach of contract (which may in an exceptional case include gain-based damages, following *A-G v Blake* [2001] 1 AC 268, HL), or seek an account of profits from the agent (which profits, as we have just seen, the agent would hold on constructive trust: *Boardman v Phipps*, above). It should be noted that the agent's duty not to use confidential information acquired in the course of the agency may extend beyond the termination of the agency relationship, although the duty will not apply once the information enters the public domain (*A-G v Blake*, above).

The no secret profit rule is designed to deter the agent from abusing his position and is strictly applied. For example, in *Boardman v Phipps* the agents were held liable to account for their profits even though they had acted honestly, the trust benefited from their actions, and the trust did not want to buy, and could not have bought, the shares. However, the agents were awarded an equitable allowance for their skill and expenditure in making the profit (cf *Guinness plc v Saunders* [1990] 2 AC 663).

(c) Duty not to accept bribes

Boston Deep Sea Fishing and Ice Co v Ansell
(1888) 39 Ch D 339, Court of Appeal

Ansell was employed as managing director of the plaintiff company. Acting on behalf of the company, Ansell contracted for the construction of certain fishing smacks, but, unknown to the company, he took a commission from the shipbuilders on the contract. Ansell also accepted bonuses from two other companies (in which he held shares) with which he had placed orders on behalf of the plaintiff company. Suspecting misconduct, the plaintiff company dismissed Ansell from office and later brought an action against him for an account of the secret commission and bonuses he had received. Reversing Kekewich J, the Court of Appeal held that the receipt of secret commission was a good ground for dismissal. Ansell was also ordered to account for his secret commission and bonuses.

Cotton LJ: ... If a servant, or a managing director, or any person who is authorized to act, and is acting, for another in the matter of any contract, receives, as regards the contract, any sum, whether by way of percentage or otherwise, from the person with whom he is dealing on behalf of his principal, he is committing a breach of duty. It is not an honest act, and, in my opinion, it is a sufficient act to shew that he cannot be trusted to perform the duties which he has undertaken as servant or agent. He puts himself in such a position that he has a temptation not faithfully to perform his duty to his employer. He has a temptation, especially where he is getting a percentage on expenditure, not to cut down the expenditure, but to let it be increased, so that his percentage may be larger. I do not, however, rely on that, but what I say is this, that where an agent entering into a contract on behalf of his principal, and without the knowledge or assent of that principal, receives money from the person with whom he is dealing, he is doing a wrongful act, he is misconducting himself as regards his agency, and, in my opinion, that gives to his employer, whether a company or an individual, and whether the agent be a servant, or a managing director, power and authority to dismiss him from his employment as a person who by that act is shewn to be incompetent of faithfully discharging his duty to his principal.

Bowen LJ: I will, first of all, deal with what is the cardinal matter of the whole case; whether the plaintiffs were justified or not in dismissing their managing director as they did. This is an age, I may say, when a large portion of the commercial world makes its livelihood by earning, and by earning honestly, agency commission on sales or other transactions, but it is also a time when a large portion of those who move within the ambit of the commercial world, earn, I am afraid, commission dishonestly by taking commissions not merely from their masters, but from the other parties with whom their master is negotiating, and with whom they are dealing on behalf of their master, and taking such commissions without the knowledge of their master or principal. There never, therefore, was a time in the history of our law when it was more essential that Courts of Justice should draw with precision and firmness the line of demarcation which prevails between commissions which may be honestly received and kept, and commissions taken behind the master's back, and in fraud of the master . . .

Now, there can be no question that an agent employed by a principal or master to do business with another, who, unknown to that principal or master, takes from that other person a profit arising out of the business which he is employed to transact, is doing a wrongful act inconsistent with his duty towards his master, and the continuance of confidence between them. He does the wrongful act whether such profit be given to him in return for services which he actually performs for the third party, or whether it be given to him for his supposed influence, or whether it be given to him on any other ground at all; if it is a profit which arises out of the transaction, it belongs to his master, and the agent or servant has no right to take it, or keep it, or bargain for it, or to receive it without bargain, unless his master knows it. It is said if the transaction be one of very old date, that in some way deprives the master of his right to treat it as a breach of faith. As the Lord Justice has pointed out, the age of the fraud may be a reason in the master's mind for not acting on his rights; but it is impossible to say that because a fraud has been concealed for six years, therefore the master has not a right when he discovers it to act upon his discovery, and to put an end to the relation of employer and employed with which such fraud was inconsistent. I, therefore, find it impossible to adopt Kekewich J's view, or to come to any other conclusion except that the managing director having been guilty of a fraud on his employers was rightly dismissed by them, and dismissed by them rightly even though they did not discover the fraud until after they had actually pronounced the sentence of dismissal . . .

That really disposes of the most important part of the dispute between the parties. But I also wish to add one word on the subject of the bonuses which he claims to be entitled to retain as received from the Hull Ice Co and the Hull Fishing Co, otherwise called the Red Cross Co. If that was a profit received by him, as it seems to me to have been, while he was agent, and arising out of the duty which he was employed to do for the company, it falls under the same branch of the law as the profits received in respect of the Shipbuilding Co. I have some little difficulty in following Kekewich J's judgment with regard to that. We may perhaps have an inaccurate note of it, but if Kekewich J is of opinion that it is the essence of a title to relief in such a case that the principal would have been able to claim as his own money, as between himself and the other party to the business transaction, the money secretly received by his agent, I do not think that is the law. It is true, as Kekewich J says, that the money which is sought to be recovered must be money had and received by the agent for the principal's use; but the use which arises in such a case, and the reception to the use of the principal which arises in such a case, does not depend on any privity between the principal and the opposite party with whom the agent is employed to conduct business—it is not that the money ought to have gone into the principal's hands in the first instance; the use arises from the relation between the principal and the agent himself. It is because it is contrary to equity that the agent or the servant should retain money so received without the knowledge of his master. Then the law implies a use, that is to say, there is an implied contract, if you put it as a legal proposition—there is an equitable right, if you treat it as a matter of equity—as between the principal and agent that the agent should pay it over, which renders the agent liable to be sued for money had and received, and there is an equitable right in the master to receive it, and to take it out of the hands of the agent, which gives the principal a right to relief in equity.

[**Fry LJ** delivered a concurring judgment.]

Novoship (UK) Ltd v Mikhaylyuk

[2012] EWHC 3586 (Comm), Commercial Court

In the course of his judgment in a case involving bribes solicited and received by an agent and various confederates in the course of arranging the charter of ships, Christopher Clarke J summarised the strict, punitive principles governing bribery of agents.

Christopher Clarke J:

104. In *Industries and General Mortgage Co Ltd v Lewis* [1949] 2 All ER 573, 575, Slade J defined a bribe as follows:

For the purposes of the civil law a bribe means the payment of a secret commission, which only means

(i)   that the person making the payment makes it to the agent of the other person with whom he is dealing;

(ii) that he makes it to that person knowing that that person is acting as the agent of the other person with whom he is dealing; and

(iii) that he fails to disclose to the other person with whom he is dealing that he has made that payment to the person whom he knows to be the other person's agent.

105. A bribe was defined even more succinctly by Leggatt J, as he then was, in *Anangel Atlas Compania Naviera SA v Ishikawajima-Harima Heavy Industries* [1990] 1 Lloyd's Rep 167 at 171, as:

A commission or other inducement which is given by a third party to an agent as such, and which is secret from his principal.

106. The essential character of a bribe is, thus, that it is a secret payment or inducement that gives rise to a realistic prospect of a conflict between the agent's personal interest and that of his principal. The bribe may have been offered by the payer or sought by the agent. There is no need to establish dishonesty or corrupt motives. This is irrebuttably presumed—*re A Debtor* [1927] 2 Ch 367 at 376 (*per* Scrutton LJ—'the court ought to presume fraud in such circumstances'). A bribe encompasses not just a payment of money but the conferring of any advantage or benefit, and may be an actual benefit or merely the promise of a benefit held out by the payer or an expectation of one. The motive for the payment or inducement (be it a gift, payment for services or

otherwise) is irrelevant. In *Fiona Trust v Privalov* [2010] EWHC 758 (Comm) at [73] Andrew Smith J contemplated that moonlighting for a person engaged in transactions with the principal might well give rise to a conflict between the agent's interest and duty and that the reward for his services might count as a bribe.

107. The payments (or other benefits) do not have to be made directly to the fiduciary. Bribes may be paid to third parties close to the agent, such as family members or discretionary trusts, or simply to those whom the agent wishes to benefit. The test is whether the payment (or other benefit) puts the fiduciary in a real (as opposed to a fanciful) position of potential conflict between interest and duty.

108. The recipient of the bribe (or the person at whose order the bribe is paid) must be someone with a role in the decision-making process in relation to the transaction in question, eg as agent, or otherwise someone who is in a position to influence or affect the decision taken by the principal. There is, however, no need to show that the payer intended the agent to be influenced by the payment or whether he was in fact influenced thereby. There is an irrebuttable presumption as to both, and that the principal has suffered damage in the amount of the bribe—*Hovenden & Sons v Milhof* (1900) 83 LT 41, 43, CA, *per* Romer LJ; *Industries & General Mortgage Co Ltd v Lewis* (above) at pp 576–8 *per* Slade J; *Mahesan v Malaysian Housing Society* [1979] AC 374, at pp 380E and 383A–C, PC; *Daraydan Holdings Ltd v Solland International Ltd* [2005] Ch 119 at [53], *per* Lawrence Collins J.

109. The payment need not be linked to a particular transaction—*Daraydan Holdings v Solland International* (above) at [53]; *Fiona Trust v Privalov* [2010] EWHC 758 (Comm) at [73] (*per* Andrew Smith J). It is sufficient if the agent is tainted by the bribery at the time of the transaction between the payer of the bribe and payee's principal. If that is so, the agent's conflict of interest means that the principal has been deprived by the other party to the transaction of the disinterested advice of his agent and is entitled to a further opportunity to consider whether it is in his interests to affirm it. It follows that subsequent transactions may be tainted by payments linked to an earlier transaction between the parties, or by a payment not linked to any particular transaction. 'If a secret payment is made to an agent, it taints future dealings between the principal and the person making it in which the agent acts for the principal or in which he is in a position to influence the principal's decisions, so long as the potential conflict of interest remains a real possibility': see *Fiona Trust* at [73].

110. The underlying rationale for the strict approach taken by the cases is that a principal is entitled to be confident that an agent will act wholly in his interests.

111. The agent/fiduciary and the payer of the bribe/secret commission are jointly and severally liable not only to account to the principal for the amount of the bribe but also in damages for fraud for any loss suffered by the principal. Consequently, the agent and the third party payer are jointly and severally liable to the principal (1) to account for the amount of the bribe in restitution as money had and received; and (2) for damages for any actual loss suffered by the principal from entering into the transaction in respect of which the bribe or secret commission was given or promised. But these are alternative remedies and the principal must elect between the two remedies prior to final judgment being entered: *Mahesan v Malaysia Government Officers' Co-operative Housing Society Ltd* [1979] AC 374, 383 (*per* Lord Diplock); *Petrotrade v Smith* [2000] 1 Lloyd's Rep 486 at 489–490 (*per* David Steel J); *Bowstead and Reynolds on Agency* (19th ed), at para 6-087....

NOTES

1. As mentioned in Christopher Clarke J's judgment in *Novoship (UK) Ltd v Mikhaylyuk* (above), in *Anangel Atlas Compañía Naviera SA v Ishikawajima-Harima Heavy Industries Co Ltd* [1990] 1 Lloyd's Rep 167 at 171, Leggatt J proposed a succinct definition of 'bribe': 'a bribe consists in a commission or other inducement, which is given by a third party to an agent as such, and which is secret from his principal'. The payment, therefore, constitutes a bribe even though it does not induce a contract between the principal of the recipient and the donor; it is the making of the payment that gives rise to a conflict of interest on the part of the recipient (*Petrotrade Inc v Smith* [2000] 1 Lloyd's Rep 486 at [16], [17], per David Steel J). The bribe may be given by the third party's agent acting in the course of his authority (*Armagas Ltd v Mundogas SA* [1986] AC 717 at 743, per Robert Goff LJ). It is irrebuttably presumed against the person giving the bribe that his motive was corrupt and against the agent that he was influenced by the bribe (see *Hovenden & Sons v Millhoff*, above; *Donegal International Ltd v Zambia* [2007] EWHC 197 (Comm), [2007] 1 Lloyd's Rep 397 at [275], per Andrew Smith J).

2.   In *Shipway v Broadwood* [1899] 1 QB 369 at 373, Chitty LJ famously said that 'the real evil is not the payment of money, but the secrecy attending it'. The burden of proving full disclosure of commission paid to an agent by a third party is on the agent. Where there is *no* disclosure the agent will be held to have received a secret commission (bribe). In some cases there may have been partial or inadequate disclosure that is sufficient disclosure to negate secrecy, and so avoid the consequences of the payment being treated as a bribe (see below), but insufficient disclosure to say that the principal's fully informed consent had been obtained, so that the agent is held to have breached his fiduciary duty by putting himself in a position where he has a conflict of interest. This was held to have been the case in *Hurstanger Ltd v Wilson* [2007] EWCA Civ 299, [2007] 1 WLR 2351, where the defendants applied to the claimant through a broker (agent) for a loan to be secured by a charge on the defendants' home. The loan documentation sent to the defendants for signature authorised payment of the broker's fee out of the loan and stated that the defendants 'understand that an amount in the sum of £295 will be debited to the loan balance being the legal costs incurred in this matter'. The claimant paid the agreed arrangement fee to the broker and also a commission of £240. The defendants later fell into arrears and the claimant brought mortgage possession proceedings. The defendants contended that the loan agreement was void or voidable by reason of the payment of the £240 from the claimant to the broker. The Court of Appeal held that this was a 'half-way house case' where there had been sufficient disclosure so that the broker had not received a secret commission, but that the defendants had not given their fully informed consent to the broker's potential conflict of interest. The court refused to order rescission of the loan agreement on the ground that such a remedy would have been unfair and disproportionate, but held instead that the claimant was liable to pay equitable compensation of £240, plus interest, to the defendants for having procured the breach of the broker's fiduciary duty.

What remedies are available to the principal if his agent should receive a bribe? See, generally, A Berg [2001] LMCLQ 27 for an excellent, detailed review.

(a)   The agent may be dismissed without notice (*Bulfield v Foamier* (1895) 11 TLR 282).

(b)   The agent will be liable to forfeit his right to commission or remuneration that he would otherwise have received (*Andrews v Ramsay & Co* [1903] 2 KB 635).

(c)   It is clear that the agent must personally account for the bribe, but does he hold it on trust for his principal? For many years, applying the decision of a strong Court of Appeal in *Lister & Co v Stubbs* (1890) 45 Ch D 1, the courts held that the principal's claim to recover the amount of the bribe was personal, not proprietary. This meant that the principal could not recover any profit made by the agent through investment of the bribe, nor could the principal gain priority over general creditors on the agent's insolvency. But there was considerable controversy as to whether *Lister & Co v Stubbs* was right or wrong (the arguments on either side are neatly summarised by PBH Birks in [1993] LMCLQ 30). Over the past two decades this question has been hotly debated by both courts and scholars.

In *A-G for Hong Kong v Reid* [1994] 1 AC 324 the Privy Council departed from *Lister & Co v Stubbs*, holding that properties purchased in New Zealand by a Crown servant (the Acting Director of Public Prosecutions for Hong Kong), using monies he had received as bribes, were held by him on constructive trust for the Crown. Lord Templeman, delivering the Board's advice, said at 331:

> When a bribe is offered and accepted in money or in kind, the money or property constituting the bribe belongs in law to the recipient. Money paid to the false fiduciary belongs to him. The legal estate in freehold property conveyed to the false fiduciary by way of bribe vests in him. Equity, however, which acts *in personam*, insists that it is unconscionable for a fiduciary to obtain and retain a benefit in breach of duty. The provider of a bribe cannot recover it because he committed a criminal offence when he paid the bribe. The false fiduciary who received the bribe in breach of duty must pay and account for the bribe to the person to whom that duty was owed. In the present case, as soon as the first respondent received a bribe in breach of the duties he owed to the Government of Hong Kong, he became a debtor in equity to the Crown for the amount of that bribe. So much is admitted. But if the bribe consists of property which increases in value or if a cash bribe is invested advantageously, the false fiduciary will receive a benefit from his breach of duty unless he is accountable not only for the original amount or value of the bribe but also for the increased value of the property representing the bribe. As soon as the bribe was received it should have been paid or transferred *instanter* to the person who suffered from the breach of duty. Equity considers as done that which ought to have been done. As soon as the bribe was received, whether in cash or in kind, the false fiduciary held the bribe on a constructive trust for the person injured. Two objections have been raised to this analysis. First it is said that if the fiduciary is in equity a debtor to the person injured, he cannot also be a trustee of the bribe. But there is no reason why equity should not provide two remedies, so long as they do not result in double recovery. If the property representing the bribe exceeds the original bribe in value, the fiduciary cannot retain the benefit of the increase in value which he obtained solely as a result of his breach of duty. Secondly, it is said that if the false fiduciary holds property representing the bribe in trust for the person injured, and if the false fiduciary is or becomes insolvent, the unsecured creditors of the false fiduciary will be deprived of their right to share in the proceeds of that property. But the unsecured creditors cannot be in a better position than their debtor. The authorities show that property acquired by a trustee innocently but in breach of trust and the property from time to time representing the same belong in equity to the *cestui que* trust and not to the trustee personally whether he is solvent or insolvent. Property acquired by a trustee as a result of a criminal breach of trust and the property from time to time representing the same must also belong in equity to his cestui que trust and not to the trustee whether he is solvent or insolvent.

When a bribe is accepted by a fiduciary in breach of his duty then he holds that bribe in trust for the person to whom the duty was owed. If the property representing the bribe decreases in value the fiduciary must pay the difference between that value and the initial amount of the bribe because he should not have accepted the bribe or incurred the risk of loss. If the property increases in value, the fiduciary is not entitled to any surplus in excess of the initial value of the bribe because he is not allowed by any means to make a profit out of a breach of duty.

Lord Templeman concluded that as *Lister & Co v Stubbs* was inconsistent with this analysis it should not be followed in future.

Although decisions of the Privy Council are not binding on English courts, so that *Lister & Co v Stubbs* remained technically binding on all courts below the House of Lords,

Lord Templeman's speech was clearly of high persuasive authority. However, the case attracted a great deal of hostile criticism (usefully summarised in K Uff, 'The Remedies of the Defrauded Principal after *Att Gen for Hong Kong v Reid*' in D Feldman and F Meisel (eds), *Corporate and Commercial Law: Modern Developments* (1996), Ch 13; but contrast the warm response given to the case by Professor Jones in R Goff and G Jones, *The Law of Restitution* (7th edn, 2007), para 33–025. Pill LJ was later to remark that this dispute has produced a literature that reveals 'passions of a force uncommon in the legal world': *FHR European Ventures LLP v Mankarious* [2013] EWCA Civ 17, [2014] Ch 1 at [61]). Leaving aside the strong technical objections to the decision (namely, the inappropriate invocation of the maxim that equity regards as done that which ought to be done), the Privy Council's failure to take proper account of the interests of the insolvent agent's unsecured creditors stands out as a particularly regrettable feature of the case (this aspect of the case was severely criticised by Professor Goode in his essay 'Proprietary Restitutionary Claims' in WR Cornish et al (eds), *Restitution: Past, Present and Future* (1998), Ch 5).

The Court of Appeal subsequently rejected the idea that the proprietary consequences of bribery should be extended to other forms of fraud (*Halifax Building Society v Thomas* [1996] Ch 217 at 228, where Peter Gibson LJ distinguished *A-G for Hong Kong v Reid* on the ground that, on the facts before him, there was no fiduciary relationship between the mortgagor and mortgagee 'but merely that of debtor and secured creditor'). The fact that proprietary relief seems only to be available in the context of a breach of fiduciary duty, and not for other wrongs, is 'a distinction which is difficult to justify' (C Rotherham [1997] CfiLR 43 at 44). Nevertheless, in *Daraydan Holdings Ltd v Solland International Ltd* [2004] EWHC 622 (Ch), [2005] Ch 119 at [86], Lawrence Collins J said (*obiter*) that he preferred *A-G for Hong Kong v Reid* to *Lister & Co v Stubbs*, and continued: 'There are powerful policy reasons for ensuring that a fiduciary does not retain gains acquired in violation of fiduciary duty, and I do not consider that it should make any difference whether the fiduciary is insolvent. There is no injustice to the creditors in their not sharing in an asset for which the fiduciary has not given value, and which the fiduciary should not have had.'

The debate was reignited by *Sinclair Investments (UK) Ltd v Versailles Trade Finance Ltd* [2011] EWCA Civ 347, [2012] Ch 453, in which the Court of Appeal declared that *Lister & Co v Stubbs* was in fact correctly decided. Lord Millett published a withering critique of *Sinclair Investments* ('Bribes and Secret Commissions Again' [2012] CLJ 583) and the ruling was more or less treated with derision by a full Federal Court of Australia (see *Grimaldi v Chameleon Mining NL (No 2)* [2012] FCAFC 6 at [569]–[574], per Finn J, who remarked that 'English law may have its own reasons for so contriving the limits to proprietary relief. We need not speculate about them'). English courts were once again obliged, sometimes reluctantly (eg *Cadogan Petroleum plc v Tolley* [2011] EWHC 2286 (Ch), [2015] WTLR 1505 at [27], per Newey J) to follow *Lister & Co v Stubbs*. Lord Millett (above, at p 614) summarised the effect of the courts' volte-face:

> *Lister v Stubbs* and *Sinclair v Versailles* are contrary to principle and authority, fail to give effect to the policy of the law, reduce English law to a state of incoherence, and leave this country in the uncomfortable position of being the only common law jurisdiction where a dishonest fiduciary is allowed to retain a profit he has made by profitably investing a bribe or otherwise exploiting the fiduciary relationship for his own benefit without the fully informed consent of his principal.

In *European Ventures LLP v Cedar Capital Partners LLC* [2014] UKSC 45, [2015] AC 250, however, the Supreme Court reconsidered the question. The case concerned an agent who, without its principal's informed consent, had accepted a €10 million secret commission from the vendor of a luxury hotel in Monaco. Lord Neuberger, who had delivered judgment in *Sinclair Investments* only two years earlier, delivered judgment on behalf of a seven-man Supreme Court. Acknowledging that '[i]n the end, it is not possible to identify any plainly right or wrong answer to the issue of the extent of the Rule, as a matter of pure legal authority' (at [32]), Lord Neuberger opted for the view that whether it concerned a bribe, secret commission, or other benefit received by the agent or simply the agent taking advantage of an opportunity that came his way as a result of the agency, the principal was entitled not merely to an equitable account in respect of the benefit but also to the beneficial ownership of the benefit: 'a bribe or secret commission accepted by an agent is held on trust for his principal' (at [46]). Such a rule, which is consistent with the fundamental principle of the law of agency that a principal is entitled to an agent's undivided loyalty, was claimed to have 'the merit of simplicity' since it applies uniformly in all situations, serves to align 'the circumstances in which an agent is obliged to account for any benefit received in breach of his fiduciary duty and those in which his principal can claim the beneficial ownership of the benefit', and conforms with elementary economics in as much as there is normally a strong possibility that the bribe or secret commission will have disadvantaged the principal (at [35]–[37]). Such a rule was also said to conform with wider policy considerations: it served to recognise that bribery, in particular, was an evil practice that undermined trust in the commercial world whilst also drawing English law into alignment with the rule that prevails in a number of other common law jurisdictions (at [45]).

It is safe to assume that, whilst academic discussion will continue, the decision of the Supreme Court in *European Ventures LLP v Cedar Capital Partners LLC* has now laid this most contentious of matters to rest.

(d) The principal may claim damages in tort for fraud against the agent bribed and the briber (they are jointly and severally liable) for any loss caused as a result of entering into the transaction in respect of which the bribe was given (see *Petrotrade Inc v Smith* [2000] 1 Lloyd's Rep 486, David Steel J; *Fyffes Group Ltd v Templeman* [2000] 2 Lloyd's Rep 643, Toulson J: an additional claim that the briber had dishonestly assisted the agent's breach of fiduciary duty failed in *Petrotrade* but succeeded in *Fyffes*: noted by C Mitchell (2001) 117 LQR 207 at 209–210). The defendant cannot reduce his responsibility merely because the principal had the opportunity to investigate or intervene, but failed to take it: there is no defence of contributory negligence, or its equivalent in equity, to a claim based on bribery (*Corporacion Nacional del Cobre de Chile v Sogemin Metals Ltd* [1997] 1 WLR 1396 at 1402, per Carnwath J). In *Mahesan S/O Thambiah v Malaysia Government Officers' Co-operative Housing Society Ltd* [1979] AC 374, the Privy Council held that as against the agent bribed, and the briber, the principal can recover the bribe through an action in restitution, and that the agent and briber are jointly and severally liable in damages for loss caused by the fraud, but that the principal must elect between these two alternative remedies before judgment (per Lord Diplock at 383). Although this decision has been strongly criticised (see A Tettenborn (1979) 95 LQR 68), it is submitted that the Privy Council were correct to put the principal to his election. To allow the principal to recover both the bribe and damages for his loss against a single defendant would allow double recovery and give the principal an undeserved 'windfall' (see C Needham (1979) 95 LQR 536). But there is no reason why the principal cannot recover the bribe from the agent and go on to recover any excess loss in damages from the briber, or vice versa.

(e) The principal may recover the bribe *and* rescind any contract he made with the third party as a consequence of the bribe being paid to his agent (*Logicrose Ltd v Southend United Football Club Ltd* [1988] 1 WLR 1256, noted by G Jones [1989] CLJ 22). The contract made with the third party is considered voidable at the election of the principal (*Hurstanger v Wilson* [2007] EWCA Civ 299, [2007] 1 WLR 2351 at [38]). On the other hand, it can be argued that where an agent accepts, or agrees to accept, a bribe he acts contrary to his principal's interests and does not have authority, actual or apparent, of his principal to enter into the contract with the third party, thereby rendering the resultant contract void (*Bowstead and Reynolds*, para 8–218). However, the fact that the contract is rendered void for lack of authority may not prevent the principal from being bound by an arbitration agreement contained within it (*Fiona Trust & Holding Corpn v Privalov* [2007] UKHL 40, [2008] 1 Lloyd's Rep 254, where the House of Lords held that the principle of separability, enacted in s 7 of the Arbitration Act 1996, required direct impeachment of the arbitration agreement before it could be set aside).

In addition to civil liability, the agent (and the briber) may also be criminally liable. The criminal law relating to bribery, which was once somewhat complex and confused, has been comprehensively overhauled by the Bribery Act 2010. This Act has introduced a range of far-reaching general bribery offences whenever someone gives or promises (s 1), requests, accepts, or agrees to accept (s 2) a 'financial or other advantage'. It might be added that there is also an offence of bribery of a foreign public official (s 6), and controversially commercial organisations can now be prosecuted for failing to prevent bribery on their behalf in order to obtain or retain business or an advantage in the conduct of business (s 7). Proceedings may only be brought under the Bribery Act with the consent of either the Director of Public Prosecutions or the Director of the Serious Fraud Office (s 10).

QUESTIONS

1. What if an agent accepts a 'bribe' but fails to keep his side of the bargain? Has the agent breached his fiduciary duty? See above and also P Millett [1993] RLR 7 at 13, fn 42.

2. Where an agent acquires an asset partly with the bribe and partly with the agent's own money, can the principal recover the whole or only part of the value of the asset? See E Peel, *Treitel's Law of Contract* (14th edn, 2015), para 16–098, referring, by analogy, to *Foskett v McKeown* [2001] 1 AC 102, where the wrongdoer was a trustee and not an agent.

(d) Duty to account

An agent is under a duty to keep the money and property of his principal separate from his own. If the agent fails to keep his principal's property separate from his own, the principal will be entitled to the entire mixed fund, unless the agent can establish any part of it as his own property (*Lupton v White* (1808) 15 Ves 432). This duty only arises where money or property is beneficially owned by the principal, so that the agent is treated as if he were a trustee of it. But in many cases this does not happen because the parties intend that the agent should be free to use the money or property received in his business (see, eg, those reservation of title clause cases considered below at pp 497–500; see, generally, *Bowstead and Reynolds*, para 6–041). In such cases, the agent will not hold money or property *qua* trustee, he will simply be liable to account for it *qua* debtor. However, where the agent is instructed to purchase property for his principal, and does so in his own name, the agent will hold that property on trust for his principal (*Lees v Nuttall* (1829) 1 Russ & M 53).

An agent must also keep accurate accounts of all transactions entered into on behalf of his principal. He must be ready at all times to produce them upon request by the principal (*Pearse v Green* (1819) 1 Jac & W 135). As Mummery LJ noted in *Fairstar Heavy Transport NV v Adkins* [2013] EWCA Civ 886, [2013] CLC 272 at [53], 'as a general rule, it is a legal incident of [the relationship of principal and agent] that a principal is entitled to require production by the agent of documents relating to the affairs of the principal'. Failure to do so means that everything will be presumed against the agent (*Gray v Haig* (1855) 20 Beav 219 at 226, per Romilly MR). The duty to keep and provide records arises out of the fiduciary nature of the principal–agent relationship and independently of any contract between them so that, unless expressly excluded by contract, it survives the termination of the contract of agency (*Yasuda Fire and Marine Insurance Co of Europe Ltd v Orion Marine Insurance Underwriting Agency Ltd* [1995] QB 174, Coleman J). Further, on the termination of the agency, the principal is entitled to have delivered up to him all documents relating to the agency which have been prepared by the agent for him: for example, in *Gibbon v Pease* [1905] 1 KB 810 an architect was ordered to deliver up plans to a house after the work had been completed and paid for. The principal's entitlement to such documents is subject to any right the agent may have to exercise a lien over them (see below, p 269).

(d) Duty not to delegate his authority

De Bussche v Alt
(1878) 8 Ch D 286, Court of Appeal

A shipowner (De Bussche) employed an agent to sell a ship in India, China, or Japan at a certain price. The agent was unable to sell the ship himself but, with the shipowner's consent, he employed a sub-agent (Alt) in Japan to do so. In fact, the sub-agent purchased the ship for himself and then resold it to a third party at a handsome profit. Affirming the judgment of Hall V-C, the Court of Appeal held the sub-agent liable to account to the shipowner for his profit.

Thesiger LJ (delivering the judgment of the court (James, Baggally, and Thesiger LJJ): . . . As a general rule, no doubt, the maxim *'delegatus non potest delegare'* applies so as to prevent an agent from establishing the relationship of principal and agent between his own principal and a third person; but this maxim when analyzed merely imports that an agent cannot, without authority from his principal, devolve upon another obligations to the principal which he has himself undertaken to personally fulfil; and that, inasmuch as confidence in the particular person employed is at the root of the contract of agency, such authority cannot be implied as an ordinary incident in the contract. But the exigencies of business do from time to time render necessary the carrying out of the instructions of a principal by a person other than the agent originally instructed for the purpose, and where that is the case, the reason of the thing requires that the rule should be relaxed, so as, on the one hand, to enable the agent to appoint what has been termed 'a sub-agent' or 'substitute' (the latter of which designations, although it does not exactly denote the legal relationship of the parties, we adopt for want of a better, and for the sake of brevity); and, on the other hand, to constitute, in the interests and for the protection of the principal, a direct privity of contract between him and such substitute. And we are of opinion that an authority to the effect referred to may and should be implied where, from the conduct of the parties to the original contract of agency, the usage of trade, or the nature of the particular business which is the subject of the agency, it may reasonably be presumed that the parties to the contract of agency originally intended that such authority should exist, or where, in the course of the employment, unforeseen emergencies arise which impose upon the agent the necessity of employing a substitute; and that when such authority exists, and is duly exercised, privity of contract arises between the principal and the substitute, and the latter becomes as responsible to the former for the due discharge of the duties which his employment casts upon him, as if he had been appointed agent by the principal himself. The law upon this point is accurately stated in *Story on Agency.* A case like the present, where a shipowner employs an agent for the purpose of effectuating a sale of a ship at any port where the ship may from time to time in the course of its employment under charter happen to be, is pre-eminently one in which the appointment of substitutes at ports other than those where the agent himself carries on business is a necessity, and must reasonably be presumed to be in the contemplation of the parties; and in the present case, we have, over and above that presumption, what cannot but be looked upon as express authority to appoint a substitute, and a complete ratification of the actual appointment of the defendant in the letters which passed respectively between *Willis & Son* and the plaintiff on the one side, and *Gilman & Co* on the other. We are, therefore, of opinion that the relationship of principal and agent was, in respect of the sale of the *Columbine,* for a time at least, constituted between the plaintiff and the defendant.

NOTES

1. An agent cannot delegate his authority to another person, or appoint a sub-agent to do some of the acts which he himself has to do, unless the agent has the express or implied consent of his principal to do so. The rule applies both where the principal places trust and confidence in the agent, and also where the principal relies on the personal skill of the agent.

2. In *De Bussche v Alt,* Thesiger LJ set out the circumstances when the consent of the principal to delegate will be implied. The performance of purely ministerial acts, which do not involve confidence or discretion, may also be delegated, for example service of a notice to quit by the solicitor of a company which was itself acting as agent (*Allam & Co Ltd v Europa Poster Services Ltd* [1968] 1 WLR 638). For the powers of a trustee to delegate, see the Trustee Delegation Act 1999 and ss 11–23 of the Trustee Act 2000, the effects of which are summarised in D Hayton, P Matthews, and C Mitchell, *Underhill and Hayton: Law Relating to Trusts and Trustees* (19th edn, 2016), paras 55.1–55.49.

3. If the agent makes an unauthorised delegation, the acts of, and payment to, the sub-agent will not bind the principal. A third party dealing with the sub-agent, however, may be able to rely on the apparent authority of the agent to delegate and thereby hold the principal bound by the sub-agent's acts. Alternatively, the principal will be bound if he ratifies the agent's unauthorised act of delegation. It should also be noted that where there has been an unauthorised delegation, the principal is not liable to the sub-agent for commission (*Schmaling v Thomlinson* (1815) 6 Taunt 147); the sub-agent has no lien against the principal (*Solly v Rathbone* (1814) 2 M & S 298); the agent will be liable to the principal for wrongful execution of his authority (*Catlin v Bell* (1815) 4 Camp 183) and may be liable for money had and received by the sub-agent (*National Employers' Mutual General Insurance Association Ltd v Elphinstone* [1929] WN 135).

What are the consequences of an authorised delegation of authority by the agent?

Calico Printers' Association Ltd v Barclays Bank Ltd
(1931) 145 LT 51, King's Bench Division

The plaintiffs sold cotton to a consignee in Beirut and sent shipping documents to Barclays Bank Ltd with instructions to insure the goods if the documents were not accepted by the consignee. Barclays Bank did not have an office in Beirut and, with the knowledge of the plaintiffs, instructed the Anglo-Palestine Bank in Beirut to act as their agents. Barclays Bank told the Anglo-Palestine Bank to insure the goods if the documents were not accepted. The Anglo-Palestine Bank did not present the shipping documents for payment and failed to insure the cotton, which was destroyed by fire. The plaintiffs then sued Barclays Bank and the Anglo-Palestine Bank for negligence. Wright J dismissed both claims, holding that the Anglo-Palestine Bank was not liable because there was no privity of contract between them and the plaintiffs, and that Barclays Bank were not liable because they could rely on an exclusion clause in their contract with the plaintiffs.

Wright J: . . . [T]o leave the goods uninsured was a gross breach of the most elementary business precautions. . . .

On this ground I should hold these defendants liable to the plaintiffs if there were privity between them and the plaintiffs, and this question must now be considered.

To support the argument that there was privity between the plaintiffs and the Anglo-Palestine Bank, reliance was especially placed on a passage from *Story on Agency*, s 201, as establishing a general principle that where the employment of a sub-agent was authorised either by express terms or by a known course of business, or some unforeseen exigency necessitating such employment, there was privity established between the principal and the sub-agent, so that the sub-agent and not the agent became directly responsible to the principal for any negligence or misconduct in the performance of the mandate. But I do not think the English law has admitted any such general principle, but has in general applied the rule that even where the sub-agent is properly employed, there is still no privity between him and the principal; the latter is entitled to hold the agent liable for breach of the mandate, which he has accepted, and cannot, in general, claim against the sub-agent for negligence or breach of duty. I know of no English case in which a principal has recovered against a sub-agent for negligence. The agent does not as a rule escape liability to the principal merely because employment of the sub-agent is contemplated. To create privity it must be established not only that the principal contemplated that a sub-agent would perform part of the contract, but also that the principal authorised the agent to create privity of contract between the principal and the sub-agent, which is a very different matter requiring precise proof. In general, where a principal employs an agent to carry out a particular employment, the agent undertakes responsibility for the whole transaction, and is responsible for any negligence in carrying it out, even if the negligence be that of the sub-agent properly or necessarily engaged to perform some part, because there is no privity between the principal and the sub-agent.

I think the rule applies to the present case. The defendants, Barclays, by accepting the employment for 74 per cent commission accepted responsibility for the whole service, including that part of it which necessarily involved the employment of a sub-agent or correspondent at Beyrout. The mere fact that he was nominated by the plaintiffs does not in my judgment affect the position; the defendants, Barclays, accepted the nomination and accepted the defendants, the Anglo-Palestine Bank, as their instrument to fulfil their contract. The case is one of most ordinary banking practice, and to accept the contention that the defendants, Barclays, were not responsible for the acts of the defendants, the Anglo-Palestine Bank, their foreign correspondents, or that there was privity between the latter and the plaintiffs, would be in my judgment to go contrary to the whole commercial understanding of a transaction like this.

The case is quite different from that put by Lord Cave LC in the case of *William H Muller & Co (London) Ltd v Lethem* ([1928] AC 34, 138 LT 241). In that case the question was whether the appellants were agents in London of a Dutch shipping company so as to be assessable to income tax in respect of business done in this country as such agents. The facts were peculiar, and one view was that the agents were directly appointed by the Dutch shipowners. Lord Cave LC said ([1928] AC at p 47, 138 LT at p 250):

> I am disposed to think that in signing both these documents the Dutch firm were acting as directors of the shipping companies, and in that capacity appointed the London firm as direct agents of those companies; but even if that be not so, and if the appointments must be held to have been made by the Dutch firm as shipping agents for the Dutch companies and not as directors—still it appears to me that they constituted the London firm direct agents of the two companies. In this connection reference may be made to the well-known judgment of Thesiger LJ in *De Bussche v Alt* (38 LT 370, (1878) 8 Ch D 286), where he pointed out that in certain cases, where the exigencies of business require it, an agent must be deemed to have authority to constitute a direct privity of contract between a substitute appointed by him and his principals. In my opinion the present case falls within that category, and the appellants were appointed and became the authorised and regular agents of the two Dutch companies in London.

For the reasons I have already indicated, I think it should not be held here that the plaintiffs gave any authority to the defendants, Barclays, to constitute a direct privity of contract between them and the Anglo-Palestine Bank; nor is my judgment on this conclusion affected by *De Bussche v Alt* (*sup.*) where a bill in equity was filed for an account in respect of secret profits made by a sub-agent for the sale of some ships. The plaintiff, the owner, consigned them for sale to a firm in the East, who appointed the defendant agent for sale in Japan. The plaintiff and the defendant corresponded about the sale; the defendant made large secret profits and was held liable to account. The court there held that the circumstances constituted an express authority to appoint a substitute apart from the complete ratification of the actual appointment, and it was accordingly held that the relationship of principal and agent was constituted as between plaintiff and defendant, at least, *pro hac vice*. But apart from the specific finding of fact that there was authority to create direct privity, the case turned on equitable principles; the sub-agent was *pro tanto* in a fiduciary position as regards the secret profits and could not retain them as against the person whom he knew to be entitled, namely, the actual principal. In a later case of a similar character, *Powell & Thomas v Evan Jones & Co* ([1905] 1 KB 11, 92 LT 430), the Court of Appeal held that there was evidence to justify the jury in finding there was privity of contract on facts which appear to me very different from those in the present case, but held also that in all the circumstances there was such a fiduciary relationship as between the sub-agent and the principal as placed the former under a personal incapacity to receive any secret reward.

I do not think the three last cited authorities require me to depart from the conclusion that I have arrived at on the facts of this case and the other authorities that I have cited. I accordingly hold that the claim against the defendants, the Anglo-Palestine Bank, fails.

[The decision of Wright J was subsequently affirmed by the Court of Appeal: (1931) 145 LT 51 at 58. There was no appeal against that part of Wright J's judgment set out above.]

NOTES

1.   The consequences of authorised delegation depend on whether there is privity of contract between the principal and the sub-agent (criticised by *Bowstead and Reynolds*, para 5–011). The existence of privity of contract turns on whether the agent was clearly authorised to create it, or whether his act in doing so was ratified by the principal. Since *Calico Printers*, the influence of *De Bussche v Alt* has waned on this issue. The general rule is that there is no privity of contract between principal and sub-agent. As Rix J said in *Prentis Donegan & Partners Ltd v Leeds and Leeds Co Inc* [1998] 2 Lloyd's Rep 326 at 332, 'the authorities show that the *De Bussche v Alt* exception is indeed an exception, and a narrow one, and the burden must be on the defendants to show some special factors…to raise an argument that the general rule makes way for the exception'. However, *De Bussche v Alt* was applied in *Velos Group Ltd v Harbour Insurance Services Ltd* [1997] 2 Lloyd's Rep 461, a decision of HHJ Hallgarten QC at the Central London County Court (Business List), where it was held that because it is necessary to use a Lloyd's broker to place insurance in the Lloyd's insurance market, the assured (principal), whose own insurance broker (agent) had used a Lloyd's broker (sub-agent) to place such insurance, could be regarded as in privity of contract with the Lloyd's broker. The correctness of that decision must be in doubt. In *Pangood Ltd v Barclay Brown & Co Ltd* [1999] Lloyd's Rep IR 405, the Court of Appeal, although seemingly without reference to the *Velos* case, rejected the notion that a Lloyd's broker was in privity of contract with the intermediate broker's principal (the assured) where the Lloyd's broker had merely been asked to obtain a quotation and subsequently to effect insurance in accordance with the terms of that quotation.

2.   If there is privity of contract between the principal and the sub-agent the appointing agent need only exercise due care and skill in the appointment of the sub-agent; he is not normally liable for the default of the sub-agent (*Aiken v Stewart Wrightson Members Agency Ltd* [1995] 1 WLR 1281). In any event, the agent will usually have included a clause in his contract with the principal excluding liability for the acts and omissions of the sub-agent (but note that such clauses may be subject to review under the Unfair Contract Terms Act 1977 and/or the Consumer Rights Act 2015: see below, p 452). Further, if there is privity, the sub-agent becomes the agent of the principal and acquires all the usual rights and duties of an agent.

3.   If there is no privity of contract between the principal and the sub-agent, the sub-agent generally owes no duty to account to the principal (*New Zealand and Australian Land Co v Watson* (1881) 7 QBD 374; cf A Tettenborn (1999) 115 LQR 655, who argues that as the sub-agent purports to act for the principal and has the power to change the principal's position, it is both just and equitable that he should be under a duty to account to him). It has also been held that, in the absence of privity of contract between them, the sub-agent could not be liable to the principal in tort for negligent performance of his work (*Calico Printers' Association v Barclays Bank Ltd*, above). It may be thought that after the landmark decisions of *Donoghue v Stevenson* [1932] AC 562 and *Hedley Byrne & Co Ltd v Heller & Partners Ltd* [1964] AC 465, a sub-agent could now be held liable to the principal for the tort of negligence, irrespective of whether there is privity of contract between them. Indeed, in *Henderson v Merrett Syndicates Ltd* [1995] 2 AC 145, another case involving the Lloyd's insurance market, the House of Lords held that Lloyd's 'managing agents' (sub-agents) owed a duty of care in tort to 'indirect names' (principals), even though there was no privity of contract between them. Despite the fact that the indirect names had employed their own agents (called 'members' agents'), who, in turn, had entered into sub-agency agreements with the managing agents, the relationship between the indirect names and the managing agents was extremely close. The managing agents held themselves out as having special expertise and thereby assumed responsibility to

the indirect names, who placed implicit reliance on that expertise. This was, however, said to be a 'most unusual' case (per Lord Goff, at 195G). Lord Goff, delivering the principal speech in the House of Lords, stressed that in other cases the court would not allow an action in tort to short-circuit the contractual structure put in place by the parties (citing as an example *Simaan General Contracting Co v Pilkington Glass Ltd (No 2)* [1988] QB 758, a case involving construction subcontracts: but now contrast *Riyad Bank v Ahli United Arab Bank (UK) plc* [2006] EWCA Civ 780, [2006] 2 Lloyd's Rep 292, where the contractual structure adopted by the parties did not exclude liability in tort to the third party). He continued (at 195H): 'It cannot therefore be inferred from the present case that other sub-agents will be directly liable to the agent's principal in tort.' Lord Goff made clear that he was dealing with a case of pure economic loss, not physical damage to property. Where an agent negligently causes physical injury to the principal or physical damage to the principal's property, it may be that the principal could sue him in tort even though there was no privity of contract between them (see generally P Cane, 'Contract, Tort and the Lloyd's Debacle' in FD Rose (ed), *Consensus Ad Idem* (1996), esp pp 111–118). But in the earlier case of *Balsamo v Medici* [1984] 1 WLR 951, Walton J held that the sub-agent was not liable in tort when he negligently paid over the proceeds of sale of the principal's car to an impostor, resulting in the principal suffering financial loss.

4.   Even if there is no privity of contract between the principal and the sub-agent, the sub-agent may still be held liable to the principal as a fiduciary for the purposes of disgorging a bribe (*Powell & Thomas v Evan Jones & Co* [1905] 1 KB 11; although, following *A-G for Hong Kong v Reid* [1994] 1 AC 324 and *European Ventures LLP v Cedar Capital Partners LLC* [2014] 3 WLR 535, that claim would now be proprietary); he may also have a lien against the principal (*Fisher v Smith* (1878) 4 App Cas 1; see below, p 269); and he may be able to rely on the appointing agent's apparent authority to claim remuneration from the principal (*Bowstead and Reynolds*, para 5–015). The principal may also be able to rely on the Contracts (Rights of Third Parties) Act 1999 to enforce a term of any contract between the agent and the sub-agent. Under s 1(1) of the Act, the principal may do this if (a) the contract expressly provides that he may, or (b) the term purports to confer a benefit on him, and there is nothing in the contract when read as a whole which indicates that the agent and the sub-agent intended otherwise.

5.   It is clear from the *Calico Printers* case that, subject to any express exclusion of liability (which will be subject to statutory control: see note 2 above), if there is no privity of contract between the principal and the sub-agent, the appointing agent will be liable to the principal for the defaults of the sub-agent (see also *Mackersy v Ramsays, Bonars & Co* (1843) 9 Cl & Fin 818; cf *Thomas Cheshire & Co v Vaughan Bros & Co* [1920] 3 KB 240 at 259, where Atkin LJ, *obiter*, suggested that the appointing agent should only be held liable if he did not exercise reasonable care in the selection of the sub-agent). The appointing agent will also be liable to the principal for money had and received by the sub-agent to the use of the principal (*Balsamo v Medici*, above). In these circumstances, the appointing agent must seek redress from the sub-agent.

QUESTIONS

1.   Pete employs Sell, It & Fast, a firm of estate agents, to sell his flat. Sell, It & Fast advertise the flat in its own shop window and also in the window of Tomkins, another firm of estate agents, with whom it has a reciprocal advertising arrangement. The advertisement states that all inquiries should be made through Sell, It & Fast. Bob sees the advertisement in Tomkins' window and contacts Sell, It & Fast to arrange to view the flat. Subsequently, Pete agrees to sell the flat to Bob and instructs his parents' solicitor, Conway, to act for him in this matter. Conway agrees to do so but, owing to his ill health, asks his old friend Drabble, a partner in another firm of solicitors, to draw up the documents needed to convey the flat to Bob. The sale of the flat is duly completed. Both Sell, It & Fast and Conway claim their agreed fees from Pete. Pete, who has just found out about the involvement of Tomkins and Drabble, now seeks your advice as to whether he has to pay both Sell, It & Fast's and Conway's fees. See *John McCann & Co v Pow* [1974] 1 WLR 1643 and *Re Becket, Purnell v Paine* [1918] 2 Ch 72.

2. Do the Commercial Agents (Council Directive) Regulations 1993 apply to sub-agencies? See *Light v Ty Europe Ltd* [2003] EWCA Civ 1238, [2004] 1 Lloyd's Rep 693: see above, p 120.

2 RIGHTS OF THE AGENT

(a) Remuneration

(i) A contractual right

With the exception of a 'commercial agent', whose position is now regulated by the Commercial Agents (Council Directive) Regulations 1993 (see below, p 266), an agent will only be entitled to remuneration from his principal for his services if the agency is contractual and there is an express or implied term of the agency contract to that effect (but see also note 4, below at p 259).

In the well-known case of *Way v Latilla* [1937] 3 All ER 759 an agent, W, had agreed with his principal, L, to send to the principal information concerning gold mines and concessions in West Africa. Although the principal had led the agent to believe that he would receive an interest in any concession obtained, no terms as to remuneration were expressly agreed between them. In the circumstances of this case, the House of Lords held that the agent was entitled to a reasonable remuneration on an implied contract to pay him a *quantum meruit*.

Lord Atkin emphasised that since the parties had not contractually agreed the share or interest that W was to receive, it was no business of the court to complete the parties' contract for them. Even had the parties agreed that W was to receive a percentage of the gross returns but had left the figure blank in their agreement, Lord Atkin insisted that 'the court could not supply the figure'. Nevertheless, since it was clear from the circumstances of this case that it had always been intended that W would receive something for his services, W was entitled to 'a reasonable remuneration on the implied contract to pay him *quantum meruit*'. In reckoning the precise sum due, if according to trade usage a particular breed of agent would normally be entitled to commission, the *quantum meruit* would be fixed after taking into account what would be a reasonable commission. In the absence of trade usage, a court could take into account what Lord Wright termed 'the communings of the parties'—although, it was stressed, these will only serve 'as evidence of the value which each of them puts upon the services'. Thus, in *Scarisbrick v Parkinson* (1869) 20 LT 175, in fixing the salary basis upon which the parties would have agreed to work in a case where their agreement was invalid under the Statute of Frauds, the court paid regard to the previous conversation of the parties in calculating the *quantum meruit*.

Lord Wright, too, declared that for courts there was 'no justification for making for the parties…a contract which they did not make themselves'. It was possible, however, to infer from the parties 'communings' in *Way v Latilla* that W was employed on the basis that he would receive a remuneration depending on results. If the information he furnished yielded profit, then he would enjoy a share in the proceeds; if the information proved unfruitful, he would not receive a remuneration. In this case, since considerable time had passed and the principal had incurred considerable costs, the precise sum of W's *quantum meruit* could be only a rough estimate. By way of a Parthian shot, Lord Wright added that the fault for this could be laid entirely at the parties' door: 'If what the court fixes is either too small or too large, the fault must be ascribed to the parties in leaving this important matter in so nebulous a state.'

Kofi Sunkersette Obu v A Strauss & Co Ltd
[1951] AC 243, Privy Council

The appellant signed an agreement to act as the respondent company's agent in West Africa in the purchase and shipment of rubber to the company in London. The agreement between the parties provided in clause 6: 'the company has agreed to remunerate my services with a monthly sum of fifty pounds', which sum was later reduced to £20 'to cover my personal and travelling expenses.…A commission is also to be paid to me by the company which I have agreed to leave to the discretion of the company'. Following termination of the appellant's employment, the respondent company brought proceedings against him claiming money which they alleged was due to the company from him as their agent. The appellant responded by entering a counterclaim for an account to be taken between them of all rubber shipped by the appellant between specified dates, and for commission on all the rubber purchased by him for the respondents. Both the first-instance court and the West African Court of Appeal dismissed the appellant's counterclaim.

Sir John Beaumont (delivering the judgment of the Board): The question in this appeal is as to the right of the appellant to commission. The appellant points out that clause 6 of the agreement contemplates that he is to get some remuneration by way of commission in addition to the £50 per month, and he contends that as the respondents have refused to pay any commission he is entitled to a reasonable commission by way of *quantum meruit* for services rendered. The appellant relied on the authority of such cases as *Bryant v Flight* (1839) 5 M & W 114 and a decision of the House of Lords in *Way v Latilla* [1937] 3 All E R 759. Only the latter case dealt with remuneration by way of a share in business introduced, and in their Lordships' opinion the earlier cases are of no assistance to the appellant. In *Way v Latilla* the agent claimed that there was an agreement to give him an interest in a concession obtained by him which by custom, or on a reasonable basis, the court was asked to define as one-third. The House of Lords rejected this claim on the ground that there was no concluded contract between the parties us to the amount of the share which the agent was to receive and it was impossible for the court to complete the contract for the parties. The House, however, held that whilst there was no concluded contract as to the amount of remuneration, it was plain that there existed between the parties a contract of employment under which the agent was engaged to do work for the plaintiff in circumstances which clearly indicated that the work was not to be gratuitous, and that the agent therefore was entitled to a reasonable remuneration on the implied contract to pay him *quantum meruit*, and the House fixed the amount to be paid.

This case again, in their Lordships' view, does not help the appellant, and, indeed, is rather against him. The right of the appellant to remuneration is governed by cl. 6 of the agreement. The sum of £50 per month was to remunerate the services of the appellant though it was to cover his personal and travelling expenses; there is therefore no question, as in *Way v Latilla*, of the services of the appellant being rendered gratuitously. Clause 6 does not provide for the payment of any further sum by way of additional remuneration for the services of the appellant on which a claim of *quantum meruit* might be founded. The only additional remuneration was to be a commission in the discretion of the respondents. The appellant claims a commission on rubber purchased or rubber shipped, but it is clear that the respondents would have to fix, not only the rate, but the basis, of the commission, and such basis might be a share of profits. The correspondence between the parties before the date of the agreement shows that it must have been in the mind of the appellant that his commission might be based on profits. In letter from the respondents to the appellant, dated October 7, 1942, the respondents said: '... your interests will be fully protected and your share of the total net profits of the entire enterprise will be made retrospective'. Again, in a letter written by the solicitors for the respondents to the appellant, dated February 2, 1943, when the solicitors were seeking from the appellant material on which to base the formal agreement which they were about to prepare, they said this: 'You further informed us that you receive a monthly remittance of £50 for expenses and that it was agreed you should share in the profits arising from the sale of rubber but that no percentage had been fixed; this percentage was in the company's discretion'.

A commission based on profits would be rendered nugatory by the absence of profits. In their Lordships' opinion the relief which the appellant claims, namely, an account and payment of commission based on rubber purchased or shipped, is beyond the competence of any court to grant. The court cannot determine the basis and rate of the commission. To do so would involve not only making a new agreement for the parties but varying the existing agreement by transferring to the court the exercise of a discretion vested in the respondents. If the appellant is not entitled to any commission it is conceded that he cannot claim an account. For these reasons their Lordships think that the judgments of the courts in West Africa were right.

Their Lordships will therefore humbly advise His Majesty that this appeal be dismissed.

NOTES

1. Whether a term as to remuneration is to be implied into the agency contract will depend on the normal rules as to the implication of terms into contracts (as set out in the standard contract law textbooks: see, eg, E Peel, *Treitel's Law of Contract* (14th edn, 2015), paras 6–033 ff and Lord Hoffmann in *A-G of Belize v Belize Telecom Ltd* [2009] UKPC 10, [2009] 1 WLR 1988, whose opinion was lauded by Lord Clarke MR in *Mediterranean Salvage & Towage Ltd v Seamar Trading & Commerce Inc* [2009] EWCA Civ 531, [2009] 2 Lloyd's Rep 639 at [8]–[9]). The rules as to implication of terms at common law are strict: a term can only be implied: (a) to give business efficacy to the contract; (b) because it is so obviously a stipulation of the agreement that it goes without saying that the parties must have intended it to form part of their contract; (c) as a standard term of a particular type of contractual relationship, for example landlord and tenant; or (d) by trade custom or usage. See also s 15 of the Supply of Goods and Services Act 1982 (contractual supplier of services to be paid a reasonable sum).

2. When a professional person is employed as an agent, and there is no express agreement as to remuneration, there is a strong presumption that he is to receive reasonable remuneration for his services (*Miller v Beal* (1879) 27 WR 403). What is reasonable may be assessed according to what is customary in the trade, profession, or business in which the agent is employed. Nevertheless, the customary rate must produce a reasonable result if it is to bind the principal (*Wilkie v Scottish Aviation Ltd* 1956 SC 198 at 205, per Lord Clyde). On the remuneration of professional agents generally, see JR Murdoch [1981] Conv 424.

3.   No term may be implied which would be inconsistent with an express term of the agency contract. In *Kofi Sunkersette Obu v A Strauss & Co Ltd*, above, it was an express term of the agency contract that the agent was to receive £50 for expenses and also commission at the discretion of the principal. No commission was paid so, relying on *Way v Latilla*, the agent had counterclaimed that he was nevertheless entitled to a reasonable commission by way of a *quantum meruit* for his services. The Privy Council rejected the claim and distinguished *Way v Latilla* on the ground that in the case before them commission was expressly provided for under the agency contract. The agency contract left the basis and rate of commission at the discretion of the principal and the Privy Council would not substitute their own discretion for that of the principal. For a similar case, see *Re Richmond Gate Property Co Ltd* [1965] 1 WLR 335. Cf *Powell v Braun* [1954] 1 WLR 401, CA.

4.   It should also be noted that an agent may be able to claim a reasonable sum on a restitutionary basis if he renders services outside a contract and those services are freely accepted by the principal, with the knowledge that they could not possibly be gratuitous (see, eg, *Michael Elliott & Partners Ltd v UK Land plc* [1991] 1 EGLR 39 at 45; cf *Fairvale Ltd v Sabharwal* [1992] 2 EGLR 27 at 28). Some of the leading writers on the law of restitution submit that this theory of free acceptance offers the best explanation of *Way v Latilla* (PBH Birks, *An Introduction to the Law of Restitution* (revised paperback edn, 1989), p 272; R Goff and G Jones, *The Law of Restitution* (7th edn, 2007), paras 23–002 and 23–003, n 9; cf A Burrows, *The Law of Restitution* (3rd edn, 2011), p 373).

5.   Where the agent's commission is provided for in the contract between principal and third party, the agent may be entitled to enforce the terms of that contract as a third party beneficiary through the Contracts (Rights of Third Parties) Act 1999. In *Nisshin Shipping Co Ltd v Cleaves & Co Ltd* [2003] EWHC 2602 (Comm), [2004] 1 Lloyd's Rep 38, Cleaves, a chartering broker, negotiated a number of charterparties on behalf of Nisshin, a shipowner. In each of the charterparties, Nisshin agreed with the charterers to pay Cleaves its commission. Each charterparty also contained an arbitration clause. Colman J held that Cleaves had the right, as a third party under the 1999 Act, to enforce Nisshin's promise to pay it commission, and that it was entitled (and bound) to do so by arbitration.

(ii) Effective cause

Unless otherwise agreed, when an agent is to be paid commission on bringing about a particular event, the agent is not entitled to that commission unless he can show that his services were the effective cause of the event.

Millar, Son & Co v Radford

(1903) 19 TLR 575, Court of Appeal

Millar, Son & Co, a firm of estate agents, were instructed by Radford to find a purchaser, or, failing a purchaser, a tenant, for his property. Millars introduced Cook, who took a seven-year lease of the property. Millars were paid their commission. Fifteen months later, without

Millars' intervention, Cook purchased the freehold from Radford. Millars then claimed commission on the sale. Upholding the decision of trial judge, the Court of Appeal rejected Millars' claim to further commission.

> **Collins MR**: . . . The claim of house agents to be entitled to commission in circumstances like the present is a claim which is often made, and is likely to continue to be made. It is, therefore, important to point out that the right to commission does not arise out of the mere fact that agents have introduced a tenant or a purchaser. It is not sufficient to show that the introduction was a *causa sine qua non*. It is necessary to show that the introduction was an efficient cause in bringing about the letting or the sale. Here the plaintiffs fail to establish what is a condition precedent to their right to commission—viz, that they have brought about the sale. It is open to the defendant in an action like this to say either that, though the plaintiffs effected a sale, they were not his agents, or that, though they were his agents, they had not effected the sale. If the defendant proves either the one or the other, the plaintiffs fail to make out their case.
>
> [**Mathew** and **Cozens-Hardy LJJ** delivered concurring judgments.]

NOTES

1.   Today, the equivalent word to 'efficient' is 'effective'. In other words, the agent must be the direct or effective cause of the event upon which his commission is to be paid: there must be no break in the chain of causation. In *County Homesearch Co (Thames & Chilterns) Ltd v Cowham* [2008] EWCA Civ 26, [2008] 1 WLR 909, where the Court of Appeal held that the express terms of the agency contract were inconsistent with an implied requirement that the agent be an effective cause of the transaction, Longmore LJ said (*obiter*, at [14]):

> The present day rationale for the implication of a term that the agent should be at least an effective cause of the transaction is thus (mainly at any rate) the need for the client to avoid the risk of having to pay two sets of commission. This is consistent with the older authorities in which the agent was claiming a second commission when his principal, who had already paid a commission for the procuring of a tenant, was asked to pay a second commission on the purchase of the property by the tenant at a later date, see the decision of the House of Lords in *Toulmin v Millar* (1887) 58 LT 96, *per* Lord Watson, and *Millar v Radford* itself in 1903.

2.   In *Toulmin v Millar* (1887) 58 LT 96, Lord Watson stated that 'in order to found a legal claim for commission there must not only be a causal, there must also be a contractual relation between the introduction and the ultimate transaction of sale'. This means, for example, that an agent instructed to find a tenant will not be entitled to commission if the person he introduces to his principal actually buys the property (*Toulmin v Millar*), and an agent instructed to find a purchaser will not be entitled to commission if he introduces a government department which goes on to acquire the property compulsorily (*Hodges & Sons v Hackbridge Park Residential Hotel Ltd* [1940] 1 KB 404). Cf *Rimmer v Knowles* (1874) 30 LT 496, where the agent employed to find a purchaser was held entitled to commission when he introduced a tenant who took a 999-year lease of the property.

3.   In *Nahum v Royal Holloway and Bedford New College* [1999] EMLR 252, the agent, an art dealer, was asked to seek out potential buyers for the principal's paintings, including one by Gainsborough and one by Constable. The principal agreed that the agent would be paid

a commission of 2½ per cent of the sale price of any one or more of the paintings sold to a buyer he introduced. The agent introduced a buyer for the Gainsborough and, after a lengthy delay, the same person also purchased the Constable. The agent was paid commission on the first sale but not on the second, as he took no part in the negotiations which led up to the second sale. The Court of Appeal held that he was entitled to commission on both sales. The court held that, subject to there being no express words of the contract requiring a different interpretation, the word 'introduce' carried with it an effective causative element in the bringing in of the purchaser to the transaction. The court stressed that it was doubtful whether it made any difference whether the agent's actions were 'an' or 'the' effective cause except, possibly, where there were two agents both with agreements entitling them to commission on the introduction of a purchaser. What the agent had to show was that it was his actions that really brought about the relation of buyer and seller between the principal and the purchaser (and the Court of Appeal found ample evidence of this in the present case). A test of causation turning on a 'factual inquiry…whether a sale is really brought about by the act of the agent', as suggested in *LJ Hooker Ltd v WJ Adams Estates Pty Ltd* (1977) 138 CLR 52 at 86, High Court of Australia, was adopted by Rix J in *Harding Maughan Hambly Ltd v Cie Européenne de Courtage d'Assurances et de Réassurances SA* [2000] CLC 524 at 548 (in the context of insurance brokers). It would seem, therefore, that it is more important to stress the word 'effective' than either the definite or indefinite article. For a review of the English, Canadian, and Australian case law on this issue, see GHL Fridman (2002) 76 ALJ 195.

4.   In *Foxtons Ltd v Bicknell* [2008] EWCA Civ 419, [2008] 2 EGLR 23 at [20], a case concerned with commission owed to an estate agent, Lord Neuberger of Abbotsbury set out the six following characteristics of effective cause:

> First, [effective cause] is 'very readily' implied, especially in a residential consumer context, unless the provisions of the particular contract or the facts of the particular case negative it (see *per* Woolf LJ in *Brian Cooper & Co v Fairview Estates (Investments)* [1987] EGLR 18, at 19H–J and *per* Longmore LJ in *County Homesearch Co (Thames & Chilterns) Ltd v Cowham* [2008] EWCA Civ 26, [2008] 1 WLR 909 at [11]). Secondly, the main reason for implying the term is to minimise the risk of a seller having to pay two commissions (see *per* Longmore LJ in *County Homesearch* at [14]). Thirdly, it is not entirely clear whether the test is '*an* effective cause' or '*the* effective cause' (see *per* Mummery LJ in *Egan Lawson Ltd v Standard Life Assurance Co* [2001] 1 EGLR 27 at 29M to 30B, . . .). Fourthly, whether an agent was the effective cause is a question whose resolution turns very much on the facts of the particular case (see, eg, *per* Nourse LJ in *John D Wood & Co v Dantata* [1987] 2 EGLR 23 at 25H and *per* Mummery LJ in *Egan Lawrence* at 29L). Fifthly, while two commissions are to be avoided, there will be cases where the terms of the relevant contracts and the facts compel such a result (as in *Brian Cooper* and *County Homesearch*). Sixthly, where the term is implied, the burden is on the agent seeking the commission to establish that he was the effective cause (see *per* Staughton LJ in *Chasen Ryder & Co v Hedges* [1993] NPC 6 at 28G).

(iii) Opportunity to earn commission

Luxor (Eastbourne) Ltd v Cooper
[1941] AC 108, House of Lords

Luxor (Eastbourne) Ltd and Regal (Hastings) Ltd (the vendors) employed Cooper, an estate agent, to find a purchaser for four of their cinemas. The vendors agreed to pay Cooper a fee of £10,000 on completion of the sale if he introduced a purchaser who bought the cinemas for not less than £185,000. Cooper introduced Burton who made an offer of £185,000 for the cinemas 'subject to contract'. The vendors, however, withdrew from the negotiations. Cooper sued the vendors for damages, claiming they had broken an implied term of his agency contract by which they undertook to do nothing to prevent his earning commission. Branson J gave judgment for the vendors and, although reversed by the Court of Appeal, his judgment was upheld by the House of Lords.

> **Lord Russell of Killowen:** A few preliminary observations occur to me. (1) Commission contracts are subject to no peculiar rules or principles of their own; the law which governs them is the law which governs all contracts and all questions of agency. (2) No general rule can be laid down by which the rights of the agent or the liability of the principal under commission contracts are to be determined. In each case these must depend upon the exact terms of the contract in question, and upon the true construction of those terms. And (3) contracts by which owners of property, desiring to dispose of it, put it in the hands of agents on commission terms, are not (in default of specific provisions) contracts of employment in the ordinary meaning of those words. No obligation is imposed on the agent to do anything. The contracts are merely promises binding on the principal to pay a sum of money upon the happening of a specified event, which involves the rendering of some service by the agent. There is no real analogy between such contracts, and contracts of employment by which one party binds himself to do certain work, and the other binds himself to pay remuneration for the doing of it...
>
> As to the claim for damages, this rests upon the implication of some provision in the commission contract, the exact terms of which were variously stated in the course of the argument, the object always being to bind the principal not to refuse to complete the sale to the client whom the agent has introduced.
>
> I can find no safe ground on which to base the introduction of any such implied term. Implied terms, as we all know, can only be justified under the compulsion of some necessity. No such compulsion or necessity exists in the case under consideration. The agent is promised a commission if he introduces a purchaser at a specified or minimum price. The owner is desirous of selling. The chances are largely in favour of the deal going through, if a purchaser is introduced. The agent takes the risk in the hope of a substantial remuneration for comparatively small exertion. In the case of the plaintiff his contract was made on September 23, 1935; his client's offer was made on October 2, 1935. A sum of £10,000 (the equivalent of the remuneration of a year's work by a Lord Chancellor) for work done within a period of eight or nine days is no mean reward, and is one well worth a risk. There is no lack of business efficacy in such a contract, even though the principal is free to refuse to sell to the agent's client.
>
> The position will no doubt be different if the matter has proceeded to the stage of a binding contract having been made between the principal and the agent's client. In that case it can be said with truth that a 'purchaser' has been introduced by the agent; in other words the event has happened upon the occurrence of which a right to the promised commission has become vested in the agent. From that moment no act or omission by the principal can deprive the agent of that vested right...
>
> My Lords, in my opinion there is no necessity in these contracts for any implication: and the legal position can be stated thus: If according to the true construction of the contract the event has happened upon the happening of which the agent has acquired a vested right to the commission (by which I mean that it is *debitum in praesenti* even though only *solvendum in futuro*), then no act or omission by the principal or anyone else can deprive the agent of that right; but until that event has happened the agent cannot complain if the principal refuses to proceed with, or carry to completion, the transaction with the agent's client.

I have already expressed my view as to the true meaning of a contract to pay a commission for the introduction of a purchaser at a specified or minimum price. It is possible that an owner may be willing to bind himself to pay a commission for the mere introduction of one who offers to purchase at the specified or minimum price; but such a construction of the contract would in my opinion require clear and unequivocal language.

Lord Wright: . . . What is in question in all these cases is the interpretation of a particular contract. I deprecate in general the attempt to enunciate decisions on the construction of agreements as if they embodied rules of law. To some extent decisions on one contract may help by way of analogy and illustration in the decision of another contract. But however similar the contracts may appear, the decision as to each must depend on the consideration of the language of the particular contract, read in the light of the material circumstances of the parties in view of which the contract is made. I shall therefore in the first instance examine the particular contract in question in the light of the material facts . . . It is important to simplify as far as possible the problem of construing commission agency agreements, especially in regard to the sale of houses and land. These are of common occurrence among all classes of the community and it is most undesirable that subtleties and complications of interpretation calculated to lead to disputes should be allowed to confuse what is ex facie a plain and simple agreement . . .

The case that the suggested term is not properly to be implied becomes, in my opinion, even clearer when account is taken of some of the more general aspects of the course of business in these matters. It is well known that in the ordinary course a property owner intending to sell may put his property on the books of several estate agents with each of whom he makes a contract for payment of commission on a sale. If he effects a sale to the client introduced by one agent, is he to be liable in damages to all the others for preventing them from earning their commission? Common sense and ordinary business understanding clearly give a negative answer. Or suppose that having employed one agent whose client has made an offer, he receives a better offer from a buyer introduced by another agent and concludes the purchase with him. It seems out of the question that he is thereby rendering himself liable in damages to the former agent. Or suppose that owing to changed circumstances he decides that he will not sell at all and breaks off negotiations with the agent's client, is he to be liable for damages to the agent? I can find no justification for such a view. I am assuming a commission contract not containing special terms such as to impose an obligation on the vendor actually to sell through the particular agent to the potential purchaser introduced by that agent. Contracts containing such terms, though not perhaps usual, are possible. But it is said that in the absence of special terms an obligation of that nature can be implied, subject, however, to the qualification that the owner retains his freedom to deal as he likes with his own and to discontinue negotiations, but only so long as in doing so he acts with reasonable excuse or just cause. I find it impossible to define these terms in this connection. If the commission agent has a right to claim commission or damages if the vendor abandons the negotiations and does not complete the sale, his doing so is a breach of contract *vis-à-vis* the agent and it is immaterial to the agent how sensible or reasonable the vendor's conduct may be from his own point of view. Such a qualified implication seems to me too complicated and artificial. The parties cannot properly be supposed to have intended it, nor can it be taken to be necessary to give business efficacy to the transaction. But I do not discuss this aspect further because, as already explained, I find no basis for the implication, whether general or qualified. And the great difficulty which the Courts have found in defining or applying the idea of 'just cause or reasonable excuse' further goes to show that it is not an implied term necessary to give business efficacy to what the parties must have intended. Nor is the suggested implication made more plausible by expressing it in a negative form as an implied term that the principal will not prevent the agent earning his commission. Such a term must be based upon something which under the contract the principal has agreed to do, of such a nature that failure to do it carries the consequence that the agent cannot earn the commission which would have become due if the principal had done what he had promised. For the purposes of the present problem this promise must be that he would complete the contract. Thus it all comes back to the same issue, namely, that there must be some breach of contract for which damages can be claimed...It may seem hard that an agent who has introduced a potential purchaser, able and willing to complete, should get nothing for what he has done, if, during the negotiations, the principal decides not to complete, according to his own pleasure and without any reason which *quoad* the agent is a sufficient excuse. But such is the express contract. And people in ordinary life do not seek the services of commission agents without a good prospect and intention of making use of them. The agent in practice takes what is a business risk. I am assuming that the commission contract is of the type exemplified in this case. The agent may, however, secure a form of contract to which what I have said does not apply. But it is necessary to reserve certain eventualities in which an agent may be entitled to damages where there is a failure to complete even under a contract like the contract in this case. For instance, if the negotiations between the vendor and the purchaser have been duly concluded and a binding executory agreement has been achieved, different considerations may arise. The vendor is then no longer free to dispose of his property. Though the sale is not completed the property in equity has passed from him to the purchaser. If he refuses to complete he would be guilty of a breach of agreement vis-à-vis the purchaser. I think, as at present advised, that it ought then to be held that he is also in breach of his contract with the commission agent, that is, of some term which can properly be implied. But that question and possibly some other questions do not arise in this case and may be reserved. Furthermore, I have been dealing with a contract in regard to the sale of real property and there may be differences where the commission agency is in regard to transactions of a different character. On the whole, however, my opinion is that the contract in question means what it says, that the simple construction is the true construction and that there is no justification for the equitable reconstruction which the Court of Appeal, following authorities which bound it, has applied. I would allow the appeal...

It may be said that...on the view which I have been propounding, the prospect of the agent getting his reward is speculative and may be defeated by the arbitrary will of the principal. That may perhaps be so in some cases. But it is I think clear that under a contract like the present the agent takes a risk in several respects; thus, for instance, the principal may sell independently of the agent to a purchaser other than the purchaser introduced by him, or where the employment is not as sole agent, he may sell through another agent. Why should not the agent take the chance also of the employer changing his mind and deciding not to sell at all? It is said that according to the term which, it is suggested, should be implied he can change his mind if he has a reasonable excuse or just cause. But then why should his freedom to dispose of his property be fettered even in this way? And what is a reasonable excuse or just cause? Is it to be decided from the point of view of the owner or from the point of view of the commission agent? It is just the difficulty of applying these vague phrases which has already led to so much litigation on this question. In my opinion the implied term is unworkable. Even in this case Branson J has taken one view and the Court of Appeal another. If the suggested implied term is discarded, a contract such as the present will be simple and workable. Commission agents may sometimes fail to get the commission that they expected, but they will be relieved from disputes and litigation. And they can always, if they desire, demand what they consider a more favourable form of contract.

[**Viscount Simon LC** and **Lord Romer** delivered concurring opinions. **Lord Thankerton** concurred with Lord Russell of Killowen's opinion.]

Company law students will be familiar with another aspect of this case, see *Regal (Hastings) Ltd v Gulliver* [1967] 2 AC 134n, HL.

NOTES

1. Unless there is an express or implied promise to the contrary in the contract of agency, the principal is free to prevent his agent from earning commission. Such a promise may be implied by trade custom, or to give business efficacy to the agency contract, or otherwise to give effect to the intentions of the parties. But as *Luxor (Eastbourne) Ltd v Cooper* illustrates, the courts are generally reluctant to imply such a promise into an agency contract. This is particularly true where, as in *Luxor*'s case itself, the implication of such a promise would restrict the principal's freedom to deal with his own property as he wished. For example, in *L French & Co Ltd v Leeston Shipping Co* [1922] 1 AC 451, a shipbroker's right to commission depended on the continuation of the charterparty he had negotiated for his principal. But the House of Lords refused to imply a term into the shipbroker's agency contract to the effect that his principal, the shipowner, could not sell his ship to the charterer, thereby bringing the charterparty to a premature end. See also *Rhodes v Forwood* (1876) 1 App Cas 256; cf *Turner v Goldsmith* [1891] 1 QB 544 (both cases are considered below at p 276); JF Burrows (1968) 31 MLR 390.

2. In *L French & Co Ltd v Leeston Shipping Co*, the shipbroker (agent) was deprived of commission because the shipowner (principal) and charterer (third party) agreed to terminate the charterparty. No term was to be implied into the agency agreement to prevent this. But a term may well be implied into the agency agreement to the effect that the principal must not break a contract negotiated by the agent with a third party and so deprive the agent of commission due on performance of that contract. In *Alpha Trading Ltd v Dunnshaw-Patten Ltd* [1981] QB 290 such a term was implied. In that case, agents negotiated a contract for the sale of cement by their principal to a third party. The principal breached the sale contract by failing to perform and settled the resulting claim made by the third party. The principal's failure to perform the sale contract prevented the agents earning commission under the terms of their agency contract. The Court of Appeal held that the principal was in breach of an implied term of the agency contract to the effect that he would not breach the sale contract with the third party so as to deprive the agents of their remuneration under the agency contract. *Alpha Trading* was followed in *Martin-Smith v Williams* [1999] EMLR 571, CA, where the principal waived future royalties on which the agent would have earned commission. But contrast *Marcan Shipping (London) Ltd v Polish Steamship Co, The Manifest Lipkowy* [1989] 2 Lloyd's Rep 138, where the Court of Appeal refused to imply a term into a collateral contract made between the agent and third party (the seller) to the effect that the *third party* would not breach a contract for the sale of a ship made between himself and the agent's principal (the buyer), and thereby deprive the agent of commission due under the agency contract made between the principal and agent.

3. In *Alpha Trading Ltd v Dunnshaw-Pattern Ltd*, Brandon and Templeman LJJ accepted that the observations of Lord Wright in *Luxor (Eastbourne) Ltd v Cooper*, although made in the context of estate agency, were capable of being applied to contracts of agency in general. However, most contracts between estate agents and vendors are unilateral, so it is probably more accurate in such cases to speak in terms of an implied collateral contract, rather than an implied term, that the vendor will not deprive the agent of commission (*Bowstead and Reynolds*, paras 7–016 and 7–035). *Aliter*, where the vendor and agent enter into a 'sole agency' agreement whereby the vendor agrees not to sell his property through another agent. Sole agency agreements are generally regarded as bilateral contracts (*Bowstead and Reynolds*, para 7–036; cf JR Murdoch (1975) 91 LQR 357 at 374–375). On estate agency agreements generally, see Fridman, pp 411–421; JR Murdoch (1975) 91 LQR 357 and *The Law of Estate Agency and Auctions* (5th edn, 2009).

(iv) Loss of right to commission

The agent will lose his right to commission if he:

(1) acts outside the scope of his actual authority (*Mason v Clifton* (1863) 3 F & F 899);

(2) acts in a manner which he knows, or ought to have known, to be unlawful (*Josephs v Pebrer* (1825) 3 B & C 639) or is otherwise dishonest (*Kelly v Cooper* [1993] AC 205 at 216–217, per Lord Browne-Wilkinson, above, p 235); or

(3) commits a serious breach of his duties as agent (*Boston Deep Sea Fishing and Ice Co Ltd v Ansell* (1888) 39 Ch D 339, above, p 241), unless the agent effects severable transactions, when he will only lose his right to commission on those transactions in respect of which he is in breach of duty (but an honest agent will not lose his right to commission where his breach does not go to the root of the contract of agency: *Hippisley v Knee Bros* [1905] 1 KB 1, above, p 240).

Unless otherwise agreed, an agent is not entitled to commission on transactions which take place after termination of the agency contract (*Crocker Horlock Ltd v B Lang & Co Ltd* [1949] 1 All ER 526). But the agent's right to commission depends upon the construction of the terms of the agency contract. The agency contract may provide that the agent's right to commission accrues before the time when the commission becomes payable. When the right arises before termination, for example when the agent secures the order, commission must be paid, even if it only becomes payable after termination, for instance when the order is executed (*Sellers v London Counties Newspapers* [1951] 1 KB 784; *Explora Group plc v Hesco Bastion Ltd* [2005] EWCA Civ 646). Particular difficulties may arise with the construction of terms providing for the payment of commission on 'repeat orders'.

(v) Commercial agents

Part III of the Commercial Agents (Council Directive) Regulations 1993 deals with the remuneration of commercial agents (as defined in reg 2(1): see above, p 119). Regulation 6(1) provides that:

> In the absence of any agreement as to remuneration between the parties, a commercial agent shall be entitled to the remuneration that commercial agents appointed for the goods forming the subject of his agency contract are customarily allowed in the place where he carries on his activities and, if there is no such customary practice, a commercial agent shall be entitled to reasonable remuneration taking into account all the aspects of the transaction.

Although reg 6(3) envisages that a commercial agent need not be remunerated by commission (it provides that regs 7–12 do not apply 'where a commercial agent is not remunerated (wholly or in part) by commission'), such agents are typically remunerated by commission. Under reg 7(1), the agent is 'entitled to commission' on:

> commercial transactions concluded during the period covered by the agency contract—
> (a) when the transactions has been concluded as a result of his action; or
> (b) where the transaction is concluded with a third party whom he has previously acquired as a customer for transactions of the same kind.

It seems that a transaction may be 'concluded as a result of his action' even though the agent was not the effective cause of the transaction—the language of the regulation may imply a laxer test. Such a conclusion might be suggested by *Moore v Piretta PTA Ltd* [1998] CLC 992, [1999] 1 All ER 174, a case on the agent's right to an indemnity under reg 17(3), where the court held (at 997–998) that it was enough that the agent was 'instrumental' in winning business for the principal and that 'a small level of involvement is sufficient and it is enough that the agent has merely contributed to bringing the new customer... the agent must have played an active role'. Such an interpretation receives support not only from the wording of reg 7(1) (b) but also from reg 8, which deals with the position of the agent's right to commission on business transacted after termination of the agency contract. Regulation 8 provides that commission is payable on any transaction '*mainly attributable* to his efforts during the period covered by the agency contract' (emphasis added) which has been entered into within a reasonable period after termination of the contract (for examples of awards of post-termination commission under reg 8, see the decisions of Morland J in *Ingmar GB Ltd v Eaton Leonard Inc* [2001] Eu LR 756; Davis J in *Tigana Ltd v Decoro Ltd* [2003] EWHC 23 (QB), [2003] Eu LR 189; HHJ Alton in *Smith v Reliance Water Controls Ltd* [2004] EWHC 1016 (QB); and HHJ Seymour QC in *Vick v Vogle Gapes Ltd* [2006] EWHC 1665 (TCC)). Whilst Davis J in *Tigana Ltd* was inclined to give 'mainly attributable to his efforts' an autonomous meaning, distinct from the common law's 'effective cause', Fulford J in *PJ Pipe & Valve Co Ltd v Audco India Ltd* [2005] EWHC 1904 (QB), [2006] Eu LR 368 at [120] observed: 'In my judgment, there is no discernible difference, certainly as applied to the facts in this case, between the two tests: "mainly attributable" and "the effective cause".'

A commercial agent is also entitled to commission where the transaction between the principal and third party was concluded in breach of an exclusive agency agreement (reg 7(2)). By reg 10(1) commission becomes due when: (a) the principal has executed the transaction; or (b) he should have done so; or (c) the third party has executed the transaction. Regulation 10(2) provides that commission becomes due at the latest when the third party has executed his part of the transaction or should have done so if the principal had executed his part of it (there can be no derogation from this provision: reg 10(4)).

QUESTION

Why do estate agents fall outside the Commercial Agents (Council Directive) Regulations 1993?

(b) Reimbursement and indemnity

An agent has a right against his principal to be reimbursed for all expenses and indemnified against all losses and liabilities incurred by him while acting within the scope of his express or implied *actual* authority.

Rhodes v Fielder, Jones and Harrison
(1919) 89 LJKB 159, King's Bench Division

A country solicitor instructed London solicitors to act as his agent in an appeal which was to be heard in the House of Lords. The London solicitors briefed counsel, who went on to win the case. The country solicitor then instructed the London solicitors not to pay counsel's fees. The London solicitors did not comply with this instruction, but paid counsel's fees and reimbursed themselves out of monies of the country solicitor in their possession. The country solicitor then brought an action against the London solicitors to recover the monies so retained.

> **Lush J**: . . . I now come to the second point taken by the plaintiffs, which is this: After the case had been heard in the House of Lords, and after consultations with counsel had been asked for and held, the plaintiff revoked the authority to the defendants to pay these fees, and it was argued that when country solicitors instruct London agents to brief counsel and, in the usual way, the agents have consultations with counsel and incur obligations towards counsel in respect of them which are fully recognized, the country solicitors can revoke their authority to their London agents to pay the counsel's fees. I can only say that to my mind such a proposition is absolutely unsustainable. It is, of course, the fact that the London agents could not be sued for these fees by counsel, but that does not dispose of the question. If they did not pay the fees they would be behaving in a way which would unquestionably place them in a serious position. I think it is right to say this, that a solicitor who has undertaken to pay fees to counsel and refuses to pay them is guilty of misconduct, and therefore it is impossible to say that it was open to the country solicitors in this case to revoke their authority. Authority for this was cited before the Master. The defendants did what they did at the request of the plaintiff, and made themselves responsible as honourable members of their profession for the payment of these fees. I think that the Master was perfectly right, and that the appeal must be dismissed.
>
> **Sankey J**: As to the second point, I so entirely agree with what has fallen from my brother Lush that I think I should be wasting public time if I said anything further. To my mind it is entirely unarguable.
>
> *Appeal dismissed.*

NOTES

1.   Where the agency is contractual, the agent's right to reimbursement and indemnity arises as an express or implied term of the contract. However, the right may be expressly excluded by the parties, or by a term implied through the custom of the trade (eg unless otherwise agreed, estate agents are not entitled to claim reimbursement for advertising expenses over and above their commission). The agent's contractual right to reimbursement and indemnity is wide. It covers not only payment of debts which are legally binding on the principal, but also payments which the agent is legally bound to make though the principal is not (*Adams v Morgan & Co* [1924] 1 KB 751) and payments which the agent is under a strong moral obligation to meet (*Rhodes v Fielder, Jones and Harrison*, above).

2.   Where the agency is gratuitous, the agent has only a restitutionary right to reimbursement of payments which he was compelled to make for the benefit of his principal and which the principal would have been ultimately liable to make himself (see, generally, C Mitchell, P Mitchell, and S Watteson, *Goff and Jones: The Law of Unjust Enrichment* (8th edn, 2011), Ch 16). However, if a gratuitous agent can rely on an equitable right to indemnity, for example as a trustee or surety, he may be able to obtain a wider indemnity than that which arises under the restitutionary remedy.

3. The agent has no right to reimbursement for expenses, or to an indemnity for losses and liabilities, incurred in any of the following circumstances:

(a) when he exceeds his actual authority (*Barron v Fitzgerald* (1840) 6 Bing NC 201), unless his unauthorised acts are subsequently ratified by his principal;

(b) as a result of the agent's breach of duty, negligence, default, or insolvency (*Lage v Siemens Bros & Co Ltd* (1932) 42 Ll L Rep 252); or

(c) in the performance of acts which the agent knows, or ought reasonably to know, are unlawful (*Re Parker* (1882) 21 Ch D 408); but the agent may be entitled to a contribution from his principal under the Civil Liability (Contribution) Act 1978.

(c) Lien

To secure his rights of remuneration, reimbursement, or indemnity, the agent may be able to exercise a lien over goods belonging to his principal which are in his possession. In general, the lien gives the agent the right to detain his principal's goods until he is paid what he is owed by the principal in respect of those goods, ie it is usually a particular lien (but see below, pp 1046–1049, as to when a general lien may arise). But the agent can only exercise a lien over his principal's goods if he lawfully acquired possession of them in the course of the agency (*Taylor v Robinson* (1818) 2 Moore CP 730), and he holds them in the same capacity as that in which he claims the lien (*Dixon v Stansfeld* (1850) 10 CB 398). Furthermore, an agent's right to exercise a lien may be excluded by the express or implied terms of the agency contract (*Wolstenholm v Sheffield Union Banking Co* (1886) 54 LT 746).

A sub-agent may also be able to exercise a lien over the principal's goods, even though the sub-agent's claims for remuneration, reimbursement, and indemnity are against the appointing agent and not the principal. To exercise such a lien the appointment of the sub-agent must have been authorised by the principal (actual or apparent authority of the appointing agent will do): see *Solly v Rathbone* (1814) 2 M & S 298, where it was held that there was no right of lien because the sub-delegation was unauthorised. So long as the sub-delegation is authorised the sub-agent may exercise his lien, even though the appointing agent may have no authority to create privity of contract between the principal and the sub-agent. Where the principal authorises sub-delegation by his agent, but the principal remains undisclosed, the sub-agent may exercise a lien over the principal's goods to secure any claim he may have against the appointing agent, so long as the claim arose before the sub-agent discovered the truth (*Mann v Forrester* (1814) 4 Camp 60). For detailed discussion of the nature of a lien, and also the way it may be acquired and lost, see below, pp 1040 ff.

QUESTION

If an agent is under a fiduciary duty not to place himself in a position where his own interests conflict with those of his principal (above, p 233), how can an agent ever exercise a lien over his principal's goods without being in breach of fiduciary duty? See *Compañía Financiera Soleada SA v Hamoor Tanker Corpn Inc, The Borag* [1980] 1 Lloyd's Rep 111 at 122, per Mustill J, reversed on other grounds [1981] 1 WLR 274.

3 TERMINATION OF AGENCY

(a) Termination of the relationship between principal and agent

Campanari v Woodburn
(1854) 15 CB 400, Court of Common Pleas

P agreed to pay A £100 if A sold P's picture. P died before the picture was sold. Unaware of P's death, A sold the picture and claimed £100 from P's administratrix. Although the administratrix confirmed the sale, she refused to pay A his commission. A then sued the administratrix for his commission.

Jervis CJ: I am of opinion that the defendant in this case is entitled to the judgment of the court. As alleged on the face of the declaration, it does not appear that the original contract between the plaintiff and the intestate conferred upon the former an authority which was irrevocable: it simply states that it was agreed between the plaintiff and the intestate that the plaintiff should endeavour to sell a certain picture of the intestate, and that, if the plaintiff succeeded in selling the same, the intestate should pay him £100. So far, therefore, as appears in the declaration, it was a mere employment of the plaintiff to do the act, not carrying with it any irrevocable authority. It is plain that the intestate might in his life-time have revoked the authority, without rendering himself liable to be called upon to pay the £100, though possibly the plaintiff might have had a remedy for a breach of the contract, if the intestate had wrongfully revoked his authority after he had been put to expense in endeavouring to dispose of the picture. In that way, perhaps, the plaintiff might have recovered damages by reason of the revocation. His death, however, was a revocation by the act of God, and the administratrix is not, in my judgment, responsible for anything. It was no fault of hers,—as in *Smout v Ibery* ((1842) 10 M & W 1)—that the contract was not carried out. It must be taken to have been part of the original compact between the plaintiff and the intestate, that, whereas, on the one hand, he would receive a large sum if he succeeded in selling the picture, so, on the other hand, he would take the chance of his authority to sell being revoked by death or otherwise. Mr Maude seems to concede, that, but for what took place subsequently to the death of the intestate, the administratrix would have been liable: but he relies upon the allegation in the declaration, that the plaintiff sold the picture, and that the sale was confirmed by the defendant as administratrix; and contends that therefore she is liable. But it seems to me that that consequence by no means follows. If the defendant as administratrix had, after the death of the intestate, ordered the sale of the picture, no doubt that would have been a new retainer, and she would have been liable to the plaintiff on a *quantum meruit*. If, with full knowledge of the contract under which the plaintiff was to receive £100 as the stipulated reward for his exertions in selling the picture, the defendant had continued the employment, and it had resulted in a sale, the £100 might have been taken by the jury as the measure of damages. But, without shewing that the defendant had any knowledge whatever of the original contract, the confirmation of the sale is relied on as a confirmation of the original contract. It is enough to say that the averment as to the confirmation of the sale by the defendant does not raise the point which Mr Maude desires to raise. That confirmation, however it might make her liable to an action for a reasonable remuneration for the plaintiff's services, clearly is not sufficient to charge the defendant either personally or in her representative character for the breach of the original contract.

Williams J: I am of the same opinion. It may be convenient to consider what the effect would have been if the declaration had omitted the averment of confirmation of the sale by the defendant. It would then have amounted to a mere statement of an agreement between the plaintiff and the intestate that the plaintiff should endeavour to sell the picture, and, if he succeeded in so doing, the intestate should pay him £100. That clearly would have been revoked by the death. In such a state of things, the mere circumstance of something having been done under the contract, does not make it irrevocable. The contract, after the death of the intestate, was not and could not be confirmed according to its terms. It is perfectly clear, that, if the count had stood without the allegation that the administratrix confirmed the sale, it would have been utterly without foundation. What, then, is the effect of that averment? There is no allegation that the contract was confirmed as between the plaintiff and the deceased; but merely an allegation that the sale was confirmed by the defendant as administratrix. That is manifestly different from an averment that the original contract was confirmed by her, with all its incidents and all its consequences. I do not think it necessary,—though I entertain no doubt on the point,—to give any opinion as to what would have been the effect, if the declaration had contained such an allegation. The utmost that can be said is, that the defendant, as administratrix, might have been liable on a *quantum meruit* for services performed by the plaintiff as her agent in relation to the sale: but she clearly could not be liable in the way in which she is sought to be charged here.

[**Crowder J** delivered a concurring judgment.]

Frith v Frith

[1906] AC 254, Privy Council

The appellant had been appointed by a power of attorney to take possession of and manage an estate owned by the respondent. The estate was mortgaged to a third party and the appellant gave a personal guarantee that he would pay the mortgage debt. Neither the mortgage debt nor the guarantee were mentioned in the power of attorney. Later the respondent revoked the appellant's authority and demanded possession of the estate from him. The appellant refused to give up possession on the ground that his authority was coupled with an interest, and was, therefore, irrevocable. The Privy Council held that the appellant's authority was revocable.

Lord Atkinson (delivering the advice of the Privy Council (Earl of Halsbury, Lord Davey, Lord Robertson, Lord Atkinson, and Sir Arthur Wilson)): . . . [I]t cannot be disputed that the general rule of law is that employment of the general character of the appellant's in this case can be terminated at the will of the employer. The proper conduct of the affairs of life necessitates that this should be so. The exception to this rule within which the appellant must bring himself, if he is to succeed, is that where 'an agreement is entered into for sufficient consideration, and either forms part of a security, or is given for the purpose of securing some benefit to the donee of the authority, such authority is irrevocable': *Story on Agency*, s 476.
  It cannot be contended that the ordinary case of an agent or manager employed for pecuniary reward in the shape of a fixed salary comes within this exception, though his employment confers a benefit upon him. And their Lordships are of opinion that the position of the appellant under the instruments appointing him attorney over this estate is in law that of an ordinary agent or manager employed at a salary, and nothing more because the authority which was conferred upon him contains no reference to the special interest in the occupation

of his post which his guarantee to Astwood might have given him, was not expressed or intended to be used for the purpose of subserving that interest, and has no connection with it. For these reasons their Lordships think that the authority given to the appellant was revocable. Several cases have been cited by the appellant's counsel in support of his . . . contention. On an examination of them it will be found that the essential distinction between this case and those cited is this, that in each of the latter power and authority were given to a particular individual to do a particular thing, the doing of which conferred a benefit upon him, the authority ceasing when the benefit was reaped, while in this case, as already pointed out, nothing of that kind was ever provided for or contemplated. In *Carmichael's Case* ([1896] 2 Ch 643) the donor of the power, for valuable consideration, conferred upon the donee authority to do a particular thing in which the latter had an interest, namely, to apply for the shares of the company which the donee was promoting for the purpose of purchasing his own property from him, and the donor sought to revoke that authority before the benefit was reaped. In *Spooner v Sandilands* ((1842) 1 Y & C Ch Cas 390) the donor charged his lands with certain debts due and to accrue due to the donees, and put the latter into the possession of those lands and into receipt of the rents and profits of them, for the express purpose of enabling the donees to discharge thereout these same debts; and it was sought to eject the donees before their debts were paid. In *Clerk v Laurie* ((1857) 2 H & N 199) a wife pledged to a bank dividends to which she was entitled to secure advances made to her husband. It was held that while the advances remained unpaid, she could not revoke the bank's authority to receive the dividends. In *Smart v Sandars* ((1848) 5 CB 895) it was decided that the general authority of a factor in whose hands goods were placed for sale, to sell at the best price which could reasonably be obtained, could not be revoked after the factor had made advances on the security of the goods to the owner of them, and while these advances remained unpaid.

Bailey and another v Angove's Pty Ltd

[2016] UKSC 47, [2016] 1 WLR 3179, Supreme Court

Lord Sumption (with whom Lords Neuberger, Clarke, Carnwath, and Hodge agreed):

THE REVOCABILITY OF AN AGENT'S AUTHORITY

6. The general rule is that the authority of an agent may be revoked by the principal, even if it is agreed by their contract to be irrevocable. The revocation is effective to terminate the agent's authority, but gives rise to a claim for damages. Powers of attorney were said by Lord Kenyon to be 'revocable from their nature': *Walsh v Whitcomb* (1797) 2 Esp 565, 566. In *Story's Law of Agency* (1864), 2nd ed, p 598, at para 463, the rule was said to be 'so plain a doctrine of common sense and common justice that it requires no illustration or reasoning to support it.' Nonetheless, its basis has never really been in doubt. An agent is empowered to commit his principal within the limits of his authority as if the principal had agreed personally. This is a confidential relationship importing a duty of loyalty, and normally of undivided loyalty, on the part of the agent. As Lord Atkinson observed, delivering the advice of the Privy Council in *Frith v Frith* [1906] AC 254, 261, to allow the agent to exercise his authority after it has been revoked would amount to the specific enforcement of a relationship which is by its nature not specifically enforceable.

7. The main exception to the general rule is the case where the agent has a relevant interest of his own in the exercise of his authority. The exception applies if two conditions are satisfied. First, there must be an agreement that the agent's authority shall be irrevocable. Secondly, the authority must be

given to secure an interest of the agent, being either a proprietary interest (for example a power of attorney given to enable the holder of an equitable interest to perfect it) or a liability (generally in debt) owed to him personally. In these cases, the agent's authority is irrevocable while the interest subsists.

8. Both conditions are now reflected in s 4(1) of the Powers of Attorney Act 1971, as regards authority conferred by a power of attorney. The first condition is perhaps self-evident, but so far as authority is required, it is supplied by the decisions of the Privy Council in *Esteban de Comas v Prost and Kohler* (1865) 3 Moo PC NS 158 and *Frith v Frith* [1906] AC 254. The second condition was established in *Walsh v Whitcomb, supra*, where the exception was said to apply in 'every case where a power of attorney is necessary to effectuate any security'. In *Smart v Sandars* (1848) 2 CB 895, 917–918, commonly regarded as the leading case, Wilde CJ, delivering the judgment of the Court of Common Pleas, declared that:

> where an agreement is entered into on a sufficient consideration, whereby an authority is given for the purpose of securing some benefit to the donee of the authority, such an authority is irrevocable. This is what is usually meant by an authority coupled with an interest, and which is commonly said to be irrevocable. But we think this doctrine applies only to cases where the authority is given for the purpose of being a security, or, as Lord Kenyon expresses it, as a part of the security; not to cases where the authority is given independently, and the interest of the donee of the authority arises afterwards, and incidentally only.

These cases demonstrate that an agreement that the agent's authority is to be irrevocable may be inferred, but not from the mere co-existence of the agency and the interest. It is necessary that the one should be intended to support the other. The exception thus stated follows from the logic of the rule. Where the parties agree that the agent is to have a personal financial interest in the performance of his agency, over and above the receipt of his remuneration, his duty of loyalty is to that extent compromised. The reason for declining to enforce his right to act for the principal therefore falls away.

9. The ambit of the exception for authority coupled with an interest is more narrowly defined by the editors of *Bowstead and Reynolds on Agency* (2014), 20th ed, para 10-007. They say that it applies

> where the notion of agency is employed as a legal device for a different purpose from that of normal agency, to confer a security or other interest on the 'agent'. In such a case it is intended that the agent use the authority not for the benefit of his principal but for his own benefit, to achieve the objects of the arrangement.

This would appear to confine the exception to cases where the authority exists solely in order to secure the agent's financial interest, and is in reality no more than the commercial equivalent of an assignment. In such a case, the editors suggest, the law of agency is not really engaged at all, because the beneficiary of the authority is only nominally an agent. In my opinion, this is too narrow. It is no doubt a fair description of the simplest cases, but I do not accept that it can be a general principle of law. At one extreme lie cases such as *Walsh v Whitcomb, supra*, where a power of attorney was granted solely to enable the grantee to satisfy a pre-existing debt owed to the agent, or *Gaussen v Morton* (1830) 10 B & C 731, where an owner of land gave a power of attorney to a creditor to sell the land to satisfy the debt. No one doubts that the exception applies in such cases. At the opposite extreme, it does not apply where the agent's only interest is a commercial interest in being able to earn his commission. The reason is that in that case, the authority is not properly speaking a security at all: *Doward, Dickson & Co v Williams & Co* (1890) 6 TLR 316; *Temple Legal Protection Ltd v QBE Insurance (Europe) Ltd* [2009] Lloyd's Rep IR 544, at [50]. But there are situations lying between these polar positions where the relationship of principal and agent is broader than the mere collection of money to satisfy the agent's debt, so that the agent may be said to act both for himself and his principal. In *Smart v Sandars, supra*, for example, the agent was a grain factor and the advances said to be secured by the agent's authority were made against the proceeds of sale of unsold grain. It is clear that the agent would have succeeded but for the fact that the advances had been made after and independently of the agency agreement so that the latter could not be construed as securing them. There is no principled reason why a true agent employed on his principal's affairs should not also be regarded as having a personal interest in the exercise of his authority sufficient to make it irrevocable. Thus although…the agent's commercial interest in continuing to act in order to earn commission is not enough to make his authority irrevocable, his interest in recovering a debt in respect of commission already earned may well be. There is no reason to distinguish a debt arising in this way from any other debt, provided that it is sufficiently clear that the parties intended that the agent's authority should secure it.

10. There are a number of special cases in which the authority of an agent has been held to be irrevocable on what appears to be a wider basis. They include the irrevocable authority conferred on the promoter of a public share offering to subscribe for shares (*In re Hannan's Empress Gold Mining and Development Co (Carmichael's Case)* [1896] 2 Ch 643), the irrevocable authority conferred by a bidder on an auctioneer of land to execute the memorandum of sale if it is knocked down to him (*Van Praagh v Everidge* [1902] 2 Ch 266, reversed on other grounds [1903] 1 Ch 434), and the irrevocable authority conferred by a Lloyd's name on his managing agent to underwrite (*Daly v Lime Street Underwriting Agencies* [1987] 2 FTLR 277, *Society of Lloyd's v Leighs* [1997] CLC 759 decided on other grounds in the Court of Appeal: *The Times*, 11 August 1997). The result in these cases was undoubtedly convenient, but they do not lend themselves to analysis along the lines discussed above. Nothing that I have said should therefore be taken to refer to them.

NOTES

1. The principal may terminate his agent's authority by revocation (whether or not this constitutes a breach of contract), so long as the agent has not already fulfilled his obligations. The agent's authority can also be terminated by the following means:

(a) execution of the agent's commission (*Blackburn v Scholes* (1810) 2 Camp 341);

(b) if the agent was appointed for a fixed period, expiry of that period (*Dickinson v Lilwal* (1815) 4 Camp 279);

(c) agreement between the principal and agent;

(d) destruction of the subject matter of the agency (*Rhodes v Forwood* (1876) 1 App Cas 256; see below, p 276);

(e) frustration of the agency rendering its performance illegal, impossible, or radically different from what the parties originally contemplated (*Marshall v Glanvill* [1917] 2 KB 87);

(f) the death, insanity, or bankruptcy of the principal or the agent, or, where the principal or agent is a company, its winding-up or dissolution (see, eg, *Pacific and General Insurance Co Ltd v Hazell* [1997] BCC 400, Moore-Bick J, provisional liquidator placed in control of corporate principal)—but cessation of the agent's business does not automatically terminate the agency relationship (*Triffit Nurseries (a firm) v Salads Etcetera Ltd* [1999] 1 Lloyd's Rep 697, Longmore J, affirmed by the Court of Appeal [2000] 2 Lloyd's Rep 74, but where doubts are cast on the question of revocation of authority by appointment of a receiver): see below, pp 1116 ff;

(g) notice of renunciation of the agency given by the agent and accepted by the principal.

2. *Irrevocable agency:*[3] an agent's authority cannot be revoked by the principal without the agent's consent, or determined by the death, insanity, or bankruptcy of the principal, in any of the following circumstances:

(a) where the authority of the agent is given by deed, or for valuable consideration, for the purpose of securing or protecting any interest of the agent (*Frith v Frith*, above; *Bailey and another v Angove's Pty Ltd*, above);

(b) where the agent's authority is given under a power of attorney which is expressed to be irrevocable and is given to secure a proprietary interest of, or the performance of an obligation owed to, the agent (so long as the interest or obligation continues): Powers of Attorney Act 1971, s 4—also note that any lasting power of attorney created under the Mental Capacity Act 2005, and any enduring power of attorney created under the Enduring Power of Attorney Act 1985 (which was repealed by the 2005 Act), is not revoked by the supervening mental incapacity of the donor (Mental Capacity Act 2005, ss 9(1), 13, 66, and Sch 4);

(c) where the agent during the currency of the agency contract has incurred personal liability in the performance of his authority for which the principal must indemnify him (see, eg, *Chappell v Bray* (1860) 6 H & N 145; *Read v Anderson* (1884) 13 QBD 779)—although these cases are usually treated as examples of irrevocable authority they are 'better regarded . . . as examples of circumstances giving rise to the right to be indemnified which in fact rests on wider [contractual, or even restitutionary] principles and which does not depend for its application on continuing authority' (*Pacific and General Insurance Co Ltd v Hazell* [1997] BCC 400 at 409–410, per Moore-Bick J, applying *Bowstead and Reynolds* (16th edn, 1995), para 10–010).

3. Termination of the agent's authority is prospective and not retrospective. Both principal and agent will be entitled to sue one another on claims which accrued before termination, for example the principal can sue the agent for the negligent performance of his duties; the agent can sue the principal for remuneration already earned. If the agency is contractual, the very act of termination, whilst effective to end the agent's actual authority, may itself give rise to a claim for breach of contract. This can occur, for instance, when the principal revokes the agent's authority without notice. In most cases where the agent is engaged under a bilateral contract (which is not for a fixed term, nor specifies a notice period), the agency will only be terminable on reasonable notice (*Martin-Baker Aircraft Co Ltd v Canadian Flight Equipment Ltd* [1955] 2 QB 556), unless the agent has committed a repudiatory breach of contract so that the principal is entitled to terminate the contract summarily (*Boston Deep Sea Fishing and Ice Co v Ansell* (1888) 39 Ch D 339, see above, p 241). But where the principal has made the agent an offer of a unilateral contract (eg as with an estate agent who is not a sole agent: *Luxor (Eastbourne) Ltd v Cooper* [1941] AC 108; above, p 261), the principal can generally withdraw his offer at will.

4. Some agency agreements are for a fixed period. The question then arises whether the principal will be in breach of the agreement if he goes out of business, or disposes of the

---

[3] See, generally, F Reynolds, 'When is an Agent's Authority Irrevocable?' in R Cranston (ed), *Making Commercial Law: Essays in Honour of Roy Goode* (1997), Ch 10.

subject matter of the agency, before the end of that period and thereby prevents the agent from earning further commission. As the following cases illustrate, the answer depends on the court's construction of the terms of the particular agency agreement in issue.

(a) *Rhodes v Forwood* (1876) 1 App Cas 256: Rhodes, a colliery owner, employed Forwood as sole agent to sell the colliery's coal in Liverpool for seven years. Rhodes sold the colliery and went out of business after four years. Forwood sued Rhodes for breach of the agency contract. The House of Lords rejected Forwood's claim holding that there was no express or implied term of the agency contract that the agreement must continue to seven years. The agency contract had been made subject to the risk that Rhodes might sell the colliery.

(b) *Turner v Goldsmith* [1891] 1 QB 544: Goldsmith, a shirt manufacturer, employed Turner for a period of five years to sell 'the various goods manufactured or sold' by Goldsmith. After two years Goldsmith's shirt factory burnt down and he closed down his business. Turner sued Goldsmith for breach of the agency contract. Reversing the judgment of the trial judge in favour of Goldsmith, the Court of Appeal refused to imply a term making the agency contract subject to the continued existence of the factory. On a true construction of the agency contract, Goldsmith could supply Turner with shirts manufactured by someone else or with other goods altogether.

For further consideration of this issue, see above, pp 261–265.

(b) Commercial agents

The Commercial Agents (Council Directive) Regulations 1993 contain detailed, and in many respects novel, provisions dealing with termination of the agency contract of a commercial agent as defined therein (see above, p 119).[4]

(i) Minimum periods of notice for termination

Where there is an agency contract for a fixed period, and it continues to be performed by both parties after the expiry of the period, reg 14 provides that it 'shall be deemed to be converted' into an agency contract for an indefinite period. Regulation 15 provides that 'where an agency contract is concluded for an indefinite period either party may terminate it by notice'. Regulation 15(2) sets out *minimum* periods of notice (the parties may agree longer periods): one month for the first year of the contract; two months for the second year commenced; and three months for the third year commenced or for the subsequent years. These minimum notice requirements do not prevent immediate termination where the contract is discharged by breach or frustration (reg 16). The breach, however, must be a repudiatory breach (*Crane v Sky In-Home Service Ltd* [2007] EWHC 66 (Ch), [2007] 1 CLC 389 at [84], per Briggs J; *Crocs Europe BV v Anderson et al (t/a Spectrum Agencies)* [2012] EWCA Civ 1400, [2013] 1 Lloyd's Rep 1).

(ii) Indemnity and compensation

Regulation 17(1) provides that on termination of his agency the commercial agent is entitled to be 'indemnified…or compensated for damage'. This entitlement results from the idea

---

[4] See, generally, *Bowstead and Reynolds*, Ch 11, RJC Munday, *Agency: Law and Principles* (3rd edn, 2016), Ch 13, and for further detail, S Saintier and J Scholes, *Commercial Agents and the Law* (2005); F Randolph and J Davey, *The European Law of Commercial Agency* (3rd edn, 2010).

that an agent may spend money, time, and effort establishing a market and goodwill for his principal, but then be deprived of the benefit of his investment through termination of his authority by a principal who seeks to deal directly with customers or employ another agent to do so (*Bowstead and Reynolds*, para 11–040). In effect, the regulations provide for the agent to be 'bought out' by his principal. The concepts of indemnity and compensation have their origins in German and French law respectively. Both concepts are new to English law, which has hitherto only been prepared to award an agent damages on termination of the agency where there has been breach of the agency contract by his principal. By contrast, the availability of an indemnity or compensation payable under the regulations is not based on fault.

Regulation 17(2) provides that 'except where the agency contract otherwise provides, the commercial agent shall be entitled to be compensated rather than indemnified'. In other words, the parties must have opted into the indemnity provisions: compensation is the default position. It will have to be shown that the contract actually does 'provide otherwise'. In *Shearman v Hunter Boot Ltd* [2014] EWHC 47 (QB), [2014] 1 CLC 240, the court declined to accept as valid an agreement which did not make clear at the time the agreement was concluded which system was to prevail: the contract merely provided that whichever system turned out to be cheapest for the principal was to apply.

According to reg 17(3), the agent is entitled to an indemnity if and to the extent that:

(a) he has brought the principal new customers or has significantly increased the volume of business with existing customers and the principal continues to derive substantial benefits from the business with such customers; and

(b) the payment of this indemnity is equitable having regard to all the circumstances and, in particular, the commission lost by the commercial agent on the business transacted with such customers.

It seems from this provision that an indemnity will only be payable where the principal continues to do business after termination of the agency agreement: in this respect compensation is more advantageous to the agent as it can apply even where the principal has ceased to trade. Furthermore, unlike a claim to compensation, there is a cap on the amount of the indemnity: it must not exceed a figure equivalent to an indemnity for one year calculated from the agent's average annual remuneration over the preceding five years or over the actual length of the agency contract if it was less than five years (reg 17(4)). However, the right to an indemnity does not preclude the agent from seeking damages from his former principal (reg 17(5)).

An agent made a successful claim for an indemnity in *Moore v Piretta PTA Ltd* [1998] CLC 992. The key issue in the case was whether the agent's entitlement should be based on his contribution to the principal's business during the entire term of his agency (seven years) or only during the period of his last written contract (one year). The judge held that the phrase 'agency contract' in reg 17(1) means the agency as a whole rather than the particular contract in place at the date of termination. He further held that an agent brings in new customers for the purposes of reg 17(3)(a) if he is instrumental in obtaining the customer's business: it does not matter that there are other factors at work. Finally, the judge emphasised that the purpose of the indemnity is to award the agent a share in the goodwill built up by his efforts: the court is determining the proper value of that goodwill; it is not assessing the agent's 'loss', so mitigation of loss is not a relevant issue.

By reg 17(6) an agent is 'entitled to compensation for the damage he suffers as a result of the termination of his relations with his principal'. For these purposes, damage is deemed to occur particularly when the termination takes place in either or both of the following circumstances, namely circumstances which:

(a) deprive the commercial agent of the commission which proper performance of the agency contract would have procured for him whilst providing his principal with substantial benefits linked to the activities of the commercial agent; or

(b) have not enabled the commercial agent to amortise the costs and expenses that he had incurred in the performance of the agency contract on the advice of his principal.

The rationale behind the post-termination payment of compensation is that the commercial agent, having worked to establish and develop the goodwill of the principal's business, has a quasi-proprietary interest in the agency and should be compensated for the loss of that interest (see C Gardiner [2007] JBL 412 at 426 ff). It is the idea of loss to the agent, and not gain to the principal, that is behind the compensation scheme. The method for calculating the compensation payable to the agent was clarified by the House of Lords in *Lonsdale v Howard & Hallam Ltd* [2007] UKHL 32, [2007] 1 WLR 2055, where Lord Hoffmann held (at [12]) that 'what has to be valued is the income stream which the agency would have generated' and (at [21]) that compensation should be calculated 'by reference to the value of the agency on the assumption that it continued'. An extended extract from this important decision appears below. (By way of additional illustrations, see also *Warren t/a On-Line Cartons and Print v Drukkerij Flack BV* [2014] EWCA Civ 993, [2015] 1 Lloyd's Rep 111, esp at [14]–[15], per Longmore LJ, and *Alan Ramsay Sales & Marketing Ltd v Typhoo Tea Ltd* [2016] EWHC 486 (Comm), [2016] 4 WLR 59 at [88] ff, per Flaux J.) There does, however, remain uncertainty as to whether compensation may be claimed in addition to any common law damages due to the agent on termination of the agency. The right to claim damages is expressly preserved by reg 17(5) in respect of an indemnity, but the regulations are silent as to the position with regard to compensation. There is nothing in the regulations to suggest that the compensation scheme overrides other remedies for breach of duty (see *Lonsdale v Howard & Hallam Ltd* [2006] EWCA Civ 63, [2006] 1 WLR 1281 at [28], per Moore-Bick LJ).

Although the indemnity or compensation provisions apply in a wide variety of circumstances (including where termination of the agency contract is due to the agent's death: reg 17(8), and also where the agency contract has expired by effluxion of time: see *Tigana Ltd v Decoro Ltd* [2003] EWHC 23 (QB), [2003] Eu LR 189 at [79], as approved by the Court of Appeal, *obiter*, in *Light v Ty Europe Ltd* [2003] EWCA Civ 1238, [2004] 1 Lloyd's Rep 693 at [32], [46], and [53]). There are a few occasions where the entitlement does not arise or is lost. According to reg 18, an indemnity or compensation will not be payable to the commercial agent where: (a) the principal terminates the agency contract because of the agent's repudiatory breach; or (b) the commercial agent himself terminates the agency contract (unless (i) such termination is 'justified by circumstances attributable to the principal', or (ii) on grounds of the age, infirmity, or illness of the agent: eg in *Abbott v Condici Ltd* [2005] 2 Lloyd's Rep 450, the agent was held to be entitled to compensation when he reached normal retirement age even though he was healthy and fit); or (c) the commercial agent, with the agreement of the principal, assigns his rights and duties under the agency contract to another person. In *Bell Electric Ltd v Aweco Appliance Systems GmbH & Co KG*, above, at [54], Elias J considered the meaning of reg 18(a) and (b) and stated that:

> [I]n my judgment the better view is that reg 18(a) and 18(b)(i) ought to be seen as the reverse sides of the same coin. In other words, the compensation is not payable if the principal terminates in circumstances which would be justifiable at common law because of the agent's conduct; but

on the other hand it is payable if the commercial agent terminates in circumstances which are justifiable at common law because of the conduct of the principal. In either case, if the innocent party affirms the contract and precludes the right to rely on the repudiatory breach, the attempt thereafter to terminate the contract, absent some fresh repudiatory breach, will not be justifiable within the meaning of the regulations.

In *Cooper v Pure Fishing (UK) Ltd* [2004] EWCA Civ 375, [2004] 2 Lloyd's Rep 518 at [15], Tuckey LJ stated that reg 18(a) only applies, and an indemnity or compensation is not payable on this ground, where two conditions are met: the principal must 'have terminated' the contract, which means he must have done something unilaterally to bring the contract to an end, and he must do this because of the agent's default. The principal's decision not to renew an agency contract which expired by effluxion of time, even where the decision was based on the agent's default, was held not to fall within reg 18(a) and so compensation was not precluded.

The commercial agent loses his right to an indemnity or compensation if within one year following termination of the agency contract he does not notify his former principal that he intends to pursue his entitlement (reg 17(9)). All the agent need do is give notice of his intention to pursue a claim under reg 17; he does not have to specify whether his claim is to an indemnity or to compensation (*Hackett v Advanced Medical Computer Systems Ltd* [1999] CLC 160 at 163).

The parties cannot contract out of regs 17 and 18 'to the detriment of the commercial agent before the agency contract expires' (reg 19). In *Crane v Sky In-Home Service Ltd* [2007] EWHC 66 (Ch), [2007] 1 CLC 389 at [93], Briggs J stated (*obiter*) that where a contract purported to exclude both indemnity and compensation, the agent would nevertheless be entitled to compensation.

Lonsdale v Howard & Hallam Ltd
[2007] UKHL 32, [2007] 1 WLR 2055, House of Lords

Lonsdale was a commercial agent in the shoe trade. In 1990 Howard & Hallam Ltd, a shoe manufacturer, appointed him as their agent to sell their Elmdale brand in southeast England. A few years later he was appointed by a German manufacturer to sell their Wendel brand in a slightly larger territory. Wendel shoes sold well, but Elmdale shoes did not. Sales, and with them Lonsdale's commission income, fell year by year. In 2003 Howard & Hallam ceased trading and duly terminated Lonsdale's agency on the appropriate notice. Lonsdale made a claim for compensation under the 1993 regulations. The trial judge found that the net annual commission was about £8,000 and assessed the appropriate measure of compensation as £5,000. The judge refused to apply the French approach to the 1986 underlying European Directive, whereby the agent was usually awarded two years' gross commission. Both the Court of Appeal and the House of Lords dismissed Lonsdale's appeal against this ruling.

Lord Hoffmann (his Lordship set out the terms of art 17 of the 1986 EC Directive on the co-ordination of the laws of the member states relating to self-employed commercial agents, and continued):
  5. It will be noticed that although the purpose of the Directive is said to be the co-ordination of the laws of the Member States relating to self-employed commercial agents, article 17 allows

Member States to choose between two different rights, one or other of which must be accorded to a commercial agent on the termination of the agency. He must be given a right to either an indemnity in accordance with article 17(2) or compensation in accordance with article 17(3). The English words 'indemnity' and 'compensation' are not very illuminating in marking the distinction between these two rights. They are both ways of dealing with the unfairness which it was thought might arise if the termination of the agency leaves the agent worse off and the principal better off than if the agency had continued. It appears that the right under article 17(2), which the draftsman has chosen to label 'indemnity', is derived from German law and is now contained in section 89b of the *Handelsgesetzbuch*. The right to 'compensation' under article 17(3) is derived from French law and is now contained in article 12 of the *Loi no 91-593 du 25 juin 1991 relative aux rapports entre les agents commerciaux et leurs mandants*. The two systems can plainly lead to different results, so that, on this point at any rate, the extent of the coordination achieved by the Directive is modest.

6. The United Kingdom chose both systems, in the sense that it allowed the parties to opt for an indemnity under article 17(2) but provided that in default of agreement the agent should be entitled to compensation under article 17(3): see regulation 17(2). In the present case the parties made no choice and Mr Lonsdale is therefore entitled to compensation under article 17(3).

7. The question in this appeal is how the compensation should be determined. But for this purpose it is necessary first to decide exactly what the agent should be compensated for. Only then can one proceed to consider how the compensation should be calculated.

8. On this first question the Directive is explicit. The agent is entitled to be compensated for 'the damage he suffers as a result of the termination of his relations with the principal.' In other words, the agent is treated as having lost something of value as a result of the termination and is entitled to compensation for this loss.

9. As this part of the Directive is based on French law, I think that one is entitled to look at French law for guidance, or confirmation, as to what it means. Article 12 of the French law says that the agent is entitled to '*une indemnité compensatrice en réparation du préjudice subi*'. The French jurisprudence from which the terms of the article is derived appears to regard the agent as having had a share in the goodwill of the principal's business which he has helped to create. The relationship between principal and agent is treated as having existed for their common benefit. They have co-operated in building up the principal's business: the principal by providing a good product and the agent by his skill and effort in selling. The agent has thereby acquired a share in the goodwill, an asset which the principal retains after the termination of the agency and for which the agent is therefore entitled to compensation: see Saintier and Scholes, *Commercial Agents and the Law* (2005) at pp 175–177.

10. This elegant theory explains why the French courts regard the agent as, in principle, entitled to compensation. It does not, however, identify exactly what he is entitled to compensation for. One possibility might have been to value the total goodwill of the principal's business and then to try to attribute some share to the agent. But this would in practice be a hopeless endeavour and the French courts have never tried to do it. Instead, they have settled upon compensating him for what he has lost by being deprived of his business. That is the '*préjudice subi*.' The French case law makes it clear that this ordinarily involves placing a value upon the right to be an agent. That means, primarily, the right to future commissions 'which proper performance of the agency contract would have procured him': see Saintier and Scholes, *op cit*, pp 187–188. In my opinion, this is the right for which the Directive requires the agent to be compensated.

11. Having thus determined that the agent is entitled to be compensated for being deprived of the benefit of the agency relationship, the next question is how that loss should be calculated. The value of the agency relationship lies in the prospect of earning commission, the agent's expectation that 'proper performance of the agency contract' will provide him with a future income stream. It is this which must be valued.

12. Like any other exercise in valuation, this requires one to say what could reasonably have been obtained, at the date of termination, for the rights which the agent had been enjoying. For this purpose it is obviously necessary to assume that the agency would have continued and the hypothetical purchaser would have been able properly to perform the agency contract. He must be assumed to have been able to take over the agency and (if I may be allowed the metaphor) stand in the shoes of the agent, even if, as a matter of contract, the agency was not assignable or there were in practice no dealings in such agencies: compare *Inland Revenue Commissioners v Crossman* [1937] AC 26. What has to be valued is the income stream which the agency would have generated.

13. On the other hand, as at present advised, I see no reason to make any other assumptions contrary to what was the position in the real world at the date of termination. As one is placing a present value upon future income, one must discount future earnings by an appropriate rate of interest. If the agency was by its terms or in fact unassignable, it must be assumed, as I have said, that the hypothetical purchaser would have been entitled to take it over. But there is no basis for assuming that he would then have obtained an assignable asset: compare the *Crossman* case. Likewise, if the market for the products in which the agent dealt was rising or declining, this would have affected what a hypothetical purchaser would have been willing to give. He would have paid fewer years' purchase for a declining agency than for one in an expanding market. If the agent would have had to incur expense or do work in earning his commission, it cannot be assumed that the hypothetical purchaser would have earned it gross or without having to do anything.

14. Mr Philip Moser, who appeared for Mr Lonsdale, objected that this method of calculation was likely to produce less than he would have been awarded by a French court. And it does appear that it is common practice for French courts to value agencies at twice the average annual gross commission over the previous three years. Mr Moser said that in stipulating that agents should receive compensation under article 17(3), the directive was adopting the French practice as Community law. This, he said, was confirmed by the report on the application of article 17 (COM(96) 364 final) which the Commission, pursuant to article 17(6), had issued in 1996. It noted that a body of case law had developed in France concerning the level of compensation. By 'judicial custom', this was fixed as two years' commission, which, they said, 'conforms with commercial practice'. However, the courts retained a discretion to award less when 'the agent's loss was in fact less.' The report said that in France the Directive had made no difference: 'pre-existing jurisprudence has continued to be applied.' In England, however, there had been difficulties of interpretation. There was, at that stage, no case law but 'the parties in practice are attempting to apply common law principles'. In particular, it was difficult to see how these principles would enable the courts to reach the figure of twice gross commission which was regularly awarded by French courts. The Commission said that there was 'a need for clarification' of article 17. But nothing has been done about it.

15. Mr Moser invited your Lordships to treat the Commission as having indorsed the French method of calculating compensation under article 17(3) as the appropriate interpretation of that article as a Community instrument. It would follow that all Member States which adopt article 17(3) would be bound to treat twice gross commission as the normal compensation for termination of an agency, subject to variation in exceptional cases in which the principal could prove that the actual loss was less or the agent could prove that it was more. If your Lordships did not accept this as the plain and obvious meaning of the Directive, he submitted that the question should be referred to the Court of Justice.

16. My Lords, I do not accept this submission, to which I think there are at least three answers. First, the Commission report was not indorsing any method of calculation as a true reflection of Community law. That was not its function. The Commission was required by article 17(6) to report on the implementation of the Article, and, if necessary, to submit proposals for amendments. It reported on the basis of information supplied by Member States and noted that the UK position

(so far as it could be ascertained in the absence of any judicial pronouncement) was different from the French. But there is no suggestion that either approach would fail to implement the directive.

17. Secondly, the provisions of article 17(3) which say what the agent is entitled to be compensated for are perfectly plain. It is the damage which he suffers as a result of the termination. The French domestic law, as I have pointed out, says exactly the same. Where French and English courts differ is in the method by which that damage is calculated. But the Court of Justice has made it clear that the method of calculation is a matter for each Member State to decide. In *Case C-465/ 04 Honeyvem Informazioni Commerciali Srl v Mariella De Zotti* [2006] ECR I-02879 at paras 34–36 the Court of Justice said:

34. ...It must be observed that although the system established by article 17 of the Directive is mandatory and prescribes a framework...it does not give any detailed indications as regards the method of calculation of the indemnity for termination of contract.

35. The Court thus held that, within that framework, the Member States may exercise their discretion as to the choice of methods for calculating the indemnity [*Case C-381/98 Ingmar GB Ltd v Eaton Leonard Technologies Inc* [2000] ECR I-9305 at para 21].

36. Therefore...within the framework prescribed by article 17(2) of the Directive, the Member States enjoy a margin of discretion which they may exercise...

18. Thirdly, it seems that commercial agencies in France operate in market conditions which are different from those prevailing in England. It would appear that in France agencies do change hands and that it is common for the premium charged on such a transaction to be twice the gross commission. Whether the judicial practice of estimating the value of the agency at twice gross commission is based upon this fact of French economic life or whether vendors of agency businesses are able to charge such a premium because the purchaser knows that he will be able to recover that amount, either from the next purchaser or from the principal on termination of the agency, is unclear. Saintier and Scholes, *op cit*, at p 187 describe it as a 'chicken-and-egg process'. There does seem to be evidence that some principals demand payment of an estimated twice gross commission in return for the grant of a commercial agency (even if they have to lend the agent the money) because they know that they will have to return this amount to the agent on termination. At any rate, whatever the origins of the practice, it would appear that twice gross commission is often the real value of an agency in France because that is what you could sell it for in the market. As the Commission significantly remarked, the French system 'conforms with commercial practice'. There is no such market in England. It would therefore appear that the difference between French and English practice exists not because their respective courts are applying different rules of law but because they are operating in different markets.

19. Mr Moser said that the adoption of anything less favourable to commercial agents than the French method of calculation would not give effect to the purpose of the Directive, which is to protect the interests of the commercial agent. No doubt this is one of its purposes: in *Page v Combined Shipping and Trading Co Ltd* [1996] CLC 1952, 1956 Staughton LJ said, with more than a touch of irony, that the directive appeared to be based upon a belief that 'commercial agents are a down-trodden race, and need and should be afforded protection against their principals.' But these are generalities which do not help one to decide what protection is sufficient to give effect to the policy of the Directive. One may however obtain a useful cross-check by considering what an agent could obtain under a system which provided him with an indemnity, since there is no doubt that this too would satisfy the policy of the directive.

20. It is a condition of the indemnity that the agent should have 'brought the principal new customers or...significantly increased the volume of business with existing customers' and that the principal 'continues to derive substantial benefits from the business with such customers': article 17(2)(a).

It follows that in a case such as the present, in which the principal went out of business and therefore derived no benefit from the customers introduced by the agent, no indemnity will be payable: see Saintier and Scholes, op cit, at p 204. In addition, article 17(2)(b) limits the indemnity to one year's commission. In the face of these provisions which will satisfy the policy of the Directive, it is impossible to argue that it requires a payment of twice gross commission whether the principal has derived any benefit from the termination or not.

21. In my opinion, therefore, the courts of the United Kingdom would not be acting inconsistently with the Directive if they were to calculate the compensation payable under article 17(3) by reference to the value of the agency on the assumption that it continued: the amount which the agent could reasonably expect to receive for the right to stand in his shoes, continue to perform the duties of the agency and receive the commission which he would have received. It remains to consider some of the English and Scottish cases in which the question has been discussed.

22. The decision of the Court of Session in *King v Tunnock Ltd* 2000 SC 424 is the only appellate case containing a full discussion of the way compensation should be calculated. Mr King sold cakes and biscuits for Tunnock Ltd. He had taken over the agency from his father in 1962. It was his full-time occupation. In 1994 the company closed its bakery and terminated the agency. The evidence was that over the previous two years he had earned gross commission amounting in total to £27,144. The sheriff held that he was not entitled to compensation because the principal, having closed the business, would not enjoy any benefits from the goodwill generated by the agent. But an Extra Division of the Court of Session reversed this interlocutor and awarded compensation in the sum of £27,144.

23. I respectfully think that the sheriff was right. In view of the closure of the business, the agency was worth nothing. No one would have given anything for the right to earn future commission on the sales of cakes and biscuits because there would be none to be sold. Nor had the principal retained any goodwill which the agent had helped to build up. The goodwill disappeared when the business closed. The reason why the business closed is not altogether clear but Mr King's low earnings for full-time work over the previous two years suggests that it was not doing well. Even if one assumes that commission would have continued at the same rate, it is hard to see why anyone should have paid for the privilege of a full-time job which earned him less than he would have been paid as a bus conductor.

24. I am bound to say that I do not find the reasoning of the Extra Division, delivered by Lord Caplan, at all convincing. He said that the agency had existed for many years and that it was likely that the agent had good relations with customers. That, no doubt, was true. But Lord Caplan then went on to say:

> In these circumstances we consider it likely that the pursuer would have expected and required a relatively high level of compensation to surrender his successful and long-established agency. The compensation would, of course, require to be tied to the commission he was earning. Thus this is a case where we can conclude, even on the limited information that is available, that the agent would have expected to receive a capital sum representing at least the total for the last two years of his earnings to be paid before he would voluntarily have given up his agency.

25. '[He] would have expected to receive . . .'. I daresay he might. But would anyone have given it to him? Lord Caplan does not seem to have considered it relevant to ask. It appears that, following *King v Tunnock Ltd*, it is standard practice for the former agent to give evidence of what he would have expected to receive for his agency. In this case, Mr Lonsdale said in a witness statement that he had been advised by an accountant that an established method of valuation was to take the gross profits and multiply them by two and a half. For the last completed accounting year before closure his gross commission was £12,239.34 and he therefore valued the business at £30,598.35.

26. Mr Lonsdale at least claimed to have the support of an accountant for his valuation, although he did not call him as a witness. But the Court of Session appears to have arrived at the figure of twice gross commission without any evidence at all. Lord Caplan said that he was 'reassured' that this would be standard compensation in France, but, for the reasons I have explained, the French practice is of no evidential value whatever.

27. *King v Tunnock Ltd* was considered by Judge Bowers (sitting as a High Court judge) in *Barrett McKenzie v Escada (UK) Ltd* [2001] EuLR 567. The judge was not attracted by the formulaic approach of the Court of Session but said (at p 575) that the point on which he agreed with Lord Caplan was that—

> one is valuing the agency and its connections that have been established by the agent at the time at or immediately before termination, and it is really a question of compensating for the notional value of that agency in the open market . . .

28. I agree that this is what compensation in article 17(3) means. My only caution is that one must be careful about the word 'notional'. All that is notional is the assumption that the agency was available to be bought and sold at the relevant date. What it would fetch depends upon circumstances as they existed in the real world at the time: what the earnings prospects of the agency were and what people would have been willing to pay for similar businesses at the time.

29. In *Tigana Ltd v Decoro* [2003] EuLR 189 the judge awarded the agent a sum equal to his commission less expenses over the 14 to 15 months during which the agency had subsisted. I would agree that prima facie the value of the agency should be fixed by reference to its net earnings because, as a matter of common sense, that is what will matter to the hypothetical purchaser. Furthermore, in the case of an agent who has more than one agency, the costs must be fairly attributed to each. He cannot simply say, as Mr Lonsdale did in this case, that the marginal cost of the Elmdale agency was little or nothing because he had to see the same customers and go to the same exhibitions for Wendel.

30. It may well be that 14 months' commission adopted by the judge was a fair valuation. But he seems to have had no evidence that anyone would have paid this figure for a comparable business. Instead, he gave (at p 221) a non-exhaustive list of 14 factors ((a) to (n)), some of them very wide-ranging indeed, which he said would require consideration. The list gives no indication of the weight to be attributed to each factor.

31. More recently, in *Smith, Bailey Palmer v Howard & Hallam Ltd* [2006] EuLR 578 Judge Overend (sitting as a High Court judge) dealt with claims by other agents who had worked for the respondent in this case. He noted that the Elmdale brand had been sold to a competitor for £550,000 and that, over the three years before the sale, 42% of the sales and distribution expenses had consisted of agent's commission. On these figures, he considered that it would be right to attribute 42% of the value of the brand to the agents. This seems to me a flawed method of calculation. First, it treats the entire value of the brand, ie the goodwill of the Elmdale name, as attributable to sales and marketing. No allowance is made for the possibility that some of the goodwill may have been attributable to the fact that the company made good shoes. Secondly, no allowance is made for the fact that the commission, which is treated as the measure of the proprietary interest of the agents in the assets of the company, is what the agents were actually paid for their services. On this theory, the advertising agents should have acquired an interest proportionate to what they were paid. Thirdly, the valuation is based entirely on cost rather than what anyone would actually have paid for the agency.

32. That brings me to the judgments in the present case. The claim was heard by Judge Harris QC in the Oxford County Court and his judgment was, if I may respectfully say so, a model of clarity and common sense. I shall extract one or two of the most important passages:

> 18. If it is kept in mind that the damage for which the agent is to be compensated consists in the loss of the value or goodwill he can be said to have possessed in the agency, then it can be

seen that valuation ought to be reasonably straightforward. Small businesses of all kinds are daily being bought and sold, and a major element in the composition of their price will be a valuation of goodwill.

19. But neither side put evidence before the court about how commercial goodwill is conventionally valued. Nor was I told upon what basis claims of this type are conventionally settled. There was no evidence at all about how commercially to value such assets. It is of course for the claimant, as a seeker of compensation, to prove the value of what he has lost.

33. The judge then found that net commission was running at about £8,000 a year, and said:

20. ...The value of that agency, the commercial value is what someone would pay for it; to acquire by assignment a business vehicle with a likely net annual income of £8,000...

22. Commonsense would indicate that few people wanting the opportunity to earn what the claimant was earning would be prepared to pay well over £20,000 for the privilege of doing so, still less would they do so in an industry in remorseless decline, and in which the likely buyers would be men of modest means...

23. Given the absence of evidence about how commercially to value goodwill, or evidence about what price in practice might have been available, the court might be thought to be justified in simply finding that the claimant has failed to prove his case...

30. This was an agency producing a modest and falling income in a steadily deteriorating environment. There is no evidence that anyone would have paid anything to buy it...I am strongly tempted to find that no damage has been established...But perhaps that conclusion, though I regard it as logical, is a little over-rigorous given that the defendant has already made a payment. Doing the best I can, I find that the appropriate figure for compensation is one of £5,000.

34. The Court of Appeal approved of this approach. After a thorough review of the authorities, Moore-Bick J quoted para 18 of the judgment (see above) and said that the judge was right in his approach. I agree. Furthermore, I do not think that the judge could have been faulted if he had simply dismissed the claim.

35. That is sufficient to dispose of the appeal, but there are three additional comments to be made. First, Mr Moser urged your Lordships not to adopt a principle which required valuation evidence. Valuations, he said, were expensive and most claims were too small to justify the cost. Moore-Bick LJ said (at [57]) that 'in most cases' the court would be likely to benefit from the assistance of an expert witness but that in some cases it might be sufficient to place all the material before the court and invite the judge to act as valuer. It seems to me that once it is firmly understood that the compensation is for the loss of the value of the agency, relatively few cases will go to court. As Judge Harris said, small comparable businesses are bought and sold every day and it should not be difficult for the parties, with the benefit of advice about the going rate for such businesses, to agree on an appropriate valuation. It should not always be necessary for them to obtain a full-scale valuation, involving the checking of income and expenditure figures and the application of the going rate to those figures. But I do not see how, if the matter does go to court, the judge can decide the case without some information about the standard methodology for the valuation of such businesses. In this case, the judge was simply invited to pluck a figure out of the air from across the Channel and rightly refused to do so. Nothing is more likely to cause uncertainty and promote litigation than a lottery system under which judges are invited to choose figures at random.

36. It may also be possible, after a period of experience in such valuations, for the court to take judicial notice of what would be the going rate in what I might call the standard

case, namely an agency which has continued for some time and in which the net commission figures are fairly stable. It should not be necessary to repeat boilerplate evidence in every case. But the judge must be reasonably confident that he is dealing with the standard case. Adjustments would be needed if, as in this case, the market was in decline or had disappeared altogether.

37. Secondly, there is the question raised by the Winemakers' Federation of Australia Inc, who were given leave to intervene and made submissions. They are concerned about the case in which the agent is able to transfer the goodwill he has created with customers to another principal: for example, to persuade the supermarkets to whom he has been selling the produce of one winery to transfer to another. In such a case the former principal would not retain the goodwill which the agent had created and it would be unfair to have to pay compensation on the basis that the agent had gone out of business.

38. In my opinion, circumstances such as these will be reflected in the process of valuation. The hypothetical purchase of the agency does not involve an assumption that the agent gives a covenant against competition. If the situation in real life is that the hypothetical purchaser would be in competition with the former agent and could not have any assurance that the customers would continue to trade with him, that would affect the amount he was prepared to pay. If it appeared that all the customers were likely to defect to the former agent (or, for that matter, to someone else), he would be unlikely to be prepared to pay much for the agency.

39. What matters, of course, is what would have appeared likely at the date of termination and not what actually happened afterwards. But I do not think that the court is required to shut its eyes to what actually happened. It may provide evidence of what the parties were likely to have expected to happen.

40. Thirdly and finally, there is the question of whether a reference should be made to the European Court of Justice. Mr Moser says that the differences in opinion between the Scottish and the English courts and between various English judges show that the law is uncertain. That is true, but what is uncertain is not the meaning of the Directive. It is clear that the agent is entitled to compensation for 'the damage he suffers as a result of the termination of his relations with the principal' and that the method by which that damage should be calculated is a discretionary matter for the domestic laws of the Member States. It is the way in which our domestic law should implement that discretion which has been uncertain and the resolution of that uncertainty is the task of this House and not the European Court of Justice.

41. I would therefore dismiss the appeal.

[Lords Bingham, **Rodger**, **Carswell**, and **Neuberger** agreed.]

S Saintier, 'Final Guidelines on Compensation of Commercial Agents'

(2008) 124 LQR 31 at 36–37

As the first ruling of the House of Lords on the method of calculation of the compensation due, this unanimous decision is of great importance. The recognition of the specificity of the loss the agent suffers on termination and the need for a clear methodology for its assessment is to be welcomed. By stating that the loss suffered is that of the agency as an asset to the agent, the court seems to accept that the basis of the payment is the expropriation of the agent's quasi-proprietary interest and not the principal's gain. This analysis, in line with French law, also recognises the different emphasis between compensation and indemnity. However, to take account of the fact that the principal's business is failing as reducing the value of the agency and therefore the value of the compensation blurs the distinction between compensation and indemnity and appears to calculate compensation by reference to existing common law principles. In fact, looking at the state of the principal's business means that in certain cases, in spite of losing the agency, the agent will be left with no compensation. Member States have some discretion in the matter, yet, given the previously mentioned different emphasis between the two options, it is not clear whether this is correct. Although the EU Commission did not consider that calculating compensation by reference to common law principles was a failure to implement the Directive, doing so may nevertheless undermine the specificity of the loss agents suffer on termination, which may be against the protective stance of the implementing text. By emphasising the domestic discretion in the calculation of compensation, their Lordships accentuate the fact that the Directive stipulated a remedy for a loss but left it to Member States to decide how that remedy is to be calculated. If the effect of such a discretion is that, on similar facts, domestic courts interpret the Directive differently, this raises wider questions as to the effectiveness of this Directive as a tool for harmonisation of European private law, a problem recognised by the European Commission, who, in its *Action Plan on a More Coherent European Contract Law* (Com (2003) 68 final) criticised the Directive for creating uncertainty (Com (2003) 68 final at para.18).

QUESTIONS

1. What are the key differences between the indemnity scheme and the compensation scheme? Do you think Lord Hoffmann was right to 'cross-check' the basis of his assessment under the compensation scheme with what the commercial agent might have recovered under the indemnity scheme?

2. How far, if at all, do you agree with Saintier's assessment that the House of Lords has taken account of common law principles?

3. Do you agree with Lord Hoffmann's view that 'once it is understood that the compensation is for the loss of the value of the agency, relatively few cases will go to court'? You should bear in mind that, in England, commercial agencies are not bought and sold on a regular basis.

(c) Termination and third parties

Drew v Nunn

(1879) 4 QBD 661, Court of Appeal

Nunn appointed his wife as his agent to purchase goods from Drew. Nunn was present when some of the goods were ordered by his wife and he paid for some of them. Nunn then became insane and was confined to an asylum. His wife, however, continued to purchase goods on his behalf from Drew, who was unaware of Nunn's insanity. When Nunn regained his sanity, he refused to pay for those goods ordered by his wife when he was in the asylum. Mellor J directed the jury that Drew was entitled to recover the price of the goods from Nunn. Nunn appealed.

Brett LJ: This appeal has stood over for a long time, principally on my account, in order to ascertain whether it can be determined upon some clear principle. I have found, however, that the law upon this subject stands upon a very unsatisfactory footing.

[His Lordship then set out the facts of the case. He continued:]

Upon this state of facts two questions arise. Does insanity put an end to the authority of the agent? One would expect to find that this question has been long decided on clear principles; but on looking into *Story on Agency*, Scotch authorities, Pothier, and other French authorities, I find that no satisfactory conclusion has been arrived at. If such insanity as existed here did not put an end to the agent's authority, it would be clear that the plaintiff is entitled to succeed; but in my opinion insanity of this kind does put an end to the agent's authority. It cannot be disputed that some cases of change of status in the principal put an end to the authority of the agent; thus, the bankruptcy and death of the principal, the marriage of a female principal, all put an end to the authority of the agent. It may be argued that this result follows from the circumstance that a different principal is created. Upon bankruptcy the trustee becomes the principal; upon death the heir or devisee as to realty, the executor or administrator as to personalty; and upon the marriage of a female principal her husband takes her place. And it has been argued that by analogy the lunatic continues liable until a fresh principal, namely, his committee, is appointed. But I cannot think that this is the true ground, for executors are, at least in some instances, bound to carry out the contracts entered into by their testators. I think that the satisfactory principle to be adopted is that, where such a change occurs as to the principal that he can no longer act for himself, the agent whom he has appointed can no longer act for him. In the present case a great change had occurred in the condition of the principal: he was so far afflicted with insanity as to be disabled from acting for himself; therefore his wife, who was his agent, could no longer act for him. Upon the ground which I have pointed out, I think that her authority was terminated. It seems to me that an agent is liable to be sued by a third person, if he assumes to act on his principal's behalf after he had knowledge of his principal's incompetency to act. In a case of that kind he is acting wrongfully. The defendant's wife must be taken to have been aware of her husband's lunacy; and if she had assumed to act on his behalf with any one to whom he himself had not held her out as his agent, she would have been acting wrongfully, and, but for the circumstance that she is married, would have been liable in an action to compensate the person with whom she assumed to act on her husband's behalf. In my opinion, if a person who has not been held out as agent assumes to act on behalf of a lunatic, the contract is void against the supposed principal, and the pretended agent is liable to an action for misleading an innocent person.

The second question then arises, what is the consequence where a principal, who has held out another as his agent, subsequently becomes insane, and a third person deals with the agent without notice that the principal is a lunatic? Authority may be given to an agent in two ways. First, it may be given by some instrument, which of itself asserts that the authority is thereby created, such as a power of attorney; it is of itself an assertion by the principal that the agent may act for him. Secondly, an authority may also be created from the principal holding out the agent as entitled to act generally for him. The agency in the present case was created in the manner last-mentioned. As between the defendant and his wife, the agency expired upon his becoming to her knowledge insane; but it seems to me that the person dealing with the agent without knowledge of the principal's insanity has a right to enter into a contract with him, and the principal, although a lunatic, is bound so that he cannot repudiate the contract assumed to be made upon his behalf. It is difficult to assign the ground upon which this doctrine, which however seems to me to be the true principle, exists. It is said that the right to hold the insane principal liable depends upon contract. I have a difficulty in assenting to this. It has been said also that the right depends upon estoppel. I cannot see that an estoppel is created. But it has been said also that the right depends upon representations made by the principal and entitling third persons to act upon them, until they hear that those representations are withdrawn. The authorities collected in *Story on Agency*, ch xviii § 481, p 610 (7th edn), seem to base the right upon the ground of public policy: it is there said in effect that the existence of the right goes in aid of public business. It is however a better way of stating the rule to say that the holding out of another person as agent is a representation upon which, at the time when it was made, third parties had a right to act, and if no insanity had supervened would still have had a right to act. In this case the wife was held out as agent, and the plaintiff acted upon the defendant's representation as to her authority without notice that it had been withdrawn. The defendant cannot escape from the consequences of the representation which he has made; he cannot withdraw the agent's authority as to third persons without giving them notice of the withdrawal. The principal is bound, although he retracts the agent's authority, if he has not given notice and the latter wrongfully enters into a contract upon his behalf. The defendant became insane and was unable to withdraw the authority which he had conferred upon his wife: he may be an innocent sufferer by her conduct, but the plaintiff, who dealt with her *bona fide*, is also innocent, and where one of two persons both innocent must suffer by the wrongful act of a third person, that person making the representation which, as between the two, was the original cause of the mischief, must be the sufferer and must bear the loss. Here it does not lie in the defendant's mouth to say that the plaintiff shall be the sufferer.

A difficulty may arise in the application of a general principle such as this is. Suppose that a person makes a representation which after his death is acted upon by another in ignorance that his death has happened: in my view the estate of the deceased will be bound to make good any loss, which may have occurred through acting upon that representation. It is, however, unnecessary to decide this point to-day.

Upon the grounds above stated I am of opinion that, although the authority of the defendant's wife was put an end to by his insanity, and although she had no authority to deal with the plaintiff, nevertheless the latter is entitled to recover, because the defendant whilst he was sane made representations to the plaintiff, upon which he was entitled to act until he had notice of the defendant's insanity, and he had no notice of the insanity until after he had supplied the goods for the price of which he now sues. The direction of Mellor J was right.

Bramwell LJ: I agree with the judgment just delivered by Brett LJ. It must be taken that the defendant told the plaintiff that his wife had authority to bind him; when that authority had been given, it continued to exist, so far as the plaintiff was concerned, until it was revoked and until he received notice of that revocation. It may be urged that this doctrine does not extend to insanity, which is not an intentional revocation; but I think that insanity forms no exception to the general law as to principal and agent. It may be hard upon an insane principal, if his agent abuses his authority; but, on the other hand, it must be recollected that insanity is not a privilege, it is a misfortune, which must not be allowed to injure innocent persons: it would be productive of mischievous consequences, if insanity annulled every representation made by the person afflicted with it without any notice being given of his malady. If the argument for the defendant were correct, every act done by him or on his behalf after he became insane must be treated as a nullity...

It has been assumed by Brett LJ that the insanity of the defendant was such as to amount to a revocation of his wife's authority. I doubt whether partial mental derangement would have that effect. I think that in order to annul the authority of an agent, insanity must amount to dementia. If a man becomes so far insane as to have no mind, perhaps he ought to be deemed dead for the purpose of contracting. I think that the direction of Mellor J was right.

Brett LJ: I am requested by Cotton LJ to state that he agrees with the conclusion at which we have arrived; but that he does not wish to decide whether the authority of the defendant's wife was terminated, or whether the liability of a contractor lasts until a committee has been appointed.

He bases his decision simply upon the ground that the defendant, by holding out his wife as agent, entered into a contract with the plaintiff that she had authority to act upon his behalf, and that until the plaintiff had notice that this authority was revoked he was entitled to act upon the defendant's representations.

I wish to add that if there had been any real question as to the extent of the defendant's insanity, it ought to have been left to the jury; and that as no question was asked of the jury, I must assume that the defendant was insane to the extent which I have mentioned. I may remark that from the mere fact of mental derangement it ought not to be assumed that a person is incompetent to contract; mere weakness of mind or partial derangement is insufficient to exempt a person from responsibility upon the engagements into which he has entered.

Blankley v Central Manchester and Manchester Children's University Hospitals NHS Trust
[2015] EWCA Civ 18, [2015] 1 WLR 4307, Court of Appeal.

The claimant, in 2002, brought a claim for damages in respect of brain damage suffered as a result of surgery at the defendant's hospital. She acted through her litigation friend since she lacked the necessary capacity to conduct her own affairs. Having regained her mental capacity in 2005, the claimant entered into a conditional fee agreement (CFA) with solicitors. In 2007, however, the Court of Protection determined that she no longer had the requisite mental capacity either to conduct her own affairs or to provide instructions to her lawyers. Accordingly, a receiver was appointed, who subsequently became a Court of Protection deputy. Once the proceedings were concluded, the solicitors submitted a bill of costs on behalf of the claimant. The defendant hospital trust denied that the costs relating to work carried out after the appointment of the receiver were recoverable, arguing that the claimant's mental incapacity had terminated the conditional fee agreement automatically by reason of frustration. Reversing the decision of the costs judge, at first instance the judge allowed the claimant's appeal, holding that the conditional fee agreement had not been terminated by frustration or otherwise. Before the Court of Appeal the defendant contended that, since the claimant's supervening incapacity had prevented her from instructing her solicitors herself, the contract of retainer had become incapable of performance and had therefore been frustrated.

Dismissing the appeal, Richards LJ (with whom McCombe and Sharp LJJ agreed) held that in the circumstances of this case the parties must have contemplated that (i) the claimant might relapse and suffer from a renewed period of incapacity during which she would be unable to give instructions personally, and (ii) in this eventuality, instructions might be given by a litigation friend, receiver, or deputy on her behalf. For this reason, the claimant's supervening incapacity to give instructions personally had not rendered the contract of retainer impossible of performance but had simply given rise to a short period of delay pending appointment of a receiver or deputy who acted in her stead, continuing to conduct proceedings on her behalf and to give instructions to the solicitors. The conditional fee agreement therefore, had not been terminated by reason of frustration. Richards LJ also made some general observations on the unsatisfactory nature of this area of law, echoing views expressed the previous year in the Supreme Court in *Dunhill v Burgin (Nos 1 and 2)* [2014] UKSC 18, [2014] 1 WLR 933.

Richards LJ: 25. The starting point for the defendant's case on the appeal... is that the supervening incapacity of a principal terminates the authority of an agent to act on the principal's behalf. That proposition is said to be derivable from *Drew v Nunn* (1879) 4 QBD 661 and was the basis on which the court proceeded in *Yonge v Toynbee* [1910] 1 KB 215, in relation to the termination of a solicitor's authority to take steps on behalf of a client to defend actions brought against him. It is submitted that the client's loss of capacity terminates the solicitor's authority to take any step on his or her behalf, so that the solicitors in this case were acting without authority (albeit in accordance with good practice) even in applying to the Court of Protection for the appointment of a receiver.

27. It is submitted [by the defendant hospital trust] that the distinction drawn by the judge between the effect of supervening incapacity on the solicitor's authority to act and its effect on the contract of retainer was wrong. A solicitor's contract of retainer is at its heart a contract of agency. If the authority to act on behalf of the client is lost, the contract giving rise to the agency cannot survive—there is nothing left of it. But the argument is put more particularly on the basis that a contract of retainer is personal in nature and depends on the ability of the client to give instructions to the solicitor. In this case the claimant's supervening incapacity created a situation in which she was unable to give instructions; and, for the purposes of the retainer, instructions could not be given on her behalf by a receiver/deputy subsequently appointed to act for her. Her inability to give instructions meant that the contract became incapable of performance and was therefore frustrated....

DISCUSSION

36. There is much to be said in favour of a fresh examination or reconsideration of the principle in *Yonge v Toynbee* [1910] 1 KB 215 and related authorities in this area. It is potentially unfair and unsatisfactory for a client's supervening incapacity to have the effect of terminating automatically the solicitor's authority to act on the client's behalf in the litigation, exposing the solicitor to the risk of liability to other parties for breach of warranty of authority in respect of steps taken in the litigation even when the solicitor is not aware of the incapacity, and depriving him of authority to take any steps to protect the client's position when he does become aware of it—to the extent that it is said that he acts without authority, albeit apparently in accordance with good practice, in applying to the court for the appointment of a deputy and/or litigation friend. One might at least expect the principle to be qualified so that (i) the solicitor retains authority to act so long as he is unaware of the incapacity and (ii) he retains authority to take necessary steps in consequence of the incapacity, including an application to the court for the appointment of a deputy and/or litigation friend, when he does become aware of it. It might also be preferable to talk in terms of 'suspension' rather than 'termination' of authority, on the basis that the solicitor's authority is restored if the client regains capacity or a litigation friend is appointed to continue the litigation on the client's behalf.

37. The present appeal, however, does not require us to re-examine the principle in *Yonge v Toynbee* or to grasp the 'hot potato' left on one side by the Supreme Court in *Dunhill v Burgin (Nos 1 and 2)* [2014] 1 WLR 933. The issue in the appeal is a much narrower one and can be resolved on the assumption that the principle in *Yonge v Toynbee* is good law. The defendant's essential case is that the claimant's supervening incapacity caused the CFA to be terminated by reason of frustration because the claimant could not give instructions to the solicitor and the contract therefore became incapable of performance. The judge rejected that case. If he was correct to do so, as in my view he was, it is unnecessary to address any underlying issues concerning the principle in *Yonge v Toynbee*.

38. The defendant's case that the CFA was frustrated depends on the proposition that the obligation to give instructions was personal to the claimant and could not be discharged by the

giving of instructions by a receiver/deputy acting on her behalf. Whilst a solicitor's retainer is in one sense a personal contract, I very much doubt whether it requires instructions to be given by the client personally even in the general run of cases. It must be commonplace for instructions to be given through an agent, such as an accountant or managing agent or a spouse. But whatever the general position, the parties must have contemplated in the particular circumstances of this case that the claimant might suffer from a further period of incapacity in which she would be unable to give instructions personally but they could be given by a litigation friend or a receiver/deputy or on her behalf. I accept Mr Spearman's submissions on that point: see para 31 above. The fact that supervening incapacity prevented the claimant from giving instructions personally did not render the contract of retainer impossible of performance; it simply gave rise to a short period of delay pending appointment of a receiver/deputy who could continue the conduct of the proceedings on the claimant's behalf and give instructions to the solicitors for that purpose.

39. I also accept Mr Spearman's submission … that if the claimant was under an obligation to give instructions personally and was unable to comply with that obligation by reason of her supervening incapacity, the situation was covered by the express terms of the CFA, which entitled the solicitors in that event to end the contract and to require payment of their basic charges and disbursements. The unattractiveness of such a result is a further indication that it cannot have been the intention of the parties that the claimant had to give instructions personally; but if that was their intention, and the situation arose in which the claimant was unable to give such instructions, the contract catered expressly for the consequences and it cannot possibly be said that this was a fundamentally different situation from anything contemplated by the contract.

40. Those points, which reflect the specific way in which the case for the claimant was argued before us on the appeal, are sufficient to show that the defendant's case that the CFA was frustrated must fail. More generally, however, I agree with the reasons given by the judge … for concluding that the CFA was not frustrated. I find no force in any of Mr Hutton's detailed criticisms of those reasons.

41. I was tempted to cut this judgment right back to a simple expression of agreement with the judge. I have taken the long route in order to deal fully with the arguments of counsel and to make clear that, notwithstanding the interesting questions thrown up by some of those arguments, the actual issue in the appeal is a narrow one and can be disposed of accordingly.

NOTES

1. Compare and contrast *Drew v Nunn* and *Yonge v Toynbee* [1910] 1 KB 215 (above, p 194, and see Notes at pp 197–199). See R Powell, *The Law of Agency* (2nd edn, 1961), pp 405–406; *Bowstead and Reynolds*, para 10–032; and E Peel, *Treitel's Law of Contract* (14th edn, 2015), para 16–110, fn 524, for ways of distinguishing these cases. It should be noted that both the agent and third party may be protected from the normal consequences of the principal's supervening mental incapacity by s 5 of the Powers of Attorney Act 1971 (above, p 198) and s 14 of the Mental Capacity Act 2005 (the Enduring Powers of Attorney Act 1985, which offered similar protection, has been repealed by the 2005 Act, but existing enduring powers of attorney are unaffected).

2. Despite occasional dicta to the contrary (eg Brett LJ in *Drew v Nunn*), it is probably the case that where the principal dies there can be no apparent authority. For as Lord Ellenborough said in *Watson v King* (1815) 4 Camp 272 at 274: 'How can a valid act be done in the name of a dead man?' Following this reasoning, it is submitted that the personal representatives of a dead principal cannot ratify any contract made on behalf of the deceased after his death

(cf *Foster v Bates* (1843) 12 M & W 226; *Campanari v Woodburn*, above, p 270; but neither case is authority against this submission: *Bowstead and Reynolds*, para 10–017; Powell, op cit, p 388, fn 7).

3. There can be no apparent authority when the principal is adjudged bankrupt. This is because when the principal is adjudged bankrupt his estate vests in the trustee in bankruptcy leaving the principal with no capacity to perform the acts which are the subject of the apparent agency. But those dealing with the agent of a bankrupt may have statutory protection under s 284(4) and (5) of the Insolvency Act 1986. Furthermore, as in cases of death or insanity of the donor of a power of attorney, a third party who deals with the donee of a power of attorney may be able to rely on s 5 of the Powers of Attorney Act 1971 to avoid the normal consequences of the donor's supervening bankruptcy.

4. Revocation of the agent's actual authority by the principal does not prevent the principal being bound by the agent's apparent authority, so long as the third party has no notice that the agency has terminated (see *Scarf v Jardine* (1882) 7 App Cas 345 at 356–357, per Lord Blackburn; see also *Curlewis v Birkbeck* (1863) 3 F & F 894). Notice given to the agent is not enough to terminate his apparent authority; notice must be given to the third party. Thus, in *AMB Generali Holding AG v SEB Trygg Liv Holding AB* [2005] EWCA Civ 1237, [2006] 1 WLR 2276, H (the agent) resigned as a director of a company (the principal) but was held to have apparent authority to bind the company to arbitration proceedings after his resignation because of a general representation from his appointment as director that he had all the usual authority of the post, and also from specific representations by the company, the effect of which survived his resignation until the third party was put on notice of it.

QUESTION

An insane principal is bound by the apparent authority of his agent, whereas the estate of a dead principal is not. What policy reasons, if any, justify this distinction?

PART III

DOMESTIC SALES LAW

Chapter 8   Introduction and definitions   297
Chapter 9   Passing of the property in the goods as between
             seller and buyer   327
Chapter 10   Transfer of title   381
Chapter 11   Seller's obligations as to quality   423
Chapter 12   Performance of the contract   455
Chapter 13   Remedies of the seller   476
Chapter 14   Remedies of the buyer   515

CHAPTER 8

INTRODUCTION AND DEFINITIONS

1 INTRODUCTION

Prior to 1893, the English law governing sale of goods was almost entirely based on case law. There were a few statutory provisions, but only a few: the two most important were the Factors Acts, discussed below at p 394, and s 17 of the Statute of Frauds 1677 (now repealed) which required written evidence for the enforcement of a contract of sale of goods to the value of over £10.[1]

Towards the end of the nineteenth century the subject was much influenced by two leading textbooks, *Blackburn on Sale* and *Benjamin on Sale*. In 1888 the celebrated statutory draftsman, Sir Mackenzie Chalmers, who had already drafted the Bills of Exchange Act 1882 (below, Chapter 19) was commissioned to draft the bill that became the Sale of Goods Act 1893. Chalmers' codification has come to be seen as a mercantile tour de force. It is a tribute to his skill that his draft is still in use, virtually unchanged, a century later, as the basis of all commercial sales[2] of goods within the UK and a very large share of the world's international sales as well. In addition, legislation based on his draft remains in force in Ireland and a great deal of the Commonwealth. Following minor amendments in 1973 and some changes made by the Unfair Contract Terms Act 1977, the Act of 1893 was consolidated and re-enacted as the Sale of Goods Act 1979, which (following further minor amendments[3]) is now the principal source of the law. All statutory references in this section will be to this Act of 1979 unless otherwise stated: it will usually be referred to simply as 'the Act'.[4]

---

[1] In this and the succeeding chapters dealing with the law of sale of goods, the following abbreviations are used in referring to standard textbooks:

Atiyah: PS Atiyah and JN Adams, *The Sale of Goods* (13th edn, 2016);
Benjamin: AG Guest et al (eds), *Benjamin's Sale of Goods* (9th edn, 2014);
Goode: RM Goode, *Commercial Law* (5th edn, 2016).

For an excellent historical survey, see M Bridge, 'The Evolution of Modern Sales Law' [1991] LMCLQ 52. More critically see also M Bridge, 'Do We Need a New Sale of Goods Act?' in J Lowry (ed), *Essays in Honour of Roy Goode* (2005).

[2] Consumer sales were once governed by the 1979 Act, but are now largely dealt with by the Consumer Rights Act 2015.

[3] By the Sale of Goods (Amendment) Act 1994, the Sale and Supply of Goods Act 1994 and the Sale of Goods (Amendment) Act 1995.

[4] In the consolidation, some minor changes of language were made from the 1893 text, and there was some renumbering of the sections—which calls for a degree of caution when reading judgments based on the former Act. However, since most sections have retained their old numbers in the new Act, cross-references will be given only where this is not the case.

2 THE SALE OF GOODS ACT AND THE GENERAL LAW

A codifying Act, such as the Sale of Goods Act 1893, is presumptively intended to *replace* the previous case law by a fresh statement, so as to preclude extensive reference to the earlier cases (see the remarks of Lord Herschell in *Bank of England v Vagliano Bros* [1891] AC 107, quoted below, p 660—a case actually on another consolidating Act, namely the Bills of Exchange Act 1882, but still in point). But in fact this principle has not always been respected, and there are many cases where judges have had regard to the former law. In some circumstances this practice is, perhaps, justified by s 62(2) of the Act, which declares that 'the rules of the common law, . . . except in so far as they are inconsistent with the provisions of the Act, . . . apply to contracts for the sale of goods'.

However, there is room for debate as to which 'rules of the common law' are 'inconsistent with the provisions of the Act'. In the leading case of *Re Wait* (below), Atkin LJ not only endorsed the *Vagliano* approach referred to above, saying ([1927] 1 Ch 606 at 631): 'Inasmuch as we are now bound by the plain language of the Code I do not think that decisions in cases before 1893 are of much value', but went on to suggest that some provisions of the Act (which Atkin LJ refers to as 'the Code') were intended to displace general provisions of the common law and equity which might otherwise be thought applicable.

Re Wait
[1927] 1 Ch 606, Court of Appeal

Wait owned 1,000 tons of wheat which was to arrive at Avonmouth from the United States on the MV *Challenger*. He agreed to sell 500 tons of this wheat to Humphries & Bobbett, who paid him the price in advance. Later, before the *Challenger* arrived, he went bankrupt. By the time that this action was brought, some of the wheat had been disposed of to other buyers, but 530 tons remained which was still in law the property of Wait (or his trustee in bankruptcy) and in his possession. Nothing had been done to identify the 500 tons which was to be used to fulfil Humphries & Bobbett's contract. The Court of Appeal (by a majority, the Chancery judge, Sargant LJ, dissenting) held that Humphries & Bobbett had no claim to any of the wheat, but could only prove in Wait's bankruptcy for the return of the price. In this passage, Atkin LJ rejected an argument that the buyers might be able to assert a claim of a proprietary nature to their share of the wheat based on principles of equity independently of the Act.

Atkin LJ: . . . I am of opinion that the claimants fail, and that to grant the relief claimed would violate well established principles of common law and equity. It would also appear to embarrass to a most serious degree the ordinary operations of buying and selling goods, and the banking operations which attend them . . .

I do not think that at any time here there was an equitable assignment which ever gave the claimants a beneficial interest in these goods. . . . Without deciding the point, I think that much may be said for the proposition that an agreement for the sale of goods does not import any agreement to transfer property other than in accordance with the terms of the Code, that is, the intention of the parties to be derived from the terms of the contract, the conduct of the parties and the circumstances of the case, and, unless a different intention appears, from the rules set out in s 18. The Code was passed at a time when the principles of equity and equitable remedies were recognized and given effect to in all our Courts, and the particular equitable remedy of specific performance is specially referred to in s 52. The total sum of legal relations (meaning by the word 'legal' existing in equity as well as in common law) arising out of the contract for the sale of goods may well be regarded as defined by the Code. It would have been futile in a code intended for commercial men to have created an elaborate structure of rules dealing with rights at law, if at the same time it was intended to leave, subsisting with the legal rights, equitable rights inconsistent with, more extensive, and coming into existence earlier than the rights so carefully set out in the various sections of the Code.

The rules for transfer of property as between seller and buyer, performance of the contract, rights of the unpaid seller against the goods, unpaid sellers' lien, remedies of the seller, remedies of the buyer, appear to be complete and exclusive statements of the legal relations both in law and equity. They have, of course, no relevance when one is considering rights, legal or equitable, which may come into existence dehors the contract for sale. A seller or a purchaser may, of course, create any equity he pleases by way of charge, equitable assignment or any other dealing with or disposition of goods, the subject-matter of sale; and he may, of course, create such an equity as one of the terms expressed in the contract of sale. But the mere sale or agreement to sell or the acts in pursuance of such a contract mentioned in the Code will only produce the legal effects which the Code states.

[**Lord Hanworth MR** delivered a concurring judgment. **Sargant LJ** dissented.]

NOTE

This case would now be decided differently, as a result of s 20A of the Act, introduced in 1995, which gives proprietary remedies to a buyer of goods forming part of a larger bulk who has prepaid the price (see below, p 335). The remarks of Atkin LJ, however, are not affected by this statutory change.

3 THE APPLICATION OF THE SALE OF GOODS ACT

The Act applies to contracts for the sale of all types of goods (though in regard to some, eg ships and aircraft, other statutes may be applicable in addition). But by s 62(4) there are excluded from its provisions on contracts of sale any contract which, although formally one of sale, is 'intended to operate by way of mortgage, pledge, charge, or other security'. An example would be where A Ltd, an industrialist based abroad, 'sold' machinery to B, a bank, for a payment of £250,000, it being agreed that B would resell it, and A buy it back, in a year's time for £275,000, and that in the meantime the machinery would continue to be possessed and used by A in its factory in England. Such a contract, even if in form a sale, would almost certainly be construed as in substance a loan on the security of the machinery; and in such a case it is obvious that terms such as the duty to supply goods of satisfactory quality would not normally be appropriate. (It may be, however, that other provisions, such as those concerning passing of title by a non-owner, would continue to apply, since they are arguably not provisions 'about contracts of sale'.)

The 1979 Act governs all commercial sales of goods between businesses. It also covers sales by a business to a consumer,[5] but with some very important exclusions: namely, the seller's duty to supply goods of the proper quality and quantity and give good title to them, the buyer's remedies for breach of these duties, and questions of the passing of risk. These latter, though previously covered by the 1979 Act, are now virtually all controlled by the provisions of the Consumer Rights Act 2015 (see s 1(5) of the 1979 Act, inserted by the 2015 Act). The 1979 Act also formally governs sales where neither party is a trader. It should be noted that in this book the overwhelming concentration will be on commercial sales, with passing reference only made to the other types.

4 DEFINITIONS

It is impossible to follow the Act properly without a clear understanding of a few key definitions, which form the basis of its whole structure. The draftsman has used these words and phrases with great precision, and it is clearly important for us also to learn to do so.

(a) 'Contract for the sale of goods'

The Act applies to 'contracts for the sale of goods', defined in s 2(1) as contracts 'by which the seller transfers or agrees to transfer the property in goods to the buyer for a money consideration, called the price'. This technically excludes some closely analogous transactions—for example, exchanges of goods, or repair contracts incidentally involving supplies of parts (though most of these are governed by similar statutory rules, referred to below at pp 312–325).

More controversially, it has also been held to exclude cases where the parties contemplate that the goods will be consumed or destroyed before the buyer has had a chance to become owner of them, on the theory that you cannot pass ownership in something that is not there. The case below, *PST Energy 7 Shipping LLC Product Shipping & Trading SA v OW Bunker Malta Ltd*, demonstrates why this may be important.

PST Energy 7 Shipping LLC Product Shipping & Trading SA v OW Bunker Malta Ltd
[2016] UKSC 23, [2016] 2 WLR 1193, Supreme Court

OWBM, a member of the OW corporate group, provided bunkers (ie heavy fuel oil) to shipowners PSTE in the Russian port of Tuapse in November 2014. The bunkers were supplied on 60 days' credit. They were also supplied on terms that no ownership passed to PSTE unless and until they were paid for, though PSTE had OWBM's consent to use them during the period of credit for powering their vessel. OWBM had obtained the bunkers from its parent company OWBAS; OWBAS in turn had obtained them from RMUK,[6] also on terms that title

---

[5] Often abbreviated to B2C. In the same way, commercial sales between businesses are often referred to as B2B.

[6] All companies are referred to by initials for brevity and clarity.

was reserved pending payment. The OW group collapsed, and OWBAS never paid RMUK. PSTE, having since consumed the bunkers (as everyone knew they would), faced demands for payment from both OWBM and RMUK; from the former for the price on the basis that it had supplied them, and from the latter for their value on the ground that at the time of consumption it had still owned them. PSTE argued that it could not be liable to OWBM for the price of the bunkers, since: (1) its contract with OWBM was governed by the Sale of Goods Act 1979; (2) OWBM had never been in a position to pass title to PSTE; and (3) under s 49(1) of the Act the price could not become payable unless and until property had passed. The Supreme Court rejected this argument, and held that PSTE was potentially liable to OWBM. This was because the contract was not in essence one for the sale of goods, since everyone envisaged that the bunkers would have been burnt and ceased to exist by the time the price became payable after 60 days. It therefore followed that s 49 was not applicable.

> **Lord Mance:**
> 26. ...[T]he contract has special features. First, they expressly provide not only for retention of title pending payment, but also expressly that, until such payment, the 'Buyer' is to be in possession of the bunkers 'solely as Bailee for the Seller'. After going on to provide that the Buyer 'shall not be entitled to use the bunkers', the terms introduce the qualification 'other than for the propulsion of the Vessel'.
> 27. The qualification clearly reflects a reality. Bunker suppliers know that bunkers are for use. If they grant relatively long credit periods combined with a reservation of title pending payment in full, it is unsurprising that they do so combined with an express qualification authorising use in propulsion, since standard terms prohibiting any use would be uncommercial or in practice, no doubt, simply ignored. [Counsel] vigorously resisted the introduction of any such considerations, on the basis that they are speculative and that the nature of a contract cannot change according to the level of certainty with which parties are to be taken to have expected that bunkers supplied might or might not be used in propulsion before payment for them was made. But OWBM's (and RMUK's) contractual terms and the assumed facts...—together with an admissible modicum of commercial awareness on the court's part about how ships operate (and in particular how owners strive to keep them operating) and about the value of credit and the likelihood that full advantage of it will be taken—all point in one direction. They demonstrate that the liberty to use the bunkers for propulsion prior to payment is a vital and essential feature of the bunker supply business.
> 28. In these circumstances, OWBM's contract with the Owners cannot be regarded as a straightforward agreement to transfer the property in the bunkers to the Owners for a price. It was in substance an agreement with two aspects: first, to permit consumption prior to any payment and (once the theory of a nanosecond transfer of property is, rightly, rejected) without any property ever passing in the bunkers consumed; and, second, but only if and so far as bunkers remained unconsumed, to transfer the property in the bunkers so remaining to the Owners in return for the Owners paying the price. But in this latter connection it is to be noted that the price does not here refer to the price of the bunkers in respect of which property was passing, it refers to the price payable for all the bunkers, whether consumed before or remaining at the time of its payment.
> 29. A contract of sale may under section 2(3) of the Act be either absolute or conditional; and under section 2(6) 'An agreement to sell becomes a sale when...the conditions are fulfilled subject to which the property in the goods is to be transferred'. Mr Crow submits on this basis that the contract can be regarded as an agreement to transfer property, conditional on the bunkers remaining unburned when payment is made. The difficulties with this submission are that:
>   i) it categorises the whole agreement by reference to only one possibility relating to only one part of the bunkers covered by the agreement, namely the possibility of at least some

> bunkers surviving unused, after 60 days or whenever payment is made. Sections 2(3) and (6) can readily be applied where there is a condition regarding the passing of property to which all the goods covered by an agreement are subject, but that is not the case here;
>
> ii) it ignores the fact that there is no condition governing the transfer of property in the bunkers used before payment—the property in bunkers consumed never passes and is never agreed to be passed; and
>
> iii) it focuses on the agreement to pass property in the bunkers surviving at the time of payment, when the agreement was a single contract to pay a single 'price' for all the bunkers sold not later than 60 days after delivery, whatever had happened to such bunkers in the meantime; the agreement is a single agreement which cannot sensibly be treated as divisible.

NOTE

See too below, p 479, for a further reference to this case.

QUESTION

If a wine merchant supplies wine to a hotel on 60 days' credit and on the basis that title is reserved until payment is made, is this a contract for the sale of goods? What if the wine was, to both parties' knowledge, provided for a wedding reception scheduled to take place in two weeks' time?

(b) 'Sale' and 'agreement to sell'

Where under a contract of sale the 'property' in the goods (a term which we may take as broadly equivalent to 'ownership') has been transferred from the seller to the buyer, the contract is called in the Act a 'sale' (s 2(4)). Where the transfer of the property is yet to take place, it is called an 'agreement to sell' (s 2(5)). The term 'contract for the sale of goods' is thus a comprehensive expression, embracing both 'sale' and 'agreement to sell'.

A sale may be seen as both a contract and a conveyance: by virtue of the contract itself, the buyer becomes the owner of the goods. An agreement to sell, in contrast, is purely a matter of obligation: ownership does not pass to the buyer until some later time.

(c) 'Goods'

The term 'goods' is defined in s 61(1) as including 'all personal chattels other than things in action and money, and in Scotland all corporeal moveables except money'; and in particular as including 'emblements,[7] industrial growing crops and things attached to or forming part of the land which are agreed to be severed before sale or under the contract of sale'. (The exclusion of money does not encompass notes or coins sold as collector's items: *Moss v Hancock* [1899] 2 QB 111.) 'Personal chattels' means 'choses in possession', essentially tangibles (see p 55 above).

---

[7] A technical term from the law of farming tenancies, denoting crops sown by the tenant which he retains the right to harvest notwithstanding any prior termination of the tenancy.

Apart from choses in action and intellectual property, it is probably right to assume that the following are not 'goods' for the purposes of the Act (though they may be 'goods', 'things', or 'articles' under other statutory definitions):

(1) electricity and other forms of pure energy;

(2) computer software and other material in written or digitised form—for example, words, music, and images (see *Southwark London Borough Council v IBM UK Ltd* [2011] EWHC 549 (TCC), but distinguish the medium on which they are stored: see *St Albans District Council v International Computers Ltd* [1996] 4 All ER 481 at 493; see S Green and D Saidov, 'Software as Goods' [2007] JBL 161 and J Adams, 'Software and Digital Content' [2009] JBL 396);

(3) databases (*Your Response Ltd v Datateam Business Media Ltd* [2014] EWCA Civ 281, [2014] CP Rep 31);

(4) information (and, *a fortiori*, even more nebulous concepts, such as an opportunity);

(5) cadavers—human tissue and bodily products (eg blood or hair) are probably 'goods', however cf *Yearworth v North Bristol NHS Trust* [2009] EWCA Civ 37, [2010] QB 1 (frozen sperm could be subject of bailment, though by statute it could not be sold).

On the other hand, the following are all 'goods' capable of being the subject matter of a contract of sale within the Act: ships, aircraft, and vehicles; animals; water, oil, and gases (even air, in the form of compressed air—compare *Britvic Soft Drinks Ltd v Messer UK Ltd* [2002] EWCA Civ 548, [2002] 2 All ER (Comm) 321 (carbon dioxide)).

As for land and things attached to it, such as buildings or pylons, the starting point is that, not being a personal chattels, these latter are not goods. But the definition of goods is artificially extended to cover land in one vital case: namely, where the subject matter of the contract comes within the words 'crops of every description and things attached to or forming part of the land which are agreed to be severed before sale or under the contract of sale'. In other words, something which would be goods when severed is not excluded merely because it forms part of the land at the time of the contract. The only possible conclusion is that where this applies the same transaction may be *both* a contract to sell land and simultaneously a contract of sale of goods under the Sale of Goods Act. Examples are contracts by a landowner to sell stone to be quarried or wheat as yet unharvested, or to give another person the right to enter upon his land and fell trees and remove the timber, pick fruit, cut hay, extract minerals, or take water, or dismantle and remove a building.[8] In relation to such contracts it may be necessary to have regard not only to the Sale of Goods Act but to mandatory provisions applicable to land sales (eg the need for writing—Law of Property (Miscellaneous Provisions) Act 1989, s 2—or the inability while property remains unsevered to pass title by mere agreement—Law of Property Act 1925, s 51). However, severance is essential. In *Saunders v Pilcher* [1949] 2 All ER 1097 a cherry orchard was sold together with its crop of ripe cherries. In an attempt to save tax, the parties purported to make separate sales of the land and the cherries. But the court held that the attempt failed. There was only one transaction—a conveyance of the land. The parties did not contemplate that the cherries would be severed *under the contract of sale*, as s 61(1) required.

The following case throws light on this issue.

---

[8] The reference in s 61(1) to 'industrial growing crops' is explained by history. Before 1893 *fructus industriales* (largely annually planted crops) could be sold as goods even while attached to the land, while *fructus naturales* (other crops such as grass or fruit) required severance. It is now clear that all crops require contemplated severance in order to be regarded as goods.

Underwood Ltd v Burgh Castle Brick & Cement Syndicate
[1922] 1 KB 343, King's Bench Division

Underwoods agreed to sell to the Syndicate a large condensing engine which was a trade fixture on their leasehold premises. As part of the contract, the sellers were to detach the engine from the land and load it onto a railway truck. It was damaged during the loading process and the buyers refused to accept it. They were held entitled to do so, since (for reasons explained below, p 341) the engine was still the seller's property at the time when it was damaged. In his judgment, Rowlatt J assumed throughout that the transaction was governed by the Sale of Goods Act, but his remarks are of interest on the general question of the sale of fixtures.

Rowlatt J: This case raises an important point under the Sale of Goods Act, 1893. This turns on the question whether the property in the engine had passed to the defendants at the time when the accident happened when the engine was being loaded. This engine weighed some thirty tons and was at the time when it was inspected by the defendants affixed to a bed of concrete by means of Lewis bolts and screwed down. By reason of its weight it had sunk into the concrete and become closely united with it, so that the operation of removing it not only involved unfastening it but taking it to pieces . . .

I think the important point is that the parties were dealing with an article which was a fixture to the premises, and that is different from the case of a loose chattel. The buyers' intention was to buy an article which would be a loose chattel when the processes of detaching and dismantling it were completed, and to convert it into a loose chattel these processes had first to be performed. The case of a tenant's fixtures seems an analogous case. It seems a safe rule to adopt that if a fixture has to be detached so as to make it a chattel again, the act of detaching has to be done before the chattel can be deliverable. The same result is arrived at if the matter be looked at a little more technically. This fixture was not personal property any more than are tenant's fixtures, but was part of the freehold, and what was sold was not personal property but a part of the realty which the sellers had a right to detach and convert into personal property. . . . In the present case the plaintiffs did not sell their right to sever, but were to sever the fixtures themselves, and when they had done so, and so produced the chattel, they were to deliver it. That was the contract if the matter is analysed. The plaintiffs contended that as between the parties the intention was that the property should pass at the time of the contract and that s 17 of the Sale of Goods Act, 1893, applied. The fallacy of that argument seems to be that it assumes that the sellers had the property in the engine at the time when the contract was made. They had not, although it is true that they had rights which reduced the rights of property of the freeholder in whom the property was to a vanishing quantity. If the property had been mortgaged it would have been no answer to the mortgagees' claim to say that in the Sale of Goods Act, 1893, there is a provision that as between buyer and seller fixtures are goods and chattels. That could not affect the property of the freeholder.

For these reasons I think that the property in this engine did not pass to the defendants at the time when the contract was made, and there must be judgment for them.

NOTES

1.   See too *Kursell v Timber Operators & Contractors Ltd* (below, p 307), which was decided many years after the Act of 1893 was passed. The judgments in this later case all treat the issue as a question of sale of goods law, to be decided by reference to the Act.

2. In *Morgan v Russell & Sons* [1909] 1 KB 357, Morgan agreed to sell the contents of three Welsh slag-heaps to Russell at 2s 3d (11p) per ton, with Russell to remove the material. Morgan failed through no fault of his to make much of the slag available. The measure of damages available to Russell depended on whether this was a contract for the sale of goods or land (under the rule in *Bain v Fothergill* (1874) LR 7 HL 158, since abolished by the Law of Property (Miscellaneous Provisions) Act 1989, s 3). The court held this to be a contract for the sale of an interest in land, rather like a licence to mine. This decision, with respect, seems doubtful. As pointed out in *Benjamin on Sale* (9th edn, 2014), para 1–098, the judgments give 'no clear indication of the point at which, or the grounds on which, this analogy is to give way to the provisions of the Act'.

3. In *Marshall v Green* (1875) 1 CPD 35, a case decided before the passing of the first Sale of Goods Act in 1893, the court was concerned to decide whether a contract to sell timber standing on the seller's land was a contract to sell the timber as goods, or an interest in land. The court plainly thought that such a contract must be one thing or the other, and that the test was 'whether the parties really looked to their deriving benefit from the land, or merely intended that the land should be in the nature of a warehouse for the trees during that period' (at 44). It would seem that this view can no longer hold water since *Underwood Ltd v Burgh Castle Brick & Cement Syndicate*, above.

(d) 'Existing goods' and 'future goods'

Section 5 divides 'goods' into two categories: (1) 'existing goods', ie goods owned or possessed by the seller, and (2) 'future goods', ie goods to be manufactured or acquired by the seller after the making of the contract of sale. It goes on to make it plain that there cannot be a 'sale' (in the statutory sense, involving an immediate conveyance) of future goods, by declaring that where a seller purports to effect a present sale of future goods, the contract operates as an agreement to sell the goods (s 5(3)).

In this distinction 'existing' clearly has a special limited meaning, since goods which are very much in existence, but not yet owned or possessed by the seller, are defined as 'future goods'. So an agreement by A to sell B existing identified machinery, which is currently owned by C but which A presently hopes to acquire from C, is a contract for 'future goods'. The reference in s 5(2) to possession of the goods ('owned *or possessed by* the seller') is, at first sight, puzzling. But some sections of the Act (eg ss 12(3), 22, 24, 25(1), and 48(2)) contemplate a sale being made by a person who has no title or a defective title, and it is probably provisions such as these which the draftsman had in mind when formulating the wording of s 5(2).

In any case, the technical classification of goods into existing or future goods is of little significance in practice.

(e) 'Specific goods', 'unascertained goods', and 'ascertained goods'

By s 61(1), 'specific goods' means goods identified and agreed on at the time a contract of sale is made. The counterpart expression used in the Act, 'unascertained goods', is curiously not defined anywhere, but must by inference mean any goods which are not specific goods: ie *not* identified and agreed on at the time the contract of sale is made.

For goods to be specific, they must be unequivocally designated at the time of the contract as the unique article or articles that the contract is concerned with. Goods may be 'specific' even if not physically present before the parties and identified only by words of description (eg 'the entire cargo of soya beans now on board the MV *Poseidon*'). If a contract is indeed for the sale of specific goods, only those particular goods can be tendered under it: in the case of the soya beans above, the buyer will be entitled to reject any beans other than those on board the *Poseidon*, even if they are just as good in every other respect.

An amendment made to s 61(1) in 1995 adds a further category: 'specific goods' now 'includes an undivided share, specified as a fraction or percentage, of goods identified and agreed on as aforesaid'. This is dealt with below.

In contrast, unascertained goods are typically (though not, as we shall see, exclusively) sold 'by description', that is, where the seller undertakes to procure for the buyer the agreed quantity of such goods, with such further characteristics as to quality, etc as may be specified—for example a 'new white 2.0 litre VW Golf GTi, 5 door' or '100 tonnes of King Edward potatoes, East Anglia grown'. In such a case the seller can fulfil his obligation by providing any car or potatoes which match the contract description. Such goods fall into three main categories: (1) generic goods sold by description, as described above; (2) goods not yet in existence, to be grown, manufactured, or obtained, such as a future crop of soya beans, or the total 2017 production of gas from Platform ABC123 in the North Sea; and (3) a part as yet unidentified out of a specific or identified bulk, for example 100 tonnes out of the 1,000 tonnes of wheat now in the seller's silo.

Contracts to sell goods known to be in a particular place can be troublesome here. Imagine A Ltd agrees to sell B Ltd 1,000 laptop computers from A's warehouse. If A has 2,000 (or for that matter 1,001) computers in its warehouse this can only be a contract for the sale of unascertained goods, since it cannot in the nature of things be clear at the time of contracting precisely which computers B is entitled to. But the converse is not necessarily true. Even if to the knowledge of the parties A has precisely 1,000 computers in its warehouse, this is not necessarily a case of specific goods. This will only be so if, properly interpreted, the contract requires A to deliver those particular computers and forbids it (for example) to sell 10 computers elsewhere, replenish its stock by a further 10, and then deliver that replenished stock to B.

The relevant time for distinguishing between specific and unascertained goods is the time the contract is concluded. If it is not clear *at that moment* what goods the buyer is entitled to, the contract is one for unascertained goods. Even if and when it becomes clear at a later stage what goods the seller is bound to deliver, this still does not make those goods 'specific'. Instead the Sale of Goods Act creates a third category for such goods, christening them 'ascertained goods'. This phrase has no statutory definition. But Atkin LJ in *Re Wait* [1927] 1 Ch 606 at 630 explained it as meaning goods which at the time of the making of the contract are unascertained but which become identified as the contract goods at some later time. For instance, in *Aldridge v Johnson* (below, p 314), the buyer, who had agreed to buy a quantity of barley, left his own sacks with the seller to be filled with barley from his bulk store. It was held that the barley became 'ascertained' (ie identified as the buyer's) as it was shovelled into his sacks, sackful by sackful, even before the total contract quantity had been measured out. In practice ascertained goods have some, but not all, the characteristics of specific goods.

The most important reason for regarding unascertained goods as essentially different from specific or ascertained goods is to be found in the rule—or at least the basic rule—contained in s 16. This states that it is not possible to transfer the property in goods to the buyer unless and until the contract goods are ascertained. This basic rule is now subject to an exception contained in s 20A, introduced in 1995 (see below, p 335). But, apart from this one exception, it remains a fundamental proposition which nothing that the parties may agree to or do or say can breach or vary. The leading cases on this point include *Re Wait*, cited above, p 298, which now falls within the exception created by s 20A, and *Kursell v Timber Operators & Contractors Ltd*.

Kursell v Timber Operators & Contractors Ltd
[1927] 1 KB 298, Court of Appeal

The contract between the parties was for the sale of all the merchantable timber growing on a certain date in a forest in Latvia, 'merchantable timber' being defined in the contract as 'all trunks and branches of trees but not seedlings and young trees of less than six inches in diameter at a height of four feet from the ground'. The buyers were to have 15 years to cut the timber. Shortly afterwards, the Latvian government passed a law nationalising the forest. The sellers argued that the property in the timber had passed to the buyers and that accordingly the consequences of the nationalisation decree fell on them. The court held, however, that the timber which was the subject of the contract of sale was not 'specific goods', since the trees answering to the contract measurements had not been identified (and could not, in fact, be identified until the time came to cut them, which could be at any time within the 15-year period); it followed that the timber was still the property of the sellers and the contract was frustrated.

> **Scrutton LJ**: What is the legal result of these facts? In the first place has the property passed? It was said that this was a contract for the sale of specific goods in a deliverable state under s 18, r 1, of the Sale of Goods Act. Specific goods are defined as goods identified and agreed upon at the time a contract of sale is made. It appears to me these goods were neither identified nor agreed upon. Not every tree in the forest passed, but only those complying with a certain measurement not then made. How much of each tree passed depended on where it was cut, how far from the ground. Nor does the timber seem to be in a deliverable state until the buyer has severed it. He cannot under the definition be bound to take delivery of an undetermined part of a tree not yet identified . . .
>
> For these reasons in my opinion the property had not passed under s 18, r 1, and, therefore, the timber was not at the risk of the purchasers.
>
> [**Lord Hanworth MR** and **Sargant LJ** delivered concurring judgments.]

Part-interests in goods (eg a one-half or one-third share in a racehorse, or a share in a specific cargo of grain) pose special problems. To a large extent these will now have been resolved by an amendment made to the definition of 'goods' in s 61(1) by s 2(2) of the Sale of Goods (Amendment) Act 1995, declaring that 'goods' includes an undivided share in goods. It is clear from s 2(2) that a contract to transfer a part-interest in goods, even as between persons who are already part-owners, is to be treated as a contract of sale of goods. However, it is obviously not easy, and in some cases not possible, to apply many of the provisions of the Act literally to a contract for the sale of a part-interest (eg those relating to delivery). The Law Commission (on whose recommendation the amendment to s 61(1) was based) took the view that any problems that might arise would normally be overcome by a finding that it was the express or presumed intention of the parties to disapply the particular statutory provision.

Where a person is owner of a proportion of an undivided bulk (eg a buyer owning a 40 per cent interest in a particular cargo of soya beans), that proportion is under s 61(1) regarded not only as goods, but as specific goods. We must therefore make a distinction between the example just given (10 tonnes out of the identified 100 tonnes of potatoes) and a contract to sell a one-tenth share in the 100 tonnes. At the completion of the first of these deals, the buyer will own 10 tonnes and the seller the remaining 90, while under the second, the two will become co-owners of the 100 tonnes in the agreed proportions.

QUESTIONS

1. Can any category of future goods ever be specific goods in the statutory sense? (Consider the example of the machinery, above, p 305.)

2. Can goods not yet in existence ever be specific goods in the statutory sense?

(f) 'The property'

The definition of a contract of sale in s 2(1) requires that the seller should transfer or agree to transfer 'the property' in goods to the buyer. In s 61(1) we are told that 'property' means 'the general property in goods, and not merely a special property'. This expression, 'special property', is sometimes used to describe the interest of a pledgee, in order to emphasise the fact that he has something more than mere possession of the goods which have been pledged. (On pledge, see below, p 1024.) A pledgee has title to an interest in the goods which he can deal with, for example by sub-pledge or assignment, and in certain circumstances he has a power of sale. But he does not have *the general property* in the goods, in the statutory sense, and so a transfer of his interest as pledgee cannot be a sale.

In loose terms, we may think of 'the property' as meaning simply 'ownership'. To be more precise, however, 'the property' which a seller transfers or agrees to transfer is his title to *the absolute legal interest* in the goods: see the article by Battersby and Preston of which an extract is cited below. A pledgee has title only to a more limited interest, which is therefore excluded from the statutory definition. For this reason, the Act will not apply to a transfer by an owner of goods to someone else of an interest less than full ownership— for example, a contract of hire or some other form of bailment, or which creates a charge over goods. Nor will it apply to the transfer of such an interest by the hirer or bailee or chargee to a third party. And since we are concerned only with the *legal* interest in goods, the Act is not concerned with transfers of beneficial ownership, such as may arise on the creation of a trust.

It does not follow, however, that a seller has to have, or to purport to transfer, a complete or perfect legal title to the goods in order to bring a transaction within the statutory definition of a 'sale of goods'. Sections 21–25 and 48(2) all deal with cases where the seller has no title, or a defective or doubtful title. And s 12(3) (a provision first inserted in 1973) expressly contemplates that a seller who has only a limited title to goods may contract to sell that title. So, a person who has found an article and has failed to trace its owner may sell his title to it as a finder. The subsection also states that a seller may contract to sell whatever title a third person may have to the goods. This might happen, for instance, when a bank which has lent on the security of goods sells them following the owner's insolvency: the bank does not contract to confer on the buyers any better title than the owner may have had. This analysis is entirely consistent with the views of Battersby and Preston referred to above: the seller here is contracting to sell such title as he (or the third person) has to an absolute legal interest in the goods, not a title to some more limited interest.

'The Concepts of "Property", "Title" and "Owner" Used in the Sale of Goods Act 1893' by G Battersby and AD Preston

(1972) 35 MLR 268 at 268–272, 288 (footnotes omitted)

A. THE THREE ELEMENTS INVOLVED IN A TRANSFER OF TANGIBLE PROPERTY

In the transfer of any tangible property, whether land or chattels, three elements are distinguishable, namely, the estate or interest which is transferred, the title to that estate or interest, and the evidence of that title.

(1) Estate or interest transferred

What rights are being transferred and what is their duration? In the context of land, the rights must be, for example, the fee simple, the residue of a 999-year lease, a life estate, or some lesser interest such as a perpetual easement. Similarly, in relation to chattels, although the range of interests recognised by the law is restricted, one needs to distinguish life interests, entailed interests and absolute interests, as well as various kinds of incumbrance. Whether the transfer involves land or chattels, therefore, its nature can be understood only when the estate or interest to be transferred is defined.

(2) Title to that estate or interest

Is there anyone who can show that the transferor's title to the estate or interest is defective? The fundamental rule of the English law of property affecting title is nemo dat quod non habet. Its effect is that, although a transfer may comply with the legal formalities required for the transfer of the interest in question, it may yet fail to take effect because the transferor has no title to transfer. It is equally possible, however, that the transferor may have a title, but one which is less than perfect. This follows from the elementary proposition of our law that title to tangible property, whether land or chattels, is relative. The title to such property is protected by the possessory actions, which require only that the plaintiff must have possession or the immediate right to possession. This principle, and the converse rule that, subject to very narrow exceptions, the defendant cannot plead *jus tertii*, mean that mere adverse possession of property confers a title which is good against all the world except a person who can prove a better title, that is to say, a person with a continuing prior title. This notion of relative title permeates our law, and is one of the key concepts in the law of property, though in sale of goods, unlike conveyancing of land, it is frequently forgotten. Given such a concept, the phrase 'owner of property' assumes significance only in relation to a particular issue with a particular person . . . The concept of absolute ownership, by which is meant an indefeasible title to the absolute interest in the particular property, is as elusive in the realm of chattels as in that of land. True, there are exceptional cases of absolute ownership: a sale of goods in market overt to a purchaser in good faith is an exception relating to chattels,[9] and in the case of land one may instance the statutory procedure by which all existing interests may be compulsorily purchased. These exceptional cases, however, in no way derogate from the general principle. In a legal system which guaranteed that all transfers would vest an indefeasible title in the transferee the distinction between title and interest would be unnecessary, but English law, adopting the nemo dat rule, does not provide such a guarantee. In any given

---

[9] No longer true, since the market overt rule was abolished by the Sale of Goods (Amendment) Act 1994.

situation, therefore, the phrase 'transfer of property' needs expanding to 'the transfer of such-and-such a title to such-and-such an interest.'

(3) Evidence of title

By what facts does the transferor of property prove his title? This question assumes great importance in transactions concerning land; in the case of transactions concerning chattels, however, there is normally no investigation of title, the transferor's possession of the chattels apparently as owner affording the only evidence. The reasons for this are not hard to find: it is extremely rare for any documentary title to exist; the transient value of most chattels means that the chain of title will usually be short; there are exceptions to the rule nemo dat quod non habet which reduce the risk of bad titles; in any event, the value of chattels must often render investigation of title something of an excess. The question of evidence of title to chattels can accordingly be forgotten.

Our basic submission, therefore, is that the two objects of currency in the English system of property and conveyancing are interests and title, and that what is dealt with in a particular transfer is a particular title to a particular interest in the property in question.

B. THE DEFINITION OF A SALE OF GOODS

With these basic points in mind, we turn to examine in more detail the nature of a sale of goods. The transaction is defined in section 1[10] of the Sale of Goods Act. Section 1(1) reads:

> A contract of sale of goods is a contract whereby the seller transfers or agrees to transfer the property in goods to the buyer for a money consideration, called the price. There may be a contract of sale between one part owner and another.

This definition is amplified in section 1(3)[11] as follows:

> Where under a contract of sale the property in the goods is transferred from the seller to the buyer the contract is called a sale; but where the transfer of the property in the goods is to take place at a future time or subject to some condition thereafter to be fulfilled the contract is called an agreement to sell.

It will be observed first that the person selling the goods is called 'the seller,' not 'the owner.' The latter term is used at the end of subsection (1) (a 'sale between one part owner and another'), but it is clear from the context that the word 'owner' is not intended to have any flavour different from the word 'seller'; just as 'the seller' is a person who sells or agrees to sell a particular title, so 'the owner' is a person who owns a particular title, and as part owner owns that title concurrently with another. These words and phrases do not, therefore, indicate the use of any concept of absolute ownership.

Secondly, it will be observed that both subsections refer to the transfer of 'property in goods.' What is the concept of 'property' here employed? It is self-evident from the context that the word 'property' is not used in the sense of the physical chattels themselves, for the word 'goods' is used for that purpose. 'Property' therefore refers in some way to the proprietary right which is transferred by the sale. In our submission, 'property' comprises the two elements distinguished earlier as being involved in any transfer of property, namely, interest and title. So far as the interest is concerned, the purpose is to define a sale as involving the transfer of the absolute legal interest in the goods (analogous to the legal fee simple estate in land), as opposed to any lesser interest. This is made clear by the definition of 'property' in section 62[12] as 'the general property in the

[10] Now s 2.
[11] Now s 2(4), (5).
[12] Now s 61.

goods and not merely a special property.' Clearly, therefore, the creation for value of a bailment, which involves the transfer merely of possession and not of the absolute interest (analogous in many ways to the grant of a lease of land), is not a sale. Equally, in our submission, the transfer for value of a life interest in goods would not be a sale as defined, but would be regarded as an assignment of that life interest. But the concept of 'property' involves also the notion of title, for a sale must involve the transfer of a particular title to the absolute interest. In this general definition of sale, however, nothing is said about the quality of that title, which may be good, bad or indifferent on the scale of relativity. Nor would one expect anything to be said about the quality of title in the definition of the transaction: it would be logically and linguistically inapposite. What section 1 of the Act really achieves, therefore, is a definition of the nature of the contract of sale of goods, and this definition is expanded into two forms: (i) 'a contract whereby the seller transfers . . . the property in goods to the buyer' (ii) 'a contract whereby the seller . . . agrees to transfer the property in goods to the buyer.' These formulations of the definition differ in that the latter separates the stages of contracting to convey and conveyance, while the former telescopes the two stages so that both contract to convey and conveyance occur simultaneously; this telescoping, however, in no way detracts from the point that contract and conveyance are independent notions. More importantly these formulations share the feature that the contract of sale of goods concerns the transfer of a title to the absolute legal interest in the goods. In exactly the same way, one could define a contract for the sale of land as 'a contract for the transfer for value of a title to the fee simple estate' (ie separating the two elements of 'property'); that is merely an explanation of the nature of the transaction, corresponding to the second of the above formulations of the definition of a contract for the sale of goods, and containing within itself no promise as to quality of title, for which the parties are left to provide, if they wish, by appropriate contractual terms. Again, one could define a gift of goods as 'a voluntary transfer of the property in goods,' this merely serving to explain the nature of the transaction, for it is in the last degree unlikely that any undertakings as to the quality of the title will be given. Our point is that in all these cases it is the nature of the transaction that is being defined, and that nature is the transfer of a title to the absolute legal interest. The title which is in fact transferred, unless the case falls within an exception to the nemo dat rule, will always be the title vested in the seller at the time of the transfer: if it is poorer than that contracted for, the seller will be liable to the buyer for breach of contract, whilst if it is better than that contracted for, the risk assumed by the buyer will be proportionately less burdensome . . .

SUMMARY

The above arguments have led to the following principal conclusions:

(1) The notion of relative title is fundamental in English law, and is the main key to understanding the proprietary concepts used in the law of sale of goods.

(2) A distinction must be drawn between title and interest, the law of sale of goods being concerned with the transfer of a title to the absolute legal interest in the goods sold.

(3) The concept of 'property' in the Sale of Goods Act, despite the limited meaning assigned to it by section 62(1), must be expanded to mean 'a title to the absolute legal interest in the goods sold,' which meaning is used consistently throughout the Act.

(4) The concept of 'title,' as used in sections 21–26 of the Act, must be expanded to take in the notion that the transfer relates to the absolute legal interest in the goods sold, with the result that 'title' bears a similar meaning to 'property' in the above sense.

(5) A contract of sale is a contract which involves the transfer of a title to the absolute legal interest, and not necessarily a good title; a transfer which excludes the implied undertakings as to good title is still a sale, and there is no bar to such exclusion as the law now stands.

(6) Care is needed in applying the exceptions to the nemo dat rule, because of the ambiguity of expressions such as 'owner' and 'good title.' A few of the exceptions have the effect of generating a new perfect title, but the majority have the much more limited effect of transferring a particular title, which may itself be defeasible, by overriding some prior transaction or interest.

The whole of this important article is particularly worthy of study.

NOTES

1. HL Ho, 'Some Reflections on "Property" and "Title" in the Sale of Goods Act' [1997] CLJ 571, makes some further pertinent observations. 'Property', he contends, is 'transaction specific', whereas 'title' is 'entity and time' specific:

Property must be analysed in the context of a particular transaction and its passing as between the buyer and the seller is not affected by the location of absolute title. Absolute title on the other hand can vest in only one entity at any particular point in time and its location has to be determined by taking into consideration all the relevant transactions.

The 'relevant transactions' would include, for instance, an event which 'feeds' a defective title so as to perfect it, and a transaction which, under an exception to the *nemo dat* principle (see below, pp 381 ff), divests the true owner of title and vests it in a buyer.

2. Professor Battersby has responded to some criticisms and elaborated some aspects of this article in the light of *National Employers Association Ltd v Jones* (below, p 419): see G Battersby, 'A Reconsideration of "Property" and "Title" in the Sale of Goods Act' [2001] JBL 1. On relativity of title to goods, see D Fox, 'Relativity of Title in Law and at Equity' [2006] CLJ 330 at 340 ff.

5 SALE OF GOODS DISTINGUISHED FROM OTHER TRANSACTIONS

There are various types of transaction which in some ways resemble contracts for the sale of goods, but do not fall within the statutory definition. This means that the Act cannot be directly applied to such contracts. However, it may be of indirect relevance, since the Act of 1893 may have codified a rule of the common law which, prior to that date, had an application wider than the sale of goods. The common law rules, in their uncodified form, may be assumed to continue to apply to these other contracts. So it may be that at least some sale of goods rules are equally applicable to contracts of barter: it is only the dearth of litigated cases on barter that prevents us from knowing how far the parallel extends. Again, in formulating legislation to govern some of these other types of transaction (eg the Supply of Goods and Services Act 1982, dealing with contracts such as leases of goods, or repair contracts under which property in certain items incidentally passes), the statutory draftsman has often modelled the new law on the Sale of Goods Act and sometimes copied its language verbatim. It would be surprising if a court were to rule that cases decided on the construction of this language in the Sale of Goods Act were not relevant guides to its meaning in the context of the later Act. However, there are a number of other contracts which it is more important to distinguish from sales of goods.

(a) Sale distinguished from gift

A gift differs from a sale because there is no consideration for the transfer of the property in the goods. This is usually an obvious matter, but in borderline cases the court may be faced with a very difficult question. For example, in the well-known case of *Esso Petroleum Ltd v Customs and Excise Comrs* [1976] 1 All ER 117, motorists were offered a 'free' medallion with each purchase of four gallons of petrol. There was a difference of judicial opinion whether the medallions were the subject of a gift or a sale, or of a contract collateral to the purchase of the petrol which fell into neither of these categories. The difference matters for a number of reasons. A giver, unlike a seller, is under no duty in respect of the quality of what is given (except that he may owe a duty of care in tort); furthermore, while ownership can pass by mere agreement in the case of sale, with a gift there must be a transfer of possession or a deed executed by the giver.

(b) Sale distinguished from barter or exchange

The Act stipulates that the consideration in a contract of sale should be in money. If it takes some other form (eg where goods are exchanged for other goods, for services, or transferred in payment of a debt), it is a contract of barter or exchange and not one of sale. A contemporary commercial example would be a counter-trade transaction, such as a supply of wheat in exchange for oil of comparable value (on which, see L Moatti, 'Countertrade in International Commercial Exchanges' (1995) 1 IBLJ 3).

The Act will not apply to such transactions: nor will statutory references to a 'sale' in other legislation (see, eg, *VFS Financial Services Ltd v JF Plant Tyres Ltd* [2013] EWHC 346 (QB), [2013] 1 WLR 2987). This may not always be important. As regards defects in the goods transferred, ss 2–5A of the Supply of Goods and Services Act 1982 provides for obligations parallel to those in ss 12–15A of the 1979 Act. Again, it is likely that many of the rules which applied to sales at common law also applied (and continue to apply) to barter. But in the absence of clear precedents we cannot be sure that this is invariably so. In particular, it remains doubtful whether ownership can pass by agreement in the case of barter, as it can in the case of sale.

Where goods are exchanged for other goods (and particularly where some money is paid by one of the parties as well), it is not always necessary or appropriate to construe the transaction as one of barter. In *Aldridge v Johnson* (below), the evidence seems to have pointed to an arrangement under which there were reciprocal *sales* of the bullocks and the barley; the prices of each were calculated and then set off against each other, and the balance of £23 was agreed to be paid in cash. In other words, there were two separate contracts of sale, and it is consistent with this analysis that sale of goods principles were applied. In *Dawson v Dutfield* (below), however (a typical 'trade-in' case), the court preferred to take the view that there was only one contract of sale, namely that by Dawsons to Dutfields of the newer lorries for £475; there was then a subsidiary arrangement that if Dutfields chose to deliver the two older lorries in part exchange, they would be allowed £225 off the price.

Aldridge v Johnson

(1857) 7 E & B 885, Court of Queen's Bench

Aldridge made a deal with Knights to exchange 32 bullocks for 100 quarters of barley, to be measured out of a larger amount lying in Knights' granary which Aldridge had inspected the day before. They valued the bullocks at £6 each (ie £192 in all) and the barley at £215, and agreed that the difference of £23 would be paid in cash. Knights took delivery of the bullocks, and Aldridge sent 200 of his own sacks, each holding half a quarter, to Knights to be filled with barley from the heap in the granary and put on the railway by Knights' men. Of the 200 sacks, 155 had been filled when, on Knights' instructions, they were emptied out into the heap again. Aldridge then learned that Knights was about to be declared bankrupt. In this action brought against Johnson, Knights' trustee in bankruptcy, Aldridge claimed the right to 100 quarters out of the barley in the heap; but the court held that only the barley in the 155 sacks had become Aldridge's property. It also held that he had not been divested of it when the sacks were emptied back into the heap. But Aldridge had no claim to the rest of the 100 quarters which had never been put into his sacks.

> **Lord Campbell CJ**: I think that no portion of what remained in bulk ever vested in the plaintiff. We cannot tell what part of that is to vest. No rule of the law of vendor and purchaser is more clear than this: that, until the appropriation and separation of a particular quantity, or significa-tion of assent to the particular quantity, the property is not transferred. Therefore, except as to what was put into the 155 sacks, there must be judgment for the defendant. It is equally clear that, as to what was put into those sacks, there must be judgment for the plaintiff. Looking to all that was done, when the bankrupt put the barley into the sacks *eo instanti* the property in each sack-full vested in the plaintiff. I consider that here was *a priori* an assent by the plaintiff. He had inspected and approved of the barley in bulk. He sent his sacks to be filled out of that bulk. There can be no doubt of his assent to the appropriation of such bulk as should have been put into the sacks. There was also evidence of his subsequent appropriation, by his order that it should be sent on. There remained nothing to be done by the vendor, who had appropri-ated a part by the direction of the vendee. It is the same as if boxes had been filled and sent on by the bankrupt, in which case it cannot be disputed that the property would pass: and it can make no difference that the plaintiff ordered the sacks to be forwarded by the vendor. As to the question of conversion, the property being in the plaintiff, he has done nothing to divest himself of it. It is not like the case of confusion of goods, where the owner of such articles as oil or wine mixes them with similar articles belonging to another. That is a wrongful act by the owner, for which he is punished by losing his property. Here the plaintiff has done nothing wrong. It was wrong of the bankrupt to mix what had been put into the sacks with the rest of the barley; but no wrong has been done by the plaintiff. That being so, the plaintiffs property comes into the hands of the defendant as the bankrupt's assignee . . . He claims all the barley, and claims all of it as being the property of the bankrupt. He therefore has converted the plaintiff s property.

> [**Coleridge**, **Erle**, and **Crompton JJ** delivered concurring judgments.]

NOTES

1. Like *Re Wait*, this case would now be affected by the new s 20A. Aldridge, as a pre-paying buyer, would be able to claim a proprietary interest in the bulk proportionate to 200 notional sackfuls, and not just 155: see below, p 335.

2.   The modern law relating to mixing (or 'confusion') of goods no longer 'punishes' a person who wrongfully mixes his own goods with someone else's by declaring them forfeited to the innocent party. The two become tenants in common of the resulting mix, with any doubts as to either quantity or quality being resolved in the innocent party's favour (*Indian Oil Corpn Ltd v Greenstone Shipping SA (Panama)* [1988] QB 345).

GJ Dawson (Clapham) Ltd v H & G Dutfield
[1936] 2 All ER 232, King's Bench Division

Dawsons, dealers in second-hand vehicles, agreed to sell Dutfields two lorries, a Leyland and a Saurer, for a combined price of £475 of which £250 was paid or credited at the time. They also agreed to allow Dutfields £225 as the trade-in price of two Leyland vehicles, which Dutfields were allowed to use while their new purchases were being overhauled, provided that they were delivered to Dawsons within a month. The Saurer turned out to be in a much worse condition than the parties expected and, after arrangements to provide another vehicle in its place had proved abortive, Dawsons sued for the balance of the price of the two lorries. It was held that they could sue for this sum and were not bound to take the other vehicles as trade-ins.

> **Hilbery J**: The first agreement was a complete one and completely executed by the plaintiffs; all that remained to be done was to be done by the defendants. The plaintiffs had discharged their duty. Further the agreement was not a severable one . . . There is no evidence of any agreement to put aside the old agreement and treat it as non-existent. There is no more than an expression by the plaintiffs of intention to placate the defendants, an expression of willingness to take back the Saurer and try and find a suitable lorry in order to ease the situation for the defendants. It was the expression of a pious—or I should say business—hope.
>
> Someone must bear the burden of a bad bargain and the loss arising from the fact that the condition of the lorry was so much worse than expected. The thing was sold as it stood, and bought after examination by people who understood that there was much to be done to it. Neither party understood how bad it was. My decision is that the plaintiffs are entitled to the balance of the purchase money in the terms of the claim, owing to the non-delivery of the two Leylands. These had to be delivered within one month and if they had so delivered them, the defendants would have been entitled so to satisfy the purchase price to the extent of £225. They did not do so and there remains £225 as part of the purchase price due to the plaintiffs. The action in such circumstances is not one in detinue, and therefore no demand is necessary. Nor are the plaintiffs bound to claim the lorries. The defendants were merely given the right to satisfy £225 of the purchase price by the delivery of the lorries within one month or thereabouts. Such an arrangement does not deprive the plaintiffs of their right to the purchase price in cash. The defendants have not delivered and there must be judgment for the plaintiffs for the balance of the purchase price.

NOTES

1.   In the United States, this problem is, sensibly, bypassed. The price in a contract of sale may be paid in money or otherwise; if it is payable in whole or part in goods, each party is a seller of the goods which he wishes to transfer (Uniform Commercial Code, s 2–304(1)).

2.   Some aspects of the contract of barter are now governed by the Supply of Goods and Services Act 1982. This Act provides for statutory terms as to title, quality, etc to be implied into contracts of barter, using much the same language as ss 12–15 of the Sale of Goods Act; but it does not deal with the question—when does the property pass?—which was vital in *Aldridge v Johnson* and might have been answered differently if the transaction had been viewed as one of pure barter.

3.   A price is payable in money (and therefore the transaction will be a sale) even where payment is effected by credit card or in some similar way: see the discussion of *Re Charge Card Services Ltd* below, p 969. But this is not so where goods are supplied in payment of a debt owed by the supplier: *VFS Financial Services Ltd v JF Plant Tyres Ltd* [2013] EWHC 346 (QB), [2013] 1 WLR 2987.

QUESTIONS

1.   If Dutfields *had* traded in the two older lorries, what would have been the nature of that second transaction—a sale, a barter, or something else? What was the consideration given by Dawsons?

2.   In the Irish case of *Flynn v Mackin* [1974] IR 101, a motor dealer agreed to supply Fr Mackin with a new car in exchange for his old car plus a cash payment of £250. No valuation or price was put by the parties on either vehicle. Was there a sale of: (a) the new car; (b) the old car; (c) neither?

(c) Sale of goods distinguished from transfer of an interest in land

There is an overlap between these categories of contract, as has been noted above (p 303).

(d) Sale distinguished from bailment

A bailment (see above, Chapter 2) involves the delivery of goods by one person to another for a limited purpose, on terms that the goods will be returned to the bailor or delivered to a third party in accordance with his instructions at the conclusion of the bailment. There is normally no likelihood that a contract of bailment will be confused with one of sale, but the question did arise in *South Australian Insurance Co v Randell* (1869) LR 3 PC 101. In that case, a farmer had delivered corn to a miller and tipped it into a common store, on terms which allowed him to claim at any time either the redelivery of an equivalent quantity of corn or the market price of such corn ruling on the day in which he made his demand. Since the identity of the corn was lost when it was delivered, and there was no obligation on the miller, if redelivery was demanded, to make the redelivery from the same store—or, indeed, from any particular source—it was held that the transaction could not be a bailment but was more in the nature of a sale. See too, more recently, the oil storage case of *Glencore International AG v Metro Trading International Inc* [2001] CLC 1732.

The distinction between sale and bailment may be blurred in some cases involving a manufacturer. For instance, components or part-finished goods may be delivered to a manufacturer, on terms that they will be combined with other goods belonging to the latter and used to make an end-product which is then either redelivered to the original supplier for a charge, or sold on to a third party for a price for which, or out of which, the seller will account to the supplier. The question whether the transaction is a bailment by the supplier of his goods to the manufacturer or one involving a transfer (perhaps a sale) of the property in his goods and a resale back to him (or a sale on to the third party) can be very complex: the answer turns essentially on the terms of the contract, but may also be influenced by such factors as whether one party has supplied the 'principal' goods, and by whether the goods supplied remain identifiable throughout the manufacturing process. Aspects of this question are discussed in Chapter 3 above; see also *Glencore International AG v Metro Trading International Inc* [2001] CLC 1732 at [189], per Moore-Bick J.

QUESTIONS

1. Would the Sale of Goods Act apply to a transaction such as that in *South Australian Insurance Co v Randell*?

2. Twenty farmers agree to rent a store owned by Bloggs, where they tip their grain into a common bulk when it is harvested in August. It is agreed that Bloggs will sell one-tenth of the total quantity on the first of each month, beginning on 1 October and ending on 1 July, and share out the proceeds (less the rent and a commission) among the farmers on a pro rata basis, proportionate to the total quantity which each has contributed. What is the nature of this arrangement? (See *Mercer v Craven Grain Storage Ltd* [1994] CLC 328, and L Smith (1995) 111 LQR 10.)

3. Imagine that a day-old chick costs £1 and the food, etc required to rear it until it is ready to lay costs £2. It can then be sold for £4.50. Consider what different arrangements might be made between A, who hatches chicks, and B, who grows foodstuffs for poultry and has the facilities for rearing them.

A contract of sale should also be distinguished from other forms of bailment, such as a contract to lease or hire goods, and a pledge.

In the commercial world, specialised forms of lease have developed, notably the 'finance lease', under which the position of the lessee is in many respects similar to that of a buyer. The finance lease can be used in relation to plant and vehicles of all sorts, ranging all the way from a photocopier to a jet airliner. In the normal case the term of the lease approximates to that of the expected working life of the goods in question, and the total of the hire charges paid by the lessee over this period is roughly equal to its capital cost plus the lessor's profit from the transaction. The lessee undertakes responsibility for the maintenance and repair of the goods, and to pay the hire charges whether the goods are in working order or not. Thus his position, though different in law, is in practical terms little different from that of a buyer who has agreed to pay the purchase price of the goods by instalments over a similar period, at the end of which they will have come to the end of their useful life. The finance lease may have tax advantages and, as a form of 'off balance-sheet accounting' may be used to enhance the appearance of a firm's financial statements.

A contract of hire-purchase is a form of bailment, but is sufficiently important to be discussed separately.

(e) Sale distinguished from hire-purchase

In a contract of hire-purchase (sometimes called 'lease-purchase'), goods are hired for a period, at the end of which the hirer may exercise an option to buy the goods, usually by making a further modest payment. In practical terms (though not in legal form), the position of the hirer under such a contract is very similar to that of a person who has agreed to buy the goods from their owner on the understanding that he is to take immediate delivery, but pay the price by instalments over a period, with property only passing on full payment (known as a 'conditional sale'). This latter contract differs from a contract of hire-purchase because the buyer is contractually bound to complete the transaction: he has 'agreed to buy' (even if in certain cases he has an option to renounce the transaction: *Forthright Finance Ltd v Carlyle Finance Ltd* [1997] 4 All ER 90, CA). The hirer under a contract of hire-purchase, in contrast, has only an option to buy, which he is free to exercise or not as he chooses; and he also commonly has the right to terminate the hiring before the expiry of the contemplated period. One might think this difference immaterial: but it is not. The reason is that a hirer under a hire-purchase agreement, unlike an instalment buyer, cannot pass title to a good faith third party purchaser under s 25(1) of the 1979 Act (see *Helby v Matthews* [1895] AC 471).

Although a hire-purchase contract is in all but name a loan on the security of the goods, if the hirer is a corporation it is nevertheless probably not registrable as a charge 'created by' the company under Part 25 of the Companies Act 2006. Furthermore, it should be noted that a contract of hire-purchase is wholly outside the scope of the 1979 Act, at least until the option to purchase is exercised (though ss 8–12 of the Supply of Goods (Implied Terms) Act 1973 imply similar terms as to the quality of the goods as appear in ss 12–15 of the Sale of Goods Act).

Notwithstanding the clear fact that in law the supplier of goods under a hire-purchase agreement is and remains their owner and is not merely the holder of a security interest in goods which he has 'sold' to the hirer, there is a strong argument for saying that in economic reality this is the case, and that it would be better if the law recognised it. The legal position is even further divorced from reality if the credit is given, not by a dealer but by a financier: for example, where machinery, having been approved by a customer, is sold by the dealer to the financier who then lets it on hire-purchase to the customer. Here the customer is in law a hirer (from a faceless institution it has no regular relations with); vis-à-vis the customer, the dealer is neither a seller nor in any direct contractual relationship at all; and the financier is a buyer who becomes the owner of the car for so long as any part of the price is outstanding!

In other jurisdictions, such as the United States, Canada, Australia, and New Zealand, general personal property security laws have been introduced (eg the US Uniform Commercial Code, Art 9, or in Australia the Personal Property Securities Act 2009 (Cth)) which assimilate into one regime all transactions that *in effect* involve the giving of security over personal chattels, regardless of their legal form. This makes unnecessary the elaborate type of legal charade described above which the technicalities of English law impose on similar transactions here. Successive reports (including the report of Professor Diamond on Security Interests in Property (1989)) recommended that there should be wholesale reform of this area of English law, along the lines of the transatlantic codes. However, the Law Commission, having initially supported the idea, later postponed reform as raising very complex and controversial issues (see Law Com No 296, *Company Security Interests* (2005), Ch 1, esp paras 1.60 ff). Since then, despite a major reform of the company charge registration system in 2013, there has been little official interest in fundamental reform of personal property security law (below, p 1085).

(f) Sale distinguished from a transaction by way of security

Among the forms of security considered later in this book are the pledge, the lien, the mortgage, and the charge: see Chapters 25 and 26. Since neither pledge nor lien involves the transfer of the property in the goods concerned, they are plainly distinguishable from a contract of sale. The same may be said of a charge: the chargor grants an interest in or over his goods in favour of the chargee, which is of a proprietary nature, but he retains the property in his own hands, and the chargee's interest is a defeasible one which is automatically terminated on payment of the debt which it secures. A mortgage resembles a sale rather more closely, in that the legal title to the goods is transferred to the creditor in order to secure the debt: the general property in the goods (to use the wording of the Act) passes to him. But whereas in a sale it passes absolutely, so that the seller has no further interest in the goods, in a mortgage it passes subject to the condition that the mortgagor is entitled to redeem—that is, to have the goods transferred back to him when the debt is paid. The parties remain in a continuing relationship of debtor and creditor, and both retain an interest in the goods during the currency of the mortgage.

Section 62(4) states that the provisions of the Act about contracts of sale do not apply to a transaction in the form of a sale which is intended to operate by way of mortgage, pledge, charge, or other security. This draws our attention to the possibility that a transaction which is to all appearances a contract of sale may in fact be intended by the parties to do no more than create a security interest in favour of the purported 'buyer': there may be a tacit understanding, or an agreement recorded in another document, that the transfer of property in the goods is only conditional and that it will be retransferred when the seller's indebtedness to the buyer has been discharged. Or the sale may be part of a composite transaction (eg a sale followed by a lease-back of the goods to the seller) which, viewed overall, is really meant to be a way of raising money on the security of the goods. In situations falling into these categories, s 62(4) means, for example, that provisions such as ss 12–15 of the Sale of Goods Act 1979 (dealing with the quality of goods) will not apply so as to make the 'seller' (borrower) liable to the financier if the goods involved are not of satisfactory quality. In practice, however, it is not this which is likely to pose legal problems, but rather the company charges legislation under Part 25 of the Companies Act 2006 and the Bills of Sale Act of 1882 (see below, p 1078); for under this latter Act (which traditionally looks to the substance rather than the form) the transaction, if it *is* held to be a security transaction, risks being declared void for non-compliance with the statute or for want of registration.

This means that the courts may be faced with the difficult task of determining the 'true intention' of the parties in many borderline cases. Occasionally it has been held that what looks like a contract of sale is in fact a concealed charge unenforceable for want of registration (eg *Re Curtain Dream plc* [1990] BCLC 925). However, such cases are rare. The sale to a financier, with or without a lease-back, is now a well-established form of transaction, especially in commercial circles, which ought nowadays to be recognised as valid in its own right (see, eg, *Eastern Distributors Ltd v Goldring* [1957] 2 QB 600, *Mercantile Credit Ltd v Hamblin* [1965] 2 QB 242, and *Welsh Development Agency v Export Finance Co Ltd* [1992] BCC 270).

(g) Sale of goods distinguished from contract for work and materials

Trebor Bassett Holdings Ltd v ADT Fire & Security Plc
[2012] EWCA Civ 1158, [2012] BLR 441, Court of Appeal

A Yorkshire confectionery factory burnt down when a small fire started and a badly designed fire suppression system failed to put it out. The suppliers of the system (ADT) sought to reduce the damages on the basis that the owners had been guilty of contributory negligence (they had omitted to take elementary anti-fire precautions, such as installing sprinklers). This was possible if the basis of the suppliers' liability was negligent design under a contract for work and materials, but not if they were strictly liable for supplying a defective system under a contract for the sale of goods on the basis of s 14 of the Sale of Goods Act 1979. The Court of Appeal upheld a judgment that damages fell to be reduced by 75 per cent for contributory negligence—ie that this was not a contract for the sale of goods.

> **Tomlinson LJ**:
>
> 42....[I]t is convenient to start with the question whether ADT should be regarded as having supplied a system which can be equated with goods so attracting the ..... implied requirement that it be of satisfactory quality or reasonably fit for the purpose.
>
> 43. Mr Roger ter Haar QC for Cadbury rightly characterised this as very largely a matter of impression, as indeed are most of the points related to the proper analysis of the obligations undertaken by ADT. In agreement with the judge, I do not regard it as either natural or accurate to regard Cadbury as having bought from ADT a system which can be equated with goods which are either of good quality or not as the case may be. I can understand that that description might possibly be apt if Cadbury had contracted to purchase, or ADT had contracted to supply, a standard kit or assembly. In such circumstances there would, ordinarily, be no element of design in order to meet specific requirements....In such circumstances it may sometimes make sense to describe the system as being of either good quality or not, provided that such an evaluation can be made without reference to the particular characteristics of the location in which it is to be or is installed or the particular characteristics of the job it is or was expected by the purchaser to do. Those matters are of no relevance to the contractual relationship. The seller simply offers a system the capacity and capability of which he will describe in such terms as he chooses consistent with the need to market the product. His liability will depend upon the descriptive words used and upon such terms as can be implied into the sale of generic goods of that description. There may in such circumstances be room to evaluate a system in terms of its inherent quality, for example because it is simply unreliable for use in the generic application for which it is sold.
>
> 44. The present is, as it seems to me, a very different situation....[T]his was not simply the supply of an off-the-shelf system or product....[T]he reasonable understanding of the parties would have been that ADT was offering to undertake the design of a system which was to be tailored 'to suit the specific requirements of the risks to be protected'. So what was offered was not a standard product to be taken off the shelf and chosen by reference to its description. If what was offered could properly be described as a product at all, which I doubt, it was at best a bespoke product in respect of which what was of importance was not so much the inherent quality of the constituent parts (which was of course required to be good) but rather their selection as being suitable for the task and the manner in which they were to be combined, located and installed in such manner as 'to suit the specific requirements of the risks to be protected'.

45. In these circumstances it is I think wholly artificial to regard ADT as having contracted to supply a system which can be equated with 'goods' and of which it can simply be asked in the abstract, was it or was it not of good quality. . . .

46. Another way of expressing the same conclusion is that it is not possible to say of the system supplied that it was in the abstract not of good quality. As Cadbury itself points out, . . . what may be a good system for one application may not be a good system for another application. That tends to suggest that the quality of the system cannot be assessed without reference to its intended or actual application. In so saying I do not overlook that in *Young and Marten Ltd v McManus Childs Ltd* [1969] 1 AC 454, Lord Upjohn observed, at page 474, that good quality and reasonable fitness for purpose are two distinct concepts 'although it very frequently happens that for any relevant purpose there is no difference between the two.' One finds an echo of this, as Mr ter Haar pointed out, in s.14(2B)(a) of the Sale of Goods Act 1979 , to the effect that in appropriate cases the quality of goods may include their fitness for all the purposes for which goods of the kind in question are commonly supplied. The point here is however that the system does not have any inherent characteristics which can be independently assessed as indicative that, as a free-standing system, it is or is not of good quality. Furthermore there are no purposes for which this system is commonly supplied. It is a one-off bespoke system, designed for one particular application. All this tends to support my view that it is not a natural or accurate use of language in this context to regard 'the system' as simply 'goods' attracting without more the well-known statutory incidents of quality and fitness for purpose. What ADT was agreeing to supply was primarily design skills and care in exercising them, not goods, and the goods which they did supply were of good quality.

. . .

49. It follows from the foregoing that Cadbury cannot in my view pray in aid the statutory implied terms. Once it is accepted, as I do, that 'the system' cannot be equated with or is not be regarded as without more 'goods', those implied terms have no relevance since it is not suggested that the equipment supplied was in itself of poor quality or reasonably unfit for the known purpose for which it was supplied.

Hyundai Heavy Industries Co Ltd v Papadopoulos
[1980] 1 WLR 1129, House of Lords

Hyundai contracted to 'build, launch, equip and complete' a 24,000 ton cargo ship and 'deliver and sell' her to a Liberian company for $14.3 million. (Perhaps significantly, the parties were described in the contract respectively as 'the builder' and 'the buyer'.) Payment of the price, which was guaranteed by Papadopoulos, was to be made by five instalments at stated stages of the work. The second instalment fell due on 15 July, but it was still unpaid on 6 September and Hyundai then exercised a contractual right to cancel the contract on the basis of this default. The question for the court to decide was whether the July instalment remained payable notwithstanding the termination of the contract. The House of Lords assumed that if the contract was one to pay periodically for services the instalment was due, since the relevant part of the services had been rendered; but that (although not without some doubt) if a contract was for sale of goods that were not in fact going to be supplied the seller could neither retain nor sue for instalments of the price (see *Dies v British & International Mining & Finance Corpn Ltd* [1939] 1 KB 724—though their Lordships had some misgivings about that decision). Their ruling was that, while the ship was in the course of construction, the contract had sufficient of the characteristics of a contract for work and materials for the latter rule to apply.

Viscount Dilhorne: Counsel for the guarantors in the instant case argued that if the buyer in the Dies case was entitled to recover an advance which had already been paid, then a fortiori the buyer in the instant case could not be liable to make an advance that was due but unpaid: if he did make it, said counsel, he would be entitled to immediate repayment of it.

I do not accept that argument. In my opinion the *Dies* case and *Palmer v Temple* (1839) 9 Ad & El 508 are both distinguishable from the present case because in both these cases the contracts were simply contracts of sale which did not require the vendor to perform any work or incur any expense on the subjects of sale. But the contract in the instant case is not of that comparatively simple character. The obligations of the buyer were not confined to selling the vessel but they included designing and building it and there were special provisions (article 2) that the contract price 'shall include payment for services in the inspection, tests, survey and classification of the vessel' and also 'all costs and expenses for designing and supplying all necessary drawings for the vessel in accordance with the specifications.' Accordingly the builder was obliged to carry out work and to incur expense, starting from the moment that the contract had been signed, including the wages of designers and workmen, fees for inspection and for cost of purchasing materials. It seems very likely that the increasing proportions of the contract price represented by the five instalments bore some relation to the anticipated rate of expenditure, but we have no information on which to make any nice comparison between the amount of expenses that the builder would have to bear from time to time, and the amounts of the instalments payable by the buyer. I do not think that such comparisons are necessary. It is enough that the builder was bound to incur considerable expense in carrying out his part of the contract long before the actual sale could take place. That no doubt is the explanation for the provision in article 10(b) of the shipbuilding contract that:

> . . . all payments under the provisions of this article shall not be delayed or withheld by the buyer due to any dispute of whatever nature arising between the builder and the buyer hereto, unless the buyer shall have claimed to cancel the contract under the terms thereof. . . .

The importance evidently attached by the parties to maintaining the cash flow seems to support my view of the contract.

There was no evidence either way as to whether the builders had in fact carried out their obligations to start designing and building the vessel, but in my opinion we must assume, in the absence of evidence or even averment to the contrary, that they had carried out their part of the bargain up till the date of cancellation.

Much of the plausibility of the argument on behalf of the guarantors seemed to me to be derived from the assumption that the contract price was simply a purchase price. That is not so, and once that misconception has been removed I think it is clear that the shipbuilding contract has little similarity with a contract of sale and much more similarity, so far as the present issues are concerned, with contracts in which the party entitled to be paid had either performed work or provided services for which payment is due by the date of cancellation. In contracts of the latter class, which of course includes building and construction contracts, accrued rights to payment are not (in the absence of express provisions) destroyed by cancellation of the contract. . . .

[**Lords Edmund-Davies** and **Fraser of Tullybelton** delivered concurring opinions. **Lords Russell of Killowen** and **Keith of Kinkel** concurred.]

NOTES

1.   There has always been a difficult—sometimes impossible—line to draw here. Is a contract to replace the tyres on a vehicle a contract to provide a service with tyres incidentally to be supplied, or a contract to sell and incidentally affix the tyres? Is a contract to provide catering

in an industrial canteen a contract to provide a catering service or a contract to sell food ready-prepared? Is a contract to write and provide bespoke software an agreement to provide computing services or a contract to sell a DVD with software embodied in it?

2. In many cases this distinction is not vital. For example, legislation now provides that where goods are supplied incidentally to a contract which is not a sale of goods contract, the same terms as to title and quality apply as if it were a contract for the sale of goods: Supply of Goods and Services Act 1982, ss 1–5A.

3. But possible differences of importance remain.

(a) Property, risk, and acceptance. It is not clear whether the rules in ss 17–20A of the Sale of Goods Act 1979 as to passing of property and risk (below, Chapter 9), or the rules in s 35 as to acceptance and rejection (below, p 469) apply in respect of goods supplied where the contract is one for work and materials.

(b) Payment and retention of the price. Insofar as services have been rendered for which the recipient has agreed to pay, the supplier can sue for the price, even if the contract is later cancelled and hence the end-product is not delivered: *Hyundai v Papadopoulos*, above. This is not true of sale of goods, where the price is payable only on delivery and acceptance. Similarly, if payment is made for services which are rendered under a contract later cancelled, such payment can normally be retained by the supplier; whereas if prepayment is made in a contract for the sale of goods and the goods are not delivered, the prepayment can be recovered on the basis of a total failure of consideration (see the later decision of the House of Lords in *Stocznia Gdanska SA v Latvian Shipping Co* [1998] 1 WLR 574).

(c) Strict liability or liability for negligence? Under the Sale of Goods Act and (in the case of incidental supplies under a contract for work and materials) under s 4 of the Supply of Goods and Services Act 1982, the goods supplied must be in fact of satisfactory quality and fit for their purpose: this is an obligation independent of fault on the supplier's part. On the other hand, in respect of a service the duty under s 13 of the 1982 Act is merely a duty of reasonable care and skill. This was the issue in *Trebor Bassett Holdings Ltd v ADT Fire & Security Plc*, above. It might be noted, however, that this can cause some fairly arbitrary results: for example, a veterinary surgeon treating a farmer's sick cow will be liable under s 4 if the drug he administers is faulty but he gives the right dose, but under s 13 if the drug is good but the dose is wrong.

4. Some of the old cases turned on s 4 of the Sale of Goods Act 1893, which (before it was repealed, to general relief, in 1954) rendered unenforceable any contract for the sale of goods for more than £10 unless evidenced in writing, but did not apply to contracts for work and materials. This could create some nice distinctions where buyers sought to renege on oral agreements by pleading s 4: for instance, compare *Robinson v Graves* [1935] 1 KB 579 (contract to paint a portrait is for work and materials) with *Marcel (Furriers) Ltd v Tapper* [1953] 1 WLR 49 (making up of extremely expensive mink coat nevertheless a contract of sale). Cases on the section need to be treated with care because of an understandable reluctance to allow defendants to escape liability on a technicality; nevertheless, the decisions remain relevant on the general point of the distinction between sale and services contracts.

5. The courts have wavered in their approach to this question of classification. In some early cases, such as *Clay v Yates* (below), what seems to have mattered was the relative importance of the two elements—the labour or the materials. Later, in cases like *Lee v Griffin* (below),

they made the issue turn on whether or not there was an end-product in the form of a chattel in which the property was transferred; elsewhere recently, in *Robinson v Graves* (below) the question was said to be determined by the 'substance' of the transaction. However, this is not always a meaningful test—a point which the court may have failed to appreciate—and the decisions which have been reached are far from consistent.

6.   The following have been held to be contracts for work and materials:

- a contract to print a book: *Clay v Yates* (1856) 1 H & N 73;

- a contract to paint a portrait: *Robinson v Graves* [1935] 1 KB 579, CA;
  In contrast, the following have been held (or assumed) to be sales of goods:

- a contract to make a set of dentures: *Lee v Griffin* (1861) 1 B & S 272;

- the supply and laying of a fitted carpet: *Philip Head & Sons Ltd v Showfronts Ltd* [1970] 1 Lloyd's Rep 140;

- the supply and installation of an animal feed hopper: *Parsons (Livestock) Ltd v Uttley Ingham & Co Ltd* [1978] QB 791, CA.

It is difficult to resist the conclusion that these decisions have been made on an impressionistic, rather than a logical, basis.

(h) Contract of sale distinguished from agency

As we saw in Chapter 4, there is again sometimes a difficult line to draw between a contract for the sale of goods and one of agency; and the question can arise both between a seller and an agent, on the one hand, and a buyer and an agent, on the other.

Suppose, first, that X is an art dealer who travels the country attending galleries and sales, and Y asks him to look out for a particular kind of picture and, if he finds one, to buy it for him. This can be done either on the basis that X buys as Y's agent, taking remuneration by way of commission, or that X himself buys the picture from its owner and resells it to Y at a profit. The difference may matter, if (for example) X fails to pay for the picture and the seller wants to sue Y. In the former case he can, while in the latter he cannot. If X and Y have not clearly spelt out the details of their arrangement, the court may be left with a difficult decision as to what was intended.

On the other hand, we may find the converse case. Z Ltd may have a showroom in which it displays Ford trucks, above which is exhibited the sign 'Sole agent for the sale of Ford trucks in the County of Whimshire'. If Z really were an agent, then a customer who bought a truck would actually be buying it from the Ford Motor Co, with Z as a mere go-between. But it is far more likely that Z is not an agent in the legal sense at all, but a retailer buying trucks from Ford to resell. Again, there is only one contract of sale in the former case, with one buyer and one seller; in the latter, two contracts of sale, and three principal parties.

It is clear that the description which the parties give to their relationship will not be decisive of its true nature in law. The use of the word 'agent' or 'agency' may be a loose, popular usage, obscuring the fact that the person in question is a buyer or a seller. The courts can have regard to several pointers, none of them in itself conclusive, in reaching a decision in a borderline case. What degree of independence does the 'middle' man have? Is he free to fix his own prices? Is he remunerated by a commission or similar payment, or by taking a profit? Does he have to account to his supplier for the payments he receives, or is he simply invoiced by the supplier for the goods he orders?

The position may be even more complicated. A person may be constituted by the same transaction as both someone who has agreed to buy goods and, in addition (eg in some 'retention of title' or *Romalpa* cases (see below, p 497)), the seller's agent to resell the goods. In the world of exporting and importing, it is common for a buyer who is based abroad to be represented in the seller's country by an agent who gives a guarantee to the seller that his principal, the buyer, will pay the price. This, as we saw above, p 117, is called a *del credere* agency; and such an agent has some of the rights given to a seller by the Sale of Goods Act— for example, the right to hold the goods under a lien until his principal, the buyer, has reimbursed him for the price (s 38(2)). Again, there is a counterpart: a *confirming agent*, an agent acting for a seller (usually based overseas) who guarantees to the buyer that his principal, the seller, will deliver the goods: see above, p 118.

(i) Sale of goods distinguished from a licence to use intellectual property

A contract for the supply of software or other intellectual property may also involve a sale of goods (eg a DVD), but a central part of the transaction will be a licence granted by the owner of the copyright in the software, who may or may not be the seller. If the seller is not the owner, there will be a separate contract between the owner and the buyer in which the seller acts as the owner's agent. In the absence of the sale of the DVD or other physical medium (eg if the DVD is merely lent or bailed), this is not a contract for the sale of goods: *London Borough of Southwark v IBM UK Ltd* [2011] EWHC 549 (TCC). (It should be noted that, at least in theory, surprisingly many 'sales' of software take this form, with a statement that the medium is bailed rather than sold.) The same presumably applies if the software is downloaded from the Internet. If the DVD is sold, there is probably a sale of goods in the case of the DVD (compare *St Albans District Council v International Computers Ltd* [1996] 4 All ER 481 at 493) and a concurrent grant of a licence to use its contents.

6 FORMATION OF THE CONTRACT OF SALE

A contract of sale, like any other contract, depends upon establishing an agreement between the parties, which usually follows from the acceptance by one party of an offer made by the other. No special rules apply to sales of goods here. One point is worth noting, however: the Act deals specifically with cases where no price is agreed. It provides as follows, in s 8:

> (1) The price in a contract of sale may be fixed by the contract, or may be left to be fixed in a manner agreed by the contract, or may be determined by the course of dealing between the parties.
> (2) Where the price is not determined as mentioned in subsection (1) above the buyer must pay a reasonable price.
> (3) What is a reasonable price is a question of fact dependent on the circumstances of each particular case.

It is clear from these provisions that the court has power to fix a reasonable price where there has been agreement on all the terms of a contract of sale other than the price. However, if the parties have purposefully left the price open, as something to be negotiated between them in the future, the court may have no option but to declare that there is as yet no binding contract. In *May & Butcher Ltd v R* [1934] 2 KB 17n, HL, an agreement to buy war surplus tentage from the Crown at prices to be agreed upon from time to time between the parties was held not to be a concluded contract. This case may be contrasted with *Hillas & Co Ltd v Arcos Ltd* (1932) 147 LT 503, HL, where the parties had already been in a contractual relationship for the supply of timber in the year 1930, and the buyers sought to exercise an option under that contract to purchase further timber in 1931. The sellers argued that this second contract was not binding because various of its terms were not fully spelt out, but the House of Lords, distinguishing *May & Butcher*, held that the uncertainty could be resolved by reference to the previous course of dealing between the parties.

It may be noted in passing that s 15 of the Supply of Goods and Services Act 1982 similarly provides for a reasonable price to be paid in a contract for the supply of a service, where no price has been otherwise fixed.

Section 9 of the Sale of Goods Act deals with the special case where the price is left to be fixed by a valuation made by a third party. Here the contract will not be binding if the third party cannot or does not make the valuation (unless he is prevented from doing so by the fault of one of the parties: s 9(2)); but if the goods have been delivered to the buyer and 'appropriated' by him, he must pay a reasonable price for them (s 9(1)). ('Appropriated' here may be taken as meaning 'dealt with in some way as if he were their owner': elsewhere in the Act, it is used in a rather more technical sense: see below, p 331.)

CHAPTER 9

PASSING OF THE PROPERTY IN THE GOODS AS BETWEEN SELLER AND BUYER

1 SIGNIFICANCE OF THE PASSING OF PROPERTY

The concept of 'the property' in the goods dominates much of the thinking in English sale of goods law—so much so that Professor Goode calls our preoccupation with the concept 'excessive' (*Commercial Law*, para 8.27). We saw when discussing s 2(4)–(5) that the Act makes a distinction between a *sale*, a completed transaction where the property has been transferred to the buyer pursuant to the contract of sale, and an *agreement to sell*, where there is an obligation to transfer the property but it has not yet been transferred.

In this chapter, we examine the concept of the passing of the property—the time at which, or the event upon which, the seller ceases to be, and the buyer becomes, the owner of the goods (or, in exceptional cases, succeeds to such title as the seller has). This event has significance for many purposes in law, the most important of which are listed below. It should be noted, however, that not all of these are fixed rules of law: some of them may be varied by agreement between the parties, and others state only a provisional or presumptive rule which may in particular situations have to give way to another which in the circumstances has an overriding effect. Subject to these qualifications, which are discussed in more detail below, we may list the following points of distinction.

Where the contract is an *agreement to sell*, and the property remains with the seller:

(1) The contract is still executory.

(2) The buyer has only rights *in personam* against the seller. The seller can exercise proprietary rights in relation to the goods (eg sue a third party in tort if the goods are wrongly detained, stolen, or damaged), but the buyer cannot: see *The Aliakmon*, below.

(3) The buyer's remedy against the seller, if he is in breach of contract, is for damages for non-delivery (s 51) (except in the rare case where specific performance is available (s 52: see below, p 527)).

(4) The seller's remedy against the buyer, if he is in breach, is for damages for non-acceptance (s 50); the seller continues to be responsible for the goods (storage charges, disposing of them if perishable, etc).

(5) A seller who has retained the property can in principle sell the goods to a different buyer and give this second buyer a good title, whereas a buyer who has not got title cannot do more than *agree to sell* them to a third party.

(6) The risk of loss is presumptively on the seller (s 20). If the goods are compulsorily purchased, or compensation becomes payable for their loss or destruction, the loss is borne by the seller, and any compensation is payable to the seller.

(7) The contract may be avoided or frustrated if the goods perish (s 7).

(8) In the event of the seller's insolvency, the buyer has no right to the goods, but only the right to prove in the insolvency for the return of any part of the price which he has paid, and for damages in respect of any loss that he has suffered: *Re Wait* (above, p 298; but note the effect of s 20A, below, p 335).

(9) In the event of the buyer's insolvency, the seller can claim back the goods even though they have been delivered to the buyer: see the *Romalpa* case (below, p 498).

(10) Any profits or increase (eg young born to livestock) belong to the seller.

Where the contract is a *sale*, and the property has passed to the buyer:

(1) The contract is executed, ie there is a conveyance as well as a contract.

(2) The buyer has rights *in rem* (proprietary rights) in relation to the goods (eg the right to sue a third party in tort if the goods are wrongly detained, stolen, or damaged).

(3) The buyer's remedies against the seller, if he is in breach, are not only for damages for non-delivery (s 51), but also lie in tort.

(4) The seller's remedies against the buyer, if he is in breach, are not only for damages for non-acceptance (s 50), but also for the contract price (s 49(1)); the buyer is left with all responsibility for the goods.

(5) A seller who has parted with title to the goods cannot save in limited circumstances pass title to a second buyer, while a buyer to whom the property in goods has passed can sell them on to a third party and give that person a good title.

(6) The risk of loss is presumptively on the buyer (s 20). If the goods are requisitioned, or compensation becomes payable for their loss or destruction, the initial loss is borne by the buyer, and any compensation is payable to the buyer.

(7) The contract is not frustrated if the goods perish.

(8) In the event of the seller's insolvency, the buyer may claim the goods: for example, *Re Blyth Shipbuilding Ltd* [1926] Ch 494.

(9) In the event of the buyer's insolvency, the seller cannot claim back any goods which have been delivered to the buyer, but can only prove in the insolvency for so much of the price as is outstanding, and also for any loss that he has suffered.

(10) Any profits or increase (eg young born to livestock) belong to the buyer.

Leigh & Sillavan Ltd v Aliakmon Shipping Co Ltd, The Aliakmon
[1986] AC 785, House of Lords

Buyers Leigh & Sillavan Ltd agreed to buy steel coils C & F Immingham, Humberside (for C & F contracts, see below, p 552). The coils were damaged by the carrier's alleged negligence while being loaded. At the time they were at the buyers' risk but under the contract property had not yet passed to the buyers. The House of Lords held that since the goods were not the buyers' property at the time when the damage was caused, their only claim was for economic loss, in respect of which the defendants owed them no duty of care.

Lord Brandon of Oakbrook: My Lords, this appeal arises in an action in the Commercial Court in which the appellants, who were the c and f buyers of goods carried in the respondents' ship, the Aliakmon, claim damages against the latter for damage done to such goods at a time when the risk, but not yet the legal property in them, had passed to the appellants. The main question to be determined is whether, in the circumstances just stated, the respondents owed a duty of care in tort to the appellants in respect of the carriage of such goods. . . .

My Lords, there is a long line of authority for a principle of law that, in order to enable a person to claim in negligence for loss caused to him by reason of loss of or damage to property, he must have had either the legal ownership of or a possessory title to the property concerned at the time when the loss or damage occurred, and it is not enough for him to have only had contractual rights in relation to such property which have been adversely affected by the loss of or damage to it.

[His Lordship examined the authorities, and continued:]

None of these cases concerns a claim by cif or c and f buyers of goods to recover from the owners of the ship in which the goods are carried loss suffered by reason of want of care in the carriage of the goods resulting in their being lost or damaged at a time when the risk in the goods, but not yet the legal property in them, has passed to such buyers. The question whether such a claim would lie, however, came up for decision in *Margarine Union GmbH v Cambay Prince SS Co Ltd (The Wear Breeze)* [1969] 1 QB 219. In that case cif buyers had accepted four delivery orders in respect of as yet undivided portions of a cargo of copra in bulk shipped under two bills of lading. It was common ground that, by doing so, they did not acquire either the legal property in, nor a possessory title to, the portions of copra concerned: they only acquired the legal property later when four portions each of 500 tons were separated from the bulk on or shortly after discharge in Hamburg. The copra having been damaged by want of care by the shipowner's servants or agents in not properly fumigating the holds of the carrying ship before loading, the question arose whether the buyers were entitled to recover from the shipowners in tort for negligence the loss which they had suffered by reason of the copra having been so damaged. Roskill J held that they were not, founding his decision largely on the principle of law established by the line of authority to which I have referred.

[His Lordship then considered and rejected a number of grounds on which it was contended that *The Wear Breeze* had been wrongly decided. He concluded that the plaintiffs had no cause of action in tort.]

[**Lords Keith of Kinkel, Brightman, Griffiths**, and **Ackner** concurred.]

NOTE

The Carriage of Goods by Sea Act 1992 would now give the buyers the right to sue the carriers in contract on the facts of *The Aliakmon* (see below, p 537), but it remains an authoritative ruling in tort.

As has already been emphasised, some of the differences between a sale and an agreement to sell which have been listed above are mere prima facie rules which are more or less heavily qualified. For instance, s 20, which declares that risk passes with the property in the goods, applies only 'unless otherwise agreed'. Many of the other propositions are qualified by further provisions of the Act. For example, although s 49(2) gives the seller a right to sue for the price once the property has passed, s 28 adds the further condition that, unless otherwise agreed, the seller must also be ready and willing to deliver the goods in exchange for the price. This means that, except where the buyer himself wrongfully refuses delivery or goods are destroyed after risk has passed, no action for the price will lie unless *both* property and possession have passed to the buyer. Further, it must be remembered that a seller who has retained possession of the goods can in some circumstances confer a good title on a second buyer even though the property may have passed to the first buyer (s 24), and that conversely a buyer who has been given possession has a corresponding power to give a good title to a sub-buyer and so defeat the original seller's title (s 25(1)). For reasons such as this, Professor Lawson in 'The Passing of Property and Risk in Sale of Goods—A Comparative Study' (1949) 65 LQR 362 argued that the significance of the concept of property was less than had traditionally been thought: the exceptions and qualifications to the 'rules' listed above were so great as virtually to eat up the rules themselves, so that 'property' should be seen as playing only a marginal, rather than a central, role in our law of sale. In the United States, the law of sale (as contained in the Uniform Commercial Code) has been drafted without using the concept of 'property' at all. This is, of course, perfectly possible, just as it would be possible to draw up the rules for the game of football without using the word 'offside'. But it does have two consequences: first, each of the 'rules' set out above (as to risk, liability to pay the price, etc) has to be separately stated, and stated in more individual and detailed terms because it is not possible to use the word 'property' as a conceptual shortcut; and, secondly, there is no convenient 'peg' on which to hang any new rule to cover a situation that the draftsman may not have thought of. (By way of example, the Act contains no rule about the right to sue third parties, the issue which arose in *The Aliakmon*, above; but the court was able to use the established concept of 'property' to resolve the matter.)

The importance of the concept of 'the property' is highlighted when we look at a further question. As a matter of rock-bottom theory, it is the property in the goods which the buyer bargains for when he enters into a contract for the sale of goods—not their possession or use or any of the other aspects of ownership. This is so not simply because that is what the definition in s 2(1) says, but because it is well established by the cases that if the buyer does *not* get the ownership that he has bargained for, he can recover the whole of the price that he has paid, as money paid on a total failure of consideration, despite the fact that he may have had the possession and use of the goods for a considerable time before this fact is discovered: see *Rowland v Divall* (below, p 459). If the buyer in such a case chose instead to frame his claim in damages, he would of course receive a smaller sum, reflecting what he had lost in practical, rather than conceptual, terms.

2 RULES FOR DETERMINING WHEN THE PROPERTY PASSES

So many issues in our sale of goods law are made to turn on the question whether the property in the goods is still vested in the seller or has passed to the buyer that it is plainly a matter of the greatest importance to identify the point in time when the property passes. The Act deals with this in ss 16–19 by a few basic rules, supplemented by a number of presumptions.

(a) The background rules

(i) *No property can pass in unascertained goods*

Sale of Goods Act 1979, s 16

> Subject to section 20A below, where there is a contract for the sale of unascertained goods no property in the goods is transferred to the buyer unless and until the goods are ascertained.

This at first sight seems obvious: until one knows what is being sold, no question can arise of the buyer becoming owner of anything. Nevertheless, it is highly significant. The significance of this rule was made clear in *Re Wait* (above, p 298), where sellers of a part cargo of wheat became bankrupt after the buyers had paid for it: whatever the parties might have intended, the result under s 16 was that the buyers were left with a useless money claim against an insolvent defendant. *Re London Wine Co (Shippers) Ltd* [1986] PCC 121, below, offers a further illustration.

Re London Wine Co (Shippers) Ltd
[1986] PCC 121, Chancery Division

London Wine had stocks of wine in various warehouses. A number of customers had contracted to buy wine of a particular description from it (eg '40 cases Volnay Santenots 1969 Domaine Jacques Prieur') and, having paid, received so-called 'Certificates of Title' describing them as 'sole and beneficial owner' of the wine in question. The company charged the buyer for storage and insurance until he collected the wine or sold it to someone else. But there was no procedure for identifying or segregating the wine sold to any particular customer.

The company had charged all its assets to its bank; the bank later appointed a receiver. The issue was whether the wine in the warehouses belonged to the bank or the customers.

The court considered separately three typical cases:

(1) those (eg that of Mr Strong) where a customer had bought the company's total stock of a particular wine at the date of the purchase;

(2) those (eg that of Mr Button) where two or more customers had bought quantities of a particular wine which, taken together, exhausted the whole of the company's stock of that wine;

(3) those (eg that of Mr Bailey) where the purchase did not exhaust the particular stock, but there had been an acknowledgement that the appropriate quantity of the particular wine was being held to the customer's order. In some of these cases, the customer had pledged his right to the wine as security for a loan—for example, a customer called Vinum Ltd had pledged its wine to a finance company called Compass, and a similar acknowledgement had been given to the pledgee.

Oliver J held that in none of these instances had the property, or any other legal or equitable interest of a proprietary nature, passed to the buyer. The bank's security interest therefore prevailed, and the buyers were simply unsecured creditors for the return of the money which they had paid.

Oliver J: . . . There, then, are the three categories with which I have to deal and the question which has arisen in each case is whether the wines which have been sold belong to the purchasers and those claiming through or under them or whether on the relevant date they remained the company's property and so became subject to the charge in the debenture which then crystallised. I should perhaps say that there is no question of stocks being insufficient to fulfil all the purchase orders so that there is no competition between purchasers *inter se* . . .

As regards the case of Mr Strong and Mr Button, Mr Wright's primary submission on their behalf is that the legal title to the goods passed and that, accordingly, the matter ends there. If, however, that is wrong, he submits first that the goods became subject to a valid and effective trust before the relevant date, and, as an alternative to this, that each purchaser had, before the relevant date, a right to specific performance of his contract and that, when the floating charge crystallised, the bank took subject to that right. These two submissions apply equally to the third category and have been adopted and expanded by Mr Stamler on behalf of the respondents Vinum and Compass and since they are, therefore, common to all cases, and, if correct, are conclusive of the whole case, they can conveniently be dealt with first.

As regards the creation of a trust, this is put in this way. On the assumption that no property passed in the goods at law—and it is not argued that this could possibly be the case in the third category represented by Mr Bailey . . .—there was, it is submitted, clearly an intention that the property should pass so far as the company had it in its power to make it do so. One has only to look at the terms of its circulars with their references to 'your wines,' to the purchaser being 'the beneficial owner' and to the company having a lien. This is reinforced when one looks at the terms of the letters of confirmation which list the quantities and types of wine and confirm that the purchaser is 'the sole beneficial owner of these wines,' and is indeed further reinforced in the case of Compass and Vinum when reference is made to the master agreements with Compass and the company where the company joins in to warrant title to the wine. By issuing these documents, the acknowledged purpose of which was to enable the purchasers to deal with their wines by sale or charge, the company, it is said, evinced the clearest possible intention to declare itself a trustee . . .

. . . Mr Wright, in his reply, put it rather differently. A trust, he said, may be constituted not merely by direct and express declaration but also by the consequences flowing from the acts of the persons themselves to which consequences the law attaches the label 'trust.' A trust, to put it another way, is the technical description of a legal situation; and where you find (i) an intention to create a beneficial interest in someone else, (ii) an acknowledgment of that intention and (iii) property in the ownership of the person making the acknowledgment which answers the description in the acknowledgment, then there is, at the date of the acknowledgment, an effective and completed trust of all the property of the acknowledger answering to that description. This is, I think, in essence the same submission as that made by Mr Stamler—he submits that where one is dealing with a homogeneous mass there is no problem about certainty. So long as the mass can be identified and there is no uncertainty about the quantitative interest of the beneficiary, the court will find no difficulty in administering the trust if it once finds the necessary intention to create an equitable interest in property of the type comprised in the mass. I think, indeed, that if the case is to be made out at all, it must be put in this way, for the submission itself is based on the premise that there are no specific or ascertained goods in which the beneficiary is interested. Were it otherwise there would be no need to invoke the concept of trust for the title would have passed under the Sale of Goods Act (as, indeed, Mr Wright submits in categories 1 and 2, it did). . . . Thus if we postulate the case of the company having in warehouse 1,000 cases of a particular wine and selling 100 cases to X the circumstances of this case indicate, it is submitted, that the company created an equitable tenancy in common between itself and X in the whole 1,000 cases in the proportions of 9/10ths and 1/10th.

It is with regret that I feel compelled to reject these submissions...I find it impossible to spell either out of the acknowledgments signed by the company or out of the circumstances any such trust as is now sought to be set up. Granted that the references to 'beneficial interest' are appropriate words for the creation of a trust; granted, even (although this I think is very difficult to spell out) that that was the company's intention, it seems to me that any such trust must fail on the ground of uncertainty of subject-matter. I appreciate the point taken that the subject-matter is part of a homogeneous mass so that specific identity is of as little importance as it is, for instance, in the case of money. Nevertheless, as it seems to me, to create a trust it must be possible to ascertain with certainty not only what the interest of the beneficiary is to be but to what property it is to attach.

I cannot see how, for instance, a farmer who declares himself to be a trustee of two sheep (without identifying them) can be said to have created a perfect and complete trust whatever rights he may confer by such declaration as a matter of contract. And it would seem to me to be immaterial that at the time he has a flock of sheep out of which he could satisfy the interest....

I turn now, therefore, to the submissions peculiar to the individual cases. Now in the case of Mr Strong, although the goods were sold by generic description, it happened that at the material time the quantity described was in the company's possession and was the only wine of that description in its possession, although it is not claimed that it could not, without undue difficulty, obtain additional quantities from elsewhere if it required to do so. Mr Wright argues that the result of this was to ascertain the goods and that the property passed; and to make this good he has to rely either upon s 17 or upon an appropriation under s 18, r 5(1) of the Sale of Goods Act. Section 16 states quite clearly that the property is not transferred to the buyer unless and until the goods are ascertained but it is not a necessary corollary of this that the property does pass to the buyer when they are ascertained. To produce that result one either has had to find an appropriation (from which an intention to pass the property will be inferred) or one has to find an intention manifested in some other way. Mr Wright relies upon what has been referred to as an 'ascertainment by exhaustion' and has drawn my attention to the decision of Roche J in *Wait & James v Midland Bank* (1926) 31 Com Cas 172.

[His Lordship referred to the facts of that case, and continued:]

The decision in that case was one of obvious common sense because in fact from November 16th onwards there were no goods from which the seller could have fulfilled the contracts except the 850 quarters. They could, no doubt, have delivered 850 quarters of Australian wheat but not 850 quarters of 'ex store Avonmouth ex Thistleros [sic].' The instant case seems to me quite different. It is not and cannot be alleged that the sale to Mr Strong was a sale of specific goods. What the company undertook to do was to deliver so many cases and bottles of the specified type of wine 'lying in bond.' This does not in my judgment link the wine sold with any given consignment or warehouse. The fact that the company had at the date of the invoice that amount of wine and that amount only is really irrelevant to the contract. No doubt it could have fulfilled the order from this wine but it could equally have fulfilled it from any other source. It is not contended that there was any act of appropriation and Mr Wright's case is that the property passed under s 17 when the usual title letter mentioning the wine described in the invoice was sent some three months later, by which date, he says, the wine was ascertained. I cannot draw that conclusion from the material before me, for it seems to me clear that the company was, under the contract, at liberty to deliver to the purchaser any bottles of wine which tallied with the description. It never has been, therefore, ... ascertained what the goods are which are covered by the contract.

The argument in relation to the second category of case is very similar. ... In my view, the company remained free to fulfil the contracts to its various purchasers from any source, as, for instance, by importing further wine of the same description. That being so, the mere fact that the company sold quantities of wine which in fact exhausted all the stocks which it held cannot, in my judgment, have had the effect of passing a proprietary interest in those stocks to the various purchasers so that they can now claim the goods collectively and ignore the bank's charge....

Accordingly, I have felt compelled, perhaps rather reluctantly, to the conclusion that I must direct: (1) that all three categories of goods described in the schedule to the summons should be dealt with by the receiver as being the property of the company on the relevant date and so subject to the floating charge and (2) that no such goods are subject to any lien or other interest having priority to the floating charge in favour of the respondent purchasers or their respective assigns or mortgagees.

NOTES

1. A similar decision was reached by the Privy Council in the case of *Re Goldcorp Exchange Ltd* [1995] 1 AC 74, PC, where investors in New Zealand were invited to buy gold from Goldcorp which Goldcorp undertook to store on the customers' behalf. Each buyer received a certificate which purported to verify the fact that he was the owner of the gold he had bought; but in fact no gold was ever appropriated to any particular purchaser. The Privy Council held that no property had ever passed at law and no equitable interest had been created.

2. Atkin LJ's opinion in *Re Wait* that there was no room at all in sale of goods law for an equitable interest to be created puts the point too strongly, for of course the parties to a contract of sale can create an equitable interest in goods by express agreement (and may even do so as a term of their sale contract, as in some of the *Romalpa* cases: see below, p 497). The real effect of *Re Wait* and *Re London Wine* is to eliminate any possibility that such an interest will be held to have arisen by inference or by operation of law.

3. Note, however, one limitation on the express creation of an equitable interest in the buyer. Although this is possible in respect of a *proportion* of a given bulk (a one-third equitable interest in the 30 cases of Château Pétrus wine in the seller's warehouse), it is not possible in respect of a given *quantity* to be taken out of that bulk (a trust of 10 cases of Château Pétrus from the bulk). This is because such a trust would fail for want of certainty as to subject matter. See Oliver J's comments above on the hypothetical farmer's two sheep; also *Hunter v Moss* [1993] 1 WLR 934 at 939–940, per Colin Rimer QC, upheld on appeal at [1994] 1 WLR 452.

4. However, it should be noted that *Re Wait* and *Re London Wine* merely require segregation of the relevant goods from the rest of the *seller's* property. Once such separation has taken place, the fact that there may be many buyers, and that the goods to be taken by each of *them* remain undifferentiated, is irrelevant. This is because s 16 is satisfied by ascertainment of shares due to multiple buyers, and property may therefore pass at law. In *Re Stapylton Fletcher Ltd* [1994] 1 WLR 1181, a case otherwise similar to *London Wine*, the sellers had followed up each sale by segregating the relevant quantity of wine from their general trading stock and placing it into separate storage. Although no steps were taken to allocate particular lots of wine to individual sales (so that, eg, where two customers had bought different quantities of the same wine the company simply transferred the aggregate amount to the other store), it was held that there had been sufficient appropriation for the property to have passed. Where customers' orders had been aggregated, they held the total amount as tenants in common.

5. Where a seller possessing a bulk sells a quantity of goods corresponding to the amount in the bulk (eg a wine merchant selling 10 cases of Château Lafite 2008 when it possesses exactly 10 cases), it is a matter of interpretation whether he intends to appropriate those particular 10 cases. For a decision where this was held to be the case, see the technical excise tax case of *Customs & Excise Comrs v Everwine Ltd* [2003] EWCA Civ 953.

(ii) Transferring property in goods forming part of an undivided bulk

Re Wait, above, caused great difficulties to those who bought, and paid for, goods to be provided from a larger bulk: in particular, as in *Re Wait* itself, the very common commercial case of buyers of part cargoes (eg 20,000 tonnes of soya beans out of the 50,000 tonnes currently on board the MV *Poseidon* en route to Rotterdam). In 1993, the Law Commissions made recommendations for the reform of the law so as to meet a number of those criticisms. These recommendations ultimately became ss 20A and 20B of the Sale of Goods Act 1979, inserted in 1995.

Section 20A requires two things: (a) a contract for the sale of a specified quantity of unascertained goods forming part of a bulk identified either in the contract or by subsequent agreement; and (b) payment of the price in whole or in part. When these factors are present, then unless the parties agree otherwise, the buyer despite s 16 becomes an owner in common of the whole of the bulk. The share he obtains is proportionate to the quantity which he has contracted to buy, discounted by any proportion of the price then unpaid. Thus, if S contracts to sell to B 3,000 tonnes of soya beans out of the 10,000 tonnes on board the MV *Poseidon*, and B has paid half of the contract price, he and the seller become co-owners of the 10,000 tonnes in the proportions 15:85. If a second buyer agrees to buy the remaining 7,000 tonnes and pays the whole price, the seller and the two buyers become tenants in common in the respective proportions 15:15:70.

Insofar as a buyer has not paid, the general rule in s 16 remains applicable: no property can pass in the goods or the corresponding proportion of the goods unless they become ascertained by severance from the bulk.

We should note that the effect of the Act is not to make the buyer the owner of any particular goods. In the example above, B becomes merely a 15 per cent part-owner of the 10,000 tonnes: he does not become the owner of any particular 1,500 tonnes of soya beans until a further act of physical separation.

Once a buyer has become a part-owner of the bulk, he may transfer his proprietary rights to a sub-buyer. The extended definition of 'goods' in s 61(1) to include an undivided share in goods makes it clear that such a transaction will be a sale of goods—indeed, of specific goods—and not a mere assignment of the first buyer's contractual rights.

Section 20A(5) and (6), taken together, state that where a buyer who has paid part only of the price takes delivery of goods from the bulk, he is deemed in the first place to have taken the goods representing his share as a part-owner. So, if B in the example above takes delivery of 1,000 tonnes of soya beans from the bulk, it is his 15 per cent share which will be proportionately reduced.

Section 20A(4) deals with the possibility that the aggregate of the shares of a number of buyers may exceed the whole of the bulk (eg because the seller has contracted to sell a greater quantity of goods than he actually has, or because part has been lost by (for example) shrinkage or theft): the undivided shares of all the buyers are reduced proportionately.

Section 20B provides as follows:

Sale of Goods Act 1979, s 20B

(1) A person who has become an owner in common of a bulk by virtue of section 20A above shall be deemed to have consented to—
  (a) any delivery of goods out of the bulk to any other owner in common of the bulk, being goods which are due to him under his contract;
  (b) any dealing with or removal, delivery or disposal of goods in the bulk by any other person who is an owner in common of the bulk in so far as the goods fall within that co-owner's undivided share in the bulk at the time of the dealing, removal, delivery or disposal.
(2) No cause of action shall accrue to anyone against a person by reason of that person having acted in accordance with paragraph (a) or (b) of subsection (1) above in reliance on any consent deemed to have been given under that subsection.
(3) Nothing in this section or section 20A above shall—
  (a) impose an obligation on a buyer of goods out of a bulk to compensate any other buyer of goods out of that bulk for any shortfall in the goods received by that other buyer;
  (b) affect any contractual arrangement between buyers of goods out of a bulk for adjustments between themselves; or
  (c) affect the rights of any buyer under his contract.

Summed up, this means that a rule of 'first come, first served' applies where a bulk is subject to partial interests under s 20A. Any person entitled may take either his share or, if he is a buyer, his full contractual entitlement: if he does so, he is protected from any liability in conversion to the others, even if as a result someone else gets less than he is entitled to. But any action by a buyer against his seller for breach of contract is preserved.

We should note that the operation of ss 20A and 20B is not confined to the case where a seller is insolvent (as in *Re Wait*), although it will very commonly be in such a situation that the new law will be invoked. A buyer who becomes a co-owner under s 20A will have other rights, such as a right to sue a third party in tort. It is also confined to the case where the goods supplied must come from a given bulk. Thus the decisions in *London Wine* and *Goldcorp*, where there was no specific bulk from which goods to fulfil the contract were to be obtained, are not affected.

For commentary on the law, see T Burns, 'Better Late than Never: The Reform of the Law on the Sale of Goods Forming Part of a Bulk' (1996) 59 MLR 260; J Ulph, 'The Sale of Goods (Amendment) Act 1995: Co-ownership and the Rogue Seller' [1996] LMCLQ 93; and on the acquisition of *equitable* interests in part of a bulk, S Worthington, 'Sorting Out Ownership Interests in a Bulk: Gifts, Sales and Trusts' [1999] JBL 1.

(iii) 'Ascertainment'

Goods which are unascertained—ie not 'identified and agreed on' at the time when the contract of sale is made (s 61(1))—will become 'ascertained' by being 'identified in accordance with the agreement after the time a contract of sale is made' (per Atkin LJ in *Re Wait* [1927] 1 Ch 606 at 630). Normally this will follow from the act of one or both of the parties or someone designated by them, for example a warehouseman. Sometimes, where the contract goods are capable of prospective identification (eg 'all the production of gas platform No 123'), ascertainment may happen automatically, when the goods come into existence. Also, occasionally, ascertainment may take place without the act of either party, 'by exhaustion'. See s 18, r 5(3), (4) of the Act:

Sale of Goods Act 1979, s 18, r 5(3), (4)

(3) Where there is a contract for the sale of a specified quantity of unascertained goods in a deliverable state forming part of a bulk which is identified either in the contract or by subsequent agreement between the parties and the bulk is reduced to (or to less than) that quantity, then, if the buyer under that contract is the only buyer to whom goods are then due out of the bulk—
   (a) the remaining goods are to be taken as appropriated to that contract at the time when the bulk is so reduced; and
   (b) the property in those goods then passes to that buyer.

(4) Paragraph (3) above applies also (with the necessary modifications) where a bulk is reduced to (or to less than) the aggregate of the quantities due to a single buyer under separate contracts relating to that bulk and he is the only buyer to whom goods are then due out of that bulk.

This provision, inserted in 1995, reflects the common law position: see *Wait & James v Midland Bank* (1926) 31 Com Cas 172 and *The Elafi* [1981] 2 Lloyd's Rep 679.

(b) The basic rule: ownership passes when intended to pass

The primary rule governing the passing of property is contained in s 17: the property in the goods is transferred at such time as the parties intend it to be transferred. Section 17(2) adds, not very helpfully, that for the purpose of ascertaining the intention of the parties, regard is to be had to the terms of the contract, the conduct of the parties, and the circumstances of the case.

An important point is that there is no requirement of physical delivery to transfer ownership: the transfer may take place by mere agreement. In this English law is in contrast with some other European systems of law. In Germany, for example, by contrast, ownership can only pass where there is also a delivery of possession: see the German Civil Code, Art 929.

Section 17 is subject to three exceptions. One is s 16, mentioned above: whatever the parties may agree, no title can pass in goods unless and until goods are ascertained, except to the extent that s 20A applies. Secondly, a seller cannot in the nature of things pass, or reserve, legal title in goods once they have ceased to exist, for example through being transmuted into something else (as in the case of resin being made into chipboard: *Borden (UK) Ltd v Scottish Timber Products Ltd* (below, p 508), or consumed, as in the case of fuel oil supplied to a ship: *PST Energy 7 Shipping LLC v OW Bunker Malta Ltd* [2016] UKSC 23, [2016] 2 WLR 1193 (above, p 300)). The third exception concerns future goods. In the nature of things there can be no transfer of title to a buyer of goods the seller does not yet himself possess, and still less to goods that do not yet exist. But a purported sale of future goods IS not without effect. Section 5(3) states that where the seller purports to effect a present sale of future goods, the contract operates as an agreement to sell the goods when obtained.

It follows that the parties are free to express an intention which is the opposite of that which would normally be inferred, and that the court will give effect to such an intention. So, for instance, in *Re Blyth Shipbuilding & Dry Docks Co Ltd* [1926] Ch 494, CA, the parties to a shipbuilding contract agreed that on payment of the first instalment of the price the property in the vessel should pass to the buyers.[1] On the builders' insolvency the buyers were held to be owners of the uncompleted vessel, even though in an ordinary case it would plainly have been expected that no property would pass until the ship was finished. Conversely, it is very common for goods to be sold and delivered on credit on the basis that no property passes until payment has been made, rather than at or about the time of delivery. Conditional sales and sales under reservation of title (below, p 497) are straightforward examples.

However, the parties' expressed intention sometimes has to be interpreted in the light of considerations of practicality or by weightier rules of law. Thus, in *Re Blyth Shipbuilding*, the court declined to give literal effect to a further provision in the contract that 'all materials appropriated' for building the vessel should also become the property of the buyers: this would have made them owners of all the unworked material and the surplus and scrap material that did not end up incorporated into the ship—a result which the parties could not have intended.

Section 17 allows the court to give effect to the implied, as well as the express, intention of the parties. In *Re Anchor Line (Henderson Bros) Ltd* [1937] Ch 1, where there was a contract to sell a crane on credit, the court inferred an intention that property should remain with the seller from the fact that there was an express clause placing the *risk* on the buyer. It reasoned that since this clause would have been unnecessary if the property had passed when the contract was made, the parties must have intended the opposite. Again, despite the normal rule that in the case of goods shipped from seller to buyer property passes on handing over to the carrier (s 18, r 5(2)), in CIF and similar contracts the inference is invariably drawn that property is not to pass unless and until the shipping documents have been handed over and accepted (below, p 545).

(c) The statutory presumptions as to passing of property: s 18

Section 17 is the formal *rule of law* relating to the passing of property. But there are many cases in which s 17 will give no guidance, because there is nothing in the express terms of their contract or the surrounding circumstances to throw light on the issue. So the Act, in s 18, sets up a series of *presumptive rules* for ascertaining the intention of the parties which the court can apply. However, we must always bear in mind the opening words of s 18 itself, echoing those of s 17, 'Unless a different intention appears . . .': the 'rules' in s 18 are no more than prima facie *presumptions as to the intention of the parties* which may be rebutted by evidence to the contrary; they are not to be regarded as rules of law.

(i) Rule 1: unconditional contracts for the sale of specific goods

Where there is an *unconditional* contract for the sale of *specific goods* which are *in a deliverable state*, r 1 states the property in the goods passes to the buyer when the contract is

---

[1] This was a common technique in the 1920s to protect vessel buyers from shipyards' all-too-common insolvency. It is no longer used: today, property in the vessel invariably passes only on delivery, with the buyer being protected instead by a bank guarantee to return instalments paid in the event of insolvency.

made; and that it is immaterial whether the time of payment or the time of delivery, or both, are postponed.

Dennant v Skinner & Collom

[1948] 2 KB 164, King's Bench Division

At an auction of cars held by Dennant, a Standard car was knocked down for £345 to a man calling himself King, who also bought five other vehicles. King falsely said that he was the son of a reputable motor dealer and, in reliance on this statement, Dennant allowed him to pay with an uncleared cheque and take the Standard car away, after signing a document acknowledging that the ownership of the vehicles would not pass to him until payment had been received under the cheque. The cheque was dishonoured on presentation. The car was later sold to Collom who resold to Skinner. Dennant claimed the return of the car, as his property; but Hallett J held that property had passed to King on the fall of the hammer, and that the subsequent purported reservation of ownership by Dennant was ineffective.

Hallett J (after dealing with a technical point based on the then criminal law): I come now to consider the second point on which the plaintiff relies, which I understand is this; that the property in the circumstances of this case did not pass until the price was paid by the cheque being in order or cash substituted for it. The circumstances in regard to that I have already stated, and it remains only to consider the law. In the first place, as I have said, I think that a contract of sale is concluded at an auction sale on the fall of the hammer. The Sale of Goods Act 1893, s 18, r 1, provides: 'Where there is an unconditional contract for the sale of specific goods, in a deliverable state, the property in the goods passes to the buyer when the contract is made, and it is immaterial whether the time of payment or the time of delivery, or both, be postponed.' Accordingly, upon the fall of the hammer the property of this car passed to King unless that prima facie rule is excluded from applying because of a different intention appearing or because there was some condition in the contract which prevented the rule from applying. In my view, this was clearly an unconditional contract of sale, and I can see nothing whatever to make a different intention appear. The only evidence upon which it was ever suggested to exist was the printed conditions, but I can see nothing in those conditions to negative an intention that the property should pass on the fall of the hammer. I think the conditions are entirely consistent with such an intention. By the Sale of Goods Act, s 28: 'Unless otherwise agreed, delivery of the goods and payment of the price are concurrent conditions,' and finally, by yet another section of the Act, namely, s 39(1)(a), an unpaid seller of goods has a lien on the goods or right to retain them for the price while he is in possession of them, and he also has a right of re-sale as limited by the Act. Passing of the property and right to possession are two different things: here the property had passed upon the fall of the hammer, but still Mr Dennant had a right to retain possession of the goods until payment was made. If, when he was ready to deliver the goods, payment was not made, he could have sued for the price, or he could have exercised powers of re-sale, and he could have secured himself by way of lien on the goods for the price, but once he chose, for reasons good, bad, or indifferent as a result of statements fraudulent or honest, to part with the possession of the vehicle by giving delivery of it, he then lost his seller's lien and no longer had a right to possession of the vehicle. . . .

In my view, therefore, the second contention for the plaintiff also fails. However, there was a third aspect of the matter and that arises out of the document which I have already read. Now the document in its terms contemplates that the ownership of the vehicle has not passed to the bidder, but, as I have already said, in my judgment it had passed upon the fall of the hammer, and if subsequently the bidder executed the document acknowledging that ownership of the vehicle would not pass to him, that could not have any effect on what had already taken place. Can it be said that this document and the transaction it records as regards payment had the effect of divesting the property from King and re-vesting it in Mr Dennant, the seller? That is the only way in which Mr Brundrit has been able to suggest it that the document assists the plaintiff. I have considered that aspect of the matter, but I do not think that such a view of the document is sound. In my view the property had passed on the fall of the hammer; the right to possession had passed when Mr Dennant, persuaded and misled by King's lies, parted with his seller's lien, and there was nothing left upon which Mr Dennant could found a claim in detinue against some third person, in this case Mr Skinner, who was thus in possession of the vehicle.

The result seems to me to be that here the sufferer from the lies of King and from the reliance which Mr Dennant unfortunately placed on him must be Mr Dennant himself and not the innocent parties who are represented by the defendant and the third party in this action. Accordingly there must be judgment for the defendant and the third party.

In order for r 1 to apply, all three of the conditions indicated by the phrases italicised on p 338 above must be met. 'Specific goods' is a term which has already been discussed (above, p 305); we proceed now to consider the concepts of 'unconditional' contract and 'deliverable state'.

Unconditional 'Unconditional' obviously means 'not subject to any conditions', but this is not very helpful, since the term 'condition' is itself notorious for the many different meanings or shades of meaning which it may have in the law of contract. (Professor Stoljar once identified 12!—see 'The Contractual Concept of Condition' (1953) 69 LQR 485.) In two early cases, *Varley v Whipp* [1900] 1 QB 513 and *Ollett v Jordan* [1918] 2 KB 41, contracts were held to be 'conditional' in the present context because the goods were defective and hence conditions implied by the Act as to conformity with description (s 13) and what is now satisfactory quality (s 14(2)) remained unfulfilled. This cannot be right, however, since if it were s 18, r 1 could never apply to defective goods (see, eg, Benjamin, para 5–019). Instead, the preferable view is that 'unconditional' means 'not subject to any condition upon the fulfilment of which the passing of the property depends'. Although this leaves us with a rather question-begging piece of reasoning—the property passes if the contract is unconditional; the contract is unconditional if there is nothing to prevent the property from passing—it will not be the only legal definition that is subject to this criticism, and is probably the best available. One example would be a contract for the sale of arms specifically made conditional on approval by a government body in the seller's state. Another example of a contract that is not unconditional in this sense is a contract for the sale of things attached to or forming part of the soil; here there will usually (and in some cases necessarily) be an implied condition that property in the goods will not pass until they have been severed from the freehold. However, as the cases of *Kursell v Timber Operators & Contractors Ltd* and *Underwood v Burgh Castle Cement* (see below) show, there may also be other grounds in such circumstances for holding that the property has not passed.

Deliverable state There is a statutory definition of 'deliverable state'. Section 61(5) provides that goods are in a deliverable state when they are in such a state that the buyer would under the contract be bound to take delivery of them. Again, there are problems with this definition. If the goods do not answer their description or are not of satisfactory quality, the buyer has the right to reject them for breach of condition (see ss 11(3), 13, 14(2) and below, Chapter 11). So it might be inferred that the property could never pass in goods which were defective in any respect such as this. But to accept this reasoning is in effect to revive the discredited arguments in *Varley v Whipp* and *Ollett v Jordan* referred to above; and in any case it is worth noting that the Act does *not* say that goods which the buyer is not bound to accept are not in a deliverable state. Although the question has not been the subject of any direct judicial ruling, it seems that goods are likely to be regarded as being in a deliverable state if nothing substantial remains to be done to them by or on behalf of the seller pending their handing over to the buyer. Professor Goode, for instance, suggests that r 1 should be read as applying 'where, *on the assumption that the goods are what they purport to be*, the seller has not, by the terms of the contract, undertaken to do anything to them as a prerequisite of the buyer's acceptance of delivery' (Goode, para 8.87). Such cases as have been reported on the meaning of 'deliverable state' have been concerned with more straightforward issues.

Kursell v Timber Operators & Contractors Ltd
[1927] 1 KB 298, Court of Appeal

See the extract from the judgment of Scrutton LJ quoted above, p 307.

Underwood Ltd v Burgh Castle Brick & Cement Syndicate Ltd
[1922] 1 KB 123, King's Bench Division

For the facts, see above, p 304.

Rowlatt J: The sale was that of a specific chattel to be delivered by the plaintiffs, but the fact that it was to be delivered by them is not the test whether the property passed. The test is whether anything remained to be done to the engine by the sellers to put it into a deliverable state; and by that I understand a state in which the thing will be the article contracted for by the buyer; I do not mean deliverable in the sense that it is properly packed or anything of that kind. It must have everything done to it that the sellers had to do to it as an article. I do not think therefore that the fact by itself that the sellers had to take the engine to pieces would postpone the time when the property passed. Many chattels have to be taken to pieces before they can be delivered—eg a sideboard or a billiard table; nevertheless the property in these passes on the sale and is not postponed until the article is actually taken to pieces and delivered. I do not, therefore, lay any stress on the fact of the engine having to be taken to pieces. I think the important point is that the parties were dealing with an article which was a fixture to the premises, and that is different from the case of a loose chattel. The buyers' intention was to buy an article which would be a loose chattel when the processes of detaching and dismantling it were completed, and to convert it into a loose chattel these processes had first to be performed. The case of a tenant's fixtures seems an analogous case. It seems a safe rule to adopt that if a fixture has to be detached so as to make it a chattel again, the act of detaching has to be done before the chattel can be deliverable.

Philip Head & Sons Ltd v Showfronts Ltd
[1970] 1 Lloyd's Rep 140, Queen's Bench Division

Showfronts contracted with Heads to supply and lay fitted carpeting for a number of rooms in an office block in Oxford St which they were refurbishing. The carpet for the largest room, a showroom measuring about 40 ft × 20 ft, had to be made from several lengths stitched together: it was very unwieldy and took up to six men to lift it. After being assembled, it was left on the premises on a Friday afternoon and stolen over the weekend. The court held that it had not been in a 'deliverable state' until it had been satisfactorily laid, and so had been the sellers' property and at their risk when stolen.

Mocatta J: The problem here is, I think, however, whether it can be said that carpeting in a deliverable state was unconditionally appropriated to the contract. That phrase is defined in s 62(4) of the statute as follows:

> Goods are in a 'deliverable state' within the meaning of this Act when they are in such a state that the buyer would under the contract be bound to take delivery of them.

There is not much assistance in the authorities as to the meaning of this phrase. It is, however, both interesting and, I think, helpful to read a passage from an opinion of Lord Blackburn in *Seath & Co v Moore* (1886) 11 App Cas 350, in which many of the points subsequently codified in the Sale of Goods Act 1893, including some of the problems which I have to deal with here, are discussed. It is true that that case was one dealing with problems arising out of a shipbuilding contract, but in this particular passage Lord Blackburn is purporting to state the relevant principles of English law in general terms. He stated in relation to the passing of property (ibid, at p 370):

> It is essential that the article should be specific and ascertained in a manner binding on both parties, for unless that be so it cannot be construed as a contract to pass the property in that article. And in general, if there are things remaining to be done by the seller to the article before it is in the state in which it is to be finally delivered to the purchaser, the contract will not be construed to be one to pass the property till those things are done. . . .

I find that passage to give valuable guidance here.

I have described as best I can the state of the carpeting subsequently stolen at the time that it came back to these premises after having been stitched up; it was plainly a heavy bundle, very difficult to move. Although I have determined that this was a contract to which the Sale of Goods Act, 1893, applied, nevertheless an important feature of it was undoubtedly the laying of the carpeting following on the planning. It seems to me that one has to consider—in each case it is a case of fact—where there is work to be done in relation to the article sold before the contractual obligations of the sellers are completed, what is the relevant importance of that work in relation to the contract when deciding whether the property has passed and in particular whether the article or goods in question is or are at a particular moment of time in a deliverable state under s 18, r 5(1). I think one is entitled to apply everyday common sense to the matter; a householder, for example, purchasing carpeting under a contract providing that it should be delivered and laid in his house would be very surprised to be told that carpeting, which was in bales which he could hardly move deposited by his contractor in his garage, was then in a deliverable state and his property.

I take the view because of the condition of this carpeting at the time it was stolen and the importance of the last stage in the obligations to be performed by the plaintiffs under this contract, that at the moment when this carpeting was stolen it had not been unconditionally appropriated to the contract in a deliverable state, and accordingly, in my judgment, the property had not passed at the moment that the carpeting was stolen. In those circumstances the plaintiffs' case must fail. . . .

NOTES

1. *Head v Showfronts* was technically concerned with s 18, r 5(1), requiring unconditional appropriation of goods 'in a deliverable state', and not with s 18, r 1. But it remains relevant to the present circumstances.

2.   It is probably true today to say that s 18, r 1 is a relatively weak presumption. Diplock LJ said in *RV Ward Ltd v Bignall* [1967] 1 QB 534 at 545 that 'The governing rule…is in section 17, and in modern times very little is needed to give rise to the inference that the property in specific goods is to pass only on delivery or payment.'

QUESTION

All goods sold in commerce today are insured. Hence where they are lost or damaged in the course of the sale an important (indeed, perhaps the most important) issue is who should insure them. Now, if A Ltd agrees unconditionally to sell B Ltd the computers currently in A's warehouse, who is in a better position to insure them pending delivery? Is it A, who knows the warehouse, the security measures, and the way the goods are stored in it, or B, who may well know none of these things? How does your answer fit in with the presumption in s 18, r 1 that property (and hence risk) pass as soon as the agreement is made?

(ii) Rule 2: specific goods to be put into a deliverable state by the seller

Where there is a contract for the sale of *specific goods* and the seller is bound to do something to the goods for the purpose of putting them into a *deliverable state*, r 2 states as a presumption that the property will not pass until the seller has done that thing and the buyer has notice that it has been done. The operation of the rule may be illustrated by two cases which have already been mentioned.

Underwood Ltd v Burgh Castle Brick & Cement Syndicate
[1922] 1 KB 123, King's Bench Division

See above, p 341.

Philip Head & Sons Ltd v Showfronts Ltd
[1970] 1 Lloyd's Rep 140, Queen's Bench Division

See above, p 341.

Typical examples might be a sale of second-hand earth-moving equipment to be refurbished by the seller, or an export sale of a specific new fire-truck to be fitted out with instructions and paperwork in the language of the country of the buyer.

In most respects, r 2 seems straightforward enough. The terms 'specific goods' and 'deliverable state' have been discussed above, at pp 305 and 338. It should be observed that it is necessary not only that the goods should be put into a deliverable state, but that the buyer must also have notice of this before the property will pass.

The one point which may cause some surprise is that the wording of the rule is restricted to acts to be performed *by the seller*. This is understandable as regards work to be done by the buyer. Since in most such cases the buyer will be bound to accept delivery whether or not the work is done, it is unlikely that such work will be a condition of the goods being in a 'deliverable state', or of the passing of property. If in *Underwood Ltd v Burgh Castle Brick & Cement Syndicate*, above, the dismantling and loading had been the buyer's affair, it would not be difficult to infer that delivery was to be taken by the buyer in situ, and that risk was to pass at latest at that point. But what if, by contrast, the job is to be done by a third party? Here, it would seem best to apply the same solution as under r 2: presumably the intention was that the transaction would be complete only once the goods had been modified as required.

(iii) Rule 3: specific goods to be weighed or measured, etc by the seller for the purpose of ascertaining the price

Where there is a contract for the sale of *specific goods* in a *deliverable state*, but the seller is bound to weigh, measure, test, or do some other act or thing to the goods for the purpose of ascertaining the price, r 3 lays down a presumption that the property in the goods will not pass until the act or thing has been done and the buyer has notice that it has been done. This is not a common situation today. But a plausible example might be a contract to sell five specific containers of scrap steel to be paid for at the rate of £x per tonne, with the seller undertaking to weigh them before collection by the buyer.

Most of the comments made in relation to r 2 apply also to r 3. The following case underlines the fact that the presumption laid down by r 3 applies only in the case where the act in question is to be performed *by the seller*.

Nanka-Bruce v Commonwealth Trust
[1926] AC 77, Privy Council

The facts appear from the judgment.

Lord Shaw (delivering the opinion of the Privy Council): This is an appeal from the judgment of the Full Court of the Gold Coast Colony[2] affirming a judgment of Beatty J without a jury.

The appellant is a planter and shipper of cocoa, carrying on business at Accra. The respondents carry on business at Accra as general exporters and importers.

One, Laing (the co-defendant with the respondents in the action), was an editor of a newspaper in Accra and a buyer and seller of cocoa. He had previously made purchases of cocoa from the appellant.

The claim of the appellant against the respondents is for damages for conversion of 160 bags of cocoa. The history of this cocoa, so far as is material to the present case, and stated neutrally, is as follows: The appellant entered into a general arrangement with Laing, under which Laing was to receive cocoa from the appellant at the price of 59s per load of 60 lbs. It was recognized that Laing would resell the cocoa to other merchants, and that when these other merchants took delivery by a transfer of the consignment notes the goods would be weighed up at their premises and the weights tested there. That operation being completed, the amount payable by Laing on the contract made with the appellant was, of course, ascertained.

On April 24, 1920, the 160 bags of cocoa were despatched by rail by the appellant to Accra under a consignment note made out in favour of Laing. Laing then acted with the goods thus: He sold them to the respondents, and handed to the respondents' representatives the railway consignment note. The respondents took delivery and, against a large debt due to them from Laing, credited him with the price at which they had purchased the goods. Laing's conduct seems unquestionably to

2 Now Ghana.

have been dishonest conduct. Both Courts have, however, found that the conduct of the respond-ents was quite honest, and that they purchased the goods for value and without any notice of any objection to, or defect in, the title of Laing, or the contract under which he had acquired the goods. Both Courts have concurrently found that Laing purchased the cocoa from the appellant. The appellant attacked this finding as erroneous in law, alleging that the weighing up of the goods must be treated as having been a condition precedent to an operative sale.

Their Lordships agree that the provision as to the weight of the goods being tested was not a condition precedent to a sale. The goods were transferred, their price was fixed, and the testing was merely to see whether the goods fitted the weights as represented, but this testing was not suspensive of the contract of sale or a condition precedent to it. To effect such suspension or im-pose such a condition would require a clear contract between vendor and vendee to that effect. In this case there was no contract whatsoever to carry into effect the weighing, which was simply a means to satisfy the purchaser that he had what he had bargained for and that the full price claimed per the contract was therefore due.

[His Lordship referred to *Cundy v Lindsay* (below, p 405), and continued:]

Applying that law their Lordships find no difficulty in affirming that these goods were de facto sold to Laing by the appellant, and that so far as the respondents were concerned they were honestly and for value bought by them from Laing. Suppose it to be the case that the appellant, defrauded by Laing, to whom he had sold the goods, could have treated the transaction as void-able on that account and sued Laing for remission accordingly, that cannot in law form a ground of impeachment as against buyers in good faith and for value from the person, like Laing, thus vested in the goods by a de facto contract.

This is an end of the case. . . .

NOTES

1. See too *Turley v Bates* (1863) 2 Hurl & C 200.

2. In *National Coal Board v Gamble* [1959] 1 QB 11 (a case concerned with a sale of *unascer-tained* goods), coal was loaded on to a lorry pursuant to a bulk contract and taken to a weigh-bridge on the seller's premises, where the lorry was found to be nearly 4 tons overladen. The driver said that he would take his chance on the overloading, took the weighbridge ticket and left the premises. He was later stopped by the police and his firm convicted of permitting the lorry to be overweight. The Divisional Court held that the Coal Board, as seller, had rightly been con-victed of aiding and abetting the driver in the commission of the offence, since until the goods had been weighed (so that the price could be ascertained) and the weighbridge ticket handed to the driver, the property in the coal remained with the seller, whose employee (the weighbridge-man) could have insisted that the excess be unloaded.

QUESTION

Once the property has passed to the buyer, the seller may in principle sue the buyer for the price (see s 49(1)). In *Nanka-Bruce* it would not have been difficult to quantify the amount which the seller could claim, because the cocoa had already been provisionally weighed. But if the buyer is to do the weighing and the goods are destroyed before the weighing has been done, how is the price to be reckoned? The following case (which turned on the fact that *risk*, as distinct from property, had passed to the buyer), gives a clue.

Castle v Playford
(1872) LR 7 Exch 98, Court of Exchequer Chamber

Castle agreed to sell to Playford a cargo of ice,[3] to be shipped to a port in the UK and paid for on arrival at the rate of £1 per ton 'weighed on board during delivery'. Under the contract, the risk lay with the buyer. The ship and cargo were lost at sea. The court ruled that the buyer was liable to pay the price which, in the circumstances, had to be an estimated price.

> **Blackburn J**: My impression is, if it were necessary to decide it now, that the effect of this contract is that the property passed; but I think it is unnecessary to decide the matter. The parties in this case have agreed, whether the property passed or not, that the purchaser should, from the time he received the bills of lading, take upon himself all risks and dangers of the seas; and, according to Mr Littler's construction, I do not see what risk he took upon himself at all, unless it was this—that he said, 'If the property perishes by the dangers of the seas, I shall take the risk of having lost the property, whether it be mine or not.'
>
> The difficulty in the court below arose in reference to the alteration of the time of payment. No doubt it was afterwards provided that payment should be made on the ship's arrival and according to what was delivered. Now here, the ship and cargo have gone to the bottom of the sea; but in the cases of *Alexander v Gardner* ((1835) 1 Bing NC 671), and *Fragano v Long* ((1825) 4 B & C 219), it was held, that if the property did perish before the time for payment came, the time being dependent upon delivery, and if the delivery was prevented by the destruction of the property, the purchaser was to pay an equivalent sum. In the present case, when the ship went down there would be so much ice on board, and, in all probability, upon an ordinary voyage so much would have melted; and what the defendant has taken upon himself to pay is the amount which, in all probability, would have been payable for the ice.
>
> [**Cockburn CJ** delivered a concurring judgment. **Mellor, Brett**, and **Grove JJ** concurred.]

(iv) *Rule 4: goods delivered on approval or on sale or return*

When goods have been delivered to a buyer 'on approval' or on 'sale or return', or other similar terms, r 4 prescribes that the property passes to the buyer:

> (a) when he signifies his approval or acceptance to the seller or does any other act adopting or approving the transaction; or
> (b) if he does not signify his approval or acceptance but retains the goods without giving notice of rejection, then, if a time has been fixed for the return of the goods, on the expiration of that time and, if no time has been fixed, on the expiration of a reasonable time.

The expressions 'on approval' or 'on sale or return' may be taken to have the same meaning in English law—namely, that the person to whom the goods have been delivered has the option of buying the goods or not as he chooses, and until he has bought them (or is deemed by r 4 to have done so), property remains with the seller. Strictly speaking, therefore, there is no

---

[3] A common (and valuable) subject of trade in the days before the advent of cheap refrigeration.

'sale' at all, but merely an option to buy, until the buyer has made his decision. In contrast, in the United States the two expressions 'on approval' and 'on sale or return' are given different meanings: there, the former term is used in the same sense as in England, but 'on sale or return' means that there *is* a sale, and the buyer becomes the owner, subject however to a condition that he may for any reason he sees fit return the goods within an agreed or a reasonable time and rescind the transaction.

If the default rule on r 4 applies, the seller's protection is very limited. This is because where the buyer sells or pledges the goods, this of itself amounts to an act 'adopting the transaction', whether or not the buyer has taken, or intends to take, any steps to pay. It follows that title passes immediately to the buyer and through him to the ultimate purchaser, as illustrated by the following case.

Kirkham v Attenborough
[1897] 1 QB 201, Court of Appeal

Kirkham, a manufacturing jeweller, delivered to Winter a quantity of jewellery on sale or return. Winter pledged some of the jewellery to Attenborough. In this action, Kirkham claimed that the goods pledged were still his property, but was unsuccessful.

Lopes LJ: The position of a person who has received goods on sale or return is that he has the option of becoming the purchaser of them, and may become so in three different ways. He may pay the price, or he may retain the goods beyond a reasonable time for their return, or he may do an act inconsistent with his being other than a purchaser. The words of the Act are difficult to construe; but it seems to me that if the recipient of the goods retains them for an unreasonable time he does something inconsistent with the exercise of his option to return them, and thereby adopts the transaction. So if he does any other act inconsistent with their return, as if he sells them or pledges them, because if he pledges them he no longer has the free control over them so as to be in a position to return them. In all these cases he brings himself within the words of the section by adopting the transaction, and the property in the goods passes to him. If that is the state of the law, applying it to this case, it is clear that the plaintiff is not entitled to recover from the defendant either the goods or their price, and the judgment in favour of the plaintiff cannot be supported.

[**Lord Esher MR** delivered a concurring judgment. **Rigby LJ** concurred.]

For the buyer to 'adopt' a transaction under r 4(a), there must be some act of election on his part (by words or conduct). It is not sufficient for the seller simply to show that the buyer is unable to return the goods. In *Elphick v Barnes* (1880) 5 CPD 321 a horse which was delivered on eight days' trial died from an illness on the third day. Lord Denman CJ, treating the contract as one of a sale on approval, said (at 326): 'Here, I think, there was no sale at the time of the horse's death, which happened without the fault of either party, and therefore that the action for goods sold and delivered must fail.'

Rule 4, like the other rules in s 18, only lays down a presumption. It is open to the parties to make any other arrangement as regards the passing of the property—for instance, that it shall not pass to the buyer until the price has been paid. This is an obvious move for the well-advised seller in the light of *Kirkham v Attenborough* (above), as appears in *Weiner v Gill*.

Weiner v Gill

[1906] 2 KB 574, Court of Appeal

Weiner, a jeweller, delivered a diamond brooch and other articles to another jeweller, Huhn, on the terms: 'On approbation. On sale only for cash or return. . . . Goods had on approbation or on sale or return remain the property of Samuel Weiner until such goods are settled for or charged.' Huhn delivered the articles to Longman who said that he had a customer for them, but in fact he pawned them with Gill.

> **Sir Gorell Barnes P**: The only question which we have to consider is whether the property in these goods had passed from the plaintiff to Huhn. As a general rule a person in the possession of goods cannot convey a better title to them than he himself has. There are exceptions to that rule, examples of which are to be found in the Factors Act 1889, and in s 25 of the Sale of Goods Act 1893. It has been argued that in the present case the defendants are protected by s 25 of the latter Act, but, having regard to the facts of the case, I do not think that that argument can be successfully maintained. In considering the question whether the property passed from the plaintiff to Huhn regard must be had to the terms of s 17 and s 18 of the Sale of Goods Act.
>
> [The President read the sections and continued:]
>
> If the present case were one falling within the terms 'on sale or return' in r 4, then the case of *Kirkham v Attenborough* [above] would no doubt be in point, because, as was said by Wightman J in *Moss v Sweet* ((1851) 16 QB 493), the meaning of a contract of sale or return is 'that the goods were to be taken as sold, unless returned within a reasonable time.' In the present case, however, we are dealing with a contract of an entirely different character, for on the face of the contract there appears a different intention as to when the property shall pass from that laid down in r 4 of s 18. The terms of the contract shew a clear intention that no property in the goods shall vest in Huhn until he has paid for them or been charged by the plaintiff for them. So that no means existed by which the buyer could exercise such an option as was indicated in r 4. The only thing he could do was to pay cash for them or to get the plaintiff to debit him with the price. That was not done, and therefore, in my opinion, the property in the goods never passed to Huhn, and consequently the defendants have no answer to the plaintiff's claim.
>
> [**Lord Alverstone CJ** and **Farwell LJ** delivered concurring judgments.]

QUESTION

Gill was in the position of a bona fide purchaser without notice of the special terms of Weiner's contract, and with no possibility of finding out about them. Should the law do more to protect such a person?

Paragraph (b) of r 4, in contrast with para (a), contemplates that the buyer under a contract on sale or return terms may sometimes become the owner of the goods by inaction. This is illustrated by the case which follows.

Poole v Smith's Car Sales (Balham) Ltd

[1962] 1 WLR 744, Court of Appeal

Both parties were car dealers. In August 1960 Poole, who was about to go on holiday, delivered a Vauxhall car to Smiths with authority to sell it, provided that he received £325, Smiths being

allowed to retain any sum received in excess of that figure. In October Poole telephoned several times and asked for the return of the car, and eventually wrote a letter on 7 November stating that if it was not returned by 10 November it would be deemed to have been sold to Smiths. The car was not returned until the end of November, when Poole refused to take it back. It had been driven for some 1,600 miles and had been badly damaged as a result of an accident sustained when two of Smiths' employees had, without authority, taken it out on a joyride. In this action Poole sued for the price, alleging that the property had passed, and was successful.

Ormerod LJ: The whole question now is whether, in the circumstances, the plaintiff is entitled to recover from the defendants either the sum of £325 as the price of goods sold and delivered, or such sum as may be proper as damages for detinue.

The plaintiff, in the first place, says that the car was sent to the defendants on sale or return, and the question which first arises to be determined is whether this was a transaction for sale or return. The judge held, that this was not a transaction having the sharply defined qualities of a contract for sale or return as envisaged by the Sale of Goods Act 1893. Mr Chedlow has raised the point that a contract for sale or return in the ordinary way is a contract where the person to whom the chattel is delivered is intending either to purchase the chattel or to send it back, whereas this was a contract where the defendants might expect to sell the car to one of their customers and if they could not sell it, then to return it, and, in those circumstances, it was not a contract for sale or return. So far as I am concerned, I am afraid I do not understand that distinction. I know of no authority for it, and in the absence of authority which is binding on this court, for my part, I would not make it. . . .

If that was the contract then the questions which arise are when and how did the property pass? It appears that we must be governed either by the express or implied intentions of the parties, or, failing those intentions, by the provisions of s 18 of the Act of 1893, and the rules there laid down. It has been contended on behalf of the plaintiff that the rule which applies here is r 4.

[His Lordship read the rule, and continued:]

The question next arises whether that particular rule which I have read applies; that is to say, whether the property has passed. Mr Chedlow has argued that that rule cannot apply, and the reason why it cannot apply is because of the first words of s 18 of the Sale of Goods Act 1893, which reads: 'Unless a different intention appears.' It was argued that on the evidence in this case it was clear that a different intention appeared, and that it was not the intention that the property should pass in the manner indicated by r 4. I think I need only say here, in dealing with Mr Chedlow's argument, that I can see nothing which warrants the conclusion that any different intention is to be discovered from the circumstances of the case.

So we are thrown back on r 4. By that rule if the parties have fixed a time for the property to pass, then the property will pass at that time. In this case there is no suggestion that any time had been fixed. Failing that, and it is a question of fact, the time for the property to pass is at the expiry of a reasonable time, and the question which arises is what is a reasonable time. . . .

It is a well-known fact that people go on holidays in the months of July, August and September. It has become obvious, I think, in recent years that when people go on holidays, they like to take their cars with them. It may be that many people, when the holidays are over, like to sell those cars and, therefore, it may be a well-recognised fact, and I think it is, that the sellers' market for secondhand motor-cars in October and November is not so good as it is before the holiday season begins or is still in its early stages. In any event, I see no reason why in these days a court should not take judicial notice of the way the market in secondhand cars is carried on and come to a conclusion as to what is a reasonable time.

For my part I am fully satisfied, both on the knowledge which has come to me in the ordinary course of life and through sitting in these courts, and from the evidence before the court in this

case, that a reasonable time had expired, certainly in November, for the return of this car; and if that reasonable time had expired, it is clear by reason of the operation of s 18 of the Act of 1893 that the property in the car had passed from the plaintiff to the defendants . . .

The position remains, therefore, that here was a car delivered on sale or return, that a reasonable time expired without the car being returned and, therefore, there must have been or must be deemed to have been a sale of the car. That being so, the defendants become liable for the purchase price.

[**Willmer LJ** delivered a concurring judgment. **Danckwerts LJ** concurred.]

QUESTION

Suppose that the car had been damaged (1) as a result of Smiths' negligence, (2) as a result of no fault by anyone, before the expiry of a reasonable time. What would the legal position be? Compare *Elphick v Barnes* (1880) 5 CPD 321.

NOTE

The case of *Atari Corpn (UK) Ltd v Electronics Boutique Stores (UK) Ltd* [1998] QB 539, CA, clarified one or two further points relating to sale or return contracts. Electronics, who were retailers, contracted with Atari for the supply of computer games on the terms 'Full sale or return until 31 January 1996'. The games did not sell well and on 19 January 1996 Electronics wrote to Atari saying that they had decided to cease stocking the goods and that the unsold goods would be placed in their central warehouse so that a detailed list could be prepared. (Electronics had a chain of retail outlets in various parts of the country and it would take some time for them to be returned to the warehouse.) It was held that the notice rejecting the unsold goods was effective (so that Electronics was not deemed to have bought them). Neither the fact that the actual quantity and identity of the unsold goods was specified in the notice, nor the fact that the goods were not physically capable of collection when the notice was issued, prevented the notice from being a valid rejection of the goods.

(v) Rule 5: unascertained goods

Rules 1–4 of s 18 are all concerned with specific goods. The only rule dealing with *unascertained* goods is r 5. It states:

> (1) Where there is a contract for the sale of unascertained or future goods by description, and goods of that description and in a deliverable state are unconditionally appropriated to the contract, either by the seller with the assent of the buyer or by the buyer with the assent of the seller, the property in the goods then passes to the buyer; and the assent may be given either before or after the appropriation is made.
>
> (2) Where, in pursuance of the contract, the seller delivers the goods to the buyer or to a carrier or other bailee . . . (whether named by the buyer or not) for the purpose of transmission to the buyer, and does not reserve the right of disposal, he is to be taken to have unconditionally appropriated the goods to the contract.

(Section 18, r 5(3) and (4), extending the definition of ascertainment, has been dealt with above: see p 336).

We have already met some of the terms used in this rule. As well as *unascertained goods* (see above, p 305) and *future goods* (above, p 305), which were dealt with in Chapter 00, the expression *deliverable state* occurs in rr 1 and 2 and has been discussed above (p 340). We are left with the concept of 'unconditionally appropriated', each part of which merits some discussion.

(a) 'Appropriated'

In r 5 'appropriation' has the connotation of a selecting or setting aside. The need for appropriation in r 5 reflects the fact that, as Lord Mustill put it in *Re Goldcorp Ltd* [1995] 1 AC 74 at 90, 'common sense dictates that the buyer cannot acquire title until it is known to what goods the title relates'. Put in another way, requiring appropriation is simply the corollary of the rule in s 16 that property cannot pass in goods so long as those goods remain unascertained.

Appropriation in this sense, it should be noted, is a necessary but not a sufficient condition of property passing: in addition to appropriation there must be an element of irrevocability. Take, for instance, *Carlos Federspiel & Co SA v Charles Twigg & Co Ltd* [1957] 1 Lloyd's Rep 240, below, p 354, where cycles representing an order from a customer were put aside labelled with the customer's name in the seller's works. Here there was an appropriation of goods, and had the contract so provided property could have passed there and then: but property did not in fact pass because under the actual terms of the contract the appropriation was not irrevocable.

A subsidiary use of the word 'appropriation' needs to be noted in the commercial context, this time one that does not bring r 5 into play at all. In a typical commodity sale contract on CIF terms (below, p 543), at some stage the seller will be bound to elect what goods he will supply for the purpose of meeting his obligations. But this goes merely to obligation and not to property. Having issued a so-called 'notice of appropriation' the seller is from that moment on bound under the contract to deliver the goods nominated and those goods only, and the buyer can reject any other goods, even if otherwise perfectly in accordance with the contract (see *Grain Union v Larsen* (1933) 46 Ll L Rep 246). Nevertheless property will generally only pass at a much later stage, for instance when shipping documents are transferred in exchange for the purchase price.

(b) 'Unconditionally'

Appropriation, as we saw above, is a necessary condition of ownership passing under r 5, but not a sufficient one. Goods must be 'unconditionally appropriated to the contract, either by the seller with the assent of the buyer or by the buyer with the assent of the seller'. Suppose that a wine merchant who has an order for a dozen cases of a particular wine for a hotel selects a box containing 12 cases of the wine from a larger quantity in its cellar with the intention of using those cases to fulfil that order: we may say that it has 'appropriated' the cases in question to the contract. But, of course, there is nothing at this stage to stop the merchant changing its mind: if a second customer urgently needed wine of the same description, the merchant could sell that customer those cases without infringing any commitment to the hotel, and then select (or even procure from elsewhere) another dozen cases to meet the original order. Hence in such a case nothing that the merchant has done by this 'appropriation' affects its ownership of the wine in question, or its ability to sell it to anyone he may choose. No subjective decision on its part, or unilateral or private act of setting aside, gives the first customer any claim to that wine. Nor would an act by the merchant such as putting the goods in a delivery van to be taken to the customer's address, or even writing the customer's

name and address on the box: these acts are all reversible or revocable, and the second customer, especially if he is in a hurry, might not mind at all being given a box with writing on it. 'Unconditional appropriation', for the purpose of r 5, must mean something more than this.

Wait v Baker
(1848) 2 Exch 1, Court of Exchequer Chamber

The facts are immaterial.

> **Parke B**: . . . It is admitted by the learned counsel for the defendant, that the property does not pass, unless there is a subsequent appropriation of the goods. The word appropriation may be understood in different senses. It may mean a selection on the part of the vendor, where he has the right to choose the article which he has to supply in performance of his contract; and the contract will shew when the word is used in that sense. Or the word may mean, that both parties have agreed that a certain article shall be delivered in pursuance of the contract, and yet the property may not pass in either case. For the purpose of illustrating this position, suppose a carriage is ordered to be built at a coachmaker's, he may make any one he pleases, and, if it agree with the order, the party is bound to accept it. Now suppose that, at some period subsequent to the order, a further bargain is entered into between this party and the coachbuilder, by which it is agreed that a particular carriage shall be delivered. It would depend upon circumstances whether the property passes, or whether merely the original contract is altered from one which would have been satisfied by the delivery of any carriage answering the terms of the contract, into another contract to supply the particular carriage—which, in the Roman law, was called *obligatio certi corporis*, where a person is bound to deliver a particular chattel, but where the property does not pass, as it never did by the Roman law, until actual delivery; although the property, after the contract, remained at the risk of the vendee, and if lost without any fault in the vendor, the vendee, and not the vendor, was the sufferer. The law of England is different: here, property does not pass until there is a bargain with respect to a specific article, and everything is done which, according to the intention of the parties to the bargain, was necessary to transfer the property in it. 'Appropriation' may also be used in another sense, and is the one in which Mr Butt uses it on the present occasion; viz where both parties agree upon the specific article in which the property is to pass, and nothing remains to be done in order to pass it. . . .

The application of the presumption contained in r 5 is illustrated by the following cases (some of which have already been discussed).

Aldridge v Johnson
(1857) 7 E & B 885, Court of Queen's Bench

See above, p 314.

Philip Head & Sons Ltd v Showfronts Ltd
[1970] 1 Lloyd's Rep 140, Queen's Bench Division

See above, p 343.

Mucklow v Mangles
(1808) 1 Taunt 318, Court of Common Pleas

Royland contracted to build a barge for Pocock. The whole of the agreed price was paid as the work progressed. When it was nearly finished, Pocock's name was painted on the stern. Two days after it had been completed, but before it was delivered, it was seized by Mangles, a sheriff's officer, who was executing a judgment against Royland. Royland was later adjudicated bankrupt. The question before the court was whether the sheriff had rightly seized the barge, or whether it had become Pocock's property. It was held that the property had not passed to Pocock.

> **Mansfield CJ**: The only effect of the payment, is, that the bankrupt was under a contract to finish the barge: that is quite a different thing from a contract of sale, and until the barge was finished we cannot say that it was so far Pocock's property, that he could have taken it away. It was not finished at the time when Royland committed the act of bankruptcy: it was finished only two days before the execution. . . .
>
> **Heath J**: . . . A tradesman often finishes goods, which he is making in pursuance of an order given by one person, and sells them to another. If the first customer has other goods made for him within the stipulated time, he has no right to complain; he could not bring trover against the purchaser for the goods so sold. The painting of the name on the stern in this case makes no difference. If the thing be in existence at the time of the order, the property of it passes by the contract, but not so, where the subject is to be made.
>
> [**Lawrence J** concurred.]

NOTE

We really need to know more facts than are stated in the report of this case. Under the law then in force, the 'commencement' of Royland's bankruptcy would have been backdated to some 'act of bankruptcy' (which is referred to by Mansfield CJ), which plainly took place between the painting of the name and the completion of the work. The title of the trustee in bankruptcy would be deemed to have vested on the date of that act of bankruptcy.

Pignataro v Gilroy
[1919] 1 KB 459, King's Bench Division

The defendants contracted to sell by sample to the plaintiff 140 bags of rice, then unascertained, and in due course notified the buyer that 125 bags were available for collection at one address and 15 at another. Despite two reminders by letter, the plaintiff did not send to collect the 15 bags for nearly a month, by which time they had been stolen. It was held that the property had passed to the plaintiff and that the risk of loss therefore lay on him.

> **Rowlatt J** (delivering the judgment of the court (Lawrence and Rowlatt JJ)): Under the above contract it would be the duty of the sellers to appropriate the goods to the contract; and if such appropriation were assented to, expressly or impliedly, by the buyer the property would have

passed. When they received the cheque for the goods and were asked for a delivery order it was right and proper for them to appropriate and place at the disposal of the buyer the goods for which he thus paid in order to effectuate a delivery or its equivalent concurrently with the receipt of the money. They did send a delivery order for the goods at Chambers' Wharf, and as to the 15 bags, told the plaintiff that they were ready, and asked that they should be taken away. It might well be contended that not only as regards the goods covered by the delivery order, but also as regards the goods at the defendants' own premises which they thus told the plaintiff were ready to be taken away in response to the plaintiff's request for a delivery order, there was an appropriation to which by asking for the delivery order the plaintiff had assented in advance. We do not think it necessary to decide this, because we think there was what amounted to an assent subsequent. If the plaintiff had replied saying that he would remove the goods the case would be precisely the same as *Rohde v Thwaites* (1827) 6 B. & C. 388. The plaintiff, however, did nothing for a month, and the question is what is the effect of that? If the goods were of the required quality it is difficult to see how the plaintiff could have dissented from the appropriation. He could not object to the place from which he was required to fetch them, because he had inspected rice lying at those premises at the time and for the purposes of this very contract. For the same reason it is not easy to see how he could have objected to their quality unless there happened to be some bags inferior to those which he had inspected. At any rate, he made no objection at all. Now it is obvious that if he made any objection he ought to do so promptly, because he could not place upon the vendors the risk involved in the continued possession of these goods, nor prolong the encumbrance of the vendors' premises. As he chose merely to say nothing for a whole month in response to an appropriation made in consequence of his own letter, we think that comes to precisely the same thing as if he had written saying he would remove them and did not. The learned judge said that there was no evidence of an appropriation with the assent of the buyer. He could only say this if he was looking for an express assent. As the assent may be implied we think that there was not only evidence of it but that it is the only inference possible upon the facts. For these reasons the appeal must be allowed, and judgment entered for the defendants. . . .

Carlos Federspiel & Co SA v Charles Twigg & Co Ltd
[1957] 1 Lloyd's Rep 240, Queen's Bench Division

Federspiel in Costa Rica agreed to buy a number of cycles from Twiggs in England and paid them the price. Under the contract, the goods were to be loaded aboard the SS *Britannica* at Liverpool. Cycles were manufactured to answer the contract and packed in crates marked with the buyers' name, and steps were taken to send the crates to Liverpool for shipment. But the sellers went into receivership before shipment took place. The buyers argued unsuccessfully that the property in the cycles had passed to them.

Pearson J: This is a case in which the contract is for the sale of unascertained goods by description, for the sale of future goods probably still to be manufactured. Afterwards certain goods were manufactured, and the sellers at one time apparently expected to use them in fulfilment of the contract. The question is whether there was an appropriation of those goods to the contract by the sellers with the assent of the buyers within the meaning of Rule 5 of s 18.

I think it is convenient just, in effect, to lay a foundation for the understanding of the exact meaning and effect of s 18 by reading a short passage from an old case, *Mirabita v Imperial Ottoman Bank* (1878) 3 Ex D 164. The relevant passage is from the judgment of Lord Justice Cotton, at p 172, where he says:

Under a contract for sale of chattels not specific the property does not pass to the purchaser unless there is afterwards an appropriation of the specific chattels to pass under the contract, that is, unless both parties agree as to the specific chattels in which the property is to pass, and nothing remains to be done in order to pass it.

[His Lordship referred to a number of other cases, including *Wait v Baker* (1848) 2 Ex 1 and *Pignataro v Gilroy* (above, p 353), and continued:]

On those authorities, what are the principles emerging? I think one can distinguish these principles. First, r 5 of s 18 of the Act is one of the rules for ascertaining the intention of the parties as to the time at which the property in the goods is to pass to the buyer unless a different intention appears. Therefore the element of common intention has always to be borne in mind. A mere setting apart or selection by the seller of the goods which he expects to use in performance of the contract is not enough. If that is all, he can change his mind and use those goods in performance of some other contract and use some other goods in performance of this contract. To constitute an appropriation of the goods to the contract, the parties must have had, or be reasonably supposed to have had, an intention to attach the contract irrevocably to those goods, so that those goods and no others are the subject of the sale and become the property of the buyer.

Secondly, it is by agreement of the parties that the appropriation, involving a change of ownership, is made, although in some cases the buyer's assent to an appropriation by the seller is conferred in advance by the contract itself or otherwise.

Thirdly, an appropriation by the seller, with the assent of the buyer, may be said always to involve an actual or constructive delivery. If the seller retains possession, he does so as bailee for the buyer. There is a passage in *Chalmers' Sale of Goods Act*, 12th edn, at p 75, where it is said:

> In the second place, if the decisions be carefully examined, it will be found that in every case where the property has been held to pass, there has been an actual or constructive delivery of the goods to the buyer.

I think that is right, subject only to this possible qualification, that there may be after such constructive delivery an actual delivery still to be made by the seller under the contract. Of course, that is quite possible, because delivery is the transfer of possession, whereas appropriation transfers ownership. So there may be first an appropriation, constructive delivery, whereby the seller becomes bailee for the buyer, and then a subsequent actual delivery involving actual possession, and when I say that I have in mind in particular the two cases cited, namely, *Aldridge v Johnson* [above, p 314], and *Langton v Higgins* (1859) 4 H & N 402.

Fourthly, one has to remember s 20 of the Sale of Goods Act, whereby the ownership and the risk are normally associated. Therefore as it appears that there is reason for thinking, on the construction of the relevant documents, that the goods were, at all material times, still at the seller's risk, that is prima facie an indication that the property had not passed to the buyer.

Fifthly, usually but not necessarily, the appropriating act is the last act to be performed by the seller. For instance, if delivery is to be taken by the buyer at the seller's premises and the seller has completed his part of the contract and has appropriated the goods when he has made the goods ready and has identified them and placed them in position to be taken by the buyer and has so informed the buyer, and if the buyer agrees to come and take them, that is the assent to the appropriation. But if there is a further act, an important and decisive act to be done by the seller, then there is prima facie evidence that probably the property does not pass until the final act is done.

Applying those principles to the present case I would say this. Firstly, the intention was that the ownership should pass on shipment (or possibly at some later date) because the emphasis is throughout on shipment as the decisive act to be done by the seller in performance of the contract. Secondly, it is impossible to find in this correspondence an agreement to a change of

ownership before the time of shipment. The letters, especially those of Aug 27 and Sept 14, which are particularly relied on by the plaintiff, do not contain any provision or implication of any earlier change of ownership. Thirdly, there is no actual or constructive delivery; no suggestion of the seller becoming a bailee for the buyer. Fourthly, there is no suggestion of the goods being at the buyer's risk at any time before shipment; no suggestion that the buyer should insist on the seller arranging insurance for them. Fifthly, the last two acts to be performed by the seller, namely, sending the goods to Liverpool and having the goods shipped on board, were not performed.

Therefore, my decision that the prima facie inference which one would have drawn from the contract is that the property was not to pass at any time before shipment, is in my view not displaced by the subsequent correspondence between the parties. It follows, therefore, that there was no appropriation of these goods and therefore the action fails.

NOTE

See too the earlier *Noblett v Hopkinson* [1905] 2 KB 214. A further powerful consideration against property having passed in this case was the fact that the agreed sale was FOB Liverpool, and in a contract to sell FOB the inference is very strong that ownership is intended to pass at the time of shipment (see *Browne v Hare* (1858) 4 H & N 822 and below, p 538).

An act of appropriation sufficient to pass the property in goods may be performed by a third party, for example a warehouseman. In such a case, the third party may be regarded as the agent of one (or possibly both) of the parties for the purpose.

Wardar's (Import & Export) Co Ltd v W Norwood & Sons Ltd
[1968] 2 QB 663, Court of Appeal

Wardar's agreed to buy from Norwoods 600 cartons of frozen ox kidneys out of a consignment of 1,500 cartons which had been imported from Argentina and were lying in a cold store in Smithfield. A driver, McBeath, employed by a firm of carriers, arrived at 8 am on an October morning to pick up the goods on behalf of Wardar's and take them to Scotland. He had a refrigerated lorry but had forgotten to turn on the refrigerating machinery. When he arrived, 600 cartons had been taken out of the store by the storage firm and placed on the pavement. McBeath handed over a delivery order and the Smithfield porters began to load the van. Loading took until noon (in part because the porters took a one-hour tea break), by which time the day was warm and some of the cartons were leaking, and the refrigeration in the van was still not fully effective. The kidneys were unfit for consumption when they arrived in Scotland. The Court of Appeal held that the loss fell on the buyers, since property and risk had passed at 8 am and the deterioration had occurred after that time.

Salmon LJ: When McBeath arrived at the cold store at 8 am on October 14, the frozen kidneys which he was to take to Scotland were there on the pavement waiting for him. There is no doubt that they had been in the cold store the day before and, indeed, had then been examined by the buyers soon after they made their oral contract of purchase. As far as the evidence goes, there was absolutely nothing the matter with the kidneys on October 13. There is no evidence as to when these 600 cartons were taken out of the cold store. It seems unlikely that they would have been left on the pavement overnight. Had they been left on the pavement overnight, it is perhaps even

more unlikely that they would all have been there in the morning. The natural inference, I think, is that they must have been taken out of the cold store at some time on the morning of October 14 prior to 8 am.

These 600 cartons were part of a consignment of 1500 cartons of frozen kidneys that had been stored in the cold store. The evidence called at the trial showed that the rest of the cartons—that is, 900 of the cartons—had also been sold, and no complaint was made in respect of them. At the time of the sale it was a sale of unascertained goods: 600 cartons were bought out of a total of 1500 cartons. This case really turns upon the question as to when the property passed to the buyers. It is plain that as a rule the goods remain at the sellers' risk until the property does pass to the buyers. After the property passes, the goods are at the buyers' risk: s 20 of the Act of 1893. There are special circumstances (of which *Sterns Ltd v Vickers Ltd* [below, p 366] is an example) when the risk may pass to the buyers even before the property has passed to them; but there are no such special circumstances here. The case depends entirely upon when the property passed.

Under r 5 of s 18, the property passes to the buyers in the case of unascertained goods, such as these, when the goods are unconditionally appropriated to the contract. At 8 am the carrier arrived; and the carrier was the buyers' agent. There were the goods, which had been left on the pavement by the sellers' agent for the purpose of fulfilling the contract. The carrier handed over the delivery note, with the clear intention that those goods should be accepted for loading; and the loading commenced.

It is unnecessary to decide the point whether there was an unconditional appropriation to the contract at the moment when the goods were put onto the pavement, which is perhaps fortunate, because we do not know precisely when that was; but, in my view, there can be no doubt that there was a clear, unconditional appropriation when the delivery order was handed over in respect of the goods which had been deposited on the pavement for loading. There is certainly no evidence that they were not then of merchantable quality. . . .

Since, however, the goods were appropriated to the contract when the delivery order was handed over and accepted in respect of the goods standing on the pavement, any deterioration that occurred thereafter was at the risk of the buyers. We know that when the goods arrived at their destination the vast bulk of them were not of merchantable quality. We also know from the driver of the lorry that he did not turn on the refrigeration, so he said, until the tea-break was taken. At any rate, the refrigeration did not become effective until 1 pm. It may not be very material, but it does not seem to me to be at all unlikely, if the goods were left in a stuffy lorry, as they were, for some hours, that the deterioration may have occurred during that time. The driver said that this was a hot day. Unless it was a very exceptional day for October 14 in this country, I cannot think that the sun had much strength in it by 8 am. In any event, none of this, I think, matters, because at 8 am these goods were appropriated to the contract and the risk of deterioration then fell on the buyers; and there is no evidence that there was any deterioration before that time . . . .

[**Harman LJ** delivered a concurring judgment. **Phillimore J** concurred.]

Paragraph (2) of r 5 deems goods to have been unconditionally appropriated to the contract when the seller has delivered them to a carrier or other bailee for the purpose of transmission to the buyer. This innocuous-looking provision is highly important in practice. This is because it means that in any case where goods are transmitted from seller to buyer by independent carrier, property (and thus inferentially risk) pass on dispatch and hence during the transit the goods are at the buyer's risk. It also means that whenever a business orders goods from a remote seller to be sent to it, risk will be on it as from dispatch and it will have to pay for the goods even if lost in transit.

For the application of r 5(2) to international sales, see below, Chapter 15.

It was unsuccessfully argued in *Wardar's* case that there had been no 'delivery' under this provision until the cartons had actually been put on the lorry; but it is plain that the court considered that delivery had taken place at the time when the delivery order was handed over by McBeath to the cold store firm and accepted.

Paragraph (2) also refers to a *reservation of the right of disposal* by the buyer—an expression which is also used, and its meaning elaborated, in s 19(1) and (2). These are perhaps rather superfluous provisions, because it is plain from the whole tenor of ss 17 and 18 that no property can pass under the contract so long as some condition remains to be fulfilled, and that an appropriation to be effective must also be unconditional; and obviously if the seller makes a stipulation that he is reserving a right of disposal even after delivery to the buyer or the carrier, the appropriation will not be unconditional. However, it does no harm for the details in question to be spelt out in the Act, and it is helpful to have it clearly stated as a prima facie rule that where goods are loaded on to a ship for the purposes of transmission to the buyer, and the seller takes the bill of lading in his own name, intending to transfer it to the buyer at some later stage (normally against payment of the price), the property is not to be taken to have passed (s 19(2)).

Finally, before leaving r 5, we should note the two new paragraphs (3) and (4), introduced by the amending Act of 1995, which deal with 'ascertainment by exhaustion'. These paragraphs, and the cases at common law on which they are based, have been discussed above, pp 337 ff. However, it should be observed that whereas the rulings at common law were primarily on the issue of *ascertainment*, the new provisions go further, and add a presumption that the goods are not only ascertained by the process of exhaustion, but *appropriated* to the contract.

3 PASSING OF PROPERTY, ACCEPTANCE, AND REJECTION

Before we leave the topic of the passing of property, it may be appropriate to ask: how is the passing of property related to acceptance of goods? That is, how does passing of property affect the question of when the buyer loses, or abandons, any right which he may have to reject the goods (eg because they are not of the contract description or quality), and finds himself confined to a damages claim? (On acceptance, see below, pp 469 ff.)

The answer is that, on principle, these two matters are entirely separate. It is thus perfectly possible for goods to be accepted before property passes. An example is where goods are delivered on reservation of title terms; here the buyer may well be regarded as having accepted the goods, and lost his right to reject them, if he keeps them for any appreciable period after delivery, but nevertheless the goods remain the seller's property for a considerable time after that. Conversely, the fact that property passes to the buyer at an early stage will not as such prevent him later rejecting the goods if they turn out to be unsatisfactory.

McDougall v Aeromarine of Emsworth Ltd
[1958] 1 WLR 1126, Queen's Bench Division

Aeromarine contracted to build for McDougall a four-ton cruiser-racer yacht for use in the 1957 yachting season. Payment of the price was to be made by five instalments. The contract contained a term (clause 8) similar to that in *Re Blyth Shipbuilding Co Ltd* (see above, p 338) by virtue of which the property in the uncompleted vessel passed to the buyer on payment of the first instalment. The yacht had defects rendering it unseaworthy when it was launched in June 1957, and these defects had not been remedied several months later when Aeromarine offered to finish the work on varied terms which McDougall was not prepared to accept. Diplock J held that the buyer was justified in rejecting the yacht and that, although the property may have passed pursuant to clause 8, it had passed only defeasibly, and had been revested in Aeromarine when McDougall rightly exercised his right to reject.

> **Diplock J**: The defendants' failure to tender the yacht for delivery in accordance with the contract by September 5 was itself, I think, a breach of condition which the plaintiff was entitled to treat as rescinding the contract. Their intimation, for that was what their offer amounted to, that they could not complete it before the end of the 1957 yachting season was a fortiori, in my opinion, a wrongful repudiation of the contract by the defendants, as was their intimation that they would only complete the contract upon terms different from those of the original contract. The plaintiff by his letter of September 19 elected to treat the defendants' wrongful repudiation of the contract as rescinding it.
>
> I hold that, in all the circumstances of the case, he was entitled to do so; but even if he were not, the defendants cannot rely on the plaintiff's purported rescission of the contract of September 19 as a wrongful repudiation on his part of the contract, thus relieving them from any further obligation to perform it, because they did not accept his repudiation but continued to hold him to the contract; and on October 30 they informed the plaintiff that they would insist either on completing the vessel on terms inconsistent with and less favourable to the plaintiff than those in the original contract, or those that they had offered in their letter of September 5, or upon delivering the vessel in its defective state with an allowance of 50 guineas off the contract price. This was, I think, yet another wrongful repudiation by the defendants of the contract, which the plaintiff was entitled to and did accept. Such part of the property, if any, in the vessel or any portion thereof as had previously vested in him under clause 8 of the contract accordingly revested then in the defendants.

As appears from *McDougall v Aeromarine of Emsworth Ltd*, above, it is sometimes possible for a buyer to reject goods even *after* the property has passed to him. In such a case, the effect of rejection is that the buyer divests himself of his ownership and causes it to revest, retroactively, in the seller. *Head v Tattersall* (below, p 364) is perhaps an early example of this: the risk, as well as the property, being deemed to have revested in the seller with retrospective effect. Two more modern cases illustrate the same principle.

Kwei Tek Chao v British Traders & Shippers Ltd
[1954] 2 QB 459, Queen's Bench Division

Buyers in Hong Kong contracted to buy from sellers in London a chemical of Swedish origin known as 'Rongalite C'. Under the contract, property passed to the buyers when the price was paid in exchange for the shipping documents: this happened on 12 November. By the time that the goods arrived in Hong Kong on 17 December, the buyers had ascertained that the goods had been shipped outside the contractual period for shipment and that the shipping documents had been forged (by a third party) to conceal this fact. Devlin J held that the buyers could reject the goods for this reason, and that they could do so even though the property had already passed to them: it must be regarded as having passed defeasibly, ie subject to a condition subsequent that in an event such as that which had happened, it could be revested in the sellers by the buyers properly exercising a right of rejection. It followed that the buyers, who had pledged the documents to their bank, had not dealt with the goods in a manner inconsistent with the sellers' ownership so as to lose their right of rejection under s 35 of the Act.

Devlin J: In *Hardy & Co v Hillerns & Fowler* [1923] 2 K.B. 490 the question which arose for decision was whether the buyers had accepted the goods under s 35. The goods had arrived, and the case showed that the time during which he had the right to examine them was still running. During that time the buyer delivered some of the goods to a sub-buyer. That was an act which was inconsistent with the ownership of the seller. . . . The court held that, notwithstanding that his time for examination was still open, the buyer could, if he chose to commit an act under s 35 such as intimating that he accepted the goods, accept them.

Mr Roskill has argued that when the goods are delivered to the buyer and he does any act in relation to them which is inconsistent with the ownership of the seller the word 'delivered' there means physical delivery of the goods from the ship. If that is so, no dealing with the documents would be within the meaning of the clause, because it would all have been done before the goods had been delivered. I cannot take that view of it. 'Delivery' as defined by the Act means a voluntary transfer of possession, and I think that it means, therefore, transfer of possession under the contract of sale. In a cif contract the goods are delivered, so far as they are physically delivered, when they are put on board a ship at the port of shipment. The documents are delivered when they are tendered. A buyer who takes delivery from the ship at the port of destination is not taking delivery of the goods under the contract of sale, but merely taking delivery out of his own warehouse, as it were, by the presentation of the document of title to the goods, the master of the ship having been his bailee ever since he became entitled to the bill of lading.

I think that the true answer may be found rather differently. Atkin LJ, in the course of his judgment in *Hardy & Co v Hillerns & Fowler*, dealt with the situation which is always a little puzzling under the cif contract: if the property passes when the documents are handed over, by what legal machinery does the buyer retain a right, as he undoubtedly does, to examine the goods when they arrive, and to reject them if they are not in conformity with the contract? Atkin LJ put forward two views for consideration. One was that the property in the goods, notwithstanding the tendering of the documents, did not pass until the goods had been examined or until an opportunity for examination had been given. The other was that it passed at the time of the tendering of the documents, but only conditionally and could be revested if the buyer properly rejected the goods. Mr Roskill argues (and I think rightly) that for the first possible view indicated by Atkin LJ no other authority can be found, and it would clearly create considerable complications. If there is no property in the goods, how can the buyer pledge them? It would provide a simple answer to the point had it arisen in this case, since there could not be a pledge. I think that the true view is that what the buyer obtains, when the title under the documents is given to him, is the property in the goods, subject to the condition that they revest if upon examination he finds them to be not in accordance with the contract. That means that he gets only conditional property in the goods, the condition being a condition subsequent. All his dealings with the documents are dealings only with that conditional property in the goods. It follows, therefore, that there can be no dealing which is inconsistent with the seller's ownership unless he deals with something more than the conditional property. If the property passes altogether, not being subject to any condition, there is no ownership left in the seller with which any inconsistent act under s 35 could be committed. If the property passes conditionally the only ownership left in the seller is the reversionary interest in the property in the event of the condition subsequent operating to restore it to him. It is that

> reversionary interest with which the buyer must not, save with the penalty of accepting the goods, commit an inconsistent act. So long as he is merely dealing with the documents he is not purporting to do anything more than pledge the conditional property which he has. Similarly, if he sells the documents of title he sells the conditional property. But if, as was done in *Hardy & Co v Hillerns & Fowler*, when the goods have been landed, he physically deals with the goods and delivers them to his sub-buyer, he is doing an act which is inconsistent with the seller's reversionary interest. The seller's reversionary interest entitles him, immediately upon the operation of the condition subsequent, that is, as soon as opportunity for examination has been given, to have the goods physically returned to him in the place where the examination has taken place without their being dispatched to third parties. The dispatch to a third party is an act, therefore, which interferes with the reversionary interest. A pledge or a transfer of documents such as that which takes place on the ordinary string contract does not. . . .

See also *J&H Ritchie Ltd v Lloyd Ltd* (below, p 472), which deals with the situation where a buyer of defective goods agrees to allow the seller to attempt to repair the defect. The property in the goods will pass to the buyer (and may already have done so) in accordance with the normal rules, but if he later lawfully exercises his right to reject them the property will revert to the seller.

4 RISK AND PROPERTY

(a) The idea of risk

The Act in various sections speaks of 'the risk' passing to the buyer, but the term 'risk' is nowhere defined. We may ask: risk of what? The parties to a contract of sale face many risks: the risk that the market value of the goods in question may go up or down, the risk that perishable goods may deteriorate, and so on. However, we may glean from the decided cases that 'the risk' that the Act is concerned with is the risk that the goods will be wholly or partly destroyed or damaged, for instance by fire or flood or the sinking of the ship on which they are being carried, or lost by theft. It is also clear that we are concerned only with events that are not attributable to the act or fault of either of the parties, or which are dealt with expressly by the terms of the contract (eg by a 'force majeure' clause).

' "Risk" in the Law of Sale' by LS Sealy
[1972B] CLJ 225 at 226–227

> . . . The truth is that risk is a derivative, and essentially negative, concept—an elliptical way of saying that either or both of the primary obligations of one party shall be enforceable, and that those of the other party shall be deemed to have been discharged, even though the normally prerequisite conditions have not been satisfied. That is to say, the legal consequences attaching to 'the risk' fall to be defined purely in terms of the parties' other duties and the corresponding rights and remedies: the seller's right to claim the price, and the buyer's right to resist payment or to demand its return; and the right to claim damages (eg for non-delivery or non-acceptance) or to resist such a claim.

What then is the effect, as between the parties, of the passing of the risk? We may summarise the position from the quotation above as follows:

(1) If the risk has passed, the buyer will have to pay the price even though he does not (and will not ever) get the goods because they have been lost or destroyed. Similarly, he must accept delivery and pay the full price even though the goods have been partly lost, or damaged. The buyer, for his part, cannot sue the seller in damages for failing to make delivery, or for delivering less than the contract quantity or damaged goods.

(2) If the risk has not passed at the time when the loss or damage happens, the seller cannot compel the buyer to pay the price, or to take delivery of any remaining goods, or of the goods in their damaged state, or sue him for damages for refusing to do so.

NOTES

1. Risk may encompass events other than destruction or deterioration. For example, if A Ltd ships goods to B Ltd on terms that risk passes on shipment (see s 18, r 5(2)) and expenses are later incurred because the goods unexpectedly have to be transhipped, those expenses are for the buyer's account. See the American decision in *Phillips Puerto Rico v Tradax Petroleum*, 782 F2d 314 (1985) (ship carrying goods impounded as unsafe when calling at intermediate port, meaning goods had to be transferred at great cost).

2. Risk may interact with the duty under s 14 to supply goods of satisfactory quality, etc (below, Chapter 11). This is because goods are not regarded as being of satisfactory quality unless, in the ordinary course of events, they will be usable for a reasonable time in the hands of the buyer. So if A Ltd ships perishable goods with a probable life of seven days to B Ltd and the voyage is likely to take eight days, A will be in breach of s 14 even though risk passed to B on shipment and the actual (and inevitable) deterioration took place after that time. See *Mash & Murrell Ltd v Joseph I Emanuel Ltd* (below, p 439) and *The Mercini Lady* [2012] EWHC 3009 (Comm), [2013] 1 Lloyd's Rep 360.

(b) Risk and s 20 of the Act

The prima facie rule relating to risk is contained in s 20(1): unless otherwise agreed, the goods remain at the seller's risk until the property is transferred to the buyer, but from and after the transfer of the property they are at the buyer's risk, whether delivery has been made to him or not.

This is, however, only the prima facie rule. *The Aliakmon* (above, p 328) is a straightforward example of the parties 'agreeing otherwise'. There, the sale was on 'C & F' terms, which meant under the conventions of international sales law that the goods were at the buyers' risk 'as from shipment'. However, it was also a term of the contract that the property was not to pass until the price had been paid. So the risk of damage was carried by the buyers even during the time when the goods remained the sellers' property. Indeed, the inference is almost invariable that in every case of sale C & F or CIF risk and property are to pass at a different time and hence s 20 of the Sale of Goods Act is implicitly excluded (below, p 545). Another instance is where goods are sold on reservation of title terms (below, p 497): although title only passes on payment, it is invariably provided that risk passes at latest on delivery.

(c) Qualifications to s 20

Subsections (2) and (3) of s 20 list two qualifications to the prima facie rule laid down by s 20(1). Under s 20(2) a party who by his own unjustified delay postpones the passing of risk cannot take advantage of that delay if the goods are damaged in the meantime. And under s 20(3), where one party is in possession of goods at the risk of the other, that party must take reasonable care of the goods. There is also a third exception not mentioned in the Act: where goods are rightfully rejected, they are it seems deemed always to have been at the risk of the seller. *Demby Hamilton & Co Ltd v Barden, Wiehe v Dennis Bros* and the pre-Sale of Goods Act case of *Head v Tattersall* respectively provide illustrations of these exceptions.

Demby Hamilton & Co Ltd v Barden
[1949] 1 All ER 435, King's Bench Division

In November 1945 Barden, a wine merchant, agreed to buy from Demby Hamilton 30 tons of apple juice, to be collected at the rate of one truckload per week by third parties to whom the juice had been sub-sold. The sellers crushed apples sufficient to fulfil this contract (the last apples they had for that season) and put the juice into barrels. If the juice had been collected punctually in accordance with the contract, deliveries would have finished in February 1946, but only two truckloads were collected after 11 December 1945, and eventually, on 7 November 1946, the sellers informed the buyer that the remaining juice had become putrid and had been thrown away. It was held that the loss lay on the buyer, because the delay in taking delivery was due to his fault.

Sellers J: The first requirement of the proviso in question [s 20(2)] is that delivery has been delayed through the fault of the buyer. I am satisfied on the facts in the present case that a good delivery, which would have avoided all loss, was delayed through the fault of the buyer, and that of the third parties. The next requirement of the proviso is that, where delivery has been delayed through the fault of the buyer, the goods are at the risk of the party in fault 'as regards any loss which might not have occurred but for such fault.' The goods referred to there must be the contractual goods which have been assembled by the seller for the purpose of fulfilling his contract and making delivery. The goods may have been defined goods, goods manufactured for the purpose of delivery, or goods which had been acquired by the seller from somebody else for the purpose of fulfilling his contract. It does not seem to me that the Act requires to be construed in any narrow sense. The real question is whether the loss which has accrued was brought about by the delay in delivery, and that must have regard to the goods which were there to be delivered. Different circumstances may arise in different cases. It may be that the seller was in a position to sell the goods elsewhere and acquire other goods for the postponed time of delivery, and if he does not do that and there is some loss in the meantime the responsibility for the loss would be held to fall upon him. Again, there may be cases (and I think this is one of them) where the seller has his goods ready for delivery and has to keep them ready for delivery as and when the buyer proposes to take them. In the present case the position is clear. The casks of apple juice which were not accepted were manufactured at the time of the contract, and the contract required that delivery should be in accordance with sample. It would have been very difficult to have obtained goods which complied with the sample unless the apples had all been crushed at the same time. They would have had to be apples from the same district and the juice from them, when obtained, would have had to be of the same maturity. The condition of apples changes. They may be unripe at one time and too ripe at another. The 30 tons of juice were goods which the sellers rightly and reasonably kept for the fulfilment of their contract. These were the last apples which the sellers had that season for crushing, and, therefore, the goods in question were goods which the sellers had awaiting delivery in fulfilment of their contract with the buyer. I have to ask myself whether this loss might not have occurred but for the fault of the buyer. I am satisfied that it would not have occurred but for his fault. There is, of course, an obligation on a seller to act reasonably, and, if possible, to avoid any loss. As to that, one or two questions arise for consideration. Was there anything the sellers could reasonably do to dispose of these goods when they still had an outstanding obligation to keep them at the disposal of the buyer and when they had to be ready and willing to deliver them when requested? If delivery had been asked for at a later date and they had let these goods go elsewhere they could not have fulfilled their contract. I do not hesitate to find (although to construe this proviso is not easy) that in a practical and business sense this loss has fallen on the sellers by reason of the fact that the buyer refused to take delivery at the proper time and postponed the date of delivery until the goods had deteriorated, and I come to the conclusion that the liability for that loss falls on the buyer . . .

Wiehe v Dennis Bros

(1913) 29 TLR 250, King's Bench Division

Wiehe in London contracted to buy a Shetland pony called 'Tiny' from Dennis Bros, intended to be presented along with a car and harness to Princess Juliana, daughter of the Queen of the Netherlands. The pony and car were to be delivered in Rotterdam in a month's time. While the pony was in the sellers' custody, a charitable ball was held at Olympia, in the course of which an unauthorised person took the pony out of its stall and led it among the dancers; but it was mishandled and suffered injuries. The sellers were held liable on the basis that they had failed to show that they had taken proper care of it as bailees pending delivery.

Scrutton J: [I]n his Lordship's view one cause of action against the defendants was that they were the bailees of the pony and that the pony was injured without their being able to give any explanation how such injuries were caused. The case therefore fell within *Bullen v Swan Electric Engraving Co* (1906) 22 TLR 275, where Mr Justice Walton said that there was in the case of a gratuitous bailee an obligation to use such care as a reasonably prudent owner would take of his own property, and also that in an action such as the present it was not sufficient for the defendants, in order to escape liability, merely to prove that the goods were not in their possession because they had been lost, but that they must prove much more than that in order to escape liability.

In this case the defendants did not satisfy the jury as to how the injuries were caused, and they had not satisfied his Lordship that they had used reasonable care. Therefore in his Lordship's opinion the defendants were liable to pay damages for the injuries to the pony which occurred while it was in their custody and as to which no satisfactory explanation had been given as to how they happened. . . .

Head v Tattersall

(1871) LR 7 Exch 7, Court of Exchequer

Head bought from Tattersall, an auctioneer, a horse described in the catalogue as having been hunted with the Bicester and Duke of Grafton's hounds. This information was incorrect. The sale contract contained a condition that 'horses not answering the description must be returned before 5 o'clock on the Wednesday evening next; otherwise the purchaser shall be obliged to keep the lot with all faults'. Head took the horse away and during the time that it was in his custody it was accidentally injured. He returned the horse in its damaged state before the 5 o'clock deadline, on the ground that it had not corresponded with its description. It was held that he was entitled to do so, and to have the whole of his money back.

> **Cleasby B:** The effect of the contract is to give the buyer an option of returning the horse in a particular event and within a specified time; and although it is clear that he might by his conduct have disentitled himself to exercise his option, he has not, in my judgment, done anything so to disentitle himself in the present case. By taking the horse away he did no more than, under his contract, he had a right to do. . . . This being so, the second question remains, whether the right given by the contract was limited, so as only to confer a right to return the horse, provided it remained in the same condition as it was in when sold. It is a sufficient answer to say, that as a time for returning the horse was expressly fixed by the contract, an accident occurring within the time from a cause beyond the plaintiff's control ought not to deprive him of his right, provided he can return the horse in some shape or other . . . Moreover, the matter may be put thus:—As a general rule, damage from the depreciation of a chattel ought to fall on the person who is the owner of it. Now here the effect of the contract was to vest the property in the buyer subject to a right of rescission in a particular event when it would revest in the seller. I think in such a case that the person who is eventually entitled to the property in the chattel ought to bear any loss arising from any depreciation in its value caused by an accident for which nobody is in fault. Here the defendant is the person in whom the property is revested, and he must therefore bear the loss. The cases cited seem to me to be beside the present question, for here there was an express condition in the contract itself giving to the purchaser an absolute right, under certain circumstances, to return the horse. I think, therefore, the plaintiff is entitled to recover.
>
> [**Kelly CB** and **Bramwell B** delivered concurring judgments.]

NOTE

See too *Kwei Tek Chao v British Traders and Shippers Ltd* [1954] 2 QB 459 at 487, where Devlin LJ said that 'what the buyer obtains, when the title under the documents is given to him, is the property in the goods, subject to the condition that they revest if upon examination he finds them to be not in accordance with the contract'. However, where non-conforming goods are delivered by the seller, the question whether the buyer has lost the right of rejection is often determined without reference to the issue of risk, and much may depend on the terms of the particular contract, the degree of non-conformity, and the nature of the event which prevents return of the goods. On this question, see AH Hudson, 'Conformity of Goods on Passing of Risk' in D Feldman and F Meisel (eds), *Corporate and Commercial Law: Modern Developments* (1996), Ch 11.

(d) Risk in unascertained goods

One further point should be made about 'risk'. It is a basic rule in English law that, save for s 20A, property cannot pass in unascertained goods (s 16: see above, p 331). But the law does not put a similar obstacle in the way when it comes to the passing of risk. The parties may, by agreement, place the risk of loss on the buyer even before the contract goods have been identified as such. This is illustrated by *Sterns Ltd v Vickers Ltd*, a case concerning a contract to sell an unascertained part out of an identified bulk.

Sterns Ltd v Vickers Ltd
[1923] 1 KB 78, Court of Appeal

The Admiralty sold to Vickers 200,000 gallons of white spirit which was being stored by the London and Thames Haven Oil Wharves Co in 'tank No 78'. Two weeks later, Vickers contracted to sell 120,000 gallons of this spirit to Sterns. Sterns resold the spirit which they had bought to Lazarus. Vickers obtained from the storage company a warrant acknowledging that 120,000 gallons of spirit were being held on Sterns' behalf, and this warrant was indorsed by Sterns to Lazarus. As Lazarus did not want to take immediate delivery of the spirit, he made his own arrangements with the company for further storage and paid them storage rent. Several months later, when Lazarus came to take the spirit, it was found to have been adulterated by being mixed with a spirit of heavier specific gravity. The Court of Appeal held that even though property in the spirit had not passed to the buyers, they had assumed the risk of loss or damage in respect of their share of the bulk spirit from the time when they accepted the storage company's warrant.

Scrutton LJ: I think Mr Thorn Drury is right in saying that as at the material time there had been no severance of the quantity purchased from the larger bulk there were no specific 120,000 gallons in which the property passed.... The acquisition of an undivided interest in a larger bulk clearly will not suffice to pass the property when the appropriation to the contract has to be made by the vendor himself. As Bayley B said in *Gillett v Hill* ((1834) 2 Cr & M 530): 'Where there is a bargain for a certain quantity' of goods 'ex a greater quantity, and there is a power of selection in the vendor to deliver which he thinks fit, then the right to them does not pass to the vendee until the vendor has made his selection, and trover is not maintainable before that is done.' Nor probably will the acquisition of such an undivided interest pass the property, so as to entitle the purchaser to sue for a conversion, in a case where the power of appropriation is, as here, in a third party. But in that latter case, whether the property passes or not, the transfer of the undivided interest carries with it the risk of loss from something happening to the goods, such as a deterioration in their quality, at all events after the vendor has given the purchaser a delivery order upon the party in possession of them, and that party has assented to it. The vendor of a specified quantity out of a bulk in the possession of a third party discharges his obligation to the purchaser as soon as the third party undertakes to the purchaser to deliver him that quantity out of the bulk. In the present case, what happened was that at the date of the contract there was a bulk larger than the quantity sold, and it was of the contract quality according to sample. A delivery warrant was issued by the Thames Haven Company undertaking to deliver that quantity from the bulk which at that time corresponded with the sample. That warrant was accepted by the purchaser and by their sub-purchaser, Lazarus, who proceeded to pay rent for the storage from the date of the warrant. In those circumstances I come clearly to the conclusion that as between the plaintiffs and the defendants the risk was on the plaintiffs the purchasers. The vendors had done all that they undertook to do. The purchasers had the right to go to the storage company and demand delivery, and if they had done so at the time they would have got all that the defendants had undertaken to sell them. What the purchasers here are trying to do is to put the risk after acceptance of the warrant upon persons who had then no control over the goods, for it seems plain that after the acceptance of that warrant the vendors would have had no right to go to the storage company and request them to refuse delivery to the purchaser. For these reasons, treating the matter as a question rather of the transfer of risk than of the passing of property—for strictly I do not think the property passed, but only a right to an undivided share in the bulk to be selected by a third person—I think the view taken by the judge below was erroneous. He seems to have considered the question of transferring the risk, and thought there was no evidence of it. With that view, I cannot agree. I think the only conclusion to be drawn from the evidence is that the risk did pass . . .

[**Bankes LJ** delivered a concurring judgment. **Eve J** concurred.]

NOTE

Sterns v Vickers was, of course, decided before the new s 20A (see above, p 335) was enacted. You may like to consider whether any of the questions which follow would be answered differently if s 20A were in force and Sterns had paid Vickers the full price.

QUESTIONS

1. Who carried the risk in respect of the other 80,000 gallons?

2. Suppose that when Lazarus came to collect the spirit which he had purchased, there had been no adulteration but 80,000 gallons had been stolen. How much would he be (a) entitled, (b) bound, to take?

3. If other spirit had been mixed with the 200,000 gallons so that the bulk was *improved* in quality, could he have claimed 120,000 gallons of it?

4. In *Healy v Howlett & Sons* [1917] 1 KB 337 Irish sellers in Co Kerry dispatched 190 boxes of mackerel by train to London, of which the buyers agreed to buy 20. The railways being inefficient then as now, the fish went bad in transit. It was held that because property had not passed the fish was at the sellers' risk and the buyers did not have to pay for their cases. Can this case be reconciled with *Sterns v Vickers*?

Risk may even pass in goods not yet appropriated to the contract in any way. Thus in *Produce Brokers Co Ltd v Olympia Oil & Cake Co Ltd* [1917] 1 KB 320 sellers agreed to sell to the buyers 6,000 tons of soya beans to be shipped from a Far East port, with risk to pass on shipment. The sellers appropriated to the contract cargo shipped on a vessel which, to their knowledge, had already sunk shortly after leaving Vladivostok. The buyers were held bound to accept it.

5 STATUTORY PROVISIONS RELATING TO PERISHING OF SPECIFIC GOODS

Sections 6 and 7 of the Act contain provisions relating to the 'perishing' of the goods which bear some relationship to the question of risk. They may be seen respectively as particular instances of the contractual doctrines of common mistake and frustration. Each section applies only to contracts for the sale of *specific* goods.

(a) Section 6: specific goods which have perished

Where there is a contract for the sale of specific goods, and the goods without the knowledge of the seller have perished at the time when the contract is made, s 6 of the Act declares that the contract is void.

(i) What amounts to 'perishing'?

The term 'perish' is not defined in the Act, but the case next cited gives a clear indication that it is to be given a broad interpretation, so as to include (for example) goods which have been stolen, or which have 'perished' in part.

Barrow, Lane & Ballard Ltd v Phillip Phillips & Co
[1929] 1 KB 574, King's Bench Division

On 11 October 1927, Phillips contracted to sell to Ballards a specific lot (or 'parcel') consisting of 700 bags of Chinese ground nuts in shell, held in the stores of a wharf company. Unknown to the parties, 109 of the bags had been stolen before the contract was made; and, after delivery had been made of 150 bags, all the rest were also stolen. Phillips sued Ballards for the price of all 700 bags. It was held that s 6 applied, since the *parcel* of 700 bags had perished when the 109 were stolen.

> **Wright J**: . . . This case raises a . . . problem, which, so far as I know, and so far as learned counsel have been able to ascertain, has never hitherto come before the Court. The problem is this: Where there is a contract for the sale of specific goods, such as the parcel of goods in this case, and some, but not all, of the goods have then ceased to exist for all purposes relevant to the contract because they have been stolen and taken away and cannot be followed or discovered anywhere, what then is the position? Does the case come within s 6 of the Sale of Goods Act, so that it would be the same as if the whole parcel had ceased to exist? In my judgment it does. The contract here was for a parcel of 700 bags, and at the time when it was made there were only 591 bags. A contract for a parcel of 700 bags is something different from a contract for 591 bags, and the position appears to me to be in no way different from what it would have been if the whole 700 bags had ceased to exist. The result is that the parties were contracting about something which, at the date of the contract, without the knowledge or fault of either party, did not exist. To compel the buyer in those circumstances to take 591 bags would be to compel him to take something which he had not contracted to take, and would in my judgment be unjust . . .
>
> A question of some difficulty arises when the goods are not lost or destroyed, but simply deteriorate in quality. Normally, this question will be determined by considering one or other of the following questions (or perhaps both: see s 33): (1) whether the seller has given any warranty as to the condition which the goods will be in at the material time (see, eg *Mash & Murrell Ltd v JI Emanuel Ltd* (below, p 439)), and (2) which party has the risk. But if the goods have deteriorated beyond the point where they cease to conform to their contract description, or are no longer of any commercial use, there is a case for saying that they have 'perished'. One English case suggests the contrary (see *Horn v Minister of Food* [1948] 2 All ER 1036, where potatoes which had rotted to a degree which made them useless even to be fed to cattle were held, obiter, not to have perished). But most writers agree that this suggestion was wrong, and it was not followed recently in New Zealand: see *Oldfield Asphalts Ltd v Grovedale*

Coolstores (1994) Ltd [1998] 3 NZLR 479 (portable building seriously damaged by fire). See too the insurance case of *Asfar & Co v Blundell* [1896] 1 QB 123, CA. Dates aboard a ship sank in the Thames and were contaminated by sea water and sewage. When salvaged, they were unfit for human consumption (but, surprisingly, still worth a considerable sum for distillation into spirit!). For insurance purposes, however, they were held a 'constructive total loss'—surely equivalent to a finding that they had 'perished' had s 6 or s 7 been in issue.

QUESTION

On Tuesday A Ltd sells B Ltd a specific truck, agreeing to deliver it on Friday. Unknown to either party the truck has been stolen on Monday. On Wednesday the truck is recovered, entirely undamaged, by the police and returned to A. Is A in breach of contract if it refuses to deliver the truck to B?

(ii) Section 6 and the common law

Section 6 was said by Chalmers himself (*The Sale of Goods* (1st edn, 1890), p 10) to have been based on the well-known House of Lords' decision at common law in *Couturier v Hastie*.

Couturier v Hastie
(1856) 5 HL Cas 673, House of Lords

A cargo of maize was shipped at Salonica[4] by Couturier in February 1848 for delivery in London. In May Hastie, acting for Couturier on a *del credere* commission (ie as an agent who assumed personal liability for the buyer's obligations: see above, p 117), contracted to sell this cargo to Callander. Unknown to either Hastie or Callander, the cargo had been sold in April by the ship's captain in Tunis, en route to London, because it was overheating. Callander refused to pay for the corn, and so Couturier sued Hastie for the price. Mr Wilde, counsel for Couturier, argued:

> The purchase here was not of the cargo absolutely as a thing assumed to be in existence, but merely of the benefit of the expectation of its arrival, and of the securities against the contingency of its loss. The purchaser bought in fact the shipping documents, the rights and interests of the vendor.

In effect, his contention was that the buyer had not bought the cargo of corn, as specific goods, but had contracted to take over the benefit of the voyage, as a venture. However, the court held, as a matter of construction, that the subject matter of the contract was the cargo. As it had not been delivered, the seller could not sue for the price.

> **Lord Cranworth LC**: Looking to the contract itself alone, it appears to me clearly that what the parties contemplated, those who bought and those who sold, was that there was an existing something to be sold and bought, and if sold and bought, then the benefit of insurance should go with it. I do not feel pressed by the latter argument, which has been brought forward very ably by

---

[4] Now Thessaloniki in northern Greece.

> Mr Wilde, derived from the subject of insurance. I think the full benefit of the insurance was meant to go as well to losses and damage that occurred previously to the 15th of May, as to losses and damage that occurred subsequently, always assuming that something passed by the contract of the 15th of May. If the contract of the 15th of May had been an operating contract, and there had been a valid sale of a cargo at that time existing, I think the purchaser would have had the benefit of insurance in respect of all damage previously occurring. The contract plainly imports that there was something which was to be sold at the time of the contract, and something to be purchased. No such thing existing, I think the Court of Exchequer Chamber has come to the only reasonable conclusion upon it, and consequently that there must be judgment given by your Lordships for the Defendants. . . .

QUESTION

Is *Couturier v Hastie* authority for the proposition stated in s 6? Or does it merely hold that when you agree to sell something you cannot claim the price if you cannot come up with the goods? What if it had been Callander suing Couturier for damages for non-delivery?

The common law background to s 6 is important because s 6 only covers goods which have perished: that is, goods which once existed but now do not. The case where goods are sold which never existed at all remains governed by the common law. This arose for decision in *McRae v Commonwealth Disposals Commission*, a decision of the High Court of Australia which some commentators have found difficult to reconcile with the statutory rule laid down by s 6.

McRae v Commonwealth Disposals Commission

(1950) 84 CLR 377, High Court of Australia

The Commission, an agency of the Australian government, advertised for sale 'an oil tanker lying on the Jourmand Reef, which is approximately 100 miles north of Samarai. The vessel is said to contain oil'. McRae agreed to buy the tanker and its contents for £285. He fitted out a salvage expedition at considerable expense and went to the advertised locality, but there was no tanker there—and in fact no reef. No such tanker had ever existed. The High Court held the Commission liable for breach of a contractual promise that there was an oil tanker at the position specified.

> **Dixon** and **Fullagar JJ** (in a joint judgment): . . . It was not decided in *Couturier v Hastie* ((1856) 5 HL Cas 673) that the contract in that case was void. The question whether it was void or not did not arise. If it had arisen, as in an action by the purchaser for damages, it would have turned on the ulterior question whether the contract was subject to an implied condition precedent. Whatever might then have been held on the facts of *Couturier v Hastie*, it is impossible in this case to imply any such term. The terms of the contract and the surrounding circumstances clearly exclude any such implication. The buyers relied upon, and acted upon, the assertion of the seller that there was a tanker in existence. It is not a case in which the parties can be seen to have proceeded on the basis of a common assumption of fact so as to justify the conclusion that the correctness of the assumption was intended by both parties to be a condition precedent to the creation of contractual obligations. The officers of the Commission made an assumption, but the plaintiffs did

not make an assumption in the same sense. They knew nothing except what the Commission had told them. If they had been asked, they would certainly not have said: 'Of course, if there is no tanker, there is no contract.' They would have said: 'We shall have to go and take possession of the tanker. We simply accept the Commission's assurance that there is a tanker and the Commission's promise to give us that tanker.' The only proper construction of the contract is that it included a promise by the Commission that there was a tanker in the position specified. The Commission contracted that there was a tanker there. 'The sale in this case of a ship implies a contract that the subject of the transfer did exist in the character of a ship' (*Barr v Gibson* (1838) 3 M & W 390)). If, on the other hand, the case of *Couturier v Hastie* and this case ought to be treated as cases raising a question of 'mistake', then the Commission cannot in this case rely on any mistake as avoiding the contract, because any mistake was induced by the serious fault of their own servants, who asserted the existence of a tanker recklessly and without any reasonable ground. There was a contract, and the Commission contracted that a tanker existed in the position specified. Since there was no such tanker, there has been a breach of contract, and the plaintiffs are entitled to damages for that breach.

Before proceeding to consider the measure of damages, one other matter should be briefly mentioned. The contract was made in Melbourne, and it would seem that its proper law is Victorian law. Section 11 of the Victorian Goods Act 1928 corresponds to s 6 of the English Sale of Goods Act [1979], and provides that 'where there is a contract for the sale of specific goods, and the goods without the knowledge of the seller have perished at the time when the contract is made the contract is void'. This has been generally supposed to represent the legislature's view of the effect of *Couturier v Hastie*. Whether it correctly represents the effect of the decision in that case or not, it seems clear that the section has no application to the facts of the present case. Here the goods never existed, and the seller ought to have known that they did not exist. . . .

[**McTiernan J** concurred.]

NOTES

1. It is possible to explain why s 6 (or rather its equivalent in the Australian state of Victoria, whose law governed this transaction) was not applied in *McRae*'s case by reference to the fact that no tanker had ever existed. But this is not the *ratio decidendi* of the judgment. The court found that the Commission had contracted to sell a ship and, as a term of that contract, *warranted that they had a ship to sell*. They were held liable to pay damages for breach of this term. This suggests that at common law a seller of specific goods is presumed to warrant that the goods exist at the time of the contract. It is only where s 6 applies—ie where the goods once existed but have since ceased to do so—that the contract is void.

2. As pointed out by Professor Atiyah (PS Atiyah, '*Couturier v Hastie* and the Sale of Non-existent Goods' (1957) 73 LQR 340), the parties to a contract on facts similar to *Couturier v Hastie* or *McRae*'s case are free to make any one of three bargains:

(a) their contract might be subject to an implied condition precedent that the goods are in existence; if they are not, neither party incurs any liability;

(b) the seller might contract (warrant) that the goods do exist; if they are not, he will be liable in damages to the buyer;

(c) the buyer may agree to take the risk that the goods may have perished prior to the contract—ie he agrees to pay for the *chance* of getting the goods.

In (a), neither party takes the risk that the goods may not exist; in (b), the seller does; in (c), the buyer does. Where this question of risk is not spelt out clearly, all are possible interpretations of the bargain which the parties have made.

QUESTIONS

1. It might be suggested that the decision in *McRae* could be better supported on the basis that, although the contract of sale itself was void under s 6, the Commission had also entered into a collateral contract with McRae in which they promised that the ship existed. Consider this suggestion.

2. A commercial seller impliedly promises that the subject matter of the contract complies with its description, is of satisfactory quality, and is reasonably fit for its purpose (see ss 13 and 14). Given that this is so, would it not be somewhat curious if he did not also promise that it existed in the first place?

3. McRae, who paid the Commission £285 for the salvage rights to a vessel and its contents worth possibly many thousands of pounds, is reported as having said: 'One often had a couple of hundred pounds on a horse on a Saturday and I might as well have a gamble on this.' Was this not a case, then, of *emptio spei*, the third of Professor Atiyah's possible contracts?

(b) Section 7: specific goods which subsequently perish

In a provision which closely parallels s 6 (above), s 7 states:

> Where there is an agreement to sell specific goods and subsequently the goods, without any fault on the part of the seller or buyer, perish before the risk passes to the buyer, the agreement is avoided.

The wording of ss 6 and 7 is similar in several places, and it is generally assumed that decisions on the meaning of any common terms (such as 'perishing') are relevant for both.

Note that s 7 is limited to *specific* goods. It is perfectly possible for *ascertained* goods to perish (for the difference between the two, see p 305 above). Imagine, for example, that A agrees on Monday to sell B 500 kg of King Edward potatoes, with delivery taking place and ownership and risk passing on Friday. On Tuesday A appropriates 500 kg of potatoes to the contract; on Wednesday the potatoes are stolen. Section 7 would not apply, since *at the time of the contract* it was not clear which potatoes B would get. It might well be, however, that the common law rules of frustration would come to A's rescue here; see below, p 372.

QUESTION

Barrow, Lane & Ballard Ltd v Phillip Phillips & Co, above, suggested that a parcel of nuts had 'perished' when roughly one-seventh of it had disappeared. Apart from s 7, would this be a case where 'a contractual obligation has become incapable of being performed because the circumstances in which performance is called for would render it a thing radically different from that which was undertaken by the contract', something which, according to Lord Radcliffe in *Davis Contractors Ltd v Fareham Urban District Council* [1956] AC 696 at 729, was essential in order to allow a party to plead frustration?

(c) 'Perishing' of unascertained goods

Both s 6 and s 7, as has been noted, apply only to specific goods. This raises the question whether unascertained goods can ever be said to have perished, and if so what the consequences are in law. Although this issue is not important with totally generic goods such as 10,000 tonnes of soya beans (since there the concept of 'perishing' in the sense of ceasing to exist makes little sense), it may matter as regards goods to be supplied from a particular store, or from a particular year's production from a given source. Imagine, for example, a contract by a wine grower in 2015 to deliver at the winery '100 cases of Château X 2016' followed by the destruction of all or part of that year's production; or a contract to sell 200 computers out of a given bulk of 500 in a warehouse, just before the destruction by fire of all or some of the contents of that warehouse.

The case *of Howell v Coupland* was concerned with a slight variant on these facts.

Howell v Coupland
(1876) 1 QBD 258, Court of Appeal

Coupland, a Lincolnshire farmer, in March 1872 contracted to sell to Howell 200 tons of Regent potatoes to be grown on specified land of Coupland's, to be delivered in the following September and October. Coupland planted potatoes on 68 acres of the land—an area sufficient in a normal season to yield over 450 tons; but the crop was struck by an unpreventable disease in August and only 80 tons were produced. Howell took delivery of the 80 tons and paid for them at the contract rate, and sued Coupland for damages for failure to deliver the balance. It was held that the failure should be excused.

> **Lord Coleridge CJ**: I am of opinion that the judgment ought to be affirmed . . . The true ground, as it seems to me, on which the contract should be interpreted . . . is that by the simple and obvious construction of the agreement both parties understood and agreed, that there should be a condition implied that before the time for the performance of the contract the potatoes should be, or should have been, in existence, and should still be existing when the time came for the performance. They had been in existence, and had been destroyed by causes over which the defendant, the contractor, had no control, and it became impossible for him to perform his contract; and, according to the condition which the parties had understood should be in the contract, he was excused from the performance. It was not an absolute contract of delivery under all circumstances, but a contract to deliver so many potatoes, of a particular kind, grown on a specific place, if deliverable from that place. On the facts the condition did arise and the performance was excused. I am, therefore, of opinion that the judgment of the Queen's Bench should be affirmed.
>
> [**James** and **Mellish LJJ**, **Baggallay J**, and **Cleasby B** delivered concurring judgments.]

QUESTIONS

1. Why would a potato merchant make a contract in March to buy potatoes as yet unplanted which would not be grown until September?

2. If a natural calamity such as frost or disease has struck one farmer's crop, it is likely to have affected others also. What would happen to the market price in such circumstances?

3. If Howell had not wanted the 80 tons, was he bound to take them? (See s 30(1).)

NOTES

1.   There has never been any doubt that *Howell v Coupland* is a correct decision, but there has been some debate as to the principle on which it should be regarded as having been based in modern law. Chalmers suggested that it demonstrated the rule in s 7 of the Act (see his *Sale of Goods* (1st edn, 1890), p 11), but this cannot be right. The goods were not 'specific goods' as defined in the Act (even though Mellish LJ did unguardedly call them 'specific'); it is also highly arguable that potatoes that never grow into recognisable tubers in the first place do not 'perish'. Nor is it easy to explain *Howell v Coupland* as a simple case of common law frustration. Frustration, where applicable, avoids the whole contract. But the court in *Howell* excused the seller only in regard to the part of the crop which had failed; and as we shall see shortly from the ruling in *HR & S Sainsbury Ltd v Street* (below), the seller is not excused from his obligation to deliver so much as he has been able to produce.

2.   In *Re Wait* (above, p 298), Atkin LJ made some interesting comments on *Howell* (see [1927] 1 Ch 606 at 631). Having pointed out that the case did not involve specific goods as defined in the Act, he said:

> The case of *Howell v Coupland* would now be covered either by s 5, sub-s 2, of the Code or, as is suggested by the learned authors of the last two editions of Benjamin on Sale, by common law principles retained by s 61, sub-s 2, of the Code.

Section 5(2) of the Act states that there may be a contract for the sale of goods, the acquisition of which depends upon a contingency which may or may not happen. In *Howell v Coupland*, the contingency was a condition implied by the court that the specified land would yield the amount of potatoes necessary to fulfil the contract. The use of an implied term in this way gives the court more flexibility than the doctrine of frustration would allow, for it makes it possible also to imply an understanding that if there is a shortfall the seller is bound to let the buyer have the smaller amount which has been produced. This was in fact the ruling in *HR & S Sainsbury Ltd v Street*.

HR & S Sainsbury Ltd v Street
[1972] 1 WLR 834, Queen's Bench Division

The facts appear from the judgment.

> **MacKenna J:** The plaintiff buyers claim damages against the defendant seller under an alleged contract for the sale of 'about 275 tons' of feed barley for delivery in August or September 1970. The defendant denies the contract. He alleges in the alternative that if he agreed to sell it was a condition precedent of his obligation to deliver that he should in 1970 harvest a crop of at least that tonnage on his farm at East Knoyle, Wiltshire, that he did not harvest such a crop but one of only 140 tons, and that his failure to harvest the larger crop excused him from the obligation to delivery any barley, even the smaller tonnage. He admittedly delivered none. The plaintiffs concede that he harvested only the smaller tonnage and further concede that they are not entitled to damages for his failure to deliver barley which he did not harvest, but assert that they are entitled to recover damages for his failure to deliver the 140 tons harvested. It is agreed that if they are entitled to recover any damages these should be computed at £7.50 per ton.

There are two questions which I must decide. (1) Did the defendant agree to sell 'about 275 tons' of feed barley to the plaintiffs? If he did, (2) was he under any obligation to deliver the 140 tons which he actually harvested? . . .

[His Lordship reviewed the evidence and concluded:]

As to the first question I find that there was a contract between the plaintiffs and the defendant for the purchase of 275 tons of feed barley (5 per cent more or less) to be grown by the defendant on his farm. . . .

As to the second, I am prepared to assume, consistently with the plaintiffs' abandonment of their claim for damages for the tonnage not in fact produced, that it was an implied condition of the contract that if the defendant, through no fault of his, failed to produce the stipulated tonnage of his growing crop, he should not be required to pay damages. It seems a very reasonable condition, considering the risks of agriculture and the fact that the crop was at the contract date still growing. But a condition that he need not deliver any if, through some misfortune, he could not deliver the whole is a very different one, and in my opinion so unreasonable that I would not imply it unless compelled to do so by authority. The way in which the parties chose the more or less conventional figure of one and a half [tons per acre] as the estimated yield of the crop is, I think, an additional reason in this case against the implication. If they had intended that a failure to achieve this optimistic tonnage would mean the end of the contract for both of them, they would have gone about the business of estimating yield in a much more cautious manner.

Mr Rawlins argued that it was reasonable that the defendant should be freed of all his obligations under the contract if without his fault he failed to produce the whole tonnage. 275 tons (5 per cent more or less) set an upper limit to the quantity which the plaintiffs could be compelled to take. It was reasonable, he said, that there should be a lower limit to the amount which the defendant could be compelled to deliver. In a year when the latter's yield was high, market prices would probably be low, and it would be a benefit to the plaintiffs not to be required to take more than an agreed tonnage at the contract price fixed in advance. In a year when the yield was low, as in the present case, it would be a benefit to the defendant if he were free to disregard his contract and to sell his crop to some other buyer at the higher market price. The contract should, if possible, be construed as giving him this freedom. I am not persuaded by the argument. The upper limit of 275 tons might in the circumstances of a particular case be beneficial to both parties. But even if it could be beneficial only to the buyer that is no reason for implying a term that the same figure shall serve as a lower limit to the seller's obligation to deliver, so that his failure to reach that figure, if blameless, would release him from the contract.

[The buyers were accordingly held to be entitled to damages. His Lordship said, in relation to *Howell v Coupland*:]

It is clear from the statement of the facts in the headnote that the case raised no question about the seller's obligation to deliver the potatoes which he had in fact produced, and clear from the last sentence quoted from the judgment of Blackburn J that it gives no support to the view that the bargain was off both as to the 120 tons and the 80. There is nothing in the judgments of the Court of Appeal which touches this question.

After the decision of *Howell v Coupland* the Sale of Goods Act 1893 was passed.

[His Lordship quoted ss 5(2), 6, 7, and 61(2) [now 62(2)] of the Act, and continued:]

The rule of *Howell v Coupland* is, I think, preserved by s 5(2). If I am wrong in that view, because the growing of a crop cannot be considered the 'acquisition' of goods within the meaning of that section, then it is preserved by s 61(2). I do not think that it is preserved by ss 6 or 7. These sections are, in my opinion, dealing with goods existing, and a crop not yet grown does not answer either description.

NOTE

There is one further problem, for which English law does not offer a wholly satisfactory solution. What if Coupland had made a second contract to sell 200 tons of potatoes to another merchant? What would be the rights of the respective parties? Or, to identify the issues more clearly, suppose that S Ltd has 200 boxes of champagne in store and in separate contracts agrees to sell '100 boxes of the champagne from our store' to B1 and the same number to B2. Before any boxes have been appropriated to either contract, thieves steal 100 boxes, leaving S able to perform one or other contract, but not both.

If the contract contains an express 'force majeure' clause exempting S from liability in the case of theft, what authority there is suggests that such a clause would allow S to apportion the remaining available champagne in any way 'which the trade would consider to be proper and reasonable—whether the basis of appropriation is pro-rata, chronological order of contracts or some other basis'—the reason being that in such a case any buyer's failure to obtain its full allocation would be 'not the seller's appropriation, but whatever caused the shortage'. See *Intertradex SA v Lesieur-Tourteaux SàRL* [1977] 2 Lloyd's Rep 146 at 155, per Donaldson J (approved by Lord Denning MR on appeal at [1978] 2 Lloyd's Rep 509 at 513).

Where there is no such clause, however, cases in other contexts suggest that in the absence of some provision in the contracts indicating that one of them should be performed first, or that each buyer should take a proportionate share of what goods are available, the seller is not excused for his failure to honour the contract that he chooses not to perform. In the language of the doctrine of frustration, this failure is 'self-induced', resulting from his own election to perform the other: see *Maritime National Fish Ltd v Ocean Trawlers Ltd* [1935] AC 524, PC and *The Super Servant Two* [1990] 1 Lloyd's Rep 1, CA (two cases on the hiring of ships). In the United States, the Uniform Commercial Code, s 2–615 offers a much fairer solution: the seller is allowed to 'prorate' his performance, ie distribute those goods which he does have available pro rata amongst the various buyers. (On prorating generally, see AH Hudson (1968) 31 MLR 535, (1978) 123 Sol Jo 137.)

(d) Impossibility of supply of generic goods

(i) Sales of generic goods

Where there is a contract to sell goods of this kind identified purely by description (the typical 'commodity sale', such as '10,000 tonnes of Portland cement'), performance may be excused by impossibility in the sense of illegality, either by English law or the law of the place of performance. See, for example, *Société Co-operative Suisse des Céréales v La Plata Cereal* (1947) 80 Ll L Rep 530. Subject to this, however, such contracts are made on the understanding that the seller undertakes the entire responsibility of ensuring the availability of the goods in question. The whole point of contracts to buy goods for forward delivery is to hedge the buyer's position against adverse movements in the market, including the risk that supplies may run out. As the extract from the *Intertradex* case (below) shows, this is part of the 'warp and woof of commerce'. The leading case is *Blackburn Bobbin Co Ltd v TW Allen & Sons Ltd*.

Blackburn Bobbin Co Ltd v TW Allen & Sons Ltd

[1918] 2 KB 467, Court of Appeal

Allens contracted to sell to the Blackburn company 70 standards of Finland birch timber (a standard is 165 cubic feet), to be delivered on rail at Hull (where Allens were based) over the period from June to November 1914. Because there had been no sailings from Finnish ports, no timber had been imported from Finland when war broke out in August of that year, and thereafter it became impossible to obtain Finnish timber either directly from Finland or from any other source. It was normal practice for merchants to import all Finnish timber direct from Finland to meet their customers' orders, and stockpiles were not held in England. The Court of Appeal, affirming McCardie J, held that Allens were not excused from their contractual obligations.

> **Pickford LJ**: The defendants contend that the contract was at an end because it was in the contemplation of both parties that the defendants should be able to supply the timber according to the ordinary method of supplying it in the trade, and that when that became impossible both parties were discharged from their obligations. . . .
>
> [His Lordship discussed a number of cases dealing with the doctrine of frustration, and continued:]
>
> In my opinion McCardie J was right in saying that the principle of these cases did not apply to discharge the defendants in this case. He has found that the plaintiffs were unaware at the time of the contract of the circumstance that the timber from Finland was shipped direct from a Finnish port to Hull, and that they did not know whether the transport was or was not partly by rail across Scandinavia, nor did they know that timber merchants in this country did not hold stocks of Finnish birch. I accept the finding that in fact the method of dispatching this timber was not known to the plaintiffs. But there remains the question, Must they be deemed to have contracted on the basis of the continuance of that method although they did not in fact know of it? I see no reason for saying so. Why should a purchaser of goods, not specific goods, be deemed to concern himself with the way in which the seller is going to fulfil his contract by providing the goods he has agreed to sell? The sellers in this case agreed to deliver the timber free on rail at Hull, and it was no concern of the buyers as to how the sellers intended to get the timber there. I can see no reason for saying—and to free the defendants from liability this would have to be said—that the continuance of the normal mode of shipping the timber from Finland was a matter which both parties contemplated as necessary for the fulfilment of the contract. To dissolve the contract the matter relied on must be something which both parties had in their minds when they entered into the contract, such for instance as the existence of the music-hall in *Taylor v Caldwell* (1863) 3 B & S 826, or the continuance of the vessel in readiness to perform the contract, as in *Jackson v Union Marine Insurance Co* (1874) LR 10 CP 125. Here there is nothing to show that the plaintiffs contemplated, and there is no reason why they should be deemed to have contemplated, that the sellers should continue to have the ordinary facilities for dispatching the timber from Finland. As I have said, that was a matter which to the plaintiffs was wholly immaterial. It was not a matter forming the basis of the contract they entered into. . . .
>
> For the reasons I have given the defendants have failed on the facts to make out their case that the contract was dissolved. The appeal will be dismissed.
>
> [**Bankes** and **Warrington LJJ** delivered concurring judgments.]

Intertradex SA v Lesieur-Tourteaux SàRL

[1977] 2 Lloyd's Rep 146, [1978] 2 Lloyd's Rep 509, Queen's Bench Division
and Court of Appeal

Intertradex contracted to sell to Lesieur-Tourteaux 800 tonnes of Mali groundnut expellers, CIF Rouen. (On CIF contracts, see below, p 543.) The sellers intended to fulfil their obligations from a consignment of 1,000 tonnes which they in turn had contracted to buy from suppliers, 'SEPOM', who (as they, but not the buyers, knew) were the sole crushers and producers of Mali groundnut expellers. The suppliers' factory at Koulikoro was ten days by rail from Abidjan, and four days from Dakar, the only export ports. The suppliers were unable to meet their commitments due to a mechanical breakdown at their factory (for which a replacement part had to be obtained from Germany) and interruptions in the supply by rail of raw materials to their factory. The sellers claimed that they were excused from performance—a view which was upheld by a board of arbitration to which the dispute was referred. Donaldson J, in a judgment affirmed by the Court of Appeal, held that they were not excused.

> **Donaldson J**: That this situation was aggravating or frustrating both for SEPOM and the sellers is not in doubt, but the legal doctrine of frustration is not based upon psychology or emotion . . .
>
> The sellers' basic obligation was to deliver the goods (or documents covering the goods) in accordance with their contract. The basic risks which they assumed were those of shortage of supply and a rise in price. It was for the assumption of these risks that they would have agreed a price which, hopefully, would have produced a profit. They have qualified this obligation by reference in cll 21 and 22 to a very wide variety of events which might place obstacles in their way. Ingenuity may suggest some concatenation of events to which these clauses do not apply, but which are of so outlandish a nature that the obligation to deliver cannot have been intended to survive in the changed circumstances. But a mere reduction in the supplies available, even from a sole supplier, due to such commonplace events as a breakdown of machinery or the inadequacies of a railway are far removed from this category. They are the warp and woof of industrial and commercial aggravation. Giving the fullest effect to the board's findings of fact and paying the fullest respect to their view of the commercial realities, in my judgment there are no possible grounds for holding the contract between the buyers and sellers to have been frustrated.

NOTES

1. *Blackburn Bobbin v Allen* and the *Intertradex* case, above, were followed and confirmed by the Court of Appeal in *CTI Group Inc v Transclear SA* [2008] EWCA Civ 856, [2008] 2 CLC 112. Indonesian sellers agreed to sell cement to buyers who wished it for the Mexican market. The closed cartel which then controlled the Mexican market then successfully pressured the Indonesian sellers' own suppliers to refuse to supply them. The buyers had to buy in replacement cement from Russia for vastly more than the contract price. There was held to be no frustration, and the sellers were held liable for large damages as a result.

2. Of course, the parties are free to make a contract for the sale of commodities of this kind on other terms. It is customary in most international sales contracts to incorporate 'force majeure' clauses designed to protect the seller against liability in such events as a failure of supply or a breakdown of transport. In fact, in *Intertradex* itself, there was such a clause, but it was held on the facts that the sellers were not able to rely on it. It should be noted, however, that the practice is to construe such clauses fairly strictly, and to resist any attempt to invoke them in cases of mere commercial difficulty, even of a high order. Representative cases are *Thames Valley Power Ltd v Total Gas & Power Ltd* [2005] EWHC 2208 (Comm), [2006] 1 Lloyd's Rep 441, and *Bunge SA v Nidera BV* [2013] EWCA 1628, [2014] 1 Lloyd's Rep 404 (appealed to the Supreme Court on other grounds [2015] UKSC 43, [2015] 3 All ER 1082). See, generally, G Treitel, *Frustration and Force Majeure* (3rd edn, 2014).

3. It is also possible for the parties to make their contract on altogether different terms, such that the 'seller' undertakes not to supply goods, but merely to use its best endeavours to procure them. If prevented by matters beyond its control from obtaining the goods, it follows that the seller is not in breach. See, for example, the old consumer case of *Monkland v Jack Barclay Ltd* [1951] 2 KB 252.

(ii) Goods to be manufactured or acquired by the seller

On principle, the same approach should normally govern contracts for the sale of goods which are to be manufactured or otherwise acquired (eg fish to be caught) by the seller. If a seller agrees to manufacture machinery for a buyer, and the machinery is destroyed by fire when 90 per cent finished, the seller has no choice but to obtain a new supply of materials and begin work all over again.

6 FRUSTRATION OF SALE OF GOODS CONTRACTS

In the discussion above, we have been concerned with the destruction of the subject matter of the contract which is, of course, one of the grounds upon which a contract can be held to be frustrated at common law. Nothing in the Act prevents the doctrine of frustration from being applied to contracts for the sale of goods where any of the other recognised grounds is relied on, for example supervening illegality, or impossibility caused by such an event as the closing of the port designated by the contract for the shipping of the goods or the sinking of the named ship in which they are to be carried.

One case where this might apply is where there is a contract to sell generic goods and goods are later appropriated to the contract, so that the seller is from that point on bound to supply those goods and no others. Imagine, for example, the example at p 372 above: A agrees on Monday to sell B 500 kg of King Edward potatoes, with delivery taking place and ownership and risk passing on Friday. On Tuesday A appropriates 500 kg of potatoes to the contract; on Wednesday the potatoes are stolen. There seems no reason why in such a case the contract should not be frustrated at common law.

We may ask one further question: what is the relation between the concept of 'risk', which we have been examining, and the doctrine of frustration? First, by definition, frustration deals with an event not contemplated by the parties and not provided for by a term of the contract. It gives way to contrary agreement. If the parties have agreed that one or the other of them shall carry the risk of accidents, or if the seller has undertaken an *absolute* obligation to supply goods of the contract description, there is no scope left for the doctrine of frustration.

Secondly, we should note that there is a difference in the respective *effects* of risk and frustration: the former exposes one party to liability, whereas frustration excuses both. Thirdly, it should be remembered that the Law Reform (Frustrated Contracts) Act 1943, which gives the court some discretionary powers to adjust the losses between the respective parties following a frustrating event, is expressly not made applicable to contracts for the sale of specific goods which, under s 7 or otherwise, are frustrated by reason of the fact that the goods have perished (s 2(5)(c) of the 1943 Act). This is in itself a statutory acknowledgement that there is no room for other solutions to a problem where the concept of risk applies.

CHAPTER 10

TRANSFER OF TITLE

1 THE RULE *NEMO DAT QUOD NON HABET*

The Sale of Goods Act distinguishes fairly sharply between 'transfer of property as between seller and buyer' and 'transfer of title'. 'Transfer of property as between seller and buyer', dealt with in ss 16–19, refers to the process by which the seller's right of ownership right passes to the buyer. In contrast, under 'transfer of title', the concern is whether a seller S who is a non-owner, or a person with a defective title, can nevertheless confer a good title on his buyer B, and in doing so defeat the claims of the true owner O (or of a person with a superior title).[1]

The attitude of the common law to this problem is unusual. Civil law countries, including nearly all continental European jurisdictions such as France and Germany, start from the position that where S is in possession of goods with the owner O's consent, a good faith purchaser from S gets good title as against O. In the common law, by contrast, the presumption goes the other way. Section 21 provides the basic rule (summed up in the ancient maxim *nemo dat quod non habet* (meaning 'no-one can transfer what he does not himself have')—or, for short, *nemo dat*), subject to any exceptions,

> where goods are sold by a person who is not their owner, and who does not sell them under the authority or with the consent of the owner, the buyer acquires no better title to the goods than the seller had.

The same, or a similar, basic rule applies (unless there are statutory or common law exceptions) to gifts, to bailments such as hire and pledge, and to the assignment of choses in action. Its importance cannot be overemphasised—even though the rule itself can be stated in a few lines, and the bulk of the discussion which is to follow will go into the exceptions at length and in some detail!

Two well-known cases illustrate the force of the *nemo dat* rule.

Farquharson Bros & Co v C King & Co
[1902] AC 325, House of Lords

Farquharsons were timber merchants who warehoused in the Surrey Commercial Docks[2] timber which they imported from abroad. They employed a clerk, Capon, who was authorised

---

[1] The abbreviations O, S, and B will be used in this sense throughout this chapter, except where they might cause confusion.

[2] The site of these was in London's Docklands, east of what is now Surrey Quays station on the East London Line.

to sign delivery orders addressed to the dock company, on the strength of which timber would be released to Farquharsons' customers. In 1896, Capon began a series of frauds. Using the name Brown, he contracted to sell timber to King & Co, saying that 'Brown' was the agent of someone called Bayley. He then issued delivery orders to the dock company directing it to deliver the appropriate quantity of Farquharsons' timber to Brown's order. As Brown, he then told the dock company to deliver timber to King & Co. Farquharsons sued King & Co in conversion, and succeeded.

Earl of Halsbury: My Lords, in this case I hesitate to speak all that is in my mind out of respect to the learned judges who have taken a different view; but for that I should have said that this was a particularly plain case in which no difficulty whatever arises. I think it might be stated compendiously in two sentences. A servant has stolen his master's goods, and the question arises whether the persons who have received those goods innocently can set up a title against the master. I believe that is enough to dispose of this case.

. . .

[H]ow has the person who has received the goods acquired a right to those goods which, it is equally not denied, originally belonged to the appellants in this case? When has the property been changed, and by what circumstances? It is impossible, I think, to answer that question except in one way. There has been no property changed: the thief could give no title whatever. The circumstances of this case shew conclusively that there is nothing to prevent this being a theft, and, it being a theft, the thief could convey no title. That disposes of the case.

Lord Lindley: Capon sold the plaintiffs' timber without their authority, and sold it to the defendants. The defendants honestly bought the timber, and they had no notice that Capon had no right to sell it; but there was no sale in market overt, and the Factors Acts do not apply. The mere fact, therefore, that the defendants acted honestly does not confer upon them a good title as against the plaintiffs, the real owners of the timber. The plaintiffs are entitled to recover the timber or its value, unless they are precluded by their conduct from denying Capon's authority to sell. (Sale of Goods Act 1893, s 21 . . .)

. . .

It is, of course, true that by employing Capon and trusting him as they did the plaintiffs enabled him to transfer the timber to any one; in other words, the plaintiffs in one sense enabled him to cheat both themselves and others. In that sense, every one who has a servant enables him to steal whatever is within his reach. But if the word 'enable' is used in this wide sense, it is clearly untrue to say, as Ashhurst J said in *Lickbarrow v Mason* [below, p 393], 'that wherever one of two innocent persons must suffer by the acts of a third, he who has enabled such third person to occasion the loss must sustain it.' Such a doctrine is far too wide; and the cases referred to in the argument . . . shew that it cannot be relied upon without considerable qualification. . . .

In the present case, in my view of it, Capon simply stole the plaintiff's goods and sold them to the defendants, and the defendants' title is not improved by the circumstance that the theft was the result of an ingenious fraud on the plaintiffs and on the defendants alike. The defendants were not in any way misled by any act of the plaintiffs on which they placed reliance; and the plaintiffs are not, therefore, precluded from denying Capon's authority to sell . . .

[**Lords Macnaghten**, **Shand**, and **Robertson** delivered concurring opinions.]

Jerome v Bentley & Co
[1952] 2 All ER 114, Queen's Bench Division

Jerome entrusted a stranger, Major Tatham, with a diamond ring on terms that if he could sell it for more than £550 he could keep any surplus for himself, and that if he had not sold it within seven days he was to return it. Twelve days later, Tatham sold the ring for £175 to Bentleys, who bought in good faith thinking that he was the owner. After Bentleys had resold the ring, Jerome sued them in conversion and succeeded, on the ground that Tatham had had no authority to sell the ring to them.

> **Donovan J**: Major Tatham belonged to no . . . well-known class of agent. He was simply a private individual, carrying on, so far as I know, no calling at all, to whom a ring had been entrusted for sale. . . . When Major Tatham sold the ring he was not the plaintiff's agent at all except, perhaps, for the purpose of safe custody of the ring. Major Tatham did more than exceed an authority to sell—he usurped it. . . .
>
> It is said here that the plaintiff gave Major Tatham the ring to sell, and if he put limitations on the authority, such as a period of seven days, he should have communicated that fact to any interested third party. I cannot help wondering how the plaintiff was to do this, for he did not know to whom out of the whole population Major Tatham would offer the ring.
>
> [His Lordship referred to a number of cases, and continued:]
>
> That brings me to the circumstances in which Major Tatham sold the ring, the subject of the present dispute. On Jan 11, 1947, his sole duty was to hand the ring back to the plaintiff, and he had no authority to deal with it in any way except for the purpose of its safe custody. He has admitted that he stole the ring as a bailee. In other words, when he entered the shop he intended fraudulently to convert the ring to his own use, and he accomplished that purpose. He then became a thief of the ring . . .
>
> It is said that, even on the footing that Major Tatham was a thief, the defendants are entitled to succeed on the dictum of Ashhurst J, in *Lickbarrow v Mason* [below, p 393]. Everything, however, depends on the construction to be put on the word 'enabled' in this passage. If I carelessly leave my front door unlocked so that a thief walks in and steals my silver, I have, in a sense, enabled him to steal it by not locking my door, but that does not prevent my recovering it from some innocent purchaser from the thief . . . 'Enabled' in this context means the doing of something by one of the innocent parties which in fact misled the other. This is clearly to be deduced from Lord Lindley's speech in *Farquharson Bros & Co v King & Co* [below, p 387]. The plaintiff here did nothing which misled the defendants. In the circumstances I hold that no property in this ring passed to the defendants, and there is nothing to prevent the plaintiff from setting up his title as against them. Therefore, I decide in his favour.

Many of the exceptions to the *nemo dat* rule reflect a concern for the bona fide purchaser in a commercial transaction. The problem faced by the courts is well put by Denning LJ in the following passage.

Bishopsgate Motor Finance Corpn Ltd v Transport Brakes Ltd
[1949] 1 KB 322, Court of Appeal

The facts are immaterial.

> **Denning LJ**: In the development of our law, two principles have striven for mastery. The first is for the protection of property: no one can give a better title than he himself possesses.

> The second is for the protection of commercial transactions: the person who takes in good faith and for value without notice should get a good title. The first principle has held sway for a long time, but it has been modified by the common law itself and by statute so as to meet the needs of our own times.

For the purposes of comparison with English law, the German Civil Code provides as follows:

> **Article 932**
>
> (1) ...[T]he person receiving a thing becomes the owner of it even where it does not belong to the transferor, unless he was not in good faith...
> (2) The transferee is not in good faith if he knows, or through gross negligence fails to realise, that the thing does not belong to the transferor.
>
> ...
>
> **Article 935**
>
> [Article 932] does not apply if the thing was stolen from, or lost by, the owner, or otherwise taken from his possession....

You may care to consider whether this is perhaps a neater solution to the problem of how to protect buyers from non-owners.

2 FIRST EXCEPTION: ESTOPPEL

At the beginning of this discussion, only part of s 21(1) was quoted. In full, the subsection reads as follows:

> Subject to this Act, where goods are sold by a person who is not their owner, and who does not sell them under the authority or with the consent of the owner, the buyer acquires no better title to the goods than the seller had, *unless the owner of the goods is by his conduct precluded from denying the seller's authority to sell*.

The word 'precluded' is more or less equivalent to 'estopped', which is perhaps a more familiar term for English lawyers (or 'personally barred', for Scottish lawyers). In essence, such estoppel when it arises will be based on an express or implied representation by O to B (or to the world at large) either: (1) that S (the person whom the Act calls 'the seller') is in fact O's authorised *agent* to sell the goods; or (2) that S is the *owner* of the goods. Many of the cases turn on the representation of an agency; and so there will necessarily be some overlap between the discussion in the present section and that in Chapter 6. There is also, at least in theory, the possibility that the owner may be in some way 'precluded' by his own negligence from denying the seller's authority to sell, but (as we shall see) this is largely an illusory concept.

Henderson & Co v Williams

[1895] 1 QB 521, Court of Appeal

The facts appear from the judgment.

> **Lindley LJ**: In this case a Liverpool sugar merchant named Grey had 150 bags of sugar belonging to him warehoused in his name in the defendant's warehouse at Goole. On June 6, 1894, Grey was induced by the fraud of one Fletcher to authorize the defendant to hold these bags of sugar according to Fletcher's order. On the same day Fletcher agreed to sell them to the plaintiffs; but before the plaintiffs paid him for them they insisted on having them transferred into their own name. This was done on June 7, and the defendant informed the plaintiffs that he held the sugar at the plaintiffs' order and disposal. Thereupon the plaintiffs paid Fletcher for the goods. Grey afterwards discovered that he had been defrauded, and he gave notice to the defendant not to part with the bags of sugar. The defendant, being indemnified by Grey, has refused to deliver them to the plaintiffs, whereupon they bring this action to recover their value. The defendant defends this action for and on behalf of Grey. . . .
>
> He contends—(1) that he is not estopped from setting up Grey's title; and (2) that his title is better than that of the plaintiffs. I am of opinion that the defendant is wrong upon the first point, even if he is right on the second. The distinct attornment by the defendant to the plaintiffs on June 7, 1894, clearly, in my opinion, estopped the defendant from denying the plaintiffs' title . . .
>
> [**Lord Halsbury LC** and **AL Smith LJ** delivered concurring judgments.]

NOTE

Henderson v Williams may be contrasted with *Farquharson Bros v King* (above). In the former, the representation as to Fletcher's authority was made directly by the owner of the sugar, Grey, to the warehouseman (his bailee), and pursuant to this the warehouseman was empowered by his attornment (see above, p 76) to inform the plaintiffs that the sugar was held at their disposal. But in the latter, there was no communication at all between Farquharsons and King & Co, either directly or through the dock company as intermediaries: indeed, King & Co thought that the timber they were buying belonged not to Farquharsons but to another firm called Bayley.

Chatfields-Martin Walter Ltd v Lombard North Central Plc

[2014] EWHC 1222 (QB), Queen's Bench Division

Chatfields bought a van from Trade Vans, which they knew was owned by a finance company, Lombard, who had let it on hire-purchase to Trade Vans. Trade Vans agreed to clear the hire-purchase debt, thus allowing Chatfields to get clear title to the van and sell it at a profit. Chatfields checked the status of the van on 22 March with HPI Ltd, a central (but non-statutory) register of hire-purchase agreements outstanding; the register showed Lombard's interest and the amount owing. Trade Vans wrote a cheque for that amount, which Chatfields passed to Lombard on 21 April. On 10 May Chatfields again checked with HPI; at Lombard's request the amount owing had been reduced to zero. Assuming all was well, Chatfields bought the van and sold it on. In fact Lombard had made a mistake; Trade Vans' cheque had not cleared, and the hire-purchase agreement was still in force. Lombard sued Chatfields in conversion. Their action failed, Leggatt J holding that Lombard had by changing the entry at HPI implicitly stated to anyone consulting the register that they no longer had any interest in the van.

Leggatt J:....

19. The HPI service, as I understand it, is structured so that the finance company can itself change the information disseminated by HPI by altering the contents of the online database. That is what was done in this case when Lombard on 22 April 2010 deleted from the database the information that was previously being displayed about its finance agreements in relation to this vehicle.

20. It seems to me that dealers using the service would reasonably assume that information entered or removed by a finance company was accurate, in just the same way as if that information had, for example, been given over the telephone. Of course information given over the telephone might turn out to have involved an error made by the particular employee who conveys it, but that is a risk which the employer takes. In the same way, it seems to me, the company (Lombard in this case) bears responsibility if information which it chooses to enter on the HPI database turns out to be inaccurate. Commerce, in general, depends on being able to act on what you are told by the other party to a transaction, provided that it is clear, without expecting to have to make independent checks of that information.

21. I therefore reject the first, most general answer which Mr. Tabari puts forward to the case advanced on this appeal.

22. Mr. Tabari, however, has two further arguments, both of which depend on more specific facts of this case. The first is that the display on the HPI database which Mr. Ebdale saw on 10 May, which showed a zero under the symbol for finance, was not a representation (or, at any rate, not an unequivocal representation) that there was no financial interest in the vehicle. It was, in effect, no more than the representation made in the Moorgate case that HPI had no record of any financial interest in the vehicle.

23. There would have been force in that submission if the number under the finance symbol had always been zero, but it is an important feature of this case that there had previously been recorded on the HPI system the three finance agreements registered by Lombard.

24. In circumstances where Lombard had previously registered agreements which had been shown on the database and then changed the information displayed so that the three was replaced by a zero, I consider that a person who—as was to be expected—checked the position before and after that change was made would reasonably have understood that there had been finance agreements (details of which had been provided) which had since been cleared. On the face of it, in my view, that was the reasonable meaning of the representation made at the time when Mr. Ebdale looked at the database on 10 May, against the background that there had previously been finance agreements registered with HPI and shown on the database.

NOTES

1. For another, older, case of implied representation that the true owner had no interest in a car, with the same result, see *Eastern Distributors Ltd v Goldring* [1957] 2 QB 600.

2. Any representation of this sort must, of course, be voluntary. Compare *Debs v Sibec Developments Ltd* [1990] RTR 91, where a Mercedes car had been stolen from Debs in the course of an armed robbery and he had been forced at gunpoint to sign a document purporting to show that he had sold the car to one of the robbers, A, for cash. On the strength of this document the car was bought by an innocent third party and resold to Sibec. The court held that no title could pass through A, and there no estoppel could be based on a representation made under duress.

3. It is perhaps a misnomer to speak of the title conferred upon B under the exception to s 21(1) as being based on an estoppel. Normally, the effect of an estoppel is limited to the two parties in question, and it is binding only on the person making the representation. But the title which B acquires under this exception is a title good against third parties and not just against O—for example, B may sue a third party in tort for wrongful interference with the goods.

4. It will be noted that s 21(1) uses the phrase 'where goods are *sold* . . .', and not some wider expression such as 'where there has been a contract to sell . . .'. In *Shaw v Metropolitan Police Comr* [1987] 1 WLR 1332 the Court of Appeal held that the word 'sold' had to be read literally and that the 'estoppel' exception did not apply where there had been only an agreement to sell. O, a student, entrusted a fraudster S with possession of his Porsche(!) and signed papers which were certainly sufficient to preclude him from denying S's authority to sell it. S delivered the car to the B on terms that no title passed until payment, and disappeared: the car was then impounded. B failed in his claim to the car. This seems right: B had not believed himself to be the owner of it, and so there was no reason to give him title by estoppel.

5. A third kind of estoppel, 'estoppel by judgment', was in issue in *Powell v Wiltshire* [2004] EWCA Civ 534, [2005] QB 117. A person claiming to be the owner of goods may be precluded from denying another person's right to sell those goods (within s 21) if a court has already held, in separate proceedings, that the latter has the better title: he is not allowed to reopen the question of ownership. However, in the case itself the buyer had bought the goods (a light aircraft) *before* judgment was given in another case declaring that his seller was not the owner, and so the estoppel exception did not apply.

Despite the above cases, estoppel is however very limited in this respect. There must be something that can be construed as a representation, made by O to B; if there is not, O prevails against B. Furthermore, the courts have resisted the temptation to say that where O negligently allows S to defraud him and sell to B, any implicit representation should be conjured out of O's negligence; still less, that the mere fact that O has voluntarily put S in possession of his goods should be regarded as any kind of representation as to S's power to deal with them.

Farquharson Bros & Co v C King & Co
[1902] AC 325, House of Lords

For the facts see above, p 382.

> **Lord Lindley**: Capon sold the plaintiffs' timber without their authority, and sold it to the defendants. . . . What have the plaintiffs done which precludes them from denying, as against the defendants, Capon's right to do what he pretended he was entitled to do? Putting the question in another form: What have the plaintiffs done to preclude them from denying, as against the defendants, Capon's right to sell to them? To answer those questions it is necessary to consider what the plaintiffs did.
>
> Capon was the plaintiffs' confidential clerk; they gave him a limited power of sale to certain customers, and a general written authority to sign delivery orders on their behalf; and the plaintiffs

sent that written authority to the dock company which stored the plaintiffs' timber. This authority would, of course, protect the dock company in delivering timber as ordered by Capon, however fraudulently he might be acting, if the dock company had no notice of anything wrong. By abusing his authority Capon made timber belonging to the plaintiffs deliverable by the dock company to himself under the name of Brown. In that name he sold it, and procured it to be delivered to the defendants. What is there here which precludes the plaintiffs from denying Capon's right to sell to the defendants?

What have the plaintiffs done to mislead the defendants and to induce them to trust Capon? Absolutely nothing. The question for decision ought to be narrowed in this way, for it is in my opinion clear that, when s 21 of the Sale of Goods Act has to be applied to a particular case, the inquiry which has to be made is not a general inquiry as to the authority to sell, apart from all reference to the particular case, but an inquiry into the real or apparent authority of the seller to do that which the defendants say induced them to buy.

. . .

It was argued that the dock company were led by the plaintiffs to obey Capon's orders and to deliver to Brown, and that the defendants were induced by the dock company to deal with Brown, or at all events to pay him on the faith of his being entitled to the timber; so that in fact the plaintiffs, through the dock company, misled the defendants. This is ingenious but unsound. Except that delivery orders were sent in the name of Brown to the defendants, and were acted on by the dock company, there is no evidence connecting the dock company with the defendants in these transactions; and the answer to the contention is that the defendants were misled, not by what the plaintiffs did nor by what the plaintiffs authorized the dock company to do, but by Capon's frauds.

It is, of course, true that by employing Capon and trusting him as they did the plaintiffs enabled him to transfer the timber to any one; in other words, the plaintiffs in one sense enabled him to cheat both themselves and others. In that sense, every one who has a servant enables him to steal whatever is within his reach. But if the word 'enable' is used in this wide sense, it is clearly untrue to say, as Ashhurst J said in *Lickbarrow v Mason* [below, p 393], 'that wherever one of two innocent persons must suffer by the acts of a third, he who has enabled such third person to occasion the loss must sustain it.' Such a doctrine is far too wide; and the cases referred to in the argument . . . shew that it cannot be relied upon without considerable qualification. . . .

In the present case, in my view of it, Capon simply stole the plaintiff's goods and sold them to the defendants, and the defendants' title is not improved by the circumstance that the theft was the result of an ingenious fraud on the plaintiffs and on the defendants alike. The defendants were not in any way misled by any act of the plaintiffs on which they placed reliance; and the plaintiffs are not, therefore, precluded from denying Capon's authority to sell . . .

[**The Earl of Halsbury LC** and **Lords Macnaghten**, **Shand**, and **Robertson** delivered concurring opinions.]

Central Newbury Car Auctions Ltd v Unity Finance Ltd
[1957] 1 QB 371, Court of Appeal

Central Newbury bought a Morris car at auction and put it on display in their showroom. Its registration book (now called a registration certificate) was in the name of a previous owner, Ashley. A distinguished-looking person calling himself Cullis agreed to take the car on hire-purchase and was allowed to take it away, together with the registration book. Three days later, a man calling himself Ashley (no doubt the same swindler who had previously called himself Cullis) sold the car to Mercury Motors, signing the transfer of ownership form on the registration book with the name of Ashley. Mercury Motors later sold the car to Unity Finance, who resisted a claim by Central Newbury to have it back. It was held that Mercury Motors were not precluded from denying the swindler's authority to sell. Note, however, Denning LJ's dissent.

Morris LJ: . . . Now it is clear that the person who purported to sell the Morris car to Mercury Motors was not the owner of the car and he did not sell it under the authority or with the consent of the owner. The suggestion is therefore that if possession of a car and of its registration book is given to someone who has no authority to sell, but who wrongly purports to sell, the true owner may lose his ownership. Perhaps, however, the suggestion is more limited and should be stated as being that if an owner negligently gives possession of a car and of its registration book to someone who has no authority to sell but who wrongly purports to sell, the true owner may lose his ownership. But the element of negligence so introduced involves and implies a duty to take care and to be circumspect in regard to one's own property. That in turn raises the question as to whom the duty is owed. So as to cover every potential purchaser it must therefore be asserted that the owner owes a duty to the whole world.

What is said in the present case is that the plaintiffs gave Cullis possession both of the car and of the registration book and were negligent in so doing: it is said, therefore, that because of their conduct in being negligent they are precluded from denying that Cullis had any authority to sell. In other words, it is said that they cannot be heard to say to the defendants that Cullis had no right to sell. Why? Not because they were deceived by Cullis into letting him have the car—but because they also let him have the registration book. This must involve that if A gives to B possession of A's car with its registration book, A cannot be heard to say that he has not given to B an 'authority to sell.' This proposition seems to me to be far-reaching and to involve giving to a registration book a significance which it does not possess.

When Cullis presented himself at Birkenhead he was a complete stranger to Mercury Motors. They accepted what he said to them. They believed that he was Mr Ashley, who was selling his own car. They, of course, did not know that the car belonged to the plaintiffs and had no sort of thought of the plaintiffs in their mind. There was no question of any kind of representation from the plaintiffs. Mercury Motors proceeded to buy because they were duped by Cullis. Cullis would not have had the registration book but for the decision of the plaintiffs to allow him to have it, but, so far as Mercury Motors were concerned, they merely had what Cullis said to them, coupled with the fact of his physical possession of the car and the registration book. If the plaintiffs are to be precluded from denying Cullis's authority to sell, it seems to me that it must be because of the mere circumstance that they gave possession of the book as well as the car to Cullis. If they had given the car and book to Cullis in circumstances which involved no criticism upon them and without any carelessness, the situation would have been exactly the same so far as Mercury Motors are concerned. Therefore, it seems to me that the plaintiffs should only lose their ownership or be precluded from asserting it if it can be said that by parting with their car and its registration book they endowed the possessor of these with an apparent authority to sell. The proposition must be that though no apparent authority to sell can be assumed from mere possession of a car, nor from mere possession of a car registration book, the possession of a car with its book carries an apparent authority to sell. If Mercury Motors can assume that Cullis had a right to sell because Cullis had the car and its book, then it seems immaterial whether the plaintiffs put Cullis into possession because they were deceived without any carelessness on their part or because they were deceived and were in some ways careless. It cannot be that ownership is lost on the basis of enduring punishment for carelessness. The improvident householder who has left a window open at night which gives easy access for a thief is not in a worse position in asserting ownership of stolen articles than is the cautious householder who has checked the secure closing of his house.

It is doubtless true that criticism, particularly when available in the light of after events and after acquired knowledge, can be levelled against the plaintiffs. But it hardly seems entirely appropriate that the criticism should come from the Birkenhead purchasers. Are the plaintiffs to be estopped by negligence while the purchasers may be negligent with impunity? Nor does it seem fitting to weigh in the balance the respective criticisms of the actions of the parties and to see in which direction the scales are tipped. . . .

Denning LJ (dissenting): I think it is quite plain that when the Newbury Auction Co. handed the Morris car to Cullis they intended to part with all their property in it. Not to Cullis, of course, but only to the finance company, but that makes no difference. They intended to part with the property just as much as if they agreed to sell it to Cullis. They intended, of course, that the transaction should go through on hire-purchase terms: but that only meant that the sale was in law to the finance company, not to Cullis. . . . So here you cannot say that the Newbury Auction Co. lost the Morris car. What they lost was the money they expected to receive from the finance company; and that was entirely their own fault because they parted with the car when they ought not to have done. . . .

The point is brought home by the fact that they handed over the log-book to Cullis. Everyone knows that the log-book is good evidence of title . . . The wise owner keeps it at home or in a place separate from the car. Thieves who steal cars know it well enough. . . . To dispose of a car without the log-book is as difficult as to dispose of land without the title deeds. In each case the thief must resort to forgery if he wishes to get rid of it to an innocent person. The Newbury Auction Co. must have been aware of the importance of the log-book. They must have known that when they handed both car and log-book over to Cullis they were arming him with complete dominion over it . . .

How, then, does the matter stand? An innocent purchaser, who buys both car and log-book, acts on the assumption that the seller is the owner of them. That is a very reasonable assumption to make, at any rate when the purchaser has checked and found that it is not on hire-purchase. Unbeknown to the purchaser, the seller is a rogue. It would be unfair and unjust to allow the original owner to go behind that assumption when he himself intended to part with the property in the car—or at any rate behaved as if he intended to part with it—and has armed the rogue with both car and log-book, and thus enabled him to dispose of them.

It is said, however, that the original owner owed no duty to the innocent purchaser. I do not agree. When the original owner handed over the car and log-book to a complete stranger, intending to part with the property in them, he ought to have foreseen the possibility that the stranger might try and dispose of them for his own benefit to someone or other. That is what does happen when you hand over goods to a stranger reserving no right to yourself. The original owner owed a duty to any person to whom the stranger might try to dispose of them. . . . Here the innocent purchaser was affected, not by any representation by the original owner, but by his conduct. and that is sufficient to work an estoppel.

[**Hodson LJ** agreed with Morris LJ.]

NOTES

1. Another case, *Mercantile Bank of India Ltd v Central Bank of India Ltd* [1938] AC 287, PC, confirms that to entrust another with possession of the *documents of title* to goods (in that case, railway receipts, which in Indian practice were treated as documents of title) can no more be relied on for the purposes of an estoppel than entrusting him with the goods themselves.

2. The fraudster in this case had agreed to take the car on hire-purchase; in other words, he was merely a hirer and had not agreed to buy it. In this latter case, a special statutory exception to the *nemo dat* rule could now be invoked (but only if the buyer is a 'private purchaser' (see the Hire-Purchase Act 1964, s 27).

QUESTION

Do you prefer the majority or the minority view in *Central Newbury Car Auctions v Unity Finance*?

Moorgate Mercantile Co Ltd v Twitchings
[1977] AC 890, House of Lords

HP Information Ltd (HPI) (the same organisation as played a part in *Chatfields-Martin Walter Ltd v Lombard North Central Plc*, p 385 above) maintained a register on which car dealers and finance companies recorded all motor-vehicle hire-purchase agreements that were notified to it by its members. At the time of the case, 98 per cent of all such hire-purchase agreements were on this record. The appellants and the respondents were both members of HPI. Moorgate had let a car on hire-purchase to a man named McLorg, who then dishonestly sold it to Twitchings. By some error or oversight, Moorgate had failed to notify HPI that the car was on hire-purchase, and so when Twitchings made an inquiry HPI informed him that no hire-purchase agreement was recorded in respect of the car. Moorgate sued Twitchings claiming damages for conversion. Twitchings pleaded in reply that Moorgate were estopped by their negligence in having failed to notify the existence of the hire-purchase agreement; and alternatively they claimed to be entitled to set off the value of the car by way of damages in negligence. The House of Lords, by a majority, held that there was no estoppel, and no liability based on negligence.

Lord Fraser of Tullybelton: The conduct of Moorgate, by which it is said to be estopped from denying McLorg's authority to sell, is its omission to register with HPI its hire purchase agreement with him. That omission is said to have been negligent and is also the basis for the counterclaim of damages for negligence. So there is no practical difference as regards this case between the defence of estoppel by conduct and the counterclaim for damages; both depend upon establishing that Moorgate's omission to register the agreement was negligent. Negative conduct or omission will of course only be negligent, in the sense of wrongful, if there was a duty to act. If Twitchings are to succeed under either head they must therefore show (a) that Moorgate owed a duty to them to take reasonable care to register the agreement, (b) that Moorgate negligently failed to perform that duty, and (c) that their negligence was the proximate or real cause of Twitchings's loss. . . .

The first question then is whether Moorgate was under such a duty to Twitchings. The mere fact that registering hire purchase agreements was a usual practice in the business of finance houses such as Moorgate will not by itself give rise to a duty on the part of Moorgate towards Twitchings to register its agreements: see *Mercantile Bank of India Ltd v Central Bank of India Ltd* [1938] AC 287, 304. The reason why it is said that the duty was owed is that both parties were members of, or subscribers to, the registration scheme operated through HPI Moorgate, as a finance house, was a full member of HPI and Twitchings, as dealers, was an affiliated member. At an earlier stage of the case it was contended on behalf of Twitchings that there had been a multi-lateral contract to which Moorgate and themselves had been parties, but that contention was not maintained in this House. The proposition here was that their common membership of the scheme created a relationship or propinquity between them which made them 'neighbours' in the sense of *Donoghue v Stevenson* [1932] AC 562, as extended by *Hedley Byrne & Co Ltd v Heller & Partners Ltd* [1964] AC 465, and so gave rise to the duty. If that proposition is right, it means that a finance house, by joining the registration scheme operated by HPI, subjected itself to a duty to other members including affiliated members, and perhaps to all users of the scheme, to take reasonable care to register all its hire purchase agreements with HPI.

[His Lordship examined the 'aims and objects' of HPI, and concluded:]

The primary purpose of the HPI scheme is, in my opinion, to provide protection to finance houses. But finance houses which are members of the scheme are under no obligation to anyone else to protect their own property by using the facilities of HPI. The owner of property is entitled to be careless with it if he likes, and even extreme carelessness with his own property will not preclude him from recovering it from a person who has bought it from someone who dishonestly purported to sell it: see *Farquharson Bros & Co v King & Co* [above, p 381], and *Swan v North British Australasian Co Ltd* (1863) 2 H & C 175. In my opinion Moorgate's conduct in not registering the hire purchase agreement with McLorg was, at worst, careless in respect of Moorgate's own property, and it was not in breach of any duty to other parties. It was quite different from the kind of conduct considered in *Eastern Distributors Ltd v Goldring* [1957] 2 QB 600, where the owner of a motor vehicle who had in effect armed a dishonest person with documents enabling him to represent himself as owner was held to be estopped from denying his authority to sell, and see also *Mercantile Credit Co Ltd v Hamblin* [1965] 2 QB 242. When Moorgate gave possession of its vehicle to McLorg on hire purchase terms, it was not doing anything of that sort. It is notorious that the person in possession of a motor vehicle is often not the owner of it, and the vehicle log book contains a warning that it is not proof of ownership of the vehicle. The very fact that dealers like Twitchings check with HPI before buying a vehicle from a stranger shows that they are well aware that possession and ownership may be separate. Accordingly, I am of opinion that when Moorgate, having given possession of their vehicle to McLorg under a hire purchase agreement, did not register the agreement with HPI, they were not in breach of any duty owed by them to Twitchings. Twitchings therefore fail to show the first of the three things that they have to establish if their defence is to be upheld. . . .

[**Lords Edmund-Davies** and **Russell of Killowen** delivered concurring opinions. **Lords Wilberforce** and **Salmon** dissented.]

NOTES

1. *Moorgate Mercantile v Twitchings* finally scotched the idea that an owner owed any general duty to buyers in general to take care to avoid them (and himself) being defrauded. It thus confirmed earlier such statements: for instance, in *Central Newbury Car Auctions Ltd v Unity Finance Ltd* (above), we saw that Morris LJ said: 'It cannot be that ownership is lost on the basis of enduring punishment for carelessness.'

2. It is worth noting that a few older authorities are in contradiction to *Moorgate Mercantile v Twitchings* and must now be regarded as highly doubtful. One is an ancient dictum of Ashhurst J in *Lickbarrow v Mason* (1787) 2 Term Rep 63 at 70:

> We may lay it down as a broad general principle that, wherever one of two innocent persons must suffer by the acts of a third, he who has enabled such third person to occasion the loss must sustain it.

This statement is notorious as having been frequently cited (not least in examination questions!), and rarely, if ever, applied: indeed, on the one occasion when it was followed without proper analysis (*Commonwealth Trust v Akotey*, below), the court almost certainly came to the wrong answer.

Commonwealth Trust v Akotey

[1926] AC 72, Privy Council

Akotey sent 1,050 bags of cocoa by rail to Laing, and sent him the consignment notes. He had previously sold cocoa to Laing, but on this occasion no agreement to sell had been concluded, Laing's offer of £2.50 a ton having been rejected as too low. Laing sold the cocoa to Commonwealth Trust, who bought in good faith. He handed over the consignment notes and was paid the price. Akotey claimed that the cocoa was still his, and sued Commonwealth Trust in conversion. The Privy Council, applying the dictum of Ashhurst J cited above, held that Akotey was estopped by his conduct from setting up his title.

> **Lord Shaw** (delivering the advice of the Privy Council): . . . It was further argued before their Lordships that although the property in the cocoa had not passed from the respondent, yet that the respondent had so acted as to estop him from setting up his title in answer to the claim of the appellants. Reliance was placed on the well-known statement of Ashhurst J in *Lickbarrow v Mason* [above], 'that wherever one of two innocent persons must suffer by the acts of a third, he who has enabled such third person to occasion the loss must sustain it.' Their Lordships are clearly of opinion that the present is a plain case for the application of that principle. There is no kind of specialty in this case such as occurred in *Farquharson Bros & Co v King & Co* [above, p 382], the parallel to which would be that the goods were delivered to Laing by the fraudulent act of respondent's agent: the goods were in fact delivered over to Laing by the direct act of the respondent himself.
>
> To permit goods to go into the possession of another, with all the insignia of possession thereof and of apparent title, and to leave it open to go behind that possession so given and accompanied, and upset a purchase of the goods made for full value and in good faith, would bring confusion into mercantile transactions, and would be inconsistent with law and with the principles so frequently affirmed, following *Lickbarrow v Mason*.

QUESTION

Was there any significant respect in which the facts of this case were different from those in *Farquharson v King* (above)? If not, which decision better represents the law? Which better serves the needs of commerce?

3 SECOND EXCEPTION: SALE UNDER THE FACTORS ACT 1889, S 2

(a) Introduction: the mercantile agent and his function

The second exception to the *nemo dat* rule is alluded to in s 21(2)(a) of the Sale of Goods Act 1979, which declares that 'nothing in this Act affects the provisions of the Factors Acts...'.

There have been Factors Acts going as far back as 1823; the latest is the Factors Act 1889. The essence of the exception to *nemo dat* which they create is that a person entrusting goods to a regular dealer for sale on his behalf should in certain cases be bound by a sale or pledge by that dealer even if the latter exceeds his authority. It has a close equivalent in the United States in the form of the doctrine of 'entrusting' in Art 2–403 of the Uniform Commercial Code.

The pivotal character in the Factors Act (which oddly enough does not use the word 'factor' except in the title[3]) is the 'mercantile agent', defined as follows in s 1(1):

> For the purposes of this Act the expression 'mercantile agent' shall mean a mercantile agent having in the customary course of his business as such agent authority either to sell goods or to consign goods for the purpose of sale, or to buy goods, or to raise money on the security of goods.

We can infer from this not very helpful definition that a mercantile agent must be someone who has a business, and who in the course of that business buys or sells goods for other people. The meat of the exception to *nemo dat* created by the Factors Act around the mercantile agent is provided by s 2(1):

> Where a mercantile agent is, with the consent of the owner, in possession of goods or of the documents of title to goods, any sale, pledge, or other disposition of the goods, made by him when acting in the ordinary course of business of a mercantile agent, shall, subject to the provisions of this Act, be as valid as if he were expressly authorised by the owner of the goods to make the same; provided that the person taking under the disposition acts in good faith, and has not at the time of the disposition notice that the person making the disposition has not authority to make the same.

Note one requirement which does not appear here: unlike ss 24 and 25(1) (dealt with in detail below, pp 407 and 412) there is no requirement that the mercantile agent deliver the goods to the purchaser.

An old but straightforward example of the operation of the Act is *Weiner v Harris*.

---

[3] The word 'factor' as an agent for sale has dropped out of commercial usage (for an entertaining history, see RJC Munday, 'A Legal History of the Factor' (1977) 6 Anglo-American LR 221). In modern business, the expression 'factoring' is used for the (wholly unrelated) phenomenon of discounting book-debts described in Chapter 23. Dealers in certain components are also often called 'factors'—eg 'motor factors', or 'electrical factors'. The word remains in limited use in Scotland to mean 'agent', especially a land agent or apartment manager.

Weiner v Harris

[1910] 1 KB 285, Court of Appeal

Weiner, a manufacturing jeweller, entrusted goods to Fisher as his agent for the purposes of sale. Fisher had a shop in Harrogate from which he sold jewellery, and he also travelled the country selling jewellery for other people. The case concerned certain items which Fisher had without Weiner's authority pledged with Harris, a Cardiff pawnbroker.

> **Cozens-Hardy MR**: . . . Then it is said that . . . this case is not within the Factors Act. It is necessary for that purpose to refer only to ss 1 and 2. Section 1, sub-s 1, says 'For the purposes of this Act the expression "mercantile agent" shall mean a mercantile agent having in the customary course of his business as such agent authority either to sell goods'—that is the only part which is material. Then s 2, sub-s 1, says this: 'Where a mercantile agent is, with the consent of the owner, in possession of goods or of documents of title to goods, any sale, pledge, or other disposition of the goods, made by him when acting in the ordinary course of business of a mercantile agent, shall . . . be valid.' Apply that first section. Many thousand pounds' worth of goods were handed over by Weiner to be dealt with on the footing of this letter. I am bound to say I cannot imagine a mercantile agent within the meaning of this section if Fisher was not. He was sent all over the country by Weiner for the very purpose of disposing of the goods upon the footing of the letter, and to say that his business was that of a shopkeeper is altogether irrelevant to any question we have to decide here . . . In my opinion . . . the defendant, having regard to the provisions of the Factors Act, has a perfectly good title to this pledge.
>
> [**Fletcher Moulton** and **Farwell LJJ** delivered concurring judgments.]

For s 2(1) to apply, all the conditions specified in the section must, of course, be satisfied. It is best to take the key phrases one by one, since many of them have been the subject of judicial consideration.

(b) 'Mercantile agent'

A mercantile agent must, as we have seen, operate a business. What sort of business? How much of a business? Is it possible to be a mercantile agent on a single occasion? After all, everyone intending to set up in business as a mercantile agent has to begin with a first transaction! The next two cases give an indication of the courts' approach to this question.

Lowther v Harris

[1927] 1 KB 393, King's Bench Division

Colonel Lowther kept furniture and antiques (including two valuable tapestries) stored in a house in Chelsea. Prior had a shop nearby from which he sold mainly glass and china. Lowther engaged Prior to seek buyers for the stored articles, but Prior was not authorised to sell anything without obtaining Lowther's approval. Customers were brought to the house to see the tapestries, and after one such visit Prior obtained Lowther's consent to remove one of the tapestries by falsely telling Lowther that he had sold it to Woodhall for £525. In fact, he had not sold the tapestry to anyone; but he later sold it to Harris for £250. Wright J held that Prior had been entrusted with possession of this tapestry as a mercantile agent, with the consequence that Harris obtained a good title under the Factors Act. (A claim in respect of the second tapestry which Prior had simply stolen and then sold to Harris failed, because it was held that Prior had never had possession of it with Lowther's consent.)

> **Wright J**: . . . Unless the defendant has a defence under the Factors Act 1889, or on the ground of common law estoppel, it is clear that he is liable in damages for conversion . . . The first question is whether Prior was a mercantile agent—that is, an agent doing a business in buying or selling, or both, having in the customary course of his business such authority to sell goods. I hold that he was. Various objections have been raised. It was contended that Prior was a mere servant or shopman, and had no independent status such as is essential to constitute a mercantile agent. It was held under the earlier Acts that the agent must not be a mere servant or shopman: *Cole v North Western Bank* ((1875) LR 10 CP 354, 372); *Lamb v Attenborough* ((1862) 1 B & S 831); *Hyman v Flewker* ((1863) 13 CBNS 519). I think this is still law under the present Act. In my opinion Prior, who had his own shops, and who gave receipts and took cheques in his own registered business name and earned commissions, was not a mere servant but an agent, even though his discretionary authority was limited. It is also contended that even if he were an agent he was acting as such for one principal only, the plaintiff, and that the Factors Act 1889, requires a general occupation as agent. This, I think, is erroneous. The contrary was decided under the old Acts in *Hyman v Flewker*, and I think the same is the law under the present Act. . . .

Budberg v Jerwood
(1934) 51 TLR 99, King's Bench Division

Baroness Marie de Budberg escaped from Bolshevik-held Russia in 1921, bringing with her a pearl necklace worth £600 which she smuggled out of the country by concealing it in her mouth. In London she decided to sell it, and entrusted it to Dr Thadee de Wittchinsky, an émigré Russian lawyer. Dr de Wittchinsky sold the necklace without the baroness's consent to Jerwood, who bought in good faith. After the death of Dr de Wittchinsky, the true facts were discovered and the Baroness sued to recover her necklace. A plea that Dr de Wittchinsky had acted as a mercantile agent failed.

> **Macnaghten J**: . . . [A] mercantile agent was a person who in the ordinary course of his business as such agent had authority to sell goods. Now, Dr de Wittchinsky was a doctor of laws, who, towards the end of his life, had a permanent residence in London and there carried on business as a lawyer advising Russians living in this country. None of the witnesses had treated him as having any other business than that of a lawyer. But it was suggested that he acted as a mercantile agent in this transaction. It was said that it was possible that a man could be a mercantile agent although he had only one customer. In support of that proposition the defendants cited *Lowther v Harris* (above). He accepted that proposition, but it was qualified to this extent, that the alleged agent must be acting in the particular transaction in a business capacity. Here it was clear that the relationship between the plaintiff and Dr de Wittchinsky was not a business relationship. There was no suggestion of remuneration, and he was acting merely as a friend. In those circumstances the Factors Act did not apply. . . .

The business must include sale on behalf of others: it is not enough that the seller S is simply a dealer in the relevant goods.

Fadallah v Pollak

[2013] EWHC 3159 (QB), Queen's Bench Division

Pollak owned a couple of generating sets stored at the premises near Birmingham of Eagle Power, from whom he had originally bought them. Pollak agreed to sell the sets back to Eagle Power on the basis that no title passed until the price was paid. Eagle Power in turn sold the sets to Fadallah; Fadallah paid Eagle Power and took constructive delivery from them. Eagle Power became insolvent without paying Pollak. The issue before HHJ Richard Seymour QC was: who owned the sets? He held that the answer was Pollak, and rejected Fadallah's argument that he could rely on the Factors Act.

> **HHJ Seymour**:
>
> 33. What was relied upon on behalf of Mr Fadallah was the provisions of Factors Act 1889 s. 2(1):—
>
> Where a mercantile agent is, with the consent of the owner, in possession of goods or of documents of title to goods, any sale, pledge or other disposition of the goods, made by him when acting in the ordinary course of business of a mercantile agent, shall, subject to the provisions of this Act, be as valid as if he were expressly authorised by the owner of the goods to make the same; provided that the person taking under the disposition acts in good faith, and has not at the time of the disposition notice that the person making the disposition has not authority to make the same.
>
> 34. That provision is obviously intended to deal with a situation in which an owner of goods has given a mercantile agent possession of goods, or of documents of title to goods, but not authority to sell them, but the mercantile agent has sold them anyway. What is critical to the operation of the sub-section is that the person purporting to sell the goods should be a mercantile agent appointed to act on behalf of the owner of the goods. The expression 'mercantile agent' is defined, for the purposes of Factors Act 1889 in s.1(1) of that Act:—
>
> The expression 'mercantile agent' shall mean a mercantile agent having in the customary course of his business as such agent authority either to sell goods, or to consign goods for the purposes of sale, or to buy goods, or to raise money on the security of goods.
>
> 35. There was no evidence before me that the business of Eagle had been that of a mercantile agent. Rather the evidence was that Eagle's business, during its existence, had been that of a buyer and seller of power generation equipment. As I have already indicated, I accept the evidence of Mr. Pollak and that of Mr. Nijim that Mr. Pollak never retained Eagle to act as his agent for the sale of any goods, and in particular not the Generating Sets. Consequently this alternative basis for the claims of Mr. Fadallah also fails.

(c) 'In possession'

The mercantile agent must be in possession of the goods. This means that a mere broker, who negotiates the sale of goods from a distance but does not handle the goods themselves, is not covered.

Note, however, that under s 2(1) the mercantile agent's possession may be, not of the goods themselves, but of 'documents of title' to those goods, defined in s 1 of the 1889 Act as

> any bill of lading, dock warrant, warehouse-keeper's certificate, and warrant or order for the delivery of goods, and any other document used in the ordinary course of business as proof of the possession or control of goods, or authorising or purporting to authorise, either by endorsement or by delivery, the possessor of the document to transfer or receive goods thereby represented.

In practical terms, documents of title fall into two classes. One is an *acknowledgement*, signed by a person in physical possession (usually a bailee, such as a warehouseman or a carrier) accepting that he holds goods for X and will deliver to X. Typical acknowledgements of this kind include a warehouseman's warrant, dock warrant, or ship's delivery order: for an example, see *Sterns Ltd v Vickers Ltd* (above, p 366). The category also includes a bill of lading, ie a document issued by a sea carrier which acknowledges that the goods in question have been received on board, and which also contains the terms of the contract of carriage: see below, p 536. The second is an order, signed by the bailor X and addressed to a warehouseman, carrier, or other bailee, instructing him to deliver the goods to a named person Y or his order.

The extension to possession of documents of title is intended to deal with the case where goods are in storage, and the mercantile agent sells or pledges a delivery order or warehouse receipt; this is to have the same effect as dealings with the goods themselves. Where goods are in sea transit the same applies to a bill of lading. It is doubtful, however, whether this applies to other transport documents such as a sea waybill, air waybill, or CMR consignment note, since these are not transferable and arguably do not evidence possession or control of the goods covered.

(d) In possession 'with the consent of the owner'

The mercantile agent must be in possession 'with the consent of the owner'. This requirement of consent is amplified by s 2(2) and (3). These state respectively that: (a) consent once given by O to possession by S is deemed to continue even if determined, unless B has notice of the determination; and (b) consent to possession of goods carries with it deemed consent to the possession of any documents of title relating to the goods which S has obtained by reason of his possession of the goods.

The cases establish that it is not sufficient that the owner should have consented to the agent having possession: he must consent to his having possession *in his capacity as mercantile agent*. The older Factors Acts used the word 'intrusted'; and the essential idea is that this 'intrusting' should be with a view to a sale, or a possible sale, by the agent—that is, for a purpose connected with his business as a selling agent. This appears from the following two extracts.

Pearson v Rose & Young Ltd
[1951] 1 KB 275, Court of Appeal

The facts are irrelevant.

> **Denning LJ**: In the early days of the common law the governing principle of our law of property was that no person could give a better title than he himself had. But the needs of commerce have led to a progressive modification of this principle so as to protect innocent purchasers....The cases show how difficult it is to strike the right balance between the claims of true owners and the claims of innocent purchasers. The way that Parliament has done it in the case of mercantile agents is this: Parliament has protected the true owner by making it clear that he does not lose his right to goods when they are taken from him without his consent, as for instance when they have been stolen from his house by a burglar who has handed them over to a mercantile agent....But

Parliament has not protected the true owner, if he has himself consented to a mercantile agent having possession of them: because, by leaving them in the agent's possession, he has clothed the agent with apparent authority to sell them; and he should not therefore be allowed to claim them back from an innocent purchaser.

The critical question, therefore, in every case is whether the true owner consented to the mercantile agent having possession of the goods. This is often a very difficult question to decide . . .

If the true owner consents to the mercantile agent having the goods for repair but not for sale, is that a consent which enables the Factors Act to operate? The answer would seem at first sight to be 'Yes', because it is undoubtedly a consent to the agent having possession. But this needs testing. Suppose, for instance, that the owner of furniture leaves it with a repairer for repair, and that the repairer happens to be a dealer as well, does that mean that the repairer can deprive the true owner of his goods by selling them to a buyer? Clearly not, if the owner did not know the repairer to be a dealer; and even if he did, why should that incidental knowledge deprive the true owner of his goods? Such considerations have led the courts to the conclusion that the consent, which is to enable the Factors Act 1889, to operate, must be a consent to the possession of the goods by a mercantile agent as mercantile agent. That means that the owner must consent to the agent having them for a purpose which is in some way or other connected with his business as a mercantile agent. It may not actually be for sale. It may be for display or to get offers, or merely to put in his showroom; but there must be a consent to something of that kind before the owner can be deprived of his goods.

[**Somervell LJ** and **Vaisey J** delivered concurring judgments.]

Astley Industrial Trust Ltd v Miller

[1968] 2 All ER 36, Queen's Bench Division

A firm called Droylesden had two businesses: hiring out cars, and dealing in them. It did not own its hire cars, but took them on hire-purchase from Astley through a dealer called Lomas. Droylesden acquired a new Vauxhall car on hire-purchase from Astley for its rental fleet, and the following day, without authority from Astley, sold it to Miller, who bought in good faith. It was held that since Droylesden had possession of the car *qua* hire-purchaser and not qua motor dealer, s 2 of the Factors Act 1889 did not apply to the transaction, and in consequence Miller was bound to return the car to Astley or pay its value.

Chapman J: . . . Counsel for the defendant has contended that . . . a person who is in fact a mercantile agent, and who has in fact possession of someone else's property with the consent of that someone else, is clothed with ostensible or apparent authority to make any sale, pledge or other disposition of it which may appeal to his lust for pecuniary gain or his urge to perpetrate a fraud. Counsel for the plaintiffs, on the other hand, has contended that there is inherent in the statutory language a fourth condition, namely, that the goods must have been entrusted by the true owner or with his permission to the mercantile agent in his capacity as a mercantile agent . . . Counsel for the defendant has disputed this interpretation of the statute on the basis that it involves reading into the statute words which are not there.

Of course, one must always construe the words of an Act of Parliament strictly; that is, with precision. . . . The meaning of words, however, does not always end at the minimal dictionary content of each word . . . Counsel for the defendant's construction would, for example, lead to this result: if

I take my car into the local garage to have a puncture repaired, or to be greased, or to have a general check-up before going on holiday, I would be at the risk of the garage not only purporting to sell it, but actually passing good title if, besides carrying out repairs and servicing for customers, they professed the business of buying and selling motor cars (whether second-hand or new). This would seem a startling conclusion....

[His Lordship referred to a number of cases, distinguished certain authorities on what is now s 24 of the Sale of Goods Act 1979, and continued:]

Accordingly, I take it to be well settled and unchallenged law that the statutory power to pass title which is vested in a mercantile agent depends on his having possession in his capacity as a mercantile agent and on the true owner having consented to his having possession in that capacity. In the present case, on the facts as I have found them, Droylesden did not have possession of the Vauxhall in their capacity as mercantile agents, nor did Lomas consent to their having possession in that capacity. Droylesden, therefore, had no power to pass title to anybody.

NOTE

See too *Lowther v Harris* (above), emphasising this point, and also *Staffs Motor Guarantee Ltd v British Wagon Co Ltd* [1934] 2 KB 305 (note, however, that the latter case, while remaining good law on the Factors Act, was later overruled on another point connected with what is now s 24 of the Sale of Goods Act 1979).

The consent of the owner for the purposes of s 2 is regarded as having been validly given, even though obtained by fraud.

Folkes v King

[1923] 1 KB 282, Court of Appeal

Folkes entrusted a car to Hudson, a mercantile agent, with a view to sale, but with instructions not to sell it for less than £575 without permission. Hudson dishonestly sold the car at once to Alvarez, who bought in good faith, for £340; after several further sales, it was eventually bought by King. Folkes sued King for the return of the car, but his claim was held barred by s 2 of the Factors Act 1889. The main issue in the case turned on the now-obsolete distinction in the criminal law between 'obtaining by false pretences' and 'larceny by a trick'. Older cases had held that there was 'consent' for the purposes of s 2 in the former case, but no 'consent' in the latter. In this case, the Court of Appeal ruled that the distinction was immaterial, and that there was 'consent' in both situations.

Scrutton LJ: . . . First on the question whether to prove larceny by a trick is a defence to the Factors Act as excluding consent of the true owner. I can understand that where by a trick there is error in the person there is no true consent and the Factors Act is excluded. But where there is agreement on the person and the true owner intends to give him possession, it does not seem to me that the fact that the person apparently agreeing to accept an agency really means to disregard the agency, and act for his own benefit, destroys the consent of the true owner under the Factors Act. That Act intended to protect a purchaser in good faith carrying out an ordinary mercantile transaction with a person in the position of a mercantile agent. It does not do so completely, for it requires the purchaser to prove that the goods were in possession of the mercantile agent 'with the consent of the owner.' But it does not require the purchaser in addition to prove that the mercantile agent agreed both openly and secretly, ostensibly and really, to the terms on which the owner transferred possession to the mercantile agent. It appears to me to be enough to show that the true owner did intentionally deposit in the hands of the mercantile agent the goods in question. It is admitted that if he was induced to deposit the goods by a fraudulent misrepresentation as to external facts, he has yet consented to give possession, and the Factors Act applies, but it is argued that if he deposits the goods in the possession of an agent who secretly intends to break his contract of agency the Factors Act does not apply. I do not think Parliament had any intention of applying the artificial distinctions of the criminal law to a commercial transaction, defeating it if there were larceny by a trick, but not if there were only larceny by a bailee, or possession obtained by false pretences.

[**Bankes LJ** and **Eve J** delivered concurring judgments.]

NOTES

1. Compare *Lowther v Harris* (above), and also *Du Jardin v Beadman Bros Ltd* [1952] 2 QB 712, where a similar interpretation was given to the expression 'consent of the seller' in s 25(1) of the Sale of Goods Act 1979 (discussed below, p 412).

2. It is still conceivable that a court would hold that a consent obtained by fraud might amount to no consent at all, if the circumstances were such as to make the owner the victim of a material mistake of identity, as in such contract cases as *Cundy v Lindsay* (1878) 3 App Cas 459). In *Folkes v King* (above), Scrutton LJ said ([1923] 1 KB 282 at 305): 'I can understand that where by a trick there is error in the person there is no true consent and the Factors Act is excluded.' Compare *Shogun Finance Ltd v Hudson* (below, p 407) and *Debs v Sibec Developments Ltd* (above, p 386) (duress).

3. In *Beverley Acceptances Ltd v Oakley* [1982] RTR 417, CA, it was held that the 'possession' and the 'disposition' referred to in s 2(1) had to be contemporaneous: it was not sufficient that the person in question had once had possession *qua* mercantile agent but had lost it prior to the purported disposition.

4. In two cases, courts put a strained interpretation on s 2 out of indulgence for car owners defrauded by dishonest dealers, by apparently holding that there had to be consent to possession not only of the car, but also of its registration certificate, for the section to apply. See *Pearson v Rose & Young Ltd* [1951] 1 KB 275 and *Stadium Finance Ltd v Robbins* [1962] 2 QB 664. These cases seem, with respect, somewhat too restrictive; in any case, even if good law they are limited in their effect to car sales.

QUESTION

Marprelate Ltd entrusted a truck to Jock, a back-street motor dealer with a reputation for dishonesty, with instructions to sell it for not less than £20,000. Jock induced Marprelate to do so by pretending to be a representative of Jockey Ltd, a well-known and reputable dealer. Jock at once sold the truck for £10,000 to Lavenham Ltd, who bought in good faith. Advise Marprelate.

(e) 'When acting in the ordinary course of business as a mercantile agent'

This phrase was explained by Buckley LJ in *Oppenheimer v Attenborough & Son* [1908] 1 KB 221 at 230–231 as follows:

> I think it means, 'acting in such a way as a mercantile agent acting in the ordinary course of business of a mercantile agent would act'; that is to say, within business hours, at a proper place of business, and in other respects in the ordinary way in which a mercantile agent would act, so that there is nothing to lead the [buyer] to suppose that anything wrong is being done, or to give him notice that the disposition is one which the mercantile agent had no authority to make.

So in *Summers v Havard* (below) it was held that there might not be a sale in the ordinary course of business where, as was obvious to the buyer, a car dealer was selling cars entrusted to him for sale in large numbers at knock-down prices in order to keep his business afloat, albeit during ordinary business hours and at business premises.

In *Stadium Finance Ltd v Robbins* [1962] 2 QB 664, it was said that the sale of a vehicle without a registration certificate might be regarded as outside the ordinary course of business. This would, of course, depend upon the circumstances: a vehicle might quite properly be sold at a time when the registration certificate had been sent to the authorities (eg to have a change of address recorded).

QUESTION

Consider the facts of *Pacific Motor Auctions Pty Ltd v Motor Credits (Hire Finance) Ltd* (below, p 408). Could the buyers in that case have relied on s 2 of the Factors Act (or its New South Wales equivalent)?

(f) 'Provided that the person taking under the disposition acts in good faith, and has not at the time of the disposition notice that the person making the disposition has not authority to make the same'

Good faith in B means, it seems, something more than mere negligence. Nevertheless actual knowledge of S's excess of authority is not necessary: it is enough if B, faced with the possibility of malpractice by S, deliberately failed to make inquiries. The requirement that B should act in good faith and without notice of any irregularity is closely tied up with the 'ordinary course of business' point which we have just discussed, for any departure from the ordinary course of business by S may well put B on notice that the circumstances are suspicious.

Summers v Havard

[2011] EWCA Civ 764, [2011] 2 Lloyd's Rep 283, Court of Appeal

Havard and Summers were both used car dealers who entrusted cars to Halfway, a Carmarthenshire motor dealer, to sell on the basis that they would share any profits with

Halfway. Halfway was clearly in financial difficulty; for this reason Havard removed all his cars from Halfway's premises. He also took away 33 cars belonging to Summers, Halfway having purported to sell them to him at rock-bottom prices. Summers sued Havard. The judge found that Halfway, in selling cheaply to Havard in an effort to remain solvent, had exceeded its authority as Summers' agent to sell cars on his behalf. He found in addition that Havard had been on notice that the sales had not been made in the ordinary course of business, had not made further inquiries, and had not acted in good faith. An appeal by Havard was unsuccessful.

Arden LJ:

15. I therefore turn to state my conclusions. As already indicated and as Mr Glasgow fairly agreed the court has to look at all the circumstances of the case in determining whether or not the conditions of section 2 of the 1889 Act, including the condition of good faith, was made out. In his judgment the judge had found that Mr Havard was aware that Halfway acted for other principals apart from himself and that he knew that some of the vehicles on Halfway's forecourt belonged to other people (see paragraph [42]). Mr Havard said in his evidence that he carried out checks—hire purchaser and outstanding finance checks—but he accepted that these checks would only show whether or not there were hire purchase payments outstanding or whether the cars had been reported as stolen or damaged; I assume therefore it was some form of insurer's record or police record that he consulted. This is my observation and not the judge's, but (insofar as we have been taken to the transcript) he did not give evidence that he had asked Halfway who owned the cars or where they had come from, or whether there had been a discussion of that nature. Mr Havard knew that Halfway was in trouble financially. Indeed, Mr Havard had put stickers on the cars which he owned so that they would not be treated as Halfway's cars. He knew that Halfway was up to 'skulduggery' and that in his words it was robbing Peter to pay Paul. He also knew that he was lending money which was, one must assume, because Halfway's bank were not prepared to lend him money in the ordinary way. He also said that he knew that there was a risk involved (see paragraph [49] of the judgment), meaning a risk that Halfway might go under. In those circumstances it is not impossible to conclude that there are circumstances in which, from the point of view of Halfway, there would be a risk of Halfway misusing property belonging to other principals.

16. In all those circumstances, in my judgment, the judge was entitled to hold that Mr Harvard knew that some of the cars in Halfway's possession did not belong to Halfway and also that Mr Havard was on notice and that he deliberately refrained from making enquiries. The judge held in strong terms that Mr Havard as good as knew about the situation but did not care. The judge went on to find that the vehicles were not sold in the ordinary course of Halfway's business. That was a contentious finding on the other ground on which permission to appeal was given. As I read the judge's judgment, the judge relied on that particular factor as part of his finding of a lack of good faith. He was using it as part of the grounds for coming to the conclusion that there was not good faith for the purposes of section 2 .

17. In my judgment the judge was entitled to come to that conclusion on the evidence before him and the findings which he made that if a person deliberately refrained from making enquiries he was not acting in good faith...

The onus of proof as regards good faith and lack of notice lies upon the buyer. Thus in *Heap v Motorists' Advisory Agency Ltd* [1923] 1 KB 577 S, a fraudster (who was assumed for the purpose of the present circumstances to have been a mercantile agent), obtained possession of O's car, worth about £210, and sold it without O's authority to B for the very low price of £110. S did not effect the sale himself, but ('apparently for reasons of prudence') used a friend,

X, to do so. Lush J held that the onus was on B to prove that they had acted in good faith and without notice of the want of authority, and that they had failed to do so.

4 THIRD EXCEPTION: SALE UNDER A VOIDABLE TITLE

Where goods are sold under a contract affected by fraud or undue influence, English law takes the view that the validity of any transfer of ownership stands or falls with that of the underlying contract. If the contract is void, it therefore follows that the person 'buying' the goods gains no title, and from that that a sub-buyer from him can be in no better position, even if he buys in complete good faith (see *Cundy v Lindsay* (below, p 405). If the contract is merely voidable for fraud, however, the title of the person buying is provisionally good, in parallel with the contract, unless and until the latter is validly avoided. Furthermore, the rule at common law was, and that under s 23 is, that if the goods have reached the hands of a good faith purchaser for value before any effective avoidance of the contract, that purchaser acquires a good and indefeasible title:

> When the seller of goods has a voidable title to them, but his title has not been avoided at the time of the sale, the buyer acquires a good title to the goods, provided he buys them in good faith and without notice of the seller's defect of title.

A similar rule applies to pledges of goods.

The commonest case in which S will have a voidable title is where he has obtained the goods from O under a contract induced by misrepresentation or fraud. Typically the fraud will consist of the use by S of a stolen credit card or cheque form in someone else's name, or forged notes or bank drafts. Normally the transaction between S and O will be voidable, even if S impersonates the owner of a stolen credit card; but sometimes it will be void. Contrast *Lewis v Averay* and *Cundy v Lindsay* below.

Lewis v Averay
[1972] 1 QB 198, Court of Appeal

Lewis, in Bristol, advertised a car for sale in a newspaper and agreed to sell it for £450 to a fraudster calling himself Greene, who claimed to be Richard Greene, a well-known film actor, and showed a Pinewood Studios pass. He allowed the fraudster to drive it away in exchange for a worthless cheque. Three days later the fraudster sold the car for £200 to Averay, who bought in good faith. The Court of Appeal held that the first sale was voidable for fraud, but not void for mistake of identity, with the result that Averay got a good title.

> **Phillimore LJ**: . . . I think the law was conveniently stated by Pearce LJ in the course of his judgment in *Ingram v Little* [1961] 1 QB 31 to which reference has already been made. He said, at p 61:
>
> > Each case must be decided on its own facts. The question in such cases is this. Has it been sufficiently shown in the particular circumstances that, contrary to the prima facie

presumption—and I would emphasise those words—a party was not contracting with the physical person to whom he uttered the offer, but with another individual whom (as the other party ought to have understood) he believed to be the physical person present. The answer to that question is a finding of fact.

Now, in that particular case the Court of Appeal, by a majority and in the very special and unusual facts of the case, decided that it had been sufficiently shown in the particular circumstances that, contrary to the prima facie presumption, the lady who was selling the motor car was not dealing with the person actually present. But in the present case I am bound to say that I do not think there was anything which could displace the prima facie presumption that Mr Lewis was dealing with the gentleman present there in the flat—the rogue. It seems to me that when, at the conclusion of the transaction, the car was handed over, the logbook was handed over, the cheque was accepted, and the receipts were given, it is really impossible to say that a contract had not been made. I think this case really is on all fours with *Phillips v Brooks* ([1919] 2 KB 243), which has been good law for over 50 years. True, the contract was induced by fraud, and Mr Lewis, when he discovered that he had been defrauded, was entitled to avoid it; but in the meanwhile the rogue had parted with the property in this motor car which he had obtained to Mr Averay, who bought it bona fide without any notice of the fraud, and accordingly he thereby, as I think, acquired a good title.

[**Lord Denning MR** and **Megaw LJ** delivered concurring judgments.]

Cundy v Lindsay

(1878) 3 App Cas 459, House of Lords

A fraudster called Blenkarn, impersonating a well-known firm named Blenkiron which carried on business in the same street, ordered linen by post from Lindsay & Co in Belfast under a deliberately scrawled signature. When the linen arrived, Blenkarn sold part of it to Messrs Cundy, who bought in good faith and without knowledge of Blenkarn's fraud. The first contract was held to be void (in modern terms, on the ground of mistake of identity), so that no title in the linen passed to Blenkarn. It followed that he could not confer any title on Cundy, who were consequently liable to Lindsay & Co in conversion.

Lord Cairns LC: My Lords, you have in this case to discharge a duty which is always a disagreeable one for any Court, namely, to determine as between two parties, both of whom are perfectly innocent, upon which of the two the consequences of a fraud practised upon both of them must fall. My Lords, in discharging that duty your Lordships can do no more than apply, rigorously, the settled and well known rules of law. Now, with regard to the title to personal property, the settled and well known rules of the law may, I take it, be thus expressed: by the law of our country the purchaser of a chattel takes the chattel as a general rule subject to what may turn out to be certain infirmities in the title. If . . . it turns out that the chattel has been found by the person who professed to sell it, the purchaser will not obtain a title good as against the real owner. If it turns out that the chattel has been stolen by the person who has professed to sell it, the purchaser will not obtain a title. If it turns out that the chattel has come into the hands of the person who professed to sell it, by a de facto [voidable] contract, that is to say, a contract which has purported to pass the property to him from the owner of the property, there the purchaser will obtain a good title, even although afterwards it should appear that there were circumstances connected with that contract, which would enable the original owner of the goods to reduce it, and to set it aside, because these circumstances so enabling the original owner of the goods, or of the chattel, to reduce the contract and to set it aside, will not be allowed to interfere with a title for valuable consideration obtained by some third party during the interval while the contract remained unreduced.

My Lords, the question, therefore, in the present case, as your Lordships will observe, really becomes the very short and simple one which I am about to state. Was there any contract which, with regard to the goods in question in this case, had passed the property in the goods from the Messrs Lindsay to Alfred Blenkarn? If there was any contract passing that property, even although, as I have said, that contract might afterwards be open to a process of reduction, upon the ground of fraud, still, in the meantime, Blenkarn might have conveyed a good title for valuable consideration to the present Appellants . . .

Now, my Lords, . . . what the jurors have found is in substance this: it is not necessary to spell out the words, because the substance of it is beyond all doubt. They have found that by the form of the signatures to the letters which were written by Blenkarn, by the mode in which his letters and his applications to the Respondents were made out, and by the way in which he left uncorrected the mode and form in which, in turn, he was addressed by the Respondents; that by all those means he led, and intended to lead, the Respondents to believe, and they did believe, that the person with whom they were communicating was not Blenkarn, the dishonest and irresponsible man, but was a well known and solvent house of Blenkiron & Co, doing business in the same street. My Lords, those things are found as matters of fact, and they are placed beyond the range of dispute and controversy in the case.

If that is so, what is the consequence? It is that Blenkarn—the dishonest man, as I call him—was acting here just in the same way as if he had forged the signature of Blenkiron & Co, the respectable firm, to the applications for goods, and as if, when, in return, the goods were forwarded and letters were sent, accompanying them, he had intercepted the goods and intercepted the letters, and had taken possession of the goods, and of the letters which were addressed to, and intended for, not himself but, the firm of Blenkiron & Co. Now, my Lords, stating the matter shortly in that way, I ask the question, how is it possible to imagine that in that state of things any contract could have arisen between the Respondents and Blenkarn, the dishonest man? Of him they knew nothing, and of him they never thought. With him they never intended to deal. Their minds never, even for an instant of time rested upon him, and as between him and them there was no consensus of mind which could lead to any agreement or any contract whatever. As between him and them there was merely the one side to a contract, where, in order to produce a contract, two sides would be required. With the firm of Blenkiron & Co of course there was no contract, for as to them the matter was entirely unknown, and therefore the pretence of a contract was a failure.

The result, therefore, my Lords, is this, that your Lordships have not here to deal with one of those cases in which there is de facto a contract made which may afterwards be impeached and set aside, on the ground of fraud; but you have to deal with a case which ranges itself under a completely different chapter of law, the case namely in which a contract never comes into existence. My Lords, that being so, it is idle to talk of the property passing. The property remained, as it originally had been, the property of the Respondents, and the title which was attempted to be given to the Appellants was a title which could not be given to them. . . .

[**Lords Hatherley** and **Penzance** delivered concurring opinions.]

NOTE

The formal distinction between *Lewis v Averay* and *Cundy v Lindsay* is that in *Lewis v Averay* Lewis intended to deal with Greene even though he thought he was Richard

Greene, whereas in *Cundy v Lindsay* Lindsay intended to deal with Blenkiron and not with Blenkarn at all. You may think that this is a distinction without a difference, as did a minority of the House of Lords in *Shogun Finance Ltd v Hudson* [2003] UKHL 62, [2004] 1 AC 919 (a case not directly concerned with s 23). The majority in that case, however (Lords Hobhouse, Phillips, and Walker) were prepared to uphold it. For further coverage you should refer to books on the law of contract, for example *Anson's Law of Contract* (30th edn, 2016), pp 289 ff.

B will only be protected under s 23 if he purchases the goods *before* the contract between S and O has been avoided. If B obtains the goods subsequently, s 23 will not help him (though s 25 may well step into the breach here: below, p 412). This means that the precise time of avoidance may be crucial. Avoidance is normally achieved by O giving notice to S, or by retaking possession from S. However, where S is a fraudster this is unlikely to be practicable. In *Car & Universal Finance Co Ltd v Caldwell* [1965] 1 QB 525, CA, it was held that, at least in exceptional circumstances, some other action on the owner's part might be sufficient. O was induced to sell a Jaguar to S by fraud. S took the car away and sold it to X; after passing through several hands, it was eventually sold several months later to B. When O discovered the fraud, and before X had bought the car, he notified the police and the AA, but predictably could not contact S, who had disappeared. The Court of Appeal held that O had effectively avoided the contract with S before the car was sold on, so that O had the right to claim the car.

NOTE

For another case where the same issue arose, see *Newtons of Wembley Ltd v Williams* (below, p 414).

QUESTION

Is it sensible that the title of a good faith purchaser B should depend on the status of a contract between O and S to which B is not party and about which B knows nothing? Most European legal systems would protect B in this situation: have another look at the provisions of German law referred to above at p 384.

5 FOURTH EXCEPTION: SALE BY SELLER CONTINUING IN POSSESSION

(a) The function of s 24

When X agrees to sell goods to Y, it is possible for the parties to agree that ownership passes immediately, even though the goods remain in X's hands: indeed, if at the time of contracting the goods are specific goods in a deliverable state, s 18, r 1 presumes that this is so (above, p 338). But this raises serious problems if X then sells and delivers those selfsame goods to Z. The logic of *nemo dat* suggests that Z gets no title since at the time X sold the goods to him X no longer owned them. But this would be disruptive of commerce and most unfair on Z: if the goods have remained all the time in X's hands, Z should not be prejudiced by a previous 'paper' sale to Y of which he has no reason to know anything at all. As a result Z receives a statutory protection under s 24:

> Where a person having sold goods continues or is in possession of the goods, or of the goods or documents of title to the goods, the delivery or transfer by that person, or by a mercantile agent acting for him, of the goods or documents of title under any sale, pledge, or other disposition thereof, to any person receiving the same in good faith and without notice of the previous sale, has the same effect as if the person making the delivery or transfer were expressly authorised by the owner of the goods to make the same.[4]

Note that LA Rutherford and IA Todd, 'Section 25(1) of the Sale of Goods Act 1893: The Reluctance to Create a Mercantile Agency' [1979] CLJ 346 draw attention to the fact that s 24 deems the *delivery or transfer* of the goods or documents to have been expressly authorised, and not the 'sale, pledge or other disposition'. In the light of this, they argue that the scope of the subsection may be more limited than has generally been assumed.

Of course, this does not mean that Y is without remedy. In most cases where X resells to Z he will be in breach of his contract with Y, and may also be liable to Y in conversion. But that is a different matter, and is not relevant to what is discussed here.

(b) The need for the seller to remain in possession

For practical reasons s 24 is limited to cases where the seller remains continuously in possession. Imagine X Ltd sells a machine to Y Ltd and delivers it: months, or even years, later Y leaves the machine with X for repairs, whereupon X sells it to Z Ltd. It would be anomalous if Z, otherwise unprotected by any exception to *nemo dat*, got title merely because it happened previously to have bought the machine from X. Nevertheless, provided X remains physically in possession, it does not matter that he may do so under some new capacity, for example as bailee for Y. These matters are discussed in *Pacific Motor Auctions Pty Ltd v Motor Credits (Hire Finance) Ltd* below.

Pacific Motor Auctions Pty Ltd v Motor Credits (Hire Finance) Ltd
[1965] AC 867, Privy Council

A car retailing firm in Sydney called Motordom held its stock of used cars under an arrangement which is sometimes called a 'display' or 'stocking' agreement and sometimes a 'floor plan'. When it bought a car, it would pay the seller in cash and then immediately resell the car to Motor Credits, who were financiers, for 90 per cent of the price it had paid. The car stayed at Motordom's premises, on display for the purposes of sale: Motor Credits owned it and Motordom was its bailee. When Motordom sold the car, it did so as agent for Motor Credits. Motordom got into financial difficulties, and Motor Credits revoked its authority to sell any further cars. Pacific Auctions, a creditor of Motordom, was owed a substantial

---

[4] It should be noted that this section is duplicated by s 8 of the Factors Act 1889, though in the latter the words 'or under any agreement for the sale, pledge or other disposition thereof' are inserted before 'to any person'. Why the duplication (which also applies to s 25(1), paralleled by s 9 of the 1889 Act)? The answer seems to be simple legislative oversight: Parliament in 1893 intended to repeal the 1889 provisions, but forgot. The difference in wording makes no difference: judges do, and you may, refer to the sections interchangeably.

amount of money, and its manager called in the evening on that same day to demand payment. When payment was not forthcoming, he bought a total of 29 cars at prices which added up to approximately the amount owed, and took them away. Motor Credits demanded the return of these cars from Pacific Auctions.

Lord Pearce (delivering the advice of the Privy Council): . . . The point under s 28(1) [of the Sale of Goods Act 1923 (NSW), equivalent to s 24 (UK)] turns on the construction of the words 'where a person having sold goods continues or is in possession of the goods.' Are those words to be construed in their full sense so that wherever a person is found to be in possession of goods which he has previously sold he can, whatever be the capacity in which he has possession, pass a good title? Or is some, and if so what, limitation to be placed on them by considering the quality and title of the seller's possession at the time when he sells them again to an innocent purchaser? . . .

The first reported question that arose about the construction of those same words is to be found in *Mitchell v Jones* ((1905) 24 NZLR 932), a case under the New Zealand Sale of Goods Act 1895. There the owner of a horse sold it to a buyer and some days later obtained it back from him on lease. Then, having possession of the horse in the capacity of lessee, he sold it a second time to an innocent purchaser. The full court held that the innocent purchaser was not protected.

Stout CJ said:

> In this case the person who sold the goods gave up possession of them, and gave delivery of them to the buyer. The relationship, therefore, of buyer and seller between them was at an end. It is true that the seller got possession of the goods again, but not as a seller. He got the goods the second time as the bailee of the buyer, and as the bailee he had no warrant, in my opinion, to sell the goods again, nor could he make a good title to them to even a bona fide purchaser.

And Williams J said that the section 'does not . . . apply where a sale has been absolutely final by delivery, and possession has been obtained by the vendee.' It has not been doubted in argument nor do their Lordships doubt that that case was rightly decided.

In 1934, however, Mackinnon J, founding on that case, put a further gloss on the statutory provision in *Staffs Motor Guarantee Ltd v British Wagon Co* [referred to above at p 400]. In April one Heap agreed with a finance company to sell his lorry to it and then to hire it from the company on hire-purchase terms. He filled up a proposal form which was accepted, and a hire-purchase agreement dated May 2 was signed. During the term of the hiring he sold it to an innocent purchaser. It seems that there was an interval between the agreement to sell and the hire-purchase agreement, but it does not appear from the report that there was any physical delivery or interruption of Heap's physical possession. Mackinnon J held that 'Heap's possession of the lorry' (at the time of the second sale) 'was not the possession of a seller who had not yet delivered the article sold to the buyer, but was the possession of a bailee under the hire-purchase agreement . . .' Although the sale had not been completed by physical delivery nor had there been interruption of the seller's physical possession, he held that the case was covered by the principle in *Mitchell v Jones*.

[His Lordship discussed certain other cases, and continued:]

It is plainly right to read the section as inapplicable to cases where there has been a break in the continuity of the physical possession. On this point their Lordships accept the observations of the judges in *Mitchell v Jones* . . . But what is the justification for saying that a person does not continue in possession where his physical possession does continue although the title under or by virtue of which he is in possession has changed? The fact that a person having sold goods is described as continuing in possession would seem to indicate that the section is not contemplating as relevant a change in the legal title under which he possesses. For the legal title by which he is in possession cannot continue. Before the sale he is in possession as an owner, whereas after the sale he is in possession as a bailee holding goods for the new owner. The possession continues unchanged but the title under which he possesses has changed. One may, perhaps, say in loose terms that a person having sold goods continues in possession as long as he is holding because of and only because of the sale; but what justification is there for imposing such an elaborate and artificial construction on the natural meaning of the words? The object of the section is to protect an innocent purchaser who is deceived by the vendor's physical possession of goods or documents and who is inevitably unaware of legal rights which fetter the apparent power to dispose. Where a vendor retains uninterrupted physical possession of the goods why should an unknown arrangement, which substitutes a bailment for ownership, disentitle the innocent purchaser to protection from a danger which is just as great as that from which the section is admittedly intended to protect him?

[His Lordship discussed the history of s 24 and its relation to various provisions in the earlier Factors Acts. He concluded:]

There is therefore the strongest reason for supposing that the words 'continues in possession' were intended to refer to the continuity of physical possession regardless of any private transactions between the seller and purchaser which might alter the legal title under which the possession was held. . . .

NOTES

1. The *Pacific Motor Auctions* case is a Privy Council decision, technically not binding in England. But the Court of Appeal in *Worcester Works Finance Ltd v Cooden Engineering Co Ltd* [1972] 1 QB 210, CA, has since adopted the same approach, as has a later Court of Appeal in *Michael Gerson (Leasing) Ltd v Wilkinson* (below, p 411), and so it can be taken as established.

2. *Pacific Motor Auctions* covers the case where X was in possession at the time of the sale to Y but later holds as mere bailee for Y. It does not cover the different situation where X was *not* in possession at the time of the sale to Y but later took delivery of the goods as bailee for Y, after which X sold to Z. See *Fadallah v Pollak*, above p 397, at [46]–[49].

Possession of documents As with the Factors Act 1889 (see above, p 394), s 24 refers not only to the case where the seller is in possession of the *goods*, but also where he is in possession of the *documents of title* to the goods. This means that if X has sold goods to Y but kept possession of a document of title relating to those goods, X has the same power to defeat Y's title and confer a good title on Z by delivering the document of title to Z as he has if he delivers the goods themselves.

(c)   The need for delivery

To be protected in the above example, Z must not only buy the goods; he must also take *delivery* of them, even if only constructively (for constructive delivery in this context, see the Australian case of *Gamer's Motor Centre (Newcastle) Pty Ltd v Natwest Wholesale Australia Pty Ltd* (1987) 163 CLR 236). This is because if he simply leaves the goods in X's hands he deserves no more protection than Y had. This requirement normally gives few problems. But it can be commercially very significant, in particular where financing is involved. Imagine X, an industrialist, sells machinery to Y and leases it back, the machinery never physically moving (this is a very common financing device). X then enters into an identical transaction with Z. If X becomes insolvent, who can claim the machinery, Y or Z? This was the issue in

Michael Gerson (Leasing) Ltd v Wilkinson, below, where the Court of Appeal applied s 24 and held that Z should prevail.

Michael Gerson (Leasing) Ltd v Wilkinson

[2001] QB 514, Court of Appeal

A company, Emshelf Ltd, sold plant and machinery to Gerson and leased it back, and then later entered into a similar sale and lease-back agreement of the same plant and machinery to State Securities. The goods remained in the physical possession of Emshelf throughout. It was held that the second sale to State defeated Gerson's title by virtue of s 24, since in order for State to be able to grant a lease-back to Emshelf there must have been a prior moment in which possession had been constructively delivered to State as buyer.

> **Clarke LJ:**
> 28. In my judgment the legal position is as set out by both Pollock & Wright and Bowstead. Thus, where a seller in possession of the goods sold acknowledges that he is holding the goods on account of the buyer in circumstances where (as Pollock & Wright put it, at p 72) he recognises the purchaser's right to possess as owner and his continuing to hold the goods thereafter as the bailee with a possession derived from that right, then (as Pollock & Wright put it, at p 73) the transaction amounts to delivery to the buyer immediately followed by redelivery to the seller as bailee and that is so whether the seller's custody is 'in the character of a bailee for reward or of a borrower'. There is a change of the character of the seller's possession when he holds the goods for the buyer and, indeed, when he subsequently becomes, say, the bailee from the buyer for reward.
> 29. [Counsel for State] submits that an application of those principles establishes a delivery by Emshelf to State and a redelivery by State to Emshelf. [Counsel for Gerson], on the other hand, submits...that there was no acknowledgement here by Emshelf of State's right of possession of the schedule 3 goods and no sufficient voluntary act of delivery by Emshelf to State. As he put it in argument, there was no time at which State could instruct Emshelf what to do with the goods and thus no time at which State could decide whether or not to lease the goods to Emshelf. For example, State could not at any stage have instructed Emshelf to deliver the goods to it or to a third party on its behalf.
> 30. It is true that there was no identifiable moment at which State could have given those instructions. However I prefer the submissions of [counsel for State] to those of [counsel for Gerson] on this point. I do not think that it is necessary to identify a moment at which the goods were delivered to State by Emshelf. The effect of the sale and leaseback arrangement was that the goods must be taken to have been delivered to State because State could not otherwise have leased them back to Emshelf....
> 31. Equally it seems to me that there was here an acknowledgement by Emshelf that it held the goods on behalf of State in the lease itself. I have already set out the relevant facts. The terms of the lease are consistent only with such an acknowledgement, since (as I have already stated) State would not otherwise have been able to lease the goods back to Emshelf. The principles set out above therefore seem to me to establish that there was a delivery and a redelivery on the facts here.
> 32. [Counsel for Gerson] submits that there was no voluntary act of transfer and that State's case fails for that reason, as the owners' case failed in the *Forsythe* case [1994] 1 WLR 1334. However, it seems to me that the making of the agreement for sale and the entering into of the lease was a sufficient voluntary act on the part of Emshelf to satisfy the requirement in section 61(1) of the Sale of Goods Act 1979 that in order to amount to 'delivery' there must be a voluntary transfer of possession from one person to another.

NOTE

As a matter of principle this result is difficult to defend. In the context of two sales by X of the same goods to Y and Z, the intent behind s 24 is that if Z takes possession but Y does not, Z should prevail. If so, then since in *Gerson v Wilkinson* both transactions took an identical form, either both transferred possession or neither did: in either case it makes no sense to say that State took possession but Gerson did not.

But on the accepted interpretation of s 24 the decision is in fact correct. To satisfy s 24 it was enough that Emshelf remained in physical control, even though by agreeing to act as bailee for Gerson it actually transferred constructive possession to Gerson; whereas the subsequent transfer of constructive possession to State sufficed to satisfy the need for a 'delivery or transfer' and thus trigger the operation of the section. A further corollary follows: if Emshelf had engaged in a third identical sale-and-leaseback transaction in favour of another third party T, State's rights would themselves be defeated and T would now prevail! Indeed, the result of *Gerson v Wilkinson* is the curious one that, in the case of repeated sale-and-leaseback transactions over the same goods in favour of innocent lenders, the last in time will always prevail.

6 FIFTH EXCEPTION: SALE BY BUYER IN POSSESSION

(a) In general

We saw above that the logic of *nemo dat* caused problems where a seller sold goods but remained in possession of them. A parallel difficulty arises in the converse case, namely, where a seller X delivers possession of goods to a buyer Y but nevertheless retains ownership of them until a later stage (a straightforward example is a clause reserving ownership in X until payment). In such a case Y has been made by X to look like an owner; from which it follows that if a sub-buyer Z buys from Y, it is unfair that—as the general *nemo dat* rule would say—Z's title should be affected by the precise terms of the contract entered into by Y with X, or the state of accounts between those parties.[5] The result is s 25(1) of the Sale of Goods Act 1979[6]:

> Where a person having bought or agreed to buy goods obtains, with the consent of the seller, possession of the goods or the documents of title to the goods, the delivery or transfer by that person, or by a mercantile agent acting for him, of the goods or documents of title, under any sale, pledge or other disposition thereof, to any person receiving the same in good faith and without notice of any lien or other right of the seller in respect of the goods, has the same effect as if the person making the delivery or transfer were a mercantile agent in possession of the goods or documents of title with the consent of the owner.[7]

---

[5] In this part of the chapter, X will consistently be used to refer to the original seller, Y to the intermediate seller without title, and Z to the ultimate good faith buyer.

[6] Rather confusingly numbered s 25(2) in the Sale of Goods Act 1893, to which a number of the older cases refer.

[7] This is similar to the Factors Act 1889, s 9, though the latter differs from s 25(1) by the inclusion of the phrase 'or under any agreement for the sale, pledge or other disposition thereof before the words 'to any person'. There is, however, no difference in meaning, and the two sections can be referred to interchangeably.

The classic application of s 25(1) is to protect purchasers from reservation of title clauses of one sort or another, as the old consumer case of *Lee v Butler* makes clear.

Lee v Butler
[1893] 2 QB 318, Court of Appeal

Mrs Lloyd agreed to take on 'hire' certain furniture from Hardy under the terms of an agreement, called a 'hire and purchase agreement', paying over a period of three months sums described as 'rent' which totalled £97 4s. It was declared that the furniture should remain the property of Hardy throughout, but that when the full £97 4s had been paid, the furniture would become the sole and absolute property of Mrs Lloyd. Mrs Lloyd, before all the instalments had been paid under the agreement, sold the furniture to Butler. Lee, who had taken an assignment of Hardy's rights under the agreement, claimed to be entitled to the goods, but the court found for Butler under the equivalent s 9 of the Factors Act 1889.

> **Lord Esher MR**: This is a very plain case, and the construction of the statute is very clear. It deals with 'Dispositions by mercantile agents' in one set of sections, and with 'Dispositions by sellers and buyers of goods' in another set of sections, in which s 9 is included. The case is clearly within that section. [His Lordship read s 9.] Mrs Lloyd had agreed by this hire and purchase agreement to buy the goods, and they were put into her possession with the consent of the owner. Mrs Lloyd sold the goods to the defendant without notice that they were not hers, and he, acting in good faith and with no notice of the plaintiff's rights, received them. Section 9 was passed to meet this very kind of case. I am of opinion that the judgment of Wright J was right, and this appeal should be dismissed.
>
> [**Kay LJ** delivered a concurring judgment. **Bowen LJ** concurred.]

NOTES

1. The key point in *Lee v Butler* is that Mrs Lloyd, though described as a 'hirer', was *bound* to complete the purchase of the goods. In other words, this was a *conditional sale* agreement, under which the seller retained the property in the goods until the whole of the agreed price had been paid.

2. *Lee v Butler* was bad news for the finance industry. In a situation where the conditional purchaser might well himself not be worth suing, it deprived the financier of recourse against the goods in the hands of a third party, thus effectively leaving it with a dead loss. The industry's response was the invention of hire-purchase, under which the hirer had similar obligations to those under *Lee v Butler*, but after paying the instalments had, in lieu of an *obligation* to buy the goods, a mere *option* to do so, normally for a nominal sum. In this situation it was argued that the hirer had not 'agreed to buy' the goods at all, with the result that what is now s 25(1) did not apply, and hence in the case of a wrongful sale by the hirer of the goods the owner could recover the goods from the innocent purchaser. In the test case of *Helby v Matthews* [1895] AC 471, the House of Lords held that this technical albeit unmeritorious argument was indeed good. This ruling has been the basis of the hire-purchase industry ever since.

3.   The law remains in this state for commercial transactions, with which this book is concerned. Two alterations apply, however, in the consumer protection context. First, in the case of conditional sale agreements governed by the Consumer Credit Act 1974 (essentially those where the buyer is an individual or small partnership rather than a company), *Lee v Butler* is reversed and the good faith buyer deprived of title (s 25(2) of the 1979 Act). And, secondly, where a hire-purchase agreement concerns a motor vehicle, the owner's title is lost when the vehicle is bought in good faith by a private (ie non-business) purchaser (see s 27 of the Hire Purchase Act 1964).

The wording of s 25(1) is intricate, and a number of parts of it need closer investigation.

(b)   'Bought or agreed to buy'

First, for a long time the words '*bought* or agreed to buy' were regarded as puzzling, because it was thought that if a person had *bought* goods he would have a good title anyway, which would enable him to sell to a sub-buyer without any need to invoke s 25(1). But in *Newtons of Wembley Ltd v Williams* it was demonstrated that the draftsman of the section had truly remarkable foresight, and that there is indeed a role for the word 'bought'.

Newtons of Wembley Ltd v Williams
[1965] 1 QB 560, Court of Appeal

On 16 June 1962 Newtons sold a car to Andrew and allowed him to take it away. Andrew's purchase was fraudulent, because he paid for the car with a worthless cheque. Newtons quickly rescinded the contract with Andrew by informing the police of what had happened (see *Car & Universal Finance v Caldwell*, above, p 407). About a month later Andrew sold the car to Biss at a then well-established market for used cars in Warren Street, London. Biss bought in good faith, albeit for cash. Biss resold the car to Williams, from whom Newtons claimed it.

> **Sellers LJ**: The title the defendant seeks to advance is the title of Biss, when Biss was the buyer, or the purported buyer, of the car from Andrew in the Warren Street market[8] on or about July 6, 1962.
>
>   Quite clearly, at common law, Andrew at that date had no title to give, and at common law Biss obtained no title. It was submitted before us that at that stage Andrew was a complete stranger in this matter, that the case is clear, and that possession should be given to the plaintiffs, or damages in lieu thereof. But in fact Andrew was not a complete stranger. Andrew had in fact the possession of the car, which had been given to him or which he had obtained when he acquired the car on the handing over of the cheque on June 15.
>
>   In those circumstances, notwithstanding the position at common law—or because of it—the defendant has relied on the Factors Act, 1889; and the question which arises in this case is whether the transaction between Andrew and Biss can be brought within the provisions of that Act.
>
>   I turn first to s 9. It is one of two sections, ss 8 and 9, dealing with dispositions by sellers and buyers of goods, s 8 dealing with the disposition by a seller remaining in possession, s 9 with disposition by a buyer obtaining possession.

---

[8] Warren Street, in the Bloomsbury district of London, was well known in the 1950s as a thriving marketplace for second-hand cars.

[His Lordship read s 9 and continued:]

Andrew had bought the goods and obtained them with the consent of the plaintiffs. He had subsequently delivered them on a sale to Biss and, if Biss was a person receiving the same in good faith and without notice of any lien or other right of the original seller, then this section provides that the transaction shall have the same effect as if the person making the delivery, ie, Andrew, were a mercantile agent in possession of the goods or documents of title with the consent of the owner. So the first part of s 9 is complied with on the facts of this case, and the question arises whether the second part, the receiving of the goods in good faith (and it is not suggested that Biss had notice of any lien or other right of the original seller), has been complied with, and whether, treating Andrew as a mercantile agent, the requirements of s 9 in that respect have been complied with.

[**Pearson LJ** delivered a concurring judgment. **Diplock LJ** concurred.]

NOTE

The importance of *Newtons of Wembley v Williams* was that Andrews was regarded as a person who had 'bought' goods even though the contract under which he bought them had subsequently been rescinded for fraud. Indeed, it may go further. Imagine that X Ltd delivers a JCB digger to Y Ltd on credit, with ownership passing straight away; but that two days later Y, being short of money, agrees with X to cancel the sale and re-vest title in X. If Y then sells the digger to Z before X has had a chance to collect it, it would seem that Z will obtain title: Y is, after all, a person who has 'bought' it, even though the contract has since been cancelled by mutual consent.

(c) 'Obtains, with the consent of the seller, possession of the goods or the documents of title to the goods'

Section 25(1) covers the situation where Y agrees to buy goods from X, later obtains possession of them, and then sells and delivers them to Z at a time when he (Y) does not have title. The order of matters is important, as shown by *Fadallah v Pollak*, already referred to above at p 397.

Fadallah v Pollak
[2013] EWHC 3159 (QB), Queen's Bench Division

Pollak owned a couple of generating sets stored at the premises near Birmingham of Eagle Power. On 17 August 2011, expecting to buy the sets from Pollak, Eagle Power 'sold' and constructively delivered the sets to Fadallah. On 30 August 2011 Pollak agreed to sell the sets to Eagle Power on the basis that no title passed until the price was paid. Fadallah paid Eagle Power but Eagle Power never paid Pollak. We dealt above with whether Fadallah could rely on s 2 of the Factors Act 1889 (p 397). Another issue was whether Fadallah could succeed on the basis that Eagle Power was a buyer in possession. HHJ Richard Seymour QC held that he could not, because the sub-sale to Fadallah had taken place *before* the agreement to buy from Pollak.

HHJ Richard Seymour QC:

54. The last alternative foundation for his claims upon which Mr. Fadallah sought to rely was the provisions of Sale of Goods Act 1979 s.25(1):—

> Where a person having bought or agreed to buy goods obtains, with the consent of the seller, possession of the goods or the documents of title to the goods, the delivery of transfer by that person, or by a mercantile agent acting for him, of the goods or documents of title, under any sale, pledge or other disposition thereof to any person receiving the same in good faith and without notice of any lien or other right of the original seller in respect of the goods, has the same effect as if the person making the delivery or transfer were a mercantile agent in possession of the goods or documents of title with the consent of the owner.

55. In the light of my finding that Mr. Pollak did not agree to re-sell the Generating Sets to Eagle until he entered into the agreement to sell on 30 August 2011, it would seem, simply as a matter of the ordinary understanding of the English language, that, in order to bring himself within Sale of Goods Act 1979 s.25(1), Mr. Fadallah would have to show that, at a point after 30 August 2011 Eagle obtained possession of the Generating Sets and delivered them to Mr. Fadallah. However, it was common ground that Eagle in fact had possession of the Generating Sets considerably earlier than 30 August 2011, and that fact seems to me to be fatal to the reliance of Mr. Fadallah upon the sub-section. Another fatal defect, in my judgment, was that, as was also common ground, delivery by Eagle to Mr. Fadallah of the Generating Sets took place constructively on or about 17 August 2011, in advance of the relevant contract between Mr. Pollak and Eagle, upon the making of full payment of the sum agreed to be paid by Mr. Fadallah to Eagle for the Generating Sets. In his closing submissions Mr. Harris sought to contend that, for the purposes of Mr. Fadallah's reliance upon Sale of Goods Act 1979 s.25(1), delivery to Mr. Fadallah of the Generating Sets had not taken place on or about 17 August 2011, whilst maintaining for the purposes of Mr. Fadallah's reliance upon Sale of Goods Act 1979 s.24, that it had. For the reasons which I have explained Mr. Harris had to contend for a delivery after 30 August 2011 in relation to the reliance upon Sale of Goods Act 1979 s.25(1), and that brought about the unhappy inconsistency in his client's positions. However, I am satisfied that the submission in his written skeleton argument that there had been a delivery on or about 17 August 2011, which Mr. Higgins did not contest, was sound.

56. Mr. Harris, in his written skeleton argument, recognised the difficulties which Mr. Fadallah faced if I reached the conclusions which I have. He sought to avoid what appeared to me to be the plain construction of Sale of Goods Act 1979 s.25(1) by raising the contention that that provision did not require that the sale pursuant to which the delivery which that sub-section contemplated took place had itself to take place after the buyer in question assumed his capacity as such. Although the argument which Mr. Harris put forward was carefully constructed, it did not seem to me to overcome the fatal objections which I have already identified. Consequently Mr. Fadallah also failed to make out his claims based on Sale of Goods Act 1979 s.25(1).

Presumably the fact that Y obtains possession from X in some capacity other than as buyer, for instance as a bailee for X, will not prevent s 25(1) applying. This is by analogy to the rule in s 24 and *Pacific Motor Auctions v Motor Credits*, above, p 408.

Note that as with s 24, possession and delivery of documents of title relating to goods has the same effect as possession and delivery of the goods themselves. An example of this process is *Carlos Soto SAU v AP Moller-Maersk AS* [2015] EWHC 458 (Comm), [2015] 1 Lloyd's Rep 537. X agreed to sell a cargo of fish to Y and transferred a bill of lading to Y, but without transferring ownership; Y in turn transferred the bill of lading to Z. Eder J held without difficulty that Z was the owner of the cargo and as such able to recover substantial damages for damage to it.

For the details of 'documents of title' in this context, see above, p 398. It should be noted that where Y agrees to buy goods represented by a document of title from X and then sells them to Z while X is still owner, there is no requirement that the document of title transferred by Y to Z be the same document as that received by Y from X. See *DF Mount Ltd v Jay & Jay (Provisions) Co Ltd* [1960] 1 QB 159.

(d) 'The delivery or transfer under any sale, pledge or other disposition'

As with s 24, delivery by Y to Z is essential for s 25(1) to apply: a mere sale without delivery will not do. Such delivery may be actual or constructive (see *Michael Gerson (Leasing) Ltd v Wilkinson (above, p 411), a case on s 24 which must equally be applicable to s 25).

However, delivery requires some voluntary act on the part of the first buyer. In *The Saetta* [1994] 1 WLR 1334 sellers sold bunkers (heavy fuel oil) to the time-charterers of a ship while reserving title until they were paid. The charterers collapsed without paying the sellers and ceased to pay hire. The shipowners terminated the charter and, as they were entitled to do under it, took over the bunkers remaining on board. Clarke J held that in the absence of any voluntary act by the charterers there had been no 'delivery' by them of the oil, that s 25(1) did not apply, and that the shipowners were liable to the sellers in conversion. It seems, however, that had the charterers entered into a separate arrangement to re-transfer the fuel rather than simply submitting to its recaption by the shipowners, the latter would have been protected. See *Angara Maritime Ltd v OceanConnect UK Ltd* [2010] EWHC 619 (QB), [2011] 1 Lloyd's Rep 61.

In *Four Point Garage Ltd v Carter* [1985] 3 All ER 12, the goods in question were delivered by the seller directly to the sub-purchaser. Simon Brown J held that s 25(1) applied, because the buyer was deemed to have taken constructive delivery of the goods and the seller to have acted as the buyer's agent in making delivery to the sub-purchaser.

It should be noted that the delivery may be pursuant to 'any sale, pledge, or *other disposition* thereof' (as with s 24). These two exceptions to the *nemo dat* rule are therefore not confined to the case of a second sale or pledge. A significant case arises where a builder who has agreed to buy materials on terms that title remains in the seller uses these materials in constructing a factory. Here there is a 'disposition' within s 25(1): the factory owner gets a good title and cannot be sued by the original seller (see the Scots decision in *Archivent v Strathclyde Regional Council* 1985 SLT 154).

But, for obvious reasons, the disposition from Y to Z must be such as would, if Y and not X were owner of the goods, have actually constituted Z owner. In *Re Highway Foods International Ltd* [1995] 1 BCLC 209, goods were sold by X to Y and sub-sold by Y to Z, in each case on terms that the seller retained title to the goods until the price had been paid. Hence, technically the arrangements between X and Y and Y and Z were agreements for sale and not sales. Neither X nor Y was ever paid. It was held that neither s 25(1) nor s 9 of the Factors Act 1889 had the effect of depriving X of its title and vesting it in Z.

(e) 'Has the same effect as if the person making the delivery or transfer were a mercantile agent in possession of the goods or documents of title with the consent of the owner'

It will be noticed that this wording differs markedly from the concluding words of s 24 (which reads 'has the same effect as if the person making the delivery or transfer were expressly authorised by the owner of the goods to make the same'). It seems to mean that a buyer has not only to prove good faith and lack of notice, but also satisfy the requirements of s 2 of the Factors Act 1889 on the assumption that the person he bought from was a mercantile agent. In particular it seems that the sale to the innocent buyer must be in the ordinary course of business. The point was discussed in *Newtons of Wembley*, already referred to.

Newtons of Wembley Ltd v Williams
[1965] 1 QB 560, Court of Appeal

The facts are given above.

Sellers LJ: The only other question which arises is how far s 9, on its true construction, takes the ultimate sub-buyer (the defendant in the present case), relying, as he does, on what happened between Andrew and Biss. The judge treated s 9 as placing Andrew in the position of a mercantile agent, but with the obligation on the defendant of establishing not only that Biss took in good faith (I leave out the other requirement of no notice of the plaintiff's rights; nothing arose on that), but also that in the transaction between Andrew and Biss (Andrew being treated as a mercantile agent in accordance with s 9), Andrew was 'acting in the ordinary course of business of a mercantile agent.' . . .

Before one takes too favourable a view for the sub-buyer and too harsh a view against the true owner of the goods as to the cases where s 9 can be invoked, one must remember that it is taking away the right which would have existed at common law, and for myself I should not be prepared to enlarge it more than the words clearly permitted and required. It seems to me that all that s 9 can be said clearly to do is to place the buyer in possession in the position of a mercantile agent when he has in fact in his possession the goods of somebody else, and it does no more than clothe him with that fictitious or notional position on any disposition of those goods. Section 2(1) makes it clear that the sub-buyer from a mercantile agent, to whom that section applies, has in order to obtain the full advantage of the subsection, to establish that the mercantile agent was acting in the ordinary course of business. . . . Counsel for the plaintiffs sought to establish that a transaction taking place in this somewhat unusual market, the street kerb in Warren Street, was, on the face of it, something which was not an ordinary business transaction in any way, by a mercantile agent or anybody else, but was to some extent suspect. But the judge had evidence about this and he said, and I think it is within the knowledge of the court, that there had been an established market in secondhand cars in this area on this very site for a long time. Although he said that he had some doubt at one time about the sale to Biss being in the ordinary course of business, for, as he pointed out, there were no business premises, the sale was in the street, and it was for cash, yet he came to the conclusion, which I think cannot be challenged, that there was in Warren Street and its neighbourhood an established street market for cash dealing in cars. When one looks at what took place in that area and finds the prospective buyer coming up and getting into contact with the prospective seller in regard to a car, with an offer and an acceptance, trial of the car and a looking over it and some questions asked and a delivery—I do not find anything to indicate that it was not in the ordinary course of business of a mercantile agent. It seems to me that the defendant has established that essential fact.

NOTES

1.   For a similar conclusion see too the Northern Irish case of *Martin v Duffy* [1985] NI 417, and also *The Saetta* [1994] 1 WLR 1334 at 1351, per Clarke J.

2.   This would seem to rule out most cases where the person making the sale was a private person, since it is not clear how a person without any business at all can be 'acting in the ordinary course of business of a mercantile agent' within s 2 of the 1889 Act. If so it is possible that the seminal case of *Lee v Butler* (above, p 4) was decided *per incuriam*.

For s 25(1) to apply Z must have been acting in good faith and without notice of any claim of X. The onus is on Z to prove this: *Fairfax Gerrard Holdings Ltd v Capital Bank plc* [2006] EWHC Civ 3439, [2007] 1 Lloyd's Rep 171.

   A further conundrum concerning s 25(1) arises from its very last word: 'with the consent of the *owner*'. In the earlier parts of the subsection, all the relevant references are to the 'seller'. At least at first sight, this would suggest that the 'owner' must be someone else: but if so, the section would have a surprising effect. Imagine X steals a truck from A and sells it to Y, whereupon Y sells and delivers it to Z. In strict logic this seems to mean that Z gets good title. Y is a person who has bought or agreed to buy the truck (from X); he has sold and delivered it to Z; Z therefore falls to be treated as if Y were a mercantile agent in possession with the consent of the owner A; from which it follows that Z will get title. The House of Lords, to much relief, rejected this construction and its bizarre consequences in *National Employers' Mutual General Insurance Association Ltd v Jones*, of which a brief extract appears below.

National Employers' Mutual General Insurance Association Ltd v Jones
[1990] 1 AC 24, House of Lords

Miss Hopkin's car was stolen in 1983. It was subsequently bought by a firm called Autochoice, which sold it to Mid-Glamorgan Motors, who resold it to Jones. When Miss Hopkin's insurers (who had been subrogated to her rights: see below, p 1099) claimed the car from Jones, he sought the protection of s 25(1). All the courts found for the insurers. The trial judge and a majority of the Court of Appeal took the view that the word 'owner' in s 25(1) had to be read as 'seller'. The House of Lords upheld the finding on a different construction: the section was to be taken as referring to a *notional* sale by a *notional* mercantile agent in possession of the goods with the consent of their *notional* owner.

Lord Goff of Chieveley: As a matter of construction of the relevant statutory provisions, therefore, I have reached the conclusion that the submission advanced by the appellant cannot be sustained. In my opinion, s 9 of the Factors Act 1889 must be read as providing that the delivery or transfer given by the intermediate transferor (B) shall have the same effect as if he was a mercantile agent in possession of the goods or documents of title with the consent of the owner who entrusted them to him (A). Such a construction is, in my opinion, to be derived from the terms of s 2(1) of the Act, to which s 9 evidently refers, and also from the legislative context which I have already discussed. The same construction must, of course, be placed upon s 25(1) of the Sale of Goods Act 1979.

[**Lords Bridge of Harwich**, **Lowry**, **Brandon of Oakbrook**, and **Griffiths** concurred.]

(f) Some final points

The following case is also of relevance, and raised some interesting incidental points.

DF Mount Ltd v Jay & Jay (Provisions) Co Ltd
[1960] 1 QB 159, Queen's Bench Division

Jays agreed to sell to Merrick 250 cartons of Australian canned peaches, part of a larger consignment owned by them and lying in the warehouse of Delta Storage Ltd, Greenwich. Merrick made it plain that he would pay the price from the monies which he would receive from his own customers when the goods had been resold. Jays made out two delivery orders addressed to Delta in favour of Merrick, one for 150 cartons and another for 100. Merrick sent the delivery orders to Delta endorsed with the words 'Please transfer to our sub-order'. Merrick then agreed to resell the 250 cartons to Mount, and received the price from Mount in exchange for a delivery order addressed to Delta and signed by Merrick. Jays were never paid by Merrick. Both Jays and Mount claimed to be entitled to the peaches, which were still in the hands of Delta. Judgment was given in favour of Mount on the ground that Jays had 'assented' to the resale under s 47(1); but the case also contains a discussion of another point relevant to the present *nemo dat* exception: does it matter that the contract goods are not identified, but unascertained?

Salmon J (holding that Jays had 'assented' to the sub-sale by Mount under s 47(1), continued): The sale of the 250 cartons was a sale of unascertained goods. In my judgment, however, there is no reason why s 47 should not apply to unascertained goods, although I respectfully agree with Pickford J that an inference can in some circumstances more readily be drawn against the seller in the case of a sale of specific goods than in the case of a sale of unascertained goods. I hold that the defendants assented to the sale of the cartons by Merrick within the meaning of s 47.

This is enough to dispose of the case, but I will deal briefly with some of the other points which have been canvassed. Mr Silkin argues that even had there been no sufficient assent by the defendants, he would be entitled to succeed under the proviso to s 47 [now s 47(2)].

NOTES

1.   While the judgment of Salmon J does refer to the fact that the goods were unascertained, the discussion is perfunctory and refers only to s 47, and not also to s 25(1).

2.   But the difficulties do not stop at this point. On Salmon J's reasoning, Mount became the owner of 'the 250 cartons' of peaches. But (assuming that there had been no appropriation by exhaustion and ignoring the complications that have since been introduced by s 20A), this ruling runs counter to the basic principle that no property can be transferred until the contract goods have been ascertained (s 16). In the event of Jays' insolvency, all the difficulties exemplified by *Re Wait* (above, p 298) would have to be faced. It is difficult to resist the conclusion that on this issue *Mount v Jay* is open to reconsideration.

QUESTION

X, the owner of 20,000 tonnes of soya beans on board the MV *Poseidon*, transfers a bill of lading relating to 10,000 tonnes to Y on terms that no title passes to Y until Y pays. Y transfers the same bill of lading to Z, who pays Y. Y then becomes insolvent without paying X. Can Z claim to be owner of a 50 per cent proportion of the cargo of the MV *Poseidon* under s 20A?

7 SIXTH EXCEPTION: SALE BY UNPAID SELLER UNDER SGA 1979, S 48

This exception to the *nemo dat* rule overlaps to some extent with s 24 (sale by seller in possession), but there are important points of difference. It is discussed with the other seller's remedies below, at p 491.

8 SEVENTH EXCEPTION: PRIVATE PURCHASE OF MOTOR VEHICLE HELD ON HIRE-PURCHASE

Part III of the Hire Purchase Act 1964 protects the title of a private purchaser of a motor vehicle held on hire-purchase. This is not covered in detail here as it is regarded as a more relevant to consumer protection than to commercial law.

9 EIGHTH EXCEPTION: SALE UNDER GENERAL POWERS OF SALE OR COURT ORDER

Section 21(2)(b) of the Sale of Goods Act states that the provisions of the Act do not affect the validity of any contract of sale under any special common law or statutory power of sale or under the order of a court of competent jurisdiction.

It is not necessary to list at length the various situations where a sale of goods may be effected without the authority of the owner under the powers referred to in this provision. It is sufficient to cite a few examples.

(1) Goods may be sold under common law powers by a pledgee: *Re Hardwick, ex p Hubbard* (see below, p 1038) and by an agent of necessity (see above, p 152).

(2) There are many statutory provisions which confer a power of sale, for example upon an unpaid seller of goods (below, p 491), or a bailee of uncollected goods (see the Torts (Interference with Goods) Act 1977, ss 12–13).

(3) In addition, the court may order a sale of goods, either under its inherent powers (eg to enforce a charge) or pursuant to the rules of court (eg to dispose of goods which are perishable or likely to deteriorate); and it may do this even against the wishes of the owner: *Larner v Fawcett* [1950] 2 All ER 727.

(4) Besides all the above, it has to be remembered that the general law of property applies in commercial law as elsewhere. For example, if an 'owner' of goods transpires to have a mere equitable interest, that interest may be overridden where the goods are sold to a good faith purchaser of a legal interest. This may be significant. For example, in *MCC Proceeds Inc v Lehman Brothers International (Europe)* [1998] 4 All ER 675 share certificates (which fell to be treated as goods) were held by trustees on bare trust for M; without M's knowledge the certificates were later pledged by the trustees to Lehman Brothers. It was held that the later pledge took precedence over M's purely equitable ownership. Again, in *Gray v Smith* [2013] EWHC 4136 (Comm), [2014] 2 All ER (Comm) 359 a racing car was bought by one Edwards as trustee for Gray, who thereby obtained an equitable title. Edwards was in fact a fraudster and sold the same car to Smith. Cooke J held that the title of Smith, as good faith buyer of the legal title, had to prevail over that of Gray.

Reform of the law In January 1994 the Department of Trade and Industry published a Consultation Document containing proposals for the reform of some of the exceptions to the *nemo dat* rule. More controversially, it also proposed that anyone who was in possession of goods with the owner's consent should have power to confer a good title on an innocent purchaser. This last suggestion, which would incidentally have brought English law closer to the system prevailing in most of Europe (see above, p 384), was nevertheless heavily criticised (see, eg, BJ Davenport, 'Consultation—How Not to Do It' (1994) 110 LQR 165); and it is unlikely that these proposals, or anything like them, will be raised again in the foreseeable future. The Law Commission briefly added transfer of title by a non-owner to its ninth programme of law reform in 2005, but by 2011 had dropped it again (see Law Com No 330, para 3.1). Indeed, the only recent change has been not an extension but a restriction of the exceptions to *nemo dat*. This was the abolition in 1994 of one exception formerly contained in s 22 of the Sale of Goods Act, the ancient rule of 'market overt', under which a buyer in a lawful market who took in good faith acquired a good title to the goods. And this only happened when in 1993 a stranger walked up to Sotheby's valuation counter in New Bond Street with a black bin bag containing a Gainsborough and a Reynolds which were immediately recognised as having been stolen some time earlier from Lincoln's Inn. Since the stranger had bought them in good faith in Bermondsey Market for the princely sums of £85 and £60, his title had to be accepted as impeccable. The art world was scandalised; and the law was smartly changed shortly afterwards.

CHAPTER 11

SELLER'S OBLIGATIONS AS TO QUALITY

1 INTRODUCTION: EXPRESS AND IMPLIED TERMS AS TO QUALITY, AND THEIR EFFECT

In very many commercial sales, the contract will lay down expressly the seller's obligations as to the characteristics and quality of the goods to be sold. Standard forms, for example those issued by the Grain and Feed Trade Association (GAFTA) for bulk commodities, very frequently contain detailed such provisions; again, contracts for the supply of oil and gas often lay down very detailed specifications indeed for what is to be supplied. Express obligations of this kind are enforced and construed according to the general rules of the law of contract. For example, these rules determine the important issue whether such obligations are conditions, warranties, or 'innominate' terms—that is, whether breach of them by the seller always allows rejection or whether the remedy for breach is made to depend on the seriousness of the breach. (An example of a term deemed to fall in the latter category was *Cehave NV v Bremer Handelsgesellschaft mbH, The Hansa Nord* [1976] QB 44, CA (term 'shipment to be made in good condition' not a condition, so buyer could not reject and then buy goods for a fraction of their price after a distress sale); and see too *RG Grain Trade LLP (UK) v Feed Factors International Ltd* [2011] EWHC 1889 (Comm), [2011] 2 Lloyd's Rep 433.)

Quite apart from such express obligations, however, ss 13–15 of the Sale of Goods Act 1979 lay down a series of *implied* obligations, which form the main subject matter of this chapter. These oblige the seller to deliver goods which comply with any description (s 13), which are of satisfactory quality and reasonably fit for their purpose (s 14), and which accord with any sample provided (s 15).

Strictly speaking ss 13–15 apply only to contracts of *sale*, and not (for example) to hire-purchase, to leases of goods, or to contracts, such as repair contracts, where goods are supplied for payment but not under a contract of sale. But this is not very important, since parallel statutory implied terms apply to such contracts. See the Supply of Goods (Implied Terms) Act 1973, ss 9–11 (hire-purchase) and the Supply of Goods and Services Act 1982, ss 3–5 (ancillary contracts) and ss 8–10 (leases of goods). The comments on ss 13–15 of the Sale of Goods Act apply by analogy to these obligations as well.

Note that a number of the cases referred to below concern consumer transactions. This is because until 2015 the same legislation applied in principle to both consumer and to business-to-business sales. Today, however, the seller's duties in consumer sales as regards quality are governed not by the 1979 Act but by the Consumer Rights Act 2015, which imposes similar (but not identical) implied obligations in such contracts. This book is a book about commercial law, and consumer transactions will not be covered in detail except where the old authorities are relevant to commercial transactions.

The terms laid down by ss 13–15 are all implied, or default, terms. Thus they may on principle be excluded or varied: see s 55(1), which states that 'where a right, duty or liability would arise under a contract of sale of goods by implication of law, it may . . . be negatived or varied by express agreement, or by the course of dealing between the parties, or by such usage as binds both parties to the contract'. In the commercial context there are limited restrictions on contracting-out, such as those contained in the Unfair Contract Terms Act 1977, which expressly makes s 55(1) subject to its provisions.[1] We shall note the effect of these restrictions later in this chapter. In addition issues can arise as to whether express provisions in a contract on quality *implicitly* exclude the ss 13–15 implied terms on the basis that they cover the same ground. This is also touched on briefly.

In relation to England and Wales, the statutory implied terms as to quality are all classified by the Sale of Goods Act as *conditions*.[2] Because it essentially reproduces legislation of 1893, the Act does not contemplate the possibility that they might be 'innominate' terms of the kind first explicitly recognised in *Hong Kong Fir Shipping Co Ltd v Kawasaki Kisen Kaisha Ltd* [1962] 2 QB 26, CA—that is, terms where the remedy for breach is made to depend on the seriousness of the breach.

The consequences of this are very significant. Section 11, setting out the definition of a condition, states that if a term is a condition any breach whatever allows the other party to treat the contract as repudiated and refuse to perform further. In the context of the quality terms, this means that any breach by the seller of the provisions of ss 13–15, however minor or inconsequential, allows the buyer to reject the goods. He may do this for any reason or no reason, unless he has waived his right, or accepted the goods. Until 1994 this right was absolute. Now, however, note needs to be taken of s 15A, inserted in 1994, which slightly qualifies it. Under this section, if the breach is so slight that it would be unreasonable to reject the goods, it is to be treated only as a breach of warranty, unless a contrary intention appears in or is to be implied from the contract.

Even since the enactment of s 15A, however, the English position remains an unusually uncompromising one, strongly preferring certainty to abstract justice. In particular, in contrast to the position in many European legal systems, and to the position under the Vienna Convention on Contracts for the International Sale of Goods (referred to below at p 533), there is no restriction of the right of rejection to substantial breaches, nor any requirement for the right to reject to be exercised in good faith or with regard to the interests of the other party.

---

[1] We do not deal here with the far more complex regime applying to exemption clauses in consumer sales, now largely contained in the Consumer Rights Act 2015.

[2] The matter is differently arranged in Scotland, to which the Sale of Goods Act also applies, and where breaches of these obligations are classed as material breaches rather than breaches of condition. But this book is concerned with the law of England and Wales.

2 THE IMPLIED CONDITION THAT THE GOODS WILL CORRESPOND WITH THEIR DESCRIPTION (S 13)

(a) General

Under s 13(1)–(3):

(1) Where there is a contract for the sale of goods by description, there is an implied term that the goods will correspond with the description.

(1A) As regards England and Wales and Northern Ireland, the term implied by subsection (1) above is a condition.

(2) If the sale is by sample as well as by description it is not sufficient that the bulk of the goods corresponds with the sample if the goods do not also correspond with the description.

(3) A sale of goods is not prevented from being a sale by description by reason only that, being exposed for sale or hire, they are selected by the buyer.

This provision has been regarded as curious. Why should the Act bother to include such a rule at all? And is it not odd that the obligation should be described as *implied* when there is surely an *express* obligation to deliver goods of the description by which they were sold? The explanation is historical. Before 1893, the date of the first Sale of Goods Act, there were no obligations as to quality as regards identified or specific goods (eg a sale of a particular horse) unless the buyer expressly stipulated for a warranty. Obligations as to quality were only implied in generic goods (eg '100 tons of King Edward potatoes'), where the qualities of the goods which the buyer was bargaining to have could be ascertained *only* by reference to the contractual description by which they were sold (and, in commercial contracts, a further term, implied by law, that they should be of 'merchantable' quality under that description (now contained in the Sale of Goods Act 1979, s 14(2)). Here a strict obligation to deliver goods of the correct type was understandably regarded as essential. Under the Act, however, the quality terms, including s 13, apply to all goods irrespective of whether they are generic or specific, and indeed even if the buyer himself has selected or inspected them (see now s 13(3)). Examples include *Grant v Australian Knitting Mills Ltd* [1936] AC 85, PC (underwear bought in a retail shop) and *Beale v Taylor* [1967] 1 WLR 1193, CA (second-hand car advertised for sale in a newspaper). These cases have led to the term 'sale by description' being given a meaning so wide as to make one wonder whether any contract of sale will be regarded as *not* being made 'by description':[3] in *Grant* Lord Wright said ([1936] AC 85 at 100):

... there is a sale by description even though the buyer is buying something displayed before him on the counter: a thing is sold by description, though it is specific, so long as it is sold not merely as the specific thing but as a thing corresponding to a description, eg woollen under-garments.

---

[3] A development partly due to the fact that before 1973 the 'satisfactory quality' term in what is now s 14(2) only applied to sales by description, and courts understandably wished to interpret the latter expression widely so as not to shut out deserving buyers of bad goods. But this restriction has now disappeared.

(b) Application

When we move out of the consumer sphere and back into the world of merchants with which this book is primarily concerned, we see that the implied condition as to correspondence with description is particularly important in contracts for the sale of generic goods, such as bulk commodities, where the buyer has only the contract description to rely on. This role is made even more important by the fact referred to above: namely, that where there is a right to reject goods, as there is under s 13, English law has always allowed it to be exercised for any reason at all (eg the fact that, even though the buyer is not prejudiced in any way, prices have fallen and he would like to buy elsewhere). This is illustrated by the two cases next cited.

Bowes v Shand

(1877) 2 App Cas 455, House of Lords

Sellers agreed to ship 600 tons of 'Madras rice, to be shipped at Madras,[4] or coast, for this port, during the months of March and/or April, 1874, *per Rajah of Cochin.*' In fact virtually all the rice was loaded in February, and a bill of lading was issued on 28 February. There was no evidence that rice shipped in February was any different from that shipped in March. The buyer rejected the cargo, and the seller sued for damages. The Court of Appeal held for the seller, but an appeal to the House of Lords was allowed.

> **Earl Cairns**: My Lords, if that [ie shipment in March–April] is the natural meaning of the words, it does not appear to me to be a question for your Lordships, or for any Court, to consider whether that is a contract which bears upon the face of it some reason, some explanation why it was made in that form, and why the stipulation is made that the shipment should be during these particular months. It is a mercantile contract, and merchants are not in the habit of placing upon their contracts stipulations to which they do not attach some value and importance, and that alone might be a sufficient answer. But, if necessary, a farther answer is obtained from two other considerations. It is quite obvious that merchants making contracts for the purchase of rice, contracts which oblige them to pay in a certain manner for the rice purchased, and to be ready with the funds for making that payment, may well be desirous both that the rice should be forthcoming to them not later than a certain time, and also that the rice shall not be forthcoming to them at a time earlier than it suits them to be ready with funds for its payment....
>
> My Lords, before leaving that part of the case, I must advert to a suggestion which was made at the Bar on behalf of the Respondents, although it does not appear to have been made in the Court below. It was suggested that even if the construction of the contract be as I have stated, still if the rice was not put on board in the particular months, that would not be a reason which would justify the Appellants in having rejected the rice altogether, but that it might afford a ground for a cross action by them if they could shew that any particular damage resulted to them from the rice not having been put on board in the months in question. My Lords, I cannot think that there is any foundation whatever for that argument. If the construction of the contract be as I have said, that it bears that the rice is to be put on board in the months in question, that is part of the description of the subject-matter of what is sold. What is sold is not 300 tons of rice in gross or in general. It is 300 tons of *Madras* rice to be put on board at *Madras* during the particular months. The construction may be shewn by evidence to be different from what I have

---

[4] Now Chennai.

supposed, but if the construction be that which I have supposed, the Plaintiff, who sues upon that contract, has not launched his case until he has shewn that he has tendered that thing which has been contracted for, and if he is unable to shew that, he cannot claim any damages for the non-fulfilment of the contract.

...

Lord Blackburn: It was argued, or tried to be argued, on one point, that it was enough that it was rice, and that it was immaterial when it was shipped. As far as the subject-matter of the contract went, its being shipped at another and a different time being (it was said) only a breach of a stipulation which could be compensated for in damages. But I think that that is quite untenable....If the description of the article tendered is different in any respect it is not the article bargained for, and the other party is not bound to take it. I think in this case what the parties bargained for was rice, shipped at *Madras* or the coast of *Madras*. Equally good rice might have been shipped a little to the north or a little to the south of the coast of *Madras*. I do not quite know what the boundary is, and probably equally good rice might have been shipped in February as was shipped in March, or equally good rice might have been shipped in May as was shipped in April, and I dare say equally good rice might have been put on board another ship as that which was put on board the *Rajah of Cochin*. But the parties have chosen, for reasons best known to themselves, to say: We bargain to take rice, shipped in this particular region, at that particular time, on board that particular ship, and before the Defendants can be compelled to take anything in fulfilment of that contract it must be shewn not merely that it is equally good, but that it is the same article as they have bargained for—otherwise they are not bound to take it.

NOTE

This case was decided at common law, but it is one of the cases on which s 13 is based, and indubitably remains good law today.

Arcos Ltd v EA Ronaasen & Son
[1933] AC 470, House of Lords

This was a contract for the sale of Russian timber cut into staves for the purpose of making cement barrels. The contract specified that the staves should be ½ inch (12.5 mm) in thickness. The buyers claimed to be entitled to reject the timber because most of the staves were thicker than half an inch, although most were not more than $9/_{16}$ of an inch (13 mm). It was found that the staves were fit for making cement barrels and merchantable under the contract specification. Even so, the House of Lords upheld the buyers' right to reject for non-conformity with the contract description.

Lord Atkin: The decisions of the learned judge and of the Court of Appeal appear to me to have been unquestionably right. On the facts as stated by the umpire as of the time of inspection only about 5 per cent of the goods corresponded with the description: and the umpire finds it impossible to say what proportion conformed at the time of shipment.

It was contended that in all commercial contracts the question was whether there was a 'substantial' compliance with the contract: there always must be some margin: and it is for the tribunal of fact to determine whether the margin is exceeded or not. I cannot agree. If the written contract specifies conditions of weight, measurement and the like, those conditions must be complied with. A ton does not mean about a ton, or a yard about a yard. Still less when you descend to minute measurements does ½ inch mean about ½ inch. If the seller wants a margin he must and in my experience does stipulate for it. Of course by recognized trade usage particular figures may be given a different meaning, as in a baker's dozen; or there may be even incorporated a definite margin more or less: but there is no evidence or finding of such a usage in the present case.

No doubt there may be microscopic deviations which business men and therefore lawyers will ignore. And in this respect it is necessary to remember that description and quantity are not necessarily the same: and that the legal rights in respect of them are regulated by different sections of the code, description by s 13, quantity, by s 30. It will be found that most of the cases that admit any deviation from the contract are cases where there has been an excess or deficiency in quantity which the Court has considered negligible. But apart from this consideration the right view is that the conditions of the contract must be strictly performed. If a condition is not performed the buyer has a right to reject.

[**Lords Buckmaster** and **Warrington of Clyffe** delivered concurring opinions. **Lords Blanesburgh** and **Macmillan** concurred.]

Decisions of this kind have since attracted some adverse comment in the House of Lords, in a case otherwise not concerned with sale of goods.

Reardon Smith Line Ltd v Yngvar Hansen-Tangen
[1976] 1 WLR 989, House of Lords

In each of two cases, defendants agreed to time-charter a supertanker then under construction as soon as she was completed. The defendants refused delivery following the oil crisis of 1974 and a collapse in shipping rates. They cited a provision in the charter giving the name of the yard and hull number of the vessel, and relied on the fact that the vessel was in fact being constructed by subcontractors in another yard under another designation. The House of Lords held that this did not justify rejection. But Lord Wilberforce had some pertinent comments on the sale of goods cases.

Lord Wilberforce: Some of these cases either in themselves (*Re Moore & Co and Landauer & Co* [1921] 2 KB 519 or as they have been interpreted (eg *Behn v Burness* (1863) 3 B & S 751) I find to be excessively technical and due for fresh examination in this House. Even if a strict and technical view must be taken as regards the description of unascertained future goods (eg commodities) as to which each detail of the description must be assumed to be vital, it may be, and in my opinion is, right to treat other contracts of sale of goods in a similar manner to other contracts generally so as to ask whether a particular item in a description constitutes a substantial ingredient of the 'identity' of the thing sold, and only if it does to treat it as a condition (see *Couchman v Hill* [1947] KB 554, 559, per Scott LJ). I would respectfully endorse what was recently said by Roskill LJ in *Cehave NV v Bremer Handelsgesellschaft mbH* [1976] QB 44, 71:

> In principle it is not easy to see why the law relating to contracts for the sale of goods should be different from the law relating to the performance of other contractual obligations, whether charterparties or other types of contract. Sale of goods law is but one branch of the general law of contract. It is desirable that the same legal principles should apply to the law of contract as a whole and that different legal principles should not apply to different branches of that law. . . .

The general law of contract has developed, along much more rational lines (eg *Hong Kong Fir Shipping Co Ltd v Kawasaki Kisen Kaisha Ltd* [1962] 2 QB 26), in attending to the nature and gravity of a breach or departure rather than in accepting rigid categories which do or do not automatically give a right to rescind, and if the choice were between extending cases under the Sale of Goods Act 1893 into other fields, or allowing more modern doctrine to infect those cases, my preference would be clear. The importance of this line of argument is that Mocatta J and Lord Denning MR used it in the present case so as to reject the appellants' argument on 'description' and I agree with them. But in case it does not appeal to this House, I am also satisfied that the appellants fail to bring the present case within the strictest rules as to 'description.'

NOTES

1. In *Re Moore & Co Ltd and Landauer & Co's Arbitration* [1921] 2 KB 519, Moore contracted to sell Landauer a quantity of Australian canned peaches, described as being packed in cases containing 30 cans each. When the goods arrived in London, they were in the right quantity and of impeccable quality; but only about half of the consignment was packed in cases of 30, the rest being in cases of 24. The buyers rejected the peaches without giving any reason; and were held by the Court of Appeal to have been entirely entitled to do so under s 13.

2. The rule epitomised by the decisions in *Bowes v Shand* and *Arcos v Ronaasen* (known in the United States as the 'perfect tender rule') has been heavily criticised on the basis that that the goods delivered were apparently in each case perfectly suitable for the buyers' purpose, and that the buyers' reason for wanting to reject them was probably that they wanted to get out of an unprofitable bargain. But there are important arguments in favour of the courts' strict approach. First, merchants put a high premium on certainty: a firm rule means that they know where they stand, whereas much delay would be caused if every case had to go to court in order to ascertain whether the deviation from the contract was significant, or what the real motives of the parties were. Secondly, more often than not, the buyers of commodities are not merchants who intend to use the goods themselves, but dealers who have bought to sell on, and who may well already have resold the goods to sub-buyers; and in such a case they will usually have resold the goods by the same description. There could well be a long chain of further subcontracts. If there is a dispute over conformity with description under the first sale, the court is not to know what use for the goods the ultimate buyer may have in mind, or whether it is such as would entitle him to reject them. Thirdly, as we shall see (below, Chapter 21) the completion of these contracts of sale is very often carried out not by the parties themselves, but by others on their behalf (eg their respective banks) by payment of the price in exchange for the shipping documents relating to the goods—possibly in a foreign country. These representatives will not be in a position to know whether goods which do not fully comply with the contract description will nevertheless be suitable for their clients' purpose (still less, their clients' sub-purchasers' purpose), and so the only workable rule has to be one calling for strict conformity. And, fourthly, it is arguable that as a matter of commercial morality it is entirely right that a seller who wishes to take advantage of what is often, owing to price volatility, a highly profitable transaction should be required to perform it to the letter or risk losing the benefit of it.

3. Businesspeople are well aware of the strictness of s 13 and often vary it. The standard GAFTA 100 contract for animal feedstuffs, for instance, says this: 'The goods are warranted free from castor seed and/or castor seed husk, but should the analysis show castor seed husk not exceeding 0.005%, the Buyers shall not be entitled to reject the goods, but shall accept them with the following allowances: 0.75% of contract price if not exceeding 0.001%, 1% of contract price if not exceeding 0.002%, and 1.50% of contract price if not exceeding 0.005%.... Should the parcel contain castor seed husk in excess of 0.005% Buyers shall be entitled to reject the parcel.'

4. The actual decision in *Arcos v Ronaasen*, above, might very well today be different because of s 15A.

(c) What forms part of the contractual 'description' of the goods?

Against the background of this discussion, we are in a better position to look a little more closely at the concept of 'sale by description', and in particular to ask which out of the many words used in reference to the goods being sold are part of their contract 'description'.

The approach of the courts will depend upon the context. In the commercial context of commodity sales, we have seen from *Re Moore & Landauer* and *Arcos v Ronaasen* (above) that words regarding the packing of the goods and their dimensions may be part of their description, and from *Bowes v Shand* that the shipment date in overseas sales almost invariably is. In *Pinnock Bros v Lewis & Peat Ltd* [1923] 1 KB 690 copra cake intended to be fed to livestock which had been adulterated with castor beans and rendered poisonous was described by Roche J as something 'which could not properly be described as copra cake at all'. And the same may be true of references to the origin of the goods, their analysis, etc: the parties can make any element or item part of the description and, if the court concludes that that was their intention, the buyer is entitled to insist that that, and that alone, is what he shall get.

However, this does not mean that everything appearing in the contract of sale which says something about the goods forms part of their description. Particularly with specific or identified goods, the courts not infrequently hold that, although descriptive words were used, the goods were not 'sold by' that description. This is clear from *Harlingdon & Leinster Enterprises Ltd v Christopher Hull Fine Art Ltd*. The issue for the court is then to decide whether the parties attached sufficient weight to the particular words as to warrant their being treated as part of the contractual description.

Harlingdon & Leinster Enterprises Ltd v Christopher Hull Fine Art Ltd
[1991] 1 QB 564, Court of Appeal

This contract concerned the sale for £6,000 of a painting described as being the work of Gabriele Münter, a painter of the German expressionist school, but which unknown to anyone was in fact a forgery worth £50 to £100. The parties were both art dealers, the buyers (but not the sellers) being specialists in this area of the art market. The Court of Appeal held that although the seller had used the words 'by Münter' in describing the painting, it had not been *sold by* that description—the buyer having relied on his own judgment in regard to this question of attribution. Accordingly, he was not liable to the buyer for breach of s 13.

Nourse LJ: The judge found that both at the time when the agreement was made and subsequently when the invoice was made out both Mr Hull and Mr Runkel [the representatives respectively of the sellers and the buyers] believed that the painting was by Münter and that, if either had not believed that, the deal would not have been made. He made the following further findings:

In my judgment Runkel must have known and accepted that Hull was disclaiming any judgment, knowledge or private information which would or could have grounded the latter's earlier statement to Braasch that he had two paintings by Gabriele Münter for sale . . . I think the only conclusion which can be drawn from the unusual facts of this case is that it was Runkel's exercise of his own judgment as to the quality of the pictures, including the factor of the identity of their painter, which induced him to enter into the agreement he made with Hull. However, I am not satisfied that without the attribution, given what followed in the circumstances in which it was made, Runkel would not have purchased the painting. If it had never been made, Runkel would never have gone to see the paintings. But when he did go and examine the painting, he considered whether it was a Münter or not; he did agree to buy it, regardless of the attribution, because he relied on his own judgment. . . . It was reliance on his own assessment and not upon anything said by a man who had gone out of his way to stress his ignorance of the paintings which led Runkel astray.

Thus did the judge find as fact that the plaintiffs did not rely on the description of the painting as one by Gabriele Münter. They relied only on their own assessment. . . . Section 13(1) of the Sale of Goods Act 1979 is in these terms:

Where there is a contract for the sale of goods by description, there is an implied condition that the goods will correspond with the description.

The sales to which the subsection is expressed to apply are sales 'by description.' Authority apart, those words would suggest that the description must be influential in the sale, not necessarily alone, but so as to become an essential term, ie a condition, of the contract. Without such influence a description cannot be said to be one by which the contract for the sale of the goods is made.

I think that the authorities to which we were referred are consistent with this view of s 13(1).

[**Slade LJ** delivered a concurring judgment. **Stuart-Smith LJ** dissented.]

NOTES

1. See too *Drake v Thos Agnew & Sons Ltd* [2002] EWHC 294 (QB), to similar effect.

2. In *Beale v Taylor* [1967] 1 WLR 1193, CA, a car was bought having been advertised in a newspaper as a 'Herald convertible, white, 1961, twin carbs'. When it transpired to be the back half of a 1961 model welded to the front half of an older one, the Court of Appeal held that the date, 1961, was part of the contract description and that the (private) buyer could invoke s 13. But whether this would apply in a commercial context is doubtful. In the unfortunately unreported *Don Commercials Ltd v Lancaster Trucks Ltd*, CA, 14 December 1994 (available on LEXIS), a DAF tractor unit bought by one Yorkshire truck dealer from another was not equivalent in power or performance to the model number ascribed to it. The Court of Appeal, following *Harlingdon & Leinster*, held that no substantial reliance had been shown and dismissed the buyer's s 13 claim.

Harlingdon & Leinster, above, concerned specific and not generic goods. Nevertheless, it is also perfectly possible for contractual statements about *generic* goods not to form part of their description within s 13. Two cases illustrate this.

Ashington Piggeries Ltd v Christopher Hill Ltd

[1972] AC 441, House of Lords

Buyers bought herring meal to be mixed into a feeding compound for mink. The contract called for 'Norwegian herring meal fair average quality of the season, expected to analyse not less than 70% protein, not more than 12% fat and not more than 4% salt.' In fact the meal contained a preservative which made it toxic to mink. The buyers succeeded in a claim against the sellers under s 14. They also argued, however, that they had a claim under s 13 because the presence of the toxin prevented it being of 'fair average quality'. This claim was held by a majority of the House of Lords to fail.

Lord Guest:

SECTION 13 OF THE SALE OF GOODS ACT 1893

The primary argument for Hill was that the whole of the clause 'Quantity and Description' was 'the description' of the goods within the meaning of section 13, the terms of which have already been quoted. It was said that 'fair average quality of the season' (f.a.q.) must be part of the description because on what has been conveniently described as the 'sandwich principle' that part of the clause dealing with expected analysis of the meal was part of the description. It therefore followed that the intervening words f.a.q. must also be part of the description. In my view, the fallacy of this argument lies in the fact that the 'expected analysis' is not part of the description. Where goods are unascertained, 'description' implies a specification whereby the goods can be identified by the buyer. Such a case was *Arcos Ltd v. E. A. Ronaasen & Son* [1933] AC 470 where the timber contracted for was precisely specified as to length, breadth and thickness. Neither f.a.q. nor the expected analysis provision identifies the goods. They prima facie indicate the quality of the goods: see *Pacific Trading Co Ltd v Wiener* (1923) 14 Ll.L.Rep. 51, 54, Roche J. There is a case where the contract was for goods 'afloat per s.s. Morton Bay due London approximately June 8'; these words were held to be part of the description (*Macpherson Train & Co Ltd v Howard Ross & Co Ltd* [1955] 1 WLR 640). But that is a different case from the present. It enabled the goods to be identified. I do not dispute that there may be cases where a qualitative description of the goods may come within the section. The case of *Varley v. Whipp* [1900] 1 QB 513 is an example of such a case. It concerned the sale of a reaping machine stated to have been new the previous year and to have been used to cut only fifty or sixty acres. This was held to be a sale by description. But in that case the description would have identified the goods as a nearly new machine.

I have reached the conclusion without much difficulty that f.a.q. is not part of the description of 'Norwegian herring meal' contained in the contract, nor is the expected analysis part of the description. Apart from the side note 'Quantity & Description' in the sales contract, I can find no justification whatever for importing f.a.q. into the description of the goods. The side note by itself cannot control the clause where the rest of the clause is clear and unambiguous.

If f.a.q. is not part of the description of the goods, then it becomes unnecessary to consider the question whether the herring meal was f.a.q. . . .

Proton Energy Group SA v Orlen Lietuva

[2013] EWHC 2872 (Comm), [2014] 1 Lloyd's Rep 100, Commercial Court

A Lithuanian oil refinery agreed to buy from a Swiss oil trader a blend of crude oils with the generic description 'CN 2710 oil blend'. To the sellers' offer that was ultimately accepted by the buyers, was attached a detailed chemical specification. The oil when delivered answered the description 'CN 2710' but did not correspond to the detailed specification. The buyers refused to accept it, citing s 13. They were held liable for breach of contract, on the basis that while the phrase 'CN 2710' went to describe the goods, the statements in the specification did not. They were terms of the contract, allowing the buyers to claim damages in the event of breach, but not part of any description.

HHJ Mackie:

57. Mr Harris submits that the specification of the product was a matter of description. He cites *Benjamin on the Sale of Goods* (8th edn):

> A buyer can refuse to receive something which is not what he promised to buy. The description of goods may be strictly interpreted with the result that a slight discrepancy may be treated as making the goods not what was stipulated for. Where goods are not what was stipulated for, they can be rejected. 11–004.

He also refers to *Ashington Piggeries v Christopher Hill Ltd* [1972] AC 441 at 503, where Lord Diplock said:

> The 'description' by which unascertained goods are sold is, in my view, confined to those words in the contract which were intended by the parties to identify the kind of goods which were to be supplied…Ultimately the test is whether the buyer could fairly and reasonably refuse to accept the physical goods proffered to him on the ground that their failure to correspond with that part of what was said about them in the contract makes them goods of a different kind from those he had agreed to buy. The key to s.13 is identification.

58. Mr Harris submits that as a matter of ordinary language and sense, the specification was a matter of description. It was a condition that the product supplied should match the specification given, and not merely a warranty. He sets out, in his written closing, a number of factors. As a non-standard product, it does not have a 'name' like petrol or diesel. Ms Isaieva had to give a 'description' of the product in order to gauge the market interest. Ms Isiaeva [sic] explains that there were such delays in selling the product because the other refineries wanted more details of the nature of the product. No refinery would purchase a cargo without knowing the specification. Mr Armalis explains that there are a wide variety of products which could be described as 'Crude Oil Mix', which are all very different. Ms Isaieva accepted that describing the product as 'oil blend': '*doesn't tell the buyer very much*' and that a buyer cannot work out how much it should pay for the product based on that information. Indeed, Proton asked Orlen whether calling the product 'Crude Oil Mix' was acceptable for it. This illustrates that the name applied to the product was a label of convenience, not something of fundamental importance.

59. Mr Karia disagrees. He submits that compliance with the specification is not an express condition of the Contract and is not implied either. It would have been uncommercial for the parties to have agreed that since it is well known in the market that contractual specifications frequently vary from the final delivered specifications in a crude oil blend for mixing, as Mr Castro confirmed in evidence. Nor did the Contract contain an implied condition to that effect. The condition implied by s.13 of the Sale of Goods Act 1979 relates only to the '*description*' of the goods, not their quality. In contrast, the specification dealt only with the Product's quality, not its description. That specification was incorporated into the Contract's 'Quality' clause, which as the name suggests dealt with quality. It was not incorporated into the 'Product' clause. Accordingly, the delivery of a product matching that specification was not a condition of the Contract (see *Ashington*, per Lord Diplock at 503–504).

60. As I see it the specification was not part of a sale by description. As Benjamin points out, in principle description and quality are different notions. The key to description is identity, as Mr

Harris himself emphasises in his citation from *Ashington*. The cases show that the distinction between the concepts is sometimes blurred and that they may overlap where, for example, a word of description identifies the quality of the product—see *Benjamin* generally between 11–011 and 11–017. I see no such blur or overlap in this case. The contract document starts by confirming a sale of Oil Blend. Clause 3 headed 'Product' describes it as 'Oil Blend...CN 2710'. That is the description of the product. Clause 4 headed 'Quality' sets out the details of the SGS Report of the analysis at the loadport. That is the quality of the product. The document and my perception of it are consistent with the commercial reality that test results at the end of a voyage may differ from those at the outset. Further if the specification had been a sale by description Proton would have had to comply with it in every respect as a condition of the deal. Of course in another deal those considerations might have been addressed in the terms of the contract but they do point to the specification being the specified quality of the oil blend CN2710 and not part of its description. Further the fact that a buyer would not purchase without knowing the specification is as much an indication of concern about quality as it is about description. The parties are always free to make the quality a condition of the deal but, unlike description, it is not implied by statute.

NOTE

According to both these decisions, things said about goods in the contract form part of the description only if they go to the *identity* of what is being sold. This is not in terms an easy test to apply: in *Hill v Ashington Piggeries*, for example, one could equally well say that the buyers in stipulating for fair average quality *had* identified what they wanted to buy: not any old herring meal, but fair average quality herring meal. One suspects that in practice the courts are doing something slightly different: namely, drawing a rough-and-ready line between the complaints of 'This isn't what I ordered' and 'This might be what I ordered, but there's something wrong with it.' The former is governed by s 13; the latter (which was the essence of the complaint in both *Hill* and *Proton*) by s 14.

3 IMPLIED TERMS AS TO QUALITY AND FITNESS IN GENERAL

Section 14 of the Sale of Goods Act 1979 contains provisions by which undertakings on the part of the seller as to the quality of the goods and their fitness for a particular purpose are implied into certain contracts of sale. However, it is most important to note that these provisions constitute *exceptions* to the general rule, under which the seller presumptively makes no undertakings. In other words, the traditional broad principal of *caveat emptor* (Latin for 'let the buyer beware') governs this aspect of the law of sale. Section 14(1) confirms this:

Except as provided by this section and section 15 below and subject to any other enactment, there is no implied term about the quality or fitness for any particular purpose of goods supplied under a contract of sale.

Note, however, that apart from statute, a term about quality or fitness may also be implied by usage (s 14(4)).

4 IMPLIED CONDITION THAT GOODS ARE OF SATISFACTORY QUALITY: S 14(2)

Section 14(2)–(2C) is as follows:

(2) Where the seller sells goods in the course of a business, there is an implied term that the goods supplied under the contract are of satisfactory quality.

(2A) For the purposes of this Act, goods are of satisfactory quality if they meet the standard that a reasonable person would regard as satisfactory, taking account of any description of the goods, the price (if relevant) and all the other relevant circumstances.

(2B) For the purposes of this Act, the quality of goods includes their state and condition and the following (among others) are in appropriate cases aspects of the quality of goods—

  (a) fitness for all the purposes for which goods of the kind in question are commonly supplied,

  (b) appearance and finish,

  (c) freedom from minor defects,

  (d) safety, and

  (e) durability.

(2C) The term implied by subsection (2) above does not extend to any matter making the quality of goods unsatisfactory—

  (a) which is specifically drawn to the buyer's attention before the contract is made,

  (b) where the buyer examines the goods before the contract is made, which that examination ought to reveal, or

  (c) in the case of a contract for sale by sample, which would have been apparent on a reasonable examination of the sample.

This is a compendious provision. A number of parts of it need detailed treatment.

(a) Sale in the course of a business

Whereas all sellers must supply goods in accordance with description (s 13) and sample (s 15), the duty to supply goods of satisfactory quality, together with that to provide goods reasonably fit for their purpose, are limited to business sellers. Where a private person sells to a business buyer or to another private person, it will be a case of *caveat emptor.*

An important question in this connection is this: does a seller sell 'in the course of a business' where its business does not normally include that of selling goods, or of selling goods of the type in question—for example, a manufacturing company selling off a superannuated company car? It is now clear that the answer is Yes, as a result of *Stevenson v Rogers* [1999] 1 All ER 613, CA. Stevenson, who had been in business as a fisherman for 20 years, sold his fishing boat, the *Jelle.* Even though this was a one-off venture and was merely incidental to the business which Stevenson carried on, it was held that the sale *was* made 'in the course of' that business so as to bring the transaction within the scope of s 14 and render him potentially liable under s 14. See too *Macdonald v Pollock (No 2)* [2011] CSIH 12, 2013 SC 22, to the same effect.

NOTE

Under s 14(5) these provisions also apply where a sale is made by a person who in the course of a business is acting as agent for another (including an undisclosed principal: see *Boyter v*

Thomson [1995] 2 AC 628, HL), except where the fact that the seller (the agent's principal) is not selling in the course of a business is known to the buyer or reasonable steps have been taken to bring this fact to the buyer's notice (s 14(5)). But where a private person sells to a business buyer or to another private person, it will be a case of *caveat emptor*.

(b) 'Satisfactory quality'

The requirement of satisfactory quality dates back to a revision of the Act in 1995. Previously the relevant term had been 'merchantable quality', a phrase which gave rise to disconcertingly variable judicial interpretations. Some early cases (eg *Jackson v Rotax Motor & Cycle Co* [1910] 2 KB 937, CA) seem to have construed it as equivalent to 'saleable' or 'resaleable' or 'saleable under that description'. A second view turned on the notion of what a reasonable buyer would accept in performance of a contract of sale of goods under that description at or about that price (*Bristol Tramways etc Carriage Co Ltd v Fiat Motors Ltd* [1910] 2 KB 831 and *BS Brown & Sons v Craiks Ltd* [1970] 1 WLR 752, HL). A third approach focused on the usual purpose for which the goods were required (see *Henry Kendall & Sons v William Lillico & Sons Ltd* [1969] 2 AC 31, HL (animal food ingredient merchantable if nutritious to cattle even though poisonous to poultry). The present provision partly reflects the recommendations in the Law Commissions' report *Sale and Supply of Goods* (Law Com No 160, Scot Law Com No 104 (Cd 137, 1987)). For a general account, see W Ervine, 'Satisfactory Quality: What Does It Mean?' [2004] JBL 684.

Satisfactory quality is now defined in s 14(2A) and (2B):

> (2A) For the purposes of this Act, goods are of satisfactory quality if they meet the standard that a reasonable person would regard as satisfactory, taking account of any description of the goods, the price (if relevant) and all the other relevant circumstances.
>
> (2B) For the purposes of this Act, the quality of the goods includes their state and condition and the following (among others) are in appropriate cases aspects of the quality of the goods—
>
> (a) fitness for all the purposes for which goods of the kind in question are commonly supplied,
> (b) appearance and finish,
> (c) freedom from minor defects,
> (d) safety, and
> (e) durability.

The principal focus is thus now on 'acceptability', judged by the standards of the reasonable person. Description, price, state, and condition are all relevant. So is fitness for normal purposes. Indeed, it is worth noting that s 14(2B)(a) refers to *all* the purposes for which such goods are commonly supplied, so that multipurpose goods (eg feedstuffs intended for use for both cattle and poultry) must now it seems be fit for all their usual uses. A few other points of principle are worth noting.

First, a buyer cannot necessarily expect top-quality goods under s 14(2). In *Jewson Ltd v Boyhan* [2003] EWCA Civ 1030, [2004] 1 Lloyd's Rep 505 a property developer building apartments bought 13 electric boilers to install in them. The boilers worked perfectly well, but did not give the flats advantageous 'home energy ratings', which was likely to discourage potential purchasers and mortgagees. The Court of Appeal held that they were nevertheless satisfactory. See too a case decided under the old law, *BS Brown & Sons v Craiks Ltd* [1970] 1

WLR 752 (buyer of a job lot of cotton cloth could expect only the minimum quality saleable under that description).

Secondly, courts are astute to limit the purposes for which goods must be fit to their ordinary purposes: goods may well be satisfactory even if unfit for particular, unusual, purposes. One example is *Jewson v Boyhan*, above; another is *Balmoral Group Ltd v Borealis (UK) Ltd* [2006] EWHC 1900 (Comm), [2006] 2 Lloyd's Rep 629 (polythene good for general purposes satisfactory, even if too brittle to make very specialised plastic tanks, which was what the buyers wanted it for).

Thirdly, expectations may vary according to the perceived quality of the product being sold. In *Clegg v Andersson* [2003] EWCA Civ 320, [2003] 1 All ER (Comm) 721 a high-class, premium-priced yacht was held unsatisfactory when delivered with a keel 800kg overweight, requiring remedial work estimated to cost about £1,680. Hale LJ said that in a case of this sort 'the customer may be entitled to expect that it is free from even minor defects, in other words perfect or nearly so'.

Fourthly, practical usability is highly important. In *Britvic Soft Drinks Ltd v Messer UK Ltd* [2002] EWCA Civ 548, [2002] 2 All ER (Comm) 321 carbon dioxide supplied to drinks manufacturers was contaminated with tiny amounts of benzene. Although the gas did not infringe the relevant British standard and, in these quantities, posed no threat whatever to health, the carbon dioxide was held of unsatisfactory quality because benzene was in principle carcinogenic and it was commercially necessary for the buyer to recall all the drinks from sale for fear of adverse publicity.

Fifthly, legal acceptability matters. In *Niblett Ltd v Confectioners Materials Co Ltd* [1921] 3 KB 387, a case decided under the old law, perfectly palatable sweets were held unsatisfactory because their packaging infringed a third party's trade mark; and in *Pears (Newark) Ltd v Omega Proteins Ltd* [2009] EWHC 1070 (Comm), [2009] 2 Lloyd's Rep 339 meat products sold as belonging to a class able to be used for manufacture of animal by-products were held unsatisfactory because under hygiene regulations they could not lawfully be used for that purpose. But practicalities are relevant here: technical illegality of use may be ignored if overwhelmingly likely to be ignored by the authorities (see *Bramhill v Edwards* [2004] EWCA Civ 403, [2004] 2 Lloyd's Rep 653).

Subparagraphs (b)–(e) seem more appropriate for sales to consumers. Nevertheless there seems no reason why (for example) a haulier buying a new lorry should not be able to expect a near-perfect model free from minor blemishes, or (*a fortiori*) a commercial purchaser of goods should not be able to complain if the goods are dangerous to him, his employees, or the public at large.

(c) Informational defects

How far can defective information, for example misleading instructions, trigger liability under s 14(2)? See *Wormell v RHM* [1986] 1 WLR 336, below, p 447 and the accompanying Notes.

(d) Exceptions

Section 14(2) provides for three exceptions, or qualifications, to liability.

Defects specifically drawn to the buyer's attention This is an obvious exception. If a seller tells a buyer about a defect before the buyer is committed to the purchase and the latter contracts nevertheless, he can hardly complain. But its limits need to be noted. The information needs to reach the buyer *before* the contract is made: subsequent information is irrelevant. Presumably general information is also intended to be excluded: a seller can hardly avoid liability by a warning in general terms that something might be wrong with the subject matter of the sale. Thirdly, it seems that information from someone *other* than the buyer, or from the seller's own knowledge, will not suffice. Here, however, it would no doubt be open to the seller to say that a buyer who actually knew of a defect before he contracted could not reasonably expect the goods to be free of that defect, and thus that the goods were of a 'standard that a reasonable person would regard as satisfactory, taking account...all the other relevant circumstances'.

Defects which an examination made by the buyer ought to have revealed This proviso was altered in 1973: previously, it appeared from the decided cases that a buyer who had only been able to make a cursory examination might be debarred from a remedy if a more thorough examination would have revealed the defect in question. This was based on the former wording of the proviso ('as regards defects which such examination ought to have revealed'). The revised wording ('as regards defects which that examination ought to reveal') makes it clear that the exception will apply only if the buyer has examined the goods and the defect ought to have been revealed by such an examination as he actually did make. See *Macdonald v Pollock* [2011] CSIH 12, 2013 SC 22 at [34]. It should be noted that this exception is only triggered at all if the buyer has made some examination. Indeed, under English law it seems, perversely, that the best legal advice for a buyer who wishes to preserve his rights as intact as possible is never to inspect goods he is thinking of buying and, if he does so, to do this as cursorily as possible!

Defects which ought to have been apparent on a reasonable examination of a sample This provision applies only in the case of a contract for sale by sample, and complements s 15(2)(c). Under the latter subsection, the seller undertakes responsibility for any defect making the quality of the goods unsatisfactory which would not be apparent on reasonable examination of the sample. Under the present provision, responsibility for any defect which would be so apparent lies with the buyer. In contrast with s 14(2C)(b), this exception applies whether or not the buyer has actually made an examination.

(e) What goods must be satisfactory?

Not only the goods but any containers and packaging supplied with them must be satisfactory, even if the latter is not sold but merely lent or bailed to the buyer. For example, if propane gas of impeccable quality is supplied in a returnable tank which explodes and causes a fire, or goods are supplied on a returnable pallet which collapses and causes the goods to be damaged, there will be a breach of s 14. See the consumer case of *Geddling v Marsh* [1920] 1 KB 668 (exploding returnable mineral water bottle). Still more, the obligation under s 14 applies to anything supplied in *purported* performance. See *Wilson v Rickett Cockerell & Co Ltd* [1954] 1 QB 598 (coal supplied with detonator embedded: not open to seller to argue that coal was impeccable and detonator not the subject of a sale). Compare too *Albright & Wilson UK Ltd v Biachem Ltd* [2002] UKHL 37, [2003] 1 CLC 637, a case under s 13 (seller agreed to supply chemical: owing to transport mix-up, wrong consignment delivered consisting of different chemical, causing massive explosion on being poured into buyer's tank: seller liable).

(f) When must goods be satisfactory?

The Sale of Goods Act requires that goods sold be satisfactory: it does not say *when* they must be satisfactory. There is little English authority on this point: but on principle the relevant time ought to be the moment when risk passes to the buyer. Such a solution connects neatly with the notion of risk, and the rule that deterioration after risk has passed is for the buyer's account (above, p 361).

This, however, needs slight adjustment in cases where goods are to be transported to the buyer, with risk passing on shipment or dispatch (see s 18, r 5, above, p 350), and transport is likely to take some time. Suppose S in the West Indies agrees to ship bananas to B in England, and the voyage lasts ten days. It will hardly do for S to be permitted to load bananas which are perfect on shipment (which is when risk passes), but which have only a week's 'shelf life' left in them, and yet still claim to have satisfied his obligation under s 14(2). It seems that in such cases S's obligation as regards satisfactory quality is implicitly extended: it is a duty to ship fruit that is good on shipment *and in addition will, in the ordinary course of things, remain good during transit and for a reasonable time thereafter.* The point is briefly dealt with in *Mash & Murrell Ltd v Joseph I Emanuel Ltd*, below.

Mash & Murrell Ltd v Joseph I Emanuel Ltd

[1961] 1 WLR 862, Queen's Bench Division (reversed by the Court of Appeal on other grounds [1962] 1 WLR 16n)

The contract was for the sale of Cyprus spring crop potatoes, C & F Liverpool, to be shipped on the SS *Ionian* from a port in Cyprus (Limassol). (On C & F contracts, see below, p 552.) When the potatoes arrived in Liverpool they were rotten and unfit for human consumption.

> **Diplock J** (found on the evidence that the potatoes when loaded at Limassol were not fit to travel to Liverpool, and said): . . . These goods being bought c & f Liverpool, the warranty as to merchantability was a warranty that they should remain merchantable for a reasonable time, the time reasonable in all the circumstances, which means a time for the normal transit to the destination, Liverpool, and for disposal after. That warranty was, in my view, broken.
>
> [The Court of Appeal ([1962] 1 WLR 16n) reversed this decision on the facts, finding that the potatoes had suffered from excess heat and lack of ventilation on the voyage. For the purpose of this finding, it assumed that the view of Diplock J correctly expressed the law.]

NOTE

See too *Cordova Land Co Ltd v Victor Brothers Inc* [1966] 1 WLR 793 at 795–796, per Winn J; also *The Mercini Lady* [2010] EWCA Civ 1145, [2010] 2 CLC 637.

(g) The place of fault

Under both s 14(2) and (3) the seller undertakes that the goods are *in fact* of satisfactory quality and fit for their purpose; not merely that he has taken reasonable care to make sure that they are. It follows that insofar as the buyer suffers loss resulting from the supply of defective goods, the question whether the seller was at fault or not is entirely irrelevant. His liability for damage is strict. See, eg, *Wren v Holt* [1903] 1 KB 610 (claim by customer against completely blameless publican when poisoned by arsenic left in beer by brewery).

What happens where the buyer is partly responsible for his own loss, for example by continuing to use goods after noticing a possible defect in them? Damages cannot be reduced under the Law Reform (Contributory Negligence) Act 1945, because that Act does not apply to strict contractual duties under the Sale of Goods Act: see *Albright & Wilson UK Ltd v Biachem Ltd* [2002] UKHL 37, [2003] 1 CLC 637 at [3], per Lord Nicholls and *Hi-Lite Electrical Ltd v Wolseley UK Ltd* [2011] EWHC 2153 (TCC), [2011] BLR 629. But there may be a solution here based on the rules of causation: see *Lexmead v Lewis*, below.

Lexmead (Basingstoke) Ltd v Lewis
[1982] AC 225, House of Lords

Lexmead sold Lewis a towing-hitch and fitted it to Lewis's Land Rover. The towing-hitch was defective, as Lewis noticed some months after buying it. Lewis nevertheless continued to use it. The result was an accident in which the hitch parted while in use and a trailer Lewis was towing ran across the road and injured X. Two other people were killed. X recovered against Lewis for negligence. Lewis (or rather his insurers, exercising his rights) sued Lexmead, alleging that Lewis's liability to X and her family resulted from Lexmead's original breach of s 14, and seeking an indemnity. The House of Lords dismissed this claim on causation grounds.

Lord Diplock: The implied warranty of fitness for a particular purpose relates to the goods at the time of delivery under the contract of sale in the state in which they were delivered. I do not doubt that it is a continuing warranty that the goods will continue to be fit for that purpose for a reasonable time after delivery, so long as they remain in the same apparent state as that in which they were delivered, apart from normal wear and tear. What is a reasonable time will depend upon the nature of the goods but I would accept that in the case of the coupling the warranty was still continuing up to the date, some three to six months before the accident, when it first became known to the farmer that the handle of the locking mechanism was missing. Up to that time the farmer would have had a right to rely upon the dealers' warranty as excusing him from making his own examination of the coupling to see if it were safe; but if the accident had happened before then, the farmer would not have been held to have been guilty of any negligence to the plaintiff. After it had become apparent to the farmer that the locking mechanism of the coupling was broken, and consequently that it was no longer in the same state as when it was delivered, the only implied warranty which could justify his failure to take the precaution either to get it mended or at least to find out whether it was safe to continue to use it in that condition, would be a warranty that the coupling could continue to be safely used to tow a trailer on a public highway notwithstanding that it was in an obviously damaged state. My Lords, any implication of a warranty in these terms needs only to be stated, to be rejected. So the farmer's claim against the dealers fails *in limine*. In the state in which the farmer knew the coupling to be at the time of the accident, there was no longer any warranty by the dealers of its continued safety in use on which the farmer was entitled to rely.

The Court of Appeal reasoned that, since there was no break in the chain of causation between negligence of the manufacturers, which consisted in the defective design of the coupling, and the plaintiffs' damage, there could be no such break between the dealers' breach of warranty, which likewise consisted in the defective design of the coupling, and the farmer's loss occasioned by his share of the liability for the plaintiffs' damage. With respect, this reasoning was erroneous. The farmer's liability arose, not from the defective design of the coupling but from his own negligence in failing, when he knew that the coupling was damaged, to have it repaired or to ascertain if it was still safe to use. The issue of causation, therefore, on which the farmer's claim against the dealers depended, was whether *his* negligence resulted directly and naturally, in the ordinary course of events, from the dealers' breach of warranty. Manifestly it did not.

5 IMPLIED CONDITION AS TO FITNESS FOR PURPOSE (S 14(3))

We have seen that the definition of 'satisfactory quality' under s 14(2) carries within it the notion that the goods sold should be fit for all the purposes for which goods of that description are *commonly* used. If the buyer wants the goods for a *particular* or *unusual* purpose, his case will be stronger if he can bring it within the wording of s 14(3).[5] This reads as follows:

Where the seller sells goods in the course of a business and the buyer, expressly or by implication, makes known . . . to the seller . . . any particular purpose for which the goods are being bought, there is an implied [condition] that the goods supplied under the contract are reasonably fit for that purpose, whether or not that is a purpose for which such goods are commonly supplied, except where the circumstances show that the buyer does not rely, or that it is unreasonable for him to rely, on the skill or judgment of the seller. . . .

(a) Sale in the course of a business

The requirement for a sale in the course of a business is exactly the same as for s 14(2). See above, p 435, for discussion.

(b) A 'particular purpose' made known to the seller

The thinking behind s 14(3) is that s 14(2) suffices in respect of 'ordinarily' defective goods, that is, goods unfit for their common purposes; but there may be a necessity exceptionally to give a remedy to the buyer who wishes to complain of unfitness for an unusual (ie 'particular') purpose (eg a buyer who buys paint for use in an unusually harsh or specialised environment). Section 14(3) exists to do this, but imposes two further requirements: the buyer must have told the seller of his requirements, and he must have relied on the latter's skill and judgment to provide goods that will satisfy it. As Clarke LJ said in *Jewson Ltd v Boyhan* [2003] EWCA Civ 1030, [2004] 1 Lloyd's Rep 505 at [68],

[T]he function of section 14(2), by contrast with section 14(3), is to establish a general standard of quality which goods are required to reach. It is not designed to ensure that goods are fit for a particular purpose made known to the seller. That is the function of section 14(3)...

[5] Confusingly, this was numbered as s 14(1) in the Act of 1893, and hence appears as such in pre-1979 decisions.

Section 14(3) still fulfils this function perfectly well. See, for example, *Cammell Laird & Co Ltd v Manganese Bronze & Brass Co Ltd* [1934] AC 402 and *BSS Group Plc v Makers (UK) Ltd (t/a Allied Services)*, below. Another, older, case is *Bristol Tramways v Fiat Motors Ltd* [1910] 2 KB 831 (buses ordered for a hilly district not up to steep climbing).

However, it now also covers a great deal else besides. This is because the words 'particular purpose' were from the start given a curiously broad interpretation. It would be natural to assume that they would be construed in a restrictive sense, confined to unusual or specialised uses—for example, perhaps, where paint was needed for some non-standard substance or surface (compare the *Cammell Laird* case (below), where a propeller was ordered for the special purpose of being fitted to a particular ship). But this did not happen. In any case where goods had a single or obvious purpose, that was consistently regarded as a 'particular' purpose. So, for instance, food was taken to have been bought for the 'particular' purpose of being eaten (*Wallis v Russell* [1902] 2 IR 585), milk to be drunk (*Frost v Aylesbury Dairy Co* [1905] 1 KB 608, CA), a hot-water bottle to be filled with hot water (*Priest v Last* [1903] 2 KB 148, CA), and a staircase to be able to be installed in a house without flouting the building regulations (*Lowe v W Machell Joinery Ltd* [2011] EWCA Civ 794, [2012] 1 All ER (Comm) 153). Moreover, if goods had more than one common purpose, each one was held to be a 'particular' purpose: see *Henry Kendall & Sons v William Lillico & Sons Ltd* [1969] 2 AC 31 (compound used for feeding both pheasants and poultry). Furthermore, in the case of common or obvious purposes the courts discounted the requirement that the seller be informed of the buyer's needs. Instead, they took it for granted that the purpose was made known to the seller by the mere act of asking for the goods.

The result is that, in most cases of goods defective in ordinary use, s 14(3) now effectively duplicates s 14(2). If a buyer buys a truck which does not work, the truck can either be said to be of unsatisfactory quality (s 14(2)) or not fit for its obvious purpose, the transport of goods (s 14(3)): the buyer can claim on either basis. This, however, raises a theoretical problem related to the exceptions to s 14(2) in s 14(2C) (defects drawn to the buyer's attention, defects apparent on examination of the goods, and defects apparent on a reasonable examination of any sample supplied). These do not expressly apply to s 14(3). However, they are probably implicit in it, in that all three factors, if present, may well show that it is unreasonable to rely on the seller's skill or judgment (see below, p 445).

Cammell Laird & Co Ltd v Manganese Bronze & Brass Co Ltd

[1934] AC 402, House of Lords

Cammell Laird had agreed to build two ships for the United Molasses Co, and had contracted with Manganese Bronze to have propellers made for these ships to designs which specified the general dimensions of the propellers but not the thickness and shaping of the blades, which it was left to Manganese Bronze, as specialist suppliers, to determine. Four propellers had to be made before two were produced which performed satisfactorily. Cammell Laird claimed damages for the delay in finishing their work caused by the fact that the first propellers supplied were defective, alleging a breach of what is now s 14(3). The House of Lords held that the defects in the propellers lay in those areas of the design where Cammell Laird had relied on Manganese Bronze's specialist skill and judgment, and upheld the claim.

Lord Macmillan: The appellants also contended that they were entitled to succeed under s 14, sub-s 1, of the Sale of Good Act 1893 [1979 Act, s 14(3)]. [His Lordship quoted the subsection and continued:]

Now there is no question that it is in the course of the respondents' business to supply ships' propellers. But there is room for argument as to whether the appellants made known to the respondents 'the particular purpose' for which the propeller was wanted. On the one hand it was contended that no particular purpose was expressed or implied which the propeller was to serve, and that if any purpose was implied it was merely the ordinary and general purpose which all ships' propellers serve—namely, as the word itself connotes, the purpose of propulsion. On the other hand it was contended that the contract disclosed that the propeller was wanted for a particular purpose—the purpose, namely, of being fitted to and working in association with the ship and engines No 972 which the appellants were building. Having regard to the decision and the reasoning in the case of *Manchester Liners Ltd v Rea Ltd* ([1922] 2 AC 74), I am of opinion that there was in the present instance sufficient disclosure of a particular purpose within the statutory meaning.

BSS Group Plc v Makers (UK) Ltd

[2011] EWCA Civ 809, Court of Appeal

BSS had supplied Makers with plumbing materials for the installation of a new plumbing system in a Cambridge pub.[6] A particular make of part, 'Uponor', was used for the project. Makers ordered more materials, specifically saying that they were for the same project. BSS supplied a different, and incompatible, type of valve. Because of the incompatibility, a connection became insecure under pressure; the pub was flooded, and Makers had to pay damages. Makers claimed an indemnity from BSS, and succeeded.

Rimer LJ:

35. Makers was using a Uponor system for its project at the property. BSS knew by 8 August 2007 that it was using such a system: BSS had in July supplied Uponor components for the project, including Uponor adaptors. It had also supplied isolating valves in July, in respect of which Mr Denman recognised that it was 'possible' that they would used with the Uponor adaptors. Makers' fax inquiry of 8 August explained on its face that the items in respect of which it was inviting a quotation were for the same project. Six of the 18 items the subject of that inquiry were expressly described as, or to be used with, 'Uponor' items. Others were not, including item seven for '15 x 22mm Ballofix valves.' It is, I consider, an irresistible inference from that fax inquiry that Makers was making known to BSS that it intended to use such valves as a device intended to regulate or control the flow of water in pipes used in the project. Moreover, it is I consider also an obvious inference that it was making known to BSS that it intended to use such valves in conjunction with the Uponor plastic pipe that BSS knew it was using. At the very least, it must have been apparent to BSS that Makers was likely so to use the valves.

36. Makers had therefore made known a particular purpose for which the valves were intended to be used; and it was likely that they would be used with the Uponor plastic pipes. Whilst I would, with respect, fall short of endorsing the judge's finding that Makers made known its purpose expressly, I consider that the judge was entitled to find, as he did, that Makers impliedly made known to BSS the purpose for which it wished to buy the valves. When on 9 August it ordered 15 of the valves for which BSS had quoted in response to the fax inquiry—BSS's own brand—it was obvious to BSS for what purpose Makers was buying them. I would uphold the judge's finding

---

[6] Not identified in the report, but said to have been the Prince Regent, in Regent Street.

that Makers made known to BSS the purpose of its request for a quotation in respect of 22mm Ballofix valves and for its subsequent order of the Boss miniball valves for which BSS had quoted.

37. Were the valves so ordered fit for that purpose? The judge found they were not because their thread was incompatible with that of the Uponor adaptors with which they were likely to be used for the purpose of sealing off the plastic Uponor pipe. In my view there is no answer to this. The valves that BSS supplied were its own brand and were specifically designed for use with copper piping. They were incompatible for use with the Uponor adaptors with which they were likely to be used. BSS's supply of its own valves appears to me to have been fairly remarkable bearing in mind that it had no basis for any assumption that Makers was going to be using any copper pipe in the project, but there is no need to say more than that. The valves that it supplied were not reasonably fit for the requisite purpose because they were incompatible with the Uponor adaptors and would be likely to (and on 24 August 2007 did) fail when used in conjunction with them.

Preist v Last

[1903] 2 KB 148, Court of Appeal

Preist bought a rubber hot-water bottle from a chemist, being told that it could withstand hot but not boiling water. Not being able to withstand even hot water, it burst and scalded Preist's wife. Preist sued for his wife's injuries (as the law then allowed him to do). He succeeded under what is now s 14(3).

Collins MR: The plaintiff, who was a draper, and had no special skill or knowledge with regard to hot-water bottles, went to the shop of the defendant, who was a chemist, and who sold such articles, and asked him for a 'hot-water bottle'; and the judge has inferred that the article was bought by the plaintiff, and sold by the defendant, for the specific purpose of being used as a hot-water bottle. The argument addressed to us with reference to the terms of s. 14, sub-s. 1, of the Sale of Goods Act, 1893, was that, the sub-section requiring that the particular purpose for which the article is purchased should be made known to the seller, this can only be done by something beyond what is contained in the recognised description of the article itself.... The argument appears to be that the purpose for which this article was sold was merely the ordinary purpose of use as a hot-water bottle, and, that being its ordinary purpose, the case is not brought within the words 'makes known to the seller the particular purpose for which the goods are required.' I do not think that this contention is sound. I think that, regard being had to the state of the law as it existed previously to the passing of the Act, the object with which those words were introduced is clear. There are many goods which have in themselves no special or peculiar efficacy for any one particular purpose, but are capable of general use for a multitude of purposes. In the case of a purchase of goods of that kind, in order to give rise to the implication of a warranty, it is necessary to shew that, though the article sold was capable of general use for many purposes, in the particular case it was sold with reference to a particular purpose. But in a case where the discussion begins with the fact that the description of the goods, by which they were sold, points to one particular purpose only, it seems to me that the first requirement of the sub-section is satisfied, namely, that the particular purpose for which the goods are required should be made known to the seller. The fact that, by the very terms of the sale itself, the article sold purports to be for use for a particular purpose cannot possibly exclude the case from the rule that, where goods are sold for a particular purpose, there is an implied warranty that they are reasonably fit for that purpose. The sale is of goods which, by the very description under which they are sold, appear to be sold for a particular purpose.

(c) 'Reasonably fit'

Goods need to be reasonably fit for the stated purpose, but not necessarily fit come hell or high water. In the Scottish case of *United Central Bakeries Ltd v Spooner Industries Ltd* [2013] CSOH 150 a conveyor belt was held reasonably fit for its stated purpose of conveying hot naan bread from an oven, even though it caught fire when, as frequently happened, the bread it carried was actually smouldering. 'The test of reasonable fitness for purpose,' said Lord Hodge, 'is a relative concept.'

(d) The 'idiosyncrasy exception'

A seller is not liable under s 14(3) insofar as the failure to satisfy the buyer's purposes is due to some unusual or idiosyncratic feature of the buyer or his property which the seller had no means of knowing about. In *Slater v Finning Ltd* [1997] AC 473, HL, a replacement camshaft was supplied by Finnings to be fitted to a marine diesel engine owned by Slater. The camshaft was of a type which worked satisfactorily in other engines but not when fitted to Slater's: there was excessive noise and considerable wear, which was attributable to some factors external to the camshaft and engine—probably the design of the boat in which it was installed. The buyer's claim under s 14(3) was unsuccessful. Lord Keith of Kinkel said (at 483):

> There is no breach of the implied condition of fitness where the failure of the goods to meet the intended purpose arises from an abnormal feature or idiosyncrasy, not made known to the seller by the buyer, in the buyer or in the circumstances of the use of the goods by the buyer. That is the case whether or not the buyer is himself aware of the abnormal feature or idiosyncrasy.

This decision followed *Griffiths v Peter Conway Ltd* [1939] 1 All ER 685, where a woman who bought a Harris tweed coat suffered dermatitis, not because the coat was unsuitable for normal wear but because she had an unusually sensitive skin. Her claim rightly failed.

(e) Reliance on the seller's skill or judgment

It is not enough that the seller knows the buyer's purpose in buying the goods. Even if the seller does know this, it may be clear from the circumstances that the seller gives no assurances and claims no expertise, and hence that the buyer is accepting the risk that what he buys may not in fact suffice for his purposes. For this reason it is also necessary for liability that the buyer reasonably relies on the seller's skill or judgment. The section in its current form (the wording was revised in 1973) eases the burden on the buyer by presuming such reliance, but leaves it open to the buyer to show either that there was no such reliance or that any such reliance was unreasonable.

Teheran-Europe Co Ltd v ST Belton (Tractors) Ltd
[1968] 2 QB 545, Court of Appeal

Belton, an English company, contracted to sell compressors to Teheran-Europe Ltd, a company incorporated in Iran (then known as Persia) and carrying on business in Tehran. The buyers made known to the sellers that the compressors were required for resale as 'new and unused' machines in Iran. An action under s 14(3) (then s 14(1)) failed because, although this 'particular purpose' had been made known to the sellers, the circumstances were not such as to show that the buyers had relied on their skill and judgment.

> **Lord Denning MR**: Now, as I read this contract, it was a contract for the sale of goods by description. These were air compressors, described as new and unused—described in the catalogue and in the correspondence. There was clearly an implied term that they should comply with the description as set out in s 13(1) of the Sale of Goods Act.
>
> So far as s 14(1) is concerned, it is quite clear that the buyers made known to the sellers that they were required for resale in Persia. In the letter of August 10, 1967, Richards Marketing Ltd wrote to S T Belton (Tractors) Ltd: 'We have now received provisional estimates for packing these units singly suitable for shipment to Khorranshahr, and cross-country transit.' Khorranshahr, as far as I understand it, is in Persia. And then in the letter of August 9, 1957, they said: 'Our clients are asking for a liberal supply of descriptive literature for advertising purposes in Iran.' So that it is quite clear that the buyers made known to the sellers that they required them for resale in Persia.
>
> But the section of the statute contains a further requirement before a condition is implied . . . The particular purpose must be made known 'so as to show that the buyer relies on the seller's skill or judgment.' That means that the buyer makes the particular purpose known to the seller in such a way that the seller knows that he is being relied upon. That cannot be said here. The sellers here did not know they were being relied on for resale in Persia. They knew nothing of conditions in Persia. The buyers knew all about those conditions. The buyers saw the machine here. They read its description. They relied upon their own skill and judgment to see that it was suitable for resale in Persia, and not on the seller's. At all events, they did not make the purpose known to the seller in such circumstances as to show him that they relied on the seller's skill and judgment. So I do not think there was an implied term that they should be fit for the purpose of being resold in Persia.
>
> [**Diplock** and **Sachs LJJ** delivered concurring judgments.]

NOTES

1.   See too *Sumner Permain & Co v Webb & Co* [1922] 1 KB 55 (tonic water sold in England for distribution in Argentina contained ingredient which meant it could not lawfully be sold there: even though seller knew purpose, no reliance on skill or judgment). In another case, *Aswan Engineering Establishment Co v Lupdine Ltd* [1987] 1 WLR 1, CA, the buyers had made known to the sellers that the plastic pails for which they were contracting were wanted 'for export'. (In fact, they were to be filled with a liquid waterproofing compound and exported to Kuwait, where they collapsed in temperatures which reached 70°C.) Lloyd LJ said that 'for export' was a purpose that 'could hardly be wider', and that the wider the purpose, the greater would be the dilution of the sellers' responsibility under s 14(3). But in any event it was held that the buyers (who had been sent a sample pail before placing their order) had not relied on the sellers' skill or judgment in any sense relevant to s 14(3). The question of reliance was also in issue in a case discussed in *Jewson v Boyhan* (p 436), where liability under s 14(3) was alleged as well as breach of the condition of satisfactory quality. It was held that the buyer had not relied on the seller to supply goods fit for his particular purpose, so that he also failed on this alternative ground.

2. There can be reliance on a seller's skill or judgment even in respect of an undiscoverable defect: a buyer may well rely on the seller's efforts to obtain and distribute only goods of proper quality. See *Frost v Aylesbury Dairy Co Ltd* [1905] 1 KB 608 (undetectably contaminated milk).

3. The fact that the seller is a monopoly, or near-monopoly, supplier militates against reliance on skill or judgment: see the Privy Council case of *Hamilton v Papakura DC* [2002] UKPC 9, [2002] 3 NZLR 308 (no reliance on municipal water supplier's skill or judgment in providing water suitable for demands of hydroponic tomatoes).

4. The *Teheran-Europe* case above was decided under the former law, which in effect required the buyer to prove that the circumstances were such as to show that he relied on the seller's skill and judgment. Section 14(3) now reverses the position, leaving it to the seller to show that the buyer did not rely on his skill and judgment, or that it was unreasonable for him to do so. However, it is likely that the same result would now be reached in each case under the revised wording.

5. In *Britvic Soft Drinks Ltd v Messer UK Ltd* (above, p 437) it was said to be sufficient for the purposes of s 14(3) that the buyer should rely on the skill and judgment of a person from whom his seller had acquired the goods. In that case carbon dioxide was bought by Britvic from Messer for the purpose of carbonating soft drinks. It was contaminated with benzene through the fault of its manufacturer, Terra, who had supplied the gas to Messer. Messer was held to be in breach of s 14(3) because Britvic had relied on the skill and judgment of Terra not to permit their product to be contaminated. This seems, with respect, a very doubtful interpretation of s 14(3), which explicitly requires reliance on the 'skill or judgment *of the seller*'.

(f) Informational defects

In *Wormell v RHM Agriculture (East) Ltd* [1986] 1 WLR 336 a farmer alleged that agricultural weedkiller of impeccable quality had been supplied with misleading instructions, that he had used it in reliance on those instructions, and that it had not worked. It was held that this claim was good, and that the instructions supplied with the goods, as much as the goods themselves, had to be correct. (An appeal was later allowed on the facts: [1987] 1 WLR 1091.) Whether this applies to 'pure' informational products such as books or maps (or satnavs) is uncertain. It would perhaps be curious if a bookseller were liable to the buyer under s 14—and, of course, liable without any proof of fault—for any misprint or error in any work he sold. See, generally, SW Hedley, 'Quality of Goods, Information, and the Death of Contract' [2001] JBL 114.

(g) What goods must be fit for purpose? When must they be fit for purpose? The place of fault in the scheme of liability

These matters are dealt with above at p 438 in connection with s 14(2). The same considerations apply to a claim under s 14(3).

6 TERMS IMPLIED IN SALES OF GOODS BY SAMPLE (S 15)

Section 15 deals with goods which are sold by sample. There are two implied conditions, set out in s 15(2):

(1) that the bulk will correspond with the sample in quality (s 15(2)(a));

(2) that the goods will be free from any defect, making their quality unsatisfactory, which would not be apparent on reasonable examination of the sample (s 15(2)(c)).

These provisions are in themselves more or less self-explanatory. The only likely surprise lies in the concept of a 'sale by sample' itself, and its legal function. The term is defined, not very helpfully, in s 15(1):

> A contract of sale is a contract for sale by sample where there is an express or implied term to that effect in the contract.

This makes it plain that it is not sufficient that the buyer should merely have seen a specimen of the goods in question; the parties must have agreed that the sale shall be a sale *by reference to* that sample.

The cases show that the function of a sample is very similar to that of a contractual description, or perhaps to supplement that contractual description. In *Drummond v Van Ingen* (1887) 12 App Cas 284 at 297, HL, Lord Macnaghten explained this function as follows:

> The office of a sample is to present to the eye the real meaning and intention of the parties with regard to the subject matter of the contract which, owing to the imperfection of language, it may be difficult or impossible to express in words. The sample speaks for itself. But it cannot be treated as saying more than such a sample would tell a merchant of the class to which the buyer belongs, using due care and diligence, and appealing to it in the ordinary way and with the knowledge possessed by merchants of that class at the time. No doubt the sample might be made to say a great deal more. Pulled to pieces and examined by unusual tests which curiosity or suspicion might suggest, it would doubtless reveal every secret of its construction. But that is not the way in which business is done in this country.

From this statement we can infer that a seller in a sale by sample does not guarantee that the bulk will comply with the sample in every possible respect: but only that it will be as like the sample as an ordinary comparison or inspection would reveal. Over and above this, the buyer must rely on the implied terms contained in s 14(2) and (3), or stipulate for an express warranty. However, there is limited further protection conferred by s 15(2)(c), which implies a condition that the goods will be free from any latent defect which makes their quality unsatisfactory. The case next cited confirms the restricted scope both of the function of a 'sale by sample' and of this latter condition.

Steels & Busks Ltd v Bleecker Bik & Co Ltd
[1956] 1 Lloyd's Rep 228, Queen's Bench Division

Steels & Busks contracted to buy from Bleecker Bik five tons of pale crepe rubber, 'quality as previously delivered'. The court construed this as a sale by sample, the 'sample' being the rubber delivered under previous contracts. Steels & Busks used the rubber to manufacture corsets, but it turned out (unlike the earlier deliveries) to contain an invisible preservative, PNP, which stained the fabric of the corsets. Sellers J held that there had been no breach of the condition implied by s 15(2)(a): the rubber was in accordance with the sample on any visual test. Nor had there been a breach of the condition as to merchantability (now satisfactory quality) implied by s 15(2)(c): this rubber was perfectly useful for commercial purposes once the staining chemical had been washed out or neutralised.

Sellers J: In assessing the quality of the goods and their state and condition on delivery, the [arbitration] Appeal Committee have applied the normal market standard and applied the normal tests. Para 8 of the award deals with the arbitrators' views:

As understood in the market, quality is determined by visual inspection of samples drawn in the wharves after rubber has been landed; such inspection extends to colour, texture, and the possibility of impurities such as specks of bark, sand, bits of cotton, and deterioration. The kind of chemical used in the preparation of rubber has never been regarded as entering into the quality of rubber. If the quality of pale crepe were to depend on the chemical preservative used, there might be as many qualities as there are preservatives; no such idea is known to the trade. 'PNP' is not a defect in rubber nor is it an adulterant or impurity. It is a preservative used, though less frequently in pale crepe than in other types of rubber, and its presence does not affect quality. We have not overlooked the statutory definition of 'quality of goods' in s 62(1) of the Sale of Goods Act [see now s 14(2B)], but we do not regard the presence of 'PNP' as a matter affecting state or condition. . . .

If the buyers are to succeed in their claim, it must, I think, only be on the ground that the 21 bales did not comply with the sample, that is, the first delivery. In one respect the bales complained of did not so comply. They contained 'PNP,' whereas the sample did not, and it was submitted that s 15(2)(a) of the Sale of Goods Act had not been complied with as the bulk did not correspond with the sample in quality.

[His Lordship quoted the section, and continued:]

Section 15(2) is not inconsistent with the view that where there is (as here) a defect not apparent on reasonable examination of the sample, the buyers' rights arise, if at all, under sub-s (2)(c) and not under sub-s (2)(a), but it is not, I think, conclusive as a matter of construction. . . .
Drummond v Van Ingen (1887) 12 App Cas 284, is the case upon which s 15 is largely based. . . .
In that case, the contract expressly provided that quality and weight should be equal to certain numbered samples; and the Earl of Selborne LC, at p 288, said this about its construction;

I think that the word 'quality' as used in the contracts, ought to be restricted to those qualities which were patent, or discoverable from such examination and inspection of the samples as, under the circumstances, the respondents might reasonably be expected to make.

In *Drummond v Van Ingen* the House of Lords was able, by giving the sample clause a restricted meaning, to hold that its terms did not exclude an implied warranty covering latent defects. It is of the essence of this reasoning that a clause of this sort does not cover latent qualities or defects at all. In that case it was the seller's argument that was defeated by this construction. But, by the same token, it is not open to a buyer to submit a sample to an analysis unusual in the trade so as to reveal in it certain attributes or qualities hitherto unsuspected, and then to require, by virtue of the sample clause alone, that the bulk should contain the same qualities. If, for example, a buyer, to use the words of Lord Macnaghten, pulls a sample of cloth to pieces and discovers by means of analysis that the dye contains a certain proportion of a certain chemical, he cannot by virtue of the same clause require that the dye in the bulk shall contain the same proportion of the same chemical. He may, of course, complain that if it does not contain that proportion, it would be unmerchantable or would fail to satisfy some other express or implied condition as to quality; but he cannot say that it breaks the condition that the bulk shall correspond with the sample in quality, for that condition is dealing only with apparent quality . . .

I am in complete agreement with that construction of s 15(2)(a), and I am grateful for that passage, which I adopt and apply here. . . .

The extent to which a sample may be held to 'speak' must depend on the contract and what is contemplated by the parties in regard to it. A sample may be analysed, X-rayed—tested to destruction. In the present case the parties were content, in accordance with the normal practice of the trade, to rely on a visual examination. Neither 'PNP' nor, I think, any other chemical in general use for coagulation and preservation or either is detectable by visual examination, and therefore the presence or absence of the chemical cannot in itself be a breach of the sample clause. . . .

The buyers had in fact used the first delivery and found it satisfactory and that no doubt resulted in the repeat orders. The crude rubber had received treatment and processing by them and revealed no defect. Such circumstances would not enlarge the liability of the sellers, as the contract remained, as far as the compliance with a sample was concerned, a contract which called for compliance in those matters revealed by visual examination and those matters only. . . .

7 CONTRACTUAL MODIFICATION OF THE SELLER'S OBLIGATIONS AS TO QUALITY

(a) Interpretation of terms modifying liability

As mentioned above, sellers in the commercial context frequently wish to do so on their own bespoke terms, which often purport to exclude entirely the terms implied under the Sale of Goods Act. Subject to the Unfair Contract Terms Act 1977 (dealt with below), this is perfectly permissible, and the courts have no hesitation in applying such clauses. Thus in *Air Transworld Ltd v Bombardier Inc* [2012] EWHC 243 (Comm) an aircraft was supplied under the following term:

> The warranty, obligations and liabilities of seller and the rights and remedies of buyer set forth in the agreement are exclusive and are in lieu of and buyer hereby waives and releases all other warranties, obligations, representations or liabilities, express or implied, arising by law, in contract, civil liability or in tort, or otherwise, including but not limited to (a) any implied warranty of merchantability or of fitness for a particular purpose, and (b) any other obligation or liability on the part of seller to anyone of any nature whatsoever by reason of the design, manufacture, sale, repair, lease or use of the aircraft or related products and services delivered or rendered hereunder or otherwise.

Cooke J brusquely dismissed the buyer's complaint that the aircraft was not of satisfactory quality. This was, he said, 'a case where the words used do encompass contractual conditions implied by law and to adopt a different construction would amount to a distortion of the words used. There is no ambiguity in the clause. There is only one meaning which can fairly be given to it. It is what the parties agreed and the parties...should be kept to their bargain.' Similarly, commodity sale contracts often state that the result of a third party inspection or certification are conclusive as to the quality of the goods even if wrong, and courts go to some lengths to uphold such clauses. See, eg, *Alfred C Toepfer v Continental Grain Co* [1974] 1 Lloyd's Rep 11; *Gill & Duffus SA v Berger & Co Inc (No 2)* [1982] 1 Lloyd's Rep 101.

However, the rule remains that such clauses must be clearly drafted; and where there is uncertainty, courts continue to lean against exclusion of liability, even where one might have thought the parties fairly clearly intended it. The next case illustrates this.

The Mercini Lady
[2010] EWCA Civ 1145, [2010] 2 CLC 637, Court of Appeal

Sellers shipped gasoil (ie kerosene) to buyers in Spain, under a contract laying down a detailed specification and then continuing 'There are no guarantees, warranties or representations, express or implied, [of] merchantability, fitness or suitability of the oil for any particular purpose or otherwise which extend beyond the description of the oil set forth in this agreement.' The buyers argued that they could reject the oil on the basis of a breach of s 14(2). The Court of Appeal held, as had the judge, that this was not precluded by the term in question, since the duty under s 14(2) was a *condition* and not a mere *warranty*.

> **Rix LJ**:
> 47. On behalf of the buyer, Mr Edey, supported by the decision of the judge, relied on a well-known line of cases which state in effect that the Sale of Goods Act implied conditions cannot be excluded without express reference to the exclusion of 'conditions'. Exclusion of guarantees, warranties or representations do not suffice. On behalf of the seller, Mr Jacobs, however, submitted that time has moved on since those cases were decided and that the attitude to the construction of exception clauses, particularly as between commercial parties, has become more realistic and less formulaic. The reference to 'guarantees, warranties or representations' was intended to be a reference to all contractual terms or pre-contractual representations of whatsoever kind.
> 48. The well-known cases are as follows. The leading decision is that of the House of Lords in *Wallis, Son & Wells v Pratt & Haynes* [1911] AC 394.
>
> ...
>
> 50. ...Lord Alverstone CJ said (at 398–9):
>
> > ...it is quite impossible to suggest that in the year 1906, when these parties made a contract whereby they required that the goods should be common English sainfoin, and the sellers put in a stipulation that they would not give any warranty, express or implied, it was intended that it was always to be understood that they were not making themselves liable in regard to any condition as to the goods or for the consequences of a breach of the condition...Within the four corners of this statute applicable to this contract we see this plain distinction between 'condition' and 'warranty'...
>
> Lord Shaw of Dunfermline said (at 399–400):
>
> > I do not think that these two commercial men meant 'warranty' in a sense of any greater refinement than the breadth if the definition in the Sale of Goods Act...it is as plain as language can make it that there are two things that are dealt with under different categories. The one is 'warranty' and the other is 'condition'...
>
> ...

58. In a recent case comment on the judge's decision ('Of FOB sales, seller's obligations and disclaimers' [2009] LMCLQ 417 at 420) Professor Andrew Tettenborn has suggested that *Wallis v Pratt* is now dated and that 'English commercial law would, it is suggested, benefit greatly' if the new trend for the interpretation of exclusion clauses ushered in by *Photo Production v Securicor* were taken to heart. I note that *Benjamin's Sale of Goods* (8th edn, 2010) refers to the jurisprudence as 'very strict' (at para. 13-025).

. . .

61. If therefore I were construing this clause untrammelled by past authority, or if such authority was plainly limited, in the way that so many decisions on the construction of individual clauses are limited, by considerations of the precise language and context of those particular clauses, I would feel it open, in the modern world, to give to clause 18 the construction which I believe that it realistically bears: that is to say, that 'guarantees' and 'warranties' are intended to cover all terms, both those which entitle the innocent party in the case of breach to treat the contract as repudiated and those which sound only in damages. As section 11(3) of the 1979 Act itself records, 'a stipulation may be a condition, though called a warranty in the contract': and clause 18 itself demonstrates that buyer's warranties there set out are treated by the contract as conditions. It might be said that what is good enough for Lord Diplock...is good enough for commercial traders. However, I am not so free. The jurisprudence extends beyond individual decisions and has become expressive of a principle, and what is more the principle also encompasses clauses very similar to clause 18. I must consider that the parties to this English law contract, foreign as both of them are and quite possibly ignorant of the consequences of their choice of language, intended to contract by reference to what English law had to say about the language which they have adopted.

NOTE

See too *Dalmare SpA v Union Maritime Ltd* [2012] EWHC 3537 (Comm), [2013] 1 CLC 59 (ship sold 'as she was' at the time of inspection; not sufficient to exclude s 14(2)). Note, however, that the standard form under which most second-hand ships are sold worldwide, known as the Norwegian Saleform, was very smartly changed after that decision. It now states explicitly: 'Any terms implied into this Agreement by any applicable statute or law are hereby excluded to the extent that such exclusion can legally be made' (Norwegian Saleform 2012, art 18). This development may cause you to draw conclusions about businesspersons' views on the courts' deliberately restrictive interpretation of exception clauses.

(b) The Unfair Contract Terms Act 1977

Except in the case of a party's own personal fraud, liability for which cannot be excluded as a matter of public policy, there are very few limits on the power of sellers dealing with commercial parties[7] to exclude the quality provisions of the Sale of Goods Act. However, there is one particular statutory limit. Under the Unfair Contract Terms Act 1977 (UCTA), s 6, liability under ss 13 (conformity with description), 14 (satisfactory quality and fitness for purpose), and 15 (conformity with sample) can be excluded or restricted only insofar as the

---

[7] With consumers it is different: see now the Consumer Rights Act 2015. But this book is not concerned with such cases.

term satisfies the 'requirement of reasonableness'. Section 7 deals in similar terms with contracts analogous to sale contracts, such as those for work and materials and barter (above, p 312). So too, under s 13 of the 1977 Act, with provisions excluding or restricting remedies in respect of such liability, or excluding or restricting rules of evidence or procedure. Examples of terms caught by this provision would be terms limiting the amount of any damages for breach, or stating that in the absence of notice of defects within seven days, goods would be conclusively presumed to be of satisfactory quality.

The 'requirement of reasonableness' is defined for the purposes of the Act generally as 'that the term shall have been a fair and reasonable one to be included having regard to the circumstances which were, or ought reasonably to have been, known to or in the contemplation of the parties when the contract was made' (UCTA, s 11(1)). More particularly, in regard to contracts for the sale of goods, the court is directed to have regard to a number of guidelines which are set out in Sch 2 to UCTA (s 11(2)). These include such matters as the relative bargaining strength of the parties, the amount of choice available to the buyer, and whether the goods were specially made or adapted to his order.

By way of illustration, in *Knight Machinery (Holdings) Ltd v Rennie* 1995 SLT 166, the inclusion of a term requiring the buyer of a printing machine to give written notice of rejection within seven days of delivery was held to be unreasonable; the machine took several days to install and defects might not be discovered until after a much longer trial period. A similar decision was *Saint Gobain Building Distribution Ltd v Hillmead Joinery (Swindon) Ltd* [2015] BLR 555. And in *St Albans City Council v International Computers Ltd* [1996] 4 All ER 481, CA, a multinational company which had supplied a computer system to a local authority to handle local taxation could not enforce a provision limiting its liability to £100,000: it was insured for £50 million and losses could be enormous.

However, where both parties are sizeable commercial concerns, the courts are today disinclined to regard terms agreed between them as unreasonable. In *Granville Oil & Chemicals Ltd v Davis Turner & Co Ltd* [2003] EWCA Civ 570, [2003] 2 CLC 418 at [31], Tuckey LJ said: 'The 1977 Act obviously plays a very important role in protecting vulnerable consumers from the effects of draconian contract terms. But I am less enthusiastic about its intrusion into contracts between commercial parties of equal bargaining strength, who should generally be considered capable of being able to make contracts of their choosing and expect to be bound by their terms.' Although this case was not strictly about sales, it remains relevant to the subject. (See too *Frans Maas (UK) Ltd v Samsung Electronics (UK) Ltd* [2004] EWHC 1502 (Comm), [2005] 1 CLC 647 at [158].)

In addition, there are two situations, vital to commercial law, where there is complete freedom of contract and the Unfair Contract Terms Act does not apply at all. One is 'international supply contracts'—a term which includes contracts for the sale of goods where the seller and buyer are based in different jurisdictions *and* one of three additional conditions applies: (1) the goods are to be carried from one state to another; (2) the acts constituting the offer and acceptance have been done in different territories; or (3) the goods are to be delivered to a territory other than that in which the offer and acceptance took place (UCTA, s 26). This is particularly significant since goods are regarded as 'carried from one state to another' even if technically delivered in State A, where they were at the time of the contract, to a buyer from State B who intends to remove them there forthwith: see *Trident Turboprop (Dublin) Ltd v First Flight Couriers Ltd* [2009] EWCA Civ 290, [2010] QB 86 (aircraft delivered in the UK to Indian buyer who flew them to India). The other is contracts which have no connection with England but which (as very commonly happens) are governed by English law because the parties have agreed that they shall be (s 27).

8 PRODUCT LIABILITY

This part of the book focuses primarily on contractual liability, something applying only between seller and buyer. (Theoretically, under the Contracts (Rights of Third Parties) Act 1999 it would be open to a seller and a buyer to agree that a third party, such as a sub-buyer, should be able to sue the seller for a breach of his contractual obligations. But this in practice hardly ever happens.) A seller or producer may, however, be liable more widely in tort.

First, under the principle of *Donoghue v Stevenson* [1932] AC 562 a seller, like anyone else, may owe a duty of care in negligence if he is at fault in selling dangerous goods. If a third party, or for that matter the buyer himself, is injured or his property damaged, he will have a cause of action. Hence in *Vacwell Ltd v BDH Chemicals Ltd* [1971] 1 QB 88 dangerous chemicals were sold improperly labelled. They caused a massive explosion in the buyers' works. Rees J held the sellers liable in negligence.

Secondly, pursuant to a European Directive (85/374/EEC), manufacturers of products and those who import them into the European Economic Area (EEA) are liable in tort without fault under Part I of the Consumer Protection Act 1987 for any defect in those products, though only in respect of personal injury and damage to property not used for business purposes (insofar, in the latter case, as the damage exceeds £275).

Since the 1987 Act is largely a consumer protection measure, this head of liability is not of great direct commercial significance (save that it is one more potential exposure which manufacturers and importers may be constrained to insure against). It may, however, be of indirect importance. Imagine a seller of a product is held strictly liable to an injured consumer under the Consumer Rights Act 2015 in respect of some defect in the product. It now has not only potential recourse under the Sale of Goods Act 1979 against its own immediate supplier, but also because of the 1987 Act a direct claim pursuant to the Civil Liability (Contribution) Act 1978 against the manufacturer or importer on the basis that the latter would also have been liable if sued by the consumer.

CHAPTER 12

PERFORMANCE OF THE CONTRACT

The Act states concisely in s 27 the duties of the parties to a sale of goods contract:

> It is the duty of the seller to deliver the goods, and of the buyer to accept and pay for them, in accordance with the terms of the contract of sale.

In addition there is one duty not mentioned in s 27, namely the duty of the seller under s 12 of the Act to give a good title to the goods he sells. These duties are the subject of this chapter.

1 DUTIES OF THE SELLER

(a) To deliver the goods

The duty to deliver is more or less self-explanatory. It is the duty of the seller to deliver the goods in accordance with the terms of the contract of sale (s 27). Unless otherwise agreed, he must be ready and willing to give possession of the goods to the buyer in exchange for the price (s 28).

The meaning of 'delivery' The term 'delivery' may be the source of some confusion, as we saw in relation to the term 'deliverable state' (above, p 340). 'Delivery', in the statutory sense, means 'voluntary transfer of possession from one person to another'. Thus, it does not necessarily mean *physical* delivery, still less 'delivery' in the popular sense of sending the goods in a vehicle to the buyer's premises (indeed, the presumptive position is that it is up to the buyer to collect the goods from the seller, not to the seller to take them to the buyer). Instead, the term 'delivery' is dependent upon the common law concept of possession, whose meaning (as we saw in Chapter 2) is rather elusive. Three forms of delivery are particularly relevant for present purposes.

   (1) Actual, or physical delivery. This means the handing over of the goods themselves, whether to a buyer, a carrier, or other person, or in a suitable case making arrangements for the buyer to collect them (as in the case of a buyer of building materials who agrees to collect them by sending a truck to pick them up and loading them on it).

(2) Symbolic delivery. This entails handing over something which symbolises the goods; for example, a bill of lading relating to goods at sea, and possibly the ignition key of a vehicle, or a key or swipe-card giving access to a locked building in which the goods are stored.

(3) Constructive delivery. This refers to a transfer of the *right* to possession of goods which are in the physical custody of a third party, and is effected by a procedure known as *attornment*, which has been described above, p 76. This, it will be recalled, involves all three parties: (a) the seller (S) must instruct the third party (T) to hold the goods to the order of the buyer (B); and (b) T must acknowledge to B that he is now holding the goods on B's behalf. In the past this was most commonly done by the issue of a *delivery order* by S addressed to T; T then acknowledged the new state of affairs by either endorsing the delivery order, or issuing a *warrant* made out in favour of B. Today the process may be done electronically, with T on S's instructions simply acknowledging that he now holds for B. Either way, the attornment will then be complete: the right to possession which was formerly vested in S will have been transferred to B, and T becomes a bailee of the goods for B. There will, however, be no effective transfer of possession in this sense without step (b) above: neither an agreement solely between S and B, nor any arrangement between S and T alone, is sufficient. This rule is confirmed by s 29(4) of the Act: for an example of its application, see *Mercuria Energy Trading Pte Ltd v Citibank NA* [2015] EWHC 1481 (Comm) especially at [73]–[77] (no 'delivery' of warehoused metal in absence of warehouse-keeper's attornment) (see also the extract referred to above at p 76).

Delivery and payment   Section 28 makes delivery and payment 'concurrent conditions', in that (absent contrary agreement) the seller must be ready and willing to give possession of the goods to the buyer in exchange for the price, and the buyer must be ready and willing to pay the price in exchange for possession of the goods. Put negatively, this means that the buyer can withhold payment unless the seller is ready to deliver, and the seller delivery unless the buyer tenders payment.

Note that s 28 says merely that the seller does not have to deliver *until* payment is forthcoming. The question whether failure to pay on time allows him to go further and refuse to deliver *at all* is dealt with by s 10(1) of the Act, stating that while the answer depends on the terms of the contract, presumptively stipulations as to time of payment are not of the essence. On the other hand, if it is made clear that payment will not be made at all, or the delay is such as to amount to a repudiation, this will allow the seller to regard the contract as being at an end.

Delivery and payment: instalment contracts   Where a buyer fails to pay, or states that he will not pay, for one or more instalments under a contract to deliver by instalments, it is a matter for interpretation of the contract whether this justifies the seller in refusing to deliver further instalments.

Withers v Reynolds
(1831) 2 B & Ad 882, Court of King's Bench

Withers, a stable-keeper, contracted to buy wheat straw from Reynolds, to be delivered at the rate of three loads per fortnight, and paid for on delivery. After about ten weeks, Withers insisted on paying for the straw one delivery in arrear. The court ruled that this was a repudiation which justified Reynolds in refusing all further performance.

Parke J: The substance of the agreement was, that the straw should be paid for on delivery. The defendant clearly did not contemplate giving credit. When, therefore, the plaintiff said that he would not pay on delivery, (as he did, in substance, when he insisted on keeping one load on hand), the defendant was not obliged to go on supplying him.

Patteson J: If the plaintiff had merely failed to pay for any particular load, that, of itself, might not have been an excuse to the defendant for delivering no more straw: but the plaintiff here expressly refuses to pay for the loads as delivered; the defendant, therefore, is not liable for ceasing to perform his part of the contract.

[**Lord Tenterden CJ** and **Taunton J** delivered concurring judgments.]

Warinco AG v Samor SpA
[1977] 2 Lloyd's Rep 582, [1979] 1 Lloyd's Rep 450, Queen's Bench Division and Court of Appeal

The facts are immaterial.

Donaldson J: It is a popular myth, which lawyers do little to dispel, that the law is a highly technical matter with mysterious rules leading to results which are contrary to commonsense. Nothing could be further from the truth, both in general and in the particular instance of the law relating to the repudiation of contracts.

If a buyer under a contract calling for delivery by instalments commits a breach of that contract before all the deliveries have been made and that breach is so serious as to go to the root of the contract—in other words, to destroy the basis of the contract—commonsense suggests that the seller should not be expected to go to the trouble and expense of tendering later instalments if he does not want to. The law so provides.

Again, if it becomes clear that the buyer will be unable to accept or to pay for later instalments, commonsense suggests that the seller should, if he wishes, be discharged from any obligation further to perform his part of the contract. The law so provides.

Finally, if a buyer acts or speaks in a manner which declares in clear terms that he will not in future perform his part of the contract, the seller should, in common sense and fairness, have the option of being discharged from further obligation under the contract. And that is the law.

But common sense also suggests that there can be borderline cases in which it is not quite so clear what should happen. The law is at a disadvantage here in that it must draw a line. The line which it draws is indicated by the question: 'Has the buyer evinced an intention to abandon or to refuse to perform the contract?'. In answering this question, the law has regard to such factors as the degree to which the delivery of one instalment is linked with another, the proportion of the contract which has been affected by the allegedly repudiatory breach and the probability that the breach will be repeated. However, these are merely part of the raw material for answering the question. They cannot be conclusive in themselves.

NOTE

See too *Mersey Steel and Iron Co Ltd v Naylor, Benzon & Co* (1884) 9 App Cas 434.

Time of delivery Goods must be delivered at the time fixed in the contract. Under s 29(3), where under the contract of sale the seller is to send the goods to the buyer, but no time for doing so is fixed, he is bound to send them within a reasonable time. What is a reasonable time is a question of fact (s 59). It is also provided that a demand or tender of delivery may be treated as ineffectual unless made at a reasonable hour—again, a question of fact (s 29(5)).

Stipulations as to the time of performance of a contractual obligation may be made 'of the essence' of the contract or not (ie may be made either conditions or warranties), as determined by the parties' agreement. Section 10(2) confirms this in relation to contracts for the sale of goods. It is therefore up to the parties to settle whether a term relating to the time of delivery is to be regarded as a condition. However, in commercial transactions, it is well established by case law that stipulations as to the time of delivery are presumptively so construed. As McCardie J said in *Hartley v Hymans* [1920] 3 KB 475 at 484, 'In ordinary commercial contracts for the sale of goods the rule clearly is that time is prima facie of the essence with respect to delivery' (see too *Macpherson Train & Co v Ross & Co* [1955] 1 WLR 640). *Bowes v Shand* (1877) 2 App Cas 455, HL, referred to above at p 426, which held that rice to be shipped 'during the months of March and/or April' could be rejected if in fact loaded in February, is another more specialised example (since, as mentioned below, delivery to a carrier for transmission to the buyer is prima facie regarded as delivery to the latter).

Place of delivery The Act says that, in the absence of some express or implied provision in the contract, the place of delivery is the seller's place of business; except that, if the contract is for specific goods, which are known when the contract is made to be in some other place, then that place is the place of delivery (s 29(2)). This means that while the question whether it is up to the seller to send the goods or the buyer to collect them depends on the terms of the contract (s 29(1)), the presumptive rule is that it is up to the buyer to collect them. On the other hand, unless otherwise agreed, the expenses of and incidental to putting the goods into a deliverable state must be borne by the seller (s 29(6)).

If the contract provides that the seller may, or must, send the goods to the buyer, delivery of the goods to a land or sea carrier for the purpose of transmission to the buyer is prima facie deemed to be a delivery of goods to the buyer (s 32(1)). Section 32 goes on to provide that any carriage contract agreed by the seller must be on reasonable terms and, if it involves sea transit, give adequate notice to the buyer to enable him to insure them during their sea transit (s 32(3)). Reflecting s 18, r 5(2) and s 20 (above, pp 350 and 362), any risk of deterioration in the goods necessarily incidental to the course of transit is to be borne by the buyer (s 33).

Quantity of goods delivered Subject to s 30(2A) (see below, p 464), the seller must deliver the exact contract quantity—neither more nor less (s 30). He cannot require the buyer to accept delivery by instalments (s 31).

This can give rise to problems in a commercial context, where delivery of exact quantities is a practical impossibility. In a delivery of 10,000 tonnes of soya beans it is impossible to avoid an excess or deficiency of a few kilograms. As a result, minimal variances are ignored (see *Shipton, Anderson & Co v Weil Bros & Co* [1912] 1 KB 574, below, p 464, where buyers valiantly but unsuccessfully sought to refuse a cargo of wheat on the basis that an overage amounting to 0.0005 per cent amounted to a breach of s 30(!)). Furthermore, commodity contracts very often avoid such difficulties by providing for fixed tolerances: for example, the standard GAFTA 100 feedingstuffs contract allows a 3 per cent tolerance either way.

The question of the buyer's right to refuse short or excessive delivery is examined in more detail below, at p 464.

(b) The duty of the seller to give good title

The seller is not merely bound to deliver the goods; he must also ensure that the buyer gets a good title to them. Subject to one statutory exception (s 12(3), discussed below), s 12(1) provides as follows:

> In a contract of sale…there is an implied term on the part of the seller that in the case of a sale he has a right to sell the goods, and in the case of an agreement to sell he will have such a right at the time when the property is to pass.

Under s 12(5A) this term is stated to be a condition. There are equivalent provisions relating to hire-purchase (Supply of Goods (Implied Terms) Act 1973, s 8) and other contracts under which ownership is to pass (Supply of Goods and Services Act 1982, s 2).

So, if goods are sold which turn out to have been stolen, or otherwise not to belong to the seller, the buyer is entitled to the return of the whole of the purchase price.

Rowland v Divall
[1923] 2 KB 500, Court of Appeal

The facts appear from the judgment.

> **Scrutton LJ**: The plaintiff purchased a car from the defendant for £334. He drove it from Brighton, where he bought it, to the place where he had a garage, painted it and kept it there for about two months. He then sold it to a third person who had it in his possession for another two months. Then came the police, who claimed it as the stolen car for which they had been looking. It appears that it had been stolen before the defendant became possessed of it, and consequently he had no title that he could convey to the plaintiff. In these circumstances the plaintiff sued the defendant for the price he paid for the car as on a total failure of consideration. Now before the passing of the Sale of Goods Act there was a good deal of confusion in the authorities as to the exact nature of the vendor's contract with respect to his title to sell. It was originally said that a vendor did not warrant his title. But gradually a number of exceptions crept in, till at last the exceptions became the rule, the rule being that the vendor warranted that he had title to what he purported to sell, except in certain special cases, such as that of a sale by a sheriff, who does not so warrant. Then came the Sale of Goods Act, which re-enacted that rule, but did so with this alteration: it re-enacted it as a condition, not as a warranty. Section 12 says in express terms that there shall be 'An implied condition on the part of the seller that . . . he has a right to sell the goods.' It being now a condition, wherever that condition is broken the contract can be rescinded, and with the rescission the buyer can demand a return of the purchase money, unless he has, with knowledge of the facts, held on to the bargain so as to waive the condition. But Mr Doughty argues that there can never be a rescission where a restitutio in integrum is impossible, and that here the plaintiff cannot rescind because he cannot return the car. To that the buyer's answer is that the reason of his inability to return it—namely, the fact that the defendant had no title to it—is the very thing of which he is complaining, and that it does not lie in the defendant's mouth to set up as a defence to the action his own breach of the implied condition that he had a right to sell. In my opinion that answer is well founded, and it would, I think, be absurd to apply the rule as to restitutio in integrum to such a state of facts. No doubt the general rule is that a

buyer cannot rescind a contract of sale and get back the purchase money unless he can restore the subject matter. There are a large number of cases on the subject, some of which are not very easy to reconcile with others. Some of them make it highly probable that a certain degree of deterioration of the goods is not sufficient to take away the right to recover the purchase money. However I do not think it necessary to refer to them. It certainly seems to me that, in a case of rescission for the breach of the condition that the seller had a right to sell the goods, it cannot be that the buyer is deprived of his right to get back the purchase money because he cannot restore the goods which, from the nature of the transaction, are not the goods of the seller at all, and which the seller therefore has no right to under any circumstances. For these reasons I think that the plaintiff is entitled to recover the whole of the purchase money as for a total failure of consideration, and that the appeal must be allowed.

Atkin LJ: I agree. It seems to me that in this case there has been a total failure of consideration, that is to say that the buyer has not got any part of that for which he paid the purchase money. He paid the money in order that he might get the property, and he has not got it. It is true that the seller delivered to him the de facto possession, but the seller had not got the right to possession and consequently could not give it to the buyer. Therefore the buyer, during the time that he had the car in his actual possession had no right to it, and was at all times liable to the true owner for its conversion. Now there is no doubt that what the buyer had a right to get was the property in the car, for the Sale of Goods Act expressly provides that in every contract of sale there is an implied condition that the seller has a right to sell. . . . The whole object of a sale is to transfer property from one person to another. . . .

It seems to me that in this case there must be a right to reject, and also a right to sue for the price paid as money had and received on failure of the consideration, and further that there is no obligation on the part of the buyer to return the car, for *ex hypothesi* the seller had no right to receive it. Under these circumstances can it make any difference that the buyer has used the car before he found out that there was a breach of the condition? To my mind it makes no difference at all. The buyer accepted the car on the representation of the seller that he had a right to sell it, and inasmuch as the seller had no such right he is not entitled to say that the buyer has enjoyed a benefit under the contract. In fact the buyer has not received any part of that which he contracted to receive—namely, the property and right to possession—and, that being so, there has been a total failure of consideration. The plaintiff is entitled to recover the £334 which he paid.

[**Bankes LJ** delivered a concurring judgment.]

NOTE

This rule can work considerable injustice, as is shown by the later case of *Butterworth v Kingsway Motors* [1954] 1 WLR 1286, where a car which was owned by a finance company and let on hire-purchase was wrongfully sold by the hirer and passed through several hands before being bought by the plaintiff, who used it for nearly a whole year before it was reclaimed by the finance company. It was held, following *Rowland v Divall*, that the plaintiff could recover all of his purchase price (£1,725) from his immediate seller because of the breach of the condition implied by s 12(1), even though he had had the use of the car for almost a year, and the far smaller sum of £175 would have been sufficient to pay off the finance company's interest in the car. Had the plaintiff been restricted to a remedy in damages, he would of course have been entitled to be paid much less.

The Law Reform Committee, in its Twelfth Report (*Transfer of Title to Chattels* (Cmnd 2958, 1967), para 36) recommended that a buyer in these circumstances should be entitled to recover no more than his actual loss, giving credit for any benefit he may have had from the goods while they were in his possession, but no action has ever been taken to implement this proposal.

QUESTION

A catering company buys ten cases of vintage Krug champagne for a wedding. All the champagne is consumed at the wedding with evident pleasure, and the catering company is paid its fee. It then becomes clear that the champagne was not the property of the sellers. Can the catering company recover the entire price from the sellers?

The statement in s 12(1) that in the case of an agreement to sell the seller must merely have the right to sell at the time when the property is to pass looks at first sight curious. It can be explained, however, on the basis that it is perfectly open to A to contract to sell to B property currently belonging to C. In such a case A no doubt hopes that he can persuade C to sell him the goods in time for him to pass title to B. Unfortunately, this can create difficulties in the case of conditional sales. In *Barber v NWS Bank plc* [1996] 1 WLR 641, CA, a buyer agreed to buy a car from a finance company under a conditional sale agreement, paying for it by instalments. The car turned out not to belong to the finance company, whereupon the buyer sought to rescind the sale. The case was not covered by s 12(1), since the finance company only had to have title at the time property was to pass, and this time had not yet come. The Court of Appeal avoided the conclusion that the buyer had to continue paying instalments on a car he might never come to own, but only by finding a further non-statutory term in the contract that the finance company would have title at the beginning, as well as at the end, of the conditional sale agreement.

It should be noted that s 12(1) (which uses the phrase 'a right to sell the goods') is wider in its scope than might be inferred from the label 'implied condition as to title' which is commonly applied to it.

First, the seller may be in breach of the section even if (because the transaction comes within an exception to the *nemo dat* rule) he is able to confer a good title on the buyer: see *Barber v NWS Bank plc* [1996] 1 WLR 641, CA. In this case the buyer could have acquired a good title under Part III of the Hire-Purchase Act 1964, but the court decreed that he could nevertheless rescind the transaction following *Rowland v Divall*. See also on this issue I Brown, 'The Scope of Section 12 of the Sale of Goods Act' (1992) 108 LQR 221, discussing *R v Wheeler* (1990) 92 Cr App R 279.

Secondly, a seller is in breach if the goods infringe an intellectual property right (eg a copyright, trade mark, or patent) belonging to a third party. This surprising result stems from the technical wording of s 12: the seller in such a case has no *right* to sell the goods (because by doing so he infringes the right of the third party), even though he has, and can pass, perfectly good title to what he sells. See *Niblett Ltd v Confectioners' Materials Co Ltd* [1921] 3 KB 387, CA.

(c) Sale of a limited title

The condition implied by s 12(1) cannot be excluded or modified in any way by the operation of an exemption clause (Unfair Contract Terms Act 1977, s 6(1)(a)), unless the contract is of a kind to which that Act does not apply at all, such as an international sale contract. This causes potential problems, however, where a seller is genuinely unsure of its title: for example, where a finance company claims title to a piece of machinery, or a work of art is alleged to have been stolen abroad at some time in the past. This issue is dealt with by s 12(3), introduced in 1973. This subsection allows a person to contract to sell merely such title to goods as he (or another person) may have, but under s 12(4) the seller must in such a case disclose all encumbrances of which he knows.

(d) The implied warranties as to freedom from encumbrances and quiet possession (s 12(2)(a) and (b))

Section 12 supplements the implied condition as to title with two implied *warranties*: first, that the goods are, and will remain, free from any undisclosed encumbrances (s 12(2)(a)) and, secondly, that the buyer will enjoy quiet and undisturbed possession (s 12(2)(b)). These are the only statutory implied terms that are characterised as warranties and not conditions. It follows that if either of these implied terms is broken, the buyer will have only a remedy in damages and will not be able to reject the goods.

The first of these covers the case where, for example, a cargo is sold that is subject to a charge or pledge in favour of a third party, such as a bank.

The second, s 12(2)(b), covers interference after the sale with the buyer's ability to possess or use the goods. An example is intervention by the seller or his agent after delivery. In *Empresa Exportadora de Azúcar v Industria Azucarera Nacional SA, The Playa Larga* [1983] 2 Lloyd's Rep 171 the seller, the Cuban state sugar trading agency, sold sugar to a buyer in Chile and shipped it on a Cuban vessel. It was held liable under s 12(2)(b) when for political reasons it later ordered the vessel to deliver the cargo elsewhere (see too *The Rio Sun* [1985] 1 Lloyd's Rep 350). Another is where a third party interferes by right, as in *Louis Dreyfus Trading Ltd v Reliance Trading Ltd* [2004] 2 Lloyd's Rep 243, where a third party with a claim against the seller successfully asserted a right in court to prevent movement of a cargo of sugar on delivery at a West African port. And so too with state actions arising out of a state of affairs existing at the time of the sale. So in *Great Elephant Corpn v Trafigura Beheer BV* [2013] EWCA Civ 905, [2013] 2 CLC 185 Teare J held, and the Court of Appeal agreed, that a seller of oil in Nigeria was in breach of s 12(2)(b) when, after certain loading irregularities had been committed by the sellers' agents, the Nigerian government prevented the vessel carrying the oil from sailing. The same may also be true where goods infringe a third party's intellectual property rights. In *Microbeads AC v Vinhurst Road Markings Ltd* [1975] 1 WLR 218, CA, road-marking machines which were the subject of the contract turned out two years later to infringe the patent of a third party who threatened proceedings against the buyer. Since the patent was not granted to the third party until after the sale, there had been no breach when the property in the goods passed to the buyer, and so it was not possible to invoke s 12(1). But the court held that a remedy lay under s 12(2)(b).

However, s 12(2)(b) is limited. Although the section read literally gives the buyer a general right to quiet possession, this must be limited to cases where that possession is disturbed by the *lawful* act of a third person with a superior title or right impairing the buyer's freedom to possess and use the goods: sellers can hardly be regarded as giving buyers an open-ended guarantee against future theft or interference by those with no claim whatever. Thus in *Great Elephant Corpn v Trafigura Beheer BV*, above, the sellers were not liable for subsequent delays to the cargo caused by entirely illegal actions by agents of the Nigerian government.

Where there has been a breach of s 12(1) (title) and the true owner reclaims the goods, there will normally be a breach of s 12(2)(b) (quiet possession) also. In *Mason v Burningham* [1949] 2 KB 545, CA, where the plaintiff bought a second-hand typewriter which turned out to have been stolen and had to be returned to its rightful owner, she could plainly have sued under s 12(1) (as in *Rowland v Divall* (above)), but chose instead to rely only on s 12(2)(b). She was awarded by way of damages not only a refund of the purchase price, but also a sum which she had reasonably (in the view of the court) paid to have the typewriter overhauled following the purchase.

Subsections (4) and (5) of s 12 apply to the case where a contract of sale is made under s 12(3)—that is, where the seller contracts to transfer a limited title. Under these subsections, modified forms of the warranties as to freedom from encumbrances and quiet possession are implied in such a contract.

QUESTION

Why do you think that the Act characterises the implied terms in s 12(2) and (3) as warranties rather than conditions?

2 DUTIES OF THE BUYER

The statutory duties of the buyer are: to take delivery (s 37(1)); to accept the goods (s 27); and to pay the price (ss 27, 28).

(a) To take delivery

The basic rules regarding the place, time, etc of delivery have already been discussed (above, p 458). If the buyer fails to take delivery at the appointed time, or the seller is ready and willing to deliver the goods and requests the buyer to take delivery, and he does not within a reasonable time after such a request take delivery, he will be liable in damages to the seller (s 37(1)). This can be commercially very significant if, for example, the seller is put to expense in warehousing the goods, or if the seller ships the goods and because of the buyer's failure to unload and collect them at the discharge port has to pay compensation ('demurrage') to the shipowner for the resulting delay to the vessel (compare *Vitol SA v Conoil plc* [2009] EWHC 1144 (Comm), [2009] 2 Lloyd's Rep 466).

If the buyer has the right to refuse to accept the goods (see below), he is equally not liable for failing to take delivery.

(b) The buyer's duty to accept the goods

Quite apart from the duty physically to take delivery, under s 27 it is the duty of the buyer to accept and pay for the goods. This is in terms uncontroversial. But two important issues arise under it. First, what are the limits of the duty to accept: in other words, in what circumstances may the buyer reject goods and/or refuse to take delivery? And, secondly, if the buyer does have the right to reject the goods, in what circumstances will he lose it?

(i) *The buyer's right to reject goods*

If the seller delivers or tenders goods which are not of the contract description, whether as regards quantity or quality, the first and most obvious remedy of the buyer will be to reject them. As we saw earlier, a right to reject may be exercised even after the property has passed to the buyer, provided that he has not 'accepted' the goods within the meaning of s 35 (*McDougall v Aeromarine of Emsworth Ltd* (above, p 358)). Section 35 is dealt with below.

If a buyer is entitled to reject goods, he may do so for any reason he likes: he is not required to act reasonably in choosing rejection rather than some other remedy. The only question is whether he has that right and, if so, whether he has lost it by waiver or acceptance. See above, p 426.

Moreover, the buyer who in fact has a good reason to reject remains entitled to do so even though he may have given a legally insufficient reason at the time. So in *Manbré Saccharine Co Ltd v Corn Products Co Ltd* [1919] 1 KB 198 sellers in the United States agreed to ship starch to buyers in England. The buyers refused the tendered documents on the basis that when they were tendered the cargo had been lost at sea. This was a clearly bad reason, since risk had passed to the buyers on shipment. The buyers were nevertheless held not to be in breach of contract. This was because the documents themselves were defective, in that no proper insurance policy had been tendered, and hence they had in fact had a perfectly good ground for rejection even though they had not referred to it at the time.

The buyer may waive his right to reject, even if the goods have not been accepted, by an unequivocal statement to that effect. See s 11(2) and, for example, *Westbrook Resources Ltd v Globe Metallurgical Inc* [2009] EWCA Civ 310, [2009] 2 Lloyd's Rep 224.

Delivery at the wrong time or place As we saw above, whether the buyer can reject goods delivered late depends on the terms of the contract (see s 10 and above, p 426 ff). As regards the place of delivery, it seems that the buyer can insist on delivery at the correct place and reject tender of delivery elsewhere. So in *Petrograde Inc v Stinnes GmbH* [1995] 1 Lloyd's Rep 142 buyers who had agreed to send a vessel to take delivery of a cargo of petrol at Antwerp were held justified in refusing to accept it in Flushing, some miles away, even though that was more convenient for them and would have involved less steaming time.

Delivery of the wrong quantity Where the seller has delivered the wrong quantity of goods, the buyer has the choice of remedies set out in s 30:

(1) in the case of a short delivery, to reject the goods or to accept them and pay at the contract rate;

(2) in the case of an excessive delivery, to reject the goods, to accept the contract quantity and reject the rest, or to accept all the goods and pay for the excess at the contract rate.

The right to reject is prima facie absolute. But there are two qualifications to it. First, the law has, in fact, always been prepared to overlook a commercially insignificant disparity (the *de minimis* exception). In *Shipton, Anderson & Co v Weil Bros & Co* [1912] 1 KB 574, already mentioned, this principle was applied: there, a cargo of 4,950 tons of wheat was overweight by 55 lbs (a difference in weight of 0.0005 per cent, or in price of 4s (20p) in £40,000, a sum to which the sellers graciously waived any claim). Secondly, s 30(2A), introduced in 1994, provides that, subject to any agreement to the contrary, a buyer may not reject the whole of the goods delivered if the shortfall or excess is so slight that it would be unreasonable for him to do so (s 30(2A)). The onus of proof is on the seller (s 30(2B)). This is likely to be a difficult burden to satisfy, and there is no reported case where s 30(2A) has been successfully invoked.

It should be noted that s 30 deals only with the contractual aspects of a wrong delivery. The question whether, and if so at what point, property passes from seller to buyer remains to be determined by ss 16 ff: see J Ulph, 'The Proprietary Consequences of an Excess Delivery' [1998] LMCLQ 4.

Delivery in instalments Section 31(1) declares that, unless otherwise agreed, the buyer of goods is not bound to accept delivery by instalments.

Behrend & Co v Produce Brokers Co
[1920] 3 KB 530, King's Bench Division

The facts appear from the judgment.

Bailhache J: In this case the sellers, by two contracts of sale . . . bound themselves to the buyers to deliver in London, ex the steamship *Port Inglis*, to the buyers' craft alongside, two separate parcels of cotton seed, one of 176 tons and the other of 400 tons. The buyers on their part had to pay for these parcels against shipping documents and to send craft to receive the goods. The buyers fulfilled both these obligations and received from the Port Inglis some fifteen tons of one parcel and twenty-two tons of the other. When these had been delivered it was discovered that the rest of the seed was lying under cargo for Hull, and the *Port Inglis* stopped delivery and left for that port, promising to return and deliver the rest of the seed. She returned in about a fortnight's time and the seed was tendered to the buyers, but the buyers had meantime informed the sellers that they regarded the departure of the *Port Inglis* with the remainder of the seed on board as a failure to deliver and a breach of contract. They kept so much of the seed as had been delivered to them and demanded repayment of so much of the contract price as represented the seed undelivered.

The umpire has decided in the buyers' favour and I am asked to say whether he was right. Everything depends upon whether the departure of the *Port Inglis* for Hull with the greater part of both parcels of seed on board was a failure to deliver, notwithstanding the promise to return and complete delivery. Both contracts between the parties are in the same terms and neither has any express provision on the subject. In my opinion, the buyer under such a contract, and where each parcel of goods is indivisible, as here, has the right to have delivery on the arrival of the steamship, not necessarily immediately or continuously; he must take his turn or the goods may be so stowed that other goods have to be discharged before the whole of the buyers' parcel can be got out. To such delays and others which may occur in the course of unloading the buyer must submit, but in the absence of any stipulation to the contrary the buyer, being ready with his craft, is entitled to delivery of the whole of an indivisible parcel of goods sold to him for delivery from a vessel which has begun delivery to him before she leaves the port to deliver goods elsewhere. If this is so the rest of the case is covered by s 30 of the Sale of Goods Act, and the buyer can either reject the whole of the goods, including those actually delivered, in which case he can recover the whole of his money; or he may keep the goods actually delivered and reject the rest, in which case he must pay for the goods kept at the contract price, and he can recover the price paid for the undelivered portion. . . . I think that the award is right.

NOTE

This right to refuse delivery by instalments can be taken very seriously. Thus a seller who agrees to sell one cargo to be discharged partly at Port A and partly at Port B cannot insist that the buyer accept separate shipments to each port: *Cobec v Toepfer* [1983] 2 Lloyd's Rep 386.

Delivery of non-conforming goods   As mentioned above (see Chapter 11), the duties laid down in ss 13–15 of the Sale of Goods Act are expressed as conditions. From this it follows that any breach by the seller of any of them, however minor, allows the buyer to reject. However, a similar restriction to that in s 30(2A) above now applies to that right: see s 15A.

Breach of a condition or serious breach of an innominate term   The right to reject will also lie if the seller has broken a condition of the contract, or has committed a serious breach of an innominate term, other than in the context of ss 13–15. An example of such a breach of condition is a tender by a seller under a contract of sale cif (see below, p 543) of non-conforming documents: as Timothy Walker said in *Soules CAF v PT Transap of Indonesia* [1999] 1 Lloyd's Rep 917, 'The documentary requirements of the contract must be strictly complied with, and the buyer is not obliged to evaluate how significant any documentary discrepancy may prove to be.' An example of a breach of an innominate term where the breach was found not serious enough was *Cehave NV v Bremer Handelsgesellschaft mbH, The Hansa Nord* [1976] QB 44, CA, where the seller of a cargo of citrus pulp pellets[1] was in breach of an express term, 'shipment to be made in good condition', but not in the view of the Court of Appeal to a degree which went to the root of the contract. Accordingly, the buyer was entitled to damages only, and not to reject the goods. See too *Tradax Internacional SA v Goldschmidt SA* [1977] 2 Lloyd's Rep 604.

The effect of rejection of the goods   If a buyer rightfully rejects goods as unsatisfactory, for example under ss 13–15 of the Sale of Goods Act, is it open to the seller to insist that the buyer accept a new tender of goods that do satisfy the contractual requirements, if this can be done within the time allowed by the contract and is not otherwise inconsistent with the contract? Section 11(3) of the Sale of Goods Act, under which a 'condition' is described as a term 'the breach of which may give rise to a right [in the buyer] *to treat the contract as repudiated*', suggests on a literal reading that the answer is No. However, the better authority is that s 11(3) need not be taken absolutely literally, and that a seller normally has the right to cure a defective tender.

Borrowman, Phillips & Co v Free & Hollis
(1878) 4 QBD 500, Court of Appeal

This case concerned a contract to buy a cargo of American maize, to be shipped between 15 May and 30 June. The sellers offered the buyers a cargo on the *Charles Platt*, but the buyers rejected this offer (it was held, by an arbitrator, rightly) because the sellers had no shipping documents. The sellers then, within the period specified by the contract, offered a second cargo on the *Maria D*, which the buyers also rejected. The sellers had to resell the cargo of the *Maria D* at a loss, and sued the buyers for damages for non-acceptance. The trial judge (Denman J) ruled that the buyers were not bound to accept the second tender once the sellers had appropriated the first cargo to the contract; but the Court of Appeal reversed this decision.

> **Brett LJ**: I now pass to the point, upon which the judgment of Denman J was given. It has been argued by the defendants' counsel that the plaintiffs could not lawfully tender the cargo of the *Maria D*, because they had already tendered that of the *Charles Platt*, and had insisted upon that

---

[1] A by-product of the orange juice industry, made from the peel, pulp, and seeds of the fruit. They go into animal feed.

tender. The doctrine of election was relied upon, and it was urged that, even if the offer of the *Charles Platt* was not of itself a sufficient election, the plaintiffs were ousted of their right to sue in this action by referring the matter to arbitration. It may be that that if the plaintiffs had recovered damages in an action for not accepting the cargo of the *Charles Platt* they could not maintain this suit; but in the present case there were no trial and judgment, it was only a reference to arbitration, whether the plaintiffs could according to mercantile usage tender the cargo of the *Charles Platt*. The question comes down to the narrow point, whether the plaintiffs are barred by the doctrine of election. For the defendants reliance has been placed upon a passage in *Blackburn on Contract of Sale*, pp 128, 129, to the effect that when in pursuance of a contract to sell unspecified goods the vendor has appropriated certain goods, he has made an election which is irrevocable; but I think that passage has nothing to do with the principle to be applied in the present case. It may be that, where goods which fulfil the terms of a contract are appropriated for sale in performance thereof, there is an election by the vendor which is irrevocable; but here the contention for the defendants is that the cargo of the *Charles Platt* was not in accordance with the contract. . . .

I have only to add that a different rule might have been applied, if the defendants had accepted the cargo of the *Charles Platt*; it is possible that the tender of the plaintiffs could not in that case have been withdrawn. I wish it however to be understood, that this is a point upon which I express no opinion.

[**Bramwell** and **Cotton LJJ** delivered concurring judgments.]

The decision in *Borrowman v Free* received support from the House of Lords in *The Kanchenjunga* [1990] 1 Lloyd's Rep 391, HL (a case not on sales, but on charterparties). See generally on this topic, A Apps, 'The Right to Cure Defective Performance' [1994] LMCLQ 525.

Breach of instalment contracts A contract of sale may provide for delivery of the goods, or payment of the price, or both, to be made by instalments. In general, such contracts will be governed by the ordinary rules of the law of contract. It may be crucial, for instance, to determine whether the contract (or, more accurately, the seller's obligation) is 'entire' or 'divisible'. An example of the former might be the sale by a mail-order company of an encyclopedia set, to be delivered to the buyer by posting one volume every month; and of the latter, the sale of 100 tonnes of coal to be delivered at the rate of 10 tonnes on the Monday of each week. The failure by the seller to deliver one volume of the encyclopedia would justify a claim by the buyer to be entitled to reject all the volumes so far received and have his money back. But a similar failure to deliver one instalment of the coal would, at the most, entitle the buyer to terminate the contract as regards *future* deliveries: there would be no question of a right to *restitutio in integrum* with retrospective effect. It is important to appreciate that the Act deals with only some points relating to instalment contracts, and leaves others (eg the distinction just made between entire and divisible obligations) to be decided by reference to the general law. Section 31(2) makes provision for one particular type of instalment contract. It states:

Where there is a contract for the sale of goods to be delivered by stated instalments, which are to be separately paid for, and the seller makes defective deliveries in respect of one or more instalments, or the buyer neglects or refuses to take delivery of or pay for one or more instalments, it is a question in each case depending on the terms of the contract and the circumstances of the case whether the breach of the contract is a repudiation of the whole contract or whether it is a severable breach giving rise to a claim for compensation but not to a right to treat the whole contract as repudiated.

It is likely that the rules stated in this subsection reflect propositions of the common law which have a wider application: for instance, similar rules would surely govern a contract for the sale of goods to be delivered by instalments which are not to be separately paid for but, perhaps, paid for in some other way. The operation of s 31(2) in practice is illustrated by the following cases.

Maple Flock Co Ltd v Universal Furniture Products (Wembley) Ltd
[1934] 1 KB 148, Court of Appeal

Maple contracted to sell to Universal 100 tons of rag flock 'to be delivered three loads per week as required'. The weekly deliveries were to be separately paid for. After 18 loads, each of one and a half tons, had been delivered, the buyers wrote purporting to cancel the remainder of the contract on the ground that an analysis of the sixteenth load had shown that its chlorine content was over eight times the government standard. The court held that this single breach did not justify termination of the contract as a whole.

Lord Hewart CJ (delivering the judgment of the court (Lord Hewart CJ, Lord Wright, and Slesser LJ)): The decision of this case depends on the true construction and application of s 31, sub-s 2, of the Sale of Goods Act 1893 . . . That sub-section was based on decisions before the Act, and has been the subject of decisions since the Act. A contract for the sale of goods by instalments is a single contract, not a complex of as many contracts as there are instalments under it. The law might have been determined in the sense that any breach of condition in respect of any one or more instalments would entitle the party aggrieved to claim that the contract has been repudiated as a whole; or on the other hand the law as established might have been that any breach, however, serious, in respect of one or more instalments should not have consequences extending beyond the particular instalment or instalments or affecting the contract as a whole. The sub-section, however, which deals equally with breaches either by the buyer or the seller, requires the Court to decide on the merits of the particular case what effect, if any, the breach or breaches should have on the contract as a whole.

[His Lordship referred to a number of decided cases, and continued:]

   With the help of these authorities we deduce that the main tests to be considered in applying the sub-section to the present case are, first, the ratio quantitatively which the breach bears to the contract as a whole, and secondly the degree of probability or improbability that such a breach will be repeated. On the first point, the delivery complained of amounts to no more than 1½ tons out of a contract for 100 tons. On the second point, our conclusion is that the chance of the breach being repeated is practically negligible. We assume that the sample found defective fairly represents the bulk; but bearing in mind the judge's finding that the breach was extraordinary and that the appellant's business was carefully conducted, bearing in mind also that the appellants were warned, and bearing in mind that the delivery complained of was an isolated instance out of 20 satisfactory deliveries actually made both before and after the instalment objected to, we hold that it cannot reasonably be inferred that similar breaches would occur in regard to subsequent deliveries. Indeed, we do not understand that the learned Judge came to any different conclusion. He seems, however, to have decided against the appellants on a third and separate ground, that is, that a delivery not satisfying the Government requirements would or might lead to the respondents being prosecuted . . . Though we think he exaggerates the likelihood of the respondents in such a case being held responsible, we do not wish to underrate the gravity to the respondents of

> their being even prosecuted. But we cannot follow the Judge's reasoning that the bare possibility, however remote, of this happening would justify the respondents in rescinding in this case. There may indeed be such cases, as also cases where the consequences of a single breach of contract may be so serious as to involve a frustration of the contract and justify rescission, or furthermore, the contract might contain an express condition that a breach would justify rescission, in which case effect would be given to such a condition by the Court. But none of these circumstances can be predicated of this case. We think the deciding factor here is the extreme improbability of the breach being repeated, and on that ground, and on the isolated and limited character of the breach complained of, there was, in our judgment, no sufficient justification to entitle the respondents to refuse further deliveries as they did.
>
> The appeal must accordingly be allowed and judgment entered for the appellants, with costs here and below, for damages for their breach of contract in refusing further deliveries.

Two other cases may be mentioned.

(1) *Robert A Munro & Co Ltd v Meyer* [1930] 2 KB 312, where there was a contract to supply 1,500 tons of meat-and-bone meal by instalments of 125 tons per month. After 631 tons had been delivered, it was discovered that all the meal delivered so far had been deliberately adulterated with cocoa husk, so that it failed to conform to its description. Wright J granted a declaration that the buyers were not bound to take delivery of any further instalments.

(2) *Regent ORG Aisenstadt und Barig v Francesco of Jermyn Street Ltd* [1981] 3 All ER 327: Regent, a firm of German clothing manufacturers, agreed to sell 62 suits to Francesco, retailers of menswear. Delivery was to be by instalments, the number and size to be at Regent's discretion. Francesco told Regent that they wished to cancel the order, but Regent insisted on continuing to make deliveries because the suits were already in production. Francesco then purported to cancel the contract on the ground that one delivery had been one suit short, relying on s 30(1) of the Act, which entitles a buyer who is tendered short delivery to reject all the contract goods. Mustill J ruled that where the contract provided for delivery to be made by instalments, s 31(2) applied to the exclusion of s 30(1), and the repudiation was wrongful in the circumstances.

NOTES

1. The statement of the law in the *Maple Flock* case may be regarded as an instance of the 'innominate term' approach to the question of breach of contract favoured by the Court of Appeal in *Hong Kong Fir Shipping Co Ltd v Kawasaki Kisen Kaisha Ltd* [1962] 2 QB 26.

2. The delivery of only one suit short in the *Regent* case (above) would, in any case, probably not now fall within s 30(1): see s 30(2A).

(ii) Acceptance and the loss of the buyer's right to reject goods

Even if the buyer has the right to reject goods, under s 11(4) he loses this right once he has 'accepted' them (or is deemed to have accepted them) in the circumstances set out in s 35. The loss of the right to reject does not affect his right to claim damages in respect of any shortfall or defect in the delivery (s 11(4)). The rules in the Sale of Goods Act governing acceptance (and the related rules as to the buyer's right to examine the goods) were extensively revised in 1994, and authorities from before that date need to be regarded with some caution.

Note that the statutory rules about acceptance discussed above apply only to sales of goods proper. There are no corresponding sections in related Acts, such as the Supply of Goods and Services Act 1982. In cases falling within the latter, the common law doctrines of affirmation and waiver will apply (R Bradgate, 'Remedying the Unfit Fitted Kitchen' (2004) 120 LQR 558).

The buyer's right to examine the goods Section 34 states that, unless otherwise agreed, when the seller tenders delivery of the goods to the buyer, he is bound on request to afford the buyer a reasonable opportunity of examining them to see if they are in conformity with the contract and, in the case of a sale by sample, of comparing the bulk with the sample. The buyer will not be deemed to have accepted the goods if he has not been given this opportunity—unless he has previously examined them (s 35(2)).

The definition of acceptance Subject to the right to examine the goods referred to above, a buyer is deemed to have accepted the goods (s 35(1) and (4)):

(a) when he intimates to the seller that he has accepted them;

(b) when the goods have been delivered to him and he does any act in relation to them which is inconsistent with the ownership of the seller; or

(c) when after the lapse of a reasonable time he retains the goods without intimating to the seller that he has rejected them.

Section 35(2) states that where goods are delivered to the buyer and he has not previously examined them, he is not deemed to have accepted them unless he has had a reasonable opportunity of examining them in order to see whether they are in conformity with the contract (and, where appropriate, with a sample). This factor is also relevant in determining whether the buyer has kept the goods for more than a reasonable time under (c) above.

Truk (UK) Ltd v Tokmakidis GmbH
[2000] 1 Lloyd's Rep 543, Bristol Mercantile Court

Truk supplied underlifts for tow-trucks. It fitted an underlift to a chassis owned by Tokmakidis and delivered the finished assembly to Tokmakidis in Germany in June 1996. Tokmakidis tried to sell the vehicle but was told by a potential purchaser in December 1996 that there might be something wrong. Following investigations, in March 1997 Truk was invited to remove the underlift in a letter which was held to amount to a rejection, and in July was informed that the underlift awaited their collection. The court held that the underlift had been validly rejected, and that it was highly relevant that the goods had been supplied with a view to a resale which might take some time.

HHJ Jack: The situation here is that the vehicle with the underlift attached could be inspected and tested on arrival in Germany. This would not have taken long. The inspection could have included whether the vehicle complied with relevant German regulations. . . . So taking inspection for the purpose of s. 35(2) and (5) in a wide sense, it could have been completed no later than the end of July.

But that would be to look at the transaction too narrowly. The most important feature is that the vehicle was not to be used by Tokmakidis but was to be resold by them. If it had been intended that the vehicle was to be used by Tokmakidis a reasonable period for rejection or acceptance would, I suggest, have been of the order of a month or two subject to any extension brought about by discussions between the parties as to remedying defects. But not only was the vehicle delivered for the purpose of resale, the contract envisaged that it might take some time, at least six months, to find a buyer: I refer to the provision that the price was to be paid by Tokmakidis on sale of the vehicle or six months after delivery, which ever was sooner.

Where goods such as machines of one kind or another are sold for the purposes of resale, and they turn out to be defective, it often happens—I would suggest more often than not, that the defect is discovered only when the sub-buyer comes to use the goods. He then rejects them and causes the buyer in turn to reject them. That is an everyday event in both consumer and non-consumer transactions. Section 35 refers to it in sub-s. (6)(b), where it is provided that acceptance shall not be deemed to have occurred merely by reason of delivery under a sub-sale. This leads to the conclusion that, where goods are sold for resale, a reasonable time in which to intimate rejection should usually be the time actually taken to resell the goods together with an additional period in which they can be inspected and tried out by the sub-purchaser. As an example, consider the position of a trader who has bought for stock an item of electrical equipment which may be sold in a week or in several months. Certainly it would usually be right in such cases at least to take account of the period likely to be required for resale. In the present case I have to decide whether the period should last at least until the date for payment—which is the earlier of the date of resale or six months from delivery. I am satisfied that in the circumstances it should. That reflects the reasonable interests of both the buyers and the sellers, and takes account of the terms of the contract itself. So I conclude that a reasonable time in which to intimate rejection had not passed when December, 1996 came...

This brings me to what we have called the second period [December 1996 onwards]. There are two further authorities which are of help.

In *Manifatture Tessile Laniera Wooltex v. Ashley Ltd* [1979] 2 Lloyd's Rep. 28 at p. 32, col. 1, a case concerned with the examination of communications between the parties after the question of defects arose, Lord Justice Megaw stated:

> The defendants were certainly reasonably entitled as an ordinary matter of commerce, especially when they were still threatened by the plaintiffs that any rejection of the goods would be a breach of contract, to make sure as to what were the goods which were defective and as to whether their sub-buyers were complaining about any of the goods which had been delivered to them.

This is relevant to the period between Dec. 9, 1996 and Mar. 2, 1997...

In *Fisher Reeves & Co Ltd. v. Armour & Co. Ltd* [1920] 3 KB 614 at p. 624 Lord Justice Scrutton stated:

> When one party to a contract becomes aware of a breach of a condition precedent by the other, he is entitled to a reasonable time to consider what he will do, and failure to reject at once does not prejudice his right to reject if he exercises it within a reasonable time....He is also entitled during that reasonable time to make enquiries as to the commercial possibilities in order to decide what to do on learning for the first time of the breach of condition which would entitle him to reject.

This is relevant to the period from Mar. 2, at least to Mar. 27, 1997...

In my judgment by his conduct in December, 1996, in particular, by refusing to pay, Mr. Tokmakidis reserved the company's position pending investigations as to what, if anything, was wrong. He was entitled to a reasonable time for that....

Once Tokmakidis had Mr. Hochscheid's report they acted reasonably promptly. In my view Walchner & Kollatz's first letter (of Mar. 27, 1997) is to be taken as a clear and unequivocal rejection. It gave Truk the option of buying the chassis by Apr. 7, 1997, and if Truk did not take that up Truk was to remove their underlift from the chassis. Either way, Tokmakidis was rejecting the underlift. Although the deadlines were extended, that position remained unchanged. Tokmakidis did nothing meanwhile to affirm the contract.

The relation between acceptance and the right to examine the goods In one case the definition of acceptance potentially clashes with the buyer's right to examine the goods: namely, where A sells goods to B, B sub-sells to C, and A delivers directly to C. If C rejects the goods vis-à-vis B, can B in turn reject vis-à-vis A? Under s 35(1)(b), B has accepted the goods, since he has done an 'act in relation to them which is inconsistent with the ownership of the seller' (ie reselling them to C); but under s 34 he has not accepted them, since he has had no chance to inspect them. Under the pre-1994 law it was held that what is now s 35(1)(b) prevailed and B had lost the right to reject (see *Hardy & Co v Hillerns & Fowler* [1923] 2 KB 490). Today, however, it is made clear by s 35(6)(b) that s 35 is subject to the overriding rule in s 34, and hence if C rejects as against B, B can in his turn reject as against A.

Partial rejection Before 1994 a seller who accepted any goods tendered automatically lost any right of rejection; even if some of the goods were acceptable and the rest defective, he could not accept the good and reject the bad. This was anomalous, and s 35A now allows partial rejection. It deals not only where part of the goods delivered are good (ie of the contract quality or description) and the rest are not, but also where the whole consignment is defective but the buyer chooses to retain some of them or is unable to return them. The section provides that, subject to any agreement to the contrary, if the buyer has a right to reject the goods by reason of a breach on the part of the seller that affects some or all of them but accepts some only of the goods, he does not by accepting them lose his right to reject the rest. However, to the extent that some of the goods delivered are in conformity with the contract, he is deemed to accept the whole of that part. So, in the case of a contract to sell 12 JCB excavators where eight of those delivered are good and four damaged, the buyer must accept the eight satisfactory machines if he accepts any at all, but he is not thereby deemed to have accepted any of the damaged ones. Nor, by accepting one damaged machine (eg because he needs it urgently), does he thereby lose the right to reject the other damaged ones.

Section 35A is subject to one qualification. Under s 35(7) where two or more items form a 'commercial unit'—that is, a unit 'division of which would materially impair the value of the goods or the character of the unit'—rejection remains an all-or-nothing affair. For example, if a retailer ordered 1,000 two-piece men's suits and the trousers were off-colour, it is highly unlikely that it would be permitted to reject them but nevertheless keep the jackets.

Where the contract is for a sale by instalments, these rules apply to the right to reject each instalment as if it were a separate contract of sale (s 35A(3)).

Requesting repair Section 35(6) (introduced in 1994) clarifies a point previously doubtful. A buyer is not deemed to have accepted the goods merely because he has asked for, or agreed to, their repair by the seller or under an arrangement with him. Thus in *Clegg v Andersson* [2003] EWCA Civ 320, [2003] 2 Lloyd's Rep 32 a yacht was sold with an overweight keel which rendered it unsatisfactory unless remedial work was done. Negotiations about this possible work took several months. It was held that the buyer had not lost his right to reject during this time. (See also the ruling of the House of Lords in *J&H Ritchie Ltd v Lloyd Ltd*, below.)

J&H Ritchie Ltd v Lloyd Ltd

[2007] UKHL 9, [2007] 1 WLR 670, House of Lords

Ritchies, a farming company based in Paisley, bought a combination seed drill and power harrow from Lloyds. Within two days of starting to use it, they had to stop work because it had developed serious vibrations. They agreed to allow the seller to take back the machine in order that it could be inspected and, if possible, repaired, and they completed their sowing operations for that season using a replacement machine provided by the sellers. It turned out that two bearings to rotors on the harrow were missing, making the equipment unsatisfactory for use. The sellers had the missing parts replaced in the next few weeks and notified Ritchies that the machine had been repaired and was ready for collection. But despite repeated requests, the sellers refused to tell Ritchies what the fault was. The buyers accordingly decided to reject the machine, and asked for the return of the price. It was held by the House of Lords (reversing the Scottish court below) that they were entitled to do so, it being necessary to imply into their agreement to allow the repair work a condition that they would be informed about the fault and what had been done to cure it.

Lord Mance:

47. Section 35(6)(a) was introduced into the Sale of Goods Act 1979 by the Sale and Supply of Goods Act 1994 to address the risk that a buyer who 'asks for, or agrees to, their repair by or under an arrangement with the seller' might, merely thereby, lose the right to reject non-compliant goods delivered to him under the contract for sale . . .

48. However, the Act does not say that such an arrangement has no effect at all. Nor could it, since the nature and effect of any arrangement is a fact-specific matter. At one end of the spectrum, one can take the example of a material, but readily identified, defect, easily curable and with no possible consequential implications (eg an obviously defective or missing part in the case of a machine not yet used). In that event, an arrangement might be made for perhaps costly and time-consuming repair by the seller which would commit the buyer outright to accepting the goods if and when they were satisfactorily repaired and returned. The arrangement would amount not to immediate acceptance (because that is the whole point of s 35(6)(a)), but to acceptance conditional upon satisfactory repair and return.

49. But that is not the present case, where the source of the problem experienced during three days' use of the harrow was unknown and could not be ascertained on superficial examination even by the seller. In consequence the arrangement actually made on 29 April 1999 did not simply involve asking for or agreeing to repair. Instead, it was arranged that the seller would take the harrow away for inspection and, if possible, repair.

50. Inspection might have shown that the problem was irreparable or so expensive to cure that the seller was not prepared to undertake any repair. In that case, the buyer could and would no doubt have rejected the harrow and drill, and would have had a claim against the seller for non-performance of the contract for sale. Or it might have shown that the problem was simple and inconsequential, in which case no doubt the harrow would have been repaired, returned and accepted by the buyer, provided of course that the repair was satisfactory. In the present case, the problem proved to be quite serious: the harrow, . . . had not been fitted with bearings which it should ordinarily have had from manufacture. Not unreasonably, as the Sheriff found, the buyer, when it eventually learned this informally, had concerns about the consequential implications for other parts of the harrow having run without these bearings for three days (on 26, 27 and 28 April 1999).

51. The circumstance giving rise to this case is that the buyer was never given the chance to comment on the seller's findings on inspection of the harrow. The next contact between seller and buyer after 29 April 1999 came only when the seller had obtained and installed new bearings. The seller at that point (on or around 17 May 1999) contacted the buyer and informed it that the harrow had been repaired and was ready for return. So it was only then that the buyer had the chance to air any concerns. The buyer not surprisingly asked what had been wrong with the

harrow, but the seller was unwilling to say. Only informally did the buyer receive information from one of the seller's employees that bearings had been missing. The buyer then asked that the seller obtain and present an engineer's report to show that there had been no consequential damage. This was refused. The buyer in these circumstances claimed on 26 May 1999 to reject the drill and harrow and to recover their price.

52. In my view, the buyer's rejection was justified. The harrow was, after its delivery to the buyer and payment of the price in March 1999, the buyer's property and at the buyer's risk, subject in each case to the buyer's right to reject it as defective. . . . The parties no doubt hoped that satisfactory repair would be possible. But in my view it was a natural implication of the arrangement made that the seller would, at least upon request, inform the buyer of the nature of the problem which required to be remedied. Indeed, I would normally have expected the seller to report such information before any repair, although it is not necessary here to decide whether the implication went so far as to require this.

53. By failing to report the result of the inspection, and by presenting the buyer with the fait accompli of repaired goods, the seller short-circuited the procedure I would have expected. By refusing to inform the buyer of the cause of the problem on request after repair, the seller was on any view in breach of the implicitly agreed procedure, and also aroused suspicion. By failing to agree to supply an engineer's report, the seller lost the opportunity to persuade the buyer to accept the goods notwithstanding the seller's failure to follow the procedure implicitly agreed.

[**Lords Hope of Craighead**, **Rodger of Earlsferry**, and **Brown of Eaton-under-Heywood** delivered concurring opinions. **Lord Scott of Foscote** concurred.]

Effect of rejection If a buyer has rightly rejected the goods, he is not bound to return them to the seller. It is sufficient if he informs the seller that he refuses to accept them (s 36). It is then up to the seller to make arrangements for (and bear the expense of) collection or disposal.

If a buyer who has rejected goods has paid all or part of the price and the seller does not make an effective substituted delivery, he may of course claim restitution of the money that he has paid. He may also claim damages for any incidental or consequential losses, provided that they are not too remote.

(c) The buyer's duty to pay the price

The buyer is bound to pay the price in accordance with the terms of the contract of sale (s 27). Unless otherwise agreed, he must be ready to do so as soon as the seller is ready and willing to give him possession of the goods in accordance with the contract (s 28, above, p 456). If he is not so ready he will be in breach of contract and potentially liable in damages.

Note, however, that presumptively under s 49(1) he cannot actually be sued for the price unless and until property has passed to him. Even if the only reason property has not passed is the buyer's own breach of contract in refusing delivery, the seller's only action is one for damages for non-acceptance: *Colley v Overseas Exporters Ltd* [1921] 3 KB 302.

There is one exception. Where the price is payable on a day certain irrespective of delivery of the goods, under s 49(2) the buyer can be sued for it as soon as that day arrives. This provision is necessary to deal with the case where a seller, for example to preserve its cashflow, stipulates for prepayment; it would be unfortunate if the seller were prevented from recovering that price as soon as it was due. Section 49(2) is itself, however, to be read subject to an implied qualification. If it is clear at the time the seller sues for the price that he cannot or will not supply the goods, then the buyer's duty to pay for them disappears: *Otis Vehicle Rentals Ltd v Ciceley Commercials Ltd* [2002] EWCA Civ 1064.

These matters are dealt with in greater detail below, in Chapter 13.

The contract may provide for payment in a foreign currency, and in this case the court has power to give its judgment in that currency: *Miliangos v George Frank (Textiles) Ltd* [1976] AC 443.

CHAPTER 13

REMEDIES OF THE SELLER

The remedies of the seller in a sale of goods transaction take, with one exception, two forms: money claims against the buyer, either for the price or for damages for breach of contract, and claims against the goods or their proceeds in order to provide security. There is one other species of claim of minor importance, namely a claim for specific performance.

1 ACTION FOR THE PRICE

The only reference in the sale of Goods Act 1979 to the seller's right to bring an action for the price appears in s 49. Under this provision he is said to be entitled to claim the price in two specified situations:

(1) where, under the contract of sale, the property in the goods has passed to the buyer, and the latter wrongfully neglects or refuses to pay according to the terms of the contract (s 49(1));

(2) where, under the contract, the price is payable on a day certain irrespective of delivery, and the buyer wrongfully neglects or refuses to pay it (s 49(2)).

Until 2016 there was room for argument that this section, which is surprisingly narrow, was exhaustive, and that whatever the contract might say, as a matter of law the seller could not sue for the price except in the two cases above. However, it has been made clear by the Supreme Court in *PST Energy 7 Shipping LLC v OW Bunker Malta Ltd* [2016] UKSC 23 at [40]–[58] that this is not so. Section 49 illustrates, but does not exhaust, the cases where the price can be claimed. There are thus some other situations where the seller may sue for the price (see Section (c) below); and in addition the parties can stipulate for further instances.

(a) Where the property has passed to the buyer (s 49(1))

For the seller to be able to sue for the price under this subsection, it is not sufficient that the property has passed to the buyer. The buyer must also have *wrongfully* neglected or refused to pay the price; his neglect or refusal will not be 'wrongful' if the price is not yet due under the terms of the contract (eg where the seller has agreed to give credit), or if the seller is in breach of certain obligations on his part (eg where s 28 applies, to be ready and willing to give possession of the goods to the buyer in exchange for the price). However, the fact that it is only due to the buyers' own default that property has not passed is irrelevant: see *Colley v Overseas Exporters Ltd*, below.

score4

score4

(b) Where the price is payable on a day certain irrespective of delivery (s 49(2))

If the contract stipulates a fixed date for payment, or a date that can be calculated by reference to some objective fact (eg 'seven days after government approval of the sale'), irrespective of delivery, the seller can sue for the price even though the property has not passed, and even though no goods have yet been appropriated to the contract. Again, however, the buyer must have wrongfully neglected or refused to pay for the goods. The reason why this provision is necessary is to allow a seller to stipulate, and where necessary sue, for prepayment on a fixed date in order to put itself in funds before it makes delivery.

The width of s 49(2) is problematical. Read literally, it only applies to a date fixed in advance by the contract in such a way that it can be determined independently of the action of either party (eg 'on 25 April' or '60 days after signing this contract'; but not '3 days after the seller gives two weeks' notice of delivery'). However, s 49(2) is essentially a cash-flow protection provision, and there is much to be said for construing it broadly rather than literally. The better authority supports this. Thus the subsection was held to cover a stage payment payable on the laying of the keel of a ship (*Workman Clark & Co Ltd v Lloyd Brazileño* [1908] 1 KB 968). And in 2015 it was said, *obiter*, to cover a payment due a certain time after delivery independently of whether the goods themselves (there fuel oil sold for consumption) were still in existence so as to allow property to pass. See Males J in *PST Energy 7 Shipping LLC v OW Bunker Malta Ltd* [2015] EWHC 2022 (Comm), [2015] 2 Lloyd's Rep 563 at [73] (the point was left undecided in the Supreme Court: [2016] UKSC 23, [2016] 2 WLR 1193).

Even where the literal requirements of s 49(2) are satisfied, it is subject to one implicit qualification. The subsection has been held not to apply, for obvious reasons, where at the time action is brought it is clear that the seller will not, or cannot, provide the goods: see *Otis Vehicle Rentals Ltd v Ciceley Commercials Ltd* [2002] EWCA Civ 1064.

(c) Where the risk has passed and the goods are lost

Despite the limited wording of s 49, there is no doubt that an action lies for the price where the risk has passed to the buyer before the property has passed and the goods are later destroyed or lost: see *Castle v Playford* (above, p 346), *Manbré Saccharine Co Ltd v Corn Products Co Ltd* (below, p 546), and *PST Energy 7 Shipping LLC v OW Bunker Malta Ltd* [2016] UKSC 23, [2016] 2 WLR 1193 at [55]–[58].

Colley v Overseas Exporters Ltd
[1921] 3 KB 302, King's Bench Division

Colley agreed to sell leather belting to the defendant company on FOB terms (see below, p 537). The contract obliged the buyers to nominate a ship on to which the seller was to make arrangements to load the goods, and provided that the price was to be paid when delivery was made to the ship. The buyers failed to nominate a ship, despite five abortive attempts, and the goods lay on the docks. It was held that the seller could not sue for the price, even though it was due to the buyer's own default that the event which would have made the price payable under the contract had not occurred.

McCardie J: This action is brought . . . to recover the sum of £985 17s 4d [£985.87] alleged to be due from the defendants to the plaintiff as the price of goods. The only question is whether that liquidated sum is due. No question arises as yet as to damages against the defendants. The case raises a point of legal interest and practical utility as to the circumstances under which the purchase price of goods can be sued for. . . .

The defendants committed no deliberate breach of contract; they suffered a series of misfortunes. They failed however to name an effective ship. The plaintiff on his part did all he could to carry out his obligations. Under these circumstances the plaintiff seeks to recover the price of the goods in question. The able argument of Mr Willes for the plaintiff rested on two well-known passages in the judgment of Lord Blackburn in *Mackay v Dick* (1881) 6 App Cas 251. The first passage is this: 'I think I may safely say, as a general rule, that where in a written contract it appears that both parties have agreed that something shall be done, which cannot effectually be done unless both concur in doing it, the construction of the contract is that each agrees to do all that is necessary to be done on his part for the carrying out of that thing, though there may be no express words to that effect.' The second passage is this: 'It would follow in point of law that the defender having had the machine delivered to him, was by his contract to keep it, unless on a fair test according to the contract it failed to do the stipulated quantity of work, in which case he would be entitled to call on the pursuers to remove it. And by his own default he can now never be in a position to call upon the pursuers to take back the machine, on the ground that the test had not been satisfied, he must, as far as regards that, keep, and consequently pay for it.' I will consider later on the facts in *Mackay v Dick*. The contention of Mr Willes before me was that inasmuch as the defendants' own fault had here prevented the goods from being put on board they were disabled from saying that the price, which would have been payable if and when the goods had actually been put on board, was not now due to the plaintiff. This is a novel and interesting submission . . .

The circumstances . . . under which a claim to the price may be made (as distinguished from a claim of damages for breach of contract) are indicated in s 49 of [the Sale of Goods] Act.

[His Lordship read the section, and continued:]

Here sub-s 2 of s 49 does not apply, as it apparently did in *Workman, Clark & Co v Lloyd Brazileño* ([1908] 1 KB 968), where the price was payable by stated instalments on stated dates. The parties before me here made no special agreement as to the payment of the price. Nor can it be said that sub-s 1 of s 49 applies here, for the property in the goods has not in fact and law passed to the buyer . . . Unless therefore the principle involved in the words of Lord Blackburn in the second passage cited from *Mackay v Dick* applies here the plaintiff will fail. Does the principle go to the extent submitted by Mr Willes? It is well to consider *Mackay v Dick*. The headnote says: 'If, in the case of a contract of sale and delivery, which makes acceptance of the thing sold and payment of the price conditional on a certain thing being done by the seller, the buyer prevents the possibility of the seller fulfilling the condition, the contract is to be taken as satisfied.' If this headnote be given its full apparent effect then the principle it suggests would be most far reaching and the results extraordinary. The facts in *Mackay v Dick* must be remembered. Concisely put they were these. By a contract in two letters the seller agreed to sell and deliver at the buyer's works a digging machine. The price of £1125 was payable after the machine had satisfactorily performed certain tests. If it failed to perform them the buyer was to remove the machine. The machine was actually delivered into the buyer's possession. Owing however to the buyer's own default it did not perform the tests. He refused to pay the price, and the seller thereupon brought his action for the £1125. The plaintiff succeeded on the principle stated by Lord Blackburn. It is to be clearly noted that a specific machine was fully deliverable by the seller to the buyer. Apparently the property in the machine actually passed to the buyer. . . .

A clear distinction exists between cases where the default of the buyer has occurred after the property has passed and cases where that default has been before the property has passed. To the former cases *Mackay v Dick* may be applied on appropriate facts. To the latter cases *Mackay v Dick* does not apply so as to enable the buyer to recover the price as distinguished from damages for breach of contract....

It follows therefore for the reasons given that the plaintiff is not entitled to recover the price of the goods in question. If he desires to claim damages he must amend his writ. On the record at present before me he cannot ask for judgment.

NOTE

See too *Stein, Forbes & Co v County Tailoring Co* (1916) 86 LJKB 448 (similar result).

(d) Contrary agreement

The other case where the seller can sue for the price outside the situations mentioned in s 49 is that of contrary agreement. See the Australian decision in *Minister for Supply v Serviceman's Cooperative Joinery Manufacturers Ltd* (1951) 82 CLR 621 at 624, per Latham CJ ('the parties may make any contract they please with respect to the payment of the price') and *PST Energy 7 Shipping LLC v OW Bunker Malta Ltd* [2016] UKSC 23, [2016] 2 WLR 1193 at [53]. One such instance is where goods are sold and the price becomes payable after the goods have been disposed of or destroyed but before title has passed (see *PST Energy*, above, at [58]). Another is where parties enter into a so-called 'take or pay' contract, common in the chemical and energy industries, under which a buyer agrees to pay periodically the price of a given quantity of some commodity whether or not he actually accepts or takes delivery of any of it (for an example where such a clause was discussed, see *M & J Polymers Ltd v Imerys Minerals Ltd* [2008] EWHC 344 (Comm), [2008] 1 CLC 276).

(e) The right to interest on the price

Section 54 preserves any right that the seller may have, apart from the Act, to claim interest on the price. The courts now have a wide statutory discretion to award interest in many cases, for example under s 35A of the Senior Courts Act 1981. In practice, interest is regularly awarded in commercial claims for debt. There is now also a statutory entitlement to interest in certain cases under the Late Payment of Commercial Debts (Interest) Act 1998. In addition to this, insofar as the price is paid late and the seller can prove actual loss resulting from the late payment, the seller can claim damages at common law: *Sempra Metals Ltd (formerly Metallgesellschaft Ltd) v Inland Revenue Commissioners* [2007] UKHL 34, [2008] 1 AC 561.

2 ACTION FOR DAMAGES FOR NON-ACCEPTANCE

The seller may bring an action against the buyer for damages for non-acceptance when the buyer has wrongfully neglected to accept and pay for the goods (s 50(1)). (The buyer has a counterpart claim against the seller for damages for non-delivery under s 51(1): see the next chapter.)

(a) The prima facie measure of damages

Section 50 goes on to state that the measure of damages is the estimated loss directly and naturally resulting, in the ordinary course of events, from the defendant party's breach of contract (s 50(2): this is essentially the rule as to remoteness of damage which contract lawyers will recognise as the 'first rule' in *Hadley v Baxendale* (1854) 9 Exch 341). It then states a presumptive 'market price' rule (s 50(3):

> Where there is an available market for the goods in question the measure of damages is prima facie to be ascertained by the difference between the contract price and the market or current price at the time or times when the goods ought to have been accepted or (if no time was fixed for acceptance) at the time of the refusal to accept.

This rule is closely connected with the general principle requiring mitigation of loss. If, when the buyer refuses to accept the goods, there is a market where other buyers are ready to take them off the seller's hands, he must mitigate by reselling to such a buyer. If he does not, the buyer will rightly be able to argue that he should not be liable for any loss due to such failure. (For a critical examination of the market price rule, see JN Adams, 'Damages in Sale of Goods' [2002] JBL 553.)

It should be noted that the primary rule here is that in s 50(2): s 50(3) is merely a presumptive way to measure the loss naturally resulting from the breach. In *Bem Dis A Turk Ticaret S/ A TR v International Agri Trade Co Ltd* [1999] All ER (Comm) 619 a consignment of tapioca was to be shipped from Thailand to Turkey but importation was banned by the Turkish government, and the buyers told the sellers not to load the ship which they had chartered. The sellers successfully sued for the cost of cancelling the hire of the ship. The Court of Appeal rejected an argument that the market price rule should be applied to prevent recovery of these consequential losses.

Section 50(3) will apply only if there is an 'available market' for the goods in question. (On the concept of a 'market', see RM Goode, 'The Concept and Implications of a Market in Commercial Law' [1991] LMCLQ 177.) There have been various judicial definitions of this term. It is sufficient to quote one, from the judgment of Jenkins LJ in *Charter v Sullivan* [1957] 2 QB 117 at 128, CA:

> I . . . will content myself with the negative proposition that I doubt if there can be an available market for particular goods in any sense relevant to s 50(3) of the Sale of Goods Act [1979] unless those goods are available for sale in the market at the market or current price in the sense of the price, whatever it may be, fixed by reference to supply and demand as the price at which a purchaser for the goods in question can be found, be it greater or less than or equal to the contract price.

So in that case, and also in the later case of *WL Thompson Ltd v Robinson (Gunmakers) Ltd* [1955] Ch 177, there was held to be no market where (this being the 1950s) the retail price of all such cars was essentially fixed by the manufacturers. Again, there is no available market if there is only one buyer potentially interested in unwanted steel (*Harlow & Jones Ltd v Panex International Ltd* [1967] 2 Lloyd's Rep 509); where machinery is so specialised that a buyer cannot be easily found (*Re Vic Mill Ltd* [1913] 1 Ch 465); or where a Boeing 757 airliner, predictably, cannot be readily disposed of at short notice (*Aercap Partners 1 Ltd v*

Avia Asset Management AB [2010] EWHC 2431 (Comm), [2010] 2 CLC 578). In *Lazenby Garages Ltd v Wright* [1976] 1 WLR 459, CA, the court took the rather surprising view that because every second-hand car was unique there could be no relevant available market, but this seems much too restrictive.

Section 50(3) states that the relevant market price is that available at the *time* of the failure or refusal to accept. It is also established by the cases that a similar test applies in regard to the *place* of the relevant market: the court asks whether a market existed for goods of the contract description at the place where the buyer ought to have taken delivery, and uses as a yardstick the price prevailing on that market.

Where s 50(3) applies, any actual profit that the seller would have made on the sale is out of account. Cooke J made the point neatly in *Glencore Energy UK Ltd v Cirrus Oil Services Ltd* [2014] EWHC 87 (Comm), [2014] 2 Lloyd's Rep 1:

> 98. . . . The contract price/market price differential is not a computation of lost profit. Lost profit is the difference between the total net cost to the seller of acquiring the goods and bringing them to market on the one hand and the net sale price that would have been achieved on the other. The difference between this measure of damages and the section 50 measure is illustrated by the different claims originally put forward in the Particulars of Claim by Glencore. The claim was first put on the basis of the difference between the net price payable by Glencore to Socar and the amount payable to it under its contract with Cirrus Oil. The alternative claim, which was the only one pursued at trial, was the claim based on section 50(2) and (3) of the Sale of Goods Act. The point is illustrated by a simple situation where the cost of the goods to the seller is £100, the on-sale price is also £100, and the market price at the time of the breach by the on-sale buyer is £50. If the buyer had accepted the goods, the seller would in fact have made no profit at all but, in accordance with section 50(2) and (3) of the Sale of Goods Act, the prima facie measure of loss is £50 because the seller is left with goods worth less than the contract price.
>
> 99. The measure of damage constituted by section 50(2) and (3) of the Sale of Goods Act was designed to compensate the seller for the loss of the bargain with the buyer by computing how much worse off the seller would be, if at the time of the breach, he had sold the goods to a substitute buyer. The measure constitutes both a ceiling and a floor to the loss claim on the assumption that the seller had gone out into the market and sold at the date of breach.

Further difficult issues may be encountered in the case of an international sale, where the buyer's breach takes place after the goods have been shipped. If there is an available market for such goods 'afloat', to which the seller can have recourse, the price on this market will be appropriate; but if there is not, the first possible place where he will be able to dispose of them will be the port of arrival. (Section 50(3) is, after all, only a prima facie rule.) Thus, in *Muller, MacLean & Co v Leslie & Anderson* (1921) 8 Ll L Rep 328, the contract was for a consignment of padlocks FOB New York, to be shipped to India. The buyers wrongly refused to accept the shipping documents after the goods had been shipped. Damages were awarded to the sellers based on the market price in India at the time of the ship's arrival.

Where there is an *anticipatory* repudiation by the buyer which is accepted by the seller, damages are prima facie to be assessed by reference to the market price at the time when the goods ought to have been accepted; however, the seller's duty to mitigate may well require him to resell as soon as possible after acceptance, especially against the background of a falling market. (If the seller does not accept the repudiation, of course, he is under no duty to mitigate until an actual breach occurs: *Tredegar Iron & Coal Co Ltd v Hawthorn Bros & Co* (1902) 18 TLR 716.)

It should be noted, however, that in the case of an anticipatory breach it is always open to the buyer to reduce damages to nil by arguing that the seller would not in the event have been able to insist on the buyer accepting the goods on the day fixed for performance. This would be the case if, for instance, events covered by a force majeure clause would have excused the buyer, or if on the evidence the seller himself could not have provided the necessary conforming goods. Compare the decisions in *Bunge SA v Nidera BV* [2015] UKSC 43, [2015] 3 All ER 1082 and *Flame SA v Glory Wealth Shipping Pte Ltd* [2013] EWHC 3153 (Comm), [2014] QB 1080 and the discussion at p 518, below, of the converse case of anticipatory breach by the seller.

Where, because there is no available market, s 50(3) does not apply, the court must fall back on the ordinary rules of the law of contract as to the assessment of damages, estimating the seller's loss as best it can. This may be nil, if for example a buyer refuses to accept a car in high demand which can immediately be sold elsewhere at the same price (*Charter v Sullivan* [1957] 2 QB 117). On the other hand, if the goods are not in demand and the seller can prove that he has made one fewer sale than he would have, an award of the lost profit is appropriate (see *Thompson v Robinson* (above)). If he has resold to a substitute buyer at a lower price, the resale price will be at least prima facie evidence by which his loss can be calculated (eg *Re Vic Mill Ltd* [1913] 1 Ch 465 and *McCandless Aircraft LC v Payne* [2010] EWHC 1835 (QB)).

(b) Further damages

Section 54 provides as follows:

> Nothing in this Act affects the right of the buyer or the seller to recover interest or special damages in any case where by law interest or special damages may be recoverable . . .

The reference to 'special damages' is best read as permitting damages to be awarded, where appropriate, by reference to the 'second rule' in *Hadley v Baxendale*: that is, losses in the specific contemplation of the parties.

It should also be remembered that under s 37(1) there may be an award of damages for failure to accept physical delivery. The seller will also be able to claim as damages the reasonable costs of reselling the goods and any incidental expenses, for example for storage, transport, etc. See above, p 463.

3 RECOVERY OR FORFEITURE OF A DEPOSIT

With sales of certain goods, such as ships and aircraft, it is not uncommon for the buyer to pay a deposit, to be forfeited if he refuses later to accept or pay for the goods. Such stipulations are enforceable in principle. See, for example, *Damon Compañía Naviera SA v Hapag-Lloyd International SA* [1985] 1 WLR 435, and, more recently, *Tandrin Aviation Holdings Ltd v Aero Toy Store LLC* [2010] EWHC 40 (Comm), [2010] 2 Lloyd's Rep 668, where Hamblen J upheld a provision for sellers of an executive jet for $31.5 million to retain a deposit of $3 million in the event of failure to accept.

If the deposit is not paid, and after it is due the buyer repudiates the contract, the seller can sue for the amount of it as an accrued debt: see *Firodi Shipping Ltd v Griffon Shipping LLC* [2013] EWHC 593 (Comm), [2013] 1 CLC 741. If the buyer's repudiation is accepted before the deposit is due, the damages available against the buyer may include the amount of the deposit: see *Damon Compañía Naviera SA v Hapag-Lloyd International SA* above.

Deposits are subject to the jurisdiction to relieve against contractual penalties, but only if so high that they are entirely disproportionate to any legitimate interest in the seller in obtaining performance of the buyer's obligation: see *Cavendish Square Holding BV v Makdessi* [2015] UKSC 67, [2015] 3 WLR 1373 at [16], [238], [291]–[292]. In practice, it seems any provision for forfeiture of a deposit is likely to be upheld unless entirely outrageous in amount.

4 SPECIFIC PERFORMANCE

Section 52 (below, p 527) allows the court to order specific performance at the suit of the buyer of goods, but not that of the seller. Nevertheless, it seems the court retains an inherent jurisdiction outside s 52 to order specific performance of a contract to buy something not otherwise easily disposable, such as a scrap ship: see *The Messiniaki Tolmi (No 2)* [1983] 2 AC 787 at 797, per Lord Roskill. Compare *P & O Nedlloyd BV v Arab Metals Co (No 2)* [2006] EWCA Civ 1717, [2007] 1 WLR 2288, where the Court of Appeal refused to strike out a claim by a carrier for specific performance of a contract by a consignee to accept contaminated scrap metal; it would seem the case would be no different with a contract of sale.

5 REMEDIES OF AN UNPAID SELLER AGAINST THE GOODS: LIEN, STOPPAGE IN TRANSIT, AND RESALE

(a) Introduction

The remedies described above are simply applications to the law of sale of ordinary principles of the law of contract. In addition, however, the Act confers additional remedies upon a seller who is unpaid in the case where ownership has passed to the buyer. These are set out in s 39(2) as follows:

(1) a *lien* on the goods (ie a right to retain them for the price while he is in possession of them);

(2) in the case of the insolvency of the buyer, a right of *stopping the goods in transit* after he has parted with the possession of them; and

(3) a *right of resale*, as limited by the Act.

Section 39(2) also states that an unpaid seller who is still the owner of the goods (ie where the property has *not* passed to the buyer) has rights analogous to the right of lien and stoppage in transit set out in s 39(1). This confirms that the rights of the seller in such a case are no less than they would be if the property had passed. It is arguable that he would in many circumstances be able to assert such rights anyway, by virtue of the fact that he is the owner of the goods; but the Act removes any doubts which there might be on the point.

The rights described in s 39(1) and elaborated in the rest of Part V of the Act are described as 'rights against the goods'. This is because they give the seller powers, in the nature of self-help remedies, which he can exercise directly against the goods in order to secure his right to be paid. For this reason, they are sometimes referred to as the seller's 'real' remedies.

A seller is an 'unpaid seller' for the purposes of s 39 in the circumstances set out in s 38(1). This will be the case when the whole of the price has not been paid or tendered, and when a bill of exchange or other negotiable instrument has been received by the seller as conditional payment and later dishonoured. A seller who has agreed to allow his buyer credit can be an unpaid seller (eg if the buyer is insolvent). Note also: (1) that a seller is 'unpaid' so long as *any part* of the price is outstanding; and (2) that if payment has been *tendered*, but refused, the seller will lose his unpaid seller's remedies.

(b) Unpaid seller's lien

The unpaid seller's *lien* is his right, if in possession, to retain possession of the goods until the price is paid or tendered, despite the fact that the goods are owned by the buyer (s 41(1)). A lien is thus a form of possessory security. As discussed more fully in Chapter 25, it is a right to *retain* goods already in the party's possession (in contrast with a pledge, which is based on a *delivery* of possession). The seller may assert his lien even though he is in possession as the buyer's bailee or agent (s 41(2)), and even though part only of the price is unpaid (s 38(l)(a)). He may exercise his lien (for the whole price, if appropriate) against part only of the goods, if he has already delivered the rest to the buyer, unless he is held to have waived his lien (s 42).

Not every unpaid seller may claim a lien: under s 41(1) the right arises only: (1) where the goods have been sold without any stipulation as to credit; (2) where any term of credit has expired; and (3) where the buyer becomes insolvent. This reflects the fact that it is normally implicit in the giving of credit that the seller should be bound to deliver without being paid.

An unpaid seller loses his lien in three circumstances (s 43(1)). One is by delivery: when the buyer or his agent lawfully obtains possession of the goods, the lien is lost. Another is by waiver. Thirdly, the seller loses his lien when he delivers the goods to a carrier for transmission to the buyer without reserving the right of disposal of the goods—a phrase which most often refers to a seller who ships goods and takes the bill of lading in his own name. Here, however, as we will see, he retains a more limited right of stoppage if the buyer becomes insolvent. In addition, of course, he will lose his lien if the price is paid or tendered; but not by reason only that he obtains a judgment for the price (s 43(2)).

Section 43(1) underlines the essential nature of the lien as a right to *retain* possession: if the unpaid seller parts with the goods, he cannot reassert his lien even if he gets back possession: *Valpy v Gibson*, below.

Valpy v Gibson
(1847) 4 CB 837, Court of Common Pleas

Brown, a merchant in Birmingham, bought cloth from Gibson. Gibson sent the cloth to Leech, Harrison & Co, shipping agents, at Liverpool, in four cases marked for shipment to

Valparaiso, requesting Leech & Co to put them on board as directed by Brown. After the goods had been loaded on to a ship, Brown's agent, Alison, ordered them to be returned to Gibson to be repacked in eight cases instead of four. Gibson was still in possession of the goods, and unpaid, when Brown was declared bankrupt. It was held that it was too late for Gibson to claim an unpaid seller's lien.

> **Wilde CJ** (delivering the judgment of the court (Wilde CJ, Coltman, Maule, and Cresswell JJ)): The right which it was contended the defendants had, as vendors in the actual and lawful possession of the goods, on the insolvency of the vendee, cannot, we think, be sustained. The goods being sold on credit, and the complete property and possession having vested in Brown, they became his absolutely, without any lien or right of the vendors attaching to them, any more than on any other property of Brown; and their delivery to the defendants to be re-packed, could not have the effect of creating a lien for the price, without an agreement to that effect. We therefore think there must be judgment for the plaintiffs.

In contrast to s 43(1), s 47 makes a converse point. A seller does *not* generally lose his lien merely because the buyer to whom property has passed has sub-sold or otherwise dealt with the goods. In other words, a seller remaining in possession can normally rest assured and concern himself with any acts of his buyer. But this is subject to exceptions. The section reads:

(1) Subject to this Act, the unpaid seller's right of lien or retention or stoppage in transit is not affected by any sale or other disposition of the goods which the buyer may have made, unless the seller has assented to it.
(2) Where a document of title to goods has been lawfully transferred to any person as buyer or owner of the goods, and that person transfers the document to a person who takes it in good faith and for valuable consideration, then
  (a) if the last-mentioned transfer was by way of sale, the unpaid seller's right of lien or retention or stoppage in transit is defeated; and
  (b) if the last-mentioned transfer was made by way of pledge or other disposition for value, the unpaid seller's right of lien or retention or stoppage in transit can only be exercised subject to the rights of the transferee.

In other words, the seller loses his rights in only two cases. One is where he has consented to the sub-sale (eg if he has sold on the basis that the buyer will pay him out of the proceeds of a sub-sale: see *Mount v Jay*, below). The other is where the buyer, having received a document of title from the seller, sells or pledges the goods to a third party by the transfer of such a document. The thinking in both cases is the same: if the seller either agrees to a sub-buyer obtaining rights prevailing over his own, or does an act causing the buyer to seem entitled to dispose of the goods freely, the rights of the sub-buyer should prevail.

Mordaunt Bros v British Oil & Cake Mills Ltd
[1910] 2 KB 502, King's Bench Division

BOCM contracted to sell various lots of boiled linseed oil to Crichton Bros, who resold it to Mordaunts. Mordaunts had paid Crichtons all or most of the price of their purchases.

Possession remained with BOCM, who had not been paid by Crichtons. Delivery orders had been sent by Crichtons to BOCM, directing BOCM to deliver to Mordaunts an amount of oil appropriate to each contract, which BOCM usually acknowledged and recorded in its books. It was held that these acts did not constitute an 'assent' by BOCM to the resale for the purposes of s 47(1).

Pickford J: It was next argued that the plaintiffs were entitled to succeed by virtue of s 47 of the Sale of Goods Act 1893, on the ground that the defendants had assented to the sales by Crichton Brothers to the plaintiffs. Several cases were cited in which it was held that unpaid vendors had assented to sub-sales so as to preclude themselves from asserting their right of lien. As a matter of fact all those cases related to sub-sales of specific goods. I am not, however, going to decide that s 47 has no application to unascertained goods; but I wish to point out that such acts as presenting to an unpaid vendor delivery orders in favour of sub-purchasers and the entry accordingly of the names of the sub-purchasers in the books of the unpaid vendor may have a different effect according as the goods are specific or unascertained. In the former case it may be more readily inferred that the unpaid vendor has assumed the position of an agent or bailee holding the goods for and on behalf of the sub-purchaser or holder of the delivery order, and the acceptance of the delivery order and entry of the holder's name in the books by the unpaid vendor might in the case of specific goods justify the inference that the unpaid vendor had accepted that position. No such inference could be drawn if the goods were not in existence, and it does not follow that because the inference may be drawn in the case of specific goods it will also be drawn in the case of goods in existence but unascertained. In my opinion the assent which affects the unpaid seller's right of lien must be such an assent as in the circumstances shews that the seller intends to renounce his rights against the goods. It is not enough to shew that the fact of a sub-contract has been brought to his notice and that he has assented to it merely in the sense of acknowledging the receipt of the information. His assent to the sub-contract in that sense would simply mean that he acknowledged the right of the purchaser under the sub-contract to have the goods subject to his own paramount right under the contract with his original purchaser to hold the goods until he is paid the purchase-money. Such an assent would imply no intention of making delivery to a sub-purchaser until payment was made under the original contract. The assent contemplated by s 47 of the Sale of Goods Act 1893, means something more than that; it means an assent given in such circumstances as shew that the unpaid seller intends that the sub-contract shall be carried out irrespective of the terms of the original contract.

Now in the circumstances of this case what was the effect of the inquiry by the plaintiffs whether the delivery orders of Crichton Brothers were 'in order' and the defendants' reply that they were? I think some light is thrown on the nature and purpose of this inquiry by the fact that the plaintiffs parted with their money before making the inquiry. Neither party regarded those inquiries as directed to the questions whether the defendants were to hold the oil as agents for the plaintiffs, renouncing any rights they might have to hold the goods till they were paid for by Crichton Brothers, and whether they were prepared to deliver to the plaintiffs and look elsewhere than to the goods themselves for any rights they might have in respect of them. Whatever might have been the effect of such an inquiry and answer in a case where specific goods were in question, I think in the present case where the goods were unascertained the inquiry and answer amounted to no more than this—that the defendants were ready to carry out the contract between themselves and Crichton Brothers with this modification, that delivery should be made to the plaintiffs instead of to Crichton Brothers, but that the delivery should be subject to all the other terms and incidents of the contract with Crichton Brothers.

DF Mount Ltd v Jay & Jay (Provisions) Co Ltd
[1960] 1 QB 159, Queen's Bench Division

Jay, owner of a large consignment of tinned peaches at a wharf, sold part of it to Merrick for resale to two of Merrick's customers. Jay sent delivery orders to Merrick; Merrick indorsed them in favour of Mount and sent them to the wharfinger. Merrick then addressed two fresh delivery orders and sent them to Mount. Mount paid Merrick, but Merrick never paid Jay and became insolvent. The case concerned which of Mount and Jay was entitled to the peaches. The court decided in favour of Mount.

Salmon J: The case raises the familiar problem—which of two innocent persons, the plaintiffs or the defendants, shall suffer for the trickery of a rogue.

The plaintiffs rely first on s 47 of the Sale of Goods Act 1893.

[His Lordship read s 47, and continued:]

There is a proviso to the section, with which I shall deal in a moment. The plaintiffs contend that the defendants assented to the sale or disposition of the 250 cartons by Merrick to the plaintiffs, and thereby lost their right as unpaid sellers to the lien which they would otherwise have had upon the cartons. The defendants contend that if they assented to the sub-sale by Merrick, their assent was not an assent within the meaning of s 47, and rely upon *Mordaunt Bros v British Oil and Cake Mills Ltd* [above]. It is clear from Pickford J's judgment in that case that the assent contemplated by s 47 means 'an assent given in such circumstances as show that the unpaid seller intends that the sub-contract shall be carried out irrespective of the terms of the original contract' and must be 'such an assent as in the circumstances shows that the seller intends to renounce his rights against the goods.' Pickford J held that there had been no such assent on the part of the sellers.

The facts of that case are, however, very different from those of the present case. There the sellers had at no time any reason to doubt the buyer's ability to pay, and were not informed of the sub-sale until after the sale was effected. Pickford J held that the sellers had assented to the sub-sale merely in the sense that they acknowledged its existence and the right of the sub-buyer to have the goods subject to their own paramount rights under the contract with the original buyer to hold the goods until paid the purchase price.

In the present case the defendants were anxious to get rid of the goods on a falling market. They knew that Merrick could only pay for them out of the money he obtained from his customers, and that he could only obtain the money from his customers against delivery orders in favour of those customers. In my view, the true inference is that the defendants assented to Merrick reselling the goods, in the sense that they intended to renounce their rights against the goods and to take the risk of Merrick's honesty. The defendants are reputable merchants and I am sure that it was not their intention to get rid of their goods on a falling market through Merrick on the basis that, if he defaulted, they could hold the goods against the customers from whom he obtained the money out of which they were to be paid. . . .

The sale of the 250 cartons was a sale of unascertained goods. In my judgment, however, there is no reason why section 47 should not apply to unascertained goods. . .

This is enough to dispose of the case, but I will deal briefly with some of the other points which have been canvassed. Mr. Silkin argues that even had there been no sufficient assent by the defendants, he would be entitled to succeed under the proviso to section 47. [His Lordship read the proviso and continued:] It is conceded that the plaintiffs took that delivery order in good faith and for valuable consideration. Mr. Noakes argues, however, that there has been no transfer by Merrick within the meaning of the proviso. The material words to consider are: '. . .where a document of title to goods has been lawfully transferred to any person as buyer,...and that person transfers the document to a person....'

It seems to me that these words confine the proviso to cases where a document is transferred to the buyer and the same document is then transferred by him to the person who takes in good faith and for valuable consideration. If Merrick had indorsed the delivery orders he received from the defendants and transferred them to the plaintiffs, the proviso would, in my judgment, have applied; but he did not do so. He sent those delivery orders to the wharf, and made out a fresh delivery order in favour of the plaintiffs.

It is strange that there appears to be no authority on this point. It is clear that the person who transfers the document of title to the buyer may originate it himself and need not have received it from some third party in order to 'transfer' it within the meaning of the proviso...In my judgment, however, on the plain language of the section, it must be that very document which is transferred by the buyer for the proviso to operate. I am conscious that this construction leads to a very artificial result, but I cannot avoid it without doing violence to the plain language of the section.

Mr. Silkin, however, also relies on section 25(2) of the Sale of Goods Act, 1893. [His Lordship read the subsection and continued:] It seems to me that the language of this subsection is less rigorous than that of the proviso to section 47 and does not compel me to hold that the subsection applies only in those cases where the buyer transfers the same document as that of which he is in possession with the consent of the seller. I would observe that there seems to be no authority on this point.

The object of the subsection is to protect an innocent person in his dealings with a buyer who appears to have the right to deal with the goods in that he has been allowed by the seller to be in possession of the goods or documents of title relating to them. In such a case the subsection provides that any transfer of the goods or documents of title by the buyer to a person acting in good faith and without notice of any want of authority on the part of the buyer shall be as valid as if expressly authorised by the seller.

In the present case the defendants sent the documents of title to Merrick with the intention that they should enable him to obtain money from his customers. With the help of these documents, which he sent to the wharf so that the wharfingers would give a reassuring reply to any inquiry that the plaintiffs might make, or at least not query any delivery order they received from the plaintiffs, Merrick managed to obtain a substantial sum of money from the plaintiffs.

In my view, the transfer by Merrick of the delivery order dated September 4 [instead of October 4] was, by virtue of section 5 (2), as valid as if expressly authorised by the defendants.

NOTE

Mount v Jay shows that there is a curious overlap between ss 25(1) and 47 of the Sale of Goods Act 1979.

QUESTIONS

1. Is it reasonable to suppose that the draftsman of the Act intended s 25(1) to be construed differently from s 47(2)?

2. Both the cases cited above accept that s 47(2) can apply to a sale of unascertained goods, which have at no stage been appropriated to the contract. Section 39(2) may give some support to this view. But could not Jays have responded to Mount's demand simply by saying that whatever peaches were still in their hands were their own property, to do what they liked

with? Is the decision in *Mount v Jay* consistent with s 16? (On this point, see the contrasting arguments of AGL Nicol (1979) 42 MLR 129 and RM Goode, *Proprietary Rights and Insolvency in Sales Transactions* (3rd edn, 2009), para 4–24.)

3. What would have been the position if Jays had become insolvent after Merrick had sub-sold to Mount and the goods had remained unascertained?

(c) Seller's right to stop the goods in transit

Sections 44–46 set out the second of the unpaid seller's 'real' remedies: to stop the goods if they are still in transit to the buyer, before they have actually reached him. For this remedy to be available, it is not sufficient that the seller should be 'unpaid'; the buyer must also have become insolvent. (For the definition of 'insolvent', see s 61(4), which makes it plain that it is 'commercial' or 'cash-flow' insolvency that matters, and not the buyer's asset position. On insolvency generally, see below, Chapter 28.)

When a seller delivers possession of the goods to a carrier (a term embracing sea, land, and air carriers equally) for transmission to the buyer and does not reserve the right of disposal, he presumptively loses both his property (s 18, r 5(2), above, p 350) and his lien (s 43(1)(a)). The right of stoppage nevertheless enables him, by communicating with the carrier, to resume possession of the goods at any time while they are in transit. It thus allows him to exercise rights similar to those that he would have under a lien. Once again, s 39(2) confirms that the same applies even if property remains in the seller. Conversely, the fact that the carrier is engaged by the buyer himself does not preclude the right of stoppage arising: see *Bethell v Clark* (1888) 20 QBD 615 at 617, per Lord Esher MR and the Australian decision in *Toll Holdings Ltd v Stewart* [2016] FCA 256 at [65], per Rares J.

Under s 45, transit, and with it the right of stoppage, continues until the earliest of: (1) delivery of the goods by the carrier to the buyer or his agent; (2) attornment by the carrier to the buyer or his agent after they have reached the appointed destination (for an example, see *Taylor v Great Eastern Rly Co* (1901) 17 TLR 394); and (3) a wrongful refusal by the carrier to deliver the goods to the buyer or his agent. But if the buyer rejects the goods and they remain in the possession of the carrier, the transit is deemed to continue, even though the seller has refused to take them back (see s 45(4)).

Under s 46, in order to exercise the right of stoppage, seller must either take actual possession of the goods, or give notice of his claim to the carrier or other person who has possession of the goods (s 46(1)–(3)). The carrier must then redeliver the goods to the seller at the latter's expense (s 46(4)). If he fails to do so, he is liable in conversion to the seller.

Like the right of lien, the seller's right of stoppage is not affected by any sub-sale which the buyer may have made, except under the circumstances outlined in s 47.

The Tigress
(1863) 32 LJPM & A 97, Court of Admiralty

Lucy & Son had sold Bushe wheat which was at sea aboard the *Tigress*, and had endorsed one copy of the bill of lading to Bushe, although they had not been paid. Bushe had become bankrupt while the wheat was still on board. Lucy & Son, purportedly exercising their right of stoppage, directed the master to deliver the wheat to themselves, and tendered payment of the freight. The ship's master refused to deliver the wheat to Lucy & Co without proof that the wheat belonged to them. It was held that he was wrong to do so: he had to assume that the seller was acting within his rights.

> **Dr Lushington**: . . . All that is necessary is for the vendor to assert his claim as vendor and owner. Were it otherwise, were the vendor obliged formally to prove his title to exercise the right of stoppage in transitu, that right would be worthless; for the validity of a stoppage in transitu depends upon several conditions. First, the vendor must be unpaid; secondly, the vendee must be insolvent; thirdly, the vendee must not have indorsed over for value. But the proof that these conditions have been fulfilled would always be difficult for the vendor—often impossible; for instance, whether the vendor is or is not unpaid may depend upon the balance of a current account; whether the vendee is insolvent may not transpire till afterwards, when the bill of exchange for the goods becomes due. . . . And, lastly, whether the vendee has or has not indorsed the bill of lading over, is a matter not within the cognizance of the vendor. He exercises his right of stoppage in transitu at his own peril, and it is incumbent upon the master to give effect to a claim as soon as he is satisfied it is made by the vendor, unless he is aware of a legal defeasance of the vendor's claim. . . . The defendant then further objects thus: assuming the plaintiffs had a right to stop in transitu, and duly asserted that right, yet the master was guilty of no breach of duty in refusing to deliver; he simply is retaining the custody of the wheat for the right owner, as soon as the claim shall be established. Now to this argument I cannot accede; for I think there are cases without number to shew that the right to stop means the right not only to countermand delivery to the vendee, but to order delivery to the vendor. Were it otherwise, the right to stop would be useless, and trade would be impeded. The refusal of the master to deliver upon demand is, in cases like the present, sufficient evidence of conversion—*Wilson v Anderton* (1830) 1 B & Ad 450. The master may indeed sometimes suffer for an innocent mistake; but he can always protect himself from liability by filing a bill of interpleader in Chancery. For these reasons, I am satisfied that this petition sufficiently shews a prima facie case of such breach of duty as renders the vessel liable in this Court, and therefore the objections must be overruled.

Reddall v Union Castle Mail Steamship Co Ltd
(1914) 84 LJKB 360, King's Bench Division

Rutherfords sold a bale of goods to Snow, knowing that he was buying for someone in South Africa. Snow instructed Rutherfords to send the goods to Union Castle's ship *Armadale Castle* at Southampton, to be marked for shipment to Algoa Bay in South Africa. Rutherfords consigned the bale by rail to Southampton as instructed, where Snow, 'in anticipation of insolvency' told the Union Co to 'stop all shipments'. In consequence, the bale did not leave with the ship, but was kept in storage at Snow's expense until it was handed to Rutherfords in response to a claim to stop in transit. Reddall, Snow's trustee in bankruptcy, sued Union Castle in conversion, and was successful: the court ruled that the transit had ceased when the buyers intercepted the goods before they had been loaded.

> **Bailhache J**: I think, upon these facts, the original transit was to Algoa Bay. The cases upon stoppage in transitu are very numerous, and, where the transit is made in stages, difficult to reconcile. I think, however, that it is true to say that, where goods are delivered by the seller or his agent to a carrier, and pass at each successive stage of the transit from the hands of one carrier to another, without the intervention of a forwarding agent, to the destination indicated by the buyer to the

seller, the transit continues until that destination is reached. It makes no difference in such a case whether an intermediate carrier receives his instructions direct from the buyer or from the seller, provided that those instructions are given to facilitate the transit of the goods upon the journey originally intended and communicated to the buyer . . .

This does not dispose of the case, because the goods were intercepted at Southampton and the journey to Algoa Bay was stopped. The buyers, not having contracted with the sellers that the goods should go to Algoa Bay, were within their rights in doing this. . . . The defendants thereafter held the goods at rent at the buyers' disposal, and would not and could not have sent them forward to Algoa Bay, or to any other destination, without fresh instructions from the buyers. I think, therefore, that, although the original transit was to Algoa Bay, that transit had been ended at Southampton, and that under the circumstances the pretended stoppage in transitu was too late, and the defendants were wrong in delivering the goods to the sellers. Where the original transitus is interrupted by the buyers, I think the test is whether the goods will be set in motion again without further orders from the buyers; if not, the transit is ended and the right to stop lost.

There will be judgment, therefore, for the plaintiff in this case.

If, when he receives notice of stoppage, the carrier has a lien on the goods for unpaid freight, the seller is liable to pay the freight, and also the costs of redelivery: *Booth Steamship Co Ltd v Cargo Fleet Iron Co Ltd* [1916] 2 KB 570, CA.

(d) Rescission and resale by the seller

Section 48 of the Sale of Goods Act runs as follows:

(1) Subject to this section, a contract of sale is not rescinded by the mere exercise by an unpaid seller of his right of lien or retention or stoppage in transit.

(2) Where an unpaid seller who has exercised his right of lien or retention or stoppage in transit re-sells the goods, the buyer acquires a good title to them as against the original buyer.

(3) Where the goods are of a perishable nature, or where the unpaid seller gives notice to the buyer of his intention to re-sell, and the buyer does not within a reasonable time pay or tender the price, the unpaid seller may re-sell the goods and recover from the original buyer damages for any loss occasioned by his breach of contract.

(4) Where the seller expressly reserves the right of re-sale in case the buyer should make default, and on the buyer making default re-sells the goods, the original contract of sale is rescinded but without prejudice to any claim the seller may have for damages.

Section 48 deals with what happens when a contract of sale becomes abortive because of the buyer's default, but the seller still has the goods on his hands. This is an important topic. The seller needs to know two things: (1) in what circumstances he will be able to resell without being in breach of contract as against the original buyer; and (2) what effect any resale will have on any rights that original buyer may have in the goods.

When may the buyer resell? Sections 48(3) and 48(4) set out the circumstances in which a seller has a right of resale: that is, when he can resell without being in breach of contract, or possibly liable in conversion to the buyer if the latter has become owner of the goods.

Section 48(1) begins by making it clear that it is not enough simply to show that the seller has exercised his right of lien or stoppage. This does not put an end to the original contract, which presumptively remains on foot. This is important. If the contract is an advantageous one for the buyer, the buyer (or its liquidator or administrator) can still tender the price and demand delivery, and sue for damages if they do not get it. Furthermore, if property has passed to the buyer, it will remain there and not re-vest in the seller.

Something more must therefore be shown in order to justify resale. The two situations in which s 48 confers such a justification are these:

(1) where an unpaid seller gives notice to the buyer of his intention to resell, and the buyer does not within a reasonable time pay or tender the price. However, no notice is required if the goods are perishable and hence a sale is urgent (see s 48(3));

(2) where the seller expressly reserves the right of resale in case the buyer should make default (s 48(4)).

It is obviously inherent in any right of the seller to resell that the previous contract and the buyer's rights under it must at that point come to an end. Section 48(4) expressly provides for this, but *RV Ward Ltd v Bignall* (below) confirms that the same rule must apply in a resale under s 48(3).

RV Ward Ltd v Bignall
[1967] 1 QB 534, Court of Appeal

On 6 May Bignall contracted to buy from Wards two cars, a Vanguard estate and a Ford Zodiac, for a total price of £850, paying a deposit of £25. Later in the same day, he refused to pay the balance or take delivery of either car. Wards the next day gave notice to him through their solicitors that if he did not complete the purchase by 11 May they would dispose of the cars. The Vanguard was later sold for £350, but the Zodiac remained unsold. In this action Wards sued Bignall, claiming (before the Court of Appeal) the balance of the contract price less the amount received for the Vanguard, together with certain expenses. The court held that by reselling the Vanguard, Wards had rescinded the whole contract, so that their only claim was for damages for non-acceptance, obliging them to bring into account the market value of the unsold Zodiac, which remained their property. The trial judge had calculated the damages at £497 10s, but on appeal this was reduced to £47 10s.

> **Sellers LJ**: The question on this part of the appeal is whether, [on the assumption that] the property passed on the sale, the Zodiac car which has not been [resold] remains the buyer's property so that the action of the plaintiffs is for the price, or whether by the sale of the Vanguard the plaintiffs have rescinded the whole contract on the buyer's breach of it so that the ownership of the Zodiac reverted back to the plaintiffs and their remedy is in damages under the statute, or, in effect, damages for non-acceptance, giving credit for what they have received from the sale of the goods or part thereof.
>
> Subsections (1) and (2) of s 48 speak clearly. Subsection (4) expressly provides: 'the original contract of sale is thereby rescinded.' That was necessary because, where the seller 'expressly reserves a right of re-sale in case the buyer should make default,' a seller who re-sold under such a contract would be applying and affirming the contract, and his action would be consistent with it. Under subs (3) no such provision of rescission is necessary, for, if an unpaid seller re-sells, he puts it out of his power to perform his contract and his action is inconsistent with a subsisting sale to the original buyer. Once there is a re-sale in accordance with s 48 by an unpaid seller in possession of the contractual goods the contract of sale is rescinded, whether the re-sale be of the whole of the goods or of part of them, and in this respect subss (3) and (4) fall into line.

As the property in the goods reverts on such a re-sale, the seller retains the proceeds of sale whether they be greater or less than the contractual price. The probability in normal trade is that the price would be less, giving rise to a claim for damages, as for non-acceptance of the goods . . .

Subsection (4) makes the resale operate as a rescission and leaves the remedy, if any loss ensues, in damages. That brings it into harmony with subs (3), which also gives a claim for damages for any loss occasioned by the original buyer's breach of contract. If the unpaid seller resells the goods, he puts it out of his power to perform his obligation under the original contract, that is, to deliver the contractual goods to the buyer. By the notice to the buyer, the seller makes payment of the price 'of the essence of the contract,' as it is sometimes put. It requires the buyer to pay the price or tender it within a reasonable time.

If he fails to do so, the seller in possession of the goods may treat the bargain as rescinded and resell the goods. The suit for damages becomes comparable to a claim for damages for non-acceptance of the goods where the property never has passed. The property has reverted on the resale, and the second buyer gets a good title. The seller resells as owner. Subsection (2) expressly gives the buyer a good title thereto as against the original buyer.

On this view of the law the plaintiffs cannot recover the price of the Zodiac, which is in the circumstances their property. They can, however, recover any loss which they have sustained by the buyer's default. The parties have sensibly agreed that the value of the Zodiac in May, 1965, was £450. The total contract price was £850, against which the plaintiffs have received £25 in cash and £350 in respect of the Vanguard, and have to give credit for £450 for the Zodiac. To the loss of £25 must be added the sum for advertising, which was admittedly reasonably incurred—£22 10s. The plaintiffs' loss was, therefore, £47 10s.

I would allow the appeal and enter judgment for £47 10s in favour of the plaintiffs in substitution for the award of the deputy judge.

Diplock LJ: Whether or not the property had passed on May 6, 1965, the seller was only liable to deliver upon payment or tender of the balance of the purchase price (see the Sale of Goods Act, s 28) and was entitled until then to retain possession, either by virtue of his lien as an unpaid seller if the property had passed (Sale of Goods Act, s 39(1)), or by virtue of his right to withhold delivery if the property had not passed (subs (2) of the same section). In either case, the unpaid seller has a right to resell the goods if he gives notice of his intention to do so and the buyer does not within a reasonable time pay or tender the price (Sale of Goods Act, s 48(3)) . . . This subsection enables a seller in possession of the goods to make time of payment of the purchase price of the essence of the contract whether the property has passed or not. The seller cannot have greater rights of resale if the property has already passed to the buyer than those which he would have if the property had remained in him.

In this court it has been contended on behalf of the seller that, when an unpaid seller who retains possession of goods the property in which has passed to the buyer exercises his statutory right of resale under s 48(3) of the Sale of Goods Act, he does not thereby elect to treat the contract as rescinded, but remains entitled to recover the purchase price from the buyer although he must give credit for the net proceeds of sale of any of the goods which he has sold. Authority for this proposition is to be found in the judgment of Finnemore J in *Gallagher v Shilcock* [1949] 2 KB 765, and the question in this appeal is whether that judgment is right or not.

Finnemore J based his conclusion on his view as to the construction of s 48 of the Sale of Goods Act, and in particular upon the contrast between the express reference in subs (4) of s 48 to the contract being rescinded when goods are resold under an express right of resale and the absence of any reference to rescission in subs (3) of s 48. With great respect, however, I think that that disregards basic principles of the law of contract, and that there is another explanation for the contrast between the two subsections.

Rescission of a contract discharges both parties from any further liability to perform their respective primary obligations under the contract, that is to say, to do thereafter those things which by their contract they had stipulated they would do. Where rescission occurs as a result of one party exercising his right to treat a breach by the other party of a stipulation in the contract as a repudiation of the contract, this gives rise to a secondary obligation of the party in breach to compensate the other party for the loss occasioned to him as a consequence of the rescission, and this secondary obligation is enforceable in an action for damages. Until, however, there is rescission by acceptance of the repudiation, the liability of both parties to perform their primary obligations under the contract continues. Thus, under a contract for the sale of goods which has not been rescinded, the seller remains liable to transfer the property in the goods to the buyer and to deliver possession of them to him until he has discharged those obligations by performing them, and the buyer remains correspondingly liable to pay for the goods and to accept possession of them.

The election by a party not in default to exercise his right of rescission by treating the contract as repudiated may be evinced by words or by conduct. Any act which puts it out of his power to perform thereafter his primary obligations under the contract, if it is an act which he is entitled to do without notice to the party in default, must amount to an election to rescind the contract. If it is an act which he is not entitled to do, it will amount to a wrongful repudiation of the contract on his part which the other party can in turn elect to treat as rescinding the contract.

Part IV of the Sale of Goods Act, ss 38 to 48, deals with the rights of an unpaid seller both before the property in the goods has passed to the buyer and after it has passed. The mere fact that a seller is unpaid does not necessarily mean that the buyer is in breach of the contract, or, if he is, that his breach is one which entitles the seller to exercise his right to treat the contract as repudiated.

[His Lordship referred to ss 39 and 48, and continued:]

If the contract provided for delivery upon a specified date, the seller's conduct in failing to deliver on that date would put it out of his power to perform one of his primary obligations under the contract if time were of the essence of the contract. It was, therefore, necessary, or at least prudent, to provide expressly that if his failure to deliver were in the mere exercise of a lien or right of stoppage in transitu it did not discharge his liability to deliver the goods upon tender of the contract price, or the buyer's liability to accept the goods and to pay for them.

Subsection (2) deals with a different topic, *videlicet*, the title of a new buyer to whom the goods are resold by the seller. If the property in the goods at the time of the resale remained in the seller, the new buyer would obtain a good title at common law and would require no statutory protection. The subsection is, therefore, limited to cases where the property in the goods at the time of resale had already passed to the original buyer, and provides that, where the seller is in possession of the goods in the exercise of his unpaid seller's lien or right of stoppage in transitu, the new buyer shall acquire a good title, and this is so whether or not the seller had a right of resale as against the original buyer.

Subsection (3) . . . is the provision of the Act which confers 'a right of resale as limited by this Act,' referred to in s 39(1)(c). The right dealt with in this subsection is a right as against the original buyer. As a stipulation as to time of payment is not deemed to be of the essence of a contract of sale unless a different intention appears from the terms of the contract (Sale of Goods Act, s 10(1)), failure by the buyer to pay on the stipulated date is not conduct by him which entitles the unpaid seller to treat the contract as repudiated. He remains liable to deliver the goods to the buyer upon tender of the contract price (Sale of Goods Act, s 28). Apart from this subsection, if the unpaid seller resold the goods before or after the property had passed to the original buyer, he would remain liable to the original buyer for damages for non-delivery if the original buyer tendered the purchase price after the resale, and if the property had already passed to the original buyer at the time of the resale he would be liable to an alternative action by the original buyer for damages for conversion. The purpose of the subsection is to make time of payment of the essence of the contract whenever the goods are of a perishable nature, and to enable an unpaid seller, whatever the nature of the goods, to make payment within a reasonable time after notice of the essence of the contract. As already pointed out, an unpaid seller who resells the goods before the property has passed puts it out of his power to perform his primary obligation to the buyer to transfer the property in the goods to the buyer and, whether or not the property has already passed, to deliver up possession of the goods to the buyer. By making the act of resale one which the unpaid seller is entitled to perform, the subsection empowers the seller by his conduct in doing that act to exercise his right to treat the contract as repudiated by the buyer, that is, as rescinded, with the consequence that the buyer is discharged from any further liability to perform his primary obligation to pay the purchase price, and becomes subject to the secondary obligation to pay damages for non-acceptance of the goods. If the contract were not rescinded by the resale the seller would still be entitled to bring an action against the buyer for the price of the goods although, no doubt, he would have to credit the buyer with the proceeds of the resale. If that were the intention of the subsection one would have expected it to provide this in express terms. That it was not the intention is, however, apparent from the words used to define the remedy of the unpaid seller who has exercised his right of resale, videlicet, to 'recover from the original buyer damages for any loss occasioned by his breach of contract.' It is, of course, well-established that where a contract for the sale of goods is rescinded after the property in the goods has passed to the buyer the rescission divests the buyer of his property in the goods.

Subsection (4) deals with the consequences of a resale by a seller, not necessarily an 'unpaid seller' as defined in s 38, made in the exercise of an express right of resale reserved in the contract on the buyer making default. If such an express right were exercisable after the property in the goods had passed to the buyer, its exercise might, on one view, be regarded as an alternative mode of performance of the seller's primary obligations under the contract, and the resale as being made by the seller as agent for the buyer. It was, therefore, necessary to provide expressly that the exercise of an express power of resale should rescind the original contract of sale. That is, in my view, the explanation of the express reference to rescission in subs (4). The absence of a similar express reference to rescission in subs (3) is no sufficient ground for ascribing to subs (3) a meaning which the actual words of the subsection would appear to contradict and which would, in my view, conflict with the general principles of the law of contract.

In the present case the unpaid seller only resold part of the goods which he had contracted to sell to the original buyer. This makes no difference, however. His primary duty under the contract was to deliver both cars to the buyer. If he delivered only one, the buyer would be entitled to reject it (Sale of Goods Act, s 30(1)). By his conduct in selling the Vanguard on May 24, 1965, the unpaid seller put it out of his power to perform his primary obligation under the contract. He thereby elected to treat the contract as rescinded. The property in the Zodiac thereupon reverted to him, and his only remedy against the buyer after May 24, 1965, was for damages for non-acceptance of the two cars, of which the prima facie measure is the difference between the contract price and their market value on May 24, 1965.

I, too, would allow this appeal, and enter judgment for the plaintiffs for £47 10s instead of £497 10s.

[**Russell LJ** concurred.]

NOTES

1. The word 'rescind' is used in varying senses in different textbooks on the law of contract. In s 48 and the judgments in *Ward v Bignall* the word 'rescind' is used as equivalent to 'terminate for breach', so far as the *contractual* position is concerned, and hence the buyer remains liable in damages to the seller for his previous non-acceptance. But 'rescind' is preferred to 'terminate' because the focus is on the destination of the *property* in the goods. It is made clear that, when a seller validly exercises a right of resale, there is a 'rescission' in the sense that the property is re-vested in him before passing to the new buyer. It follows that if the resale is made for a higher price, the seller may keep it all (*Commission Car Sales (Hastings) Ltd v Saul* [1957] NZLR 144).

2. We may infer from the judgments in this case the following additional points.

(a) A resale of *part* of the goods operates to rescind the whole contract.

(b) An unpaid seller's right of resale is said to be 'as limited by this Act' (s 39(1)(c)). But this should not be taken to mean that the right of resale is limited to those cases where he has exercised his right of lien or stoppage in transit. There could, for instance, be a right of resale reserved by the terms of the contract of sale in specified events, as in some of the *Romalpa* cases (see below, p 497). Alternatively, the buyer could be in breach of his obligation to pay the price on the agreed date, in a case where time has been made of the essence of the contract. Section 48 does not have the effect of excluding or restricting any right of resale which the seller may have at common law.

(c) Section 48(4) applies whether the seller is an unpaid seller or not (eg it would apply to a term in a contract whereby a seller could resell goods which a buyer paid for but then failed to collect by a given date).

(e) Effect of resale by an unpaid seller

Sections 48(3) and 48(4) deal with the question when a seller acts rightfully in reselling; in other words, whether he escapes liability in damages to the first buyer. Section 48(2) deals with a different question: namely, if an unpaid seller resells, does he pass good title to the new buyer even if title had earlier passed to the previous buyer? The section gives the answer Yes: it states that where an unpaid seller who has exercised his right of lien or retention or stoppage in transit resells the goods, the second buyer acquires a good title to them as against the original buyer. This seems to apply even where the resale is otherwise wrongful and makes the seller liable to the original buyer: for example, where the seller exercises a right of lien over non-perishable goods and then resells them *without* first giving notice to the buyer.

There is a degree of overlap between this provision and s 24 (sale by seller in possession, above, p 407), and in some cases a sale by an unpaid seller will pass title under either. But there are important differences. Most significantly, s 24 only applies to a buyer in good faith: that is, a buyer who does not know of the interest of the previous buyer. There is no such requirement under s 48, for the obvious reason that an unpaid seller must be able to dispose of the goods even where the buyer knows the full facts. Secondly, under s 48 there is no need for delivery: a mere agreement to pass title to the new buyer suffices. Other minor differences include the facts that: (1) s 48(2), unlike s 24, applies only where an unpaid seller 'has exercised his right of lien or retention or stoppage in transit'; and (2) s 24 operates for the benefit not only of a sub-buyer, but also someone who takes under a pledge or other disposition of the goods, while s 48 applies only to a resale.

NOTE

In the opinion of Lord Diplock in *Ward v Bignall*, s 48(2) applies—and is needed—only where the property in the goods has passed to the buyer. Where a seller who has *retained* the property resells the goods, he can confer a good title on the second buyer by virtue of his ownership, and there is no need to invoke s 48(2). The seller may, however, still be liable to the first buyer for breach of contract. Since s 24 also speaks only of a person who has *sold* goods, we may infer that a person who has retained title to the goods (ie only agreed to sell them) can confer a good title on a second purchaser by virtue of his ownership and does not need to invoke the provisions of that section.

QUESTION

S agrees to sell to B1 goods currently stored in W's warehouse. S retains the property in the goods but gives B1 a delivery order addressed to W. Not having been paid by B1, S resells the goods to B2, telling him that he has been let down by a previous buyer, B1. S gives B2 a delivery order. The following day, B1 contracts to sell the goods to X, and endorses his delivery order over to X. Who is entitled to the goods: (1) before any delivery order is presented to W; (2) if B2 presents his delivery order to W before X; (3) if X presents his delivery order to W before B2?

6 RETENTION OF TITLE CLAUSES

(a) What is a retention of title clause?

Since the passing of title under a contract for the sale of goods depends on the terms of the contract (s 17), it is axiomatic that a clause in a contract of sale may stipulate that the seller retains title to the goods until a stated event has happened, and in particular until he has been paid the price. Further, this may be done even though possession of the goods is given to the buyer: see ss 2(3) and 19(3).

The term 'retention of title clause' has, however, come to have a special connotation. Very large numbers of sellers include as part of their standard terms a clause postponing the passing of title until payment of the price, but use them in tandem with further provisions of some complexity. These typically deal with such matters as the buyer's duty to store the goods separately and distinguishably from its own; a limited licence given to the buyer to use or consume the goods in the ordinary course of its business; provisions allowing the buyer to resell the goods only as the seller's agent and/or trustee; terms about keeping any proceeds of such sales separate from the buyer's own funds; and so on.

The object of contracts of this sort is essentially to create a security interest over the goods sold, rather like a mortgage or charge, to secure the seller's claim to the price. Thus if the buyer becomes insolvent, the seller hopes to be able to lay claim not only to the goods themselves (if the buyer still has them), but also to any cash proceeds, any claims against sub-buyers for the price if they have been resold, and possibly anything made out of them. The seller may also have in mind claiming the original goods in the hands of third party purchasers.

Security interests in general are dealt with in Chapter 24 below. However, in English practice retention of title clauses are formally part of sale of goods law, and for that reason are dealt with in this chapter. In other jurisdictions, it should be noted, a more functional (and perhaps logical) approach is followed. In the United States, for example, the law relating to security interests applies to 'a transaction, *regardless of its form*, that creates a security interest in personal property or fixtures by contract' (see Uniform Commercial Code, Art 9–109(a)(1)). Again, in Australia s 12 of the Personal Property Securities Act 2009 (Cth) defines a security interest as 'an interest in personal property provided for by a transaction that, *in substance*, secures payment or performance of an obligation (without regard to the form of the transaction or the identity of the person who has title to the property)' and goes on to say expressly that it includes 'a conditional sale agreement (*including an agreement to sell subject to retention of title*)'. See generally RM Goode, *Commercial Law in the Next Millennium* (1998), Ch 3.

Retention of title clauses are commonly called '*Romalpa* clauses' after the case below, in which they first came to the attention of the English courts.

Aluminium Industrie Vaassen BV v Romalpa Aluminium Ltd

[1976] 1 WLR 676, Queen's Bench Division and Court of Appeal

AIV, a Dutch company, supplied aluminium foil to Romalpa in England on AIV's standard terms of trading, parts of which are quoted in the judgment of Mocatta J. Romalpa went into receivership owing AIV £122,239. The receiver had in his possession unprocessed aluminium foil worth £50,000 and £35,152 representing the proceeds of sub-sales of foil which had been made by Romalpa. It was held: (1) that AIV's claim to the unprocessed foil prevailed over that of the receiver, because AIV had effectively retained title to it; and (2) that AIV was entitled to the money representing the proceeds of sub-sales on the basis of the doctrine of equitable tracing established in *Re Hallett's Estate* (1880) 13 Ch D 696, CA.

> **Mocatta J**: [His Lordship referred to the clause and continued] The first sentence of the clause reads as follows:
>
> > The ownership of the material to be delivered by AIV (that is the plaintiffs) will only be transferred to purchaser when he has met all that is owing to AIV, no matter on what grounds.
>
> I read the remainder of the clause in view of its somewhat elaborate nature and of subsequent issues arising:
>
> > Until the date of payment, purchaser, if AIV so desires, is required to store this material in such a way that it is clearly the property of AIV. AIV and purchaser agree that, if purchaser should make (a) new object(s) from the material, mix this material with (an)other object(s) or if this material in any way whatsoever becomes a constituent of (an)other object(s) AIV will be given the ownership of this (these) new object(s) as surety of the full payment of what purchaser owes AIV. To this end AIV and purchaser now agree that the ownership of the article(s) in question, whether finished or not, are to be transferred to AIV and that this transfer of ownership will be considered to have taken place through and at the moment of the single operation or event by which the material is converted into (a) new object(s), or is mixed with or becomes a constituent (an)other object(s). Until the moment of full payment of what purchaser owes AIV purchaser shall keep the object(s) in question for AIV in his capacity of fiduciary owner and, if required, shall store this (these) object(s) in such a way that it (they) can be recognized as such. Nevertheless, purchaser will be entitled to sell these objects to a third party within the framework of the normal carrying on of his business and to deliver them on condition that—if

AIV so requires—purchaser, as long as he has not fully discharged his debt to AIV shall hand over to AIV the claims he has against the buyer emanating from this transaction.

[His Lordship decided that the clause applied to the course of dealing between the parties, and that AIV's claims succeeded. The defendants appealed.]

Roskill LJ: . . . Are the plaintiffs entitled to the proceeds of sales to sub-purchasers now held by the receiver? We were told both by Mr Price and by Mr Lincoln that the receiver received these moneys after he had entered into his receivership from sales made by the defendants to sub-purchasers before that date. The receiver, properly if I may say so, kept those moneys separate; as we were told that there is no complication arising of those moneys having become mixed with other moneys, because they were always kept separate. There was no suggestion that the sub-sales in question were other than authorised by the plaintiffs or that the sub-purchasers concerned did not acquire a valid title to the several quantities of foil which each of them bought. The sole question is whether, on the facts and on the true construction of the bargain, including the general conditions, between the plaintiffs and the defendants, the plaintiffs are entitled to trace and recover those proceeds of the sub-sales, upon the well-known principles laid down in the judgment of Sir George Jessel MR in *Re Hallett's Estate*. . . .

The critical question is whether there was a fiduciary relationship between the plaintiffs and the defendants which entitles the plaintiffs successfully to claim these moneys in the way and upon the footing which I have just described. Mr Price strenuously argued that the bargain between the parties was a perfectly ordinary bargain, creating the ordinary contractual relationship of seller and buyer, with the consequence that if the buyers—that is to say the defendants—became insolvent before payment for the goods was made by them to the sellers,—that is, the plaintiffs—the sellers were left with their ordinary contractual or, as he put it, personal remedy as unsecured creditors of the buyers, and that there was no additional proprietary remedy (again to borrow his language) available to them justifying their seeking to trace and recover the proceeds of the sub-sales which had come from the sub-purchasers into the hands of the receiver.

It seems to me clear that, but for the provisions of clause 13—which have to be read in conjunction with the other relevant clauses I have mentioned—this would be the position. The individual contracts were for delivery ex the plaintiffs' works in Holland, and, apart from special provisions, in English law at least—as already stated, there is no evidence of Dutch law and therefore we must apply English law to these contracts—both property and risk would have passed to the defendants upon such delivery.

But clause 13 plainly provides otherwise. The defendants as sellers were to retain the property in the goods until all—and I underline 'all'—that was owing to them had been paid. . . . It is obvious, to my mind, that the business purpose of the whole of this clause, read in its context in the general conditions, was to secure the plaintiffs, so far as possible, against the risks of non-payment after they had parted with possession of the goods delivered, whether or not those goods retained their identity after delivery. I unhesitatingly accept that part of Mr Lincoln's submission. In the case of unmanufactured goods this was to be achieved by the plaintiffs retaining the property until all payments due had been made, to which were added the special rights given by clause 25. In the case of mixed or manufactured goods, more elaborate provisions were made and indeed were obviously required if the avowed object of clause 13 were to be achieved in the case of the latter class of goods. The plaintiffs were to be given the ownership of these mixed or manufactured goods as 'surety' for 'full payment.' 'Surety' I think in this context must mean, as Mr Lincoln contended yesterday, 'security.' This is as between the defendants and the plaintiffs, and it is not necessary to consider how far this provision would protect the plaintiffs against adverse claims, at any rate in this country, by third parties. Further, the clause later provides that until 'full payment' is made the defendants shall keep the mixed goods for the plaintiffs as 'fiduciary owners'—not perhaps the happiest of phrases but one which suggests, at least to an English lawyer, that in relation to mixed or manufactured goods there was produced what in English law would be called a fiduciary relationship in this respect. The clause goes on to give to the defendants an express power of sale of such goods, and the right to deliver them; and adds an obligation upon the defendants, if required by the plaintiffs so to do, to assign (to use English legal language) to the plaintiffs the benefit of any claim against a sub-purchaser so long as the defendants have not fully discharged all their indebtedness to the plaintiffs . . .

The burden of Mr Lincoln's argument was, first, that all goods dealt with in pursuance of clause 13 were, until all debts were discharged, the plaintiffs' goods which the defendants were authorised to sell on the plaintiffs' behalf and for the plaintiffs' account but only within the framework of clause 13. Since the goods were the plaintiffs', the defendants remained accountable to the plaintiffs for them or for their proceeds of sale, so long as any indebtedness whatever remained outstanding from the defendants to the plaintiffs. Hence the creation of the fiduciary relationship upon which Mr Lincoln sought to rely. The burden of Mr Price's argument was, as already stated, that the clause created in the first part no more than the ordinary debtor/creditor, buyer/seller, relationship, and that nothing in the second part justified placing additional fiduciary obligations upon the defendants in respect of unmanufactured goods, referred to in the first part of the clause.

[His Lordship held that clause 13 impliedly authorised Romalpa to sell the unmanufactured, as well as the manufactured, goods, on terms that they were accountable to AIV for the proceeds of sale. He continued:]

I see no difficulty in the contractual concept that, as between the defendants and their sub-purchasers, the defendants sold as principals, but that, as between themselves and the plaintiffs, those goods which they were selling as principals within their implied authority from the plaintiffs were the plaintiffs' goods which they were selling as agents for the plaintiffs to whom they remained fully accountable. If an agent lawfully sells his principal's goods, he stands in a fiduciary relationship to his principal and remains accountable to his principal for those goods and their proceeds. A bailee is in like position in relation to his bailor's goods. What, then, is there here to relieve the defendants from their obligation to account to the plaintiffs for those goods of the plaintiffs which they lawfully sell to sub-purchasers? The fact that they so sold them as principals does not, as I think, affect their relationship with the plaintiffs; nor (as at present advised) do I think—contrary to Mr Price's argument—that the sub-purchasers could on this analysis have sued the plaintiffs upon the sub-contracts as undisclosed principals for, say, breach of warranty of quality.

It seems to me clear . . . that to give effect to what I regard as the obvious purpose of clause 13 one must imply into the first part of the clause not only the power to sell but also the obligation to account in accordance with the normal fiduciary relationship of principal and agent, bailor and bailee. Accordingly, like the judge I find no difficulty in holding that the principles in *Hallett's* case are of immediate application, and I think that the plaintiffs are entitled to trace these proceeds of sale and to recover them, as Mocatta J has held by his judgment.

It is ironic that the starting point for this major modern commercial development was not a high-powered collaboration between the best brains in the City and the Temple, but a rather poor translation into English of a document drafted by a Dutch lawyer! It is perhaps also significant, with hindsight, that this seminal case came before a commercial court in which some key issues of an equitable nature were not argued. The same cannot be said of the second leading case in the series, *Re Bond Worth Ltd* (below), where the hearing lasted for 15 full days and over 90 authorities were cited in argument.

(b) The commercial and legal background

It is necessary to understand something of the way in which companies normally finance their operations. Most companies depend upon borrowing to maintain their cash-flow. When a company borrows, and more particularly when it borrows on overdraft from a bank, it is usually required to give security in the form of a general *floating charge* to the bank. Such a charge (explained more fully below, p 1070) allows the company to carry on its business without interference from the bank, unless and until it defaults; but if it does default (eg if its overdraft is run up beyond the agreed limit), the bank can take control of all of the company's assets by appointing a receiver—an insolvency practitioner whose role it is to enforce the bank's security—or an administrator (see below, Chapter 28). In the context of goods sold under retention of title to an insolvent company, the contest is in practice nearly always between the seller and a bank holding a general floating charge over the company's assets.

But for two factors mentioned below—Part 25 of the Companies Act 2006 and the terms of the floating charge—there is no difficulty over a seller retaining title to the goods or any proceeds of them by a suitably explicit clause. As regards the goods themselves, we have already said that s 17 of the Sale of Goods Act gives parties carte blanche to delay passing of title as long as they wish. As regards proceeds of the goods, these may be manufactured proceeds (eg carpets made out of fibre), money proceeds (money paid by third party buyers standing to the company's credit), or debt proceeds (debts owing by third parties who have bought the goods from the company on credit in a bank account). Although the seller cannot claim *legal title* to any of these, an explicit agreement by the buyer to create security over an asset of this sort in favour of the seller for good consideration will automatically create an *equitable charge* over it (ie a proprietary right created by a debtor in favour of another person empowering the latter to look to specified property of the debtor for satisfaction of the debt). This charge, arising out of the maxim that equity regards as done that which ought to be done, will be immediately effective if the asset is already in the hands of the buyer; and as regards future assets of the buyer, will attach to them as and when they come into its hands. (See *Holroyd v Marshall* (1862) 10 HLC 191, *Tailby v Official Receiver* (1888) 13 App Cas 523, and RM Goode, *Commercial Law* (5th edn, 2016), Ch 26. This matter is discussed at greater length below at p 1068.)

Companies Act 2006, Part 25   So far so good. However, the first factor that causes difficulty here arises from Part 25 of the Companies Act 2006, stating that a charge created by a UK company over any of its assets is ineffective in insolvency unless registered (s 859H). Since registration of every retention of title sale at the Companies Registry is neither practicable nor cost-effective, it follows that insofar as a retention of title clause entails the buyer company creating a charge over its assets, it is ineffective (an example being *Re Bond Worth*, below). When will this be so? The important wording is that of s 859A, referring to the case where a company 'creates a charge'. This implies a disposition by the company of a property interest; conversely, it excludes the case where the company never had any interest in the asset to start with. Hence where, under a contract of sale of goods, the seller uses s 17 of the Sale of Goods Act to reserve to itself the entire legal property in the goods until the price is paid, there is no charge *created* by the buyer, since it has never owned the property concerned at all (see *Clough Mill Ltd v Martin* [1985] 1 WLR 111 and *Re Highway Foods International Ltd* [1995] 1 BCLC 209). However, it was held in *Re Bond Worth* that a purported transfer of legal title to goods coupled with reservation of an equitable interest amounts to a transfer of the entire interest followed by a regrant of the equitable interest, and thus to a charge created by the buyer. Similarly, an agreement aimed at giving rise to a charge over any *other* property, such as cash or debt proceeds, will generally amount to a charge created by the buyer. And the same goes for an agreement concerning manufactured proceeds of goods sold, since as a matter of law most manufacture involves not the reappearance of ingredients in a new form, but the disappearance of the original raw materials and the emergence of an entirely new thing (*Borden v STP*, below). Had an argument along these lines been fully explored in the *Romalpa* case itself, the outcome (at least as regards the proceeds of sale of the foil) might well have been different.

How, then, can a seller ever claim a valid interest over the proceeds of goods sold? The clue comes in the doctrine of tracing embodied in *Re Hallett's Estate* (1880) 13 Ch D 696, mentioned in the *Romalpa* case. Under this doctrine, where a trustee or fiduciary entrusted with an asset obtains property in exchange for it, that property belongs to the beneficiary as a matter of law and not by virtue of any grant by the fiduciary (see *Tatung (UK) Ltd v Galex Telesure Ltd* (1989) 5 BCC 325 at 334, per Phillips J and *Clough Mill Ltd v Martin* [1985] 1 WLR 111 at 119, per Robert Goff LJ). It follows that insofar as the seller can show that the buyer held the goods as its trustee or fiduciary, it may be able to show an equitable interest in any proceeds that is not caught by Part 25 of the 2006 Act. Provisions aimed at doing this include: (1) terms requiring the buyer to keep the goods separate from other goods, perhaps also stipulating that he shall hold the goods as bailee for the seller; (2) terms seeking to confer upon the seller proprietary rights in relation to the proceeds of any sale of the goods, including terms which require the buyer to sell such goods as the seller's agent, to keep such proceeds separate from other monies, to hold them on a fiduciary basis, to pay them into a special account, etc; and (3) similar provisions with relation to goods which may be manufactured by B and which incorporate the goods which S has sold.

It should be noted that the above discussion affects only UK-registered companies. Since 2013, charges created by companies registered abroad, including in other EU states, are not affected by Part 25 of the Companies Act 2006. It follows that, subject to what is said below about the terms of any floating charge, retention of title clauses can be enforced against foreign-registered companies according to their terms over both goods and any proceeds.

Terms of a floating charge Apart from Part 25 of the Companies Act 2006, where the buyer is a company which has already given a floating charge over all of its assets, present and future, to its bank, that charge will almost always include a term (a 'negative pledge clause') which prohibits the company from creating any other charge ranking ahead of that of the bank. If the seller has actual or constructive notice of this term (which under the rules of company law and current practice he probably has, since the presence of a 'negative pledge' clause is a particular that will appear on the register), any attempt on his part to create a prior charge in his own favour is likely to be doomed to fail. And so he will avoid at all costs making any concession that the contract of sale involves a charge.

It follows from the above that in any reservation of title case, two issues arise. First, what is the interpretation of the clause, and what interest, if any, does it create in the goods or their proceeds? Secondly, does the clause amount to a charge created by the buyer (assuming the buyer is a UK company)?

(c) The application of the law to retention of title clauses

The first case cited below illustrates the issues concerned with the interpretation of the clause.

Re Peachdart Ltd

[1984] Ch 131, Chancery Division

Leather was supplied by Freudenbergs to Peachdart to be made into handbags, on terms that until payment of the price the sellers retained ownership in the leather and the right to trace their interest into any proceeds of sale of the leather or of goods made out of it, by virtue of a fiduciary relationship created between the buyer and sellers. Vinelott J held, however, that the sellers' interest was lost once the leather had been appropriated in the handbag-making process.

Vinelott J: Turning to the partly or wholly manufactured handbags and the proceeds of sale of those sold before the receiver was appointed, Mr Littman's submission was shortly as follows. It was said that under the terms of the bailment of each parcel of leather supplied by Freudenbergs pending payment in full of the price for that parcel the company as bailee was entitled to use the leather in the manufacture of handbags, a process which involved cutting and shaping and sewing a piece of leather and attaching to it hinges, handles, clasps and the like, in the course of which the piece of leather would remain identifiable throughout. The thread and attachments which were, it was said (and I do not think it is disputed) of comparatively minor value, then became the property of Freudenbergs as accessories to the leather. Thus the company remained a bailee of the hand-bags throughout the process of manufacture, and when the company sold the handbag it sold it (as in *Romalpa*) as agent for Freudenbergs, and was accordingly accountable to Freudenbergs as owner for the entire proceeds of sale. Freudenbergs was not entitled to a mere charge. Mr Littman instanced as an analogy a sportsman who having shot a rare animal takes the skin to a leather worker and instructs him to make it into a game bag. There the property in the skin would remain with the sportsman notwithstanding that the skin would undergo many operations and would have thread and other material added to it. He distinguished the *Borden* case on the ground that in that case the resin was inevitably consumed and destroyed as a separate substance when used in the manufacture of chipboard. The title retention clause accordingly did not purport to vest the property in the chipboard in the vendor, and if it had done so the vesting could only have been by way of equitable transfer of something not in existence when the resin was sold.

To my mind it is impossible to suppose that in the instant case, even assuming in Freudenbergs' favour that the company became a bailee of the leather when it was first delivered to it, the parties intended that until a parcel of leather had been fully paid for the company would remain a bailee of each piece of leather comprised in the parcel throughout the whole process of manufacture, that Freudenbergs should have the right until the parcel had been fully paid for, to enter the company's premises and identify and take away any partly or completely manufactured handbag derived from it, and that on the sale of a completed handbag the company would be under an obligation to pay the proceeds of sale into a separate interest bearing account and to keep them apart from their other moneys and not employ them in the trade.

It may be that, as Mr Littman asserts, an expert in the leather trade could identify each handbag whether partly or completely manufactured as made from a skin comprised in a particular parcel of leather. But after a handbag had been sold it would be impossible to do so. There is nothing in the conditions of sale which requires the company to keep a record of handbags sold so as to identify those of which it was a bailee and agent of Freudenbergs. No such records were in fact kept and there is nothing in the evidence which suggests that the parties contemplated that they would be. Indeed on the facts of this case it would be impossible for Freudenbergs now to prove that the handbags sold by the company but not paid for when the receiver was appointed were in fact made out of leather comprised in any of the parcels to which the unpaid invoices relied on by Freudenbergs relate. It seems to me that the parties must have intended that at least after a piece of leather had been appropriated to be manufactured into a handbag and work had started on it (when the leather would cease to have any significant value as raw material) the leather would cease to be the exclusive property of Freudenbergs (whether as bailor or as unpaid vendor) and that Freudenbergs would thereafter have a charge on handbags in the course of manufacture and on the distinctive products which would come into existence at the end of the process of manufacture (the value of which would be derived for the most part from Mr Launer's reputation and skill in design and the skill in his workforce). The charge would in due course shift to the proceeds of sale. That I accept does some violence to the language of clause 11(b) in so far as that clause provides that, 'The property in the whole or such other goods shall be *and remain* with the seller' (my emphasis). I do not think that those words compel the conclusion that the company was to be a mere bailee throughout the whole process of manufacture until the purchase price of the relevant parcel had been paid, and that on a sale before that time it would be no more than an agent for Freudenbergs. The language is, I think, consistent with the view that once the process of manufacture had started so that in the course of manufacture work and materials provided by the company would result in the leather being converted into (that is incorporated in or used as material for) other goods of a distinctive character the property in those other goods would vest in Freudenbergs only as security for any outstanding balance of the price of the relevant parcel of leather. What the draftsman has done is to elide and I think confuse two quite different relationships, that of bailor and bailee, with a superimposed contract of sale (or of vendor and purchaser) on the one hand and that of chargor and chargee on the other hand.

Mr Littman conceded, and I think he must concede, that if Freudenbergs had no more than a charge on the partly completed and completed handbags the charge was void for non-registration. It was also void as regards the book debts against the bank, which under the debenture had a prior fixed charge. . . .

NOTES

1. NE Palmer, *Bailment* (3rd edn, 2009), para 3–066 suggests that Vinelott J perhaps too readily (given the clear wording of the contract) rejected the argument that the leather would remain the sellers' property after it had been made into handbags. Unlike the resin in the *Borden* case (below, p 508), which ceased to exist at all, the leather here was still the dominant constituent in the end-product. However, in the more recent case of *Modelboard Ltd v Outer Box Ltd* [1993] BCLC 623, it was held that cardboard which had been made into cardboard boxes had ceased to be 'the goods' (ie the cardboard) which had been the subject of the original sale, and so it is not likely that this argument would have prevailed. (The *result* in *Peachdart* can, however, be justified on other grounds, for there was no provision in the contract requiring either that the handbags made from Freudenberg's leather should be kept separate from other handbags or that the proceeds of sale of such handbags should similarly be kept separate.)

2. In *Re Andrabell Ltd* [1984] 3 All ER 407 Airborne supplied travel bags to Andrabell, a retailer, on terms that ownership should not pass to Andrabell until it had paid Airborne the 'total purchase price'. When Andrabell went into liquidation, Airborne claimed to be entitled to certain bags which were in its possession and to monies, allegedly representing the proceeds of sale of bags, which Airborne had paid into its general bank account. In view of the following facts, Peter Gibson J held that no fiduciary relationship had been created, since: (a) the passing of the property in the bags was postponed only until full payment was made for the particular consignment, rather than Andrabell's total indebtedness; (b) there was no provision requiring the bags to be stored separately; (c) there was no express acknowledgement of a fiduciary relationship, and no provision that Airborne should have the benefit of the sub-sales; (d) Andrabell was not constituted Airborne's agent to resell; (e) there was no obligation to keep the proceeds of sale separate from other moneys; and (f) the contracts provided for a 45-day period of credit, during which time Andrabell was free to use the proceeds of any sub-sales in any way that it liked. In the absence of a fiduciary relationship, he said, the parties had to be treated simply as creditor and debtor, and there was no duty to account. Nor could Airborne claim any of the bags.

3.   In *Chaigley Farms Ltd v Crawford, Kaye & Grayshire Ltd* [1996] BCC 957 it was held that livestock which had been delivered by a farmer to an abattoir for slaughter on terms that they should remain the farmer's property until paid for lost their identity as the contract 'goods' when the living animals became carcasses of meat. The case was decided simply on this point: there was no difficulty in identifying the carcasses as those to which the contract related. The judge conceded that he was probably not giving effect to the intention of the parties, but said that there was 'an inescapable difference between a live animal and a dead one, particularly a dead one minus hide or skin, offal, etc not sold on as butcher's meat'. This may be contrasted with a New Zealand decision where the opposite conclusion was reached at first instance on similar facts: *Re Weddell New Zealand Ltd* (1996) 5 NZBLC 104,055. (On appeal, however, the decision was reversed on other grounds: see [1997] 2 NZLR 455.) In another New Zealand decision, *Pongakawa Sawmill Ltd v New Zealand Forest Products Ltd* [1992] 3 NZLR 304, logs sold to a sawmilling company were held not to have lost their identity and to have remained the seller's property even after they had been sawn into timber.

QUESTION

Assuming that all the bags in Andrabell's possession were identifiable as having been supplied by Airborne, why did the claim for return of the bags fail? Could Airborne have succeeded if the contract had been differently worded?

The next cases raise in various forms the issue of whether a retention of title clause gives rise to a registrable charge.

Re Bond Worth Ltd
[1980] Ch 228, Chancery Division

'Acrilan' artificial fibre was supplied by Monsanto to Bond Worth for use in the manufacture of carpets. The contract of sale provided that 'equitable and beneficial ownership' of the Acrilan should remain in the sellers until the price had been paid, or until prior resale, in which case Monsanto's beneficial ownership was to attach to the proceeds of the resale. It was also stipulated that Monsanto should have the equitable and beneficial ownership in any products made out of the fibre. Slade J held that these provisions were consistent only with the creation of a floating charge, and that the transaction was void for non-registration as a charge under the Companies Act.

Slade J: I turn to consider the relevant contracts. In my judgment at least the following points are fairly clear:

(1) They were absolute contracts for the sale of goods within the meaning of s 1(2) of the Sale of Goods Act 1893, though this is not to say that they did not comprise other features in addition.

(2) The legal title or property in the Acrilan fibre comprised in any one of the contracts passed to Bond Worth when the fibre was delivered to Bond Worth: see s 18, rule 1 of the Sale of Goods Act 1893. In using the term 'property' in this context I refer to the general property in the goods (which is the definition given to the word in s 62(1) of that Act) and not merely a special property, such as that possessed by a bailee.

(3) The risk in the goods likewise passed to Bond Worth on delivery. This followed not only from s 20 of the Sale of Goods Act 1893, but also from the opening words of sub-clause (a) of the retention of title clause. Thus if, after delivery, the goods had been stolen or destroyed before Bond Worth had had the opportunity to use them in any way, Bond Worth would nevertheless have had to pay the full purchase price for them.

(4) Though sub-clause (a) of the retention of title clause provided that 'equitable and beneficial ownership' in the goods would remain with Monsanto until full payment for the whole amount of the relevant order had been received or until prior resale, it was manifestly not the intention to confer on or reserve to Monsanto all the rights which would normally be enjoyed by a *sui juris* person, having the sole beneficial title to property, as against the trustee holding the legal title. Mr Sears, on behalf of Monsanto, expressly conceded and affirmed that Monsanto would not, by virtue of its so called 'equitable and beneficial ownership,' have had the right to call for re-delivery of the goods, at any rate so long as Bond Worth was not in default under its payments. Bond Worth, on the other hand, was to have far-reaching rights even before payment to deal with the goods, which would not normally be possessed by a trustee holding the legal title therein on behalf of one sole, sui juris beneficiary.

(5) Even during the period before full payment had been received by Monsanto and notwithstanding the provisions relating to 'equitable and beneficial ownership,' Bond Worth were to be at liberty to sell all or any part of the goods and to transfer the property therein to a purchaser. The words 'until prior resale,' in sub-clause (a) of the retention of title clause, render the implication of such authority to resell inevitable. They go far beyond the provisions of s 25(1) of the Sale of Goods Act 1893 which empower a buyer of goods in possession after sale in some circumstances, even without the authority of his vendor, to resell and pass a good title to a purchaser on a resale, but confer no authority on him to effect such resale, as between him and his vendor.

(6) The parties nevertheless intended that if Bond Worth were to resell all or any part of the goods at a time when Monsanto had not yet been paid the full price due under the order, Monsanto's 'equitable and beneficial ownership,' whatever that meant, would attach to the proceeds of sale or to the claim for such proceeds.

(7) Even during the period before full payment had been received by Monsanto and notwithstanding the provisions relating to 'equitable and beneficial ownership,' Bond Worth were to be at liberty to use the goods for the purposes of manufacture. . . .

(8) The parties nevertheless intended that if, by virtue of such last-mentioned use, the goods should become constituents of or be converted into other products, the retention of title clause should attach to such other products as if they had been the original subject matter of the sale . . .

Thus far, the position would seem to me reasonably clear. The real difficulty arises concerning the meaning and legal effect, if any, of the provisions in the retention of title clause concerning 'equitable and beneficial ownership.' If the contracts embody something more than a mere sale, what is this additional feature? What is the nature of the relationship beyond a mere vendor-purchaser relationship between Monsanto and Bond Worth that comes into existence by virtue of the provisions relating to 'equitable and beneficial ownership'?

In *Aluminium Industrie Vaassen BV v Romalpa Aluminium Ltd* [above, p 498], to which I shall have to refer in greater detail later, it was expressly admitted that the retention of title clause had the effect of making the defendants bailees of the relevant goods while in their possession until all money owing had been paid, . . . On the different facts of the present case, however, there can be no question of a bailor-bailee relationship, since it is common ground that the property in the Acrilan fibre passed to Bond Worth at latest when it was delivered, while it is of the essence of a bailment that the general property in the goods concerned remains in the bailor, while only a special property passes to the bailee, which entitles him to exercise certain possessory remedies. Nor can the relationship be one of agency, since the documents contain no suggestion that Bond Worth is to be regarded as an agent and the rights which by necessary implication are given to it deal with the goods on its own behalf are quite inconsistent with a principal-agent relationship.

In these circumstances, I think it plain that, if the retention of title clause operated to create any effective rights at all for the benefit of Monsanto, such rights can only have been rights either (i) by way of a trust under which Monsanto was the sole beneficiary or (ii) by way of a trust under which Monsanto had a charge in equity over the relevant assets to secure payment of the unpaid purchase price. No possible third alternative has occurred to me.

[His Lordship examined the authorities, and continued:]

The implicit authority and freedom of Bond Worth to employ the relevant raw materials, products and other moneys as it pleased and for its own purposes during the subsistence of the operation of the retention of title clause were in my judgment quite incompatible with the existence of a relationship of Bond Worth as trustee and Monsanto as beneficiary solely and absolutely entitled to such assets, which is the relationship asserted.

I have, however, already indicated that this is not my own view of the effect, if any, of the retention of title clause when properly construed, but that such effect, if any, is a declaration of trust by Bond Worth in respect of the relevant assets by way of equitable charge to secure repayment of the moneys from time to time owing in respect of the relevant order.

[Since no particulars of this charge had been registered, it was held ineffective against creditors under what is now Part 25 of the Companies Act 2006.]

NOTES

1. In the course of his judgment, Slade J said ([1980] Ch 228 at 248):

In my judgment, any contract which, by way of security for the payment of a debt, confers an interest in property defeasible or destructible upon payment of such debt, or appropriates such property for the discharge of the debt, must necessarily be regarded as creating a mortgage or charge, as the case may be. The existence of the equity of redemption is quite inconsistent with the existence of a bare trustee-beneficiary relationship.

This passage has been frequently quoted in later cases.

2.   Although Monsanto, by the terms of the contracts, purported to *retain* equitable and beneficial ownership in the goods, Slade J held that the contract had to be construed as taking effect in two steps: there was first a *sale* of the entire property in the fibre to Bond Worth, which was then 'followed by a security, *eo instanti*, given back by Bond Worth to the vendor, Monsanto'. Bond Worth had therefore *created* a charge, which brought the transaction within the registration requirements of the Companies Act. *Bond Worth* was later followed on this point in *Stroud Architectural Systems Ltd v John Laing Construction Ltd* [1994] BCC 18.

Borden (UK) Ltd v Scottish Timber Products Ltd
[1981] Ch 25, Court of Appeal

Bordens sold resin to Scottish Timber, on terms that the property in the resin was not to pass to the buyers until payment had been made for all goods supplied to them by Bordens. The resin was bought to be mixed with hardeners and wood chippings and made into chipboard (an irreversible process), and was normally used within two days. Bordens were owed over £300,000 when the buyers went into receivership. They claimed to be entitled to trace their proprietary interest in the resin into the finished chipboard and the proceeds of sale of the chipboard. The Court of Appeal held, however, that the resin ceased to exist as such once it was used in making the chipboard, and that the sellers lost their title to it in consequence.

> **Buckley LJ**: It is common ground that it was the common intention of the parties that the defendants should be at liberty to use the resin in the manufacture of chipboard. After they had so used the resin there could, in my opinion, be no property in the resin distinct from the property in the chipboard produced by the process. The manufacture had amalgamated the resin and the other ingredients into a new product by an irreversible process and the resin, as resin, could not be recovered for any purpose; for all practical purposes it had ceased to exist and the ownership in that resin must also have ceased to exist.
>
> The [retention of title] condition does not expressly deal with any property in the chipboard, or create any equitable charge upon the chipboard, produced by the manufacture. If any term is to be implied, that must be a term which is necessary to give the contract business efficacy, but it must also be a term which the court can see unambiguously to be a term which the parties would have inserted into their contract had they thought it appropriate to express it. If no such term can be identified, then the court may have to conclude that the contract was inept to achieve any valuable, practical result in that respect.
>
> Is it possible here to imply any term giving the plaintiffs a proprietary interest in the chipboard manufactured by the defendants, or giving the plaintiffs an equitable charge upon that chipboard?
>
> Common ownership of the chipboard at law is not asserted by the defendants; so the plaintiffs must either have the entire ownership of the chipboard, which is not suggested, or they must have some equitable interest in the chipboard or an equitable charge of some kind upon the chipboard. For my part, I find it quite impossible to spell out of this condition any provision properly to be implied to that effect.
>
> It was impossible for the plaintiffs to reserve any property in the manufactured chipboard, because they never had any property in it; the property in that product originates in the defendants when the chipboard is manufactured. Any interest which the plaintiffs might have had in the chipboard must have arisen either by transfer of ownership or by some constructive trust or equitable charge, and, as I say, I find it impossible to spell out of this condition anything of that nature.

Mr Mowbray, in a very valiant argument, has contended that he can achieve his end by relying upon the doctrine of tracing. But in my judgment it is a fundamental feature of the doctrine of tracing that the property to be traced can be identified at every stage of its journey through life, and that it can be identified as property to which a fiduciary obligation still attaches in favour of the person who traces it.

In the present case, in the circumstances that I have described of the resin losing its identity in the chipboard, I find it impossible to hold that the resin can be traced into the chipboard, or to any other form of property into which the chipboard might at any time be converted. Accordingly, it seems to me that the doctrine of tracing is inapplicable to a case such as this. . . .

[**Bridge** and **Templeman LJJ** delivered concurring judgments.]

Hendy Lennox (Industrial Engines) Ltd v Grahame Puttick Ltd
[1984] 1 WLR 485, Queen's Bench Division

Lennox had supplied Puttick, who manufactured electric generators, with diesel engines under contracts which reserved their title as sellers until full payment of the price. The engines were incorporated into generating sets which would then be sold to Puttick's customers; but each engine remained identifiable by its serial number and could easily be unbolted from the generating set. Puttick went into receivership at a time when three generating sets were in its possession. Two sets were in a deliverable state and Staughton J held that the property in them had passed to Puttick's customers, so that Lennox's claim to the two engines concerned was lost; but since the third set was not in a deliverable state (although its engine had been affixed) he held that Lennox could assert a proprietary claim to retake that engine.

Staughton J: I am aware that until very recently the radio and radar apparatus on a ship was commonly hired by the shipowner rather than bought by him. No doubt it was attached to the ship; but I do not suppose that it thereby became the property of the shipowner or his mortgagee. Nor in my judgment would an engine which was the property of A become the property of B merely because B incorporated it in a generator set otherwise composed of his own materials.

Those reflections and the facts of this case persuade me that the proprietary rights of the sellers in the engines were not affected when the engines were wholly or partially incorporated into generator sets. They were not like the Acrilan which became yarn and then carpet (the *Bond Worth* case), or the resin which became chipboard (*Borden's* case), or the leather which became handbags (the *Peachdart* case) . . . They just remained engines, albeit connected to other things.

Clough Mill Ltd v Martin
[1985] 1 WLR 111, Court of Appeal

Clough Mill, spinners of yarn, sold yarn to Heatherdale, a manufacturer of fabrics, on terms which included the following (as the first and fourth sentences respectively of condition 12):

However, the ownership of the material shall remain with the seller, which reserves the right to dispose of the material until payment in full for all the material has been received by it in accordance with the terms of this contract or until such time as the buyer sells the material to its customers by way of bona fide sale at full market value. . . .

If any of the material is incorporated in or used as material for other goods before such payment the property in the whole of such goods shall be and remain with the seller until such payment has been made, or the other goods have been sold as aforesaid, and all the seller's rights hereunder in the material shall extend to those other goods.

The Court of Appeal held that Clough Mill could claim to be the owner of unused yarn which was in Heatherdale's possession when it went into receivership.

Sir John Donaldson MR: . . . Section 95 of the Companies Act 1948 [a predecessor of Part 25 of the Companies Act 2006] provides:

(1) . . . every charge created . . . by a company . . . shall, so far as any security on the company's property . . . is conferred thereby, be void against the liquidator and any creditor of the company [unless registered] . . .

Accordingly s 95 can only apply if (a) the company creates a charge, and (b) that charge confers a security on the company's property.

The plaintiff's demands upon the defendant related solely to unused and unsold yarn and it is quite clear that if the first sentence of condition 12 had stood alone, s 95 would have had no application. The agreement between the plaintiff and the buyer involved the plaintiff retaining property in the goods. It did not involve the buyer conferring a charge on any property, but still less on its own property.

The argument that the object of the exercise was to give the plaintiff security for the price of the yarn does not of itself advance the matter. Just as it is possible to increase the amount of cash available to a business by borrowing, buying on hire-purchase or credit sale terms, factoring book debts or raising additional share capital, all with different legal incidents, so it is possible to achieve security for an unpaid purchase price in different ways, with different legal consequences. The parties have chosen not to use the charging method in relation to unused yarn.

Fortunately we do not have to decide whether the fourth sentence of condition 12 creates a charge to which s 95 of the Act of 1948 would apply. I say 'fortunately,' because this seems to me to be a difficult question. If the incorporation of the yarn in, or its use as material for, other goods leaves the yarn in a separate and identifiable state, I see no reason why the plaintiff should not retain property in it and thereby avoid the application of s 95. However, in that situation I should have though that the buyer was clearly purporting to create a charge on the 'other goods' which would never have been the plaintiffs goods. I say 'purporting,' because those goods might them-selves remain the property of another supplier in consequence of the inclusion of the equivalent of the first sentence of condition 12 in the relevant sale contract. If, on the other hand, the incorpora-tion of the yarn created a situation in which it ceased to be identifiable and a new product was created consisting of the yarn and the other material, it would be necessary to determine who owned that product. If, and to the extent that, the answer was the buyer, it seems to me that the fourth sentence would create a charge.

For present purposes I am content to assume that in some circumstances the fourth sentence of condition 12 would indeed give rise to a charge to which s 95 of the Act of 1948 would apply, but they are not the circumstances which exist in the instant appeal and I see no reason to distort the plain language of the first sentence on the false assumption that the parties must be deemed to have intended that the same legal framework should apply both before and after the yarn was made up into other goods.

There remains one other aspect which creates problems, but again is not, I think, determinative of this appeal. The first sentence of condition 12 retains property in all the material to which the contract relates until the price of that material has been paid in full. Thus if three-quarters of the yarn had been paid for, the plaintiffs would retain ownership of, and have a right to resell, all the material. Such a resale would be likely to realise more than was owed by the buyer. What happens then? I am inclined to think that the word 'until' in the phrase 'reserves the right to dispose of the material until payment in full for all the material has been received' connotes not only a temporal, but also a quantitative limitation.

In other words, the plaintiff can go on selling hank by hank until they have been paid in full, but if thereafter they continue to sell, they are accountable to the buyer for having sold goods which, upon full payment having been achieved, became the buyer's goods.

NOTES

1. In *Specialist Plant Services Ltd v Braithwaite Ltd* [1987] BCLC 1, CA, sellers supplied parts and materials for the purposes of repairing a machine owned by Braithwaite. The contract contained a provision that the supplier should be given ownership of the machine 'as surety for the full payment' of what the customer owed. This was held to create a charge.

2. In *E Pfeiffer Weinkellerei-Weineinkauf GmbH & Co v Arbuthnot Factors Ltd* [1988] 1 WLR 150 and *Compaq Computer Ltd v Abercorn Group Ltd* [1991] BCC 484, goods (respectively wines and computing equipment) were supplied on retention of title terms to a retailer who sold or leased them to customers. The supplier purported to reserve title to the goods, and also a proprietary interest in the monies representing the proceeds of the sub-sales and leases, until the price of the goods was paid; and its claim in each case was against these monies. Since the suppliers' claim was only in respect of so much of the proceeds as was necessary to satisfy the outstanding price, the court held that the contracts amounted to an equitable assignment of the proceeds by way of charge, which was inconsistent with the fiduciary relationship on which a proprietary claim would be based; and because no charge had been registered, the suppliers could not succeed. (The suppliers also failed on a second ground, namely that the proceeds had been assigned to a factoring house which was held to have priority: see below, p 914.)

3. In *Tatung (UK) Ltd v Galex Telesure Ltd* (1988) 5 BCC 325 television and video equipment was sold to a retailer on terms which authorised the goods to be resold or let on hire to customers, but which purported to reserve title in the goods to the suppliers and to confer on them rights to the proceeds of sale or hire of the goods until the purchase price and any other sums owing to the suppliers had been paid. Since the suppliers' interest in the proceeds was defeasible upon payment of whatever the retailers owed to the suppliers, it was held that the contract created rights by way of security rather than an absolute interest.

4. Cases are rare indeed in which sellers under retention of title clauses have succeeded in claiming an interest in any kind of proceeds. One such, however, is the New Zealand decision in *Len Vidgen Ski & Leisure Ltd v Timaru Marine Supplies (1982) Ltd* [1986] 1 NZLR 349, where it was held that a ski shop owed fiduciary duties to its wholesaler in relation to goods supplied and had to account for proceeds of sale in its hands. In *Associated Alloys Pty Ltd v CAN 001 452 106 Pty Ltd* (2000) 202 CLR 558 the Australian High Court (which, prior to legislation in 2009, applied the common law rules) upheld the effectiveness of a 'proceeds subclause' and ruled that it did not involve the creation of a charge. The clause in question provided that if the buyer should use the goods that were subject to a retention of title provision in a manufacturing or similar process, the buyer should hold 'such part of the proceeds of such process as relates to the goods' in trust for the seller, the 'part' in question being equal in dollar terms to the amount owing by the buyer to the seller at the time of the receipt of the proceeds. In other words (assuming that no part of the price had been paid), the proceeds of any sale of the product should be held on trust for the seller and the buyer in proportions which reflected the value of their respective inputs.

(d) Retention of title clauses and the right to sue for the price

Presumptively a seller has no right to recover the price unless and until ownership has passed: Sale of Goods Act 1979, s 49(1). It seems to follow that where a seller under retention of title sues for the price at the end of the period of credit, ownership will pass to the buyer as and when he pays the amount of the judgment (compare *Standard Chartered Bank v Dorchester LNG* [2014] EWCA Civ 1382, [2014] 2 CLC 740 at [37]). It is always possible, however, to provide that the price is payable at some other time, such as 60 days after delivery, independently of the passing of title, and indeed independently of whether the buyer still has the goods at all. In such a case, it seems that s 49(1) is implicitly excluded: see *PST Energy 7 Shipping LLC v OW Bunker Malta Ltd* [2016] UKSC 23, [2016] AC 1034 at [58].

(e) Retention of title and third parties

Can a seller under a retention of title clause claim the goods in the hands of third parties to whom they have been supplied?

As regards the goods themselves, the answer is normally No, because the buyer under such a clause is almost invariably a buyer in possession, and hence the third party is able to invoke the exception to *nemo dat* in s 25(1) of the Sale of Goods Act 1979 (above, p 412). Thus in *Angara Maritime Ltd v OceanConnect UK Ltd* [2010] EWHC 619 (QB), [2011] 1 Lloyd's Rep 61 sellers supplied fuel oil to the charterers of a ship under retention of title: later the charter was terminated and the ship, with much of the fuel still on board, was returned to the owners who gave the charterers credit for the fuel concerned. The owners were held protected by s 25(1). So too in the very common situation where a builder's merchant supplies materials under retention of title to a construction company which incorporates it in a client's building: the building owner is protected as an innocent purchaser from any claim by the builder's merchant. See the Scots decision in *Archivent Ltd v Strathclyde Regional Council* 1985 SLT 154.

However, third parties are not always protected. Section 25(1) requires a *delivery* by the buyer in possession, connoting a voluntary act on its part. In *The Saetta* [1994] 1 WLR 1334, a similar case to *Angara v OceanConnect*, above, a charter was terminated for non-payment of hire and the shipowners simply took over the bunkers (which had again been supplied on retention of title terms) without any act on the charterers' part. Clarke J held that the oil still belonged to the suppliers, and in consequence the owners' act amounted to the tort of conversion as against them.

Furthermore, s 25(1) also requires a sale to the third party: a mere agreement to sell is not enough. In *Re Highway Foods International Ltd* [1995] 1 BCLC 209 meat was sold by A to B and resold by B to C. Each contract reserved title to the seller until the price was paid. It was held that the sub-sale (since, strictly speaking, it was only an agreement to sell) did not confer a good title on C: see above, p 417.

As regards proceeds, there is little authority. But since the interest of the seller in the proceeds of goods sold under retention of title is invariably equitable, it must follow that any good faith buyer of a legal interest in those proceeds must prevail.

NOTE

Retention of title provisions are in widespread use, but in practice they provide sellers with rather less protection that might be expected—not because many cases are taken to court and the provision struck down as an unregistered charge, but for more down-to-earth reasons. Among the major obstacles standing in the way of a seller seeking to assert his title we may list: the difficulty in proving that the retention of title provision was incorporated into the contract of sale; problems of obtaining access to the buyer's premises or other place where the goods are believed to be in order to identify them; the question of distinguishing the seller's goods from those supplied by others, or those that have been paid for from those that have not; and the risk that the goods may have lost their identity, for example through being used in a manufacturing process, or that they may have been sold. See on these issues, Professor S Wheeler, *Retention of Title Clauses: Impact and Implications* (1991).

(f) Reform of the law of retention of title

It is clear from the cases that the theoretical basis of many of the customary *Romalpa* terms—at least the more elaborate ones—is unclear, and that much uncertainty would be avoided if this topic were made the subject of clarifying legislation. But views differ as to the best course to be taken.

There are some who argue that the law should be changed so that, regardless of contractual form, all retention of title clauses should be deemed to create a charge and require registration. This would, of course, suit the banks, who would almost always be able to enforce their own charges in priority. (See above, p 501.) The Diamond Report of 1989 (*A Review of Security Interests in Property* (HMSO, 1989)) took this view (see para 9.3.2); so initially did the Law Commission (*Consultation Paper on Registration of Security Interests: Company Charges and Property other than Land* (Law Com CP No 164 (2002)), para 7.24), but the latter body then sidelined the proposal as better dealt with as part of a general reform of the law on the acquisition of title from non-owners (Report on *Company Security Interests* (Law Com No 296 (2005)), para 21), a project itself then dropped. The 2013 reforms of the law on company securities duly made no mention of retention of title.

There is, moreover, a counter-argument which stresses the commercial importance and utility of *Romalpa* terms as they are, and the need to take account of these factors rather than ignore them. There is a working 'retention of title' regime of this kind in many other European countries with a large trade with the UK; and indeed the most recent European jurisdiction to reform the law on this subject, Belgium (see *Loi du 11 juillet 2013 sur le gage*, in force from 2017), introduced a registration system but pointedly did not include retention of title clauses in it.

QUESTIONS

1. In *Borden (UK) Ltd v Scottish Timber Products Ltd*, Templeman LJ said ([1981] Ch 25 at 42):

> Unsecured creditors rank after preferential creditors, mortgagees and the holders of floating charges and they receive a raw deal: see *Business Computers Ltd v Anglo-African Leasing Ltd* [1977] 1 WLR 578, 580. It is not therefore surprising that this court looked with sympathy on an invention designed to provide some protection for one class of unsecured creditors, namely unpaid sellers of goods: see *Aluminium Industrie Vaassen BV v Romalpa Aluminium Ltd* [1976] 1 WLR 676, although there is no logical reason why this class of creditor should be favoured as against other creditors such as the suppliers of consumables and services.

Do you agree that there is 'no logical reason' for this distinction? If so, what attitude should the law take?

2. Many retention of title clauses expressly allow sales of the goods affected in the ordinary course of business. The result is that ordinary third party buyers acquire ownership even if they know that the goods are subject to retention of title. It would be possible to pass legislation extending this, and saying that such permission should be implied in all retention of title clauses notwithstanding any agreement to the contrary. Would this be a good idea?

CHAPTER 14

REMEDIES OF THE BUYER

1 INTRODUCTION

This topic is relatively straightforward, largely restating principles of the general law of contract in the specialised field of sale of goods. The remedies which will be dealt with here are threefold: (1) damages; (2) the recovery of money paid for a consideration that has totally failed; and (3) specific performance and injunctions.

2 BUYER'S ACTION FOR DAMAGES FOR NON-DELIVERY

The buyer's right to sue the seller for damages for non-delivery closely parallels the seller's action for damages for non-acceptance (s 50: see above, p 479). Section 51 provides:

> (1) Where the seller wrongfully neglects or refuses to deliver the goods to the buyer, the buyer may maintain an action against the seller for damages for non-delivery.
> (2) The measure of damages is the estimated loss directly or naturally resulting, in the ordinary course of events, from the seller's breach of contract.
> (3) Where there is an available market for the goods in question the measure of damages is prima facie to be ascertained by the difference between the contract price and the market or current price of the goods at the time or times when they ought to have been delivered or (if no time was fixed) at the time of the refusal to deliver.

Although it is often said that the prima facie measure of damages for non-delivery is the difference between the contract and the market price, a look at the above shows that the fundamental measure is that in s 51(2), the estimated loss directly or naturally resulting (a measure itself based on the remoteness rule in *Hadley v Baxendale*: see *Patrick v Russo-British Grain Export Co Ltd* [1927] 2 KB 535 at 538, per Salter J). The measure in s 51(3) is merely a special case of the general measure in s 51(2).

Bunge SA v Nidera BV
[2015] UKSC 43, [2015] 3 All ER 1082, Supreme Court

The facts, which are not relevant at this stage, appear in the further extract below at p 520.

Lord Sumption:

14. The fundamental principle of the common law of damages is the compensatory principle, which requires that the injured party is 'so far as money can do it to be placed in the same situation with respect to damages as if the contract had been performed': *Robinson v Harman* (1848) 1 Exch 850, 855 (Parke B). In a contract of sale where there is an available market, this is ordinarily achieved by comparing the contract price with the price that would have been agreed under a notional substitute contract assumed to have been entered into in its place at the market rate but otherwise on the same terms.

15. Section 51 of the Sale of Goods Act 1979 provides:

[His Lordship set out the section:]
Section 50 contains corresponding provisions for non-acceptance by the buyer.

16. Sections 50 and 51 reproduce the corresponding provisions of the Sale of Goods Act 1893, and reflect common law principles which had already been established at the time of the earlier Act. Section 51(2) states the compensatory principle in the context of a seller's non-delivery. Subsection (3) states the prima facie measure of damages where there is an available market, but it is not so much a rule as a technique which is prima facie to be treated as satisfying the general principle expressed in subsection (2).

(a) Measure where available market: s 51(3)

As with damages under s 50 (see above, p 479), the rule is that, where there is a market, the price prevailing there is prima facie to be used to ascertain the measure of damages, with the place and time when the delivery ought to have been made being the relevant time and place for the reckoning of it. The actual profit that would have been made by the buyer is out of account.

Williams v Reynolds
(1865) 6 B & S 495, Court of Queen's Bench

The facts appear from the judgment.

Blackburn J: The plaintiff and the defendants entered into a contract on the 1st April, by which the defendants agreed to sell 500 piculs of China cotton at 16¾d [about 7p] per lb, guaranteed fair, to be delivered in August, so that the defendants had all that month to supply a certain quantity of cotton, answering the description given, at a certain price. At the end of August they had failed to fulfil their contract. And if the case stood there, the measure of damages would have been the difference between the contact price of 16¾d and the market price at the end of August, the latest time for delivery, which was 18¼d [about 8p].

The question is, whether the plaintiff is entitled to recover a further sum, this being a contract, not for the delivery of specific cotton, but of cotton of a particular description . . . The additional facts here are that, on the 25th May, nearly two months after the original contract and three months before its completion, the plaintiff made a contract to supply Mayall & Anderson, at Liverpool, with the same quantity and quality of cotton at 19¾d [about 9p], to be delivered in August. If the defendants had fulfilled their contract the plaintiff would have handed over the cotton to his purchasers, and would have gained a considerable profit by the transaction. It was argued that because this purchase was made on the Liverpool Cotton Exchange, where all persons know that cotton is bought on speculation to sell again, the defendants would be aware that the plaintiff would enter into a fresh contract, relying on the performance by them of their contract, and that the nonfulfilment of it would occasion the breach of the second contract, and so the loss of profit by the resale would be natural consequence of the defendants' breach of contract. . . . I cannot see that loss of profit from a contract subsequently made by the purchaser . . . follows as a natural consequence from the original seller's breach of contract. Though the purchaser might naturally rely on the seller's contract to enable him to fulfil his own, it is not necessary that he should do so; and if the seller was a slippery customer it would be imprudent to do it: in that case the purchaser would, as a prudent man, go into the market and supply himself from thence. Here the plaintiff had reason to rely on the defendants, but that does not entitle him to throw upon them the loss of the profit he would have made.

[**Crompton** and **Shee JJ** delivered concurring judgments.]

NOTES

1. This case was decided at common law, but clearly reflects the principle codified in s 51(3). Incidentally, a picul is a traditional Chinese measure of weight, about 60 kg.

2. The same principle applies in the converse case where the seller would have resold for *less* than the market value: the damages will not be reduced on that account. See *Williams Bros v ET Agius Ltd* [1914] AC 510.

3. In a sale on CIF terms (see below, p 543), the seller may be in breach either of his duty to deliver the proper documents relating to the goods, or of his duty to deliver the goods at the destination port (or both). In the former case, there may be a difficulty in fixing the time and place by reference to which the existence of an available market is to be determined. Sometimes, it will be possible to buy equivalent goods already afloat, and the relevant time will then be that when the proper documents ought to have been delivered. Failing this, the appropriate time may be that when the goods ought to have been delivered at their destination, and this will also then be the relevant place. But the buyer may, by virtue of his duty to mitigate his loss, be obliged to contract to buy comparable goods at the place of destination as soon as he rejects the documents, and this will bring forward the date for fixing the market price: see *C Sharp & Co Ltd v Nosawa & Co* [1917] 2 KB 814.

4. The concept of 'an available market' is similar, though not identical, to that applicable in cases of non-acceptance. It connotes relatively quick availability of very similar goods. They need not be identical: if ordinary electronic goods of Brand X are not delivered there may be an available market if one can get Brand Y equipment with a similar function (*Air Studios (Lyndhurst) Ltd v Lombard North Central Plc* [2012] EWHC 3162 (QB), [2013] 1 Lloyd's Rep 63 at [93], per Males J). But there is normally no market in specialised goods available only to special order from one manufacturer (*M & J Marine Engineering Services Co Ltd v Shipshore Ltd* [2009] EWHC 2031 (Comm)) or only intermittently (*Glencore Energy UK Ltd v Transworld Oil Ltd* [2010] EWHC 141 (Comm), [2010] 1 CLC 284 (crude oil obtainable only occasionally)). And there is no market in one-off or rare goods, such as a high-class limited edition Porsche: *Hughes v Pendragon Sabre Ltd* [2016] EWCA Civ 18, [2016] 1 Lloyd's Rep 311.

QUESTION

Why do we deny the claimants in cases like *Williams v Reynolds* recovery of their full losses? You may care to look at *Patrick v Russo-British Grain Export Co Ltd* [1927] 2 KB 535.

Most cases on s 51(3) concern past breach: but the same rules apply to anticipatory breach, where the seller unequivocally repudiates the contract before delivery is due. Nevertheless, three special rules apply here. First, once the seller's repudiation has been accepted, the buyer's duty to mitigate his loss may oblige him to accept lower damages if he fails to buy against a rising market. Secondly, the reference to the time of 'refusal to deliver' means not the time of repudiation, but the time delivery might notionally have been demanded had there been no repudiation. Thirdly, where the repudiation is accepted, account may be taken of later events between the time of acceptance and the time fixed for delivery that would have deprived the claimant of his right to delivery.

Melachrino v Nickoll & Knight
[1920] 1 KB 693, King's Bench Division

Melachrino agreed in two separate contracts to sell Egyptian cotton seed to Nickoll & Knight, to be shipped to London on the SS *Asaos*, expected to arrive between 10 January and 10 February 1917. The sellers repudiated the contracts on 14 December 1916, and the buyers accepted their repudiation on the same day. On 14 December the market price of cotton seed was above the contract price; for the whole of the period between 10 January and 10 February it was below it. The court held that the buyer was entitled to only nominal damages.

> **Bailhache J**: Upon these facts the question arises: Are the buyers' damages to be fixed with reference to the market prices on December 14, 1916, or with reference to the prices ruling at the time when the goods might be expected to be delivered? If the former the damages are substantial, if the latter nominal. The arbitrators have assessed the damages as at the date of the anticipatory breach.
>
> . . .
>
> [T]he prima facie measure of damages is said to be the difference between the contract price and the market price at the time the goods ought to have been delivered—in this case the period between January 10 and February 10, 1917. In a constantly fluctuating market and if the prices during that period had ruled higher than the contract prices there might have been some difficulty in determining the proper price to be taken, but in this case that point does not arise, as at all times between those dates the market prices were below the contract prices.
>
> Section 51 does not in terms deal with an anticipatory breach, and in the case of a breach by effluxion of time it is clear that it makes no difference to the measure of damages whether a buyer goes into the market or is content to take the difference in price without troubling to buy against the defaulting seller. The question to be decided is whether the same rule applies in the case of an anticipatory breach.
>
> . . .
>
> Immediately upon the anticipatory breach the buyer may bring his action whether he buys against the seller or not.
>
> It is the duty of the buyer to go into the market and buy against the defaulting seller if a reasonable opportunity offers. This is expressed by the phrase 'It is the buyer's duty to mitigate damages.' In that event the damages are assessed with reference to the market price on the date of the

repurchase. If the buyer does not perform his duty in this respect the seller is none the less entitled to have damages assessed as at the date when a fresh contract might and ought to have been made.

As a corollary to this rule the buyer may if he pleases go into the market and buy against the seller: as he is bound to do so to mitigate damages, so he is entitled to do so to cover himself against his commitments or to secure the goods. In that case again the damages are assessed with reference to the market price at the date of the repurchase.

It is also settled law that when default is made by the seller by refusal to deliver within the contract time the buyer is under no duty to accept the repudiation and buy against him but may claim the difference between the contract price and the market price at the date when under the contract the goods should have been delivered.

Further, in the case of an anticipatory breach [accepted by the buyer] the contract is at an end and the defaulting seller cannot take advantage of any subsequent circumstances which would have afforded him a justification for non-performance of his contract had his repudiation not been accepted.

In logical strictness it would appear to follow that equally the defaulting seller cannot take advantage of a fall in the market before the due date for delivery to escape liability for damages.

It looks therefore at first sight as though the date at which the difference between the contract price and the market price ought to be taken for the assessment of damages when the buyer does not buy against the seller should follow by analogy the rule adopted where the buyer goes into the market and buys, or where the breach is failure to deliver at the due date and should be at or about the date when the buyer intimates his acceptance of the repudiation though he does not actually go into the market against the seller. If so, in this case, the date would be about December 14, when the buyer claimed arbitration and so the arbitrators have found.

As against this line of reasoning, it must be remembered that the object of damages is to place a person whose contract is broken in as nearly as possible the same position as if it had been performed. This result is secured by measuring damages either at the date of the repurchase, in the case of repurchase on an anticipatory breach, or at the date when the goods ought to have been delivered when there is no anticipatory breach whether there is a repurchase or not. In these cases the buyer gets a new contract as nearly as may be like the broken contract and the defaulting seller pays the extra expense incurred by the buyer in restoring his position.

Where however there is an anticipatory breach but no buying against the defaulting seller, and the price falls below the contract price between the date of the anticipatory breach and the date when the goods ought to have been delivered, the adoption of the date of the anticipatory breach as the date at which the market price ought to be taken would put the buyer in a better position than if his contract had been duly performed. He would if that date were adopted be given a profit and retain his money wherewith to buy the goods if so minded on the fall of the market. It would be in effect, to use a homely phrase, to allow him to eat his cake and have it. Perhaps it is better to avoid figures of speech however picturesque and to say, to make a profit from the anticipatory breach while the contract if duly performed would have shown a loss—a position which is I think irreconcilable with the principles upon which damages are awarded as between buyer and seller.

In my opinion the true rule is that where there is an anticipatory breach by a seller to deliver goods for which there is a market at a fixed date the buyer without buying against the seller may bring his action at once, but that if he does so his damages must be assessed with reference to the market price of the goods at the time when they ought to have been delivered under the contract. If the action comes to trial before the contractual date for delivery has arrived the Court must arrive at that price as best it can.

To this rule there is one exception for the benefit of the defaulting seller—namely, that if he can show that the buyer acted unreasonably in not buying against him the date to be taken is the date at which the buyer ought to have gone into the market to mitigate damages. . . .

The result in this case is that the damages are nominal.

Tai Hing Cotton Mill Ltd v Kamsing Knitting Factory
[1979] AC 91, Privy Council

Tai Hing contracted to sell 1,500 bales of cotton yarn to Kamsing at HK$1335 per bale, delivery to be made as required by the buyers on giving one month's notice. In July 1973, when 424 bales remained undelivered, the sellers wrote to the buyers repudiating the contract. The buyers for some months pressed the sellers to continue to deliver supplies, but eventually on 28 November 1973 they issued a writ claiming damages for breach. The market price of cotton was $3,300 per bale in August 1973 but fell steadily from September 1973 onwards. The Privy Council held that the sellers' repudiation was not a 'refusal to deliver' within s 51(3), since they remained bound to deliver until the repudiation was accepted; rather, this was a case of an anticipatory breach which was not accepted until 28 November; that this was the latest date on which the buyers could have given the sellers notice requiring delivery of all the outstanding bales; and that accordingly damages should be assessed by reference to the market price one month after that, ie on 28 December 1973.

Bunge SA v Nidera BV
[2015] UKSC 43, [2015] 3 All ER 1082, Supreme Court

Sellers agreed to sell Russian milling wheat to be shipped from a Russian Black Sea port between 23–30 August 2010. The contract contained a clause excusing the sellers in the event of state prohibitions on export. On 5 August Russia prohibited the export of agricultural products from 15 August until the end of the year. On 9 August the seller purported to cancel the contract relying on the clause and the prohibition. This amounted to an anticipatory breach, because such prohibitions were often lifted shortly after being imposed and there was no overwhelming likelihood that this one would still be in effect during the agreed shipment period. The buyers accepted the breach and sued for damages under a clause in the contract that, it was held, essentially applied s 51(3). The sellers argued that damages should be nominal because in the event the prohibition was not lifted before the shipment date, and hence the buyers would not have been entitled to any wheat anyway. The buyers contended that this fact should be out of account. The Supreme Court decided in favour of the sellers.

> **Lord Toulson**:
>
> 78. The broad principle... is that where a contract is discharged by reason of one party's breach, and that party's unperformed obligation is of a kind for which there exists an available market in which the innocent party could obtain a substitute contract, the innocent party's loss will ordinarily be measured by the extent to which his financial position would be worse off under the substitute contract than under the original contract.
>
> 79. The rationale is that in such a situation that measure represents the loss which may fairly and reasonably be considered as arising naturally, ie according to the ordinary course of things, from the breach of contract (*Hadley v Baxendale*). It is fair and reasonable because it reflects the wrong for which the guilty party has been responsible and the resulting financial disadvantage to the innocent party at the date of the breach. The guilty party has been responsible for depriving the innocent party of the benefit of performance under the original contract (and is simultaneously released from his own unperformed obligations). The availability of a substitute market enables a market valuation to be made of what the innocent party has lost, and a line thereby to be drawn under the transaction.

80. Whether the innocent party thereafter in fact enters into a substitute contract is a separate matter. He has, in effect, a second choice whether to enter the market—similar to the choice which first existed at the time of the original contract, but at the new rate prevailing (the difference being the basis of the normal measure of damages). The *option* to re-enter or stay out of the market arises from the breach, but it does not follow that there is a causal connection between the breach and his *decision* whether to re-enter or to stay out of the market, so as to make the guilty party responsible for that decision and its consequences. The guilty party is not liable to the innocent party for the adverse effect of market changes after the innocent party has had a free choice whether to re-enter the market, nor is the innocent party required to give credit to the guilty party for any subsequent market movement in favour of the innocent party. The speculation which way the market will go is the speculation of the claimant.

. . .

82. There are three important things to note about measurement of damages by reference to an available market. First it presupposes the existence of an available market in which to obtain a substitute contract. Secondly, it presupposes that the substitute contract is a true substitute. The claimant is not entitled to charge the defendant with the cost of obtaining superior benefits to those which the defendant contracted to provide. Thirdly (and in the present case most importantly), the purpose of the exercise is to measure the extent to which the claimant is (or would be) financially worse off under the substitute contract than under the original contract.

83. Depending on the nature of the market, cases in which this method is appropriate may include an anticipatory repudiatory breach of a one-off contract of sale, a contract of sale in instalments or a period contract. A single unconditional contract of purchase or sale of a commodity in the futures market is an example of the first. The accepted repudiation by the buyer or seller amounts to the premature closing out of the transaction. The innocent party can then use the market to put himself back in the same position at a price which will reflect the market's assessment of the value of the contract. . . .

84. However, in this case the lost contract and its hypothetical substitute were subject to automatic cancellation unless the Russian government ban was lifted, and the extent to which the buyers were worse off by loss of the original contract could not be measured by a simple comparison of the contract price with the price of a hypothetical substitute contract.

85. The fundamental compensatory principle makes it axiomatic that any method of assessment of damages must reflect the nature of the bargain which the innocent party has lost as a result of the repudiation. In this case the bargain was subject to a high risk of cancellation. Leaving aside for the purposes of this discussion the sellers' offer to reinstate the contract, what the buyers lost was the chance of obtaining a benefit in the event of the export ban being lifted before the delivery period, only in which case would the contract have been capable of lawful performance. In *The Golden Victory* [[2007] 2 AC 535] Lord Bingham observed, uncontroversially, that although it may be difficult to calculate a loss prospectively, an injured party can recover damages for the loss of a chance of obtaining a benefit. He also acknowledged that the market value of a contract may be reduced if terminable on an event which 'the market' judges to be likely but not certain. But how is the chance to be valued if there is no market risk index to which the court can refer? (In this case the Appeal Board merely found that there 'was a possibility that the ban might be lifted or relaxed in some way'.) The assessment would have to be made by the arbitrator or judge doing the best he can.

86. Should the assessment be made on the facts as known at the date of the assessment or should the tribunal apply a retrospective assessment of how the chances would have appeared at the date of the repudiation? I see no virtue in such circumstances in the court attempting some

form of retrospective assessment of prospective risk when the answer is known. To do so would run counter to the fundamental compensatory principle. In *The Golden Victory* Lord Bingham acknowledged that the saying 'you need not gaze into the crystal ball when you can read the book' is in many contexts a sound approach in law as in life. He did not consider that approach to be appropriate in that particular context because of the available market rule. I have given my reasons for not regarding that rule as apt for the circumstances of this case . . .

NOTE

Bunge v Nidera allowed the repudiating seller to defend the buyer's action under s 53(1)(c) on the basis that subsequent *events* would have excused it from liability for non-delivery when the time came for the wheat to be shipped. The same thing will also apply where it is clear that the *buyer himself* would not have been in a position to insist on the seller's performance. Imagine, for example, that a contract is concluded in January for the seller to deliver to the buyer ten JCB excavators in June; imagine also that the contract is repudiated by the seller, and the repudiation accepted, in February, whereupon the buyer sues for damages. Since a buyer cannot insist on delivery unless it tenders the price (see s 28, above, p 456), it is open to the seller to reduce damages to a nominal level if it can show that the seller could not or would not have come up with the money in June. See *Flame SA v Glory Wealth Shipping Pte Ltd* [2013] EWHC 3153 (Comm), [2014] QB 1080 (not a case about sale of goods, but clearly applicable to it).

(b) Measure where no available market: s 51(2)

Where there is no available market for goods of the contract description, the court must make its own assessment of the amount of the buyer's loss. It may, for instance, have regard to price movements in other, comparable markets (eg *The Arpad* [1934] P 189, where there was no available market for Romanian wheat, but the price of wheat generally had fallen), or, if a sub-sale by the buyer was within the reasonable contemplation of the parties, the buyer's lost profit on reselling or processing the goods (*Patrick v Russo-British Grain Export Co Ltd* [1927] 2 KB 535; *The Marine Star* [1994] 2 Lloyd's Rep 629). Where goods cannot be exactly duplicated, the cost of comparable or similar goods gives a guide: see *Air Studios (Lyndhurst) Ltd v Lombard North Central Plc* [2012] EWHC 3162 (QB), [2013] 1 Lloyd's Rep 63 (similar second-hand electronics) and *Hughes v Pendragon Sabre Ltd* [2016] EWCA Civ 18, [2016] 1 Lloyd's Rep 311 (a limited-edition Porsche with equivalent but not identical features to that not supplied). In *The Alecos M* [1991] 1 Lloyd's Rep 120, CA, the contract was for the sale of a second-hand ship 'including spare propeller'; but no spare propeller was delivered. To manufacture a propeller would have cost $121,000. In the absence of proof that the buyers genuinely intended to buy a spare propeller if none was delivered under the contract, the court upheld a ruling that they should not be awarded damages under s 51 equivalent to the replacement cost, but only a notional scrap value of $1,100. There may have been 'rough justice' in this decision, but it is open to criticism: see GH Treitel, 'Damages for Non-Delivery' (1991) 107 LQR 364.

Where near equivalent goods are bought, any resulting savings in ongoing costs are relevant. In *Thai Airways International Public Co Ltd v KI Holdings Co Ltd* [2015] EWHC 1250 (Comm) German aircraft seats bought by an airline to replace Japanese ones not supplied by a seller in breach of contract were much more expensive. But they saved fuel costs because they were less heavy. The fuel savings were deducted from the damages.

In addition to any damages available for non-delivery under s 51(2) or (3), there is little doubt that the buyer can claim any further consequential losses he may have suffered, provided they are not too remote. Examples include lost profits on resale (*Patrick v Russo-British Grain Co* [1927] 2 KB 535), or damages paid to a sub-buyer (*Grébert-Borgnis v Nugent* (1884) LR 15 QBD 85). Note that s 54, preserving claims for 'special damages', preserves the right to claim any losses falling within the second limb of *Hadley v Baxendale*, that is, claims for loss within the contemplation of the parties.

3 BUYER'S ACTION FOR DAMAGES FOR LATE DELIVERY

The Act contains no provision relating to the assessment of damages when the seller fails to deliver on the due date but the buyer accepts them when they are tendered late. The issue therefore falls to be determined an ordinary contractual principles. If the goods are bought for possible immediate resale on the spot market,[1] the prima facie measure of the buyer's loss is the difference in the market price on the two dates: thus, if the market is rising, he will get substantial damages, while if it is falling, he will have suffered no loss. (See *Wertheim v Chicoutimi Pulp Co* [1911] AC 301 (where, however, the claim failed for other reasons) and *Galaxy Energy International Ltd v Murco Petroleum Ltd* [2013] EWHC 3720 (Comm), [2013] 2 CLC 1007; and compare *Koufos v C Czarnikow Ltd, The Heron II* [1969] 1 AC 350, HL, where late delivery was made by a carrier.)

If the goods are not bought for sale, it is up to the buyer to prove what loss, if any, he has suffered as a result of the late delivery.

Contigroup Companies, Inc v Glencore AG
[2004] EWHC 2750 (Comm), [2005] 1 Lloyd's Rep 241, Commercial Court

Glencore bought a shipload of LPG gas from Contichem, which it sold on to Petrochina for its use. The gas was delivered to Petrochina a few days late. Glencore settled a claim from Petrochina for lost profits of about $170,000, and sued Contichem for this sum. The claim succeeded.

> **Ian Glick QC**:
> 80. It was urged upon me that the proper measure of damages in the absence of an available market is the difference between the value of the cargo at the time when it should have been delivered and its value at the time of actual delivery. In my judgment to try to calculate damages on that basis would be entirely artificial. The loss suffered by Petrochina and passed back ultimately to Glencore did not result from any change in the value of butane. It resulted from Petrochina being short of butane and as a result losing profits. The question is whether Glencore can recover damages for having compensated Petrochina for this loss.

---

[1] The spot market is the market for goods to be delivered and paid for there and then, at the then ruling price.

81. The position is in my judgment is as follows:

(a) Contichem knew that Glencore was a trader and that it would probably resell Lot 2. Such a resale might be to another trader, to a retailer, or indeed to an end user.

(b) Glencore did resell Lot 2, to Glencore International which in turn sold it to Petrochina, a retailer.

(c) On the facts of this case, the interposition of Glencore International is of no consequence. The sale to it was on terms back to back to the sale contract, and any claim for a breach of contract against Glencore International caused by a breach of contract by Contichem would inevitably be passed back to Glencore. The position is the same as if Glencore had resold direct to Petrochina.

(d) Given that Glencore was likely to resell Lot 2, the parties must have contemplated that if Contichem delivered late, that was likely to put Glencore in breach on any sub-sale (for which purpose, for the reasons given, I include the sub-sale to Petrochina).

(e) There was no available market on which Glencore could acquire a substitute cargo. If it is necessary to do so, I find that it must have been within the contemplation of the parties to the sale contract that, if the nominated vessel was late, Glencore would be unable to acquire substitute goods. The parties certainly must have realised when they made the sale contract that, if Glencore found itself looking for 21,000 metric tons of butane at the port of discharge because the nominated vessel had failed to arrive in time it would have precious little chance of finding them. But even on the basis that Glencore would be given, as it was, 12 or 13 days' warning of the breach, the parties must have appreciated Glencore would probably be unable to find substitute butane. Indeed, it is noticeable that Contichem does not seem to have made any attempt itself to find a substitute cargo to enable it to comply with the sale contract. Doubtless it knew then, and earlier at the time of the sale contract, that such an attempt would be fruitless.

(f) It follows that it must also have been in the contemplation of the parties that, if delivery was delayed, Glencore would have to compensate a sub-buyer for any loss (including of course loss of profit) it suffered as a result of that delay.

(g) Glencore (albeit through Glencore International) did have to compensate such a sub-buyer.

(h) The compensation in question was that provided for in the settlement. That compensation was wholly referable to the delay, and the settlement itself was reasonable.

82. Accordingly, Glencore is in my judgment entitled to damages in the sum of US$172,899.67 and to set off those damages against Contichem's claim for the balance of the purchase price of Lot 2.

NOTE

See too the well-known case of *Victoria Laundry (Windsor) Ltd v Newman Industries Ltd* [1949] 2 KB 528, CA, where the claimants recovered the profits which they had foreseeably lost during the period of the delay, which was itself a case of late delivery in a sale of goods contract.

4 THE BUYER'S ACTION FOR DAMAGES FOR BREACH OF WARRANTY

Section 53 sets out a series of propositions about the buyer's remedies where there has been a breach of warranty by the seller, or where the buyer has elected (or is compelled) to treat a breach of condition as a breach of warranty. He may sue for damages: in addition he may 'set up against the seller the breach of warranty in diminution or extinction of the price' (s 53(1)). The measure of damages (again, echoing the rule in *Hadley v Baxendale* (1854) 9 Exch 341) is the estimated loss directly and naturally resulting, in the ordinary course of events, from the breach of warranty (s 53(2)).

The measure of damages for breach of a warranty of quality is stated to be prima facie the difference between the value of the goods at the time they were delivered to the buyer and the value they would have had if they had fulfilled the warranty (s 53(3)). In such a case, the fact that there has been a sub-sale of the goods is normally irrelevant (*Slater v Hoyle & Smith Ltd* [1920] 2 KB 11, CA). Exceptionally, in *Van Den Hurk v Martens & Co Ltd* [1920] 1 KB 850, where it was known that the goods had been resold to a sub-buyer abroad and that they were to be dispatched to him unopened and without any examination, the court substituted the market price at the time and place of the second delivery abroad as being more appropriate for the assessment of damages than the time and place of delivery under the principal contract.

However, it has to be remembered that the 'difference in value' test, like the 'market price' formula in cases of non-delivery, is only a prima facie rule. If it is clear that the claimant's real loss resulting in the ordinary course of things is different, that figure may be awarded. The case of *Bence Graphics International Ltd v Fasson UK Ltd* [1998] QB 87 demonstrates that it may not take a great deal to displace s 53(3). The plaintiffs here had contracted to buy vinyl film on which they printed words and numbers and which was then sold on to end-users for affixing to sea-borne containers. The film was not up to scratch because the writing soon became illegible. Remarkably, few of the end-users made any complaint or claim. On the assumption that the film, as delivered, had no market value, the plaintiffs could have been awarded damages of over £500,000, but in fact all that they stood to lose was a mere £22,000 plus whatever was needed to compensate the few complaining end-users. The Court of Appeal declined to apply the 'difference in value' yardstick and held that the buyers could recover only their actual loss, in effect applying the basic *Hadley v Baxendale* principles to the exclusion of s 53(3).

Conversely, in *Saipol SA v Inerco Trade SA* [2014] EWHC 2211 (Comm), [2015] 1 Lloyd's Rep 26 Saipol bought a shipload of sunflower oil contributed to by a number of sellers: Inerco supplied about 18 per cent of it. The whole cargo was contaminated. Field J rejected a plea that Inerco's liability was limited to the diminution in value of its 'share' under s 53(3) and held Inerco liable for the value of the whole cargo.

NOTE

Some end-users of Bence's product may have chosen not to sue them because they did not want to damage the goodwill which had been built up between them in the course of a long business relationship. Alternatively, some may have taken their future business else-where, causing Bence to lose profits. Yet Fasson was paid in full for a worthless product—a half-million-pound windfall. This may trouble you. See GH Treitel, 'Damages for Breach of Warranty of Quality' (1997) 113 LQR 188 and C Hawes, 'Damages for Defective Goods' (2005) 121 LQR 389. And compare the Australian decision in *Clark v Macourt* [2013] HCA 56, (2013) 253 CLR 1. Sperm straws were sold to a fertility clinic which, owing to a breach of warranty, were unusable and worthless. But the clinic lost nothing, because its clients paid separately for sperm straws bought elsewhere. The High Court of Australia nevertheless followed the lead of *Slater v Hoyle* and awarded the would-be value of the sperm straws.

In practice, in most claims for damages for breach of warranty it is consequential losses that are most important. Substandard goods very often cause damage or injury, or harm to the buyer's reputation with its own customers, out of all proportion to the value of the goods. A straightforward example, mentioned in Chapter 11 above, is *Britvic Soft Drinks Ltd v Messer UK Ltd* [2002] EWCA Civ 548, [2002] 2 Lloyd's Rep 368, where contaminated gas sold to soft drink manufacturers led to a very costly recall programme. Consequential losses for breach of warranty are assessed on ordinary contractual principles: *H Parsons (Livestock) Ltd v Uttley Ingham & Co Ltd* [1978] QB 791, CA—again, a sale of goods case which has a leading place in the contract syllabus.

In *Saipol SA v Inerco Trade SA*, above, where a composite cargo contributed to by five separate sellers was contaminated, Field J held that each seller was liable in full for all the loss caused by the contamination, subject to a right to contribution from the other sellers.

5 THE BUYER'S RIGHT TO RECOVER THE PRICE OF GOODS NOT DELIVERED, OR VALIDLY REJECTED

A buyer who pays in advance and does not receive the goods contracted for, or who validly rejects and returns those goods, is entitled at common law to sue the seller for the return of any sums paid. This is not a claim for damages, but a claim on the restitutionary (or 'unjust enrichment') basis of total failure of consideration. It is based on the idea that the seller cannot be allowed to keep both the money and the goods. Of course the buyer may *also* have a parallel claim for damages for this purpose: if A pays B £5,000 for goods which B in breach of contract fails to deliver, A has a prima facie claim for damages of £5,000, which is the loss he has suffered. Nevertheless, the right to rely on a total failure of consideration is important for two reasons.

First, it may yield more than an action for damages. Imagine that goods are agreed to be sold for £10,000 but not delivered; that the buyer prepays the £10,000; and that the market price at the time fixed for delivery is only £8,000. If the buyer sues for damages he recovers his loss, which is £8,000. But if he sues for the return of his money on the basis of failure of consideration he recovers the full £10,000 (compare the share sale case of *Wilkinson v Lloyd* (1845) 7 QB 27). Alternatively, imagine that a seller fails to provide good title to construction machinery; after the buyer has had three months' use of the machinery, it has to be given up to the true owner. In an action for damages under s 12 of the Sale of Goods Act the value of that use must be deducted: in an action for money paid for a failed consideration it does not. See *Rowland v Divall*, above, p 459.

Secondly, there may be cases where the buyer has no right of action for damages at all. If, for example, an agreement to sell goods contains a clause excusing the seller from liability if prevented from delivering them by governmental action, the buyer who prepays may well not have any claim in damages in the event of non-delivery: but he will always retain a right to the return of his money on the basis of failure of consideration.

Furthermore, it does not matter for these purposes that the buyer himself may be in breach of contract. In *Newland Shipping and Forwarding Ltd v Toba Trading FZC* [2014] EWHC 661 (Comm) a buyer made advance payments for deliveries of gasoil (a form of diesel fuel) from Turkmenistan: but when it failed to pay on time for deliveries made, the seller cancelled the contract. Leggatt J nevertheless allowed the buyer to recover its prepayments; the seller would, he pointed out, be unjustly enriched if permitted not to deliver the gasoil but nevertheless to keep monies prepaid by the buyer.

Although the practice is to refer to a *total* failure of consideration, it is well established that where a buyer prepays in full but the seller short delivers, it is open to the buyer to rely on failure of consideration to recover a proportionate part of what he has paid: see, eg, *Behrend v Produce Brokers Ltd* [1920] 3 KB 530.

6 SPECIFIC PERFORMANCE

(a) Jurisdiction to order specific performance

Section 52(1) expressly empowers the court, in an action by a buyer for breach of contract for failure to deliver *specific or ascertained goods*, to order (if it thinks fit) that the contract be performed specifically, without giving the seller the option of retaining the goods on payment of damages. We saw earlier in *Re Wait* [1927] 1 Ch 606, CA (above, p 298), that a person who had contracted to buy *unascertained* goods could not invoke this provision, at least for so long as the goods remained unascertained.

Can the court grant specific performance outside s 52, ie in the case of unascertained goods? Atkin LJ thought not in *Re Wait*, above (see pp 629–634 of the report). But today it seems accepted that it can, as the case below demonstrates.

Thames Valley Power Ltd v Total Gas & Power Ltd
[2005] EWHC 2208 (Comm), [2006] 1 Lloyd's Rep 441, Commercial Court

TVPL agreed with the owners of Heathrow Airport (HAL) to supply and run a major gas-powered heating facility. Under a gas supply agreement (GSA) Total agreed to supply TVPL with gas over a 15-year period from mid-1995. This was therefore a contract for the supply of unascertained goods, not within s 52. In 2005, when the agreement had five years to run, Total alleged that because the price of gas had risen exponentially a force majeure clause in the contract excused all further deliveries. The court rejected this argument. Towards the end of the case Clarke J discussed the appropriateness of an order of specific performance.

> **Clarke J**:
>
> 58. I turn then to consider whether or not on the footing that Total are not entitled to invoke force majeure, TVPL are entitled to specific performance or damages. In the light of the position taken by Total, it is sufficient for TVPL's purposes if they are entitled to damages since Total have indicated that, in that event, they will continue to supply under the terms and conditions of the GSA....
>
> ...
>
> 63. In those circumstances it is not strictly necessary for me to consider whether this is a case for specific performance or injunctive relief to the same effect, but, if it is, I answer the question in the affirmative. It would in my view be entirely unjust that TVPL should be confined to a remedy in damages. The basis of the GSA was that TVPL would be assured of a source of supply from a

first-rank supplier at an agreed price for a 15-year term in order that they might in turn contract with HAL for a similar term. To confine them to a claim in damages would deprive them of substantially the whole benefit that the contract was intended to give them.

64. There is a further difficulty: if the contract is to be treated as remaining on foot but with Total in continuing breach, TVPL will not be in a position to seek or secure another long-term source of supply, since Total may if the market turns, claim to resume supplies under the agreement. If, as they may therefore be driven to do, TVPL treat Total's refusal to supply as repudiatory, they would then be faced with the almost impossible task in calculating any damages of predicting over a five-year period

(a) the state of the gas market, in order to calculate the price that TVPL will have to pay its new supplier or suppliers; and

(b) the changes in the several indices [indicating the price TVPL would have had to pay if Total had carried on supplying].

Last but by no means least—if TVPL is compelled to pay gas at market prices it may, unless the shortfall is quickly made up by the payment of damages, become insolvent as early as the beginning of 2006.

65. Accordingly, subject to any further argument on the form of the order, I propose

(a) to refuse a stay and to dismiss Total's application dated August 26;

(b) to declare that on the true construction of the Gas Supply Agreement, Total was not entitled to serve on TVPL the notice pursuant to special condition 15 contained in the letter of July 5, 2005;

(c) to declare that in the event that in reliance on that notice Total were to fail to supply TVPL with any gas pursuant to the GSA, TVPL would be entitled to damages and an order by way of specific performance.

NOTE

See too *Sky Petroleum Ltd v VIP Petroleum Ltd* [1974] 1 WLR 576, where a petrol supplier threatened in apparent breach of contract to cut off supplies to a garage at a time when, owing to world conditions, petrol was almost unobtainable elsewhere. This again was a contract to sell unascertained goods. Goulding J referred to the supposed bar on specific performance of such contracts, and said: '[T]he ratio behind the rule is, as I believe, that under the ordinary contract for the sale of non-specific goods, damages are a sufficient remedy. That, to my mind, is lacking in the circumstances of the present case. The evidence suggests, and indeed it is common knowledge that the petroleum market is in an unusual state in which a would-be buyer cannot go out into the market and contract with another seller, possibly at some sacrifice as to price. Here, the defendants appear for practical purposes to be the plaintiffs' sole means of keeping their business going, and I am prepared so far to depart from the general rule as to try to preserve the position under the contract.'

(b) The discretion to order specific performance

Specific performance is a discretionary remedy. It is as a rule not granted in respect of goods of an ordinary description which the buyer intends to resell (see *Cohen v Roche* [1927] 1 KB 169 (where the 'ordinary' goods were in fact 'eight genuine Hepplewhite chairs'!) and *Société des Industries Metallurgiques SA v Bronx Engineering Co Ltd* [1975] 1 Lloyd's Rep 465 (machinery)). But, as the case cited in the previous paragraph indicates, this attitude may now be open to challenge if there is no other source of supply reasonably open to the buyer.

By contrast, orders of specific performance have been made in respect of ships, of a design especially suited to the buyer's needs (*Behnke v Bede Shipping Co Ltd* [1927] 1 KB 649 and *The Star Gazer* [1985] 1 Lloyd's Rep 370) and antiques (*Taylor v Hamer* [2002] EWCA Civ 1130, [2003] 1 P & CR DG60). There is no doubt they are available for works of art (*Falcke v Gray* (1859) 4 Drewry 651); and it seems they will also be available for large constructions such as drilling-rigs (*International Finance Corpn v DSNL Offshore Ltd* [2005] EWHC 1844 (Comm), [2007] 2 All ER (Comm) 305).

PART IV

INTERNATIONAL SALES

Chapter 15   International sales   533

CHAPTER 15

INTERNATIONAL SALES

1 INTRODUCTION

There is more than one way in which a sale of goods contract may have an international element—for example, the seller and buyer may be in different jurisdictions, or the contract may contemplate that the goods are to be carried from one country to another. We are concerned in this section particularly with the latter: that is, sale contracts that involve the transport of the goods from one country to another. These will not necessarily be the countries in which the seller and buyer are respectively based—indeed, they may be based anywhere, even in the same country.[1] A contract of this kind exposes the parties to greater risks than a purely domestic sale: physical risks associated with transport and the extra handling; financial risks, such as movements in exchange rates; political (and even war) risks; and legal risks if a judgment or award has to be enforced in a foreign country. Some of these risks can be covered by insurance. Others may be avoided by careful drafting of the sales contract. Much uncertainty can be resolved if the parties use one of the standard contract forms of the relevant trade association, which have been tried and tested over the years, for example the GAFTA forms of the Grain and Feed Trade Association, or those of the London Metal Exchange. There are also standard international terms of trade, such as INCOTERMS 2010 (see below).

This chapter is concerned with the rules of English law affecting international sales as they affect buyer and seller. (It will not cover, except peripherally, the law of carriage: that is, the relation between buyers and sellers on the one hand, and carriers on the other.) Although this may seem a parochial approach, it should be remembered that a surprisingly large proportion of international trade is carried on under contracts governed by English law by choice of the parties.

With a few exceptions (notably the applicability of the Unfair Contract Terms Act 1977—see above, p 452), the English rules on international sales are the same as those for domestic sales. Today this is an unusual approach. More than 80 of the world's nearly 200 states, including importantly the United States, Canada, Brazil, Russia, China, Australia, New Zealand, and most EU members, are signatories to the UN Convention on Contracts for the International Sale of Goods (known as the CISG or Vienna Convention), setting out a regime of detailed rules for international sales based on both common law and civil law models, entirely separate from the national provisions on domestic sales.[2] However, the UK

---

[1] eg no less than four of the largest international oil and commodity dealers—Glencore, Vitol, Trafigura, and Mercuria, many of whom feature in these pages—are Swiss-based.

[2] An earlier attempt at introducing uniform rules, the 1964 Hague Convention relating to a Uniform Law on International Sales, failed to gain substantial support. The UK did ratify it, but on the basis that it would apply only where the parties positively chose it (see the Uniform Laws on International Sales Act 1967). It is in effect a dead letter.

has deliberately not ratified this Convention, largely because of a feeling that compared with English law it is apt to introduce an excessive degree of uncertainty into the law of contract. We will not refer to it further in any detail.

For further reading on this, see I Schwenzer, *Commentary on the Convention on the International Sale of Goods* (4th edn, 2016); L D'Arcy (ed), *Schmitthoff's Export Trade* (11th edn, 2007), Ch 14; N Hofmann, 'Interpretation Rules and Good Faith as Obstacles to the UK's Ratification of the CISG and to the Harmonization of Contract Law in Europe' (2010) 22 Pace Intl L Rev 141. Decisions on the CISG are collected at a website specifically maintained for that purpose: see http://www.cisg.law.pace.edu.

2 TYPICAL EXPORT TRANSACTIONS AND INCOTERMS

The parties to an international contract of sale are free to make any arrangement they choose as regards delivery, risk, and the other incidents of the transaction. (The Unfair Contract Terms Act 1977 does not generally apply because of ss 26 and 27: above, p 453.) In practice, the contract is likely to fall under one or another of a series of recognised heads, listed below. In listing these we will use the designations of INCOTERMS 2010, a set of international rules for the interpretation of trade terms promulgated by the International Chamber of Commerce (ICC). These have no official force in English law, but may be incorporated in sale contracts by the parties, and in addition are sometimes referred to as persuasive authorities by the English courts.

EXW (Ex Works [named place])

> Goods to be collected by the buyer from the seller's premises or another place (ie works, factory, warehouse). No duty on the seller to load.

FAS (Free Alongside [port of shipment])

> Seller to deliver alongside a ship nominated by the buyer at the named port of shipment.

FOB (Free on Board [port of shipment])

> Seller to put goods on board a ship nominated by the buyer at the named port of shipment.

FCA (Free Carrier [named place])

> Seller to deliver goods into custody of a land or air carrier nominated by the buyer at the named place.

CFR (Cost and Freight [named port of destination]. In England normally referred to as C & F)

> Seller to arrange carriage by sea to named port of destination, pay freight, obtain the bill of lading and shipping documents, and transfer the documents to the buyer.

CPT (Carriage Paid to [named place of destination])

> Seller to arrange carriage by land or air to named destination, pay freight, and transfer any relevant documents to buyer.

CIF (Cost, Insurance and Freight [named port of destination])

> Seller to arrange carriage by sea to named port of destination, pay freight, and insure goods in transit.

CIP (Carriage Paid to [named place of destination])

> Seller to arrange carriage by land or air to named destination, pay freight, insure goods in transit, and transfer any relevant documents to buyer.

DAP (Delivered at Place [named place]. In England, where sea carriage involved, this is often known as 'ex ship' or 'arrival')

> Seller to arrange to carry goods, by any mode of transport, to the named place and put the goods at the buyer's disposal there, ready for unloading by buyer. Buyer to unload and (if sale international) clear for import.

DAT (Delivered at Terminal [named terminal])

> Seller to arrange to carry goods, by any mode of transport, to a named container terminal and put the goods at the buyer's disposal there, ready for collection by buyer. Buyer to clear for import.

DDP (Delivery Duty Paid [named destination])

> Goods to be delivered by seller at named place of destination, duty paid.

The above terms, as will be seen, begin with the least burdensome to the seller. It will also be noticed that some (eg CIF) are appropriate only to sales involving carriage by sea. Some (eg FCA) are appropriate only to land or air carriage, or to multimodal transport (eg transport between two inland places using both sea and land transport). Others (eg DAP) can be used in connection with any type of transport. Most can be used, not only with individual cargoes (eg five JCB excavators), but also with bulk cargoes (eg 10,000 tonnes of soya beans) and containerised cargo. See, generally, G Oduntan, ' "C.I.F. Gatwick" and Other Such Nonsense Upon Stilts: Incoterms and the Law, Jargon and Practice of International Business Transactions' (2010) 21 ICCLR 214.

Because these designations have no official status, it is always possible for the parties to vary their incidents by agreement. For example, while a CIF contract presumptively requires a bill of lading to be transferred to the buyer, it is not unusual for parties to agree that a sea waybill be used instead (on which, see p 537 below). It is also possible that there may be a conflict between the name given by the parties to a contract and its actual terms. For example, a contract may be headed 'CIF' but its terms be consistent only with some other type of contract. If so, it is open to a court to disregard the heading and treat the contract according to the parties' real intention. An example is *Comptoir d'Achat et de Vente du Boerenbond Beige S/A v Luis de Ridder Ltda, The Julia*, below, p 553.

3 SALES INVOLVING SEA CARRIAGE

For many reasons, it makes best sense to begin with contracts where the goods are to be carried by sea. These are the traditional export–import transactions and so the ones for which well-established legal rules have evolved. Non-marine transactions use many of the same ideas, and can then be dealt with later in the light of contracts involving sea carriage.

Because of the time which it takes for goods to travel by sea, and also because of the practice of repeated sales of bulk commodities such as oil or soya beans before their arrival at destination, it is particularly necessary in this type of transaction for the parties to be able to make arrangements to deal with goods while afloat and, in addition, in order to finance the deal, to give effective security over those goods to banks and other lenders. To meet these problems, two developments have taken place.

First, performance of the contract is largely documentary. Traditionally, for example, CIF contracts are performed by the seller handing over three documents. These are:

(1) the bill of lading (see below);.

(2) the commercial invoice—this is an invoice itemising the goods sold and describing them in a way which makes it possible to identify them as the contract goods, or as answering to the description of the contract goods;

(3) a marine insurance document—this must be expressed in such a way as to make it clear that it covers the goods specified for the whole of the voyage covered by the bill of lading. When the bill of lading is transferred from one person to another, the policy of insurance will be assigned at the same time.

Other documents which may be required under particular contracts may include certificates of origin; certificates of quality or inspection certificates (important because there usually will be no opportunity for the buyer or any later sub-purchasers to inspect the goods until after they have reached their destination); and export and/or import licences.

Secondly, one particular document, the bill of lading, has been elevated to a position of special symbolic importance, to the point where for many purposes it is treated in law as representing the goods themselves: for instance, 'delivery' of the goods can be effected by handing it over. This is referred to in greater detail in the next paragraphs.

The bill of lading   The bill of lading is a document with a threefold purpose, issued by or on behalf of the sea carrier to the consignor of the goods, or to someone nominated by him, shortly after the goods have been loaded.

First, it acknowledges the fact that the goods have been received, describing them in an itemised list, and evidences the fact that they have been loaded in apparent good order and condition. (If not, the defect is noted—eg that some barrels were leaking—and the bill is then called a 'claused', as distinct from a 'clean', bill. It will then be difficult to dispose of because ordinary contracts of sale require a bill of lading to be 'clean'.)

Secondly, it contains the terms of the contract of carriage, and identifies loading port and destination.

Thirdly, it is regarded in law as a 'document of title'. This means three things. (1) It evidences the rights of possession and ownership in respect of the goods. This is recognised in s 19(2) of the Sale of Goods Act 1979, which states that 'Where goods are shipped, and by the bill of lading the goods are deliverable to the order of the seller or his agent, the seller is prima facie to be taken to reserve the right of disposal'—in other words, it is presumed that property does not pass unless and until the seller transfers the bill of lading to the buyer. (2) It is regarded as a substitute for the goods as regards possession, such that possession or delivery of it is treated in law as possession or delivery of the goods themselves. Hence the requirement of a transfer of possession in order to create a valid pledge is satisfied by delivery of the bill of lading (*Barber v Meyerstein* (1870) LR 4 HL 317). (3) Delivery of the goods at their destination must be made against, and only against, the surrender of the bill (*Sze Hai Tong Bank v Rambler Cycle Co* [1959] AC 576; *Motis Exports Ltd v Dampskibsselskabet AF 1912 A/S* [2000] 1 All ER (Comm) 91).

A bill of lading may be made out in different ways. An 'order bill' is made out to a named person 'or order'. A 'straight bill' is made out to a named person only (often accompanied by a statement that the document is 'not transferable' or 'non-negotiable').[3] In the first case, the rights to the goods covered by the bill may be transferred from one holder to another by indorsing and delivering the document. In the second case, no rights can be transferred in this way, and hence the goods can only be delivered to the named consignee.

Note that, despite superficial similarities to a bill of exchange, a bill of lading is never a *negotiable instrument* in the sense discussed in Chapter 18. A transferee can never acquire a better title than that of the preceding holder by virtue merely of taking it in good faith.

Delivery of a bill of lading can transfer not only the rights in the goods it represents, but also the holder's contractual rights against the carrier under the contract of carriage. This is provided for by s 2 of the Carriage of Goods by Sea Act 1992 (replacing s 1 of the Bills of Lading Act 1855). The result is that not only the shipper, but the consignee and anyone to whom the bill of lading has been transferred, obtains a right to sue the carrier in respect of any breach of the contract of carriage: for example, damage to the cargo through the provision of an unseaworthy ship, or losses due to delayed delivery. In addition, if anyone who is thus entitled asserts his contractual rights against the carrier, under s 3 of the 1992 Act he assumes the corresponding contractual duties—although these liabilities will cease if the bill is transferred to another holder: *Borealis AB v Stargas Ltd* [2001] UKHL 17, [2002] 2 AC 205.

The bill of lading is to be contrasted to another document used in carriage by sea, the sea waybill. Very widely used where sale of the goods at sea is not expected and much preferred by the shipping industry, this is unlike the bill of lading in that it is non-transferable, is not a document of title, and need not be surrendered to obtain delivery of the goods. Nevertheless it has similarities to the bill of lading, in that it acts as a receipt and normally embodies the terms of the contract of carriage. Under the Carriage of Goods by Sea Act 1992 the consignee named in a sea waybill has the same right to enforce the terms of the contract of carriage as a transferee of a bill of lading.

Bills of lading and sea waybills traditionally cover port-to-port transport. They are, however, also issued in respect of multimodal transport where the sea leg of the transport forms the major part of the distance travelled (eg carriage of machinery from Düsseldorf in Germany to Canberra in Australia, incorporating sea carriage from Rotterdam to Sydney and trucking elsewhere). Although the matter has not been definitively resolved, it seems that such documents, which refer to themselves as negotiable bills of lading or waybills as the case may be, probably have the legal characteristics of their port-to-port equivalents. See A Tettenborn, 'Bills of Lading, Multimodal Transport Documents, and Other Things' in B Soyer and A Tettenborn (eds), *Carriage of Goods by Sea, Land and Air* (2013), Ch 7.

In this book, we shall look in a little detail at four of the more common of the traditional marine standard form contracts: FOB, FAS, CIF, and DAP or 'ex ship'. For further information, reference may be made to L D'Arcy (ed), *Schmitthoff's Export Trade* (11th edn, 2007).

4 FOB CONTRACTS

The contract on FOB ('free on board') terms is one of the 'mainstream' export transactions for which detailed rules have been very fully worked out over the years. There can be a wide variety of FOB arrangements, but we shall concentrate on a contract on 'classic' or 'strict' FOB

---

[3] Theoretically it can be made out to 'bearer', or to a named person 'or bearer'; but this hardly ever happens in contemporary practice.

terms. Here, the seller undertakes not just to get the goods *to* the ship, but to bear the cost of loading them *on to* her. But it is the buyer's business to make all arrangements regarding the shipping and insurance of the goods. The buyer also bears all the risk of problems on the voyage, such as delay in unloading (*Profindo Pte Ltd v Abani Trading Pte Ltd* [2013] SGHC 10, [2013] 1 Lloyd's Rep 370). The contract will state, typically: 'FOB, Rotterdam, shipment in August', or, perhaps, 'FOB, August shipment, Dutch or Belgian port' (in the latter case the choice of port is presumptively the buyer's: *Boyd v Louca* [1973] 1 Lloyd's Rep 209). The seller must hold itself ready to put the goods on any ship nominated by the buyer at the nominated port during August. The first step is taken by the buyer, who has the right (and the duty) to find a suitable ship and nominate it. He may voyage-charter an entire ship, if the goods are enough to constitute a whole cargo, or book space on a general cargo ship for less than a ship-load.[4] The seller must then have the goods ready to ship at that time and place and load them. After loading, the carrier (or more commonly its agent) gives the seller a document called a 'mate's receipt', acknowledging receipt of the goods, itemised as to quantity and description, and confirming their apparent order and condition; later it prepares, signs, and hands the seller a bill of lading made out in the buyer's name. (Alternatively, the contract may provide for the seller to procure the bill of lading, in which case it will retain the mate's receipt and have the bill of lading issued in its own name and receive payment in exchange for the bill itself.) If the bill is made out to the seller, it will be a party to the contract of carriage; and it will also have 'reserved the right of disposal' in regard to the goods, which will normally prevent the property from passing to the buyer until the bill is transferred to him (s 18, r 5(2); s 19(1), (2)). For an example of a case where the seller reserved the right of disposal see *The Ciudad de Pasto*, below.

In this case, the rules as to rejection of the cargo are the same as in CIF contracts: that is, the buyer may reject the bill of lading if not in order, and in addition may reject the goods themselves in respect of any defect not apparent from the bill of lading itself. *See Aston FFI (Suisse) SA v Louis Dreyfus Commodities Suisse SA* [2015] EWHC 80 (Comm), [2015] 1 Lloyd's Rep 413, and *Kwei Tek Chao v British Traders*, below.

The critical moment in an FOB contract occurs when the goods go on board the ship: in old practice by 'crossing the ship's rail' while suspended from a crane or derrick, more commonly today by passing a point ('flange') in a pipe from shore to ship (eg in the case of oil or grain) or being placed on board (in the case of a container). At this point risk invariably passes (*Browne v Hare* (1858) 4 H & N 822), and property may pass also unless the seller has 'reserved the right of disposal' (eg by retaining the bill of lading), or the contract goods are unascertained, or the contract provides otherwise.

Under an FOB contract of this traditional type, the seller's and buyer's duties may thus be listed as follows.

The seller's duties will typically include:

- to supply the goods, with evidence of conformity with contract;
- to deliver the goods on board the ship, at the place and time stipulated by the contract or nominated by the buyer;
- to obtain the export licence;
- to bear all costs up to and including loading (across the ship's rail);

---

[4] He may alternatively enter into a 'slot charter' as regards a container ship: ie a reservation of one or more container spaces on the relevant vessel.

- to provide documents evidencing delivery to the ship, certificate of origin, etc;
- to cooperate with the buyer in procuring the bill of lading and other documentation;
- to give notice to the buyer to enable him to insure the goods during their sea transit (see s 32(3)).

The buyer's duties are as follows:

- to procure a suitable ship or shipping space and give the seller due notice of the ship and place and time of loading;
- to pay the price;
- to bear all costs subsequent to the goods passing the ship's rail;
- to bear the costs of procuring all documentation, including the bill of lading and certificate of origin.

Variations on the 'classic' FOB contract are very common. In the 'extended' FOB contract, the seller takes on the additional responsibilities of making the shipping and insurance arrangements. This he will do on behalf of the buyer, who therefore bears the risk of any increase in shipping and insurance rates after the contract of sale is concluded. It may be more convenient for the parties to arrange matters this way, especially where the goods sold do not amount to a complete cargo. The seller is often better placed to deal with exporting agencies in his own country—or he may be in the exporting business himself. Of course, every additional duty which the seller undertakes is likely to be reflected in the price which he charges the buyer.

Some of the cases which have been cited in earlier chapters were concerned with contracts made on FOB terms—for example, *Colley v Overseas Exporters Ltd* (above, p 477) and *Carlos Federspiel & Co SA v Charles Twigg & Co Ltd* (above, p 354). The case which follows contains a useful description of this type of contract, and shows the importance in law of the moment when the goods go on board the ship.

Pyrene Co Ltd v Scindia Navigation Co Ltd

[1954] 2 QB 402, Queen's Bench Division

This case turned on a technical point of carrier's liability under what are now the Hague–Visby Rules appended to the Carriage of Goods by Sea Act 1971, which need not concern us here. But it contains a useful summary of the incidents of a FOB contract.

> **Devlin J**: The contract of sale provided for delivery fob London, the price including dock and harbour dues and port rates to be paid by the seller; and further expressly provided that freight was to be engaged by the buyer, who was to give due notice to the seller when and on board what vessel the goods were to be delivered. Payment was to be made twenty-one days after delivery and after receipt of certain documents for which the contract called, such as invoice, inspection certificate, etc, and of the dock company's or mate's receipt. In the special circumstances of this case and because of delay in shipment, payment was in fact made in advance, but on the terms that that should not affect the seller's obligations as to delivery. As I have said, it was agreed that the property did not pass till delivery over the ship's rail.
>
> ...
>
> The fob contract has become a flexible instrument. In what counsel called the classic type as described, for example, in *Wimble, Sons & Co v Rosenberg & Sons* [1913] 3 KB 743, the buyer's

duty is to nominate the ship, and the seller's to put the goods on board for account of the buyer and procure a bill of lading in terms usual in the trade. In such a case the seller is directly a party to the contract of carriage at least until he takes out the bill of lading in the buyer's name. Probably the classic type is based on the assumption that the ship nominated will be willing to load any goods brought down to the berth or at least those of which she is notified. Under present conditions, when space often has to be booked well in advance, the contract of carriage comes into existence at an earlier point of time. Sometimes the seller is asked to make the necessary arrangements; and the contract may then provide for his taking the bill of lading in his own name and obtaining payment against the transfer, as in a cif contract. Sometimes the buyer engages his own forwarding agent at the port of loading to book space and to procure the bill of lading; if freight has to be paid in advance this method may be the most convenient. In such a case the seller discharges his duty by putting the goods on board, getting the mate's receipt and handing it to the forwarding agent to enable him to obtain the bill of lading. The present case belongs to this third type; and it is only in this type, I think, that any doubt can arise about the seller being a party to the contract.

NOTE

See too, for another useful summary, *The El Amria* [1982] 2 Lloyd's Rep 28 at 32, per Donaldson LJ.

The question of the passing of title in a contract FOB is a matter for the interpretation of the contract: it can be either when the goods are loaded, or when the bill of lading (if issued to the seller) is transferred.

The Ciudad de Pasto
[1988] 1 WLR 1145, Court of Appeal

Cartons of prawns were shipped FOB from South America to Japan. The carriers issued bills of lading which provided for delivery to the order of Vikingos. Eighty per cent of the price was paid by the buyers, Colombia; it was understood that the bill of lading would be transferred when the remaining 20 per cent was paid. The goods were found to be damaged on discharge, allegedly because of the negligence of the carriers at a time when the bills of lading had not been transferred. The buyers, Colombia, sued the carriers in tort. The question whether they could succeed depended on whether Colombia owned the prawns at the time. Hobhouse J held that they did. The Court of Appeal reversed his decision.

Purchas LJ: ... Parliament has provided a statutory, if prima facie, presumption as to how the intention of the parties as to the passing of property should be resolved.

The relevant sections of the Sale of Goods Act 1979 have already been cited in the judgment of Staughton L.J. and it is unnecessary for me to repeat them here. The vital section, however, is section 19(2) and, purely for the sake of reference, I refer to that only:

Where goods are shipped, and by the bill of lading the goods are deliverable to the order of the seller or his agent, the seller is prima facie to be taken to reserve the right of disposal.

The question which faced the judge was whether that prima facie position had been disturbed by the inadequate evidence placed before him.

In addition, the authority of the speech of Lord Wright in *Ross T. Smyth and Co. Ltd. v. T. D. Bailey, Son and Co* (1940) 45 Com Cas 292 already cited by Staughton LJ and the passage cited at pp. 300–301 lends support to this presumption where the seller reserves or retains for himself the right of payment by cash against documents. The judge approached this problem in this way: [1987] 2 Lloyd's Rep. 392, 399:

> The next issue I have to consider is the issue of title to sue. The plaintiffs have alleged that they have the title to sue … This is based upon the allegation that the plaintiffs, or one or other of them, was the owner of the goods at all material times while they were in the care and custody of the defendants.… Despite the unsatisfactory nature of the plaintiffs' evidence I am prepared to find on the balance of probabilities that the title in the relevant goods passed to Colombia Fisheries on shipment and remained in them until after the completion of discharge at Yokohama.

It is at this point of the judge's judgment that, like Staughton L.J., regretfully I find myself unable to follow him in drawing that inference. I therefore direct my attention to see where the difference has arisen. The judge said, at pp. 399–400:

> The relevant dispute before me centred upon whether it was right to conclude that title had passed to Colombia Fisheries at the time of shipment at Cartagena or only at some later, unidentified time. The clear inference is that Colombia Fisheries bought the goods on f.o.b. terms. Therefore unless there was a breach of the agreement, or some failure on the part of their sellers to perform their agreement, the title in the goods should have been passed to Colombia Fisheries at the time of shipment.

The inference which the judge has drawn from the statements before him under the Civil Evidence Act 1968 that the goods were bought on f.o.b. terms has not been challenged on appeal. In citing that as one of the leading inferences on which the judge inferred that the property passed on shipment, it is difficult not to conclude that at this point in his judgment Homer must have nodded in overlooking the fact that in an f.o.b. contract it is still open to the seller to reserve to himself the right of disposal of the goods the subject matter of the contract. If it were otherwise it is unlikely that the judge would have referred to that particular aspect of the case at that point in his judgment. I now turn again to the judgment where reference is made to section 19(2) of the Act of 1979, at p. 400:

> I was asked by the defendants to infer that Vikingos had not passed the title to Mitsui U.S.A. on shipment because of the terms in which Vikingos took the bills of lading, which were to their own order. Prima facie taking bills of lading in such a form is an indication that the shipper wishes to reserve the right of disposal of the goods and not at that time to pass the property in the goods to any other person. No reliance before me was placed upon any difference between any foreign legal system and English law and the parties among other things referred me to the Sale of Goods Act and the well known passage in Lord Wright's speech in *Ross T. Smyth and Co. Ltd. v. T. D. Bailey, Son and Co* (1940) 45 Com.Cas. 292; [1940] 3 All E.R. 60. However in each case it is a question of evaluating all the evidence of the parties' conduct including all the contracts which they have made in order to see whether they have intended that the general property should not pass on shipment. In the present case I do not consider that I should conclude that Vikingos were intending not to perform their obligation to pass the property in the goods on shipment.

There again, with respect to the judge, he has returned to the error which, in my judgment, he made in the application of the accepted fact that the contract was on f.o.b. terms to the problem of deciding when the property in the goods should pass. He continued then to this finding, which was based on that erroneous inference, at p. 400:

> The correct inference is in my judgment that they were at most merely reserving a special property in order to facilitate the operation of the letter of credit mechanism for payment. Vikingos would have a lien on the bills of lading until they were paid and thereafter the bankers would have a lien. But there is no reason why the general property should not pass down the line to Colombia Fisheries. Further it would be extravagant that the general property should not pass seeing that Vikingos had already been paid 80 per cent. of the value of the goods prior to shipment and were only interested in collecting the balance of 20 per cent.

In my judgment, there was simply no evidence from which secondary inferences could be drawn which would entitle the departure from the prima facie presumption arising from the form in which the bills of lading were drawn....

So far as Mr. Howard's courageous attempt to take the path of avoiding the impact of section 19(2) of the Act of 1979 is concerned, whilst accepting that the inference apparently drawn by the judge from the fact that the contract was on f.o.b. terms was not one that he was entitled to draw, I find myself in agreement with Staughton L.J. that I cannot follow Mr. Howard's able and attractive submissions along that path. In particular, I adopt with gratitude the analysis that Staughton L.J. has given of the point based on the so-called 'red clause,' that Vikingos had already been paid 80 per cent. of the value of the goods prior to shipment. In my judgment, that is an aspect which has little or no impact on the general evidence necessary if a party is to avoid the prima facie presumption contained in section 19(2).

For those reasons and for the reasons already given by Staughton L.J. I agree that this appeal should be allowed.

5   FAS CONTRACTS

'FAS' stands for 'free alongside ship'. An FAS contract is essentially the same as a strict FOB contract, save that the seller's duty is merely to get the goods alongside the ship nominated by the buyer,[5] rather than into or onto her. Since the loading is to be carried out by the buyer, no question can arise of any documents being issued by the carrier to the seller. Typically, the seller's duties might include the following:

- to supply the goods, with evidence of conformity with the contract;
- to deliver the goods alongside the ship, at the place and at or within the time stipulated by the contract or nominated by the buyer;
- to give the buyer notice of the above;
- to provide a certificate of origin;
- to cooperate with the buyer in obtaining other necessary documentation, for example an export licence.

---

[5] Because the seller has to deliver *alongside* the vessel, this is not suitable for container traffic, where delivery is made at a terminal in the port area, but not alongside the carrying vessel.

The buyer, for his part, will have the following duties:

- to procure a ship, or shipping space, and give the seller due notice of the name of the ship and the place and time of loading;
- to pay the price;
- to bear all the costs of loading from alongside ship;
- to bear the costs of procuring all documentation, including the export licence, bill of lading, etc.

Property, possession, and risk will normally pass to the buyer on delivery—ie when the goods have been placed alongside the ship so that they can be taken on board. 'Alongside' may mean (depending upon the custom of the particular port) on the docks, in a lighter, etc.

6 CIF CONTRACTS

These are a further 'classic' export sale form. In a CIF contract, the buyer looks to the seller to make the whole of the shipping arrangements, including those relating to insurance (from which it follows that any increase—or reduction—in shipping or insurance rates after the sale contract is concluded is for the seller's account). The buyer takes delivery of the goods symbolically, commonly while they are at sea, by taking over the shipping documents relating to the consignment—comprising, at least, the bill of lading, commercial invoice, and insurance document. As will become apparent, what the buyer bargains for is, in a certain sense, to take over a whole commercial *venture*.

In contrast with an FOB contract, which specifies the port of loading, a CIF contract specifies the port of arrival: thus, if goods are sold on terms 'CIF Hamburg', the seller undertakes to provide goods which are destined to arrive at that port. Most CIF contracts are for commodities of some sort, such as crude oil or sugar or grain—in legal terms, unascertained goods sold by description. It will be no concern of the buyer how the seller finds the goods to meet its contract. The seller may ship the goods itself. But in practice cargoes of this sort are sold repeatedly while at sea;[6] hence, the majority of sellers will be commodity dealers who have themselves bought afloat. Conversely, the majority of buyers will never take delivery, but will sell the cargo on, still afloat.

The seller's duties are essentially:

- to ship at the agreed port of shipment goods of the contract description (or procure goods afloat which have been so shipped);
- if it ships the goods itself, to procure a contract of sea carriage by which the goods will be delivered to the contract destination, and obtain a bill of lading relating to them. If it buys afloat, it will obtain the bill of lading from its own seller.
- if it ships the goods itself, to insure them under an insurance contract which will be available for the benefit of the buyer and to obtain a policy or other document to that effect. If it buys afloat, it will again obtain the necessary document from its own seller;

---

[6] Cases are common where the same cargo is bought and sold 20 times over or more.

- to procure a commercial invoice in conformity with the contract;
- to tender these documents, plus any others required under the contract, to the buyer (or his agent or bank).

The buyer's duties will be:

- to accept the documents, if they are in conformity with the contract, and pay the price;
- to take delivery of the documents, and (unless it resells still afloat) to accept and take delivery of the goods at the agreed destination, and pay all unloading costs;
- (unless it resells still afloat) to pay customs and other duties at the port of arrival;
- (unless it resells still afloat) to procure any necessary import licence.

Presumptively the seller must pay the freight (and hence any bill of lading must bear the clause 'freight prepaid'). In practice, however, the freight is often deducted from the overall price and left to be paid by the buyer when the ship has reached its destination.

(a) The importance of the shipping documents

The key feature of the CIF contract is the role played by the documents in the performance of the contract. Once the buyer has had these documents delivered in a way which effectively transfers or assigns to it the rights which they embody, it can assert his title to the goods (since property normally passes on delivery of the bill of lading), and with it, the right to possession; it can demand delivery of the goods at the port of arrival, and sue a wrongdoer in tort if the goods are wrongfully damaged or lost or detained; it has contractual rights against the carrier, if the goods are missing, damaged, delayed, or misdelivered; and it has the right to claim on the policy of insurance in the event of loss or damage. The buyer thus takes over from the seller the whole *package* of rights and liabilities which make up the commercial venture. This means that it is bound to go through with the deal—to pay the price and take up the documents, when tendered—even though the goods may have been lost (see the *Manbré Saccharine* case, below). However, since the buyer has only the documents to go on, the law rightly says that it is bound to complete by taking up the documents only if they are strictly in conformity with the contract (this is also shown by the *Manbré Saccharine* case). The commercial invoice, the bill of lading, and the insurance policy must describe the goods in the same terms as the contract description; the quantities must tally, as must the date of shipment; the contract of carriage must be a reasonable one (and so, eg, not allow carriage on deck where this is inappropriate (*Geofizika DD v MMB International Ltd* [2009] EWHC 1675 (Comm), [2010] 1 Lloyd's Rep 458; reversed on the facts [2010] EWCA Civ 459, [2010] 2 Lloyd's Rep 1)). Both the contract of carriage and the insurance document must cover the whole of the period during which the goods are in transit. Unless the contract provides otherwise, the level of cover under the insurance document probably has to be minimal ICC cover—ie Institute Cargo Clauses A (this is stated expressly in INCOTERMS 2010). Although one antique authority states that an actual insurance policy must be tendered (*Diamond Alkali Export Corpn v Bourgeois* [1921] 3 KB 443), modern practice is to use a certificate issued by the insurer which is expressly stated to give rights to any transferee. The insurance document must be provided even if the voyage has been safely completed, for the documentation may turn out to be necessary later if an unforeseen claim should arise (eg see *Orient Co v Brekke & Howlid* [1913] 1 KB 531).

As we saw above, if documents are in any way not in order the buyer can reject them. If he accepts them notwithstanding, he loses the right to reject the cargo for any defect apparent from them: so if on a contract for 10,000 tonnes of soya beans the bill of lading states that only 9,500 tonnes were loaded, the buyer by accepting the documents loses the right to reject for short delivery. But it may be that there is a right to reject the cargo not apparent from a perusal of the documents: a hidden defect making the goods unsatisfactory on shipment, perhaps, or a misstatement in the bill of lading as to the date of shipment. To deal with this problem, the buyer under a CIF contract is held to have two rights of rejection (*Kwei Tek Chao v British Traders*, below, p 551). If the documents are not in order, he may refuse to take them up; and even after he has accepted the documents, he has a further right to reject the goods if the cargo proves not to be in conformity with the contract. Conversely, if the buyer rejects the documents when they are apparently in order, the seller may elect to treat this as a repudiation on the part of the buyer, and is relieved from the duty of delivering the goods themselves (*Berger v Gill & Duffus*, below, p 552).

In a CIF contract the property in the goods and the right to possession normally pass to the buyer when the documents are handed over. But the *risk* is deemed to have passed retrospectively 'as from' shipment. This may mean that he has to pay the price and take up the documents even though the goods have been lost: *Manbré Saccharine Co Ltd v Corn Products Co Ltd* (below). He will, however, succeed to such rights as the seller may have against the carrier and insurer in such a case.

Ross T Smyth & Co Ltd v TD Bailey, Sons & Co

(1940) 67 Ll L Rep 147, House of Lords

The facts are immaterial.

Lord Wright: The contract in question here is of a type familiar in commerce, which is described as a c.i.f. contract. The initials indicate that the price is to include cost, insurance and freight. It is a type of contract which is more widely and more frequently in use than any other contract used for purposes of seaborne commerce. An enormous number of transactions, in value amounting to untold sums, are carried out every year under c.i.f. contracts. The essential characteristics of this contract have often been described. The seller has to ship or acquire after that shipment the contract goods, as to which if unascertained he is generally required to give a notice of appropriation. On or after shipment he has to obtain proper bills of lading and proper policies of insurance. He fulfils his contract by transferring the bills of lading and the policies to the buyer. As a general rule he does so only against payment of the price, less the freight, which the buyer has to pay. In the invoice which accompanies the tender of the documents on the 'prompt,' that is, the date fixed for payment, the freight is deducted for this reason. In this course of business the general property in the goods remains in the seller until he transfers the bills of lading.

These rules, which are simple enough to state in general terms, are of the utmost importance in commercial transactions. I have dwelt upon them perhaps unnecessarily because the judgment of the Court of Appeal might seem to throw doubt on one of their most essential aspects. The property which the seller retains while he or his agent or the banker to whom he has pledged the documents retains the bills of lading, is the general property, not a special property by way of security. But in general the importance of the retention of the property is not only to secure payment from the buyer but for purposes of finance. The general course of international commerce involves the practice of raising money on the documents so as to bridge the period between shipment and the time of obtaining payment against documents. These credit facilities, which are of the first importance, would be completely unsettled if the incidence of the property were made a matter of doubt. By mercantile law the bills of lading are the symbols of the goods. The general property in the goods must be in the seller if he is to be able to pledge them. The whole system of commercial credits depends on the seller's ability to give a charge on the goods and the policies of insurance. A mere unpaid seller's lien would for obvious reasons be inadequate and unsatisfactory. . . .

NOTES

1. The presumption enunciated here, that property passes on the taking up of the bill of lading, is of course a mere presumption arising from ss 17 and 19 of the Sale of Goods Act. Property may, if so intended, pass after the taking up of the bill of lading (eg *Carlos Soto SAU v AP Moller-Maersk AS* [2015] EWHC 458 (Comm), [2015] 1 Lloyd's Rep 537), or before (*The Albazero* [1977] AC 774, where seller and buyer were part of the same corporate group and so there was no element of credit risk).

2. Any presumption as to passing of title with the transfer of the bill of lading is subject to the overriding provision in s 16 and the classic ruling in *Re Wait* (above, p 298). In consequence, problems may arise in the case of goods shipped in bulk for several buyers—for example, where a seller ships 10,000 tonnes of soya beans as a complete cargo and then contracts to sell 1,000 tonnes to each of ten separate purchasers. Even if the carrier (as is common) issues multiple bills of lading in respect of the goods (eg ten bills each relating to 1,000 tonnes), the delivery of such a bill to a buyer cannot pass ownership to him in the traditional sense. However, the difficulties have now been largely sidestepped. Under s 2 of the Carriage of Goods by Sea Act 1992 each buyer, even if not owner, obtains contractual rights against the carrier. Furthermore, if he has paid, he now becomes a co-owner with the seller (and/or other buyers) of the entire bulk; a status which protects him in the event of the seller's bankruptcy and entitles him to sue wrongdoers in tort. But insofar as buyers have not paid all or any part of the price, s 16 continues to apply.

Manbré Saccharine Co Ltd v Corn Products Co Ltd
[1919] 1 KB 198, King's Bench Division

Under two separate contracts, Corn Products sold starch and corn syrup to Manbré Saccharine on terms CIF London. Goods answering the contract description were shipped aboard the SS *Algonquin*, which was sunk by a torpedo or mine on 12 March 1917. The sellers tendered the documents relating to the goods on 14 March, but the buyers refused to take them up or pay the price. It was held that they were bound to do so, and that this was a breach of contract.

McCardie J: The first question arising can be briefly stated as follows: Can a vendor under an ordinary cif contract effectively tender appropriate documents to the buyer in respect of goods shipped on a vessel which at the time of tender the vendor knows to have been totally lost? . . .
I conceive that the essential feature of an ordinary cif contract as compared with an ordinary contract for the sale of goods rests in the fact that performance of the bargain is to be fulfilled by delivery of documents and not by the actual physical delivery of goods by the vendor. All that

the buyer can call for is delivery of the customary documents. This represents the measure of the buyer's right and the extent of the vendor's duty. The buyer cannot refuse the documents and ask for the actual goods, nor can the vendor withhold the documents and tender the goods they represent. The position is stated with weight and clearness in the treatise on charterparties by Scrutton LJ, 8th edn, p 167, in the notes to article 59 as follows: 'The best way of approaching the consideration of all questions on cif sales is to realise that this form of the sale of goods is one to be performed by the delivery of documents representing the goods—ie, of documents giving the right to have the goods delivered or the possible right, if they are lost or damaged, of recovering their value from the shipowner or from underwriters. It results from this that various rules in the Sale of Goods Act 1893, which is primarily drafted in relation to the sale and delivery of goods on land, can only be applied to cif sales *mutatis mutandis*. And there may be cases in which the buyer must pay the full price for delivery of the documents, though he can get nothing out of them, and though in any intelligible sense no property in the goods can ever pass to him—ie, if the goods have been lost by a peril excepted by the bill of lading, and by a peril not insured by the policy, the bill of lading and the policy yet being in the proper commercial form called for by the contract.'

In *Arnhold Karberg & Co v Blythe, Green, Jourdain & Co* [1916] 1 K.B. 495, Scrutton LJ, when a judge of first instance, described a cif contract as being a sale of documents relating to goods and not a sale of goods. But when the Court of Appeal considered that case Bankes LJ and Warrington LJ commented on the language of Scrutton J and indicated their view that a cif contract is a contract for the sale of goods to be performed by the delivery of documents. But I respectfully venture to think that the difference is one of phrase only. For in reality, as I have said, the obligation of the vendor is to deliver documents rather than goods—to transfer symbols rather than the physical property represented thereby. If the vendor fulfils his contract by shipping the appropriate goods in the appropriate manner under a proper contract of carriage, and if he also obtains the proper documents for tender to the purchaser, I am unable to see how the rights or duties of either party are affected by the loss of ship or goods, or by knowledge of such loss by the vendor, prior to actual tender of the documents. If the ship be lost prior to tender but without the knowledge of the seller it was, I assume, always clear that he could make an effective proffer of the documents to the buyer. In my opinion it is also clear that he can make an effective tender even though he possess at the time of tender actual knowledge of the loss of the ship or goods. For the purchaser in case of loss will get the documents he bargained for, and if the policy be that required by the contract, and if the loss be covered thereby, he will secure the insurance moneys. The contingency of loss is within and not outside the contemplation of the parties to a cif contract. I therefore hold that the plaintiffs were not entitled to reject the tender of documents in the present case upon the ground that the *Algonquin* had, to the knowledge of the defendants, sunk prior to the tender of documents. This view will simplify the performance of cif contracts and prevent delay either through doubts as to the loss of ship or goods or through difficult questions with regard to the knowledge or suspicion of a vendor as to the actual occurrence of a loss.

NOTES

1. In this case the appropriation took place before the goods were lost, when the seller shipped the particular goods which were to answer the contract. A more difficult question arises where the seller *appropriates* to the contract goods which have been shipped some time previously and which it knows have since been lost. Is the buyer bound to accept these documents? The question is not free from difficulty. It might seem that the answer must be no, and indeed that a seller who acted in this way was almost fraudulent. The better view, however, is that the buyer is bound. This is because it is inherent in a CIF contract that the seller is not bound to insure the goods against all events, but only against the usual risks. If a seller duly does this and the goods are then lost through an uninsured peril, to deny the seller the right to insist that the buyer accept the documents relating to those goods would leave the loss with the seller and contradict the latter's limited duty to insure. This solution was accepted in *Produce Brokers Co Ltd v Olympia Oil & Cake Co Ltd* [1917] 1 KB 320, but partly on the basis of a found custom to that effect.

For contrasting views see JD Feltham, 'The Appropriation to a CIF Contract of Goods Lost or Damaged at Sea' [1975] JBL 273 and *Benjamin on Sale* (9th edn, 2014), para 19–084.

2. In fact the seller lost in *Manbré Saccharine* because it had failed to tender insurance documents. Indeed, even if the documents had been tendered they would still have been bad tender because the policy covered not simply the cargo destined to the buyers but a good deal of other cargo as well. This is not permissible because of the possible conflict of interests between different buyers.

3. The case is also authority that CIF buyers 'are not, by their rejection of the tender on an insufficient ground, precluded from supporting the rejection on other and valid grounds' (per McCardie J at 204). The buyers here had not, at the time of rejection, raised the point about the insurance documents.

Hindley & Co Ltd v East India Produce Co Ltd
[1973] 2 Lloyd's Rep 515, Commercial Court

Sellers agreed to sell buyers 80 tons of jute to be shipped at Bangkok, C & F Bremen (C & F is CIF without the insurance element—see below—but nothing turns on the difference). They bought a bill of lading and other documents relating to goods apparently shipped, and transferred these to the buyers. On arrival, it transpired that for some unexplained reason no goods had been shipped and the bill of lading had been issued in error. The buyers sued the sellers for damages, and won.

Kerr J: The sellers' submissions can be summarized as follows: They submit that there is no liability because contracts of sale on c.i.f. or c. & f. terms are contracts for the sale of documents or to be performed by the delivery of documents. They point out that the bill of lading was in all respects proper on its face, that they themselves relied on the truth of its contents, and that they had no reasonable or any means of checking the accuracy of its contents.

They also point out—and in my view this must be a crucial limb of their argument—that they were not the shippers of these goods, but merely parties in a string who were on any view unconnected with whatever may have been the circumstances which gave rise to the issue of this bill of lading without any goods having been shipped.

Finally they contend that in the circumstances the buyers have a remedy against the carriers and submit that the buyers should be confined to that remedy and should have no remedy against the sellers, who were on any view innocent of what may have happened.

In my judgment none of these considerations can avail the sellers, and the award in favour of the buyers is correct. The reported cases and text-books contain many authoritative statements defining or describing the obligations of sellers under c.i.f. or c. & f. contracts. I do not propose to add to these save in so far as is necessary for present purposes. It is sufficient to say that a seller under such contracts has what can broadly be described as a duality of obligations relating respectively to the goods which are the subject-matter of the contract and the documents covering the goods which have to be tendered to the buyer. On the facts of the present case I consider that the sellers are in breach of both these aspects of their obligation.

I will deal first with the aspect relating primarily to the goods. The obligation of the seller under this type of contract is either to ship or to procure the shipment of goods of the contract description under a proper contract of affreightment, and to do so in accordance with any terms of the contract relating to their shipment as regards, for instance, time and place of shipment. Alternatively, the seller's obligation, if he does not himself ship or procure the shipment, is to procure documents—and in this connection one is referring to a bill of lading or a number of bills of lading—which cover such goods so shipped. In either event the obligation of the seller is thereafter to deliver such documents to the buyer.

I need only refer to a few passages which deal with the seller's obligations relating to the goods, but most of these appear to have had in mind the position of sellers who are also the shippers. There is for instance the classic passage in the judgment of Mr. Justice Hamilton (as he then was) in *Biddell Brothers v. E. Clemens Horst Co* [1911] 1 KB 214, at p. 220, where he said:

> … A seller under a contract of sale containing such terms [—and he was dealing with a c.i.f. contract—] has firstly to ship at the port of shipment goods of the description contained in the contract; secondly to procure a contract of affreightment, under which the goods will be delivered at the destination contemplated by the contract; thirdly to arrange for an insurance under the terms current in the trade which will be available for the benefit of the buyer; fourthly to make out an invoice … and finally to tender these documents to the buyer [—I am not quoting the passage in full because the further details do not matter—]

That well-known passage was cited with approval by Lord Justice Warrington in *Arnhold Karberg & Co v Blythe, Green Jourdain & Co* in the Court of Appeal, [1916] 1 K.B. 495, at p. 513. That case and other cases also show that it is an over-simplification to say that a c.i.f. contract is merely a contract for the sale of documents. It is, as Lord Justice Bankes put it in that case (at p. 510, with whom Lord Justice Warrington agreed at p. 514) a contract for the sale of goods to be performed by the delivery of documents.

Another passage in which that part of the seller's obligation which relates to the shipment of the goods is stressed is to be found in the speech of Lord Wright in *Ross T. Smyth & Co Ltd v. T. D. Bailey, Son & Co* (1940) 67 Ll.L.Rep. 147, at p. 156; [1940] 3 All E.R. 60, at p. 67;. He there said:

> The contract in question here is of the type familiar in commerce and is described as a c.i.f. contract. The initials indicate that the price is to include cost, insurance and freight. It is a type of contract which is more widely and more frequently in use than any other contract used for purposes of sea-borne commerce. An enormous number of transactions, in value amounting to untold sums, are carried out every year under c.i.f. contracts. The essential characteristics of this contract have often been described. The seller has to ship or acquire after the shipment the contract goods, as to which, if unascertained, he is generally required to give a notice of appropriation. On or after shipment, he has to obtain proper bills of lading and proper polices of insurance. He fulfils his contract by transferring the bills of lading and the policies to the buyer …

Turning to the text-books, there are only two to which I propose to refer. In what is now vol. 5 of *British Shipping Laws*, dealing with c.i.f. and f.o.b. contracts, one has in the first part an up-dated version of the well-known work of Mr. Justice Kennedy (as he then was), on c.i.f. contracts. In par. 1 on p. 3 of that work one finds the following description of the seller's obligations.

> Under this form of contract the seller performs his obligations by shipping, at the time specified in the contract or, in default of express provision in the contract, within a reasonable time,

goods of the contractual description in a ship bound for the destination named in the contract, or by purchasing documents in respect of such goods already afloat, and by tendering to the buyer, as soon as possible after the goods have been destined to him, the shipping documents.

Similarly, in the 17th edition of *Scrutton on Charter-Parties and Bills of Lading*, at p. 173 there is the following note on c.i.f. contracts:

In a contract for the sale of goods upon 'c.i.f.' terms, the contract, unless otherwise expressed, is for the sale of goods to be carried by sea, and the seller performs his part by shipping goods of the contractual description on board a ship bound to the contractual destination, or purchasing afloat goods so shipped, and tendering, within a reasonable time after shipment, the shipping documents, to the purchaser [—then there should be a comma—] the goods during the voyage being at the risk of the purchaser....

It follows from all these passages—and is indeed a matter of elementary law—that a c. & f. or c.i.f. contract is to be performed by the tender of documents covering goods which have been shipped either by the seller or by someone else in accordance with the terms of the contract. If no goods have in fact been shipped the sellers have not performed their obligation. I cannot see any basis for the distinction which the sellers here seek to draw between a seller who is also the shipper and a seller who is not the shipper. At the date of the contract it may well be unknown which means of performance the particular seller will employ, and in an ordinary c.i.f. or c. & f. contract, as in the present case, there will be nothing in the contract which restricts his choice between the two alternative methods of performance.

Since there was no shipment of any goods in the present case, either by these sellers or by anyone else, this is in my judgment sufficient to enable the buyers to succeed in recovering damages for breach of that part of the sellers' obligations.

Hansson v Hamel & Horley Ltd
[1922] 2 AC 36, House of Lords

Hansson agreed to sell 350 tons of Norwegian cod guano to Hamel & Horley CIF Kobe or Yokohama. Since there were no ships running directly from Norway to these Japanese ports, the guano was sent on a local ship, the *Kiev*, from Braatvag in Norway to Hamburg and there transshipped to the *Atlas Maru* for the ocean voyage to Japan. After the *Atlas Maru* had sailed, the seller tendered to the buyers in purported performance of his contract a bill of lading, which related only to the 'ocean' leg of the transport. The buyers were held entitled to insist on 'continuous documentary cover', ie documentary evidence of a contract or contracts of carriage covering both legs of the journey and the period of transshipment, and to reject this tender.

Lord Sumner: A cf and i [CIF] seller, as has often been pointed out, has to cover the buyer by procuring and tendering documents which will be available for his protection from shipment to destination, and I think that this ocean bill of lading afforded the buyer no protection in regard to the interval of thirteen days which elapsed between the dates of the two bills of lading and presumably between the departure from Braatvag and the arrival at Hamburg . . .

When documents are to be taken up the buyer is entitled to documents which substantially confer protective rights throughout. He is not buying a litigation, as Lord Trevethin (then A T Lawrence J) says in the *General Trading Co's Case* ((1911)16 Com Cas 95, 101). These documents have to be handled by banks, they have to be taken to be such as can be retendered to sub-purchasers, and it is essential that they should so conform to the accustomed shipping documents as to be reasonably and readily fit to pass current in commerce. I am quite sure that, under the circumstances of this case, this ocean bill of lading does not satisfy these conditions. It bears notice of its insufficiency and ambiguity on its face: for, though called a through bill of lading, it is not really so. It is the contract of the subsequent carrier only, without any complementary promises to bind the prior carriers in the through transit. . . . As things stood, the buyer was plainly left with a considerable lacuna in the documentary cover to which the contract entitled him . . .

[**Lords Buckmaster**, **Atkinson**, **Wrenbury**, and **Carson** concurred.]

Kwei Tek Chao v British Traders & Shippers Ltd
[1954] 2 QB 459, Queen's Bench Division

Chemicals were sold CIF Hong Kong, to be shipped in London in October. In fact they were shipped in November, but owing to a fraud which was nothing to do with the sellers the bills of lading transferred to the buyers said the goods had been shipped in October. On arrival the buyers stored the goods for some months, having lost their original planned sub-sale and the market being then in free fall. On discovering the facts they sued the sellers for damages for tendering a misdated bill of lading, claiming that had they known the true facts they would have rejected the goods and avoided their losses. One issue turned on whether, having accepted the documents, they could later have rejected the goods.

Devlin J: Here, therefore, there is a right to reject documents, and a right to reject goods, and the two things are quite distinct. A c.i.f. contract puts a number of obligations upon the seller, some of which are in relation to the goods and some of which are in relation to the documents. So far as the goods are concerned, he must put on board at the port of shipment goods in conformity with the contract description, but he must also send forward documents, and those documents must comply with the contract. If he commits a breach the breaches may in one sense overlap, in that they flow from the same act. If there is a late shipment, as there was in this case, the date of the shipment being part of the description of the goods, the seller has not put on board goods which conform to the contract description, and therefore he has broken that obligation. He has also made it impossible to send forward a bill of lading which at once conforms with the contract and states accurately the date of shipment. Thus the same act can cause two breaches of two independent obligations.

However that may be, they are distinct obligations, and the right to reject the documents arises when the documents are tendered, and the right to reject the goods arises when they are landed and when after examination they are found not to be in conformity with the contract. There are many cases, of course, where the documents are accepted but the goods are subsequently rejected. It may be that if the actual date of shipment is not in conformity with the contract, and the error appears from the documents, the buyer, by accepting the documents, not only loses his right to reject the documents, but also his right to reject the goods, but that would be because he had waived in advance reliance on the date of shipment. This case confirms that the buyer has two rights to reject: he may refuse to take up the documents if they are not in conformity with the contract, and he may reject the goods even after having accepted the documents, if he later discovers a breach on the seller's part.

NOTE

For a similar earlier case, see *James Finlay & Co Ltd v NV Kwik Hoo Tong HM* [1929] 1 KB 400.

Berger & Co Inc v Gill & Duffus SA
[1984] AC 382, House of Lords

Bergers contracted to sell to Gill & Duffus 500 tonnes of Argentine bolita beans CIF Le Havre. The contract provided for payment to be made against shipping documents, and also that a certificate given by independent assessors (GSC) as to the quality of the beans at the port of discharge should be final. The ship first unloaded only 445 tonnes at Le Havre, and overcarried the remaining 55 tonnes to Rotterdam. This part of the consignment reached Le Havre some two weeks later. Meantime, the buyers twice rejected the documents, on grounds relating to the certificate of quality as regards the 445 tonnes which the House of Lords held to be unfounded. The buyers were accordingly guilty of a repudiatory breach which, it was held, discharged the sellers from their obligation to deliver the 55 tonnes and debarred the buyers from any right that they might have had to reject the goods. In consequence, the buyers were held liable in damages for non-acceptance in respect of the entire 500 tonnes.

QUESTION

Sections 15A and 30(2A) of the Sale of Goods Act state that a buyer who is not a consumer may not reject the goods on the grounds (respectively) that they do not conform with their contract description or that the wrong quantity has been delivered, where the breach is so slight that it would be unreasonable for him to reject. Suppose that there is such a breach in a CIF contract as regards: (1) the goods as described in the documents; or alternatively (2) the goods themselves on arrival at their destination: should the buyer be able to reject the documents or the goods?

7 VARIANTS OF THE CIF CONTRACT

The basic principles applicable to a CIF contract apply with the necessary modifications to contracts where the seller agrees to pay to unload the goods (CIF free out) or the buyer agrees to pay for some extra items such as commission (CIF & C). The same is true of the C & F contract (often called by its INCOTERMS name of CFR), where it is the buyer rather than the seller who has the responsibility of arranging the insurance cover. (One reason for this may be that the laws of the buyer's country require it to take out insurance with a local insurer, or possibly with a state-owned insurance agency, in order to save foreign exchange.) It is more likely that a C & F contract will be one which contemplates that the seller is an exporter who will procure and dispatch the goods, rather than one which can be fulfilled by buying goods already afloat, since in the latter case there will be insurance cover in place which it assumed the buyer will take over.

8 DAP CONTRACTS (SOMETIMES CALLED 'EX SHIP' OR 'ARRIVAL' CONTRACTS)

Under a contract of this description, the buyer is bound to pay the price only if actual delivery of the goods is made at the port of delivery, the seller bearing all costs up to but not including unloading costs and import duties. Property and risk will pass with delivery of possession. It is not sufficient that the seller tenders a valid set of shipping documents: the buyer is entitled to the goods, not just the documents; and if the seller cannot procure the delivery of the goods from the ship, it has not fulfilled its obligations.

Comptoir d'Achat et de Vente du Boerenbond Beige S/A v Luis de Ridder Ltda, The Julia
[1949] AC 293, House of Lords

Rye was sold to a Belgian company under a contract expressed to be on terms 'CIF Antwerp', but which was held to be an 'arrival' contract. While the goods were at sea, the buyer paid the price in exchange for documents which included a delivery order, but the ship was prevented from unloading at Antwerp when the Germans invaded Belgium. The goods were unloaded at Lisbon instead. The buyers claimed their money back, alleging a total failure of consideration; the sellers argued in reply that the delivery of the documents was at least part performance, which was enough to defeat the buyer's claim. It was held that since the contract, as an 'arrival' contract, required actual delivery to be made at Antwerp, the consideration had totally failed.

Lord Porter: My Lords, this is an appeal [from] a judgment of the Court of Appeal affirming by a majority the judgment of Morris J who upheld an award of an umpire stated in the form of a special case under the Arbitration Acts 1889 to 1934. The arbitration arose out of a contract for the sale of rye by the respondents (the sellers) to the appellants (the buyers). The buyers, who were the claimants in the arbitration, asked for the refund of the purchase price paid by them under the contract on the ground that the consideration had wholly failed. The question for your Lordships' consideration is whether there was such a total failure of consideration.

The learned judge in agreement with the umpire, as I understand him, regarded the contract as a cif contract modified to some extent, but not altered in its essential characteristics. The buyers had, in his view, entered into a contract for the purchase of documents or, more accurately, for the purchase of a parcel of rye, the fulfilment of which was to be implemented by the handing over of documents. The documents, he considered, might be varied at the option of the sellers, who would fulfil their contract if they chose to tender a delivery order instead of a bill of lading, and a certificate instead of a policy of insurance. Even the stringency of these obligations he regarded as reduced by the practice of the parties with the result that delivery order meant an instruction to their own agents (countersigned, it is true, by those agents) and a certificate of insurance which was never tendered to or held on behalf or at the disposal of the buyers. The delivery order, Morris J considered, 'doubtless possessed commercial value.' In other words, the buyers were purchasers of documents and had received that for which they stipulated, ie, the usual delivery order and a certificate of insurance which would compel or incite the sellers to recover any loss from underwriters and pay it over to the buyers.

My Lords, the obligations imposed upon a seller under a cif contract are well known …

The strict form of cif contract may, however, be modified: a provision that a delivery order may be substituted for a bill of lading or a certificate of insurance for a policy would not, I think, make the contract concluded upon something other than cif terms, but in deciding whether it comes within that category or not all the permutations and combinations of provision and circumstance must be taken into consideration. Not every contract which is expressed to be a cif contract is such . . . In the present case therefore it is not as if a usual form of delivery order had been given and accepted or an insurance certificate covering the parcel was in the hands of Van Bree as agents for the buyers, nor can a solution be found in the mere designation of the contract as cif . . . The true effect of all its terms must be taken into account, though, of course, the description cif must not be neglected. It is true, no doubt, to say that some steps had been taken towards the performance of this contract, eg, the goods had been shipped, an invoice sent, the customary so-called delivery order had been transmitted and that delivery order amongst its provisions contained a declaration by the sellers' agents, Belgian Grain and Produce Co Ltd that they gave a share of the present delivery order of $4,973 in a certificate of insurance. But the taking of steps towards performance is not necessarily a part performance of a contract. The question is whether the purchaser has got what he is entitled to in return for the price. Of course, if the buyers paid the sum claimed in order to obtain the delivery order and the share purported to be given by it in the certificate of insurance, the contract would have been performed in part at least, but I do not so construe the contract, even when illuminated by the practice adopted by the parties. That practice seems to me rather to show that the payment was not made for the documents but as an advance payment for a contract afterwards to be performed. With all due respect to the learned judge and the Master of the Rolls, I can see no sufficient reason for supposing . . . that the delivery order had some commercial value. . . . There was no evidence of commercial value and the document itself was merely an instruction by one agent of the sellers to another . . . The document appears to me to be no more than an indication that a promise already made by the sellers would be carried out in due course, but in no way increases their obligations or adds to the security of the buyers.

My Lords, the object and the result of a cif contract is to enable sellers and buyers to deal with cargoes or parcels afloat and to transfer them freely from hand to hand by giving constructive possession of the goods which are being dealt with. Undoubtedly the practice of shipping and insuring produce in bulk is to make the process more difficult, but a ship's delivery order and a certificate of insurance transferred to or held for a buyer still leaves it possible for some, though less satisfactory, dealing with the goods whilst at sea to take place. The practice adopted between buyers and sellers in the present case renders such dealing well nigh impossible. The buyer gets neither property nor possession until the goods are delivered to him at Antwerp, and the certificate of insurance, if it enures to his benefit at all, except on the journey from ship to warehouse, has never been held for or delivered to him. . . .

The vital question in the present case, as I see it, is whether the buyers paid for the documents as representing the goods or for the delivery of the goods themselves. The time and place of payment are elements to be considered but by no means conclusive of the question: such considerations may, on the one hand, indicate a payment in advance or, on the other, they may show a payment postponed until the arrival of the ship, though the property in the goods or the risk have passed to the buyer whilst the goods are still at sea, as in *Castle v Playford* [above, p 346]. But the whole circumstances have to be looked at and where, as, in my opinion, is the case here, no further security beyond that contained in the original contract passed to the buyers as a result of payment, where the property and possession both remained in the sellers until delivery in Antwerp, where the sellers were to pay for deficiency in bill of lading weight, guaranteed condition on arrival and made themselves responsible for all averages, the true view, I think, is that it is not a cif contract even in a modified form but a contract to deliver at Antwerp. Nor do I think it matters that payment is said to be not only on presentation but 'in exchange for' documents. There are many ways of carrying out the contract to which that expression would apply, but in truth whether the payment is described as made on presentation of or in exchange for a document, the document was not a fulfilment or even a partial fulfilment of the contract: it was but a step on the way. What the buyers wanted was delivery of the goods in Antwerp. What the sellers wanted was payment of the price before that date, and the delivery of the documents furnished the date for payment, but had no effect on the property or possession of the goods or the buyers' rights against the sellers. If this be the true view there was plainly a frustration of the adventure—indeed the sellers admit so much in their pleading—and no part performance and the consideration had wholly failed. The buyers are accordingly entitled to recover the money which they have paid. . . .

[**Lords Simonds**, **du Parcq**, **Normand**, and **MacDermott** delivered concurring opinions.]

QUESTION

Why do you think that the buyer in *The Julia* was so keen to insist that the contract was ex ship (ie DAP) rather than CIF, as claimed by the seller?

NOTE

DAP contracts, as they are now referred to in INCOTERMS, may be used not only for contracts to ship goods, but for contracts where goods are to be transported by land, air, or multimodally. As mentioned above, there is a variant on DAP applicable only to land or multimodal transport, namely DAT (delivered at terminal). This is particularly appropriate to container traffic.

9 FCA, CIP, AND SIMILAR CONTRACTS

It is worth remembering that a declining proportion of world trade is carried under the kind of port-to-port shipment contracts referred to above. Especially within Europe (including to and from the UK), a great deal is carried by truck or train (or inland waterway). Small high-value consignments increasingly travel wholly or partly by air. Furthermore, where goods have to be transported from seller to buyer, transport is increasingly arranged door-to-door, on a multimodal basis. A consignment of electronics being sent from China to England is likely to be collected from the seller's premises, consolidated elsewhere in a container, trucked containerised to a port, carried by sea to a port in the UK, and trucked to the buyer's premises. For these, contracts arrangements such as FOB and CIF are inappropriate, if only because: (1) there is no equivalent of the bill of lading, with its particular legal effects, outside carriage by sea; and (2) in any case repeated sales of goods in transit are unlikely except in the maritime context.

For this reason, business has developed, and the ICC acknowledged, rough equivalents in FCA (free carrier) and CIP (carriage and insurance paid).

A FCA (free carrier) contract is in many ways similar to a FOB contract. It is up to the buyer to provide the transport unless otherwise agreed, and to ensure that the carrier is in a position to pick up the goods at the agreed place; it is then the seller's function to get the goods there. However, under INCOTERMS 2010 (which, in the absence of much authority in England, are likely to inform any decision), the seller's duty is not to load the goods, except where the place of delivery is its own premises: instead, it need merely put them at the disposal of the carrier. (If there are alternative places of delivery, the seller is entitled *and bound* to select between them (*Zenziper Grains v Bulk Trading Corpn* [2001] CLC 496).) Export formalities and charges are for the seller's account. As for documentation, the seller must obtain and provide to the buyer proof that the goods have reached the carrier, and then give the buyer all reasonable assistance in obtaining any necessary transport documents (eg air waybills, combined transport documents, or in the European context CMR consignment notes for carriage by road). Risk, and probably property, pass when the goods are placed at the disposal of the carrier (Sale of Goods Act, s 18, r 5).

CIP (carriage and insurance paid) is the non-marine equivalent of CIF. As with CIF, it requires the seller to arrange carriage of the goods to the buyer and insure them in transit. Because (with the possible exception of multimodal transport with a large sea element) there is no land equivalent of the bill of lading by which possession and rights of the carrier can be transferred, it is unlikely that the seller can buy goods already en route.

The contract of carriage must be on whatever terms are customary in the trade. In practice, in the European context, this would seem to require dispatch under the rules of the Convention on the Contract for the International Carriage of Goods by Road (CMR) or the Uniform Rules Concerning the Contract for International Carriage of Goods by Rail (CIM), the international conventions relating to transborder carriage by road or rail. For carriage by air, virtually all transborder carriage will in any case be governed by Warsaw Convention 1929 or the Montreal Convention 1999 (whichever is applicable). As for multimodal transport, a contract compatible with the ICC/UN Conference on Trade and Development (UNCTAD) rules would seem to be required. Any transport document obtained must be made available to the buyer, together with a commercial invoice. For the details of these carriage regimes, which are not dealt with in this book, see *Schmitthoff's Export Trade* (11th edn, 2007), Chs 17 and 18.

Insurance requirements are dealt with by INCOTERMS in some detail. Insofar as not inconsistent with the terms of the contract, the seller's duty is to insure the goods for 110 per cent of invoice value, on the basis of minimum Institute Cargo Clauses cover: ie Institute Cargo Clauses C.[7] For the same reasons as with CIF contracts, the cover must extend over the whole transit (*Lindon Tricotagefabrik v White & Meacham* [1975] 1 Lloyd's Rep 384).

Property and risk pass, it would seem, on handing over to the carrier: see Sale of Goods Act, s 18, r 5(2) and *Glaxo Group Ltd v Dowelhurst Ltd*, below.

Glaxo Group Ltd v Dowelhurst Ltd
[2004] EWCA Civ 290, [2005] ETMR 104, Court of Appeal

The claimants marketed trade-marked drugs. They sold a consignment to Senegal, which they shipped in France CIP Dakar (the capital of Senegal). Some of these drugs reached the European market, apparently after re-import by the defendants from Africa. The claimants sued the defendants for trade mark infringement. One defence raised was that the drugs had been marketed, that is sold to a buyer who was free to do as it pleased, within the European Economic Area (EEA), and hence that the trade mark owners had 'exhausted' their rights. The Court of Appeal held that this was an arguable defence, on the basis that by shipping goods in France CIP Dakar the claimants had transferred ownership to the buyers there and then.

---

[7] The Institute Cargo Clauses are standard clauses for the insurance of cargo, published by the Institute of London Underwriters and in use worldwide. See, for a useful summary, *Schmitthoff's Export Trade* (11th edn, 2007), paras 19–18 ff.

Jacob LJ:

37. There is another reason for so doing at this stage. The deputy judge held that they were delivered to the customer (L'Afrique aide L'Afrique) by the vendor's agent—'as if the claimants had carried the goods to Dakar in Senegal themselves'. On that basis he held that Glaxo did not put the goods on the EEA market and there was no exhaustion defence.

39.... The contract was 'CIP Dakar.' Mr Burkill took us to the definition of CIP which is to be found in an ICC publication. This says:

'Carriage and Insurance paid to ...' means that the seller delivers the goods to the carrier nominated by him but the seller must in addition pay the cost of carriage necessary to bring the goods to the named destination. This means that the buyer bears all risks and any additional costs occurring after the goods have been so delivered. However, in CIP the seller also has to procure insurance against the buyer's risk of loss or damage to the goods during the carriage.

So, submitted Mr Burkill, even though the seller has to pay the insurance and pays the cost of carriage, it does not follow that the property in the goods does not pass before delivery at the destination. Risk (and perhaps property) passes when the goods are delivered to the carrier. So the buyer can, if he choses, redirect the goods. If that is right then, submits Mr Burkill, the buyer has been given the right of subsequent disposal within the EEA and the goods are in free circulation. The position is rather like the host paying for the guest's taxi—it leaves the guest free not to take the taxi if he so pleases.

40. This analysis seems at least arguable. And Mr Leaver did not answer it specifically. It is fit to go to trial. In these circumstances there is no need to go to Mr Burkill's other point which was based on a particular clause in the LAL contract. The deputy judge rejected it, and, if it had been the only point, I would have done so too.

10 PAYMENT IN INTERNATIONAL SALES TRANSACTIONS

In earlier times, payment in international contracts of sale was commonly effected by bill of exchange: the seller would draw a bill on the buyer for the price and transmit it and the bill of lading to him together (a 'documentary bill': see below, p 768); and the understanding was that the buyer would take up the bill of lading only if he accepted the bill of exchange or honoured it by payment (see Sale of Goods Act 1979, s 19(3)).

This method has been largely superseded, however, and is now little used. Instead, other methods are used. A surprising number of sales are on open account: that is, on simple credit, with the seller taking the risk of the buyer's insolvency. Another common method of payment is bank collection. The seller hands over documents giving access to the goods to his bank, and arranges for the bank (or its agent in the buyer's country) to present the documents to the buyer only against payment, or against a guaranteed bill of exchange. More recently, there has arisen the 'bank payment obligation', under which the buyer's bank agrees with the seller that against certain authenticated electronic messages from the seller it will automatically transfer funds into the seller's account. For further details of these methods of payment, see H Bennett, 'Bank Collections, Privity of Contract, and Third Party Losses' (2008) 124 LQR 532 and K Vorpeil, 'Bank Payment Obligations: Alternative Means of Settlement in International Trade' [2014] IBLJ 41.

Still very significant, however, is payment by letter of credit. If this is envisaged, it will usually be a term of the contract that the buyer will procure the opening of a confirmed letter of credit in the seller's favour before the goods are shipped (a requirement which has been construed as a condition of the contract: *Trans Trust SPRL v Danubian Trading Co Ltd* [1952] 2 QB 297).

Payment by banker's commercial letter of credit is considered in detail below, in Chapter 21. In practice, the working of the system depends upon two fundamental rules. The first is the doctrine of strict compliance: the bank is entitled to reject the shipping documents if not in strict conformity with the contract: *Equitable Trust Co of New York v Dawson Partners Ltd* (below, p 779); *JH Rayner & Co Ltd v Hambro's Bank Ltd* (below, p 780). The second is the autonomy of the credit: the bank must pay against the documents if they are in order, regardless of any later instructions from the buyer, his bankruptcy, suspicions regarding the validity of the underlying sale transaction, etc (*Urquhart Lindsay & Co Ltd v Eastern Bank Ltd* [1922] 1 KB 318; *Hamzeh Malas & Sons v British Imex Industries Ltd* (below, p 786)).

11 INTERNATIONAL SALES: THE FUTURE

The classic export-sale transactions described in this chapter—CIF and FOB—and the legislation and case law associated with them are actually rather limited in scope. They are ideally suited to contracts dealing with contracts for the sale of bulk commodities, such as grain and minerals, which are to be dispatched by sea carriage on a voyage of some distance. Elsewhere they raise difficulties. They are not suitable except for carriage by sea: hence this book spends a little time on other trade terms such as CIP, and also says something about multimodal transport.

And even with sea carriage, the classic rules cause problems. Ships are faster than they used to be; bills of lading have often to be repeatedly handled not only by buyers and sellers but by banks. The result is that cargoes often reach their destination well before the bill of lading arrives. Delaying the carrying vessel for days while waiting for a bill of lading is commercially unacceptable; this in turn means that if the cargo is to be collected on arrival the consignee must provide an inconvenient (and expensive) bank guarantee to indemnify the carrier against any possible liability for delivery without production of the bill of lading. Hence practices are changing fast. For instance, sea waybills (documents made out in the name of the consignee) and freight forwarders' receipts are frequently preferred to bills of lading because, although they offer less legal protection, the consignee can take delivery of the goods simply on proof of identity without having to produce physically the relevant document.

Furthermore, moves are under way to eliminate—or at least reduce—the traditional reliance on paper in international sales. Many countries, for example, now allow customs declarations to be made by means of electronic messages. Again, the use of documents like sea waybills rather than bills of lading has the added advantage that they can be transmitted electronically, since nothing turns on the possession of the actual piece of paper—indeed, the waybill may never exist in paper form.

The one area of difficulty is in regard to the bill of lading. Efforts have been made to give paperless procedures attributes which match the negotiability of the bill of lading have met with only partial success. The three best-known, which are now accepted by some shipowners and their P&I Clubs,[8] are BOLERO (Bill of Lading Electronic Registry Organisation), ess-DOCS, and E-Title. All involve centralised computerised registries where the terms of the contract of carriage and the rights of consignors, consignees, and intermediate parties are securely recorded, and instructions regarding the transfer of ownership, etc are given by the parties concerned using agreed authentication procedures. The main obstacle to the more widespread use of a system of this sort is that most legislation, and all the relevant international treaties, continue to assume the existence of a bill of lading in paper form, and so the new procedures can only be put in place by private contractual arrangements.[9]

Section 1(5) of the Carriage of Goods by Sea Act 1992 paves the way for an extension of the provisions of that Act to cases where electronic means are used in place of documents of carriage: the Secretary of State is empowered to make regulations adapting the statute accordingly. So far no such regulations have appeared.

On the move towards paperless trading, see D Faber [1996] LMCLQ 232; C Pejovic, 'Documents of Title in Carriage of Goods by Sea' [2001] JBL 461; MA Clarke, 'Transport Documents: Their Transferability as Documents of Title; Electronic Documents' [2002] LMCLQ 356; and 'The Long March to Dematerialised International Trade Documentation' (2015) 5 JIBFL 321. More generally see M Goldby, 'Electronic Presentations and Documents in International Trade and Carriage (eUCP etc.)' in B Soyer and A Tettenborn, *International Trade and Carriage of Goods* (2016).

---

[8] A P&I Club is essentially a shipowner's mutual liability insurer in respect of, among other things, cargo claims.
[9] A proposed convention on transport of goods wholly or partly by sea, the Rotterdam Rules 2009, goes some way to dealing with the problem, but thus far has not attracted much support.

PART V

PAYMENT METHODS

Chapter 16	Modern payment systems	563
Chapter 17	Payment cards	624
Chapter 18	Negotiable instruments	644
Chapter 19	Bills of exchange	659
Chapter 20	Cheques and other instruments	727

CHAPTER 16

MODERN PAYMENT SYSTEMS

1 INTRODUCTION

Payment is a fundamental aspect of commercial transactions.[1] Payment in the legal sense has been defined as 'a gift or loan of money or any act offered and accepted in performance of a money obligation' (C Proctor, *Goode on Payment Obligations in Commercial and Financial Transactions* (3rd edn, 2016), p 9). Any act accepted by the creditor in performance of a money obligation can constitute payment. Payment may be made by the delivery of physical money (ie coins and bank notes by way of legal tender) from the debtor to the creditor. However, payment by the physical delivery of money can be both risky and expensive, incurring transport and insurance costs, as well as loss of interest during transit. These difficulties have led to the development of various forms of payment mechanisms and payment systems. Professor Benjamin Geva, one of the leading commentators in this area, has defined the concept of payment mechanism and payment system in the following terms (B Geva, *The Law of Electronic Funds Transfers* (looseleaf), s 1.03[l]; and see also B Geva, 'The Concept of Payment Mechanism' (1986) 24 Osgoode Hall LJ 1):

> Any machinery facilitating the transmission of money which bypasses the transportation of money and its physical delivery from the payor to the payee is a payment mechanism. A payment mechanism facilitating a standard method of payment through a banking system is frequently referred to as a payment system. Payment over a payment mechanism is initiated by payment instructions, given by the payor or under the payor's authority, and is often referred to as a transfer of funds.

In modern business practices, particularly where large sums are involved, and in international transactions, payment is usually made by the transfer of funds from the bank account of the debtor to that of the creditor. In such cases the creditor agrees to accept a claim against his bank in substitution for his claim against his original debtor.

---

[1] The main student textbooks dealing with this subject are EP Ellinger, E Lomnicka, and CVM Hare, *Ellinger's Modern Banking Law* (5th edn, 2011), Ch 13; E McKendrick, *Goode on Commercial Law* (5th edn, 2016), Ch 17; R Cranston, *Principles of Banking Law* (2nd edn, 2002), Chs 8–10. For an international perspective, see B Geva, *The Law of Electronic Funds Transfers* (looseleaf); for an excellent comparative treatment, see B Geva, *Bank Collections and Payment Transactions—Comparative Study of Legal Aspects* (2001); and for an historical review, see B Geva, *The Payment Order of Antiquity and the Middle Ages* (2011).

Payment through the use of a funds transfer system is not payment by legal tender. As the creditor's claim against his bank is subject to a credit risk (even banks can fail), and to the offsetting of the claim with a counterclaim, the creditor must consent to payment in this way if it is to amount to discharge of the original debt. The creditor's consent may be express or implied, for example from the fact that he has provided the debtor with his bank account number on his invoice or stationery (but transfer of funds to an account other than the one stipulated will not constitute payment or even a valid tender of payment: *PT Berlian Laju Tanker TBK v Nuse Shipping Ltd* [2008] EWHC 1330 (Comm), [2008] 1 CLC 976 at [67]). The mere fact that the creditor has a bank account is not in itself to be construed as evidencing his tacit consent to accept payment into that account (*Customs and Excise Comrs v National Westminster Bank plc* [2002] EWHC 2204 (Ch), [2003] 1 All ER (Comm) 327, applying *TSB Bank of Scotland plc v Welwyn Hatfield District Council* [1993] 2 Bank LR 267: see below, p 619). Nevertheless, the courts have shown themselves willing to construe the terms of commercial agreements to allow for payment through the transfer of funds between bank accounts. In *Tenax Steamship Co Ltd v Reinante Transoceanica Navigation SA, The Brimnes* [1973] 1 WLR 386, affirmed [1975] 1 QB 929, CA, under the terms of a charterparty the debtor agreed to pay the creditor $51,000 'in cash in US currency'. Brandon J held that 'cash must be interpreted against the background of modern commercial practice' and 'cannot mean only payment in dollar bills or other legal tender of the United States'. His Lordship held that, in this context, payment 'in cash' meant 'any commercially recognised method of transferring funds the result of which is to give the transferee the unconditional right to the immediate use of the funds transferred'. Brandon J's formulation was later approved by the House of Lords in *A/S Awilco of Solo v Fulvia SpA di Navigazione of Cagliari, The Chikuma* [1981] 1 WLR 314 with substitution of 'unfettered or unrestricted' for 'unconditional' as the adjective before 'right'. Much depends on the context in which the payment obligation arises. Thus, in the context of a customer withdrawing money from his bank account the court will not imply the customer's agreement to waive his right to payment in cash, however large the amount (*Libyan Arab Foreign Bank v Bankers Trust Co* [1989] QB 728, where Staughton J ordered the bank to pay its customer US$292 million in cash!).

2 THE NATURE OF A FUNDS TRANSFER

The relationship between a bank and its customer is that of debtor and creditor with regard to the balance in the customer's bank account (*Foley v Hill* (1848) 2 HLC 28 at 36, per Lord Cottenham). When the account is in credit, the customer is the creditor and the bank the debtor; when the account is overdrawn, the roles are reversed.

Payment by funds transfer involves the adjustment of balances on the accounts of the payer and the payee. The payer's account is debited and the payee's account is credited. Thus, the debt owed to the payer by his bank is extinguished or reduced *pro tanto* (or, where the account is overdrawn, his liability to the bank increased) by the amount of the transfer to the payee, whilst the debt owed to the payee by his own bank is increased (or, where the account is overdrawn, his liability is reduced) by the same amount. Property rights are not transferred between accounts (see the extract below). The receipt of a payment message from the payer, or from the payee acting under the payer's authority, leads to the adjustment of the separate property rights (ie choses in action) of the payer and payee against their own banks.

R v Preddy

[1996] AC 815, House of Lords

The defendants were charged with obtaining or attempting to obtain mortgage advances from building societies and other lending institutions by deception contrary to s 15(1) of the Theft Act 1968. The defendants had deliberately given false information when they submitted their mortgage applications. In cases where the advances were approved, they were paid, not in cash, but by the CHAPS electronic transfer of funds from the bank account of the lending institution to the account of the defendant (or his solicitor). In each case payment instructions were transmitted over a computer-to-computer telecommunications link between the bank of the lending institution and the bank of the defendant (or his solicitor), which resulted in a debit entry in the former's bank account and a corresponding credit entry in the latter's bank account. Net settlement between the banks took place at the end of each day over their accounts held at the Bank of England. The key question for the House of Lords was whether this process meant that the defendants had 'obtain[ed] property belonging to another' as required by s 15(1). Reversing the Court of Appeal ([1995] Crim LR 564), the House of Lords held that it did not, which resulted in the defendants' convictions being quashed.

Lord Goff of Chieveley: . . . I now turn to the first question which your Lordships have to consider, which is whether the debiting of a bank account and the corresponding crediting of another's bank account brought about by dishonest misrepresentation amount to the obtaining of property within section 15 of the Act of 1968.

Under each count, one of the appellants was charged with dishonestly obtaining, or attempting to obtain, from the relevant lending institution an advance by way of mortgage in a certain sum. In point of fact it appears that, when the sum was paid, it was sometimes paid by cheque, sometimes by telegraphic transfer, and sometimes by the CHAPS (Clearing House Automatic Payment System) system. However in the cases where the sum was paid by cheque the appellants were not charged with dishonestly obtaining the cheque. A useful description of the CHAPS system is to be found in the Law Commission's Report, *Criminal Law: Conspiracy to Defraud* (1994) (Law Com No 228), p 39, n 83. It involves electronic transfer as between banks, and no distinction need be drawn for present purposes between the CHAPS system and telegraphic transfer, each involving a debit entry in the payer's bank account and a corresponding credit entry in the payee's bank account.

The Court of Appeal in the present case concentrated on payments by the CHAPS system. They considered that the prosecution had to prove that the relevant CHAPS electronic transfer was 'property' within section 15(1) of the Act of 1968. They then referred to the definition of property in section 4(1) of the Act as including 'money and all other property, real or personal, including things in action and other intangible property;' and they concluded, following the judgment of the Court of Appeal in *Reg v Williams (Jacqueline)* (unreported), 30 July 1993, that such a transfer was 'intangible property' and therefore property for the purposes of section 15(1).

The opinion expressed by the Court of Appeal in *Reg v Williams* on this point was in fact obiter. The case related to a mortgage advance, the amount having been paid by electronic transfer. The court however concluded that a sum of money represented by a figure in an account fell within the expression 'other intangible property' in section 4(1), and that the reduction of the sum standing in the lending institution's account, and the corresponding increase in the sum standing to the credit of the mortgagor's solicitor's account, constituted the obtaining of intangible property within section 15(1).

In holding that a sum of money represented by a figure in an account constituted 'other intangible property,' the court relied upon the decision of the Privy Council in *Attorney-General of Hong Kong v Nai-Keung* [1987] 1 WLR 1339, in which an export quota surplus to a particular exporter's requirements, which under the laws of Hong Kong could be bought and sold, was held to constitute 'other intangible property' within section 5(1) of the Hong Kong Theft Ordinance (Laws of Hong Kong, 1980 rev. c. 210) (for present purposes identical to section 4(1) of the English Act of 1968). I feel bound to say that that case, which was concerned with an asset capable of being traded on a market, can on that basis be differentiated from cases such as the present. But in any event, as I understand the position, the Court of Appeal were identifying the sums which were the subject of the relevant charges as being sums standing to the credit of the lending institution in its bank account. Those credit entries would, in my opinion, represent debts owing by the bank to the lending institution which constituted choses in action belonging to the lending institution and as such fell within the definition of property in section 4(1) of the Act of 1968.

My own belief is however that identifying the sum in question as property does not advance the argument very far. The crucial question, as I see it, is whether the defendant obtained (or attempted to obtain) property *belonging to another.* Let it be assumed that the lending institution's bank account is in credit, and that there is therefore no difficulty in identifying a credit balance standing in the account as representing property, ie a chose in action, belonging to the lending institution. The question remains however whether the debiting of the lending institution's bank account, and the corresponding crediting of the bank account of the defendant or his solicitor, constitutes obtaining of that property. The difficulty in the way of that conclusion is simply that, when the bank account of the defendant (or his solicitor) is credited, he does not obtain the lending institution's chose in action. On the contrary that chose in action is extinguished or reduced pro tanto, and a chose in action is brought into existence representing a debt in an equivalent sum owed by a different bank to the defendant or his solicitor. In these circumstances, it is difficult to see how the defendant thereby obtained *property belonging to another*, ie to the lending institution.

Professor Sir John Smith, in his commentary on the decision of the Court of Appeal in the present case [1995] Crim LR 564, 565–566, has suggested that 'Effectively, the victim's property has been changed into another form and now belongs to the defendant. There is the gain and equivalent loss which is characteristic of, and perhaps the substance of, obtaining.' But even if this were right, I do not for myself see how this can properly be described as obtaining property belonging to another. In truth the property which the defendant has obtained is the new chose in action constituted by the debt now owed to him by his bank, and represented by the credit entry in his own bank account. This did not come into existence until the debt so created was owed to him by his bank, and so never belonged to anyone else. True, it corresponded to the debit entered in the lending institution's bank account; but it does not follow that the property which the defendant acquired can be identified with the property which the lending institution lost when its account was debited. In truth, section 15(1) is here being invoked for a purpose for which it was never designed, and for which it does not legislate.

I should add that, throughout the above discussion, I have proceeded on the assumption that the bank accounts of the lending institution and the defendant (or his solicitor) are both sufficiently in credit to allow for choses in action of equivalent value to be extinguished in the once case, and created in the other. But this may well not be the case; and in that event further problems would be created, since it is difficult to see how an increase in borrowing can constitute an extinction of a chose in action owned by the lending institution, or a reduction in borrowing can constitute the creation of a chose in action owned by the defendant. It may be that it could be argued that in such circumstances it was the lending institution's bank whose property was 'obtained' by the defendant' but, quite apart from other problems, that argument would in any event fail for the reasons which I have already given. For these reasons, I would answer the first question in the negative.

Lord Jauncey of Tullichettle: My Lords, these cases turn upon the words 'belonging to another' in section 15(1) of the Theft Act 1968. In applying these words to circumstances such as the present there falls to be drawn a crucial distinction between the creation and extinction of rights on the one hand and the transfer of rights on the other. It is only to the latter situation that the words apply.

It would be tempting to say that the appellants by deception obtained money belonging to the lenders and therefore offences have been committed. That however would be to adopt a simplistic approach ignoring the nature of the precise transactions which are involved. I start with the proposition that the money in a bank account standing at credit does not belong to the account holder. He has merely a chose in action which is the right to demand payment of the relevant sum from the bank. I use the word money for convenience but it is of course simply a sum entered into the books of the bank. When a sum of money leaves A's account his chose in action *quoad* that sum is extinguished. When an equivalent sum is transferred to B's account there is created in B a fresh chose in action being the right to demand payment of that sum from his bank. Applying these simple propositions to the cases where sums of money are transferred from the lender's account to the account of the borrower or his solicitor either by telegraphic transfer or by CHAPS the lender's property which was his chose in action in respect of the relevant sum is extinguished and a new chose in action is created in the borrower or his solicitor. Thus although the borrower has acquired a chose in action *quoad* a sum of money of equal value to that which the lender had right, he has not acquired the property of the lender which was the latter's right against his own bank. It follows that section 15(1) has no application to such a situation. The position is, of course, even more obvious if the lender's account is in debit at the time of transfer in which event he has no right to demand payment of the sum transferred.

[**Lord Mackay of Clashfern LC**, **Lord Slynn of Hadley**, and **Lord Hoffmann** concurred.]

NOTES

1. It is something of a misnomer to speak of the 'transfer' of funds as there is no actual transfer of coins or banknotes from the payer to the payee. In *Foskett v McKeown* [2001] 1 AC 102 at 128, Lord Millett stressed that '[n]o money passes from paying bank to receiving bank or through the clearing system (where the money flows may be in the opposite direction). There is simply a series of debits and credits which are causally and transactionally linked.' (See also *Customs and Excise Comrs v FDR Ltd* [2000] STC 672 at [37], CA and *Dovey v Bank of New Zealand* [2000] 3 NZLR 641 at 648, New Zealand Court of Appeal.) Moreover, there is no assignment to the payee of any debt that may be owed to the payer by his own bank (*Libyan Arab Foreign Bank v Bankers Trust Co* [1989] QB 728 at 750, per Staughton J). *Preddy* involved a credit transfer, but the same principle also applies in the case of a debit transfer (for the distinction between credit and debit transfers, see below). Thus, payment by direct debit does not operate to vest in the payee any rights of the payer against his own bank (*Mercedes-Benz Finance Ltd v Clydesdale Bank plc* [1997] CLC 81, Outer House of the Court of Session) and s 53(1) of the Bills of Exchange Act 1882 expressly provides that a bill of exchange (including a cheque, which is a debit instrument), of itself, does not operate as an assignment of funds in the hands of the drawee bank available for the payment thereof (see also *Deposit Protection Board v Dalia* [1994] 2 AC 367 at 400, HL). In each case it is probably more accurate to speak in terms of the *transfer of value*, rather than the transfer of funds, from payer to payee (see David Fox's useful note on *Preddy* in [1996] LMCLQ 456 at 459).

2.   Some advances were paid by telegraphic transfer, but the House of Lords held that no distinction need be drawn for present purposes between the CHAPS system (details of which are set out below, p 582) and telegraphic transfers (see Lord Goff above). In some cases advances were made by cheque, but the House of Lords were not asked whether a s 15(1) offence had been committed in these circumstances. However, Lord Goff stated (*obiter*) that no offence would have been committed under the section because again there had been no obtaining of property belonging to another. As Lord Goff emphasised (at 835–837), when a payee deceives a drawer into drawing a cheque in his favour, the payee does not obtain a chose in action belonging to the drawer against his own bank (for the cheque does not constitute a chose in action in the hands of the drawer), the payee acquires a new chose in action, namely his right of action against the drawer on the cheque. The High Court of Australia has declined to follow *Preddy* on this point (*Parsons v R* (1999) 73 ALJR 270 at 277, 'a cheque has characteristics which render it more than a chose in action held by the payee against the drawer'). English courts have also distinguished *Preddy* when the property offence involves a cheque rather than a funds transfer (see, eg, *R v Adams* [2003] EWCA Crim 3620 at [17]–[20]). See further R Hooley, 'Payment in a Cashless Society' in BAK Rider (ed), *The Realm of Company Law* (1998), pp 240–241, where the issue of theft of the piece of paper constituting the cheque itself, touched on by Lord Goff in *Preddy*, is also considered.

3.   *Preddy* exposed an important lacuna in the criminal law. The Law Commission acted quickly and in its report, *Offences of Dishonesty: Money Transfers* (Law Com No 243), published on 10 October 1996, only three months after *Preddy* was decided, proposed, inter alia, a new s 15A of the Theft Act 1968 introducing a specific offence of 'obtaining a money transfer by deception'. Lord Goff introduced the Law Commission's draft bill into the House of Lords on 24 October 1996, and it was enacted as the Theft (Amendment) Act 1996 on 18 December 1996. In fact, both s 15 and s 15A of the Theft Act 1968 have since been repealed by the Fraud Act 2006, which creates a new offence of 'fraud' (s 1). The new offence includes fraud by false representation (s 2), which does not require the defendant to have obtained 'property belonging to another'.

QUESTION

Would the defendants in *Preddy* have obtained 'property belonging to another' if the building society had paid out the mortgage advance in bank notes?

3 TERMINOLOGY

There had been some attempt to standardise the terminology in this area. This has arisen from the influence of Art 4A of the US Uniform Commercial Code (adopted in 1989) and the UNCITRAL Model Law on Credit Transfers (1992). The Prefatory Note to Art 4A of the Uniform Commercial Code uses the following terminology to describe a funds transfer operation:[2]

---

[2] The idea of citing the Prefatory Note for this purpose comes from Professor Sir Roy Goode: see (now) E McKenrick, *Goode on Commercial Law* (5th edn, 2016), p 505.

X, a debtor, wants to pay an obligation owed to Y. Instead of delivering to Y a negotiable instrument such as a check or some other writing such as a credit card slip that enables Y to obtain payment from a bank, X transmits an instruction to X's bank to credit a sum of money to the bank account of Y. In most cases X's bank and Y's bank are different banks. X's bank may carry out X's instruction by instructing Y's bank to credit Y's account in the amount that X requested. The instruction that X issues to its bank is a 'payment order'. X is the 'sender' of the payment order and X's bank is the 'receiving bank' with respect to X's order. Y is the 'beneficiary' of X's order. When X's bank issues an instruction to Y's bank to carry out X's payment order, X's bank 'executes' X's order. The instruction of X's bank to Y's bank is also a payment order. With respect to that order, X's bank is the sender, Y's bank is the receiving bank, and Y is the beneficiary. The entire series of transactions by which X pays Y is known as the 'funds transfer'. With respect to the funds transfer, X is the 'originator', X's bank is the 'originator's bank', Y is the 'beneficiary' and Y's bank is the 'beneficiary's bank'. In more complex transactions there are one or more additional banks known as 'intermediary banks' between X's bank and Y's bank. In the funds transfer the instruction contained in the payment order of X to its bank is carried out by a series of payment orders by each bank in the transmission chain to the next bank in the chain until Y's bank receives a payment order to make the credit to Y's account.

It should be noted, however, that Art 4A restricts the term 'fund transfer' to credit transfers and excludes debit transfers from its scope. The terms 'originator' and 'beneficiary' make more sense in the context of a credit transfer, where the originator of the first payment order will be the payer, than they do for a debit transfer, where the originator of the first payment order will often be the payee, for example as happens with a direct debit (although a cheque, also a debit instrument, is drawn by the payer). By contrast, the EU's Payment Services Directive (2007/64/EC), implemented in the UK through the Payment Services Regulations 2009 (SI 2009/209, as amended), and its recent successor, the revised Payment Services Directive (or PSD2) (2015/2366/EU), extend to both credit and debit transfers and adopt the more flexible (and less confusing) terminology of 'payer' and 'payee', instead of 'originator' and 'beneficiary', as well as 'payer's bank' and 'payee's bank', instead of 'originator's bank' and 'beneficiary's bank'. In this chapter, the same European-based terminology is used throughout.

4 CREDIT/DEBIT TRANSFERS

Funds transfer operations can be classified as either credit transfers or debit transfers according to the way payment instructions are communicated to the payer's bank.

With a *credit transfer* the payer instructs his bank to cause the account of the payee, at the same or another bank, to be credited. The payer's instruction may be for an individual credit transfer, for example by bank giro credit (see below, p 581) or CHAPS payment (see below, p 582), or for a recurring transfer of funds under a standing order (standing orders are instructions given by a customer to his bank to make regular payments of a fixed amount to a particular payee). On receipt of the payer's instruction, the payer's bank will debit the payer's account, unless the payer has provided his bank with some other means of reimbursement, and credit the payee's account where it is held at the same bank, or, where the payee's account is held at another bank, forward instructions to the payee's bank, which will credit the payee's account.

With a *debit transfer* the payee conveys instructions to his bank to collect funds from the payer. These instructions may be initiated by the payer himself and passed on to the payee, for example as happens with the collection of cheques (see below, p 730); alternatively, they may be initiated by the payee himself pursuant to the payer's authority, as happens with direct debits where the payer signs a mandate authorising his bank to pay amounts demanded by the payee (the payee's failure properly to implement a correctly completed direct debit mandate might constitute a breach of an implied term of the underlying contract between them, or even a breach of a duty of care in tort owed by the payee to the payer: *Weldon v GRE Linked Life Assurance Ltd* [2000] 2 All ER (Comm) 914). On receipt of instructions from the payee, the payee's bank usually provisionally credits the payee's account with the amount to be collected and forwards instructions to the payer's bank, which will debit the payer's account. The credit to the payee's account becomes final when the debit to the payer's account becomes irreversible.

The movement of payment instructions and funds in both credit and debit transfers is illustrated by Figure 16.1.

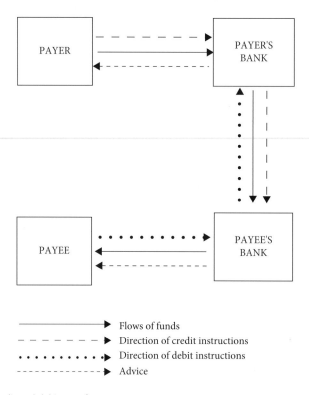

Flows of funds
Direction of credit instructions
Direction of debit instructions
Advice

Figure 16.1 Credit and debit transfers

The payer's order to his bank to make a credit transfer to the payee (whether by standing order mandate, bank giro credit, CHAPS payment order, letter, facsimile, or telex, etc) is not a negotiable instrument (*Tenax Steamship Co Ltd v Brimnes (Owners of), The Brimnes* [1915] QB 929 at 949 at 969, CA: funds transfer order given by telex). There is no mercantile custom that credit transfer orders are capable of being transferred from one person to another by delivery (or indorsement and delivery), or that they give the bona fide purchaser for value a title which is free from the defects of title of prior parties, which are the two essential requirements for a negotiable instrument (*Crouch v Crédit Fonder of England* (1873) LR 8 QB 374 at 381–381, per Blackburn J: see below, p 649, and on negotiable instruments generally, see Chapter 18 below). The same applies in the case of debit transfer orders, save where the debit transfer is effected by a cheque, which may be a negotiable instrument (although most cheques issued in the UK are not negotiable instruments because they are crossed 'account payee' and, therefore, not transferable: see below, p 727). Yet despite the fact that credit and debit transfer instructions are not afforded the status of negotiable instruments, the courts nevertheless seem prepared, as a matter of modern commercial practice, to regard payment by at least one form of funds transfer operation, namely by direct debit, as having certain characteristics normally associated with payment by negotiable instrument (see the next case).

Esso Petroleum Co Ltd v Milton
[1997] 1 WLR 1060, Court of Appeal

Esso owned two garages operated and managed by Milton under licence. Under the terms of two licence agreements, one for each garage, Milton was obliged to purchase all his petrol supplies from Esso and pay for them on or before delivery by direct debit. Milton was forbidden to sell petrol at prices greater than those notified to him by Esso. Towards the end of 1995 Esso instructed Milton to cut petrol prices in the face of stiff pricing competition and it also increased his site rentals. Milton complained that this made his operations unprofitable and, in order to put pressure on Esso, he cancelled his direct debit mandate when almost £170,000 was owing to Esso for petrol supplied. Esso applied for summary judgment under RSC Ord 14 (now see the Civil Procedure Rules 1998, Part 24). Milton admitted the claim, but alleged that the increasingly stringent financial terms which Esso had imposed amounted to a repudiatory breach of contract, and he counterclaimed damages which he sought to set off in equity in extinction of his debt to Esso. The first-instance judge dismissed Esso's application for summary judgment, but Esso successfully appealed on two grounds. The first was that Milton's counterclaim, even if good, would not give rise to an equitable set-off. The second was that no set-off or counterclaim is available where payment was made, or agreed to be made, by direct debit.

Simon Brown LJ (dissenting): … I turn, therefore, to Esso's arguments as to why such a counterclaim, being for an unliquidated sum and accordingly available only by way of equitable set-off, is not in the present circumstances available to the defendant. These arguments are first that the defendant is in the same position as had he countermanded payment by cheque; a claim following a cancelled direct debit mandate is, Esso submit, equivalent to a claim upon a dishonoured cheque to which elementarily a mere right of equitable set-off can never constitute a defence (the direct debit argument)….

The direct debit system is increasingly commonly used and its essential nature is well-known. Those unfamiliar with the system will find it conveniently described in *Chitty on Contracts*, 27th ed. (1994), vol. 2, pp. 336 et seq., paras. 33–302 et seq.

Esso submit that the closest analogy with the system would be for the intending purchaser to provide a number of signed blank cheques to be presented by the supplier upon delivery of the goods or services contracted for. In neither case, they point out, can the creditor prevent the debtor from countermanding his instruction to the bank and in neither does the bank itself assume a direct payment obligation to the creditor. Thus the creditor in both cases is exposed to the risk of non-payment through the debtor countermanding his instructions. The central

question presently arising is whether under the direct debit scheme the debtor should be entitled to escape the specially restrictive rules as to the stay of judgments and the scope of defences
which apply with regard to dishonoured cheques. In submitting not, Mr. Hapgood relies upon
the well known authority of *Nova (Jersey) Knit Ltd. v. Kammgarn Spinnerei G.m.b.H.* [1977] 1
W.L.R. 713 where the House of Lords by a four to one majority overturned the Court of Appeal's
decision ([1976] 2 Lloyd's Rep. 155) which had allowed a plaintiff's action upon a dishonoured
bill of exchange to be stayed pending the resolution of the defendant's counterclaim for unliquidated damages. Lord Wilberforce said, at p. 721:

> When one person buys goods from another, it is often, one would think generally, important
> for the seller to be sure of his price: he may (as indeed the appellants here) have bought the
> goods from someone else whom he has to pay. He may demand payment in cash; but if the
> buyer cannot provide this at once, he may agree to take bills of exchange payable at future
> dates. These are taken as equivalent to deferred instalments of cash. Unless they are to be
> treated as unconditionally payable instruments (as in the Act, section 3, says 'an unconditional
> order in writing'), which the seller can negotiate for cash, the seller might just as well give
> credit. And it is for this reason that English law (and German law appears to be no different)
> does not allow cross-claims, or defences, except such limited defences as those based on
> fraud, invalidity, or failure of consideration, to be made. I fear that the Court of Appeal's
> decision, if it had been allowed to stand, would have made a very substantial inroad upon the
> commercial principle on which bills of exchange have always rested.

Mr. Hapgood points out that almost no cheques today are in fact negotiable instruments: virtually all are crossed 'account payee only.' The creditors' expectations, he submits, are the same
irrespective whether the debtor is to pay by cheque or, as commercially now is found to be
generally more convenient, by direct debit. The differences between the two means of payment
are, he submits, for present purposes, technical and immaterial. Mr. Hapgood also refers to a
judgment of my own in *Esso Petroleum Co. Ltd. v. Craft (unreported), 1 February 1996; Court
of Appeal (Civil Division) Transcript No. 47 of 1996* in which, refusing the defendant's ex parte
application in this court for leave to appeal against summary judgment in circumstances not
dissimilar to the present (save only that counterclaim there was for damages for alleged short
deliveries in the past rather than future loss of profits), I said:

> Payment for that [the particular delivery giving rise to the claim for £16,000 odd] was due
> under a direct debit arrangement, a liability equivalent to that arising upon a dishonoured
> cheque which, in turn, is to be treated as akin to cash.

As the first instance judgment in that case ((unreported), 15 June 1995) records, however, it
was: 'common ground that the status of a direct debit … is similar to a cheque or other bill of
exchange.' Whether that was rightly conceded is, of course, the very point at issue upon this
appeal.

Mr. Soole submits that the position here is quite unlike that arising when a cheque is countermanded. In the first place, Esso's claim here is one for the price of goods sold and delivered,
not upon a dishonoured cheque. And that is no mere technicality: the defendant in this case
gave no specific instruction to his bank to pay for these particular deliveries. It is one thing, Mr.
Soole submits, to cancel a general direct debit mandate; quite another to countermand payment
of a signed cheque. Esso's argument, he submits, overlooks the central distinction between the
(debtor's) bank mandate and the (creditor's) request for payment submitted pursuant to it. The
mandate does not constitute a cheque, not least because it is not an instruction to pay 'a sum
certain in money' as required by the Bills of Exchange Act 1882 (45 & 46 Vict c. 61). And the
request, so far from being a signed instrument equivalent to cash provided by the debtor, is
drawn rather by the creditor.

In short, submits Mr. Soole, the defendant is really in no different position than had he agreed to pay for deliveries by cash or cheque and then declined to do so. What he did was to dishonour a promise, not a cheque. His termination of the mandate gives Esso no rights independently of the licence agreement. Before expressing my own conclusions upon this important point it is, I think, worth setting out verbatim the final written formulation of Esso's argument:

Esso's propositions of law

Payment by direct debit is equivalent to payment by cash. Accordingly: (1) In an action for the recovery of a debt (a) the defence of set-off is not available to a defendant who has wrongfully countermanded a direct debit instruction to his bank; and (b) execution of judgment will not be stayed pending the trial of a counterclaim. (2) Countermand is wrongful if the defendant has expressly or impliedly promised to pay the debt by direct debit. (3) The plaintiff must plead and prove (a) the consideration for the debt; (b) the defendant's agreement to pay the debt by direct debit; and (c) the dishonour of the direct debit. (4) As in an action by the payee of a dishonoured cheque against the drawer, it is a good defence for the defendant to prove fraud inducing the issue of the direct debit or its invalidity (for example, on the ground that it was issued without the defendant's authority).

By way of oral elaboration of those propositions Mr. Hapgood doubted whether the word 'wrongfully' was strictly required in paragraph (1) (in which event paragraph (2) would be unnecessary); explained that the reference in paragraph (2) to an implied promise was included to enable a future decision to be reached upon whether the opening of a direct debit mandate itself gives rise to a promise to pay by that system (such decision being unnecessary in the present case); accepted a variation suggested by Sir John Balcombe that there be added to paragraph (2) the words 'and the plaintiff had not received notice of countermand of the direct debit at the time when consideration moved from him;' and explained that paragraph (3)(a) reflected his recognition of the fact that, unlike the position with cheques, in direct debit cases there is no presumption of consideration in favour of the plaintiff.

Powerfully argued although Esso's case was on this issue, and commercially convenient although no doubt it would be in many, perhaps most, instances to place direct debit arrangements on the same footing as cheques, I find myself ultimately unpersuaded by the argument.

By no means all direct debit cases are akin to actions on a cheque—that, indeed, is reflected in the very complexity of Esso's final formulation of their argument. Of course there will be occasions when a direct debit arrangement is stipulated and accepted by the supplier, just like a cheque, as an alternative to a demand for cash payment. But that will not invariably be so and I have no doubt that many direct debit arrangements are nowadays entered into for the settlement of transactions effected on credit rather than in substitution for cash transactions. I may have a charge account at a store which routinely allows its customers 28 days credit. Were I for convenience to enter into an agreement to pay my account by periodic direct debit payments, that surely ought not to deny me my basic credit entitlement nor limit the scope of such defences as would otherwise be available to me were some purchase to prove unsatisfactory. Similarly with service providers.

There are, of course, certain obvious similarities between cheques and direct debit arrangements just as there are obvious differences too. I find the similarities insufficient to justify deciding as a matter of policy and principle that for Order 14 purposes the two are equivalent. Nor indeed does such an extension of the special rule for enforcing claims on dishonoured cheques seem to me commercially necessary—to avoid, as Mr. Hapgood sought to submit, the supplier having to insist on payment by cash or cheque before delivery. Instead, a supplier intent on achieving by direct debit a position equivalent to that of the holder of a cheque can do so—as, indeed, by their third argument Esso assert they have—by expressly excluding equitable rights of set-off.

Thorpe LJ: … [O]n the direct debit argument, I would hold for the plaintiffs. Whilst I am conscious of difficulties and dangers involved in such an extension, I believe that it is consistent with the principle stated by Lord Wilberforce in *Nova (Jersey) Knit Ltd. v. Kammgarn Spinnerei G.m.b.H.* [1977] 1 W.L.R. 713, 721 in the passage cited by Simon Brown L.J. Where goods are effectively sold for cash the seller should have the security that cash brings when for mutual convenience the parties have adopted the banking mechanism in general usage for the transfer of cash from one account to another. Twenty years ago that was still by cheque. Theoretically the tanker driver could demand a signed cheque on arrival for an amount to be written in when ascertained by completion of the fuel delivery. But that is only theory. The defendant's annual petrol purchases under the licence agreements amounted to about £5m., and, as the evidence established, Esso's daily collection through the direct debit system for all petrol sales varies between £9m. and £20m. The modern mechanism for handling what are effectively cash sales on that scale is the direct debit system. So it seems to me that it is a natural evolution rather than an extension of the *Nova Knit* principle to hold that the seller of goods for cash transferred by the direct debit mechanism should be in no worse position than if he had accepted a cheque on delivery. Mr. Hapgood's formulation emerged in reply and was then modified in argument. No doubt it requires further consideration and perhaps further modification but I would accept the fundamental principle for which he contends.

Balcombe LJ: … I agree with Thorpe L.J. and would allow the appeal also on the ground of the direct debit argument. This is essentially a question of policy. As the evidence in the case discloses—and it is a fact of which we can take judicial notice—modern commercial practice is to treat a direct debit in the same way as a payment by cheque and, as such, the equivalent of cash. The fact that a cheque is, technically, a negotiable instrument, is for this purpose irrelevant; in any case modern practice is to require payment by cheque crossed 'A/C Payee only,' which is not negotiable. It is its equivalence to cash which is the essential feature of a direct debit and which makes relevant Lord Wilberforce's explanation for the reason why a defence of set-off is not normally allowed in the case of a claim based on a bill of exchange: see *Nova (Jersey) Knit Ltd. v. Kammgarn Spinnerei G.m.b.H.* [1977] 1 W.L.R. 713, 721—the passage is cited in full in the judgment of Simon Brown L.J. I accept that the precise circumstances in which a payment by direct debit will preclude a defence of set-off may require to be worked out as further cases show different combinations of fact but, like Thorpe L.J., I accept the fundamental principle that, in general, a payment by direct debit for goods or services received should preclude a defence of set-off.

NOTE

If the majority (Thorpe LJ and Sir John Balcombe) are right on this point, and there must be considerable doubt that they are (see the extract below), their reasoning could also be applied to payment made, or agreed to be made, by other forms of credit and debit transfer between bank accounts, for example by standing order.

'Pay Now, Sue Later"—Direct Debits, Set-Off and Commercial Practice' by A Tettenborn
(1997) 113 LQR 374 at 375–377

With the greatest respect to the majority, it is submitted that the direct debit aspect of the decision is hard to support.

To begin with, there is an issue of legal principle. In seeking to equiparate direct debiting arrangements with cheques and bills of exchange, the majority view takes no account of one crucial juridical difference between them. Where goods or services are paid for by cheque, not one but two contracts are in existence: one on the cheque itself, the other arising out of the underlying transaction. The contracts are discrete, and the payee may sue on either: but, as Pollock CB pointed out in *Warwick v Nairn* (1855) 10 Exch 762 at p. 764, the rule precluding set-off only applies to the former. But this analysis simply cannot apply to payments by direct debit. There is no such thing as an action on a direct debit; there is no separate contact contained in a direct debit apart from the underlying contract of sale—or whatever. As Simon Brown LJ pertinently observed (at p. 601), the plaintiffs in *Esso v Milton* were suing for goods sold and delivered, no more, no less: and if this is so it is difficult to see any legal reason to deny the defendants their ordinary rights of set-off which they would have in any other contract of sale.

Not only is the majority decision hard to justify on principle: it is also difficult to support commercially or as a matter of policy. *Pace* Thorpe LJ it is suggested that the origin of, and justification for, the special rules relating to negotiable instruments do not lie in their use as convenient payment mechanisms to obviate the necessity of transferring cash. They lie instead in the transferability of such instruments as commercial paper (a point which, incidentally, explains why the anti-set-off rule applies equally to promissory notes, which are not really payment mechanisms at all, but are nevertheless transferable in the market). If it is envisaged that the holder of a cheque or bill of exchange may want to transfer or discount it for cash, it makes good commercial sense to make it as effective an instrument as possible by limiting severely the factors which may go to impugn the obligation to pay contained in it. But no such argument can apply to direct debits, which are not, and never were intended to be, readily transferable: they are merely a convenient means of arranging for the transfer of funds to the payee. From which it must follow that there is no need to extend to him the jealous and peculiar protection afforded to the holder of a bill of exchange.

Nor, despite its initial attractiveness, is there (with respect) much in a further argument advanced by Thorpe LJ; that since direct debits are set up as a quick and easy means of payment of regular bills, it would be unfair to deprive the payee of the assurance of prompt and full payment which such arrangements give him. The answer to this is straightforward: if the supplier of goods or services wants such an assurance (as well he may), he can always have it by the simple expedient of stipulating in his contract that payments are to be made without deduction or set-off. (Indeed, Esso argued that they had done just this in *Esso v Milton* by virtue of one of the terms of their contract, but in the event it was held that the relevant clause was not sufficiently explicit to have this effect.) But there is, it is submitted, no demonstrated need to go further and say that such a stipulation is implicit in the nature of direct debits themselves . . .

It remains to mention one more general issue. As Thorpe LJ pointed out (at p 606), the point that cheques are transferable negotiable instruments, whereas direct debits are not, has one logical weakness. Whatever may have been the position in the nineteenth century, when the rule 'pay now and sue the payee later' grew up, today in practice nearly all cheques are non-transferable because they bear the words 'account payee' on their face (see S.81A of the Bills of Exchange Act 1982). Yet, as his Lordship observed, the 'pay now and sue later' rule still applies to them in full force; and if so, why not equally to non-transferable direct debits?

Now, his Lordship's premise is clearly right: but his conclusion is, it is respectfully submitted, a little perverse. If cheques today are indeed just a convenient (non-transferable) means of switching cash balances from one account to another, the logical answer is surely not to extend the 'pay now, sue later' rule but to restrict it: that is, to make cheques more like other means of payment, and not *vice versa*. If we are to recognise changing commercial practice, as we clearly should, there must now be a powerful case for taking cheques outside the rule entirely, so as to limit it to promissory notes and bills of exchange proper where it belongs. Indeed, one might even go further and question whether cheques should continue to come under the regime of the Bills of Exchange Act at all, since any similarity between a modern-day cheque and a traditional bill of exchange is pretty tenuous. But that raises large issues of banking law and practice well beyond the purview of this note.

5 CLEARING AND SETTLEMENT

(a) Clearing

Payment effected through a payment system is initiated by payment instructions given by the payer, or someone else acting with his authority (the payee), to his own bank. In cases where the payment is not 'in-house' (see below), the payer's instructions will lead to further payment instructions passing between the payer's bank and the payee's bank, sometimes through the intermediation of other banks. The process of exchanging payment instructions between participating banks is known as clearing. Clearing may take place through a series of bilateral exchanges of payment instructions between banks, but in the UK it is more common for clearing to take place multilaterally through a centralised clearing house.

Payment systems are classified as either paper-based or electronic depending on the medium used for inter-bank communication of payment instructions (B Geva, *The Law of Electronic Funds Transfers* (looseleaf), s 1.03[4]). In a paper-based funds transfer system the paper embodying the payment instruction is physically transferred from one bank to another, for example by direct courier or at a centralised clearing house. The cheque and credit clearing are paper-based funds transfer systems (see below, p 730). By contrast, with an electronic funds transfer system the inter-bank communication of payment instructions is by electronic means, for example by magnetic tape, disc, or, more usually, telecommunication link. The major inter-bank electronic funds transfer systems in the UK are the services operated by BACS Payment Schemes Ltd, called BACS, the payment system run by CHAPS Clearing Co Ltd, called CHAPS, and the Faster Payments Service operated by the Faster Payments Scheme Ltd (see below, p 582).

(b) Settlement

Where the payer and the payee have accounts at the same bank, the transfer of funds between the two accounts will usually involve a simple internal accounting exercise at the bank (known as an 'in-house' transfer). The payer's account is debited and the payee's account is credited. The position will be different where the payer's account and the payee's account are held at different banks (known as an 'inter-bank' transfer). In such cases an inter-bank payment instruction will pass from bank to bank, sometimes from the payer's bank directly to the payee's bank, otherwise via intermediary banks which each issue their own payment instruction to the next bank down the chain, until a payment instruction finally reaches the payee's bank. Each inter-bank payment instruction must be paid by the bank sending the instruction to the bank receiving it. It is this process whereby payment is made between the banks themselves of their obligations *inter se* which is known as settlement.

Settlement can occur on either a bilateral or multilateral basis. Bilateral settlement occurs where the bank sending the payment instruction and the bank receiving it are correspondents, meaning that each holds an account with the other. Settlement is effected through an adjustment of that account. Multilateral settlement involves the settlement of accounts of the sending bank and the receiving bank held at a third bank. The third bank could be a common correspondent of the two banks, ie one where they both have accounts; alternatively, and more typically, the third bank could be a central bank. The fact that settlement is usually effected across accounts held at the central bank means that payments involving a particular currency are usually routed through the country of that currency, for instance a transfer of US dollars from a payer in London to a payee in Zurich will usually be settled in New York. But note that with the introduction of the single European currency, the euro, in 1999— the UK has not joined the single currency—the linkage between currency and country is removed for inter-bank payments in euro within the EU.

Settlement may be either gross or net. With gross settlement the sending and receiving banks settle each payment order separately without regard to any other payment obligations arising between them (see Figure 16.2 below). This is usually done on a real-time basis, with settlement across the accounts of participating banks held at the central bank as each payment instruction is processed. With net settlement the mutual payment obligations of the parties are set off against each other and only the net balance paid. This process occurs periodically with net balances being settled either at the end of the day ('same-day' funds) or on the following day ('next-day' funds).

Net settlement may be either bilateral or multilateral. (The text which follows is only concerned with payment netting and not with the netting of contractual commitments, for example as carried out in a variety of contracts such as foreign exchange contracts, repurchase agreements, securities trades, and derivatives.) In a bilateral net settlement system a participant's exposure is measured by reference to its net position with regard to each individual counterparty and not by reference to the system as a whole (see Figure 16.3 below). In a multilateral net settlement system a participant's position is measured by reference to its net position with regard to all other participants in the system as a whole. As a result, each participant with end up as a net net debtor or a net net creditor in relation to all other participants in the system. Multilateral netting may arise through direct determination of multilateral net positions (see Figure 16.4 below) or indirectly by netting the net bilateral positions and thereby obtaining net net positions (see Figure 16.5 below). In each case settlement follows the multilateral netting process (see Figure 16.6 below).

The process of gross and net settlement is illustrated in the following diagrams (reproduced with kind permission of Mario Giovanoli from his chapter 'Legal Issues Regarding Payment and Netting Systems' in JJ Norton, C Reed, and I Walden (eds), *Cross-Border Electronic Banking: Challenges and Opportunities* (1st edn, 1995), Ch 9).

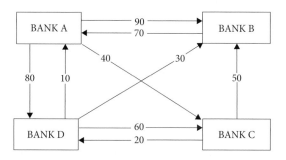

Number of payments: 9
Total volume of transactions: 450

Figure 16.2 Gross payments without netting

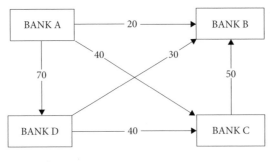

Number of payments: 6
Total volume of transactions: 250

Figure 16.3 Bilateral netting (bilateral net positions)

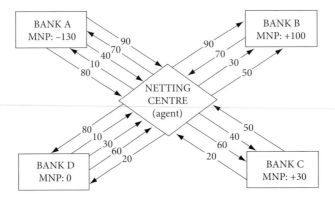

Figure 16.4 Multilateral netting—1. Netting phase (2 systems) Direct multilateral netting: direct determination of multilateral net positions (MNP)

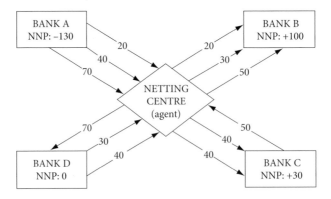

Figure 16.5 Indirect multilateral netting: determination of 'net-net' positions (NNP) by netting the net bilateral positions

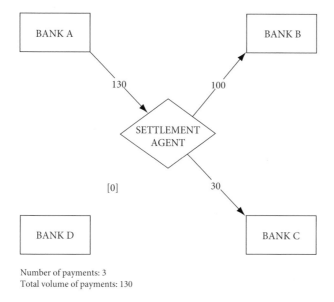

Number of payments: 3
Total volume of payments: 130

Figure 16.6 Multilateral netting—2. Settlement phase

There are a number of advantages to be gained from net settlement: it reduces the number and value of inter-bank settlement operations, this leads to reduced transaction costs, liquidity is maintained, and it reduces insolvency losses provided netting withstands insolvency. On the other hand, net settlement does result in exposure to several types of risk, including receiver risk (R Sappideen, 'Cross-Border Electronic Funds Transfers through Large Value Transfer Systems, and the Persistence of Risk' [2003] JBL 584 at 589 and 593). A bank receiving a payment instruction from another bank participating in a payment system usually makes funds available to its own customer before it has itself been placed in funds on completion of the multilateral net settlement at the end of the day (assuming the receiving bank turns out to be a net creditor). Thus, the receiving bank carries the risk that it might never be placed in funds. Furthermore, acting on its customer's instruction, the receiving bank might itself pass on the payment instruction down a chain of banks. The failure of one bank to make payment may mean that the other banks in the chain cannot meet their own payment commitments. This is known as systemic risk.

There are various ways to reduce systemic risk in settlement systems through the introduction of appropriate prudential safeguards, for example same-day (as opposed to next-day) settlement; net bilateral receiver limits (credit caps); net sender limits (debit caps); appropriate membership criterion; real-time monitoring of net balances; and schemes which guarantee settlement even if one party defaults.

In order to reduce systemic risk in payment systems which operate on the basis of payment netting, and to minimise the disruption caused by insolvency proceedings against a participant in a payment or securities settlement system, the European Parliament and Council adopted Directive 98/26/EC on settlement finality in payment and securities settlement systems ([1998] OJ L166/45). The Directive provides, inter alia, that: (1) transfer orders and netting are to be legally enforceable and binding on third parties, even in the event of insolvency proceedings, provided the transfer orders were entered into the system before the moment of opening of the insolvency (art 3(1)); (2) there is to be no unwinding of a netting because of the operation of national laws or practice which provide for the setting aside of contracts and transactions concluded before the moment of opening of insolvency proceedings (art 3(2)); (3) a transfer order is not to be revoked by a participant in a system, nor by a third party, from the moment defined by the rules of that system (art 5); and (4) insolvency proceedings are not to have retrospective effect on the rights and obligations of a participant arising from, or in connection with, its participation in a system earlier than the moment of opening of such proceedings (art 7). The moment of opening of insolvency proceedings is the moment when the relevant judicial or administrative authority handed down its decision (art 6(1)).

The UK has implemented the Directive through the Financial Markets and Insolvency (Settlement Finality) Regulations 1999 (SI 1999/2979) (for an excellent summary, see LS Sealy [2000] CifLR 221). The Regulations apply only to systems which are accorded designation by a 'designating authority'. In its capacity as a designating authority, the Bank of England has granted the five major payment systems operating in the UK—namely, the cheque clearing system, the credit clearing system, BACS, CHAPS, and the Faster Payments Service—designated system status (for brief descriptions of these payment systems, see p 581 below). Part III of the Regulations largely displaces the rules of insolvency law, giving precedence to the proceedings of the relevant designated system.

Nevertheless, concern about systemic risk in large-value transfer systems led the EU central banks to adopt the principle that Member States should each develop their own real-time gross settlement system for large-value payments. The UK made CHAPS a real-time gross settlement system in April 1996 (see below, p 582). The various real-time gross settlement systems of Member States of the EU are now connected by TARGET2, which is the payment system arrangement allowing high-value payments in euro to be made in real-time both domestically and across borders within the EU (UK banks also have a range of other euro payment mechanisms available to them). With real-time gross settlement, receiver risk is significantly reduced as no intra-day credit is granted to participants in the system. However, lack of credit means that participants must have funds available at the central bank to meet their payment obligation before they can send payment instructions. This reduces liquidity and can lead to gridlock (ie the system cannot get going until participants have received sufficient credits from other participants), although this can be avoided through the central bank offering secured overdraft facilities to participating banks ('daylight overdrafts') or entering into repurchase arrangements. The effectiveness and robustness (whether before insolvency or on insolvency) of arrangements of this nature have been strengthened by the European Parliament and Council Directive 2002/47/EC on financial collateral arrangements ([2002] OJ L168/43), implemented in the UK through the Financial Collateral Arrangements (No 2) Regulations 2003 (SI 2003/3226).

6 CLEARING SYSTEMS AND CLEARING RULES

The term 'clearing system' can be used in one of two senses:

> In its narrow sense, 'clearing system' is a mechanism for the calculation of mutual positions within a group of participants ('counterparties') with a view to facilitating the settlement of their mutual obligations on a net basis. In its broad sense, the term further encompasses the settlement of the obligations, that is, the completion of payment discharging them.
>
> (B Geva, 'The Clearing House Arrangement' (1991) 19 Can BLJ 138)

A clearing system is operated by an organisation known as a clearing house. The banks which participate in a clearing system (known in the UK as 'clearing banks') are members of the clearing house. They are bound by the rules of the clearing house through a multilateral contract (although administrative procedures and technical specifications set out in the rules may not be intended to be legally binding). The multilateral contract may arise where the member contracts with the clearing house to conform to the rules; the member is then deemed to have contracted with all other members on the terms of its individual undertaking (on the same principle as applied in *Clarke v Dunraven, The Satanita* [1897] AC 59). Alternatively, the members of the clearing system may agree together to abide by the system's rules. The rules must be interpreted against the background of the manner and operation of the particular clearing system. Any interpretation of the rules must also be in accordance with the nature of the rules themselves (see R Cranston, *Principles of Banking Law* (2nd edn, 2002), pp 281–282).

A customer of a clearing bank may be bound by, and able to rely on, the clearing house rules against his own bank through an implied term of the banker–customer contract (it is always open for the clearing house rules to be expressly incorporated into a bank's contract with its customer but this is unlikely in practice). The customer is taken to have contracted with reference to the reasonable usage of bankers, including those clearing house rules which represent such reasonable usage (*Hare v Henty* (1861) 10 CBNS 65; *Tayeb v HSBC Bank plc* [2004] EWHC 1529 (Comm), [2004] 4 All ER 1024 at [57]; *Tidal Energy Ltd v Bank of Scotland plc* [2014] EWCA Civ 1107, [2014] 2 CLC 124 at [48]–[49], [59], and see below, p 589). However, where clearing house rules derogate from the customer's existing rights, the usage codified in the rules will be deemed unreasonable and will not bind the customer without his full knowledge and consent (*Barclays Bank plc v Bank of England* [1985] 1 All ER 385 at 394; see also *Turner v Royal Bank of Scotland plc* [1999] 2 All ER (Comm) 664, CA). In order to rely on the clearing house rules against a member bank other than his own bank, the customer would have to bring himself within the ambit of the Contracts (Rights of Third Parties) Act 1999, which may prove difficult, not least because the member banks may have 'contracted out' of the Act (as occurs, eg, with the CHAPS Rules, r 11.1.1). Agency arguments are likely to prove equally problematical.

There are the five major clearing systems in the UK. Each system is run by an independent company supported by Payments UK, which is the trade association representing the UK payments industry. Since 1 April 2015 retail payments systems in the UK are regulated by a new Payment Systems Regulator established under s 40 of the Financial Services (Banking Reform) Act 2013. The main clearing systems are as follows:

(1) the cheque clearing system (operated by the Cheque and Credit Clearing Co Ltd), which is used for the physical exchange of cheques, although the introduction of cheque imaging under new Part 4A of the Bills of Exchange Act 1882, inserted by s 13 of the Small Business, Enterprise and Employment Act 2015, will eliminate the need for the physical exchange of cheques through clearing (see below, p 733);

(2) the credit clearing system (also run by the Cheque and Credit Clearing Co Ltd), which is a paper-based credit transfer system used for the physical exchange of high-volume, low-value, credit collections such as bank giro credits: new legislation allowing for cheque imaging (see immediately above) also extends to other paper instruments such as bank giro credits (see s 89B of the Bills of Exchange Act 1882, inserted by s 13 of the Small Business, Enterprise and Employment Act 2015);

(3) BACS (operated by BACS Payment Schemes Ltd), which provides a high-volume, low-value, bulk electronic clearing service for credit and debit transfers, including standing orders, direct debits, wages and salaries, pensions, and other government benefits;

(4) CHAPS (operated by the CHAPS Clearing Co Ltd), which is an electronic real-time gross settlement credit transfer system for sterling, normally used for high-value transfers.

(5) Faster Payments Service (operated by the Faster Payments Scheme Ltd), which offers a near real-time facility for internet and telephone transfers between bank accounts, with standing orders processed on a same-day basis.

Save for CHAPS, which is a real-time gross settlement system, the other clearing systems are multilateral net settlement systems with settlement of balances across the participants' accounts held at the Bank of England at the end of each day, or several times each day for the Faster Payments Service.

There are also other payment networks, for example the Visa and MasterCard networks, which handle various types of payment cards (see below, Chapter 17).

7 DUTIES OF THE BANKS INVOLVED IN A FUNDS TRANSFER

(a) Payment Services Regulations 2009

The Payment Services Regulations 2009 (PSRs; SI 2009/209), introduced a new regulatory regime for payment services from 1 November 2009. The PSRs implement the EC Payment Services Directive (2007/64/EC), which has itself recently been replaced by a revised Directive on Payment Services (PSD2) (2015/2366/EU). EU Member States have two years to introduce the new Directive into their own national laws, although the UK's position is uncertain following the 23 June 2016 referendum decision to leave the EU.

The PSRs impose conduct of business requirements on payment services (incorporating both payment transactions and the operation of payment accounts) that are within scope. To be within the scope of the regulations, the payment services must be provided from an establishment maintained by a payment service provider or its agent in the UK, the payment service providers of both the payer and the payee must be located within the European Economic Area (EEA), and the transaction or payment account must be in either euro or sterling or another Member State currency (regs 33(1), 51(1): but rules relating to value date and availability of funds in reg 73 apply regardless of whether both payer and payee are located within the EEA). The PSRs' conduct of business rules cover both the information to be provided to the payment service user (Part 5), and the rights and obligations of payment service users and providers (Part 6). Parts 5 and 6 apply to entirely domestic payment transactions (which probably includes entirely 'in-house' transfers, and also where the payer and the payee are the same person) and also cross-border payments. Any breach of the requirements of Part 5 or 6 is actionable by a 'private person' who suffers loss as a result of the contravention, subject to the defences and other incidents applying to actions for breach of statutory duty (reg 120(1): for the definition of 'private person', see reg 120(3)).

Two limitations on the extent of the PSRs are of vital importance. First, the PSRs only extend to electronic means of payment; they do not apply to cash-only transactions directly between payer and payee or to paper-based transactions such as cheques (Sch 1, Part 2, (f), (g)). Secondly, except where the payment service user is a consumer, a micro-enterprise, or a charity (as defined in reg 2(1), and for the definition of 'consumer', see p 639 below), payment service providers may contract out of most conduct of business requirements (regs 33(4), 51(3)). For example, in *Tidal Energy Ltd v Bank of Scotland plc* [2013] EWHC 2780 (QB), [2013] 2 CLC 407 at [21] (affirmed [2014] EWCA Civ 1107, [2014] 2 CLC 124), the PSRs were excluded by a clause in the bank's terms and conditions which governed the claimant's account.

The wide scope of the PSRs mean that they are likely to apply to most domestic electronic funds transfer within the UK, and to a large number of international electronic funds transfers from the UK to other EU Member States. Insofar as a payment transaction falls outside the scope of the PSRs, for example because of the currency of the transfer or because of contracting out, it will be necessary to consider the position at common law. In respect of electronic funds transfers falling within their scope, the PSRs do not expressly preserve the remedies that the parties might otherwise have had at common law. Whether this means that the PSRs establish an exclusive remedial regime when applicable must await judicial determination.

(i) Payer's bank

Under the PSRs the payer's bank is strictly liable for non-execution or defective execution of a payment order whether initiated by the payer or by the payee (regs 75 and 76). But the payer's bank must have been provided with the correct 'unique identifier' which identifies the payee and the payee's account. Where the 'unique identifier' is incorrect, the payer's bank is not liable for non-execution or defective execution of the payment transaction (under reg 75 or 76), but must instead make reasonable efforts to recover the funds involved in the payment transaction (reg 74(2)). In *Tidal Energy Ltd v Bank of Scotland plc* [2013] EWHC 2780 (QB), [2013] 2 CLC 407 at [22] (affirmed [2014] EWCA Civ 1107, [2014] 2 CLC 124 without reference to this point), HHJ Havelock-Allan QC said (*obiter*) that if the PSRs had applied to a CHAPS transfer made to the wrong payee (the PSRs did not apply because they had been expressly excluded by the bank's terms and conditions), the payer's bank would not have been liable under reg 75 as the 'unique identifier' provided by the payer was incorrect, because there was a mismatch between (1) the payee's name, and (2) the account number and sort code, so that reg 74(2) would have applied.

Where a payment order is initiated by the payer, as with a CHAPS transfer or a standing order, the payer's bank is liable to the payer for the correct execution of the payment transaction unless it can prove to the payer that the correct amount was received by the payee's bank on time (reg 75(2)). The general rule is that the payer's bank must ensure that the amount of the payment transaction is credited to the account of the payee's bank by the end of the business day following receipt of the payment order (reg 70(1)). If the payer's bank is liable, it must refund the amount of the defective or non-executed transaction to the payer without undue delay, and, where applicable, restore the debited payment account to the state it would have been in had the transaction not occurred at all (reg 75(4); unless force majeure applies: reg 79). Where a payment order is initiated by the payee, as with direct debits, the payer's bank will be liable to refund the payer the amount of the direct debit payment, and if necessary re-credit the payer's account, if the payee's bank has been able to prove that it carried out its end of the payment transaction properly, ie it has sent the payment instruction (in the correct amount and within the correct timescale) and the correct payee's details to the payer's bank, so that failure to receive the correct amount of funds within the correct timescale lies with the payer's bank rather than with the payee's bank (reg 76(2), (5): unless force majeure applies: reg 79). The payer can also claim for any charges and any interest incurred as a result of the non-execution or defective execution of the payment transaction (reg 77). In order to obtain the redress stated above (under regs 75, 76, and 77), the payer must notify the payer's bank without delay, and in any event no later than 13 months after the debit date, on becoming aware of any unauthorised or incorrectly executed payment transactions (reg 59(1): reg 59(2) relieves the payment service user of this obligation if his bank has failed to comply with various information requirements in Part 5). The payer's bank is given a right of recourse, which applies where the non-execution or defective execution of a payment transaction is 'attributable' to the payee's bank or an intermediary bank (reg 78).

A payment transaction must be authorised, which means that the payer must have given his consent to the execution of the payment transaction or to the execution of a series of payment transactions of which the payment transaction forms part (reg 55(1)). The payer may have given his consent before or, if agreed, after the execution of the payment transaction, and it must be in a form, and in accordance with the procedure, agreed between the payer and the payer's bank (reg 55(2)). The payer's bank is liable to the payer for execution of an unauthorised payment transaction and it must refund the amount of the unauthorised payment to him (reg 61(a)). If the unauthorised payment has been debited from the payer's account, the payer's bank must restore the debit to that account (reg 61(b)). (For burden of proof and circumstances where the payer may be held liable for unauthorised payment transactions, see p 640 below.) In order to claim a refund or restoration of his account following an unauthorised payment transaction, the payer must notify his bank without delay on becoming aware of the unauthorised nature of the transaction and, in any event, this must be done no later than 13 months after the debit date (reg 59(1), and see above for reg 59(2) exception). The payer may also be entitled to a refund from the payer's bank where an authorised payment transaction is initiated by or through the payee, as with a direct debit, where the payer did not specify the exact amount of the payment when initially authorising the direct debit and the amount of the payment 'exceeded the amount that the payer could reasonably have expected taking into account the payer's previous spending pattern, the conditions of the framework contract and the circumstances of the case' (reg 63(2)).

(ii) Payee's bank

Part 6 of the PSRs contains provisions relating to the rights and obligations of the payee's bank in the provision of payment services that are within scope (for scope of PSRs, see above, p 582).

First, in the case of a direct debit, the payee's bank must transmit the payment order to the payer's bank within the time limits it has agreed with the payee (reg 70(6)). The payee's bank must then credit the amount of the payment to the payee's account following its receipt of the funds (reg 70(5)). The payee's bank must ensure that the amount of the payment is at the payee's disposal immediately after that amount has been credited to the payee bank's account (reg 73(2)). The transferred funds must start to earn interest by the end of the business day upon which the payee's bank received those funds (reg 73(1)).

Secondly, the payee's bank must ensure that the full amount of the payment is transferred to the payee and that no charges are deducted from that amount (reg 68(1)), unless charges have been agreed (reg 68(2)). In the case of a direct debit, the payee's bank is liable to reimburse the payee for any unauthorised charges deducted from the amount transferred (reg 68(3)(b)).

Thirdly, in the case of the incorrect execution of a payment order initiated by the payer, if the payer's bank can prove that the funds were transferred to the payee's bank within the relevant time limits (see above, p 583), responsibility for the non-execution or defective execution of the payment transaction shifts to the payee's bank, which must then immediately make available to the payee a sum equivalent to the amount of the transfer and, where applicable, credit the corresponding amount to the payee's account (reg 75(5)). Where the payment transaction is initiated by the payee, the payee's bank is liable to the payee for the correct transmission of the payment order to the payer's bank within the relevant time limits (reg 76(2); the payee's bank must transmit the relevant payment order within the time limits agreed between the payee and his bank: reg 70(6)). Where the payee's bank is so liable, it must immediately re-transmit the payment order to the payer's bank (reg 76(3)), and it must, on request, make immediate efforts to trace the payment transaction and notify the payee of the outcome (reg 76(4)). It remains open to the payee's bank to prove that it correctly transmitted the payment order to the payer's bank in time, and in such a case liability for the non-execution or defective execution of the payment transaction shifts to the payer's bank, which must refund the amount of the payment to the payer and, where necessary, re-credit his account (reg 76(5)). The payee can also claim for any charges and any interest incurred as a result of the non-execution or defective execution of the payment transaction (reg 77). However, in order to obtain the redress stated above, the payee must notify the payee's bank without delay, and in any event no later than 13 months after the debit date, on becoming aware of any incorrectly executed payment transactions (reg 59(1), and see above for reg 59(2) exception). The payee's bank will not be liable for an incorrectly executed transfer where the unique identifier (eg the payer's account number, sort code, or bank details) provided by the payee is incorrect, although the bank must make reasonable efforts to recover the funds involved in the transaction (reg 74(2), and see above, p 583). The payee's bank can also avoid liability in cases of force majeure (reg 79). The payee's bank is given a right of recourse where the non-execution or defective execution of a payment transaction is 'attributable' to the payer's bank or an intermediary bank (reg 78).

(iii) Intermediary banks

Regulation 78 of the PSRs provides as follows:

> Where the liability of a payment service provider ('the first provider') under regulation 75 or 76 is attributable to another payment service provider or an intermediary, the other payment service provider or intermediary must compensate the first provider for any losses incurred or sums paid pursuant to those regulations.

Liability may be avoided where the payer provided an incorrect 'unique identifier' (identifying the payee and his account) (reg 74, and see above, p 583), or in a case of force majeure (reg 79).

QUESTION

How does the position of an intermediary bank under the PSRs differ from that under the common law?

(b) At common law

(i) Payer's bank

(a) Relationship with payer

The payer's bank must comply with the payer's mandate, ie the payment instructions received from the payer. But the doctrine of strict compliance, encountered in letters of credit cases (see below, p 778), has been held not to apply to payment instructions received from the payer (*Royal Products Ltd v Midland Bank Ltd* [1981] 2 Lloyd's Rep 194). Under the common law, the payer's bank will usually be precluded from debiting the payer's account when acting outside its mandate. Sometimes the court will be required to interpret the terms of the payer's mandate and it may be able to rely on banking practice to do so, at least where the practice is known or reasonably available to both the payer and the bank (*Tidal Energy Ltd v Bank of Scotland plc* [2014] EWCA Civ 1107, [2014] 2 CLC 124: the judgments, even of the majority, are not easy to reconcile, but all three Lords Justices appear to have agreed that there can be reliance on banking practice for the purposes of interpretation where the practice was known or reasonably available to both the bank and its customer). As well as complying with the payer's mandate, the payer's bank owes the payer a duty to act with reasonable care and skill in and about the execution of his payment instructions. Both issues arose in the next case.

Royal Products Ltd v Midland Bank Ltd
[1981] 2 Lloyd's Rep 194, Queen's Bench Division

The plaintiffs (Royal Products), a Maltese company, instructed the defendant bank (Midland) to transfer £13,000 by cable from their current account with Midland in the UK to their account with the Bank of Industry, Commerce and Agriculture Ltd (BICAL) in Malta. Midland regularly employed the Bank of Valletta (National) in Malta as its correspondent and so telexed National instructing it to transfer £13,000 to BICAL. Although National was aware that BICAL was facing liquidity problems at the time, National made the transfer of £13,000 to BICAL and notified BICAL that that amount was to be credited to Royal Products' account. The following day BICAL collapsed and Royal Products failed to receive any of its funds, which had already been debited by Midland from Royal Products' account in the UK. Royal Products brought an action against Midland claiming the return of £13,000 or damages. Two of Royal Products' main claims were (1) that National were their agents, owing and having broken certain duties and obligations of a fiduciary nature for breach of which Midland were liable, and (2) even if National were not their agents, Midland were vicariously liable for the negligence of National, who acted as Midland's agents (it was not alleged that Midland were in breach of duty themselves). Webster J rejected these claims and gave judgment for Midland.

> **Webster J**: . . . The question whether [Royal Products] make good any of these claims depends in the first instance on the terms of their instructions to Midland and on the implications of law arising out of those instructions.

THE INSTRUCTIONS AND THEIR IMPLICATIONS

Royal Products' instructions were contained in a letter dated Nov 23, 1972, which must have been delivered by hand to Midland on that day. They read:

> *Account No 30039748*
>
> Will you please transfer by full rate cable the sum of £13,000 to our Account No 008516 with the Bank of Industry, Commerce & Agriculture Ltd, Commercial House, South Street, Valetta, Malta. Your cable charges are to be for our account.

The background to these instructions is important. When the instructions were given, Royal Products were, as I have said, a customer of Midland, having a current account with them, and they were also a customer of BICAL, having a current account with that bank also; and they had given similar instructions before. It is also in my view relevant to note that Midland took, as I infer, no fee from the transaction. By letter dated Nov 24, 1972, they wrote to Royal Products:

> We have to advise you that in accordance with your request of 23rd instant, we have arranged by cable for the following payment to be effected.
>
> | | |
> |---:|:---|
> | *Beneficiary* | Yourselves |
> | *Amount* | £13,000 |
> | *Charges* | £10.00 |
>
> *Total amount of* £13,010.00 is being debited to your Company's Account.

When similar instructions had been given on previous occasions Midland had transferred the credit direct, without using the services of National, and this was the first occasion on which they had used those services for this particular purpose in relation to Royal Products. There is no evidence before me as to the manner in which Royal Products contemplated that the transfer would be effected by Midland, but in a letter written on Oct 1, 1979, during the course of these proceedings, in answer to a request by Midland's solicitors, Royal Products' solicitors wrote saying that they admitted that Midland 'were entitled to use the services of the National Bank of Malta as sub agents'. I conclude that Royal Products did not mind how the transfer was effected provided that it was effected, or at least initiated, forthwith, that is to say by a cable sent on the same day, Nov 23. Nor was any evidence adduced as to what Royal Products expected of BICAL if the instructions were implemented and I infer, from the surrounding circumstances which I have mentioned and from the nature of the instructions, that they expected no more than that, when credit or payment was received, the sum should forthwith be credited to Royal Products' current account with BICAL. It was Midland, not Royal Products, who inserted in their instructions to National the words 'for advice credit Royal Products', meaning, as I find, that BICAL were to advise Royal Products of the credit, and, although that fact is consistent with the fact that Royal Products may have expected to be informed when their account was credited, it is not sufficient, in my view, to enable Royal Products' instructions to be read as if they included such a requirement. I return to this point later in this judgment.

What, then, are the legal implications of those instructions? How are they to be regarded, as a matter of law? In my judgment they are to be regarded simply as an authority and instruction, from a customer to its bank, to transfer an amount standing to the credit of that customer with that bank to the credit of its account with another bank, that other bank being impliedly authorized by the customer to accept that credit by virtue of the fact that the customer has a current account with it, no consent to the receipt of the credit being expected from or required of that other bank, by virtue of the same fact. It is, in other words, a banking operation, of a kind which is often carried out internally, that is to say, within the same bank or between two branches of the same bank and which, at least from the point of view of the customer, is no different in nature or quality when, as in the present case, it is carried out between different banks. I use the word 'operation' advisedly, in an attempt to distinguish and exclude a contract, for in my judgment the instructions did not bring into existence, as between Royal Products and Midland, any separate or distinct contract of any kind. In this respect, therefore, the circumstances of this case differ from those of *Calico Printers' Association v Barclays Bank Ltd. and the Anglo-Palestine Co Ltd* (1930) 38 Lloyd's Rep 105; [1930] 36 Com Cas 71, where the defendant bank took ¼ per cent, commission (see Mr Justice Wright at pp 110 and 80), although in other respects to which I will allude later it seems to me that the principle to be derived from the judgment of Mr Justice Wright in that case can be applied to the present one.

Given that this was an ordinary banking operation, as I hold that it was, it follows that in carrying out its part of the transaction Midland owed Royal Products a duty to use reasonable care and skill: see *Selangor United Rubber Estates Ltd v Cradock and Others (No 3)*, [1968] 2 Lloyd's Rep 289; [1968] 2 All ER 1073, and *Karak Rubber Co Ltd v Burden and Others (No 2)*, [1972] 1 Lloyd's Rep 73; [1972] 1 All ER 1210 and that they would be vicariously liable for the breach of that duty by any servant or agent to whom they delegated the carrying out of the instructions. Midland, therefore, would be liable to Royal Products for National's negligence, if any, in that respect. But in my judgment National owed no duty of any kind direct to Royal Products. Although Midland were entitled, as Royal Products later admitted, to execute the instructions by using the services of National as their correspondents, Royal Products had given Midland no authority which would have had the effect of creating privity of contract between them and National, which was the principle applied by Mr Justice Wright in *Calico Printers* case so as to exclude privity of contract between the plaintiffs and the 'sub-agent' in that case. In my judgment, therefore, National are not to be regarded as having been agents of Royal Products and did not, therefore, owe them any of the duties, including a fiduciary duty, owed by an agent to his principal.

It follows from what I have said that in my view the relevant law is accurately stated in the following passages from the *Law of Banking* by Lord Chorley, 6th edn at p. 374:

> The substantial difference between the branch and the correspondent is that while the former is managed by the servants of the banker acting under his supervision and control, the latter is independently in business and acts only on occasion as an agent and at his discretion. The fact that the correspondent is a legal entity independent of the banker who employs him does not, however, mean that there exists any contractual relationship between him and the banker's customers on whose business he is being employed . . . As between the customer and his banker, however, the latter is liable for the acts of his correspondent in exactly the same way and within the same limits as for those of his managers and servants, for it is immaterial to the customer whether the banker operates through a branch or through a correspondent, unless, of course, the banker expressly stipulates that he is not to be so liable.

Finally, before turning to the subsequent facts and while still considering the implications of Royal Products' original instructions, it is necessary to decide what had to be done to enable Midland, or National, to contend that those instructions had been fulfilled. Unless there is any authority which compels me to decide otherwise, I would hold that Midland had carried out Royal Products' instructions when it had enabled Royal Products to draw on or otherwise use the amount of credit transferred, which Royal Products would have been able to do once Midland had, in one way or another and either directly or indirectly, made funds available to BICAL to the extent of £13,000 and had notified BICAL that that sum was to be credited to the account of Royal Products. Mr Tugendhat on behalf of Royal Products advanced two arguments in relation to this question which I should mention at this stage. First, in reliance on *Rekstin v Severn Sibirsko and the Bank for Russian Trade*, [1933] 1 KB 47, he submitted that the instructions had not been complied with until BICAL had assented to the receipt of the credit. I reject that submission. In the first place the facts in that case were a long way from the facts in the present case. This is a case of the transfer of a customer's credit from one of his banks to another. *Rekstin's* case was one in which a judgment debtor sought to transfer an amount standing to the credit of its current account at a bank to the current account of another customer of that bank, a customer which enjoyed diplomatic immunity and to which it, the judgment debtor, owed nothing. I respectfully agree with the comment made by Mr Justice Kerr in *Momm and Others v Barclays Bank International Ltd* [1976] 3 All ER 588 at p 597, when he said that in his view that decision should be confined to its special facts.

Secondly he submitted, as a general proposition, that the doctrine of strict compliance was to be applied to the instructions given in this case so that, if they were not strictly complied with, National was precluded from contending that they had been complied with at all. I reject that contention if Mr Tugendhat means (which I suspect that he does not) that there was some duty on Midland or National which required them to do more than comply with Royal Products' instructions as those instructions are to be construed as a matter of law. I reject the submission also if by it he means that in construing those instructions I should, as a matter of law or banking practice, give a legal implication to each detail of them, for it seems to me that the doctrine which would lead to that result has little application to the facts of the present case, having received its first authoritative recognition by Lord Sumner in *Equitable Trust Co of New York v Dawson Partners Ltd* (1926) 27 Lloyd's Rep 49, in the context of confirmed credits. It may be that that doctrine has been or should be applied to all documentary credits; but the transaction in this case is not a 'documentary credit' within the meaning of that expression contained in the Uniform Custom and Practice for Documentary Credits . . .

I conclude, therefore, that no authority precludes me from holding, as I do, that in order to comply with Royal Products' instructions Midland were required, in the present case by National, their agents, to make funds available to BICAL in one way or another to the extent of £13,000 and to notify BICAL that that sum was to be credited to the account of Royal Products.

[Webster J went on to hold on the facts that Midland had complied with Royal Products' instructions and that National had not been negligent in making the transfer to BICAL when it did.]

Tidal Energy Ltd v Bank of Scotland plc
[2014] EWCA Civ 1107, [2014] 2 CLC 124, Court of Appeal

Tidal Energy Ltd owed £217,781 to one of its suppliers called Designcraft Ltd. Tidal instructed Bank of Scotland (BOS) to pay the debt. Tidal used one of the bank's standard printed CHAPS Transfer Forms to instruct BOS to make the transfer to an account number 13027309 at Barclays Bank with sort code 20-16-12. The receiving customer's name (Designcraft Ltd) and the receiving bank (Barclays) were correctly identified on the transfer form, but the bank account number and the sort code were incorrect. Unknown to Tidal, it had been fraudulently given an account number that belonged to a third party unconnected with Designcraft Ltd. The payment was executed through the CHAPS system on the same day as the instruction was given. Barclays, acting in accordance with banking practice, did not check the name on the account to confirm that it was Designcraft's account. The money was credited to the third party's account and Tidal's account at BOS was debited. When Tidal discovered the fraud it commenced proceedings against BOS, alleging that BOS had not carried out its instructions on the transfer form and seeking to be re-credited with the sum lost. HH Judge Havelock-Allen QC, sitting in the High Court, gave judgment for BOS. The judge accepted the bank's evidence of normal banking practice that execution of CHAPS transfers was done on the basis of bank account number and sort code only and not on the basis of the name of the payee (which was only included on the CHAPS Transfer Form for anti-money laundering and counter-terrorism purposes). Tidal appealed.

Lord Justice Floyd (dissenting): …

21. Does banking practice invariably form part of the relevant background for interpreting a contract or other instrument between the bank and its customer? The bank's skeleton argument referred to the statement of Willes J in *Hare v Henty* (1861) 10 CB NS 65, 77 that 'A man who employs a banker is bound by the usages of bankers'. Like all generalisations, care must be taken in its application to individual circumstances. The narrow issue in *Hare v Henty* was whether a banker receiving a cheque from a customer had a duty to transmit it to the paying bank for presentation on the day on which he received it, or whether it had until the following day to do so. Instead of transmitting the cheque directly to the paying bank, as had previously been the practice, the presenting bank had used the recently established country clearing house. The use of the clearing house had resulted in delay as compared with the earlier practice, with the result that the cheque had not been paid, and the customer claimed damages in negligence or contract. Erle CJ held that the remitting bank's duty to transmit the cheque was defined by earlier authority, *Rickford v Ridge* (1810) 2 Camp 537, and allowed the presenting bank until the following day. He said that that rule would apply in the case in point unless 'circumstances exist from which a contract or duty on the part of the banker to present earlier … can be inferred'. No such circumstances arose at the relevant time, as the practice of using the clearing house necessarily involved a delay. Willes J's observation about the practice of bankers was made in the course of argument, and did not form part of a judgment. The case is not authority for any general proposition that a contract with a bank must always be construed by reference to banking practice, far less banking practice not known to the customer.

22. In *Barclays Bank plc v Bank of England* [1985] 1 All ER 385, a decision of Bingham J as a judge of the Commercial Court appointed as an arbitrator, the court had to determine the time and place at which a bank presenting a cheque for payment through the clearing system was discharged of its responsibility towards its customer. Although Bingham J cites Willes J's statement in *Hare v Henty* at paragraph 17 of his award, he does so, firstly, in a passage which set out the respondent's argument, which he went on to reject. It was contended for the respondent that delivery at the clearing house was, by agreement or by usage of the banks, treated as equivalent to presentation and therefore amounted to a waiver of the normal obligation to present at the paying bank. Bingham J rejected the contention that there was any agreement to treat delivery at the clearing house as dispensing with the need for presentation at the bank. In a concluding, and *obiter*, passage of his judgment he said that if the drawer was to lose any right which he possessed 'as a result of a private agreement between banks for their own convenience the very strongest proof of his knowledge and assent would be needed'. He also said:

> In deciding whether presentation in a given way, as through the clearing house, is a proper and reasonable discharge of the presenting banker's duty to his customer, reference to the ordinary usage and practice of bankers is very relevant, and likely in most cases to be decisive (see, for example, *Hare v Henty* (1861) 10 CB NS 65, 142 ER 374, *Prideaux v Criddle* (1869) LR 4 QB 455), but the usage and practice contended for here, even if proved, could not without more derogate from the presenting bank's duty to its customer.

23. Those passages distinguish, in my judgment correctly, between the use of banking practice to decide whether a bank has complied with a duty imposed on it by contract, and the use of such practice, if unknown to the customer, to inform the meaning of the contract itself. Of course, if the practice is known or reasonably available to both customer and bank, then its use for interpretation is uncontroversial. Where that is not so, banking practice cannot in

my judgment have a bearing on deciding the meaning and scope of the authority granted to the bank.

24. The evidence before the judge did not show that there was material reasonably available to the customer to show how CHAPS worked, and in particular to inform him of the fact that CHAPS did not use the account name. Mr Johnson's evidence stressed the difference between the relationships between the banks 'in the Bank to Bank space' and those between the banks and their customers when he said that the CHAPS Scheme Rules 'do not articulate how the Bank should transact with its customers'. His evidence as to banking practice was obtained as a result of Tidal's Part 18 request. The bank made no attempt to establish that the relevant aspect of the operation of CHAPS was known outside banking circles. One document which mentioned the practice 'Payment Services Regulations—Industry Best Practice' was not targeted at consumers. In fact it states that it focuses on direct members, that is to say those members of the Payments Council who have direct access to the technical infrastructure, and not on payment service providers or indirect members. The judge was of course entitled to accept Mr Johnson's evidence about the practice. He was not in my judgment entitled to hold that it established that the practice was reasonably available to customers.

25. Mr Cox [counsel for BOS] did not seriously seek to support the judge's additional reliance on the bank's suggestion that the beneficiary's name might be required in order to comply with anti-money laundering or counter-terrorism rules. The suggestion that the user of the transfer form would make a connection between the reference to those matters in section 2 and the requirement for the name of a beneficiary in section 1 is quite unrealistic. For reasons similar to those I have given, such knowledge, possessed only by the bank, would not be part of the admissible background.

26. One comes back, therefore, to the circumstances in which, pursuant to the transfer form, the bank is authorised to debit Tidal's account with the amount specified on the form. Section 2 of the form expressly asks the bank to 'debit *the payment*' from Tidal's account. Both sides agreed that the bank could not validly debit the payment from Tidal's account unless the payment was made. What for the purposes of this form constitutes a payment? ...

34. To my mind, on the proper construction of this form, a payment cannot be said to be made until funds are credited into an account which conforms to the four identifiers which the customer is required to give in section 1 of the form: sort code, bank name, account number and customer name. It seems to me to be plain, as I think it did to the judge, that the first three of these are essential indicators of when a payment has been made. I can see no rational criterion for excluding the fourth identifier—customer name. Indeed, so far as the customer is concerned at least, it could be said to be the most important. The judge expressly found that the identity of the beneficiary was important to Tidal and noted that the customer could be forgiven if he thought that the account name mattered, given that the transfer form included a box for naming the beneficiary and mentions the 'payee'. If that is the case, then the reaction of the reasonable person to the language used in the form is the same. There is nothing whatever in the form, or the admissible background, to alert the reasonable person to the fact that, in routing the payment, account would be taken of some but not all of the identifiers, and in particular that no account would be taken of the name. Tidal was of course consenting to the use of the CHAPS system (or indeed any other payment method which the Bank decided on) to carry out its instructions, but Tidal was not agreeing that the bank could carry out those instructions in a way which allowed it to disregard any of the identifiers, least of all the name of the beneficiary.

35. I agree that it is not reasonable to expect the bank to ensure that a payment to Design Craft has been made, if by that one means that there has been, in fact, a proper discharge of the legal obligation which Tidal had to pay them. It is, however, entirely reasonable for a customer to expect the bank to obtain an acknowledgment that a credit has been made to an account

conforming to all (and not just some) of the identifiers given on the transfer form, when he is given nothing to make him believe the contrary.

36. It follows that on the construction of the form which I consider to be correct, the bank has no right to debit the customer's account when a transfer is made to an account having the correct sort-code and account number but a different account name. The customer has the right to prevent the bank from debiting his account except when the payment is made to an account matching the four identifiers. Nothing in the private arrangements between the banks as to how they manage CHAPS payments between themselves, such as their decision to disregard the beneficiary name, can add to or derogate from that right.

37. Lurking beneath the submissions in this case is a suggestion that, if we were to decide the case against the bank, it would undermine the CHAPS system. I cannot accept that this is so for a number of reasons. Firstly, the bank could deal with the matter by drawing attention to the relevant aspect of the system on their CHAPS transfer forms, or when they accept oral instructions, if they do, to make a CHAPS transfer. In those circumstances it would be clear that a 'payment' in accordance with the instruction would be made provided only that the sort code, bank and account number coincided with those on the form. If, for commercial reasons, they prefer not to take this simple step, then the risk that there will be a percentage of transfers for which a customer may subsequently claim to be reimbursed is a risk which the bank voluntarily undertakes. In that connection there was some material before the judge that the banks did at one time operate a process of manual checking when a CHAPS transfer exceeded £50,000. The abandonment of the manual checking process was no doubt based on an assessment of the risk which the bank was prepared to take.

38. Although this is an appeal from a summary judgment, neither side suggested that it turned on the test for summary judgment. The bank expressly accepted that if the instruction was an instruction to pay Design Craft rather than Barclays, then it would have no defence. In my judgment it is clear that the bank only had authority to debit Tidal's account if a payment was made which complied with the four identifiers on the transfer form. I would, for my part, have allowed the appeal and granted summary judgment to Tidal on its claim.

Lord Justice Tomlinson: …

39. I have read in draft the judgments prepared by Floyd LJ and by Lord Dyson MR. I find myself in the invidious position of having to choose between them.

40. When I first read the papers in this case, it seemed to me likely that the loss would properly lie with Tidal, for it was Tidal which was defrauded into believing that the account information with which it supplied the bank corresponded to an account held by its supplier, Designcraft Limited. That instinctive answer however simply begs the question as to the proper construction of the instruction given by Tidal to the bank, and by the end of the hearing I was more or less persuaded that that instruction should be construed as Floyd LJ has done.

41. Even so, I remained troubled by two aspects of this conclusion. The first, which I sought to explore with counsel at the hearing, relates to the possible lack of correspondence between the 'Receiving (beneficiary) sort code' as advised by the bank's customer (or sending (remitter)) and the 'Receiving (beneficiary) bank and branch', as advised by the bank's customer. What is the position if the customer supplies the correct sort code but wrongly believes that it belongs to a branch of Barclays whereas it in fact relates to a branch of Lloyds? Given that the hallmark of CHAPS payments is speed, is it really intended that payment should not be made but only that, within the designated maximum execution time, the bank should inform its customer of its refusal or inability so to do? That could have serious consequences for the customer, bearing in mind that CHAPS is frequently used where time for payment is of the essence. The question may be more starkly posed. As set out by Floyd LJ at paragraph 6 above, the bank's standard form invited the customer to supply both receiving bank name and receiving bank branch. As

it happens Tidal here filled in that box with the single entry 'Barclays'. As it also happens the bank branch uniquely identified by sort code 20–16–12 is Barclays' branch at Bury St Edmunds. But suppose Tidal knew that its supplier, Designcraft, is based in Newmarket and wrongly assumed that its account was held at Barclays' branch in that town. Should payment not be made because the customer had identified the wrong branch of Barclays by name of location, albeit it had identified the right branch by sort code?

42. Similar questions arise in relation to the 'Receiving (beneficiary) customer name'. The form was in this case completed in manuscript capital letters. Subject to what I point out below, what was here written was 'DESIGN CRAFT LTD'. Leaving aside that this company apparently calls itself Designcraft Ltd rather than Design Craft Ltd, what would be the position if, contrary to Tidal's belief, Designcraft was not a limited company, or if its account was simply designated Designcraft rather than Designcraft Ltd? Who is to be the arbiter of whether any discrepancy is significant, or if it requires payment not to be made? One can think of many examples of plausible misrendering of the beneficiary's name, likewise of many examples where the beneficiary's name and the name attached to its bank account may not correspond.

43. It may be that something has here been lost in the photocopying, but as it happens in the present case only a person familiar with the English language would readily realise that the beneficiary name here written was 'DESIGN CRAFT LTD' for what is written more closely resembles 'DCSIGN CRAFT LTD'. This has caused no problem here, but one can readily conceive of cases in which poor handwriting could inadvertently be misleading as to the identity of the intended beneficiary.

44. In short, and on reflection, I can see grave difficulties arising if payment may only be made where there is correspondence with all four identifiers. Sort code and account number are alone sufficient to identify the intended destination of the payment and conformity therewith requires only mechanical checking without the need for the exercise of any subjective judgment.

45. The normal banking practice of which Mr Johnson here gave evidence therefore comes as no surprise. Whether the average bank cashier who accepts over the counter instructions to effect a CHAPS transfer is aware of it is another matter, as is, I think, whether the average customer, corporate or otherwise, is aware of it either. A contract cannot be construed against the background of facts which are neither known nor reasonably ascertainable.

46. In that regard it is I consider little short of astonishing that the judge was asked to resolve this question, and we are asked to determine this appeal, without the benefit of seeing the CHAPS Scheme Rules and associated Reference Documents. Disclosure was, incredibly to my mind, resisted by the bank on the ground that these documents 'set out the service provided by CHAPSCo in the Bank to Bank space, i.e. they articulate the obligations of members, CHAPSCo and the Bank of England when sending payments between member banks. They do not articulate how the Bank should transact with its customers'. Mr Johnson, who made this statement, went on however to say 'CHAPSCo does not prescribe the basis on which the payments are processed by the members of the scheme following the receipt of the payment, apart from stating that the payment should be processed within the maximum inward payment transmission time of 1.5 hours'. In my view this important reservation alone rendered the CHAPS Scheme Rules and associated Reference Documents relevant to the bank's pleaded contention that 'it is normal banking practice for banks to process payments through CHAPS on the basis of the payee's account number and sort code and not the name of the payee'—Defence, paragraph 8.1. As the Master of the Rolls has demonstrated, and as I allude to above, the feature of the CHAPS system that it is intended to achieve rapid payment is key to the proper construction of the mandate. Moreover, the 'designated maximum execution time for a CHAPS transfer' is referred to in the terms and conditions on the reverse side of the bank's standard form instruction, a point to which I return below. However, as I understand it the appellant did not persist in its request for disclosure.

47. The bank adduced no evidence as to how a customer, as opposed to a payment services provider, could find out about the practice described by Mr Johnson. Whilst I am inclined to think that the Master of the Rolls must be right in his observation that the CHAPS practice of clearing banks would have been reasonably available to the Appellant and any other customer who wished to use the CHAPS payments system, the bank can hardly complain if I harbour reservations as to the enthusiasm or accuracy with which any enquiry would have been met.

48. All this notwithstanding, I reach the same conclusion as the Master of the Rolls. At paragraph 59 the Master of the Rolls suggests that, 'subject to any contrary express terms, a customer who uses CHAPS is taken to contract on the basis of the banking practice that governs CHAPS transactions.' Given my lingering concerns as to the ease with which a customer could ascertain that practice, and the paucity of the evidence in this case, I would prefer to put the point a little differently. In my judgment, the customer's instruction made by execution of this specific 'CHAPS transfer' request form, and in particular the giving of the confirmation 'You are hereby authorised to effect these instructions ... by transmission through the Clearing House Automated Payments System' was an instruction to make a payment transfer in accordance with the current CHAPS Scheme Rules and as the CHAPS transfer system is currently operated in accordance with the usual practice adopted by the participating clearing bankers. A question might arise if the usual banking practice is unreasonable or otherwise inimical to the nature of the instruction, but no such question arises here as the practice described by Mr Johnson cannot, as I have endeavoured to show, be said to be unreasonable. My lingering belief that a customer might have needed to show some persistence in order successfully to find out the usual banking practice does not deter me from construing the mandate in the way I do. After all, by agreeing to clause 4 of the Terms and Conditions on the reverse of the form, the customer agreed that in the event of refusal of the bank to execute a CHAPS transfer it would be informed 'within the designated maximum execution time for a payment transaction of this type' without any explanation of what that designated maximum execution time is. Furthermore, the customer agreed that, having been so informed together with the bank's reasons for refusal, and the procedure for rectifying any factual errors that led to the refusal, the bank's obligation in such event would then be to 'make the CHAPS transfer within the designated maximum execution time for a payment transaction of this type after the reasons for stopping it cease to exist'.

49. The Master of the Rolls at paragraph 60 suggests that most customers would not be interested in obtaining information as to how CHAPS works in practice, and would be content if the CHAPS transfer is executed in accordance with normal banking practice. I agree. In my judgment the proper analysis is that the customer, by execution of the form, authorised the bank to execute the transfer in accordance with usual banking practice, thereby rendering that practice the contractual method of performance. That conclusion is in no way dependent upon the nature of the practice being reasonably available to the appellant and to any other customer. My conclusion is simply that the customer authorised execution in accordance with usual banking practice, whatever that might be, subject possibly to questions of reasonableness which do not here arise.

50. Accordingly, I would dismiss the appeal.

Lord Dyson MR: ...

51. The facts have already been sufficiently stated by Floyd LJ. I can, therefore, come immediately to the reasons why I respectfully disagree with his conclusion.

52. The question raised in this case is what is the proper construction of the CHAPS transfer form. In particular, did it authorise the Bank of Scotland ('the bank') to debit the appellant's account (i) only when the payment was made to an account matching all four 'identifiers' (sort code, bank name, account number and customer name) or (ii) only when the payment was

made to the first three identifiers. Floyd LJ favours (i); the judge favoured (ii). I agree with the judge essentially for the reasons that he gave.

53. CHAPS is an electronic bank to bank same day payment scheme for payments made within the UK in sterling. Up to 50% of UK GDP flows through the CHAPS payment system each day: see *Paget's Law of Banking* (13th edn) paragraph 17.8. Floyd LJ has summarised some of the evidence as to CHAPS banking practice which was given by Mr Johnson and was accepted by the judge. Mr Johnson was a Customer & Domestic Manager within the bank's Electronic Payments team. In my view, the judge was plainly entitled to accept his evidence.

54. I would emphasise the following. CHAPS is run by the CHAPS Clearing Company Limited ('CHAPSCo'). CHAPSCo does not prescribe the basis on which payments are processed by the members of the scheme, apart from stating that payments should be processed within the maximum inwards payment transmission time of 1.5 hours. Since at least 2007, all of the major UK clearing banks have processed and routed electronic payments to a customer's account, including CHAPS payments, on the basis of sort code (or bank identifier code) and account number, but not account or beneficiary name. This is reflected by the Payment Council's guidance note entitled 'Payment Services Regulations—Industry Best Practice' which states 'payments executed via CHAPS are processed on sort code and account number—"the unique identifier"'. Banks are expected to process the vast majority of CHAPS payments on a 'straight-through' basis (i.e. without manual checks) in order to meet the short time-scale that is the hallmark of CHAPS. Mr Johnson says at paragraph 14 of his first witness statement:

> I believe that the CHAPS members use this system of account number and sort code primacy because it maximises the number of payments which go straight through the system without delay. 'Straight-through processing' is fundamental to payments as customers operate in a real-time world and their accounts are credited in near real-time. CHAPS payments are usually high value payments and are treated as urgent so speed of credit is important. Whilst it is open for the receiving CHAPS member (in this case Barclays) to scrutinise every payment instruction which they receive, to check that the beneficiary name entered by the paying member matches the name of the beneficiary account or account holder, I believe it would be economically impossible to do so if they are also to fulfil their obligations to process CHAPS payments, within the maximum inward payment transmission time of 1.5hrs.

55. The evidence of Mr Johnson (paragraph 15 of his first statement) is that:

> Although it is my experience that as a matter of normal banking practice, beneficiary name is not used as a primary means by which a payment is routed through CHAPS, the Financial Action Task Force Recommendations requires members of CHAPS, for anti-money laundering and counter-terrorist purposes, to include the beneficiary name when making payments via wire transfers, including CHAPS.

56. In my view, the critical question in this case is whether the banking practice described by Mr Johnson can be relied on in order to construe the transfer form.

57. Floyd LJ has referred to the statement by Willes J in *Hare v Henty* (1861) 10 CB NS 65, 77: 'A man who employs a banker is bound by the usages of bankers'. I accept that this statement was made in the course of argument and did not form part of the judgment. But it was applied by Bingham J in *Barclays Bank plc v Bank of England* [1985] 1 All ER 385 at paragraph 26 of his award, as Floyd LJ points out at paragraph 22 above. In *Paget* at paragraph 17.46, the editors say:

> A customer of a clearing bank may be bound by, and able to rely on, the clearing house rules against his own bank through an implied term of the bank-customer contract. The customer is taken to have contracted with reference to the reasonable usage of bankers, including those clearing house rules which represent such reasonable usage.

58. The authorities cited in support of this passage include *Hare v Henty*. They also include *Tayeb v HSBC Bank plc* [2004] EWHC 1529 (Comm); [2005] 1 CLC 866 in which Colman J said at paragraph 57:

> Equally, if a customer opens an account of a kind which is of a kind [*sic*] into which CHAPS transfers can be made, that customer is entitled to assume that, if a transfer is made for the credit of that account, the bank will operate the account in accordance with the CHAPS Rules, but subject always to such course as may in the circumstances be required for the purpose of compliance with the 1988 Act and the Regulations and Guidelines.

59. Floyd LJ distinguishes these authorities on the basis that there is a material difference between (i) the use of banking practice to decide whether a bank has complied with its contractual duty and (ii) the use of such practice, if unknown to the customer, to inform the meaning of the contract itself (paragraph 23). He suggests (or at least implies) that banking practice may be relevant to (i), but not to (ii). I respectfully disagree. In my view, it may be relevant to both. Subject to any contrary express terms, a customer who uses CHAPS is taken to contract on the basis of the banking practice that governs CHAPS transactions. On the evidence which the judge accepted, there is a clear and settled practice that the receiving bank in a CHAPS transaction does not check the beneficiary's name for correspondence with the other identifiers. There are good commercial reasons why this practice is adopted: see paragraphs 62 and 63 below.

60. In any event, the distinction which Floyd LJ seeks to draw may not matter in the present case. That is because he accepts that, if the existence of the practice is known or reasonably available to both the customer and the bank, then 'its use for interpretation is uncontroversial' (paragraph 23). Even if this formulation is correct, I do not agree that the evidence did not show that 'there was material reasonably available to the customer to show how CHAPS worked, and in particular to inform him of the fact that CHAPS did not use the account name' (paragraph 24). The practice that at the material time the bank name, sort code and account number were the 'unique' identifiers was not a secret. It was not a practice, knowledge of which was only available to bankers. It is a practice which has been adopted since at least 2007. It is mentioned in the *Payment Services Regulations—Industry Best Practice*. The fact that this document is targeted at payment services providers does not mean that its contents are not reasonably available to customers. Any customer who wishes to find out in detail about how CHAPS works in practice can do so either by asking the bank for information or seeking information on-line. I would expect that most customers would not be interested in obtaining such information, and they would be content if the CHAPS transfer is executed in accordance with usual banking practice. But even if that is wrong, the important point is that the CHAPS practice of clearing banks would have been reasonably available to the appellant and any other customer who wished to use the CHAPS payments system.

61. Even if a banking practice is not reasonably available to the customer, the court should still be astute to avoid a construction of the contract which is inconsistent with business common sense. As Lord Steyn said in *Mannai Investment Co Ltd v Eagle Star Life Assurance Co Ltd* [1997] CLC 1124; [1997] AC 749 at page 1140; 771:

> In determining the meaning of the language of a commercial contract ... the law ... generally favours a commercially sensible construction. The reason for this approach is that a commercial construction is more likely to give effect to the intention of the parties. Words are therefore interpreted in the way in which a reasonable commercial person would construe them.

62. In my judgment, the construction sought by the appellant produces a result which is not reasonable and not commercially sensible (and therefore unlikely to have been intended by the parties) for the following reasons. First, the object of the CHAPS system is to achieve rapid (maximum of 1.5 hours) payment. That is why customers choose to use this system of electronic

payment. Secondly, the court should lean against a construction which involves imposing a requirement on a receiving bank which would frustrate the customer's wish to have the money transferred within 1.5 hours. If the beneficiary's name has to be checked within this period for correspondence with the other identifiers, the evidence is that this would be economically impossible to do.

63. Thirdly, the appellant's construction places on the remitting bank an obligation, in effect, to guarantee correspondence between the beneficiary name and the account number even though it has no control (i) over the care with which its customers complete the transfer form and (ii) over the way the receiving bank processes its incoming CHAPS payments. As regards this second point, Mr Johnson says at paragraph 16 of his first statement that, where the beneficiary account resides with another CHAPS member bank, there is no possibility for the remitting bank to check and verify the account number or name of the beneficiary: such information is confidential to the payee and is not disclosed as a matter of routine by receiving banks to remitting banks. In my view, the appellant's construction is unreasonable and makes no business sense. I see no reason why the remitting bank should assume responsibility for the accuracy of the name of the beneficiary entered by the customer on the form or for its correspondence with the other identifiers.

64. Floyd LJ says that the remitting bank could make it clear on the form that a 'payment' in accordance with the instruction will be made provided only that the sort code, bank and account number (but not the name) coincides with those on the form. I accept that this could be done. But that possibility should not distract us from the question of construction that lies at the heart of this appeal.

65. For the reasons that I have given, I would dismiss this appeal. I should add that I agree with Floyd LJ that, for the reasons that he gives at paragraphs 27 to 29, the transfer form should not be construed as an instruction to pay the receiving bank.

NOTES

1.   There are subtle differences between the judgments handed down by the majority.

(a) Lord Dyson (at [52]) held that BOS were authorised to debit Tidal's account only when the payment was made to an account matching the sort code, bank name, and account number supplied by Tidal. On the other hand, Tomlinson LJ (at [41]) saw potential problems where the sort code and the name of the bank differed and so (at [44]) held that the sort code and the account number alone were the key identifiers. This apparent divergence of opinion is unfortunate as some uncertainty remains in a case where the payee bank's name and sort code do not match.

(b) Lord Dyson's reasoning (at [59]) is based upon the implicit incorporation of banking practice governing CHAPS transactions into the contract between the bank and its customer. It is an application of the dicta of Willes J in *Hare v Henty* (1861) 10 CB (NS) 65 at 77, that '[a] man who employs a banker is bound by the usages of bankers'. On the other hand, Tomlinson LJ preferred to rely on the fact that the CHAPS transfer form made express reference to transmission using CHAPS, which made it an instruction to make the transfer in accordance with current CHAPS rules and practice. Lord Dyson's approach appears to depend upon the practice being known to the customer, or at least reasonably available to him, whereas Tomlinson LJ's approach does not.

2.   As a result of these inconsistencies, it is worth remembering Floyd LJ's suggestion (at [37]) that banks could protect themselves by making it clear on the CHAPS Transfer Form, or when they accepted oral instructions to make a CHAPS transfer, that a 'payment' in

accordance with the instruction was to be made provided only that the sort code, bank and account number coincided on the form. This was something that Lord Dyson (at [64]) also accepted could be done.

3.   HHJ Havelock-Allan QC held at first instance (see [2013] EWHC 2780 (QB), [2013] 2 CLC 407 at [22]) that the PSRs did not apply to the transfer because they had been expressly excluded by the bank's terms and conditions. What would have been the result in this case if the PSRs had applied (see above, p 583)?

4.   The case is noted by G McMeel [2015] LMCLQ 1 and TKC Ng (2015) 131 LQR 202.

QUESTIONS

1.   Is the legal relationship between the payer and his bank one of principal and agent?

2.   What is the legal relationship between the payer's bank and any intermediary bank it employs?

3.   What is the legal relationship between the payer's bank and the payee's bank? That of principal/agent, or one of principal/principal?

(b) Relationship with payee

The contractual duty of care owed by the payer's bank to the payer does not extend to the payee. There is no contractual link between them, although where the payee is himself a customer of the payer's bank, the bank *in its capacity as the payee's bank* will owe him a contractual duty of care. The Contracts (Rights of Third Parties) Act 1999 is unlikely to assist the payee in this regard. The payer's bank may well have expressly excluded the operation of the Act in the terms agreed with the payer and it is doubtful, even where there is no express exclusion, that within the context of the transaction as a whole the payer and his bank intended to confer an enforceable benefit on the payee. In the normal course of events, the payer's bank will not owe the payee a duty of care in tort (see the next case).

Wells v First National Commercial Bank
[1998] PNLR 552, Court of Appeal

The plaintiff lent money to a Spanish company, secured by a charge on property held by that company in Spain, and by four postdated bills of exchange issued personally in favour of the plaintiff by U and W, who were owners of the company. The bills of exchange were subsequently dishonoured. The plaintiff commenced proceedings on the bills, those proceedings reaching the stage where either judgment was entered or the plaintiff was entitled to enter judgment. Meanwhile the defendant bank agreed to provide new finance to the company, in return for a first charge on the Spanish property. In order to persuade the plaintiff to release the charge on the property, and in consideration for not entering judgment and/or enforcing judgment in the proceedings on the bills of exchange, the company issued irrevocable instructions to the defendant bank to pay 1 million pesetas to discharge the charge on the property, and to pay a further £275,000 to the plaintiff's solicitors in respect of the sums owing on the bills of exchange. The bank acknowledged receipt of those instructions, knowing that the plaintiff was the intended beneficiary of the payment. There was no direct communication between the bank and the plaintiff. The bank failed to make the transfer. The plaintiff started proceedings against the bank claiming breach of a tortious duty of care. The plaintiff argued that the bank owed him a duty of care because of the irrevocable nature of the payment instructions and the fact that the bank knew that the plaintiff was the intended beneficiary of the transfer. On the bank's application, the judge struck out the plaintiff's claim as disclosing no cause of action. The Court of Appeal dismissed the plaintiff's appeal against that decision.

Evans LJ: . . . After noting those preliminary difficulties the judgment proceeds to consider the question whether this was, as counsel had put it, a duty situation as between the plaintiff and the defendants. That is to say, a situation where a person, placed as the bank was after receiving and acknowledging irrevocable instructions from its customer, owed a duty of care to the beneficiary or intended beneficiary of the payment which it was instructed to make.

The learned judge first referred to *Hedley Byrne* (*Hedley Byrne and Co Ltd v Heller and Partners Ltd* [1964] AC 465). He said that counsel, Mr Pawlak, had not contended before him that the present case could be brought within orthodox *Hedley Byrne* principles. There may have been some misunderstanding and before us Mr Colin Ross-Munro [leading counsel for the plaintiff] has submitted, first, that a claim can be made out under what is called the orthodox *Hedley Byrne* principle. The learned judge then went on to consider what the situation would be if the plaintiffs contentions were correct. He said this, page 8:

If such a duty of care exists in tort towards the third party, it would have very considerable ramifications for banks. It is a commonplace for banks to be requested by their customers to pay monies to third parties. Indeed, every ordinary cheque drawn on a bank in favour of a named payee is such a request. If the bank wrongly fails to pay the cheque, it may incur a liability to its customer, the drawer. But, I do not believe it has ever been suggested that the bank would also incur a liability to the named payee of an ordinary cheque in the tort of negligence, even if the bank had previously told the customer that it would honour the cheque on presentation.

Mr Ross-Munro submits, first, that the learned judge in that passage failed to record or take account of the distinction between revocable and irrevocable instructions by the customer to the bank. Whilst he is prepared to accept that it might be difficult to establish a duty of care where the instructions were revocable, he submits that it is essential to the plaintiffs argument that in this case the instructions were expressed to be irrevocable.

Mr Ross-Munro, secondly, refers to the passage in the current edition of *Paget's Law of Banking* (11th edn), where there is a passage at page 295 which I should read:

The relationship with payee
    The paying bank's contractual duty of care and skill does not extend to the payee . . . However, it has been suggested that the paying bank owes the payee a tortious duty of care so as to make the bank liable to the payee for its negligence.

That is followed by a reference to recent House of Lords decisions in *Henderson v Merrett Syndicates Ltd* [1995] 2 AC 145 and *White v Jones* [1995] 2 AC 207. The learned editor continues:

It might be possible to establish such a duty of care under the *Hedley Byrne* principle which was explained in terms of assumption of responsibility by the defendant. It could be argued that the paying banks' assumption of responsibility to its own customer, the payer, should be extended to the intended beneficiary of the payment, the payee. If so this would create a new category of special relationship to which the law attaches a duty of care to prevent economic loss.

Among the footnotes to that passage is the following, No 19:

Arora, *Electronic Banking and the Law,* (2nd edn 1993), p 149. Although Dr Arora's reliance on *Anns v Merton London Borough Council* [1978] AC 728 is misplaced as the case was overruled by the House of Lords in *Murphy v Brentwood District Council* [1991] 1 AC 398.

That proposition of law is essentially the one for which Mr Ross-Munro contends in this case. He submits that the burden on the plaintiff is merely to show that the contention is arguable. He enlists of the support of that leading textbook, with the gloss that he emphasises that in the present case the instructions were irrevocable and he goes no further than to submit that a duty of care arises when the instructions are such.

Returning to the judgment, the judge referred to the further House of Lords' decision in *Caparo Industries plc v Dickman* [1990] 2 AC 605 and accurately, as I would say, summarises the effect of that decision in the following passage:

> However, since that decision it is now well-established that for there to be duty to take reasonable care to avoid damage of a particular type (here, pecuniary not physical loss) towards a particular person or category of persons mere foreseeability of damage is not enough. There must also be such a direct and close relationship between the parties as constitutes a relationship of 'proximity' and, in addition, the situation must be one where it is fair, just and reasonable for the law to impose the duty of the scope contended for. In the present case, it is not suggested that there had been any dealing of any sort, or indeed any communication at all, between the Bank and Mr Wells when the Bank received and accepted the letter of instruction of September 29, 1989 from its customer, Granfe.

The learned judge then proceeded to consider the plaintiff's submissions as to *Henderson v Merrett*, on which he commented as follows:

> The *Merrett* case was one where, as Lord Goff put it at page 180G, 'the plaintiff entrusts the defendant with the conduct of his affairs'. I do not believe that the relationship between a Lloyd's managing agent and a Name bears any comparison at all with the situation as it was between the Bank and Mr Wells.

Having referred to *White v Jones* the learned judge said this:

> In my view *White v Jones* is far removed from providing any support, even by analogy, for the [plaintiff's] proposition . . .

In neither of those passages did the learned judge refer to the distinction between revocable and irrevocable instructions and, again, Mr Ross-Munro submits that by failing to note that distinction the learned judge failed to deal with the plaintiff's essential argument.

The learned judge's final conclusion was this:

> I do not think that either *White v Jones* or the *Merrett* case provide any support for the proposition that, on the facts pleaded, the Bank owed towards Mrs Wells a duty of care to pay the £275,000 as directed in Granfe's letter of instruction of September 29, 1989. In my view, it is unarguable that merely by accepting a client's instructions to pay money to a third party a bank incurs a duty in tort towards the third party to comply, or more accurately to take reasonable care to comply, with the client's instructions. A duty of care towards the third party does not arise simply because the bank knows his identity. . . . If I were to say that there was a duty of care on the present pleaded facts, it would not be an 'incremental' step but, rather, 'a massive extension': cf the observations of Brennan J in the Australian case, *Sutherland Shire Council v Heyman* (1985) 60 ALR 1 at 43 cited with approval by both Lord Bridge and Lord Oliver in *Caparo* [1990] 2 AC 605 at 618D, and 633G–634A.

For my part I must say that I agree entirely both with the learned judge's reasoning and with his conclusion. Mr Ross-Munro's submission that the learned judge failed to take account of the difference between revocable and irrevocable instructions is, of course, a formidable submission. Mr Ross-Munro emphasises that he need show only that the plaintiff's case is arguable, in other words not bound to fail. He emphasises, as already stated, that this is an area of the law which can be said to be in a state of transition, with the narrow 3–2 majority in the House of Lords in *White v Jones*. He submits that the ingredients for establishing a duty of care are all present, whether one adopts the strict *Hedley Byrne* approach or the more general approach shown by *Caparo* and *White v Jones*.

As regards *Hedley Byrne*, he says that there was 'a special relationship' between the bank as payer and the plaintiff as payee. The bank could certainly foresee that the plaintiff as the intended beneficiary of the payment would incur loss if the payment was not made. He emphasises that on a strict application of *Hedley Byrne* no question arises as to whether the imposition of duty of care would be fair, reasonable and just.

However, his second submission, relying upon the more general ground, is that when foreseeability of financial loss is established and, what is more, loss to the individual plaintiff, then there is no reason why it is not fair, just and reasonable for the bank to owe a duty of care to the payee, just as it owes a contractual duty to its customer to make the payment when it becomes due. He submits that the lack of authority is no bar to his submission, referring to the passage in *Paget* which I have already read. He submits, therefore, that the plaintiff's case is clearly arguable and that the plaintiff should be allowed to take the matter to trial.

These are attractive submissions but I do not find them cogent. *Henderson* was a case where there was a commercial situation where the necessary relationship was found to exist. In *White v Jones* the speeches of Lords Goff and Browne-Wilkinson, who with Lord Nolan formed the majority, show that the duty of care was held to exist in that case only because it was an exceptional case. The head note reads as follows:

> . . . the assumption of responsibility by a solicitor to his client, who had given instructions for the drawing up of a will for execution, extended to an intended beneficiary under the proposed will in circumstances where the solicitor could reasonably foresee that a consequence of his negligence might result in the loss of the intended legacy without either the testator or his estate having a remedy against him; and that, accordingly, in the circumstances the plaintiffs were entitled to the relief sought.

In my view that summary is amply justified by speeches of Lord Goff at page 268, letter C, a passage which I need not read, and Lord Browne-Wilkinson at pages 275–276. I should refer to Lord Nolan's agreement also. In both of those speeches emphasis was laid, first, upon the particular responsibility of a solicitor as a professional man acting in those circumstances on instructions to draw up a will in favour of a third party beneficiary, and, secondly, upon the fact that if the beneficiary had no right to claim and the testator was unable to recover substantial damages for breach of contract or in tort, then it would follow that the solicitor's negligence, which had in fact caused loss to the plaintiff, would not result in his being held liable for that loss. That is not the case here because there was a chain of agreements or contracts on the facts alleged between the plaintiff and the Granfe company and Mr Urquhart and Mr Waddy, under which the plaintiff would seem to have an unanswerable claim.

It seems to me that *White v Jones* can be taken as authority for two propositions which are helpful to Mr Ross-Munro. The first is that the fact that a duty arises under a contract made by the defendant with a party other than the plaintiff does not mean that a duty of care owed to the plaintiff cannot arise. Similarly, and secondly, the fact that there is no relationship between the plaintiff and the defendant is not necessarily a fatal bar to the plaintiffs claim. I should also refer, before leaving *White v Jones*, to a passage in the dissenting speech of Lord Mustill at page 279, letter D, where he said this:

> This is certainly not to deny that where the act or omission complained of occurs between persons who have deliberately involved themselves in a network of commercial or professional contractual relations, such for example as may exist between the numerous parties involved in contracts for large building or engineering works, the contractual framework

may be so strong, so complex and so detailed as to exclude the recognition of delictual duties between parties who are not already connected by contractual links: see for example *Pacific Associates Inc v Baxter* [1990] 1 QB 993. This aspect of the law is far from being fully developed and I need not explore it here.

Lord Browne-Wilkinson who formed a member of the majority at page 274 letter D said this:

(I should add that I agree with my noble and learned friend, Lord Mustill, that this factor should not lead to the conclusion that a duty of care will necessarily be found to exist even where there is a contractual chain of obligations designed by the parties to regulate their dealings.)

The present is not a case of complex or detailed contractual agreements, nevertheless it is a commercial situation where the relationships between the various parties are governed by contracts between themselves.

The question which arises is how to apply these authorities in the present case. The crucial factor, in my view, is that the plaintiff does not allege any dealings or even any communication between himself and the bank. If there was any such communication then he would know about it, therefore the absence of any such allegation in the pleadings can be taken to indicate that no such communication took place. It seems to me that the plaintiff fails under the orthodox *Hedley Byrne* principle because he fails to show that there was any relationship between himself and the bank. The question whether it was a special relationship, or as Lord Devlin put it in *Hedley Byrne*, whether it was a situation 'equivalent to contract' simply does not arise. This is not merely semantic or a play upon words. The fact that there must be some relationship for the *Hedley Byrne* decision to apply goes a long way to explain the difficulties which were faced by the House of Lords in *White v Jones*. Lord Keith of Kinkel and Lord Mustill both found it impossible to hold that the law could recognise or impose a duty of care in the circumstances of that case. The majority did hold that such a duty of care existed on the grounds which have already been referred to.

It seems to me that those grounds clearly were regarded by them as exceptional. The two most significant factors were those to which I have referred: non-availability of any effective remedy either for the beneficiary or for the testator's estate if no duty of care was imposed; and, secondly, the peculiar status of the solicitor when preparing a will. Neither of those factors is present here.

So the question becomes, 'can this also, at least arguably, be regarded as an exceptional case?' It seems to me that almost inevitably the answer must be 'no'. The plaintiff contends for a duty of care which, if it arises here, would arise in the course of an everyday commercial transaction and would go a long way to revolutionise English Banking Law. I agree with the judge's comment that such a duty would not be incremental. I would say that it would be a massive sea change in the regulation of liabilities in a commercial context such as this. The very fact that the facts relied upon are the basic ones to which I have referred, that is to say, a bank is given irrevocable instructions by its customer to make a payment to a third party, prevents the plaintiff from saying that this is an exceptional case. Mr Ross-Munro in my view contends for a duty of care in a case which from both the banking and the legal points of view is common place and certainly no exceptional. It follows from that, in my view, that the plaintiff cannot contend for a duty of care in the present situation in the light of the recent House of Lords authorities to which I have referred. The case is not exceptional, it is a straightforward commercial situation where the duty of care has never been held to exist and where there are no grounds for creating an exception to the basic rule, recognised and established by the House of Lords.

I should add this in deference to Mr Ross-Munro's emphasis upon the fact that the instructions here were 'irrevocable'. It seems to me that even if the instructions were expressed as being irrevocable, nevertheless the bank and its customer could agree to vary that contract. It would be entirely up to them whether to do so or not, unless rights had been acquired by third parties which is the very point in issue in the present case.

Mr Ross-Munro finally submitted that even if the instructions were changed by agreement between the bank and its customer the bank would remain liable to the original intended payee, even though its fresh instructions were to make the payment elsewhere. It seems to me that that exposes the fact that the submission cannot be right. In my judgment the fact that the instructions are expressed as irrevocable does not assist the submission that the bank came under a duty of care.

Finally, I would add this: if the plaintiff had communicated with the bank then it could be, I say no more, a situation which was in Lord Devlin's words 'equivalent to contract'. It may be that in such a situation it would be arguable that a *Hedley Byrne* duty would arise. It would arise from the relationship which in fact was established between them. But here the plaintiff did not have any dealings with the bank, he dealt only with Mr Urquhart and Mr Waddy. He undoubtedly has remedies against them, first, under the bills of exchange and secondly on the pleaded facts for breach of the contract or agreement, if contract there was, between him and them.

Finally, although it may be superfluous, I emphasise that the only allegation made in the present case is the tortious claim for breach of the alleged duty of care. There is no allegation of any contractual claim express or implied. In those circumstances, in my judgment, the conclusion was right and the appeal should be dismissed.

[**Hutchison** and **Mantell LJJ** concurred.]

NOTE

In *National Westminster Bank Ltd v Barclays Bank International Ltd* [1975] QB 654 at 662, Kerr J held that a drawee (paying) bank did not owe a duty of care to the payee when deciding whether to honour a cheque presented for payment. However, the drawee bank may owe the payee of a cheque a duty to act carefully and honestly under the *Hedley Byrne* principle when advising the payee of its reasons for dishonouring the cheque (*TE Potterton Ltd v Northern Bank Ltd* [1995] 4 Bank LR 179, Irish High Court: criticised by EP Ellinger [1995] JBL 583–585).

QUESTION

In *White v Jones* [1995] 2 AC 207 (where the House of Lords held by a majority that a solicitor who accepts instructions to draft a will owes a duty of care to the intended beneficiary and may be liable to him in tort if he does not implement the testator's instructions within a reasonable time), their Lordships seemed much influenced by the fact that, without the imposition of the duty of care, the intended beneficiary would have suffered a loss without a remedy. Do you think it would have made any difference in *Wells v First National Commercial Bank* if the plaintiff had been left without an alternative remedy? Would the bank have been liable to the company for failing to make the transfer?

(ii) Payee's bank

In the case of a debit transfer, such as a payment by direct debit, where the payee pulls funds from the payer's account, the payee's bank is acting as an agent of the payee in the collection process. (Because most cheques are crossed 'account payee', and therefore non-transferable, the collecting bank will now rarely collect a cheque on its own behalf: see below, p 741.) The position is less certain in the case of a credit transfer. The cases suggest that the payee's bank again acts as an agent of the payee.

Mardorf Peach & Co Ltd v Attica Sea Carriers Corpn of Liberia, The Laconia
[1977] AC 850, House of Lords

The Laconia was time-chartered by the appellants (the owners) to the respondents (the charterers) on the New York Produce Exchange form, under the terms of which hire was to be paid in cash in US currency semi-monthly in advance 'to the owners . . . into their bank account with First National City Bank of New York, 30 Moorgate, London, EC2 to the credit of OFC Account No 705586'. The seventh instalment of hire fell due on 12 April, a Sunday when London banks were closed. At about 3 pm on Monday 13 April the charterers' London bank delivered a payment order for the hire instalment to the owners' bank, where it was accepted and dealt with in the usual way. The bank informed the owners that the payment order had been received, but were instructed to return it at once. When the owners then tried to invoke a forfeiture clause in the charterparty on the grounds of late payment of hire (it was conceded by the charterers that the due date for payment of this instalment was Friday 10 April, as London banks were closed on Saturday and Sunday), the charterers argued that their breach had been waived through acceptance of the late tender by the owners' bank acting as the owners' agents. The House of Lords, reversing a majority decision of the Court of Appeal in favour of the charterers, rejected this contention and gave judgment for the owners.

Lord Wilberforce (held that a right of withdrawal had accrued to the owners under the terms of the forfeiture clause in the charterparty and continued): . . .

This leaves the second question, which is whether the right of withdrawal was waived by the owners. The submission of the charterers was that on Monday, April 13, 1970, before the owners purported to withdraw the ship, they accepted the charterers' late payment of the instalment and so affirmed the contract. The arbitrators found that there had not been any waiver, so that the charterers must undertake the task of showing that, upon the facts found, the only possible conclusion must have been there had.

In order to understand the argument, it is necessary to go into the facts in some detail. At about 3 p.m., at which time London banks closed for the day, a messenger from the Midland Bank, acting for the charterers, delivered to the owners' bank, the First National City Bank, 34, Moorgate, London ('FNCB'), a 'payment order' for the amount of the seventh instalment. A payment order is a document issued by one bank to another under a scheme (LCSS) by which banks maintain dollar suspense accounts in which they credit or debit each other with sums in dollars and make periodical settlements. As between banks, a payment order is the equivalent of cash, but a customer cannot draw upon it. The amount must first be credited to his account, but he can, of course, make special arrangements for earlier drawing. At about 3.10 or 3.15 p.m. the payment order was received and stamped in the sorting office of FNCB. It was then taken to the transfer department. There an official called an editor wrote on the face of the order the formula CR ADV & TT Lausanne, an instruction (to be carried out elsewhere in the bank) meaning 'credit advice and telegraphic transfer Lausanne.' Not perhaps quite simultaneously, but at about the same time, another official telephoned to the owners' agents and said that the bank had received a payment order for the amount of the hire: this was in accordance with instructions received by the bank earlier in the day from the owners' agents. This official was immediately told to refuse the money and to return it. Thereupon the editor deleted the annotation he had made on the payment order and wrote on it. 'Beneficiary has refused payment. Advise remitter by phone.' There was no direct evidence that this was done but such may be presumed. The next day FNCB sent to the Midland Bank a payment order for the same amount as that which the Midland Bank had sent the previous day.

My Lords, much ingenuity and effort was used in order to show that this series of actions, or some part of it, constituted acceptance and waiver by the owners of the right to withdraw. But in my opinion it did not approach success. Although the word 'waiver,' like 'estoppel,' covers a variety of situations different in their legal nature, and tends to be indiscriminately used by the courts as a means of relieving parties from bargains or the consequences of bargains which are thought to be harsh or deserving of relief, in the present context what is relied on is clear enough. The charterers had failed to make a punctual payment but it was open to the owners to accept a late payment as if it were punctual, with the consequence that they could not thereafter rely on the default as entitling them to withdraw. All that is needed to establish waiver, in this sense, of the committed breach of contract, is evidence, clear and unequivocal, that such acceptance has taken place, or, after the late payment has been tendered, such a delay in refusing it as might reasonably cause the charterers to believe that it has been accepted.

My Lords, if this is, as I believe, what would have to be proved in order to establish a waiver in the situation under review, it must be obvious that the facts in the present case do not amount to it. Looked at untechnically, the facts were that the money was sent to the bank, taken into the banking process or machinery, put in course of transmission to the owners, but rejected by the latter as soon as they were informed of its arrival and as soon as they were called upon, or able, to define their position. Put more technically, the bank, though agents of the owners, had a limited authority. It is not necessary to decide whether, in general, and in the absence of specific instructions, bankers in such situations as these have authority to accept late payments—on this matter I regard *The Brimnes* [1975] QB 929 as a special case where an inference to this effect may have been justified on the facts and the observations of the Lords Justices (in particular of Cairns LJ at p 972) as directed to that situation. But here it is clear that the bankers had no such authority and still less any authority to make business decisions as to the continuance or otherwise of the charterparty but that per contra they had express instructions to refer the matter to the owners' agents. On this basis they receive the order (they clearly had no right to reject it out of hand), and, while provisionally starting to process it into the owners' possession, at the same time seek the owners' directions in accordance with the owners' previous instructions. On those directions, they arrest the process and return the money. The acts of the editors—the annotation on the payment order—were internal acts (Brandon J, of a similar situation in *The Brimnes* [1973] 1 WLR 386, 411 called them 'ministerial,' ie acts done without any intention or capacity to affect legal relations with third parties), not irrevocable, but provisional and reversible acts, consistent with an alternative decision of the customer which might be to accept or reject. The customer chose to reject, he did so as rapidly as the circumstances permitted, and he could have given no ground to the charterer for supposing that the payment had been accepted. The charterer did not act upon any such supposition.

The pattern of action is to me so clear that I do not find it necessary to decide the rather technical question whether, as regards the owners, there was payment 'in cash' as required by the charterparty, or not. Whatever it was it was not punctual payment, and not accepted in waiver of the unpunctuality. I think then that there is no basis on which the arbitrators' finding against waiver can be attacked.

[**Lord Simon of Glaisdale** delivered a judgment concurring with Lord Wilberforce.]

Lord Salmon: . . . Much was sought to be made in argument on behalf of the charterers of the small amount of ministerial work which had been done inside FNCB before the Midland Bank had been informed that the payment was being returned. To my mind none of this even approached a waiver. I doubt whether even if the processing of the payment order had been completed and the owners' account had been credited with the full amount of the payment order before that amount was returned to the Midland Bank on the following day, a finding of waiver could have been justified.

Undoubtedly the owners held out FNCB, indeed they were designated in the charter, as the owners' agents to receive and accept the *punctual* payment of any hire due under the charter.

The charterers had defaulted in payment of the hire due on April 10 when they tendered it to FNCB at about 3 p.m. on Monday, April 13. There is nothing to suggest that that bank was familiar with the terms of the charter or knew whether or not the charterers were in default. Certainly it was not within the banker's express or implied authority to make commercial decisions on behalf of their customers by accepting or rejecting late payments of hire without taking instructions. They did take instructions and were told to reject the payment. They did so and returned it to the charterers on the following day which on any view must have been within a reasonable time. If the bank had kept the payment for an unreasonable time, the charterers might well have been led to believe that the owners had accepted payment. This would have amounted to a waiver of their right to withdraw the vessel. But nothing of the kind happened in the present case.

Clearly if the charterers had paid the hire in US dollar bills on April 10 just before the bank closed, this would have been a punctual cash payment. No doubt a certain amount of processing or paper work has to be done even in relation to a cash payment before it finds its way as a credit into the haven of the customer's account. If the cash is paid into the bank just before it closes on a Friday afternoon it is unlikely, if not impossible, that the customer could have drawn it out before the bank closed for business that afternoon. The customer would probably have had to wait for payment until the following Monday morning. No doubt certain valued customers would be admitted to a bank after banking hours and allowed to cash a cheque even against moneys received on their account but which had not yet passed through the books. There is however no legal obligation on a bank to cash a cheque after banking hours. There has been a great deal of argument as to whether payment of the hire by a payment order just before the bank closed on Friday, April 10 would have amounted to a good payment under the charter. The point does not however arise for decision and I prefer to express no concluded view about it. As at present advised however I am inclined to think that, for the reasons I have indicated, there is no real difference between a payment in dollar bills and a payment by payment orders which in the banking world are generally regarded and accepted as cash.

Lord Fraser of Tullybelton: . . . There remains the second question of whether the bank accepted the payment and, by accepting it, operated a waiver of the owners' right. The argument in favour of waiver by acceptance was based on the arbitrators' finding that 'The FNCB began to deal with the order in the usual way by making the relevant entries in their books.' When this finding is analysed in the light of the agreed notes of additional facts, it comes to mean that acceptance occurred after the payment order had been passed from the sorting office in the FNCB, to their transfer department, when an official called an editor marked the payment order 'CR ADV and TT Lausanne' (short for 'credit advice and telegraphic transfer Lausanne'). That was an instruction to other people in the FNCB to transfer the sum in the payment order to a bank in Lausanne as previously instructed by the owners. But about the same time another person in the transfer department telephoned to the owners who instructed that the payment be refused. The marking 'CR ADV and TT Lausanne' was then deleted by the editor who also wrote on the payment order 'Beneficiary had refused payment. Advise remitter by phone.' There is no finding that the Midland Bank was in fact advised by phone. In all probability that would be done about 15.30 hours or soon after but I do not think anything turns on whether it was done or not.

In my opinion, the marking of the payment order in the way I have mentioned, even if accompanied by entries in the books concerning the LCS scheme, cannot have operated to waive the owners' right of withdrawal. I reach that opinion on two grounds. In the first place, the bank was, in my opinion, the agent of the owners only to receive payments for hire but it had no authority, actual or ostensible, to waive the owners' rights. It was the nominated place at which the hire was to be paid; its function in receiving payment was, in the phrase used in *The Brimnes* [1975] QB 929, merely ministerial. It was suggested that the position of the bank was the same as that of the estate agents in *Central Estates (Belgravia) Ltd v Woolgar (No 2)* [1972] 1 WLR 1048, but in my opinion that is wrong because the estate agents had the full authority to manage the property on behalf of the owner. The bank had no such authority. A decision on whether to exercise a right of withdrawing a vessel or to waive the right may be a difficult decision involving consideration of many variable facts, including the state of the freight market and the exact position of the ship at the time, and it would be unreasonable to expect the bank to make the decision. It would also, I think, be unreasonable to expect the owners to instruct the bank in advance before the hire has been received. A reasonable time must be allowed for the bank, after it has received the hire, to take instructions from the owners and a reasonable time for that purpose would certainly extend from 15.00 hours until 18.55 hours. In the second place, the actions of the editor in marking the payment order in the FNCB transfer office were not of a character that could have operated as a waiver of the owners' rights of withdrawal. A waiver would have required an overt action. These were private acts internal to the bank. They were not communicated to the charterers, nor did they have any 'impact' on them, if I may borrow the word used by Russell LJ in *London and County (A & D) Ltd v Wilfred Sportsman Limited* [1971] Ch 764, 782. Moreover, the marking of the payment order did not in my opinion demonstrate a final decision by the editor or by anyone acting for the owners to accept the hire; on the contrary, it was done at about the very time when another person in the same department, who must I think have acted to the knowledge of the editor concerned, was telephoning to the owners for instructions whether to accept the hire or not. I therefore conclude that no waiver occurred at that time.

[**Lord Russell of Killowen** delivered judgment in favour of the owners on the ground that none of the dealings with the payment order constituted an unequivocal act of acceptance on behalf of the owners so as to constitute a waiver.]

NOTES

1. There are three good reasons why the payee's bank should be deemed to act as the payee's agent in a credit transfer (but for a contrasting view, see R King (1982) 45 MLR 369).[3] First, if the payee's bank is not acting as the payee's agent then the payer's bank transfers funds to someone who is not authorised to receive them. The transfer of funds to an unauthorised person would not discharge the payer's underlying indebtedness to the beneficiary (*Customs and Excise Comrs v National Westminster Bank plc* [2002] EWHC 2204 (Ch), [2003] 1 All ER (Comm) 327: see below, p 619). Secondly, treating the payee's bank as the payee's agent is consistent with the rule that payment is complete as between payer

---

[3] The first two reasons given in the text are drawn from B Geva, *Bank Collections and Payment Transactions— Comparative Study of Legal Aspects* (2001), p 296.

and payee on receipt of funds and before a credit is posted to the payee's account. Thirdly, failure to regard the payee's bank as the payee's agent draws an unnecessary distinction between payment by credit transfer and payment by debit transfer so far as completion of payment is concerned.

2.   The payee's bank owes a contractual duty of care and skill to its customer, the payee. But does it owe a similar duty to the payer of a funds transfer? There is no privity of contract between the payee's bank and the payer and it is submitted that a contractual claim by the payer based on s 1(1) of the Contracts (Rights of Third Parties) Act 1999 is unlikely to succeed as no term of the bank–customer contract between the payee and his own bank purports to confer a benefit on the payer (s 1(1)(b)). Could a duty of care arise in tort? In *Royal Bank of Canada v Stangl* (1992) 32 ACWS (3d) 17, a Canadian decision, the payee's bank was held liable to its sender (a correspondent bank) in negligence for the failure to clarify the contents of a payment order instructing payment into an account that did not belong to the named payee. But English law appears to be different. In *Abou-Rahman v Abacha* [2005] EWHC 2662 (QB), [2006] 1 All ER (Comm) 247, the defendant bank received two payments made by the victims of a fraud with instructions to credit the account of a customer called 'Trust International'. In fact the bank credited the account of an entity called 'Trusty International', which was controlled by the fraudsters. Treacy J, sitting in the English High Court, refused to follow *Stangl* and held that a payee's bank does not owe a duty of care to a non-customer payer of a funds transfer to pay money received only to the payee identified in the payer's instructions, or to clarify any discrepancies in those instructions as to the payee's identity with the payer. The judge reminded himself that the case before him was concerned purely with economic loss and that the common law was reluctant to impose a duty of care save in special circumstances. The decision of Treacy J was later upheld by the Court of Appeal, although there was no appeal on this particular issue: [2006] EWCA Civ 1492, [2007] 1 Lloyd's Rep 115.

3.   A different question arises in respect of the liability of the payee's bank to the payee when that bank refuses to accept a transfer of funds into his account. This will turn on the terms of the contract between the payee and his bank. In *Tayeb v HSBC Bank plc* [2004] EWHC 1529 (Comm), [2004] 4 All ER 1024, Colman J held that when a customer opens an account with his bank, which is capable of receiving incoming CHAPS electronic funds transfers, the bank engages that it will accept into his account all CHAPS transfers which comply with the CHAPS Rules and which are otherwise in accordance with the terms of the account (for CHAPS transfers, see p 582 above). In this case, the payee's bank became suspicious of the origin of funds that had been transferred into its customer's account using CHAPS and, without its customer's consent, returned those funds to the payer's bank. Colman J held that the bank was indebted to its customer in the amount of the sum transferred. The judge took account of the CHAPS Rules and held that a CHAPS transfer was ordinarily irreversible once the receiving bank had authenticated the transfer, sent an acknowledgement informing the sending bank that the transfer had been received, and credited the funds to its customer's account. However, Colman J added that there was an appropriate analogy with the practice in relation to documentary credits where, at the time of presentation of documents, a bank with cogent evidence of fraud can decline to make payment to the beneficiary (see below, p 789), and that the same exception was likely to apply in respect of illegal transactions (see below, p 802). But mere suspicion as to the origin of the transferred funds did not present the bank with a justifiable reason for returning those funds to the transferor without the customer's consent.

QUESTIONS

1. If the payee's bank does not act as the payee's agent in a credit transfer operation, does it act as agent for the payer or his bank?

2. If the payee's bank does act as the payee's agent for the purposes of receiving a credit transfer, how can this be reconciled with their underlying debtor/creditor relationship?

3. What remedy does a payer have at common law where the payer's bank has sent accurate payment instructions to the payee's bank but the payee's bank has mistakenly credited funds to the wrong account?

(iii) Intermediary bank

Where the payer's bank does not have a correspondent (account) relationship with the payee's bank it must employ an intermediary bank to effect the transfer. Intermediary banks may be employed in domestic funds transfers, but they are used more commonly in international funds transfers (as illustrated by the next case). Sometimes both the payer's bank and the payee's bank will each have to employ their own intermediary bank in the same transaction. An intermediary bank employed by the payer's bank acts as its agent, and one employed by the payee's bank acts as that bank's agent. It is often important to ascertain on whose behalf an intermediary bank acts as this may determine such matters as whether the payer can revoke his payment instruction and the time of completion of payment.

Royal Products Ltd v Midland Bank Ltd
[1981] 2 Lloyd's Rep 194, Queen's Bench Division

See above, p 586.

NOTE

The position of an intermediary bank under the common law appears to differ from that under the PSRs (see above, p 585) in two ways. First, liability of an intermediate bank under the common law turns on its negligence, whereas under the PSRs the bank's liability appears to be strict (reg 78: but, according to reg 79, subject to a force majeure defence). Secondly, the common law limits the payer's bank or the payee's bank to recoupment of losses from the intermediary bank that it actually instructed, whereas the PSRs appear to offer the payer's bank or the payee's bank a right of action against the intermediary bank responsible for the loss (or, to use the language of reg 78, to which the loss is 'attributable'), even though there is no direct contractual link between the two banks.

8 COUNTERMAND

(a) Under the Payment Services Regulations 2009

Regulation 55(3) of the PSRs (see above, p 582) provides that the payer's consent to a payment transaction can be withdrawn at any time before the point at which the payment order can no longer be revoked under reg 67 (reg 55(4) deals with withdrawal of consent to the execution of a series of payment transactions). Regulation 67 provides as follows:

(1) Subject to paragraphs (2) to (5), a payment service user may not revoke a payment order after it has been received by the payer's payment service provider.

(2) In the case of a payment transaction initiated by or through the payee, the payer may not revoke the payment order after transmitting the payment order or giving consent to execute the payment transaction to the payee.

(3) In the case of a direct debit, the payer may not revoke the payment order after the end of the business day preceding the day agreed for debiting the funds.

(4) Where a day is agreed under regulation 65(4), the payment service user may not revoke a payment order after the end of the business day preceding the agreed day.

(5) At any time after the time limits for revocation set out in paragraphs (1) to (4), the payment order may only be revoked if the revocation is—

    (a) agreed between the payment service user and its payment service provider; and

    (b) in the case of a payment transaction initiated by or through the payee, including in the case of a direct debit, also agreed with the payee.

(6) A framework contract may provide for the payment service provider to charge for revocation under this regulation.

In general terms, the time of receipt of a payment order is the time at which the payment order, given directly by the payer or indirectly by or through the payee, is received by the payment service provider (reg 65(1), subject to exceptions).

(b) Under the common law

The payer's bank is under a duty to obey its customer's countermand. Notice of countermand must be clear and unambiguous (*Westminster Bank Ltd v Hilton* (1926) 136 LT 315), and it must be brought to the actual (not constructive) knowledge of the bank (*Curtice v London City and Midland Bank Ltd* [1908] 1 KB 293). Unless otherwise agreed, notice of countermand must be given to the branch of the payer's bank where the account is kept (*London, Provincial and South-western Bank Ltd v Buszard* (1918) 35 TLR 142).

As the payer's bank acts as the payer's agent for the purpose of executing his payment instruction, the general rule is that the payer, as principal, may countermand that instruction before it has been executed by the payer's bank, his agent (*Campanari v Woodburn* (1854) 15 CB 400). However, a principal may not revoke his agent's authority after the agent has commenced performance of his mandate and incurred liabilities for which the principal must indemnify him (*Warlow v Harrison* (1859) 1 E & E 309 at 317, per Martin B).

The general principles to be applied, in the absence of express contract, when determining the availability of countermand of an payer's payment instruction in a funds transfer operation, have been summarised by Professor Cranston in the following terms:[4]

---

[4] R Cranston, 'Law of International Funds Transfers in England' in W Hadding and UH Schneider (eds), *Legal Issues in International Credit Transfers* (1993), p 233.

Firstly, a customer who instructs its bank to hold funds to the disposal of a third party can countermand at least until the time when the funds have been transferred or credit given to the transferee (*Gibson v Minet* (1824) 130 ER 206). Secondly, a customer who instructs its bank to transfer funds to a third party cannot revoke from the moment the bank incurs a commitment to the third party (*Warlow v Harrison* (1859) 1 E & E 309). Thirdly—and this is the typical case—a customer who instructs its bank to pay another bank to the order of a third party cannot revoke once the payee bank has acted on the instructions. This may be a point prior to crediting the payee's account (*Astro Amo Compania Naviera SA v Elf Union SA, The Zographia M* [1976] 2 Lloyd's Rep 382). In all cases, it is irrelevant, from the point of view of revocation, whether the third party has been informed.

Applying these general principles to the typical case where there is a payer's bank and a payee's bank involved in the funds transfer operation, the customer's payment instruction is irrevocable once the payee's bank accepts the payment order from the payer's bank either by returning an acceptance message or by acting on the payment order in some other way, for example by debiting an account of the payer's bank held by the payee's bank or by making a decision unconditionally to credit the payee's account. Where the payer's bank and the payee's bank employ intermediary banks to act on their behalf, as would be the case where neither bank is a member of the relevant clearing system, countermand is no longer possible once the payment order has passed from the payer's side to the payee's side of the payment chain and has been accepted by an intermediary bank acting on behalf of the payee's bank, for example by it sending a further payment order on to the payee's bank or another intermediary bank acting on its behalf.

To avoid uncertainty as to the customer's right of countermand, the payer's bank may include in its contract with the payer an express provision stipulating that the payer may not countermand his payment instruction after a certain point in the payment process. Thus, for example, it is usually made a term of issue of any credit or charge card, debit card, or digital cash card (see below, Chapter 17) that the cardholder is prohibited from countermanding payment effected through the use of the card. Alternatively, the payer may be bound by the rules of the payment system used to make the transfer where those rules represent banking usage. It is well established that a 'man who employs a banker is bound by the usage of bankers': the usage becomes an implied term of the bank–customer contract (*Hare v Henty* (1861) 10 CBNS 65, 142 ER 374 at 379: and see also the discussion in *Tidal Energy Ltd v Bank of Scotland plc* [2014] EWCA Civ 1107, [2014] 2 CLC 124, above, p 589). But the customer must know of, and consent to, the usage where it deprives him of a right (*Barclays Bank plc v Bank of England* [1985] 1 All ER 385 at 394). Revocation of payment instructions will usually be a matter provided for, expressly or by implication, in the rules of the payment system used to effect the transfer).

9 COMPLETION OF PAYMENT

We are here concerned with completion of payment as between payer and payee. Determining the time of completion of payment as between payer and payee can be important in certain circumstances, for example where the payer attempts to revoke a payment instruction (although a payment instruction may become irrevocable before payment is made, in theory at least, it cannot be revoked after completion of payment as between the payer and the payee);

where the death, liquidation, or bankruptcy of the payer terminates the bank's authority to pay; where the contract between payer and payee requires payment to be made strictly on the due date; where it is necessary to determine the time of payment for taxation purposes, or for the calculation of interest; or where there is a failure of one of the banks involved. The issue is considered in detail in J Vroegop, 'The Time of Payment in Paper-Based and Electronic Funds Transfer Systems' [1990] LMCLQ 64, and also by B Geva in his article 'Payment into a Bank Account' [1990] 3 JIBL 108 and in his book *Bank Collections and Payment Transactions—Comparative Study of Legal Aspects* (2001), pp 270–289.

We have seen that payment usually involves the transfer of money, or the performance of some other act, tendered and accepted in discharge of a money obligation (above, p 563). Money means cash, ie coins and bank notes, but the creditor may agree to accept payment by means of a funds transfer into his bank account in fulfilment of an obligation to pay money. In a commercial transaction it should not be difficult to imply the creditor's consent to accept payment by this method, especially where he furnishes the debtor with details of his account to enable to the transfer to take place. By agreeing to payment by funds transfer, the creditor (payee) agrees to accept a right of action against his own bank in lieu of his right of action against his debtor (payer). This substitution of one debtor for another is equivalent to payment by cash and discharges the underlying money obligation between the payer and the payee. Unless the creditor and the debtor have agreed otherwise, completion of payment between them occurs when this substitution takes place.

The precise time of substitution may be difficult to determine. In general, payment by funds transfer will be deemed to be complete when the payee is given an unfettered or unrestricted right against his own bank to the immediate use of the funds transferred (*Tenax Steamship Co Ltd v Reinante Transoceanica Navigation SA, The Brimnes* [1973] 1 WLR 386 at 400, per Brandon J; affirmed [1975] 1 QB 929, CA; *A/S Awilco of Solo v Fulvia SpA di Navigazione of Calgiari, The Chikuma* [1981] 1 WLR 314 at 319, HL: see above, p 564). Various attempts have been made to identify the precise moment at which the payee is given an unfettered or unrestricted right against his own bank to the immediate use of the funds transferred. It is submitted that this occurs, and payment is made between payer and payee, when the payee's bank decides to make an unconditional credit to the payee's account, assuming that the bank has the payee's actual or ostensible authority to accept the transfer on his behalf (the leading case is *Momm (t/a Delbrueck & Co) v Barclays Bank International Ltd* [1977] QB 790, an extract from this case appears below; but see also *Tenax Steamship Co Ltd v Brimnes (Owners), The Brimnes* [1975] QB 929, CA; *Libyan Arab Foreign Bank v Bankers Trust Co* [1989] QB 728, 750; *Libyan Arab Foreign Bank v Manufacturers Hanover Trust Co (No 2)* [1989] 1 Lloyd's Rep 608). It does not matter that the payee's bank has yet to credit the payee's account (*The Brimnes*, above; *Momm*, above; cf *Eyles v Ellis* (1827) 4 Bing 112) or notify him of the transfer (*Eyles v Ellis*, above; *Momm*, above; cf *Rekstin v Severo Sibirsko AO* [1933] 1 KB 47 at 57, 62). Where both payer and payee have accounts at the same bank (an 'in-house' transfer) the bank has the assurance of knowing whether the payer has funds in his account to meet the transfer before it decides to make the unconditional credit to the payee's account. In some cases where the payer and payee have accounts at separate banks (an 'inter-bank' transfer), the payee's bank will require to be put in funds by the payer's bank (or an intermediary bank acting on its behalf) before it will reach a decision to make an unconditional transfer. However, in other cases the payee's bank may be prepared to reach its decision to make an unconditional credit to the payee's account before it is put in funds by the payer's bank, for example where the payer's bank and the payee's bank are correspondents. In each case, once the payee's bank has made its decision to credit the payee's account unconditionally the bank accepts the payee as its creditor for the amount in question and is substituted for the payer as the payee's debtor. Payment has then been made as between the payer and the payee.

Momm and Others (trading as Delbrueck & Co) v Barclays Bank International Ltd
[1977] QB 790, Queen's Bench Division

Herstatt Bank, a German bank, as part of a currency exchange transaction with the plaintiffs, ordered a London branch of the defendants to transfer £120,000 from its account held at that branch to the plaintiffs' account, also held at the same branch, 'value June 26, 1974'. Although Herstatt's account was overdrawn at the time, the defendants decided to make the transfer and set in motion the appropriate computer processes to carry it out. Later that day it was announced that Herstatt Bank had ceased trading and was going into liquidation, but no further action was taken by the defendants that day and processing of the payment from Herstatt to the plaintiffs was completed by the defendants' central computer that night. The following day the defendants reversed the transfer. When the plaintiffs later discovered what had happened they claimed that the transfer was irrevocable and that the defendants had wrongly debited their account. Kerr J gave judgment for the plaintiffs.

Kerr J: . . . The issue in the present case is shortly whether the debit in Herstatt's account of £120,000 on June 26, 1974, and a corresponding credit in the plaintiffs' account on the same day, which were processed by the central computer overnight but reversed on the following day, constituted a completed payment on the first day, followed by an unauthorised debit on the second day, or whether no completed payment was ever made. The defendants contend that for either or both of two reasons there was no completed payment. First, because no advice note was sent, or other communication made, to the plaintiffs before the credit on their account was reversed. Secondly, because the defendants maintain that the decision to credit the plaintiffs' account was only provisional on the 26th, and that the final decision against making the payment was made on the 27th by reversing the entries. The latter submission is made in particular in the context of a number of recent shipping cases to which I shall have to return, in which the time of decision was treated as the relevant time.

I must next complete the history. As already mentioned, on June 25, 1974, pursuant to their contract, Herstatt instructed the defendants' branch to transfer the sum of £120,000 'value June 26' to the plaintiffs' account at this branch, and also gave instructions for two out-payments on the same day totalling £15,000. This telex was submitted to Mr Bass [assistant manager of the bank's inward sterling transfer department] at about midday on the 26th. The reason for consulting him was that on the morning of the 26th the computerised balance of Herstatt's account at the close of business on the previous day showed a debit of about £4,650. This fact in itself had caused no concern to anyone, since there had been no communication about it between Mr Delf [manager in the bank's International Division], Mr Dunn [manager of the bank's inward sterling transfer department] or Mr Bass. Nor had there been any communication with Herstatt about it, as there had been on previous occasions when they had been overdrawn. This is perhaps not surprising, since there had been considerable movements on Herstatt's account during the previous days without any resulting debit balances. A transfer from the plaintiffs of £150,000 and to the plaintiffs of £160,000 had taken place between these parties on June 24. But since Herstatt's account was overdrawn on the morning of the 26th, though only to a small extent, the telex instructions for further payments totalling £135,000 'value June 26' were referred to Mr Bass.

He had to make a decision. He could comply with the instructions or refuse to comply with them wholly or in part, or he could consult Mr Delf. His difficulty was, as on every such occasion, that he could not know whether or to what extent these payments would be covered by credits coming in during the day. In fact, though he did not then know it, £140,000 was received for Herstatt's credit at some unknown time on the same day. However, there were also some smaller further debits, with the result that the opening debit balance of about £4,650 rose to about £15,350 by the end of the day. But in the context of the history of the account as a whole over the last six months, this was by no means alarming, and in itself hardly significant. At any rate, and in all the circumstances not surprisingly, Mr Bass decided to allow the payments to be 'actioned' without reference to higher authority. He accordingly gave instructions that all three payments, the in-house transfer of £120,000 and the two out-house payments of £10,000 and £5,000 respectively, were to be made. Banker's payments for the latter two sums were prepared and despatched. As regards the £120,000, the appropriate computer processes were set in motion to debit Herstatt's account, credit the plaintiffs' account and produce the corresponding advice notes.

Now, Mr Bass said in evidence that he distinguished in his mind between the out-house payments of £15,000 and the in-house transfer of £120,000. He said that he decided to 'action' the latter payment only on a provisional basis. This is where it is necessary to choose one's words with care in determining what Mr Bass's mental process was, in so far as this may be relevant. It was in no way an unusual situation. Mr Bass and Mr Dunn, as well as Mr Delf, were continuously making decisions of this kind several times a day. They were fully conscious of the importance of making payments on the 'value' day. There was nothing unusual or particularly difficult about this decision; indeed, Mr Bass did not even refer it to Mr Delf. I think that his decision to sanction the transfer without reference to Mr Delf may to some extent have been influenced by the thought at the back of his mind that if it should unexpectedly appear from the balance on the following morning that this payment had remained substantially uncovered by credits during the day, and if Herstatt were then unable to provide some satisfactory explanation or promise to remedy the situation quickly, there was always the possibility of reversing the entries on the following day. Mr Bass had this at the back of his mind in relation to all substantial in-house payments which might produce an impermissible overdraft. However, on my impression of the witnesses and of the evidence as a whole, it was only to this very limited extent that Mr Bass, or for that matter Mr Dunn or Mr Delf, would have regarded the transfer as 'provisional.' Thus, the plaintiffs would have been allowed to draw against it at once. If they had inquired whether the payment had been made, they would have been given an affirmative and not an equivocating answer, and I do not accept the evidence in so far as it suggested otherwise. No instructions would have been accepted from Herstatt to revoke the payment after the computerisation processes had begun. To express the position in legal terms, I do not accept that this was merely a conditional transfer in the sense that whether or not it stood depended on what might or might not happen on the following morning. It was an unconditional transfer, but subject to the remote possibility of the entries being reversed on the following day. This possibility, however remote and indeed unprecedented in the case of a banking customer, merely had the effect that the decision whether or not to make certain in-house payments was somewhat easier than in relation to corresponding out-house payments. But apart from this, the decision-making process itself, and all the physical processes in 'actioning' such payments on the 'value' date, were precisely the same.

However, at about 4.15 p.m. on June 26 it was announced that Herstatt had ceased trading and were going into liquidation. But for this, this action would never have seen the light of day. Mr Delf got to hear about it shortly thereafter by telephone from Germany. His recollection is that he then gave instructions either to Mr Dunn or to Mr Bass that the entries relating to the transfer of £120,000 should be reversed *on that day*. I emphasise these words because he emphasised them in the way in which he gave his evidence, and he clearly recognised the importance of arriving at a final position on the 'value' date itself. However, neither Mr Dunn nor Mr Bass had any recollection of this having happened. I cannot accept the accuracy of Mr Delf s recollection on this point. Both Mr Dunn and Mr Bass only heard about Herstatt's failure when they read about it in the press early the following morning. They then spoke to Mr Delf on the telephone. Even then, as I am satisfied on their evidence, the position remained fluid for some little time while further inquiries were being made. At first the only decision was to hold up the despatch of the advice notes concerning the debit and credit of the £120,000. Shortly thereafter Mr Delf gave instructions for the entries to be reversed, and this was done by instructing the computer to debit the plaintiffs' account and to credit Herstatt's account with £120,000 on June 27. Mr Delf also gave instructions that the relevant pages in the statements of Herstatt and the plaintiffs should be retyped before being sent to them, omitting the original entries and their reversals. In so far as it might be relevant, though in my view it is not, I find that none of this would have happened if Herstatt had not ceased trading and if there had merely been a debit balance of about £15,350 on their account on the morning of the 27th. The reason why it was done was that the defendants did not wish an unauthorised debit balance to appear in Herstatt's account at the time when they went into liquidation.

The subsequent events are of little importance. The plaintiffs made various inquiries directed to ascertain whether or not the £120,000 had been paid. They were told that it had not, 'due to the present position of Herstatt's account.' However, when they asked to see the branch's internal records, the photostat copies of the ledger sheets relating to their account were at once sent to them without any prevarication. These clearly showed the original entries on the 26th and their reversal on the 27th, but for some reason these passed unnoticed. It was only several months later, when the plaintiffs came to see photostat copies of Herstatt's ledger sheets which had apparently equally readily been sent to Herstatt, that they realised what had happened. They then brought this action.

The issue is whether or not a completed payment had been made by the defendants to the plaintiffs on June 26. This is a question of law. If the answer is 'Yes,' it is not contested that the plaintiffs have a good cause of action. If there were no authorities on this point, I think that the reaction, both of a lawyer and a banker, would be to answer this question in the affirmative. I think that both would say two things. First, that in such circumstances a payment has been made if the payee's account is credited with the payment at the close of business on the value date, at any rate if it was credited intentionally and in good faith and not by error or fraud. Secondly, I think that they would say that if a payment requires to be made on a certain day by debiting a payor customer's account and crediting a payee customer's account, then the position at the end of that day in fact and in law must be that this has either happened or not happened, but that the position cannot be left in the air. In my view both these propositions are correct in law.

The only authorities which are of any assistance are those concerning so-called in-house payments. The oldest of them was decided by the Court of Common Pleas nearly 150 years ago. It is indistinguishable on its facts, unless the process of computerisation has changed the law, which the defendants do not contend. It was an action between payor and payee, but it was rightly not suggested, if there was a completed payment as between them, that the position could be different as between the customers and the bank. In *Eyles v Ellis* (1827) 4 Bing 112, the plaintiff and the defendant had accounts at the same bank. The plaintiff sued the defendant for rent. The defendant contended that he had paid it. What happened was that the defendant instructed his banker to transfer the amount of the rent to the plaintiff's account on a Friday, October 8, the banker having omitted to do so on a previous occasion. The defendant's account was then overdrawn, but the banker complied with the defendant's instructions on that Friday by transferring the amount in his books from the defendant's account to the plaintiffs account. On the same day the defendant wrote to the plaintiff to inform him that the mistake had been rectified, but this letter did not reach the plaintiff until the Sunday.

Meanwhile the banker failed on the intervening Saturday. The short judgment of the court was given by Best CJ at pp 113–114, and is worth quoting in full:

> The learned serjeant was right in esteeming this a payment. The plaintiff had made the Maidstone bankers his agents, and had authorised them to receive the money due from the defendant. Was it then paid, or was that done which was equivalent to payment? At first, not; but on the 8th a sum was actually placed to the plaintiffs account; and though no money was transferred in specie, that was an acknowledgment from the bankers that they had received the amount from Ellis. The plaintiff might then have drawn for it, and the bankers could not have refused his draft.

The rest of the court concurred.

Eyles v Ellis has been referred to with apparent approval in a number of subsequent cases, and its correctness has never been questioned: see *per* Lopes LJ in *In re Land Development Association* (1888) 39 ChD 259, 271; *per* Sankey J in *British and North European Bank Ltd v Zalzstein* [1927] 2 KB 92, 96, 98 and *per* Mocatta J in *Zim Israel Navigation Co v Effy Shipping Corpn* [1972] 1 Lloyd's Rep 18, 33. The important feature of the case for present purposes is that the payment was held to be complete when the payee's bank account was credited and before the payee had had any notice that this had happened.

I then turn to a case on which Mr Staughton strongly relied on behalf of the defendants. This was *Rekstin v Severo Sibirsko Gosudarstvennoe Akcionernoe Obschestvo Komseverputj and the Bank for Russian Trade Ltd* [1933] 1 KB 47, a decision of the Divisional Court and the Court of Appeal. The facts were very unusual. I will refer to the first defendants, a Russian trading organisation, as 'Severo' and to the second defendant as 'the bank.' The plaintiffs had obtained a judgment against Severo who had an account at the bank. Severo clearly wished to prevent the plaintiffs from levying execution against the moneys in that account. A Russian trade delegation with diplomatic immunity also had an account at the bank. Severo therefore decided, without the knowledge or consent of the delegation, to close their account and to transfer all the moneys in it to that of the delegation. Severo so instructed the bank by letter. On receipt of the letter a clerk of the bank made the necessary book entry to close Severo's account and also prepared a slip preparatory to crediting the delegation's account with the equivalent sum. However, the corresponding credit entry in the delegation's account had not been made when the plaintiffs served on the bank a garnishee order nisi in respect of their judgment against Severo. In so far as the headnote of the report suggests that all relevant entries had then been made to credit the delegation's account, it is inaccurate. The following three questions arose. (1) Was the mere notice to the bank to close Severo's account sufficient to bring to an end the relation of banker and customer between Severo and the bank? This was answered in the negative, because the bank continued to owe the moneys in the account to Severo until it had either paid them to Severo or to their order. (2) Was the mandate to the bank to transfer the moneys to the account of the trade delegation still revocable in the circumstances? This was answered in the affirmative and is relevant to the present case. (3) If so, did the garnishee order operate as a revocation? This was also answered in the affirmative and is irrelevant here.

It is not easy to extract from the judgments any clear ratio decidendi underlying the answer to the second issue. Mr Staughton submitted that the ratio was simply that payment to the trade delegation had not been completed, because it had not received any notice of the payment. This was said in *Continental Caoutchou and Gutta Percha Co v Kleinwort Sons & Co* (1903) 8 Com Cas 277, where money was paid to the defendant bank under a mistake by the payor of which the payee was aware. It was held that in those circumstances the payor could recover the money from the bank as money received to the payor's use, a result which might well have followed even after the bank had given notice of the mistaken payment to the payee. However, at any rate in the absence of any mistake, a requirement of notice to the payee would be in direct conflict with *Eyles v Ellis*, 4 Bing 112, which does not appear to have been cited in either of these cases and is not referred to in the judgments. I cannot accept this analysis of the effect of the decision in the *Rekstin* case [1933] 1 KB 47. I think that the majority of the judgments show that the decision was based on either or both of two grounds. First, that there had been no final appropriation of the money to the credit of the trade delegation. Secondly, and evidently of greater importance in the minds of the members of the two courts, the fact that the trade delegation knew nothing of the proposed trans-fer, that there was no transaction between Severo and the delegation underlying it, and that the delegation had accordingly never assented to its account being credited with these moneys. Both these reasons distinguish the case from the present one. In my view this decision should be treated as confined to its special facts. As Mr Tapp [counsel for the plaintiffs] submitted, I think that it merely decided that payment by means of an in-house transfer has not taken place if the payee has not assented to it, and perhaps also if the transfer has not been completed. I therefore reject Mr Staughton's submission that for present purposes the *Rekstin* case decides that there could not have been any completed payment to the plaintiffs unless and until an advice note recording the credit to their account had been despatched to them or had been received by them. Mr Staughton preferred to rely on the time of despatch rather than on the time of receipt, because the evidence showed, as indeed one knows from one's own experience, that in practice some days may elapse before an account holder receives notice of a debit or credit to his account. But in my view the time of despatch would in any event be logically unjustifiable as the relevant time. If notice to the account holder is required, then it seems to me that only the receipt of the notice will do. However, apart from the fact that this would be wholly inconsistent with *Eyles v Ellis*, 4 Bing 112 such a rule would create all sorts of commercial difficulties and would also put a large question-mark against the point of time up to which a payor could countermand his instructions. What would happen, for instance, if he instructed the bank to revoke notice of the payment to the payee by telex or telephone between the despatch of the advice note by post and its receipt? The evidence showed, in my view rightly as a matter of law, that the defendants would not have accepted countermand-ing instructions from Herstatt once the process of crediting the plaintiffs' account had been set in motion pursuant to Herstatt's telex instructions.

This analysis of the legal position is strongly supported by one of the recent shipping cases to which I have already referred. They all concerned situations in which charterers made or purported to make a late payment of time-charter hire and the shipowners claimed to have validly withdrawn the vessel from the charterers' service before the payment was made. The issue was accordingly always a race between the effective time of payment and the time of withdrawal. The only one of these cases which is of direct assistance for present purposes is *The Brimnes* [1975] QB 929, since this concerned an in-house payment. The relevant facts were as follows. The charterers' bankers, Hambros, were instructed to pay the hire to the shipowners' bankers, MGT in New York, where Hambros also had an account. To pay the hire, Hambros instructed MGT by telex to transfer the appropriate amount from Hambros's account to that of the owners. The position was complicated by the fact that the owners had previously assigned the hire to MGT with the result that there was some difference of opinion in the Court of Appeal whether MGT were acting as payees or as the owners' bankers in receiving the hire, but this is irrelevant for present purposes. All the members of the Court of Appeal clearly considered that payment was complete when MGT decided to credit the shipowners' account and acted on that decision. In a later case, which concerned an out-house payment before a differently constituted Court of Appeal, *Mardorf Peach & Co Ltd v Attica Sea Carriers Corpn of Liberia* [1976] QB 835, this point was taken a little further by making it clear that the time of payment was the time when the bank accepted the payment order and decided to act on it, irrespective of the time which had to elapse before the bank's internal accounting processes had been completed.

Mr Staughton's answer to *The Brimnes* [1975] QB 929 was that it was neither argued nor necessary to argue that the time of payment was later than the time when the bank decided to act on the instructions to credit the shipowners' account and began to act on that decision, and that this point was also not argued in any of the other cases. This is correct. He also relied on a passage in the judgment of Megaw LJ at p 964 where he said that 'the time of payment could not be earlier than the time when MGT made their decision to debit Hambros' account . . .' But taking the judgments as a whole, it is clear that it never occurred to anyone that notice to the payee was an essential ingredient of a completed payment. Both *Eyles v Ellis*, 4 Bing 112 and the *Rekstin* case [1933] 1 KB 47 were cited in argument, but neither was mentioned in the judgments. The judgments are wholly consistent with *Eyles v Ellis* but do not in any way reflect what Mr Staughton seeks to extract from the *Rekstin* case. I therefore conclude that the authorities clearly support the contention that payment in the present case was complete when Mr Bass decided to accept Herstatt's instructions to credit the plaintiffs' account and the computer processes for doing so were set in motion. Indeed, the present case is a fortiori to *The Brimnes* [1975] QB 929 and *Mardorf Peach & Co Ltd v Attica Sea Carriers Corpn of Liberia* [1976] QB 835, because these processes were in fact completed before the defendants purported to revoke the payment by reversing the entries on the following morning.

This only leaves one further point with which I have to some extent already dealt. The defendants' witnesses said that they acted on the basis that the following morning was to be treated as an extension of the 'value' day, because the final balances for that day are not available from the computer until then, and because they always had in mind the possibility of being able to reverse the entries. I cannot accept this. A day is a day. For banking purposes it ends at the close of working hours, and otherwise at midnight. Commerce requires that it should be clearly ascertainable by the end of the day whether a payment due to be made on that day has been made or not. Whether this has happened or not cannot be held in suspense until the following morning. In this case the payment was made on the due day. What happened on the following morning was that the defendants made an unauthorised reverse payment by the plaintiffs to Herstatt.

The defendants suggest that this result will send their system into disarray. But I do not see why, even if this were relevant. It is no more difficult to decide whether to make an in-house payment than an out-house payment; nor to set the necessary processes in motion if the payment is to be made. The consequences of an affirmative decision should be the same in both cases. The only result will be that the defendants will no longer be able to rely, as against their own payee customers, on the possibility of having second thoughts on the following morning.

It follows that this action succeeds and that there will be judgment for the plaintiffs.

NOTES

1.   Kerr J gave judgment for the plaintiffs on the ground that, as between Herstatt and the plaintiffs, the payment was complete the moment the defendant bank decided to credit the plaintiffs' account and initiated the internal payment process. Kerr J also held, following banking practice, that 'a payment has been made if the payee's account is credited with the payment at the close of business on the value date, at any rate if it was credited intentionally and in good faith and not by error or fraud'. This offers a fallback position where it is not possible to identify precisely when a 'decision' is made to make payment. However, in some cases the posting of a credit to the payee's account may not be conclusive proof of payment (eg the credit may only be provisional). Where it is difficult to identify a 'decision' to make payment a better approach, particularly suitable where funds are available to the payee's bank, is to apply a 'hypothetical positive response' test (see B Geva, 'Payment into a Bank Account' [1990] 3 JIBL 108 at 112–115; and see also B Geva, *Bank Collections and Payment Transactions* (2001), pp 282–289). Under this test payment is complete as between payer and payee at the first point in time when the payee would have been told, if he had contacted the bank, that his account was to be credited.

2. In *Momm v Barclays Bank International Ltd*, Kerr J emphasised that the transfer was complete when the bank decided to credit the plaintiffs' account *and initiated the computer process for making the transfer*. However, it is submitted that initiation of the payment process is not essential to completion of the transfer. Initiation of the mechanical accounting process merely provides objective evidence that a decision to credit the payee's account has been made, evidence which may be available from other sources. However, the bank must decide to make an *unconditional* credit to the payee's account for the payment to be complete, as a provisional or conditional credit would allow for its subsequent reversal (see, eg, *Sutherland v Sutherland v Royal Bank of Scotland plc* [1997] 6 Bank LR 132; *Holmes v Governor of Brixton Prison* [2004] EWHC 2020 (Admin), [2005] 1 All ER 490). In *Momm*, this did not present a problem as the case involved an in-house transfer at a bank holding the payer's funds, but in other cases the bank may be unsure of being put in funds and so decide to make a provisional credit to the payee's account pending the arrival of funds.

QUESTION

Alan, who owes Bert £100 for work done, provides his own bank (A Bank) with the name of Bert's bank (B Bank) and branch, as well as Bert's bank account number, which Bert had previously given him, and instructs A Bank to transfer £100 from his own account into Bert's account held at B Bank. As A Bank and B Bank are correspondent banks, A Bank sends an email to B Bank in the following terms: 'Please credit £100 immediately to Bert's account, and debit our account with you accordingly.' B Bank's computer is programmed in such a way that whenever it receives a credit transfer request by email from A Bank it automatically generates an email in reply agreeing to do as instructed. Such a reply is automatically sent by B Bank to A Bank in this case. However, B Bank has two customers called Bert, and before it has the chance to check which one is meant to receive the credit, B Bank goes into liquidation. Has Alan made payment to Bert? Would it make any difference if B Bank had mistakenly credited £100 to the wrong account just before going into liquidation?

10 UNWANTED PAYMENTS

Mardorf Peach & Co Ltd v Attica Sea Carriers Corpn of Liberia, The Laconia
[1977] AC 850, House of Lords

See above, p 604.

Customs and Excise Comrs v National Westminster Bank plc
[2002] EWHC 2204 (Ch), Chancery Division

The claimants, the Commissioners of Customs and Excise (the Customs and Excise), were under a statutory obligation to repay overpaid value added tax (VAT) to the taxpayer, Car Disposals Ltd (CDL). CDL wrote to the Customs and Excise informing them that 'the cheque be paid direct to our solicitors . . . for them to bank into their client account. The reason [we] make this request is that we are experiencing difficulties with our bank.' Despite this request, the Customs and Excise paid in error a sum representing the amount of overpaid VAT into CDL's account with the defendant bank, National Westminster Bank (NatWest), which duly credited CDL's account with the money, thereby reducing CDL's existing overdraft. On discovering this, CDL complained to the Customs and Excise, which paid CDL a second time by transfer to their solicitors as originally requested. Meanwhile, the Customs and Excise asked NatWest to repay the sum paid to them by mistake. NatWest refused to do so. The Customs and Excise commenced proceedings. NatWest's defence was that the payment had been made for good consideration, which was a recognised defence to recovery of a claim for recovery of a mistaken payment (see below, p 708). NatWest claimed that it was authorised to accept payment on behalf of CDL and, therefore, the payment discharged the Customs and Excise's debt to CDL. The Customs and Excise denied that payment in a manner contrary to CDL's instructions constituted discharge of the debt.

Judge Rich QC (sitting as a judge of the High Court): ...

6. The mistake alleged in the Particulars of Claim is that 'the claimants in error overlooked CDL's letter of instruction, dated 15th October 1998, and acted under a mistaken belief or assumption that CDL had authorised the defendant to accept payment of the VAT refund from the claimants.' If Mr Wilson is right that the defendant was authorised to accept payment, then the mistake alleged was not made, but he accepts that at the least the Customs and Excise were mistaken in believing that they had been authorised to make payment to the bank and counsel are, therefore, agreed that the issue to be determined by the court is as to the authority of the bank and its consequent effects of the discharge of the claimant's debt to CDL.

7. In *TSB (Scotland) v Welwyn & Hatfield District Council* [1993] 2 Bank LR 267, Hobhouse J made a distinction between what he called the ministerial or physical act of delivery of money and payment of a debt. The case concerns a preliminary issue between Welwyn and Brent, as third party, which the judge defined at page 471 as: 'What suffices to discharge the liability of the recipient of money paid in under an ultra vires contract to make restitution to the payer of the money.'

8. Brent had paid the capital sum so obtained into Welwyn's bank account. The judge held that: 'What Brent had to show for the purpose of their defence is the same as that necessary to provide a defence to a claim in debt.' Counsel are agreed that the Customs and Excise statutory duty to repay overpaid VAT is to be treated as a contractual debt. Accordingly, the judgment is precisely in point as to whether the present claimants would, after their payment to the bank, have had a defence to a claim by CDL for the payment which, in fact, they did make to CDL's solicitors.

9. The judge explained at page 271:

To discharge a debt there must have been an accepted payment of that debt, not a mere receipt by the creditor of the sum of money. The late Dr Francis Mann at page 75 of the *Legal Aspect of Money*, says: 'No creditor is under any legal duty to accept any payment, and no debtor can force any payment of any kind upon his creditor without the latter's consent, express or implied, precedent or subsequent. All the debtor can do is make an unconditional tender of the relevant sum to the creditor. If the creditor accepts the sum the liability of the debtor is appropriately discharged or reduced. If the creditor refuses to accept the tender, the debtor may, providing that he remains ready and willing to pay the relevant sum and pays it into court if action is brought against him, raise a defence of tender to the creditor's claim in respect of the debt. The unaccepted tender, therefore, does not discharge the debt, but it provides the debtor with a protection in respect of costs and against any award of interest.' Brent do not rely on any defence of tender in this case since they have on a subsequent occasion declined to pay the relevant sum and when sued instead of paying the sum into court have disputed their liability altogether. The defence of Brent is a defence of payment before action brought.... The physical or ministerial aspect of payment involves the delivery of money by one person to another. Where the two persons meet face to face and the debtor seeks to hand to the creditor legal tender, the physical act of delivery, in the absence of some misrepresentation or mistake, will not be achieved without the concurrence of the debtor. Where the relevant contract or the terms of the debt require payment to be made in a particular way as, for example, by payment into an identified account at a particular branch of a named bank, the payment will be effected by payment into that account. Prior authority has been given to discharge the debt or other obligation in that way. The debtor has authorised the bank, or other relevant person, to receive and accept the money on his behalf. No further act of concurrence or assent is required from the debtor. The creditor discharges his obligation by making the contractual payment in the contractually stipulated way.

10. In the particular circumstances of that case the judge held that there had been no prior authority for Brent to discharge its liability by payment into Welwyn's bank account, but held that by keeping the money for three weeks and making use of it to earn interest Welwyn had accepted the payment. It does, therefore, in my judgment, constitute authority for the proposition that unsolicited payment to a creditor's bank account will not constitute payment of a debt unless accepted as such. It is no part of the bank's case in this present case that there was any acceptance by CDL.

11. Mr Wilson suggests that the TSB case could be distinguished on the basis that it was the particular dealings between Brent and Welwyn which made specific authorisation necessary, but realistically accepting the impossibility of such distinction, he invited me to say that the case proceeded on an unwarranted concession, recorded at the bottom of page 272 as follows: 'Brent accept that they have to show something more than that the money was paid into an account which was solely under the control of Welwyn to prove an effective payment which would satisfy the criteria for a common-law defence of payment.' The passages which I have already cited from the judgment of Hobhouse J show that this was not a matter of concession; it was part of the reasoning of the judge which Brent felt bound to accept.

12. Mr Wilson submits that such acceptance is inconsistent with the accepted definition of the scope of a bank's relationship with its customer which Atkin LJ gave in *Joachimson (N) (a firm) v Swiss Bank Corporation* [1921] 3KB 110 p127, when he said: 'I think there is only one contract made between the bank and its customer. The terms of that contract involve obligations on both sides and require careful statement. They appear upon consideration to include the following provisions. The bank undertakes to receive money and collect bills for its customers' account. The proceeds so received are not to be held in trust for the customer, but the bank borrows the proceeds and undertakes to repay them.' I do not need to read any more of the definition. Mr Wilson says that that undertaking to receive money and collect bills means that the customer must be taken to have authorised a bank so to do. I accept that, but once the distinction between receiving money and collecting bills or collecting bills (the ministerial act) is distinguished from acceptance of payment it can be seen that this dictum is not inconsistent with the requirement to show something more in the form of prior authorisation to prove an effective payment.

13. Mr Wilson referred me to a decision of Kerr J in *Momm v Barclays Bank* [1977] QB 790, but it is not, I think, of assistance because there had been a direction by the creditor to pay into the particular bank account in that case.

14. In *Royal Products Limited v Midland Bank* [1981] 2 Ll.L.R. 194, Webster J is recorded as having held that a bank was impliedly authorised by its customer to accept a credit 'by virtue of the fact that the customer had a current account with it', but this was said in the context of an instruction to one bank, of which the plaintiff was a customer, to transfer funds to another

bank, of which it was also a customer. It was, as the judge said at 198: 'A banking operation of the kind which is often carried out internally, that is to say within the same bank or between two branches of the same bank, which at least from the point of view of the customer is no different in nature or quality when, as in the present case, it is carried out between different banks.'

15. In my judgment, the judge's analysis of the position in that case cannot justify the conclusion that a bank is impliedly authorised to accept a credit from a third party as payment to its customer, albeit it is its function and duty to accept delivery of funds to have such effect in law as may be determined between the parties. I conclude, therefore, that there is no general rule which enables Mr Wilson to say that the defendant is, merely by virtue of holding a current account for CDL, authorised to receive payment from the Customs and Excise on CDL's behalf so as to discharge their debt to CDL. No specific authorisation is suggested....

20.... I, therefore, give judgment to the claimant for £44,454,53 as asked.

NOTES

1.   In *TSB Bank of Scotland plc v Welwyn Hatfield District Council and Council of the London Borough of Brent* [1993] 2 Bank LR 267, Hobhouse J held that a payee would be deemed to have accepted an unauthorised payment made into his account where he dealt with the transferred funds as his own. In that case the issue before the court was whether an inter-bank transfer of funds by one local authority into the account of another local authority amounted to payment of an underlying restitutionary liability. Hobhouse J held that, despite initial protestations, retention of the money for three weeks, use of the money, and eventual return of the money without interest amounted to acceptance of tender by the payee local authority and, therefore, payment.

2.   In *TSB Bank of Scotland plc v Welwyn Hatfield District Council and Council of the London Borough of Brent* (above), the payee local authority was at all times aware that the unauthorised payment had been made into its account. This may not always be the case. In *HMV Fields Properties Ltd v Bracken Self Selection Fabrics Ltd* 1991 SLT 31, a Scottish case, a landlord served the Scottish equivalent of a notice of forfeiture on his tenant for breach of various covenants in the lease. The tenant refused to move out and arbitration proceedings were commenced. Meanwhile, the tenant continued to pay rent by bank giro credit transfer into the landlord's bank account, something which the landlord did not notice for several weeks. When the rent payments eventually came to the landlord's attention it returned them to the tenant, again using the bank giro credit transfer system. On appeal from the arbitration it was held by the First Division of the Inner House of the Court of Session that the landlord was not barred from forfeiture by reason of having accepted rent. It was held that 'acceptance' was a question of fact and, despite the landlord's initial delay of several weeks before returning the rent, there had been no acceptance here. In this case the payee had no knowledge of the payment being made into the account, whereas in the *TSB Bank of Scotland* case the payee was fully aware of the payment.

3.   In *Dovey v Bank of New Zealand* [2000] 3 NZLR 641, D instructed his bank (BNZ) in New Zealand to transfer funds to 'my account' at a bank (BCCI) in Luxembourg. In fact D had no account with BCCI. BNZ purported to execute the transfer by instructing its agent bank in London to transfer funds to BCCI's agent bank in London. Payment was made between the agent banks at 10 am on a day about a week later, but at 1 pm on the same day liquidators were appointed to BCCI. In an inadequately pleaded claim against BNZ, D alleged that the bank was in breach of contract because it had not completed his instructions. D alleged that the

transaction was incomplete because BCCI had not formally opened an account for him and so had to be treated as holding the funds as agent for BNZ. The New Zealand Court of Appeal showed little hesitation in rejecting that claim. It held that by nominating the bank to which the funds were to be transferred, D gave the bank authority to accept funds on his behalf, even though the bank had yet to open an account for him. There was nothing more BNZ could have done to complete the transaction. Tipping J, delivering the judgment of the court, added (at [26]) that: '[i]f the receiving bank does not have the payee's authority to receive the money, it is treated as acting pro tanto as the paying bank's agent until that authority is received or the transaction reversed'.

QUESTION

Why would a payee of a funds transfer not want to receive those funds into his bank account?

CHAPTER 17

PAYMENT CARDS

1 INTRODUCTION

Payment through the use of plastic payment cards continues to increase in popularity.[1] In 2015 payment cards were used in the UK to make 17 billion transactions totalling £856 billion. Statistics published by the UK Cards Association for 2015 show that there were 175.6 million cards in issue in the UK made up of 59 million credit cards, 5.7 million charge cards, 98.8 million debit cards, and 12.2 million ATM-only cards (http://www.theukcardsassociation.org.uk).

Contactless cards are becoming increasing popular and account for 49 per cent of all cards in issue. Contactless payment is made through the tap of a card on (or by waving it over) a reader, without requiring a personal identification number or signature. Contactless terminals use an antenna so that at the touch of certain credit, debit, or pre-paid cards, bank details are securely transmitted to complete the purchase up to a limit of £30 in the UK. The increased availability of mobile payment technology is likely to see contactless payments shifting from cards to smartphones.

2 TYPES OF PAYMENT CARD

The main types of payment card in general circulation in the UK are the following.

(1) **Credit (and charge) cards**—which enable the holder to whom such a card is issued to obtain goods and services without payment in cash or by cheque, and to obtain cash. A credit card gives the holder a revolving credit facility with a monthly credit limit. The cardholder does not have to settle his account in full at the end of each month but has the option to take extended credit, subject to an obligation to make a specified minimum payment each month. Amounts outstanding at the end of a set period commencing with the date of the monthly statement sent by the card-issuer to the cardholder attract interest charged on a daily basis. Unlike a credit card, the primary function of a charge card is to facilitate payment, rather than to provide a credit facility. The holder of a charge card must normally settle his account in full within a specified period after the date of a monthly statement sent by the card-issuer to the cardholder. Delinquent accounts may be charged a sum equal to interest, but this is described

---

[1] See EP Ellinger, E Lomnicka, and CVM Hare, *Ellinger's Modern Banking Law* (5th edn, 2011), Ch 14; M Smith and P Robertson, 'Plastic Money' in M Brindle and R Cox (eds), *Law of Bank Payments* (4th edn, 2010), Ch 4.

by the card-issuer as 'liquidated damages' for failure by the cardholder to honour the terms of card membership. Credit and charge cards may be 'two-party' cards, which means the card is issued by shops and stores for the purchase of their own goods and services. Alternatively, they may be 'three-party' cards issued by banks, building societies, credit card and finance companies, etc for the purchase of goods and services from participating retailers (in fact a fourth party, the 'merchant acquirer', is also often involved in the transaction: see below, p 633). In the UK most 'three-party' and 'four-party' cards operate through the Visa and MasterCard networks (credit cards) and the American Express and Diners Club networks (charge cards).

(2) **Debit cards**—debit card payments are made using EFTPOS ('electronic funds transfer at point of sale') systems. The major EFTPOS debit card schemes in operation in the UK are run by Visa (Visa Debit and Visa Electron) and MasterCard (Debit MasterCard and Maestro). In a typical retail transaction, the cardholder presents the retailer with a plastic debit card that incorporates a microchip which holds information relating to the cardholder's current bank account (but note that in some cases the cardholder may use his debit card to make a purchase over the telephone or via the internet when he will simply provide the retailer with his card details). The card is inserted into a card reader installed at the retailer's point of sale terminal and the retailer enters the amount of the transaction into his terminal (see Section 1 above for 'contactless' cards). The cardholder is then invited to insert his personal identification number (PIN) into the machine. Where the transaction is over a given amount the retailer's terminal will seek authorisation from the authorisation centre of the cardholder's bank to accept the card, although the precise circumstances where authorisation is required will vary according to the rules of each EFTPOS system. The PIN acts as the cardholder's mandate to his bank to debit his account and credit the retailer's account, and a message to this effect is transmitted, via one of the EFTPOS networks, to the cardholder's bank and the retailer's bank. The message may be transmitted either directly to the EFTPOS network or stored at the retailer's terminal for transmission in batch mode at the close of business that day. When the cardholder's bank and the retailer's bank have received their respective debit and credit instructions over the network, the cardholder's and retailer's accounts will be adjusted accordingly. Where an EFTPOS system operates online it is technically possible for the transmission of the debit/credit message from the retailer's terminal, and adjustments of accounts at the cardholder's and retailer's banks, to be virtually instantaneous.

Credit card transactions may also be executed using EFTPOS terminals or contactless payment readers, for example Visa and MasterCard operate such systems. But with most credit (and charge) card schemes a separate card account is opened for the customer with debits made against that account. The cardholder will then make payments into the account from a current account with a bank by cheque, direct debit, or sometimes even by standing order. By contrast, a debit card operates directly on the cardholder's current account, to which debits are posted as the card is used to pay for goods and services (or to obtain cash), and a corresponding credit is made to the account of the supplier who has accepted payment by debit card (a debit card may also be used to obtain cash from a supplier who offers a 'cashback facility'). Thus, debit cards perform a similar function to that performed by cheques, and it is not surprising that the increased use of debit cards has contributed, together with the increased use of direct debit payments, to a significant drop in the number of cheque transactions in recent years.

(3) **ATM cards**—which give customers access (when used in conjunction with their PIN) to Automated Teller Machines (ATMs). The first ATMs introduced in the UK in 1967 only dispensed cash. ATMs now provide a variety of services. Typically, a customer can use an

ATM to withdraw cash from his account, make a balance inquiry, order a bank statement, order a cheque book, change his PIN, pay bills, and accept deposits. An ATM card can only be used in the ATMs of the card-issuing bank and the ATMs of other banks with whom the issuing bank has reached a reciprocal agreement. Reciprocal agreements were introduced to provide shared ATM networks giving customers access to their accounts via any ATM within the network. A number of ATM networks were established, namely, the FOUR BANKS, MINT, and LINK networks. All UK ATM owners have since joined the LINK network and the FOUR BANKS and MINT networks have closed. There are also a number of international ATM networks, for example the Visa and MasterCard networks.

(4) **Multifunctional cards**—often a single card will have several functions, for example debit cards usually also operate as ATM cards. For the purpose of legal analysis, each function must be examined separately.

Banks are also starting to make **'electronic money'** cards available to customers in certain areas. Electronic money, which may be designated in a wide range of currencies including pounds sterling, is designed to mimic the essential features of cash payment, namely that transfer of possession of physical cash transfers ownership of the cash and immediately discharges the debt owed by the transferor to the transferee. Electronic money systems are either smart card systems, where electronic value is stored in a microchip on a smart card, or software-based systems where tokens or coins are stored in the memory of a computer. The 'value', 'tokens', or 'coins' take the form of digital information. Electronic money allows payment to be made simply by transferring digital information directly between debtor and creditor so that value is transferred immediately upon delivery. In some systems the recipient of electronic money can immediately use it to pay for other goods or services. Other systems require the token to be deposited in a bank account or with the issuer who will then issue a token of equivalent value or credit the value to an account.

Electronic money systems depend on various contractual relationships for legal effect. Electronic money is issued by an 'issuer' or 'originator' (a private company) to banks participating in the scheme that pay for it in real funds. Participating banks re-issue electronic money to customers by charging their electronic money card, or the memory of their computer in a software system, with digital information representing the value purchased from the bank by the customer (usually through a debit to their account). There is a contractual relationship between the electronic money issuer and the participating banks and between those banks and their own customers. However, for an electronic money scheme to work, holders of electronic money must be confident that the electronic money issuer will ultimately be liable to redeem the digital cash for real value. The legal basis for this has yet to be established but one possible explanation is to treat electronic money systems as giving rise to a series of standing offers of unilateral contracts, or through reliance on the Contracts (Rights of Third Parties) Act 1999 where the electronic issuer and participating banks have not contracted out of the Act (see further, R Hooley, 'Payment in a Cashless Society' in BAK Rider (ed), *The Realm of Company Law—A Collection of Papers in Honour of Professor Leonard Sealy* (1998), p 245).

Electronic money must be distinguished from **virtual currencies** such as Bitcoin, which is a decentralised scheme maintained by peer-to-peer networks that authenticate and maintain a public ledger of Bitcoin transactions (see further TA Anderson [2014] JIBLR 428; E Chan [2014] BJIBFL 398). Electronic money is a digital representation of fiat currency (which is what we generally think of as money, ie the legal tender of a particular jurisdiction) and is used for electronic transfers of value denominated in fiat currency. By contrast, Bitcoins are not issued or controlled by a third party such as a corporate entity or a government.

Bitcoin gains acceptance as a store of value and means of exchange simply from a consensus amongst its community of users. Significantly, issuers of electronic money are regulated by the Financial Conduct Authority under the Electronic Money Regulations 2011 (SI 2011/99) (implementing the second Electronic Money Directive 2009/110/EC), but these regulations do not purport to extend to Bitcoin (see P Susman [2016] BJIBFL 150). For an analysis of the legal aspect of virtual currencies which addresses issues of legal uncertainty in the context of their development as a medium of exchange, see the report of the Financial Markets Law Committee, 'Issues of legal uncertainty arising in the context of virtual currencies' (July 2016), published at http://www.fmlc.org.

QUESTIONS

1. Electronic money has proved less popular with consumers than originally envisaged. Why do you think that is so?
2. What are the risks associated with the use of virtual currencies?

3 CONTRACTUAL NETWORKS

(a) Credit and charge cards

Re Charge Card Services Ltd
[1989] Ch 497, Court of Appeal

Charge Card Services Ltd ('the company') ran a fuel card scheme for the purchase of petrol and other fuels from approved garages with the use of charge cards issued by the company. The company went into creditors' voluntary liquidation owing substantial sums to garages which had supplied fuel in return for vouchers signed by fuel card holders. There were also substantial sums owing to the company from cardholders who had purchased fuel with the use of their fuel cards before the date of the liquidation. Under a factoring agreement the company had assigned all its receivables to Commercial Credit Services Ltd. A dispute arose between the unpaid garages and the factoring company as to which of them was entitled to the monies owed to the company by the cardholders. Millett J's first-instance decision (at [1987] Ch 150), that the factoring company was entitled to the monies on the ground that a cardholder's payment obligation to the garage was absolutely, not conditionally, discharged by use of the fuel card, was upheld on appeal.

Sir Nicolas Browne-Wilkinson V-C: . . . The case raises fundamental questions as to the legal character of credit card sales. It is therefore convenient, before turning to the specific questions argued, to set out what, in my judgment, are the normal features of credit card or charge card transactions, there being no relevant distinction between charge cards and credit cards for present purposes.

1. THE GENERAL FEATURES OF CREDIT CARD TRANSACTIONS

(A) There is an underlying contractual scheme which predates the individual contracts of sale. Under such scheme, the suppliers have agreed to accept the card in payment of the price of goods purchased: the purchasers are entitled to use the credit card to commit the credit card company to pay the suppliers. (B) That underlying scheme is established by two separate contracts. The first is made between the credit company and the seller: the seller agrees to accept payment by use of the card from anyone holding the card and the credit company agrees to pay to the supplier the price of goods supplied less a discount. The second contract is between the credit company and the cardholder: the cardholder is provided with a card which enables him to pay the price by its use and in return agrees to pay the credit company the full amount of the price charged by the supplier. (C) The underlying scheme is designed primarily for use in over-the-counter sales, ie sales where the only connection between a particular seller and a particular buyer is the one sale. (D) The actual sale and purchase of the commodity is the subject of a third bilateral contract made between buyer and seller. In the majority of cases, this sale contract will be an oral, over-the-counter sale. Tendering and acceptance of the credit card in payment is made on the tacit assumption that the legal consequences will be regulated by the separate underlying contractual obligations between the seller and the credit company and the buyer and the credit company. (E) Because the transactions intended to be covered by the scheme would primarily be over-the-counter sales, the card does not carry the address of the cardholder and the supplier will have no record of his address. Therefore the seller has no obvious means of tracing the purchaser save through the credit company. (F) In the circumstances, credit cards have come to be regarded as substitutes for cash; they are frequently referred to as 'plastic money.' (G) The credit card scheme provides advantages to both seller and purchaser. The seller is able to attract custom by agreeing to accept credit card payment. The purchaser, by using the card, minimises the need to carry cash and obtains at least a period of free credit during the period until payment to the card company is due.

2. THE PARTICULAR FEATURES OF THIS SCHEME

In the present case, the fuel card scheme run by the company contained all those features. The scheme and the contracts in which it is contained draws a distinction between the account holder and the cardholders, the former being the company or person who contracts with the company, the latter being the persons authorised by the account holder to use the card. The distinction is of no significance in the present case and I will refer to both classes as 'the cardholder.' It merely reflects the fact that many account holders were haulage and fleet operators rather than individuals.

The underlying scheme is constituted by two bilateral contracts, viz: (a) The contract between the garage and the company ('the franchise agreement'). By the franchise agreement the garage undertook to honour the company's fuel card. There were two different ways in which the garage could claim payment: nothing turns on the difference between them. The company in effect undertook that on receipt of vouchers signed by the cardholders together with a claim form, payment of the price (less commission) would be made to the garage within five days at the latest, (b) The contract between the cardholder and the company ('the subscriber agreement'). There is a major issue as to the proper construction of the subscriber agreement to which I will have to revert. In essence, the cardholder authorised the company to pay for fuel supplied to the cardholder and to debit the cardholder. The company was to send to the cardholder a monthly statement of the amount debited and the cardholder was bound to pay to the company within 14 days the full amount shown owing in the statement.

In addition there was a third contract ('the forecourt agreement') made between the cardholder and the garage. This contract came into existence when the cardholder bought fuel at the garage. It was necessarily an oral agreement. In the present case, the forecourt agreement has a special feature not to be found in the majority of credit card purchases. At a self-service garage, the petrol is put into the tank by the purchaser/cardholder before there is any contact between him and the staff of the garage. It is common ground that the contract for the sale of the petrol is made at that stage, the garage having made an open offer to sell at pump prices which is accepted by the motorist putting petrol in the tank. Having done so, the motorist then goes to pay for the petrol and produces the fuel card. That is the first time at which the garage knows that payment is to be made not in cash but by using the card. There is a dispute between the parties whether, in those circumstances, the purchaser ever becomes liable to the garage to satisfy the price by payment in cash.

3. THE ISSUES

The following principal points were argued, (a) Commercial Credit contended that self-service forecourt sales do not at any stage give rise to a primary obligation on a fuel card holder to pay cash for the petrol. It is said that the garage makes an open offer, by exhibiting the fuel card sign on the forecourt, that it will accept payment either in cash or by means of the card. Therefore, it is said, there is no primary obligation to pay cash which can revive when the company fails to honour the fuel card. The judge rejected this contention [1987] Ch 150, 164. I find it unneces-sary to decide the point since, on the view I take of the case, it makes no difference, (b) Is there a general principle of law that whenever a method of payment is adopted which involves a risk of non-payment by a third party there is a presumption that the acceptance of payment through a third party is conditional on the third party making the payment, and that if he does not pay the original obligation of the purchaser remains? (c) If there is no such general principle, was the acceptance of the fuel card by garages merely conditional payment or was it an absolute payment? (d) Mr Potts, for the garages, put forward an alternative argument. He submitted that on the true construction of the subscriber agreement the cardholder was only liable to pay the company if and when the company had paid the garage. On this basis he submitted that since the company had not paid the garages the sums recovered from the cardholders by the liquidator ought either to be applied in paying the garages or alternatively should be returned to the cardholders since the cardholders were never liable to pay either the garages or the com-pany. On the view which I have formed on the construction of the subscriber agreement (see at 5. below) this point does not arise for decision. I will deal with points (b) and (c) in turn.

4. IS THERE A GENERAL PRESUMPTION OF CONDITIONAL PAYMENT?

Mr Potts' argument is founded on the law applicable to cheques, bills of exchange and letters of credit. It is common ground that where a debt is 'paid' by cheque or bill of exchange, there is a presumption that such payment is conditional on the cheque or bill being honoured. If it is not honoured, the condition is not satisfied and the liability of the purchaser to pay the price remains. Such presumption can be rebutted by showing an express or implied intention that the cheque or bill is taken in total satisfaction of the liability: see *Chitty on Contracts*, 25th edn (1983), vol 1, pp 800–802, paras 1436 et seq; *Sayer v Wagstaff* (1844) 14 LJ Ch 116; *In re London, Birmingham and South Staffordshire Banking Co Ltd* (1865) 34 Beav 332; *In re Romer & Haslam* [1893] 2 QB 286; *Allen v Royal Bank of Canada* (1925) 95 LJPC 17 and *Bolt & Nut Co (Tipton) Ltd v Rowlands Nicholls Co Ltd* [1964] 2 QB 10.

There is a similar presumption applicable to payments made by means of letters of credit. If the seller does not receive payment under the letter of credit, it is presumed that the buyer is still liable to pay the price although this presumption can be rebutted by express or implied agree-ment to the contrary: see *WJ Alan &. Co Ltd v El Nasr Export and Import Co* [1972] 2 QB 189, 212B, *per* Lord Denning MR and, at p 221E, *per* Stephenson LJ; *Maran Road Saw Mill v Austin Taylor & Co Ltd* [1975] 1 Lloyd's Rep 156 and *E D & F Man Ltd v Nigerian Sweets & Confectionery Co Ltd* [1977] 2 Lloyd's Rep 50.

Like the judge (see [1987] Ch 150, 166A), I cannot detect from the authorities any such general principle as Mr Potts suggests which is applicable to all cases where payment is to be effected through a third party. The cases on cheques and bills of exchange do not contain any reference to such a principle. They are all cases where there was an obligation to pay a sum of money which predated the tendering of the cheque. The principle applied is that the obligation to discharge the pre-existing debt has not been satisfied unless the creditor has expressly or impliedly agreed to accept the cheque or bill in final satisfaction.

When a similar rule was applied to letters of credit in *WJ Alan & Co Ltd v El Nasr Export and Import Co* [1972] 2 QB 189, Lord Denning MR, with whom Stephenson LJ agreed, did not treat the matter as decided by any existing general principle of law. He described the question as one of construction to be determined in the light of the consequences: see p 209D. He then considered the consequences of treating a letter of credit as being an absolute or a conditional payment in the light of the circumstances affecting the type of commercial transaction in which letters of credit are used. He reached the conclusion that in those circumstances payment by letters of credit should be treated as conditional. Although he referred to the position as being analogous to that applicable to cheques and bills of exchange, he did not treat those cases as establishing any such general principle as Mr Potts relies on.

In my judgment, there is no such general principle. Each method of payment has to be considered in the light of the consequences and other circumstances attending that type of payment. When, as with credit cards, a new form of payment is introduced applicable to new sets of circumstances, it is necessary to consider whether such payment should be treated as absolute or conditional in the light of the consequences and circumstances of such new type of payment, not according to any general principle.

5. WAS THE ACCEPTANCE OF THE FUEL CARD BY THE GARAGES CONDITIONAL OR ABSOLUTE PAYMENT?

The answer to this question must depend on the terms of the forecourt agreement since this is the only contract made between the garage and the cardholder. The terms on which the garage accepted payment from the cardholder must be determined by the only contract to which they are parties. To determine the terms of the forecourt agreement is not an easy task. Such agreement is at best oral and, in the majority of cases, not even that. The sale contract is made by putting the fuel in the tank before the parties have met: tender of the card and the making out of the signature of the voucher for the sale is often conducted in complete silence. Moreover, although both garage and cardholder are in general aware that some underlying contract exists between the garage and the company and between the cardholder and the company, neither the garage nor the cardholder is aware of the exact terms of the contract to which they are not a party. Therefore the terms of the forecourt agreement have to be inferred from the surrounding circumstances known to the parties.

At the time of the sale, it is almost inconceivable that either party addressed its mind to the question. 'What will be the position if the company does not pay the garage?' At one stage in the argument, both parties were contending that *The Moorcock* test (see *The Moorcock* (1889) 14 PD 64) should be applied to determine what term should be implied in the agreement. If such test were to be applied, one would be looking for a term that any reasonable garage proprietor and cardholder would have agreed should be the result. On such a test, it is most unlikely that any term could properly be implied. But, in my judgment, this is not the right test since in a case such as the present there has to be *some* term regulating the legal effect of the acceptance of the card. The law has to give an answer to the problem. In my judgment, the correct approach in such a case is that the court should seek to infer from the parties' conduct and the surrounding circumstances what is the fair term to imply: this approach became common ground between the parties.

A sale using the fuel card for payment did not, in my judgment, differ in any material respect from an ordinary credit card sale. The one peculiarity of the transaction: viz. that the contract for sale of the petrol took place when the tank was filled and not, as in a supermarket, at the till, does not make any relevant difference. The question remains, on what terms did the supplier accept the card in payment?

Although neither party to the forecourt agreement knew the exact terms of the other party's contract with the company, both parties were aware of the underlying contractual structure. The customer/cardholder knew that, if he signed the voucher, the supplier/garage would be entitled to receive a payment for the petrol which would fully discharge the customer's liability for the price: depending on his sophistication, the customer/cardholder might or might not have known that the company would deduct commission in paying the garage. On the other side, the garage knew that on signing the voucher the cardholder rendered himself liable to the company to pay to the company the price of the petrol. Before entering into the forecourt agreement, both parties had entered into their respective contracts with the company and their underlying assumption must have been that on completion of the sale of the petrol by use of the fuel card, the parties' future rights and obligations would be regulated by those underlying contracts. In the majority of cases, the garage had no record of the address of the customer and no ready means of tracing him.

To my mind, all these factors point clearly to the conclusion that, quite apart from any special features of the fuel card scheme, the transaction was one in which the garage was accepting payment by card in substitution for payment in cash, ie, as an unconditional discharge of the price. The garage was accepting the company's obligation to pay instead of cash from a purchaser of whose address he was totally unaware. One way of looking at the matter is to say that there was a quasi-novation of the purchaser's liability. By the underlying scheme, the company had bound the garage to accept the card and had authorised the cardholder to pledge the company's credit. By the signature of the voucher all parties became bound: the garage was bound to accept the card in payment; the company was bound to pay the garage; and the cardholder was bound to pay the company. The garage, knowing that the cardholder was bound to pay the company and knowing that it was entitled to payment from the company which the garage itself had elected to do business with, must in my judgment be taken to have accepted the company's obligation to pay in place of any liability on the customer to pay the garage direct.

In the present case, there are two additional features which point the same way. First, under the franchise agreement, the company undertook to provide a guarantee of its obligations to the garage. This undertaking unhappily was not honoured. But the inclusion of the term in the franchise agreement provides some support for the view that, in the event of the company being unable to pay, the garage was looking for payment, not to the customer, but to the guarantor lying behind the company.

Secondly, there is a feature of great importance which may or may not be common to all credit card sales. Mr Potts in effect accepted that neither party could have envisaged that the cardholder/customer would have to pay twice: once to the company and again to the garage. To avoid this result, he submitted that the acceptance of the card by the garage was conditional on *either* the company paying the garage *or* the cardholder paying the company. A condition to that effect is wholly different to that applicable in the case of cheques or letters of credit. I find it an impossible condition to imply. I fully see the force of implying a condition that payment is conditional on the actual discharge of the price by a third party: such condition is based on the fundamental premise that a seller expects to be paid for the goods sold. But I can see no reason for implying a condition that the seller is not to be so paid if the buyer has discharged another obligation to a different party. In truth, the suggestion of this additional condition is merely a forensic device designed to avoid what everyone looking at the transaction feels, viz. that in no circumstances can the result be that the cardholder has to pay both the garage and the company.

[The Vice-Chancellor then examined the particular features of the subscriber agreement in issue and held that they supported his conclusion that payment by credit or charge card is normally to be taken as an absolute, not a conditional, discharge of the cardholder's liability. He continued:]

I do not find the analogy with cheques at all close or helpful. Payments by cheque involve the unilateral act of the buyer and his agent, the bank on which the cheque is drawn. The buyer's basic obligation to pay the price is sought to be discharged through a third party, the bank, which is in no contractual relationship with the seller. Moreover, the seller has had no say in the selection of the bank. It is very far from the position in a credit card sale where the seller has agreed to rely on the credit of the credit card company and there is a pre-existing contractual obligation on the credit card company to pay the supplier quite separate from any obligation of the buyer.

The analogy with letters of credit is much closer. In both, there are three parties to the arrangement and, once the letter of credit is issued, the bank is contractually bound to pay on the presentation of the documents. But the whole commercial context of the two types of transaction is totally different. The letter of credit is primarily an instrument of international trade issued pursuant to an individually negotiated contract of considerable substance made in writing: the credit card is used for small, over-the-counter transactions between strangers there being, at best, an oral agreement and more often an agreement by conduct. In the case of credit card sales, the seller does not even know the address of the purchaser, which makes it hard to infer an intention that he will have a right of recourse against the purchaser. It is normally the buyer, not the seller, who selects the bank issuing the letter of credit: if, unusually, the seller does select the bank, this factor may rebut the presumption of conditional payment by letter of credit: see *WJ Alan & Co Ltd v El Nasr Export and Import Co* [1972] 2 QB 189, 210A. In contrast, in a credit card transaction the seller has decided long before the specific supply contract is made whether or not to accept the cards of the credit card company and has entered into an overall contract with it, under which the seller is obliged to accept the card and the credit card company is bound to pay him. With letters of credit, the issuing bank is the agent of the buyer and not the seller and it is the buyer who pays for the facility: in credit card transactions the credit card company is in a contractual relationship with both but it is the seller who pays for the facility by allowing the deduction of the commission. These differences are, in my judgment, so fundamental that the law affecting letters of credit is not of great assistance in deciding what law should apply to credit card transactions.

Accordingly, I agree with the judge, and broadly for the same reasons, that the cardholder's obligations to the garages were absolutely, not conditionally, discharged by the garage accepting the voucher signed by the cardholder and that accordingly the appeal should be dismissed. I reach this conclusion with satisfaction since I think it reflects the popular perception of the role of credit cards in modern retail trade as 'plastic money.'

[**Nourse** and **Stuart-Smith LJJ** concurred.]

NOTES

1.   *Re Charge Card Services Ltd* involved a simplified card scheme with a single card-issuer. By contrast, numerous banks and other financial institutions issue Visa and MasterCard credit (and debit) cards in the UK. Each scheme has its own master agreement which operates as a binding contract between the participating banks and other financial institutions (see *Sainsbury's Supermarkets Ltd v MasterCard Inc* [2016] CAT 11 at [6]–[10] and [42]–[82] for a review of the MasterCard scheme). The master agreement provides for such matters as the form of the card, card authorisation procedures, and settlement between participating financial institutions. Under the master agreement, participating financial institutions generally become entitled to issue cards in their own name to their customers, and to admit suppliers to the scheme so as to entitle them to accept cards in payment for goods and services supplied by them. A supplier contracts with a 'merchant acquirer', a financial institution giving the supplier admission to the scheme (the merchant acquirer is often the supplier's own bank, so long as it is a participant in the particular scheme). Admission to the scheme will be on the merchant acquirer's own terms and conditions (see *Lancore Services Ltd v Barclays Bank plc* [2009] EWCA Civ 752, [2010] 1 All ER 763). By this contract, the supplier is authorised and obliged to accept all cards issued under the scheme in payment for goods or services, and the merchant acquirer agrees to pay to the supplier the value of the goods or services supplied, less a handling charge, provided the supplier has complied with certain stipulated conditions (eg he has obtained specific transaction authorisation if the price is over a stated ceiling). For each transaction the supplier transmits both card and transaction details to the merchant acquirer over an EFTPOS system. The merchant acquirer then pays the supplier as agreed. Under the terms of the master agreement, the merchant acquirer obtains reimbursement from the participating financial institution which issued the card used in the transaction (unless they happen to be one and the same). It may be the case that some or all of the participating financial institutions' services, performed as 'issuer' or 'merchant acquirer' or both, are 'outsourced' to separate companies (for a clear explanation of how outsourcing operates, see *Customs and Excise Comrs v FDR Ltd* [2000] STC 672 at [11]–[19], per Laws LJ).

2. Where a credit or charge card is issued by a store for the purchase of its own goods or services, there may only be one contractual relationship, namely that between the store and the customer; however, in-store cards are often issued by a separate company which is a subsidiary of the retailer.

3. In *Re Charge Card Services Ltd* [1987] Ch 150, Millett J, at first instance, analysed the true nature of the consideration for the goods or services supplied when payment is to be obtained by the supplier by the use of a credit or charge card. His Lordship stated (at 164) that:

> Three possibilities have been canvassed. The first is that the consideration for the supply is not the price (which is to be paid by the card-issuing company, a stranger to the contract of supply) but production of the card and signature of a voucher. I reject this analysis, which is quite unrealistic. Production of the card and signature of a voucher are not the consideration itself but the means of obtaining it. Moreover, a sale of goods requires a monetary consideration: see section 2(1) of the Sale of Goods Act 1979. This analysis would thus lead to the conclusion that, where payment is to be made by credit or charge card, the contract of supply is not a sale of goods, with the result that the statutory conditions and warranties are not implied. The second possibility which has been suggested is that there is a sale of goods, but the contract is a tripartite contract under which the consideration for the supply to the cardholder is the undertaking of the card-issuing company to pay the price to the supplier. I reject this analysis, which confuses the result of all the arrangements made with the legal means employed to achieve it. On the use of the card, there is no tripartite agreement, but three separate bilateral contracts come into operation. In my judgment, the true consideration in the contract of supply is the price, to be satisfied by the cardholder, by means of the card if he wishes.

4. *Re Charge Card Services Ltd* was followed in *Customs and Excise Comrs v Diners Club Ltd* [1989] 2 All ER 385, CA.

(b) Debit card

The debit card schemes which operate in the UK generate the same types of contractual relations as arise with credit and charge card transactions. What is set out above in relation to credit and charge cards can equally be applied to debit cards. Debit card transactions involve four discrete contractual relationships, namely those between: (1) cardholder and supplier (further explained in *Debenhams Retail plc v Customs and Excise Comrs* [2005] EWCA Civ 892, [2005] STC 1155); (2) card-issuing bank and cardholder (giving the cardholder authority to use the card and the card-issuing bank authority to debit the cardholder's account with the amount of any card transaction entered into); (3) supplier and merchant acquirer (obliging the supplier to accept all cards issued under the scheme in payment for goods or services and containing the merchant acquirer's undertaking to pay the supplier for the value of good and services supplied: cf *Do-Buy 925 Ltd v National Westminster Bank plc* [2010] EWHC 2862 (QB), where the merchant acquirer was held entitled to withhold payment); and (4) the participating banks and financial institutions themselves (covering various matters including, most importantly, the means of transfer of funds from one institution to another). See *Sainsbury's Supermarkets Ltd v MasterCard Inc* [2016] CAT 11 at [6]–[10] (in outline) and [42]–[82] (in detail) for a review of the MasterCard scheme.

The general consensus is that payment by debit card should be treated like payment by credit or charge card and constitute absolute, and not conditional, discharge of the underlying indebtedness (see, eg, EP Ellinger, E Lomnicka, and CVM Hare, *Ellinger's Modern Banking Law* (5th edn, 2011), p 660; *Paget's Law of Banking* (14th edn, 2014), para 25.38). Although debit cards perform a payment function similar to that performed by cheques, which only constitute conditional payment, there is an important distinction between them. Payment by cheque does not give the supplier the benefit of the drawee bank's undertaking to pay, whereas payment by debit card (like credit and charge cards) gives the supplier a direct payment undertaking from the bank or other financial institution which admitted him into the scheme. It is the fact that the cardholder knows that use of the card means that a third party becomes obliged to pay the supplier that prevents the cardholder from countermanding his payment instruction once he has entered his PIN into the supplier's point of sale terminal (in fact the terms of the contract between the card-issuing bank and the cardholder usually expressly preclude countermand from this point in time).

(c) ATM cards

Where an ATM card is used to withdraw cash from an ATM operated by the card-issuing bank there will be only one contractual relationship involved, as the issuer and the supplier of cash is one and the same. However, we have already noted that banks which issue ATM cards are usually members of the UK's ATM network (called the LINK network) allowing customers to use their cards in any ATM operated by other banks and financial institutions which are members of that network. The ATM network is held together by a master agreement between the network members.

Where a cardholder uses an ATM card issued by his own bank to withdraw cash from a machine operated by another bank within the same network, there is some uncertainty as to whether the cardholder and the bank whose ATM is used enter into a direct contractual relationship or whether the bank acts merely as the agent of the cardholder's own bank (the relationship between the banks themselves was examined in *Royal Bank of Scotland Group plc v Customs and Excise Comrs* [2002] STC 575, Second Division, Inner House, Court of

Session). It is arguable that there is a unilateral contract between the cardholder and the bank whose ATM is used, which comes into existence in a similar way to the unilateral contract which arises when a supplier accepts a cheque card. The distinction becomes important when assessing whether an ATM card is a 'credit-token' for the purposes of the Consumer Credit Act 1974 (see below).

4 THE REGULATION OF CONTRACTUAL RELATIONSHIPS

Resolution of any dispute between cardholder and card-issuer, cardholder and supplier, supplier and card-issuer (or other financial institution which has admitted him to the scheme), and between the financial institutions which are members of the particular payment card scheme, will normally depend on the terms of the contract governing the relevant contractual relationship in issue. The point can be neatly illustrated by the following case. In *Tony Mekwin MTV & Co v National Westminster Bank plc* [1998] CCLR 22, when the plaintiff attempted to use his National Westminster Business MasterCard at a service station the attendant was not satisfied that the cardholder's signature matched the one on the card and so contacted the relevant MasterCard office which informed him that, although the card had not been reported stolen, if the signature did not match the one on the card then the card was to be retained. In fact the attendant had made a mistake and the plaintiff was offered the return of his card the next day. However, the plaintiff refused to have the card back and instead started proceedings against the defendant card-issuing bank alleging breach of contract in ordering retention of the card. The county court judge found in favour of the bank and the Court of Appeal dismissed the plaintiff's application for leave to appeal from that decision. Aldous LJ examined the card-issuing contract and pointed to the clause which stated: 'All cards are and remain the property of the bank at all times. The business is responsible for recovering and returning all cards issued to it if the bank or its agent so requests.' He held that there was nothing in the agreement which prevented the bank retaining the card if, for some reason, it should be suspicious that the person presenting it was not the person to whom it had been issued. The card was the property of the bank and not of the plaintiff.

(a) The unfair terms legislation

The card-issuing contract and the merchant agreement by which a supplier becomes a member of a particular scheme will generally be on the card-issuer/bank's written standard terms of business. Where the card-issuing contract is with a 'consumer' cardholder (see below for definition, which excludes a company), it will be caught by Part 2 of the Consumer Rights Act 2015, and most of its terms assessed as to their fairness. Where the card-issuing contract is with a non-consumer cardholder, for example a company, it will be caught by the Unfair Contract Terms Act 1977, and terms which can broadly be described as 'exclusion' or 'limitation' clauses in the contract will be assessed as to their reasonableness. Similar exclusion or limitation clauses in a merchant agreement will also be caught by the 1977 Act, but not by the 2015 Act as a supplier will not fall within the definition of 'consumer' set out in s 2 of that Act ('an individual acting for purposes that are wholly or mainly outside that individual's trade, business, craft or profession'). The 1977 Act may protect a supplier trying to escape the effect of a particularly draconian term in his agreement with the bank or other financial institution which admitted him to the card scheme (eg there is some controversy as to whether the 'charge back' clause in a merchant agreement, which, inter alia, makes the supplier liable when goods and services are obtained by a fraudster in a 'card not present' transaction, is invalid as unfair and unreasonable under the Unfair Contract Terms Act 1977 (see Brownsword and MacGowan at [1997] NLJ 1806; the response by S Ward at [1998] NLJ 7; and Brownsword and MacGowan's reply at [1998] NLJ 133)).

(b) The Consumer Credit Act 1974

The Consumer Credit Act 1974 may be relevant when considering the relationship between card-issuer and cardholder (for an extremely useful review of this area, see M Smith and P Robertson, 'Plastic Money' in M Brindle and R Cox (eds), *Law of Bank Payment* (4th edn, 2010), paras 4–060 ff). So far as payment cards are concerned, the Consumer Credit Act 1974, where it is applicable (as to which, see below), is relevant in three respects.

(1) Section 66 of the Act excludes the cardholder from liability under a credit-token agreement for use of a credit-token unless the credit-token has been previously accepted by the cardholder (either by signature of the card itself, or of a receipt for the card, or by first use of the card). Under s 51 of the Act it used to be an offence to give a person an unrequested credit-token (although this provision did not apply to replacements for cards already issued). Section 51 was repealed in 2014 when consumer credit regulation was transferred from the Office of Fair Trading to the Financial Conduct Authority (FCA), and its provisions were essentially replaced by FCA rules in the FCA Handbook (see Consumer Credit Sourcebook (CONC) 2.9—breach of which is not a criminal offence). Notwithstanding the repeal of s 51, it continues to have effect for the purposes of the Payment Services Regulations 2009, reg 52(a), so that it continues to apply in relation to regulated credit agreements in place of reg 58(1)(b) of those regulations.

(2) The Act imposes limits on the cardholder's liability for unauthorised use of the card by a third party (see below, Section 5).

(3) The Act imposes liability on the card-issuer for the supplier's breach of contract or misrepresentation in relation to goods or services paid for with the card (see below, Section 6).

'Credit-token' and 'credit-token agreements' Section 14(1) of the Act defines a credit-token to mean a card, cheque, voucher, coupon, stamp, form, booklet, or other document or thing given to an individual (ie not a company) by a person carrying on a consumer credit business, who undertakes:

> (a) that on production of it (whether or not some other action is also required) he will supply cash, goods and services (or any of them) on credit, or
>
> (b) that where, on the production of it to a third party (whether or not any other action is required), the third party supplies cash, goods and services (or any of them), he will pay the third party for them (whether or not deducting any discount or commission), in return for payment to him by the individual.

(Where s 14(1)(b) applies a deemed provision of credit arises under s 14(3).)

A credit-token agreement is defined by s 14(2) as a regulated agreement for the provision of credit in connection with the use of a credit-token.

There is some controversy as to which payment cards fall within the definition of a 'credit-token' and which are issued under 'credit-token agreements'. We shall look at each of the main types of payment cards in turn, remembering that each separate function of a multifunction card must be considered in the context of the Consumer Credit Act 1974.

(1) **Credit cards**—there is no doubt that credit cards fall within the statutory definition of a 'credit-token' whether they be 'two-party' cards, 'three-party' cards, or even 'four-party' cards (*OFT v Lloyd's TSB Bank plc* [2006] EWCA Civ 268, [2007] QB 1: no appeal on this issue before the House of Lords). However, a credit card can only be issued under a credit-token agreement where the contracting cardholder is an individual (ie not a company).

(2) **Charge cards**—generally, these are treated no differently to credit cards, save that they are exempt from the 'connected lender' liability under s 75 of the Act (see below, Section 6).

(3) **Debit cards**—the position with regard to debit cards is much less certain. It has been argued by some commentators that debit cards are not credit-tokens unless issued in connection with an overdraft facility (RM Goode, *Consumer Credit Law and Practice* (looseleaf), paras 1C[25.83]–[25.85]), and that, even if debit cards are credit-tokens, they are not issued under credit-token agreements (M Smith and P Robertson, 'Plastic Money' in M Brindle and R Cox (eds), *Law of Bank Payments* (4th edn, 2010), para 4–074, who argue that there is insufficient connection between the use of a debit card and the provision of credit to satisfy the s 14(2) definition of a credit-token agreement). However, we submit that a debit card falls within the definition of a credit-token set out in s 14(1)(b) of the 1974 Act because the card enables the cardholder to obtain goods or services from suppliers against the card-issuer's undertaking to pay those suppliers by way of debit from the cardholder's account. The fact that the supplier may have been admitted to the debit card scheme by a bank or other financial institution other than the card-issuing bank does not alter the situation. We further submit that the agreement under which a debit card is issued normally falls within the definition of a credit-token agreement set out in s 14(2); the link between the use of the debit card and the provision of credit being made through the operation of s 14(3) of the Act. Section 14(3) deems credit to have been given to the debit cardholder, which is drawn on whenever the card is used to obtain cash, goods, or services from a third party. The issue awaits judicial determination.

It is clear that if the cardholder has an overdraft facility then insofar as the card may be used to obtain goods or services from a supplier on credit, there will be a debtor-creditor-supplier agreement for unrestricted use credit and the issuer of the card will be subject to 'connected lender' liability under s 75 of the Consumer Credit Act 1974. But in an EFTPOS transaction, the EFTPOS arrangements between the suppliers and the card-issuers do not themselves give rise to a debtor–creditor–supplier agreement (s 187(3A) of the Consumer Credit Act 1974, as amended by s 89 of the Banking Act 1989), and so the card-issuer will not (merely because of those arrangements) be subject to liability under s 75 of the 1974 Act (see Section 6 below). Insofar as a debit card may be used to obtain cash, it will be a debtor–creditor agreement for unrestricted use credit. Insofar as the agreement allows the cardholder to overdraw on a current account, Part V of the Consumer Credit Act 1974 will apply, as modified in relation to such overdraft agreements by implementation of the Consumer Credit Directive 2008/48/EC through a series of statutory instruments.

(4) **ATM cards**—like debit cards, ATM cards can give rise to some uncertainty. An ATM card issued by a bank for use only in its own ATMs, and which only allows the customer to withdraw cash when his account is in credit, is not a credit-token. However, a card which can be used to make withdrawals against an overdraft facility or other form of credit is a

credit-token under s 14(1)(a) of the Consumer Credit Act 1974. Some ATMs function on the basis of the balance at the close of the day preceding the transaction. This may allow the customer to withdraw cash when his account is actually overdrawn. Although it has been argued that an ATM card is a credit-token in these circumstances (by Professor Lomnicka in EP Ellinger, E Lomnicka, and CVM Hare, *Ellinger's Modern Banking Law* (5th edn, 2011), p 666), the bank does not *undertake* to provide credit to the customer and so this conclusion must be doubted (all the more strongly where the terms of issue prohibit using the card when the account is, or will become, overdrawn). Where a bank issues an ATM card which can be used to make withdrawals from the machines of other banks and building societies under a shared ATM scheme, the card is probably a credit-token, unless the cash-dispensing bank or building society acts merely as the agent of the card-issuing bank (see above, p 634). But for a strongly argued case the other way, see Professor Lomnicka in *Ellinger's Modern Banking Law* (above), at p 666.

Although an ATM card may constitute a credit-token, it does not automatically follow that the agreement under which the card was issued will be a credit-token agreement. Where an ATM card can be used to withdraw cash from an account in debit, the card will only be issued under a credit-token agreement if there is sufficient connection between the card and the agreement to provide credit. This probably means that there will be no credit-token agreement within the meaning of s 14(2) unless the provision of an overdraft facility was actually a term of the agreement pursuant to which the ATM card was issued (M Smith and P Robertson, 'Plastic Money' in M Brindle and R Cox (eds), *Law of Bank Payments* (4th edn, 2010), para 4–075). The position may be different where the ATM card can be used to withdraw cash from machines of other banks and building societies under a shared ATM scheme. Unless the cash-dispensing bank or building society is simply regarded as being an agent of the card-issuing bank, the ATM card will be a credit-token under s 14(l)(b) and there will be a deemed provision of credit to the cardholder through the operation of s 14(3) of the 1974 Act. Credit is thereby provided in connection with the use of the ATM card and the agreement under which the card was issued would meet the s 14(2) definition of a credit-token agreement.

Until the issue is judicially resolved, there is likely to be some controversy as to whether an **electronic money (or digital cash) card** falls within the definition of a credit-token set out in s 14(1) of the Consumer Credit Act 1974. It could be argued that an electronic money card falls within para (b) of s 14(1), because the card enables the cardholder to obtain goods or services from a supplier who is himself entitled to demand conversion of 'electronic money' into real cash (ie into coins and bank notes, or into a credit to the supplier's bank account) by the card-issuer or merchant acquirer who admitted the supplier into the scheme. However, we submit that electronic money cards are more likely to be held to fall outside the statutory definition of a credit-token. There are two reasons for this. First, an electronic money card is a form of pre-payment card, whereby the cardholder pays for the card on issue. In no real sense is credit extended to him. Secondly, the words 'in return for payment to him by the individual' in s 14(l)(b) implies that the card-issuer undertakes to pay the supplier, with a right then to be reimbursed by the cardholder. By contrast, where an electronic money card is used to pay a supplier the card-issuer has already received payment from the cardholder in advance of the transaction. The fact that the cardholder may have used an overdraft facility to purchase the electronic money card in the first place does not affect the status of the card itself. The source of value must be distinguished from the issuance of the card.

(c) Payment Services Regulations 2009

When compared to the Consumer Credit Act 1974, there is greater certainty as to the application of the Payment Services Regulations 2009 (PSRs; SI 2009/209), to the range of payment cards considered in this chapter. The PSRs are relevant to credit cards, charge cards, debit cards, ATM cards, and electronic money cards (although exclusions operate for store cards issued by a retailer for use in its store and electronic money cards that can only be used in a limited number of outlets: PSRs Sch 1, Part 2, para 2(k)). Card-issuing agreements are 'framework contracts' for the purposes of the PSRs. Part 5 of the PSRs specifies certain information that must be provided by the card-issuer to the cardholder. Part 6 of the PSRs sets out the rights and obligations of the card-issuer and the cardholder, and in the next section of this chapter we shall consider those provisions of the PSRs that provide cardholders with protection for unauthorised use of their payment cards. There is scope for the card-issuer to contract out of all of the information provisions in Part 5 and most of the provisions in Part 6 (but some are mandatory: see especially regs 56–59, 61), but not where the 'payment services user' is a 'consumer', a 'micro-enterprise', or a 'charity' as defined in the PSRs (for definitions, see reg 2(1), which, inter alia, defines a 'consumer' as 'an individual … acting for purposes other than a trade, business or profession'). It is also important to note that if payment cards are issued under 'regulated agreements' within the meaning of the Consumer Credit Act 1974, the PSRs' consumer protection provisions are generally excluded insofar as they would otherwise duplicate provisions of the consumer credit regime (regs 34 and 52), and they are considerably modified in relation to certain 'low value payment instruments' (regs 35 and 53). There are special provisions in relating to unauthorised use of electronic money cards (reg 53(3)).

5 LIABILITY FOR UNAUTHORISED TRANSACTION

(a) Consumer Credit Act 1974

In certain circumstances the cardholder may be able to argue that his payment card is a 'credit-token' (the Consumer Credit Act 1974 (CCA), s 14(1): see Section 4(b) above), issued to him under a 'credit-token agreement' (CCA, s 14(2): see Section 4(b) above), and that his liability for unauthorised use should be limited under ss 83 and 84 of the CCA, in effect, to a maximum of £50 prior to notification to the card-issuer that the card is lost, stolen, or otherwise liable to misuse (the cardholder will not be liable for misuse of a card that is lost or stolen before being 'accepted' by him: s 66). On the other hand, the cardholder can be held liable for all loss occasioned through use of the card by a person who acquired possession of it with his consent (s 84(2)). However, after the card-issuer has been so notified in accordance with the provisions of s 84, the cardholder will not be liable for further loss arising from use of the card (s 84(3)). Moreover, where the Act applies and the cardholder claims that the use of his card was unauthorised, then under s 171(4)(b) of the CCA it is for the card-issuer to prove either that the use was authorised, or that the use occurred before the card-issuer had been given notice as stated above.

The protection offered by ss 83 and 84 of the CCA only applies to payment cards issued under credit-token agreements. Credit cards and charge cards are issued under credit-token agreements when issued to an individual (including a sole trader or small partnership). But there is some controversy as to whether debit cards and ATM cards are protected by these provisions (see Section 4(b) above). Electronic money cards are probably not covered by the protection offered by ss 83 and 84 (see Section 4(b) above).

(b) Payment Services Regulations 2009

Part 6 of the PSRs provides cardholders with protection against unauthorised use of a wider range of payment cards than is offered by the Consumer Credit Act 1974 (which may well only extend to credit cards and charge cards: see Section 4(b) above). Where the 1974 Act applies to the unauthorised use of a payment card issued under the terms of a regulated consumer credit agreement, certain regulations within the PSRs are disapplied and ss 66, 83, and 84 of the Act apply instead. However, the protection afforded by the PSRs is significant because they extend to payment cards that may not be caught by the CCA, for example debit cards, ATM cards, and electronic money cards.

Except in relation to agreements that are regulated by the CCA, where an executed payment transaction is not properly authorised, the card-issuer must immediately refund the amount of the unauthorised payment transaction to the cardholder and, where applicable, restore the debited payment account to the state it would have been in had the unauthorised payment transaction not taken place (PSRs, reg 61). In order to claim a refund or restoration of his account, the cardholder must notify the card-issuer without delay on becoming aware of the unauthorised nature of the transaction and, in any event, this must be done not later than 13 months after the debit date (reg 59(1), but not, according to reg 59(2), if the card-issuer had failed to comply with various information requirements in Part 5 of the PSRs). The onus is on the card-issuer to prove that the transaction was 'authenticated' (which is defined to mean the use of any procedure to verify the use of the card, including its personal security features: reg 60(2)), accurately recorded, and not affected by a technical breakdown or some other deficiency (reg 60(1)). The mere use of the card is not of itself necessarily sufficient to prove either that the transaction was authorised by the cardholder or that he acted fraudulently or failed with intent or gross negligence to keep his personal security features safe (reg 60(3)). These card-issuer obligations apply in relation to regulated agreements covered by the CCA (see *Ellinger's Modern Banking Law*, above, pp 675–677).

Regulation 57 places the cardholder under several express obligations, including that he must 'take all reasonable steps' to keep his personalised security features (eg his PIN) safe (reg 57(2)) and to notify the card-issuer 'in the agreed manner and without undue delay' once he has become aware of the loss, theft, misappropriation, or unauthorised use of the card (reg 57(1)(b)). Again, these obligations also apply even with regard to credit tokens covered by the CCA (see *Ellinger's Modern Banking Law*, above, pp 675–677). Except in the case of agreements that are regulated by the CCA, the cardholder is liable for all losses incurred in respect of an unauthorised payment transaction where he has (1) acted fraudulently, or (2) has with intent or gross negligence failed to comply with reg 57 (reg 62(2)), otherwise the cardholder's liability is limited to £50 at most (reg 62(1)). In certain circumstances, the non-fraudulent cardholder will not be liable for any losses incurred in respect of an unauthorised payment transaction, namely where the losses arose after notification to the issuer of the loss, theft, misappropriation, or unauthorised use of the card, where the issuer failed to provide him with the appropriate means for notification and where the card was used in connection with a 'distance contract' (other than an 'excepted contract': 'distance contract' and 'excepted contract' have the meanings given in the Consumer Protection (Distance Selling) Regulations 2000 (SI 2000/ 2334), regs 3, 5) (PSRs, reg 62(3)).

The card-issuer may contract out of most of the provisions in Part 6 of the PSRs (but some are mandatory: see especially regs 56–59, 61), but not where the 'payment services user' is a 'consumer', a 'micro-enterprise', or a 'charity' as defined in the PSRs (see Section 4(c) above).

6 CONNECTED LENDER LIABILITY

Section 75(1) of the CCA provides that 'if a debtor under a debtor-creditor-supplier agreement falling within section 12(b) or (c) of the Act has, in relation to a transaction financed by the agreement, any claim against the supplier in respect of a misrepresentation or breach of contract, he shall have a like claim against the creditor, who, with the supplier, shall accordingly be jointly and severally liable to the debtor'.[2] A 'like claim' does not include a right to rescind the credit agreement on the ground that the debtor is entitled to rescind the underlying supply contract, but the debtor can still rescind the credit agreement on the ground that it includes an implied term that it is conditional upon the survival of the supply agreement (*Durkin v DSG Retail Ltd* [2014] UKSC 21, [2014] 1 WLR 1148). In the context of payment cards, s 75 applies both to 'three-party' credit card transactions, where the cardholder uses a card to pay for goods/services from a supplier recruited to the scheme by the card-issuer, and to 'four-party' credit card transactions, where the supplier is recruited by a merchant acquirer who is not the card-issuer (*Office of Fair Trading v Lloyds TSB Bank plc* [2006] EWCA Civ 268, [2007] QB 1: there was no appeal on this point to the House of Lords; see also *Bank of Scotland v Truman* [2005] EWHC 583 (QB), [2005] CCLR 3, where a fifth party acted as agent for the supplier when processing credit card transactions). It does not apply to purchases made using a 'two-party' credit card (which fall under s 12(a), not s 12(b) or (c), of the Act), or a charge card (which is exempted by s 75(3)(c) of the CCA), or an EFTPOS debit card (which is expressly excluded from the operation of s 75 by s 187(3A) of the Act: as explained at p 637 above), or an ATM card (again, not a debtor–creditor–supplier agreement), or an electronic money card (again, not a debtor–creditor–supplier agreement). Where s 75 applies, so as to make the credit card-issuer liable to the cardholder who has contracted with the issuer (where an additional non-contracting cardholder uses the card s 75 does not apply), then the card-issuer is entitled to be indemnified by the supplier, subject to any agreement between them (s 75(2)). The cardholder has a claim against the issuer even if, in entering the transaction with the supplier, he has exceeded his credit limit or otherwise contravened the credit agreement (s 75(4)).

There is an important limitation to the availability of a s 75 claim against a card-issuer. By virtue of s 75(3), s 75(1) does not apply to a claim so far as the claim relates to any single item with a cash price not exceeding £100 or over £30,000 (the section also does not apply to a claim under a non-commercial agreement, but in practice this will never be the case in respect of a credit card agreement). (Where the cash value of goods or services is over £30,000 there

---

[2] For a comparative analysis of connected lender liability as part of consumer protection law in the UK, North America, and the EU, see EZ Lomnicka, 'Connected Lender Liability' in EZ Lomnicka and CGJ Morse (eds), *Contemporary Issues in Commercial Law—Essays in Honour of Professor AG Guest* (1997), pp 93–116.

may be creditor liability under s 75A of the CCA ('linked credit agreements') where there is a claim for breach of contract (only) against the supplier and the debtor has taken steps to exhaust his remedies against the supplier. There are a number of other qualifying conditions set out in s 75A.) However, it should be noted that a claim may be made where a credit card is used to make part payment of less than £100 in respect of an item priced over £100. It has been unclear for some time as to whether s 75(1) extends to a claim by a cardholder in respect of a transaction made abroad with a foreign supplier when the supply transaction is governed by a foreign law. In *Office of Fair Trading v Lloyds TSB Bank plc* [2007] UKHL 48, [2008] 1 AC 316, the House of Lords held that s 75(1) does indeed apply to foreign transactions (but for unresolved issues, see C Hare [2008] LMCLQ 333 at 338). Their Lordships felt that such an interpretation was consistent with the principles that lay behind the recommendation of the Crowther Committee on Consumer Credit in 1971 that there should be connected lender liability in future consumer credit legislation (which appeared as s 75(1) in the 1974 Act). Lord Mance (at [29]) considered that, in relation to overseas transactions, there was an even greater discrepancy than in domestic transactions between the cardholder's ability to pursue suppliers on the one hand and the ease with which card-issuers could obtain redress through contractual and commercial ties which Crowther contemplated would link them together. His Lordship concluded that '[c]ard issuers' ability to bear irrecoverable losses and so "spread the burden" exists in relation to both overseas and domestic transactions'. It remains the case, however, that the cardholder must still be able to prove that he has a valid claim under the foreign law against the foreign supplier in respect of misrepresentation or breach of contract if he is to have a claim against the UK card-issuer under s 75(1). For a critical assessment of the applicability of s 75 to credit card transactions, see C Bisping [2011] JBL 457.

The other important connected lender liability provision set out in the Consumer Credit Act 1974 is that found in s 56. By virtue of s 56(2), where negotiations ('antecedent negotiations') are conducted with the debtor (ie the cardholder who contracts with the card-issuer) by the supplier in relation to a transaction financed or proposed to be financed by a debtor–creditor–supplier agreement within s 12(b) or (c) (ie by a 'three-party' or 'four-party' credit card), they are deemed to be conducted by the supplier ('the negotiator') in the capacity as agent of the creditor (ie the card-issuer) as well as in his actual capacity. Through this provision the card-issuer may become liable for any pre-contractual misrepresentation by the supplier, quite apart from the provisions of s 75 (see *Scotland v British Credit Trust Ltd* [2014] EWCA Civ 790, [2015] 1 All ER (Comm) 401). In fact s 56 appears to be broader in its application than s 75 in at least two respects. First, s 56 is not restricted by any monetary limitations as found in s 75(3). Secondly, whereas s 75 is limited to imposing liability on the creditor for the supplier's breach of contract or misrepresentation, there is no such limitation where the supplier is deemed to have conducted negotiations as the creditor's agent under s 56. Thus, Professor Goode highlights the significance of s 56 where the supplier has delivered, in advance of the transaction being completed or paid for (ie while 'antecedent negotiations' as still taking place), dangerous goods which cause physical damage to the cardholder's property (RM Goode, *Consumer Credit Law and Practice* (looseleaf), para IC[32.19]).

QUESTION

Joe applies for and obtains a credit card from his bank, Trust Bank Ltd, which he uses to purchase a dishwasher from Eleco Stores at a cost of £500. After two weeks the dishwasher malfunctions, due to a design fault, and floods his kitchen causing considerable damage. When Joe goes round to Eleco Stores to complain, he finds that it has closed down.

Advise Joe as to any remedy he may have against his bank.

How, if at all, would it affect your answer in each of the following alternative scenarios:

(1) Joe paid £450 in cash and £50 using his credit card;

(2) the dishwasher had been purchased by Joe's wife, Sue, using a second credit card issued to her by the bank under the terms of its agreement with Joe;

(3) Joe had applied for his card in the name of his company, JJ Contractors Ltd;

(4) Eleco Stores had not been recruited to the credit card scheme by Trust Bank, but by a different merchant acquirer;

(5) Joe had used his credit card to buy the dishwasher from a store in France.

CHAPTER 18

NEGOTIABLE INSTRUMENTS

1 INTRODUCTION

As you enter the world of negotiable instruments you could be forgiven for thinking that you are travelling back in time.[1] The modern world is dominated by the microchip and instantaneous telecommunication networks which have allowed the development of electronic payment systems capable of transferring vast sums around the globe at the touch of a button. Negotiable instruments are at the other end of the spectrum. The tangible nature of the instrument (a piece of paper) dominates the intangible right to payment embodied in the instrument. Transfer of the right to payment requires physical delivery of the instrument itself. This can be a slow and cumbersome process. Negotiable instruments seem to be redolent of a bygone age.

However, negotiable instruments merit our attention for two important reasons. First, they are still used as a method of making payment in the commercial world, especially in the area of international trade (see below, Chapter 21). Bills of exchange, one type of negotiable instrument, were for centuries the principal method of payment in international trade. Their popularity stemmed from the fact that they combine the characteristics of negotiability (see below, p 648) and autonomy (see below, p 655). Today, electronic payment mechanisms mean that bills of exchange are less commonly used, but they remain important in trade with a number of countries, particularly in Africa, the Indian sub-continent, and the Pacific (M Brindle and R Cox (eds), *Law of Bank Payments* (4th edn, 2010), para 6–004). The second reason for examining the law relating to negotiable instruments is because it encapsulates many of the fundamental principles and concepts of commercial law in general:

---

[1] See, generally, E McKendrick, *Goode on Commercial Law* (5th edn, 2016), Part 3. For detailed analysis, see AG Guest, *Chalmers and Guest on Bills of Exchange, Cheques and Promissory Notes* (17th edn, 2009); N Elliott, J Odgers, and JM Phillips, *Byles on Bills of Exchange and Cheques* (29th edn, 2013). J Barnard Byles, who wrote the first edition of his treatise of the law of bills of exchange in 1829, was responsible for what may be the only bills and notes joke. He is said to have named his horse 'Bills' so that as he rode up people could say 'Here comes Byles on Bills'! (JS Rogers, *The Early History of the Law of Bills and Notes: A Study of the Origins of Anglo-American Commercial Law* (1995), p 7: and see *Rogers* generally for historical development, together with B Geva, *The Payment Order of Antiquity and the Middle Ages: A Legal History* (2011), Ch 11). For an outstanding comparative treatment of the subject, see EP Ellinger, 'Negotiable Instruments' in U Drobnig (ed), *International Encyclopedia of Comparative Law* (2000), Vol IX, Ch 4.

- Mercantile custom and usage has been, and remains, an important influence in this area. It was, after all, the fact that the common law refused to recognise the transferability of a debt that led commercial men to embody the debt in a chattel (a piece of paper) and render the debt transferable through transfer of the chattel.

- Nowhere is certainty more prized than in the law relating to negotiable instruments. In *Carlos v Fancourt* (1794) 5 Term Rep 482 at 486, Ashhurst J stated that '[c]ertainty is a great object in commercial instruments; and unless they carry their own validity on the face of them, they are not negotiable . . .'. This requirement ensures that negotiable instruments are freely negotiable and saleable and it lies at the heart of the definition of a bill of exchange contained in s 3(1) of the Bills of Exchange Act 1882.

- Protection of the bona fide purchaser for value is paramount. It is a fundamental principle of the law relating to negotiable instruments that the bona fide holder for value of a negotiable instrument is able to acquire a better title than that of his transferor. Negotiable instruments represent a major exception to the *nemo dat* rule (see above, Chapter 10, Section 1). The marketability of the instrument is enhanced through the protection afforded to the good faith purchaser.

2 DEFINITION OF A NEGOTIABLE INSTRUMENT

There is no statutory definition of the term 'negotiable instrument'. Any definition must be drawn from the common law. To define the term, the concepts of 'instrument' and 'negotiability' require separate consideration.

(a) Instrument

An instrument is a document which physically embodies a payment obligation so that the possessor of the instrument (following any necessary indorsement in his favour) is presumed to be entitled to claim payment of the money it represents. It has been described as 'a document of title to money' (E McKendrick, *Goode on Commercial Law* (5th edn, 2016), p 517) and must be distinguished from a document of title to goods, such as a bill of lading. To be a document of title to money an instrument must contain an undertaking to pay a sum of money (eg as in a promissory note) or an order to another to pay a sum of money to the person giving the order or a third person (eg as in a bill of exchange). Alternatively, the undertaking or order may relate to the delivery of a security for money (*Goodwin v Robarts* (1876) 1 App Cas 476). A document which is primarily a receipt for money, even if coupled with a promise to pay it, is not an instrument (*Akbar Khan v Attar Singh* [1936] 2 All ER 545, PC; applied in *Claydon v Bradley* [1987] 1 All ER 522, CA).

If an instrument is made payable to bearer, or if it is made payable to a specified person or his order and it has been indorsed (ie signed on the back) by or with the authority of that person, it is described as being 'in a deliverable state'. The possessor, otherwise known as the 'holder', of an instrument in a deliverable state is presumed to be entitled to payment of the money due under it. This is because the instrument embodies the contractual right to payment and that right is transferable by mere delivery.

'The Nature of the Negotiable Instrument' by A Barak
(1983) 18 Israel LR 49 at 53–55, 57–58, 60–63, 65

III. THE NEGOTIABLE INSTRUMENT AS A CHATTEL

(a) Rights on and to the negotiable instrument

In discussing the negotiable instrument one refers not only to rights on it, but also to rights in, or to it. While this is not accurate terminology from a strictly juridical point of view, it does reflect the proprietary character of the negotiable instrument. The negotiable instrument is a physically tangible thing, and just as one speaks of ownership of, or title to, a chair or a car, so one can speak of ownership of a negotiable instrument. . . .

(b) Consequences of the proprietary nature of the negotiable instrument

The negotiable instrument is, then, seen to be a chattel. Its owner has the same powers as the owner of any other property. He can retain possession of it, sell it, transfer it, give it away as a gift, destroy it, or alter it. These actions may, of course, affect the very ownership of the instrument or its value. When the owner of the instrument has possession of it, there is a unity of ownership and possession. This, however, is not essential and the two can equally well be in separate hands. For example, an instrument to the order of A is stolen from him. A remains the owner, but the thief has possession. When possession is unlawfully separated from ownership, the law of conversion comes into operation and gives the owner—who is entitled to immediate possession—the right to demand restitution of the instrument or its value. But, of course, possession can also be separated from ownership lawfully when, for example, the owner delivers it into the custody of another person for safekeeping or as a deposit. . . .

(c) The negotiable instrument as a special kind of chattel

It cannot be denied that the negotiable instrument is unlike other chattels. One does not refer to it as a chattel naturally and as a matter of course. Its proprietary nature is not its most important side, for its inherent value as a chattel is negligible. The real value of the negotiable instrument lies in the obligations it embodies. A legal system in which the proprietary nature of the negotiable instrument is hardly stressed at all is conceivable. It is not absolutely essential to dwell on the instrument's proprietary qualities. Reference to it as a chattel in the common law countries is for the purpose of attaining certain results. Just as a chattel can be transferred from hand to hand, so too can a negotiable instrument be transferred, since it is itself a chattel. However, it embodies an obligation and, by transferring the chattel, one transfers the obligation as well. Thus, it was possible to transfer the obligation embodied in a negotiable instrument at a time when ordinary obligations could not, as a rule, be transferred.

> The common law did not recognize the transferability of a debt, but accepted that the owner of a chattel could sell, pledge or deliver it to someone else at will. If the debt be given the outward appearance of a chattel, why should it not be transferable just as a chattel is? Why should such a debt not be subject to the law of property which allows a chattel to be transferred from hand to hand without difficulty? While the law remained steadfast in its refusal to allow the transfer of debts, men of commerce came to grasp that, by giving a debt the qualities of a chattel, the problem of freely transferring it would be solved. [Sussman, *The Law of Bills of Exchange* (6th edn, 1983), p 4.]

Today, reference to the negotiable instrument as a chattel has further consequences—for example, the possibility of resorting to the law of conversion when the instrument is taken from its owner unlawfully . . .

IV. THE NEGOTIABLE INSTRUMENT AS AN OBLIGATION

(a) The negotiable instrument as a new and independent obligation

In most cases bills are drawn in the course of commercial transactions between the parties. When A draws a bill to the order of B the reason generally is that A owes B money, either on account of a loan which B has given him, or of goods supplied to him by B. In cases of this kind, the instrument is evidence of the existence of A's liability to B. The obligation does not derive from the instrument itself, but from the initial transaction between the two. However, the instrument is not merely a piece of evidence. A's signature on it creates a new and independent obligation, whereby A is liable to B and to any person to whom B transfers the instrument. This obligation is in addition to—and often even in place of—that deriving from the initial transaction. Accordingly, if a bill, given by A to B as a conditional discharge of the initial transaction, is dishonoured, B has two causes of action: one on the initial transaction between him and A; the other on the obligation created by the instrument itself. Insofar as the former is concerned, the instrument is no more than written evidence. As for the latter, the initial transaction constitutes the consideration. Thus, by virtue of the signatures on it, the negotiable instrument creates a new and independent obligation, completely different from the obligation deriving from the initial transaction. Moreover, the instrument does not only give rise to one single obligation; there are as many obligations as there are signatures on it—some of them primary obligations, some secondary.

(b) The negotiable instrument as a contract

The wording of the Bills of Exchange Ordinance clearly indicates that the obligation on a bill is a contract. This contract, however, is—it will be noted—unilateral, not bilateral. There is no mutual exchange of undertakings and only one party is liable on such a contract; the rules of offer and acceptance do not apply to it. True, the contract on a negotiable instrument is not complete until the instrument is delivered 'in order to give effect thereto'; but delivery is not the same as acceptance of an offer in the law of contract.

Frequently, a negotiable instrument is made within the framework of a bilateral contract. For example, A undertakes to sell goods to B and in consideration B gives A a bill. That is a bilateral contract; but the bill has an existence of its own. Once it has been made, an additional contract arises—that on the bill itself. If B fails to pay the bill, A will generally have two contractual remedies—one based on the bilateral contract, the other on the bill. There is, of course, a close connection between the two contracts: payment of the bill discharges the bilateral contract; failure on the part of A to perform his undertaking under the bilateral contract may provide B with a defence to an action brought on the bill. But this connection must not be allowed to blur the material difference between the two or hide the fact that the bill has a separate existence of its own as a unilateral contract.

(c) Consequences of the contractual nature of the negotiable instrument

Subject to the special rules which follow from the negotiability of the instrument, the obligation on it is just like any other contractual obligation to pay a certain sum of money. Thus, capacity to incur liability as a party to a bill is coextensive with capacity to contract. Events which invalidate contracts generally, also invalidate liability on a bill. Defences available under the general law of contract, such as duress, fraud, failure of consideration and so on, are equally a part of the law of negotiable instruments. It is a well-known fact that the plea of *non est factum*, so common in the law of contract, was first raised in a case concerning a negotiable instrument. The contractual nature of the negotiable instrument is similarly reflected in the application of the doctrine of consideration. A number of legal systems, in which consideration is essential for the creation of contractual liability, make consideration a prerequisite of liability on a negotiable instrument too—since that liability is itself a form of contractual liability. On the other hand, systems in which consideration is not one of the elements of the contract, and which require no more than *causa* for example, are found to forgo the need for consideration and make do with *causa* in the case of liability on a negotiable instrument too.

Since the obligations on a negotiable instrument are contractual obligations, there is nothing to prevent the guarantor known to the general law of contract being used in this connection. And, indeed, the ordinary rules applicable to the relations between guarantor and the person to whom he gives the guarantee do apply in the case of negotiable instruments as well. These obligations are, moreover, themselves divisible into principal and secondary obligations, the latter being by way of guarantee for the performance of the former. Accordingly, the relations between the two are governed by the general rules of guarantee.

Again, the fact that the obligations we are considering are contractual obligations, which—by their very nature—are transferable, means that, in principle, there is no reason why they cannot be transferred from one person to another in accordance with the rules of assignment applicable to ordinary contractual obligations. And, in fact, this is the position in English Law . . .

(d) The negotiable instrument as a special kind of contract

While the obligation on a negotiable instrument is of a contractual nature, what characterises it is the fact that it is 'negotiable'. Accordingly, apart from being transferable under the general law of contract, it can be transferred in the special manner established by the law merchant—namely, by negotiation . . .

(b) Negotiability

The holder may not be the 'true owner' of the instrument. The true owner is the person entitled to the property in and possession of the instrument against all others. But the true owner may have lost the instrument, or it may have been stolen from him. The 'holder' of the instrument would be the finder or the thief who is in possession of it (assuming the instrument is in a deliverable state). Figure 18.1 illustrates how one person can be the 'true owner' and another the 'holder' of a stolen instrument (note that the instrument is in a deliverable state because it is made payable to bearer).

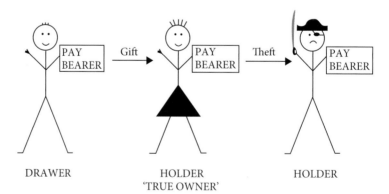

Figure 18.1 'True owner' and 'holder'

In Figure 18.1, the true owner has a superior title to the instrument and, relying on the fact that the instrument is a chattel, she can sue the holder in conversion. However, should the instrument reach the hands of a holder who gave value for the instrument, in good faith and without notice of the defect in the title of his transferor, that person takes an indefeasible title to the instrument. The true owner has no claim against her. But the instrument must be a *negotiable* instrument for the bona fide purchaser to take an indefeasible title to it. Figure 18.2 illustrates how a bona fide purchaser for value (called a 'holder in due course' in the Bills of Exchange Act 1882) may take possession of a stolen instrument and acquire a better title than her transferor.

DRAWER   HOLDER   HOLDER   HOLDER IN DUE COURSE
'TRUE OWNER'   (NO TITLE)   (BONA FIDE PURCHASER FOR
VALUE WITHOUT NOTICE OF
DEFECT IN TITLE)

Figure 18.2 Negotiability

It is its capacity to be acquired free from defects in the title of prior parties which character-ises an instrument as 'negotiable' in the strict sense of the word.

Crouch v Credit Foncier of England
(1873) LR 8 QB 374, Court of Queen's Bench

> **Blackburn J**: In the present case the plaintiff has taken upon himself the burden of establishing both that the property in the debenture passed to him by delivery, and that the right to sue in his own name was transferred to him.
>
> The two propositions are very much connected, but not identical. The holder of an overdue bill or note may confer the right on the transferee to sue in his own name, but he conveys no better title than he had himself. So the assignee of a Scotch bond, which is assignable by the law of Scotland, may sue in his own name in the courts of this country: see *Innes v Dunlop* ((1800) 8 Term Rep 595); but he has not a better title than those from whom he took the bond, unless, perhaps, if the contract is by the law of Scotland not merely assignable but also negotiable. As to this, in *Dixon v Bovill* ((1856) 3 Macq 1 at 16), Lord Cranworth, then Lord Chancellor, in delivering the judgment of the House of Lords in a Scotch case as to iron scrip notes, says, 'I have no hesitation in saying, that independently of the law merchant and of positive statute, within neither of which classes do these scrip notes range themselves, the law does not, either in Scotland or in England, enable any man by a written engagement to give a floating right of action at the suit of any one into whose hands the writing may come, and who may thus acquire a right of action better than the right of him under whom he derives title'.
>
> But the two questions go very much together; and, indeed, in the notes to *Miller v Race* ((1758) 1 Burr 452, 1 Smith LC (13th edn, 1929), pp 452, 533), where all the authorities are collected, the very learned author says: 'It may therefore be laid down as a safe rule that where an instrument is by the custom of trade transferable, like cash, by delivery, and is also capable

of being sued upon by the person holding it *pro tempore*, then it is entitled to the name of a *negotiable instrument*, and the property in it passes to a bona fide transferee for value, though the transfer may not have taken place in market overt. But that if either of the above requisites be wanting, ie, if it be either not accustomably transferable, or, though it be accustomably transferable, yet, if its nature be such as to render it incapable of being put in suit by the party holding it *pro tempore*, it is not a *negotiable instrument*, nor will delivery of it pass the property of it to a vendee, however bona fide, if the transferor himself have not a good title to it, and the transfer be made out of market overt.'

Bills of exchange and promissory notes, whether payable to order or to bearer, are by the law merchant negotiable in both senses of the word. The person who, by a genuine indorsement, or, where it is payable to bearer, by a delivery, becomes holder, may sue in his own name on the contract, and if he is a bona fide holder for value, he has a good title notwithstanding any defect of title in the party (whether indorser or deliverer) from whom he took it . . .

NOTES

1.   According to Blackburn J a negotiable instrument has two characteristics, namely: (1) it is 'transferable, like cash, by delivery' (which assumes it is in a deliverable state) so that the transferee can enforce the rights embodied in it in his own name; and (2) the transferee, being a bona fide holder for value, can acquire a better title to it than that of his transferor.

2.   By contrast, a bill of lading in a deliverable state is transferable by delivery and so can be described as 'negotiable' in one sense of the word. But it is not 'negotiable' in the strict sense as it cannot pass a title free from equities of prior parties: *Kum v Wah Tat Bank Ltd* [1971] 1 Lloyd's Rep 439 at 446, per Lord Diplock, PC. Cf C Debattista, *Sale of Goods Carried by Sea* (2nd edn, 1998), paras 3–15 to 3–27, who argues that a bill of lading can be described as 'negotiable' in the strict sense of the word because, under the Factors Act 1889 and ss 24 and 25 of the Sale of Goods Act 1979, its transferee may be able to take a better title to the goods it represents than his transferor had. For a comprehensive rebuttal of Debattista's theory, see A Tettenborn [1991] LMCLQ 538 at 541–542. However, note that under s 47(2) of the Sale of Goods Act 1979 a bona fide transferee for value of a bill of lading may defeat an unpaid seller's right of stoppage in transit even though the right of stoppage may have been valid against his transferor.

3.   The distinction between using the term 'negotiable' to mean 'transferable' and using it in its strict sense was made clear by Bowen LJ in *Simmons v London Joint Stock Bank* [1891] 1 Ch 270 at 294 when he said that:

A negotiable instrument payable to bearer is one which, by the custom of trade, passes from hand to hand by delivery, and the holder of which for the time being, if he is a *bona fide* holder for value without notice, has a good title, notwithstanding any defect of title in the person from whom he took it. A contractual document in other words may be such that, by virtue of its delivery, all the rights of the transferor are transferred to and can be enforced by the transferee against the original contracting party, but it may yet fall short of being a completely negotiable instrument, because the transferee acquires by mere delivery no better title than his transferor.

See s 8(1) of the Bills of Exchange Act 1882, and s 6(2) of the Cheques Act 1957, for examples of when the term 'negotiable' is used only in the sense of 'transferable'.

(c) A composite definition

In summary, a 'negotiable instrument' is a document of title embodying rights to the payment of money or a security for money, which, by custom or legislation, is: (1) transferable by delivery (or by indorsement and delivery) in such a way that the holder *pro tempore* may sue on it in his own name and in his own right; and (2) a bona fide transferee for value may acquire a good and complete title to the document and the rights embodied therein, notwithstanding that his predecessor had a defective title or no title at all (adopted from DV Cowen and L Gering, *Cowen on the Law of Negotiable Instruments in South Africa* (5th edn, 1985), Vol 1, p 52).

QUESTIONS

1.   Negotiable instruments are one of the most important exceptions to the *nemo dat* rule. Why should they be given such a privileged status? See Chafee (1918) 31 Harvard LR 1104 at 1146.

2.   Can the bona fide transferee for value of a non-negotiable instrument ever take the instrument free from defects in the title of his transferor? See *Goodwin v Robarts* (1876) 1 App Cas 476 at 489, HL; *Easton v London Joint Stock Bank* (1886) 34 Ch D 95 at 113–114, CA; *Colonial Bank v Cady and Williams* (1890) 15 App Cas 267 at 285, HL.

3 HOW INSTRUMENTS COME TO BE NEGOTIABLE

There are two ways in which documents may come to be recognised as negotiable instruments: (1) statute; and (2) mercantile usage.

(a) Statute

In most, perhaps all, cases statutory recognition of negotiability merely confirms previous judicial acceptance of a mercantile usage which recognised an instrument as negotiable. For example, bills of exchange and cheques were accepted as negotiable by the courts before they were recognised as such by the Bills of Exchange Act 1882.

There has been some debate as to whether the Promissory Notes Act 1704 made promissory notes negotiable when that had not previously been the case, or whether it was merely declaratory of the law as it stood before Lord Holt's landmark decision in *Clerke v Martin* (1702) 2 Ld Raym 757. In that case Lord Holt held that a promissory note payable to order was not a bill of exchange, and was, therefore, not negotiable. He said:

> . . . that this note could not be a bill of exchange. That the maintaining of these actions upon such notes, were innovations upon the rules of the common law; and that it amounted to the setting up a new sort of specialty, unknown to the common law, and invented in Lombard Street, which attempted in these matters of bills of exchange to give laws to Westminster Hall. That the continuing to declare upon these notes upon the custom of merchants proceeded from obstinacy and opinionativeness, since he had always expressed his opinion against them, and since there was so easy a method, as to declare upon a general *indebitatus assumpsit* for money lent, etc . . .

Most commentators have interpreted this decision as wrong and have held the 1704 Act to be declaratory of the case law as it existed prior to *Clerke v Martin* (for a judicial statement to this effect, see *Goodwin v Robarts* (1875) LR 10 Exch 337 at 350, per Cockburn CJ delivering the judgment of the Exchequer Chamber). But Professor Holden has argued that Lord Holt's decision was correct and that promissory notes had not been recognised as negotiable prior to his decision (J Milnes Holden, *The History of Negotiable Instruments in English Law* (1955), pp 79–84). If Holden is right then the 1704 Act was constitutive of negotiability. (For a strong defence of Lord Holt, see JS Rogers, *The Early History of the Law of Bills and Notes: A Study of the Origins of Anglo-American Commercial Law* (1995), pp 179–186.)

(b) Mercantile usage

Instruments may be regarded as negotiable through judicially recognised mercantile usage.

Goodwin v Robarts

(1875) LR 10 Exch 337, Exchequer Chamber

Through his stockbroker Goodwin purchased certain Russian and Hungarian government scrip. The scrip promised to give the bearer, after all instalments had been paid, a bond for the amount paid, with interest. Goodwin allowed his stockbroker to retain possession of the scrip and the stockbroker fraudulently pledged it with the defendant bankers as security for a loan. The stockbroker went bankrupt and the bankers sold the scrip. Goodwin brought an action against the bankers to recover the amount realised on the sale. The bankers argued that through mercantile usage such scrip had been treated as negotiable by delivery so that Goodwin had lost his title to it. The judgment of the Exchequer Chamber was delivered by Cockburn CJ.

> **Cockburn CJ**: . . . The substance of [the defendants'] argument is, that, because the scrip does not correspond with any of the forms of the securities for money which have been hitherto held to be negotiable by the law merchant, and does not contain a direct promise to pay money, but only a promise to give security for money, it is not a security to which, by the law merchant, the character of negotiability can attach.
>
> Having given the fullest consideration to this argument, we are of opinion that it cannot prevail. It is founded on the view that the law merchant thus referred to is fixed and stereotyped, and incapable of being expanded and enlarged so as to meet the wants and requirements of trade in the varying circumstances of commerce. It is true that the law merchant is sometimes spoken of as a fixed body of law, forming part of the common law, and as it were coeval with it. But as a matter of legal history, this view is altogether incorrect. The law merchant thus spoken of with reference to bills of exchange and other negotiable securities, though forming part of the general body of the lex mercatoria, is of comparatively recent origin. It is neither more nor less than the usages of merchants and traders in the different departments of trade, ratified by the decisions of Courts of law, which, upon such usages being proved before them, have adopted them as settled law with a view to the interests of trade and the public convenience, the Court proceeding herein on the well-known principle of law that, with reference to transactions in the different departments of trade, Courts of law, in giving effect to the contracts and dealings of the parties, will assume that the latter have dealt with one another on the footing of any custom or usage prevailing generally in the particular department. By this process, what before was usage only, unsanctioned by legal decision, has become engrafted upon, or incorporated into, the common law, and may thus be

said to form part of it. 'When a general usage has been judicially ascertained and established,' says Lord Campbell, in *Brandao v Barnett* ((1846) 12 Cl & Fin 787 at 805), 'it becomes a part of the law merchant, which Courts of justice are bound to know and recognise.'

[Cockburn CJ then traced the history of how bills of exchange, promissory notes, bankers' notes, exchequer bills, and cheques came to be regarded as negotiable and continued:]

It thus appears that all these instruments which are said to have derived their negotiability from the law merchant had their origin, and that at no very remote period, in mercantile usage, and were adopted into the law by our Courts as being in conformity with the usages of trade; of which, if it were needed, a further confirmation might be found in the fact that, according to the old form of declaring on bills of exchange, the declaration always was founded on the custom of merchants.

Usage, adopted by the Courts, having been thus the origin of the whole of the so-called law merchant as to negotiable securities, what is there to prevent our acting upon the principle acted upon by our predecessors, and followed in the precedents they have left to us? Why is it to be said that a new usage which has sprung up under altered circumstances, is to be less admissible than the usages of past times? Why is the door to be now shut to the admission and adoption of usage in a matter altogether of cognate character, as though the law had been finally stereotyped and settled by some positive and peremptory enactment?

[Cockburn CJ then distinguished several cases relied on by Goodwin and continued:]

We must by no means be understood as saying that mercantile usage, however extensive, should be allowed to prevail if contrary to positive law, including in the latter such usages as, having been made the subject of legal decision, and having been sanctioned and adopted by the Courts, have become, by such adoption, part of the common law. To give effect to a usage which involves a defiance or disregard of the law would be obviously contrary to a fundamental principle. And we quite agree that this would apply quite as strongly to an attempt to set up a new usage against one which has become settled and adopted by the common law as to one in conflict with the more ancient rules of the common law itself . . .

If we could see our way to the conclusion that, in holding the scrip in question to pass by delivery, and to be available to bearer, we were giving effect to a usage incompatible either with the common law or with the law merchant as incorporated into and embodied in it, our decision would be a very different one from that which we are about to pronounce. But so far from this being the case, we are, on the contrary, in our opinion, only acting on an established principle of that law in giving legal effect to a usage, now become universal, to treat this form of security, being on the face of it expressly made transferable to bearer, as the representative of money, and as such, being made to bearer, as assignable by delivery. This being the conclusion at which we have arrived, the judgment of the Court of Exchequer will be affirmed.

[The House of Lords upheld the judgment of the Court of Exchequer Chamber and approved the *ratio decidendi* of that decision: (1876) 1 App Cas 476.]

NOTES

1. Compare the willingness of Cockburn CJ to ratify mercantile usage with the unwillingness of Lord Holt to do the same in *Clerke v Martin* (above, p 651). WS Holdsworth remarked that one of the effects of *Clerke v Martin*, and its statutory reversal in the Promissory Notes Act 1704, was to teach the courts that 'they could not wholly ignore approved mercantile custom; that they must adapt their rules to such customs; that in fact there were cases in which Lombard Street must be allowed to give laws to Westminster Hall' (WS Holdsworth,

A History of English Law (5th edn, 1942), Vol VIII, p 176). Chorley went so far as to say that Cockburn CJ's statements on the judicial recognition of mercantile usage 'should be inscribed in letters of gold in every Court handling commercial litigation': (1932) 48 LQR 51 at 55.

2. Even if the usage is of recent origin the courts will still recognise it (*Bechuanaland Exploration Co v London Trading Bank Ltd* [1898] 2 QB 658). As Bigham J stated in *Edelstein v Schuler & Co* [1902] 2 KB 144 at 154:

> . . . but it is to be remembered that in these days usage is established much more quickly than it was in days gone by; more depends on the number of the transactions which help to create it than on the time over which the transactions are spread . . .

3. Before a court will recognise an instrument as negotiable through mercantile usage the following conditions must be satisfied:

(a) the usage must be 'reasonable, certain and notorious': *Devonald v Rosser & Sons* [1906] 2 KB 728 at 743, per Farwell LJ, CA;

(b) the usage must be general and not 'a custom or habit which prevails only in a particular market or particular section of the commercial world': *Easton v London Joint Stock Bank* (1886) 34 Ch D 95 at 113, per Bowen LJ, CA; reversed on a different point sub nom *Sheffield (Earl of) v London Joint Stock Bank* (1888) 13 App Cas 333; and

(c) the instrument's terms must not be incompatible with negotiability (eg not marked 'non-negotiable') nor stated to be transferable by some method other than delivery: *London and County Banking Co Ltd v London and River Plate Bank Ltd* (1887) 20 QBD 232 at 239, per Manisty J.

QUESTION

Unless recognised as negotiable by statute or mercantile usage, an instrument cannot be made negotiable simply by an express specification to that effect in its terms (*Crouch v Credit Fonder of England* (1873) LR 8 QB 374 at 386, per Blackburn J). Why? What advantage would there be in recognising such an instrument as negotiable?

4 TYPES OF NEGOTIABLE INSTRUMENT

Negotiable instruments include the following documents:

(1) bills of exchange;

(2) cheques;

(3) promissory notes;

(4) bank notes;

(5) treasury bills;

(6) banker's drafts;

(7) dividend warrants;

(8) share warrants;

(9) bearer scrip;

(10)   bearer debentures;

(11)   bearer bonds;

(12)   floating rate notes;

(13)   certificates of deposit.

The following documents are not negotiable instruments:

(1)   bills of lading;

(2)   dock warrants;

(3)   delivery orders;

(4)   postal or money orders;

(5)   registered share certificates;

(6)   registered debentures;

(7)   insurance policies;

(8)   IOUs.

The list is not closed. New instruments may be recognised as negotiable at any time through statute or mercantile usage.

5 ADVANTAGES OF A NEGOTIABLE INSTRUMENT

Before 1874 the assignment of a promise to pay money was not permitted (apart from limited exceptions) at common law. It was the refusal of the common law to allow the transfer of promises to pay money which contributed to the use of negotiable instruments to achieve that end. Only with the enactment of s 25(6) of the Supreme Court of Judicature Act 1873 have promises to pay money been generally assignable at law (since repealed and substantially re-enacted by s 136 of the Law of Property Act 1925: see below, Chapter 22). However, there remain a number of distinct advantages in embodying a payment obligation in a negotiable instrument and transferring it by delivery (or delivery and indorsement) rather than merely assigning the obligation under the 1925 Act. These advantages can be summarised as follows:

(1)   the transferee of a negotiable instrument can sue in his own name, even though there has been no assignment in writing, or notice to the obligor or even if the transfer is not absolute, as required for assignments under the statute; and

(2)   the transferee of a negotiable instrument who takes it for value and in good faith acquires a good title free from equities, whereas an assignee under the statute always takes subject to equities.

The ease with which a negotiable instrument can be transferred, and the security of title which it can provide, means it can be readily sold to raise cash before the payment obligation on the instrument becomes due.

Even if the payee does not intend to transfer the payment obligation there are advantages in receiving payment by means of a negotiable instrument. As the instrument embodies its own payment obligation divorced from the underlying transaction from which it originates, payment under the instrument, at least in theory, becomes certain, regardless of any breach of that underlying transaction. The principle of autonomy of the payment obligation, central to the marketability of the instrument, will benefit even the original payee. This has led bills of exchange to be treated as cash ensuring that in most cases the courts will give summary judgment on the instrument and refuse to stay execution of that judgment pending trial of any counterclaim.

Cebora SNC v SIP (Industrial Products) Ltd

[1976] 1 Lloyd's Rep 271, Court of Appeal

The plaintiffs entered into a distribution agreement with the defendants whereby the defendants were given the exclusive right to sell the plaintiffs' products in the UK. In payment of the price of products supplied by the plaintiffs under this agreement, the defendants drew five bills of exchange. Following disputes between the parties, the defendants gave instructions that the bills should be dishonoured. The plaintiffs applied for summary judgment on the bills and the defendants counterclaimed for non-delivery of goods, delivery of defective goods, and loss of profit. The District Registrar entered judgment for the plaintiffs and refused the defendants' application for a stay of execution pending trial of their counterclaim. May J dismissed the defendants' appeal, as did the Court of Appeal (Buckley and Stephenson LJJ, and Sir Eric Sachs).

Sir Eric Sachs: Any erosion of the certainties of the application by our Courts of the law merchant relating to bills of exchange is likely to work to the detriment of this country, which depends on international trade to a degree that needs no emphasis. For some generations one of those certainties has been that the bona fide holder for value of a bill of exchange is entitled, save in truly exceptional circumstances, on its maturity to have it treated as cash, so that in an action upon it the Court will refuse to regard either as a defence or as grounds for a stay of execution any set off, legal or equitable, or any counterclaim, whether arising on the particular transaction upon which the bill of exchange came into existence, or, a fortiori, arising in any other way. This rule of practice is thus, in effect, pay up on the bill of exchange first and pursue claims later . . .

In my judgment, the Courts should be really careful not to whittle away the rule of practice by introducing unnecessary exceptions to it under the influence of sympathy-evoking stories, and should have due regard to the maxim that hard cases can make bad law. Indeed, in these days of increasing international interdependence and increasing need to foster liquidity of resources, the rule may be said to be of special import to the business community. Pleas to leave in Court large sums to deteriorate in value while official referee scale proceedings are fought out may well to that community seem rather divorced from business realities, and should perhaps be examined with considerable caution.

Nova (Jersey) Knit Ltd v Kammgarn Spinnerei GmbH

[1977] 2 All ER 463, House of Lords

An English company and a German company set up a partnership in Germany. The English company sold machines to the German company to be used for the partnership and the German company issued bills of exchange for the price. The English company brought an action on the bills. The German company sought to bring a defence and counterclaim for unliquidated damages for mismanagement of the partnership and defects in the machines.

The House of Lords (Lord Wilberforce, Viscount Dilhorne, Lords Salmon, Fraser, and Russell) held the German company liable to pay the bills in full without set-off or counterclaim. By a majority (Lord Salmon dissenting), their Lordships refused a stay of execution of the judgment based on an arbitration agreement contained in the underlying contract.

Lord Wilberforce: . . . When one person buys goods from another, it is often, one would think generally, important for the seller to be sure of his price: he may (as indeed the appellants here) have bought the goods from someone else whom he has to pay. He may demand payment in cash; but if the buyer cannot provide this at once, he may agree to take bills of exchange payable at future dates. These are taken as equivalent to deferred instalments of cash. Unless they are to be treated as unconditionally payable instruments (as the Bills of Exchange Act 1882, s 3, says 'an unconditional order in writing'), which the seller can negotiate for cash, the seller might just as well give credit. And it is for this reason that English law (and German law appears to be no different) does not allow cross-claims, or defences, except such limited defences as those based on fraud, invalidity, or failure of consideration, to be made . . .

Lord Russell of Killowen: . . . It is in my opinion well established that a claim for unliquidated damages under a contract for sale is no defence to a claim under a bill of exchange accepted by the purchaser: nor is it available as set-off or counterclaim. This is a deep rooted concept of English commercial law. A vendor and purchaser who agree upon payment by acceptance of bills of exchange do so not simply upon the basis that credit is given to the purchaser so that the vendor must in due course sue for the price under the contract of sale. The bill is itself a contract separate from the contract of sale. Its purpose is not merely to serve as a negotiable instrument, it is also to avoid postponement of the purchaser's liability to the vendor himself, a postponement grounded upon some allegation of failure in some respect by the vendor under the underlying contract, unless it be total or quantified partial failure of consideration . . .

NOTES

1.   It is clear from *Nova (Jersey) Knit* that cross-claims for unliquidated damages cannot be set up in answer to a claim on a bill of exchange. But certain other defences may be available. A total failure of consideration, or a quantified (liquidated) partial failure, may be relied on as a defence against immediate parties and against a subsequent holder who is not a holder for value. A total failure of consideration would arise, for example, where a commercial buyer, who had paid for good by drawing a bill of exchange in favour of the seller, rejected all the goods on delivery because they were not of satisfactory quality and/or fit for their purpose (see Sale of Goods Act 1979, s 14(2), (3)). A quantified (liquidated) partial failure of consideration would arise, for example, where some of the delivered goods were rejected and others were not (see Sale of Goods Act 1979, s 35A). The defence would operate to the extent of the value of the goods that had been rejected. Another defence that could be raised against an immediate party to the bill, or against a remote party who is not a holder in due course, is where the validity of the instrument can be called into question because, for example, its issue was induced by conspiracy or misrepresentation (*SAFA Ltd v Banque Du Caire* [2000] 2 All ER (Comm) 567, CA; *Solo Industries UK Ltd v Canara Bank* [2001] EWCA Civ 1059, [2001] 2 All ER (Comm) 217). In each case, the availability of a defence depends on the status of the holder claiming to enforce the bill (as to which, see below, Chapter 19, Section 5).

2.   Although treated as the equivalent of cash, a bill of exchange is not legal tender and, subject to any agreement or usage to the contrary, a creditor is only obliged to accept legal tender, ie cash, in payment of a debt (*Gordon v Strange* (1847) 1 Exch 477). If a bill of exchange,

promissory note, or cheque is accepted in payment of a debt it depends on the intention of the parties as to whether it is taken in absolute or conditional payment of the debt. In *Re Charge Card Services Ltd* [1989] Ch 497 at 511, CA, Browne-Wilkinson V-C stated that:

> It is common ground that where a debt is 'paid' by cheque or bill of exchange, there is a presumption that such payment is conditional on the cheque or bill being honoured. If it is not honoured, the condition is not satisfied and the liability of the purchaser to pay the price remains. Such presumption can be rebutted by showing an express or implied intention that the cheque or bill is taken in total satisfaction of the liability . . .

For further statements to the same effect, see *Crockfords Club Ltd v Mehta* [1992] 1 WLR 355 at 366, CA; *Homes v Smith* [2000] Lloyd's Rep Bank 139 at [35], CA.

QUESTIONS

1. Is there any advantage to a creditor in accepting payment by negotiable instrument as opposed to cash? If so, would this enable a debtor to argue that payment by negotiable instrument provided its own consideration to support the creditor's agreement to accept a lesser sum in settlement of an undisputed debt? See *D & C Builders v Rees* [1966] 2 QB 617, CA. See also McLauchlan (1987) 12 NZULR 259 and *James Cook Hotel Ltd v Canx Corporate Services Ltd* [1989] LRC (Comm) 518 (New Zealand).

2. If a negotiable instrument is used to pay a debt and, when in the creditor's hands, the instrument is accidentally destroyed before its maturity, can the creditor return to the debtor demanding payment of the debt?

CHAPTER 19

BILLS OF EXCHANGE

1 THE USE OF BILLS OF EXCHANGE

Bills of exchange are used much less today than they once were. Modern electronic funds transfer mechanisms have become the preferred method of payment in many commercial transactions. The most common type of bill of exchange is a cheque. Cheques are still used in large (albeit decreasing) numbers, but they are invariably drawn 'account payee' or 'a/c payee', with or without the word 'only', which means that they cannot be transferred by the named payee and so have lost the characteristic of negotiability (see above, Chapter 18, and below, Chapter 20).

Nevertheless, bills of exchange remain important as a method of payment in international trade (see below, Chapter 21). Bills of exchange are frequently used where a seller of goods allows his overseas buyer a period of credit but needs access to funds in the interim. The seller draws a bill of exchange in his own favour on the buyer or, more usually, on a bank that has undertaken to pay under the terms of a documentary credit. As a credit period has been agreed, the bill will be payable at a future date, for example 90 or 180 days after sight. The seller then presents the bill for acceptance by the buyer or, in the case of a documentary credit transaction, by the bank. Once the bill has been accepted, the seller does not have to wait until it matures to receive funds. He can take advantage of the negotiable character of the bill and discount (sell) it to his own bank for an immediate (but reduced) cash payment. The seller's own bank is left to collect payment from the buyer, or other party that has accepted liability, on maturity of the instrument. In certain cases, the seller will obtain an advance on the bill from his own bank before acceptance and leave it to the bank to present the bill for acceptance and for payment.

2 THE BILLS OF EXCHANGE ACT 1882

The primary source of the law of bills of exchange is the Bills of Exchange Act 1882 (BEA). The Act was drafted by Sir Mackenzie Chalmers, who also drafted the Sale of Goods Act 1893 and the Marine Insurance Act 1906. It is a masterpiece of statutory draftsmanship.

The Preamble to the BEA states that it was intended 'to codify the law relating to Bills of Exchange, Cheques and Promissory Notes' (although it also altered the common law in a number of respects). The way the courts interpret a codification statute of this nature is revealed in the following extract.

Bank of England v Vagliano Bros

[1891] AC 107, House of Lords

The facts appear below, p 667. The case turned on the meaning of s 7(3) of the BEA. The Court of Appeal had qualified the wording of the subsection by introducing a limitation to be found in the common law.

> **Lord Herschell**: My Lords, with sincere respect for the learned Judges who have taken this view, I cannot bring myself to think that this is the proper way to deal with such a statute as the Bills of Exchange Act, which was intended to be a code of the law relating to negotiable instruments. I think the proper course is in the first instance to examine the language of the statute and to ask what is its natural meaning, uninfluenced by any considerations derived from the previous state of the law and not to start with inquiring how the law previously stood, and then, assuming that it was probably intended to leave it unaltered, to see if the words of the enactment will bear an interpretation in conformity with this view.
>
> If a statute, intended to embody in a code a particular branch of the law, is to be treated in this fashion, it appears to me that its utility will be almost entirely destroyed, and the very object with which it was enacted will be frustrated. The purpose of such a statute surely was that on any point specifically dealt with by it, the law should be ascertained by interpreting the language used instead of, as before, by roaming over a vast number of authorities in order to discover what the law was, extracting it by a minute critical examination of the prior decisions, dependent upon a knowledge of the exact effect even of an obsolete proceeding such as a demurrer to evidence. I am of course far from asserting that resort may never be had to the previous state of the law for the purpose of aiding in the construction of the provisions of the code. If, for example, a provision be of doubtful import, such resort would be perfectly legitimate. Or, again, if in a code of the law of negotiable instruments words be found which have previously acquired a technical meaning, or been used in a sense other than their ordinary one, in relation to such instruments, the same interpretation might well be put upon them in the code. I give these as examples merely; they, of course, do not exhaust the category. What, however, I am venturing to insist upon is, that the first step taken should be to interpret the language of the statute, and that an appeal to earlier decisions can only be justified on some special ground.
>
> One further remark I have to make before I proceed to consider the language of the statute. The Bills of Exchange Act was certainly not intended to be merely a code of the existing law. It is not open to question that it was intended to alter, and did alter it in certain respects. And I do not think that it is to be presumed that any particular provision was intended to be a statement of the existing law, rather than a substituted enactment.

NOTES

1. The Act does not, in general, extend to negotiable instruments other than bills of exchange, cheques, and promissory notes (although see BEA, s 95 and Cheques Act 1957, s 5).

2. Lord Herschell gave examples of when it would be legitimate to examine the common law as an aid to construction of the provisions of the BEA. The common law remains relevant in many other ways. This is emphasised by A Barak in the following extract.

'The Nature of the Negotiable Instrument' by A Barak

(1983) 18 Israel LR 49 at 69–70

> . . . [S]everal different sets of rules apply to the negotiable instrument: since it is a chattel—the general law applicable to chattels (such as sales and torts); since it is an obligation—the general law

of obligations (for example the rules as to capacity); and since it is a negotiable paper—the special rules applicable to such instruments. In most countries, the law of negotiable instruments is normally confined to that latter body of rules. Israel's Bills of Exchange Ordinance deals almost entirely with the bill as a negotiable instrument; it makes virtually no reference at all to the bill as a chattel or an obligation. Those aspects of the bill are covered by the general law. Hence, one can draw a distinction between the law of negotiable instruments in the strict sense and the law of negotiable instruments in the broad sense. The former deals with the bill as a negotiable paper and, as said, is usually to be found in special legislation. The latter deals with the bill as a chattel and an obligation and is usually to be found in the general law. The parallel existence of the two has been possible because legislation on negotiable instruments was never intended to provide an exhaustive list of the rules of law dealing with such instruments. From the time of the very earliest legislation in this field it has been clear that, alongside the special rules governing the bill as a negotiable instrument, the ordinary rules relating to it as a chattel and an obligation continue to apply . . .

NOTES

1. Israel's Bills of Exchange Ordinance is based on the English BEA and so Barak's comments are equally relevant to the 1882 Act.

2. Section 97(2) of the BEA provides that: 'The rules of common law including the law merchant, save in so far as they are inconsistent with the express provisions of this Act, shall continue to apply to bills of exchange, promissory notes, and cheques.'

3. An example of the general law applicable to chattels relevant to bills is the tort of conversion. This is the remedy usually, but not always, available to the true owner of a stolen bill. An example of the general law of obligations applicable to bills is the doctrine of consideration. In this case the Act expressly imports the common law rules as s 27(1)(a) of the BEA states that valuable consideration for a bill may be constituted by any consideration sufficient to support a simple contract.

QUESTION

Lord Herschell's restrictive method of interpreting a codifying statute has not always been followed by the courts (eg *Ashington Piggeries Ltd v Christopher Hill Ltd* [1972] AC 441). What are its disadvantages?

3 DEFINITION OF A BILL OF EXCHANGE

Section 3 of the BEA defines a bill of exchange as follows:

(1) A bill of exchange is an unconditional order in writing, addressed by one person to another, signed by the person giving it, requiring the person to whom it is addressed to pay on demand or at a fixed or determinable future time a sum certain in money to or to the order of a specified person, or to bearer.

(2) An instrument which does not comply with these conditions, or which orders any act to be done in addition to the payment of money, is not a bill of exchange.

The person who draws the bill and gives the order to pay is called the 'drawer'. The person upon whom the bill is drawn, and who is thereby ordered to pay, is called the 'drawee'. When the drawee indicates his willingness to pay, he is then called the 'acceptor'. The person identified in the bill as the person to or to whose order the money is to be paid is called the 'payee', or, if the bill is drawn payable to bearer, and he is in possession of the bill, the 'bearer'. A bill payable to order is negotiated (meaning transferred) by the indorsement of the payee (or of a subsequent transferee) completed by delivery. The person indorsing the bill is called the 'indorser' and the person to whom it is indorsed, the 'indorsee'. A bill payable to bearer is negotiated by mere delivery. The payee or an indorsee of a bill who is in possession of it, or the bearer, is called the 'holder'.

Figures 19.1 and 19.2 are examples of instruments that fall within the statutory definition of a bill of exchange. The accompanying notes should help you identify the relevant parties to the instruments.

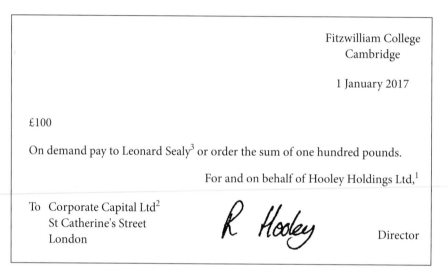

Figure 19.1 Bill of exchange payable on demand

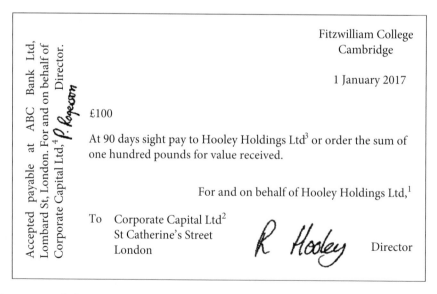

Figure 19.2 Bill of exchange payable at a future date

NOTES

1. The 'drawer'.
2. The 'drawee'.
3. The 'payee' (when the bill is delivered to him he becomes the first 'holder').
4. The 'acceptor' (when the 'drawee' has accepted the bill he is then called the 'acceptor').

An instrument must comply with all the requirements set out in s 3(1) of the BEA if it is to be a bill of exchange.

- *Unconditional* The order given by the drawer to the drawee must be unconditional. An order to pay 'provided funds are available', or out of a particular fund, would not be a bill.

- *Writing* The order to pay must be in writing, which includes print (BEA, s 2). The bill does not have to be drawn on any particular material, and there is one famous example of a cheque being drawn on the side of a cow! There is some uncertainty as to whether an electronic communication, such as an email or an electronic data interchange (EDI) message, can satisfy a statutory requirement for writing. Section 8 of the Electronic Communications Act 2000 empowers the appropriate minister to amend the statute book, by statutory instrument, to authorise or to facilitate the use of electronic communication and storage. No order has yet been made with regard to bills of exchange. But exercise of this power alone would not facilitate the introduction of an electronic bill of exchange. The definition of a bill of exchange in s 3(1) of the BEA includes a number of paper-based concepts, the cumulative effect of which means that the definition cannot be satisfied by electronic communications (this is also the conclusion of the Law Commission in its Advice to Government, *Electronic Commerce: Formal Requirements in Commercial Transactions* (December 2001), para 9.5). Provision has recently been made for cheques (and similar instruments) to be presented for payment by providing the bank upon which the cheque is drawn with an electronic image of the front and back of the cheque instead of the physical cheque itself (BEA, ss 89A–89F, as inserted by the Small Business, Enterprise and Employment Act 2015, s 13). The electronic image of the cheque becomes the equivalent of the original physical cheque, but only for the purposes of presentation for payment (see below, p 733).

- *Addressed by one person to another* If the drawer draws the instrument on himself, it is not a bill of exchange but the holder of such an instrument has the option of treating it either as a bill of exchange or as a promissory note (BEA, s 5(2)). The instrument is a bill of exchange where the drawer names himself as the payee.

- *Signed by the person giving it* The drawer must sign the bill personally or through an agent. If the signature of the drawer is forged or placed on the bill without his authority, the signature is 'wholly inoperative', although certain estoppels may arise as against the drawer (BEA, s 24) and against the acceptor (BEA, s 54(2)(a)) and any indorser (BEA, s 55(2)(b)). It is arguable that where the drawer's signature is forged, then the instrument is not a bill at all. If it becomes possible to have an electronic bill of exchange through ministerial order made under the Electronic Communications Act 2000 (see above), an electronic signature will inevitably be valid, although as the law currently stands electronic signatures have been recognised as effective with regard to a number of other statutes: see, for example, *Lindsay v O'Loughnane* [2010] EWHC 529 (QB), [2012] BCC 153 at [95] (Statute of Frauds Amendment Act 1928, s 6); *Pereira Fernandes SA v Mehta* [2006] EWHC 813 (Ch), [2006] 1 WLR 1543 at [29] (Statute of Frauds 1677, s 4); *Golden*

Ocean Group Ltd v Salgaocar Mining Industries Pvt Ltd [2012] EWCA Civ 265 (Statute of Frauds 1677, s 4); *Bassano v Toft* [2014] EWHC 377 (Ch) at [43] (Consumer Credit Act 1974, s 60(1)).

- *On demand or at a fixed or determinable future time* By s 10(1) of the BEA, a bill is payable on demand: (a) which is expressed to be payable on demand, or at sight, or on presentation; or (b) in which no time for payment is expressed. By s 11 of the BEA, a bill is payable at a fixed or determinable future time: (a) if it is expressed to be payable at a fixed period after date or sight; or (b) on or at a fixed period after the occurrence of a specified event which is certain to happen, though the time of happening may be uncertain. It is vital that the time of payment is certain according to the terms of the bill. This renders the bill saleable. Where time of payment is not certain from the face of the instrument it will not be treated as a bill of exchange. Thus, an instrument drawn payable *by* a specified date does not fall within the statutory definition because the acceptor has the option of paying before that date (*Claydon v Bradley* [1987] 1 All ER 522, CA, following *Williamson v Rider* [1963] 1 QB 89, CA, criticised by AH Hudson (1962) 25 MLR 593 at 596–596), and an instrument expressed to be payable on a contingency is not a bill, and the happening of the event does not cure the defect (BEA, s 11). However, the courts are prepared to overcome faulty expressions in an instrument where the true meaning is obvious despite the defect. In *Hong Kong & Shanghai Banking Corpn Ltd v GD Trade Co Ltd* [1998] CLC 238, the Court of Appeal inserted a '/' between the words 'acceptance' and 'sight' and held the instrument to be a bill of exchange payable at '90 days after acceptance/sight'. This had the effect of making the bill payable at a fixed period after the date of sight (ie presentation for acceptance), whether it was actually accepted or not (an instrument payable on, or a fixed period after, acceptance is not a bill of exchange because acceptance by the drawee is a contingency: *Korea Exchange Bank v Debenhams (Central Buying) Ltd* [1979] 1 Lloyd's Rep 548, CA). Their Lordships also tentatively suggested (without deciding the issue) that acceptance of a bill not previously negotiated, in terms which unequivocally stated that it was payable on a specified day, cured any uncertainty as to the date of maturity of the bill as originally drawn. Alternatively, it might be possible to treat the terms of the acceptance as turning the instrument into a promissory note (*Novaknit Hellas SA v Kumar Bros International Ltd* [1998] CLC 971, CA).

- *A sum certain in money* 'Money' includes legal tender and foreign currency (including the euro). A sum payable is a sum certain even though required to be paid with interest, or by stated instalments, or according to an indicated rate of exchange or a rate of exchange to be ascertained as directed on the bill (BEA, s 9(1)).

- *To or to the order of a specified person or to bearer* Where a bill is not payable to bearer, the payee must be named or otherwise indicated therein with reasonable certainty (BEA, s 7(1)). Payment to the holder of an office for the time being (eg 'Treasurer of the Cambridge University Law Society') is permissible (BEA, s 7(2)). Where the payee is a fictitious or non-existent person the bill may be treated as payable to bearer (BEA, s 7(3): see below, p 666). An instrument drawn payable to 'cash or order' is not a bill of exchange, as it is not payable to a specified person or to bearer (*Orbit Mining and Trading Co Ltd v Westminster Bank Ltd* [1963] 1 QB 794, CA). But a bill drawn payable to 'cash or bearer' would appear to be a valid bill payable to bearer (*Grant v Vaughan* (1764) 3 Burr 1516), as is a bill payable to 'X or bearer' (*MK International Development Co Ltd v Housing Bank* [1991] 1 Bank LR 74, CA). In *Chamberlain v Young and Tower* [1893] 2

QB 206, an instrument drawn 'pay to . . . order' was construed as being a valid bill payable 'to my order' so as to give effect to the drawer's clear intention to create a negotiable instrument. It is a moot point whether an instrument drawn 'pay . . . . or order' is a valid bill. The words 'or order' negative any inference that it is payable to bearer (cf *Wookey v Pole* (1820) 4 B & Ald 1). Despite a number of early nineteenth-century cases holding that such an instrument was not a bill of exchange (*R v Richards* (1811) Russ & Ry 193; *R v Randall* (1811) Russ & Ry 195), it is generally accepted that an instrument drawn 'pay . . . . or order' would now be construed as payable 'to myself or order' (see *Chalmers and Guest on Bills of Exchange* (17th edn, 2009), para 2–049; EP Ellinger, E Lomnicka, and CVM Hare, *Ellinger's Modern Banking Law* (5th edn, 2011), p 404; cf *Byles on Bills of Exchange and Cheques* (29th edn, 2013), para 3–008). In the Scottish case of *Henderson, Sons & Co Ltd v Wallace and Pennell* (1902) 40 SLR 70, Lord Traynor treated an instrument drawn 'pay . . . . or order' as a promissory note. However, the issue was left undecided in *Chamberlain v Tower and Young* and in *North and South Insurance Corpn v National Provincial Bank* [1936] 1 KB 328.

An unsigned document cannot be a bill of exchange but a signed document, though failing to comply with all the requirements of s 3(1) of the BEA, may be converted into a bill of exchange where the signatory (the drawer, the acceptor, or an indorser) delivers it to another person in order that the missing details may be completed by him. Such a document is an 'inchoate' instrument. The person who takes delivery of an inchoate instrument has prima facie authority to fill it up as a complete bill and to rectify any omission of any material particular, for example the amount or the name of the payee (BEA, s 20(1)). In order that the instrument, when completed, may be enforceable against a person who became a party to it prior to its completion, it must be filled up within a reasonable time and strictly in accordance with the authority given (BEA, s 20(2)). Not surprisingly, given the need to encourage the marketability of bills of exchange, where a completed instrument is negotiated to someone who takes it in good faith and for valuable consideration (ie a holder in due course), that person may enforce the bill against anyone who became a party to it prior to its completion even where it turns out that the bill was not completed within a reasonable time or in accordance with the authority given (BEA, s 20(2)).

Even if the holder of the bill cannot rely on the inchoate instrument provisions set out in s 20 of the BEA, he may be able to argue that the person who signs a negotiable instrument in blank, or while it is otherwise incomplete, is estopped from denying the validity of the completed instrument against him if he has acted to his detriment in reliance upon it (*Lloyds Bank Ltd v Cooke* [1907] 1 KB 794, CA). In *Wilson and Meeson v Pickering* [1946] KB 422, the Court of Appeal emphasised that this type of estoppel was confined to the case of negotiable instruments so that a cheque which had lost its negotiability because it had been crossed 'not negotiable' (see BEA, s 81) fell outside its ambit (cf *Mercantile Credit Co Ltd v Hamblin* [1965] 2 QB 242 at 274–275, 278–279).

4 TRANSFER OF A BILL OF EXCHANGE

We have already seen how the payee of a bill of exchange payable at a future time may discount the bill, ie sell it at a reduced rate, before it matures in order to raise immediate cash (see above, Section 1). The payee must 'negotiate' the bill to the purchaser and give him legal title to the sum payable under it. The same bill could, in theory, be negotiated many times down a chain of different people, for example from A to B, from B to C, from C to D, etc.

By s 31(1) of the BEA, 'a bill is negotiated when it is transferred from one person to another in such a manner as to constitute the transferee the holder of the bill'. In this section the word 'negotiated' is used to mean 'transferred', whether or not such transfer is free from equities of prior parties. The actual mode of transfer depends on whether the bill is a bearer bill or payable to order.

(a) Bearer bills

Bearer bills are transferred by delivery, ie through the transfer of possession, whether actual or constructive, from one person to another (BEA, s 31(2)). A bill of exchange is payable to bearer in any of the following circumstances:

- When it is expressed to be so payable, ie 'Pay bearer' (BEA, s 8(3)).

- When the only or last indorsement is an indorsement in blank (BEA, s 8(3)). An indorsement in blank occurs when the indorser simply signs the bill without specifying an indorsee (BEA, s 34(1)) and is to be contrasted with a special indorsement which occurs when the indorser specifies the person to whom, or to whose order, the bill is to be payable (BEA, s 34(2)). The back of the bill reproduced as Figure 19.1, above, appears as Figure 19.3. This shows a special indorsement by the payee (Sealy) and an indorsement in blank by the indorsee (Prichard).

Figure 19.3 Back of bill of exchange reproduced as Figure 19.1

NOTES

5. Special endorsement.

6. Indorsement in blank.

- Where the payee is a fictitious or non-existing person the bill may be treated as payable to bearer (BEA, s 7(3)). By virtue of s 34(3) of the BEA, this provision is extended to the case where an indorsee under a special indorsement is a fictitious or non-existent person so that the bill can then be treated as having been indorsed in blank. The next case is the leading authority on whether the payee is fictitious.

Bank of England v Vagliano Bros
[1891] AC 107, House of Lords

Vagliano Brothers regularly accepted bills drawn on them by their foreign correspondent in Odessa, Vucina. Glyka, a clerk employed by Vagliano Brothers, forged Vucina's signature as drawer on a number of such bills. The bills were drawn payable to the order of C Petridi & Co, a firm carrying on business in Constantinople, which had been the payee of some genuine bills previously drawn by Vucina upon Vagliano Brothers. In ignorance of the forgery, Vagliano Brothers accepted these bills payable at the Bank of England. Glyka then forged the indorsement of C Petridi & Co and obtained payment from the Bank of England in the name of a fictitious indorsee. The issue was whether the Bank of England was entitled to treat the bills as payable to bearer and debit Vagliano Brothers' account with the amount of their acceptances. The House of Lords by a majority (Lords Bramwell and Field dissenting) held that the Bank of England had been entitled to do so.

Lord Herschell: . . . If I am right in thinking that in the case of a payee who is a fictitious person (whatever be the meaning of that expression) a bill may, as against the acceptor, be treated by a lawful holder as payable to bearer whether the acceptor knew of the fiction or not, why should this right and liability differ according as the name inserted as payee be a creature of the imagination or correspond to that of a real person, the drawer in neither case intending a person so designated to receive payment, and in each case himself indorsing the bill in the name of the nominal payee before putting it into circulation? I am at a loss for any reason why this distinction should exist. It is true that there is this difference between the two cases—that in the one an indorsement by the named payee is physically impossible, whilst in the other it is not. But I do not think this difference affords a sound basis for a distinction between the respective rights and liabilities of the drawer, acceptor, and holder. It seems to me that it would in each case be reasonable, and on the same grounds, that the acceptor should be liable to the holder of the bill, indemnifying himself out of the funds of the drawer or obtaining reimbursement from him . . .

Do the words, 'where the payee is a fictitious person,' apply only where the payee named never had a real existence? I take it to be clear that by the word 'payee' must be understood the payee named on the face of the bill; for of course by the hypothesis there is no intention that payment should be made to any such person. Where, then, the payee named is so named by way of pretence only, without the intention that he shall be the person to receive payment, is it doing violence to language to say that the payee is a fictitious person? I think not. I do not think that the word 'fictitious' is exclusively used to qualify that which has no real existence. When we speak of a fictitious entry in a book of accounts, we do not mean that the entry has no real existence, but only that it purports to be that which it is not—that it is an entry made for the purpose of pretending that the transaction took place which is represented by it. . . .

I have arrived at the conclusion that, whenever the name inserted as that of the payee is so inserted by way of pretence merely, without any intention that payment shall only be made in conformity therewith, the payee is a fictitious person within the meaning of the statute, whether the name be that of an existing person, or of one who has no existence, and that the bill may, in each case, be treated by a lawful holder as payable to bearer.

I have hitherto been considering the case of a bill drawn by the person whose name is attached to it as drawer, whilst the bills which have given rise to this litigation were not drawn by Vucina, who purported to be the drawer, his name being forged by Glyka. I think it was hardly contended on behalf of the respondents that this made any difference. The bills must, under the circumstances, as against the acceptor, be taken to have been drawn by Vucina, and if they have been made payable to a fictitious person within the meaning of the statute, I do not think it is open to question that they may, as against the acceptor, be treated as payable to bearer, in every case in which they could have been so treated if Vucina had drawn them. If, in the present case, Vucina had himself drawn the bills and inserted the name of C Petridi & Co as payees, as a mere pretence without intending any such persons to receive payment, it follows from what I have said that in my opinion they would have been bills whose payee was a fictitious person, and I do not think they can be regarded as any the less so, in view of the circumstances under which the name of C Petridi & Co was inserted.

Lord Macnaghten: On behalf of the bank, it was pointed out that these pretended bills, being duly accepted and regular and complete on the face of them, were presented for payment apparently in due course; and it was said that although no doubt at the time they were taken to be payable to order, and to be duly indorsed by the payee, yet when it turns out that the payee was a fictitious person, they may be treated as payable to bearer, and so the payment is justified though all the indorsements are inoperative.

On behalf of Vagliano Bros, it was contended that a bill payable to a fictitious person is not payable to bearer unless the acceptor is proved to have been aware of the fiction; and further, it was contended that nothing but a creature of the imagination can properly be described as a fictitious person. I do not think that either of these contentions on behalf of the respondents can be maintained.

Before the Act of 1882, the law seems to have been, as laid down by Lord Ellenborough in *Bennett v Farnell* ((1807) 1 Camp 130 at 180), that 'a bill of exchange made payable to a fictitious person or his order, is neither in effect payable to the order of the drawer nor to bearer, unless it can be shewn that the circumstances of the payee being a fictitious person was known to the acceptor.' The Act of 1882, s 7, sub-s 3, enacts that, 'Where the payee is a fictitious or non-existing person, the bill may be treated as payable to bearer.' As a statement of law before the Act that would have been incomplete and inaccurate. The omission of the qualification required to make it complete and accurate as the law then stood seems to shew that the object of the enactment was to do away with that qualification altogether. The section appears to me to have effected a change in the law in the direction of the more complete negotiability of bills of exchange—a change in accordance, I think, with the tendency of modern views and one in favour of holders in due course, and not, so far as I can see, likely to lead to any hardships or injustice.

Then it was said that the proper meaning of 'fictitious' is 'imaginary.' I do not think so. I think the proper meaning of the word is 'feigned' or 'counterfeit.' It seems to me that the 'C Petridi & Co' named as payees on these pretended bills were, strictly speaking, fictitious persons. When the bills came before Vagliano for acceptance they were fictitious from beginning to end. The drawer was fictitious; the payee was fictitious; the person indicated as agent for presentation was fictitious. One and all they were feigned or counterfeit persons put forward as real persons, each in a several and distinct capacity; whereas, in truth, they were mere make-believes for the persons whose names appeared on the instrument. They were not, I think, the less fictitious because there were in existence real persons for whom these names were intended to pass muster.

[Lord Halsbury LC and Lords Selbourne, Watson, and Macnaghten based their opinions mainly on the ground that Vagliano Brothers had misled the Bank of England into making the payments and so the bank was not to be held responsible for them. However, as an additional ground for their opinions Lord Halsbury LC and Lord Watson, together with Lord Morris, held that s 7(3) was to be interpreted as interpreted by Lords Herschell and Macnaghten.]

NOTES

1. The only genuine signature on these 'bills' was that of Vagliano Brothers as acceptor. The drawer's and payee's signatures were forgeries. As s 3(1) of the BEA requires the drawer's signature to appear on the bill, and Vucina had not signed these bills, they could not fall within the statutory definition of a bill of exchange. This was recognised by Lord Halsbury LC (at 116) and by Lords Watson (at 134), Macnaghten (at 160), and Morris (at 162). As s 7(3) of the BEA states that '. . . *the bill* may be treated as payable to bearer', the subsection would appear to have little relevance to the 'bills' in the *Vagliano* case. Lords Watson (at 134) and Macnaghten (at 160) stated that as the instruments were not genuine bills of exchange, s 7(3) was not intended to apply to them (see also JR Adams (1891) 7 LQR 295 at 295–296). Lord Halsbury LC (at 116 and 120) overcame this difficulty by holding that Vagliano Brothers, as acceptor, were estopped from denying that the instrument was a valid bill. Lords Herschell (at 154) and Morris (at 162–163) appear to concur with that view. The estoppel operates at common law and prevents the acceptor from asserting against a bona fide holder for value without notice that the drawer's signature was forged (it is not a statutory estoppel under BEA, s 54(2)(a)—can you see why?). The estoppel will operate against the acceptor so that the instrument, upon which the drawer's signature has been forged, is deemed to be a bill of exchange. Section 7(3) will then treat the bill as payable to bearer if the forger did not intend the named payee to receive payment.

2. The drawer's intention is, therefore, of utmost importance when deciding whether a payee is fictitious. That this should be so seems anomalous in a case like *Bank of England v Vagliano Bros.* The editors of *Ellinger's Modern Banking Law* (5th edn, 2011), p 405, fn 134, observe that whilst such emphasis on the intention of the drawer:

. . . is supportable in the case of cheques in which the drawer determines the tenor of the bill and is, in effect, the main party to be charged in the event of its dishonour, it is difficult to see that the principle in *Vagliano* is appropriate in the case of bills of exchange. In such an instrument, the main obligor is the acceptor rather than the drawer: BEA 1882, s 54. If an acceptor, such as the claimants in *Vagliano*, intends the instrument to be payable to a designated payee, such as P & Co in *Vagliano*, why should the court be guided by the intention of a person whose name does not even appear on the bill of exchange, as was the case with the forger, G, in *Vagliano*? This argument is reinforced in the case of a bill of exchange because the order to pay the bill is given to the designated bank, such as the defendants in *Vagliano*, by the acceptor!

3. Focusing on the drawer's intention means that if the drawer does intend the named payee to receive payment that payee is not fictitious, even though the drawer may have been fraudulently induced into drawing the bill in that way. Such a bill falls outside s 7(3) of the BEA and remains payable to order. This was held to have occurred in the following cases.

- In *Vinden v Hughes* [1905] 1 KB 795, a fraudulent clerk made out cheques to certain well-known customers and persuaded Vinden, his employer, to sign the cheques even though no money was in fact owing to those customers. The employee then forged the customers' signatures and sold the cheques to Hughes for cash. Hughes passed the cheques through his own bank account, and had the proceeds placed to his credit. Warrington J held that Vinden believed he owed money to his customers when he signed the cheques as drawer and intended those customers to receive their proceeds. So far as Vinden was concerned at that time, the names of the customers/payees had not been inserted as a mere pretence and, therefore, they were not fictitious persons. Vinden could, therefore, recover the proceeds of the cheques from Hughes because the clerk's forged indorsements were wholly ineffective and did not entitle Hughes to receive payment of those proceeds.

• In *North and South Wales Bank v Macbeth* [1908] AC 137, White fraudulently induced Macbeth to draw a cheque in favour of Kerr or order. Kerr was an existing person, and Macbeth, who had been misled by the fraud, intended him to receive the proceeds of the cheque. White then forged Kerr's indorsement and paid the cheque into his account with the appellant bank who received payment of it. Macbeth sued the bank for conversion of the cheque. The House of Lords held that s 7(3) of the BEA did not apply as, although misled, Macbeth intended Kerr or his transferee to receive the proceeds of the cheque. This meant the cheque was payable to order and without Kerr's genuine indorsement the bank was not entitled to receive payment of it.

4. Who is the drawer for these purposes? In *Vinden v Hughes*, the employer signed the cheques as drawer, the fraudulent clerk merely induced him to do so. But where an employee, with authority to sign cheques, does so with the intention that the named payee should not receive payment, should the employee's intention be attributed to his employer? In *Boma Manufacturing Ltd v Canadian Imperial Bank of Commerce* (1996) 140 DLR (4th) 463, Supreme Court of Canada, a bookkeeper employed by two associated companies was authorised to sign cheques drawn on the companies' bank accounts. Over a period of time the bookkeeper signed a number of cheques payable to existing employees of the companies, but without the intention that they should receive payment. In fact the bookkeeper forged the indorsement of the named payee on each cheque and paid it into one of her accounts at the defendant (collecting) bank. On discovering the fraud, the companies brought an action in conversion against the defendant bank and the issue arose as to whether the bank took the cheques as a holder in due course giving it a complete defence to the claim. The bank could only be a holder in due course if the named payees were fictitious and the cheques deemed payable to bearer under the Canadian equivalent to s 7(3) of the BEA. However, a majority of the Supreme Court held that the payees were not fictitious payees, and the cheques were not payable to bearer, so that the bank had no defence to the action in conversion. Iacobucci J, delivering the judgment of a seven-judge majority, held that it is the intention of the drawer, in the sense of the one from whose account the cheque is drawn, which is significant for the purposes of s 7(3), not the intention of the signatory of the cheque (although in some cases the drawer and the signatory may be one and the same person). In this case the companies were the drawers and it was to be presumed that they intended the named payees to receive the proceeds of the cheques. The intention of the bookkeeper could not be attributed to the companies: she was simply the signatory and, as she was neither a director nor other officer of the companies, she could not be described as the directing mind of the companies. La Forest and McLachlin JJ dissented on the ground that the intention of the signatory should be attributed to the companies. Although the bookkeeper acted beyond the ambit of her actual authority when she prepared and signed the cheques, the dissenting minority held that in the eyes of a third party she would have had apparent authority to sign the cheques as she was an acknowledged signing officer of the companies. The minority judges also justified their decision on policy grounds arguing that by focusing on the intention of the actual signatory there would be a more efficient allocation of risk of loss between the drawer of a fraudulent cheque and the collecting bank, especially where it is an employee of the drawer which perpetrates the fraud, as the employer is in the best position to control fraud within his own organisation and will usually carry insurance to cover the loss. It is submitted that there is much to commend this approach, but it should be noted that similar policy arguments were rejected by the Privy Council in *Tai Hing Cotton Mill Ltd v Liu Chong King Bank Ltd* [1986] AC 80 (a customer is under no duty to take reasonable precautions in the conduct of his business to prevent forged cheques being presented to the bank for payment). For strong persuasive criticism of the majority's decision in *Boma*, see B Geva (1997) 28 CBLJ 177, especially at 192–196.

5. The intention of the drawer is irrelevant if the payee is non-existing. For example, the drawer may have intended the named payee to receive payment but, unknown to the drawer, that payee may have died before the bill is issued. The problem arose in *Clutton v Attenborough & Son* [1897] AC 90 where a clerk, employed by Clutton, induced his employer to draw cheques payable to one George Brett by falsely representing that a person of that name was entitled to payment for certain work done for Clutton. The clerk obtained possession of the cheques, indorsed them in the name of George Brett, and negotiated them to Attenborough & Son who gave value for them in good faith. The House of Lords held that as the cheques fell within s 7(3) of the BEA they were to be treated as payable to bearer and so Attenborough & Son were entitled to receive their proceeds. Lord Halsbury LC noted rather abruptly that 'it has in this case never been suggested that on the face of these instruments the name of George Brett is anything other than the name of a non-existing person'. Despite the possibility that there was at least one person in the world called George Brett when Clutton signed the cheques, the 'George Brett' named as payee did not exist because there was no person of that name who had done work for Clutton. Clutton did not know that George Brett did not exist. However, if the drawer knows that the payee does not exist then he cannot intend payment to be made to him. In these circumstances (eg a cheque drawn payable to 'Ivanhoe'), the payee will be both a fictitious and non-existent person.

6. There is no practical difference whether the payee is fictitious or non-existent, as s 7(3) of the BEA treats them both in exactly the same way. The subsection is important because it circumvents the effects of s 24 of the BEA. By s 24, a forged or unauthorised signature is treated as wholly inoperative. This means that if the payee's or indorsee's signature is forged any subsequent possessor of the instrument will not be an 'indorsee' and, therefore, not a 'holder' within the definition contained in s 2 of the BEA. However, if the bill is treated as payable to bearer, any forged indorsement is irrelevant because the possessor of a bearer bill will be, in any event, a 'holder' within the statutory definition. A 'holder' who has given value can enforce the bill and an acceptor who pays such a holder gets a good discharge under s 59 of the BEA. Where a bill is payable to order, payment to a person who has acquired it through or under a forged indorsement will not constitute a discharge because payment has not been made to a holder and so has not been made in due course as required by s 59. If the acceptor's bank pays someone who is not capable of giving the acceptor a good discharge then it acts in breach of mandate and may not debit its customer's account. If the acceptor's bank pays a 'holder' then it acts within its mandate (because the acceptor is discharged) and may debit its customer's account. This explains why it was so important in *Bank of England v Vagliano Bros* for the bank to establish that the bills in question were payable to bearer. Given that the payee's signature had been forged, only if the bill was payable to bearer could the acceptor be discharged from his liability and the bank act within its mandate. But see JR Adams (1891) 7 LQR 295, who questions whether the discharge of Vagliano Brothers was a relevant issue given that the drawer's signature was a forgery.

7.   Finally, note that s 7(3) of the BEA is permissive and not peremptory in its wording, ie '. . . the bill *may* be treated as payable to bearer'. It may be possible, therefore, to draw a bill using words prohibiting its transfer, or indicating an intention that it should not be transferred, which prevent the bill being treated as payable to bearer under s 7(3). For example, a bill drawn 'Pay X only' would not be treated as payable to bearer under s 7(3), even where X was a fictitious or non-existent person, nor would a cheque crossed 'account payee' or 'account payee only', as such a cheque is non-transferable under s 81A(1) of the BEA.

QUESTIONS

1.   If a bill of exchange is drawn 'pay cash or order', is it treated as payable to bearer under s 7(3) of the BEA?

2.   In *Vinden v Hughes* the clerk used the names of existing customers as payees and s 7(3) of the BEA was held not to apply. The loss occasioned by the clerk's fraud, therefore, fell on the third party, Hughes. If the clerk had simply invented names of non-existing customers then s 7(3) would have applied and the loss would have fallen on the employer, Vinden. Is it reasonable that the third party's rights should depend upon the nature of the misrepresentation made by the person who has induced the drawer to issue the instrument? If not, how should the third party's rights be determined? Should they turn on the fault of the drawer? (See the dissent of Laskin CJC in *Royal Bank of Canada v Concrete Column Clamps (1961) Ltd* (1976) 74 DLR (3d) 26 at 31–32, Supreme Court of Canada; also the dissent of La Forest and McLachlin JJ in *Boma Manufacturing Ltd v Canadian Imperial Bank of Commerce* (1997) 140 DLR (4th) 463 at 495–496.)

(b) Order bills

A bill payable to the order of a specified payee is transferred by indorsement of the payee, or the holder to whom the bill has been specially indorsed, and delivery of it (BEA, s 31(3)). A bill is payable to order in any of the following circumstances.

- When it is expressed to be so payable, for example 'Pay J Smith or order', or when it is payable to a particular person, for example 'Pay J Smith', so long as the bill does not contain words prohibiting transfer or indicating an intention that it should not be transferable (BEA, s 8(4)).

- When the only or last indorsement on the bill is in blank (and, therefore, the bill is payable to bearer) and the holder inserts above the indorsement in blank a direction to pay the bill to or to the order of himself or some other person, ie he converts the indorsement in blank into a special indorsement (BEA, s 34(4)). For example, the bill of exchange appearing in Figures 19.1 and 19.3 (see above, pp 662 and 666), could be converted back into an order bill if Prichard delivers it to Hooley and he inserts the words 'Pay R Hooley or order' above Prichard's signature. It seems to follow from the policy behind s 34(4) that a bill originally drawn payable to bearer may also be converted into a order bill by the execution of a special indorsement (EP Ellinger, E Lomnicka, and CVM Hare, *Ellinger's Modern*

Banking Law (5th edn, 2011), pp 403–404). However, in *Miller Associates (Australia) Pty Ltd v Bennington Pty Ltd* (1975) 7 ALR 144 at 149, Supreme Court of New South Wales, Sheppard J held that such a bill remains payable to bearer regardless of the 'indorsement'. Sheppard J appeared to be of the opinion that as a bill drawn payable to bearer can be transferred by mere delivery, the signature of a holder of such a bill is irrelevant to its transfer and is not, therefore, an indorsement within the meaning of the Act (cf WJ Chappenden (1981) 55 ALJ 135 at 137). Professors Goode and McKendrick adopt the same view as Sheppard J, although they note that the holder's signature will expose him to the same liabilities imposed on an indorser under s 55(2) (see *Goode on Commercial Law* (5th edn, 2016), p 533, fn 59). The issue remains open.

By s 31(4) of the BEA, where a holder of a bill payable to his order transfers it for value without indorsing it, the transfer gives the transferee such title as the transferor had in the bill, and the transferee in addition acquires the right to have the indorsement of the transferor. In these circumstances the transferee is placed in the position of an assignee of an ordinary chose in action and takes subject to equities of prior parties. If the transferor does indorse the bill he will be liable on it as an indorser but, as the indorsement only takes effect from that time, the transferee will take the instrument subject to any defect of title of which he has become aware between the date of the transfer and the date of the indorsement (see *Whistler v Forster* (1863) 14 CBNS 248).

(c) Destruction of transferability

Under s 8(1) of the BEA, a bill is 'negotiable' (meaning 'transferable' in this section) when drawn, unless it contains words prohibiting transfer, or indicating an intention that it should not be transferable. If the bill is drawn so that it is not transferable then only the original payee can enforce it. However, a non-transferable instrument still appears to fall within the definition of a bill of exchange set out in s 3(1) of the BEA (cf JK Macleod (1997) 113 LQR 133 at 149–157). It is obvious that if the bill is not transferable then it is not 'negotiable' in the technical sense of the word (ie it cannot be acquired free from defects of title of prior parties). The reverse is not necessarily true. A bill which is not 'negotiable', in the technical sense of the word, can still be transferable.

Hibernian Bank Ltd v Gysin and Hanson
[1939] 1 KB 483, Court of Appeal

The Irish Casing Co Ltd drew a bill of exchange payable three months after date 'to the order of the Irish Casing Co Ltd only the sum of £500 effective value received'. The bill was also crossed 'not negotiable'. After acceptance by the defendants the bill was indorsed by the drawers and transferred to the plaintiffs for value. On presentation for payment by the plaintiffs, as indorsees and holders for value, the bill was dishonoured. The defendants claimed that by its wording the bill was not transferable. Lewis J held that the words 'not negotiable' meant that the bill was not transferable or negotiable and gave judgment for the defendants. The Court of Appeal affirmed his decision.

Slesser LJ: . . . I am unable to see, construing the document as indicating the intention of the parties, that there was any acceptance of the bill except upon the basis that it was 'not negotiable.' If that be so, then it is difficult to see how the plaintiffs in this case can show any title to sue at all, because it is by reason, and by reason only, of the bill being capable of being transferred in such a manner as to constitute them the holders of the bill that they have any title to sue. If the matter ended there, and the only words for consideration were the words 'not negotiable,' then I think the case would clearly fall within s 8, sub-s 1, of the Act, which provides that 'when a bill contains words prohibiting transfer, or indicating an intention that it should not be transferable, it is valid as between the parties thereto, but is not negotiable.' Section 81 of the Act, defining the words 'not negotiable,' is in terms limited to cheques, and cannot be extended to bills not cheques to alter the natural meaning. But it is said that those words 'not negotiable' must be read subject to the other words, that the bill is payable 'to the order of the Irish Casing Co Ltd, only,' and Mr Murphy [counsel for the plaintiffs] seeks, as I understand him, to reconcile those words by saying that the bill is not negotiable after the order has been given by the Irish Casing Company, and that the absence of negotiability does not exclude the giving of the first order by the Irish Casing Company. I am unable to accept that construction. I think that the words 'not negotiable' are affirmative and govern the whole tenor of the instrument. The matter then comes to this, that either the words 'Not negotiable—Pay to the order of the Irish Casing Company only' make the whole instrument really no bill at all, or some other and more limited meaning must be given to the words 'To the order of the Irish Casing Company only.'

The surrounding circumstances of the case support a view which my brother Clauson has suggested and which has been adopted by Mr Willink [counsel for the defendants], that those words 'To the order of the Irish Casing Co Ltd, only,' are, so to speak, words of convenience, requiring payment to an agent of the Irish Casing Company, but do not, when they are read subject to the words 'not negotiable' amount to constituting the bill a bill payable to order within the meaning of s 8 at all. Fry LJ in *National Bank v Silke* ([1891] 1 QB 435 at 439) says that he is 'inclined to think that s 8 divides bills into three classes—bills not negotiable, bills payable to order, and bills payable to bearer.' In my view, adopting that classification, this is a bill 'not negotiable,' and when Fry LJ goes on to say 'so that a bill payable to order must always be negotiable,' he supports, I think, my conclusion that, in so far as this bill is not negotiable, it is not a bill payable to order within the meaning of the Bills of Exchange Act, and must have some lesser and more conditional effect. I think that that effect may be carried out by limiting it to cases where the order is merely for money to be paid to some one as agent for or for the purposes of the Irish Casing Company, and no more. In that view the instrument does not become irreconcilable or impossible of interpretation. It remains a non-negotiable instrument drawn by the Irish Casing Company Ltd, and accepted by the defendants, but limited as to its effect as between those two parties. It is not transferable; it produces no rights of action in the Hibernian Bank at all . . .

[**Clauson** and **Du Parcq LJJ** concurred.]

NOTES

1. In *Hibernian Bank v Gysin and Hanson*, the Court of Appeal held that where a bill (not a cheque) is drawn: 'Pay to the order of X only' and is crossed 'not negotiable', it is not transferable. But what if the words 'not negotiable' had been omitted from the bill? Neither the Court of Appeal, nor Lewis J, gave much thought as to whether the word 'only' was effective in itself to override the statement that the bill was to be payable to order. The editors of *Byles on Bills of Exchange and Cheques* (29th edn, 2013), para 8–005, submit that it did do this and that the case could have been decided on the basis of the fact that the bill was drawn in favour of the payee 'only', without involving the question of the effect of the words 'not negotiable'. A bill drawn 'Pay X only' is certainly non-transferable.

2. What if a bill (not a cheque) is drawn: 'Pay X or order' and crossed 'not negotiable'. Can it be transferred? Professor Guest submits that such words would probably be construed as indicating an intention that the bill should not be transferable within s 8(1) of the BEA, although he accepts the possibility that the words 'not negotiable' might be regarded as an error and have no legal effect (*Chalmers and Guest on Bills of Exchange* (17th edn, 2009), para 14–033). The reasoning of the Court of Appeal, and Lewis J, in the *Hibernian Bank* case strongly supports Professor Guest's submission that the words 'not negotiable' are decisive of the issue. But the issue turns on which words ('Pay X or order' or 'not negotiable') are the best evidence of the drawer's intention.

3. The holder of a crossed cheque bearing the words 'not negotiable' cannot take a better title than his transferor, although the cheque remains transferable (BEA, s 81). A crossed cheque bearing across its face the words 'account payee' or 'a/c payee', either with or without the word 'only', is non-transferable (BEA, s 81A(1)).

4. Deletion of the words 'or order' on a printed standard form bill of exchange does not restrict the transferability of the instrument. This is because under s 8(4) of the BEA a bill payable to a particular person is payable to that person's order in any event. The deletion of the words 'or order' would have no practical effect. If the bill was to be made non-transferable the word 'only' should be inserted after the name of the payee.

5. If a bill is 'negotiable' (meaning 'transferable') when drawn it will remain so until it is restrictively indorsed or discharged by payment or otherwise: see BEA, ss 35, 36(1), and 59.

QUESTIONS

1. A standard printed form of an uncrossed cheque states 'Pay . . . or order'. The drawer inserts X's name between the words 'Pay' and 'or order' and adds the words 'not negotiable' to the cheque. Is the cheque transferable? Would your answer be different if the cheque had been drawn in these terms on a blank piece of paper?

2. If a standard printed form of order cheque is drawn 'Pay X only or order', is it transferable?

5 PERSONS ENTITLED TO THE BENEFIT OF THE OBLIGATION ON THE BILL

The right to enforce payment of a bill lies with its 'holder', defined by s 2 of the BEA as 'the payee or indorsee of a bill or note who is in possession of it, or the bearer thereof'. A holder may sue on the bill in his own name (BEA, s 38(1)). Moreover, payment to the holder, within the terms of s 59(1) of the BEA, discharges the bill. Where a bill is stolen, the acceptor is not obliged to pay the thief (as he has no title to the instrument), but a thief in possession of a stolen bearer bill is still a 'holder', and an acceptor who pays the thief gets a good discharge, so long as he does so in good faith and without notice of the defect in title (BEA, s 59(1)). But mere possession is not enough to render a thief the holder of a stolen order bill, and a thief cannot become the holder of a stolen order bill through a forged indorsement (BEA, s 24). Payment made to a thief in possession of a stolen order bill would not discharge the acceptor's liability on the bill.

The BEA recognises three categories of holder: a 'mere holder', a 'holder for value', and a 'holder in due course'. Closely linked to the last category is a holder who derives his title through a holder in due course and who is himself not party to any fraud or illegality affecting the bill. The rights of the holder depend on the category into which he falls. A mere holder is at the bottom of the scale, a holder for value in the middle, and a holder in due course at the top.

(a) Mere holder

A mere holder is a holder otherwise than for value, who does not claim title to the bill through a holder in due course. His rights are limited. He can transfer the bill through indorsement and/or delivery, present it for payment, sue on it in his own name, and give a good discharge to a drawee or acceptor whose payment is otherwise in due course. But the real weakness of the position of a mere holder who does not himself give consideration for the bill, or is not deemed to have done so (under s 27(2) of the BEA), is that he can be met by the defence of absence or failure of consideration, whether his claim is against an immediate or remote party (these terms are explained below, p 679).

(b) Holder for value

The liabilities of the drawer, acceptor, and indorser of a bill are contractual in nature. Section 21(1) of the BEA specifically refers to their 'contract on the bill'. This means not only that those persons must have the capacity to contract on the bill (BEA, s 22) but also that consideration has been provided for their contractual 'engagement' on the bill (BEA, ss 54(1), 55(1)(a), (2)(a)). The same pre-conditions apply to the maker's contractual engagement on a promissory note (BEA, s 88(1)). That said, every party whose signature appears on a bill is prima facie deemed to have become a party to it for value (BEA, s 30(1)).

Whether 'value' has in fact been given for a bill is determined by s 27 of the BEA. Section 27(1) provides that valuable consideration for a bill may be instituted by: (a) any consideration sufficient to support a simple contract; (b) an antecedent debt or liability, this being deemed valuable consideration whether the bill is payable on demand or at a future time. As the next case illustrates, the antecedent debt or liability in question must be that of the promisor or drawer, maker, or negotiator of the instrument, and not of a third party.

Oliver v Davis
[1949] 2 KB 727, Court of Appeal

Davis borrowed £350 from Oliver and gave him a postdated cheque for £400. Later, he told his fiancée's sister, Miss Woodcock, that he was in difficulty about repaying Oliver, and as a result Miss Woodcock drew a cheque for £400 in favour of Oliver. Before the cheque was presented Miss Woodcock learnt that Davis was already married and stopped her cheque. When sued by Oliver on the cheque, Miss Woodcock contended that there had been no consideration for it. Oliver succeeded before Finnemore J, but Miss Woodcock succeeded on appeal.

Evershed MR: Section 27, sub-s 1 of the Bills of Exchange Act 1882, on which the whole argument turns, is in these terms: 'Valuable consideration for a bill may be constituted by (a) Any consideration sufficient to support a simple contract; (b) An antecedent debt or liability. Such a debt or liability is deemed valuable consideration whether the bill is payable on demand or at a future time.' It is pointed out by Mr Lawson that para (b), referring to an antecedent debt or liability, is on the face of it something distinct in subject-matter from para (a), which refers to considerations sufficient to support a simple contract. I think for myself that the proper construction of the words in (b) 'An antecedent debt or liability' is that they refer to an antecedent debt or liability of the promisor or drawer of the bill and are intended to get over what would otherwise have been prima facie the result that at common law the giving of a cheque for an amount for which you are already indebted imports no consideration, since the obligation is past and has been already incurred. On the facts of this case it may not be strictly necessary to express a concluded view on that matter. But the case in this court of *Crears v Hunter* ((1887) 19 QBD 341) (which, though decided after the date of the Act of 1882, related to the law in regard to bills of exchange which the Act generally codified) including the argument addressed to the court on behalf of the defendant, in my judgment strongly supports the view that 'an antecedent debt or liability' ought so to be construed. This at any rate is plain—that if the antecedent debt or liability of a third party is to be relied upon as supplying 'valuable consideration for a bill,' there must at least be some relationship between the receipt of the bill and the antecedent debt or liability. And for practical purposes it is difficult to see how there can be any distinction between a case in which there is a sufficient relationship for this purpose between the bill and the antecedent debt or liability and a case in which, as a result of that relationship, there is in the ordinary sense a consideration passing from the payee to the drawer of the bill. Otherwise the creditor might recover both on the debt from the third party and on the cheque from the drawer . . .

Somervell LJ: . . . [T]he antecedent debt or liability in s 27, sub-s 1(b) is a debt or liability due from the maker or negotiator of the instrument and not from a third party. That being so, in this case the plaintiff cannot rely on (b). He cannot say: 'Because there was an antecedent debt or liability from the third party, therefore I am entitled to succeed.' *Crears v Hunter*, in my opinion, makes it clear that when dealing with a negotiable instrument given in respect of a debt of a third party, consideration has to be found such as is now referred to in s 27, sub-s 1(a), namely, consideration sufficient to support a simple contract. If that is right, the plaintiff has here to show a consideration sufficient to support a simple contract . . .

Denning LJ: . . . Section 27, sub-s 1(b) of the Act . . . does not apply to a promise to pay an antecedent debt or liability of a third party. In such a case in order that the promise may be enforced there must be shown a consideration which is sufficient to support a simple contract.

NOTES

1.   What 'consideration sufficient to support a simple contract' could have been provided by Oliver? If he had promised to forbear from suing Davis, or had actually forborne from suing him at the express or implied request of Miss Woodcock, then he would have provided consideration for the cheque (*Alliance Bank v Broom* (1864) 2 Drew & Sm 289; *Fullerton v Provincial Bank of Ireland* [1903] AC 309). This would have provided *present* consideration under s 27(1)(a), not consideration arising out of the antecedent debt or liability of Davis under s 27 (1)(b). Where the person taking the bill or cheque is an employee (or other agent) he must have authority from his employer (or other principal) to release the liability of the debtor in exchange for the instrument (*AEG (UK) Ltd v Lewis* [1993] 2 Bank LR 119, CA).

2.   Certain dicta of Evershed MR may have gone somewhat further than the opinion expressed by Somervell and Denning LJJ. He stated that the antecedent debt or liability of a third party could be relied on as providing consideration if there was 'some relationship between the receipt of the bill and the antecedent debt or liability'. What did he mean by 'some relationship'? Could it mean something other than actual forbearance, or a promise to forbear, to sue? A more flexible approach to consideration was taken in *Autobiography Ltd v Byrne* [2005] EWHC 213 (Ch), where a wife drew a cheque on a joint account with her husband to meet a debt of a company in which they were both shareholders, and of which the husband was a director. The cheque was held to be sufficiently supported by consideration because in the 'commercial context' of the cheque not being intended to be a gift, consideration had moved to the wife in that it was 'unrealistic to suggest that no benefit was conferred on Mrs Byrne given her interest in the Company'. But the case was readily distinguished in *Lomax Leisure Ltd (in liquidation) v Miller* [2007] EWHC 2508 (Ch), where it was held that cheques drawn by liquidators of an insolvent company, for the purpose of making a dividend payment to that company's creditors, were not supported by consideration because the liquidators did not stand to gain personally by making the payment and were merely performing what they reasonably considered to be their statutory functions. It is submitted, therefore, that there is little scope for application of the wider dicta of Evershed MR by the English courts, which have consistently adopted the orthodox position that the antecedent debt or liability referred to under s 27(1)(b) cannot be that of a stranger (see, eg, *Oliver v Davis*, above; *Hasan v Willson* [1977] 1 Lloyd's Rep 431 at 441, per Robert Goff J; *MK International Development Co Ltd v Housing Bank* [1991] 1 Bank LR 74 at 78–79, per Mustill LJ). As Professor Guest submits: 'This may be justified on the ground that, as between immediate parties [see below], consideration—whether present or past—must move from the promisee' (*Chalmers and Guest on Bills of Exchange* (17th edn, 2009), para 4–023).

3.   Professors Goode and McKendrick argue that, save in relation to a bill taken as security for an existing debt, it is a misconception to regard s 27(1)(b) as an exception to the common law rule as to past consideration (*Goode on Commercial Law* (5th edn, 2016), pp 536–537). This is because it was established by Lush J in *Currie v Misa* (1875) LR 10 Exch 153 at 163–164 that a negotiable instrument is given for value when it is offered, and accepted, as conditional payment of an existing debt. This leaves open the question: why should the same rule not equally apply where the debt is that of a third party?

By s 27(2) of the BEA where value has at any time been given for a bill, the holder is deemed to be a holder for value as regards the acceptor and all parties to the bill who became parties prior to such time. In other words, a holder can be a 'holder for value' despite not having given value himself and, relying on the status afforded to him by s 27(2), he can sue a party to the bill who did not receive value, so long as some other party to the bill in the chain between them gave value. Take Figure 19.4 as an example.

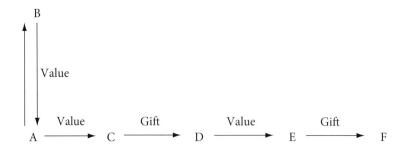

Figure 19.4 Holder for value

An order bill payable at a future date is drawn by A on B and accepted by B as payment for goods supplied to him by A. A, who is the named payee, indorses the bill to C for value. C then indorses it to D as a gift. D indorses the bill to E for value. E indorses it to F as a gift. Relying on s 27(2), F (a donee) can sue the acceptor (B) and all parties to the bill who became parties before E gave value, including C who received no value himself.

There are two important limitations on the operation of s 27(2). First, a holder can rely on the subsection to make himself a holder for value as against a remote party but not as against an immediate party. As between immediate parties, consideration must move from the promisee (*Churchill and Sim v Goddard* [1937] 1 KB 92 at 110, per Scott LJ; *Hasan v Willson* [1977] 1 Lloyd's Rep 431 at 442, per Robert Goff J). 'Immediate' parties are those that have dealt directly with each other, for example by an agreement to sell or supply goods or services, or to purchase or discount the instrument. All other parties are 'remote'. For example, in Figure 19.4, F and D are remote parties, but F and E are immediate parties, which explains why F (a donee) cannot sue E on the bill. Secondly, s 27(2) envisages value being given by a party to the bill and not by a stranger. Nevertheless, these assertions must be considered against the *obiter dictum* of Danckwerts LJ in the next case.

Diamond v Graham

[1968] 1 WLR 1061, Court of Appeal

To induce Diamond to lend £1,650 to Herman, Graham drew a cheque for £1,665 in favour of Diamond. In return, Herman drew a cheque for £1,665 in favour of Graham and Diamond made the loan to Herman. Later, Graham's cheque in favour of Diamond was dishonoured when presented for payment. When sued on the cheque, Graham argued that Diamond was not a holder for value because no value had passed directly between Diamond and himself, as drawer.

> **Danckwerts LJ**: Prima facie, of course, a bill of exchange is presumed to be for value, and the onus is upon the drawer of the cheque to show that it was not for value, and the discussion which has taken place before us has really revolved round the provisions of s 27(2) of the Bills of Exchange Act, which says:
>
>> Where value has at any time been given for a bill the holder is deemed to be a holder for value as regards the acceptor and all parties to the bill who become parties prior to such time.
>
> The contention of Mr Tibber on behalf of the defendant is that Mr Diamond was not a holder for value because no value had passed directly between him and Mr Graham, the drawer; I think that was the effect of his argument.
>
> There is one thing that I have not mentioned, I think, and that is that when Mr Graham drew the cheque in favour of Mr Diamond, Mr Herman drew his own cheque for the amount and gave it to Mr Graham, but unfortunately Mr Herman's cheque was dishonoured, and I gather that he has since become bankrupt.
>
> It seems to me that in presenting the argument which he did, Mr Tibber was giving a meaning which the words of s 27(2) do not bear, and is not in accordance with the words of that subsection. There is nothing in the subsection which appears to require value to have been given by the holder as long as value has been given for the cheque, and in the present case it seems to me that double value was given for the cheque first of all by Mr Herman, who gave his own cheque to Mr Graham in return for Mr Graham drawing a cheque in favour of Mr Diamond, and as it appears to me further value was given by Mr Diamond when he thereupon released his cheque

to Mr Herman, and consequently there was clearly value for the cheque given, and therefore Mr Diamond was a holder for value. It seems to me, therefore, the defence fails, the plaintiff succeeds, and the appeal must be dismissed . . . .

Diplock LJ: . . . Here there clearly passed between Mr Diamond and Mr Herman 'consideration to support a simple contract.' Was that consideration given for a bill? A bill is defined by s 3(1) in these terms: . . .

Plainly this was a bill, an unconditional order in writing, and it was for the bill that consideration was given to Mr Herman. 'Holder' is defined in s 2: ' "Holder" means the payee or indorsee of a bill or note who is in possession of it.' Mr Diamond was plainly the payee of the bill who acquired possession of it as the result of the consideration which he gave to Mr Herman. It seems to me that clearly he falls within all the requirements of the section.

I should add that Mr Graham became a party to the bill 'prior to such time.' Section 21, which deals with delivery, in sub-s (3) says:

Where a bill is no longer in the possession of a party who has signed it as drawer . . . a valid and unconditional delivery by him is presumed until the contrary is proved.

Mr Tibber has argued, as my Lord has said, that one must not read the words in their literal meaning, but subject to a qualification that it applies only where the consideration has passed directly between one party to the bill and another party to the bill. I can see nothing in the authorities which requires that qualification, and I can see nothing in common sense or justice which requires that qualification in circumstances (though they must be rare) such as existed in this case.

I too would dismiss the appeal.

Sachs LJ: I agree. Not only has the defendant got nowhere near establishing that he did not become a party for value to this cheque, but upon the evidence it is abundantly clear to my mind that there was valuable consideration given for it within the meaning of s 27(1)(a), and in addition that the value was given for it within the meaning of s 27(2).

Accordingly the appeal must be dismissed.

NOTES

1. In *Churchill and Sim v Goddard* [1937] 1 KB 92 at 110 Scott LJ held that '. . . as between immediate parties, the defendant is entitled to prove absence of consideration moving from the plaintiff as a defence to an action on the bill . . '. The accuracy of this statement of law was thrown into doubt by Danckwerts LJ's *obiter dictum* in *Diamond v Graham* that there was nothing in s 27(2) 'which appears to require value to have been given by the holder as long as value has been given for the cheque'. However, Danckwerts LJ's interpretation of s 27(2) was subsequently doubted by Roskill LJ in *Pollway Ltd v Abdullah* [1974] 1 WLR 493 at 497 and in *Hasan v Willson* [1977] 1 Lloyd's Rep 431 at 442 Robert Goff J observed that:

. . . If Lord Justice Danckwerts is to be understood as having stated that, as between immediate parties to a bill, valid consideration may move otherwise than from the promisee, then I have to say, with the greatest respect, that I find it impossible to reconcile this statement with the analysis of the law by the Court of Appeal in *Oliver v Davis*.

See also J Thornley [1968] CLJ 196 and S Scott (1969) 15 McGill LJ 487.

2. In *Diamond v Graham*, Herman was not a party to the cheque yet this did not stop Danckwerts LJ holding that Diamond was a holder for value under s 27(2). The question arose in *MK International Development Co Ltd v Housing Bank* [1991] 1 Bank LR 74, CA, where, following instructions from one of their customers, the Housing Bank drew a bill of exchange payable to 'MK International or bearer' and debited their customer's account accordingly. The bill was first handed to their customer, who then delivered it to MK International. The Court of Appeal held that as the customer gave value for this bearer bill and held it as bearer, MK International could rely on s 27(2) as holders for value. However, Mustill LJ also considered whether MK International could have relied on s 27(2) if the customer had not been a party to the bill. Mustill LJ (at 80) expressed a tentative opinion that s 27(2) was:

> . . . not to be read as envisaging value being provided by strangers to the instrument, but rather as a special provision, directed to the position of a holder who wishes to establish that he is a holder for value in good faith without notice and must as a first step show that he is a holder for value; and it relieves him of the necessity to show that he himself gave value. But it does not alter the requirement created by s 27(1) that some party to the instrument must have done so.

Mustill LJ's comments were made at an interlocutory stage of the proceedings. He acknowledged that his remarks on s 27(2) constituted *obiter dicta* and emphasised that he did not want any court seized of the action to regard his decision as foreclosing its decision on this 'new' point.

3. Section 27(2) states that a holder is deemed to be a holder for value as regards the acceptor 'and all parties to the bill who became parties prior to [the time when value had been given for the bill]'. In *Diamond v Graham* it appears from Danckwerts LJ's judgment that when Graham drew his cheque in favour of Diamond, Herman simultaneously drew his cheque in favour of Graham. The precise sequence of events is not clear from the report. As Graham's liability as drawer would only be complete and irrevocable when the bill was delivered to Diamond (BEA, s 21(1)), it seems likely that he received Herman's cheque, and hence value, before that time. However, in *MK International Development Co Ltd v Housing Bank* [1991] 1 Bank LR 74, when the issue arose of the simultaneous provision of value for a cheque at the time it was drawn, Staughton LJ held (at 82) that '[i]t cannot be right that s 27(2) does not cover the case where a person becomes a party to the bill and receives value simultaneously'.

Rights of a holder for value A holder for value, like any other holder, has the right to sue on the bill in his own name (BEA, s 38(1)). But there is controversy as to the defences that can be raised against him. Two things are certain. First, a holder for value, like a holder in due course, takes the bill subject to 'real' defences, ie those founded on the invalidity of the bill itself (eg forgery of a signature, lack of contractual capacity). Secondly, a holder for value, unlike a holder in due course, takes the bill subject to the defects in title of prior parties (eg fraud, duress, force, or illegality connected with the issue, acceptance or negotiation of the bill). In short, a holder in due course may get a better title than his transferor, whereas a holder for value gets no better title (*Arab Bank Ltd v Ross* [1952] 2 QB 216, 229, CA). The uncertainty relates to how far a holder for value takes the bill subject to personal defences of prior parties, ie those defences that are not founded on the bill itself but arise out of the relationship between the parties themselves (eg the defence of total or partial (liquidated) failure of consideration for the bill through non-performance of the underlying transaction; the right to avoid liability on the bill on the ground that its delivery was induced by misrepresentation). A holder in due course takes the bill free from personal defences available to prior parties as between themselves (BEA, s 38(2)), and so it seems to follow that a holder for value, a less protected and privileged category of holder, takes the bill subject to personal defences of prior parties, unless he is also a holder in due course (the BEA is silent on the issue). This is the position whether the holder for value is immediate or remote to the party raising the personal defence, except that a defence based on absence or failure of consideration is only available as between immediate parties and is unavailable against a remote holder for value (but contrast B Geva [1980] CLJ 360).

QUESTION

The Report of the Review Committee on Banking Services Law and Practice (Cm 622, 1989, paras 8.14–8.16; rec 8(4)) recommended that the need for consideration as a test of the negotiability of negotiable instruments should be abolished. The Review Committee felt that the requirement produced unnecessary complications when used to distinguish between the various types of holders and was unnecessary evidence of an intention to create legal relations. What 'unnecessary complications' could the Review Committee have been referring to? Other than the need for consideration, what evidence is there to show that a party to a bill intends to enter into legal relations? The government's subsequent White Paper on banking services did not take up this recommendation on consideration (Cm 1026, 1990).

(c) Holder in due course

A holder in due course is in a protected and privileged position. He holds the bill free from any defects of title of prior parties, and also from mere personal defences available to prior parties amongst themselves (BEA, s 38(2)). Every holder of a bill is prima facie presumed to be a holder in due course (BEA, s 30(2)). To rebut this presumption, the defendant must prove that the requirements for holder in due course status, set out in s 29(1) of the BEA, have not been satisfied. However, if it is shown that the bill was drawn, accepted, or negotiated as a result of fraud, duress, force, or fear, or illegality, then the claimant can only benefit from the presumption of holder in due course status if he can prove that, following the alleged fraud or illegality, value was given in good faith for the bill (BEA, s 30(2)).

Section 29(1) of the BEA defines a holder in due course as:

> a holder who has taken a bill, complete and regular on the face of it, under the following conditions; namely,
>
> (a) That he became the holder of it before it was overdue, and without notice that it had been previously dishonoured, if such was the fact:
>
> (b) That he took the bill in good faith and for value, and that at the time the bill was negotiated to him he had no notice of any defect in the title of the person who negotiated it.

A person seeking enforce a bill as a holder in due course must satisfy each of requirements set out in s 29(1) of the BEA.

(i) He must be a holder of the bill

But a payee cannot be a holder in due course despite the fact that he is listed as a holder in s 2 of the BEA (see above, p 675).

RE Jones Ltd v Waring and Gillow Ltd

[1926] AC 670, House of Lords

A rogue, by fraud, induced the appellants to draw two cheques, one for £2,000 and another for £3,000, payable to the order of the respondents (who were totally innocent of the fraud). The rogue tendered the cheques to the respondents in payment of his existing indebtedness to them. Subsequently, the respondents raised an objection to the signature on the cheques and returned the cheques to the appellants. The appellants then issued the respondents with a new cheque for £5,000. On discovering the fraud the appellants claimed repayment of the proceeds of the cheque from the respondents. By a majority (Viscount Cave LC and Lord Atkinson dissenting), the House of Lords gave judgment for the appellants.

Viscount Cave LC: My Lords, it was contended on behalf of the respondents that they were 'holders in due course' of the cheque for £5000 within the meaning of s 21, sub-s 2, of the Bills of Exchange Act 1882, and entitled on that ground to retain the proceeds of the cheque. I do not think that the expression 'holder in due course' includes the original payee of a cheque. It is true that under the definition clause in the Act (s 2) the word 'holder' includes the payee of a bill unless the context otherwise requires; but it appears from s 29, sub-s 1, that a 'holder in due course' is a person to whom a bill has been 'negotiated,' and from s 31 that a bill is negotiated by being transferred from one person to another and (if payable to order) by indorsement and delivery. In view of these definitions it is difficult to see how the original payee of a cheque can be a 'holder in due course' within the meaning of the Act. Section 21, sub-s 2, which distinguishes immediate from remote parties and includes a holder in due course among the latter, points to the same conclusion. The decision of Lord Russell in *Lewis v Clay* ((1897) 67 LJQB 224) was to the effect that the expression does not include a payee; and the opinion to the contrary expressed by Fletcher Moulton LJ in *Lloyds Bank v Cooke* ([1907] 1 KB 794) does not appear to have been accepted by the other members of the Court of Appeal. This contention therefore fails.

[On the issue of whether the respondents were holders in due course, the majority (**Lords Shaw of Dunfermline**, **Sumner**, and **Carson**) delivered opinions concurring with that of the Lord Chancellor. **Lord Atkinson** concurred.]

NOTES

1.   As a payee cannot be a holder in due course, he cannot be deemed to be one under s 30(2) of the BEA. However, the editors of *Byles on Bills of Exchange and Cheques* (29 edn, 2013) state that *RE Jones Ltd v Waring and Gillow* 'did not, specifically, at any rate, reduce the rights of a payee-holder for value below those of a holder in due course. Moreover, it is submitted that the decision did not affect the rights of the payee-holder for value whatever they may be' (para 18–031). It appears that if the issue or acceptance of a bill is affected by the fraud or duress of a third party, that can only be raised as a defence against the original payee who has taken the bill in good faith and for value, if the party sued on the bill can prove that when the payee took it he had notice of the defect (*Talbot v Von Boris* [1911] 1 KB 854, CA; followed by Robert Goff J in *Hasan v Willson* [1977] 1 Lloyd's Rep 431 at 444; as approved and applied in *Dextra Bank & Trust Co Ltd v Bank of Jamaica* [2002] 1 All ER (Comm) 193 at [22], PC). When assessing whether the payee had notice of the third party's fraud, etc, the court should take account of the wider circumstances in which the transaction had taken place, including whether there had been previous, similar transactions which the payee knew to be fraudulent (*Abbey National plc v JSF Finance & Currency Exchange Co Ltd* [2006] EWCA Civ 328 at [41]–[44]). Note how the burden of proof rests on the party sued

and not the payee, as would be the case if s 30(2) applied (see *Chalmers and Guest on Bills of Exchange* (17th edn, 2009), paras 4–085 and 5–073).

2. The payee can be given the rights of a holder in due course under s 29(3) of the BEA where the bill is negotiated from the payee to an indorsee, who is a holder in due course, and later renegotiated back to the original payee by that indorsee (*Jade International Steel Stahl and Eisen GmbH & Co KG v Robert Nicholas (Steels) Ltd* [1978] QB 917, CA: see below, p 690).

(ii) *The bill must be complete and regular on its face (which includes the back of the bill)*

The incompleteness or irregularity of the bill stands as a warning to the holder. No matter how honest he is, the holder of such a bill cannot acquire a better title than his transferor.

(a) Incomplete bill

A bill is considered incomplete if any material detail is missing, for example the name of the payee, the amount payable, or any necessary indorsements (omission of the date does not render the bill incomplete unless the date is necessary to fix the maturity of the bill).

If the bill is incomplete in a material respect (ie it is an inchoate instrument), the holder has the right to complete it, so long as this is done within a reasonable time and strictly in accordance with the authority given (BEA, s 20: see above, p 665). There is authority to suggest that this enables the holder to convert himself retrospectively into a holder in due course (*Glenie v Bruce Smith* [1908] 1 KB 263 at 268–269, and other cases cited in *Chalmers and Guest on Bills of Exchange* (17th edn, 2009), para 4–052). The bootstraps nature of this approach makes it unattractive. Moreover, it conflicts with the express wording of s 29(1) of the BEA, which requires the holder to have 'taken' a bill that is complete and regular on its face if he is to be a holder in due course. This does not stop a holder completing the bill and then negotiating it to another holder who takes it as a holder in due course, but it would seem to prevent the first holder from elevating himself to that status.

By s 2 of the Cheques Act 1957 if a collecting bank takes for value a cheque payable to order (ie not a non-transferable cheque, such as one crossed 'account payee') without the cheque having been indorsed to it, the cheque will be treated as indorsed in blank and, therefore, payable to bearer. Notwithstanding the omission of the indorsement the cheque is transferable by mere delivery and the bank can take it as a holder in due course (*Midland Bank Ltd v RV Harris Ltd* [1963] 1 WLR 1021 at 1024–1025; *Westminster Bank Ltd v Zang* [1966] AC 182 at 190).

(b) Irregular bill

A bill is considered irregular if it contains a feature that would reasonably put the holder on inquiry. For example, a bill will not be regular on its face if an indorsement is irregular.

Arab Bank Ltd v Ross
[1952] 2 QB 216, Court of Appeal

Ross was the maker of two promissory notes naming a Palestine firm, 'Fathi and Faysal Nabulsy Company', as payees. One of the partners in that firm indorsed the notes 'Fathi and Faysal Nabulsy' (the word 'Company' being omitted) and discounted them to the Arab Bank. The issue arose whether the notes were 'complete and regular on [their] face' so that the Arab

Bank could succeed with a claim against Ross as holders in due course under s 29. The Court of Appeal held that the indorsements were irregular and that the Arab Bank were not holders in due course. Nevertheless, the bank were held entitled to succeed with their claim on the notes as a holders for value.

Denning LJ: The first question in this case is whether the Arab Bank Ltd were holders in due course of the promissory note, and that depends on whether, at the time they took it, it was 'complete and regular on the face of it' within s 29 of the Bills of Exchange Act 1882. Strangely enough, no one doubts that the 'face' of a bill includes the back of it. I say strangely enough, because people so often insist on the literal interpretation of Acts of Parliament, whereas here everyone agrees that the literal interpretation must be ignored because the meaning is obvious. The meaning is that, looking at the bill, front and back, without the aid of outside evidence, it must be complete and regular in itself.

Regularity is a different thing from validity. The Act itself makes a careful distinction between them. On the one hand an indorsement which is quite invalid may be regular on the face of it. Thus the indorsement may be forged or unauthorized and, therefore, invalid under s 24 of the Act, but nevertheless there may be nothing about it to give rise to any suspicion. The bill is then quite regular on the face of it. Conversely, an indorsement which is quite irregular may nevertheless be valid. Thus, by a misnomer, a payee may be described on the face of the bill by the wrong name, nevertheless, if it is quite plain that the drawer intended him as payee, then an indorsement on the back by the payee in his own true name is valid and sufficient to pass the property in the bill (*Leonard v Wilson* ((1834) 2 Cr & M 589); *Bird & Co v Thomas Cook & Son Ltd* ([1937] 2 All ER 227); *Hadley v Henry* ((1896) 22 VLR 230)), but the difference between front and back makes the indorsement irregular unless the payee adds also the misnomer by which he was described on the front of the bill. This is what he eventually did in *Leonard v Wilson*.

Regularity is also different from liability. The Act makes a distinction between these two also. On the one hand a person who makes an irregular indorsement is liable thereon despite the irregularity. Thus, if a payee, who is wrongly described on the front of the bill, indorses it in his own true name, the indorsement is irregular, but he is liable to any subsequent holder and cannot set up the irregularity as a defence; or, if he is rightly described on the front of the bill, but indorses it in an assumed name, the indorsement is irregular but he is liable thereon as if he had indorsed it in his own name: see s 28(1) and s 55(2) of the Act. Conversely, a regular indorsement will not impose liability if it is forged or unauthorized. Thus, where a firm is the payee, but is described in an unauthorized name which is substantially different from its real name, an indorsement by one partner in that name does not impose liability on the other partners: *Kirk v Blurton* ((1841) 9 M & W 284). It would be otherwise if the name was substantially the same: *Forbes v Marshall* ((1855) 11 Exch 166).

Once regularity is seen to differ both from validity and from liability, the question is when is an indorsement irregular? The answer is, I think, that it is irregular whenever it is such as to give rise to doubt whether it is the indorsement of the named payee. A bill of exchange is like currency. It should be above suspicion. But if it is asked: When does an indorsement give rise to doubt? I would say that that is a practical question which is, as a rule, better answered by a banker than a lawyer. Bankers have to consider the regularity of indorsements every week, and every day of every week, and every hour of every day; whereas the judges sitting in this court have not had to consider it for these last 20 years. So far as I know the last occasion was in *Slingsby's* case ([1932] 1 KB 544).

The Law Merchant is founded on the custom of merchants, and we shall not go far wrong if we follow the custom of bankers of the City of London on this point. They have given evidence that they would not accept the indorsements in this case as a regular indorsement. They said that if a bill is made payable to 'Fathi and Faysal Nabulsy Company' they would not accept an indorsement 'Fathi and Faysal Nabulsy.' I think there is good sense in their view. For aught they know, in Palestine the word 'company' may be of vital significance. It may there signify a different legal entity, just as the word 'limited' does here (*Bank of Montreal v Exhibit and Trading Co* ((1906) 11 Com Cas 250), or it may signify a firm of many partners and not merely two of them. I agree with the bankers that this indorsement does give rise to doubt whether it is the indorsement of the named payee. It was, therefore, irregular . . .

The truth is, I think, that the bankers adopted this strict attitude both in their own interests and also in the interests of their customers. It would be quite impossible for them to make inquiries to see that all the indorsements on a bill are in fact genuine; but they can at least see that they are regular on the face of them: see *Bank of England v Vagliano* ([1891] AC 107 at 157), per Lord Macnaghten. That is some safeguard against dishonesty. It is a safeguard which the bankers have taken for the past 120 years at least, and I do not think we should throw any doubt today on the correctness of their practice.

I do not stay to discuss the regularity of indorsements by married women or titled folk, except to say that titles and descriptions can often be omitted without impairing the regularity of the indorsement. The word 'company' in this case is not, however, mere description. It is part of the name itself. It was suggested that an indorsement in Arabic letters would be regular. I cannot accept this view. The indorsement should be in the same lettering as the name of the payee; for otherwise it could not be seen on the face of it to be regular. My conclusion is, therefore, that this promissory note, when it was taken by the Arab Bank Ltd, was not complete and regular on the face of it. They were not, therefore, holders in due course.

[**Somervell** and **Romer LJJ** delivered concurring judgments.]

(iii) The bill must not be overdue at the time of transfer

A time bill (payable on a particular day) is overdue if not presented for payment on the day it falls due. A demand bill is overdue when it appears on its face to have been in circulation for an unreasonable length of time, which is a question of fact in each case (BEA, s 36(3)).

(iv) The holder must have no notice of previous dishonour

The dishonour may be for non-payment or for non-acceptance. What constitutes 'notice' is considered below.

(v) The holder must have taken the bill without notice and in good faith

Section 29(1) of the BEA contains separate requirements that:

(a) when he takes the bill the holder does not have notice of any previous dishonour for non-acceptance or for non-payment;
(b) at the time the bill was negotiated to him the holder does not have notice of any defect in the title of the person who negotiated it; and
(c) the holder takes the bill in good faith.

The expression 'notice' in s 29(1) means either actual knowledge of a fact or suspicion that something is wrong coupled with a wilful disregard of the means of knowledge. It does not include 'constructive knowledge' (see above, p 33). By s 90 of the BEA, the expression 'good faith' is defined in terms of the holder's honesty and not his negligence. Notice and good faith are linked. Failure to discover a defect in the title of the transferor because of lack of care is not dishonest but deliberately turning a blind eye to suspicious circumstances is.

Jones v Gordon

(1877) 2 App Cas 616, House of Lords

To defraud their creditors, S drew and G accepted a number of bills of exchange. Four of the bills, with an overall face value of £1,727, were purchased by J for £200. J knew that G was in financial difficult, but he refrained from contacting certain people who he knew could give him information as to G's financial affairs. The House of Lords held that J was not a bona fide purchaser who could take the bills free of defects in title as he was deemed to have known of the fraud.

Lord Blackburn: . . . [M]y Lords, I think it is right to say that I consider it to be fully and thoroughly established that if value be given for a bill of exchange, it is not enough to shew that there was carelessness, negligence, or foolishness in not suspecting that the bill was wrong, when there were circumstances which might have led a man to suspect that. All these are matters which tend to shew that there was dishonesty in not doing it, but they do not in themselves make a defence to an action upon a bill of exchange. I take it that in order to make such a defence, whether in the case of a party who is solvent and *sui juris*, or when it is sought to be proved against the estate of a bankrupt, it is necessary to shew that the person who gave value for the bill, whether the value given be great or small, was affected with notice that there was something wrong about it when he took it. I do not think it is necessary that he should have notice of what the particular wrong was. If a man, knowing that a bill was in the hands of a person who had no right to it, should happen to think that perhaps the man had stolen it, when if he had known the real truth he would have found, not that the man had stolen it, but that he had obtained it by false pretences, I think that would not make any difference if he knew that there was something wrong about it and took it. If he takes it in that way he takes it at his peril.

But then I think that such evidence of carelessness or blindness as I have referred to may with other evidence be good evidence upon the question which, I take it, is the real one, whether he did know that there was something wrong in it. If he was (if I may use the phrase) honestly blundering and careless, and so took a bill of exchange or a bank-note when he ought not to have taken it, still he would be entitled to recover. But if the facts and circumstances are such that the jury, or whoever has to try the question, came to the conclusion that he was not honestly blundering and careless, but that he must have had a suspicion that there was something wrong, and that he refrained from asking questions, not because he was an honest blunderer or a stupid man, but because he thought in his own secret mind—I suspect there is something wrong, and if I ask questions and make farther inquiry, it will no longer be my suspecting it, but my knowing it, and then I shall not be able to recover—I think that is dishonesty. I think, my Lords, that that is established, not only by good sense and reason, but by the authority of the cases themselves.

[**Lords O'Hagan** and **Gordon** delivered concurring judgments.]

NOTE

J paid £200 for bills with a total value of £1,727. This caused Lord Blackburn to note at 631–632 that:

. . . since the repeal of the Usury Laws we can never inquire into the question as to how much was given for a bill, and if [J's vendor] was in such a position that he could have proved against the estate it would have been no objection at all that he conveyed these bills to another for a nominal amount, that he sold bills nominally amounting to £1,727 for £200. Although I think that could not have been inquired into, yet the amount given in comparison with the apparent value is an important piece of evidence guiding us to a conclusion as to whether or not it was a bona fide transaction.

In *MK International Development Co Ltd v Housing Bank* [1991] 1 Bank LR 74, CA, Mustill LJ (at 79) noted Lord Blackburn's remarks in *Jones v Gordon* and continued:

> . . . It may also be the law that where the bill is given as the price of an indivisible obligation the maker cannot complain even as against an immediate party that the obligation was not worth the amount of the bill, ie that he made a bad bargain: unless perhaps the consideration is so trifling as not to be consideration at all: see *Young v Gordon* (1896) 23 R 419.

(vi) The holder must take the bill for value

If a holder is deemed to be a holder for value under s 27(2) of the BEA (see above, p 678), can he establish 'that he took the bill . . . for value' under s 29(1)(b) and so become a holder in due course? Two cases suggest he can. In *MK International Development Co Ltd v The Housing Bank* [1991] 1 Bank LR 74 at 80, Mustill LJ clearly thought, albeit *obiter* only, that a holder in due course did not have to provide value himself but that he could rely on s 27(2). In *Clifford Chance v Silver* [1992] 2 Bank LR 11, the Court of Appeal held that a cheque received by the claimant solicitors as stakeholders (ie without themselves giving value for it) was nevertheless held by them as holders in due course because they were deemed to be 'holders for value' pursuant to s 27(2). But in neither case does it appear that the Court of Appeal considered the views of the majority of commentators who believe that it is necessary for a person claiming to be a holder in due course under s 29(1) to have given value personally: see, for example, J James, *Richardson's Guide to Negotiable Instruments* (8th edn, 1991), p 77; B Geva [1980] CLJ 360 at 364; *Chalmers and Guest on Bills of Exchange* (14th edn, 1991), p 274 (now 17th edn, 2009, para 4–057). It remains strongly arguable that the phrase 'he took the bill in good faith and for value' in s 29(1)(b) implies that a holder in due course must give value personally (see E McKendrick, *Goode on Commercial Law* (5th edn, 2016), p 540). The issue is considered further by LP Hitchens in [1993] JBL 571. A holder relying on s 27(2) does not give value personally; by contrast, a holder relying on s 27(3) does. Section 27(3) of the BEA deems a person to be a holder for value of a bill over which he has a lien. A holder who is deemed by s 27(3) to be a holder for value will be a holder in due course if the other conditions set out in s 29(1) are also satisfied (*Barclays Bank Ltd v Astley Industrial Trust Ltd* [1970] 2 QB 527 at 539).

(a) Rights of a holder in due course

Cebora SNC v SIP (Industrial Products) Ltd

[1976] 1 Lloyd's Rep 271, Court of Appeal

See above, p 656.

NOTES

1.   Under s 38(2) of the BEA, a holder in due course holds the bill free from any defects of title of prior parties, as well as from mere personal defences available to prior parties amongst themselves, and may enforce payment against all parties liable on the bill. Section 29(2) of the BEA provides that 'the title of a person who negotiates a bill is defective when he obtained the bill, or its acceptance, by fraud, duress, or force or fear, or other unlawful means, or for an illegal consideration, or when he negotiates it in breach of faith, or under such circumstances as amount to fraud'. Thus, the title of the person negotiating the bill may be defective as a result of either the circumstances in which he acquired the bill, or those in which he transferred it. In addition, it may be due to a defect in the title of a prior party. The s 29(2) list of 'defects of title' is probably not exhaustive (see Geva [1980] CLJ 360 at 363). The expression 'mere personal defences' is not defined in the BEA and covers defences not founded on the bill itself but arising out of the relationship between the parties themselves. It appears to include matters of set-off or counterclaim and general contractual defences, such as any misrepresentation inducing the contract on the bill. There is some controversy as to whether absence or failure of consideration is a mere personal defence or a defect of title (see above, pp 681–682).

2.   Although the holder in due course is not subject to defects of title or mere personal defences of prior parties, there are 'exceptional circumstances', as referred to by Sir Erich Sachs in the *Cebora* case, when a bill will not be treated as cash in the hands of such a holder. They are as follows:

(a)   when there are 'real' or 'absolute' defences arising from the invalidity of the bill itself, or the invalidity of the defendant's apparent contract on the bill (eg contractual incapacity, forged or unauthorised signature, *non est factum*): *Chalmers and Guest on Bills of Exchange* (17th edn, 2009), para 5–070;

(b)   when the holder in due course sues as agent or trustee for another person, or when he sues wholly or in part for another person, as any defence or set-off available against that person is available *pro tanto* against the holder: see *Barclays Bank Ltd v Aschaffenburger Zellstoffwerke AG* [1967] 1 Lloyd's Rep 387, CA;

(c)   when the holder in due course does not comply with his duties as to presentment for acceptance and/or payment, or when he fails to comply with the proper procedure on dishonour (see below, Section 8).

3.   In the context of 'regulated' consumer credit and consumer hire agreements (unless they are non-commercial agreements), s 123(1) of the Consumer Credit Act 1974 prohibits the taking of negotiable instruments, other than banknotes or cheques, in discharge of amounts payable by the debtor or hirer or by a surety. Section 123(3) prohibits the taking of any negotiable instrument (including cheques) as a security for an amount payable under such an agreement. Under s 125(1) a person who takes a negotiable instrument in contravention of s 123(1) or (3) is not a holder in due course, and is not entitled to enforce the instrument. However, the transferee of a negotiable instrument from such an owner or creditor can be a holder in due course and is entitled to enforce the instrument (s 125(4)). Even a transferee who is not a holder in due course can enforce such an instrument as the contravention of s 123(1) or (3) is probably not a defect of title within s 29(2) of the 1882 Act (*Chalmers and Guest on Bills of Exchange* (17th edn, 2009), paras 4–070 and 4–071). In these circumstances the person forced to pay on the instrument is entitled to be indemnified by the owner or creditor (s 125(3)).

QUESTION

Why did Parliament seek to restrict the use of negotiable instruments in the manner set out in ss 123–125 of the Consumer Credit Act 1974?

(d) Holder in due course by derivation

Section 29(3) of the BEA provides that a holder (whether for value or not) who derives his title to a bill through a holder in due course, and who is not himself a party to any fraud or illegality affecting it, has all the rights of a holder in due course as regards the acceptor and all parties to the bill prior to that holder. It has even been held that a person who draws a bill in his own favour can benefit from s 29(3) where the bill is negotiated from him, as payee, to an indorsee, who is a holder in due course, and later renegotiated back to the original payee by that indorsee.

Jade International Steel Stahl und Eisen GmbH & Co KG v Robert Nicholas (Steels) Ltd

[1978] QB 917, Court of Appeal

Jade drew a bill of exchange, payable to themselves or order, on Nicholas for the price of steel supplied by them to Nicholas. Jade indorsed the bill and discounted it to a German bank (Sparkasse), who discounted it to another German bank, and they, in turn, discounted it to Midland Bank. Each bank took the bill as a holder in due course. Midland Bank presented the bill to Nicholas for acceptance. Nicholas accepted the bill but later dishonoured it when presented for payment owing to a dispute about the quality of the steel supplied by Jade. Midland Bank then indorsed the bill in blank and, as each bank exercised its rights of re-course, the bill was passed back down the line until it reached Jade, whose account Sparkasse had debited with its amount. Jade then brought an action on the bill against Nicholas, who raised the defective quality of the steel as a defence. The issue was whether, under s 29(3) of the BEA, Jade could claim the benefits of holder in due course status enjoyed by the banks. Donaldson J held Jade were entitled to summary judgment on the bill. His decision was upheld on appeal.

Cumming-Bruce LJ: So the short point which is raised as the first point on this appeal is whether in those circumstances the drawer/payee to whom the bill was delivered pursuant to the Midland Bank or Sparkasse's right of recourse is properly to be regarded as a holder who derives his title to the bill through a holder in due course, within the meaning of s 29(3) of the Act.

The submission of Mr Bowsher is that when the plaintiffs recovered the bill pursuant to the Sparkasse Bank's right of recourse they did not thereby derive their title to the bill through the Sparkasse Bank, or through any of the other indorsers, but that it came back to them in their initial capacity as drawer pursuant to their liability as drawer under s 47(2) of the Act. Thus, he submits, that whether or not it is right within the meaning of the subsection to regard the plaintiffs at that stage as holders they were not holders who derived their title through a holder in due course. Initially as drawers they derive title from nobody. When they negotiated the bill in the first instance they then lost their title. All that was left was their liability under s 47(2), the liability to a right of recourse against them in their capacity as drawers. And so the submission is that the words of s 29(3) ought to be read strictly so as to limit the meaning of the words 'derive title to the bill' to those situations in which the bill is negotiated, what I would call on its way upwards, from the original drawer to indorser and subsequent indorsers . . .

I see the force as a matter of mercantile practice of the submission of Mr Bowsher that there is not any good commercial reason to deprive the defendants of the contractual rights that they initially had before they discounted the bill merely because in the last stages of the story when the bill was being dishonoured it comes back into the drawer's hands pursuant to the right of recourse of a party to whom the bill has been negotiated. The question which in the absence of authority I do not find perfectly straightforward is whether it can be right to place a restricted meaning on the apparently clear words of the subsection so as to exclude these plaintiffs from a capacity which at first sight they have, namely, a holder deriving title to the bill from a holder in due course; and faced with the words of the statute I am persuaded that there is not sufficient reason shown for placing upon those words the restricted meaning for which he contends.

I remain, which may be only a reflection of my inexperience, surprised that in the year 1977, one hundred years almost since this section was placed on the Statute Book, that the point does not appear ever to have come up for decision and is without authority.

For the reasons that I have stated on the first point, which is the only point that has been argued, I would agree that the appeal should be dismissed.

Geoffrey Lane LJ: It seems to me that once the drawers/payees (the plaintiffs in this case) have discounted the bill to the Sparkasse (Sparkasse then becoming the holders in due course), they lose the capacity which they had as immediate parties to the bill as drawers. Then when in the effluxion of time they once again become holders of the bill in the way that I have described, it is in that new fresh capacity of holders via the Sparkasse and the other bank that their situation must be judged. It is unreal as I see it to regard them as having a dual capacity. Indeed, it is something of a logical difficulty to see how they could. I repeat, when they discounted the bill they lost the benefit of their original capacity, and the guise under which they held it on the second occasion becomes the dominating guise for the purpose of deciding whether or not the judge was in a position to consider the question of discretion . . .

On the first ground I would dismiss this appeal.

[**Stephenson LJ** delivered a concurring judgment.]

NOTES

1. This decision has the surprising result that a gratuitous payee, who can bring himself within s 29(3), can enforce the bill as though he were a holder in due course (and see the other criticisms of J Thornley [1978] CLJ 236).

2. It is immaterial that the holder in due course by derivation knows of any fraud or illegality when he takes the bill, so long as he is not party to it. Similarly, his knowledge of defects in the title of prior parties is also irrelevant (*Insurance Corpn of Ireland plc v Dunluce Meats Ltd* [1991] NI 286). But s 29(3) only gives the holder in due course by derivation the same rights as the holder in due course through whom he derived his title as against the acceptor and all parties to the bill prior to that holder. This means that if the holder in due course by derivation took the bill as a gift from the holder in due course he could not sue that holder as he had not provided consideration for the bill (although he could sue the acceptor and prior parties). Further, as certain 'real' defences are available against a holder in due course (eg contractual incapacity, forged or unauthorised signature, *non est factum*), they will also be available against a holder in due course by derivation.

6 LIABILITY ON THE BILL OF EXCHANGE: GENERAL PRINCIPLES

It has already been noted that the liability created by a bill of exchange is contractual (see above, p 676). However, the drawer, acceptor, or indorser will only be liable on the bill if:

(1) he has capacity to contract;

(2) his contract on the bill is complete and irrevocable; and

(3) he has signed the instrument as such.

(a) Capacity to contract

By s 22(1) of the BEA, capacity to incur liability as a party to a bill is determined by the general law relating to capacity to contract. If a drawer, acceptor, or indorser has no capacity to contract, he is not liable on the bill. With the abolition of the *ultra vires* rule insofar as it affects third parties, a company will rarely be able to plead against a holder of a bill that it does not have capacity to contract (see the Companies Act 2006, s 39(1)). However, the fact that one party does not have the capacity to contract does not, in itself, release other parties from liability on the bill. Section 5(2) of the BEA provides that where the drawee has no capacity to contract, the holder may treat the instrument, at his option, either as a bill of exchange or as a promissory note.

(b) Complete and irrevocable contract

By s 21(1) of the BEA, every contract on the bill is incomplete and revocable until delivery of the bill. Section 2 of the BEA defines 'delivery' as the transfer of possession, actual or constructive, from one person to another. However, the acceptor's contract can also become complete and irrevocable if he gives notice to, or according to, the directions of the person entitled to the bill that he has accepted it. If the bill is in the hands of a holder in due course a valid delivery of the bill by all parties prior to him, so as to make them liable to him, is conclusively presumed (BEA, s 21(2), and see *Clifford Chance v Silver* [1992] 2 Bank LR 11, CA). The same conclusive presumption also applies in favour of a holder in due course by derivation (*Insurance Corpn of Ireland plc v Dunluce Meats Ltd* [1991] NI 286). If the bill is in the hands of a holder, who is not a holder in due course, there is a rebuttable presumption that there was a valid and unconditional delivery by the drawer, acceptor, or indorser (BEA, s 21(3)). In such a case, in order to be effectual the delivery must be made either by or under the authority of the party drawing, accepting, or indorsing the bill (BEA, s 22(2)(a)). For example, if a drawer draws a bill in favour of a named payee and puts it in his desk, and the bill is later stolen by a thief who hands it to the named payee, the drawer would not be liable since he never authorised delivery at all (remember, the payee cannot be a holder in due course: *RE Jones Ltd v Waring & Gillow Ltd* [1926] AC 670: see above, p 683). By contrast, in *Dextra Bank & Trust Co Ltd v Bank of Jamaica* [2001] UKPC 50, [2002] 1 All ER (Comm) 193, the Privy Council held that there had been an effectual delivery where the drawer authorised his agent to deliver the bill to the payee by one method (personal delivery by the agent) but the agent effected physical delivery by another method (agent used an intermediary to effect delivery). Delivery was held to be effectual, even though not made in the prescribed manner, because the payee had given value and did not know of the method of delivery prescribed. The Privy Council stated (at 200) that any other result seemed 'neither just nor consistent with the objective of achieving maximum certainty in mercantile transactions'.

(c) Signature essential to liability

Under s 23 of the BEA, a person is liable as drawer, acceptor, or indorser of a bill only if he has signed it as such. Particular issues arise when a bill is signed by an agent.

(i) Liability of the principal

Section 91(1) of the BEA provides that a bill does not have to be signed in a person's own hand 'but it is sufficient if his signature is written thereon by some other person by or under his authority'. The agent will usually sign the bill in his own name and add words to his signature indicating that he signs for and on behalf of a principal, but a simple signature of the principal in the hand of the agent will suffice. In either case the principal will be bound if the agent has his actual (express or implied) or apparent (or ostensible) authority to sign. However, if the agent acts outside the bounds of his actual authority and signs by procuration (eg 'per procurationem', 'per pro' or 'pp'), the principal is not bound by the signature. This is the effect of s 25 of the BEA, which provides that a signature by procuration operates as notice to third parties that the agent's authority is limited so that the principal will only be liable on signatures within the actual limits of the agent's authority. Even a holder in due course will be put on notice by such a signature and will not be able to enforce the bill against the principal if the agent has exceeded his authority (*Morison v London County & Westminster Bank Ltd* [1914] 3 KB 356 at 367, per Lord Reading CJ). Unfortunately, the effect of s 25 means that a principal who has misled a third party, by holding his agent out as having authority, will avoid liability simply because of the form of the agent's signature. This will occur even if the third party has no reasonable opportunity to check the agent's authority. It is not clear whether s 25 extends to all forms of representative signature (eg signatures 'for' or 'on behalf of' the principal). Protection of the third party would suggest that a narrow interpretation of the section is to be preferred.

(ii) Liability of the agent

An agent may be held personally liable on the bill if he signs it in his own name unless he makes it quite clear that he is signing only in his capacity as agent. By s 26(1) of the BEA, where a person signs a bill as drawer, indorser, or acceptor, and adds words to his signature, indicating that he signs for or on behalf of a principal, or in a representative capacity, he is not personally liable on the bill, but merely describing himself as an agent, or as filling a representative character, does not exempt him from personal liability. Thus, where an agent signs the bill in his own name and adds words to his signature such as 'per pro', 'for', or 'on behalf of' the principal, he will not be personally liable on the bill, but merely adding words to his signature such as 'agent', 'director', or 'secretary', does not exempt him from personal liability. However, the courts are generally reluctant to impose personal liability on agents.

Bondina Ltd v Rollaway Shower Blinds Ltd
[1986] 1 All ER 564, Court of Appeal

Mr Ward, a company director, signed a cheque by placing his signature (without additional words) below the pre-printed name of the company as drawer. At the bottom of the cheque there was a pre-printed line of figures designating the number of the cheque, the branch of the bank, and the number of the account which was the company's account. The director denied he was personally liable on the cheque.

> **Dillon LJ**: Counsel for the plaintiffs founds himself on s 26 of the Bills of Exchange Act 1882, which provides by sub-s (1):
>> Where a person signs a bill as drawer, indorser, or acceptor, and adds words to his signature, indicating that he signs for or on behalf of a principal, or in a representative character, he is not personally liable thereon; but the mere addition to his signature of words describing him as an agent, or as filling a representative character, does not exempt him from personal liability.

> Counsel for the plaintiffs says that Mr Ward has merely signed a printed form of cheque and has not added any relevant words to his signature. As it seems to me, however, when Mr Ward signed the cheque he adopted all the printing and writing on it; not merely the writing designating the payee and the amount for which the cheque was drawn, if that had been written out for him and not by himself, but also the printing of the company's name and the printing of the numbers which designate the company's account. The effect of this is to show that the cheque is drawn on the company's account and not on any other account. It is not a case of a joint liability of several people. It shows plainly, as I construe it, looking no further than the form of the cheque itself, that the drawer of the cheque was the company and not Mr Ward . . .
>
> [**Sir George Waller** delivered a concurring judgment.]

If there is doubt as to whether a signature on the bill or note is that of the principal or of the agent, then the construction most favourable to the validity of the instrument is adopted (BEA, s 26(2)).

Rolfe Lubell & Co (a firm) v Keith

[1979] 1 All ER 860, Queen's Bench Division

The plaintiffs would only supply goods to GF Ltd if bills of exchange drawn in payment were personally indorsed by two officers of the company. The bills were accepted by the company and indorsed by the managing director and company secretary who placed their signatures within a rubber-stamped box on the back of the bill, so that it read 'For and on behalf of GF Ltd, X (*signature*) director, Y (*signature*) secretary'. The plaintiffs brought an action against the director claiming he was personally liable on the bills.

> **Kilner-Brown J**: . . . In the instant case the form of signature as acceptors on the face of the bill and as indorser on the back of the bill is precisely the same. The two defendants signed for and on behalf of the company and made the company liable on the bill as acceptor. By signing in similar form on the back of the bill they produced what counsel for the plaintiffs described as a mercantile nonsense. An indorsement on the back of a bill amounts to a warrant that the bill will be honoured and imposes in certain circumstances a transfer of liability to the indorser. No one can transfer liability from himself to himself. The only way in which validity can be given to this indorsement is by construing it to bind someone other than the acceptor. As soon therefore as it becomes obvious that the indorsement as worded is meaningless and of no value there is a patent ambiguity which allows evidence to be admitted to give effect to the intentions of the parties . . .
>
>   On the evidence I find as a fact that the first defendant agreed personally to indorse the bills; that his signature is evidence of that agreement and consequently a valid indorsement in a personal capacity and that he is personally liable on the two bills which were dishonoured on presentation. It follows that in my judgment the words 'for and on behalf of the company' are of no significance in so far as the relationship between the plaintiffs and the first defendant are concerned; they do not vary or amend a clear agreement personally to indorse and thereby to warrant and assume liability for the default of the company. The signature is the relevant and significant act.

If the agent signs the bill simply using his principal's name, or if he signs it in his own name but indicating that he accepts no personal liability, then, whether he acts with or without authority, he will not be personally liable on the bill. However, if the agent acts without authority he may be liable in tort for deceit or for breach of warranty of authority.

(iii) *Signatures on company bills, cheques, and promissory notes*

(a) Section 51 of the Companies Act 2006

Under s 51(1), where a contract purports to be made by a company, or by a person as agent for a company, at a time when the company has not been formed, then subject to any agreement to the contrary the contract has effect as a contract entered into by the person purporting to act for the company or as agent for it, and he is personally liable on the contract accordingly. Even though the person signing a bill, cheque, or promissory note adds words to his signature indicating that he signs for and on behalf of a principal, or in a representative capacity, he will still be personally liable on the instrument if he purports to draw, accept, make, or indorse the instrument on behalf of a company which has not been formed (*Phonogram Ltd v Lane* [1982] QB 938, CA).

(b) Repeal of s 349(4) of the Companies Act 1985

Under s 349(4) of the Companies Act 1985, if a director or other officer of a company signed or authorised to be signed on behalf of the company any bill of exchange, promissory note, cheque, or order for money or goods in which its name was not mentioned in legible characters, he was liable to a fine; and he was further personally liable to the holder of the bill etc for the amount of it (unless it was fully paid by the company). The courts applied this subsection strictly so that directors or other officers of the company were held liable where the company's name was misstated even to a relatively minor degree (see, eg, *Fiorentino Comm Giuseppe Srl v Farnesi* [2005] EWHC 160 (Ch), where the company's name was stated as 'Portofino Collections (London)' instead of 'Portofino Collections (London) Ltd' on a cheque), although where the misstatement was attributable to the holder of the bill of exchange etc, that holder was estopped from holding the company's signatory liable (*Durham Fancy Goods Ltd v Michael Jackson (Fancy Goods Ltd)* [1968] 2 QB 839, CA).

Section 349(4) could operate harshly, especially on junior employees of the company, and several commentators, including the original authors of this book (see 3rd edn, p 536), called for its repeal. The Company Law Review took the same view in its *Final Report* (2001), and s 349(4) was later repealed by the Companies Act 2006. The Company, Limited Liability Partnership and Business (Names and Trading Disclosures) Regulations 2015 (SI 2015/17) now require every company to disclose its registered name on (inter alia) its bills of exchange, promissory notes, endorsements, and order forms (reg 24(1)(b)), and also on cheques purporting to be signed by or on behalf of the company (reg 24(1)(c)). Under s 83 of the Companies Act 2006, if legal proceedings are brought by a company to enforce a contract made in the course of a business in respect of which the company was, at the time the contract was made, in breach of these regulations, the legal proceedings will be dismissed if the defendant shows: (a) that he has a claim against the company arising out of the contract which he has been unable to pursue because of the breach of the regulations, or (b) that the company's breach of the regulations has caused him to suffer financial loss in connection with the contract, unless (in either case) the court is satisfied that it is just and equitable to permit the proceedings to continue. The company and any officer of the company may be subject to a criminal penalty for breach of the regulation (reg 28(1), and Companies Act 2006, s 84).

(d) Forged or unauthorised signatures

Section 24 of the BEA provides that where a signature on a bill is forged or placed on it without the authority of the person whose signature it purports to be, the forged or unauthorised signature is wholly inoperative, and no right to retain the bill, discharge it, or enforce it can be acquired through or under that signature, unless the party against whom it is sought to retain it or enforce payment of the bill is precluded (ie estopped) from setting up the forgery or want of authority. The section also provides that it does not affect the ratification of an unauthorised signature not amounting to a forgery. But what is a forgery?

Forgery and Counterfeiting Act 1981

Section 1

A person is guilty of forgery if he makes a false instrument, with the intention that he or another shall use it to induce somebody to accept it as genuine, and by reason of so accepting it to do or not to do some act to his own or any other person's prejudice.

Section 9

(1) An instrument is false for the purposes of this Part of the Act—

. . .

    (d) if it purports to have been made in the terms in which it is made on the authority of a person who did not in fact authorise its making in those terms; . . .

(2) A person is to be treated for the purposes of this Part of this Act as making a false instrument if he alters an instrument so as to make it false in any respect (whether or not it is false in some other respect apart from that alteration).

NOTE

Section 9(1)(d) of the Forgery and Counterfeiting Act 1981 superseded s 1 of the Forgery Act 1913, which was drafted in similar terms. In *Kreditbank Cassel GmbH v Schenkers Ltd* [1927] 1 KB 826 a branch manager of the defendant company, without authority and fraudulently, drew and indorsed bills on behalf of the company for his own benefit. The Court of Appeal held that the company was not liable on the bills as they were forgeries within the Forgery Act 1913 and the claimants could not rely on the rule in *Turquand*'s case (1856) 6 E & B 327 (the rule that persons dealing with a company are not bound to inquire into its indoor management and will not be affected by irregularities of which they had no notice) because that rule did not apply where the bills were forgeries. It would appear, therefore, that a fraudulent unauthorised signature amounts to a forgery and cannot be ratified (*Brook v Hook* (1871) LR 6 Exch 89). Yet this cannot be what was intended by s 24 which distinguishes between unauthorised signatures (which are ratifiable) and forged signatures (which are not ratifiable). The explanation appears to be that when the Bills of Exchange Act 1882 was passed the Forgery Act 1861 was in force and that Act did not treat an unauthorised signature as a forgery (see *Morison v London County and Westminster Bank Ltd* [1914] 3 KB 356 at 366, CA). Consistent with what appears to have been Parliament's intention when the Bills of Exchange Act 1882 was passed, it is submitted by Professor Guest, in *Chalmers and Guest on Bills of Exchange* (17th edn, 2009), para 3–047, that the definition of forgery now contained in the Forgery and Counterfeiting Act 1981 should not be applied to s 24 of the BEA (cf E McKendrick, *Goode on Commercial Law* (5th edn, 2016), p 559: there is no reason why a signature on behalf of another without his authority should not be ratified even though it is a forgery as defined by the 1981 Act). Yet even if the 1981 Act's definition of forgery is applied to the 1882 Act, it is submitted that, so far as ratification is concerned, the distinction between forged and unauthorised signatures, emphasised by s 24, should be maintained. This is because a true forger does not act, or purport to act, under the authority of the person whose signature he forges and so his signature cannot be ratified; whereas an unauthorised signature can be ratified when the agent purports to act on behalf of a principal.

Greenwood v Martins Bank Ltd
[1933] AC 51, House of Lords

A husband opened an account in his sole name with the respondent bank. His wife forged his signature on various cheques and drew money out of this account. The husband found out about the forgeries but was persuaded by his wife to say nothing. The husband remained silent for eight months and when he finally decided to tell the bank of his wife's action she shot herself. The husband brought an action against the bank to recover the sums paid out of his account on the cheques to which his signature had been forged.

Lord Tomlin: . . . Now it may be said at once that there can be no question of ratification or of adoption in this case. The necessary elements for ratification were not present, and adoption as understood in English law requires valuable consideration, which is not even suggested here.

The sole question is whether in the circumstances of this case the respondents are entitled to set up an estoppel.

The essential factors giving rise to an estoppel are I think:

(1) A representation or conduct amounting to a representation intended to induce a course of conduct on the part of the person to whom the representation is made.

(2) An act or omission resulting from the representation, whether actual or by conduct, by the person to whom the representation is made.

(3) Detriment to such person as a consequence of the act or omission.

Mere silence cannot amount to a representation, but when there is a duty to disclose deliberate silence may become significant and amount to a representation.

The existence of a duty on the part of the customer of a bank to disclose to the bank his knowledge of such a forgery as the one in question in this case was rightly admitted.

The respondents' case is that the duty ought to have been discharged by the appellant immediately upon his discovery in October, 1929, and that if it had been then discharged they could have sued the appellant's wife in tort and the appellant himself would have been responsible for his wife's tort. They claim that his silence until after his wife's death amounted in these circumstances to a representation that the cheques were not forgeries and deprived the respondents of their remedy.

[Lord Tomlin emphasised that the husband had known of his wife's actions for some months and continued:]

The appellant's silence, therefore, was deliberate and intended to produce the effect which it in fact produced—namely, the leaving of the respondents in ignorance of the true facts so that no action might be taken by them against the appellant's wife. The deliberate abstention from speaking in those circumstances seems to me to amount to a representation to the respondents that the forged cheques were in fact in order, and assuming that detriment to the respondents followed there were, it seems to me, present all the elements essential to estoppel. Further, I do not think that it is any answer to say that if the respondents had not been negligent initially the detriment would not have occurred. The course of conduct relied upon as founding the estoppel was adopted in order to leave the respondents in the condition of ignorance in which the appellant knew they were. It was the duty of the appellant to remove that condition however caused. It is the existence of this duty, coupled with the appellant's deliberate intention to maintain the respondents in their condition of ignorance, that gives its significance to the appellant's silence. What difference can it make that the condition of ignorance was primarily induced by the respondents' own negligence? In my judgment it can make none. For the purposes of the estoppel, which is a procedural matter, the cause of the ignorance is an irrelevant consideration.

[**Lords Atkin, Warrington, Thankerton,** and **Macmillan** concurred in Lord Tomlin's opinion and the husband's appeal was dismissed.]

NOTES

1. This was a case of estoppel by representation. Estoppel may also arise by negligence as where a customer of a bank draws a cheque in such a way as to facilitate the fraud or forgery: see *London Joint Stock Bank v Macmillan* [1918] AC 777, HL. *Greenwood v Martins Bank Ltd* was a case where the estoppel prevented the person charged with liability on the bill from relying on the forgery of his own signature. Such a common law estoppel may also prevent a party to the bill from asserting that the signature of another party to the bill is forged or unauthorised: see *Bank of England v Vagliano Bros*, above, p 667.

2. In a case like *Greenwood v Martins Bank Ltd*, the customer must have actual knowledge of the forgery, or have deliberately turned a blind eye, to be in breach of duty. Constructive knowledge, in the sense that the customer had knowledge of circumstances which would cause a hypothetical reasonable customer to discover the fraud, is not enough (*Price Meats Ltd v Barclays Bank plc* [2000] 2 All ER (Comm) 346; *Patel v Standard Chartered Bank* [2001] Lloyd's Rep Bank 229).

3. Although a forged signature cannot be ratified, it may be adopted. This would occur, for example, if a customer's signature on a cheque is forged but he subsequently agrees that his bank may debit his account with the cheque. Whether adoption is an example of estoppel by representation or derives from a separate contractual promise, which must be supported by its own consideration, is undecided. In *Greenwood v Martins Bank Ltd*, Lord Tomlin clearly saw it falling into the category of contractual promise. But a forged signature cannot be adopted if the consideration for accepting responsibility for the forged signature is a promise not to prosecute the forger; such consideration is unlawful as being contrary to public policy (*Brook v Hook* (1871) LR 6 Exch 89; *Newell v Royal Bank of Canada* (1997) 147 DLR (4th) 268, Nova Scotia Court of Appeal). Whether the adoption of a person's forged indorsement on a bill would give that person rights against prior parties, as opposed to simply making him liable to subsequent parties, has not been addressed by the courts.

A person in possession of an order bill bearing a forged or unauthorised indorsement cannot be a holder in due course (nor any other form of 'holder') of that bill and has no right to enforce it against any person who became a party to the bill prior to the forgery (see above, p 671). However, if after the forged or unauthorised indorsement, the bill is subsequently indorsed, then, under s 55(2)(b) of the BEA the subsequent indorsers will be precluded from denying to a holder in due course the genuineness and regularity in all respects of the previous indorsements. In this context, the term 'holder in due course' must be taken to include a person who would, but for the forged or unauthorised indorsement, have been a holder of the bill. Figure 19.5 provides an example. An order bill is stolen from C, the first indorsee. The thief forges C's indorsement and delivers the bill to D. D then indorses the bill and delivers it to E, who takes it in good faith for value and without notice of the forgery. E would not be able to hold A, B, or C liable on the bill as he is not a holder of the bill as against them (this is the effect of BEA, s 24). But E could hold D liable on the bill relying on the estoppel contained in s 55(2)(b).

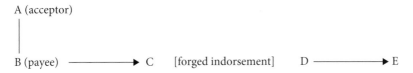

Figure 19.5 Forged indorsements

Similarly, under s 54(2)(a) of the BEA the acceptor will be precluded from denying to a holder in due course the genuineness of the drawer's signature.

(e) Material alteration

Forgery of a signature or an unauthorised signature on the bill must be distinguished from material alteration of the bill. Section 64 of the BEA deals with the situation where a bill is materially altered, for example any alteration of the date, the sum payable, the time of payment, the place of payment, and, where a bill has been accepted generally, the addition of a place of payment without the acceptor's assent. The effect of any material alteration of a bill without the assent of all parties liable thereon, is to avoid the bill, except as against the party who himself made, authorised, or assented to the alteration, and subsequent indorsers (BEA, s 64(1)). However, s 64(1) contains the important proviso that where an alteration is not apparent, a holder in due course may avail himself of the bill as if it had not been altered and may enforce payment of it according to its original tenor.

In *Smith v Lloyds TSB Bank plc* [2001] QB 541, see below, p 743, the Court of Appeal held that, on a true construction of s 64(1), a cheque (a form of bill of exchange) which had been materially altered by a fraudulent third party was no longer a cheque but, subject to the qualifications in the section, a worthless piece of paper. This was the effect of the word 'avoided' in the section. Thus, there could be no cause of action for damages in conversion for the face value of such an instrument because it no longer represented a chose in action for that amount. Section 64(1) is said to be an application of the rule in *Pigot's Case* (1614) 11 Co Rep 26b, which is to the effect that any material alteration, not approved by all the parties to the original document, made to a deed or other instrument after the execution of that instrument or deed is rendered void (*Habibsons Bank Ltd v Standard Chartered Bank (Hong Kong) Ltd* [2010] EWCA Civ 1335, [2011] QB 943 at [28]).

7 LIABILITY ON THE BILL: SPECIFIC PARTIES

(a) Overview

Sections 53–58 of the BEA deal with the liability of specific parties on the bill. Liability on the bill is confined to those who have signed the bill. We have already seen that a person is liable as drawer, acceptor, or indorser of a bill only if he has signed it as such (BEA, s 23). The party signing the bill incurs liability to subsequent parties for its payment (and certain statutory estoppels may also be raised against him). This enables the current holder of the bill to claim against any or all of the prior parties to the bill. Where a party liable on the bill has paid the holder, that party can himself recover the amount of the bill from his predecessors (BEA, s 57). Ultimate liability for payment rests with the acceptor (unless the bill is an accommodation bill, when it will lie with the party accommodated: see below, Section 7(c)). In other words, the party primarily liable on the bill is the acceptor and the drawer and indorsers are in a position analogous to that of sureties.

Figure 19.6 illustrates the flow of rights on a bill of exchange (liabilities are incurred only to subsequent parties and so flow in the opposite direction). In Figure 19.6, an order bill is drawn by A (the seller of goods) in favour of B (his supplier) and accepted by X (who buys the goods from A). The bill is negotiated (for value) from B to C, from C to D, and from D to E, each party indorsing and delivering the bill to the next in the chain. Should X fail to pay the bill on its maturity, the current holder, E, may claim against all prior parties (A, B, C, D, and X) or any of them. E may choose to sue D because D is well known to him, but he does not have to do so. D may be insolvent and so E could decide to sue C instead. Once C had paid E, C can similarly choose to bring a claim against all or any of his predecessors (A, B, and X). The process goes on with each party, having paid the bill, being entitled to recover against his predecessors. X stands at the end of the chain. He is acceptor and has no one against whom to claim.

X	A	B	C	D	E
Acceptor	Drawer	Payee/Indorser 1	Indorser 2	Indorser 3	Holder

Figure 19.6 Rights on the bill

(b) Liability of the drawee

Section 53(1) of the BEA provides that a bill of exchange, of itself, does not operate as an assignment of funds which the drawer has in the hands of the drawee and that, unless he accepts the bill, the drawee is not liable on the instrument. The drawing of a bill of exchange imposes no obligation upon the drawee to accept or pay the bill (*Credit Lyonnais Bank Nederland NV v Export Credit Guarantee Department* [1998] 1 Lloyd's Rep 19 at 39, per Hobhouse LJ). But this does not prevent the drawee being bound by some extrinsic contractual obligation to accept the bill or pay the sum due on it, for example banks used to issue cheque guarantee cards which provided an undertaking to any supplier of goods or services to the cardholder that it would honour its customer's cheques (the practice of issuing cheque guarantee cards in the UK was abandoned in 2011).

(c) Liability of the acceptor

The acceptor of a bill, by accepting it, engages that he will pay it according to the tenor of his acceptance (BEA, s 54(1)). He is the person primarily liable on the bill. Sometimes the acceptor acts as a surety for another person who may or may not be a party to the bill. In such a case, the bill is called an 'accommodation bill' and the person primarily liable on the bill is the person accommodated and not the acceptor. This is important because with an accommodation bill payment in due course by the person accommodated will discharge the bill (BEA, s 59(3)), whereas the usual rule is that only payment in due course by the drawee or acceptor will discharge the bill (BEA, s 59(1) and (2)).

Various statutory estoppels are raised against the acceptor by virtue of his acceptance. Section 54(2) of the BEA provides that the acceptor is precluded from denying to a holder in due course:

(a) the existence of the drawer, the genuineness of his signature, and his capacity and authority to draw the bill;

(b) in the case of a bill payable to drawer's order, the then capacity of the drawer to indorse, but not the genuineness or validity of his indorsement;

(c) in the case of a bill payable to the order of a third person, the existence of the payee and his then capacity to indorse, but not the genuineness or validity of the indorsement.

(d) Liability of the drawer

By s 55(1) of the BEA, the drawer of a bill by drawing it:

(a) engages that on due presentment it shall be accepted and paid according to its tenor, and that if it be dishonoured he will compensate the holder or any indorser who is compelled to pay it, provided that the requisite proceedings on dishonour be duly taken;

(b) is precluded from denying to a holder in due course the existence of the payee and his then capacity to indorse.

(e) Liability of an indorser

By s 55(2) of the BEA, the indorser of a bill by indorsing it:

(a) engages that on due presentment it shall be accepted and paid according to its tenor, and that if it be dishonoured he will compensate the holder or a subsequent indorser who is compelled to pay it, provided that the requisite proceedings on dishonour be duly taken;

(b) is precluded from denying to a holder in due course the genuineness and regularity in all respects of the drawer's signature and all previous indorsements;

(c) is precluded from denying to his immediate or a subsequent indorsee that the bill was at the time of his indorsement a valid and subsisting bill, and that he had then a good title thereto.

When a bill has been accepted for value, the relationship between the drawer and indorsers on the one hand and the acceptor on the other is analogous, therefore, to that of suretyship. This explains why the drawer and any indorser are discharged from liability if the requisite proceedings on dishonour are not followed (see below, Section 8). It also ensures that they are entitled to the equities of a surety, although in the case of an indorser this will only accrue when the bill has been dishonoured (*Duncan, Fox & Co v North and South Wales Bank* (1880) 6 App Cas 1 at 18–19, HL, per Lord Blackburn).

(f) Liability of a quasi-indorser

Only a holder of a bill can be an indorser. Nevertheless, where a person who is not a holder signs the bill he may incur liabilities. Section 56 of the BEA provides that 'where a person signs a bill otherwise than as drawer or acceptor, he thereby incurs the liabilities of an indorser to a holder in due course'. Thus, the 'quasi-indorser', or 'anomalous indorser', as he is described, will be liable to *subsequent* parties in the event of dishonour by non-acceptance or non-payment. The quasi-indorser usually signs the bill to accommodate or guarantee the liabilities of another party to the bill.

Civil law jurisdictions generally recognise the concept of an *aval*, a form of suretyship undertaken by the indorsement of a bill of exchange which renders the surety liable to subsequent *and prior* holders in the event of default by the party for whose account it is given. But English law does not recognise a guarantee given by way of an *aval* (*G & H Montague GmbH v Irvani* [1990] 2 All ER 225, CA). A quasi-indorser can only be held liable to prior parties in one of two ways. First, through a specific guarantee given in writing by the quasi-indorser which complies with the requirements of s 4 of the Statute of Frauds (1677). Secondly, where the intention to give a guarantee is clear from extrinsic evidence, by enabling a person who is already a party to the bill to take it from the quasi-indorser, insert his own indorsement above that of the quasi-indorser (relying on BEA, s 20: see above, p 665), and then claim on the bill as a 'holder' against the quasi-indorser as an 'indorser' (*Gerald McDonald & Co v Nash & Co* [1924] AC 625, HL). The desire to remedy a perceived injustice has meant that the courts have been prepared to overlook the strict requirement of s 31(3) of the BEA that an indorsement is completed by delivery. As Professors Goode and McKendrick point out, a payee would not have parted with the bill to the quasi-indorser after completing the bill by indorsing it with his own signature above that of the quasi-indorser (E McKendrick, *Goode on Commercial Law* (5th edn, 2016), p 546, fn 148).

(g) Liability of a transferor of a bearer bill

The holder of a bearer bill who transfers it by mere delivery is not liable on the bill for he has not signed it (BEA, s 58(2)). If he signs the bill he incurs all the liabilities of an indorser. But the transferor of a bearer bill by mere delivery may incur liability *outside* the bill for on transfer he warrants to his immediate transferee (provided the transferee is a holder for value), that the bill is what it purports to be, that he has a right to transfer it, and that he is not aware of any fact which renders it valueless (BEA, s 58(3)). The fact that the claim is for breach of warranty arising outside the bill means that: (a) it is not for the amount of the bill but for damages or restitution of money paid on a total failure of consideration; and (b) the transferor may be able to meet the claim with a counterclaim on the underlying contract. The holder of a bearer bill who indorses the bill incurs all the liabilities of an indorser.

(h) Exemption and limitation of liability

Under s 16(1) of the BEA, the drawer and any indorser may negative or limit his liability to the holder by an express stipulation on the bill to that effect. The most an acceptor can do to limit his liability is to give a qualified acceptance to the order of the drawer contained in the bill, for example by making his acceptance conditional, or for part only of the amount for which the bill is drawn, or by agreeing to pay only at a particular place (BEA, s 19). If the acceptor purports to exclude his liability completely he would not be deemed to have accepted the bill at all. The holder may reject a qualified acceptance and treat the bill as dishonoured for non-acceptance (BEA, s 44(1)). If the holder takes a qualified acceptance, then, unless the drawer or an indorser has expressly or impliedly authorised the holder to take such an acceptance, the holder must give notice to the drawer and any indorser, who (except in a case of a partial acceptance) may decline to be bound by it and be discharged from his liability on the bill (BEA, s 44(2), (3)).

QUESTION

Barak states that s 58 of the BEA (or rather its Israeli equivalent) 'is no more than a repetition of the general law of sale and its place is there, not in the law of negotiable instruments' (A Barak, 'The Nature of the Negotiable Instrument' (1983) 18 Israel LR 49 at 70). Is s 58, therefore, a redundant provision?

8 ENFORCEMENT OF THE BILL

(a) Dishonour by non-acceptance and non-payment

A demand bill is simply presented for payment. The drawee's failure to pay a demand bill duly presented for payment constitutes dishonour by non-payment (BEA, s 47(1)). By contrast, a term bill must first be presented for acceptance if the drawee is to become liable on the bill. The drawee's failure to accept the bill constitutes dishonour by non-acceptance (BEA, s 43(1)). Where a bill has been dishonoured for non-acceptance it is not necessary to go on and present it for payment. The holder has the right (subject to giving notice of dishonour) to proceed immediately against the drawer and any prior indorser (BEA, s 43(2)). Where the bill is accepted by the drawee it must be presented for payment on its maturity. Failure to pay the bill at maturity constitutes dishonour for non-payment (BEA, s 47(1)).

(b) Presentment for acceptance

As a general rule, it is not necessary for the holder to present a bill for acceptance. An acceptor is not an essential party to a bill: the holder of an unaccepted bill may still proceed against the drawer and any prior indorser. On the other hand, the bill must be presented for acceptance when its terms so require, where the bill is drawn payable elsewhere than at the residence or place of business of the drawee, or where presentment is necessary to fix the maturity date of the instrument, for example where the bill is payable 'X days after sight' (BEA, s 39). When a bill payable after sight is negotiated, the holder must either present it for acceptance or negotiate it within a reasonable time; failure to do so discharges the drawer and all indorsers prior to that holder (BEA, s 40).

(c) Presentment for payment

As we have seen, there is no need to present a bill for payment when it has already been dishonoured for non-acceptance. In other cases, unless waived or excused, presentment for payment is essential. If the bill is not duly presented, the drawer and indorsers will be discharged from liability on the bill (BEA, s 45). They are discharged from liability whether or not they have been prejudiced by the omission (although the drawer of a cheque is only discharged to the extent he has suffered actual damage: BEA, s 74). But, where the bill is accepted generally, presentment is not required to preserve the liability of the acceptor on the bill (BEA, s 52(1)). On the other hand, by the terms of a qualified acceptance the acceptor may stipulate that presentment for payment is required, for example at the acceptor's bank.

A bill must be 'duly' presented for payment. Section 45 of the BEA contains detailed rules as to the time and place of presentment. For example, a term bill must be presented for payment on the day it falls due (BEA, s 45, r (1)). As the next case illustrates, presentment the day before or the day after the due date is not due presentment.

Yeoman Credit Ltd v Gregory
[1963] 1 WLR 343, Queen's Bench Division

The plaintiffs drew two bills of exchange on a company called Express Coachcraft Ltd which accepted them, payable at National Provincial Bank Ltd. The defendant was a director of Express Coachcraft Ltd and indorsed the bills as surety. One bill was a 'fixed date' bill payable on 9 December, the other was an 'on demand' bill. Before the plaintiffs presented the bills they were informed by Mr Thornton, a director of Express Coachcraft Ltd, that the bills should be presented at a branch of Midland Bank where there were funds to meet them. The plaintiffs noted this instruction in pencil on the bills. The bills were presented for payment at Midland Bank on 9 December but the bank refused to meet them. They were then presented to National Provincial Bank on 11 December but that bank also dishonoured them.

Megaw J: The two bills which were presented in December were a 'fixed date' bill for £2,000 and an 'on demand' bill for £900. The date for payment of the 'fixed date' bill was December 9, 1959. Section 45, r (1), of the Bills of Exchange Act 1882, provides: 'Where the bill is not payable on demand, presentment must be made on the day it falls due.' Now presentment was made on December 9, the date when this bill fell due, to Midland Bank Ltd, because of the pencil notation on it. In my view, that cannot be treated as being a proper presentment of a bill which was drawn as payable at a different bank at a different place, and I am quite unable to say that that is in any way altered by the fact that, as the result of a telephone conversation, the pencil notation had been made on it and the plaintiffs had been told that it was to be presented at a different place and there, and there only, to be met. Certainly it cannot be a circumstance which could in any way affect the rights or liabilities of the defendant unless it was established that he knew and had consented to those instructions being given to the plaintiffs. What Mr Collins [credit controller of the plaintiffs] quite clearly ought to have done, and what I am sure in retrospect he realises that he ought to have done, was, after that telephone conversation, to have gone to the defendant and to have gone to all indorsers and said: 'I have had this information. Will you please, with our consent, alter the bill so as to put a different place of payment on it, and each of you indicate on the bill your consent to that alteration?' If that had been so, the matter would have been in order. But, whatever may be said about an estoppel in relation to Coachcraft or in relation to Mr Thornton, that cannot apply to the defendant. So far as the defendant is concerned, he was entitled to have the bill presented on December 9 to the named bank, National Provincial Ltd. That was not done. It was presented at the named bank on the following day. That was a bad presentment, and the result of that, under s 45, r (1), of the Act of 1882, is that, without any proof that the defendant was in any way prejudiced by that late presentation, he is excused from liability on the bill. No question arises here—I do not think that any question was sought to be raised by the plaintiffs—under s 46(1) of the Act of 1882 with regard to the excuse of delay in making presentment for payment. If it had been raised, there would, in my view, have been no facts which would have justified any bringing in of that subsection against the defendant. Accordingly, the claim for the bill for £2,000 fails.

With regard to the other bill, for £900, it being a bill payable on demand, that question of time of presentment does not arise. Counsel for the defendant has contended that it was a bad presentment for payment none the less, because of the pencil writing of a different bank on it. In my judgment, that is not a valid contention, and I say no more about it.

NOTES

1. There are some nineteenth-century cases which have been interpreted as authority for the proposition that failure to present a bill for payment not only discharges the drawer and indorsers on the bill but also deprives the holder of his right to sue on the underlying contract for which the bill was given (see, eg, *Soward v Palmer* (1818) 8 Taunt 277; *Peacock v Pursell* (1863) 14 CBNS 728; and *Byles on Bills of Exchange & Cheques* (29th edn, 2013), para 12–004). Professors Goode and McKendrick maintain that this line of authority does not support this supposed rule (E McKendrick, *Goode on Commercial Law* (5th edn, 2016), p 552, fn 179). In any event it is questionable whether such a draconian rule represents the law today (Goode, above, p 552; *Chalmers and Guest on Bills of Exchange* (17th edn, 2009), para 6–042). Professors Goode and McKendrick submit that the appropriate solution is to treat the drawer as discharged from liability on the underlying contract to the extent that he has suffered prejudice by the non-presentment.

2. By s 45(2) of the BEA, a bill payable on demand must be presented for payment within a reasonable time after its issue in order to render the drawer liable, and within a reasonable time after its indorsement in order to render the indorser liable. But by s 74 of the BEA, where a *cheque* is not presented for payment within a reasonable time of its issue, the drawer is only discharged to the extent of the actual damage suffered by him through the delay (for the special rules relating to the place and method of presentation of cheques, see below, p 733). However, s 45(2) of the BEA continues to apply in relation to an indorser of a cheque, who will be discharged if the cheque was not presented for payment within a reasonable time of its issue even if he was not prejudiced by the delay (cf *King and Boyd v Porter* [1925] NI 107). As to the liability of the maker and indorsers of a promissory note, if it is not duly presented for payment, see ss 86, 87, and 89 of the BEA.

(d) Notice of dishonour

Where the bill has been dishonoured for non-acceptance or non-payment, the holder must within a reasonable time give notice of dishonour to the drawer and any prior indorser of the bill. Unless notice is excused, failure to give notice of dishonour discharges the drawer and prior indorsers from liability on the bill (BEA, s 48). However, notice given by the holder enures for the benefit of all subsequent holders and also for the benefit of all prior indorsers who have a right of recourse against the party to whom it was given (BEA, s 49, r (3)). For example, where B draws a bill on A payable to C, which C indorses to D, notice given by D (holder) to B (drawer) will enure for the benefit of C (indorser). C can sue B where C is given due notice from D and, in consequence, has a right of recourse against B. Moreover, notice given by or on behalf of an indorser entitled to give notice enures for the benefit of the holder and all indorsers subsequent to the party to whom notice is given (s 49, r (4)). In the example just given, if D gives notice to C (and it is often the case that the holder only gives notice to his immediate indorser), but C gives notice to B, that notice will enure for the benefit of D, and D can sue both B and C.

It is not necessary to give notice of dishonour for non-payment to the acceptor (BEA, s 52(3)); he is, after all, the party who has dishonoured the bill. Notice of dishonour is also dispensed with in several other cases (BEA, s 50(2)). As regards the drawer, two situations where notice is dispensed with should be mentioned as they arise reasonably frequently, especially with regard to cheques (BEA, s 50(2)(c)). First, where the drawee or acceptor owes the drawer no duty to accept or pay the bill (eg where the drawer of a cheque has insufficient funds in his account to cover payment and the drawee bank has not agreed to give him an overdraft facility). Secondly, where the drawer has countermanded payment. Finally, it should be noted that the rights of a holder in due course are protected even though a previous holder has failed to give notice of dishonour for non-acceptance (BEA, s 48, r (1)).

(e) Protesting a foreign bill

In the case of a foreign bill, that is a bill that is not or does not on the face of it purport to be both drawn and payable within the British Islands or drawn within the British Islands upon some resident therein, dishonour by non-acceptance or non-payment must be duly protested, ie formally established by a notarial act (BEA, s 51(2)).

9 DISCHARGE OF THE BILL

Discharge of the bill must be distinguished from discharge of a party to the bill. A discharged bill is treated as exhausted so that no party can sue or be sued on the instrument. A party to a bill may be discharged from liability, but others may still remain liable on the instrument. For example, where the bill is paid by an indorser or the drawer, the party making the payment and all subsequent parties are discharged from liability, but the bill is not discharged and may be enforced against prior parties.

A bill may be discharged by any one of the following methods:

- payment in due course, that is to say payment at or after maturity of the bill by or on behalf of the drawee or acceptor to the holder in good faith and without notice that his title to the bill is defective (BEA, s 59(1));

- the acceptor becoming the holder of the bill in his own right at or after maturity of the bill (BEA, s 61);

- express waiver by the holder of his rights against the acceptor at or after maturity of the bill (BEA, s 62);

- intentional cancellation of the bill by the holder or his agent when this is apparent from the bill itself (BEA, s 63); and

- in certain circumstances, material alteration of the bill without the assent of the parties liable on it (BEA, s 64: see above, p 699).

When a bill is paid, the person making payment has the right to call on the holder to deliver it up to him immediately (BEA, s 52(4)). Should he not take delivery of the bill, there is a risk that it will remain in circulation and be transferred to a third party. Does the acceptor of a discharged bill, or the maker of a discharged note, incur any liability to the person to whom it has been transferred? The next case addresses the issue.

Glasscock v Balls

(1889) 24 QBD 13, Court of Appeal

As security for a debt, the defendant gave to W a promissory note payable on demand to W's order. On becoming further indebted to W, the defendant executed a mortgage in favour of W to secure all his indebtedness, including the debt already secured by the promissory note. W then transferred the mortgage to H and received from him a sum equal to the amount of the defendant's total indebtedness to W. As security for a debt owed by W to the plaintiff, W indorsed and delivered the promissory note to the plaintiff who took it without knowledge of the previous transactions. The plaintiff's claim on the note against the defendant was upheld by Lord Coleridge CJ. The defendant appealed.

> **Lord Esher MR:** In this case the plaintiff sues the maker of a promissory note payable on demand as indorsee. It was admitted that the plaintiff was indorsee of the note for value without notice of anything that had occurred. The plaintiff cannot be said to have taken the note when overdue, because it was not shewn that payment was ever applied for, and the cases shew that such a note is not to be treated as overdue merely because it is payable on demand and bears date some time back. Under such circumstances prima facie the indorsee for value without notice is entitled to recover on the note. It lies on the defendant to bring the case within some recognised rule which would prevent such an indorsee from recovering upon the note. . . . If a negotiable instrument remains current, even though it has been paid, there is nothing to prevent a person to whom it has been indorsed for value without knowledge that it has been paid from suing . . . [T]he note here has not been paid. Nothing has happened which would prove a plea of payment. Something has happened which would entitle the maker to certain rights as against the payee, but which is not payment of the note. The maker might be entitled to an injunction to prevent the payee from suing on the note, but there has not been a payment of the note. It was said by the defendant's counsel that the note was extinguished. I cannot say I understand the meaning of the term 'extinguished' as used in the argument. I never heard of a plea of extinguishment of a bill or note . . . No other principle could be suggested by the defendant under which the case could be brought, and therefore it must come under the general principle that the maker of the note, having issued it and allowed it to be in circulation as a negotiable instrument, is liable upon it to an indorsee for value without notice of anything wrong. For these reasons I think the appeal must be dismissed.
>
> [**Lindley LJ** delivered a concurring judgment. **Lopes LJ** concurred.]

NOTES

1. Even though W applied the money received from H in satisfaction of the defendant's indebtedness, the note was not discharged by payment in due course. Payment had not been made by the maker of the note, nor had it been made to the holder as required by s 59(1) of the BEA.

2. Lord Esher's remarks as to the rights of a holder in due course who takes a negotiable instrument after it has been paid are clearly *obiter dicta*. In any event, if a bill, or note, is payable at a fixed date and the holder transfers it after maturity, the transferee could not be

a holder in due course as he would take the instrument after it had become overdue (BEA, s 29(1)(a)). The issue seems, therefore, to arise only with regard to a bill, or note, payable on demand which will not be overdue unless it has been in circulation for an unreasonable period of time (BEA, s 36(3)). Even then, the holder of a discharged bill, or note, will probably not be a holder in due course. Section 36(1) of the BEA provides that a bill that has been discharged for payment or otherwise ceases to be negotiable (applied to promissory notes by BEA, s 89(1)). Professor Guest convincingly argues that this seems to rule out the possibility of such a bill subsequently being 'negotiated' to a holder in due course as required by s 29(1) (b) of the Act (*Chalmers and Guest on Bills of Exchange* (17th edn, 2009), para 8–003; cf L Kadirgamar (1959) 22 MLR 146).

3. If an order bill is indorsed and transferred after discharge, the indorser will be precluded by s 55(2)(c) of the BEA from denying to his immediate or subsequent indorsee that the bill was at the time of his indorsement a valid and subsisting bill. If a bearer bill is transferred after discharge, the transferor will be liable to his transferee for value for breach of warranty under s 58(3) of the BEA.

10 MISTAKEN PAYMENT

What happens if the drawee or acceptor of an order bill pays someone who has taken the bill under a forged or unauthorised indorsement? As the payee will not be a 'holder' (due to BEA, s 24), the bill is not discharged by payment (subject to the special protection given to bankers, see Chapter 20). The true owner can turn to the drawee/acceptor for payment forcing the latter to attempt to recover their original payment from the erroneous payee as money paid under a mistake of fact. Similar problems arise if a drawee banker pays a cheque after the drawer has countermanded his original order to pay. If the recipient knew of the mistake as to the facts at the time he received the payment he will be ordered to make restitution (*Kendal v Wood* (1870) LR 6 Exch 243). But what if the payment was received in good faith and in ignorance of the mistake?

Barclays Bank Ltd v WJ Simms, Son & Cooke (Southern) Ltd
[1980] QB 677, Queen's Bench Division

The first defendants contracted to do certain building works for a housing association. On the issue of an interim certificate of completion of some of the work, the association sent the first defendants a cheque for £24,000 drawn on the plaintiffs. At all times there were sufficient funds in the housing association's account held with the plaintiffs to meet the cheque. The following day the National Westminster Bank, exercising its powers under a debenture, appointed the second defendant as receiver over the property and assets of the first defendants. On hearing of the receiver's appointment, the association instructed the plaintiffs not to pay the cheque. Due to a clerical error, the plaintiffs overlooked the stop order and paid the cheque when presented by the receiver. The plaintiffs demanded repayment of the £24,000 from the defendants.

Robert Goff J: . . . This case raises for decision the question whether a bank, which overlooks its customer's instructions to stop payment of a cheque and in consequence pays the cheque on presentation, can recover the money from the payee as having been paid under a mistake of fact. The point is one on which there is no decision in this country; and it is a point, I was told, of considerable importance to bankers, not only because it is an everyday hazard that customers' instructions may be overlooked, but because modern technology, rather than eliminating the risk, has if anything increased it ...

1 THE PRINCIPLES ON WHICH MONEY IS RECOVERABLE ON THE GROUND THAT IT HAS BEEN PAID UNDER A MISTAKE OF FACT

[After reviewing, inter alia, the decisions of the House of Lords in *Kleinwort Sons & Co v Dunlop Rubber Co* (1907) 97 LT 263; *Kerrison v Glyn, Mills, Currie & Co* (1911) 81 LJKB 465; and *RE Jones Ltd v Waring and Gillow Ltd* [1926] AC 670, his Lordship continued:]

From this formidable line of authority certain simple principles can, in my judgment, be deduced: (1) If a person pays money to another under a mistake of fact which causes him to make the payment, he is prima facie entitled to recover it as money paid under a mistake of fact. (2) His claim may however fail if (a) the payer intends that the payee shall have the money at all events, whether the fact be true or false, or is deemed in law so to intend; or (b) the payment is made for good consideration, in particular if the money is paid to discharge, and does discharge, a debt owed to the payee (or a principal on whose behalf he is authorised to receive the payment) by the payer or by a third party by whom he is authorised to discharge the debt; or (c) the payee has changed his position in good faith, or is deemed in law to have done so.

To these simple propositions, I append the following footnotes:

(a) *Proposition 1*. This is founded upon the speeches in the three cases in the House of Lords, to which I have referred. It is also consistent with the opinion expressed by Turner J in *Thomas v Houston Corbett & Co* [1969] NZLR 151, 167. Of course, if the money was due under a contract between the payer and the payee, there can be no recovery on this ground unless the contract itself is held void for mistake (as in *Norwich Union Fire Insurance Society Ltd v Wm H Price Ltd* [1934] AC 455) or is rescinded by the plaintiff.

(b) *Proposition 2 (a)*. This is founded upon the dictum of Parke B in *Kelly v Solari*, 9 M & W 54. I have felt it necessary to add the words 'or is deemed in law so to intend' to accommodate the decision of the Court of Appeal in *Morgan v Ashcroft* [1938] 1 KB 49, a case strongly relied upon by the defendants in the present case, the effect of which I shall have to consider later in this judgment.

(c) *Proposition 2 (b)*. This is founded upon the decision in *Aiken v Short*, 1 H & N 210, and upon dicta in *Kerrison v Glyn, Mills, Currie & Co*. However, even if the payee has given consideration for the payment, for example by accepting the payment in discharge of a debt owed to him by a third party on whose behalf the payer is authorised to discharge it, that transaction may itself be set aside (and so provide no defence to the claim) if the payer's mistake was induced by the payee, or possibly even where the payee, being aware of the payer's mistake, did not receive the money in good faith: cf. *Ward & Co v Wallis* [1900] 1 QB 675, 678–679, *per* Kennedy J.

(d) *Proposition 2 (c)*. This is founded upon the statement of principle of Lord Loreburn LC in *Kleinwort, Sons & Co v Dunlop Rubber Co* 97. I have deliberately stated this defence in broad terms, making no reference to the question whether it is dependent upon a breach of duty by the plaintiff or a representation by him independent of the payment, because these matters do not arise for decision in the present case. I have however referred to the possibility that the defendant may be deemed in law to have changed his position, because of a line of authorities concerned with negotiable instruments which I shall have to consider later in this judgment, of which the leading case is *Cocks v Masterman* (1829) 9 B & C 902.

(e) I have ignored, in stating the principle of recovery, defences of general application in the law of restitution, for example where public policy precludes restitution.

(f) The following propositions are inconsistent with the simple principle of recovery established in the authorities: (i) that to ground recovery, the mistake must have induced the payer to believe that he was liable to pay the money to the payee or his principal; (ii) that to ground recovery, the mistake must have been 'as between' the payer and the payee. Rejection of this test has led to its reformulation (notably by Asquith J in *Weld-Blundell v Synott* [1940] 2 KB 107 and by Windeyer J in *Porter v Latec Finance (Qld) Pty Ltd* (1964) 111 CLR 177, 204) in terms which in my judgment mean no more than that the mistake must have caused the payment …

2 WHERE A BANK PAYS A CHEQUE DRAWN UPON IT BY A CUSTOMER OF THE BANK, IN WHAT CIRCUMSTANCES MAY THE BANK RECOVER THE PAYMENT FROM THE PAYEE ON THE GROUND THAT IT WAS PAID UNDER A MISTAKE OF FACT?

It is a basic obligation owed by a bank to its customer that it will honour on presentation cheques drawn by the customer on the bank, provided that there are sufficient funds in the customer's account to meet the cheque, or the bank has agreed to provide the customer with overdraft facilities sufficient to meet the cheque. Where the bank honours such a cheque, it acts within its mandate, with the result that the bank is entitled to debit the customer's account with the amount of the cheque, and further that the bank's payment is effective to discharge the obligation of the customer to the payee on the cheque, because the bank has paid the cheque with the authority of the customer.

In other circumstances, the bank is under no obligation to honour its customer's cheques. If however a customer draws a cheque on the bank without funds in his account or agreed overdraft facilities sufficient to meet it, the cheque on presentation constitutes a request to the bank to provide overdraft facilities sufficient to meet the cheque. The bank has an option whether or not to comply with that request. If it declines to do so, it acts entirely within its rights and no legal consequences follow as between the bank and its customer. If however the bank pays the cheque, it accepts the request and the payment has the same legal consequences as if the payment had been made pursuant to previously agreed overdraft facilities; the payment is made within the bank's mandate, and in particular the bank is entitled to debit the customer's account, and the bank's payment discharges the customer's obligation to the payee on the cheque.

In other cases, however, a bank which pays a cheque drawn or purported to be drawn by its customer pays without mandate. A bank does so if, for example, it overlooks or ignores notice of its customer's death, or if it pays a cheque bearing the forged signature of its customer as drawer, but, more important for present purposes, a bank will pay without mandate if it overlooks or ignores notice of countermand of the customer who has drawn the cheque. In such cases the bank, if it pays the cheque, pays without mandate from its customer; and unless the customer is able to and does ratify the payment, the bank cannot debit the customer's account, nor will its payment be effective to discharge the obligation (if any) of the customer on the cheque, because the bank had no authority to discharge such obligation.

It is against the background of these principles, which were not in dispute before me, that I have to consider the position of a bank which pays a cheque under a mistake of fact. In such a case, the crucial question is, in my judgment, whether the payment was with or without mandate. The two typical situations, which exemplify payment with or without mandate, arise first where the bank pays in the mistaken belief that there are sufficient funds or overdraft facilities to meet the cheque, and second where the bank overlooks notice of countermand given by the customer. In each case, there is a mistake by the bank which causes the bank to make the payment. But in the first case, the effect of the bank's payment is to accept the customer's request for overdraft facilities; the payment is therefore within the bank's mandate, with the result that not only is the bank entitled to have recourse to its customer, but the customer's obligation to the payee is discharged. It follows that the payee has given consideration for the payment; with the consequence that, although the payment has been caused by the bank's mistake, the money is irrecoverable from the payee unless the transaction of payment is itself set aside. Although the bank is unable to recover the money, it has a right of recourse to its customer. In the second case, however, the bank's payment is without mandate. The bank has no recourse to its customer; and the debt of the customer to the payee on the cheque is not discharged. Prima facie, the bank is entitled to recover the money from the payee, unless the payee has changed his position in good faith, or is deemed in law to have done so. . . .

3 IF A BANK PAYS A CHEQUE UNDER A MISTAKE OF FACT, IN WHAT CIRCUMSTANCES HAS THE PAYEE A GOOD DEFENCE TO THE BANK'S CLAIM TO RECOVER THE MONEY, ON THE PRINCIPLE IN *COCKS v MASTERMAN*?

The authorities on this topic have recently been analysed by Kerr J in *National Westminster Bank Ltd v Barclays Bank International Ltd* [1975] QB 654, an analysis which I gratefully adopt and which makes it unnecessary for me to burden this judgment with a full analysis of the authorities. The case before Kerr J was concerned with a claim by the plaintiff bank to recover from the defendant bank a sum paid by it on a forged cheque presented by the defendant bank on behalf of a customer for special collection, which the plaintiff bank had paid to the defendant bank in ignorance of the forgery, and the defendant bank had then credited to its customer's account. A principal question in the case was whether the plaintiff bank was estopped from claiming repayment by a representation, in honouring the cheque, that the cheque was genuine. Kerr J, in holding that the bank made no such representation and was not so estopped, considered the line of cases, commencing with the decision of Lord Mansfield in *Price v Neal* (1762) 3 Burr 1354, in which payments of bills of exchange which contained forged signatures had been held irrecoverable on a number of grounds. The early cases on the topic culminated in the leading case of *Cocks v Masterman*. In that case the plaintiff bankers paid a bill which purported to have been accepted by their customer, in ignorance of the fact that the acceptance was forged—a fact they did not discover until the day after payment. It was held by the Court of King's Bench that they could not recover the money from the defendants, the holders' bankers. Bayley J, who delivered the judgment of the court, said, at pp 908–909:

> . . . we are all of opinion that the holder of a bill is entitled to know, on the day when it becomes due, whether it is an honoured or dishonoured bill, and that, if he receive the money and is suffered to retain it during the whole of that day, the parties who paid it cannot recover it back. The holder, indeed, is not bound by law (if the bill be dishonoured by the acceptor) to take any steps against the other parties to the bill till the day after it is dishonoured. But he is entitled so to do, if he thinks fit, and the parties who pay the bill ought not by their negligence to deprive the holder of any right or privilege. If we were to hold that the plaintiffs were entitled to recover, it would be in effect saying that the plaintiffs might deprive the holder of a bill of his right to take steps against the parties to the bill on the day when it becomes due.

The principle to be derived from this case is probably that, if the plaintiff fails to give notice on the day of payment that the bill contained a forged signature and that the money, having been paid in ignorance of that fact, is being claimed back, the defendant is deprived of the opportunity of giving notice of dishonour on the day when the bill falls due, and so is deemed to have changed his position and has a good defence to the claim on that ground. But, whatever the precise basis of the defence, it is clearly founded on the need for the defendant to give notice of dishonour; and it can therefore have no application where notice of dishonour is not required. Thus in *Imperial Bank of Canada v Bank of Hamilton* [1903] AC 49, it was held by the Privy Council that the defence had no application to an unendorsed cheque in which the amount of the cheque had been fraudulently increased by the drawer after it had been certified. The cheque was regarded as a total forgery, and not as a negotiable instrument at all. Lord Lindley, who delivered the advice of the Board, said, at p 58:

> The cheque for the larger amount was a simple forgery; and Bauer, the drawer and forger, was not entitled to any notice of its dishonour by non-payment. There were no indorsers to whom notice of dishonour had to be given. The law as to the necessity of giving notice of dishonour has therefore no application. The rule laid down in *Cocks v Masterman*, and recently reasserted in even wider language by Mathew J in *London and River Plate Bank Ltd v Bank of Liverpool Ltd* [1896] 1 QB 7, has reference to negotiable instruments, on the dishonour of which notice has to be given to some one, namely, to some drawer or indorser, who would be discharged from liability unless such notice were given in proper time. Their Lordships are not aware of any authority for applying so stringent a rule to any other cases. Assuming it to be as stringent as is alleged in such cases as those above described, their Lordships are not prepared to extend it to other cases where notice of the mistake is given in reasonable time, and no loss has been occasioned by the delay in giving it.

Likewise, in *National Westminster Bank Ltd v Barclays Bank International Ltd*, Kerr J held that the defence had no application in the case which he had to consider of a wholly forged cheque, which was also not a negotiable instrument at all . . .

It is therefore a prerequisite of the application of the defence that the defendant should be under a duty to give notice of dishonour. The provisions regarding notice of dishonour in the Bills of Exchange Act 1882 are contained in ss 48 to 50 of the Act. In s 50(2) are set out the circumstances in which notice of dishonour is dispensed with. For present purposes, the relevant provision is contained in s 50(2)(c), which provides (inter alia) that notice of dishonour is dispensed with, as regards the drawer, where the drawer has countermanded payment. It follows that in the case of a simple unendorsed cheque, payment of which is countermanded by the drawer, notice of dishonour is not required; and in such a case the payee cannot invoke the defence established in *Cocks v Masterman*.

It is to be observed that, in *Imperial Bank of Canada v Bank of Hamilton*, Lord Lindley described the rule laid down in *Cocks v Masterman* as a stringent rule. It is not merely stringent, but very technical. It is possible that if, in due course, full recognition is accorded to the defence of change of position, there will be no further need for any such stringent rule and the law can be reformulated on a more rational and less technical basis. Whether the law will hereafter develop in this way remains to be seen.

4 APPLICATION OF THE FOREGOING PRINCIPLES TO THE PRESENT CASE

In the light of the above principles, it is plain that in the present case the plaintiff bank is entitled to succeed in its claim. First, it is clear that the mistake of the bank, in overlooking the drawer's instruction to stop payment of the cheque, caused the bank to pay the cheque. Second, since the drawer had in fact countermanded payment, the bank was acting without mandate and so the payment was not effective to discharge the drawer's obligation on the cheque; from this it follows that the payee gave no consideration for the payment, and the claim cannot be defeated on that ground. Third, there is no evidence of any actual change of position on the part of either of the defendants or on the part of the National Westminster Bank; and, since notice of dishonour is not required in a case such as this, the payee is not deemed to have changed his position by reason of lapse of time in notifying them of the plaintiffs error and claiming repayment.

I must confess that I am happy to be able to reach the conclusion that the money is recoverable by the plaintiff bank. If the bank had not failed to overlook its customer's instructions, the cheque would have been returned by it marked 'Orders not to pay,' and there would have followed a perfectly bona fide dispute between the association and the receiver on the question, arising on the terms of the building contract, whether the association was entitled to stop the cheque—which ought to be the real dispute in the case. If the plaintiff bank had been unable to recover the money, not only would that dispute not have been ventilated and resolved on its merits but, in the absence of ratification by the association, the plaintiff bank would have had no recourse to the association. Indeed, if under the terms of the building contract the money had not been due to the defendant company, non-recovery by the plaintiff bank would have meant quite simply a windfall for the preferred creditors of the defendant company at the plaintiff bank's expense. As however I have held that the money is recoverable, the situation is as it should have been; nobody is harmed, and the true dispute between the association and the receiver can be resolved on its merits.

NOTES

1. The mistaken payer may seek to recover his mistaken payment from the payee by means of a common law action for money had and received. The modern approach is to refer to the action as a 'personal claim in restitution at common law' (*Westdeutsche Landesbank Girozentrale v Islington London Borough Council* [1996] AC 669 at 683, per Lord Goff). The claim is founded on the unjust enrichment of the payee at the expense of the payer. The payer's mistake renders the enrichment of the payee unjust because it vitiates the payer's intention to transfer the benefit to him. Reversal of that unjust enrichment lies at the heart of the claim. (But a mistake is different from ignorance, inadvertence, and misprediction as to the future: *Pitt v Holt* [2013] UKSC 26, [2013] 2 WLR 1200 at [104], per Lord Walker.)

2. Until recently, English law only allowed a common law action to recover money paid by mistake where the mistake was of fact and not where it was of law (the origin of the mistake of law rule was *Bilbie v Lumley* (1802) 2 East 469). In *Kleinwort Benson Ltd v Lincoln City Council* [1999] 2 AC 349, the House of Lords held (by a 3:2 majority) that the mistake of law rule no longer formed part of English law. It is now settled that a cause of action at common law is available for money paid under a mistake of law (*Deutsche Morgan Grenfell Group plc v Inland Revenue Comrs* [2006] UKHL 449, [2007] 1 AC 558 at [62], per Lord Hope). Following the decision of the House of Lords in *Sempra Metals Ltd v Inland Revenue Comrs* [2007] UKHL 34, [2007] 3 WLR 354, it is also settled that a court has jurisdiction at common law to award compound interest where the claimant seeks a restitutionary remedy for the time value of money paid under a mistake of fact or law.

3. In *Lloyds Bank plc v Independent Insurance Co Ltd* [2000] QB 110, a customer paid a cheque into his bank and, because he owed a similar sum to a third party, instructed the bank to transfer that sum to the third party as soon as possible. The bank agreed to do this but only on condition that the cheque had first cleared as there were insufficient funds in the account to make the transfer otherwise. However, before the cheque cleared the money was transferred by inter-bank electronic transfer into the payee's bank account by mistake. On discovering the error the bank sought to recover the payment from the payee. Applying para 2(b) of Goff J's classification in *Barclays Bank v Simms*, the Court of Appeal held that the bank was not entitled to restitution of a transfer of funds which had been made with its customer's authority to discharge a debt owed by that customer to the payee. The payment had been made with the customer's actual authority and, because it discharged his debt to the third party, had been made for good consideration. It was the bank, not its customer, which had imposed the qualification that the transfer was not to be made before the cheque cleared. The bank had acted within its mandate.

4.   As a specific technical defence turning on the holder's prejudice in not being able to give notice of dishonour to prior parties, the rule in *Cocks v Masterman* is flawed. Section 50(1) of the BEA provides that delay in giving notice of dishonour is excused where the delay is caused by circumstances beyond the control of the party giving notice, and is not imputable to his default, misconduct, or negligence. If the holder gives notice of dishonour when informed that the payment was made in mistake of the facts then, under s 50(1), he should not be prejudiced by the delay in giving such notice.

5.   For as long as English law did not recognise any general defence of change of position, the rule in *Cocks v Masterman* had to be based on the technical ground of failure to give notice of dishonour. In *Barclays Bank v Simms*, Robert Goff J recognised that this could all change if full recognition was accorded to the general defence. This came with *Lipkin Gorman v Karpnale Ltd* [1991] 2 AC 548 where the House of Lords finally recognised that a general defence of change of position in good faith is available against restitutionary claims based on unjust enrichment of the defendant. Although their Lordships were at pains to point out that they did not wish to define the scope of the defence in abstract terms, but to let it develop on a case-by-case basis, Lord Goff did emphasise (at 580) 'that the defence is available to a person whose position has so changed that it would be inequitable in all the circumstances to require him to make restitution, or alternatively to make restitution in full'. This would mean that if the holder, who had been wrongly paid, had actually suffered prejudice because, for example, he had lost an immediate right of recourse against a prior party who had since become insolvent, the defence of change of position would apply. Insofar as the rule in *Cocks v Masterman* can be justified on this wider ground it should now be regarded as a specific application of the general defence.

6.   In *Lipkin Gorman* (above) Lord Goff stressed that the mere fact that the recipient has spent the money received, in whole or in part, does not render it inequitable that he should be called upon to repay 'because the expenditure might in any event have been incurred by him in the ordinary course of things' (at 580). If the recipient is to succeed with a defence of change of position he must have incurred expenditure which he would not otherwise have incurred or have otherwise acted in such a way as to render it unjust that he should now be compelled to refund the payment. Where the recipient has purchased goods or services, the benefit of which he still retains, he might still be held to have been unjustly enriched to their value as a result of the payment. For example, the recipient may have used the mistaken payment to purchase a car that remains in his possession (*Lipkin Gorman*, above, at 560), or shares that have increased in value (*Crédit Suisse (Monaco) SA v Attar* [2004] EWHC 374 (Comm) at [98]), or land that he still retains (*Campden Hill Ltd v Chakrani* [2005] EWHC 911 (Ch) at [87]).

7.   The Court of Appeal had to consider the availability of the defence of change of position in *Scottish Equitable plc v Derby* [2001] EWCA Civ 369, [2001] 2 All ER (Comm) 274. In that case, the claimant life assurance company miscalculated the defendant's pension entitlement, which resulted in him receiving a significant overpayment. The Court of Appeal upheld the trial judge's decision that the claimant was entitled to recover the overpayment, save for a relatively small sum spent by the defendant on making modest improvements to his lifestyle. The Court of Appeal stressed two points with regard to the defence of change of position. First, that for the defence to apply there must be a causal link between the recipient's change of position and the mistaken payment which makes it inequitable for the recipient to be

required to make restitution. Moreover, the defence was to be available not only to those who had detrimentally relied on the mistaken payment but also to those who had suffered some other misfortune, for example the innocent recipient of a payment which is later stolen from him, so long as the misfortune could be causally linked to the mistaken receipt. The court appeared to give tacit approval to a 'but for' test of causation. Secondly, it was held that a court should not apply too demanding a standard of proof when an honest recipient says that he has spent an overpayment by improving his lifestyle, but cannot produce any detailed accounting. The defence was not to be limited, as it is in Canada and some of the states of the United States, to specific identifiable items of expenditure.

8. It was held by Clarke J in *South Tyneside Metropolitan Borough Council v Svenska International plc* [1995] 1 All ER 545 that the defence of change of position was only available where the defendant had changed his position after receipt of the enrichment. In other words, anticipatory change of position was not sufficient to raise the defence. This restrictive interpretation of the defence has been heavily criticised (see, eg, A Jones [1995] Conv 490). The requirement that the change of position must follow receipt of the enrichment seems unnecessary. It should be enough that the two are causally linked in some way. It is not surprising, therefore, to find that the Privy Council has since indicated that the defence should extend to anticipatory change of position. In *Dextra Bank & Trust Co Ltd v Bank of Jamaica* [2001] UKPC 50, [2002] 1 All ER (Comm) 193, Lords Bingham and Goff, delivering the advice of the Privy Council in a case where payment was held to be made as a result of a misprediction as to a future event (and so not recoverable) and not as a result of a mistake, stated *obiter* that anticipatory expenditure was enough to raise the defence. Their Lordships reasoned that by the time a claim in unjust enrichment was brought to trial, the defendant would merely want to retain the benefit that *ex hypothesi* he already had received. Moreover, so long as there was a sufficient causal connection between receipt of the enrichment and the expenditure, the injustice of requiring the defendant to make restitution was the same whether the defendant incurred an exceptional expenditure before or after receiving the enrichment. In *Commerzbank AG v Gareth Price-Jones* [2003] EWCA Civ 1663 at [38] and [64], the Court of Appeal followed *Dextra Bank* and held that a change of position in anticipation of an enrichment was to be treated in the same way as one that came afterwards. More recently, anticipatory reliance was endorsed by Henderson J in *Test Claimants in the FII Group Litigation v HMRC* [2014] EWHC 4302 (Ch) at [243] and by Simon J in *T & L Sugars Ltd v Tate & Lyle Industries Ltd* [2015] EWHC 2696 (Comm) at [137].

9. The change of position defence is only open to someone who has changed his position in good faith. In *Lipkin Gorman* [1991] 2 AC 548 at 580, Lord Goff considered that it was 'plain that the defence is not open to one who has changed his position in bad faith, as where the defendant has paid away the money with knowledge of the facts entitling the plaintiff to restitution; and it is commonly accepted that the defence should not be open to a wrongdoer'. But dishonesty, in the sense of knowledge that one is transgressing ordinary standards of honest behaviour, is not the sole criterion of the right to invoke the defence of change of position. In *Niru Battery Manufacturing Co v Milestone Trading Ltd* [2002] EWHC 1425 (Comm), [2002] 2 All ER (Comm) 705 at [135], Moore Bick J held that lack of good faith was a concept 'capable of embracing a failure to act in a commercially acceptable way and sharp practice of a kind that falls short of outright dishonesty as well as dishonesty itself'. The judge was upheld on appeal, where the Court of Appeal stressed that the key question was whether it would be inequitable or unconscionable to deny restitution ([2003] EWCA Civ 1446, [2004] QB 985 at [148]–[149], [162], [182]–[185], [192]). This approach can be criticised for being

too wide and imprecise, moving away from the narrow question of bad faith to the wider one of whether it is inequitable to allow the defence (see Birks (2004) 120 LQR 373 at 377; Virgo [2004] CLJ 276 at 278). But a more principled approach was restored in *Abou-Rahmah v Abacha* [2006] EWCA Civ 1492, [2007] 1 Lloyd's Rep 115, where Arden and Pill LJJ, at [84] and [102] respectively, focused only on the defendant's conduct at the time of the change of position and not on the general nature of the defendant's conduct (the latter approach being favoured by Rix LJ at [58]). Bad faith does not include negligence (*Dextra Bank*, above, at [45]; *Niru Battery*, above, at [33], CA) or incompetence (*Jeremy D Stone Consultants Ltd v National Westminster Bank* [2013] EWHC 208 (Ch) at [247]). On the other hand, where a change of position involves illegality, the change of position will not be taken into account, unless the illegality is very minor (*Barros Mattos Junior v MacDaniels Ltd* [2004] EWHC 1188 (Ch), [2004] 3 All ER 299). The defence is also not available where the defendant took the risk of his position changing (*Haugesund Kommune v Depfa ACS Bank* [2010] EWCA Civ 579, [2012] 2 WLR 199: recipient of payment made under void loan contract took risk that money would have to be repaid). For detailed coverage, see E Bant, *The Change of Position Defence* (2009).

10. Other grounds for denying a restitutionary claim for money paid under a mistake include:

(a) if the payee presented the instrument as agent and, without notice of the claim, has since remitted the proceeds to his principal, the payer can only look to the principal, and not the agent, for repayment (*Buller v Harrison* (1777) 2 Cowp 565 at 568)—but the defence is only available to a bank that has received a mistaken payment and credited it to its customer's account when that credit is irreversible (*Jones v Churcher* [2009] EWHC 722 (QB), [2009] 2 Lloyd's Rep 94 at [77]); and

(b) if the payer is estopped by representation from alleging that he made the payment under a mistake (although mere payment of money cannot in itself constitute a representation which will estop the payer from recovering payment: *Re Jones Ltd v Waring and Gillow Ltd* [1926] AC 670, HL; *Philip Collins Ltd v Davies* [2000] 3 All ER 808 at 825, Ch D).

In *Lipkin Gorman v Karpnale Ltd* [1991] 2 AC 548 at 578, Lord Goff suggested that the defence of an agent who has paid over money might be based on change of position. This seems wrong. Payment over is a separate defence which is well established with its own rules. It is based on the fact that the agent recipient is a mere conduit pipe for the money, which is treated as paid to the principal, not to the agent, so that the principal, not the agent, is the proper party to be sued (*Portman Building Society v Hamlyn Taylor Neck (a firm)* [1998] 4 All ER 202 at 207, per Millett LJ; *Jones v Churcher*, above, at [77]; *Jeremy D Stone Consultants Ltd v National Westminster Bank*, above, at [244]). The relationship between the two defences is considered further by Elise Bant in 'Payment Over and Change of Position: Lessons from Agency Law' [2007] LMCLQ 225.

The estoppel defence is said to differ from the change of position defence in two respects: (a) it depends on a representation by the person making the payment whereas the change of position defence does not; and (b) it gives a total defence to the claim whereas the change of position defence only provides a *pro tanto* defence. The broad extent of the estoppel defence has recently proved unpopular with the courts and the recipient has only been permitted to retain the amount of his detrimental reliance (*Scottish Equitable plc v Derby* [2001] EWCA Civ 369, [2001] 3 All ER 818; *National Westminster Bank plc v Somer International (UK) Ltd* [2001] EWCA Civ 970, [2002] 1 All ER 198). The future of the defence is uncertain.

11. Professor Goode has been particularly critical of *Barclays Bank v Simms*. In 'The Bank's Right to Recover Money Paid on a Stopped Cheque' (1981) 97 LQR 254 at 255–256, he writes:

> . . . the defendants ought to have succeeded on two grounds, neither of which appears to have been argued. The first is that whilst the countermand of payment terminated the bank's *actual* authority to pay the cheque, the payee was entitled to rely on the bank's continued *apparent* authority to make payment, so that this was effective to discharge the drawer's liability to the payee on the cheque. The second is that a payee who gives up a cheque on which he has a valid claim in exchange for payment inevitably suffers a change of position, for he no longer has the instrument in his hands, and any claim he wishes to pursue against the drawer will have to be on the original consideration, not on the cheque, so that he loses valuable rights. It will further be argued that if the claim had been dismissed the rights of the parties could then have been adjusted by reference to the principle of subrogation, without unjust enrichment of the drawer or unjust detriment to the bank.

Not everyone agrees with Professor Goode's assessment of the case. In 'Unauthorised Payment and Unjustified Enrichment in Banking Law' in FD Rose (ed), *Restitution and Banking Law* (1998), Ch 1, Justice van Zyl (Judge of the Cape High Court) writes in fairly blunt terms:

> There is not the slightest merit in these submissions and it is not surprising that they were not argued. If the bank has no authority to pay out a cheque it certainly cannot have 'apparent' authority to do so, unless the suggestion is that the bank misrepresented that it had authority. Furthermore . . . payment without authority can under no circumstances discharge the underlying agreement between the drawer and payee or have any legal effect on it whatever. The second argument must likewise be rejected since it is based on the faulty premise that the unauthorised payment discharged the drawer's indebtedness to the payee.

An argument based on the bank's apparent authority to pay was firmly rejected by the Court of Appeal in *Lloyds Bank plc v Independent Insurance Co Ltd* [1999] 1 All ER (Comm) 8, an electronic funds transfer case (see Note 3 above), on the grounds that: (a) there was no holding out that the bank had authority to make the payment; and (b) there was no reliance by the payee on the bank having authority to pay.

Nevertheless, there remains strong academic support for the view that a payment made to discharge another's debt and accepted as so doing by the payee creditor should be regarded as discharging the debt irrespective of the consent of the debtor (A Burrows, *The Law of Restitution* (3rd edn, 2011), p 209 and Ch 17). Further, in *B & H Engineering v First National Bank of SA Ltd* 1995 (2) SA 279 (A), the Appellate Division (now the Supreme Court of Appeal) in South Africa held that payment of a countermanded cheque by the drawee bank discharges the underlying debt between drawer and payee, so that the drawee bank has no claim against the payee for mistaken payment but is left with a restitutionary claim against the drawer based on his unjust enrichment at the bank's expense (the decision is strongly criticised by Justice van Zyl (above), pp 22–26). Similarly, in the United States, the Uniform Commercial Code denies direct recovery by the bank which made the mistaken payment against a payee who took the cheque in good faith and for value: the bank is subrogated to the rights of the payee or holder in due course of the cheque against the drawer, or those of the drawer against the payee, so as to prevent unjust enrichment (Uniform Commercial Code, s 4–407).

The approach taken by the Supreme Court of Appeal in South Africa and by the Uniform Commercial Code in the United States has the superficial attraction of leaving the mistaken bank with a claim for unjust enrichment against its own customer, the drawer, when it is denied recovery against the payee. However, the bank will not necessarily recover all of its mistaken payment from the drawer as the bank is merely subrogated to the payee's claim against him and the drawer may have a defence to some or all of that claim (eg where the drawer stops the cheque because the payee has delivered defective goods). It is submitted that the bank should not be drawn into that dispute but should be allowed to recover its mistaken payment from the payee and withdraw from the scene, leaving the drawer and payee to fight it out amongst themselves (the solution suggested by Professor Birks in 'The Burden on the Bank' in FD Rose (ed), *Restitution and Banking Law* (1998), p 217).

Tracing at common law Sometimes a mistaken payer will first have to trace at common law before he can bring a personal claim for money had and received. Tracing will be necessary in two cases: (1) when making a claim to a substituted asset acquired with the enrichment; and (2) in order to maintain a claim against a remote recipient, ie when the claimant's property was received by the defendant from a third party, rather than having been subtracted directly from the claimant (see PBH Birks, 'Overview' in PBH Birks (ed), *Laundering and Tracing* (1995), pp 300–305; LD Smith, 'Tracing and Electronic Funds Transfers' in FD Rose (ed), *Restitution and Banking Law* (1998), pp 121–131). In each case tracing merely serves an evidential purpose, identifying the path of value from the claimant to the defendant, and does not give rise to a cause of action or remedy in itself (*Boscawen v Bajwa* [1995] 4 All ER 769 at 776, per Millett LJ; *Foskett v McKeown* [2001] 1 AC 102 at 128, per Lord Millett). As the next case illustrates, difficulties arise where payment is made through the banking system, which entails a series of more or less complex substitutions.

Agip (Africa) Ltd v Jackson
[1991] Ch 547, Court of Appeal

An authorised signatory of the plaintiff (Agip) signed a payment order instructing Agip's Tunisian bankers, Banque du Sud, to transfer US$518,000 to a named payee. Zdiri, Agip's chief accountant, fraudulently altered the name of the payee to Baker Oil Services Ltd, a company controlled by the defendant chartered accountants, which held a US dollar account at Lloyds Bank in London. On receipt of the altered payment order, Banque du Sud debited Agip's account and telexed Lloyds Bank in London to credit Baker Oil's account. Banque du Sud also telexed its correspondent bank, Citibank, in New York and instructed it to credit Lloyds Bank through the New York clearing system. As New York is five hours behind London, Lloyds Bank took a delivery risk and credited Baker Oil's account before being placed in funds through the New York clearing system. Later the money was debited from Baker Oil's account and transferred to an account in the name of the defendants. Acting on their clients' instructions, the defendants transferred all but US$45,000 to unknown parties. At first instance Millett J held that Agip had an equitable proprietary claim to the US$45,000 and was entitled to compensation for the defendants' knowing assistance in a breach of trust; but he rejected Agip's alternative claims based on the receipt of money either at common law (see below) or in equity (because the defendants had received the money as agents and not for their own benefit). The Court of Appeal upheld Millett J's decision on the equitable proprietary claim and the claim for compensation for knowing assistance in a breach of trust. The Court of Appeal dismissed Agip's appeal on the common law action for money had and received. There was no appeal on Millett J's decision to reject the equitable receipt claim.

Fox LJ: . . .

THE RIGHT TO SUE

Agip's claim was for money paid under a mistake of fact. The defendants' contention was that Agip had disclosed no title to sue. The basis of that contention was that the relationship between banker and customer was one of debtor and creditor. When the customer paid money into the bank, the ownership of the money passed to the bank. The bank could do what it liked with it. What the bank undertook to do was to credit the amount of the money to the customer's account, and to honour his drafts or other proper directions in relation to it. Thus, it was said, when Banque du Sud paid Baker Oil it had no authority to do so on behalf of Agip because the order for payment was forged. Further, the Banque du Sud paid with its own money.

In terms of the mechanism of payment, what happened was no different from what would have happened if the order was not forged but genuine. Banque du Sud paid the collecting bank and debited Agip's account at Banque du Sud. In practical terms the Banque du Sud paid with Agip's money in both cases and, indeed, in both cases intended to do so. In both cases the substance of the matter was that money standing to the credit of Agip's account was paid to a third party in accordance with the order or supposed order, as the case may be, of Agip. The direction was to pay from Agip's account. To say that the payment was made out of the Banque du Sud's own funds, while true as far as it goes, only tells half the story. The banker's instruction is to pay from the customer's account. He does so by a payment from his own funds and a corresponding debit. The reality is a payment by the customer, at any rate in a case where the customer has no right to require a re-crediting of his account. Nothing passes in specie. The whole matter is dealt with by accounting transactions partly in the paying bank and partly in the clearing process.

It does not advance the matter to say that the Banque du Sud had no mandate from Agip to make the payment at Agip's expense. What actually happened was that Banque du Sud did so. Moreover, when Agip sued Banque du Sud in the Tunisian courts—and I take it that Tunisian law was the proper law of the banking relationship between Agip and Banque du Sud—to have its account re-credited, it failed to obtain that relief. In those circumstances, to regard Agip as not having paid Baker Oil is highly unreal. Banque du Sud had no intention of paying with its own money. The substance of its intention, which it achieved, was to pay with Agip's money. The order, after all, was an order to pay with Agip's money. I agree, therefore, with the view of Millett J [1990] Ch. 265, 283h that 'the fact remains that the Banque du Sud paid out the plaintiffs' money and not its own'. If Banque du Sud paid away Agip's money, Agip itself must be entitled to pursue such remedies as there may be for its recovery. The money was certainly paid under a mistake of fact.

It was said that the difference between this case and a case where the bank paid with the authority (though given under a mistake of fact) of the customer, was that, in the latter case, the bank paid as agent of the customer and that, accordingly, either the principal or agent could sue. Thus, it was contended that where, as here, there was a claim to recover money paid by mistake of fact, the mistake must be that of the plaintiff or of his agent. That, it was contended, could not be established here. There was no mistake by Agip, which was simply the victim of a fraud. The only mistake was that of Banque du Sud, which paid in the mistaken belief that it had Agip's authority to do so. Banque du Sud, it was said, did not pay as the agent of Agip because it had no authority to pay. In *Westminster Bank Ltd v Hilton* (1926) 43 TLR 124, 126, Lord Atkinson said:

> It is well established that the normal relation between a banker and his customer is that of debtor and creditor, but it is equally well established that *quoad* the drawing and payment of the customer's cheques as against money of the customer's in the banker's hands the relation

is that of principal and agent. The cheque is an order of the principal's addressed to the agent to pay out of the principal's money in the agent's hands the amount of the cheque to the payee thereof.

The defendants, as I understand it, would accept the proposition as to agency but say that Banque du Sud did not pay as agent of Agip because of lack of authority. The order was forged. It seems to me, however, Banque du Sud plainly intended to pay as agent of Agip. Thus, it paid in accordance with the order as presented to it and debited Agip's account accordingly. There was no reason why it should do anything else. The order as presented to it appeared perfectly regular.

But, accepting the intention, can the Banque du Sud properly be regarded as having paid as agent of Agip? The defendants say the absence of authority concluded the point against Agip. The judge met that by saying that Banque du Sud had general authority from Agip to debit the account in accordance with the instructions. That is correct but it was said that there were no instructions because the order was bad. I do not feel able to accept that. The order emanated from within Agip; it was properly signed and the amount had not been altered. Banque du Sud had no reason at all to doubt its authenticity. The Tunisian court refused to order Banque du Sud to re-credit Agip's account. For practical purposes, therefore, the order was given effect to according to its tenor as if it were a proper order. Everything that was done (i.e. the payments and the debit) stands good so far as the banking transaction is concerned. Agip cannot recover from Banque du Sud. And Banque du Sud does not seek to recover from Baker Oil. It seems to me, therefore, that the order must be regarded as having been paid by Banque du Sud as agent for Agip. That, however, does not alter the circumstance that it was money paid under a mistake of fact. The defendants accepted that a principal could recover where there was either (i) mistaken payment by an authorised agent within his instructions or (ii) mistaken payment in breach of instructions by using money entrusted to the agent by the principal. The present case can be brought within, at any rate, the first of these.

The judge referred to the decision in *Colonial Bank v Exchange Bank of Yarmouth, Nova Scotia* (1885) 11 App Cas 84, 91. In that case it was held that the bank had a sufficient interest to recover the money, if only to obtain relief from the consequences of its liability to its customer. Millett J thought the decision was inconsistent with any suggestion that, far from being the wrong plaintiff, the bank was the only plaintiff. The present point, however, was not before the Privy Council in that case and I think the decision gives only limited assistance.

Looking at the whole matter, however, it seems to me that the judge correctly concluded that Agip's right to sue was made out.

TRACING AT COMMON LAW

The judge held that Agip was not entitled to trace at law. Tracing at law does not depend upon the establishment of an initial fiduciary relationship. Liability depends upon receipt by the defendant of the plaintiffs money and the extent of the liability depends on the amount received. Since liability depends upon receipt the fact that a recipient has not retained the asset is irrelevant. For the same reason dishonesty or lack of inquiry on the part of the recipient are irrelevant. Identification in the defendant's hands of the plaintiff's asset is, however, necessary. It must be shown that the money received by the defendant was the money of the plaintiff. Further, the very limited common law remedies make it difficult to follow at law into mixed funds. The judge's view [1990] Ch 265, 286 of the present case was that the common law remedy was not available. He said:

> The money cannot be followed by treating it as the proceeds of a cheque presented by the collecting bank in exchange for payment by the paying bank. The money was transmitted by telegraphic transfer. There was no cheque or any equivalent. The payment order was not a

cheque or its equivalent. It remained throughout in the possession of the Banque du Sud. No copy was sent to Lloyds Bank or Baker Oil or presented to the Banque du Sud in exchange for the money. It was normally the plaintiffs' practice to forward a copy of the payment order to the supplier when paying an invoice but this was for information only. It did not authorise or enable the supplier to obtain payment. There is no evidence that this practice was followed in the case of forged payment orders and it is exceedingly unlikely that it was. Nothing passed between Tunisia and London but a stream of electrons. It is not possible to treat the money received by Lloyds Bank in London or its correspondent bank in New York as representing the proceeds of the payment order or of any other physical asset previously in its hands and delivered by it in exchange for the money.

Agip relied upon the decision of the Court of Appeal in *Banque Belge pour L'Etranger v Hambrouck* [1921] 1 KB 321. In that case what happened was that Hambrouck was a cashier employed by Pelabon. By fraud he possessed himself of cheques purporting to be drawn by Pelabon but in fact without Pelabon's authority. The cheques (which purported to be drawn to the order of Hambrouck himself or to his order) were crossed so payment had to be made through a bank. Hambrouck, therefore, opened an account with Farrow's Bank at Richmond. He endorsed the cheques and paid them into that account. Farrow's Bank cleared them through the London and South Western Bank which collected the amount of the cheques and placed them to the credit of Hambrouck's account. It seems that no funds were paid into that account other than the amount of the forged cheques: see *per* Atkin LJ at p 331. Hambrouck was living with Mademoiselle Spanoghe to whom he paid various sums of money out of his bank account with Farrow's. Mile Spanoghe paid them into a deposit account of her own in the London Joint City and Midland Bank. No other sums were at any time placed in that deposit account. Certain sums were drawn out for Hambrouck's defence. The balance, £315, was the subject of the action. The Court of Appeal held that Banque Belge was entitled to recover it Bankes LJ at p 328, and Atkin LJ, at p 334, saw no objection to a claim at common law. After having referred to Lord Ellenborough's judgment in *Taylor v Plumer* (1815) 3 M & S 562, Atkin LJ said, at pp 335–336:

I notice that in *Sinclair v Brougham* [1914] AC 398,419 Lord Haldane LC in dealing with this decision says: 'Lord Ellenborough laid down, as a limit to this proposition, that if the money had become incapable of being traced, as, for instance, when it had been paid into the broker's general account with his banker, the principal had no remedy excepting to prove as a creditor for money had and received,' and proceeds to say 'you can, even at law, follow, but only so long as the relation of debtor and creditor has not superseded the right in rem.' The word above 'as for instance' et seq. do not represent and doubtless do not purport to represent Lord Ellenborough's actual words; and I venture to doubt whether the common law ever so restricted the right as to hold that the money became incapable of being traced, merely because paid into the broker's general account with his banker. The question always was, Had the means of ascertainment failed? But if in 1815 the common law halted outside the bankers' door, by 1879 equity had had the courage to lift the latch, walk in and examine the books: *In re Hallett's Estate* (1879) 13 Ch.D 696. I see no reason why the means of ascertainment so provided should not now be available both for common law and equity proceedings. If, following the principles laid down *In re Hallett's Estate*, it can be ascertained either that the money in the bank, or the commodity which it has bought, is 'the product of, or substitute for, the original thing,' then it still follows 'the nature of the thing itself.' On these principles it would follow that as the money paid into the bank can be identified as the product of the original money, the plaintiffs have the common law right to claim it, and can sue for money had and received. In the present case less difficulty than usual is experienced in tracing the descent of the money, for substantially no other money has ever been mixed with the proceeds of the fraud.

Bankes LJ at p 328, while accepting that tracing at common law was permissible, took a narrower position. He said that there was no difficulty about tracing at law because the money which the bank sought to remove was capable of being traced because the appellant (Mile Spanoghe) never paid any money into the bank except money which was part of the proceeds of Hambrouck's fraud and all the money standing to the credit of the account was now in court. Scrutton LJ at p 330, thought that tracing at common law was probably not permissible because the money had changed its identity when paid into the account at Farrow's. He felt, however, that the Banque Belge could trace in equity and that its claim succeeded.

Now, in the present case, the course of events was as follows. (1) The original payment order was in December signed by an authorised signatory. (2) The name of the payee was then altered to Baker Oil. (3) The altered order was then taken to Banque du Sud who complied with it by debiting the account of Agip with $518,822.92 and then instructing Lloyds Bank to pay Baker Oil. Banque du Sud also instructed Citibank in New York to debit its account with Citibank and credit Lloyds Bank with the amount of the order. (4) Lloyds Bank credited the money to Baker Oil's account on the morning of 7 January. (5) On 8 January, Lloyds Bank in pursuance of instructions from Baker Oil transferred the $518,822.92, which was the only sum standing to the credit of Baker Oil's account, to an account in the name of Jackson & Co. (6) Immediately before the transfer from Baker Oil, Jackson & Co's account was $7,911.80 in credit. In consequence of the transfer it became $526,734.72 in credit.

The inquiry which has to be made is whether the money paid to Jackson & Co's account 'was the product of, or substitute for, the original thing.' In answering that question I do not think that it matters that the order was not a cheque. It was a direction by the account holder to the bank. When Atkin LJ referred in the *Banque Belge* case to the 'original money' he was, I assume, referring to the money credited by Banque Belge (the plaintiff) to Hambrouck's account. Money from that account was the only money in Mile Spanoghe's deposit account. It was not, therefore, difficult to say that the money in issue (ie the residue of Mile Spanoghe's account) could be identified as the product of the original money. There were no complexities of tracing at all. Everything in Mile Spanoghe's account came from Hambrouck's account and everything in Hambrouck's account came from the credit in respect of the fraudulent cheque.

The position in the present case is much more difficult. Banque du Sud can be regarded as having paid with Agip's money but Lloyds Bank, acting as directed by Banque du Sud, paid Baker Oil with its own money. It had no other and, accordingly, took a delivery risk. It was, in the end, put in funds, but it is difficult to see how the origin of those funds can be identified without tracing the money through the New York clearing system. The money in the present case did get mixed on two occasions. The first was in the New York clearing system and the second was in Jackson & Co's own account. The judge held that the latter was of no consequence. I agree. The common law remedy attached to the recipient of the money and its subsequent transposition does not alter his liability. The problem arises at an earlier stage. What did Jackson & Co receive which was the product of Agip's asset? Baker Oil was controlled for present purposes by Jackson & Co but Baker Oil was paid by Lloyds Bank which had not been put in funds from New York. It was subsequently recouped. But it is not possible to show the source from which it was recouped without tracing the money through the New York clearing system. The judge said [1990] Ch 265, 286:

> Unless Lloyds Bank's correspondent bank in New York was also Citibank, this involves tracing the money through the accounts of Citibank and Lloyds Bank's correspondent bank with the Federal Reserve Bank, where it must have been mixed with other money. The money with which Lloyds Bank was reimbursed cannot therefore, without recourse to equity, be identified as being that of the Banque du Sud.

I respectfully agree with that view. Accordingly, it seems to me that the common law remedy is not available.

I should add this. Atkin LJ's approach in the *Banque Belge* case amounts virtually to saying that there is now no difference between the common law and equitable remedies. Indeed, the common law remedy might be wider because of the absence of any requirement of a fiduciary relationship. There may be a good deal to be said for that view but it goes well beyond any other case and well beyond the views of Bankes and Scrutton LJJ. And in the 70 years since the *Banque Belge* decision it has not been applied. Whether, short of the House of Lords, it is now open to the courts to adopt it I need not consider. I would in any event feel difficulty in doing so in the present case where, as I indicate later, it seems to me that the established equitable rules provide an adequate remedy in relation to this action . . .

[**Butler-Sloss** and **Beldam LJJ** concurred.]

NOTES

1. Did Agip really have title to sue? The Court of Appeal held that 'in practical terms' the bank had paid Baker Oil with Agip's money, but in legal terms payment was with the bank's own money. A bank which pays outside its mandate has no right to debit its customer's account and, if a bank cannot debit its customer's account, it must be paying with its own money and not that of its customer. In the *Agip* case the Court of Appeal appears to have been influenced by the fact that Agip had unsuccessfully brought proceedings against Banque du Sud in Tunisia to have its account re-credited (see E McKendrick [1991] LMCLQ 378 at 379–381).

2. It is a well-established rule that it is not possible to trace money at law through a mixed fund (see, eg, *Taylor v Plumer* (1815) 3 M & S 562 at 575, per Lord Ellenborough CJ; *Re Diplock* [1948] Ch 465 at 518, per Lord Greene MR; cf LD Smith, *The Law of Tracing* (1997), pp 162–174). The common law can only trace through clean substitutions (see, eg, *Trustees of the Property of FC Jones & Sons (a firm) v Jones* [1997] Ch 159). This rule prevents common law tracing when money is paid into a bank account which has also received other credits. The rule was fatal to Agip's attempt to trace at common law because the Court of Appeal expressly approved of Millett J's reasoning at first instance that Agip's funds were mixed with other funds during the clearing process in New York (see also *Bank of America v Arnell* [1999] Lloyd's Rep Bank 399 at 405, per Aikens J). However, this reasoning seems to misconstrue what happens in a clearing process, where transactions are accounted for individually and the only mixing is in the settlements, which are generally irrelevant (LD Smith, *The Law of Tracing* (1997), pp 252–255; see also LD Smith, 'Tracing and Electronic Funds Transfer' in FD Rose (ed), *Restitution and Banking Law* (1998), pp 131–134, who argues that it is not necessary to trace through a clearing system where the banks involved in the payment process are all acting as agents for one side or the other). The decision in *Agip* is also difficult to reconcile with *Banque Belge pour l'Etranger v Hambrouck* [1921] 1 KB 321 (above), where the plaintiffs were held to be entitled to trace despite the fact that the cheques which Hambrouck had obtained by fraud had been cleared through the clearing system in London (see E McKendrick [1991] LMCLQ 378 at 383–384; cf P Millett (1991) 107 LQR 71 at 73). In *BMP Global Distribution Inc v Bank of Nova Scotia* [2009] 1 SCR 504, the Supreme Court of Canada, following *Banque Belge* and distinguishing *Agip*, recognised that the mixing of cheque proceeds in the clearing system did not prevent the drawee bank that had paid out on a forged cheque from tracing those funds at law (noted by D Fox [2010] CLJ 28).

3.   Millett J's reasoning at first instance that it is not possible to trace at law where money is transferred using electronic means does not appear to have found favour with the Court of Appeal (see the *obiter* remarks of Fox LJ). However, Millett J was later followed on this point by Tuckey J in *Bank Tejarat v Hong Kong and Shanghai Banking Corpn* (CI) Ltd [1995] 1 Lloyd's Rep 239, and the issue cannot be considered closed. This is unfortunate as there is no good reason why the transfer of funds by electronic means should be treated any differently from the transfer of funds by cheque (ie where there is a tangible asset), where common law tracing is allowed. Distinctions that are made between the electronic transfer of funds and payment by a tangible asset, such as a cheque, fail to appreciate that what is traced is not the physical asset but the value inherent in it (*Foskett v McKeown* [2001] 1 AC 102 at 128, per Lord Millett; *Relfo Ltd v Varsani* [2014] EWCA Civ 360, [2015] 1 BCLC 14 at [60], per Arden LJ: but contrast T Cutts (2016) 79 MLR 381 for an explanation based on the intention of the transacting parties and not the tracing of value). There are also sound policy reasons for a uniform approach to this issue. The point is made the editors of *Ellinger's Modern Banking Law* (5th edn, 2011), p 305, in the following blunt terms:

> Modern banking requires fast and efficient money transmission systems to transfer funds between bank accounts both domestically and internationally. In terms of the value of payments, electronic funds transfer systems are the dominant systems in use. It is unacceptable that the English common law is incapable of operating in this modern environment. The only people to gain from this unsatisfactory state of affairs are criminals and other money launderers who use electronic funds transfer systems to shift their ill-gotten gains around the globe.

Tracing in equity It may benefit a mistaken payer to trace the mistaken payment in equity and seek an equitable proprietary remedy against its recipient. This will be of real value to the payer where the recipient is insolvent, as priority may be obtained over his general creditors. The court may grant an equitable proprietary remedy through the imposition of an equitable charge, lien, constructive trust, or by subrogation. Equitable tracing may also be invoked with the aim of seeking a personal equitable remedy based on unconscionable receipt (sometimes called 'knowing receipt'). The remedy is not proprietary because it involves only a personal liability to account or to compensate (*Williams v Central Bank of Nigeria* [2014] UKSC 10, [2014] AC 1189). This personal remedy, unlike a proprietary one, does not depend upon continued retention of the payment by the defendant.

Generally speaking equitable tracing rules are more flexible than common law tracing rules, and it is possible in equity to trace through a mixed fund (so, eg, equitable tracing was possible in *Agip (Africa) Ltd v Jackson* [1991] Ch 547, above). But there are important restrictions on the right to trace in equity. First, the general rule is that it is not possible to trace money which has ceased to exist, for example by being paid into an overdrawn bank account, or an account which has subsequently become overdrawn, even though the account may later return into credit (*Bishopsgate Investment Management Ltd v Homan* [1995] Ch 211, CA). However, in *Brazil v Durant International Corpn* [2015] UKPC 35, the Privy Council endorsed the concept of so-called 'backward tracing' which makes it possible, for example, to trace through an overdrawn account where, according to Lord Toulson (at [40]), the claimant can 'establish coordination between the depletion of the trust fund and the acquisition of an asset which is the subject of the tracing claim, looking at the whole transaction, such as to warrant the court attributing the value of the interest acquired to the misuse of the trust fund'. Secondly, the right to trace in equity has been held to be dependent on the establishment of a fiduciary relationship between the claimant and the defendant, or between the claimant and a third party through whose hands the money passes, and that the claimant has an equitable interest in the relevant property (*Re Diplock* [1948] Ch 465, CA; *Bank of America v Arnell* [1999] Lloyd's Rep Bank 399, per Aikens J). The need for a fiduciary relationship has been widely criticised and seems irrational given that tracing is merely a process of identification and not a right or remedy. The requirement is likely to be jettisoned when the Supreme Court next has to address the issue head-on (*Foskett v McKeown* [2001] 1 AC 102 at 128–129, per Lord Millett).

The requirement of a fiduciary relationship is satisfied, for example, where a payment made by or on behalf of an employer or principal is misapplied by his employee or agent in breach of fiduciary duty (eg as in *Agip (Africa) Ltd v Jackson* [1991] Ch 547, above). Nevertheless, in order to satisfy the requirement of a fiduciary relationship, the courts have sometimes 'discovered' fiduciary relationships, not because the relationship in question was of the sort that would normally attract the imposition of fiduciary duties, but because the courts have wanted to allow the claimant to take advantage of equitable tracing rules (C Mitchell, P Mitchell, and S Watterson, *Goff and Jones' Law of Restitution* (9th edn, 2016), para 7–18, who say that this is to 'debase the currency of the fiduciary concept'). In fact dicta of Lord Browne-Wilkinson in *Westdeutsche Landesbank Girozentrale v Islington London Borough Council* [1996] AC 669 at 716, clearly states that when property is obtained by fraud, whether or not in breach of fiduciary duty, equity imposes a constructive trust on the fraudulent recipient so that the property is recoverable and traceable in equity (cf PBH Birks [1996] RLR 3 at 10, who asserts, somewhat optimistically, that this dicta eliminates the requirement of a fiduciary relationship as a prerequisite of equitable tracing). Thus, according to Lord Browne-Wilkinson, money stolen from a bank account can be traced in equity. However, in *Box v Barclays Bank plc* [1998] Lloyd's Rep Bank 185 at 201, Ferris J stated *obiter* that Lord Browne-Wilkinson could not have intended to include all cases of fraud within this principle. Ferris J drew a distinction between transactions which were void, where the principle applied, and those which were merely voidable, where it did not. A similar point was made by Potter LJ in *Twinsectra Ltd v Yardley* [1999] Lloyd's Rep Bank 438 at 461 (the case went on appeal to the House of Lords but this issue was not considered further: see [2002] 2 AC 164). It has been suggested by Buxton LJ in *Sinclair Investment Holdings SA v Versailles Trade Finance Ltd* [2005] EWCA Civ 722, [2006] 1 BCLC 60 at [53], that Lord Browne-Wilkinson 'was dealing with the theoretical explanation of the doctrine of tracing' when he said that where property is obtained by fraud equity imposes a constructive trust on the fraudulent recipient. Arden LJ said (at [43]), agreeing with Rimer J in *Shalson v Russo* [2003] EWHC 1637 (Ch), [2005] 2 WLR 1213, that 'the normal position is that title to the stolen moneys does not vest in the thief'.

It has been held that a payment under mistake constituted the recipient a trustee of the money mistakenly paid. In *Chase Manhattan Bank NA v Israel-British Bank (London) Ltd* [1981] Ch 105, money was paid by mistake by the plaintiff bank to the defendant bank, which subsequently became insolvent and went into liquidation. Goulding J granted a declaration that the defendant bank became trustee for the plaintiff bank of the money mistakenly paid. Goulding J reasoned that 'a person who pays money to another under a factual mistake retains an equitable property in it and the conscience of that other is subjected to a fiduciary duty to respect his proprietary right' (at 119). This reasoning has since been strongly criticised (*obiter*) by Lord Browne-Wilkinson in *Westdeutsche Landesbank Girozentrale v Islington London Borough Council* [1996] AC 669 at 714–715 (a case where money was paid under a void contract) and also by Lord Millett, writing extra-judicially, in 'Restitution and Constructive Trusts' in W Cornish et al (eds), *Restitution—Past, Present and Future* (1998), p 212. *Chase Manhattan* seems no longer to represent good law (Aikens J refused to follow it in *Bank of America v Arnell* [1999] Lloyd's Rep Bank 399 at 406). There is no basis for the contention that, in the ordinary course, a person retains an equitable (or any) interest in money paid away. Nevertheless, Lord Browne-Wilkinson did concede that, despite Goulding J's faulty reasoning, *Chase Manhattan* may well have been rightly decided. The recipient bank had known of the mistake made by the paying bank within two days of the receipt of the money. Lord Browne-Wilkinson concluded (at 715):

> Although the mere receipt of money, in ignorance of the mistake, gives rise to no trust, the retention of the moneys after the recipient bank learned of the mistake may well have given rise to a constructive trust.

This seems to require actual knowledge on the part of the recipient (*Papamichael v National Westminster Bank plc* [2003] 1 Lloyd's Rep 341 at 373), but it has also been suggested that an objective test of unconscionability ought to be adopted (*Fitzalan-Howard (Norfolk) v Hibbert* [2009] EWHC 2855 (QB) at [49]).

There are a number of defences which may be raised to an equitable proprietary claim. In commercial transactions, an equitable proprietary claim will often be defeated by the defence of bona fide purchaser for value without notice (but not change of position: *Foskett v McKeown* [2001] 1 AC 102 at 129, per Lord Millett). But the bona fide purchaser defence will not be available where the defendant has either actual or constructive notice of the claimant's proprietary rights at the time the property was received (*Crédit Agricole Corpn and Investment Bank v Papadimitriou* [2015] UKPC 13, [2015] 2 All ER 974, where the Privy Council stated that constructive notice can arise either where a reasonable person with the attributes of the defendant would have appreciated on the facts already available to it that the rights of the claimant to the fund probably existed, or that a defendant, in this case a bank, must make inquiries if such facts as are known to 'the bank would give the reasonable banker in the position of the particular banker serious cause to question the propriety of the transaction' (at [20], per Lord Clarke)). Other defences include laches (delay) and acquiescence.

QUESTIONS

1.   A trustee of a pension fund borrows money from his bank to buy a yacht and later repays the loan using money stolen from the fund. Can the stolen money be traced into the yacht? Contrast the views of L Smith [1995] CLJ 290 (in favour of so-called 'backward tracing') and M Conaglen (2011) 127 LQR 432 (against it), and then read *Brazil v Durant International Corpn* [2015] UKPC 35 (Privy Council allowed 'backward tracing' where the various steps were part of a 'coordinated scheme').

2.   'There is no merit in having distinct and different tracing rules at law and in equity, given that tracing is neither a right nor a remedy but merely the process by which the plaintiff establishes what has happened to his property and makes good his claim that the assets which he claims can properly be regarded as representing his property' (*Trustees of the Property of FC Jones & Sons (a firm) v Jones* [1997] Ch 159 at 171–172, per Millett LJ; for similar dicta, see *Foskett v McKeown* [2001] 1 AC 102 at 128–129, per Lord Millett). Is it time to recognise just one tracing regime? See PBH Birks, 'The Necessity of a Unitary Law of Tracing' in R Cranston (ed), *Making Commercial Law* (1997), Ch 9.

CHAPTER 20

CHEQUES AND OTHER INSTRUMENTS

1 CHEQUES

A cheque is defined by s 73 of the Bills of Exchange Act 1882 (BEA) as 'a bill of exchange drawn on a banker payable on demand'. Section 73 also states that except as otherwise provided in the part of the BEA relating to cheques (ss 73–82), the provisions of that Act applicable to bills of exchange payable on demand apply to cheques.

All cheques are bills of exchange, and the s 73 definition of a cheque must be read together with that of a bill of exchange set out in s 3 of the BEA (above, p 661). However, it has long been recognised that a cheque has, in truth, very different characteristics from those of a bill of exchange (see, eg, *Ramchurn Mullick v Luchmeechund Radakissen* (1854) 9 Moo PCC 46 at 69–70, per Parke B). First, a cheque, being payable on demand, is intended as an instrument which will immediately be paid, whereas a bill of exchange is frequently drawn payable at a future date and is intended as a credit instrument. Secondly, unlike bills of exchange, cheques are not, and are not intended to be, accepted by the bank on which they are drawn. A bank which refuses or fails to pay a cheque incurs no liability to the payee or other holder of the cheque, whose remedy is to sue the drawer. Thirdly, while bills of exchange are often negotiated and the subject of indorsement over to third parties, modern banking law and practice means that cheques are rarely transferred to third parties, beyond the payee. Since the Cheques Act 1992 introduced s 81A(1) into the BEA, to the effect that crossed cheques marked 'account payee' or 'a/c payee', with or without the word 'only', are not transferable, UK banks now almost invariably supply their customers with cheque forms which are crossed and pre-printed with the words 'account payee', so that the cheque is valid only as between the parties to it. It follows that the vast majority of cheques issued in the UK are not negotiable instruments but merely payment orders directing the bank to pay the amount of the cheque to the named payee. This has led one leading commentator to conclude that much of the 'old learning' relating to the negotiability and indorsement of cheques should be jettisoned; that cheques should now be analysed along with other payment methods in the context of the ordinary law governing the banker–customer relationship; and that, at least in the context of the typical account-payee cheque, bills of exchange law should no longer be allowed to dominate the discussion (R Cranston, *Principles of Banking Law* (2nd edn, 2002), p 258). There is much truth in this statement, but it is submitted that it would be premature to ditch all the 'old learning' on negotiability, indorsement, and the BEA, not least because it remains possible for the drawer, before or at the time of issuing a cheque, to delete, and so cancel, the words 'account payee' printed on the cheque, so that the cheque becomes transferable and payable to order or bearer as the case may be. Those payees without bank accounts may well ask the drawer to do this to enable them to transfer the cheque to a friend who has a bank account so that the cheque may be collected through that account (the particular problems facing the 'unbanked' payee of an 'account payee' cheque are explored by JK Macleod in (1997) 113 LQR 133).

Modern banking law and practice make it high time for the law of cheques to be severed from the BEA and dealt with in separate legislation, as with the Australian Cheques and Payment Orders Act 1986 (in 1998 the Act was amended and renamed the Cheques Act 1986). However, there is probably little prospect of parliamentary time being set aside for wholesale reform of the law dealing with cheques (some minor legislative reform has recently allowed cheques to be presented for payment using digital imaging: see below, p 733). The use of cheques as a means of payment has been in decline for more than 20 years, falling from 4 billion cheques written in 1990 to 558 million cheques written in 2015, with electronic payment mechanisms, especially direct debits (see below, p 570) and debit cards (see below, p 625), being preferred alternatives to payment by cheque (source: Cheque & Credit Clearing Company website at http://www.chequeandcredit.co.uk). The decline in use has been such that in December 2009 the Payments Council, the industry body then responsible for oversight of payment mechanisms in the UK, announced that the central clearing for cheques would be closed in 2018 (note that a new independent Payment Systems Regulator, set up under the Financial Services (Banking Reform) Act 2013, became fully operational on 1 April 2015). There was a significant body of opposition to that decision, especially from charities and groups representing the elderly, who continue to use cheques and are familiar with the way they operate. In July 2011, the Payments Council reversed its decision and announced that cheques would continue to be available for so long as the banks' customers needed them.

(a) Crossed cheques

A cheque is crossed when two parallel transverse lines are drawn across its face. This is a general crossing and means that the cheque must be presented for payment through a bank account (BEA, s 76(1), sometimes the words 'and company', or an abbreviation of those words, are inserted between the parallel lines but this adds nothing). The holder of a crossed cheque cannot present it in person for cash. Sometimes the name of a bank will be written on the face of the cheque. This is a special crossing and means that the cheque must be presented for payment through the named bank (BEA, s 76(2)).

A transferee of a crossed cheque which is also marked 'not negotiable' cannot acquire a better title than his transferor had, although the cheque remains transferable (BEA, s 81). An *uncrossed* cheque marked 'not negotiable' is probably non-transferable (*Hibernian Bank Ltd v Gysin and Hanson* [1939] 1 KB 483; cf *National Bank v Silke* [1891] 1 QB 435 at 438; and see AG Guest, *Chalmers and Guest on Bills of Exchange* (17th edn, 2009), para 14–035). Crossed cheques marked 'not negotiable' and uncrossed cheques are hardly ever seen today.

In 1992, following the enactment of the Cheques Act 1992, which introduced s 81A(1) into the BEA, where a cheque is crossed and bears across its face the words 'account payee' or 'a/c payee', either with or without the word 'only', the cheque is non-transferable and is only valid as between the parties to it, ie the drawer and the payee. Today virtually all cheque forms supplied by UK banks to their customers are crossed and pre-printed 'account payee'. Only the named payee can be the holder of such a cheque. Figure 20.1 shows a crossed cheque marked 'account payee'.

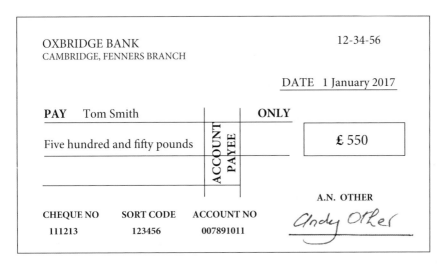

Figure 20.1 Cheque crossed 'Account Payee'

Who can cross a cheque? By s 77 of the BEA 1882, only the drawer, holder, and certain bankers may cross a cheque. A holder may cross an uncrossed cheque or alter a previous crossing by making it more restrictive, for example turning a general crossing into a special crossing (BEA, s 77(2), (3), and (4)). A banker to whom a cheque is specially crossed may cross it to another banker for collection (BEA, s 77(5)). If an uncrossed cheque, or a cheque crossed generally, is sent to a banker for collection, he may cross it specially to himself (BEA, s 77(6)). A crossing authorised by the 1882 Act is a material part of the cheque and it is unlawful to obliterate or, except as authorised by the Act, to add to or to alter the crossing (BEA, s 78). Obliteration or unauthorised alteration of the crossing engages s 64 of the Act and voids the cheque except as provided by that section (see above, p 699). However, in those rare cases where a cheque form is not pre-printed with an 'account payee' crossing, the payee of a crossed cheque is probably entitled after issue to add the words 'account payee' to the cheque (making it non-transferable) and this would not be a material alteration or contravene s 78 of the Act (AG Guest, *Chalmers and Guest on Bills of Exchange* (17th edn, 2009), para 8–083).

The bank on which a cheque is drawn (ie the bank where the drawer keeps his account) must be careful to pay in accordance with the crossing. The crossing is part of the mandate and failure to adhere to it prevents the bank from debiting the drawer's account (*Bellamy v Majoribanks* (1852) 7 Exch 389 at 404; *Bobbett v Pinkett* (1876) 1 Ex D 368 at 372). Moreover, s 79(2) of the BEA provides that the bank will be liable to the 'true owner' of the cheque for any loss incurred owing to the cheque having been paid contrary to the crossing, for example where a thief steals a crossed cheque from the payee and the bank allows the thief to present it for payment over the counter. If the true owner is the drawer he will have no claim since he can require the bank to reinstate his account (*Channon v English, Scottish & Australian Bank* (1918) 18 SR (NSW) 30 at 38). Section 79(2) goes on to protect the drawer's bank against a claim by the true owner, and allows the bank to debit the drawer's account, where the cheque does not appear: (1) to be crossed; or (2) to have had a crossing which has been obliterated; or (3) to have a crossing which has been added to or amended in an unauthorised manner, provided that the bank acted in good faith and without negligence.

QUESTIONS

1.   What are the benefits of crossing a cheque?

2.   Are any of the following cheques transferable ? See AG Guest, *Chalmers and Guest on Bills of Exchange* (17th edn, 2009), para 14–039.

(a)   An uncrossed cheque marked 'account payee only'.

(b)   A crossed cheque drawn (in handwriting) 'Pay X or order', but bearing the pre-printed words 'account payee' across its face.

(c)   A crossed cheque drawn (in handwriting) 'Pay Bearer', but bearing the pre-printed words 'account payee' across its face.

(d)   A crossed cheque drawn (in handwriting) 'Pay X or bearer', but bearing the pre-printed words 'account payee' across its face.

(b) The clearing system

A cheque is a debit instrument. It must be presented for payment to the paying bank, which is the bank on which it is drawn (ie where the drawer keeps his account). The collecting bank is the bank whose customer is the payee or other holder of the cheque and which is entrusted with collection of the amount of the cheque on the customer's behalf and the crediting of it to his account. The cheque clearing system facilitates this process by enabling the bulk presentation of cheques from collecting banks to paying banks in order that they may be paid or dishonoured.

Not all cheques need to be presented for payment through the clearing system. Cheques drawn on the same or a different branch of the payee's bank do not go through the clearing. Where the cheque is uncrossed it need not go through the clearing because it may be presented in person by the payee for payment in cash over the counter of the branch of the paying bank on which it is drawn. Only crossed cheques need be presented for payment through a bank, and even then it is possible for a crossed cheque to be presented for payment without using the clearing system. This applies where the cheque is specially presented by the collecting bank, at the request of the payee, directly to the branch of the paying bank on which it is drawn. However, in practice most cheques are presented for payment through the cheque clearing system.

Barclays Bank plc v Bank of England
[1985] FLR 209, Commercial Court

> **Bingham J** (sitting as judge arbitrator): . . . The origins of the clearing house as it exists today can be traced back to a device adopted by bank employees in the 18th century, largely (as it would seem) for their own convenience. During the early years of the 18th century the banks employed walk clerks whose task it was to call at other banks in the City and the West End of London to present cheques for payment and obtain cash in exchange. As the use of cheques increased so this task became increasingly laborious. As a result a practice grew whereby, instead of visiting other banks on foot, the clerks would meet at a central point, exchange cheques and settle the difference between the total exchanged. To begin with, the meeting place was unofficial and unrecognised, but the advantages of this central exchange were obvious and in due course a room was hired and, in 1833, a building erected on the present site. The respondent entered the clearing house in 1864....

I start with the case where a customer of a bank (the presenting or collecting bank) delivers to the presenting bank for collection and credit to his account a cheque drawn on another bank (the paying bank) by a person having an account at a branch of the paying bank, the cheque being eligible for handling through the general clearing but ineligible for handling through the town clearing. The steps which will normally follow are these:

(1) The cheque will be stamped (crossed) on receipt by the branch which receives it. The amount will normally be credited to the customer's account forthwith. The customer will not, however, receive value for the cheque on that date: thus the customer cannot without agreement withdraw the sum prior to clearance, he will not earn interest or (if overdrawn) be relieved of his obligation to pay interest and it will not rank as a credit for purposes of calculating bank charges. The credit is provisional in the sense that it will be reversed if the cheque is dishonoured or not satisfactorily cleared and there is in any event a delay before it will become fully effective.

(2) The branch which receives the cheque will in most cases encode it, by adding the sum payable under it in magnetisable ink to the cheque number, branch reference number and account number which are already printed on the bottom of it. At the end of the banking day the branch will sort out the cheques received during the day into bundles, one bundle for each bank whose cheques have been received.

(3) These bundles will be collected from the branch during the evening of that day or early in the morning of the following day and taken to the clearing department of the presenting bank. If the encoding has not for any reason been done at the branch it will be done there, early on the day following receipt of the cheque at the branch. All the bundles received by the presenting bank from all its branches will then be amalgamated and placed in boxes labelled with the name of the bank on which they are drawn, the paying bank. They will also be checked to ensure that the cheques are all facing the same way, have the magnetisable ink characters at the bottom, are free of staples and are unfolded. They will be subject to no other inspection.

(4) The cheques so sorted will then be taken in closed boxes to the clearing house, where they are either handed over to employees of the various paying banks or placed in racks reserved for those banks. The boxes are not opened and the cheques themselves are not the subject of consideration or inspection, which would be quite impracticable given that the cheques so handled run to several millions each day. (Sometimes the exchange or delivery may take place not at the clearing house but at the clearing department of the paying bank, but it is not suggested that this variation of practice gives rise to any difference of principle).

(5) From the clearing house the cheques will be taken to the clearing department of the paying bank, whose employees then feed all the cheques received for payment into reader-sorter machines. This process performs a number of functions. First, it sorts the cheques received into bundles for each of the paying bank's branches on which cheques have been drawn (and, for some branches, further sorts the cheques according to account number or customer's name). Secondly, it checks the totals charged against the paying bank in the clearing by the various presenting banks which have delivered cheques for payment, making necessary corrections. Thirdly, it records the magnetisable references on the cheques sorted, so that this information can be transmitted to the computer centre where branch accounts are maintained. From this information a computer projection is (or is in some cases) made showing the state of customers' accounts at the end of the next day if the cheques are paid and no further transactions occur, but no alteration is made to the accounts themselves. No consideration is given to the validity or payability of a cheque at this stage. Thus a cheque obviously defective, for example because it is unsigned, will not be weeded out but will be treated in the same way as all other cheques.

(6) Having been sorted, the cheques drawn on each branch will be delivered to that branch, so as to arrive during the night of the day on which they were received from the presenting bank or early the following morning. On the opening of the branch each cheque received overnight

for payment will be inspected and considered by an officer of the branch to determine whether the cheque is technically in order (properly signed and dated, with numbers and figures corresponding, without unsigned alteration, and so on) and whether there is any reason (such as lack of funds, countermand or injunction) why the cheque should not be honoured. In the case of cheques for small amounts, or large and respected customers issuing large numbers of cheques, the process of inspection and consideration may be abbreviated, but the process described is the norm. If the cheque is to be paid, it is cancelled and the drawer's account is debited at the end of that working day. The debit projected by the computer will then take effect. If the cheque is not to be paid, it will be sent by first class post at the end of that working day to the branch at which it was delivered for collection and the computer projection entry will be reversed. Under rules agreed between the banks with seats in the clearing house, to which I must return, this step must be taken on the day the cheque is received at the branch, save in the case of inadvertence, when a delay until the next day is permitted. A telephone call will in that case be made to the branch at which the cheque was received for collection.

(7) At the end of each working day the claimants settle between themselves by paying net balances between them. This is done by means of daily transfers to and from accounts maintained by each of them with the respondent [ie the Bank of England]. Such settlements comprise differences established in the general clearing carried out by their clearing departments on the preceding day and in the town clearing on that day, in each case on the assumption that all the cheques received for payment will be honoured. Dishonoured or unpaid cheques are the subject of later adjustment.

NOTES

1. Since 1985 the cheque clearing system for England and Wales has been run by the Cheque and Credit Clearing Co Ltd, which operates with administrative support from UK Payments Administration Ltd (the Cheque and Credit Clearing Co is also responsible for the Scottish cheque clearing which takes place in Edinburgh). The cheque clearing takes place in Milton Keynes (having moved there from London in September 2003). It is conducted by the Cheque and Credit Clearing Co on behalf of its settlement members and in accordance with its own system rules (but there is also a growing amount of direct exchange of cheques on a bilateral basis at the premises of the collecting or the paying bank). Member banks and building societies are known as settlement members because they must maintain settlement accounts at the Bank of England. Where a non-member bank or building society wishes to use the clearing it must employ the services of a member to act as its agent. A separate town clearing system, for the same day clearing of high-value cheques drawn on and paid into City branches of participating banks, was abolished in February 1995. In January 1999 the Cheque and Credit Clearing Co Ltd set up a clearing system for cheques drawn in euros; the system is generally the same as that for the clearing of sterling cheques.

2. Bingham J describes a 'clearing cycle' that took three banking days after receipt of the cheque. For example, the proceeds of a cheque paid into the payee's account on Monday would not finally be credited to the payee's account, for the purposes of gaining interest or reducing his overdraft, until Thursday. This delay was criticised and, following the recommendations of the payment systems taskforce set up by the Office of Fair Trading, the banks agreed to reform the clearing process. From November 2007, the payee of a UK sterling cheque has been entitled to interest (if the account bears interest) or credit, if overdrawn, on the proceeds after a maximum of two days from deposit of the cheque, to withdraw the proceeds after a maximum of four days, and to know the fate of the cheque after a maximum of six days, ie after six days the customer is protected from loss if the cheque is subsequently dishonoured and the money cannot be reclaimed back without their consent unless they are knowingly party to fraud (this is sometimes referred to as the '2-4-6' cheque clearing time-scale: the timescale is altered to '2-6-6' for cheques paid into savings accounts).

3.   The collecting bank owes a duty to its customer to present for payment all cheques deposited for collection (*Hare v Henty* (1861) 10 CBNS 65). Presentment is governed by s 45 of the BEA. Section 45 provides that a bill of exchange must be duly presented for payment, and that failure to do so discharges the drawer and indorsers. The bill must be presented 'at the proper place' (BEA, s 45(3)). In the case of a cheque the courts have interpreted this requirement to mean that the cheque must be physically presented for payment at the branch of the bank on which it is drawn and that presentment by electronic means (ie truncation) would not comply with the requirements of s 45 (*Barclays Bank plc v Bank of England* [1985] 1 All ER 385 at 386, per Bingham J). However, following an earlier recommendation of the Review Committee on Banking Services Law and Practice (Cm 622, 1989), rec 7(8)), which was accepted by the government (White Paper (Cm 1026, 1990), Annex 5, paras 5.11–5.13), the BEA was amended in November 1996 to allow for 'cheque truncation', ie the presentation of a cheque by electronic transmission of essential 'code-line' information about the cheque. However, significant infrastructural costs, and the declining use of cheques, meant that a fully truncated cheque clearing system was never developed in the UK. Most of the 1996 amendments have recently been repealed by s 13 of the Small Business, Enterprise and Employment Act 2015 (but not s 74A of the 1882 Act, which allows for a bank upon which a cheque is drawn to specify the place for presentation of the cheque). Section 13 of the 2015 Act introduces a new Part 4A (ss 89A–F) into the BEA which allows for a cheque to be cleared through presentation of an electronic image of the front and back of the cheque in place of presentation of the physical cheque itself. This would, for example, enable a customer to take a photograph of her cheque on her smartphone and pay it into her bank electronically via the bank's mobile banking app. Cheque imaging, as the process is called, will speed up the clearing process, reducing it from six to two days, ie 1-2-2 rather than 2-4-6 (see Note 2 above).

(c) Protection of the paying bank

'Bank's liability for paying fraudulently issued cheques' by EP Ellinger
(1985) 5 OJLS 293 at 293–294

1. INTRODUCTION

In recent years there has been an abundance of cases in which dishonest employees have perpetrated frauds by misusing their employer's cheque book. By now some well defined patterns have emerged. There are cases in which the employee obtains a signature executed on a blank or on a partly completed cheque and then fills the instrument in improperly or changes a 'material detail' (within s 64 of the Bills of Exchange Act 1882, the 'BEA') by making the instrument payable to himself or by raising its amount.

   Other frauds include the theft of instruments payable to the employer and their payment into the employee's personal account either under a forged indorsement (see, eg, *Orbit Mining and Trading Co v Westminster Bank Ltd* [1963] 1 QB 794) or by the imaginative means of opening an account under a suitable fictitious name. By the same token, the employee may steal cheques issued by his employer to a genuine client and pay them to the credit of an account surreptitiously opened by him in the true payee's name. (See, eg, *Marfani & Co Ltd v Midland Bank Ltd* [1968] 1

WLR 956; *Lumsden & Co v London Trustee Savings Bank* [1971] 1 Lloyd's Rep 114). The last and most crude type of fraud is the forgery of the employer's signature as drawer by the employee (for a remarkable case in recent years see *National Bank of New Zealand v Walpole & Patterson Ltd* [1975] 2 NZLR 7).

In all three types of case, the drawee bank honours the instrument in breach of its authority. In the first type of case, the cheque is vitiated when the material detail is altered (s 64 BEA). In addition, the bank pays an excessive amount or meets the demand of a person other than the intended payee. In the second case, it pays a cheque under a forged indorsement of the payee, which does not transfer the instrument (*Lacave v Crédit Lyonnais* [1897] 1 QB 148). The bank therefore does not comply with the drawer's instruction to pay the instrument to the 'holder' (given when the cheque is drawn to order: BEA, s 8).

It is clear that bankers are unable to recognize a fraud involving a forged indorsement. The signature of the payee or of the holder is unknown to them. A protection was conferred on them for the first time under s 19 of the Stamp Act 1853, which provided the model for the current provision: s 60 of the BEA. (Section 19 is still in force in respect of instruments which, being outside the scope of the BEA, are not governed by s 60; the bankers' draft—drawn on himself—is an example; *Capital and Counties Bank Ltd v Gordon* [1903] AC 240, 250–1; *Charles v Blackwell* (1877) 2 CPD 151, 159.) In cases of this type, the best advice that can be given to the customer (or 'true owner') is to sue the collecting bank. That bank is liable in conversion, unless it has collected the cheque in good faith, without negligence and for a customer (in which case it is protected by s 4 of the Cheques Act 1957.)

In the other two types of fraud, the customer's rights against his own bank depend on common law doctrines. His argument would usually be that the bank paid the cheque without having the mandate to do so. This is particularly so where the customer's signature as drawer was forged. (That the bank's liability is not based on its failure to recognize the customer's signature has been clear since *Cocks v Masterman* (1858) 18 CB 273.) (That he could also sue the collecting bank, see *Chitty on Contracts* (25th edn, 1983) § 2463 and authorities there cited.)

The customer's action against his own bank usually assumes the form of an application for a declaration that the bank is not entitled to debit his account with the forged items. The bank has two possible defences. The one is based on negligence and on estoppel. Fundamentally, it asserts that the frauds or forgeries were occasioned by the customer's own carelessness, which involved a breach of a duty of care owed by him to the bank. It is said that he is, accordingly, precluded from disputing the debits involved. The other, frequently related defence, is based on the customer's failure to detect the frauds through his periodic statements. In some cases these statements include counterfoils which the customer is expected to return to the bank with an indication of any unwarranted debits.

Both defences have been considered by English and Commonwealth authorities. Traditionally, the first defence has been upheld only where the customer's carelessness was directly related to the drawing of the cheque. The second defence has been unsuccessful in England. It has been held consistently that the customer does not owe a contractual duty to peruse his statements or, in earlier days, his passbook. In Canada, where such a duty is undertaken by the customer at the time of the opening of the account, the law has taken a different course.

NOTES

1. In the circumstances identified by Professor Ellinger the drawee or paying bank (the 'paying bank') cannot debit its customer's account if it honours the cheque. There is no mandate to debit the account. Where the bank does wrongly debit the account, the customer's cause of action against the bank only accrues, and the limitation period starts to run, when he makes a demand for repayment of the amount wrongly debited and such payment is refused (*National Bank of Commerce v National Westminster Bank plc* [1990] 2 Lloyd's Rep 514). If the bank can trace the recipient of the money wrongfully paid, it may have a remedy against him for money paid under a mistake of fact (*National Westminster Bank Ltd v Barclays Bank International Ltd* [1975] QB 654). But the collecting bank will have a defence to the paying bank's restitutionary claim where it has already paid the money over to its customer in ignorance of the paying bank's claim (see above, p 716).

2. Furthermore, the paying bank may also be liable to the true owner of the cheque in conversion (*Smith v Union Bank of London* (1875) LR 10 QB 291 (affirmed 1 QBD 31); *Bavins Jnr and Sims v London and South Western Bank Ltd* [1900] 1 QB 270 at 278; cf *Charles v Blackwell* (1877) 2 CPD 151 at 162–163: see also EP Ellinger, E Lomnicka, and CVM Hare, *Ellinger's Modern Banking Law* (5th edn, 2011), pp 488–492). The value of the cheque is deemed to be its face value and the true owner can recover damages of that amount (*Morison v London County and Westminster Bank Ltd* [1914] 3 KB 356 at 365, CA; the rule is rightly described as a 'legal fiction' by Lord Nicholls in *OBG Ltd v Allan* [2007] UKHL 21, [2007] 2 WLR 920 at [227]–[228], and Amy Goymour [2011] LMCLQ 67 can find no coherent justification for it). However, where the cheque has been materially altered, the measure of damages is not the face value: the cheque is avoided under s 64(1) of the BEA and becomes a worthless piece of paper (*Smith v Lloyds TSB plc* [2001] QB 541, CA: see below, p 743). The true owner is the person with an immediate right to possession of the cheque (*Marquess of Bute v Barclays Bank Ltd* [1955] 1 QB 202). In cases of misappropriation, the identity of the true owner depends on whether the cheque has been delivered by the drawer to the payee. Problems sometimes arise where a cheque is stolen in the post. The authorities are unclear as to whether a cheque which is sent by post is delivered where it is posted or where it is received (see N Elliott, J Odgers, and JM Phillips, *Byles on Bills of Exchange and Cheques* (29th edn, 2013), para 22–015; AG Guest, *Chalmers and Guest on Bills of Exchange* (17th edn, 2009), para 2–151). If it is uncertain whether a cheque was misappropriated whilst in the hands of the drawer or the payee, by s 21(3) of the BEA the payee will be deemed to have received a valid and unconditional delivery of the cheque, and hence be the true owner, until the contrary is proved (*Surrey Asset Finance Ltd v National Westminster Bank plc* (2000) The Times, 30 November; permission to appeal refused [2001] EWCA Civ 60).

3. *Common law defences of the paying bank* Even if the bank has paid a cheque in the circumstances outlined by Professor Ellinger, it may still debit its customer's account in the following circumstances:

(a) the customer may be estopped by representation or negligence from relying on a forged or unauthorised signature (see above, pp 696 ff, and also B Geva (1998) 114 LQR 251 at 258 ff), or he may be held to have adopted or ratified it (see above, p 698);

(b) if there is a forged or unauthorised indorsement of a cheque payable to bearer (either because it was drawn payable to bearer, or because it has been indorsed in blank, or because it was drawn payable to a fictitious or non-existent payee), the bank can pay the bearer and debit the customer's account, if payment was made in good faith and without notice of any defect of the bearer's title to the cheque, because payment to the bearer of such a cheque is payment in due course which discharges the instrument (BEA, s 59);

(c) if the cheque has been materially altered after issue by a person other than the drawer and without his authority or consent, the paying bank cannot take advantage of the proviso to s 64(1) of the BEA (see above, p 699) as it is not a holder in due course (*Slingsby v District Bank Ltd* [1931] 2 KB 588 at 600; affirmed [1932] 1 KB 544); nor is the bank entitled to debit its customer's account when the amount of the cheque has been fraudulently raised on the basis that the customer's mandate is still good for the original amount (BEA, s 64(1) as applied in *Yorkshire Bank plc v Lloyds Bank plc* [1999] 2 All ER (Comm) 153 at 156, and in *Smith v Lloyds TSB plc* [2000] 2 All ER (Comm) 693 at 703, CA: see below, p 743); but the bank may be able to argue that the customer is estopped by his negligence from questioning the debit if the alteration is due to the customer's failure to take usual and reasonable precautions when drawing the cheque (*London Joint Stock Bank Ltd v Macmillan* [1918] AC 777); and

(d) if the payment discharges the customer's prior indebtedness to the recipient of the payment, the bank may be subrogated to the rights of that recipient and debit its customer's account accordingly (*B Liggett (Liverpool) Ltd v Barclays Bank Ltd* [1928] 1 KB 48; cf *Re Cleadon Trust Ltd* [1939] Ch 286; *Crantrave Ltd v Lloyds TSB Bank plc* [2000] QB 917; *Swotbooks.com Ltd v Royal Bank of Scotland plc* [2011] EWHC 2025 (QB)).

But note that a customer does not owe his bank a duty at common law to take reasonable care to run his business in such a way that the risk of cheque fraud is reduced or eliminated (*Tai Hing Cotton Mill Ltd v Liu Chong Hing Bank Ltd* [1986] AC 80, PC: but see the criticisms of C Hare (2012) 23 JBFLP 182). The bank may be able to impose a specific duty on a customer to check his bank statements by means of a clear and unambiguous express verification clause (*Tai Hing* at 106; but such a clause is likely to face problems with review under the Unfair Contract Terms Act 1977, s 13(1)(c), when the customer is a non-consumer, and the Consumer Rights Act 2015, s 63(1) and Sch 2, Part 1, para 20, when the customer is a consumer).

4. *Statutory defences* There are three statutory defences available to the paying bank:

(a) Section 60 of the Bills of Exchange Act 1882 provides that a banker who pays in good faith and in the ordinary course of business a cheque (crossed or uncrossed) drawn on him payable to order on which the indorsement of the payee or any subsequent indorsement is forged or unauthorised is deemed to have paid it in due course. But s 60 cannot apply to cheques crossed 'account payee' as such cheques are non-transferable (BEA, s 81A(1)) and, therefore, cannot be payable to order as required by the section.

(b) Section 80 of the BEA provides that where a banker upon whom a crossed cheque (including a cheque which under s 81A of the Act or otherwise is not transferable) is drawn pays the cheque to another banker in good faith and without negligence and in accordance with the terms of the crossing, the banker paying the cheque, and, if the cheque has come into the hands of the payee, the drawer, are respectively entitled to the same rights and are placed in the same position as if payment had been made to the true owner thereof. Although s 80 is limited to crossed cheques paid to a banker (s 60 is not), it is not limited to cheques payable to order (s 60 is so limited). Section 80 will apply if the cheque bears a forged or unauthorised indorsement, but it will not protect the paying bank if the drawer's signature has been forged or made without his authority as the instrument is not then a cheque at all, for the signature is wholly inoperative (BEA, s 24) so that the instrument does not meet the requirements of a bill of exchange (BEA, s 3(1)). Neither will the section protect the paying bank where the cheque has been 'materially altered' so as to be caught by s 64(1). The effect of the material alteration is to render the instrument void with the result that it is no longer a cheque but a worthless piece of paper (*Smith v Lloyds TSB Bank plc* [2001] QB 541 at 557, per Pill LJ, see below, p 743).

A banker is not to be treated for the purposes of s 80 as having been negligent *by reason only* of his failure to concern himself with any purported indorsement of a cheque which under s 81A(1) of the BEA or otherwise is not transferable (s 81A(2)). In other words, the paying bank can normally ignore any purported indorsement on the cheque, as it is the responsibility of the collecting bank to ensure that a non-transferable cheque is collected only for the account of the named payee. But, as Professor Guest rightly points out, there may be additional circumstances, for example, where the paying bank is reliably informed that the cheque has been stolen from the payee (assuming the drawer has not, or has not yet, countermanded payment), in which it might be negligent for a bank to pay a non-transferable cheque bearing a purported indorsement without first satisfying itself that it was in fact being paid to the person entitled to receive it (AG Guest, *Chalmers and Guest on Bills of Exchange* (17th edn, 2009), para 14–028). By s 5 of the Cheques Act 1957 the protection offered by s 80 extends to certain other crossed instruments, analogous to cheques, referred to in s 4(2)(b), (c), and (d) of the 1957 Act.

(c) Section 1 of the Cheques Act 1957 provides that where a bank in good faith and in the ordinary course of business pays a cheque drawn on it which is not indorsed or is irregularly indorsed, the bank does not, in doing so, incur any liability by reason only of the absence of, or irregularity in, indorsement, and the bank is deemed to have paid the cheque in due course. (An irregular indorsement is one which on its face does not sufficiently correspond with the payee or named indorsee, eg where a cheque drawn 'Pay D Hooley' is indorsed 'R Hooley'.) However, in its memorandum of 23 September 1957, the Committee of London Clearing Bankers (CLCB) stated that paying banks should require indorsement of cheques cashed over the counter and of cheques with receipt forms attached to them. The practice laid down in the memorandum has remained unaltered. If a bank pays a cheque without an indorsement as required by the CLCB memorandum, it would not be acting in the ordinary course of business and would forfeit the protection of s 1 of the Cheques Act 1957.

If the paying bank can bring itself within the protection of any of these statutory provisions it may debit its customer's account with the sum paid. If the bank can rely on s 80 of the 1882 Act or s 1 of the 1957 Act it will also have a defence against any action brought against it by the true owner. Whether the bank will have a defence against an action by the true owner if it can only bring itself within s 60 of the 1882 Act remains unclear (E McKendrick, *Goode on Commercial Law* (5th edn, 2016), p 601 and AG Guest, *Chalmers and Guest on Bills of Exchange* (17th edn, 2009), para 8–053, recognise the defence; EP Ellinger, E Lomnicka, and CVM Hare, *Ellinger's Modern Banking Law* (5th edn, 2011), p 491 and R Bradgate, *Commercial Law* (3rd edn, 2000), para 30.2.3, appear to reject the defence). However, the modern practice of banks providing their customers with pre-printed 'account payee' (non-transferable) cheque forms has rendered both s 60 of the BEA and s 1 of the Cheques Act 1957 defences of marginal relevance as such cheques are not payable to order and do not require indorsement.

Carpenters' Co v British Mutual Banking Co Ltd
[1938] 1 KB 511, Court of Appeal

The plaintiffs kept an account with the defendant bank. The plaintiffs' clerk (B) also held an account with the defendant bank. Over a period of time B misappropriated cheques drawn by the plaintiffs payable to the order of various tradesmen who had supplied goods to them. He also procured cheques to be drawn by the plaintiffs in favour of tradesmen who had not supplied goods. In both cases B forged the indorsement of the payees and paid the cheques into his account. The plaintiffs brought an action against the defendant bank for the amount of the cheques. Branson J found as a fact that the defendant bank did not act without negligence and so had lost the protection of s 82 of the BEA (now s 4 of the Cheques Act 1957), but that they had paid the cheques in good faith and in the ordinary course of business and, notwithstanding their negligence, they were protected by s 60 of the 1882 Act. The plaintiffs appealed.

Greer LJ: . . . In the present case what happened was that when the cheques were presented to the defendant bank they had never ceased to be the property of the drawers, the Carpenters' Company, as they had never in fact been indorsed by the payees. The defendant bank was then asked by Blackborow to receive the cheques, and to place the amounts to the credit of his private account with it. This the bank did, and by so doing it in my judgment converted the cheques to its own use and became liable to the Carpenters' Company, the drawers of the cheques, for the face value of the cheques.

In my judgment s 60 of the Bills of Exchange Act 1882 only protects a bank when that bank is merely a paying bank, and is not a bank which receives the cheque for collection. In my judgment the learned judge was wrong in treating the defendant bank as if the bank had merely been a paying bank, and in failing to apply the law of conversion to the facts proved before him. The sole question which he had to decide was whether the bank was protected by s 82 of the Bills of Exchange Act from its liability for conversion of the cheques. He treated s 82 as applicable to the defendant bank, but decided that it had not proved that it received payment without negligence, but on the contrary he decided that it was negligent . . .

It remains to say something with reference to the questions discussed in the judgment as to the effect of s 19 of the Stamp Act 1853. I agree with the view to which Slesser LJ called attention in the course of the argument that s 60 of the Bills of Exchange Act 1882 must be treated as inconsistent, so far as cheques are concerned, with the provisions of s 19 of the Stamp Act 1853 and the sole duty of the Court after the passing of the Bills of Exchange Act is to apply s 60 of that Act. The observations of Stirling LJ in *Gordon v London, City & Midland Bank* ([1902] 1 KB 242) were made per incuriam, as they refer to s 19 of the Stamp Act as if it had been part of the Bills of Exchange Act.

I have just referred to the mistake made by Stirling LJ in *Gordon's* case, but the case calls for consideration from another point of view. The cheques in that case belonged to various classes, but they were all crossed cheques. Class No 4 related to crossed cheques drawn on one branch of the defendant bank and handed to another branch for collection. As to these cheques it was held by the Master of the Rolls, Sir Richard Henn Collins, though with some difficulty, that though the defendant bank was a collecting bank as well as a paying bank, it was protected from liability by reason of s 60 of the Bills of Exchange Act. I find it a little difficult to follow the logic of this reasoning, because the bank was no less a collecting bank because it was collecting from one of its branches for the customer and paying the money so collected for the benefit of the fraudulent presenter of the cheque; but, be this as it may, it seems to me that the actual decision does not bind me in the present case inasmuch as there was an express finding of the jury on which the Court of Appeal acted that the bank acted without negligence. It seems to me impossible to say in the present case that the bank acted without negligence. Branson J has expressly found that it acted negligently, and it cannot, therefore, in my judgment, be heard to say when acting negligently that it was acting in the ordinary course of business within the meaning of s 60 of the Bills of Exchange Act 1882. The finding in this case that the bank acted negligently in my judgment distinguishes this case from *Gordon's* case. I note that by para 7 of the statement of claim the action was based alternatively on negligence. I think on this ground the decision in *Gordon's* case is not an authority on which we are bound to decide that the bank having acted negligently is excused by reason of s 60 of the Bills of Exchange Act 1882 from the consequences of its negligence . . .

For the reasons above stated I am of opinion, though with some hesitation, that the learned judge was wrong in holding that the bank was entitled to the protection of s 60 of the Bills of Exchange Act, and the appeal will be allowed with costs, and judgment entered for the Carpenters' Company for the face value of all the cheques received by the bank and passed to the credit of Blackborow during the six years preceding the issue of the writ.

Slesser LJ: In this case the critical question arises whether or not the defendants have wrong-fully received the proceeds of the plaintiffs' cheques and converted them. In so far as they received the plaintiffs' cheques at Blackborow's request and credited their customer Blackborow with the proceeds, which were at all times the property of the plaintiffs, they appear to me to have acted, albeit wrongly, as a receiving bank as well as in the capacity of a paying bank.

As paying banker they may well be protected by s 60 of the Bills of Exchange Act 1882 in so far as they acted in good faith, which is not disputed, and in the ordinary course of business. Branson J has come to the conclusion that in all the facts of this case, which I do not repeat, they did so act in the ordinary course of business. It was argued by Mr Schiller that in so far as the learned judge has held that they failed to show that they acted without negligence within the meaning of s 82 of the Bills of Exchange Act that therefore they cannot be held to have acted in the ordinary course of business. I do not agree; negligence does not necessarily preclude the protection of s 60, a view made clear in the case of the other requirement, of good faith, by s 90 of the same Act, which in terms provides that 'a thing is deemed to be done in good faith, within the meaning of this Act, where it is in fact done honestly, whether it is done negligently or not.' This provision is helpful, I think, in deciding whether an admittedly negligent act can be done in the ordinary course of business. In *Vagliano's* case ([1891] AC 107 at 117) Lord Halsbury LC, speaking of the alleged negligence of bankers evidenced by the pursuit of an unusual course of business, says: 'I should doubt whether . . . it would be possible to affirm that any particular course was either usual or unusual in the sense that there is some particular course to be pur-sued when circumstances occur, necessarily giving rise to suspicion.' Branson J points out in his judgment in the present case that there was nothing in the steps taken by the bank which was not in the ordinary course of business, and I agree with him.

Bissell & Co v Fox Bros & Co ((1885) 53 LT 193), which the learned judge cites, was a case decided under s 19 of the Stamp Act 1853, which section has no limitation of reference to pay-ments in the ordinary course of business and therefore is of no assistance on that question in the present case. (See also the dicta of Stirling LJ in *Gordon's* case ([1902] 1 KB 242), which also can only refer to s 19 of the Stamp Act 1853.) That section, I think, is impliedly repealed by s 60 of the Bills of Exchange Act 1882, in the case of bills of exchange and cheques: see Lord Lindley in *Capital & Counties Bank v Gordon* ([1903] AC 240 at 251). But though I am of opinion that the Stamp Act 1853 is not here applicable, I think that the judge was entitled to hold on the facts that s 60 of the Bills of Exchange Act 1882, applied to this case, and therefore it follows that the bankers as payers are to be deemed to have paid the bill in due course notwithstanding that the indorsement has been forged, and I so treat them.

As receiving bank, however, unless protected by statute, they were guilty of conversion and liable in trover or for money had and received, for they dealt with the cheques which, for the want of a payee, were still the property of the plaintiffs in a manner inconsistent with the plain-tiffs' rights as the true owners. See Lord Lindley in *Capital & Counties Bank v Gordon* ([1903] AC 240); Collins MR in the same case ([1902] 1 KB 242); *Morison v London County & Westminster Bank Ltd* ([1914] 3 KB 356 at 365 and 379), per Lord Reading CJ and per Phillimore LJ; *Lloyds Bank Ltd v EB Savory & Co* ([1933] AC 201 at 228), per Lord Wright.

As to the protection of the Bills of Exchange Act 1882, s 82; I think that the judge was entitled as a question of fact to find that the bank had failed to show that they had acted without negligence . . .

I agree with Greer LJ that in so far as Collins MR and the rest of the Court in *Gordon's* case held that s 82 of the Bills of Exchange Act 1882 applied, and that there was no negligence, the observations of the Master of the Rolls and those of Stirling LJ as to the effect of s 60 or s 82 were obiter and are not binding in this case on a finding that there was negligence, and the protection of s 82 cannot be invoked by the bank at all.

It follows, therefore, that, on the finding of the learned judge that the bank have failed to prove that they acted without negligence, they are liable to the true owner in conversion, and that this appeal succeeds.

MacKinnon LJ (dissenting): . . . It is said that in paying them they acted negligently, and for that reason they cannot be said to have paid in the ordinary course of business. I do not agree with that contention. A thing that is done not in the ordinary course of business may be done negligently; but I do not think the converse is necessarily true. A thing may be done negligently and yet be done in the ordinary course of business . . .

[His Lordship felt bound to follow *Gordon v Capital & Counties Bank* [1902] 1 KB 242 and, therefore, would have dismissed the appeal.]

NOTES

1. When does the bank pay in the ordinary course of business? The general rule is that the payment must accord with the mode of transacting business which is adopted by the banking community at large (*Australian Mutual Provident Society v Derham* (1979) 39 FLR 165 at 173). For example, if the bank closes at 3.00 pm and yet pays a cheque at 3.05 pm, it still acts in the ordinary course of business, as banks may pay cheques within a reasonable margin of time after their advertised time for closing (*Baines v National Provincial Bank Ltd* (1927) 96 LJKB 801). But payment will not be in the ordinary course of business if, for example, the bank pays a crossed cheque over the counter (*Smith v Union Bank of London* (1875) LR 10 QB 291; affirmed 1 QBD 31 at 35) or pays an order cheque bearing an irregular indorsement (*Slingsby v District Bank Ltd* [1932] 1 KB 544 at 565–566) although, because of s 1 of the Cheques Act 1957, the irregularity in the indorsement will no longer render the paying bank liable.

2. Professor Guest prefers the view taken by Slesser and Mackinnon LJJ to that of Greer LJ on the question of whether the bank can pay in the ordinary course of business when it acts negligently (AG Guest, *Chalmers and Guest on Bills of Exchange* (17th edn, 2009), para 8–051). The same view has been taken by courts in Australia (*Smith v Commercial Banking Co of Sydney Ltd* (1910) 11 CLR 667 at 677, 688) and in South Africa (*Stapleberg v Barclays Bank* 1963 (3) SA 120). However, the opposite view is taken by Lord Chorley (*Law of Banking* (6th edn, 1974), p 93) and by Professor Holden (*The History of Negotiable Instruments in English Law* (1955), pp 227–228). Professor Holden even goes so far as to say that 'any suggestion that bankers who act negligently are (or can be) acting within "the ordinary course of business" is a gratuitous insult to the very fine body of men and women who are responsible for the day-to-day conduct of British banking' (op cit, p 228)! The Jack Committee also went against the view of Slesser and MacKinnon LJJ. Following criticism that the various statutory defences available to the paying banker 'overlap in considerable measure and in some respects their interrelationship is unclear' (E McKendrick, *Goode on Commercial Law* (5th edn, 2016), p 601), the Jack Committee recommended that these

various statutory protections should be brought together and each should be made subject to the condition that the bank has acted 'in good faith and without negligence' (Report, rec 7(5)). The government of the day accepted this recommendation (White Paper (Cm 1026, 1990), Annex 5, para 5.9), but no reform followed.

QUESTIONS

1. How does the protection offered to the paying bank by s 60 of the BEA differ, if at all, from that offered by s 80 of the Act?

2. A draws a cheque in favour of B. Due to B's carelessness the cheque is stolen from B by C, who fraudulently alters the payee's name to his own. The cheque is duly paid by A's bank when presented for payment by C's bank. Can A's bank debit A's account? Does A's bank have any claim in negligence against B for failing to keep the cheque safe? See *Yorkshire Bank plc v Lloyds Bank plc* [1999] 2 All ER (Comm) 153.

(d) Protection of the collecting bank

The collecting bank (defined above, p 730) owes its customer a duty to collect the cheque promptly and, once collected, to credit the customer's account with the amount, whether the cheque is payable to the customer himself or to a third party who has indorsed it to the customer. The holder of the cheque is himself obliged to present it for payment within a reasonable time of issue or indorsement to him to be sure he can recover in full from the drawer (BEA, s 74(1)) or indorser (BEA, s 45(2)). In either case, when considering what is a reasonable time regard must be had to the usage of the trade and of bankers (BEA, s 45(2) and s 74(2)). The fact that the vast majority of cheques drawn on one bank and collected by another are presented for payment through the cheque clearing system (above, p 730) means that a court would undoubtedly have regard to all reasonable rules of practice of the clearing system when deciding what was a reasonable time (see E McKendrick, *Goode on Commercial Law* (5th edn, 2016), p 590).

It is almost invariably the case today that where a cheque is delivered to a bank for collection the bank receives the cheque as agent for the customer for the purposes of collecting it on the customer's behalf (but the proceeds are not held on trust for the customer; the bank merely incurs a commitment to credit the customer's account with an equivalent amount: *Emerald Meats (London) Ltd v AIB Group (UK) Ltd* [2002] EWCA Civ 460). For these purposes, the collecting bank's customer may be another domestic or foreign bank using the collecting bank as its agent to gain access to the cheque clearing system (see *Importers Co Ltd v Westminster Bank Ltd* [1927] 2 KB 297; *Honourable Society of the Middle Temple v Lloyds Bank plc* [1999] 1 All ER (Comm) 193; *Linklaters (a firm) v HSBC Bank plc* [2003] EWHC 1113 (Comm), [2003] 2 Lloyd's Rep 545). In theory the collecting bank could give the customer value for the cheque and collect the cheque, to the extent of the value given, on its own behalf as a holder for value, but the fact that UK banks now almost invariably issue cheque forms to their customers which are crossed and pre-printed with the words 'account payee', thereby making the cheque non-transferable (BEA, s 81A(1)), means that this is very rare indeed for a collecting bank cannot become the holder of a non-transferable cheque (see R Hooley [1992] CLJ 432).

If the collecting bank collects a cheque for anyone other than the true owner, the bank may be liable to the true owner for conversion of the cheque (for who is the 'true owner' of a cheque, see p 735 above). For the purposes of an action in conversion, the cheque is deemed to have a value equal to the amount for which it is drawn. The fiction in that rule is evident when one considers a cheque drawn by an impecunious customer on an account which is heavily overdrawn (see EP Ellinger, E Lomnicka, and CVM Hare, *Ellinger's Modern Banking Law* (5th edn, 2011), pp 684–685; see also *OBG Ltd v Allan* [2007] UKHL 21, [2007] 2 WLR 920 at [227]–[228], per Lord Nicholls). The rule has been rejected where the cheque has been materially altered by an unauthorised person: in *Smith v Lloyds TSB Group plc* [2001] QB 541 (see below), the Court of Appeal held that such a cheque is a 'worthless piece of paper'. Alternatively, the amount received for the cheque may be recovered from the bank by the true owner as money had and received. In theory the collecting bank may have a right of indemnity or recourse against its customer, but in practice this may prove worthless (but see *Honourable Society of the Middle Temple v Lloyds Bank plc* (above), where an English clearing bank was held entitled to claim a full indemnity from the overseas bank that had instructed it to act as the collecting agent of the overseas bank: applied in *Linklaters (a firm) v HSBC Bank plc* (above), where Gross J held that the fact the collecting agent was also the paying bank was of no significance to its claim for a complete indemnity and that there was no room for just and equitable apportionment between the two banks under the Civil Liability (Contribution) Act 1978 as this solution was inherently uncertain and carried with it a much increased risk of litigation). As the collecting bank will have a defence to the restitutionary claim for money had and received if it has already paid the proceeds of the cheque over to its customer in good faith and in ignorance of the claim (see above, p 716), the most common form of action brought by the true owner against the bank is an action in conversion.

Recent legislative reforms allowing for the collection of a cheque through transmission of a digital image of the cheque seek to place liability for fraud or error on the shoulders of the collecting bank. The government considered that the collecting bank, which collects the digital image and introduces it into the clearing system, was best placed to implement measures to make the system secure, detect security risks at the earliest stage, and reduce fraud in the system. Section 13 of the Small Business, Enterprise and Employment Act 2015 inserts a new Part 4A into the BEA to allow for the electronic presentation of cheques by the collecting bank to the drawee bank for payment (see above, p 733). Under new s 89E(1), the Treasury may by regulations make provision for the 'responsible banker' to compensate any person for any loss of a kind specified by the regulations which that person incurs in connection with electronic presentation or purported electronic presentation of a cheque or other relevant instrument. The Explanatory Notes to the Small Business, Enterprise and Employment Act 2015 explain that such regulations could, for example, provide for a claim by the drawer of the cheque or the bank that paid the cheque where the payment was made to the wrong account because of a defect in the image, or where the image had been created fraudulently. The term 'responsible banker' is defined in subs (3) to mean: (a) the banker who is authorised to collect payment of the instrument on a customer's behalf; or (b) if the holder of the instrument is a banker, that banker. It should be noted that, under subs (5), the regulations may make provision for: (a) the responsible banker to be required to pay compensation irrespective of fault (ie strict liability); and (b) the amount of compensation to be reduced by virtue of anything done, or any failure to act, by the person to whom compensation is payable (ie contributory negligence). Subsection (6) makes it clear that if a bank has to pay compensation under the regulations, it is not prevented from making a claim against another party for a contribution towards compensation.

Smith v Lloyds TSB Bank plc; Harvey Jones Ltd v Woolwich plc
[2001] QB 541, Court of Appeal

These were conjoined appeals. In *Smith*, the Insolvency Service drew a cheque crossed 'A/C Payee Only' in favour of the Inland Revenue. The cheque was issued at the request of the claimants, who were the joint liquidators of a company in creditors' voluntary winding up. The cheque was stolen from the offices of the Inland Revenue and the name of the payee was fraudulently altered to 'Joseph Smitherman' and paid into an account at Lloyds. The cheque was cleared before the fraud was discovered and the claimants sued Lloyds (the collecting bank) for its conversion.

In *Jones*, the claimant company was the payee of a banker's draft issued by Woolwich. The draft was stolen, the name of the payee was fraudulently altered, and the draft was paid into an account with the National Westminster Bank. The claimant sued Woolwich (the paying bank) in conversion.

In both cases, it was accepted that the alteration of the payee's name was a 'material alteration' within the meaning of s 64(1) of the BEA. Conflicting decisions were reached at first instance. In *Smith*, it was held that the claimants were only entitled to nominal damages because the cheque had been avoided by the material alteration. In *Woolwich*, it was held that Woolwich was liable for the full face value of the draft. The Court of Appeal held that the claimants in both cases were only entitled to nominal damages.

Pill LJ: These appeals raise questions as to the possible liabilities in conversion of a bank to the true owner of a cheque or banker's draft for the full value of the instrument where the instrument has been fraudulently altered by the deletion of the name of the true payee and substitution of the name of a false payee prior to collection and payment. In *Smith v Lloyds TSB Group plc* ('the Lloyds action') the claimants appeal against the decision of Blofeld J [2000] 1 WLR 1225 dated 29 June 1999 whereby it was ordered, following the hearing of a preliminary issue of law, that the claimants were entitled to no more than nominal damages for the conversion by Lloyds, as the collecting bank, of a cheque which had been fraudulently altered. In *Harvey Jones Ltd v Woolwich plc* ('the Woolwich action'), the bank appeals against a decision of Judge Hallgarten QC dated 8 June 1999 whereby it was ordered that the true owner of a banker's draft was entitled to damages in conversion for the full face value of a fraudulently altered draft which had been converted by it as paying bank. In each case the bank relied upon section 64 of the Bills of Exchange Act 1882.

...

THE STATUTE
Section 64(1) of the Bills of Exchange Act 1882 provides:

Where a bill or acceptance is materially altered without the assent of all parties liable on the bill, the bill is avoided except as against a party who has himself made, authorised, or assented to the alteration, and subsequent indorsers. Provided that, where a bill has been materially altered, but the alteration is not apparent, and the bill is in the hands of a holder in due course, such holder may avail himself of the bill as if it had not been altered, and may enforce payment of it according to its original tenor.

...

THE COMMON GROUND AND THE ISSUES
The issues in these appeals are narrowed by the common ground which exists. (1) Authority binding on this court establishes that both a collecting bank and a paying bank may in certain circumstances be liable in the tort of conversion by collecting or paying a cheque for or to

someone other than the true owner. (2) In both appeals, the banks accept that they converted the relevant piece of paper. (3) Section 80 of the 1882 Act does not protect a bank which pays on a forged instrument, for example a cheque on which the signature of the drawer has been forged, or an instrument which was once valid but has been avoided by material alteration. The paying bank is not entitled to debit its customer and bears the loss itself. (4) Both the alteration to the name of the payee on the cheque in the Lloyds action and the draft in the Woolwich action were 'material alterations' within the meaning of section 64 of the 1882 Act. (5) In these appeals, no party comes within the exception in or the proviso to section 64(1) of the 1882 Act. (6) Neither alteration was apparent on the face of the document and the failure of the bank to recognise the change in name was not in either case negligent.

In each case, it was alleged that the bank had converted the claimant's cheque. In the Lloyds action, the claim was also based on money had and received. Blofeld J recorded that it was accepted that no separate issue of law arose on that claim. At that stage the claim was kept open on the facts but the claimants now concede that, on the facts of this case, there is no claim for money had and received.

I accept Mr Hapgood's formulation of the main issue in the appeals:

> Where a cheque or banker's draft is fraudulently altered by deleting the name of the true payee and substituting the name of a different payee, and the cheque or draft is then collected and paid, is the paying bank and/or the collecting bank liable in conversion for the full value of the instrument, or is the measure of damage nominal on the ground that the material alteration renders the instrument a nullity by virtue of section 64 of the 1882 Act?

Conversion is an interference with goods inconsistent with the owner's right to possession. Cheques are goods for this purpose. Both defendant banks admit that they converted the relevant piece of paper, the cheque form.

By a legal fiction, a valid cheque is deemed to have a value equal to its face amount. This rule was explained by Scrutton LJ in *Lloyds Bank Ltd v Chartered Bank of India, Australia and China* [1929] 1 KB 40, 55–56:

> Conversion primarily is conversion of chattels, and the relation of bank to customer is that of debtor and creditor. As no specific coins in a bank are the property of any specific customer there might appear to be some difficulty in holding that a bank, which paid part of what it owed its customer to some other person not authorised to receive it, had converted its customer's chattels; but a series of decisions ... culminating in *Morison v London County and Westminster Bank Ltd* [1914] 3 KB 356 and *A L Underwood Ltd v Bank of Liverpool* [1924] 1 KB 775, have surmounted the difficulty by treating the conversion as of the chattel, the piece of paper, the cheque under which the money was collected, and the value of the chattel converted as the money received under it: see the explanation of Phillimore LJ in *Morison's* case.

In *Morison v London County and Westminster Bank Ltd* [1914] 3 KB 356, 379 Phillimore LJ stated:

> That the damages for such conversion are (at any rate where the drawer has sufficient funds to his credit and the drawee bank is solvent) the face value of the cheques is ... so well established that it is not necessary to inquire into the principle which may underlie the authority. But the principle probably is that, though the plaintiff might at any moment destroy the cheques while they remained in his possession, they are potential instruments whereby the sums they represent may be drawn from his bankers, and, if they get into any other hands than his, he will be the loser to the extent of the sums which they represent. It may be also that any one who has obtained its value by presenting a cheque is estopped from asserting that it has only a nominal value.

...

SLINGSBY v DISTRICT BANK LTD

Each side contends that an authoritative ruling in its favour emerges from the judgment of Scrutton LJ in *Slingsby v District Bank Ltd* [1932] 1 KB 544. That was the last of three actions by the executors of an estate who wished to invest £5,000 in war stock and employed a firm of stockbrokers, John Prust & Co. The executors drew a cheque on their account at a branch of the District Bank, the payees being expressed to be 'John Prust & Co or order'. It was duly signed by the executors and left with a solicitor, Cumberbirch, a partner in the firm Cumberbirch & Potts. Cumberbirch fraudulently added the words 'per Cumberbirch & Potts' in the space between the words John Prust & Co and the words 'or order'. He then indorsed the cheque 'Cumberbirch & Potts' and paid it into the account, at a branch of Westminster Bank, of a company in which he had an interest. The cheque was dealt with in the usual way in that the account of the company with the Westminster Bank was credited and the account of the executors with the District Bank was debited.

The executors failed in their first action against the *Westminster Bank (Slingsby v Westminster Bank Ltd* [1931] 1 KB 173), which is not material for present purposes, on the ground that the bank was protected by section 82 of the 1882 Act. They failed in a second action against Westminster Bank, the collecting bank, also heard by Finlay J (*Slingsby v Westminster Bank Ltd* [1931] 2 KB 583), on the ground that there had been a material alteration by Cumberbirch of the cheque, which had therefore ceased to be a valid cheque and there had been no conversion of any money of the executors. An action against District Bank, the paying bank, succeeded, the Court of Appeal (*Slingsby v District Bank Ltd* [1932] 1 KB 544) upholding a decision of Wright J [1931] 2 KB 588. The parties are in issue as to the grounds upon which the court found against District Bank and as to the effect of the court's decision upon the judgment of Finlay J in the earlier action.

Finlay J stated in *Slingsby v Westminster Bank Ltd* [1931] 2 KB 583 that the facts were simple and not really in dispute. Both sides agreed that the alteration to the cheque was a material alteration with the result that, under section 64 of the Bills of Exchange Act 1882, the cheque was avoided. The judge accepted the submission that the cheque was by reason of the alteration a mere valueless piece of paper. He stated, at p 586:

> I have come to the conclusion that [the bank's] submission is right and ought to prevail. It seems clear that the document, when it came into the hands of the defendant bank, was not a valid cheque at all. It had been avoided by the material alteration made in it. This being so, it seems to me that no action can be brought upon it against the defendants. They have not dealt either with a cheque or the money of the plaintiffs, and on this short ground I think this action must fail.

Miss Simmons [counsel for the claimants in the Lloyd's action] accepts that, if that is a correct statement of the law, the claim against Lloyds fails.

Finlay J twice stated in his judgment that, if that view was correct, the question of negligence did not arise but he none the less considered the conduct of the collecting bank in detail and concluded that there was no negligence and the bank was entitled to the protection of section 82 of the 1882 Act. There was nothing to suggest that further inquiry ought to have been made. It was not disputed that the indorsement was a proper one.

Wright J [1931] 2 KB 588 tried the action against the paying bank in the following year. In the *District Bank* action the validity of the indorsement was not admitted. Wright J held that the indorsement was an improper indorsement. Wright J went on to consider and reject several distinct claims that defences arose. Defences were claimed under section 60 of the 1882 Act, the proviso to section 64(1), section 80, as well as defences by reason of the conduct of the executors and by reason of the liability of Cumberbirch's employers for his fraud. The effect of section 64 does not appear to have been in issue and was stated briefly by the judge. Having held that the alteration was a material alteration within the meaning of section 64(1) Wright J stated, at p 599:

> But under the section just cited, the alteration avoids the cheque, subject to the proviso. The defendants cannot charge the plaintiffs with a payment made, however innocently, on a void instrument, or a payment for which they cannot show a mandate from the plaintiffs to pay; the only mandate by the plaintiffs was to pay John Prust & Co simpliciter, whereas the defendants paid on the simple indorsement of Cumberbirch & Potts, and in any case on an apparent mandate deviating in respect of the description of the payee.

That view of the effect of section 64 is consistent with the view expressed by Finlay J in the earlier case.

Delivering the leading judgment in the Court of Appeal [1932] 1 KB 544, Scrutton LJ considered three issues: whether Westminster Bank had been negligent, the effect of the indorsement and the effect of section 64. He dealt with them in that order, though it would appear that it was Finlay J who took the logical course of dealing with section 64 first because, if the cheque was a worthless piece of paper, the claim against Westminster Bank was bound to fail and that against District Bank, for debiting its customer's account, was bound to succeed. Scrutton LJ expressed, in strong terms, his disagreement with the finding of Finlay J in the earlier action that Westminster Bank had not been negligent. It was when dealing with the second issue, that is whether the indorsement was a proper one, that Scrutton LJ cited in full the view of Finlay J on the effect of section 64. However, the statement by Finlay J had nothing to do with the point Scrutton LJ was then considering, the propriety of the indorsement. That point had not been in issue before Finlay J. Having cited the passage, Scrutton LJ stated, at p 558:

> I cannot understand this. There are, of course, difficulties as to how in law you should deal with money claimed by a customer from a bank because the bank has collected it from the customer's bank on a document which does not authorise such collection, but I thought that all those difficulties had been settled by the decision in *Morison's* case [1914] 3 KB 356, followed by this court in *Underwood's* case [1924] 1 KB 775; in the *Lloyds Bank* case [1929] 1 KB 40; and in Reckitt *v Midland Bank Ltd*, lately affirmed in the House of Lords [1933] AC 1. *Slingsby v Westminster Bank Ltd* [1931] 2 KB 583 is, in my opinion, wrongly decided and should not be followed by any court in preference to these decisions of the Court of Appeal.

Only then did Scrutton LJ consider the effect of section 64. He stated [1932] 1 KB 544, 559:

> But the legal result of these facts begins earlier than indorsement. This cheque, having been signed by the executors in a form which gave Cumberbirch no rights, was fraudulently altered by Cumberbirch before it was issued and, it was not disputed, altered in a material particular, by the addition of the words 'per Cumberbirch & Potts'. The cheque was thereby avoided under section 64 of the Bills of Exchange Act. A holder in due course might not be affected by an alteration not apparent, such as this alteration. But counsel for the District Bank did not contend that the Westminster Bank were holders in due course, and I am clear they were not. They could not therefore justifiably claim on the District Bank, and the cheque when presented to the District Bank was invalid, avoided, a worthless bit of paper, which the District Bank was under no duty to pay. This invalidity comes before any question of indorsement.

Scrutton LJ went on to repeat his conclusion that the cheque was not properly indorsed and concluded this section of his judgment, stating, at p 559: 'The protection given by sections 80 and 82 is excluded in my opinion by the fact that the alteration has made the paper a null and void document, no longer a cheque.' Scrutton LJ concluded his judgment by stating that he might have been content to adopt the careful judgment of Wright J, with which he substantially agreed.

Greer LJ also stated, at p 562, that 'Under the provisions of section 64 of the Act the cheque was rendered void except as therein stated.' The defect in the cheque which rendered it invalid was on the face of the cheque and not merely in the indorsement. Romer LJ, at p 565, listed the six questions which appeared to him to arise from the appeal and expressed his agreement with the conclusions of Wright J. I find it significant that Romer LJ did not identify the effect of section 64 as being an issue in the appeal.

Miss Simmons understandably relies strongly upon the apparent rejection by Scrutton LJ of Finlay J's statement in the *Westminster Bank* case of the effect of section 64. However I have come to the conclusion that the apparent disapproval was based upon a wholly uncharacteristic and, with great respect, most unexpected misreading by Scrutton LJ of the judgment of Finlay J in the earlier action. Scrutton LJ expressed in strong terms his disagreement with Finlay J on the negligence issue. He then dealt with the indorsement issue, which had first been raised only in the *District Bank* case, but cited from Finlay J's judgment in *Slingsby v Westminster Bank Ltd* [1931] 2 KB 583 a passage dealing not with indorsement, but with section 64. That Scrutton LJ was dealing with the indorsement issue at that stage and not section 64 is illustrated by his reference to the *Morison* line of cases, which deals with other types of dishonesty and not material alteration which is covered by section 64. When going on to deal specifically with the effect of section 64, Scrutton LJ expressed views entirely consistent with those of Finlay J.

It is submitted that, when stating, at p 559, that Westminster Bank could not claim against District Bank, Scrutton LJ was distinguishing between the position of the banks as against each other and the position of the customer of the paying bank as against the collecting bank. It is also submitted that Judge Hallgarten QC was right to find that, underlying Scrutton LJ's approach, was the feature that, so far as the claimants in the Woolwich action, as owners, were concerned, the cheque continued to have its face value. In my judgment Scrutton LJ's reasoning upon section 64 is not susceptible to those interpretations.

The effect of section 64 was in my view not seriously in issue in the *District Bank* action. Wright J dealt with it briefly and in conformity with the view of Finlay J. All members of the Court of Appeal expressed agreement with Wright J, Greer LJ stating that under the provisions of section 64 the cheque was rendered void and Romer LJ setting out the questions arising upon the appeal without mentioning a question on section 64.

CONCLUSION

My conclusions can in the event be stated briefly. In my judgment the effect of the presence of the word 'avoided' in section 64(1) of the 1882 Act is that the materially altered cheque or draft is, subject to the qualifications in the section, a worthless piece of paper. The words of Scrutton LJ when dealing with the legal effect of the material alteration of the cheque in that case are to be taken at face value. The piece of paper is no longer a cheque and no action can be brought upon it as a cheque. The cheque is invalidated and no distinction can be drawn between parties who, but for the material alteration, would have had contractual rights based on the cheque. No party can bring an action for damages in conversion for its face value because it no longer represents a chose in action for that amount.

In the case of a cheque, the customer of the paying bank is protected because the bank, which bears the risk, cannot debit the customer's account. In the case of a banker's draft, the customer's account is debited when the draft is issued to him. He has the benefit of a bill drawn by the bank itself, which he may require to satisfy business requirements, but once he has it he assumes the relevant risk as he would assume the risk if he drew bank notes which are stolen. It does not follow from the fact that the paying bank will normally issue a replacement draft, if the invalidity is discovered before the collecting bank credits the wrong account, that the materially altered draft is valid. The paying bank will have suffered no loss and may issue a replacement draft as a matter of good business practice, or possibly contractual obligation. The likelihood of such action does not, however, render valid what section 64 has rendered invalid.

Moreover the consequence of invalidity cannot in my judgment be avoided by alleging an estoppel. The cheque is rendered invalid by section 64 and, by presenting it under normal banking arrangements, the collecting bank was not asserting its validity.

I would dismiss the appeal in the Lloyds action and allow the appeal in the Woolwich action.

[**Potter LJ** delivered a concurring judgment. **Sir Murray Stuart-Smith** concurred.]

QUESTIONS

1. The cheque in *Smith* was not transferable because it was crossed 'A/C Payee only'. In the case of a transferable cheque, rare though such cheques are these days, the cheque could reach the hands of a holder in due course who could, if the material alteration was not apparent, enforce the cheque according to its original tenor. What is the value of such a cheque?

2. A collecting bank is usually protected from liability for conversion of a cheque by s 4 of the Cheques Act 1957 where it has acted without negligence (see below, p 752). Does that statutory protection extend to liability for conversion of a cheque which has been materially altered? What if a materially altered cheque has passed through the hands of a holder in due course before it is converted by the collecting bank?

(e) What defences can a collecting bank raise to a claim in conversion?

(i) Holder in due course

As UK banks now almost invariably issue their customers with cheque forms which are crossed and pre-printed with the words 'account payee', thereby making the cheque non-transferable (BEA, s 81A(1)), the holder in due course defence will rarely be available to a collecting bank. The collecting bank cannot become a holder in due course, or indeed any other type of holder, of a non-transferable cheque when it is not the named payee (the requirements for holder in due course status are set out in BEA, s 29(1), and are considered in detail above, p 682). In consequence, the holder in due course defence need only be considered in those relatively rare cases where a cheque is uncrossed, or where the words 'account payee' are absent or have been deleted by the drawer of the cheque. Where the collecting bank can establish holder in due course status it acquires an overriding title to the cheque and proceeds.

Westminster Bank Ltd v Zang
[1966] AC 182, House of Lords

Tilley was the managing director and controlling shareholder of Tilley's Autos Ltd. Zang asked him to finance his gambling. Tilley gave Zang £1,000 in cash, which belonged to the company, and received from Zang a cheque for £1,000 drawn in favour of 'J Tilley or order'. Without indorsing the cheque, Tilley paid it into the company's account at the bank. The paying-in slip used by Tilley reserved the right of the bank, at its discretion, to postpone payment of cheques drawn against uncleared effects. When presented, the cheque was dishonoured. The bank returned the cheque to Tilley who commenced an action on the cheque against Zang but that action was later dismissed for procedural reasons. The cheque was then returned to the bank which commenced its own action for dishonour against Zang. The bank claimed as holder in due course and holder for value. Roskill J gave judgment for the bank but this was reversed by the Court of Appeal. The bank appealed to the House of Lords.

Viscount Dilhorne: . . . 'Holder' is defined by s 2 of the Bills of Exchange Act 1882, as meaning 'the payee or indorsee of a bill or note who is in possession of it, or the bearer thereof.' As the appellants had received the cheque from Mr Tilley without indorsement by him, they did not become holders of the cheque within the meaning of s 2 of the Bills of Exchange Act 1882.

In 1957 the Cheques Act was passed with the object of reducing the labour involved and the time taken by collecting and paying banks in ensuring not only that each cheque was indorsed but also that the indorsement corresponded with the name of the payee on the face of the cheque. Section 2 deals with the rights of collecting banks in respect of cheques not indorsed by holders and reads as follows:

A banker who gives value for, or has a lien on, a cheque payable to order which the holder delivers to him for collection without indorsing it, has such (if any) rights as he would have had if, upon delivery, the holder had indorsed it in blank.

The appellants relied upon this section and sought to establish (1) that the holder had delivered the cheque to them, (2) that it had been delivered to them for collection and (3) that they had given value for it or had a lien upon it. . . .

The first question, namely, whether the holder of the cheque had delivered it to the bank, was answered by the Court of Appeal in the affirmative. In my opinion, it is clear that Mr Tilley was, when he delivered the cheque to the bank, the holder of it within the meaning of s 2 of the Bills of Exchange Act 1882.

Much argument was directed to the second question, namely: was the cheque delivered to the bank for collection? It was argued for the respondent that 'collection' in s 2 of the Cheques Act was to be interpreted as meaning collection for payment into the payee's account when the payee is named on the cheque; and that as the appellants had received the cheque unindorsed with the direction that it was to be paid into the account of Tilley's Autos Ltd, they could not rely upon s 2 . . .

Production of a paid cheque indorsed by the payee is very strong evidence of receipt by the payee. By dispensing with the requirement of indorsement on all 'order' cheques, the Cheques Act deprived the drawer of ability to establish receipt by the payee in this way. He might, it is true, be able to secure evidence from the payee's bank if it had been credited to the payee's account, but, if it was credited to the account of some other person, it appears that it would be very difficult, if not impossible, for the drawer to establish into whose account it had gone and that it had been credited to that account on the instructions of the payee. So if 'collection' in s 2 is confined to meaning collection for the payee's account only, the drawer of the cheque not indorsed by the payee may still be able to prove receipt by the payee.

It can safely be assumed that it was not the intention of Parliament, when providing for relief from the need for indorsement, materially to prejudice the position and rights of the collecting and paying banks and of drawers of cheques. Section 1 provides protection for the paying banks. If the prescribed conditions are satisfied, s 2 gives the collecting banks the same rights in respect of an unindorsed cheque as in respect of an indorsed one. Section 4 provides protection for collecting banks and s 3 gives some protection to the drawer. That section provides that an unindorsed cheque which appears to have been paid by the banker on whom it is drawn is evidence of the receipt by the payee of the sum payable by the cheque.

The acceptance of a paid unindorsed cheque as evidence of its receipt by the payee of the sum payable by the cheque does not appear to be as cogent evidence of receipt by the payee as production of a paid cheque indorsed by him. But this is, in my opinion, no ground on which one would be entitled to construe s 2 in the way contended for by the respondent. I regard the language of that section as clear and unambiguous. I can see nothing in the section nor in the other sections of the Act from which it is to be inferred that 'collection' in s 2 means collection only for the payee's account. If that had been the intention of Parliament, it could easily have been expressed. If the protection given to the drawer by s 3 is inadequate, that is a matter for Parliament to rectify.

It is apparently the practice of the banks, which inadvertently was not followed in this case, to require the indorsement of a cheque by the payee when it is to be credited to some account other than that of the payee.

In my view, Mr Tilley handed in the cheque for collection and the appellants received it for collection. To bring themselves within s 2 it is not necessary for the appellants to show that it was after collection to be credited to the payee's account. In my opinion, the second question should be answered in favour of the appellants in the affirmative.

The next question for consideration is whether the appellants gave value for the cheque. They claimed in their statement of claim that by crediting the cheque to the account of Tilley's Autos Ltd, and by reducing the company's overdraft by £1,000 they had done so. Alternatively, they claimed that it was to be implied from the course of dealing between them and Tilley's Autos Ltd, that there was an agreement whereby Tilley's Autos Ltd were entitled to draw against uncleared effects and they alleged that this agreement amounted to their giving value for the cheque.

The claim that they gave value by crediting the cheque to the account of Tilley's Autos Ltd does not appear to have been pursued before Roskill J or in the Court of Appeal. The evidence was to the effect that although the cheque was credited to the account of Tilley's Autos Ltd with the result that the overdraft was reduced by £1,000, nonetheless the bank charged interest on the amount of the uncleared cheque for four days pending its clearance. They thus did not charge interest on £1,000 on the overdraft but charged it on the cheque. In these circumstances, it is hard to see that by crediting it to the account and reducing the overdraft the bank gave value for it . . .

The account of Tilley's Autos Ltd was described as a 'swinging' account, sometimes substantially in credit and sometimes heavily overdrawn. In 1960 the limit on the overdraft was £2,000. In January, 1962, it was raised to £3,500. Tilley's Autos Ltd were, however, allowed to overdraw considerably in excess of this limit; for instance, the bank statements show that the overdraft on April 5 of £2,978 15s 10d rose to £4,902 15s 9d at the close of business on April 26, and throughout most of April the overdraft was in excess of the limit.

Mr Silburn [the branch manager] was asked whether, if the overdraft was near the limit of £3,500 and a cheque for £1,000 came in drawn by Tilley's Autos Ltd, he would have paid it, if the only thing to meet it was uncleared effects. His answer was that if the account was in bad odour, he would not.

If there had been an agreement of the character alleged, then Mr Silburn would have been bound to meet a cheque for £1,000 drawn by Tilley's Autos Ltd if there was an uncleared cheque of that amount credited to the account, even though the account at the time of the presentation of the cheque drawn by Tilley's Autos Ltd was overdrawn to the limit which Mr Silburn was prepared to allow. The words printed on the paying-in slip also negative the existence of any such implied agreement.

Danckwerts LJ expressed the view that, if the bank did in fact allow the customer to draw against the uncleared cheque for £1,000 before it was cleared, this amounted to giving value for it. Salmon LJ expressed the same opinion. He pointed out that there was no finding that the bank did honour any cheque drawn against the uncleared cheque for £1,000 and said that on the evidence of the bank manager and of the ledger sheet it was difficult to see how any such finding could have been made. Danckwerts LJ said that he felt some doubt as to the right deduction to be made from the accounts . . .

Evidence was not given that cheques drawn by the company and presented between April 27 and May 2 were only honoured in consequence of the uncleared effects.

In the circumstances, I agree with the opinion of Salmon LJ. In my opinion, the bank did not establish that they had in fact allowed Tilley's Autos Ltd to draw against the cheque for £1,000.

It follows that the bank has failed to establish the facts necessary to support their contentions that they had given value. No such agreement as alleged is to be implied and no cheque was shown to have been honoured in consequence of the payment in of the cheque for £1,000 . . .

For these reasons, in my opinion, the appeal fails and should be dismissed.

[**Lord Reid** delivered a concurring judgment. **Lords Hodson**, **Upjohn**, and **Wilberforce** concurred.]

NOTES

1. When the case was before the Court of Appeal, Zang successfully argued that by returning the cheque to Tilley the bank had lost both its lien over the cheque, which arose because of an existing overdraft, and also its status as 'holder'. When Tilley returned the cheque to the bank after his abortive attempt to sue Zang, the bank did not take the cheque as a 'holder' as it was not indorsed by Tilley and s 2 of the 1957 Act no longer applied as the bank did not receive the cheque for collection, nor did the bank give value for it, when it took the cheque from Tilley for the second time: [1966] AC 182 at 202–203, 207, 211. This point was not considered by the House of Lords.

2. If the bank collects as agent for its customer, can it ever collect as a holder for value on its own account? The question was answered by Milmo J in *Barclays Bank Ltd v Astley Industrial Trust Ltd* [1970] 2 QB 527 at 538, when he said:

I am unable to accept the contention that a banker cannot at one and the same time be an agent for collection of a cheque and a holder of that cheque for value. It seems to me that the language of s 2 of the Cheques Act 1957 negatives this proposition since it presupposes that a banker who has been given a cheque for collection may nevertheless have given value for it. It is, moreover, a commonplace occurrence for a banker to allow credit to a customer against an uncleared cheque. A banker who permits his customer to draw £5 against an uncleared cheque for £100 has given value for it but is it to be said that in consequence he is no longer the customer's agent for the collection of that cheque? I readily accept that if a banker holds a cheque merely—and I emphasise the word 'merely'—as his customer's agent for collection he cannot be a holder for value and still less a holder in due course; but that is an entirely different proposition.

In this case the bank successfully argued that it had a lien on five cheques paid into the bank because of the payee's existing overdraft. Milmo J held that 'the holder of a cheque who has a lien on it is by virtue of s 27(3) [of the BEA] deemed to have taken that cheque for value within the meaning of s 29(l)(b) to the extent of the sum for which he has a lien' (at 539). As the bank had acted in good faith and without notice of any defect in the payee's title, it held the cheques as a holder in due course.

3. If the collecting bank can establish itself as a holder for value, or holder in due course, it can sue the drawer in its own name should the cheques be dishonoured on presentation for payment (as happened in *Midland Bank Ltd v RV Harris Ltd* [1963] 1 WLR 1021). But a bank cannot be a holder in due course of a crossed cheque marked 'not negotiable' (BEA, s 81). Neither, as we have seen, can it be a holder in due course, nor any other type of holder, of a non-transferable cheque paid in for collection (above, p 748). Furthermore, the bank cannot be a holder in due course if its customer's title depends on a forged signature or indorsement (BEA, s 24).

(ii) Cheques Act 1957, s 4

Section 4(1) of the Cheques Act 1957 provides as follows:

> Where a banker, in good faith and without negligence—
>
> (a) receives payment for a customer of an instrument to which this section applies; or
> (b) having credited a customer's account with the amount of such an instrument, receives payment thereof for himself;
>
> and the customer has no title, or a defective title, to the instrument, the banker does not incur any liability to the true owner of the instrument by reason only of having received payment thereof.

The section applies to a cheque (and also to certain other instruments identified in Note 2 below) and protects the collecting bank from claims for conversion of the cheque and also for money had and received (*Capital and Counties Bank Ltd v Gordon* [1903] AC 240, HL). However, s 4 would not provide a collecting bank with a defence to a claim that by collecting the cheque on behalf of a customer the bank was liable as a constructive trustee, for 'unconscionable (or knowing) receipt' or 'dishonest assistance', where it turned out that the customer was acting in breach of trust. Nor would s 4 assist a collecting bank where (exceptionally) it paid cash for the cheque instead of crediting the customer's account.

To avail itself of the protection afforded by s 4, the collecting bank must be able to prove that it acted in good faith and without negligence. Often good faith is presumed and negligence is in issue. Negligence is judged against the objective standard of the reasonable banker (*Marfani & Co Ltd v Midland Bank Ltd* [1968] 1 WLR 956 at 973, CA; *Linklaters (a firm) v HSBC Bank plc* [2003] EWHC 1113 (Comm), [2003] 2 Lloyd's Rep 545 at [106]). A failure by the bank properly to identify its customer when opening the account is likely to be held to be negligent (and the bank must also have proper procedures for identifying, and verifying the identity of, its customers as required by the Money Laundering Regulations 2007 (SI 2007/2157)). Similarly, there may be negligence in the collecting of the cheque itself, for example in the absence of special circumstances, it would generally be negligent to collect payment of an 'account payee' cheque for someone other than the named payee without further inquiry because such a cheque is non-transferable (BEA, s 81A(1)). In each case the inquiry is fact-sensitive and current banking practice is highly relevant to the issue of negligence. Rix LJ makes this point in the next case, *Architects of Wine Ltd v Barclays Bank plc* [2007] EWCA Civ 239, [2007] 2 Lloyd's Rep 471.

Architects of Wine Ltd v Barclays Bank plc
[2007] EWCA Civ 239, Court of Appeal

The claimant, Architects of Wine Ltd (AoW Ltd), a Cayman Islands company, sold a scheme for investing in wine futures into the American market. AoW Ltd was a subsidiary of another

Cayman Islands company, Paradigm Holdings Ltd. A third company, Architects of Wine UK Ltd (AoW UK), was another subsidiary of Paradigm.

By March 2004, AoW Ltd was facing difficulties with the US regulatory authorities. A number of orders were made against it. Its bankers in the Cayman Islands, and their US correspondents, stopped accepting payments and/or collecting cheques for AoW Ltd from its customers. AoW Ltd then couriered cheques received from its customers to the UK, where they were paid into AoW UK's sterling and (after June 2004) dollar accounts held at the defendant bank, Barclays Bank plc (the bank). By early September, approximately 400 cheques to the value of US$1.3 million had been paid into AoW UK's accounts in this way. None of these cheques were payable to AoW UK and, although the cheques were not printed 'a/c payee only', there was no evidence that they had been indorsed to AoW UK.

In October 2004, AoW Ltd went into liquidation. The liquidators of AoW Ltd commenced proceedings against the bank, alleging strict liability for conversion of the cheques, and applied for summary judgment. The bank relied on s 4 of the Cheques Act 1957 in its defence. David Steele J gave summary judgment in favour of AoW Ltd. He held that the s 4 defence was not open to the bank because it had 'fallen well short of establishing any realistic prospect of success on the issue of negligence'. The bank appealed. It submitted that Mr Penny, an employee of the bank who was an expert on banking practice, had presented unchallenged evidence to the court of current banking practice which showed that a 'sufficient' (not absolute) match of the names of payee and account holder was good compliance and that, in the light of that evidence, the judge had been wrong to say that the bank had no realistic prospect of sustaining the burden of its case that it acted without negligence. The Court of Appeal allowed the bank's appeal.

Rix LJ: ...

THE AUTHORITIES

3. We were provided with a substantial selection of relevant authorities on section 4 and its statutory predecessors. Many of them concern the payment by rogues into personal accounts of cheques drawn on their company, employers or other principals and which they had stolen or created without authority. Factually, such cases are rather far from the present. Nevertheless, as often in this area of the law, the leading case of *Marfani & Co Ltd v. Midland Bank Ltd* [1968] 1 WLR 956 is well worth consulting, not for its facts (which concerned a rogue who opened a new account under a false name with the help of an incorrect reference from a valued customer) but for its statements of general principle.

4. Thus Diplock LJ said this about section 4 (at 972/974):

It is, however, in my view, clear that the intention of the subsection and its statutory predecessors is to substitute for the absolute duty owed at common law by a banker to the true owner of a cheque not to take any steps in the ordinary course of business leading up to and including the receipt of payment of the cheque, and the crediting of the amount of the cheque to the account of his customer, in usurpation of the true owner's title thereto a qualified duty to take reasonable care to refrain from taking any such step which he foresees is, or ought reasonably to have foreseen was, likely to cause loss or damage to the true owner.

The only respect in which this substituted statutory duty differs from a common law cause of action in negligence is that, since it takes the form of a qualified immunity from a strict liability at common law, the onus of showing that he did take such reasonable care lies upon the defendant banker. Granted good faith in the banker (the other condition of the immunity), the usual matter with respect to which the banker must take reasonable care is to satisfy himself that his own customer's title to the cheque delivered to him for collection is not defective, i.e., that no other person is the true owner of it. Where the customer is in possession of the cheque at the time of delivery for collection and appears upon the face of it to be the 'holder', i.e., the payee or indorsee or the bearer, the banker is, in my view, entitled to assume that the customer is the owner of the cheque unless there are facts which are, or ought to be, known to him which would cause a reasonable banker to suspect that the customer was not the true owner.

What facts ought to be known to the banker, i.e., what inquiries he should make, and what facts are sufficient to cause him reasonably to suspect that the customer is not the true owner, must depend upon current banking practice, and change as that practice changes. Cases decided 30 years ago, when the use by the general public of banking facilities was much less widespread, may not be a reliable guide to what the duty of a careful banker in relation to inquiries, and as to facts which should give rise to suspicion, is today. [at 972] ...

What the court has to do is to look at all the circumstances at the time of the acts complained of and to ask itself: were those circumstances such as would cause a reasonable banker possessed of such information about his customer as a reasonable banker would possess, to suspect that his customer was not the true owner of the cheque? [at 973] ...

In all actions of the kind with which we are here concerned, the banker's customer has in fact turned out to be a fraudulent rogue, and attention is naturally concentrated upon the duty of care which was owed by the banker to the person who has in fact turned out to be the true owner of the cheque. We are always able to be wise after the event, but the banker's duty fell to be performed before it, and the duty which he owed to the true owner ought not to be considered in isolation. At the relevant time, the true owner was entitled to take into consideration the interests of his customer, who, be it remembered, would in all probability turn out to be honest, as most men are, and his own business interests, and to weigh those against the risk of loss or damage to the true owner of the cheque in the unlikely event that he should turn out not to be the customer himself. [at 974]

5. Diplock LJ added this about the evidence of the practice of bankers (at 975):

The only evidence of the practice of bankers was given by the manager and the securities clerk of the branch in question of the defendant bank. No evidence that the general practice of other bankers differed from that adopted by the defendant bank was called by the plaintiff company, although they knew well in advance of the trial, as a result of searching interrogatories, exactly what steps the defendant bank had taken, and what inquiries they had made. It seems a reasonable inference that what the defendants did in the present case was in accordance with current banking practice. Nield J accepted that it was, and Mr Lloyd has not sought to argue the contrary. What he contends is that this court is entitled to examine that practice and to form its own opinion as to whether it does comply with the standard of care which a prudent banker should adopt. That is quite right, but I venture to think that this court should be hesitant before condemning as negligent a practice generally adopted by those engaged in banking business.

6. One of the tests of what is negligent that has been sounded in the authorities relates to what is out of the ordinary course of business. Thus in *Commissioners of Taxation v. English, Scottish and Australian Bank Limited* [1920] AC 683 (PC) at 688, Lord Dunedin, giving the opinion of the Privy Council, approved (with the addition of the words in italics cited below) the statement of Isaacs J in the High Court of Australia in *Commissioners of State Savings Bank v. Permewan, Wright & Co* 19 CLR 457, 478 that—

the test of negligence is whether the transaction of paying in any given cheque [*coupled with the circumstances antecedent and present*] was so out of the ordinary course that it ought to have aroused doubts in the bankers' mind, and caused them to make inquiry.

7. That test was to be applied by 'the standard to be derived from the ordinary practice of bankers, not individuals' (at 689). Isaacs J's test was again approved by this court in *Lloyds Bank Limited v. The Chartered Bank of India, Australia and China* [1929] 1 KB 40, at 59 (Scrutton LJ) and 72 (Sankey LJ). In this connection, we have been reminded, as a counterpoint to what Diplock LJ said in *Marfani* at 974, of what Scrutton LJ said in *A L Underwood Ltd v. Bank of Liverpool & Martins* [1924] 1 KB 775 at 793 of unusual circumstances: 'If banks, for fear of offending their customers will not make inquiries into unusual circumstances, they must take with the benefit of not annoying their customer the risk of liability because they do not inquire.'

8. For these purposes, it is relevant to consider the nature of the employee of the bank before whom the cheque in question will come for action. If a cheque will only come before a cashier, then the question of negligence has to be applied to the role of a cashier. In *Lloyds Bank v. The Chartered Bank* at 72 Sankey LJ also approved of what Bailhache J had said in *Ross v. London County Westminster and Parr's Bank* [1919] 1 KB 678, 685, viz—'I must attribute to the cashiers and clerks of the defendants the degree of intelligence and care ordinarily required of persons in their position to fit them for the discharge of their duties. It is therefore necessary to consider whether a bank cashier of ordinary intelligence and care on having these cheques presented to him by a private customer of the bank would be informed by the terms of the cheques themselves that it was open to doubt whether the customer had a good title to them.'

9. In many circumstances, however, the conduct of a careful banker's business will mean that the supervision or knowledge of a manager (of some or other level of seniority) will be relevant, for example on the occasion of the opening of an account for a new customer. In this connection consideration may have to be given to the vastness of a modern bank's enterprise. Cheques without number have to be handled by clerical staff or even by wholly automatic processes. What is the bank's duty then in terms of negligence? One answer was given in *Honourable Society of the Middle Temple v. Lloyds Bank plc* [1999] 1 All ER (Comm) 193 at 228 (per Rix J):

> When, however, the cheque emerges from that multitude and is referred by the clerical staff to management, albeit only as a result of an inquiry after fate, it seems to me that different considerations come into play. The cheque is no longer a mere item following a course in a factory-like process. It no longer becomes impracticable to give it individual attention, or the attention of management. It is referred for just such individual attention, even if the cause of referral is something collateral.

10. In this connection, Mr Michael Black QC on behalf of the claimant respondent, AoW Ltd, now in liquidation, submitted that all aspects of a bank's knowledge about a customer are to be assumed to be accumulated in every employee of the bank, so that a bank cannot rely on any division of knowledge between department and department. For these purposes he relied on a passage in *Lloyds Bank Limited v. E B Savory and Company* [1933] AC 201 at 213, per Lord Buckmaster. He submitted that a fortiori in the era of computers and information technology, banks could not rely on ignorance as between different departments or officials of a bank. I take the point about computer and information technology. The observations of Lord Buckmaster, however, were dealing with a different problem, viz where the system adopted by the bank made it impossible to achieve what it was acknowledged a proper system of checking the contents of a cheque ought to do. I do not think that it follows that Mr Black's submission is correct, and we have not been referred to an authority which supports it. If it were correct, it would be a very big point. It might be said against it, that it would be liable to make banking impossible. In any event I do not think that such a proposition could be adopted without evidence of current banking practice.

11. I referred above to Diplock LJ's dictum from *Marfani* of the inappropriateness of simply being wise after the event. That of course is a standard insight in the context of a duty of reasonable care. In this connection we were also referred to what Sankey LJ said in *Lloyds Bank v. Chartered Bank* at 73, that—'a bank cannot be held to be liable for negligence merely because they have not subjected an account to a microscopic examination. It is not to be expected that the officials of banks should also be amateur detectives.'

12. In sum, I would for present purposes underline the following matters as being indicated by these authorities. The section 4 qualified duty does not require an assumption of negligence, just because a bank bears the burden of showing that it took reasonable care. The enquiry is fact sensitive. Current banking practice is highly relevant to the issue of negligence. A bank's evidence about its practice is, especially if unchallenged, relevant evidence of the current practice of bankers. A court is not bound by such evidence, but it will be hesitant to reject it. Notice of what is so out of the ordinary course of events as to arouse doubts in a banker's mind or put him on enquiry is a relevant test of negligence, and may make the proof of the taking of reasonable care very difficult. However, the courts should be wary of hindsight or of imposing on a bank the role of an amateur detective. Ultimately, these principles were not in dispute. I therefore turn to the facts of the case.

...

DISCUSSION AND DECISION

56. In my judgment there is force in [counsel for the bank's] criticisms of the judge's decision to give summary judgment against the bank. One issue related to the process by which cashiers at the Regent Street branch and processors at ICO [where cheques were sent by the branch] accepted the cheques as sufficiently matching the name of the customer's account, AoW UK. Although the judge may have been sceptical, he was not I think entitled to reject out of hand, or to disregard, as he appears to have done, the bank's evidence that the current banking practice was that a sufficient match was acceptable and that the names in question did in fact sufficiently match. That evidence was unchallenged. It seems to me to raise an arguable case, a realistic prospect of a defence, based on the absence of negligence at this stage. I agree that it might have been better to have had more detailed evidence about how the practice of a sufficient match operates with respect to company names: Mr Penny's examples, while apposite, related to personal names. The problem of similar corporate names within a group must be a widespread one. All of us, I suspect, know from our own experience about how imprecise we sometimes are about writing exactly the right name on our cheques, and how very frequently we may leave off everything but the trading name itself, eg Marks & Spencer, or Prudential. How is this problem dealt with? How do banks and their customers ensure that the cheques reach the right accounts, especially where there may often be several associate companies which are candidates? In the present case, however, the bank and a fortiori its cashiers knew of only one company, Architects of Wine (UK) Limited. It did not have to choose between that and its foreign associate, Architects of Wine Ltd. The point that 41 batches totalling some 400 cheques went through without raising a problem is at least double edged.

57. The 'sufficient match' issue is primarily for the cashiers and their ICO equivalents. Unless there is something on the face of the cheque which ought to give those employees of the bank notice of a problem which, if they cannot resolve themselves, they ought to bring to the notice of more senior officials, the cheques will pass this check and then enter the numberless queue of cheques being processed.

58. A second issue, therefore, is whether, despite the similarity of the names, there were aspects of the cheques themselves which ought, at least arguably without further knowledge of the business of the customer, to have alerted the cashiers and ICO of something wrong. The judge relied

on the fact that the cheques were all dollar cheques, in sums averaging $3,000, and that about 10 per cent of them gave the payee's address in the Cayman Islands. I certainly understand the argument: but Mr Penny's evidence is again that such matters would not have suggested anything out of the ordinary such as would deprive the bank of its defence. That evidence, as it seems to me, raises a real defence with real prospects. It is plain that English companies do bank foreign currency cheques, and the branches have remittance forms for such foreign currency cheques which can list up to 50 of them on a single form. Once a dollar account is opened, the position changes again: for the operators at ICO would expect a customer with a dollar account to have dollar cheques for collection. It does not seem to me that an average of $3,000 (or even the higher values of some of the cheques) is obviously out of the way for a company dealing with quality wines by mail order. There is no evidence that that is so, or that these values were out of the ordinary course of the value of cheques banked by AoW UK. I note that in 2002 the company had had a banking turnover of £3.3 million, and in 2003 of £2.5 million. Why should not this company have marketed its wines by mail order in the United States? Or have a billing address, a PO Box number it should be noted, in the Cayman Islands? Should cashiers have alerted senior officials simply because of a change of business? Should a proper banking system be designed to throw up, for referral to a more senior official, any such change in the currency of payment? Perhaps so, even though Mr Penny says otherwise. However, that seems to me to be a question for trial.

...

61. In sum, although AoW Ltd may have a strong case to make at trial, a matter on which I make no comment at all, it is an untested case. At present, the bank's evidence is unchallenged, and I agree with [counsel for the bank] that the court is not in a position to reject it as raising no realistic prospect of a good defence, even bearing in mind as I do that it is the bank that bears the burden of showing that it acted with reasonable care.

62. The judge thought otherwise. In this court, I think it is necessary to have considerable respect for the views of an experienced commercial judge that a defendant has not met the test of providing evidence of a defence with a real prospect of success at trial. The commercial court prides itself justifiably on its ability to distinguish the speculative but doomed claim which should be given its quietus sooner rather than later; or to identify the specious if colourable defence, which does not merit a trial. However, I do not regard the bank's defence, on the present state of the evidence, as either speculative or specious. On the contrary, I think that there is some justification in the bank's concern, expressed in submission, that if this summary judgment were to stand, then, on the basis of the judge's judgment that the bank fell "well short" of raising a proper defence for trial, this bank, and its competitors, would, for reasons which it is not easy to define or restate in advance of a judgment following trial, be required substantially to revisit what are said, expressly in the case of Barclays, and inferentially in the case of its competitors, to be their procedures and current banking practice.

CONCLUSION

63. I would therefore allow this appeal.

[**Sir Mark Potter P** and **Wilson LJ** agreed.]

NOTES

1. In *Honourable Society of the Middle Temple v Lloyds Bank plc* [1999] 1 All ER (Comm) 193, an English clearing bank collected a stolen account payee cheque as collecting agent for a foreign bank located in Istanbul. Rix J held the English bank to have been negligent and unable to rely on the s 4 defence against the true owner's action for conversion of the cheque. His Lordship distinguished between a bank acting as collecting agent for a domestic bank and one acting on behalf of a foreign bank. Rix J held that a bank acting as collecting agent for a domestic bank was entitled to assume that the domestic bank knew of its responsibilities under the Cheques Act 1992, so that the agent would not be negligent in leaving it to that bank to ensure that the cheque was being collected for the named payee, unless there was something exceptional which brought the cheque to the agent's notice. By contrast, Rix J held that a bank acting as a collecting agent for a foreign bank was not entitled to make the same assumption, so that the agent would be negligent if it had failed to inform the foreign bank of its responsibilities under the 1992 Act, as Lloyds had failed to do in this case. However, Rix J also held that whilst negligence of the English bank deprived it of a s 4 defence, it did not constitute a breach of duty to the foreign bank because (at 225): 'an English clearing bank has no duty to its foreign correspondent banks to advise them of every aspect of English banking law'. The English agent bank was held to be entitled to a full indemnity from its foreign principal. Gross J applied Rix J's judgment in *Linklaters (a firm) v HSBC Bank plc* [2003] EWHC 1113 (Comm), [2003] 2 Lloyd's Rep 545, holding that it made no difference that, in the case before him, the collecting agent was also the paying bank.

2.   Section 4(2) of the 1957 Act extends the protection afforded by s 4(1) to the collection of cheques and certain other instruments, for example conditional orders for payment, instruments drawn payable to 'cash or order', interest and dividend warrants, 'cheques' requiring a receipt, bankers' drafts. Section 3 of the Cheques Act 1992 has amended s 4(2) to include within the definition of 'cheques' those cheques which under s 81A(1) of the BEA (see above, p 727) or otherwise are not transferable. However, it appears that an instrument in the form of a cheque to which the drawer's signature is a forgery is not a cheque and is not within s 4. Similarly, an unauthorised material alteration of a cheque avoids the instrument and has the effect of rendering it a worthless piece of paper (*Smith v Lloyds TSB Group plc* [2001] QB 541, CA; see above, p 743). Thus, a materially altered 'cheque' would also fall outside s 4, although the risk to the collecting bank is minimal as the true owner would not be able to recover more than nominal damages for conversion of the instrument.

3.   By s 4(3) of the 1957 Act the collecting bank will not be treated for the purposes of s 4(1) as having been negligent by reason only of its failure to concern itself with absence of, or irregularity in, indorsement of a cheque or other instrument specified in s 4(2). However, a memorandum of the Committee of London Clearing Bankers (23 September 1957) stated that indorsement would still be required if: (a) the instrument was tendered for an account other than that of the ostensible payee (unless it was specially indorsed to the customer for whose account it was tendered); or if (b) the payee's name was misspelt or he was incorrectly designated and there were circumstances to suggest that the customer was not the person to whom payment was intended to be made; or if (c) an instrument payable to joint payees was tendered for credit of an account to which all were not parties. If a collecting bank did not comply with the memorandum, and that failure was material, it would be unable to establish that it acted without negligence as it would have failed to comply with standard banking practice. The practice established by the memorandum had remained in effect and the consequence of material non-compliance remains the same.

4.   The bank may be both the paying and collecting bank, as where both the drawer of a cheque and the person presenting it for payment maintain an account at the same branch or different branches of the drawee bank. In such a case, the bank as paying bank may rely the protection conferred by s 60 or s 80 of the BEA, but as collecting bank it must rely on s 4 of the Cheques Act 1957 (*Carpenter's Co v British Mutual Banking Co Ltd* [1938] 1 KB 511 (above, p 737)). The bank is acting in two capacities and it cannot escape liability incurred in one capacity by setting up what may be a complete defence in the other.

(iii) Banking Act 1979, s 47

Section 47 of the Banking Act 1979 provides as follows:

> In any circumstances in which proof of absence of negligence on the part of a banker would be a
> defence in proceedings by reason of section 4 of the Cheques Act 1957, a defence of contributory
> negligence shall also be available to the banker notwithstanding the provisions of section 11(1) of
> the Torts (Interference with Goods) Act 1977.

(iv) Other defences

It is open to the collecting bank to plead in its defence to an action in conversion that: (1) the
proceeds actually reached the true owner, the payment discharged a debt of the true owner,
or the true owner benefitted from the payment in some other way (*B Liggett (Liverpool) Ltd
v Barclays Bank Ltd* [1928] 1 KB 48); or (2) the true owner ratified the unauthorised transaction or is estopped from alleging the conversion (*Bank of Montreal v Dominion Gresham
Guarantee and Casualty Co Ltd* [1930] AC 659 at 666); or (3) the true owner's claim was itself
tainted with illegality (*Thackwell v Barclays Bank plc* [1986] 1 All ER 676).

QUESTIONS

1. Alan banked with the Cambridge branch of NE Bank plc. Using a chequebook supplied
by the Cambridge branch, Alan drew a crossed cheque in favour of Bill or order. Bill indorsed
the cheque specially to Chris for value. Daniel stole the cheque from Chris, forged Chris's
signature on the back, and delivered it to Ethel in payment of a debt. Ethel took it to her bank,
the Oxford branch of NE Bank plc, who obtained payment of the cheque from Alan's branch
and credited Ethel's account with the proceeds. Advise the parties.

2. What would have been the position in the preceding question if the cheque had been
crossed 'account payee'?

3. Is the term 'negligence', as found in s 4 of the Cheques Act 1957, something of a misnomer? Does the collecting bank owe a duty of care to the true owner of a cheque? Would
a collecting bank have acted 'without negligence' for the purposes of s 4 if its carelessness
had no causative effect on the loss suffered by the true owner of a stolen cheque? Contrast
A Malek and J Odgers (eds), *Paget's Law of Banking* (14th edn, 2014), para 27.23, citing, inter
alia, *Marfani & Co Ltd v Midland Bank Ltd* [1968] 1 WLR 956 at 976, CA; *Hon Soc of the
Middle Temple v Lloyds Bank plc*, [1999] 1 All ER (Comm) 193 at 226, with M Brindle and R
Cox (eds), *Law of Bank Payments* (4th edn, 2010), para 7–160, citing, inter alia, *Thackwell v
Barclays Bank plc* [1986] 1 All ER 676 at 684.

2 PROMISSORY NOTES

The definition of a promissory note is set out in s 83(1) of the BEA as follows:

> A promissory note is an unconditional promise in writing made by one person to another signed
> by the maker, engaging to pay, on demand or at a fixed or determinable future time, a sum certain
> in money, to, or to the order of, a specified person or to bearer.

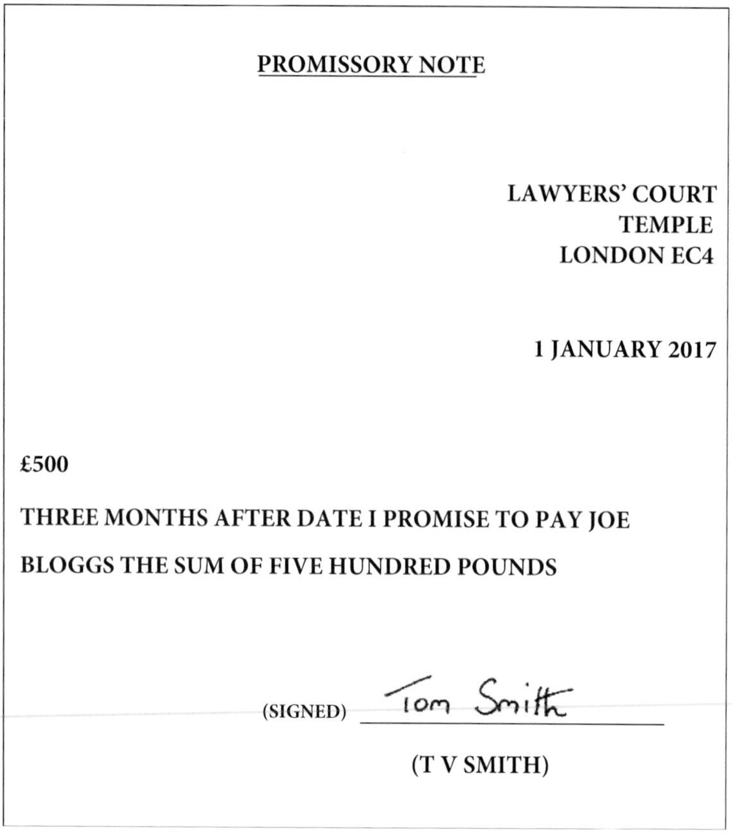

PROMISSORY NOTE

LAWYERS' COURT
TEMPLE
LONDON EC4

1 JANUARY 2017

£500

THREE MONTHS AFTER DATE I PROMISE TO PAY JOE
BLOGGS THE SUM OF FIVE HUNDRED POUNDS

(SIGNED) *Tom Smith*

(T V SMITH)

Figure 20.2 Promissory note

An example of a promissory note appears as Figure 20.2.

Section 83(1) requires a promissory note to contain a promise to pay. As the next case illustrates, a mere acknowledgement of indebtedness, although it contains an implied promise to pay, is not enough.

Akbar Khan v Attar Singh
[1936] 2 All ER 545, Privy Council

The plaintiff deposited the sum of Rs43,900 with the defendants and received a deposit receipt which stated that 'this amount to be payable after two years. Interest at the rate of Rs5.40 per cent per year to be charged'. The document was stamped as a receipt. The issue before the Privy Council was whether this document was a deposit receipt or a promissory note.

Lord Atkin (delivering the advice of the Board): . . . It is indeed doubtful whether a document can properly be styled a promissory note which does not contain an undertaking to pay, not merely an undertaking which has to be inferred from the words used. It is plain that the implied promise to pay arising from an acknowledgment of a debt will not suffice, for . . . an IOU is not a promissory note, though of the implied promise to pay there can be no doubt . . .

Their Lordships prefer to decide this point on the broad ground that such a document as this is not and could not be intended to be brought within a definition relating to documents which are to be negotiable instruments. Such documents must come into existence for the purpose only of recording an agreement to pay money and nothing more, though of course they may state the consideration. Receipts and agreements generally are not intended to be negotiable, and serious embarrassment would be caused in commerce if the negotiable net were cast too wide. This document plainly is a receipt for money containing the terms on which it is to be repaid. It is not without significance that the defendants who drew it, and who were experienced moneylenders did not draw it on paper with an impressed stamp as they would have to if the document were a promissory note, and that they affixed a stamp which is sufficient if the document is a simple receipt. Being primarily a receipt even if coupled with a promise to pay it is not a promissory note.

NOTES

1. This ruling of Lord Atkin has been applied by the Court of Appeal in *Claydon v Bradley* [1987] 1 WLR 521 at 526, 528.

2. An IOU is not a promissory note, but merely evidence of indebtedness. Similarly, bankers' negotiable certificates of deposit are not promissory notes as they merely acknowledge receipt of a deposit, but they are negotiable by custom. Floating rate notes are also negotiable by custom, but they are not promissory notes as the sum payable is not certain. By contrast, sterling commercial paper, issued by financial institutions other than banks, usually takes the form of a promissory note payable to bearer (see R MacVicar (1986) 2 JIBFL 40) and Bank of England bank notes are promissory notes payable to bearer on demand (although it is pointless to present bank notes for payment as bank notes are also legal tender and the holder would only receive other bank notes in exchange). Further, by s 5(2) of the BEA, where in a bill of exchange the drawer and drawee are the same person, or where the drawee is a fictitious person or a person not having capacity to contract, the holder may treat the instrument, at his option, either as a bill of exchange or as a promissory note. For example, the recipient of a banker's draft (an order to pay drawn by a branch of a bank on its head office or another branch of the same bank) may treat the instrument as a promissory note and thereby normally be relieved of the need to present it for payment in order to render the maker liable (BEA, s 87(1)).

3. By s 89(1) of the BEA, subject to certain qualifications contained in ss 83–89, the provisions of the 1882 Act relating to bills of exchange apply, with the necessary modifications, to promissory notes. By s 89(2) of the Act, the maker of a promissory note is deemed to correspond with the acceptor of a bill, and the first indorser with the drawer of an accepted bill payable to his own order. As the maker is deemed the acceptor, s 89(3) states that the provisions of the Act relating to presentment for acceptance and to acceptance do not apply.

4. What are promissory notes used for? In international trade they are mainly used in forfaiting transactions where the importer will make a promissory note (supported by bank guarantees) which the exporter will indorse (without recourse) to a forfaiter at a discount. The forfaiter bears the credit risk, and economic and political risks, and must obtain payment of the instrument, or rediscount it in the secondary market (see below, p 854). In domestic trade, promissory notes serve two functions. First, they provide added security if they are made by a debtor or hirer. They give the creditor or lessor the advantage of being able to bring an action by summary procedure and prevent the maker of the note raising certain defences which would be available if an action was brought on the underlying transaction (a principle affirmed in

Cardinal Financial Investments Corpn v Central Bank of Yemen [2001] Lloyd's Rep Bank 1 at 3, CA). As this may place the debtor or hirer in a worse position if sued on the note than if sued on the underlying transaction, ss 123 and 124 of the Consumer Credit Act 1974 precludes the taking of promissory notes in respect of regulated consumer credit and consumer hire agreements (see above, p 689). Secondly, as with international trade, they facilitate the refinancing of transactions in that the notes may be discounted to a financial institution. Unlike the assignment of a chose in action which is made subject to equities, the negotiation of a promissory note can pass a title free from any defects in the title of previous parties.

3   BANKER'S DRAFTS

A banker's draft is an order to pay drawn by one branch of a bank on its head office or on another branch of the same bank. It is not a bill of exchange (or a cheque) because it is not drawn by one person on another as required by s 3(1) of the BEA (see above, p 661). The instrument is in fact treated as a promissory note made and issued by the bank (*Commercial Banking Co of Sydney v Mann* [1961] AC 1 at 7). However, the holder of a banker's draft has the right to treat it either as a bill of exchange or as a promissory note (BEA, s 5(2)). The bank is protected in the case of such instruments by ss 1 and 4 of the Cheques Act 1957 (ss 1(2)(b), 4(2)(d)) and, in the case of crossed drafts, the provisions of the BEA (especially s 80) relating to crossed cheques (Cheques Act 1957, s 5).

Banker's drafts are sometimes used to make payment in commercial transactions where the supplier of goods or services wants to be sure that he will get paid (eg a car dealer will demand that his purchaser pays the price, or its balance where a deposit was paid earlier, by banker's draft before he will release the car to him). A banker's draft is generally treated as equivalent to cash to the extent that the only risk is that of the insolvency of the bank. However, the supplier, who is usually the named payee on the draft (virtually all banker's drafts issued by UK banks are now crossed 'account payee', and so are not transferable because of s 81A(1) of the BEA), cannot be absolutely certain of payment under a banker's draft as the bank may be able to refuse to pay the draft, or seek to recover money already paid out as money paid by mistake, on the ground that the issue of the draft was obtained by the fraud of its customer (the recipient of the supplier's goods or services), or that the consideration given by its customer for the issue of the draft has failed. English law remains uncertain on these issues, but *RE Jones v Waring & Gillow Ltd* [1926] AC 670 (above, p 683), on the fraud issue, and *Hasan v Willson* [1977] 1 Lloyd's Rep 431 (above, p 680), on the failure of consideration issue, seem to support the bank's case in these circumstances (but for persuasive arguments to the contrary, see A Tettenborn [1998] RLR 63; see also B Geva (1994) 73 Can Bar Rev 21). Exactly the same issues also affect anyone who accepts payment by a building society cheque.

4   TRAVELLERS' CHEQUES

Travellers' cheques are sometimes used by businessmen and holidaymakers as a means of payment or of acquiring cash when travelling abroad. Travellers' cheques are purchased from banks or their agents. They come in a number of different forms, but in each case the travellers' cheque must be signed by the traveller when issued to him ('the signature') and countersigned by him when he cashes or negotiates the instrument ('the countersignature'). The most common types of travellers' cheque are: (1) where the issuing bank promises to pay a certain amount of money to the payee (whose name is left blank) provided the signature and countersignature correspond; (2) where one or more directors of the issuing bank order the bank to pay a certain amount of money to the payee (whose name is left blank) provided the signature and countersignature correspond; and (3) where the traveller gives an order, as drawer, to the issuing bank to pay to his own order provided the instrument is duly countersigned by him. In each case the travellers' cheque is treated as containing an undertaking by the issuing bank to pay the amount stated in the instrument (normally the undertaking is express). However, as payment is made conditional on the signature and countersignature being by the same person, the instrument in any of the three forms set out above cannot be a bill of exchange, cheque, or promissory note within the meaning of ss 3(1), 73, and 83 of the BEA (contrast Stassen (1978) 95 SALJ 180 at 182–183, who argues that the countersignature is only a means of identification; and also Ottolenghi [1999] JBL 22 at 35). However, there is little doubt that, as a result of modern mercantile custom, travellers' cheques are treated as negotiable instruments throughout the world. This means that the general principles of the law of negotiable instruments apply, with necessary modifications, to travellers' cheques. For a detailed analysis of the law relating to travellers' cheques, see Ellinger (1969) 19 Univ of Toronto LJ 132; Stassen (1978) 95 SALJ 180; Frohlich (1980) 54 ALJ 388; *Chitty on Contracts* (32nd edn, 2015), Vol II, paras 34–17 1ff.

QUESTIONS

1. Adam purchased a number of travellers' cheques from B Bank. He did not sign or countersign the cheques when he collected them as he was in a hurry to get to the airport. At the airport Adam found that his plane had been delayed and so he decided to do some last-minute shopping. Despite a number of notices warning passengers not to leave their baggage unattended, Adam left his rucksack on a seat in the departure lounge while he went to browse in a nearby bookshop. Adam spent nearly an hour in the bookshop and on his return to the departure lounge he found that the rucksack had been opened and his travellers' cheques taken. Adam immediately cancelled his holiday and returned to B Bank demanding a refund for the stolen travellers' cheques. B Bank refused to give a refund relying on a clause printed on the inside of the plastic wallet, which had contained his travellers' cheques, which stated that the traveller had a right to a refund so long as he 'properly safeguarded each cheque against loss or theft'. Advise Adam. Compare *Braithwaite v Thomas Cook Travellers Cheques Ltd* [1989] QB 553, with *Fellus v National Westminster Bank plc* (1983) 133 NLJ 766 and *El Awadi v Bank of Credit and Commerce International SA Ltd* [1990] 1 QB 606.

2. In fact it was Chris who had stolen Adam's travellers' cheques. After stealing the cheques, Chris immediately signed them in his own name. He then went to a local department store where he used the cheques to pay for some jewellery. Before tendering the cheques in payment, Chris countersigned them in the presence of the shop assistant. The department store now seeks payment of the cheques from B Bank. Advise the bank.

PART VI

THE FINANCING OF INTERNATIONAL TRADE

Chapter 21   The financing of international trade   767

CHAPTER 21

THE FINANCING OF INTERNATIONAL TRADE

There are various ways to pay for goods sold under an international sales contract. The method chosen for any particular transaction will greatly depend on the seller's confidence in the integrity and solvency of the overseas buyer, as well as on the bargaining strengths of the respective parties. Where the seller has such confidence in the buyer, he may be prepared to supply goods on open account. Here the seller extends a fixed period of credit to the buyer, say 28 days after shipment, before payment has to be made. It is common and cheap, but there is a clear risk of non-payment by, or insolvency of, the buyer. Where the seller lacks confidence in the honesty or solvency of the buyer, he may insist that payment is made through the intervention of one or more banks. This increases the cost of the transaction for the buyer as the bank will usually charge a fee for its services. Traditionally, the two most common methods of payment which involve banks have been the collection of documentary bills (now little used) and payment under documentary credits. But now the Bank Payment Obligation offers the seller a new means to mitigate the risks of non-payment and insolvency associated with open account transactions.

The move towards increased automation of the payment process in international trade (related to the development of electronic bills of lading) has led to the introduction of a new payment method called the Bank Payment Obligation (BPO), which is an irrevocable and independent undertaking given by one bank (the Obligor Bank, which is usually the buyer's bank) to another bank (the Recipient Bank, which must be the seller's bank) that payment will be made after successful electronic matching of data supplied by the seller (eg commercial, transport, and insurance information about the shipment) against that agreed between the buyer and the seller. The BPO is transmitted electronically between the participating banks using the SWIFT messaging system, and it is the SWIFT system, and not the banks themselves, which automatically checks data supplied by the seller and submitted to the system by the seller's bank. The payment undertaking in a BPO is made between the two banks and, unlike what happens with a documentary credit, the seller has no direct claim against the bank that gave the undertaking (the seller's claim is against the seller's bank according to the terms of any separate contractual agreement that the seller will usually have entered into with the seller's bank, but this bilateral agreement is not part of the BPO itself). Uniform Rules for Bank Payment Obligations were published by the International Chamber of Commerce (ICC) in 2013 (ICC Publication No 750E). Payment using a BPO is faster and cheaper than that using a documentary credit. It remains to be seen whether the BPO will be widely adopted and eventually replace documentary credits in international trade transactions. For detailed analysis of the BPO, see DJ Hennah, *The ICC Guide to the Uniform Rules for Bank Payment Obligations* (ICC Publication No 751E); K Vorpeil, 'Bank Payment Obligations: Alternative Means of Settlement in International Trade' [2014] IBLJ 41.

1   DOCUMENTARY BILLS

A 'documentary bill' is a bill of exchange to which the bill of lading (or other document of title) is attached.[1] The seller will send a documentary bill to the buyer to ensure that the buyer does not take up the bill of lading, which gives him a right of disposal of the goods, without first accepting or paying the bill of exchange as previously agreed between the parties. If the buyer fails to accept or pay the bill of exchange (depending on whether it is a term or sight bill), he is bound to return the bill of lading to the seller and, if he wrongfully retains the bill of lading, the property in the goods does not pass to him (Sale of Goods Act 1979, s 19(3)). However, this method of payment does not prevent a buyer, who has dishonoured the bill of exchange, from passing title to the goods to a third party under one of the exceptions to the *nemo dat* rule: in particular, under s 9 of the Factors Act 1889 or s 25 of the Sale of Goods Act 1979 (*Cahn & Mayer v Pockett's Bristol Channel Steam Packet Co Ltd* [1899] 1 QB 643, CA).

To avoid the risk of a fraudulent buyer passing title to the goods to a third party, the seller may instruct his own bank (the 'remitting bank') to deliver the bill of lading, and other shipping documents, to the buyer in his own country and, as a precondition to the release of those documents, collect the price from him, ie by acceptance or payment of the bill of exchange. If the remitting bank does not have an office in the buyer's country, it may instruct a local bank (the 'collecting bank') to perform this task as its agent. In this situation, according to general principles of agency law, there is privity of contract between the seller and the remitting bank, and also between the remitting bank and the collecting bank, but not between the seller and the collecting bank, unless the seller contemplates that a sub-agent will be employed *and* authorises the remitting bank to create privity of contract between himself and the collecting bank (*Calico Printers' Association Ltd v Barclays Bank Ltd* (1931) 145 LT 51 (above, p 252), affirmed on appeal without reference to this point: at 58). Relations between the seller and the remitting bank, and between the remitting bank and the collecting bank, will usually be governed by the ICC's *Uniform Rules for Collections* (the latest revision is URC 522, published in 1995). The seller is a party to a collection governed by URC 522, but the Rules do not create privity of contract between seller and collecting bank (*Grosvenor Casinos Ltd v National Bank of Abu Dhabi* [2008] EWHC 511 (Comm); cf *Bastone & Firminger Ltd v Nasima Enterprises (Nigeria) Ltd* [1996] CLC 1902 at 1908, per Rix J, who saw the point as fully arguable: and see also the analysis of both cases by Howard Bennett in (2008) 124 LQR 532). The Rules only apply if incorporated into the contracts by the parties, whether expressly or by course of dealings or simply by the international custom and practice of bankers (*Harlow & Jones Ltd v American Express Bank Ltd* [1990] 2 Lloyd's Rep 343 at 349, per Gatehouse J; *Minories Finance Ltd v Afribank Nigeria Ltd* [1995] 1 Lloyd's Rep 134 at 139, per Longmore J).

In most cases the remitting bank will discount the bill of exchange before acceptance or payment by the buyer. A bill of exchange is discounted when the bank credits the seller's

---

[1] See, generally, EP Ellinger and H Tjio, 'Uniform Rules for Collections' [1996] JBL 382; *Benjamin's Sale of Goods* (9th edn, 2014), paras 22–032 ff.

account with the full amount of the bill (less banking charges) or when the bank agrees to advance to the seller a percentage of the face value of the bill but withholds the balance until the bill is paid by the buyer. This has the advantage of releasing funds to the seller at an earlier date than if he waited for the bill of exchange to mature. But the remitting bank will usually retain a right of recourse against the seller: if the buyer dishonours the bill of exchange by non-acceptance or non-payment, the bank can sue the seller on the bill. This highlights the real disadvantage, from the seller's point of view, of payment under a documentary bill which is collected by, or discounted to, a bank: the buyer may accept the bill of exchange so that the bill of lading will be released to him, yet the seller has no assurance that the buyer will pay when the bill matures. Documentary credits provide a solution to this problem.

QUESTIONS

1. From the buyer's point of view, what are the advantages of payment by means of a documentary bill?

2. Does the remitting bank become a party to the bill of exchange by discounting it for the seller? What would be the practical significance of the remitting bank becoming a party to the bill? See *Barclays Bank Ltd v Aschaffenburger Zellstoffwerke AG* [1967] 1 Lloyd's Rep 387; *Barclays Bank Ltd v Astley Industrial Trust Ltd* [1970] 2 QB 527 at 538–539.

2   DOCUMENTARY CREDITS

Documentary credits are a common method of payment in international sales.[2] However, modern trade practice shows that documentary credits are being supplanted by open account (above, p 767) as a means of settling international trade transactions. The decline in use of documentary credits is likely to continue with the development of the BPO (above, p 767).

(a) The function and operation of documentary credits

A documentary credit represents a bank's assurance of payment against presentation of specified documents. The seller stipulates in the contract of sale that payment is to be by documentary credit. The buyer then gets his bank to issue the credit in favour of the seller, so that the seller has the bank's independent payment undertaking. This has two advantages from the seller's point of view. First, subject to the solvency of the bank, the seller is certain of payment under the credit provided he can present conforming documents to the bank and comply with any other terms of the credit. Secondly, where the credit is transferable, the seller can use it to finance his own acquisition of the goods.

---

[2] The leading textbooks on this subject are *Benjamin's Sale of Goods* (9th edn, 2014), Ch 23; P Ellinger and D Neo, *The Law and Practice of Documentary Letters of Credit* (2010); A Malek and D Quest, *Jack: Documentary Credits* (4th edn, 2009) and R King, *Gutteridge and Megrah's Law of Bankers' Commercial Credits* (8th edn, 2001). For excellent comparative studies, see B Kozolchyk, 'Letters of Credit' in *International Encyclopedia of Comparative Law*, Vol IX, Ch 5 and EP Ellinger, *Documentary Letters of Credit—A Comparative Study* (1970).

A documentary credit transaction normally operates as follows (assuming the underlying transaction is one of sale).

- The seller and the overseas buyer agree in the contract of sale that payment shall be made under a documentary credit.

- The buyer (acting as the 'applicant' for the credit) requests a bank in his own country (the 'issuing' bank) to open a documentary credit in favour of the seller (the 'beneficiary') on the terms specified by the buyer in his instructions.

- The issuing bank opens an irrevocable credit (below, p 775; revocable credits are now rare) and by its terms undertakes to pay the contract price or to incur a deferred payment undertaking and pay at maturity, or to accept a bill of exchange drawn by the beneficiary and pay at maturity, provided that the specified documents (that is to say, the transport document, such as a bill of lading, the policy of insurance, the invoice, and other documents specified in the credit, eg certificates of origin, certificates of quality, and packing lists) are duly tendered and any other terms and conditions of the credit are complied with.

- The issuing bank may open the credit by sending it direct to the seller; alternatively, as happens in most cases, the issuing bank may arrange for a bank in the seller's country (the 'advising' or 'correspondent' bank) to advise the seller that the credit has been opened.

- The issuing bank may also ask the advising bank to add its 'confirmation' to the credit. If the bank agrees to add its confirmation, and it may be under no obligation to do so, the advising bank (now called the 'confirming' bank) gives the seller a separate payment undertaking in terms similar to that given by the issuing bank and the seller benefits from having the payment obligation localised in his own country.

- The seller ships the goods and tenders the required documents (often through his own bank, which acts as his agent) to the advising bank (acting as the nominated bank[3]) or confirming bank. If the documents conform to the terms of the credit, the advising bank (as a nominated bank[4]) or confirming bank will pay the contract price, or incur a deferred payment undertaking and pay at maturity, or accept a bill of exchange and pay at maturity, or negotiate a bill of exchange drawn for the price, and seek reimbursement from the issuing bank.

- Before releasing the documents to the buyer, the issuing bank will in turn seek payment from him. If the buyer is not in a position to pay without first reselling the goods, the issuing bank may release the documents to him under a 'trust receipt', thereby giving the buyer access to the goods on arrival without destroying the bank's security interest in the goods and in the proceeds of sale.[5]

---

[3] 'Nominated bank' means the bank authorised in the credit to honour or negotiate or, in the case of a freely available credit, any bank (UCP 600, arts 2 and 6(a)).

[4] Unless a nominated bank is the confirming bank, an authorisation to honour or negotiate does not impose any obligation on that nominated bank to do so, except when expressly agreed to by that nominated bank and so communicated to the beneficiary (UCP 600, art 12(a)). Receipt or examination and forwarding of documents by a nominated bank that is not a confirming bank does not make that nominated bank liable to honour or negotiate (UCP 600, art 12(c)).

[5] But the use of a 'trust receipt' may not give the bank complete protection: see *Lloyds Bank Ltd v Bank of America* [1938] 2 KB 147, noted below at p 1033. See generally EP Ellinger, 'Trust Receipt Financing' [2003] JIBLR 305.

(b) The contracts arising out of a documentary credit transaction

(i) The contractual network

A documentary credit transaction is held together by a series of interconnected contractual relationships. First, there is the underlying contract of sale between the seller and the buyer. Secondly, when the issuing bank agrees to act on the instructions of the buyer a contract comes into existence between them. Thirdly, when a correspondent bank agrees to act on the instructions of the issuing bank, and advises or confirms the credit, there is a contractual relationship between the issuing bank and its correspondent. Finally, the payment undertakings given to the seller by the issuing and confirming banks in a documentary credit transaction are contractual in nature (despite the fact that they do not readily comply with some of the general principles of contract law: see Section (ii) below). As Figure 21.1 illustrates, in relation to a confirmed irrevocable credit, there are five contractual relationships involved (Lord Diplock identified four contractual relationships in *United City Merchants (Investments) Ltd v Royal Bank of Canada, The American Accord* [1983] 1 AC 168 at 181–183 (below, p 790), omitting to refer to the contract between the issuing bank and the seller; but see *Bank of Baroda v Vysya Bank Ltd* [1994] 2 Lloyd's Rep 87 at 90, per Mance J; *Bank of Credit & Commerce Hong Kong Ltd (in liquidation) v Sonali Bank* [1995] 1 Lloyd's Rep 227 at 237, per Cresswell J).

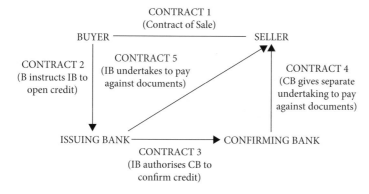

Figure 21.1 The parties to a confirmed irrevocable credit

(ii) The nature of the banks' undertakings

When the credit is irrevocable and confirmed, the issuing and confirming banks each give contractual undertakings to the seller to pay (or pay, accept, or negotiate bills of exchange) according to the terms of the credit. Yet it is far from clear as to what, if any, consideration is provided by the seller in support of these payment undertakings. Various attempts have been made to find consideration moving from the seller, or otherwise explain the legal basis of the banks' undertakings. It has been argued, for example, that consideration for the credit is the seller's agreement to present shipping documents to the bank or, alternatively, that the credit becomes binding as a result of the seller's reliance on it, such reliance either constituting acceptance of an offer giving rise to a unilateral contract or making the bank's undertaking binding by estoppel.

None of these theories stands up to rigorous analysis (see RM Goode, 'Abstract Payment Undertakings' in P Cane and J Stapleton (eds), *Essays for Patrick Atiyah* (1991), p 218). Of the two theories highlighted, Professor Goode rightly points out that: (1) the seller makes no promise to the bank to produce the shipping documents; and (2) the idea that reliance of the seller makes the bank's promise binding is irreconcilable with the commercial understanding of the credit as irrevocable from the moment it is communicated to the seller. The enactment of the Contracts (Rights of Third Parties) Act 1999, which allows third parties (the beneficiary under the credit) to enforce rights conferred on them in other people's contracts (the contract between the applicant and the issuing bank), does not take the matter any further forward. Article 4(a) of the UCP 600 provides that the beneficiary cannot avail himself of the contract between the banks or between the applicant and the issuing bank, and this would be effective to exclude the operation of the Act (Contracts (Rights of Third Parties) Act 1999, s 1(2)). In *Petrologic Capital SA v Banque Cantonale de Genève* [2012] EWHC 453 (Comm) at [52]–[56], it was held, using analogous reasoning, that an applicant for a letter of credit was unable to rely on the 1999 Act to enforce a jurisdiction clause contained in the credit. It is also very likely that a third party cannot enforce a credit incorporating UCP 600 as an undisclosed principal (*Taurus Petroleum Ltd v State Oil Marketing Co of the Ministry of Oil, Republic of Iraq* [2013] EWHC 3494 (Comm), [2014] 1 Lloyd's Rep 432 at [21], per Field J (*obiter*): the issue was not addressed by the Court of Appeal, [2015] EWCA Civ 835, [2016] 1 Lloyd's Rep 42).

Probably the best explanation is that the undertakings of the banks are binding through mercantile usage (*Hamzeh Malas & Sons v British Imex Industries Ltd* [1958] 2 QB 127 at 129, per Jenkins LJ (below, p 786); see also Goode in *Essays for Patrick Atiyah*, above, pp 222–225). It would appear, therefore, that documentary credits are an exception to the doctrine of consideration (as is expressly recognised by the US Uniform Commercial Code (1995 Revision), s 5–105). In any event, whatever the theoretical basis for the binding effect of the bank's undertaking, it is most unlikely in practice that an issuing or confirming bank would attempt to avoid payment under the credit on the technical ground of lack of consideration. The bank's commercial reputation would be irreparably damaged if it tried to take the point.

(c) The Uniform Customs and Practice for Documentary Credits

The Uniform Customs and Practice for Documentary Credits (UCP) is a set of rules governing the use of documentary credits. It was first published by the ICC in 1933 and has been revised six times since then. The latest revision is UCP 600, which came into effect on 1 July 2007 (noted by EP Ellinger [2007] LMCLQ 152).[6] UCP 600 replaces the 1993 revision (UCP 500). Unless stated otherwise, all references in this chapter are to UCP 600. A supplement to UCP 600 (called the eUCP) deals with the electronic presentation of documents. The UCP has been adopted by bankers and traders throughout the world. It has been described as 'the

---

[6] The ICC Commission on Banking Technique and Practice meets regularly to consider problems which arise in relation to the application of the UCP. It has produced a number of booklets containing its opinions on the UCP. In 1997, the ICC established a dispute resolution procedure whereby disputes relating to trade-finance related instruments, including documentary credits which incorporate the UCP, can be referred to a panel of experts (see *DOCDEX Rules—Rules for Documentary Credit Dispute Resolution Expertise*, 2015 Revision). Opinions of the ICC Banking Commission and DOCDEX decisions provide the English courts with evidence of international banking practice, which they can use to interpret the UCP.

most successful harmonizing measure in the history of international commerce' (RM Goode [1992] LMCLQ 190).

In most countries, including the UK, the UCP does not have the force of law. The parties are free to incorporate all or any of the UCP rules into their contracts and, if incorporated, the UCP will govern all aspects of documentary credit arrangements except the relationship between the applicant and the beneficiary under the underlying contract, for example between buyer and seller where the underlying contract is one of sale, as this contract does not usually incorporate the UCP. Article 1 of UCP 600 provides that the UCP 'are rules that apply to any documentary credit . . . when the text of the credit expressly indicates that it is subject to those rules'. Nevertheless, it has been argued that, even in the absence of express incorporation, the UCP may be incorporated as a matter of business practice because it is so widely used by banks all over the world (E McKendrick, *Goode on Commercial Law* (5th edn, 2016), pp 1032-1033, citing, by analogy, *Harlow and Jones Ltd v American Express Bank Ltd* [1990] 2 Lloyd's Rep 343 at 349, a case on the Uniform Rules for Collections). However, given the wording of UCP 600, express incorporation is advised. The eUCP must be expressly incorporated into the credit if it is to apply (eUCP, art e1(b)). Incorporation of the eUCP has the effect of incorporating the UCP into the credit without express incorporation of the UCP (eUCP, art e2(a)). Where the eUCP applies, its provisions prevail to the extent that they would produce a result different from the application of the UCP (eUCP, art e2(b)).

The UCP may be expressly modified or excluded by the terms of the credit (UCP 600, art 1). In cases where there is no such express exclusion, the courts will endeavour to construe the express terms of the credit so as to avoid conflict with the rules of the UCP (*Forestal Mimosa Ltd v Oriental Credit Ltd* [1986] 1 WLR 631 at 639, CA). If there is conflict between the express terms of the credit and the UCP, the former will prevail over the latter (*Royal Bank of Scotland plc v Cassa di Risparmio Delle Provincie Lombard* [1992] 1 Bank LR 251 at 256, CA).

When construing the provisions of the UCP, the English courts 'seek to give effect to the international consequences underlying the UCP' (*Glencore International AG v Bank of China* [1996] 1 Lloyd's Rep 135 at 148, per Sir Thomas Bingham MR). In *Fortis Bank SA/NV v Indian Overseas Bank* [2011] EWCA Civ 58, [2011] 2 Lloyd's Rep 33 at [29], Thomas LJ said:

> In my view a court must recognize the international nature of the UCP and approach its construction in that spirit. It was drafted in English in a manner that it could easily be translated into about 20 different languages and applied by bankers and traders throughout the world. It is intended to be a self-contained code for those areas of practice which it covers and to reflect good practice and achieve consistency across the world. Courts must therefore interpret it in accordance with its underlying aims and purposes reflecting international practice and the expectations of international bankers and international traders so that it underpins the operation of letters of credit in international trade. A literalistic and national approach must be avoided.

This must be right as the UCP does not have its origins in English law but represents international custom and practice. The UCP is a prime example of the impact of commercial custom and usage on the development of commercial law.

(d) Definition and types of credits

The terms 'documentary credit', 'banker's commercial credit', and 'commercial letter of credit' are synonymous. But documentary credits are only one type of letter of credit. Letters of credit may also be used in transactions which do not involve payment against the presentation of documents. Such letters of credit are called 'open' or 'clean' credits (see, eg, *Re Agra and Masterman's Bank, exp Asiatic Banking Corpn* (1867) 2 Ch App 391). Open credits do not fall within the scope of the UCP and so we shall not be concerned with them in this chapter.

Article 2 of UCP 600 defines a documentary credit ('credit') as 'any arrangement, however named or described, that is irrevocable and thereby constitutes a definite undertaking of the issuing bank to honour a complying presentation'. This marks an important change from UCP 500 which covered both revocable and irrevocable credits. But revocable credits are rare in practice and so the change is not unexpected. Article 2 also contains a definition of 'honour', which means 'to pay at sight if the credit is available by sight payment; to incur a deferred payment undertaking and pay at maturity if the credit is available by deferred payment; to accept a bill of exchange ("draft") drawn by the beneficiary and pay at maturity if the credit is available by acceptance'. Article 2 defines a 'complying presentation' of documents as one 'that is in accordance with the terms and conditions of the credit, the applicable provisions of [the UCP] and international standard banking practice'.

The parties to the underlying contract, which we shall continue to assume to be a contract of sale, should choose whether the credit is to be available by sight payment, by deferred payment, by acceptance, or by negotiation. Their choice must be reflected in the terms of the credit (UCP, art 6(b)).

- *Sight payment or sight credit*—the bank undertakes to pay the seller (the beneficiary under the credit) on presentation of the specified documents. It usually calls on the seller to draw a sight bill of exchange (above, p 662) on the issuing bank, advising bank, or another bank and for him to present it with the documents for immediate payment.

- *Deferred payment credit*—the bank undertakes to pay the seller at some future date determined in accordance with the terms of the credit, for example '180 days from shipment'. Where a future payment by the bank is to be made other than against an accepted bill of exchange (acceptance credit), the credit is known as a deferred payment credit. A deferred payment credit can be discounted before its maturity date by the discounting bank taking an assignment of the beneficiary's rights under the credit. But under the rules of assignment, defences, and cross-claims that can be raised against the beneficiary (as assignor) are normally available against the discounting bank (as assignee). In other words, there is a risk when a deferred payment credit is discounted before maturity that the discounting bank's claim to payment on maturity will be defeated by a defence that would have been available against the beneficiary. The risk was highlighted by *Banco Santander v Bayfern Ltd* [2000] 1 All ER (Comm) 776 where a confirming bank discounted its own deferred payment undertaking and fraud in the documents was discovered prior to the maturity date. The Court of Appeal held that the issuing bank was not obliged to reimburse the confirming bank. The *Banco Santander* decision was not popular with the banking community. It placed the risk of fraud in a deferred payment credit on the discounting bank. UCP 600 was meant to deal with the problem and shift the risk of fraud back to the issuing bank (thereby reversing the outcome in a case like *Santander*). Article 12(b) provides that, by nominating a bank to accept or incur a deferred payment undertaking, an issuing bank gives the nominated bank authority to prepay or purchase a draft accepted or a deferred payment undertaking incurred by that bank. This deals with the question of authorisation, but it is doubtful that art 12(b) protects a discounting bank that takes an assignment of the beneficiary's rights under the credit before maturity (see D Horowitz [2008] JBL 508).

- *Acceptance credit*—the bank undertakes to accept bills of exchange drawn on it by the seller. The bill will usually be a time bill payable at a future date (above, p 662) so that by accepting the bill the bank agrees to pay the face value of the bill on maturity to the party presenting it. Between acceptance and maturity the seller may discount the bill to his own bank for cash. Negotiation of the bill of exchange to a bank that is invariably acting in good faith ensures the discounting bank takes free of any defences or cross-claims that can be raised by the issuing bank against the beneficiary. The commercial benefits of discounting have made acceptance credits an extremely popular form of credit in international sales.

- *Credit available by negotiation*—the credit may be available by negotiation with a bank nominated in the credit (or with any bank if the credit so provides). Article 2 of UCP 600 defines 'negotiation' to mean the purchase by the nominated bank of bills of exchange ('drafts') drawn on a bank other than the nominated bank (eg the issuing bank), and/or documents under a complying presentation, by advancing or agreeing to advance funds to the beneficiary on or before the banking day on which reimbursement is due to the nominated bank. This enables the beneficiary to obtain funds without delay by selling the documents to the nominated bank (and so it is only of practical use to the beneficiary where payment under the credit is not immediate). A nominated bank that has honoured or negotiated a complying presentation and forwarded the documents to the issuing bank is entitled to reimbursement from the issuing bank (UCP 600, art 7(c); and on the requirement to forward the documents to the issuing bank, see *Société Générale SA v Saad Trading* [2011] EWHC 2424 (Comm), [2011] 2 CLC 629). However, the term 'negotiation' is sometimes used in a different sense, namely where the undertaking contained in the credit is extended to third parties (including a negotiating bank) as well as the beneficiary, so that the third party may purchase the documents and present them to the issuing bank in its own right. Credits of this type are called 'negotiation credits' and should be contrasted with credits 'available by negotiation' in the sense described above (and also contrasted with 'straight credits' where the issuing bank's payment undertaking is directed solely to the seller). UCP 600 has made the practice of using 'negotiation credits' virtually redundant for if, under a credit incorporating UCP 600, it is intended that the beneficiary should be able to obtain payment by selling the documents to any bank, then the credit should be made freely available by negotiation (A Malek and D Quest, *Jack: Documentary Credits* (4th edn, 2009), para 2.19).

(i) Revocable and irrevocable credits

Where the credit is revocable, the issuing bank is free to modify or cancel it at any time without notice to the beneficiary (see, eg, *Cape Asbestos Co Ltd v Lloyds Bank Ltd* [1921] WN 274, where the seller shipped goods in ignorance of the prior cancellation of the credit). All the issuing bank is required to do is reimburse any other bank that has already paid the credit. Revocable credits are rare and tend only to be found where the parties are not interested in security (eg they are members of the same group of companies), but where they are concerned to save costs. UCP 600 only applies to irrevocable credits; it does not apply to revocable credits (above, p 774). If the parties to the underlying contract want to use a revocable credit, they should make the credit subject to UCP 500, an earlier version of the UCP, which does extend to such credits. A credit that does not indicate whether it is revocable or irrevocable will be deemed to be irrevocable (UCP 600, art 3).

An irrevocable credit constitutes a definite undertaking of the issuing bank that it will honour the credit, provided that there is a complying presentation of the documents specified in the credit (UCP 600, arts 2 and 7(a)). Except as otherwise provided by art 38 of the UCP (transferable credits), an irrevocable credit cannot be modified or cancelled after it has been communicated to the seller (beneficiary) without the consent of the seller, issuing bank, and confirming bank (if any) (UCP 600, art 10(a)). If the underlying contract of sale is silent as to whether the credit should be revocable or irrevocable, art 3 of UCP 600 cannot be used to argue that the credit must be irrevocable. However, because a revocable credit offers no security to the seller, there is a strong presumption that the parties intend the credit to be irrevocable. Irrevocable credits are the norm.

(ii) Confirmed and unconfirmed credits

A confirmed credit is one to which the advising bank has added its own definite undertaking to honour or negotiate the credit, provided there is a complying presentation of the documents specified in the credit (UCP 600, arts 2 and 8(a)). The credit is unconfirmed when the advising bank has not provided such an undertaking. The advising bank does not incur any liability to the seller (beneficiary) if the credit is unconfirmed (see UCP 600, art 12(a) and (c)). The issuing bank may ask the advising bank to confirm the credit but, subject to prior agreement between them, the advising bank is under no obligation to do so (UCP 600, art 9(a)). To avoid the risk of being held liable to pay the seller, with no right of reimbursement from the issuing bank, an advising bank will, in practice, only confirm an irrevocable credit. If the advising bank, in adding its 'confirmation', reserves a right of recourse against the seller, its undertaking does not constitute a confirmation (*Wahbe Tamari & Sons Ltd v Colprogeca-Sociedade Geral de Fibras, Cafes e Products Colonias Lda* [1969] 2 Lloyd's Rep 18 at 21).

Sometimes the advising bank will be asked by the beneficiary to confirm the credit. Should the advising bank accede to that request and add its confirmation (called a 'silent confirmation'), it will not qualify as a confirming bank within UCP 600 because it does not act upon the authorisation or request of the issuing bank, but this does not affect a nominated bank's right of reimbursement under the credit as a non-confirming nominated bank (*Benjamin's Sale of Goods* (9th edn, 2014), para 23–021). On the other hand, where the issuing bank permits the advising bank to confirm the credit at the beneficiary's request and expense, the advising bank is treated as a confirming bank for the purposes of UCP 600 (*Fortis Bank SA/NV v Indian Overseas Bank* [2009] EWHC 2303 (Comm), [2010] 1 Lloyd's Rep 227 at [59]–[60]).

(iii) Revolving credits

A revolving credit allows the seller (beneficiary) to present documents and obtain payment as often as he wants during a credit period, so long as the overall financial limit specified in the credit is not exceeded. As each payment is made, the buyer automatically replenishes the sum that has been drawn down under the credit. A revolving credit is particularly useful when the contract of sale contemplates delivery of goods by instalments.

(iv) Transferable and non-transferable credits

Documentary credits are either transferable or non-transferable. A transferable credit allows the seller (the original beneficiary of the credit) to transfer the rights embodied in the credit to a third party, for example his own supplier. Article 38 of UCP 600 sets out a number of conditions which must be met if the credit is to be transferable. Chief amongst these are the requirements that the transferring bank must expressly consent to the extent and manner of the transfer (art 38(a)), *and* that the credit must be expressly designated as 'transferable' by the issuing bank (art 38(b)). In *Bank Negara Indonesia 1946 v Lariza (Singapore) Pte Ltd* [1988] AC 583, the Privy Council held that, for the purposes of what is now art 38(a), the transferring bank's consent 'has to be an express consent made after the request [for transfer] and it has to cover both the extent and manner of the transfer requested' (at 599, per Lord Brandon). This means that a bank may issue a transferable credit and, if it is a credit where no other bank is involved, later refuse to allow the transfer at will. The decision has been rightly criticised for reducing the usefulness of the transferable credit for financing supply transactions (CM Schmitthoff [1988] JBL 49 at 53).

The term 'transfer' is somewhat misleading. A documentary credit is not a negotiable instrument which can be transferred from one person to another by indorsement and delivery. In practice what happens when the first beneficiary (the seller) wants to transfer the credit to the second beneficiary (usually the seller's own supplier) is that he returns the credit to the transferring bank, which at the first beneficiary's request issues a new credit to the second beneficiary for the whole or part of the amount of the original credit. Where the first beneficiary transfers only a part of the credit, the balance remains payable to him. Unless otherwise stated in the credit, a transferable credit can be transferred only once (UCP 600, art 38(d)). This means that the second beneficiary is not able to transfer part of the credit in favour of his supplier, but it does not prevent the first beneficiary from transferring part of the credit to several different people, so long as the aggregate of the sums transferred does not exceed the amount of the credit and partial shipments and partial drawings are not prohibited under the credit (UCP 600, art 38(d) and (g)).

When a credit is transferred the second beneficiary is substituted to the rights and obligations of the first beneficiary (the seller) under the credit. This means that the second beneficiary can obtain payment under the credit by tendering the specified documents in his own name (the transferring bank must be careful not to reveal information about the transaction underlying the transfer to the applicant for the credit which could cause loss to the first beneficiary: see *Jackson v Royal Bank of Scotland* [2005] UKHL 3, [2005] 1 All ER (Comm) 337, where the transferring bank was held liable in damages to the first beneficiary for breach of its duty of confidentiality when it inadvertently sent the second beneficiary's invoice to the applicant, thereby revealing the size of first beneficiary's mark-up, and caused the applicant to terminate his business relationship with the first beneficiary; see further, CVM Hare [2005] LMCLQ 350). This distinguishes transfer from assignment (see below, Chapter 22). The proceeds of a credit can be assigned to a third party even though the credit is not stated to be transferable (UCP 600, art 39). But assignment does not transfer the right of performance (see A Ward and G McCormack [2001] JIBL 138). This means that even after assignment of the proceeds of the credit, the seller must still present the specified documents to the bank, or the assignee must do so on the seller's behalf.

(v) Back-to-back credits

Under a back-to-back credit arrangement the seller will use the credit opened in his favour by the buyer as security for the issue of a second credit (the back-to-back credit) in favour of the seller's own supplier. Save for those terms relating to price and time for presentation of documents, the two credits will be identical in their terms. If the seller banks with the bank which advised him of the opening of the buyer's credit, he will usually ask that bank to issue the back-to-back credit in favour of his own supplier.

(vi) Standby credits

See below, p 839.

See below, p 839.

QUESTIONS

1.   Are documentary credits negotiable instruments?

2.   From the point of view of both the seller and the buyer, what are the advantages and disadvantages of payment being made through an unconfirmed credit? See CM Schmitthoff [1957] JBL 17 at 18.

3.   What are the commercial functions of transferable credits and back-to-back credits? See *Ian Stack Ltd v Baker Bosley Ltd* [1958] 2 QB 130 at 138.

(e) Fundamental principles

(i) Strict compliance

English common law adopts the principle of strict compliance.[7] This requires that tendered documents must strictly comply with the terms of the credit. In the words of Viscount Sumner in *Equitable Trust Co of New York v Dawson Partners Ltd* (1927) 27 Ll L Rep 49 at 52: '[t]here is no room for documents which are almost the same, or which will do just as well.' The principle may be justified on several grounds. First, the banks involved in checking the documents can only be expected to be familiar with banking practices and not the commercial practices and terminology of the parties to the underlying contract which may be reflected in the terms of the credit itself. The bank cannot take on responsibility to decide which documents fulfil the underlying commercial purpose of the parties and which do not. Secondly, the banks act (at least in part) as agents of the applicant and must remain within the terms of their principal's mandate to be sure of reimbursement. In summary, for the protection of the issuing (or confirming) bank and the applicant, the bank is only obliged to pay against strictly conforming documents, and is only entitled to reimbursement if the terms of the credit have been strictly complied with.

The principle of strict compliance applies to all contracts arising out of a documentary credit transaction: the underlying contract (but see below); the contract between the applicant and the issuing bank; the contract between the issuing (and confirming) bank and the beneficiary; and the contract between the issuing and correspondent bank. There is some evidence in other jurisdictions that the degree of strictness varies according to the particular contract in issue (see B Kozolchyk in *International Encyclopedia of Comparative Law*, Vol IX, pp 82–83). In the United States, for example, some courts have applied a strict compliance standard in respect of the contract between the bank and the beneficiary but only a substantial compliance standard in the contract between the applicant and the issuing bank (*Transamerica Delaval Inc v Citibank NA*, 545 F Supp 200, 203–204 (SDNY 1982); *Far Eastern Textile Ltd v City National Bank and Trust*, 430 F Supp 193, 196 (SD Ohio 1977)). On the other hand, it seems that such a 'bifurcated standard' has not attracted wide acceptance and that 'in the overwhelming majority of US cases . . . the appropriate standard (has been held to be) the strict compliance standard' (G McLaughlin, 'The Standard of Strict Documentary Compliance in Letter of Credit Law: An American Perspective' (1990) 1 JBFLP 81). Critics of the bifurcated approach stress that '[n]othing less than strict compliance appears workable as

---

[7]   On compliance generally, see E Adodo, *Letters of Credit: The Law and Practice of Compliance* (2014).

a standard for document checkers within banks' (R Buckley, 'Documentary Compliance in Documentary Credits: Lessons from the UCC and the UCP' (2002) 1 Journal of International Commercial Law 69 at 75; cf J Dolan, 'Letter of Credit Disputes Between Issuer and Customer' (1989) 105 Banking LJ 380; 'A Principled Exception to the Strict Compliance Rule in Trilateral Letter of Credit Transactions' (2003) 18 BFLR 245).

Under English law there is little evidence of the courts applying a substantial compliance standard as opposed to a strict compliance standard. Such evidence as there is relates to the underlying contract and not to the various contracts that arise out of the credit itself.

Moralice (London) Ltd v ED and F Man
[1954] 2 Lloyd's Rep 526

The seller tendered documents to the bank showing shipment of 499.7 metric tons of sugar. The credit called for documents showing shipment of 500 metric tons. McNair J held that the bank was entitled to reject the documents as the *de minimis* rule did not apply as between the bank and the beneficiary seller, nor did it apply as between the buyer and his bank. (Note that art 30(b) of UCP 600 now provides for certain tolerances as to the quantity of goods: +/- 5 per cent subject to a number of exceptions.)

Bunge Corpn v Vegetable Vitamin Foods (Pte) Ltd
[1985] 1 Lloyd's Rep 613

Neill J held (at 616) that while the *de minimis* rule did not apply as between a bank and a beneficiary of a letter of credit, the rule did apply as between the buyer and the seller (the underlying contract was one of sale). He held that there was no breach of contract by the buyers when there were minor differences between the credit as opened and that stipulated in the contract of sale. There had been 'substantial compliance' with the contract of sale. This reasoning can be justified on the ground that, as between the seller and the buyer, what is involved is not a credit relationship, but simply one based on the underlying contract of sale.

The following cases illustrate how the principle of strict compliance has been applied by the English courts to the various relationships arising out of the credit.

(a) Bank v Applicant

Equitable Trust Co of New York v Dawson Partners Ltd
(1927) 27 Ll L Rep 49

The credit called for payment against certain documents including 'a certificate of quality to be issued by experts'. The seller tendered a certificate of quality issued by a single expert. The seller was paid. When the issuing bank tendered the certificate to the buyers, they refused to pay on grounds of non-compliance with the credit. In fact, the seller had been fraudulent and shipped mainly rubbish to the buyers. The House of Lords (by a 4:1 majority) ruled in favour of the buyers. Viscount Sumner stated (at 52) that:

> [t]here is no room for documents which are almost the same, or which will do just as well. Business could not proceed securely on any other lines. The bank's branch abroad, which knows nothing officially of the details of the transaction thus financed, cannot take upon itself to decide what will

> do well enough and what will not. If it does as it is told, it is safe; if it declines to do anything else, it is safe; if it departs from the conditions laid down, it acts at its own risk.

The same approach was recently taken in *Swotbook.com v Royal Bank of Scotland plc* [2011] EWHC 2025 (QB) at [24] (a bank v applicant case): but note that the issuing bank's application form contained a deemed compliance clause (payment by the bank was deemed to be conclusive evidence of its liability to make the payment) which was challenged by the applicant in its pleadings as unreasonable under s 3 of the Unfair Contract Terms Act 1977 (the clause was not relied on at trial and so the issue was not considered further).

(b) Beneficiary v Bank

JH Rayner & Co Ltd v Hambro Bank Ltd
[1943] KB 37

The credit referred to the shipment of 'Coromandel groundnuts' but the seller tendered a bill of lading for 'machine-shelled groundnut kernels' and an invoice for 'Coromandel groundnuts'. Although it was well known in the trade that 'Coromandel groundnuts' were the same thing as 'machine-shelled groundnut kernels', the Court of Appeal held the bank entitled to reject the bill of lading for non-compliance with the terms of credit. Mackinnon LJ stated (at 41) that '. . . it is quite impossible to suggest that a banker is to be affected with knowledge of the customs and customary terms of every one of the thousands of trades for whose dealings he may issue a letter of credit'.

(c) Bank v Bank

Bank Melli Iran v Barclays Bank DCO
[1951] 2 Lloyd's Rep 367

Bank Melli opened an irrevocable credit which was confirmed by Barclays Bank. The credit called for the tender of documents evidencing shipment of 'sixty new Chevrolet trucks'. The documents tendered by the seller included an invoice which described the trucks as 'in new condition', a certificate which described them as 'new, good, Chevrolet . . . trucks', and a delivery order describing them as 'new (hyphen) good'. Barclays Bank accepted the documents, paid the seller, and debited Bank Melli's account accordingly. Bank Melli claimed Barclays were in breach of mandate by paying against non-conforming documents. McNair J held that the descriptions in the tendered documents were inconsistent with each other and that the tender was bad. However, he went on to hold that Bank Melli had subsequently ratified the actions of its agent, Barclays Bank, who were entitled to reimbursement.

The wording of the credit is of paramount importance when determining whether there has been compliance with its terms. Even an apparently trivial discrepancy will justify rejection of the documents if the credit is specific as to that requirement.

Seaconsar Far East Ltd v Bank Markazi Jomhouri Islami Iran
[1993] 1 Lloyd's Rep 236

A confirmed irrevocable credit stipulated that all documents presented to the bank should bear the letter of credit number and the buyer's name. The seller presented documents to the advising bank and claimed payment. The advising bank refused to pay relying on the fact that one of the documents, the list of the goods shipped, did not carry the letter of credit number or the buyer's name. On the seller's application for leave to serve proceedings on the issuing bank out of the jurisdiction, the Court of Appeal, by a majority, held that the tender was clearly bad and refused leave. Lloyd and Beldam LJJ rejected submissions that the omission was trivial and that, in any event, it could be cured by reference to the other tendered documents which all carried the necessary particulars. Their Lordships emphasised that neither of these arguments could apply when the credit clearly and expressly required each document to contain the necessary particulars. Stuart-Smith LJ, dissenting, thought that the seller's case was not 'unworthy of consideration'. The House of Lords later reversed the Court of Appeal on other grounds and gave the seller leave to serve out of the jurisdiction (see [1994] 1 AC 438). When the case later came back to the Court of Appeal on its merits (see [1999] 1 Lloyd's Rep 36), the fact that there were discrepancies in the tendered documents was admitted. Sir Christopher Staughton, delivering the only reasoned judgment of the court, observed (at 38) that 'the discrepancies in the documents do not appear to be of any great significance. But that is neither here nor there. It is hornbook law for bankers that the documents must appear on their face to be precisely in accordance with the terms and conditions of the credit.'

On the other hand, the courts are willing to overlook a trivial defect in the tendered documents where there is a patent typographical error, or other obvious slip or omission.

Seaconsar Far East Ltd v Bank Markazi Jomhouri Islami Iran
[1993] 1 Lloyd's Rep 236

> **Lloyd LJ:** It would not, I think, help to attempt to define the sort of discrepancy which can properly be regarded as trivial. But one might take, by way of example, *Bankers Trust Co v State Bank of India* [1991] 2 Lloyd's Rep 443, where one of the documents gave the buyer's telex number as 931310 instead of 981310.

(Note that under art 14(j) of UCP 600 contact details (fax, telephone, email, and the like) stated as part of the beneficiary's and the applicant's address are now to be disregarded unless they are of the applicant and appear as part of the consignee or notify party details on a transport document.)

Hing Yip Hing Fat Co Ltd v Daiwa Bank Ltd
[1991] 2 HKLR 35

The Supreme Court of Hong Kong held that there had been a patent typographical error, and no discrepancy, when a document tendered to the issuing bank by the beneficiary gave the name of the applicant for the credit as 'Cheergoal Industrial Limited', when it should have been 'Cheergoal Industries Limited'.

But where it is not clear whether the departure from the detail set out in the credit was a draftsman's error or not, the discrepancy justifies the rejection of the documents (see, eg, *Bulgrains & Co Ltd v Shinhan Bank* [2013] EWHC 2498 (QB) at [24], where the claimant beneficiary was identified in the credit as 'Bulgrains Co Ltd' and in the tendered commercial invoice as 'Bulgrains & Co Ltd', and it was held 'that there was a discrepancy as to name that was not clearly and demonstrably simply a typographical error and was material'). It is sometimes difficult to draw a clear line between the two types of case.

There is evidence that the English courts have moved away from a 'mirror image' approach to strict compliance which had been the favoured approach for many years (see above).

Kredietbank Antwerp v Midland Bank plc
[1999] 1 All ER (Comm) 801

The credit specified 'Draft survey report issued by Griffith Inspectorate at port of loading'. The claimant accepted a draft survey report signed on behalf of Daniel C Griffith (Holland) BV, which was described as a 'member of the worldwide inspectorate group'. The defendant rejected the document on the ground that it was not issued by 'Griffith Inspectorate'. The Court of Appeal held that the document was conforming. Evans LJ began by citing those cases where the courts had drawn a line between 'trivial' discrepancies and those which require the bank to reject the tendered documents (see above). He continued (at 806):

> For these reasons, the requirement of strict compliance is not equivalent to a test of exact literal compliance in all circumstances and as regards all documents. To some extent, therefore, the banker must exercise his own judgment whether the requirement is satisfied by the documents presented to him.

The case illustrates that whilst the English courts continue to apply the strict compliance rule, they do not take a mechanical or robotic approach to documentary compliance. Of course, how far a court can move away from strict literal compliance remains governed by the precise wording of the credit. On the other hand, the case in no way implies that the English courts require a bank to exercise its judgment as to whether the tendered document fulfils the same commercial purpose as the document called for in the credit. A bank cannot be expected to know the commercial practices of the parties.

The strict compliance rule is commercially convenient in that it enables banks to make quick decisions about the documents presented to them. In fact, it is estimated that approximately 70 per cent of documents initially presented to banks are discrepant (Introduction to UCP 600, p 11). In many cases discrepancies are easily remedied by the seller and the documents represented to the bank. The seller usually has time to do this because the bank must specify all of the discrepancies in a notice of rejection which must be given no later than the close of the fifth banking day following receipt of the documents (UCP 600, art 16(c)(ii) and (d)). In other cases, the discrepancies are waived by the buyer. But this may not always happen. The strict compliance rule allows documents to be rejected for insubstantial discrepancies. This may facilitate or encourage what has been described as 'bad faith rejection of documents'. Although the bank may approach the buyer for waiver of the discrepancy, it may not be in the buyer's wider commercial interests to agree to this, for example where the market has fallen and he can now obtain the same goods at a lower price. However, in *Glencore International AG v Bank of China* [1996] 1 Lloyd's Rep 135 at 153, Sir Thomas Bingham MR observed:

> [t]he judge described the Bank of China's argument as 'very technical' and observed that it might appear to lack merit. Both comments are apt. But a rule of strict compliance gives little scope for recognizing the merits.

A 'mirror image' interpretation of the strict compliance rule is probably unworkable in practice. Rejection of tendered documents becomes the norm. Bankers have recognised this for some time. This has led the ICC to promote a more flexible approach to documentary compliance. There were signs of this in UCP 500 and many of the changes introduced by UCP 600 are designed to move away from 'mirror image' compliance of tendered documents with the credit towards a 'functional standard of documentary verification' that allows the credit to function as a payment instrument, something it cannot do when so many documents are rejected on first tender.

The ICC's philosophy is enshrined in the definition of a 'complying presentation' which can be found in art 2 of UCP 600 (see above, p 774). It will be recalled that a complying presentation is one in accordance with, inter alia, 'international standard banking practices'. A bank cannot be expected to know the commercial practices of the parties to the underlying contract but it can be expected to be aware of the standards of international banking practice (*Kredietbank Antwerp v Midland Bank plc* [1999] 1 All ER (Comm) 801 at 804, per Evans LJ: 'The professional expertise of a trading bank includes knowledge of the UCP rules and of their practical application'). The ICC has detailed relevant practices in a publication called the *International Standard Banking Practice for the Examination of Documents under UCP 600* (2013 revision, ICC Publication No 745) (ISBP). The ISBP will be relevant when an issue of banking practice comes before the courts. In *Crédit Industriel et Commercial v China Merchants Bank* [2002] EWHC 973 (Comm), [2002] 2 All ER (Comm) 427 at [62], David Steel J considered that the opinions of the ICC Banking Commission were entitled to considerable weight, and we can add that the same must also be said of the ISBP. But the ISBP merely represents one source of international standard banking practice: it is not the exclusive source. Expert evidence can still be relied upon by the parties to a dispute to establish a local or regional banking practice which may be at odds with that found in the ISBP (see EP Ellinger [2007] LMCLQ 152 at 159).

The latest revision of the UCP contains a number of new provisions which are designed to ensure that tendered documents are not rejected for overly technical reasons. Two examples can be taken from art 14 of UCP 600.

- Sub-article 14(d) provides that data in a document, when read in context with the credit, the document itself, and international standard banking practice, need not be identical to, but must not conflict with, data in that document, any other stipulated document, or the credit. Documents need not be mirror images of each other, but merely that they must not be inconsistent.

- Sub-article 14(f) provides that if a credit requires presentation of a document other than a transport document, insurance document, or commercial invoice, without stipulating by whom the document is to be issued or its data content, banks will accept the document as presented if its content appears to fulfil the function of the required document and otherwise complies with sub-art 14(d). Sub-article 14(f) seems to take data content out of the equation when there is no stipulation as to what it should be. For example, if the credit calls for an inspection certificate without more, the condition will be satisfied if an inspection certificate is presented even if it does not 'pass' the goods. If the buyer wants tender of an inspection certificate which states that the goods have passed inspection, then he must specify this in his application to the issuing bank to open the credit and the credit must be issued in those terms.

Under English common law, if the descriptions of the goods in the documents read as a whole comply with the description in the credit that is sufficient unless the credit specifies otherwise or there are inconsistencies between the tendered documents. Article 18(c) of UCP 600 provides that the description of the goods in the commercial invoice must correspond with the description in the credit. Article 14(e) of UCP 600 provides that in all other documents, the goods may be described in general terms not inconsistent with the description of the goods in the credit. Both requirements were previously to be found in art 37(c) of UCP 500. Whether the requirements of art 37(c) had been met was at issue in the following cases.

Glencore International AG v Bank of China
[1996] 1 Lloyd's Rep 135

The issuing bank argued that the description of the goods (aluminium ingots) contained in the commercial invoice ('Origin: Any Western brand—Indonesia (Inalum Brand)') was inconsistent with that in the credit ('Origin: Any Western brand'). The Court of Appeal rejected that argument on the basis that the description in the commercial invoice fell within the broad generic nature of the description in the credit.

Packing lists and other specified documents were tendered by the beneficiary and negotiating bank to the issuing bank, but the issuing bank claimed that the packing lists were discrepant as they did not describe the goods as required by the credit. The Court of Appeal rejected this argument, as it required each document to be examined in isolation, and held that the packing lists and other tendered documents formed a set of documents which should be read and considered together, the linkage between the documents being clear and exact and devoid of discrepancy (but it remains the case that the goods must still be properly *identified* in each document: *Banque de l'Indochine et de Suez SA v JH Rayner (Mincing Lane) Ltd* [1983] QB 711 at 732, CA).

Crédit Agricole Indosuez v Chailease Finance Corpn
[2000] 1 All ER (Comm) 399

The underlying contract related to the sale of a ship. The bank claimed: (1) that the tendered bill of sale and signed acceptance of sale, which stated that delivery had taken place on 21 August 1998, did not comply with the terms of the letter of credit, which required the documents to state a delivery date within 17–20 August; and (2) that, because of the difference in the stated dates of delivery, the description of the vessel in the tendered documents was inconsistent with that in the letter of credit. The Court of Appeal held that the tendered documents were not discrepant. As to (1), the court held that the letter of credit did not state that the documents had to show that the vessel had been delivered within a range of dates. As to (2), the court agreed (*obiter*) with the trial judge that, on a true construction of the credit, the words 'for delivery . . . during 17–20 August 1998' were not part of the description of the goods. In any event, the court held that as there was ample descriptive information in the acceptance and the bill of sale which made clear that the vessel delivered and accepted was the vessel the subject of the sale agreement, so that the date of actual delivery stated, ie one day beyond the range of dates, did not render the description of the vessel in the documents inconsistent with the description of the goods in the credit.

The basic rule is that original documents must be tendered to the bank, unless the credit calls for copy documents. But, in a world dominated by the word processor and the photocopier, there has been uncertainty as to what constitutes an original document, uncertainty that has been reflected in the case law. So far as UCP 500 was concerned, the relevant article was art 20(b):

> Unless otherwise stipulated in the credit, banks will also accept as an original document(s), a document(s) produced or appearing to have been produced:
>
> i. by reprographic, automated or computerized systems;
> ii. as carbon copies;
>
> provided that it is marked as original and, where necessary, appears to be signed. A document may be signed by handwriting, by facsimile signature, by perforated signature, by stamp, by symbol, or by other mechanical or electronic method of authentication.

In *Glencore International AC v Bank of China* [1996] 1 Lloyd's Rep 135, the Court of Appeal held that whilst an original handwritten or originally typed document was acceptable, a signed photocopy of a word processed document was not an 'original' document and could be rejected on presentation unless 'marked as original' as required by art 20(b) of UCP 500. Dicta in *Glencore* even suggested that, on a true interpretation of art 20(b), a word processed document was not an original document and could be rejected unless 'marked as original'. The issue arose in *Kredietbank Antwerp v Midland Bank plc* [1999] 1 All ER (Comm) 801, where the Court of Appeal held that so long as the word processed document was *clearly* an original document—'in the sense that it contains the relevant contract, and which is not itself a copy of some other document'—it should be treated as such. Both decisions were reviewed by Steel J in *Crédit Industriel et Commercial v China Merchants Bank* [2002] EWHC 973 (Comm), [2002] 2 All ER (Comm) 427. In this case it was unclear how the relevant documents had been produced but the judge held that the issuing bank was not entitled to reject them as not being original documents. Steel J held that it was appropriate to apply the ICC's Policy Statement published on 12 July 1999. In essence, the Policy Statement embodied the general principle upheld in the *Kredietbank* case, namely that art 20(b) did not apply to a document which appeared on its face to be an original. For these purposes, an original would include a photocopy if it was hand signed by the issuer, or if it was produced on original stationery rather than blank paper. In *Glencore*, the documents were photocopies produced on blank paper but signed. Under the Policy Statement, these documents would be treated as originals.

This would now also be the position under UCP 600 which addresses the problem in art 17 as follows:

> a. At least one original of each document stipulated in the credit must be presented.
> b. A bank shall treat as an original any document bearing an apparently original signature, mark, stamp or label of the issuer of the document, unless the document itself indicates that it is not an original.
> c. Unless a document indicates otherwise, a bank will also accept a document as an original if it:
>   i.   appears to be written, typed, perforated or stamped by the document issuer's hand; or
>   ii. appears to be on the document issuer's original stationery; or
>   iii. states that it is original, unless the statement appears not to apply to the document presented.

Article 17 goes on to permit the presentation of either originals or copies if a credit requires presentation of copies of documents (UCP 600, art 17(d)). In addition, if a credit requires presentation of multiple documents by using terms such as 'in duplicate', 'in two fold', or 'in two copies', this can be satisfied by the presentation of at least one original and the remaining number in copies, except when the document itself indicates otherwise (UCP 600, art 17(e)).

QUESTION

Which approach to the doctrine of documentary compliance better promotes commercial certainty: the 'mirror image' approach (evident in the English cases) or the 'functional standard of verification' approach (promoted by the ICC)?

(ii) Autonomy of the credit

A documentary credit is separate from and independent of the underlying contract between the seller and the buyer, and the relationship between the issuing bank and the buyer.[8] In general, therefore, the seller's breach of the underlying contract is no defence to the issuing bank (or to the confirming bank). It is irrelevant to the performance of the credit that the buyer alleges, for example, that the shipped goods are not of satisfactory quality, or fit for their purpose, or that there has been a shortfall in delivery. By the same token, the issuing bank cannot refuse to honour its undertaking just because of the buyer's failure to put it in funds.

The principle of autonomy of the credit is enshrined in the UCP. Article 4(a) of UCP 600 provides that '[a] credit by its nature is a separate transaction from the sale or other contract on which it may be based. Banks are in no way concerned with or bound by such contract, even if any reference whatsoever to it is included in the credit.' The autonomy rule is also linked to the principle, to be found in art 5, that in credit operations '[b]anks deal with documents and not with goods, services or performance to which the documents may relate'. Similarly, art 34 makes clear that in credit operations banks have no responsibility for anything other than conformity of the documents to the credit.

The English courts have applied the principle of autonomy of the credit on numerous occasions. The following case illustrates the point.

Hamzeh Malas & Sons v British Imex Industries Ltd
[1958] 2 QB 127, Court of Appeal

Jordanian buyers (the plaintiffs) agreed to purchase from British sellers (the defendants) a quantity of steel rods, to be delivered in two instalments. Payment for each instalment was to be by two confirmed letters of credit. The buyers duly opened the two credits with the Midland Bank Ltd. The sellers delivered the first instalment and were paid under the first credit. The buyers then complained that that instalment was defective and sought an injunction to restrain the sellers from drawing on the second credit. Donovan J refused to grant the injunction and the buyers appealed against that order.

---

[8] See, generally, N Enonchong, *The Independence Principle of Letters of Credit and Demand Guarantees* (2011); see also R Goode, 'Abstract Payment Undertakings and the Rules of the International Chamber of Commerce' (1995) 39 Saint Louis Univ LJ 725 and 'Abstract Payment Undertakings in International Transactions' (1996) 22 Brooklyn J Int'l L 1.

Jenkins LJ stated the facts and continued: It appears that when the first consignment of steel rods arrived they were, according to the plaintiffs, by no means up to contract quality and many criticisms were made on that score. That is a matter in issue between the parties. In the meantime the plaintiffs wish to secure themselves in respect of any damages they may be found to be entitled to when this dispute is ultimately tried out, by preventing the defendants from dealing with this outstanding letter of credit. Mr Gardiner [counsel for the plaintiffs], in effect, treats this as no more than part of the price, a sum earmarked to pay for the goods bought under the contract, which the plaintiffs have become entitled to repudiate; and he says that the defendants ought, accordingly, to be restrained from dealing with the amount of this letter of credit. He points out that he is not seeking any order against the bank, but merely against the defendants.

We have been referred to a number of authorities, and it seems to be plain enough that the opening of a confirmed letter of credit constitutes a bargain between the banker and the vendor of the goods, which imposes upon the banker an absolute obligation to pay, irrespective of any dispute there may be between the parties as to whether the goods are up to contract or not. An elaborate commercial system has been built up on the footing that bankers' confirmed credits are of that character, and, in my judgment, it would be wrong for this court in the present case to interfere with that established practice.

There is this to be remembered too. A vendor of goods selling against a confirmed letter of credit is selling under the assurance that nothing will prevent him from receiving the price. That is of no mean advantage when goods manufactured in one country are being sold in another. It is, furthermore, to be observed that vendors are often reselling goods bought from third parties. When they are doing that, and when they are being paid by a confirmed letter of credit, their practice is—and I think it was followed by the defendants in this case—to finance the payments necessary to be made to their suppliers against the letter of credit. That system of financing these operations, as I see it, would break down completely if a dispute as between the vendor and the purchaser was to have the effect of 'freezing,' if I may use that expression, the sum in respect of which the letter of credit was opened.

I agree with Mr Gardiner that this is not a case where it can be said that the court has no jurisdiction to interfere. The court's jurisdiction to grant injunctions is wide, but, in my judgment, this is not a case in which the court ought, in the exercise of its discretion, to grant an injunction. Accordingly, I think this application should be refused.

Sellers LJ: I agree, but I would repeat what my Lord has said on jurisdiction. I would not like it to be taken that I accept, or that the court accepts, the submission if it was made, as I think it was, that the court has no jurisdiction. There may well be cases where the court would exercise jurisdiction as in a case where there is a fraudulent transaction.

Pearce LJ: I agree.

NOTES

1. The courts have consistently defended the autonomy principle on the ground that irrevocable documentary credits are 'the life-blood of international commerce' which 'must be allowed to be honoured, free from interference by the courts. Otherwise, trust in international commerce could be irreparably damaged' (*RD Harbottle (Mercantile) Ltd v National Westminster Bank Ltd* [1978] QB 146 at 155–156, per Kerr J: below, p 846). The commercial value of the documentary credit system lies in the fact that payment under the credit is virtually assured. Certainty of payment is of paramount importance to the business community and so irrevocable credits are treated like cash by the courts.

2. The autonomy rule is not absolute. The most important exception to the rule is where there is fraud on the part of the beneficiary or his agent in relation to the presentation of documents to the bank. Nevertheless, even in cases of fraud the bank must pay the holder in due course of a bill of exchange accepted by the bank under the terms of the credit on the ground that the bill creates an autonomous contract independent of the documentary credit itself (*Discount Records Ltd v Barclays Bank Ltd* [1975] 1 All ER 1071). The fraud exception is considered in greater detail below.

3. In *Sirius International Insurance Corpn (Publ) v FAI General Insurance Co Ltd* [2003] EWCA Civ 470, [2003] 1 All ER (Comm) 865, the Court of Appeal held that the principle of autonomy did not mean that a beneficiary could draw on a letter of credit when it had expressly agreed not to do so unless certain conditions were satisfied and those conditions had not been met. In this case, the restrictions were contained in a separate agreement made between the beneficiary (Sirius) and the applicant (FAI). May LJ held (at [27]) that:

> although those restrictions were not terms of the letter of credit, and although the bank would have been obliged and entitled to honour a request to pay which fulfilled its terms, that does not mean that, as between themselves and FAI, Sirius were entitled to draw on the letter of credit if the express conditions of this underlying agreement were not fulfilled. They were not so entitled.

The Court of Appeal were also of the opinion that if draw-down was attempted in these circumstances, a court would be likely to grant an injunction restraining the beneficiary from drawing on the letter of credit in breach of express conditions contained in the separate agreement. It should be noted that fraud was not alleged against Sirius and so the case does not fall within the fraud exception to the autonomy principle considered in the next section. The House of Lords later reversed the Court of Appeal's decision on the ground that the express conditions to draw-down had been satisfied. Their Lordships found it unnecessary to examine arguments about the autonomy principle: [2004] UKHL 54, [2004] 1 WLR 3251.

4. The *Sirius* case raises important questions about the extent of the autonomy principle. There must be some concern as to how far it undermines the principle and its consequential benefits of commercial certainty. However, the English courts have not shown themselves willing to embrace the wider principle of 'unconscionable demand' which has gained judicial support in Singapore in the area of independent guarantees (see P Ellinger and D Neo, *The Law and Practice of Documentary Letters of Credit* (2010), pp 319 ff). It is not entirely clear what constitutes unconscionability, although it seems to be something more than unfairness and less than fraud, nor as to the standard of proof required to obtain injunctive relief on this ground (see Ganotaki [2004] LMCLQ 148 at 152). The uncertainty that this creates is obvious. Nevertheless, there have been dicta in recent English cases which suggest that the previous reluctance to apply a concept of 'unconscionability' may not last forever (see, especially, the dicta of Potter LJ in *Montrod Ltd v Grundkötter Fleischvertriebs* [2001] EWCA Civ 1954, [2002] 1 WLR 1975 at [59] (below, p 794), and also that of Judge Thornton QC, sitting as a deputy High Court judge, in *TTI Team Telecom International Ltd v Hutchison 3G UK Ltd* [2003] EWHC 762 (TCC), [2003] 1 All ER (Comm) 914 at [37]).

5. The concept of 'unconscionability' might find acceptance in the area of independent guarantees, which perform a security function as opposed to a payment function. In *Simon Carves Ltd v Ensus UK Ltd* [2011] EWHC 657 (TCC), [2011] BLR 340, Akenhead J granted an injunction restraining a beneficiary from seeking payment under a performance bond on

the ground that the issuing bank had a strong case that, as between it and the beneficiary, the bond was null and void pursuant to the terms of the underlying contract. Akenhead J said (at [33]) that:

> in principle, if the underlying contract, in relation to which the bond has been provided by way of security, clearly and expressly prevents the beneficiary party to the contract from making the demand under the bond, it can be restrained by the Court from making a demand under the bond.

Akenhead J tentatively thought that this might constitute a second type of exception (the other being fraud) to the general principle that the court will not act to prevent a beneficiary calling on a demand guarantee or performance bond. In *Doosan Babcock Ltd v Comercializadora de Equipos y Materiales Mabe Limitada* [2013] EWHC 3201 (TCC), [2014] BLR 33, Edwards-Stuart J said (at [36]) that Akenhead J's judgment 'has extended the law, but in my view it has done so adopting a principled and incremental approach that does not undermine the general principles applicable to making a call on a bond'. It has recently been stressed that in order to obtain injunctive relief 'it must be positively established that the beneficiary was not entitled to draw down under the underlying contract' (*MW High Tech Projects UK Ltd v Biffa Waste Services Ltd* [2015] EWHC 949 (TCC) at [34], per Stuart-Smith J).

(iii) Autonomy and the fraud exception

(a) Fraud in relation to the tendered documents

The classic statement of the fraud exception to the autonomy principle is to be found in the judgments of Lord Diplock in *United City Merchants (Investments) Ltd v Royal Bank of Canada* [1983] 1 AC 168 (below). Lord Diplock began by affirming the principle that with credits the parties deal in documents and not in goods, and that a bank is obliged to pay if on their face the documents presented conform to the credit notwithstanding that the bank may know of a dispute between the buyer and the seller as to the underlying contract of sale. He continued (at 183):

> To this general statement of principle as to the contractual obligations of the confirming bank to the seller, there is one established exception: that is where the seller, for the purposes of drawing on the credit, fraudulently presents to the confirming bank documents that contain, expressly or by implication, material representations of fact that to his knowledge are untrue.

Lord Diplock explained the rationale for the fraud exception in terms of an application of the maxim *ex turpi causa non oritur actio* or, in plain English, 'fraud unravels all'. The courts will not allow their process to be used by a dishonest person to carry out a fraud. In *Czarnikow-Rionda Sugar Trading Inc v Standard Bank London Ltd* [1999] 1 All ER (Comm) 890 at 914, when considering a claim for an injunction against an issuing bank and the need to find a substantive cause of action against the party to be restrained, Rix J said that Lord Diplock's reference to the *ex turpi causa* principle 'may appropriately be viewed as an authoritative expression of the source in law of the implied limitation on a bank's mandate'. More recently, in *Mahonia Ltd v JP Morgan Chase Bank* [2003] EWHC 1927 (Comm), [2003] 2 Lloyd's Rep 911 at [39], Colman J held that the *ex turpi causa* explanation 'accords more comfortably with principle and is therefore to be preferred'.

United City Merchants (Investments) Ltd v Royal Bank of Canada, The American Accord

[1983] 1 AC 168, House of Lords

English sellers sold manufacturing equipment to Peruvian buyers and agreed to invoice for the order at twice the correct price, to enable the buyers to evade Peruvian exchange control regulations. Payment was to be made by confirmed irrevocable credit, and this was issued by the buyers' bank and confirmed by Royal Bank of Canada. The goods were shipped on 16 December 1976. However, the credit specified that the last day for shipment was 15 December 1976 and so the carriers' agent fraudulently issued a bill of lading showing shipment to have been made on 15 December. The sellers knew nothing of this fraud. On presentation of the documents the confirming bank refused to pay on the ground that it had information suggesting that shipment had not taken place on the day stated in the bill of lading. The sellers (strictly, the assignees of their rights under the credit) sued the confirming bank under the credit.

Mocatta J held that, as the sellers were innocent of the fraud of the carriers' agent, the bank was wrong to refuse payment of documents which, on their face, appeared to be in order. But, in a second judgment, he held that, because of the breach of Peruvian exchange control regulations, the credit was rendered unenforceable under the Bretton Woods Agreements Order in Council 1946. The Court of Appeal dismissed the sellers' appeal on the ground that whilst it was possible to divide the credit and allow payment for that half of the invoice price which did not infringe the exchange control regulations, the bank had been entitled to rely on the fraud of the carriers' agent and refuse payment of any sum. The sellers appealed.

Lord Diplock:

THE DOCUMENTARY CREDIT POINT

My Lords, for the proposition upon the documentary credit point, both in the broad form for which counsel for the confirming bank have strenuously argued at all stages of this appeal and in the narrower form or 'halfway house' that commended itself to the Court of Appeal, there is no direct authority to be found either in English or Privy Council cases or among the numerous decisions of courts in the United States of America to which reference is made in the judgments of the Court of Appeal in the instant case. So the point falls to be decided by reference to first principles as to the legal nature of the contractual obligations assumed by the various parties to a transaction consisting of an international sale of goods to be financed by means of a confirmed irrevocable documentary credit. It is trite law that there are four autonomous though interconnected contractual relationships involved. (1) The underlying contract for the sale of goods, to which the only parties are the buyer and the seller; (2) the contract between the buyer and the issuing bank under which the latter agrees to issue the credit and either itself or through a confirming bank to notify the credit to the seller and to make payments to or to the order of the seller (or to pay, accept or negotiate bills of exchange drawn by the seller) against presentation of stipulated documents; and the buyer agrees to reimburse the issuing bank for payments made under the credit. For such reimbursement the stipulated documents, if they include a document of title such as a bill of lading, constitute a security available to the issuing bank; (3) if payment is to be made through a confirming bank the contract between the issuing bank and the confirming bank authorising and requiring the latter to make such payments and to remit the stipulated documents to the issuing bank when they are received, the issuing bank in turn agreeing to reimburse the confirming bank for payments made under the credit; (4) the contract between the confirming bank and the seller under which the confirming bank undertakes to pay to the seller (or to accept or negotiate without recourse to drawer bills of exchange drawn by him) up to the amount of the credit against presentation of the stipulated documents.

Again, it is trite law that in contract (4), with which alone the instant appeal is directly concerned, the parties to it, the seller and the confirming bank, 'deal in documents and not in goods,' as art 8 of the Uniform Customs [1974 Revision; now art 5, UCP 2007 Revision] puts it. If, on their face, the documents presented to the confirming bank by the seller conform with the requirements of the credit as notified to him by the confirming bank, that bank is under a contractual obligation to the seller to honour the credit, notwithstanding that the bank has knowledge that the seller at the time of presentation of the conforming documents is alleged by the buyer to have, and in fact has already, committed a breach of his contract with the buyer for the sale of the goods to which the documents appear on their face to relate, that would have entitled the buyer to treat the contract of sale as rescinded and to reject the goods and refuse to pay the seller the purchase price. The whole commercial purpose for which the system of confirmed irrevocable documentary credits has been developed in international trade is to give to the seller an assured right to be paid before he parts with control of the goods that does not permit of any dispute with the buyer as to the performance of the contract of sale being used as a ground for non-payment or reduction or deferment of payment.

To this general statement of principle as to the contractual obligations of the confirming bank to the seller, there is one established exception: that is, where the seller, for the purpose of drawing on the credit, fraudulently presents to the confirming bank documents that contain, expressly or by implication, material representations of fact that to his knowledge are untrue. Although there does not appear among the English authorities any case in which this exception has been applied, it is well established in the American cases of which the leading or 'landmark' case is *Sztejn v J Henry Schroder Banking Corpn* 31 NYS 2d 631 (1941). This judgment of the New York Court of Appeals was referred to with approval by the English Court of Appeal in *Edward Owen Engineering Ltd v Barclays Bank International Ltd* [1978] QB 159 [below, p 845], though this was actually a case about a performance bond under which a bank assumes obligations to a buyer analogous to those assumed by a confirming bank to the seller under a documentary credit. The exception for fraud on the part of the beneficiary seeking to avail himself of the credit is a clear application of the maxim *ex turpi causa non oritur actio* or, if plain English is to be preferred, 'fraud unravels all.' The courts will not allow their process to be used by a dishonest person to carry out a fraud.

The instant case, however, does not fall within the fraud exception. Mocatta J found the sellers to have been unaware of the inaccuracy of Mr Baker's notation of the date at which the goods were actually on board *American Accord*. They believed that it was true and that the goods had actually been loaded on or before December 15 1976, as required by the documentary credit.

Faced by this finding, the argument for the confirming bank before Mocatta J was directed to supporting the broad proposition: that a confirming bank is not under any obligation, legally enforceable against it by the seller/beneficiary of a documentary credit, to pay to him the sum stipulated in the credit against presentation of documents, if the documents presented, although conforming on their face with the terms of the credit, nevertheless contain some statement of material fact that is not accurate. This proposition which does not call for knowledge on the part of the seller/beneficiary of the existence of any inaccuracy would embrace the fraud exception and render it superfluous.

My Lords, the more closely this bold proposition is subjected to legal analysis, the more implausible it becomes; to assent to it would, in my view, undermine the whole system of financing international trade by means of documentary credits.

It has, so far as I know, never been disputed that as between confirming bank and issuing bank and as between issuing bank and the buyer the contractual duty of each bank under a confirmed irrevocable credit is to examine with reasonable care all documents presented in order to ascertain that they appear *on their face* to be in accordance with the terms and conditions of the credit, and, if they do so appear, to pay to the seller/beneficiary by whom the documents have been presented the sum stipulated by the credit, or to accept or negotiate without recourse to drawer drafts drawn by the seller/beneficiary if the credit so provides. It is so stated in the latest edition of the Uniform Customs. It is equally clear law, and is so provided by art 9 of the Uniform Customs [1974 Revision; now UCP 2007 Revision, art 34], that confirming banks and issuing banks assume no liability or responsibility to one another or to the buyer 'for the form, sufficiency, accuracy, genuineness, falsification or legal effect of any documents.' This is well illustrated by the Privy Council case of *Gian Singh & Co Ltd v Banque de l'Indochine* [1974] 1 WLR 1234 [below, p 820], where the customer was held liable to reimburse the issuing bank for honouring a documentary credit upon presentation of an apparently conforming document which was an ingenious forgery, a fact that the bank had not been negligent in failing to detect upon examination of the document.

It would be strange from the commercial point of view, although not theoretically impossible in law, if the contractual duty owed by confirming and issuing banks to the buyer to honour the credit on presentation of apparently conforming documents despite the fact that they contain inaccuracies or even are forged, were not matched by a corresponding contractual liability of the confirming bank to the seller/beneficiary (in the absence, of course, of any fraud on his part) to pay the sum stipulated in the credit upon presentation of apparently conforming documents. Yet, as is conceded by counsel for the confirming bank in the instant case, if the broad proposition for which he argues is correct, the contractual duties do not match. As respects the confirming bank's contractual duty to the seller to honour the credit, the bank, it is submitted, is only bound to pay upon presentation of documents which not only appear on their face to be in accordance with the terms and conditions of the credit but also do not in fact contain any material statement that is inaccurate. If this submission be correct, the bank's contractual right to refuse to honour the documentary credit cannot, as a matter of legal analysis, depend upon whether *at the time of the refusal* the bank was virtually certain from information obtained by means other than reasonably careful examination of the documents themselves that they contained some material statement that was inaccurate or whether the bank merely suspected this or even had no suspicion that apparently conforming documents contained any inaccuracies at all. If there be any such right of refusal it must depend upon whether the bank, when sued by the seller/beneficiary for breach of its contract to honour the credit, is able to prove that one of the documents did in fact contain what was a material misstatement.

It is conceded that to justify refusal the misstatement must be 'material' but this invites the query: 'material to what?' The suggested answer to this query was: a misstatement of a fact which if the true fact had been disclosed would have entitled the buyer to reject the goods; date of shipment (as in the instant case) or misdescription of the goods are examples. But this is to destroy the autonomy of the documentary credit which is its raison d'être; it is to make the seller's right to payment by the confirming bank dependent upon the buyer's rights against the seller under the terms of the contract for the sale of goods, of which the confirming bank will have no knowledge.

Counsel sought to evade the difficulties disclosed by an analysis of the legal consequences of his broad proposition by praying in aid the practical consideration that a bank, desirous as it would be of protecting its reputation in the competitive business of providing documentary credits, would never exercise its right against a seller/beneficiary to refuse to honour the credit except in cases where at the time of the refusal it already was in possession of irrefutable evidence of the inaccuracy in the documents presented. I must confess that the argument that a seller should be content to rely upon the exercise by banks of business expediency, unbacked by any legal liability, to ensure prompt payment by a foreign buyer does not impress me; but the assumption that underlies reliance upon expediency does not, in my view, itself stand up to legal analysis. Business expediency would not induce the bank to pay the seller/beneficiary against presentation of documents which it was not legally liable to accept as complying with the documentary credit unless, in doing so, it acquired a right legally enforceable against the buyer, to require him to take up the documents himself and reimburse the bank for the amount paid. So any reliance upon business expediency to make the system work if the broad proposition contended for by counsel is correct, must involve that as against the buyer, the bank, when presented with apparently conforming documents by the seller, is legally entitled to the option, *exercisable at its own discretion and regardless of any instructions to the contrary from the buyer*, either (1) to take up the documents and pay the credit and claim reimbursement from the buyer, notwithstanding that the bank has been provided with information that makes it virtually certain that the existence of such inaccuracies can be proved, or (2) to reject the documents and to refuse to pay the credit.

The legal justification for the existence of such an independently exercisable option, it is suggested, lies in the bank's own interest in the goods to which the documents relate, as security for the advance made by the bank to the buyer, when it pays the seller under the documentary credit. But if this were so, the answer to the question: 'to what must the misstatement in the documents be material?' should be: 'material to the price which the goods to which the documents relate would fetch on sale if, failing reimbursement by the buyer, the bank should be driven to realise its security.' But this would not justify the confirming bank's refusal to honour the credit in the instant case; the realisable value on arrival at Callao of a glass fibre manufacturing plant made to the specification of the buyers could not be in any way affected by its having been loaded on board a ship at Felixstowe on December 16, instead of December 15, 1976 . . .

The proposition accepted by the Court of Appeal as constituting a complete defence available to the confirming bank on the documentary credit point has been referred to as a 'half-way house' because it lies not only halfway between the unqualified liability of the confirming bank to honour a documentary credit on presentation of documents which upon reasonably careful examination appear to conform to the terms and conditions of the credit, and what I have referred to as the fraud exception to this unqualified liability which is available to the confirming bank where the seller/beneficiary presents to the confirming bank documents that contain, expressly or by implication, material representations of fact that to his own knowledge are untrue; but it also lies half way between the fraud exception and the broad proposition favoured by the confirming bank with which I have hitherto been dealing. The half-way house is erected upon the narrower proposition that if any of the documents presented under the credit by the seller/beneficiary contain a material misrepresentation of fact that was *false to the knowledge of the person who issued the document* and intended by him to deceive persons into whose hands the document might come, the confirming bank is under no liability to honour the credit, even though, as in the instant case, the persons whom the issuer of the document intended to, and did, deceive included the seller/beneficiary himself.

My Lords, if the broad proposition for which the confirming bank has argued is unacceptable for the reasons that I have already discussed, what rational ground can there be for drawing any distinction between apparently conforming documents that, unknown to the seller, in fact contain a statement of fact that is inaccurate where the inaccuracy was due to inadvertence by the maker of the document, and the like documents where the same inaccuracy had been inserted by the maker of the document with intent to deceive, among others, the seller/beneficiary himself? Ex hypothesi we are dealing only with a case in which the seller/beneficiary claiming under the credit *has* been deceived, for if he presented documents to the confirming bank with knowledge that this apparent conformity with the terms and conditions of the credit was due to the fact that the documents told a lie, the seller/beneficiary would himself be a party to the misrepresentation made to the confirming bank by the lie in the documents and the case would come within the fraud exception, as did all the American cases referred to as persuasive authority in the judgments of the Court of Appeal in the instant case.

The American cases refer indifferently to documents that are 'forged or fraudulent,' as does the Uniform Commercial Code that has been adopted in nearly all states of the United States of America. The Court of Appeal reached their half-way house in the instant case by starting from the premiss that a confirming bank could refuse to pay against a document that it knew to be forged, even though the seller/beneficiary had no knowledge of that fact. From this premiss they reasoned that if forgery by a third party relieves the confirming bank of liability to pay the seller/beneficiary, fraud by a third party ought to have the same consequence.

I would not wish to be taken as accepting that the premiss as to forged documents is correct, even where the fact that the document is forged deprives it of all legal effect and makes it a nullity, and so worthless to the confirming bank as security for its advances to the buyer. This is certainly not so under the Uniform Commercial Code as against a person who has taken a draft drawn under the credit in circumstances that would make him a holder in due course, and I see no reason why, and there is nothing in the Uniform Commercial Code to suggest that a seller/beneficiary who is ignorant of the forgery should be in any worse position because he has not negotiated the draft before presentation. I would prefer to leave open the question of the rights of an innocent seller/beneficiary against the confirming bank when a document presented by him is a nullity because unknown to him it was forged by some third party; for that question does not arise in the instant case. The bill of lading with the wrong date of loading placed on it by the carrier's agent was far from being a nullity. It was a valid transferable receipt for the goods giving the holder a right to claim them at their destination, Callao, and was evidence of the terms of the contract under which they were being carried.

But even assuming the correctness of the Court of Appeal's premiss as respects forgery by a third party of a kind that makes a document a nullity for which at least a rational case can be made out, to say that this leads to the conclusion that fraud by a third party which does not render the document a nullity has the same consequence appears to me, with respect, to be a non sequitur, and I am not persuaded by the reasoning in any of the judgments of the Court of Appeal that it is not.

Upon the documentary credit point I think that Mocatta J was right in deciding it in favour of the sellers and that the Court of Appeal were wrong in reversing him on this point.

[That part of Lord Diplock's opinion dealing with the Bretton Woods point is set out below, p 802.]

[**Lords Fraser of Tullybelton**, **Russell of Killowen**, **Scarman**, and **Bridge of Harwich** concurred.]

In *United City Merchants*, the bill of lading in question contained a false statement but that did not affect the essential validity of the document. It remained a valid transferable receipt for the goods giving the holder a right to claim them at their destination. But what if an innocent seller tenders a document that is a 'nullity' in the sense that it was forged or executed without the authority of the person by whom it purports to be issued? Although Lord Diplock left the issue open in the *United City Merchants* case, it has been addressed by the Court of Appeal.

Montrod Ltd v Grundkötter Fleischvertriebs GmbH
[2001] EWCA Civ 1954, [2002] 1 WLR 1975, Court of Appeal

The underlying contract was a contract of sale of goods (pork) made between a German seller (GK) and a Russian buyer. The letter of credit, opened by the issuing bank (SBC) in favour of the seller, provided for payment of drafts 45 days after presentation of documents. One of the documents to be presented under the credit was an inspection certificate signed by the applicant for the credit (Montrod), a finance company employed by the buyer to facilitate the purchase. This was a device to ensure that Montrod was put in funds by the buyer before it incurred liability as applicant under the credit. However, the fraudulent buyer informed the seller that it should sign the inspection certificate on behalf of Montrod. The seller, honestly believing that it had Montrod's authority to sign the certificate, did so and presented the duly signed certificate under the credit. The pork was delivered to the buyer in Moscow. Between the date of presentation and the date of payment, it became clear that Montrod had not given its authority for the seller to sign the certificate. Montrod disputed the seller's right to payment and the issuing bank's right to reimbursement on the ground that the certificate was a 'nullity'. The first instance judge (reported at [2001] 1 All ER (Comm) 368) held that the seller, whom he found to be innocent of the fraud, was entitled to payment under the credit, and that the issuing bank was entitled to reimbursement from Montrod. The Court of Appeal upheld the decision.

Potter LJ: . . .

56. I consider that the judge was correct in the decision to which he came. The fraud exception to the autonomy principle recognised in English law has hitherto been restricted to, and it is in my view desirable that it should remain based upon, the fraud or knowledge of fraud on the part of the beneficiary or other party seeking payment under and in accordance with the terms of the letter of credit. It should not be avoided or extended by the argument that a document presented, which conforms on its face with the terms of the letter of the credit, is none the less of a character which disentitles the person making the demand to payment because it is fraudulent *in itself*, independently of the knowledge and bona fides of the demanding party. In my view, that is the clear import of Lord Diplock's observations in the *Gian Singh* case [1974] 1 WLR 1234, 1238, and in the *United City Merchants* case [1983] 1 AC 168, 183–188, in which all their Lordships concurred. As I understand it, Lord Diplock was of the view that a seller/beneficiary who was ignorant of forgery by a third party of one of the documents presented, or of the fact that the document contained a representation false to the knowledge of the person who created it, should not be in a worse position than someone who has taken a draft drawn under a letter of credit in circumstances which rendered him a holder in due course. While he left open the position in relation to a forged document where the effect of the forgery was to render the document a 'nullity', there is nothing to suggest that he would have recognised any nullity exception as extending to a document which was not forged (ie fraudulently produced) but was signed by the creator in honest error as to his authority; nor do I consider that such an exception should be recognised.

57. That being so, I do not consider that the fact that in this case it was the seller/beneficiary himself who created the document said to be a nullity should *of itself* disentitle him to payment, assuming (as the judge found) that such creation was devoid of any fraudulent intent and was effected in the belief that GK enjoyed the authority of Montrod, as applicant for the credit, to sign and issue the certificate. Although the circumstances were highly unusual, they may none the less be regarded as no more than an illustration of the wide variety of circumstances in which documents come into existence in a commercial context which do not necessarily reflect the factual situation but which parties may none the less employ as a convenient means of progressing a particular transaction. If, in the circumstances of a multipartite transaction, a seller/beneficiary is indeed led to believe that he has authority to create and present a certificate of inspection for the purpose of triggering payment by letter of credit, I do not see why he should be regarded as any less entitled to payment in accordance with UCP 500 than in a case where he receives from a third party a document regular on its face which has, unknown to him, been created without authority.

58. In my view there are sound policy reasons for not extending the law by creation of a general nullity exception. Most documentary credits issued in the United Kingdom incorporate the UCP

by reference. Various revisions of the UCP have been widely adopted in the USA and by United Kingdom and Commonwealth banks. They are intended to embody international banking practice and to create certainty in an area of law where the need for precision and certainty are paramount. The creation of a general nullity exception, the formulation of which does not seem to me susceptible of precision, involves making undesirable inroads into the principles of autonomy and negotiability universally recognised in relation to letter of credit transactions. In the context of the fraud exception, the courts have made clear how difficult it is to invoke the exception and have been at pains to point out that banks deal in documents and questions of apparent conformity. In that context they have made clear that it is not for a bank to make its own inquiries about allegations of fraud brought to its notice; if a party wishes to establish that a demand is fraudulent it must place before the bank evidence of clear and obvious fraud: see *Edward Owen Engineering Ltd v Barclays Bank International Ltd* [1978] QB 159; cf *Turkiye Is Bankasi AS v Bank of China* [1996] 2 Lloyd's Rep 611, 617 per Waller J. If a general nullity exception were to be introduced as part of English law it would place banks in a further dilemma as to the necessity to investigate facts which they are not competent to do and from which UCP 500 is plainly concerned to exempt them. Further such an exception would be likely to act unfairly upon beneficiaries participating in a chain of contracts in cases where their good faith is not in question. Such a development would thus undermine the system of financing international trade by means of documentary credits.

59. I have concluded that there is and should be no general nullity exception based upon the concept of a document being fraudulent *in itself* or devoid of commercial value. I would only add, with reference to Lord Diplock's reservation, that I would not seek to exclude the possibility that, in an individual case, the conduct of a beneficiary in connection with the creation and/ or presentation of a document forged by a third party might, though itself not amounting to fraud, be of such character as not to deserve the protection available to a holder in due course. In this connection, I note the reference by Mocatta J in the *United City Merchants* case [1979] 1 Lloyd's Rep 267 to 'personal fraud' or '*unscrupulous conduct*' on the part of the seller presenting documents for payment, a remark upon which Lord Diplock made no adverse comment when approving the original judgment on the documentary credit point. In this connection, we have had brought to our attention the decision of the High Court of Singapore in *Lambias (Importers and Exporters) Co Pte Ltd v Hong Kong and Shanghai Banking Corpn* [1993] 2 SLR 751, in which the defendant bank rejected documents tendered under a letter of credit which included a quality and weight inspection certificate required to be countersigned by a named individual. The court held that the certificate contained discrepancies which entitled the bank to refuse the documents tendered and went on to find that the inspection certificate was in any event a nullity in that, not only did it fail to state the particulars of the goods and their quality and weight, but that, having been issued by the beneficiary instead of the applicant, it had been countersigned by an impostor. Having considered the observations, and in particular the reservation, of Lord Diplock in the *United City Merchants* case [1983] 1 AC 168 and the particular facts before the court in relation to the plaintiffs, who had themselves introduced the countersignatory to the bank as the person named, Goh Phai Cheng JC observed [1993] 2 SLR 751, 765–766:

> The law cannot condone actions which, although not amounting to fraud per se, are of such recklessness and haste that the documents produced as a result are clearly not in conformity with the requirements of the credit. The plaintiffs in the present case are not guilty of fraud, but they were unknowingly responsible for having aided in the perpetration of the fraud. In such a case where the fraud was discovered even before all other documents were tendered, I think it is right and proper that the plaintiffs should not be permitted to claim under the letter of credit.

60. While such a finding was not necessary to the outcome of the case, it fell within the reservation of Lord Diplock in the *United City Merchants* case and has certain attractions. However, it is

not necessary for us to decide in this case whether it is correct. This is a case where the judge found neither recklessness, haste, nor blame in the conduct of GK. Furthermore, in the *Lambias* case the bank rejected the documents as non-compliant, whereas in this case SCB accepted the documents as compliant, having raised Montrod's observations and reservations with Fibi before it did so. Fibi in turn accepted the documents when sent to them, making clear to Montrod that payment would be made unless a court order to prevent it were obtained.

61. In those circumstances, I consider that GK were entitled to payment and I would affirm the decision of the judge....

Sir Martin Nourse:
81. I agree with the judgment of Potter LJ and with the orders proposed by him.

Thorpe LJ:
82. I agree.

NOTES

1. It seems, therefore, that presentation to the bank of a forged or unauthorised document is to be treated in exactly the same way as presentation of a genuine document containing false information. In both cases the seller is entitled to payment under the credit unless he knew of the fraud at the time of presentation of the document to the bank (*Group Josi Re v Walbrook Insurance Co Ltd* [1996] 1 WLR 1152 at 1161, per Staughton LJ, 'it is the time of presentation that is crucial.'). Nevertheless, it remains a cause of some unease that the seller, however innocent himself, becomes entitled to payment through tender of a document that carries a deliberately false shipping date, when tender of a document giving the true shipping date could have been rejected as discrepant (as in *United City Merchants*), or though tender of a document that was, in effect, a worthless piece of waste paper (as in *Montrod*). Both decisions have been strongly criticised: see RM Goode, 'Abstract Payment Undertakings' in P Cane and J Stapleton (eds), *Essays for Patrick Atiyah* (1991), pp 228–233 (on *United City Merchants*) and R Hooley [2002] CLJ 279 (on *Montrod*). See also K Donnelly [2008] JBL 316; P Todd [2008] LMCLQ 547; J Ren [2015] JBL 1.

2. A nullity exception has been recognised in Singapore.

Beam Technology (MFG) PTE Ltd v Standard Chartered Bank
[2003] 1 SLR 597, Court of Appeal (Singapore)

The appellant sellers contracted to sell electronic components to buyers who obtained a letter of credit from their bank in favour of the sellers. The respondent bank was the confirming bank of the credit. Under the terms of the credit, a clean air waybill was needed to draw on the credit. The buyers notified the sellers that the air waybill would be issued by their freight forwarders, 'Link Express (S) Pte Ltd'. When the sellers presented the documents required to draw on the credit, the confirming bank rejected the documents on the ground that the air waybill was a forgery because 'Link Express (S) Pte Ltd' did not exist. The bank applied to the court for a determination of the question of law whether it was entitled to refuse to make payment when the air waybill was a forgery known to the bank. For the purposes of the application it was agreed that the sellers were not privy to the forgery.

Chao JA (delivering the judgment of the court):

31. In summary, the current position of the law would appear to be this. The House of Lords in *United City Merchants* had left open the question whether there is a nullity exception although at the Court of Appeal all the three members of the quorum thought there was. In *Montrod*, the Court of Appeal (of a different quorum) was inclined to the view that, apart from the traditional fraud exception (ie fraud or knowledge of fraud on the part of the beneficiary or other party seeking payment), there was no separate nullity exception. In any case, even if there was such a nullity exception, it held that the certificate issued by the seller in *Montrod* in honest belief that he had the authority of the applicant of the letter of credit could not be a nullity. Perhaps another way of differentiating *Montrod* from the present case is that there the certificate required was not an essential document but one touching on the question as to the quality of the goods sold. In short, there is no definite authority on point, although the views of the Court of Appeal in *United City Merchants* are no doubt highly persuasive.

32. It seems to us that the issue must be approached on first principles. It is clear that the obligation of the issuing/confirming bank towards the beneficiary is independent and separate from the contractual obligations between the seller and the buyer, and the obligation to pay is absolute irrespective of any dispute that may arise between the seller and the buyer. As far as the confirming or negotiating bank is concerned, their duty is only to verify whether what appears on the documents conforms with what is required by the credit. If there is prima facie compliance, the bank is authorised to pay and may claim reimbursement from the issuing bank notwithstanding that a document tendered may subsequently turn out to be a forgery: *Gian Singh*. This is to protect the bank and to ensure the smooth flow of international trade and the avoidance of delay. But we are unable to see why such a rule should also lead to the result that if the confirming or negotiating bank, from whatever source, is able to establish within the prescribed seven-day limit that a material document tendered is a forgery, being null and void, the bank is, nevertheless, obliged to pay.

33. While the underlying principle is that the negotiating/confirming bank need not investigate the documents tendered, it is altogether a different proposition to say that the bank should ignore what is clearly a null and void document and proceed nevertheless to pay. Implicit in the requirement of a conforming document is the assumption that the document is true and genuine although under the UCP 500 and common law, and in the interest of international trade, the bank is not required to look beyond what appears on the surface of the documents. But to say that a bank, in the face of a forged null and void document (even though the beneficiary is not privy to that forgery), must still pay on the credit, defies reason and good sense. It amounts to saying that the scheme of things under the UCP 500 is only concerned with commas and full stops or some misdescriptions, and that the question as to the genuineness or otherwise of a material document, which was the cause for the issue of the LC, is of no consequence.

34. As the judge below observed, UCP 500 does not provide that a bank is obliged to accept a document which is a nullity notwithstanding that the time prescribed under art 14 for the bank to reject the document has not expired. Thus the nullity exception which we postulate is a limited one and would not have given rise to the sort of problems which Potter LJ had expressed concern (at 274):

> If a general nullity exception were to be introduced as part of English law it would place banks in a further dilemma as to the necessity to investigate facts which they are not competent to do and from which UCP 500 is plainly concerned to exempt them.

We are not in any way suggesting that the bank is obliged to investigate into any document tendered. The nullity exception would only permit a bank to refuse payment if it is satisfied that a material document is a nullity.

35. Here, we would like to refer to the following comments of Professor R M Goode in an article in Centre Point entitled 'Reflections on Letters of Credit–1', where he, in discussing the position of the bona fide plaintiff, said:

Is a plaintiff who seeks to enforce a letter of credit affected by forgery of the documents or other fraud in the transaction if he himself acted in good faith? There is a remarkable dearth of authority on this question. Let us start with the beneficiary. He himself has a duty to tendering forged documents which are in order, and the fact that he acted in good faith in tendering forged documents is thus irrelevant. This fundamental point appears to have been overlooked by Mr Justice Mocatta in *The American Accord* when he held that the beneficiary was entitled to collect payment despite the insertion of a fraudulent shipping date on the bill of lading, since the fraud had been committed by the loading broker who was the agent of the carrier, not of the seller/beneficiary. But this, with respect, is not to the point. The beneficiary under a credit is not like a holder in due course of a bill of exchange; he is only entitled to be paid if the documents are in order. A fraudulently completed bill of lading does not become a conforming document merely because the fraud is that of a third party.

36. It is our opinion that the negotiating/confirming bank is not obliged to pay if it has established within the seven-day period that a material document required under the credit is forged and null and void and notice of it is given within that period. While we recognise that there could be difficulties in determining under what circumstances a document would be considered material or a nullity, such a question can only be answered on the facts of each case. One cannot generalise. It is not possible to define when is a document a nullity. But it is really not that much more difficult to answer such questions than to determine what is reasonable, an exercise which the courts are all too familiar with.

(b) Fraud in the underlying transaction

The fraud in the *United City Merchants* case was documentary fraud, ie fraud in relation to the tendered documents. Does the fraud exception apply where the documents presented are truthful but there is fraud in the underlying transaction? There is no English authority that expressly decides the point (although the much criticised majority decision of the Court of Appeal in *Themehelp Ltd v West* [1996] QB 84 lends support to an extension of the fraud exception to fraud in the underlying transaction). By contrast, s 5–109(a) of revised art 5 of the US Uniform Commercial Code refers to 'material fraud by the beneficiary on the issuer or the applicant' (the phrase 'fraud in the transaction' was expressly used in s 5–114 of the original version of art 5). The Supreme Court of Canada has also endorsed the wider scope of the exception. In *Bank of Nova Scotia v Angelica-Whitewear Ltd* [1987] 1 SCR 59 at 83, Le Dain J expressly referred to dicta of Lord Denning in *Edward Owen Engineering Ltd v Barclays Bank Ltd* [1978] QB 159—'the request for payment is made fraudulently in circumstances when there is no right to payment'—as suggesting that it was not intended to limit the fraud exception to documentary fraud. Extending the fraud exception to fraud in the underlying transaction is consistent with Lord Diplock's view that 'fraud unravels all', ie the court will not permit a beneficiary to obtain payment in reliance on his own wrongdoing. As the authors of one of the leading textbooks on documentary credits observe: 'it would be odd if the bank were obliged to pay an obviously fraudulent beneficiary only because fraud did not manifest itself in false documents' (A Malek and D Quest, *Jack: Documentary Credits* (4th edn, 2009), para 9.26). On the other hand, Professor Dolan, a leading US commentator, warns against the courts engaging in a wide-ranging fraud inquiry which would undermine the independence of letters of credit (JF Dolan, 'Tethering the Fraud Inquiry in Letter of Credit Law' (2006) 21 BFLR 479 at 489–490). He calls on the courts to be sure the applicant's allegations involve the beneficiary's attempt to take the proceeds of a credit when he has no honest belief in his right to them, and refuse to elevate underlying contract disputes into letter of credit fraud disputes (at 502).

(c) Established fraud and the bank's right of reimbursement

Where the fraudulent conduct of the beneficiary or other person presenting the documents is clear and obvious to the bank, then the bank should not pay against the documents and it will not be entitled to reimbursement from the applicant or other instructing party. As Rix J said in *Czarnikow-Rionda Sugar Trading Inc v Standard Bank London Ltd* [1999] 1 All ER (Comm) 890 at 914: 'I do not see how payment in the face of fraud can be a mere matter of discretion by a bank: it must be either within its mandate or not, and either a matter of obligation or not'. If the bank refuses to pay, it must be able to prove at the subsequent trial of the action that there was fraud on the part of the seller at the time of presentation of the documents. It is not enough for the bank to refuse to pay on the ground that it had evidence from which a reasonable banker would think that there had been fraud of the seller, whether or not fraud actually existed in fact (*Society of Lloyd's v Canadian Imperial Bank of Canada* [1993] 2 Lloyd's Rep 579 at 581). Where the bank pays, and the buyer later disputes its right to reimbursement on the ground that the fraud was clear and obvious to the bank, the buyer must prove either that the bank was actually aware of the fraud (eg where the beneficiary admits it), or else reckless, in that the only realistic inference to be drawn by the bank was that the demand was fraudulently made (see *Turkiye Is Bankasi AS v Bank of China* [1996] 2 Lloyd's Rep 611; affirmed [1998] 1 Lloyd's Rep 250, CA).

(d) Injunctions

Usually the bank when faced with clear evidence of fraud will invite the buyer to apply to the court for an injunction. To maintain the status quo until the trial the buyer will seek an interlocutory injunction. This may be obtained against the bank to restrain it from honouring the credit or against the seller to prohibit presentation of documents for payment or negotiation of the drafts (although where the bank has accepted a draft drawn by the seller, and the draft has already been negotiated to a holder in due course, the bank must pay at maturity: *Discount Records Ltd v Barclays Bank Ltd* [1975] 1 All ER 1071). In practice it is notoriously difficult for a buyer to prevent payment of an irrevocable credit on grounds of fraud as the courts have shown a marked reluctance to interfere with the smooth running of the system of documentary credits. As Sir John Donaldson MR stated in *Bolivinter Oil SA v Chase Manhattan Bank* [1984] 1 Lloyd's Rep 251 at 257:

> The wholly exceptional case where an injunction may be granted is where it is proved that the bank knows that any demand for payment already made or which may thereafter be made will clearly be fraudulent. But the evidence must be clear, both as to the fact of fraud and as to the bank's knowledge. It would certainly not normally be sufficient that this rests upon the uncorroborated statement of the customer, for irreparable damage can be done to a bank's credit in the relatively brief time which must elapse between the granting of such an injunction and an application by the bank to have it discharged.

It may be argued that an injunction against the beneficiary prohibiting him from making a call on the credit does not interfere with the operations of international commerce and that, in consequence, a mere allegation of fraud on the part of the beneficiary ought to be enough for the court to grant injunctive relief. Although this approach found favour with a majority of the Court of Appeal in *Themehelp Ltd v West* [1996] QB 84 (a performance bond case), it was soundly condemned by Staughton LJ (*obiter*) in *Group Josi Re v Walbrook Insurance Co Ltd* [1996] 1 WLR 1152 at 1161–1162 and by Rix J in *Czarnikow-Rionda Sugar Trading Inc v Standard Bank London Ltd* [1999] 1 All ER (Comm) 890 at 913. An injunction restraining a beneficiary from making a call on the credit should be granted only to the extent that the facts justify the granting of an injunction against the bank restraining payment (see, further, A Mugasha, 'Enjoining the Beneficiary's Claim on a Letter of Credit or Bank Guarantee' [2004] JBL 515).

According to *American Cyanamid v Ethicon Ltd* [1975] AC 396, an applicant for an interlocutory injunction must establish that: (1) he has a seriously arguable claim against the party he is seeking to restrain; and (2) the balance of convenience is in favour of the grant of an injunction. Moreover, by reason of *The Siskina* [1979] AC 210, an injunction can only be granted in aid of a substantive cause of action against the person to be restrained. The buyer seeking to restrain a bank from paying under a documentary credit, or his seller from calling on the credit, will rarely be able to meet all these requirements and his application for an interlocutory injunction will usually fail.

First, the buyer will have to establish a substantive cause of action against the person to be restrained (*Czarnikow-Rionda Sugar Trading Inc v Standard Bank London Ltd* [1999] 1 All ER (Comm) 890 at 914; cf *Group Josi Re v Walbrook Insurance Co Ltd* [1996] 1 WLR 1152 at 1160). The problem is where the bank to be restrained is the confirming bank as there is no contractual relation between the applicant for a credit and the confirming bank, and the chances of establishing a duty of care in tort are slim on the current state of the authorities. By contrast, the applicant has a contract with the issuing bank, and an injunction to restrain the issuing bank from paying by itself or its agents should prevent payment by an advising bank that has not confirmed the credit because it acts as the issuing bank's agent. Secondly, the burden of proof of fraud is high, even at the interlocutory stage, as it must be clearly established that the only realistic inference is: (1) that the beneficiary could not honestly have believed in the validity of its demands under the credit; and (2) that the bank was aware of the fraud (*Alternative Power Solution Ltd v Central Electricity Board* [2014] UKPC 31, [2015] 1 WLR 697 at [59], per Lord Clarke, applying *United Trading Corpn SA v Allied Arab Bank Ltd* [1985] 2 Lloyd's Rep 554n at 561, per Ackner LJ). Thirdly, in documentary credit disputes the balance of convenience is usually against the granting of an injunction, for if the injunction is granted the bank may suffer damage to its reputation if fraud is not proved at trial, whilst if the injunction is refused, and fraud is later proved at trial, the applicant will suffer no loss as the bank's claim against him for reimbursement will fail. Only in the most exceptional circumstances will the balance of convenience favour the grant of an injunction (*Czarnikow-Rionda Sugar Trading Inc v Standard Bank London Ltd,* above, at 916; *Alternative Power Solution Ltd v Central Electricity Board*, above, at [79]).

(e) Freezing orders

A buyer unable to prevent payment of the credit on grounds of fraud may still be able to obtain an order to restrain the seller from removing the proceeds of the credit from the jurisdiction or otherwise dealing with them within the jurisdiction (called a freezing order). The order catches the proceeds of the credit as and when received by the seller. It does not prevent payment under the credit, and so the buyer does not have to bring himself within the fraud exception. In exceptional circumstances, a court may grant a worldwide freezing order, but it is unlikely that an English court would grant an order affecting money paid under a documentary credit by a bank abroad (A Malek and D Quest, *Jack: Documentary Credits* (4th edn, 2009), para 9.80). In appropriate cases the court may combine a freezing order with an ancillary order requiring the proceeds of the credit to be paid into court (*Themehelp Ltd v West* [1996] QB 84 at 103, per Evans LJ). But where the credit is to be paid abroad, it would be an unjustified interference with the operation of the credit to order the bank to pay the money into an account in England (*Britten Norman Ltd v State Ownership Fund of Romania* [2000] 1 Lloyd's Rep Bank 315).

QUESTIONS

1.   In *Montrod Ltd v Grundkötter Fleischvertriebs GmbH* [2001] EWCA Civ 1954, [2002] 1 WLR 1975, Potter LJ considered that there were 'sound policy reasons' for rejecting a general nullity exception to the autonomy of the credit. What were those reasons? Are they sound? Do they also undermine Potter LJ's tentative (*obiter*) suggestion that a non-fraudulent beneficiary might be refused payment on tender of apparently conforming documents where he acts recklessly, in haste, or is otherwise blameworthy?

2.   Why is it so difficult for a buyer who suspects fraud on the part of the seller to obtain an injunction to restrain the bank from paying the seller under the terms of a documentary credit?

(iv) Autonomy and illegality

A documentary credit may itself be illegal where its issue is prohibited or because of some supervening prohibition. This does not affect the autonomy principle because the credit is illegal in itself rather than because of illegality in the underlying transaction. There is also a growing body of English case law in favour of an illegality exception to the autonomy principle where there is illegality in the underlying transaction which *taints* the documentary credit transaction. This is a true exception to the autonomy principle because the illegality is in the underlying transaction and not in the documentary credit transaction itself. See generally, N Enonchong, 'The Autonomy Principle of Letters of Credit: An Illegality Exception?' [2006] LMCLQ 404; N Enonchong, *The Independence Principle of Letters of Credit and Demand Guarantees* (2011), Ch 8.

United City Merchants (Investments) Ltd v Royal Bank of Canada, The American Accord
[1983] 1 AC 168, House of Lords

The facts appear above, p 790.

> **Lord Diplock:** The Bretton Woods point arises out of the agreement between the buyers and the seller collateral to the contract of sale of the goods between the same parties that out of the payments in US dollars received by the sellers under the documentary credit in respect of each instalment of the invoice price of the goods, they would transmit to the account of the buyers in America one half of the US dollars received.
>
> The Bretton Woods Agreements Order in Council 1946, made under the Bretton Woods Agreements Act 1945, gives the force of law in England to art VIII s 2(b) of the Bretton Woods Agreement, which is in the following terms:

Exchange contracts which involve the currency of any member and which are contrary to the exchange control regulations of that member maintained or imposed consistently with this agreement shall be unenforceable in the territories of any member . . .

My Lords, I accept as correct the narrow interpretation that was placed upon the expression 'exchange contracts' in this provision of the Bretton Woods Agreement by the Court of Appeal in *Wilson, Smithett & Cope Ltd v Terruzzi* [1976] QB 683. It is confined to contracts to exchange the currency of one country for the currency of another; it does not include contracts entered into in connection with sales of goods which require the conversion by the buyer of one currency into another in order to enable him to pay the purchase price. As was said by Lord Denning MR in his judgment in the *Terruzzi* case at p 714, the court in considering the application of the provision should look at the substance of the contracts and not at the form. It should not enforce a contract that is a mere 'monetary transaction in disguise.'

I also accept as accurate what was said by Lord Denning MR in a subsequent case as to the effect that should be given by English courts to the word 'unenforceable.' The case, *Batra v Ebrahim*, is unreported, but the relevant passage from Lord Denning's judgment is helpfully cited by Ackner LJ in his own judgment in the instant case: [1982] QB 208, 241F–242B. If in the course of the hearing of an action the court becomes aware that the contract on which a party is suing is one that this country has accepted an international obligation to treat as unenforceable, the court must take the point itself, even though the defendant has not pleaded it, and must refuse to lend its aid to enforce the contract. But this does not have the effect of making an exchange contract that is contrary to the exchange control regulations of a member state other than the United Kingdom into a contract that is 'illegal' under English law or render acts undertaken in this country in performance of such a contract unlawful. Like a contract of guarantee of which there is no note or memorandum in writing it is unenforceable by the courts and nothing more.

Mocatta J, professing to follow the guidance given in the *Terruzzi* case [1976] QB 683, took the view that the contract of sale between the buyers and the sellers at the inflated invoice price was a monetary transaction in disguise and that despite the autonomous character of the contract between the sellers and the confirming bank under the documentary credit, this too was tarred with the same brush and was a monetary transaction in disguise and therefore one which the court should not enforce. He rejected out of hand what he described as a 'rather remarkable submission' that the sellers could recover that half of the invoice price which represented the true sale price of the goods, even if they could not recover that other half of the invoice price which they would receive as trustees for the buyers on trust to transmit it to the buyer's American company in Florida. He held that it was impossible to sever the contract constituted by the documentary credit; it was either enforceable in full or not at all.

In refusing to treat the sellers' claim under the documentary credit for that part of the invoice price that they were to retain for themselves as the sale price of the goods in a different way from that in which he treated their claim to that part of the invoice price which they would receive as trustees for the buyers, I agree with all three members of the Court of Appeal the learned judge fell into error.

I avoid speaking of 'severability,' for this expression is appropriate where the task upon which the court is engaged is construing the language that the parties have used in a written contract. The question whether and to what extent a contract is unenforceable under the Bretton Woods Agreement Order in Council 1946 because it is a monetary transaction in disguise is *not* a question of construction of the contract, but a question of the substance of the transaction to which enforcement of the contract will give effect. If the matter were to be determined simply as a question of construction, the contract between the sellers and the confirming bank constituted by the documentary credit fell altogether outside the Bretton Woods Agreement; it was not a contract to exchange one currency for another currency but a contract to pay currency for documents which included documents of title to goods. On the contrary, the task on which the court is engaged is to penetrate any disguise presented by the actual words the parties have used, to identify any monetary transaction (in the narrow sense of that expression as used in the *Terruzzi* case [1976] QB 683) which those words were intended to conceal and to refuse to enforce the contract to the extent that to do so would give effect to the monetary transaction.

In the instant case there is no difficulty in identifying the monetary transaction that was sought to be concealed by the actual words used in the documentary credit and in the underlying contract of sale. It was to exchange Peruvian currency provided by the buyers in Peru for US $331,043 to be made available to them in Florida; and to do this was contrary to the exchange control regulations of Peru. Payment under the documentary credit by the confirming bank to the sellers of that half of the invoice price (viz $331,043) that the sellers would receive as trustees for the buyers on trust to remit it to the account of the buyer's American company in Florida, was an essential part of that monetary transaction and therefore unenforceable; but payment of the other half of the invoice price and of the freight was not; the sellers would receive that part of the payment under the documentary credit on their own behalf and retain it as the genuine purchase price of goods sold by them to the buyers. I agree with the Court of Appeal that there is nothing in the Bretton Woods Agreements Order in Council 1946 that prevents the payment under the documentary credit being enforceable to this extent.

[**Lords Fraser of Tullybelton**, **Russell of Killowen**, **Scarman**, and **Bridge of Harwich** concurred.]

Group Jose Re v Walbrook Insurance Co Ltd

[1996] 1 WLR 1152, Court of Appeal

The plaintiff reinsurers entered into a number of reinsurance contracts with the defendant insurance companies (referred to as 'the stamp companies'), who acted through their agent (Weavers). To ensure that the stamp companies paid all their premiums over to the plaintiffs, and did not retain any part of them as a reserve against claims, the plaintiffs opened letters of credit in favour of the stamp companies, which provided for payment on presentation of debit notes stating that the plaintiffs were liable for the amounts in question under the reinsurance contracts. Later the plaintiffs claimed that the reinsurance contracts were void because of their own illegality in carrying on an insurance business without statutory authorisation and applied for injunctions restraining the stamp companies and their agent from presenting documents for payment under the letters of credit. The Court of Appeal (Staughton, Rose, and Saville LJJ) held that performance of the reinsurance contracts by the reinsurers was not illegal and refused to grant the injunctions. Staughton LJ alone considered what would have been the effect of illegality of the reinsurance contracts on the letters of credit.

Staughton LJ:

CAN A LETTER OF CREDIT BE AFFECTED BY ILLEGALITY OF THE UNDERLYING TRANSACTION?

The reinsurers put their case in this way: (i) the underlying reinsurance contracts were illegal; (ii) directly or by way of taint, this rendered the letter of credit contracts illegal or at least unenforceable; (iii) therefore it would be fraudulent for the stamp companies and Weavers to claim payment under the letters of credit.

That seems to me unnecessarily complicated. Surely one can stop after stage (ii), without bringing fraud into it. I say that because in my judgment illegality is a separate ground for nonpayment under a letter of credit. That may seem a bold assertion, when Lord Diplock in the *United City*

Merchants case [1983] 1 AC 168, 183 said that there was '*one* established exception.' But in that very case the House of Lords declined to enforce a letter of credit contract in part for another reason, that is to say the exchange control regulations of Peru as applied by the Bretton Woods Agreements Order in Council 1945 (SR & O 1946 No 36). I agree that the Bretton Woods point may well have been of a kind of its own, and not an indication that illegality generally is a defence under a letter of credit. But it does perhaps show that established fraud is not necessarily the only exception.

It seems to me that there must be cases when illegality can affect a letter of credit. Take for example a contract for the sale of arms to Iraq, at a time when such a sale is illegal. The contract provides for the opening of a letter of credit, to operate on presentation of a bill of lading for 1,000 Kalashnikov rifles to be carried to the port of Basra. I do not suppose that a court would give judgment for the beneficiary against the bank in such a case. Would illegality, like fraud, have to be clearly established and known to the bank before it could operate as a defence, or a ground for restraining payment by the bank? That is not an altogether easy question, but I am inclined to think that it would. If the legality of the payment is merely doubtful, it may be that the bank would not be restrained. But whether in a *United City Merchants* type of case, if illegality were clearly proved at trial, it would be a defence that it was not clear at the time when the documents were presented for payment is even more of a problem.

Turning to the present case, if the reinsurance contracts are illegal, and if the letters of credit are being used as a means of paying sums due under those contracts, and if all that is clearly established, would the court restrain the bank from making payment or the beneficiary from demanding it? In my judgment the court would do so. That would not be because the letter of credit contracts were themselves illegal, but because they were being used to carry out an illegal transaction. I hesitate to enter upon a discussion of what is *turpis causa*, or what is taint. Since *Tinsley v Milligan* [1994] 1 AC 340 the two categories of *turpis causa* that I identified and the Court of Appeal upheld in *Euro-Diam Ltd v Bathurst* [1990] 1 QB 1 no longer survive. The public conscience test is gone, and one is left (I suppose) with the *Bowmakers* principle (*Bowmakers Ltd v Barnet Instruments Ltd* [1945] KB 65): the defence succeeds if 'the plaintiff seeks to, or is forced to, found his claim on an illegal contract or to plead its illegality in order to support his claim' (Kerr LJ [1990] 1 QB 1, 35).

That is what the stamp companies and Weavers would have to do in this case, if the contracts of insurance are illegal. In order to operate the letters of credit they must present a debit note to the bank. That debit note must be one 'covering the liability for outstanding loss reserves under your umbrella quota share facilities.' In my opinion, and Mr Rokison does not dispute this, it must say so in terms. On this hypothesis they would be founding on an illegal contract, that is the contract of reinsurance.

Mr Rokison argues that whatever was due to be paid under the reinsurance contracts has already been paid—by the opening of the letter of credit. In one sense that is true; *WJ Alan & Co Ltd v El Nasr Export and Import Co* [1972] 2 QB 189 decided that the opening of a letter of credit, like the giving of a cheque, was or could be conditional payment of money due under a contract, so that nothing remained due from the debtor unless and until the letter of credit or the cheque failed. But that does nothing whatever to convince me that the obligation of the bank to pay under the letters of credit is altogether free of taint from any obligation of the reinsurers which it superseded.

NOTE

Clarke J, deciding the same case at first instance ([1996] 1 Lloyd's Rep 345), held that the letters of credit were not void or unenforceable. His reasoning ran as follows (at 352): (1) the letter of credit represented a contract separate from the underlying reinsurance contract; (2) the opening of the letter of credit was conditional payment under the reinsurance contract; (3) in presenting the documents to the bank the stamp companies would not be carrying on the business of insurance prohibited by the statute and nor would the bank in paying under the letters of credit; and (4) nor would the stamp companies and the bank be aiding and abetting the carrying on by the reinsurers of unauthorised insurance business. As can be seen from the final paragraph of the extract taken from Court of Appeal's decision, Staughton LJ expressly rejected Clarke J's reasoning. However, Colman J returned to the issue in the next case.

Mahonia Ltd v JP Morgan Chase Bank
[2003] EWHC 1927 (Comm), [2003] 2 Lloyd's Rep 911, Commercial Court

Mahonia Ltd (Mahonia), JP Morgan Chase Bank (Chase), and Enron North America Corporation (ENAC), a subsidiary of Enron Corporation, entered into three swap transactions. Under these arrangements US$350 million was paid by Chase to Mahonia and the same sum from Mahonia to ENAC. Six months later ENAC was to pay Chase US$355.9 million. The overall effect of the circularity of these three swaps was that ENAC was to receive the use of US$350 million for six months and that Chase was to be paid by ENAC an additional US$5.9 million. In order to secure its exposure, Chase required ENAC to procure the issue of standby letters of credit by way of security. One such credit in the amount of US$165 million was provided by the London branch of West LB AG ('the Bank').

Following ENAC's filing for Chapter 11 (a US insolvency procedure), the swap arrangements fell into default and Chase made demand upon the Bank under the letter of credit. The Bank declined to pay on grounds of illegality. The substance of the Bank's case on illegality was that: (1) the swaps were a 'cosmetic' device to provide Enron with a loan of US$350 million from Chase that Enron did not have to record in its accounts as a debt; and (2) the omission to show the loan in Enron's accounts was contrary to US securities law and was intended to defraud. On this basis, so the Bank argued, the letter of credit for US$165 million was rendered illegal and/or was unenforceable on grounds of public policy.

Colman J dismissed the claimant's application to strike out the illegality defence and for summary judgment in respect of that defence. He stated that the letter of credit was created for the purpose of forming part of the basis of transactions (the swaps) which were illegal under US law because they had an illegal purpose. The judge held that it did not make any difference that the purpose was unlawful, not under English law, but under the law of a friendly foreign state. He also held that it made no difference that the illegal purpose was known only to the claimant and not to the Bank until long after the demand for payment had been presented.

Colman J:
    63. In order to investigate the enforceability of the letter of credit it is first necessary to identify what function it had in relation to the assumed illegal purpose of the three swaps. That function was to provide security to Chase in case the planned circulation of funds was interrupted by the failure of ENAC to pay Mahonia, the beneficiary under the letter of credit. If ENAC failed to pay Mahonia, then the money would not get back to Chase and the circularity which was an essential feature of the structure of the overall transaction would be broken, with the source of the funding (Chase) remaining out of its money.

64. The transaction is therefore similar in many ways to one in which the underlying contract is illegal to the knowledge of both parties and therefore unenforceable by either and where one of the parties to it procures an innocent third party to provide to the other a bond which pays against a certificate that the underlying contract has not been performed. Leaving aside the additional feature of a letter of credit, the authorities discussed in paragraphs (21 to 27) above support the proposition that the innocent third party could rely by way of defence on the underlying illegality. The position would be no different if the underlying contract were legal on its face but entered into for an illegal purpose or if the underlying contract were illegal because it required the carrying out of an act in the United States which was unlawful there or was for the purpose of the carrying out of such an act. Does it make any difference that the security was provided by means of a documentary letter of credit confirmed by a bank innocent of the illegality of the underlying transaction, but which has clear evidence of that illegality at the time when it ought otherwise to pay?

65. As appears from the authorities discussed earlier in this judgment, the impregnability of letters of credit is a consequence of the need to insulate them from the transaction in relation to which they have been utilised as security. That is because they have a special function in international trade which requires that their integrity and irrevocability should not be interfered with unless an ex turpi causa defence can be clearly proved by the bank, as for example in a case of fraud such as to be found in *Sztejn v. J Henry Schroder Banking Corporation* [31 NYS 2d 631 (1941)]. As a matter of public policy the courts will not permit their process to be used to obtain the benefit of an unlawful act. In such a case the policy of the law in withholding its process from the enforcement of benefits derived from an unlawful act displaces the otherwise impregnable nature of the letter of credit. Does that policy extend to a case like the present where the unlawfulness consists not in a fraud on the bank but in the purpose for which the letter of credit has been procured?

66. I am bound to say that I have found the reasoning of Clark J. in the *Group Josi* case … strongly persuasive resting, as it does, on the insulation of the opening and negotiation of the letter of credit from the unlawful carrying on of insurance business. He was able to distinguish between conduct prohibited by the legislation and conduct collateral to that unlawful conduct. Only the latter would have to be relied upon in order to enforce the letters of credit. In that case however the letters of credit were not an integral part of the unlawful conduct. They were simply a facility provided subsequently to the entering into of the illegal contracts which assisted performance in a manner not specifically rendered illegal. Where, however, the letter of credit plays from the outset an integral part in the illegal transaction, there is, as I see it, a very different situation, when it comes to enforcement for the court's process is then deployed for the purpose of giving effect to an essential part of the illegal scheme.

67. Although in *United City Merchants*, supra, Lord Diplock expressly stated that the underlying sale contract and letters of credit were not rendered *illegal* by the Bretton Woods Order in Council, the underlying sale contract was certainly *prohibited* and thereby rendered unenforceable. However, the conclusion that the letter of credit was also rendered unenforceable was derived from the proper construction of the Order in Council which required the court to go behind contracts which on their proper construction, when taken in isolation, were not exchange contracts but which were a disguise for a prohibited monetary transaction. Accordingly, that case is an example of a letter of credit which because of its cosmetic purpose was directly rendered unenforceable by legislation. Unlike Staughton LJ. I therefore am unable to derive from that case any very significant assistance on this point.

68. However, there is a real conflict between on the one hand the well-established principle that contracts lawful on their face which are entered into in furtherance of an illegal purpose will be unenforceable at the suit of the party having knowledge of that purpose at the time of contracting

and on the other hand the policy of the law reflected in all the letter of credit cases of preserving the impregnability of the letter of credit save where the bank has clear evidence of an ex turpi causa defence such as fraud. This conflict is not, in my judgment, a matter which can be resolved simply by postulating the separate nature of the letter of credit and applying reasoning similar to that in the *Bowmakers* case. Thus, like Staughton LJ. in *Group Josi* ..., at page 362 I find it almost incredible that a party to an unlawful arms transaction would be permitted to enforce a letter of credit which was an integral part of that transaction even if the relevant legislation did not on its proper construction render ancillary contracts illegal. To take an even more extreme example, I cannot believe that any court would enforce a letter of credit to secure payment for the sale and purchase of heroin between foreign locations in which such underlying contracts were illegal. On the other hand, there is much to be said for the view that the public policy in superseding the impregnability of letters of credit where there is an unlawful underlying transaction defence may not be engaged where the nature of the underlying illegal purpose is relatively trivial, at least where the purpose is to be accomplished in a foreign jurisdiction. The problems which arise from attempting to reconcile conflicting considerations of public policy may well give rise to uncertain consequences, as illustrated in relation to the finality of New York Convention arbitration awards in *Westacre Investments Inc v. Jugoimport—SDPR Holding Co* [1999] QB 740. It would, however, be wrong in principle to invest letters of credit with a rigid inflexibility in the face of strong countervailing public policy considerations. If a beneficiary should as a matter of public policy (*ex turpi causa*) be precluded from utilising a letter of credit to benefit from his own fraud, it is hard to see why he should be permitted to use the courts to enforce part of an underlying transaction which would have been unenforceable on grounds of its illegality if no letter of credit had been involved, however serious the material illegality involved. To prevent him doing so in an appropriately serious case such as one involving international crime could hardly be seen as a threat to the lifeblood of international commerce.

69. In the present case, I have therefore come to the conclusion that on the assumed facts there is at least a strongly arguable case that the letter of credit cannot be permitted to be enforced against the defendant bank. That represents at the very least a realistic prospect of success for the Bank's defence based on this point. Furthermore, the conclusion as to whether enforcement is permissible at least arguably depends on the gravity of the illegality alleged. Although on the pleaded case that appears to be considerable, the uncertainty of this area of law is such that this is an issue which ought to be determined by reference to the evidence before the court at trial and not merely on assumptions derived from the pleaded defence. Moreover, I have also concluded, as I have sought to explain, that the fact that the Bank did not have clear evidence of such illegality at the date when payment had to be made would not prevent it having a good defence on that basis if such clear evidence were to hand when the court was called upon to decide the issue. For this purpose I proceed on the basis that it now has sufficiently clear evidence as expressed in the pleading.

70. Accordingly, the claimant's application to strike out the illegality defence and for summary judgment in respect of that defence will be dismissed.

NOTES

1.   These proceedings involved an application to strike out a defence and for summary judgment. Due to the interlocutory nature of the application, the court proceeded on the basis that the factual matters asserted by the defendant bank were true. At the full trial of the action, Cooke J held that there was no illegality which affected the transaction ([2004] EWHC 1938 (Comm)). However, Cooke J added (*obiter*, at [432]), expressly following the reasoning of Colman J, that the autonomy of a documentary credit does not prevent it being tainted with illegality of the underlying transaction.

2. Charles Proctor considers that the illegal objectives alleged to be at issue in the *Mahonia* case fell within the fraud exception because those activities were designed to mislead the investing public (see 'Enron, Letters of Credit and the Autonomy Principle' [2004] JIBFL 204 at 207):

> The *Mahonia* decision does, however, break new ground . . . In virtually every case in which the fraud exception had previously been pleaded, the arrangements included either fraud against the issuing bank itself or, more usually, against the seller/applicant for the credit. In contrast, *Mahonia* involved a fraud against the financial and securities markets and the investing public generally.

Proctor makes the point that the fraud was not committed against ENAC because it was party to the fraud. He also argues that the Bank was only a target of the fraud in a very marginal way. He continues:

> In this respect, it may be argued that *Mahonia* has broadened the fraud exception, in the sense that a fraud may fall within the principle even though it is perpetrated against the public as a whole, rather than merely as against a party to the credit. Nevertheless, the ultimate decision seems to be entirely consistent with . . . the principle '*ex turpi causa*'.

Do you agree?

3. As well as cases of fraud and (to a lesser extent) illegality, there are other circumstances when the court will allow the bank to withhold payment to the beneficiary under the credit after conforming documents have been tendered. These circumstances arise when:

- the credit is procured by misrepresentation of the beneficiary enabling the bank to rescind the credit *ab initio* (*SAFA Ltd v Banque Du Caire* [2000] 2 All ER (Comm) 567, CA): misrepresentation by the applicant for the credit would not vitiate the credit, but if the misrepresentation was fraudulent, and the beneficiary was an accomplice to that fraud, so that there was a conspiracy between them, the bank can refuse payment (*Solo Industries UK Ltd v Canara Bank* [2001] EWCA Civ 1059, [2001] 2 All ER (Comm) 217);
- there is a fundamental mistake which renders the credit void *ab initio*, for example where the credit is issued to the wrong person who is aware of the mistake;
- the bank's duty to pay is frustrated or suspended through supervening illegality or governmental action;
- the bank may set off against the sum due to the beneficiary a liquidated sum due from the beneficiary to the bank (*Hongkong and Shanghai Banking Corpn v Kloeckner & Co AG* [1990] 2 QB 514). The bank may also have a right of set-off against an assignee of the proceeds of the credit, so long as the liquidated sum due to the bank from the assignee, which the bank seeks to set off against the proceeds of the credit, accrued before notice of assignment was received by the bank (*Marathon Electrical Manufacturing Corpn v Mashreqbank PSC* [1997] CLC 1090).

These circumstances are considered further by Professor Goode in 'Abstract Payment Undertakings' in P Crane and J Stapleton (eds), *Essays for Patrick Atiyah* (1991), pp 225–234.

(f) The contracts arising out of a documentary credit transaction

Earlier in this chapter we listed the contractual relationships arising out of a confirmed irrevocable documentary credit transaction (see above, p 771). Each contract will now be examined in detail.

(i) The contract of sale

(a) The credit to comply with the contract of sale

The buyer must ensure the credit is issued in the form prescribed by the contract of sale.

Garcia v Page & Co Ltd

(1936) 55 Ll L Rep 391, King's Bench Division

By a contract dated 27 May 1935, Page & Co sold 2,000 tons of ammonium sulphate to Garcia in Spain, shipment to be during the first half of September 1935. The contract required Garcia 'to open immediately a confirmed credit in London' in favour of Page & Co. There was considerable delay before the credit was opened. On 22 August Page & Co wrote to Garcia stating that if the credit was not received in London by 24 August the contract would be cancelled. The credit was opened on 24 August but not notified to Page & Co until 26 August. Further, the credit did not comply with that provided for in the contract of sale. Page & Co repudiated the contract. A satisfactory credit was opened on 3 September but Page & Co maintained their repudiation. The dispute came before Porter J on a case stated from the arbitrator.

During the course of counsels' submissions, Porter J stated that he was satisfied that the provision with regard to the opening of the credit was a condition precedent in the sense that the sellers would not ship unless it was arranged.

Porter J (when giving judgment): . . . In my view, under the original contract there was a contract by which a confirmed credit in the terms specified was a condition precedent, and it had to be opened immediately. That means that the buyer must have such time as is needed by a person of reasonable diligence to get that credit established. I cannot myself believe that to get that credit established a reasonable time would be from May 27 until Aug 22 or Aug 27—whichever date you like to take. But just as I think that that was a condition precedent, so I think it is open to either of the parties, with the consent of the other, to prolong the time; and once you have put an end to the reasonable or particular time you have to allow another reasonable time from the moment you say: 'Now I demand you to fulfil that condition.'

To me it is clear, as at present advised, that up to Aug 22 the sellers were not demanding that the stipulation with regard to the confirmed credit should be immediately fulfilled. On the other hand, they were constantly urging that the matter should be taken in hand and I think making it quite plain that the step ought to be taken as speedily as possible. Then, on Aug 22, they did demand that the matter should be put in hand by the 24th. Whether Aug 24 was a reasonable time does not matter for this purpose. Starting from Aug 22, the buyer ought to have a reasonable time, having regard to all the circumstances of the case, to fulfil it.

To decide whether he had may involve a certain amount of evidence, which the arbitrator may take, of surrounding facts and circumstances—such as the difficulty Spaniards have in creating credits in this country by a particular date. I am not particularly impressed, though it is a matter for the arbitrator, with the difficulties, because some sort of credit was established by Aug 26. However, that is a matter to be taken into account. I think that is all the arbitrator has to find.

I say that because it has been urged upon me that I should take into consideration the fact that when the proper credit was finally established, three days of the time the sellers had for shipment had already elapsed. That is quite true, but I do not think that that seriously helps the case, because the delay that took place up to Aug 22 was with their consent; and if with their consent there were two or three days lost it would be part of their consent that that delay should take place.

For these reasons, I think the case should go back to the arbitrator in order that he may determine whether after Aug 22 the buyer had a reasonable time; and, as I say, the costs will be reserved.

Glencore Grain Rotterdam BV v Lebanese Organisation for International Commerce
[1997] CLC 1274, Court of Appeal

The plaintiff sellers concluded a FOB contract for the sale of wheat to the defendant buyers, by which the latter had to make payment by an irrevocable letter of credit. The credit opened, however, required tender of documents including a full set of marine bills of lading marked 'freight pre-paid'. The sellers rejected the credit and refused to load the wheat. The Court of Appeal held that the sellers were entitled to do so as the buyers had breached the contract of sale by failing to open a letter of credit conforming with the sale contract.

Evans LJ: The first issue, therefore, is whether the buyers under a sale contract on what are described as, normal fob terms are entitled to open a letter of credit which requires the sellers to present 'freight pre-paid' bills of lading if they are to receive payment from the buyers' bank. Absent any special agreement, the sellers are entitled to see a conforming letter of credit in place before they begin shipment of the goods, and then their obligation is to ship the contract goods on board the vessel provided by the buyers, for carriage on whatever terms as to freight and otherwise the buyers have agreed with the shipowner. The sellers are expressly free of any obligation to pay freight (special terms apart, fob is the antithesis of c & f—cost and freight) and in the normal course they cannot be sure before shipment that the shipowner will issue freight pre-paid bills of lading, unless they are prepared if necessary to pay the amount of freight themselves, or unless some other guaranteed payment mechanism is already in place. I would put the matter broadly in that way, because it may be that an undertaking from the shipowner himself, or a third party guarantee of the payment of freight following due shipment of the goods, would suffice. It is unnecessary to consider that aspect further in the present case, because all that was offered by the buyers was their own assurance that the freight would be paid, by them or on their behalf. It is abundantly clear, in my judgment, that the buyers' own assurance cannot be enough to serve as a guarantee to the sellers that 'freight pre-paid' bills of lading will be issued when shipment is complete. That would mean, as the judge pointed out, that the security of a bank guarantee for the payment of the price, which is what the letter of credit mechanism provides, would be destroyed. I therefore agree with the judge's observations that the buyers' contention, that the letter of credit terms were in conformity with the contract, is contrary both to the underlying concept of the fob contract (subject always to what special terms may be agreed in a particular case) and to the essential commercial purpose of the letter of credit machinery.

The buyers' submission is that there were special features which entitled the board to reach the conclusion that the buyers were entitled to require freight pre-paid bills in this case. In my judgment, the board's conclusion that the buyers were so entitled 'provided that they did indeed ensure that such freight was paid by the completion of loading' is open to the objections set out by the judge. More generally, Mr Havelock-Allan refers to certain specific facts. The sellers knew that Hoboob, the receivers and sub-buyers, had bought on c & f terms and themselves required freight pre-paid bills. The named vessel was time-chartered to the buyers, and so they were entitled to instruct the master to issue 'freight pre-paid' bills (*The Nanfri* [1979] AC 757). The buyers gave their assurance (though not until 29 March, after the dispute had arisen) that the freight would be paid before the bills were issued 'without any problem'. But none of this, in my judgment, justifies the implication of a term which, for the reasons stated above, would be wholly at variance with the express terms of the fob sale in fact agreed.

In this context, the buyers referred to the judgment of Robert Goff J in *Ficom v Sociedad Cadex Ltda* [1980] 2 Ll Rep 118 at p. 131, which was quoted by the judge. This judgment distinguishes between implying a term in the sale contract and, on the other hand, establishing what the parties agreed should be the terms of the letter of credit issued or to be issued under that contract. The latter process may result in a letter of credit agreement which supplements or even varies the terms originally agreed. This is demonstrated in the present case by the agreement to vary the shipment date to include the month of April. But I do not consider that it is relevant to the question in issue. The freight pre-paid requirement, unless it was a term of the sale contract itself, was introduced by the buyers and immediately rejected by the sellers. The buyers maintained their requirement on 29 March and it is of the essence of their case that the sellers made no further reference to it before the contract came to an end. The sellers thereafter did not act inconsistently with their previous refusal, and their silence on this matter cannot be regarded as an acceptance of the buyer's demand: *Allied Marine Transport Ltd v Vale do Rio Doce Navegacas SA ('The Leonidas D')* [1985] 1 WLR 925 per Robert Goff LJ at pp. 936–937. In short, the buyers cannot allege that there was a fresh agreement as regards this term of the letter of credit which had the effect either of supplementing or varying the requirements of the sale contract.

For these reasons, as well as those given more succinctly by Longmore I, in my judgment the buyers were not entitled to require the sellers to procure and produce freight pre-paid bills of lading in order to receive payment under the letter of credit opened by them. It follows that the buyers failed to open a letter of credit conforming with the sale contract and, subject to the question of waiver considered below, they were thereby in breach of contract.

[**Nourse LJ** and **Sir Ralph Gibson** concurred.]

NOTES

1. *Garcia v Page & Co Ltd* illustrates that the buyer's obligation to have a documentary credit opened in favour of the seller is usually a condition precedent to the seller's obligation to deliver the goods (cf M Clarke [1974] CLJ 260 at 264–269). Provision of the documentary credit is a condition precedent to any obligation on the part of the seller to perform any aspect of the loading operation which is the seller's responsibility (*Kronos Worldwide Ltd v Sempra Oil Trading Sarl* [2004] EWCA Civ 3, [2004] CLC 136 at [19], per Mance LJ). But the opening of the credit may be construed as a condition precedent to the contract of sale itself (*Trans Trust SPRL v Danubian Trading Co Ltd* [1952] 2 QB 297 at 304, CA), or the contract of sale may impose an obligation on the seller which is a condition precedent to the opening of the credit (*Knotz v Fairclough Dodd and Jones Ltd* [1952] 1 Lloyd's Rep 226).

2. If the buyer opens a credit which does not comply with the terms of the contract of sale, he may remedy the defect if there is still time before the credit is required (*Kronman & Co v Steinberger* (1922) 10 Ll L Rep 39 at 40, per Greer J). But if the buyer fails to open the credit in time, or does not remedy a defective credit in time, he commits a repudiatory breach which entitles the seller to treat the contract of sale as discharged (*Dix v Grainger* (1922) 10 Ll L Rep 496 at 496–497, per Bailhache J) and claim damages for breach of contract (on the basis of *Hadley v Baxendale* (1854) 9 Exch 341, 156 ER 145). The seller will be able to claim damages for loss of profit on the transaction if, at the time the contract was made, such loss was within the reasonable contemplation of the parties as the probable consequence of the breach (*Trans Trust SPRL v Danubian Trading Co Ltd*, above; *Ian Stach Ltd v Baker Bosley Ltd* [1958] 2 QB 130 at 145). A buyer who fails to open a credit may be able to defend the seller's claim for damages on the ground that it would have been illegal to have opened the credit (*Soeximex SAS v Agrocorp International Pte Ltd* [2011] EWHC 2743 (Comm), [2012] 1 Lloyd's Rep 52).

3. The seller may decide to ship the goods despite the buyer's failure to open the credit on the due date or in its specified form. In *Panoutsos v Raymond Hadley Corpn of New York* [1917] 2 KB 473, a series of shipments of flour was to be paid for by confirmed bankers' credit. The buyer opened an unconfirmed credit. The sellers knew of this defect but still made some shipments before repudiating the contract. The Court of Appeal held that the non-conformity of the credit had been waived by the sellers and that the waiver could only be revoked if reasonable notice was given to the buyer (at 477–478). But in other cases the seller may be deemed to have agreed to a variation of the contract thus preventing him from changing his mind, even on reasonable notice. Variation, unlike waiver, will only be valid if supported by consideration. Identifying whether a contractual requirement has been waived or varied may prove difficult and will depend on the circumstances of each case. See, for example, *WJ Alan & Co Ltd v El Nasr Export and Import Co* [1972] 2 QB 189, where Lord Denning MR decided the case on grounds of waiver of the seller's strict rights under the contract, whereas Megaw and Stephenson LJJ decided it on grounds of variation of the contract. The case is exhaustively examined by M Clarke [1974] CLJ 260.

(b) The time of opening of the credit

Where the contract of sale provides a date for the opening of the credit, the buyer must open the credit by that date. If the contract of sale stipulates that the credit must be opened 'immediately', the buyer has such time as is needed by a person of reasonable diligence to open such a credit (*Garcia v Page & Co Ltd*, above, p 810). But what if no time is stipulated?

Pavia & Co SpA v Thurmann-Nielsen
[1952] 2 QB 84, Court of Appeal

A CIF contract for the sale of shelled Brazilian groundnuts provided for payment by confirmed irrevocable credit and for shipment in the period from 1 February to 30 April 1949 at the sellers' option. The buyers did not open the credit until 22 April. The sellers claimed damages for breach of contract by delay in opening the credit. Affirming the decision of McNair J, the Court of Appeal upheld the sellers' claim.

> **Somervell LJ:** . . . Speaking for myself, I would have no doubt, apart from any question arising with regard to export licences, that under this contract the obligation of the buyers was prima facie to open the credit on February 1 and to have it opened and available as from that date . . .
>
> The argument, which was very clearly put by Mr Widgery [counsel for the buyers], was on these lines: Normally, delivery and payment are concurrent conditions. You do not really need the credit until you are ready to deliver and have got your bills of lading, when you can go round to the bank and get

your money. That is the object of it, to see that the seller can get immediate payment. He read to us, as he read to the learned judge below, certain cases in which Scrutton LJ pointed out (as, of course, I accept) that the main object of the credit system is that the seller may get his money when he has shipped his goods and, at any rate, in some forms of credit the buyer gets an interval of time before he has to meet bills. Whether under this particular form of credit there would be any interval of time between the time of its operation and the time when the buyer had to put his bank in credit I do not know, and to my mind it does not matter. I am quite clear that Scrutton LJ was not addressing himself to the problem which is at present before us. My view is that the contract would be unworkable if, as suggested by Mr Widgery, the buyer under it was under no obligation until a date, which he could not possibly know, and which there is no machinery for his finding out, namely, when the seller actually has the goods down at the port ready to be put on to the ship. There are no words in the contract which would justify us in arriving at that result and there is no reason why we should imply any such term into this contract. I do not think it is a question of implication. I think when a seller is given a right to ship over a period and there is machinery for payment, that machinery must be available over the whole of that period. If the buyer is anxious, as he might be if the period of shipment is a long one, not to have to put the credit machinery in motion until shortly before the seller is likely to want to ship, then he must put in some provision by which the credit shall be provided 14 days after a cable received from the seller, or the like. In the absence of any provision of that kind, I think the answer which the judge gave to the question posed is plainly right, and the appeal should be dismissed.

Denning LJ: The question in this case is this: In a contract which provides for payment by confirmed credit, when must the buyer open the credit? In the absence of express stipulation, I think the credit must be made available to the seller at the beginning of the shipment period. The reason is because the seller is entitled, before he ships the goods, to be assured that, on shipment, he will get paid. The seller is not bound to tell the buyer the precise date when he is going to ship; and whenever he does ship the goods, he must be able to draw on the credit. He may ship on the very first day of the shipment period. If, therefore, the buyer is to fulfil his obligations he must make the credit available to the seller at the very first date when the goods may be lawfully shipped in compliance with the contract. I agree with the answer given by McNair J. The appeal should be dismissed.

[**Roxburgh J** concurred.]

NOTES

1. In *Sinason-Teicher Inter-American Grain Corpn v Oilcakes and Oilseeds Trading Co Ltd* [1954] 1 WLR 1394, a CIF contract for the sale of barley provided for shipment during October–November 1952. The buyers agreed to give the sellers a guarantee that the bank would take up the shipping documents on first presentation. The contract did not stipulate a time when the buyers should give the guarantee but when the buyers had failed to provide it by 10 September the sellers cancelled the contract. Affirming the decision of Devlin J, the Court of Appeal held that the sellers had been wrong to cancel the contract as the buyers had not been in default at that time. In an *obiter dictum* Denning LJ stated (at 1400):

We were referred to *Pavia & Co SpA v Thurmann-Nielsen.* I agree with what Devlin J said about that case. It does not decide that the buyer can delay right up to the first date for shipment. It only decides that he must provide the letter of credit at latest by that date. The correct view is that, if nothing is said about time in the contract, the buyer must provide the letter of credit within a reasonable time before the first date for shipment. The same applies to a bank guarantee: for it stands on a similar footing.

2.   In *Ian Stach Ltd v Baker Bosley Ltd* [1958] 2 QB 130, an FOB contract for the sale of steel plates provided for payment by confirmed irrevocable credit and for shipment during August–September 1956 at the buyers' option. The buyers failed to open the credit by 1 August and Diplock J held them to be in breach of contract. It was argued that as the buyer stipulates the shipping date under a 'classic fob contract' (see above, p 537), the credit need only be opened a reasonable time before the date of shipment fixed by the buyer. Diplock J rejected that argument on grounds of uncertainty and held that the prima facie rule was that credit must be opened at the latest by the earliest shipping date (and to the same effect, see *Glencore Grain Rotterdam BV v Lebanese Organisation for International Commerce* [1997] 4 All ER 514; *Kolmar Group AG v Traxpo Enterprises Pvt Ltd* [2010] EWHC 113 (Comm), [2010] 2 Lloyd's Rep 653). Diplock J observed (at 141) that Denning LJ's statement in the *Sinason-Teicher* case, that the credit must be provided a reasonable time before the first date for shipment, was *obiter* and that the other Lords Justices in that case did not express any view on the matter. Diplock J did not expressly adopt Denning LJ's formulation, but he did not dissent from it either. In fact there is much to be said in favour of Denning LJ's approach, for a shipper cannot be expected to make instantaneous shipping arrangements, and if he does not receive the credit until the day before the start of the shipment period he is likely to lose the benefit of the first few days of that period (see E McKendrick, *Goode on Commercial Law* (5th edn, 2016), p 1045, fn 172).

3.   If the contract of sale specifies a shipment date, and not a period of shipment, the buyer must open the credit a reasonable time before that date (*Plasticmoda SpA v Davidsons (Manchester) Ltd* [1952] 1 Lloyd's Rep 527 at 538, per Denning LJ).

4.   A documentary credit becomes irrevocable upon issue; that is, upon its release from the control of the issuing bank or confirming bank, irrespective of the time that it is delivered to or received by the beneficiary (UCP 600, arts 7(b) and 8(b)). However, for the purpose of determining whether the buyer has complied with its obligations under the contract of sale, the credit may be considered to be 'opened' only when it is communicated to the beneficiary (*Bunge Corpn v Vegetable Vitamin Foods (Private) Ltd* [1985] 1 Lloyd's Rep 613 at 617, per Neill J). In each case, it will be a question of construction of the contract concerned (R King, *Gutteridge and Megrah's Law of Bankers' Commercial Credits* (8th edn, 2001), para 4–48, fn 132). The buyer will be liable for any delay in opening the credit, even if it was caused by circumstances beyond his control (*AE Lindsay & Co Ltd v Cook* [1953] 1 Lloyd's Rep 328 at 355, per Pilcher J).

QUESTION

Where an FOB or CIF contract does not specify the date by which the credit must be opened, but does specify a period of shipment, when must the buyer open the credit? Contrast *Goode on Commercial Law*, above, p 1045 and A Malek and D Quest, *Documentary Credits* (4th edn, 2009), para 3.23.

(c) Expiry date and place for presentation

Article 6(d)(i) of UCP 600 provides that a credit must state an expiry date for presentation and that an expiry date stated for honour or negotiation will be deemed to be an expiry date for presentation. A presentation by or on behalf of the beneficiary must be made on or before the expiry date (art 6(e)). Article 6(d)(ii) provides that the place of the bank with which the credit is available is the place for presentation (and that the place for presentation under a credit available with any bank is that of any bank). A place for presentation other than that of the issuing bank is in addition to the place of the issuing bank. Further, art 14(c) of UCP 600 provides that a presentation including one or more original transport documents must be made by or on behalf of the beneficiary not later than 21 days after the date of shipment (but in any event not later than the expiry date of the credit).

The expiry date of the credit or the last day for presentation of documents may be extended by the operation of art 29, which applies where a time limit would otherwise expire on a day on which the bank to which presentation is to be made is closed (other than for reasons specified in art 36, eg Acts of God, riots, civil commotions, etc). Article 29(a) extends the time limit to the next succeeding day on which the bank is open. Under art 29(b), a bank which accepts documents on the next succeeding banking day must provide a statement that the documents were presented within the time limits extended under art 29(a). In *Bayerische Vereinsbank Aktiengesellschaft v National Bank of Pakistan* [1997] 1 Lloyd's Rep 59, a confirming bank, which had accepted documents on the next succeeding banking day, failed to supply the issuing bank with the necessary statement. Mance J held that presentation of the statement was not a condition precedent to the confirming bank's right of reimbursement, but that the confirming bank would be liable to pay damages to the issuing bank if the latter suffered any resultant loss (eg where omission of the statement caused delay in payment of the issuing bank by the buyer).

(d) The credit as payment

Unless otherwise agreed, payment by documentary credit constitutes conditional payment of the price. As Lord Denning MR stated (*obiter*) in *WJ Alan & Co Ltd v El Nasr Export and Import Co* [1972] 2 QB 189 at 212:

> . . . I am of the opinion that in the ordinary way, when the contract of sale stipulates for payment to be made by confirmed irrevocable letter of credit, then, when the letter of credit is issued and accepted by the seller, it operates as conditional payment of the price. It does not operate as absolute payment.
>
> It is analogous to the case where, under a contract of sale, the buyer gives a bill of exchange or a cheque for the price. It is presumed to be given, not as absolute payment, nor as collateral security, but as conditional payment. If the letter of credit is honoured by the bank when the documents are presented to it, the debt is discharged. If it is not honoured, the debt is not discharged: and the seller has a remedy in damages against both banker and buyer.

For reasons supporting this view, see M Clarke [1974] CLJ 260 at 274–276. See also *ED & F Man Ltd v Nigerian Sweets & Confectionery Co Ltd* [1977] 2 Lloyd's Rep 50 at 56–57, per Ackner J; *Maran Road Saw Mill v Austin Taylor & Co Ltd* [1975] 1 Lloyd's Rep 156 at 159–160, per Ackner J (noted (1977) 40 MLR 91); and *Re Charge Card Services Ltd* [1989] Ch 497 at 516 (above, p 627).

When the contract of sale specifies that payment is to be by documentary credit the seller must present the documents to the bank. He cannot 'short-circuit' the credit and present documents directly to the buyer and claim payment from him (*Soproma SpA v Marine & Animal By-Products Corpn* [1966] 1 Lloyd's Rep 367 at 385–386, per McNair J). However, if the bank defaults, for example by becoming insolvent, the seller can normally claim payment from the buyer by tendering documents directly to him (*Soproma*, at 386). This stems from the fact that in most cases the credit only operates as conditional payment. As Ackner J said in *ED & F Man Ltd v Nigerian Sweets & Confectionery Co Ltd*, above, at 56: 'The [buyers'] liability to the sellers was a primary liability. This liability was suspended during the period available to the issuing bank to honour the drafts and was activated when the issuing bank failed.' Alternatively, the seller can sue the buyer for damages for breach of contract.

(ii) The contract between buyer and issuing bank

(a) The issuing bank must adhere strictly to the terms of the buyer's instructions

The buyer will usually sign and complete the issuing bank's standard documentary credit application form, which usually incorporates the UCP. This constitutes an offer of a unilateral contract which the issuing bank accepts when it issues the credit. The application form sets out the buyer's instructions in relation to the credit. The issuing bank must adhere strictly to the terms of the buyer's instructions. This means that the issuing bank must ensure that the credit issued to the seller complies with the instructions set out in the application form and that payment, acceptance, or negotiation is effected only on presentation of documents which comply with the terms of the credit. Only then will the issuing bank be entitled to reimbursement from the buyer. Where the buyer's instructions are ambiguous, the issuing bank will be entitled to be reimbursed if it construes them reasonably. The point is illustrated by the next case.

Midland Bank Ltd v Seymour

[1955] 2 Lloyd's Rep 147, Queen's Bench Division

Seymour contracted to purchase a large quantity of feathers from Hong Kong sellers. Payment was to be by confirmed irrevocable credit. The credit was issued by the Midland Bank after receiving instructions from Seymour given on the bank's pro forma application form. Seymour had instructed the bank to make the credit 'available in Hong Kong'. On presentation of the shipping documents, the Midland Bank accepted, and later paid, various bills of exchange drawn by the sellers. But the sellers were fraudulent and had shipped rubbish. Seymour refused to reimburse the bank, raising various defences to the bank's claim for payment. One defence was that the documents tendered did not conform to the credit as the bill of lading did not state the description, quantity, and price of the goods (although such information was contained in other tendered documents, eg the invoice, which were consistent with the bill of lading). Another defence was that the bank had not complied with its mandate by issuing a credit which provided for acceptance of drafts in London instead of Hong Kong. Devlin J gave judgment for the bank on its claim.

   Devlin J held that the sellers had presented conforming documents as the credit was to be construed as requiring the presentation of a set of documents which were consistent between themselves, and which, when read together, provided a statement of the description, quantity, and price of the goods. He held that the credit did not require each individual document to provide such information.

> **Devlin J** continued: But if I had not reached that conclusion . . . I should have arrived at the same result on another ground. In my judgment, no principle is better established than that when a banker or anyone else is given instructions or a mandate of this sort, they must be given to him with reasonable clearness. The banker is obliged to act upon them precisely. He may act at his peril if he disobeys them or does not conform with them. In those circumstances there is a corresponding duty cast on the giver of instructions to see that he puts them in a clear form. Perhaps it is putting it too high for this purpose to say that it is a duty cast upon him. The true view of the matter, I think, is that when an agent acts upon ambiguous instructions he is not in default if he can show that he adopted what was a reasonable meaning. It is not enough to say afterwards that if he had construed the documents properly he would on the whole have arrived at the conclusion that in an ambiguous document the meaning which he did not give to it could be better supported

than the meaning which he did give to it. If I am wrong in adopting the construction that Mr Diplock gives to this document, I am quite clear that at the best it is ambiguous. It is impossible to say that the document specifies in reasonably clear terms that the bill of lading has to contain the description and quantity.

That argument is met to some extent by Mr Mocatta when he points out that the form which was filled up is not Mr Seymour's own form but is the bank's form; and he relies upon what I think may be called the *contra proferentes* principle on which a person who prepares a form is responsible for any ambiguities that it contains, or must suffer for it. In my judgment, that principle does not apply in this case. It applies (or would apply) if there were some exception, as for example in one of the conditions or clauses on the back of the document which was inserted for the benefit of the bank. If there were some exception there, no doubt the principle would apply.

But this is not a case of that type. This is a printed document which shows the sort of thing that the bank wants, but it is left to the applicant for the credit to fill it up in what way he wants; and if he thinks there is some ambiguity in it there is no difficulty, so far as I can see, in his filling it up in a way to make it clear. For example, if he wanted plainly to specify that the bill of lading should contain the full description, I cannot see that there would be any difficulty in his doing so, or that the bank could conceivably object if he did so. The bank do not care what the bill of lading is or is not required to contain. It cannot matter to them so long as they are told clearly what it is that they have to look for.

[On the issue whether the bank had exceeded its mandate Devlin J continued:]

I have not to determine whether the Midland Bank is in breach by failing to create facilities in Hongkong. If they did so fail, and if it was in breach, it has caused no damage, because the seller has never tried to make use of that. The point is whether the bank is authorized to pay or accept only in Hongkong. . . . If it was authorized so to pay, then although the place of payment may be commercially immaterial, the bank has exceeded its mandate and cannot recover. It is a hard law sometimes which deprives an agent of the right to reimbursement if he has exceeded his authority, even though the excess does not damage his principal's interests. The corollary, which I have already noted in the judgment I delivered earlier, is that the instruction to the agent must be clear and unambiguous.

The mandate to the bank in this case does not make the place of availability expressly exclusive, and I do not think it ought lightly to be assumed that it was intended to be expressly exclusive. Let me take a simple example, uncomplicated by a letter of credit. A, who does business in London, arranges that his debt to X at Edinburgh will be discharged by his agent B, whose place of business is also in London. If matters were left there, X would, in accordance with the ordinary rule, have to come to London to collect his money. But it might well be that A would tell his agent B that he was to travel to Edinburgh to pay X there. If he did, and if before B went to Edinburgh X happened to come to London and call for the money and B paid it, it would be a strong thing to say that B could not debit A. It would be held in such a case as that, I think, that the naming of Edinburgh was merely an additional convenience made for the benefit of X, if he wanted to take advantage of it. So here I think the naming of Hongkong is additional and not exclusive. If it were not named, the drafts would have to be presented at the Midland Bank's place of business in London. That might not be convenient to the seller, and so there is a request for additional facilities in the place where the seller does business … In my judgment, acceptance in London was within the terms of the mandate to the bank in this case.

NOTES

1. The reason for the rule relating to ambiguous or unclear instructions given by the buyer to his bank is best stated by Lord Diplock in *Commercial Banking Co of Sydney Ltd v Jalsard Pty Ltd* [1973] AC 279 at 286, PC:

The banker is not concerned as to whether the documents for which the buyer has stipulated serve any useful commercial purpose or as to why the customer called for tender of a document of a particular description. Both the issuing banker and his correspondent bank have to make quick decisions as to whether a document which has been tendered by the seller complies with the requirements of a credit at the risk of incurring liability to one or other of the parties to the transaction if the decision is wrong. Delay in deciding may in itself result in a breach of his contractual obligations to the buyer or to the seller. This is the reason for the rule that where the banker's instructions from his customer are ambiguous or unclear he commits no breach of his contract with the buyer if he has construed them in a reasonable sense, even though upon the closer consideration which can be given to questions of construction in an action in a court of law, it is possible to say that some other meaning is to be preferred.

2. But the rule has its limits. In *European Asian Bank AG v Punjab and Sind Bank (No 2)* [1983] 1 WLR 642 at 656, Goff LJ said that 'a party relying on his own interpretation of the relevant document must have acted reasonably in all the circumstances in so doing. If instructions are given to an agent, it is understandable that he should expect to act on those instructions without more; but if, for example, the ambiguity is patent on the face of the document it may well be right (especially with the facilities of modern communication available to him) to have his instructions clarified by his principal, if time permits, before acting upon them'. See also, above, pp 127–128.

3. In *European Asian Bank AG v Punjab and Sind Bank (No 2)*, above, Goff LJ pointed out that it was not strictly correct to refer to the issuing bank as the agent of the buyer, as Devlin J had done in *Midland Bank Ltd v Seymour*. Goff LJ was right, for the issuing bank does not contract with the seller on the buyer's behalf: the bank enters into a separate contract with the seller as principal. This does not alter the rule that the issuing bank, like an agent, is entitled to give ambiguous instructions a reasonable construction, but it does mean that it is probably more accurate to refer to the buyer's informed acceptance of an unauthorised act of the issuing bank (eg acceptance of non-conforming documents) as waiver of the bank's breach of mandate rather than as ratification of the act itself. The nature of the relationship between the issuing bank and the confirming bank, and the effect of ambiguous instructions passing between them, is considered below at p 823.

(b) The issuing bank must examine the tendered documents to determine whether they appear on their face to constitute a complying presentation

Uniform Customs and Practice for Documentary Credits
(2007 Revision, ICC Publication No 600)

ARTICLE 14

Standard of Examination of Documents

a. A nominated bank acting on its nomination, a confirming bank, if any, and the issuing bank must examine a presentation to determine, on the basis of the documents alone, whether or not the documents appear on their face to constitute a complying presentation.

b. A nominated bank acting on its nomination, a confirming bank, if any, and the issuing bank shall each have a maximum of five banking days following the day of presentation to determine if a presentation is complying. This period is not curtailed or otherwise affected by the occurrence on or after the date of presentation of any expiry date or last day for presentation.

Gian Singh & Co Ltd v Banque de l'Indochine
[1974] 1 WLR 1234, Privy Council

Banque de l'Indochine opened an irrevocable documentary credit on the instructions of Gian Singh & Co Ltd (the customer) to finance the purchase of a fishing vessel. The credit required the tender of a certificate signed by Balwant Singh, holder of Malaysian Passport E-13276, certifying that the vessel had been correctly built and was in a condition to sail. The certificate was tendered but the signature of Balwant Singh was a forgery, as was the passport presented to the bank for inspection. The bank accepted the documents and debited its customer's account with the sum paid to the beneficiary. The customer sued the bank claiming that its account had been wrongly debited. The Court of Appeal in Singapore gave judgment for the bank. The Privy Council dismissed the customer's appeal against that decision.

Lord Diplock (delivering the advice of the Privy Council (Lords Wilberforce, Diplock, Cross of Chelsea, and Kilbrandon and Sir Harry Gibbs)): The fact that a document presented by the beneficiary under a documentary credit, which otherwise conforms to the requirements of the credit, is in fact a forgery does not, of itself, prevent the issuing bank from recovering from its customer money paid under the credit. The duty of the issuing bank, which it may perform either by itself, or by its agent, the notifying bank, is to examine documents with reasonable care to ascertain that they appear on their face to be in accordance with the terms and conditions of the credit. The express provision to this effect in article 7 of the Uniform Customs and Practice for Documentary Credits [1962 Revision] does no more than re-state the duty of the bank at common law. In business transactions financed by documentary credits banks must be able to act promptly on presentation of the documents. In the ordinary case visual inspection of the actual documents presented is all that is called for. The bank is under no duty to take any further steps to investigate the genuineness of a signature which, on the face of it, purports to be the signature of the person named or described in the letter of credit.

The instant case differs from the ordinary case in that there was a special requirement that the signature on the certificate should be that of a person called Balwant Singh, and that that person should also be the holder of Malaysian passport no. E-13276. This requirement imposed upon the bank the additional duty to take reasonable care to see that the signature on the certificate appeared to correspond with the signature on an additional document presented by the beneficiary which, on the face of it, appeared to be a Malaysian passport No E-13276 issued in the name of Balwant Singh. The evidence was that that is what the notifying bank had done when the certificate was presented. The onus of proving lack of reasonable care in failing to detect the forgery of the certificate lies upon the customer. In their Lordships' view, in agreement with all the members of the Court of Appeal, the customer did not succeed in making out any case of negligence against the issuing bank or the notifying bank which acted as its agent, in failing to detect the forgery.

NOTES

1. Unlike art 13(a) of UCP 500, and unlike art 7 of the 1962 UCP Revision, referred to by Lord Diplock in *Gian Singh*, art 14(a) of UCP 600 does not expressly state that the bank must conduct its examination 'with reasonable care'. The drafters of UCP 600 considered that a general reference to reasonable care was unnecessary as UCP 600, supplemented by ISBP (above, p 783), adopted a significantly more detailed approach to compliance (G Collier, *Commentary on UCP 600* (2007, ICC Publication No 680), p 62). A presentation of documents either complies or it does not comply: if it does not, a bank that honours or negotiates is not entitled to reimbursement and cannot claim such entitlement on the basis that it exercised reasonable care in examining the documents (*Benjamin's Sale of Goods* (9th edn, 2014), para 23–094).

2.   Article 14(a) of UCP 600 calls for documents to be examined only 'on their face'. The bank does not have to engage in mathematical calculations in order to check compliance (*Crédit Industriel et Commercial v China Merchants Bank* [2002] EWHC 973 (Comm), [2002] 2 All ER (Comm) 427). The superficial nature of the examination is reinforced by art 34 of UCP 600, which provides that 'a bank assumes no liability or responsibility for the form, sufficiency, accuracy, genuineness, falsification or legal effect of any document'.

3.   Related UCP provisions:

- UCP 600, art 14(b), provides that the issuing bank, confirming bank, or nominated bank, each has a maximum of five banking days following the day of presentation of documents to determine if the presentation is complying (see further, below at p 825);

- UCP 600, art 14(g), states that a document presented but not required by the credit is to be disregarded and may be returned to the presenter;

- UCP 600, art 14(h), provides that non-documentary conditions are to be ignored. A non-documentary condition would be where the credit contains a reference to goods being of 'US origin'. This condition will be ignored unless the credit also calls for one of the tendered documents—most likely the certificate of origin—to indicate compliance with that condition.

4.   Where the buyer has been the victim of a fraud of the seller (eg the seller ships rubbish, tenders complying documents, and receives payment), the buyer must reimburse the issuing bank and pursue the seller for breach of the contract of sale and/or deceit. The buyer might have a claim against the issuing bank in negligence for failing to advise on the transaction, for example as to the need for an inspection certificate from a reliable third party, but such a claim will only succeed where the facts show that the bank has undertaken a duty to advise, which will be rare, or the bank has actually given misleading advice. In *Midland Bank Ltd v Seymour*, above, p 817, the bank was held liable on Seymour's counterclaim for contractual negligence because it failed to pass on certain adverse information about the Hong Kong sellers after being instructed by Seymour to make inquiries. However, the bank was only ordered to pay nominal damages as Seymour had suffered no loss as a result of this breach. See also *Commercial Banking Co of Sydney Ltd v Jalsard Pty Ltd* [1973] AC 279, PC.

5.   General comments:

(a)   If the issuing bank fails to comply with the buyer's instructions with regard to the opening of the credit or as to the acceptance or rejection of documents presented to it, the buyer is under no obligation to accept the documents from the bank and is not obliged to reimburse the bank for any payment made to the beneficiary (the buyer will then be taken to have 'abandoned' the goods to the issuing bank, in whom they will then vest: see E McKendrick, *Goode on Commercial Law* (5th edn, 2016), pp 1046–1047). Further, the bank may be liable to the buyer for any loss sustained by him as a result of the bank's breach of contract.

(b) The UCP exonerates the issuing bank from liability for matters beyond its control. Article 35 protects the bank against liability for the consequences arising out of delay and/or loss in transit of messages and for errors in the translation and/or interpretation of messages. But it is submitted that art 35 does not exempt the issuing bank from liability for its own negligence (A Malek and D Quest, *Jack: Documentary Credits* (4th edn, 2009), para 4.17). Article 36 of UCP 600 excludes liability for force majeure events. Article 37 is particularly important because it exonerates the issuing bank from all liability for the errors of any correspondent bank employed by the issuing bank to give effect to the instructions of the buyer (applicant). But again it is submitted that this immunity does not extend to the issuing bank's own negligence (Malek and Quest, above, paras 4.21–4.25). Moreover, art 37 does not require the buyer to accept and pay for documents which failed to comply with his instructions: the sole effect of art 37 is to prevent a buyer holding an issuing bank liable for damage caused to the buyer by the action of the correspondent bank instructed by the issuing bank (*Crédit Agricole Indosuez v Generate Bank (No 2)* [1999] 2 All ER (Comm) 1016 at 1024, Steel J; cf *Société Générale SA v Saad Trading* [2011] EWHC 2424 (Comm), [2011] 2 CLC 629 at [49]–[53], where documents when presented were compliant and not discrepant). Nevertheless, art 37 may still prove harsh on the buyer when the correspondent bank employed by the issuing bank (ie the advising bank or the confirming bank) has been negligent, for there is no clear way to make the correspondent bank directly liable to him (there is no privity of contract and no duty of care in tort: although it was suggested in *United Trading Corpn SA v Allied Arab Bank* [1985] 2 Lloyd's Rep 554n, CA, that the correspondent bank owes a duty of care to the buyer, this was later doubted in *GKN Contractors Ltd v Lloyds Bank plc* (1985) 30 BLR 48, CA). Article e12 of the eUCP contains additional disclaimers where documents are tendered electronically.

The issuing bank may include exemption clauses in its contracts which are wider than those included in the UCP. For example, it is common to find exemption clauses in which the applicant agrees to be bound by the issuing bank's determination of the regularity of the documents. Professor Ellinger submits that no attempt should be made to discourage the use of such clauses as freedom of contract must be respected (EP Ellinger, 'The UCP 500: Considering a New Revision' [2004] LMCLQ 30 at 41). Nevertheless, the English courts can usually subject such clauses to a test of reasonableness as the application form used by the applicant to request the opening of a credit is commonly a pro forma supplied by the issuing bank which contains the bank's standard terms and conditions (Unfair Contract Terms Act 1977, s 3). The question of reasonableness was raised, but not pursued, by the applicant in *Swotbook.com v Royal Bank of Scotland plc* [2011] EWHC 2025 (QB) at [24] (above, p 780).

QUESTION

Does acceptance of conforming documents by the issuing bank preclude the buyer from rejecting the goods if they prove defective on arrival? What if the defect was apparent on the face of the documents? See E McKendrick, *Goode on Commercial Law* (5th edn, 2016), p 1046.

(iii) The contract between the issuing bank and the advising or confirming bank

Bank Melli Iran v Barclays Bank DCO
[1951] 2 Lloyd's Rep 367, King's Bench Division

The facts appear above, p 780.

McNair J: In my judgment, both on the construction of the documents under which the credit was established and in principle, the relationship between Bank Melli, the instructing bank, and Barclays Bank, the confirming bank, was that of principal and agent. This relationship was held to exist in substantially similar circumstances in *Equitable Trust Co of New York v Dawson Partners Ltd* ((1927) 27 Ll L Rep 49) (see per Viscount Cave LC at p 52, Lord Sumner at p 53, and Lord Shaw of Dunfermline at p 57), and the existence of this relationship is implicit in the judgments of the Court of Appeal in *J H Rayner & Co Ltd v Hambro's Bank Ltd* ([1943] KB 37). I accept as accurate the statement of Professor Gutteridge KC in his book on Bankers' Commercial Credits, at p 51, that 'as between the issuing banker' (in this case Bank Melli) 'and the correspondent' (in this case Barclays Bank) 'the relationship is, unless otherwise agreed, that of principal and agent . . .' On the facts of this case I find no agreement to the contrary.

NOTES

1.   Where the advising bank is instructed to advise the beneficiary of the opening of the credit and/or receive and inspect the documents, it acts merely as the agent of the issuing bank (*Bank Melli Iran v Barclays Bank DCO*, above). Where the advising bank is instructed to confirm the credit, and does so as a confirming bank, it acts in a dual capacity. The relationship between the issuing bank and the confirming bank is that of principal and agent, and yet the confirming bank gives its own payment undertaking to the beneficiary as principal, not as agent for the issuing bank (see *Bank of Baroda v Vysya Bank Ltd* [1994] 2 Lloyd's Rep 87 at 90, per Mance J). This may explain why, in *Crédit Agricole Indosuez v Muslim Commercial Bank Ltd* [2000] 1 All ER (Comm) 172 at 180, Sir Christopher Staughton, sitting the Court of Appeal, said that:

> there is not *in law* an agency relationship between an issuing bank and a confirming bank ... But in terms of commerce the confirming bank is the correspondent of the issuing bank, and acts for the issuing bank in order to do what the issuing bank is not present to do for itself. That is in my respectful opinion sufficient to attract the rule that an agent is to be excused for acting on a reasonable, even if ultimately wrong, interpretation of his principal's instructions.

2.   Under art 7(c) of UCP 600, an advising bank (if a nominated bank) or confirming bank, which pays the beneficiary against the tender of compliant documents, may claim reimbursement from the issuing bank. In order to claim reimbursement, the advising or confirming bank must forward the tendered (and compliant) documents to the issuing bank. In *Société Générale SA v Saad Trading* [2011] EWHC 2424 (Comm), [2011] 2 CLC 629 at [44], Teare J held that if documents forwarded to the issuing bank are not compliant, then the issuing bank is not obliged to reimburse the forwarding bank even if that bank considers them to be compliant. Teare J added (at [45]–[46]) that *all* documents tendered to the advising or confirming bank must be forwarded to the issuing bank: discretion on the part of that bank

as to which documents to forward would be contrary to the principle of strict compliance. So long as the tendered documents are regular on their face, the advising or confirming bank will be entitled to reimbursement even if the documents turn out to be forged or false (UCP 600, art 34). Payment against obviously discrepant documents does not give the advising or confirming bank a right of reimbursement unless the issuing bank has irrevocably waived its entitlement to insist on payment only against conforming documents (as was held to have occurred in *Habib Bank Ltd v Central Bank of Sudan* [2006] EWHC 1767, [2006] 2 Lloyd's Rep 413 at [49], per Field J). The reimbursement obligation may be performed directly by the issuing bank itself or indirectly through an intermediary bank, which is in turn reimbursed by the issuing bank (an intermediary bank will often be a US bank when the currency of the credit is US dollars). Such bank-to-bank reimbursements are regulated by art 13[9] and, when incorporated into the relevant contracts, by the ICC's Uniform Rules for Bank-to-Bank Reimbursement under Documentary Credits (2008 Revision, ICC Publication No 725).

3. The advising or confirming bank must adhere strictly to the issuing bank's instructions if it is to claim its right of reimbursement (the receipt of ambiguous instructions is considered in Note 1 above). Where that bank suspects fraud on the issuing bank it is under a duty to inquire and will commit a breach of duty to the issuing bank, its principal, if it fails to do so (cf *Standard Bank London Ltd v Bank of Tokyo Ltd* [1995] 2 Lloyd's Rep 169 at 176, per Waller J, where Standard Bank London, which was in the position of both advising bank *and beneficiary*, was held to owe no duty to investigate the transaction for the benefit of the issuing bank and to owe no duty to warn the issuing bank of any facts that may be discovered).

4. Sometimes one bank ('the instructing bank') may ask another bank ('the correspondent issuer') to issue a credit in its own name. In such a case, only the correspondent issuer gives a payment undertaking to the beneficiary; there is no direct relationship between the instructing bank and the beneficiary. The correspondent issuer is entitled to reimbursement from the instructing bank. For cases of this type see *National Bank of Egypt v Hannevig's Bank Ltd* (1919) 1 Ll L Rep 69 and *Scandinaviska Akt v Barclays Bank* (1925) 22 Ll L Rep 523.

QUESTION

Intra Bank issues an irrevocable documentary credit in favour of Slicker. The credit is advised through Agro Bank. Agro Bank advises Slicker that payment will be made on the tender of certain documents to Intra Bank. Contrary to Intra Bank's instructions, Agro Bank omits to inform Slicker that the tendered documents must include a certificate of origin of the goods shipped. Slicker tenders documents, but not a certificate of origin, to Intra Bank. Relying on this omission, Intra Bank refuses to pay Slicker. Advise Slicker as to his rights, if any, against Intra Bank. Slicker, hearing that Intra Bank is almost insolvent, also seeks your advice as to any rights he may have against Agro Bank.

(iv) *The contracts between the banks and the seller*

(a) Examination of documents and complying presentations

The issuing bank and the confirming bank each undertake to the seller (as the beneficiary of the credit) that payment will be made if conforming documents are duly presented (UCP 600, arts 7(a) and 8(a)). The rights and duties of the banks to examine the documents, the

---

[9] Should the intermediary bank fail to make reimbursement, the issuing bank remains liable to reimburse the bank which has paid the beneficiary (UCP 600, art 13(b)(iii), (c)).

time for starting the settlement process where the tendered documents are in order, and the procedures to be adopted where the tendered documents are defective, are set out in arts 14, 15, and 16 of UCP 600 respectively.

We have already seen that banks must examine all tendered documents to determine, on the basis of the documents alone, whether or not the documents appear on their face to constitute a complying presentation, ie whether they constitute a presentation in accordance with the terms and conditions of the credit, the applicable provisions of the UCP and international standard banking practice (UCP 600, art 14(a): above, p 819).

The issuing bank, the confirming bank, and any other nominated bank acting on its nomination (including an advising bank) each has a maximum of five banking days following the day of presentation to determine if the presentation is complying (UCP 600, art 14(b): above, p 819). UCP 500 was differently worded. Article 13(b) of UCP 500 gave the bank a reasonable time, not to exceed seven banking days, to examine the documents and make the determination. But this led to considerable uncertainty as to what constituted a 'reasonable time', which could be less than seven banking days. UCP 600 brings greater certainty with the removal of the reference to a reasonable time and its replacement by a fixed period of five banking days following the date of presentation.

Article 15(a) of UCP 600 provides that the issuing bank must honour the credit when it determines that a presentation is complying. When a confirming bank determines that a presentation is complying, it must honour or negotiate and forward the documents to the issuing bank (art 15(b)). When a nominated bank determines that a presentation is complying and honours or negotiates, it must forward the documents to the confirming bank or issuing bank (art 15(c)).

Some problems of interpretation remain.

'The New UCP 600—Changes to the Tender of the Seller's Shipping Documents under Letters of Credit' by C Debattista
[2007] JBL 329 at 339

Thus, for example, what if a bank decides on the second day that the documents are compliant? Can the seller insist on payment on that second day or must he or she wait until the fifth day for payment? Article 14(b) gives the bank five banking days 'to determine if a presentation is complying'. Article 15(a), however, says that '*when* an issuing bank determines that a presentation is complying, it must honour' (emphasis added) and Art. 15(b) and (c) applies the same rule to confirming and nominated banks. Moreover, Art. 16(d) states that the notice of its refusal to pay must be given:

... by telecommunication or, if that is not possible, by other expeditious means *no later than* the close of the fifth banking day following the day of presentation. (emphasis added)

It is at least arguable that while Art. 14(b) gives each bank five banking days to decide *whether* to pay, Art. 15 says that it must pay immediately it comes to that decision and that Art. 16(d) requires the greatest expedition possible. The consequence would be that a bank proven by the beneficiary to have waited for the fifth day would be in breach of its duty to pay the beneficiary and would be liable towards the beneficiary, for example, for interest on the sum due.

The same issue may cause problems for the buyer. If the bank were to pay on the second day, and if the goods are lost or damaged on the fourth day in a sale contract concluded on a 'delivered' basis, is it open to the buyer to complain that the bank had paid the sum under the credit before it was obliged to—and that therefore the bank should indemnify the buyer for the costs of recovering the price from the seller in a foreign jurisdiction—and possibly for the price itself in case of the seller's default? Again, here, it is at least arguable that Art. 14(b) does not *require* the bank to wait five days: it simply gives it five days to examine the documents *if it needs five days*. The consequence would be that a bank is entitled, as far as the buyer it concerned, to pay on the second day if it rightly decides then that the documents comply—and that the bank is entitled to do so without risk of liability towards the buyer.

(b) Waiver of discrepancies

Where an issuing bank, confirming bank, or a nominated bank acting on its nomination determines that a presentation does not comply, it may refuse to honour or negotiate the credit (UCP 600, art 16(a)). On the other hand, the discrepancies in the documents may be minor or immaterial and the applicant, keen to get hold of the goods, may be prepared to waive them. Article 16(b) facilitates this process by providing that:

> When an issuing bank determines that a presentation does not comply, it may in its sole judgment approach the applicant for a waiver of the discrepancies. This does not, however, extend the period mentioned in sub-art 14(b).

Three points should be noted. First, the decision whether to approach the applicant for a waiver is at the sole discretion of the issuing bank. The applicant has no legal remedy against the issuing bank if it rejects non-compliant documents without having approached him. Secondly, art 16(b), does not permit re-examination of the documents by the applicant with a view to finding further discrepancies. In *Bankers Trust Co v State Bank of India* [1991] 2 Lloyd's Rep 443, the Court of Appeal held that it was for the bank and not the applicant to make the decision as to whether or not the documents were discrepant (see also *Bayerische Vereinsbank Aktiengesellschaft v National Bank of Pakistan* [1997] 1 Lloyd's Rep 59 at 69–70, per Mance J). Thirdly, if the applicant is to be approached for a waiver, the whole process must be completed, and the issuing bank must make its decision whether or not to accept the documents, within the maximum period of five banking days following presentation (the position was less certain under the wording of UCP 500, art 13(b) (above, p 825): see R Buckley, 'Documentary Compliance in Documentary Credits: Lessons from the UCC for the UCP' (2002) 1 Journal of International Commercial Law 69 at 88–89).

(c) Notice of rejection

Article 16(c) of UCP 600 states that when the issuing bank, the confirming bank, or a nominated bank acting on its nomination, decides to refuse to honour or negotiate a credit, it must give a single notice to that effect to the presenter (ie the beneficiary, bank, or other party that makes a presentation of documents under a credit). The notice must state that the bank refuses to honour or negotiate the credit (UCP 600, art 16(c)(ii)). It was said in *Bulgrains & Co Ltd v Shinhan Bank* [2013] EWHC 2498 (QB) at [32]–[33] that failure to state in the notice that the bank refuses to honour or negotiate the credit may be cured by a second notice correcting the defect, provided the bank does not rely on any new discrepancies (a proposition rejected as inconsistent with UCP 600 in *Benjamin's Sale of Goods* (9th edn, 2014), para 23–191). Article 16(d) says that the rejection notice must be given by telecommunication or, if that is not possible, by other expeditious means no later than the close of the fifth banking day following the day of presentation. This provision is more tightly worded than the equivalent provision in UCP 500. Article 14(d)(i) of UCP 500 required notice to be given 'without delay but no later than the close of the seventh banking day following the day of receipt of the documents'. Under UCP 600 there can be no arguments as to whether the notice was given 'without delay' (eg in *Bayerische Vereinsbank Aktiengesellschaft v National Bank of Pakistan* [1997] 1 Lloyd's Rep 59 at 70, Mance J held that a bank did not act 'without delay' when sending a notice of rejection by DHL courier, when telex and fax facilities were also available). The net effect of arts 14(b) and 16(d) of UCP 600 seems to be that a bank has a maximum of five banking days following presentation of the documents to determine if the presentation is compliant, but that the longer it takes to make its determination, the less time it has available to it to give a notice of rejection to the applicant. If the bank fails to comply with the five (banking) day maximum period, it will not have served a proper notice which satisfies art 16(d) and, because of the effect of art 16(f) of UCP 600 (below), will be precluded from claiming that the documents do not comply with the credit (J Ulph, 'The UCP 600: Documentary Credits in the Twenty-first Century' [2007] JBL 355 at 364).

The notice of rejection must state the discrepancies in respect of which the document is being rejected. There has been some doubt as to whether a bank would be estopped from later raising further discrepancies not identified in the original rejection notice. The position at common law is that, absent special circumstances raising a true estoppel, the bank will not be prevented from relying upon discrepancies which were not listed in the original rejection notice (*Kydon Compañía Naviera SA v National Westminster Bank Ltd, The Lena* [1981] 1 Lloyd's Rep 68 at 79). But the position was thought to be different under the UCP (see *Hing Yip Hing Fat Co Ltd v Daiwa Bank Ltd* [1991] 2 HKLR 35 at 45–51). The 1993 revision of the UCP clarified the issue by stating, for the first time, that the notice must specify *all* discrepancies in respect of which the bank refused the documents (UCP 500, art 14(d)(ii)). Article 16(c)(ii) of UCP 600 retains the requirement, although it does so in slightly different language: the bank must give a 'single notice' of rejection to the presenter and that notice must state 'each discrepancy in respect of which the bank refuses to honour or negotiate'. If the bank fails to comply with this requirement, or any other requirement of art 16, it is precluded from claiming that the documents do not constitute a complying presentation (UCP 600, art 16(f)). This seems to mean the bank may be precluded from raising a new objection when documents are re-tendered by the seller having cured the defects identified in the original notice of rejection (but note that in *Paget's Law of Banking* (14th edn, 2014), para 36.19, it is submitted that there is no such preclusion in the normal course of events).

Under art 14(d)(i) of UCP 500 a bank which refused documents had also to state in its rejection notice whether it was holding the documents at the disposal of, or was returning them to, the presenter. The purpose of this provision was that, as soon as the documents had been rejected, they should be put back in circulation. However, problems arose where a bank served a rejection notice and at the same time approached the applicant for a waiver of the discrepancies, and if such waiver was received released the documents without further notice. In *Crédit Industriel et Commercial v China Merchants Bank* [2002] EWHC 973 (Comm), [2002] 2 All ER (Comm) 427, the issuing bank's notice of rejection was held to be bad where it ended with the words: 'Should the disc[repancy] being accepted by the applicant, we shall release the documents to them without further notice to you unless yr instructions to the contrary received prior to our payment. Documents held at yr risk for yr disposal.' Steel J considered (at [68]) that the conditional nature of the rejection was not saved by the potential for acceptance of contrary instructions prior to payment, particularly where no notice was to be given. The message constituted a continuing threat of conversion of the claimant's documents. However, art 16 of UCP 600 contains additional options designed to avoid banks sitting on discrepant documents. Under art 16(c)(iii) the rejection notice must state that the bank:

> (a) holds the documents pending further instructions from the presenter; or
> (b) holds the documents until it receives a waiver from the applicant and agrees to accept it, and receives further instructions from the presenter prior to agreeing to accept a waiver; or
> (c) is returning the documents; or
> (d) is acting in accordance with instructions previously received from the presenter.

In *Fortis Bank SA/NV v Indian Overseas Bank* [2011] EWCA Civ 58, [2011] 2 Lloyd's Rep 33 at [41]–[45], Thomas LJ interpreted art 16(c)(iii) of UCP 600 to include within it a requirement that the bank must act in accordance with the statement contained in the rejection notice with reasonable promptness. In that case the issuing bank's failure to return the documents with reasonable promptness was held, applying art 16(f), to preclude the bank from claiming that the documents did not constitute a complying presentation. In related proceedings (*Fortis Bank SA/NV v India Overseas Bank* [2011] EWHC 538 (Comm), [2011] 2 Lloyd's Rep 190), J Hirst QC, sitting as a deputy High Court judge, held (at [35]) that 'in the absence of special extenuating circumstances, a bank which failed to dispatch the documents within three working days would have failed to act with reasonable promptness'.

According to art 16(f), if the issuing bank or confirming bank fails to act in accordance with the provisions of art 16, it is precluded from claiming that the documents do not constitute a complying presentation. But the article makes no reference to the position of a nominated bank. However, if a nominated bank is employed by the issuing bank or confirming bank to take up and examine the documents on its behalf, the nominated bank's failure to comply with art 16 will bar the issuing bank or confirming bank from claiming that the documents are not conforming (see EP Ellinger [1997] 3 (No 2) DCI 9).

(d) Payment under reserve

Banque de l'Indochine et de Suez SA v JH Rayner (Mincing Lane) Ltd
[1983] QB 711, Court of Appeal

An irrevocable credit was opened by a Djibouti bank and confirmed by the plaintiff bank (the confirming bank). The defendant sellers tendered documents to the confirming bank but the bank considered them to be defective for various reasons which the sellers were informed of. However, the confirming bank agreed to pay the sellers 'under reserve'. When the issuing bank, on the buyer's instructions, rejected the documents, the confirming bank demanded repayment from the sellers. The Court of Appeal affirmed Parker J's decision that the documents were defective but disagreed with his analysis of the effect of a payment under reserve.

> **Sir John Donaldson MR:** It seems that it is not unusual for a confirming bank to be asked to pay on documents which in its view do not fully comply with the terms of the letter of credit. The bank then has to decide whether (a) to refuse payment, (b) to pay, taking an indemnity from the beneficiary in respect of any loss or damage resulting from the deficiency in the documentation or (c) to pay the beneficiary 'under reserve.' Which course is adopted depends upon the extent and

importance of the deficiencies as perceived by the confirming bank, the likelihood of the bank at whose request the credit was opened ('the issuing bank') and that bank's customer refusing to accept the correctness of any payment to the beneficiary and the credit worthiness, and value attached by the paying bank to the goodwill, of the person seeking to draw on the letter of credit. It is a tribute to the standing of JH Rayner (Mincing Lane) Ltd, the defendants, in the City of London that, notwithstanding the bank's conviction that the documents were seriously defective, they paid them 'under reserve.'

The use of the expression 'payment under reserve,' as denoting the character of a payment, is, we were told, widespread and would undoubtedly serve a very useful purpose if it had a defined and generally accepted meaning. Unfortunately it seems that it has not. If this is correct, banks will be most unwise to use it without at the same time stating precisely what they mean by it. In the longer term the International Chamber of Commerce, who are the authors and guardians of the Uniform Customs and Practice for Documentary Credits might like to turn their minds to this problem when undertaking the next revision. Meanwhile we have to determine what the parties meant by the expression when they used it on this occasion.

It is common ground that it relates to the circumstances in which the beneficiary can be called upon to repay the money which he has been paid under the letter of credit. The competing submissions are that (1) the money is repayable on demand if the issuing bank, in reliance upon some or all of the deficiencies alleged by the confirming bank, declines to reimburse the confirming bank or to ratify the payment, the beneficiary then being left to sue the confirming bank; (2) money is repayable if, but only if, the circumstances in (1) exist and the beneficiary accepts that the documentation was defective or this is established in a suit brought by the confirming bank against the beneficiary. If (2) is correct, the only effect of the qualification upon the payment, albeit an important effect, is that the beneficiary cannot resist an order for repayment on the basis that the payment itself had been made under a mistake of law. This was the submission accepted by the judge and his reasons appear in his judgment ante, pp 716D–717E; [1982] 2 Lloyd's Rep 476, 479.

The point is clearly one of difficulty. Mr Saville [counsel for the plaintiffs] characterised the view of the judge as 'a lawyer's view' as contrasted with 'a commercial view' and I think that this is right. It depends for its validity upon the parties having had it well in mind that money payable under a mistake of law is irrecoverable and wishing to do no more than eliminate this defence. This seems to me to be an improbable premise, when the parties are a commercial bank and a commodity merchant. As I see it, the dialogue to be imputed to the parties goes something like this:

Merchant: 'These documents are sufficient to satisfy the terms of the letter of credit and certainly will be accepted by my buyer. I am entitled to the money and need it.'

Bank: 'If we thought that the documents satisfied the terms of the letter of credit, we would pay you at once. However, we do not think that they do and we cannot risk paying you and not being paid ourselves. We are not sure that your buyer will authorise payment, but we can of course ask.'

Merchant: 'But that will take time and meanwhile we shall have a cash flow problem.'

Bank: 'Well the alternative is for you to sue us and that will also take time.

'*Merchant:* 'What about your paying us without prejudice to whether we are entitled to payment and then your seeing what is the reaction of your correspondent bank and our buyer?'

Bank: 'That is all right, but if we are told that we should not have paid, how do we get our money back?'

Merchant: 'You sue us.'

Bank: 'Oh no, that would leave us out of our money for a substantial time. Furthermore it would involve us in facing in two directions. We should not only have to sue you, but also to sue the issuing bank in order to cover the possibility that you might be right. We cannot afford to pay on those terms.'

Merchant: 'All right. I am quite confident that the issuing bank and my buyer will be content that you should pay, particularly since the documents are in fact in order. You pay me and if the issuing bank refuses to reimburse you for the same reason that you are unwilling to pay, we will repay you on demand and then sue you. But we do not think that this will happen.'

Bank: 'We agree. Here is the money "under reserve." '

Kerr LJ: . . . What the parties meant, I think, was that payment was to be made under reserve in the sense that the beneficiary would be bound to repay the money on demand if the issuing bank should reject the documents, whether on its own initiative or on the buyer's instructions. I would regard this as a binding agreement made between the confirming bank and the beneficiary by way of a compromise to resolve the impasse created by the uncertainty of their respective legal obligations and rights. For present purposes it is then unnecessary to go further and decide whether such a demand would only be effective if the grounds of the rejection included at least one of the grounds on which the confirming bank had relied in refusing to pay otherwise than under reserve. But I incline to the view that this should be implied, since the agreement to pay and accept the money under reserve will have been made against the background of these grounds of objection.

In the present case the issuing bank in fact rejected the documents on grounds which included at least one of the grounds of objection which had been raised by the plaintiffs. It therefore follows that the judgment in favour of the plaintiffs must in any event be upheld.

[**Sir Sebag Shaw** concurred.]

NOTES

1. If the issuing bank or the confirming bank fails to pay against presentation of compliant documents under a documentary credit payable at sight, the seller (as the beneficiary under the credit) may sue in debt to recover the face value of the credit, provided he is willing and able to transfer the documents to the bank against payment (*Standard Chartered Bank v Dorchester LNG (2) Ltd* [2014] EWCA Civ 1382, [2016] QB 1 at [51]–[52], per Moore-Bick LJ, subject to the right to claim any consequential losses as damages; but for an unusual case where the beneficiary expressly contracted out of any right to direct payment to itself or to its order, and was left with a non-proprietary right to damages for any failure by the issuing bank to pay a specified sum, the third party being the sole creditor of the issuing bank under the credit, see *Taurus Petroleum Ltd v State Oil Company of the Ministry of Oil, Republic of Iraq* [2015] EWCA Civ 835, [2016] 1 Lloyd's Rep 42 at [54] and [55]–[64]). If the seller is not willing or able to hand over the documents, the seller's claim is for damages (and not in debt) for wrongful failure to honour the credit (*Standard Chartered Bank v Dorchester LNG (2) Ltd*, above). As the bank's failure to honour the credit is not merely a failure to pay money, but also an act which interferes with performance of the underlying contract of sale, the court will, in an appropriate case (eg where the seller elects to treat the contract of sale as repudiated), assess damages against the bank on a similar basis to those awarded for breach of the buyer's obligation to accept delivery under the contract of sale (see E McKendrick, *Goode on Commercial Law* (5th edn, 2016), p 1067, citing *Urquhart, Lindsay & Co Ltd v Eastern Bank Ltd* [1922] 1 KB 318 at 324–325). Where the seller sues for damages, he is under a duty to mitigate his loss, and it is also necessary for him to establish a causal link between the bank's breach of contract and the loss he has suffered (*Fortis Bank SA/NV v India Overseas Bank* [2011] EWHC 538 (Comm), [2011] 2 Lloyd's Rep 190 at [43]). Where the seller suffers loss because the bank has delayed in making payment, he may recover that loss from the bank so long as it is not too remote (*Ozalid Group (Export) Ltd v African Continental Bank* [1979] 2 Lloyd's Rep 231 at 233). If the bank fails to honour a bill of exchange which it has previously accepted, the seller will sue the bank on the bill of exchange itself.

2. Where payment is not made 'under reserve', can the bank recover money paid to the seller against non-conforming documents?

(a) *Where there is fraud* Where the bank has paid against forged or fraudulent documents and is unable to obtain reimbursement from the applicant or other instructing party, for example if the applicant is insolvent or if it is found that the bank should not have paid because the fraud was apparent or the documents were discrepant, it can attempt to recover the payment from the beneficiary. The claim is for restitution of money paid under a mistake of fact (*Bank Russo-Iran v Gordon Woodroffe & Co Ltd* (1912) 116 Sol Jo 921, per Browne J, cited with apparent approval by Lord Denning MR in *Edward Owen Engineering Ltd v Barclays Bank International Ltd* [1978] QB 159 at 169–170). Change of position is a recognised defence to a claim for recovery of a mistaken payment (for details, see above, p 714). The scope of the defence is still uncertain but it was made clear by Lord Goff in the leading authority on the subject, *Lipkin Gorman v Karpnale* [1991] 2 AC 548, that the defence would not be available to someone who changed his position in bad faith. This explains why the defence is not available to the fraudulent beneficiary who has paid away the proceeds of the credit. But it will usually be available to any bank that has presented documents and collected payment under the credit for the fraudulent beneficiary and then paid over those proceeds to the fraudster (but not in *Niru Battery Manufacturing Co v Milestone Trading Ltd* [2003] EWCA Civ 1446, [2004] 1 All ER (Comm) 193 (noted by Ellinger (2005) 121 LQR 51), where the bank that had received the proceeds of the credit had grounds for believing that the payment may have been made by mistake but failed to make inquires of the issuing bank that had made the mistaken payment).

The bank will also have a claim for damages in deceit against the beneficiary and any third party who has issued a document knowing that it contains a false statement and that it is to be presented to the bank under the credit (*KBC Bank v Industrial Steels (UK) Ltd* [2001] 1 All ER (Comm) 409; *Komercni Banka AS v Stone and Rolls Ltd* [2002] EWHC 2263 (Comm), [2003] 1 Lloyd's Rep 383). The bank may be able to make a recovery from the beneficiary or third party even where it is itself guilty of fraudulent conduct, provided that it does not have to rely on that conduct in support of its claim (*Standard Chartered Bank v Pakistan National Shipping Corpn (No 2)* [2000] 1 All ER (Comm) 1, CA, where the confirming bank falsely represented to the issuing bank that the documents had been presented in time but was still held entitled to recover damages in deceit from the carrier that had issued a bill of lading falsely stating that the goods had been shipped within the shipping period). There is no defence of contributory negligence in the case of deceit (*Standard Chartered Bank v Pakistan National Shipping Corpn (No 2)* [2002] UKHL 43, [2002] 2 All ER (Comm) 931, HL).

(b) *Cases not involving fraud* Where the bank has paid against non-conforming documents because of its own mistake it is unlikely to be able to recover the money so paid. Any restitutionary claim would probably be defeated by defences of change of position or estoppel (at least as against claims made by the issuing or confirming banks: claims by those banks would also be barred by art 16(f) of UCP 600—see above, p 828).

(c) *Bills of exchange* If the bank negotiates a bill of exchange drawn by the seller on the buyer, who later dishonours the bill, it might be possible for the bank, as holder or indorser, to claim a right of recourse against the seller under s 43(2) or 47(2) of the Bills of Exchange Act 1882. But there is some uncertainty as to whether such a right of recourse applies to a bill drawn under a credit (see D Sheehan, 'Rights of Recourse in Documentary (and Other) Credit Transactions' [2005] JBL 326). The issue is no longer a live one under UCP 600, as art 6(c) provides that a credit must not be issued available by a draft drawn on the applicant (buyer).

(d)   It should be noted that in the United States a bank may have a right of action against the seller for breach of warranty relating to the fraud or forgery of the tendered documents (s 5–110(a) of the Uniform Commercial Code, 1995 Revision). English law might be prepared to imply a similar warranty in the case of fraud or forgery but not in the case of a non-fraudulent presentation of documents (*Benjamin's Sale of Goods* (9th edn, 2014), para 23–279; A Malek and D Quest, *Jack: Documentary Credits* (4th edn, 2009), para 5.99; cf E McKendrick, *Goode on Commercial Law* (5th edn, 2016), p 1066 and RM Goode [1980] JBL 443 at 445–446).

(g) The governing law of documentary credits

Standard forms of documentary credits do not normally state a choice of law. The English courts must decide upon the governing law of the credit (or of any of the other contractual relationships that arise under a documentary credit transaction) through the application of a detailed series of presumptions that, for contracts concluded on or after 17 December 2009, are to be found in article 4 of Regulation (EU) No 593/2008 on the Law Applicable to Contractual Obligations ('the Rome I Regulation), which replaced the EEC Convention on the Law Applicable to Contractual Obligations 1980 ('the Rome Convention').

In the absence of choice, the contract arising out of the documentary credit transaction (whether it be between issuing bank and beneficiary, confirming bank and beneficiary, issuing bank and confirming bank, or between issuing bank and applicant) will be presumed to be governed by the law of the habitual residence of the bank, under art 4(1)(b) of the Rome I Regulation. This means that the law of the place of central administration of the bank will apply (Rome I Regulations, art 19(1)), unless the contract is concluded in the course of the operations of a branch, agency, or any other establishment, when the law of the place of that branch, agency, or other establishment will apply (Rome I Regulation, art 19(2)). In the case of contracts formed in respect of a documentary credit, this could lead to different laws governing the various related contracts. This would be commercially undesirable as it could, for example, lead to the beneficiary's position against the issuing bank and the confirming bank being governed by a different law (R Fentiman, *International Commercial Litigation* (2nd edn, 2015), para 5.96). However, the governing law may be displaced under art 4(3) of the Rome I Regulation. In this respect, an English court should take account of recital (20), which provides that:

> In order to determine that country, account should be taken, *inter alia*, of whether the contract in question has a very close relationship with another contract or contracts.

This should enable a court to avoid applying different laws to the various related contracts arising out of a documentary credit transaction and to apply the law of the country where payment is to be made against presentation of the documents (Fentiman, above, para 5.97).

This was the approach taken by the English courts when applying the Rome Convention, as is evident from the next extract (although it should be noted that the displacement provision in art 4(3) of the Rome I Regulation is narrower in scope than the displacement provision in art 4(5) of the Rome Convention).

Bank of Baroda v Vysya Bank Ltd
[1994] 2 Lloyd's Rep 87, Queen's Bench Division

Aditya, an Indian importer, agreed to purchase a consignment of pig iron through the London office of Granada, an Irish exporter. Aditya instructed Vysya Bank, its bank in India, to open a documentary credit in favour of Granada. The credit was opened and, though initially advised through National Westminster Bank in London, was later confirmed by Bank of Baroda's City of London office. Bank of Baroda paid Granada against tender of documents, which were sent on to Vysya Bank. The credit provided for reimbursement through Citibank in New York. Vysya Bank informed Bank of Baroda that it had already mailed reimbursement instructions to Citibank and authorised Bank of Baroda to claim reimbursement from that bank. However, Vysya Bank subsequently withdrew this authorisation on the ground that the cargo shipped had been the subject of two different sets of bills of lading. Bank of Baroda commenced proceedings in London against Vysya Bank claiming damages for breach of contract between itself as confirmer and Vysya Bank as the issuing bank. The issue before the Commercial Court was whether Bank of Baroda should be given leave to issue and serve a writ on Vysya Bank out of the jurisdiction on the ground that the contract between the two banks was governed by English law (Rules of the Supreme Court, Ord 11, r (l)(d): see now Civil Procedure Rules, Part 6, which is in similar terms to those rules formerly contained in RSC Ord 11, r 1(1)). Mance J gave leave.

Mance J: . . . I shall start with the issue of the governing law which arises under 0.11, r. 1 (1)(*d*) (iii). This is of some general importance, since it involves the application to international letters of credit of the Rome Convention as enacted by the Contracts (Applicable Law) Act, 1990. It was common ground before me in view of the wide provisions of s. 2(1) of the Act and art. 3(1) of the Rome Convention that the proper law of the present contract, however it was made, must be determined in accordance with the Convention. So it is necessary to examine the provisions of art. 4 which read:

1. To the extent that the law applicable to the contract has not been chosen in accordance with Article 3, the contract shall be governed by the law of the country with which it is most closely connected. Nevertheless, a severable part of the contract which has a closer connection with another country may by way of exception be governed by the law of that other country.

2. Subject to the provisions of paragraph 5 of this Article, it shall be presumed that the contract is most closely connected with the country where the party who is to effect the performance which is characteristic of the contract has, at the time of conclusion of the contract, his habitual residence, or, in the case of a body corporate or unincorporate, its central administration. However, if the contract is entered into in the course of that party's trade or profession, that country shall be the country in which the principal place of business is situated or, where under the terms of the contract the performance is to be effected through a place of business other than the principal place of business, the country in which that other place of business is situated . . .

5. Paragraph 2 shall not apply if the characteristic performance cannot be determined, and the presumptions in paragraphs 2, 3 and 4 shall be disregarded if it appears from the circumstances as a whole that the contract is more closely connected with another country.

The relevant presumption is contained in par. 2. It raises the question: what is 'the performance which is characteristic of the contract' made between Vysya and Bank of Baroda? Bank of Baroda says that the answer is the addition of its confirmation to the credit and the honouring of the liability accepted thereby. Vysya says that this fails to distinguish the contract between Vysya and Bank of Baroda as confirming banker and Granada as beneficiary. In Vysya's submission the performance which is characteristic of the contract between Vysya and Bank of Baroda is the former's obligation to pay the latter upon presentation of conforming documents.

There are several different contractual relationships which can be identified in a situation such as the present. Leaving aside the underlying sale contract, there are contracts between (i) the buyer and the issuing bank, (ii) the issuing bank and the confirming bank, (iii) the confirming bank and the seller and (iv) the issuing bank and the seller. The last two relationships co-exist, giving a beneficiary two banks which he may hold responsible for payment. As the Uniform Customs put it in art. 10(b):

> When an issuing bank authorizes or requests another bank to confirm its irrevocable credit and the latter has added its confirmation, such confirmation constitutes a definite undertaking of such bank (the confirming bank), in addition to that of the issuing bank, provided that the stipulated documents are presented and that the terms and conditions of the credit are complied with: . . .

Article 11 (d) provides:

> By nominating a bank other than itself, or by allowing for negotiation by any bank, or by authorizing or requesting a bank to add its confirmation, the issuing bank authorizes such bank to pay, accept or negotiate, as the case may be, against documents which appear on their face to be in accordance with the terms and conditions of the credit, and undertakes to reimburse such bank in accordance with the provisions of these articles.

As between issuing bank and confirming bank the relationship is one of agency, although as against the beneficiary the confirming bank commits itself as principal (see *Jack on Documentary Credits* at pars. 5.33 and 5.53). This is consistent with the language of authorization and request used in these articles, even though it is possible that the confirming bank can also rely on art. 16 of the Uniform Customs as against an issuing bank. That the relationship is one of agency is also shown by the language used in the instant case when Bank of Baroda was instructed, whether one looks at Bank of Baroda's or Vysya's account of the making of the contract. . . .

Both these accounts of the making of the contract between Vysya and Bank of Baroda identify the confirmation as the object or focus of the contract. They confirm the appropriateness of the general conclusion, at which I would anyway arrive, that under a contract between an issuing bank and a confirming bank the performance which is characteristic of the contract is the adding of its confirmation by the latter and its honouring of the obligations accepted thereby in relation to the beneficiary. The liability on the part of the issuing bank to reimburse or indemnify the confirming bank is consequential on the character of the contract; it does not itself characterize the contract.

The fact that reimbursement was to be claimed and made in New York is doubly insignificant, being probably a mere matter of convenience because this was a dollar credit and in any event unrelated to any country whose law could conceivably govern (cf *European Asian Bank v Punjab and Sind Bank* [1981] 2 Lloyd's Rep. 651, 656 per Mr Justice Robert Goff).

Additional confirmation of these conclusions is provided by the text of the report on the Rome Convention by Professors Giuliano and Lagarde to which reference may be made under s. 3(3) of the Act. The report points out that in bilateral or reciprocal contracts the counter-performance by one of the parties in a modern economy usually takes the form of money. It says:

This is not, of course, the characteristic performance of the contract. It is the performance for which the payment is due, i.e. depending on the type of contract, the delivery of goods, the granting of the right to make use of an item of property, the provision of a service, transport, insurance, banking operations, security, etc., which usually constitutes the centre of gravity and the socio-economic function of the contractual transaction.

A little later the report goes on:

Thus, for example, in a banking contract the law of the country of the banking establishment with which the transaction is made will normally govern the contract. . . . To take another example, in an agency contract concluded in France between a Belgian commercial agent and a French company, the characteristic performance being that of the agent, the contract will be governed by Belgian law if the agent has his place of business in Belgium.

In conclusion, Article 4(2) gives specific form and objectivity to the, in itself, too vague concept of 'closest connection' . . .

For each category of contract, it is the characteristic performance that is in principle the relevant factor in applying the presumption for determining the applicable law, even in situations peculiar to certain contracts, as for example in the contract of guarantee where the characteristic performance is always that of the guarantor, whether in relation to the principal debtor or the creditor.

In this passage the first sentence contemplates the straightforward situation of a banking contract or transaction with or involving a single branch or office of a bank; in the present case, even if the contract was concluded in India its whole focus was upon Bank of Baroda's City of London branch acting as confirming banker under the credit advised to the beneficiary in London. The reference to an agent instructed to undertake his activity in a particular country is directly relevant. Also of some assistance by way of analogy (though not exact since a confirming bank does not act as guarantor of the issuing bank but assumes separate liabilities in identical terms) is the comment that the performance characteristic of a guarantee is always the guarantor's performance (*i.e.* the giving and honouring of the guarantee) whether one looks at his contract with the creditor or the debtor. The same is in my view true of a confirming bank's performance (the addition and honouring of its confirmation), whether one looks at its contract with the beneficiary or with the issuing bank.

It follows in the present case, looking at the position of Bank of Baroda in relation to the confirmation given to Granada, that the performance characteristic of Bank of Baroda's contract with Vysya, however made, was the addition and honouring of its confirmation of the credit in favour of Granada. That performance was to be effected through Bank of Baroda's City of London office, viz 'a place of business other than [its] principal place of business' and so by the express terms of art. 4(2) the presumption is that English law governs the contract between Vysya and Bank of Baroda. For reasons which will further appear below, any wider examination of the circumstances under art. 4(5) simply confirms the application of English law.

[Mance J then considered what was the governing law of the contract between the beneficiary and the confirming bank, and the governing law of the contract between the beneficiary and the issuing bank where the credit is confirmed (or unconfirmed but advised by an agent bank):]

So far I have focused on the contract between Vysya and Bank of Baroda which is the contract immediately in issue. It is relevant to consider the matter more widely, as the arguments before me did, and in this context to consider the proper laws of other contracts involved in the present situation. Whether one looks at art. 4(2) or at art. 4(5) of the Rome Convention, the contract of confirmation between Bank of Baroda's City of London branch as confirming bank and Granada as beneficiary was clearly governed by English law. Even if one ignores the clear application of the presumption in art. 4(2) to that contract, the reasoning in such cases as *European Bank v Punjab Bank* [1981] 2 Lloyd's Rep 651 at pp 656–657 per Mr Justice Robert Goff is as relevant when determining the closeness of connection with any country under art. 4(5) as it was for the purposes of the similar common law test. A suggestion that English law did not, as between beneficiary and confirming bank, govern a credit confirmed through the London branch of a foreign bank for payment in London would be wholly uncommercial.

Vysya submits however that, although Granada's contract as beneficiary with Bank of Baroda as the confirming bank is subject to English law, Granada's parallel contract with Vysya as the issuing bank falls as a result of the Rome Convention (and contrary to the previous common law position) to be regarded as subject to Indian law. It submits that the contract between the buyer and Vysya in India must also be subject to Indian law. In its submission different legal systems govern different contracts involved in the present situation and there is no particular incongruity in holding that the contract between the two Indian banks is subject to Indian law.

I do not think that I need consider to what law the contract between Atiya and Vysya might, even prima facie be subject, if one were to analyse it under English law by reference to the Contracts (Applicable Law) Act. Not only is there practically no information before the Court at all about that contract, it is on any view quite separate from any contract between the banks or the banks and the beneficiary.

A point of importance is involved in the submission that the contract between Granada as beneficiary and Vysya as issuing bank is subject to Indian law. That would mean that, by force of the Contracts (Applicable Law) Act [1990], one and the same credit is here governed by two different laws, and that the applicable law varies according to the bank against which the beneficiary decides to enforce the credit. If the beneficiary enforces the credit against the Bank of Baroda, English law applies, and presumably (whatever the governing law of the contract between confirming and issuing banks) Bank of Baroda can then claim reimbursement from Vysya in respect of liabilities which it has incurred subject to English law. However if the beneficiary chooses to pursue the issuing bank direct, Indian law applies. Counsel for Vysya contemplated this with equanimity as a necessary result of the Contracts (Applicable Law) Act, but I do not. In my judgment it would involve precisely the same wholly undesirable multiplicity of potentially conflicting laws to which Mr Justice Ackner drew attention in his reasoning in *Offshore International SA v Banco Central SA* [1976] 2 Lloyd's Rep 402 at p. 404, col. 1; [1977] 1 WLR 399 at p 401. He there rejected a suggestion that an unconfirmed credit opened by a Spanish company through a New York bank for payment at that bank in New York was subject to Spanish law. In concluding for the purposes of the common law test that the 'closest and most real connection' was with New York law, Mr Justice Ackner said:

> . . . I am satisfied that Mr Yorke was correct in his contention that very great inconvenience would arise, if the law of the issuing bank were to be considered as the proper law. The advising bank would have constantly to be seeking to apply a whole variety of foreign laws. Indeed it is very difficult to follow exactly what would flow from Mr Alexander's submission, if the advising bank was (as was not the case) to confirm the letter or credit.

In the present case Bank of Baroda did confirm the credit (whether it or National Westminster Bank strictly performed the function of 'advising bank' is neither here nor there), and the wholly undesirable difficulties mentioned in the last sentence of Mr Justice Ackner's reasoning would be unavoidable on Vysya's submissions.

As between the beneficiary and Vysya, the position under art. 4(2) is that there is a presumption that Indian law applies. This presumption applies, although the performance which is characteristic of the contract is the issue of the letter of credit in London which was to be and was effected in London through National Westminster, initially at least as advising bank, with Bank of Baroda later adding its confirmation. Although such performance was to take place in London, art. 4(2) refers one back, prima facie, to India as the place of Vysya's central administration.

In my judgment this is a situation where it would be quite wrong to stop at art. 4(2). The basic principle is that the governing law is that of the country with which the contract is most closely connected (art. 4(1)). Art. 4(2) is, as stated in Professors Giuliano and Lagarde's report, intended to give 'specific form and objectivity' to that concept. In the present case the application of art. 4(2) would lead to an irregular and subjective position where the governing law of a letter of credit would vary according to whether one was looking at the position of the confirming or the issuing bank. It is of great importance to both beneficiaries and banks concerned in the issue and operation of international letters of credit that there should be clarity and simplicity in such matters. Article 4(5) provides the answer. The Rome Convention was not intended to confuse legal relationships or to disrupt normal expectations in the way which is implicit in Vysya's submissions. Under art. 4(5) the presumptions in art. 4(2), (3) and (4) are to be

> . . . disregarded if it appears from the circumstances as a whole that the contract is more closely connected with another country.

I accept that the presumptions are to be applied unless there is valid reason, looking at the circumstances as a whole, not to do so. But I note and consider that there is force in the comment in *Dicey and Morris on The Conflict of Laws* (12th edn) at pp 1137–1138:

> Inevitably the solution of individual cases will depend on the facts, but in principle it is submitted that the presumption may be most easily rebutted in those cases where the place of performance differs from the place of business of the party whose performance is characteristic of the contract.

The present situation provides in my judgment a classic demonstration of the need for and appropriateness of art. 4(5). I conclude that English law applies to the contract between Vysya and Granada.

The fact that the credit was to be confirmed by Bank of Baroda's City of London branch highlights the need for art. 4(5) and its applicability in this case. But I should not be taken as suggesting that the conclusion would be any different if the credit had been an unconfirmed credit to be opened and advised on Vysya's behalf in London through National Westminster or Bank of Baroda's City branch available for negotiation here. I agree with the editors of *Dicey and Morris* that the application of the law of the place of performance would in such a case still be likely to result, by application of art. 4(5), as it did applying common law principles: *Dicey and Morris* pp 1238–1239 illustration 4; and cf *Offshore International SA v Banco Central SA*, [1976] 2 Lloyd's Rep 402; [1977] 1 WLR 399; where the 'very great inconvenience' of any other conclusion in the case of an unconfirmed credit was the direct subject of Mr Justice Ackner's comments which I have already cited.

I therefore conclude that the letter of credit was governed by English law as between the beneficiary and each of the banks. On this basis, it would be wholly anomalous if English law were not also to govern the contract between Vysya and Bank of Baroda and in my opinion it does. As between Bank of Baroda and Vysya the application of the presumption arising under art. 4(2) accords with good sense and sound policy and there is therefore no reason to depart from it.

It follows that Bank of Baroda has made out its case for saying that the Court had jurisdiction to grant leave to issue and serve the writ out of the jurisdiction under the first head of O. 11, r. 1(1)(d).

[Mance J exercised his general discretion whether or not to permit service out of the jurisdiction in favour of Bank of Baroda on the ground that the facts and the evidence showed England to be the most appropriate forum to resolve the dispute. The principles to be applied when exercising such discretion are set out in *Spiliada Maritime Corpn v Cansulex Ltd* [1987] AC 460, HL, as applied in *Lubbe v Cape plc* [2000] 1 WLR 1545.]

NOTES

1.   In *Marconi Communications International Ltd v Pt Pan Indonesia Bank* Ltd [2005] EWCA Civ 422, [2005] 2 All ER (Comm) 325, both the issuing bank and the confirming bank were located in Indonesia. The beneficiary was advised of the opening of the credit through a third bank located in London. The Court of Appeal held that there was a good arguable case that the contract between the beneficiary and the confirming bank was governed by English law. There was held to be valid reason and commercial logic why, rather than simply applying the presumption in art 4(2) of the Rome Convention, which would have pointed to Indonesian law as the law of the place of characteristic performance of the contract, art 4(5) of the Rome Convention should be applied to the contracts between the beneficiary and the issuing bank and the confirming bank. Their Lordships (at [66]) relied on the fact that the credit was opened in London through the advising bank and contemplated payment of the beneficiary in sterling in London by the advising bank as negotiating bank authorised to make payment to the beneficiary against tender of conforming documents. Christopher Hare has rightly criticised this decision on the ground that the Court of Appeal gave too little weight to the presumption in art 4(2) (C Hare [2005] LMCLQ 417 at 419). He submits (at 420) that the credit was freely negotiable and that the fact the advising bank in London was simply one of any number of banks at whose counters negotiation might have occurred ought not to have been sufficient per se to displace the presumption in art 4(2). Moreover, as the Court of Appeal also indicated (at [67]) that the contract between the confirming bank and the issuing bank would have been governed by Indonesian law through the application of art 4(2), the application of art 4(5) to the relationship between beneficiary and issuing/confirming banks led to the commercially undesirable result of different laws being applied to various relationships arising out of the same letter of credit transaction (Hare, at 422–423).

2.   The law governing the debt created by a letter of credit may not be the same as the law governing the bank's contractual promise to pay under the credit. A debt is governed by the law of the place where it is situated (the *lex situs*). The general rule is that a debt is situated at the place where it is properly recoverable or can be enforced, which is usually where the debtor resides. However, in *Taurus Petroleum Ltd v State Oil Co of the Ministry of Oil, Republic of Iraq* [2015] EWCA Civ 835, [2016] 1 Lloyd's Rep 42, the Court of Appeal held, following *Power Curber International Ltd v National Bank of Kuwait SAK* [1981] 1 WLR 1233, that letters of credit are to be treated differently, and that the *lex situs* of a debt contained in a letter of credit is the place where the payment is to be made. In *Taurus*, two letters of credit were issued by the London branch of a French bank. The credits were unusually worded and contained a promise by the issuing bank to make payment into the bank account of a third party in New York. Although the issuing bank's promise to the beneficiary to make payment to the third party, which gave the beneficiary only a non-proprietary right to damages, was governed by English law (under art 4(1)(b) or 4(2) of the Rome I Regulation), the Court of Appeal held that the debts owed by the issuing bank to the third party under the letters of credit were governed by the law of New York as the law of the place where the credits were payable. The issue was important because the English courts do not have jurisdiction to make a third party debt order (ie an order of the court granted to a judgment creditor, which attaches to funds held by a third party, eg a bank, that owes money to the judgment debtor, eg the bank's customer) in respect of a debt situated outside England unless the law applicable in its situation would recognise the English order as discharging the liability of the third party to the judgment debtor (*Société Eram Shipping Co Ltd v Internationale de Navigation* [2004] 1 AC 260). Nevertheless, the question remains whether it makes commercial sense to have an exceptional rule that applies to the *lex situs* of a debt created by a letter of credit, which allows the governing law of that debt to be different from, and potentially inconsistent with, the governing law of the credit itself.

3   STANDBY CREDITS, PERFORMANCE BONDS, AND GUARANTEES

Standby credits, performance bonds, and guarantees have a different function to that of documentary credits. Whereas the function of documentary credits is to provide payment for goods and services against documents, the function of the instruments considered in this section is to provide security against default in performance of the underlying contract. Although standby credits, performance bonds, and demand guarantees may be used to secure the performance of the buyer and (more usually) the seller under an international sale contract (see, eg, *State Trading Corpn of India Ltd v M Golodetz Ltd* [1989] 2 Lloyd's Rep 277), they are more often found in international construction contracts where the overseas employer requires financial security from a reputable third party (usually a bank) against the contractor defaulting in his performance of the contract.

(a)   Standby credits

A standby letter of credit is similar to an ordinary documentary credit in that it is issued by a bank and embodies an undertaking to make payment to a third party (the beneficiary) or to accept bills of exchange drawn by him, provided the beneficiary tenders conforming documents. But, whereas a documentary credit is a primary payment mechanism for discharge of the payment obligation contained in the underlying contract (ie the issuing or confirming bank is the first port of call for payment), the standby credit is given by way of security with the intention that it should only be drawn on if the party by whom the work should be done, or the goods or services provided, (the principal) defaults in the performance of his contractual obligations to the beneficiary (see RM Goode, 'Abstract Payment Undertakings' in P Cane and J Stapleton (eds), *Essays for Patrick Atiyah* (1991), pp 212–213, 220; and also RM Goode [1992] LMCLQ 190 at 192–193).

The liability of a bank under a standby credit is intended to be secondary to that of the principal (although, technically, the form of the credit makes the bank's liability primary) and the credit performs the same security function as would be provided by a bank guarantee (see E McKendrick, *Goode on Commercial Law* (5th edn, 2016), p 1086). But, unlike a guarantee, a standby credit may be called upon by tendering any specified documents without the beneficiary having to prove actual default by the principal, for example the specified document may be simply a demand from the beneficiary or a statement from him that the principal is in default. Fraudulent calling on the credit is prohibited but, as we have already seen with regard to documentary credits (above, pp 800-801), this is notoriously difficult to establish.

Standby credits are covered by the UCP (subject to its incorporation by the parties), and the principles of autonomy of the credit and strict compliance apply to standby credits as they do to documentary credits in general. However, the UCP is generally regarded as being ill-suited to the security nature of standby credits, and so the American Institute of International Banking Law and Practice produced a separate set of rules called the International Standby Practices (ISP98) (ICC Publication No 590), which came into effect on 1 January 1999. Standby credits can be issued subject to the UCP or ISP98, depending on the will of the parties.

(b) Performance bonds and guarantees

Although the terms 'performance bond' and 'performance guarantee' may be used to denote a true contract of suretyship, they are now more often used to refer to instruments which are similar in form and function to standby credits (when they are sometimes called 'on demand' performance bonds or demand guarantees—hereafter collectively referred to in this text as 'demand guarantees'). The bank which issues a demand guarantee agrees to make payment on production of a written demand by the beneficiary, or his written declaration that the principal has defaulted. The beneficiary need only demand payment, he does not have to prove that the principal has defaulted in performance of the underlying contract. Sometimes the terms of the demand guarantee require that the demand is accompanied by specific documents, such as a certificate from an independent third party indicating the principal has defaulted or that payment is otherwise due. This requirement can lead to uncertainty as to whether the instrument is a true demand guarantee (where the liability of the issuer is primary) or a suretyship guarantee (where the liability of the surety is secondary and turns on proof of default on the part of the principal). Guidance on how to resolve the issue can be found in the next case extract (taken from Longmore LJ's judgment in *Wuhan Guoyu Logistics Group Co Ltd v Emporiki Bank of Greece SA*). The demand guarantee may be issued by a bank in the principal's country direct to the beneficiary located overseas (a three-party demand guarantee), or it may be issued by a local bank in the beneficiary's country against the counter-guarantee of the principal's bank (a four-party demand guarantee). In either case the principal's bank will require a counter-indemnity from its customer.

Wuhan Guoyu Logistics Group Co Ltd v Emporiki Bank of Greece SA
[2012] EWCA Civ 1629, [2012] 2 CLC 986, Court of Appeal

The claimant seller operated a shipyard in China. The seller agreed to construct two ships for a Liberian buyer. The buyer was obliged to pay for the ships by instalments. The second instalment was to be paid when the ships had reached a certain stage of construction. That payment was supported by an instrument described as a 'Payment Guarantee' issued by the defendant Greek bank. Under the terms of the instrument the defendant bank agreed to: 'irrevocably, absolutely and unconditionally guarantee, as the primary obligor and not merely as surety, the due and punctual payment by the Buyer of the second instalment of the Contract Price.' The instrument further provided that: 'in the event that the Buyer fails to punctually pay the second instalment guaranteed hereunder …, then, upon receipt by us of your first written demand … we shall immediately pay to you or your assignee the unpaid second instalment.' The seller issued an invoice for the second instalment and written demand for payment, together with a certificate stating the relevant construction stage had been reached (the completion of cutting of the first 300 metric tons of steel). The buyer disputed whether the construction stage had been reached. The seller then made a demand under the Payment Guarantee. The buyer disputed the payment was due and the defendant bank refused to make payment. The seller applied for summary judgment. Christopher Clarke J held that the instrument was a suretyship guarantee and refused to grant summary judgment. The seller appealed. The Court of Appeal reversed the judge and held that the instrument was a demand guarantee.

Longmore LJ:

22. The judge decided that the document was a traditional guarantee and not an 'on-demand' bond. I mean no disrespect to the judge whatever when I say that the judgment is an exhausting document. Entirely understandably he found it necessary, in order to resolve this question of construction, to cite no less than 20 authorities and deliver a judgment of 93 paragraphs. Beatson J needed to cite a similar number of authorities in *Meritz v Jan de Nul* [2011] 2 CLC 842. But something has surely gone wrong if this comparatively simple question of construction requires such lengthy consideration. It is a problem of our system of precedent, that as more and more cases get decided, it seems to be necessary for judges at first instance to consider each case and determine how near or how far the document in question differs from the document construed in each past case. The commercial community deserves better than this, if better can be done.

23. The judge did not find this case particularly easy and neither do I. The difficulty, as so often in these cases, is that there are pointers in different directions. The following points might be thought to favour a conclusion that the document is a traditional guarantee:

(i) the document is called a 'payment guarantee' not an 'on-demand bond';

(ii) clause 1 says that the Bank guaranteed 'the due and punctual payment by the Buyer of the 2nd instalment';

(iii) clause 2 describes the second instalment as being payable (in terms different from article 3(b) of the shipbuilding contract) five days after completion of cutting of the first 300 metric tons of steel of which a written notice is to be given with a certificate countersigned by the buyer;

(iv) clause 3 guarantees the due and punctual payment of interest;

(v) clause 4 imposes an obligation on the Bank to pay 'in the event that the Buyer fails punctually to pay the second instalment';

(vi) clause 7 says that the guarantor's obligation is not to be affected or prejudiced by any variations or extensions of the terms of the shipbuilding contract or by the grant of any time or indulgence.

24. Conversely the following points might be thought to favour a conclusion that the document is an 'on-demand' bond:

(i) clause 4, which is the clause which requires payment by the Bank, provides that:

(a) payment is to be made on the seller's first written demand saying that the buyer has been in default of the payment obligation for 20 days; and

(b) payment is to be made 'immediately' without any request being made to the seller to take any action against the buyer;

(ii) clause 7 provides that the Bank's obligations are not to be affected or prejudiced by any dispute between the seller and the buyer under the shipbuilding contract or by any delay by the seller in the construction or delivery of the vessel;

(iii) clause 10 provides a limit to the guarantee of US$10,312,500 representing the principal of the second instalment plus interest for a period of 60 days; it is thus not envisaged that there will be any great delay in payment after default as there will be if (as in the present case) there is a dispute about whether the second instalment has ever became due.

25. In deciding whether the document is a traditional 'see to it' guarantee or an 'on-demand' guarantee, it would be obviously absurd to say that there are six pointers in favour of the former and only four pointers in favour of the latter and it must therefore be the former. But if the law does not permit boxes to be ticked in this way, commercial men will need some assistance from the courts in determining their obligations. The only assistance which the courts can give in practice is to say that, while everything must in the end depend on the words actually used by the parties, there is nevertheless a presumption that, if certain elements are present in the document, the document will be construed in one way or the other.

26. It is exactly this kind of assistance that the editors of *Paget's Law of Banking* have endeavoured to provide. In the 11th edition of that work these words appeared under the heading of 'Contract of suretyship v. demand guarantee':

> Where an instrument (i) relates to an underlying transaction between the parties in different jurisdictions, (ii) is issued by a bank, (iii) contains an undertaking to pay 'on demand' (with or without the words 'first' and/or 'written') and (iv) does not contain clauses excluding or limiting the defences available to a guarantor, it will almost always be construed as a demand guarantee.
>
> ...
>
> In construing guarantees it must be remembered that a demand guarantee can hardly avoid making reference to the obligation for whose performance the guarantee is security. A bare promise to pay on demand without any reference to the principal's obligation would leave the principal even more exposed in the event of a fraudulent demand because there would be room for argument as to which obligations were being secured.

27. The words 'will almost always be' amount to a presumption which was by then fully justified by the Court of Appeal authorities, *Howe Richardson v Polimex* [1978] 1 Ll Rep 161, *Owen v Barclays Bank* [1978] QB 159 and *Esal (Commodities) Ltd v Oriental Credit Ltd* [1985] 2 Ll Rep 546. It is enough to quote from the judgment of Lord Denning MR in *Owen* at page 170H–171C:

> So, as one takes instance after instance these performance guarantees are virtually promissory notes payable on demand. So long as the ... customers make an honest demand, the banks are bound to pay: and the banks will rarely, if ever, be in a position to know whether the demand is honest or not. At any rate they will not be able to prove it to be dishonest. So they will have to pay.
>
> All this leads to the conclusion that the performance guarantee stands on a similar footing to a letter of credit. A bank which gives a performance guarantee must honour that guarantee according to its terms. It is not concerned in the least with the relations between the supplier and the customer; nor with the question whether the supplier has performed

his contracted obligation or not; nor with the question whether the supplier is in default or not. The bank must pay according to its guarantee, on demand, if so stipulated, without proof or conditions. The only exception is when there is clear fraud of which the bank has notice.

Such has been course of decision in all the cases there have been this year in our courts here in England.

And from the judgment of Ackner LJ in *Esal* at page 549:

... a bank is not concerned in the least with the relations between the supplier and the customer nor with the question whether the supplier has performed his contractual obligation or not, nor with the question whether the supplier is in default or not, the only exception being where there is clear evidence both of fraud and of the bank's knowledge of that fraud.

In *Siporex v Banque Indosuez* [1986] 2 Ll Rep 146, 158 Hirst J was able to say:

All three of the leading Court of Appeal cases are the strongest authority in favour of the proposition that the bank guarantor is not and should not be concerned in any way with the rights and wrongs of the underlying transaction. This is also the case in relation to letters of credit, with which all the authorities draw a very close analogy ...

I, of course, accept Mr Hallgarten's submissions that every bond has to be construed in accordance with its terms, and there can be no blind categorization of its character or blind assumption of the obligations which it creates. However, I can see nothing whatsoever in the present performance bond to differentiate it from a number of those quoted in the authorities (particularly that in the *Esal* case) or to justify a departure from the general principles laid down in those cases.

I also consider it is extremely important that, for such a frequently adopted commercial transaction, there should be consistency of approach by the courts, so that all parties know clearly where they stand.

28. Paget's presumption was in due course *approved by this court in Caja de Ahorros v Gold Coast Ltd* [2002] CLC 397, para. 16, where the document was held to be an on-demand guarantee although (as in this case) the fourth element of the presumption was absent but the others were present.

29. The fact is that guarantees of the kind before the court in this case are almost worthless if the Bank can resist payment on the basis that the foreign buyer is disputing whether a payment is due. That would be all the more so in a case such as the present when the buyer can refuse to sign any certificate of approval which may be required by the underlying contract.

[**Rimer** and **Tomlinson LJJ** agreed.]

NOTES

1. It is generally accepted that the correct categorisation of a demand guarantee or a suretyship guarantee depends upon construction of the instrument. The modern approach to the construction of a commercial contract is objective and contextual, which goes beyond the four corners of the agreement itself and takes into account the wider background to the contract (the classic statement of the modern principles of construction was provided by Lord Hoffmann in *Investors Compensation Scheme Ltd v West Bromwich Building Society*

[1998] 1 WLR 896 at 912–913: see above, p 21). This is illustrated by *Rainy Sky SA v Kookmin* [2011] UKSC 50, [2012] 1 All ER (Comm) 1, where the Supreme Court construed the ambiguous terms of an advanced payment bond (APB), which was issued by the ship-builder's bank, in accordance with the commercial purpose of the bond, and held that it allowed the buyer to demand payment under the bond on the shipbuilder's insolvency. In *Rainy Sky*, the Supreme Court had to construe the terms of the APB in order to ascertain whether or not the bank was obliged to pay, rather than to characterise the nature of the instrument itself, nevertheless, the same objective and contextual approach to construction applies for the purposes of categorisation of an instrument as a demand guarantee or a suretyship guarantee.

2. In *Wuhan*, Longmore LJ clearly considered that the analysis provided in *Paget* should be applied flexibly, as the instrument in that case contained a clause waiving defences based on any variation or extensions of the terms of the underlying shipbuilding contracts (a clause that would normally be found in a suretyship contract because the obligations of the surety may be discharged by transactions between the creditor and the principal debtor), and yet it was still categorised as a demand guarantee. The same result followed in *Spliethoff's Bevrachtingskantoor BV v Bank of China Ltd* [2015] EWHC 999 (Comm) at [71] and [81], in *Caterpillar Motoren GmbH v Mutual Benefits Assurance Co* [2015] EWHC 2304 (Comm) at [21] and [27], and in *South Lanarkshire Council v Aviva Insurance Ltd* [2016] CSOH 83 at [26].

3. In *Marubeni Hong Kong & South China Ltd v The Government of Mongolia* [2005] EWCA Civ 395, [2005] 2 All ER (Comm) 289 at [28], Carnwath LJ said that cases where documents are issued by banks which are 'described as, or assumed to be, performance bonds ... provide no useful analogy for interpreting a document which was not issued by a bank and which contains no overt indication of an intention to create a performance bond or anything analogous to it'. In *Vossloh Aktiengesellschaft v Alpha Trains (UK) Ltd* [2010] EWHC 2443 (Ch), [2011] 2 All ER (Comm) 307 at [36], the judge, Sir William Blackburne, suggested that, because Vossloh was not a bank, there was a strong presumption that its payment obligations did not constitute a demand guarantee. However, the clear language of the instrument itself may result in an instrument issued by a non-bank party being charac-terised as a demand guarantee: see, for example, *IIG Capital LLC v Van Der Merwe* [2008] EWCA Civ 542, [2008] 2 Lloyd's Rep 187; *ABM Amro Commercial Finance plc v McGinn* [2014] EWHC 1674 (Comm); *Caterpillar Motoren GmbH v Mutual Benefits Assurance Co* [2015] EWHC 2304 (Comm). In *Meritz Fire & Marine Insurance Co Ltd v Jan de Nul NV* [2011] EWCA Civ 827, [2011] 2 Lloyd's Rep 379 at [19], the Court of Appeal stated that the express incorporation of the ICC's Uniform Rules for Demand Guarantees (URDG) into advance payment guarantees issued by an insurance company (and not a bank: see also *South Lanarkshire Council v Aviva Insurance Ltd* [2016] CSOH 83 at [25] '[w]here ... the granter is a bank or other financial institution whose business includes the granting of financial instruments for a fee') made it 'extremely difficult' for the insurers to argue that the instruments were suretyship guarantees. In *WS Tankship II BV v Kwangju Bank Ltd* [2011] EWHC 3103 (Comm) at [123], Blair J said that incorporation of the URDG into a guarantee was likely to be conclusive as to the nature of the instrument but that its omission was in itself a neutral factor. The same can probably be said of an instrument that expressly incorporates the uniform rules for standby credits called International Standby Practices (ISP98).

Edward Owen Engineering Ltd v Barclays Bank International Ltd
[1978] QB 159, Court of Appeal

The plaintiffs, English suppliers, contracted with Libyan buyers to supply and erect glass-houses in Libya. The plaintiffs agreed to provide the buyers with a performance bond for 10 per cent of the contract price and the buyers agreed to open a confirmed irrevocable credit in their favour. The plaintiffs instructed an English bank, the defendants, to provide the bond against their counter-guarantee. The defendants instructed the Umma Bank in Libya to issue the bond, undertaking to pay the amount 'on demand without proof or conditions'. Umma Bank then issued the bond. But the buyers failed to open a confirmed irrevocable documentary credit as agreed and so the plaintiffs terminated the supply contract. Nevertheless, the buyers went on to claim payment under the performance bond from Umma Bank, who in turn claimed payment from the defendants. The plaintiffs sought an injunction to restrain the defendants from paying. An interim injunction was granted by Boreham J but later discharged by Kerr J. The plaintiffs appealed.

Lord Denning MR: A performance bond is a new creature so far as we are concerned. It has many similarities to a letter of credit, with which of course we are very familiar. It has been long established that when a letter of credit is issued and confirmed by a bank, the bank must pay it if the documents are in order and the terms of the credit are satisfied. Any dispute between buyer and seller must be settled between themselves. The bank must honour the credit. That was clearly stated in *Hamzeh Malas & Sons v British Imex Industries Ltd* [1958] 2 QB 127, Jenkins LJ, giving the judgment of this court, said, at p 129: . . . [see above, p 786].

To this general principle there is an exception in the case of what is called established or obvious fraud to the knowledge of the bank. The most illuminating case is of *Sztejn v J Henry Schroder Banking Corpn* 31 NYS 2d 631 (1941) which was heard in the New York Court of Appeals. After citing many cases Shientag J said, at p 633:

It is well established that a letter of credit is independent of the primary contract of sale between the buyer and the seller. The issuing bank agrees to pay upon presentation of documents, not goods. This rule is necessary to preserve the efficiency of the letter of credit as an instrument for the financing of trade.

He said, at p 634, that in that particular case it was different because:

on the present motion, it must be assumed that the seller has intentionally failed to ship any goods ordered by the buyer. In such a situation, where the seller's fraud has been called to the bank's attention before the drafts and documents have been presented for payment, the principle of the independence of the bank's obligation under the letter of credit should not be extended to protect the unscrupulous seller.

That case shows that there is this exception to the strict rule: the bank ought not to pay under the credit if it knows that the documents are forged or that the request for payment is made fraudulently in circumstances when there is no right to payment.

I would in this regard quote the words of Browne J in an unreported case when he was sitting at first instance. It is *Bank Russo-Iran v Gordon Woodroffe & Co Ltd* ((1972) 116 Sol Jo 921). He said:

In my judgment, if the documents are presented by the beneficiary himself, and are forged or fraudulent, the bank is entitled to refuse payment if it finds out before payment, and is entitled to recover the money as paid under a mistake of fact if it finds out after payment.

But as Kerr J said in this present case:

> In cases of obvious fraud to the knowledge of the banks, the courts may prevent banks from fulfilling their obligation to third parties.

Such is the law as to a confirmed letter of credit. How does it stand with regard to a performance bond or a performance guarantee? Seeing that it is a guarantee of performance—that is, a guarantee that the supplier will perform his contracted obligations—one would expect that it would be enforced in such a case as this: suppose the English supplier had been paid for the goods and had delivered them, but that the Libyan customer then discovered that they were defective and not up to contract or that they had been delayed. The Libyan customer could then claim damages for the breach. But instead of coming to England to sue for the breach, his remedy would be to claim payment under the guarantee—of the 10 per cent or the 5 per cent of the price—as liquidated damage, so to speak. He claims payment from the Umma Bank. The Umma Bank pay him 'on first request.' They claim on Barclays Bank International. Then Barclays pay 'on first demand without proof or conditions.' And Barclays claim against the English suppliers, the payment being 'conclusive evidence.'

It is obvious that that course of action can be followed, not only when there are substantial breaches of contract, but also when the breaches are insubstantial or trivial, in which case they bear the colour of a penalty rather than liquidated damages: or even when the breaches are merely allegations by the customer without any proof at all: or even when the breaches are non-existent. The performance guarantee then bears the colour of a discount on the price of 10 per cent or 5 per cent, or as the case may be. The customer can always enforce payment by making a claim on the guarantee and it will then be passed down the line to the English supplier. This possibility is so real that the English supplier, if he is wise, will take it into account when quoting his price for the contract.

Take the case one stage further. The English supplier is not in default at all. He has not shipped the goods because he has not been paid. The Libyan customer has not provided the confirmed letter of credit. It is still open to the Libyan customer to make some allegation of default against the English supplier—as for instance not doing the preliminary work or not being ready and willing—and on that allegation to claim payment under the performance guarantee. On that request being made, payment will be made by the banks down the line: and be made by them 'on demand without proof or conditions.'

So, as one takes instance after instance, these performance guarantees are virtually promissory notes payable on demand. So long as the Libyan customers make an honest demand, the banks are bound to pay: and the banks will rarely, if ever, be in a position to know whether the demand is honest or not. At any rate they will not be able to prove it to be dishonest. So they will have to pay.

All this leads to the conclusion that the performance guarantee stands on a similar footing to a letter of credit. A bank which gives a performance guarantee must honour that guarantee according to its terms. It is not concerned in the least with the relations between the supplier and the customer; nor with the question whether the supplier has performed his contracted obligation or not; nor with the question whether the supplier is in default or not. The bank must pay according to its guarantee, on demand, if so stipulated, without proof or conditions. The only exception is when there is a clear fraud of which the bank has notice.

Such has been the course of decision in all the cases there have been this year in our courts here in England. First of all, there was *RD Harbottle (Mercantile) Ltd v National Westminster Bank Ltd* [1978] QB 146 before Kerr J. The judge considered the position in principle. I would like to adopt a passage from his judgment, p 761E–G.

> It is only in exceptional cases that the courts will interfere with the machinery of irrevocable obligations assumed by banks. They are the life-blood of international commerce. Such obligations

are regarded as collateral to the underlying rights and obligations between the merchants at either end of the banking chain. Except possibly in clear cases of fraud of which the banks have notice, the courts will leave the merchants to settle their disputes under the contracts by litigation or arbitration . . . The courts are not concerned with their difficulties to enforce such claims; these are risks which the merchants take. In this case the plaintiffs took the risk of the unconditional wording of the guarantees. The machinery and commitments of banks are on a different level. They must be allowed to be honoured, free from interference by the courts. Otherwise, trust in international commerce could be irreparably damaged.

Since that time there has been before Donaldson J and afterwards in this court *Howe Richardson Scale Co Ltd v Polimex-Cekop and National Westminster Bank Ltd* ([1915] 1 Lloyd's Rep 161). In that case Roskill LJ spoke to the same effect. He said [at p 165]:

Whether the obligation arises under a letter of credit or under a guarantee, the obligation of the bank is to perform that which it is required to perform by that particular contract, and that obligation does not in the ordinary way depend on the correct resolution of a dispute as to the sufficiency of performance by the seller to the buyer or by the buyer to the seller as the case may be under the sale and purchase contract; the bank here is simply concerned to see whether the event has happened upon which its obligation to pay has risen.

So there it is: Barclays Bank International has given its guarantee—I might almost say its promise to pay—to Umma Bank on demand without proof or conditions. They gave that promise, the demand was made. The bank must honour it. This court cannot interfere with the obligations of the bank . . .

I would therefore dismiss this appeal.

Browne LJ: I agree that this appeal should be dismissed for the reasons given by Lord Denning MR. Kerr J in *Harbottle (Mercantile) Ltd v National Westminster Bank Ltd* [1978] QB 146 and this court in the *Howe Richardson* case ([1978] 1 Lloyd's Rep 161) treated a bank's position under a guarantee or performance bond of the type given by Barclays Bank to the Umma Bank as being very similar to the position of a bank which has opened a confirmed irrevocable credit, and I have no doubt that this is right.

Geoffrey Lane LJ: The law applicable in these circumstances is conveniently set out, as Lord Denning MR and Browne LJ have indicated, by Roskill LJ in the recent decision in *Howe Richardson Scale Co Ltd v Polimex-Cekop and National Westminster Bank Ltd* ([1978] 1 Lloyd's Rep 161). The passage already cited by my brethren is followed by these words of Roskill LJ:

The bank takes the view that that time has come and that it is compelled to pay; in my view it would be quite wrong for the court to interfere with Polimex's apparent right under this guarantee to seek payment from the bank, because to do so would involve putting upon the bank an obligation to inquire whether or not there had been timeous performance of the sellers' obligations under the sale contract.

In the present case Mr Ross-Munro [counsel for the suppliers] submits that, since this document between the two banks is expressed to be a guarantee, the bank is under no liability to pay prima facie unless, first of all, there is a principal debtor and, secondly, some default by the principal debtor in his obligations under his contract with the seller. Since, he submits, no such default on the part of the sellers is suggested, the guarantee does not come into effect. The answer to that appears to me to be this. Although this agreement is expressed to be a guarantee, it is not in truth such a contract. It has much more of the characteristics of a promissory note than the characteristics of a guarantee . . .

The only circumstances which would justify the bank not complying with a demand made under that agreement would be those which would exonerate them under similar circumstances if they had entered into a letter of credit, and that is this, if it had been clear and obvious to the bank that the buyers had been guilty of fraud. Mr Ross-Munro, conceding that that is the situation, endeavours to show that indeed fraud is clear and obvious here, that the bank knew about it, and accordingly he is entitled to succeed.

The way he seeks to establish fraud is this. He points to the undoubted fact that the buyers in Libya have failed to reply to any of the requests for a proper confirmed letter of credit according, Mr Ross-Munro submits, to the terms of the contract and, moreover, have failed to produce any suggestion of any default or breach of contract on the part of the sellers in England which would possibly justify a demand that the performance guarantee be implemented.

I disagree that that amounts to any proof or evidence of fraud. It may be suspicious, it may indicate the possibility of sharp practice, but there is nothing in those facts remotely approaching true evidence of fraud or anything which makes fraud obvious or clear to the bank. Thus there is nothing, it seems to me, which casts any doubt upon the bank's prima facie obligation to fulfil its duty under the two tests which I have set out.

It may be harsh in the result, but the sellers must have been aware of the dangers involved or, if they were not, they should have been aware of them, and either they should have declined to accept the terms of the performance bond or else they should have allowed for the possibility of the present situation arising by making some adjustment in the price.

I agree that the appeal should be dismissed.

Cargill International SA v Bangladesh Sugar and Food Industries Corpn
[1996] 2 Lloyd's Rep 524, Queen's Bench Division

The plaintiff sellers agreed to sell a consignment of sugar to the defendant buyers. The sellers provided the buyers with an unconditional performance bond which was issued by the Dhaka branch of Banque Indosuez (the bank). The underlying contract of sale provided that the performance bond was liable to be forfeited if the sellers failed to fulfil any of the terms and conditions of the contract and also if any loss or damage occurred to the buyers as a result of the fault of the sellers. Shipment was made by the sellers, but rejected by the buyers who alleged, inter alia, that delivery was late. The sellers then applied for an injunction restraining the buyers from calling on the bond and a declaration that the buyers were not entitled to make a call on the bond or to retain any money so received on the ground that they had suffered no loss since the market for sugar had fallen and the buyers had replaced the rejected sugar at less than the contract price. On the assumption that the sellers were in breach of the contract of sale, Morison J ordered the trial of certain preliminary issues, including whether the buyers were entitled to make a call for the full amount of the performance bond and, if so, whether they were entitled to retain all the monies received by them.

Morison J: I start with the commercial purpose of a performance bond. There is a wealth of authority concerned with the question whether and in what circumstances an interlocutory injunction may be granted (1) against the bank which issued the bond to restrain it from paying in accordance with its terms; (2) against the beneficiary of the bond to prevent it from calling the bond.

The Court will not grant an injunction in either case unless there has been a lack of good faith. The justification for this lies in the commercial purpose of the bond. Such a bond is, effectively, as valuable as a promissory note and is intended to affect the 'tempo' of parties' obligations in the sense that when an allegation of breach of contract is made (in good faith), the beneficiary can call the bond and receive its value pending the resolution of the contractual disputes. He does not have to await the final determination of his rights before he receives some moneys. On an application for an injunction, it is, therefore, not pertinent that the beneficiary may be wrong to have called the bond because, after a trial or arbitration, the breach of contract may not be established; otherwise, the Court would be frustrating the commercial purpose of the bond. The concept that money must be paid without question, and the rights and wrongs argued about later, is a familiar one in international trade, and substantial building contracts. A performance bond may assume the characteristics of a guarantee, especially, if not exclusively, in building contracts, where the beneficiary must show, as a prerequisite for calling on the bond, that by reason of the contractor's non-performance he has sustained damage: *Trafalgar House Construction (Regions) Ltd. v. General Surety & Guarantee Co. Ltd.,* [1996] 1 A.C. 199.

However, it seems to me implicit in the nature of a bond, and in the approach of the Court to injunction applications, that, in the absence of some clear words to a different effect, when the bond is called, there will, at some stage in the future, be an 'accounting' between the parties in the sense that their rights and obligations will be finally determined at some future date. The bond is not intended to represent an 'estimate' of the amount of damages to which the beneficiary may be entitled for the breach alleged to give rise to the right to call. The bond is a 'guarantee' of due performance. If the amount of the bond is not sufficient to satisfy the beneficiary's claim for damages, he can bring proceedings for his loss. As far as I am aware, and no case was cited to me to suggest otherwise, the performance bond is not intended to supplant the right to sue for damages. Indeed, such a contention would conflict with what I believe to be the commercial purpose of these instruments. Mr. Hossain submitted that the buyer's rights were exhausted when the bond was called, but he could give no support for the proposition; and he had, I think, no satisfactory explanation as to why his clients should have wished so to restrict their damages. The bond could be called in any number of circumstances, at least some of which could have caused his clients losses substantially, in excess of the bond value. If he were right, then, presumably, the beneficiary would decline to call the bond; yet serious loss caused by a breach of contract was the very event for which the bond was required and given in the first place, I reject, entirely, his submission on this point, both as being without legal foundation and as lacking in commercial good sense.

Therefore, the question arises as to why, if the beneficiary can sue to recover what he has actually lost, the seller (in this case) should not be able to recover any overpayment. It would seem, in principle, correct that if a performance bond does not exhaust one party's rights it should not exhaust the rights of the other party.

What I perceive to be correct in principle, is fortified by authority. In *State Trading Corporation of India Ltd. v. E. D. & F. Man (Sugar) Ltd. and The State Bank of India*, July 17, 1981, transcript, Lord Denning, M.R. said this (in an injunction case):

> I may say that performance bonds fulfil a most useful role in international trade. If the seller defaults in making delivery, the buyer can operate the bond. He does not have to go to far away countries and sue for damages, or go through a long arbitration. He can get the damages at once which are due to him for breach of contract. The bond is given so that, on notice of default being given, the buyer can have his money in hand to meet his claim for damages for the seller's non-performance of contract. If he receives too much, that can be rectified later at an arbitration. The courts must see that these performance bonds are honoured.

If the Court had considered that an 'overpayment' could not be recovered, its approach to the grant of injunctive relief might have been different. Almost all cases where such relief has been sought are ones where the plaintiff is saying that there has been no breach, or that he has the benefit of some exclusion clause, or that the other contracting party has not suffered any loss. None of these contentions will suffice, partly because, I think, the Court always recognized that the bonds affected the 'tempo' of the parties' obligations but not their substantive rights.

Support may also be found in two Australian cases. In the first, *Australasian Conference Association Ltd. v. Mainline Constructions Pty. Ltd. (in liquidation),* [1978] 141 C.L.R. 335 the question before the Court was whether the employer under a building contract made with a builder (Mainline) which subsequently went into liquidation was entitled to pay sub-contractors out of the performance bond moneys which it had called, and been paid by the builder's bank. It was the bank's position, inter alia, that the employer was obliged to account to it for any surplus after the sub-contractors had been paid off. The employer conceded that it was not entitled to retain any surplus, and the Court clearly believed that to be correct, as did the other two parties. The Court's conclusion was that the issue had to be determined by reference to the contract between the employer and Mainline; it concluded that the surplus should be released to Mainline and not to the bank. In a subsequent building case (an injunction case) *Woodhall Ltd. v. Pipeline Authority and Another,* [1979] 141 C.L.R. 443, the Court held that the beneficiary was entitled to call the bond but that once paid, the "money must be held as security for the contractor's due and faithful performance of the work". Both these cases lend (limited) support for the proposition that moneys paid under a performance bond are designed to be used in accordance with the provisions of the contract and that any surplus is for the account of the party which provided the bond....

In the 4th edition of Benjamin's Sale of Goods, at par. 23–218, there is the following passage:

> As the making of an excessive demand is, basically, a breach of the beneficiary's underlying contract, the amount ought to be regarded as repayable to the account party rather than to the bank.

The learned editors assume that the overpayment may be recovered and infer that the only question is whether the account party [the seller] or the bank is entitled to receive the repayment. They rely upon the two Australian cases as supporting the conclusion that it is the account party and not the bank which is entitled to the moneys.

As a matter of general principle, therefore, in the light of the commercial purpose of such bonds, the authorities to which I have referred and the textbook comments, I take the view that if there has been a call on a bond which turns out to exceed the true loss sustained, then the party who provided the bond is entitled to recover the overpayment. It seems to me that the account party may hold the amount recovered in trust for the bank, (where, for example, the bank had not been paid by him) but that does not affect his right to bring the claim in his own name. In the normal course of events, the bank will have required its customer to provide it with appropriate security for the giving of the bond, which would be called upon as soon as the bank was required to pay. On the facts of this case, no question of a trust or agency will arise. In principle, I take the view that the account party is always entitled to receive the overpayment since his entitlement is founded upon the contract between himself and the beneficiary.

I turn therefore to the contract between the parties. Under cl. 13 the bond was—

> ... liable to be forfeited ... if the Seller fails to fulfil any of the terms and conditions of this contract ... and also if any loss/damage occurs to the Buyer due to any fault of the seller.

It seems to me that on a proper construction of this clause, there is no indication that it was the parties' intention that the bond would either satisfy the whole of the buyer's damages (see above) or prevent the seller from recovering any overpayment. The word 'forfeit' might be apt to suggest that once called, the bond moneys had 'gone' for good. But if it had been the intention of the parties to produce a result whereby the buyer could both call on the bond and sue for damages, whereas the seller forfeited his right to any overpayment then much plainer words would have been required to take this case away from the general principles as I perceive them to be. That being so, it seems to me that treating the two parts of the clause disjunctively, and treating the right to forfeit as arising if either there was a breach or if any loss or damage occurred to the buyer due to any fault of the seller (which might not be a breach) would make commercial good sense.

The buyer is stipulating clearly that, as between himself and the seller, all he needs to show to be entitled to call on the bond was a breach of contract; he need not show damage (although damage will almost always follow); if, on the other hand, say through a misrepresentation by the seller, damage was caused to the buyer then the right to call the bond was conferred by the second half of the clause. But in either event, there will be an 'accounting' at trial or arbitration to ensure that the buyer has not been underpaid or overpaid....

The basis upon which recovery may be made in respect of an overpayment is, I think, contractual rather than quasi, contractual. It seem to me that it is necessary to imply into the contract that moneys paid under the bond which exceeded the buyer's actual loss would be recoverable by the seller. I am content to adopt Mr. Males' formulation of the term which is to be implied into the sale contract, as a matter of necessity or on the basis that the implication of such a term was so obvious that its incorporation in the contract went without saying:

> ... that the buyer will account to the Seller for the proceeds of the bond, retaining only the amount of any loss suffered as a result of the Seller's breach of contract.

It is unnecessary to consider the interesting argument advanced on penalty. Had I been persuaded that there was a term of the contract between the parties which enabled the buyer to call on the bond when he had suffered no damage, and to retain the moneys, I would have held the provision to have been penal. In *Workers Trust Bank Ltd. v. Dojap Ltd.*, [1993] A.C. 573 at p. 582 Lord Browne Wilkinson said:

> There is clear authority that in a case of a sum paid by one party to another under the contract as security for the performance of that contract, a provision for its forfeiture in the event of non-performance is a penalty from which the court will give relief by ordering repayment of the sum so paid, less any damage actually proved to have been suffered as a result of non-completion: *Commissioner of Public Works v. Hills* [1906] A.C. 368.

[The decision of Morison J was upheld by the Court of Appeal: [1998] 1 WLR 461. There was no appeal against the judge's reasoning that it is implicit in the nature of a performance bond that in the absence of clear contractual words to a different effect there will be an accounting between the parties at some stage after the bond has been called: Potter LJ noted (at 465) that he had himself approved Morison J's reasoning in *Comdel Commodities Ltd v Siporex Trade SA* [1997] 1 Lloyd's Rep 424 at 431. The issue on appeal was whether the references to forfeiture in the underlying contract of sale indicated that the parties intended to oust the usual implication as to any subsequent accounting between the parties. The Court of Appeal held that it did not and that the reference to forfeiture referred only to the position as between the buyers and the bank, and not as between the buyers and the sellers.]

NOTES

1. Since the *Edward Owen* case, the courts have continued to treat demand guarantees on a similar footing to documentary credits: see, for example, *Intraco Ltd v Notis Shipping Corpn, The Bhoja Trader* [1981] 2 Lloyd's Rep 256; *Bolivinter Oil SA v Chase Manhattan Bank* [1984] 1 WLR 392; *Turkiye Is Bankasi AS v Bank of China* [1998] 1 Lloyd's Rep 250; but contrast *Potton Homes Ltd v Coleman Contractors (Overseas) Ltd* (1984) 28 BLR 19 at 27–29. As Professor RM Goode has stated ([1992] LMCLQ 190 at 192):

> Demand guarantees share with documentary credits the characteristic of being abstract payment undertakings, that is to say, they are promises of payment which are considered binding upon

communication to the beneficiary without the need for acceptance, consideration, reliance, or solemnity of form, and are separate from and independent of the underlying contract.

The fact that a documentary credit is a primary payment mechanism, whereas a demand guarantee is intended as a secondary obligation, must not, of course, be overlooked (Goode, above, p 193).

2. The autonomous nature of a demand guarantee makes it vulnerable to abusive calling (see N Enonchong [2007] LMCLQ 83). Although the fraud exception applies, it is notoriously difficult to establish: see, for example, *Harbottle (Mercantile) Ltd v National Westminster Bank* [1978] QB 146; *State Trading Corpn of India Ltd v ED & F Man (Sugar) Ltd* [1981] Com LR 235; *GKN Contractors Ltd v Lloyds Bank plc* (1985) 30 BLR 48; *Turkiye Is Bankasi AS v Bank of China* [1998] 1 Lloyd's Rep 250; and, generally, see above, pp 789–802. It is no easier to obtain an injunction to restrain the beneficiary from making demand than it is to obtain an injunction to prevent the bank paying out under the demand guarantee after the demand has been made: see the strong *obiter dictum* of Staughton LJ in *Group Josi Re v Walbrook Insurance Co Ltd* [1996] 1 WLR 1152 at 1161–1162, and also that of Rix J in *Czarnikow-Rionda Sugar Trading Inc v Standard Bank London Ltd* [1999] 1 All ER (Comm) 890 at 913, criticising the majority decision of the Court of Appeal in *Themehelp Ltd v West* [1996] QB 84. The starting point is that the court will not grant an interlocutory injunction without clear evidence of fraud or lack of good faith on the part of the beneficiary (*TTI Team Telecom International Ltd v Hutchison 3G UK Ltd* [2003] EWHC 762 (TCC), [2003] 1 All ER (Comm) 914). In *Simon Carves Ltd v Ensus UK Ltd* [2011] EWHC 657 (TCC), [2011] BLR 340, Akenhead J granted an injunction restraining a beneficiary from seeking payment under a performance bond on the ground that the issuing bank had a strong case that, as between it and the beneficiary, the bond was null and void pursuant to the terms of the underlying contract. This was not a case of fraud and, as we have already seen, it may constitute a further exception to the autonomy principle (see above, p 789). In any event, the issuing bank will not be obliged to pay on a demand guarantee if it is tainted by illegality (*Group Josi Re v Walbrook Insurance Co Ltd*, above, at 1163–1164, per Staughton LJ; *Mahonia Ltd v JP Morgan Chase Bank* [2003] EWHC 1927 (Comm), [2003] 2 Lloyd's Rep 911 at [68], per Colman J) or some other vitiating factor applies, for example the bank issued the demand guarantee as a result of a conspiracy between, or misrepresentation by, its customer and the beneficiary (*Solo Industries UK Ltd v Canara Bank* [2001] EWCA Civ 1059, [2001] 2 All ER (Comm) 217; see also *SAFA Ltd v Banque Du Caire* [2000] 2 All ER (Comm) 567, CA). In cases of abusive calling, the principal probably stands a better chance of obtaining a freezing injunction (formerly known as a *Mareva* injunction) restraining the beneficiary from using the funds he has received in payment of the demand guarantee, than he does of obtaining an injunction to prevent payment in the first place (*Intraco Ltd v Notis Shipping Corpn, The Bhoja Trader* [1981] 2 Lloyd's Rep 256). In appropriate cases the court may combine a freezing injunction with an ancillary order requiring the proceeds of the demand guarantee to be paid into court (*Themehelp Ltd v West* [1996] QB 84 at 103, per Evans LJ). But where the demand guarantee is to be paid abroad, it would be an unjustified interference with the operation of the instrument to order the bank to pay the money into an account in England (*Britten Norman Ltd v State Ownership Fund of Romania* [2000] 1 Lloyd's Rep Bank 315).

3. In *Banque Saudi Fransi v Lear Siegler Services Inc* [2006] EWCA Civ 1130, [2007] 1 All ER (Comm) 67, the Court of Appeal held that where a bank has paid the beneficiary under a demand guarantee and claims against the principal on a counter-indemnity, summary judgment will be given in favour of the bank unless the principal can show that there is a real prospect of proving at trial that the beneficiary had not honestly believed that he had the right to make the demand and that the bank had been aware of this. Arden LJ reasoned (at [18]) that the test was different from the one that applied in the case of a claim against a bank on a demand guarantee or letter of credit (where it had to be shown that there was a real prospect that the 'only realistic inference' was fraud), because the giver of a counter-indemnity, unlike the bank, was unlikely to be in a position to know by the time of the summary judgment application whether the fraud exception applied. The test is therefore lower than that which applies when a summary claim is brought against the bank on a demand guarantee, but Arden LJ (at [20]) still described it as 'a high hurdle to meet', and the principal was held not to have satisfied the test in the instant case. By contrast, in *Enka Insaat Ve Sanayi AS v Banca Popolare dell'Alto Adige SpA* [2009] EWHC 2410 (Comm) at [24]–[25], the test applied by Teare J when deciding whether to give summary judgment against a bank on a demand guarantee (the claim was not on a counter-indemnity) was whether there was a real prospect that the bank would establish at trial that the only realistic inference was that the beneficiary did not honestly believe in the validity of the demand.

4. The principle of strict compliance applies to demand guarantees. There had been some uncertainty as to whether the principle applies with the same rigour to demand guarantees as it does to documentary credits, but the correct position would seem to be that outlined by Staughton LJ on appeal in *IE Contractors Ltd v Lloyds Bank plc* [1990] 2 Lloyd's Rep 496 at 500–501, namely, that while there may be more scope for interpreting the demand guarantee as not requiring the demand to follow any particular form, it is in all cases a question of construction of the terms of the guarantee and that, once construed, the requirements of the instrument must be strictly complied with. This approach was adopted by Teare J in *Sea-Cargo Skips AS v State Bank of India* [2013] EWHC 177 (Comm), [2013] 2 Lloyd's Rep 477, who held that a demand made by a buyer under a refund guarantee issued by the shipbuilder's bank did not trigger the bank's liability because the demand did not make clear on its face that it was being made because of delay in the construction of the ship, as opposed to delay in delivery of the ship to the buyer, as was required by the terms of the refund guarantee when properly construed. The key point is that the issuer of a demand guarantee needs to know whether, on the face of the demand, its obligation to pay had been triggered. More recently, Stuart-Smith J stressed in *Lukoil Mid-East Ltd v Barclays Bank plc* [2016] EWHC 166 (TCC) at [17] that 'it is the terms of the guarantee itself that will determine the formal requirements, if any, with which a demand must comply in order to be valid', but concluded (at [33]) that the particular wording that appeared in the demand guarantee before him (that the bank's obligation to pay under the demand guarantee was conditional on there having been no amendment of the underlying construction contract between beneficiary and principal 'impacting the timely performance of the Works under the Contract') were 'an historical relic that [had] washed up in a modern Bank Guarantee' and served no useful commercial purpose, with the result that, in the absence of clear words making it a requirement of the demand, the beneficiary did not have to include a statement to that effect when calling for payment under the demand guarantee.

5. There is an implied term in the contract between the beneficiary and the principal that the beneficiary will account to the principal to the extent of any overpayment that arises as a result of a call on the demand guarantee (*Cargill International SA v Bangladesh Sugar and Food Industries Corpn*, above). The amount is due to the principal as a debt, whether or not the principal has indemnified either the paying bank or the indemnifier of the paying bank (*Tradigrain SA v State Trading Corpn of India* [2005] EWHC 2206 (Comm), [2006]

1 All ER (Comm) 197 at [26], per Christopher Clarke J). The obligation to account arises when the fact of the overpayment has been established either by agreement or judgment (per Christopher Clarke J, *obiter*, in *Tradigrain* at [28]). There is no implied term in the demand guarantee itself that there will be repayment if any part of a demand is later found to be excessive (*Uzinterimpex JSC v Standard Bank plc* [2008] EWCA Civ 819, [2008] 2 Lloyd's Rep 456 at [16]–[25]). In *Wuhan Guoyu Logistics Co Ltd v Emporiki Bank of Greece SA* [2013] EWCA Civ 1679, [2014] 1 Lloyd's Rep 273, the Court of Appeal held that money paid by a bank to the beneficiary under a demand guarantee was not held in trust by the beneficiary for the bank when, between the beneficiary making the demand in good faith (in other words, this was not a case of fraud) and payment being made to the beneficiary, it was conclusively determined by a final arbitration award that the event which purportedly triggered the demand had not in fact occurred. Tomlinson LJ (at [29]) also expressed the tentative view that the existence of the beneficiary's contractual obligation to account to the principal for an overpayment under a demand guarantee was inconsistent with the creation of *any* trust affecting the money in the hands of the beneficiary, including a trust in favour of the principal.

6. The ICC has promulgated rules designed to provide a fair balance between the competing interests of the principal, beneficiary, and those banks involved in the issue of demand guarantees: see the ICC's *Uniform Rules for Demand Guarantees* (URDG) (2010, ICC Publication No 758) for the most recent version. The Uniform Rules only apply if adopted by the parties concerned. See, generally, G Affaki and R Goode, *Guide to ICC Uniform Rules for Demand Guarantees URDG 758* (2011, ICC Publication No 702E). A further choice of rules for the parties is offered by the *International Standby Practices* (ISP98) (ICC Publication No 590), drafted by the American Institute of International Banking Law and Practice, which came into effect on 1 January 1999. ISP98 has the same scope as the URDG and applies to independent guarantee instruments issued subject to it (the relationship between the URDG and ISP98 is examined by in Affaki and Goode's *Guide* at paras 579–580). In 1995, the United Nations General Assembly adopted the UNCITRAL Convention on Independent Guarantees and Standby Letters of Credit. Unlike the URDG and ISP98, which do not have the force of law, but are of a contractual nature requiring the consent of the parties, the UN Convention, as an international treaty, has become the law in all the countries that have ratified it. The Convention covers much of the same ground as the URDG, although it also deals with the power of courts to grant injunctions restraining presentation or payment, something which falls outside the URDG. The Convention came into force on 1 January 2000, though it has not been widely adopted. The UK has no plans to ratify or accede to the Convention.

7. For ascertainment of the governing law applicable to demand guarantees and counter-indemnities under the Rome I Regulation on the law applicable to contractual obligations (Regulation (EC) No 593/2008), which applies to contracts concluded as from 17 December 2009, see N Enonchong [2015] LMCLQ 194.

4 OTHER FINANCING METHODS

There are a number of other methods of financing international trade. They include the following.

(a) Forfaiting

Forfaiting is a type of non-recourse finance which assists the export seller's cash flow whilst giving the buyer a period of credit. The seller draws a term bill of exchange on the buyer, the bill being drawn 'without recourse' to himself. The bill is accepted by the buyer and backed by the buyer's bank, which may either execute an aval on the bill (see above, pp 701–702) or give a separate guarantee. The seller may then indorse the bill 'without recourse' and discount it to his own bank (the forfaiter). Alternatively, the buyer may make a promissory note which is guaranteed by his bank before being indorsed 'without recourse' by the seller and sold to the forfaiter. The advantage of this form of finance from the seller's point of view is that he receives an immediate payment of the cash value of the bill or note (less the usual charges and a discount fee) without recourse should the buyer default on payment. However, the forfaiter has the aval or guarantee of the buyer's bank to fall back on if the bill or note is dishonoured by non-payment. Usually, the forfaiter will itself sell the bill or note on into the *à forfait* market. The ICC and the International Forfaiting Association have produced a set of standard rules called the Uniform Rules for Forfaiting (URF 800), which came into effect on 1 January 2013.

(b) International factoring

See below, p 1003.

(c) International financial leasing

A financial leasing arrangement is a three-party transaction. The lessee negotiates with a supplier to supply goods (usually capital items such as ships, aircraft, or heavy equipment). The lessee also negotiates with a lessor (a bank or finance house) which purchases the goods from the supplier and leases them to the lessee. The lease is for the period of the anticipated working life of the asset and rentals are structured so as to amortise the capital cost of the equipment and give the lessor a return on capital (RM Goode [1987] JBL 318 and 399).

The UNIDROIT Convention on International Financial Leasing (1988), in force in only a limited number of states (and not the UK), governs certain types of financial leasing arrangements, namely those where:

(1) the lessee selects the goods and the supplier without relying primarily on the skill and judgment of the lessor;

(2) the supplier knows that the equipment is being acquired by the lessor in connection with a leasing arrangement; and

(3) the rentals are calculated to amortise the capital cost of the equipment (art 1(2)).

The UNIDROIT Convention applies where the lessor and the lessee have places of business in different states and either all three parties (lessor, lessee, and supplier) have places of business in Contracting States, or both the supply contract and the lease arrangement are governed by the law of a Contracting State (art 3(1)). The most important feature of the UNIDROIT Convention is that it shifts responsibility for the non-delivery, late delivery, or delivery of non-conforming equipment from the lessor to the supplier (see arts 8, 10, and 12(5)). This reflects the fact that the lessor has only a financial interest in the transaction. The UNIDROIT Convention formed the basis of the 2008 UNIDROIT Model Law on Leasing, which is designed for developing countries and countries in transition to a market economy. The model law is broader than the UNIDROIT Convention in that it covers operating leases as well as financial leases, and applies to domestic as well as cross-border transactions. The 2001 Cape Town Convention on International Interests in Mobile Equipment and its associated Aircraft Protocol are also of major importance in the field of leasing. Unlike the UNIDROIT Convention, the Cape Town Convention is not confined to cross-border leasing or to financial leasing agreements. The Cape Town Convention and the Aircraft Protocol were ratified by the UK in 2015.

For further discussion of the 1988 UNIDROIT Convention and the UNIDROIT model law, see R Goode, H Kronke, and E McKendrick, *Transactional Commercial Law: Text, Cases, and Materials* (2nd edn, 2015), Ch 12, and also Ch 14 for coverage of the 2001 Cape Town Convention and Aircraft Protocol.

(d) Confirming houses

Where an overseas buyer uses the services of a confirming house in the seller's country, and the confirming house makes itself liable to the seller for the price, the confirming house provides, in effect, non-recourse finance to the seller (see above p 118).

5 EXPORT CREDIT GUARANTEES

The seller may insure himself against loss arising from the overseas buyer's failure to pay the price. He can do this by taking out an export credit guarantee (available from government and private agencies). An export guarantee covers such risks as the buyer's insolvency (commercial risk) and his inability to accept the goods or pay the price due to circumstances beyond his control, for example government orders (political risk). Export guarantees may also assist the seller to secure finance from his bank. For detailed discussion, see *Benjamin's Sale of Goods* (9th edn, 2014), Ch 25.

PART VII

ASSIGNMENT AND RECEIVABLES FINANCING

Chapter 22   Assignment of choses in action   859
Chapter 23   Receivables financing   948

CHAPTER 22

ASSIGNMENT OF CHOSES IN ACTION

1 INTRODUCTION

Mixed claims have been made about the subject of this chapter: the assignment of choses in action. Lord Millett once wrote that '[a] large part of corporate wealth is tied up in debts, and these ought to form an ideal basis for short-term financing'. But, he added, '[t]he obvious commercial importance of the subject, however, is exceeded only by the complexity and confusion of the law which governs it': (1991) 107 LQR 679 at 679. Without passing comment on the law on the subject, Lady Hale has spoken of its importance in noting that '[t]he buying and selling of choses in action is, of course, commonplace. Debts are regularly traded at a discount so that the creditor can obtain some of what he is entitled to while passing on the risks of litigation to others. Businesses are regularly sold with the benefit of their claims as well as their liabilities' (*Massai Aviation Services Ltd v Attorney-General for the Bahamas* [2007] UKPC 12 at [18]).

The modern rules and principles of assignment are the product mainly of steady developments rather than sudden shocks. Those developments occurred over a long period, and especially from the seventeenth century onwards. Incremental developments in the judge-made law can be expected to continue. Commerce will continue to present new promise and new pitfalls. As legal advisors apply their ingenuity to those situations for their clients, the law of assignment can be expected to adjust and develop further.

One effect of the steady development of the law over prolonged periods is that the modern law of assignment presents itself as an amalgam of logic, practicality, and history. More than in many areas of commercial law, the law of assignment rewards those with the agility to move between those three forms of reason. In particular, since the common law historically did not permit assignment, while equity did, the relations of law and equity are basal features of the modern law of assignment.

Because an assignment is a transaction, it must have subject matter: there must be an existing, assignable chose in order for a transaction by assignment to occur. The chapter therefore considers in turn: (1) what 'choses in action' and 'assignments' are; (2) the requirements that there be an existing and assignable chose in action or right; (3) the requirement that a person who holds an existing assignable chose in action intend to assign it; (4) whether and when a rule of legal formality requires writing to be made; (5) whether and when notice of the assignment is required; (6) the effects of assignment as between the parties thereto; and (7), finally, obstacles to the enforcement of an assigned chose in action.

2 'CHOSE IN ACTION' AND 'ASSIGNMENT'

(a) Chose in action defined

'The History of the Treatment of Choses in Action by the Common Law' by WS Holdsworth
(1920) 33 Harvard LR 967 at 967–968

'All personal things are either in possession or action. The law knows no *tertium quid* between the two.'[1] It follows from this that the category of choses in action is in English law enormously wide, and that it can only be defined in very general terms. This is clear from the terms of the definition given by Channell J in *Torkington v Magee*,[2] which is generally accepted as correct. It runs as follows: '"Chose in action" is a known legal expression used to describe all personal rights of property which can only be claimed or enforced by action, and not by taking physical possession.' In fact the list of choses in action known to English law includes a large number of things which differ widely from one another in their essential characteristics. In its primary sense the term 'chose in action' includes all rights which are enforceable by action—rights to debts of all kinds, and rights of action on a contract or a right to damages for its breach; rights arising by reason of the commission of tort or other wrong; and rights to recover the ownership or possession of property real or personal. It was extended to cover the documents, such as bonds, which evidenced or proved the existence of such rights of action. This led to the inclusion in this class of things of such instruments as bills, notes, cheques, shares in companies, stock in the public funds, bills of lading, and policies of insurance. But many of these documents were in effect documents of title to what was in substance an incorporeal right of property. Hence it was not difficult to include in this category things which were even more obviously property of an incorporeal type, such as patent rights and copyrights. Further accessions to this long list were made by the peculiar division of English law into common law and equity. Uses, trusts, and other equitable interests in property, though regarded by equity as conferring proprietary rights analogous to the rights recognised by law in hereditaments or in chattels, were regarded by the common law as being merely choses in action.

FOOTNOTES:

1 *Colonial Bank v Whinney* (1885) 30 Ch D 261, 285, per Fry LJ, whose dissenting judgment was upheld by the House of Lords (1886) 11 App Cas 426.

2 [1902] 2 KB 427, 430 (see below, pp 907–909).

NOTES

1. Holdsworth said that category of choses in action is enormously wide. However, the phrase 'chose in action' is not always used in that wide sense. It is sometimes used to refer only to primary and secondary rights arising in contract and tort. More narrowly again, it is sometimes used to mean only *assignable* rights arising in contract and tort; when used in this narrower sense, a contrast may be drawn between choses in action (assignable rights) and 'mere rights of action' or 'personal rights of action' (non-assignable rights). The meaning depends on the context. See G Tolhurst, *The Assignment of Contractual Rights* (2nd edn, 2016), Ch 2.

2. Wide definitions of chose in action can be useful when describing the various forms of intangible property which are the location of considerable wealth and social value. However,

such wide definitions can falsely suggest that a single set of rules of assignment applies to the assignment of all kinds of choses in action. In fact, the rules of assignment differ according to the nature of the particular kind of right. For example, because copyright is a statutory privilege enforceable against all the world, while contractual debts are enforceable only against the debtor, different assignment rules naturally apply to each: see Turner [2011] LMCLQ 462.

3.   A primary division between the various sorts of choses in action is between legal choses in action and equitable choses in action. Legal choses in action are those which before the Supreme Court of Judicature Act 1873 entered force on 1 November 1875 could be enforced by action at law. Equitable choses in action are those which would have been enforceable only by a suit in equity before that date. The distinction between legal and equitable choses in action is made in *Snell's Equity* (33rd edn, 2015), para 3–01:

> A chose may be legal (ie formerly enforceable in a court of law), such as a debt, bill of exchange, policy of insurance, sweepstake ticket or share in a company; or it may be equitable (ie formerly enforceable only by a suit in equity), such as a legacy, a legatee's rights in an unadministered estate, a share in a trust fund, surplus proceeds of sale in the hands of a mortgagee, or a right to relief against forfeiture of a lease for non-payment of rent.

While this distinction reflects differences of procedure and enforceability, for example, the particular rules of assignment depend on further distinctions. This chapter concentrates on the assignment of legal choses in action arising from transactions (mainly, but not only, contracts) and torts (so far as rights in tort may be assigned).

4.   Rights and remedies are inextricably linked in English law. As Browne-Wilkinson V-C said in *Spain v Christie, Manson & Woods Ltd* [1986] 3 All ER 28 at 35: 'in the pragmatic way in which English law has developed, a man's legal rights are in fact those which are protected by a cause of action. It is not in accordance, as I understand it, with the principles in English law to analyse rights as being something separate from the remedy given to an individual'. But, while the existence of a remedy or remedies is an essential condition for the existence of a chose in action, that does not mean that the remedies are property in themselves, capable of assignment separately from the chose. This was confirmed by the House of Lords in *Investors Compensation Scheme Ltd v West Bromwich Building Society* [1998] 1 All ER 98. Their Lordships held that a claim to rescission of a mortgage is a right of action, but not a chose in action or part of a chose in action which the owner can assign separately from his property. On the other hand, a right to damages is a chose in action which can be assigned. It followed that there was no objection to a clause in the Investors Compensation Scheme claim form by which investors assigned a right to damages against a building society to the Investors Compensation Scheme Ltd, but which did not assign (because legally impossible) a right to rescission of the investors' mortgages with the building society.

5.   Periodic attempts are made to include new items in the category of choses in action. In *Goel v Pick* [2006] EWHC 833 (Ch), [2007] 1 All ER 982, Sir Francis Ferris held (at [20]) that a car owner's ability to apply to the Driver and Vehicle Licensing Authority (DVLA), to ask for the transfer of a vehicle registration mark (a VRM) from one vehicle to another (the car owner cannot require the DVLA to do so), could not be described as a chose in action and, even if it could be so described, it was not capable of being 'assigned', as distinct from being exercised in accordance with the relevant regulations made under statute that govern the transfer of VRMs. The VRM was 'an item of property only in a very qualified sense'.

6. More recently, the Court of Appeal has said (in *obiter dicta*) that rights to sue for personal injury resulting from negligence—which previously were purely personal (non-assignable) rights—may now be assignable in an appropriate case: *Simpson v Norfolk & Norwich University Hospital NHS Trust* [2011] EWCA Civ 1149, [2012] QB 640. As a result, have rights to sue for personal injury in negligence become choses in action?

(b) Assignment defined

The following dictum of Windeyer J in *Norman v Federal Comr of Taxation* (1963) 109 CLR 9, High Court of Australia, is often cited to explain the meaning of 'assignment':

> Assignment means the immediate transfer of an existing proprietary right, vested or contingent, from the assignor to the assignee. Anything that in the eye of the law can be regarded as an existing subject of ownership, whether it be a chose in possession or a chose in action, can to-day be assigned, unless it be excepted from the general rule on some ground of public policy or by statute.

For example, A purchases goods from B on deferred payment credit. B needs finance. B assign's A's debt to C in return for immediate payment from C. When payment from A falls due, A pays C instead of B. The effect of the assignment is to transfer B's payment entitlement to C. A is the debtor, B the assignor, and C the assignee.

Although Windeyer J dissented on the facts of *Norman*, his analysis of principle is authoritative. Referring to Windeyer J's analysis, Dixon CJ—who was in the majority—managed to say: 'I do not know that there is anything contained in it with which I am disposed to disagree'.

3 EXISTING AND ASSIGNABLE CHOSES IN ACTION

Since an assignment is an immediate transfer of an existing chose in action or proprietary right, the plainest grounds on which to challenge an alleged assignment is that there was no existing chose in action when the purported assignment was made, or that the existing chose in action was unassignable at the time (and possibly never assignable).

Whether at law or in equity, only existing proprietary rights (including existing choses in action) can be assigned. Future choses in action (including a mere expectancy or *spes successionis*) cannot be assigned. The purported assignment for value of a future chose in action may in fact reveal an intention, not to assign immediately, but to agree to assign future choses in action if and when they come into existence and vest in the would-be assignor. Although agreements to assign future property are not an assignment, they, too, are commercially important.

(a) Present and future choses in action

A right to recover damages can arise when a right to sue for breach of contract, or the commission of a tort, is upheld by a court, which enters judgment for the claimant. Until the judgment is entered, the claimant has an existing right of action. But that right to recover damages will be a future chose in action unless and until a court enters judgment for the claimant. This distinction is important where the cause of action is not assignable. In *Glegg v Bromley* [1912] 3 KB 474, CA, a wife agreed to assign to her husband the proceeds of her action against the defendant for slander. A bare cause of action in the form of a right to sue for slander is prohibited by the law. However, the proceeds of an action in slander may be assigned, at least when the assignee has no right to influence the course of the proceedings. At the time of the agreement, the proceeds of Mrs Glegg's action represented *future* property, since judgment had not yet been given. There was no assignment of the cause of action itself.

A chose in action in the form of a debt can be an existing chose in action even though it is not presently payable.

G & T Earle Ltd v Hemsworth RDC
(1928) 44 TLR 758, Court of Appeal

A firm of contractors agreed to build certain cottages for Hemsworth RDC. By the terms of the building contract, as subsequently varied, each month the contractors were to be paid 90 per cent of the value of all work completed by them as certified by the architects. The remaining 10 per cent of the value of the work completed was to be held in a retention fund which was to be paid to the contractors on the issue of the architects' final certificate. During the course of the building work the contractors purported to assign to the plaintiffs 'all moneys now or hereafter to become due to us from the Hemsworth Rural District Council for retention money'. At the time of the assignment all the retention fund had accrued but the architects had not issued their final certificate. The issue before the Court of Appeal was whether the money standing to the credit of the retention fund was an existing chose in action or a mere expectancy at the time of the purported assignment. Affirming the decision of Wright J, the Court of Appeal held that it was an existing chose. In the only reasoned judgment delivered in the Court of Appeal, Scrutton LJ stated that 'where the thing assigned arises out of an existing contract, although it may not become payable until a later date than the assignment, it is a debt or other legal thing in action which can be assigned and sued for without joining the assignor as a party'. As the retention money had already been earned when the assignment took place it represented an existing chose in action, even though the time of actual payment had yet to accrue.

The distinction between present and future choses in action has been likened to the difference between a tree and its fruit.

Shepherd v Federal Taxation Comr
(1965) 113 CLR 385, High Court of Australia

The taxpayer was the grantee of certain letters patent relating to castors. He granted to C a licence to manufacture the castors and, in return, C agreed to pay him royalties directly in proportion to the number of castors manufactured. By deed the taxpayer then purported to assign by way of gift absolutely and unconditionally to certain named persons all his 'right title and interest in and to an amount equal to ninety per cent of the income which' might accrue during a period of three years under the licence agreement. The High Court of Australia (Barwick CJ and Kitto J; Owen J dissenting) held that on its true construction the deed constituted a present assignment of an existing chose in action. The majority accepted that the taxpayer had assigned his existing contractual right to future royalties, even though the quantum of the royalties had yet to be ascertained. As Kitto J said (at 396): 'The tree, though not the fruit, existed at the date of the assignment as a proprietary right of the appellant of which he was competent to dispose; and he assigned ninety per centum of the tree.' There was certainty at the time of the assignment that the contractual relationship between the patentee and the licence was not terminable at the whim of the obligor during the period for which the assignment was to operate.

The distinction between existing and future choses in action was difficult to draw in the following case.

Norman v Federal Comr of Taxation
(1963) 109 CLR 9, High Court of Australia

By a deed dated 21 December 1956, the taxpayer attempted an assignment by way of gift. He wished to give his wife all the interest to be derived from the sum of £3,000 which was part of a sum deposited by him on loan at interest with a named firm. The loan was not for a fixed term; the firm was free to repay part or all of it at any time without notice. By the same deed the taxpayer purported to assign dividends to which he might be entitled arising from estates in which he had a beneficial interest. In 1957 the trustees of these estates transferred to the taxpayer his proportion of certain shares and he was registered as the shareholder. During the year ending 30 June 1958, £450 was paid by way of interest on the loan of £3,000 and dividends amounting to £460 were paid on the shares. The Commissioner claimed that these sums remained the income of the taxpayer and assessable to tax in his hands. The taxpayer argued that because of the deed of assignment the interest and dividend payments were part of his wife's income and not his own. By a majority (McTiernan and Windeyer JJ dissenting) the High Court of Australia held that the assignment of the interest and the dividend payments was ineffective.

Menzies J: . . . It is common ground that the assignment did not operate as a legal assignment of interest or the taxpayer's right to it, and the real question is whether there was an effectual equitable assignment of a right to interest. I do not think there was because what was assigned was not an existing right but was no more than a right which might thereafter come into existence and so could not be effectually assigned in equity without consideration.

In general future property was not assignable at common law: *Lunn v Thornton* ((1845) 1 CB 379) but in equity after-acquired property was assignable for value according to the principles stated by Lord Macnaghten in *Tailby v Official Receiver* ((1888) 13 App Cas 523) but only for value notwithstanding the assignment was by deed: *Re Ellenborough* ([1903] 1 Ch 697). If then interest that may arise under a contract has the character of a future rather than an existing right, the deed, lacking consideration, was not effective to entitle the assignee to the interest in question as and when it became due and payable. I regard interest which may accrue in the future upon an existing loan repayable without notice as having the character of a right to come into existence rather than of a right already in existence and I do not regard *G & T Earle (1925) Ltd v Hemsworth RDS* ((1928) 44 TLR 758), upon which Mr Bright for the taxpayer relied, as any authority to the contrary. In that case no more was decided than that an assignment of a specific fund retained under a building contract which did not become payable until an architect's certificate was given, which happened after the date of the assignment, was a good legal assignment of a chose in action. As Wright J, the learned trial judge, said in a judgment fully approved by the Court of Appeal:—'I find there was a specific fund . . . In my judgment the retention moneys represented moneys actually earned at the date of the certificate, though in fact these retention moneys, as their name indicates, were to be held as a sort of security and in any case subject to having set off against them any cross-claims, which would reduce the amount when the final settlement came and the final certificate was issued. The retention moneys, therefore, were only future in the sense that they were not payable until some future date' ((1928) 44 TLR 605 at 609). An accruing debt arising out of contract, though not payable at the date of the assignment, was, it was held, assignable at law. One other observation upon the applicability of that case to the present may be made, that is, it is not to be assumed that every right that can now be assigned at law without consideration pursuant to s 25(6) of the Judicature Act and corresponding legislation can also be assigned in equity voluntarily. Thus if, as seems to be generally accepted, . . . the section extends to future debts and not merely debts not presently payable, in equity as distinct from the Judicature Act, the effectiveness of voluntary assignment remains limited to existing rights and interests. See *Tailby v Official Receiver* ((1888) 13 App Cas 523) and *Re McArdle* ([1951] Ch 669 at 676), per Jenkins LJ.

[For the same reason as that given by Windeyer J (below) and because of a specific provision of Australian tax legislation, Menzies J held that the dividend payments remained assessable to tax in the hands of the taxpayer.]

Windeyer J (dissenting): . . . In *Lampet's Case* ((1612) 10 Co Rep 46b at 48a), Coke spoke of 'the great wisdom and policy of the sages and founders of our law, who have provided that no possibility, right, title, nor thing in action, shall be granted or assigned to strangers, for that would be the occasion of multiplying of contentions and suits'. It was a somewhat unsophisticated view of legal rights that led the common lawyers to classify choses in action and debts with mere possibilities, and to condemn all assignments of them as leading to maintenance.

Assignment means the immediate transfer of an existing proprietary right, vested or contingent, from the assignor to the assignee. Anything that in the eye of the law can be regarded as an existing subject of ownership, whether it be a chose in possession or a chose in action, can to-day be assigned, unless it be excepted from the general rule on some ground of public policy or by statute. But a mere expectancy or possibility of becoming entitled in the future to a proprietary right is not an existing chose in action. It is not assignable, except in the inexact sense into which, again to use Maitland's words, lawyers slipped when it is said to be assignable in equity for value.

The distinction between a chose in action, which is an existing legal right, and a mere expectancy or possibility of a future right is of cardinal importance in this case, as will appear. It does not, in my view, depend on whether or not there is a debt presently recoverable by action because presently due and payable. A legal right to be paid money at a future date is, I consider, a present chose in action, at all events when it depends upon an existing contract on the repudiation of which an action could be brought for anticipatory breach.

The common law doctrine that debts and other choses in action were not assignable never applied to Crown debts; and, by the influence of the law merchant, bills of exchange and promissory notes were outside it. And it was never accepted in equity. 'Courts of equity from the earliest times thought the doctrine too absurd for them to adopt' said Buller J in 1791 in the course of a vigorous condemnation of it: *Master v Miller* ((1791) 4 Term Rep 320 at 340). Furthermore he said that already at common law it had been 'so explained away that it remains only an objection to the form of the action in any case'. Blackstone had said 'this nicety is now disregarded': *Commentaries*, ii, 442. In *Balfour v Sea Fire Life Assurance Co* ((1857) 3 CBNS 300 at 308), Willes J said that the doctrine had long been exploded 'as everyone must know'. What had happened was that the common law rule came to be circumvented in various ways. One was by novation. Another was by the assignor giving a power of attorney to the assignee to sue the debtor at law in the assignor's name, without having to render an account: the history of this has been narrated at length by Mr Bailey in learned articles in the *Law Quarterly Review* vols 47 and 48. And courts of equity would come to the assistance of the assignee if the assignor refused to do whatever was necessary to enable the assignee to get the benefit of the assignment. Thus a recalcitrant assignor would be required, on having an indemnity for his costs, to permit his name to be used in an action to recover the debt; or an assignor would be restrained from receiving the debt for himself, as for example in *L'Estrange v L'Estrange* ((1850) 13 Beav 281). Because the assistance of equity was available, it was generally not needed. The common law courts recognized that an assignee might sue in the assignor's name. So that in 1849 it could be said that 'the courts of law have adopted the doctrines of the court of chancery in regard to assignments of choses in action'; so much so that 'In ordinary cases, where the plaintiff has an easy remedy by suing in the name of the assignor, the court (scil. the Court of Chancery) will not entertain jurisdiction, but leave the party to his remedy at law': *Spence, Equitable Jurisdiction of the Court of Chancery*, vol 2, pp 853, 854; and see *Roxburghe v Cox* ((1881) 17 Ch D 520), Dicey, *Parties to an Action* (1870) pp 66–72. Therefore, as the Chief Justice observed during the hearing of this case, it is somewhat misleading to say, as is often said, that before the Judicature Act the common law would not allow assignments of legal choses in action. Long before 1873 the development of common law processes and the impact of equity had pushed the common law prohibition of the assignment of choses in action back into history. Nevertheless the original doctrine survived, to this extent that, until the Judicature Act 1873, s 25(6), and the corresponding statutory provisions in Australia and elsewhere came into operation, an assignee of a legal debt could not in his own name bring an action against the debtor to recover the debt. The original creditor must be the plaintiff on the record. He remained in law the owner of the chose in action. What the provision of the Judicature Act 1873, did was to render unnecessary the previous circumlocutions. Debts and other legal choses in action were made directly assignable by the statutory method. But this, while it simplified assignments, has not simplified the law surrounding them, as the argument in this case showed . . .

[I]t was said a thing which is not yet in existence cannot be the subject of an equitable assignment except for consideration. That, as I have said, is undoubtedly so. It is true too that the interest, to the extent of £450, that the deed assigned was not due and payable at the date of the deed. But a contract to pay a sum of money on a future day, call it interest or what you will, calculable in amount according to conditions presently agreed, is in my view a presently existing chose in action. As between the parties to a contract of money lent at interest the borrower is simply a debtor who must pay a sum or sums (called interest) that he has, for good consideration (the forbearance of the creditor) contracted to pay to his creditor at the time or times stipulated. Why should not the creditor before the date when this debt becomes due and payable, assign his right to receive payment on the due date? He could assign the whole under the statute: *Walker v Bradford Old Bank Ltd* ((1884) 12 QBD 511). Why not part in equity? What he assigns is not, it seems to me, a right to arise in the future but a present contractual right to be paid at a future date a sum of money, to be calculated in the agreed manner: cf *Lett v Morris* ((1831) 4 Sim 607). In *Brice v Bannister* ((1878) 3 QBD 569 at 573), Lord Coleridge CJ said 'that a debt to become due is a chose in action, is clear'. Interest on money lent is recoverable by action at law as a debt separate from the principal, as the common *indebitatus* count for interest shows: . . .

But it was urged this case is not like a case of a loan for a fixed term. What was owing might, it is pointed out, have been repaid by the partnership, or reduced below £3,000, after the date of the deed of assignment and before 1st July 1957. As a matter of law, no doubt that is so. But it does not, I think, follow that the taxpayer had for that reason no assignable right. He had a present right to be paid interest at a future date on the money he had lent, unless in the meantime the loan was repaid. The taxpayer assigned the benefit of this contract, to the extent of £450 to become due conditionally in 1958, to his wife by the deed of 1956. I consider that the deed was an effectual equitable assignment . . .

I turn now to the second matter, the sum of £460 . . .

Is a dividend that may become payable in the future upon shares presently held something that can be assigned in equity? Is it a present chose in action or a mere possibility? Is it property in existence, or something not in existence and therefore not capable of being assigned in the absence of consideration? I think it is the latter. The court will not compel directors to declare a dividend: *Bond v Barrow Haematite Steel Co* [1902] 1 Ch 353. A dividend is not a debt until it is declared. Until then it is in the eye of the law a possibility only. When it is declared it becomes a debt for which a shareholder who is on the register at the date of the declaration may sue. The companies paid the dividends to the registered holder of the shares, the taxpayer. They knew nothing of the purported assignment. Depending perhaps in some cases on their articles of association, they might have paid the dividends directly to the taxpayer's wife had they been directed by him to do so. But, in the absence of consideration, such a direction would have been merely a revocable mandate, not an assignment. Dividends that may be declared are to my mind quite unlike the interest that will become due according to an existing contract of loan if the loan be not repaid.

[**McTiernan J** (dissenting) gave a similar judgment to that of Windeyer J. **Dixon CJ** delivered a judgment similar to that of Menzies J. **Owen J** concurred with Menzies J.]

The principle as to contracts terminable at will has been recognised in English law.

Re Adams

[2004] EWHC 2379 (Admin), Administrative Court

The question was whether certain rights of Mr Adams were 'realisable property' for the purposes of the provisions for confiscation orders against criminals under the Criminal Justice Act 1988. (See now the Proceeds of Crime Act 2002.) 'Realisable property' was defined to mean 'any property held by the defendant' and 'property' was defined to include money and all other property, whether real or personal, heritable or movable, including choses in action and other intangible or incorporeal property. The contract was for consultancy services to be performed by Mr Adams to a company referred to as Burgon. In return, Burgon was to pay an annual fee of £52,000. The consultancy contract was summarily terminable by either party.

Lightman J:

7. The Consultancy Contract is a chose in action but, since it is a contract for the provision of services where the identity of the provider is of the essence, the chose is personal to the parties to it and not assignable. It is accordingly not realisable property. It is also not realisable because it is summarily determinable by Burgon at any time.

8. In my judgment the entitlement under the Consultancy Contract to payment for services to be provided in the future under the Consultancy Contract is not a present chose in action. It arises if the Consultancy Contract is not determined and if the services required of Mr Adams are provided: such conditional and future entitlement plainly is not property, let alone realisable property, of Mr Adams. The position is very different from the situation when the defendant is owed a debt or has a contractual right to receive a payment on a future date or is entitled to a

contingent beneficial interest under a will (compare *Re Walbrook and Glasgow* (1994) 15 Cr App R (S) 783). The law cannot be said to be entirely clear, but on principle and in accordance with the balance of authority there is no existing chose in action where there is a contract, but it is uncertain whether anything will become due under it in the future: see Chitty on Contracts 29th ed, vol 1 para 19-029 and *Norman v. Federal Commissioner of Taxation* (1963) 109 CLR 9. The position is a fortiori in a case such as the present where the contract is summarily terminable, its duration is totally uncertain and any liability of Burgon subsists only at its will. In any event the 'chose' (if it is a 'chose') is scarcely realisable and can have no substantial realisable value.

NOTES

1.   In his book *Legal Aspects of Receivables Financing* (1991), Dr Oditah summarises the distinction made by English law between existing and future receivables as follows (pp 28–29):

English law draws an arbitrary distinction between existing and future receivables on the one hand, and future receivables and other contingent liabilities, on the other. All contractual rights are vested from the moment when the contract is made, even though they may not be presently enforceable, whether because the promisee must first perform his own part of the bargain, or because some condition independent of the will of either party (such as the elapsing of time) has to be satisfied. The result is that English law treats as existing debts not only those which have been *earned* by the promisee, whether or not presently payable, but also those which are *unearned*. The basis for the inclusion of unearned rights to payment in the category of *existing* receivables even where the contract is wholly executory is that they *grow out of a present obligation*. So it is that for a long time the courts have treated as existing or present receivables a legal right to be paid only at a future date if it depends upon an existing contract on the repudiation of which an action could be brought for an anticipatory breach. The contract is the *tree*, the future debts which *may* arise, the fruits. The unearned debts are *potential* and hence existing. But in so lumping earned (even though not presently payable) debts and unearned, albeit potential, debts, as existing debts, the common law has, in a somewhat extravagant fashion, destroyed the vital distinction between *rights in esse* and *rights in potentia*. Thus, a right to interest under a fixed-term loan, future rent from existing leases, sums payable under an existing construction contract, royalties payable under an existing copyright, freight payable under a signed bill of lading, and sums payable for goods or services not yet delivered or rendered, are all present receivables. Uncertainty as to the amount payable is immaterial. Similarly the fact that under some of these contracts nothing may be earned because the right is conditional on counter-performance is not considered important.

2.   In *Marathon Electrical Manufacturing Corpn v Mashreqbank PSC* [1997] CLC 1,090 at 1,095 (ChD), Mance J (as he then was) said Dr Oditah's description of the rationale of the authorities may have force 'but the principle which [the authorities] establish appears to me to embrace any contract under which payments may be received, provided at least that it is not terminable at will'. Is any qualification of Dr Oditah's analysis necessary in the light of the analysis of contracts terminable at will in *Norman*, *Shepherd*, and *Re Adams*?

3.   In *Shepherd's* case, the majority distinguished *Norman v Federal Comr of Taxation* as a case where the putative assignor had no existing right to future interest payments because interest would only be payable if the loan remained in existence and the taxpayer had no right to keep it in existence in the future as the debtor firm had the right to repay the loan whenever it wished. There was no such uncertainty in *Shepherd* itself.

(b) Existing non-assignable choses in action

A right—or, if used in a wide sense, a chose in action—may exist and yet not be assignable. Here, in particular, familiarity with some points of legal history is of especial use. Lawyers today recognise three groups of unassignable rights or choses in action. (See A Tettenborn, 'Problems in Assignment Law: Not Out of the Wood?' in A Burrows and E Peel (eds), *Contract Formation and Parties* (2010), Ch 9.)

First, those the assignment of which would be contrary to (high) public policy. Public policy prohibits the assignment of the salary of a public officer, paid from central (not local) funds. For example, in *Arbuthnot v Norton* (1846) 5 Moo PCC 219 it was held that a judge could not assign his salary. The nature of the public policy involved is explored by DW Logan (1945) 61 LQR 240. Statute may prohibit assignment. When it does, it may be taken to do so for reasons of high public policy: for example, social security benefit is not assignable (Social Security Administration Act 1992, s 187); a right to a pension under an occupational pension scheme cannot be assigned other than in favour of a widow, widower, or dependant (Pensions Act 1995, s 91). Most importantly, the doctrines of maintenance and champerty are a source of 'a principle of public policy designed to protect the purity of justice and the interests of vulnerable litigants' (*Giles v Thompson* [1994] 1 AC 142 at 164). Maintenance is the supporting of litigation in which the supporter has no legitimate concern without just cause or excuse. Champerty is simply maintenance coupled with an agreement that the maintainer is to share in the recoveries of the litigation. Maintenance and champerty have been said to render choses in action unassignable. Certainly the unassignability of entire species of rights or choses in action has been attributed to these doctrines. But an attempted assignment of any type of chose in action—even a claim to a simple debt—will be contrary to public policy and ineffective where it can be proved independently and distinctly that the object or purpose of the assignment was champertous. While the effect of finding that an attempted assignment was tainted with maintenance or champerty will be to prevent that particular assignment, it may be more strictly correct to view maintenance and champerty as attacking particular attempted transactions rather than rendering whole species of choses in action unassignable.

Secondly, so-called bare rights to litigate. Rights to sue for damages in tort or for breach of contract relate to harm to a particular person. Contractual obligations arise from an undertaking between particular persons. Obligations to pay damages for breach of contract arise upon failure to perform those personal undertakings, and to pay damages compensating for the loss peculiar to the disappointed party. In tort, rights of action are personal in relating to the claimant's body, belongings, economic welfare, and so on. Obligations to pay damages in tort are, again, peculiar to the victim of the tort. Legally, all such rights to sue for damages are prima facie unassignable as 'bare' rights to litigate: they are bare because they are not clothed with some proprietary or other—normally commercial—interest so as to lend them an assignable character.

Thirdly, those arising from an instrument evincing an intention that rights arising therefrom shall not be assignable. This intention may be found from the terms themselves. For instance, a bilateral contract may provide that the rights thereunder of one or both parties shall not be assignable—at all, or without the prior consent of the other party. Such provisions will not deprive an agreement between the 'assignor' and a putative assignee of all effect. However, where the original contract is aptly drafted, an attempt to assign a right arising therefrom will be ineffective (*Linden Gardens Trust Ltd v Lenesta Sludge Disposals Ltd and St Martin's Property Corpn Ltd v Sir Robert McAlpine & Sons Ltd* [1994] 1 AC 85, HL: see below) but ineffective as against the debtor (*Helstan Securities Ltd v Hertfordshire County Council*

[1978] 3 All ER 262). In the absence of such drafting, an intention that contractual rights shall be unassignable may be found from all the circumstances of the transaction, as where a contract which involves personal skill or confidence. Contractual rights of performance by employees (*Nokes v Doncaster Amalgamated Collieries Ltd* [1940] AC 1014, although special employment legislation now allows for novation of employment contracts on the transfer of a business by sale, other disposition or by operation of law, eg on insolvency) and authors and publishers (*Devefi Pty Ltd v Mateffy Pearl Nagy Pty Ltd* [1993] RPC 493) have been held unassignable on that basis.

In the early days of the common law, however, *all* rights were unassignable as a matter of public policy. Few exceptions ever developed at common law. The common law judges did come to admit: (1) assignments by and to the Crown; (2) assignment of annuities; (3) assignment of certain negotiable instruments under the law merchant (now mostly regulated by statute); and (4) of course, assignment of particular choses in action in accordance with the provisions of special statutory enactments (eg assignment of shares in a company under the Companies Act 2006, s 544 and Part 21; assignment of policies of life insurance under the Policies of Assurance Act 1867, s 1; assignment of copyright under the Copyright, Designs and Patents Act 1988, s 90). Since the seventeenth century the courts of equity have always permitted and given effect to assignments of choses in action. Such an assignment is called an 'equitable assignment' and it will pass an equitable, though not a legal, right to the chose in action.

The structure of the modern law is most readily seen by bearing this historical development in mind. Three features may be emphasised. First, the doctrines of maintenance and champerty have been beaten into retreat by legislation and the liberality of the judges. Secondly, the loci of these developments were the courts of equity. Equitable doctrine developed to permit assignment in many cases. The common law's objections to assignment weakened, but the common law judges never as such abandoned the general rule that choses in action cannot be assigned at common law. Thirdly, because that rule of the judge-made common law has not been displaced by developments in the judge-made law itself, it remains part of the structure of the modern law. Assignments in the modern law depend on equitable principles and—as will be seen—on strengthening of equitable assignments into 'legal' assignments by means of legislation: Law of Property Act 1925, s 136 (re-enacting s 25(6) of the Supreme Court of Judicature Act 1873). As Lord Lindley explained in *Tolhurst v Associated Portland Cement Manufacturers (1900) Ltd* [1903] AC 414 at 424, that legislation provides a procedure for making and enforcing assignments that would have been permitted in equity before the Act was made. It does not authorise assignments—such as champertous assignments—which were unenforceable in equity before the legislation was made (see also *Manchester Brewery Co v Coombs* [1901] 2 Ch 608 at 619).

(i) Maintenance and champerty

Maintenance and champerty were crimes and torts from the medieval period onwards. The policy of the law required transactions savouring of either to be treated similarly severely. Hence the role of maintenance and champerty in the law of assignment. As Hobhouse LJ said in *Camdex International Ltd v Bank of Zambia* [1998] QB 22 at 29: 'what is objectionable is the trafficking in litigation'.

Though the crimes and torts of maintenance and champerty were abolished by s 14 of the Criminal Law Act 1967, in the law of transactions maintenance and champerty remain contrary to public policy. But the extent of the policy of the law has not remained fixed.

Hobhouse LJ spoke with understatement when he added (at 29) that, 'the modern approach is not to extend the types of involvement in litigation which are considered objectionable'. In truth, the area in which these doctrines operate has shrunk. In *Giles v Thompson* (at 153), Lord Mustill stated that, in practice, maintenance and champerty are now to be found in only two areas: (1) as the source of the rule which forbids a solicitor from accepting payment for professional services on behalf of a claimant calculated as a proportion of the sum recovered by the defendant (although Parliament has since accepted the concept of conditional fees for all civil proceedings except family proceedings: see ss 58 and 58A of the Courts and Legal Services Act 1990); and (2) as the ground for denying recognition to the assignment of a 'bare cause of action'. It is (2) which concerns us here, an area which Lord Mustill described (at 153) 'as having achieved an independent life of its own'. An assignment of a bare cause of action in contract or tort is not permitted, unless the assignee has an appropriate interest in the litigation (although see YL Tan (1990) 106 LQR 656 at 664–668 as to whether tort claims may be assigned at all). The next case is the leading one in this area.

Trendtex Trading Corpn v Crédit Suisse
[1982] AC 679, House of Lords

The plaintiffs, Trendtex (T), sold cement to an English company (CIF Lagos) with payment to be made under a letter of credit issued by the Central Bank of Nigeria (CBN). CBN failed to honour the letter of credit and T sued CBN for breach of contract. The defendants, Crédit Suisse (CS), who had provided T with financial assistance in connection with the cement contract, guaranteed T's legal costs of the proceedings against CBN. CS saw the proceedings as providing its only prospect of recovering the money owed to it by T. In return, T assigned its right of action against CBN to CS by way of security. T was successful before the Court of Appeal but CBN obtained leave to appeal to the House of Lords. T now owed US$1.5 million to CS. At this juncture, T entered into an agreement with CS whereby T assigned any residual interest in its claim against CBN to CS outright to CS. T further agreed that CS could reassign the right of action to a purchaser of its choice: the agreement recited that CS had received an offer from a third party to buy the right of action for US$800,000. Five days later CS reassigned the right of action to a third party for US$1.1 million and five weeks after that the third party settled with CBN for US$8 million. T was suspicious of these arrangements and claimed that the agreement and assignment were void as they savoured of maintenance and champerty. The Court of Appeal (Lord Denning MR, Bridge and Oliver LJJ) upheld the assignment. T appealed.

Lord Wilberforce: . . . If no party had been involved in the agreement of January 4, 1978, but Trendtex and Crédit Suisse, I think that it would have been difficult to contend that the agreement, even if it involved (as I think it did) an assignment of Trendtex's residual interest in the CBN case, offended against the law of maintenance or champerty. As I have already shown, Crédit Suisse had a genuine and substantial interest in the success of the CBN litigation. It had, and I do not think that the legitimacy of its action was challenged, guaranteed the previous costs. It had by the documents of September 6 and November 26, 1976, taken a security interest in the litigation or its proceeds. To carry this a stage further by a surrender of Trendtex's residual interest (if this was the effect of the agreement of January 4, 1978) would, in my view, have been lawful, though a question might have arisen (and indeed may arise) whether, after Crédit Suisse had been satisfied as creditors, Trendtex could claim the return to it of any surplus. The possibility of this could not invalidate the agreement; it would arise under it, and clearly fall within the exclusive jurisdiction clause.

The vice, if any, of the agreement lies in the introduction of the third party. It appears from the face of the agreement not as an obligation, but as a contemplated possibility, that the cause of action against CBN might be sold by Crédit Suisse to a third party, for a sum of US $800,000. This manifestly involved the possibility, and indeed the likelihood, of a profit being made, either by the third party or possibly also by Crédit Suisse, out of the cause of action. In my opinion this manifestly 'savours of champerty,' since it involves trafficking in litigation—a type of transaction which, under English law, is contrary to public policy.

Lord Roskill: . . . My Lords, before considering these submissions in any detail it is necessary to recall that the Criminal Law Act 1967 by s 13(1) abolished the crimes of maintenance and champerty and by s 14(1) provided that neither should any longer be actionable as a tort. But s 14(2) further provided that these provisions should not affect any rule of law as to the cases in which a contract was to be treated as contrary to public policy or otherwise illegal. It therefore seems plain that Parliament intended to leave the law as to the effect of maintenance and champerty upon contracts unaffected by the abolition of them as crimes and torts.

My Lords, it is clear, when one looks at the cases upon maintenance in this century and indeed towards the end of the last, that the courts have adopted an infinitely more liberal attitude towards the supporting of litigation by a third party than had previously been the case. One has only to read the classic judgment of Danckwerts J affirmed by the Court of Appeal, in *Martell v Consett Iron Co Ltd* [1955] Ch 363 to see how this branch of the law has developed and how the modern view of sufficiency of interest has come about. My Lords, learned counsel cited to your Lordships many of the cases on maintenance which are there discussed. For my part I think no further review of them is necessary today. I would only emphasise the importance when reading them of distinguishing between the use of the word maintenance to denote *lawful* maintenance and the use of that word to denote what was then both a crime and a tort.

My Lords, one of the reasons why equity would not permit the assignment of what became known as a bare cause of action, whether legal or equitable, was because it savoured of maintenance. If one reads the well known judgment of Parker J in *Glegg v Bromley* [1912] 3 KB 474, 490, one can see how the relevant law has developed. Though in general choses in action were assignable, yet causes of action which were essentially personal in their character, such as claims for defamation or personal injury, were incapable of assignment for the reason already given. But even so, no objection was raised to assignments of the proceeds of an action for defamation as in *Glegg v Bromley*, for such an assignment would in no way give the assignee the right to intervene in the action and so be contrary to public policy: see Fletcher Moulton LJ, at pp 488–489.

My Lords, just as the law became more liberal in its approach to what was *lawful* maintenance, so it became more liberal in its approach to the circumstances in which it would recognise the validity of an assignment of a cause of action and not strike down such an assignment as one only of a bare cause of action. Where the assignee has by the assignment acquired a property right and the cause of action was incidental to that right, the assignment was held effective. *Ellis v Torrington* [1920] 1 KB 399 is an example of such a case. Scrutton LJ stated, at pp 412–413, that the assignee was not guilty of maintenance or champerty by reason of the assignment he took because he was buying not in order to obtain a cause of action but in order to protect the property which he had bought. But, my Lords, as I read the cases it was not necessary for the assignee always to show a property right to support his assignment. He could take an assignment to support and enlarge that which he had already acquired as, for example, an underwriter by subrogation: see *Compania Colombiana de Seguros v Pacific Steam Navigation Co* [1965] 1 QB 101. My Lords, I am afraid that, with respect, I cannot agree with the learned Master of the

Rolls [1980] QB 629, 657 when he said in the instant case that 'The old saying that you cannot assign a "bare right to litigate" is gone.' I venture to think that that still remains a fundamental principle of our law. But it is today true to say that in English law an assignee who can show that he has a genuine commercial interest in the enforcement of the claim of another and to that extent takes an assignment of that claim to himself is entitled to enforce that assignment unless by the terms of that assignment he falls foul of our law of champerty, which, as has often been said, is a branch of our law of maintenance. For my part I can see no reason in English law why Crédit Suisse should not have taken an assignment to themselves of Trendtex's claim against CBN for the purpose of recouping themselves for their own substantial losses arising out of CBN's repudiation of the letter of credit upon which Crédit Suisse were relying to refinance their financing of the purchases by Trendtex of this cement from their German suppliers.

My Lords, I do not therefore think that Mr Brodie [counsel for Trendtex] is correct in criticising the judgment of Oliver LJ ([1980] QB 629) on the ground that the learned Lord Justice failed to distinguish between the interest necessary to support an assignment of a cause of action and the interest which would justify the maintenance of an action by a third party. I think, with respect, that this submission involves over-analysis of the position. The court should look at the totality of the transaction. If the assignment is of a property right or interest and the cause of action is ancillary to that right or interest, or if the assignee had a genuine commercial interest in taking the assignment and in enforcing it for his own benefit, I see no reason why the assignment should be struck down as an assignment of a bare cause of action or as savouring of maintenance.

But, my Lords, to reach that conclusion and thus to reject a substantial part of Mr Brodie's argument for substantially the same reasons as did Oliver LJ does not mean that at least article 1 of the agreement of January 4, 1978, is not objectionable as being champertous, for it is not an assignment designed to enable Crédit Suisse to recoup their own losses by enforcing Trendtex's claim against CBN to the maximum amount recoverable. Though your Lordships do not have the agreement between Crédit Suisse and the anonymous third party, it seems to me obvious, as already stated, that the purpose of article 1 of the agreement of January 4, 1978, was to enable the claim against CBN to be sold on to the anonymous third party for that anonymous third party to obtain what profit he could from it, apart from paying to Crédit Suisse the purchase price of US $1,100,000. In other words, the 'spoils,' whatever they might be, to be got from CBN were in effect being divided, the first US $1,100,000 going to Crédit Suisse and the balance, whatever it might ultimately prove to be, to the anonymous third party. Such an agreement, in my opinion, offends for it was a step towards the sale of a bare cause of action to a third party who had no genuine commercial interest in the claim in return for a division of the spoils, Crédit Suisse taking the fixed amount which I have already mentioned. To this extent I find myself in respectful disagreement with Oliver LJ.

[**Lord Fraser of Tullybelton** delivered a concurring judgment. **Lords Edmund-Davies** and **Keith of Kinkel** concurred in the judgments of Lords Wilberforce and Roskill.]

[Their Lordships went on to order the action be stayed. They held that, as the agreement was governed by Swiss law, it was for the Swiss courts to decide what effect the invalidity of the assignment under English law had on the agreement as a whole.]

NOTES

1. In *Trendtex*, Lord Roskill held that the assignment from T to CS did not savour of maintenance. But because CS had a genuine commercial interest in the enforcement of T's claim, he held the assignment to be champertous: it facilitated the sale of a bare cause of action to a third party who had no genuine commercial interest in the claim in return for a division of

the 'spoils' between CS and the third party. This leaves open a question. May an assignee of a right to sue, who *has* a genuine commercial interest in the claim, nevertheless profit from the assignment? In *Brownton Ltd v Edward Moore Inbucon Ltd* [1985] 3 All ER 499, the Court of Appeal (Sir John Donaldson MR, Lloyd LJ, and Sir John Megaw) held that if the assignee has a genuine commercial interest it was not fatal to the validity of the assignment that he may be better off as a result of it, or that he might make a profit out of it (see also *Massai Aviation Services Ltd v Attorney-General for the Bahamas* [2007] UKPC 12 at [17]). However, Sir John Megaw (at 506) did consider that an excessive level of profit might indicate that the commercial interest was not genuine (see also *Advanced Technology Structures Ltd v Cray Valley Products Ltd* [1993] BCLC 723, CA). Lloyd LJ (at 509) left open the question whether any profit would be returnable by the assignee to the assignor. If the assignment is out and out, not by way of security, it is difficult to see why the assignee should return any profit to the assignor. For further comment on *Trendtex*, see J Thornely [1982] CLJ 29. On champerty generally, see YL Tan (1990) 106 LQR 656; A Walters (1996) 112 LQR 560; G McMeel [2004] LMCLQ 483 at 494–498.

2.   When does an assignee have a 'genuine commercial interest'? A genuine commercial interest may, of course, arise from commercial transactions. In *Brownton Ltd v Edward Moore Inbucon Ltd*, above, the plaintiff sued the first defendant alleging that it had negligently advised the plaintiff to purchase an unsuitable computer. The second defendant supplied the computer and the plaintiff sued it for breach of contract. The first defendant settled with the plaintiff and took an assignment of the plaintiff's right of action against the second defendant. The Court of Appeal held that the first defendant had a genuine commercial interest in taking the assignment as: (a) the contracts between the plaintiff and the first and second defendants arose out of same transaction; and (b) the first and second defendants had been sued in respect of the same damage to the plaintiff so that any sum recovered from the second defendant would have gone to reduce the sum recoverable from the first defendant. But in *Bourne v Colodense Ltd* [1985] ICR 291 a 'commercial interest' was found where the relevant rights did not arise in trade or commerce. The Court of Appeal held the defendant to have a 'commercial interest' in enforcing the plaintiff's rights against his (the plaintiff's) union (see YL Tan (1990) 106 LQR 656 at 664). The plaintiff unsuccessfully sued the defendant for personal injuries caused by negligence. As the plaintiff's union had agreed to pay the plaintiff's costs, the trial judge ordered the plaintiff to pay the defendant's costs. When the union refused to pay the costs the defendant applied to the court for the appointment of a receiver. The receiver would sue in the plaintiff's name to realise the plaintiff's claim towards the satisfaction of the costs due to the defendant. The Court of Appeal held that the defendant clearly had a commercial interest in the enforcement of such rights as the plaintiff had against his union: unless he could enforce those rights, the defendant would have had a worthless order for costs. (It has subsequently held that a judge has power to order a person who finances an unsuccessful claimant to pay the defendant's costs pursuant to the Senior Courts Act 1981, s 51: *Aiden Shipping Co Ltd v Interbulk Ltd* [1986] AC 965.) In effect, the Court of Appeal regarded the defendant's 'financial interest' as its 'commercial interest' to satisfy the *Trendtex* test. Is this a paradox? Or is a 'genuine commercial interest' merely one kind of interest sufficient to justify an assignment of an otherwise bare right to litigate?

3.   Most of the modern authorities on maintenance and champerty relate to rights that are (or, but for the identification of a relevant interest, would be) bare rights to litigate. However the distinctness of maintenance and champerty is well illustrated by *Camdex International Ltd v Bank of Zambia* [1998] QB 22, in which an attempted assignment of a debt—the

paradigm of the assignable chose in action—was alleged to be champertous. A financial crisis meant that the defendant bank was unable to repay deposits of Kuwaiti dinars (KD) 20 million made by its customer, the Central Bank of Kuwait. Anticipating that the debt would not be recovered without litigation, the Central Bank of Kuwait assigned it absolutely to the plaintiff under s 136 of the Law of Property Act 1925 in return for a payment of KD 4 million. The defendant bank did not dispute its indebtedness to the Central Bank of Kuwait, nor the amount of the debt, but disputed the validity of the assignment on the ground that it was tainted by champerty. The Court of Appeal upheld the assignment of the debt as a valid assignment of a species of property, which carried with it the right to prosecute the cause of action closely related to that property. The payment of KD 4 million was held to represent a proper commercial valuation of the debt as the defendant bank was insolvent and unable to pay its debts. Hobhouse LJ summarised the law relating to the assignment of debts as follows (at 39):

> An assignment of a debt is not invalid even if the necessity for litigation to recover it is contemplated. Provided that there is a bona fide debt, it does not become unassignable merely because the debtor chooses to dispute it. Suing on an assigned debt is not contrary to public policy even if the assignor retains an interest. What is contrary to public policy and ineffective is an agreement which has maintenance or champerty as its object; such a consequence will not be avoided by dressing up a transaction which has that character and intent as an assignment of a debt. But, because the assignment of a debt itself includes no element of maintenance and is sanctioned by statute, any objectionable element alleged to invalidate the assignment has to be proved independently and distinctly in the same way as any other alleged illegality has to be proved in relation to a contract which is on its face valid.

(ii) Bare rights of action

As well as to immunise a transaction from the considerations of high public policy embodied by the doctrines of maintenance and champerty, identifying a sufficient 'interest' under the principles in *Trendtex* will also cause bare rights of action to become assignable. A narrow conceptual problem arises. Strictly, the bare right may cease to be bare when such an interest is identified; the right may owe its assignability to its no longer being bare. But whether bare rights become assignable when coupled with such an interest, or become assignable because they become clothed with some relevant 'interest', may not be crucial. More important are the points that: (1) rights of damages not clothed with such an interest are bare and, therefore, prima facie unassignable; and (2) that unassignability can be overcome by identifying a relevant interest.

Equuscorp Pty Ltd v Haxton
(2012) 246 CLR 498, High Court of Australia

> **French CJ, Crennan and Kiefel JJ**: The primary judge found that Rural's rights to claim for restitutionary relief were assigned by the Deed. His Honour did so on the unexamined premise that the rights were assignable. In the Court of Appeal, Dodds-Streeton JA, after a careful review of the authorities, correctly concluded that they offered no clear guidance on the question. Her Honour held that the better view was that the rights were assignable. In so holding, she recognised that the nature of the restitutionary right, informed by equitable considerations and

subject to defences such as change of position, could pose difficulties for an assignee. These, however, were problems which would affect the availability and nature of the remedy, rather than constituting an absolute barrier to assignment.

Gummow and Bell JJ point out in their joint reasons that it might be said that Rural's claims against the respondents for money had and received only accrued when the respondents pleaded the unenforceability of the loan agreements in their defences. As their Honours observe, however, the provision of value by Equuscorp under the asset sale agreement would have overcome the difficulty that the claims were mere expectancies at the time the Deed was executed. The questions which remain are whether such claims are assignable and whether they were the subject of assignment.

The respondents submitted that a claim for money had and received is not a 'chose in action' but a 'bare right of action' and therefore not assignable. The concept of the chose in action has a tangled historical background, linked closely to questions of assignability which, in turn, reflected logical concerns about the personal nature of contractual and delictual rights and policy concerns about maintenance (Holdsworth, 'The History of the Treatment of *Choses* in Action by the Common Law', (1920) 33 *Harvard Law Review* 997, especially at 1015–1016). OR Marshall, writing in 1950, observed that historically the question whether something was a chose in action was independent of the question whether it was assignable (Marshall, *The Assignment of Choses in Action*, (1950) at 24). Then confusion arose:

> A thing in action is not assignable; that which is not assignable is a thing in action. This is a vicious circle. There is no test for determining a chose in action or assignability apart from their interrelation. (footnote omitted)

Marshall argued that the assignability of choses in action depended upon a positive common law prohibition which has gradually been relaxed. That the relaxation did not extend to tortious actions was, he suggested, a survival of the objection that the subject matter of a grant must be certain.

In *Campbells Cash and Carry Pty Ltd v Fostif Pty Ltd*, Gummow, Hayne and Crennan JJ observed that ((2006) 229 CLR 386 at 428 [74]; [2006] HCA 41):

> The distinction between the assignment of an item of property and the assignment of a bare right to litigate was regarded as fundamental to the application of the law of maintenance and champerty. But drawing that distinction was not always easy. And it was a distinction whose policy roots were not readily discernible, the undesirability of maintenance and champerty being treated as self-evident. (footnotes omitted)

In *Ellis v Torrington* [1920] 1 KB 399, Scrutton LJ referred to the common position of Courts of Law and Equity in opposition to the assignment of 'a bare right of action, a bare power to bring an action' (at 411). Such an assignment was seen 'as offending against the law of maintenance or champerty or both' (at 411). That opposition was qualified however (at 411):

> [E]arly in the development of the law the Courts of equity and perhaps the Courts of common law also took the view that where the right of action was not a bare right, but was incident or subsidiary to a right in property, an assignment of the right of action was permissible, and did not savour of champerty or maintenance.

The attenuated role of maintenance and champerty in relation to assignability was acknowledged by Lord Mustill in *Giles v Thompson* [1994] 1 AC 142 who spoke of them as maintaining a living presence in only two respects, first as the source of the rule against contingency fees and, secondly, as the ground for denying recognition to the assignment of a 'bare right of action'. Of the latter, Lord Mustill said it was, in his opinion, 'best treated as having achieved an independent life of its own' (at 153).

The criteria for assignability of causes of action were widened by the decision of the House of Lords in *Trendtex Trading Corporation v Credit Suisse*. The non-assignability of a bare right to litigate was still treated as a fundamental principle. Nevertheless, Lord Roskill said ([1982] AC 679 at 703):

> But it is today true to say that in English law an assignee who can show that he has a genuine commercial interest in the enforcement of the claim of another and to that extent takes an assignment of that claim to himself is entitled to enforce that assignment unless by the terms of that assignment he falls foul of our law of champerty, which, as has often been said, is a branch of our law of maintenance.

The application of criteria of assignability to restitutionary claims has remained uncertain. However, as is pointed out in Smith, *The Law of Assignment* (2007) at [12.106]:

> [a]s with tortious causes of action, restitutionary claims can arise independently of any prior relationship between the parties. That said, a restitutionary claim can be so intertwined with a contract, that a legitimate interest may be easy to establish. (footnote omitted)

The author points out that the question has received very little consideration either in the case law or in text books.

Australian authority on the assignability of restitutionary rights is sparse. In *Mutual Pools & Staff Pty Ltd v The Commonwealth* (1994) 179 CLR 155, Mason CJ observed, without elaboration, that a claim for restitution of taxes mistakenly paid was not based on a contractual right and was not assignable (at 173). On the other hand, Brennan J referred to a debt owed by the Commonwealth under an agreement or in restitution as 'a common law chose in action vested in the plaintiff and assignable by it' (at 176).

A restitutionary claim for money had and received under an unenforceable loan agreement is inescapably linked to the performance of that agreement. If assigned along with contractual rights, albeit their existence is contestable, it is not assigned as a bare cause of action. Neither policy nor logic stands against its assignability in such a case. The assignment of the purported contractual rights for value indicates a legitimate commercial interest on the part of the assignee in acquiring the restitutionary rights should the contract be found to be unenforceable. Equuscorp fell into the category of a party with a genuine commercial interest in the restitutionary rights. Notwithstanding the difficulties that may attend the claims having regard to particular circumstances and defences which might affect their vindication, the better view is that adopted by the Court of Appeal, namely, that the restitutionary claims were assignable. The question that next arises is whether they were assigned.

[**French CJ, Crennan and Kiefel JJ** held that the drafting of the deed of assignment was inapt to apply to rights to sue for money had and received and that, in any event, statute prevented such restitutionary rights from arising at all. **Gummow and Bell JJ** also thought no such restitutionary rights arose, but that, if they had, the wording of the deed of assignment would have applied to them. **Heydon J** dissented, holding that restitutionary rights arose and that the deed of assignment was apt to assign those rights to the intended assignee.]

NOTES

1. The courts are usually generous in their interpretation of what constitutes a genuine commercial interest. This raises the question of whether the requirement serves any useful purpose. It has been argued by Professor Tettenborn, following the US model, that it would be better if all intangible rights were prima facie freely assignable, with restrictions on assignment only where there were good substantive or policy-based reasons for imposing them, for example where there was a non-assignment clause in the underlying contract (see

below), or in cases of the assignment of personal injury actions, when the personal injury claimant might not be in the best position to bargain unsupervised (see A Tettenborn, 'Assignment of Rights to Compensation' [2007] LMCLQ 392).

2.   The status of a right as a bare right to litigate appears to be diminishing. In *Simpson v Norfolk & Norwich University Hospital NHS Trust* [2011] EWCA Civ 1149, [2012] QB 640, the Court of Appeal said it was unnecessary to decide whether a right to sue in the tort of negligence for personal injury could be assigned. However, the court opined that the principles in *Trendtex* apply such that a right to sue for personal injury in tort is not by definition unassignable. The *Equuscorp* case applies the *Trendtex* principles to a restitutionary claim for money had and received. Do these cases establish a presumption of assignability of bare rights of action?

(iii) Rights intended to be unassignable

Linden Gardens Trust Ltd v Lenesta Sludge Disposals Ltd and St Martin's Property Corpn Ltd v Sir Robert McAlpine & Sons Ltd
[1994] 1 AC 85, House of Lords

These were consolidated appeals heard together by the Court of Appeal (1992) 57 BLR 57 and House of Lords. In the *Linden Gardens* case, Stock Conversion and Investment Trust plc ('Stock Conversion'), the lessee of part of a building, engaged a building contractor to remove asbestos from those premises under a standard JCT building contract, clause 17 of which stipulated expressly that Stock Conversion, the employer, 'shall not without written consent of the contractor assign this contract'. When executing the work the contractor allegedly committed various breaches of contract. Stock Conversion then sold its leasehold interest in the premises to Linden Gardens Trust Ltd ('Linden Gardens') at full market value, and later purported to assign all its rights of action under the building contract to them, although it did not obtain the contractor's consent before doing so. As the full extent of the contractor's breaches became clear, Linden Gardens spent considerable sums remedying them. Linden Gardens, as assignee, then sought to recover its loss by suing the contractor for breach of the building contract. Stock Conversion, the assignor, was not a party to that action.

The facts of the *St Martin's* case were similar. Here a building contractor was engaged by St Martin's Property Corporation Ltd ('Corporation'), the lessee of a building site, to build shops, offices, and flats on the site under a standard JCT building contract, clause 17 of which was in the same terms as clause 17 in the *Linden Gardens* case. Before the contractor started work, Corporation sold its leasehold interest in the site at full market value to an associate company, St Martin's Property Investments Ltd ('Investments'), and simultaneously purported to assign the benefit of the building contract to them (although without first obtaining the contractor's consent). Subsequently, the contractor allegedly breached that contract causing loss to the new lessee of the site, Investments. That the contractor's breaches occurred after assignment distinguishes the facts of the *St Martin's* case from those of the *Linden Gardens* case, as does the fact that in the *St Martin's* case the assignor (Corporation) was a party to the action brought by the assignee (Investments) against the contractor.

In both cases the contractors pleaded that they were not liable in damages to the purported assignees (Linden Gardens and Investments) because Clause 17 made both assignments ineffective. This point is dealt with by Lord Browne-Wilkinson in the extract which immediately follows. In the *St Martin's* case, the contractor also pleaded that whilst the original contracting party, Corporation, was entitled to sue, it could not recover any more than nominal damages because it had suffered no loss.

Lord Browne-Wilkinson: . . .

(1) DOES CLAUSE 17 PROHIBIT THE ASSIGNMENT OF THE BENEFIT OF BUILDING CONTRACTS?

Staughton LJ (dissenting on this point) held that on its true construction clause 17 did not prohibit the assignment by the employer of the benefit of the building contract. It was urged before your Lordships on behalf of Linden Gardens and Investments that his views were correct.

The argument runs as follows. On any basis, clause 17 is unhappily drafted in that it refers to an assignment of 'the contract.' It is trite law that it is, in any event, impossible to assign 'the contract' as a whole, ie including both burden and benefit. The burden of a contract can never be assigned without the consent of the other party to the contract in which event such consent will give rise to a novation. Therefore one has to discover what the parties meant by this inelegant phrase. It is said that the intention of the parties in using the words 'assign this contract' is demonstrated by clause 17(2) which prohibits both the assignment of the contract by the contractor without the employer's consent and the sub-letting of any portion of the works without the consent of the architect. In clause 17(2), the contractor is only expressly prevented from subletting 'any *portion* of the works.' Yet it must have been the party's intention to limit the contractor's rights to sublet the *whole* of the works. Accordingly, the words in clause 17(2) 'assign this contract' have to be read as meaning 'sublet the whole of the works.' If that is the meaning of the words 'assign this contract' in clause 17(2) they must bear the same meaning in clause 17(1), which accordingly only prohibits the employer from giving substitute performance and does not prohibit the assignment of the benefit of the contract.

Like the majority of the Court of Appeal, I am unable to accept this argument. Although it is true that the phrase 'assign this contract' is not strictly accurate, lawyers frequently use those words inaccurately to describe an assignment of the benefit of a contract since every lawyer knows that the burden of a contract cannot be assigned: see, for example, *Nokes v Doncaster Amalgamated Collieries Ltd* [1940] AC 1014, 1019–1020. The prohibition in clause 17(2) against subletting 'any portion of the works' necessarily produces a prohibition against the subletting of the whole of the works: any subletting of the whole will necessarily include a subletting of a portion and is therefore prohibited. Therefore there is no ground for reading the words 'assign this contract' in clause 17(1) as referring only to subletting the whole. Decisively, both clause 17(1) and (2) clearly distinguish between 'assignment' and 'subletting:' it is therefore impossible to read the word 'assign' as meaning 'sublet.' Finally, I find it difficult to comprehend the concept of an employer 'subletting' the performance of his contractual duties which consist primarily of providing access to the site and paying for the works.

Accordingly, in my view clause 17(1) of the contract prohibited the assignment by the employer of the benefit of the contract. This, by itself, is fatal to the claim by Investments (as assignee) in the *St Martins* case.

(2) DOES CLAUSE 17(1) PROHIBIT THE ASSIGNMENT OF ACCRUED RIGHTS OF ACTION?

The majority in the Court of Appeal drew a distinction between an assignment of the right to require future performance of a contract by the other party on the one hand and an assignment of the benefits arising *under* the contract (eg to receive payment due under it or to enforce accrued rights of action) on the other hand. They held that clause 17 only prohibited the assignment of the right to future performance and did not prohibit the assignment of the benefits arising under the contract, in particular accrued causes of action. Therefore, in the *Linden Gardens* case, where all the relevant breaches of contract by the contractors pre-dated the assignment, an assignment to *Linden Gardens* of the accrued rights of action for breach was not prohibited. In contrast, in the *St Martins* case, where all the breaches of contract occurred after the date of the assignment, the majority of the Court of Appeal held that it was a breach of clause 17 to seek to transfer the right to future performance.

This distinction between assigning the right to future performance of a contract and assigning the benefits arising under a contract was largely founded on a Note entitled 'Inalienable Rights?' by Professor RM Goode (1979) 42 MLR 553 on *Helstan Securities Ltd v Hertfordshire County Council* [1978] 3 All ER 262. In that case a contract contained a clause prohibiting the contractor from assigning the contract 'or any benefit therein or thereunder.' The contractors assigned to the plaintiffs the right to a liquidated sum of money then alleged to be due to the contractors under the contract. Croom-Johnson J held that the plaintiffs, as assignees, could not sue the employers to recover the sum of money.

In his Note, Professor Goode rightly pointed out that where a contract between A and B prohibits assignment of contractual rights by A, the effect of such a prohibition is a question of the construction of the contract. There are at least four possible interpretations, viz, (1) that the term does not invalidate a purported assignment by A to C but gives rise only to a claim by B against A for damages for breach of the prohibition; (2) that the term precludes or invalidates any assignment by A to C (so as to entitle B to pay the debt to A) but not so as to preclude A from agreeing, as between himself and C, that he will account to C for what A receives from B: *In re Turcan* (1888) 40 ChD 5; (3) that A is precluded not only from effectively assigning the contractual rights to C, but also from agreeing to account to C for the fruits of the contract when received by A from B; (4) that a purported assignment by A to C constitutes a repudiatory breach of condition entitling B not merely to refuse to pay C but also to refuse to pay A.

Professor Goode then expressed the view that construction (2) (being the *Helstan* case itself) was permissible and effective but that construction (3) to the extent that it purported to render void not only the assignment as between B and C but also as between A and C was contrary to law.

I am content to accept Professor Goode's classification and conclusions, though I am bound to say that I think cases within categories (1) and (4) are very unlikely to occur. But Professor Goode's classification provides no warrant for the view taken by the majority of the Court of Appeal in the present case: he does not discuss or envisage a case where a contractual prohibition against assignment is to be construed as prohibiting an assignment by A to C of rights of future performance but does not prohibit the assignment by A to C of 'the fruits of performance' eg accrued rights of action or debts. Professor Goode only draws a distinction between the assignment of rights to performance and the assignment of rights under the contract in two connections: first, in dealing with the effect of a prohibited assignment as between the assignor and the assignee (in categories (2) and (3)): secondly, in dealing with contracts for personal services. In the latter, he rightly points out that, although an author who has contracted to write a book for a fee cannot perform the contract by supplying a book written by a third party, if he writes the book himself he can assign the right to the fee—the fruits of performance. He expressly mentions that such right to assign the fruits of performance can be prohibited by the express terms of the contract.

However, although I do not think that Professor Goode's article throws any light on the true construction of clause 17, I accept that it is at least hypothetically possible that there might be a case in which the contractual prohibitory term is so expressed as to render invalid the assignment of rights to future performance but not so as to render invalid assignments of the fruits of performance. The question in each case must turn on the terms of the contract in question.

The question is to what extent does clause 17 on its true construction restrict rights of assignment which would otherwise exist? In the context of a complicated building contract, I find it impossible to construe clause 17 as prohibiting only the assignment of rights to future performance, leaving each party free to assign the fruits of the contract. The reason for including the contractual prohibition viewed from the contractor's point of view must be that the contractor wishes to ensure that he deals, and deals only, with the particular employer with whom he has chosen to enter into a contract. Building contracts are pregnant with disputes: some employers are much more reasonable than others in dealing with such disputes. The disputes frequently arise in the context of the contractor suing for the price and being met by a claim for abatement of the price or cross-claims founded on an allegation that the performance of the contract has been defective. Say that, before the final instalment of the price has been paid, the employer has assigned the benefits under the contract to a third party, there being at the time existing rights of action for defective work. On the Court of Appeal's view, those rights of action would have vested in the assignee. Would the original employer be entitled to an abatement of the price, even though the cross-claims would be vested in the assignee? If so, would the assignee be a necessary party to any settlement or litigation of the claims for defective work, thereby requiring the contractor to deal with two parties (one not of his choice) in order to recover the price for the works from the employer? I cannot believe that the parties ever intended to permit such a confused position to arise.

Again, say that before completion of the works the employers assigned the land, together with the existing causes of action against the contractor, to a third party and shortly thereafter the contractor committed a repudiatory breach? On the construction preferred by the Court of Appeal, the right to insist on further performance, being unassignable, would have remained with the original employers whereas the other causes of action and the land would belong to the assignee. Who could decide whether to accept the repudiation, the assignor or the assignee?

These possibilities of confusion (and many others which could be postulated) persuade me that parties who have specifically contracted to prohibit the assignment of the contract cannot have intended to draw a distinction between the right to performance of the contract and the right to the fruits of the contract. In my view they cannot have contemplated a position in which the right to future performance and the right to benefits accrued under the contract should become vested in two separate people. I say again that that result could have been achieved by careful and intricate drafting, spelling out the parties' intentions if they had them. But in the absence of such a clearly expressed intention, it would be wrong to attribute such a perverse intention to the parties. In my judgment, clause 17 clearly prohibits the assignment of any benefit of or under the contract.

It follows that the purported assignment to Linden Gardens without the consent of the contractors constituted a breach of clause 17. The claim of Linden Gardens as assignee must therefore fail unless it can show that the prohibition in clause 17 was either void as being contrary to public policy or, notwithstanding the breach of clause 17, the assignment was effective to assign the chose in action to Linden Gardens.

(3) IS A PROHIBITION ON ASSIGNMENT VOID AS BEING CONTRARY TO PUBLIC POLICY?

It was submitted that it is normally unlawful as being contrary to public policy to seek to render property inalienable. Since contractual rights are a species of property, it is said that a prohibition against assigning such rights is void as being illegal.

This submission faces formidable difficulties both on authority and in principle. As to the authorities, in *In re Turcan*, 40 ChD 5, a man effected an insurance policy which contained a term that it should not be assignable in any case whatever. He had previously covenanted with trustees to settle after-acquired property. The Court of Appeal held that although he could not assign the benefit of the policy so as to give the trustees the power to recover the money from the insurance company, he could validly make a declaration of trust of the proceeds which required him to hand over such proceeds to the trustees. This case proceeded, therefore, on the footing that the contractual restriction on assignment was valid. In *Helstan Securities* [1978] 3 All ER 262 Croom-Johnson J enforced such a prohibition. In *Reed Publishing Holdings Ltd v Kings Reach Investments Ltd* (unreported), 25 May 1983; Court of Appeal (Civil Division) Transcript No 231 of 1983, the Court of Appeal had to consider an application to join as a party to an action an assignee of the benefit of a contract which contained a prohibition on such assignment. One of their grounds for refusing the application was that by reason of the prohibition the assignment was of no effect.

In none of these cases was the public policy argument advanced. But they indicate a long-term acceptance of the validity of such a prohibition which is accepted as part of the law in *Chitty on Contracts*, 26th edn (1989), Vol 1, p 883, para 1413. We were referred to a decision of the Supreme Court of South Africa, *Paiges v Van Ryn Gold Mines Estates Ltd* 1920 AD 600 in which it was expressly decided that a term prohibiting a workman from assigning his wages was not contrary to public policy. In Scotland a covenant against assigning a lease of minerals (which was treated simply as a contract) was held not to infringe public policy: *Duke of Portland v Baird and Co* (1865) 4 Macph 10. We were referred to certain cases in the United States, but they give no unequivocal guidance.

In the face of this authority, the House is being invited to change the law by holding that such a prohibition is void as contrary to public policy. For myself I can see no good reason for so doing. Nothing was urged in argument as showing that such a prohibition was contrary to the public interest beyond the fact that such prohibition renders the chose in action inalienable. Certainly in the context of rights over land the law does not favour restrictions on alienability. But even in relation to land law a prohibition against the assignment of a lease is valid. We were not referred to any English case in which the courts have had to consider restrictions on the alienation of tangible personal property, probably because there are few cases in which there would be any desire to restrict such alienation. In the case of real property there is a defined and limited supply of the commodity, and it has been held contrary to public policy to restrict the free market. But no such reason can apply to contractual rights: there is no public need for a market in choses in action. A party to a building contract, as I have sought to explain, can have a genuine commercial interest in seeking to ensure that he is in contractual relations only with a person whom he has selected as the other party to the contract. In the circumstances, I can see no policy reason why a contractual prohibition on assignment of contractual rights should be held contrary to public policy.

To avoid doubt, I must make it clear that I have been considering only the validity of a restriction which prohibits assignments which have the effect of bringing the assignee into direct contractual relations with the other party to the contract. I have not been considering Professor Goode's category (3), ie an attempt by contractual term to prevent one party making over the fruits of the contract to a third party. Professor Goode expresses the view that if the prohibition seeks to prevent the assignor from binding himself to pay over such fruits to the assignee, such prohibition is pro tanto void. I express no view on that point.

(4) ARE THE ASSIGNMENTS (ALTHOUGH PROHIBITED) EFFECTIVE TO TRANSFER THE CAUSES OF ACTION TO THE ASSIGNEES?

It was submitted that, even though the assignments were in breach of clause 17, they were effective to vest the causes of action in the assignees, ie Professor Goode's category (1). This argument was founded on two bases: first, the decision in *Tom Shaw and Co v Moss Empires*

Ltd (1908) 25 TLR 190; second, the fact that an assignment of a leasehold term in breach of a covenant against assignment is effective to vest the term in the assignee.

In the *Tom Shaw* case an actor, B, was engaged by Moss Empires under a contract which prohibited the assignment of his salary. B assigned 10 per cent, of his salary to his agent, Tom Shaw. Tom Shaw sued Moss Empires for 10 per cent, of the salary joining B as second defendant. Moss Empire agreed to pay the 10 per cent, of the salary to Tom Shaw or B, as the court might decide ie in effect it interpleaded. Darling J held, at p 191, that the prohibition on assignment was ineffective: it could 'no more operate to invalidate the assignment than it could to interfere with the laws of gravitation.' He gave judgment for the plaintiffs against both B and Moss Empires, ordering B to pay the costs but making no order for costs against Moss Empires.

The case is inadequately reported and it is hard to discover exactly what it decides. Given that both B and Moss Empires were parties and Moss Empires was in effect interpleading, it may be that the words I have quoted merely indicate that as between the assignor, B and the assignee Tom Shaw, the prohibition contained in the contract between B and Moss Empires could not invalidate B's liability to account to Tom Shaw for the moneys when received and that, since B was a party, payment direct to Tom Shaw was ordered. This view is supported by the fact that no order for costs was made against Moss Empires. If this is the right view of the case, it is unexceptional: a prohibition on assignment normally only invalidates the assignment as against the other party to the contract so as to prevent a transfer of the chose in action: in the absence of the clearest words it cannot operate to invalidate the contract as between the assignor and the assignee and even then it may be ineffective on the grounds of public policy. If on the other hand Darling J purported to hold that the contractual prohibition was ineffective to prevent B's contractual rights against Moss Empires being transferred to Tom Shaw, it is inconsistent with authority and was wrongly decided.

In the *Helstan Securities* case [1978] 3 All ER 262 Croom-Johnson J did not follow the *Tom Shaw* case and held that the purported assignment in breach of the contractual provision was ineffective to vest the cause of action in the assignee. That decision was followed and applied by the Court of Appeal in the *Reed Publishing Holdings* case, 25 May 1983: see also *In re Turcan*, 40 ChD 5.

Therefore the existing authorities establish that an attempted assignment of contractual rights in breach of a contractual prohibition is ineffective to transfer such contractual rights. I regard the law as being satisfactorily settled in that sense. If the law were otherwise, it would defeat the legitimate commercial reason for inserting the contractual prohibition, viz., to ensure that the original parties to the contract are not brought into direct contractual relations with third parties.

As to the analogy with leases, I was originally impressed by the fact that an assignment of the term in breach of covenant is effective to vest the term in the assignee: *Williams v Earle* (1868) LR 3 QB 739,750; *Old Grovebury Manor Farm Ltd v W Seymour Plant Sales and Hire Ltd (No 2)* [1979] 1 WLR 1397. However, Mr Kentridge in his reply satisfied me that the analogy is a false one. A lease is a hybrid, part contract, part property. So far as rights of alienation are concerned a lease has been treated as a species of property. Historically the law treated interests in land, both freehold and leasehold, as being capable of disposition and looked askance at any attempt to render them inalienable. However, by the time of Coke covenants against the assignment of leases had been held to be good, because the lessor had a continuing interest in the identity of the person who was his tenant: *Holdsworth, A History of English Law*, 2nd edn, Vol III (1914), p 85 and Vol VII (1937), p 281. The law became settled that an assignment in breach of covenant gave rise to a forfeiture, but pending forfeiture the term was vested in the assignee. In contrast, the development of the law affecting the assignment of contractual rights was wholly different. It started from exactly the opposite position, viz, contractual rights were personal and not assignable. Only gradually did the law permitting assignment develop: *Holdsworth*, Vol VII, pp 520–521 and 531 etc. It is therefore not surprising if the law applicable to assignment of contractual rights differs from that applicable to the assignment of leases.

Therefore in my judgment an assignment of contractual rights in breach of a prohibition against such assignment is ineffective to vest the contractual rights in the assignee. It follows that the claim by Linden Gardens fails and the *Linden Garden* action must be dismissed.

[Lords Keith of Kinkel, Bridge of Harwich, Griffiths, and **Ackner]** all agreed with Lord Browne-Wilkinson on this issue.]

NOTES

1. Debtors often include 'non-assignment' clauses in their contracts restricting or absolutely prohibiting the assignment of their debts (see, generally, G McCormack [2000] JBL 422; G McMeel [2004] LMCLQ 483; PG Turner [2008] LMCLQ 308 at 325–326; M Smith and N Leslie, *The Law of Assignment* (2nd edn, 2013), Ch 35; G Tolhurst, *The Assignment of Contractual Rights* (2nd edn, 2016), pp 190–299). The reasons are various.

- The debtor may value the personal qualities of the other contracting party. A seller of goods may have personal confidence in his buyer's ability to keep his business going and pay the seller for goods sold on credit: *Cooper v Micklefield Coal and Lime Co Ltd* (1912) 107 LT 457 (inferred, not express, intention). In *Don King Productions Inc v Warren* [2000] Ch 291, a case concerning boxing promotion, the identity of the promoter was crucial to the boxer and explained the presence of a non-assignment clause. In *Linden Gardens*, above, Lord Browne-Wilkinson explained that a contractor may wish to deal with a particular employer and no other because 'building contracts are pregnant with disputes: some employers are more reasonable than others in dealing with such disputes'.

- The debtor may wish to retain, up to the very date of the discharge of the debts, rights of set-off and the right of raising counterclaims based on different liabilities (certain new 'equities' may not be set up after notice of assignment).

- The debtor may wish to avoid the risk of making the error of paying twice owing to an oversight of a notice of assignment or having to pay more than one creditor if there is an assignment of part of a debt.

2. Intentions that contractual rights shall not be freely assignable have long generated litigation: for example, *Lynch v Dalzell* (1729) 4 Bro PC 431; Turner [2008] LMCLQ 308 at 311–313; and, in Canada, *McKillop & Benjafield v Alexander* (1912) 45 SCR 551. The recent agitation of questions about such intentions appears to be due to a perhaps late realisation that the effect of 'non-assignment clauses' depends on the construction of the particular clause: see *Devefi Pty Ltd v Mateffy Pearl Nagy Pty Ltd* [1993] RPC 493 at 506. Among other things, construction determines whether the clause deprives the rights within its terms of assignability, as Lord Browne-Wilkinson explained in *Linden Gardens* (see further *British Energy Power & Trading Ltd v Credit Suisse* [2007] EWHC 1428 (Comm), [2007] 1 Lloyd's Rep 427, per Langley J; affirmed on other grounds [2008] EWCA Civ 53, [2008] 1 Lloyd's Rep 413 (clause purporting to render contractual rights unsusceptible of a declaration of trust)). It also determines which contractual rights are subject to the clause and how absolute the restriction is.

3. Attempts to confine generally expressed restrictions on assignment to only some of the rights arising under a contract have tended to be unsuccessful. *Linden Gardens* is an example; see also *Helstan Securities Ltd v Hertfordshire County Council* [1978] 3 All ER 262; *Barbados*

Trust Co v Bank of Zambia [2007] EWCA Civ 148, [2007] 1 Lloyd's Rep 495 (below, pp 891–899). However, in *Flood v Shand Construction Ltd* (1996) 54 Con LR 125, the clause in question was construed as merely extending to the assignment of 'personal' rights of performance and not to the debts arising. The clause in question was expressed to prohibit the assignment by the subcontractor of the benefit of the subcontract without the other party's consent, but permitted assignment of 'any sum which is or may become due and payable to him under this Sub-Contract'. The Court of Appeal construed the clause as prohibiting the assignment of the right to claim damages or other sums that were not yet due or payable and needed to be established as due and payable by litigation or arbitration or contractual machinery, but as permitting the assignment of the right to recover sums which were already due, ie essentially debts.

4.   That a restriction on assignment will not necessarily be absolute is clear from the authorities. The chose in action may be assignable to certain persons, but not to others. The permitted persons may be named or described by their required characteristics: for example, *Argo Fund Ltd v Essar Steel Ltd* [2006] EWCA Civ 241, [2006] 2 Lloyd's Rep 134 (assignment permitted only to an entity which was 'a bank or other financial institution'). Or, rather than prohibit assignment absolutely, it may be prohibited subject to obtaining the obligor's consent. In *Hendry v Chartsearch Ltd* [1998] CLC 1382, a clause in a contract prohibited assignment without the debtor's prior consent 'which shall not be unreasonably withheld'. (See also *Greymouth Gas Kaimiro Ltd v Swift Energy New Zealand Ltd* [2010] NZSC 117, [2011] 1 NZLR 289 at [10]–[11], [18]–[20].) The assignor company went ahead and purported to assign various causes of action against the debtor arising under the contract. The assignor did not obtain the debtor's consent thereto. The assignee (the chairman and a shareholder of the assignor) later submitted that this omission did not make the assignment ineffective against the debtor because the debtor's consent to the assignment could have not reasonably been refused. Evans LJ preferred to leave the point open, although he thought it arguable that the debtor could object to the validity of the assignment on the ground that he could have reasonably refused consent in the present case (because the corporate assignor could have been required to give security for costs in an action against the debtor, whereas the assignee, as an individual, could not). Henry and Millett LJJ dealt with the assignee's main submission head-on. They held that where an assignment of contractual rights is prohibited without the prior written consent of the other party (such consent not to be unreasonably refused), then there could be no valid assignment until after: (a) written consent had been granted; or (b) the court had declared that the consent had been unnecessarily refused. According to Henry LJ (at 1393):

> [t]he suggestion that the assignor can validly assign in breach of his contract without ever seeking prior consent by asserting that, as such consent could not reasonably be refused, so it is unnecessary, seems to me to be a recipe to promote uncertainty and speculative litigation.

Millett LJ went on to hold that as the contract in question required the assignor to obtain the *prior* consent of the other party, retrospective consent, if given, might operate as a waiver, but could not amount to the consent required by the contract. The proper course was for the assignor to ask for consent to a new assignment and to wait until it was given or unreasonably refused before proceeding to make it. This view was applied by Gloster J in *CEP Holdings v Steni AS* [2009] EWHC 2447 (QB) and Cooke J in *BG Global Energy Ltd v Talisman Sinopec Energy UK Ltd* [2015] EWHC 110 (Comm) at [78]–[79]. Estoppels may operate against an obligor's denial that an instrument purporting to assign a chose in action is valid, even though the obligor did not consent to the assignment: *Orion Finance Ltd v Crown Management Ltd* [1994] 2 BCLC 607.

(iv) Overcoming unassignability

Unassignability can be overcome or avoided. The hurdles of maintenance and champerty, and the deficiencies of bare rights to litigate, may be avoided where an intended assignee holds a relevant interest sufficient to justify an assignment of them. Practically, a partial method of overcoming unassignability is to have the parties agree to deal with the *proceeds* of the unassignable rights, or benefits *arising under* a contract, rather than the unassignable rights themselves. As Professor Goode has stated in (1979) 42 MLR 553 at 555 with regard to contracts drafted to restrict assignability: 'What is non-transferable is the duty to perform, not the fruits of performance.' An agreement to deal with the proceeds of unassignable choses in action will be given effect in equity as a contract to assign the chose if and when it comes into existence and comes into the hands of the assignor (*Raiffeisen Zentralbank Osterreich AG v Five Star General Trading LLC* [2001] EWCA Civ 68, [2001] QB 825 at [80]–[81]).

The law is best summarised by Windeyer J in *Norman v Federal Comr of Taxation* when he said (at 24) that:

> . . . in equity a would-be present assignment of something to be acquired in the future is, when made for value, construed as an agreement to assign the thing when it is acquired. A court of equity will ensure that the would-be assignor performs this agreement, his conscience being bound by the consideration. The purported assignee thus gets an equitable interest in the property immediately the legal ownership of it is acquired by the assignor, assuming it to have been sufficiently described to be then identifiable. The prospective interest of the assignee is in the meantime protected by equity. These principles, which now govern assignments for value of property to be acquired in the future, have been developed and established by a line of well-known cases, of which *Holroyd v Marshall* (1862) 10 HL Cas 191; *Collyer v Isaacs* (1881) 19 Ch D 342; *Tailby v Official Receiver* (1888) 13 App Cas 523; and *Re Lind, Industrials Finance Syndicate v Lind* [1915] 2 Ch 345, are the most important.

An assignment of a bare cause of action is valid if made by a trustee in bankruptcy or by the liquidator of a company under their statutory powers of sale: Insolvency Act 1986, s 314(1), Sch 5, Pt II, para 9 (bankruptcy); Insolvency Act 1986, ss 165(2), 167(1), Sch 4, Pt III, para 6 (liquidation). For example, in *Ramsey v Hartley* [1977] 1 WLR 686, the Court of Appeal allowed a trustee in bankruptcy to sell the bankrupt's right of action back to the bankrupt himself. However, in a series of cases examining the scope of a liquidator's statutory powers, it has been held that the statutory exemption does not extend to the assignment of a cause of action conferred exclusively on the liquidator (*Re Ayala Holdings Ltd (No 2)* [1996] 1 BCLC 467—attempt by liquidator to assign rights under the Companies Act 1985, s 395 (see now the Companies Act 2006, s 874) and the Insolvency Act 1986, s 127) or an assignment of the proceeds of such an action (*Re Oasis Merchandising Services Ltd* [1998] Ch 170, CA—attempt by liquidator to assign proceeds of a wrongful trading action under the Insolvency Act 1986, s 214). In neither case is there a sale of 'the company's property' as required by the terms of the statutory exemption. It has also been held that the statutory exemption does not extend to assignments of the proceeds of litigation *made in return for the assignee agreeing to fund the action* (*Grovewood Holdings plc v James Capel & Co Ltd* [1995] Ch 80, the correctness of which was rightly doubted by the Court of Appeal in *Re Oasis Merchandising* (at 179–180): if the proceeds of an action can properly be described as an asset of the company, then surely they fall within the blanket immunity given by the statutory exemption). By contrast, in *Norglen Ltd v Reeds Rains Prudential Ltd* [1999] 2 AC 1, the House of Lords held that an assignment of a cause of action by a liquidator under his statutory powers was not invalid even if it: (1) enabled the company to benefit indirectly from legal aid which was available to the assignee (an individual) when it was not available to the company (the company benefited indirectly because the assignee had agreed to share the proceeds of the cause of action with it); and (2) deprived the defendant in an action of the right to apply for security for costs against the company.

Whether 'non-assignment' clauses should be overridden is controversial. Whilst there are considerations in favour of the validity of non-assignment clauses, there are counter-vailing arguments which support the principle of free assignability of debts. It has been said that a debt is a form of property and, as such, should be freely alienable, unless there is a clear expression of contrary intention in the underlying contract between the assignor and the debtor (*Barbados Trust Co v Bank of Zambia* [2007] EWCA Civ 148, [2007] 1 Lloyd's Rep 495 at [43], per Waller LJ, and at [88], per Rix LJ). From a commercial point of view, non-assignment clauses affect the marketability of debts and therefore the validity of receivables financing. Such considerations have prevailed in the United States, where the Uniform Commercial Code renders non-assignment clauses ineffective (rev art 9–406(d)), and this approach has influenced the drafting of international conventions (see the UNIDROIT Factoring Convention, art 6 and the UNCITRAL Convention on Receivables Financing, art 11) and UNIDROIT's statement of principles applicable to international commercial contracts (see UNIDROIT *Principles of International Commercial Contracts* (2004), art 9.1.9). Section 1 of the Small Business, Enterprise and Employment Act 2015 confers power to make regulations to invalidate such restrictions in contracts affecting certain receivables. As at the date of writing, that power has not been exercised. For competing views on the freedom to assign debts, see P Zonneveld (2007) 6 JIBFL 313 and T Prime (2008) 2 JIBFL 71.

4　INTENTION TO ASSIGN

Statute may effect a compulsory assignment by operation of law. In all other cases, however, assignment depends on finding that the holder of a chose in action expressed an intention to assign it to another. Since assignments share some features of other forms of transaction, intention to assign must be distinguished from intention to deal with a chose in action by other means.

(a)　Intention to assign

William Brandt's Sons & Co v Dunlop Rubber Co Ltd

[1905] AC 454, House of Lords

Merchants agreed with a bank, by which they were financed, that buyers of goods sold by the merchants should pay the price directly to the bank. When goods had been sold, the bank forwarded to the buyers notice in writing that the merchants had made over to the bank the right to receive the purchase money and requested the buyers to sign an undertaking to remit the purchase money to the bank. The buyers returned the acknowledgement to the bank but then paid a third party by mistake. The bank sued the buyers and the question arose whether there had been an equitable assignment.

> **Lord Macnaghten** held that even without consideration of the notice sent to the buyers there was clear evidence of an equitable assignment between the merchants and the bank (at 460) and continued: The statute [s 25(6) of the Judicature Act 1873; now s 136 of the Law of Property Act 1925] does not forbid or destroy equitable assignments or impair their efficacy in the slightest degree. Where the rules of equity and the rules of the common law conflict, the rules of equity are to prevail. Before the statute there was a conflict as regards assignments of debts and other choses in action. At law it was considered necessary that the debtor should enter into some engagement with the assignee. That was never the rule in equity. It 'is certainly not the doctrine of this Court,' said Lord Eldon, sitting in Chancery in *Ex p South* ((1818) 3 Swan 392). In certain cases the Judicature Act places the assignee in a better position than he was before. Whether the present case falls within the favoured class may perhaps be doubted. At any rate, it is wholly immaterial for the plaintiffs' success in this action. But, says the Lord Chief Justice, 'the document does not, on the face of it, purport to be an assignment nor use the language of an assignment.' An equitable assignment does not always take that form. It may be addressed to the debtor. It may be couched in the language of command. It may be a courteous request. It may assume the form of mere permission. The language is immaterial if the meaning is plain. All that is necessary is that the debtor should be given to understand that the debt has been made over by the creditor to some third person. If the debtor ignores such a notice, he does so at his peril. If the assignment be for valuable consideration and communicated to the third person, it cannot be revoked by the creditor or safely disregarded by the debtor. I think that the documents which passed between Brandts [the bank] and the company [the buyers] would of themselves . . . have constituted a good equitable assignment.
>
> [**Lord James** delivered a concurring judgment. **The Earl of Halsbury LC** and **Lord Lindley** concurred.]

NOTES

1. Intention to assign is ascertained objectively. In *Re Gillott's Settlements* [1934] Ch 97, a man positively wished not to assign his entitlement to receive the income of a trust in the form of a marriage settlement. His entitlement was expressed to last until (inter alia) he should assign it. In exchange for a loan from a third party he covenanted that, while money should remain owing under the agreement, he should pay any income received from the trust into a specified bank account within three days of receiving it. That money was to be used in paying the debts and repaying the loan; the remaining money was, relevantly, to be handed to the man. Maugham J held that the covenants in the loan agreement expressed intention on the man's part to assign his entitlement to the trust income. The man's entitlement was thereby forfeited.

2. An intention to assign may be shown by conduct alone. The conduct must, presumably, be probative of an intention to assign. 'It must be possible to identify some act on the assignor's part from which his intention then and there to divest himself — in favour of the assignee — of the right or interest to be assigned, on the terms which have been agreed, can be inferred': *Finlan v Eyton Morris Winfield* [2007] EWHC 914 (Ch), [2007] 4 All ER 143, per Blackburne J. *Coulter v Chief of Dorset Police* [2003] EWHC 3391 (Ch), [2004] 1 WLR 1425 is a difficult decision on this point. It was held that the benefit of a judgment had been assigned in equity by a retiring chief constable to his successor. Patten J acknowledged the need for there to be 'a sufficient expression of an intention to assign' and held that the resignation of the existing office-holder, and the assumption of office by his successor, was 'a sufficient outward manifestation of an intention that the successor office holder should obtain the benefit held on trust by a predecessor, for there to be an equitable assignment of the benefit of the judgment'. Can retiring from office be considered probative evidence of an intention to assign the benefit of a chose in action? The judge invoked the maxim that equity considers as done that which ought to be done. That maxim is normally invoked to deny effect to a defendant's plea that he breached a legally enforceable obligation to do some act. Whether the retiring chief constable owed such an obligation, however, raised questions about the nature of Crown offices which were not argued in this case. An appeal was dismissed on grounds that made it unnecessary to consider these points: [2004] EWCA Civ, [2005] 1 WLR 130.

(b) Intention to deal otherwise

Intention to assign must be distinguished from intention to deal by other means.

(i) Revocable mandate (agency)

An assignment must be distinguished from a revocable mandate given by a creditor to a third party authorising him to collect payment from the debtor and also from a revocable mandate to the debtor directing him to pay the third party. Assignment is irrevocable. Thus, an intention to assign may only be found where the intention to deal is irrevocable. Payment by cheque does not as such evidence intention to assign: a cheque is only a revocable mandate and not the assignment of any money standing to the credit of the drawer in his bank account (Bills of Exchange Act 1882, s 53(1); *Hopkinson v Forster* (1874) LR 19 Eq 74; *Deposit Protection Board v Dalia* [1994] 2 AC 367 at 400). When a creditor gives a third party a power of attorney to sue the debtor in the creditor's name without having to account to the creditor (see, eg, *Gerard v Lewis* (1867) LR 2 CP 305), that alone does not evince an intention to assign: the creditor may generally revoke his power of attorney. Only where the intention is irrevocably that the third party should benefit can the creditor have intended to assign. For discussion of when the creditor's mandate will be revocable and when it will be irrevocable, see AP Bell, *Modern Law of Personal Property in England and Ireland* (1989), pp 370–371.

(ii) Novation

Assignment involves the transfer of existing proprietary rights without the consent of the debtor, and it involves the transfer only of existing rights not contractual liabilities. As Lord Browne-Wilkinson emphasised in *Linden Gardens Trust Ltd v Lenesta Sludge Disposals Ltd* [1994] 1 AC 85 at 103: 'the burden of a contract can never be assigned without the consent of the other party to the contract in which event such consent will give rise to a novation'. Novation involves a new party becoming substituted to the position of the old. But the new party assumes rights and obligations equivalent to those of the departing party, rather than acquiring the rights and obligations of the departing party as such. Novation and assignment thus depend on different intentions. In particular, novation cannot be achieved through a unilateral expression of intention. A novation requires the consent of all parties (*Rasbora Ltd v JCL Marine Ltd* [1977] 1 Lloyd's Rep 645). The new contract must be supported by consideration moving from the new promisee (*Tatlock v Harris* (1789) 3 Term Rep 174 at 180). See further *Olsson v Dyson* (1969) 120 CLR 365 at 368, per Windeyer J, and, for a debate touching closely on novation, CH Tham [2010] LMCLQ 38; A Trukhnatov [2010] LMCLQ 551; CH Tham [2010] LMCLQ 559.

(iii) Attornment by fundholder

A result similar to that achieved by assignment can be achieved where a fundholder acknowledges that he holds a fund for a third party. If a creditor causes a fundholder debtor to acknowledge that it holds for a third party—ie attorns to the third party—the third party may sue the fundholder for money had and received. This has been possible since the middle of the nineteenth century: *Griffin v Weatherby* (1868) LR 3 QB 753. The transferee need not provide consideration for the fundholder's promise as his remedy is restitutionary and not contractual. The relevant intention is expressed by the fundholder rather than the creditor as assignor.

It was always accepted that only a fundholder could attorn to a third party in this way; a transferee could only enforce a promise made by a mere debtor (ie not holding a fund) if the transferee had supplied consideration for the promise to pay (*Liversidge v Broadbent* (1859) 4 H & N 603). However, in *Shamia v Joory* [1958] 1 QB 448, Barry J rejected this limitation (*Liversidge v Broadbent* not being cited to him) holding that if a creditor asks his debtor to pay a third party, and the debtor agrees to do so, and informs the third party of his agreement, then the third party is entitled to sue the debtor even though he supplied no consideration for the debtor's promise. The decision has been described as 'unsound' and has been subjected to sustained criticism (see JD Davies (1959) 75 LQR 220 at 231–233; cf E Peel, *Treitel's Law of Contract* (14th edn, 2015), para 15–004). Even if *Shamia v Joory* is correct, attornment differs from assignment in that it requires the consent of the debtor; it does not arise through a unilateral expression of intention by the creditor.

(iv) Declaration of trust

In *Don King Productions Inc v Warren* [2000] Ch 291 at 319-320, Lightman J stated that:

> A declaration of trust in favour of a third party of the benefit of obligations or the profits obtained from a contract is different in character from an assignment of the benefit of the contract to that third party: see *Devefi Pty Ltd v Mateffy Pearl Nagy Pty Ltd* [1993] RPC 493 at 505.

An intention to assign is an intention to transfer a chose in action, by ceasing any longer to hold it (but see J Edelman and S Elliott (2015) 131 LQR 228). Intention to hold on trust, on the other hand, involves an intention to continue to hold a chose in action, but henceforth to hold it on trust for another or others.

In *Don King* that distinction was pivotal. An express prohibition on assignment contained in the terms of the contract between assignor and debtor, and the personal nature of that contract (a promotion and management contract between a boxer (debtor) and his manager/promoter (assignor)), prevented assignment of the benefit of the contract: however, Lightman J held (at 319–320) that the purported assignor held the benefit of the contract on trust for the purported assignee who acquired an equitable interest in it:

> Whether the contract contains a provision prohibiting such a declaration of trust must be determined as a matter of construction of the contract. Such a limitation upon the freedom of the party is not lightly to be inferred and a clause prohibiting assignments is prima facie restricted to assignments of the benefit of the obligation and does not extend to declarations of trust of the benefit . . .

Despite the fact that the difference between assigning a right and having someone else own the beneficial interest in it under a trust seems marginal (see A Tettenborn [1998] LMCLQ 498 at 500), Lightman J's decision was upheld on appeal: see [2000] Ch 291.

The distinction between assignment and declaration of trust, and the forms of intention necessary to effect each type of dealing, was agitated further in the next case in the light of criticisms of *Don King* made in A Tettenborn [1998] LMCLQ 498 and [1999] LMCLQ 353 and PG Turner, 'Charges of Unassignable Rights' (2004) 20 JCL 97. In the extract below, the Court of Appeal addresses intention to assign and intention to declare a trust, as well as consequential matters of how any intended trust could operate in the face of the proven intention that the chose in action involved in the case should not be freely assignable.

Barbados Trust Co v Bank of Zambia

[2007] EWCA Civ 148, [2007] 1 Lloyd's Rep 495, Court of Appeal

Bank of Zambia (BoZ) borrowed a large sum of money from a group of banks. Article 12.01(A) of the loan agreement provided that 'each bank may at any time assign all or part of it rights and benefits . . . to any one or more banks or other financial institutions . . . provided that any such assignment may only be effective if . . . the prior written consent of [BoZ] shall have been obtained . . .' Part of BoZ's debt was assigned to Bank of America (BoA), which then assigned the debt to a third party. Subsequently, the third party assigned the debt to Barbados Trust Co (BT). BT wanted to bring proceedings against BoZ to recover the debt but it turned out that the assignments to the third party and to BT were ineffective because neither entity was a 'bank or other financial institution' within art 12.01(A). To get round the problem of title to sue, BoA declared itself a trustee of its interest in the debt in favour of BT. BoA did not itself want to bring proceedings against BoZ and so BT joined BoA to the proceedings as second defendant relying on the procedure, endorsed by Lord Wright in *Vandepitte v Preferred Accident Insurance Corpn of New York* [1933] AC 70 at 79, of the beneficiary suing in its own name, naming the trustee as a defendant, where the trustee refused to sue in its own name.

BoZ admitted the debt, but defended the claim on the following bases: (1) that the assignment to BoA had not been with the prior consent of BoZ; and (2) that BT was not entitled to sue as beneficiary, naming BoA as defendant, on the ground that the declaration of trust was simply a prohibited assignment in another name. Langley J decided issue (1), the prior written consent point, in favour of BT, but issue (2), the declaration of trust point, in favour of BoZ: [2006] 1 Lloyd's Rep 723. BT appealed issue (2), and BoZ appealed issue (1). The Court of Appeal (by a majority) dismissed BT's claim on the ground that the assignment to BoA had not been with the prior consent of BoZ. Then, in a series of *obiter* statements, their Lordships stated that the prohibition on assignment contained in art 12.01(A) did not extend to a declaration of trust. However, there was some disagreement between their Lordships as to whether, if BoA had had title to the debt owed by BoZ, BT, as the beneficiary of the trust declared by BoA, was entitled to bring proceedings against BoZ in its own name, joining BoA as a defendant, under the *Vandepitte* procedure. Waller LJ thought BT could rely on the *Vandepitte* procedure; Hooper LJ thought it could not. Rix LJ thought that 'on balance' the *Vandepitte* procedure was available to BT but felt that further evidence would have been required as to whether the declaration of trust was 'merely a device' to bring before the court a claim which BoA would otherwise have allowed to become time-barred. If a mere 'device', Rix LJ felt that it was doubtful whether equity would enforce the trust.

Waller LJ: . . . The issue that arises in this case can be put in these terms. (1) If BoA had attempted to assign the debt to BT by a legal assignment and BT had sued, BoZ would have been entitled to have refused to pay BT, since it was not a bank or financial institution and since consent had not been obtained. . . . (2) If BoA were to declare a trust of the proceeds when received and then sue for the debt in its own name, since BoZ could have no interest in the proceeds once in BoA's hands, BoZ would have no answer to BoA's claim and BoA would have to answer to BT's claim once it had received the proceeds. (3) If, however, BoA declares a trust in the right to the debt in favour of BT, and if BoA does not sue, will the court hold, by virtue of the fact that BT sues in its own name, joining BoA as a Defendant, that the Declaration of Trust is simply an assignment in another name, enabling BoZ to refuse to pay, or will the court hold that, since BT's only remedy in order to enforce the trust between it and BoA is to sue in its own name joining BoA, the effect is to put BoZ in the same position as if BoA itself had sued?

It is important to bear in mind when considering the above questions that what has for shorthand been referred to as the *Vandepitte* short cut is a matter of *procedure* to enable a beneficiary under a trust to obtain what he is beneficially entitled to in a situation in which the trustee will not sue—will not sue for what the trustee is legally entitled to but which if he succeeds he must hold for the beneficiary. It would be understandable if the court would not allow the procedure to be misused to obtain rights that the beneficiary is not otherwise entitled to, but otherwise if the beneficiary has an unanswerable right under a trust and the trustee has an unanswerable claim, why should the court's procedure not be available to enable the rights to be established or brought to fruition? The focus ultimately has to be on which contract governs the entitlement of the beneficiary and the true construction of that contract.

As my Lord, Rix LJ, pointed out during the argument it is necessary to take matters in stages. To spell out the stages consideration has to be given to the following questions. First what is the proper construction of art 12? Does it seek to prohibit a declaration of trust by the legal owner of a debt, BoA, in favour of BT without the consent of BoZ? Does art 12 seek to prohibit BoA suing BoZ on the debt once the declaration of trust in favour of BT has been entered into ie would BoZ have any answer to a claim by BoA once the declaration of Trust has been entered into? If BoZ would have no answer to a claim by BoA, does art 12 seek to prohibit BT using the *Vandepitte* procedure if BoA refuses to sue? If the declaration of Trust is valid as between BoA and BT is it a term of that declaration of Trust that BoA will not sue in its own name and if so what difference would that make? On the assumption that so far the answers are in favour of BT being able to sue with BoA joined as a Defendant, are the circumstances such that the court will hold that the use of the *Vandepitte* procedure should not be available in this case?

[His Lordship then referred to *Don King Productions Inc v Warren* [2000] Ch 291, and the articles by Tettenborn and Turner (see p 891) criticising that decision, and continued:]

All the above articles are helpful in seeking to answer the questions that have to be considered in this case, but at the end of the day each case must be considered by reference to its own context and by reference to the terms of the agreements or contracts, the subject of the case.

The most important and thus the first question to consider is the true construction of art 12. It seems to me that if an embargo was to be placed on a participating bank declaring a trust in relation to sums due or creating a charge over sums due, words could have been used so as to make that clear, . . . As regards Mr Handyside's [counsel for BoZ] submission that a declaration of trust was in effect an 'equitable assignment', I would for my part accept that if it was it would be caught by the prohibition—the word assignment includes assignments both legal and equitable. But a declaration of trust is not an equitable assignment. An equitable assignment if in writing can be converted into a legal assignment under s 136 of the Law of Property Act and that is simply not true of a declaration of trust. The language of art 12 does not in terms include within the prohibition a declaration of trust, and it seems to me that since one is concerned with the question whether a restriction should be placed on the transfer of a piece of property, an acknowledged debt, the court should be slow to contemplate that the parties ever intended such to be within the prohibition.

If, however, that were wrong, I am not sure it is a complete answer in this case because I cannot see how BoZ would by reference to art 12 have any answer to a claim by BoA simply because they had declared a trust of the right to a debt or the proceeds of the debt in favour of a third party, about the existence of whom BoZ was unaware and to whom thus BoZ had not consented. It would thus still leave open two questions, first whether, despite having no answer to a claim by BoA, art 12 prevents the use of the *Vandepitte* procedure by BT, or, if not, the second question, whether the court should allow use of the *Vandepitte* procedure so as to enable BT to enforce its rights against BoA.

It is said that BoZ has, by art 12, a right to decree by whom it should be sued and that to allow the bringing of an action using the *Vandepitte* procedure on an acknowledged debt would be to allow interference in BoZ's contract with its lenders under the facility. This argument seems to me to be a false one. The procedure is 'procedure' and it simply provides a short cut to prevent litigation under which BoA could be forced to sue followed by an action under which BoA sues. In other words albeit BT is the Claimant, it is as if BoA were Claimant seeking to recover that which is due in law which they will then hold for BT. There is thus no interference by BT. In any event to construe suing on an acknowledged debt as interfering in BoZ's contract with its lenders seems to me far fetched. Thus art 12, on its true construction, does not, in my view, prevent the use of the *Vandepitte* procedure.

What then should be the attitude of the court? In that regard one should first consider the terms of the Declaration of Trust. The Declaration of Trust certainly does not provide in terms for BoA not being prepared to sue in its own name, nor is any assistance to be gained from the letters which preceded the declaration in that regard. The Declaration recognises that BT will sue, but it also seems to recognise that there does exist the very situation in which the *Vandepitte* procedure should be available in normal circumstances.

That brings me to the final question, which is whether, if as I am now assuming, art 12 contains some prohibition on alienability, what attitude should the court take to the use of the *Vandepitte* procedure? In my view procedure is then to enable BT to enforce its rights against BoA. It is not a measure of substantive law which might affect the asset, the subject of the declaration of trust. There is no reason why the court should hold that BoZ should be entitled to a defence which it would not have had if some longer and more tortuous form of procedure, compelling BoA to sue, were used. The court has to recognise that it is concerned in this instance both with the enforcement of the trust declared as between BoA and BT as well as with the contract as between BoA and BoZ. I see no reason for the court not to assist BT or any reason why it should provide BoZ with a defence which BoZ does not have against BoA.

Rix LJ: . . .

ISSUE (3): DOES ARTICLE 12 PROHIBIT A DECLARATION OF TRUST IN RESPECT OF THE FRUITS OF THE FACILITY? . . .

That is a question of construction, and one on which the judge ultimately came to rule in favour of BoZ. Thus at para 54 of his judgment he expressed the functional and practical view that, if art 12.01(A) did not prohibit a declaration of trust, then its prohibition on assignment:

> would achieve very little. Any Bank could declare itself to be a trustee of the Asset for any third party which could then claim the Asset in, in substance, the same way as if it were an assignee,

(ie by making use of the *Vandepitte* procedure). And at para 73 he concluded, after a review of the authorities, that art 12.01(A) as a matter of construction ('the real key to this claim was the construction and effect of art 12.01(A)') did prohibit declarations of trust as well as assignments.

His reasoning at this point is succinct, but his ground, as I understand it, is that as the practical effect of the former was the same as the latter, ie to permit third parties, through the *Vandepitte* procedure, to come into direct relations with the obligor under a contract to which the third parties were strangers, therefore the original parties to the Facility must have intended, by their reference to assignment, to prohibit declarations of trust as well.

In my judgment, however, the question of construction must ultimately be kept separate from the different question of what effect will be given to the contractual term which prohibits an assignment and/or declaration of trust as the case may be. I accept that the practical effects which may (or may not) be achievable through the route of the *Vandepitte* procedure may enter as a background factor into the question of construction, ie the objectively understood intentions of the parties, but the questions are nevertheless distinct.

On the question of construction, then, there is in my judgment good authority for the proposition that a failed assignment may take effect as a declaration of trust between its immediate parties. This is certainly true so far as a declaration of trust which is limited to the *proceeds of a claim (or the fruits of a contract) when received*. The leading authority for this is *In re Turcan* (1888) 40 Ch D 5, 58 LJ Ch 101, 37 WR 70, as approved in *Linden Gardens* itself, where Lord Browne-Wilkinson said this (at 106F):

> As to the authorities, in *In re Turcan*, 40 ChD 5, a man effected an insurance policy which contained a term that it should not be assignable in any case whatever. He had previously covenanted with trustees to settle after-acquired property. The Court of Appeal held that although he could not assign the benefit of the policy so as to give the trustees the power to recover the money from the insurance company, he could validly make a declaration of trust of the proceeds, which required him to hand over such proceeds to the trustees.

That reflects Lord Browne-Wilkinson's acceptance of the second of Professor Goode's four possible interpretations of a prohibition of assignment, discussed as a 'question of the construction of the contract' at 104E/F, thus:

> (2) that the term precludes or invalidates any assignment by A to C (so as to entitle B to pay the debt to A) but not so as to preclude A from agreeing, as between himself and C, that he will account to C for what A receives from B: *In re Turcan* . . .

Similarly, but perhaps more broadly, Lord Browne-Wilkinson said (at 108D):

> a prohibition on assignment normally only invalidates the assignment as against the other party to the contract so as to prevent a transfer of the chose in action: in the absence of the clearest words it cannot operate to invalidate the contract as between the assignor and the assignee and even then it may be ineffective on the grounds of public policy.

Lord Browne-Wilkinson there appears to be contemplating a declaration of trust relating to a chose of action, and not merely proceeds when received.

[His Lordship noted that this broader approach had been applied by Lightman J, at first instance, in the *Don King* case, and continued:]

In these circumstances, my conclusions under this issue are as follows. The fact that a prohibition on assignment between A and B cannot allow a third party, C, as A's purported assignee, to bring a direct contractual claim against B is not in dispute. It was held in *Linden Gardens* to be the consequence of the contractual prohibition. As Lord Browne-Wilkinson said (at 108F):

> Therefore the existing authorities establish that an attempted assignment of contractual rights in breach of a contractual prohibition is ineffective to transfer such contractual rights. I regard the law as being satisfactorily settled in that sense. If the law were otherwise, it would defeat the legitimate commercial reason for inserting the contractual prohibition, viz,

to ensure that the original parties to the contract are not brought into direct contractual relations with third parties.

The ineffectiveness of the assignment in breach of a prohibition on assignment is understandable. It is not merely a matter of contract but of property. Although the would-be assignor has legal title to property in the form of a chose in action, he lacks the power, because of the terms on which the property is held, to transfer that property so as to entitle the transferee to exercise those contractual rights himself against the other party to the contract. However, he does not lack the power to render himself a trustee in equity of the property concerned. He would only do that if the prohibition on assignment extended as far as prohibiting a declaration of trust.

There is, however, nothing in art 12.01(A) to suggest that the limitations on assignment go as far as preventing the contract between would-be assignor and assignee taking effect as between those two as a declaration of trust, and a fortiori nothing to prevent a personal contract between them.

. . .

ISSUE (5): DOES USE OF THE *VANDEPITTE* PROCEDURE MEAN THAT BoA IS NOT TO BE REGARDED AS A CLAIMANT, OR IS IT OTHERWISE INEFFECTIVE OR ILLEGITIMATE TO USE THAT PROCEDURE TO REDUCE THE DEBT INTO POSSESSION? . . .

I would therefore consider that the effect of the *Vandepitte* procedure is that, although the trustee is nominally a Defendant, his real role as a party is to ensure that, through his presence, his legal right can be properly before the court for adjudication, just as though he was, as he should be if he is indeed a trustee for the Claimant, a Claimant himself. There is support for that in *Harmer v Armstrong* [1934] Ch 65 (CA) at 88, 103 LJ Ch 1, [1933] All ER Rep 778 where Lawrence LJ said:

> The right of a beneficiary in such a case as the present, however, is to enforce the agreement according to its tenor, that is to say in favour of the Defendant Armstrong, and not in favour of the Plaintiff beneficiaries.

In these circumstances, the ultimate question is whether, in circumstances where there has been a prohibition on assignment, and the legal owner declines himself to claim, the law will permit the beneficiary of a trust to make use of the *Vandepitte* procedure in order to reduce a debt into possession. This it seems to me is not itself a question of construction, but of legal principle.

In *Don King*, which was admittedly a case between trustee and beneficiary and not between the original parties to the contracts containing prohibitions on assignment, Lightman J and this court considered that the mere possibility that a declaration of trust might bring in its train the use or attempted use of the *Vandepitte* procedure against other parties in whose favour those prohibitions had been agreed did not prevent the arrangements between the litigants themselves from having effect. On the other hand the law would not permit the *Vandepitte* procedure to be used to curtail the protection for which the parties to a contract had stipulated by means of a prohibition of assignment.

Lightman J said (at 321C/D):

> (1) If one party wishes to protect himself against the other party declaring himself a trustee, and not merely against an assignment, he should expressly so provide. That has not been done in this case.
> (2) The applicable principles of trust law in this situation are the basic principles and those (and only those) whose rationale have application in this commercial context: see *Target Holdings Ltd v Redferns* [1996] AC 421, 436. The courts will accordingly be astute to

disallow use of the procedural short-cut sanctioned in the *Vandepitte* case [1933] AC 70 in a commercial context where it has no proper place. A beneficiary cannot be allowed to abrogate the fullest protection that the parties to the contract have secured for themselves under the terms of the contract from intrusion into their contractual relations by third parties.

In this court *Morritt LJ* said (at 335H/336C, para 26):

In that case [*In re Turcan*], as the House of Lords considered in *Linden Gardens Trust Ltd v Lenesta Sludge Disposals Ltd* [1994] 1 AC 85, 106, the court gave effect to the intention of the parties by means of a declaration of trust. But, it is objected, the existence of such a trust would enable one partner to interfere in the management of the personal contract made by a third party with the other partner. I do not agree. The other partner cannot insist on rendering vicarious performance of the personal obligations arising under the contract. Rules and procedures designed to enable a beneficiary to sue in respect of a contract held in trust for him would not be applied so as to jeopardise the trust property. As Lord Browne-Wilkinson observed in *Target Holdings Ltd v Redferns* [1996] AC 421, 435:

> in my judgment it is in any event wrong to lift wholesale the detailed rules developed in the context of traditional trusts and then seek to apply them to trusts of quite a different kind. In the modern world the trust has become a valuable device in commercial and financial dealings. The fundamental principles of equity apply as much to such trusts as they do to the traditional trusts in relation to which those principles were originally formulated. But in my judgment it is important, if the trust is not to be rendered commercially useless, to distinguish between the basic principles of trust law and those specialist rules developed in relation to traditional trusts which are applicable only to such trusts and the rationale of which has no application to trusts of quite a different kind.

It is possible to read these passages as saying that the *Vandepitte* procedure has no place in the commercial sphere. That, however, would not accord with my understanding of what Lightman J and Morritt LJ were saying. It would also be inconsistent with established lines of cases in the commercial field, such as the trust found in a charterparty in favour of the shipbroker. I understand these passages as saying that the law would not permit rules and procedures, such as the *Vandepitte* procedure, to be misused in the commercial context where inappropriate. Lightman J appears to have particularly in mind contractual stipulations against intrusion into the business affairs of the original contractual parties, whereas Morritt LJ seems to be focusing on personal obligations. The contracts in *Don King* were of both kinds: many had prohibition of assignment clauses, but all of them were contracts of a personal kind, for they concerned the management of boxers.

An example of the courts being cautious in certain circumstances about the use of the *Vandepitte* procedure may be found in *Harmer v Armstrong* [1934] Ch 65 at 88/89.

. . .

What is a court to do in such circumstances? It seems to me that there is a tension between (a) the interests of those whose contracts, either because they are of an inherently personal nature or because of agreed restrictions on alienability, should not readily be intruded upon by strangers to them, (b) the interests of those who seek to arrange their affairs on the basis of holding property in trust for others, and (c) the public interest, which is concerned to see that contracts are performed, that the beneficiaries of trusts are protected, and that financial assets are not too readily made inalienable especially where markets regularly provide liquidity for the trading of them. If a prohibition on assignment carried all before it, destroying all alienability whatever the circumstances, even to the extent of making it impossible for beneficial interests to be protected in any circumstances in the absence of the legal owner as a formal Claimant, it seems to me that the public interest in freedom of contract and the freedom of markets could be severely prejudiced.

Some illustrations can be given. In *Linden Gardens* at 107/108 the case of *Tom Shaw and Co v Moss Empires Ltd* (1908) 25 TLR 190 was considered. Lord Browne-Wilkinson said:

> In the *Tom Shaw* case an actor, B, was engaged by Moss Empires under a contract which prohibited the assignment of his salary. B assigned 10% of his salary to his agent, Tom Shaw. Tom Shaw sued Moss Empires for 10% of the salary joining B as Second Defendant. Moss Empires agreed to pay the 10% of the salary to Tom Shaw or B as the court might decide ie in effect it interpleaded. Darling J held, at p 191, that the prohibition on assignment was ineffective: it could 'no more operate to invalidate the assignment than it could interfere with the laws of gravitation'. He gave judgment for the Plaintiffs against both B and Moss Empires, ordering B to pay the costs but making no order for costs against Moss Empires.
>
> The case is inadequately reported and it is hard to discover exactly what it decides. Given that both B and Moss Empires were parties and Moss Empires was in effect interpleading, it may be that the words I have quoted merely indicate that as between the assignor, B, and the assignee Tom Shaw, the prohibition contained in the contract between B and Moss Empires could not invalidate B's liability to account to Tom Shaw for the moneys when received and that, since B was a party, payment direct to Tom Shaw was ordered. This view is supported by the fact that no order for costs was made against Moss Empires. If this is the right view of the case, it is unexceptionable: a prohibition on assignment normally only invalidates the assignment as against the other party to the contract so as to prevent a transfer of the chose in action: in the absence of the clearest words it cannot operate to invalidate the contract as between the assignor and the assignee and even then it may be ineffective on the ground of public policy. If on the other hand Darling J purported to hold that the contractual prohibition was ineffective to prevent B's contractual rights against Moss Empires being transferred to Tom Shaw, it is inconsistent with authority and was wrongly decided.

I have already cited most of the penultimate sentence of that passage out of its context (at para 31 above).

What is going on here? The contract concerned was certainly a personal one, akin to a contract for the writing of a book, but the salary, like the fee for the book, was something separate, the fruits of the contract. However, there was an express prohibition on assignment of those fruits. There was nevertheless a purported assignment, which took effect only as a declaration of trust to account for the moneys when received. Only the would-be assignee, the beneficiary of that trust, sued, but he adopted the *Vandepitte* procedure and joined the would-be assignor, the actor, as Second Defendant. Moss Empires did not mind whom it paid, and in effect interpleaded. It had no defence in substance, other than the prohibition on assignment. That point was taken by the actor, who presumably wished to receive the assigned salary himself. The case therefore illustrates the operation of the *Vandepitte* procedure, despite a failed assignment, on the basis of a declaration of trust and suit by the beneficiary. Would it have made any difference if Moss Empires had not effectively interpleaded? That is possible, on the ground that Moss Empires thereby waived the prohibition in its favour. However, another way of looking at the matter is that in any event the actor, although Defendant, was treated as a Claimant. It would be very unattractive (in the absence of a prohibition on a declaration of trust) if a party who owed his agent a percentage of his earnings, and made a declaration of trust in his favour as security, could prevent his agent recovering simply by declining to claim.

Another example is illustrated by the two cases considered by the House of Lords under the report in *Linden Gardens*. Both concerned construction contracts containing prohibitions on assignment. In the first case, *Linden Gardens* itself, the would-be assignor was not joined as a Defendant, and the assignee Claimant therefore lost (at 109C). In the second case, *St Martins*

Property Corporation Ltd v Sir Robert McAlpine Ltd, both the assignor and the assignee claimed, being sister companies within the same group. There was therefore no problem about the title to sue, which remained in the assignor company (at 109F). The main issue there, however, was whether that company had suffered any more than nominal damages, since the loss had been suffered by the assignee company which, because of the prohibition on assignment, lacked its own cause of action. However, the House of Lords was unwilling for the claim to disappear in this way into a black hole, and found an analysis, based on the concept that the assignor company entered into the contract for the benefit of future third parties to whom the property development had been sold and who might thus suffer from defective performance of the contract, which enabled the assignor to recover substantial damages for the assignee. Justice was done, but, if the case was looked at in an overall way, it could be said that the law permitted the problems of a stranger assignee to intrude into the contractual relationship despite the prohibition of assignment. If therefore a purely functional approach had been adopted, on the basis that the assignor could only recover for its own loss, the claim would have failed despite the presence of the assignor as Claimant. In such circumstances, would it have mattered if the assignor and assignee companies had not been in the same group, but in different enterprises, so that in practical terms the assignee would have been the sole Claimant and the assignor would have been joined under the *Vandepitte* procedure as a Second Defendant? I think not.

A third example is an agency contract under which the agent earns commission. Such a contract is both a personal contract and one in which a non-assignment clause is often found, for good commercial reasons. While the contract is on foot it would be entirely understandable that no stranger to that contract should, through assignment, be permitted to intrude upon it. However, suppose the agent becomes insolvent and as a result the contract is brought to an end. The relationship is over, as is any ongoing performance of the contract. However, there is outstanding commission due to the agent. The liquidator has no interest in pursuing a claim he does not understand. He sells the claim to the former managers of the insolvent agent, who have formed a new company. The assignee brings a claim against the debtor principal, joining the liquidator as Defendant. Can the debtor say that he is to answer only if the liquidator is a Claimant rather than a Defendant? That is most unattractive. See *Explora Group plc v Hesco Bastion Ltd* [2005] EWCA Civ 646.

A fourth example of a somewhat different nature is that of the subrogated insurer who sues in his insured's name. If he sues under a contract containing a non-assignment clause, he will not be affected by it. The claim is that of the insured, and there has been no assignment. However, functionally the insured has been paid and has no interest in the claim, and the litigation is conducted entirely by the underwriter for his own benefit, who thus intrudes on his insured's contract with the Defendant. No one would suggest, however, that the non-assignment clause should be given effect because the law of subrogation functionally achieves a result whereby a stranger to the contract can intrude on it.

A closely related example is that of factored invoices. A non-assignment clause will create difficulties for the factoring company. However, it would be highly undesirable if customers could totally prevent their suppliers from factoring their book debts by the device of a non-assignment clause. If the supplier has no interest in suing and has to be joined as a Defendant, is that case crucially different from the case where the supplier is prevailed upon to sue together with the factoring company?

For these reasons, if I had decided issue (1) in favour of finding that BoA had a good legal title to the debt, I would, on balance, have been in favour of saying that, on the facts of this case as far as they appear and on the submissions we have heard, the *Vandepitte* procedure could be used to recover into BoA's possession, for the benefit of BT, a debt which on that hypothesis would have been an acknowledged debt owned by BoA. As it is, I do not have to make a final decision on this ultimate issue. That is perhaps just as well, as the argument on appeal has both far outstripped the evidence with which the parties had come to court in the first place and at the same time failed to focus on the particular facts before the court. Thus we know little about the real considerations which have affected the relationships in this case. Moreover, there was no immediate relationship between BoA and BT to support the declaration of trust, which does not arise out of a failed assignment directly between BoA and BT. It might therefore have been said that that declaration was merely a device to bring before the court, at the instance of BT, a claim which BoA would otherwise have allowed to become time-barred. On that hypothesis, I would be doubtful that equity would enforce the trust.

Hooper LJ: . . . I start with an example. D enters into a contract with A, giving A certain benefits. D agrees with A that A can assign the benefits to anyone other than C. He distrusts C and wants to have nothing to do with him. Notwithstanding this, A assigns the benefits to C. A declines to sue D. C then invokes the *Vandepitte* procedure and brings an action against A and D. Thus D is facing C across the court—something which D had insisted should not happen. I would find it surprising if English law permits this to happen. I would find it surprising if the only way that D could have prevented this happening was by including a further term in his contract with A. I accept that it might gladden the heart of lawyers if the law is that D could have prevented this happening by the inclusion (on legal advice) of a further term in his contract with A.

This example is not this case, but it has similarities. As Langley J said, it is not hard to fathom the commercial realities of a restricted assignment clause such as that found in art 12. In para 10, he wrote:

> Any covenant against or restrictive of assignment is intended to ensure that the original parties to the contract are not brought into direct contractual relations with third parties save to any extent expressly permitted by the covenant. Any borrower, but particularly a central bank, may be concerned to ensure that its affairs and obligations are known and owed to and only enforceable by established and authorised institutions.

. . .

Whilst I agree with Rix LJ (para 90) that the art 12.01(A) limitations on assignment do not prevent BoA from creating a declaration of trust in favour of BT (as it purported to do by the documents set out by Waller LJ at paras 22 and following), I disagree with the proposition which finds favour with Waller LJ (and with Rix LJ 'on balance'), that the terms of art 12.01(A) permit BT to bring the claim against BoZ. The clause prevents an assignment to a body such as BT and must therefore be construed so as to prevent BT from enforcing the debt directly against BoZ. The clause cannot be circumvented by the device of a declaration of trust and the use of the *Vandepitte* procedure. To require those who draft contracts of this kind to take steps to avoid the device used by BoA and BT to get round the non-assignment clause would be unduly onerous and, as I have said, would only benefit lawyers.

NOTES

1. How does the reasoning in *Barbados Trust Co* suggest that a legal assignment may be made of a chose in action the assignability of which is restricted by the terms of the contract from which it arises? The court gave close consideration to the requirement of consent expressed in the contract. However, they did not consider (and were not required to consider) a further argument: that obtaining consent would merely make the chose in action assignable in equity; a legal assignment could only occur if the requirements of s 136 of the Law of Property Act 1925 were then also complied with: Turner [2008] LMCLQ 306.

The interaction of the requirements of the contract and the requirements of the statute will be critically important in some cases.

2. Waller LJ considered what would have been the position had he been wrong and art 12.01(A) had prohibited both an assignment and a declaration of trust. He declared (at [45]) that the *Vandepitte* procedure was merely a procedural shortcut allowing the beneficiary to obtain what he was entitled to when the trustee refused to act, thereby avoiding unnecessary litigation under which the trustee would be forced to sue followed by an action under which the trustee sued. The beneficiary would be the actual claimant but it would be as if the trustee were the claimant seeking to recover that which was due in law and which would then be held by the trustee for the beneficiary. Crucially, his Lordship considered that there would be no interference by the beneficiary, and that the beneficiary would not be given rights to which he was not already entitled (see [29] and [45]). Professor Tolhurst, writing in [2007] LMCLQ 278, acknowledges that 'there is doctrinal force in the approach of Waller LJ' but goes on to make the pragmatic observation that 'by recognizing a declaration of trust, which is operational before the fruits of the contract are in the hands of the trustee, then the [debtor] by virtue of the *Vandepitte* procedure becomes, to some extent, subject to the whims of a third party, which is what the prohibition is designed to prevent. The ensuing litigation is not driven by the trustee, even though it may be said that it is the trustee's claim, as it is the legal title holder.' See also PG Turner [2008] CLJ 23.

3. The diversity of the opinions expressed in the *Don King* and *Barbados Trust Co* cases has left uncertainty over some basic questions as to the operation of clauses that restrict the assignability of choses in action: see J Edelman and S Elliott (2015) 131 LQR 228; G Tolhurst and J Carter [2014] CLJ 405; M Bridge (2016) 132 LQR 437.

5 WRITING

Writing is of differing importance according to whether an assignment of a chose in action is to be equitable or is to pass a legal title in the chose to the assignee. In this section, the exceptional rules developed by the common law to allow legal assignment in particular cases—as to Crown debts, bills of exchange, and promissory notes—will be put to one side. The discussion will concentrate exclusively on legal choses in action which, before the courts of common law and equity were administratively fused into the Supreme Court of Judicature in 1875, were recognised as assignable in a court of equity but not in a court of common law.

(a) The choice between equitable and legal assignment

From the development of the law, it follows that commercial parties (or the legal advisors) may wish to consider whether to attempt an equitable assignment or a legal assignment. The decision may seem obvious. To pass legal title in a chose is to pass something greater than a title in equity. After a legal assignment, the assignee may demand performance directly from the debtor or obligor (against whom the assigned chose in action is enforceable) and do so, in or out of litigation, without the law requiring the assignor to be involved. After an equitable assignment, in contrast, the assignor retains the legal title to the chose in action. In order to sue the obligor to judgment, the assignee must therefore join the assignor—who, legally, still owns the assigned chose in action—to the proceedings.

Though equitable assignments may have shortcomings, an assignor and an assignee may prefer their assignment to lie in equity only. They may not wish to establish a direct relationship between the obligor and the assignee. It may be more efficient or otherwise preferable that the debtor continue to deal with the assignor, as where an assignor bank wishes to continue to service its relationship with borrowers who are its customers—rather than to confuse its customers by requiring them to pay a third party assignee, to the possible prejudice of bank–customer relations.

(b) Equitable assignment

Equitable assignments are straightforward to make. An equitable assignment of a legal chose in action need not be in writing, nor in any particular form. In *Phelps v Spon-Smith & Co* [2001] BPIR 326 at [34], Mr Peter Whiteman QC, sitting as a deputy High Court judge, summarised the position as follows:

> It is well established that it is not necessary for an equitable assignment to follow any particular form. What is necessary, however, is that there should be an intention to assign, that the subject-matter of the assignment should be so described as to be capable of being identified at the time of the alleged assignment and that there should be some act by the assignor showing that he is transferring the chose in action to the (alleged) assignee.

The deputy judge called for a 'broad approach' to what constitutes such an 'act' and gave as examples 'a letter or an oral statement'. Nonetheless, he did stress that 'there must be an "act" which establishes clearly the nature of the transaction'. As Lord Macnaghten said in the classic case, *William Brandt's Sons & Co v Dunlop Rubber Co Ltd* [1905] AC 454 at 462, the assignment 'may be couched in the language of command. It may be a courteous request. It may assume the form of mere permission. The language is immaterial if the meaning is plain.' On the other hand—and although assignment of equitable choses in action are outside the scope of this book—an equitable assignment of an equitable chose in action must be in writing if it falls within s 53(1)(c) of the Law of Property Act 1925.

(c) Legal assignment

Until legislation was made, legal assignments of choses in action were not possible outside the narrow exceptions for Crown debts, bills of exchange, and the like. The Policies of Marine Assurance Act 1868 provides for legal assignment of marine insurance policies. However, more general provision for legal assignment was to wait until 1875, when s 25(6) of the Supreme Court of Judicature Act 1873 gained force. That section provided in general terms for the assignment of choses in action at law. It was repealed and substantially re-enacted by s 136 of the Law of Property Act 1925. An assignment under s 136 is called a 'statutory' or 'legal' assignment and it will pass the legal right to the chose in action. If there is a legal assignment of a legal or equitable chose in action the assignee may bring an action to enforce the chose in his own name and he does not have to join the assignor as a party to the action.

> (1) Any absolute assignment by writing under the hand of the assignor (not purporting to be by way of charge only) of any debt or other legal thing in action, of which express notice in writing has been given to the debtor, trustee or other person from whom the assignor would

have been entitled to claim such debt or thing in action, is effectual in law (subject to equities having priority over the right of the assignee) to pass and transfer from the date of such notice—

(a) the legal right to such debt or thing in action;

(b) all legal and other remedies for the same; and

(c) the power to give a good discharge for the same without the concurrence of the assignor:

Provided that, if the debtor, trustee or other person liable in respect of such debt or thing in action has notice—

(a) that the assignment is disputed by the assignor or any person claiming under him; or

(b) of any other opposing or conflicting claims to such debt or thing in action;

he may, if he thinks fit, either call upon the persons making claim thereto to interplead concerning the same, or pay the debt or other thing in action into court under the provisions of the Trustee Act 1925.

The advantages of legal assignment may therefore be obtained only where a relevant assignment 'by writing under the hand of the assignor' is made, and where 'express notice in writing has been given'. The topic of notice will be considered in the following section. The requirement that an assignment—or, strictly, an instrument *of* assignment—be in writing under the hand of the assignor is uncomplicated. The assignor himself must sign the assignment; it is not sufficient for someone other than the assignor to sign in the assignor's name even if that other person is the assignor's agent signing with the assignor's authority: *Technocrats International Inc v Fredic Ltd* [2004] EWHC 692 (QB) at [53]. In that case, Field J held there to be no assignment under s 136 where the assignor's wife signed an assignment in his name and with his authority, though there was an equitable assignment as the husband's intention to assign was sufficiently manifest.

However, a rather full body of case law has grown in relation to this question: which assignments will be legal assignments when the writing required by s 136 is made?

(i) Selected equitable assignments may be converted into legal assignments

It will be recalled that, as Mance LJ put it in *Raiffeisen Zentralbank Osterreich AG v Five Star General Trading LLC* [2001] EWCA Civ 68, [2001] QB 825 at [62], 'Prior to the … Supreme Court of Judicature Act 1873 … choses or things in action were assignable if at all only in equity. The statute provisions of … section 136 of the 1925 Act must be seen against the background.' Professor Tolhurst has suggested that the cases betray a division between those which see the legislation as operating 'procedurally' and those which see the legislation as having a 'substantive' operation: G Tolhurst, *The Assignment of Contractual Rights* (2nd edn, 2016), Ch 5. Whatever the resolution of that debate, there are several statements in the cases to indicate that the legislation appears to operate by allowing selected equitable assignments to be converted into legal assignments. For instance, in the *Five Star General Trading* case, Mance LJ said (at [62]) that '[t]he operation of section 136 depends upon there *having been* an "absolute assignment" of a "debt or other legal thing in action" and upon express notice in writing being given to (in this case) the insurers' (emphasis added); see also *Snell's Equity* (32nd edn, 2015), para 3–012.

In the events of the real world, there may be little separation in time between the making of an equitable assignment and—assuming all other requirements are met—its conversion into a legal assignment by giving written notice. However, to understand the operation of the section, it is necessary to appreciate that it operates upon selected equitable assignments and converts those into legal assignments by attaching to them the features set out in s 136—for example, by giving the legal assignee the power to give the debtor a good discharge for its payment of the assigned debt. It follows, too, that—as Lord Macnaghten said in *William Brandt's* case (at 461), 'The statute does not forbid or destroy equitable assignments or impair their efficacy in the slightest degree.' But except for the selected forms of assignment specified in s 136, all other equitable assignments of legal choses in action will lie only in equity: they cannot be 'converted' into legal assignments under the section.

(ii) Absolute assignment

Absolute assignments made in equity come within the statute. An absolute assignment is one by which the assignor has transferred his entire interest in the chose to the assignee. However, as the next case shows, the courts have construed 'absolute assignment' in s 136 mindful of the consequences a wide construction of the phrase would have on debtors.

Durham Bros v Robertson
[1898] 1 QB 765, Court of Appeal

Under the terms of a building contract building contractors agreed to build certain houses for Robertson and take a lease of them. The contract also gave the contractors the option of paying an increased ground rent in consideration of which they were to receive from Robertson a sum of £1,080. Later the contractors purported to assign the £1,080 to the plaintiffs by letter in the following terms: 'In consideration of money advanced from time to time we hereby charge the sum of £1,080, being the agreed price for £60 per annum ground-rent which will become due to us from John Robertson . . . on the completion of the above buildings as security for the advances, and we hereby assign our interest in the above-named sum until the money with added interest be repaid to you.' The plaintiffs gave notice of the assignment to Robertson and an action was started by them to recover the sum due. Robertson claimed that there had not been a valid assignment under s 25(6) of the Judicature Act 1873 (now s 136 of the Law of Property Act 1925). The Court of Appeal agreed with him.

Chitty LJ: . . . To bring a case within the sub-section transferring the legal right to sue for the debt and empowering the assignee to give a good discharge for the debt, there must be (in the language of the sub-section) an absolute assignment not purporting to be by way of charge only. It is requisite that the assignment should be, or at all events purport to be, absolute, but it will not suffice if the assignment purport to be by way of charge only. It is plain that every equitable assignment in the wide sense of the term as used in equity is not within the enactment. As the enactment requires that the assignment should be absolute, the question arose whether a mortgage, in the proper sense of the term, and as now generally understood, was within the enactment. In *Tancred v Delagoa Bay and East Africa Rly Co* ((1889) 23 QBD 239) there was an assignment of the debt to secure advances with a proviso for redemption and reassignment upon repayment. It was there held by the Divisional Court (disapproving of a decision in *National Provincial Bank v Harle* ((1881) 6 QBD 626), that such a mortgage fell within the enactment. It appears to me that the decision of the Divisional Court was quite right. The assignment of the debt was absolute: it purported to pass the entire interest of the assignor in the debt to the mortgagee, and it was not an assignment purporting to be by way of charge only. The mortgagor-assignor had a right to redeem, and on repayment of the advances a right to have the assigned debt reassigned to him. Notice of the reassignment pursuant to the sub-section would be given to the original debtor, and he would thus know with certainty in whom the legal right to sue him was vested. I think that the principle of the decision ought not to be confined to the case where there is an express provision for reassignment. Where there is an absolute assignment of the debt, but by way of security, equity would imply a right to a reassignment on redemption, and the sub-section would apply to the case of such an absolute assignment. In a well-known judgment of the Exchequer Chamber in *Halliday v Holgate* ((1868) LR 3 Exch 299), the late Willes J, in delivering the judgment of the Court, distinguished between lien, pledge, and mortgage, and spoke of a mortgage as passing the property out and out. A mortgage is not mentioned in the enactment; but where there is an absolute assignment of the debt, the limiting words as to a charge only are not sufficient to exclude a mortgage . . .

The assignment before us complies with all the terms of the enactment save one, which is essential: it is not an absolute but a conditional assignment. The commonest and most familiar instance of a conditional assurance is an assurance until JS shall return from Rome. The repayment of the money advanced is an uncertain event, and makes the assignment conditional. Where the Act applies it does not leave the original debtor in uncertainty as to the person to whom the legal right is transferred; it does not involve him in any question as to the state of the accounts between the mortgagor and the mortgagee. The legal right is transferred, and is vested in the assignee. There is no machinery provided by the Act for the reverter of the legal right to the assignor dependent on the performance of a condition; the only method within the provisions of the Act for revesting in the assignor the legal right is by a retransfer to the assignor followed by a notice in writing to the debtor, as in the case of the first transfer of the right. The question is not one of mere technicality or of form: it is one of substance, relating to the protection of the original debtor and placing him in an assured position.

It is necessary to refer to *Brice v Bannister* ((1878) 3 QBD 569). In that case there was an assignment of £100 out of money due or to become due to the assignor under a contract to build a ship, with an express power to give a good discharge to the debtor. Lord Coleridge CJ held that the assignment was within the 25th section. The Court of Appeal decided the case quite apart from the Act. Cotton LJ expressly decided the case on the ground of equitable assignment. That is shewn by the opening sentence of his judgment, where he says that the letter was a good equitable assignment. Bramwell LJ reluctantly assented to this view. Brett LJ dissented, but on general principles. So soon as it was ascertained that there was a good equitable assignment, with power to give a discharge, it became unnecessary to consider whether it fell within the Act or not. In *Ex p Nichols* ((1883) 22 Ch D 782 at 787) the present Master of the Rolls, referring to this decision, treated the assignment as an equitable assignment. He said that the decision was founded on the principle that the right of an equitable assignment of a debt cannot be defeated by a voluntary payment by the debtor to the assignor. The decision of Lord Coleridge CJ in *Brice v Bannister*, that the case fell within the 25th section, appears to me to be open to question. The assignment purported to be by way of charge only. It was a direction to pay the £100 out of money due or to become due. No doubt it purported to be a charge of an unredeemable sum of £100; but still it was a charge. The section speaks of an absolute assignment of any debt or other chose in action. It does not say 'or any part of a debt or chose in action.' It appears to me as at present advised to be questionable whether an assignment of part of an entire debt is within the enactment. If it be, it would seem to leave it in the power of the original creditor to split up the single legal cause of action for the debt into as many separate legal causes of action as he might think fit. However, it is not necessary to decide the point in the present case, and I leave it open for future consideration.

[**AL Smith** and **Collins LJJ** concurred.]

NOTES

1.   Assignment by way of security for a debt can be absolute. In *Burlinson v Hall* (1884) 12 QBD 347, DC, debts were assigned to the plaintiff on trust that he should receive them and out of them pay himself a sum due to him from the assignor, and pay the surplus to the assignor. Day J stated:

> I think this is an 'absolute assignment.' It is said that it is an assignment of a security for payment of the debt, and that the moment that purpose is answered the surplus will belong to the assignee. But still the assignment is, in terms, absolute. Not indeed absolute as a sale, but absolute as contradistinguished from conditional, an assignment giving a title there and then. This deed does so. True, if the debt due from the assignor were paid off, the assignor might be entitled to have the subject-matter of the assignment re-assigned to him. But the right of the assignee to whom it is assigned is absolute. No person can control him in dealing as he thinks fit with that which was assigned to him.

The same point was made by the Court of Appeal in *Bovis International Inc v Circle Ltd Partnership* (1995) 49 Con LR 12, where Millett LJ stated (at 29): 'an assignment does not cease to be absolute merely because it is given by way of security and is subject to an express or implied obligation to reassign on redemption'.

2.   On its face, the assignment in *Durham Bros* was absolute: although the assignor was automatically to regain title to the assigned chose in action once the secured debt was discharged, the entirety of the title to the chose had been assigned to the assignee. Why, according to the Court of Appeal, would the assignment have been come within s 136 if all the facts were the same except that the assignee was to reassign the assigned debt, rather than the chose reverting automatically to the original assignor? The difference probably has to be explained in terms of inconvenience. Where an absolute assignment occurs under s 136, the debtor is then only concerned with the assignee's rights and can pay the assignee without fear of the assignor later asserting rights in the chose against him. However, if the chose in action has reverted to the original assignor without the debtor's knowledge, then the debtor is not safe in paying the assignee: that would be inconvenient. When a statute can be construed in two ways, one of which gives rise to inconvenience, courts often presume that Parliament intended the construction whose effects are the more convenient. The Court of Appeal in *Durham Bros* effectively applied that principle. That is, the judges thought that, because Parliament would not have intended debtors and obligors to be left worse off by s 136, the apparently absolute assignment in that case was, nevertheless, not an absolute assignment within the meaning of what is now s 136.

3.   An assignment of the unpaid balance of a debt can be assigned under the statute: *Harding v Harding* (1886) 17 QBD 442. That is distinguishable from a partial assignment in that the latter is intended to pass only part of the right to payment. To assign the right to payment of an unpaid balance, however, is to assign not only part of a right.

(iii) Assignments by way of charge

Section 136 expressly contrasts absolute assignments and those purporting to be by way of charge only. The latter may take effect in equity but fall outside s 136. The difference was expressed by Denman J in *Trancred v Delagoa Bay and East Africa Rly Co* (1889) 23 QBD 239 at 239, DC: 'a document given "by way of charge" is not one which absolutely transfers the property with a condition for re-conveyance, but is a document which only gives a right to payment out of a particular fund or particular property, without transferring that fund or property'.

Hughes v Pump House Hotel Co Ltd
[1902] 2 KB 190, Court of Appeal

Hughes, a building contractor, assigned to his bank all monies due or to become due under a building contract with the defendants. The assignment stated that it was '[i]n consideration of [the bank] continuing a bank account with [Hughes] . . . and by way of continuing security to [the bank] for all moneys due or to become due to [the bank] from [Hughes]'. Notice of the assignment was given to the defendants. Subsequently, Hughes brought an action against the defendants to recover sums due under the building contract. On a preliminary issue, Wright J held that the assignment was not absolute but by way of charge only. The defendants appealed.

Mathew LJ: . . . In every case of this kind, all the terms of the instrument must be considered; and, whatever may be the phraseology adopted in some particular part of it, if, on consideration of the whole instrument, it is clear that the intention was to give a charge only, then the action must be in the name of the assignor; while, on the other hand, if it is clear from the instrument as a whole that the intention was to pass all the rights of the assignor in the debt or chose in action to the assignee, then the case will come within s 25, and the action must be brought in the name of the assignee . . . What, then, is the effect of the assignment? It seems to me clear from its terms that the intention was to pass to the assignees complete control of all moneys payable under the building contract, and to put them for all purposes in the position of the assignor with regard to those moneys. That being so, I think, unless there be some difficulty created by the decisions on the subject, this instrument may be properly described as an absolute assignment, because it is one under which all the rights of the assignor in respect of the moneys payable under the building contract were intended to pass to the assignees, and not one which purports to be by way of charge only. The learned judge appears to have been of opinion that the assignment was not absolute, but purported to be by way of charge only, because the object was that it should be a continuing security for such amount as might from time to time be due from the assignor to the assignees. But, if that were the true criterion, it might equally well be argued that a mortgage is not an absolute assignment, because under a mortgage it may become necessary to take an account in order to ascertain how much is due; but, though a mortgage is only a security for the amount which may be due, it is nevertheless an absolute assignment because the whole right of the mortgagor in the estate passes to the mortgagee.

Cozens-Hardy LJ: . . . If, on the construction of the document, it appears to be an absolute assignment, though subject to an equity of redemption, express or implied, it cannot in my opinion be material to consider what was the consideration for the assignment, or whether the security was for a fixed and definite sum, or for a current account. In either case the debtor can safely pay the assignee, and he is not concerned to inquire into the state of the accounts between the assignor and the assignee: nor does it matter that the assignee has obtained a power of attorney, and a covenant for further assurance from the assignor. Both these elements were found in *Burlinson v Hall* ((1884) 12 QBD 347). The real question, and, in my opinion, the only question, is this: Does the instrument purport to be by way of charge only? It remains to apply these principles to the document of March 7, 1901. In my opinion that document is an absolute assignment, and does not purport to be by way of charge only. It assigns all moneys due or to become due under the contract. It follows that the plaintiff, Hughes, has no right of action, and that the order of Wright J must be discharged.

NOTE

Where an assignment is equitable because it operates by way of charge only, the assignor must be joined as a party to the action to enforce the chose.

(iv) Partial assignments

Equity permits part of a debt to be assigned, but partial assignments fall outside s 136 of the Law of Property Act 1925: *Re Steel Wing Co* [1921] 1 Ch 349 at 354; *Williams v Atlantic Assurance Co* [1933] 1 KB 81 at 100; *Deposit Protection Board v Dalia* [1994] 2 AC 367 at 392; *Raiffeisen Zentralbank Osterreich AG v Five Star General Trading LLC* [2001] EWCA Civ 68, [2001] QB 825 at [60], [75]. The distinction between partial assignments and charges is narrow where the chose in action is a debt. If the creditor assigns part of the debt by way of security, the creditor will retain an equity of redemption and the assignee—the grantee of the security—will be satisfied, if the security requires to be enforced, by receiving payment from the fund paid or payable by the debtor. But the same is true if the creditor grants a charge over the debt! Nevertheless, the distinction between charges and partial assignments is real outside that peculiar situation. An assignor may assign part of a debt outright; that is, other than by way of security.

Oddly, when the cases have explained that partial assignments are outside s 136, they have sometimes been put beyond the reach of s 136 by the words 'not purporting to be by way of charge only' (eg *Durham Bros v Robertson* [1898] 1 QB 765 at 769). Since partial assignments are not necessarily by way of charge, it would appear to be more sound to say that partial assignments are not 'absolute' within the special meaning of that term as used in s 136.

The suggestion that partial assignments are outside s 136, not because they are charges, but because they are not 'absolute' assignments, appears to be consistent especially with the reasoning in *Durham Bros v Robertson*. The Court of Appeal there explained that a debtor would be prejudiced if the creditor could split up the debt any number of times and thereby expose the debtor to numerous actions at common law by the assignees of the various parts (*Durham Bros v Robertson* [1898] 1 QB 765 at 774). There could be conflicting decisions if the existence and amount of the debt were in dispute (*Re Steel Wing Co*, above, at 357). These risks do not arise from partial assignments in equity, where the assignee cannot sue for that part of the debt which has been assigned without joining the assignor. Nor, in equity, can the assignor sue for the balance without joining the assignee (*Walter & Sullivan Ltd v J Murphy & Sons Ltd* [1955] 2 QB 584). It is not apparent that these matters were grappled with by the Court of Appeal in its account of partial assignment in *Kapoor v National Westminster Bank plc* [2011] EWCA Civ 1083, [2012] 1 All ER 1201; see PG Turner [2012] CLJ 270.

(v) Equitable choses under s 136

It has been said that s 136 (like s 25(6) of the Judicature Act 1873 before it) applies not only to legal choses in action, but also to equitable choses in action. This view has been attributed to the judgment of Channell J in the following case.

Torkington v Magee
[1902] 2 KB 427, Divisional Court

Magee contracted with Rayner to sell him a reversionary interest in certain funds under a settlement. Rayner by deed assigned his interest in the contract to Torkington and notice in writing of the assignment was given to Magee. Torkington alleged that Magee had broken the contract and brought an action for damages, as assignee, in his own name. The issue before Channell J was whether the executory contract of purchase of the reversionary interest was assignable under s 25 of the Judicature Act 1873 as a 'legal chose in action' (now a 'legal thing in action' in s 136 of the Law of Property Act 1925).

> **Channell J:** . . . We have, therefore, to consider the meaning of the expression 'other legal chose in action' in sub-s 6 of s 25 of the Judicature Act 1873. In order to arrive at this meaning, I think it necessary to consider what is the object of the Act, and of the particular section of the Act in which the words are to be found. The Act provided for the amalgamation of the then existing superior Courts of Law and Equity with a view to the administration in the new Court of one system of law in place of the two systems previously known as Law and Equity, and the general scope of the Act was to enable a suitor to obtain by one proceeding in one Court the same ultimate result as he would previously have obtained either by having selected the right Court, as to which there frequently was a difficulty, or after having been to two Courts in succession, which in some cases he had to do under the old system. The 25th section provided what was to be the rule in future in cases where previously the two systems differed . . . 'Chose in action' is a known legal expression used to describe all personal rights of property which can only be claimed or enforced by action, and not by taking physical possession. It is an expression large enough to include rights which it can hardly have been intended should be assignable by virtue of the sub-section in question, as, for instance, shares, which can only be transferred as provided by the Companies Acts. It is probably necessary, therefore, to put some limit upon the generality of the words; . . . I think the words 'debt or other legal chose in action' mean 'debt or right which the common law looks on as not assignable by reason of its being a chose in action, but which a Court of Equity deals with as being assignable.' That is the point of difference or variance between the rules of equity and common law which it is intended to deal with by this sub-section. Further, by the words of the sub-section itself the assignment is to be effectual in law, subject to all the equities which would have been entitled to priority over the rights of the assignee if this Act had not been passed. This seems to mean that the cases dealt with are cases where the assignee had some right before the Act—that is to say, where the right of the assignee had previously been recognised by a Court of Equity . . . Now, the question we have to consider in the present case is whether an executory contract of purchase under which each party has rights and responsibilities, but of which there had been no breach at the date of the assignment, so that at that date no action could be brought upon the contract, but which, if occasion should ever arise to enforce it, must of necessity be enforced by action, is assignable by this sub-section as a 'legal chose in action.' That it is a legal chose in action, and was so at the date of the assignment, cannot be denied; but the question is whether it is so within the meaning of the words as used in the sub-section. I think it is, because it is a case in which the assignee would, at any rate after giving notice of the assignment, have had rights if the Act had not been passed. The Court of Equity would undoubtedly have recognised his right, and would have treated the assignor as being trustee for his assignee, and they would have given to the assignee all the rights and remedies as against his assignor which they gave to a *cestui que* trust against his trustee, and would have given to him as against the other party to the contract all the rights and remedies which they gave to a *cestui que* trust against a third person dealing with his trustee in reference to the subject of the trust after notice of the trust . . . I may mention, not as an authority, but in explanation of the view I take, that I myself in *Marchant v Morton, Down & Co* ([1901] 2 KB 829 at 832) have held that this sub-section is merely machinery; that it enables an action to be brought by the assignee in his own name in cases where previously he would have sued in the assignor's name, but only where he could so sue. I think that in the

present case, where there was a contract of sale which gave the purchaser an equitable interest in the property contracted to be sold, the assignment and notice gave the assignee a legal right to sue, not only for specific performance if he had a case for it, but also for damages if he either was driven or elected to take that remedy. I think, therefore, that the appeal should be allowed, and judgment be entered for the plaintiff for £100. The Chief Justice and Mr Justice Darling concur in this judgment.

[The decision of the Divisional Court was reversed on other grounds by the Court of Appeal in [1903] 1 KB 644.]

NOTES

1. The strongest statement of the proposition that equitable choses in action fall within s 136 is probably to be found in the judgment of Younger J in *Re Pain* [1919] 1 Ch 38. His Lordship derived the doctrine from the judgment of Channell J in *Torkington v Magee*. Does the reasoning of Channell J support Younger J's interpretation?

2. The question whether equitable choses can be assigned under s 136 may appear moot since absolute equitable assignments of equitable choses (which alone fall within s 136) already enabled the assignee to sue in his own name without joining the assignor and did not need consideration. However, if equitable choses come within s 136, the question has practical significance since that would appear to render equitable assignment more difficult than it was before the Judicature Acts entered into force.

3. The High Court of Australia has, in *obiter dicta*, adopted the view that equitable choses in action fall within the local equivalent of s 136, but that compliance with s 136 is not mandatory for equitable assignments: *Federal Commissioner of Taxation v Everett* (1980) 143 CLR 440 at 447. Does the language of s 136 support such a reading? Assuming that this reading is correct, will it be to the advantage of parties to assignments of equitable interests to make their transaction under s 136?

4. Professor Tolhurst argues that s 136 does not apply to equitable choses in action, with one exception. Suppose that A makes an absolute equitable assignment of a common law debt to B but the writing requirements of s 136 are not fulfilled; B then assigns its entire interest to C which in turn assigns its entire interest to D. Tolhurst writes (at para 5.07):

> Clearly, the assignments to C and D are assignments of equitable choses in action. However, if the assignments to C and D are assignments of the assignor's entire interest then the end result is that D owns the right that was once vested in B which, in terms of characterization, is the equitable ownership of the promise made by the debtor to A. The result is that B and C effectively drop out of the picture so that there is only a tripartite relationship left. If B could have given notice to the debtor for the purposes of making the assignment legal, then there seems no reason why D (who took an equitable assignment of an equitable interest) cannot now give notice, render the assignment legal and vest in D the legal right to the chose.

Would those dealings between B and C and then C and D be equitable assignments of an equitable chose in action, as Professor Tolhurst assumes they would be?

(vi) Statutory exception

An assignment may be required in order to create a 'financial collateral arrangement' over 'financial instruments' such as shares and bonds, and 'cash' that is held in a bank account or 'a similar claim for the repayment of money', including money market deposits and sums payable or received under various operations in financial markets (but not a simple debt incurred in other circumstances). In the making of that legal assignment, the requirement under s 136 of the Law of Property Act that the assignment be signed by the assignor or on the assignor's authority (to the extent that an agent's signature is sufficient), does not apply: Financial Collateral Arrangements (No 2) Regulations 2003 (SI 2003/3226), reg 4(3). Given that those regulations were made to assist the informal making of transactions, an interesting question is whether the regulation was necessary so far as assignments of legal choses in action are concerned. Lord Macnaghten's statement that the provision now made in s 136 'does not forbid or destroy equitable assignments or impair their efficacy in the slightest degree' (*William Brandt's Sons & Co v Dunlop Rubber Co Ltd* [1905] AC 454 at 461) appears to be in point.

6 NOTICE

The giving of notice affects the legal relations as between the parties to assignments. Questions naturally arise. Is notice necessary in order to assign a chose in action? Will an assignment of a legal chose in action be effective without notice? What, if any, differences are found in the requirements and effects of notice at law and in equity? In approaching these questions, it is important to bear in mind the functions of notice. The functions are several. After an assignment, a debtor may pay the assignor rather than the assignee. The debtor's position may be determined by whether the debtor has received valid notice of the assignment. Next, an assignor may—counter-intuitively, it may at first seem—assign the one chose in action more than once. As between rival assignees each of whom claims the benefit of the assignment, notice will be determinative. Further, after an assignment the debtor may acquire a claim against the assignor which the debtor wishes to press against the assignee. To a large extent, notice determines whether the debtor may do so.

Because notice has several functions, the simple question—'Is notice necessary?'—is unhelpful. For one purpose, notice may be necessary. But unless a litigant's success depends on showing that that notice was validly given, generally speaking it will be possible to say that notice is unnecessary.

(a) Equitable assignment

(i) What amounts to notice

James Talcott Ltd v John Lewis & Co Ltd
[1940] 3 All ER 592, Court of Appeal

A creditor (the North American Dress Co Ltd) placed the following notice on its invoices by means of a rubber stamp: 'To facilitate our accountancy and banking arrangements, it has been agreed that this invoice be transferred to and payment in London funds should be made to James Talcott Ltd . . .'. The defendant debtor ignored the notice and paid the creditor. The plaintiff (as assignee) sued the debtor for payment of the sum alleged to be assigned. Macnaghten J dismissed the claim. The plaintiff appealed but the Court of Appeal, by a majority, dismissed the appeal.

MacKinnon LJ: . . . One may have a notice to a debtor from his creditor asking him to pay the money to a third party. The terms of it may be such as to indicate that it is to be paid to that third party because that third party has, by virtue of an assignment, become the person entitled to receive it. On the other hand, it may be a request to pay the debt to a third party, not because that third party has a right to it, but because, as a matter of convenience, the creditor desires that it shall be paid to that third party as his agent to receive it in respect of the right of the creditor still surviving to receive the debt himself. Plainness of meaning is necessary in order that the debtor who has received a notice to pay a third party shall be rendered liable to pay the money over again if he disregards the notice. The language is immaterial if the meaning is plain, but that plain meaning must be that the debt and the right to receive it have been transferred to the third party. It is not merely that I have made some arrangement by which I request another to pay this money to the third party as my agent. The question is whether this stamped clause put upon the invoices did amount to a plain intimation to the first defendants that the right to receive this money had been transferred to the plaintiffs.

First of all, it is not a notice sent by the plaintiffs at all. If it were sent direct by the plaintiffs to the first defendants, the mere fact that it emanated from them would go some little way to indicate that they were doing so pursuant to a right of theirs. I do not say that there is very much in that, but the fact that it is stamped on their own invoice by the North American Dress Co Ltd makes it a communication from them, and not a communication from John Lewis & Co Ltd to the plaintiffs. The words are these:

> To facilitate our accountancy and banking arrangements, it has been agreed that this invoice be transferred to and payment in London funds should be made to James Talcott, Ltd . . . Errors in this invoice must be notified to James Talcott, Ltd immediately.

It would have been so simple for James Talcott Ltd to give a correct notice, 'This debt has been assigned to us,' or to insist that the North American Dress Co Ltd should in clear terms give that intimation, that it is a matter of extreme wonder and speculation why this stamp should have been couched in this extremely vague and obscure language.

We have been told (I think that it appears from one of the letters) that the wording of this extraordinary sentence was actually settled by counsel. I can only conceive that it was couched in this obscure language to conceal the fact that the North American Dress Co Ltd were carrying on their business with borrowed money, and had assigned to the plaintiffs the money to which they themselves were entitled.

The words begin—and they are the first words to be read by anybody who did read them— 'To facilitate our accountancy and banking arrangements . . .'. The word 'our' suggests that it is still a debt due to the North American Dress Co Ltd and that it is only a matter of their internal business arrangements. It is true that the words go on 'it has been agreed,' and it is suggested that that must mean an agreement between the North American Dress Co Ltd and the plaintiffs, though I do not know why it should. There is nothing to show that it has been agreed between those parties. There are the vague, uncertain words 'it has been agreed.' Then it goes on to say 'that this invoice be transferred to.' It is suggested that those words in themselves ought to be taken to mean that the debt due upon this invoice shall be assigned, but they do not say so. The invoice is transferred:

> . . . and payment in London funds should be made to James Talcott Ltd . . . Errors in this invoice must be notified to James Talcott Ltd immediately.

As I have said, it is not enough to make the debtor liable to pay over again if he has creditors, if he has merely received a notice that he is to pay to some other party merely as agent for his creditor. He is not bound to pay over again unless he has received a sufficiently plain notice that the right to receive the money has been transferred to the third party, so that he will at his peril neglect that notice and neglect the right of the third party. I think that this notice stamped on the invoice was ambiguous. I think that it is equally consistent with being merely a request to pay to the plaintiffs, as agents of the creditor to receive the money, and it does not indicate sufficiently clearly that there has been an assignment of the debt to the plaintiffs so that they should become the real creditors of the first defendants, be the only persons entitled to be paid the money. That was the view taken by Macnaghten J, with the result that he dismissed the claim. I think that his decision was right, and that this appeal fails.

Goddard LJ (dissenting): I have the misfortune to differ from MacKinnon LJ and Macnaghten J. I do so only with great hesitation, but, as I have formed a very clear opinion, assisted, I may say, by the very clear and forcible argument of counsel for the appellants, I think that I must express my opinion of dissent. The law of this country allows a creditor to assign his debt to a third party. If the debtor receives notice of that assignment, he must pay the assignee. If he pays the assignor, he does so at his peril. If the assignor does not account to the assignee for the money, the debtor will have to pay a second time. Notice may be given by the assignor or by the assignee. For myself, I think that the fact that the notice is given by the assignor may strengthen the position, as far as the debtor is concerned, in this way. I should not draw any inference which is adverse by reason of the fact that it is given by the assignor, because, if the debtor gets a notice from B telling him to pay B the money he owes to A, he will naturally want to know if he is safe in doing so, and he will apply to A, the assignor. If he gets a notice from the assignor, then, of course, he can safely pay, because he will be paying in accordance with the directions of his creditor.

I do not say that this is an easy case, and I think that much clearer words could have been used, but, in my opinion, the words are clear enough to indicate the position to John Lewis & Co Ltd, if they ever thought about it. Probably the reason why they did not pay the plaintiffs was that they ignored the notice and never thought about it. I think that it is enough to tell them that the plaintiffs had a charge on, or were interested in, the money, and, therefore, for my part, I would allow this appeal.

Du Parcq LJ: . . . A notice to pay a debt to a third person may be given in words which show that there has been an assignment of the debt. It may be given in words which show that there has not been an assignment of the debt. It may be given in words which leave it in doubt whether or not there has been an assignment of the debt. If those words are in the first category, the plaintiffs succeed. If the words are in either of the other categories, the plaintiffs fail. I say either of the other categories, because it is not enough that the notice should be capable of being understood to mean that the debt is assigned. It must be plain and unambiguous, and not reasonably capable, when read by an intelligent business man, of a contrary construction.

NOTES

1. In deciding whether a notice is clear and unambiguous the court must construe it in context. In *Colonial Mutual General Insurance Co Ltd v ANZ Banking Group (New Zealand) Ltd* [1995] 1 WLR 1140, a mortgagee asked the insurer of mortgaged property to note its interest in an insurance policy taken out in the mortgagor's name. The Privy Council held (at 1145) that 'in the context of a notice to an insurance company by a mortgagee of the insured property, the language of the notice was plain and unambiguous' and was effective to give the insurer notice of the assignment of the proceeds of the policy from the mortgagor to the mortgagee. This anticipates the modern approach to the construction of unilateral notices and commercial contracts later set out in *Mannai Investment Ltd v Eagle Star Life Assurance Co Ltd* [1997] AC 749 and seemingly countless subsequent cases.

2. Though no specified form of notice is required, in *Herkules Piling Ltd v Tilbury Construction Ltd* (1992) 32 Con LR 112 at 121, Hirst J said 'that there must be some kind of formal notification by the assignee, or possibly by the assignor on his behalf, to the debtor' in order for the debtor to receive notice. His Lordship held that the debtor did not receive notice of assignment when he received a copy of the contract of assignment from the assignor on discovery in arbitration proceedings, and rejected as wrong a submission that the debtor must or may pay the assignee where he learns by some other credible means that the money does not or may not belong to the assignor but to the assignee. It may be accepted that this is a kind of 'formal' notification. The gist of the matter would appear to be that the giver of notice must intend to do so in order for it to be valid notice for the purposes of assignment. Accidental discovery of the fact of the assignment will not suffice.

(ii) Passing of title to the chose in action in equity

Notice to the debtor is not essential in order for the equitable title to a legal chose in action to be assigned validly to the assignee.

Gorringe v Irwell India Rubber and Gutta Percha Works
(1886) 34 Ch D 128, Court of Appeal

As the defendants were indebted to H & Co, they wrote to them agreeing to hold a sum due from C & Co to H & Co's disposal until the balance of their indebtedness to H & Co was repaid. Before notice of this equitable assignment was given to C & Co, a petition was presented to wind up the defendants, who were subsequently put into liquidation. The liquidator took out a summons to determine whether the money due from C & Co belonged to the defendants or to H & Co. Bacon V-C held that there had been no assignment to H & Co as there had been no notice given to the debtor before the commencement of the winding up. H & Co appealed to the Court of Appeal which allowed the appeal.

> **Cotton LJ**: . . . It is contended that in order to make an assignment of a *chose in action*, such as a debt, a complete charge, notice must be given to the debtor. It is true that there must be such a notice to enable the title of the assignee to prevail against a subsequent assignee. That is established by *Dearle v Hall* [(1823) 3 Russ 1: below, pp 914-916], but there is no authority for holding this rule to apply as against the assignor of the debt. Though there is no notice to the debtor the title of the assignee is complete as against the assignor.
>
> [**Bowen** and **Fry LJJ** delivered concurring judgments.]

(iii) Obligor performs in favour of the assignor

This problem typically arises where the obligor is a debtor. If the debtor pays the original creditor (or gives the creditor a negotiable instrument) before receiving notice of the assignment, the debtor will be under no obligation to pay the assignee (*Bence v Shearman* [1898] 2 Ch 582). If, however, the debtor disregards the notice and pays the assignor, the debtor is not discharged and remains liable to pay the assignee (*Brice v Bannister* (1878) 3 QBD 569).

 Beyond this, the law is obscure to the point of being 'perhaps the least satisfactory part of assignment law': G Tolhurst, *The Assignment of Contractual Rights* (2nd edn, 2016), para 8.06. It is especially unclear whether, after a partial assignment of a debt, the debtor may obtain a good discharge from the assignee of that part of the debt. Simon Brown LJ said, dissenting, in *Deposit Protection Board v Dalia* [1994] 2 AC 367 at 382, that even after notice the debtor remains liable to the equitable assignor. (The actual decision of the Court of Appeal was reversed on other grounds [1994] 2 AC 367 at 391.) Expressly empowering an assignee to give a good discharge can avoid the problem: *Durham Bros v Robertson* [1898] 1 QB 765 at 770. Otherwise, the only safe course for the unsure debtor may be to interplead: JD Heydon, MJ Leeming, and PG Turner, *Meagher, Gummow and Lehane's Equity: Doctrines and Remedies* (5th edn, 2015), para 6–525.

(iv) Claims between rival assignees—the rule in Dearle v Hall

Where there are two successive equitable assignments of the same chose in action, the rule in *Dearle v Hall*, which originally related to competing equitable assignments, regulates priorities. Under this rule an assignee for value who is first to give notice to the debtor, trustee, or fundholder takes priority, unless he knew of the earlier assignment when he took his assignment.

Dearle v Hall
(1823) 3 Russ 1, Court of Chancery

Brown, a beneficiary, assigned his interest by way of security first to Dearle and then to Sherring. The trustees were not given notice of the assignments. Some years later Brown assigned his interest to Hall. Before purchasing the interest, Hall made inquiries of the trustees and they indicated that the interest was unencumbered. Hall gave the trustees notice of his assignment. Subsequently, Dearle and Sherring gave the trustees notice of their assignments.

> **Sir Thomas Plumer MR:** . . . The ground of this claim is priority of title. They [Dearle and Sherring] rely upon the known maxim, borrowed from the civil law, which in many cases regulates equities—*'qui prior est in tempore, potior est in jure'* ['first in time, first in right']. If, by the first contract, all the thing is given, there remains nothing to be the subject of the second contract, and priority must decide. But it cannot be contended that priority in time must decide, where the legal estate is outstanding. For the maxim, as an equitable rule, admits of exception, and gives way, when the question does not lie between bare and equal equities. If there appears to be, in respect of any circumstance independent of priority of time, a better title in the *puisne* purchaser to call for the legal estate, than in the purchaser who precedes him in date, the case ceases to be a balance of equal equities, and the preference, which priority of date might otherwise have given, is done away with and counteracted. The question here is,—not which assignment is first in date,—but whether there is not, on the part of Hall, a better title to call for the legal estate than Dearle or Sherring can set up? or rather, the question is, Shall these Plaintiffs now have equitable relief to the injury of Hall?
>   What title have they shown to call on a court of justice to interpose on their behalf, in order to obviate the consequences of their own misconduct? All that has happened is owing to their negligence (a negligence not accounted for) in forbearing to do what they ought to have done, what would have been attended with no difficulty, and what would have effectually prevented all the mischief which has followed. Is a Plaintiff to be heard in a court of equity, who asks its interposition on his behoof, to indemnify him against the effects of his own negligence at the expense of another who has used all due diligence, and who, if he is to suffer loss, will suffer it by reason of the negligence of the very person who prays relief against him? The question here is not, as in *Evans v Bicknell* ((1801) 6 Ves 174), whether a court of equity is to deprive the Plaintiffs

of any right—whether it is to take from them, for instance, a legal estate, or to impose any charge upon them. It is simply, whether they are entitled to relief against their own negligence. They did not perfect their securities; a third party has innocently advanced his money, and has perfected his security as far as the nature of the subject permitted him: is this Court to interfere to postpone him to them?

They say, that they were not bound to give notice to the trustees; for that notice does not form part of the necessary conveyance of an equitable interest. I admit, that, if you mean to rely on contract with the individual, you do not need to give notice; from the moment of the contract, he, with whom you are dealing, is personally bound. But if you mean to go further, and to make your right attach upon the thing which is the subject of the contract, it is necessary to give notice; and, unless notice is given, you do not do that which is essential in all cases of transfer of personal property. The law of England has always been, that personal property passes by delivery of possession; and it is possession which determines the apparent ownership. If, therefore, an individual, who in the way of purchase or mortgage contracts with another for the transfer of his interest, does not divest the vendor or mortgagor of possession, but permits him to remain the ostensible owner as before, he must take the consequences which may ensue from such a mode of dealing. That doctrine was explained in *Ryall v Rowles* ((1750) 1 Ves Sen 348, 1 Atk 165), before Lord Hardwicke and three of the Judges. If you, having the right of possession, do not exercise that right, but leave another in actual possession, you enable that person to gain a false and delusive credit, and put it in his power to obtain money from innocent parties on the hypothesis of his being the owner of that which in fact belongs to you. The principle has been long recognised, even in courts of law. In *Twyne's* case ((1602) 3 Co Rep 80), one of the badges of fraud was, that the possession had remained in the vendor. Possession must follow right; and if you, who have the right, do not take posession, you do not follow up the title, and are responsible for the consequences.

'When a man,' says Lord Bacon (*Maxims of the Law*, max 16), 'is author and mover to another to commit an unlawful act, then he shall not excuse himself by circumstances not pursued.' It is true that a chose in action does not admit of tangible actual possession, and that neither Zachariah Brown nor any person claiming under him were entitled to possess themselves of the fund which yielded the £93 a year. But in *Ryall v Rowles* the Judges held, that, in the case of a chose in action, you must do every thing towards having possession which the subject admits; you must do that which is tantamount to obtaining possession, by placing every person, who has an equitable or legal interest in the matter, under an obligation to treat it as your property. For this purpose, you must give notice to the legal holder of the fund; in the case of a debt, for instance, notice to the debtor is, for many purposes, tantamount to possession. If you omit to give that notice, you are guilty of the same degree and species of neglect as he who leaves a personal chattel, to which he has acquired a title, in the actual possession, and under the absolute control, of another person.

Is there the least doubt, that, if Zachariah Brown had been a trader, all that was done by Dearle and Sherring would not have been in the least effectual against his assignees; but that, according to the doctrine of *Ryall v Rowles*, his assignees would have taken the fund, because there was no notice to those in whom the legal interest was vested? In that case it was the opinion of all the Judges, that he who contracts for a chose in action, and does not follow up his title by notice, gives personal credit to the individual with whom he deals. Notice, then, is necessary to perfect the title,—to give a complete right *in rem*, and not merely a right as against him who conveys his interest. If you are willing to trust the personal credit of the man, and are satisfied that he will make no improper use of the possession in which you allow him to remain, notice is not necessary; for against him the title is perfect without notice. But if he, availing himself of the possession as a means of obtaining credit, induces third persons to purchase from him as the actual owner, and they part with their money before your pocket-conveyance is notified to them, you must be postponed. In being postponed, your security is not invalidated: you had priority, but that priority has not been followed up; and you have permitted another to acquire a better title to the legal possession. What was done by Dearle and Sherring did not exhaust the thing (to borrow the principle of the civil law) but left it still open to traffic. These are the principles on which I think it to be very old law, that possession, or what is tantamount to possession, is the criterion of perfect title to personal chattels, and that he, who does not obtain such possession, must take his chance.

I do not go through the cases which constitute exceptions to the rule, that priority in time shall prevail. A man may lose that priority by actual fraud or constructive fraud; by being silent, for instance, when he ought to speak; by standing by, and keeping his own security concealed. By such conduct, even the advantage of possessing the legal estate may be lost . . .

On these grounds, I think that the plaintiffs have not shewn a title to call on a court of equity to interpose in their behalf, and to take the fund from an individual who has used due diligence, in order to give it to those whose negligence has occasioned all the mischief. There is no equality of equities between the defendant Hall, and the plaintiffs . . .

The bill, therefore, must be dismissed, but, as against Hall, without costs. I do not make the plaintiffs pay costs to Hall, because they may have been losers without any intention to commit a fraud, and I am unwilling to add to their loss. Constructive fraud is the utmost that can be imputed to them.

[On appeal, Lord Lyndhurst LC affirmed the Master of the Rolls' judgment.]

NOTES

1. The rule 'in'—or, rather, developed from—*Dearle v Hall* initially applied only to interests in personalty (which, under the doctrine of conversion, included trusts of sale of land). The judges extended the rule to apply to assignments of legal choses in action generally. By statute, the rule now also applies to dealings with interests in real property held on trust: s 137(1) of the Law of Property Act 1925. The statutory extension does not apply to assignments of legal choses in action. Notice of an assignment of such a chose in action need not be written. However, under the statutory extension of *Dearle v Hall*, s 137 of the Law of Property Act 1925 provides:

(3) A notice, otherwise than in writing, given to, or received by, a trustee after the commencement of this Act as respects any dealing with an equitable interest in real or personal property, shall not affect the priority of competing claims of purchasers in that equitable interest.

2. In its developed form, the rule in *Dearle v Hall* has several requirements, including the following.

- Notice is only effective of assignments that have occurred. Notice of agreements to assign future choses in action is ineffective: *Re Dallas* [1904] 2 Ch 385.

- Only an assignee who has given value for its assignment may benefit from the rule. A volunteer may not: *Justice v Wynne* (1860) 121 Ch R 289 at 304–305, per Brady LC; *United Bank of Kuwait plc v Sahib* [1997] Ch 107 at 119–120, per Chadwick J, affirmed on appeal at 130, without comment on this point.

- The assignee must be without notice of any prior assignment. Even the constructive notice which comes of being put on inquiry will disable an assignee from gaining priority over a rival assignee under the rule in *Dearle v Hall*: *Spencer v Clarke* (1878) 9 Ch D 137. In fact, there is no express reference to this proviso in *Dearle v Hall* itself, but it has been emphasised by the courts on numerous occasions since (see, eg, *Re Holmes* (1885) 29 Ch D 786 at 789, per Cotton and Lindley LJJ; *Ward v Duncombe* [1893] AC 369 at 384, per Lord Macnaghten). The proviso has been described as 'a rule of good sense' based on 'the ordinary morality of the matter' (*Rhodes v Allied Dunbar Pension Services* [1987] 1 WLR 1703 at 1708, per Harman J, reversed on appeal at [1989] 1 WLR 800, without affecting this statement; but contrast J de Lacy (1999) 28 Anglo-Am LR 87 and 197, who questions the origins of the proviso and calls for its rejection).

• The debtor or fundholder must also lack notice of any prior assignment.

• The assignee must take for its own benefit, not as an agent or trustee for another: see *Compaq Computers* (below).

3.   Where the rule in *Dearle v Hall* does not apply, the ordinary equitable rule of priority applies: where the equities are equal, the first in time prevails (*Re Dallas* [1904] 2 Ch 385).

4.   The rule has shifted some way since *Dearle v Hall* itself. Sir Thomas Plumer MR sought to justify his decision on two grounds: the conduct of the competing assignees and the need for notice to perfect an equitable assignment. Today, neither ground can be used to justify the rule in *Dearle v Hall*. In *Foster v Cockerell* (1835) 3 Cl & Fin 456 the House of Lords disregarded the conduct of the competing assignees and gave priority to the assignee who was the first to give notice to the trustees. In *Ward v Duncombe* [1893] AC 369 at 392, Lord Macnaghten stressed that notice was not needed to perfect the title of an equitable assignee. He also said (at 391): 'I am not sure that the doctrine rests upon any very satisfactory principle.' Has the law accepted this doctrine at the expense of other, superior principles?

5.   The rule in *Dearle v Hall* is open to numerous criticisms. Two deserve special mention. First, it is an arbitrary rule in that it can be relied on by an assignee who has given value, but not by a volunteer. Secondly, by ignoring the reasons for failure to give notice, it can cause considerable injustice. (See F Oditah (1989) 9 OJLS 521 at 525–527.) For such reasons, the courts are usually reluctant to extend the application of the rule (eg it does not apply to successive dealings in company shares: *Macmillan Inc v Bishopsgate Investment Trust plc (No 3)* [1995] 3 All ER 747 at 761–762, per Millett J; affirmed on other grounds [1996] 1 All ER 585). In the next case, an attempt was made to limit the rule in *Dearle v Hall* in reliance on an equitable trump card: the defence of bona fide purchase for value without notice of an equity.

Compaq Computer Ltd v Abercorn Group Ltd
[1991] BCC 484, Chancery Division

Compaq, a manufacturer of computers and computer products, appointed Abercorn as an authorised dealer and supplied it with computer products on standard terms which reserved title in the products to Compaq until payment of the price. It was further provided that Abercorn would hold the goods as 'bailee and agent' for Compaq and would strictly account to Compaq for the full proceeds thereof received from third parties and keep a separate account of all such proceeds or monies. Abercorn then entered into a written invoice-discounting agreement with Kellock, pursuant to which it assigned to Kellock nearly £400,000 owed by customers under sub-sales of Compaq products. Notice in writing of each of these assignments was given by Kellock to the relevant debtor. On Abercorn's subsequent receivership, a dispute arose between Compaq and Kellock as to which of them was entitled to be paid the proceeds of the sub-sales.

Mummery J held that on its true construction the terms of the agreement between Compaq and Abercorn operated by way of a charge over the proceeds of the sub-sales and that charge was void for non-registration under Part XII of the Companies Act 1985 (cognate provisions are now to be found contained in Part 25 of the Companies Act 2006: see below, pp 977–980). On that ground alone, Kellock were entitled to the proceeds of the sub-sales. However, on the assumption that he was wrong on that issue, his Lordship then considered whether Kellock's rights as assignee took priority over Compaq's equitable interest in the proceeds of the sub-sales.

Mummery J: I deal first with the arguments on the rule in *Dearle v Hall* ((1823) 3 Russ 1). It was accepted by Compaq that if the rule did apply, Kellock would enjoy priority. Two arguments were advanced on behalf of Compaq as to why the rule in *Dearle v Hall* did not apply.

The first argument was that the rule did not apply because the subject-matter in question consisted of legal choses in action, ie debts owing to Abercorn by subpurchasers of Compaq products. It was contended that the rule is confined to equitable choses in action and to other equitable interests including, after 1926, equitable interests in land—see s 137(1) of the Law of Property Act 1925 . . .

In brief, Compaq's submission was that it is the equitable nature of the property dealt with and not the equitable nature of the dealing with it—for example, by way of assignment—which attracts the rule.

It is, however, established on the authorities that the rule in *Dearle v Hall* applies to equitable assignments of legal choses in action. In *Pfeiffer* [*E Pfeiffer Weinkellerei-Weineinkauf GmbH & Co v Arbuthnot Factors Ltd* [1988] 1 WLR 150] at p 163 Phillips J said:

> The rule in *Dearle v Hall* is an exception to the general principle that equitable interests take priority in the order in which they are created. The rule applies to dealings with equitable interests in any property and, in particular, to equitable assignments of legal choses in action.
>
> Under the rule, priority depends upon the order in which notice of the interest created by the dealing is given to the person affected by it, ie, in the case of assignments of a debt, the debtor.

He went on to note that counsel conceded that if the rights asserted by the plaintiff were rights conferred by equitable assignment, the rule in *Dearle v Hall* must apply. The judge applied the rule because he held that such security rights as were conferred upon the plaintiff by the agreement were conferred by equitable assignment.

That passage in the judgment of Phillips J was criticised in argument before me. It was submitted that counsel had wrongly made a concession. I disagree. In my judgment, the view of Phillips J and the concession made by counsel receives full support from earlier authorities, including *Dearle v Hall* itself at p 58.

[His Lordship then referred to the following cases, namely: *Gorringe v Irwell India Rubber & Gutta Percha Works* (1886) 34 Ch D 128 at 132, per Cotton LJ (see above, p 913) and, at 135, per Bowen J; *Ward and Pemberton v Duncombe* [1893] AC 369 at 383 ff, per Lord Macnaghten; *Marchant v Morton, Down & Co* [1901] 2 KB 829 at 831, per Channell J; and *BS Lyle Ltd v Rosher* [1959] 1 WLR 8 at 16, per Lord Morton and, at 14, per Viscount Kilmuir LC. He continued:]

Those formulations of the rule both appear to accept its applicability to an equitable assignment of a legal chose in action, such as a debt. I therefore reject the submission that the rule in *Dearle v Hall* cannot apply to this case because the relevant dealings were with debts.

The second argument advanced on behalf of Compaq against the application of the rule in *Dearle v Hall* was that the rule only applies in the case of successive assignments of equitable interests already created and not to the case of the creation of a new equitable interest—for example, by way of a declaration of trust. For this proposition reliance was placed on *Hill v Peters*

[1918] 2 Ch 273 at p 279, where Eve J referred to the observations of Lord Macnaghten [in *Ward and Pemberton v Duncombe* [1893] AC 369 at 383] as to the undesirability of doing anything to extend the doctrine of *Dearle v Hall* to cases which were not already covered by it, and stated:

> The principle on which the rule in *Dearle v Hall* is founded, which regards the giving of notice by the assignee as the nearest approach to the taking of possession, has no application, in my opinion, to the beneficiary who has no right to possession himself, and who can only assert his claim to receive through his trustee.

In *Lyle v Rosher* there was argument about the correctness of the opinion expressed by Eve J on the distinction between a declaration of trust and an equitable assignment. No opinion on that question was expressed by four members of the House of Lords. Lord Reid, however, discussed the point and expressed the view at p 22 that,

> to apply the rule in *Dearle v Hall* to defeat the rights of a cestui que trust would introduce an exception to the general law.

—and he concluded at p 23:

> I think that it would be an innovation in the law of England to require a cestui que trust for his own protection to give notice of the trust in his favour to the person who holds the fund.

On the basis of those observations it was submitted on behalf of Compaq that the rule in *Dearle v Hall* did not apply because, as already submitted in argument on the charge point, Abercorn never became beneficially entitled to the proceeds of sale of Compaq products; by virtue of Abercorn's fiduciary obligations, the beneficial interest in those proceeds vested automatically in Compaq. There was, therefore, no assignment by Abercorn, by way of charge or otherwise, of the proceeds of sale. They were the subject of a trust in favour of Compaq which determined when the price of the Compaq products and other sums owing were paid. There was no equitable assignment of a chose in action to compete with the assignment made by Abercorn in favour of Kellock and, if there was only one assignment, there was no room for the application of *Dearle v Hall*.

In my judgment, assuming that there is a distinction between the creation of a trust and an equitable assignment, Compaq's argument fails on the construction of the terms and conditions of the dealer agreement. No bare trust of the proceeds of sale was created in favour of Compaq. An equitable assignment may be effected by an agreement between a debtor and a creditor that the debt owing shall be paid out of a specific fund coming to the debtor—see the speech of Lord Wilberforce in *Swiss Bank Corpn v Lloyds Bank Ltd* [1982] AC 584 at p 613A–E.

In my view, there was such an agreement in this case. In cl 8.3 and cl 8.3.2 Abercorn and Compaq in substance agreed that the debts owing by Abercorn to Compaq would be paid out of a specific fund coming to Abercorn, namely the proceeds of the subsales of Compaq products to Abercorn's customers. That was an equitable assignment of the proceeds of sale. I have held on the charge point that that assignment was by way of charge, registrable and void for want of registration. If I am wrong on that point and the assignment was not by way of charge, it was nevertheless an equitable assignment to which the rule in *Dearle v Hall* can apply when determining whether or not it enjoys priority over another equitable assignment of the same debt or fund . . . Kellock had by virtue of the discounting agreement and assignments made pursuant to it priority over Compaq in respect of the proceeds of sale of the Compaq products supplied on the terms and conditions of the dealer agreement.

I should, however, briefly deal with the other argument advanced by Kellock: that it was a purchaser for value of the legal title to the debts without notice of any prior equitable interest of Compaq and therefore took free of any such interest. Paragraph (3) of the schedule requires me to assume that Kellock did not have notice or knowledge of Compaq's terms and conditions . . .

Kellock's submission was that it was a bona fide purchaser for value of the debts without notice of Compaq's interest at the time of the purchase and that it therefore enjoyed priority over any interest that Compaq might have by way of retention of title, charge or equitable interest. Reliance was placed on *Pitcher v Rawlins* (1872) 7 Ch App 259 at pp 268–269 where James LJ said:

. . . according to my view of the established law of this Court, such a purchaser's plea of a purchase for valuable consideration without notice is an absolute, unqualified, unanswerable defence, and an unanswerable plea to the jurisdiction of this Court.

Taylor v Blakelock (1886) 32 Ch D 560 was also cited along with *Thorndike v Hunt* (1859) 3 De G & J 563 to demonstrate the strength of the position of a purchaser for value in contrast to the position of a volunteer.

[He went on to consider an argument that the rule in *Dearle v Hall* had no application to assignment to which s 136 of the Law of Property Act 1925 applies: see below, pp 927-928.]

NOTES

1.   Strong arguments have been made in favour of the bona fide purchaser rule when there is competition between a statutory assignee and an equitable assignee, see F Oditah (1989) 9 OJLS 521, supported by JD Heydon, MJ Leeming, and PG Turner, *Meagher, Gummow and Lehane's Equity: Doctrines and Remedies* (5th edn, 2015), paras 8–095 to 8–215. But the arguments raised by Dr Oditah were effectively rejected by Mummery J in *Compaq Computers Ltd v Abercorn Group Ltd*, who followed the decision of Phillips J in *E Pfeiffer Weinkellerei-Weinenkauf GmbH & Co v Arbuthnot Factors Ltd* [1988] 1 WLR 150. For similar rejection of the bona fide purchaser rule in this context, see DW McLauchlan (1980) 96 LQR 90 at 92–93; J Farrar and G McLay, 'The Interface of Floating Charges, Romalpa Clauses and Credit Factoring' in J Prebble (ed), *Dimensions in Business Finance Law* (2nd edn, 1992), Ch 3.

2.   Assuming that a seller's reservation of title clause gives him an equitable right to trace into the proceeds of sub-sales held by the buyer, is priority between the seller and an assignee of the buyer's book debts governed by the rule in *Dearle v Hall*? There is no clear answer to this question. It has been argued by DW McLauchlan that there is no room for the rule when the buyer holds the proceeds on trust for the seller. He argues that the rule in *Dearle v Hall* is restricted to competing assignments and does not apply in a situation when one of the interests is an equitable tracing right arising by operation of law ((1980) 96 LQR 90 at 95 ff). But Professor Goode counters that argument by stating that as it is the seller who chooses the form of his interest, by imposing an accounting obligation in the sale contract, and as he knows that the buyer may sell the debts arising from sub-sales to a bona fide purchaser, then the seller has no cause to complain if the rule in *Dearle v Hall* is applied against him (Goode, above, at 752, fn 69). Might not the requirement that the notice relate to an assignment that has occurred also be in point (*Re Dallas*), at least where the seller's reservation of title clause in truth relates to future book debts? In *Compaq Computer Ltd v Abercorn Group Ltd*, Mummery J avoided having to answer such questions by holding that the accounting obligation in the sale contract gave rise to an equitable assignment and not a bare trust. For a general discussion of reservation of title clauses and priorities, see G McCormack, *Reservation of Title* (2nd edn, 1995), Ch 9; and F Oditah, *Legal Aspects of Receivables Financing* (1991), pp 149–154.

(v) Equities

Notice prevents further 'equities' arising between the debtor or obligor, on the one hand, and the assignor, on the other hand. Otherwise those equities will bind the assignee and weaken the assignee's ability to demand performance (eg by payment) in full from the obligor. These equities mainly consist of cross-claims and, especially, set-offs. This subject will be discussed under a subsequent heading (pp 943-947).

(vi) Notice to assignee?

This requirement has proved troublesome to writers more than to commercial parties, since it is rare that an intended assignee does not know of the planned assignment to him. In *Timpson's Executors v Yerbury* [1936] 1 KB 645 at 658, Lord Wright MR said that 'communication from assignor to assignee either directly or indirectly is a necessary condition of an assignment', and in *Shamia v Joory* [1958] 1 QB 448 at 460, Barry J found that an equitable assignment of a legal chose in action had not occurred 'because there was no evidence that notice of the assignment had in fact been given to [the intended assignee]'. Though these statements seem quite clear, the position they describe is peculiar. A voluntary transfer by declaration of trust of a legal chose does not require notice to, or prior agreement of, the assignee: *Middleton v Pollock* (1876) 2 Ch D 104. A voluntary assignment of an *equitable* chose in action may take effect without the assignee first receiving notice: *Donaldson v Donaldson* (1854) Kay 711; *Re Way's Trusts* (1864) 2 De GJ & S 365 at 371–372. And in *Standing v Bowring* (1885) 31 Ch D 282, the Court of Appeal spoke in general terms of a principle that a gift may be made without the donee's consent (subject to disclaimer or repudiation upon the donee's learning of the gift). If legal choses in action may not be assigned without the assignee first having notice thereof, the position is unique.

Seeing the anomaly, writers have said notice ought not to be required to assign a legal chose equitable: M Smith and N Leslie, *The Law of Assignment* (2nd edn, 2013), paras 13.73–13.76; JD Heydon, MJ Leeming, and PG Turner, *Meagher, Gummow and Lehane's Equity: Doctrines and Remedies* (5th edn, 2015), para 6–430. Strictly, however, the point is yet to be decided. One authority cited in support (*Grey v Australian Motorists & General Insurance Co Pty Ltd* [1976] 1 NSWLR 669 at 673) decides the point with respect to legal assignment only (expressly leaving aside the position in equity, at 672, albeit questionably). Certain other authorities cited in support merely repeat the established position that the assignment of *equitable* choses in action does not depend on the assignee having notice: *Donaldson v Donaldson*, above; *Re Way's Trusts*, above; *Comptroller of Stamps (Vic) v Howard-Smith* (1936) 54 CLR 614 at 622; *UTC Ltd (in liq) v NZI Securities Australia Ltd* (1991) 4 WAR 349 at 356. And *Standing v Bowring*, while expressed generally, was a case in which, as Cotton LJ put it (at 288), 'the transfer of stock in the public funds is regulated by Act of Parliament' and a 'statutory mode of transfer' applied, rather than equitable principles.

But it seems sufficiently clear that there is no general rule that an equitable assignment of a legal chose in action depends on notice to the intended assignee. In terms of authority, the principal decisions relied on in support of such a general rule were decisions regarding equitable choses in action (*Morrell v Wootten* (1852) 16 Beav 197; *Re Hamilton* (1921) 124 LT 737; *Timpson's Executors v Yerbury*), not legal choses in action. In terms of analysis of principle, the concern of the courts has in any case been with whether an irrevocable intention to assign has been expressed. In *Re Hamilton* the Court of Appeal held that a lack of notice to an intended assignee caused there to be no assignment because 'the authority remained simply a bare authority, which is revocable, and can be revoked, and … is not an assignment'. In *Timpson's Executors v Yerbury*, the conclusion to which Lord Wright MR was led by his concern that no communication had been intended to, or received by, the putative assignee was that 'there is no evidence of intention to assign at all' (at 659). Although *Morrell v Wootten* has been read as authority that notice to, or the prior agreement of, the assignee is necessary for an effective assignment of a legal chose (*Snell's Equity* (33rd edn, 2015), para 3–017), it is instead authority for a more favourable proposition discussed earlier: that, where a fundholder attorns to a third party, the third party may sue the fundholder for money had and received. Since attornment depends on communication to the attornee, 'it is absolutely necessary that the order should be communicated to the intended payee' (at 302, per Sir John Romilly MR).

It seems open to a court, therefore, to hold that, once an intention to assign is expressed— that being an irrevocable intention—no further notice to, or agreement of, the assignee is necessary before an equitable assignment of a legal chose in action may occur.

(b) Legal assignment

It would be consistent with the purpose and legislative history of s 136 of the Law of Property Act 1925 to expect that, except so far as the section modifies them, on its true legal con-struction, the equitable principles of assignment apply equally to assignments made under the section. That is, the section operates to convert selected equitable assignments into legal assignments: except so far as that process of conversion alters the equitable incidents of the assignment, one might expect them to be the same. To a large extent, the courts have held that to be so. But not in every case.

(i) What amounts to notice

Written notice of the assignment must be given to the debtor if the assignment is to fall within s 136 of the Law of Property Act 1925. What constitutes effective notice for this purpose?

WF Harrison & Co Ltd v Burke
[1956] 1 WLR 419, Court of Appeal

Mrs Burke entered into a hire-purchase agreement with a finance company whereby she hired a refrigerated counter on immediate payment of £30 and 24 instalments of £8 9s 6d a month, until a total of £233 8s was paid. Only the £30 was paid. By an assignment dated 7 December 1954, the finance company purported to assign to the plaintiffs the sum of £203 8s as 'now legally due and owing' to them from Mrs Burke. On 6 December 1954, the day before the assignment was executed, a letter, purporting to be a notice of assignment, was drawn up by the plaintiffs, dated 6 December 1954 and addressed to Mrs Burke. The letter stated that 'We hereby give you notice that by an indenture dated Dec 6, 1954, the debt amounting to £203 8s owing by you to [the finance company] has been assigned to us absolutely and the debt is now due and owing to us.' The letter was posted on 8 December and received by Mrs Burke on 9 December.

Denning LJ: . . . The whole question in this case, as it comes before us, is whether that is a valid notice of assignment such as to transfer to Harrisons the legal right to sue for the debt. I ought to point out at once that the sum owing at that date of December 7, 1954, was not £203 8s, as stated in the assignment, but only the instalments which had then accrued due—£33 18s, and so the notice of assignment did not give the right figure for the debt. Further, apart from that, it gives the wrong date of the assignment: it said that the indenture was dated December 6, 1954, whereas the only assignment produced to the court is one dated December 7, 1954. The question is whether that error in giving the date of the assignment makes the notice bad.

In 1899, in *Stanley v. English Fibres Industries Ltd.* (1899) 68 LJQB 839, it was held by Ridley J. that if the date given for the assignment is bad, the notice does not comply with the requirements of the statute. I find myself in agreement with that decision. It is only necessary to read section 136 of the Law of Property Act, 1925, to realize that the notice in writing of the assignment is an essential part of the transfer of title to the debt, and, as such, the requirements of the Act must be strictly complied with, and the notice itself, I think, must be strictly accurate—accurate in particular in regard to the date which is given for the assignment; and even though it is only one day out, as in this case, the notice of assignment is bad.

I need not say anything about the amount of the debt, which in this case was put at £203 8s when it was in fact only £33 18s; but, as at present advised, I should have thought the notice of assignment ought to state the debt accurately too, because, after all, we are dealing with a transfer of title and the requirements of the Act must be strictly complied with. I find myself in agreement with the judgment of the county court judge that the assignee in this case did not prove a right or title in himself to this debt in accordance with the statute, and I think the appeal must fail.

Morris LJ: I agree. A question might be raised in regard to the assignment itself, which is an assignment of the debts or sums of money referred to in the schedule. The schedule refers to a debt owing from Mrs. Burke of £203. At the date of the assignment there was not a debt of £203. But we have not had argument in regard to the validity of the assignment itself, and so I express no opinion in regard to it. We have been concerned with the question as to whether there has been a valid notice in writing of the assignment. The section requires express notice in writing, and the section provides that after the giving of 'express' notice in writing, the assignment 'is effectual in law ... to pass and transfer from the date of such notice—(a) the legal right to such debt or thing in action,' etc.

Now, my Lord has read the terms of the notice in writing in this case, and it refers to the debt amounting to £203. If this is a good notice in writing, it would seem to be a notice as from the date of which there would be a 'legal right to such debt,' namely, a debt of £203. But there was not a debt of £203.

But again I do not think it necessary to decide this case on a consideration of the points that arise in regard to that aspect of the matter. I think the case can be decided by reference to the question of the date. The notice is dated December 6. Whether the purported assignment was good or not, it was not in existence on December 6. The purported assignment came into existence on December 7. But it seems to me that it is necessary to comply with the section, and I think that a notice given on December 6 purporting to be a notice in reference to an assignment dated December 6, when there was no such assignment in existence, was, therefore, not a good notice to enable the assignment that came into existence the following day to be effectual to pass the legal right to the debt assigned. I therefore agree that the judge came to a correct conclusion.

Parker LJ: I also agree.

Van Lynn Developments Ltd v Pelias Construction Co Ltd
[1969] 1 QB 607, Court of Appeal

The defendants were overdrawn at their bank. The plaintiffs paid off that indebtedness and took an assignment of the debt from the bank. The plaintiffs' solicitors then sent a letter to the defendants in the following terms: 'We have been instructed by our above-named clients to apply to you for the payment of a sum of £5,296 19s 5d outstanding to them following the assignment of the debt to them by National Provincial Bank Ltd. Notice of this assignment has already been given to you . . .'. In fact, no such notice had been given and the question arose whether the solicitors' letter was itself a notice of assignment such as to satisfy the statute.

Lord Denning MR: . . . What is a sufficient notice of assignment? There are only two or three cases on the subject. There is the case of *Stanley v English Fibres Industries Ltd* ((1899) 68 LJQB 839), which was accepted and applied by this court in *W F Harrison & Co Ltd v Burke* ([1956] 1 WLR 419). Those cases show that, if a notice of assignment purports to identify the assignment by giving the date of the assignment, and that date is a wrong date, then the notice is bad. The short ground of those decisions was that the notice with a wrong date was a notice of a non-existing document. Assuming those cases to be correct, they leave open the question whether it is necessary to give the date of the assignment. Test it this way: Suppose the mistaken sentence were omitted in this letter so that it ran: 'We have been instructed by our above-named clients to apply to you for the payment of a sum of £5,296 19s 5d outstanding to them following the assignment of the debt to them by the National Provincial Bank Limited.' Would that be a good notice, even though it gives no date for the assignment? I think it would. I think the correct interpretation of this statute was given by Atkin J in *Denney, Gasquet and Metcalfe v Conklin* ([1913] 3 KB 177 at 180). It is quite plain from his judgment that no formal requirements are required for a notice of assignment. It is sufficient if it brings

> to the notice of the debtor with reasonable certainty the fact that the deed does assign the debt due from the debtor so as to bind the debt in his hands and prevent him from paying the debt to the original creditor.

It seems to me to be unnecessary that it should give the date of the assignment so long as it makes it plain that there has in fact been an assignment so that the debtor knows to whom he has to pay the debt in the future. After receiving the notice, the debtor will be entitled, of course, to require a sight of the assignment so as to be satisfied that it is valid, and that the assignee can give him a good discharge. But the notice itself is good, even though it gives no date.

This notice does, however, go on to make an inaccurate statement. It says that, 'Notice of this assignment has already been given to you.' But, as Davies LJ said in the course of the argument, that is merely an inaccurate surplusage. It can be ignored.

Davies LJ: . . . [I]t is very interesting to notice . . . what was the unsuccessful argument by Mr Croom-Johnson for the defendants [in *Denney, Gasquet and Metcalfe v Conlin* [1913] 3 KB 177]. According to the report, he submitted (at 179) that:

> In order to be valid the notice must expressly state (1) that there has been an assignment; (2) the names and addresses of the assignees so that the debtor may be in a position to seek out the new creditors created by the assignment for the purpose of paying the debt; and (3) what has been assigned.

The present document does show all that. It sets out the amount of the debt assigned by the bank to the plaintiffs and claims that that should be paid forthwith. It seems to me that, leaving out of consideration the last sentence of the first paragraph of that letter, it is a perfectly satisfactory notice of assignment in every respect, and that its validity cannot be destroyed by the inaccurate statement in the second sentence of that paragraph.

I agree, for the reasons which my Lord has given, that this appeal should be dismissed.

Widgery LJ: . . . The statute only requires that information relative to the assignment shall be conveyed to the debtor, and that it shall be conveyed in writing. That fact is fully demonstrated by the judgment of Atkin J to which reference has already been made. Once it is appreciated that the section requires no more, it becomes obvious that the objection to the notice in this case, that it was not intended as a notice but merely to record the fact that notice had already been given, must fail. The letter of June 27 in my judgment undoubtedly contains the necessary particulars and it matters not in the slightest that the writer did not think when he wrote the letter that he was performing the function of giving notice under the section.

So far as the argument based on failure to give the date of the assignment is concerned, it seems to me it would be very undesirable to attach to this procedure technicalities which are not mentioned in the statute and which are not necessary to give effect to it. The notice is a notice given by the assignee for his own protection. It is given by the assignee in order to prevent the debtor continuing to deal with the assignor. It is clearly necessary that the debtor should be given information which tells him that an assignment has been made, which identifies the debt, and which sufficiently identifies the assignee. I see no reason at all why other and irrelevant information should be required as a feature of the notice. It is said that in some instances the debtor would want to know the date of the assignment. For my part I find it very difficult to visualise a case in which the date would have any relevance at all so far as the debtor was concerned, and I would certainly regard it as a retrograde step to require, as a general rule, that the notice should specify the date of the assignment. I would therefore dismiss this appeal.

NOTES

1.   The net result of these two decisions is that a notice without a date of assignment can be valid, whereas one with an incorrect date (which is superfluous information) is necessarily invalid. Is that difference founded on a substantial distinction?

2.   It cannot be said that all signs point towards Denning LJ's destination. In *Harrison v Burke*, Morris LJ appears to have adopted a less restrictive interpretation of s 136 than did Denning LJ. Denning LJ considered that any inaccuracy in the notice would vitiate it, whereas Morris LJ's judgment rests on the narrower ground that the notice is only vitiated if the date of the assignment recorded on the notice antedates the actual date of the assignment. Although in *Van Lynn Developments* Lord Denning MR held fast to the position he had taken in *Harrison v Burke* as Denning LJ, the principles on which he decided each case are rather at odds with one another. He decided *Van Lynn Developments* on the ground that the notice would be effective provided that it brought 'to the notice of the debtor with reasonable certainty the fact that the deed does assign the debt due from the debtor so as to bind the debt in his hands and prevent him from paying the debt to the original creditor'. May not the debtor gain this notice even while the date is incorrectly stated in the notice? Furthermore, holding a notice invalid simply because it specifies the incorrect date of the assignment goes against the analogous principles of construction of unilateral notices served under contractual rights as set down by the House of Lords in *Mannai Investment Co Ltd v Eagle Star Life Assurance Co Ltd* [1997] AC 749. In that case, a notice served by a tenant on his landlord to exercise a break clause in a commercial lease specified the wrong date from which it was to operate under the terms of the clause. A majority of the House of Lords nevertheless held the notice to be effective. Lords Steyn, Hoffmann, and Clyde (Lords Goff and Jauncey dissenting) held that the issue turned on how a reasonable recipient would have understood the notice, taking into account the relevant objective 'context' or circumstances. (In *Mannai* it was clear that the reasonable recipient of the notice, knowing the terms of the lease, would have been in no doubt that the tenant wished to determine the lease under the relevant break clause.) Applying the same approach to a notice served on

a debtor under s 136 of the Law of Property Act 1925, it would seem that where the notice specifies the wrong date of the assignment it may still be valid if the reasonable recipient of such a notice would nevertheless realise that he should stop dealing with the assignor and pay the assignee, for then the notice has achieved its purpose (as specified by Widgery LJ in *Van Lynn Developments Ltd v Pelias Construction Co Ltd* [1969] 1 QB 607 at 615).

3.   The key question to arise in these cases is: what is the proper construction of s 136? Denning LJ in *Harrison v Burke* said that '[i]t is only necessary to read section 136 of the Law of Property Act, 1925, to realize that the notice in writing of the assignment is an essential part of the transfer of title to the debt, and, as such, the requirements of the Act must be strictly complied with, and the notice itself, I think, must be strictly accurate'. In order for a legal assignment to occur, the Act makes it essential that there be an absolute assignment, that it be made in writing under the assignor's hand, that express notice of it be given in writing to the debtor, and so on. Where any of those requirements is not ful-filled, no legal assignment will occur: the assignment will rest in equity. To that extent the section is 'strict'. However, to conclude that the express written notice of the assignment must be strictly correct is arguably to read into the statutory text a requirement which is not there.

4.   Notice of an equitable assignment need not be express notice in writing, whereas notice under s 136 must be. Subject to that difference, it is arguable that the requirements of a notice under s 136 are no different in principle from the requirements of a notice in equity. That argument appears to be consistent with the basis and legislative history of the provi-sion. Indeed, the principles on which the Court of Appeal decided *Van Lynn Developments* are, it seems, identical to the equitable principles of notice, which merely require that the assignment is clearly brought to the attention of the debtor, trustee, or fundholder (see, eg, *Whittingstall v King* (1882) 46 LT 520).

5.   In *Curran v Newpark Cinemas Ltd* [1951] 1 All ER 295, below, p 928, the Court of Appeal appears to have accepted that the written notice to the debtor could also constitute the assign-ment in writing itself. For another decision to the same effect, see *Cossill v Strangman* [1963] NSWR 1695, Supreme Court of New South Wales.

(ii) Passing of title to the chose in action at law

Equitable title to a legal chose in action may pass without notice first being given to the debtor. The cases and the legislative history suggest that a 'legal' assignment of a legal chose in action is any of certain select types of equitable assignment which has been converted into a legal chose in action by complying with the requirements of s 136 of the Law of Property Act 1925. Notice as required by the statute—express notice in writing 'given to the debtor, trustee or other person from whom the assignor would have been entitled to claim such debt or thing in action'—is essential if legal title to a legal chose in action is to pass to an assignee.

(iii) Obligor performs in favour of the assignor

Where an assignment compliant with the requirements of s 136 of the Law of Property Act 1925 has occurred except that express written notice as required by the section has not yet been served on the debtor, the debtor is safe in paying the original creditor and assignor. Once effective notice has been given, the section provides that 'the power to give a good discharge' for the 'debt or thing in action' is in the assignee.

(iv) Claims between rival assignees—the rule in Dearle v Hall

The next case required the court to consider whether, and to what extent, the rule in *Dearle v Hall* applies to legal assignments made under s 136 of the Law of Property Act 1925.

Compaq Computer Ltd v Abercorn Group Ltd

[1991] BCC 484, Chancery Division

The facts of the case are set out above, p 917. After considering arguments as to the rule in *Dearle v Hall* with respect to equitable interests and equitable assignments, Mummery J considered a further argument that the rule has no application under s 136 of the Law of Property Act 1925.

Mummery J: ... The paramount plea of the bona fide purchaser for value without notice of an equitable interest in a debt or other legal thing in action has to be considered, however, in the context of s 136(1) of the Law of Property Act 1925 ... The effect of that section was considered by Phillips J in *Pfeiffer* [*E Pfeiffer Weinkellerei-Weineinkauf GmbH & Co v Arbuthnot Factors Ltd* [1988] 1 WLR 150] at p 162. He accepted the submission that the effect of s 136(1) and of the earlier section which it replaced (s 25(6) of the Supreme Court of Judicature Act 1873) was that it enabled the assignee to acquire a title which has all the procedural advantages of legal title, but so far as priorities are concerned his position is no better than if the assignment had been effected prior to those Acts. Phillips J said at p 162:

> It follows that, even if the assignment is effected for value without notice of a prior equity, priorities fall to be determined as if the assignment had been effected in equity, not in law.

That view was challenged but the judge held that it was supported by the views expressed by Channell J on s 25(6) of the 1873 Act in *Marchant v Morton, Down & Co* at p 832. No distinction was drawn in that case or in *Pfeiffer* between an assignment for value and a voluntary assignment.

It was submitted on behalf of Kellock that the conclusion of Phillips J on this point was wrong, particularly in not recognising a distinction between an assignee for value and a volunteer. I was referred to *Read v Brown* (1888) 22 QBD 128, a case not cited in *Pfeiffer*, for the proposition that s 25(6) of the 1873 Act gave to the assignee of a debt more than the mere right to sue for it. Lord Esher MR said at 131:

> ... it gives him the debt and the legal right to the debt ...

He rejected the contention that the provision only affected procedure and confirmed that the words meant what they said, ie they transferred the legal right to the debt as well as the legal remedies for its recovery. He said at p 132:

> The debt is transferred to the assignee and becomes as though it has been his from the beginning; it is no longer to be the debt of the assignor at all, who cannot sue for it, the right to sue being taken from him; the assignee becomes the assignee of a legal debt and is not merely an assignee in equity, and the debt being his, he can sue for it, and sue in his own name.

It was submitted that if this is correct, the matter of priorities is not as stated by Phillips J in *Pfeiffer*. I was referred to obiter comments of Robert Goff J in *Ellerman Lines Ltd v Lancaster Maritime Co Ltd* [1980] 2 Lloyd's Rep 497 at p 503 that:

> ... a legal assignment ... ranks before any equitable interest, even a prior equitable interest, unless the assignee had actual or constructive notice of the equitable interest at the time of the assignment.

> I was also referred to obiter remarks of Viscount Finlay in *Performing Right Society Ltd v London Theatre of Varieties Ltd* [1924] AC 1 at p 19 to the effect that:
>
> > There may possibly be cases in which a person who has made an equitable assignment might by a subsequent assignment have transferred the legal interest in the same work to a purchaser for value without notice, whose title would prevail over the merely equitable right, and such a possibility is one reason for the rule of making the legal owner a party.
>
> Those authorities were not cited to Phillips J in *Pfeiffer* but I have not been convinced by the arguments advanced on behalf of Kellock that he came to the wrong conclusion in holding that, even if there is a legal assignment for value without notice of a prior equity, priorities fall to be determined as if the assignment had been effected in equity. Section 136(1) provides that the assignment is 'subject to equities having priority over the right of the assignee'. The effect of those words is to create, in the case of a statutory assignment of a chose in action, an exception to the general rule that an equity will not prevail against a bona fide purchaser of a legal estate for value without notice of the prior equity. If that is so, in the hands of Abercorn, the assignor to Kellock, the rights of action against the subpurchasers which it assigned to Kellock were subject to an earlier equitable assignment of those same rights to Compaq and Kellock therefore took subject to that prior equity. Unless the rule in *Dearle v Hall* were applicable, the result would be determined by the ordinary rule as to priorities, ie the basic rule of the order of creation where the merits are equal. The rule in *Dearle v Hall* apart, Kellock could not put itself in a stronger position than Abercorn as against Compaq by giving notice of the assignment from Abercorn to the subpurchasers and by then seeking to rely on the statutory assignment thereby completed to take in priority to the equity of Compaq.
>
> As I have mentioned, it is not necessary to form a final view on this point in order to answer the points of law raised by way of preliminary issue. As at present advised, however, I would follow the decision of Phillips J in *Pfeiffer.*

(v) Equities

Section 136(1) of the Law of Property Act 1925 provides that assignments within its terms 'are effectual in law (subject to equities have priority over the right of the assignee) to pass and transfer' the legal right to the chose in action, all remedies for the same, and the power to give a good discharge for the same. Those equities include equitable set-offs (discussed below, p 944): *Compaq Computers*, above.

(vi) Notice to assignee?

The possibility that notice to the assignee might be required in order for an equitable assignment to be made of a legal chose was considered above (p 921). Is the position any different under s 136 of the Law of Property Act 1925?

Curran v Newpark Cinemas Ltd
[1951] 1 All ER 295, Court of Appeal

Curran obtained judgment against Newpark Cinemas for a debt and costs. The debt was paid but the costs remained outstanding so Curran procured the issue of a garnishee summons against a debtor of Newpark Cinemas. The debtor opposed the summons claiming that, before being served with the summons, Newpark Cinemas had already given the debtor written notice that 'pursuant to the arrangements for valuable consideration which we, Newpark Cinemas Ltd, have made with Barclays Bank Ltd, we give you irrevocable directions, instructions and authority to pay to the said Barclays Bank Ltd . . . all moneys payable to us. . . . This authority and instructions can be varied or cancelled only by a document duly signed on behalf of Barclays Bank Ltd . . .' No notice of assignment had been given by the bank to the debtor and there was no evidence that the bank had been given notice of the document sent by Newpark Cinemas to the debtor. The county court judge held there had been no valid assignment of the debt to the bank. The debtor appealed to the Court of Appeal (Somervell, Jenkins, and Birkett LJJ).

Jenkins LJ read the judgment of the court: . . . It is, no doubt, true that s 136(1) does not require any particular form of assignment, or that the notice given to the debtor should necessarily have been given by the assignee. The sub-section does, however, clearly postulate that, whatever its form, there should be a document amounting to an absolute assignment by writing under the hand of the assignor. Given such an assignment, and given the requisite notice to the debtor, the assignment (to put it shortly) is to operate as a legal assignment of the debt in question. Section 136(1), however, does not provide that a document which would not, independently of the sub-section or its predecessor (Supreme Court of Judicature Act 1873, s 25(6)), have operated as an absolute assignment at law or in equity is to have the force of an absolute assignment for the purposes of the sub-section. The document here relied on is the direction and authority, which in point of form is not an assignment to the bank of the debt in question but merely a direction to the garnishees to pay the debt in question to the bank. On the footing that there had, in fact, been no prior agreement with the bank to give such a direction, and that the bank had not been notified of the fact that such a direction had been given, we think the result would follow that the direction and authority, though expressed to be irrevocable except with the consent of the bank, could in fact have been revoked by the judgment debtors at any time as amounting to no more than an arrangement between the judgment debtors and the garnishees in which they alone were concerned and which, in the absence of any such agreement or notification, conferred no interest in the debt on the bank. If that is right, then we think that the contention of counsel for the garnishees to the effect that the mere production by the garnishees of the direction and authority, without proof of any agreement with, or notice to, the bank, sufficed in itself to establish an absolute assignment of which express notice had been given to the garnishees, and hence a legal assignment by virtue of s 136(1), necessarily fails.

[The Court of Appeal held that whilst there was no evidence that the bank had not been given notice of the direction and authority, there was prima facie evidence of an assignment in that the notice to the debtor referred to prior arrangements with the bank. The garnishee order was set aside and the case remitted to the county court with a view to the bank being ordered to appear and state its claim.]

Grey v Australian Motorists & General Insurance Co Pty Ltd
[1976] 1 NSWLR 669, Court of Appeal of New South Wales

Grey was a car repairer. The defendant was an insurance company which indemnified motorists against the costs of having their vehicles repaired. Grey claimed the cost of repair of six vehicles from the defendant. The defendant claimed that Grey was not the proper plaintiff as he had previously assigned the debts in question to a finance company. It was alleged that Grey had assigned the debts by completing a number of standard forms of assignment supplied by the finance company which stated that Grey 'irrevocably directs payment of this account direct to the absolute assignee thereof [the finance company]'. The completed forms had been sent to the defendant to obtain payment but there was no evidence that the finance company had notice of or assented to the assignments. A central issue before the

Court of Appeal was whether there could be a statutory assignment under s 136 (or rather its Australian equivalent) when no notice of the assignment had been given to the assignee. The Court of Appeal (Samuels and Mahoney JJA; Glass JA dissenting) held that there had been a statutory assignment of the debts.

Glass JA (dissenting): . . . There is little authority on the question whether the operation of the section depends on the assent of the purported assignee. It is clear that a transfer of property made in proper form vests the title in the transferee at once, notwithstanding his lack of knowledge: *Standing v Bowring* ((1885) 31 Ch D 282). His remedy, if he wishes to reject the gift, is to transfer it back. Accordingly, the absence of consent cannot invalidate the assignment. His Honour ruled, however, that an assignment uncommunicated to the assignee cannot be absolute within the meaning of the section. He relied in this respect upon the following passage in the judgment of Asprey JA in *International Leasing Corpn (Vic) Ltd v Aiken* ((1967) 85 WNNSW 766 at 793): '. . . there can be no effective *absolute* assignment of a debt as between an assignor and an assignee within the meaning of s 12 unless and until the assignee has had notice of the assignment executed by the assignor and has assented to it (see *Rekstin v Severo Sibirsko etc and Bank of Russian Trade Ltd* ([1933] 1 KB 47); Jenks' *English Civil Law*, 4th edn, vol 2, para 1626, pp 890–892; see also *Curran v Newpark Cinemas Ltd* ([1951] 1 All ER 295), where both the last-mentioned case and *Standing v Bowring* were referred to; and cf *Norman v Federal Comr of Taxation* ((1963) 109 CLR 9 at 29), per Windeyer J. An assignment of a debt uncommunicated to the assignee can only be a conditional assignment, that is to say, predicated upon the condition that if the assignee repudiates it when it is brought to his notice, there would be without more, an automatic revesting of the legal ownership of the debt in the assignor.'

With great respect to his Honour, I cannot agree that his proposition is supported by authority in the general terms in which it is formulated. *Rekstin's* case depends upon the special rules governing the relationship of banker and customer. Jenks quoted *Rekstin's* case; and *Curran's* case, to which I shall later refer, stands upon different ground. An absolute assignment is to be contrasted with a conditional assignment. A conditional assignment is an assignment which becomes operative or ceases to be operative upon the happening of an event: *Durham Bros v Robertson* ([1898] 1 QB 765 at 773). Accordingly, an assignment of a chose in action, until a loan is repaid is conditional: ibid. But an assignment of a debt with a proviso for redemption and reassignment upon repayment of a loan is absolute: *Tonered v Delagoa Bay and East Africa Rly Co* ((1889) 23 QBD 239). A distinction is clearly drawn between a reassignment occurring by force of the original transaction (conditional), and a reassignment which depends upon a further assurance (absolute). These authorities, as well as *Standing v Bowring* and the language of the section, and, in my view, inconsistent with the general proposition that an assignment, otherwise absolute in its terms, must operate conditionally where the assignee, not having been consulted, has the right to reassign . . .

In *Curran v Newpark Cinemas Ltd* the court had before it a direction to a second party to pay money to a bank which had not been communicated to the bank. It was held that the document relied on failed to establish an absolute assignment to the bank, because the direction to pay recorded in it could have been revoked at any time by the party giving it, in the absence of evidence that the bank had been notified or had agreed to the arrangement. The document before us takes a different form. . . . In *Curran's* case the assignment was subject to a condition subsequent.

[However, Glass JA went on to hold that the assignments were conditional on other grounds and, therefore, outside the statute.]

Samuels JA: . . . *Curran's* case is distinguishable from the present one. There, Jenkins LJ, as he then was, emphasized that the document in question was not in form an assignment, but 'merely a direction to the garnishees to pay a third party (ie the bank) ...' and could only answer the description of an assignment 'if and when communicated to the bank, as, until so communicated, it was revocable by the judgment debtors at any time and, therefore, not absolute'. The authority referred to is *Rekstin's* case. His Lordship went on to say that, although s 136(1) of the Law of Property Act 1925 (the equivalent of s 12 of the Conveyancing Act) did not require any particular form of assignment, it did however 'clearly postulate that, whatever its form, there should be a document amounting to an absolute assignment by writing under the hand of the assignor. Given such an assignment, and given the requisite notice to the debtor, the assignment (to put it shortly) is to operate as a legal assignment of the debt in question'. Accordingly, I would read that judgment (which was the judgment of the court) as having no application to a case where the document relied on is in form an assignment which would, independently of statute, have operated as an absolute assignment at law or in equity. The distinction relevant for present purposes is really that between an assignment and a mere revocable mandate or authority . . .

Finally, and perhaps most importantly, s 12 sets out the requirements of an effective statutory assignment. It provides that the assignment must be absolute and in writing and stipulates for express notice to the debtor. But it does not mention notice to the assignee, much less the necessity for his consent; nor are either of these stipulations to be found in s 136 of the Law of Property Act 1925 (Imp.). And they did not appear in s 25(6) of the Judicature Act 1873 (Imp.) which s 136 replaced. According to s 12, the conditions to be satisfied if an assignment is to derive validity from the statute are that it must be absolute, in writing and written notice must be given to the debtor. If, in addition, notice to the assignee were required, one would have expected the statute to prescribe it.

[**Mahoney JA** decided the case on the basis that Grey had admitted that the debts had been assigned.]

NOTE

A simple, or simplistic, contrast between *Curran* and *Grey* might be to say that notice to the assignee is required for a statutory assignment in England, but not in Australia. However, the difference in the cases evidently turns on a narrower point: in what circumstances a court will find, as a fact, that a putative assignor intended to assign—ie immediately and irrevocably to transfer the relevant chose in action—to an assignee where the assignee was unaware of the proposed transaction.

7 EFFECTS OF ASSIGNMENT

(a) Equitable assignment

(i) Title and procedure

The Assignment of Contractual Rights by G Tolhurst
(2nd edn, 2016), para 4.05

Historically, for an equitable assignee of a legal right to enforce the legal right the action had to be brought by the assignee in the name of the assignor. If the assignor refused to allow its name to be used the assignee could, if the assignment was for valuable consideration, file a bill in equity and, upon giving an indemnity as to costs, obtain an injunction allowing the assignor's name to be used in a suit at law to recover the assigned debt. The action had the appearance of one brought by the assignor. Even today, because the assignor remains the legal owner of the debt, he or she [retains] a cause of action.

Roberts v Gill

[2011] 1 AC 240, Supreme Court

In this case, principles of assignment were exposed in the course of resolving questions about limitation periods and deceased estates. The claimant commenced proceedings to recover damages for the tort of negligence from two firms of solicitors. He claimed as a beneficiary of his late grandmother's estate and in his own right. The limitation period expired. He thereafter made an application in which he asserted new claims which, under s 35 of the Limitation Act 1980, would be fresh claims still within time. In the application, he sought to continue the claims in his personal capacity and as a derivative action on behalf of the deceased estate. Permission to amend his claim depended, inter alia, on showing exceptional circumstances that would justify his bringing the derivative action, rather than (as is normally the case) it being brought by an executor. The trial judge held that there were no special circumstances. The Court of Appeal held that there were special circumstances but refused leave to amend for other reasons. In the Supreme Court, it was held that there were no special circumstances. In delivering their reasons, the Justices of the Supreme Court referred to the similar requirement in the law of assignment that an equitable assignee may only sue a third party obligor in special circumstances.

> **Lord Collins of Mapesbury JSC**: ... [I]f an equitable assignee sues a third party, the assignor must be joined as a defendant: *EM Bowden's Patents Syndicate Ltd v Herbert Smith & Co* [1904] 2 Ch 86, 91, per Warrington J; *William Brandt's Sons & Co v Dunlop Rubber Co Ltd* [1905] AC 454, 462, per Lord Macnaghten; *Performing Right Society Ltd v London Theatre of Varieties Ltd* [1924] AC 1, 13–14, 19–20, 29, per Viscount Cave LC, Viscount Finlay, Lord Sumner; *Vandepitte v Preferred Accident Insurance Corpn of New York* [1933] AC 70, 79, per Lord Wright; *Harmer v Armstrong* [1934] Ch 65, 82, per Lord Hanworth MR.
>
> But it is not an invariable rule: *Performing Right Society Ltd v London Theatre of Varieties Ltd* [1924] AC 1, 14 ('there may be special cases where it will not be enforced' per Viscount Cave LC). In that decision it was held that an equitable assignee may obtain interlocutory relief but was not entitled to obtain a final injunction without joining the legal owners. Viscount Cave LC said, at p 14:
>
>> That an equitable owner may commence proceedings alone, and may obtain interim protection in the form of an interlocutory injunction, is not in doubt; but it was always the rule of the Court of Chancery, and is, I think, the rule of the Supreme Court, that, in general, when a plaintiff has only an equitable right in the thing demanded, the person having the legal right to demand it must in due course be made a party to the action ... Further, under Order XVI, r 11, no action can now be defeated by reason of the misjoinder or non-joinder of any party; but this does not mean that judgment can be obtained in the absence of a necessary party to the action, and the rule is satisfied by allowing parties to be added at any stage of a case. Subject to these observations, I think that the general rule is still operative ...
>
> *William Brandt's Sons & Co v Dunlop Rubber Co Ltd* was a case in which an assignee was allowed to proceed to judgment without joining the assignor. That was because the whole focus of the litigation was on the question whether instructions given by the bank's customer to purchasers of rubber to pay its bank direct amounted to an equitable assignment of debts, so that the bank could sue for their recovery. The bank sued the purchasers directly without joining its customer, the assignor. The fact that the assignor was not a party seems to have been overlooked until the House of Lords held that there had been an equitable assignment. Lord Macnaghten said, at p 462:

> Strictly speaking, [the sellers], or their trustee in bankruptcy, should have been brought before the court. But no action is now dismissed for want of parties, and the trustee in bankruptcy had really no interest in the matter. At your Lordships' bar the Dunlops disclaimed any wish to have him present, and in both courts below they claimed to retain for their own use any balance that might remain after satisfying Brandts.

> Lord James said, at p 464: 'The defect in the parties to the suit can be remedied.'

> In more modern times it has been held that, although the practice was to join the assignor, the requirement is a procedural one, the absence of which can be cured. The assignor must be joined before a final judgment can be obtained by the assignee, but the action is validly constituted without joinder, so that if the assignee sues without joining the assignor, the action is in time for the purposes of limitation: *Central Insurance Co Ltd v Seacalf Shipping Corpn (The Aiolos)* [1983] 2 Lloyd's Rep 25, 34, per Oliver LJ; *Weddell v JA Pearce & Major* [1988] Ch 26, 40, per Scott J; and cf *Robinson v Unicos Property Corpn Ltd* [1962] 1 WLR 520, 525–526, per Holroyd Pearce and Harman LJJ; *Three Rivers District Council v Governor and Company of the Bank of England* [1996] QB 292, 309, 313, per Peter Gibson LJ. For criticism see GJ Tolhurst, 'Equitable Assignment of Legal Rights: A Resolution to a Conundrum' (2002) 118 LQR 98, 111–116.

> What distinguishes these cases from the present one is that in the case of an equitable assign-ment the assignee is the true owner and the assignor is a bare trustee ... [I]t is plain that, other than in the most exceptional circumstances such as existed in *William Brandt's Sons & Co v Dunlop Rubber Co Ltd* [1905] AC 454, even in the case of an equitable assignment the assignee cannot proceed to judgment without joining the assignor.

> [**Lord Rodger of Earlsferry JSC**, **Lord Walker of Gestingthorpe JSC**, and **Lord Clarke of Stone-cum-Ebony JSC** agreed with Lord Collins on this point. **Lord Hope of Craighead DPSC** delivered (at [84]) short reasons consistent with this reasoning of Lord Collins.]

NOTES

1. A deal has been made of situations in which joinder did not occur at the outset of pro-ceedings, or at all, as showing that joiner is not 'essential' (eg *Kapoor v National Westminster Bank plc* [2011] EWCA Civ 1083, [2012] All ER 1201). In *William Brandt's* case the assignor was not joined; Lord Macnaghten said that 'strictly' it or its trustee in bankruptcy should have been joined, and then glossed over the matter: Smith (2008) 124 LQR 517. In the *Performing Right Society* case, as Lord Collins explained, the assignee was permitted to seek an interim injunction without joining the assignor, but was not permitted to obtain a permanent injunc-tion without joining the assignor. Does the fact that joinder is not always essential allow it to be said that joinder is never essential, or that it should never be so?

2. Another instructive account of the principles of assignment may be found in the Court of Appeal's decision in *Three Rivers District Council v Bank of England* [1996] QB 292 at 299, CA, noted by M Leeming (1995) 111 LQR 549; A Tettenborn [1995] CLJ 499.

(ii) Partial assignment

Kapoor v National Westminster Bank plc
[2011] EWCA Civ 1083, [2012] All ER 1201, Court of Appeal

The question in this case was whether an equitable assignee of part of a debt was entitled to vote at a meeting of the creditors of the debtor. The debtor's financial circumstances were febrile. He wished there to be a meeting of creditors in the hope they would approve an individual voluntary agreement (or IVA), by which he would repay his various debts according to an agreed plan. On the basis of the relevant provisions of the Insolvency Act 1986 and the Insolvency Rules 1986, the Court of Appeal held on the facts that the partial assignee was not entitled to vote at the creditors' meeting. Although it was unnecessary to do so, the Court of Appeal also discussed the effect of partial assignments in equity.

> **Etherton LJ**: ... There is no good reason of policy or principle for the courts to refuse to recognise the title of the undisputed equitable assignee of part of a debt, and every good reason for the courts to refuse to recognise the bare legal title of the assignor, except where the assignor is a trustee for the assignee and expressly suing as such or the assignee joins in the proceedings. As the Court of Appeal in *Three Rivers* [*District Council v Bank of England* [1996] QB 292] said, that approach is entirely consistent with section 49 of the Senior Courts Act 1981 ... [T]he consistent line of authority, binding on this court, is that the equitable assignee of a debt, and not the equitable assignor, has the substantive legal right to sue for the assigned debt. Although there is a procedural requirement that the assignee should join the assignor in order to protect the debtor from successive actions and to prevent conflicting decisions, even that procedural requirement will not apply or may be dispensed with by the court in appropriate circumstances, most particularly where those concerns do not apply.

NOTES

1.   Professor Tolhurst has demonstrated that the line between 'substance' and 'procedure' is not without problems in relation to equitable assignment or, indeed, assignment under s 136 of the Law of Property Act 1925. The reasoning of Etherton LJ in *Kapoor* suggests a simple division between the bare title to a chose in action, and the substantive benefit thereof. Does that division fail to account for the realities of the cases (such as those discussed by Lord Collins in *Roberts v Gill*) or is Etherton LJ's division a progressive clarification of the law? Consider the Court of Appeal's judgments in *Deposit Protection Board v Dalia* [1994] 2 AC 367, CA, and see PG Turner [2012] CLJ 270.

2.   On occasion it will suit a partial assignee of a chose in action to assert that the legal title to the chose is illusory. Will such assertions always be in the interests of a partial assignee?

(iii) Options

A particular question as to the effect of an equitable assignment between the parties is: may the equitable assignee exercise an option to renew a contract given that the legal title to the relevant chose in action remains vested in the assignor? In *Warner Bros Records Inc v Rollgreen Ltd* [1976] QB 430, the Court of Appeal held that an equitable assignee of an option to renew a contract for services (a legal chose), who had not given notice of his assignment to the other contracting party, could not exercise the option. Roskill LJ said (at 443) that the only right that can be created in such circumstances in the equitable assignee is the right against the assignor 'who thenceforth becomes the trustee of the benefit of the option for the assignee'. The decision has been criticised on the ground that it fails to distinguish between substantive rights arising in equity out of assignments and the procedure for their enforcement; or between assignments and agreements to assign (E Peel, *Treitel's Law of Contract* (14th edn, 2015), para 15–022, fn 93): that is, once the assignee has the substantive benefit of the chose in action, it ought to be recognised that the assignee holds substantive entitlements directly of the obligor. It may be that the discussion of this point distracts from another question of substance: whether, as a matter of construction of the option, the offer contained therein may only be exercised by the grantee of the option, or whether it may also be exercised by an assignee of the grantee. The answer to that question could conceivably deprive analysis of the equities of assignor and assignee of its importance.

(b) Legal assignment

The relations of the parties to an assignment under s 136 of the Law of Property Act 1925 are those set out in the section itself, subject to any elaborations made by the parties in their agreements among themselves. The obligor becomes liable to perform to the assignee, rather than the assignor. The assignee becomes entitled to receive performance to issue a good receipt to the debtor upon receiving payment sufficient to discharge a debt assigned to the assignee. Upon an obligor's failure to perform, s 136 entitles the assignee to all legal and other remedies available to enforce the relevant obligation.

(c) General

(i) No compliance with 'non-assignment' clause

The force of Lord Browne-Wilkinson's reasoning in *Linden Gardens Trust Ltd v Lenesta Sludge Disposals Ltd* [1994] 1 AC 85 (above) is that the effect of a clause restricting assignment is in the first instance a matter of construction. Did the parties intend that choses in action arising from their contract should nevertheless be assignable but that the assigning party should be liable for damages? Did the parties intend that the chose should be unassignable, and that an attempt to assign it should constitute a repudiatory breach of contract? His Lordship thought these possibilities 'very unlikely' (at 104). Unlikely agreements are, nevertheless, made.

More likely, Lord Browne-Wilkinson thought, is that parties will have intended that the chose in action should be unassignable—or, more accurately perhaps, that the chose should be assignable only in accordance with any provisions therefor in the contract. Whether an attempted assignment constitutes a breach is then a question of fact and intention. Sometimes, the drafting of a non-assignment clause provides that an attempt to assign choses in action arising from the contract constitutes a breach of contract. The clause in *Hendry v Chartsearch Ltd* [1998] CLC 1382 did not so provide. Millett LJ held (at 1394) that where an ordinary commercial contract provides that a party should not be entitled to assign the benefit of the agreement without the debtor's prior consent, a purported assignment in the face of that prohibition does not constitute a breach of the assignor's contract with the debtor, let alone a repudiatory breach of contract, so that the assignor could later go back to the debtor for his consent to a new assignment.

What remedy does an assignee have against his assignor where the assignment is ineffective against the debtor because of a non-assignment clause? The relationship between the assignor and an assignee for value remains a contractual one. Save where the terms of their agreement amounts to a declaration of trust in favour of the assignee of the benefit of the assignor's contract with the debtor, the purported assignment does not amount to the legal or equitable transfer of any proprietary interest to the assignee (*R v Chester and North Wales Legal Aid Area Office, ex p Floods of Queensferry Ltd* [1998] 2 BCLC 436 at 442–443 at 445, CA—where it was expressly held that the corporate assignor had not declared itself a trustee of its cause of action against the debtor; applied in *Bawejem Ltd v MC Fabrications Ltd* [1999]

1 All ER (Comm) 377, CA). In many cases it will be possible for the assignee to bring a breach of contract claim against the assignor where the assignor has failed to obtain the debtor's consent to the assignment: *Linden Gardens Trust Ltd v Lenesta Sludge Disposals Ltd* [1994] 1 AC 85 at 109–110. However, where the assignor becomes insolvent after the purported assignment and receives payment from the debtor, the assignee will need to assert a proprietary claim against the assignor in order to take priority over his other creditors. In some cases the assignee may be able to rely on the assignor's conduct as amounting to a declaration of trust of the proceeds of the debt in favour of the assignee (see *Re Turcan* (1888) 40 Ch D 5, cited without disapproval by Lord Browne-Wilkinson in *Linden Gardens* at 106: see above). Although an equitable assignor is often described as a 'trustee' or 'constructive trustee' for the assignee, it would be unsafe to assume that that 'trust' or 'constructive' trust confers proprietary claims on the assignee. Cf *GE Crane Pty Ltd v Federal Commissioner of Taxation* (1971) 126 CLR 177, per Menzies J.

(ii) Assignee cannot recover more than assignor

An assignee cannot recover more from the debtor than the assignor could have done had there been no assignment. The principle is of limited scope. It is designed to ensure that the debtor is no worse off as a result of the assignment; it does not enable the debtor to rely on the fact of the assignment in order to escape liability for his breach of contract. The next case illustrates the point.

Offer-Hoar v Larkstore Ltd (Technotrade Ltd, Part 20 defendants)
[2006] EWCA Civ 1079, [2006] 1 WLR 2926, Court of Appeal

Starglade Ltd commissioned Technotrade Ltd, which offered geo-technical site investigation and engineering services, to produce a soil inspection report on a sloping site in Hythe, Kent that Starglade owned. The report showed that the site was satisfactory for a proposed housing development. Starglade used the report to gain full planning permission. Starglade then sold the site to Larkstore, a property development company. Larkstore engaged contractors to carry out building works on the site. While the building works were being carried out, a landslip occurred causing damage to adjacent properties uphill from the site. The owners of those uphill properties alleged that the landslip was caused by the building works. Extensive stabilisation works had to be undertaken by Larkstore. Larkstore then took a statutory assignment of Technotrade's site inspection report from Starglade 'together with all the benefit and interest and rights of Starglade in and under the report and the right to enforce the same'. The owners of the damaged uphill properties commenced proceedings against Larkstore, which itself started Part 20 proceedings against Technotrade, relying on the assignment of the cause of action as the basis of a contractual claim for damages for breach. A number of preliminary points were raised for determination by Wilcox J, but only one substantial issue survived for determination by the Court of Appeal. The issue was whether Larkstore was able, by virtue of the assignment from Starglade, to recover the loss allegedly suffered by it, even though Starglade had not suffered substantial damage while it was entitled to the benefit of the contract with Technotrade and when the cause of action arose and even though the landslip causing the damage occurred before the assignment to Larkstore. It was assumed for the determination of the preliminary issues that there had been a breach of contract by Technotrade in respect of the soil inspection report. Judge David Wilcox determined the issue in favour of Larkstore: [2005] EWHC 2742 (TCC). Technotrade appealed.

Mummery LJ:

THE ISSUE

This appeal is against a ruling on a preliminary issue in Part 20 proceedings. The litigation arises from a dispute about liability for the substantial physical damage and financial loss resulting from building operations on a residential development site.

The main issue turns on the legal effect of the assignment of a cause of action for breach of contract. Is the assignee of the cause of action entitled to recover from the contract-breaker damages for loss, which occurred after the transfer of the development site by the assignor to the assignee, but before the assignment of the cause of action, in a larger sum than the assignor would have recovered?

One possible answer to this question would produce 'a legal black hole.' The expression cropped up in argument. The whole topic of assignment, including possible 'black holes', is of special interest to practitioners in construction law and their clients. A 'black hole' scenario would occur when loss is suffered in consequence of a breach of contract, but the contract-breaker's position is that no-one is legally entitled to recover substantial damages from him.

The question was well put in a Note in the Law Quarterly Review (1994) 110 LQR 42 at p 44; I N Duncan Wallace QC)—

> ... whether ... a contract-breaker can avoid an otherwise inescapable liability in damages as a result of the accident of the transfer of the property and assignment of the benefit of the relevant ... contract to a third party, either by arguing that the original contracting party or assignor, having parted with the property at full value, has suffered no loss and that the assignee cannot be in a better position, or conversely that an assignee, in a case where he alone can sue, has paid a reduced price, equally suffering no loss. In other words, does the accident of transfer and assignment create a 'legal black hole' into which the right to damages disappears, leaving the contract-breaker with an uncovenanted immunity?

It will be necessary to consider the leading authorities on the effect of the assignment of a cause of action for breach of contract on the liability of the contract-breaker to the assignee for damages, notably the case of *Linden Gardens Trust v Lenesta Sludge Disposals* [1994] 1 AC 85 and (in the Court of Appeal) 57 BLR 57 (*Linden Gardens*). We have been referred to valuable discussions of the decision in an extended case note in the Law Quarterly Review by Mr I N Duncan Wallace QC: (1994) LQR Vol 110 at pp 42–55 and in an article in the Construction Law Journal by Mr John Cartwright — (1993) 9 Const LJ pp 281–296.

The 'black hole' question arises here in the context of the assignment of a contract claim for an allegedly negligent soil inspection report obtained by the original owner of a building site for residential development. After the site ceased to be in the ownership of the company which obtained the report, a landslip occurred in the course of building operations by the contractor, who was engaged by the purchaser of the site from the original owner. The cause of action in respect of the report had not, however, been assigned when the site was sold. It was assigned only after the landslip. The assignment was made nearly 5 years after the site itself had changed hands.

. . .

ASSIGNMENT POINT: GENERAL PRINCIPLES

The perceived problem of the effect of the assignment on the assignee's right to recover substantial damages is temporal in origin. It arises from the particular order in which the following events occurred: the breach of contract by Technotrade, the transfer of ownership of the Site by Starglade to Larkstore, the damage caused by the landslip after the transfer, and the assignment of the cause of action by Starglade to Larkstore, which occurred years after the transfer of the Site.

There are 3 relevant points of time.
1) The time of the breach of contract by Technotrade. The contractual cause of action against Technotrade arose when Starglade was the owner of the Site. Starglade was only entitled to recover nominal damages at that time. No substantial damage could be established until the occurrence of the landslip in October 2001.
2) The time of the landslip. Larkstore was the owner of the Site at the time when the landslip occurred and substantial damage was suffered. Starglade was still entitled to the chose in action, but it was not entitled to recover substantial damages, as it had ceased to own the Site. Larkstore owned the Site and suffered substantial damage, but was not entitled to recover damages form Technotrade for breach of contract, because it had no contract with Technotrade and, at that time, had no assignment from Starglade of the benefit of its contract, rights of action and remedies for breach of contract.
3) The time of the assignment. Starglade could not, it was submitted, assign to Larkstore more than it had. It did not have a claim for substantial damages against Technotrade in contract, as it had ceased to own the Site before the assignment and before the landslip.

The answer to the perceived problem of a limit on the damages which Larkstore, as assignee, is entitled to recover from Technotrade is to be found, in my judgment, in an analysis of the cause of action itself. In this case the cause of action was the right to sue Technotrade for breach of contract in respect of the preparation of the soil inspection report on the Site. The cause of action was complete in December 1998 when Technotrade produced the soil report for Starglade.

It is accepted that the report and the rights of action and remedies in respect of it were assignable and were not personal to Starglade. It is also accepted that, although the damages which Starglade could have recovered at the date when the cause of action was complete would have been no more than nominal damages, Starglade, if it had remained the owner of the Site, would have been entitled to claim and, if able to prove, recover substantial damages for the landslip which occurred in October 2001.

The remedy in damages for breach of contract is not limited to the loss that could have been proved at the date when the breach occurred and the cause of action first arose. Subject to factual and legal issues of causation, remoteness, quantum and limitation of actions, there is a remedy in damages against the contract breaker for loss which occurs after the cause of action has accrued. A cause of action may arise years before any substantial damage occurs, as, for example, in the case of negligent advice on title. There is no legal principle which protects the contract-breaker by excluding his liability for substantial damage that occurs after the initial breach of contract.

What difference, if any, can an assignment of the cause of action make to the remedies available to the assignee against the contract-breaker? A statutory assignment in writing under section 136 of the Law of Property Act 1925, of which express notice has been given, as was done in this case, is effectual in law to pass and transfer from the date of notice the legal right to the thing in action and 'all legal and other remedies for the same.' The statutory assignment is expressly made 'subject to equities having priority over the right of the assignee.'

Mr Friedman QC (who did not appear in the court below) submitted on behalf of Technotrade that the assignment makes a crucial difference. His broad submission was that the only losses that Larkstore is entitled to claim by virtue of the assignment of the cause of action are the losses that Starglade could itself have recovered from Technotrade at the time of the assignment. As the assignment of the cause of action took place after Starglade had parted with the Site to Larkstore and the substantial damage occurred before the assignment of the cause of action to Larkstore, Starglade and therefore Larkstore had no right to claim and recover substantial damages for loss resulting from the landslip.

In its defence to the Part 20 Particulars of Claim Technotrade pleaded that Starglade's rights of action are of no assistance to Larkstore, as Starglade has suffered no losses (paragraph 31). It is pleaded in paragraph 30—

(i) The well established principle that an assignee of a chose in action (here Larkstore) cannot recover more than the assignor (here Starglade) has lost, is applicable on the particular facts of this claim, which it is averred does not fit within any of the exceptions to the said principle. Starglade has suffered no loss and Larkstore is not entitled to put itself in any better position than the principal to the contract which it has purported to assign.

The scope of the principle pleaded is discussed generally in *Chitty on Contracts* (29th Edition-2004) Ch 19—

19–073 Assignee cannot recover more than assignor

19–073 A further aspect of the idea that an assignee takes an assignment 'subject to equities' is the principle that an assignee cannot recover more from the debtor than the assignor could have done had there been no assignment. For example, in *Dawson v. Great Northern & City Railway Co* the assignment of a statutory claim for compensation for damage to land did not entitle the assignee to recover extra loss suffered by reason of a trade carried on by him, but not the assignor, that the assignor would not have suffered.

19–074 The application of this principle has given rise to particular difficulty in relation to building contracts or tort claims for damage to buildings. Say, for example, a building is sold at full value along with an assignment to the purchaser of claims in contract or tort in relation to the building. The building turns out to need repairs as a result of a breach of the builder's contract with the assignor (whether that breach is prior, or subsequent, to the sale to the as- signee) or of a tort (damaging the building prior to the sale). The assignee pays for the repairs. It might be argued that the assignor in that situation has suffered no loss so that, applying the governing principle that the assignee cannot recover more than the assignor, the assignee has no substantial claim. If correct, '… the claim to damages would disappear … into some legal black hole, so that the wrong-doer escaped scot-free.' Acceptance of the argument would also nullify the purpose of the governing principle which is to avoid prejudice to the debtor and not to allow the debtor to escape liability.

19–075 Perhaps not surprisingly, therefore, that argument was rejected by the House of Lords in a Scottish delict case. And the problem has been circumvented in England by the courts' recognition that, where a third party is, or will become, owner of a defective or dam- aged property, there is an exception to the general rule that a contracting party can recover damages for its own loss and not for the loss of a third party. Where the exception applies, the contracting party (the assignor) is entitled to substantial damages for the loss suffered by the third party (the assignee): by the same token, an award of substantial damages to the assignee does not infringe the principle that the assignee cannot recover more than the assignor.

APPLICATION OF PRINCIPLES

Applying this concise account of the legal principles to the particular circumstances of this case, it is, in my judgment, fallacious to contend that Larkstore cannot recover substantial damages from Technotrade, even if it can prove that Technotrade was in breach of contract and otherwise liable for them.

The contention is based on the propositions that Starglade (the assignor) had only suffered nominal damages at the date of the assignment, because it no longer owned the Site, and that Larkstore (the assignee) could not acquire by assignment from Starglade any greater right than Starglade had against Technotrade.

As I see it, that is not the true legal position. What was assigned by Starglade to Larkstore was a cause of action for breach of contract against Technotrade and the legal remedies for it. It was not an assignment of 'a loss', as Mr Friedman described it in his attempt to persuade the court that the amount of the loss recoverable by Larkstore was limited by what loss had been suffered by Starglade, in this case nil. The assignment included the remedy in damages for the cause of action. The remedy in damages for breach of contract is not, in principle, limited to the loss suffered as at the date of the accrual of the cause of action or as at any particular point of time thereafter.

The principle invoked by Technotrade that the assignee cannot recover more than the assignor does not assist it on the facts of this case. The purpose of the principle is to protect the contract-breaker/debtor from being prejudiced by the assignment in having, for example, to pay damages to the assignee which he would not have had to pay to the assignor, had the assignment never taken place. The principle is not intended to enable the contract-breaker/debtor to rely on the fact of the assignment in order to escape all legal liability for breach of contract.

In this case the assignment of 23 February 2004 did not, in itself, prejudice Technotrade by exposing it to a claim for damages by Larkstore, which Starglade could not have brought against Technotrade. The assignment of the cause of action by Starglade to Larkstore was a delayed consequence of the earlier sale of the Site. It completed the transaction. If Starglade had not sold the Site to Larkstore, it would not have assigned the cause of action against Technotrade to Larkstore and it could have recovered substantial damages against Technotrade for the landslip. The increased exposure of Technotrade for damages for breach of contract was a consequence of the landslip after the cause of action arose. It was not a consequence of the assignment of the cause of action, which was made to enable Larkstore to step fully into the shoes of Starglade following on the earlier sale of the Site.

Indeed, if Mr Friedman's arguments were accepted, far from being prejudiced by the assignment, Technotrade would improve its position as a result of it. Technotrade would escape all potential contractual liability for the damage caused by the landslip. It would have ceased to be liable to Starglade, which no longer owned the Site. It would not be liable to Larkstore, which did own the site, but the liability to Larkstore would be subject to the Starglade limit proposed by Mr Friedman, which would cancel any claim against Technotrade for substantial damages. By a legal conjuring trick worthy of Houdini the assignment would free Technotrade from the fetters of contractual liability. The position would be that the contract-breaker would be liable to no-one for the substantial loss suffered in consequence of the breach. As a matter of legal principle and good sense, this cannot possibly be the law, and fortunately the authorities cited in argument and discussed below do not compel the court to reach such a result.

Mr Friedman submitted that there was no 'legal black hole' or conjuring trick here. He contended that the parties did not contemplate that any one other than Starglade would or might suffer loss in consequence of a breach of contract by Technotrade in respect of the report. Technotrade's retainer was on the basis that it was Starglade who would be carrying out the development of the Site. Losses have been suffered by Larkstore because it chose not to seek any form of warranty from Technotrade, did not engage its own geo-technical advisers and relied on the Technotrade report without obtaining the consent of Technotrade for a purpose for which it had not been written.

In my judgment, these arguments amount to no more than an ingenious attempt to deny what has been correctly conceded, namely that the report and the causes of action in respect of it were assignable by Starglade. There was no express prohibition against assignment. No prohibition can be implied from any special circumstances. It was not argued, for example, that the contract between Starglade and Technotrade was of a personal nature and therefore unassignable.

THE AUTHORITIES

Mr Friedman's submissions on the assignment point are not supported by the authorities cited by him to show that the judge had misunderstood or misapplied the correct legal principles. Although the cases were discussed at length in the skeleton arguments and at the hearing, I propose to deal with them quite briskly.

Dawson v. Great Northern and City Railways Company [1905] 1 KB 260 at 272–274 per Stirling LJ was cited for the proposition that the assignee was not entitled to recover any greater amount of compensation than the assignor could have recovered. The width of the general proposition has to be read in context. In that case compensation under the Lands Clauses Consolidation Act 1845 was not payable to the assignee for 'damage to her trade stock' (as distinct from structural damage to premises requiring re-instatement works which did not increase the burden on the defendants), because that was compensation for an item that could not have been recovered by the assignor from the defendants. The assignor did not trade in the stock in question and could not have made a claim for compensation for that item.

GUS Property Management Limited v. Littlewoods Mail Order Stores Limited 1982 SLT 583 was also cited for Lord Keith's statement at p 537–538 that

> ... the basic question at issue is whether in this action the Pursuers are really seeking to pursue against the Defenders a claim or claims which the [assignor] could have pursued at the date of the [assignment] ... the only relevant loss which by virtue of the [assignment] the Pursuers could claim title to recover is loss suffered by the [assignor] for which the [assignor] could at the date of the [assignment] have sought reparation.

The speech of Lord Keith was considered in *Linden Gardens*. We heard very detailed submissions on the speech of Lord Browne-Wilkinson in the House of Lords (with which the other members of the Appellate Committee concurred) and on the judgments in the Court of Appeal.

The judge was criticised by Mr Friedman for relying on the following passage in the judgment of Staughton LJ in 57 BLR 57 at p 80–81—

> That brings me to the last point to be considered in connection with assignment of choses in action. Where the assignment is of a cause of action for damages, the assignee must of course have a sufficient proprietary right, or a genuine commercial interest, if the assignment is not to be invalid. It is no longer in issue in these appeals that the assignees had such a right in each case; we heard no argument to the contrary from the contractors. But it is said that in such a case the assignee can recover no more as damages than the assignor could have recovered.
>
> That proposition seems to me well founded. It stems from the principle already discussed, that the debtor is not to be put in any worse position by reason of the assignment. And it is established by *Dawson v. Great Northern & City Railway Co* [1905] 1 KB 260; see also *GUS Property Management Ltd v. Littlewoods Mail Order Stores Ltd* 1982 SLT 533 by Lord Keith of Kinkel at page 538, cited later in this judgment [pp 89–90]. But in a case such as the present one must elucidate the proposition slightly: the assignee can recover no more damages than the assignor could have recovered if there had been no assignment, *and if the building had not been transferred to the assignee.*

As I read the judgments of the other members of the court (Kerr LJ at pp 97–98 and Nourse LJ at p 66), it is reasonably clear that they agreed with what Staughton LJ said on this point in the passage cited and on pp 91–92.

Although the House of Lords overturned the decision of the Court of Appeal on the issue of the effect of the prohibition against assignment, I do not read the speech of Lord Browne-Wilkinson, which did not directly address the issue, as questioning the ruling of the Court of Appeal on the question whether an assignee could recover no more damages than the assignor could have recovered. It was unnecessary for the House to consider the assignee's remedies for breach of contract in view of its decision that the prohibition against assignment rendered the assignments ineffective.

The judgment of Staughton LJ was rightly relied on by the judge. I am respectfully of the view that the ruling of Staughton LJ on this point is correct as a matter of legal principle and good sense, and ought to be followed by this court in this case. It completely disposes of the argument raised in the defence of Technotrade that Larkstore is not entitled to claim substantial damages from Technotrade, because its assignor, Starglade, had suffered no loss, having parted with the Site before the landslip occurred and before the assignment of its cause of action to Larkstore.

I must, however, make it clear that the only point raised in this case at this preliminary stage is whether Larkstore had, by virtue of the assignment, a right to sue Technotrade for substantial damages for breach of contract in respect of loss claimed to have been suffered by it in consequence of the landslip at the Site. There is no question before this court, nor was there below, as to the proper measure or quantum of damages, which Larkstore is entitled to recover against Technotrade. We have heard no argument on it and I express no views on that aspect of the case.

. . .

CONCLUSION

I would dismiss the appeal on the assignment point.

[**Rix LJ** delivered a concurring judgment in which he elaborated on some of the points made by Mummery LJ. **Peter Smith J** concurred without giving further reasons.]

NOTES

1. The key reasoning was given by Mummery LJ when he said (at [41]) that '[w]hat was assigned by Starglade to Larkstore was a cause of action for breach of contract against Technotrade and the legal remedies for it. It was not an assignment of "a loss" . . .' The occurrence of loss or damage is not an essential ingredient of a cause of action for breach of contract. In *Technotrade*, the breach occurred before the sale of the site and the loss occurred after the sale, but before the assignment. In *Linden Gardens Trust Ltd v Lenesta Sludge Disposals Ltd* [1994] 1 AC 85 (see above), the breach and the loss—though not the financial cost of remedying the loss—both occurred before the sale and the assignment. Rix LJ said (at [77]) that 'this difference is not crucial'.

2. In *Technotrade*, the first-instance judge held that the assignment did not enable Larkstore to make a claim in tort for negligence against Technotrade. The cause of action in tort did not arise until the damage had occurred and damage was an essential ingredient of the cause of action in tort. The damage occurred after the sale of the site. There was, therefore, no cause of action in tort for Starglade to assign at the date of the assignment. The Court of Appeal did not address this issue. But, it is to be remembered, a claim in tort is generally non-assignable.

3. Rix LJ was keen to stress that the right to damages arising from the cause of action assigned by Starglade to Larkstore would be subject to the rules of causation and remoteness (see [77]–[78] and [87]). For example, on the question of causation, Larkstore might have to demonstrate that the landslip caused by its site development would also have occurred had the site been developed by Starglade, and, on the question of remoteness, it might have to show that the original parties reasonably contemplated that the cause of action might be assigned to an entity such as Larkstore (see Chee Ho Tham [2007] LMCLQ 286 at 289–290, from which these examples are taken).

4. In *Technotrade*, there was no question of Starglade claiming in respect of Larkstore's loss as there was no term of the contract between Starglade and Technotrade that prohibited the assignment to Larkstore. But where there is an effective non-assignment clause, as was the case in *St Martin's Property Corpn Ltd v Sir Robert McAlpine Ltd* [1994] 1 AC 85, the courts have had to show some ingenuity to allow the assignor to recover substantial damages which represent the assignee's, and not his own, loss (see *Technotrade*, above, at [80]–[83]). The courts have been keen to avoid 'legal black holes', where loss is suffered as a result of a breach of contract, but the contract-breaker's position is that no one is legally entitled to recover substantial damages from him.

(d) Other consequences of assignment

It may be necessary to register the assignment. Under s 344 of the Insolvency Act 1986, where a person engaged in any business makes a general assignment of existing or future book debts, or any class of them, and is subsequently adjudged bankrupt, the assignment will be void against the trustee of the bankrupt's estate as regards book debts which were not paid before the presentation of the bankruptcy petition, unless the assignment had been registered under the Bills of Sale Act 1878. As to registration of a charge on the book debts of a company, see below, p 977.

8 OBSTACLES TO ENFORCEMENT

An assignee may find that he has acquired a chose in action to the enforcement of which there are obstacles.

(a) Assignee takes subject to equities

(i) *The general rule*

The general rule is misleadingly expressed around notice. Equities arising before notice of an assignment is given to the obligor are said to bind the assignee. Equities arising thereafter are said not to bind the assignee. This general rule applies both to equitable and to statutory assignments under s 136 of the Law of Property Act 1925. However, the rule requires further explanation. The giving of notice prevents some subsequent equities from becoming enforceable at the expense of the assignee's position, but not all equities. There are some equities to which assignees take subject regardless of the time at which the equities arise.

(ii) *Equities to which assignees are always subject*

Assignees are always subject, for example, to 'flaws' in their title. Two varieties of such flaw are common. First, if the chose in action arises from a contract that was procured by common law fraud, the assignee will take subject to the assignor's (or the obligor's) entitlement to rescind the contract. Rescission extinguishes the chose in action from its base: *Athenaeum*

Life v Pooley (1859) 3 De G & J 294. Notice as such will not prevent this, save where the giving of notice amounts to a waiver of a right to rescind and, thus, to an affirmation of the contract. Secondly, assignees take subject to one type of equitable set-off: 'transaction set-off', as it is sometimes called, or 'substantive equitable set-off'. The traditional test for substantive equitable set-off suggests why assignees are always subject thereto: where A's title to claim a payment from B is 'impeached' by B's entitlement to claim payment from A, A will, in equity, be restrained from claiming payment of the full sum owed at law by B to A. A, of course, may be an obligor and B may be the obligee and assignor: whether A receives notice of B's assignment to C after *or before* A's cross-claim arises against B, the assignee, C, will be subject to the set-off. See G Tolhurst, *The Assignment of Contractual Rights* (2nd edn, 2016), Ch 8 and *Bibby Factors Northwest Ltd v HFD Ltd* [2015] EWCA Civ 1908, [2016] 1 Lloyd's Rep 517 at [31].

(iii) Equities stopped by notice

The equities stopped by notice are chiefly those relating to the state of the account between the obligor and the assignor.

Business Computers Ltd v Anglo-African Leasing Ltd
[1977] 1 WLR 578, Chancery Division

The plaintiffs sold two computers to the defendants under two separate transactions. At 29 May 1974, £10,587.50 remained owing by the defendants to the plaintiffs under these transactions. By a third transaction, the plaintiffs sold another computer to the defendants and then leased it back from them under a hire-purchase agreement. Under the terms of the hire-purchase agreement, the plaintiffs were to pay the defendants monthly instalments payable on the 18th of each month. The 13th instalment due on 18 May was not paid, nor were any subsequent instalments. On 13 June 1974, debenture holders appointed a receiver over the plaintiffs under the terms of a floating charge. This crystallised the charge which had the effect of assigning the sums owed by the defendants to the debenture holders. Notice of the assignment was given to the defendants on 17 June. The receiver claimed the debt of £10,587.50 from the defendants who tried to set off against it: (1) the 13th instalment due on 18 May (which the receiver conceded); and (2) damages of £30,000 under the terms of the hire-purchase agreement which the receiver had repudiated on 31 July and which repudiation was accepted by the defendants on 8 August.

Templeman J: . . . Set off has been allowed against an assignee in a variety of circumstances. In *Biggerstaff v Rowan's Wharf Ltd* [1896] 2 Ch 93 a debtor who became entitled to a liquidated claim against a company before a floating charge crystallised was allowed to set off the liquidated claim against the debt after the debenture crystallised. This decision does not assist the defendants because in the present case no claim liquidated or otherwise for £30,000 arose on or before June 17 when the defendants received notice that the debentures had crystallised.

In *Christie v Taunton, Delmard, Lane and Co* [1893] 2 Ch 175 a debtor was allowed to set off against an assignee a debt from the assignor which accrued due before the date of the assignment but was not payable until after the assignment. In the present case the defendants on June 17, 1974, when they received notice of the assignment completed by the appointment of the receiver did not possess a claim for £30,000 payable then or on any subsequent date. That claim only arose in August 1974.

In *Government of Newfoundland v Newfoundland Rly Co* (1888) 13 App Cas 199 a debtor sued by an assignee for a sum payable pursuant to a contract between the debtor and the assignor was allowed to set off a claim for unliquidated damages made by the debtor against the assignor for breach of the same contract by the assignor. This case also does not assist the defendants because the debt owed by the defendants for £10,587.50 arose under different and separate contracts from the hire purchase agreement under which the defendants' claim for £30,000 has now arisen.

In *Watson v Mid Wales Rly Co* (1867) LR 2 CP 593 a debtor sued on a bond by the assignee of the bond was not allowed to set off arrears of rent which accrued due from the assignor to the debtor after the assignment under a lease made before notice of the assignment. Bovill CJ said, at p 598:

> No case has been cited to us where equity has allowed against the assignee of an equitable chose in action a set off of a debt arising between the original parties subsequently to the notice of assignment, out of matters not connected with the debt claimed, nor in any way referring to it . . . In all the cases cited . . . some qualification occurred in the original contract, or the two transactions were in some way connected together, so as to lead the court to the conclusion that they were made with reference to one another.

In the present case, the claim of the defendants under the hire purchase agreement for £30,000 arose subsequently to notice of the assignment of the debt of £10,587.50 and the transactions out of which the claim and the debt arose respectively were separate and not connected in any way. Set off is therefore not available by the defendants against the assignees, the debenture holders.

In *Re Pinto Leite and Nephews, exp Visconde des Olivaes* [1929] 1 Ch 221 a debtor owed £100,000 payable in January 1932 and the original creditor, after assigning the debt on March 2, 1926, became liable to the debtor for £15,000 as a result of a contract entered into between the debtor and the creditor prior to the assignment. There was no connection between the debt of £100,000 and the contract under which the £15,000 became owing. The debtor was not allowed to set off the £15,000 liability against the debt of £100,000 claimed by the assignee. Clauson J said, at p 233:

> It is, of course, well settled that the assignee of a chose in action ... takes subject to all rights of set off which were available against the assignor, subject only to the exception that, after notice of an equitable assignment of a chose in action, a debtor cannot set off against the assignee a debt which accrues due subsequently to the date of notice, even though that debt may arise out of a liability which existed at or before the date of the notice; but the debtor may set off as against the assignee a debt which accrues due before notice of the assignment, although it is not payable until after that date:

and, at p 236:

> when the debt assigned is at the date of notice of the assignment payable in future, the debtor can set off against the assignee a debt which becomes payable by the assignor to the debtor after notice of assignment, but before the assigned debt becomes payable, if, but only if, the debt so to be set off was *debitum in praesenti* at the date of notice of assignment.

In the present case the £30,000 claim did not accrue due until after the date of notice of the assignment and cannot therefore be set off.

I was referred to *Bankes v Jarvis* [1903] 1 KB 549, but that case only decided that a debtor could set off against a trustee for the creditor all claims which at the date of the action could have founded a set off against the creditor beneficiary. See also *Hanak v Green* [1958] 2 QB 9, 24 where the decision in *Bankes v Jarvis* was supported on the ground that 'There was a close relationship between the dealings and transactions which gave rise to the respective claims.' No such close relationship was put forward in the present case.

I was referred to *N W Robbie & Co Ltd v Witney Warehouse Co Ltd* [1963] 1 WLR 1324, but that case only decided that a debtor cannot after notice of an assignment of his debt by his creditor improve his position as regards set off by acquiring debts incurred by the assignor creditor to a third party. I have already referred to *George Barker (Transport) Ltd v Eynon* [1974] 1 WLR 462, but that case only decided that if a receiver after his appointment took the benefit of a contract entered into before his appointment, he could not dispute a lien conferred by that contract but not exercised until after the appointment. The defendants in the present case cannot invoke this principle. The contracts under which the debt of £10,587.50 became payable were completed before the receiver was appointed, apart from the payment now sought against the defendants. I was also referred to *Rother Iron Works Ltd v Canterbury Precision Engineers Ltd* [1974] QB 1. In that case, pursuant to a contract made before the appointment of a receiver, a debtor delivered goods to the company and the goods were accepted by the receiver. The debtor was allowed to set off the price of the goods against his debt to the company because the receiver could not take the benefit of the contract without the burden. He was not entitled to the debt and to the goods and to keep the purchase price. A similar point does not arise in the present case.

The result of the relevant authorities is that a debt which accrues due before notice of an assignment is received, whether or not it is payable before that date, or a debt which arises out of the same contract as that which gives rise to the assigned debt, or is closely connected with that contract, may be set off against the assignee. But a debt which is neither accrued nor connected may not be set off even though it arises from a contract made before the assignment. In the present case the claim for £30,000 did not accrue before June 17, 1974, when the defendants received notice of the appointment of the receiver and thus notice of the completed assignment of the debt of £10,587.50 to the debenture holders and there was no relevant connection between the transactions which gave rise to the claim and to the debt respectively.

NOTES

1. Defences which the debtor could have raised against the assignor, and cross-claims arising out of, or closely connected with, the transaction which gave rise to the chose being assigned, can be set up by the debtor against the assignee whether they arise before or after the debtor receives notice of the assignment. Defences include any claim that the original transaction giving rise to the chose has been vitiated by illegality, mistake, fraud, or other misrepresentation (*Graham v Johnson* (1869) LR 8 Eq 36). Such cross-claims may be liquidated or unliquidated but they must be so closely connected with the transaction that gave rise to the assigned chose that it would be inequitable not to allow a set-off (*Bim Kemi AB v Blackburn Chemicals Ltd* [2001] EWCA Civ 457, [2001] 2 Lloyd's Rep 93; *Government of Newfoundland v Newfoundland Rly Co* (1888) 13 App Cas 199, PC). However, it appears that at least one category of tort claim is not to be regarded as closely connected with the transaction giving rise to the chose assigned. In *Stoddart v Union Trust Ltd* [1912] 1 KB 181, the Court of Appeal held that a claim for damages for fraudulently inducing the debtor to enter into the contract with the assignor could not be set up against the assignee unless the debtor rescinded the contract. The decision may be criticised on the ground that it draws an unnecessary distinction between a claim for damages for fraud and a claim for damages for breach of contract: A Tettenborn [1987] Conv 385.

2. A cross-claim arising out of some other transaction which is independent of that which gave rise to the chose being assigned may be set off by the debtor against the assignee only if: (a) it is a debt or other liquidated sum; *and* (b) it accrued before notice of assignment is given to the debtor (see, eg, *Marathon Electrical Manufacturing Corpn v Mashreqbank PSC* [1997] 2 BCLC 460—Mance J held assignment of proceeds of a letter of credit to be subject to collecting bank's (debtor's) right of set-off where assignor's indebtedness to the bank accrued before notice of assignment had been received). Unless there is contrary agreement between the assignor and the debtor, there can be no set-off if the claims are unconnected and one or both is unliquidated (see, eg, *De Mattos v Saunders* (1872) LR 7 CP 750). There is also no set-off where the cross-claim is subject to an arbitration clause (*Glencore Grain Ltd v Argos Trading Co Ltd* [1999] 2 All ER (Comm) 288, CA).

3. The debtor may use his cross-claim to reduce or extinguish the assignee's claim for the sum assigned. Where the cross-claim is for an amount exceeding the sum assigned, the debtor cannot recover the excess from the assignee as he himself has committed no wrongdoing (*Young v Kitchin* (1878) 3 Ex D 127). The debtor must look to the assignor for the excess. For similar reasons, a debtor cannot recover back a payment already made to the assignee on the ground that the payment was made for a consideration that had totally failed. For example, in *Pan Ocean Shipping Ltd v Creditcorp Ltd, The Trident Beauty* [1994] 1 All ER 470, the House of Lords held that the assignee of freight payable in advance under the terms of a charterparty was not liable to return hire paid to it by the debtor (the charterer) when the assignor (the shipowner) failed to supply the ship. The liability to repay the unearned hire remained with the assignor. But what if the assignor is insolvent? The injustice of this decision is evident when one considers that had the debtor not paid the assignee in advance he could have relied on the 'subject to equities' rule to set up the assignor's failure to perform as a complete defence to any claim by the assignee for payment. Tolhurst submits that the debtor had a reasonable expectation that the nature of the right assigned, a right to payment conditional on provision of the ship, would be respected by the assignee, so that denial of that reasonable expectation without good cause was unconscionable ([1999] CLJ 546 at 560–561).

4. The 'subject to equities' rule does not apply in the following circumstances: (a) if the assigned debt is created by contract, the contract may provide, by an express or implied term, that the assignee takes free of equities (*Re Blakely Ordnance Co* (1867) 3 Ch App 154 at 159–160); and (b) if the debt is embodied in a negotiable instrument, a person who purchases the instrument in good faith, before its maturity, and without notice of any defect in the title of the holder or of previous dishonour, will take it free from equities (Bills of Exchange Act 1882, ss 29(1) and 38(2)). There is also authority for the view that the assignee is only liable to equities available against the original assignor, not to those available against an intermediate assignee (*The Raven* [1980] 2 Lloyd's Rep 266 at 273, Parker J; *Re Milan Tramways Co* (1884) 25 Ch D 587 at 593, CA). However, it has been argued that where the claim or defence against the intermediate assignee arose after the first assignment it should be available in a claim by a subsequent assignee (E Peel, *Treitel: The Law of Contract* (14th edn, 2015), para 15–043).

CHAPTER 23

RECEIVABLES FINANCING

1 GENERAL INTRODUCTION

This chapter is concerned with the raising of money on the strength of receivables. The term 'receivable' is not defined in English law. In general terms, it is a commercial expression referring to money that is receivable in the performance and discharge of a legal obligation. In this chapter 'receivable' will be used more particularly to mean 'account receivable' which is 'the right to payment of a sum of money, whether presently or in the future, for goods supplied, services rendered or facilities made available, being a right not embodied in a negotiable instrument' (L Gullifer, *Goode on Legal Problems of Credit and Security* (5th edn, 2013), para 3–01). The terms 'receivables' and 'book debts' are often used interchangeably. Unlike 'receivables', the term 'book debts' has been the subject of legal definition (see below, p 980). However, as Dr Oditah has pointed out, the term 'receivables' is wider than 'book debts': it includes book debts but is not limited to them (*Legal Aspects of Receivables Financing* (1991), p 19).

A simple contract debt is a *pure* receivable or 'account receivable'. If the debtor tenders a bill of exchange or promissory note in payment of the debt then the negotiable instrument is referred to as a *documentary* receivable. This is because the negotiable instrument embodies an independent payment obligation which, at least in a general sense, acts in substitution for the payment obligation arising out of the underlying pure receivable. In consequence, a security expressed to be granted over 'receivables' without qualification would cover both pure receivables and negotiable instruments tendered in payment by the obligor, assuming the grantor of the security uses 'receivables' in the ordinary commercial sense (*Siebe Gorman & Co Ltd v Barclays Bank Ltd* [1979] 2 Lloyd's Rep 142). On the other hand, negotiable instruments tendered as *security* for payment, but not as payment, in no sense act as a substitute for the underlying pure receivable. They are not to be classified as documentary receivables (see Oditah, above, pp 26–27).

(a) 'Receivables financing' defined

Commercial parties holding receivables may use those to obtain finance. In so doing, they rely on the rules and principles of assignment of choses in action. Receivables financing is of considerable economic importance.

Legal Aspects of Receivables Financing by F Oditah

(1991), p 2

The expression 'receivables financing' is ambiguous.[1] In this book, however, the expression is used to denote any arrangement by which money is raised on the strength of contractual receivables. Receivables form an integral part of the assets of every trading company. Mortgage and charge debts, car loans, insurance premiums, credit card debts, secured consumer loans, equipment loans, freights (including sub-freights), rentals from real and personal property, debts for goods sold or services rendered, are all receivables. So important is this category of liquid assets that Macleod was compelled to write over a hundred years ago:

> . . . if we were asked—who made the discovery which has most deeply affected the fortunes of the human race? We think, after full consideration we might safely answer—the man who first discovered that a debt is a saleable commodity.[2] When Daniel Webster said that credit has done more a thousand times to enrich nations than all the mines of the world, he meant discovery that a debt is a saleable chattel.[3]

A hundred years on, nothing has diminished the importance of receivables as a basis for raising money. If anything, the indications are to the contrary. In developed economies the bulk of corporate wealth is locked up in debts. The recycling of these valuable assets as well as their utilisation in the provision of working capital is the primary focus of this book. As would be expected both the recycling and utilisation take a variety of forms. Receivables could be, and frequently are, discounted either privately or in the money markets. Also they may be, and often are, assigned or charged as security for a loan, or an overdraft or other revolving credit facility. Between discounting and security lies a third possibility—outright assignment in discharge or reduction of a pre-existing debt, very little known and almost completely ignored in discussions of forms and patterns of receivables financing. There could also be more complex combinations of these. Normative arguments as to which form is better are not useful because there is no absolute, universal objective criterion by reference to which their relative merits may be ascertained. A number of considerations are relevant to the choice of any one form. The technique chosen will normally reflect the desire to give the company a financing package tailored to meet its own particular circumstances and needs.

FOOTNOTES:

1 In one sense receivables financing means financing the creation of contractual receivables. This is usually the sense in which the related expression 'stock-in-trade financing' is used. Since every going concern necessarily generates receivables, the financing of receivables would in this sense be the financing of an enterprise. The expression, however, has a narrower meaning, namely, the raising of money on the strength of receivables.

2 Macleod *Principles of Economical Philosophy* (2nd edn, 1872), p 481, cited in I Gilmore *Security Interests in Personal Property* (1965), p 213, n 7.

3 Macleod *Elements of Economics* (1881), p 327, cited in I Gilmore, op cit, p 213, n 7.

(b) Financing techniques: sale or charge

A trader who wishes to convert receivables into cash may employ either of two techniques. He can sell them or he can mortgage (or charge) them as security for a loan, overdraft, or other form of revolving credit. A species of sale occurs where an outright assignment is made in discharge or reduction of a pre-existing debt (Oditah, above, p 33). No sale occurs where receivables are assigned in repayment of an advance made under a financing agreement: the advance was not a payment of a price for purchasing of the receivables (Oditah, above, p 71).

A sale of receivables often takes the form of an assignment of a trader's book debts to the financier ('factor') under a factoring agreement. It could also involve the block discounting of hire-purchase or credit sale agreements. However, other 'sale' mechanisms may also be used, such as a sale and agency agreement, as was used in *Welsh Development Agency v Export Finance Co Ltd* [1992] BCLC 148. These forms and mechanisms will be further explained below.

How do matters stand from the financier's side of such arrangements? A financier who advances cash to a trader may take a mortgage of, or charge over, the trader's receivables as security. A mortgage of a debt is an assignment (equitable or statutory) of it upon terms, express or implied, that it is to be reassigned to the transferor when the obligation which it secures has been discharged. Before reassignment the mortgagee has a proprietary interest in the debt. A charge on a debt (which can only be an *equitable* charge) is a mere incumbrance giving the chargee a preferential right to, but not ownership of, the debt. However, the default provisions in the charge usually confer on the chargee: (1) a power of attorney to convert the charge into a mortgage by executing an assignment in the name of the chargor; and (2) a power to appoint a receiver. According to Dr Oditah, '[t]hese powers diminish to vanishing point, any remaining distinction between a charge and a mortgage' (above, at p 96); at any rate, the drafting employed by the parties may attach no great significance to the distinction, though a distinction exists. For further consideration of the distinction between a mortgage and a charge, see RM Goode [1984] JBL 172; and below, Chapter 26.

Securitisation of receivables is a major source of finance for institutional investors. It can be contrasted with factoring which is mainly used to provide finance for the manufacturing sector. Securitisation involves raising finance by packaging together large numbers of receivables (eg receivables arising from residential mortgages, finance leases, hire-purchase agreements, conditional sale agreements, and trade relationship) and then selling them to a special-purpose company. Typically, the special-purpose company raises the purchase price through loan notes issued in the securities market. The loan notes are secured on the receivables. The difference between the interest rate paid to the noteholders and that paid on the original loan by the borrower represents the transferor's profit margin. As securitisation involves either an outright sale or a sale coupled with a sub-charge, it will not be given separate consideration in this chapter. For further details, see PR Wood, *Project Finance, Securitisations, Subordinated Debt* (2nd edn, 2007), Chs 6–9.

(c) Sale and security

In determining whether a security has been created, the courts look to the substance and not merely to the form of the transaction. The language used by the parties is not to be disregarded, but is not necessarily conclusive of the character of a transaction.

(i) *Importance of the distinction*

The distinction between transactions of sale of, and security over, receivables is important in several respects. As will be seen from Romer LJ's judgment in *Re George Inglefield Ltd* [1933] Ch 1, which is quoted in the case next set out below, three significant differences are that: (1) whereas a mortgagor is entitled to the return of the mortgaged asset by paying the sum due, a vendor is not entitled to the return of the asset sold by returning the purchase money; (2) a mortgagee who realises mortgaged property must account for any surplus above what it is owed, whereas a buyer who resells an asset is not accountable for the profit; and (3) if a mortgagee's realisation of mortgaged property yields insufficient money to discharge the secured debt, the mortgagee may sue the mortgagor for the balance; but a purchaser who resells for less than its costs may not sue the vendor for the difference.

In addition:

(1) a sale of receivables need not be registered (but see the Insolvency Act 1986, s 344, avoiding general assignments of book debts by a bankrupt); a 'charge' over a company's receivables must be registered (below, p 976);

(2) even if registered, a mortgage of, or charge over, a company's receivables may be set aside on the company's administration or liquidation because it is deemed a transaction at an undervalue, a preference, an extortionate credit bargain, a floating charge created during the relevant time, or an attempt to defraud creditors (see the Insolvency Act 1986, ss 238, 239, 244, 245, 423–425; considered below, Chapter 28); a sale is unlikely to be avoided on any of these grounds, save that it could be reopened if the level of 'discount' given to the financier is deemed to be extortionate (see F Oditah, *Legal Aspects of Receivables Financing* (1991), p 43);

(3) a sale of receivables is liable to *ad valorem* duty on the instruments by which the sale is effected and VAT; a loan secured by a mortgage or charge is not liable to stamp duty and is exempt from VAT;

(4) the creation of additional debt or security may be prohibited by the terms of an existing debenture but a sale would fall outside such a restriction (although it is now usual for the terms of a prohibition to extend to all forms of dealing with the company's receivables).

(ii) Drawing the distinction

Welsh Development Agency v Export Finance Co Ltd
[1992] BCLC 148, Court of Appeal

The defendant (Exfinco) provided finance to a company called Parrot Corp Ltd (Parrot) which sold computer floppy disks to overseas buyers. The finance was provided under the terms of a Master Agreement whereby Parrot first sold the floppy disks to Exfinco and then resold the same disks to overseas buyers as Exfinco's agent. The sale to Exfinco was at a discount to the resale price as Exfinco would pay Parrot in advance of receiving payment from the overseas buyers. Later Parrot created a charge over its book debts in favour of the plaintiff (WDA). When Parrot went into receivership, WDA claimed that monies owed by the overseas buyers to Parrot were subject to its charge (which had been duly registered under the Companies Act 1985; see now s 859A of the Companies Act 2006). Exfinco claimed to be entitled to these monies as payment for the goods which it owned and which had been sold on its behalf by Parrot as its agent. One of the main issues was whether the Master Agreement had created a charge on the assets of Parrot which was void for non-registration under s 395 of the Companies Act 1985 (a similar provision is now to be found in s 859H of the Companies Act 2006). Exfinco claimed that the Agreement effected a sale of goods and not a charge on the goods. Reversing Browne-Wilkinson V-C, the Court of Appeal held that the Master Agreement effected a sale of goods and gave judgment for Exfinco.

Dillon LJ: … I turn then to issue 2: were the transactions under the master agreement by way of sale or secured loan?

It is not suggested that the master agreement was in any sense a sham or that its terms did not represent the true agreement between the parties. Moreover it is not suggested in this case, as it was in *Lloyds & Scottish Finance Ltd v Cyril Lord Carpet Sales Ltd* ([1992] BCLC 609), that in what they actually did the parties had departed from what was provided for by the master agreement, and that therefore they ought to be treated as having made some fresh agreement by conduct in the place of the master agreement.

What is said is that in determining the legal categorisation of an agreement and its legal consequences the court looks at the substance of the transaction and not at the labels which the parties have chosen to put on it.

This is trite law, but it is law which has fallen to be applied in different types of cases where different factors are the relevant factors for consideration. It is therefore not surprising that the words used by eminent judges in different cases in applying the principle do not all fit very harmoniously together.

Thus the task of looking for the substance of the parties' agreement and disregarding the labels they have used may arise in a case where their written agreement is a sham intended to mask their true agreement. The task of the courts there is to discover by extrinsic evidence what their true agreement was and to disregard, if inconsistent with the true agreement, the written words of the sham agreement. This is discussed in the judgments of Diplock and Russell LJJ in *Snook v London and West Riding Investments Ltd* [1961] 1 All ER 518, [1967] 2 QB 786 and is exemplified by some of the cases cited in *Street v Mountford* [1985] AC 809 and *AG Securities v Vaughan* [1990] 1 AC 417 where in an endeavour to set up a licence to occupy, rather than a tenancy of, residential accommodation the landlord had introduced into the agreement terms purportedly reserving to himself a right to introduce further occupants which were plainly inconsistent with the real intention.

But the question can also arise where, without any question of sham, there is some objective criterion in law by which the court can test whether the agreement the parties have made does or does not fall into the legal category in which the parties have sought to place their agreement. One can see that in the comments of Lord Templeman in *Street v Mountford* [1985] AC 809 at 824 on the case of *Shell-Mex and BP Ltd v Manchester Garages Ltd* [1971] 1 WLR 612, where the defendant had been allowed to use a petrol company's filling station for the purposes of selling petrol, and the question was whether the transaction was a licence or a tenancy. Lord Templeman said that the agreement was only personal in its nature and therefore a licence if it did not confer the right to exclusive occupation of the filling station, since no other test for distinguishing between a contractual tenancy and a contractual licence appeared to be understandable or workable.

In the present case Mr Moss QC asserts for WDA that there are, on the authorities, clearly laid down criteria for what is a charge, that all those criteria are present in the present case in the master agreement, and that the master agreement is therefore necessarily as a matter of law a charge, whatever the parties may have called it or thought it was.

He relies in particular on the passage in the judgment of Romer LJ in *Re George Inglefield Ltd* [1933] Ch 1 at 27–28 where Romer LJ sets out what he regarded as the essential differences between a transaction of sale and a transaction of mortgage or charge. These were three, viz:

> [i] In a transaction of sale the vendor is not entitled to get back the subject-matter of the sale by returning to the purchaser the money that has passed between them. In the case of a mortgage or charge, the mortgagor is entitled, until he has been foreclosed, to get back the subject-matter of the mortgage or charge by returning to the mortgagee the money that has passed between them, [ii] . . . if the mortgagee realises the subject-matter of the mortgage

for a sum more than sufficient to repay him, with interest and the costs, the money that has passed between him and the mortgagor he has to account to the mortgagor for the surplus. If the purchaser sells the subject-matter of the purchase, and realizes a profit, of course he has not got to account to the vendor for the profit, [iii] . . . if the mortgagee realizes the mortgaged property for a sum that is insufficient to repay him the money that [has been] paid to the mortgagor, together with interest and costs, then the mortgagee is entitled to recover from the mortgagor the balance of the money . . . If the purchaser were to resell the purchased property at a price which was insufficient to recoup him the money that he had paid to the vendor . . . he would not be entitled to recover the balance from the vendor.

But these indicia do not have the clarity of the distinction between a tenancy and a licence to occupy, viz that it must be a tenancy if the grantee has been given exclusive occupation of the property in question. In particular it is clear from *Re George Inglefield Ltd,* and the *Lloyds & Scottish* case, (a) that there may be a sale of book debts, and not a charge, even though the purchaser has recourse against the vendor to recover the shortfall if the debtor fails to pay the debt in full and (b) that there may be a sale of book debts, even though the purchaser may have to make adjustments and payments to the vendor after the full amounts of the debts have been got in from the debtors. As to the latter see especially the judgment of Lord Hanworth MR in *Re George Inglefield Ltd* [1933] Ch 1 at 20.

In my judgment there is no one clear touchstone by which it can necessarily and inevitably be said that a document which is not a sham and which is expressed as an agreement for sale must necessarily, as a matter of law, amount to no more than the creation of a mortgage or charge on the property expressed to be sold. It is necessary therefore to look at the provisions in the master agreement as a whole to decide whether in substance it amounts to an agreement for the sale of goods or only to a mortgage or charge on goods and their proceeds.

[**Ralph Gibson LJ** delivered a similar judgment.]

Staughton LJ:

SALE OR CHARGE?

(a) The test

We were referred to a bewildering array of authority on this topic, some of it by no means easy to reconcile. The problem is not made any easier by the variety of language that has been used: substance, truth, reality, genuine are good words; disguise, cloak, mask, colourable device, label, form, artificial, sham, stratagem and pretence are 'bad names', to adopt the phrase quoted by Dixon J in *Palette Shoes Pty Ltd v Krohn* (1937) 58 CLR 1 at 28. It is necessary to discover, if one can, the ideas which these words are intended to convey.

One can start from the position that statute law in this country, when it enacts rules to be applied to particular transactions, is in general referring to the legal nature of a transaction and not to its economic effect. The leading authority on this point, albeit in a case from Malaya, is the advice of Lord Devlin in *Chow Yoong Hong v Choong Fah Rubber Manufactory Ltd* [1962] AC 209 at 216:

> There are many ways of raising cash besides borrowing . . . If in form it is not a loan, it is not to the point to say that its object was to raise money for one of them or that the parties could have produced the same result more conveniently by borrowing and lending money.

See too the *Crowther Committee's Report on Consumer Credit* (Cmnd 4596 (1971)) para 1.3.6, where it was said that the existing law was deficient because:

> It lacks any functional basis: distinctions between one type of transaction and another are drawn on the basis of legal abstractions rather than on the basis of commercial reality.

There are in my opinion two routes by which this principle can be overcome. The first, which I will call the external route, is to show that the written document does not represent the agreement of the parties. It may, if one wishes, then be called a sham, a cloak or a device. The second is the internal route, when one looks only at the written agreement, in order to ascertain from its terms whether it amounts to a transaction of the legal nature which the parties ascribe to it. These two routes are described, for example, by Lord Hanworth MR in *Re George Inglefield Ltd* [1933] Ch 1 at 19, 23, by Maugham LJ in *Re Lovegrove* [1935] Ch 464 at 496, and by Knox J in *Re Curtain Dream plc* [1990] BCLC 925 at 937. (I express no view on the way that Knox J described the second route or the result which he reached; an appeal is pending.)

The Welsh Agency do not rely on the external route in this case. They disclaim any argument that the master agreement was a sham. It is not therefore necessary for me to consider the external route in any detail, except for the purpose of showing what this appeal is *not* about. One can show that the written document does not reflect the agreement of the parties by proving a collateral agreement, or at least a common intention, to that effect. Or there may be proof of a subsequent variation, as was argued in *Lloyds & Scottish Finance Ltd v Cyril Lord Carpets Sales Ltd* ([1992] BCLC 609) . . .

There was here no sham, no collateral agreement or common intention to be bound by different terms, and no subsequent variation to that effect. So I can leave the external route, and turn to an internal consideration of the master agreement itself. This must be carried out on the basis that the parties intended to be bound by its terms, and by nothing else.

If one part of the agreement purports to create a particular legal transaction, it may happen that other provisions are inconsistent with such a transaction. The task of the court is then to ascertain which is the substance, the truth, the reality. That was plainly the approach of Lord Herschell LC in *McEntire v Crossley Bros Ltd* [1895] AC 457 at 463–466, where there are repeated references to inconsistency. See also the speech of Lord Watson where he said ([1895] AC 457 at 467):

> The duty of a Court is to examine every part of the agreement, every stipulation which it contains, and to consider their mutual bearing upon each other; but it is entirely beyond the function of a Court to discard the plain meaning of any term in the agreement unless there can be found within its four corners other language and other stipulations which necessarily deprive such term of its primary significance.

Mr Moss argued that the court is free to disregard the label which the parties have attached to a transaction. If by label one means the description which is found on the backsheet, or even in a preamble or a recital, I can see that it should be given little if any weight. A label can also be found elsewhere. Thus in *Street v Mountford* [1985] AC 809, Mrs Mountford agreed 'to take' a furnished room; the references to 'licence' in the agreement were in truth labels and nothing more. 'Licence' was the name by which the agreement described itself. And in *AG Securities v Vaughan* [1990] 1 AC 417 at 444 Bingham LJ said that:

> . . . the true legal nature of a transaction is not to be altered by the description the parties choose to give it.

In my judgment the correct process, when one is following the internal route, is to look at the operative parts of the document, in order to discover what legal transaction they provide for. If some parts appear to be inconsistent with others in this respect, a decision must be made between the two. This is what I understand by ascertaining the substance of the transaction. The cases on whether an agreement provides for a licence or tenancy—*Street v Mountford, AG Securities v Vaughan* and *Asian v Murphy (Nos I and 2)* [1990] 1 WLR 766—do not in my opinion overturn this well-established doctrine. Nor does the decision of the majority of this court in *Gisborne v Burton* [1989] QB 390. There it was held, with reference to the Agricultural Holdings Act 1948, that one must look at the scheme of a preordained series of transactions as a whole, instead of concentrating on each pre-ordained step individually. The doctrine of revenue law, derived from *W T Ramsay Ltd v IRC* [1982] AC 300 and other cases, was thus extended to private transactions. I do not need to consider whether it should also be extended to this case; there is no series of transactions here, but only the one master agreement.

It can be said that Exfinco have adopted their method of business because their customers wished to avoid the registration provisions of the Companies Act, and the appearance of loans in their balance sheets. But one should not, from sympathy for creditors or rather for a debenture holder, overthrow both established law and recognised methods of providing finance for trade and industry.

NOTES

1. The classic formulation of the sham doctrine is found in *Snook v London and West Riding Investments Ltd* [1967] 2 QB 786, where Diplock LJ said (at 802) that a 'sham':

> means acts done or documents executed by the parties to the 'sham' which are intended by them to give to third parties or to the court the appearance of creating between the parties legal rights and obligations different from the actual legal rights and obligations (if any) which the parties intend to create. One thing I think, however, is clear in legal principle, morality and the authorities (see *Yorkshire Railway Wagon Co v Maclure* (1882) 21 Ch D 309 and *Stoneleigh Finance Ltd v Phillips* [1965] 2 QB 537), that for acts or documents to be a 'sham', with whatever legal consequences follow from this, all the parties thereto must have a common intention that the acts or documents are not to create the legal rights and obligations which they give the appearance of creating.

The *Snook* definition of a sham has been cited with approval in many cases (see, eg, *IRC v McGuckian* [1997] 1 WLR 991 at 1001, per Lord Steyn; *Norglen Ltd v Reeds Rains Prudential Ltd* [1999] 2 AC 1 at 13, per Lord Hoffmann). However, in *Hitch v Stone* [2001] EWCA Civ 63, [2001] STC 214 at [63], Arden LJ indicated that the *Snook* definition related only to one particular type of sham. She developed the point in *Bankway Properties Ltd v Pensfold-Dunsford* [2001] EWCA Civ 528, [2001] 1 WLR 1369, where there could be no finding of a *Snook*-type sham because the parties (landlord and tenant) had no common intention to disguise the true nature of the transaction. Instead Arden LJ (but not Pill LJ, the other member of the court) relied on a second type of sham that she said did not depend on 'common intention' but operated: (a) where there was legislation that it was impossible to contract out of; and (b) the court inferred from the evidence (i) that a party never intended to exercise or enforce a right given to him by a particular clause in the contract and (ii) that the purpose of the clause was to make it appear that the contract was of a type which was outside the legislation.

2. It is rare for an agreement or document to be held a sham. In *National Westminster Bank plc v Jones* [2001] 1 BCLC 98 at [59] (affirmed [2002] 1 BCLC 55 without discussion of the issue), Neuberger J explained why:

> In one sense, lawyers find it difficult to grapple with the concept of sham, presumably on the basis that, subject to questions of mistake . . . there is a very strong presumption indeed that parties intend to be bound by the provisions of agreements into which they enter, and, even more, intend the agreements they enter into to take effect. . . . Because a finding of sham carries with it a finding of dishonesty, because innocent third parties may often rely upon the genuineness of a provision or an agreement, and because the court places great weight on the existence and provisions of a formally signed document, there is a strong and natural presumption against holding a provision or a document a sham.

3. Several comments can be made about the various statements made by Dillon and Staughton LJJ in the *Exfinco* case.

- The statement made by Staughton LJ that statute law usually focuses on the legal nature of a transaction and not on its economic effect must now be considered in the light of the dicta of Lord Hoffmann in *MacNiven v Westmoreland Investments Ltd* [2001] UKHL 6, [2003] 1 AC 311. In that case, which involved the interpretation of tax legislation, Lord Hoffmann said that a term in legislation must first be construed to see whether it was intended to refer to a legal concept or a commercial concept. There seems no doubt according to what Lord Hoffmann said in *MacNiven* (at [33]) that this distinction between juristic and commercial concepts is not confined to tax legislation. If this approach were adopted generally by the courts, there would be a real risk that title finance arrangements could be recharacterised according to their economic function and not their legal nature for some purposes. Moreover, there would be considerable uncertainty as to whether a term in a statute referred to commercial concepts as opposed to purely legal ones. It does seem, however, that when Part 25 of the Companies Act 2006 refers to a 'charge', it refers to a purely legal concept: see Graham [2014] JBL 175 and, on cognate earlier legislation, see *Lloyds & Scottish Finance Ltd v Cyril Lord Carpet Sales Ltd* [1992] BCLC 609 at 616, per Lord Wilberforce. However, the House of Lords later downplayed Lord Hoffmann's distinction between legal concepts and commercial concepts. In *Barclays Mercantile Business Finance Ltd v Mawson (Inspector of Taxes)* [2004] UKHL 51, [2005] 1 AC 684, another case involving the interpretation of tax legislation, Lord Nicholls delivered the opinion of a bench which included Lord Hoffmann himself. Their Lordships said (at [38]) that they did not think that Lord Hoffmann's distinction between legal concepts and commercial concepts was intended to provide a substitute for a close analysis of what the statute meant. It certainly did not justify the assumption that an answer could be obtained by classifying all concepts *a priori* as either 'commercial' or 'legal' for that 'would be the very negation of purposive construction'.

- The internal route is also sometimes called the 'four corners' approach (see *McEntire v Crossley Bros Ltd* [1895] AC 457 at 467, per Lord Watson). The idea is that, in searching for the substance of an agreement, the court construes the wording of the agreement as a whole. It does not ignore the plain meaning of a term unless there can be found within the four corners of the agreement other language which necessarily deprives the term of its primary significance. But it is not literally true to say that only the contractual document itself must be examined. The court may, along the internal route, have regard to the surrounding circumstances and other relevant factors outside the document in accordance with the normal rules relating to the construction of contracts generally. In *Re Spectrum Plus Ltd (in liquidation)* [2005] UKHL 41, [2005] 2 AC 680, where a clause that purported to create a fixed charge over the chargor's book debts was contained in a standard form bank debenture, the House of Lords adopted a similarly broad approach to contract construction. Lord Walker stated (at [159]) that '[t]he wish to achieve legal certainty by the use of a standard precedent cannot override the need to construe any document in its commercial context'. It seems that even the conduct of the parties after execution of the agreement may be relevant to the issue of characterisation of their agreement (see *Agnew v IRC* [2001] UKPC 28, [2001] 2 AC 710 at [48], per Lord Millett), although, as this runs against a well-established principle of contract interpretation (see, eg, *Whitworth Street Estates Ltd v Miller* [1970] AC 583 at 603, per Lord Reid), the point is controversial (see *Re Spectrum Plus Ltd*, above, at [160], per Lord Walker; and also S Atherton and RJ Mokal (2005) 26 Company Lawyer 10 at 16–18).

- The inquiry in some cases is perhaps more burdensome than it need be. The source of difficulty is an assumption that there is, or ought to be, just one criterion by which to discriminate between legal categories. Thus, Dillon LJ referred to an 'objective criterion in law by which the court can test whether the agreement the parties have made does not fall into the legal category in which the parties have sought to place their agreement'. In *Exfinco*, finding a criterion for distinguishing a sale from a charge was not easy to identify as 'there is no one clear touchstone' (per Dillon LJ). In other contexts, a criterion may be easier to identify. The right to exclusive occupation is recognised as the central characteristic of a lease which distinguishes it from a licence (*Street v Mountford* [1985] AC 809, HL). The chargor's right to deal with the charged asset for its own account is recognised as the badge of a floating charge and is inconsistent with a fixed charge (*Agnew v IRC*, above, at [13], per Lord Millett; *Re Spectrum Plus Ltd*, above, at [106]–[107], [111]–[112], per Lord Scott, and at [138]–[140], per Lord Walker). But often the distinction between legal concepts depends on the presence and absence of *criteria*, not a criterion. Thus, in *Orion Finance Ltd v Crown Financial Management Ltd* [1996] 2 BCLC 78 at 84–85, Millett LJ stressed that there was no single objective criterion by which it is possible to determine whether a transaction is one of sale and repurchase or of security. In such circumstances, to commence a search for a criterion may be to posit a task more difficult than it need be.

- It is submitted that Lord Millett's approach to characterisation in *Agnew* is broadly similar to the internal approach adopted by the Court of Appeal in the *Exfinco* case (for the contrary view, see A Berg [2003] JBL 205). In *Exfinco*, the Court of Appeal held that, absent a sham, the court would ignore the labels used by the parties if the rights and obligations created by the documents were inconsistent with those labels. But how is a court to do this unless it knows what the labels mean? It is not possible to ascribe legal meaning to a transaction without legal concepts through which the parties' expressed intentions are understood. This is why Dillon LJ referred to the need for some objective criterion in law by which the court could test the agreement the parties had made. In essence, in following this approach the court is doing no more than that outlined by Lord Millett in *Agnew*: (a) construing the agreement to ascertain the intention of the parties as to their respective rights and obligations; and (b) measuring those rights and obligations against the objective legal criterion of the type of transaction in issue.

4. An option to repurchase is treated differently from an equity of redemption. As Millett LJ emphasised in *Orion Finance Ltd v Crown Financial Management Ltd* [1996] 2 BCLC 78 at 84:

> The transaction may take the form of a sale with an option to repurchase, and this is not to be equated with a right of redemption merely because the repurchase price is calculated by reference to the original sale price together with interest since the date of sale. On the other hand, the presence of a right of recourse by the transferee against the transferor to recover a shortfall may be inconsistent with a sale, but it is not necessarily so, and its absence is not conclusive.

In factoring and block discounting agreements the vendor is usually placed under an obligation to repurchase a factored or discounted receivable which cannot be recovered from the debtor for any reason, including the insolvency of the debtor, but such repurchase or recourse arrangements do not create an equity of redemption and do not turn a sale of receivables into a secured loan (*Olds Discount Co Ltd v John Playfair Ltd* [1938] 3 All ER 275; *Lloyds and Scottish Finance Ltd v Cyril Lord Carpets Sales Ltd* [1992] BCLC 609, HL). This is because the obligation to repurchase in a factoring or block discounting agreement only arises on the happening of an uncertain future event (non-recovery from the debtor), whereas an absolute obligation to repurchase ought to lead to the conclusion that the purported sale is only a sham masking a mortgage or charge which is in reality the substance of the transaction (F Oditah, *Legal Aspects of Receivables Financing* (1991), pp 38–39).

5. Ingenious and poor drafting can incline a court to 'recharacterise' a transaction more readily than the drafting may strictly require. On one view, that is implied by the High Court of Australia's decision on whether a contract expressed to establish trust over the proceeds of book debts was in truth a 'charge': *Associated Alloys Pty Ltd v ACN 001 452 106 Pty Ltd (in liq)* [2000] HCA 25, (2000) 202 CLR 588. Diverging from English judicial opinion, the High Court held that, because the agreement would be commercially effective if 'trust' meant 'trust', the fact that the arrangement did not engage the requirement to register charges of a company's book debts was no sign that the parties did not mean what their agreement said. See also *Palgo Holdings Pty Ltd v Gowans* [2005] HCA 28, (2005) 221 CLR 249 ('pledge', 'pawn').

6. For further discussion of the process of recharacterisation: see A Berg, 'Recharacterisation' [2001] JIBFL 346; A Berg, 'Recharacterisation after Enron' [2003] JBL 205; R Hooley, 'Recharacterisation' in D Neo, TH Wu, and M Hor (eds), *Lives in the Law: Essays in Honour of Peter Ellinger, Koh Kheng Lian & Tan Sook Yee* (2007), pp 30–51.

7. If the terms of the financing agreement consistently indicate a sale, and this is not a sham, will the courts take into account that a financier's real function is the lending of money when assessing whether the transaction is really one of loan secured by a charge? See *Olds Discount Co Ltd v Cohen* [1938] 3 All ER 281n.

8. If the financing agreement provides for the sale of receivables, will the courts hold the agreement to be a sham if it can be shown that the parties operated the agreement in a manner different from that envisaged in it? See *Lloyds and Scottish Finance Ltd v Cyril Lord Carpets Sales Ltd* [1992] BCLC 609, HL.

2 FINANCING BY SALE

Financing by sale may be done by means of factoring or by block discounting.

(a) Factoring

Assignment lies at the heart of factoring. It is important, therefore, to keep in mind the general law relating to the assignment of choses in action when considering factoring arrangements (see above, Chapter 22). However, when negotiable paper is discounted before maturity, the discounting is by negotiation and not by assignment.

'Some Aspects of Factoring Law—1: The Acquisition of Rights in the Receivables' by RM Goode
[1982] JBL 240 at 240–241

STRUCTURE OF A FACTORING TRANSACTION

Factoring is a transaction by which one person (the supplier or 'client') supplying goods or services to trade customers on short-term credit assigns the resulting receivables to another, the factor, upon terms that the assignment is to be notified to the debtors[1] and the factor is to collect in the receivables direct, assume responsibility for the maintenance of the relevant accounts and, within agreed limits, bear the risk of default in payment by customers. Factoring is thus a useful method of improving the supplier's liquidity. This could be done either by selling the receivables outright, or by mortgaging or charging them. Hitherto, factoring has almost invariably been carried out by way of outright sale, thus avoiding the need to register an assignment of receivables as a charge on book debts.[2]

Receivables which the factor is prepared to purchase without recourse are termed 'approved' receivables. These are receivables arising from transactions specifically approved by the factor or falling within an agreed limit authorised to be given to a particular customer. It is usual for factoring to be conducted on a 'whole turnover' basis, that is to say, the client offers or assigns all his receivables to the factor. Those which are not approved (termed 'unapproved' receivables) are purchased on a recourse basis. The factor thus provides a collection and accounting service and, as regards approved receivables, credit protection. In addition, instead of deferring payment for the receivables until the date they mature[3] ('maturity factoring') the factor will normally agree to allow the client to draw up to 80 per cent of the price in advance, charging the client a discount for the period the factor is out of his money.

Relations between the factor and the client are governed by a master agreement, the factoring agreement, which incorporates detailed undertakings and warranties by the client in relation to the receivables and the underlying contracts. Breach of these in relation to any receivable will usually render that receivable unapproved and entitle the factor to debit back the price.

FOOTNOTES:

1. Usually by a notice of assignment stamped on the invoice. Notification is what distinguishes full factoring from invoice discounting (or non-notification factoring). The latter is a pure financial facility.
2. Under [Part 25] of the Companies Act [2006]. Where the client is a sole trader or partnership firm, the assignment will usually be registrable [under s 344 of the Insolvency Act 1986].
3. Or, in the case of approved receivables, the date of the customer's insolvency, if this occurs before maturity.

NOTES

1. There are two types of agreement commonly used by factors. Factoring may take place under a 'whole turnover' agreement whereby the client agrees to sell, and the factor agrees to buy, all the client's receivables. The receivables vest in the factor as they come into existence. By contrast, factoring can also take place under a 'facultative' agreement which provides for the client to offer receivables for sale to the factor at agreed intervals and for acceptance of each offer by the factor as regards those receivables he is willing to purchase. The factor is under no obligation to purchase such receivables as are offered to him.

2. The facultative agreement simply provides a set of putative terms which will govern specific transactions as and when they are entered into (RM Goode [1982] JBL 240 at 241). Under a facultative agreement, receivables vest in the factor only when he has accepted the client's offer to sell.

3. The whole turnover and facultative agreements just described convey property—ie debts—from the client to the factor. They are assignments. However, they operate only as equitable assignments.

(b) Future receivables

The common law has long set itself against the idea that the transfer of future property (or after-acquired property) creates proprietary rights even after acquisition of the property by the transferor. The common law usually requires some new act of transfer after acquisition to vest a proprietary interest in the transferee. The position is different in equity. The next case is the landmark decision in this area.

Holroyd v Marshall
(1862) 10 HL Cas 191, House of Lords

T mortgaged mill machinery to secure his indebtedness to H. The mortgage deed (later registered as a bill of sale) contained a covenant by the mortgagor that all machinery placed in the mill in addition to, or in substitution for, the original machinery should be subject to the mortgage. The mortgagor did sell and exchange some of the original machinery, and introduced new machinery. The issue was whether the mortgagee had an interest in respect of the new machinery purchased and introduced after the date of the deed, which prevailed over subsequent execution creditors of the mortgagor. The House of Lords held that the mortgagee had a prevailing equitable interest in the new machinery.

> **Lord Westbury LC:** My Lords, the question is, whether as to the machinery added and substituted since the date of the mortgage the title of the mortgagees, or that of the judgment creditor, ought to prevail. It is admitted that the judgment creditor has no title as to the machinery originally comprised in the bill of sale; but it is contended that the mortgagees had no specific estate or interest in the future machinery. It is also admitted that if the mortgagees had an equitable estate in the added machinery, the same could not be taken in execution by the judgment creditor.
>
> The question may be easily decided by the application of a few elementary principles long settled in the Courts of Equity. In equity it is not necessary for the alienation of property that there should be a formal deed of conveyance. A contract for valuable consideration, by which it is agreed to make a present transfer of property, passes at once the beneficial interest, provided the contract is one of which a Court of Equity will decree specific performance. In the language of Lord Hardwicke, the vendor becomes a trustee for the vendee; subject, of course, to the contract being one to be specifically performed. And this is true, not only of contracts relating to real estate, but also of contracts relating to personal property, provided that the latter are such as a Court of Equity would direct to be specifically performed. . . .
>
> There can be no doubt, therefore, that if the mortgage deed in the present case had contained nothing but the contract which is involved in the aforesaid covenant of Taylor, the mortgagor, such contract would have amounted to a valid assignment in equity of the whole of the machinery and chattels in question, supposing such machinery to have been in existence and upon the mill at the time of the execution of the deed.
>
> But it is alleged that this is not the effect of the contract, because it relates to machinery not existing at the time, but to be acquired and fixed and placed in the mill at a future time. It is quite true that a deed which professes to convey property which is not in existence at the time is as a conveyance void at law, simply because there is nothing to convey. So in equity a contract which engages to transfer property, which is not in existence, cannot operate as an immediate alienation merely because there is nothing to transfer.
>
> But if a vendor or mortgagor agrees to sell or mortgage property, real or personal, of which he is not possessed at the time, and he receives the consideration for the contract, and afterwards

becomes possessed of property answering the description in the contract, there is no doubt that a Court of Equity would compel him to perform the contract, and that the contract would, in equity, transfer the beneficial interest to the mortgagee or purchaser immediately on the property being acquired. This, of course, assumes that the supposed contract is one of that class of which a Court of Equity would decree the specific performance. If it be so, then immediately on the acquisition of the property described the vendor or mortgagor would hold it in trust for the purchaser or mortgagee, according to the terms of the contract. For if a contract be in other respects good and fit to be performed, and the consideration has been received, incapacity to perform it at the time of its execution will be no answer when the means of doing so are afterwards obtained.

Apply these familiar principles to the present case; it follows that immediately on the new machinery and effects being fixed or placed into the mill, they became subject to the operation of the contract, and passed in equity to the mortgagees, to whom Taylor was bound to make a legal conveyance, and for whom he, in the meantime, was a trustee of the property in question.

There is another criterion to prove that the mortgagee acquired an estate or interest in the added machinery as soon as it was brought into the mill. If afterwards the mortgagor had attempted to remove any part of such machinery, except for the purpose of substitution, the mortgagee would have been entitled to an injunction to restrain such removal, and that because of his estate in the specific property. The result is, that the title of the Appellants is to be preferred to that of the judgment creditor.

[**Lord Wensleydale** concurred. **Lord Chelmsford** delivered a concurring judgment.]

Holroyd v Marshall concerned goods. *Tailby v Official Receiver* extended the principle of *Holroyd v Marshall* to future book debts.

Tailby v Official Receiver
(1888) 13 App Cas 523, House of Lords

I compounded with his creditors. At F's request, T signed promissory notes in favour of those creditors and paid a large sum to them. T took from I a bill of sale as counter-security. The bill of sale assigned (inter alia) 'all the book debts due and owing or which may during the continuance of this security become due and owing to the said mortgagor'. The bill also contained a power of attorney and a proviso that if the mortgagor on demand failed to pay the amount due, the mortgagee could take possession and sell the mortgaged property. On I's bankruptcy an issue arose as to whether the assignment of future book debts generally, without any delimitation as to time, place, or amount, was too vague to be upheld. Reversing the judgment of the Court of Appeal, the House of Lords upheld the validity of the assignment.

Lord Watson: ... The rule of equity which applies to the assignment of future choses in action is, as I understand it, a very simple one. Choses in action do not come within the scope of the Bills of Sale Acts, and though not yet existing, may nevertheless be the subject of present assignment. As soon as they come into existence, assignees who have given valuable consideration will, if the new chose in action is in the disposal of their assignor, take precisely the same right and interest as if it had actually belonged to him, or had been within his disposition and control at the time when the assignment was made. There is but one condition which must be fulfilled in order to make the assignee's right attach to a future chose in action, which is, that, on its coming into existence, it shall answer the description in the assignment or, in other words, that it shall be capable of being identified as the thing, or as one of the very things assigned. When there is no uncertainty as to its identification, the beneficial interest will immediately vest in the assignee. Mere difficulty in ascertaining all the things which are included in a general assignment, whether in esse or in posse, will not affect the assignee's right to those things which are capable of ascertainment or are identified. Lord Eldon said in *Lewis v Madocks* ((1803) 8 Ves 156): 'If the Courts find a solid subject of personal property they would attach it rather than render the contract nugatory.'

In the case of book debts, as in the case of choses in action generally, intimation of the assignee's right must be made to the debtor or obligee in order to make it complete. That is the only possession which he can attain, so long as the debt is unpaid, and is sufficient to take it out of the order and disposition of the assignor. In this case the appellant's right, if otherwise valid, was, in any question with the respondent, duly perfected by his notice to Wilson Brothers & Co before Izon became a bankrupt.

The learned judges of the Appeal Court were unanimously of opinion that the description of book debts in the assignment of Tyrell is 'too vague,' and it is upon that ground only that they have held the assignment to be invalid. The term which they have selected, in order to express what they conceived to be the radical defect of the assignment, is susceptible of at least two different meanings. It may either signify that the description is too wide and comprehensive, without implying that there will be any uncertainty as to the debts which it will include, if and when these come into existence, or it may signify that the language of the description is so obscure that it will be impossible, in the time to come, to determine with any degree of certainty to what particular debts it was intended to apply. In the latter sense the description of future book debts in the mortgage of 1879 does not incur the imputation of vagueness. No one has suggested that the expression 'book debt' is indefinite; and it is, in my opinion, very clear that every debt becoming due and owing to the mortgagor, which belongs to the class of book debts (a fact quite capable of ascertainment), is at once identified with the subject-matter of the assignment.

The ground of decision in the Appeal Court was obviously this: that the description of future debts is 'too vague,' in the sense of being too wide and comprehensive, inasmuch as it embraces debts to become due to the mortgagee in any and every business which he may think fit to carry on. If it had been limited to debts arising in the course of the business of packing-case manufacturer, in which Izon was engaged at the date of the mortgage, the Master of the Rolls was, as then advised, prepared to hold that the description would not have been too vague. Upon that point the other members of the Court express no definite opinion, Lindley LJ merely remarking, 'I do not say that an assignment of future book debts must necessarily be too vague.' All of their Lordships were evidently under the impression that they were deciding the case according to a well-established equitable doctrine, which Lopes LJ traces to *Belding v Read* ((1865) 3 H & C 955).

It is unnecessary for the purposes of this case to consider how far a general assignment of all after-acquired property can receive effect, because the assignment in question relates to one species of property only. I have been unable to discover any principle upon which the decision of the Court of Appeal can be supported, unless it is to be found in *Belding v Read* ((1865) 3 H & C 955). That case arose in a Court of Common Law, and, with all deference to the very learned judges who decided it, I am bound to say that, in my opinion, they misapprehended the doctrine laid down by Lord Westbury in *Holroyd v Marshall* ((1862) 10 HL Cas 191), which was not new doctrine, but, as the noble Lord explicitly stated, was the mere enunciation of elementary principles long settled in Courts of Equity. It is possible that the learned judges were misled by the reference which the noble Lord makes to specific performance, an illustration not selected with his usual felicity. Not a single decision by an Equity Court was cited to us, prior in date to *Belding v Read,* which gives the least support to the opinions expressed in that case, and I venture to doubt whether any such decision exists. It is true that judges on the equity side of the Court have, in one or two instances, deferred to the views expressed in *Belding v Read,* which they assumed to be an authoritative exposition of the law applied by this House in *Holroyd v Marshall,* but these views conflict with the previous cases in equity, to which Lord Westbury referred as establishing a well-known and elementary principle. In *Bennett v Cooper* ((1846) 9 Beav 252), Lord Langdale MR gave effect to an equitable mortgage by a debtor of 'all sums of money then or thereafter to become due to him, and all legacies or bequests which had already or might thereafter be given or bequeathed to him or his wife, by any person whomsoever.' I cannot understand upon what principle an assignment of all legacies which may be bequeathed by any person to the assignor is to stand good, and effect is to be denied to a general assignment of all future book debts. As Cotton LJ said, in *Re Clarke* ((1887) 36 Ch D 348 at 353): 'Vagueness comes to nothing if the property is definite at the time when the Court is asked to enforce the contract.' A future book debt is quite as capable of being identified as a legacy; and in this case the identity of the debt, with the subjects assigned, is not matter of dispute. When the consideration has been given, and the debt has been clearly identified as one of those in respect of which it was given, a Court of Equity will enforce the covenant of the parties, and will not permit the assignor, or those in his right, to defeat the assignment upon the plea that it is too comprehensive.

I am accordingly of opinion that the order appealed from ought to be reversed, and the judgment of the Divisional Court restored.

Lord Macnaghten: . . . The claim of the purchaser was rested on well-known principles. It has long been settled that future property, possibilities and expectancies are assignable in equity for value. The mode or form of assignment is absolutely immaterial provided the intention of the parties is clear. To effectuate the intention an assignment for value, in terms present and immediate, has always been regarded in equity as a contract binding on the conscience of the assignor and so binding the subject-matter of the contract when it comes into existence, if it is of such a nature and so described as to be capable of being ascertained and identified . . .

My Lords, I should wish to say a few words about *Holroyd v Marshall* ((1862) 10 HL Cas 191), because I am inclined to think that *Belding v Read* ((1865) 3 H & C 955) is not the only case in which Lord Westbury's observations have been misunderstood. To understand Lord Westbury's judgment aright, I think it is necessary to bear in mind the state of the law at the time, and the point to which his Lordship was addressing himself. *Holroyd v Marshall* laid down no new law, nor did it extend the principles of equity in the slightest degree. Long before *Holroyd v Marshall* was determined it was well settled that an assignment of future property for value operates in equity by way of agreement, binding the conscience of the assignor, and so binding the property from the moment when the contract becomes capable of being performed, on the principle that equity considers as done that which ought to be done, and in accordance with the maxim which Lord Thurlow said he took to be universal, 'that whenever persons agree concerning any particular subject, that, in a Court of Equity, as against the party himself, and any claiming under him, voluntary or with notice, raises a trust:' *Legard v Hodges* ((1792) 1 Ves 477). It had also been determined by the highest tribunals in the country, short of this House—by Lord Lyndhurst as Lord Chancellor in England, and by Sir Edward Sugden as Lord Chancellor in Ireland—that an agreement binding property for valuable consideration had precedence over the claim of a judgment creditor. Some confusion, however, had recently been introduced by a decision of a most eminent judge, who was naturally less familiar with the doctrines of equity than with the principles of common law. In that state of things, in *Holroyd v Marshall,* in a contest between an equitable assignee and an execution creditor, Stuart VC decided in favour of the equitable assignee. His decision was reversed by Lord Campbell LC in a judgment which seemed to strike at the root of all equitable titles. Lord Campbell did not hold that the equitable assignee obtained no interest in the property the subject of the contract when it came into existence. He held that the equitable assignee did obtain an interest in equity. But at the same time he held that the interest was of such a fugitive character, so shadowy, and so precarious, that it could not stand against the legal title of the execution creditor, without the help of some new act to give it substance and strength. It was to this view, I think, that Lord Westbury addressed himself; and by way of shewing how real and substantial were equitable interests springing from agreements based on valuable consideration, he referred to the doctrines of specific performance, illustrating his argument by examples. One of the examples, perhaps, requires some qualification. That, however, does not affect the argument. The argument is clear and convincing; but it must not be wrested from its purpose. It is difficult to suppose that Lord Westbury intended to lay down as a rule to guide or perplex the Court, that considerations applicable to cases of specific performance, properly so-called, where the contract is executory, are to be applied to every case of equitable assignment dealing with future property. Lord Selborne has, I think, done good service in pointing out that confusion is sometimes caused by transferring such considerations to questions which arise as to the propriety of the Court requiring something or other to be done in specie (*Wolverhampton and Walsall Rly Co v London and North Western Rly Co* ((1873) LR 16 Eq 433)). His Lordship observes that there is some fallacy and ambiguity in the way in which in cases of that kind those words 'specific performance,' are very frequently used. Greater confusion still, I think, would be caused by transferring considerations applicable to suits for specific performance—involving, as they do, some of the nicest distinctions and most difficult questions that come before the Court—to cases of equitable assignment or specific lien where nothing remains to be done in order to define the rights of the parties, but the Court is merely asked to protect rights completely defined as between the parties to the contract, or to give effect to such rights either by granting an injunction or by appointing a receiver, or by adjudicating on questions between rival claimants.

The truth is that cases of equitable assignment or specific lien, where the consideration has passed, depend on the real meaning of the agreement between the parties. The difficulty, generally speaking, is to ascertain the true scope and effect of the agreement. When that is ascertained you have only to apply the principle that equity considers that done which ought to be done if that principle is applicable under the circumstances of the case. The doctrines relating to specific performance do not, I think, afford a test or a measure of the rights created.

[**Lord Herschell** delivered a concurring judgment. **Lord FitzGerald** upheld the appeal on different grounds.]

NOTES

1. The interpretation in *Tailby v Official Receiver* of Lord Westbury's earlier reference to specific performance is highly significant to the factoring of future receivables. *Tailby* decides that specific performance in a strict sense is not necessary in order to generate equitable interests in assignees of future debts once those debts come into existence. Provided the consideration moving from the creditor is executed and not executory—ie the creditor has actually advanced his money to the debtor, and not merely promised to do so—the creditor is entitled to specific performance once property identifiable as the subject matter of the contract is acquired by the debtor. In other words, specific performance in the strict sense may be necessary to give further effect to an assignment, but is not the test of whether the assignment has occurred.

2. Lord Macnaghten honoured Lord Selborne by saying that the latter had done good service in pointing out that 'specific performance' can denote two different forms of equitable relief: relief in respect of executory contracts and relief in respect of executed contracts. Two points arise. First, is it possible to say that the efficacy of an assignment of future receivables depends in no sense on the specific enforceability of the agreement to assign them? In this regard, it is notable that even an assignment of an existing debt requires no formal step in equity beyond expression of intention to assign. By definition, there is no unperformed step the taking of which a court could order by decreeing specific performance. Would specific performance be a necessary remedy if the parties agreed that an assignment of debts should be made by one of them to the other by means of a deed executed in particular terms? Secondly, is it important that further meanings of 'specific performance' and 'specific enforceability' have been identified in connection with the creation of equitable interests? See Turner (2012) 128 LQR 582; JD Heydon, MJ Leeming, and PG Turner, *Meagher, Gummow and Lehane's Equity: Doctrines and Remedies* (5th edn, 2015), para 6–055; *Golden Mile Property Investments Pty Ltd (in liq) v Cudgegong Australia Pty Ltd* [2015] NSWCA 100, (2015) 89 NSWLR 237.

3. In the context of the factoring of receivables, future receivables can only be factored under a whole turnover agreement. Under the terms of such an agreement, the factor is obliged to purchase future receivables. Undertaking that obligation constitutes the provision (or execution) of valuable consideration. As soon as future receivables (within the description of the agreement) come into existence and vest in the client, the equitable interest therein vests in the factor as the intended assignee.

4. However, the factor faces a number of disadvantages if future receivables are assigned to it and those receivables have not yet come into existence:

(a) it cannot intervene in actions concerning the property to which it is not yet entitled;

(b) it cannot give notice of its assignment to secure priority against other assignees until there is some debtor to whom effective notice can be given (*Re Dallas* [1904] 2 Ch 385);

(c) it cannot give notice of its assignment to the debtor so as to stop the debtor's equities enforceable against the assignor until the debt has come into existence (Oditah, op cit, pp 239–240; compare S Mills, N Ruddy, and N Davidson, *Salinger on Factoring* (5th edn, 2006), paras 9–22 to 9–25);

(d) if the receivable comes into existence as a result of post-liquidation performance of an underlying contract by the client or its liquidator, the 'disposition' of the receivable under the terms of a pre-liquidation factoring agreement will be void unless the court orders otherwise (Insolvency Act 1986, s 127).

5. Future receivables cannot be factored under a facultative agreement. This is because the factor is under no obligation to purchase the receivables offered to him and so provides no consideration to support a valid assignment of future receivables. Only after the receivables have come into existence can the client offer them to the factor. If the factor purchases any receivable offered to him an equitable assignment will take place at that stage.

(c) Block discounting

Lloyds & Scottish Finance Ltd v Cyril Lord Carpets Sales Ltd
[1992] BCLC 609, House of Lords (the case was decided in 1979)

The facts are irrelevant.

> **Lord Scarman**: Block discounting is a well-known service offered by certain finance houses to traders who do a substantial business by way of hire-purchase or credit-sale agreements with their customers. Though there are variations of detail, the essential feature of the service

is that in return for an immediate advance the trader sells to the finance house at a discount his interest in the agreements he has with his customers. The trader gives the house his guarantee of due performance by his customers of their obligations. He includes a number, often a very large number, of hire-purchase or credit-sale agreements in each discounting transaction: hence the City's name 'block discounting' for this type of transaction. The service is similar to many other financial services offered in the City of London and elsewhere—an immediate advance of money against documents, which are purchased at a discount. It is an adaptation of the historic business of discounting bills and notes to the particular circumstances of the hire-purchase and credit-sale trade. The finance house looks only to the discount for its profit. Once the trader has met his commitment for the advance and the discount charge (out of the moneys received or receivable from his customers whose debts he has sold), the finance house is content that the trader should keep for himself whatever else is collected from the customers.

Of course the facility offered is money. The finance house advances money in reliance upon obligations which have not yet matured. But is it the lending of money? The question was answered (at first instance) 40 years ago. If the transaction be genuine and not a sham to cover something different, the judges held it to be a sale, not a loan. The three cases in which this answer was given have stood over the years unchallenged—and are, no doubt, the basis of City practice. They are *Re George Inglefield Ltd* [1933] Ch 1; *Olds Discount Co Ltd v Cohen* [1938] 3 All ER 281n and *Olds Discount Co Ltd v Playfair Ltd* [1938] 3 All ER 275.

NOTES

1. A block discounting agreement is essentially facultative. It provides a set of terms upon which blocks of receivables may later be sold by a dealer to the finance company. Each sale constitutes a separate transaction by which blocks of debt are equitably assigned to the finance company. Under the terms of the master agreement the dealer gives the finance company a power of attorney to execute a legal assignment, should this prove necessary.

2. In the case of a block discounting agreement, it is usual not to give notice of the assignment of the debt to the dealer's customers. The dealer collects the debt as agent of the finance company. From the dealer's point of view, this has the advantage of allowing the dealer to retain control over his debts and maintain a relationship with his customers. From the finance company's point of view, block discounting saves it the costs associated with debt collection.

3. Yet block discounting is inherently riskier for the finance company than notification factoring.

(a) If a customer pays the dealer, then the customer is discharged from its debt, whether or not the dealer pays the finance company.

(b) The dealer is under no obligation to account to the finance company for payments received from his customers, nor is he obliged to segregate such payments from his other resources (although under the terms of the master agreement the dealer will have guaranteed payment by the hirers or credit buyers and will have secured that guarantee by accepting a series of bills of exchange, or issuing promissory notes, payable to the finance company). Contrast this with factoring, where the client has been said to receive the proceeds on trust for the factor (*GE Crane Pty Ltd v Federal Commissioner of Taxation* (1971) 126 CLR 177, High Court of Australia) and where the client will be liable for conversion if it misappropriates any cheque, or other negotiable instrument, paid to it (*International Factors Ltd v Rodriguez* [1979] QB 351).

(c) The finance company is at risk of loss of priority to another assignee who gives notice to the hirer or credit buyer (although under the terms of the master agreement the dealer usually undertakes not to assign, charge, or otherwise encumber any receivable assigned to the finance company).

(d) If the finance company does collect the debt itself, it takes the debt subject to all defences and rights of set-off which have accrued between the customer and the dealer in the period up to when the customer receives notice of the assignment.

(d) Nature of financier's discount

A financier's discount is typically set by reference to a fitting rate of interest for the duration of the agreement. In the next case, the Court of Appeal considered whether the nature of the financier's discount was, accordingly, a charge of interest.

Welsh Development Agency v Export Finance Co Ltd
[1992] BCLC 148, Court of Appeal

The facts appear above, p 951.

Dillon LJ: The essence of the transaction when a trader raises finance by factoring book debts or block discounting hire-purchase agreements is that the trader sells the book debts to a finance company for a price which is necessarily discounted from the full aggregate face value of the debts. It is discounted, primarily, because the trader will be getting an immediate payment, while the finance company will have to wait for the debts to come in from the debtors and they may well not be presently payable. Indeed with hire-purchase agreements the debt will be payable by the hirer by instalments over what may be a considerable period. The rate of discount will also no doubt take into account the risk the finance company is assuming that the debtor will fail to pay the debts . . .

It is normal, therefore, that the rate of discount for the finance company will be calculated by reference to the appropriate rate of interest for the period for which the finance company is out of its money. It has been normal for the amount of discount to be calculated once and for all; it will be actually received by the finance company when the finance company receives payment of the book debt from the debtor, or from the vendor under rights of recourse for the finance company against the vendor. If the vendor has guaranteed to the finance company that the debtor will pay the debt punctually, and the debtor does not pay punctually, it may well be that the finance company could claim damages from the vendor, to be measured by a computation of interest over the period for which it has been kept out of its money in excess of the period on which the calculation of the amount of the finance company's discount was based.

The classic exposition by Lord Devlin in *Chow Yoong Hong v Choong Fah Rubber Manufactory Ltd* [1962] AC 209 at 217, of the difference between interest and discounts is as follows:

When payment is made before due date at a discount, the amount of the discount is no doubt often calculated by reference to the amount of interest which the payer calculates his money would have earned if he had deferred payment to the due date. But that does not mean that discount is the same as interest. Interest postulates the making of a loan and then it runs from day to day until repayment of the loan, its total depending on the length of the loan. Discount is a deduction from the price *fixed once and for all at the time of payment.* (My emphasis.)

Lord Wilberforce made a statement to the same effect—that discount is fixed and paid once and for all whereas interest accrues from day-to-day—in the *Lloyds & Scottish* case after citing from Lord Devlin's opinion in *Chow Yoong Hong*. Lord Wilberforce also referred to statements in *Willingale (Inspector of Taxes) v International Commercial Bank Ltd* [1978] AC 834 at 841, 843 by Lord Salmon and by Lord Fraser of Tullybelton to the effect that, unlike interest, discount is not earned and does not accrue from day-to-day.

NOTES

1. In *Welsh Development Agency* the discount was not fixed but fluctuating. It was closely tied to the average period taken by all overseas buyers to pay. However, Dillon LJ held that this did not convert the discount into interest on a loan and did not negate the transaction as being one of sale and purchase.

2. Factors may also make an 'administration charge' if they provide administrative services such as ledger administration, debt collection, and credit protection. However, there is evidence that some factors make this charge even when these additional services are not provided (eg *Re Charge Card Services Ltd* [1987] Ch 150 at 171).

(e) The financier's security

Whether finance is provided under a factoring or block discount agreement, the financier usually obtains one or more of the following types of security against the client or dealer (hereafter collectively referred to as the 'client').

(i) Guarantees and indemnities

An ordinary indemnity clause in a factoring agreement will provide that a client shall indemnify the factor and keep it indemnified against any claim of whatsoever nature by a customer against the client or the factor. Block discounting agreements may contain more elaborate provisions. Dr Oditah has noted that these guarantees and indemnities 'afford personal security to the factor [and block discounter] although when combined with a right to set off damages and loss against the retention fund, could, no doubt, prove powerful' (F Oditah, *Legal Aspects of Receivables Financing* (1991), p 51).

(ii) A right of recourse

The right of recourse found in a factoring or block discounting agreement does not create an equity of redemption giving rise to a mortgage of, or charge over, a debt (see above, p 957). It, too, is a personal security, not a proprietary security.

(iii) A right of retention

Such a right appears in the next case.

Re Charge Card Services Ltd

[1987] Ch 150, Chancery Division

Charge Card Services Ltd (the company) entered into an invoice discounting agreement by which it agreed to factor its receivables to Commercial Credit Services Ltd (the factor). The relevant provisions of the agreement were as follows.

- By clause 3(a) the factor could require the company to repurchase any receivable in certain specified circumstances (eg if the debtor disputed liability).
- By clause 3(c) the company guaranteed payment by every debtor and agreed to indemnify the factor against loss caused by the debtor's failure to pay.
- By clause 4 the purchase price payable by the factor to the company was the gross amount payable by the debtor less any discount allowable and less a discount charge calculated in the manner prescribed by standard condition 3.
- By clause 6 the factor's obligation to pay was made subject to the right of debits and right of retention set out in standard condition 3.
- By clause 10 (read with clause 11) the factor had the option of determining the agreement on the company going into insolvent liquidation, whereupon the company was obliged to repurchase at face value so much of any receivable purchased by the factor as then remained outstanding. At the date of the trial the factor had not exercised this option.
- By standard condition 3A the factor had to maintain a current account which would be credited with (inter alia) the purchase price of each receivable and which would be debited with (inter alia) the amount of any receivables which the factor had required the company to repurchase, inter alia, under clause 3(a) (but not under clause 10).
- By standard condition 3B the factor was to remit to the company or its order any balance for the time being standing to the credit of the current account less any amount which the factor in its absolute discretion decided to retain as security for:
  - (i) any claims or defences against the company;
  - (ii) any risk of non-payment by a debtor; and
  - (iii) any amount prospectively chargeable to the company as a debit under standard condition 3A.

The company went into insolvent liquidation and a dispute arose between its liquidator and the factor as to the validity of the factor's right of retention under standard condition 3B. Millett J upheld the validity of the factor's right.

Millett J: It was submitted on behalf of the company that the right of retention was expressly reserved by Commercial Credit as security for its prospective rights of set off, and that in consequence it constituted a charge on book debts created by the company which was void against the liquidator for want of registration under s 95 of the Companies Act 1948 [now s 859H of the Companies Act 2006] . . .

In my judgment, and leaving aside for the moment the possible claim under clause 10, the short answer to these submissions is that Commercial Credit's right of retention under standard condition 3B(iii) in respect of any amount prospectively chargeable to the company as a debit to the current account is a matter not of set off but of account. In *Halesowen Presswork & Assemblies Ltd v National Westminster Bank Ltd* [1971] 1 QB 1, Buckley LJ said, at p 46:

Where the relationship of the banker and customer is a single relationship such as I have already mentioned, albeit embodied in a number of accounts, the situation is not, in my judgment, a situation of lien at all. A lien postulates property of the debtor in the possession or under the control of the creditor. Nor is it a set-off situation, which postulates mutual but independent obligations between the two parties. It is an accounting situation, in which the existence and amount of one party's liability to the other can only be ascertained by discovering the ultimate balance of their mutual dealings.

Counsel for the company put forward a sophisticated analysis of the various provisions of the agreement to show that, despite the wording of clause 4, the discounting charge was not integral to the ascertainment of the purchase price but, like the administration charge, a true contra item. In my judgment, however, the crucial factor is not the definition of the purchase price, but the extent of Commercial Credit's obligation to pay. This is to be found in clause 6, and it is an obligation to pay, not the purchase price, which is merely a credit in the current account, but the balance shown on the current account subject to the right of retention. The right of retention thus constitutes a contractual limitation on the company's right to require payment of the balance on the current account. It is an essential safeguard against overpayment since, except at the end of the month when the discounting and administration charges are debited, and in the unlikely event of there being no bad debts at all, the balance on the current account can never represent the true amount owing by Commercial Credit. The sum made payable by clause 6, therefore, is in effect a provisional payment only and represents the best estimate that can be made at the time of the true state of account between the parties.

In my judgment, this is not a case of set off at all, for there are no mutual but independent obligations capable of being quantified and set off against each other. There are reciprocal obligations giving rise to credits and debits in a single running account, a single liability to pay the ultimate balance found due on taking the account, and provisions for retention and provisional payment in the meantime.

If this analysis is correct, it also provides an answer to the company's claim that the right of retention in standard condition 3B(iii) constitutes a registrable charge, for there is no relevant property capable of forming the subject matter of the charge. The only asset which the company could charge is its chose in action, ie the right to sue Commercial Credit for the sum due under the agreement, but this already contains within it the liability to suffer a retention. Counsel for the company naturally stressed the fact that the right of retention is expressed to be by way of security, but that is of no avail if, as I hold, it secures Commercial Credit, not against default by the company in the performance of its obligations, but against overpayment by itself.

This still leaves the company's liability to repurchase outstanding receivables at face value if Commercial Credit serves a notice of termination under clause 10. The purchase price payable by the company in this event is not available to be debited to the current account under standard condition 3A(ii), but Commercial Credit has the right to retain money to meet it under standard condition 3B(i). It has been conceded before me that this is a true right of set off. Accordingly, as well as in case I am wrong in my analysis of the other rights of retention, I must deal with the company's contentions that the right of retention in standard condition 3B is a registrable charge on the company's book debts and that in so far as it gives a right of set off in respect of sums only contingently due from the company at the date of liquidation it goes beyond what is permitted by s 31 of the Bankruptcy Act 1914 [now s 323 of the Insolvency Act 1986; and r 4.90 of the Insolvency Rules 1986].

If the right of retention constitutes a charge, there is no doubt that it is a charge on book debts and is a charge created by the company. But is it a charge at all? The sum due from Commercial Credit to the company under the agreement is, of course, a book debt of the company which the company can charge to a third party. In my judgment, however, it cannot be charged in favour of Commercial Credit itself, for the simple reason that a charge in favour of a debtor of his own indebtedness to the chargor is conceptually impossible.

Counsel for the company conceded that a debt cannot be assigned in whole or in part to the debtor, since such an assignment operates wholly or partially as a release. Likewise, it was conceded, it cannot be made the subject of a legal or equitable mortgage in favour of the debtor, since this requires a conveyance or assignment by way of security, and this operates as a conditional release. But, it was submitted, an equitable charge need involve no conveyance or assignment of property, so that any objection on this ground falls away.

[His Lordship then examined the requirements for the creation of an equitable charge as set out in *Palmer v Carey* [1926] AC 703 at 706–707 and in *National Provincial and Union Bank of England v Charnley* [1924] 1 KB 431 at 449–450 and continued:]

Thus the essence of an equitable charge is that, without any conveyance or assignment to the chargee, specific property of the chargor is expressly or constructively appropriated to or made answerable for payment of a debt, and the chargee is given the right to resort to the property for the purpose of having it realised and applied in or towards payment of the debt. The availability of equitable remedies has the effect of giving the chargee a proprietary interest by way of security in the property charged.

It is true, therefore, that no conveyance or assignment is involved in the creation of an equitable charge, but in my judgment the benefit of a debt can no more be appropriated or made available to the debtor than it can be conveyed or assigned to him. The objection to a charge in these circumstances is not to the process by which it is created, but to the result. A debt is a chose in action; it is the right to sue the debtor. This can be assigned or made available to a third party, but not to the debtor, who cannot sue himself. Once any assignment or appropriation to the debtor becomes unconditional, the debt is wholly or partially released. The debtor cannot, and does not need to, resort to the creditor's claim against him in order to obtain the benefit of the security; his own liability to the creditor is automatically discharged or reduced.

In *Halesowen Presswork & Assemblies Ltd v National Westminster Bank Ltd* [1971] 1 QB 1, 46 Buckley LJ, in a passage subsequently approved in the House of Lords [1972] AC 785 by Viscount Dilhorne, at p 802, Lord Simon of Glaisdale at p 808, and Lord Cross of Chelsea, at p 810, stated that he could not understand how it could be said with any kind of accuracy that the bank had a lien upon its own indebtedness to its customer. It is true that this comment was made in relation to a lien rather than a charge, and a lien unlike a charge can only attach to tangible property. But the reason why it was said that the bank did not have a lien on the credit balance in its customer's current account was clearly based on the identity of the parties rather than the particular character of the security given.

Counsel for the company relied on *Ex p Caldicott* (1884) 25 Ch D 716, in which a partner deposited money with a bank by way of security for the indebtedness of his firm. The Court of Appeal held that the bank was not required to value its security before proving for its debt against the firm. It was, however, not necessary to decide whether the deposit created a charge; it was sufficient that it did not create a security on the joint estate.

It does not, of course, follow that an attempt to create an express mortgage or charge of a debt in favour of the debtor would be ineffective to create a security. Equity looks to the substance, not the form; and while in my judgment this would not create a mortgage or charge, it would no doubt give a right of set off which would be effective against the creditor's liquidator or trustee in bankruptcy, provided that it did not purport to go beyond what is permitted by s 31 of the Bankruptcy Act 1914 [now s 323 of the Insolvency Act 1986; and r 4.90 of the Insolvency Rules 1986.]

[Although the case went to the Court of Appeal ([1989] Ch 497), there was no appeal on this part of Millett J's judgment.]

NOTE

The suggestion by Millett J that 'charge-backs'—or charges-back—were conceptually impossible came as something of a surprise to the banking world, where it was common practice for banks to take charges over their customers' deposits (which constitute debts owed by the bank to its customer) as security. However, there was some Australian authority in favour of the conceptual impossibility of such a charge (*Broad v Stamp Duties Comr* [1980] 2 NSWLR 40; see *Re the Estate of McClure* (1947) 48 SR (NSW) 93 at 96), and Professor Goode has been a consistent advocate of this approach (eg RM Goode, *Legal Problems of Credit and Security* (1st edn, 1982), pp 86–87; (1998) 114 LQR 178. In (1989) 15 Mon LR 361 at 368, Professor Goode wrote:

> . . . a debt is a species of property only as between the creditor and a third party taking an assignment or charge. In the relationship between creditor and debtor the debt is merely an obligation. As creditor I do not own the debt, I am owed it. Accordingly as against the debtor I have nothing to assign or charge back to him.

On the other hand, Millett J's dictum has been subjected to severe criticism from the majority of academic writers: see PR Wood (1987) 8 Co Law 262 and *English and International Set-Off* (1989), paras 5–134 to 5–181; DE Allan (1989) 15 Mon LR 337; and F Oditah [1992] JBL 541 at 555–562. The critics argue that a debt can be 'property' as between the creditor and the debtor, at least when it is charged back to the creditor as security. They point to cases like *Re Jeavons, ex p Mackay, ex p Brown* (1873) 8 Ch App 643 (better reported in (1873) 42 LJ(NS) Bankruptcy 68), where an argument that a debtor cannot have a charge on royalties due from him was rejected by the Court of Appeal. The critics reject the argument that a charge-back is conceptually impossible because a debtor cannot sue himself by emphasising that a debt constitutes more than a right to sue and that examples can be found of the courts upholding unenforceable debts (eg *Curwen v Milburn* (1889) 42 Ch D 424). They deal with the argument that a charge-back is impossible because it would involve a merger of the security interest and the liability, by pointing out that merger is dependent on the intention of the parties, and that merger would not occur provided it was made clear that it was not intended. Less persuasively, perhaps, the critics cite the Legal Risk Review Committee's recommendation that there should be legislation to make it clear that charges-back are permitted under English law (Final Report of the Legal Risk Review Committee, October 1992).

Millett J's dictum in *Charge Card* was endorsed in dicta of the Court of Appeal in *Re Bank of Credit and Commerce International SA (No 8)* [1996] Ch 245 but did not survive the following appeal.

Re Bank of Credit and Commerce International SA (No 8)
[1998] AC 214, House of Lords

BCCI, a bank which was now in liquidation, had made a loan to a company. To secure the loan the person controlling the company had deposited funds with BCCI and signed a letter charging the funds with the repayment of the company's debt. The depositor did not guarantee payment of the loan or accept any other form of personal liability. The issue was whether BCCI's liquidators could recover the full amount of the loan from the company, leaving the depositor to prove for his deposit as an unsecured creditor, or whether the deposit could be set off against the company's liability for the loan. The Court of Appeal, upholding Rattee J, held that there could be no set-off because there was no mutuality between the claims sought to be set off (as required by the Insolvency Rules 1986, r 4.90). The borrowing company owed the amount due to BCCI (the loan), but the amount due from BCCI (the deposit) was owed to the depositor, who himself owed BCCI nothing since he had not given any personal guarantee. The House of Lords affirmed the decision of the Court of Appeal.

The charge-back point arose because it was argued by the company that although the depositor purported to create a charge over his deposit, this was legally ineffective for this purpose (charges-back being conceptually impossible), and so the only way in which the letter could operate as an effective security, which was what the parties intended, was if it was construed as imposing personal liability on the depositor for the company's indebtedness.

Lord Hoffmann: . . .

(B) IN RE CHARGE CARD SERVICES LTD

The Court of Appeal rejected the argument that the letter was ineffective unless construed as imposing personal liability. They accepted Mr McDonnell's [counsel for the borrowing company and the depositor] submission that, by reason of conceptual impossibility, it could not operate as a charge over the deposit. But they said that it could provide perfectly good security by virtue of the contractual provisions in the third paragraph which limited the right to repayment of the deposit and made it what is sometimes called a 'flawed asset.' I agree and could stop there without commenting on the question of whether a charge is conceptually impossible or not. But the point has been very fully argued and should, I think, be dealt with.

The doctrine of conceptual impossibility was first propounded by Millett J in *In re Charge Card Services Ltd* [1987] Ch 150, 175–176 and affirmed, after more extensive discussion, by the Court of Appeal in this case. It has excited a good deal of heat and controversy in banking circles; the Legal Risk Review Committee, set up in 1991 by the Bank of England to identify areas of obscurity and uncertainty in the law affecting financial markets and propose solutions, said that a very large number of submissions from interested parties expressed disquiet about this ruling. It seems clear that documents purporting to create such charges have been used by banks for many years. The point does not previously appear to have been expressly addressed by any court in this country. Supporters of the doctrine rely on the judgments of Buckley LJ (in the Court of Appeal) and Viscount Dilhorne and Lord Cross of Chelsea (in the House of Lords) in *Halesowen Presswork & Assemblies Ltd v Westminster Bank Ltd* [1971] 1 QB 1; [1972] AC 785. The passages in question certainly say that it is a misuse of language to speak of a bank having a lien over its own indebtedness to a customer. But I think that these observations were directed to the use of the word 'lien,' which is a right to retain possession, rather than to the question of whether the bank could have any kind of proprietary interest. Opponents of the doctrine rely upon some 19th century cases, of which it can at least be said that the possibility of a charge over a debt owed by the chargee caused no judicial surprise.

The reason given by the Court of Appeal [1996] Ch 245, 258 was that 'a man cannot have a proprietary interest in a debt or other obligation which he owes another.' In order to test this proposition, I think one needs to identify the normal characteristics of an equitable charge and then ask to what extent they would be inconsistent with a situation in which the property charged consisted of a debt owed by the beneficiary of the charge. There are several well known descriptions of an equitable charge (see, for example, that of Atkin LJ in *National Provincial and Union Bank of England v Charnley* [1924] 1 KB 431, 449–50) but none of them purports to be exhaustive. Nor do I intend to provide one. An equitable charge is a species of charge, which is a proprietary interest granted by way of security. Proprietary interests confer rights in rem which, subject to questions of registration and the equitable doctrine of purchaser for value without notice, will be binding upon third parties and unaffected by the insolvency of the owner of the property charged. A proprietary interest provided by way of security entitles the holder to resort to the property only for the purpose of satisfying some liability due to him (whether from the person providing the security or a third party) and, whatever the form of the transaction, the owner of the property retains an equity of redemption to have the property restored to him when the liability has been discharged. The method by which the holder of the security will resort to the property will ordinarily involve its sale or, more rarely, the extinction of the equity of redemption by foreclosure. A charge is a security interest created without any transfer of title or possession to the beneficiary. An equitable charge can be created by an informal transaction for value (legal charges may require a deed or registration or both) and over any kind of property (equitable as well as legal) but is subject to the doctrine of purchaser for value without notice applicable to all equitable interests.

The depositor's right to claim payment of his deposit is a chose in action which the law has always recognised as property. There is no dispute that a charge over such a chose in action can validly be granted to a third party. In which respects would the fact that the beneficiary of the charge was the debtor himself be inconsistent with the transaction having some or all of the various features which I have enumerated? The method by which the property would be realised would differ slightly: instead of the beneficiary of the charge having to claim payment from the debtor, the realisation would take the form of a book entry. In no other respect, as it seems to me, would the transaction have any consequences different from those which would attach to a charge given to a third party. It would be a proprietary interest in the sense that, subject to questions of registration and purchaser for value without notice, it would be binding upon assignees and a liquidator or trustee in bankruptcy. The depositor would retain an equity of redemption and all the rights which that implies. There would be no merger of interests because the depositor would retain title to the deposit subject only to the bank's charge. The creation of the charge would be consensual and not require any formal assignment or vesting of title in the bank. If all these features can exist despite the fact that the beneficiary of the charge is the debtor, I cannot see why it cannot properly be said that the debtor has a proprietary interest by way of charge over the debt.

The Court of Appeal said that the bank could obtain effective security in other ways. If the deposit was made by the principal debtor, it could rely upon contractual rights of set-off or combining accounts or rules of bankruptcy set-off under provisions such as rule 4.90. If the deposit was made by a third party, it could enter into contractual arrangements such as the limitation on the right to withdraw the deposit in this case, thereby making the deposit a 'flawed asset.' All this is true. It may well be that the security provided in these ways will in most cases be just as good as that provided by a proprietary interest. But that seems to me no reason for preventing banks and their customers from creating charges over deposits if, for reasons of their own, they want to do so. The submissions to the Legal Risk Review Committee made it clear that they do.

If such charges are granted by companies over their 'book debts' they will be registrable under section 395 and 396(1)(e) of the Companies Act 1985 [now replaced by s 859A of the Companies Act 2006 for charges created on or after 6 April 2013]. There is a suggestion in the judgment of the Court of Appeal that the banking community has been insufficiently grateful for being spared the necessity of registering such charges. In my view, this is a matter on which banks are entitled to make up their own minds and take their own advice on whether the deposit charged is a 'book debt' or not. I express no view on the point, but the judgment of my noble and learned friend, Lord Hutton, in *Northern Bank Ltd v Ross* [1990] BCC 883 suggests that, in the case of deposits with banks, an obligation to register is unlikely to arise.

Since the decision in *In re Charge Card Services Ltd* [1987] Ch 150 statutes have been passed in several offshore banking jurisdictions to reverse its effect. A typical example is section 15A of the Hong Kong Law Amendment and Reform (Consolidation) Ordinance (c 23), which I have already mentioned. It reads:

For the avoidance of doubt, it is hereby declared that a person ('the first person') is able to create, and always has been able to create, in favour of another person ('the second person') a legal or equitable charge or mortgage over all or any of the first person's interest in a chose in action enforceable by the first person against the second person, and any charge or mortgage so created shall operate neither to merge the interest thereby created with, nor to extinguish or release, that chose in action.

There is similar legislation in Singapore (section 9A of the Civil Law Act (c 43)); Bermuda (the Charge and Security (Special Provisions) Act 1990 (c 53)) and the Cayman Islands (the Property (Miscellaneous Provisions) Law 1994 (No 7 of 1994)). The striking feature about all these provisions is that none of them amend or repeal any rule of common law which would be inconsistent with the existence of a charge over a debt owed by the chargee. They simply say that such a charge can be granted. If the trick can be done as easily as this, it is hard to see where the conceptual impossibility is to be found.

In a case in which there is no threat to the consistency of the law or objection of public policy, I think that the courts should be very slow to declare a practice of the commercial community to be conceptually impossible. Rules of law must obviously be consistent and not self-contradictory; thus in *Rye v Rye* [1962] AC 496, 505, Viscount Simonds demonstrated that the notion of a person granting a lease to himself was inconsistent with every feature of a lease, both as a contract and as an estate in land. But the law is fashioned to suit the practicalities of life and legal concepts like 'proprietary interest' and 'charge' are no more than labels given to clusters of related and self-consistent rules of law. Such concepts do not have a life of their own from which the rules are inexorably derived. It follows that in my view the letter was effective to do what it purported to do, namely to create a charge over the deposit in favour of BCCI. This means that the foundation for Mr McDonnell's argument for implying a personal obligation disappears.

[**Lords Goff**, **Nicholls**, **Hope**, and **Hutton** concurred.]

NOTE

It is not surprising that Lord Hoffmann's (highly persuasive) *obiter dictum* upholding charges-back was welcomed by bankers and their advisers (see, eg, R Calnan (1998) 114 LQR 174). However, academic commentators have pointed to various weaknesses in Lord Hoffmann's reasoning, and concluded that 'the decision would appear to be based more on practical and commercial considerations than on strongly held views about legal theory' (J Lipton (1998) 9 JBFLP 101 at 109; see also G McCormack [1998] CfiLR 111; S McCracken, *The Banker's Remedy of Set-Off* (2nd edn, 1998), pp 205–206; Turner (2004) 15 JBFLP 148 and 235). Professor Goode has maintained his opposition to charges-back, criticising Lord Hoffmann for undermining so fundamental a concept as the distinction between property and obligation for no good reason—he points to the fact that there are other ways for a bank to take security over its customer's deposits, for example through a flawed asset or contractual set-off (see R Goode (1998) 114 LQR 178). Unfortunately, the distinction between property and obligation was not addressed by Lord Hoffmann. Nevertheless, even Professor Goode was forced to accept that the tide has turned in favour of charges-back and that conceptual and policy problems 'must yield to business practice and legislative developments designed to accommodate it' (RM Goode, *Legal Problems of Credit and Security* (3rd edn, 2003), para 3–12, citing, inter alia, art 4 of the EC Directive on financial collateral arrangements (Directive 2002/47/EC dated 5 June 2002) which requires Member States to ensure that on the occurrence of an enforcement event cash collateral may be realised by setting off the amount against or applying it in discharge of the relevant financial obligations); and now L Gullifer, *Goode on Legal Problems of Credit and Security* (5th edn, 2013), para 3–12.

(f) Registration

Insolvency Act 1986, s 344

(1) The following applies where a person engaged in any business makes a general assignment to another person of his existing or future book debts, or any class of them, and is subsequently *adjudged* [made][1] bankrupt.

(2) The assignment is void against the trustee of the bankrupt's estate as regards book debts which were not paid before the [making of the bankruptcy application or (as the case may be) the] presentation of the bankruptcy petition, unless the assignment has been registered under the Bills of Sale Act 1878.

(3) For the purposes of subsections (1) and (2)—

(a) 'assignment' includes an assignment by way of security or charge on book debts, and

(b) 'general assignment' does not include—

(i) an assignment of book debts due at the date of the assignment from specified debtors or of debts becoming due under specified contracts or

(ii) an assignment of book debts included either in a transfer of a business made in good faith and for value or in an assignment of assets for the benefit of creditors generally.

(4) For the purposes of registration under the Act of 1878 an assignment of book debts is to be treated as if it were a bill of sale given otherwise than by way of security for the payment of a sum of money; and the provisions of that Act with respect to the registration of bills of sale apply accordingly with such necessary modifications as may be made by rules under that Act.

FOOTNOTE:

1. In this extract the word 'adjudged' is to be repealed, and the words in square brackets in sub-ss (1)–(2) are to be inserted and to enter force, as from a date yet to be appointed under the Enterprise and Regulatory Reform Act 2013, s 71(3), Sch 19, paras 1, 37.

NOTES

1.   What are 'book debts'? See below, p 980.

2.   Section 344 only applies to a general assignment of book debts by a natural person who is subsequently adjudged bankrupt. It does not apply, therefore, to any such assignment made by a company: although a company can become insolvent and be liquidated, a company cannot be adjudged bankrupt.

3.   Registration does not constitute notice to the debtor and does not guarantee the priority of the assignment over subsequent interests (L Gullifer, *Goode on Legal Problems of Credit and Security* (5th edn, 2013), paras 3–23 to 3–38).

3 FINANCING BY SECURED TRANSACTIONS

(a) Generally

A factor may secure the financing transaction in a number of ways. For example, negotiable paper may be pledged with the factor. Title may be retained by the factor in a sale and resale agreement. The factor may even claim a right to trace the proceeds of authorised sub-sales (see above, p 497), and the client's debtor may even attorn to the factor (see above, p 890). However, the most common forms of security taken by the factor are mortgages and equitable charges (see below, p 1059).

Problems related to taking a mortgage of, or equitable charge over, a debt will be considered further in this section. In particular, when do registration requirements apply? The answers to that question require consideration of such matters as the nature of 'book debts' and the interesting if notorious differences between 'fixed charges' and 'floating charges' of a company's property.

(b) Registration of 'charges' on a company's property

The regime for registration of charges created by a company over its property is set out in Part 25 of the Companies Act 2006. As a result of amendments to Part 25 made by the Companies Act 2006 (Amendment of Part 25) Regulations 2013 (SI 2013/600), the registration requirements of charges differ according to their date of creation. Those created before 6 April 2013 are subject ss 860, 861, and 874, as set out below. Those created on or after 6 April 2013 are subject to simpler provisions discussed below. These will be referred to as the 'old regime' and the 'new regime' for convenience.

(i) Old regime

Under the old—but continuing—regime, not every category of charge is affected. However, a charge over book debts (s 860(7)(f)) and all floating charges on the company's property (s 860(7)(g)) are caught by the legislation. The main consequence of non-registration is that the charge-holder will lose his priority in an insolvency (s 874(1)).

Companies Act 2006, ss 860, 861, and 874

> **860 Charges created by a company**
> (1) A company that creates a charge to which this section applies must deliver the prescribed particulars of the charge, together with the instrument (if any) by which the charge is created or evidenced, to the registrar for registration before the end of the period allowed for registration.
> (2) Registration of a charge to which this section applies may instead be effected on the application of a person interested in it.
> (3) Where registration is effected on the application of some person other than the company, that person is entitled to recover from the company the amount of any fees properly paid by him to the registrar on registration.
> (4) If a company fails to comply with subsection (1), an offence is committed by—
>   (a) the company, and
>   (b) every officer of it who is in default.

(5) A person guilty of an offence under this section is liable—

    (a) on conviction on indictment, to a fine;

    (b) on summary conviction, to a fine not exceeding the statutory maximum.

(6) Subsection (4) does not apply if registration of the charge has been effected on the application of some other person.

(7) This section applies to the following charges—

    (a) a charge on land or any interest in land, other than a charge for any rent or other periodical sum issuing out of land,

    (b) a charge created or evidenced by an instrument which, if executed by an individual, would require registration as a bill of sale,

    (c) a charge for the purposes of securing any issue of debentures,

    (d) a charge on uncalled share capital of the company,

    (e) a charge on calls made but not paid,

    (f) a charge on book debts of the company,

    (g) a floating charge on the company's property or undertaking,

    (h) a charge on a ship or aircraft, or any share in a ship,

    (i) a charge on goodwill or on any intellectual property.

861 Charges which have to be registered: supplementary

(1) The holding of debentures entitling the holder to a charge on land is not, for the purposes of section 860(7)(a), an interest in the land.

(2) It is immaterial for the purposes of this Chapter where land subject to a charge is situated.

(3) The deposit by way of security of a negotiable instrument given to secure the payment of book debts is not, for the purposes of section 860(7)(f), a charge on those book debts.

(4) For the purposes of section 860(7)(i), 'intellectual property' means—

    (a) any patent, trade mark, registered design, copyright or design right;

    (b) any licence under or in respect of any such right.

(5) In this Chapter—

  'charge' includes mortgage, and

  'company' means a company registered in England and Wales or in Northern Ireland.

874 Consequence of failure to register charges created by a company

(1) If a company creates a charge to which section 860 applies, the charge is void (so far as any security on the company's property or undertaking is conferred by it) against—

    (a) a liquidator of the company,

    (b) an administrator of the company, and

    (c) a creditor of the company,

  unless that section is complied with.

(2) Subsection (1) is subject to the provisions of this Chapter.

(3) Subsection (1) is without prejudice to any contract or obligation for repayment of the money secured by the charge; and when a charge becomes void under this section, the money secured by it immediately becomes payable.

NOTE

There is no need to register a charge over financial collateral where reg 4(4) of the Financial Collateral Arrangements (No 2) Regulations 2003 (SI 2003/3226) applies. That provides that the registration requirement contained in s 860 of the Companies Act 2006 does not apply (if it would otherwise do so) to a security financial collateral arrangement ('a security FCA'), or any charge created or otherwise arising under a security FCA. Financial collateral includes 'cash' that is held in a bank or other account or 'a similar claim for the repayment of money' (reg 3). To qualify as a security FCA, the financial collateral must be 'in the possession or under the control of the collateral-taker' (reg 3). In the case of a charge-back, when the bank is the chargee of an account held with itself, the need for 'control' means that the account must be kept 'blocked', ie the chargor is prevented from drawing on the account (see H Beale, M Bridge, L Gullifer, and E Lomnicka, *The Law of Personal Property Security* (2007), para 10.46). In the past, where a bank took a charge-back over its customer's account balance as part of a 'triple cocktail' (a charge-back, a flawed asset arrangement, and a contractual right of set-off), the normal practice would have been to register. It now appears that, where cash is charged as part of a security FCA, registration is unnecessary where the chargor and the chargee are not natural persons.

(ii) New regime

The new charge registration regime is simpler by comparison. All charges created by a company are registrable, save those listed in s 859A(6). The regime applies to charges created on or after 6 April 2013.

Companies Act 2006, ss 859A and 859H

859A Charges created by a company

(1) Subject to subsection (6), this section applies where a company creates a charge.

(2) The registrar must register the charge if, before the end of the period allowed for delivery, the company or any person interested in the charge delivers to the registrar for registration a section 859D statement of particulars.

(3) Where the charge is created or evidenced by an instrument, the registrar is required to register it only if a certified copy of the instrument is delivered to the registrar with the statement of particulars.

(4) 'The period allowed for delivery' is 21 days beginning with the day after the date of creation of the charge (see section 859E), unless an order allowing an extended period is made under section 859F(3).

(5) Where an order is made under section 859F(3) a copy of the order must be delivered to the registrar with the statement of particulars.

(6) This section does not apply to—

(a) a charge in favour of a landlord on a cash deposit given as a security in connection with the lease of land;

(b) a charge created by a member of Lloyd's (within the meaning of the Lloyd's Act 1982) to secure its obligations in connection with its underwriting business at Lloyd's;

(c) a charge excluded from the application of this section by or under any other Act.

(7) In this Part—

'cash' includes foreign currency,

'charge' includes—

(a) a mortgage;

(b) a standard security, assignation in security, and any other right in security constituted under the law of Scotland, including any heritable security, but not including a pledge, and

'company' means a UK-registered company.

> **859H Consequence of failure to deliver charges**
>
> (1) This section applies if—
>   (a) a company creates a charge to which section 859A or 859B applies, and
>   (b) the documents required by section 859A or (as the case may be) 859B are not delivered to the registrar by the company or another person interested in the charge before the end of the relevant period allowed for delivery.
> (2) 'The relevant period allowed for delivery' is—
>   (a) the period allowed for delivery under the section in question, or
>   (b) if an order under section 859F(3) has been made, the period allowed by the order.
> (3) Where this section applies, the charge is void (so far as any security on the company's property or undertaking is conferred by it) against—
>   (a) a liquidator of the company,
>   (b) an administrator of the company, and
>   (c) a creditor of the company.
> (4) Subsection (3) is without prejudice to any contract or obligation for repayment of the money secured by the charge; and when a charge becomes void under this section, the money secured by it immediately becomes payable.

NOTES

1. Whereas the old regime under Part 25 of the Companies Act 2006 was virtually identical to provisions under the Companies Act 1985, and retained the imperfections of the old, the new regime under the 2006 Act breaks with the former provisions. Failure to register a charge is no longer an offence. Whereas the only registrable charges under the old regime were those enumerated in the Act, all charges under the new regime are registrable with few exceptions. On the other hand, the new regime continues to turn on the creation of a 'charge'. One commentator has said that this 'represents a victory of form over substance and leaves the United Kingdom's registration system out of line with that of most other major Anglo-Saxon jurisdictions': Graham [2014] JBL 175 at 192. The consequences of non-registration on the enforceability of a charge remain the same as under the old regime.

2. The term 'charge' is used in different sense under s 136 of the Law of Property Act 1925 and under both the old and new regimes of Part 25 of the Companies Act 2006. This may be seen from consideration of a mortgage of a chose in action. Such an assignment may be treated as 'absolute' under s 136; it can fall outside the exclusion of assignments 'purporting to be by way of charge only'. By contrast, 'charge' for the purposes of Part 25 of the Companies Act 2006 includes not only charges in the s 136 sense, but also mortgages: an assignor will have granted a charge over a debt if the assignor retains any interest in the nature of an equity of redemption as against the assignee: see s 859A(7)(a).

(c) What is a 'book debt'?

Although the new charge registration regime does not refer to book debts, the old regime does so. The definition of 'book debt' therefore remains of importance for charges created before 6 April 2013.

Independent Automatic Sales Ltd v Knowles & Foster

[1962] 1 WLR 974, Chancery Division

The plaintiff company carried on a business of manufacturing and dealing in automatic machines. For that purpose it obtained finance from the defendant merchant banking firm whereby it was agreed that bills of exchange and other documents belonging to the plaintiff and deposited with the defendant should be pledged to the defendant as continuing security for the payment of all liabilities of the plaintiff to the defendant. The plaintiff then deposited 53 hire-purchase agreements with the defendant as security for a loan. Each agreement included a provision whereby the hirer, on exercising his option to terminate or return the machine, was liable for not less than one half of the purchase price. On the plaintiff's liquidation, the liquidator claimed delivery of the hire-purchase agreements and an account of all money received under them on the ground that the charge created by the deposit of the agreements was void against him for non-registration under s 95 of the Companies Act 1948 (an earlier version of ss 860, 861, and 874 of the Companies Act 2006 (old regime)), since the debts arising under the agreements were 'book debts' within s 95(2)(e) of the 1948 Act.

> **Buckley J:** In my judgment, the charge constituted by the deposit of one of these agreements was a charge upon each and all of the benefits of the company under that agreement. If those benefits included any rights which can properly be described as 'book-debts' the charge was, in part at least, a charge on book-debts and therefore registrable under the section.
>
> Nearly 100 years ago in *Shipley v Marshall* ((1863) 14 CBNS 566) the Court of Common Pleas considered the meaning of the term 'book-debts' as used in s 137 of the Bankruptcy Act 1861. Erle CJ said (at 570): 'By "book-debts," the legislature doubtless intended to describe debts in some way connected with the trade of the bankrupt: and I am inclined to give the term a wider range. But it is enough to say that this was a debt connected with and growing out of the plaintiff's trade.' Williams J said (at 571): 'The words of s 137 are no doubt as Mr Griffits has pointed out, authorising the assignees to sell the "book-debts due or growing due to the bankrupt, and the books relating thereto." This, it is said, can only mean debts which are actually entered in some book kept by the bankrupt in the course of his trade. I cannot, however, accede to that construction. I think the meaning of the statute is, that the assignees shall dispose of all debts due to the bankrupt in respect of which entries could be made in the ordinary course of his business: otherwise, a debt by accident omitted to be entered would not pass by the assignment.' Byles J said (at 573): 'It is said that "book-debts" must mean debts which are entered in the trade-books of the bankrupt. I agree with my Brother Williams that they must be such debts as are commonly entered in books.' And a little later he said: 'Suppose the trader kept no books, or was blind and could not write, and did not choose to incur the expense of keeping a clerk or book-keeper,—upon the construction contended for by the defendant, there could be no book-debts which could be made the subject of sale and assignment under s 137 of the Bankruptcy Act 1861. That surely would not be a very sensible construction to put upon the statute.'
>
> So far as I am aware, no more precise definition of the meaning of the term 'book-debts' has ever been attempted judicially and I shall not attempt one. *Shipley v Marshall*, I think, establishes that, if it can be said of a debt arising in the course of a business and due or growing due to the proprietor of that business that such a debt would or could in the ordinary course of such a business be entered in well-kept books relating to that business, that debt can properly be called a book-debt whether it is in fact entered in the books of the business or not . . .
>
> Mr Bagnall [counsel for the defendants] has further argued that any debts which could arise under the agreements could only have come into existence after the date of the deposit. I will

assume, as seems probable, that at that date all the amounts payable on the signing of the agreements had been paid and that no instalments of hire rent were in arrear. Mr Bagnall's submission was that in these circumstances there would at the date of the deposit have been no book-debts in existence and that, since he says one cannot charge what does not exist, the deposits did not per se constitute any charge on book-debts, although he conceded that if and when a book-debt came into existence under any of the agreements that book-debt would immediately become charged by reason of the deposit. He contends that s 95 does not on its true construction require a charge on future book-debts to be registered and that 'book-debts' in sub-s (2)(e) means only existing book-debts . . .

I think that there are two answers to this argument. First, for the reason I have already given, I am of opinion that upon the true interpretation of the form of agreement used in this case the hirer became liable immediately upon the agreement coming into operation to the extent of his minimum liability under it notwithstanding that some part of that liability was to be discharged by future payments and that the debts so constituted were existing book-debts at the date of the deposit. The proposition that when the agreements were deposited there were no book-debts in existence which could be charged is, in my judgment, untenable.

Secondly, in my judgment, a charge on future book-debts of a company is registrable under s 95. That it is competent for anyone to whom book-debts may accrue in the future to create an equitable charge upon those book-debts which will attach to them as soon as they come into existence is not disputed. (See *Tailby v Official Receiver* ((1888) 13 App Cas 523.) That such a charge can accurately be described as a charge on book-debts does not appear to me to be open to question. Such a charge would not, of course, be effective until a book-debt came into existence upon which it could operate. Nevertheless, I think it would be accurate to speak of the charge being created at the date of the instrument, deposit or other act giving rise to it, for no further action on the part of the grantor would be required to bring the charge to life. A charge on book-debts, present and future, is not an unusual form of security in the commercial world, and it would seem to me strange if such a charge were registrable (as it undoubtedly is) and a charge confined to future book-debts were not. I find nothing in the language of s 95 requiring me to read sub-s (2)(e) in so restricted a way as to confine it to a charge on existing book-debts . . .

Accordingly, in my judgment, the charges created by the deposit of 53 agreements were registrable under s 95, and, not having been registered, they are void as against the plaintiff liquidator. There will be a declaration that the charges are void as against the plaintiff liquidator, and an order for the delivery up of the agreements.

Paul and Frank Ltd v Discount Bank (Overseas) Ltd
[1967] Ch 348, Chancery Division

The plaintiff company had completed a letter of authority to an export credit guarantee organisation (ECG) authorising it to pay the defendant discount bank any monies which might become payable under an exchange insurance policy. On the plaintiff's liquidation, the liquidator claimed that the letter of authority was void under s 95 of the Companies Act 1948 (an earlier version of ss 860, 861, and 874 of the Companies Act 2006), as an unregistered charge on a book debt of the company.

After hearing the accountancy evidence, Pennycuick J held that even after ECG had accepted liability for a claim and the amount of the claim had been ascertained, the right to payment under the ECG policy would not in practice have been entered in the books of the plaintiff company.

Pennycuick J continued: I turn now to s 95 of the Companies Act 1948 . . . Looking at the matter for a moment apart from authority, I do not think that in ordinary speech one would describe as a 'book-debt' the right under a contingency contract before the contingency happens. By 'contingency contract' in this connection I mean contracts of insurance, guarantee, indemnity and the like. However, this point is not free from authority, and I have been referred to two cases as to what is meant by a 'book-debt.' . . .

Counsel on both sides have addressed their arguments in great part to the nature of the company's right at the date when the contingency under the policy occurred, or alternatively the date when the liability of ECG was accepted and the amount ascertained. Even if this is the true test, the findings on accountancy practice which I have made would conclude the case in favour of the defendants. But I do not think that this is the true test. Section 95 requires registration of a charge on book-debts within 21 days of creation. It seems to me that, in order to ascertain whether any particular charge is a charge on book-debts within the meaning of the section, one must look at the items of property which form the subject matter of the charge at the date of its creation and consider whether any of those items is a book-debt. In the case of an existing item of property, this question can only be answered by reference to its character at the date of creation. Where the item of property is the benefit of a contract and at the date of the charge the benefit of the contract does not comprehend any book-debt, I do not see how that contract can be brought within the section as being a book-debt merely by reason that the contract may ultimately result in a book-debt. Here the ECG policy admittedly did not comprehend any book-debt at the date of the letter of authority, and that seems to me to be an end of the matter.

Mr Sutcliffe, for the plaintiffs, contended that a contract requires registration under paragraph (e) if at any time it may result in a book-debt. If this were right, the section would be of wide scope and would cover a charge on any possible contract which might produce a money obligation unless it could be shown that the obligation, even when admitted and quantified, was such as would not commonly be entered in the books of a company.

Mr Sutcliffe relied on another principle laid down by Buckley J in *Independent Automatic Sales Ltd v Knowles & Foster* ([1962] 1 WLR 974). After holding that upon the true interpretation of the hire-purchase agreement 'the hirer became immediately liable to the extent of his minimum liability under it notwithstanding that some part of that liability is to be discharged by future payments,' Buckley J went on as follows . . .

[His Lordship quoted the passage cited above, p 981, and continued:]

Mr Wheeler, for the first defendant, and Mr Bateson, for the second defendant, unless I misunderstood them, found it difficult to resist Mr Sutcliffe's contention on this point, except by saying that the second proposition of Buckley J is wrong. I confess that I do not share that difficulty. If a charge upon its proper construction covers future debts, in the sense of debts under a future contract which, when that contract comes to be made, will constitute book-debts, eg an ordinary contract for the sale of goods on credit, I see no reason why paragraph (e) should not be fairly applicable to the charge; and that, I think, is all that Buckley J says. It by no means follows, it seems to me, that paragraph (e) applies to an existing contract which does not comprehend a book-debt merely by reason that that contract may result in a book-debt in the future. Nor did Buckley J say so.

I prefer to rest my decision on the ground which I have indicated. But, as I have said, if indeed the test were the character of ECG's obligation when liability is admitted and the amount ascertained, then the plaintiffs' claim would fail on the facts, namely, the evidence of accountancy practice.

NOTES

1. Does a charge created by a company over its bank account before 6 April 2013 require to be registered under s 860 of the Companies Act 2006 as a charge over a 'book debt'? Probably not, as the debt owed by the bank to the company, its customer, will not have arisen in the company's ordinary course of business, unless the company ran an investment business and the deposit was made by way of investment. However, the cases do not provide any clear guidance on this issue—see *Re Brightlife Ltd* [1987] Ch 200; *Re Permanent Houses (Holdings) Ltd* (1988) 5 BCC 151 at 154; and *Northern Bank Ltd v Ross* [1990] BCC 883, NICA—although in *Re Bank of Credit and Commerce International SA (No 8)* [1998] AC 214 at 227, Lord Hoffmann hinted, without deciding the issue, that a charge over a company's deposits with its bank need not be registered. His reasoning has been strongly criticised by J Upton (1998) 9 JBFLP 101 at 112–114, and also by G McCormack [1998] CfiLR 111.

2. Fixed charges over future book debts are registrable (*Independent Automatic Sales*), whereas fixed charges over contingent debts are not (*Paul and Frank*). This means that a book debt which arises from an existing contract will be non-registrable if the debt is contingent, whereas a book debt arising from a non-existent contract will be registrable if the debt is not contingent. However, this distinction, as drawn by Pennycuick J in *Paul and Frank*, has been the subject of considerable criticism, see F Oditah, *Legal Aspects of Receivables Financing* (1991), pp 30–32; E Ferran, *Mortgage Securitisation—Legal Aspects* (1992), pp 77–80. Furthermore, in *Contemporary Cottages (NZ) Ltd v Margin Traders Ltd* [1981] 2 NZLR 114, High Court of New Zealand, Thorp J has held (at 126) that:

> There seems to me to be a basic conflict between the proposition that registration may be required in respect of a debt not existing at the time of the charge, and the concept that the test is to be the character of the property assigned and charged at the date of the creation of the charge. I prefer the proposition which lies behind the judgment of Buckley J, ie, that the charge over future book debts is created at the time of the execution of an appropriate assignment pursuant to *Tailby's* case, to distinguishing between book debts which arise from existing contracts and book debts which arise from non-existent contracts on any basis which makes charges over the latter registrable but charges over the former not registrable. That consequence, which is necessarily involved in the proposal by Pennycuick J, is one which seems to me, with respect, to indicate the illogicality of the distinction.

3. In *Re Brush Aggregates Ltd* [1983] BCLC 320, RAK Wright QC, sitting as a deputy judge, held that a charge on future debts which might arise under a contract already in existence at the date of the charge would be registrable as a fixed charge on book debts. As a matter of construction of the terms of the assignment, the deputy judge distinguished *Paul and Frank* as a case involving the assignment by way of security of a contingent contractual right (non-registrable), as opposed to an assignment by way of security of any money which might become due under that contract (registrable). However, considerable doubt has been expressed as to whether the distinction drawn by the deputy judge has any substance to it (see E Ferran, p 79).

(d) Distinguishing fixed from floating charges over book debts

The leading authorities on the distinction—or, better, the distinctions—between fixed and floating charges are decisions in the effect of dealings with book debts. The two main authorities are decisions on a form of security construed and characterised by the Court of Appeal in *Re New Bullas Trading Ltd* [1994] 1 BCLC 485. The character of this security, and thus the distinctions between fixed and floating charges of book debts, remained controversial until the Privy Council's consideration of the matter in *Agnew v Commissioner of Inland Revenue (Re Brumark Investments Ltd)* [2001] UKPC 28, [2001] 2 AC 710 was in turn considered by the House of Lords in *National Westminster Bank plc v Spectrum Plus Ltd (Re Spectrum Plus Ltd)* [2005] UKHL 41, [2005] 2 AC 680. The Privy Council could not overrule *New Bullas*, but considered the case to be wrongly decided. The House of Lords could, of course, overrule it and did so in *Spectrum Plus*.

In *New Bullas*, a company had granted a charge over book debts which was expressed to be a fixed charge over the uncollected book debts and a floating charge over their proceeds. The Court of Appeal, overruling Knox J, held that there were commercial advantages for both parties to these arrangements and that the parties were free to agree to such terms. Accordingly, it upheld the wording of the charge instrument as having the effect of making the charge over the uncollected debts a fixed charge. The case was the subject of sustained criticism. Professor Goode, (1994) 110 LQR 592, maintained that it is not possible to create separate security interests over a debt and its proceeds: all that is possible is to have a single, continuous security interest which moves from debt to proceeds. Professor Worthington, (1997) 113 LQR 563, while not supporting the view that a book debt and its proceeds constitute an indivisible asset, considered that the wrong conclusion had been reached in *New Bullas* because the security arrangement had left the chargor free to remove the charged assets from the ambit of the security without recourse to the chargee.

In the event, Professor Worthington's view was upheld. In order for a charge over book debts to be characterised as fixed, *both* the uncollected book debts *and* their proceeds after collection must be under the control of the charge-holder.

Agnew v Commissioner of Inland Revenue (Re Brumark Investments Ltd)
[2001] 2 AC 710, [2001] UKPC 28, Privy Council

Brumark had given security over its book debts to its bank, Westpac, in terms which purported to make the debts subject to a fixed charge so long as they were uncollected but a floating charge over the proceeds once they had been collected and received by the company. (These terms were virtually identical to those in *New Bullas*.) The company was free to collect the debts for its own account and to use the proceeds in its business. It went into receivership and the receivers collected the outstanding debts. Fisher J at first instance held that, as uncollected debts, they were subject to a fixed charge (as the parties had agreed) and, as such, not subject to the claims of the company's preferential creditors. The New Zealand Court of Appeal, declining to follow *New Bullas*, held that the fact that the company was free to collect the debts for its own account (and so remove them from the bank's security) was inconsistent with the charge being a fixed charge. It was accordingly a floating charge and the preferential creditors had a prior claim to the proceeds. This ruling was affirmed by the Privy Council.

> **Lord Millett** (delivering the opinion of the Judicial Committee): The question in this appeal is whether a charge over the uncollected book debts of a company which leaves the company free to collect them and use the proceeds in the ordinary course of its business is a fixed charge or a floating charge.
>
> [His Lordship set out the facts and the terms of the debenture and continued:]

The question is whether the company's right to collect the debts and deal with their proceeds free from the security means that the charge on the uncollected debts, though described in the debenture as fixed, was nevertheless a floating charge until it crystallised by the appointment of the receivers. This is a question of characterisation. To answer it their Lordships must examine the nature of a floating charge and ascertain the features which distinguish it from a fixed charge . . .

[His Lordship traced the history of the floating charge, referring to cases from *Re Panama, New Zealand and Australian Royal Mail Co* (1870) 5 Ch App 318, CA, to *Re Cosslett (Contractors) Ltd* [1998] Ch 495, CA, emphasising in particular the following passage from the judgment of Vaughan Williams LJ in *Re Yorkshire Woolcombers Association Ltd* [1903] 2 Ch 284 at 295:

> but what you do require to make a specific security is that the security whenever it has once come into existence, and been identified or appropriated as a security, *shall never thereafter at the will of the mortgagor cease to be a security. If at the will of the mortgagor he can dispose of it and prevent its being any longer a security, although something else may be substituted more or less for it, that is not a 'specific security'* (Emphasis added.)]

[His Lordship referred to the wording of the debentures in this case and in *New Bullas* and continued:]

The intended effect of the debenture was the same in each case. Until the charge holder intervened the company could continue to collect the debts, though not to assign or factor them, and the debts once collected would cease to exist. The proceeds which took their place would be a different asset which had never been subject to the fixed charge and would from the outset be subject to the floating charge.

The question in *New Bullas*, as in the present case, was whether the book debts which were uncollected when the receivers were appointed were subject to a fixed charge or a floating charge. . . .

The principal theme of the judgment, however, was that the parties were free to make whatever agreement they liked. The question was therefore simply one of construction; unless unlawful the intention of the parties, to be gathered from the terms of the debenture, must prevail. It was clear from the descriptions which the parties attached to the charges that they had intended to create a fixed charge over the book debts while they were uncollected and a floating charge over the proceeds. It was open to the parties to do so, and freedom of contract prevailed.

Their Lordships consider this approach to be fundamentally mistaken. The question is not merely one of construction. In deciding whether a charge is a fixed charge or a floating charge, the court is engaged in a two-stage process. At the first stage it must construe the instrument of charge and seek to gather the intentions of the parties from the language they have used. But the object at this stage of the process is not to discover whether the parties intended to create a fixed or a floating charge. It is to ascertain the nature of the rights and obligations which the parties intended to grant each other in respect of the charged assets. Once these have been ascertained, the court can then embark on the second stage of the process, which is one of categorisation. This is a matter of law. It does not depend on the intention of the parties. If their intention, properly gathered from the language of the instrument, is to grant the company rights in respect of the charged assets which are inconsistent with the nature of a fixed charge, then the charge cannot be a fixed charge however they may have chosen to describe it. . . . In construing a debenture to see whether it creates a fixed or a floating charge, the only intention which is relevant is the intention that the company should be free to deal with the charged assets and withdraw them from the security without the consent of the holder of the charge; or, to put the question another way, whether the charged assets were intended to be under the control of the company or of the charge holder.

[His Lordship considered and rejected an argument which had been upheld by the Court of Appeal in *New Bullas*: that the book debts did not cease to be subject to the charge at the will of the company but that they ceased to be subject to the charge because that was what the parties had agreed in advance when they entered into the debenture. He also rejected as irrelevant a distinction which Fisher J had drawn between a power on the part of the company to *dispose* of the debts (eg by factoring them) and a power to *consume* them (by realising them). He continued:]

Their Lordships turn finally to the questions which have exercised academic commentators: whether a debt or other receivable can be separated from its proceeds; whether they represent a single security interest or two; and whether a charge on book debts necessarily takes effect as a single indivisible charge on the debts and their proceeds irrespective of the way in which it may be drafted.

Property and its proceeds are clearly different assets. On a sale of goods the seller exchanges one asset for another. Both assets continue to exist, the goods in the hands of the buyer and proceeds of sale in the hands of the seller. If a book debt is assigned, the debt is transferred to the assignee in exchange for money paid to the assignor. The seller's former property right in the subject matter of the sale gives him an equivalent property right in its exchange product. The only difference between realising a debt by assignment and collection is that, on collection, the debt is wholly extinguished. As in the case of alienation, it is replaced in the hands of the creditor by a different asset, viz its proceeds.

The Court of Appeal saw no reason to examine the conceptual problems further. They held that, even if a debt and its proceeds are two different assets, the company was free to realise the uncollected debts, and accordingly the charge on those assets (being the assets whose destination was in dispute) could not be a fixed charge. There was simply no need to look at the proceeds at all . . .

If the company is free to collect the debts, the nature of the charge on the uncollected debts cannot differ according to whether the proceeds are subject to a floating charge or are not subject to any charge. In each case the commercial effect is the same: the charge holder cannot prevent the company from collecting the debts and having the free use of the proceeds. But is does not follow that the nature of the charge on the uncollected book debts may not differ according to whether the proceeds are subject to a fixed charge or a floating charge; for in the one case the charge holder can prevent the company from having the use of the proceeds and in the other it cannot. The question is not whether the company is free to collect the uncollected debts, but whether it is free to do so for its own benefit . . .

To constitute a charge on book debts a fixed charge, it is sufficient to prohibit the company from realising the debts itself, whether by assignment or collection. If the company seeks permission to do so in respect of a particular debt, the charge holder can refuse permission or grant permission on terms, and can thus direct the application of the proceeds. But it is not necessary to go this far. As their Lordships have already noted, it is not inconsistent with the fixed nature of a charge on book debts for the holder of the charge to appoint the company its agent to collect the debts for its account and on its behalf. The *Siebe Gorman* case [below, p 991] merely introduced an alternative mechanism for appropriating the proceeds to the security. The proceeds of the debts collected by the company were no longer to be trust moneys but they were required to be paid into a blocked account with the charge holder. The commercial effect was the same: the proceeds were not at the company's disposal. Such an arrangement is inconsistent with the charge being a floating charge, since the debts are not available to the company as a source of its cash flow. But their Lordships would wish to make it clear that it is not enough to provide in the debenture that the account is a blocked account if it is not operated as one in fact . . .

Their Lordships consider that the *New Bullas* case was wrongly decided.

National Westminster Bank plc v Spectrum Plus Ltd (Re Spectrum Plus Ltd)
[2005] UKHL 41, [2005] 2 AC 680, House of Lords

Spectrum Plus Ltd ('Spectrum') opened a current account at National Westminster Bank plc ('the bank'), obtained an overdraft facility of £250,000 and, on 30 September 1997, executed a debenture to secure its indebtedness to the bank. The security created by the debenture was expressed to include:

> A specific charge [of] all book debts and other debts . . . now and from time to time due or owing to [Spectrum]' (para 2(v)) and 'A floating security [of] its undertaking and all its property assets and rights whatsoever and wheresoever present and/or future including those from the time being charged by way of specific charge pursuant to the foregoing paragraphs if and to the extent that such charges as aforesaid shall fail as specific charges but without prejudice to any such specific charges as shall continue to be effective (para 2 (vii)).

Paragraph 5 of the debenture supported the grant of the charge over book debts:

> With reference to the book debts and other debts hereby specifically charged [Spectrum] shall pay into [Spectrum's] account with the bank all moneys which it may receive in respect of such debts and shall not without the prior consent in writing of the bank sell factor discount or otherwise charge or assign the same in favour of any other person or purport to do so and [Spectrum] shall if called upon to do so by the bank from time to time execute legal assignments of such book debts and other debts to the bank.

After the opening of the current account in September 1997, Spectrum collected book debts, paid them into its current account, and drew on the account as it wished for its business purposes. The overdraft limit was never exceeded but the account was never in credit.

Spectrum's business fortunes did not prosper and on 15 October 2001 it went into voluntary liquidation. The issue that came before the courts was whether the charge over book debts was a fixed charge, which it was expressed to be, or merely a floating charge. If it was a floating charge Spectrum's preferential creditors were entitled to have their debts paid out of the proceeds of the book debts in priority to the bank (Insolvency Act 1986, s 175). If it was not a floating charge the preferential creditors had no such priority and the bank would be entitled to the whole of the proceeds.

In *Siebe Gorman & Co Ltd v Barclays Bank* [1979] 2 Lloyd's Rep 142, Slade J had held that a similarly worded debenture created a fixed charge over book debts. Reversing Sir Andrew Morritt V-C at first instance [2004] Ch 337, the Court of Appeal [2004] Ch 337, held that the restrictions imposed by the debenture (and the restrictions imposed by the Siebe Gorman debenture) had been sufficient to justify the categorisation of the charge as a fixed charge. The Revenue and Customs Commissioners and the Secretary of State for Trade and Industry, as parties subrogated to the preferential creditors, appealed to the House of Lords.

> **Lord Scott**: . . .
>
> #### WHAT IS A FLOATING CHARGE?
>
> It is helpful in answering this question to bear in mind the juridical history of floating charges and the reasons why a degree of statutory intervention became necessary. By the middle of the 19th century industrial and commercial expansion in this country had led to an increasing need by

companies for more capital. Subscription for share capital could not meet this need and loan capital had to be raised. But the lenders required security for their loans. Traditional security, in the form of legal or equitable charges on the borrowers' fixed assets, whether land or goods, could not meet the need. The greater part of most entrepreneurial companies' assets would consist of raw materials, work in progress, stock-in-trade and trade debts. These were circulating assets, replaced in the normal course of business and constantly changing. Assets of this character were not amenable to being the subject of traditional forms of security. Equity, however, intervened. *Holroyd v Marshall* (1862) 10 HLC 191 was a case in which a debtor had purported to grant a mortgage not only over his existing machinery but also over all the machinery which, during the continuance of the security, should be placed in his mill. The question arose whether the equitable title of the chargee in respect of new machinery that had been placed in the mill prevailed over the rights of a judgment creditor of the chargor/debtor. Could the chargee assert an equitable interest in the new machinery? Lord Campbell LC held that he could not. But the House of Lords reversed the decision, holding that

> . . . immediately on the new machinery and effects being fixed or placed in the mill, they became subject to the operation of the contract, and passed in equity to the mortgagees (per Lord Westbury at p 211)

and that

> . . . in equity it is not disputed that the moment the property comes into existence, the agreement operates on it (per Lord Chelmsford at p 220).

Holroyd v Marshall opened the way to the grant by companies of security over any class of circulating assets that the chargor company might possess. Acceptance that it was possible to do this became established by the 1870s. In *In re Panama New Zealand and Australian Royal Mail Co* (1870) 5 Ch App 318 the company simply charged its 'undertaking and all sums of money arising therefrom'. Gifford LJ held, at p 322, that 'undertaking' meant

> . . . all the property of the company, not only which existed at the date of the debenture, but which might afterwards become the property of the company.

He said also that the word 'undertaking'

> . . . necessarily infers that the company will go on, and that the debenture holder could not interfere until either the interest which was due was unpaid, or until the period had arrived for the payment of his principal, and that principal was unpaid.

(see also *In re Florence Land and Public Works Co* [1878] 10 Ch D 530, 540).

The two features mentioned by Gifford LJ became the hallmark of the new form of security, namely, (1) a charge on the chargor company's assets, or a specified class of assets, present and future and (2) the right of the chargor company to continue to use the charged assets for the time being owned by it and to dispose of them for its normal business purposes until the occurrence of some particular future event. In *In re Colonial Trusts Corporation* (1879) 15 Ch D 465 Jessel MR referred to this form of security as a 'floating security' (see at pp 468, 469 and 472) and in *Moor v Anglo-Italian Bank* (1879) 10 Ch D 681, 687 he contrasted the new form of security with a 'specific charge' on the property of the company.

By the last decade of the 19th century this form of security, Jessel MR's 'floating security', had become firmly established and in regular use. This new form of security, the floating charge, did not derive from statute. It had been bred by equity lawyers and judges out of the needs of the commercial and industrial entrepreneurs of the time. But the new form of security, notwithstanding its convenience for both borrowers and lenders, had its drawbacks for others. Those dealing with a company could not tell whether its circulating assets were subject to a charge that, if the company became insolvent or ceased business, would allow a debenture holder to 'step in and sweep off everything' (Lord Macnaghten in *Salomon v Salomon & Co Ltd* [1897] AC 22, 53). And if a debenture holder did 'step in and sweep off everything' there would be nothing left for unsecured creditors including, in particular, the company's employees to whom wages arrears might be owing.

Statutory intervention began in 1897 with the Preferential Payments in Bankruptcy Amendment Act. Where a company was being wound-up or was in receivership ss 2 and 3 of the 1897 Act gave preferential creditors, a class which included employees as well as Crown creditors, priority over the chargee under a floating charge, so far as payment of debts out of the assets subject to that charge was concerned. Preferential creditors had priority anyway over ordinary creditors and the sections did not disturb the priority over ordinary creditors to which the charge holder was entitled by virtue of the charge. These statutory provisions, with very little alteration, are now to be found in ss 40 (receivership) and 175 (winding-up) of the Insolvency Act 1986. And in 1900 further statutory interventions required floating charges to be registered: (see now ss 395 and 396, Companies Act 1985) and provided for floating charges created by an insolvent company within a short period before the commencement of its winding-up to be invalid except to the extent of new money provided by the chargee (see now s 245 Insolvency Act 1986). The statutes which first introduced these reforms did not attempt any definition of a 'floating charge'. Nor have any of their statutory successors done so. The expression has been taken to be self-explanatory. It bears the meaning attributed to it by judicial decision. But the judicial process over the years whereby the concept of a 'floating charge' has been developed must, in my opinion, keep in mind the mischief that these statutory reforms were intended to meet and, in particular, that on a winding-up or receivership preferential creditors were to have their debts paid out of the circulating assets, sometimes referred to as 'ambulatory' assets, of the debtor company in priority to a debenture holder with a charge over those assets.

The classic and frequently cited definition of a floating charge is that which was given by Romer LJ in the Court of Appeal in the *Yorkshire Woolcombers Association* case [1903] 2 Ch 284, 295.

> I certainly think that if a charge has the three characteristics that I am about to mention it is a floating charge.
>
> (1) If it is a charge on a class of assets of a company present and future; (2) if that class is one which, in the ordinary course of the business of the company, would be changing from time to time; and (3) if you find that by the charge it is contemplated that, until some further step is taken by or on behalf of those interested in the charge, the company may carry on its business in the ordinary way as far as concerns the particular class of assets I am dealing with.

But it is important to notice that Romer LJ prefaced his definition with a qualification. He said—

> I certainly do not intend to attempt to give an exact definition of the term 'floating charge', nor am I prepared to say that there will not be a floating charge within the meaning of the Act, which does not contain all the three characteristics . . .

The case came to this House under the name *Illingworth v Houldsworth* [1904] AC 355. In short *ex tempore* speeches their Lordships upheld the Court of Appeal. Lord Macnaghten described the case as 'clear' and offered the following definition of a floating charge in contrast to a 'specific charge'—

> A specific charge, I think, is one that without more fastens on ascertained and definite property or property capable of being ascertained and defined; a floating charge, on the other hand, is ambulatory and shifting in its nature, hovering over and so to speak floating with the property which it is intended to affect until some event occurs or some act is done which causes it to settle and fasten on the subject of the charge within its reach and grasp (p 358).

And a few years later Buckley LJ in *Evans v Rival Granite Quarries Ltd* [1910] 2 KB 979, 999 similarly contrasted a 'floating security' with a 'specific security.'

> [A floating security] is not a specific security; the holder cannot affirm that the assets are specifically mortgaged to him. The assets are mortgaged in such a way that the mortgagor can deal with them without the concurrence of the mortgagee. A floating security is not a specific mortgage of the assets, plus a licence to the mortgagor to dispose of them in the course of his business, but is a floating mortgage applying to every item comprised in the security, but not specifically affecting any item until some event occurs or some act on the part of the mortgagee is done which causes it to crystallise into a fixed security.

It is in the nature of commercial lenders to want the most effective security that they can get. It is in the nature of commercial borrowers to want to be able to carry on the business for the purposes of which they are borrowing money with as much freedom from restrictions imposed by their lenders that negotiation can achieve for them. But the lenders are usually in the stronger bargaining position and able to stipulate the terms to be included in the debenture which will constitute their security. So it is not in the least surprising to find attempts by lenders to obtain fixed charges as security rather than floating charges, thereby avoiding the need, if financial misfortune were to visit their borrowers, to yield priority to preferential creditors and also avoiding possible vulnerability under s 245 of the 1986 Act or its statutory predecessors. And it is not surprising to find borrowers agreeable to co-operate in these attempts provided their ability to carry on business in the normal way were not unduly impeded.

There was never any doubt that it was possible to create a fixed charge over a specific, ascertained book debt. And *Tailby v Official Receiver* (1888) 13 App Cas 523 established that an assignment of future book debts would be effective to vest in the assignee an equitable interest in the future debts at the moment they became owing to the assignor. So there was no reason why a debenture should not be expressed to assign to the debenture holder, by way of security, the company's future book debts. But the question would still remain whether such an assignment, not being an out-and-out assignment as in *Tailby v Official Receiver* but an assignment by way of security, could be said to constitute a fixed security.

There was nothing much that the lenders could do about the third of the characteristics that Romer LJ had regarded as typical of floating charges. Most commercial borrowers would be unlikely to agree to grant charges over their circulating assets that did not enable them to use those assets for their normal business purposes. So it was natural for the quest for fixed charges to be concentrated on the prominence given by Lord Macnaghten in the *Yorkshire Woolcombers* case to the characteristic of a fixed charge as being a charge on 'ascertained and definite property.' As soon as a book debt is incurred and becomes owing to the chargor it constitutes an item of 'ascertained and definite' property and would qualify as a possible object of a fixed charge. So a debenture expressed to grant a fixed charge over present and future book debts would be capable of creating a fixed charge over all such debts as and when they accrued due to the chargor company. Slade J so held in *Siebe Gorman* and no-one has suggested that in that respect he was wrong.

Moreover, the debenture could fortify the apparently fixed character of the charge by including a provision entitling the chargee to call for a formal written assignment by the chargor of the debts as they accrued. Such an assignment unaccompanied by written notice to the debtor would constitute the chargee equitable proprietor, and not simply equitable chargee, of the debt. The appearance of a fixed security would be fortified. It is not surprising, therefore, to find debentures containing provisions of this sort. The *Siebe Gorman* debenture did so. So did the Bank's debenture in the present case. But the intention of the parties that the charge over book debts created and fortified in this way would be a fixed charge has to take account also of

Romer LJ's third characteristic of a floating charge, namely, that until some further step by way of intervention is taken by the chargee the chargor company can use the assets in question for its normal business purposes and, in using them, remove them from the security. The fact that a valid fixed charge over present and future book debts is capable of being created does not answer the essential question whether a fixed charge over assets that remain at the disposal of the chargor can be created.

Slade J in *Siebe Gorman* [1979] 2 Lloyd's Rep 142, 158 inclined to the opinion that if the chargor of book debts, having collected the book debts,

> . . . [had] had the unrestricted right to deal with the proceeds of any of the relevant book debts paid into its account, so long as that account remained in credit . . . the charge on such book debts could be no more than a floating charge.

Hoffmann J in *In re Brightlife Ltd* [1987] Ch 200, 209, in a passage cited with approval by Lord Millett in *Agnew v Commissioners of Inland Revenue* [2001] 2 AC 710, 723, said that the significant feature of the *Brightlife* debenture was that the company was free to collect its debts and pay the proceeds into its bank account. He went on

> Once in the account, they would be outside the charge over debts and at the free disposal of the company. In my judgment a right to deal in this way with the charged assets for its own account is a badge of a floating charge and is inconsistent with a fixed charge.

Similar conclusions were expressed in *In re Keenan Bros Ltd* [1986] BCLC 242 in the Supreme Court of Ireland and by Tompkins J in the *Supercool Refrigeration* case [1994] 3 NZLR 300, in New Zealand.

The Privy Council in the *Agnew* case agreed with these decisions. Lord Millett pointed out, in para 13 of the Board's opinion, that Romer LJ's first two characteristics, although typical of a floating charge, were not distinctive of it. They were not necessarily inconsistent with a fixed charge. It was the third characteristic, Lord Millett said, which was the hallmark of a floating charge and distinguished it from a fixed charge.

I respectfully agree. Indeed if a security has Romer LJ's third characteristic I am inclined to think that it qualifies as a floating charge, and cannot be a fixed charge, whatever may be its other characteristics. Suppose, for example, a case where an express assignment of a specific debt by way of security were accompanied by a provision that reserved to the assignor the right, terminable by written notice from the assignee, to collect the debt and to use the proceeds for its (the assignor's) business purposes, ie, a right, terminable on notice, for the assignor to withdraw the proceeds of the debt from the security. This security would, in my opinion, be a floating security notwithstanding the express assignment. The assigned debt would be specific and ascertained but its status as a security would not. Unless and until the right of the assignor to collect and deal with the proceeds were terminated, the security would retain its floating characteristic. Or suppose a case in which the charge were expressed to come into existence on the future occurrence of some event and then to be a fixed charge over whatever assets of a specified description the chargor might own at that time. The contractual rights thereby granted would, in my opinion, be properly categorised as a floating security. There can, in my opinion, be no difference in categorisation between the grant of a fixed charge expressed to come into existence on a future event in relation to a specified class of assets owned by the chargor at that time and the grant of a floating charge over the specified class of assets with crystallisation taking place on the occurrence of that event. I endeavoured to make this point in *In re Cosslett (Contractors) Ltd* [2001] UKHL 58, [2002] 1 AC 336, 357, para 63. Nor, in principle, can there be any difference in categorisation between those grants and the grant of a charge over the specified assets expressed to be a fixed charge but where the chargor is permitted until the occurrence of the specified event to remove the charged assets from the security. In all these cases, and in any other case in which the chargor remains free to remove the charged assets from the security, the charge should, in principle, be categorised as a floating charge. The assets would have the circulating, ambulatory character distinctive of a floating charge.

The debenture in the *New Bullas Trading* case [1994] 1 BCLC 485, had features which illustrate the ingenuity of equity draftsmen in seeking to produce for their clients fixed charges out of circumstances that would normally be associated with floating charges. The debenture was expressed to grant the chargee a fixed charge over the company's present and future book debts. The chargee was entitled to demand that the debts be assigned to it, but never in fact made any such demand. The chargee was entitled to give the chargor instructions as to how the chargor should deal with its book debts, but apparently never in fact gave any such instructions, at any rate none prior to liquidation. The debenture left the chargor free to collect the debts and required the chargor to pay into a specified bank account all money it received in payment of the debts. The debenture then provided that on payment of the money into the bank account the fixed charge would be released and replaced by a floating charge over the money in the account. The obvious intention of these provisions was that on the occurrence of a crystallisation event, eg liquidation, the uncollected book debts at that time would be subject to the fixed charge notwithstanding that if the debts had been paid prior to the crystallisation event the collected money would have been subject to only a floating charge. The preferential creditors would then enjoy no priority over the debenture holder so far as the uncollected debts were concerned.

Nourse LJ could see no reason in law to prevent the parties from providing for a fixed charge on book debts while uncollected but a floating charge on the money collected. He referred at p 492 to the question and answer posed by Lord Macnaghten in *Tailby v Official Receiver* 13 App Cas 523, 545—

> Between men of full age and competent understanding ought there to be any limit to the freedom of contract but that imposed by positive law or dictated by considerations of morality or public policy? The limit proposed is purely arbitrary, and I think meaningless and unreasonable.

These reservations, he thought, supported the view that it was open to contracting parties, if they wished to do so, to provide for a fixed charge on uncollected book debts but a floating charge on the money received in payment of those debts.

Lord Millett expressed the Board's disagreement with Nourse LJ's reasoning and conclusion. Essentially Lord Millett challenged the notion that the security rights granted over a book debt could be any greater than the rights, if any, granted over the money received in payment of the debts (see [2001] 2 AC 710, para 46). If a book debt were to be charged as security but with an accompanying provision that any money received from the debtor in payment of the debt would belong to the chargor, the so-called 'charge', whether expressed to be a fixed charge or a floating charge, would not be a security at all. It would not constitute a possible source for the repayment of the allegedly secured debt. As Lord Millett said, it would be worthless. If the accompanying provision were, instead, to say that any money received from the debtor would be subject to a floating charge, that provision would, in my opinion, necessarily describe and limit the nature of the charge over the receivable debt. And if the charge were to be expressed to be a fixed charge as respects the receivable debt but a floating charge as respects the money received from the debtor there would be an internal contradiction in the formulation of the charge. Since the essential value of a book debt as a security lies in the money that can be obtained from the debtor in payment it seems to me that Lord Millett was right in concluding that such a security should be categorised as a floating security and that *New Bullas* [1994] 1 BCLC 485 was wrongly decided.

In my opinion, the essential characteristic of a floating charge, the characteristic that distinguishes it from a fixed charge, is that the asset subject to the charge is not finally appropriated as a security for the payment of the debt until the occurrence of some future event. In the meantime the chargor is left free to use the charged asset and to remove it from the security. On this point I am in respectful agreement with Lord Millett. Moreover, recognition that this is the essential characteristic of a floating charge reflects the mischief that the statutory intervention to which I have referred was intended to meet and should ensure that preferential creditors continue to enjoy the priority that s 175 of the 1986 Act and its statutory predecessors intended them to have.

DID THE BANK'S DEBENTURE CREATE A FIXED CHARGE OR ONLY A FLOATING CHARGE?

If, as I think, the hallmark of a floating charge and a characteristic inconsistent with a fixed charge is that the chargor is left free to use the assets subject to the charge and by doing so to withdraw them from the security, how should the charge over book debts granted by the bank's debenture be categorised? The following features of the debenture and the arrangements regarding the bank account into which the collected debts had to be paid need to be taken into account.

1. The extent of the restrictions imposed by the debenture ...
2. The rights retained by Spectrum to deal with its debtors and collect the money owed by them ...
3. Spectrum's right to draw on its account with the bank into which the collected debts had to be paid, provided it kept within the overdraft limit ...
4. The description 'fixed charge' attributed to the charge by the parties themselves.

Restrictions on Spectrum's right to deal with its uncollected book debts go very little way, in my opinion, in supporting the characterisation of the charge as a fixed charge for the reasons I have given in criticising the *New Bullas* decision. It is restrictions on the use that Spectrum could make of the payments made by its debtors that are important. I have already cited the passage at p 158 from Slade J's judgment in *Siebe Gorman* [1979] 2 Lloyd's Rep 142, 158 ... and need not repeat it. It makes the same point.

Moreover, the restrictions on Spectrum's right to deal with its uncollected book debts did not enable the bank to realise its security over those uncollected book debts. The bank could not have sold the book debts without first taking some step or steps that would have given it the power to do so. In effect a crystallisation event would, I think, have had to take place. The value of the uncollected book debts as a security lay always in the money that could be obtained from the debtors in payment of those debts.

The bank's debenture required all payments of book debts received by Spectrum to be paid into its account with the bank. The money once received by the bank would become the bank's money and in return Spectrum's account would be credited with the amount that had been received. Whether the account was for the time being in credit or in debit the result of each payment would be the accrual to Spectrum of the right to withdraw from the account a corresponding amount for its normal business purposes.

An attempt has been made to justify the categorisation of the charge as a fixed charge by looking no further than the receipt by the bank, through the operation of the clearing system, of the proceeds of the cheques from Spectrum's debtors that were paid in by Spectrum. The consequent crediting of Spectrum's account with amounts equal to the proceeds of the cheques and Spectrum's ability to draw on that account for its business purposes is not inconsistent, it is suggested, with the categorisation of the charge over the book debts as a fixed charge. This is the point being made by the Master of the Rolls in para 94 of his judgment. ...

It was a point pressed before your Lordships by Mr Moss QC, counsel for the bank. Your Lordships should not, in my opinion, accept this argument. It seeks to perpetuate what I regard as the *New Bullas* heresy, namely, that the categorisation of a charge over book debts can ignore the rights of the chargor over the money received in payment of those debts. The expression 'floating charge' has never been a term of art but is an expression invented by equity lawyers and judges to describe the nature of a particular type of security arrangement between lenders and borrowers. The categorisation depends upon the commercial nature and substance of the arrangement, not upon a formalistic analysis of how the bank clearing system works. If part of the arrangement is that the chargor is free to collect the book debts but must pay the collected money into a specified bank account, the categorisation must depend, in my opinion, on what, if any, restrictions there are on the use the chargor can make of the credit to the account that reflects each payment in.

The bank's debenture placed no restrictions on the use that Spectrum could make of the balance on the account available to be drawn by Spectrum. Slade J in *Siebe Gorman* [1979] Lloyd's Rep 142, 158 thought it might make a difference whether the account were in credit or in debit. I must respectfully disagree. The critical question, in my opinion, is whether the chargor can draw on the account. If the chargor's bank account were in debit and the chargor had no right to draw on it, the account would have become, and would remain until the drawing rights were restored, a blocked account. The situation would be as it was in *Re Keenan Bros Ltd* [1986] BCLC 242. But so long as the chargor can draw on the account, and whether the account is in credit or debit, the money paid in is not being appropriated to the repayment of the debt owing to the debenture holder but is being made available for drawings on the account by the chargor.

Slade J said that the debenture in the *Siebe Gorman* case

> . . . creat[ed] in equity a specific charge on the proceeds of [the book debts] as soon as they are received and consequently prevents the mortgagor from disposing of an unencumbered title to the subject matter of such charge without the mortgagee's consent, even before the mortgagee has taken steps to enforce its security. (p 159)

But it is very difficult to see what feature of the arrangement between chargor and bank chargee in *Siebe Gorman* justified this conclusion. The debenture was on all fours with the debenture in the present case. There is nothing in the report of the case to suggest that the bank account into which the chargor had to pay the collected book debts was other than, as here, a normal bank current account on which the chargor could draw for its normal business purposes. In considering the cited passage it seems to me worth noting that the issues that Slade J had to decide in the *Siebe Gorman* case did not include the question whether the charge over book debts was a fixed charge or a floating charge. The main issue in the case was one of priority as between the bank chargee on the one hand and a subsequent assignee of the charged book debts on the other. This issue turned on notice. Did the subsequent assignee have notice of the bank's charge and the provision barring subsequent assignments? If the subsequent assignee did have notice, the bank would have priority. If not, the subsequent assignee would have priority. The categorisation of the charge did not matter.

Slade J in *Siebe Gorman*, Nourse LJ in the *New Bullas* case, and Mr Moss QC in his submission on behalf of the bank in the present case, attributed considerable significance to the labels that the parties to the debenture had chosen to attribute to the charge over book debts. Mr Moss indeed argued that a debenture expressed to grant a fixed charge thereby limited by necessary implication the ability of the chargor to deal with the charged assets. He argued that Spectrum had no right without the consent of the bank to draw on the account into which the cheques received by Spectrum in payment of its book debts had to be paid. This limitation was, he said, an inevitable result of the grant by the debenture of the fixed charge. This argument, my Lords, puts the cart before the horse. The nature of the charge depends on the rights of the chargor and chargee respectively over the assets subject to the charge. The moneys in the bank account were assets subject to the charge. If the account had been treated as a blocked account, so long as it remained overdrawn, it would be easy to infer from a combination of that treatment and the description of the charge as a fixed charge that Spectrum had no right to draw on the account until the debit on the account had been discharged. But the account was never so treated. The overdraft facility was there to be drawn on by Spectrum at will. In the operation of the account there was never a suggestion that Spectrum needed to obtain the bank's consent before writing a cheque. The bank could, by notice, have terminated the overdraft facility, required immediate repayment of the indebtedness and turned the account into a blocked account. Pending such a notice, however, Spectrum was free to draw on the account. Its right to do so was inconsistent with the charge being a fixed charge and the label placed on the charge by the debenture cannot, in my opinion, be prayed-in-aid to detract from that right.

The correct conclusion, in my opinion, is that the debenture, although expressed to grant the bank a fixed charge over Spectrum's book debts, in law granted only a floating charge. I think the Vice-Chancellor, save for the precedent point, was correct in his reasoning and his conclusion.

Lord Walker:

[His Lordship began by outlining some of the problems associated with the development of the floating charge, in particular the fact that third parties might be misled by the chargor's 'false wealth' and that there is no statutory definition of a 'floating charge'. He continued:]

UPGRADING THE SECURITY TO A FIXED CHARGE

These difficulties have not diminished over the years. Sections 2 and 3 of the 1897 Act (now re-enacted, with a refinement as to timing, as ss 175(2)(b) and 40(2) respectively of the Insolvency Act 1986) make a floating charge more precarious as a security. Banks and other large commercial lenders have therefore tried, for understandable reasons, to upgrade their security by imposing fixed (and not merely floating) charges on parts of a trading customer's circulating capital, especially book debts. This chapter of commercial history has been described by Professor Sir Roy Goode QC, *Legal Problems of Credit and Security*, 3rd ed. (2003) pp 121–123. In practice, most standard forms of debenture make the charge extend not just to book debts but to all present and future 'book debts and other debts', the extent of which expression was considered by Hoffmann J in *In re Brightlife Ltd* [1987] Ch 200, 204–5; but nothing turns on that in this appeal. In considering the practical effect of charges on debts it should be borne in mind that money paid into a trading company's bank account will not necessarily represent the proceeds of debts of any description, especially if the trader is a retailer making a large number of cash sales, either over the counter or on a 'cash with order' basis.

Banks and their advisers have had some success in their efforts to upgrade their security. It is quite clear that a fixed charge on book debts, present and future, is conceptually possible. That was the most important point decided (or at any rate confirmed) by Slade J in *Siebe Gorman & Co Ltd v Barclays Bank Ltd* [1979] 2 Lloyd's Rep 142, and the Crown, the appellant in this appeal, does not seek to cast any doubt on that general proposition. The Crown challenges the decision on a much narrower point, that is the correct construction of the particular form of debenture which was before the Court. But that narrow point is itself of considerable general importance because the Siebe Gorman form has become a precedent and has been widely used, either in precisely the same words or in very similar words, by numerous banks.

In *Siebe Gorman*, Slade J decided that the form of debenture before him did on its true construction restrict the borrower, R H McDonald Ltd ('McDonald') in making use of the proceeds of collected debts in the ordinary course of its business. Slade J clearly accepted that, in the absence of such a restriction, the charge on debts could not as a matter of law have been more than a floating charge, even though the parties described it as a fixed (or specific) charge. He said at p 158,

> if I had accepted the premise that [McDonald] would have had the unrestricted right to deal with the proceeds of any of the relevant book debts paid into its account, so long as that account remained in credit, I would have been inclined to accept the conclusion that the charge on such book debts could be no more than a floating charge.

The Crown has little quarrel with that, except perhaps for the adjective 'unrestricted.'

THE ESSENTIAL DIFFERENCE

This passage brings us close to the issue of legal principle, that is the essential difference between a fixed charge and a floating charge. Under a fixed charge the assets charged as security are permanently appropriated to the payment of the sum charged, in such a way as to give the chargee a proprietary interest in the assets. So long as the charge remains unredeemed, the assets can be released from the charge only with the active concurrence of the chargee. The chargee may have good commercial reasons for agreeing to a partial release. If for instance a bank has a fixed charge over a large area of land which is being developed in phases as a housing estate (another example of a fixed charge on what might be regarded as trading stock) it might be short-sighted of the bank not to agree to take only a fraction of the proceeds of sale of houses in the first phase, so enabling the remainder of the development to be funded. But under a fixed charge that will be a matter for the chargee to decide for itself.

Under a floating charge, by contrast, the chargee does not have the same power to control the security for its own benefit. The chargee has a proprietary interest, but its interest is in a *fund* of circulating capital, and unless and until the chargee intervenes (on crystallisation of the charge) it is for the trader, and not the bank, to decide how to run its business. There is a detailed and helpful analysis of the matter, with full citation of authority, in Professor Sarah Worthington's *Proprietary Interests in Commercial Transactions* (1996) pp 74–77; see also her incisive comment on this case ('An Unsatisfactory Area of the Law—Fixed and Floating Charges Yet Again') in (2004) 1 International Corporate Rescue 175. So long as the company trades in the ordinary way (a requirement emphasised by Romer LJ in the *Yorkshire Woolcombers case* [1903] Ch 284, 295, and by the Earl of Halsbury on appeal in the same case, [1904] AC 355, 357–8) the constituents of the charged fund are in a state of flux (or circulation). Trading stock is sold and becomes represented by book debts; these are collected and paid into the bank; the trader's overdraft facility enables it to draw cheques in favour of its suppliers to pay for new stock; and so the trading cycle continues.

I have drawn attention to Slade J's reference to an 'unrestricted' right to deal with the proceeds of collected debts. It is clear that not every restriction on a trader's freedom of action is a badge of a fixed charge: see *Brightlife* [1987] Ch 200, 209. A prohibition on factoring or otherwise dealing with uncollected debts does not prevent the trader from collecting the debts itself. But if the terms of the debenture were such as to require the trader to pay all its collected debts into the bank and to prohibit the trader from drawing on the account (so that the account is blocked), a charge on debts, described as a fixed or specific charge, would indeed take effect as such (see *Re Keenan Brothers Ltd* [1986] BCLC 242, a decision of the Supreme Court of Ireland, followed by Morritt J in *William Gaskell Group Ltd v Highley* [1994] 1 BCLC 197). In those circumstances the chargee would be in control, prior to crystallisation, and the trader would be unable to trade in the ordinary way without the chargee's positive concurrence. In *Agnew*, Lord Millett pointed out ([2001] 2 AC 710, 730, para 48) that it was not enough to provide in the debenture for an account to be blocked, if it was not in fact operated as a blocked account.

Both sides agree that the label of 'fixed' or 'specific' (which I take to be synonymous in this context) cannot be decisive if the rights created by the debenture, properly construed, are inconsistent with that label. There is a fairly close parallel (first drawn, I think, by Hoffmann J in *Brightlife* [1987] Ch 200, 209 and often repeated) with the important distinction, in land law, between a lease and a licence: see the decision of this House in *Street v Mountford* [1985] AC 809. The distinction is clear in principle although landlords (in framing letting agreements) and banks (in framing debentures) may produce legal documents in a form which makes the principle difficult to apply. Whether or not it is appropriate to describe this by some disparaging term such as camouflage, it is the court's duty to characterise the document according to the true legal effect of its terms, as has been very clearly explained by Lord Millett in *Agnew* [2001] 2 AC 710, 725–726, para 32. In each case there is a public interest which overrides unrestrained freedom of contract. On the lease/licence issue, the public interest is the protection of vulnerable people seeking living accommodation. On the fixed/floating issue, it is ensuring that preferential creditors obtain the measure of protection which Parliament intended them to have. This public interest is unaffected by the changes in the classes of preferential creditors made by s 251 of the Enterprise Act 2002.

In my opinion Slade J did not, in *Siebe Gorman*, make any significant error in stating the general principles which apply. But he did not correctly construe the debenture which was before him in that case, and his decision on its construction has had surprisingly far-reaching consequences.

[His Lordship was critical of the *Siebe Gorman* decision and continued:]

POSTCRIPT [sic]: DRAFTSMEN'S PRECEDENTS AND COLLATERAL TRANSACTIONS

Judges considering this area of the law have often commented on the convenience (in point of legal certainty) of using standard-form clauses, the meaning of which has already been determined by the court. For instance Knox J observed in *Ex p Copp* [1989] BCLC 13, 25:

> this is a type of transaction in respect of which judicial precedent is a particularly valuable guide to the commercial adviser. It is one of the main justifications for the doctrine of precedent that the adviser can, if he can rely on precedent, give reliable advice to his clients, and it is trite law that that is a particularly cogent consideration in regard to property transactions of one sort or another.

Requirements for particulars of floating charges to be registered publicly, and for a company's register of debentures to be open for inspection, suggest that Parliament intended that the existence and scope of any floating charge should be ascertainable by the general public, at least in theory (doubts as to how the system works in practice were expressed by Lord Hoffmann in the *Cosslett case*, [2001] UKHL 58, [2002] 1 AC 336, 347–8, para 19).

These considerations might be thought to lead to the conclusion that everything relevant to the characterisation of a charge should be apparent on the face of the formal debenture, without further inquiry. That was, as I understand it, one of the reasons why Knox J, in *Ex p Copp*, declined to look at evidence about an agreed overdraft limit, regarding it as a 'collateral arrangement'. Knox J may have been right in his view that it was unnecessary to receive evidence about an overdraft limit (which may change from time to time) but he took the wrong approach as to the effect of the debenture itself, as the Vice-Chancellor rightly concluded ([2004] Ch 337, 355, para 40). The form of debenture showed that the recycling of book debts was 'not only permitted but envisaged' and it contained no relevant restriction on that being done in the ordinary course of business.

In practice banks use printed standard forms of debenture in simple cases, and City solicitors no doubt have more sophisticated forms, suitable for very large transactions, in their word-processing libraries. It is most desirable that any form of secured debenture, whether simple or complicated, should contain all the terms necessary for its correct characterisation, without resort to any side-letters or other less formal documents (as in the Australian case of *Hart v Barnes* (1982) 7 ACLR 310, mentioned in *Agnew* at para 23). But the fact is that when a bank takes a charge there will normally be at least three documents in play: the debenture creating the charge, the bank's facility letter offering a term loan or an overdraft, and the bank's general terms and conditions. Sometimes there will be more documents that are relevant. I would not rule out the possibility that in some (probably rare) cases all this documentation might have to be taken into account, in its proper commercial context, in determining whether a charge 'as created' was a fixed or floating charge.

In one of the earliest cases on floating charges, *In re Florence Land and Public Works Co* (1878) 10 Ch D 530, 537, Sir George Jessel MR said,

> The question we have to decide must be decided, like all other questions of the kind, having regard to the surrounding circumstances under which the instrument was executed, and especially the respective positions of the parties who were the contracting parties, to carry out whose agreement that instrument was executed.

Cozens-Hardy LJ made similar observations in *Yorkshire Woolcombers* [1903] 2 Ch 284, 297. Many of the later cases have emphasised the need for the court to look at the commercial realities of the situation. The wish to achieve legal certainty by use of a standard precedent cannot override the need to construe any document in its commercial context.

It is also necessary to bear in mind Lord Millett's warning in *Agnew* [2001] 2 AC 710, 730, para 48, that formal provision for a blocked account is not enough 'if it is not operated as one in fact.' Lord Millett did not expand on this point, which may raise difficult questions as to what Staughton LJ, in *Welsh Development Agency v Export Finance Co Ltd* [1992] BCLC 148, 186–7, referred to as 'external' and 'internal' routes to the construction of commercial documents. This point is discussed in an article by Stephen Atherton and Rizwaan Jameel Mokal in (2005) 26 Company Lawyer 10, 16–18. These difficulties suggest to me that the expedient mentioned in the postscript to the judgment of the Master of the Rolls (para 99), although no doubt appropriate and efficacious in some commercial contexts, may not provide a simple solution in every case.

On the topic of overruling long-standing decisions which have been relied on by commercial lenders, and on the further topic of prospective overruling, I am in full and respectful agreement with the opinions of my noble and learned friends, Lord Nicholls of Birkenhead and Lord Hope. I would allow this appeal and hold, without any sort of temporal restriction, that *Siebe Gorman* was wrongly decided on the issue of construction.

[**Lord Nicholls**, **Steyn**, and **Brown** and **Baroness Hale** delivered concurring judgments.]

NOTES

1. The starting assumption in *Agnew* and *Spectrum Plus* was that the drafting 'converted' a fixed charge into a floating charge at the time when a receivable (which was subject to a fixed charge) was paid, thus yielding 'proceeds' (which were subject to a floating charge). Was that starting assumption correct? As to other, uncollected receivables, the charge—created by an instrument of charge—remained fixed. It has been argued that a more straightforward analysis might have been possible. According to this argument, the charge was both fixed and floating from the outset. The 'fixed' terms of the charge applied to receivables; the 'floating' terms applied to the proceeds. On that view, the drafting would have failed to avoid the claims of preferential creditors to assets held subject to a floating charge from the time of the charge's creation. That argument has been augmented to suggest that, as things were, their Lordships adopted 'anti-avoidance' reasoning: Lord Scott grounded his anti-avoidance reasoning in statutory interpretation, while Lord Walker grounded his anti-avoidance reasoning in interpretation of the contract: Turner [2006] Sing JLS 200.

2. *Re Spectrum Plus Ltd* was a test case. The debenture was in the bank's standard form and many other banks and other commercial lenders had taken security over their borrowers' book debts using a similar form of debenture. In *Siebe Gorman*, Slade J had endorsed this form of debenture as creating a fixed charge. Imagine the consternation of the lending community when it was told that this long-standing decision, which had for many years been relied on when formulating and using standard form charges on book debts, had been overruled on this point. In *Re Spectrum Plus* the bank even went so far as to ask the House of Lords to overrule *Siebe Gorman* prospectively, leaving undisturbed charges granted before their decision. Their Lordships refused to do this on the ground that banks and other commercial lenders were sophisticated operators who could not have been lulled into a false sense of security by what was a first-instance decision, so that *Siebe Gorman* could not have been regarded as finally and definitively settling the law. Moreover, their Lordships felt that if their decision was given only prospective effect, it would result in preferential creditors in many existing liquidations being deprived of priority which Parliament intended they should have.

3. *Re Spectrum Plus Ltd* has left banks and other commercial lenders with the thorny question of how to prevent borrowers exercising control over the proceeds of the book debts. Requiring the proceeds of the book debts to be paid into a blocked account is an effective way to ensure that the lender retains control (so long as the account is operated as such) but it comes at a price. Borrowers will usually require quick and easy access to those funds for their day-to-day working capital requirements. Lenders will not want to take on the administrative burden of having to consent to each and every withdrawal from the 'blocked account'. In the Court of Appeal, Lord Phillips had said (at [99]) that: 'it would seem beyond dispute that a requirement to pay book debts into a blocked account will be sufficient restriction to render a charge over book debts a fixed charge, even if the chargor is permitted to overdraw on another account, into which from time to time transfers are made from the blocked account'. In the House of Lords, Lord Walker commented (at [160]) that although the expedient would be 'appropriate and efficacious in some commercial contexts', it 'may not provide a simple solution in every case'. This level of uncertainty is commercially undesirable. Perhaps it is time for banks and other lenders to accept that fixed charges over book debts are, in practical terms, a thing of the past. Financiers may find that they have to settle for a floating charge over book debts in most cases.

4. The relevance of the conduct of the parties after the debenture has been executed raises a number of difficult issues. In *Agnew*, Lord Millett (at [48]) thought that 'it is not enough to provide in the debenture that the account is a blocked account if it is not operated as one in fact'. This seems to run against the well-established rule that the meaning and construction of a contract cannot be reconsidered by post-contractual events (*James Miller & Partners Ltd v Whitworth Estates (Manchester) Ltd* [1970] AC 583). The difficulties raised by Lord Millett's dictum were recognised by Lord Walker in *Spectrum Plus* (at [160]).

5. Numerous casenotes and articles have been written on the *Spectrum Plus* decision. The following are particularly useful: C Hare [2005] LMCLQ 440; D Capper (2006) 6 JCLS 447. See also J Getzler and J Payne (eds), *Company Charges: Spectrum and Beyond* (2006).

4 OTHER DOCTRINES AFFECTING ASSIGNED RECEIVABLES

The general principles of assignment, as discussed in Chapter 22, apply to assignments of receivables. What follows is consideration of points particular to commercial transactions in the form of assignments of receivables.

(a) Equities

Unlike a mortgagee of a debt, a chargee does not own the charged debt. This has led Professor Goode to submit that giving notice of the charge to the debtor does not prevent the debtor's right of set-off building up against the debt ([1984] JBL 172 at 174). Cf F Oditah, *Legal Aspects of Receivables Financing* (1991), pp 95–96, 245–246. If Professor Goode is correct, the chargee would be placed in a worse position than that of an assignee, who can stop equities accumulating by giving the debtor notice of assignment. But in practice this distinction is rarely encountered. This is because a charge over receivables usually contains a power to convert it into a mortgage through execution of an assignment by the chargee in the name of the chargor. Therefore, for the purposes of set-off, a charge may be equated with an assignment (L Gullifer, *Goode on Legal Problems of Credit and Security* (5th edn, 2013), para 3–21).

(b) The rule in *Dearle v Hall*

The discussion of *Dearle v Hall* found in Chapter 22 also applies to assignments of receivables. For the purpose of the notice requirement of that rule, registration of an assignment as a charge under Part 25 of the Companies Act 2006 is insufficient to give the assignee priority under the first limb of the rule in *Dearle v Hall*: the debtor cannot be expected to search the register. However, it may constitute sufficient notice to deny an assignee the ability to rely on the rule in *Dearle v Hall*. The criticisms of *Dearle v Hall* generally have been re-expressed specifically with regard to receivables financing (see JS Ziegel (1963) 41 Can Bar Rev 54 at 109–110; RM Goode (1976) 92 LQR 528 at 566; DM McLauchlan (1980) 96 LQR 90 at 98; F Oditah, *Legal Aspects of Receivables Financing* (1991), p 140).

Report of the Committee on Consumer Credit (Chairman: Lord Crowther)
(Cmnd 4596, 1971), Vol 2, p 579

It is doubtful whether any system of priorities can be provided which will do justice in all situations. Certainly existing rules of law fall far short of the ideal. For example, if a debt is assigned to A and afterwards the assignor fraudulently assigns the same debt to B who takes in good faith then if B is the first to give notice to the debtor he gains priority under the rule in *Dearle v Hall*. This rule implicitly assumes that notice to the debtor is equivalent to notice to the second assignee. But this will not in fact be the case unless the second assignee, before giving value, makes enquiries of the debtor to see whether he has had notice of a prior assignment. In the financing of receivables such enquiries would be quite impracticable and the second assignee would not give notice to the debtors, or indeed have occasion to communicate with them, until after he had taken his assignment and paid the price. Moreover the rule in *Dearle v Hall* does not provide a secured party with any machinery for protecting a security interest in future receivables due from future debtors.

(c) Priority conflicts between factor and chargee

A company which has given a floating charge over its assets remains at liberty to deal with those assets in the ordinary course of its business. This means that a factor who later purchases the company's receivables takes priority over the earlier floating charge, even though he did so with knowledge of the charge. The position is otherwise where the factor has notice of the prior crystallisation of the charge or of a provision prohibiting the factoring of receivables contained in the charge instrument itself. Provisions prohibiting the factoring of receivables are now commonly found in charge instruments and so the prudent factor should secure a waiver from the chargee before entering into the factoring agreement. See especially Nolan (2004) 120 LQR 108.

Where the factoring agreement precedes the floating charge, priority depends on whether it is a whole turnover agreement or a facultative agreement. Where money has been advanced by the factor under a whole turnover agreement, the receivables vest automatically in the factor when they come into existence and are not caught by the floating charge. On the other hand, in the case of a facultative agreement the receivables only vest in the factor once they come into existence and have been offered to and accepted by the factor, ie there is a binding contract for their sale and purchase: until then the factor will be bound by notice of crystallisation of the charge or a prohibition against the factoring of receivables contained in the charge instrument.

5 REFORM

As Professor Goode has noted: 'In economic terms, a sale of receivables with recourse is virtually indistinguishable from a loan on the security of the receivables, for in both cases the trader receives money now and has to repay it himself, or ensure payments by debtors, later' (E McKendrick, *Goode on Commercial Law* (4th edn, 2009), p 787). As we have already seen, a major distinction between a sale and a loan secured on a company's book debts is that only the latter must be registered under Part 25 of the Companies Act 2006 (old or new regime). Registration protects any third party who subsequently deals with the company and who would otherwise be unaware that the company's book debts were encumbered. However, if the financing arrangement is structured as a sale with a right of recourse, the finance company is fully secured and yet others dealing with the company are ignorant of the fact.

This anomaly has been criticised: see, especially, the *Report of the Crowther Committee on Consumer Credit* (Cmnd 4596, 1971), Chs 4 and 5, and also Professor Diamond's report entitled *A Review of Security Interests in Property* (HMSO, 1989), paras 18.2–18.3. The Law Commission has revisited the issue and, in 2005, recommended that there should be a scheme of electronic 'notice-filing' for charges created by companies (Law Com Report No 296, *Company Security Interests*). It recommended that the sale of receivables of the kind which factoring and discounting agreements cover should be brought within the 'notice-filing' scheme. This would mean that sales of receivables by companies would have to be registered to be valid on insolvency. Their priority would be determined by the date of filing. None of these recommendations was taken up in the reform of company law through the Companies Act 2006 or the amendments of the charge registration provisions of that Act as made by the descriptively named Companies Act 2006 (Amendment of Part 25) Regulations 2013 (SI 2013/600). However, s 1 of the Small Business, Enterprise and Employment Act

2015 confers power to make regulations to invalidate such restrictions in contracts affecting certain receivables. As at the date of writing, that power has not been exercised.

6 INTERNATIONAL FACTORING

A factoring agreement is considered to be 'international' when the factor's client (as supplier of goods or services) and the person responsible for the payment of goods and services are situated in different states. In these circumstances, factoring is used to finance international trade. A common practice is for the supplier to enter into a factoring agreement with a factor in his own country (the 'export factor'). The export factor then enters into an arrangement with correspondent factors (the 'import factors') in the countries of the supplier's customers. The import factors accept the credit risk of the debtors situated in their own country and are responsible for collection. The export factor sub-assigns the purchased debt to the import factors. At all times, the import factor is responsible to the export factor and the export factor is responsible to the supplier. Rights of recourse may be exercised along that chain. This method of international factoring is known as a 'two factor' system.

Other methods of international factoring include:

(1) the 'single factor' system, where the export factor does not use an import factor for routine collections but only for the collection of seriously overdue debts or on the debtor's insolvency;

(2) 'direct import factoring', where the supplier simply factors the debt to a factor in the importing country;

(3) 'direct export factoring' where the export factor handles the functions of the import factor using correspondents to assist with collections in the debtor's country.

Reflecting the growing importance of international factoring, the International Institute for the Unification of Private Law (UNIDROIT) adopted a draft Convention on international factoring in May 1988. The Convention, known as 'The Unidroit Convention on International Factoring', aims to 'facilitate international factoring, while maintaining a fair balance of interests between the different parties involved in factoring transactions' (in the words of the Preamble to the Convention). However, the Convention has been criticised for its limited scope. It does not cover domestic factoring arrangements nor does it deal with the relationship between the factor and the supplier (which is governed by domestic law). It also fails to address the questions of priority of competing claims to receivables and ignores difficult questions of conflict of laws raised by international factoring.

In December 2001 the United Nations General Assembly adopted the text of the UNCITRAL Convention on the Assignment of Receivables in International Trade. The five ratifications of states required in order to bring the Convention into force were not made. But the 'principles' of the Convention were incorporated into the UNCITRAL Legislative Guide on Secured Transactions (2007)—to which only Liberia has acceded at the time of writing. The Convention and the Legislative Guide deal mainly with property issues, including priority upon default or insolvency of any one of the participants. They also deal with some contractual issues by way of default rules that apply in the absence of agreement between the parties. They permit the assignment of future receivables and the assignment of receivables in bulk.

PART VIII

COMMERCIAL CREDIT AND SECURITY

Chapter 24   Introduction   1007
Chapter 25   Possessory security   1024
Chapter 26   Non-possessory security   1059

INTRODUCTION

1 COMMERCIAL CREDIT

Credit plays an important role in the world of commerce. Let us take the sale of goods as an example. The seller may have to borrow money from his bank to finance the expansion of his business so that he can obtain the buyer's order and supply the goods as required. The bank loan is a form of credit. On the other hand, the buyer may be unwilling or unable to pay for the goods in advance or on delivery and require a period of credit from the seller. The buyer may even need to sell the goods himself before he can pay his supplier. In these circumstances, the seller may provide the credit himself by deferring payment, or he may accept payment by means of a bill of exchange payable at a future date. The extent to which the seller is willing to accommodate the buyer will greatly depend on the bargaining strengths of the parties. But a seller who has accommodated the buyer by allowing him credit may be unwilling or unable to wait until the credit period expires before receiving funds locked up in the debt he is owed. In such circumstances, he may sell the debt to a factoring company, or discount the bill of exchange to a bank or discount house, for immediate cash. Alternatively, he may borrow on the strength of those receivables (see above, Chapter 23).

So far we have considered the means by which the seller provides credit to the buyer. However, the seller may be unwilling to do this. The seller may prefer to sell the goods to a third party, such as a finance house, and leave it to the third party to supply the goods to the buyer on credit terms, for example through hire-purchase, conditional sale, credit sale, or finance leasing. Alternatively, the buyer may simply borrow money from a commercial lender and use the loan to pay the seller.

But no matter who provides credit, or how, the creditor will usually require some form of security. For example, the seller may reserve title in the goods or demand that payment is made by irrevocable documentary credit; the bank or factoring company may require security over other property belonging to the borrower; the finance house may ask for a third party guarantee. In all these cases the creditor is trying to ensure that he is not left high and dry should the debtor fail before making payment. In certain cases, the creditor may even insure himself against such loss (see above, p 856).

(a) Credit defined

The term 'credit' is used in many different senses. For example, it may be used to describe someone's financial standing (eg 'his credit is good'); alternatively, it may be used in a legal sense, such as to describe some form of financial accommodation. In this chapter, we shall be concerned with credit in the sense of financial accommodation, that is, 'the provision of a benefit (cash, land, goods, services or facilities) for which payment is to be made by the recipient in money at a later date' (E McKendrick, *Goode on Commercial Law* (5th edn, 2016), p 625; cf the Consumer Credit Act 1974, s 9(1), and the Financial Services and Markets Act 2000 (Regulated Activities) Order 2001 (the 'RAO'; SI 2001/ 544), as amended, art 60L, which defines credit as including 'a cash loan, and any other form of financial accommodation').

(b) The forms of credit

There are two forms of credit: loan credit and sale credit. *Loan credit* is granted where money is lent to the debtor on terms that it must be repaid to the creditor, together with interest, in due course, for example as with a bank loan or overdraft. *Sale credit* is granted where the debtor is allowed to defer payment of the price of goods and services supplied, for example as with conditional sale, hire-purchase, and credit sale agreements. It used to be important to distinguish between loan credit and sale credit because of the different regulatory regimes which applied to each (eg the Moneylenders Acts never applied to instalment selling and hire-purchase). However, insofar as a transaction is now caught by the Consumer Credit Act 1974 the distinction between the two forms of credit has become irrelevant in this context. But the distinction remains relevant in other contexts, for instance a company's borrowing powers may be restricted by its articles of association, or it may breach the terms of a debenture given to its bankers by further borrowing, yet in both cases the company remains free to purchase goods and services on sale credit.

A distinction must also be made between *fixed-sum credit* and *revolving credit*. Fixed-sum credit is granted where the debtor receives a fixed amount of credit which must be repaid in a lump sum or by instalments over a period of time. Non-instalment loans, hire-purchase agreements, and conditional sale agreements are all examples of fixed-sum credit. By contrast, revolving credit is granted where the debtor is allowed a credit facility which he may draw on as and when he pleases, up to an overall credit limit. The debtor may then restore the facility in whole or in part as he repays the creditor. A bank overdraft provides a good example of revolving credit: as the bank executes its customer's payment instructions, the available balance of the overdraft decreases; as amounts are paid to the credit of the account, the available balance of the overdraft increases. Both fixed-sum credit and revolving credit may be purchase money (eg where a customer purchases a car for cash advanced direct from the finance house to the car dealer and where goods and services are purchased by credit card) or non-purchase money (eg a bank loan for general purposes).

(c) The Consumer Credit Act 1974

The Consumer Credit Act 1974 regulates credit agreements entered into by an 'individual' ('the debtor'), which includes small partnerships (three partners or less) and unincorporated associations but not corporations. All such credit agreements are prima facie covered by the Act irrespective of the amount involved (a previous financial limit of £25,000 was removed by the Consumer Credit Act 2006, s 2). However, certain types of credit agreement are exempt from regulation under the 1974 Act (see RAO, arts 60C–60HA), these include those agreements where credit is supplied to a natural person who is a 'high net worth' borrower (ie someone with an annual net income of £150,000 or more and/or with net assets—excluding their primary residence and certain other assets—to the value of £500,000 or more) and is secured on land or is in excess of £60,260 (RAO, art 60H, but note exceptions in art 60HA to comply with the Mortgage Credit Directive 2014/17/EU), or where the credit exceeds £25,000 and the agreement is entered into 'wholly or predominantly' for the borrower's 'business purposes' (RAO, art 60C(3)–(7)) (but note that even these two types of agreement are not exempt from ss 140A–140C of the 1974 Act which enables debtors to challenge unfair relationships with creditors). A credit agreement not made by the creditor in the course of a business carried on by him (called a 'non-commercial agreement') is also exempt from most of the provisions of the Act.

Where the Consumer Credit Act 1974 applies it regulates such matters as the form, contents, terms, and enforcement of the credit agreement. Wherever credit is provided to a small partnership or to an unincorporated trader it will be important to consider the effect of the Act on the transaction. This is particularly so where the credit provided is for more than £25,000, because the business purposes exemption only applies where the credit exceeds that sum (remembering also that where the debtor is a natural person, the 'high net worth' exemption might apply). Nevertheless, despite the significant changes made to the consumer credit regime by the Consumer Credit Act 2006, the 1974 Act is still primarily concerned with *consumer* protection, and so we do not intend to consider its provisions any further at this stage.

QUESTIONS

1. List the principal institutions granting commercial credit. See RM Goode, *Consumer Credit Law: Law and Practice* (looseleaf), para 1A[2.3].

2. 'The provision of credit for trade and industry stimulates production and encourages enterprise. Credit also tides individuals and companies over difficult times' (F Oditah, *Legal Aspects of Receivables Financing* (1991), p 1). Can you think of any other motives for demanding credit? Is the provision of credit always a good thing?

2 SECURITY

(a) The nature and purpose of security

In 1985 Professor Diamond was asked by the Minister for Corporate and Consumer Affairs to examine the need for alteration of the law relating to security over property other than land. His report was published by the Department of Trade and Industry in 1989 and is entitled A *Review of Security Interests in Property*. In the extract which follows, Professor Diamond considers the nature and purpose of security.

A Review of Security Interests in Property by Professor AL Diamond
(1989), paras 3.1–3.3

THE NATURE OF SECURITY

3.1 There are two types of security. One type is often known as personal security. This is where a person who is not otherwise liable under a contract between the debtor and the creditor enters into a separate contract with the creditor under which he assumes some form of liability to ensure that the creditor does not lose (or loses less than he otherwise might) if the debtor fails to perform his contractual obligations. The debtor's contractual obligations may involve the payment of money, but this is not necessarily the case: they may require the performance of any kind of act. Personal security may take the form of a guarantee, caution or indemnity, or may be known as a performance bond. This report is not concerned with this form of security.

3.2 The other type of security is security over property. This is a right relating to property, the purpose of which is to improve the creditor's chance of getting paid or of receiving whatever else the debtor is required to do by way of performance of the contract. It is this type of security—security over property other than land—which is the subject matter of this report. Such security may be possessory, where the creditor takes possession of the subject matter of the security, or non-possessory.

THE PURPOSE OF SECURITY

3.3 As stated in the last paragraph, the purpose of security is to improve the creditor's chance of obtaining performance of the contract with the debtor. In particular, the taking of security may have any one or more of the following effects:

(a) Coercion

In most situations the last thing the creditor wants is to have to enforce his security. His prime objective is that the contract he has entered into with the debtor should be performed. The debtor's fear that the security may be enforced, or a threat by the creditor to enforce the security, will often be enough to ensure that a debtor who is having difficulty in fulfilling all his contracts will give priority to performance in favour of the secured creditor.

(b) Insolvency

If the debtor is unable to meet all his obligations, the creditor with security will usually be in a better position than unsecured creditors, for he will be able to look to the security which, if it has sufficient value, will enable him to receive money on its disposal. In some situations the agreement creating the right by way of security will enable the creditor to appoint a receiver in specified circumstances.

(c) Execution or diligence

Another creditor may, usually after obtaining a judgment against the debtor, attempt to seize the debtor's property by way of execution or diligence, or a landlord may, without obtaining a judgment, distrain on the debtor's goods or sequestrate the debtor's goods for rent. The holder of security will hope to exercise his rights against the property subject to the security and to prevent seizure by or on behalf of the other creditor.

(d) Sale

If the debtor purports to sell the subject matter of the security interest, the question arises whether the holder of the security interest can assert his rights as against the buyer or whether he can, in the alternative or in addition, lay claim to the proceeds of the sale in the debtor's hands.

(e) General

The above may be summed up in Professor Goode's words: 'All forms of real security . . . confer on the secured creditor at least two basic real rights: the right of pursuit, and the right of preference. The secured party can follow his asset, and its products and proceeds, into the hands of any third party other than one acquiring an overriding title by virtue of some exception to the *nemo dat* rule; and the secured party is entitled to look to the proceeds of the asset to satisfy the debt due to him in priority to the claims of other creditors.' [now E McKendrick, *Goode on Commercial Law* (5th edn, 2016), p 693.] Professor Goode continues: 'Other real rights are available for the enforcement of the security, depending on the nature of the security interest. These are: the retention or recovery of possession of the asset; sale of the asset; foreclosure; and an order vesting legal title in the secured creditor.'

NOTES

1. A creditor holding personal security has merely a personal claim against the third party guarantor (as well as against the original debtor). Personal security can also be given by the debtor himself on a collateral undertaking by way of security, for example on a bill of exchange. The weakness of personal security is that its value depends on the continued solvency of the third party. If the third party is made bankrupt, or goes into liquidation, the creditor is only left with a right to prove for a dividend in competition with other unsecured creditors.

2. By contrast, a creditor holding real security (or 'security over property' as Professor Diamond describes it) can rely on his right of preference to ensure priority over other creditors in the event of the debtor's bankruptcy or liquidation. As Professor DE Allan has observed ((1989) 15 Mon LR 337 at 343):

> . . . the principal value of traditional security is to give the creditor a preferred position in the insolvency or liquidation of the debtor. The major fear of creditors is the insolvency of the debtor and the risk that the creditor will have to line up and share pari passu with all other creditors. Security provides a means whereby, in the event of this catastrophe, the secured party can make off with the assets against which he is secured and satisfy his claim in full outside the bankruptcy.

But what benefits a creditor holding real security (hereafter referred to as 'a secured creditor') may hinder the debtor and unsecured creditors generally. Professor Allan continues (at 343):

> This privileged position [ie of the secured creditor] . . . is at variance with a legal policy manifested in the bankruptcy and winding-up legislation of seeking the rehabilitation of the debtor and, where that is not possible, of providing an even-handed distribution among creditors of all types. It concedes to any secured creditor the right to withdraw the assets against which he is secured and virtually to determine unilaterally that the debtor shall be put into bankruptcy or liquidation without reference to whether the situation of the debtor is salvageable and without regard to the interests of other creditors. The position is particularly acute so far as the unsecured creditors are concerned . . .

Some of Professor Allan's concerns have been met by statutory intervention. In particular, the Insolvency Act 1986, Sch B1, paras 43 and 44, impose restrictions on the secured creditor's right to enforce his security where a petition has been presented for an administration order, or the company has gone into administration, without leave of the court or the administrator's consent (see the landmark decision of the Court of Appeal in *Re Atlantic Computer Systems plc* [1992] Ch 505 for guidance on the principles governing the exercise of the court's discretion). Such intervention evidences a modest shift of balance away from secured creditors and back towards the principle of *pari passu* (or even-handed) distribution (MG Bridge [1992] JBL 1 at 17). However, the extent to which insolvency law should generally look to redistribute assets from secured to unsecured creditors, in the interests of equality, raises important policy questions (see F Oditah (1992) 108 LQR 459 at 472; R Goode, 'Proprietary Rights and Unsecured Creditors' in BAK Rider (ed), *The Realm of Company Law: A Collection of Papers in Honour of Professor Leonard Sealy* (1998), pp 183–197). The moratorium provisions are disapplied in relation to financial collateral arrangements (ie security interests over financial collateral such as bank accounts, debt and equity securities, and credit claims by banks that grant credit in the form of loans) in order to prevent systemic risk and promote the certainty of such arrangements (Financial Collateral Arrangements (No 2) Regulations 2003 (SI 2003/3226), as amended, reg 8).

3. What justifies placing a secured creditor in such a privileged position? This question has generated a vast body of literature, especially in the United States (see, eg, the collection of papers published in (1997) 82 Cornell Law Review 1279–1567). A number of theories have been advanced which seek to justify the privilege on grounds of economic efficiency (see A Schwartz (1981) 10 Journal of Legal Studies 1 for a general review; see also TH Jackson and AT Kronman (1979) 88 Yale LJ 1143). None of them is entirely convincing. Probably the best explanation for the priority given to secured creditors over other creditors is that real security makes credit accessible to many debtors who, in the absence of such security, would be unable to obtain unsecured finance. As Dr Oditah explains (F Oditah, *Legal Aspects of Receivables Financing* (1991), p 18):

> . . . the law recognises and gives effect to the priority of secured creditors because security makes available funds which may otherwise be employed elsewhere, or made available only on terms which the average debtor can ill afford. This may or may not be perceived as detrimental to unsecured creditors of a common debtor, but it can scarcely be shown to be at their expense. Indeed a secured creditor has already paid for his priority through receipt of a lower return on his investment. On the other hand, unsecured creditors have already been paid for allowing this priority and they receive a higher rate of return because of their lower priority position. Since most creditors are free to select the terms on which they would lend, there is no compelling argument based on considerations of fairness for adopting one legal rule rather than the other.

Nevertheless, academic studies in the UK reveal a growing hostility towards secured credit on grounds of unfairness and inefficiency (see, eg, V Finch (1999) 62 MLR 633; and see also RJ Mokal (2002) 22 OJLS 686 for a strongly argued case that the pendulum has swung too far). Moreover, there is the potential for conflict between the interests of secured creditors and a modern corporate 'rescue culture' that seeks to assist companies in times of financial difficulty rather than allow secured creditors to scupper plans for survival through enforcement of their security (see, generally, Milman and Mond, *Security and Corporate Rescue* (1999)). The Enterprise Act 2002 reflects this rescue culture. Two of its provisions illustrate the point. First, s 250 of the Enterprise Act 2002 (inserting s 72A(1) into the Insolvency Act 1986) provides that, with certain exceptions, a floating charge holder may no longer appoint an administrative receiver over the corporate debtor's assets and thereby undermine the prospect of reorganisation of the company through administration. Secondly, s 252 of the Enterprise Act 2002 (inserting s 176A into the Insolvency Act 1986) revives a recommendation of the Cork Committee (Cmnd 8338 (1982), paras 1538 ff) that a prescribed amount of the company's 'net property' (the amount of the company's property that, but for s 176A itself, would have been available for distribution to a floating chargee) must be paid into a fund for unsecured creditors (50 per cent of the first £10,000 of the company's net property, followed by 20 per cent of the remainder, but with the overall distribution to be made from the fund capped at £600,000). The prevailing rescue culture is also manifest in the statutory reversal of *Buchler v Talbot (Re Leyland Daf)* [2004] UKHL 9, [2004] AC 298, where the House of Lords held that general liquidation expenses were not payable out of assets subject to a floating charge (see the Companies Act 2006, s 1282, inserting s 176ZA into the Insolvency Act 1986). Administration expenses were not affected by *Buchler v Talbot*, which continued to be paid out of floating charge assets, so that until that decision was reversed secured creditors had an incentive to push for liquidation rather than administration.

Whatever the strengths and weaknesses of the arguments for and against secured credit, there can be little doubt that it is here to stay, at least for the foreseeable future (M Bridge (1992) 12 OJLS 333 at 341). To abolish the system of secured credit would be futile, for, as Professors Jackson and Kronman have pointed out (op cit, p 1157), 'if the law denied debtors the power to prefer some creditors over others through a system of security agreements, a similar network of priority relationships could be expected to emerge by consensual arrangement between creditors'. The rights given to secured creditors provide a simpler and more efficient system for organising priorities than would arise out of such a complex web of priority agreements between creditors.

4. Security can be taken over both tangible and intangible property. In the past security was mainly taken over tangible property, that is land and goods. Security over tangible property remains important as is evidenced by the 2001 Convention on International Interests in Mobile Equipment governing security, retention of title, and leasing interests in aircraft, space objects, and railway rolling stock (see RM Goode [2000] LMCLQ 161). Security can also be taken over documentary intangibles such as documents of title to goods, negotiable instruments, and negotiable securities. Today, however, the greatest wealth is tied up in pure intangible property, including receivables (debts) and investment securities (eg shares and bonds) held in dematerialised form on electronic clearing and settlement systems. The ability to take security over pure intangible property is of paramount importance in the modern business world.

QUESTION

Is a secured creditor always ensured priority over other creditors on the debtor's bankruptcy or liquidation? What if two creditors hold security over the same property?

(b) Real security and security interest

In *Bristol Airport plc v Powdrill* [1990] Ch 744 at 760, Browne-Wilkinson V-C, without claiming it was comprehensive, accepted the following description of (real) security:

> Security is created where a person ('the creditor') to whom an obligation is owed by another ('the debtor') by statute or contract, in addition to the personal promise of the debtor to discharge the obligation, obtains rights exercisable against some property in which the debtor has an interest in order to enforce the discharge of the debtor's obligation to the creditor.[1]

The essential feature of real security is that it gives the holder of the security a proprietary claim over assets of the debtor (or a third party) to secure payment of a debt or other obligation. Real security means security in a *res* (or asset). It involves the *grant* to the creditor of an *interest* in one or more assets of the debtor (or a third party) to *secure* the debtor's obligations. The interest conferred may be full legal ownership or some lesser property right in the asset, but in all cases it must have been given to secure the discharge of a debt or other obligation of the debtor (or a third party) (*Re Cosslett (Contractors) Ltd* [1998] Ch 495 at 508, per Millett LJ). A creditor granted an interest in such circumstances is described as having a 'security interest' (see, generally, L Gullifer, *Goode on Legal Problems of Credit and Security* (5th edn, 2013), Ch 1).

As a consequence of the grant of his interest, the secured creditor acquires those rights which inhere in the asset and which, therefore, can be exercised against third parties generally. Such 'real' rights include the rights of pursuit and preference. However, these real rights must be distinguished from rights of pursuit and preference conferred on the creditor by agreement with the debtor (or third party) independently of the creation of any property interest in the asset. In such circumstances, the rights of pursuit and preference will only bind the parties to the particular agreement and not third parties generally (see RM Goode (1989) 15 Mon LR 361 at 363–364, replying to the contrary argument presented by DE Allan (1989) 15 Mon LR 337 at 346). However, equity blurs the distinction between rights *in* an asset (real rights) and rights *to* an asset (personal rights). Because equity treats as done that which ought to be done, most agreements to give security in an asset will be treated as proprietary in nature, ie as if the agreements were actual transfers (RM Goode (1987) 103 LQR 433 at 437–438; F Oditah (1992) 108 LQR 459 at 470).

Only four types of consensual security (ie created by agreement between the parties) give a creditor a security interest: pledge, contractual lien, mortgage, and charge (*Re Cosslett (Contractors) Ltd* [1998] Ch 495 at 508, per Millett LJ: see also L Gullifer, *Goode on Legal Problems of Credit and Security* (5th edn, 2013), paras 1–46 to 1–56; and (1989) 15 Mon LR 361 at 362; cf F Oditah, *Legal Aspects of Receivables Financing* (1991), pp 5–11; DE Allan (1989) 15 Mon LR 337 at 348). Other types of consensual security are regarded as quasi-security (see below). Furthermore, in certain circumstances real security may arise automatically by operation of law. The main category of real security arising by operation of law is the lien (other than the contractual lien). Pledges, common law liens (including contractual liens), and the principal statutory lien (the unpaid seller's lien) are all possessory securities, ie the creditor takes possession of the subject matter of the security (see below, Chapter 25). Mortgages, charges, equitable liens, and maritime liens are non-possessory securities (see below, Chapter 26).

---

[1] Of course, the property of a third party can also be made available by way of security.

(c) Quasi-security

Real security can be contrasted with quasi-security. Although quasi-security is intended to fulfil a security function, it does not give the creditor a security interest because it does not involve rights *in* an asset which bind third parties generally (RM Goode (1989) 15 Mon LR 361 at 362). Examples of such quasi-security include: contractual set-off, subordination agreements, flawed assets, and negative pledge clauses in unsecured financing (see L Gullifer, *Goode on Legal Problems of Credit and Security* (5th edn, 2013), paras 1–18 ff).

Hire-purchase agreements, conditional sale agreements, and retention of title clauses (although again fulfilling security functions) are also regarded as quasi-securities. Although in the case of these security devices the creditor does have a right in the asset, it is a right which he retains and not one which the debtor grants to him. Only real rights created by the debtor (not retained by the creditor) are regarded as rights by way of security. This distinction was established by the House of Lords in *McEntire v Crossley Bros Ltd* [1895] AC 457, and was restated by their Lordships' House in *Armour v Thyssen Edelstahlwerke AG* [1991] 2 AC 339 (on appeal from the Inner House of the Court of Session (Scotland)). In *Armour v Thyssen*, sellers claimed redelivery of steel supplied under a contract of sale containing an 'all monies' reservation of title clause. Receivers of the buyers resisted the claim arguing that the clause constituted an attempt, ineffective under Scots law, to create a right of security over corporeal movables without transfer of possession, and that the property in the steel passed to the buyers on delivery. The House of Lords upheld the seller's claim on the ground that the buyers had not created a security over the goods in favour of the seller. Lord Jauncey of Tullichettle stated that '[i]t is of the essence of a right of security that the debtor possesses in relation to the property a right which he can transfer to the creditor, which right must be retransferred to him on payment of the debt'. As the contract of sale reserved property in the seller until payment of all debts due, the buyers 'had no interest of any kind whatsoever in the particular goods . . . [and] . . . were never in a position to confer on the [sellers] any subordinate right over the steel . . .' (per Lord Keith of Kinkel). See also RM Goode (1989) 15 Mon LR 360 at 362 (who argues that if the debtor has neither an interest in the asset *nor the power to dispose of it* he cannot give it in security); cf F Oditah, *Legal Aspects of Receivables Financing* (1991), pp 5–8; and DE Allan (1989) 15 Mon LR 337 at 348–349).

(d) How is the creation of real security to be determined?

There are a number of reasons why it is important to distinguish real security from quasi-security. In general, quasi-security does not require registration under the Bills of Sale Acts 1878–1891 or under Part 25 of the Companies Act 2006 (but see also the Insolvency Act 1986, s 344: above, p 976), whereas certain types of real security (especially consensual non-possessory real security) must be registered under one or other of these statutes, or possibly under some other Act (eg as with land, shares, ships, etc). There are other reasons for making the distinction, for example where an agreement creates a security interest in law the debtor has a right to redeem and an interest in any surplus following repossession and sale by the creditor (see L Gullifer, *Goode on Legal Problems of Credit and Security* (5th edn, 2013), para 1–03). Should a functionally-based notice-filing system for security over personal property ever be introduced into the UK, many (but not all) types of quasi-security would become registrable (see Section 2(g) below for the current state of the reform process). This would eliminate one of the reasons for distinguishing real security from quasi-security but the other reasons for making the distinction would remain important (see G McCormack [2003] LMCLQ 80 at 91–92).

When determining whether real security has been created the court must identify an intention to create a security interest coupled with an agreement in a form which brings this intention into effect (RM Goode (1989) 15 Mon LR 360 at 364). It is sometimes difficult to ascertain the precise legal form of an agreement which fulfils a security function, but it is well established that the court must look at the *substance* of the transaction and not the labels the parties have chosen to give it. This is illustrated by the next case.

Welsh Development Agency v Export Finance Co Ltd
[1992] BCLC 148, Court of Appeal

See above, p 951.

NOTE

See Notes above, pp 955-958.

(e) Attachment, perfection, and priorities

The process of creating an effective security interest can be broken down into three stages: attachment, perfection, and priorities.[2] You should keep these three stages in mind when reading Chapters 25 and 26 on possessory and non-possessory security.

(i) Attachment

Attachment is the process by which a security interest is created as between the creditor and the debtor. The effect of attachment is that the security interest fastens on the asset offered as security so as to give the creditor rights *in rem* against the debtor personally, though not against third parties.[3]

In order for a security interest to attach to an asset, otherwise than by operation of law, the following conditions must be satisfied.[4]

(a) There must be an agreement to create a security interest. Leaving aside the pledge and contractual lien (see below), a valid agreement is enough to create a security interest in equity (ie a mortgage or charge) so long as the following conditions—as well as those contained in sub-paras (b) to (d) below—are fulfilled. First, the agreement must be valid and enforceable as a contract, so it must be supported by consideration and comply with any necessary formalities. Secondly, the particular requirements for recognition of a security interest by a court of equity must be fulfilled: the agreement must manifest an intention to create a present security (*Palmer v Carey* [1926] AC 703), the creditor

---

[2] This tripartite scheme is advocated by Professor Sir Roy Goode and Professor Louise Gullifer, two of the leading exponents of English security law: L Gullifer, *Goode on Legal Problems of Credit and Security* (5th edn, 2013), Ch 2; see also E McKendrick, *Goode on Commercial Law* (5th edn, 2016), Chs 23 and 24.

[3] *Goode on Legal Problems*, para 2–02; *Goode on Commercial Law*, p 694, where it is acknowledged that the term 'attachment' is derived from art 9 of the US Uniform Commercial Code.

[4] Taken from *Goode on Legal Problems*, paras 2–03 to 2–10; see also *Goode on Commercial Law*, pp 698-703.

must have advanced his money (*Rogers v Challis* (1859) 27 Beav 175), the property must be sufficiently identifiable (*Tailby v Official Receiver* (1888) 13 App Cas 523), and the conditions of attachment expressly or implicitly specified by the agreement itself must be fulfilled (so a floating charge, though a present security, will not attach until crystallisation: see below, p 1075)—but where the specified event is a mere contingency which may or may not occur then unless the contingency is simply the debtor's acquisition of an interest in the asset the agreement will not by itself be enough to create a security interest.[5]

In the case of a legal mortgage there must be actual transfer by way of security and compliance with any statutory requirements as to form (see below, p 1060) but, as Professors Goode and Gullifer note, 'these are not conditions of attachment of a security interest, merely additional steps needed to convert an equitable security into a legal security' (see L Gullifer, *Goode on Legal Problems of Credit and Security* (5th edn, 2013), para 2–04). However, a pledge requires delivery of actual or constructive possession to the creditor for attachment to take place. Possession is also essential for a contractual lien, although in this case the lienee retains possession of goods that were delivered to him for some other purpose.

(b) The asset must be identifiable as falling within the scope of the security agreement, either because it has been so identified in the agreement or because it has become identified by being later set aside and appropriated to the agreement by an unconditional act of appropriation made in accordance with the agreement. So a security interest cannot be effective if the asset which is prospectively the secured property has not been identified. In the case of security over tangible property, the process is the same as for the identification of goods which are the subject of a contract of sale (see above, p 330). In the case of security over intangible property, there is greater scope for the identification of an asset that remains part of an undivided fund. There is no need for precise identification of the asset, it is enough that it is identifiable as falling within the terms of the security agreement, for example a debtor can charge *all* his existing and future book debts (*Tailby v Official Receiver* (1888) 13 App Cas 523) or even *all* his assets (*Re Kelcey* [1899] 2 Ch 530; *Syrett v Egerton* [1957] 3 All ER 331).

(c) The debtor must have either a present interest in the asset or power to dispose of the asset as security by virtue of some exception to the *nemo dat* rule (see above, Chapter 10). The grant of security over 'future property' (see below) creates only an inchoate security interest, but when the debtor acquires an asset falling within the after-acquired property clause the security interest attaches to the asset with effect from the date of the agreement, unless the parties have agreed otherwise (as in the case of a floating charge).

(d) There must be some current obligation of the debtor to the creditor which the asset is designed to secure (although it is possible to create security to secure an obligation owed to someone other than the grantee of the security: *Re Lehman Brothers International (Europe) (In Administration)* [2012] EWHC 2997 (Ch), [2014] 2 BCLC 295 at [43] and [44]). If there is no current indebtedness, there can be no attachment. If an advance is made and then repaid, attachment ceases, though it will revive with effect from the date of the security agreement if a new advance is later made pursuant to that agreement.

---

[5] *Goode on Legal Problems*, paras 2–09 and 2–15; *Goode on Commercial Law*, p 699; but contrast T Chen-Han (2002) 2 JCLS 191.

Attachment occurs when all these conditions are satisfied and, unless otherwise agreed, takes effect retrospectively from the date of the security agreement, regardless of the order in which the conditions were fulfilled.[6]

(ii) Perfection

Perfection of a security interest involves the taking of any additional steps prescribed by law for the giving of notice of the security interest so as to bind third parties.[7] Without perfection an attached security interest will only bind the debtor, but after perfection it will also bind third parties, unless the interest is displaced by a particular priority rule.

The main methods of perfection are where there is registration of the security interest at Companies House under ss 895A ff of the Companies Act 2006 (where the interest is created by a company), or in the Bills of Sale Act register under the Bills of Sale Acts 1878–1882 (where the interest is created by a person who is not a company, which includes unincorporated businesses such as sole traders and unincorporated partnerships). Failure to register makes the security interest ineffective against other secured creditors and in the debtor's insolvency (Companies Act 2006, s 859H; Bills of Sale Act (1878) Amendment Act 1882, s 8).

Reform of the Companies Act 2006 in 2013 means that all charges (including mortgages) created by a company are now registrable (Companies Act 2006, s 859A). There are a few categories of security interests created by a company that are not registrable, including security interests which arise by operation of law (most of these being possessory liens, but the category also includes non-possessory equitable liens), security interests which are security financial collateral arrangements within the meaning of reg 3 of the Financial Collateral Arrangements (No 2) Regulations 2003 (SI 2003/3226, as amended) (where the security taker must have possession or control over the financial collateral), and security interests where the holder is in actual or constructive possession of the asset, as with pledges or liens. In such cases there is no general requirement for perfection of the security interest.[8] On the other hand, where a security interest is taken over a debt or interest in a fund, the giving of notice to the debtor or fundholder could be said to be a form of public notice and, therefore, a means of perfection (see above, Chapters 22 and 23). But notice to the debtor or fundholder does not dispense with any requirement to register, unless the security interest falls within the Financial Collateral Arrangements (No 2) Regulations 2003, or is otherwise exempt from registration.

(iii) Priorities

Priority rules declare the ranking of the security interest in relation to rival claims over the debtor's assets.[9] These rules have evolved at common law and in equity, and will apply unless restricted by statute. They apply equally to tangible and intangible property. The most important priority rules have been summarised by Professor Goode as follows:[10]

> (a) a person cannot in general transfer a better title than he himself possesses, so that, in general, priority among competing interests is determined by the order of their creation; but
> (b) a legal estate or interest is preferred to an equitable interest; accordingly,

---

[6] *Goode on Legal Problems*, para 2–11; *Goode on Commercial Law*, p 698.
[7] *Goode on Legal Problems*, para 2–16; *Goode on Commercial Law*, p 694.
[8] *Goode on Legal Problems*, para 2–16.
[9] *Goode on Commercial Law*, p 694.
[10] *Goode on Commercial Law*, pp 724-726 (footnotes omitted). See also *Goode on Legal Problems*, Ch 5.

(c) while as between competing equitable interests the first in time prevails, if the holder of the second interest, having advanced his money without notice of the first, gets in the legal title, he obtains priority;

(d) the priority of successive assignees of a debt or other chose in action is determined by the order in which the assignments are made except that an assignee who takes without prior notice of an earlier assignment and is the first to give notice of assignment to the debtor has priority over the earlier assignee;

(e) both legal and equitable interests acquired for value and without notice prevail over mere equities; and

(f) one whose interest derives from the holder of an indefeasible title can shelter behind that title, even if taking with notice of an earlier title or if taking otherwise than for value, unless he committed or assisted in the wrongdoing by which that earlier title was lost.

These principles are supplemented by the following subsidiary, but nonetheless important, rules:

(1) Even the holder of a legal estate or interest will lose his priority where:
  (a) he has connived at or participated in a fraud as the result of which the later interest was acquired without notice of the prior legal title; or
  (b) he has held out the debtor, or permitted the debtor to hold himself out, as the unencumbered owner of the asset or as authorized to deal with it free from the security interest; or
  (c) he has by his gross negligence in failing to obtain or, possibly, to retain, the title deeds enabled the debtor to deal with the asset as if it were not encumbered by the security interest.

(2) The holder of a floating charge is postponed to the grantee of a subsequent fixed charge unless this is taken with notice of a negative pledge clause in the floating charge.

(3) Normal priority rules may be displaced by agreement between the competing interests. So a first mortgagee may agree to have his interest subordinated to that of the second mortgagee. Such subordination agreements are not uncommon and do not require the consent of the debtor.

(4) There are special rules governing the ability of a secured party, after the grant of a subsequent encumbrance, to tack advances or further advances ranking in priority to the later encumbrances.

(5) Discharge of a security interest automatically promotes junior security interests. So if Blackacre is mortgaged in first to A, then to B, then to C, and the mortgage in favour of A is discharged, B becomes the first mortgagee, C the second mortgagee.

(f) Security over future property

Future property is property which does not exist or in which the debtor has no proprietary interest at the time of giving the security. It must not be confused with *potential* property which is to grow out of an asset in which the debtor has an interest at the time of giving the security, for example milk from a cow or sums payable in the future under an existing building contract.[11]

---

[11] *Goode on Commercial Law*, pp 701-702.

Potential property is regarded as existing (not future) property (see above, p 701). The grant of security over the potential property is treated as the present assignment of existing property, although the security cannot be asserted until the potential property actually comes into existence.

The common law has long set itself against the idea that an agreement to give security over future property could create proprietary rights. So far as the common law is concerned, there must be a new act of transfer, after acquisition of the property by the debtor, for proprietary rights to vest in the creditor. The position is different in equity, which treats as done that which ought to be done. There, so long as the prerequisites for the recognition of a security interest by a court of equity have been satisfied (as to which, see above, p 1016), an agreement to give security over future property is treated as a present, but inchoate, security which fastens on the property as soon as it is acquired by the debtor without the need for a new act of transfer (see the landmark decision of the House of Lords in *Holroyd v Marshall* (1862) 10 HL Cas 191, above p 960, as interpreted by their Lordships' House in *Tailby v Official Receiver* (1888) 13 App Cas 523, above p 961). Attachment of the security interest takes effect retrospectively relating back to the time of the security agreement (*Tailby v Offical Receiver*, above; *Re Lind* [1915] 2 Ch 345), unless the parties have agreed otherwise (so crystallisation of a floating charge is not retrospective).

(g) Reform

The law regulates transactions according to their legal form rather than their economic substance or function. Real security and quasi-security fulfil the same security function but they are regulated differently because of their form. The problems which the 'form over substance' approach can lead to are highlighted by Professor Diamond in the following extract from his report.

A Review of Security Interests in Property by Professor AL Diamond
(1989), paras 8.2.1–8.2.11

> ### 8.2 DEFECTS IN THE PRESENT LAW
>
> 8.2.1 *(a) Obstacles to security.* Having concluded that legal obstacles to the creation of security interests where both parties are contracting in the course of a business should be kept to the minimum necessary, how far does the present law reflect this policy? In England and Wales I can sum up the present position as being one where a security interest can be taken in almost anything, provided an appropriate method is used, but that it is not always clear what the most appropriate method is. . . .
>
> 8.2.3 For reasons I am coming to, I think English law is in urgent need of reform . . .
>
> 8.2.4 *(b) The law lacks a functional basis.* The English law of security is divided into rigid compartments, making the law fragmented and incoherent. Transactions essentially similar in nature are treated in very different ways. This has the effect of complicating the legal issues quite unnecessarily . . .
>
> 8.2.5 This can cause problems when an attempt is made to create a security interest, for a method must be chosen appropriate to the property concerned and the effect that is desired. There are, for example, many cases in the law reports where the parties adopted the form of a sale followed by a hire-purchase agreement only to find that, perhaps for reasons of timing, perhaps

for other reasons, it totally failed to take effect—in England and Wales because the Bills of Sale Acts had not been complied with . . .

8.2.6 It can also cause problems at the stage of enforcement, for different forms of security interest may have very different consequences. In England and Wales the difference between the equitable rules governing mortgages and the common law or statutory rules governing hire-purchase agreements, for example, can be striking. If goods subject to a mortgage or charge are seized and sold, and fetch more than the amount owed by the debtor to repay the loan with interest and costs, the excess belongs to the debtor. If the goods were subject to a hire-purchase agreement, however, the creditor can keep the excess.

8.2.7 *(c) Complexity.* The compartmentalisation of the law just referred to inevitably gives rise to a law that is complex and uncertain. In England and Wales the old division between common law and equity, parallel systems administered in separate courts before 1876, still looms large in the field of security law. For example, an innocent purchaser, who buys goods not knowing of any security interest in them, may be in a radically different position according to whether the security interest of which he is unaware was equitable or legal. In a case concerning charterparties (*Re Welsh Irish Ferries Ltd* [1986] Ch 471) the judge had to consider whether a contractual 'lien' was a charge registrable under the Companies Act and for this purpose had to explore the effect in equity of a non-statutory assignment of contractual rights. (See too *The Annangel Glory* [1988] 1 Lloyd's Rep 45.)

8.2.8 The complexity of the law leads to difficulty, and perfectly legitimate business activities are in consequence attended with unnecessary expense and delay. The complications may be disastrous for a party who gets it wrong. What should and could be a routine business activity may involve complicated documentation or uncertainty. Particularly difficult are the rules relating to the secured creditor's right to the proceeds of the subject matter of the security if it is sold.

8.2.9 Because issues are decided by reference to rules that evolved for different purposes, the law is capable of acting unfairly and may fail to hold a just balance as between the parties. In some cases creditors have found that they lose the protection that they intended to obtain, and sometimes debtors are harshly treated because of the failure of the law to recognise their true position as a party who has given security. Although any legal rule is capable of producing the wrong result in a particular fact situation, the present law is notably defective. The rules vary widely according to distinctions which have no commercial or rational significance.

8.2.10 *(d) Priorities.* Because there are so many different ways of achieving similar economic ends, it is difficult to reconcile competing interests. This causes problems in determining priorities and leads to fortuitous differences in insolvency. There is no logical plan for ranking conflicting claims, . . . The uncertainty of the effect of some clauses in contracts for the sale of goods seeking to retain title can make it difficult for a receiver or liquidator to discover what are in effect security interests.

8.2.11 *(e) Purchasers.* Particularly unfortunate is that the effect of security interests on purchasers may be difficult to ascertain. I have already referred to the effect of the differences between legal and equitable rules in the law of England and Wales. In addition, there is inadequate protection for the purchaser of property subject to a security interest of which he was unaware, and perhaps could not discover. Such purchasers are put at risk and inadequately protected by the law. It may even be difficult for them to secure speedy legal advice because of the fragmentation of the law and the varieties of security interest that are possible.

NOTE

These criticisms of the current law led Professor Diamond (in Part II of his Report) to recommend the introduction of a functionally-based electronic notice-filing system which would apply to all types of consensual security interests. The new system was to be based closely on art 9 of the US Uniform Commercial Code (revised in 2001) and the Personal Property Security Acts introduced in several Canadian provinces. New Zealand, Australia, and even Jersey have introduced similar reforms. Under these proposals the term 'security interests' was to be given a functional definition so as to catch both real security, such as mortgages and charges, and also quasi-security, such as retention of title devices. The new notice-filing system was to replace the bills of sale registers and the registration of charges under the Companies Act. The date of filing a 'financing statement' (with minimum particulars) would be the relevant date for determining the priority of competing security interests (but not for possessory security interests). The first to file would win the priority race. Under this system it would even be possible to file an entry before the security interest was actually created so that, for example, a financing statement could be filed in the course of negotiations for a loan.

Professor Diamond was not the first to call for reform of English personal property security law. Similar proposals were made in Part 5 of the Report of the Crowther Committee on Consumer Credit (Cmnd 4596, 1971) and later endorsed by the Cork Committee in its review of insolvency law and practice (Cmnd 8558, 1982). Professor Sir Roy Goode advocated reform of personal property security law as part of his proposals for an English Commercial Code to parallel the Uniform Commercial Code of the United States (see his Fullagar Memorial Lecture, reprinted in (1988) 14 Mon LR 135). None of these proposals generated sufficient government interest to get them onto the statute book. However, in 1998 the Secretary of State for Trade and Industry launched a wide-ranging and fundamental review of company law. This led to the Company Law Review Steering Group publishing a Final Report in 2001 which recommended the adoption of a notice-filing system for company charges. However, as the Steering Group had not had time to consult over the details, it recommended that the matter be referred to the Law Commission. As an alternative to its proposal for notice-filing, the Steering Group recommended a number of changes to the existing registration system.

The Law Commission published a first consultation paper (LC CP No 164) in 2002. This provisionally proposed a notice-filing system for company charges (defined to include mortgages), with associated priority rules, and explained how the scheme might be extended to apply also to quasi-security interests, including retention of title devices and outright sales of receivables. The responses to the consultation paper were mixed and more detail was called for. The Law Commission then published a consultative report (LC CP No 176) in 2004, which provisionally proposed a scheme based on the Saskatchewan Personal Property Security Act 1993, together with certain elements of art 9 of the revised Uniform Commercial Code. The proposal proved controversial. The Financial Law Committee of the City of London Law Society, amongst others, was particularly concerned that the Law Commission's provisional proposal to register and recharacterise quasi-security would make the law less flexible and more complex than it is at present, would create greater uncertainty, would provide less information to those dealing with companies, and would place unnecessary restraints on freedom of contract in business transactions, as well as being costly to implement (see R Calnan, 'The Reform of Company Security Interests' [2005] JIBFL 25). This resulted in the Law Commission's Final Report (LC Report No 296) being far less radical. In its Final Report, the Law Commission recommended that an electronic notice-filing system (and associated priority rules) be introduced for company charges and the outright sale of receivables, but that it should not be applied to quasi-security without further study. Furthermore, the Law Commission thought that further work was necessary before even its limited recommendations could be extended to charges created by unincorporated business debtors.

In July 2005 the Department of Trade and Industry published a consultation document based on the Law Commission's proposals. The responses to that consultation showed there was a lack of consensus of support for the Law Commission's proposals. The demands of parliamentary time meant that the Companies Act 2006 contained no major reform of the law on company charges. Part 25 of the 2006 Act (as originally enacted) reproduced the substance of Part XII of the Companies Act 1985.

In 2010, the Department for Business, Innovation and Skills (BIS) started a consultation process regarding more widespread reform of the registration process. Eventually, new regulations were brought into force that apply to all company charges created after 6 April 2013 (the Companies Act 2006 (Amendment of Part 25) Regulations 2013 (SI 2013/600), inserting ss 859A–859Q into the Companies Act 2006). The new regime introduced three main reforms: (1) it replaced the previous list of registrable interests with a provision making all charges registrable, with limited exceptions; (2) it changed the registration system from a mandatory one (which was backed by criminal sanctions) to one which is optional and registration lies at the discretion of the company; and (3) it provided for a new scheme enabling registration to be done electronically. But the 2013 reforms did not introduce a functionally-based electronic notice-filing system which would apply to all types of consensual security interests.

Proposals for secured transaction law reform continue to be made: compare and contrast those made by the Secured Transactions Law Reform Project, set up by Professor Sir Roy Goode (http://securedtransactionslawreformproject.org), with those of the City of London Law Society Secured Transaction Reform Project, chaired by Richard Calnan (http://www.citysolicitors.org.uk/attachments/article/121/Secured%20Transactions%20Code%20-%20Discussion%20draft.pdf). See generally, H Beale, M Bridge, L Gullifer, and E Lomnicka, *The Law of Security and Title-Based Financing* (2nd edn, 2012), Ch 23; J de Lacy (ed), *The Reform of UK Personal Property Security Law: Comparative Perspectives* (2010). The Law Commission published a consultation paper in September 2015 proposing abolition of the Bills of Sale Acts regime and its replacement with a universal scheme of 'goods mortgages', with special rules for vehicles and a revised regime for book debt loans (LC CP No 225). A final Law Commission report on Bills of Sale (No 369) was published on 12 September 2016.

Three international initiatives stand out. First, in 1994, the European Bank for Reconstruction and Development (EBRD) published a Model Law on Secured Transactions. The EBRD Model Law has been partially adopted in a number of states in Eastern Europe. Secondly, the Cape Town Convention on International Interests in Mobile Equipment 2001 entered into force on 1 April 2004. The Convention applies to security interests in airframes, aircraft engines, helicopters, railway rolling stock, and space assets, as designated in the relevant Protocol. The UK ratified the Convention and the Aircraft Protocol in 2015. Thirdly, on 1 July 2016, UNCITRAL adopted a new model law on secured transactions. The model law is based on UNCITRAL's Legislative Guide on Secured Transactions (2007) and its Supplement on Security Rights in Intellectual Property (2010). Successful completion of the UNCITRAL project may accelerate reform of English secured transactions law.

CHAPTER 25

POSSESSORY SECURITY

1 PLEDGE

(a) What is a pledge?

Coggs v Bernard
(1703) 2 Ld Raym 909, Court of King's Bench

Holt CJ (describing various types of bailment): The fourth sort is, when goods or chattels are delivered to another as a pawn, to be a security to him for money borrowed of him by the bailor; and this is called in Latin *vadium*, and in English a pawn or a pledge . . .

As to the fourth sort of bailment, viz *vadium* or a pawn, in this I shall consider two things; first, what property the pawnee has in the pawn or pledge, and secondly for what neglects he shall make satisfaction. As to the first, he has a special property, for the pawn is a securing to the pawnee, that he shall be repaid his debt, and to compel the pawner to pay him. But if the pawn be such as it will be the worse for using, the pawnee cannot use it, as cloaths, etc but if it be such, as will be never the worse, as if jewels for the purpose were pawn'd to a lady, she might use them. But then she must do it at her peril, for whereas, if she keeps them lock'd up in her cabinet, if her cabinet should be broke open, and the jewels taken from thence, she would be excused; if she wears them abroad, and is there robb'd of them, she will be answerable. And the reason is, because the pawn is in the nature of a deposit, and as such is not liable to be used. And to this effect is Ow 123. But if the pawn be of such a nature, as the pawnee is at any charge about the thing pawn'd, to maintain it, as a horse, cow, etc then the pawnee may use the horse in a reasonable manner, or milk the cow, etc in recompense for the meat. As to the second point Bracton 99 b gives you the answer. *Creditor, qui pignus accepit, re obligatur, et ad illam restituendam tenetur; et cum hujusmodi res in pignus data sit utriusque gratia, scilicet debitoris, quo magis ei pecunia crederetur, et creditoris quo magis ei in tuto sit creditum, sufficit ad ejus rei custodiam diligentiam exactam adhibere, quam si praestiterit, et rem casu amiserit, securus esse possit, nee impedietur creditum petere.* In effect, if a creditor takes a pawn, he is bound to restore it upon the payment of the debt; but yet it is sufficient, if the pawnee use true diligence, and he will be indemnified in so doing, and notwithstanding the loss, yet he shall resort to the pawnor for his debt. Agreeable to this is 29 Ass 28, and *Southcote's* case is. But indeed the reason given in *Southcote's* case is, because the pawnee has a special property in the pawn. But that is not the reason of the case; and there is another reason given for it in the Book of Assize, which is indeed the true reason of all these cases, that the law requires nothing extraordinary of the pawnee, but only that he shall use an ordinary care for restoring the goods.

But indeed, if the money for which the goods were pawn'd, be tender'd to the pawnee before they are lost, then the pawnee shall be answerable for them; because the pawnee, by detaining them after the tender of the money, is a wrong doer, and it is a wrongful detainer of the goods, and the special property of the pawnee is determined. And a man that keeps goods by wrong, must be answerable for them at all events, for the detaining of them by him, is the reason of the loss. Upon the same difference as the law is in relation to pawns, it will be found to stand in relation to goods found.

Halliday v Holgate
(1868) LR 3 Exch 299, Exchequer Chamber

Willes J: . . . There are three kinds of security: the first, a simple lien; the second, a mortgage, passing the property out and out; the third, a security intermediate between a lien and a mortgage— viz, a pledge—where by contract a deposit of goods is made a security for a debt, and the right to the property vests in the pledgee so far as is necessary to secure the debt. It is true the pledgor has such a property in the article pledged as he can convey to a third person, but he has no right to the goods without paying off the debt, and until the debt is paid off the pledgee has the whole present interest.

NOTES

1. The essential characteristics of a pledge are that: (a) it is created by contract; (b) possession of the property pledged (or of documents of title thereto) must be delivered (actually or constructively) to the pledgee; (c) the pledgor has a right of redemption on discharge of the debt or obligation secured—the pledgee has no right of foreclosure; and (d) the pledgee is given a 'special property' in the subject matter of the pledge, including a power of sale at common law, which he can assign or sub-pledge. Usually, a pledge secures repayment of a debt but, in principle, there is no reason why it should not secure the performance by the pledgor of some other obligation.

2. Although the pledgee is given special property in the goods pledged, he does not become the general owner of the goods. This led Lord Mersey in *The Odessa* [1916] 1 AC 145 at 158–159, to question whether it was appropriate to describe the pledgee's 'interest' in the goods as a form of property at all. However, even if the pledgee is described as having merely 'a special interest' in the pledged goods, it is, nevertheless, an interest of proprietary significance. As Professor NE Palmer has observed in his treatise on bailment (*Bailment* (3rd edn, 2009), para 22–004):

The pledgee, eg, has an inherent right of sale; and the interests distributed by the pledge (to wit, the pledgor's reversion and the pledgee's special property) are capable of surviving both a sale of the chattel by the pledgor, and its repledge by the pledgee, respectively. Further, in common with other varieties of bailment, the pledgee's possession entitles him to exercise the proprietary and possessory remedies against a third party wrongdoer, and to recover at common law damages calculated according to the full value of the goods (or the full cost of their depreciation) as if he were the owner.

In *Mathew v TM Sutton Ltd* [1994] 4 All ER 793, Chadwick J held that, in view of the nature of a pledge, a pledgee who sells unredeemed chattels for more than the sum owed by the pledgor holds the surplus as a fiduciary on trust for the pledgor. The judgment implies that the fiduciary relationship existed from the time of the original delivery. It seems to follow from this decision that the pledgee would also hold any surplus as a fiduciary on trust for the pledgor: (a) where he sues a third party wrongdoer and recovers, by virtue of his possessory title, a sum greater than the amount secured by the pledge; and (b) where he insures the goods for their full value and recovers from the insurer an amount greater than the secured debt (see All ER Annual Review 1994, pp 26–28).

3. At common law, the terms 'pledge' and 'pawn' were used interchangeably, although the pledge of a bill of lading was never described as a 'pawn' (*Halsbury's Laws of England* (5th edn, 2011 reissue), Vol 4, para 189, n 1). Under the Pawnbrokers Acts 1872–1960 (now repealed), the term 'pledge' referred to the goods and 'pawn' to the act of delivery or receipt of the goods. Under s 189(1) of the Consumer Credit Act 1974, the term 'pawn' means any article subject to a pledge and 'pledge' means the pawnee's rights over an article taken in pawn. The 'pawnee' is the recipient of the goods and the 'pawnor' is the person who delivered them to the pawnee.

(b) Delivery

Official Assignee of Madras v Mercantile Bank of India Ltd
[1935] AC 53, Privy Council

A firm of merchants (the merchants) purchased groundnuts and transported them to Madras by rail. For each consignment of groundnuts the merchants obtained a railway receipt from the railway companies. The receipt entitled the named consignee, or indorsee, to obtain delivery of the groundnuts from the railway companies. The merchants then raised loans against the consignments by sending, inter alia, the railway receipts, duly indorsed in blank, to the respondent bank. On the insolvency of the merchants, the Official Assignee of Madras, in whom their property vested by reason of the insolvency, disputed whether the bank had taken a valid pledge of the groundnuts. The issue before the Privy Council was whether the pledging of railway receipts was a pledge of the goods represented by them or merely a pledge of the actual documents. The Privy Council held that under the relevant Indian legislation the railway receipts were documents of title to the goods and that the owner of the goods could pledge the goods by pledging the documents of title. The Privy Council affirmed the judgment of the High Court of Madras in favour of the bank. But the Privy Council also emphasised that if the case had been governed by English law the result would have been different.

> **Lord Wright** (delivering the advice of the Privy Council): But the arguments advanced on behalf of the appellant have sought to treat the matter as concluded by the history and present state of the relevant law in England, which will now be briefly summarized. At the common law a pledge could not be created except by a delivery of possession of the thing pledged, either actual or constructive. It involved a bailment. If the pledgor had the actual goods in his physical possession, he could effect the pledge by actual delivery; in other cases he could give possession by some symbolic act, such as handing over the key of the store in which they were. If, however, the goods were in the custody of a third person, who held for the bailor

so that in law his possession was that of the bailor, the pledge could be effected by a change of the possession of the third party, that is by an order to him from the pledgor to hold for the pledgee, the change being perfected by the third party attorning to the pledgee, that is acknowledging that he thereupon held for him; there was thus a change of possession and a constructive delivery: the goods in the hands of the third party became by this process in the possession constructively of the pledgee. But where goods were represented by documents the transfer of the documents did not change the possession of the goods, save for one exception, unless the custodier (carrier, warehouseman or such) was notified of the transfer and agreed to hold in future as bailee for the pledgee. The one exception was the case of bills of lading, the transfer of which by the law merchant operated as a transfer of the possession of, as well as the property in, the goods. This exception has been explained on the ground that the goods being at sea the master could not be notified; the true explanation may be that it was a rule of the law merchant, developed in order to facilitate mercantile transactions, whereas the process of pledging goods on land was regulated by the narrower rule of the common law and the matter remained stereotyped in the form which it had taken before the importance of documents of title in mercantile transactions was realized. So things have remained in the English law: a pledge of documents is not in general to be deemed a pledge of the goods; a pledge of the documents (always excepting a bill of lading) is merely a pledge of the ipsa corpora of them; the common law continued to regard them as merely tokens of an authority to receive possession. . . .

The common law rule was stated by the House of Lords in *William McEwan & Sons v Smith* ((1849) 2 HL Cas 309). The position of the English law has been fully explained also more recently in *Inglis v Robertson* ([1898] AC 616) and in *Dublin City Distillery Ltd v Doherty* ([1914] AC 823). But there also grew up that legislation which is compendiously described as the Factors Acts, the first in 1823, then an Act in 1825, then an Act in 1842, then an Act in 1877, and finally, the Act in 1889 now in force. The purpose of these Acts was to protect bankers who made advances to mercantile agents: that purpose was effected by means of an inroad on the common law rule that no one could give a better title to goods than he himself had. The persons to whom the Acts applied were defined as agents who had in the customary course of their business as such authority to sell goods or to consign goods for sale or raise money on the security of goods; in the case of such persons thus intrusted with possession of the goods or the documents of title to the goods, the possession of the goods or documents of title to the goods was treated in effect as evidence of a right to pledge them, so that parties bona fide and without notice of any irregularity advancing money to such mercantile agents on the goods or documents were held entitled to a good pledge, even though such mercantile agents were acting in fraud of the true owner. Section 3 of the Factors Act 1889, provides that 'a pledge of [the] document[s] of title to goods shall be deemed to be a pledge of the goods.' It has been held that this section only applies to transactions within the Factors Act: *Inglis v Robertson*.

Thus the curious and anomalous position was established that a mercantile agent, acting it may be in fraud of the true owner, can do that which the real owner cannot do, that is, obtain a loan on the security of a pledge of the goods by a pledge of the documents, without the further process being necessary of giving notice of the pledge to the warehouseman or other custodier and obtaining the latter's attornment to the change of possession. But it is obvious that the ordinary process of financing transactions in goods is much facilitated by ability to pledge the goods by the simple process of pledging the documents of title. It need not be repeated that bills of lading stand apart, nor need it be observed here that some warehousing companies have, by means of private Acts, assimilated their warrants or delivery orders to bills of lading for this purpose.

NOTES

1. As delivery of possession lies at the heart of a pledge, only chattels which are capable of actual, constructive, or symbolic delivery can be pledged. Intangible property, such as information, cannot be pledged (see, for analogous reasoning, *Your Response Ltd v Datateam Business Media Ltd* [2014] EWCA Civ 281, [2015] QB 41 at [15]–[16] and [23], where the Court of Appeal refused to allow a common law possessory lien to be taken over an electronic database on the ground that it is not possible to take possession, ie physical control, of intangible property (see further below, p 1041); see also N Palmer and A Hudson, 'Pledge' in N Palmer and E McKendrick (eds), *Interests in Goods* (2nd edn, 1998), p 635). This means, for example, that bearer bonds (negotiable instruments) may be pledged (*Carter v Wake* (1877) 4 Ch D 605) but not the choses in action (the shares) represented by share certificates (*Harrold v Plenty* [1901] 2 Ch 314). For reasons of public policy, certain other chattels may not be pledged, for example firearms, ammunition, military, naval, and airforce equipment, equipment issued to those in the territorial army reserve or Royal Auxiliary Air Force, and Social Security cards, or used stamps therefor. In each case the prohibition arises under statute.

2. Delivery by means of the pledge of a bill of lading amounts to a pledge of the goods themselves so long as the goods are identified in the bill of lading (see Note 4 below). The bill of lading is the only document recognised by the common law as a document of title to goods (see, generally, R Aikens, R Lord, and M Bools, *Bills of Lading* (2nd edn, 2015); S Dromgoole and Y Baatz, 'The Bill of Lading as a Document of Title' in N Palmer and E McKendrick (eds), *Interests in Goods* (2nd edn, 1998), Ch 22). Documents other than bills of lading may be recognised as documents of title to goods at common law by local mercantile custom. A pledge of other documents relating to goods (not being documents of title at common law) operates as a pledge only of the documents themselves and not the actual goods. This includes documents which are documents of title under s 1(4) of the Factors Act 1889, such as delivery orders, delivery warrants, and warehouse receipts. However, where a mercantile agent (but not others) pledges such a document of title, the pledge of the document of title is deemed to be a pledge of the goods (Factors Act 1889, s 3, as interpreted by the House of Lords in *Inglis v Robertson* [1898] AC 616). See H Beale, M Bridge, L Gullifer, and E Lomnicka, *The Law of Security and Title-Based Financing* (2nd edn, 2012), para 5.34.

3. In *Meyerstein v Barber* ((1866) LR 2 CP 38; affirmed sub nom *Barber v Meyerstein* (1870) LR 4 HL 317) it was argued that delivery of an exhausted bill of lading (as to which, see AH Hudson (1963) 26 MLR 442) only operated as an *agreement* to pledge goods and not as an actual pledge effected by the symbolic delivery of the goods themselves. The Court of Common Pleas held that the bill of lading was not exhausted and so delivery of the goods represented by the document had been made to complete the pledge. However, Willes J stated *obiter* that: '. . . a mere contract to pledge even specific goods, and even if money is actually advanced upon the faith of the contract, is not sufficient to carry the legal property in the goods ... such a transaction amounts only to an authority to take possession of the goods . . .'. By contrast, in *Hilton v Tucker* (1888) 39 Ch D 669, where money was lent pursuant to an agreement that the borrower would deliver certain goods into the lender's possession but the goods were not delivered until a month after the loan had been made, Kekewich J held that with a pledge of goods it was not essential that the loan and delivery of possession should be contemporaneous. His Lordship held that it was

enough if possession was delivered within a reasonable time of the loan in pursuance of the contract to pledge. But if delivery does not take place, Willes J's dictum in *Meyerstein v Barber* would apply.

4. In *Official Assignee of Madras v Mercantile Bank of India Ltd*, Lord Wright stated that there would be constructive delivery of goods held by a third person on behalf of the pledgor if that third person attorned to the pledgee. Constructive delivery will also take place when the goods are in the possession of the pledgor and he contracts to continue to hold them as bailee for the pledgee and not on his own account as owner (*Meyerstein v Barber* (1866) LR 2 CP 38 at 52, per Willes J). In *Dublin City Distillery Ltd v Doherty* [1914] AC 823 at 852, Lord Parker of Waddington stated that the pledgor's agreement to hold the goods on behalf of the pledgee '. . . operates as a delivery of the goods to the pledgee and a redelivery of the goods by the pledgee to the pledger [sic] as bailee for the purposes mentioned in the agreement'. The delivery/redelivery theory can also be used to explain what happens when a third person attorns to the pledgee. But the theory only works if specific goods are pledged. If the goods are part of an undivided bulk, then according to Hope JA in *Maynegrain Pty Ltd v Compafina Bank* [1982] 2 NSWLR 141 at 149 (reversed on another ground (1984) 58 ALJR 389, PC):

> . . . an attornment in respect of an undifferentiated portion of a larger quantity of goods does not operate as a delivery of some severed portion of the goods and a redelivery of that portion to the attornor; it operates as if such a delivery and redelivery had been effected, the attornor being estopped from denying the necessary severance and appropriation by virtue of the attornment itself, and no doubt in many cases because the attornee has acted to his prejudice on the basis of the attornment. It is, however, irrelevant that the attornee knows that in fact no severance or appropriation has taken place.

The difference between a pledge effected by a true attornment and one arising through an estoppel is that the former gives the pledgee proprietary rights whereas the latter only gives him personal ones (and does not really constitute a pledge at all). The distinction is of vital importance where third party rights are involved. In *Re London Wine Co (Shippers) Ltd* [1986] PCC 121, a sale of goods case where no property passed, an estoppel argument was raised by the pledgees of various buyers to defeat a bank with a floating charge over the seller's assets. Oliver J held that the buyers obtained no 'title by estoppel' and so there were no proprietary rights that they could pass on themselves to the pledgees. The same principle applies to the 'pledge' of a bill of lading which relates to unascertained goods forming part of a bulk. The pledgee cannot acquire constructive (or symbolic) possession of the goods, or obtain proprietary rights thereto, as the goods are not identified: the 'pledge' only operates as an estoppel against the carrier. However, since the enactment of the Sale of Goods (Amendment) Act 1995, introducing ss 20A and 20B into the Sale of Goods Act 1979, the situation may be different as regards the pledge of a bill of lading by a prepaying buyer of goods forming part of a bulk. The 1995 Act gives the prepaying buyer a proprietary interest in an undivided share of the bulk and, although the point is not specifically addressed in the Act, there seem to be no good policy reasons for denying the proprietary effect of a pledge of that interest (see L Gullifer [1999] LMCLQ 93 at 102–104; cf N Palmer and A Hudson, 'Pledge' in N Palmer and E McKendrick (eds), *Interests in Goods* (2nd edn, 1998), p 625). Further legislation is probably required to clarify the issue.

Wrightson v McArthur and Hutchisons (1919) Ltd
[1921] 2 KB 807, King's Bench Division

In consideration of the plaintiff allowing the first defendant more time to pay for goods, the second defendant (the company) set aside certain specified goods in two rooms on its premises which were locked up and the keys handed to the plaintiff, no other goods being in those rooms. In a subsequent letter to the plaintiff, the company stated that: 'The goods to be locked up, the keys in your possession, and you to have the right to remove same as desired.' On the company's liquidation, an issue arose as to whether the letter evidenced a charge. If so, the security, being unregistered, was void against the liquidator. On the other hand, if the security was a pledge completed by delivery of possession of the goods without reference to the letter, then it was valid as not requiring registration (see below, p 1040). Rowlatt J upheld the validity of the security.

> **Rowlatt J:** The point to which this case is now reduced is whether the circumstance that the rooms, the keys of which were delivered, were within the defendants' premises, prevents the delivery of the keys conferring possession of the contents of the rooms. If the keys delivered had been the outside key of the whole warehouse containing these goods I should have felt no difficulty, nor should I have felt any difficulty had the key been of an apartment or receptacle in the premises of a third party as was the case in *Hilton v Tucker* ((1888) 39 Ch D 669). On the other hand if, the rooms being in the defendants' premises, the keys had been given without the licence to go and remove the goods at any time I should have thought it clear that possession of the goods did not pass. It would be merely a case of the goods remaining in the defendants' possession with the security that they should not be interfered with, but without any power of affirmative control at the free will of the plaintiff. It would be like the case of furniture left in a locked room in a house that is let furnished, where the lessor has no right to enter except upon reasonable notice and at reasonable times. The actual question has to be considered in the light of the principle that delivery of a key has effect not as symbolic delivery, but as giving the actual control. This was the view expressed by Lord Hardwicke in *Ward v Turner* ((1752) 2 Ves Sen 431), where he says the key is the means of coming at the possession. The matter was fully discussed in the light of all the cases in *Pollock and Wright on Possession in the Common Law*, p 61 and following pages. In *Hilton v Tucker*, already referred to, in a judgment delivered since the date of that work, Kekewich J observes 'that the delivery of the key in order to make constructive possession must be under such circumstances that it really does pass the full control of the place to which admission is to be gained by means of the key.' If I might criticise that statement my criticism would only be as to the propriety of the use of the word 'constructive' in the connection in question.
>
> I think therefore there can be no doubt as to the true principle, and the difficulty is in its application. There are two cases in which delivery of the key of a box in a house has been held to confer possession of the contents. The first was *Jones v Selby* ((1710) Prec Ch 300), referred to by Lord Hardwicke in *Ward v Turner* above mentioned, the other was *Mustapha v Wedlake* ([1891] WN 201), but in both those cases both parties were living in the house and therefore the person receiving the delivery could not be expected to take away the box, but could hold possession of it in the house. It has never been held, so far as I know, that delivery of the key of a box which the deliverer retains in his own house, where the other party does not live, passes possession of the contents. Upon the whole, however, I think that in the case before me the possession was transferred, having regard to the fact that a licence to come and make the necessary entry to use the key was also conferred, a licence which it seems to me could not be revoked. The door into the building would be open in business hours, and the mere fact that the plaintiff might wrongfully be excluded from

the whole building does not, I think, affect the matter. If the key had been given him with the intention to pass to him the possession of the room itself upon a demise of it, I cannot doubt that possession would pass. I see no difference when the key is given to pass possession not of the room, but of the chattels. The key guards both in the same way.

NOTES

1. In *Hilton v Tucker* (1888) 39 Ch D 669, pursuant to an agreement with the pledgee, the pledgor hired a room in a building belonging to a third party and stored certain prints and engravings there. The pledgor then wrote to the pledgee informing him that the third party held the key to the room 'which I place entirely at your disposal'. Kekewich J held that the prints and engravings had been constructively delivered to the pledgee even though the pledgor continued to have access to the room (via a duplicate key). Although the pledgee must usually be given exclusive control of the pledged chattels, Kekewich J stressed that in this case the 'laxity in the control of the room' was irrelevant as the pledgor had only a limited right of access (to clean the room and list the chattels) and at all times had acknowledged that his right was subject to the pledgee's paramount control. The issue appears to turn on whether the deliveror really intends to relinquish possession of the chattels to the deliveree. It should also be noted that the question of whether the pledgee needed the third party's permission to pass through the building (to gain access to the room) was not raised in *Hilton v Tucker*. The question was also ignored by Rowlatt J in *Wrightson v McArthur and Hutchisons (1919) Ltd*. As Andrew Bell has observed: 'In general, a key will not confer possession if the third party has not agreed to grant access to persons other than the deliveror' (AP Bell, *Modern Law of Personal Property in England and Ireland* (1989), pp 47–48).

2. In *Dublin City Distillery Ltd v Doherty* [1914] AC 823 whisky was kept in a bonded warehouse over which the distillery company and the Inland Revenue had joint control. In particular, the warehouse had two locks; the distillery company held the key to one lock and the Revenue held the key to the other. The distillery company purported to pledge the whisky to the respondent by entering the transaction into its books and by issuing invoices and warrants to the respondent. The House of Lords held that there had been no constructive delivery of the whisky and, therefore, no pledge. Lord Atkinson held that the warrants issued by the distillery company did not entitle the respondent to delivery of the whisky without further attornment to him (at 847–848; and Lord Sumner at 862–865; cf Lord Parker of Waddington at 853). When reviewing the law relating to constructive delivery, Lord Atkinson accepted that it could take place by delivery of the key to a store or house but doubted 'whether, owing to the dual control over this whisky exercised by the distillers and the Revenue officer, it would not be necessary in the present case that both keys should be delivered' (at 843–844). Lord Parker of Waddington viewed the question of dual control somewhat differently. He held that dual control meant that the distillery company and the Revenue had joint possession of the whisky so that the respondent could not take delivery from either one of them without the consent of the other (at 857–858).

QUESTIONS

1. Why was the pledgee's licence to enter the pledgor's premises held to be irrevocable in *Wrightson v McArthur and Hutchinson (1919) Ltd* (above)? See Bell, op cit, pp 48–49.

2.   On the issue of 'exclusive control', how can *Hilton v Tucker* be distinguished from *Dublin City Distillery Ltd v Doherty*?

3.   Does transfer of a key constitute actual, constructive, or symbolic delivery of the chattels to which it gives access? Compare ACH Barlow (1956) 19 MLR 394 with Bell, op cit, p 58.

(c) Re-delivery

Reeves v Capper
(1838) 5 Bing NC 136, Court of Common Pleas

W, the master of a ship, pledged his chronometer to C as security for a loan. Pursuant to the terms of the loan agreement, C returned the chronometer to W for use on a specific voyage. After the voyage W pledged the chronometer to R. R claimed that the original pledge had been destroyed when C had parted with possession of the chronometer by redelivering it to W. Tindal CJ held that this redelivery did not destroy the pledge.

> **Tindal CJ**: . . . [W]e agree entirely with the doctrine laid down in *Ryall v Rolle* ((1750) 1 Atk 165), that in the case of a simple pawn of a personal chattel, if the creditor parts with the possession he loses his property in the pledge: but we think the delivery of the chronometer to Wilson under the terms of the agreement itself was not a parting with the possession, but that the possession of Captain Wilson was still the possession of Messrs Capper. The terms of the agreement were, that 'they would allow him the use of it for the voyage:' words that gave him no interest in the chronometer, but only a licence or permission to use it, for a limited time, whilst he continued as their servant, and employed it for the purpose of navigating their ship. During the continuance of the voyage, and when the voyage terminated, the possession of Captain Wilson was the possession of Messrs Capper; just as the possession of plate by a butler is the possession of the master; and the delivery over to the Plaintiff was, as between Captain Wilson and the Defendants a wrongful act, just as the delivery over of the plate by the butler to a stranger would have been; and could give no more right to the bailee than Captain Wilson had himself. We therefore think the property belonged to the Defendants, and that the rule must be made absolute for entering the verdict for the Defendants.

NOTES

1.   Whether the pledgor holds as owner or as bailee after the goods are redelivered to him turns on the intention of the parties. An agreement to hold the goods for a special purpose indicates such an intention. This type of agreement is commonly found in international trade finance. After the importing buyer has pledged the bill of lading and other shipping documents as security for an advance from his bank, he may later be allowed to take back those documents to enable him to sell the goods and pay off the bank. To ensure that the bank maintains its constructive possession of the goods represented by the documents, it will only release the documents to the buyer under a letter of trust or a trust receipt. By the terms of such a letter or receipt, the buyer undertakes that in consideration of the release of the documents to him he will hold them on trust for the bank, will use them to sell the goods as the bank's agent, and will hold the goods themselves until sale, and the proceeds after sale, on trust for the bank. The effect of the letter of trust or trust receipt is to preserve the bank's pledge over the documents and goods (*North Western Bank Ltd v John Poynter, Son & Macdonalds* [1895] AC 56, HL). See, further, EP Ellinger, 'Trust Receipt Financing' [2003] JIBLR 305.

2. The pledge will be preserved if the pledgor takes the goods without permission or obtains redelivery by fraud (*Mocatta v Bell* (1857) 24 Beav 585). However, when redelivery is obtained by fraud the pledgee's rights may be lost against a subsequent pledgee or purchaser who takes the pledged chattels bona fide, for value and without notice. In *Babcock v Lawson* (1880) 5 QBD 284, the pledgors, who were merchants, obtained redelivery of the pledged goods by fraudulently misrepresenting to the pledgees that they had sold the goods and that the pledgees would be paid from the proceeds of sale. Upon redelivery, the pledgors obtained an advance from the defendants and deposited the goods with them. The Court of Appeal held that as the pledgees had parted with their special property in the goods to the pledgors, they could not recover the goods from the defendants who had obtained them bona fide and for good consideration. An important feature of this case was that, because of the fraud, the pledgees intended to divest themselves of their special property in the pledged goods. But what if the goods, or documents of title to the goods, are redelivered to the pledgor for a special purpose other than sale? Should the pledgee be bound by any subsequent sale or pledge, or should the *nemo dat* rule apply?

3. A similar problem to that discussed in Note 2 above arises when the pledgee redelivers goods to the pledgor under the terms of a trust receipt. In *Lloyds Bank Ltd v Bank of America* [1938] 2 KB 147, the pledgee bank returned bills of lading to the pledgor, against a trust receipt, so that the pledgor could sell the goods and pay the bank off out of the proceeds. Instead of selling the goods, the pledgor repledged them to a second bank. It was held that the second bank got a good title as against the first bank by virtue of s 2 of the Factors Act 1889 (see above, p 394). The Court of Appeal held that for the purposes of s 2, the pledgee was deemed the (joint) 'owner' of the goods. But s 2 will only apply if, inter alia, the pledgor is a mercantile agent and the goods, or documents of title to the goods, were entrusted to him in that capacity (*Astley Industrial Trust Ltd v Miller* [1968] 2 All ER 36).

4. Both *Babcock v Lawson* and *Lloyds Bank v Bank of America* can be distinguished as cases where the pledgees intended to divest themselves of their special property in the goods and redelivered the goods to the pledgor for that purpose. But where a pledgee intends to retain his special property, and redelivers the goods, or the documents of title to the goods, to the pledgor for a purpose other than disposition, his rights are not to be defeated by an unauthorised disposition by the pledgor, so long as the pledgee has not in some other way lent himself to the transaction, for example through an estoppel by representation (*Mercantile Bank of India Ltd v Central Bank of India Ltd* [1938] AC 287, PC). This may seem harsh on a third party who buys, or takes a pledge, from the pledgor in good faith and without notice.

5. In *Bassano v Toft* [2014] EWHC 377 (QB), [2014] ECC 14, the pledgor delivered her antique viola to the pledgee as security by way of pledge for a loan. The pledgee gave the viola to its agent for safekeeping and under strict instructions not to allow access to, or movement of, the viola without consent of the pledgee. The agent did not abide by the terms of those instructions and, without the pledgee's consent, gave the viola to a third party dealer in musical instruments to enable it to be played by a potential buyer. The pledgor alleged that the pledgee had lost its security interest in the viola: (a) when it was delivered to the agent; or

(b) when it was delivered by the agent to the third party dealer. Popplewell J gave judgment for the pledgee. At [57], he summarised the law as follows:

> The pledgee's special interest, whether or not properly described as proprietary in nature, may be defeated by a superior property interest held by someone other than the pledgor, such as that of a true owner from whom the pledgor had derived no good title, or a subsequent bona fide purchaser for value without notice of the pledge (see *Babcock v Lawson* (1880) 5 QBD 284 *per* Bramwell LJ at 286). But in the absence of a superior property claim by a third party, the pledgee's special interest is not lost by parting with possession of the chattel unless he does so in circumstances which constitute a voluntary surrender of his interest. What is required is a voluntary surrender of his special interest as pledgee, rather than simply a surrender of physical possession. The voluntary surrender of possession will not be treated as a surrender of his special interest as pledgee unless the circumstances of such surrender are inconsistent with the preservation of that special interest. If the loss of possession is involuntary, or where voluntary, consistent with an intention to preserve his special interest, such interest is not thereby lost.

Popplewell J held (at [58]): (a) the pledgee had transferred custody (but not possession, in the legal sense) of the viola to its agent, who held the instrument as bailee for the pledgee; and (b) delivery of the viola by the agent to the third party dealer was unauthorised and did not constitute a voluntary surrender by the pledgee of its special interest, just as the owner's special interest in *Reeves v Capper* was not destroyed by the master's unauthorised transfer of the chronometer to Reeves.

6.   A pledge of goods (or of a document of title thereto) would not be registrable under the notice-filing scheme for company charges proposed by the Law Commission in its Final Report, *Company Security Interests* (LC Report No 296) published in 2005 (see above, p 1022). However, under the Law Commission's proposals, where a pledgor is given possession of pledged goods (or a document of title) under a trust receipt, the pledge will become registrable unless the goods (or document of title) are returned to the pledgee's possession within 15 business days (see draft reg 22(4) of the draft regulations annexed to the Law Commission's Final Report). This proposal proved to be controversial and was not implemented.

QUESTION

Swell agrees to lend £1,000 to Tight, an artist, on the security of some of Tight's pictures, and Tight accordingly places these in an empty shed in his garden, locks the shed, and sends the only key to Swell with a letter stating that Swell can enter and remove the pictures whenever he wishes. Consider the rights of the parties in the following alternative circumstances.

(1) Tight, pretending that he wishes to show the pictures to an admirer, obtains the key from Swell for an hour. Tight removes a picture and sells it to Swap.

(2) The roof of the shed springs a leak and Swell, on learning of this, hands Tight the key and asks him to cover up the pictures. Tight takes the opportunity to remove a picture and sell it to Flint.

(3) Tight had previously stolen the pictures from Otto, who now looks to recover them from Swell. See s 11(2) of the Torts (Interference with Goods) Act 1977.

(d) Re-pledge by the pledgee

Donald v Suckling

(1866) LR 1 QB 585, Court of Queen's Bench

The pledgor deposited debentures with Simpson as security for the payment, at maturity, of a bill of exchange indorsed by the pledgor and discounted by Simpson. *Before* maturity of the bill, Simpson pledged the debentures to the defendant to secure a loan which exceeded the amount secured by the original pledge. The pledgor sought to recover the debentures from the defendant, by a claim in detinue, without tendering the amount of the original debt. The Court of Queen's Bench (Shee J dissenting) held that he was not entitled to do so.

Mellor J: . . . The question thus raised by this plea is, whether a pawnee of debentures, deposited with him as a security for the due payment of money, at a certain time, does, by repledging such debentures and depositing them with a third person as a security for a larger amount, before any default in payment by the pawnor, make void the contract upon which they were deposited with the pawnee, so as to vest in the pawnor an immediate right to the possession thereof, notwithstanding that the debt due by him to the original pawnee remains unpaid. . . .

In a contract of pledge for securing the payment of money, we have seen that the pawnee may sell and transfer the thing pledged on condition broken; but what implied condition is there that the pledgee shall not in the meantime part with the possession thereof to the extent of his interest? It may be that upon a deposit by way of pledge, the express contract between the parties may operate so as to make a parting with the possession, even to the extent of his interest, before condition broken, so essential a violation of it as to revest the right of possession in the pawnor; but in the absence of such terms, why are they to be implied? There may possibly be cases in which the very nature of the thing deposited might induce a jury to believe and find that it was deposited on the understanding that the possession should not be parted with; but in the case before us we have only to deal with the agreement which is stated in the plea. The object of the deposit is to secure the repayment of a loan, and the effect is to create an interest and a right of property in the pawnee, to the extent of the loan, in the goods deposited; but what is the authority for saying that until condition broken the pawnee has only a personal right to retain the goods in his own possession?

In *Johnson v Stear* ((1863) 15 CBNS 330), one Cumming, a bankrupt, had deposited with the defendant 243 cases of brandy, to be held by him as a security for the payment of an acceptance of the bankrupt for £62 10s, discounted by the defendant, and which would become due January 29, 1863, and in case such acceptance was not paid at maturity, the defendant was to be at liberty to sell the brandy and apply the proceeds in payment of the acceptance. On the 28th January, before the acceptance became due, the defendant contracted to sell the brandy to a third person, and on the 29th delivered to him the dock warrant, and on the 30th such third person obtained actual possession of the brandy. In an action of trover, brought by the assignee of the bankrupt, the Court of Common Pleas held that the plaintiff was entitled to recover, on the ground that the defendant wrongfully assumed to be owner, in selling; and although that alone might not be a conversion, yet, by delivering over the dock warrant to the vendee in pursuance of such sale, he 'interfered with the right which the bankrupt had on the 29th if he repaid the loan'; but the majority of the Court (Erie CJ, Byles and Keating JJ) held that the plaintiff was only entitled to nominal damages, on the express ground, 'that the deposit of the goods in question with the defendant to secure repayment of a loan to him on a given day, with a power to sell in case of default on that day, created *an interest and a right of property in the goods, which was more than a mere lien*; and the wrongful act of the pawnee *did not annihilate the contract between the parties nor the interest of the pawnee in the goods* under that contract.' From that view of the law, as applied to the circumstances of that case, Mr Justice Williams dissented, on the ground 'that the bailment was terminated by the sale before the stipulated time, and consequently that the title of the plaintiff to the goods became as free as if the bailment had never taken place.' Although the dissent of that most learned judge diminishes the authority of that case as a decision on the point, and although it may be open to doubt whether in an action of trover the defendant ought not to have succeeded on the plea of not possessed, and whether the plaintiffs only remedy for damages was not by action on the contract, I am nevertheless of opinion that the substantial ground upon which the majority of the Court proceeded, viz that the 'act of the pawnee did not annihilate the contract, nor the interest of the pawnee in the goods,' is the more consistent with the nature and incidents of a deposit by way of pledge. I think that when the true distinction between the case of a deposit, by way of pledge, of goods, for securing the payment of money, and all cases of lien, correctly so described, is considered, it will be seen that in the former there is no implication, in general, of a contract by the pledgee to retain the personal possession of the goods deposited; and I think that, although he cannot confer upon any third person a better title or a greater interest than he possesses, yet, if nevertheless he does pledge the goods to a third person for a greater interest than he possesses, such an act does not *annihilate the contract of pledge* between himself and the pawnor; but that the transaction is simply inoperative as against the original pawnor, *who upon tender of the sum secured immediately becomes entitled to the possession of the goods*, and can recover in an action for any special damage which he may have sustained by reason of the act of the pawnee in repledging the goods; and I think that such is the true effect of Lord Holt's definition of a 'vadium or pawn' in *Coggs v Bernard* [above, p 1024]; although he was of opinion that the pawnee could in no case use the pledge if it would thereby be damaged, and must use due diligence in the keeping of it, and says that the creditor is bound to restore the pledge upon payment of the debt, because, by detaining it after the tender of the money, he is a wrongdoer, his special property being determined; yet he nowhere says that the misuse or abuse of the pledge before payment or tender annihilates the contract upon which the deposit took place.

If the true distinction between cases of lien and cases of deposit by way of pledge be kept in mind, it will, I think, suffice to determine this case in favour of the defendant, seeing that no tender of the sum secured by the original deposit is alleged to have been made by the plaintiff; and considering the nature of the things deposited, I think that the plaintiff can have sustained no real damage by the repledging of them, and that he cannot successfully claim the immediate right to the possession of the debentures in question.

I am therefore of opinion that our judgment should be for the defendant.

Blackburn J: . . . Now I think that the subpledging of goods, held in security for money, before the money is due, is not in general so inconsistent with the contract, as to amount to a renunciation of that contract. There may be cases in which the pledgor has a special personal confidence in the pawnee, and therefore stipulates that the pledge shall be kept by him alone, but no such terms are stated here, and I do not think that any such term is implied by law. In general all that the pledgor requires is the personal contract of the pledgee that on bringing the money the pawn shall be given up to him, and that in the meantime the pledgee shall be responsible for due care being taken for its safe custody. This may very well be done though there has been a subpledge; at least the plaintiff should try the experiment whether, on bringing the money for which he pledged those debentures to Simpson, he cannot get them. And the assignment of the pawn for the purpose of raising money (so long at least as it purports to transfer no more than the pledgee's interest against the pledgor) is so far from being found in practice to be inconsistent with or repugnant to the contract, that it has been introduced into the Factors Acts, and is in the civil law (and according to *Mores v Conham* ((1610) Owen 123) in our own law also) a regular incident in a pledge. If it is done too soon, or to too great an extent, it is doubtless unlawful, but not so repugnant to the contract as to be justly held equivalent to a renunciation of it.

Cockburn CJ: I think it unnecessary to the decision in the present case to determine whether a party, with whom an article has been pledged as a security for the payment of money, has a right to transfer his interest in the thing pledged (subject to the right of redemption in the pawnor) to a third party. I should certainly hesitate to lay down the affirmative of that proposition. Such a right in the pawnee seems quite inconsistent with the undoubted right of the pledgor to have the thing pledged returned to him immediately on the tender of the amount for which the pledge was given. In some instances it may well be inferred from the nature of the thing pledged,—as in the case of a valuable work of art,—that the pawnor, though perfectly willing that the article should be intrusted to the custody of the pawnee, would not have parted with it on the terms that it should be passed on to others and committed to the custody of strangers. It is not, however, necessary to decide this question in the present case. The question here is, whether the transfer of the pledge is not only a breach of the contract on the part of the pawnee, but operates to put an end to the contract altogether, so as to entitle the pawnor to have back the thing pledged without payment of the debt. I am of opinion that the transfer of the pledge does not put an end to the contract, but amounts only to a breach of contract, upon which the owner may bring an action,—for nominal damages if he has sustained no substantial damage; for substantial damages, if the thing pledged is damaged in the hands of the third party, or the owner is prejudiced by delay in not having the thing delivered to him on tendering the amount for which it was pledged.

NOTES

1. Subject to Mellor J's caveat that a prohibition on repledge may be imposed by an express term in the contract, or might be implied by virtue of the special character of the goods in exceptional cases, the Court of Queen's Bench held in *Donald v Suckling* that a repledge by the pledgee does not destroy the original pledge, even if made before the pledgor's default and for a sum exceeding that secured by the original pledge. Similarly, the original pledge is not destroyed where the pledgee sells the goods prematurely (*Halliday v Holgate* (1868) LR 3 Exch 299), although deliberate destruction of the goods would destroy it (*Cooke v Haddon* (1862) 3 F & F 229, 176 ER 103, pledgee drank wine). However, premature sale of the pledged goods, or a sub-pledge for an amount greater than that secured by the original pledge, is wrongful and may render the pledgee liable for breach of contract (see dicta of Blackburn J and Cockburn CJ in *Donald v Suckling* at 616–617 and 618; cf Mellor J at 608, who seems to have proceeded on the basis that the repledge was not a breach). The issue was left open in *Halliday v Holgate*, although a dictum of Willes J (at 302) suggests that the pledgor may have a claim for damage to his reversionary interest where he suffers actual loss through wrongful dealing with the pledged chattel before his debt is paid off, for example where the pledgee wrongfully sells goods worth more than the sum owed by the pledgor and the goods are now effectively irrecoverable (see A Tettenborn [1994] CLJ 326 at 333–334).

2. If the pledgor tenders payment to the pledgee he may demand the return of the pledged chattel. The pledgee is thereby divested of his special property in the chattel and the pledgor is given an immediate right to possess it. This right allows the pledgor to bring an action in conversion against a sub-pledgee who has taken a sub-pledge for an amount greater than that secured by the original pledge, or the purchaser of a chattel wrongfully sold by the pledgee, should the sub-pledgee or purchaser refuse to return the chattel to the pledgor. In both cases the wrongful nature of the disposition renders it ineffective: the sub-pledgee cannot demand additional payment from the pledgor nor can the purchaser claim ownership. But for so long as the original pledgee has a special property in the pledged chattel, the pledgor has no immediate right to possession and so cannot bring an action in conversion (*Halliday v Holgate*, above, at 302–303). This explains why it was so important for the pledgor in *Donald v Suckling*, who had not tendered payment, to establish that the original pledgee had been divested of his special property in the debentures.

3. If the pledgor sells the goods while they are still subject to the pledge, the buyer can sue the sub-pledgee in conversion if he refuses to deliver up the goods after the buyer has tendered the amount owed, under the original pledge, to the original pledgee (*Franklin v Neate* (1844) 13 M & W 481). The buyer cannot sue the original pledgee for breach of the contract of pledge as he is not privy to that contract.

4. The modes of terminating the pledge are:

(a) tender of the amount due;

(b) pledgee redelivering possession of the chattel to the pledgor without reservation (see above, p 1032);

(c) pledgee accepting some alternative security or other discharge of the debt;

(d) 'annihilation' of the contract of pledge (see above).

Sale of the subject matter of the pledge on the pledgor's default is also a form of termination.

(e) Realisation

Re Hardwick, ex p Hubbard
(1886) 17 QBD 690, Court of Appeal

The facts are irrelevant.

> **Bowen LJ:** . . . A special property in the goods passes to the pledgee in order that he may be able—if his right to sell arises—to sell them. In all such cases there is at Common Law an authority to the pledgee to sell the goods on the default of the pledgor to repay the money, either at the time originally appointed, or after notice by the pledgee.

The Odessa
[1916] 1 AC 145, Privy Council

The facts are irrelevant.

> **Lord Mersey:** . . . If the pledgee sells he does so by virtue and to the extent of the pledgor's ownership, and not with a new title of his own. He must appropriate the proceeds of the sale to the payment of the pledgor's debt, for the money resulting from the sale is the pledgor's money to be so applied. The pledgee must account to the pledgor for any surplus after paying the debt.

He must take care that the sale is a provident sale, and if the goods are in bulk he must not sell more than is reasonably sufficient to pay off the debt, for he only holds possession for the purpose of securing himself the advance which he has made. He cannot use the goods as his own. These considerations show that the right of sale is exercisable by virtue of an implied authority from the pledgor and for the benefit of both parties. It creates no *jus in re* in favour of the pledgee; it gives him no more than a *jus in rem* such as a lienholder possesses, but with this added incident, that he can sell the property *motu proprio* and without any assistance from the Court.

NOTES

1. Unlike a mortgagee, a pledgee has no right of foreclosure (*Carter v Wake* (1877) 4 Ch D 605). Unless the contract or statute otherwise provides, the pledgee has no right to become the owner of the pledged goods on default by the pledgor. The pledged goods must either be redeemed or sold.

2. In *Mathew v TM Sutton Ltd* [1994] 4 All ER 793, Chadwick J held that the pledgee holds any surplus after realisation of the pledged chattel as a fiduciary on trust for the pledgor. There the pledgor of unredeemed silver and jewellery successfully claimed that the pledgee was bound to pay him equitable interest on the surplus proceeds. Chadwick J held that because of the nature of a pledge, whereby ownership of the property remains in the pledgor subject only to the 'special interest' to which the pledgee is entitled for the purpose of protecting and realising his security, there is a fiduciary relationship between pledgor and pledgee and the pledgee holds the surplus 'upon trust' for the pledgor.

3. As the pledge is only collateral security for the pledgor's debt, if sale of the pledged chattel does not realise the amount lent on it the pledgee may bring an action for the deficit (*Jones v Marshall* (1889) 24 QBD 269, per Lord Coleridge CJ).

4. If a pledge or pawn is caught by the terms of the Consumer Credit Act 1974, redemption and sale are strictly controlled by the terms of that Act (see below).

QUESTION

If the pledgee holds surplus proceeds of sale of the pledged chattel on trust for the pledgor, what happens to the surplus if the pledgee becomes insolvent before paying it over to the pledgor?

(f) Statutory control

(i) *Consumer Credit Act 1974*

Section 189(1) of the Consumer Credit Act 1974 defines a 'pawn' as 'any article subject to a pledge' and a 'pledge' as 'the pawnee's rights over an article taken in pawn'. The definitions are circular. Sections 114–122 of the 1974 Act contain special provisions relating to articles taken in pawn under a regulated agreement (see above, p 1008). When the 1974 Act applies:

(1) a pawn-receipt must be given in the prescribed form, informing the pawnor of his rights (s 114(1));

(2) the pawnee cannot sell the pawn within six months of the pawning (s 116(1)) and even then he must give the pawnor notice of his intention to sell and inform him of the asking price (s 121(1));

(3) ownership of an unredeemed pawn passes to the pawnee automatically at the end of a six-month redemption period where the pawn is security for fixed sum credit not exceeding £75, or running account credit on which the credit limit does not exceed £75 (s 120(1)(a)).

But note that ss 117–122 do not apply to: (a) a pledge of documents of title, or of bearer bonds; or (b) to a non-commercial agreement (s 114(3)).

Implementation of the Consumer Credit Directive 2008/48/EC resulted in significant changes being made to the 1974 Act and the regulations made thereunder. Pawn agreements fall outside the Directive but, in order to maintain a coherent regime, protections that can be found in the Directive have mostly (but not entirely) been extended to pawn agreements.

(ii) Registration

A pledge which takes effect on delivery of a chattel, or document of title thereto, does not require registration under the Bills of Sale Acts 1878–1891 (*Re Hardwick, ex p Hubbard* (1886) 17 QBD 690) or the Companies Act 2006 (*Wrightson v McArthur and Hutchisons (1919) Ltd* [1921] 2 KB 807). The possessory nature of a pledge means that third parties are put on notice of the pledgee's rights without the need for registration. On the other hand, a mere agreement to make a pledge, without any delivery of the chattel or document of title thereto, is registrable (*Dublin City Distillery Ltd v Doherty* [1914] AC 823 at 854, per Lord Parker of Waddington).

(iii) Insolvency Act 1986

Although there is no case directly on the point, it is submitted that a pledge would fall within the definition of 'security' contained in s 248(b) of the Insolvency Act 1986. This is of particular significance when a pledge is taken over a company's property and that company is subsequently made the subject of an administration order (explained below, p 1111). In these circumstances, no steps could be taken to enforce the pledge except with the consent of the administrator or the leave of the court (Insolvency Act 1986, Sch B1, para 43). For the application of the Insolvency Act 1986, Sch B1, para 43, to a possessory lien, see below, p 1054.

2 LIEN

(a) What is a lien?

Hammonds v Barclay
(1802) 2 East 227, Court of King's Bench

> **Grose J**: . . . A lien is a right in one man to retain that which is in his possession belonging to another, till certain demands of him the person in possession are satisfied.

Tappenden v Artus

[1964] 2 QB 185, Court of Appeal

The facts appear below, at p 1049.

> **Diplock LJ:** The common law remedy of a possessory lien, like other primitive remedies such as abatement of nuisance, self-defence or ejection of trespassers to land, is one of self-help. It is a remedy *in rem* exercisable upon the goods, and its exercise requires no intervention by the courts, for it is exercisable only by an artificer who has actual possession of the goods subject to the lien. Since, however, the remedy is the exercise of a right to continue an existing actual possession of the goods, it necessarily involves a right of possession adverse to the right of the person who, but for the lien, would be entitled to immediate possession of the goods. A common law lien, although not enforceable by action, thus affords a defence to an action for recovery of the goods by a person who, but for the lien, would be entitled to immediate possession.

NOTES

1. Grose J has provided the classic definition of a common law (or possessory) lien. Like a pledge, a common law lien depends on possession of the goods (or other tangible property—but there can be no common law possessory lien over intangible property as such property cannot be the subject of possession in any physical sense: see *Your Response Ltd v Datateam Business Media Ltd* [2014] EWCA Civ 281, [2015] QB 41, where the Court of Appeal, following *OBG Ltd v Allan* [2007] UKHL 21, [2008] 1 AC 1, held that it was not possible to exercise a common law possessory lien over an electronic database), although a lien depends on the *retention* of possession of goods previously delivered to the lienee in some other capacity, whereas a pledge requires a *delivery* of possession as security (*Re Cosslett (Contractors) Ltd* [1998] Ch 495 at 508, per Millett LJ). Furthermore, unlike a pledge, a common law lien merely gives a personal right of retention to the person (the lienee) in possession of goods belonging to another (the lienor) (*Legg v Evans* (1840) 6 M & W 36 at 42, per Parke B). This means that the lienee, in contrast to the pledgee, cannot dispose of his interest and, at common law, he has no implied right to sell the goods which are the subject matter of the lien (*Donald v Suckling* (1866) LR 1 QB 585 at 604, 610, 612; cf N Palmer and A Hudson, 'Pledge' in N Palmer and E McKendrick (eds), *Interests in Goods* (2nd edn, 1998), p 636, citing *Vered v Inscorp Holdings Ltd* (1993) 31 NSWLR 290, New South Wales Supreme Court, where an accountant's lien over his client's papers was assigned to a third party along with the debt).

2. There are four main types of lien: (a) common law; (b) statutory; (c) equitable; and (d) maritime. The most important statutory lien is the unpaid seller's lien (Sale of Goods Act 1979, ss 41–43; above, p 484). Like the common law lien, a statutory lien such as the unpaid seller's lien is a possessory lien. (For other examples of statutory liens, see the Consumer Credit Act 1974, ss 70(2), 73(5). Statute may create rights similar to a lien, for example under s 88 of the Civil Aviation Act 1982 an airport has the right to detain an aircraft for unpaid airport charges and aviation fuel supplied: *Bristol Airport plc v Powdrill* [1990] Ch 744.) By contrast, equitable and maritime liens are non-possessory liens. An equitable lien is analogous to an equitable charge (see generally, H Beale, M Bridge, L Gullifer, and E Lomnicka, *The Law of Security and Title-Based Finance* (2nd edn, 2012), paras 6.140 ff). The lien of the unpaid vendor of land is the most common example of this type of lien, although it is also possible for an equitable lien to arise in relation to personalty (see, eg, *International Finance Corpn v DSNL Offshore Ltd* [2005] EWHC 1844 (Comm), [2007] 2 All ER (Comm) 305: lien of purchaser in contract for work and materials in relation to oil rig equipment). However, unless expressly agreed by the parties, an equitable lien will not arise in relation to a contract for the sale of goods as the Sale of Goods Act provides an exhaustive code as to the legal effects of the contract (*Re Wait* [1927] 1 Ch 606 at 639, per Atkin LJ (see above, p 298); *International Finance Corpn v DSNL Offshore Ltd*, above, at [49], per Colman J). A maritime lien is a right of action *in rem* against a ship and freight for payment due under a contract, for the cost of salvage or for damage caused by a ship (*The Law of Security and Title-Based Finance*, above, paras 6.164–6.167).

3.   The remainder of this chapter will concentrate on the common law lien. Unless expressly stated otherwise, all references in this chapter to a 'lien' should be read as references to that type of lien.

QUESTIONS

1.   Given that we live in a 'digital age', is there a case to be made for a change in the law to allow for the exercise of a common law possessory lien over intangible property such as an electronic database or digital currency, for example Bitcoin? See *Your Response Ltd v Datateam Business Media Ltd* [2014] EWCA Civ 281, [2015] QB 41 at [9]–[10] and [27], per Moore-Bick LJ, and see also *Re Lehman Brothers International (Europe) (in administration)* [2012] EWHC 2997 (Ch) at [34], per Briggs J.

2.   If you think it should be possible to take a common law possessory lien over intangible property such as an electronic database or digital currency, should it be treated as a registrable charge for the purposes of s 859A of the Companies Act 2006 (see *Your Response Ltd v Datateam Business Media Ltd*, above, at [39], per Davis LJ)? If not, how would third parties be made aware of it?

(b) Possession

Forth v Simpson
(1849) 13 QB 680, Court of Queen's Bench

The owner of race horses stabled them with a trainer to be trained and kept. From time to time the horses, by order of the owner, were sent to run at different races, where the owner selected and paid the rider. The trainer claimed a lien over the horses for the cost of training and keep.

> **Lord Denman CJ:** I have little doubt that the care and skill employed by a trainer upon a race horse are of such a nature as would, on general principles, give a right of lien. But it is essential to a lien that the party claiming it should have had the right of continued possession. In the present case there was no right of continued possession; for the owner of the horses might, at his own pleasure, have sent them to any race, and to be ridden by any jockey of his own selection. The circumstances of this case, therefore, make it like the case of a livery stable keeper; for it is immaterial whether the owner's possession be more or less, if he has a right to assert it at all, and to interrupt the possession of the party claiming the lien.

Coleridge J: I also have no doubt that the skill and labour of a trainer are a good foundation for a lien; because he educates an untaught animal, and otherwise adapts it for a particular purpose, and thereby greatly improves its value. But it is a well established principle that, without the right of continuing possession, there can be no right of lien. Now a good test of the existence of such right of possession is to consider in whose possession the race horse is when it is employed in doing that for which it has been trained. The evidence shewed that the horse, during the race, was in the owner's possession, and in his possession rightfully and according to usage or contract. The horse, before the race, is placed for convenience in the stable of the trainer; but during the race it is in the care of the jockey nominated by the owner. It appears too that, if, on any occasion, the jockey were selected by the trainer, the trainer, *pro hac vice*, would have only the delegated authority of the owner. I think it is part of the understanding that the owner shall have the possession and control of the horse to run at any race. This is quite inconsistent with the trainer's continuing right of possession.

[**Patteson** and **Erie JJ** delivered concurring judgments.]

NOTES

1. In *Forth v Simpson*, Coleridge J stated that it was part of the 'understanding' that the owner was to have possession of the horses. This illustrates that the terms of any agreement between the creditor and the debtor can prevent a lien arising. Another example of the parties' agreement being inconsistent with the existence of a lien is where the creditor extends a period of credit to the debtor (*Wilson v Lombank Ltd* [1963] 1 WLR 1294). In such cases the intention of the parties prevents a lien arising.

2. For a valid lien to arise there must have been a voluntary delivery of possession by the debtor to the creditor (*Re Cosslett (Contractors) Ltd* [1998] Ch 495 at 508–509, CA—no lien where employer exercised contractual right to take possession of plant and materials against the will of the contractor). Possession must not be obtained by force or other tortious means (*Bernal v Pim* (1835) 1 Gale 17), nor must it arise as a result of fraud or any other kind of misrepresentation (*Madden v Kempster* (1807) 1 Camp 12). Furthermore, as a general rule no lien will arise from wrongful possession resulting from the act of a debtor who is not the owner of the goods (see below, pp 1049 ff, for the rule and its exceptions).

3. For cases on loss of possession, see below, pp 1055 ff.

(c) How does a lien arise?

A common law possessory lien arises by operation of law (*Re Bond Worth Ltd* [1980] Ch 228 at 250, per Slade J). Unlike a pledge, it does not depend upon the express or implied agreement of the parties. However, it is also possible to create a possessory lien by contract where none would otherwise arise. These are called contractual liens. Many standard form contracts now include provision for a contractual lien where a lien might otherwise arise by operation of law. A contractual lien supersedes or excludes a lien arising by operation of law, and the rights of the parties are governed purely by the contractual terms (*Fisher v Smith* (1878) 4 App Cas 1, HL). The lienee may also be given a contractual power of sale: this does not convert a contractual lien into an equitable charge (*Trident International Ltd v Barlow*

[1999] 2 BCLC 506, CA; *Jarl Tra AB v Convoys Ltd* [2003] EWHC 1488 (Comm), [2003] 2 Lloyd's Rep 459), nor a pledge (*Marcq v Christie Manson & Woods Ltd (t/a Christies)* [2003] EWCA Civ 731, [2003] 3 All ER 561 at [41]).

This section will concentrate on particular liens arising by operation of law (ie by judicially recognised usage). A particular lien gives the lienee the right to retain a chattel until all charges *incurred in respect of that chattel* have been paid. By contrast, a general lien gives the lienee the right to retain a chattel until all claims against the lienor are satisfied, *whether or not those claims arise in respect of the retained chattel*. General liens are considered below, pp 1046 ff.

Hatton v Car Maintenance Co Ltd
[1915] 1 Ch 621, Chancery Division

The owner of a motor car entered into an agreement with the defendant company whereby the company agreed to maintain the vehicle, supply a driver, and do any necessary repairs. An amount having become due by the owner under the agreement, the company took possession of the car and claimed a lien on it for the amount due. Sargant J rejected the company's claim.

Sargant J: Now it is clear that the amount to be paid is not merely for the repair of the car, but is for the wages of the chauffeur and the supply of petrol and oil, and that kind of thing, and therefore it is an inclusive lump sum.

It was said by Mr Crossfield [counsel for the defendant] that whenever an article is repaired, the repairer gets a lien on the article for the amount of his charges. Well, I do not dissent at all from that view of the law, assuming that the repairer gets the article in his shop for the purpose of repair and by that repair improves it, as he would ordinarily do. But certainly I cannot find anything in the authorities which have been cited to me to show that, if what the contractor does is not to improve the article but merely to maintain it in its former condition, he gets a lien for the amount spent upon it for that maintenance. The cases with regard to horses seem to point entirely the other way, because it is clear that a jobmaster has no lien at all for the amount of his bill in respect of feeding and keeping a horse at his stable, whereas, on the other hand, a trainer does get a lien upon a horse for the improvement which he effects to the horse in the course of training it for a race. A case was cited to me by Mr Crossfield with regard to the extent of the lien of an innkeeper, but I do not think that has really any application to the present case. Here all that was to be done by the contractor was for the purpose of maintaining the car in the condition in which it was sent to him, and in my judgment he would have no lien, that is no common law lien, in respect of the amount owing to him for that service.

That really would be sufficient to dispose of the case, but I think I ought also to express my opinion that, on the cases cited to me, even if he had such a lien originally, that lien would be lost by virtue of the arrangement under which the owner was to be at liberty to take the car away, and did take the car away, as and when she pleased. The existence of a lien seems to me to be inconsistent with an arrangement under which the article is from time to time taken entirely out of the possession and control of the contractor, for I cannot think that the fact that the chauffeur was to be deemed to be the servant of the company was intended to have the effect, or had the effect, of leaving the car in the possession of the company. I think that clause was inserted for quite other and fairly obvious reasons.

Re Southern Livestock Producers Ltd

[1964] 1 WLR 24, Chancery Division

By an agreement with a pig company, a farmer agreed to 'care for' a herd of pigs and super-vise the breeding of the herd. The company supplied boars for the latter purpose. On the company's liquidation, the farmer claimed a lien over the pigs to cover outstanding sums expended in feeding and caring for the herd. Pennycuick J rejected the farmer's claim.

Pennycuick J: The authorities which I have cited bind me in this court. It is perfectly clear that unless the bailee can establish improvement he has no lien. If this matter were free from authority it would, I think, be tempting to draw the line in rather a different place so as to cover the case where a person by the exercise of labour and skill prevents a chattel from deteriorating in con-tradistinction to improving it. The obvious example is feeding of animals which would otherwise die; but other examples come to mind. It seems to me to be illogical that a kennel keeper should have a lien for the expense of stripping a dog, but not for that of boarding it. However, it is quite impossible for me at this time of day to introduce that sort of modification into a well-established principle.

Turning now to the facts of the present case, the first step is to look again at the agreement. What the farmer undertakes to do under that agreement is to care for a specified number of pigs and piglets. The word 'care' received a definition in the recital. The word means 'house feed care for and arrange for the proper servicing and farrowing of' the sows and gilts concerned, and also the piglets farrowed by the sows and gilts. Mr Figgis, who appears for the liquidator, accepts the position that under that agreement the farmer was required to employ, and did employ, labour and skill . . . But, says Mr Figgis, the agreement does not provide for any improvement upon the subject-matter of the agreement, namely, the pigs and their litters. I have come to the conclusion that I must accept this argument. The operations comprised in the definition of 'care' add up precisely to 'care' in the ordinary sense of that word and do not seem to me to go in any respect beyond it. It is of great importance to observe in this connection that the company is under obliga-tion to supply the boars for the service of the sows. The position would be different if the farmer had to supply the boars. In that case it appears from *Scarfe v Morgan* ((1838) 4 M & W 270) that the farmer would have a lien in respect of service charge, provided he could identify this item.

Mr Sunnucks, for the farmer, contends that one must look at the herd of pigs as a whole and that the agreement provides for the improvement of the herd as a whole by the production of litters. I agree that one must look at the herd as a whole and not pig by pig, and that is, indeed, accepted by Mr Figgis. But when one does look at the herd as a whole, one finds that the pro-duction of litters results from the natural properties of the sows in co-operation with the boars supplied by the company, and I do not think this production of litters could fairly be described as an improvement effected by the farmer. What the farmer does is merely to look after the herd as it increases from other causes.

I say again that I am not altogether attracted by the argument on behalf of the liquidator, and I should be glad if I were able to draw the line in a manner rather more generous to the person claiming a lien. But it seems to me that to do so in the way in which I am asked so to do by Mr Sunnucks would be to make an unjustifiable inroad upon well-established principles. I do not think it is legitimate to say that a person improves a flock or herd of animals merely by supervising its natural increase, however much skill and care is involved in that process.

I would add that, even if there were an element of improvement in this respect—that is, super-vising the production of litters—the farmer would find himself in this difficulty because under the terms of the agreement it would be impossible to apportion the sums expended by him between the ordinary upkeep on the one hand and the improvement on the other hand.

NOTES

1.   Where goods are entrusted to a person to do work on them, that person will have a lien for the work done, provided that he improves the goods (which has been held to include the undertaking of research relating to the goods which increases their financial and cultural value, even though the goods themselves remain unchanged: *Spencer v S Franses Ltd* [2011] EWHC 1269 (QB)). The lien is called an improver's (or artificer's) lien and it is a particular lien (although, exceptionally, an improver may be able to assert a lien over a part of a composite chattel, or one of a group of chattels, even though he has not worked on that part or on that particular chattel in the group, for example 'a car repairer could exercise a lien on the spare tyre for work carried out on the engine', per Lloyd J in *The Ijaolo* [1979] 1 Lloyd's Rep 103 at 116; much depends on whether the contract was entire: see *Palmer on Bailment* (3rd edn, 2009), paras 15–072 to 15–089). The lien only arises when the work is complete (*Pinnock v Harrison* (1838) 3 M & W 532). However, if the owner of the goods prevents completion by withdrawing his instructions, the improver is entitled to a lien for his charges in respect of that part which is actually completed (*Lilley v Barnsley* (1844) 1 Car & Kir 344).

2.   A particular lien can also arise where a person is under a legal obligation to perform services, for example a common carrier or an innkeeper. A common carrier (not a private carrier) has a lien for his carriage charges as they become due, ie when the goods arrive at their destination. An innkeeper's lien extends over the belongings the guest brings into the inn (which includes a hotel: Hotel Proprietors Act 1956, s 1((1)) and secures the amount of his bill for food and lodging (*Matsuda v Waldorf Hotel Co Ltd* (1910) 27 TLR 153). However, the lien does not affect the clothes the guest is wearing at any particular moment (*Sunbolf v Alford* (1838) 3 M & W 248), neither does it extend to any vehicle (or any property left therein) or any horse or other live animal or its harness or other equipment (Hotel Proprietors Act 1956, s 2(2)). See, generally, G McBain, 'Abolishing the Strict Liability of Hotelkeepers' [2006] JBL 705, esp at 739–749.

QUESTIONS

1.   Does a warehouseman enjoy a common law lien (general or particular) in respect of his storage charges? See *Gordon v Gordon* [2002] EWCA Civ 1884 (must be a lien arising from contract); see also *Palmer on Bailment* (3rd edn, 2009), paras 14.098–14.099.

2.   B agrees to restore A's painting for £100. A delivers the painting to B's studio. Before the restoration is complete A demands the return of his picture. Advise B as to whether: (a) he may keep the painting until A pays for the work actually done; and (b) he may ignore the demand, complete the restoration, and claim the £100. See *Hounslow London Borough Council v Twickenham Garden Developments Ltd* [1971] Ch 233 at 253; and contrast *Bolwell Fibreglass Pty Ltd v Foley* [1984] VR 97 at 111 (both cases are discussed in *Palmer on Bailment*, above, para 15.084) .

(d) General liens

General liens may arise either by express agreement or as a common law right arising from general usage. As the next case illustrates, general liens are discouraged by the courts.

Rushforth v Hadfield

(1805) 6 East 519, Court of King's Bench

A common carrier retained a bankrupt's goods, after the cost of carriage of those goods had been paid, on the ground that he had a right to retain the goods until the cost of carriage of other goods was paid. The assignee of the estate of the bankrupt brought an action in trover against the carrier to recover the value of his goods. The common carrier claimed a general lien arising from a general usage of the trade. At the trial the jury gave a verdict for the carrier; which was moved to be set aside as a verdict against the law and evidence.

Lawrence J: I agree that there ought to be a new trial. Common carriers are every day attempting to alter the situation in which they have been placed by the law. At common law they are bound to receive and carry the goods of the subject for a reasonable reward, to take due care of them in their passage, and to deliver them in the same condition as when they were received: but they are not bound to deliver them without being paid for the carriage of the particular article, and therefore they have a lien to that extent. Of late years however they have been continually attempting to alter their general character by special notices on the one hand to diminish their liability, and on the other hand by extending their lien. But what evidence have we in this case to say that their common law situation is altered? To do that it must be shewn that both parties have consented to the alteration: the carrier cannot alter his situation by his own act alone. It is said that a general lien is convenient to the parties concerned: I do not say that it may not be so, but it must arise out of the contract of the parties. It may be convenient enough for the customer to say, that in consideration that you, the carrier, will give up your right to stop each particular parcel of goods for the price of the carriage, I will agree that you may stop any one parcel of my goods for the carriage price of all together. But still this must be by contract between them; and usage of trade is evidence of such a contract. And where such a usage is general, and has been long established so as to afford a presumption of its being commonly known, it is fair to conclude that the particular parties contracted with reference to it. Then, if in this case there had been evidence of a usage so uniform and frequent as to warrant an inference that the parties contracted with reference to it, it should have been left to the jury to infer that it was part of their contract.

Le Blanc J: . . . General liens are a great inconvenience to the generality of traders, because they give a particular advantage to certain individuals who claim to themselves a special privilege against the body at large of the creditors instead of coming in with them for an equal share of the insolvent's estate. All these general liens infringe upon the system of the bankrupt laws, the object of which is to distribute the debtor's estate proportionably amongst all the creditors, and they ought not to be encouraged. But I do not mean to say that a usage in trade may not be so general and well established as to induce a jury to believe that the parties acted upon it in their particular agreement; and I cannot say that such an agreement would not be good in law. . . . The instances of detainer by carriers for their general balance which were proved at the trial were very few and recent with a view to found so extensive a claim. . . . Without saying therefore that there may not be such a usage as that insisted on, I am clearly of opinion that there should be a new trial in order to have the case submitted to the jury on its true ground, which it does not appear to have been upon the last trial.

[**Lord Ellenborough CJ** and **Grose J** delivered concurring judgments.]

[At the new trial the jury gave a verdict for the plaintiff; which was moved to be set aside.]

Rushforth v Hadfield

(1806) 7 East 224, Court of King's Bench

Lord Ellenborough CJ: It is too much to say that there has been a general acquiescence in this claim of the carriers since 1775, merely because there was a particular instance of it at that time. Other instances were only about 10 or 12 years back, and several of them of very recent date. The question however results to this, what was the particular contract of these parties? And as the evidence is silent as to any express agreement between them, it must be collected either from the mode of dealing before practised between the same parties, or from the general dealings of other persons engaged in the same employment, of such notoriety as that they might fairly be presumed to be known to the bankrupt at the time of his dealing with the defendants, from whence the inference was to be drawn that these parties dealt upon the same footing as all others did, with reference to the known usage of the trade. But at least it must be admitted that the claim now set up by the carriers is against the general law of the land, and the proof of it is therefore to be regarded with jealousy. In many cases it would happen that parties would be glad to pay small sums due for the carriage of former goods, rather than incur the risk of a great loss by the detention of goods of value. Much of the evidence is of that description. Other instances again were in the case of solvent persons, who were at all events liable to answer for their general balance. And little or no stress could be laid on some of the more recent instances not brought home to the knowledge of the bankrupt at the time. Most of the evidence therefore is open to observation. If indeed there had been evidence of prior dealings between these parties upon the footing of such an extended lien, that would have furnished good evidence for the jury to have found that they continued to deal upon the same terms. But the question for the jury here was, whether the evidence of a usage for the carriers to retain for their balance were so general as that the bankrupt must be taken to have known and acted upon it? And they have in effect found either that the bankrupt knew of no such usage as that which was given in evidence, or knowing, did not adopt it. And growing liens are always to be looked at with jealousy, and require stronger proof. They are encroachments upon the common law. If they are encouraged the practice will be continually extending to other traders and other matters. The farrier will be claiming a lien upon a horse sent to him to be shod. Carriages and other things which require frequent repair will be detained on the same claim; and there is no saying where it is to stop. It is not for the convenience of the public that these liens should be extended further than they are already established by law. But if any particular inconvenience arise in the course of trade, the parties may, if they think proper, stipulate with their customers for the introduction of such a lien into their dealings. But in the absence of any evidence of that sort to affect the bankrupt, I think the jury have done right in negativing the lien claimed by the defendants on the score of general usage.

Le Blanc J: This is a case where a jury might well be jealous of a general lien attempted to be set up against the policy of the common law, which has given to carriers only a lien for the carriage price of the particular goods. The party therefore who sets up such a claim ought to make out a very strong case. But upon weighing the evidence which was given at the trial, I do not think that this is a case in which the Court are called upon to hold out any encouragement to the claim set up, by overturning what the jury have done, after having the whole matter properly submitted to them.

[**Grose** and **Lawrence JJ** delivered concurring judgments.]

NOTES

1. The following have been held to have general liens as a matter of usage: solicitors (*Ismail v Richards Butler (a firm)* [1996] QB 711; *Bentley v Gaisford* [1997] QB 627, CA); bankers (*Brandao v Barnett* (1846) 3 CB 519); factors (*Baring v Corrie* (1818) 2 B & Ald 137);

stockbrokers (*Re London & Globe Finance Corpn* [1902] 2 Ch 416); and insurance brokers (*Hewison v Guthrie* (1836) 2 Bing NC 755; *Eide UK Ltd v Lowndes Lambert Group Ltd* [1998] 1 All ER 946, CA). Accountants only enjoy a particular lien over the books of account, files, and papers of their clients (*Woodworth v Conroy* [1976] QB 884, CA, although Lawson LJ suggests at 890, without deciding the point, that they may enjoy a wider lien than this).

2. The right to exercise a lien (general or particular) is not enforceable in all circumstances. Section 246(2) of the Insolvency Act 1986 renders a lien unenforceable to the extent that its enforcement would deny possession of any books, papers, or other records to an insolvency office-holder (an administrator, liquidator, or provisional liquidator of a company) (see below, Chapter 28). There is also authority in relation to solicitors (*Re Capital Fire Insurance Association* (1883) 24 Ch D 408) and accountants (*DTC (CNC) Ltd v Gary Sargeant & Co (a firm)* [1996] 2 All ER 369) which makes it clear that they are not to exercise a lien over books or documents of a client company which are required by statute or by its articles of association to be kept at a particular place, or to be available for a specific purpose such as inspection.

QUESTIONS

1. Why was there such hostility to general liens in *Rushforth v Hadfield*?

2. How may a general lien be 'convenient to the parties concerned' (per Lawrence J, above)? See AP Bell, *Modern Law of Personal Property in England and Ireland* (1998), pp 142–143.

(e) Liens and third parties

Tappenden v Artus
[1964] 2 QB 185, Court of Appeal

T allowed A to use a van pending completion of a hire-purchase agreement between them. It was a condition of the bailment that A should tax and insure the vehicle at his own expense. The van broke down and A took it to the defendants' garage for repair. Shortly afterwards T withdrew his permission for A to use the van and demanded its return. The defendants refused to deliver up the van until paid for their work. At first instance, T succeeded in his action against the defendants for the return of the van and damages for its retention. The defendants appealed to the Court of Appeal (Willmer and Diplock LJJ).

> **Diplock LJ** (delivering the judgment of the court): Since a common law lien is a right to continue an existing actual possession of goods (that is to say, to refuse to put an end to a bailment) it can only be exercised by an artificer if his possession was lawful at the time at which the lien first attached. To entitle him to exercise a right of possession under his common law lien adverse to the owner of the goods, he must thus show that his possession under the original delivery of the goods to him was lawful—*Bowmaker Ltd v Wycombe Motors Ltd* ([1946] KB 505)—and continued to be lawful until some work was done by him upon the goods. Where, therefore, as in the present case, possession of the goods was originally given to the artificer not by the owner himself, but by a bailee of the owner, the test whether the artificer can rely upon his common law lien as a defence in an action for detinue brought against him by the owner is whether the owner authorised (or is estopped as against the artificer from denying that he authorised) the bailee to give possession of the goods to the artificer. This, it seems to us, is the test which, after some

vacillation, is laid down by the modern authorities. It is as a result of applying this test that the cases which have been cited to us fall upon one side or other of the line . . .

These cases, all of which fall upon one side of the line, seem to us to do no more than support the propositions that where no question of ostensible authority arises, (1) the mere fact of delivery of possession of goods by an owner to a bailee does not of itself give the bailee authority to deliver possession of the goods to a third party; and (2) that whether the bailee has such authority depends in each case upon the purpose of the bailment and terms of the contract (if any) under which the goods are bailed to him.

The latter proposition was most clearly stated in the judgment of Collins J in the Divisional Court case of *Singer Manufacturing Co v London & South Western Rly Co* ([1894] 1 QB 833), a case which falls on the other side of the line. This passage, although it was not the ratio decidendi of the other member of the court, has been repeatedly cited with approval, and is the foundation of the modern law on this topic. In that case a man who was in possession under a hire-purchase agreement of a Singer sewing machine placed it in a railway cloakroom during the time that the hiring was in existence and, the hiring having come to an end, the owners of the machine claimed it from the railway company, who set up a warehouseman's lien. In his judgment Collins J said this: 'I think in this case the lien may also be rested on another ground; and that is, that the person who deposited this machine was, as between himself and the owner of it, entitled to the possession of it at the time he deposited it. He was entitled to it under a contract of hire, which gave him the right to use it, I presume, for all reasonable purposes incident to such a contract, and among them, I take it, he acquired the right to take the machine with him if he travelled, and to deposit it in a cloakroom if he required to do so. In the course of that reasonable user of the machine, and before the contract of bailment was determined, he gave rights to the railway company in respect of the custody of it. I think those rights must be good against the owners of the machine, who had not determined the hire-purchase agreement at the time that those rights were acquired by the railway company.'

This, in our view, lays down the correct test for determining what authority is conferred by the owner of goods upon the bailee to part with possession of the goods when the purpose of the bailment is the use of the goods by the bailee. He is entitled to make reasonable use of the goods, and if it is reasonably incidental to such use for the bailee to give possession of them to a third person in circumstances which may result in such person acquiring the common law remedy of lien against the goods, the bailee has the authority of the owner to give lawful possession of the goods to the third person. This is not strictly an 'implied term' in *The Moorcock* ((1889) 14 PD 64) sense of the contract between the bailor and the bailee. The grant of authority to use goods is itself to be construed as authority to do in relation to the goods all things that are reasonably incidental to their reasonable use. If the bailor desires to exclude the right of the bailee to do in relation to the goods some particular thing which is reasonably incidental to their reasonable use, he can, of course, do so, but he must do so expressly.

In the case of a bailment for use, therefore, where there is no express prohibition upon his parting with possession of the goods (and no question of ostensible authority arises), the relevant inquiry is whether the giving of actual possession of the goods by the bailee to the person asserting the common law lien was an act which was reasonably incidental to the bailee's reasonable use of the goods. This was the inquiry in *Williams v Allsup* ((1861) 10 CBNS 417) a ship's mortgage case where there was no express provision requiring the mortgagor to keep the ship in repair. Willes J there said (at 427): 'By the permission of the mortgagees the mortgagor has the use of the vessel. He has, therefore, a right to use her in the way in which vessels are ordinarily used. Upon the facts which appear on this case, this vessel could not be so used unless these repairs had been done to her. The state of things, therefore, seems to involve the right of the mortgagor to get the vessel repaired,—not on the credit of the mortgagees, but upon the ordinary terms, subject to the shipwright's lien. It seems to me that the case is the same as if the mortgagees had been present when the order for the repairs was given. To that extent I think the property of the mortgagees is impliedly modified.' It was also the inquiry in *Keene v Thomas* ([1905] 1 KB 136) a hire-purchase case, in which there was an express provision requiring the hirer to keep a dog-cart in repair, and in *Green v All Motors Ltd* ([1917] 1 KB 625), another hire-purchase case, in which there was a similar obligation on the hirer to keep a car in repair. But Scrutton LJ, citing *Williams v Allsup* and *Singer Manufacturing Co v London & South Western Rly Co*, put the decision upon the broader ground with which we concur (at 633): 'The law is clear. The hirer of a chattel is entitled to have it repaired so as to enable him to use it in the way in which such a chattel is ordinarily used. The hirer was therefore entitled, without any express authority from the owner, to have the motor car repaired so as to enable him to use it as a motor car is ordinarily used.'

Albemarle Supply Co v Hind & Co ([1928] 1 KB 307), which was also cited, is on a different point, namely, the ostensible authority of the bailee. It was another case of a hire-purchase agreement, but the agreement contained a term which expressly excluded the hirer's right to create a lien on the vehicles in respect of repairs. The artificer to whom possession of the vehicles was delivered for the purpose of repair was aware that the vehicles were bailed to the hirer under a hire-purchase agreement, but was not aware of the express exclusion of his right to create a lien. It was held that vis-à-vis the artificer the owner had given the hirer ostensible authority to give possession of the vehicles to the artificer for the purpose of effecting repairs, and could not rely upon a secret limitation upon the terms upon which the hirer was authorised to do so, that is, upon terms excluding the artificer's common law remedy of lien. It was a case where the owner was estopped from denying that he had conferred on his bailee authority to give up possession of the vehicles to the artificer on the ordinary terms, and thus subject to the ordinary remedy of lien.

The actual decision in that case is not germane to the present appeal, for the artificer here relies solely upon the actual authority conferred by the bailor on the bailee, and not upon any ostensible authority in excess of that actual authority . . .

Finally, there is *Bowmaker Ltd v Wycombe Motors Ltd*. It was another hire purchase case in which, however, the bailment to the hirer had been lawfully determined before he delivered possession of the vehicle to the artificer. Since the hirer's possession of the vehicle was itself unlawful, it followed that he could not then confer any lawful possession upon the artificer upon which the artificer could base his claim to a lien. But there is a passage in the judgment of Goddard LJ which summarises with his usual accuracy and clarity the true ratio decidendi of the cases. He said this ([1946] KB 505 at 509): 'So, too, it has been held in the cases to which our attention has been called, more especially *Green v All Motors Ltd* and *Albemarle Supply Co Ltd v Hind & Co* that in the case of a motor car where it is necessary that the motor car should be kept in running condition and repair during the time the hire-purchase agreement is current and valid, the hirer has a right to take it and get it repaired and, if he does so the repairer can exercise an artificer's lien on it, because at the time when the motor car was left with him he, the hirer, had the right, whether you call it by implied authority or by legitimate authority, to use that car in all reasonable ways, and among those ways was a right to get the car repaired and kept in running order. Therefore he was placing it with the repairer with the implied consent of the owner and the artificer's lien on that account will prevail against the owner. These cases have also held, and quite understandably, that an arrangement between the owner and the hirer that the hirer shall not be entitled to create a lien, does not affect the repairer. A repairer has a lien although the owner has purported to limit the hirer's authority to create a lien in that way. That seems to me to depend upon this: Once an artificer exercises his art upon a chattel, the law gives the artificer a lien upon that chattel which he can exercise against the owner of the chattel if the owner of the chattel has placed it with him or has authorised another person to place it with him. If I send my servant with my chattel to get it repaired, the artificer will get the lien which the law gives him on that chattel although I may have told my servant that he is not to create a lien. The fact is that the lien arises by operation of law because the work has been done on the chattel.'

To this statement of principle we would only add the rider that the latter part of it which deals with ostensible authority should be understood as restricted to cases where the artificer has no express notice of the limit upon the authority of the person to whom the owner has given possession of the chattel.

Mr Forbes [counsel for the plaintiff] has argued that this principle is limited to bailments under contracts of hire purchase where there is a liability on the hirer to keep the goods in repair. We cannot accept this. *Williams v Allsup* was not a hire purchase case at all; the *Singer Company's* case was concerned with a warehousemen's lien, not with an artificer's lien. We think that Mr Hammerton [counsel for the defendants] is right in his contention that, at any rate if there is consideration for the bailment, the principle applies to all cases where the purpose of the bailment of goods is their use by the bailee.

In the present case the purpose of the bailment of the Dormobile van was clearly for use on the roads by the bailee. Mr Forbes has submitted that it was a gratuitous bailment, made in anticipation of the bailee's entering into a hire-purchase agreement in respect of the van. We do not think this is right. It was a term of the bailment that the bailee, not the bailor, should license the van at his own expense and insure it upon comprehensive terms. This was in fact done in the bailee's own name although it does not appear whether or not this was a term of the prior arrangement as to licensing and insurance. There was thus good consideration in law for the bailment, and it is unnecessary to consider what the position would have been if the bailment had been purely gratuitous.

It is a statutory offence to use a motor vehicle on the highway which is in an unroadworthy condition. If the van should become unroadworthy during the period of the bailment the bailee could not use it for the purposes of the bailment unless he were to have it repaired. In the ordinary way, save in the case of minor adjustments, a motor vehicle can be repaired only by delivering possession of it to an expert mechanic to effect the repairs; and in our view the giving of actual possession of a motor vehicle to an artificer for the purpose of effecting repairs necessary to render it roadworthy is an act reasonably incidental to the bailee's reasonable use of the vehicle. If the bailor desires to exclude the bailee's authority to do this, he must do so expressly . . .

Different considerations would apply to repairs which were not necessary to make the van roadworthy, for the execution of such repairs might not be reasonably necessary to the reasonable use of the van by the bailee, which was the purpose of the bailment; but there is no suggestion in the evidence that any of the repairs in respect of which the lien was claimed were not necessary to make the van roadworthy.

We are, therefore, of opinion that the artificer was entitled to a common law lien upon the van in respect of the repairs which he effected, and he is entitled to assert that lien against the bailor because the bailor gave the bailee authority to give lawful possession of the van to the artificer for the purpose of effecting such repairs as were necessary to make the van roadworthy.

For these reasons we allow this appeal.

NOTES

1.   Why did the hire-purchaser have ostensible or apparent authority to bind the owner with a lien in *Albemarle Supply Co Ltd v Hind & Co* [1928] 1 KB 307 (below, p 1055) but not in *Bowmaker Ltd v Wycombe Motors Ltd* [1946] KB 505? Merely allowing the hirer to have possession of the vehicle would not of itself be enough to bring into operation the doctrine of estoppel (see above, p 388). However, in *Albemarle* the hire-purchaser had garaged the

vehicles with the defendants over a long period with the apparent sanction of the owner (at least the owner did not interfere with this arrangement). Although not explicit in their Lordships' reasoning, it is probable that the Court of Appeal found the necessary representation in this conduct of the owner (this is how the case was explained by Isaacs and Higgins JJ in *Fisher v Automobile Finance Co of Australia Ltd* (1928) 41 CLR 167 at 177 and 180, High Court of Australia). On the other hand, in the *Bowmaker* case the hire-purchaser took the vehicle to the garage for a one-off repair. There was no representation of authority by the owner.

2. There are other exceptional cases when wrongful possession resulting from the act of a third party may nevertheless bind the owner.

(a) A mercantile agent, seller, or buyer in possession of goods may by wrongful disposition bind the owner (Factors Act 1889, ss 2, 8, and 9 and Sale of Goods Act 1979, ss 24 and 25).

(b) If the person claiming the lien is obliged by law to receive the goods, for example a common carrier or an innkeeper, he is not affected by the wrongful disposition by the depositor (see, eg, *Marsh v Police Comr* [1945] KB 43, where the Court of Appeal held the Ritz Hotel entitled to exercise a lien over stolen goods brought onto its premises by a guest). Whilst an innkeeper's lien is not affected by the fact that the innkeeper knows the goods are not the property of the guest (*Robins & Co v Gray* [1895] 2 QB 501), it is unlikely that a court would allow an innkeeper to exercise a lien over goods he knew to be stolen.

(c) The lien is claimed in respect of a negotiable instrument received in good faith and without notice of any dishonour (Bills of Exchange Act 1882, s 27(3)).

QUESTION

Rook hired a car from Bishop, stole a quantity of jewellery from King's shop, and drove off in the car, which he then negligently damaged against a wall. He left the car at Queen's garage for repair, pledged one necklace to Pawn for £60, and took the rest of the stolen jewellery to Castle's hotel, where he stayed until he was arrested three weeks later. Queen, Pawn, and Castle now refuse to surrender the car and the jewellery unless they are paid, respectively, £80 for repairing the car, £60 for the necklace, and £200 for hotel charges. Advise Bishop and King. What is the position if Bishop had originally bought the car from Queen and still owes Queen £50 of the purchase price?

(f) Enforcement

(i) *Generally*

We have already established that, as a general rule, a common law lien cannot be enforced by sale (above, p 1041). However, a lienee may be given a power of sale in the following circumstances:

(1) by contract;

(2) by trade usage (see *Re Tate, ex p Moffatt* (1841) 2 Mont D & De G 170);

(3) by statute, for example s 1 of the Innkeepers Act 1878 (innkeeper's right of sale); ss 12 and 13 of the Torts (Interference with Goods) Act 1977 (bailee's right of sale of uncollected goods); s 48 of the Sale of Goods Act 1979 (unpaid seller's right of resale).

Additionally, on the application of any party to a cause or matter, a court has power under Pt 25.1(c)(v) of the Civil Procedure Rules (CPR) to order the sale of any property (including land) which is the subject of a claim or as to which any question may arise on a claim and which is of a perishable nature or which for any other good reason it is desirable to sell quickly. In *Larner v Fawcett* [1950] 2 All ER 727, the Court of Appeal exercised this power on the interlocutory application of a race horse trainer claiming a lien over the respondent's horse to cover outstanding charges. The court emphasised that the power of sale under what is now Pt 25.1(c)(v) of the CPR could be exercised even though the common law lienee has no power of sale at law or in equity. The court went on to hold that it was proper to make such an order for sale in this case on the grounds that: (1) the horse was 'eating its head off at the trainer's expense'; and (2) the owner had unreasonably delayed in requesting its return. The proceeds of sale were ordered to be paid into court to abide the result of the action.

(ii) Insolvency Act 1986

Section 246(2) of the Insolvency Act 1986 provides that a lien or other right to retain possession of any books, papers, or other records of a company is unenforceable to the extent that its enforcement would deny possession of any books, papers, or other records to an insolvency office-holder (an administrator, liquidator, or provisional liquidator of a company). But the section does not apply where a lien is claimed 'on documents which give a title to property and are held as such' (s 246(3)). Thus, in *Re Carter Commercial Developments Ltd* [2002] BPIR 1053, solicitors owed fees by a corporate client that was later placed into administration were held entitled to assert a lien over title deeds to the client's land.

In *Bristol Airport plc v Powdrill* [1990] Ch 744, the Court of Appeal held (*obiter*) that the exercise of a possessory lien over a company's property was included within the statutory definition of 'security' contained in s 248(b) of the Insolvency Act 1986 and, therefore, was caught by what is now para 43 of Sch B1 of that Act. When an administration order is made in respect of a company (see below, p 1111), 'no . . . steps may be taken to enforce any security over the company's property . . . except with the consent of the administrator or with permission of the court' (Insolvency Act 1986, Sch B1, para 43: see further above, Chapter 24, Section 2). This could create a number of practical problems for someone claiming a lien over the company's property when an administrator has been appointed, for example is the lien holder liable to damages in conversion if he refuses to hand over the goods to the administrator pending an application to the court for leave? Woolf LJ attempted to deal with a number of these problems when he said (at 768):

> You are not taking steps to enforce a security unless by relying on the security you are preventing the administrator doing something to . . . [a] chattel in which he has an interest which he would otherwise be entitled to do. Taking first the case of the ordinary repairer who is entitled to retain goods until his charges are paid. Unless and until someone who is entitled to possession of those goods seeks to obtain possession of the goods, the lien holder does not take steps to enforce his lien. The security which is given to the lien holder entitles him to refuse to hand over the possession of the goods, but until he makes an unqualified refusal to hand over the goods he has not in my judgment taken steps to enforce the security for the purposes of [what is now Sch B1, para 43] of the Act of 1986 . . . I would not regard a person who is otherwise entitled to a lien as enforcing that lien if he does not make an unqualified refusal to hand over the goods to an administrator but instead indicates to the administrator that unless the administrator consents to his exercising his right to detain, he will apply promptly to the court for leave and does so. In my view such conduct would not amount to taking steps to enforce the lien within the meaning of [what is now Sch B1, para 43] of the Act of 1986.

Browne-Wilkinson V-C agreed with Woolf LJ; Staughton LJ did not express an opinion as to the correctness of Woolf LJ's dicta.

In *London Flight Centre (Stansted) Ltd v Osprey Aviation Ltd* [2002] BPIR 1115, a creditor, who was unsecured at the date the debtor went into administration, asserted a contractual lien over one of the debtor's aircraft that happened to come into its possession after that date. Hart J held that the creditor was not entitled to enforce the lien which it had acquired post-administration and thereby gain priority over unsecured creditors and undermine the purposes for which the administration order was made. Hart J stated (at 1125) that 'a possessory lien which the court will not allow to be enforced is an oxymoron. It is no lien at all'.

(g) Termination of lien

Albemarle Supply Co Ltd v Hind and Co
[1928] 1 KB 307, Court of Appeal

B hired three taxicabs from the plaintiffs under hire-purchase agreements. The agreements required B to keep the cabs and their equipment in good repair but prohibited him from selling, pledging, or parting with possession of them without the plaintiffs' consent, and from creating a lien on them in respect of repairs. For a number of years B garaged the cabs, and two other cabs, with the defendants who serviced them and carried out necessary repairs. The defendants knew of the hire-purchase agreements but were not aware of their terms. B's account then fell into arrears, but the defendants allowed him to take the cabs from their garage each day on condition that the cabs continued 'in pawn' and were returned to the garage each night. B then fell into arrear with his hire-purchase instalments and the plaintiffs terminated the agreements and demanded the three cabs from the defendants. The defendants claimed a lien over the three cabs for the balance of their general account for all five cabs due from B. The balance of account included the cost of rent, washing, oil, and petrol, which would not be the subject of a repairing lien.

Scrutton LJ: The plaintiffs' first line of attack on the lien claim was a clause in their hire-purchase agreement providing that 'the hirer shall not have or be deemed to have any authority to pledge the credit of the owners for repairs to the vehicle or to create a lien upon the same in respect of such repairs.' This Court in *Green v All Motors Ltd* ([1917] 1 KB 625) has held that the mere knowledge by the repairer that there is a hire-purchase agreement without knowledge of its exact terms relating to the car which he repairs does not deprive him of his lien. The owner leaving the cab in the hands of a man who is entitled to use it gives him an implied authority to have it repaired with the resulting lien for repairs. Rowlatt J had held in a previous case, and the judge below in the present case followed his decision, that a contractual limitation of authority not communicated to the repairer does not limit the implied authority derived from the hirer's being allowed to possess and use the car. I agree with this view; if a man is put in a position which holds him out as having a certain authority, people who act on that holding out are not affected by a secret limitation, of which they are ignorant, of the apparent authority. The owners can easily protect themselves by requiring information as to the garage where the cab is kept, and notifying the garage owner that the hirer has no power to create a lien for repairs. They will thus escape the lien, though they may not get their cab repaired.

The plaintiffs next contended that any lien was lost because the cabs went out of the possession of the garage each day to ply for hire. The defendant proved an agreement with Botfield at a time when the lien existed, that the cabs should go out for hire each day on the terms that they should be returned to the garage each night, the lien continuing while the cabs were in possession of the garage. I do not think any plying for hire under this agreement prevented the lien, if any, from continuing, and in my view repair of a damaged cab, though it may be described as 'maintenance,' gave rise to a repairer's lien.

It was next said that the lien for repairs was lost inasmuch as it was originally claimed for a larger amount and a different cause than the right one. I have considered the numerous authorities cited, and in my view the law stands as follows: A person claiming a lien must either claim it for a definite amount, or give the owner particulars from which he himself can calculate the amount for which a lien is due. The owner must then in the absence of express agreement tender an amount covering the lien really existing. If he does not, unless excused, he has no answer to a claim of lien. He may be excused from tendering (1) if he has no knowledge or means of knowledge of the right amount; (2) if the person claiming the lien for a wrong cause or amount makes it clear that he will not release the goods unless his full claim is satisfied, and that claim is wrongful. The fact that the claim is made for more than the right amount does not matter unless the claimant gives no particulars from which the right amount can be calculated, or makes it clear that he insists on the full amount of the right claimed: see *Scarfe v Morgan* ((1838) 4 M & W 270); *Dirks v Richards* ((1842) 4 Man & G 574); *Huth & Co v Lamport* ((1886) 16 QBD 735 at 736), *per* Lord Esher; and *Rumsey v North Eastern Rly Co* ((1863) 14 CBNS 641 at 651 and 654), *per* Erle CJ and Willes J.

In the present case the accounts handed to the plaintiffs show the items relating to the repairs to each cab, and the plaintiffs did not tender because they thought their agreement prevented the creation of a lien, not because they could not ascertain what repairs were done. I do not think the defendants ever pinned themselves definitely to a demand for the whole sum.

[**Lord Hanworth MR** and **Sargant J** delivered concurring judgments (although Sargant J did not address the issue of loss of possession).]

NOTES

1.   Professor Norman Palmer notes that '[t]he loss of possession is a question of fact but the effect upon the lien itself is one of law . . . the question is whether the change of circumstances, and the intentions accompanying it, are inconsistent with the further continuance of the lien' (*Palmer on Bailment* (3rd edn, 2009), para 15–081). In *Albemarle Supply Co Ltd v Hind and Co*, the intention of the parties was expressed in the terms of their agreement for the release of the cabs. An intention to maintain the lien may also be implied (see *Allen v Smith* (1862) 12 CBNS 638, where the lien was not lost when a guest took a horse out of an innkeeper's stable intending to return it). But where there is no evidence of a contrary intention (as in the great majority of cases), loss of possession will terminate the lien (see, eg, *Pennington v Reliance Motor Works Ltd* [1923] 1 KB 127).

2.   In *Pennington v Reliance Motor Works Ltd*, above, E agreed with the plaintiff to rebuild his car. Without the plaintiff's authority, E subcontracted the work to the defendants. The defendants completed the work and returned the car to E, who delivered it back to the plaintiff. The defendants were not paid by E. When the plaintiff later delivered his car to the defendants for further repairs, the defendants claimed a lien on it for the earlier work done for E. McCardie J held that there was no lien as the plaintiff gave no authority, express or implied, to E to create one and no custom of the trade was proved. He also held, in the alternative, that even if there had been a lien it had been lost when the defendants parted with possession of the car to E. As McCardie J stated: '. . . the defendants allowed E to take possession of the car not for any limited purpose, but in the belief that he would get payment from [the plaintiff], and would pay them as soon as he could'. But contrast *Euro Commercial Leasing Ltd v Cartwright and Lewis* [1995] 2 BCLC 618, where Evans-Lombe J held that solicitors with a general lien over client's money in a client account lost that lien when the money was transferred to the solicitors' office account without an order of court, contrary to what is now Insolvency Act 1986, Sch B1, para 43, but that when the error was discovered, and an equivalent sum repaid into the client's account, a 'fresh general lien' attached to the money in the account so reconstituted (for these purposes the judge assumed that money paid back into the client's account became the client's property, although he expressed some doubt about this). His Lordship considered that cases on loss of innkeepers' liens and improvers' liens through loss of possession of the relevant chattel were not analogous to a case of a solicitor's general lien. As one commentator has observed, 'though the judge did not say so, a ground of distinction seems to have been that the accounts were not choses in possession, as was the case in the old authorities, but debts, choses in action' (A Hudson, 'Solicitors' Liens' in N Palmer and E McKendrick (eds), *Interests in Goods* (2nd edn, 1998), p 651). It is well established that a solicitor is allowed a lien over money in his client account (*Loescher v Dean* [1950] Ch 491), unless the reason the money is there is inconsistent with a lien arising, for example it is there for a particular purpose (*Withers LLP v Rybak* [2011] EWCA Civ 1419, [2012] 1 WLR 1748 at [22]).

3.   Therefore, a lien may be terminated by the following means:

(a) a loss of possession to the lienor (or to a third party, as the lienee then loses his immediate right to possession and will be unable to redeliver to the lienor: *Mulliner v Florence* (1878) 3 QBD 484 at 489; cf s 48(2) of the Sale of Goods Act 1979);

(b) waiver of the necessity of making a tender (as outlined by Scrutton LJ in *Albemarle Supply Co Ltd v Hind and Co* (above, p 1055), and, recently, by Thirlwall J in *Spencer v S Franses Ltd* [2011] EWHC 1269 (QB) at [264]–[267]);

(c) payment or tender of the amount due.
    It may also be lost by:

(d) accepting alternative security in substitution for the lien (save that taking bills of exchange as alternative security usually only suspends the lien so that it will revive on dishonour—*Stevenson v Blakelock* (1813) 1 M & S 535);

(e) a wrongful sale (*Mulliner v Florence* (1878) 3 QBD 484) or other act of conversion (eg using the goods subject to the lien: *Rust v McNaught and Co Ltd* (1918) 144 LT Jo 440, CA).

Furthermore, the holder of a general lien will be held to have abandoned it if he agrees to release the goods merely on payment of sums due in respect of those goods alone (*Morley v Hay* (1828) 3 Man & Ry KB 396).

QUESTIONS

1.   Distinguish *Forth v Simpson* (above, p 1042) from *Albemarle Supply Co Ltd v Hind and Co.*

2.   Would the decision in *Pennington v Reliance Motor Works Ltd* have been different if: (a) E had obtained delivery from the defendants by stating (untruthfully) that he had instructed the plaintiff to pay the defendants directly (see *Wallace v Woodgate* (1824) 1 C & P 575); or, alternatively, (b) when returning the car to E, the defendants had expressly reserved a right to retake the goods? (See Bell, op cit, p 147.)

(h) Registration

As a common law lien is a possessory security it does not require registration by virtue of the Bills of Sale Acts 1878–1882, nor does it fall under the new, optional company charge registration regime set out in ss 859A ff of the Companies Act 2006 (*Trident International Ltd v Barlow* [1999] 2 BCLC 506, CA, decided under the old mandatory registration regime, where it was held that the fact the lienee had a contractual power of sale did not turn a contractual general lien into a registrable charge; see also *Jarl Tra AB v Convoys Ltd* [2003] EWHC 1488 (Ch), [2003] 2 Lloyd's Rep 459). But a contractual right to take possession of the debtor's goods in satisfaction of a debt will be characterised as a charge (*Re Cosslett (Contractors) Ltd* [1998] Ch 495 at 509–509, CA; *Online Catering Ltd v Acton* [2010] EWCA Civ 58, [2011] QB 204 at [22]–[23]).

3 REFORM

The Law Commission published its Final Report, *Company Security Interests*, in 2005 (LC Report No 296). The Law Commission recommended that there should be a scheme of electronic 'notice-filing' for charges created by companies (for further details, see p 1022 above). However, the Law Commission recommended that, with two exceptions, a 'pledge' (which the Law Commission defined to include a contractual possessory lien) was to fall outside the new notice-filing scheme (para 3.17). The reason for this exclusion is that where there is actual possession by the creditor, the existence of the pledge would be evident to third parties, and hence a 'false wealth' risk—where assets that may appear to be owned by the debtor are in fact subject to securities in favour of other parties—would not apply. Similarly, where the creditor has constructive possession of the goods that are in the hands of a third party who has attorned to the creditor, the existence of the pledge would soon be found out. However, the situation is different where the goods are in the hands of the debtor and the debtor attorns to the creditor. It would be difficult for the third party to find out that the debtor's apparent possession was subject to the creditor's security in the absence of any requirement to register. Thus, the Law Commission recommended that such attornments should be registrable under a notice-filing system (para 3.21). For similar reasons, the Law Commission also recommended that where the debtor was given possession of the pledged goods under a trust receipt, the pledge would become registrable unless the goods were returned to the creditor's possession within 15 business days (para 3.25). Liens arising by operation of law, for example a repairer's lien, would not require registration (para 3.27). The reform of company law which took place in 2006, and again in 2013, did not incorporate any of these recommendations (see further, p 1023 above).

CHAPTER 26

NON-POSSESSORY SECURITY

1 MORTGAGE

(a) Mortgage defined

Santley v Wilde
[1899] 2 Ch 474, Court of Appeal

> **Lindley MR**: . . . [A] mortgage is a conveyance of land or an assignment of chattels as a security for the payment of a debt or the discharge of some other obligation for which it is given. This is the idea of a mortgage: and the security is redeemable on the payment or discharge of such debt or obligation, any provision to the contrary notwithstanding.

Downsview Nominees Ltd v First City Corpn Ltd
[1993] AC 295, Privy Council

> **Lord Templeman:** A mortgage, whether legal or equitable, is security for repayment of a debt. The security may be constituted by a conveyance, assignment or demise or by a charge on any interest in real or personal property. An equitable mortgage is a contract which creates a charge on property but does not pass a legal estate to the creditor. Its operation is that of an executory assurance, which, as between the parties, and so far as equitable rights and remedies are concerned, is equivalent to an actual assurance, and is enforceable under the equitable jurisdiction of the court. All this is well settled law and is to be found in more detail in the textbooks on the subject . . .

NOTES

1. A mortgage involves the transfer of ownership of property from the mortgagor (the debtor or a third party) to the mortgagee (the creditor) as security for a debt or other obligation (although this no longer remains true for a legal mortgage of land which, since

1926, must be made either by demise for a term of years or by charge by way of legal mortgage: Law of Property Act 1925, ss 85, 86).[1] A mortgage may be either legal or equitable. It may be of real or personal property.[2] As a mortgage does not require the delivery of possession of the mortgaged property, that property can be tangible or intangible (ie choses in action can be mortgaged).

2. A legal mortgage of personal property is a transfer of legal title to the mortgagee with an express or implied proviso for retransfer on redemption.[3] As future property cannot generally be transferred at common law, a legal mortgage usually involves the present transfer of property to which the transferor holds the legal title at the date of the transfer.

3. The mode of creating a legal mortgage of personal property varies according to the subject matter of the mortgage (the following summary is based on L Gullifer, *Goode on Legal Problems of Credit and Security* (5th edn, 2013), para 1–13).

- A legal mortgage of goods may be oral but if in writing and given by an individual it must be made by deed and in accordance with the form and other requirements of the Bills of Sale Acts 1878 and 1882 (see below, pp 1078 ff), and if made by a company it may be registered under s 859A of the Companies Act 2006, with failure to register a registrable charge rendering it void against the administrator, liquidator, or any (secured) creditor of the company under s 859H of the 2006 Act (see below, pp 1080 ff). The legal mortgage of certain types of goods must also be in a prescribed form and registered in a specialist register, for example a mortgage of a registered ship must be entered in the register of ship mortgages, a mortgage of a registered aircraft must be entered in the register of aircraft mortgages.

- A legal mortgage of a debt or other chose in action is effected by assignment in writing under the hand of the assignor with written notice of the assignment being given to the debtor (thereby complying with the Law of Property Act 1925, s 136; see above, p 901), or alternatively by novation, and in the case of documentary intangibles there is the option of negotiation by delivery together with any necessary indorsements.

- A legal mortgage of registrable intellectual property rights is effected by entry in the relevant register (ie the register of patents, the register of trade marks, or the register of designs: but there is no registration of copyright).

- A legal mortgage of registered securities, such as shares and bonds, is effected by novation through entry of a transfer on the issuer's register or the CREST register, and by delivery of possession with intent to transfer ownership in the case of bearer securities. A legal mortgage cannot be taken over intermediated (indirectly held) securities as the interest of the mortgagor is equitable.

4. The nature of an equitable mortgage was considered in the next case.

---

[1] In unregistered land, legal mortgages are created either by the grant of a leasehold interest or the creation of a legal charge. In registered land, the only legal mortgage is a registered legal charge (Land Registration Act 2002, s 23(1)(a)).

[2] As the mortgage of land is dealt with in the casebooks on land law, we shall concentrate on the mortgage of personal property (defined above, p 54).

[3] A mortgagor is said to have an 'equity of redemption' entitling him to redeem or recover the property even though he has failed to pay at the appointed time. The equity of redemption may be determined by release, lapse of time, sale, and foreclosure (*Fisher and Lightwood's Law of Mortgage* (14th edn, 2014), para 1.9).

Swiss Bank Corpn v Lloyds Bank Ltd

[1982] AC 584, Court of Appeal

The plaintiff bank agreed to lend foreign currency to IFT to enable it to buy shares and loan stock in FIBI, an Israeli bank. Under clause 3(b) of the loan agreement, IFT agreed to observe all the conditions attached to the Bank of England consent which had been obtained for the loan under the Exchange Control Act 1947 (since repealed). The conditions were, inter alia, that on acquisition the FIBI securities should be held in a separate account and that repayment of the loan was to be made from the proceeds of sale of those securities. The plaintiff bank claimed to be an equitable chargee of the FIBI securities or the proceeds of sale thereof. Browne-Wilkinson J upheld the claim but was reversed on appeal.

Buckley LJ: We are not concerned here with a charge on an equitable interest in property but with an equitable charge upon property in the legal ownership of the party creating the charge.

An equitable charge may, it is said, take the form either of an equitable mortgage or of an equitable charge not by way of mortgage. An equitable mortgage is created when the legal owner of the property constituting the security enters into some instrument or does some act which, though insufficient to confer a legal estate or title in the subject matter upon the mortgagee, nevertheless demonstrates a binding intention to create a security in favour of the mortgagee, or in other words evidences a contract to do so. . . . From the way in which the judge dealt with the matter in his judgment it is, I think, clear that he was applying his mind to the question whether the circumstances of the case gave rise to an equitable charge by way of mortgage. The argument in this court has also proceeded upon the same lines, but I must not overlook the possibility of the existence of an equitable charge which is not of the nature of a mortgage.

The essence of any transaction by way of mortgage is that a debtor confers upon his creditor a proprietary interest in property of the debtor, or undertakes in a binding manner to do so, by the realisation or appropriation of which the creditor can procure the discharge of the debtor's liability to him, and that the proprietary interest is redeemable, or the obligation to create it is defeasible, in the event of the debtor discharging his liability. If there has been no legal transfer of a proprietary interest but merely a binding undertaking to confer such an interest, that obligation, if specifically enforceable, will confer a proprietary interest in the subject matter in equity. The obligation will be specifically enforceable if it is an obligation for the breach of which damages would be an inadequate remedy. A contract to mortgage property, real or personal, will, normally at least, be specifically enforceable, for a mere claim to damages or repayment is obviously less valuable than a security in the event of the debtor's insolvency. If it is specifically enforceable, the obligation to confer the proprietary interest will give rise to an equitable charge upon the subject matter by way of mortgage.

It follows that whether a particular transaction gives rise to an equitable charge of this nature must depend upon the intention of the parties ascertained from what they have done in the then existing circumstances. The intention may be expressed or it may be inferred. If the debtor undertakes to segregate a particular fund or asset and to pay the debt out of that fund or asset, the inference may be drawn, in the absence of any contra indication, that the parties' intention is that the creditor should have such a proprietary interest in the segregated fund or asset as will enable him to realise out of it the amount owed to him by the debtor: compare *Re Nanwa Gold Mines Ltd* [1955] 1 WLR 1080 and contrast *Moseley v Cressey's Co* (1865) LR 1 Eq 405 where there was no obligation to segregate the deposits. But notwithstanding that the matter depends upon the intention of the parties, if upon the true construction of the relevant documents in the light of any admissible evidence as to surrounding circumstances the parties have entered into a transaction the legal effect of which is to give rise to an equitable charge in favour of one of them over property of the other, the fact that they may not have realised this consequence will not mean that there is no charge. They must be presumed to intend the consequence of their acts.

In the present case the loan agreement contained no express requirement that IFT should charge the FIBI securities or the fruits of the borrowing by way of mortgage to secure repayment of the loan. Such intention must be found, if at all, by implication.

A binding obligation that a particular fund shall be applied in a particular manner may found no more than an injunction to restrain its application in another way, but if the obligation be to pay out of the fund a debt due by one party to the transaction to the other, the fund belonging to or being due to the debtor, this amounts to an equitable assignment *pro tanto* of the fund: see *Rodick v Gandell* (1852) 1 De GM & G 763, 777 and *Palmer v Carey* [1926] AC 703, 706–707:

> This is but an instance of a familiar doctrine of equity that a contract for valuable considera-tion to transfer or charge a subject matter passes a beneficial interest by way of property in that subject matter if the contract is one of which a court of equity will decree specific performance.

With this in mind I address myself to the construction and effect of clause 3(b) of the loan agree-ment. It is said that by that subclause IFT covenanted with the plaintiff that all the requirements of the Bank of England from time to time would be observed by IFT during the continuance of the agreement. Accordingly, it is said that IFT covenanted that the loan should be repaid out of the sale proceeds of the securities in the 'relative loan portfolio' (see condition (vii)) and out of no other source save in so far as those sale proceeds should fall short of being sufficient. So, it is said, the relevant loan portfolio, which by the terms of the Bank of England permission was required to be kept as a separate fund distinct from any other foreign currency securities owned by IFT, should be the primary source for repayment of the loan. Therefore, it is contended, the parties have manifested an intention that the plaintiff should have such a proprietary interest in the FIBI securities or any other fruits of the borrowing into which they might be converted from time to time as would enable the plaintiff to realise out of that property, so far as it should suffice, any amount required to repay the loan.

Mr Parker has conceded that IFT was only obliged by clause 3(b) of the loan agreement to observe such requirements of the Bank of England as might be in force from time to time. The Bank of England could have waived or rescinded condition (vii) at any time. He accepts that the equitable charge which the plaintiff claims was consequently a precarious one. The fact that an equitable charge may be precarious, however, is not in my view necessarily a sufficient ground for holding that there is no such charge. A mortgage of a terminable lease would be a precarious security, vulnerable to determination of the lease by the landlord, but I can see no reason why such a lease should not be capable of being the subject matter of a mortgage, if a mortgagee of it could be found. In the present case, however, it is not the continued existence of the subject matter which is precarious; it is those very terms of the contract which are alleged to give rise to the equitable charge, that is to say, the Bank of England conditions requiring segregation of the fruits of the borrowing and repayment of the loan thereout, which might have been terminated or waived by the Bank of England at any time during the continuance of the agreement. The Bank of England might at any time have permitted repayment of the loan out of some other fund, and in that event the plaintiff could have had no ground of complaint about the loan being so discharged. A security of this kind, if capable of constituting a security at all, would, it seems to me, be so precarious that one would need very clear indications that the parties intended, or must be taken to have intended, to enter into such an arrangement by way of security, particularly where the relevant agreement contains an express charge on another subject matter. In my judgment, however, clause 3(b) of the agreement was incapable, upon its true construction, of constituting any security or creating any equitable charge. So far as it consisted of a covenant, it required IFT to observe the requirements of the Bank of England during the continuance of the agreement. It was directed to ensuring that the loan should not become tainted with any illegality by reason of any failure to comply with those requirements, such as they might be from time to time. In this respect it is, I think, significant that the covenant is linked with the warranty contained in the same sub-clause, which is obviously directed to the legality of the transaction at the date of the agreement. The covenant is, in my opinion, in substance a negative one, viz not to do anything which might invalidate the bargain between the parties; but, although some argument was addressed to us based upon this negative quality, it is not that which weighs with me. What is to my mind important is that there is here no obligation to repay the loan out of the fruits of the borrowing in any event; the covenant merely requires IFT to repay the loan in a manner approved by the Bank of England. No doubt the plaintiff could have objected to repayment in any manner not so approved and could have obtained an injunction restraining such repayment, if this would have served any useful purpose; but the covenant does not, in my judgment, confer upon the plaintiff any specifically enforceable right to have the loan repaid out of the FIBI securities or out of any other fruits of the borrowing. It consequently did not, in my judgment, give rise to an equitable charge by way of mortgage.

[**Brandon** and **Brightman LJJ** concurred.]

[The decision of the Court of Appeal was affirmed by the House of Lords [1982] AC 584 at 604.]

NOTES

1. An equitable mortgage of personal property is a transfer of an equitable title to the mortgagee, or a declaration of trust in his favour, with an express or implied proviso for retransfer or termination of the trust on redemption.

2. An equitable mortgage can arise as follows:

(a) by a present mortgage of an equitable interest (eg a second mortgage of goods when the first mortgage is legal—the second mortgage will be equitable as the owner divests himself of his legal title by the first mortgage thereby leaving himself only with an equity of redemption); or

(b) by an agreement to give a legal or equitable mortgage, so long as it is supported by consideration and can be specifically enforced (see *Swiss Bank Corpn v Lloyds Bank Ltd*, above, p 1061; *Thames Guaranty Ltd v Campbell* [1985] QB 210 at 218; affirmed [1985] QB 210, CA)—the agreement may be express or implied and may even be based on the intention to create a legal mortgage which is ineffectual for want of proper form.

3. An agreement to mortgage after-acquired property can only operate as a contract to assign the property when it is acquired. A debtor's agreement to mortgage his after-acquired property will give the creditor an equitable interest in the property as soon as it is acquired by the debtor, so long as the creditor has actually advanced the money (ie the consideration is executed) and the property is described sufficiently to be identifiable when acquired (see the landmark decision of the House of Lords in *Holroyd v Marshall*

(1862) 10 HL Cas 191, above, p 960; as explained in the equally important case of *Tailby v Official Receiver* (1888) 13 App Cas 523, HL, above, p 961). The consideration must be executed because equity will not decree specific performance of a contract to borrow and lend money (*Roger v Challis* (1859) 27 Beav 175).

4.   An equitable mortgage of personal property, not being of an equitable interest in such property (which must be in writing under the Law of Property Act 1925, s 53(l)(c)), can be oral (contrast this with an equitable mortgage of land, which must be in writing signed by or on behalf of the parties: Law of Property (Miscellaneous Provisions) Act 1989, s 2(1); an equitable mortgage can no longer be created solely by deposit of the title deeds: *United Bank of Kuwait plc v Sahib* [1997] Ch 107, CA). However, any security (including a mortgage) provided in relation to a regulated (consumer credit or consumer hire) agreement by a third party (when it must be provided at the express or implied request of the debtor or hirer) is required by s 105(1) of the Consumer Credit Act 1974 to be expressed in writing (s 105(6) confines s 105(1) to security provided by third parties).

5.   In *Palmer v Carey* [1926] AC 703 at 706–707, Lord Wrenbury, delivering the advice of the Privy Council, held that a contractual agreement that a specific fund be applied in a particular way could found an injunction to restrain its application in another way but that for a security interest to arise there must also be a specifically enforceable obligation on the debtor to pay the debt out of the fund. The bank's claim to a security interest failed in *Swiss Bank Corpn v Lloyds Bank Ltd* because the loan agreement did not require the loan to be repaid out of the proceeds of sale of the borrower's securities. Similarly, in *Flightline Ltd v Edwards* [2003] EWCA Civ 63, [2003] 1 WLR 1200, where a creditor agreed to discharge a freezing order on funds being paid on the debtor's behalf into a bank account held in the joint names of the parties' solicitors, the Court of Appeal held that the creditor had no valid charge over the monies standing to the credit of the account because it was not a term of the agreement that any judgment obtained by the creditor had to be satisfied out of the monies in the account. In *Re TXU Europe Group plc* [2003] EWHC 1305, [2004] 1 BCLC 519, a company agreed with its senior executives that they would continue to be entitled to final salary pensions, despite the cap on earnings that could be used for such assessments under the Finance Act 1989. The company set up a fund which would match the extent to which the pensions were not funded by the Inland Revenue-approved scheme. It was clear that the fund was intended to be the source from which the pension obligations would be met, but it was held that the senior executives had no specifically enforceable rights to look to the fund to satisfy their pension claims and did not have a charge over the fund.

(b) Enforcement

The mortgagee may sue the mortgagor on his personal covenant to pay the debt.[4] In addition the mortgagee has a number of *in rem* remedies where the mortgagor is in default.

(i) Foreclosure

Foreclosure extinguishes the equity of redemption of the mortgagor, and all persons claiming through him, and vests the mortgaged property absolutely in the mortgagee. This gives

---

[4] Sometimes a person may provide real security for another's debts without undertaking any personal liability himself (as in *Re Conley* [1938] 2 All ER 127).

the mortgagee a windfall where the value of the mortgaged property exceeds the secured debt. But foreclosure also extinguishes the residue of the secured debt so that if, after foreclosure, the secured property turns out to be worth less than the secured debt the mortgagee cannot pursue the mortgagor for the shortfall. Unlike the remedy of sale under a power of sale (see below), or appropriation of financial collateral under the Financial Collateral Arrangements (No 2) Regulations 2003 (SI 2003/3226; as amended) (see below, p 1067), foreclosure requires a court order. Foreclosure proceedings are usually prolonged, the court being keen to give the mortgagor every opportunity to redeem, and hence are very rare (*Palk v Mortgage Services Funding plc* [1993] Ch 330 at 336, per Sir Donald Nicholls V-C). The Privy Council has even gone so far as to describe the remedy of foreclosure as 'obsolescent' (*Cukurova Finance International Ltd v Alfa Telecom Turkey Ltd* [2009] UKPC 19, [2009] 3 All ER 849 at [13]).

(ii) Sale

Stubbs v Slater
[1910] 1 Ch 632, Court of Appeal

P, being indebted to the defendant stockbrokers, deposited with them as security a certificate for 390 shares, and signed a blank transfer of the same. After sending P repeated notices that they would have to sell the shares if the debt was not paid, the defendants sold the shares. P sued the defendants for wrongful conversion of the shares, alleging inter alia that the sale was bad because the notices demanded more than was owed. The Court of Appeal held that in the circumstances the defendants had reasonably exercised their implied power of sale as mortgagees.

> **Cozens-Hardy MR** referred to his own judgment in *Harrold v Plenty* [1901] 2 Ch 314 and continued: . . . This then was a transaction of mortgage and not a transaction of pledge. It was a transaction of mortgage, in which there was no express power of sale given, but which by law involves and implies a right in the mortgagee to sell after giving reasonable notice. I need scarcely pause to say that the notice here was reasonable, if ever there was reasonable notice. Then the matter came before the Court of Appeal in 1902 in *Deverges v Sandeman, Clark & Co* ([1902] 1 Ch 579). There it was laid down that in the case of a mortgage by deposit of shares there is an implied power to sell, if no time is fixed, upon giving reasonable notice, and the only point decided in that case was whether or not the notice was reasonable. Nothing else was there decided except that the general principle applicable to transactions of this kind was for the first time laid down by the Court of Appeal. In the course of my judgment, which I refer to only because I see no reason to change the view which I there expressed, I say this: 'Although a mistake as to the amount due may destroy the effect of the notice, as between pledgor and pledgee—*Pigot v Cubley* ((1864) 15 CBNS 701)—I think that is not the law as between mortgagor and mortgagee. In order to restrain a mortgagee from selling in the absence of fraud, it is not sufficient to contest the amount due on the mortgage. The mortgagor must pay into Court, or tender to the mortgagee, the amount claimed to be due.' I there referred to *Pigot v Cubley*, saying that a mistake as to the amount due might destroy the effect of the notice as between pledgor and pledgee. I have looked at that case again and as at present advised I can find nothing in the judgment in the Court which bears out the last sentence in the head-note, which says that 'a notice that he'—ie, the pledgee—'will sell unless an excessive sum be paid immediately, is not such a notice as will justify the sale.' But, however that may be, it seems to me that in a mortgage as distinguished from a pledge that head-note affords no ground for the contention that a mortgagee has not a power of sale after giving reasonable notice unless the notice specifies with precise

accuracy the amount due on the mortgage. I see no ground for making any exception from the general law in this particular class of mortgage. There was here alleged to be due on the mortgage the sum of £69 odd. That being so, and there having been abundant applications for payment, I am clearly of opinion that the mortgagee had a perfect right to sell these shares.

[**Buckley J** delivered a concurring judgment. **Joyce J** concurred.]

NOTES

1. By s 101(1) of the Law of Property Act 1925, where the mortgage is made by deed, a mortgagee is given a statutory power to sell the mortgaged property when the mortgage money has become due (but, under s 103, the power of sale is not exercisable unless the mortgagor has failed to pay the mortgage money after three months' notice in writing, or the mortgagor has fallen at least two months in arrears on payments of interest, or there has been a breach by the mortgagor of an obligation contained in the mortgage agreement or the Law of Property Act 1925). This power applies to any mortgage of any property made by deed, save those to which the Bills of Sale Acts apply (see AP Bell, *Modern Law of Personal Property in England and Ireland* (1989), p 187; and below, p 1077). However, in *Re Morritt, ex p Official Receiver* (1886) 18 QBD 222 at 241–242, Lopes LJ held (Lord Esher MR concurring) that a power of sale was to be implied into a mortgage within the Bills of Sale Act (1878) Amendment Act 1882, by virtue of s 7 of that Act.

2. *Stubbs v Slater* is a case where a mortgagee of intangible property was held to have a common law power of sale. Whether a mortgagee of tangible property has such a common law power of sale is not clear. In *Re Morritt, ex p Official Receiver* (1886) 18 QBD 222 at 233, Cotton LJ held that a mortgagee of personal chattels, which are in his possession, had a common law power of sale (Lindley and Bowen LJJ concurred). But in the same case Fry LJ, dissenting, held that a power of sale was not to be implied by law into a mortgage of chattels (at 235). See also *Deverges v Sandeman, Clark & Co* [1902] 1 Ch 579 at 589, where Vaughan Williams LJ questioned whether a mortgagee of personal chattels had a common law power of sale. For contrasting treatment of this issue, compare Crossley Vaines, *Personal Property* (5th edn, 1973), p 447, with Bell, op cit, p 187.

3. An express power of sale will usually be inserted into a well-drafted mortgage of real or personal property. Even if the mortgagee has no express or implied power of sale, he may apply to the court for an order for sale (Law of Property Act 1925, s 91).

4. Where the mortgagee sells secured property he owes the mortgagor (and others interested) equitable duties to act in good faith, not to use his rights and powers for improper or ulterior purposes (*Worwood v Leisure Merchandising Services Ltd* [2002] 1 BCLC 249; *Meretz Investments NV v ACP Ltd* [2006] EWHC 74 (Ch), [2006] 3 All ER 1029 at [314]: mixed motives are fine so long as one of which is a genuine purpose of recovering, in whole or in part, the amount secured by the mortgage), and to take reasonable care to obtain a proper price (*Downsview Nominees Ltd v First City Corpn Ltd* [1993] AC 295; *PK Airfinance SARL v Alpstream AG* [2015] EWCA Civ 1318, [2015] 2 WLR 875 at [198]–[221], [245]–[250]). However, the mortgagee owes no general duty of care in dealing with the secured property: he is free to exercise his powers as he chooses, ie he has a free choice as to the timing of the sale (*Downsview Nominees Ltd v First City Corpn Ltd*, above; *Silven Properties Ltd v Royal Bank* *of Scotland plc* [2003] EWCA Civ 1409, [2004] 1 WLR 997 at [14]; *Den Norske Bank ASA v Acemex Management Co Ltd* [2003] EWCA Civ 1559, [2004] 1 Lloyd's Rep 1 at [23]). The mortgagee is under no duty to preserve his security unless and until he takes possession of it (*AIB Finance Ltd v Debtors* [1998] 2 All ER 929, CA, although Nourse LJ said (at 937) that it may be possible to conceive of circumstances in which a mortgagee could come under a duty to cooperate with the mortgagor in procuring a sale of a mortgaged property and business as a going concern at a proper price before taking possession). Any surplus following sale will be held for the mortgagor, but the mortgagor remains liable for any shortfall on his express covenant for payment contained in the mortgage deed (*Bristol & West plc v Bartlett* [2002] EWCA Civ 1181, [2003] 1 WLR 284; held that save for exceptional cases, which could not be envisaged at present, claims for a mortgage debt are governed by s 20 of the Limitation Act 1980, which means that the mortgagee has 12 years from accrual of the cause of action to sue for the principal of the debt but only six years to sue for interest; see also *West Bromwich BS v Wilkinson* [2005] UKHL 44, [2005] 1 WLR 2303).

(iii) Appointment of a receiver

When a mortgage is made by deed a court has power to appoint a receiver over the mortgaged property (Law of Property Act 1925, ss 101, 109). However, in most cases the mortgage contains an express power of appointment. A receiver, like the holder of the security who has appointed him, owes a duty to act in good faith and, if he decides to sell the charged property, a limited duty to take reasonable care to obtain a proper price. In the *Downsview Nominees* case (above) the Privy Council dismissed an argument that a receiver owes a more general duty of care to the chargor or to a guarantor of his debt, but this view has been since qualified by the ruling of the Court of Appeal in *Medforth v Blake*, discussed below, p 1121.

(iv) Possession

A mortgagor who defaults is liable to surrender his right to remain in possession of the mortgaged property. Where a mortgage is a security bill of sale for the purposes of the Bills of Sale Act (1878) Amendment Act 1882, there is an implied right of seizure, which is required by the Act to be exercised within certain limits (see ss 7 and 13: discussed below). Where the Consumer Credit Act 1974 applies the seizure will be subject to the 'default notice' provisions of that Act (ss 87–89: discussed below), and the right of seizure under the 1882 Act will be restricted accordingly (s 7A of the 1882 Act).

(v) Appropriation of financial collateral

The Financial Collateral Arrangements (No 2) Regulations 2003 (SI 2003/ 3226; as amended), implementing the Financial Collateral Directive 2002/47/EC, establish a new regime for taking and enforcement of financial collateral arrangements. The main changes which the Directive required to be made to English law concerned the abolition of the requirement to register charges (some other formalities are also dispensed with) and the disapplication of those provisions of insolvency law which restricted the rights of the creditor with security over financial collateral.

The regulations apply to any written security or title-transfer financial collateral arrangement (key definitions are found in reg 3(1)), where both the collateral provider and the collateral taker are 'non-natural persons', for example two corporates (questions have been raised as to whether the regulations are *ultra vires*, most recently in *USA v Nolan* [2015] UKSC 63, [2015] 3 WLR 1105 at [67]–[69] (*obiter*), but the issue is likely to become redundant with the recent coming into force of ss 255–256 of the Banking Act 2009, which allow HM Treasury to provide that the regulations, and anything done under or in reliance on them, be treated as effective despite any lack of *vires*). The regulations are designed to limit risk in financial transactions where money credited to an account (or similar), securities, and claims for repayment of a loan made by a bank or credit institution, are used as collateral under security and title-transfer structures.

The regulations have introduced a right of 'appropriation' as a new, self-help remedy allowing, in the event of default, for the realisation of collateral held under a security financial collateral arrangement without court order, so long as the power of appropriation has been included in the security financial collateral arrangement (reg 17). The collateral taker appropriates the collateral by becoming absolute owner, which, effectively, operates as a sale of the collateral by the collateral taker to itself. In order to protect the collateral provider, the collateral taker must value the collateral in a commercially reasonable manner and account to the collateral provider for any surplus (reg 18(2)). The collateral provider remains liable to pay any shortfall where the value of the collateral is insufficient to meet the secured obligation (reg 18(3)). Appropriation can be of the absolute legal title (if the mortgage is legal) or the absolute equitable title (if the mortgage is equitable), but there must be some overt act evidencing the collateral taker's intention to appropriate, which is communicated to the collateral provider (*Cukurova Finance International Ltd v Alfa Telecom Turkey Ltd* [2009] UKPC 19, [2009] 1 CLC 701 at [35]: equitable mortgagee of shares (taker) appropriated by sending a letter asserting full beneficial ownership to the mortgagor (provider)). In an exceptional case, the court may be prepared to protect the mortgagor's equity of redemption by ordering relief against forfeiture on terms (*Cukurova Finance International Ltd v Alfa Telecom Turkey Ltd* [2013] UKPC 2 and [2013] UKPC 20, both reported at [2015] 2 WLR 875).

QUESTION

What are the differences between 'foreclosure' of a mortgage and 'appropriation' of financial collateral held under a security financial collateral arrangement (pursuant to the Financial Collateral Arrangements (No 2) Regulations 2003)?

2 EQUITABLE CHARGE

(a) Equitable charge defined

Swiss Bank Corpn v Lloyds Bank Ltd
[1982] AC 584, Court of Appeal

Buckley LJ: An equitable charge which is not an equitable mortgage is said to be created when property is expressly or constructively made liable, or specially appropriated, to the discharge of a debt or some other obligation, and confers on the chargee a right of realisation by judicial process, that is to say, by the appointment of a receiver or an order for sale . . .

Re Cosslett (Contractors) Ltd

[1998] Ch 495, Court of Appeal

> **Millett LJ:** It is of the essence of a charge that a particular asset or class of assets is appropriated to the satisfaction of a debt or other obligation of the chargor or a third party, so that the chargee is entitled to look to the asset and its proceeds for the discharge of the liability.

Re Bank of Credit and Commerce International SA (No 8)

[1998] AC 214, House of Lords

> **Lord Hoffmann**: A charge is a security interest created without any transfer of title or possession to the beneficiary. An equitable charge can be created by an informal transaction for value (legal charges may require a deed or registration or both) and over any kind of property (equitable as well as legal) but is subject to the doctrine of purchaser for value without notice applicable to all equitable interests.

NOTES

1.   In *Re Bond Worth Ltd* [1980] Ch 228 at 250, Slade J stated that: 'The technical difference between a "mortgage" or "charge", though in practice the phrases are often used interchangeably, is that a mortgage involves a conveyance of property subject to a right of redemption, whereas a charge conveys nothing and merely gives the chargee certain rights over the property as security for the loan.' As a charge is a mere encumbrance and does not convey ownership of property, it can only arise in equity (and so is called an 'equitable charge') or by statute (as is the case with a charge by way of legal mortgage over land: Law of Property Act 1925, ss 85–87). A charge over personal property must be equitable, it cannot be legal.

2.   Since a charge, unlike a mortgage, does not involve a conveyance of a proprietary interest, a chargee cannot foreclose or take possession. The remedy of the chargee is to apply to the court for an order for sale or for the appointment of a receiver. In practice, however, there is little difference between a mortgage and a charge as it is usual for the instrument creating the charge to provide expressly that the chargee has the rights of a mortgagee. Note, however, that if the charge is a floating charge secured over the whole or substantially the whole of the company's property, then the chargee may no longer appoint an administrative receiver (Insolvency Act 1986, s 72A; but subject to certain limited exceptions in ss 72B–72H: major capital market and financial market transactions, utility transactions, and public–private finance transactions).

3.   In general, a charge must be created by agreement which must be supported by consideration (see above, pp 1016-1017). An agreement for value for an equitable charge will be treated as an equitable charge (*Tailby v Official Receiver* (1888) 13 App Cas 523 at 549, per Lord Macnaghten). As a charge creates an equitable interest, and does not transfer such an interest, it falls outside s 53(1)(c) of the Law of Property Act 1925 and so may be oral. If the charge extends to future property it must be given for value (a deed is not enough) and the property must be sufficiently described to be identifiable when acquired (see the important decisions of the House of Lords in *Holroyd v Marshall,* above, p 960, and *Tailby v Official Receiver*, above, p 961). It is also possible to create an equitable charge by declaration of trust (see *Re Bond Worth Ltd* [1980] Ch 228 at 250; cf *Carreras Rothman Ltd v Freeman Mathews Treasure Ltd* [1985] Ch 207 at 227).

(b) Fixed and floating charges

(i) *The nature of fixed and floating charges*

> A specific charge, I think, is one that without more fastens on ascertained and definite property or property capable of being ascertained and defined; a floating charge, on the other hand, is ambulatory and shifting in its nature, hovering over and so to speak floating with the property which it is intended to affect until some event occurs or some act is done which causes it to settle and fasten on the subject of the charge within its reach and grasp . . .
>
> *(Illingworth v Holdsworth* [1904] AC 355 at 358, per Lord Macnaghten)

A fixed (or 'specific') charge is a charge created over identified property which prevents the debtor dealing with the property without first paying off the indebtedness secured by the charge or obtaining the chargee's consent. If the debtor does not do this before transferring the property, the transferee will take the property subject to the charge, unless he is a bona fide purchaser for value without notice. Future property may be made the subject of an agreement to charge, provided the agreement is for value and the future property is sufficiently described as to be identifiable when acquired by the chargor. Once the property is acquired by the chargor it automatically becomes subject to the charge (see the landmark House of Lords' decision of *Holroyd v Marshall* (1862) 10 HL Cas 191, above, p 960). Until then the security interest is inchoate, but on acquisition of property by the chargor it bites, taking effect retrospectively from the date of the security agreement (see *Tailby v Official Receiver* (1888) 13 App Cas 523, another important House of Lords' decision, above, p 961).[5]

By contrast, a floating charge 'hovers' over a changing fund of assets, including assets acquired by the debtor after the creation of the charge. Under a floating charge the debtor is at liberty to deal with the charged assets in the ordinary course of the debtor's business, and does so free from the charge. Only upon the happening of certain events, such as the appointment of a receiver or insolvency, is the floating charge said to 'crystallise' and become fixed on the assets then comprising the fund or subsequently acquired by the debtor. At that point the debtor has no further right to deal with the charged assets.

It is not possible in English law for individual borrowers to give a floating charge over their assets, because to do so would infringe the Bills of Sale Acts of 1878 and 1882 (and in particular it would be impossible to meet the requirement that the goods affected be specifically described in a schedule to the instrument). But the Bills of Sale Acts do not apply to companies, and so it is possible for a company to grant a floating charge over some or all of its assets, both present and future. This allows a company to give security over assets which are continually turned over or consumed and replaced in the ordinary course of business, for example over fluctuating assets such as stock-in-trade, raw materials, and book debts. The form of business organisation called a Limited Liability Partnership (LLP), being a body corporate, can also borrow on the security of a floating charge (see the Limited Liability Partnerships Act 2000).

The essential characteristics (if not a complete definition) of the floating charge, and the distinction between a floating charge and a fixed charge, appear from the cases which follow.

---

[5] However, the agreement may evince a contrary intention, as in the case of a floating charge. Crystallisation of a floating charge is not retrospective: only *qua* floating security does the charge relate back to the date of the security agreement (see E McKendrick, *Goode on Commercial Law* (5th edn, 2016), p 704 fn 61).

Agnew v Commissioner of Inland Revenue (Re Brumark Investments Ltd)

[2001] UKPC 28, [2001] 2 AC 710, Privy Council

The facts and a longer extract appear on p 985.

> **Lord Millett**: The most celebrated, and certainly the most often cited, description of a floating charge is that given by Romer LJ in *Re Yorkshire Woolcombers Association Ltd* [1903] 2 Ch 284, 295:
>
>> I certainly do not intend to attempt to give an exact definition of the term 'floating charge' nor am I prepared to say that there will not be a floating charge within the meaning of the Act , which does not contain all of the three characteristics that I am about to mention, but I certainly think that if a charge has the three characteristics that I am about to mention, it is a floating charge. (1) If it is a charge on a class of assets of a company present and future; (2) if that class is one which, in the ordinary course of business of the company, would be changing from time to time; and (3) if you find that by the charge it is contemplated that, until some future step is taken by or on behalf of those interested in the charge, the company may carry on its business in the ordinary way as far as concerns the particular class of assets I am dealing with.
>
> This was offered as a description and not a definition. The first two characteristics are typical of a floating charge but they are not distinctive of it, since they are not necessarily inconsistent with a fixed charge. It is the third characteristic which is the hallmark of a floating charge and serves to distinguish it from a fixed charge. Since the existence of a fixed charge would make it impossible for the company to carry on business in the ordinary way without the consent of the charge holder, it follows that its ability to [do] so without such consent is inconsistent with the fixed nature of the security.

National Westminster Bank plc v Spectrum Plus Ltd (Re Spectrum Plus Ltd)

[2005] UKHL 41, [2005] 2 AC 680, House of Lords

The facts and a longer extract appear on p 988.

> **Lord Scott**: I respectfully agree. Indeed if a security has Romer LJ's third characteristic I am inclined to think that it qualifies as a floating charge, and cannot be a fixed charge, whatever may be its other characteristics. . . . In my opinion, the essential characteristic of a floating charge, the characteristic that distinguishes it from a fixed charge, it that the asset subject to the charge is not finally appropriated as a security for the payment of the debt until the occurrence of some future event. In the meantime the chargor is left free to use the charged asset and to remove it from the security.

Evans v Rival Quarries Ltd

[1910] 2 KB 979, Court of Appeal

The facts are irrelevant.

> **Buckley LJ**: . . . A floating charge is not a future security; it is a present security which presently affects all the assets of the company expressed to be included in it. On the other hand, it is not a specific security; the holder cannot affirm that the assets are specifically mortgaged to him. The

> assets are mortgaged in such a way that the mortgagor can deal with them without the concurrence of the mortgagee. A floating security is not a specific mortgage of the assets, plus a licence to the mortgagor to dispose of them in the course of his business, but is a floating mortgage applying to every item comprised in the security, but not specifically affecting any of item until some event occurs or some act on the part of the mortgagee is done which causes it to crystallize into a fixed security.

NOTES

1. When determining whether a security is a fixed or floating charge the courts will look to the substance rather than the form of the transaction: the parties' description of the charge as one or the other is not conclusive (*Re Armagh Shoes Ltd* [1984] BCLC 405).

2. It is the third feature identified by Romer LJ in *Re Yorkshire Woolcombers Association Ltd* (which appears in the *Agnew* extract above)—the ability to deal in the ordinary course of business free from control by the chargee—which has come to be recognised as the most essential characteristic of a floating charge. In *Re Spectrum Plus Ltd*, the House of Lords held that, in characterising a charge as fixed or floating, the key element is the freedom of the chargor company to use the assets in the ordinary course of its business, and not the nature of the assets charged. This means that a charge is fixed only if the chargor is legally obliged to preserve the charged assets, or (if drafted very strictly) their permitted substitutes, for the benefit of the chargee (the question of whether a charge can be fixed where there is a right of substitution remains controversial after *Re Spectrum Plus Ltd*: see H Beale, M Bridge, L Gullifer, and E Lomnicka, *The Law of Security and Title-Based Financing* (2nd edn, 2012), paras 6.120–6.127). In every other case, the charge will be floating. In order for a charge over book debts to be characterised as fixed, both the uncollected book debts and their proceeds after collection must be under the control of the chargee. This requires not just that the chargee has a right to take control of the proceeds, but an actual ongoing control over the collected proceeds (*Agnew v CIR* at [48]; *Spectrum* at [55]–[58], [116]–[119], [140]). There is no doubt that following *Re Spectrum Plus Ltd*, the ability of a company to grant a fixed charge over its circulating assets, such as its stock-in-trade or its book debts, has been severely curtailed.

3. The ability of the chargor company to deal with the charged assets in the ordinary course of its business means that it can create security interests that have priority to the floating charge. The priority rules are such that: (a) a subsequent fixed legal or equitable charge takes priority over an earlier floating charge (*Wheatley v Silkstone and Haigh Moor Coal Co* (1885) 29 Ch D 715); (b) a company which has given a floating charge over its assets cannot create a second floating charge over the *same* assets to rank in priority to the original floating charge (*Re Benjamin Cope & Sons Ltd* [1914] 1 Ch 800); and (c) a company which has given a floating charge over its assets may create a second floating charge over *part* of those assets ranking in priority to the original floating charge, provided the power to create such a charge is reserved in the earlier charge (*Re Automatic Bottle Makers Ltd* [1926] Ch 412, CA). In an attempt to avoid subsequent charges taking priority, the floating charge will usually contain a provision that restricts the right of the company to create charges that have priority to or rank equally with the floating charge (called a negative pledge clause). The clause will only be effective to retain priority where the subsequent chargee has notice (actual or constructive) of it, and not merely notice of the charge (*English & Scottish Mercantile Investment Co Ltd v Brunton* [1892]

2 QB 700, CA). Following the 2013 reforms of the company charges registration regime, the registrable particulars of a floating charge now include whether or not there is a negative pledge clause (Companies Act 2006, s 859D(2)(c)), and so it seems that those who could reasonably be expected to search the register, for example most secured lenders, will be taken to have constructive notice of such clauses (L Gullifer, *Goode on Legal Problems of Credit and Security* (5th edn, 2013), paras 2.25–2.31: but uncertainty remains, see P Graham [2014] JBL 175 at 191–192). Notice subjects the subsequent chargee to a personal equity in favour of the floating chargee and this gives the latter priority even though the subsequent security interest was created before crystallisation of the floating charge. It is submitted that the decision of Morritt J in *Griffiths v Yorkshire Bank Ltd* [1994] 1 WLR 1427, that a negative pledge clause only operates as a matter of contract and not of property, so that a second floating charge has priority if crystallising first, even if taken with notice of a negative pledge clause in the first floating charge, must be wrong (Neuberger J refused to follow it in *Re H & K Medway Ltd* [1997] 1 WLR 1422). It is certainly inconsistent with the underlying assumption in *English & Scottish Mercantile Investment Co Ltd v Brunton* (see E McKendrick, *Goode on Commercial Law* (5th edn, 2016), p 764, fn 91).

QUESTION

To secure further borrowing facilities, X Ltd creates a floating charge over its present and future assets in favour of A Bank. The charge contains a negative pledge clause. Later, wishing to purchase a new factory, X Ltd approaches B Bank for a loan. B Bank agrees to make the loan, subject to it taking a mortgage (ie legal charge) over the factory to rank in priority to any other security. X Ltd agrees to this and the loan is made, factory purchased, and mortgage executed all within a couple of days. At all material times B Bank was aware of A Bank's floating charge and had actual knowledge of the negative pledge clause. Shortly afterwards X Ltd went into liquidation and the floating charge 'crystallised'. Advise the liquidator as to whether A Bank's charge or B Bank's mortgage has priority. See *Abbey National Building Society v Cann* [1991] 1 AC 56, HL; and see also R Boadle [2014] LMCLQ 76.

(ii) Fixed and floating charges: why the distinction matters

(1) Property subject to a fixed charge cannot be dealt with without the charge-holder's consent; in contrast, the chargor under a floating charge may deal with the charged assets in the ordinary course of business without special authorisation.

(2) A floating charge-holder has a relatively low ranking in the priority order of creditors, and in particular ranks below preferential creditors (now primarily employees since the Enterprise Act 2002 abolished Crown preference) in a receivership or winding up of the chargor company (Insolvency Act 1986, ss 40, 175(2)(b), Sch B1, para 65(2) and Sch 6, paras 8–12); but the holder of a fixed charge may have recourse to his security without regard to any other claims.

(3) A floating charge created in the run-up to the chargor company's liquidation or administration may be subject to avoidance under s 245 of the Insolvency Act 1986; a fixed charge only if it involves a preference (considered below, p 1130).

(4) The chargee's interest in property that is subject to a fixed charge is immune from set-offs, execution, distress, and garnishment; but if the charge is a floating charge, it may be vulnerable to such claims because of the chargor's freedom to trade prior to crystallisation

(see, eg, *Biggerstaff v Rowan's Wharf Ltd* [1896] 2 Ch 93, CA, where it was held that prior to crystallisation the company's unsecured creditors could set off debts due by the company against sums which they owed it).

(5) A floating charge is subordinated to the costs and expenses of administration and liquidation (Insolvency Act 1986, Sch B1, paras 70 and 99, and s 176ZA, inserted by the Companies Act 2006, s 1282, reversing *Re Leyland Daf Ltd, Buchler v Talbot* [2004] UKHL 9, [2004] 2 AC 298, which denied priority to liquidation expenses).

(6) For charges created after 15 September 2003, the holder of a qualifying floating charge in respect of a company's property may no longer appoint an administrative receiver of the company (Insolvency Act 1976, s 72A, inserted by s 250 of the Enterprise Act 2002). There are a limited number of exceptions: major capital market and financial market transactions, utility transactions, and public–private finance transactions (Insolvency Act 1986, ss 72B–72H). The holder of a fixed charge has never been able to appoint an administrative receiver. The appointment of an administrative receiver prevents the company being put into administration (which brings with it an almost total moratorium on the enforcement of secured and unsecured claims against the company).

(7) On insolvency, a prescribed percentage of floating charge (but not fixed charge) asset realisations must be set aside to pay the company's unsecured creditors (see Insolvency Act, s 176A, and the Insolvency (Prescribed Part) Order 2003 (SI 2003/2097), art 3 and also below, p 1137).

(8) A company administrator needs court approval to dispose of property subject to a fixed charge, but property subject to a floating charge may be freely disposed of, subject to the chargee's priority being transferred to the proceeds acquired from the disposition of the charged property (Insolvency Act 1986, Sch B1, paras 70–71).

NOTES

1. Section 251 of the Insolvency Act 1986 defines a 'floating charge' as 'a charge which, as created, was a floating charge'. This definition closes a loophole that existed prior to 1986 (exploited in *Re Brightlife Ltd* [1987] Ch 200). The loophole enabled the holder of a floating charge to evade the statutory rules which cut down the effectiveness of a floating charge by showing that the floating charge had crystallised and become a fixed charge before commencement of the liquidation or other relevant statutory date.

2. There are fewer distinctions to be made between a floating charge and a fixed charge when the floating charge is created or otherwise arises under a security financial collateral arrangement ('security FCA'), pursuant to the Financial Collateral Arrangements (No 2) Regulations 2003 (SI 2003/3226; as amended) (see above, p 1067). To qualify as a security FCA the financial collateral must be 'in the possession or under the control of the collateral-taker' (reg 3(1)). 'Possession' is defined in such a way as to allow for the substitution of collateral of the same or greater value or the withdrawal of excess collateral (reg 3(2)), inserted by SI 2010/2993. This means that some (but not all) floating charges will fall within the regulations (and it should be noted that 'security interest' is defined in reg 3(1) to include 'a charge created as a floating charge', so long as the financial collateral is in the possession or control of the collateral taker, subject to rights of substitution and withdrawal). In *Gray v G-T-P Group Ltd* [2010] EWHC 1772 (Ch), [2011] 1 BCLC 313 at [58], Vos J did not rule out the possibility that examples exist of floating charges falling within the regulations, and in *Re Lehman Brothers International (Europe) (in administration)* [2012] EWHC 2997 (Ch) at [135], Briggs J said that it was obvious that they did, but in neither case were any examples provided. Professor Hugh Beale submits that there are two types of floating charge that fall within the regulations: (1) when the charge is one which would be categorised as floating only because the chargor has the right to substitute collateral and withdraw excess collateral; and (2) (more controversially) where the charge has crystallised, and the collateral taker has taken any practical steps as may be necessary to prevent the collateral provider from dealing with the securities or other financial collateral (H Beale, M Bridge, L Gullifer, and E Lomnicka, *The Law of Security and Title-Based Financing* (2nd edn, 2012) at para 3.63; cf LC Ho [2011] JIBLR 151 at 163, and Beale's response, above, at para 3.68). The regulations are particularly relevant to banks, securities firms, and other takers of financial collateral in the banking, derivatives, foreign exchange, securities, and commodities trading and repo, prime brokerage, and related financial markets. This is a specialist area and, for detailed analysis, students are directed to Chapter 3 of H Beale, M Bridge, L Gullifer, and E Lomnicka, *The Law of Security and Title-Based Financing* (2nd edn, 2012). For present purposes, it is enough to note that because of the regulations: (1) s 859A (charges created by a company) and s 859H (consequences of failure to register charges created by a company) of the Companies Act 2006 do not apply (if they would otherwise do so) to a security FCA, or any charge created or otherwise arising under it (reg 4); and (2) certain provisions of insolvency law, relating to the enforcement of FCAs, are disapplied, including the moratorium on administration, the avoidance of a floating charge under s 245 of the Insolvency Act 1986, the requirement to pay preferential creditors out of floating charge assets, and the requirement to pay a share of floating charge assets to the fund for unsecured creditors (Part 3 of the Regulations).

(iii) Crystallisation of a floating charge

A floating charge[6] will crystallise, and become a fixed charge attaching to the assets of the company at that time: (1) when a receiver is appointed; (2) when the company goes into liquidation (since the licence to deal with the assets in the ordinary course of business will then necessarily terminate); (3) when the company ceases to carry on business (*Re Woodroffes (Musical Instruments) Ltd* [1986] Ch 366) or sells its business (*Re Real Meat Co Ltd* [1996] BCC 254); (4) in the case where the debenture empowers the charge-holder to convert the floating charge into a fixed charge by giving the company 'notice of conversion', and such a notice is given (*Re Woodroffes (Musical Instruments) Ltd*, above); and (5) where an event occurs which under the terms of the debenture causes 'automatic' crystallisation.

The last ground depends upon there being a provision in the document creating the charge which states that the charge will crystallise on the happening of some particular event—for example, if a creditor of the company levies execution against its property, or if the company should give security over assets covered by the charge to a third party without the charge-holder's consent.

There has been much controversy over automatic crystallisation clauses, both as to their legality and as to whether, as a matter of policy, their use should be prohibited or subjected to restrictions by law (see, generally, H Beale, M Bridge, L Gullifer, and E Lomnicka, *The Law*

---

[6] Part of this text is taken from S Worthington, *Sealy and Worthington's Text, Cases, and Materials in Company Law* (11th edn, 2016), pp 641-642.

of Security and Title-Based Finance (2nd edn, 2012), para 6.84). Nevertheless, there is clear authority both in England and overseas upholding the effectiveness of an automatic crystal-lisation clause (for England, see *Re Brightlife Ltd* [1987] Ch 200 at 214–215, per Hoffmann J; for Australia, see *Fire Nymph Products Ltd v The Heating Centre Property Ltd* (1992) 7 ACSR 365; for New Zealand, see *Re Manurewa Transport Ltd* [1971] NZLR 909, *DFC Financial Services Ltd v Coffey* [1991] 2 NZLR 513, *Covacich v Riordan* [1994] 2 NZLR 502: although the New Zealand and Australian cases are now inapplicable in those countries after the com-ing into force of the New Zealand Personal Property Securities Act 1999 and the Australian Personal Property Securities Act 2009).

NOTES

1. Does the chargee have a proprietary interest in the charged assets before crystallisation of a floating charge? There are at least three alternative theories. First, the chargee may have no proprietary interest at all prior to crystallisation; the floating charge is simply an agreement to grant a charge at some time in the future (ie on crystallisation). This is known as the 'mort-gage of future assets theory' and is espoused by Dr Gough (see WJ Gough, *Company Charges* (2nd edn, 1996), Ch 13). The second theory is that the chargee holds some proprietary rights before crystallisation, but these are rights in a 'fund' and not in specific assets (see R Goode, *Commercial Law* (3rd edn, 2004), pp 677–680; *Re Spectrum Plus Ltd* [2005] UKHL 41, [2005] 2 AC 680 at [139], per Lord Walker). The third theory is that the chargee's interest is the same whether it is a fixed charge or an uncrystallised floating charge, although in the case of a float-ing charge there is a licence to deal with the assets which terminates on crystallisation (see S Worthington, *Proprietary Interests in Commercial Transactions* (1996), pp 82–100). It has been suggested that 'the last [theory] is the simplest, since the courts have come to view that the very essence of the difference between fixed and floating charges is the chargor's ability lawfully to deal with charged assets, not some difference in the interest held by the chargee' (A Burrows (ed), *Principles of English Commercial Law* (2015), para 8.95).

2. Crystallisation converts a floating charge into a fixed charge which attaches to all assets subject to the charge (including, if the charge instrument so provides, future assets). From that point in time the company loses its freedom to deal with the assets subject to the charge in the ordinary course of its business. The general rule is that post-crystallisation the floating charge has priority over subsequent interests. But a subsequent purchaser or chargee without notice of crystallisation might still be able to obtain priority ahead of the floating charge-holder by relying on the ostensible authority of the company to deal with its property in the ordinary course of business (see L Gulllifer, *Goode on Legal Problems of Credit and Security* (5th edn, 2013), para 5–51).

3. In *Re Brightlife Ltd* [1987] Ch 200, Hoffmann J regarded crystallisation as being a matter of agreement between the parties. On this reasoning there seems no reason why the parties should not later agree to 'decrystallise' a crystallised charge and enable the chargor to deal with its assets again. Such agreement would only be possible where the chargee remained in control of the chargor company's business, which would not be the case where the company was in receivership or liquidation. Some commentators argue that a new floating charge is created on decrystallisation (see, eg, R Grantham [1997] CFILR 53; CH Tan [1998] CFILR 41), others argue that decrystallisation simply removes the restriction on the chargor's dealing power and that the *same* charge refloats (see, eg, RM Goode (1994) 110 LQR 592 at 604). The issue is important as a new floating charge would require registration if it is not to be void as against an administrator, liquidator, or any (secured) creditor of the company (under s 859H of the Companies Act 2006).

3 EQUITABLE LIEN

Unlike a common law lien, an equitable lien is a non-possessory security. It is similar to an equitable charge in that it attaches to property belonging to another until certain specific claims have been satisfied. It gives the holder of the equitable lien the same remedies as a chargee, namely to apply to the court for an order for sale or for the appointment of a receiver. However, unlike a charge, which is created by agreement of the parties, an equitable lien arises by operation of law[7] and, as a result, is not required to be registered under the Bills of Sale Acts 1878 and 1882 or registrable under s 859A of the Companies Act 2006. The most common examples of an equitable lien are the lien of the unpaid vendor of land to secure the purchase price (*Mackreth v Symmons* (1808) 15 Ves 329, 33 ER 778) and the lien of the purchaser to secure repayment of his deposit if the transaction is not completed (*Rose v Watson* (1864) 10 HL Cas 672). There is some uncertainty as to the scope of the equitable lien.[8] It may be exercised in relation to the sale and purchase of intangible personal property (*Re Stucley* [1906] 1 Ch 67), but not in relation to the sale and purchase of goods (*Re Wait* [1927] 1 Ch 606 at 636 and 639, per Atkin LJ; *Transport & General Credit Co Ltd v Morgan* [1939] Ch 531 at 546, per Simonds J).

4 STATUTORY CONTROL

(a) Protection of third parties

The statutory requirement that non-possessory security interests must be registered—a legal requirement under the Bills of Sale Acts 1878 and 1882, and a practical requirement under Chapter A1 of Part 25 of the Companies Act 2006 given the sanction for non-registration—provides a prospective creditor (ie a third party) with the opportunity to establish whether the debtor has already encumbered the property in his possession. Without registration the non-possessory security interest would be hidden and the prospective creditor could be misled as to the creditworthiness of the debtor (cf F Oditah [1992] JBL 541 at 542–543). Furthermore, registration may also benefit a creditor by enabling him to publicise his own non-possessory security interest and so reduce the chances of the encumbered asset being disposed of by the debtor to a bona fide third party purchaser without notice of it, and who might, therefore, take priority over it (RM Goode (1984) 100 LQR 234 at 238–239).

---

[7] A maritime lien is also a non-possessory security interest arising by operation of law. It is a right of action *in rem* against a ship and her cargo for the cost of salvage or for damage caused by the ship. For details, see H Beale, M Bridge, L Gullifer, and E Lomnicka, *The Law of Security and Title-Based Financing* (2nd edn, 2012), paras 6.164–6.167.

[8] See, generally, H Beale, M Bridge, L Gullifer, and E Lomnicka, *The Law of Security and Title-Based Financing* (2nd edn, 2012), paras 6.140–6.163; J Phillips, 'Equitable Liens—A Search for a Unifying Principle' in N Palmer and E McKendrick (eds), *Interests in Goods* (2nd edn, 1998), Ch 39; S Worthington, *Proprietary Interests in Commercial Transactions* (1996), Ch 9; S Worthington, 'Equitable Liens in Commercial Transactions' [1994] CLJ 263; I Hardingham, 'Equitable Liens for the Recovery of Purchase Money' (1985) 15 MULR 65.

Non-possessory security interests may be registrable under the Bills of Sale Acts 1878 and 1882 (if given by individuals), or under Chapter A1 of Part 25 of the Companies Act 2006 (if given by companies). We shall concentrate on registration under these statutes, although it should be noted that registration may also be required for certain types of property (eg ships and aircraft) in other specialised registers.

(i) Bills of Sale Acts

The Bills of Sale Act 1878 and the Bills of Sale Act (1878) Amendment Act 1882 (as amended) require, inter alia, the registration of bills of sale.[9] It should be noted at once that any security issued by a company is excluded from the operation of these Acts (s 17 of the 1882 Act; and *Online Catering Ltd v Acton* [2010] EWCA Civ, [2011] QB 204 at [23], [36]).

According to Lord Esher MR in *Mills v Charlesworth* (1890) 25 QBD 421 at 424: 'A bill of sale, in its ordinary meaning, is the document which is given where the legal property in the goods passes to the person who lends money on them, but the possession does not pass'. This common law description of a bill of sale has been considerably extended by the Bills of Sale Acts 1878 and 1882. For the purposes of the 1878 and 1882 Acts, the term 'bill of sale' is defined to include a much broader class of documents relating to 'personal chattels' than is the case at common law (see s 4 of the 1878 Act, which lists the various documents; also s 3 of the 1882 Act). Those documents falling within the statutory definition divide into three broad categories: (1) instruments transferring legal or beneficial ownership of personal chattels; (2) instruments conferring a right to take possession of personal chattels as security for any debt; and (3) agreements by which a right in equity to any personal chattels, or to any charge or security thereon, is to be conferred. In general, all written mortgages and charges relating to personal chattels fall within the statutory definition of a bill of sale and are caught by the Bills of Sale Acts (but not equitable liens, which arise by operation of law and not by agreement).

As a bill of sale is defined in terms of documents, oral transactions fall outside the definition and are not caught by the Bills of Sale Acts. The same applies to transactions whereby the transferee's rights are completed by delivery without reference to any document, for example a pledge or possessory lien (*Charlesworth v Mills* [1892] AC 231 at 235, HL). Furthermore, s 4 of the 1878 Act excludes certain documents from the definition of 'bill of sale'. In particular, 'transfers of goods in the ordinary course of business of any trade or calling' and bills of lading are excluded from the statutory definition. Intangible property is excluded from the definition of 'personal chattels' (s 4 of the 1878 Act) so that, for example, an assignment of book debts would not be caught by the Bills of Sale Acts (although s 344 of the Insolvency Act 1986 makes a general assignment of book debts by way of security registrable under the 1878 Act; see above, p 976). After-acquired property has been held to constitute personal chattels for the purpose of the Bills of Sale Acts (*Welsh Development Agency v Export Finance Co Ltd* [1991] BCLC 936 at 956, per Browne-Wilkinson V-C (reversed by the Court of Appeal on another ground [1992] BCLC 148), disapproving Lord Macnaghten's dictum to the contrary in *Thomas v Kelly* (1888) 13 App Cas 506 at 521). This means that agreements conferring a right in equity over after-acquired goods, under the rule in *Holroyd v Marshall* (1862) 10 HL Cas 191 (above, p 960), are caught by the Bills of Sale Acts.

There are two types of bills of sale, namely, those given as security for the payment of money ('security bills') and those which are given otherwise than as security for the payment

---

[9] For detailed coverage, see H Beale, M Bridge, L Gullifer, and E Lomnicka, *The Law of Security and Title-Based Financing* (2nd edn, 2012), paras 11.03 ff.

of money ('absolute bills'). The 1878 Act applies to both absolute and security bills so long as they confer on the holder or grantee a power to seize or take possession of any personal chattels comprised in or made subject to the bill (s 3 of the 1878 Act). However, with regard to security bills, the 1878 Act must be read together with the 1882 Act. The 1882 Act applies only to security bills and provides that any provisions in the 1878 Act which are inconsistent with the 1882 Act are repealed as to such bills of sale (s 15 of the 1882 Act).

The 1878 Act sets out a scheme for the registration of bills of sale of personal chattels which remain in the possession of the grantor. Under this scheme all such bills of sale must be attested and registered within seven days of their execution, and failure to do so renders the bill void against the chargor's other creditors or their representatives (s 8 of the 1878 Act; see *Online Catering Ltd v Acton*, above, at [25]). But if a security bill of sale is not attested and registered within seven days of execution (and does not truly state the consideration for which it was given), that renders the bill 'void in respect of the personal chattels comprised therein' against the whole world, including the grantor (s 8 of the 1882 Act; see *Online Catering Ltd v Acton*, above, at [25]). This means that the security granted by the bill becomes unenforceable, although any other covenant in the bill remains enforceable, for example the grantor's covenant as to payment (*Heseltine v Simmons* [1892] 2 QB 547 at 553–554, CA). To maintain the registration, it must be renewed every five years (s 11 of the 1878 Act). A transfer or assignment of a registered bill of sale need not be registered (s 10 of the 1878 Act).

Registration is a cumbersome process. It is regulated by the 1878 Act which provides that the bill of sale, with every schedule or inventory thereto annexed or therein referred to, and a true copy of the bill and of every schedule or inventory and of every attestation of the execution of such bill, together with an affidavit containing certain required particulars, must be presented to the registrar (a master of the Supreme Court, Queen's Bench Division); and the copy of the bill of sale and the original affidavit must be filed with him. Every security bill must have annexed to it a schedule containing an inventory of the personal chattels comprised in the bill of sale. To ensure that this schedule of chattels is accurate, and that no creditor consulting the registered copy of the bill of sale is misled, failure to include a specific description of an item in the schedule renders the bill void as regard to it, except as against the grantor himself (s 4 of the 1882 Act). The accuracy of the schedule annexed to a security bill is further maintained by s 5 of the 1882 Act which, in general, renders a bill of sale void, except as against the grantor, in respect of any chattels specifically described in the schedule of which the grantor was not the true owner at the time of the execution of the bill of sale (see *Lewis v Thomas* [1919] 1 KB 319, where a person who held goods on hire-purchase was held not to be their true owner). In practice, s 5 of the 1882 Act prevents an individual giving a floating charge over future property (see *Chapman v Wilson* [2010] EWHC 1746 (Ch) at [100]–[101], per Vos J) .

Registration does not of itself constitute notice to third parties (*Joseph v Lyons* (1884) 15 QBD 280 at 286, CA). It remains possible for a bona fide purchaser from the grantor, without notice of the prior bill of sale, to acquire a good title and override that of the grantee (although in the case of a security bill this will only be possible if the title acquired by the original grantee is purely equitable or the original grantee is estopped from asserting his legal title). If the subsequent disposition of the goods by the grantor is itself a registrable bill of sale, priority will generally be governed by s 10 of the 1878 Act. Under s 10 of the 1878 Act, the date of registration governs priority between two or more bills of sale comprising, in whole or in part, any of the same chattels. With regard to security bills, this general rule applies in the following cases: (1) as between two registered security bills; and (2) where an absolute bill is granted after the grant of a security bill. If a security bill is granted after an absolute bill (whether registered or not) the security bill will be void, except as against the grantor, under s 5 of the 1882 Act.

(ii) Companies Act 2006

Sealy and Worthington's Text, Cases, and Materials in Company Law by S Worthington
(11th edn, 2016), pp 627–631 (footnotes omitted)

STATUTORY REQUIREMENTS

Part 25 of CA 2006 imposes on companies a statutory obligation to register particulars of charges which they have created over their property. Following a long history of failed attempts at reforming the law in this area (see later), the existing rules have finally been modified, although perhaps not greatly, with the aim of delivering a more modern regime which will save time and cost for those using it. The Department of Business, Innovation and Skills suggests the cost savings could be of the order of £22 million per annum. The reforms were made by way of the Companies Act 2006 (Amendment of Part 25) Regulations 2013, which repealed CA 2006 Pt 25, Chs 1 and 2, replacing them with Ch A1, which came into force on 6 April 2013.

This requirement to register charges was first imposed by the Companies Act 1900. Up until the 2013 changes, the approach adopted was to list the types of charges which were required to be registered. Not every category of charge was affected— fixed charges over shares or negotiable instruments, for instance, escaped the net—although the list was always fairly comprehensive, and included all floating charges. Under the new rules, there is no longer a prescribed list. On the contrary, s 859A quite simply states that the section will apply 'where a company creates a charge', subject only to three exceptions set out in s 859A(6). The hope is that this will reduce the uncertainty surrounding which charges must be registered. Section 859B provides parallel provisions for charges given to support a series of debentures. But note that it is only charges *created by the company* which come within Pt 25: a charge created by operation of law, such as an unpaid vendor's lien over land which is the subject of a contract of sale, is outside the scope of the Act.

For every charge created by a company, CA 2006 s 859A does not make it mandatory for the parties to register the charge (as the previous rules had, with criminal sanctions to back up the rule), but instead compels the registrar to register the charge *if* the parties deliver the appropriate instruments and details to the registrar within the specified time (basically 21 days, but see ss 859E and 859F). Either the company or the charge holder (or 'any person interested in the charge', s 859A(2)) may see to the registration, and would be well advised to do so if there is any risk that the company will default. The change from compulsion to permission may be immaterial, however, as the consequence of failure to register is that the charge is void on precisely the occasions when it is most needed: see 'Effect of failure to register' [below].

If a company acquires property which is already subject to a charge, particulars of the charge may similarly be delivered for registration (s 859C).

Where the charge (eg a charge over land or a ship) requires registration under other legislation, that does not provide a reason for non-compliance with CA 2006 Pt 25, unless the other Act excludes the application of the CA 2006 provisions (see s 859A(6)).

CERTIFICATE OF REGISTRATION

On registration, a certificate is issued which must state the unique reference code allocated to the charge (s 859I(4)). Under s 859I(6), the certificate is 'conclusive evidence that the documents required by the section concerned were delivered to the registrar before the end of the relevant period allowed for delivery.'

This is far more specific than its predecessor, which simply stated that the certificate was 'conclusive evidence that the requirements of this Chapter as to registration have been satisfied'. Earlier cases suggested the force of the certificate—and of the register— was assured even where the certificate was inaccurate (*Re Mechanisations (Eaglescliffe) Ltd* [1966] Ch 20), or the facts on which the certificate was based were untrue (eg where the charge instrument is falsely dated: *Re CL Nye Ltd* [1971] Ch 442), or the charge was registered by mistake (*Ali v Top Marques Car Rental Ltd* [2006] EWHC 109 (Ch)). The effect was that notwithstanding that the details on the register were incorrect, and people inspecting the register would be misled, the certificate would be conclusive proof that the statutory requirements had been met. As a consequence, the *actual* charge as created by the company would be deemed to be duly registered, and would have to be observed by the company's creditors and its liquidator or administrator, notwithstanding creditors who may have been misled as to the company's true position. And because the certificate was conclusive evidence that the requirements had been met, it was impossible to have proceedings for judicial review of the registrar's decision.

Despite all this, the conclusiveness of the certificate was seen as a crucial benefit of the registration system, and a proposed downgrading of it was in large measure the reason for the unpopularity of certain proposed 1989 reforms. The new rules seem to have worked around this.

EFFECT OF FAILURE TO REGISTER

If particulars are not registered within 21 days of the creation of the charge (a date defined in s 859E, attempting to provide for both English and Scottish securities), or such longer period as allowed by the court (s 859F, see the following section), then CA 2006 s 859H declares the *security* to be void against the liquidator, administrator and any creditor of the company (s 859H(3)), although the personal obligation remains and, indeed, the money secured becomes immediately payable (s 859H(4)).

The nature of this sanction of 'partial voidness' should be noted. First, it is only the *security* that is avoided, not the underlying obligation, which remains good as an unsecured debt. Secondly, the charge is void only as against the persons mentioned and not, for instance, *inter partes*, or against an execution creditor. And the chargee may dispose of the property in exercise of a power of sale and give a good title to the purchaser, even though the charge is 'void'.

EXTENSION OF THE REGISTRATION PERIOD AND RECTIFICATION OF THE REGISTER

CA 2006 s 859F enables applications to court to extend the 21-day registration period. The court may make whatever orders it sees as just and expedient provided certain pre-conditions are satisfied (s 859F(2)), including that it is just and equitable to grant relief. This replicates predecessor rules, so see *Barclays Bank plc v Stuart Landon Ltd* [2001] EWCA Civ 140, CA, for a discussion of the factors to be considered by the court when dealing with an application for late registration of a charge created by a company which was close to liquidation.

In analogous circumstances, and subject to the same conditions, s 859M enables the court to make an order rectifying the register where there has been an omission or mis-statement, and s 859N provides the court with a discretion to replace the instrument or debenture where there has been an omission, mistake or defect.

REGISTRATION, PRIORITY AND CONSTRUCTIVE NOTICE OF REGISTERED CHARGES

Registration does not of itself confer priority or give any protection to a charge holder, although of course, as noted previously, non-registration has almost fatal consequences for the security. Instead, priority as between different charges over the same property is determined by the ordinary rules of law. Thus, for example, a legal charge will normally have priority over an equitable charge, a fixed charge over a floating charge (because of their terms) and, as between two equitable charges, the earlier in time will prevail. So, if a company were to create a charge in favour of A on the first of the month, and then give an identical charge over the same property to B on the 10th, registering particulars on the 15th, B (who had searched the register on the 10th and found it clear) could in all innocence believe that he has a first charge, only to discover later that A has a charge which ranks ahead of his own, so long as it has been registered within the statutory 21 days. B is deemed to have notice of the earlier charge provided A files for registration within the statutory 21-day period. (This is referred to in the Company Law Review (CLR) as 'the 21-day invisibility problem'. It could be eliminated if 'notice filing' were introduced, although even then there could be a gap between the time when a document is delivered to Companies House and the time when it is recorded on the register.)

The doctrine of constructive notice has not been abolished in regard to particulars of charges held by the registrar, and so everyone dealing with a company is deemed to have notice of those particulars which are required by statute to be registered. These are defined in s 859D, and include the date of creation of the charge, the nature of the charge (fixed or floating), the amount secured, short particulars of the property charged, and the persons entitled to the charge, and, by way of change from the earlier rules, whether the charge includes a 'negative pledge' clause (ie a provision by which the company undertakes not to create other charges ranking in priority to or *pari passu* with the charge; see s 859D(2)(c)).

This change in the rules on negative pledges eliminates the problem illustrated in *Siebe Gorman & Co Ltd v Barclays Bank Ltd* [1979] 2 Lloyd's Rep 142, Ch (overruled in *Spectrum*, but not on this issue). Under the predecessor rules, details of negative pledges were not mandatory, but a practice developed of including such details in the registered particulars. In *Siebe Gorman*, it was held that the constructive notice doctrine did not extend to such additional information, but only to those matters which the Act prescribed, and so a searcher would be taken to know of such a clause only if he had *actual* notice of it. The point always remained controversial, with little persuasive authority or argument.

Section 859L contains provision for entering on the register a 'statement' that the debt secured by a charge has been satisfied or some or all of the property charged has been released from the security. But there is no obligation to register this information under the existing law.

COMPANY'S OWN REGISTER OF CHARGES

Under the old rules, the company itself was also required to keep a register of charges. Since this register was required to cover every kind of charge, not only those which were registrable, the obligations were potentially very burdensome. They were also largely pointless, since neither the validity of the charge nor any question relating to priority was affected by a failure to observe these requirements, and in practice the related criminal sanctions were never invoked. This may explain why the new rules no longer require companies to keep their own registers, but merely demand that companies keep copies of the full instruments available for inspection (s 859Q).

FURTHER REFORM OF THE REGISTRATION SYSTEM

The need for some sort of registration system is almost universally accepted, but the present system, which has changed little for over a century, despite the various 2013 changes, has long been thought to be deficient. Almost 25 years ago, changes were made to the Companies Act 1989 that were intended to sweep away the old law and replace it with a completely new regime containing provisions which would reduce the burden on Companies House but at the same time give rather less protection to persons who relied on the registration system. Those proposed reforms met with such opposition from business and professional circles that the government was dissuaded from bringing the regime into operation. Instead, a consultation process was begun which envisaged retaining the earlier CA 1985 provisions, but introducing some modifications. That idea was subsequently overtaken by the decision to set up the CLR, which published its own consultation document seeking views on possible ways forward. Following that, the Law Commission was asked to examine the whole of the law on the registration, perfection and priority of company charges, and to consider the case for a new registration system. It was also asked to consider whether such a system should be extended to quasi-securities (retention of title agreements, etc), and to securities created by individuals as well as companies.

The Law Commission, looking to have changes included in CA 2006, made various recommendations, including adoption of a notice-filing system (see later) for company charges (see *Company Security Interests* (Law Com No 296, 2005)). The government then issued a further consultation document (*The Registration of Companies' Security Interests (Company Charges): The Economic Impact of the Law Commissions' Proposals*, 2005). This received a rather negative response, and so all the issues were parked, subject to still further discussions and deliberations before any decision could be taken on what ought to be done. The latest 2013 reforms fall far short of counting as movement on this front. Their biggest changes are simply the elimination of the list of registrable charges in favour of making all charges registrable, and also including public notification on the register of negative pledge clauses.

This rocky road to reform might be seen as both surprising and disappointing. Both the Crowther Committee (which was concerned with reform of the law on consumer credit: Cmnd 4596, 1971) and Professor Diamond in his report (*A Review of Security Interests in Property* (1989)) categorically recommended that this country should follow the lead of the United States and Canadian jurisdictions in setting up an entirely new system of registration for all personal property security interests, whether created by individuals or companies, on the model of Art 9 of the American Uniform Commercial Code. This would make a separate regime for company charges unnecessary. The same conclusion was reached independently by reform bodies in other Commonwealth jurisdictions, such as Australia and New Zealand—each of which has now implemented this major change. But, sadly, there seems to be little enthusiasm for any such reform in the UK, despite the most recent consultation responses in its favour.

What is different about these other regimes? Article 9 of the Uniform Commercial Code is at the same time a more comprehensive system and yet a simpler and more flexible one: it governs all transactions which *in effect* create a security, whatever their form (including, eg, hire-purchase agreements and sales on retention of title (*Romalpa* [above] terms), and works on the principle of 'notice filing'. Priority as between competing registered securities is governed simply by the time of filing of the notice of such security: the security filed first has priority over all that follow. It gives better protection—first, for security holders, in that registration confers priority over others who may claim interests in the same property; secondly, for those intending to take security who, by filing a notice, can cover their position provisionally until the security is completed or the charge attaches; and, thirdly, for those seeking to rely on searches of the register, who can take the record at its face value.

NOTE

Regulation 4(4) of the Financial Collateral Arrangements (No 2) Regulations 2003 (SI 2003/3226; as amended), provides that s 859A (charges created by a company) and s 859H (consequences of failure to register charges created by a company) of the Companies Act 2006 do not apply (if they would otherwise do so) to a security financial collateral arrangement, or any charge created or otherwise arising under a security financial collateral arrangement. Thus, where the regulations apply, there is no need to register a charge over 'financial collateral', which is defined to mean cash held in a bank account (or similar), securities (eg shares and bonds), and 'credit claims' (meaning the benefit of loans made available by credit institutions such as banks) (reg 3). For an explanation of the regulations, see above, p 1067 and p 1074.

(iii) Insolvency Act 1986

There are controls in the Insolvency Act to protect third parties in the event of any unlawful preference or transaction at an undervalue (ss 238, 239, 339, 340): see below, pp 1130 ff.

(b) Protection of debtors

Where security is given by an individual (usually the principal debtor) there are statutory controls which protect him against harsh and unreasonable terms and oppressive enforcement of the security. Such protection is to be found in the Bills of Sale Act (1878) Amendment Act 1882 (as amended) and the Consumer Credit Act 1974. Neither statute affords protection to companies who are principal debtors or who have given security to secure the debt of another person. Companies are regarded as having sufficient bargaining strength to look after their own interests (although this must be doubted when the company is small and heavily indebted to a lender who demands further security).

(i) Bills of Sale Acts

Unlike the Bills of Sale Act 1878, which is concerned with the protection of creditors, the Bills of Sale Act (1878) Amendment Act 1882 is primarily concerned with the protection of the grantor of a security bill (*Manchester, Sheffield and Lincolnshire Rly Co v North Central Wagon Co* (1888) 13 App Cas 554 at 560, per Lord Herschell). Pursuant to s 9 of the 1882 Act, a bill of sale made or given by way of security for the payment of money by the grantor thereof is rendered void unless made in accordance with the form prescribed by the Act. Every bill of sale made or given in consideration of any sum under £30 is also rendered void (s 12 of the 1882 Act). In both cases the security itself, and any personal covenant contained in the bill, is rendered unenforceable (*Davies v Rees* (1886) 17 QBD 408, CA; *Bassano v Toft* [2014] EWHC 377 (QB), [2014] ECC 14 at [13]). A covenant in the bill for the repayment of principal and interest will be unenforceable but the money lent will be recoverable as money had and received, together with reasonable interest (*North Central Wagon & Finance Co Ltd v Brailsford* [1962] 1 WLR 1288; see also *Bradford Advance Co Ltd v Ayers* [1924] WN 152).

The 1882 Act also prohibits the grantee of a security bill seizing the chattels to which it relates unless: (1) the grantor is in default, or fails to comply with any obligation necessary for maintaining the security; (2) the grantor becomes bankrupt, or suffers the goods to be distrained for rent, rates, or taxes; (3) the grantor fraudulently removes or allows the goods to be removed from the premises; (4) the grantor fails to comply with a written request for his last receipts for rents, rates, and taxes; (5) execution has been levied against the grantor's goods. Even then the seizure may be made subject to the 'default notice' provisions of the Consumer Credit Act 1974 (s 7A of the 1882 Act; also see below). The goods may not be removed by the grantee within five days of seizure (s 13 of the 1882 Act) thereby giving the grantor the opportunity to apply to the court for relief (s 7 of the 1882 Act).

(ii) Consumer Credit Act 1974

A bill of sale that falls within the consumer credit regulatory regime, set out in the Consumer Credit Act 1974, must comply with the provisions of that Act as well as those of the Bills of Sale Act (1878) Amendment Act 1882. This is of particular relevance to para (1) of s 7 of the 1882 Act, which entitles the grantee of a bill of sale to take possession of the chattels assigned '[i]f the grantor shall make default in payment of the sum or sums of money thereby secured at the time therein provided for payment, or in the performance of any covenant or agreement contained in the bill of sale and necessary for maintaining the security'. By s 7A(1) of the 1882 Act (inserted by the Consumer Credit Act 1974), para (1) of s 7 does not apply to a default relating to a bill of sale given by way of security for the payment of money under a regulated agreement to which s 87(1) of the Consumer Credit Act 1974 applies (which requires the service of a 'default notice' on the debtor before the creditor can be entitled, by reason of any breach by the debtor of a regulated agreement, inter alia, to recover possession of any goods): (1) unless the restriction imposed by s 88(2) of that Act (preventing certain action before expiry of time for remedying the default) has ceased to apply to the bill of sale; or (2) if, by virtue of s 89 of that Act, the default is to be treated as not having occurred.

For detailed discussion of the consumer credit regime, see E Lomnicka, *Encyclopedia of Consumer Credit Law* (looseleaf).

QUESTION

The use of bills of sale has grown dramatically in recent years, from 2,840 registered in 2001 to 52,483 in 2014. This is due to the increasing use of 'logbook loans', whereby a borrower uses their current motor vehicle as security, by transferring ownership to the logbook lender. Logbook loans account for over 90 per cent of all bills of sale registered.

How adequately do the Bills of Sale Acts 1878 and 1882 protect the logbook borrowers? How could the law be usefully reformed? For suggestions, see Law Commission Report, *Bills of Sale* (No 369, 2016).

5 REFORM

See above, pp 1020 ff and 1083.

PART IX

PRINCIPLES OF INSURANCE LAW

Chapter 27   Insurance   1089

INSURANCE

1 INTRODUCTION

(a) Description

In a contract of insurance one party undertakes, in return for a consideration paid by the other, to pay a sum of money or provide some equivalent benefit to the other *if* a specified event should happen, or *when* such an event should happen, or to make payments to the other *until* such an event should happen, the essence of the arrangement being that it is either uncertain whether, or uncertain when, the event will occur.[1] The contract is commonly known as (and recorded in) a 'policy' (at least if it is in writing), the parties are called respectively 'the insurer' (or 'underwriter') and 'the insured' (or 'assured' or 'policyholder'), and the consideration is referred to as 'the premium'.

Contracts of insurance may be subdivided into two categories: (1) *indemnity insurance*, where the undertaking is to provide the insured with an indemnity against a possible future loss or liability—for example, damage to property caused by fire, or a motorist's liability in tort to a third party who may be injured by his driving; and (2) *contingency insurance*, where the promise is to pay a specified sum on the happening of a named event—for example, a personal injury or (in a life policy) death. In the latter case, the insurer contracts to pay a predetermined sum when the person whose life is insured dies, and the sum is payable irrespective of the value of the life that is lost. Another form of contingency insurance is a contract of annuity, where the premium is a lump sum paid in advance and the insurer agrees to make regular periodic payments of a fixed amount until the death of the person concerned. In the same way, if an insurer in a personal injury policy promises to pay the insured £10,000 if he should lose the sight of an eye, he must pay that sum without regard to the loss to the insured that that injury actually represents.

It is of the essence of a contract of insurance that the event insured against be uncertain, either in the sense that it may or may not occur, or that the time of the occurrence is uncertain. Thus, a policy of insurance on goods will not normally protect the insured against depreciation or fair wear and tear, or against losses arising from some internal or inherent cause, such as the deterioration of perishable goods (commonly referred to technically as

---

[1] Specialist textbooks include J Birds, *Modern Insurance Law* (9th edn, 2014); MA Clarke, *The Law of Insurance Contracts* (looseleaf and online); and R Merkin QC, *Colinvaux's Law of Insurance* (11th edn, 2016).

'inherent vice'). These events are not sufficiently uncertain. Nor will it be construed as covering events brought about by the deliberate act of the insured himself (eg loss caused by fraud or arson on his part). There is, in addition, a further reason why an insured is debarred from recovering on an insurance in events such as his own fraud or arson, namely the general constraints of public policy.[2]

(b) Insurable interest

One further element, an essential requirement of a contract of insurance, and which distinguishes it from a wagering contract, is that the event upon which the insurer's liability depends must be one in which the insured has an *insurable interest*—that is to say, the event must, at least prima facie, be one which is adverse to the insured's interests. A person cannot, as a rule, insure a stranger's house against fire, because he does not stand to lose anything if it is burnt down; but if he is a mortgagee of the property, this gives him an insurable interest. In the same way, a person normally cannot take out a life policy on the life of someone else, but he could do so if the latter were a key employee in his business.[3]

(c) Statutes

Parts of the law governing contracts of insurance are regulated by statute. Thus, the Life Assurance Act 1774 (which is not in fact confined to life insurance but extends also to some other forms of insurance) defines an insurable interest for some purposes, and the Third Parties (Rights against Insurers) Act 1930 allowed claims to be made directly against an insurer (eg by the victim of a motoring accident) where the insured is insolvent. It has now been replaced for this purpose by the Third Parties (Rights against Insurers) Act 2010. The law of *marine insurance* (the insurance of ships, their cargoes, and freight) is largely codified by the Marine Insurance Act 1906. But for the purposes of this chapter, we concentrate on the general principles of insurance law, which are based mainly on the common law as modified by the Consumer Insurance (Disclosure and Representations) Act 2012, which applies to consumer insurance contracts (as defined in s 1), and, as from 12 August 2016, by the Insurance Act 2015, which principally (but not exclusively) affects the law relating to non-consumer insurance contracts.[4]

(d) Authorisation

Persons wishing to carry on business as insurers must be authorised to do so by the Financial Conduct Authority (FCA), under powers delegated to it by the Treasury pursuant to the

---

[2] See *Gray v Barr* [1971] 2 QB 554, CA.

[3] See *Macaura v Northern Assurance Co* [1925] AC 619, HL. However, it has not been followed in some Commonwealth decisions. In this country, too, there are signs that the courts now take a broader view: if a person has a 'factual expectation' that he may suffer consequential loss following a fire or other insured peril which damages property owned by someone else, he may be regarded as having a sufficient interest to insure against the risk. For example, a subcontractor in a building contract may have such an interest in the works as a whole because he could lose the opportunity to complete his contract: *Petrofina (UK) Ltd v Magnaload Ltd* [1984] QB 127.

[4] As this is a book about commercial (and not consumer) law, we concentrate on non-consumer contracts in this chapter.

Financial Services and Markets Act 2000 and regulations made thereunder, or by the equivalent authority in some other EU Member State. There is provision also under this legislation for compensating persons who suffer loss as a result of the failure of financial services providers (including those carrying on insurance business) to meet claims, and for the establishment of a Financial Ombudsman Scheme to resolve disputes which may arise between providers and their customers. The former Insurance Ombudsman Bureau, established in 1981, was incorporated as a division within the Scheme.[5]

In 1977 the insurance industry, through the Association of British Insurers and the General Insurance Standards Council, introduced a measure of self-regulation by the publication of non-statutory codes of practice. These 'Standards of Insurance Practice' obliged insurers to adopt a user-friendly approach and not to rely on some of the more technical points of law in their dealings with private customers. The Ombudsman has regularly applied these standards when dealing with the cases before him. In January 2005 these non-statutory codes were replaced by Conduct of Business Rules and guidance notes issued by the Financial Services Authority (which was the financial services regulator at the time), and in January 2008 by the Insurance Conduct of Business Sourcebook currently issued by the FCA.[6] The UK has also implemented the EC Insurance Mediation Directive (Directive 2002/92/EC) which confers on the FCA power to regulate insurers and their intermediaries when selling insurance and handling claims. Once again, the Directive draws a distinction between commercial customers and individual customers (including some small businesses) and gives greater protection to the latter. The Insurance Mediation Directive has recently been updated by the Insurance Distribution Directive 2016/97/EU with EU Member States having until 23 February 2018 to implement the new Directive.

2   FORMATION OF THE CONTRACT

(a) Insurance: a contract *uberrimae fidei*

A contract of insurance is the paradigm case of a contract *uberrimae fidei*—a contract of the utmost good faith. The insurer is unlikely to know anything about the insured or the nature of the risk for which cover is sought, apart from such information as it is given by the insured. Accordingly, the insured was required at common law to disclose to the insurer in advance of the contract all material facts known to him, facts of which he was fully aware.

In *Joel*[7] M had taken out life insurance without disclosing that she had suffered from mental illness; but this was a fact of which she was unaware because she believed that it was no more than depression following influenza. Fletcher Moulton LJ said: 'You cannot disclose what you do not know.'[8] This obligation may be extended, in the case of an insured in a business context, to facts which he ought to know; but there is no similar rule of deemed knowledge as regards a private individual.

---

[5] On the work of the Insurance Ombudsman, see W Merricks, 'The Jurisprudence of the Ombudsman' [2001] JBL 532.
[6] For a full account of these developments, see G McMeel [2005] LMCLQ 186.
[7] *Joel v Law Union & Crown Insurance Co* [1908] 2 KB 863, CA.
[8] At 884.

A major change was made by the Insurance Act 2015.[9] According to s 3, the common law requirement of disclosure of material information was replaced by a duty to make a fair presentation of the risk. Subsection (3) states:

> A fair presentation of the risk is one—
>
> (a) which makes the disclosure required by subsection (4),
> (b) which makes that disclosure in a manner which would be reasonably clear and accessible to a prudent insurer, and
> (c) in which every material representation as to a matter of fact is substantially correct, and every material representation as to a matter of expectation or belief is made in good faith.

Subsection (4) states:

> The disclosure required is a follows, except as provided in subsection (5)—
>
> (a) disclosure of every material circumstance which the insured knows or ought to know, or
> (b) failing that, disclosure which gives the insurer sufficient information to put a prudent insurer on notice that it needs to make further enquiries for the purpose of revealing those material circumstances.

Subsection (5) provides:

> In the absence of enquiry, subsection (4) does not require the insured to disclose a circumstance if—
>
> (a) it diminishes the risk,
> (b) the insurer knows it,
> (c) the insurer ought to know it,
> (d) the insurer is presumed to know it, or
> (e) it is something as to which the insurer waives information.[10]

The duty of utmost good faith has been modified (not abolished) by the 2015 Act.[11] But the draconian rule that an insurer can avoid a policy on the ground that utmost good faith has not been observed by the insured has been abolished (s 14(1)). Instead, the 2015 Act has introduced proportionate remedies for any failure in the duty of fair presentation that were neither deliberate nor reckless (s 8 and Sch 1).

---

[9] Part 2 (ss 2–8) of the 2015 Act applies to non-consumer contracts only (s 2(1)), and the parties may contract out of these provisions unless their contract is to settle a claim arising under a non-consumer insurance contract (ss 16–17). Under the Consumer Insurance (Disclosure and Representations) Act 2012, the duty of disclosure no longer applies to consumer insurance contracts: instead, a consumer insured is only under an obligation to take reasonable care not to make misrepresentations to the insurer.

[10] Ss 4–6 contain detailed provisions for determining the 'knowledge' of the insured and the insurer for the purposes of s 3(4) and s 3(5) respectively.

[11] The Explanatory Notes to the Insurance Act 2015 indicate that 'good faith will remain a general interpretative principle' (para 117).

(b) Disclosure

Disclosure means, as in the past, communication of certain information (material information) to a certain person (the right person in the insurance company).[12] The right person is the person in the company underwriting the risk (or to some other agent of the insurer who can be expected to pass the information to that person).

As regards material information, the common law rule about what is material for this purpose has not been changed by the 2015 Act. A fact is material if known to the applicant at the time of contract and one which would affect the judgment of a reasonable man, which, in the typical insurance case, means the prudent insurer.[13] It need not have been decisive in its effect, it is enough that the representation was 'actively present' to the mind of the representee (the insurer), when deciding to conclude the contract of insurance.

(c) Controversial cases

One controversial issue is rumour. Even a rumour or suspicion that proves to be unfounded may affect the judgment of a prudent insurer—for example, where a person is being questioned by the police in connection with a burglary—and may have to be disclosed. In one marine case,[14] a ship, the *North Star*, had been damaged by an explosion. The loss would have been covered by a 'war risks' policy but the insurers declined liability because the shipowner, when taking out the insurance, had not disclosed the fact that its two controlling shareholders were facing fraud charges in courts in Greece and Panama. The charges were entirely false, but the court accepted expert evidence that the mere fact that they had been brought would have been considered material by a prudent insurer, so that the non-disclosure justified the insurers in rejecting the claim. The insurer has a similar duty.[15]

Another controversial instance is declinature. In *Glicksman*,[16] G and his partner had insured the stock of their tailoring business against burglary with the respondent company; but the company declined liability when a burglary occurred, on the ground that G had not disclosed at the time when he applied for the cover that another insurance company had once declined to grant him insurance. An arbitrator found as a fact that this information was material, and in consequence the House of Lords (albeit with reluctance) held that the insurer's refusal to accept liability was justified. At common law it was possible for insurers to stipulate that answers to certain questions shall be the 'basis of the insurance' and thus material;[17] but this possibility was prohibited by s 9(2) of the Insurance Act 2015 (in relation to non-consumer insurance but it is regarded as unacceptable practice generally[18]).

A further contentious instance concerns the significance of the insurers' questions. In *Woolcott*,[19] Woolcott's house was destroyed in a fire. The insurer refused payment because when W had applied for the insurance cover he had not disclosed the fact that he had

---

[12] *Hadenfayre Ltd v British National Insurance Society Ltd* [1984] 2 Lloyd's Rep 393.
[13] *Smith v Chadwick* (1882) 20 Ch D 27 at 44–45, per Jessel MR (CA).
[14] *North Star Shipping Ltd v Sphere Drake Insurance plc* [2006] EWCA Civ 378, [2006] 2 All ER (Comm) 65.
[15] *Banque Financière de la Cité SA v Westgate Insurance Co Ltd* [1991] 2 AC 249, HL.
[16] *Glicksman v Lancashire & General Assurance Co Ltd* [1927] AC 139, HL.
[17] See, eg, *Dawsons v Bonnin* [1922] 2 AC 413.
[18] Consumer Insurance (Disclosure and Representations) Act 2012, s 6(2), renders such clauses ineffective when they appear in consumer insurance contracts.
[19] *Woolcott v Sun Alliance and London Insurance Ltd* [1978] 1 Lloyd's Rep 629.

convictions for robbery and other offences some 12 years previously. He did not volunteer this information to the building society through which the insurance was taken out, and he was not asked any question about his character on the application form, although the judge accepted that he would have answered such a question truthfully, if he had been asked. The judge referred to the opinion of MacKenna J in *Lambert*,[20] that the absence of a proposal form and hence of any questions from the insurer did not modify in any degree the duty of disclosure. The duty was to disclose such facts as a reasonable or prudent insurer might have treated as material, whether asked or not. Woolcott was in breach of this duty. On the other hand, the judge thought that the fact that a specific question has been put to the insured in a proposal is usually sufficient to satisfy the court that the matter that it deals with is material.

Many contracts of insurance are effected on the basis of a form which the applicant is required to complete beforehand, and in this he will usually be asked a number—often a considerable number—of questions. The fact that specific questions are put to the insured in this way does not displace his obligation to make disclosure under the doctrine of *uberrima fides*. Thus, in *Glicksman*'s case (above), a question on the proposal form asked whether other insurers had at any time refused to give cover to the insured. No insurer had ever refused cover to the *partnership*, and so it was possible for Glicksman and his partner to answer this question truthfully in the negative; but even so, they remained under their common law duty under the doctrine of *uberrima fides* to disclose the fact that Glicksman himself had once been refused insurance.

(d) Good faith

The leading case on good faith, at least on the part of non-professional applicants, is *Economides*.[21] A student aged 21, E, took out insurance cover with the Commercial Union (CU) for the contents of his flat, on the basis of a CU form in which he stated that the full cost of replacing these items was £12,000 and that the total value of valuables did not exceed one-third of the sum insured. He declared on the form that the statements were to the best of his knowledge and belief, true, and complete. Subsequently, his parents came to live with him and, at his father's suggestion, the cover was increased to £16,000. Some months later the flat was burgled and jewellery belonging to his mother was stolen, jewellery which was worth over £30,000. The CU sought to avoid liability under the policy on the grounds of misrepresentation and non-disclosure. The Court of Appeal held that for a policy of household insurance an applicant was only under an obligation to be honest and that his belief, if made in good faith, should be deemed to be honest. E had acted honestly and accordingly the policy could not be avoided on either ground.

The CU did not argue that the goods should have been professionally valued but that relying, however honestly, on his father's opinion was not enough; this argument was rejected.

Finally, many contracts of insurance purport to impose an express duty to inform the insurer if the circumstances change materially during the currency of the policy and these have been enforced.[22]

---

[20] *Lambert v Cooperative Insurance Society Ltd* [1975] 2 Lloyd's Rep 485 at 487, CA.
[21] *Economides v Commercial Union* [1998] QB 587, CA.
[22] See, eg, *Hussain v Brown (No 1)* [1996] 1 Lloyd's Rep 627, CA.

3 CONTENT AND INTERPRETATION OF THE CONTRACT

(a) The risk and exceptions

It is obviously of central importance in any contract of insurance to identify the nature and scope of the risk which the policy covers. Although this is purely a matter of construction of the particular contract, many standard terms have, over time, been the subject of judicial rulings which allow the task of construction to be approached with a reasonable degree of certainty. Thus, the meaning of words such as 'accident', 'all risks', 'fire', 'loss' (and 'consequential loss'), and 'natural causes' have been discussed in many authoritative cases, which are cited in some detail in the leading manuals of insurance law. Even so, such words may admit of different shades of meaning which have to be examined in the particular case: in *Gray v Barr*,[23] for instance, there was a difference of opinion among the judges on the question whether Gray's death had been caused by an 'accident'.

One well-known rule of construction which may be of particular relevance in relation to insurance contracts is the *contra proferentem* rule—that any ambiguity in a document is to be construed in the sense least favourable to the person who has drawn it up, usually the insurer.[24]

We should also bear in mind when ascertaining the scope of the risk covered by the policy that the courts in recent years have abandoned the traditional 'strict' approach to the construction of written contracts in favour of a 'contextual' approach which allows the court to have regard to the factual background and to accept evidence as to the 'wider' matrix of facts of which knowledge may be attributed to the parties when the contract was drawn up.[25] This approach has been adopted in quite a number of recent claims based on contracts of insurance—inevitably at some cost in legal certainty.

The risk may be defined both affirmatively by words such as 'fire' or 'accident' which specifically describe it, and also by words of exception or limitation which exclude liability in particular cases.

(b) Conditions and warranties

The law of insurance, anomalously, has traditionally used the term 'warranty' in a sense rather different from its use in the general law of contract. A warranty in insurance cases is an undertaking given by the insured which forms the very basis of the contract, one the breach of which releases the insurer from liability, rather than merely giving rise to a claim in damages. In other words, it is used in a way which to some extent resembles the term 'condition' in other branches of the law. However, the decision of the House of Lords in *The Good Luck*[26] has pointed up a subtle but important distinction: the breach of a condition in the general law of contract does not of itself avoid or terminate the contract, but merely gives the party

---

[23] Above. See also *Dhak v Insurance Co of North America (UK) Ltd* [1996] 1 WLR 936, CA.
[24] See, eg, *Lancashire County Council v Municipal Insurance Ltd* [1997] QB 897, CA.
[25] See the *Investors Compensation Scheme* case [1998] 1 WLR 896, HL; and *BCCI v Ali* [2001] UKHL 8. See also above, Chapter 1, Section 4(a).
[26] *Bank of Nova Scotia v Hellenic Mutual War Risks Association (Bermuda) Ltd* [1992] 1 AC 233, HL.

who is not in breach the right to terminate it, if he so elects; in contrast, in insurance law, if the insured gives a warranty and this is broken, the insurer is *automatically* discharged from liability unless the insurer decides to waive the breach. So if an insured warrants the accuracy of a statement in the application, and it proves to have been untrue, the insurer is discharged from liability under the policy *ab initio*. Alternatively, if circumstances change *during* the currency of the policy which cause the warranty to be breached, the insurer is discharged from liability under the policy from that time on.

However, the word 'condition' also has a role to play in insurance contracts. Thus, the policy may make it a condition of the insurer's liability in respect of a particular loss that the insurer is given notice of the relevant event within 14 days of its occurrence. Here, the term 'condition' is used in much the same way as in the general law of contract.

Where a warranty is not complied with, the insurer at common law could avoid liability even though the breach of warranty had no connection with the loss.[27] However, the common law position in regard to warranties has been mitigated by regulatory codes and statute. The Insurance Conduct of Business Sourcebook (ICOBS) applies to all 'non-investment insurance contracts' (ie general insurance contracts or 'pure protection contracts') other than reinsurance contracts and the mediation by intermediaries of 'contracts of large risks' (marine, aviation and transport, credit and surety, and other commercial risks) where the risk is located outside the European Economic Area (EEA) or it is located within the EEA but brokered for a commercial customer. The rules are published in the FCA Handbook. ICOBS 8.1.2 forbids a 'rejection of a consumer policyholder's claim ..., except where there is evidence of fraud, if it is ... (3) for breach of warranty or condition unless the circumstances are connected to the breach ...'

Most importantly, the Insurance Act 2015, which for these purposes applies to both consumer and non-consumer insurance contracts, provides that '[a]ny rule of law that breach of a warranty (express or implied) in a contract of insurance result in the discharge of the insurer's liability under the contract is abolished' (s 10(1)). Where there has been a breach of warranty, the insurer has no liability under the insurance contract in respect of any loss occurring, or attributable to something happening, after the breach of warranty but before the breach has been remedied (s 10(2)). This means that the insurer will remain liable in respect of losses occurring before the breach of warranty, or after the breach has been remedied, if capable of remedy (s 10(4)). The insurer cannot rely on a breach of warranty to suspend its liability under the insurance contract (as provided for in s 10(2)) where (a) because of a change of circumstances, the warranty ceases to be applicable to the circumstances of the contract; (b) compliance with the warranty is rendered unlawful by any subsequent law, or the insurer waives the breach (s 10(3)). Sections 15–17 allow the parties to contract out of s 10, but stricter controls apply in the case of consumer insurance contracts than in respect of non-consumer insurance contracts.

Another difficult question which has arisen in many cases is whether the insured warrants only that a state of facts is true at the time he makes it, or that it *will continue to be true* throughout the currency of the cover. Again, this is basically a question of construction, but the task of the court is made easier by the existence of a wealth of relevant precedents.[28]

---

[27] See, eg, *Conn v Westminster Motor Ins Assn Ltd* [1966] 1 Lloyd's Rep 407, CA.
[28] See *Woolfall & Rimmer Ltd v Moyle* [1942] 1 KB 66 at 71, CA.

(c) Consumer protection

Note that under Part 2 of the Consumer Rights Act 2015 (replacing the Unfair Terms in Consumer Contracts Regulations 1999 (SI 1999/2083)) a term which is held to be 'unfair' will not be binding on an insured who is a consumer (s 62(1)). However, the scope of the Act in an insurance context is limited by the fact that a term will not be assessed for unfairness if it specifies the main subject matter of the contract, provided that it is transparent (meaning it is expressed in plain and intelligible language and, if in writing, legible) and prominent (meaning that it is brought to the consumer's attention in such a way that an average—reasonably well-informed, observant, and circumspect—consumer would be aware of the term); and it is arguable that every term in an insurance contract which serves to define or limit the risk is part of its 'main subject matter'. It is likely, therefore, that (apart from the 'transparent and prominent' requirement), the Act can only be invoked in relation (for example) to a term requiring notice of a claim to be given within a specified time, and not to any of the warranties, exceptions, and limitations which are discussed above. Moreover, that part of the Act that restricts terms which purport to exclude or restrict liability for negligence has no application to insurance contracts (ss 65, 66(1)(a)). More importantly, perhaps, the Competition and Markets Authority and certain other 'regulators', including the Consumers' Association, are given powers to monitor the use of unfair terms and to obtain undertakings or injunctions to control or prevent their use (s 70 and Sch 3).

4 LIABILITY OF THE INSURER

(a) Notice

In principle, the insured is entitled to payment of the sum assured on the happening of the event that has been insured against. But in practice most policies stipulate that the insured should give notice of the event and details of his loss within a specified time, and (depending upon the construction of the contract) it may be a condition precedent to the insurer's liability that this requirement is strictly adhered to.

(b) The onus of proof

The burden of proving that the event which has occurred is covered by the policy and, in a policy of indemnity, that he has suffered loss or damage, is on the insured; but where the insurer seeks to avoid liability on the ground that the claim is covered by an exception the onus is normally shifted to the insurer. This will be the case also where the insurer claims to be entitled to avoid liability on any other ground, such as fraud.

The standard of proof is the civil standard of the balance of probabilities. Moreover, the insured is required to show that the event was the 'proximate' cause of his loss—often a difficult issue, but of course one which is not confined to this branch of the law. The court is sometimes willing to take a broad approach: thus, where loss or damage is caused to goods by water as a result of action taken to prevent a fire from spreading, the loss has been treated as caused by the fire.[29] In contrast, where goods were stolen during an air raid, it was held that

---

[29] *Symington & Co v Union Insurance Society of Canton* (1928) 97 LJKB 646, CA.

it was not the air raid but the theft which was the cause of the loss—the air raid had merely facilitated it.[30]

In indemnity insurance, the onus is also on the insured to prove the quantum of his loss, except where the parties have agreed the value of the insured property under the terms of the policy. It may also be agreed as a term of the contract that the insurer will pay only for any loss in excess of a specified sum; or that the insured will bear a proportionate part of the loss if the property is insured for less than its full value (sometimes called an 'average' clause); or that a person who has insured the same risk with more than one insurer will be entitled to claim only a rateable proportion of his loss from any one insurer.

A claim under a contract of indemnity insurance is, by definition, limited to the amount of the insured's actual loss.[31]

(c) Reinstatement

Although the insurer's liability is normally to pay the insured a sum of money to reimburse him for his loss, the contract may give the insurer the option of reinstating the property. Thus, if a building is wholly or partly destroyed by fire, the insurer may have it rebuilt or repaired instead of paying the value of the loss. If the insurer does so elect, it must then reinstate the property whether the cost is greater or less than the sum insured. In certain cases, an insured or other interested person is entitled to *require* an insurance company to apply the policy monies towards reinstating an insured building which is destroyed or damaged by fire, but this statutory obligation extends only to expending the amount of the policy monies and no more.[32]

(d) Insurer's liability to third parties

A policy may be expressed in terms that the insurer agrees to indemnify parties other than the insured (eg a policy taken out by a building company which extends to employees and subcontractors for liabilities incurred by them in carrying out a construction contract). Prior to the enactment of the Contracts (Rights of Third Parties) Act 1999, the doctrine of privity of contract created difficulties if a third party sought to enforce such a contract directly against the insurer. But this Act now gives such a party the right to do so, provided that the contract purports to confer a benefit on him and he is expressly identified in the contract by name, as a member of a class, or as answering to a particular description.

Where a policy covers an insured against his liability to third parties (as in motor vehicle and employer's liability insurance), problems may arise if the insured is insolvent or is for some reason unable to enforce the policy—for example, if it is a company which has been wound up and dissolved. In such circumstances the third party, such as the victim of a motor accident caused by the insured's negligence, may be prejudiced. In the case of an insolvency, he would rank as an ordinary unsecured creditor and any money claimed under the policy would go into the general pool of assets, while if the insured company has been dissolved he would succeed only if he was able to have the company reinstated by court

---

[30] *Winicofsky v Army & Navy General Assurance Association Ltd* (1919) 88 LJKB 1111.
[31] *Castellain v Preston* (1883) 11 QBD 380, CA.
[32] See s 83 of the Fires Prevention (Metropolis) Act 1774 (which is not confined in its application to the 'metropolis').

order. The Third Parties (Rights against Insurers) Act 1930 was passed in order to deal with this sort of problem: as its name suggests, it gives the victim a right to proceed directly against the insurer. But that Act deals mainly with insolvency situations and is not comprehensive, so the Law Commissions recommended that the law should be reformed: the law is now to be found in the Third Parties (Rights against Insurers) Act 2010, which came into force on 1 August 2016 and which repeals the 1930 Act. Where, however, both the policyholder's insolvency and liability to a third party occurred before 1 August, the 1930 Act remains applicable.

5 RIGHTS OF THE INSURER

An insurer who has reimbursed the insured for his loss under an indemnity policy thereby acquires three rights: salvage, subrogation, and contribution.

(a) Salvage

Where an insurer has compensated an insured for the total loss of insured property, all rights to the property are ceded by operation of law to the insurer, who thereby becomes their owner. Thus, if a car is so damaged that it is uneconomic to repair it (a 'constructive total loss') and the insurer pays its owner its full value, the insurer can exercise this right of salvage in respect of the wrecked property and sell it for what it will fetch.[33]

(b) Subrogation

The doctrine of subrogation has its basis in the principle of unjust enrichment. It has two aspects. One is the rule that an insured cannot ever receive more than a full indemnity for his loss, and if he does receive more, he is accountable to the insurer for the excess.[34] The second is that an insurer who has indemnified his insured is entitled to succeed to all the rights of the latter—as it is commonly put, to 'stand in his shoes'—and so he may, for instance, sue any third party who is liable to the insured for the loss in an action in tort or contract. For this purpose, the insurer may use the insured's name in the litigation.[35]

The insured, for his part, may not do anything which prejudices the insurer's right of subrogation, for example grant a release to a tortfeasor or compromise his claim, without the insurer's consent.

(c) Contribution

Where an insured has taken out more than one policy of indemnity insurance in respect of the same risk, any one insurer who has met a claim for the loss in full is entitled to claim contribution in equity on a rateable basis from the other insurers.

---

[33] Cf *Holmes v Payne* [1930] 2 KB 301.
[34] *Castellain v Preston* (1883) 11 QBD 380, CA.
[35] See *Lister v Romford Ice & Cold Storage Co Ltd* [1957] AC 555, HL.

6 MARINE INSURANCE

The law of insurance has its origins in the early days of seafaring, and most of its principles were worked out first in relation to the risks associated with ships and their cargoes and the loss of freight which the carrier would sustain if a ship should fail to complete its voyage. The law governing contracts of marine insurance was codified by statute in the Marine Insurance Act 1906. In some respects, marine insurance law has developed its own rules; but, broadly speaking, its principles are indicative of those of insurance law generally, and judges in non-marine cases do quite often refer to marine insurance decisions and even to the Act itself for guidance. In this chapter, no special attention has been paid to those topics where marine insurance law has different rules—for example, that a contract of marine insurance must be recorded in writing. It is thought sufficient in a work of this nature to deal with the subject of insurance generally, and to add the warning that if an issue of marine insurance is involved, a specialist work should be consulted.[36]

7 INSURANCE CLAIMS

(a) Introduction

Claims must be submitted in the right way, to the right person or office, containing correct and truthful information.

Most contracts require and regulate the written notice of loss to the insurer to start a claim. However, claims at Lloyd's, London, are submitted by the relevant Lloyd's broker by means of an electronic claims file (ECF) and through the Claims Loss Advice and Settlement System (CLASS).

The claimant must be the insured, or a person acting on his behalf, and not a third party.[37] The claim must be sent to (and brought to the attention of) the correct person in the insurance company.

For example, it is sufficient to post the claim to the insurer at a particular place, such as the head office of the insurance company, if that is what is required by the policy. However, it may be sufficient to give it to a local agent for transmission to head office, if given to the agent in time for it to reach head office in the normal course of business.

(b) Time

Notice (which initiates claims) must be given within the time required by the policy or, if none, within a reasonable time.[38] Time runs from the insured event, such as the loss, accident, or occurrence.

For example, where an insurer of cash in transit excluded liability for loss not notified 'within 14 days of its occurrence', it was not liable for periodic embezzlement of the money

---

[36] See, eg, FD Rose, *Marine Insurance: Law and Practice* (2nd edn, 2012).
[37] *Barratt v Davies* [1966] 2 Lloyd's Rep 1, CA.
[38] *Hadenfayre Ltd v British National Insurance Society Ltd* [1984] 2 Lloyd's Rep 393.

over several months prior to the last 14 days, even though notice was given as soon as the insured discovered the loss.[39]

As regards what is reasonable, notice must also be in time for the insurer to test the genuineness of claims before the evidence is obscured,[40] and to minimise loss (and thus the amount to be paid).[41]

The legal consequences of late notice depend on construction: whether the requirement is: (1) a condition precedent to indemnity, which is unlikely unless the words 'condition precedent' have been used; (2) a suspensive condition barring payment until notice is given; or (3) a minor duty, breach of which does not prevent recovery.[42] If notice is late, these rules apply and the claim may be ineffective even if the insurer is not prejudiced thereby.[43]

(c) Claims content

After the initial notice of a claim, the insurer must indicate, if necessary, what further particulars are required. Commonly insurers respond simply by sending a standard claim form for the claimant to complete. The claimant must prove (on the balance of probabilities) the insured event, and the amount or extent of the loss claimed.[44]

(d) Fraudulent claims

A claim is fraudulent where the insurer proves a substantially false (and material) statement by the claimant: one made (1) knowingly; or (2) without belief in its truth; or (3) recklessly, careless whether it be true or false. A claim is substantially false (a question of fact) where, for example, it is considerably exaggerated in amount (and not just a miscalculation or innocent overestimate).[45]

A material statement is one material to the insurer's decision to pay—the amount to be paid, the identity of the payee, or whether to pay anyone at all. Thus, arguably, the claimant who presents false evidence to bolster a true claim, or conceals irrelevant facts, that he finds embarrassing, does not make a material misstatement: the insurer would have paid anyway.[46]

A controversial example of the latter is the 'fraudulent device', now referred to as a 'collateral lie': where 'the insured believes that he has suffered the loss claimed, but seeks to improve or embellish the facts surrounding the claim, by some lie' later on.[47]

In *The DC Merwestone*,[48] Popplewell J applied the notion of fraudulent device rule but also commented that it was important that the rule:

> should not itself be allowed to be used as an instrument of injustice… I would be strongly attracted to a materiality test which permitted the court to look at whether it was just and proportionate

---

[39] *Adamson & Sons v Liverpool & London & Globe Ins Co Ltd* [1953] 2 Lloyd's Rep 355.
[40] *Re Coleman's Depositories and Life & Health Assurance Assn* [1907] 2 KB 798, CA.
[41] See *The Vainqueur José* [1979] 1 Lloyd's Rep 557.
[42] *K/S Merc-Scandia XXXXII v Certain Lloyd's Underwriters* [2001] Lloyd's Rep IR 802, CA.
[43] See *Pioneer Concrete (UK) Ltd v National Employers' Mutual* [1985] 2 All ER 395 at 400.
[44] *Welch v Royal Exchange* [1939] 1 KB 294 at 315, CA.
[45] Cf *Nsubuga v Commercial Union* [1998] 2 Lloyd's Rep 682 and *Galloway v GRE* [1999] Lloyd's Rep IR 209 at 214, CA.
[46] *K/S Merc-Scandia XXXXII v Certain Lloyd's Underwriters* [2001] EWCA Civ 1275.
[47] *Agapitos v Agnew* [2003] QB 556 at [30], CA.
[48] *Versloot Dredging v HDI-Gerling* [2013] EWHC 1666 (Comm), [2013] 2 Lloyd's Rep 131, affirmed [2014] EWCA Civ 1349, [2015] Lloyd's Rep IR 115.

> to deprive the assured of his substantive rights, taking into account all the circumstances of the case. The blunt instrument of a relatively inflexible test of materiality, reminiscent of the old latin tag 'fraus omnia corrumpit', must surely be capable of yielding to a more proportionate response, which can meet the varying circumstances of each case.

On appeal to the Supreme Court,[49] the majority endorsed the reservation of Popplewell J, holding that, if causation was irrelevant to the application of the fraudulent claim rule, some connection had to exist between the fraudulent device (which the court called the collateral lie) and the claim, unless the rule was to part company with rationality. The fraudulent claims rule applied to a wholly fabricated claim. It applied to an exaggerated claim. However, it did not apply to a lie which the true facts, once admitted or ascertained, showed to have been immaterial to the insured's right to recover. The extension of the fraudulent claims rule to lies which were found to be irrelevant to the recoverability of the claim was a step too far. It was disproportionately harsh to the insured and went further than any legitimate commercial interest of the insurer could justify. It led naturally to anomalous consequences.

(e) The consequences of fraud

Absent a provision to that effect, in the past it has been assumed that in the case of fraud the insurer could terminate cover and refuse to pay; this was confirmed by the Insurance Act 2015:

> If the insured makes a fraudulent claim …—
>
> (a) the insurer is not liable to pay the claim,
> (b) the insurer may recover from the insured any sums paid by the insurer to the insured in respect of the claim, and
> (c) in addition, the insurer may by notice to the insured treat the contract as having been terminated with effect from the time of the fraudulent act.[50]

Moreover, money wasted by the insurer investigating a claim may be recoverable as damages.[51]

(f) Claims enforcement

Claims may be enforced by courts with jurisdiction, which is regulated mainly by EU legislation. Special rules regulate all insurance contracts except reinsurance contracts which are treated as normal commercial contracts.[52]

---

[49] [2016] UKSC 45.

[50] Insurance Act 2015, s 12(1). Further, according to s 12(2), where 'the insurer does not treat the contract as having been terminated, it may refuse all liability to the insured under the contract in respect of [loss] occurring after the time of the fraudulent act'. The parties may contract out of the effect of s 12 under ss 15–17, which impose stricter controls on contracting out for consumer insurance contracts than for non-consumer insurance contracts.

[51] *Haywood v Zurich Insurance Co plc* [2016] UKSC 48.

[52] See Regulation (EU) No 1215/2012 of 12 December 2012 (the recast EU Brussels I Regulation), which applies to proceedings instituted on or after 10 January 2015, and replaces Council Regulation (EC) No 44/2001 of 22 December 2000 (the Brussels I Regulation).

PART X

INSOLVENCY LAW

Chapter 28   Insolvency   1105

INSOLVENCY

1 INTRODUCTION

The law relating to the bankruptcy of individuals goes back to a statute of Henry VIII in 1542. The concern of this early legislation (which applied only to persons engaged in trade) was to establish a procedure for the realisation and orderly distribution of the debtor's property among his creditors generally: the fate of the person himself—and still less the question of his rehabilitation into the world of commerce—was not thought to be important. We do not need to look further than the pages of Dickens to discover that in as late as Victorian times people who could not pay their debts were treated little better than criminals, even when their insolvency was due purely to misfortune. There were, it is true, major steps taken to ameliorate the position by the Bankruptcy Acts of 1883 and 1914, but the regime remained a fairly harsh one and the 'stigma of bankruptcy' something that it was never easy to shake off.

Corporate insolvency law, by comparison, dates only from the first companies legislation of 1844. And in stark contrast with the position in bankruptcy, the individuals concerned have usually been able to escape with relative impunity by taking advantage of the principle of limited liability.

Until the reforms of 1985–1986 there was separate legislation for bankruptcies and corporate insolvencies, although some of the principles of bankruptcy law were extended to companies by the operation of a general 'incorporation' provision in the Companies Act.

The initiative for change came from the report of the Review Committee on Insolvency Law and Practice (Cmnd 8558, 1982), commonly known as the 'Cork Committee' after its chairman, Sir Kenneth Cork. This committee recommended that the law should be streamlined and modernised and that bankruptcy law and corporate insolvency law should be integrated and brought rather more into line with each other. This would involve a relaxation of the harsher aspects of bankruptcy law, with a much greater emphasis on the restoration of the debtor to a normal role in the community, and at the same time a tightening up in those areas of corporate insolvency law which had formerly lent themselves to abuse. These recommendations were largely implemented by the Insolvency Act 1985; but very little of this Act was brought into force. Instead, it was almost immediately superseded by the Insolvency Act 1986—a consolidating measure which brought together the new legislation of 1985 and large parts of the Companies Act. In the remainder of this chapter, the Insolvency Act 1986 is referred to as 'IA 1986' and section numbers refer to that Act.

The 1986 Act has since been amended, mainly by the Insolvency Act 2000 and the Enterprise Act 2002. The latter Act made significant changes to both bankruptcy law and the law governing corporate insolvencies. A sharper distinction was made between bankruptcies which were due to misfortune (and in particular consumer cases) and those resulting from irresponsible or fraudulent conduct. On the one hand, it was made easier for a non-culpable debtor to obtain an early discharge and resume a normal life, while on the other hand a guilty bankrupt could be subjected to restrictions on his activities for up to 15 years. In the corporate sphere, secured creditors holding a floating charge over all or substantially all of a company's assets were no longer permitted to enforce their charge by appointing a receiver but were required instead to use the administration regime (shifting the focus towards the possible rehabilitation of the business), and at the same time it was made possible to put a company into administration by a simpler procedure which did not require an application to court. In addition, the long-standing rule which gave priority to Crown debts in an insolvency was abolished.

Further amendments to the legislation have been made by the Enterprise and Regulatory Reform Act 2013 (introducing an out-of-court procedure for debtor applications in bankruptcy), the Deregulation Act 2015 (streamlining procedures and eliminating formalities), and the Small Business, Enterprise and Employment Act 2015 (continuing the increased focus on rehabilitation but at the same time increasing the sanctions for irresponsible conduct).

Two other measures have introduced a degree of order into the administration of insolvencies which contain a cross-border element—for example, where the debtor (individual or corporate) has assets or creditors in more than one country. The first, Regulation (EU) No 2015/848 on Insolvency Proceedings, applies throughout the EU (except for Denmark, which has an opt-out). The Regulation requires the insolvency to be administered primarily by main proceedings in the Member State where the debtor has his (or its) principal base, and by ancillary proceedings in other states, and coordinates and regulates the relationship between the two. At the same time it provides that the proceedings in every jurisdiction, and the authority of the liquidator or other office-holder in the proceeding, be recognised without any formality throughout the EU. The second is a piece of purely domestic legislation, the Cross-Border Insolvency Regulations 2006 (SI 2006/1030), which provide for recognition in Great Britain of the validity of foreign insolvency proceedings instituted anywhere in the world, and the authority of their office-holders, without the need for formal court proceedings. The Regulations are based on the Model Law on Cross-Border Insolvency which was adopted by the UN Commission on International Trade Law (UNCITRAL) in 1997 and has since become part of the law in over 40 countries. The enactment of the Regulations was, of course, a unilateral step: a more general international regime will only come into place as other countries follow suit.

2 THE BASIC OBJECTIVES OF INSOLVENCY LAW

We may summarise the basic objectives of insolvency law as follows.

In the bankruptcy of individuals:

- to protect the insolvent from harassment by his creditors;
- to enable him to make a fresh start, especially in less blameworthy cases;
- to have him reduce his indebtedness by making such contribution from his present resources and future earnings as is just, taking into account his personal circumstances and the claims and needs of his family.

In corporate insolvency:

- where possible, to preserve the business, or the viable parts of it (but not necessarily the *company*);
- where it is considered that the principle of limited liability has been abused, to impose personal liability and other sanctions on those responsible.

In both forms of insolvency:

- to ensure that all creditors participate *pari passu* (ie on an equal footing) in the estate, except insofar as they may have priority as secured creditors or a statutory right to preference;
- to ensure that secured creditors deal fairly in realising and enforcing their security, vis-à-vis both the debtor and the other creditors;
- to investigate impartially the reasons for failure and to see that such disabilities and penalties as are appropriate are imposed, in the interests of society;
- where the assets of the insolvent have been improperly dealt with prior to the onset of insolvency (eg so as to remove them from the estate, or give a preference to some creditors at the expense of others), to recoup the assets for the benefit of the general estate.

The importance of the *pari passu* principle is shown by the following case.

British Eagle International Airlines Ltd v Cie Nationale Air France
[1975] 1 WLR 758, House of Lords

Many of the world's airlines are members of IATA (the International Air Transport Association). A 'clearing house' scheme was set up under which the debts and credits between one airline and another arising from carrying each other's passengers and cargo were not settled directly but were pooled through IATA. A balance was struck each month and the net sum due was then paid by IATA to each airline or vice versa, as appropriate. British Eagle went into liquidation at a time when it was a net debtor to the scheme as a whole, but if the scheme was ignored it was a net creditor as between itself and Air France. The House of Lords, by a majority, held that the clearing house arrangement was contrary to public policy, in that the parties to it were contracting out of the statutory regime which would apply in a liquidation.

Lord Cross of Chelsea: . . . What the respondents are saying here is that the parties to the 'clearing house' arrangements by agreeing that simple contract debts are to be satisfied in a particular way have succeeded in 'contracting out' of the provisions contained in [IA 1986, s 107] for the payment of unsecured debts 'pari passu.' In such a context it is to my mind irrelevant that the parties to the 'clearing house' arrangements had good business reasons for entering into them and did not direct their minds to the question how the arrangements might be affected by the insolvency of one or more of the parties. Such a 'contracting out' must, to my mind, be contrary to public policy. The question is, in essence, whether what was called in argument the 'mini liquidation' flowing from the clearing house arrangements is to yield to or to prevail over the general liquidation. I cannot doubt that on principle the rules of the general liquidation should prevail. I would therefore hold that notwithstanding the clearing house arrangements, British Eagle on its liquidation became entitled to recover payment of the sums payable to it by other airlines for services rendered by it during that period and that airlines which had rendered services to it during that period became on the liquidation entitled to prove for the sums payable to them . . .

[**Lords Diplock** and **Edmund-Davies** concurred. **Lords Morris of Borth-y-Gest** and **Simon of Glaisdale** dissented.]

NOTE

Although the *British Eagle* ruling remains authoritative for the purposes of the general law, it has been recognised that in practice, in the interests of expediency, such 'clearing house' and 'pooling' arrangements perform a useful function in the financial, banking, and securities settlement markets. Accordingly, legislation has been passed directing that contracts of this nature made between the participants on these markets are to have effect, to the exclusion of the normal rules of insolvency law: see, for example, the Companies Act 1989, Part VII, the Financial Markets and Insolvency Regulations 1991 (SI 1991/880), and the Financial Markets and Insolvency (Settlement Finality) Regulations 1999 (SI 1999/2979).

Similar reasoning underlies another well-established principle, commonly referred to as the 'anti-deprivation' rule. It is unlawful for the parties to a contract to agree that an asset belonging to one of them shall, in the event of his bankruptcy, cease to belong to him and be automatically vested in the other one. In *Ex parte Mackay* (1873) 8 Ch App 643 A, who owed B money, gave B security for the debt over half of the royalties due to him under a patent, with the proviso that if A became bankrupt the security should be extended to the whole of the royalties. This provision was held to be void.

3 THE VARIOUS DEFINITIONS OF INSOLVENCY

There is no single meaning of the term 'insolvent'. It is important to distinguish between three different definitions of this unhappy state—or, rather, at least three, since these are broad-brush distinctions and any one of them may have variations on points of detail.

'Balance-sheet' insolvency The first test of insolvency has regard to the person's assets and liabilities, and looks to see whether there is, overall, a net surplus or a deficit. If there is a deficit, that person is insolvent. A company with investments which have fallen in value may become 'insolvent' within this definition, even though it is currently trading satisfactorily and paying its way.

'Commercial' insolvency   This test is not concerned with the asset position, but with liquidity. It is sometimes also called 'practical' insolvency or insolvency on a 'cash-flow' basis. The person concerned may have substantial assets, but is unable to pay his debts as they fall due. This could be so of a company, for instance, which has its wealth tied up in property that is not readily realisable (eg in out-of-season stock, or half-finished products), or which has overspent on research and development for a new project which is still on the drawing-board.

'Ultimate' insolvency   Here we are concerned with the final outcome of events. The debtor's assets have been sold for what they will fetch—perhaps in a forced sale, on a break-up basis—and the costs of realisation and of administering the estate are brought into account. If his creditors have received less than 100p in the pound, we can say that the estate was insolvent. Many a person who could very reasonably have claimed to be solvent if his assets were valued on a going-concern basis may prove, in the event, to be insolvent in this sense if the worst happens.

Insolvency, as such, has very few legal consequences. So, for instance, the fact that a person who is a party to a contract becomes insolvent does not amount to a repudiation of the contract or entitle the other party to terminate it, unless the contract so provides. Occasionally, however, rights may be affected by *statute* because a party has become insolvent—for example, in a sale of goods, an unpaid seller is given the right to stop the goods in transit if the buyer has become insolvent (see above, p 489). But it is usually only as a consequence of some *insolvency procedure* that the legal position changes—for example, when an individual has been declared bankrupt, or a company has gone into liquidation, administration, or receivership.

Where 'insolvency' is a precondition for the operation of a provision in a statute or a contract or other document, it is obviously important to determine in which of the various senses the term is to be construed. Thus, in the Sale of Goods Act 1979, a person is deemed to be insolvent 'if he has either ceased to pay his debts in the ordinary course of business or he cannot pay his debts as they become due' (s 61(4)); and so the seller's right of stoppage in transit referred to above will arise if the buyer is 'insolvent' in a 'commercial' sense. In contrast, the question whether a director can be held liable for 'wrongful trading' (see below, p 1133) depends in part on whether there was a 'reasonable prospect that the company would avoid going into insolvent liquidation'; and for this purpose IA 1986 prescribes a 'balance sheet' test (s 214(6)). Plainly, the relevant definition must be examined closely in each case.

4 INSOLVENCY PROCEDURES

(a) Individual insolvency

When an individual becomes insolvent, a choice of statutory procedures is available.

County court administration order made under the County Courts Act 1984, Part VI. (These orders should not be confused with administration orders made in relation to insolvent companies under Part II of IA 1986 (see below, p 1111).) An order may be made against a person who cannot pay the whole of a judgment debt and whose total indebtedness is not more than £5,000. A moratorium comes into effect and an officer of the court supervises the payment of the debts of such creditors as are known by instalments out of the debtor's income.

Individual voluntary arrangement (IVA) (IA 1986, Part VIII). This is a scheme of voluntary arrangement of a fairly informal kind, supervised by a professional insolvency practitioner. A moratorium can be sought from the court, staying all enforcement proceedings while the supervisor of the scheme and the creditors consider proposals to resolve the position, for instance by a compromise, which can be made binding on all creditors if supported by a prescribed majority.

Debt relief order (DRO) (IA 1986, Part 7A). This procedure was introduced to allow an individual debtor who has few or no assets (not exceeding £1,000) and little disposable income (not more than £50 per month, following deduction of normal household expenses) and unsecured debts not exceeding £20,000 to be relieved of those liabilities without the formalities of bankruptcy or an IVA. The debtor must not currently be bankrupt or subject to any other form of insolvency procedure or have been subject to a DRO within the last six years.

The court is not involved. An application for a DRO is made online to the Official Receiver through an 'approved intermediary' (an experienced debt advisor) or a 'competent authority' (eg a Citizens Advice Bureau), who certifies that the debtor is eligible and lists the debts which qualify to be covered by the order. The DRO protects the debtor from enforcement action by the creditors concerned for a moratorium period of 12 months, and at the end of that period those debts are written off. There are necessarily various statutory safeguards against abuse, and in particular the court is empowered to make a debt relief restrictions order (DRRO), on the application of the Official Receiver, which imposes limitations on the debtor's freedom to obtain credit, etc similar to those which apply to an undischarged bankrupt, and can last for up to 15 years. As an alternative to a DRRO, the Official Receiver may accept a debt relief restrictions undertaking (DRRU) from the individual concerned.

Bankruptcy application (IA 1986, ss 263H–263O). There has been a major change here. Before April 2016 every bankruptcy application had to be made by petition to the court and the person concerned was made bankrupt by court order. New sections introduced into IA 1986 by the Enterprise and Regulatory Reform Act 2013 have removed the need for individual debtors seeking their own bankruptcy to go through the court procedure. Instead, an application is made electronically to a new official called an Adjudicator, who makes the decision. This will result in considerable saving in costs. But a court order is needed where the application is made by a creditor.

Bankruptcy order (IA 1986, Part IX). A bankruptcy order may be made against a person on the petition of one or more creditors whose debts total at least £5,000, on the ground that he 'appears either to be unable to pay or to have no reasonable prospect of being able to pay' his debts. A 'commercial' rather than a 'balance-sheet' test of insolvency is thus applied. A debtor will be deemed unable to pay his debts if he has failed to pay a debt within three weeks after being served with a formal statutory demand for payment, or if execution has been issued against him and has been returned unsatisfied. An order will not be made on the basis of a debt which is the subject of a bona fide dispute; nor will the court resolve such a dispute in the bankruptcy proceedings—the parties must litigate the matter elsewhere in the normal way.

The Official Receiver (a government officer attached to the court) takes charge of the bankrupt's assets until an independent insolvency practitioner is appointed trustee. On his appointment, the bankrupt's assets vest in the trustee. He has the responsibility of administering the bankrupt's estate, realising the available assets, and applying them, so far as they will go, towards satisfying the creditors. Certain creditors are entitled to be paid in priority: primarily employees, for up to £800 unpaid wages. (For full details, see IA 1986, Sch 6.) (Formerly, the Crown was also entitled to priority, up to certain limits, for unpaid PAYE taxes, VAT, and NI contributions, but this was abolished by the Enterprise Act 2002.) The rules in this respect are identical, or nearly so, to those which apply in a company liquidation, as are those relating to transactions at an undervalue, preferences, and transactions defrauding creditors which are discussed below, at pp 1130-1133. The bankrupt is entitled to keep tools, books, vehicles, etc necessary for his employment and furniture, clothing, and household equipment necessary for use by him and his family.

During the currency of a bankruptcy, the bankrupt is subject to a number of disabilities— for example, he may not be a company director—and there are restrictions upon his obtaining credit. But it is now the policy of the law that this situation should not continue for any long period: unless there has been some impropriety, or the person has been bankrupt more than once, a *discharge in bankruptcy* becomes effective automatically after one year (at least in most cases). Once a bankrupt is discharged, all his pre-bankruptcy debts are deemed to have been satisfied, and he is free to live a normal life again. Until the Enterprise Act 2002 came into force in 2004, the normal duration of a bankruptcy had been three years, but that Act introduced a distinction between debtors who had been guilty of culpable wrongdoing and those who had not, and reduced the period for the latter.

This reflected a general policy which recognises that many bankruptcies (and particularly those involving consumers or persons in a small way of business) are the consequence of bad luck or poor judgment rather than anything seriously blameworthy, and which seeks to give such debtors a 'fresh start'. In contrast, there is now a power for the court to make a 'bankruptcy restrictions order', similar to a director disqualification order (see the Company Directors Disqualification Act 1986), where fraudulent or irresponsible conduct by the debtor has caused him to become insolvent. Such an order can last after his discharge from bankruptcy and will prevent him from acting as a company director, impose restrictions on obtaining credit, etc for up to 15 years. As an alternative to a court order, he may give a bankruptcy restrictions undertaking to the Secretary of State, which has the same effect.

(b) Corporate insolvency

Again, a range of procedures is available.

Company voluntary arrangement (CVA) (IA 1986, Part I). This is a procedure introduced by the Act of 1986. It is similar in many respects to the individual voluntary arrangement. Once again, a qualified insolvency practitioner is brought in to put proposals to a meeting of the company's creditors and, if they agree to its terms, to supervise the scheme. In contrast with an IVA, there was no provision in IA 1986 as originally enacted enabling a moratorium to be put in place while the proposal for a CVA was being put together and considered by the company's creditors. This was a weakness in the law and was the main reason why the CVA was relatively little used in practice. However, since 1 January 2003, s 1 of and Sch A1 to IA 2000 have been in force—provisions (in quite astonishing detail) which now allow the directors of a company who propose a CVA to take steps to obtain a moratorium while the arrangement is being formulated and put before the creditors for approval. This protection is restricted to 'small' private companies (as defined by the Companies Act 1985, s 247(3)), and is not available for certain categories of company (eg banks and insurance companies), for companies which are already subject to some other insolvency procedure, and for a company which has had the benefit of a similar moratorium in the previous 12 months. In practice, the administration procedure (below) is commonly preferred since it is less formal and more flexible. But it may also be used as a method of exit from an administration, as a step towards rehabilitation.

Administration (IA 1986, Part II). This is another innovation dating from the 1986 reforms. As with a CVA, the affairs of the company are placed under the control of an insolvency practitioner, without putting it into liquidation, but instead of pursuing a plan agreed at a meeting of the company's creditors, the administrator's role and the objectives which he must seek to achieve are primarily laid down by statute. Under Part II as originally enacted, a company could only be put into administration by an order of the court, and the procedure was formal and relatively slow and expensive. In consequence, it was not used as often as might have been expected. One reason was that the law at that time allowed the holder of a floating charge over the company's general assets to veto an administration and put the company into receivership instead—more accurately, into 'administrative' receivership (see below). Since this could be done very speedily and the receiver could normally carry out his functions independently of the court, it was naturally more likely to be preferred.

But with the enactment of the Enterprise Act 2002, everything was stood on its head. Part II was replaced and a new administration regime introduced which in most cases did not require the participation of the court (and the associated formality, delay, and expense). At the same time a new s 72A was inserted into IA 1986 which (with a few exceptions) prohibited the holder of a floating charge from appointing an administrative receiver. So if a charge-holder wishes to enforce his security against the company's property, he must now normally use the administration procedure. However, the whole process of putting a company into administration has been simplified and streamlined, and the statutory purposes of an administration have been redefined so as to include 'realising property in order to make a distribution to one or more secured or preferential creditors', so that in many ways the disadvantages of administration when compared with receivership have been eliminated or reduced.

The thinking that prompted this change in the law was that, whereas administration is a procedure designed to take into account the interests of all parties—shareholders, creditors, and everyone else concerned in the business and its possible survival—the principal function of a receiver is to look after the interests of the creditor who has appointed him, usually by realising sufficient assets to pay off the secured debt. As we shall see, a receiver owes only very limited duties to have regard to the interests of the company itself or any of its stakeholders. The object of the reforms contained in the Enterprise Act 2002 was to promote more of a 'rescue' culture, making the survival of the company's business, so far as that could be achieved, a primary objective, and it was believed that this could best be done by making greater use of the administration procedure. In addition, the statutory purposes of an administration were reformulated so as to give greater emphasis—indeed, priority—to the survival of the company's business while at the same time making suitable provision, as noted above, to ensure that the security rights of floating changes were respected in the administration.

The current Part II is to be found in Sch B1 to IA 1986, inserted by the Enterprise Act 2002. A company may be put into administration by an out-of-court procedure by: (1) the company itself or its directors; or (2) the holder of a floating charge secured over all or substantially all of the company's assets. This is done simply by filing a notice of appointment of the administrator and other prescribed documents with the court: it is not involved in any judicial capacity (although it is given some back-up and supervisory powers). Other persons (eg an unsecured creditor) are still able to have a company put into administration, but only by obtaining a court order. Although the charge-holder no longer has the power to block an administration, various rules ensure that he is kept informed of steps taken by other parties and can, for instance, have an insolvency practitioner of his own choosing appointed to act instead of or in addition to some other nominee. But all administrators are now required to perform their functions with the same objectives, ranked in priority as follows:

(1) rescuing the company as a going concern;

(2) achieving a better result for the company's creditors as a whole than would be likely if the company were wound up;

(3) realising property in order to make a distribution to secured or preferential creditors.

So even if it is a charge-holder who has made the appointment, his interests now have to be subordinated to objects (1) and (2) if either of them is thought to be achievable.

An administrator has wide statutory powers, which are set out in IA 1986, Sch 1. In addition he may, with the leave of the court, dispose of assets which are in the company's possession but which are owned by others (eg machines which the company has on lease or hire-purchase, or goods which it has contracted to buy on 'retention of title' terms) or which are subject to security interests in favour of other parties (Sch B1, paras 70–72). This plainly makes it easier for an administrator to sell the business on a going-concern basis, and prevents the owner or security-holder from being obstructive if such a sale is proposed. Any order which the court makes under s 15 will, of course, include provision for the person concerned to be paid the value of his interest out of the proceeds of sale of the property.

It is unlikely that, in many cases, the first statutory objective of rescuing the company as a going concern will be regarded as achievable—still less achieved, particularly since it is a prerequisite to an appointment that the company should be insolvent (or, where it is a charge-holder who initiates the procedure, that the security should have become enforceable). However, the appointment of an administrator brings about a moratorium binding on all creditors which will allow a breathing space for him to try to find additional or alternative finance or in some other way restore vitality to the enterprise so that control can be handed back to the directors. A more likely outcome is that the company's *business* or the profitable parts of it will be sold for a better sum than would be likely in a liquidation, so achieving the second statutory purpose. It is only when neither of these objectives is considered likely to be fulfilled that the administrator may proceed to enforce a charge-holder's security.

On his appointment, the administrator calls for a 'statement of affairs' of the company to be prepared by one or more of its officers, and on the strength of this information it is his duty to formulate proposals for achieving the purpose of the administration and to summon meetings of the creditors to consider them with a view to their approval. If they are approved, it is then his duty to seek to carry them out. He is empowered to take custody or control of the company's property and to do anything necessary for the management of its business and property.

But in all too many cases there will be no future for the enterprise and the only option will be to close it down. The Act spells out a straightforward procedure enabling the administration to proceed seamlessly to a liquidation (usually with the same insolvency practitioner becoming liquidator) or, in the worst case, where the company is hopelessly insolvent, empowering the administrator to have it dissolved without further formality.

One advantage that administration has over receivership is that, since it is a 'collective' procedure intended to look after the interests of all the insolvent company's creditors, and since it has the backing of the court, it is much more likely to be recognised by a foreign court, in any jurisdiction where the institution of receivership is unknown.

A recent innovation (undoubtedly something unanticipated by the legislators) has been the introduction of the 'pre-pack' administration. Here, a company on the verge of insolvency engages an insolvency practitioner to prepare the ground for the sale of the company's business, or the viable parts of it, to a third party, with a view to clinching the transaction immediately after the company is put into administration, usually with the same person as administrator. This procedure bypasses the statutory provisions which require an administrator to give various notices, hold meetings, etc—formalities which take a considerable amount of time.

The main advantage of the pre-pack is thus the saving of time and expense and the avoidance of possibly adverse publicity which the statutory formalities would involve. The continuity of the business may preserve goodwill and save jobs, securing a better price. However, two aspects of the procedure have given rise to some concern: most likely, there will be insufficient funds for the company's unsecured creditors to receive any dividend and, secondly, they will usually have had no advance notice of the pre-arranged sale and no opportunity to have a say in the decision-making process. These circumstances are all the more likely to arouse suspicion where, as in many cases, the sale is to the existing management or other 'connected' persons. These concerns attracted considerable public comment and have led to the imposition by government of an extra-statutory code of practice which binds insolvency practitioners to provide creditors with specified information at the earliest opportunity.

The pre-pack has now been accepted as legitimate in a good number of reported cases. It is most appropriate where the insolvency is such that there will be no surplus available for distribution to the unsecured creditors and the proposed sale is likely to be more advantageous than what might have been raised if all the statutory formalities had been followed.

The next case is unusual in that an application was made by a secured creditor to have an administrator appointed by a court order when he could have made the appointment himself out of court. In this way he was able to see off the threat of a challenge by a third party.

Bank of Scotland plc v Targetfollow Property Holdings Ltd
[2010] EWHC 3606 (Ch), [2013] BCC 817, Chancery Division

The company was in debt to its bank and had defaulted on a loan, and it was indisputably insolvent. The bank applied for the appointment of an administrator by the court, fearing that if it had made the appointment itself extra-judicially, another creditor, CI Ltd, would challenge it. In the event, CI did not seek to intervene in the court proceedings and the judge held that the case for an appointment had been made out.

> **David Richards J**: The company is part of a substantial property investment and development group. ... That group is indebted to the bank in a substantially larger sum than the amount due from the company with which I am concerned today. ... The term facility which the bank had granted to the company matured on July 22, 2010, at which point a sum of £89 million-odd became due. It was not paid by the company. This failure constituted an immediate event of default under the terms of the loan agreement.
>
> The company had granted to the claimant a debenture which conferred a number of forms of security in favour of the bank. ...The debenture conferred on the bank an express right to appoint a receiver. ... In addition there is a floating charge over the company's undertaking and assets in favour of the bank. The debenture ... expressly confers upon the bank the right to appoint an administrator pursuant to para.14 of Sch.B1 [of IA 1986]. The bank could have taken the step itself of appointing administrators of the company, pursuant to the powers to which I have just referred, and it continues to be entitled to do so. ... The reason why it has not taken that straightforward step is because another ... secured creditor of the company, a company called CI Ltd, had in correspondence claimed that under the terms of an inter-creditor deed which it entered into with the bank and the company, primarily to agree priorities between those secured creditors, it had a contractual right to consultation before the bank took any step to appoint administrators. It threatened to challenge the appointment of administrators.
>
> The bank disputed the position taken by CI Ltd, but decided that the best way of dealing with it was to issue the application for the appointment of administrators so that the arguments being advanced by CI Ltd could then be litigated and decided in that application, rather than have an out-of-court appointment disrupted by proceedings brought by CI Ltd. It seems to me that this was an entirely sensible course for the bank to adopt in these particular circumstances. In the event, it appears to have been unnecessary because CI Ltd has not appeared on this application to raise its arguments or to oppose the appointment of administrators.
>
> The application is therefore made for an administration order under para.10 of Sch.B1 by the bank, in its capacity as a creditor of the company, pursuant to para.12(1)(c). Under para.11 of Sch. B1 the court may make an administration order in relation to the company only if it is satisfied of

two matters. The first is that the company is, or is likely to become, unable to pay its debts. There is, again, no issue as to this…. The second precondition is that the administration order is reasonably likely to achieve the purpose of administration. That refers back to para.3 of Sch.B1, which sets out the purposes or objectives of administration, which are: (a) rescuing the company as a going concern, or (b) achieving better result for the company's creditors as a whole than would be likely if the company were wound up without first being in administration, or (c) realising property in order to make a distribution to one or more secured, or preferential, creditors. The subsequent provisions of para.3 make it clear that that is a set of objectives and purposes in, as it were, diminishing importance. That is to say that the administrator must first seek to achieve (a) unless it was not reasonably practicable or would not achieve as good a result as (b) for the creditors as a whole. If (b) is also not reasonably practicable, he may seek to achieve (c).

[His Lordship then said that while there was insufficient evidence for him to be sure that condition (a) was satisfied, conditions (b) and (c) had been met, and exercised his discretion to make the administration order.]

Receivership, and in particular administrative receivership (IA 1986, Part III). The term receiver is a word that is used in a number of contexts, some of which have no necessary connection with insolvency. The court, for instance, has an inherent jurisdiction to appoint a person to act as a receiver in order to protect and preserve property which is the subject of litigation—for example, in relation to partnership property pending the resolution of a partnership dispute. It may also appoint a receiver to enforce a charge or other security by taking control of the charged assets and, if appropriate, selling them.

We shall not be concerned in this section with the special rules that apply to receivers appointed by the court, but will look only at the type of receiver who is appointed *out of court*, by the holder of a charge, to enforce the security by taking control of the charged assets on behalf of the charge-holder and, in most cases, to realise the assets and apply the proceeds in or towards paying off the charge. It has been customary for a century or more for the instrument which creates a charge to include among its terms a power for the charge-holder to appoint a receiver in this way. The power will normally be exercisable if there is some default on the part of the debtor or if an event occurs which puts the security in jeopardy. A receiver may be appointed to enforce either a fixed charge or a floating charge—or, for that matter, a security which combines both; but our interest will be centred mainly on the receiver who is appointed to enforce a floating charge which has been granted by a company over its undertaking and all of its assets, present and future.

Shamji v Johnson Matthey Bankers Ltd shows that the holder of a charge is entitled to have regard to his own interests in deciding whether to appoint a receiver: he owes no duty of care to the chargor or any guarantors.

Shamji v Johnson Matthey Bankers Ltd
[1986] BCLC 278, [1991] BCLC 36, Chancery Division and Court of Appeal

A group of companies owed the defendant bank (JMB) £21 million, secured by mortgage debentures. JMB was pressing for the loan to be repaid, but had allowed the group 21 days to try to obtain alternative finance, and had agreed to extend this period by a further 14 days if it was satisfied that the refinancing negotiations were proceeding in a proper and expeditious manner. JMB appointed receivers within this 14-day period. The plaintiff alleged that JMB in taking this step had been in breach of a duty of care towards the group and its guarantors, but the court held that no such duty was recognised in law.

> **Hoffmann J:** Counsel for the defendants said under the terms of the security documents as pleaded in the statement of claim, JMB had a contractual right to appoint a receiver at any time after demanding payment. In the absence of bad faith, the bank could not owe the mortgagors or guarantors a duty of care in deciding whether to exercise that right. It might owe some duty in the way in which the right was exercised (eg it might owe a duty to take reasonable care not to appoint an incompetent) but not as to whether it was exercised or not.
>
> [His Lordship referred to a number of cases, and continued:]
>
> It is clear, however, that in the case of a conflict between the interests of the mortgagor and mortgagee, any duty of care which the mortgagee owes to the mortgagor is subordinated to his right to act in the protection of his own interests. As Salmon LJ said in the *Cuckmere Brick Co* case ([1971] 2 All ER 633 at 643, [1971] Ch 949 at 965):
>
> > If the mortgagee's interests, as he sees them, conflict with those of the mortgagor, the mortgagee can give preference to his own interests . . . .
>
> The appointment of a receiver seems to me to involve an inherent conflict of interest. The purpose of the power is to enable the mortgagee to take the management of the company's property out of the hands of the directors and entrust it to a person of the mortgagee's choice. That power is granted to the mortgagee by the security documents in completely unqualified terms. It seems to me that a decision by the mortgagee to exercise the power cannot be challenged except perhaps on grounds of bad faith. There is no room for the implication of a term that the mortgagee shall be under a duty to the mortgagor to 'consider all relevant matters' before exercising the power. If no such qualification can be read into the security documents, I do not think that a wider duty can exist in tort. . . .
>
> [The Court of Appeal affirmed this judgment, [1991] BCLC 36.]

The term 'receiver' was originally used to describe a person appointed to receive the *income* (eg rents) yielded by the property in question—hence the name. When the receiver's function was extended to include taking charge of the property itself, and perhaps selling it, the name was not changed. But where the property included a business which it was important to keep on foot as a going concern, it was necessary to ensure also that there was continuity of management while the receiver was in office; and so (whether the appointment was made by the court or by the charge-holder) in these cases a *manager* as well as a receiver would be appointed—or, more commonly, the same individual would be appointed as a *receiver and manager*. It is evident that such an appointment will invariably be appropriate where the charge extends to the whole or part of the debtor company's undertaking. In practice, most receivers' powers include a power to manage; and IA 1986, s 29(1) reflects this by stating that a 'receiver' includes a receiver or manager of the property of a company, and also a receiver or manager of part of the property of a company. (Section 29(2) goes on to define a particular category of receiver—an 'administrative receiver'—who is given special statutory powers and duties. But the Enterprise Act 2002 has now imposed a ban on the appointment of an administrative receiver (apart from a few exceptions), and a charge-holder is obliged to appoint an administrator instead.)

Apart from the special case of administrative receivership, there is little legislation governing receivers: IA 1986 prohibits a body corporate or an undischarged bankrupt from acting as a receiver (ss 30, 31), and parts of the Law of Property Act 1925 dealing with mortgages may be relevant in some cases; but otherwise everything is left to the common law. A receiver usually has extensive powers conferred by the charge document under which he has been appointed and the instrument of appointment itself. It will be provided that in the exercise of these powers he shall be deemed to act as the agent of the company (and not of the charge-holder who has appointed him) although this deemed agency will cease if the company should go into liquidation.

This is, however, an anomalous form of 'agency'. It does have the effect of ensuring that liabilities incurred by the receiver are met from the company's assets and not from those of the security-holder, but the company has few, if any, of the normal rights and powers of a principal—for example, the power to give directions to the agent, or to remove him from office.

The receiver's responsibilities are focused primarily on the interests of the charge-holder whom he represents. His function may be simply to sell up some or all of the company's assets and apply them towards clearing the charge-holder's debt, with little or no regard to the consequences for the other creditors, employees, shareholders, and, indeed, the business itself. But he may, alternatively, be appointed with the responsibility of managing the business for a time, in the hope that the company will trade its way out of a bad patch, or will find a new source of finance, or at the very least that its undertaking can be sold on a going-concern rather than a break-up basis, in whole or in part, and so fetch a better price. Whatever his function, however, the interests of the charge-holder who has appointed him come first, as the following cases illustrate.

Gomba Holdings UK Ltd v Homan

[1986] 1 WLR 1301, Chancery Division

This case was a sequel to *Shamji v Johnson Matthey Bankers Ltd* (above, p 1115). After the receivers had sold assets realising some £11 million, and while negotiations were taking place to make further sales, Shamji claimed to have entered into an agreement with an undisclosed third party which would provide funds to pay off the remainder of the debt owed by his group of companies to the bank. In these proceedings, the companies sought an order requiring the receivers not to dispose of further assets without first giving the companies five days' notice, and a further order compelling the receivers to disclose information about actual and pending sales. Hoffmann J refused both orders.

Hoffmann J: . . . I shall consider first motion 3 to restrain the receivers from entering into any commitments to dispose of assets unless they have first given the plaintiffs five working days' written notice of the details of any such proposed commitment. Mr Cullen submitted that pending the proposed redemption, the balance of convenience favoured such an order because the sale of an asset without notice to the plaintiffs might upset the arrangements with the unknown third party. This may be true, although I think there are other matters which also enter into the balance of convenience. But the primary difficulty is that I can see no arguable cause of action which could entitle the plaintiffs to such relief. The security documents give the receivers an unrestricted right to sell at any time. Until actual redemption or at least a valid tender of the redemption price, these powers continue to exist. The fact that the plaintiffs claim that they will shortly be able to redeem cannot give them a right in law to restrict the powers granted to the receivers.

Even if there were a cause of action, I do not think that the balance of convenience would favour an injunction. The receivers are entitled to take the view that they should continue with realisations on the assumption that redemption may not take place. No doubt the receivers will exercise a commercial judgment in the matter. But an enforced delay of five working days or even the need to reveal the proposed transaction to the plaintiffs may cause the loss of an advantageous sale. As against this possibility of loss, the plaintiffs are unable to offer anything in support of a cross-undertaking in damages. I therefore dismiss motion 3.

Most of the three-day hearing of these motions was taken up with discussion of motion 1 for information. The cases do not provide very much guidance on the extent of the duty of a receiver and manager of the property of a company to provide information to the directors during the currency of the receivership. A receiver is an agent of the company and an agent ordinarily has a duty to be ready with his accounts and to provide his principal with information relating to the conduct of his agency. But these generalisations are of limited assistance because a receiver and manager is no ordinary agent. Although nominally the agent of the company, his primary duty is to realise the assets in the interests of the debenture holder and his powers of management are really ancillary to that duty: *Re B Johnson & Co (Builders) Ltd* [1955] Ch 634, 644–645 . . .

There are, I think, certain principles which can be deduced from what the parties may be supposed to have contemplated as the commercial purpose of the power to appoint a receiver and manager. The first is that the receiver and manager should have the power to carry on the day to day process of realisation and management of the company's property without interference from the board. As Lord Atkinson said in *Moss SS Co Ltd v Whinney* [1912] AC 254, 263, the appointment of a receiver:

> entirely supersedes the company in the conduct of its business, deprives it of all power to enter into contracts in relation to that business, or to sell, pledge, or otherwise dispose of the property put into the possession, or under the control of the receiver and manager. Its powers in these respects are entirely in abeyance.

This relationship between the receivers and the company would suggest that the board may be entitled to periodic accounts but cannot, merely because it is the board and the receivers are agents of the company, demand current information about the conduct of the business . . .

The second principle which can be deduced from the nature of receivership is that, in the absence of express contrary provision made by statute or the terms of the debenture, any right which the company may have to be supplied with information must be qualified by the receiver's primary duty to the debenture holder. If the receiver considers that disclosure of information would be contrary to the interests of the debenture holder in realising the security, I think he must be entitled to withhold it and probably owes a duty to the debenture holder to do so. The company may be able to challenge the receiver's decision on the ground of bad faith or possibly that it was a decision which no reasonable receiver could have made, but otherwise I think that the receiver is the best judge of the commercial consequences of disclosing information about his activities.

[His Lordship discussed the evidence, and concluded:]

The history of this case, both before and after the appointment of the receivers, is a chronicle of unfulfilled assurances by Mr Shamji that someone was just about to provide the money to pay his debts to the bank. In my judgment the receivers were under no obligation to provide any information until they had firmer evidence that there was a realistic prospect of redemption . . .

Downsview Nominees Ltd v First City Corpn Ltd
[1993] AC 295, Privy Council

Glen Eden Motors Ltd (GEM) had executed a debenture creating a first charge in favour of the Westpac bank and a debenture creating a second charge to First City Corporation

(FCC). GEM had been trading at a loss when the debt due to FCC became payable, and FCC appointed receivers, who decided that it was necessary to sell GEM's assets. They removed Pedersen, the manager of GEM, from office. Pedersen consulted Russell, who controlled Downsview, a finance company, and as a result: (1) Downsview took an assignment of the Westpac debenture; (2) it appointed Russell receiver under that debenture; (3) Russell then took control of GEM's assets, displacing the FCC receivers; and (4) Pedersen was reinstated as manager. Russell announced that it was his intention that GEM should trade its way out of its difficulties. FCC and its receivers warned Russell that in their view this course was likely to result in further losses, which would damage the company and FCC as the lower-ranking debenture-holder, and they offered to pay off the whole of the money owed under the Westpac debenture. But Downsview refused this offer, and Russell and Pedersen continued to run the company, which lost a further $500,000. The Privy Council held Downsview and Russell liable in damages for breaches of their duty to use their powers as chargee and receiver for proper purposes; but they also confirmed two important points: (1) that a receiver's duties are owed primarily, if not exclusively, to the security-holder who has appointed him, and this is inconsistent with the existence of a duty of care in law owed to the company or other creditors; and also (2) that his powers are conferred upon him solely for the purpose of securing the repayment of his appointor's debt, so that if either the company or any other interested party offers to pay off the debt, he must accept that offer and discharge this, his only, function.

Lord Templeman (delivering the opinion of the Privy Council) dealt with a number of points and continued: The nature of the duties owed by a receiver and manager appointed by a debenture holder were authoritatively defined by Jenkins LJ in a characteristically learned and comprehensive judgment in *Re B Johnson & Co (Builders) Ltd* [1955] Ch 634, 661–663. Jenkins LJ said:

> . . . The primary duty of the receiver is to the debenture holders and not to the company. He is receiver and manager of the property of the company for the debenture holders, not manager of the company. The company is entitled to any surplus of assets remaining after the debenture debt has been discharged, and is entitled to proper accounts. But the whole purpose of the receiver and manager's appointment would obviously be stultified if the company could claim that a receiver and manager owes it any duty comparable to the duty owed to a company by its own directors or managers.
>
> In determining whether a receiver and manager for the debenture holders of a company has broken any duty owed by him to the company, regard must be had to the fact that he is a receiver and manager—that is to say, a receiver, with ancillary powers of management—for the debenture holders, and not simply a person appointed to manage the company's affairs for the benefit of the company . . . The duties of a receiver and manager for debenture holders are widely different from those of a manager of the company. He is under no obligation to carry on the company's business at the expense of the debenture holders. Therefore he commits no breach of duty to the company by refusing to do so, even though his discontinuance of the business may be detrimental from the company's point of view. Again, his power of sale is, in effect, that of a mortgagee, and he therefore commits no breach of duty to the company by a bona fide sale, even though he might have obtained a higher price and even though, from the point of view of the company, as distinct from the debenture holders, the terms might be regarded as disadvantageous.
>
> In a word, in the absence of fraud or mala fides . . . the company cannot complain of any act or omission of the receiver and manager, provided that he does nothing that he is not empowered to do, and omits nothing that he is enjoined to do by the terms of his appointment . . .

In the present case the evidence of the second defendant himself and the clear emphatic findings of Gault J [1989] 3 NZLR 710, 749, which have already been cited, show that the second defendant [Russell] accepted appointment and acted as receiver and manager

> not for the purpose of enforcing the security under the Westpac debenture but for the purpose of preventing the enforcement by the plaintiffs of the [FCC] debenture.

This and other findings to similar effect establish that, *ab initio* and throughout his receivership, the second defendant did not exercise his powers for proper purposes. He was at all times in breach of the duty, which was pleaded against him, to exercise his powers in good faith for proper purposes.

Gault J rested his judgment not on breach of a duty to act in good faith for proper purposes but on negligence. He said, at pp 744, 747:

> on an application of negligence principles, a receiver owes a duty to the debenture holders to take reasonable care in dealing with the assets of the company . . . [The first defendant's] position is merely a specific example of the duty a mortgagee has to subsequent chargeholders to exercise its powers with reasonable care . . .

Richardson J, delivering the judgment of the Court of Appeal [1990] 3 NZLR 265, 278–280, agreed that duties of care in negligence as defined by Gault J were owed by the second defendant as receiver and manager and by the first defendant as first debenture holder to the plaintiffs as second debenture holders. . . .

The general duty of care said to be owed by a mortgagee to subsequent encumbrancers and the mortgagor in negligence is inconsistent with the right of the mortgagee and the duties which the courts applying equitable principles have imposed on the mortgagee. If a mortgagee enters into possession he is liable to account for rent on the basis of wilful default; he must keep mortgage premises in repair; he is liable for waste. Those duties were imposed to ensure that a mortgagee is diligent in discharging his mortgage and returning the property to the mortgagor. If a mortgagee exercises his power of sale in good faith for the purpose of protecting his security, he is not liable to the mortgagor even though he might have obtained a higher price and even though the terms might be regarded as disadvantageous to the mortgagor. *Cuckmere Brick Co Ltd v Mutual Finance Ltd* [1971] Ch 949 is Court of Appeal authority for the proposition that, if the mortgagee decides to sell, he must take reasonable care to obtain a proper price but is no authority for any wider proposition. A receiver exercising his power of sale also owes the same specific duties as the mortgagee. But that apart, the general duty of a receiver and manager appointed by a debenture holder, as defined by Jenkins LJ in *Re B Johnson & Co (Builders) Ltd*, leaves no room for the imposition of a general duty to use reasonable care in dealing with the assets of the company. The duties imposed by equity on a mortgagee and on a receiver and manager would be quite unnecessary if there existed a general duty in negligence to take reasonable care in the exercise of powers and to take reasonable care in dealing with the assets of the mortgagor company . . .

The liability of the second defendant in the present case is firmly based not on negligence but on the breach of duty. There was overwhelming evidence that the receivership of the second defendant was inspired by him for improper purposes and carried on in bad faith, ultimately verging on fraud. The liability of the first defendant does not arise under negligence but as a result of the first defendant's breach of duty in failing to transfer the Westpac debenture to the first plaintiff at the end of March 1987. It is well settled that the mortgagor and all persons having any interest in the property subject to the mortgage or liable to pay the mortgage debt can redeem. It is now conceded that the first plaintiff was entitled to require the first defendant to assign the Westpac debenture to the first plaintiff on payment of all moneys due to the first defendant under the Westpac debenture . . .

The first defendant was from the end of March 1987 in breach of its duty to assign the Westpac debenture to the first plaintiff. If that debenture had been assigned, the second defendant would have ceased to be the receiver and manager and none of the avoidable losses caused by the second defendant would have been sustained . . .

NOTE

Prior to the ruling in this case, it had been accepted as a result of several decisions that a secured creditor and any receiver acting on his behalf was under a duty of care towards the debtor and others interested (eg a guarantor of the debt) when exercising a power of sale, and perhaps more generally: *Cuckmere Brick Co Ltd v Mutual Finance Ltd* [1971] Ch 949, CA; *Standard Chartered Bank Ltd v Walker* [1982] 1 WLR 1410, CA. It is clear that in the *Downsview* ruling the Privy Council wished emphatically to deny that any such duty of care was recognised by the law, except in the very limited case of the actual conduct of the sale of the charged property. However, in the case next cited, the Court of Appeal seems to have been just as anxious to keep open the possibility of finding a duty of care in other circumstances— more particularly in the management of the debtor company's business.

Medforth v Blake

[2000] Ch 86, [1999] 3 All ER 97, Court of Appeal

Medforth was a pig farmer on a large scale: his annual turnover was over £2 million. He ran into financial difficulties and his bank appointed receivers, who ran the business for four and a half years, until Medforth was able to find funding elsewhere and pay off the bank. Although he had repeatedly told the receivers that they could claim large discounts from the suppliers of feedstuffs, amounting to some £1,000 a week, they failed to do so. The court held that the receivers owed a duty (subject to their primary duty to the bank) to manage the business with due diligence, and that for breach of this duty they were liable to compensate Medforth.

Sir Richard Scott V-C: . . . As a Privy Council case, the *Downsview Nominees* case is not binding but, as Mr. Smith submitted, it is a persuasive authority of great weight. But what did it decide as to the duties owed by a receiver/manager to a mortgagor? It decided that the duty lies in equity, not in tort. It decided that there is no general duty of care in negligence. It held that the receiver/manager owes the same specific duties when exercising the power of sale as are owed by a mortgagee when exercising the power of sale. Lord Templeman cited with approval the *Cuckmere Brick* case [1971] Ch 949 test, namely, that the mortgagee must take reasonable care to obtain a proper price . . .

The *Cuckmere Brick* case test can impose liability on a mortgagee notwithstanding the absence of fraud or mala fides. It follows from the *Downsview Nominees* case and *Yorkshire Bank plc v Hall* [1999] 1 WLR 1713 that a receiver/manager who sells but fails to take reasonable care to obtain a proper price may incur liability notwithstanding the absence of fraud or mala fides. Why should the approach be any different if what is under review is not the conduct of a sale but conduct in carrying on a business? If a receiver exercises this power, why does not a specific duty, corresponding to the duty to take reasonable steps to obtain a proper price, arise? If the business is being carried on by a mortgagee, the mortgagee will be liable, as a mortgagee in possession, for loss caused by his failure to do so with due diligence. Why should not the receiver/manager, who, as Lord Templeman held, owes the same specific duties as the mortgagee when selling, owe comparable specific duties when conducting the mortgaged business? It may be that the particularly onerous duties constructed by courts of equity for mortgagee in possession would not be appropriate to apply to a receiver. But, no duties at all save a duty of good faith? That does not seem to me to make commercial sense nor, more importantly, to correspond with the principles expressed in the bulk of the authorities . . .

I do not accept that there is any difference between the answer that would be given by the common law to the question what duties are owed by a receiver managing a mortgaged property to those interested in the equity of redemption and the answer that would be given by equity to that question. I do not, for my part, think it matters one jot whether the duty is expressed as a common law duty or as a duty in equity. The result is the same. The origin of the receiver's duty, like the mortgagee's duty, lies, however, in equity and we might as well continue to refer to it as a duty in equity.

In my judgment, in principle and on the authorities, the following propositions can be stated. (1) A receiver managing mortgaged property owes duties to the mortgagor and anyone else with an interest in the equity of redemption. (2) The duties include, but are not necessarily confined to, a duty of good faith. (3) The extent and scope of any duty additional to that of good faith will depend on the facts and circumstances of the particular case. (4) In exercising his powers of management the primary duty of the receiver is to try and bring about a situation in which interest on the secured debt can be paid and the debt itself repaid. (5) Subject to that primary duty, the receiver owes a duty to manage the property with due diligence. (6) Due diligence does not oblige the receiver to continue to carry on a business on the mortgaged premises previously carried on by the mortgagor. (7) If the receiver does carry on a business on the mortgaged premises, due diligence requires reasonable steps to be taken in order to try to do so profitably . . .

[His Lordship accordingly ruled that the trial judge had rightly held the receivers liable for breach of duty.]

[**Swinton Thomas** and **Tuckey LJJ** concurred.]

The above cases emphasise the essential difference between a receivership and other forms of insolvency procedure, such as administration or liquidation. An administrator or liquidator is appointed to act in the interests of all the parties who are concerned in the insolvency, and to hold the balance between the various competing interests. A receiver, in contrast, is concerned only with the enforcement of his appointor's security. It is not his role to see to the payment of any other creditors—indeed, if there is a surplus in his hands after realising the security he must hand it over to the company (*Re GL Saunders Ltd* [1986] 1 WLR 215). This, at least, is the traditional position, and it remains true for all receivers except those appointed to enforce a *floating* charge. Here, statute has made some exceptions. First, s 40 of IA 1986 requires that where a receiver is appointed to enforce a floating charge, certain debts which would be entitled to preference in a liquidation (eg some debts owed to employees—and, until this privilege was abolished by the Enterprise Act 2002, various debts owed to the Crown) must be paid in priority to the claims of the charge-holder. A receiver who fails to do so is personally liable to the creditors concerned (*IRC v Goldblatt* [1972] Ch 498). Secondly, under s 176A of IA 1986 where a company has gone into receivership (or into liquidation or administration) and its property is subject to a floating charge, the receiver or other office-holder is obliged to set aside a 'prescribed part' of the proceeds of realisation of that property for the benefit of the company's unsecured creditors, and prohibited from distributing anything from that fund to the charge-holder unless the unsecured creditors have been paid in full. This innovation also was one of the changes made by the 2002 Act.

Before leaving the topic of receivership, we should look briefly at *administrative receivership*, a statutory subcategory introduced by IA 1986. An administrative receiver is a receiver appointed by the holder of a floating charge secured over all, or substantially all, of a company's assets (s 29(2)). The Act requires such a receiver to be a qualified insolvency practitioner, and confers on him an extensive range of powers but at the same time imposes a number of duties (eg to give information and make reports to the company and its creditors). Most of the receivers appointed after IA 1986 came into force came within this category, and a considerable body of case law developed. But in a switch of policy the use of administrative receivership was banned by the Enterprise Act 2002 except for a few special cases, such as electricity and other utility companies, and the holder of such a floating charge is now obliged to put the company into administration in order to enforce his security. An administration, in contrast with a receivership, must be conducted in the interest of the company's creditors as a whole, and not primarily for the benefit of the security-holder.

Taken together, the changes to the law made by the Enterprise Act 2002 have radically transformed the practice in regard to the enforcement of floating charges by the banks and other commercial lenders. Under the law as it formerly stood, the holder of an all-assets charge could enforce his security with little regard for the interest of anyone else, except for those unsecured creditors entitled to priority, of which the most substantial was usually the Crown. In practice, this often meant that the Crown's claims and the secured debt swallowed up everything that there was of the company's assets, with nothing for its general creditors. A charge-holder now has to use the administration procedure, where the satisfaction of his debt ranks last among the objectives that the administrator is required to try to achieve. The Crown has lost its preferential status, but this is balanced by the priority given to the unsecured creditors as a whole in respect of the 'prescribed part' of the realisations. But there have been some gains, and not just for charge-holders. The legislators realised that the administration procedure established by the 1986 Act was too slow and cumbersome to be used for the enforcement of an all-assets security, where speedy and decisive action is often required, and so a more streamlined out-of-court procedure was devised to meet this need; and in the event the same procedure was made available for the company itself and its directors. As a result, administration is now the most popular insolvency procedure, displacing not only receivership but also the less flexible CVA and even, to some degree, creditors' voluntary liquidations.

Winding up (IA 1986, Part IV). Winding up, or liquidation, is a procedure which anticipates the dissolution of a company—its ceasing to exist as a corporate entity. An insolvency practitioner is appointed to act as liquidator, with the task of closing down or selling off the company's business, realising all of its assets, paying off its creditors, and, if there is a surplus remaining, distributing it amongst those who are entitled to it under the company's constitution. It is possible that he may keep the business going for a while, but he will do this only with a view to its ultimate sale—rehabilitation is not within a liquidator's terms of reference! The company need not, of course, be insolvent, but the legislation treats every liquidation as a form of insolvency procedure and deals with the whole subject in the Insolvency Act. There are two ways of bringing a liquidation about: by resolution of the company itself (called a 'voluntary' liquidation), and by court order (a 'compulsory' liquidation). We shall deal with each of these in turn.

A *voluntary winding up* may take two forms. If the directors of the company are able to certify that all of its creditors will be paid in full, the liquidation proceeds under the control of the members and is called a 'members' voluntary winding up'. If they cannot do this, control of the liquidation passes to the creditors and it is known as a 'creditors' voluntary winding up'. Either way, a qualified insolvency practitioner is appointed liquidator to administer the winding up.

He has very wide powers, which are set out in IA 1986, Sch 4. The court is not normally involved, but it does have advisory and back-up powers which can be invoked if necessary. When he has completed his administration and distributed all the monies in his hands, the liquidator makes his final account to the members or the creditors, and sends a return to the Registrar of Companies. The company is automatically dissolved three months later.

A *winding up by the court*, or 'compulsory' winding up, results from a court order, which is normally made on the petition of the company itself or one or more of its members or creditors. One of the grounds on which an order may be made is that the company is unable to pay its debts (IA 1986, s 122(1)(f)). For this purpose, a 'commercial' test of insolvency is prima facie the appropriate one, but the Act provides, alternatively, that a company may be deemed to be unable to pay its debts if it is insolvent on a 'balance-sheet' basis (s 123(2)). A company will also be deemed insolvent (as is the case in bankruptcy) if it has failed to comply with a statutory demand for payment of a debt of £750 or more, or if execution against it has been returned unsatisfied (s 123(1)). The Official Receiver takes charge of the company's assets and affairs and either he or an insolvency practitioner agreed on by the members and/or the creditors acts as liquidator, and the administration then proceeds on a basis largely similar to a voluntary liquidation, except that the liquidator is responsible to the court and more immediately under its control.

Assets in the liquidation   In contrast with the position in bankruptcy, the assets in a liquidation are not vested in the liquidator but remain vested in the company. But all control passes from the directors and shareholders to the liquidator.

The assets available to the liquidator include all the property which is beneficially owned by the company at the time when it goes into liquidation. This will exclude assets in the possession of the company which belong to someone else (eg goods which have been supplied to it on 'retention of title' terms: see above, p 499). It will also exclude property which the company holds on trust for another person. Rather surprisingly, the courts have, on occasion, found a trust to exist in circumstances which would ordinarily be regarded as having created a debtor–creditor relationship and not a trust. We look at two examples in the cases which follow.

Re Kayford Ltd
[1975] 1 WLR 279, Chancery Division

Kayfords carried on a mail-order business. Its directors were worried about the financial position of its principal supplier, and consulted the company's accountants. They advised the directors to open a separate bank account and to pay all prepayments made by Kayfords' customers from then on into this new account, and to draw money from it only as the relevant goods were delivered to the customer. When the suppliers became insolvent, Kayfords' own financial position became impossible and it also went into liquidation. The court held that the money in the account did not belong to the company but was held on trust for Kayfords' customers.

Megarry J: . . . The question for me is whether the money in the bank account . . . is held on trust for those who paid it, or whether it forms part of the general assets of the company. Mr Heyman appears for the joint liquidators, . . . and he has contended that there is no trust, so that the money forms part of the general assets of the company and thus will be available for the creditors generally. On the other hand, Mr Kennedy appears for a Mr Joels, who on December 12 paid the company £32.20 for goods which have not been delivered; and a representation order is sought on behalf of all others whose moneys have been paid into the bank account, some 700 or 800 in number. I make that order. Mr Kennedy, of course, argued for the existence of an effective trust. I may say at the outset that on the facts of the case Mr Heyman was unable to contend that any question of a fraudulent preference arose. If one leaves on one side any case in which an insolvent company seeks to declare a trust in favour of creditors, one is concerned here with the question not of preferring creditors but of preventing those who pay money from becoming creditors, by making them beneficiaries under a trust . . .

Now there are clearly some loose ends in the case. Nevertheless, despite the loose ends, when I take as a whole the affidavits of Mr Wainwright, Mr Kay and Mr Hall (the bank manager) I feel no doubt that the intention was that there should be a trust. There are no formal difficulties. The property concerned is pure personalty, and so writing, though desirable, is not an essential. There is no doubt about the so-called 'three certainties' of a trust. The subject-matter to be held on trust is clear, and so are the beneficial interests therein, as well as the beneficiaries. As for the requisite certainty of words, it is well settled that a trust can be created without using the words 'trust' or 'confidence' or the like: the question is whether in substance a sufficient intention to create a trust has been manifested.

In *Re Nanwa Gold Mines Ltd* [1955] 1 WLR 1080 the money was sent on the faith of a promise to keep it in a separate account, but there is nothing in that case or in any other authority that I know of to suggest that this is essential. I feel no doubt that here a trust was created. From the outset the advice (which was accepted) was to establish a trust account at the bank. The whole purpose of what was done was to ensure that the moneys remained in the beneficial ownership of those who sent them, and a trust is the obvious means of achieving this. No doubt the general rule is that if you send money to a company for goods which are not delivered, you are merely a creditor of the company unless a trust has been created. The sender may create a trust by using appropriate words when he sends the money (though I wonder how many do this, even if they are equity lawyers), or the company may do it by taking suitable steps on or before receiving the money. If either is done, the obligations in respect of the money are transformed from contract to property, from debt to trust. Payment into a separate bank account is a useful (though by no means conclusive) indication of an intention to create a trust, but of course there is nothing to prevent the company from binding itself by a trust even if there are no effective banking arrangements.

Accordingly, of the alternative declarations sought by the summons, the second, to the effect that the money is held in trust for those who paid it, is in my judgment the declaration that should be made. . . . I should, however, add one thing. Different considerations may perhaps arise in relation to trade creditors; but here I am concerned only with members of the public, some of whom can ill afford to exchange their money for a claim to a dividend in the liquidation, and all of whom are likely to be anxious to avoid this. In cases concerning the public, it seems to me that where money in advance is being paid to a company in return for the future supply of goods or services, it is an entirely proper and honourable thing for a company to do what this company did, upon skilled advice, namely, to start to pay the money into a trust account as soon as there begin to be doubts as to the company's ability to fulfil its obligations to deliver the goods or provide the services. I wish that, sitting in this court, I had heard of this occurring more frequently; and I can only hope that I shall hear more of it in the future.

NOTE

In this case, Megarry J accepted that there was no question of a fraudulent preference, under the law as it then stood. This was undoubtedly correct, for fraudulent preference required proof of a dishonest intention on the part of the company that the creditor or creditors concerned would have an advantage in a subsequent liquidation. Under IA 1986, s 239, however, the concept of 'fraudulent preference' has been replaced by 'preference', and the requirement to show dishonesty has been eliminated: see below, p 1130. It is likely that this point would need reconsideration under the new law if the facts of *Re Kayford Ltd* were to occur again.

Barclays Bank Ltd v Quistclose Investments Ltd
[1970] AC 567, House of Lords

Rolls Razor Ltd was in serious financial difficulties. It had declared a dividend on its ordinary shares, but did not have the funds to pay it. With the knowledge of its bank, it agreed to borrow some £209,000 from Quistclose (the respondents) on the understanding that the money would be used only for the purpose of paying the dividend. The loan was made and the money paid in to the bank, but before the shareholders had been paid their dividend Rolls Razor went into liquidation. The House of Lords held that the bank held the £209,000 on a resulting trust for Quistclose.

> **Lord Wilberforce**: . . . Two questions arise, both of which must be answered favourably to the respondents if they are to recover the money from the bank. The first is whether as between the respondents and Rolls Razor Ltd the terms upon which the loan was made were such as to impress upon the sum of £209,719 8s 6d a trust in their favour in the event of the dividend not being paid. The second is whether, in that event, the bank had such notice of the trust or of the circumstances giving rise to it as to make the trust binding upon them.
>
> It is not difficult to establish precisely upon what terms the money was advanced by the respondents to Rolls Razor Ltd. There is no doubt that the loan was made specifically in order to enable Rolls Razor Ltd to pay the dividend. There is equally, in my opinion, no doubt that the loan was made only so as to enable Rolls Razor Ltd to pay the dividend and for no other purpose. This follows quite clearly from the terms of the letter of Rolls Razor Ltd to the bank of July 15, 1964, which letter, before transmission to the bank, was sent to the respondents under open cover in order that the cheque might be (as it was) enclosed in it. The mutual intention of the respondents and of Rolls Razor Ltd, and the essence of the bargain, was that the sum advanced should not become part of the assets of Rolls Razor Ltd, but should be used exclusively for payment of a particular class of its creditors, namely, those entitled to the dividend. A necessary consequence from this, by process simply of interpretation, must be that if, for any reason, the dividend could not be paid, the money was to be returned to the respondents: the word 'only' or 'exclusively' can have no other meaning or effect.
>
> That arrangements of this character for the payment of a person's creditors by a third person, give rise to a relationship of a fiduciary character or trust, in favour, as a primary trust, of the creditors, and secondarily, if the primary trust fails, of the third person, has been recognised in a series of cases over some 150 years.
>
> [His Lordship referred to a number of authorities and continued:]
>
> The second, and main, argument for the appellant was of a more sophisticated character. The transaction, it was said, between the respondents and Rolls Razor Ltd, was one of loan, giving rise to a legal action of debt. This necessarily excluded the implication of any trust, enforceable in equity, in the respondents' favour: a transaction may attract one action or the other, it could not admit of both.
>
> My Lords, I must say that I find this argument unattractive. Let us see what it involves. It means that the law does not permit an arrangement to be made by which one person agrees to advance money to another, on terms that the money is to be used exclusively to pay debts of the latter, and if, and so far as not so used, rather than becoming a general asset of the latter available to his

creditors at large, is to be returned to the lender. The lender is obliged, in such a case, because he is a lender, to accept, whatever the mutual wishes of lender and borrower may be, that the money he was willing to make available for one purpose only shall be freely available for others of the borrower's creditors for whom he has not the slightest desire to provide.

I should be surprised if an argument of this kind—so conceptualist in character—had ever been accepted. In truth it has plainly been rejected by the eminent judges who from 1819 onwards have permitted arrangements of this type to be enforced, and have approved them as being for the benefit of creditors and all concerned. There is surely no difficulty in recognising the coexistence in one transaction of legal and equitable rights and remedies: when the money is advanced, the lender acquires an equitable right to see that it is applied for the primary designated purpose (see *Re Rogers* (1891) 8 Morr 243 where both Lindley LJ and Kay LJ recognised this): when the purpose has been carried out (ie the debt paid) the lender has his remedy against the borrower in debt: if the primary purpose cannot be carried out, the question arises if a secondary purpose (ie, repayment to the lender) has been agreed, expressly or by implication: it if has, the remedies of equity may be invoked to give effect to it, if it has not (and the money is intended to fall within the general fund of the debtor's assets) then there is the appropriate remedy for recovery of a loan. I can appreciate no reason why the flexible interplay of law and equity cannot let in these practical arrangements, and other variations if desired: it would be to the discredit of both systems if they could not. In the present case the intention to create a secondary trust for the benefit of the lender, to arise if the primary trust, to pay the dividend, could not be carried out, is clear and I can find no reason why the law should not give effect to it.

[**Lords Reid**, **Morris of Borth-y-Gest**, **Guest**, and **Pearce** concurred.]

Other cases in which a relationship was held not to be that of debtor and creditor but to involve a trust include *Carreras Rothmans Ltd v Freeman Mathews Treasure Ltd* [1985] Ch 207; *Chase Manhattan Bank NA v Israel-British Bank (London) Ltd* [1981] Ch 105; *Neste Oy v Lloyds Bank plc* [1983] 2 Lloyd's Rep 658; and *Twinsectra Ltd v Yardley* [2002] UKHL 12, [2002] 2 AC 164; contrast *Swiss Bank Corpn v Lloyds Bank Ltd* [1982] AC 584, HL, where the opposite conclusion was reached.

The liquidator may *disclaim* any asset which is unsaleable or fettered with onerous liabilities, and any unprofitable contract (IA 1986, ss 178 ff). A person who is disadvantaged by a disclaimer is left to prove for his losses as a creditor in the liquidation.

Avoidance of antecedent transactions The assets available for distribution by the liquidator may be augmented as a result of the operation of a number of special statutory provisions (sometimes referred to as 'claw-backs'), under which transactions that have taken place in the period immediately prior to the liquidation may be set aside. The language of each of these provisions is complex and calls for careful study; in the present chapter we can only describe them in outline.

First, s 127 of IA 1986 provides that, in a winding up by the court, any disposition of the company's property made after the filing of a petition for winding up is void, unless the court otherwise orders. This means that if a company has paid off a debt, given security over its property to a creditor, or sold an asset (even for full value) during this 'twilight' period before it goes into liquidation, it is automatically avoided unless the court agrees that it should be upheld. The leading case of *Re Gray's Inn Construction Co Ltd* (below) sets out some of the factors which the court will take into account in deciding whether to exercise this discretion. It also held, perhaps surprisingly, that both payments by a company *into* its bank account and drawings made by the company *out* of its account were 'dispositions' within the meaning of the section.

In a similar provision, executions issued against the property of a company after the commencement of the winding up are declared to be void by s 128 of IA 1986.

Re Gray's Inn Construction Co Ltd
[1980] 1 WLR 711, Court of Appeal

An order was made to wind up the company on 9 October 1972, on the basis of a petition which had been presented on 3 August. The bank allowed the company to continue to use its bank account while the hearing of the petition was pending. The court, varying the judgment of Templeman J in the court below, ruled: (1) that both payments into and payments out of the account were 'dispositions' of the company's property within s 127; and (2) that the bank ought to have become aware of the fact that a petition had been presented at some date before 15 August. In the exercise of its discretion, it allowed transactions made before that date to stand, but declined to validate those which had been effected later. The extract cited below indicates the factors which the court is likely to take into account in exercising its discretion under the statute.

> **Buckley LJ**: . . . It is a basic concept of our law governing the liquidation of insolvent estates, whether in bankruptcy or under the Companies Acts, that the free assets of the insolvent at the commencement of the liquidation shall be distributed rateably amongst the insolvent's unsecured creditors as at that date . . . In a company's compulsory winding up [this] is achieved by s 227 [of the Companies Act 1948, equivalent to IA 1986, s 127]. There may be occasions, however, when it would be beneficial, not only for the company but also for its unsecured creditors, that the company should be enabled to dispose of some of its property during the period after the petition has been presented but before a winding up order has been made. An obvious example is if the company has an opportunity by acting speedily to dispose of some piece of property at an exceptionally good price. Many applications for validation under the section relate to specific transactions of this kind or analogous kinds. It may sometimes be beneficial to the company and its creditors that the company should be enabled to complete a particular contract or project, or to continue to carry on its business generally in its ordinary course with a view to a sale of the business as a going concern. In any such case the court has power under s 227 of the Companies Act 1948 to validate the particular transaction, or the completion of the particular contract or project, or the continuance of the company's business in its ordinary course, as the case may be. In considering whether to make a validating order the court must always, in my opinion, do its best to ensure that the interests of the unsecured creditors will not be prejudiced. Where the application relates to a specific transaction this may be susceptible of positive proof. In a case of completion of a contract or project the proof may perhaps be less positive but nevertheless be cogent enough to satisfy the court that in the interests of the creditors the company should be enabled to proceed, or at any rate that proceeding in the manner proposed would not prejudice them in any respect. The desirability of the company being enabled to carry on its business generally is likely to be more speculative and will be likely to depend on whether a sale of the business as a going concern will probably be more beneficial than a break-up realisation of the company's assets. In each case, I think, the court must necessarily carry out a balancing exercise . . . Each case must depend upon its own particular facts.
>
> Since the policy of the law is to procure so far as practicable rateable payments of the unsecured creditors' claims, it is, in my opinion, clear that the court should not validate any transaction or

series of transactions which might result in one or more pre-liquidation creditors being paid in full at the expense of other creditors, who will only receive a dividend, in the absence of special circumstances making such a course desirable in the interests of the unsecured creditors as a body. If, for example, it were in the interests of the creditors generally that the company's business should be carried on, and this could only be achieved by paying for goods already supplied to the company when the petition is presented but not yet paid for, the court might think fit in the exercise of its discretion to validate payment for those goods.

Where a third party proposes to enter into a transaction with a company which is liable to be invalidated under [s 127 of the Companies Act 2006], the third party can decline to do so until the company has obtained a validating order, or it might itself seek a validating order, or it can enter into the transaction in anticipation of the court making a retroactive validating order at a later date. In the present case the bank adopted the last course. A third party who does that takes the risk of the court refusing to make the order.

It may not always be feasible, or desirable, that a validating order should be sought before the transaction in question is carried out. The parties may be unaware at the time when the transaction is entered into that a petition has been presented; or the need for speedy action may be such as to preclude an anticipatory application; or the beneficial character of the transaction may be so obvious that there is no real prospect of a liquidator seeking to set it aside, so that an application to the court would waste time, money and effort. But in any case in which the transaction is carried out without an anticipatory validating order the disponee is at risk of the court declining to validate the transaction. It follows, in my view, that the parties when entering into the transaction, if they are aware that it is liable to be invalidated by the section, should have in mind the sort of considerations which would influence the court's decision.

A disposition carried out in good faith in the ordinary course of business at a time when the parties are unaware that a petition has been presented may, it seems, normally be validated by the court . . . unless there is any ground for thinking that the transaction may involve an attempt to prefer the disponee, in which case the transaction would probably not be validated. In a number of cases reference has been made to the relevance of the policy of ensuring rateable distribution of the assets . . .

But although that policy might disincline the court to ratify any transaction which involved preferring a pre-liquidation creditor, it has no relevance to a transaction which is entirely post-liquidation, as for instance a sale of an asset at its full market value after presentation of a petition. Such a transaction involves no dissipation of the company's assets, for it does not reduce the value of those assets. It cannot harm the creditors and there would seem to be no reason why the court should not in the exercise of its discretion validate it. A fortiori, the court would be inclined to validate a transaction which would increase or has increased, the value of the company's assets, or which would preserve, or has preserved, the value of the company's assets from harm which would result from the company's business being paralysed.

[**Goff LJ** and **Sir David Cairns** concurred.]

NOTE

Not all of the observations in this case have gone without criticism. Professor Goode has argued, convincingly, that a payment made by a company which is debited to an account with its bank which is already overdrawn does not, without more, involve any disposition of the company's property (*Principles of Corporate Insolvency Law* (4th edn, 2011), para 13–131). And in *Re Barn Crown Ltd* [1994] 2 BCLC 186 it was held that there is no 'disposition', but only an adjustment of entries in the statements recording the accounts between customer and banker, when cheques belonging to the company are paid into an account which is already in credit. This decision, also, has been criticised by Professor Goode (para 13–133): if the bank were to become insolvent, the money would be lost, and so there must have been a 'disposition'. More recently, in *Hollicourt (Contracts) Ltd v Bank of Ireland* [2001] Ch 555, [2001] 1 All ER 289, CA, it has been held that where a bank meets a cheque drawn by its customer (whether the account is in credit or overdrawn) it does so merely as the customer's agent, so that, while there is clearly a disposition by the customer in favour of the payee, there is no disposition to the bank itself—as had been assumed in *Gray's* case.

It should be noted that ss 127 and 128 are applicable in all compulsory liquidations, whether or not the company is insolvent.

A second set of statutory provisions (which apply in liquidations of all types) allows the court to order the avoidance of transactions which have taken place prior to the commencement of the winding up—that is, even before the petition is presented or the resolution for winding up is passed. Most of these provisions apply also in an administration. They include the following.

- *Transactions at an undervalue* (IA 1986, s 238). Where a company has made a gift of property or has parted with property for an inadequate consideration, within two years of the commencement of the winding up, at a time when the company was unable to pay its debts, the court may make an order annulling the transaction.

- *Preferences* (IA 1986, s 239). Where a company has given a preference to a particular creditor (ie paid his debt or done some other act which would put him in a better position in the event of the company's insolvency) within six months (or, in certain cases, two years) prior to the commencement of the liquidation, at a time when the company was unable to pay its debts, the court may order that it be struck down. It is necessary to show that the company was influenced by a desire to prefer the creditor.

- *Transactions defrauding creditors* (IA 1986, s 423). If a company has entered into a transaction at an undervalue at any time for the purpose of putting assets beyond the reach of a creditor or potential creditor, it may be avoided by order of the court.

- *Extortionate credit transactions* (IA 1986, s 244). A transaction involving the giving of credit to the company which was entered into within three years prior to the winding up may be set aside or varied by the court if its terms are deemed extortionate.

- *Floating charges* (IA 1986, s 245). No order of the court is required in this case. A floating charge created by a company within the period of 12 months (or, where the chargee is a person 'connected with' the company, such as a director or another company in the same group, two years) prior to the commencement of its winding up is declared by this section to be invalid, unless: (1) 'new value', in the form of money paid or goods or services supplied, was given to the company in consideration of the charge; or (2) where the chargee is not a 'connected person', the company was solvent at the relevant time. In other words, where the statutory conditions apply, a floating charge may not be taken during the period immediately prior to an insolvent liquidation to secure an existing debt. A fixed charge is not caught by s 245, although it may be struck down as a preference if the requirements of s 239 are satisfied. (For the definition of 'connected person'—which is relevant also for the purposes of some of the other sections referred to above—see IA 1986, ss 249, 435.)

The operation of some of these provisions is illustrated by the cases which follow.

Re MC Bacon Ltd

[1990] BCLC 324, Chancery Division

The company had carried on business profitably as an importer and wholesaler of bacon until it lost its main customer. Its fortunes then rapidly dwindled and it soon had to be wound up. This action was brought to challenge a debenture which had been given to its bank on the alternative grounds that it was a transaction at an undervalue (IA 1986, s 238), or a preference (s 239); but Millett J held that it was neither. It was not a transaction at an undervalue because the giving of security had neither depleted the company's assets nor diminished their value, and it was not a preference because the directors' motive in giving the charge had not been to prefer the bank but to keep the company trading.

Millett J: . . .

VOIDABLE PREFERENCE

So far as I am aware, this is the first case under the section and its meaning has been the subject of some debate before me. I shall therefore attempt to provide some guidance.

The section replaces s 44(1) of the Bankruptcy Act 1914, which in certain circumstances deemed fraudulent and avoided payments made and other transactions entered into in favour of a creditor 'with a view of giving such creditor . . . a preference over the other creditors'. Section 44(1) and its predecessors had been construed by the courts as requiring the person seeking to avoid the payment or other transaction to establish that it had been made 'with the dominant intention to prefer' the creditor.

Section 44(1) has been replaced [by IA 1986, s 239] and its language has been entirely recast. Every single word of significance, whether in the form of statutory definition or in its judicial expression, has been jettisoned. 'View', 'dominant', 'intention' and even 'to prefer' have all been discarded. These are replaced by 'influenced', 'desire', and 'to produce in relation to that person the effect mentioned in sub-s (4)(b)'.

I therefore emphatically protest against the citation of cases decided under the old law. They cannot be of any assistance when the language of the statute has been so completely and deliberately changed. It may be that many of the cases which will come before the courts in future will be decided in the same way that they would have been decided under the old law. That may be so, but the grounds of decision will be different. What the court has to do is to interpret the language of the statute and apply it. It will no longer inquire whether there was 'a dominant intention to prefer' the creditor, but whether the company's decision was 'influenced by a desire to produce the effect mentioned in sub-s (4)(b)'.

This is a completely different test. It involves at least two radical departures from the old law. It is no longer necessary to establish a *dominant* intention to prefer. It is sufficient that the decision was *influenced* by the requisite desire. That is the first change. The second is that it is no longer sufficient to establish an *intention* to prefer. There must be a *desire* to produce the effect mentioned in the subsection.

This second change is made necessary by the first, for without it it would be virtually impossible to uphold the validity of a security taken in exchange for the injection of fresh funds into a company in financial difficulties. A man is taken to intend the necessary consequences of his actions, so that an intention to grant a security to a creditor necessarily involves an intention to prefer that creditor in the event of insolvency. The need to establish that such intention was dominant was essential under the old law to prevent perfectly proper transactions from being struck down. With the abolition of that requirement intention could not remain the relevant test. Desire has been substituted. That is a very different matter. Intention is objective, desire is subjective. A man can choose the lesser of two evils without desiring either.

It is not, however, sufficient to establish a desire to make the payment or grant the security which it is sought to avoid. There must have been a desire to produce the effect mentioned in the subsection, that is to say, to improve the creditor's position in the event of an insolvent liquidation. A man is not to be taken as *desiring* all the necessary consequences of his actions. Some consequences may be of advantage to him and be desired by him; others may not affect him and be matters of indifference to him; while still others may be positively disadvantageous to him and not be desired by him, but be regarded by him as the unavoidable price of obtaining the desired advantages. It will still be possible to provide assistance to a company in financial difficulties provided that the company is actuated only by proper commercial considerations. Under the new regime a transaction will not be set aside as a voidable preference unless the company positively wished to improve the creditor's position in the event of its own insolvent liquidation.

There is, of course, no need for there to be direct evidence of the requisite desire. Its existence may be inferred from the circumstances of the case just as the dominant intention could be inferred under the old law. But the mere presence of the requisite desire will not be sufficient by itself. It must have influenced the decision to enter into the transaction. It was submitted on behalf of the bank that it must have been the factor which 'tipped the scales'. I disagree. That is not what sub-s (5) says; it requires only that the desire should have influenced the decision. That requirement is satisfied if it was one of the factors which operated on the minds of those who made the decision. It need not have been the only factor or even the decisive one. In my judgment, it is not necessary to prove that, if the requisite desire had not been present, the company would not have entered into the transaction. That would be too high a test.

It was also submitted that the relevant time was the time when the debenture was created. That cannot be right. The relevant time was the time when the decision to grant it was made. In the present case that is not known with certainty. . . . But it does not matter. If the requisite desire was operating at all, it was operating throughout.

[His Lordship then ruled that the directors' motive had not been a desire to prefer the bank in the event of a liquidation, but to keep the company trading. He continued:]

TRANSACTION AT AN UNDERVALUE

Section 238 of the 1986 Act is concerned with the depletion of a company's assets by transactions at an undervalue.

[His Lordship read s 238(4) and continued:]

The granting of the debenture was not a gift, nor was it without consideration. The consideration consisted of the bank's forbearance from calling in the overdraft and its honouring of cheques and making of fresh advances to the company during the continuance of the facility. The applicant relies therefore on para (b).

To come within that paragraph the transaction must be (i) entered into by the company; (ii) for a consideration; (iii) the value of which measured in money or money's worth; (iv) is significantly less than the value; (v) also measured in money or money's worth; (vi) of the consideration provided by the company. It requires a comparison to be made between the value obtained by the company for the transaction and the value of consideration provided by the company. Both values must be measurable in money or money's worth and both must be considered from the company's point of view.

In my judgment, the applicant's claim to characterise the granting of the bank's debenture as a transaction at an undervalue is misconceived. The mere creation of a security over a company's assets does not deplete them and does not come within the paragraph. By charging its assets the company appropriates them to meet the liabilities due to the secured creditor and adversely affects the rights of other creditors in the event of insolvency. But it does not deplete its assets or diminish their value. It retains the right to redeem and the right to sell or remortgage the charged assets. All it loses is the ability to apply the proceeds otherwise than in satisfaction of the secured debt. That is not something capable of valuation in monetary terms and is not customarily disposed of for value.

In the present case the company did not suffer that loss by reason of the grant of the debenture. Once the bank had demanded a debenture the company could not have sold or charged its assets without applying the proceeds in reduction of the overdraft; had it attempted to do so, the bank would at once have called in the overdraft. By granting the debenture the company parted with nothing of value, and the value of the consideration which it received in return was incapable of being measured in money or money's worth.

Counsel for the applicant (Mr Vos) submitted that the consideration which the company received was, with hindsight, of no value. It merely granted time and with it the opportunity to lose more money. But he could not and did not claim that the company ought to have received a fee or other capital sum in return for the debenture. That gives the game away. The applicant's real complaint is not that the company entered into the transaction at an undervalue but that it entered into it at all.

In my judgment, the transaction does not fall within sub-s (4), and it is unnecessary to consider the application of sub-s (5) which provides a defence to the claim in certain circumstances.

CONCLUSION
In my judgment, the granting of the debenture to the bank was neither a voidable preference nor a transaction at an undervalue and I dismiss the application.

The third broad head under which the company's assets may be augmented in a liquidation is by making personal claims against the company's former officers and others for compensation for breach of duty or for contribution on some other ground. The relevant sections of IA 1986 are s 212 (misfeasance), s 213 (fraudulent trading), and s 214 (wrongful trading). The latter two provisions were extended in 2015 to apply also in an administration.

- *Misfeasance* (IA 1986, s 212). This provision does not create a new head of liability but simply provides a summary procedure by which the liquidator may recover property or claim compensation from the company's former officers on the grounds of accountability, misfeasance, or breach of duty.

- *Fraudulent trading* (IA 1986, s 213). If, in the course of winding up, it is found that any business of the company has been carried on with intent to defraud creditors or for any fraudulent purpose, the court may order that those who were knowingly parties to this wrongdoing should contribute such sums as it thinks proper to the company's assets. For the purposes of this provision, actual dishonesty must be shown (*Re Patrick & Lyon Ltd* [1933] Ch 786).

- *Wrongful trading* (IA 1986, s 214). A director or former director of a company in insolvent liquidation may be ordered to contribute personally to the assets in the hands of the liquidator if he knew, or ought to have concluded, that there was no reasonable prospect that it would avoid going into insolvent liquidation and failed to take every step with a view to minimising the potential loss to the company's creditors that he ought to have taken.

The following cases illustrate the fraudulent and wrongful trading sections.

Bank of India v Morris

[2005] EWCA Civ 693, [2005] BCC 739, Court of Appeal

BCCI was a large international banking group active in over 40 countries which collapsed with massive losses in 1991. Many investors sustained heavy losses. The case was concerned with six inter-bank transactions between BCCI and the Bank of India (BoI) which, on the face of things, appeared to be normal but in fact were part of a dishonest scheme designed by officers of BCCI to conceal heavy trading losses. The liquidators sued BoI alleging that it had (in the words of s 213) been 'knowingly a party to the carrying on of the business of BCCI with intent to defraud creditors of BCCI or for any fraudulent purpose'. The case turned on the question whether those at BoI responsible for entering into the transactions knew that they were assisting BCCI to commit a fraud on its creditors. The trial judge found that the relevant person had a suspicion that this was the case and deliberately avoided inquiring further, turning a blind eye. The Court of Appeal confirmed that this was sufficient to implicate BoI in the fraudulent trading.

Jetivia SA v Bilta (UK) Ltd

[2015] UKSC 23, [2016] AC 1, Supreme Court

Bilta, an English company, had been used by its directors to commit what are known as 'carousel' frauds, involving the buying and selling of 'carbon credits' and using offshore companies in transactions which were not liable to VAT in England. The net result was to render Bilta liable to pay output VAT to the Revenue and the Revenue liable to refund input VAT to another company. Bilta was put into liquidation owing the Revenue £38 million, but it had no assets and so (as had been intended all along) the debt could not be paid. The liquidator brought proceedings under s 213 against the directors, who were all based overseas. In a preliminary application the directors pleaded that the case should be struck out: (1) on the ground of illegality, because Bilta itself was party to the alleged fraud; and (2) because s 213 did not have extra-territorial effect, so that the directors were out of the reach of English law. Both pleas failed: (1) because Bilta was the victim of the fraud and not a party to its commitment; and (2) on the construction of the statute.

Re Produce Marketing Consortium Ltd (No 2)

[1989] BCLC 520, Chancery Division

The company (PMC) was in the business of fruit importers and distributors. Its directors, David and Murphy, had continued to run the business when they ought to have known that it was insolvent and heading inevitably towards liquidation. They were ordered to make a payment of £75,000 to the liquidator.

> **Knox J**: . . . Section 214 of the 1986 Act . . . reads, so far as is material, as follows:
>
> (1) Subject to subsection (3) below, if in the course of the winding up of a company it appears that subsection (2) of this section applies in relation to a person who is or has been a director of the company, the court, on the application of the liquidator, may declare that the person is to be liable to make such contribution (if any) to the company's assets as the court thinks proper.

(2) This subsection applies in relation to a person if— (a) the company has gone into insolvent liquidation, (b) at some time before the commencement of the winding up of the company, that person knew or ought to have concluded that there was no reasonable prospect that the company would avoid going into insolvent liquidation, and (c) that person was a director of the company at that time . . .

(3) The court shall not make a declaration under this section with respect to any person if it is satisfied that after the condition specified in subsection (2)(b) was first satisfied in relation to him that person took every step with a view to minimising the potential loss to the company's creditors as (assuming him to have known that there was no reasonable prospect that the company would avoid going into insolvent liquidation) he ought to have taken.

(4) For the purposes of subsections (2) and (3), the facts which a director of a company ought to know or ascertain, the conclusions which he ought to reach and the steps which he ought to take are those which would be known or ascertained, or reached or taken, by a reasonably diligent person having both—(a) the general knowledge, skill and experience that may reasonably be expected of a person carrying out the same functions as are carried out by that director in relation to the company, and (b) the general knowledge, skill and experience that that director has.

(5) The reference in subsection (4) to the functions carried out in relation to a company by a director of the company includes any functions which he does not carry out but which have been entrusted to him . . .

The first question is whether it appears that sub-s (2) applies to Mr David and Mr Murphy. There is no question but that they were directors at all material times and that PMC has gone into insolvent liquidation. The issue is whether at some time after 27 April 1986 and before 2 October 1987, when it went into insolvent liquidation, they knew or ought to have concluded that there was no reasonable prospect that PMC would avoid going into insolvent liquidation. It was inevitably conceded by counsel for the first respondent that this question has to be answered by the standards postulated by sub-s (4), so that the facts which Mr David and Mr Murphy ought to have known or ascertained and the conclusions that they ought to have reached are not limited to those which they themselves showing reasonable diligence and having the general knowledge, skill and experience which they respectively had, would have known, ascertained or reached but also those that a person with the general knowledge, skill and experience of someone carrying out their functions would have known, ascertained or reached.

The 1986 Act now has two separate provisions; s 213 dealing with fraudulent trading . . . and s 214 which deals with what the sidenote calls 'wrongful trading'. It is evident that Parliament intended to widen the scope of the legislation under which directors who trade on when the company is insolvent may, in appropriate circumstances, be required to make a contribution to the assets of the company which, in practical terms, means its creditors.

Two steps in particular were taken in the legislative enlargement of the court's jurisdiction. First, the requirement for an intent to defraud and fraudulent purpose was not retained as an essential . . .

I pause here to observe that at no stage before me has it been suggested that either Mr David or Mr Murphy fell into this category.

The second enlargement is that the test to be applied by the court has become one under which the director in question is to be judged by the standards of what can reasonably be expected of a person fulfilling his functions, and showing reasonable diligence in doing so. I accept the submission of counsel for the first respondent in this connection, that the requirement to have regard to the functions to be carried out by the director in question, in relation to the company in question, involves having regard to the particular company and its business. It follows that the general knowledge, skill and experience postulated will be much less extensive in a small company in a modest way of business, with simple accounting procedures and equipment, than it will be in a large company with sophisticated procedures.

Nevertheless, certain minimum standards are to be assumed to be attained. Notably there is an obligation laid on companies to cause accounting records to be kept which are such as to disclose with reasonable accuracy at any time the financial position of the company at that time: see the Companies Act 1985, s 221(1) and (2)(a) . . .

As I have already mentioned, the liquidator gave evidence that the accounting records of PMC were adequate for the purposes of its business. The preparation of accounts was woefully late, more especially in relation to those dealing with the year ending 30 September 1985 which should have been laid and delivered by the end of July 1986.

The knowledge to be imputed in testing whether or not directors knew or ought to have concluded that there was no reasonable prospect of the company avoiding insolvent liquidation is not limited to the documentary material actually available at the given time. This appears from s 214(4) which includes a reference to facts which a director of a company ought not only to know but those which he ought to ascertain, a word which does not appear in sub-s (2)(b). In my judgment this indicates that there is to be included by way of factual information not only what was actually there but what, given reasonable diligence and an appropriate level of general knowledge, skill and experience, was ascertainable. This leads me to the conclusion in this case that I should assume, for the purposes of applying the test in s 214(2), that the financial results for the year ending 30 September 1985 were known at the end of July 1986 at least to the extent of the size of the deficiency of assets over liabilities.

Mr David and Mr Murphy, although they did not have the accounts in their hands until January 1987, did, I find, know that the previous trading year had been a very bad one. They had a close and intimate knowledge of the business and they had a shrewd idea whether the turnover was up or down. In fact it was badly down in that year to £526,459 and although I have no doubt that they did not know in July 1986 that it was that precise figure, I have no doubt that they had a good rough idea of what it was and in particular that it was well down on the previous year. A major drop in turnover meant almost as night follows day that there was a substantial loss incurred, as indeed there was. That in turn meant again, as surely as night follows day, a substantial increase in the deficit of assets over liabilities.

That deals with their actual knowledge but in addition I have to have regard to what they have to be treated as having known or ascertained and that includes the actual deficit of assets over liabilities of £132,870. This was £80,000 over Mr David's personal guarantee. It was a deficit that, for an indefinite period in the future could not be made good even if the optimistic prognostications of level of turnover entertained by Mr David and Mr Murphy were achieved.

Counsel for the first respondent was not able to advance any particular calculation as constituting a basis for concluding that there was a prospect of insolvent liquidation being avoided. He is not to be criticised for that for in my judgment there was none available. Once the loss in the year ending 30 September 1985 was incurred PMC was in irreversible decline, assuming (as I must) that the respondents had no plans for altering the company's business and proposed to go on drawing the level of reasonable remuneration that they were currently receiving . . .

The next question which arises is whether there is a case under s 214(3) for saying that after the end of July 1986 the respondents took every step with a view to minimising the potential loss to the creditors of PMC as, assuming them to have known that there was no reasonable prospect of PMC avoiding insolvent liquidation, they ought to have taken. This clearly has to be answered No, since they went on trading for another year . . .

I am therefore driven to the conclusion that the court's discretion arises under s 214(1) . . .

In my judgment the jurisdiction under s 214 is primarily compensatory rather than penal. Prima facie the appropriate amount that a director is declared to be liable to contribute is the amount by which the company's assets can be discerned to have been depleted by the director's conduct which caused the discretion under sub-s (1) to arise. But Parliament has indeed chosen very wide words of discretion and it would be undesirable to seek to spell out limits on that discretion.

[His Lordship reviewed the facts, and ordered David and Murphy to make a contribution of £75,000.]

Administration of the estate The company's creditors 'prove' for their debts in the liquidation by submitting a claim in a prescribed form to the liquidator, which he may admit in whole or in part or reject, subject to an appeal to the court. Contingent and future liabilities are admitted at an estimated or discounted value. A creditor who is also indebted to the company normally has the right to set off his indebtedness against his claim and either prove for the balance or account for it to the liquidator: thus, to the extent that he can exercise this right, his claim is paid off in full. The House of Lords, in *National Westminster Bank Ltd v Halesowen Presswork & Assemblies Ltd* [1972] AC 785, HL, held that the right of set-off is a mandatory feature of insolvency law which is not capable of being waived or varied by contract.

A *secured creditor* may exercise his right to have recourse to the security independently of the liquidation. If there is a surplus after realising the security, he must account for it to the liquidator; if a shortfall, he may prove for the outstanding balance. Alternatively, he may elect to surrender his security and prove for the whole of his debt as an unsecured creditor.

The Act provides that certain debts shall be paid in priority to those of other creditors (and to those of the holder of any floating—but not fixed—charge) in the winding up (IA 1986, ss 175, 386, and Sch 6). The list of preferential debts is the same as applies in bankruptcy, administration, and receivership. It is now much shorter because the preferential position of the Crown was abolished by s 176A: see above, p 1123. Those entitled include employees, for arrears of wages and other entitlements up to a limit of four months or £800—a sum which is overdue for an increase to reflect over three decades' inflation. Secondly, a 'prescribed part' of the net proceeds of realisation of the company must be set aside for the benefit of its unsecured creditors, in priority to any floating charge-holder. (The amount prescribed is 50 per cent of the first £10,000, plus a further 20 per cent of the remainder, up to a maximum prescribed part of £600,000.)

The *order of application of assets* is as follows: (1) expenses of the liquidation; (2) preferential debts; (3) the prescribed part; (4) debts secured by a floating charge; (5) unsecured debts; (6) debts payable to members of the company in their capacity as members (eg unpaid dividends): IA 1986, s 74(2)(f)). Any surplus remaining after satisfaction of all the company's liabilities is payable to the members in accordance with their respective rights and liabilities. If the assets are insufficient to pay the debts of any category of creditor in full, the claims of all those in that category abate proportionately.

INDEX

acceptance credit
   documentary credits 775
acceptance of goods
   passing of property 358–9
   performance contract 463–74
account payee cheques 728
account of profits 239–41
account receivable *see*
       receivables financing
'acting in the ordinary course of
       business'
   sale under Factors Act 1889 402
action for the price
   interest 479
   introduction 476
   price payable on fixed date,
      where 476
   property has passed,
      where 476
   risk has passed, where 477–9
actual authority
   express 127–9
   implied 129–32
   meaning 127
administration orders
   company 1111–37
   individual 1109
administrative
      receivership 1115–23
agency
   see also **agent, duties of;**
      agent, rights of;
      disclosed agency;
      remuneration of agent;
      termination of agency;
      undisclosed agency
   account by agent 249–50
   actual authority
      express 127–9
      implied 129–32
      meaning 127
   apparent authority
      alteration of position 145
      generally 132–7
      reliance 144–5
      representation 137–44
      subsequent conduct of
         principal 145–6
   assignment of choses in
      action 889

auctioneers 117
authority of agent
   actual authority 127–32
   apparent authority 132–46
   introduction 113
   operation of law, by 152–8
   ratification 158–67
   usual authority 146–51
bailment 114
bribes 241–9
brokers 117
care and skill of agent 225–30
commercial agents 119–22
commission agents 118
competition law 122–3
confirming houses 118
conflicts of interest 233–9
counsel 117
creation of 125–226
definitions
   generally 107–13
del credere **agent** 117–18
delegate authority, duty not
     to 250–5
directors 117
distinction from other
     relationships
   bailment 114
   distributorship 115
   franchising 115
   independent
      contractors 116
   sale 114–15
   servants 116
   trusts 114
distributorship 115
estate agents 117
EU law
   commercial agents 119–22
   competition law 122–3
factors 117
fiduciary duties of agent
   account 249–50
   bribes 241–9
   conflicts of interest 233–9
   generally 230–3
   secret profits 239–41
franchising 115
Geneva Convention 1983 123–4
harmonisation of laws 123–4

indemnification of
     agent 267–9
independent contractors 116
legal concept
   definitions of
      agency 107–13
   distinction from other
      relationships 114–16
   EU law 119–22
   harmonisation of
      laws 123–4
   types of agent 117–18
lien 269
necessity, of 152–8
non-delegation of
     authority 250–5
obedience of instructions by
     agent 224–5
operation of law, authority
     by 152–8
partners 117
performance of undertaking by
     agent 224–5
ratification
   effect 163–7
   generally 158–9
   requirements 158–63
reimbursement of agent 267–9
relations between agent and
     third party
   disclosed agency 179–99
   undisclosed agency 223
relations between principal
     and agent
   agent's duties 224–56
   agent's rights 256–69
   introduction 224
   termination of agency 270–6
relations between principal
     and third party
   disclosed agency 168–79
   undisclosed agency 200–23
sale 114–15
sale of goods 324–5
secret profits 239–41
servants 116
solicitors 117
trusts 114
types of agent 117–18
usual authority 146–51

agent, duties of
    account, to 249–50
    bribes 241–9
    care and skill 225–30
    conflicts of interest 233–9
    delegation 250–5
    fiduciary
        account 249–50
        bribes 241–9
        conflicts of interest 233–9
        generally 230–3
        secret profits 239–41
    non-delegation of
        authority 250–5
    obedience of
        instructions 224–5
    performance of
        undertaking 224–5
    secret profits 239–41
agent, rights of
    see also **remuneration**
        of agent
    indemnity 267–9
    lien 269
    reimbursement 267–9
agreement to sell
    meaning 302
    passing of property 327–8
alteration of position
    apparent authority 145
alternative dispute
        resolution (ADR)
    functions of commercial
        law 12–14
American Uniform
        Commercial Code
    nature of commercial law 5
apparent authority
    alteration of position 145
    generally 132–7
    reliance 144–5
    representation 137–44
    subsequent conduct of
        principal 145–6
appointment of receiver
    mortgage 1067
appropriation of goods
        from bulk
    perishing of goods 372
approval, goods on
    passing of property 346–50
arbitration
    functions of commercial
        law 12–13
'Arrival' contracts 552–5
ascertained goods 305–8
assignment

    see also **assignment of choses**
        in action; equitable
        assignment; legal
        assignment
    receivables financing 950
assignment of choses in action
    agency 889
    assignment, meaning of 862
    attornment 890
    bare rights of action 875–8
    champerty 870–85
    charges 905–7
    chose in action, meaning
        of 860–2
    conversion of equitable
        assignment to legal
        assignment 902–3
    Dearle v Hall, rule in 914–20
    debtors 913–14
    declaration of trust 890–900
    definitions
        assignment 862
        chose in action 860–2
    effect
        assignee cannot
            recover more than
            assignor 936–43
        book debts 943
        equitable assignment 931–5
        legal assignment 935
        non-compliance with non-
            assignment clause 935–6
        registration 943
    enforcement
        assignees take subject to
            equities 943–7
        cross-claims 946–7
        equities stopped by
            notice 944–7
        fraud 943–4
        obstacles 943–7
        rescission 943–4
        subject to equities rule 947
    existing non-assignable choses
        in action 869–87
    future choses in action 862–8
    intention
        assign, to 887–9
        attornment 890
        declaration of trust 890–900
        novation 889–90
        revocable mandate 889
    introduction 859
    maintenance 870–5
    non-assignable choses
        champerty 870–5
        maintenance 870–5

    notice
        equitable
            assignment 910–22
        generally 910
        legal assignment 922–31
    novation 889–90
    obligor performs in favour of
        assignor 913–14
    overcoming
        unassignability 886–7
    partial assignment 907
    passing of title 913
    present choses in action 862–8
    revocable mandate 889
    rights intended to be
        unassignable 878–86
    rival assignees, claims
        between 914–20
    writing
        choice between legal
            and equitable
            assignment 900–1
        equitable assignment 901
        generally 900
        legal assignment 901–10
ATM cards
    connected lender
        liability 641–2
    generally 634–5
    liability for unauthorised
        transaction 639–41
attornment 76–8
auctioneers
    agency 117
authority of agent
    actual authority
        express 127–9
        implied 129–32
        introduction 125–6
    apparent authority
        alteration of position 145
        generally 132–7
        reliance 144–5
        representation 137–44
        subsequent conduct of
            principal 145–6
    introduction 127, 768
    necessity, of
        generally 152–8
        requirements 152–8
    operation of law, authority
        by 152–8
    ratification
        effect 163–7
        generally 158–9
        requirements 158–63
    usual authority 146–51

autonomy of the credit
  fraud exception
    freezing orders 801
  generally 786–9
  injunctions 800–1
  reimbursement right 800
avoidance of antecedent
    transactions
  winding up 1127–37

back-to-back credit
  documentary credits 777
bailment
  agency 114
  bailee's liability 97–9
  burden of proof 100–1
  contractual 99
  generally 69–72
  gratuitous 99
  involuntary 99
  requirements 94–6
  sale of goods 316–17
  third parties 101–3
  types 92–4
balance-sheet insolvency
  generally 1108
bank notes
  negotiable instruments 654
Bank Payment Obligation (BPO)
  generally 767–8
  SWIFT 767
banker's drafts
  generally 762
bankruptcy
  generally 1110
barter 313–16
bearer bills 666–72
bearer bonds
  negotiable instruments 555
bearer debentures
  negotiable instruments 655
bearer scrip
  negotiable instruments 654
beneficiary's rights under a trust
  property rights 68
bills of exchange
  bearer bills 666–72
  capacity to contract 692
  complete and irrevocable
    contract 692
  definition 661–5
  destruction of
    transferability 673–5
  discharge 706–8
  dishonour by
    non-acceptance 703
  documentary bills 768

  enforcement 703–6
  dishonour by
    non-acceptance 703
  notice of dishonour 705–6
  presentment for
    acceptance 703
  presentment for
    payment 703–5
  protesting foreign bill 706
  forged signature 696–9
  holder in due course
    complete and regular on its
      face 684–6
    generally 682
    holder of the bill 681–4
    no notice of previous
      dishonour 686
    not overdue at time of
      transfer 686
    rights of 688–9
    take for value 688
    without notice and in good
      faith 686–8
  holder in due course by
    derivation 689–91
  holder for value 676–82
  liability 691–9
    capacity to contract 692
    complete and irrevocable
      contract 692
    drawee, of 700
    drawer, of 701
    exemption 702–3
    indorser, of 701
    introduction 691
    limitation of 702–3
    overview 699–700
    parties
      acceptor, of 700–1
      quasi-indorser, of 701–2
    signature of bill 693–5
    transferor of bearer bill,
      of 702
  material alteration 699
  mere holder 676
  mistaken payment 708–26
  notice of dishonour 706
  obligation 675–82
  order bills 672–3
  persons entitled to benefit to
    obligation
    generally 675–6
    holder in due course 682–91
    holder in due course by
      derivation 689–91
    holder for value 676–82
    mere holder 676

  presentment for
    acceptance 703
  presentment for
    payment 703–5
  protesting foreign bill 706
  signature
    agent's liability 693–5
    Companies Act 1985,
      s 349(4), under 695
    Companies Act 2006, s 51,
      under 695
    company bills, etc. 695
    forgery of 696–9
    introduction 694–5
    material alteration 699
    principal's liability 692–3
    signature on company bills
    unauthorised 696–9
  statutory basis 659–61
  transfer 666–72
  transferability
    bearer bills 666–72
    destruction of 673–5
    order bills 672–3
  unauthorised
    signature 696–9
  use 659
bills of lading
  negotiable instruments,
    relationship with 655
  personal property,
    representing 55
bills of sale
  non-possessory security
    protection of debtors 1084
    protection of third
      parties 1077–84
block discounting
  financier's discount 965–7
  financier's security
    generally 968–76
  generally 965–7
  registration 976
book debts 984–1000
breach of trust 90
breach of warranty of authority
  disclosed agency
    (agent/third party
    relationship) 194–200
Brexit implications 51–3
bribes
  civil liability 241–9
  criminal liability 249
  generally 241–9
  remedies 245–9
brokers
  agency 117–18

buyer in possession, sale
    by 412–21
buyer's remedies (sale of goods)
    damages for breach of
        warranty 524–6
    damages for late
        delivery 523–4
    rejection of goods 526–7
    specific performance 483

capacity to contract
    bills of exchange 692
care and skill, duty of
    agents 225–30
carriage paid contracts
    international sales 555–7
certificate of deposit
    negotiable instruments 655
champerty 870–5
change of position
    apparent authority 145
CHAPS
    credit/debit transfer 569–76
charge cards
    connected lender liability 641–2
    generally 624–5
    liability for unauthorised
        transaction 639–41
charges
    see also **equitable charges;
        fixed charges; floating
        charges**
    assignment of choses in
        action 905–7
    receivables financing
        'book debt' 980–4
        generally 977–80
        registration 977–84
chattels
    personal property 55
cheque cards
    connected lender
        liability 641–2
    liability for unauthorised
        transaction 639–41
cheques
    clearing system 730–3
    collecting bank, protection
        of 748–59
    conversion 742
    crossed
        account payee 728
        general 728–9
    defences by collecting
        bank 748–59
    Banking Act 1979, s 47,
        under 759

Cheques Act 1957, s 4,
    under 752–8
    holder in due course 748–52
    electronic presentation 742
    introduction 727–8
    negotiable instruments 654
    paying bank, protection
        of 733–41
    statutory basis for 728–9
choses in action
    see also **assignment of choses
        in action**
    definition 860–2
    personal property 55, 84–9
CIF contracts 543–52
    introduction 543–4
    shipping documents 544–52
    variants 552
CIP contracts 556
clearing
    cheques 730–3
    funds transfer 576
    rules 580–2
    system 580–2
CMR Convention 555–6
co-ownership
    personal property 67
codification of commercial
    law 4–6, 15, 44–6
collecting bank, protection of
    defences 748–59
commercial agents
    see also **agency**
    factors 402
    generally 119–22
    minimum periods of
        notice 276
    remuneration 266–7
    termination of agency 276–87
commercial claims
    meaning 11
Commercial Court
    functions of commercial
        law 12–13
commercial credit
    consumer credit
        legislation 1008–9
    definition 1007–8
    fixed-sum credit 1008
    forms 1008
    introduction 1007
    loan credit 1008
    revolving credit 1008
    sale credit 1008
commercial law
    challenges in the 21st
        century 47–51

codification 44–6
concepts 36–44
definition 3
dispute resolution 12, 47–8
equity's role in 28–33, 39–41
function 8–14
historical development
    commercial codification 15
    consumerism 15–16
    harmonisation of national
        laws 18–20
    lex mercatoria 14–15
meaning 3
nature 3–8
philosophy 36–44
public law 33–6
sources
    contracts 20–2
    custom and usage 22–4
    EU law 25–6
    international
        conventions 26–7
    model laws 28
    national legislation 24–5
    uniform laws 28
    uniform trade terms 28
commission
    'effective cause' of event 259–61
    loss of right 251–2
    opportunity to earn 261–5
commission agents
    agency 118
commission due to agent
    bribes 244–5
compensation
    commercial agents 276–87
competition law
    agency 122–3
conditions and warranties
    (insurance) 1095
conduct of principal
    apparent authority 145–6
confirmed credits
    documentary credits 776
confirming houses
    agency 118
    financing of international
        trade 856
conflicts of interest 233–9
connected lender liability
    payment cards 641–2
consent of the owner
    sale under Factors
        Act 398–401
constructive trusts
    see also **fraud on bank**
    secret profits 239–41

consumer credit legislation
commercial credit 1008–9
non-possessory security 1085
payment cards
ATM cards 634–5
charge cards 627–33
credit cards 627–33
introduction 624
types of card 624–7
pledge 1039–40
consumer protection
insurance contracts 1097
consumer sales 330
consumerism
development of commercial
law 15–16
contract debt 950
contract of sale (documentary
credits)
credit as payment 816
credit in prescribed
form 810–13
examination of
documents 819–22
expiry date of credit 815–16
time of opening of
credit 813–15
contract for the sale of
goods 300–2
contractual documents 20–2
contribution
insurance contracts 1099
conversion
protection of collecting
bank 759
copyright
personal property 55–6
corporate insolvency
administration order
(company) 1111–15
receivership 1115–23
voluntary
arrangements 1109, 1111
winding up
administration of
estate 1137
assets in the
liquidation 1124–37
avoidance of antecedent
transactions 1127–37
compulsory 1124
court, by 1124
extortionate credit
transactions 1130
floating charges 1130
generally 1123–4
preferences 1130

transactions at an
undervalue 1130
transactions defrauding
creditors 1130
correspondence with
description 425–34
cost, insurance and freight
(CIF) contracts *see* CIF
contracts
counsel
agency 117
countermand, honouring
a 609–11
credit cards
connected lender
liability 641–2
generally 627–33
introduction 624–5
liability for unauthorised
transaction 639–41
credit sale agreements
receivables financing 949–50
criminal liability
bribes 249
crossed cheques
account payee 728
general 728–9
not negotiable 728
crystallisation
floating charges 1075–7
custom and usage
concept of commercial law 40
lien 1044, 1053
negotiable instruments 22–4,
645, 652–4

damages
bribes 241–9
buyer's remedies (sale
of goods)
breach of warranty 524–6
late delivery 523–4
non-acceptance of
goods 479–82
DAP contracts 552–5
de facto **possession**
personal property 71
Dearle v Hall, **rule in**
assignment of choses in
action 914–20
receivables financing 1001
debit cards
connected lender liability 641–2
generally 634
introduction 625
liability for unauthorised
transaction 639–41

debt relief orders 1109–10
debts
personal property 55–6
declaration of trust
assignment of choses in
action 890–900
deeds
disclosed agency (agent/third
party relationship) 190–1
defects in goods
satisfactory quality 437
deferred payment
documentary credits 774
del credere **agent**
agency 117–18
delegate authority, duty not
to 250–5
deliverable state
passing of property 340–1
delivered ex ship
contracts 552–5
delivery
bills of lading 655
goods
buyer's duty 463
instalment contracts 456–7
payment 456–7
time of delivery 458
pledge 1026–32
description, sale by 425–34
directors
agency 117
discharge
bills of exchange 706–8
disclosed agency
agent/third party relationship
action by agent
directly 191–4
breach of warranty of
authority 194–200
deeds 190–1
fictitious principals 191
foreign principals 191
general rule 168–71
negotiable instruments 191
non-existent principals 191
oral contracts 188–90
statutory liability 191
written contracts 182–8
principal/third party
relationship
defences 174–5
election 175–9
general rule 168–71
merger 175–9
set-off 174–5
settlement with agent 171–4

dishonest assistance
   breach of fiduciary duty,
      in 90–1
dispute resolution
   functions of commercial
      law 12, 47–8
distributorship
   agency 115
dividend warrants
   negotiable instruments 654
dock warrants
   negotiable instruments 655
documentary bills
   financing of international
      trade 768–9
documentary credits
   acceptance credit 775
   appearance of compliance
      on the face of the
      documents 819–22
   autonomy 786–9
   back-to-back credits 777
   confirmed credits 776
   contract between banks and
      seller 824–32
   contract between buyer and
      issuing bank 817–22
   contract of sale 810–16
   contracts arising out of
      transaction
      contract between banks and
         seller 824–32
      contract between buyer and
         issuing bank 817–22
      contract between issuing
         bank and advising
         bank 823–4
      contract of sale 810–16
   contractual network 771
   nature of banks'
      undertakings 771–2
   contractual network 771
   deferred payment 774
   definition 773
   fraud exception
      freezing orders 801
      generally 789–802
      injunctions 800–1
      reimbursement right 800
   function 769–70
   illegality 802–9
   irrevocable credits 775–6
   nature of banks'
      undertakings 771–2
   negotiation credit 775
   non-transferable credits 776–7
   notice of rejection 826–7

   operation 769–70
   payment at sight 774
   principles 777–810
   revocable credits 775–6
   revolving credits 776
   strict compliance
      bank v applicant 779–80
      bank v bank 780–6
      beneficiary v bank 780
      generally 778–86
   transferable credits 776–7
   types
      back-to-back credits 777
      confirmed credits 776
      introduction 769
      irrevocable credits 775–6
      non-transferable
         credits 776–7
      revocable credits 775–6
      revolving credits 776
      transferable credits 776–7
      unconfirmed credits 776
   unconfirmed credits 776
   Uniform Customs and
      Practice 772–3
   waiver of discrepancies 826
documentary intangibles
   personal property 55
documents of title
   bills of lading as 536
   buyer in possession and 416
   Factors Act and 397
   seller in possession and 408–10
domestic sales *see* **sale of goods**

e-commerce 46–7, 50–1
economic law 25
election
   disclosed agency 175–9
   undisclosed agency 213–17
electronic documentation
   international sales, in 558
electronic signatures
   future of commercial law 50
encumbrances, freedom from
   implied terms in sales of
      goods 462–3
enforcement
   bills in exchange
      dishonour by
         non-acceptance 703
      notice of dishonour 705–6
      presentment for
         acceptance 703
      presentment for
         payment 703–5
      protesting foreign bill 706

   lien 1053–5
   mortgage
      appointment of receiver 1067
      foreclosure 1064–5
      possession 1067
      sale 1065–7
equitable assignment
   see also **assignment of choses
      in action**
   champerty 870–5
   Dearle v Hall, rule in 914–20
   maintenance 870–5
   non-assignable choses
      champerty 870–5
      maintenance 870–5
   notice to assignee 921–2
   notice to debtor 913–14
   requirements
      notice to assignee 921–2
      notice to debtor 913–14
equitable charges
   creation 1068–9
   debtors, protection of
      Bills of Sale Acts,
         under 1084–5
      Consumer Credit Act 1974,
         under 1085
      introduction 1084
   definition 1068–9
   third parties, protection of
      Bills of Sale Acts,
         under 1078–80
      Companies Act 2006,
         under 1080–4
      introduction 1077
equitable choses in action
   generally 860–2
equitable liens
   non-possessory security 1077
equitable ownership
   acquisition and transfer 68–9
   generally 68–9
equity
   generally 28–33
   trusts 89–91
estate agents
   agency 117
estoppel
   forged signatures on bills of
      exchange 696–9
   judgment, by 387
   nemo dat rule 381–4
   settlement with agent 174
EU law 25–6
   agency
      commercial agents 119–22
      competition law 122–3

Brexit implications 51–3
sources of law 25–6
eUCP
examination of
documents 822
introduction 772
ex ship contracts 552–5
examination of goods
satisfactory quality 438
exchange of goods 314
existing goods
sale of goods 305
export credit guarantees
financing of international
trade 856
extortionate credit transactions
winding up 1130

factoring
facultative agreement 959
financier's discount 967–8
future receivables 960–5
international factoring 1003
receivables financing 958–9
factors
agency 117
Factors Act 1889
'acting in the ordinary course
of business' 402
'acts in good faith' 402–4
conditions 394–404
generally 394–404
mercantile agents 394–7
in possession 397–8
'with the consent of the
owner' 398–401
facultative agreement
factoring 959
FA encumbrances, freedom from
implied terms in sales of
goods 462–3
FAS contracts 542–3
FCA contracts 555–7
fictitious principals
disclosed agency (agent/third
party relationship) 191
fiduciary duties of agent
account 249–50
bribes 241–9
conflicts of interest 233–9
generally 230–3
secret profits 239–41
financier's discount 967–8
financing of international trade
Bank Payment
Obligation (BPO)
generally 767–8

confirming houses 856
documentary bills 768–9
documentary credits
autonomy 789–802
contracts arising 810–32
contractual network 771
definition 773
governing law 832–9
illegality 802–9
nature of banks
undertakings 771–2
operation 769–70
principles 777–810
strict compliance 778–86
types 773–8
Uniform Customs and
Practice 772–3
export credit guarantees 856
financial leasing 855–6
forfaiting 854–5
guarantees 840–54
performance bonds 840–54
standby credits 839–40
fixed charges
characteristics 1068–9
debtors, protection of
Bills of Sale Acts,
under 1084–5
Consumer Credit Act 1974,
under 1085
introduction 1084
distinction from floating
charges
importance of 1073–5
importance of
distinction 1073–5
meaning 1068–9
nature 1070–3
fixed-sum credit
commercial credit 1008
flexibility
functions of commercial
law 8–14
floating charges
characteristics 1068–9
crystallisation 1075–7
debtors, protection of
Bills of Sale Acts,
under 1084–5
Consumer Credit Act 1974,
under 1085
introduction 1084
distinction from fixed charges
importance of 1073–5
importance of
distinction 1073–5
meaning 1070–7

nature 1070–3
winding up 1130
floating rate notes 655, 761
FOB contracts 537–42
force majeure
passing of property 361
foreclosure
mortgage 1064–5
foreign principals
disclosed agency (agent/third
party relationship) 191
forfaiting
financing of international
trade 954–5
forgery
bills of exchange 696–9
cheques 742
formation of contract
sale of goods 325–6
franchising
agency 115
fraud
cheques 742
documentary bills 768
documentary credits
freezing orders 801
generally 799–800
injunctions 800–1
reimbursement right 800
free on board contracts *see*
**FCA contracts; FOB
contracts**
international sales 555–7
freezing orders
documentary credits 801
frustration
passing of property
and 379–80
funds transfer
banks' duties
common law 586–609
intermediary bank 609
payee's bank 603–9
payer's bank 586–603
Payment Services
Regulations 2009 582–5
clearing 576
common law duties of
bank 586–609
completion of payment 611–19
countermand 609–11
intermediary bank,
duties of 609
introduction 564
nature of 564–8
terminology 568–9
unwanted payments 619–23

future goods
meaning 305
future receivables, factoring
of 960–5

GAFTA
international sales 533
garnishee orders *see* **third party**
debt orders
general lien 1046–9
generic goods
perishing 376–9
Geneva Convention 1983
agency 123–4
gifts
sale of goods and 313
good faith
Factors Act and 402–4
philosophy of commercial
law 38, 41–3
goods
definition 302–5
goodwill
personal property 55
governing law
documentary credits 832–9
guarantees
international trade
financing 840–54

harmonisation of
national laws
agency 123–4
generally 18–20
hire-purchase
nemo dat rule and 421
sale of goods and 317–18
historical development of
commercial law
commercial codification 15
consumerism 15–16
harmonisation of national
laws 18–20
lex mercatoria 14–15
holder in due course
complete and regular on its
face 684–6
generally 682
holder of the bill 682–4
no notice of previous
dishonour 686
not overdue at time of
transfer 686
protection of collecting
bank 748–52
rights of 688–9
take for value 688

without notice and in good
faith 686–8
holder in due course by
derivation 689–91
holder for value 676–82

illegality
documentary credits 802–9
implied terms in sales of goods
description, sale by 425–34
encumbrances, freedom
from 462–3
fitness for purpose 434, 441–7
introduction 423–4
quality, as to 423–4
sample, sale by 448–50
satisfactory quality 423–4
incomplete bill
bills of exchange 684
INCOTERMS
international sales and 533
indemnities
agents
commercial agents 276–87
generally 267–9
lien 269
independent contractors
agency 116
injunctions
documentary credits 800–1
secret profits 239–41
insolvency
administration orders 1109
administrative
receivership 1115–23
'balance-sheet'
insolvency 1108
bankruptcy order 1110–11
basic objectives 1106–8
'commercial' insolvency 1108
corporate insolvency
administration
order 1111–15
administrative
receivership 1115–23
receivership 1115–23
voluntary
arrangement 1111
winding up 1123–37
debt relief orders 1109–10
definitions
'balance-sheet' 1108
'commercial' 1108
generally 1108–9
'ultimate' 1108–9
individual insolvency
administration order 1109

bankruptcy order 1110–11
voluntary
arrangements 1109
introduction 1105–6
legal consequences 1108
procedures
corporate 1111–37
individuals 1108–9
receivership 1115–23
'ultimate' insolvency 1108–9
voluntary arrangements
corporate 1111
individual 1109
winding up
administration of
estate 1137
assets in the
liquidation 1124–37
avoidance of antecedent
transactions 1127–37
court, by 1124
extortionate credit
transactions 1130
floating charges 1130
generally 1122–4
preferences 1130
transactions at an
undervalue 1130
transactions defrauding
creditors 1130
instalment contracts
acceptance of delivery
under 456–7
insurance contracts
authorisation 1090–1
conditions and
warranties 1095
consumer protection 1097
content and interpretation
conditions and
warranties 1095
consumer protection 1097
risk 1095
contribution 1099
disclosure 1093
formation 1091–4
good faith 1094
insurable interest 1090
insurer's liability 1097–9
insurer's rights 1099
introduction 1089–91
marine insurance 1100
material questions 1093
notice 1097
onus of proof 1097–8
questions, insurer's 1093–4
reinstatement 1098